ENCYCLOPEDIA OF RELIGION

SECOND EDITION

ENCYCLOPEDIA OF RELIGION

10

SECOND EDITION

NECROMANCY
•
PINDAR

LINDSAY JONES
EDITOR IN CHIEF

MACMILLAN REFERENCE USA
An imprint of Thomson Gale, a part of The Thomson Corporation

THOMSON
GALE

Detroit • New York • San Francisco • San Diego • New Haven, Conn. • Waterville, Maine • London • Munich

THOMSON
GALE

Encyclopedia of Religion, Second Edition

Lindsay Jones, Editor in Chief

For more information, contact
Macmillan Reference USA
An imprint of Thomson Gale
27500 Drake Rd.
Farmington, Hills, MI 48331-3535
Or you can visit our Internet site at
http://www.gale.com

LIBRARY OF CONGRESS CATALOGING-IN-PUBLICATION DATA

Encyclopedia of religion / Lindsay Jones, editor in chief.— 2nd ed.
p. cm.
Includes bibliographical references and index.
ISBN 0-02-865733-0 (SET HARDCOVER : ALK. PAPER) —
ISBN 0-02-865734-9 (V. 1) — ISBN 0-02-865735-7 (v. 2) —
ISBN 0-02-865736-5 (v. 3) — ISBN 0-02-865737-3 (v. 4) —
ISBN 0-02-865738-1 (v. 5) — ISBN 0-02-865739-X (v. 6) —
ISBN 0-02-865740-3 (v. 7) — ISBN 0-02-865741-1 (v. 8) —
ISBN 0-02-865742-X (v. 9) — ISBN 0-02-865743-8 (v. 10)
— ISBN 0-02-865980-5 (v. 11) — ISBN 0-02-865981-3 (v. 12) — ISBN 0-02-865982-1 (v. 13) — ISBN 0-02-865983-X (v. 14) — ISBN 0-02-865984-8 (v. 15)
1. RELIGION—ENCYCLOPEDIAS. I. JONES, LINDSAY, 1954-

BL31.E46 2005
200'.3—dc22 2004017052

This title is also available as an e-book.
ISBN 0-02-865997-X
Contact your Thomson Gale representative for ordering information.

Printed in the United States of America
10 9 8 7 6 5 4 3 2 1

EDITORS AND CONSULTANTS

Harvard Forum on Religion and Ecology
Ecology and Religion

JOSEPH HARRIS
Francis Lee Higginson Professor of English Literature and Professor of Folklore, Harvard University
Germanic Religions

URSULA KING
Professor Emerita, Senior Research Fellow and Associate Member of the Institute for Advanced Studies, University of Bristol, England, and Professorial Research Associate, Centre for Gender and Religions Research, School of Oriental and African Studies, University of London
Gender and Religion

DAVID MORGAN
Duesenberg Professor of Christianity and the Arts, and Professor of Humanities and Art History, Valparaiso University
Color Inserts and Essays

JOSEPH F. NAGY
Professor, Department of English, University of California, Los Angeles
Celtic Religion

MATTHEW OJO
Obafemi Awolowo University
African Religions

JUHA PENTIKÄINEN
Professor of Comparative Religion, The University of Helsinki, Member of Academia Scientiarum Fennica, Finland
Arctic Religions and Uralic Religions

TED PETERS
Professor of Systematic Theology, Pacific Lutheran Theological Seminary and the Center for Theology and the Natural Sciences at the Graduate Theological Union, Berkeley, California
Science and Religion

FRANK E. REYNOLDS
Professor of the History of Religions and Buddhist Studies in the Divinity School and the Department of South Asian Languages and Civilizations, Emeritus, University of Chicago
History of Religions

GONZALO RUBIO
Assistant Professor, Department of Classics and Ancient Mediterranean Studies and Department of History and Religious Studies, Pennsylvania State University
Ancient Near Eastern Religions

SUSAN SERED
Director of Research, Religion, Health and Healing Initiative, Center for the Study of World Religions, Harvard University, and Senior Research Associate, Center for Women's Health and Human Rights, Suffolk University
Healing, Medicine, and Religion

LAWRENCE E. SULLIVAN
Professor, Department of Theology, University of Notre Dame
History of Religions

WINNIFRED FALLERS SULLIVAN
Dean of Students and Senior Lecturer in the Anthropology and Sociology of Religion, University of Chicago
Law and Religion

TOD SWANSON
Associate Professor of Religious Studies, and Director, Center for Latin American Studies, Arizona State University
South American Religions

MARY EVELYN TUCKER
Professor of Religion, Bucknell University, Founder and Coordinator, Harvard Forum on Religion and Ecology, Research Fellow, Harvard Yenching Institute, Research Associate, Harvard Reischauer Institute of Japanese Studies
Ecology and Religion

HUGH URBAN
Associate Professor, Department of Comparative Studies, Ohio State University
Politics and Religion

CATHERINE WESSINGER
Professor of the History of Religions and Women's Studies, Loyola University New Orleans
New Religious Movements

ROBERT A. YELLE
Mellon Postdoctoral Fellow, University of Toronto
Law and Religion

ERIC ZIOLKOWSKI
Charles A. Dana Professor of Religious Studies, Lafayette College
Literature and Religion

ABBREVIATIONS AND SYMBOLS USED IN THIS WORK

abbr. abbreviated; abbreviation
abr. abridged; abridgment
AD *anno Domini,* in the year of the (our) Lord
Afrik. Afrikaans
AH *anno Hegirae,* in the year of the Hijrah
Akk. Akkadian
Ala. Alabama
Alb. Albanian
Am. *Amos*
AM *ante meridiem,* before noon
amend. amended; amendment
annot. annotated; annotation
Ap. *Apocalypse*
Apn. *Apocryphon*
app. appendix
Arab. Arabic
ʿArakh. *ʿArakhin*
Aram. Aramaic
Ariz. Arizona
Ark. Arkansas
Arm. Armenian
art. article (pl., arts.)
AS Anglo-Saxon
Asm. Mos. *Assumption of Moses*
Assyr. Assyrian
A.S.S.R. Autonomous Soviet Socialist Republic
Av. Avestan
ʿA.Z. *ʿAvodah zarah*
b. born
Bab. Babylonian
Ban. Bantu
1 Bar. *1 Baruch*
2 Bar. *2 Baruch*
3 Bar. *3 Baruch*
4 Bar. *4 Baruch*
B.B. *Bavaʾ batraʾ*
BBC British Broadcasting Corporation
BC before Christ
BCE before the common era
B.D. Bachelor of Divinity
Beits. *Beitsah*
Bekh. *Bekhorot*
Beng. Bengali
Ber. *Berakhot*
Berb. Berber
Bik. *Bikkurim*
bk. book (pl., bks.)
B.M. *Bavaʾ metsiʿaʾ*
BP before the present
B.Q. *Bavaʾ qammaʾ*
Brāh. *Brāhmaṇa*
Bret. Breton
B.T. Babylonian Talmud
Bulg. Bulgarian
Burm. Burmese
c. *circa,* about, approximately
Calif. California
Can. Canaanite
Catal. Catalan
CE of the common era
Celt. Celtic
cf. *confer,* compare
Chald. Chaldean
chap. chapter (pl., chaps.)
Chin. Chinese
C.H.M. Community of the Holy Myrrhbearers
1 Chr. *1 Chronicles*
2 Chr. *2 Chronicles*
Ch. Slav. Church Slavic
cm centimeters
col. column (pl., cols.)
Col. *Colossians*
Colo. Colorado
comp. compiler (pl., comps.)
Conn. Connecticut
cont. continued
Copt. Coptic
1 Cor. *1 Corinthians*
2 Cor. *2 Corinthians*
corr. corrected
C.S.P. Congregatio Sancti Pauli, Congregation of Saint Paul (Paulists)
d. died
D Deuteronomic (source of the Pentateuch)
Dan. Danish
D.B. Divinitatis Baccalaureus, Bachelor of Divinity
D.C. District of Columbia
D.D. Divinitatis Doctor, Doctor of Divinity
Del. Delaware
Dem. *Demaʾi*
dim. diminutive
diss. dissertation
Dn. *Daniel*
D.Phil. Doctor of Philosophy
Dt. *Deuteronomy*
Du. Dutch
E Elohist (source of the Pentateuch)
Eccl. *Ecclesiastes*
ed. editor (pl., eds.); edition; edited by

'Eduy. *'Eduyyot*
e.g. *exempli gratia,* for example
Egyp. Egyptian
1 En. *1 Enoch*
2 En. *2 Enoch*
3 En. *3 Enoch*
Eng. English
enl. enlarged
Eph. *Ephesians*
'Eruv. *'Eruvin*
1 Esd. *1 Esdras*
2 Esd. *2 Esdras*
3 Esd. *3 Esdras*
4 Esd. *4 Esdras*
esp. especially
Est. Estonian
Est. *Esther*
et al. *et alii,* and others
etc. *et cetera,* and so forth
Eth. Ethiopic
EV English version
Ex. *Exodus*
exp. expanded
Ez. *Ezekiel*
Ezr. *Ezra*
2 Ezr. *2 Ezra*
4 Ezr. *4 Ezra*
f. feminine; and following (pl., ff.)
fasc. fascicle (pl., fascs.)
fig. figure (pl., figs.)
Finn. Finnish
fl. *floruit,* flourished
Fla. Florida
Fr. French
frag. fragment
ft. feet
Ga. Georgia
Gal. *Galatians*
Gaul. Gaulish
Ger. German
Giṭ. *Giṭṭin*
Gn. *Genesis*
Gr. Greek
Ḥag. *Ḥagigah*
Ḥal. *Ḥallah*
Hau. Hausa
Hb. *Habakkuk*
Heb. Hebrew
Heb. *Hebrews*
Hg. *Haggai*
Hitt. Hittite
Hor. *Horayot*
Hos. *Hosea*
Ḥul. *Ḥullin*
Hung. Hungarian
ibid. *ibidem,* in the same place (as the one immediately preceding)
Icel. Icelandic
i.e. *id est,* that is
IE Indo-European
Ill. Illinois
Ind. Indiana
intro. introduction
Ir. Gael. Irish Gaelic
Iran. Iranian
Is. *Isaiah*
Ital. Italian
J Yahvist (source of the Pentateuch)
Jas. *James*
Jav. Javanese
Jb. *Job*
Jdt. *Judith*
Jer. *Jeremiah*
Jgs. *Judges*
Jl. *Joel*
Jn. *John*
1 Jn. *1 John*
2 Jn. *2 John*
3 Jn. *3 John*
Jon. *Jonah*
Jos. *Joshua*
Jpn. Japanese
JPS Jewish Publication Society translation (1985) of the Hebrew Bible
J.T. Jerusalem Talmud
Jub. *Jubilees*
Kans. Kansas
Kel. *Kelim*
Ker. *Keritot*
Ket. *Ketubbot*
1 Kgs. *1 Kings*
2 Kgs. *2 Kings*
Khois. Khoisan
Kil. *Kil'ayim*
km kilometers
Kor. Korean
Ky. Kentucky
l. line (pl., ll.)
La. Louisiana
Lam. *Lamentations*
Lat. Latin
Latv. Latvian
L. en Th. Licencié en Théologie, Licentiate in Theology
L. ès L. Licencié ès Lettres, Licentiate in Literature
Let. Jer. *Letter of Jeremiah*
lit. literally
Lith. Lithuanian
Lk. *Luke*
LL Late Latin
LL.D. Legum Doctor, Doctor of Laws
Lv. *Leviticus*
m meters
m. masculine
M.A. Master of Arts
Ma 'as. *Ma'aserot*
Ma 'as. Sh. *Ma' aser sheni*
Mak. *Makkot*
Makh. *Makhshirin*
Mal. *Malachi*
Mar. Marathi
Mass. Massachusetts
1 Mc. *1 Maccabees*
2 Mc. *2 Maccabees*
3 Mc. *3 Maccabees*
4 Mc. *4 Maccabees*
Md. Maryland
M.D. Medicinae Doctor, Doctor of Medicine
ME Middle English
Meg. *Megillah*
Me 'il. *Me'ilah*
Men. *Menaḥot*
MHG Middle High German
mi. miles
Mi. *Micah*
Mich. Michigan
Mid. *Middot*
Minn. Minnesota
Miq. *Miqva'ot*
MIran. Middle Iranian
Miss. Mississippi
Mk. *Mark*
Mo. Missouri
Mo'ed Q. *Mo'ed qaṭan*
Mont. Montana
MPers. Middle Persian
MS. *manuscriptum,* manuscript (pl., MSS)
Mt. *Matthew*
MT Masoretic text
n. note
Na. *Nahum*
Nah. Nahuatl
Naz. *Nazir*
N.B. *nota bene,* take careful note
N.C. North Carolina
n.d. no date
N.Dak. North Dakota
NEB New English Bible
Nebr. Nebraska

Ned. *Nedarim*
Neg. *Nega'im*
Neh. *Nehemiah*
Nev. Nevada
N.H. New Hampshire
Nid. *Niddah*
N.J. New Jersey
Nm. *Numbers*
N.Mex. New Mexico
no. number (pl., nos.)
Nor. Norwegian
n.p. no place
n.s. new series
N.Y. New York
Ob. *Obadiah*
O.Cist. Ordo Cisterciencium, Order of Cîteaux (Cistercians)
OCS Old Church Slavonic
OE Old English
O.F.M. Ordo Fratrum Minorum, Order of Friars Minor (Franciscans)
OFr. Old French
Ohal. *Ohalot*
OHG Old High German
OIr. Old Irish
OIran. Old Iranian
Okla. Oklahoma
ON Old Norse
O.P. Ordo Praedicatorum, Order of Preachers (Dominicans)
OPers. Old Persian
op. cit. *opere citato,* in the work cited
OPrus. Old Prussian
Oreg. Oregon
'Orl. *'Orlah*
O.S.B. Ordo Sancti Benedicti, Order of Saint Benedict (Benedictines)
p. page (pl., pp.)
P Priestly (source of the Pentateuch)
Pa. Pennsylvania
Pahl. Pahlavi
Par. *Parah*
para. paragraph (pl., paras.)
Pers. Persian
Pes. *Pesahim*
Ph.D. Philosophiae Doctor, Doctor of Philosophy
Phil. *Philippians*
Phlm. *Philemon*
Phoen. Phoenician
pl. plural; plate (pl., pls.)
PM *post meridiem,* after noon
Pol. Polish
pop. population
Port. Portuguese
Prv. *Proverbs*
Ps. *Psalms*
Ps. 151 *Psalm 151*
Ps. Sol. *Psalms of Solomon*
pt. part (pl., pts.)
1Pt. *1 Peter*
2 Pt. *2 Peter*
Pth. Parthian
Q hypothetical source of the synoptic Gospels
Qid. *Qiddushin*
Qin. *Qinnim*
r. reigned; ruled
Rab. *Rabbah*
rev. revised
R. ha-Sh. *Ro'sh ha-shanah*
R.I. Rhode Island
Rom. Romanian
Rom. *Romans*
R.S.C.J. Societas Sacratissimi Cordis Jesu, Religious of the Sacred Heart
RSV Revised Standard Version of the Bible
Ru. *Ruth*
Rus. Russian
Rv. *Revelation*
Rv. Ezr. *Revelation of Ezra*
San. *Sanhedrin*
S.C. South Carolina
Scot. Gael. Scottish Gaelic
S.Dak. South Dakota
sec. section (pl., secs.)
Sem. Semitic
ser. series
sg. singular
Sg. *Song of Songs*
Sg. of 3 *Prayer of Azariah and the Song of the Three Young Men*
Shab. *Shabbat*
Shav. *Shavu'ot*
Sheq. *Sheqalim*
Sib. Or. *Sibylline Oracles*
Sind. Sindhi
Sinh. Sinhala
Sir. *Ben Sira*
S.J. Societas Jesu, Society of Jesus (Jesuits)
Skt. Sanskrit
1 Sm. *1 Samuel*
2 Sm. *2 Samuel*
Sogd. Sogdian
Soṭ. *Soṭah*
sp. species (pl., spp.)
Span. Spanish
sq. square
S.S.R. Soviet Socialist Republic
st. stanza (pl., ss.)
S.T.M. Sacrae Theologiae Magister, Master of Sacred Theology
Suk. *Sukkah*
Sum. Sumerian
supp. supplement; supplementary
Sus. *Susanna*
s.v. *sub verbo,* under the word (pl., s.v.v.)
Swed. Swedish
Syr. Syriac
Syr. Men. *Syriac Menander*
Ta' an. *Ta'anit*
Tam. Tamil
Tam. *Tamid*
Tb. *Tobit*
T.D. *Taishō shinshū daizōkyō,* edited by Takakusu Junjirō et al. (Tokyo,1922–1934)
Tem. *Temurah*
Tenn. Tennessee
Ter. Terumot
Ṭev. Y. *Ṭevul yom*
Tex. Texas
Th.D. Theologicae Doctor, Doctor of Theology
1 Thes. *1 Thessalonians*
2 Thes. *2 Thessalonians*
Thrac. Thracian
Ti. *Titus*
Tib. Tibetan
1 Tm. *1 Timothy*
2 Tm. *2 Timothy*
T. of 12 *Testaments of the Twelve Patriarchs*
Ṭoh. *ṭohorot*
Tong. Tongan
trans. translator, translators; translated by; translation
Turk. Turkish
Ukr. Ukrainian
Upan. *Upaniṣad*
U.S. United States
U.S.S.R. Union of Soviet Socialist Republics
Uqts. *Uqtsin*
v. verse (pl., vv.)
Va. Virginia
var. variant; variation
Viet. Vietnamese

viz. *videlicet,* namely
vol. volume (pl., vols.)
Vt. Vermont
Wash. Washington
Wel. Welsh
Wis. Wisconsin
Wis. *Wisdom of Solomon*
W.Va. West Virginia
Wyo. Wyoming

Yad. *Yadayim*
Yev. *Yevamot*
Yi. Yiddish
Yor. Yoruba
Zav. *Zavim*
Zec. *Zechariah*
Zep. *Zephaniah*
Zev. *Zevaḥim*

* hypothetical
? uncertain; possibly; perhaps
° degrees
+ plus
– minus
= equals; is equivalent to
× by; multiplied by
→ yields

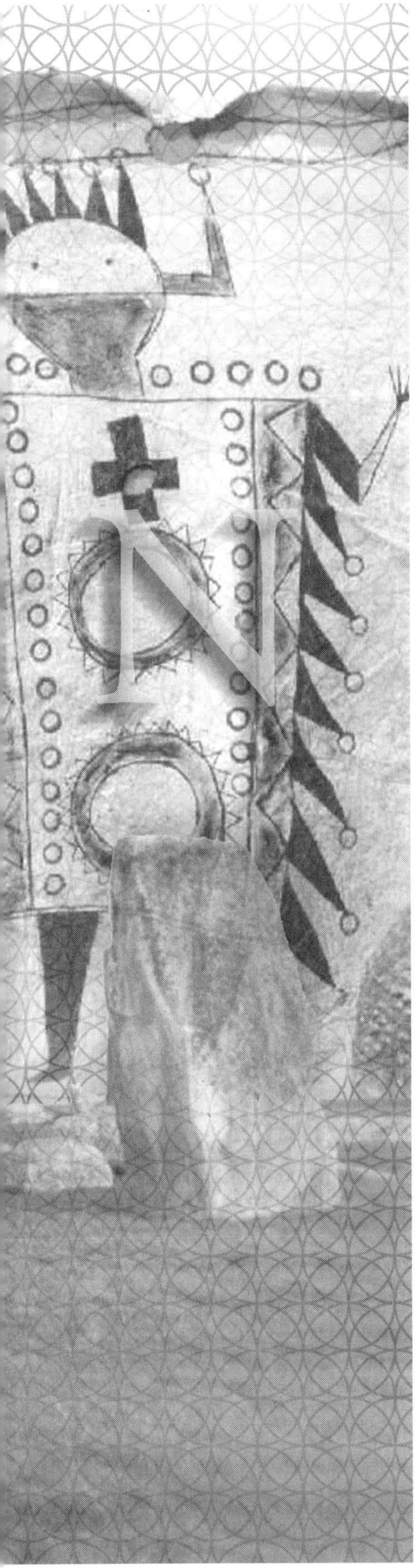

N

CONTINUED

NECROMANCY, the art or practice of magically conjuring up the souls of the dead, is primarily a form of divination. The principal purpose of seeking such communication with the dead is to obtain information from them, generally regarding the revelation of unknown causes or the future course of events. The cause of the death of the deceased who is questioned may be among the facts sought.

More generally, necromancy is often considered synonymous with black magic, sorcery, or witchcraft, perhaps because the calling up of the dead may occur for purposes other than information seeking, or because the separation of divination from its consequences is not always clear. There is also a linguistic basis for the expanded use of the word: the term *black art* for magic appears to be based on a corruption of *necromancy* (from Greek *necros,* "dead") to *nigromancy* (from Latin *niger,* "black").

Limited to the practice of magical conjuration of the dead, necromancy does not include communication employing mediums, as in spiritualism or spiritism. Nor does it include encounters with the souls of the departed during the spirit journeys of shamans, apparitions of ghosts, or communications in dreams, with the possible exception of those in dreams resulting from incubation.

Divination is undoubtedly a universal phenomenon found in all cultures. In the form of necromancy, however, it is relatively infrequent, though widespread. Only limited descriptions and documentation of the phenomenon are available, and only for certain periods and regions. Necromancy presupposes belief in both a form of life after death and the continued interest of the dead in the affairs of the living. As such it may well be associated with complex funerary and postfunerary customs and with ancestor worship.

TECHNIQUES OF NECROMANCY. Necromancy is a theme often found in myths, legends, and literary works. Such texts may describe communications with the dead or state their messages, but they seldom provide information on actual techniques that might have been employed in a given community. With regard to classical antiquity, Greek and Roman accounts deal with cases described in myth and legend, but there is no evidence of actual

CLOCKWISE FROM TOP LEFT CORNER. Thai bronze Buddha in meditation under a *nāga.* *[©Michael Freeman/Corbis]*; A lion-headed Imdugud bird above two stags in a twenty-fifth-century BCE Mesopotamian relief from the temple of Ninhursaga. British Museum, London. *[©Erich Lessing/Art Resource, N.Y.]*; Detail of an Apache "Kan" god painted on a warrior's cloak. Smithsonian Institution, Washington, D.C. *[©Werner Forman/Art Resource, N.Y.]*; Stonehenge. Wiltshire County, England. *[©Roger Ressmeyer/Corbis]*; Double-headed Neolithic idol, 5000–2000 BCE. Historical Museum, Targoviste, Romania. *[©Erich Lessing/Art Resource, N.Y.]* .

necromantic practices, whether in inscriptions or in documentation of specific historic events. More generally, where actual descriptions exist of rites in other societies rather than fabulous accounts or rumors and accusations, inquiries are connected with burial and burial preparation. Here the questioning of the corpse may concern the cause of death and the identification of a murderer. Other necromantic practices involve rites at the grave site with the use of the name or some part of the deceased, often his or her skull. The response may be in the form of an utterance produced by the diviner, either in a trance state or through ventriloquism. It may also be revealed in the form of a sign; this may involve the interpretation of an omen or the drawing of lots.

The concept of necromancy is of limited utility for at least two reasons. First, it is linked to its history in the Western tradition and therefore difficult to employ in analyzing beliefs and practices of other cultures with different traditions. Second, necromancy is also only one of several types of divinatory practices, and these tend to shade into each other. For both of these reasons the term is of limited value in cross-cultural research, and it is not generally utilized in modern ethnographic studies.

NECROMANCY IN ANTIQUITY. The ancient Greeks believed that the dead had great prophetic powers and that it was possible to consult them by performing sacrifices or pouring libations at their tombs. Such offerings were also part of the funerary and postfunerary ceremonies. The legendary visit of Odysseus to Hades to consult the seer Tiresias, as described in Book 11 of the *Odyssey*, has also been classified as an instance of necromancy. Various other classical texts include references to formal oracles of the dead; however, these generally speak of practices not among Greeks but in remote locations or among barbarians. They cannot be considered reliable reports of actual practices.

Most information on necromancy among Nordic and Germanic peoples comes from the sagas. A number of references appear, for example, in the Eddas. Odin (Óðinn) is, among other things, god of the dead, and in one account he awakens a dead prophetess in order to consult her. It is not known whether or not such conjurations took place. Interpretation of the movement of rune-inscribed sticks appears to have been practiced. Necromancy was only one of numerous techniques of divination and one considered to be particularly dangerous, especially when the dead were not family members. It appears to have been prohibited even prior to the conversion of these peoples to Christianity.

Necromancy appears to have been unknown, or at least unreported, among the Etruscans and in the earlier periods of Roman history. It may have been introduced with other Hellenistic and Oriental divinatory and magic practices, all of which were prohibited by Augustus (63 BCE–14 CE). Like other forms of divination and magic, which might include the use of poisons, necromancy was perceived as a potential political tool, dangerous in a world of personal power and ambition. The emperors, however, surrounded themselves with diviners of all sorts. The concerns of medieval Christianity with necromancy and magic have their roots in this period as well as in biblical prohibitions.

Numerous divinatory techniques are mentioned in the Bible. The account of the so-called Witch of Endor (*1 Sm.* 28) is frequently cited as an example of necromancy and of the prohibitions attached to it (cf. *Deuteronomy, Leviticus,* and *Isaiah*). Necromancy is mentioned in the Talmud among other divinatory practices. Although it is severely condemned, several examples are cited. The practice appears to have been rare, but it left its trace in rabbinic sources and medieval Jewish magical beliefs, perhaps reinforced by the beliefs of the Christians among whom the Jews lived. Magical beliefs, many of pre-Christian origins, continued throughout the Middle Ages.

LATE MEDIEVAL AND RENAISSANCE NECROMANCY. The primary use of the term refers to the period between the late Middle Ages and the early Renaissance. This was a time of great social and political instability and change. It was also the time when fear of and persecution of witches took hold in Europe. In England the several shifts between Catholicism and Protestantism were linked to fears of resistance and repression.

One of the crimes of which witches were accused was necromancy, conjuring up the dead as well as (or with the help of) the devil. It was in this context that the term *necromancy* came to be used as synonymous with *demonic magic;* that is, magic performed with the devil's assistance. It no longer referred exclusively or even principally to magic using bodies of the dead or conjuring up the spirits of the dead. There are two major sources of information about these beliefs and practices. These are the instructions used by witch-hunters and exorcists, on the one hand, and the surviving manuals and books of magic, on the other. Possession of such books itself was a basis for prosecution. The introduction of printing and the resulting availability of books to a larger number of people were in part responsible for the wider diffusion of such texts.

Manuals such as the *Munich Book of Necromancy,* which dates from the fifteenth century, are rich sources of information on the general subject of the magic of the period. The *Munich Book* contains detailed information of what magicians claimed to be able to do and said they actually did. Interestingly, this concerns not only specifics on how to gain magical powers through conjurations, and about the spirits that could be conjured up, but also provides information on various forms of stage magic, particularly illusionist experiments that could be performed for entertainment, such as producing the appearance of banquets, horses, and castles. Some aspects of modern illusionist stage magic seem to have a long tradition behind them.

Reading and owning books in themselves gave rise to suspicions, and the possession of such books of magic was often sufficient for a person to be accused and prosecuted for necromancy. Suspect books were confiscated and burned. Lower-level clergy (men with some literacy) were frequently accused of practicing necromancy by the use of books. Women, who were less likely to be literate, seem generally not to have been suspected of manual-based necromantic practices. Rather, they were accused of using spells, of making pacts with the devil, and of having animal familiars. The fear of black magic and legislation against it often reflected anxiety over its possible use for political purposes. An example is King James's 1604 decree of death for anyone using the body of a dead person or any of its parts for purposes of magic. This fear is also seen in writings of the period. Shakespeare's *Macbeth* shows witches conspiring to practice necromancy: they collect body parts on a battlefield, and in Act IV they use the dead to prophecy.

NECROMANCY IN ARCHAIC CULTURES. Spanish chronicles, composed shortly after the conquest of Peru, record that the Inca had two special classes of diviners who consulted the dead, one group specializing in dealing with mummies of the dead and another consulting various spirit beings and their representations, which the Spaniards referred to as idols. The reports are written from the perspective of sixteenth-century Spaniards at a time when, in their own country, the Inquisition searched out necromancers and others considered sorcerers and heretics.

In the Huon Gulf region of New Guinea, throughout the nineteenth century and prior to the arrival of missionaries, all deaths were attributed to magic. The identification of the sorcerer who had caused the death was carried out by a diviner, who conjured the spirit of the deceased into one of several types of objects. It was then questioned, and "yes" or "no" responses were obtained from the motion of the object. The most common object used was a stunned eel, whose convulsions were interpreted as "yes" responses. Other objects might be an upturned shell or a piece of bamboo held in the hand. The movements of these objects were subject to some manipulations, and the answers were often used to confirm suspicions held by popular opinion.

In Haiti a tradition exists that is derived from both European influences of the colonial period and West African traditions. As part of postfunerary rites of Vodou initiates, one of the two souls with which every person is endowed is removed from a temporary sojourn underwater and settled in a family shrine. During this ceremony the soul is questioned on various matters of interest. At a later time it may be called into a jar for purposes of consultation. Like conversations with the dead in parts of Africa, as, for instance, among the Zulu, this process appears to involve ventriloquism by the performing ritual specialist. It is also believed that sorcerers can send the spirit of one or more dead persons into the body of a victim to cause illness and eventual death if appropriate counter-rites are not performed. These involve the identification of both the dead and the sender. The diagnostic process may involve the direct questioning of the dead using the patient as a medium or by scrying (water gazing) or using other divinatory techniques. The Haitian example suggests the difficulty in drawing clear lines between sorcery, divination, diagnosis, and healing—that is, between rituals with positive or negative intent, or even among the various divinatory techniques. As a result it is doubtful that the term *necromancy* is used appropriately for any of these practices.

From the perspective of research methods, it is important to distinguish between studies based on written sources, often of a fragmentary nature, and ethnographic studies of living people, their beliefs, and their customs. In contrast to written sources, living people can be observed and questioned, so a larger context for their understandings can be discerned.

The term *necromancy* has changed meaning in the course of time. The practices described as necromantic were seen as the very essence of evil in the period of the Renaissance. Calling up the dead to question them, as described in Greek literature and myth, was not necessarily evil but might be concerned with decision making about the future and practical matters. How the dead are understood as potentially active in the world of the living has varied not only from culture to culture but also from period to period. Distinctions are often made between those who died a natural death and those who did not. In modern times, faith healing by means of calling on the help of the dead has been referred to as necromancy in the United States. This gives the term a different meaning, unrelated to black magic. As interest in various aspects of the occult has seen a revival in the United States, curiosity about necromancy has also grown.

SEE ALSO Divination.

BIBLIOGRAPHY

Callaway, Henry. *The Religious System of the Amazulu in the Zulu Language with Translation into English and Notes in Four Parts* (1870). Africana Collectanea, vol. 35. Cape Town, South Africa, 1970.

Caquot, André, and Marcel Leibovici, eds. *La divination.* 2 vols. Paris, 1968.

Caro Baroja, Julio. *The World of the Witches.* Translated by O. N. V. Glendinning. Chicago, 1964.

Godwin, William. *Lives of the Necromancers.* London, 1834.

Hogbin, Herbert Ian. *The Island of Menstruating Men: Religion in Wogeo, New Guinea.* Scranton, Pa., 1970.

Hughes, Pennethorne. *Witchcraft* (1952). Baltimore, 1965.

Institoris, Heinrich, and Jakob Sprenger. *The Malleus Maleficarum of Heinrich Kramer and James Sprenger* (1928). Translated by Montague Summers. New York, 1971.

Junod, Henri A. *The Life of a South African Tribe.* 2d ed., rev. and enl. 2 vols. London, 1927. The 1912 first edition has been reprinted, New Hyde Park, N.Y., 1962.

Kieckhefer, Richard. *Forbidden Rites: A Necromancer's Manual of the Fifteenth Century.* Stroud, U.K., 1997.

Métraux, Alfred. *Voodoo in Haiti.* New York, 1959.

Trachtenberg, Joshua. *Jewish Magic and Superstition: A Study in Folk Religion.* New York, 1939; reprint, New York, 1982.

Williams, Charles. *Witchcraft.* New York, 1941; reprint, New York, 1959.

Wills, Garry. *Witches and Jesuits: Shakespeare's Macbeth.* New York, 1995.

ERIKA BOURGUIGNON (1987 AND 2005)

NEGRITO RELIGIONS

This entry consists of the following articles:

AN OVERVIEW
NEGRITOS OF THE PHILIPPINE ISLANDS
NEGRITOS OF THE ANDAMAN ISLANDS
NEGRITOS OF THE MALAY PENINSULA

NEGRITO RELIGIONS: AN OVERVIEW

The term *Negrito* (Spanish for "little Negro") has been used by some Western scholars to indicate those inhabitants of the Malay Peninsula, the Philippine Islands, and the Andaman Islands (off the coast of Myanmar) who are characterized by small stature, dark skin, curly hair, and generally "negroid" facial features. Scholars disagree regarding a possible genetic connection between these small and widely separated populations. The traditional view is that they are all remnants of a single ancient race that was once widespread in Southeast Asia but has now been largely exterminated or absorbed by more powerful and populous immigrant groups. A second view, put forward by some biological anthropologists, is that the distinctive features of the Negritos are examples of "parallel evolution," similar physical changes among unrelated local populations resulting from their common adaptation to the tropical rain forest. Although plausible hypotheses have been advanced as to why that environment might favor "negritoid" characteristics, it is still not clear why such features have not arisen in similar environments elsewhere, such as the Amazon Basin of South America. The genetic relationship between the Asiatic Negritos, then, remains an open question.

The cultures of the various Negrito groups have many similarities, but whether these are due to a common ancestral culture, to contact between the different groups, or to parallel adaptations to similar environments is often unclear. Before 1900 almost all Negritos lived by hunting and gathering, supplemented in some places by small-scale trade in forest products. Their hunting-gathering economy produced such social consequences as small living groups, a lack of wealth accumulation, and informal leadership. Most groups were also nomadic, although the rich environment of the Andaman coast permitted its inhabitants to become partially sedentary.

The religions of the Andamanese, the Semang (Malayan Negritos), and the Philippine Negritos have many features in common, some very general but others highly specific and undoubtedly due to contact or common origin. The similarities are most striking with respect to deity conceptions and the corresponding prohibitions and rituals. The most personified and individualized deities are those associated with weather, especially destructive storms. Most groups have deities responsible for making thunder, and even some of the names given them are similar: Karei in the Malay Peninsula, Kayai and Kadai in the Philippines, and Tarai in the Andamans. These beings are thought to bring thunderstorms as punishment for breaking prohibitions against such diverse acts as incest and burning leeches. The Semang and some of the Philippine groups attempt to avert the storms by offering their own blood to the thunder god. Such common features are striking, but they form only part of each group's religion. In other respects their beliefs and rituals diverge, sometimes so radically as to place even the common features in different lights. For this reason it is best to treat the religions of the Andamanese, Semang, and Philippine Negritos as separate entities, although certain similarities will be apparent.

BIBLIOGRAPHY

The most complete survey and comparison of the cultures of the Asiatic Negritos is Paul Schebesta's three-volume work *Die Negrito Asiens* (Vienna, 1952–1957). Comprising volumes 6, 12, and 13 of "Studia Instituti Anthropos," Schebesta's work has been partially translated into English by Frieda Schütze for the Human Relations Area Files (New Haven, Conn., 1962). The great bulk of this material is based on Schebesta's extensive fieldwork among the Semang. A similar, although much briefer, comparison can be found in Marcelino N. Maceda's *The Culture of the Mamanua (Northeast Mindanao) as Compared with That of the Other Negritos of Southeast Asia,* 2d ed. (Cebu City, Philippines, 1975), which takes the Philippine Negritos as its point of departure. A valuable article pointing out the religious similarities among the three divisions of Negritos is John M. Cooper's "Andamanese-Semang-Eta Cultural Relations," *Primitive Man* (now *Anthropological Quarterly*) 13 (April 1940): 29–47. William C. Boyd's "Four Achievements of the Genetical Method in Physical Anthropology," *American Anthropologist* 65 (April 1962): 243–252, provides a useful introduction to the opinion on the question of whether the Asiatic Negritos constitute a single race or represent parallel adaptations to similar environments.

KIRK ENDICOTT (1987 AND 2005)

NEGRITO RELIGIONS: NEGRITOS OF THE PHILIPPINE ISLANDS

The Negritos of the Philippines comprise approximately twenty-five widely scattered ethnolinguistic groups totaling an estimated fifteen thousand people. They are assumed to be the aboriginal inhabitants of the archipelago. Many of these Negrito groups still live by hunting and gathering, trading wild meat and forest products to the Filipino farmers around them in exchange for rice or corn. They also practice some marginal cultivation.

The traditional religion of all Philippine Negritos is animism. Today, most of them remain animists, although some of their beliefs have been modified by Roman Catholic Christianity.

One salient feature of Negrito religion is its noticeable lack of systematization. Consequently, it has a secondary place in Negrito ideology. Because the animistic beliefs and practices of Philippine Negritos are individualistic and sporadic, they exert less control over the people's daily lives than do the religious systems of other, non-Negrito animistic societies in the Philippines. Likewise, the minor function of religion in most Philippine Negrito cultures contrasts markedly with the important role of religion among the Negritos of Malaysia, which is reported by Kirk Endicott in *Batek Negrito Religion* (Oxford, 1979).

Nevertheless, there is a universal belief among Philippine Negritos in a spirit world, containing many classes of supernatural beings. These beings are seen to have some influence over processes of nature, as well as over the health and economic success of humans. Negritos especially have a preoccupation with malignant ghosts of deceased humans. Most Negritos also hold to a belief in a supreme deity. Scholars have debated the question of whether this "monotheism" is of pre-Hispanic origin or is merely the result of Christian influences.

AGTA RELIGION. The Agta, or Dumagat, of northeastern Luzon are typical of the least acculturated Philippine Negrito societies. They show little inclination to adapt to the dominant Roman Catholic religion of their peasant Filipino neighbors. The Agta believe in a single high god and in a large number of supernatural spirit beings that inhabit their surrounding natural environment. Depending on the class of spirit, these various beings live in trees, underground, on rocky headlands, or in caves.

There are two general classes of spirit beings in the Agta worldview: *hayup* ("creature") and *bélet* or *anito* ("ghost"). The latter are always malignant. Ghosts are wandering disembodied souls of deceased humans. The ghosts of recently deceased adult relatives are especially feared, as they are prone to return to the abode of their family during the night, causing sickness and death.

There are several varieties of *hayup* creatures. Although these are nonhuman, they are bipedal and may appear in human form. Most varieties of *hayup* beings are malignant; others are neutral, and a few can be called upon for help in curing disease.

AGTA SHAMANS. In Aurora province, 8 percent of Agta adults are shamans, of whom two out of ten are women. They practice only white magic. A shaman (*bunogen*) is defined by the Agta as an individual who has a familiar spirit "friend" (*bunog*) who aids him or her in diagnosing and treating disease. The primary role of shamans is curing. They do not practice black magic. (Agta do not practice sorcery, although they are aware of the custom among other Filipino societies.) Shamans may treat their patients with herbal medicines and simple prayers to their spirit "friends." For difficult cases, they may conduct a séance. In such cases, shamans will enter into a trance state, chanting prayers over the patient until they are possessed by their familiar spirits. These chants are not in the normal Agta language but are sung in a form of glossolalia.

It would be incorrect to say that Agta worship the spirits in their environment. Rather, they fear them, and placate them. The Agta do not have a sacrifical system as do other Philippine tribal groups, but they do occasionally offer small gifts to the *hayup* spirits if they are taking something from the forest. These gifts may consist of a few grains of rice, a few ounces of honey, or just a piece of thread from a man's G-string. In some areas, when a new garden is cleared a shaman may set up a small table with spirit offerings of betel quid or food.

Agta religious practices are done haphazardly, when it is convenient, and usually on an individual basis. Most such practices revolve around the prevention or treatment of illness. Agta have only a vague interest in the afterlife, the realm of the dead, creation of the world, immortality, or the future. They do not seek religious experiences. Rather, it is the chronic fear of sickness and death that activates Agta religious behavior. While it would be wrong to say that religion is unimportant to the Agta, it does play a lesser role in their culture than it does in other animistic groups.

BIBLIOGRAPHY

There are to date no complete studies on any of the religious systems of any Philippine Negrito society. Brief sketches appear, however, in many of the more general descriptions of such groups. Much of this material on such religious systems is reviewed in *A Primer on the Negritos of the Philippines,* compiled by Daisy Y. Noval-Morales and James Monan (Manila, 1979).

Three other important sources, which attempt to generalize on Philippine Negrito religions, are John M. Garvan's *The Negritos of the Philippines* (Vienna, 1964), edited by Hermann Hochegger; Marcelino N. Maceda's *The Culture of the Mamanua (Northeast Mindanao) as Compared with That of the Other Negritos of Southeast Asia,* 2d ed. (Cebu City, Philippines, 1975); and a three-volume work in German by Paul Schebesta, *Die Negrito Asiens* (Vienna, 1952–1957).

New Sources

Rae, Navin K. *Living in a Lean-To: Philippine Negrito Foragers in Transition.* Ann Arbor, 1990.

Rahman, Rudolf. "The Nocturnal Prayer Ceremonies of the Negritos of the Philippines." *Philippine Quarterly of Culture and Society (Cebu City)* 26, nos. 1–2 (1998): 192–211.

Shimizu, Hiromu. "Communicating with Spirits: A Study of the Manganito Seance among the Southwestern Pinatubo Negritos." *East Asian Cultural Studies (Tokyo)* 22, nos. 1–4 (1983): 129–167.

THOMAS N. HEADLAND (1987)
Revised Bibliography

NEGRITO RELIGIONS: NEGRITOS OF THE ANDAMAN ISLANDS

The Andaman Negritos are extremely primitive hunter-gatherers representing a prelithic stage of cultural development. They fall into two separate divisions, the Great Andamanese and the Onge-Jarawa-Sentinelese. As a result of colonization and the introduction of syphilis and other diseases, the Great Andamanese tribes have already become extinct; only a hybrid group of some twenty-eight individuals survives on a tiny islet called Strait Island. The Jarawa and the Sentinelese live in complete isolation and eschew all external contacts. Consequently, nothing is known about their religion. The remaining tribe, the Onge, lives on Little Andaman Island.

The universe as conceived by the Onge is a multilayered structure with Little Andaman at its center. There are six layers above Little Andaman and six layers below, and each is inhabited by a different class of spirit. These spirits are neither divine nor immaterial. They eat, drink, marry, multiply, and die just like human beings. The most important among them are the *onkoboykwe*, a class of benevolent spirit inhabiting the first layer above Little Andaman, and the *eaka*, a class of harmful spirit living immediately beneath the island. Above the Onge universe there is a limitless void and below there is Kwatannange, the primary sea, which is full of turtles.

The sun, moon, stars, and clouds are believed to be the creation of the *onkoboykwe*. The Onge do not personify and worship the heavenly bodies. There are two monsoons in the Andamans, the southwest and the northeast; spirits living in distant islands across the sea send the monsoonal winds.

The Onge believe that one's life after death depends on how a person has met his death. If he dies of illness, he becomes an *eaka* and goes below the earth. If an Onge is killed by a wild boar, by snakebite, or by a fall from a tree, he becomes an *onkoboykwe* and lives above the sky. If drowned, he becomes a sea spirit.

The Onge hold that all non-Negrito people are the spirits of dead Onges. The term *inene* is collectively applied to them. In the event of death from illness, one day before the emergence of *eaka* from the dead body, another miniature human form called *embekete* comes out from the corpse and swims across the sea to the land of *inene* where he soon transforms himself into another *inene*. Thus, according to the Onge, we the outsiders were Onge in our previous birth. The belief in the existence of two spirits, *embekete* and *eaka*, in one individual probably emanated from their attempts to rationalize the origin of non-Negritos and find a place for them in their scheme of the universe.

From the fragmentary data that are available on the religion of the Great Andamanese, it appears that they, like the Onge, believed in different classes of spirit living above the sky, below the earth, and in the sea. There is, however, an important difference between the Great Andamanese and the Onge. The former believed that the sun was the wife of the moon and that the stars were their children, whereas the Onge hold that the sun and the moon are flat, disc-shaped, inanimate things created by the *onkoboykwe*. Concepts of a superior spirit or high god, heaven and hell, virtue and sin, are conspicuously absent among the Andaman Negritos.

Bibliography

Although the literature on the religious life of the Andamanese Negritos is small, the reader may profitably consult John M. Cooper's "Andamanese-Semang-Eta Cultural Relations," *Primitive Man* (now *Anthropological Quarterly*) 13 (April 1940): 29–47.

New Sources

Basu, Badal Kumar. *The Onge, Negrito Hunter-Gatherers of Little Andaman.* Calcutta, 1990.

Ghosal, Samit. "Past and Present of the Negrito Tribes in the Andaman Islands: A Critical Appraisal." *Journal of the Anthropological Survey of India (Calcutta)* 43, no. 1–2 (1994): 25–30.

Sudarsen, V., and D. Venkatesan. "Life Cycle Ceremonies among the Onge of Little Andaman." In *Religion and Society in South India: A Volume in Honour of Prof. N. Subba Reddy*, edited by V. Sudarsen, G. Prakash Reddy, and M. Suryanarayana, pp. 163–173. Delhi, 1987.

PRANAB GANGULY (1987)
Revised Bibliography

NEGRITO RELIGIONS: NEGRITOS OF THE MALAY PENINSULA

The Negritos of the Malay Peninsula, who are generally called the Semang in the literature, numbered about two thousand in 1974. They live in small groups scattered about the foothills in the northern half of the peninsula (4°N–6°30′N; 100°E–103°E). They speak a number of related languages in the Mon-Khmer language family. Until about 1950 most of the Semang were nomadic hunter-gatherers. The staple of their diet was wild yams, and their main source of meat was arboreal animals—monkeys, gibbons, squirrels, and birds, which they hunted with blowpipes and poisoned darts. They also carried on some trade with neighboring Malay farmers, exchanging such forest produce as rattan and resins for iron tools, salt, cloth, and cultivated foods. They lived in camps of five to fifteen related nuclear families, moving every week or two when the local resources were exhausted. Each family was politically independent, the only leadership in a group being the informal influence of a particularly wise or persuasive person. Since 1950 well over half the Semang have settled down, often under the direction of government agencies, and adopted shifting agriculture. Yet even in these changed conditions, they have clung to their traditional religion, which has served as an important symbol of their ethnic identity.

In the cosmology of the Semang, the land forms a disk that is surrounded and underlaid by sea. It rests on the back of a giant snake, called Naga', which by shifting position can cause eruptions of water from underground. The firmament is a solid dome or series of layers, on top of which live the benevolent superhuman beings, called *chinoi* in the west and *hala'* in the east, who bring the seasonal fruit blossoms to earth. After death the shadow-souls of the Semang are believed to join these beings, on top of the firmament or on an island in the western sea. A stone pillar rises at the center of the world and reaches the firmament. Near its top is a cave, the home of the thunder god. The thunder god, whom most Semang groups call Karei, is generally regarded as male—sometimes a single being and sometimes a pair of brothers. The Semang believe that Karei causes thunderstorms to punish persons who have broken prohibitions against disruptive or disrespectful behavior. Karei is aided by a female earth deity, sometimes pictured as a pair of sisters, who is occasionally identified with the earth-supporting snake.

The rituals of the Semang are few and simple. The best-known rite is the blood sacrifice—throwing blood from the leg to the thunder god and earth deity—which is used to avert thunderstorms. Most groups also have singing and dancing sessions in which they thank the superhuman beings for the fruit and request their general support. These sessions may culminate in trancing and journeys of the shadow-soul to the haunts of the superhumans. Among the western Semang, a shaman may perform a séance in a special hut called a *panoh*, in which he calls down the *chinoi*. Semang rituals are intended to promote the fecundity of nature and to avert the dangers of their forest world.

BIBLIOGRAPHY

We are fortunate to have several reliable and detailed sources of information on the religions of the Semang. The most extensive is Paul Schebesta's *Die Negrito Asiens: Religion und Mythologie* (Vienna, 1957), which has been partially translated into English by Frieda Schütze for the Human Relations Area Files (New Haven, 1962). This work, volume 13 of "Studia Instituti Anthropos," focuses especially on the Jahai and other groups of the north-central and northwestern parts of the Malay Peninsula. Schebesta gives a fascinating popular account of his fieldwork and findings in *Among the Forest Dwarfs of Malaya*, translated by Arthur Chambers (London, 1928). Ivor H. N. Evan's *The Negritos of Malaya* (Cambridge, 1937) also contains a great deal of material on Semang religion. It is based on numerous visits to Semang groups in all parts of the peninsula between 1913 and 1932. For a detailed account of the religion of a Semang group from the east-coast state of Kelantan, see my book *Batek Negrito Religion: The Worldview and Rituals of a Hunting and Gathering People of Peninsular Malaysia* (Oxford, 1979).

New Sources

Endicott, Kirk. "The Batek of Malaysia." In *Endangered Peoples of Southeast and East Asia*, edited by Leslie E. Sponsel, pp. 101–121. Westport, Conn., 2000.

KIRK ENDICOTT (1987)
Revised Bibliography

NEHEMIAH (mid-fifth century BCE), or, in Hebrew, Neḥemyah; a governor of Judah in the Persian period, known for rebuilding the walls of Jerusalem. In the twentieth year of the reign of Artaxerxes I (445 BCE), Nehemiah received a commission from the Persian king to return to Judah and take on the task of rebuilding the walls of Jerusalem. The *Book of Nehemiah* gives an account of his activity in the first-person style of memoirs. It begins with his reception of distressing news from the homeland while he is in the royal service in Susa. This leads to his petitioning the king for support in repairing the walls and gates of Jerusalem and to his appointment as governor to carry out the task. In spite of opposition from Sanballat, governor of Samaria, and other local authorities of the region, the work is successfully completed. With the walls rebuilt, the city was repopulated with settlers from the countryside.

Nehemiah is credited also with social and religious reforms. He is presented as showing concern for the poor while maintaining a modest administration. In his second term as governor, which is not precisely dated, Nehemiah carried out a series of religious reforms having to do with Temple regulations and provisions for the priests, observance of the Sabbath, and the dissolution of mixed marriages. These reforms emphasize a tradition of religious conservatism and concern for ethnic purity that eventually leads to the Samaritan schism.

Nehemiah 8–9, having to do with the mission of Ezra, does not properly belong to the "memoirs" source and has seriously confused the historical relationship between Ezra and Nehemiah. It seems preferable to view Ezra's activity as subsequent to that of Nehemiah, building on the latter's work of restoration.

Nehemiah is recognized by tradition (*Sir.* 49:13) and by modern scholarship as largely responsible for restoring Jerusalem to a place of political prominence and semiautonomy with a chance to grow into a city of destiny.

SEE ALSO Ezra.

BIBLIOGRAPHY

For the historical treatments of Nehemiah, one should compare John Bright's *A History of Israel*, 3d ed. (Philadelphia, 1981), and Peter R. Ackroyd's *Israel under Babylon and Persia* (Oxford, 1970). See also the commentary by Jacob M. Myers in *Ezra, Nehemiah*, vol. 14 of the Anchor Bible (Garden City, N. Y., 1965).

New Sources

Eskenazi, Tamara Cohn. *In an Age of Prose: A Literary Approach to Ezra-Nehemiah.* Atlanta, Ga., 1988.

JOHN VAN SETERS (1987)
Revised Bibliography

NEMBUTSU SEE NIANFO

NEO-HASIDISM SEE JEWISH RENEWAL MOVEMENT

NEOLIN, known as the Delaware Prophet; a religious leader active among the Ohio Delaware Indians in the 1760s. Neolin (whose name means "the enlightened") was one of several Delaware prophets who arose in the latter part of the eighteenth century along the Susquehanna and Allegheny rivers in Pennsylvania and the Cuyahoga and Muskingum rivers in Ohio. The teachings of the prophet were widely known throughout the tribes of the frontier. Pontiac, the famed Ottawa chief, saw in the prophet's message divine authority for his own attempts to unite the frontier tribes. Through Pontiac, Neolin affected the policies of nearly twenty tribes from Lake Ontario to the Mississippi, including among them the Ojibwa, Ottawa, Potawatomi, Seneca, Huron, Miami, Shawnee, and Delaware. Pontiac may have tempered Neolin's message somewhat by affirming the rights of the French and opposing the British. Nevertheless, whatever setbacks the British suffered during the 1760s west of the Alleghenies were the result not only of Pontiac's leadership but also of the appeal of the Delaware Prophet's message.

This message came from a great dream-vision journey of the prophet to the mountain home of the Master of Life, or Great Spirit. The Master instructed him to tell the people that they must give up their drunkenness, sexual promiscuity, internecine fighting, witchcraft, and medicine songs dedicated to the evil spirit. In addition, they were to cast off all of the influences of the whites and return to hunting with bow and arrow. Ritually, they were to purify themselves through sexual abstinence and the use of emetics, and they were to reinstitute sacrifices. These reforms would result in a revitalization of their power that would enable them to drive the whites from the continent.

The Master of Life also gave the prophet a stick on which was written a prayer, in native hieroglyphs, to be recited by all of his followers every morning and evening. John Heckewelder, a Moravian missionary who lived with the Delaware at this time, reported seeing a map used by the prophet in his preaching. In the center of the map was a square that represented the dwelling place of the Great Spirit. This land, full of game and forests, had been the goal of the soul's journey after death. Now, however, it was all but inaccessible because of the barriers set by the whites, and only a very few souls could reach that land. Most fell into the hands of the evil one when attempting to overcome these barriers and were taken to his land of emaciated game animals and parched soil.

East of the inner square the prophet had drawn a map of the lands formerly occupied by the Delaware but now in the control of the British. Once the Delaware had dwelt beside the ocean and in the coastal areas, where they hunted, farmed, and fished with great delight. Then they allowed the Europeans to settle, gave away or sold their land, and became dependent on the white people's goods. The result of their own follies and English acquisitiveness was migration, fragmentation, and deterioration. If they followed the instructions of the prophet, however, they could have their land and their old ways back again.

Neolin played an essential role in helping his people interpret their situation. In Neolin's image of heaven, the Delaware saw their own recently lost state. In his image of the evil spirit's land, the Delaware perceived the despoiled land of the white settlements. The entry into paradise was not only a difficult eschatological event, it necessitated a historical expulsion of the whites. A further dimension of Neolin's message was not always grasped by Pontiac, that is, that the Great Spirit had allowed the whites to control the land and had taken away game animals as a punishment for the immorality of the Indians. Neolin's map depicted not only the barriers on earth and in heaven but also within the hearts of the people. They had corrupted themselves by their dependence on the whites. More importantly, the increasing dependence on the whites eroded the Indians' previous dependence on the spirit-forces of forest, field, stream, and sky. Only a spiritual purification and moral reform could give them the inner strength to cut loose from the whites and supply them with the capacity to enter again into the paradisal state they had abandoned. The prophet interpreted the social and historical situation using the religious symbolism of death and rebirth. His paradigm allowed for no compromise. This rite of passage from a state of degeneration and chaos to one of rebirth and a new order could not be entered halfheartedly. Nor could it be successful if halted before completion. The recovery of lost innocence and the regaining of lost land were intimately linked.

The prophet had faced squarely the problem that confronted his people, a problem that would continue to confront Native Americans: how does a people recover its identity and pride in the face of social, cultural and economic deterioration and a calculatingly aggressive foe? Yet, Neolin's answer was not necessarily wrong; it came, however, too late. Nevertheless, it was a course that others would follow, even when they knew it was too late, for it seemed to them the only honorable course to take.

BIBLIOGRAPHY

Gregory Evan Dowd's *A Spirited Resistance: The North American Indian Struggle for Unity, 1745–1815* (Johns Hopkins, 1992) masterfully interprets Neolin and other prophets of the era within the context of the Indian worldview and the pressures from Euro-American expansion. Neolin's mission is situated within the context of other Delaware revitalization movements in Anthony F. C. Wallace's "New Religions among the Delaware Indians, 1600–1900," *Southwestern Journal of Anthropology* 12 (1956): 1–21. A paraphrase of Pontiac's version of the prophet's teaching recorded by Robert Navarre, a Frenchman witnessing the siege of Detroit, may be found in Henry R. Schoolcraft's *Algic Researches,* vol. 1 (New York, 1839), pp. 239–248. The prophet's teachings as summarized by a Moravian missionary may be found in John Heckewelder's *History, Manners and Customs of the Indian Nations* (1819; rev. ed., 1876; reprint, New York, 1971). A standard if occasionally biased account of the life of Pontiac and the influence on and use by him of the Delaware Prophet's teaching is Howard H. Peckham's *Pontiac and the Indian Uprising* (Princeton, 1947).

DONALD P. ST. JOHN (1987 AND 2005)

NEOLITHIC RELIGION comprises the religious concepts, cults, and rituals of the early farming communities that sprang up throughout the world in the Early Holocene period (8000–3000 BCE). Unlike the Paleolithic and Mesolithic periods of prehistory, the Neolithic period was characterized by climatic conditions, very similar to those of the present, that directed human activity chiefly to the soil and its fruits. Attention that previously had been focused on stone now shifted to earth, which became not only the basic raw material but a multivalent symbol. These preoccupations gave rise to a specific ideology, to sedentary ways of life and the construction of permanent settlements, to the domestication of plants and animals, and to important technological inventions such as pottery making—developments identified as the basic achievements of the "Neolithic Revolution."

The association of complex ideas and numerous activities with earth was not, however, a process completed rapidly. It took Neolithic communities centuries to learn to use earth as a new material and to find it more necessary, more valuable, and more meaningful than stone. Since, in the Paleolithic and Mesolithic periods, not only everyday activities but complex religious beliefs, cults, rituals, and probably myths were also associated with stone, this "Neolithic Revolution" may be defined, from the point of view of the history of religions, as a gradual process of the desacralization of stone and the sacralization of earth.

Because the basic achievements of the Neolithic period were attained neither simultaneously nor in a particular area only, the chronological and territorial boundaries of the Neolithic world are very flexible. Its beginnings date from the eighth millennium BCE at the earliest, but only in a few comparatively limited and mutually distant territories (in Asia: Palestine, northern Mesopotamia, Thailand, and Japan; in Europe: Crete, Thessaly, and the central Danubian region). It was only in the period between 6500 and 5000 BCE that the Neolithic cultures established themselves and began to expand and influence one another (in the Near East, northern China, southeastern Europe, and the western Mediterranean). The period between 5000 and 3000 BCE was a particularly dynamic one; while Neolithic cultures in the Near East and southeastern Europe began to disintegrate, others began to emerge and take root in northern Africa, southwestern Europe, India, Mesoamerica, and Peru.

Neolithic cultures differed not only in their chronology but, much more important for the study of religion, in their basic content: their methods of production, technological skills, social relations, and achievements in art. The earliest ware was produced in Japan by the Jomon culture during the eighth millennium BCE, long before communities of that region had mastered the cultivation of plants and the domestication of animals. Finds from the Spirit Cave in northern Thailand, however, suggest that the beginnings of the Neolithic period in southeastern Asia (the Hoa Binh culture of the ninth and eighth millennia BCE) was characterized by the cultivation of leguminous plants; pottery was made only from the end of the seventh millennium, and general farming was practiced beginning in the fourth millennium. In northern Mesopotamia, the beginnings of the Neolithic period were marked by the domestication of sheep (as evident at Zawi Chemi during the Shanidar phase, c. 8000 BCE), and in Palestine (Jericho, eighth millennium BCE) and Anatolia (Hacilar, seventh millennium BCE), by the cultivation of grain. In the Iron Gate region of Europe (the Lepenski Vir culture), dogs and pigs were domesticated and grain was cultivated as early as the seventh millennium BCE. These two basic achievements of the "Neolithic Revolution" were fully utilized only in the middle of the sixth millennium BCE.

The Neolithic world was not uniform but, as these diverse developments indicate, varied and very dynamic. It is therefore necessary to modify the general assessment of the period as one in which the economy was limited to farming, social relations were limited to tribal organization and the matriarchate, and religion was confined to a fertility cult and the worship of a supreme female deity (Magna Mater, Mother Earth, and the like). One cannot really speak of a Neolithic religion, but only of Neolithic religions. Lack of evidence that might enable people to define each of these religions does not justify generalization or neglect.

Archaeological artifacts, which constitute the main sources for the study of Neolithic religions, for the most part still lie buried; those that are known are usually fragmented and ambiguous. The material at our disposal documents chiefly the places and objects used for cult and ritual purposes within these religions, rather than the words and gestures that were their most essential and explicit expressions. Two other major obstacles preclude a fuller reconstruction of Neolithic religions: large areas of the world (parts of Australia, South America, and the Pacific islands) are still archaeologically unexplored, and evidence concerning the other spheres of Neolithic life with which religion was closely associated, such as the economy, social relations, and art, is fragmentary.

Attempts have been made to compensate for these limitations and to use, as clues to the meaning of Neolithic religious concepts, cults, and rituals, ethnographic materials related to the psychology and behavior of farmers, the mythology of ancient civilizations, and the scientific reconstruction of the earliest known Indo-European and Semitic languages. Although the usefulness of these approaches should not be denied, the most reliable method is to study the religion of Neolithic communities on the basis of what has been discovered in their settlements and graves. The most relevant of these finds are cultic places and objects, ritual instruments, remains of sacrifices, and various symbols. However, these material expressions of the religious consciousness of Neolithic communities have not been discovered in all Neolithic cultures; in some, they have been documented only sporadically. Accordingly, this narrows down even more the chronological and territorial boundaries within which it is possible to study the origin, distinctive traits, and evolution of Neolithic religious conceptions.

The fullest evidence for the study of Neolithic religion comes from Asia Minor and Europe, the two regions that have been best explored. Within this large territory, which extends from the Persian Gulf and the Caspian Sea to Denmark and the British Isles, three religious spheres can be distinguished: the Near East, southeastern Europe, and the western Mediterranean with northwestern Europe. The remaining regions of Europe either were under the direct influence of these spheres or, as in northeastern Europe, were inhabited by hunting-gathering communities that held on to the traditional religious concepts of the Paleolithic and Mesolithic periods. The latter was also true of communities inhabiting the forest zone of northern Asia, primarily Siberia.

In spite of the scarcity of relevant archaeological finds, three religious spheres can also be distinguished in southern and eastern Asia: the Malay archipelago, northern China and Manchuria, and the Japanese islands with Korea. The inhabited regions of central Asia probably did not constitute a separate religious zone. In Africa, only two Neolithic religious spheres can be distinguished, one in northern Africa and the other in the Nile Valley. Nothing is known of developments south of the Sahara. The situation is similar in the New World, where only one sphere of Neolithic religion, comprising Middle America and the coastal zone of Peru, is known.

Of the nine religious spheres that may be distinguished on the map of the Neolithic world, those in Asia Minor and southeastern Europe were the earliest, the most long-lived, and the most influential. Future investigations will probably show that Neolithic religions in southeastern and eastern Asia were much more specific and influential than present evidence suggests. In the western Mediterranean area and in northwestern Europe, religion acquired specific traits at an early date but began to radiate far and wide only in the Late Neolithic. The other Neolithic religions appeared comparatively late and were mainly of brief duration and local importance.

The Near East. The Neolithic religion of the Near East originated between 8300 and 6500 BCE in the zone of the so-called Fertile Crescent (Palestine, Syria, northern Iraq, and Iran). It flourished between 6500 and 5000 BCE in Anatolia, and disintegrated between 5000 and 3000 BCE in the lowlands of Mesopotamia.

Evidence of a sedentary way of life, a basic trait of the Neolithic period, is clearly discerned in the Natufian culture, which developed in Palestine and Syria between 10,000 and 8300 BCE. Excavations of Natufian settlements have yielded indirect evidence of the use and cultivation of grain (for example, stone mortars, pestles, and sickles). Such evidence, together with the remains of dogs, marks the Natufian as the dawn of Neolithic culture in the Near East (the so-called Proto-Neolithic). Although no objects of an undoubtedly sacred character have been discovered at Natufian sites, it is nevertheless possible to form some idea, on the basis of surviving houses, graves, and art objects, of the religious concepts, cults, and rituals extant in this period.

No cult places have been found in Natufian settlements, with the possible exception of the remains of a large oval structure discovered in Jericho. Its isolated location on virgin soil beside a spring indicates that this may have been a cult site visited at certain times of the year.

That all of the figural representations belonging to this culture were carved from pebbles suggests beliefs associated with water and its creative potential. These representations include schematized human heads from Ain Mallaha and Al-Oued and an "erotic" statuette from Ain Sakhri showing an embracing couple, perhaps illustrating the concept of the "holy marriage." Sexual attributes are not marked on any of the figures, and the relationship of the sexes is expressed in an allusive way: the large stone mortars with circular recipients in their middles probably represent the female principle, as the phallus-shaped stone pestles probably represent the male principle.

These mortars, used for the grinding of grain, were sometimes sunk into the floor of circular houses, next to the hearth (as at Ain Mallaha). They were also frequently associated with burials and used either as grave markers (Wadi Fallah) or as altars around which graves were arranged in a semicircle (Al-Oued). Frequent burial of the dead in pits used for the storage of grain, and the occasional building of hearths above graves (Ain Mallaha) or in cemeteries (Nahal Oren), emphasizes a close connection between the dead and the processes of providing, keeping, and preparing grain food. There is also evidence to suggest some link between certain animals, the dead, and the underworld: for example, a grave in Ain Mallaha contained a human skull framed with the horns of a gazelle; another grave at the same site contained the skeleton of a dog; and seven human skulls, each accompanied by an equid's tooth, were found in Erq el-Ahmar. These finds may indicate that the Natufians believed that ancestors provided all the basic sources of food, that they looked after plants and animals and caused them to multiply.

Evidence of a cult of ancestors is also found in the complex funeral customs of the Natufians, especially in their burial of detached skulls, sometimes grouped in fives or nines. At Ain Mallaha, two graves lay beneath a circle of stone with a diameter of two and one-half meters; upon it a quadrangular hearth was built. A skull and two uppermost vertebrae lay on the hearth, an indication perhaps of human sacrifice. This structure and a hearth in the cemetery at Nahal Oren, with a deposit of ashes one-half meter thick, present reliable evidence of a chthonic cult. Here were altars on which sacrifices were offered to the heroic dead or to the forces governing the underworld. There is, however, no evidence of a transition from the chthonic to an agrarian cult in the Proto-Neolithic period.

Throughout the entire zone of the Fertile Crescent, the period between 8300 and 6500 BCE saw the appearance of villages in which cereals were cultivated and animals domesticated, as is now known through the discovery of remains of barley, wheat, sheep, goats, and pigs at scattered sites. Pottery was very rare, and therefore this period has been termed the Pre-Pottery Neolithic. The number of finds associated with religion is comparatively large, but they were discovered chiefly in Palestine, Syria, and northern Mesopotamia.

The traditional cult of ancestors, manifested primarily in the detachment and special treatment of skulls, developed further, culminating between 7500 and 6500 BCE. Complete burials or detached skulls, sometimes placed in special structures, were discovered beneath the floors of houses in almost all sites from this period. In Mureybet, skulls were placed on clay benches along the walls of the houses, so that they were always within reach. In Jericho, a skull might be covered with a kind of plaster, and then a face, sometimes with individualized features, was modeled upon it. Evidence of the same practice exists at Beisamoun and Tell Ramad (both in Syria), where each plastered skull was placed on a clay support in the form of a seated human figure.

Cult centers discovered in Palestine (Jericho and Beida), in the upper Euphrates Valley (Mureybet), and in western Iran (Ganjadareh) provide more detailed evidence for the religion of the Pre-Pottery Neolithic. In Jericho, two rooms and a structure are supposed to have served cult purposes, primarily because of their unusual shapes: a room with a niche in which a block of volcanic rock stood on a stone support was discovered in a house; a pit filled with ashes was found in the middle of another house, which suggests that some ritual was performed in that place; finally, figurines representing oxen, goats, and, perhaps, pigs were found in a large structure with wooden posts placed in an unusual arrangement. In Beida, a group of three enigmatic oval structures, located some fifty meters distant from the settlement and approached by a paved path, were explored. In the middle of the central structure, a large block of sandstone was set upright; a large slab with a parapet built around the edge lay against the southern wall, and a triangular basin, made of a large slab and partly filled with ashes, soot, and charred animal bones (probably the remains of a sacrifice or a ritual feast), was found outside the wall. In Ganjadareh a room with a niche containing fixed, superimposed rams' skulls was found in the middle of the Neolithic village, and in Mureybet rooms were discovered in which horns of wild oxen, perhaps bucrania (sometimes flanked by the shoulder blades of oxen or asses), were embedded in the walls.

These rooms were mostly house shrines, for they were directly linked with dwelling rooms. Only the group of three oval structures in Beida and the building with wooden posts in Jericho might have been communal shrines. The cult objects from these shrines suggest that the powers venerated in them had not yet acquired an anthropomorphic shape and that their presence was expressed by aniconic forms, mostly by upright stones or the heads of bulls or rams. Two finds only, dating from the very end of the Pre-Pottery Neolithic, might be associated with anthropomorphic deities. These are the remains of three plastered human statues from Jericho and the deposit of at least ten human statues, 80 to 90 centimeters high, and twelve busts, 30 to 45 centimeters high, found in Ain Ghazal (Palestine). The Jericho statues make up a group representing a man, a woman, and a child, possibly a divine triad. The Ain Ghazal statues have stylized bodies but individualized heads; one of them represents a man, and the others have female breasts.

The meaning of these statues, and of the busts that were found surrounding them, is difficult to decipher. Since miniature clay figurines of pregnant women, often deliberately damaged, were also found in Ain Ghazal, we may surmise that the small anthropomorphic figurines were used in fertility rites or in some chthonic-agrarian cult; the larger statues may have been representations of particular deities and therefore objects of the greatest veneration.

The cults performed in individual households became clearly distinct from those in the care of the broader community or of persons specially chosen by the community (priests and priestesses) only in the period of the full consolidation of the Neolithic culture, between 6500 and 5000 BCE. A gap between the sacred and the profane opened during this time, as is evidenced by the very limited number of sacred objects, mainly fragmented anthropomorphic and zoomorphic figurines, found in villages from this period, in conjunction with their high concentration in some settlements; this causes people to speak of religious centers.

The best example of such a center is Çatal Hüyük in Anatolia, where fourteen building horizons, dating from 6300 to 5400 BCE, were discovered. Each of these levels consists of dwelling rooms linked with storage spaces and shrines, of varying size, that contain sacred representations (reliefs and frescoes), stone and clay figurines, and graves of privileged members of the community, possibly priests and priestesses. A certain consistency in the arrangement of representations on walls suggests the existence of a coherent religious concept or myth in which the character and mutual relationship of superior powers were clearly defined. We may assume that the reliefs depicted the divine powers, the frescoes described the sacred activities (religious ceremonies, sacrifices, and ritual scenes), and the statuettes represented the chief actors in the myth. Scenes associated with the world of the dead were always shown on the northern and eastern walls of the shrines, scenes related to the giving of birth were depicted on the western walls, and representations of the goddess and the bull appeared on all of the walls. The most common motifs used in the reliefs were bulls heads and the so-called "twin goddesses," whereas most of the frescoes depicted bulls and vultures. In addition, there were various other symbols, such as representations of the human head, the boar's head, and the female breast. Viewed as a whole, these complex motifs represent the confrontation between the creative powers (the bulls, the twin goddesses) and the destructive forces (the boars, the vultures), and the opposition of birth and death or light and darkness. The statuettes express a similar opposition: they are representations of the great female deity (sometimes in her positive and sometimes in her negative aspect) and of the goddess's son or male consort.

Representations of the same female deity were discovered in the Neolithic settlement of Hacilar (southwestern Anatolia), dating from around 5500 BCE. Statuettes, modeled in a naturalistic way and frequently colored, represent a young or mature woman, naked or clothed, in a standing, seated, or reclining position, sometimes with a child or an animal in her lap or arms. Plastered bulls' heads, as well as stone amulets in the shape of bulls' heads, were also found, but there were no shrines. Some houses, however, had niches with stone slabs, a type of which had a human face with large eyes incised on it. These may have been figures of ancestors, household spirits, the guardians of the family. The later settlements of Hacilar, dating from 5400 to 5000 BCE, yielded two shrines associated with the cult of the dead, standardized feminine statuettes, almost violin-shaped masculine figurines, and anthropomorphic and zoomorphic ritual vessels. Over the following two millennia, the number of figurines decreased, but painted pottery became very common, and its decoration frequently incorporated basic religious concepts.

At the beginning of the fifth millennium BCE, Anatolia lost its importance, and the centers of culture and spiritual life were transferred to Mesopotamia, Khuzestan, and the Transcaspian lowlands. The intensive migratory movements, exploitation of new materials (copper and gold), and increased exchange of goods transformed the traditional religion in almost all of the regions of the Near East and led, at the end of the fourth millennium BCE, to the disintegration of all Neolithic cultures. Although a number of distinct and frequently unrelated cultures emerged in the period between 5000 and 3000 BCE, the religion of this period was characterized by three general features: the separation of the world of the living from the world of the dead, as manifested in the increasing practice of burying the dead in special cemeteries outside the settlements; the separation of cult centers from dwellings and the establishment of communal shrines; and the abandonment of figural representations of deities and the tendency to suggest their potency and activity by means of abstract symbols, signs, and ornaments.

All these traits already are evidenced clearly in the cultures from the first half of the fifth millennium BCE. In northern Mesopotamia (the Halaf-Hassuna-Samarra cultures), the dead were buried mainly outside the settlements, and only children were interred beneath the floors of houses or shrines. Anthropomorphic figurines either disappeared or underwent a change in significance. The number of feminine figurines was comparatively large in the Samarra and Halaf cultures, and costly materials (for example, alabaster) were frequently used for their manufacture, but they were usually placed in graves. Shrines from this period can be identified by their special position in the settlement rather than by their decoration or by the objects found in them. In Eridu (southern Mesopotamia), the shrine formed the nucleus around which the settlement was built; in Pessejik and Dashliji (Transcaspian lowlands), shrines were distinguished not only by their size and rich decoration but also by their position.

In the cultures of the second half of the fifth and the fourth millennium BCE, the processes manifested earlier developed further. In the Al-Ubayyid culture, there is evidence of monumental temples on platforms and of cult places separated from settlements. Some temples (for example, the temple from Layer VIII in Eridu) already resembled ziggurats. No statues or figurines of deities were found in these temples, but there were altars around which rites, probably similar to those shown on the seals of the Gawra type (processions, ritual dances, the adorning of altars, and the like), were performed. Burials were made in cemeteries separated from settlements (Tell Arpachiya, Eridu, Al-Ubayyid), and grave goods included both feminine and masculine figurines as well as a type of figurine representing a woman with a child in her arms. These figurines did not represent deities; rather, they were instruments used in funerary rites. It is obvious that deities became remote and abstract toward the end of the Neolithic period. The religion of the Al-Ubayyid culture, as well as that of other contemporaneous cultures of the Near East, was basically transcendental. In this respect, it anticipates the religion of the early urban civilization of Mesopotamia.

SOUTHEASTERN EUROPE. The Neolithic religion of southeastern Europe was based on local traditions and the religion of the Epi-Paleolithic hunting-gathering communities, the presence of which is attested on numerous sites from Peloponnese to the northern fringe of the Pannonian plain, and from the western shores of the Black Sea to the Alps and the eastern coast of the Adriatic. As early as the twelfth millennium BCE, this extensive territory was incorporated into the sphere of the Mediterranean Gravettian culture, in whose religion the most important artifacts were pebbles colored with red ocher and engraved objects of bone and antler. When the climate became gradually warmer at the end of the ninth millennium BCE, the Tardi-Gravettian culture began to disintegrate. This disintegration had different consequences in different regions: in the southwestern part of the Balkan Peninsula, the traditional culture was impoverished and gradually became extinct; in the Aegean and, particularly, in the Danubian region, it became richer, developing, between 7000 and 6500 BCE, into the culture of the first farming communities.

As in the Near East, the beginning of the Neolithic culture in the Danubian region and the Aegean was marked by a sedentary way of life. The first permanent open-space settlements appeared at the beginning of the eighth millennium BCE, in the central part of the Danubian valley, on low river terraces near large whirlpools abounding in fish. The local Epi-Paleolithic culture began to change rapidly and, at the end of the same millennium, evolved into the Proto-Neolithic Lepenski Vir culture. The shrines of this culture were associated not only with the earliest monumental sculptures in Europe but also with the first achievements in the domestication of plants and animals.

The earliest settlements of the Lepenski Vir culture were small. No places used for cult purposes were discovered in them, but finds did include ritual instruments and pebbles colored with red ocher. Later settlements, dating from the beginning of the seventh millennium BCE, yielded varied material. Some contained a number of specialized implements and a great quantity of bones of fish and game animals, whereas others (for example, Lepenski Vir and Hajdučka Vodenica) had shrines, sculptures made of very large boulders, and graves containing evidence of complex funerary rites. This turning of human faculties toward different goals led, on the one hand, to the transition from a gathering economy to a food-producing one, and, on the other hand, to the appearance of monumental sculptures and the cults and myths associated with them.

A total of 147 dwelling places were discovered at Lepenski Vir, the religious center for the entire central Danubian region between 7000 and 6500 BCE. About fifty of them had small shrines, each consisting of a rectangular hearth surrounded by large stone slabs embedded in a floor made of limestone mortar, an altar with a circular or ellipsoid recipient, and anywhere from one to five sculptures made of large boulders. Directly against the stones surrounding the hearth, one to fifteen triangular openings were sunk into the floor, framed with small slabs of red stone and, sometimes, with human mandibles.

All of these dwelling places with shrines had a uniform ground plan in the form of a truncated sector of a circle, with an angle of about sixty degrees. Skeletons of infants (from one to five) were found beneath the floors, and secondary or partial burials (consisting mainly of skulls) were made within the shrines. In each shrine, the hearth structure and the altar lay on an axis extending from east to west, whereas the dead and the sculptures had a north-south orientation. This fixed orientation implies a clear division of the world. The shrines probably reproduced the world's structure, and the sculptures, both abstract and figural, probably illustrated the myth of its creation. Abstract sculptures were more numerous, and the intertwining on their surfaces of rounded, "female" signs with open, "male" ones suggests the idea of continuous fertilization. The figural sculptures probably represent only what was born out of that intertwining: hybrid, fishlike beings, water spirits, lords of the great river, and primeval ancestors. Regardless of how we interpret these stone figures, their close association with the hearth (on which food was prepared for the living and where sacrifices were offered to the dead) shows that the religion of the Lepenski Vir culture was based on the cult of the domestic hearth.

In the period when religion and art in this region reached their apogee, two major advances were made in the sphere of economy: the cultivation of some sorts of grain and the domestication or selection of some animals (dogs, pigs, deer) were mastered, so that the Lepenski Vir culture assumed the traits of the Pre-Pottery Neolithic. The uniform character of its shrines and sculptures shows that all ancestral knowledge was combined into an integral system and incorporated into cult, myth, and ritual.

In the middle of the seventh millennium BCE, in the period when the cultivation of plants and the keeping of animals were taken out of the ritual context, the Lepenski Vir culture lost its specific traits and developed into the culture of the earliest Danubian farmers, the so-called Starčevo-Körös-Cris culture. Concurrently or a few centuries later, Early Neolithic cultures appeared, either autonomously or as a result of acculturation, in other regions of southeastern Europe as well. However they came into being, an almost uniform sacred world, centered again on the domestic hearth, established itself throughout the whole of southeastern Europe as early as around 6000 BCE.

The sixth millennium was a period of stabilization for Neolithic cultures in southeastern Europe. The most creative regions were Thessaly-Macedonia (the Proto-Sesklo and Sesklo cultures), the Danubian region (the Starčevo culture) and the Maritsa Valley (the Karanovo culture). No shrines have been discovered in any of these regions; the only possible exception is a building in Nea Nikomedeia (Aegean Macedonia), which, because of its large dimensions, was probably a shrine. Some houses in northwestern Macedonia (in Porodin, Madzare, and Zelenikovo) had stoves next to which stood richly decorated clay tables (perhaps altars) and sometimes also clay models of houses with head-shaped chimneys or breast-shaped roofs. These finds, as well as the considerably more modest models of houses from Thessaly and the Danubian region, suggest that the entire house was considered to be under the protection of a household deity.

Anthropomorphic figurines, mostly representing pregnant women, were common only in Thessaly, Macedonia, and the Danubian region, usually at places where utensils for everyday use were also found. Feminine figurines were the more numerous, but they are not earlier than masculine ones. Zoomorphic figurines (mostly representations of oxen and deer) were produced in great numbers, as were amulets, each in the shape of a stylized bull's head. Types of sacrifices can be deduced on the basis of several finds in Crete and Thessaly, where narrow, deep pits filled with ashes, animal bones, and occasional anthropomorphic figurines have been found. These were probably places where sacrifices were offered to chthonic deities, and the figurines were probably placed there as substitutes for human sacrifice, indications of which are evident only in the hilly and marginal areas of southeastern Europe. The cult of the dead was not particularly important. The deceased were buried in contracted position in various places—in the settlements, outside them, or in caves. They were buried without rich gifts and without any fixed orientation. The idea of death apparently did not play an important role in the life of the Neolithic communities of southeastern Europe.

The fifth millennium BCE was the period of the flowering of Neolithic cultures in southeastern Europe, especially in the inland regions of the Balkan Peninsula and in the Pannonian plain, where the Vinča culture was dominant. There were no essential innovations in the religious sphere, but the traditional elements of religious life became more clearly defined and more numerous. There is no evidence of shrines; cultic life was still associated with households, especially with the rooms for the storage and grinding of grain or for the preparation of food. Rooms with bucrania on the walls and an abundance of cult objects have been found on several sites of the Vinča culture. The geographical distribution of these sites shows that in the entire territory of the Vinča culture, covering some 120,000 square kilometers, there were only five or six large settlements that were major religious centers. Vinča itself was certainly one of them, for each change in the sacred objects produced in it was reflected in the surrounding territory up to about one hundred kilometers in diameter. Several thousand anthropomorphic figurines and hundreds of ritual vases, amulets, and various cult instruments have been found at Vinča.

The anthropomorphic figurines were very varied and included naked and clothed human figures, figures in flexed, kneeling, or seated positions, two-headed figures, figures of musicians, and masked figures. Some scholars have seen in them representations of particular deities, such as the Great Goddess, the Bird and Snake Goddess, the Pregnant Vegetation Goddess, and the Year God. But these figurines were not found in ritual contexts, and the differences in their appearances probably resulted from aesthetic rather than religious considerations. Only about five percent of them are clearly defined as feminine or masculine. All examples whose place of discovery is known have been associated with various elements of the household (for instance, the stove, the hearth, the guern, the weaving loom, and the storage pit) or with particular domestic activities. A number of figurines have been found in graves but these are exceptions confined to some local cultures (for example, the Hamangia culture in Dobruja). The fact that they were commonly found together with objects of everyday use, and that they had frequently been fragmented and discarded, suggests that they lost their value once the ritual had been performed and the desired end achieved. These figurines were probably held to incorporate the powers presiding over the household, granary, flocks, or farmed land. The relationship between these powers and the community seems to have been direct, so that the religion of this period was, in fact, a popular one. It was manifested in the performance of rites associated with rain, sowing, reaping, the seasons of the year, birth, sickness, and death, rather than with the veneration of particular deities.

The discovery of copper and gold in the Carpathian Mountains at the end of the fifth millennium BCE, and the later inroads of nomads from the southern Russian steppes, caused a crisis in the old values and goals; as a result, traditional shrines lost some of their importance. In the fourth millennium BCE, the centers of sacred life were transferred to the eastern part of the Balkan Peninsula (the Boian-Gumelnita culture) and to Moldavia and the southwestern Ukraine (the Cucuteni-Tripol'e culture). It was only in this period of crisis that special attention was devoted to the dead—separation of cemeteries from settlements, fixed orientation of burials, exceptionally rich funerary gifts—and that special rooms in the houses were set apart for cult purposes. The cult of the bull continued to be practiced (shrines with bucrania, amulets in the form of bulls' heads) as did the cult of the household hearth (concentration of sacred objects, especially of anthropomorphic figurines, around a stove used for baking bread).

At Căscuiareke (Romania), however, a shrine was found that contained evidence of the cult of the sacred pillar and, possibly, of the sun. A group of miniature clay objects (altars, stools, figurines in positions of adoration, and ritual vessels) with painted decoration (concentric circles, triangles, and spirals) representing the sun and other celestial bodies was discovered at Ovcharevo (Bulgaria). Similar ornaments found on painted ware suggest that religious thought was primarily directed to the sky and was concerned with cosmogony. These ornaments consist of ideograms for the sun, moon, four sides of the world, heavenly spheres, earth, air, fire, and the like. Later they came to include human, animal, and fantastic figures (giants with two pairs of arms, winged dogs, and so on); one may thus surmise that a special mythology was being evolved in southeastern Europe during the fourth millennium BCE. This mythology could not be fully developed: in the middle of the fourth millennium BCE, southeastern Europe was overrun by nomadic horsemen who destroyed the shrines of local farming communities and paralyzed their creativity.

OTHER REGIONS. The separate religious spheres of the Neolithic world were the western Mediterranean with northwestern Europe; the Sahara; the Nile Valley; China; Japan; and Middle America. The hunting-gathering communities of Italy, the Iberian Peninsula, and the adjacent islands became acquainted with the main achievements of the "Neolithic Revolution" at the end of the seventh millennium BCE, but they mostly continued to live in caves and rock shelters and to hold on to ancient customs. In coastal districts and the adjacent hinterlands the preoccupation with earth was first established through pottery making rather than farming. Something of the spiritual life of these communities is reflected in the ornaments on their pottery, which includes such motifs as wavy lines, flamelike patterns, and crescents. These motifs may have symbolized objects of the greatest veneration—the moon, sun, and sea—and may be taken as evidence of the cult of waters and celestial bodies.

In the fifth millennium BCE, influences from the Aegean began to modify the culture of the Apennine Peninsula, while the Iberian peninsula saw the beginning of processes that in time led to the emergence, throughout western and northwestern Europe, of cultures characterized by megalithic tombs for collective burial (such as dolmens, passage graves, and gallery graves) and by sacred architecture consisting of large stone uprights (menhirs) set in parallel alignments or in circles (cromlechs). These were the basic forms, but some other types of sacred stone structures were built in other regions, for example, shrines with a U-shaped plan in Denmark and temples with niches and a central courtyard in Malta. The dominant cult was that of ancestors. Highly stylized idols with large eyes in the form of rosettes (the "all-seeing goddess") have been found in megalithic graves in Spain and Portugal. Special places for sacrificial offerings have also been discovered at certain sites, such as the cemetery in Los Millares, Spain. Gravestones were frequently decorated with abstract engravings and reliefs, more rarely, with representations of snakes, oxen, or double-edged axes. At the end of the Neolithic period, some upright gravestones were modeled in the form of human figures (statue menhirs).

All these megalithic shrines were surrounded by the graves of ancestors; since they were placed far apart, it is certain that they marked sites at which large groups of farming communities gathered on special occasions. The gigantic cromlech Stonehenge (southern England), as well as the alignment of stone monuments in Carnac (Brittany, France), must have attracted thousands of believers who gathered to establish contact with ancestral or divine powers. Malta, with its numerous temples, was probably a holy island (*isola sacra*) to which believers came from all parts of the world to be initiated into the mysteries of the Great Goddess, whose colossal fragmented statue has been discovered under one of the temples. Each Maltese temple has a ground plan in the form of a uterus or the silhouette of the Great Goddess. Figurines with deformed bodies and representations of the so-called sleeping ladies found in these temples suggest that they were also healing places and oracles where believers could, through a period of sojourn (incubation), obtain cures for the body or soul. The very act of walking through these uterus-shaped temples, between alignments, or through the circles of cromlechs had the significance of an initiation.

The religion of the Neolithic populations of Africa was based on quite different concepts and cults. The predominantly pastoral communities of the Sahara left rock paintings and drawings that usually represent oxen or human figures in the position of adoration. Farther east, in Egypt, the first farming communities paid greatest attention to their dead and to the Nile. The earliest Neolithic graves (middle of the fifth millennium BCE) already had a fixed orientation. The dead were buried facing east, with grains of wheat in their mouths (the Merimde culture). In some cases, models of boats and anthropomorphic figurines made of clay or ivory were placed in graves (the Badari culture). Vases from the second half of the fourth millennium BCE (the Naqada II culture) show processions of decorated boats, probably depicting the rite of offering sacrifice to the Nile.

The Neolithic religion in the countries of the Far East also had distinct features. The Yang-shao culture of China seems to have fostered the cult of ancestors and fertility. Judging from motifs on painted ware, an important role was also accorded to the cult of evergreen trees (fir and cypress) and, perhaps, mountaintops. A significant role was accorded as well to the dynamic forces of the universe and cosmic radiation, which influence nature and the destiny of man. The Neolithic population of Japan, which had long remained in complete isolation, also left some traces of its religion. They include enigmatic stone circles—the so-called sundials, with a radius of up to forty-five meters—and figurines with large protruding eyes and stone phalli, sometimes of large dimensions. These represent mere fragments of a Neolithic religion based on the worship of stone, the sun, and the phallus.

The Neolithic religions of the Malay archipelago and of Mesoamerica must have been equally specific, since the development of a Neolithic culture in these regions was specific and autonomous. The archaeological evidence is, however, so slender that it does not permit poeple to form any definite conclusions about the religious ideas of Neolithic communities in these areas.

SEE ALSO Agriculture; Ancestors; Earth; Goddess Worship; Hieros Gamos; Megalithic Religion; Metals and Metallurgy; Prehistoric Religions.

BIBLIOGRAPHY

No comprehensive account of Neolithic religion has yet been written. The general surveys of prehistoric religion devote comparatively little space to Neolithic religion and present only the material from the Neolithic sites in Europe and the Near East; see, for example, E. O. James's *Prehistoric Religion* (London, 1957), Johannes Maringer's *The Gods of Prehistoric Man* (New York, 1960), and Étienne Patte's *Les hommes préhistoriques et la religion* (Paris, 1960). Some new and stimulating ideas concerning Neolithic religion have been introduced by Karl J. Narr in the chapter "Kunst und Religion der Steinzeit und Steinkupferzeit," in his *Handbuch der Urgeschichte*, vol. 2 (Bern, 1975), pp. 655–670, and by Mircea Eliade in *A History of Religious Ideas*, vol. 1 (Chicago, 1978), pp. 29–52 and 114–124.

A rich and systematic collection of documents for the study of Neolithic religion is provided by Hermann Müller-Karpe in his *Handbuch der Vorgeschichte*, vol. 2 (Munich, 1968). Several books discuss, in a rather uncritical way, the problem of the meaning of anthropomorphic and zoomorphic figurines in the Neolithic world: Olaf Höckmann's *Die menschengestaltige Figuralplastik der südosteuropäischen Jungsteinzeit und Steinkupferzeit*, 2 vols. (Hildesheim, 1968); Marija Gimbutas's *The Goddesses and Gods of Old Europe, 6500–3500 B.C.*, rev. ed. (London, 1982); Elena V. Antonova's *Antropomorfnaia skul'ptura drevnikh zemledel'tsev Perednei i Srednei Azii* (Moscow, 1977); and Nándor Kalicz's *Clay Gods* (Budapest, 1980). A correct methodological approach to these problems is demonstrated by Peter J. Ucko in "The Interpretation of Prehistoric Anthropomorphic Figurines," *Journal of the Royal Anthropological Institute* 92 (January-June 1962): 38–54, and in his *Anthropomorphic Figurines from Egypt and Neolithic Crete with Comparative Material from Prehistoric Near East and Mainland Greece* (London, 1968).

The great spiritual centers of the Neolithic world are outlined in detail in Kathleen M. Kenyon's *Digging Up Jericho* (London, 1957), James Mellaart's *Çatal Hüyük* (London, 1967), Jacques Cauvin's *Religions néolithiques de Syro-Palestine* (Paris, 1972), and my own book *Europe's First Monumental Sculpture: New Discoveries at Lepenski Vir* (London, 1972). A. Rybakov's "Kosmogoniia i mifologiia zemledel'tsev eneolita," *Sovetskaia arkheologiia* 1 (1965): 24–47 and 2 (1965): 13–33, is an important contribution to understanding the semantics of pottery decoration. The Neolithic shrines of southeastern Europe are discussed by Vladimir Dumitrescu in "Édifice destiné au culte découvert dans la couche Boian-Spantov de la station-tell de Căsciorele," *Dacia* (Bucharest) 15 (1970): 5–24; by Henrieta Todorova in "Kultszene und Hausmodell aus Ovčarevo," *Thracia* (Sofia) 3 (1974): 39–46; and by Marija Gimbutas in "The Temples of Old Europe," *Archaeology* 33 (November-December 1980): 41–50. Megalithic monuments have been the subject of many recent monographs and papers; however, they discuss the problems of the systematization, distribution, and chronology of these monuments rather than their religious meaning. There are no comprehensive studies of Neolithic religion in eastern and southeastern Asia, although some attention has been devoted to the significance of ornamentation on the pottery of the Yang-shao culture and of figurines from the Jomon period.

New Sources

Cauvin, Jacques. *The Birth of the Gods and the Origins of Agriculture.* Cambridge, 2000.

Gimbutas, Marija Alseikaite, and Miriam Robbins Dexter. *The Living Goddesses.* Berkeley, 1999.

North, John David. *Stonehenge: Neolithic Man and the Cosmos.* London, 1996.

DRAGOSLAV SREJOVIĆ (1987)
Translated from Serbo-Croatian by Veselin Kostić
Revised Bibliography

NEOORTHODOXY. *Neoorthodoxy* is the term used mainly in the English-speaking world to designate a theological movement within Protestantism that began after World War I as a reaction to liberal theology and broadened into diverse attempts to formulate afresh a theology of the Word of God grounded in the witness of holy scripture and informed by the great themes of the Protestant Reformation. Since its leaders had no interest in producing a new orthodoxy along the lines either of seventeenth-century Protestant scholasticism or of twentieth-century fundamentalism, the neoorthodox movement could more accurately be called neo-Reformation theology, but the former term has prevailed in common usage.

In its broadest sense *neoorthodoxy* is an umbrella term that includes a number of diverse but related theologies and theologians. Among them are dialectical theology, or "theology of crisis" in Switzerland and Germany (Karl Barth, Emil Brunner, Friedrich Gogarten, Rudolf Bultmann); motif research at Lund, Sweden (Gustaf Aulén, Anders Nygren); reconstructionist theology in Scotland (John Baillie, Donald M. Baillie, Thomas F. Torrance); and realistic theology, or Christian realism, in the United States (Reinhold Niebuhr, H. Richard Niebuhr, Paul Tillich). Related to these are a multitude of others who, from the 1920s to the 1950s, joined in the tasks of overcoming the weaknesses perceived in liberalism and of finding a more adequate way of expressing the gospel of Jesus Christ in the social setting of the twentieth century.

Because of its emphasis on the Bible as the written witness to God's self-revelation and on the church as the locus of God's continuing revelation, neoorthodoxy provided stimulus and support for two significant parallel developments: the biblical theology movement, which strove to express the unity of scripture, and the ecumenical movement, which was established to foster church unity.

The characteristic themes of neoorthodoxy, as well as its divergent emphases, are found in two prophetic books that shocked theological communities in Europe and America and sparked the neoorthodox movement. The first was the publication in 1919 of *Der Römerbrief (The Epistle to the Romans)* by Karl Barth (1886–1968); the second was the appearance in 1932 of *Moral Man and Immoral Society*, by Reinhold Niebuhr (1892–1971). Both men had had extensive experience in the parish ministry (Barth in the Swiss village of Safenwil, Niebuhr in the American industrial city of Detroit), direct encounter with movements advocating the social responsibility of the churches (Barth with Swiss religious socialism, Niebuhr with the American Social Gospel), education in the liberal tradition (Barth at Berlin and Marburg, Niebuhr at Eden and Yale), probing intellects, and powerful personalities. Barth's commentary on Romans was written with the problem of the preacher in mind; he discovered the message of God's sovereign grace that declares divine judgment upon all human pretension, especially that of bourgeois society and its religion of human perfectibility. Niebuhr's book was written with the problem of the ethicist in mind; he probed the difference between the social behavior of individuals and that of social groups, in light of the Reformation doctrines of sin and justification by faith. Barth's theology tended to move from God to humanity, Niebuhr's from humanity to God; they found their common ground in the centrality of Jesus Christ.

Neoorthodoxy erupted as a fresh theological movement during the period of social upheaval caused by World War I and the Great Depression. Liberal assumptions about human goodness and historical progress were shaken, if not destroyed, by the sudden outbreak of evil in the midst of a modern civilization that had considered itself enlightened and humane. Liberal theology was closely allied with German idealistic philosophy, and therefore assumed a basic continuity between the human and the divine. God was to be found in human consciousness, in the human sense of morality, and in the progressive evolution of human society toward the kingdom of God. Belief in the immanence of the divine within the human self and in world history led to an optimistic view of human progress and a focusing of theological attention upon the religious experience of individual Christians and the historical experience of the religious community. The result was a blending of Christian perspectives with those of so-called modern, scientific society. Liberalism tried to hold on to the Christian tradition while adjusting it to the changing worldview; modernism, a more radical option, accepted the worldview of science and then attempted to reclaim as much of Christianity as possible. As Karl Barth and his colleagues discovered in the midst of a culture in crisis, both liberalism and modernism inevitably distorted biblical faith and the theology of the Protestant reformers.

Barth began to study Paul's *Letter to the Romans* because of his disillusionment with the theology and ethics of his liberal theological professors in Germany, especially after one "black day" in August 1914 when he learned that they, together with other intellectuals, had declared their support for Kaiser Wilhelm's war policy. In Paul's letter to the Romans Barth discovered what he later referred to as "the strange new world within the Bible," a world concerned not with the right human thoughts about God but with the right divine thoughts about humans, not with what people should say about God but with what God says to people, not with how people can find God but with the way God has taken to find people. The Bible speaks not of human religious experience but of God—God's sovereignty, God's glory, God's incomprehensible love, God's covenant with humankind, sealed once and for all in Jesus Christ.

Barth likened the 1919 edition of his commentary on *Romans* to the unexpected ringing of a church bell at night. It awakened the theological world, especially in postwar Germany, and won Barth an invitation to teach theology at the university at Göttingen. He accepted the position in 1922; the same year he published a completely rewritten, more radical second edition of *The Epistle to the Romans.*

Other theologians had come to similar conclusions about the inadequacy of liberal theology. In 1923 another Swiss Reformed pastor, Eduard Thurneysen (1888–1974), and a German Lutheran pastor, Friedrich Gogarten (1887–1967), joined Barth in publishing the journal *Zwischen den Zeiten* (Between the times) as the organ of their movement. Soon another Swiss pastor, Emil Brunner (1889–1966), and a German Lutheran New Testament professor, Rudolf Bultmann (1884–1976), began contributing articles to the journal. All of these prominent collaborators eventually attained professorships, so that the neoorthodox movement, which had begun in the pastorate, gradually reached the universities. From there its influence spread abroad, especially to Scandinavia and Scotland, and then to the United States. Between the two world wars, neoorthodoxy was the dominant force in Protestant theology and was influential in Roman Catholic and Orthodox circles as well. Despite serious theological divisions that caused them to cease publishing *Zwischen den Zeiten* in 1933, the originators of the movement and their followers remained united in their opposition to certain elements of liberalism and in their commitment to a theology of the Word of God.

Since neoorthodoxy began as a reaction within liberal theology and at first intended to provide a mere corrective, it is not surprising that the movement retained some of its liberal heritage: respect for the scientific method of investigating the natural world, acceptance of historical-critical research on the Bible, and aversion to metaphysics and natural theology. Nevertheless, the following characteristic emphases of neoorthodoxy were all formulated in opposition to positions common in liberal theology:

1. the transcendence and otherness of God instead of God's immanence in nature and history, and thus a fundamental discontinuity between the divine and the human that can be overcome by God alone;
2. divine revelation rather than human religious experience as the source of the knowledge of God, and thus the Word of God—incarnate in Jesus Christ, attested in scripture, and proclaimed in the church—as the seat of authority for Christian thought and action;
3. the Christ of faith rather than the Jesus of history as the basis and/or object of Christian faith, and thus the acceptance of the conclusion of the eschatological interpretation of the New Testament that the quest for "the historical Jesus" is fruitless and unnecessary;
4. the meaning of history as hidden and thus not to be viewed as a progressive movement in which humans cooperate in the building of the kingdom of God; rather, Christ provides the only clue to history's ultimate meaning, and the kingdom of God is an eschatological event that depends solely upon the action of God;
5. sin as a rebellion against God caused by the abuse of human freedom rather than a result of human ignorance or failure to curb natural impulses; thus, the self-centeredness and alienation resulting from sin cannot be overcome by education but only by an act of divine forgiveness that calls forth repentance and new life.

Behind the rise of neoorthodoxy lay a number of factors. First was the general cultural crisis of Western bourgeois society that was reflected in two world wars. The nineteenth century's optimistic view of the future, based on scientific advances, evolutionary theory, and idealistic philosophy, was seriously undermined by historical events. There were other important factors as well: scholarly investigations of the New Testament that established apocalyptic eschatology as the framework for interpreting Jesus and his message of the kingdom of God and viewed the Gospels as products of the early church for preaching and worship rather than as biographies of Jesus; the thesis of Martin Kähler (1835–1912) that church and faith are dependent not on the results of historical inquiry into the life of the so-called historical Jesus but on the preaching of the early church's kerygma of the risen Christ, who is known in faith; the renaissance of interest in the study of the theology of the Protestant reformers, especially of Luther; the writings and preaching of Christian socialists (on the continent, Christoph Blumhardt, Leonhard Ragaz, Hermann Kutter; in America, Walter Rauschenbusch); the literary explorers of the ambiguity of human existence, such as Fyodor Dostoevsky (1821–1881) and, above all, Søren Kierkegaard (1813–1855), the Danish "father of existentialism," whose writings were first translated during the early decades of the twentieth century; and the personalistic philosophy of Ferdinand Ebner (1882–1931) and Martin Buber (1878–1965), who insisted that God always remains a subject with whom humans can have an I-Thou, but never an I-It, relationship.

All these factors supported the neoorthodox attack on the nineteenth century's legacy of anthropocentric religion and helped to turn the church's attention to the God of the Bible, who is "wholly other" than the world and whose word enters the world "from outside" and never comes under the control of humans—not even in the sphere of religion. Inspired by his biblical studies, by the religious socialists' critique of present-day society in the light of God's coming kingdom, and by Kierkegaard's message of the infinite qualitative difference between the eternal God and finite, sinful humanity, Barth led the attack on the pious religiosity and cultural captivity of the church. He emphasized the "Godness" of God (God is not "man writ large"), the difference between the Word of God and the word of humans, and the judgment (*Krisis*) that God's word pronounces on human pretension and hypocrisy, whether in civil or religious affairs. Barth stressed that God pronounces a No to human sinfulness, but in and through that No comes the unexpected and incomparable Yes of God's mercy and forgiveness. This word of judgment and grace, which breaks into the world "from above," he insisted, can be understood by humankind in history only in a dialectical manner, and this in two senses: first, as the dialectical relation between eternity and time, and, second, as the dialectical movement from God's No to God's Yes.

Barth's appeal to revelation and his attack on the psychologism and historicism of liberal theology generated early support from Gogarten, Brunner, Bultmann, and even Tillich (1886–1965), but it soon became evident that they disagreed with Barth's stringent opposition to natural theology and with what some considered to be an unwarranted supernaturalism. Each in his own way declared the dialectic to be not between two separate worlds (God's and ours) but within human existence (unfaith and faith, the "old man" and the new). Thus each affirmed the necessity of incorporating into theology an analysis of human existence prior to faith, whether it be based on a personalist philosophy of I-Thou relationships (Gogarten), on the phenomenon of human "respondability" as the formal image of God that remains even in sinful humanity (Brunner), or on a human "preunderstanding" derived from existentialist philosophy (Bultmann and Tillich). In response, Barth, who in his early work had agreed that God's self-revelation was "the answer to human existence," determined henceforth to free his theology from any dependence on an analysis of the "existential question of man" and to base it solely on God's self-revelation in *one* man: Jesus Christ.

Subsequent events in Germany tended to confirm Barth's suspicion of any theology that appealed to a revelation of God "outside Christ," in the natural order or in history. With the rise of Nazism, the so-called German Christians hailed the advent of Hitler and his policies as a new revelation of God. Their attempt to blend Nazism with Christianity was decisively repudiated at a meeting of the representatives of the Lutheran and Reformed traditions at Barmen in 1934, when it was declared that the Christian church must listen to Jesus Christ as the one Word of God, and to him alone.

Barth's split with Gogarten over the latter's initial support of the German Christians led to the cessation of publication of *Zwischen den Zeiten* in 1933, and the following year Barth repudiated Brunner's call for the development of a Christian natural theology. Thenceforth this group of "dialectical theologians," who had found their closest unity in what they opposed, followed their own paths toward mature theological positions that in many respects differed markedly and yet in the broad perspective of theological history still shared the basic characteristics of neoorthodoxy.

Barth's *Kirchliche Dogmatik* (Church dogmatics), consisting of thirteen volumes originally published between 1932 and 1967, represents the premier intellectual expression of neoorthodoxy. In it Barth conducted a critical examination of the church's present teaching in the light of the scriptural attestation to God's self-revealing Word become flesh in the man Jesus of Nazareth. While not relinquishing his earlier stress on the deity of God, Barth more and more centered his focus on the "humanity of God," that is, on the triune God's covenental relationship with humankind that is fulfilled in Jesus Christ, in whose person one encounters both the true God as humanity's loyal partner and the true human being as God's loyal partner. God and humankind are thus reconciled in Christ, and those who respond to God's word of free, self-giving love become participants in Christ's earthly, historical body—the church—and witnesses of the Word to the world. Barth's biblical, Christ-centered theology reinterprets for today all of the doctrinal themes of classic Protestantism: God's sovereign grace, the lostness of humankind, Christ's reconciling deed, and renewed life under the rule of God.

Brunner, whose apologetic, or "eristic," interest on behalf of the church's mission was expressed in a number of theological and ethical monographs, ultimately summarized his theology in a three-volume *Dogmatik* (1946–1960), which is representative of neoorthodox thinking. He emphasized that for sinners who are living in contradiction to their true being, truth comes in the personal encounter with the Word of God that evokes the response of faith and new life in the church, which he considered to be a spiritual community rather than an institution.

Unlike Barth and Brunner, both of whom were in the Swiss Reformed tradition, Bultmann and Gogarten were German Lutherans who, ostensibly guided in their thinking by Luther and the apostle Paul, emphasized the nonobjective character of the revelatory event of faith. For Bultmann, whose *Theologie des Neuen Testaments* (1948–1953) sets forth a demythologized, or existentialist, interpretation of the New Testament, the event of faith produces a new self-understanding that enables the believer to live authentically in the present. Gogarten, who after World War II produced a number of significant books on the relation of Christian faith to secularism, proposed in his magnum opus, *Der Mensch zwischen Gott und Welt* (1952), that the Christian gospel itself leads to a secularizing of the world insofar as it depopulates the world of its "principalities and powers" and calls humans to assume the responsibility of ordering and caring for the world as mature sons and daughters of God.

Echoes of continental neoorthodoxy in Great Britain were strongest in Scotland, where John Baillie (1886–1960) entered into the debate between Barth and Brunner over natural theology in his book *Our Knowledge of God* (1939); his brother Donald M. Baillie (1887–1954) wrote a profound essay on incarnation and atonement, entitled *God Was in Christ* (1948), in which these doctrines were interpreted as "paradoxes of faith." In Swedish Lutheranism, neoorthodoxy is represented by two studies: the seminal treatise of Anders Nygren (1890–1978), *Eros och Agape* (1930, 1936), in which Nygren stressed the radical difference between *agapē* as God's self-giving love and eros as human love fueled by desire; and the monograph of Gustaf Aulén (1879–1977), *Den kristna försoningstanken* (1930), translated as *Christus Victor*, which argued for the superiority of the classic view of the atonement held by Irenaeus and Luther over Latin and moral-influence theories.

Reinhold Niebuhr and his brother H. Richard Niebuhr (1894–1962), both Christian ethicists, led the neoorthodox battle against liberalism in the United States. Influenced by the Augustinian-Lutheran understanding of the profundity of sin, Reinhold Niebuhr probed the Christian understanding of humankind in his two volumes, *The Nature and Destiny of Man* (1941, 1943). His realism regarding sin, especially as it is manifested in the structures of society, plus his keen sense of God's action in history, made his writings significant for both church and political constituencies. H. Richard Niebuhr in his best-known book, *Christ and Culture* (1951), applied his knowledge of sociology and theology to illuminate the relationship between faith and culture. The thought of both Niebuhrs was enriched by their association with Tillich, who emigrated to America in 1933. In his three-volume *Systematic Theology* (1951–1963), Tillich attempted to correlate the questions raised in modern culture with the answers provided in the Christian tradition.

By the end of the 1950s the influence of neoorthodoxy had begun to wane. Critics questioned its sharp separation of sacred history from world history, its pronounced discontinuity between Christianity and humanity's secular experience, its seeming lack of interest in the historical Jesus, its tendency to collapse eschatology into Christology, its failure to address sufficiently the challenge of world religions, and the inadequacy of its answers to the ethical problems of a nuclear age. In spite of these questions, however, all subsequent theology has acknowledged its enormous indebtedness to neoorthodoxy, realizing that it can ignore the neoorthodox legacy only at its own peril.

SEE ALSO Barth, Karl; Brunner, Emil; Bultmann, Rudolf; Modernism, article on Christian Modernism; Niebuhr, Reinhold; Protestantism; Tillich, Paul Johannes.

BIBLIOGRAPHY

Important primary resources regarding the beginnings of neoorthodoxy, beyond Karl Barth's *Epistle to the Romans*, translated by Edwyn C. Hoskyns (Oxford, 1933) and Reinhold Niebuhr's *Moral Man and Immoral Society* (New York, 1932), mentioned above, are the following: *The Beginnings of Dialectic Theology*, vol. 1, edited by James M. Robinson and translated by Keith R. Crim and Louis De Grazia (Richmond, 1968); Karl Barth's *The Word of God and the Word of Man*, translated by Douglas Horton (New York, 1928); Brunner's *The Theology of Crisis* (New York, 1929); Rudolf Bultmann's *Faith and Understanding*, vol. 1, edited by Robert W. Funk and translated by Louise Pettibone Smith (New York and Evanston, Ill., 1969); Reinhold Niebuhr's *An Interpretation of Christian Ethics* (New York, 1935); and Paul Tillich's *The Religious Situation*, translated by H. Richard Niebuhr (New York, 1932).

The best systematic expressions of neoorthodox theology are found in the following works: Karl Barth's *Church Dogmatics*, 13 vols. plus index, edited by G. W. Bromiley and T. F. Torrance (Edinburgh, 1936–1977); H. Emil Brunner's *Dogmatics*, 3 vols., translated by Olive Wyon (vols. 1–2) and David Cairns (vol. 3) (Philadelphia, 1950–1962); Gustaf Aulén's *The Faith of the Christian Church*, translated from the fifth Swedish edition by Eric H. Wahlstrom (Philadelphia, 1960); Paul Tillich's *Systematic Theology*, 3 vols. (Chicago, 1951–1963); Reinhold Niebuhr's *The Nature and Destiny of Man*, 2 vols. (New York, 1941, 1943); and Rudolf Bultmann's *Theology of the New Testament*, 2 vols., translated by Kendrick Grobel (New York, 1951, 1955).

Distinguished writings on particular themes are Gustaf Aulén's *Christus Victor: An Historical Study of the Three Main Types of the Idea of the Atonement*, translated by A. G. Hebert (1931; reprint, New York, 1969); Anders Nygren's *Agape and Eros*, pt. 1, *A Study of the Christian Idea of Love*, and pt. 2, *The History of the Christian Idea of Love*, translated by Philip S. Watson (London, 1932, 1939; rev. in 1 vol., Philadelphia, 1953); Friedrich Gogarten's *The Reality of Faith: The Problem of Subjectivism in Theology*, translated by Carl Michalson et al. (Philadelphia, 1959); and Donald M. Baillie's *God Was in Christ: An Essay on Incarnation and Atonement* (New York and London, 1948).

Of the innumerable secondary resources regarding neoorthodoxy and its theologians, the following are recommended as lucid and fair interpretations: James D. Smart's *The Divided Mind of Modern Theology: Karl Barth and Rudolf Bultmann, 1908–1933* (Philadelphia, 1967); Nels F. S. Ferré's *Swedish Contributions to Modern Theology* (New York, 1939); Mary Frances Thelen's *Man as Sinner in Contemporary American Realistic Theology* (New York, 1946); John B. Cobb, Jr.'s *Living Options in Protestant Theology: A Survey of Methods* (Philadelphia, 1962); Christof Gestrich's *Neuzeitliches Denken und die Spaltung der dialektischen Theologie: Zur Frage der natürlichen Theologie* (Tübingen, 1977); James C. Livingston's *Modern Christian Thought: From the Enlightenment to Vatican II* (New York, 1971), chaps. 11, 12, and 15; Alasdair I. C. Heron's *A Century of Protestant Theology* (Philadelphia, 1980), chaps. 3–6; and the essays on individual theologians in *A Handbook of Christian Theologians*, edited by Dean G. Peerman and Martin E. Marty (Cleveland, 1965).

New Sources

Cross, Terry L. *Dialectic in Karl Barth's Doctrine of God.* New York, 2001.

Dorrien, Gary J. *The Baritone Revolt in Modern Theology: Theology without Weapons.* Louisville, 2000.

Gilkey, Langdon Brown. *On Niebuhr: A Theological Study.* Chicago, 2001.

Hart, John W. *Karl Barth vs. Emil Brunner: The Formation and Dissolution of a Theological Alliance.* New York, 2001.

Schuurman, Douglas James. *Creation, Eschaton, and Ethics: The Ethical Significance of the Creation-Eschaton Relation in the Thought of Emil Brunner and Jürgen Moltmann.* New York, 1991.

Warren, Heather A. *Theologians of a New World Order: Reinhold Niebuhr and the Christian Realists.* New York, 1997.

Webster, John, ed. *The Cambridge Companion to Karl Barth.* Cambridge, U.K., and New York, 2000.

JOHN D. GODSEY (1987)
Revised Bibliography

NEOPAGANISM. The term *Neopagan* covers a wide variety of traditions that include re-creations of ancient Celtic Druidism (a British organization of sun worshippers who gathered in sacred groves), Wicca or Witchcraft, ceremonial magic, and neoshamanism (revivals of ecstatic journeys into the spirit world in indigenous and pre-Christian cultures). Neopaganism's historical origins lie in nineteenth-century religious movements such as Theosophy, folk practices such as tarot and astrology, studies in folklore and anthropology, the theatrical rituals of an Edwardian occult group called the Order of the Golden Dawn, and the countercultural milieu of North America in the 1960s. Neopagans' images of god and goddess emerged from nineteenth-century British folklore and literature and were influenced by the armchair anthropology of scholars like Sir James Frazer (1854–1941), author of the sweeping *Golden Bough* (1890), and the mythology of Robert Graves (1895–1985), author of *The White Goddess* (1948). In Europe, contemporary pagan organizations usually claim a lineage that is ancient and unbroken, often tied to nationalism and ethnic pride. American, Canadian, British, and Australian "Neopagan" communities differ in that they have been influenced by feminist and environmentalist movements and are self-conscious revivals created to be egalitarian and individualistic.

HERITAGE. Neopagans tend to emphasize newness, creativity, imagination, and invention over tradition, creed, established doctrine, and institutionalized religion, but they also claim ancient traditions as their heritage. Neopaganism did not emerge directly from ancient pagan cultures, even though a few Neopagans would argue that their religion descended through the centuries from a pre-Christian goddess religion. According to scholarly consensus, there is no direct lineage from ancient goddess cultures to Neopaganism. Contemporary Pagans (*pagan* was originally a term that referred to non-Christians or country dwellers) are "neo" in the sense that they are revising and updating what they can learn from ancient traditions to meet the needs of modern people. They believe that, in some aspects of life, ancient cultures have much to teach contemporary people, such as respect for the earth and maintaining a balance between humans and nature. They search for alternatives to the gods they were raised with by looking to Asian and Native American religions, and they claim that spiritual beings from other cultures are more accessible to humans than the Western monotheistic god.

The various forms of Neopaganism share a desire to revive ancient pre-Christian nature religions. In the process of creating new religions in the cast of old ones, Neopagans borrow from Native American and other available religious cultures. They tend to be tolerant of eclectic uses of other cultures' myths and traditions, but borrowing from Native American religions has been more controversial. Some Neopagans, for instance, argue that "white people" should only borrow myths and deities from their "own" cultural heritage, such as Witchcraft or ancient Druidism of the British Isles. Druids, for instance, often learn ancient Celtic languages and focus on their roles as caretakers of the woods. Neopagans who are intrigued by specific ancient cultures look to Tibetan, Greek, West African, Roman, and Egyptian pantheons. They find ritual texts, usually in translation, and fashion their rituals after mythological stories, such as the descent of the goddess Persephone into the underworld. Neopagans dressed as Aphrodite and Dionysos put in appearances at

Neopagan festivals, and festival rituals encourage participants to explore divine archetypes from ancient pantheons of deities.

Witches, or "Wiccans," form the largest religious culture under the Neopagan umbrella and include, at one extreme, separatist feminist Witches who worship a great goddess in women-only covens, and at the other, traditional Gardnerian Witches who worship a god and a goddess together, claim to have the oldest lineage, and pass down their rituals from teachers to students who are instructed to perform them in exactly the same way. Gardnerian rituals emphasize the dual nature of divinity in the form of a paired god and goddess. An increasingly common kind of Witch is the man or woman who is an "eclectic Witch" or "Wiccan" and borrows from British traditional Witchcraft as well as from a variety of other religious cultures. Witches are sometimes trained and initiated through covens, but they are also self-taught or guided by correspondence courses and books, like Raymond Buckland's (1934–) *Complete Book of Witchcraft* (1986), which includes lists of ritual tools, directions for how to make ritual robes, simple explanations of Witchcraft's moral principles, and guidelines for basic rituals. Do-it-yourself Witchcraft has to some extent replaced traditional covens that included several levels of initiation. Another popular Neopagan title derived from traditional Wiccan teachings is the feminist Witch Starhawk's *The Spiral Dance* (1979), which encourages individuals to tailor their rituals to suit personal needs and preferences and includes sections on herbal charms, chants, blessings, spells, and myths.

Witches have only a few beliefs that almost all of them adhere to, and these include "The Witches Rede: An it harm none, do what you will" and "The Law of Threefold Effect," the belief that any action a person commits will return to that person threefold. These beliefs, or similar versions of them, are also held by other Neopagans, such as ceremonial magicians and Druids, who share Witchcraft's or Wicca's origins in early twentieth-century British magical groups.

Ceremonial magicians, another important community of Neopagans, are more likely to turn to late-nineteenth- and early twentieth-century occultists for inspiration, especially the writings of the British occultist Aleister Crowley (1875–1947) and the Order of the Golden Dawn (started in 1888), which included the Irish writer William Butler Yeats (1865–1939) among its members. Ceremonial magic also draws heavily on Qabbalah, a Jewish mystical tradition. Ceremonial magicians may blend these traditions with their own interests in religious cultures as diverse as Haitian vodou and Tibetan Buddhism, while others stay within the bounds of organizations like the Ordo Templi Orientis (OTO), which Crowley joined in 1912 and which involves lengthy study and specific rites of initiation. Where ceremonial magicians emphasize their Golden Dawn heritage, Witches identify with the work of the English civil servant Gerald Gardner (1884–1964), whose novel, *High Magic's Aid* (1949), and pseudo-anthropological study of a coven, *Witchcraft Today* (1954), are founding documents for contemporary Witchcraft that have influenced many other Neopagans as well.

Although organizations like the OTO and Gardnerian Witchcraft offer structured guidelines for their members and levels of initiation based on the secret societies of the Freemasons, many Neopagans choose to create their own spiritual practice by drawing on information from a rich array of teachers and traditions. Hierarchical structures were common in the earliest Neopagan groups and still characterize some contemporary Neopagan communities, but by the twenty-first century many ritual groups had become more loosely structured and egalitarian. Elders are still acknowledged for their wisdom and experience but not viewed as all-powerful. One of the ways in which American Neopagans adapt religious traditions of the past and other cultures is to make them more democratic and inclusive, and this is particularly evident in the new rituals they create.

RITUALS. Ritual is the touchstone of Neopagan religious identity and community. Neopagans honor the cycles of nature with rituals at new and full moons and on eight seasonal festivals, including the solstices and equinoxes. Regular rituals are often held in small groups for any number of purposes, including healing and personal spiritual growth. Rituals are usually held in circles and are facilitated by ritual leaders, who explain the purpose of the ritual, invite deities or spirits to be present, monitor the group's energy, and end the ritual in such a way that everyone returns to a normal state of consciousness. Ritual spaces are generally oriented in relation to the four cardinal directions and feature altars that hold statues of deities and symbols of water, air, fire, and earth. Neopagans also periodically hold rituals to mark life passages, including death rites, baby blessings, and marriage vows. Rituals and festivals held as seasonal celebrations include retellings of ancient myths, theater, ritual performances, music, feasting, and storytelling.

Because of their interest in bringing back the past, Neopagans perform Egyptian rites based on ancient texts, dress like Renaissance mages, and engage in Yoruba divination, replicating the original as best they can. In 1993 large numbers of Neopagans attended a festival in Nashville, Tennessee, to honor the goddess Athena, whose statue there is the largest indoor statue in the Western world (according to a report in the Neopagan magazine *Green Egg*). The reconstructed ancient Greek games included a ritual to pay tribute to Athena. Rites of Spring, a Neopagan gathering that is held annually in western Massachusetts, hosts a "Medieval Feast," during which medieval music is played and festivalgoers are served by "wenches" dressed in period costumes. Some men and women have become Neopagans as a result of their interest in historical reenactment and are involved with the Society for Creative Anachronism (SCA), a medieval reenactment society. Historical re-creation and science fiction, especially Robert Heinlein's (1907–1988) *Stranger in a Strange Land* (1961), contribute to the colorful aesthetics of Neopagan rituals and gatherings.

CONNECTION TO NATURE. Because of their close identification of deity with nature, Neopagans often travel from cities and towns to worship in the woods and to establish nature sanctuaries to honor their gods. Several Neopagan organizations have established retreats and sanctuaries, where stone altars and ritual circles are constructed in the woods to facilitate interactions between Neopagans and the natural world. Circle Sanctuary in southwestern Wisconsin is a prominent Neopagan organization that in the 1980s bought land specifically set aside for the enjoyment of the Neopagan community as a retreat and sanctuary from the outside world. Gatherings and other ritual events held at the sanctuary include caring for the land, planting flowers, and learning about local edible plants and the healing properties of herbs. Lothlorien in southern Indiana was also established as a Neopagan retreat and, like Circle, is open to people of all faiths as long as they are tolerant of others. Named after the novelist J. R. R. Tolkien's land of the elves, the Neopagan Lothlorien is envisioned as a magical place, where spiritual beings are free to roam, and it is accessible to humans who treat the land properly. Nature sanctuaries are one way that Neopagans put their religious ideas into practice, because these sites are set up to facilitate ongoing relationships among humans, spiritual beings, and nature.

BELIEFS. Neopagans create rituals and establish nature sanctuaries to provide what they see as much-needed alternatives to other available religious options. They believe their special role is not to maintain tradition, though there may be some who try to do this, but rather to change self and society. They practice "magic" with the understanding that it means changing consciousness in accordance with will, thus taking charge of their lives instead of relying on institutional religions. Because they begin with the assumption that the self is sacred or divine, Neopagans place the responsibility for change with each individual. Even when social and political structures are seen to need changing, the self and not the institution is the agent and locus of change.

Many Neopagans see the self as flawed and the world in which they live as desperately in need of transformation, but their approaches to cultural change vary. According to some Neopagan authors, destructive ways of relating to each other, ongoing interpersonal and global violence, and environmental devastation are some of the ills that need to be addressed as personal healing takes place. That said, it is important to point out that such beliefs do not necessarily lead to social and political activism in Neopagan communities. Neopagans participate in a range of activist activities. On one end of the spectrum is the entirely private pursuit of transformation, in which one consults information in books and on the Internet for guidance. At the other end is involvement with public protest actions, such as the Neopagans who marched as a "living river" at the World Bank meeting protests in Ottawa in 2001 and a group of Witches that gave an "earth-based blessing" when they joined other religious groups at the School of Americas Protest in Columbus, Georgia, that same month. Some Neopagans publicly challenge the American status quo, while others focus inward on personal changes. In contrast, some Neopagans are not pacifists or countercultural activists but instead feel comfortable serving in the military.

Regardless of their political preferences, Neopagans generally have a tendency to privilege internal over external authority and experience over belief. They focus on self-exploration as the best route to truth and knowledge. The explosion of information available on the Internet and in bookstores makes it seem unnecessary to rely on religious elders, though they are still sought out for their ritual experience, charismatic presence, and detailed knowledge of specific traditions. The process of self-exploration through techniques that shift one's consciousness, such as meditation and visualization, is similar across the diverse forms of Neopaganism. Neopagan religious practices are flexible and can be personalized to fit individual needs. This is in part because of how Neopagans understand the relationship between human and divine. Starhawk, for example, teaches that the goddess who guides human beings dwells in the earth and in the world all around. According to her view, the goddess looks at "each of us unique and natural as a snowflake, each of us her own star, her Child, her lover, her beloved, her Self" (Starhawk, 1979, p. 29). This belief, commonly echoed by other Neopagans, is that the self has all the necessary resources for spiritual advancement and that the divine is within as well as without. It is this view that, in part, accounts for the diversity of religious identities among Neopagans.

Neopagan beliefs and practices highlight the centrality of the relationship between humans and nature. An important element of Neopagan theology is the belief in immanence, the idea that divinity permeates the world and runs through other humans, the earth, and all living beings. For some Neopagans, divine power is personified by a great goddess or the planet Gaia, and for others divinity is polytheistic—assorted deities are available to help and teach humans. They may be seen as spirits or gods and goddesses representing the forces of nature or anthropomorphized into archetypes that represent particular aspects of human personality, such as the "wild man" or the "trickster." Neopagans are likely to reject monotheistic understandings of deity, except for those who worship one great goddess or remain nominally Christian or Jewish and believe in one god. Deities are typically identified with forces of nature—the earth goddess Gaia is one example—and the four elements—earth, air, water, and fire—are almost always invoked in Neopagan rituals. Another popular Neopagan deity is the god Pan, who emerged as an archetype in mid-twentieth-century Britain and was incorporated into the magical subculture in the form of a "horned god," paired with a goddess derived from Artemis and other Greek deities. Many Neopagans continue to interact with the god and goddess, while others have returned to Pan in his Greek form. Morning Glory Zell, a Neopagan elder and representative of the Church of All Worlds, explains in her article "Pan" that "our word *panthe-*

ism is derived from that idea, that all Nature is God and that God is all Nature" (Zell, 1994, p. 13).

Neopagans enjoy intimate and highly personalized relationships with spiritual beings. They frequently make contact with the spirit world or another level of reality and communicate with deities through home altars and group rituals. Spiritual beings are approached for help with everyday concerns, like finding jobs and lovers, as well as more generally for spiritual growth and global healing. Neopagans assert that their spirituality is based on experience and a direct relationship with deities. Images of deities are gateways to an experience of other realities, and meditating on them is meant to transport the meditator into another state of consciousness or onto the "astral" plane, an unseen dimension of reality. Because Neopaganism is decentralized and has no founding text or teacher, participants vary greatly in how they understand their interactions with the gods and spirits. Spiritual beings can be images that "take you someplace" or friendly guides leading seekers on spiritual journeys, but what they have in common is being accessible to humans rather than distant.

The Internet has played an important role in popularizing Neopagan traditions and making them accessible to seekers everywhere. Websites for Neopagan organizations abound and are designed to guide the uninitiated to information on the strange religion they heard about in the news. The website of the Covenant of the Goddess, a national ecumenical Neopagan organization, includes resources for teenagers, families, and solitary practitioners as well as schedules of events taking place throughout the country. Websites for Neopagan communities like Circle Sanctuary and the Church of All Worlds have similar content, with the addition of resources on religious freedom and religious persecution, such as Circle's Lady Liberty League. Neopagan Internet discussions have been in existence since the early 1990s, a reflection of the disproportionate technoliteracy among Neopagans. Such groups remain one of the important ways that Neopagans, especially young Neopagans, stay in contact with others who share their spiritual concerns.

Most Neopagans believe in reincarnation (rebirth—the continuity of the soul through many lives) and karma (derived from the Hindu belief that the condition to which each soul is reborn is the result of good or bad actions performed in previous lives), and they look to past lives to help them understand the present. In order to heal wounds from the past and past lives and to live more fully in the present, some Neopagans engage in holistic healing practices, such as herbal therapies, aura cleansing, psychic healing, and massage and other types of body work. Healing practices tend to be focused on cleansing and purifying the self and healing old and new physical and emotional wounds. The goal of these practices is to usher in a more peaceful, tolerant, healthy, and spiritually enlightened society. They consult astrologers and tarot cards, the *I ching* (a type of Chinese divination), and other divinatory techniques for guidance in life choices and to further self-knowledge. They appropriate the spiritual riches of other religious cultures, including Tibetan, Hindu, Taoist, Buddhist, Egyptian, Native-American, and even some Christian beliefs and practices. They put statuettes of the Buddha or Hindu and Egyptian deities on their home altars alongside pentacles, candles, crystals, and goddess figurines. In these ways Neopagans attempt to synthesize new religious identities from the old and the new, drawing from tradition as well as the imagination.

See Also Wicca.

Bibliography

Adler, Margot. *Drawing down the Moon: Witches, Druids, Goddess-Worshippers, and Other Pagans in America Today* (1979). Boston, 1986. The National Public Radio reporter's journalistic account of a wide variety of Neopagan organizations. A general introduction to people, organizations, and central issues of belief and practice in Neopaganism

Buckland, Raymond. *Buckland's Complete Book of Witchcraft.* St. Paul, Minn., 1986. A how-to book for Witches and Neopagans by one of the important founders of Witchcraft in the United States. The book includes directions for setting up altars, making ritual tools, and conducting ritual practices.

Gardner, Gerald B. *Witchcraft Today.* London, 1954. A founding document for contemporary Witchcraft that describes Gardner's knowledge of a folk religion of the English countryside that venerated nature and worshipped a god and a goddess.

Griffin, Wendy, ed. *Daughters of the Goddess: Studies of Healing, Identity, and Empowerment.* Walnut Creek, Calif., 2000. This edited volume includes essays by both scholars and participants on a variety of Neopagan and feminist spiritual practices.

Harvey, Graham. *Contemporary Paganism: Listening People, Speaking Earth.* New York, 1997. A scholarly overview of Neopagan beliefs and practices with a focus on Neopaganism in Great Britain.

Hutton, Ronald. *The Triumph of the Moon: A History of Modern Pagan Witchcraft.* Oxford, and New York, 1999. An exhaustive history of the origins, leading figures, beliefs, and practices of Neopaganism from 1800 to the late 1990s.

Luhrmann, T. M. *Persuasions of the Witch's Craft: Ritual Magic in Contemporary England.* Cambridge, Mass., 1989. A psychological anthropologist reports on her experiences as a participant-observer with an emphasis on psychological explanations for magical beliefs.

Magliocco, Sabina. *Neo-Pagan Sacred Art and Altars: Making Things Whole.* Jackson, Miss., 2001. In this book the folklorist Magliocco describes the role of the arts in Neopagan ritual life and showcases photographs of a wide range of Neopagan altars and artwork.

Pike, Sarah M. *Earthly Bodies, Magical Selves: Contemporary Pagans and the Search for Community.* Berkeley, Calif., 2001. An ethnography of Neopagan rituals and festivals, including discussion of rituals, self-identity, sacred space, and conflicts between Neopagans and other religious cultures.

Salomonsen, Jone. *Enchanted Feminism: Ritual, Gender, and Divinity among the Reclaiming Witches of San Francisco.* London and New York, 2002. The Norwegian theologian Salomonsen focuses on the theology, feminist ideals, and ritual life of one important Neopagan organization.

Starhawk. *The Spiral Dance: A Rebirth of the Ancient Religion of the Great Goddess.* San Francisco, 1979. A description of the basic beliefs and practices of a feminist version of Witchcraft by the Neopagan leader and social activist Starhawk. One of the first Neopagan books to achieve widespread popularity and to function as a kind of sacred text for many women and men discovering Neopaganism for the first time.

Zell, Morning Glory. "Pan." *Green Egg* 27 (1994): 12–13. An essay by one of the leaders of the Neopagan organization the Church of All Worlds that explores the deep connection Neopagans feel between divinity and nature.

SARAH PIKE (2005)

NEOPLATONISM is the Platonic philosophy interpreted by Plotinus (205–270 CE), systematized in his *Enneads* and further developed by others through the sixth century. From the first century BCE, the "divine Plato" had been revived as the supreme religious and theological guide by pagan Middle Platonists; simultaneously Neo-Pythagorean philosophers were active. Plotinus was receptive to both these theistic and apophatic (negative) schools. He liked the Middle Platonist teaching of the transcendence of a Supreme Mind and Being called *theos* (God) possessing the Platonic Forms as divine Ideas. These Ideas became the basis for kataphatic (positive) theology and a doctrine of divine providence for a later period, not for Plotinus.

Realizing that unity must always precede plurality, however, Plotinus taught that the First Principle of reality, the One, or Good, transcends being and thought and is ineffable, indefinable, thereby contradicting Middle Platonism. This theory, original with Plotinus, was repeated by his pagan successors, especially Iamblichus and Proclus, but not by Porphyry.

Conflict between Christians and pagan philosophers began in the second century with an anti-Christian treatise of the Platonist Celsus, to which the Christian theologian Origen responded in the third century; the opposition continued with Porphyry's fourth-century treatise *Against the Christians.* Yet Origen considered philosophy and Plato as natural defenders of some Christian doctrines. By openness to Greek culture but not to Classical Greek religion, the Cappadocian fathers who succeeded Origen fruitfully related Hellenism to Christianity, with increased ability to discuss Christianity with educated pagans.

The Neoplatonic One, or Good, was the object of religious aspiration. It was described as transcendent, infinite, overflowing goodness and spiritual freedom, and reachable through mystical experience. The One pours love (*eros*) into all souls, a love leading each soul, aided by intellectual and moral effort, to mystical union with their Source. The One is present everywhere, and whenever one turns within to identify with one's higher, true self, there is opportunity for a mystical union. Plotinus had frequent mystical experiences (IV.8.1). Neoplatonists separated their pagan philosophy from pagan worship, allowing intellectual Christians to be philosophically educated and yet remain orthodox believers. Nevertheless, one cannot assume that all borrowing between Christians and pagans came from the Christian side. Plotinus's teacher, Ammonius, was reputed to have once been a Christian. In the third century CE the goal of philosophy became more explicitly religious, but according to human reason. The philosopher's role was to guide his followers, without using religious myths and oracles as premises, to the experience of the divine. Christians thereby found in Neoplatonism a purer notion of God than was available in Classical Greek religion.

The *Enneads* present an ordered structure of living reality eternally proceeding from the One and descending in continuous stages from the Divine Intellect, with its living forms, intelligences, through Soul, ruling through World Soul to the forms of bodies, made from formless matter. No dualism here.

DEVELOPMENT OF NEOPLATONIC THEORIES. Post-Plotinian Neoplatonism developed in four stages, largely through modifying the Plotinian structure.

1. The first stage is the teaching of the disciples, Porphyry, Amelius, and Eustochius. Most influential was Porphyry (c. 234–c. 305), who taught a more monistic philosophy than that of Plotinus by conflating the hypostases into a unity of being, life, intelligence, thus departing from Plotinian subordinationism.
2. The fourth-century Syrian and Pergamene schools were influenced by the teaching of Iamblichus (d. 326) that theurgy (ritual magic), invoking demons rather than philosophizing, was the way to God. Iamblichus and followers rejected Plotinus's doctrine of the undescended part of the soul and stressed a need for divine help to reach the Intelligible World. Julian the Apostate (332–363) sought to downgrade Christianity when as a two-year sole Roman emperor he declared Iamblichus's version of Neoplatonism to be the State religion.
3. During the predominance of the fifth and sixth century Athenian school, Neoplatonism became the official teaching of Plato's Academy, the chief member being Proclus (410?–485), who continued pagan worship against imperial policy. For Proclus, theurgy, rather than philosophy, brought salvation to souls. The last head of the Academy when Justinian closed it in 529 was Damascius.
4. The Neoplatonism of the Athenian school was influential over the Alexandrian school (fifth and sixth centuries) of commentators on Plato's and Aristotle's psychology and logic. Both schools depended on Iamblichus. The Alexandrians, however, preferred philosophical scholarship to theurgy.

Early Christian Thought. Plotinus and the Christian Origen, who studied under Ammonius (Saccas), influenced the Cappadocian fathers—Basil of Caesarea, Gregory of Nazianzus, Gregory of Nyssa—who saw Christianity and its mission as the fulfillment of Classical Greek education (*paideia*). Reading the Bible rather than classical Greek literature, they believed, would mold humankind into the form of Christ. Like Neoplatonists, the Eastern Church valued the material world as a theophany, or manifestation of the divine.

Proclus influenced the fifth-century thinker known under the name of the apostle Paul's first Athenian convert, Dionysius the Areopagite, as well as Michael Psellus (1018–1078?), who stimulated the eleventh-century Byzantine renaissance. At the Council of Florence (1438), called to unite Eastern and Western churches, George Plethon (1360–1450), from the Platonic school at Mistra, inspired Cosimo de' Medici to open a Platonic academy in Florence. Its head, Marsilio Ficino (1433–1499), translated Platonic dialogues and the *Enneads* into Latin and wrote commentaries to harmonize Platonic and Chaldean traditions with Christianity. Some scholars consider the Renaissance to have been more Neoplatonic than Platonic, with Aristotle also influential. After the fall of Constantinople (1453), the literary tradition of the Byzantine East was brought to Italy by Greek scholars. The Christian humanism of Erasmus is rooted in the theology of the Greek fathers.

Islamic Neoplatonism. The Alexandrian School, moving to Antioch in 720 CE and to Baghdad in 900, was active with commentaries on Plato and Aristotle. The Arabic interpretation of these two thinkers was affected by two works, purported to be by Aristotle but actually based on the writings of Plotinus and Proclus. The so-called *Theology of Aristotle* was mainly composed of extracts of *Enneads* IV–VI; the *Liber de causis,* attributed to Aristotle, reproduced parts of Proclus's *Elements of Theology.* Accepting the two pseudo works of Aristotle as authentic led the Arabic philosophers to interpret Neoplatonically the actual texts of Aristotle. They interpreted Aristotle's First Principle as an efficient as well as final cause of the world. This helped Muslims to harmonize philosophy with the Qur'ān. Later, under the influence of Ibn Rushd (Averroës), some Muslim philosophers separated philosophy from religion, holding that one could contradict the other. This is the so-called double-truth theory.

Neoplatonism in the Middle Ages. Marius Victorinus (fourth century) in his work on the Trinity against the Arian heresy conflated the Porphyrian triad of Being, Life, Intelligence into Absolute Being at rest and in motion, expressed infinitively as *to einai* (Esse) (To Be), a triad discoverable in the *Sentences* of Porphyry and in the anonymous *Commentary on the Parmenides,* considered by Pierre Hadot (*Porphyre et Victorinus,* 1968) to be authored by Porphyry. Both the *Sentences* and the Parmenides *Commentary* were influenced by the *Chaldaean Oracles* as well as by Middle Platonism. Through Victorinus's translation of some Neoplatonic works (Plotinus/Porphyry) into Latin, Augustine became aware of the spirituality of human souls and of God, thus freeing him from Manichaean materialism. Some Porphyrian positions on the divine triad and on the body-soul union impressed Augustine. In the *City of God* Augustine seems to take Porphyry's version of Neoplatonism as the empire's main pagan philosophy. Boethius was familiar with texts of both Victorinus and of Proclus.

Until Plato's dialogues *Meno* and *Phaedo* were translated into Latin in the twelth century, the western medieval world had a Middle Platonic view of Platonism, their awareness of Platonism coming only from Chalcidius's fourth-century commentary on the *Timaeus,* greatly influenced by Numenius. An indirect influence of Neoplatonism upon medieval thought came through Augustine, Dionysius the Areopagite, and Boethius.

In medieval Jewish thought, Neoplatonism is evident in the Qabbalah and in the teachings of Shelomoh ibn Gebirol (Avicebron) (1021–1058), who developed Plotinus's views on intelligible matter. Maimonides (1135/8–1204) accepted Neoplatonic negative theology while remaining predominantly Aristotelian.

Only in the twelth century also did the West recover the complete Aristotle through translations of the Arabic texts into Latin. But among these texts was the *Theology of Aristotle* (*Enneads*) and *Liber de causis* (Proclus's), attributed by the Arabs to Aristotle. In translating Aristotle's texts, these translators would assume a harmony between them and these two pseudo-texts. Therefore, in the thirteenth century William of Moerbeke translated from the original Greek Aristotle's works. But he also translated Proclus's *Elements of Theology* and his commentaries on the *Parmenides* and *Timaeus.* These translations enabled Thomas Aquinas to identify the *Liber de causis* as non-Aristotelian. This freed Aristotle from the Neoplatonic additions and interpretations of the Muslims. Neoplatonism reached Thomas Aquinas chiefly through Augustine, Dionysius, Boethius, and Proclus. Meister Eckhart (c.1260–1327) embraced Neoplatonism, as indicated by his distinction between God and the unknowable godhead as well as by his doctrine of the uncreated element in the soul. Also influenced by Neoplatonism and Dionysius were the other Rhineland mystics, Tauler (c. 1300–1361) and Suso (1295–1366), as were Nicholas of Cusa and Giordano Bruno.

Neoplatonism in Modern Thought. Neoplatonism may be lurking in the background of Descartes's philosophy of consciousness, although Plotinus made room for a subconscious and superconscious activity as more significant than ordinary consciousness. Neoplatonism is present in the Cambridge Platonists, Henry More (1614–1687) and Ralph Cudworth (1617–1688), as well as in Berkeley's *Siris.* It is detectable in Spenser, Coleridge, Blake, and Yeats. It is evident in Spinoza's monism and in Leibniz's monadism. In the nineteenth century Schelling learned from Plotinus, and Hegel from Proclus. In the twentieth century Bergson attempted the reconciliation of Plotinus's philosophy of soul with modern science.

Only in the nineteenth century was Plato recognized for his authentic thought and clearly distinguished from Plotinus and his followers who were henceforth called Neoplatonists. Neoplatonism was the first philosophical theology based on religious experience. Although it gave mixed messages regarding the value of the body and the material world, its cosmic religion—the veneration of star-gods—entailed respect for the sensible world. Neoplatonism benefited religion by adocating interiority, negative theology, and both God's transcendence and immanence as ground for mystical experience. Christians and Jews freely borrowed Neoplatonic principles to express revealed truths, those accessible to reason. This made possible dialogue with educated nonbelievers. The presence of an intellectual Greek culture in the empire gave to Christian teaching, expressed in contemporary philosophical concepts, some universality. Christians saw human wisdom as God's own natural revelation before divine Revelation through the Law and the prophets and the teachings of Christ.

Christianity was not Hellenized, but with divine Revelation guiding the choice of Greek concepts, Christianity, at first a Jewish sect, became a world religion. Christians respected the Greek classical tradition, as did the Romans. Through the Christian classicists of the fourth century, such as Augustine in the West and the Cappadocians in the East, classical culture and literature survived and was made available to the future. Philosophy was enriched by Neoplatonic reasoning, but philosophy as a human activity was without saving power. Neither does it even claim to give positive knowledge of an ineffable God. But since "faith seeks understanding," philosophy, and especially Neoplatonic philosophy, contributes greatly to that understanding.

See Also Plotinus.

Bibliography

Armstrong, A. Hilary, ed. *The Cambridge History of Later Greek and Early Medieval Philosophy.* Cambridge, U.K., 1957, 1970.

Armstrong, A. Hilary, and Robert A. Markus. *Christian Faith and Greek Philosophy.* London, 1960. The tension and interplay of revealed doctrine and philosophical ideas, a dialogue that continues.

Blumenthal, Henry J., and Robert A. Markus, eds. *Neoplatonism and Early Christian Thought: Essays in Honor of A. H. Armstrong.* London, 1981. Emphasis on Plotinus's dialogue with his contemporaries, the Neoplatonic background of Augustine, and the encounter between later Neoplatonism and the Christian tradition.

Dodds, E. R. *Pagan and Christian in an Age of Anxiety.* Cambridge, U.K., 1965.

Gersh, S. *Middle Platonism and Neoplatonism: The Latin Tradition.* 2 vols. Notre Dame, Ind., 1986.

Hadot, Pierre. *Porphyre et Victorinus.* Paris, 1970.

Harris, R. Baine, ed. *The Significance of Neoplatonism.* Albany, N.Y., 1976.

Harris, R. Baine, ed. *Neoplatonism and Indian Thought.* Albany, N.Y., 1982.

Lloyd, A. C. *The Anatomy of Neoplatonism.* Oxford, 1990.

O'Meara, Dominic J., ed. *Neoplatonism and Christian Thought.* Norfolk, Va., 1981.

Smith, A. *Porphyry's Place in the Neoplatonic Tradition.* The Hague, 1974.

Victorinus, Marius. *Theological Treatises on the Trinity.* Translated by M. T. Clark. Washington, D.C., 1984.

Wallis, Richard T. *Neoplatonism.* London, 1972. Discusses the interrelationships of all the Neoplatonic schools of thought.

Wallis, Richard T., and J. Bregman, eds. *Neoplatonism and Gnosticism.* Albany, N.Y., 1992.

Whittaker, Thomas. *The Neo-Platonists: A Study in the History of Hellenism,* 4th ed. Hildesheim, 1928, 1968. Before Wallis's book, this was the only survey of Neoplatonism.

Mary T. Clark (1987 and 2005)

NERGAL

NERGAL was a Mesopotamian god of the underworld. *Nergal* (properly, *Nerigal)* is a phonetic rendering of the Sumerian *Enirigal(a)* ("lord of the big city [i.e., the underworld]"). Nergal was also called Meslamtaea ("one who comes out of the Meslam [temple]"). His consort was Ereshkigal ("queen of the big place [i.e., the underworld]"). How he came to be king of the underworld is described in the Akkadian myth *Nergal and Ereshkigal.* His cultic center was Cuthah, in central Babylonia, where his consort was Laz (Akk., *la asu,* "no exit [i.e., the underworld]"), also called Mamma, Mammi, and Mammitum. Because of the complete identity of Nergal with Cuthah, that city's name became synonymous with the underworld.

The myth of *Nergal and Ereshkigal* is preserved in three versions, the first coming from Tell El-Amarna, with two later versions from Sultantepe and Uruk. The story of how Nergal became the husband of Ereshkigal begins with the decision of the heavenly gods to hold a banquet and to send their messenger Kaka to the underworld, so that Ereshkigal (for whom it is impossible to go up to heaven, just as it is impossible for the heavenly gods to descend to the underworld) can receive her due portion of the banquet foods. Kaka makes the journey, presents himself to the gatekeeper, and asks him to open the gate. The latter welcomes him, lets him pass through the seven gates of the underworld, and takes him to see Ereshkigal. Kaka bows before the queen of the underworld and passes on the message he has been given.

Ereshkigal is given greetings from the heavenly gods, and Kaka tells her that the gods of the heavenly pantheon are well. After these conventional greetings the queen of the underworld appoints Namtar to go to heaven to retrieve her portion of the food. After a lacuna in the text, the god Ea severely chastises Nergal for being disrespectful to the messenger from the underworld by not bowing down before him like all the other gods. After another lacuna, we are told Nergal's reply, which is unfortunately fragmentary, but which seems to concern a plan by which Nergal must descend to the underworld, where he would "split his divine character in two." Ea agrees that Nergal should go to the kingdom of Ereshkigal, and advises Nergal not to enter the underworld with hostile intent, but to go to the forest beforehand and cut down various kinds of wood to make a throne to offer to the gods Anu, Ningizzida, and Ea himself. Nergal carries out the orders, builds a throne, and decorates it green, gold, and yellow. Not satisfied with this, Ea further advises Nergal to accept nothing that is offered to him in the underworld, no throne, no food, and no drink, but above all not to look lustfully upon Ereshkigal.

After a gap in the text, there is a description of Nergal's journey to the underworld, which is portrayed as a dark, terrifying place. When he arrives, the gatekeeper makes Nergal wait while he gets instructions. Despite the fragmentary state of the text it is clear that Ereshkigal directs Namtar to identify the newcomer; Namtar looks at the god and recognizes that it is the same one who had offended him. For the first time, Namtar calls the newcomer *Erra* rather than *Nergal*, and speaks about him not in the singular but the plural. Expressing unease, Ereshkigal orders Namtar to let "the gods Erra" enter. Erra passes through the seven gates of the underworld, then comes into the presence of Ereshkigal, immediately bowing down before her. Following his greeting, she offers him a throne, as well as food and drink, and finally, after taking a bath, she shows him her beautiful body. Mindful of Ea's advice, Erra refuses the various offers and does not allow himself to be seduced by the beauty of the goddess.

The next passage is fragmentary and difficult to reconstruct. When the text becomes readable again, the situation is completely reversed: Nergal/Erra gives in to the seductions of Ereshkigal and lies with her for six days. On the seventh day the god tells his lover that he wants to return to heaven for a short time, much to her disappointment. After he has decided upon this course of action, Nergal/Erra goes to the gates of the underworld and gains his freedom through trickery. He returns to heaven, where the gods ask Ea to give him a deformed body, so that Ereshkigal, who will certainly look for him, will be unable to recognize him.

Meanwhile Ereshkigal, unaware that her lover has fled, orders that her house be cleaned in preparation for the wedding, by which the "imprisoned" god will be given a specific role in the underworld. Namtar informs her that all these preparations are pointless because the god from heaven left her realm at dawn. Ereshkigal is in complete despair and laments at length for the love she has lost and the outrage she has suffered. She then orders Namtar to go to heaven and bring back her lover, and furthermore to convey to the gods of heaven the threat that, if this does not happen, she will open the gates of the underworld and let the dead emerge and overrun the earth.

When Namtar enters heaven for the second time, he is welcomed by Ea and the gods bow down before him, but he is unable to identify the sacrilegious god from those present. Namtar returns to the queen and tells her of a strange, bald, cross-eyed, deformed god amongst the divine assembly. Ereshkigal realizes that this is a trick by Ea and sends her herald to seize and bring back the deformed god. The previous scene is repeated: Namtar looks at the gods, one by one, but without success. Meanwhile, Nergal/Erra tries to persuade Ea to have Namtar drink divine water and clean his body, obviously intending to make him one of the heavenly gods.

After another lacuna the text resumes with a conversation between Nergal/Erra and Namtar, from which we learn that the fate of the heavenly god is sealed and he must return to the underworld. Ea apparently chooses the talismans that the god should take with him. Nergal/Erra descends the long stairway of heaven and requests entrance to the underworld, but at each gate the gatekeeper takes a talisman from the visitor. As soon as the god arrives in the presence of Ereshkigal, he smiles at her, then he pulls her from the throne and lies with her again for six days, just as he did during the first visit. On the seventh day, the heavenly gods realize that Nergal/Erra is inextricably bound to the underworld, and An summons his envoy and sends him to Ereshkigal with a message that seems to confirm the new arrangement for the future.

Based upon careful study of two versions of the story, Silvia Maria Chiodi (1998) draws the conclusion that Nergal never actually enters the underworld, but rather his twin brother Erra does so. When the god from heaven goes back to the underworld for the second time, Namtar carefully examines the newcomer, and at this point the scribe inserts a very important piece of information. The god whom Namtar is looking at is not called Nergal, as might be expected, but Erra: "Namtar went and from behind the gate he looked at Erra." Namtar becomes as pale as a tamarisk cutting when he sees Erra, the god who had offended him and had not bowed down before him when he visited heaven. Namtar then rushes to Ereshkigal and reveals the newcomer's identity with these words: "The gods who offended me, now went down to the land of no return."

The use of the plural in reference to Erra in the Uruk version is problematic. This is not an error, however, but probably a device to allow the audience to understand that a god, who is in fact a double, is crossing the threshold of the underworld. In other words, Nergal, in order to try and escape the laws of the underworld, was split in two and became "the Erra," even if he apparently remains a single being. Furthermore, the name that the writer chooses for the god is interesting. He could easily have said that the "gods Nergal" were crossing the threshold of the underworld, but instead prefers, at this precise point in the story, to change the name, as if he wanted to indicate further the change in the status of the god. Besides, if Erra were simply a synonym for Nergal, it would be hard to understand why the person responsible for the myth should swap the two names at this critical moment of the narrative. The Uruk editor uses the plural at this point as well, which fits what was stated previously when he described "the gods" who turned up in the underworld: "now *they* went down to the land of no return."

SEE ALSO Heaven and Hell; Mesopotamian Religions, overview article; Underworld.

BIBLIOGRAPHY

Burns, John B. "Namtaru and Nergal." *Vetus testamentum* 43 (1993): 1–25.

Chiodi, Silvia Maria. "Studi Mesopotamici I: Nergal un dio doppio." *Rivista di studi fenici* 26 (1998): 3–20.

Gurney, Oliver R. "The Sultantepe Tablets, VII: The Myth of Nergal and Ereshkigal." *Anatolian Studies* 10 (1960): 105–137.

Hunger, Hermann. *Spätbabylonische Texte aus Uruk.* Berlin, 1976.

Hutter, Manfred. *Altorientalische Vorstellungen von der Unterwelt: Literar- und religionsgeschichtliche Überlegungen zu "Nergal und Ereshkigal."* Freiburg, Germany, 1985.

Lambert, Wilfred G. "Studies in Nergal." *Bibliotheca orientalis* 30 (1973): 355–363.

Lambert, Wilfred G. "The Theology of Death." In *Death in Mesopotamia,* edited by Bendt Alster, pp. 23–66. Copenhagen, 1980.

Pettinato, Giovanni. *Nergal ed Ereshkigal: Il poema assiro-babilonese degli Inferi.* Rome, 2000.

Saporetti, Claudio. *Nergal ed Ereshkigal: Una storia d'amore e di morte.* Pisa, Italy, 1995.

von Weiher, Egbert. *Der babylonische Gott Nergal.* Neukirchen-Vluyn, Germany, 1971.

DAVID MARCUS (1987)
GIOVANNI PETTINATO (2005)
Translated from Italian by Paul Ellis

NERSĒS OF CLA

NERSĒS OF CLA (1101–1173), also known as Nersēs Clayatsi and Shnorhali; theologian, catholicos, and saint of the Armenian church. Born in the province of Tlouk' in Cilician Armenia (the central part of southern Turkey), Nersēs lost his father at an early age. Together with his elder brother Grigor, he was entrusted to the guardianship of his maternal granduncle, the catholicos Grigor II Vekayaser who commended them to the Monastery of Shoughri. Grigor's successor then placed them under the tutelage of the monk Stepanos Manouk, a renowned scholar and theologian.

Ordained a celibate priest when he was seventeen years old, Nersēs was consecrated a bishop at the age of thirty-five. He then served his church and nation in numerous capacities, including contributing to the establishment of peace in Cilician Armenia. Endowed with a keen mind and a Christian spirit, he became the architect in developing intercommunion and reconciliation between the Armenian and the Greek churches. Following the death of his brother, the catholicos Grigor, Nersēs was consecrated catholicos of the Armenian church in 1166. He died in 1173 and was buried in Hromcla.

Nersēs is considered one of the great literary figures in the ecclesiastical history of the Armenian church. He composed prayers, liturgical songs, and chants, sometimes written acrostically (consisting of thirty-six verses after the order of the Armenian alphabet or according to the alphabetical arrangement that spells his name). Uniquely impressive is Nersēs's prayer, Havatov Khosdovaneem (I Confess with Faith), currently available in thirty-six languages. Chief among his literary achievements is *Vipasanoutyoun,* a novel in poetic form; *Voghb Yedesyo* (Lamentation of Edessa); and commentaries on the first five chapters of the *Gospel of Matthew,* Gregory of Nyssa's discourse *On Evil,* and the discourse of the Neoplatonist Armenian philosopher David the Invincible. Also renowned is *Toukht Enthanrakan,* an exhortation on Christian behavior and a treatise on pastoral theology. It also supplies information concerning the hierarchy of the Armenian church, the stratification of society, and the manner of life in twelfth-century Cilician Armenia.

Nersēs always struggled to maintain the autocephalicity of the Armenian church, defining the important issues facing church unity in eight letters to the Byzantine emperor Manuel I Comnenus (c. 1122–1180). Nersēs remarked that unity cannot come by imposing royal force but through love, tolerance, and humility, thus indirectly warning the Byzantines not to impose their Chalcedonian faith on other churches. He saw the truths of Christianity in the unity of its parts, since no single church may consider the Christian faith its sole possession. His approach regarding unity was slowly finding adherents when his death halted the progress of further negotiations.

Nersēs dominated the thought and orientation of the Armenian church in twelfth-century Cilician Armenia, thus crowning its silver age in literary achievements. In due time, Nersēs received the appellation Shnorhali ("grace-filled") in recognition of his deep Christian faith and accomplishments.

BIBLIOGRAPHY

Nersēs's *Hisous Vordi* (Constantinople, 1824), written in 1152, is a reproduction of the Old and New Testaments in poetic form, containing episodes from church history and ending with the events that are to ensue during the second coming of Christ. It is available in English, translated by Jane S. Wingate, as *Jesus Son* (New York, 1947). *Toukht Enthanrakan* is available in classical Armenian (Jerusalem, 1871) and in vernacular Armenian translated by Anoushavan Vardapet Danialian (Beirut, 1977). For discussion of Nersēs's life, see volume 30 (1973) of the Armenian journal *Echmiadzin.* Mal'achia Ormanian's *Azgapatowm,* 3 vols. (1912–1927; reprint, Beirut, 1959–1961), is a comprehensive study of the Armenian church as well as of the politics of the Armenian nation. Of particular relevance to the study of Nersēs are paragraphs 927, 931, 936, 939, 944, 948–953, 961–992.

AVAK ASADOURIAN (1987)

NERSĒS THE GREAT, a saint of the Armenian church and chief bishop of Armenia from circa 353 to 373. During his youth Nersēs was brought up and educated in Caesarea Mazaca (modern-day Kayseri, Turkey). He was married and served as a chamberlain in the court of King Arshak II of Armenia. Because the office of bishop of Armenia was the patrimony of the family of Gregory the Illuminator, Nersēs's great-great-grandfather, Nersēs was chosen chief bishop and returned to Caesarea to receive episcopal ordination from the metropolitan bishop of that city. He called a council of bishops at Ashtishat, where his see was located. The council established general discipline in the Armenian church and set rules and regulations. At Nersēs's urging, provisions were made to found hospices for the sick, to open schools, to build hospitals, and to establish other benevolent institutions.

The fifth-century sagas of P'awstos Buzand refer to a rift between Nersēs and King Arshak that brought about the downfall of the bishop. The reason for the conflict is said to have been the immoral conduct of the king, who had his Greek wife poisoned and his nephew killed, and then married the latter's wife. The actual reason for the rift, however, was probably political. Nersēs represented the pro-Byzantine faction in Armenia. He had headed a delegation to Constantinople in the mid-fourth century and had reinforced the alliance between the Byzantine empire and his sovereign, who remained faithful to the empire until the treaty of 363, when the emperor Jovian agreed not to interfere in the internal affairs of Armenia and left the country exposed to the Persians. Nersēs was forced to abdicate from his office and was immediately replaced by another bishop, who was probably the candidate of the pro-Persian faction in Armenia. Nersēs reappeared as chief bishop circa 370, when the Byzantines succeeded in restoring the kingdom of Armenia and placed Pap, son of Arshak II, on the throne. During his second tenure of office, Nersēs participated in a council of bishops held at Caesarea in 372. He came into conflict with King Pap, presumably because of the latter's Arian leanings. The king is said to have poisoned Nersēs. This detail, however, is not supported by most sources. Nersēs probably died from natural causes.

BIBLIOGRAPHY

The major source for Nersēs's life is the fifth-century compilation of legends by P'awstos Buzand, *Buzandaran patmut'iwnk'* (Venice, 1889). These are also available in French as volume 1 of Victor Langlois's *Collections des historiens anciens et modernes de l'Arménie* (Paris, 1868) and in German, translated by Max Lauer as *Des Faustus von Byzanz Geschichte Armeniens* (Cologne, 1879). Other useful sources are Mal'achia Ormanian's *The Church of Armenia*, 2d rev. ed. (London, 1955), and Nina Garsoïan's "Quidam Narseus? A Note on the Mission of Nersēs the Great," in *Armeniaca* (Venice, 969).

KRIKOR H. MAKSOUDIAN (1987)

NESTORIAN CHURCH. The proper name of the church that is called Nestorian or Assyrian is the Ancient Church of the East. *Nestorian* is an appellation dating from the fifth century and *Assyrian* from the nineteenth. By *East* is meant those ancient territories lying east of the former Byzantine empire comprising modern-day Iraq, Persia, and the southeastern part of Turkey. These territories had their religious center at Edessa (Orhoi in Syriac), known as Urfa in present-day Turkey. Edessa was the capital of a small Syriac-Aramaic principality ruled by Syriac toparchs (rulers or princes), known also as Abgarites. According to the *Doctrine of Addai*, a late fourth-century church document attributed to Thaddaeus (known in Aramaic as Addai, one of the seventy evangelists and the twin of the apostle Thomas), Thaddaeus, following the Resurrection and at the behest of Christ, went to Edessa and healed its toparch, Abgar V (d. 50 CE). Thaddaeus stayed to preach the gospel, made converts, and ordained his disciple, ʿAggai, a bishop. He then journeyed to and preached the gospel in Mesopotamia, southern Turkey, Iraq, and southwestern Persia.

By the second century, Christianity had spread throughout the East, from Najran in southwestern Arabia, through southern Turkey and Iraq, to southwestern Persia. In the third century, Christianity also spread to the island of Socotra in the Indian Ocean and to Riyordashīr, the capital of Fars in extreme southern Persia, as well as to the Sasanid capital of Seleucia-Ctesiphon, where the bishopric was founded under Phafa. By the latter part of the fifth century, the bishops of Seleucia-Ctesiphon (by that time followers of Nestorius) were claiming that the see had been established by Thaddaeus and his disciple Mari.

The bishop (metropolitan) of Seleucia-Ctesiphon was recognized as being under the jurisdiction of the patriarch of Antioch. At a synod convened in 410 by Marutha of Miya-farqin, who was sent by the emperor and the patriarch, the metropolitan of Seleucia-Ctesiphon was made a catholicos (a church position higher than a metropolitan and lower than a patriarch). Given the authority to ordain bishops in the name of the patriarch of Antioch, and using his new powers to advantage, the catholicos was able to bring under his jurisdiction all the dioceses in the East except the metropolitan see of Riyordashīr. This see remained independent until the ninth century when Catholicos Timothy I (d. 823) brought it under his aegis after offering its metropolitan some special privileges.

Meanwhile, under the Sasanid kings Shāpūr II (309–379) and his brother Ardashīr II (379–383) the Ancient Church of the East suffered persecution and martyrdom because of its ties to the Byzantines whom the Persians considered enemies. Persecution continued sporadically until the conquest of Persia by the Arabs in the first part of the seventh century.

In the first half of the fifth century the Church of the East was rocked by a theological controversy so serious that it resulted in schism. This was the so-called Nestorian controversy. Nestorius, a Syrian by origin, became patriarch of Constantinople in 428. Fully developing the theological implications of the school of Antioch, he taught that Jesus Christ had two distinct natures: divine and human. Nestorius was condemned at the Council of Ephesus in 431 but his teaching spread, and by 451 most of the eastern part of the Church of the East had become "Nestorian," rejecting the Council of Ephesus. By 451 the Nestorians were almost completely cut off from the rest of the patriarchate of Antioch, and Nestorians controlled the see of Seleucia-Ctesiphon.

Between 484 and 486 Bishop Bar Sauma convened several councils that issued new canons for the foundation of the new Nestorian church. Those bishops in the East who did not accept Nestorian teachings met in 487 and ordained Accacius as their catholicos. However, through threats and coercion by Bar Sauma and his group, Accacius yielded to the Nestorians. What gave added strength to the Nestorians in the East is that many students of the celebrated school of Edessa became Nestorian partisans. When the emperor Zeno, in retaliation, closed it in 489, many of these Nestorian students left for Persia, where they spread their beliefs under the protection of the Persian state. Thus, the Church of the East came also to be known as the Persian church. By 498, at the Council of Seleucia, the Nestorians severed forever their ties with the patriarchate of Antioch.

After the Arab conquest of Iraq in the beginning of the seventh century, the Nestorians, like other Christians, became *dhimmīs* under the protection of the Muslims. Under the Abbasid caliphs (750–1258) the Nestorians enjoyed relative peace, and in 762 their catholicoi moved their see to Baghdad, the Abbasid capital. In Baghdad, the Nestorians were the first to promote Greek science and philosophy by translating Greek texts into Syriac and then into Arabic. They were highly favored by the caliphs and were the first to introduce Greek medicine into Baghdad.

Although the Nestorians were generally favored, there were times when they, like other Christians, were persecuted or humiliated by the caliphs. The Nestorian church generally prospered until the fall of Baghdad to the Mongols in 1258, when the widespread disruption in the Middle East drained its vitality. The Nestorian catholicoi left Baghdad and settled in northern Iraq (Kurdistan) in the vicinity of Mosul and Alqosh.

The most detrimental effect of the Muslim conquest on the Nestorian church in the countries lying between Persia and China was that its missionary activity, begun among the Mongols, Turks, and Chinese, was cut off. Eventually the early blossom of Christianity in China died. The inscriptions in both Syriac and Chinese on the stone at Chou-chih, fifty miles southwest of Sian Prefecture, China, containing a long list of Nestorian clergymen, is evidence of the expansion of the Nestorian church in China. Nestorianism also reached the coast of Malabar in South India and made converts among the Christians there. The new converts used the Syriac liturgy and honored the memory of Nestorius and Theodore of Mopsuestia. From 1599 to 1663 they were reconverted to Roman Catholicism through the efforts of Jesuit missionaries. Many however returned to Nestorianism when the power and influence of the Portuguese empire began to fade.

In the fifteenth century the small Nestorian community on the island of Cyprus joined the church of Rome. Power struggles within the ecclesiastical hierarchy of the mother Nestorian church also caused large segments of it to join Rome. The struggle in the East began in 1450 when the catholicos, Shimon Baṣīdi, restricted the election of future catholicoi to men of his own family. This interdiction continued for the next hundred years. After the death of the catholicos in 1551, a group of Nestorians who opposed his successor met in Mosul and chose a monk, Yūḥanna (John) Sūlāqa, to send to Rome to be ordained. Arriving in Rome, Sūlāqa professed the Roman Catholic faith before Pope Julius III, who ordained him a bishop and then a catholicos in April 1553. It is most likely that it was Julius who gave the name *Chaldean* (in reference to ancient Chaldea) to Sūlāqa and his followers; thus was born the "Chaldean" church. Sūlāqa returned to Diyarbakır, Turkey, where he made few converts. He was assassinated by the Kurdish chief of ʿAmadiyya, allegedly at the instigation of his rival, Shimon Bār Māma. Several catholicoi served at Diyarbakır, not all of whom were ordained by popes and whose loyalty to Rome was dubious.

About this time, a Nestorian bishop, Shimon Dinbah, united his congregation with Rome, and the Chaldeans made him their catholicos. He moved his seat from Diyarbakır to Urmia in northern Persia where many Nestorians lived. In 1670 one of his successors renounced the church of Rome, returned to Nestorianism, and was accepted as catholicos by the Nestorian catholicoi, one in Urmia and the other in Alqosh.

In the middle of the eighteenth century a Nestorian bishop, Mar Yūsuf (Joseph) of Diyarbakır, joined the church of Rome and was ordained by the pope as a successor to the line of Sūlāqa as catholicos of the Chaldeans in Diyarbakır. In 1778 a Nestorian bishop, Yūḥanna (John) Hormizd, embraced Roman Catholicism and began to contend for the office of catholicos with his cousin, Mar Eliyya XI of Alqosh. Rome could not ordain Hormizd catholicos of the Chaldean community because Mar Yūsuf was already catholicos in Diyarbakır. When Yūsuf died in 1779, Rome entrusted the Chaldean church to his nephew, Augustine Hindi. Finally, after long waiting and through the machinations of Roman Catholic missionaries, Hormizd was confirmed by Pope Pius VIII as the catholicos of the Chaldean community. By then most of the Nestorians of the plains of Mosul had become Roman Catholics. Since then, the Nestorian community has retreated into the mountains of Kurdistan.

Since 1820 the Protestant churches in the West have taken a rather special interest in the Nestorian communities of the East. The American Presbyterian church became the first to organize missions among them when, in 1830, the Presbyterian Board of Missions sent the first missionaries. The mission headquarters were located in Urmia, where there were doctors as well as a printing press.

The Church of England became involved with the Nestorians when in 1842, George P. Badger, chaplain of the East India Company, was sent to Iraq. He wrote two volumes (published in 1852) on the Nestorians and their church. The interest of the Church of England continued until after World War I and the establishment of the national government of Iraq (1921).

For more than a hundred years (1830–1933), the Nestorian community in Kurdistan and Iraq suffered continuous tragedies. Being Christians they were always prey to Kurdish chieftains, who plundered their villages. The activity and existence of Western missionaries among the Nestorians most probably motivated the Kurds and their patrons, the Ottomans, to agitate against them.

The outbreak of World War I saw the Nestorians hopeful of an eventual Allied victory. This happy consequence would certainly alleviate the persecution aimed at them by both Kurds and Ottomans. Encouraged by the Russian advance into eastern Turkey in 1915, the Nestorians revolted against the Turks and assisted the Russians. But when the Bolshevik revolution erupted and Russia withdrew from the war in 1917, they were in great danger. Consequently, about twenty thousand Nestorians struggled to reach the British lines in Iraq to avoid reprisal by Kurds and Ottomans. With fear of reprisal haunting the rest of the Nestorians of Urmia, in the summer of 1918 some hundred thousand of them attempted to reach the Kermānshāh-Qazvīn region, which was then under British occupation. Less than half made it through; the rest were rounded up and settled by the British authorities in the mountains of northern Iraq.

As a result of their association with the British, the Nestorians ("Assyrians") developed nationalistic feelings. They asserted that the northern part of Iraq, the ancient land of Athur, was their ancestral and rightful home. They fostered the hope of an independent Assyrian state in Iraq. This dream was probably encouraged by minor British army officers, and, in 1919, a group of Assyrians, including many from the United States, submitted a petition to the peace conference in Paris outlining their nationalistic aspirations. There was no response.

After the establishment of national rule in Iraq in 1921, the Iraqi government granted autonomy in internal and religious affairs to the Nestorian community (in northern Iraq) led by their catholicos, Mar Ishā Shimon XXI. But Mar Shimon, barely thirteen years old, was ill advised by members of his household and demanded complete independence from Iraq on the premise that northern Iraq was the ancestral land of the Assyrians. This demand was not acceptable to either Iraq or Britain. The Iraqi government tried to dissuade Mar Shimon from acting as if he were head of a state within a state but failed. Finally, in 1933 it notified the Assyrians either to behave as Iraqi citizens or leave. About a thousand Assyrians decided to leave and crossed the Euphrates into Syria, which was occupied by the French. The French authorities turned them back, where they faced an Iraqi army force. A stray shot was fired, and the Iraqi army used the occasion to massacre most of the Nestorian contingent. Subsequently, Mar Shimon was stripped of his Iraqi nationality and deported to Cyprus. From Cyprus he went to England, and then to the United States, where he became an American citizen.

In 1973 Mar Shimon resigned because of a conflict with his community over his violation of some church rules. After his death in 1975, he was succeeded by Mar Ḥānania Dinkha IV, who was installed in London in 1976 as catholicos patriarch of the Assyrian Church of the East. The Assyrian community, which numbered about 500,000 in 1980, still has many members living in Iraq and Iran, but their greatest concentration is in the United States, especially in Chicago, Illinois. This latter group is mostly composed of immigrants who left Iraq after 1933 and their descendants.

The Nestorian church in the latter part of the twentieth century forms the extreme eastern branch of the Syriac-speaking church of Antioch. Its liturgical language is Syriac-Aramaic with a distinct dialect and script. It recognizes only the first two ecumenical councils and rejects the Council of Ephesus, which condemned Nestorius. Its rite is the Old Eastern Syriac rite, and it has three main liturgies: those of the evangelist Thaddaeus and his disciple Mari, of Nestorius, and of Theodore of Mopsuestia. Other liturgies, such as those of Bar Sauma, Narsai, and Diodore of Tarsus, are presumed lost. The liturgy begins with the practical making and baking of the bread for communion but does not contain the words of institution. The communion is given in both elements, bread and wine. The hierarchy consists of the catholicos, also called patriarch, who always takes the name Mar Shimon. Under him come the metropolitans, bishops, priests, and deacons. The church is essentially iconoclastic, although the Cross is revered. Through the vicissitudes of time, schism, persecution, and apostasy, this once grand church of the East has been reduced to a tiny community, living for the most part in a Western diaspora. It has become a member of the World Council of Churches.

See Also Christianity, article on Christianity in Asia; Nestorianism; Nestorius; Theodore of Mopsuestia.

Bibliography

Perhaps the most important ancient source on the theological teaching and views of Nestorius is the *Bazaar of Heracleides*, translated by Godfrey R. Driver and Leonard Hodgson (Oxford, 1925). Other sources are the "Opera and Literae" of Cyril of Alexandria in *Patrologia Graeca*, edited by J.-P. Migne, vols. 126–127 (Paris, 1859); the *Acts of the Council of Ephesus* in *Sacrorumounciliorum nova et amplissima collec-*

tio, edited by Giovanni Domenico Mansi, vols. 4 and 5 (Florence and Venice, 1758–1798); Giuseppe Simone Assemani's *Bibliotheca Orientalis,* vol. 3, pt. 2 (Rome, 1728); and Friedrich Loofs's *Die Fragmente des Nestorius* (Halle, 1905) and *Nestorius and His Place in the History of Christian Doctrine* (Cambridge, 1914).

The earliest sources on the Nestorian catholicoi are *The Chronicle of Mshiha Zkha,* in *Sources syriaques,* edited by Alphonse Mingana (Leipzig, 1907); *Chronique de Michel le Syrien,* edited by Jean-Baptiste Chabot (Paris, 1890); Bar Hebraeus's *Chronicon ecclesiasticum,* 3 vols., edited by J. B. Abbeloos and T. J. Lamy (Paris, 1872–1877); and *Chronique de Seert, histoire nestorienne* (in Arabic and French), edited by Addai Scher, in *Patrologia Orientalis,* vol. 4 (Paris, 1907).

For the role of the Nestorians in spreading Christianity among the Turks, Mongols, and Chinese, see Alphonse Mingana's "The Early Spread of Christianity in Central Asia and the Far East," *Bulletin of the John Rylands Library* 9 (1925): 297–371; Adolf von Harnack's *The Mission and Expansion of Christianity in the First Three Centuries,* vol. 2, 2d ed. (New York, 1908); and *The Nestorian Monument: An Ancient Record of Christianity in China, with Special Reference to the Expedition of Frits V. Holm,* edited by Paul Carus (Chicago, 1909). For the Nestorians in India, consult John D. Macbride's *The Syrian Church in India* (Oxford, 1856) and William J. Richards's *The Indian Christians of St. Thomas, Otherwise Called the Syrian Christians of Malabor* (London, 1908).

For the general history of the Nestorians, old and modern, see Asahel Grant's *The Nestorians, or The Lost Tribes* (1841; reprint, Amsterdam, 1973) and *History of the Nestorians* (London, 1855); George Percy Badger's *The Nestorians and Their Rituals,* 2 vols. (London, 1852); Henry Holme's *The Oldest Christian Church* (London, 1896); Jerome Labourt's *Le christianisme dans l'empire perse sous la dynastie sassanide, 224–632* (Paris, 1904); William A. Wigram's *An Introduction to the History of the Assyrian Church, or The Study of the Sassanid Empire, 100–640 A. D.* (London, 1910); George David Malech's *History of the Syrian Nation and the Old Evangelical-Apostolic Church of the East* (Minneapolis, 1910); Adrian Fortesque's *The Lesser Eastern Churches* (1913; reprint, New York, 1972); William C. Emhardt and George M. Lamsa's *The Oldest Christian People: A Brief Account of the History and Traditions of the Assyrian People and the Fateful History of the Nestorian Church* (1926; reprint, New York, 1970); Eugène Tisserant's "Nestorienne (L'église)," in *Dictionnaire de théologie catholique,* edited by Alfred Vacant and Eugène Mangenot (Paris, 1931), vol. 2; George Graf's *Geschichte der christlichen arabischen Literatur,* "Bibliotica Apostolica Vaticana," vol. 2 (Rome, 1947); and John Joseph's *The Nestorians and Their Muslim Neighbors: A Study of Western Influence on Their Relations* (Princeton, 1961).

New Sources

Coakley, J. F. *The Church of the East and the Church of England: A History of the Archbishop of Canterbury's Assyrian Mission.* Oxford, 1992.

Ferguson, Everett, Michael P. McHugh, and Frederick W. Norris. *The Encyclopedia of Early Christianity.* New York, 1990.

Hill, Henry, comp. and ed. *Light from the East: A Symposium on the Oriental Orthodox and Assyrian Churches.* Toronto, 1988.

Kannookadan, Pauly. *The East Syrian Lectionary: An Historico-Liturgical Study.* Rome, 1991.

Moffett, Samuel Hugh. *A History of Christianity in Asia,* Vol. I: *Beginnings to 1500.* San Francisco, Calif., 1992.

Thottakara, Augustine, ed. *East Syrian Spirituality.* Rome, 1990.

Yousif, Patros. *An Introduction to East Syrian Spirituality.* Rome, 1989.

MATTI MOOSA (1987)
Revised Bibliography

NESTORIANISM is a doctrinal position on the nature of Jesus Christ. In its extreme form the doctrine has been condemned by Christian councils, but the ideas associated with Nestorianism have come to represent one of the two main traditions of Christological thought in Christianity and have been ably defended and articulated by successive generations of Christian thinkers. The name goes back to Nestorius, a patriarch of Constantinople in the early fifth century who was deposed at the Council of Ephesus in 431 and exiled to Egypt in 436. Nestorius was not, however, an original thinker, and the theological views that came to be associated with his name had arisen late in the fourth century among Christian thinkers in eastern Asia Minor and Syria (in the vicinity of ancient Antioch), notably Diodore of Tarsus and Theodore of Mopsuestia. The distinctive features of Nestorianism can be made clear by contrasting it with another tradition of thought associated with the city of Alexandria in Egypt.

After the councils of Nicaea (325) and Constantinople (381), the majority of Christians affirmed that Christ was fully God and was one with God the Father, creator of the world. The question then arose of the relation between this divine Son of God, the eternal Logos, and the human person Jesus of Nazareth who lived in the first century and is portrayed in the Gospels of the New Testament. The Alexandrian theologians, led by Cyril of Alexandria (d. 444), taught that Jesus Christ was the eternal Logos under the conditions of humanity. All the actions predicated of Jesus (e.g., human birth, growth in wisdom, suffering, and death) were predicated of the divine Logos as well. The Antiochene theologians (the forerunners of Nestorianism) believed that Jesus Christ was the result of a union between the divine Son of God and the man Jesus. They explained this union by analogy with the Jewish prophets, outstanding men on whom the spirit of God descended, except that in the case of Christ, God indwelt as in a Son, and the union between God and the Son was inseparable and perfect.

In the early fifth century these two ways of thinking, Alexandrian and Antiochene, clashed over the issue of whether Mary was *theotokos,* the one who gave birth to God, or *christotokos,* the bearer of Christ. After Nestorius became bishop of Constantinople, one of his priests, without Nestorius's objection, criticized the concept of *theotokos* as theologically erroneous. He urged the use of the term *christotokos,* which conformed to the Antiochene way of thinking of Mary as having given birth to the man Jesus, not to the eternal son of God. The term *theotokos,* however, had begun to be used by Christians and had the sanction of recent tradition. To Cyril of Alexandria, as well as to the bishop of Rome, denial of the concept of *theotokos* implied that Mary was not the Mother of God, and hence that God had not become human in the birth of Jesus Christ and that Mary was simply the mother of an exceptional man. Nestorius appeared to teach that there were two persons in Christ, the man Jesus and the divine Son of God. A flurry of theological polemics and political maneuvering ensued. In 430 Celestine, bishop of Rome, condemned Nestorius, and a year later Cyril presided over the Council of Ephesus, which also anathematized him. Emperor Theodosius supported the decision.

Nestorius's writings survive only in fragments, except for an obscure work, *Bazaar of Heracleides,* discovered in 1895 in a Syriac translation from the original Greek. Nestorius wrote the *Bazaar* some years after the controversy as a defense against the charges of his opponents.

Nestorianism, however, is not to be identified with the teaching of Nestorius, though he is venerated by the Nestorian church (i.e., the church of eastern Syria and Persia). Nestorius's supporters thought that their views were vindicated by the Council of Chalcedon in 451. During the course of the fifth century, they constituted themselves as an independent Christian body, with a school in Edessa under the leadership of Ibas, bishop of Edessa (435–457) and an ecclesiastical center and see of the patriarch (who is called *catholicos*) at Seleucia-Ctesiphon on the Tigris River. A small body of Nestorians has survived into modern times.

Under the leadership of distinguished theologians such as Babai the Great (d. 628), the Nestorians forged an alternative to the way of thinking about Christ that had become normative for most Christians in the East and West. They believed that the dominance of the Alexandrian tradition, with its stress on Christ's unity with God, jeopardized the integrity of his human nature. One of their favorite biblical texts was *Luke* 2:52, "Jesus increased in wisdom and in stature, and in favor with God and man," a passage that is extremely difficult to interpret if one does not allow genuine human growth in Jesus. Other texts came from passages in *Hebrews* (2:10, 3:1–2) that suggest that Jesus had become perfect by what he had accomplished as a human being. Long after the ancient disputes a systematic presentation of Nestorian theology was written by Abdisa (d. 1318), metropolitan of Nisibis, in *The Book of the Pearl.*

See Also Nestorian Church; Nestorius.

Bibliography

Abramowski, Luise, and Alan E. Goodman, eds. *A Nestorian Collection of Christological Texts.* 2 vols. Cambridge, 1972.

Grillmeier, Aloys. *Christ in Christian Tradition.* Atlanta, 1975.

Grillmeier, Aloys, and Heinrich Bacht, eds. *Das Konzil von Chalkedon: Geschichte und Gegenwart.* 3 vols. Würzburg, 1951–1954.

Robert L. Wilken (1987)

NESTORIUS (381?–451?), Christian bishop after whom was named one of the major heresies concerning the doctrine of Christ. The figure of Nestorius is much less significant than the teachings associated with his name and the theological developments after his deposition. He was born in Germanicia in Cilicia, a Roman province in southeastern Asia Minor (modern-day Turkey). In the Syrian city of Antioch, he distinguished himself by his asceticism and skill in preaching. When the clergy of the capital city of Constantinople could not agree on a replacement for the patriarch Sisinnius, the emperor invited Nestorius to accept the post. As bishop he was zealous in stamping out heresy, particularly Arianism and Novatianism. He soon became embroiled in controversy, however, initially because of the preaching of his assistant Anastasius, a presbyter he had brought with him from Syria, but later through his own lack of judgment.

Nestorius criticized the term *theotokos* ("God bearer"), a slogan for the idea that Mary, in giving birth to Jesus Christ, had given birth to God. He preferred *christotokos* ("bearer of Christ," i.e., the human being Jesus Christ). Since the term *theotokos* had become a sign of orthodox teaching, Nestorius's imprudence made him vulnerable to the charge of heresy, as his opponents swiftly recognized. Cyril of Alexandria, the ambitious patriarch of a rival see and the exponent of the theological ideas behind the concept of *theotokos,* obtained copies of Nestorius's sermons and initiated proceedings against him.

Nestorius was deposed, and in 436, after spending several years in a monastery in Constantinople, he was exiled to Egypt, where he remained for the rest of his life. He lived until the Council of Chalcedon (451), which he and others saw as a vindication of his views and a repudiation of Cyril. Nestorius was not, however, rehabilitated. His name has been associated with the view that there are two separate persons in Christ, the one divine and the other human (orthodox teaching is that there were two "natures"), but his theological contribution is insignificant. Of his writings a few sermons remain, as well as some fragments from theological works and an amorphous and difficult book, *Bazaar of Heracleides,* a defense of his views written long after the controversy and discovered in 1895 in a Syriac translation from the original Greek. He is revered by the Nestorian church, and his tomb in Egypt was venerated by his followers for centuries.

See Also Nestorian Church; Nestorianism.

Bibliography

Driver, G. R., and Leonard Hodgson, eds. and trans. *Nestorius: The Bazaar of Heracleides.* Oxford, 1925.

Loofs, Friedrich. *Nestoriana: Die Fragmente des Nestorius.* Halle, Germany, 1905.

Scipioni, Luigi I. *Nestorio e il concilio di Efeso.* Milan, 1974.

ROBERT L. WILKEN (1987)

NETHERWORLD SEE UNDERWORLD

NETS SEE WEBS AND NETS

NEUMANN, ERICH

NEUMANN, ERICH (1905–1960), German-Israeli analytical psychologist and writer. Neumann's upbringing in Berlin was Jewish but not orthodox; he was influenced, nevertheless, by Hasidism, in response perhaps to his strong mystical leaning. Long before the rise of Hitler, Neumann was drawn to the Zionist ideal of the renewal of Jewish life in Palestine. At the University of Erlangen, he earned his Ph.D. degree with a dissertation on J. A. Kanne, a mystical philosopher of the time of the Enlightenment who, although a Christian, had been deeply influenced by Jewish esoteric thought. In his youth Neumann wrote a novel, *Der Anfang* (The Beginning), a story of self-fulfillment, which was partially published in 1932. He also wrote poetry and literary essays, notably on Franz Kafka and biblical themes.

Neumann's growing interest in psychology led to his choice of profession; he started medical training and completed his studies in 1933, but Nazi restrictions blocked his qualifying as a physician. In 1958, however, the University of Hamburg awarded Neumann an M.D. degree *in absentia,* having accepted his book *Die Ursprungsgeschichte des Bewusstseins* (1949, translated as *The Origins and History of Consciousness,* 1954) as his thesis. Neumann opted for immigration to Palestine in 1934, pausing on the way in Zurich for a period of analysis and study with C. G. Jung. Gerhard Adler has written: "Here, in Jung's approach, he found the dynamic focus of his various interests and gifts. Analytical psychology provided the instrument that helped him to translate his creative insight into practical work with other people, and for them" (preface to Neumann's *Creative Man: Five Essays,* 1979, p. xiii).

In Palestine, Neumann devoted himself to building a practice and to pursuing studies that, after the enforced isolation of World War II, brought forth an enormous burst of creative work. He revisited Europe only in 1947, for a family holiday in Ascona, Switzerland, where he had two crucial encounters—with Olga Froebe-Kapteyn, the director of the Eranos Conferences, and with John D. Barrett, the editor of the Bollingen Series. Neumann lectured the following year at Eranos on "mystical man" and at each of the conferences thereafter as keynote speaker. His last lecture there was delivered in 1960, shortly before his death. In 1948 he was awarded a Bollingen Foundation fellowship, which continued for twelve years and supported his copious literary activity.

The Origins and History of Consciousness aims to illustrate archetypal stages in the development of human consciousness by interpreting basic mythologems drawn from several religious traditions. Neumann argues that individual consciousness passes through the same developmental stages that mark the history of human consciousness. Published in the same year, *Tiefenpsychologie und neue Ethik* (1949, translated as *Depth Psychology and a New Ethic,* 1969) demonstrates the impact that the idea of psychological wholeness had made on Neumann, on whom self-realization seemed to impose a new ethical outlook and an obligation beyond conventional ethical concepts. The book aroused controversy; Jung commented, "If Neumann recommends the 'inner voice' as the criterion of ethical behavior instead of the Christian conscience . . . [he] stands on the best footing with very many Christian mystics" (*Letters,* vol. 1, 1973, p. 519). *The Great Mother* (1955), a study of the archetypal feminine, is based on images from numerous cultures that were collected in Froebe-Kapteyn's Eranos Archive. Feminine psychology here becomes a focus of Neumann's interest, vying for priority with the psychology of creative art. Both concerns are effectively blended in *The Archetypal World of Henry Moore* (1959). In his later years, essays, lectures, seminars, and analytical training preoccupied Neumann, and he produced no more longer works.

When an illness he had was diagnosed as terminal in October 1960, Neumann returned from London to Israel, where he died a month later, leaving many projects unfinished. In Gerhard Adler's words, "Neumann was the one truly creative spirit among the second generation of Jung's pupils, the only one who seemed destined to build on Jung's work and to continue it" (preface to Neumann's *Creative Man: Five Essays,* 1979, p. xv).

BIBLIOGRAPHY

Neumann's longer writings in English translation are the following: *Depth Psychology and a New Ethic* (New York, 1969); *The Origins and History of Consciousness* (New York, 1954); *The Great Mother,* 2d ed. (New York, 1963); *Amor and Psyche: The Psychic Development of the Feminine* (New York, 1956); *The Archetypal World of Henry Moore* (New York, 1959); and *The Child* (New York, 1973). An Eranos lecture, "Art and Time," was included in *Papers from the Eranos Yearbooks,* vol. 3, edited by Joseph Campbell (New York, 1957), pp. 3–37. Essays by Neumann on Leonardo da Vinci, Marc Chagall, and creative transformation are collected in *Art and the Creative Unconscious* (New York, 1959), and essays on Kafka, Chagall, Trakl, Freud, and Jung appear in *Creative Man: Five Essays* (Princeton, 1979).

The journal *Analytische Psychologie* (Basel) 11 (1980) devoted a double issue (nos. 3–4) to Neumann in commemoration of his seventy-fifth birthday. It contains articles, letters of Neumann and Jung, and a list of publications in German.

New Sources

Giskin, Howard. "Art as Transcendence: Seeing the Divine through the Creative Act in Taoism and Erich Neumann." *Studia Mystica* 15, no. 4 (1992): 99–110.

Neumann, Erich. *The Fear of the Feminine and Other Essays on Feminine Psychology.* Princeton, N.J., 1994.

Neumann, Erich. *The Place of Creation: Six Essays.* Princeton, N.J., 1999.

Weiler, Gerda. *Der enteignete Mythos: Eine feministische Revision der Archetypenlehre C.G. Jungs und Erich Neumanns.* Frankfurt/Main; New York, 1991.

WILLIAM MCGUIRE (1987)
Revised Bibliography

NEUROSCIENCE AND RELIGION

This entry consists of the following articles:

AN OVERVIEW
NEUROEPISTEMOLOGY
NEUROTHEOLOGY

NEUROSCIENCE AND RELIGION: AN OVERVIEW

Neuroscience is the study of the nervous system, including the brain, spinal cord, and peripheral systems. As a discipline, it reached maturity only in the twentieth century. Developments in brain-scanning technologies, in particular, have revolutionized neuroscience, and it can only be expected that the existing and growing body of literature will continue to expand. As neuroscience develops, its findings are increasingly seen to have implications for religious worldviews and the study of religion.

HISTORY. Awareness of the nervous system and its role in the human body dates back at least to the Roman physician Galen (third century BCE), who understood movement to be controlled by the nerve cords extending through the body. By the end of the eighteenth century, the major anatomical features of the brain were known, as well as the central relationship of mind and brain. This knowledge was most famously reflected in the work of René Descartes (1596–1650), who understood the motions of the body to be controlled by mechanistic animal spirits originating from the brain, connected to the nonmaterial mind through the pineal gland.

It was not until the mid- to late nineteenth century that neuroscience began to emerge as a separate discipline, thanks to new experimental techniques and the increasing refinement of the microscope. It came to be realized that the central building block of the brain and nervous system was the neuron, a kind of cell that appeared designed to communicate by electrical impulses. In addition, studies in functional neuroanatomy had begun to associate specific forms of brain damage with specific kinds of mental deficits. Paul Broca (1824–1880), for instance, showed that damage to a region in the left hemisphere of the brain (now known as Broca's area) resulted in the inability to produce speech. Findings of this kind were capitalized on for dubious purposes, most notably the pseudo-science of phrenology, but the work of Broca and his colleagues has since been well substantiated.

Despite these advances, neuroscience did not truly become established until after World War II. This progress was made possible, in part, by the large number of war casualties, who made ideal test subjects for neuroscientists studying the relationship between brain and thought. The period of the 1950s through the 1970s was one of tremendous growth, particularly in the area of functional neuroanatomy and in the understanding of the basic functioning of the neuron. By the 1980s these findings began to come together to make a coherent whole. This process was abetted by the use of computational models for understanding the brain and mind and by the use of new scanning technologies (most notably magnetic resonance imaging, or MRI) that allowed images of living brains and, eventually, imaging of the brain in action, enabling neuroscientists to see what areas of the brain become active during specified tasks.

For most of this history, religion has rarely been the subject of theorizing by neuroscientists, but this is not to say that there were no interactions between neuroscience and religion. Descartes's mechanistic understanding of the brain and body can be understood to fall within the context of a larger, religious worldview. The important discoveries about the nervous system made by Hermann von Helmholtz (1821–1894)—showing, among other things, that it takes time for nerve signals to communicate over distances—were driven by his materialistic convictions. Furthermore, two of the twentieth century's most famous psychologists of religion, Sigmund Freud and William James, both had significant exposure to the advances in neuroscience in their day. Religious beliefs (or the lack of them) thus played an important background role in shaping the field of neuroscience, while the findings of neuroscience (real or putative) were sometimes used to justify positions about religion.

CURRENT CHARACTER OF NEUROSCIENCE. Knowledge of the brain and how it works grew enormously in the second half of the twentieth century and into the twenty-first, so much so that the U.S. Congress designated the 1990s as the "decade of the brain" to commemorate and further brain research. It is now estimated that the brain is composed of approximately 100 billion nerve cells. In turn, each nerve cell is typically connected to 3,000 to 10,000 other nerve cells, and it has been suggested that there are on the order of 100 trillion such connections. It is important to note the staggering complexity that this implies: that there are more neuron connections than there are stars in the Milky Way Galaxy. Neurons communicate by sending electronic impulses facilitated by chemical reactions that are still not fully understood. Chemicals known as neurotransmitters play an essential role in this communication. Imbalances in neurotransmitter production and uptake play important roles in some forms of mental illness (such as schizophrenia, Parkinson's disease, and depression) and altered states of consciousness (due, for instance, to drug use).

Much of the functional organization of the brain has been mapped out. It is now known that, for most individuals, the majority of language processing occurs in the left hemisphere of the brain. Visual processing occurs in the occipital lobe in the rear, motor control is centered along the midline of the brain, and complex rational thought seems to be concentrated in the frontal and prefrontal cortexes immediately behind the forehead. Emotional responses seem to be controlled by a collection of brain structures known as the limbic system. In many cases the correspondence between a specific behavioral ability and the specific area of the brain responsible for it has been mapped out in considerable detail. When damage to an area of the brain occurs, the corresponding ability is lost, sometimes permanently and sometimes with counterintuitive results. Prosopognosia (the inability to recognize faces) is the result of one such instance of brain damage. People with this condition are unable to tell one face from another, even though they may recognize people by other means (e.g., by the sound of their voice or the clothes that they are wearing).

It has become common among some scientists to compare the mind and brain to a computer. Though this metaphor has proven useful in some ways, it is also exceedingly misleading in others. Individual neurons function somewhat analogously to the individual logic gates of a computer chip, but there is no central processor as is typical on modern desktop computers. A closer analogy has been computers that utilize decentralized parallel distributed processing (PDP) or neural networks, and it has been shown that individual neuronal groups are capable of such processing. However, the analogy between brains and computers has been a contentious one, with some neuroscientists utilizing computational metaphors and others strongly denying any such link.

Among recent areas of development, three may be seen as particularly important. First, a growing body of research has helped to reveal the centrality of emotion in brain processing and cognition. Research by Antonio Damasio (1994) has shown that rational thought and emotion are not completely distinct from one another, and to think rationally one must have a proper repertoire of emotional responses as well. This has contributed to a move away from thinking of the brain as simply a computer-like thinking machine. Second, research in brain development is helping to show how the brain comes to organize itself in relation to its environment. The brain goes through dramatic changes in the early periods of childhood, and there is good evidence that the brain continues to change in subtle ways throughout a person's life. The prefrontal cortex (responsible for reasoning) continues in its development through late adolescence. Increasing knowledge of genetics is also beginning to illuminate the ways in which specific genes influence brain development, suggesting the potential for providing links between assemblies of genes and specific human behaviors. Furthermore, individual neurons have been shown to be exceedingly plastic, changing their receptivity to communication from and to other neurons throughout one's life. Third, some research has indicated the possibility of brain-machine interfaces in the not-so-distant future. Magnetic fields, for instance, can be used to stimulate specific areas of the brain, either for research or therapeutic purposes (to alleviate depression, for instance). Work with rhesus monkeys has shown that a machine interface can be used to control a mechanical device by a thought command alone, suggesting help for individuals with physical disabilities but also raising questions about the relationship of human beings and machines.

Neuroscience, the Mind-Body Relation, and Personhood. There are a number of ways in which neuroscience might be said to relate to or have an impact on religious traditions and religious thinking. The most obvious concerns the relationship of mind to body. Religious beliefs about the nature and relation of the mind and the body have been varied and complex. In the earliest forms of Judaism, Christianity, and Islam, the tendency was to think of persons as wholes, distinguishing between body and spirit but maintaining their essential unity. As a result, these traditions looked forward to a resurrection of the dead that united (or reunited) spirit and body. Later thought, especially in the Christian tradition, was profoundly influenced by Platonism, with the result that emphasis was placed on the survival of an immortal soul separate from the body. This distinction was accentuated by later Christian philosophers and theologians, most notably Réne Descartes. Other religious traditions have subscribed to quite variant understandings of the human person and mind-body relationship. Hinduism speaks of the *ātman*, or self, but sometimes in quite different ways than the monotheistic traditions (as is most obviously reflected in the Upanishads and the Advaita Vedanta tradition). Buddhism has historically subscribed to a doctrine of *anātman*, or no-self, and so has traditionally denied the existence of a soul in any straightforward sense.

As a science, neuroscience does not address the broader question of mind and body, although its findings can be said to have consequences for particular religious views. Neuroscience does seem to rule out any straightforward account of mind-body dualism. Damage to the brain leads to loss of cognitive function, often in fairly predictable ways. Such potential damage is not limited to motor functions, but can also affect higher-order thinking and emotional response. Brain damage or alteration of brain chemistry can lead sometimes to rather profound alterations of personality. It should be noted that this damage affects not simply the behavior of the individual but one's subjective experience as well. Someone who suffers a stroke and is afflicted with temporary aphasia (the inability to speak) because of brain damage is not simply prevented from speaking the words. When recovered, they will testify they were unable to even think of the words (or think in words) while having the disability. With a few, early, and prominent exceptions (most notably Wilder Penfield and John Eccles, two of the more famous neuroscientists of the twentieth century), few neuroscientists now count themselves dualists, and most would argue that mind and body are intimately linked.

It is important to note, however, that neuroscientists remain perplexed by the phenomenon of consciousness. Beginning in the late 1980s, neuroscientists began to consider consciousness as a legitimate subject of inquiry. Most efforts at explanation have been devoted to the function of consciousness rather than its very nature. Philosopher David Chalmers (1997) has usefully distinguished between the "easy problems" of consciousness and the "hard problem." The easy problems deals with cognitive functions associated with consciousness (such as attention, bodily representation, and the ability to think about one's thoughts and so be self-conscious), but they do not tell us why there is a subjective quality to consciousness at all. This latter question, to date, remains better suited to philosophy than science, and it may be permanently so.

Beyond the mind-body relationship, neuroscience may be seen to have repercussions for more general understandings of personhood. Research into the physical factors linked to specific behaviors and personality, particularly when tied to advances in developmental biology and behavioral genetics, stand to have fairly profound implications for doctrines of free will and the meaning and nature of personal transformation. The advent of subtle, personality-altering drugs such as Prozac and the increasing trend toward diagnosing and using drugs to treat personality variants such as attention deficit disorder (ADD) reveals the complex relationship of person, biology, and environment in ways that have implications for religious doctrines of health and happiness. Such implications have, to date, led to little in the way of religious reflection, but will become increasingly important in the coming decades.

NEUROSCIENCE AND RELIGIOUS EXPERIENCE. A recent area of neuroscientific exploration has been the nature of religious experience itself and its possible roots in the brain. There has been a long tradition of scientific speculation on the nature of religious experience. For much of its history, when neuroscience has on rare occasion turned its attention to the topic of religious experience, the tendency has been to associate it with one or another form of mental illness. William James, for instance, chided medical materialists (as he called them) for attempting to reduce religious experience to mental illness. One early favorite candidate has been temporal lobe epilepsy, which has been known to produce in some individuals profound religious experiences prior to the onset of seizures. The Russian novelist Fyodor Dostoevsky is probably the most famous example of this phenomenon. Knowledge of such instances has been used by some neuroscientists (Robert Persinger in 1987, for example) as a general explanation for religious experience. Research by V. S. Ramachandran (Ramachandran and Blakeslee, 1998) has shown this to be unlikely, however, as religious individuals with no epilepsy seem to respond differently in tests using religious imagery than individuals with temporal lobe epilepsy.

Beginning in the 1990s, some neuroscientists turned their attention to Buddhist meditation as a subject of research. Meditation has proven to be a congenial subject of research because it is largely stationary, predictable, and has a base of willing test subjects. The primary concern of this research has been to link meditational states with heightened or lowered activity in specific regions of the brain. Research done by Eugene D'Aquili and Andrew Newberg (1999) has shown that such meditation consistently correlates with heightened activity in some areas of the brain (the prefrontal cortex, for instance) and lowered activity in others (most specifically areas in the parietal lobes associated with spatial orientation). D'Aquili and Newberg theorize that it is the alteration of these brain states that leads to the particular experiences (e.g., a sense of unity and a loss of distinction between self and other) that meditation is traditionally said to give rise to.

There are deep divides as to how to interpret such research. Some argue that studies that correlate brain states with religious experiences show that these religious experiences are not real, i.e., religious experiences are nothing but a form of brain dysfunction or even mental illness with no basis in any kind of higher reality. On this account, religious experience is necessarily illusory in character, and such research can be taken as evidence for a more general reductive account of religion. D'Aquili and Newberg, however, have argued that their research shows that religious experience is part of the normal functioning of the brain and should not be characterized as a form of mental illness, as has often been the case in psychology. They also argue that the implications of such research are not reductive. Rather, they claim, it should be admitted that the realities such brain states reveal are just as real as those of ordinary experience, and so one should not be privileged over the other.

Some important limitations of these studies should be noted. To date, the studies done have been small, involving few subjects, thus raising the probability of error or variant results in further trials. In addition, it is important to note that meditational practices vary from tradition to tradition, and what holds true for one form of meditational practice may not hold true for all. Furthermore, it would be a mistake to suppose that religious experiences arising from meditation can simply and straightforwardly be used as a model for explaining all religious experiences. Religious experience is diverse and complex, and there are likely multiple factors involved.

NEUROSCIENCE, UNIQUENESS, AND DIGNITY. Issues of uniqueness and human dignity may also be raised by neuroscience and its related fields. Evidence reveals that human beings evolved from ape-like ancestors approximately six million years ago. There is now a significant amount of fossil data with which to construct key aspects of this evolutionary history, although the details remain contentious and ongoing discoveries have revealed the complexity of the evolutionary links. The evidence does show, however, a gradual rise in cranial size from very old fossils like *Australopithecus afarensis* (about five million years ago with brain size equivalent to that of a modern chimpanzee) to *Homo erectus* to *Homo sapiens.* Because the brains themselves are not preserved, brain development can only be inferred from the size and shape of the brain case and other physiological clues. One important issue has been determining when the brain reached its current state of development, with some suggesting that changes were still taking place as recently as 40,000 years ago (about the time that we see some of the first cave art).

Greater understanding of the minds and brains of other animals may also provoke religious reflection. Research with dolphins and apes (particularly chimpanzees and bonobos) in particular has shown sometimes surprising intellectual abilities. A dolphin brain is about the size of a human brain, although its different organization suggests that it would be a mistake to assume this to mean equivalent intellectual ability. Although their brains are smaller than ours, chimpanzees are capable of some symbolic communication and are capable of recognizing themselves in a mirror (an ability comparatively rare among animals), which has been taken to suggest some level of self-consciousness. Moreover, genetic studies indicate that chimpanzees share up to 98 percent or more of their genes with human beings.

The extent to which these findings will be important for religious belief will clearly vary from tradition to tradition. Monotheistic traditions have been much more inclined to insist on an absolute division between human beings and animals than, for instance, Hinduism and Buddhism. Distinctions are observed, however, even in these latter traditions. From a neuroscientific perspective, any claim of an absolute divide between human beings and animals would be difficult to support, especially when evolutionary histories are taken into account. Rather, it seems much more likely that a continuum exists, albeit one with important leaps along the way.

Bibliography

Andresen, Jensine, ed. *Religion in Mind: Cognitive Perspectives on Religious Belief, Ritual, and Experience.* Cambridge, U.K., 2001.

Chalmers, David. *The Conscious Mind: In Search of a Fundamental Theory.* New York, 1997.

Churchland, Patricia Smith. *Neurophilosophy: Toward a Unified Science of the Mind/Brain.* Cambridge, Mass., 1986.

Damasio, Antonio. *Descartes' Error: Emotion, Reason, and the Human Brain.* New York, 1994.

D'Aquili, Eugene G., and Andrew B. Newberg. *The Mystical Mind: Probing the Biology of Religious Experience.* Minneapolis, Minn., 1999.

Gazzaniga, Michael S., Richard B. Ivry, and George R. Mangun. *Cognitive Neuroscience: The Biology of the Mind.* 2d ed. New York, 2002.

Persinger, Michael A. *Neuropsychological Bases of God Beliefs.* Westport, Conn., 1987.

Peterson, Gregory R. *Minding God: Theology and the Cognitive Sciences.* Minneapolis, Minn., 2002.

Ramachandran, V. S., and Sandra Blakeslee. *Phantoms in the Brain: Probing the Mysteries of the Human Mind.* New York, 1998.

Russell, Robert J., Nancey Murphy, Theo C. Meyering, and Michael Arbib. *Neuroscience and the Person: Scientific Perspectives on Divine Action.* Chicago, 1999.

Gregory R. Peterson (2005)

NEUROSCIENCE AND RELIGION: NEUROEPISTEMOLOGY

Neuroepistemology is a relatively new discipline that considers questions of the theory of knowledge in terms of the structure and function of the brain. In order to consider neuroepistemology, it is necessary to review how the human brain organizes sensory input and how it "constructs" the subjective representation of reality that is called knowledge. The process by which the brain enables a perception of reality lies at the heart of neuroepistemology and provides a unique perspective for the scientific, philosophical, and theological evaluation of reality.

Primary Epistemic States. The various perceptions of reality can be grouped into several primary *epistemic states.* A primary epistemic state may be defined as the state in which a person has an experience and interpretation of reality. Such primary epistemic states can be considered along three neurocognitive dimensions: (1) sensory perceptions of objects or things that can be manifested as either multiple discrete things or a holistic union of all things; (2) cognitive relationships between objects or things that are either regular or irregular; and (3) emotional responses to the objects or things that are either positive, negative, or neutral. The emotional responses do not refer to the usual feelings of happiness, sadness, and so on, but to the overall emotional approach of a person to his or her reality. It is likely that one's overall affective response to reality is to a large degree set by the brain's limbic system, which includes such structures as the amygdala, hippocampus, and hypothalamus. Furthermore, scholars such as Antonio Damasio (1999) have suggested that emotional responses, even in relation to the body's perceptions, play a critical role in the human experience of reality. It is also important to mention that each of these parameters is set along a continuum. In other words, one's reality may be based primarily on multiple discrete objects, but it may also include some holistic attributes.

Based upon the dimensions described above, nine possible primary epistemic states that are internally consistent can be considered. These nine states should actually be considered a continuum of states with those mentioned below as nodal points along the continuum.

1. Multiple discrete reality—regular relationships—neutral affect
2. Multiple discrete reality—regular relationships—positive affect
3. Multiple discrete reality—regular relationships—negative affect
4. Multiple discrete reality—irregular relationships—neutral affect

5. Multiple discrete reality—irregular relationships—positive affect
6. Multiple discrete reality—irregular relationships—negative affect
7. Unitary being—neutral affect
8. Unitary being—positive affect
9. Unitary being—negative affect

Unitary being cannot be perceived as having either regular or irregular relationships since relationships can only be considered to exist between discrete independent things, and in unitary being there are no discrete independent things that can be related to each other. Furthermore, it might be argued that unitary being cannot be associated with affect until after an individual actually has the experience of unitary being. Thus, the final three states might ultimately be considered one; for the purposes of this entry, however, it will be helpful to maintain the symmetry of these states.

The first six primary epistemic states could all be considered to represent the experience of a reality with multiple discrete objects. In other words, a person in one of these states perceives individual and independent objects in that reality. These objects can be related to other objects in terms of time, space, causality, or many other possible relationships.

Neurophysiologically, there are specific brain structures that appear to underlie the ability to order reality along these different relationships. In particular, the parietal lobe, in conjunction with the temporal and frontal lobes, appears to play a critical role in the perception of spatial and temporal orientation, as well as the establishing of causal relationships between objects and events. The first three primary epistemic states refer to realities in which there are regular relationships between things. Thus, these relationships are logical and have a logical ordering. It may be said that these regular relationships are predictable and allow for a consistent understanding of reality.

Baseline reality. This regularity helps scientists understand what is typically called *reality* or *baseline reality.* Baseline reality generally carries a neutral affect and refers to that state in which there are discrete objects with regular relationships. This is the primary epistemic state that most people are in most of the time. Furthermore, few individuals would question the fundamental reality (or the sense of that reality) of the state that they are usually living within. It is precisely because this state appears certain while an individual is in it that it can be called a primary epistemic state. In fact, most people would consider this state to be the true reality, with nothing beyond this reality.

Cosmic consciousness. The second primary epistemic state is one in which there are discrete objects with regular relationships between objects, but an overwhelmingly positive affect. It is a state associated with an elated sense of being and joy, in which the universe is perceived to be fundamentally good. There is a sense of purposefulness to all things and to humankind's place within the universe. This purposefulness is not derived logically, it is simply intuited because of the positive emotional state. The onset of this state is usually sudden and is often described as a conversion experience, especially in religious thought. In psychiatric literature, Richard Bucke called this state "Cosmic Consciousness"; it is characterized by overwhelming happiness, comprehension, universal understanding, and love. Although this state may have a sudden onset, it can last for many years and even for the person's entire life. This state of Cosmic Consciousness is a primary epistemic state because the person perceives this understanding of the universe as fundamentally real (it is not an illusion) and sometimes will look with a sense of pity at those who have only the baseline perception of reality. People in this state are not psychotic, nor do they have any emotional or mental disorder. They perceive objects and relationships between objects in the universe in the same way as those in baseline reality. They simply have a different emotional understanding of this perception.

Negative reality. The third primary epistemic state is comprised of discrete objects with regular relationships, but it is associated with a profoundly negative affect. It is a state of exquisite sadness and futility, as well as the sense of the incredible smallness of humankind within the universe and the suffering inherent in the human condition. In this state, the universe may be understood as one vast pointless machine without purpose or meaning. In the full-blown state, people often seek psychiatric help because of the extreme depression associated with this state, even though they perceive this state to be fundamentally real. Essentially, they are asking to be taught to think in an "illusory" way so that they can survive. They are not asking to be restored to reality. As with Cosmic Consciousness, this overly negative state can last many years. However, people do revert back to baseline reality and anecdotal evidence suggests that reversion occurs more frequently from the negative state than from the positive state, perhaps because the negative state is in many ways incompatible with survival from a psychological perspective.

Irregular relationships. The next three states are associated with discrete objects and beings, but contain irregular relationships between the objects in that reality. Thus, the time, space, and causal relationships between various objects are distorted, bizarre, and unpredictable. Examples of this type of state include dreams, drug-induced states, and schizophrenia. Further, the state of irregular relationships can be associated with negative, positive, or neutral affect. For example, the experience of using LSD or other hallucinogenic drugs can either be incredibly elating or profoundly disturbing. Quite literally, these states can be described as either heaven or hell. Schizophrenia is similar in that the bizarre patterns of relationships between objects can be associated with negative, positive, or neutral emotion, and patients can suffer from both a mood disorder and psychotic symptoms. In these cases, the patient may be extraordinarily depressed while also experiencing delusions or hallucinations.

All of these states involving discrete being are perceived as real while the person is in them. Of course, once an individual lapses into another primary epistemic state, he or she recognizes the original state as an illusion, delusion, or hallucination. This judgment is consistent with the nature of primary epistemic states, for once a person has entered into a different primary state, they perceive the new state as real. It is the nature of a primary epistemic state to perceive that state as reality. A person would therefore necessarily understand what they remember from a drug experience or from a dream as an illusion or a distortion.

Unitary states. The final three states involve the experience of a totally unitary reality. There is no point in referring to regular or irregular relationships regarding the primary epistemic states of unitary being, since there are no discrete objects that can be related to each other. In unitary being there is no sense of individual objects, there is no self–other dichotomy, and everything is perceived as undifferentiated, unified oneness. Thus, the state of unitary being can be divided into three possible states that include positive, negative, or neutral affect. However, even these emotional perspectives can be considered only after the fact, since while an individual is actually in a unitary state, there theoretically can be no distinction between objects, including even emotions.

This unitary state has been studied to some degree using neuroimaging of individuals in meditation or prayer. The results of early studies appear to support the original neurophysiological model suggested by Eugene d'Aquili and Andrew Newberg (1993), in which the experience of unitary states may be associated with the deafferentation, or blocking of sensory input, into the areas of the brain typically responsible for the perception and ordering of reality. However, more studies will need to be performed to better differentiate the neurophysiological correlates of the primary epistemic states, including that of unitary being.

GOD AND THE WHOLE. The experience of reality associated with unitary being yields the subjective perception of absolute and total unity of being without a temporal dimension. Reality is perceived as "ultimate wholeness" without any admixture of fragmentation. When absolute unitary and atemporal being is perceived as suffused with positive affect after the fact, it is generally perceived as personal (d'Aquili, 1982). This perceived experience of unitary atemporal being is interpreted in most world religions as either a direct perception of God or as the *unio mystica* of the Christian tradition, which, though a manifestation of God, is not considered a revelation of God's innermost nature. The experience transcends any perception of multiple, discrete being, and the awareness of the subject-object difference is obliterated. The unitary experience is ineffable, but it is frequently interpreted (when experienced with strong positive affect) in terms that express a union with, or a direct experience of, God.

The experience of ultimate wholeness does not have to be theistically labeled. It can be understood philosophically (usually with neutral affective valence) as an experience of the absolute, the ultimate, or the transcendent. In the Buddhist tradition the experience (also with neutral affective valence) is interpreted as the "void," or *nirvāṇa,* and is generally expressed as impersonal. It is also theoretically possible to enter into a state of unitary being associated with negative affect. However, there are no references to this type of experience in any religious, philosophical, or psychological literature. It may be that such a state is not neurophysiologically possible. Perhaps it cannot come about because the experience of all things as an undifferentiated oneness is so powerfully positive and integrative that it cannot be perceived in negative terms. At worst (so to speak) unitary being can be perceived neutrally. It may be argued that such a state of unitary being with negative affect is incompatible with life, the brain, or the mind. Thus, until actual evidence can be brought forward to demonstrate the existence of this theoretical state, it must be assumed that it is just that, theoretical.

It is also interesting that the perception of the logical opposite of ultimate wholeness—that is, ultimate fragmentation—does not seem to be possible. For anything to be known at all, however chaotic it may be, some sense of wholeness or form must be perceived or imposed. The post hoc description of ultimate wholeness may be of an experience of a personal God or of a completely nonpersonal experience of total being, but in any case the experience is always interpreted as absolutely transcendent, or ultimate, or in some sense beyond ordinary experience.

Whether or not the phenomenon is interpreted as the experience of God or as the experience of a philosophical absolute tends to depend on the a priori conceptual frame of the individual having the experience. But there can be no doubt as to the reality of the unitary experience for those few who have had it; furthermore, these people are absolutely certain of the experience's objective reality. This experience, for those individuals, contains at least the same subjective conviction of reality as does the subjective conviction of the reality of the external world. Although it is true philosophically that we cannot prove the existence of the external world as perceived (or even of the external world at all) based upon a completely neuropsychological perspective, nonetheless each of us carries a subjective and pragmatic certainty of its existence. The experience of absolute unity carries to the subject the same, or perhaps even a greater, degree of certainty of its objective reality. Research indicates that this is true even in people whose orientation is materialist, reductionist, or atheistic prior to the experience of absolute unitary being.

As noted above, it seems likely from recent research that the experience of unitary being arises from the integrated functioning of several brain structures resulting in the deafferentation of orienting areas such as the parietal lobe. These parts of the brain may have evolved to yield such transcendent experiences, or perhaps such experiences are merely a byproduct of cortical machinery that evolved for other purposes. In any case, the experience of absolute unity can be described in terms of the evolution of the present structure and function of the central nervous system. An important point is that such an explanation, while legitimate from a scientific perspective, in no way alters the subjective sensation of the objective reality of the experience. So strong is this feeling of objective reality that, for most people, even a detailed neuroepistemological analysis does not alter the conviction that something objectively real has been experienced. For those few who have experienced both realities—the reality of the day-to-day world (and objective science) on one hand and the reality of transcendent unitary states on the other—the problem is not one of trying to decide which reality is real. These people feel that they know both are real. Rather, the problem is one of reconciling the two drastically different and seemingly contradictory perceptions of reality.

Several important neuroepistemological issues can now be considered: the meaning of what it is to know at all; the nature and consequence of the certainty of reality, however reality is perceived; and the neurophysiological limitations and constraints on knowing anything whatsoever. To consider the meaning of knowing is to be forced into the heart of subjective experience, of which objective reality is but a subset (and science but a subset of this subset). It is probably impossible to resolve the conflict between the two realities as experienced. Given the phenomenology of the experience, it is clearly impossible to undercut the certainty of the "absolute" in those people who have experienced it. Research indicates that they cannot be dissuaded from their conviction of the objective reality of absolute unity no matter how often the adaptive value of the transcendence-generating parts of the brain is pointed out to them. Science is a product of the everyday world, but the experience of an absolute unitary state is an experience of another world, and this world is essentially cut off from the world of discrete reality (unlike hallucinations and delusions, which are epistemically part of the world of discrete, transient being). It would seem, therefore, that the absolute unitary state, whatever its significance may be in post hoc religious description, has in itself an epistemological status equivalent to baseline everyday reality and, at least from a neuroepistemological perspective, must be dealt with accordingly.

Unitary State Versus Baseline Reality. To simplify the issue somewhat, it is helpful to contrast the unitary state with baseline reality. In such an exercise there is no question that the unitary state wins out as being experienced as "more real." People who have experienced unitary being, and this includes some very learned and previously materialistically oriented scientists, regard such a state as being more fundamentally real than baseline reality. Even the memory of it is, for them, more fundamentally real. When individuals who have had this experience are interviewed, there is no doubt that it, and even the memory of it, carries a greater sense of fundamental reality than that generated by their experiences of day-to-day living.

To further clarify this point, compare four characteristics of baseline reality (coherent lucid consciousness) with the hyperlucid consciousness of unitary being (called *hyperlucid* here since it is perceived as more clear and more real than other primary epistemic states of reality). Baseline reality demonstrates the following four fundamental properties:

1. A strong sense of the reality of what is experienced.
2. Endurance of that reality through very long periods of time, usually only interrupted by sleeping.
3. The sense that when elements in baseline reality disappear from all forms of sensory detection, they have ceased to be.
4. High cross-subjective validation both for details of perception and core meaning (in other words, other people corroborate one's perceptions of the world—reality is a collective hunch).

The essential characteristics of hyperlucid unitary being are the following:

1. An extremely strong sense of reality, to the point of its being absolutely compelling under almost all circumstances.
2. Endurance for short periods of time relative to the sense of time of baseline reality.
3. A sense of its underlying persistence and continued existence even when the perception of the overall state has ended.
4. High cross-subjective validation for core perceptions; moderate to low cross-subjective validation for perceptual detail in those hyperlucid states where discrete being is perceived (as in near-death experiences).

It is probably impossible to determine whether the hyperlucid unitary state or baseline reality is more "real" (i.e., which state represents the ultimate objective reality without making gratuitous and unsubstantiated assumptions). Clearly, baseline reality has some significant claim to being ultimate reality. However, unitary being is so compelling that it is difficult to write off assertions of its reality. Actually, for individuals having experienced unitary being, it seems virtually impossible to negate that experience, no matter what level of education or sophistication such individuals may have. This being the case, it is a misguided reductionism to state that because hyperlucid unitary consciousness can be understood in terms of neuropsychological processes, it is therefore derivative from baseline reality. Indeed the reverse argument might just as well be made. Neuropsychology can give no answer as to which state is more real, baseline reality or hyperlucid unitary consciousness (often experienced as God). It may be most accurate to state that each is real in its own way and for its own adaptive ends.

The essential characteristic of different states of reality are eventually reducible only to the strength of the sense of reality, the *phantasia catalyptica* of the Stoics or the *Anwesenheit* (compelling presence) of certain modern German philosophers. A vivid sense of reality may be the only thing that can be used to help determine what is really real until someone discovers a method for going beyond the brain's perception of reality. This conclusion may not be epistemologically satisfying, but at this time all alternatives seem untenable.

Therefore, the brain can be conceived of as a machine that operates upon whatever it is that fundamental reality may be, and the brain produces, at the very least, two basic versions. One version is a world of discrete beings, usually baseline reality, and the other version is the perception of unitary being, usually experienced as God. Both perceptions are accompanied by a profound subjective certainty of their objective reality. Whatever is prior to the experience of either unitary being or the baseline reality of everyday life is in principal unknowable, since that which is in any way known must be translated, and in this sense transformed by the brain.

BIBLIOGRAPHY

Damasio, Antonio R. *The Feeling of What Happens: Body and Emotion in the Making of Consciousness.* New York, 1999.

d'Aquili, Eugene G. "Senses of Reality in Science and Religion: A Neuroepistemological Perspective." *Zygon* 17 (1982): 361–364.

d'Aquili, Eugene G., and Andrew B. Newberg. "Religious and Mystical States: A Neuropsychological Model." *Zygon* 28 (1993): 177–200.

Gazzaniga, Michael S. *The Bisected Brain.* New York, 1970.

Gazzaniga, Michael S., ed. *The New Cognitive Neurosciences.* Cambridge, Mass., 2000.

Luria, Aleksandr R. *Higher Cortical Functions in Man.* Translated by Basil Haigh. New York, 1966; 2d rev. ed., 1980.

Luria, Aleksandr R. *The Working Brain: An Introduction to Neuropsychology.* Translated by Basil Haigh. New York, 1973.

Newberg, Andrew B., Eugene G. d'Aquili, and Vince P. Rause. *Why God Won't Go Away: Brain Science and the Biology of Belief.* New York, 2001.

EUGENE G. D'AQUILI (1987)
ANDREW B. NEWBERG (2005)

NEUROSCIENCE AND RELIGION: NEUROTHEOLOGY

Neurotheology is an emerging field of study that seeks to integrate in some manner cognitive neuroscience with religion and theology. Its development as a field is attested to by significant interest in both the academic and lay population. Neurotheology is multidisciplinary in nature and includes the fields of theology, religious studies, religious experience, philosophy, cognitive science, neuroscience, psychology, and anthropology. Each may contribute to neurotheology, and conversely, neurotheology may ultimately contribute to each of these fields.

Individuals engaged in neurotheology can help develop theoretical models of the neurophysiological mechanisms of brain activity during religious and spiritual practices, such as meditation, prayer, or ritual. This analysis also includes the spiritual or religious experiences associated with such practices, as well as those that arise spontaneously, such as near-death experiences. The overall purpose of this area of neurotheology is to generate a substantial theoretical base from which to explore the other aspects of religious and spiritual phenomena. Models typically build upon both the known neuropsychological and neuroscientific literature to determine exactly how various brain structures function both individually and as an integrated whole. Models typically include not only general brain function but changes in a variety of neurotransmitter and hormonal systems. An analysis of various types of neuropsychiatric disorders, such as schizophrenia or temporal lobe epilepsy, as they relate to religious and spiritual phenomena, must also be considered as a way of helping to understand various aspects of religious experience. The work of Andrew Newberg and Eugene d'Aquili, for example, demonstrates one method for developing a complex integrated model in which various aspects of brain function are correlated with religious experiences. The brain structures that have already been shown to be involved in religious practices such as meditation or prayer include the frontal lobes (involved in attention focusing and emotional processing), the limbic system (part of the temporal lobes and involved in emotional responses), the parietal lobe (involved in spatial and body orientation), the thalamus (a main sensory relay), and the hypothalamus (regulating basic body functions, hormones, and the immune system).

EMPIRICAL TESTING OF RELIGIOUS EXPERIENCE. Once theoretical models of religious and spiritual experiences are developed, they provide a hypothetical framework from which significant empirical testing can be performed. Much of the theoretical and empirical work depends upon a strong neuroscientific background with regard to how the brain functions in general, and then how such functioning can be applied to religion and theology. The brain must handle tremendous amounts of sensory, cognitive, and emotional information to provide human beings with a reasonable representation of the "external world." It may be helpful to simplify the understanding of how the brain abstracts elements of meaning from various input by considering basic approaches to organizing this information. Such basic brain functions have sometimes been called *cognitive modules* or *cognitive operators.* Cognitive modules refer to brain structures with specific functions for manipulating input into the brain. Cognitive operators typically refer to more generalized brain functions that operate on input with the understanding that there are underlying brain structures or groups of structures that subserve such functions. A partial list of the cognitive operators initially developed by d'Aquili that are relevant to neurotheology are given below. It should be noted that a number of brain-imaging studies, including studies of positron emission tomography (PET), single photon emission computed tomography (SPECT), and functional magnetic resonance imaging (fMRI), have demonstrated more specifically how the brain processes input along a variety of different functions.

(1) The causal operator permits reality to be viewed in terms of causal sequences of abstract elements.

(2) The abstractive operator permits the formation of a general concept from the perception of empirical individuals.

(3) The binary operator permits the extraction of meaning by ordering abstract elements into dyads involving varying degrees of polarity so each pole of the dyad derives meaning from contrast with the other pole.

(4) The formal quantitative operator permits the abstraction of quantity per se from the perception of empirical individuals, generating arithmetic and mathematics.

(5) The emotional value operator permits an affective valence to be assigned to various elements of perception and cognition.

(6) The holistic operator permits reality to be viewed as a whole or as a gestalt. It is responsible for the generation of absolute unitary being discussed in the second part of this article.

The causal operator has much scientific support and likely resides at the junction of the superior temporal and inferior parietal lobes (Pribram and Luria, 1973; Mills and Rollman, 1980). The abstractive operator likely resides in the region of the left inferior parietal lobe, most likely near the angular gyrus, and forms an important part of the language axis (Luria, 1966; Joseph, 1996). The binary operator may arise near the region of the inferior parietal lobe in close proximity to the area that underlies the ability to formally quantitate objects (Dahaene, 2000). However, with regard to quantitation, evidence suggests that the left hemisphere is more associated with specific mathematical functions, whereas the right appears better equipped for comparing numbers. In terms of the emotional value operator, much evidence for the importance of emotions in human behavior and reason has come from the research of Antonio Damasio (1994, 1999). His somatic marker hypothesis suggests that emotions are critical in helping human beings make decisions and think rationally. Furthermore, emotions appear necessary to assign relative value to all of the other products of the cognitive operators. Evidence for the holistic operator derives from studies that have explored the functions of the right hemisphere, demonstrating more holistic applications to perceptions and problem solving (Nebes and Sperry, 1971; Gazzaniga and Hillyard, 1971; Gazzaniga, 2000). Other physiological information relevant to the study of religious experiences may be provided by measuring parameters, including blood pressure, heart rate, and reaction times. Future studies will likely measure the effects of various hormones and neurotransmitters as they relate to the religious practices and experiences.

Religious Experience and Health. Another area within neurotheology is the study of the health-related effects of religiousness and religious experiences. A number of studies have shown positive (and sometimes negative) effects of religion on physical and mental health (Koenig, 1998, 2001). In general, studies have linked religiousness with an overall lower mortality rate and specific decreases in the incidence of cardiac disease, liver disease, and some types of cancer. Studies of mental health have shown that religion is a primary source of coping for many individuals, and practices such as meditation and prayer may have beneficial effects on depression and anxiety. On the other hand, some studies have indicated that, when an individual has a conflicted perspective of religion or perceives God as punishing them, there can be negative outcomes. Furthermore there are many examples of religious-type behaviors associated with cults and other groups in which there is a negative worldview often ending in mass suicides. While many more clinical studies need to be performed, an understanding of the associated physiological and neurophysiological effects of religiousness and religious experience may help provide a clearer link to health. This area of neurotheology can help clarify why religion is sometimes a positive force and sometimes a negative force in an individual or community's life.

The Scope of Neurotheology. One of the criticisms of neurotheology is that the field focuses too much on individual religious experiences, particularly the mystical ones, people have and that it does not take into account the other aspects of religions. For neurotheology to achieve its full potential as a field of study, it is important for any investigator to understand the complexity and diversity of experiences that are religious or spiritual. In other words, religion is much more than just the experiences that individuals can have, especially the strong mystical experiences that are not common. Religions typically have many different rituals, holidays, and cognitive, emotional, and behavioral components that all can be evaluated from a neuropsychological perspective. Even issues such as forgiveness, love, or altruism can be considered from a neuropsychological perspective to gain better insight into how and when such feelings and behaviors take place. It is this ability to explore the neuropsychological basis of such concepts that can ultimately be a strength of neurotheology.

Finally, neurotheology must be able to address theological concepts. The cognitive operators mentioned above, as well as other aspects of brain function, can be utilized to consider a wide variety of theological concepts (d'Aquili and Newberg, 1999). In neurotheology this analysis is based somewhat on an interpretation of religious myth and ritual and how these elements affect or are affected by the human brain. For example, the causal operator described above may play a prominent role in the conception of God as the fundamental cause of all things. The binary operator is crucial to developing concepts such as good and evil, justice and injustice, and even humankind and God. These opposites are a focal point of many myth structures and are of fundamental importance in religion and theology. The quantitative abilities of the brain may help explain why numbers have had such important meaning in the human understanding of most religions, with specific numbers having a special status. Thus certain quantities and numbers have special religious meaning depending on the particular tradition. The holistic operator is likely to be deeply tied to the notion of God as infinite and inclusive of all things. Furthermore, the holistic functions of the brain appear particularly tied to the mystical experiences in which an individual perceives a union with God or ultimate reality.

It is important to state that these brain functions do not necessarily constrain the reality of a particular concept but may have an important impact on the human understanding of these issues. As an example, one might consider the notion of God as the fundamental cause of all things. It can be asked whether or not such a conception is related to the human brain's ability to perceive causality. If an individual had damage to the areas of the brain responsible for perceiving causality, he or she may no longer perceive God from a causal perspective. God might be perceived as the fundamental love in the universe rather than the cause. Again, such a perception would not alter what God's actual nature is, only the human perception of this nature.

The emotional elements of religion are also an important aspect of neurotheological analysis because a variety of emotions are fundamental to religions and religious experience. The autonomic nervous system (in conjunction with the hypothalamus) that regulates basic body functions, such as heart rate, blood pressure, and hormones, and the limbic system that regulates basic emotional responses can produce a wide variety of complex feelings. Religious concepts pertaining to love, joy, envy, or awe are likely associated with concomitant changes in these components of the nervous system. Neurotheology seeks to study the relationship between the nervous-system structures and such elements of religions and religious experiences.

Neurotheology may also have a special status because neurology is universal in the sense that all human beings have brains that function in a similar manner. The challenge for future neurotheological development is to evaluate the similarities and differences among individual brain functions, as well as the phenomenological differences both within and across religious traditions. Neurotheology has the opportunity to explore religion and theology on a broad scale and on an individual level. It has also been argued that neurotheology may provide a basis for a metatheology and even a megatheology. A metatheology comprises both the general principles describing, and implicitly the rules for constructing, any concrete theological system. In and of itself, a metatheology is devoid of theological content, because it consists of rules and descriptions about how any and all specific theologies are structured. A metatheology must evaluate how and why foundational, creation, and soteriological myths are formed; how and why such myths are elaborated into complex theological systems; and how and why the basic myths and certain aspects of their theological elaborations are objectified in the motor behavior of ceremonial ritual. A megatheology, on the other hand, should contain content of such a universal nature that it could be adopted by most, if not all, of the world's great religions as a basic element without any serious violation of their essential doctrines. Since brain function is universal and necessarily has an impact on how human beings understand and practice religion, a fully developed neurotheology may provide a basis for a megatheology.

Overall, neurotheology seeks to facilitate a dialogue between religion and science with the eventual goal of helping to integrate these perspectives around the nexus of neuropsychology. That neuropsychology provides some universal perspective on human behavior and thought that can also be utilized in an approach to the study of religions and theology lies at the heart of neurotheology. Furthermore neurotheology seeks to integrate theoretical development, empirical studies, and philosophical and theological interpretation. Neurotheology as a field of study thus holds many opportunities for expansion and may play a critical role in future theological and religious study.

BIBLIOGRAPHY

Dahaene, S. "Cerebral Basis of Number Processing and Calculation." In *The New Cognitive Neurosciences*, edited by Michael S. Gazzaniga, pp 987–998. Cambridge, Mass., 2000.

Damasio, Antonio R. *Descartes' Error: Emotion, Reason, and the Human Brain.* New York, 1994.

Damasio, Antonio R. *The Feeling of What Happens: Body and Emotion in the Making of Consciousness.* New York, 1999.

D'Aquili, Eugene G. "The Myth-Ritual Complex: A Biogenetic Structural Analysis." *Zygon* 18 (1983): 247–269.

D'Aquili, Eugene G., and Andrew B. Newberg. "Religious and Mystical States: A Neuropsychological Model." *Zygon* 28 (1993): 177–200.

D'Aquili, Eugene G., and Andrew B. Newberg. *The Mystical Mind: Probing the Biology of Religious Experience.* Minneapolis, Minn., 1999.

Gazzaniga, Michael S. *The Bisected Brain.* New York, 1970.

Gazzaniga, Michael S., ed. *The New Cognitive Neurosciences.* Cambridge, Mass., 2000.

Gazzaniga, Michael S., and S. A. Hillyard. "Language and Speech Capacity of the Right Hemisphere." *Neuropsychologia* 9 (1971): 273–280.

Joseph, Rhawn. *Neuropsychiatry, Neuropsychology, and Clinical Neuroscience.* Baltimore, Md., 1996.

Koenig, Harold G., ed. *Handbook of Religion and Mental Health.* San Diego, Calif., 1998.

Koenig, Harold G., Michael E. McCullough, and David B. Larson, eds. *Handbook of Religion and Health.* New York, 2001.

Luria, Aleksander R. *Higher Cortical Functions in Man.* New York, 1966.

Luria, Aleksander R. *The Working Brain.* New York, 1973.

Mills, L., and G. B. Rollman. "Hemispheric Asymmetry for Auditory Perception of Temporal Order." *Neuropsychologia* 18 (1980): 41–47.

Nebes, R. D., and R. W. Sperry. "Hemispheric Deconnection Syndrome with Cerebral Birth Injury in the Dominant Arm Area." *Neuropsychologia* 9 (1971): 249–259.

Newberg, Andrew B., Eugene G. d'Aquili, and Vince P. Rause. *Why God Won't Go Away: Brain Science and the Biology of Belief.* New York, 2001.

Pribram, K. H., and Aleksander R. Luria, eds. *Psychophysiology of the Frontal Lobes.* New York, 1973.

ANDREW B. NEWBERG (2005)

NEW AGE JUDAISM See JEWISH RENEWAL MOVEMENT

See JEWISH RENEWAL MOVEMENT

NEW AGE MOVEMENT.

"New Age" was originally a buzzword that achieved widespread popularity in Europe and the United States during the 1980s. It referred to a wide array of spiritual practices and beliefs perceived as "alternative" from the perspective of mainstream Western society. To many observers, the increasing visibility of "things New Age" in the media and popular culture conveyed the impression of something radically new: the birth of a grassroots movement of social and spiritual innovation, prophesying a profound transformation of Western society that some claimed would culminate in a vastly superior culture—the "Age of Aquarius."

The phenomenon that came to be known as the New Age movement during the last two decades of the twentieth century actually had its immediate roots in the counterculture of the 1960s and some of its immediate predecessors, while its fundamental ideas had much more ancient origins. New Age religion is neither something completely new nor just a revival—or survival—of something ancient. While its fundamental ideas have origins that can be traced far back in history, these ideas are interpreted and put to use in a manner that makes New Age a manifestation par excellence of postmodern consumer society. In order to gain a balanced view of the New Age movement, we therefore need to consider both dimensions: its historical foundations as well as its specific modernity.

THE NEW AGE MOVEMENT IN A STRICT SENSE (1950S–1970S). The immediate roots of the New Age movement may seem surprising at first. Shortly after World War II, popular curiosity was attracted by unexplained phenomena in the sky referred to as unidentified flying objects (UFOs). In various places in Western Europe and the United States, study groups were formed by people who wanted to investigate these phenomena, and some of those groups rapidly proceeded to take on cultic characteristics. Typically, such groups believed that UFOs were in fact spaceships inhabited by intelligent beings from other planets or other dimensions of outer space. Representing a superior level of cultural, technological, and spiritual evolution, they now made their appearance to herald the coming of a New Age. The Earth was entering a new evolutionary cycle that would be accompanied by a new and superior kind of spiritual consciousness. However, since the present cultures of humanity were thoroughly corrupted by materialism, they would resist this change. As a result, the transition to a new cycle of evolution would necessitate the destruction of the old civilization by violent causes such as earthquakes, floods, diseases, and the like, resulting in global economic, political, and social collapse. Those individuals whose consciousness was already in tune with the qualities of the new culture would be protected in various ways and would survive the period of cataclysms. In due time they would become the vanguard of the New Age, or Age of Aquarius: an age of abundance, bliss, and spiritual enlightenment when humanity would once again live in accordance with universal cosmic laws.

These beliefs were inspired by occultist teachings of various provenance, but especially by the writings of the Christian Theosophist Alice Bailey (1880–1949) and, in some respects, the anthroposophical metaphysics of the German visionary Rudolf Steiner (1861–1925). In 1937, Alice Bailey "channeled" a spiritual prayer known as "The Great Invocation," which is still used by some New Age adherents to invoke the New Age and which reflects the pronounced Christian elements that still informed the occultist millenarianism of the early New Age movement. These elements would remain prominent during the second, countercultural stage of its development. During the 1960s, the basic belief system and millenarian expectations of the UFO groups were adopted by various utopian communities, the most famous of which is the Findhorn community in Scotland. The members of these communities were trying to live in a new way, in tune with the laws of nature and the universe. They were trying, in the spirit of "The Great Invocation," to be "Centers of Light," or focal points in a network from which spiritual illumination would eventually spread out and encompass the globe.

In the attitude of these early New Agers, represented by popular spokespeople such as David Spangler (b. 1945) or George Trevelyan (1906–1996), there can be seen an important change from the perspectives of the 1950s UFO groups. Whereas the pronounced apocalypticism of the latter entailed an essentially passive attitude of "waiting for the great events" that would destroy the old civilization and usher in a New Age, utopian communities of the 1960s, such as Findhorn, increasingly emphasized the importance of an activist, constructive attitude: Spangler noted in *The Rebirth of the Sacred:* "Instead of spreading warnings of apocalypse, let Findhorn proclaim that the new age is already here, in spirit if not in form, and that anyone can now cocreate with that spirit so that the form will become manifest" (London, 1984, pp. 34–35). This became the perspective typical of the New Age movement of the 1960s and its sympathizers in later decades.

THE CULTIC MILIEU. This early New Age movement, born in the context of the postwar UFO cults and flowering in the spiritual utopianism of the 1960s and 1970s, was only one manifestation of the countercultural ferment of the times. More generally, this ferment found expression in a widespread "cultic milieu" (Campbell, 1972) in Western society: a diffuse phenomenon consisting of individuals who feel dissatisfied with mainstream Western culture and religion and are looking for alternatives. This cultic milieu proved to be fertile soil for a plethora of new religious movements of various provenance. Some of these movements took the form of relatively stable social entities, including an internal hierarchy of power and authority, definite doctrines and rules of conduct, clearly defined boundaries between members and nonmembers, claims of exclusive truth, and so on. Other movements were more ephemeral and fluid, with relatively few demands on members and an inclusive and tolerant attitude. The latter type of cultic groups may come into existence quickly and vanish as quickly again, and their membership may sometimes be very small. Members may participate in several such groups at the same time—displaying an activity known as "spiritual shopping"—without feeling committed to making a choice in favor of one at the expense of the other. This type of spiritual activity is most characteristic of the development of the "cultic milieu" that spawned and supported the New Age movement of the 1980s.

It is helpful to distinguish the latter movement from the original New Age movement described above. The spiritual perspectives associated with the UFO cults of the 1950s and the utopian communities of the 1960s and 1970s may collectively be referred to as the New Age movement in a strict sense (Hanegraaff, 1996/1998, pp. 94–103). This movement is characterized by a broadly occultist metaphysics (with special prominence of the forms of Theosophy founded by Alice Bailey and, to some extent, Rudolf Steiner), a relatively strong emphasis on community values and a traditional morality emphasizing altruistic love and service to humanity, and a very strong millenarian emphasis focused on the expectation of the New Age. This New Age movement "in a strict sense" still exists, but its membership is rather strongly dominated by the baby-boomer generation and tends to be perceived as somewhat old-fashioned by new-generation New Agers. By the end of the 1970s this New Age movement in a strict sense came to be assimilated as merely one aspect within the much more complex and widespread phenomenon that may be referred to, by way of contrast, as the New Age movement in a general sense.

THE NEW AGE MOVEMENT IN A GENERAL SENSE (1980S–1990S). This New Age movement in a general sense may be defined as the cultic milieu having become conscious of itself, by the end of the 1970s, as constituting a more or less unified movement (although not a New Religious Movement in the normal sense of the word; Hanegraaff, 1996/1998, p. 17). In other words, people who participated in various "alternative" activities and pursuits began to consider themselves as part of an international invisible community of like-minded individuals, the collective efforts of whom were destined to change the world into a better and more spiritual place. American sociologist Marilyn Ferguson referred to this phenomenon as the Aquarian Conspiracy: a "leaderless but powerful network" working to bring about radical change (Ferguson, 1980, p. 23). Physicist Fritjof Capra saw it as the "rising culture" destined to replace the declining culture of the modern West (Capra, 1982, p. 419). But eventually what they were referring to came to be known as the New Age movement: by the late 1970s and early 1980s the term *New Age* was adopted from the specific occultist-millenarian movement known under that name and came to be applied as a catchall term for the much more extensive and complex cultic milieu of the 1980s and beyond. This is how the New Age movement in a strict sense was absorbed into the New Age movement in a general sense.

This development has been a cause of concern for some representatives of the original movement, who perceived in it a cheapening of the idea of a New Age. While the original New Age movement had been carried by high-minded idealism and an ethic of service to humanity, the movement of the 1980s quickly developed into an increasingly commercialized "spiritual marketplace" catering to the tastes and whims of an individualistic clientele. While the original movement had espoused a reasonably coherent theosophical metaphysics and philosophy of history, the movement of the 1980s seemed to present a hodgepodge of ideas and speculations without a clear focus and direction. While the excited expectation of a radical New Age dominated the earlier movement, this expectation ceased to be central to the movement of the 1980s, which, in spite of its name, tends to concentrate on the spiritual development of the individual rather than of society. The development might also be described in terms of cultural geographics: while the original movement was England-based and relied upon occultist traditions that had long been influential there, the new movement was dominated by the so-called metaphysical and New Thought traditions typical of American alternative culture. The move from community-oriented values to individual-centered ones is a reflection of that development.

Indeed, the New Age movement in a general sense has been dominated by American cultural and spiritual ideas and values, and the most important spokespersons have been Americans. While many names could be mentioned, two stand out as symbolic of the 1980s and the 1990s, respectively. During the 1980s the most vocal representative of the New Age idea may have been the movie actress Shirley MacLaine. Her autobiographies, published between 1983 and 1989, in which she describes her spiritual quest, and the television miniseries *Out on a Limb* based upon the first of these books, encapsulate the essential perspective of the New Age movement of the 1980s. For the 1990s the same thing may be said of the best-sellers of James Redfield: *The Celestine Prophecy,* with its accompanying *Celestine Workbook,* and a succession of follow-up volumes capitalizing on the success of the first one. While MacLaine's autobiographies were certainly easy to read, Redfield's books carried the New Age perspective to a new level of simplicity, thereby broadening the potential market for New Age beyond the audiences already reached by earlier authors.

These developments contributed to the fact that by the beginning of the 1990s more and more people attracted to alternative spirituality began to distance themselves from the label New Age, which they perceived as loaded with unwanted associations. During the 1980s it was still possible to investigate the New Age movement (in a general sense) simply by questioning people who identified themselves as involved in New Age; during the 1990s participants increasingly refused to identify themselves as such, preferring vague and noncommittal terms such as "spirituality." It is a mistake to conclude from this, as has sometimes been done, that the New Age movement is declining or vanishing. Rather, the movement has been moving away from its traditional status as a "counterculture" that proclaims the New Age in a gesture of rejecting the values of the "old culture." Attempts to replace the term *New Age* by a term such as *spirituality* fit within a new strategy of adaptation and assimilation instead of rejection and confrontation, as a result of which the New Age movement is now securing its place as an increasingly professionalized spiritual wing *within* the cultural mainstream.

SECULARIZED ESOTERICISM. From the perspective of intellectual history, the basic ideas of New Age religion have their origins in the traditions referred to as modern Western Esotericism, which took shape since the early Renaissance. The foundational worldviews of Western esoteric religiosity were thoroughly transformed, however, under the impact of various processes of modernization since the eighteenth century, resulting in a new phenomenon that may be referred to as secularized Esotericism and that comprises "all attempts by esotericists to come to terms with a disenchanted world or, alternatively, by people in general to make sense of Esotericism from the perspective of a disenchanted secular world" (Hanegraaff, 1996/1998, p. 422). Although there is a risk of terminological confusion, the term *occultism* will be used below as a synonym for secularized Esotericism.

The first signs of a secularization of Western Esotericism may be perceived in the perspectives of Swedish visionary Emanuel Swedenborg (1688–1772) and German physician Franz Anton Mesmer (1734–1815), both of whom exerted an incalculable influence on the history of Esotericism during the nineteenth and twentieth centuries. Theurgical practices, spiritual manifestations, and psychic phenomena of a type already present in some esoteric societies of the later eighteenth century as well as in the popular practice of magnetic healing achieved mass popularity in the second half of the nineteenth century in the movement known as Spiritualism. Spiritualism provided a context within which a plethora of more or less sophisticated occultist movements came into existence. Among these manifestations of alternative religiosity, the Theosophical Society founded in 1875 by Helena P. Blavatsky (1831–1891) and Henry Steel Olcott (1832–1907) is certainly the most important in terms of its influence, and the basic metaphysical system of modern theosophy may be considered the archetypal manifestation of occultist spirituality at least until far into the 1970s. In addition, popular practices of magnetic healing, also referred to as mesmerism, reached the United States as early as 1836 and spread widely in the following decades, eventually providing a popular basis for the emergence of the so-called New Thought movement of the later nineteenth century. Each one of these various currents—Spiritualism, modern theosophy, and the American New Thought movement—has taken on a multitude of forms, and their representatives have mingled and exchanged ideas and practices in various way. The result of all this alternative religious activity was the emergence, during the nineteenth century, of an international "cultic milieu" with its own social networks and literature; relying on an essentially nineteenth-century framework of ideas and beliefs, this cultic milieu has continued and further developed during the twentieth century, eventually to provide the foundation after World War II for the emergence of the New Age movement.

The occultist or secularized esoteric milieu of the nineteenth and twentieth centuries differs from traditional Western Esotericism in at least four respects, which are crucial for understanding New Age religion. First, Esotericism was originally grounded in a worldview where all parts of the universe were linked by invisible networks of noncausal correspondences and a divine power of life was considered to permeate the whole of nature. Although esotericists have continued to defend such holistic view of the world as permeated by invisible forces, their actual statements demonstrate that they came to compromise in various ways with the mechanical and disenchanted world models that achieved cultural dominance under the impact of scientific materialism and nineteenth-century positivism. Accordingly, secularized Esotericism is characterized by hybrid mixtures of traditional esoteric and modern scientistic-materialist worldviews: while originally the religious belief in a universe brought forth by a personal God was axiomatic for Esotericism, eventually this belief succumbed partly or completely to popular scientific visions of a universe answering to impersonal laws of causality. Even though the laws in question may be referred to as spiritual, nonetheless they tend to be described according to models taken from science rather than religion.

Second, the traditional Christian presuppositions of modern Western Esotericism were increasingly questioned and relativized because of new translations of Asian religious texts and the emergence of a "comparative study of the religions of the world." Asian religions began to display missionary activities in Western countries, and their representatives typically sought to convince their audience by using Western terms and concepts to present the spirituality of religions such as Hinduism and Buddhism. Conversely, since esotericists had always believed that the essential truths of esoteric spirituality were universal in nature and could be discovered at the heart of all great religious traditions East and West, it was natural for them during the nineteenth century to incorporate Asian concepts and terminology into already-existing Western esoteric frameworks. One excellent example is the concept of *karma* that Blavatsky adopted from Hinduism as a welcome alternative to Christian concepts of divine providence, whereas Blavatsky's essential understanding of reincarnation depended on Western esoteric rather than Asian sources (see discussion in Hanegraaff, 1996/1998, pp. 479–482).

Third, the well-known debate between Christian creationism and the new theories of evolution became highly relevant to esotericists as well, and in this battle they generally took the side of science. But although popular evolutionism became a crucial aspect of Esotericism as it developed from the nineteenth into the twentieth century, and although this evolutionism was generally used as part of a strategy of presenting occultism as scientifically legitimate, the actual types of evolutionism found in this context depended less on Darwinian theory than on philosophical models originating in German Idealism and Romanticism. The idea of a universal process of spiritual evolution and progress, involving human souls as well as the universe in its entirety, is not to be found in traditional Western Esotericism but became fundamental to almost all forms of nineteenth- and twentieth-century Esotericism.

Finally, the emergence of modern psychology (itself dependent partly on mesmerism and the Romantic fascination with the "night-side of nature") has had an enormous impact on the development of Esotericism from the second half of the nineteenth century on. While psychology could be used as an argument against Christianity and against religion generally by arguing that God or the gods are merely projections of the human psyche, it also proved possible to present Western esoteric worldviews in terms of a new psychological terminology. Most influential in this respect was Swiss psychiatrist Carl Gustav Jung (1875–1961), whose spiritual perspective was deeply rooted in the esoteric and occult currents of German Romantic *Naturphilosophie* but whose theories could be used to present that spirituality as a scientific psychology. Apart from Jung, the pop psychology of the American New Thought movement has been a major influence on the mixtures of occultism and psychology typical of New Age spirituality (Hanegraaff, 1996/1998, pp. 482–513).

POSTMODERN SPIRITUALITY: THE RELIGION OF THE SELF. To the four main aspects of the secularization of Western Esotericism, perhaps a fifth one may be added that became dominant only after World War II and is fully characteristic of the New Age movement of the 1980s and 1990s: the impact of the capitalist market economy on the domain of spirituality. Increasingly, the New Age movement has taken the shape of a spiritual supermarket where religious consumers pick and choose the spiritual commodities they fancy and use them to create their own spiritual syntheses, fine-tuned to their strictly personal needs. The phenomenon of a spiritual supermarket is not limited to the New Age movement only but is a general characteristic of religion in (post)modern Western democracies. Various forms of New Age spirituality are competing with more traditional forms of religion (including the Christian churches as well as other great religious traditions such as Islam or Buddhism) and with a great number of so-called new religious movements. However, in this universal battle for the attention of the consumer, the New Age movement enjoys certain advantages over most of its competitors, which seem to make it the representative par excellence of the contemporary spirituality of the market. Whereas most other spiritual currents that compete for the attention of the consumer in modern society take the form of (at least rudimentary) organizations, enabling their members to see themselves as part of a religious community, New Age spirituality is strictly focused on the individual and his or her personal development. In fact, this individualism functions as an in-built defense mechanism against social organization and institutionalization: as soon as any group of people involved with New Age ideas begins to take up "cultic" characteristics, this very fact already distances them from the basic individualism of New Age spirituality. The more strongly they begin to function as a cult, or even as a sect, the more other New Agers will suspect that they are becoming a church (that is, that they are relapsing into what are considered old-fashioned patterns of dogmatism, intolerance, and exclusivism), and the less they will be acceptable to the general cultic milieu of New Age spirituality. Within the present social context of a democratic free market of ideas and practices, the New Age's strict emphasis on the self and on individual experience as the only reliable source of spiritual truth, the authority of which can never be overruled by any religious dogma or considerations of solidarity with communal values, functions as an effective mechanism against institutionalization of New Age religion into a religion. This essential individualism makes the New Ager into the ideal spiritual consumer. Except for the very focus on the self and its spiritual evolution, there are no constraints a priori on a New Ager's potential spiritual interests; the fact that every New Ager continually creates and re-creates his or her own private system of symbolic meaning and values means that spiritual suppliers on the New Age market enjoy maximum opportunities for presenting him or her with ever-new commodities.

As indicated above, that New Age as a spiritual supermarket caters to an individualistic clientele primarily interested in personal growth and development is not only a fact of social observation but also reflects beliefs that are basic to the movement. At the symbolic center of New Age worldviews, one typically finds not a concept of God but, rather, the concept of the (higher) Self, so that New Age spirituality has indeed sometimes been dubbed Self Religion (Heelas). The symbolism of the self is linked to a basic mythology, which narrates the growth and development of the individual soul through many incarnations and existences in the direction of ever-increasing knowledge and spiritual insight. Strict concentration on personal spiritual development rather than on communal values is therefore not considered a reflection of egoism but, rather, of a legitimate spiritual practice based on listening to your own inner guidance: only by following one's inner voice may one find one's way through the chaos of voices that clamor for attention on the spiritual supermarket and find one's personal way to enlightenment.

A final remark is in order about the question of a globalization of New Age religion beyond the confines of Western democracies. From what has been said, it will be clear that New Age religion is a product of specific historical developments in Western culture and that its present manifestations are impossible to separate from the internal dynamics of (post)modern consumer societies. Furthermore, as a movement that owes its identity to a consistent pattern of criticism directed against certain dominant aspects of mainstream Western culture, it is difficult even to imagine New Age religion existing in non-Western societies. It has often been claimed that New Age is spreading to continents other than North America and Europe (such as Africa, South America, or Asia); but on closer scrutiny one discovers that scholars who describe such processes of alleged acculturation tend to use the term *New Age* in a too vague and intuitive sense, and that they are usually speaking of the spread, not of New Age religion, but of various Western new religious movements to non-Western societies (Hanegraaff, 2001). To the extent that non-Western cultures and societies resist socioeconomic pressures tending toward a global Americanization, there is no particular reason to refer to new forms of spiritual syncretisms that may emerge on their soil as New Age religion; this is true regardless of whether or not these syncretisms happen to owe something to the influence of Western New Age ideas. Rather, such local new spiritualities must be considered as products of the specific culture and society in question, and one should not prejudge the question of whether—and if so, to what extent—they can be compared to the Western phenomenon of New Age religion.

WHITHER THE NEW AGE? For quite some time now, it has been claimed by scholars and critics that the days of the New Age movement are numbered, that the New Age is over, or that the movement has already yielded to a follow-up phenomenon sometimes referred to as the Next Age. Whether this is true depends very much on one's definition. There are indeed clear signs that New Age religion is losing its status as a countercultural movement and is now increasingly assimilated by the mainstream of society. Such a development is anything but surprising: rather, it may be seen as the predicable result of commercial success. From one perspective, the fact that New Age is developing from a distinct counterculture to merely a dimension of mainstream culture may indeed be interpreted as the end of the New Age movement as we have known it; but from another one, it may be seen as reflecting the commonsense fact that New Age is developing and changing, just like any other religious movement known to history. The idea of a decline of New Age is largely the result of optical illusion. There are some indications that the phenomenon of specialized New Age bookstores is declining, but at the same time one notices a substantial increase of spiritual literature on the shelves of bookstores. Likewise, specialized New Age centers for healing and personal growth predictably become less necessary to the extent that at least a part of their therapeutic services are becoming more acceptable in mainstream medical and psychological contexts. One might well interpret such developments as reflecting not the decline of the New Age movement but, precisely, its development from a countercultural movement set apart from the mainstream to a significant dimension of the spiritual landscape of contemporary Western society in general.

Whether or not the label New Age will eventually survive, there is no evidence that the basic spiritual perspectives, beliefs, and practices characteristic of the movement of the 1980s and 1990s are losing popular credibility. Quite the contrary: all the evidence indicates that they are becoming more acceptable to great numbers of people in contemporary Western societies, whether or not the latter identify themselves as "New Agers." Again, the phenomenon is anything but surprising, for the highly individualized approach to spirituality traditionally referred to as New Age simply accords too well with the demands of the contemporary consumer culture in a democratic society where citizens insist on their personal autonomy in matter of religion.

That the social dynamics of postmodern consumer society happen to favor a particular type of religion (referred to above as secularized Esotericism) is a fact of recent history, but once again it is not a surprising one. That traditional forms of religion—the Christian churches and their theologies—are in decline at least in the contemporary Western European context is a generally known fact. The vogue of postmodern relativism indicates that the grand narratives of progress by science and rationality are shaken as well. If more and more people feel that traditional Christianity, rationality, and science are no longer able to give sense and meaning to human existence, it is to be expected that a spiritual perspective based on personal revelations by means of *gnosis* or personal religious experience will profit from the circumstances (Van den Broek and Hanegraaff, 1996/1998, pp. vii–x). As long as the grand narratives of the past fail to regain their hold over the population while no new ones are forthcoming, and as long as Western democratic societies continue to emphasize the supreme virtue of individual freedom, the "self religion" traditionally known as New Age will remain a force to be reckoned with.

SEE ALSO Blavatsky, H. P.; Esotericism; Jung, C. G.; New Religious Movements, article on New Religious Movements and Millennialism; New Thought Movement; Occultism; Olcott, Henry Steel; Spiritualism; Swedenborg, Emanuel; Swedenborgianism; Theosophical Society; UFO Religions.

BIBLIOGRAPHY

Bednarowski, Mary Farrell. *New Religions and the Theological Imagination in America.* Bloomington and Indianapolis, Ind., 1989. Probably the first book to take New Age theologies seriously.

Bochinger, Christoph. *"New Age" und moderne Religion: Religionswissenschaftliche Analysen,* Gütersloh, 1994. The most ambitious study of the German context; it interprets New Age as a "phantom" created by book publishing enterprises rather than an actual "religious movement."

Campbell, Colin. "The Cult, the Cultic Milieu, and Secularization." *A Sociological Yearbook of Religion in Britain* 5 (1972): 119–136. A classic article that made theoretical and terminological distinctions essential to an adequate analysis of the New Age movement.

Capra, Fritjof. *The Turning Point: Science, Society, and the Rising Culture.* New York, 1982.

Corrywright, Dominic. *Theoretical and Empirical Investigations into New Age Spiritualities.* Oxford and New York, 2003. One of the most recent sociological studies.

Ferguson, Marilyn. *The Aquarian Conspiracy: Personal and Social Transformation in the 1980s.* Los Angeles and New York, 1980.

Hammer, Olav. *Claiming Knowledge: Strategies of Epistemology from Theosophy to the New Age.* Leiden and Boston, 2001. Analyzes in depth the argumentative strategies by which contemporary esotericists seek to present their beliefs as "reasonable."

Hanegraaff, Wouter J. *New Age Religion and Western Culture: Esotericism in the Mirror of Secular Thought.* Leiden, 1996; Albany, N.Y., 1998. The most complete study of New Age beliefs and their historical backgrounds.

Hanegraaff, Wouter J. "New Age Spiritualities as Secular Religion: A Historian's Perspective." *Social Compass* 46, no. 2 (1999): 145–160. Discusses further aspects of New Age not treated in Hanegraaff 1996/1998.

Hanegraaff, Wouter J. "Prospects for the Globalization of New Age: Spiritual Imperialism versus Cultural Diversity." In *New Age Religion and Globalization,* edited by Mikael Rothstein, pp. 15–30. Aarhus, 2001. Analyzes what is at stake in studying the spread of New Age ideas to non-Western contexts.

Hanegraaff, Wouter J. "Spectral Evidence of New Age Religion: On the Substance of Ghosts and the Use of Concepts." *Journal of New Age Studies* 1 (2004). Discusses theoretical and methodological issues suggested by recent social-science studies of New Age.

Heelas, Paul. *The New Age Movement: The Celebration of the Self and the Sacralization of Modernity.* Cambridge, Mass., 1996. The best sociological study of New Age.

Spangler, David. *Emergence: The Rebirth of the Sacred.* New York, 1984.

Sutcliffe, Steven J. *Children of the New Age: A History of Spiritual Practices.* London and New York, 2003. Methodologically problematic and unreliable as regards the general New Age movement, but contains good discussions of the England-based "New Age in a strict sense."

York, Michael. *The Emerging Network: A Sociology of the New Age and Neo-Pagan Movements.* Lanham, Md., and London, 1995. The first book-length sociological study of New Age.

WOUTER J. HANEGRAAFF (2005)

NEW CALEDONIA RELIGION is best known from the work of Maurice Leenhardt, a former Protestant missionary (Société des Missions Évangéliques Pratique de Paris), who was Marcel Mauss's successor as professor of comparative religions at the École Pratique des Hautes Études.

Because each local group (*mwaro*) in New Caledonia is linked with an animal or plant or other natural phenomenon, Western observers have described the religion of the island as "totemism." Though this term is now less fashionable than it was in the period from 1880 to 1940, it can still, for convenience' sake, be applied to the New Caledonia religious system. The local groups have divided among themselves all the aspects of nature that either can be utilized or need to be feared, with each group becoming the master of a particular aspect. Within each group, one of the members of the most junior line, referred to as the group's "master," is in charge of performing the ritual that will protect or benefit all the *mwaro.* Thus, the master of the yam ensures a good crop over the whole of the valley. Along the sea one finds masters of the trade winds, the shark, the whale, or the mosquito, while masters of the thunder are to be found nearer the mountain range.

Each master not only ensures prosperity and wards off natural disasters, but also controls the specific sickness thought to be linked with the totemic entity assigned to him. If someone is ailing, word is sent to a seer, who divines the cause of the sickness. A messenger is then sent to the master in charge of the force responsible for the sickness. The master prays and gives the necessary herbal remedies to the patient; many of these medications are quite effective in treating at least those illnesses that were not brought by Europeans.

The natures of the New Caledonia gods are complex, and Leenhardt spent considerable time attempting to understand them. R. H. Codrington, in *The Melanesians* (1891), distinguished two principal types of gods: those who were once human and those who have never been human. The New Caledonians, however, make no linguistical distinction, both types of gods being referred to either as *bao* or *due.* The two kinds of deities are linked in the figure of Teê Pijopac, a god who has himself never been human but who controls the subterranean or submarine land of the dead, where all must go. According to local belief, the dead reach the entrances to this land by following ridges that lead down to the sea. At one of these entrances, known as Pucangge (near Bourail), the goddess Nyôwau examines all those who wish to enter to make sure that their left earlobe is pierced. She pierces any unpierced lobe with the mussel-shell knife that she also uses to peel yams.

There is constant communication between the living and the dead. The dead can be seen and spoken with when needed. They can be called upon to help in a crisis such as sickness or war, or to favor the results of family labors. Myths speak of the living going to the land of the dead and of the dead acting in the land of the living. There are, for example, various versions of a myth in which a loving husband attempts to bring his young wife back from the land of the dead. He either succeeds in his quest through the help of a bird (a common link for communication with the dead), or he fails. Among the stories about people from the underworld acting among the living there are those that describe an unsuspecting husband who might find, for example, that his new wife snores at night, or that she is double-jointed, both of which are characteristics of people from the underworld. There are also numerous versions of a myth about a goddess, usually Toririhnan, who, after drowning the pregnant wife of a chief, disguises herself as the wife by filling her belly with pots. The true wife, however, is saved by a miracle and taken away to a distant island. Later, this woman returns with her grown sons; their identity is revealed, and the usurper is killed.

Other gods preside over agriculture, such as Kapwangwa Kapwicalo, who protects irrigated taro terraces in the Gomen area, or Toririhnan, who causes it to rain each time she blows her nose at the top of the Hienghène Valley. There are also a great number of gods whose function is the protection of a given clan, protection that is often traced back to the clan's mythical origin. Gods can have sexual relations with humans, an event that either can have terrifying consequences—such as the death of the mortal or the turning backward of his head—or can resemble normal human sexual acts. Myths in which families trace their origins to instances of intercourse between gods and humans record both types of occurrences.

Indeed in Melanesia, as in Polynesia, all genealogies have divine origins, and although the religion of New Caledonia is totemistic in appearance there is no available evidence that any of the kinship groups believe that they are descended from the animal species or natural phenomenon with which they are spiritually associated. These totem entities—called *rhë re* (sg., *rhë e*)—represent the "spiritual belonging" of the group and are passed along through the male line. When a woman marries outside of her totem group, her *rhë e* is sometimes said to follow her. This does not mean, however, that the *rhë e* has left its original abode; because mythical beings are understood to be ubiquitous they are thought to be able to dwell in the two places at once.

There are occasions on which the *rhë re* and the *bao* (who were formerly human) meet. Such a meeting will take place in part of the landscape that is outside of human control, such as the bush, the forest, or the mountain range. The dead, those *bao* who were formerly human, can merge with the *rhë e* that is linked with their clan. Thus, for example, if thunder is associated with a particular group, the rumbling of the thunder is also the voice of the dead of that clan. Also in accordance with this pattern, no ancestor of the octopus group, for example, will appear in the form of a shark, unless they have what early authors referred to as "linked totems," that is, clusters of symbols all of which are linked to a certain *mwaro*. In some cases a group's *rhë e* will manifest itself in various forms depending on the setting: thus, for some chiefly families of the so-called Naacuwe-Cidopwaan group the *rhë e* takes the form of a lizard if seen inland, but becomes a water-snake on the beach, or a shark in the sea, and is also thought of as a masked male dancer said to emerge from the sea.

Missionaries who worked among the New Caledonians attempted to find the natives' idols in order to destroy them; they discovered objects resembling idols that had been carefully preserved by clan leaders over the course of centuries. Pierre Lambert (1900) has published illustrations of some of these items. They are stones of various shapes about which little is actually known except that they turn up from time to time in yam gardens, are linked with the clan's totem entity, and are in some way connected with success in farming, fishing, weather control, and so forth, as were the thunderstones (meteorites) of the Europeans of old. It has been observed that when these artifacts are used as repositories of the divine presence for sacramental purposes—and not as representations of gods—they can be replaced if lost or confiscated. This provision allows for the indefinite preservation of this type of link with the divine.

It is important to recognize that the mythical systems of the hundreds of different clans are highly diversified, a diversity that appears most clearly in the origin myths of the various groups. Some clans believe their spiritual origin to be the mountain that is called Souma (in the Ajië language) or Caumyë (in the Paici language). The vernacular texts obtained by Leenhardt demonstrated that the mountain had a connection with the creation of mankind and that its importance stems from the gods who live in the various principal mountains. For instance, Ka To Souma, the god associated with Souma, guards one of the possible entrances to the subterranean land of the dead. So great is the respect for, and fear of, this god that his proper name (Gomawe or Kavere) is never uttered. Other clans, usually those living near the watershed, claim a spiritual link with one or another of the forms of thunder. These different forms are grouped in distinctive ways according to the local theology, thereby giving each clan a powerful mythical protector. Clans can thus be classified according to their myths; conversely, mythical beings in charge of protecting the various clans may be classified according to the patrilineal marriage moieties with which they are associated in the Paici area or, in the north, according to the political phratries to which they belong.

The nearby Loyalty Islands (Uvéa, Lifou, and Maré) present a different set of problems. Although the inhabitants have been Christians for a century and a half (twice as long as the natives of New Caledonia proper) sacred groves still exist there, the old deities are remembered, and the cult of the dead continues to surface from time to time. However, the distribution of mythical beings among the families of the islands is significantly different from what prevails in New Caledonia. One essential aspect of the religion of the Loyalty Islands is that direct relations with the invisible world are the prerogative of the oldest established clans. These privileged clans, called *ten adro* (on Lifou), *wäi* (on Uvéa), or *èlè-tok* (on Maré), act as hosts to visiting gods. It is this status as host to the gods that provides legitimacy to the chiefly lines of today. The senior clans are also, however, the wardens of the invisible road along which the dead travel, eventually diving into the sea and reaching the island of Heo (Beautemps-Beaupré), where the entrance to the world of the dead is located. At the court of each of the paramount chiefs, a special person (called Atesi on Lifou and, on Maré, Acania) has the role of being the representative of these clans. He acts as their intermediary, for neither they nor their yams can enter a chief's house since their presence would endanger his life. On these islands there is thus a formalized distinction between families having the privilege of communicating with the divine world—each *ten adro* has its own god, to which only it can pray—and those who must be satisfied with praying to their own dead. The latter use diviners to discover whom they must negotiate with in order to ward off any invisible power which is causing injury to the clan.

See Also Codrington, R. H.; Leenhardt, Maurice.

Bibliography

The oldest, but still quite illuminating, work on the subject of New Caledonia religion is R. P. Gagnère's *Étude ethnologique sur la religion des Néo-calédoniens* (Saint-Louis, France, 1905). It vividly describes the man and lizard cult relation in the Pouebo area of northeastern New Caledonia. Pierre Lambert's *Moeurs et superstitions des Néo-calédoniens* (Nouméa, New Caledonia, 1900) is interesting, although Lambert is at times less than accurate in his descriptions of the religions of the Belep Islands in the north and the Isle of Pines in the south. The monumental, two-volume *Ethnologie der Neu-Caledonier und Loyalty-Insulaner* (Munich, 1929) by the Swiss ethnographer Fritz Sarasin contains an indispensable atlas. The classic works in the field are Maurice Leenhardt's two volumes: *Notes d'ethnologie néo-calédonienne* (Paris, 1930) and *Documents néo-calédoniens* (Paris, 1932). Admired for their precision at the time of their publication, Leenhardt's books are full of information, and continue to be valuable research tools. My own contributions to the subject include the following: *Structure de la chefferie en Mélanésie du sud* (Paris, 1963), *Mythologie du masque en Nouvelle-Calédonie* (Paris, 1966), *Des multiples niveaux de signification du mythe* (Paris, 1968), and *Naissance et avortement d'un messianisme* (Paris, 1959). Recent publications in the field include Marie-Joseph Dubois's *Mythes et traditions de Maré, Nouvelle Calédonie: Les Elètok* (Paris, 1975) and Alban Bensa and Jean-Claude Rivière's *Les chemins de l'alliance: L'organisation sociale et ses représentations en Nouvelle-Calédonie* (Paris, 1982).

New Sources

Lenormand, Maurice H., and Léonard Drilë Sam. *Lifou: Origine des Chefferies de la Zone de Wé: Quelques Éléments de la Société Traditionnelle.* Nouméa, 1993.

Métais, Eliane. *Au Commencement Était la Terre: Réflexions sur un Mythe Canaque d'Origine.* Talence, France, 1988.

Jean Guiart (1987)
Revised Bibliography

NEW GUINEA RELIGIONS [FIRST EDITION].

Any summary of traditional religions in New Guinea must address itself to two issues: the people's subjective view of the phenomena, and outside observers' arbitrary definitions of them, which are often at odds with each other. Melanesians as a whole appear to have no collective term for religion as a separate cultural category in their own languages, so that it is difficult to specify the limits of inquiry. In their eyes, however important to them, "religion" is merely one facet of their generalized sociocultural system. The foreign observer has to select and concentrate on those features that most closely resemble religion in his own society. It must also be asked what the foreign observer's most appropriate approach to the study of religion would be. During the last hundred-odd years anthropology has been rich in definitions of religion, three of which—the intellectualist, the economic or technological, and the social—dominated field inquiry. Before I survey New Guinea religions, I will consider the theoretical relevance of these three approaches, especially with regard to their one common tenet: the strict dichotomy between religion and magic.

For E. B. Tylor and James G. Frazer, writing in the last third of the nineteenth century, religion was man's belief in superior spirit-beings (such as gods and ghosts), whom he had to placate by means of prayer and sacrifice, whereas magic was his belief that he himself, ideally without the aid of spirit-beings, could use sympathetic techniques to control nonpersonalized occult forces. Although this approach is consistent with the great intellectual importance New Guineans attach to religion and magic, the dichotomy it posits between religion and magic often cannot be substantiated. Many New Guinea rituals are designed not to placate spirit-beings but to place them in morally binding relationships which leave them no option but to comply with human wishes. Indeed, some sympathetic techniques are believed to derive their power from spirit-beings, who gave them to mankind. Clearly, this definition would continually produce unsatisfactory hybrid forms.

Bronislaw Malinowski, whose approach derived from fieldwork in the Trobriand Islands (now part of Papua New Guinea) during World War I, distinguished religion from magic on the basis of the ends sought by those engaged in a ritual. A religious rite, on Malinowski's view, is an end in itself with no obviously pragmatic objective, while the aim of magic, vitally important for economic production, is "always clear, straightforward, and definite." Although its stress on economic affairs is quite correct, this approach pays too little attention to a people's intellectual life. Again, Malinowski's dichotomy between religion and magic is not supported by later research in New Guinea: virtually every ritual observed and described has a specific end in view, which those performing it can explain without difficulty.

Finally, Émile Durkheim, in the early twentieth century, differentiated religion from magic on the grounds of the human personnel holding particular beliefs and performing particular rites. Religion was seen as social and cohesive: its beliefs symbolize and validate, and its rituals reinforce, the social order. Magic is individual and isolative: its beliefs and rituals do not symbolize or reinforce any social collective. Once again, this approach has two weaknesses. Although its reference to society is justified, it tends to reduce religion to an oblique and almost secular replica of the social order at the expense of human economic and cognitive interests. As will appear, most New Guineans would reject this. Furthermore, Durkheim's dichotomy between religion and magic also cannot be sustained. In virtually every New Guinea society, even if they are not privy to all its secrets, all its members share and more or less endorse its beliefs, and the personnel involved in any ritual depends on the number of people necessary to carry it out efficiently. This varies according to each situation.

Although none of these approaches on its own offers a comprehensive answer to the problem or a convincing distinction between religion and magic, with due modification each makes a contribution. It is possible to select from them and combine those features that make sense in New Guinea. At the outset it is wise to dismiss the idea of a dichotomy between religion and magic and retain a single concept, religion, of which magic forms a part. Thus from Tylor and Frazer, I adopt the principle of intellectualism, which stresses religion's contribution to a people's mental life by helping them interpret the world around them. With Malinowski, I emphasize religion's role in the economic system. With Durkheim, I examine religion's relation to society.

Broadly I define traditional religion as man's beliefs about and putative interaction with what Westerners call "the supernatural" or "the transcendental," although, as I shall argue, these terms have little relevance to New Guinea. To explain this I shall outline the total cosmic order that the people conceive to exist: its general structure, the types and location of spirit-beings within it, and its dynamics, especially the methods by which humans believe that they communicate with spirit-beings to consolidate their own interests.

The General Structure of the Cosmos. New Guineans' conceived cosmic order has two parts: the empirical—the natural environment, its economic resources (including animals), and its human inhabitants; and the nonempirical—spirit-beings, nonpersonalized occult forces, and, sometimes, totems. Theoretically it has three analytically separate systems: men in relation to the natural environment and its resources, or the economic system; relationships among human beings themselves, or the sociopolitical system; and men in relation to spirit-beings, occult forces, and totems, or religion. In fact, these systems interdepend, so that it is essential to understand how religion impinges on economic and social life and, in so doing, how it contributes to intellectual life and leadership.

The traditional economic and sociopolitical systems of New Guinea must be summarized, insofar as religion directly relates to them. The whole of New Guinea (Papua New Guinea and Irian Jaya) has about a thousand distinct language groups, each one virtually a separate society. The economic system is generalized: most of the people are settled agriculturalists with few specialized skills apart from religious ritual, which a limited number of adult males (the leaders) monopolize. Without specialized occupational groups, social structure has to be based on kinship, marriage, and descent, although even within this broad framework there is much variation. Some groups are congeries of relatively large phratries or tribes, while others consist of small clans or even lineages. Some have over 100,000 members and others as few as 150.

Diversity of social structures is paralleled in religions, which, although based on common principles, show a degree of heterogeneity. In general terms, most New Guineans recognize the following kinds of spirit-beings: autonomous creative or regulative spirit-beings (deities or culture heroes); autonomous noncreative or malevolent spirit-beings (demons, tricksters, and pucks); and spirits of the dead. Many also recognize clan totems and practice sympathetic magic. Variations of belief are most marked with respect to deities and spirits of the dead. Some peoples, such as the Huli and the Kainantu of the Highlands, claim relatively few gods, to each of whom they attribute multiple creative or regulative functions. Others, such as the inhabitants of the southern Madang Province littoral and Karkar Island, have a few major deities and a large number of minor ones with limited powers. Yet others, such as the Mae Enga of the Highlands and the peoples inland from Madang, believe in many deities, no one of whom has primacy and each of whom has only one creative or regulative function. Again, although belief in ghosts is ubiquitous, some peoples (especially Highlanders) distinguish between the recent and remote dead, while others (especially those on the coast) do not. One group inland from Madang, the Garia, assert that after three generations ghosts turn into fruit bats or pigeons and cease to have any religious significance.

Yet despite this heterogeneity, New Guineans appear to hold one concept in common, that the cosmos is essentially a finite physical realm with, as hinted, almost no supernatural or transcendental attributes. Gods, ghosts, demons, and totems are superhuman but terrestrial. They are more powerful than humans but still corporeal, taking human or animal form with normal physical attributes. They normally live on the earth in special sanctuaries near human habitations. There are a few exceptions, such as the Mae Enga sky people, who live in the clouds but who are in easy contact with the earth. This stress on earthliness gives New Guinea religions a quality of nearness and immediacy lacking in some of the higher religions, as is especially apparent in ritual. The significance of this will emerge later.

The Function of Religion. As the criticism of Tylor and Frazer's approach indicates, it is inadequate to concentrate on the form of New Guinea religions, as if they were purely philosophical systems; it is necessary to consider also their functions. Melanesians believe that they have inherited a generally predictable cosmic order, which is anthropocentric and materialistic. It exists for man's benefit, and its material resources (crops, livestock, and artifacts) are concomitants of his existence. Hence religion has two principal functions. First, myths (regarded as the source of ultimate truth) explain and thereby validate the cosmic order. Second, just as the fulfillment of obligations between human beings maintains the secular social structure, the observance of ritual duties assures men that superhuman beings will guarantee the success of their major undertakings and protect the cosmic order from unforeseeable dangers.

Religion, therefore, is a technology, and, more particularly, ritual is man's means of contacting superhuman beings so as to exploit it. Ritual techniques, which I describe later on, again tend to vary. For deities they may involve placation, bargaining, coercion, or striking moral relationships through invocation or esoteric spells. Sympathetic magic, sometimes used on its own, is said to be more effective if taught to men by gods. For demons ritual is based on placation and bargaining, although some say it is futile and will never use it. Ritual directed at spirits of the dead is usually an expression of honor, often involving mourning, feasting, and music. For totems there is no specific ritual but only avoidance behavior: taboos against harming, killing, and eating. As indicated, ritual knowledge is the prerogative mainly of leaders or big men. Women have limited access to it, and then principally to contraceptive and abortifacient techniques. Yet although Melanesians use ritual to approach superhuman beings, there are grounds for believing that they regard it as a substitute for face-to-face interaction. Many of them have assumed that their first European visitors were either deities or ghosts appearing in their midst, but there is no evidence that they performed ritual in their honor. Rather, they engaged in ordinary social behavior, offering food, and trying to create beneficial exchange relationships.

Throughout New Guinea the use of myth and ritual to explain and maintain the cosmic order is uneven. The people tend to ignore the aspects of it that they can take for granted and concentrate on those that involve risk and cause anxiety. I shall examine this in the context of the economic and sociopolitical systems and then discuss religion's role in the intellectual system.

The natural environment and economic resources. Not many New Guinea religions are greatly concerned with the natural environment as a whole. Except for occasional volcanic eruptions and droughts it is never seriously threatened, so that the people do not fear for its continuance. Hence elaborate accounts of its origin and rituals to preserve it are rare. In most cases there are only short, albeit sometimes explicit, statements to the effect that the earth always existed or suddenly came into being in some miraculous way.

Mythology and ritual are generally more detailed and complex for the economic system, which, for reasons given below, is more uncertain and thus needs to be buttressed. Whether the people attribute creation to few or many deities is irrelevant. Except in the few societies that do not acknowledge deities, there is normally a myth cycle or set of discursive myths telling how specific gods and goddesses invented economic resources —staple crops, pigs, dogs, wild animals, and important artifacts—and gave them to human beings.

Yet, as is implicit in the foregoing argument, explanation and validation on their own, however necessary, are not enough. People also want knowledge that they can use to their advantage, knowledge that will make sure that economic resources do not fail. Crops may wither, livestock remain barren, and newly made artifacts prove faulty. Ritual should eliminate these risks. It is performed for both the relevant deities and spirits of the dead.

The performance for economic ends of ritual in honor of the dead is very common in New Guinea. Specifically, it consists of formal keening at funerals, food offerings, dancing, and the celebration of the male cult (which I shall discuss later). In response, ghosts are said to help their living descendants by protecting gardens from wild pigs and landslides, helping hunters find game, bringing presents, and, especially in dreams, by giving messages about impending events. These ceremonies are particularly important among peoples who either do not acknowledge deities, or have no elaborate ritual for propitiating them. Yet there are two differences in this context. First, as noted, Highlanders tend to distinguish between the recent and remote dead. They regard the recent dead as minatory—interested mainly in punishing transgressors—and expect economic benefits from the remote dead, to whom, with the exception of mortuary ceremonies, they address their rituals. Most seaboard peoples, who do not hold this belief, honor the recent dead, many of whom they remember as living persons. Second, there are different interpretations of the likely responses of the dead to the rituals performed in their honor. Some Highlanders, noted for their general aggressiveness, are said to apply to ghosts the same techniques they apply to the living: bargaining and bribery, in which the aim is to manipulate and curb pugnacious egalitarian rivals. Ghosts are said to respond in kind. Seaboard peoples are less assertive. Their view is that ritual should create strong ties between men and ghosts; as long as men fulfill their obligations, ghosts should automatically reciprocate.

The sociopolitical order. Likewise, total sociopolitical systems receive irregular treatment in religion. Some groups (for example, the Mae Enga, the Kainantu people, and the inhabitants of Wogeo Island) have myths that attribute society's existence and forms to their deities. Others, like the Ngaing, do not. They see no need to validate the social order in its entirety: they are unaware that any other kind of social order exists, and theirs is not threatened by conquest from outside or revolution from within. Nevertheless such peoples are by no means unconcerned about society; they implicitly realize that it has sensitive areas—key institutions, groups, and relationships that must be buttressed at all costs. Thus the Ngaing have war gods, who protect their bush groups, their main political units, and a myth of origin for the male cult, which binds together the inhabitants of a whole locality, as described below.

In this context, spirits of the dead are most important. They validate the social order in a number of ways. Among the Garia, the life of the dead replicates that of human beings. Ghosts build and live in ordinary settlements with their kin; they plant gardens and celebrate exchanges. Again, throughout New Guinea, ghosts are the ultimate custodians of their living descendants' land rights, a vital component of the social system, and they punish trespass. Yet it is above all the ceremonies of the male cult—exchanges of pigs, food, and valuables coupled with feasting and dancing to solemnize birth, initiation, marriage, and death—that induce ghosts to preserve and strengthen the sociopolitical order.

The primary function of the male cult is the initiation of boys into manhood. After they are about ten years old, boys in adjacent settlements are assembled, segregated from women, placed under the supervision of adult males (especially leaders) in a cult house, and given special instruction. They are taught the rudiments of myths and ritual. They observe stringent taboos and are subjected to a physical ordeal that may include beating, scarification, penile incision, or forced nose bleeding. Thereafter they are returned to village life. The severity of initiation appears to correlate with society's pattern of male-female relations. In general, men are dominant in both secular and ritual affairs. Where this is particularly marked, as in the eastern Highlands and among the Ilahita Arapesh (in the East Sepik Province) and the Garia, initiation is either traumatic or protracted over many years and stresses sexual antagonism. Where women are less subordinate, male initiation rites are less exacting and less shrouded in secrecy and may be paralleled, as on Manam and Wogeo islands and among the Ngaing, by special puberty rites for girls. Nevertheless, despite these differences of emphasis, in most of New Guinea boys during their initiation are said to be under special protection of the spirits of the dead, who guarantee their safety, health, physical maturity, and ability to attract wives and thereby perpetuate society. The male cult has also a latent function: it promotes the solidarity of the clans or other local units that must assemble all the wealth going out in exchange and reaffirms the kinship or marriage relationships, which link these groups and provide the network for its distribution.

The last two important aspects of religion in the context of the sociopolitical order are (1) religion's impingement on moral obligation, and (2) the role of sorcery. Once again, the relationship between religion and moral obligation has no standard pattern: for some groups it is an important issue, but for others it is not. Thus the Huli insist that their primary god Datagaliwabe enjoined moral precepts on them, while the Kai-nantu people have a secondary mythology devoted to the inculcation of ethics, and the Manus of the Admiralty Islands believe themselves to be under the continual surveillance of the dead, who punish the infringement of any rule. In other societies, such as the Wogeo and the Ngaing, good conduct is said to be enforced only by secular sanctions.

Belief in sorcery is virtually universal. The art has many forms: contagious magic (theft and destruction of personal leavings such as cast-off clothing, hairclippings, or excrement); projection of missiles into a victim; figurative removal and replacement of a victim's head or entrails; and actual immobilization of a victim by inserting slivers of bamboo (or, nowadays, lengths of wire) into vital parts of his body. With possible exception of the last example, which is in fact physical murder, the efficacy of sorcery is guaranteed by the performance of ritual, often to harness the power of a deity or familiar spirit.

It is difficult to state precisely the reasons for belief in sorcery. The degree to which a religion does or does not uphold the moral code and to which it is or is not intellectually elaborated seems to be irrelevant. Sorcery is found in societies whose religions either stress or ignore ethics and are either closely or loosely articulated. Hence it is wiser to consider two issues: the forces that promote belief in sorcery and the intellectual climate that allows it to flourish.

Belief in sorcery is motivated by personal anxiety. This is immediately intelligible in societies that have weak group structures and unstable, ever-changing patterns of local organization—for example, the Dobu (of Papua), Huli, Tangu, and Garia. As individuals continually move in and out, settlement and neighborhood populations are never permanent. A person can never be sure where his friends and foes are. Unless he can attribute illness or bad luck to an angry god, ghost, or demon, he will search for a human enemy lurking in his locality. Yet, by way of contrast, belief in sorcery is found also in societies with territorial organizations based on stable, permanently localized descent groups. Possibly sorcery has come to be regarded as more important than it was since modern centralized government banned traditional warfare, leaving it as the only way to relieve feelings of aggression.

There appear to be two prerequisites for an intellectual climate in which the belief in sorcery will thrive. First, the belief must be integrated with other aspects of religion, taking a normal place in both myth and ritual. Thus the Garia believe that the god Yeyaguliba invented it and taught men his secret names as spells to make it effective. From a technical point of view, sorcery is no different from agricultural ritual. Second, the belief helps solve the perpetual emotional and cognitive problem of death. Thus, although the Garia claim that the goddess who first gave birth to human beings was responsible also for human mortality, they regard this as a sufficient explanation only in the case of old people. The young should not die. Sorcery, by offering the solution of the hidden enemy, at least removes the agony of an impenetrable riddle.

Leadership and the intellectual system. Myth and ritual are for many New Guineans the principal means of understanding the cosmic order and maintaining their central position in it. Everyday experience largely endorses their certitude of the truth of religion. Normally crops do mature, livestock and human beings reproduce their kind, and artifacts meet their owners' expectations. The rituals used are obviously effective, so that their acquisition is an essential prerequisite of leadership. Big men are those who "know": they are experts in mythology and, particularly, in harnessing the power of gods and spirits of the dead that will ensure the success of their followers' purely secular activities. Secular skills are "knowledge" but at a low level: they are something anybody can acquire by imitation. It takes a special kind of man, however, to master "true knowledge," the religious secrets that are the core of the instruction given boys during initiation. Thereafter, those who aspire to leadership must undergo a long and exacting apprenticeship under acknowledged experts until they are accepted as qualified practitioners. Yet it would be false to conclude from this that the people's thought is mystical. Rather, it is pragmatic, even mundane, because of their conviction that the cosmos is a purely terrestrial realm. Gods and ghosts live on the earth, and their interaction with men and women in response to ritual is not illusory but as real as cooperation among human beings themselves.

Inevitably, the intensity of intellectual commitment to religion is not found to be consistent throughout New Guinea. The peoples of the northeastern seaboard and hinterland from Lae to Bogia typify the paradigm I have sketched. Traditionally they have always been theologians, and it is significant that they have provided many of the leaders of the Christian churches since Papua New Guinea's independence in 1975. Others, such as the Ilahita Arapesh, are perhaps more skeptical. Yet about one area there has been particular controversy. The first anthropologists in the Highlands after World War II depicted its peoples as if they had relatively little interest in religion—that is, the Highlanders were portrayed as hard-working and secular-minded with leaders who relied for their positions more on tough negotiation and military prowess than on ritual expertise. The early absence of cargoism, so prevalent on the seaboard, seemed to confirm their argument. Recently, however, we have been forced to reconsider it. There are now more numerous outbreaks of the cargo cult as well as Pentecostalism and other eccentric quasi-Christian movements. This suggests that, even allowing for random differences of degree, the dominantly secular image of all the peoples in the Highlands is unjustified and may have been the result of uncritical addiction to the Durkheimian social approach to the study of religion at the time the field research was carried out. Certainly the issue is unresolved. Yet it is still justifiable to conclude that for the great majority of New Guineans religion has been not merely an important part but the very quintessence of their sociocultural systems. It represents the final rationale of their cosmic experience.

SEE ALSO Cargo Cults.

BIBLIOGRAPHY

Allen, M. R. *Male Cults and Secret Initiations in Melanesia.* Melbourne and London, 1967. The most detailed general analysis of initiatory ceremonies for males in New Guinea so far published. A standard text.

Baal, Jan van. *Dema.* The Hague, 1966. An important Irian Jaya ethnography, including a detailed account of traditional religion.

Berndt, Ronald M. *Excess and Restraint.* Chicago, 1962. A general ethnography of the Kainantu people of the Papua New Guinea Highlands. Provides background to Berndt's essay in Lawrence and Meggitt (1972).

Burridge, Kenelm. *Tangu Traditions.* Oxford, 1969. A thorough study of a New Guinea people's traditional mythology.

Fortune, Reo F. *Sorcerers of Dobu* (1932). Rev. ed. New York, 1963. An early and classic analysis of religion and sorcery in a traditional Papuan society.

Hogbin, Ian. *The Island of Menstruating Men: Religion in Wogeo, New Guinea.* Scranton, Pa., 1970. Another important account of a traditional religion, written nearly forty years after the field work was done.

Lawrence, Peter. "Statements about Religion: The Problem of Reliability." In *Anthropology in Oceania,* edited by Lester R. Hiatt and Chandra Jayawardena, pp. 140–154. Sydney, 1971. A discussion of the difficulty of assessing the validity of personal belief in and commitment to religion in New Guinea.

Lawrence, Peter. "Religion and Magic." In *Encyclopaedia of Papua and New Guinea,* edited by Peter Ryan, pp. 1001–1012. Melbourne, 1972. A general introduction to traditional religions in New Guinea. Reprinted in *Anthropology in Papua New Guinea,* edited by Ian Hogbin (Melbourne, 1973), pp. 201–226.

Lawrence, Peter. *The Garia.* Melbourne and Manchester, 1984. An analysis of a traditional cosmic system in New Guinea, with emphasis on religion.

Lawrence, Peter, and M. J. Meggitt, eds. *Gods, Ghosts, and Men in Melanesia* (1965). Oxford, 1972. A symposium of essays on a number of traditional religions in New Guinea and Vanuatu. The best collection available.

McArthur, Margaret. "Men and Spirits in the Kunimaipa Valley." In *Anthropology in Oceania,* edited by Lester R. Hiatt and Chandra Jayawardena, pp. 155–189. Sydney, 1971.

Tuzin, Donald F. *The Voice of the Tambaran: Truth and Illusion in Ilahita Arapesh Religion.* Berkeley, 1980. A detailed and sophisticated analysis of a New Guinea traditional religion. Pays special attention to male initiation rites and the problem of individual belief and commitment.

Williams, Francis E. *Orokaiva Society.* Oxford, 1930. An early monograph that provides much valuable information about traditional religion.

Williams, Francis E. *Drama of Orokolo.* Oxford, 1940. Williams's most mature work; a carefully documented account of an elaborate ceremonial and ritual complex in western Papua. A classic.

PETER LAWRENCE (1987)

NEW GUINEA RELIGIONS [FURTHER CONSIDERATIONS]. Since Peter Lawrence wrote on the indigenous religions of New Guinea—the area encompassing Papua New Guinea and Papua (formerly Irian Jaya)—for the first edition of the *Encyclopedia of Religion* (1987), further studies have been undertaken providing an even greater wealth of material concerning myth, ritual, knowledge, morality, and religious innovation in New Guinea. More attention has been given to personal experiences such as dreams, trance, and spirit possession. Moreover, the religious landscape has continued to change as a result of political and economic innovations and through interaction with Christianity. New religious movements, many emphasizing relationship to the Holy Spirit, have emerged. At the same time, changing approaches and emphases in anthropology and religious studies have influenced the ways that scholars understand religion. For instance, feminism has occasioned a new look at rituals for the making of men and women, while transcultural studies have suggested that the movements earlier labeled *cargo cults* may have been misnamed.

Lawrence outlined three approaches to the study of New Guinea religions, which he called the intellectualist, the economic or technological, and the social. He stressed intellectualist approaches and defined traditional religion as "beliefs about and putative interaction with what Westerners call the 'supernatural' or the 'transcendental'." He outlined the general structure of the cosmos in New Guinean societies as three interrelating systems: people in relation to the natural environment and its resources (the economic system), relationships among human beings themselves (the sociopolitical system), and people in relation to spirit beings, occult forces, and totems (religion). He saw myth and ritual as means of explaining and maintaining the cosmic order. Most scholars accept this framework. However, more recent works have emphasized the significance of place (Munn, Rumsey and Weiner), religion as an ecological process (Rappaport), and fertility as focus of both practical and symbolic work (Meigs). Scholars have attended to the construction of gender (Gillison, Herdt, Lutkehaus and Roscoe, Tuzin) and to personal experience, consciousness, and sentiment (Herdt and Stephen, Feld, Schieffelin, Lohmann). Some have looked on religion as a process of exchange (MacDonald) or reciprocity (Trompf). A number of scholars have explored Christianity in New Guinean contexts (Barker, Robbins) and given attention to new religious movements.

INSIDERS AND OUTSIDERS. Most studies of New Guinea religions that reach publication are the work of outsiders. However, indigenous religions and local forms of Christianity have also been studied by insiders, mainly by those with theological, pastoral, and social commitments. Some of their research and reflections have been published as journal articles within New Guinea and have found their way into sermons, workshops, and speeches. A number of B.D. and M.A. theses and Ph.D. dissertations written by New Guineans explore the relationship of indigenous religion and Christianity and the value of land. For example, in 1995 Benny Giay, a Papuan pastor who has been active in opposition to the Freeport-McMoran mine, submitted his Ph.D. dissertation for Vrije Universiteit in Amsterdam on the topic "Zakheus Pakage and his Communities: Indigenous Religious Discourse, Sociopolitical Resistance, and Ethnohistory of the Me of Irian Jaya." He dwelt on the passionate hopes of Pakage (1920–1970) of establishing a reciprocity between indigenous wisdom and Christian wisdom and of integrating Dutch development plans with the work of local Me communities, hopes that were thwarted both by the mission agency and Dutch authorities.

Religious studies has been taught in the History Department at the University of Papua New Guinea since 1972, first by lecturers from overseas and then by Papua New Guineans. It is also taught at the University of Goroka and Divine Word University in Madang. Moreover, the theological seminaries in both Papua New Guinea and Papua give attention to the study of indigenous religions in relation to Christianity. The mainline churches tend to look on indigenous religions as a preparation for the Christian gospel, while fundamentalist groups have a more negative evaluation of indigenous religions. The outsiders who study New Guinea religions include social scientists (mainly anthropologists), historians of religion, and theologians. Some missionary scholars (e.g., Mantovani, Gesch, Zöllner, Gibbs) are trained in social sciences or religious studies as well as in theology.

ECOLOGY AND PLACE. Roy Rappaport's fieldwork among the Tsembaga Maring in the highlands of Papua New Guinea in the 1960s led him to develop an ecological theory of religion. In the first edition of *Pigs for the Ancestors* in 1968 he argued that the ritual cycle that culminates in large scale pig kills is a homeostatic mechanism regulating the relationship of pig populations to other environmental factors such as human energy, land use, and warfare. He maintained that when pig herds reach a size at which pigs become a hindrance, invading gardens and requiring large amounts of food and human attention, then people decide to kill them, conceptualizing their action as killing pigs for the ancestors. A second edition of the book, in 1984, placed more stress on the reciprocity of ecological order and ritual order, allowing that culture may drive ecological processes, which in turn may sustain culture. In *Ecology, Meaning, and Religion*, published in 1979, Rappaport elaborated his theory of religion as an ecological process. Shortly before his death, in 1997, he completed *Ritual and Religion in the Making of Humanity*, in which he explores the significance of ritual for relating human beings to nature.

Several anthropologists, including Roy Wagner, have given attention to the religious importance of land. The intrusion of mining companies in both Papua New Guinea and Papua has led local communities to reassert claims to land in terms of ancestral cosmologies. Confrontations over land have provided occasion for researchers to consider the impact of mining on local ecosystems and to give attention to the narratives in which peoples tell of the journeys of culture heroes and ancestors who shaped their place and their way of life. The edited volume *Emplaced Myth* (Rumsey and Weiner, 2001) provides several case studies from Papua New Guinea and others from Aboriginal Australia that reflect on space and place in local and regional domains and on environmental ethics in times of change. Papua New Guineans Simeon Namunu and Bernard Narokobi assert that the relationship to land is a religious issue with which Christians should concern themselves. Pamela Stewart and Andrew Strathern's *Remaking the World: Myth, Mining, and Ritual Change among the Duna of Papua New Guinea* (2002) considers the ways in which a community reconstructs its place and way of life.

FERTILITY AND GENDER. While there are no universally acceptable definitions of gender and marriage, all cultures have ideas about sexual difference, female/male complementarity, and fertility, which they take as models for thinking about human and cosmic relationships. Early work by Margaret Mead and Gregory Bateson pointed to the social and cosmological significance of gender in the Pacific. In New Guinea the relationship of woman and man is often seen as homologous to the work of gardening, to the arrangement of village space, and to roles in traditional exchanges. Early anthropologists in the highlands recorded antagonism between the sexes in many societies, and later studies that described the "making of men" elaborated on notions of masculinity and the ritual means of achieving it (Barth, Herdt, Tuzin). The "making of women," which is a matter for ritual in some societies (Lutkehaus and Roscoe) has received less attention.

In her work on the Hua, Anna Meigs focuses on the concept of *nu* or "vital essence" of a person or thing and the ways it can be increased or depleted, leading her to explore ideas about food and sexual activity. In New Guinea, fertility—of crops, of sea creatures, of forest animals and domestic animals, and of people—is a desired outcome of personal and group rituals. The juxtaposition of male and female elements in ritual is part of the management of a gendered world.

RELIGIOUS EXPERIENCE. Michele Stephen and Gilbert Herdt have taken a lead in the study of personal religious experience in New Guinea. In their introduction to *The Religious Imagination in New Guinea* (1989) they say that they see the "inner world of religious experience as emerging from an interaction between individual experience and culture, mediated by autonomous imagination" (p. 4). The contributors to their volume explore altered states of consciousness in dreams, trances, possession, spirit mediumship, sorcery, witchcraft, prophetism, and shamanism. While recognizing cultural variation the editors point to psychological universals underlying it and assert that each person must "create his or her own cultural world through the process of imagination" (p. 235). They urge that altered states of consciousness be taken seriously as modes of cognition.

Another important contribution to the study of subjective experience is *Dream Travelers* (2003), edited by Roger Ivar Lohmann, which brings together case studies from New Guinea, aboriginal Australia, and Indonesia to make a case that dreams are, in some not well-understood sense, ways to knowledge.

RECIPROCITY. Peter Lawrence understood the indigenous religions of New Guinea to consist of beliefs about, and putative interaction with, the supernatural. The understanding of religion as an extension of social interaction beyond the human community to include gods, ghosts, and a variety of nonhuman beings works well for New Guinea and for traditions that posit the presence of such beings. It accords with Marcel Mauss's ideas on gift exchange. Human beings make gifts to the gods; the gods respond with benefits for human beings. Or human beings neglect the ancestral ghosts, and they respond by afflicting their living kin.

Garry Trompf, who taught at the University of Papua New Guinea in the 1970s and served as professor of history there from 1983 to 1985, developed an approach to religion that he called a logic of retribution. He was concerned not only with positive reciprocity but also with revenge and with the explanation of events in terms of praise and blame or in terms of reward and punishment. This logic may be seen in indigenous traditions, and it is also possible to see it in the moral reflections of Christian communities in New Guinea.

CHRISTIANITY AND NEW RELIGIOUS MOVEMENTS. From the latter part of the nineteenth century, when the Netherlands, Germany, and Great Britain divided the large island of New Guinea among themselves, missionaries arrived, first in the coastal areas and much later in the highland regions, to preach the Christian message. As a result, at the beginning of the twenty-first century some 90 percent of the population of Papua New Guinea claimed to be Christian, and in Papua the large majority of the indigenous people were also Christian. Since Indonesia took over Papua from the Dutch in 1962, the presence of government officials and the resettlement of landless people from other parts of Indonesia, especially from Java, have brought Islam to the region. However, Islam has remained more the religion of government officers and new settlers than of the indigenous peoples.

The study of New Guinea's forms of Christianity was first of all the concern of missiologists and other theologians who were concerned with whether, and how, God might speak through indigenous religions. As more and more New Guineans became Christians, Christianity in a variety of denominational forms became part of the cultures that anthropologists came to New Guinea to study. In tracing the transition from indigenous religion to Christianity, some see the new religion being incorporated into the indigenous cosmos, but indigenous religion and Christianity may also appear as competing moral discourses. For example, Joel Robbins, in his study of the Urapmin of the West Sepik, says he observed "the interplay between two cultures that are operative in the same place at the same time" (2004, p. 6). In considering the changes experienced by the Urapmin, who had never been directly missionized, Robbins tells how they first experienced the law introduced in the colonial period by Australian patrol officers and found themselves deficient in relation to it, how they decided in the 1960s to send young men to study with Baptist missionaries in neighboring communities, and how they underwent a charismatic renewal, and adopted a Christianity focused on human sinfulness and millennial expectation. The Urapmin, he concludes, have opted for a hybrid culture that leaves them with a sense of moral failure but also with an openness to change.

Peter Lawrence's *Road Belong Cargo* (1964), a study of cargo cults in the Madang area of Papua New Guinea, became a classic for the study of social and religious change. Hundreds of religious movements, some resembling the "cargo cult" documented by Lawrence and others appealing to the Holy Spirit for empowerment, have emerged in New Guinea. In writing of the God Triwan movement in the Enga province of Papua New Guinea, a movement that has remained within the Catholic Church, Philip Gibbs regards it as part of a process of inculturation of the gospel.

It seems likely that future studies will grapple not only with what is referred to within New Guinea as "traditional" religion—religion that is practiced to some extent, yet in many places is more a tale that is told about the ways of the ancestors—but also with the Christianities that occupy a powerful position in personal and communal life.

SEE ALSO Cargo Cults; Christianity, article on Christianity in the Pacific Islands; Melanesian Religions; Oceanic Religions; Rappaport, Roy A.

BIBLIOGRAPHY

Barker, John., ed. *Christianity in Oceania: Ethnographic Perspectives.* Lanham, Md., 1990.

Barth, Fredrik. *Ritual and Knowledge Among the Baktaman of New Guinea.* Oslo and New Haven, 1975.

Feld, Steven. *Sound and Sentiment: Birds, Weeping, Poetics, and Song in Kaluli Expression.* Philadelphia, 1982; 2d ed., 1990.

Gesch, Patrick F. *Initiative and Initiation: A Cargo Cult-Type Movement in the Sepik Against Its Background in Traditional Village Religion.* Saint Augustin, Germany, 1985.

Gibbs, Philip. "The God Triwan Movement: Inculturation Enga Style." *Catalyst* 34, no. 1 (2004): 3–24.

Gillison, Gillian. *Between Culture and Fantasy: A New Guinea Highlands Mythology.* Chicago, 1993.

Godelier, Maurice. *The Enigma of the Gift.* Translated by Nora Scott. Chicago, 1999.

Goldman, L. R., and C. Ballard. *Fluid Ontologies: Myth, Ritual, and Philosophy in the Highlands of Papua New Guinea.* Westport, Conn., 1998.

Habel, Norman C., ed. *Powers, Plumes, and Piglets: Phenomena of Melanesian Religion.* Bedford Park, South Australia, 1979.

Hayward, Douglas James. *Vernacular Christianity among the Mulia Dani: An Ethnography of Religious Belief among the Western Dani of Irian Jaya, Indonesia.* Lanham, Md., 1997.

Herdt, Gilbert, and Michele Stephen, eds. *The Religious Imagination in New Guinea.* New Brunswick, N.J., 1989.

Herdt, Gilbert H., ed. *Rituals of Manhood: Male Initiation in Papua New Guinea.* Berkeley, 1982.

Kamma, Freerk C., collector and trans. *Religious Texts of the Oral Tradition from Western New-Guinea (Irian Jaya).* Leiden, 1975.

Lattas, Andrew. *Cultures of Secrecy: Reinventing Race in Bush Kaliai Cargo Cults.* Madison, Wis., 1998.

Lawrence, Peter. *Road Belong Cargo: A Study of the Cargo Movement in the Southern Madang District, New Guinea.* Melbourne, 1964.

Lohmann, Roger Ivar. *Dream Travelers: Sleep Experiences and Cultures in the Western Pacific.* New York, 2003.

Lutkehaus, Nancy C., and Paul B. Roscoe, eds. *Gender Rituals: Female Initiation in Melanesia.* New York, 1995.

MacDonald, Mary N. *Mararoko: A Study of Melanesian Religion.* New York, 1991.

Mantovani, Ennio, ed. *An Introduction to Melanesian Religions: A Handbook for Church Workers.* Goroka, Papua New Guinea, 1984.

Meigs, Anna S. *Food, Sex, and Pollution: A New Guinea Religion.* New Brunswick, N.J., 1984.

Merrifield, William R., Marilyn Gregerson, and Daniel C. Ajamiseba, eds. *Gods, Heroes, Kinsmen: Ethnographic Studies from Irian Jaya, Indonesia.* Jayapura, Irian Jaya, and Dallas, Tex., 1983.

Munn, Nancy. *The Fame of Gawa: A Symbolic Study of Value Transformation in a Massim (Papua New Guinea) Society.* New York, 1986; reprint, Durham, N.C., 1992.

Namunu, Simeon B. "Melanesian Religion, Ecology, and Modernization in Papua New Guinea." In *Indigenous Traditions and Ecology: The Interbeing of Cosmology and Community,* edited by John A. Grim, pp. 249–280. Cambridge, Mass., 2001.

Narokobi, Bernard. *The Melanesian Way.* Port Moresby, Papua New Guinea, 1983.

Rappaport, Roy. *Pigs for the Ancestors: Ritual in the Ecology of a New Guinea People.* Rev. ed. New Haven, 1984.

Robbins, Joel. *Becoming Sinners: Christianity and Moral Torment in a Papua New Guinea Society.* Berkeley, 2004.

Rumsey, Alan, and James Weiner, eds. *Emplaced Myth: Space, Narrative, and Knowledge in Aboriginal Australia and Papua New Guinea.* Honolulu, 2001.

Schieffelin, Edward L. *The Sorrow of the Lonely and the Burning of the Dancers.* Saint Lucia, Queensland, Australia, 1977.

Stewart, Pamela J., and Andrew Strathern. *Remaking the World: Myth, Mining, and Ritual Change Among the Duna of Papua New Guinea.* Westport, Conn., 2002.

Trompf, G. W. *Melanesian Religion.* Cambridge, U.K., 1991.

Trompf, G. W. *Payback: The Logic of Retribution in Melanesian Religions.* Cambridge, U.K., 1994.

Tuzin, Donald. *The Cassowary's Revenge: The Life and Death of Masculinity in a New Guinea Society.* Chicago, 1997.

Wagner, Roy. *Habu: The Innovation of Meaning in Daribi Religion.* Chicago, 1972.

Zöllner, Siegfried. *The Religion of the Yali in the Highlands of Irian Jaya.* Translation and synopsis by Jan A. Godschalk. Goroka, Papua New Guinea, 1988.

MARY N. MACDONALD (2005)

NEWMAN, JOHN HENRY (1801–1890), Anglican and Roman Catholic controversialist and cardinal.

LIFE AND WORKS. Newman was born in London. He was raised an Anglican, but in 1816, under evangelical influence, he underwent a profound religious experience that transformed his understanding of his faith. The same year he entered Trinity College, Oxford, and in 1822 was elected a fellow of Oriel College. There, formative contacts with the so-called Noetics Edward Hawkins and Richard Whately, who freely applied logic to traditional Christian doctrines, introduced him to rationalist analysis of religious concerns. After 1828 illness, bereavement, and personal friendships with Richard Hurrell Froude, John Keble, and Edward Bouverie Pusey drew him toward the high church tradition. At this time he began to read the documents of the patristic church; this interest led to the publication of *The Arians of the Fourth Century, Their Doctrine, Temper and Conduct as Exhibited in the Councils of the Church* (1833) and *The Church of the Fathers* (1833–1836).

Newman was ordained an Anglican priest in 1825 and was appointed vicar of the university church Saint Mary the Virgin, where he gained fame as a preacher. His sermons there were collected in *Parochial and Plain Sermons* (8 vols., 1834–1843), *Sermons Preached before the University of Oxford on Faith and Reason, 1826–1843* (1843), and *Sermons Bearing on Subjects of the Day* (1843).

In 1833 Newman traveled to the Mediterranean. He fell ill in Sicily, and there experienced a special vocation, which he expressed in the words "I have a work to do in England."

In September 1833, with publication of the first *Tract for the Times*, Newman launched the Oxford Movement, a high church movement within Anglicanism that emphasized Catholic elements in the Church of England and continuity with the early church. Editor of the series, he contributed twenty-nine tracts. During this period, he also wrote two important works: *Lectures on the Prophetical Office of the Church Viewed Relatively to Romanism and Popular Protestantism* (1837), which argued for the via media, or foundational position, of the Church of England as true representative of the unbroken tradition of the Fathers; and a theological masterpiece, *Lectures on Justification* (1838). In 1841 his *Tract 90*, in which he tried to give a Catholic interpretation of the Thirty-nine Articles, touched off national alarm and was censured by the university and condemned by twenty-four Anglican bishops.

Research in patristics, together with his philosophy of development, at last led Newman to conclude that his *via media* existed only on paper and that the Anglican church was in fact schismatic. In 1841 he retired to Littlemore, near Oxford; he resigned the care of Saint Mary's in 1843 and his Oriel fellowship in 1845. That year he confirmed his position in *An Essay on the Development of Christian Doctrine.* In the same year he converted to Roman Catholicism. After study at the College of Propaganda Fide in Rome, Newman was ordained a Catholic priest and entered the Congregation of the Oratory. Upon his return to England he founded an oratory at London and another at Birmingham, which in 1852 was transferred to nearby Edgbaston. There Newman remained until his death.

As a Catholic preacher and controversialist Newman wrote a novel, *Loss and Gain, the Story of a Convert* (1848); two collections of talks, *Discourses Addressed to Mixed Congregations* (1848) and *Lectures on Certain Difficulties Felt by Anglicans in Submitting to the Catholic Church* (1850); and a masterpiece of defensive controversy, *Lectures on the Present Position of Catholics in England* (1851), which occasioned the Achilli trial in which Newman was prosecuted for libel. In 1851 he accepted the rectorship of the Catholic University of Dublin, but he resigned in 1859, believing that he had been unsuccessful in attaining his goals. His university publications, however, are among the best achievements of English prose: *Discourses on the Scope and Nature of University Education* (1852) and *Lectures and Essays on University Subjects* (1859), later published as *Idea of a University and Office and Work of Universities. Callista, a Sketch of the Third Century* (1855) reflects his own path from conscience to steadfast Christian faith.

In 1859 Newman founded the Oratory School and accepted the editorship of *The Rambler*, a magazine opposed by the Catholic bishops, in which Catholic laity and converts independently judged ecclesiastical affairs. Newman, who sympathized with the cause of lay emancipation and education, contributed to the magazine his famous article "On Consulting the Faithful in Matters of Doctrine." This article was delated to Rome and, at the request of his bishop, Newman resigned the editorship in October 1859. He lived under the cloud of suspicion until his *Apologia pro vita sua* (1864), written in response to attacks by Charles Kingsley, at once won over public opinion. Henceforth Newman actually became the main authority in Catholic public affairs. Roman mistrust, manipulated by Cardinal Henry Manning, defeated his last attempt to found a Catholic college at Oxford in 1865, but Ambrose St. John, an Oratorian and his dearest friend, in 1867 cleared him of suspicion in Rome. Newman answered E. B. Pusey's criticism of the Roman Catholic cult of Mary in his *Letter to Rev. E. B. Pusey on his Recent Eirenicon* (1866).

Although invited, Newman refused to assist at the First Vatican Council. He believed in the pope's infallibility but strongly opposed its definition as unripe and inopportune. But when former prime minister William Gladstone attacked Catholics for being unable to remain loyal British subjects, Newman countered by giving, on solid theological grounds, the now generally accepted minimizing interpretation of papal infallibility in his *Letter to the Duke of Norfolk on Occasion of Mr. Gladstone's Recent Expostulation* (1875).

Newman revealed his deepest Catholic feelings in his longest poem, *The Dream of Gerontius* (1865), and presented his basic philosophical ideas on the working of the human mind in his *Essay in Aid of a Grammar of Assent* (1870). His last important publication was the "Preface to the Via Media" (1877), the introduction to a new edition of his main Anglican controversial writings. In 1877 he was elected the first honorary fellow of Trinity College. Pope Leo XIII created him cardinal deacon of San Giorgio in Velabro in 1879. He died on August 11, 1890, and was buried at Rednal.

THOUGHT. Newman's thought reflects the nature and development of his individual personality. An introverted and self-conscious man, he engaged in constant self-analysis, assimilating scholarship and personal experience to germinate the religious and philosophical insights that characterize his work. Hence his writings manifest those opposing forces and tendencies that made his mind "from opposition grow"—reason versus imagination, love of detail versus comprehensiveness, doubt versus certitude, faith versus sight, reserve versus frankness, emotionalism versus self-control, strategy versus honesty. These conflicting tendencies gave rise to a false image of Newman as sentimental, resentful, paradoxical, mysterious, and even deceitful, but in their integration they yield a thinker of greater complexity and genius, whose worldview combines the consistency of a logical system with the organic wholeness and beauty proper to a work of poetic imagination. This view was grounded in two basic religious experiences: that of conscience as the inner witness of God, and that of the material world's merely relative reality, which directs the soul to communication with an invisible world.

Conscience. For Newman, conscience is an original and irreducible "moral sense"; by it, without logical medium, people instinctively discriminate the morally good and bad in concrete situations. Its essential characteristic, through which it differs from all other inner spiritual senses (such as the sense of beauty), is an adjoined yet distinct "sense of duty" grasping the unconditional demand of doing the good and avoiding the evil. As such, conscience bears witness to the inner presence of an omniscient and almighty master. But it must develop from an implicit and confused feeling to an explicit and distinct apprehension and assent. Conscience may be silenced, although never extinguished, through infidelity and thoughtlessness. It grows in clarity and scope through faithfulness and attention, so that the inner voice of nature becomes recognized beyond doubt as an echo of the voice of God.

Sacramentality. At first doubting the reality of the exterior material world, Newman came to recognize its genuine reality as an instrumental one. The material world is the medium of communication between the soul and the invisible world of God and his heavenly court. Hence, Newman believed that God revealed himself in and through the visible historical world and that people communicate with him through sacramental actions.

First principles. Three principles derive from the experience of conscience and of world as sacramental medium. These ruled Newman's thought and judgment in all matters.

The principle of providence. All things and events—visible and invisible, natural and historical—are part of an almighty creator's universal providence. All are directed to one end: the manifestation of the creator's justice (reflected in the painful experiences of a bad conscience) and of his goodness (reflected in the joyful experiences of a good conscience). Newman's concept of God, stressing providence, has as counterpart his concept of the universe as a process of constant development. To be, to live, is to develop.

The principle of nature. God governs all things in conformity with their nature. Hence the supreme universal rule and method in the attempts to know the truth and to act rightly and adequately is to consider "the nature of the things" and to submit to what is required by "the nature of the case."

The principle of analogy. The universe as governed by God is a unity of extreme diversity. Unity implies conformity of part to part; diversity implies degrees of similarity. Hence Newman generally justifies a judicious use of argument from analogy and fittingness.

Epistemology. In accordance with the principle of nature, Newman's epistemology rests on a descriptive analysis of the nature of the mind and its actual operational patterns. The logic of the human mind cannot be established *a priori*; rather, mind must be scrutinized in all its complexity; one must ask how the mind generally proceeds in its quest for truth, and how it actually attains to certitude. The mind is spontaneously, instinctively, aware of an objective world of particular things, persons, and events. It apprehends the meaning of propositions about them and assents to these propositions if it feels them to rest upon convincing grounds. Inference is this movement of mind from premise to conclusion.

Assent is real (termed also "imaginative") when the meaning grasped strikes the imagination as a concrete reality, rousing the individual's powers of affection and action. Assent is notional when the meaning grasped conveys to the intellect alone combinations of general concepts. These two aspects may and should go together, giving the mind depth and holding power combined with breadth and clarity of view. Inference differs from assent in that inference is by its nature conditional and admits of degrees, whereas assent is by its nature unconditional and does not admit of degrees.

Inference is either formal or informal. Formal inference is deduction from general principles and can neither prove its first principles nor reach conclusions regarding concrete states of affairs. This gap must be bridged by informal inference, at its most spontaneous and implicit termed "natural" inference. An individual mind, at the convergence of independent probabilities, indications, and clues—often too numerous and too subtle to be exhaustively analyzable—grasps the concrete pattern of evidence and its conclusion *per modum unius*, by an act of intuitive comprehensive imagination. Newman calls this mental power the "illative sense." It is a power of judgment, in part a gift of nature, in part the result of experience and exercise. As a power of concrete, and not merely notional, judgment, it may depend upon mastery in a specific field of endeavor.

Newman's account of inference stresses its status as mental attitude; it is an attitude toward the conclusion as following from its premises. Likewise, Newman contrasts certitude with certainty. Certainty pertains to propositions in their formal interrelation; certitude pertains to the living mind in exercise of the illative sense.

Theology and the sciences. Reality is one, but complex. The conceptual knowledge of reality is one in its ultimate aim, but by virtue of its abstractive nature, knowledge necessarily divides into an increasing number of sciences treating various parts and aspects of the whole. The intellect can neither take in the whole nor adequately reconstruct it by addition and composition of all the available sciences. Each science has its own principles and methods imposed by the nature of the subject matter. Hence a certain amount of disagreement between scientific views is inevitable. The clash between the exact sciences and theological science may be expected. Scientists will easily imagine that their conclusions are irreconcilable with faith, for the experiences with which theology starts are rather elusive, whereas the data of the exact sciences are clearer and more compelling; moreover, the prevailing methods of the exact sciences are inductive, whereas those of theology are deductive.

As truth is one, the very evolution of scientific investigation may be expected to solve the difficulties that it raises. Hence, total freedom, tolerance, dialogue, mutual esteem, and understanding should govern the relationship between all the sciences in their living coexistence.

Faith. For Newman, faith is both objective and subjective. As objective, faith is a doctrinal system of revealed truths, articulated in plain human language, inadequate yet true. This is the principle of dogma, which Newman sternly opposed to all forms of religious or theological liberalism. It is contained in scripture, gradually clarified in the life of the church under the guidance of divine providence (the Holy Spirit), in the course of history confirmed, at least in its essentials, by its magisterium, and proposed as a condition of ecclesiastical membership by its present authority. In the end, Newman saw this Catholic position as being in the nature of a church called to survive substantially in the flux of historical experience.

As subjective, faith is acceptance of dogma combined with a personal surrender to the realities signified by dogma, that is, real apprehension and assent. It is a gift of God's "illuminating grace," yet justified by reason.

Influence. During his years in the Anglican church, Newman was the most influential leader of the Oxford Movement, defining the position of Anglo-Catholicism in the Church of England and deepening the life of devotion through his sermons. In the Roman Catholic church his controversial writings, especially his *Apologia,* fostered among the British people a better knowledge of and higher esteem for his religion and his coreligionists. Moreover, his minimizing theological attitude in matters of faith and his critical open-mindedness with regard to difficulties and disagreements prepared that spirit of dialogue and conciliation in the Roman Catholic church that characterizes so much of contemporary theological thought and is believed to have strongly influenced the spirit of the Second Vatican Council.

Perhaps Newman's most important influence is that which his ideas increasingly exercise on contemporary thought, especially through his pioneering investigations into the nature and workings of the human mind in the individual (*Grammar of Assent*) and in society (*Development of Christian Doctrine*). Further, his *Idea of a University* has become a classic in intellectual education and the philosophy of the sciences. In this last regard it is widely known that Newman influenced Alfred North Whitehead.

Bibliography

A complete bibliography of works by Newman and concerning him is available in *Newman-Studien,* a serial publication of the Internationales Cardinal-Newman-Kuratorium (Nuremberg, 1948–). For works on Newman, see Vincent F. Blehl's *John Henry Newman: A Bibliographical Catalogue of His Writings* (Charlottesville, Va., 1978). John R. Griffin's *Newman: A Bibliography of Secondary Studies* (Fort Royal, Va., 1980) is an almost complete list of publications on Newman, comprising more than 2,500 entries. The main posthumous documents are *John Henry Newman: Autobiographical Writings,* edited by Henry Tristam (New York, 1957); *The Philosophical Notebook of John Henry Newman,* 2 vols., edited by Edward J. Sillem (New York, 1970); *The Theological Papers of John Henry Newman: On Faith and Certainty,* edited by Hugo M. de Achaval and J. Derek Holmes (Oxford, 1976); and *The Letters and Diaries of John Henry Newman,* 26 vols., edited by Thomas Gornall (London, 1973–). The best comprehensive study is Henry Tristam and F. Bacchus's "Newman," in *Dictionnaire de théologie catholique* (Paris, 1903–1950). The most complete biography, though lacking quotations of sources, is Meriol Trevor's *Newman: Light in Winter,* 2 vols. (New York, 1962).

J. H. Walgrave (1987)

NEW RELIGIOUS MOVEMENTS

This entry consists of the following articles:

NEW RELIGIOUS MOVEMENTS: AN OVERVIEW

Scholars adopted the term *new religious movements* (NRMs) in order to avoid the pejorative connotations of the popularly used term *cult*. Although the word *cult* originally referred to an organized system of worship (and is still used in that sense by scholars in several disciplines), *cult* began to take on negative connotations in popular discourse in the 1960s and 1970s, when a variety of unconventional religions appeared in North America. The word conveyed a stereotype that prevented objective research into these religions; moreover, NRMs were so different from one another that it was impossible to generalize about them. Instead, NRM scholars preferred to investigate each new religion separately without imposing the filter of a stereotype. Beginning in the 1970s, people called "deprogrammers" began illegally kidnapping NRM members and attempting to undo their alleged "brainwashing," curtailing their civil liberties in the process. As a result, many NRM scholars began to advocate freedom of religion for NRMs. While scholars admit that some members of NRMs have committed abusive and illegal acts (as have members of mainstream religions and people who have no religious commitments), they advise that law enforcement agencies exercise discipline when investigating claims of wrongdoing, rather than overreacting.

New religious movements emerge from humans' creativity and capacity for religious expression, providing spiritual meaning and social connection for their members, just as mainstream religious groups do. Contemporary NRMs manifest the increasing pluralism associated with greater ease of global travel and communications.

NRMs provide arenas for theological and social experimentation. Some of these experiments are successful and result in lasting religious organizations that exert broad cultural and theological influences. Some experiments are less successful, resulting in small groups that are not influential or lasting. A few produce groups whose beliefs and practices are deemed utterly abhorrent by the wider society.

NRMs exist in varying degrees of tension within their respective religious and cultural contexts. To survive for the long-term, however, this tension must not become too great, and may indeed be mitigated over time. On the other hand, some degree of tension with society can attract converts who are dissatisfied with the spirituality and practices of mainstream religious institutions.

NRMs may be alternative in terms of theology, leadership, authority structures, gender roles, family and sexual relationships, and religious practices.

DIVERSITY OF NEW RELIGIOUS MOVEMENTS. The term *new religious movements* covers many types of religious movements and groups: religions that were introduced into a culture by missionary representatives from world religions abroad, such as the International Society for Krishna Consciousness (ISKCON) or other Asian-based religions with converts in the West, as well as Christian groups in China and Japan; religious groups that were brought into new cultural contexts by recent immigrants, such as Muslims in the West; groups that evolved out of a more established tradition, such as the Branch Davidians, which emerged from Seventh-day Adventism; reconfigurations of religious themes in traditional religions, such as Kurozumikyō, Tenrikyō, and other new religions in Japan; revivals of suppressed religious traditions, such as contemporary Pagan movements in eastern Europe; creative mergings of diverse religious traditions, such as the African Independent Churches (AICs; often called African Initiated Churches), which combined Christianity with African beliefs and modes of worship, or the New Age movement's blend of different religions and spiritualities; imaginative and syncretistic re-creations of preexisting religious traditions, such as Neopaganism in North America; organizations that coalesced around new formulations of teachings found in alternative religious traditions, such as the Theosophical Society, which grew out of the Western Esoteric tradition and borrowed from virtually all the world's religions; or millennial movements that formed in response to new cultural conditions or oppression (such as the Ghost Dance movement among Plains Native Americans in the nineteenth century) or innovations (such as the UFO movement known as the Raelians). However innovative they may be, NRMs always utilize elements of earlier religious traditions as building blocks to construct their new theologies, practices, and organizations.

NRMs are diverse in terms of their authority, organizational structures, and levels of commitment required of their members. For example, ISKCON in the 1960s and 1970s demanded much from its participants and had a communal structure; on the other hand, the Theosophical Society has organizational structures on the local, national, and international levels, is not communal for the most part, and does not require prospective members to pledge a large commitment of resources. Falun Gong is a network of like-minded people, and the New Age movement is an alternative milieu in which people move from one group or teacher to another, appropriating what works for them as individuals. Some NRM members may make significant investments of time, money, identities, marriages, families, and careers to a group, only to find out later that leaving the group involves very high "exit costs." These exit costs may make it difficult for them to leave the group, even if they would like to. Many other NRM members, however, attend their alternative group and imbibe its worldview only sporadically, enjoying the socializing once or twice a week, much the way members of mainstream religions attend their churches, synagogues, and mosques.

NRMs also vary in terms of their size and influence. Many NRMs have remained small, localized groups, while others have become large denominations, such as the Church of Jesus Christ of Latter-day Saints (Mormons) and Church of Christ, Scientist (Christian Science). A few NRMs have become world religions, such as Buddhism, Christianity, and Islam. Many others remain diffuse milieus containing many individuals and groups, such as Western Esotericism. Often, a NRM gives birth to its own movement, as additional groups and teachers continue the process of splitting off to form separate organizations, while continuing to contribute to an environment of shared ideas and practices, such as the Theosophical and the New Thought movements.

New religious movements also have different modes of origination. Many NRMs have been founded by prophets with new revelations, or messiahs who claim to have the superhuman power to create a millennial collective salvation; many others consist of movements of people who have contributed to an alternative worldview, such as Christian Identity.

New religions provide social spaces for experimentation in alternative theologies, gender roles, sexual relations, leadership structures, and group organization. Some of these experiments, such as free love and polygamy, have not been successful in the West because the wider society condemned and opposed them. Other experiments have succeeded and influenced mainstream society, such as theologies that emphasize the divine feminine, or imagine God to be both male and female, or view the ultimate reality as a neuter and impersonal force, counteracting the patriarchal conception of God. These alternative theological conceptions, such as the Christian Science Father-Mother God, the Wiccan Great Goddess, or the Theosophical impersonal ultimate, have influenced—directly or indirectly—mainstream Christian theologies; they have prefigured theological innovations in mainstream denominations. NRMs have experimented with women's religious leadership and feminist gender roles; consequently, many mainstream religious institutions have promoted women's equality and leadership. Yet many NRMs have opted to institutionalize patriarchal gender roles and traditional conceptions of God, often in reaction to changes in society and religion.

New religions scholars will continue to observe a particular new religious movement and the changes that occur as the new group matures, as long as the worldview, practices, and organization remain alternative, unconventional, somewhat marginal, and in some degree of tension with the mainstream cultural context. Thus, some NRMs will continue to be studied by NRM scholars well past the time they are no longer "new." The tension with the mainstream society may arise due to alternative theology or worldview, practices, organization, leadership, gender roles, sexual practices, or other factors.

New Religions Studies. New religions studies became an emerging field in the late 1960s and 1970s, when numerous unconventional religions attracted attention from the general public. In the early twenty-first century, this maturing field has produced scholarly analysis and many insights important to the study of religions.

Investigation into new religions is an extension of the comparative and interdisciplinary study of religions. The study of new religions is the study of *religions* in all their diversity and creativity. Many NRM studies have focused on Western cultural contexts, but the field is increasingly becoming international in scope, examining numerous religious movements emerging from, and finding themselves in tension with, different cultures.

New religions studies is interdisciplinary. Most contributors to the field have been historians of religions and sociologists. Scholars who contribute to NRM studies also belong to the fields of psychology, anthropology, folklore, and linguistics.

Contexts Conducive To Producing NRMs. Any context may produce NRMs, because nonconformists and innovators exist in any culture. Certain contexts, however, involving cultural disruption, change, and a high degree of exchange of ideas and people, seem particularly conducive to producing NRMs.

New religions have arisen in various times and places as a result of the migration of peoples and the exchange of ideas. This process has been accelerated in today's world due to the relative ease of travel and worldwide communication by electronic means, including the Internet. The United States, and Japan from the nineteenth century on, have been particularly fertile grounds for the creation of new religions, as people in both countries have confronted the changes affecting work, family, technology, values, and the mobility of peoples throughout the world associated with modernity and postmodernity. Growth in the number of new religions is one characteristic of the world's increasing pluralism.

Oppressive contexts, in which an invading colonial power possessing advanced technology and military advantage seizes the land and wealth of an indigenous people, disrupts their traditional way of life, and causes loss of life, are ripe for spawning new religious movements. A colonial power will import its own religion into the new context, where it will be adapted to the values, concepts, and practices of the indigenous culture, giving rise to new religious movements such as the numerous African Independent Churches or the Latin American folk Catholic movements and Pentecostal churches. Millennial movements with new prophets and messiahs are likely to emerge among indigenous peoples desperate for liberation from their oppressors and difficult conditions. Some of these movements may be revolutionary, such as Cuscat's War (1867–1870) in Mexico, led by the Mayan prophet Pedro Díaz Cuscat, while others may promote the expectation of salvation by divine intervention, such as the Ghost Dance movement among Plains Native Americans in the late nineteenth century. Many millennial movements reacting to poverty and oppression have set up separate communities, such as Joaseiro do Norte in Brazil or Nueva Jerusalén in Mexico.

Newly opened or liberating contexts can also give rise to a proliferation of NRMs. For instance, the demise of the

Soviet Union at the end of the 1980s created contexts in Russia, the former Soviet states, and eastern Europe that were very receptive to the importation of NRMs, the resurgence of indigenous Pagan religious expressions, and the creation of new religions. The fall of communism as a dominant worldview and state structure in these areas left a vacuum of meaning that people quickly filled.

CHARISMATIC LADERS AND THE BRAINWASHING DEBATE. Members of the general public, attempting to explain why people join strange religious groups with unusual beliefs and behaviors, have often resorted to what James T. Richardson has called "the myth of the omnipotent leader" and the corresponding "myth of the passive, brainwashed follower" (cited in Wessinger, *How the Millennium Comes Violently*, 2000, 273–274). In subscribing to these perspectives, however, citizens forget that the beliefs and practices of any religion appear to be bizarre from the outsider's vantage point. Instead, people in the mainstream assume that the so-called "charismatic leader" wields an invisible and irresistible power over his or her brainwashed followers.

Charisma. *Charisma,* in the popular sense, refers to the characteristics of an attractive individual gifted with excellent communications skills, but historians of religions and sociologists use the term to designate a different quality often found in religious leaders. In a religious studies and sociological sense, *charisma* refers to an attribute possessed by an individual whom people believe has access to an unseen source of authority, such as revelation from God, angels, spirits, ancestors, or even extraterrestrials. The source of the authority is unseen, so people either believe or reject the claim. Charisma is socially constructed. If no one believes the individual's claim, then he or she does not have charisma in this sense. No one can become a charismatic leader without the support and allegiance of believers, and the followers can withdraw their faith in the leader at any time.

Not all NRMs are founded or led by charismatic leaders, but this type of leadership is common in the first generation of a movement. Thereafter, authority usually becomes "routinized" (Weber, 1946) into offices that people may obtain by an institutionalized credentialing process.

Given that followers can withdraw allegiance, Thomas Robbins and Dick Anthony (1995), following Max Weber, have pointed to the inherent instability of charismatic leadership. The leader may go to great lengths to continue to win the faith of followers. If such faith is forthcoming, the charismatic leader may be emboldened to demand even greater actions demonstrating commitment, involving sacrifices in relation to family, sexuality, property, and even acts of violence. If followers carry out acts of coercion and violence in support of the leader and the leader's vision, he or she can then exert totalitarian control, making it very difficult for people to leave the group. Examples of leaders possessing charisma whose followers carried out coercive actions with varying degrees and scopes of influence include Jim Jones (1931–1978) of the Peoples Temple and Jonestown, Asahara Shōkō (b. 1955) of Aum Shinrikyō, and Adolf Hitler (1889–1945). Although Adolf Hitler may appear to have been solely a political leader, he was also the messiah of a revolutionary millennial movement (see below), and he claimed to be destined by "Nature" to lead the Germans into a collective salvation called the "Third Reich."

Many NRMs, such as the Theosophical Society, have democratic structures of authority. These democracies often develop after the death of a charismatic founder. Also, it is important to note that many, probably most, charismatic leaders *do not* become totalitarian and do not lead their believers into disaster.

Brainwashing Debate. Most social scientists studying NRMs have concluded that indoctrination practices in NRMs are not inherently different from those practiced in mainstream institutions, such as families, schools, churches, the military, and prisons. They reject the concept that anyone's will can be overcome by a mysterious power of "mind control" or "brainwashing." This is not to say that social and interpersonal influence techniques are not present, as they are in all social situations. Although most NRMs do not use coercive practices to retain members, a few have. An NRM cannot become coercive, however, without the willing complicity of at least some of its members.

An example of an NRM that actively attempted to practice brainwashing is Aum Shinrikyō, the criminal Japanese new religion active in the late 1980s through the mid-1990s. Aum devotees kidnapped, imprisoned, starved, drugged, subjected to electric shocks, and abused people in attempts to convert them. None of these people became believers, although many of them were severely injured or killed. On the other hand, Aum members who willingly went through socialization processes, such as listening to the guru's lectures, working long hours for the organization, listening to audiotaped affirmations, and enduring immersions in cold water and hot water as ascetic practices, were committed believers. The contrast between these two types of people illustrates that socialization processes are most effective when the individual willingly participates in them.

People join new religions for numerous reasons: the worldview makes sense to them; they find benefits in the religious practices; they have preexisting affective bonds with family members and friends who are members; they like the people and the alternative community and "family" they have found; the group offers a sense of belonging and social support; they enjoy the adventure offered in terms of travel and new lifestyles; the new religion enables them to live out their commitments to values and beliefs that were inculcated by their upbringing; they like the roles of men and women; they become emotionally attracted to the leader for various reasons; membership offers therapeutic benefits in dealing with personal problems and life transitions.

The rapid turnover of membership that is common to most NRMs disproves the brainwashing theory, which claims that people are unable to resist the mesmerizing influence exerted by a charismatic leader. For instance, The Family (formerly the Children of God) had about fifty-seven thousand people join during its first twenty-five years, but only about three thousand adult members remained at the end of that time (See statistics on NRMs summarized in Richardson 2003 and Palmer 2003). People leave a new religion when they lose faith or become disenchanted with the group and its lifestyle and leadership.

NEW RELIGIONS AND SCRIPTURES. New religions offer new interpretations of traditional scriptures, such as the Bible and the Qurʾān, and often produce their own scriptures.

The scriptures of established religious traditions are so internally diverse that, for centuries, leaders, prophets, messiahs, and ordinary people have offered new interpretations of them; these new readings have often led to the formation of new movements.

The founders of new religions claiming divine revelation often produce new scriptures themselves, while sometimes people's written memories of these individuals become new scriptures. For example, Joseph Smith, Jr. claimed to have translated a text engraved on golden tablets, which became known as the Book of Mormon, a scripture important to Mormons (along with the Bible).

New interpretations of established scriptures and the production of new scriptures is an important part of the creativity of religion-making. In the twenty-first century, additional scriptures may be found in nonwritten media, such as movies, videos, audiotapes, CDs, and websites. Whatever the medium, scriptures address the meaning and purpose of life and provide advice on proper living. Scriptures convey a worldview in which meaningful human life is possible.

WOMEN AND GENDER ROLES IN NRMS. Many NRMs experiment with gender roles and sexuality. Some NRMs enforce conservative patriarchal gender roles (such as the Unification Church and the Twelve Tribes), many are attractive primarily to heterosexuals, others welcome people of all sexual orientations (such as the Raelians), some encourage free love within the group (such as The Family, Raelians, and the followers of Rajneesh in the 1970s), while others promote celibacy (such as the Shakers and the Brahma Kumaris).

A conservative NRM that follows the Bible or the Qurʾān (such as the Twelve Tribes and the Nation of Islam, respectively) may encourage traditional heterosexual marriages and male headship of the family. Some NRMs have experimented with polygamy, such as the nineteenth-century Latter-day Saints (Mormons) and contemporary Mormon splinter groups. The Branch Davidians practiced celibacy for ordinary members, but their leader, David Koresh (1959–1993), took numerous wives, with whom he had children to fulfill his interpretations of biblical prophecies.

Other NRMs promote equality for women and do not restrict women to the roles of wife and mother. Often, these religions welcome people of all sexual orientations, such as the Raelian group. Neopaganism has been particularly woman-affirming in its emphasis on a Great Goddess, multiple goddesses, and the sacredness of Earth.

When patriarchal religious institutions are dominant in the mainstream, women's religious leadership is necessarily exercised on the margins of society in unconventional religions. Women have founded new religions, and women in NRMs have been acknowledged as being prophets, messiahs, theologians, and philosophers. For instance, Mother Ann Lee (1736–1784), who in the late eighteenth century founded the Shakers—which promoted women's liberation through men and women living together in celibate communities—was regarded by the Shakers as the "Second Appearing of Christ in female form." Helena P. Blavatsky (1831–1891), an unconventional Russian world traveler, articulated the philosophical basis for Theosophy and claimed to be in touch with enlightened masters via psychic means. Mary Baker Eddy (1821–1910) received a healing and revelation that led her to write her magnum opus, *Science and Health, With Key to the Scriptures* (1875) and found the Church of Christ, Scientist.

Scholar Mary Farrell Bednarowski (1980) has pointed out that NRMs founded by women or that have women as leaders often develop a view of God that either promotes a divine feminine, perhaps balanced with a divine masculine aspect of God, or sees the ultimate reality as impersonal.

CHILDREN IN NEW RELIGIONS. Children are a highly sensitive topic with respect to NRMs, and the scholarly study of children in NRMs is just beginning. Children in NRMs are often the subjects of custody battles between the parent who is a member and the parent who is not a member or who has left the group. People in mainstream society often fear for the welfare of children in NRMs because of their unorthodox practices and beliefs. Under these circumstances, exaggerated allegations are often made about the treatment of children in NRMs. Sometimes there is a real basis for these concerns, but often there is not. For instance, authorities have seized children from two alternative Christian groups, the Twelve Tribes and The Family, only to have to return them later when no evidence of abuse could be produced. On the other hand, the leader of the Nuwaubian Nation of Moors was convicted in 2004 for sexually abusing children, and the International Society for Krishna Consciousness in the late 1990s and early 2000s had to confront the damage caused by abuse of children placed in ISKCON boarding schools. The highly publicized pedophilia scandal in the Roman Catholic Church in the early 2000s reminds us that abuse of children can occur in mainstream religions and not only in the unconventional ones.

Fears about children in NRMs can lead to overreactions from law enforcement officials. The two assaults against the Branch Davidians in 1993 by federal agents purportedly were motivated by concerns about the safety of the children, but their actions resulted in the deaths of twenty-three children under the age of fifteen (including two who were born in the fire when their pregnant mothers died and then died themselves), five teenagers over fifteen, eighteen people in their twenties, and their parents. A number of the young women who died in the fire were the mothers of the eighteen children who were eight years old or younger who died with them. In the Branch Davidian case, the matter of child abuse did not fall under federal jurisdiction. The Branch Davidians had been investigated for child abuse by Texas authorities and the case was closed for lack of evidence. While the allegations of severe corporal punishment remain unsubstantiated, David Koresh was, in fact, having sex with underage girls with the permission of their parents, and the girls were bearing his children.

Religiously committed parents want their children to be raised in the lifestyle they deem best according to their deeply held beliefs. This is the case for parents who belong to mainstream, as well as marginal, religions. Difficulties arise when the values of parents in unconventional religions diverge radically from the values of mainstream society.

Sometimes parents in a new religion hold to a faith so strongly that they permit their daughters to be married at early ages, as with the Branch Davidians and contemporary polygamous Mormons. On rare occasions, strongly committed parents may kill their children to achieve an ultimate goal by collective suicide, which occurred at Jonestown in 1978 and with the Solar Temple in 1994 and 1995.

The vast majority of parents in NRMs do not go to these extremes, however. Scholars recognize the need for additional research into the benign situations of children in NRMs, as well as in the cases where harm was done. Close scholarly examinations of children in NRMs will likely reveal complex situations possessing both positive and negative features.

MILLENNIALISM. The religious patterns that scholars term *millennialism*—belief in an imminent transition to a collective salvation (either earthly or heavenly) effected by a supernatural or superhuman agent—are ideal for promoting new religious movements. Persuading people that a catastrophic destruction of the world is imminent, and that salvation can be found only among the "elect" who join the new religion and have faith in its prophet or messiah and his or her message, is a powerful factor in motivating people to convert. Likewise, an anticipation of an imminent, nonviolent, progressive transformation into a new age in accordance with a divine plan can motivate people to join the movement to facilitate the collective salvation. Millennial beliefs are often, but not always, found in new religious movements.

NEW RELIGIONS AND VIOLENCE. It is well known that members of dominant religious traditions often commit violence or become caught up in violence While the vast majority of NRMs do not become involved in violence, some have been involved in spectacular cases of violence. Excluding the inevitable isolated incidents caused by deranged individuals, religious violence is typically *interactive* in nature. The quality of the interactions of people in mainstream society—law enforcement agents and other government officials, reporters, psychologists and social workers, citizens, concerned relatives, and anticultists—with members of a new religion helps determine whether or not tragic violence occurs. It is seldom only the believers who contribute to a situation that culminates in violence, although their actions and the content of their faith certainly do affect the overall scenario.

Assaulted NRMs. Members of NRMs do not always initiate the violence; sometimes, they are attacked by others. When members of a new religious movement are assaulted, they may or may not fight back. The early Christians did not fight back when they were assaulted. Some of the early Christians, as well as some Falun Gong practitioners in the early twenty-first century, may have deliberately put themselves in danger of being harmed by the state. Conversely, the Branch Davidians tried to defend themselves in 1993.

Fragile NRMs. A few new religions become fragile in reaction to internal weaknesses and experiences of opposition from society. Members of a fragile NRM initiate violence to preserve their endangered religious goal. Their violence may be directed outwardly against perceived enemies, inwardly against members, or both. Jonestown in Guyana (1978); the Solar Temple in Switzerland, Quebec, and France (1994, 1995, 1997); Aum Shinrikyō in Japan (1995); and Heaven's Gate in the United States (1997) are examples of fragile groups. The Movement for the Restoration of the Ten Commandments of God (MRTCG) (2000), a Catholic Marian apparition group in Uganda involved in the deaths of about 780 people, also may have been a fragile millennial group.

Revolutionary NRMs. The most dangerous NRMs are the ones that are revolutionary. These are usually revolutionary millennial movements seeking to achieve a collective salvation on Earth. They use violence to try to overthrow what they see as the corrupt order to create a new one. The Taiping Revolution in China from 1850 to 1864 and the German Nazis in the twentieth century can be seen as revolutionary NRMs. Al-Qāʿidah is a contemporary example of a revolutionary NRM. Even in the cases of revolutionary NRMs, however, the quality of interactions of people in mainstream society with nonbelievers is crucial for stimulating the believers' sense of being persecuted, thus confirming their convictions that revolutionary violence is needed to achieve a collective salvation for those who are identified as worthy of being included in the "elect."

Dualism. A dualistic outlook usually contributes to episodes of violence involving new religious movements. An extreme dualism entails a rigid perspective of good versus evil, or of us versus them. But dualism is not restricted to religious believers. In these interactive conflicts, dualism can usually be discerned in the worldviews of reporters, anticult activists, law enforcement agents, politicians, and government officials. Among the religious believers, the dualism is often associated with a millennial outlook that expects catastrophic destruction before salvation is achieved for the elect.

GOVERNMENTAL OPPOSITION TO NRMS: FREEDOM OF RELIGION ISSUES. It is a serious matter when a religion is called a "cult" or "sect" by a government and the general public. Labeling a group with the pejorative term *cult* or an equivalent term promotes opposition, discrimination, and even persecution of the believers, with possible disastrous consequences. The believers become dehumanized by the pejorative label, and outsiders may believe it is morally right to exterminate them.

Scholarship on the Branch Davidian conflict in 1993 indicates that federal agents were motivated in great part by the "cult" stereotype to carry out two assaults against the community. The media depicted the Branch Davidians as "cultists" during the fifty-one-day siege; as a result, much of the American public approved of the gas-and-tank assault carried out by the Federal Bureau of Investigation that resulted in the deaths of seventy-four Branch Davidians. In all, eighty Branch Davidians and four law enforcement agents died in what was later determined to be an unnecessary conflict. David Koresh had consistently expressed his willingness to cooperate with authorities, from the initial investigations to the fiery end, provided the Branch Davidians were permitted to remain faithful to their biblical concerns.

During 1999 and the early 2000s, Falun Gong was the most visible among many persecuted religious groups in the People's Republic of China. Falun Gong adherents, who practiced a form of *qigong* (exercises designed to enhance *qi*, or life force), surprised officials in the Chinese Communist Party in 1999 by coordinating a protest gathering of more than ten thousand people near the Beijing residence of the highest party leaders. Despite being labeled an "evil cult" and outlawed, Falun Gong practitioners continued to assert their right to freedom of religion by practicing their *qigong* exercises in public places, such as Tiananmen Square, where they were arrested. Reportedly, hundreds of Falun Gong practitioners died in custody. All of the official forces of the People's Republic of China, including the media, were mobilized in the repression of Falun Gong practitioners.

In the mid- to late 1990s, France and Belgium issued reports and passed laws against *sectes,* the pejorative term equivalent to *cults.* Minority religions of all types unfortunate enough to be included on the lists of *sectes* were subjected to harassment and surveillance by law enforcement agents, and members lost jobs and suffered other civil disabilities.

Russia and former Soviet republics in the late 1990s and early 2000s took steps to curtail the legal rights of minority religious groups and to favor traditional historical churches, such as the Russian Orthodox Church in Russia and the Armenian Apostolic Church in Armenia. In 2004, the city of Moscow banned the religious activities of Jehovah's Witnesses, including holding meetings and services in private homes. In Turkmenistan, all religions other than approved Islam and Russian Orthodoxy were banned; members of all other religions were treated harshly.

The ideologies of the American anticult and countercult (evangelical Christian) movements have been exported to other countries, where the anticult/countercult perspective is utilized to curtail religious freedoms and justify state-sponsored repression and violence against unconventional religious groups. Phillip Charles Lucas (2004) points out that the right to freedom of religion needs to be balanced with the concern that some religious groups may be engaged in illegal and harmful activities. The "cult" stereotype promoted by the anticult and countercult movements has promoted religious bigotry and has led to extreme actions on the part of authorities in various countries.

When authorities suspect illegal activities on the part of NRM members, they should conduct a careful investigation and ensure that the actions of law enforcement agents conform to reasonable and moderate procedures to avoid causing unnecessary harm. Furthermore, law enforcement agents should consult with credentialed scholars of religions.

NRMs are religions. They represent the creativity of the human spirit. They are novel, alternative, and unconventional in their cultural contexts, and thus they live in some degree of tension with society. At the same time, they express the universal human yearning for contact with the sacred, and in this regard they are neither novel nor unusual. Because they are religions-in-formation, the study of them sheds light on all religions, as well as on the perpetual human quest for meaning.

New religions studies is focused on emergent, alternative, and unconventional religions in any given cultural context, thus it is interdisciplinary in approach and multicultural in scope. Because of the cultural opposition that often confronts NRMs, scholars in the field also study social control efforts directed against NRMs. The field represents an important extension of the study of religions in all their diversity.

SEE ALSO African Religions, article on New Religious Movements; Anticult Movements; Aum Shinrikyō; Blavatsky, H. P.; Brainwashing (Debate); Branch Davidians; Charisma; Christian Identity Movement; Christian Science; Cults and Sects; Eddy, Mary Baker; Esotericism; Falun Gong; Family, The; Ghost Dance; Heaven's Gate; International Society for Krishna Consciousness; Jehovah's Witnesses; Jones, Jim; Jonestown and Peoples Temple; Koresh, David; Law and Religion, article on Law and New Religious Movements; Lee, Ann; Mormonism; Movement for the Restoration of the Ten Commandments of God; Nation of Islam; Neopaganism; New Age Movement; New Thought Movement; Raëlians; Shakers; Smith, Joseph; Sōka Gakkai; Taiping; Theosophical Society; Twelve Tribes; UFO Religions; Unification Church; Wicca.

BIBLIOGRAPHY

Barker, Eileen. "Perspective: What Are We Studying? A Sociological Case for Keeping the '*Nova*.'" *Nova Religio: The Journal of Alternative and Emergent Religions.* 8, no. 1 (2004): 88–

102. Barker, a sociologist, argues for defining a new religion as being a first-generation group consisting of converts, and that the cultural antagonism directed toward NRMs is a consequence of their being novel.

Bednarowski, Mary Farrell. "Outside the Mainstream: Women's Religion and Women's Religious Leaders in Nineteenth-Century America." *Journal of the American Academy of Religion* 48 (1980): 207–231. Groundbreaking essay that illuminates factors which promote ongoing women's religious leadership in unconventional religions.

Bromley, David G. "Perspective: Whither New Religions Studies: Defining and Shaping a New Area of Study." *Nova Religio: The Journal of Alternative and Emergent Religions* 8, no. 2 (2004). In a discussion of the sociological development of New Religions Studies (NRS) as an emerging interdisciplinary area of study, Bromley argues that mainstream religions are characterized by congruence or alignment with the dominant culture, while NRMs are characterized by a lack of alignment and are therefore in tension with the dominant culture, values, and institutions.

Campbell, Colin. "The Cult, the Cultic Milieu, and Secularization." *A Sociological Yearbook of Religion in Britain* 5 (1972): 119–136. Reprinted in *The Cultic Milieu: Oppositional Subcultures in an Age of Globalization.* Edited by Jeffrey Kaplan and Heléne Lööw, 12–25. Walnut Creek, Calif., 2002. Campbell describes a milieu of "seekership" among alternative ideas and practices associated with the Western Esoteric tradition or Occultism, and often associated with the Theosophical and New Age movements, which has incorporated influences from Asian religions.

Dawson, Lorne L. *Comprehending Cults: The Sociology of New Religious Movements.* Oxford, 1998. Excellent sociological treatment of the main issues relating to new religions, including typologies, causes of NRMs, conversion, the brainwashing debate, violence, and cultural significance.

Dawson, Lorne L. "Who Joins New Religious Movements and Why: Twenty Years of Research and What Have We Learned?" In *Cults and New Religious Movements: A Reader,* pp. 116–130. Edited by Lorne L. Dawson. Oxford, 2003. Helpful summary of conclusions found in social scientific literature on why people join new religious movements

Ellwood, Robert S. *Introducing Religion: From Inside and Outside.* 3rd ed. Englewood Cliffs, N.J., 1993. A pioneering scholar of new religions offers a focused treatment of "emergent religion" on pages 129–133.

Ellwood, Robert S. "Nazism as a Millennialist Movement." In *Millennialism, Persecution, and Violence: Historical Cases,* pp. 241–260. Edited by Catherine Wessinger. Syracuse, N.Y., 2000. Discussion of German Nazism as a revolutionary millennial movement.

Gallagher, Eugene V. "Introduction." *The New Religious Movements Experience in America.* Westport, Conn., 2004. Excellent introduction to the study of NRMs in America and the issues involved, such as deprogramming, freedom of religion, the brainwashing theory, and typologies.

Lucas, Phillip Charles. "The Future of New and Minority Religions in the Twenty-First Century: Religious Freedom Under Siege." In *New Religious Movements in the 21st Century: Legal, Political, and Social Challenges in Global Perspective,* edited by Phillip Charles Lucas and Thomas Robbins, pp. 341–357. New York, 2004. The important conclusion to a significant set of essays on the status of new religious movements in different countries and parts of the world.

Melton, J. Gordon. "Perspective: Toward a Definition of 'New Religion.'" *Nova Religio: The Journal of Alternative and Emergent Religions* 8, no. 1 (2004): 73–87. Melton, a historian of religions, opts for understanding a new religious movement as being any religion that is assigned fringe status by the dominant religions in any given culture because of significantly different beliefs and practices.

Miller, Timothy, ed. *When Prophets Die: The Postcharismatic Fate of New Religious Movements.* Albany, N.Y., 1991. A collection of essays on a variety of NRMs examining the processes of "routinization of charisma" after the death of the founding charismatic leader.

Miller, Timothy. "Introduction." In *America's Alternative Religions,* edited by Timothy Miller, pp. 1–10. Albany, N.Y., 1995. Miller, a historian of religions, opts for the term "alternative" to describe NRMs, and emphasizes that NRMs are not inherently inferior to mainstream religions.

Needleman, Jacob. *The New Religions.* New York, 1970. Probably the first title to use the term "new religions," Needleman studies Asian religions in the United States, especially California, that attracted attention in the late 1960s.

"*Nova Religio* Symposium: Falun Gong." *Nova Religio: The Journal of Alternative and Emergent Religions* 6, no. 2 (April 2003). A collection of eight scholarly articles on the history and practice of Falun Gong, and its conflict with the government of the People's Republic of China.

Palmer, Susan Jean. *Moon Sisters, Krishna Mothers, Rajneesh Lovers: Women's Roles in New Religions.* Syracuse, N.Y., 1994. Examines women's roles in a variety of NRMs—International Society for Krishna Consciousness, Rajneesh movement, Unification Church, Institute of Applied Metaphysics, Messianic Community (Twelve Tribes), Raelian movement, Institute for the Development of the Harmonious Human Being, The Family—paying particular attention to gender roles and sexual expressions.

Palmer, Susan J. "Women's 'Cocoon Work' in New Religious Movements: Sexual Experimentation and Feminine Rites of Passage." In *Cults and New Religious Movements: A Reader,* pp. 245–56. Edited by Lorne L. Dawson. Oxford, 2003. This summary of gender roles for women in a variety of NRMs proposes that women's temporary membership in an NRM serves as a rite of passage.

Palmer, Susan J., and Charlotte E. Hardman, eds. *Children in New Religions.* New Brunswick, N.J., 1999. The first collection of scholarly articles on children in new religions.

Puttick, Elizabeth. "Women in New Religious Movements." In *Cults and New Religious Movements: A Reader,* pp. 230–44. Edited by Lorne L. Dawson. Oxford, 2003. Illuminating discussion of women's gender roles and expressions of sexuality in "traditionalist" (patriarchal) new religions and more liberal "personal development" new religions; includes discussion of issues of abuse and sexual abuse of women.

Richardson, James T. "A Critique of 'Brainwashing' Claims about New Religious Movements." In *Cults and New Religious*

Movements: A Reader, pp. 160–66. Edited by Lorne L. Dawson. Oxford, 2003. A social scientific critique of the brainwashing theory as scientifically unfounded and self-serving to proponents.

Robbins, Thomas, and Dick Anthony. "Sects and Violence: Factors Enhancing the Volatility of Marginal Religious Movements." In *Armageddon in Waco: Critical Perspectives on the Branch Davidian Conflict.* Edited by Stuart A. Wright, pp. 236–59. Chicago, 1995. Discusses the precariousness of charismatic authority in addition to other factors that can contribute to violence involving a new religion.

Robbins, Thomas, and David Bromley. "Social Experimentation and the Significance of American New Religions: A Focused Review Essay." *Research in the Social Scientific Study of Religion.* 4 (1992): 1–28. Discusses NRMs as "laboratories of social experimentation," which can produce innovations that later will be incorporated into mainstream religions and societies.

Weber, Max. "The Social Psychology of the World Religions." In *From Max Weber: Essays in Sociology*, pp. 267–301, especially 297. Translated and edited by H. H. Gerth and C. Wright Mills. New York, 1946. Early discussion, first published in 1922–1923, of the process of "routinization" of charisma.

Wessinger, Catherine, ed. *Women's Leadership in Marginal Religions: Explorations Outside the Mainstream.* Urbana, Ill., 1993. An examination of the factors in certain new religions that have promoted women's religious leadership after the death of the founder (often a woman).

Wessinger, Catherine, ed. "Introduction: Going Beyond and Retaining Charisma: Women's Leadership in Marginal Religions." In *Women's Leadership in Marginal Religions: Explorations Outside the Mainstream.* Edited by Catherine Wessinger, 1–19. Urbana, Ill., 1993. In addition to discussing the factors that support ongoing religious leadership by women in alternative religions, examines some different ways a religion may be considered "marginal" to the mainstream cultural contexts.

Wessinger, Catherine, ed. *Millennialism, Persecution, and Violence: Historical Cases.* Syracuse, N.Y., 2000. Studies millennialism in a variety of cultures and time periods to elucidate the connection between millennial beliefs and episodes of violence.

Wessinger, Catherine, ed. *How the Millennium Comes Violently: From Jonestown to Heaven's Gate.* New York, 2000. Case studies of NRMs and millennial groups from 1978 involved in dramatic incidents of violence.

Benjamin D. Zablocki, "Exit Cost Analysis: A New Approach to the Scientific Study of Brainwashing," *Nova Religio: The Journal of Alternative and Emergent Religions* 1, no. 2 (1998): 216–49. Discussion of "exit costs" considered by people choosing whether to stay in or leave a religious group.

CATHERINE WESSINGER (2005)

NEW RELIGIOUS MOVEMENTS: HISTORY OF STUDY

In the 1970s a new subfield in academia developed around the study of what was termed *new religions.* Though minority religions had regularly populated the fringes of Western culture throughout history, a host of new religious movements had appeared in North America at the end of the 1960s and incited public controversy. Parents of the young adults who had joined many of these groups mounted fierce battles against what they termed *cults.* In order to present a more balanced view, early research efforts began, initially in the San Francisco Bay metropolitan area, to explore these groups from an academic perspective. At the time, it was assumed by some that the sudden burst of new religions was merely a passing phenomenon, particularly related to the social unrest of the 1960s. The long-term role of the many diverse movements was more fully understood only after their growth continued over several decades. Still in its relative infancy, the study of new religions was dramatically affected by the murder/suicides that occurred at Jonestown, Guyana, in November 1978.

NEW RELIGIONS STUDIES. The contemporary study of new religions grew from two roots: the study of cults (or in Europe, sects) through the early twentieth century, and the burst of new religious life in Japan following World War II. Through the late nineteenth century, observers of the trends in American religion realized that pluralism was altering the Christian community and that a number of "heretical" expressions were demanding a place on the spiritual landscape. By the end of the century, the first book had appeared that labeled some of these diverse religions "cults." Then, through the first half of the twentieth century, scholars and church leaders tried to discover why people would forsake traditional religions for these obviously false new religious expressions. Among these movements in question were Spiritualism, Mormonism, Theosophy, Christian Science, and New Thought. At the same time a variety of Christian literature denouncing the different groups would begin to circulate as part of an effort to stop their growth and keep Christians from straying toward them.

Simultaneously, with the growth of religious pluralism, both the psychology and sociology of religion developed as distinctive areas of concentration within the emerging social sciences. Pioneering scholars would attempt overviews of the different new religions. Favored targets were commonly independent African American groups such as Father Divine's Peace Mission and the Church of God and Saints of Christ; proselytizing Christian sectarian groups including Jehovah's Witnesses and Seventh-day Adventists; and alternative religions with distinctive practices, among them Spiritualism and Christian Science. The new Pentecostal movement with its unfamiliar practice of speaking in tongues spread across America just as observers were trying to make sense of Spiritualist séances, metaphysical healing, and occult fortunetelling.

The first generation of scholarly comment on new religions range from the rather empathetic remarks of William James in his classic, *The Varieties of Religious Experience* (1902), to the caustic ridicule heaped on the Pentecostals by

James' Harvard College colleague, George B. Cutten, in his *Speaking with Tongues: Historically and Psychologically Considered* (1927).

Prior to the 1950s, the study of "cults" was a fringe topic. Only a few scholars showed any long-term interest in the subject, and only a handful of Christian scholars wrote more than a single book on the topic. Among the few titles that attempted to go beyond a negative reductionist approach to the various groups and adopt, with relative success, an understanding of them as valid religious expressions that needed to be understood in their own right were Elmer T. Clark's *The Psychology of Religious Awakening* (1929); Louis R. Binder's *Modern Religious Cults and Society* (1933); and Arthur Huff Fauset's *Black Gods of the Metropolis: Negro Religious Cults of the Urban North* (1944). Among those who denounced the heretical teachings of the groups was Reformed Church minister Jan Karel Van Baalen, whose *Chaos of the Cults* first appeared in 1938. His somewhat careful study of the teachings of the "cults" was motivated by a desire to show how untenable they were in the light of Protestant orthodoxy.

The largely negative approach to the alternative religious groups was firmly established in the 1930s. The search for a rationale to explain why religious groups, outside of the limited pluralism marked by the major American denominations, could attract a following—albeit a minority one—dominated scholarly writing of the era. Attraction to the new religions was seen as a product of economic, social, and educational deprivation, if not actually linked to ill-defined psychological disturbances.

Transition. A transition from the earlier, more negative approach to new religions occurred in the two decades following World War II. In England, sociologist Bryan Wilson (1926–2004) began to look at what he termed sectarian religion. Following a format already applied to the more familiar churches, both state-sponsored and free, Wilson began to explore the different behavior and theologies proposed by individual sects and ask questions about the social organization of those groups then visible in England, North America, and Africa. His work, published in several books through the 1960s, led to a system of classifying sects according to the variant paths to salvation they outlined for their members:

conversionist,
revolutionist,
introversionist,
manipulationist,
thamaturgical,
reformist,
and utopian.

In a similar vein, church historian Elmer Clark, surveying American groups, classified them according to their dominant organizational thrust, thus finding sects that were:

pessimistic (or adventist),
perfectionist (or subjectivist),
charismatic (or pentecostal),
communistic,
legalistic (or objectivists),
egocentric (the New Thought groups),
and esoteric (or mystical).

It is to be noted that both Wilson and Clark developed their classification schema apart from the emerging distinction between sect and cult, and both included in their discussion some groups that would later be seen as sects (Salvation Army, Christadelphians) and those thought of as "new religions" (Christian Science, Jehovah's Witnesses) under the single rubric of sects. This approach had the benefit of allowing consideration of some otherwise orthodox Christian groups that evidenced out-of-the-ordinary behavior, such as speaking in tongues, contemporary revelations, communalism, and apocalypticism.

Joining Wilson and Clark was Marcus Bach, one of the first faculty members of the University of Iowa's pioneering religious-studies department. Bach was the first to teach a class on new religions and to invite members of the groups under discussion to come into his class and speak to students. He would go on to author a number of books with catchy titles, such as *Strange Sects and Curious Cults* (1906), that nevertheless offered the general public a factual and empathetic entrance into the life of groups such as the Amish, the Doukhobors, the Hutterites, and Father Divine's Peace Mission.

Whereas Clark's and Bach's influence was largely through their books, Wilson emerged as the teacher of a new generation of British scholars, mostly sociologists, who began in the 1970s to make the study of new religions their primary research field. His students, including Roy Wallis, and others inspired by his example, such as Eileen Barker and James Beckford, would arrive on the scene just as interest turned to emerging studies about Japan and its religious sects.

As a new generation of scholars in North America and Europe were absorbing Clark and Wilson, the Japanese religious community was in some turmoil. Nearly a century of suppression of Japan's diverse religions ended decisively with the introduction of American-style religious freedom in 1945. Over the next decade, a number of religious groups appeared seemingly out of nowhere. Attempting to make some sense of the phenomena, scholars soon discovered three different types of groups: some that had assumed a low profile during the Meiji era; others that had disbanded but were reconstituted after 1945; and a few that were entirely new. Scholars also saw that new groups were emerging at a steady pace. During the 1960s, Western scholars of Japanese religion like Harry Thomsen and H. Neill McFarland produced the first English-language texts about the *shin shūkyō,* or "new religions" of Japan.

The Emergence of New Religions Study. The books from Japan offered Western scholars a much-needed tool: a new language with which to discuss the numerous, outside-the-mainstream alternative religions that had become their focus in the 1970s. At this time, some older, unfamiliar religious groups joined a number of recently introduced movements to create a new alternative religious milieu, and many found the term borrowed from the Japanese, "new religions," appropriate to describe these recently visible movements elsewhere. Scholars sought distance from the older terms of "sect"—which in Europe had been used to describe so many groups that it hindered analysis—and "cult," which had in America taken on a decidedly negative connotation. While not altogether fitting terms, "new religion" and "new religious movement" (NRM) nevertheless gradually replaced the previous terminology, especially the term *cult.*

Leading the way in the appropriation of Japanese religious studies in the English-speaking world was Robert S. Ellwood, who emerged in the 1970s as one of the leading new religions scholars. He drew upon his own training in Eastern religions to produce a set of early theoretical texts including *Religious and Spiritual Groups in Modern America* (1973), *The Eagle and the Rising Sun: Americans and the New Religions of Japan* (1974), and *Alternative Altars: Unconventional and Eastern Spirituality in America* (1979), and an early study of Tenrikyo (a Japanese new religion) in 1982.

A secondary origin for the term *New Religion* has also been suggested. In 1970, San Francisco Bay Area scholar Jacob Needleman authored a book titled *The New Religions,* which his colleagues began to use to describe the emergence of so many unfamiliar alternative religions within the counterculture at the end of the 1960s. Needleman found special significance in Zen Buddhism, the followers of Meher Baba, Subud, Transcendental Meditation, Krishnamurti, Tibetan Buddhism, and G. I. Gurdjieff. He also went beyond the largely descriptive work from Japan, and invited readers to consider the philosophical/theological questions about the nature of genuine spirituality.

In the mid-1970s, a group of scholars in the Bay Area became the center for the initial studies of new religions, and a number of books flowed from a well-funded project they initiated. The works most closely associated with the study are *The New Religious Consciousness* (1977), edited by Charles T. Glock and Robert N. Bellah; Robert Wuthnow's *Experimentation in American Religion* (1978); and Steven Tipton's *Getting Saved from the Sixties* (1982). In 1977, the Graduate Theological Union in Berkeley, California, received a Rockefeller Grant that allowed the school to host a large conference on new religious movements, the papers of which appeared in 1978 as *Understanding the New Religions,* edited by Jacob Needleman and George Baker. *Understanding the New Religions* summarized the consensus prior to the deaths at Jonestown that would set a whole new agenda for scholars.

As scholars in both England and the United States pursued their initial studies of the new religions, a second important social phenomenon was also emerging: the cult awareness movement. This movement was fueled by in part by the large number of college-age youths who had joined various new religions, and the subsequent concern of parents that their sons and daughters were too deeply involved in what were viewed as cult-like movements. Parents found some early support from various psychological counselors, lawyers, and law-enforcement officials. Through the 1970s, scholars followed the development of the cult awareness movement with some concern relative to its effects on issues of religious freedom, concerns that were heightened by the introduction of coercive deprogramming. Members of a spectrum of new religions were being taken into custody, held against their will, and placed under rather strong psychological pressure to renounce and withdraw from the group they had joined.

The leadership of the cult awareness movement sought justification for the necessity of kidnapping and deprogramming the offspring of concerned parents. Such a rationale appeared during the trial of millionaire heiress Patty Hearst in 1976. Hearst's lawyer, F. Lee Bailey (1933–), argued that Hearst, who had participated in a bank robbery some months after being captured and held by the Symbionese Liberation Army, had been brainwashed. Though unable to prevent her conviction, two of the psychologists that had worked with Bailey, Louis J. West (1925–1999) from the University of California-Los Angeles and Margaret Singer (1921–2003), a psychologist in private practice in Berkeley, began to apply the same argument to members of the new religions—that they were being brainwashed and, in effect, held against their will. They found additional support from Massachusetts psychiatrist John Clark (1926–1999).

The reality of the Jonestown deaths in 1978, and the introduction of the brainwashing hypothesis into the conversations would dominate new religions studies for the next decade. The debate would go on largely without the participation of the primary exponents of brainwashing, for West, Singer, and Clark rarely appeared at scholarly gatherings to defend their ideas, and they did not respond directly to their scholarly critics. In fact, discussion of the issues was substantially hindered because the primary statements concerning the reputed brainwashing in the new religions were made in hard-to-retrieve court depositions and testimony. Despite the obstacles, by the mid-1980s a consensus had been reached in the major relevant academic associations that brainwashing, as articulated primarily in court by Margaret Singer, had no basis in fact. That position was argued by the likes of psychologists Dick Anthony and Newton Maloney, sociologists Eileen Barker, Tom Robbins, and James T. Richardson, and others.

The brainwashing issue would lead to the establishment of a Task Force within the American Psychological Association to prepare a statement concerning the new approach to brainwashing. That Task Force's 1987 report was unanimously rejected by the reviewers. The publicizing of the rejection letter largely ended the debate over brainwashing in academia and several years later, with supportive documents by Dick Anthony and Rutgers psychiatrist Perry London, the idea and its exponents failed to make their case convincingly before the court, most notably in the case of *United States v. Fishman* (1990), in which a former Scientologist claimed his "brainwashing" in Scientology as a factor leading to his embezzling bank funds. Though the idea of brainwashing still appears in the occasional court case, new religions in North America no longer fear accusations of brainwashing as a major concern and the practice of coercive deprogramming was largely replaced with non-coercive exit counseling. (Brainwashing ideas remain alive in some European countries like France and Spain and deprogramming still occurs in Japan.)

The brainwashing controversy, though a diversion from the agenda set in the 1970s for studying new religions, had several important effects. Firstly, it brought a number of people to the field, and during the 1980s the Association for the Sociology of Religion, the Society for the Scientific Study of Religion, and the American Academy of Religion developed tracks for papers on new religions. At the same time, as a significant percentage of research on new religions was devoted to dealing with the controversy, a relatively small number of new religions became the focus of numerous studies. These groups, less than two dozen in number, had been threatened with legal action due to accusations of brainwashing. As a result, the majority of the new religions were looked at only cursorily. The early neglect of the hundreds of new religions also meant that the development of overall understandings of the field initially lagged.

The decisive rejection of brainwashing as a theory by the scholarly associations and the courts had its most dramatic impact on the cult awareness community. Unable to call upon its stable of experts to defend its actions, a court rendered a $1 million judgment against the Cult Awareness Network following a deprogramming incident in Seattle in 1995, forcing it into bankruptcy and dissolution. By this time, the majority of new religious movements scholars had moved on to other concerns. Professionals who supported the brainwashing theory subsequently launched personal attacks against major new religions scholars whom they labeled "cult apologists." Attempts to revive the brainwashing theory in the late 1990s by several sociologists have found little positive response from the majority of scholars who study new religions.

PICKING UP THE STUDY. While the brainwashing controversy in the 1980s diverted significant energy, new religions studies did continue, and through the 1970s and 1980s considerable progress was made. Among the most important trends was the gradual dismantling of the definition of "cult/new religion" which scholars had been using since the 1950s. Sociologists such as J. Milton Yinger had suggested back then that cults were small, ephemeral groups, led by a charismatic leader to whom a cosmic status and/or various supernatural abilities had been assigned, and which operated in a different theological world than that of the dominant mainstream religions.

As early as 1969, Geoffrey Nelson's work on British Spiritualism pointed out that new religions were not ephemeral, one-generation phenomena. A variety of subsequent work pointed out that the role of charismatic leaders had been overestimated (Miller, 1991). In this regard, scholars undercut one of the most persistent ideas about new religions: that the death of a founder was a major trauma that tended to cause his or her group to fragment or dissolve entirely. This notion was further dispelled as many new religions passed through their first generation, were seen to splinter over a variety of reasons, but managed the death of their founder with relative ease. In like measure, the other elements of the old definition did not fit many of the prominent new religions of the 1970s and 1980s.

Since the beginning of the twenty-first century, scholars such as David G. Bromley, Eileen Barker, and J. Gordon Melton have turned their attention to reconstructing definitions of the new religions. Bromley has emphasized their nature as breaking with the dominant religious culture of the society and their alienation from its power structures. Barker has emphasized the special characteristics that first-generation religious groups tend to share. Melton has emphasized the manner in which new religions, in spite of their obvious innovations, tend to perpetuate the life of older religious traditions out of which they had emerged. Thus contemporary definitions of new religions see them as groups that operate both socially and culturally outside the mainstream of society while seeking to continue or revitalize an older tradition. During their first generation they tend to share certain characteristics relative to leadership, membership profiles, and a response to basic organizational imperatives, though operating out of different theologies and advocating different practices.

ADDITIONAL DEVELOPMENTS. While much energy was placed on discussing brainwashing, the field of new religions studies matured along several contemporaneous parallel tracks in the latter half of the twentieth century. One of the first manifestations of this maturity was the publication of significant reference books in the 1970s, which were needed to support the emerging new field of study. The regularly updated *Encyclopedia of American Religions,* which includes an entry on all of the new religions known to be operating in North America, was first published in 1979 and was in its seventh edition just a quarter-century later. Through the 1980s, Garland Publishing issued a set of bibliographies on new religions, culminating in two outstanding volumes by John Saliba which covered research in the social and psychological sciences (1987, 1990). Meanwhile, in Japan scholars associated with the Association for the Study of Religion and Society produced an expansive dictionary of Japanese new religions, *Shinshûkyô jiten* (1990).

Specialized reference works on new religions appeared as well. These include works by Peter Clark (*A Bibliography of Japanese New Religious Movements,* 1999); James R. Lewis (*The Encyclopedia of Cults and New Religions,* 2002); and

Christopher Partridge (*New Religions: A Guide,* 2004). Massimo Introvigne and his colleagues at the Center for Studies on New Religions in Turin, Italy, compiled a large volume on religions that, like its American counterpart, covered all the new religions operating in Italy (*Encyclopedia delle Religioni in Italia,* 2001). In a singularly important volume, in 1993 David Bromley and Jeffrey Hadden compiled a set of papers from a broadly representative set of new religions scholars surveying the field, *The Handbook on Cults and Sects in America.*

Parallel to the development of reference works in the scholarly study of new religions was the rise in the number of academic conferences in the field. In the 1980s, several such conferences were sponsored by the Unification Church, though later abandoned by the Church in favor of other programs. Through the rest of that decade, the various academic societies concerned with religion, especially the Society for the Scientific Study of Religion and the American Academy of Religion, created space on their annual programs for papers on new religions. In 1989, the Center for Studies on New Religions began to sponsor annual international conferences that alternated between Europe and the Americas. Within a decade these conferences were attracting between one and two hundred attendees.

The Institute for the Study of American Religion (ISAR), founded in 1968, was the first research facility founded to focus upon what would later be called new religions. In the 1980s, however, similar institutes would also emerge, most noticeably the Center for the Study of New Religions (1982), headed by Peter Clarke at Kings College, London; the Information Network Focus on Religious Movements (INFORM, 1988), headed by Eileen Barker and headquartered at the London School of Economics; and the aforementioned Center for Studies of New Religions (CESNUR, 1988) in Turin, Italy. These centers would, through the 1990s, give birth to a spectrum of institutes and study centers across Europe. Several research centers emerged in Japan as well.

The work of these centers includes the archiving of materials produced by and about the new religions. The largest such archive is included in the American Religions Collection that began in 1985 with the deposit of ISAR's library and files at the Davidson Library at the University of California's Santa Barbara campus. CESNUR houses a similar collection in Turin. Other equally valuable collections, many with local emphases, were under development in the first decade of the twenty-first century. Of particular interest are the specialized collections housed by organizations such as the Jonestown Institute, founded by Rebecca Moore and Fielding McGehee III, in San Diego, which has gathered an extensive collection related to the Peoples Temple.

Fields within Fields. New religions studies emerged and continues to exist in contested space. It examines religions that challenge society's dominant religious institutions. Along with questions about the legitimacy of many new religions have been questions about the legitimacy of academic study of some controversial groups. Several well-known groups advocate ideas and practices that the general public perceives to be beyond merely "different"; they are strange in the extreme and even threatening to the social order and individual well-being. A few groups have been involved in violent incidents involving multiple homicides and/or suicides. A number have engaged in illegal activities, from fraud to smuggling to confidence schemes. At the same time, groups in different countries have been subjected to government regulation and even suppression despite their lack of direct association with harmful or illegal activity. Above and beyond their being targeted by cult awareness groups, because of their fringe-like status NRMs have occasionally been caught up in waves of social panic and become victims of guilt by association.

Through the last decades of twentieth century, the study of new religions proceeded within the context of a steady stream of public controversy, and the lines between research and the response to such controversy was often blurred. In the mid-1980s, for example, new religions scholars were called upon to deal with a wave of interest in Satanism. Prompted by the rise of the Church of Satan in San Francisco in the 1960s, the study of Satanism had been part of the first phase of NRM studies in the 1970s. In the 1980s, however, hundreds of claims emerged that a widespread, secretive Satanic movement characterized by the ritual abuse of children existed. The primary evidence for this movement proved to be a set of reports by people undergoing psychological counseling. In the course of such counseling, they began to "remember" events from their childhood and teen years that they had forgotten. At the same time, similar reports were emerging among UFO investigators of alien abductions and medical examinations. Both appeared in the context of widespread attention to the problem of child abuse and new legislative initiatives aimed at its prevention.

Given the inability of law-enforcement officials and investigative reporters to find corroborative evidence of widespread Satanism, new religions scholars, with their own knowledge of the world of religious Satanism, rather quickly reached a consensus on the falsity of such reports, at least relative to their satanic content. Their findings, published in books by Jean La Fontaine in the United Kingdom and Jeffrey S. Victor, James T. Richardson, Joel Best, and David Bromley in the United States, contributed significantly to ending the public controversy.

The late 1990s saw a rising level of attention to millennialism, a perennial subject within new religions, and the possible role that the arrival of the twenty-first century would have on different religious groups. Millennial beliefs have often been associated with intense confrontations between new religions and society; two oft-quoted precedents were the sixteenth-century Anabaptists at Münster, Germany, and the Fifth Monarchy Men in England. New considerations of millennialism were provided by a group within the American

Academy of Religions and several other research projects, such as the Boston-based Center for Millennial Studies. Initial speculation on the confluence of millennialism and violence was followed by closer analysis of the more widespread and peaceful millennial movements, especially in the wake of the non-event of the end of the millennium in 1999.

Interest in Satanism and millennialism closely paralleled the subject that became the major focus of NRM studies after the end of the brainwashing controversy: violence. The incident involving Jim Jones's Peoples Temple at Jonestown, Guyana, in 1978 had generated some interest in violence, but was seen as a singular incident with little reference to the larger world of new religions. The Peoples Temple, however interesting otherwise, had been a congregation in a large Christian denomination, the Disciples of Christ, and its membership was predominantly older African Americans. In contrast, many new religions, especially the more controversial ones, consisted largely of Caucasian young adults.

The issue of violence and new religions, however, changed considerably after the deaths of the majority of the members of the Branch Davidians at Mount Carmel, their church center near Waco, Texas, in 1993. In 1994, an all-day symposium on violence and new religions was held in conjunction with the Society for the Scientific Study of Religion's annual fall meeting. As facts about the role played by associates of the Cult Awareness Network in both the initiation of the raid on Mount Carmel and the conduct during the subsequent fifty-one-day siege, new religions scholars became more vocal in attempting to communicate with law-enforcement officials, especially those within the Federal Bureau of Investigation (FBI), in hopes of averting any future reoccurrence. Eventually, a series of meetings were held, the FBI began to send observers to the annual meetings of the American Academy of Religion, and numerous individual contacts between FBI agents and individual scholars took place.

The changes that flowed from the Branch Davidian incident occurred in the context of a set of subsequent episodes of violence involving groups such as the Solar Temple in Switzerland, France, and Quebec (1994, 1995, 1997), Aum Shinrikyō in Japan (1995), Heaven's Gate in the United States (1997), and the Movement for the Restoration of the Ten Commandments of God in Uganda (2000). Each of these occurrences, unique in their own right, generated significant reconsideration of the possible connection between life within new religions and these large-scale violent events. Taking the lead in such reconsideration was Catherine Wessinger, who proposed new ways of looking at the role of millennialism and called attention to the fragility and instability within some groups that pushed them toward violent confrontations. Wessinger's *How the Millennium Comes Violently* (2000) set the stage for a second round of discussions brought together by David G. Bromley and J. Gordon Melton and published in 2002 as *Cults, Religion & Violence.* Between the appearance of the two books, a heretofore little known radical Islamist group, al-Qā'idah, in its attack on the Pentagon in Washington, D.C., and New York City's World Trade Center towers on September 11, 2001, provided the foundation for future ongoing discussions. Contributing to the Bromley-Melton volume was John R. Hall, who continued his seminal discussion of the close association of religion in general to violence as also developed in two books, *Gone from the Promised Land: Jonestown in American Cultural History* (1987), one of the more perceptive volumes on Jonestown, and *Apocalypse Observed: Religious Movements and Violence in North America and Europe and Japan* (2000), a book he co-authored with Philip D. Schuyler and Sylvaine Trinh.

LEGAL PERSPECTIVES. Through the 1970s and 1980s, scholars assumed that new religions were an American concern, a peculiar product of the social unrest of the 1960s, especially in California. Such attitudes began to change by the end of the 1980s as the widespread presence of new religions in Europe and other parts of the world was recognized, and as the history of the gradual rise of religious pluralism throughout the world in the nineteenth and twentieth centuries was more fully documented. And as the spread of a more radical religious pluralism was recognized, new religions became the target of numerous legal actions.

In the 1970s, questions about the legitimacy of the new religions were raised by associations of parents in the United States whose members were angry at their sons and daughters who had been swept into an alternative religious life, often at the cost of hoped-for careers in business or the professions. Their search for a solution to their dilemma provided the context for the emergence of deprogramming and the brainwashing ideas that supported it. Proponents of brainwashing charged that the new religions took away the ability of recruits to make informed choices about joining. Some went so far as to suggest that new religions were not religions (in any legal sense) at all, but were merely con games in which leaders brainwashed and exploited members for personal financial gain.

Legal cases between new religions and their detractors began in the 1970s, and by the end of the decade it was determined that civil court provided the best venue for litigating parental concerns. Then, during the 1980s, a number of multimillion-dollar lawsuits were filed against new religions by former group members who had been deprogrammed; they sought redress and damages as a result of having undergone brainwashing. While almost all the judgments were reversed on appeal, juries seemed eager to deliver a series of decisions against unpopular new religions such as the Church of Scientology, the Church Universal and Triumphant, the International Society for Krishna Consciousness, and the Unification Church.

Deprogramming, brainwashing, and the court cases of the 1980s provided an abundance of material for legal speculation. James T. Richardson, a professor at the University of Nevada with degrees and appointments in both sociology and law, emerged in the early 1980s as the leading scholar offering legal reflections on new religions. His 1983 book, *The Brainwashing/Deprogramming Controversy: Sociological, Psychological, Legal, and Historical Perspectives,* co-edited with David G. Bromley, is an important document of the era. Subsequently Richardson has remained at the forefront of writing about and focusing dialogue on the legal status of new religions globally.

During the 1990s, with the new legal era brought on by the Fishman decision in the United States, much of the legal news on new religions shifted to Europe, where, as James Beckford so ably noted in his 1985 text, *Cult Controversies,* intense debates (minus the brainwashing element) paralleled those in the United States. But then, following the Solar Temple deaths in 1994, the French government moved first to establish a parliamentary commission that in 1996 issued a report condemning a number of new religions, and some 172 groups were placed on a list of "sects." The primary accusation was their practicing "mental manipulation," a term that signaled the introduction of brainwashing theory into Europe from the United States. A year later the Canton of Geneva, in French-speaking Switzerland, issued a similar decree, followed by a 600-page report from Belgium, which singled out some 189 groups. The Belgian document included, somewhat surprisingly for American scholars, the Young Women's Christian Association, the Assemblies of God, and the Quakers.

These first reports were then followed by a second wave of reports from, among others, the General Direction of the Police with the Italian Ministry of Internal Affairs, the commission established by the German parliament, and the government of Sweden. The more reflective tone of these documents backed away in part from the brainwashing theory and found little that was sinister in new religions overall. Meanwhile in France, Belgium, and several other countries, steps were taken to stop the progress of new religions by the establishment of official cult observatories, and in the case of France the passing of a series of anticult laws.

The dialogues within the government of Western Europe were followed by discussions and an array of actions in the lands of the former Soviet bloc of nations, where in the wake of the fall of the Soviet Union, new religions had quickly and visibly proliferated. Governments found themselves caught between the still-dominant voices of religious secularists, leaders of older churches asking for the return of pre-Communist privileges, and demands for the implementation of Western-style religious freedoms. The different governments made an array of accommodations to these voices that found common ground in their dislike of the missionaries of the new religions. Meanwhile, new religions studies have emerged as a prominent focus of post-Soviet countries in Eastern and Central Europe.

The changes in Europe continue to provide fertile ground for scholars of new religions who, sharing a bias toward religious freedom as the foundational issue, have written extensively about the prospects and promises in the post-Soviet era. Many of these insights have been drawn together in two edited volumes: Phillip Charles Lucas and Thomas Robbins' *The Future of New Religions in the 21st Century* (2004), and James T. Richardson's *Regulating Religion: Case Studies from Around the Globe* (2004).

FAMILY LIFE. As first-generation new religions, whose membership consisted almost totally of young adult converts, evolved into second-generation new religions, concern was expressed about children born and raised in such settings. Critics suggested a range of potential problems, including their alienation from culture and society to their being physically and psychologically harmed by growing up in a cult milieu. Concern was punctuated by occasional reports of child abuse, usually the beating of a minor by a group leader who was not the child's parent. On a rare occasion, a child died as a result of such beatings.

However, the situation of children in new religions gained a new level of attention in the early 1990s when widespread charges of sexual abuse emerged around The Family, a group that had earlier called itself the Children of God. In the early 1990s, Family homes in several countries, most notably France, Spain, Argentina, and Australia, were raided and the minors taken into custody by child-welfare officials while legal charges were prepared against the adults. A series of lengthy court proceedings followed, culminating in a child-custody case in England. Though the defendants in each of the cases stemming from the raids were found not guilty, and the Family-member mother in the child-custody case retained legal custody, it emerged that in the 1980s a number of young people—overwhelmingly teenage women—had been molested while in Family homes. The Family, however, between the time the molestations had occurred and the court cases, had taken steps to change the environment that permitted such abuse and, as it happened, those taken into custody in the raids were not the individuals accused of molesting the minors. The revelations of the Family's problems were followed by similar disclosures coming out of the International Society of Krishna Consciousness, which in the 1970s had operated a school in Texas that included pedophiles on its staff.

The British custody dispute, which became the lengthiest legal case in the history of Britain's family court system, called attention to the variant roles assumed by women and children in some new religions with strong male hierarchical organizations. However, even prior to this time, scholars had noticed that new religions had become an arena for women who were shut out of traditional leadership roles in older Christian and Jewish groups to exercise their leadership skills. One such study is Catherine Wessinger's *Women's Leadership in Marginal Religions: Explorations outside the Mainstream* (1993).

It would be Canadian new religions scholar Susan J. Palmer, however, an expert witness in the Family's British court case, who would in the mid-1990s seize the issue of women's and children's diverse life within new religions and launch a collaborative effort with other concerned scholars to pursue study of the issue. Turning first to the role of women, she wrote *Moon Sisters, Krishna Mothers, Rajneesh Lovers: Women's Roles in New Religions* (1994) and then several years later, with co-editor Charlotte E. Hardeman, issued *Children in the New Religions* (1999).

WESTERN ESOTERICISM. As the twenty-first century began, a new issue has been placed on the agenda of new religions scholars by Sorbonne professor Antoine Faivre: Western Esotericism. Esoteric/metaphysical/occult groups have been considered in new religions studies from the beginning. One of the earliest popular essays in new religions, Colin Campbell's "The Cult, the Cultic Milieu and Secularization" (1972), grew out of his observation of the British occult community, and a large number of writings appeared in the 1990s which attempted to understand the New Age movement. The problem in writing about such groups, in spite of early works such as J. Stillson Judah's *The History and Philosophy of the Metaphysical Movements in America* (1967) and additional works on the common history of such movements, has been their tendency to treat esoteric bodies as isolated organizations without a history prior to their particular founding.

Faivre, and those who gathered around him such as Joscelyn Godwin and Wouter Hanegraaff, have compiled a picture of an alternative religious impulse in the West that has had a near-continuous presence at least since the second century CE and has grown steadily over the last four centuries. In fact, the largest percentage of the new religions—including Theosophical Society, Scientology, Wicca, New Age (1970s and 1980s) and Post-New Age (1990s to the present) groups—are generally contemporary manifestations of the Esoteric tradition.

Of the world's major religious movements, the Western Esoteric tradition has remained the least known, in large part due to its role as a losing competitor to Christianity, resulting in its dismissal as serious religion in recent centuries. The modern revival of Esotericism can be traced to the beginning of the sixteenth century and the development of a Christian Qabbalah by Johann Rauchlin (1455–1522). Its subsequent history can be traced through Rosicrucianism, Speculative Freemasonry, the Swedenborgian movement, the Mesmerist and Magnetist movements, neo-Templarism, Spiritualism, Ceremonial Magic, Theosophy and its many offshoots (Alice Bailey, I AM), Wicca, and most recently the New Age Movement.

In the mid-1980s Faivre founded the Association pour la Recherche et l'Information sur l'Esotericisme and its journal *ARIES*. In the late 1990s, with Faivre nearing retirement, the association's work was transferred to Amsterdam, where Hanegraaff headed a new department of esoteric studies. By this time, the field had grown exponentially, and early in the new century, two new structures arose to perpetuate esoteric studies both in England (Alternative Spiritualities and New Age Studies, or ASANAS) and North America (Association for the Study of Esotericism).

Western Esoteric studies now exists as a subfield its own right. When it concentrates on Esoteric history, it resonates the least with new religions studies. Yet because all contemporary esoteric groups would fall under the rubric of "new religion," when Western esoteric studies turns its attention to the twentieth century, the two fields are almost indistinguishable.

CONCLUSION. In the first four decades of its existence, the academic field of new religions grew from a handful of scholars who in the 1960s decided that these interesting groups then proliferating on the fringes of Japanese, North American, and European societies were important enough to enjoy more than sporadic cursory glances. At the onset of the twenty-first century there were several hundred scholars around the world who were devoting the majority of their research time to this field of inquiry. To a certain extent, the progress since the 1960s can be traced in the series of new religions text books produced over the decades by Robert Ellwood (1973), David Bromley and Anson Shupe (1981), Gordon Melton and Robert Moore (1982), Melton (1986, 1992), Timothy Miller (1995), Eileen Barker (1989), John Saliba (1995, 2003), William Sims Bainbridge (1998), James R. Lewis (1998), Lorne Dawson (1998), and most recently, Stephen J. Hunt (2003).

The study of new religions has been a bulwark in countering the more extreme conclusions of secularization theory, offered new approaches for governments in dealing with controversial groups that have disturbed the social quiet of some societies, and has begun to see the naturalness of the emergence of innovative religious experiments as societies grow and change. Born in part in the times of social turmoil in postwar Japan and the generation of Baby Boomers coming of age in America, new religions studies has expended considerable energy to map the presence of NRMs through time and space, indicating their steady emergence through the nineteenth and twentieth centuries. In the process, more than a thousand new religions operating in the West have been documented and several dozen examined in considerable depth.

In the process, some consensus has been reached concerning issues such as brainwashing, Satanism, and the fact of religious pluralism as part of the long-term future of contemporary society, though, as a young field of inquiry, far more questions have been posed and remain to be posed than have been answered.

SEE ALSO Anticult Movements; Brainwashing (Debate); Branch Davidians; Cults and Sects; Esotericism; Heaven's Gate; Jonestown and Peoples Temple; Millenarianism, overview article; Secularization; Unification Church.

BIBLIOGRAPHY

Listed below is a highly selective list of some of the important titles produced by scholars of new religions. Many of the textbooks cover much of the same ground though differing whether from a social science (Bainbridge, Barker, Dawson) or religious studies (Ellwood, Lewis, Melton, Saliba) perspective. Many of the volumes are anthologies, chosen for the spectrum of opinion they present on a problem of high interest in the field of new religions studies (Bromley and Melton, Palmer and Hardmann, Richardson). Finally, a set of foundational studies in Western esotericism have been cited (Faivre, Godwin, Judah).

Bainbridge, William Sims. *The Sociology of Religious Movements.* New York, 1997.

Barker, Eileen. *The Making of a Moonie: Choice or Brainwashing?* New York, 1984.

Barker, Eileen. *New Religious Movements: A Practical Introduction.* London, 1989.

Bromley, David G., and James T. Richardson, eds. *The Brainwashing/Deprogramming Controversy.* Lewiston, N.Y., 1983.

Bromley, David G., and Jeffrey Hadden. *The Handbook on Cults and Sects in America.* Greenwich, Conn., 1993.

Bromley, David G., and J. Gordon Melton, eds. *Cults, Religion and Violence.* New York, 2002.

Clark, Elmer T. *Small Sects in America.* Nashville, Tenn., 1949.

Clarke, Peter B. *Bibliography of Japanese New Religions, with Annotations and an Introduction to Japanese New Religions at Home and Abroad.* Richmond, U.K., 1999.

Dawson, Lorne L. *Comprehending Cults: The Sociology of New Religious Movements.* Toronto, Ont., 1998.

Ellwood, Robert S. *Religious and Spiritual Groups in Modern America.* Englewood Cliffs, N.J., 1973.

Ellwood, Robert S. *The Eagle and the Rising Sun: Americans and the New Religions of Japan.* Philadelphia, 1974.

Faivre, Antoine. *Theosophy, Imagination, Tradition: Studies in Western Esotericism.* Albany, N.Y., 2000.

Godwin, Joscelyn. *The Theosophical Enlightenment.* Albany, N.Y., 1994.

Hunt, Stephen J. *Alternative Religions: A Sociological Introduction.* Aldershot, U.K. 2003.

Introvigne, Massimo, et al. *Enciclopedia delle religioni in Italia.* Turin, 2001.

Judah, J. Stillson. *The History and Philosophy of the Metaphysical Movements in America.* Philadelphia, 1967.

Lewis, James R. *Cults in America.* Santa Barbara, Calif., 1998.

Melton, J. Gordon. *Encyclopedia of American Religions.* 7th ed. Detroit, Mich., 2003.

Miller, Timothy, ed. *When Prophets Die: The Post Charismatic Fate of New Religious Movements.* Albany, N.Y., 1991.

Miller, Timothy, ed. *America's Alternative Religions.* Albany, N.Y., 1995.

Needleman, Jacob. *The New Religions.* New York, 1969.

Nelson, Geoffrey K. *Spiritualism and Society.* London, 1969.

Palmer, Susan J., and Charlotte E. Hardman, eds. *Children in New Religions.* New Brunswick, N.J., 1999.

Richardson, James T. *Regulating Religion: Case Studies from around the Globe.* New York, 2003.

Saliba, John A. *Psychiatry and the Cults: An Annotated Bibliography.* New York, 1987.

Saliba, John A. *Social Science and the Cults: An Annotated Bibliography.* New York, 1990.

Van Baalen, Jan Karel. *The Chaos of Cults.* Grand Rapids, Mich., 1938.

Wessinger, Catherine. *How the Millennium Comes Violently: From Jonestown to Heaven's Gate.* New York, 2000.

Wilson, Bryan. *Sects and Society: A Sociological Study of Three Religious Groups in Britain.* London, 1961.

Wilson, Bryan, and Jamie Cresswell, eds. *New Religious Movements: Challenge and Response.* London, 1999.

J. GORDON MELTON (2005)

NEW RELIGIOUS MOVEMENTS: SCRIPTURES OF NEW RELIGIOUS MOVEMENTS

Because new religious movements often generate suspicious or hostile reactions from representatives of the status quo, substantial scholarly attention has been devoted to their processes of leadership, recruitment, and conversion, as well as to other forms of interaction between new groups and their social environments. While such encounters do shape both the public images and self-understandings of new religious movements, they are not their only religious activities.

Many new religious movements have produced substantial bodies of literature that amplify their self-definitions, establish ritual practices and moral codes, elaborate their mythic visions of humanity and the cosmos, and reconstruct history. That literature is read, heard, studied, preached, debated, interpreted, enacted, and implemented in the daily lives of members. The texts derive their authority both from the claimed experiences of founders or other influential figures within the group and from members' acceptance of the texts as particularly revelatory. When people within a group treat a religious text as central for their understandings of themselves and the world in which they live, they elevate it above other quotidian forms of communication and accord it, at least implicitly, the status of scripture. In new religious movements, as in other religious groups, texts are made into "scriptures" by the claims that are made for them, the recognition of those claims, and the uses to which the texts are put. The scriptural status of texts is always in the process of construction. Oral teaching and informal written communications may be viewed as authoritative, and through their repeated use they may move towards a more formalized status as scripture. Even texts definitively asserted to be authoritative are subject to successive re-interpretations. Since scriptures are texts that are deemed authoritative and revelatory by a specific religious community, the process of scriptural formation in new religious movements is no different than it is in more established ones. Although individual writings frequently contain assertions about their own authority, they only function as scripture when those claims are acknowledged and acted upon by those who receive and use them.

MAKING NEW SCRIPTURES. As new religious movements strive to secure their legitimacy, defend themselves against their cultural opponents, and attract the interest of potential members, they address what they see as the religious inadequacies of their particular social environments. Because the Western concept of scripture, as embodied by the Christian Bible, has been so widely diffused throughout the world, new religious movements frequently identify the errors or limitations that they perceive in the dominant interpretations of the Bible. In their own writings they propose the necessary corrections, supplements, or replacements. Accordingly, interpretation of the Bible is often the vehicle by which new religious movements assert both their novelty and their continuity with a hallowed past. Their novelty is what makes new religious movements worth attention, but their continuity with the past is what guarantees their gravity. Similar dynamics are at work when new religious movements confront other scriptures or collections of religiously authoritative texts, such as the Qurʾān or widely revered Hindu texts like the *Bhagavadgītā*. Reinterpretations of familiar scriptural texts transform their meanings for new religious communities even as they leave their scriptural status intact. The specific procedures by which new interpretations are constructed, including spiritual or allegorical readings, historical contextualization, and philological commentary, are often no different than those employed by more mainstream interpreters of scriptural texts, but the meanings that they produce reinforce new groups' status as dramatic departures from parent bodies or as distinctive, freestanding innovations.

The production of scriptural texts within new religious movements takes two distinctive but overlapping forms. One is new readings of familiar texts. Those readings are expressed in a variety of forms, including detailed commentaries, meandering meditations, loose glosses, and direct appropriations of specific scriptural models, such as creation stories, law codes, ethical admonitions, or prayers. The second form is the production of new scriptures. Movements that directly address a scriptural heritage can produce books that aspire to the status of "new Bibles" either by supplementing or replacing the older scriptures. Other movements strive to establish the utterances or writings of a founder as supremely authoritative. In either case, the new scriptural texts codify a novel vision of what it means to be human, how to establish proper relations with other humans and the divine, and how to achieve the goals of human life.

Whatever form the writings take, they are grounded on specific claims to authority. Ever conscious of their own novelty, new religious movements take great care to lay out the experiences and insights that sanction their innovations. Founders and influential exegetes articulate the experiences that authorize their distinctive messages and establish them as trustworthy and true. Their new ways of seeing are frequently stimulated by intimate encounters with the divine but also can result from the consistent application of rational intelligence to familiar problems.

NEW VISIONS: DIVINE ENCOUNTERS. The founders of many new religions describe dramatic, unbidden encounters with the divine. For example, on December 13, 1973, Claude Vorhilon (b. 1946), a French journalist and racecar driver, came upon what he took to be a UFO. One of its occupants soon informed Vorhilon that he had been chosen to bring to humankind the message of the extraterrestrial "Elohim," the true creators of life on earth. Vorhilon was given the name "Raël" and was charged with preparing the earth to receive emissaries from the Elohim, who would then share their incredibly advanced technology. As the name *Elohim* suggests, Vorhilon's encounter with the extraterrestrials led him to a dramatic rereading of the creation story in *Genesis*. That reinterpretation of scripture plays a crucial role in the books that have become the guiding texts of the Raëlian movement.

Similarly, on Easter morning 1936, Sun Myung Moon (1920–) experienced a vision of Jesus that led him to a thoroughgoing revision of history. *Divine Principle*, first published in English in 1973, and the central scriptural text of the Unificationist movement that grew out of Moon's Easter experience, provides a new account of biblical history from the creation and fall through the career of Jesus to the imminent arrival of a new messiah who will gather humanity into a single loving family in accordance with God's original wishes. More than a century earlier, in 1820 in upper New York state, a series of visions sparked the founding of the Church of Jesus Christ of Latter-day Saints and the promulgation of a new holy book, the *Book of Mormon* (1830). That new Bible, it was claimed, would dispel confusion about which of the many competing Christian sects held the truth by communicating God's message with unprecedented clarity. Also, in the 1980s Elizabeth Clare Prophet (b. 1939), who succeeded her husband Mark Prophet (1918–1973) as leader of the Church Universal and Triumphant, published four volumes of *The Lost Teachings of Jesus* (1986), which are based on over thirty years of communications from Jesus directly to both of the Prophets. The texts build on the Prophets' claim that Jesus spent substantial time in India and surrounding areas during his so-called lost years, and they align his recovered teachings with those of the Prophets' Church Universal and Triumphant.

In each of these instances a prophetic figure's direct encounter with the divine led to both the formation of a new religious movement and to the publication of new authoritative texts. The books written by Claude Vorhilon and Mark and Elizabeth Prophet correct misreadings of the biblical tradition and supplement the tradition with new material. In a fuller fashion, the texts produced by Sun Myung Moon and Joseph Smith stand on their own as authoritative documents that incorporate, repair, and advance the message of the Christian scriptures. In each instance the new texts derive their authority from their authors' extraordinary experiences. The founder and the book confirm each other's status with reference to the same divine source.

A. C. Bhaktivedanta Swami Prabhupada's (1896–1977) claim to authority for his *Bhagavad-Gita As It Is* (1968) displays an interesting variation. Although he contends that the *Bhagavadgītā* summarizes all of Vedic literature and that it should be the one common scripture for the entire world, Prabhupada denies that he is offering any interpretation of it. His claim to present the text without any distorting interpretation is founded on his conviction that Lord Kṛṣṇa himself speaks in the text and that a line of thirty-two teachers that culminates with Prabhupada himself has accurately preserved the true meaning of the text. Although Prabhupada's contact with the divine is thus mediated by a "disciplic succession," its authorizing power is maintained.

NEW VISIONS: RATIONAL SYSTEMS. Texts can achieve scriptural status without appeal to such divine encounters, however. The Church of Scientology, for example, accepts the writings of its founder, L. Ron Hubbard (1911–1986), as scripture even though he claimed no privileged intimacy with the divine. Hubbard attributed his insights instead to a deep immersion in the problems of human psychology. His first major work on the human mind, *Dianetics: The Modern Science of Mental Health* (1950), relies on what Hubbard saw as rigorous, scientific study rather than any special religious inspiration. As Hubbard's system of Dianetics developed into Scientology and came to be identified explicitly as a religion, he still claimed that the processes of his "technology" for achieving mental health were universally accessible and not restricted to religious adepts. Insight, rather than inspiration, yielded the principles of Scientology.

Anton LaVey (1930–1997), founder of the Church of Satan and author of *The Satanic Bible* (1969), made a similar claim for the principles of his counter-religion. While avowing that the time had definitely come for a new religion that would unmask the hypocrisies of Christianity, LaVey staked no claim to a personal religious vision. Like Hubbard, LaVey credited the discovery of his system simply to the rigorous application of rational thought. With a clear-eyed appreciation of true human nature, a love of ritual and pageantry, and a flair for mockery, LaVey's *Satanic Bible* promulgated a gospel of self-indulgence that, he argued, anyone who dispassionately considered the facts would embrace. Although contemporary Satanism remains an amorphous conglomeration of practices, beliefs, and attitudes, LaVey's new Bible remains a touchstone for many in the broad movement. That *The Satanic Bible* and Hubbard's writings could still achieve scriptural status without dependence upon divine revelation emphasizes that members of a group elevate books to scriptural status by adopting them as lenses through which they view themselves, their group, and the cosmos.

NEW READINGS: CREATION. Although they cover a wide range of topics, new readings of familiar scriptural texts often focus on both the creation of human life and its ultimate end. In *The Message Given to Me by Extraterrestrials* (1975) and *Let's Welcome Our Fathers from Space* (1979), Raël asserts that the term *Elohim,* which has long been understood as one of the names of God, really means "those who came from the sky," a race of superior beings with advanced knowledge of genetics. The Raëlians' story of the origins of humankind transforms any previous understandings of human nature and destiny based on *Genesis,* replaces the Bible's linear sense of time with a perpetual cycle of creations, and lends a newfound urgency and authority to scientific activity. The Raëlians' new reading of *Genesis* both remakes the past and charts a new future in which Raël's prophecy will determine the fate of the planet.

In the *Divine Principle* of the Unificationist movement, the focus shifts from the creation of human beings to the subsequent fall. In its presentation, Adam and Eve failed to observe God's commandments to be fruitful, to multiply and fill the earth, and to subdue the earth and have dominion over it (*Gn.* 1:28). In a singular assertion, the *Divine Principle* traces that failure to Eve's adulterous relations with Satan. Eve's and Adam's failings kept them from reaching the state of perfection that God had intended for them. Subsequently, God's desire for men and women to form loving families by uniting with each other and with God has been continually undermined by the aftershocks of the Fall. God's attempts to restore the original state of humankind by raising up prophets and potential messiahs, particularly Jesus of Nazareth, has met with only limited success. The *Divine Principle's* new vision of human history sets the stage for the mission of Reverend Moon, who in the last days brings a revelation that offers humankind the chance to return to an Edenic state. Indispensable both for an understanding of the course of history and the transformative mission of Reverend Moon, the *Divine Principle* functions as a scriptural text that provides fundamental orientation and direction for Unificationist thought and action.

Like Claude Vorhilon and Sun Myung Moon, Mary Baker Eddy (1821–1910) drew new meaning out of the traditional *Genesis* story. For Vorhilon and Moon, extraordinary interactions with superior beings inspired their new visions of the creation story, while Eddy owed her new comprehension of the meaning of *Genesis* to a transforming experience of spiritual healing that led her to assert the unreality of matter and the primacy of the spiritual. For Eddy, like the Raëlians, the traditional interpretations of *Genesis* produce only a false picture of God. Eddy views the first creation story in *Genesis* 1:1–2:3 as an authoritative description of how a wholly incorporeal God created, through mind alone, a universe of ideas, including immortal humans, all without the slightest taint of materiality. Correspondingly, she concludes that the material creation of Adam out of dust and the breath of God in *Genesis* 2:7 must be a lie. Through her interpretation, which is included in *Science and Health with Key to the Scriptures* (1875), Eddy makes *Genesis* address the distinctive theological concerns of Christian Science. Other readings of the text then become part of the history of human error. Read through the lenses supplied by Eddy the Bible speaks in a new voice and proclaims an unanticipated and surprising message for a new audience. *Science and Health* takes its place alongside, if not above, the Bible as an authoritative text for the Christian Science community.

In the later days of the People's Temple, the Reverend Jim Jones (1931–1978) offered one of the most dramatic rereadings of *Genesis* in a new religious movement. As he departed further from his Protestant roots and edged closer to addiction and madness, Jones began to see the Bible as a problem to overcome. He indicted the King James Version as a Bible of slaveholders and a source of oppression rather than liberation. To counteract its influence Jones proposed a contemporary Gnostic redeemer myth in which the God of the Bible was seen to be merely a just God, with limited powers and unsavory human characteristics. Acting as a Gnostic redeemer, Jones brought his followers news of a God beyond the Bible who would teach them their true identities. In Jones's treatment, the authority of the Bible was thoroughly overturned and his own pronouncements, given in speeches and sermons but never codified in writing, took the Bible's place and functioned as scripture for the members of the People's Temple.

NEW READINGS: THE END OF THE WORLD. Leaders of new religious movements have applied similar ingenuity to imagining the end of the world. For example, after experiencing an ascent into the heavens in 1985, David Koresh (1959–1993) claimed that he himself was the Lamb of God mentioned in *Revelation* 4 and 5 as the only one able to open a scroll sealed with seven seals. Koresh argued, like many Christian millennialists, that every book of the Bible found its fruition in *Revelation* and that its apocalyptic message could only be comprehended through the agency of the Lamb of God. As a result, Koresh's oral teachings, along with their distillation in his unfinished written commentary on the seven seals, became essential for his students who sought the apocalyptic meaning of scripture; Koresh's teachings had the authority, if not the form, of scripture.

Like Koresh, Asahara Shōkō (b. 1955), the founder of Aum Shinrikyō, came to identify himself as a character from the Bible, the promised "comforter" of John's gospel. As he experienced mounting opposition to his movement and as he viewed the end of the world as growing ever nearer, Asahara devoted progressively more attention to the apocalyptic visions of the book of *Revelation* and to his own role in the unfolding apocalypse. In his teachings, speeches, and published materials, Asahara assimilated the New Testament to the teachings of what he identified as "original Buddhism," and he constructed a synthetic scenario of the imminent end. As with Koresh, Asahara's readings of *Revelation* set the biblical text in a radically new interpretive frame—Asahara simultaneously appropriated *Revelation* as a scriptural text for his own movement and certified his own teaching as being of equal authority.

The legal responses to Aum's murderous release of sarin gas in the Tokyo subway in 1995 ended Asahara's public career as a teacher and transformed the movement that he founded; the legal responses also truncated the processes of textual interpretation and production that marked Aum's brief lifespan. As with Koresh's teaching, Asahara's production of texts was limited to a relatively short period. Because new religious movements are particularly malleable in their early days, and because many quickly dissolve or fade away, the procedures by which texts achieve authoritative status for their communities are not often fully played out. When new religions achieve some institutional stability, it is easier to chart the fluctuating prestige of particular texts and interpretive strategies and to identify which texts consistently maintain authoritative or even canonical status.

NEW SCRIPTURES. Some texts produced by new religious movements explicitly claim for themselves the status of scripture. One of the most provocative examples is LaVey's *Satanic Bible.* By presenting as a Bible his hodgepodge of historical research, dogmatic pronouncements, obscure invocations, and both playful and serious critiques of Christianity, LaVey suggests a religious dynamic that virtually any other title would not. By naming his book a "bible," LaVey identifies a target that he intends to supplant and a status to which he aspires. Although LaVey never developed supporting structures in the Church of Satan to reinforce the status of *The Satanic Bible,* this text remains a primary gateway into the diffuse world of contemporary Satanism.

The Holy Piby (1924), one of the texts that inspired the development of Rastafarianism in Jamaica in the early 1930s, also insists on its scriptural status. It claims to be a holy book given to the prophet Athlyi by an angel named Douglas. Following closely the model of the Christian scriptures, *The Holy Piby* begins with an account of a seven-day creation, moves to the divine commissioning of a prophet and lawgiver, provides historical accounts of the doings of God's chosen people, records prayers and creedal statements, and even devotes a section to recounting "the facts of the apostles." A later reprint of the text hails it as the black man's Bible. *The Holy Piby* was designed to be the scriptural text of the short-lived Afro Athlican Constructive Church, but it also helped foster the pervasive biblical consciousness of the Rastafarian movement.

The amorphous contemporary New Age movement and its various precursors also offer a rich trove of texts claiming scriptural authority. In the late nineteenth century, John Ballou Newbrough published a first (1882) and then a revised (1891) version of the *Oahspe: A New Bible in the Words of Jehovih and His Angel Embassadors,* which he claimed to have produced by angelically directed automatic typing. *Oahspe* offers an elaborate cosmology with descriptions of myriad gods and heavens, a history of the planet earth, revised versions of many biblical stories, ethical guidelines, and predictions about the future. The book serves as the scripture for the Faithist movement, which still claims adherents. Comparable in scope is *The Urantia Book,* attributed to an array of superhuman personalities and first published in 1955. Other similar works include *A Course in Miracles* (1975), the result of Helen Shucman's automatic writing under the reputed direction of Jesus, and the material communicated through human "channels" by various disincarnate entities, such as the teachings of Ramtha spoken by J. Z. Knight or those of Lazaris voiced by Jach Pursel.

These texts join Eddy's *Science and Health*, the voluminous writings of Hubbard, and the Church of Jesus Christ of the Latter-day Saints' *Book of Mormon* (1830), *Doctrine and Covenants* (1835), and *Pearl of Great Price* (1851) as substantial bodies of scripture that have been composed over the past two hundred years. The drive towards articulating a clear and compelling self-definition, defining an appropriate way of life, and situating individuals in historical and cosmic contexts that animates the production of texts in any religious tradition is fully shared by new religious movements. Their founders eagerly express the new visions of human life that they have achieved either through their own diligent labors or through their privileged contact with supernatural beings. The followers attracted by those new messages see in the founder's words precious insights that must be preserved, studied, and communicated to others. Through multiple discrete interactions, both founders and followers sift through their common cache of wisdom and distill from it the statements and stories that matter most; they make (and remake) scripture from both oral and written materials that, they earnestly believe, will stand the test of time. Once made, their scriptures are then continually probed by various forms of exegesis for the inexhaustible wisdom that they are held to contain.

SEE ALSO Aum Shinrikyō; Branch Davidians; Christian Science; Church Universal and Triumphant; Eddy, Mary Baker; Hubbard, L. Ron; International Society for Krishna Consciousness; Jones, Jim; Jonestown and Peoples Temple; Koresh, David; Mormonism; New Age Movement; Prabhupada, A. C. Bhaktivedanta; Raëlians; Rastafarianism; Satanism; Scientology; Smith, Joseph; Unification Church.

BIBLIOGRAPHY

Primary Texts

The Book of Mormon. Salt Lake City, 1920.

Anonymous. *A Course in Miracles.* Tiburon, Calif., 1975.

Anonymous. *Oahspe: A New Bible in the Words of Jehovih and His Angel Embassadors.* 2 vols. New York, 1882.

Anonymous. *The Urantia Book.* Chicago, 1955.

Eddy, Mary Baker. *Science and Health with Key to the Scriptures.* Boston, 1875.

Koresh, David. "The Seven Seals of the Book of Revelation." In *Why Waco? Cults and the Battle for Religious Freedom in America,* by James D. Tabor and Eugene V. Gallagher, pp. 189–203. Berkeley, 1995.

LaVey, Anton Szandor. *The Satanic Bible.* New York, 1969.

Lazaris (Jach Pursel). *The Sacred Journey: You and Your Higher Self.* Orlando, Fla., 1987,

Prabhupada, A. C. Bhaktivedanta Swami. *Bhagavad-Gita As It Is.* Los Angeles, 1983.

Prophet, Elizabeth Clare. *The Lost Teachings of Jesus.* 4 vols. Livingston, Mont., 1986.

Raël (Claude Vorhilon). *The Message Given to Me by Extra-Terrestrials.* Tokyo, 1986.

Ramtha (J. Z. Knight). *The Ancient Schools of Wisdom: A Collection of Teachings.* Yelm, Wash., 1996

Rogers, Shepherd Robert Athlyi. *The Holy Piby.* Chicago, 2000; reprint of 1924 edition.

Secondary Works

Barlow, Philip L. *Mormons and the Bible: The Place of the Latter-day Saints in American Religion.* Oxford, 1991. Sets the origin, spread, and use of the Mormon scriptures within the context of broadly diffused knowledge about the Bible in the pre-Civil War United States.

Denny, Frederick M., and Rodney L. Taylor, eds. *The Holy Book in Comparative Perspective.* Columbia, S.C., 1985. Essays on the formation and use of holy books in various traditions, with a specific contribution on the dynamics of scriptures in the Mormon tradition.

Gallagher, Eugene V. "'Not Yours, But Ours': Transformations of the Hebrew Bible in New Religious Movements." In *Sacred Text, Secular Times: The Hebrew Bible in the Modern World,* edited by Leonard Jay Greenspoon and Bryan F. Le Beau, pp. 87–102. Omaha, Neb., 2000. Analysis of the appropriation of the Hebrew Bible in Christian Science, the Unification Church, and early Rastafarianism.

Givens, Terryl L. *By the Hand of Mormon: The American Scripture that Launched a New World Religion.* Oxford, 2002. Focuses on the *Book of Mormon* in the context of Joseph Smith's prophetic career and broader cultural trends, its claims to present ancient history, and its nature as a theological resource; this volume also examines the arguments of both Mormons and non-Mormons about the book's authority, coherence, and cultural impact.

Graham, William A. *Beyond the Written Word: Oral Aspects of Scripture in the History of Religion.* Cambridge, U.K., 1987. Focuses on the uses of scriptures in the lives of religious communities and employs a broadly comparative approach, though it does not directly address new religious movements.

Levering, Miriam, ed. *Rethinking Scripture: Essays from a Comparative Perspective.* Albany, N.Y., 1989. Includes essays by W. C. Smith and William Graham that summarize the arguments of their longer works, and offers comparative materials from Buddhist, Hindu, and Jewish traditions.

Smith, Jonathan A. "Sacred Persistence: Towards a Redescription of Canon." In *Approaches to Ancient Judaism: Theory and Practice,* edited by William Scott Green, pp. 11–28. Missoula, Mont., 1978. Develops "canon" as a broadly useful comparative category.

Smith, Wilfred Cantwell. *What Is Scripture? A Comparative Approach.* Minneapolis, 1993. Despite scant attention to the scriptural products of new religious movements, a comprehensive inquiry into the processes by which texts are made into and treated as "scriptural."

Stein, Stephen J. "America's Bibles: Canon, Commentary, and Community." *Church History* 64 (1995): 169–184. Focuses on the formation and use of scriptural texts in new religious movements in the United States, with special attention to the *Book of Mormon, Science and Health with Key to the Scriptures,* and other nineteenth-century texts.

EUGENE V. GALLAGHER (2005)

NEW RELIGIOUS MOVEMENTS: NEW RELIGIOUS MOVEMENTS AND WOMEN

Whether they arise from within a given culture or find their way into it by multiple means of importation, new religions take many different forms and play a variety of social, spiritual, economic, and political roles. They provide arenas of resistance to prevailing cultural and religious beliefs, practices, and values. They sometimes foster restoration, as members see it, of earlier, more authentic expressions of religious piety or offer visions of as-yet-unrealized possibilities for the future. New religions offer their members support, often communal, for developing and living out alternatives to established theological worldviews, dominant economic systems, and monogamous marriage. They are pivotal sites for the adjudication of cultural and religious tensions with the capacity to respond more quickly to those tensions than is often the case with long-established religious traditions. They hold together sometimes-conflicting manifestations of innovation and conservation, critique and construction, protest against some cultural norms and compliance with others. Given these functions, it is not surprising that new religions are often subjects of conflict, anger, and suspicion.

These multifaceted dynamics are particularly evident in the area of gender and gender relationships and with significant consequences for the roles of women. New religions formulate questions and convictions about femaleness and its bearing upon how women might achieve spiritual fulfillment, salvation, or enlightenment; about the relative spiritual significance of female and male bodies for the proper operating of the universe and the prospering of the human community; and about whether women and men are helpmates, hindrances, or of no ultimate consequence to each other on the spiritual path, however defined.

Since the last third of the twentieth century, scholars of religion have become increasingly aware of the extent to which new religions provide insights into larger questions about women and religion. Are there beliefs, practices, and organizational structures along with historical and cultural factors that tend either to promote or stand in the way of women's leadership and full participation, not only in new religions but also in religion in general? Are there discernible patterns to explain why, historically, women have achieved more public prominence in new religions than in the established traditions? When given the opportunity, do women exercise religious authority in distinctively different ways from men? Are women more drawn to one kind of religious worldview than another? Do female, androgynous, or nonpersonal images of the sacred necessarily ensure equal access of women to authority or, as Catherine Wessinger suggests in *Women's Leadership in Marginal Religions*, do these have to be under girded by institutional structures and demands from the broader culture for women's equality?

Scholarly works about women and new religions have increasingly revealed that there are no all-encompassing answers to these questions. In some new religions, gender as an essential aspect of being human is de-emphasized, thereby taking down traditional gender-related bars to women's leadership and opening up new possibilities for women to exercise publicly acknowledged positions of authority. In others, femaleness and maleness are intensified, understood in cosmically significant ways that require a new religion to foster women leaders as a way of reflecting the female nature of the divine or the importance of the feminine principle in the workings of universe. There are yet other new religions that insist upon traditional gender roles to the extent that they would ordinarily circumscribe women's access to public prominence. Nonetheless, there may be demonstrations of charismatic power by women in these groups sufficient in the power and respect they generate to override the community's reluctance to grant women public authority if they are also willing to satisfy traditional expectations for marriage and motherhood. There are, by contrast, new religions that discourage women from living out traditional female roles in a physical sense and instead offer romantic and maternal fulfillment with opportunities for "spiritual" wifehood or motherhood.

Both the complexity and the variety of new religions and the roles of women within them require reference to a multiplicity of examples and a resistance to the temptation to over-generalize. Studies of women in new religions have been emerging since the 1980s; they work to avoid ultimately unsupportable conclusions about cause-and-effect relationships between beliefs and particular forms of religious organization and practice and their consequences for the participation or exclusion of women. To see any new religion as either a paradise of freedoms and possibilities for women or a sinkhole of restrictions and degradations is to miss the nuances of the realities women live out in new religions. An exploration of selected new religions from the seventeenth, eighteenth, nineteenth, and twentieth centuries demonstrates, nonetheless, at least some general patterns. This essay focuses on historical context and inter-relationships between religious ideas and institutional forms and practices as they affect women. Ambiguities, ironies, and paradoxes are often in evidence as new religions negotiate combinations of resistance to and compliance with social and religious expectations concerning women's nature, women's bodies, and women's roles.

QUAKERS IN THE SEVENTEENTH AND EIGHTEENTH CENTURIES. The Quakers demonstrate a compelling example of a new religious movement that emerged in protest against Puritanism and Anglicanism in England and America, and whose theology and minimalist system of governance were conducive to the public leadership of women. The title of a 1666 tract, "Women's Speaking Justified, Proved, and Allowed by the Scriptures, all such as speak by the Spirit and Power of the Lord Jesus," suggests that Quaker approval of women preachers and teachers found legitimation through two primary means. One was a rejection of biblical passages that admonished women to keep silent in church and to submit to the familial, governmental, and religious authority of men. The other emerged from the theological claim of an inner light, a sacred presence, dwelling within every person and upon whose authority anyone could speak. Quakers rejected a doctrine of the fall that rendered women morally unequal to men for the sin of Eve. They opposed what they called exterior religion and priestly authority, and emphasized lay ministry. Taken together, these characteristics removed traditional scriptural and theological bars to women's public leadership. They foreshadow strategies for empowering women that women would use again in the nineteenth and twentieth centuries to argue for women's ordination in the mainline denominations.

Women Preachers in the Eighteenth Century. Two eighteenth-century women founders of new religions offer instances not only of women's leadership, but also of the significance of alternative interpretations of "body" and sexuality. Influenced by the evangelical preaching of George Whitefield (1714–1770) and her own Quaker upbringing, Jemima Wilkinson (1752–1819) rose from a near-death vision in 1776 to acclaim herself the genderless "Publick Universal Friend," commissioned by God to preach and to redeem the world. Wilkinson is a good example of the lone, charismatic woman who achieves a singular fame as the founder of a short-lived new religion. Wilkinson advocated celibacy and de-emphasized her female body by dressing in clergymen's robes. Both reviled and praised as a woman in the pulpit, Wilkinson's fame seems to have come at the cost of her "femaleness," a trade-off that is in evidence in numerous other new religions of later centuries.

Ann Lee (1736–1784), an Englishwoman who emigrated to the United States in 1774, extended the practice of celibacy and the separation of women and men to form the foundation for the communal religion she established, the United Society of Brethren, or Shakers, a new religion that reached its apex in the years before the American Civil War. Mother Ann's theological claims about the male and female nature of the godhead and original sin as the result of sexual intercourse fostered the eventual construction of nineteen Shaker communities across New York, New England, and into Ohio and Kentucky after Lee's death, and the further development of her ideas about the Shakers as a saved community. There are gender conflicts and ironies evident in Shakerism as it grew after Mother Ann's death. There were a number of major attractions for women: a female founder; a deity imaged as both female and male; economic security and a form of family life free from the dangers of childbirth; and the opportunity to participate in a theoretically egalitarian, male/female leadership that was required to serve the spiritual and material needs of celibate men and women who lived separately within their communities. Shaker women had the opportunity to express themselves in ecstatic visions, teaching, domestic arts, and aesthetic/religious outpourings of dancing and painting. At the same time, Shaker work roles were gender-based with women having responsibility for domestic chores. There were also gender-based leadership tensions and conflict over control of ecstatic, female-related religious experiences in contrast to more orderly male expressions. In addition, males primarily articulated Shaker theology.

Women in Five Nineteenth-Century New Religions. A survey of five new religions with their origins in the nineteenth century, two of them communal, reveals the variety of circumstances, theological ideas, and religious forms and practices that, at one level, afforded women radically countercultural ways of participating in religious life and, at another level, paradoxically, circumscribed and interpreted their activities, self-understandings, and religious experiences in gender-traditional ways that reflected values in the larger culture. In effect, these examples function to offer a dialogue about an array of roles available for women in new religions, as well as the theological and structural foundations and eschatologically oriented community goals that supported them. They suggest how new religions participate in the always-in-process cultural project of working out women's roles and, by implication, men's. They also demonstrate the extent to which new religions see the bringing about of the kingdom of God on Earth, however defined, as predicated on bringing about right relations between the sexes.

Mormon women found themselves participating in a religious community that began to practice polygamy, a policy instituted almost twenty years after founder Joseph Smith's (1805–1844) visions in the 1820s led to the founding of the Church of Jesus Christ of Latter-day Saints and the publication of the *Book of Mormon* in 1830. Polygamy, based according to Smith on the model of biblical patriarchs, stirred up animosity among some of Smith's followers, and more intensely among outsiders, but it functioned to expand and solidify kinship ties and therefore group loyalty in Mormonism. The practice of polygamy, which was prosecuted by the U.S. government and outlawed by the Mormon Church in 1890, is by no means the only distinctive aspect of nineteenth-century Mormonism, but debate persists in contemporary scholarship and within the Mormon community about the relative benefits and restrictions of polygamy for women. As an alternative to monogamous marriage, did polygamy offer women more or less autonomy and opportunity for self-fulfillment, greater or fewer options for significant authority within Mormon communities? There is general agreement that Mormon women experienced more freedom in general in the early frontier-based years of the movement during the time that polygamy was practiced, and that Mormon assimilation into the American mainstream has brought with it a restriction of women's authority to the roles of wife and mother. At the same time, contemporary Mormon feminists are reclaiming earlier forms of authority, healing among them. They have reinstituted an influential nineteenth and early twentieth-century women's newspaper, now called *Exponent II*, and they are engaged in theological reconstructions of women-oriented images of divinity through the vehicle of "Heavenly Mother."

The Oneida Perfectionists, an upstate New York community founded by John Humphrey Noyes (1811–1886) that existed between 1848 and 1880, engaged in another alternative to monogamous marriage. "Complex marriage" was designed to foster the solidarity of the group and to eliminate what Noyes considered the divisiveness of exclusive sexual relationships in order to bring about the kingdom of God on Earth. Noyes's patriarchal stance dominated the authority structure of Oneida. The privilege of participation in community governance, of choice in the matter of sexual partners, and permission to bear children were meted out according to a hierarchical criterion called "ascending and descending fellowship." Ambiguities, ironies, and contradictions abounded for Oneida women. Noyes was scornful of nineteenth-century women's rights advocates and articulated views about male superiority. He was just as convinced that social disorder could be eliminated and right relationships restored between God and humankind and between the sexes by doing away with the excesses of female bondage to domesticity and male enslavement to isolating capitalist endeavors. Women at Oneida enjoyed greater freedom of dress and access to education than women in the mainstream culture. Because childrearing was turned over to the community after the first year, women experienced both liberation and deprivation in this respect, according to documents left by community members. Contemporary scholarship is divided on whether Oneida offered women liberation or repression, greater or lesser status. There is evidence to support both interpretations, and, as Lawrence Foster suggests in *Women, Family, and Utopia*, the most compelling evidence will take both interpretations into account.

Spiritualism emerged as a cultural movement with minimal organization in 1848, not founded by a particular person but in response to doubts fostered by the growing prestige of science as the primary arbiter of ultimate truth in combination with reactions against Calvinist theology among Protestants. The catalyzing events were the rappings heard and interpreted by two young girls, Kate and Margaret Fox, as evidence that the spirits of the dead were attempting to contact the living with physical evidence that life survived the death of the body. There followed a burgeoning of possibilities for women without prescribed credentials to assume careers as Spiritualist mediums and to preach and teach publicly. In combination with the development of an optimistic, progressive, anti-clerical theology derived from sources as varied as Swedenborgianism and Transcendentalism, Spiritualists fostered a progressive politics that engaged issues like abolition, divorce reform, and women's rights. In addition, mediumship proved to be good training for public work on behalf of women's suffrage later in the nineteenth century. Scholars have also pointed to the fact that female mediums, unlike most male mediums, frequently spoke in trance under spirit guidance rather than directly as a conscious or unconscious means to fend off claims that they were challenging propriety by speaking publicly. Male protectors often managed them and both exploited and were exploited by stereotypes of women as passive, sensitive agents of higher spiritual forces.

Theosophy, founded in 1875 by Helena P. Blavatsky (1831–1891), a Russian emigree, and Colonel Henry Steel Olcott (1832–1907), both one-time Spiritualists, embraced an eclectic worldview, the "Ancient Wisdom," that combined Eastern and occult thought, and rejected both Christian orthodoxy and scientific materialism, and understood itself as gathering together the essential truths of all the world's religions. Theosophy offered an immanental doctrine of the sacred—a spark of the divine in every atom of the universe—that gave women as well as men direct access to spiritual authority. It promoted hopeful doctrines of human nature, among them a theosophical form of *karma* that held that human souls could be born into either female or male bodies, depending upon the lessons needed in a particular lifetime. Theosophy offered women models of strong female leadership in addition to Madame Blavatsky, including Annie Besant (1847–1933), Katherine Tingley (1847–1929), and Alice Bailey (1880–1949). Twenty-first-century scholarship such as that of Joy Dixon has begun to demonstrate the extent to which British Theosophical women were involved in progressive politics and rejected a privatized occult spirituality that excluded participation in political culture. Generally speaking, Theosophy attracted educated middle- and upper-class women whose spiritual needs were not being met by prevailing Christian orthodoxies and who found outlets for their spiritual gifts, religious experiences, and psychic needs in Theosophy.

Mary Baker Eddy (1821–1910), founder of the Church of Christ Scientist, better known as Christian Science, provided yet another option for women as both participants and leaders in a new religious movement. Christian Science was grounded in an absolutist metaphysical claim based on Eddy's own healing experience in 1866—that there is no ultimate reality in matter—and upon which she based not only a new theology, but a healing system and a church structure. Eddy published the first of many versions of *Science and Health with Key to the Scriptures* in 1866. Christian Science offered women positions as teachers and practitioners and promulgated a theology that denied the reality of the physical body and its ultimate relevance, whether female or male. It understood sin, sickness, suffering, and evil as illusions based in the mistaken conviction that matter is real. For Christian Science, the site of struggle for achieving health and social transformation was "mind," an arena obviously open to women who had little opportunity for active, public involvement in institutional religion, politics, or the marketplace.

Bridging the Nineteenth and the Twentieth Centuries. The direct and indirect influence of Christian Science and Theosophy, along with different kinds of spiritual healing and esotericism, proliferated during the late nineteenth and early twentieth centuries as there emerged a constellation of new religions categorized variously as "harmonial" religion, the "metaphysical" traditions, and, more pejoratively, the positive thinking religions. Typically, these religions integrated philosophical idealism with distinctive, often called "spiritual," interpretations of Christianity. Among the most famous names associated with these movements are Ursula Gestefeld and Emma Curtis Hopkins of New Thought, Myrtle Fillmore, who, along with her husband Charles, founded the Unity School of Christianity, and Alice Bailey of the Arcane School. These movements were not reluctant to institutionalize leadership positions for women, and they drew large numbers of women members. Their theological worldviews promulgated ideas that women have been drawn to historically. They revolted against what they saw as rigid forms of creedal Christianity, de-emphasized the doctrine of original sin, and held to hopeful understandings of human nature such as a belief in the divinity of the inner self. These religions often combined elements of both Eastern and Western religious thought and were characterized by an emphasis on healing, both spiritual and physical. They typically held to the power of thought or mind to changes one's consciousness, often by tapping into other levels of reality, and thereby to change one's circumstances as well. There are many examples, however, of these traditions giving over institutional power to men as they moved into the second and third generations of existence and became more assimilated to patterns in mainstream American and British culture.

TWENTIETH-CENTURY NEW RELIGIONS. The twentieth century continued to offer a great variety of possibilities for women in new religions. Charismatic, pentecostal preaching and healing women in the earlier part of the century, among them Aimee Semple McPherson (1890–1944), founder of the International Church of the Foursquare Gospel, Alma B. White (1862–1946), a Methodist preacher and founder of the Pillar of Fire Church, and Mother Leafy Anderson (c. 1887–1927), founder of the Black Spiritualist churches, continued to overcome disapproval of women preachers by force of their personal power. Growing numbers of Eastern religions began to find their way into Western culture in greater numbers beginning in the 1960s and provided new communities, practices, and forms of leadership for women. Feminist/goddess spirituality, an outgrowth of the women's movement and based in the authority of women's distinctive bodily and religious experiences and rituals, came into prominence as well, beginning in the 1960s. The constellation of ideas and practices that came to be called the New Age movement, many of whose themes overlap with Theosophy and feminist spirituality, also attracted large numbers of women and women leaders. Like their nineteenth-century forerunners, these religions offered women ways to experiment with new religious ideas, practices and images, often female, of the sacred and with alternative models of family and community and expressions of sexuality.

BUDDHISM AS A NEW RELIGION IN AMERICA. An ancient religion in the East, but relatively new to the West, Buddhism offered Western women new spiritual opportunities and has itself been changed by the process of responding to calls for a feminist Buddhism, a Buddhism "beyond patriarchy," as Buddhist scholar and practitioner Rita Gross (1943 –) puts it. Highly cognizant of anti-female assumptions in traditional Buddhism about women's bodies and women's nature, an increasing number of Buddhist feminists who have become teachers and leaders—Gross, Charlotte Joko Beck, Joanna Macy, Jan Willis, Anne Klein, Sandy Boucher, Lekshe Tsomo—have found in Buddhism itself sources to combat its own anti-woman entrenchments. Buddhism's non-theism, its emphasis on impermanence, its various female images of power, its teachings that insist on the ultimate irrelevance of gender, and its focus on the primacy of experience are all resources from which women Buddhists draw to foster female leadership, a more Earth-centered practice of Buddhism, and innovations in the teaching of Buddhism.

THREE TWENTIETH-CENTURY RELIGIONS OF EASTERN ORIGIN. Other, newer forms of Eastern religions have also attracted Western women, three in particular that have emerged since the middle of the twentieth century. Looked at comparatively, they offer women very different possibilities for both traditional relational roles and alternatives to Western marriage traditions that illustrate what can appear to the cultural mainstream as paradoxical, unappealing, and even dangerous combinations of freedom and restriction.

The Unification Church, better known as the Moonies, was founded in 1954 by Korea's Reverend Sun Myung Moon (1920–). Unificationism's complex theology of restoration assumes that Jesus Christ accomplished a spiritual, but not a physical, redemption. It is in living out the tightly structured, family based, husband-wife sexuality modeled by Moon and his wife that the edenic pre-fall condition of the world will be restored. Unification women have access to a wide range of roles, mostly ordered sequentially: careers often involving work for the church, arranged marriages followed by several years of celibate sisterhood to their husbands, and, eventually, children who may be left in the care of others while the parents work elsewhere for the church. The domestic sphere is valued as one of ultimate spiritual significance and the value of the marriage relationship in bringing about the salvation of the world cannot be overestimated. One of the early leaders and theologians of the movement was Oon Young Kim (1915–1990), a female professor at Ewha University in Seoul and the first Unification missionary to the West.

The International Society for Krishna Consciousness, known also as ISKCON and Hare Krishna, came to America from India in 1965. The society and its male founder, Swami Prabhupada (1896–1977), attracted young counterculture members. Unlike the male/female sexual complementarity assumed by Unificationists, ISKCON espouses a radical body/spirit split that holds bodies to be illusion but nonetheless assumes male spiritual superiority. At the same time, the security of a highly ordered sexual life and the comfort and support of the women's ashram is appealing to the women of ISKCON, and there is evidence to suggest that women exercise significant power indirectly, a pattern common in traditionally male-dominated religions.

Another new religion of Indian origin, the Rajneesh movement, now known as Osho, originated with Bhagwan

Shree Rajneesh (1931–1990) in an ashram in Poona, India, in the 1970s. Its most famous site in the West was Rajneeshpuram in Oregon, disbanded in 1985 in the midst of scandals and church/state tensions. In contrast with marriage-based movements, Rajneesh encouraged women to have nonexclusive sexual relationships with men. These were regarded as gateways to spiritual experiences and gave women both the freedom and the responsibility to avoid traditional roles of wife and mother, develop identities as "lovers," and assume positions of leadership. This movement offers an excellent forum for exploration of issues dealing with women's relationships to male gurus and of the question of what distinctions need to be drawn between sexual freedom and exploitation in religions that make connections between overtly physical rather than metaphorical sexual expression related to the sacred.

FEMINIST SPIRITUALITY. Unlike highly structured family and communally oriented new religions, feminist spirituality has been developing since the second wave of feminism emerged in the 1960s as a loosely organized, very widespread cultural movement movement. However many varieties exist within the movement, there is a discernible woman-oriented worldview often grounded in female images of God or devotion to the Goddess or goddesses. However imaged, the divine is understood as radically immanent in every aspect of reality. Earth- and nature-related rituals affirm both the spiritual relevance and the physical reality of the world and celebrate women's bodies and bodily rhythms, in contrast with some nineteenth-century groups that denied the ultimate reality of the body. Feminist spirituality is broad enough to encompass manifestations as wide-ranging as Neopaganism and Wicca and groups that identify themselves with Judaism and Christianity. The movement as a whole places great emphasis on spiritual healing from what members describe as the scars of male-dominated religion and culture. Feminist spirituality continues to develop ethical stances related particularly to environmentalism and peace.

CONCLUSION. Scholarly and popular speculations abound about women's motivations for joining new religious movements. No one explanation suffices, since women offer many, many reasons for their attractiveness, even if, as sociological data indicate, women who join new religions do not necessarily stay in them forever. Those reasons almost always include the appeal of theological claims and ways of living that are more coherent with women's own experiences, religious and otherwise, than those offered by the established religious traditions or the secular culture. They encompass, as well, possibilities for expression of women's charismatic gifts and leadership abilities along with the freedom to explore individual psychological strengths or deficits that find outlets and compensations in new religions. There is also the draw of economic security and community, along with opportunities for sexual relationships outside monogamous marriage, or, communally validated celibacy, or communal suppot for traditional monogamous marriages. All of these may figure in one combination or another in women's joining—or founding—new religious movements.

SEE ALSO Besant, Annie; Blavatsky, H. P.; Buddhism, article on Buddhism in the West; Christian Science; Eddy, Mary Baker; Feminist Theology; Fillmore, Charles and Myrtle; Gender and Religion; Hopkins, Emma Curtis; International Society for Krishna Consciousness; Lee, Ann; Mormonism; Neopaganism; New Thought Movement; Noyes, John Humphrey; Olcott, Henry Steel; Prabhupada, A. C. Bhaktivedanta; Quakers; Rajneesh; Shakers; Smith, Joseph; Spiritualism; Swedenborgianism; Theosophical Society; Tingley, Katherine; Unification Church; Wicca.

BIBLIOGRAPHY

Bednarowski, Mary Farrell. "Outside the Mainstream: Women's Religion and Women Religious Leaders in Nineteenth-Century America." *Journal of the American Academy of Religion* 48 (1980), 207–231. An analysis of four theological and social characteristics that fostered women's leadership in Shakerism, Spiritualism, Theosophy, and Christian Science.

Braude, Ann. *Radical Spirits: Spiritualism and Women's Rights in Nineteenth-Century America.* Boston, 1989. A comprehensive study of nineteenth-century American Spiritualism's origins, teachings, and advocacy for numerous social reforms, particularly women's rights.

Chmielewski, Wendy E., Louis J. Kern, and Marlyn Klee-Hartzell, eds. *Women in Spiritual and Communitarian Societies in the United States.* Syracuse, N.Y., 1993. Essays detailing the variety of women's experiences in spiritual and communitarian societies from the eighteenth through the twentieth centuries.

Dixon, Joy. *Divine Feminine: Theosophy and Feminism in England.* Baltimore and London, 2001. A study of the relationship between esoteric religion and feminist social reform movements in late nineteenth- and early twentieth-century England.

Eller, Cynthia. *Living in the Lap of the Goddess: The Feminist Spirituality Movement in America.* New York, 1993. A detailed description and interpretation of the variety of beliefs, practices, rituals, and appeals of contemporary goddess-related feminist spirituality.

Foster, Lawrence. *Women, Family, and Utopia: Communal Experiments of the Shakers, the Oneida Community, and the Mormons.* Syracuse, N.Y., 1991. A historical study of the complexities of male-female relationships in three communal societies and of the multiple and distinctive ways they addressed the changing roles of women, the nature of family, and the impact of sexuality.

Gill, Gillian. *Mary Baker Eddy.* Reading, Mass., 1998. An interpretation of Mary Baker Eddy as neither saint nor sinner but a woman whose considerable gifts as theologian and leader had few outlets in the society in which she lived.

Gross, Rita M. *Soaring and Settling: Buddhist Perspectives on Contemporary Social and Religious Issues.* New York, 1998. Academic essays with significant autobiographical content by a leading scholar in American feminist Buddhism.

Humez, Jean M., ed. *Mother's First-Born Daughters: Early Shaker Writings on Women and Religion.* Bloomington and Indianapolis, 1993. A collection of primary sources by Shaker women from 1780–1851 with a general introduction and introductions to each of four sections by the editor.

Jacobs, Janet L. *Divine Disenchantment: Deconverting from New Religions.* Bloomington and Indianapolis, 1989. An exploration of members' diverse reasons for leaving new religions with attention to issues of gender.

Judah, J. Stillson. *The History and Philosophy of the Metaphysical Movements in America.* Philadelphia, 1967. An interpretation of the origins and beliefs of metaphysical religions, among them Spiritualism, Theosophy, New Thought, and Christian Science, with a fifteen-point list of pervasive characteristics in the introduction.

Knott, Kim. "Men and Women, or Devotees? Krishna Consciousness and the Role of Women." In *Women in the World's Religions Past and Present,* edited by Ursula King, pp. 111–128. New York, 1987.

Lewis, James R., and J. Gordon Melton, eds. *Perspectives on the New Age.* Albany, N.Y., 1992. Essays, some of which emphasize gender, with multiple approaches to the academic study of the New Age Movement including suggestions for future research.

Palmer, Susan Jean. *Moon Sisters, Krishna Mothers, Rajneesh Lovers: Women's Roles in New Religions.* Syracuse, N.Y., 1994. A study of the multiplicity of women's roles in seven contemporary new religions.

Puttick, Elizabeth. *Women in New Religions: In Search of Community, Sexuality and Spiritual Power.* New York, 1997. An interpretation of both the liberating and oppressive characteristics of new religions for women with emphasis on alternative approaches to sexuality and the sacred.

Salomonsen, Jone. *Enchanted Feminism: The Reclaiming Witches of San Francisco.* London and New York, 2002. In-depth study of the community and new spiritual tradition set up by Starhawk and her friends.

Sered, Susan Starr. *Priestess, Mother, Sacred Sister: Religions Dominated by Women.* New York and Oxford, 1994. A comparative anthropological, historical, social study of the meanings of "women's religion" in the context of twelve religions from around the world.

Ursenbach, Maureen, and Lavina Fielding Anderson, eds. *Sisters in Spirit: Mormon Women in Historical and Cultural Perspective,* foreword by Jan Shipps. Urbana, 1987. Essays by Mormon women scholars that integrate Mormon history and women's history to explore the identities of Mormon women both past and present.

Wessinger, Catherine, ed. *Women's Leadership in Marginal Religions: Explorations outside the Mainstream.* Urbana and Chicago, 1993. Essays about social and theological characteristics that, by contrast with those in mainstream religions, have fostered women's leadership in nineteenth- and twentieth-century new religions.

Mary Farrell Bednarowski (2005)

NEW RELIGIOUS MOVEMENTS: NEW RELIGIOUS MOVEMENTS AND CHILDREN

In the 1960s and 1970s the religions classified as "cults" or "new religious movements" (NRMs) were largely populated with people in their late teens and early twenties. Often characterized as rebellious youth, disenchanted "dropouts" who had rejected the values of mainstream religion and culture to create their own counterculture and protest movements, few of them had children or other responsibilities. Their enthusiasm for Asian mysticism, new forms of psychotherapy, or new fervent expressions of evangelical Christianity led them to join exciting new religions in the hope of experiencing the numinous, finding the authentic self, or transforming the world and themselves. This religious resurgence occurred in both America and Europe. By the 1980s and 1990s the demographic picture worldwide had changed dramatically. The young seekers had matured into middle age, and children had become a significant feature of most NRMs.

Children and their views about the religions they belong to have been neglected by academics in the study of religion generally but especially in studies looking at NRMs. Their significance is, however, without question. Their impact has been noted by various sociologists of religion; their involvement in drawing sectarian religious groups away from isolation and toward assimilation was described by Richard Niebuhr in *The Social Sources of Denominationalism* in 1929. More recently, in his article "Why Religions Movements Succeed or Fail" (1996), Rodney Stark commented that the second generation is key to the success or failure of new religious movements. Without doubt, the arrival of a second generation, often in large numbers, is key to understanding how many of these new movements undergo organizational transformations and changes to their practices. Retaining the second generation is crucial to many of these groups. In some new religions, such as The Family (previously known as Children of God), second-generation members now outnumber the first generation, and they are highly active in participating and developing the future of the movement. The success coming to groups retaining their second generation can be seen in some of the older sects, such as the Mormons and Hutterites, who solved the problem of increasing membership by breeding new members. Whereas in the 1980s there were about four hundred Hutterites in North America, now there are nearer thirty thousand, and the claim is they still retain 98 percent of their offspring. In contrast, some new religions are struggling; not managing to increase membership by proselytizing, they clearly need to retain their second generation. For example, the Unification Church (better known as "the Moonies") and the International Society for Krishna Consciousness (ISKCON) had fewer adult members at the end of the twentieth century than they did in the 1970s. For new movements like Neopaganism, retaining the second generation is not an issue; the ideal is for the spiritual path to be one of individual choice.

The wave of children born into the new religious movements has created new challenges. The responses to the problems of raising this new generation have taken a rich variety of forms; not surprisingly, given the radical nature of these parents, not all of their parenting solutions have been conventional. For the insiders—the adult members of NRMs—the main issues have been child raising, education, and how best to incorporate the second generation in their active religious lives. How far should their religion remain a religion of converts, and how far should they adapt to accommodate the new generation? For those watching from the outside, particularly those who felt they had little access to inside information, children added a new dimension and a focus of concern, which was easily fueled by the negative stereotyping of NRMs as "dangerous cults" by the anticult movement and the media. The three issues that have preoccupied the public, the media, and concerned outsiders are, firstly, child abuse (including mental and sexual abuse and neglect); secondly, child custody cases and the difficult issue of the "best interests of the child"; and thirdly, child socialization and education. The article will deal with each of these in turn.

CHILD ABUSE. One crucial significance of children in NRMs is the role they play in the fight against cults. As James T. Richardson points out in "Social Control of New Religions: From 'Brainwashing' Claims to Child Sex Abuse Allegations," children have become the new weapon for anticultists in the battle against NRMs now that the brainwashing weapon has lost its potency (Richardson, 1999, p. 172). Accusations about child abuse in new religious movements have become the "ultimate weapon" used in attempts to control new religious movements. After the Jonestown murders-suicides in 1978, there was an explosion of negative media stories about "cults," and accusations of child abuse increased. The reason for this was that so-called cultic groups, according to anticultists, are disposed to abuse children. In their view all cult parents are extremists, obsessed with personal salvation or creating a heaven on earth, dependent on a leader and now unable to think critically and independently.

Moreover, because they are portrayed as working in exploitative conditions, they must have little time for family. Kaj Moos in *Save Our Children* describes cult children as simply "an imposition upon their emotionally fragile, dependent parents," which tends to "lead toward a path of child abuse, for the cultist parent is regressed and unable to cope with the parenting demands and need of children" (Moos, 1993, p. 12). According to Moos, "cult children" are raised in organizations predisposed toward abusive practices. Michael Langone, editor of the *Cultic Studies Journal*, is more cautious in his writing and as such has been influential in arguing that cults have a particular capacity to harm children physically and psychologically. In *Recovery from Cults: Help for Victims of Psychological and Physical Abuse* (1993), Langone argues that it is their absolutist ideology that provides a rationalization for child abuse and makes them different from Catholics, Baptists, or Episcopalians. Their ideology, he argues, compels harsh physical discipline and the rejection of medical intervention and supports physical isolation and resistance to investigations of child abuse, the members using religious beliefs to justify their ideology and isolation (Langone, 1993, pp. 327–329). Langone makes this case while at the same time admitting it is hard to draw conclusions specifically linking cultic groups and child abuse because of the lack of evidence.

At the close of the twentieth century, scholars cited a lack of evidence to support anticult groups' claims of child abuse, and research had not demonstrated a causal link between NRMs and victims of child abuse. To give one example, the theosophically inspired group the Church Universal and Triumphant (CUT) received particularly hostile media and anticult attention after the Branch Davidian tragedy, calling it one of America's "top cults." Concern was raised about the well-being of children in this group, perceived as socially and religiously deviant. From their research described in *Church Universal and Triumphant in Scholarly Perspective* (1994), Lawrence Lilliston and Gary Shepherd were able to identify certain problem areas in the relationship between adults and youth: some small-scale delinquent acts by a few young people such as "joyriding, shoplifiting"; some "off the Ranch" pregnancies after associating with outsider boys; more generally a resistance to strict church prohibition against music with a heavy beat (especially rock and roll); and some teen dissatisfaction, characterized by feeling ignored and ridiculed by outsiders, particularly when preparation was made in the 1990s for nuclear war. The church made some changes in the 1990s, however, to address parenting problems. Realizing that intense commitment to organizational jobs in the church was affecting parent-child relationships, the church gave staff with children more time; parenting skills were encouraged and parenting workshops introduced; youth antidrug programs and ties to national youth programs were established. Researchers were impressed by the openness of the parents to exposing children to a diversity of religious views and by their respect for free choice. They described CUT children as having high but realistic standards, as self-reliant, and as having appropriate dependency attitudes and strong feelings of competence and confidence in their ability. Reporting that the parents were resigned to the fact that most of the children would become religious defectors, they in fact concluded that the church may have introduced new structures that could increase the loyalty of the second generation. Though previously charged with isolation, lack of parenting skills, and other concerns expressed by Langone and Moos, the Church Universal and Triumphant introduced changes that led observers to view the organization more favorably.

The notion put forward by Langone and others seeking to control "cults"—that NRMs, unlike other religions such as Catholicism, are predisposed to child abuse—is not supported by the evidence. Anson Shupe, editor of *Wolves within the Fold: Religious Leadership and Abuses of Power*, points out that Catholic priests "have preyed upon literally hundreds of young victims" (Shupe, 1998, p. 5). A survey by the National Review Board (February 2004) revealed that from 1950 to 2002 in the United States, 4,450 Catholic priests were accused of sexual abuse of minors. With such evidence it is no longer appropriate to suspect new religions as being any more or less likely to breed sexual abuse. Children raised in NRMs are not more likely to be abused than those raised in any other religion, but in the case of NRMs, the religious group and its ideology or structure are usually blamed rather than individuals. The Catholic Church has tried to separate individual abuse from any connection with the social structure or practices of the church. There is research, described by contributors to Shupe's volume, to suggest that, in fact, there may be problems when the total economic structure and power of a group rests on male, unmarried clergy.

Careful scrutiny of the child abuse accusations against NRMs reveals that many of the allegations have been concerned with harsh discipline and corporal punishment. This is a highly controversial area, the rights and wrongs of "smacking" being hotly debated. The new tide of opinion against any form of physical punishment of children makes the adoption of the more disciplinarian view more controversial. Over the years theories of socially and politically acceptable discipline have varied greatly. The quotation from *Proverbs* (13:24), "he who spares the rod hates his child," is central to one theory, advocated, for example, by James Dobson in his book *Dare to Discipline* (1970). According to this theory, children need to be taught strong self-discipline and self-control, which are best encouraged by strong disciplining of the child, including the use of corporal punishment. This is still the theory favored by some mainstream evangelical Christians worldwide and by some Christian NRMs, such as The Family.

The more liberal attitudes of later child-care experts, such as Dr. Spock or the "modern" Penelope Leach, are supported by liberal, secular, and New Age parents. In the past two decades countries have in general become more liberal. The United Nations Convention on the Rights of the Child, adopted in 1989 and ratified by every country in the world except the United States and Somalia, makes it clear that children should be protected from all forms of physical and mental violence, injury, or abuse (Article 19.1). It states that any form of discipline should take into account the child's human dignity. Nevertheless, in the United Kingdom there still exists a Victorian law allowing a defense in terms of reasonable chastisement allowing parents to hit children when they can claim the punishment was justified. Laws were passed to abolish spanking in British state schools in 1986 and in privately funded schools in 1998; it is still permitted in some states in the United States. Nowhere is it allowed in Scandinavia; Sweden banned smacking thirty years ago. The question of whether parents should be restricted from hitting their children will become increasingly an issue between religious conservatives and liberals. It is not an issue that is limited to new religious movements.

One of the better-known cases involving accusations about severe corporal punishment involved the Northeast Kingdom Community Church, a fundamentalist Christian sect that was the object of much controversy in the 1980s and that was described by George Robertson in "Island Pond Raid Begins New Pattern" (1994) and by Vanessa Malcarne and John Burchard in "Investigations of Child Abuse/Neglect Allegations in Religious Cults: A Case Study in Vermont" (1992). The Messianic Communities, also known as the Twelve Tribes, continue to have problems in France and Germany on issues of homeschooling and discipline. These and other groups advocating strict discipline and openly supporting corporal punishment believe it is in the children's best interests, sometimes even to "break the will" of the child. The Community in Island Pond in Vermont is a strongly fundamentalist community, homeschooling their children and disciplining them with a stick for minor disobediences and adult strikes for more serious offenses. In 1984 the community was raided, and more than a hundred adults and 112 children were taken into custody. Although all the children were returned to their parents, the techniques for the allegations of abuse, as George Robertson (1994) points out, worked for the anticult movement—the raids made headline news, highlighting the allegations of abuse, but the children's return was hardly mentioned. What is striking is that in 2004 the Vermont community continued its strict fundamentalist lifestyle and lived without conflict with its neighbors.

Some children have suffered from severe corporal punishment. The famous American case is that of the twelve-year-old boy in the House of Judah who died as the result of beatings at a camp. Children raised in belief systems that advocate severe physical punishment in some cases are defenseless against the group if they live within a closed community. However, no evidence has as yet been produced to show that children in new religious movements are more likely to be harmed than children in other institutions or mainstream society. The Institute for the Study of American Religion carried out a survey in 1986 exploring reports of child abuse in cults and concluded that beliefs about corporal punishment and strict discipline could lead to violent tendencies in children. But the survey also concluded that such behavior "did not come from the major non-conventional religions (that is, those identified as cults in the public mind) but from conservative evangelical Christian groups" (Melton, 1986, pp. 255, 258).

It could be argued that many of the accusations of child abuse by anticultists have in themselves led to abuse of children. Accusations about child abuse were made against the Family in Argentina, France, Spain, Australia, Peru, Norway, and the United Kingdom. Worldwide raids on the Family homes made front-page news as the allegedly abused children were dragged from their parents in the night, with scarcely a mention of their return after no abuse could be found in any of the children in any of the countries. Some of the officials' treatment of the children of the Family might on the other hand be seen to constitute abuse. In Australia social services took more than 190 children away from parents who were members of the Family in 1992, but within a few days all were returned. Based on similarly false information, children in France and Spain were kept in custody and separated from their mothers for weeks or months. In all cases courts dismissed the charges. A few of the key anticult figures who instigated some of these raids (Rick Ross, for example) also used child abuse allegations against David Koresh and the Branch Davidians.

It should be noted in terms of child abuse that there is a particularly complex relationship between gender, age, power, and spirituality. Particularly difficult is the relationship of guru and disciple, or priest and child, with the enormous potential for religious exploitation. For example, Elizabeth Puttick has commented that the master-disciple relationship was a profound experience for many Rajneesh followers with "little evidence of sexual exploitation of female disciples by Osho" (Puttick, 1999, p. 102). But problems of authority and misuse of power did arise in the International Society for Krishna Consciousness (ISKCON). There were cases of child abuse and instances of second-class child care. In June 2000 children of ISKCON filed a federal complaint naming ISKCON and its governing body as defendants. In *Betrayal of the Spirit* (2001) Nori Muster describes how the worst abuses took place between 1971 and 1986 in the Dallas boarding school, the West Virginia boarding school in New Vrindavan, and in the Vrindavana (India) boarding school. The scandals about child abuse in ISKCON, with the leaders' focus on attaining spiritual objectives rather than looking after their children in schools and child-care facilities, have played a large part in destroying the second generation's trust in this movement. Many of the second generation, who now mostly attend non-ISKCON schools, are critical of some of the fanaticism of the first generation, as Burke Rochford describes in "Reactions of Hare Krishna Devotees to Scandals of Leaders' Misconduct" (1998). Another article by Rochford, "Education and Collective Identity" (1999), analyzes how the second-generation members hold on to their identity as Krishna devotees but have a less-strong collective ISKCON identity. Incidents of underage sex in the early years of The Family have also been documented by James Chancellor in *Life in the Family: An Oral History of the Children of God* (2000). David Koresh, the leader of the Branch Davidians, is cited as having sexual relations with underage girls to create a new spiritual lineage. There are concerns about children in Christian Science, which has been criticized for promoting faith healing and neglecting children in need of medical attention. In the United States adults can either seek medical attention to deal with a physical disorder, or they can use faith healing or alternative medicine. If a child dies from not receiving medical attention, however, parents can face criminal charges. In "Christian Science Spiritual Healing, the Law, and Public Opinion" (1992), James Richardson and John Dewitt argue that concern about the welfare of children has at times overridden concern about parental rights and freedom of religion.

What is dangerous about an approach that accepts that certain organizations like NRMs are predisposed toward abusive practices is that there is then little need to explore in depth any particular NRM to see the reality of whether child abuse is occurring. Anticultists see unchecked information from ex-members about the totalitarian nature and lifestyle of the organization as sufficient. If a group can be defined as a "destructive cult" or an "extreme cult," detailed evaluations of the religious group are not needed to make allegations of child abuse. In France, where there is a governmental preference for listening to the "victims" of sects and to the anticultists who deal with the practical problems of these victims rather than taking an academic viewpoint, very little scholarly work is being undertaken, and an anticult scare continues. In 1996 the French National Assembly declared a list of 172 groups, including Jehovah's Witnesses, Mormons, Catholic charismatics, evangelicals, and Quakers, as potentially dangerous. In Belgium a similar parliamentary report produced in 1997 declared 189 sects potentially dangerous. Sweden has been critical of the attitudes expressed in these reports, and the report of the Swedish Government's Commission on New Religious Movements (1998), "In Good Faith: Society and the New Religious Movements," gives a far more balanced view of the needs of children in unconventional religions and calls for more research:

> The right of parents to bring up their children in accordance with their faith and convictions is above dispute, but it has to be balanced against the knowledge that there are children who suffer harm in new religious movements. . . . The Commission considers it essential that children living in closed groups should have the same form of support, protection and rights as other children. At the same time it is important that children growing up in these movements should not be stigmatized.

Unfortunately not all governments have been as open-minded. A new law introduced by the French parliament in June 2000 was Europe's toughest antisect legislation to date. It allows judges to order the dissolution of a sect if members are convicted of a criminal offence. It bans sects from advertising. It has also made "mental manipulation" a crime. Targeting youth, such as touting for new members near schools or offering children's Sunday school by any church, is now illegal in France.

Allegations of child abuse over the last two decades have been used very effectively against particular NRMs. In those countries in Europe where brainwashing and mind-control claims are still accepted and experts are sought among anticultists (e.g., France, Belgium), it seems likely that those who want to hinder the activities of any NRM will in the last resort use child abuse accusations to persuade the local authorities to act.

FREEDOM OF RELIGION AND THE BEST INTERESTS OF THE CHILD. It is a standard principle of child welfare law and policy that the "best interests" of a child should be promoted. Article 13.1 of the United Nations Convention on the Rights of the Child (1989) states that "in all actions concerning children . . . the best interests of the child shall be a primary consideration." Key articles of the convention also stress the need to respect both "the right of the child to freedom of thought, conscience and religion" (Article 14.1) and "the rights and duties of parents in providing religious and moral guidance to their children in a manner consistent with the evolving capacities of the child" (Article 14.2). These principles have been welcomed by religious groups of all kinds, mainstream and minority religions, because they indicate that the United Nations has no interest in preventing parents from bringing up their children within a religious tradition and endorses freedom of religion.

The main difficulty for courts in Europe or the United States lies in the precarious balance between these two notions: freedom of religion and the best interests of the child. From research on court cases dealing with the custody of a child with one parent in a so-called cult or minority religion, Anthony Bradney, in "Children of a Newer God," says there is no doubt that because courts rely on evidence and arguments given by the parties involved, some judgments have been swayed by incomplete evidence and anticult "experts" (Bradney, 1999, p. 215). How this balance is achieved in the United States and in Europe is well documented in the articles by Bradney, Richardson, and Michael Homer in *Children in New Religions* (1999), although much research is still to be undertaken on the European interpretation of these principles in custody cases. It is already clear, however, that how a particular country views NRMs, cults, or sects has an impact on the legal process and on child custody cases. Custody cases may not actually assess the quality of parenting in any new religious group because very often the judges are as ignorant about NRMs as are members of the public. As Bradney has discussed *in Religions, Rights, and Laws*, although courts in the United Kingdom are supposed to be neutral about religious matters, some parents have lost custody of their child or children "precisely because of their religion" (Bradney, 1993, p. 49). As yet it is not clear how the French or Belgian reports advocating anticult laws or indeed any of those commissioned by European governments will affect the courts and the custody of children in NRMs.

Socialization and Education in NRMs: From Detachment to Affirmation. All societies and all new religious movements attach considerable importance to the upbringing of their children, but what practices are perceived as being most conducive to the general good (including the welfare of the children themselves) are often strikingly different. The alternative childhoods to be found in NRMs can be usefully understood according to the Weberian perspective offered by Roy Wallis in *The Elementary Forms of the New Religious Life* (1984), from the "world-rejecting" to the "world-affirming." These "ideal types" focus on "how a movement orients itself toward the social world into which it emerges" (Wallis, 1984, p. 4).

At one end of the spectrum, children are raised in movements rejecting the world, emphasizing the polluting, permissive, evil, contaminating aspects of the mainstream, which could harm their own children, seen as sinless and vulnerable. Examples can be found in Sahaja Yoga, the Family, the Unification Church, and ISKCON. Boundaries are maintained between the movement and the outside. For example, separate sets of clothes are kept by Family members; purification rituals like foot soaking and meditation are carried out by Sahaja Yoga children after school to negate any negative vibrations picked up at school. Practices and lifestyles are emphasized to help children participate in building the new kingdom or to become spiritually pure. As one Family/Children of God publication commented, "If the millennium is that close, it's all the more reason to get these kids trained in a hurry" (*Teen Rev.*, no. 7, 1986), hence the importance of teaching the very young to be toilet trained and to read and write and the importance of learning Scriptures. These world-rejecting groups create alternative childhoods that emphasize the importance of growing up within a saved community, and therefore the emphasis is on detachment from worldly life. If they are not living in communes, members of these groups emphasize socialization into their values and practices in weekend gatherings, camps, or ashrams. World-rejecting movements often create their own forms of homeschooling, particularly for preteens, not wanting their children to be exposed to the vice-ridden, secular schools of the outside world. CUT and the Family homeschool using the Montessori approach and education philosophies that stress precocious acquisition of reading skills (such as those of Glenn Doman). The more conservative of these groups attempt to revive paternal authoritarianism and strong discipline. These children, like adults, have a prescribed role to play; toys and books are carefully supervised because children can be led astray by the devil, who may try to tempt them through the wrong kind of music or unsupervised TV or try to tempt them into losing their innocence.

At the other end of the spectrum are those NRMs emphasizing the importance of affirming the individual ("self" religions, such as the Human Potential Movement, Damanhur, Scientology, Transcendental Meditation, Rajneesh). The emphasis in raising children must be to help them fill their potential, especially their inner spirituality, and find ways to cope with the world and its stresses. Many of these groups are less obviously "religious," have less dogmatic ideas, and are more highly individualized, emphasizing children's empowerment and affirming individual children's goals and values. Child socialization and education in the mainstream is criticized for being an outdated conventional institution. Children need to be emancipated from the narrow bondage of an educational system that focuses solely on the intellect and a future accepting the materialistic values associated with capitalism. For these more countercultural movements, schooling should emphasize creativity, intuition, and natural intelligence. One must maintain faith in the goodness of children and their potential. Strong discipline and punishment, far from being advocated, are seen as creating fear and a distance between the generations, preventing emotional growth, self-actualization, personal responsibility, and maturity. Children in many of the Eastern-influenced groups, such as Transcendental Meditation, Sathya Sai Baba, Ananda Marga, School of Economic Science, and Western Buddhist Order, learn early on to meditate, and in response their parents may face condemnation and accusations of indoctrination or exploitation.

As Wallis noted, empirical examples will only approximate to these ideal types and may well combine elements of both (Wallis, 1984, p. 5). Although in terms of beliefs and organization a group may be world-rejecting, in terms of the ideal childhood envisaged it may have elements of both detachment from the world and the importance of developing potential power and self-actualization. For example, the international movements of Rajneesh (now Osho), Sahaja Yoga, or Damanhur in Italy, all world-rejecting movements, see the outside world as contaminating, its mainstream schools and patriarchal nuclear-family structures as the root of Western bad habits and neurosis; the alternative is to be found in communal living, detached from the rest of the world. At the same time, there are strong world-affirming elements; correct child-rearing practices are seen as crucial in helping Rajneesh children attain their full potential (Puttick, 1999), and the New Age Damanhurians involve their children in "harmonization," a form of yoga to restore human beings to their original and authentic condition (Introvigne, 1999).

CONCLUSIONS. The significance of studying children in NRMs began to be taken seriously when they were consistently used by anticultists to bolster their attacks on movements. Since then, however, much of the debate has focused on countering these attacks, and the literature on children is heavily weighted with discussions on child abuse, child custody cases, and the indoctrination of children. Although the debates have furthered the understanding of children in new religious movements, the focus on these areas to the exclusion of others has led to a distorted picture of children in NRMs.

In the academic research there is general agreement that although children in NRMs may have unusual childhoods, which in itself can produce difficulties for children, the majority are not worse off in NRMs than children whose parents belong to mainstream religions. Yet the literature focusing on scandals leaves an impression of deviancy. For research on children to progress there needs to be less focus on the scandals and more attention on understanding the impact of children on any religious movement. Wider research is needed on how children develop spiritually, how they gain meaning and order from the religious and cultural patterns in which they live, and what children think about religion and spirituality whether they grow up in new religious movements or the mainstream. There is need for a great deal more research to confront the stereotypical negative attitude to these children's lives by actually looking at what goes on. Children do change religions, but exactly how they change both organizational patterns and religious practices is still little explored. It is important to emphasize the diversity of the systems of meaning in terms of which children give form, order, and direction to their lives within new religions. It will be seen here, however, that the key issues that have influenced the popular view of children in NRMs are ones that are not fundamentally different from the issues involved in raising children in mainstream religions: issues of child abuse, child custody, and the precarious balance of religious freedom, parental rights, and the "best interests of the child" with the extent to which children are "indoctrinated" or "freely choose" the views of their parents. One sad consequence of imposing restrictions on NRMs, on reducing freedom of religion, is a reduced tolerance of diversity.

SEE ALSO Anticult Movements; Brainwashing (Debate); Branch Davidians; Christian Science; Church Universal and Triumphant; Cults and Sects; Family, The; Hutterian Brethren; International Society for Krishna Consciousness; Jehovah's Witnesses; Jonestown and Peoples Temple; Koresh, David; Mormonism; Neopaganism; Quakers; Sai Baba Movement; Scientology; Transcendental Meditation; Twelve Tribes; Unification Church.

BIBLIOGRAPHY

Bradney, Anthony. *Religions, Rights, and Laws.* Leicester, U.K., 1993. British law professor analyzes the legal attitude to religion and laws pertaining to religion in Britain. Looking at case studies, he questions that courts are neutral in regard to religious issues.

Bradney, Anthony. "Children of a Newer God." In *Children in New Religions,* edited by Susan J. Palmer and Charlotte E. Hardman, pp. 210–223. New Brunswick, N.J., and London, 1999.

Chancellor, James. *Life in the Family: An Oral History of the Children of God.* Syracuse, N.Y., 2000. An insider's personal view of the history of the Children of God, backed up by rigorous research.

Homer, Michael. "The Precarious Balance between Freedom of Religion and the Best Interests of the Child." In *Children in New Religions,* edited by Susan J. Palmer and Charlotte E. Hardman, pp. 187–209. New Brunswick, N.J., and London, 1999.

Introvigne, Massimo. "Children of the Underground Temple: Growing up in Damanhur." In *Children in New Religions,* edited by Susan J. Palmer and Charlotte E. Hardman, pp. 138–149. New Brunswick, N.J., and London, 1999.

Langone, Michael. *Recovery from Cults: Help for Victims of Psychological and Physical Abuse.* New York, 1993. Edited by an anticultist, the book is intended as a practical reference book for mental health professionals dealing with cults, psychological manipulation, and "mind control," including special sections on children and cults and the ritualistic abuse of children in day-care centers.

Malcarne, Vanessa, and John Burchard. "Investigations of Child Abuse/Neglect Allegations in Religious Cults: A Case Study in Vermont." *Behavioural Sciences and the Law* 10 (1992): 75–88.

Markowitz, A., and D. A. Halperin. "Cults and Children. The Abuse of the Young." *Cultic Studies Journal* 1 (1984): 143–155.

Melton, Gordon. *Encyclopedic Handbook of Cults in America.* New York and London, 1986. Useful and detailed reference book on NRMs, including bibliographies on each movement.

Muster, Nori. *Betrayal of the Spirit: My Life in the Hare Krishna Movement.* Urbana, Ill., 1997. One woman's account of living in ISKCON. Critical of the movement, she examines scandals of child abuse in ISKCON schools and schisms that forced most original members to leave.

Niebuhr, Richard. *The Social Sources of Denominationalism.* New York, 1929. A sociological study of religion and denominational divisions identifying the change across generations from sectarian to denominational religious life.

Palmer, Susan J., and Charlotte E. Hardman, eds. *Children in New Religions.* New Brunswick, N.J., and London, 1999. Essays examining the impact children have on NRMs and their chances of surviving in the future, discussing how movements socialize children, and addressing the legal and human rights issues, including child abuse allegations worldwide.

Puttick, Elizabeth. "Osho Ko Hsuan School: Educating the 'New Child.'" In *Children in New Religions,* edited by Susan J. Palmer and Charlotte E. Hardman, pp. 88–107. New Brunswick, N.J., and London, 1999.

Richardson, James. "Social Control of New Religions: From 'Brainwashing' Claims to Child Sex Abuse Allegations." In *Children in New Religions,* edited by Susan J. Palmer and Charlotte E. Hardman, pp.172–186. New Brunswick, N.J., and London, 1999.

Richardson, James, and John Dewitt. "Christian Science Spiritual Healing, the Law, and Public Opinion." *Journal of Church and State* 34 (1992): 550–561. An article that examines legal cases involving Christian Scientists whose children have died as a result of spiritual healing, leading to a church response altering policy and practice.

Robertson, George. "Island Pond Raid Begins New Pattern." In *Sex, Slander, and Salvation: Investigating the Family/Children of God,* edited by James R. Lewis and Gordon Melton, pp. 153–158. Palo Alto, Calif., 1994.

Rochford, E. Burke. "Child Abuse in the Hare Krishna Movement: 1971–1986." *ISKCON Communications Journal* 6 (1998): 43–69.

Rochford, E. Burke. "Reactions of Hare Krishna Devotees to Scandals of Leaders' Misconduct." In *Wolves within the Fold,* edited by Anson Shupe, pp. 101–117. New Brunswick, N.J., 1998.

Rochford, E. Burke. "Education and Collective Identity: Public Schooling of Hare Krishna Youths." In *Children in New Religions,* edited by Susan Palmer and Charlotte E. Hardman, pp. 29–50. New Brunswick, N.J., and London, 1999.

Shupe, Anson. *Wolves within the Fold: Religious Leadership and Abuses of Power.* New Brunswick, N.J., 1998. A collection of articles dealing with what Shupe terms "clergy malfeasance," that is, the abuse of power by religious authorities and religious leaders at the expense of followers.

Stark, Rodney. "Why Religions Movements Succeed or Fail." *Journal of Contemporary Religion* 11, no. 2 (1996): 133–146. An essay expanding Stark's 1987 theory of why religious groups succeed or fail and applying it to sects as well as new religions.

United Nations. *United Nations Convention on the Rights of the Child.* Available from http://www.unhchr.ch/html/menu3/b/k2crc.htm.

Wallis, Roy. *The Elementary Forms of the New Religious Life.* London, 1984. An analytic comparison of types of NRMs by a British sociologist illustrating the characteristics of each type from actual movements.

CHARLOTTE E. HARDMAN (2005)

NEW RELIGIOUS MOVEMENTS: NEW RELIGIOUS MOVEMENTS AND MILLENNIALISM

The religious patterns that scholars term *millennialism* or *millenarianism* are noteworthy among new religious movements (NRMs). While many NRMs are not oriented toward a millennial outlook, millennialism is often found in the early stages of a religion. A millennial worldview is well suited to motivating people to convert to completely new religions, accept the spiritual guidance of new teachers, and build new communities. The millennial expectation of an imminent transition to a new order of existence represents a rejection of the status quo, thereby putting millennialists in tension with mainstream society; tension with society also characterizes new religious movements in general. Millennialists are often not involved in violence, but in some significant cases millennialists become caught up in dynamics leading to violence: they may initiate violent acts or be assaulted by opponents in the dominant society. While the term *millennialism* is derived from Christianity, millennial religious patterns can be found in diverse religious traditions in many times and places.

DEFINING MILLENNIALISM. The terms *millennialism* or *millenarianism* come from *millennium,* meaning one thousand years. These terms originate in Christianity with the statement in the New Testament *Book of Revelation* (Apocalypse) that the rule of Christ on earth will last one thousand years (*Rev.* 20:1–4). Scholars now apply the terms to several common religious patterns found in many religions.

Based on his study of medieval Christian revolutionary millennial movements, Norman Cohn defined *millennialism* as expecting a salvation that is:

> (a) collective, in the sense that it is to be enjoyed by the faithful as a collectivity; (b) terrestrial, in the sense that it is to be realized on this earth and not in some otherworldly heaven; (c) imminent, in the sense that it is to come both soon and suddenly; (d) total, in the sense that it is utterly to transform life on earth, so that the new dispensation will be no mere improvement on the present but perfect itself; (e) miraculous, in the sense that it is to be accomplished by, or with the help of, supernatural agencies. (Cohn, 1970, Introduction)

The study of new religious movements reveals the need to modify this definition of millennialism in several ways to make it more accurately descriptive. Many millennialists expect a heavenly collective salvation, and many believe in agencies that should more accurately be called "superhuman," which includes the supernatural.

While many millennialists are expecting an earthly collective salvation, many others are expecting a heavenly collective salvation, or both. If the earthly collective salvation is utterly disproved, then it is easy for millennialists to shift to pinning their hopes on a heavenly salvation. This was the case with the Solar Temple, which committed group murders and suicides in Switzerland, Quebec, and France in 1994, 1995, and 1997. When their hope for a transition to an earthly New Age was disproved, they undertook to make a "transit" to a heavenly salvation on another planet.

Heaven's Gate, which committed a group suicide near San Diego, California, in 1997, never expected an earthly salvation. The Heaven's Gate "class" members saw earthly human existence as irredeemable, they believed there would be imminent apocalyptic violence "to spade under" the human "plants" growing in this earthly "garden," and their goal was to "exit" their physical "vehicles" to attain a type of heavenly salvation on the "mother ship." They believed they would attain eternal, neuter extraterrestrial bodies, travel among the galaxies on flying saucers, and guide evolution on other planets.

Contemporary NRMs also demonstrate that many believers may no longer understand as being supernatural or miraculous the agencies causing the transition to the collective salvation. Increasingly in NRMs, extraterrestrials, space aliens, and UFOs are taking on the roles formerly attributed to God, Satan, angels, and devils. The similarity is that these are all superhuman beings who are normally unseen but are believed to contact certain people. For UFO millennialists, the transition to the collective salvation will take place according to natural laws and be influenced by superhuman agents.

Reflecting the results of NRM studies, millennialism is here defined as involving belief in an imminent transition to a collective salvation, either earthly or heavenly, accomplished by superhuman agencies. The collective salvation is understood as eliminating the unpleasant limitations of the human condition.

Millennial patterns can be called either *catastrophic millennialism* or *progressive millennialism*. Catastrophic millennialism expects a violent transition to the collective salvation. Progressive millennialism is characterized by a strong belief in progress, a confidence that things are getting better. These two patterns are not mutually exclusive; believers can shift from one to the other. Catastrophic millennialism seems most prevalent among people who feel persecuted, although the teachings of a religious tradition also promote these beliefs. Progressive millennialism reflects optimism about the future. The Holy Order of MANS, originating among 1960s hippies in California, is an example of an NRM that was initially oriented toward a progressive New Age millennialism but whose catastrophic millennial expectations increased when it experienced opposition from the anticult movement and as it adopted Eastern Orthodox Christianity. Conversely, an NRM that has catastrophic millennial ideas and is in opposition to society can put these ideas on the back burner and begin to highlight progressive millennial ideas as its members and organization feel more comfortable in society.

Catastrophic Millennialism. The majority of scholarly writings on millennialism are actually studies of catastrophic millennialism, or *apocalypticism*, because this type of millennialism is prone to dramatic episodes of failure: a predicted salvation event fails to occur, or sometimes the believers become involved in horrifying episodes of violence. Catastrophic millennialism, the belief in an imminent catastrophic transition to the collective salvation orchestrated by superhuman agencies, is very common in NRMs. Catastrophic millennialism has a pessimistic view of society and human beings; humans are so evil and corrupt that the old order must be destroyed so the new order can be created. A rigid dualistic outlook may be associated with catastrophic millennialism: things are seen in terms of good versus evil, which often translates into a sense of us versus them. Catastrophic millennialism expects, and may provoke, conflict. In the history of Christianity, this type of millennialism has been called "pre-millennialism" because the belief is that Christ will return *first*, destroy evil, resurrect the dead, judge everyone, and then create the millennial kingdom, either earthly or heavenly.

Catastrophic millennialism has the power to motivate people to convert to entirely new religions, even when there is social and familial opposition. Belief that the world will be destroyed very soon and that the only access to salvation is through this new religion provides a great incentive to disregard the stigma of joining the new group.

Religions that start out as catastrophic millennial movements may remain small, such as the Branch Davidians; they may achieve notable success in becoming international movements with millions of members, such as the Church of Jesus Christ of Latter-day Saints (Mormons); and a few may become diverse world religions, such as Christianity and Islam. A religious tradition that did not begin as a millennial movement may develop millennial movements within it later, such as the Buddhist hope for the coming of the Maitreya Buddha. Messianism may be added later if it was missing in the early versions of the millennial expectations, as in subsequent expectations in Islam of a coming savior figure called the *mahdī*.

The gospels in the New Testament depict Jesus (c. 4 BCE–c. 30 CE) as an apocalyptic prophet and messiah, who predicted imminent catastrophic destruction and the descent of the Son of man from heaven before that generation died out (Matthew 24). The earliest revelations given to Muhammad (570–632) predicted an imminent "Day of Clamor" in which the sun, moon, and stars would fall from the sky, the earth would shake, graves would open, the dead would be resurrected, and everyone would be judged, some going to heaven and others going to hell (Qur'ān 101:11; see also *sūrah* 56:1–74; 77; 81:1–14; 82:1–19; 84:1–12; 99:1–8).

Progressive millennialism. Progressive millennialism is an optimistic view of human nature and the possibility of society to improve. Progressive millennialism is the belief that the imminent transition to the collective salvation will occur through human effort in harmony with a divine or superhuman plan. The guiding agent may be divine, such as God or angels, but is often superhuman, as in extraterrestrials, ascended masters, or earthly masters with superhuman powers, as in the Theosophical and New Age movements. The progressive millennial belief is that humans can create the collective salvation if they cooperate with the guidance of the divine or superhuman agencies. In Christianity this pattern has been called "post-millennialism" because the belief is that Christians must work according to God's plan to create God's kingdom on Earth, and then Christ will return. Christian progressive millennialism has been manifested in the Protestant Social Gospel movement and in the post–Vatican II Roman Catholic orientation toward having a "special option for the poor" and working for social justice.

A Range of Behaviors. A range of behaviors is associated with both catastrophic millennialism and progressive millennialism. At one end of the spectrum, millennial movements are benign: catastrophic millennialists await divine intervention to destroy the world and, at the most, engage in intense proselytizing and may separate themselves from sinful society; progressive millennialists perform social work to improve society and may also attempt to build communities as forerunners of the ideal society. Katherine Tingley's (1847–1929) Point Loma Theosophical community in California from 1900 to 1942 is an example of the latter.

Further in on the belief and behavior spectrum are millennialists who arm themselves for protection. Catastrophic millennialists, such as Christian Identity believers and the Branch Davidians, may arm themselves for protection during the anticipated tribulation period; if they are attacked they will fight back. Progressive millennialists who arm themselves for protection are a logical possibility, but examples of this pattern have not yet been identified and studied.

Interestingly, at the extreme end of the spectrum, both catastrophic millennialists and progressive millennialists are violent revolutionaries whose goal is to overthrow the old order and create the new. The connection between catastrophic millennialism and a revolutionary outlook is apparent; the old order is seen as being so corrupt that people feel called to participate in violent events to destroy it. The numerous medieval Christian revolutionary millennial movements studied by Cohn exemplify this perspective. David Cook (2002) has suggested that early Islamic military expansion was, in part, a way to extend the Muslim faith to more people before the anticipated end of the world one hundred years after the establishment of the Muslim community. Robert Ellwood (2000), Richard Salter (2000), and Scott Lowe (2000) have suggested that there have been revolutionary progressive millennial movements, as represented by the Nazis, the Khmer Rouge, and Mao Ze-dong's movement. These Nazis and Communists believed in progress so fervently that they stopped at nothing to speed progress up "to an apocalyptic rate" (Ellwood, 2000, p. 253) to create their collective salvation.

When catastrophic millennialists and progressive millennialists become revolutionary, they have more in common with each other than with catastrophic and progressive millennialists on the benign end of the spectrum. Revolutionary millennialists of both types possess rigid dualistic perspectives, seeing things in terms of good versus evil, of us versus them, and they do not hesitate to kill many people to achieve their ends.

Charisma, Leaders, and Followers. From the perspective of religious studies, individuals who are believed to have access to revelation from an unseen source of authority (God, angels, saints, ancestors, masters, extraterrestrials) are said to have "charisma." Charisma is socially constructed. If no one believes a person's claimed access to revelation, he or she does not have charisma. The person has charisma only if others believe the claim.

Both prophets and messiahs have charisma. Catastrophic and progressive millennial movements may or may not have prophets and/or messiahs. Some millennial movements, such as Christian Identity, may arise out of a widely shared millennial expectation without one exceptional person taking on the prophetic or messianic role for the whole movement, although there may be numerous people predicting the imminent transition to the collective salvation.

An inner circle of believers around a prophet or messiah become "secondary leaders." They help empower the prophet or messiah to positions of authority in their movement. The secondary leaders and the rank-and-file members can withdraw their faith in the charismatic leader at any time. Thus, the charismatic leader is under constant pressure to maintain his or her position by avoiding disconfirmation of prophecies and authority in the eyes of the believers.

Prophet. A prophet is someone who is believed to receive revelation from an unseen source of authority. Prophets often predict the imminent coming of the millennial kingdom, or they may predict the imminent appearance of a messiah. Muhammad was an apocalyptic prophet warning of the imminent Day of Sorting Out (Qur'ān 77). According to the gospels, Jesus also served as one who warned of God's imminent destruction and judgment (*Matt.* 25). John the Baptist was a prophet of the imminent appearance of the messiah. Joseph Smith Jr. (d. 1844) was the founding prophet of the Church of Jesus Christ of Latter-day Saints. Annie Besant (1847–1933) of the Theosophical Society was a progressive millennial prophet of the imminent coming of the "New Civilization" and the "World-Teacher" who would accomplish it.

Messiah. A messiah (Hebrew, "anointed") is a prophet, because he or she is believed to receive revelation, but the messiah is more than a prophet, because he or she is believed to have the superhuman power to create the collective salvation. Jesus is regarded as the messiah (christ) by Christians. Mother Ann Lee (1736–1784) was seen by the Shakers as the "Second Appearing of Christ in female form"; the Heavenly Father and Holy Mother Wisdom had a son and daughter, Jesus and Ann Lee. The Branch Davidians see David Koresh (1959–1993) as the messiah who will destroy evil in the catastrophic endtime events; like the earliest Christians, the most committed Branch Davidians are expecting Koresh's imminent return. Asahara Shōkō (b. 1955) of Aum Shinrikyō was seen as an enlightened Buddha and the suffering Lamb of Christianity—as the messiah who would create a Buddhist millennial kingdom called Shambhala. The young J. Krishnamurti (1895–1986) was groomed to function as the messiah in Annie Besant's progressive millennial movement in the early twentieth century; she taught that he would be the World-Teacher who would present a teaching that would raise humanity to an awareness of universal unity and move the world into the New Civilization.

A millennial movement does not necessarily have to have a messiah. The passages in the Qurʾān about the Day of Clamor do not mention a messiah; Allah will bring about the endtime events all by himself.

Secondary leaders. Secondary leaders, the inner circle, are crucial for validating the authority of the prophet or messiah. They may even receive some revelation themselves, but usually the prophet or messiah will attempt to restrict claims of charisma to himself or herself. The decisions made by secondary leaders can help determine the trajectory of the movement, whether it will be benign or become totalitarian and violent.

The inner circle of young white leaders around Jim Jones (1931–1978) of Peoples Temple colluded with him to fabricate healings and other miracles, and they helped facilitate the group murders and suicides on November 18, 1978, in Jonestown, Guyana. The inner circle of scientists, doctors, and others around Asahara Shōkō made Aum Shinrikyō into an organization that committed numerous murders and developed a variety of weapons of mass destruction before committing the sarin gas attack on the Tokyo subways in 1995. The inner circle of men around Adolf Hitler helped create a totalitarian, aggressive state that killed millions in its quest to create a millennial kingdom, the Third Reich, for the pure German *völk* (folk).

Secondary leaders can also help direct a millennial group into a direction to lessen conflict with society and become more democratic. In the 1990s the inner circle around Elizabeth Clare Prophet (b. 1939) of the Church Universal and Triumphant helped steer the church away from authoritarianism and catastrophic prophecies to create a denominational structure with shared authority. Apostle Elbert Spriggs (b. 1937), founder of the Twelve Tribes in the 1970s attracting countercultural Christians, takes a low-key approach to leadership, which is shared among elders and other community leaders.

Followers. The followers have crucial roles to play in determining the direction of a millennial movement. They have autonomy and choose whether or not to think critically about their leaders' teachings and projects. Followers choose whether to cooperate in authoritarian schemes leading to totalitarian organization and coercion, or whether they insist on accountability from their leaders. They can choose to withdraw their faith in the leader's charisma at any time. However, once a group has gone so far down the path of attempting to exercise totalitarian control over followers, it can be very difficult to leave. Additionally, if the believer has committed a great deal to the group in terms of lifestyle, sexuality, relationships, family attachments, livelihood, identity, and even crimes, then the very high "exit costs" can discourage a person from choosing to leave.

NATIVIST MILLENNIAL MOVEMENTS. A distinctive form of millennialism has been called "nativist movements" or sometimes "revitalization" movements. These movements consist of people who feel they are being oppressed by a foreign colonizing government that is destroying their traditional way of life and is removing them from their land. They long for a return to an idealized past, which they remember as having been perfect. Numerous nativists who have been exposed to the Christian Bible identify with the story in the Old Testament of the Israelites' liberation from bondage, and may even call themselves Israelites, such as the *Israelitas* (the Israelites of the New Universal Covenant) of Peru whose messiah is Ezequiel Ataucusi Gamonal. Nativists may be either catastrophic millennialists or progressive millennialists, or they may shift between catastrophic and progressive expectations.

Nativists have the same range of behaviors discussed above. They may await divine intervention to remove their oppressors and bring prosperity. They may believe that certain purifying and magical acts will stimulate the divine intervention, as in the Xhosa Cattle-Killing movement in 1856 in South Africa, or the Ghost Dance movement among nineteenth-century Native Americans. Nativists may engage in active rebellion, such as the rebellion in Java against the Dutch in 1825–1830 led by Prince Dipanagara, who was believed to be the *Ratu Adil*, the awaited "Just King," and the rebellion of Burmese against the British in 1930–1932, led by Saya San, who was believed to be the Buddhist righteous king or even the Maitreya Buddha. Both Dipanagara and Saya San were believed to be destined to establish perfect reigns of happiness after the oppressors were removed. The diverse Pai Marire movement among the Maori in New Zealand in the nineteenth century had several prophets and demonstrated different approaches. Some people attempted to build their perfect society apart from their oppressors; others carried out revolution.

AVERTIVE APOCALYPTICISM. A distinctive form of catastrophic millennialism may be termed avertive apocalypticism. A prophet will make predictions of imminent destruction but also say that the catastrophe may be averted if people convert, live moral lives, and practice certain spiritual techniques.

In the late 1980s and early 1990s, avertive apocalypticism was the major theme of Elizabeth Clare Prophet of the Church Universal and Triumphant, who stressed that nuclear Armageddon could be averted through vigorous practice of verbal "decrees" calling on the protective powers of the ascended masters.

Avertive apocalypticism is an important theme in many Marian apparitions, such as the Bayside apparitions in New York City given to Veronica Leuken beginning in 1968 until her death in 1995. According to the Bayside apparitions, God's imminent chastisement by World War III, nuclear war, and a great fireball can be averted if people return to God's ways and believe and practice as good Catholics. The faithful can protect themselves from the catastrophic events by means of talismans such as crucifixes, scapulars, rosaries, religious medals, saints' statues, and praying the Hail Mary.

Tensions between Millennialists and Society. The millennial vision represents a challenge to the current order. Society may be rejected as sinful, or millennialists may direct their energies toward transforming it, or they may become revolutionaries to overthrow the status quo. The values and lifestyles of millennialists are often very different from those of the dominant society. People in mainstream society may find millennialists' lifestyles and new religious commitments to be offensive and take punitive actions. The two characteristics found to be most offensive are the claim of a new revelation by a new prophet or messiah and unconventional sexual lifestyles.

Americans in the late eighteenth century found the new revelation of Mother Ann Lee and the celibate, separate lifestyle and unusual worship of the Shakers to be offensive. Ann Lee and her followers were subjected to repeated beatings and harassment. On one occasion Ann Lee and two secondary leaders were physically expelled from Massachusetts by a mob.

In the nineteenth century both the claim that Joseph Smith Jr. had received a new revelation and scripture and the polygamy practiced by Smith and other Mormons were offensive to the American public. Smith and his brother died at the hands of a mob in Carthage, Illinois, in 1844, and there were numerous acts of violence against Mormons even after most of them relocated to Utah. (In 2004 the state of Illinois apologized to Mormons for the violence against their ancestors.) The church officially ended the practice of polygamy in 1890, but pockets of fundamentalist Mormons still live in marginal communities.

A group called the Children of God, now known as the Family, was formed in the late 1960s. Its members practice free love among their communities, which in the past sometimes included children. By the late 1980s members of the Family reformed their sexual activities to exclude children while maintaining their free-love ethic between consenting adults. They stopped a controversial practice initiated in the 1970s called "flirty fishing," in which women became "fishers of men" by using sexual relations as a recruiting tool. Nevertheless, the Family homes in various countries continue to be subjected to raids by authorities suspecting child abuse, but the children are typically returned to their parents when the charges are found to be baseless.

David Koresh's claim to be the apocalyptic Christ, his polygamy, which included sexual relations with underage girls with the permission of their parents, and his weapons stockpiling put the Branch Davidians in great tension with authorities and citizens, a situation that ended with disastrous results in 1993. Koresh's activities were based on his interpretation of prophecies in the Bible. Koresh taught that the Branch Davidians would be called upon to fight and die in Armageddon predicted to occur in Israel in 1995. He also taught that he was a messiah destined to have children who would be the twenty-four Elders (*Rev.* 4:4 ff.) who would help rule God's kingdom. Fourteen of Koresh's children and their mothers were among the twenty-three children who died in the fire that resulted from the tank and CS (tear) gas assault on April 19, 1993, carried out by agents of the Federal Bureau of Investigation (FBI).

Millennialism and Violence. Most millennialists are peaceful. Some become caught up in dynamics leading to violence. Millennialists are not necessarily the ones who initiate the violence. Millennial groups that become involved in violence may be assaulted millennial groups, fragile millennial groups, or revolutionary millennial movements. These categories are not mutually exclusive; they indicate the primary characteristics of a group at the time the violence occurred. A group may shift from one category to another according to circumstances and may possess aspects of multiple categories at the time of the violence.

Assaulted millennial groups. Millennial groups have been assaulted in many times and places because of their tension with the dominant society. They are assaulted because people in the wider society perceive them as being dangerous. Examples of assaulted millennial groups include: a band of Lakota Sioux massacred at Wounded Knee, South Dakota, in 1890 by U.S. soldiers who were frightened by the Ghost Dance movement; a group of black South Africans calling themselves "Israelites," who refused to move from crown land, fired upon by white South African police in 1921; the Branch Davidians, who were assaulted twice in 1993 by American federal agents, first by agents of the Bureau of Alcohol, Tobacco, and Firearms in an unnecessary "dynamic entry," and then by FBI agents with tanks and CS gas, who first waged psychological warfare against them during a fifty-one-day siege; the Mormons in the nineteenth century who were repeatedly attacked by civilians and authorities across the United States and had an extermination order issued against them by the governor of Missouri in 1838; Rastafari (called Dreads) in Dominica who in 1974 were subjected to a shoot-on-sight order; and in the new temporal millennium, Falun Gong practitioners in the People's Republic of China, who were repeatedly arrested, with many of them dying in custody, for asserting their right to freedom of religion and practicing their *qigong* exercises in public. The early Christians may also be regarded as members of an assaulted millennial movement. It is not unusual for leaders of millennial movements to be executed by the state—for example, Jesus and the Bab (d. 1850), one of the foundational prophets of Bahā'ī from Iran—or imprisoned like Bahá'u'lláh (1817–1892), the other Bahā'ī prophet-founder.

Fragile millennial groups. A fragile millennial movement initiates violence as a final effort to preserve the ultimate concern, the millennial goal on which believers are focused. Jonestown in Guyana in 1978, Solar Temple in Switzerland in 1994, Aum Shinrikyō in Japan in 1995, Heaven's Gate in the United States in 1997, and probably the Movement for the Restoration of the Ten Commandments of God in Uganda in 2000 were fragile millennial groups.

A fragile millennial group is suffering from an accumulation of stresses, some internal to the group, such as dissent, money problems, illness of the leader, threats to the leader's credibility, failure to accomplish goals set by the leader, combined with stresses coming from outside the group, such as vocal apostates, investigations by authorities, lawsuits, hostile neighbors, concerned family members, negative press, and pressures from anticult groups. In some cases the stresses may be primarily internal to the group; in other cases the stresses may come primarily from outside the group. Usually there is a combination of endogenous and exogenous factors that threaten the millennial goal. Instead of giving up their ultimate concern, members of fragile millennial groups opt to commit violence to preserve it. They may choose to attack and kill perceived enemies. They may choose to commit group suicide to preserve the cohesiveness of the group (if that was their ultimate concern, as with the Jonestown residents) or to go to a type of heavenly salvation (Solar Temple, Heaven's Gate). They often direct the violence both outwardly and inwardly.

Revolutionary millennial movements. Revolutionary millennial movements carry out violence to overthrow the old order to create the new. If they become socially dominant, they cause massive violence, such as the Nazis, the Khmer Rouge in Cambodia, and the Taiping Rebellion in China in 1850–1864, which caused 20 million deaths and for a time established the Taiping capital at Nanjing. If the revolutionary movement is not socially dominant, some participants will undertake terrorist acts. Examples are to be found in the diffuse Euro-American nativist (white supremacist) movement in the United States, which includes Identity Christians, racist Neopagans, secular survivalists, and disaffected former military men, such as Timothy McVeigh, who committed the Oklahoma City bombing in 1995. With September 11, 2001, al-Qāʿidah became the most visible portion of a diffuse revolutionary Islamist movement aimed at creating the true Islamic state as its millennial goal.

CONCLUSION. Millennial movements express the human longing for the elimination of suffering for a group of people, the collective salvation. The millennial longing has sparked new religions since the time of Zoroaster, dating perhaps as early as 1000 BCE, through Jesus, Muhammad, and many other prophets and founders of new religious movements.

As a millennial movement becomes more accommodated to society, its millennial expectation may move to the background and the sense of imminence diminish. This is what Jacqueline Stone (2000) calls "managed millennialism." But the millennial prophecies will be preserved in scriptures to be utilized by subsequent prophets, messiahs, and believers searching for meaning and hope, who will initiate even more new religious movements.

SEE ALSO Anticult Movements; Aum Shinrikyō; Besant, Annie; Branch Davidians; Christian Identity Movement; Church Universal and Triumphant; Falun Gong; Family, The; Heaven's Gate; Holy Order of MANS; Jones, Jim; Jonestown and Peoples Temple; Koresh, David; Krishnamurti, Jiddu; Lee, Ann; Mormonism; Nation of Islam; New Age Movement; Point Loma Theosophical Community; Prophet, Mark and Elizabeth Clare; Shakers; Smith, Joseph; Temple Solaire; Theosophical Society; Tingley, Katherine; Transcendental Meditation; Twelve Tribes; UFO Religions; Unarius Academy of Science; Zoroastrianism.

BIBLIOGRAPHY

Adas, Michael. *Prophets of Rebellion: Millenarian Protest Movements against the European Colonial Order.* Chapel Hill, N.C., 1979. Excellent comparison of case studies of revolutionary nativist movements.

Ashcraft, W. Michael. *The Dawn of the New Cycle: Point Loma Theosophists and American Culture.* Knoxville, Tenn., 2002. One of the few in-depth studies of a progressive millennial community.

Barkun, Michael. *Religion and the Racist Right: The Origins of the Christian Identity Movement.* Chapel Hill, N.C., 1997. Definitive history of Christian Identity and its roots in British Israelism.

Cohn, Norman. *The Pursuit of the Millennium: Revolutionary Millenarians and Mystical Anarchists of the Middle Ages.* Rev. ed. Oxford, 1970. Classic study of millennialism with focus on medieval revolutionary Christian movements.

Cook, David. "Suicide Attacks or 'Martyrdom Operations'; in Contemporary Jihad Literature." *Nova Religio: The Journal of Alternative and Emergent Religions* 6, no. 1 (2002): 7–44. Illuminating discussion of the scriptural, historical, and sociological roots of the contemporary practice of suicide attacks by radical Muslims. An appendix contains a translation of "Last Night" instructions found in the luggage of Muhammad Atta, the leader of the September 11, 2001, terrorists.

Ellwood, Robert. "Nazism as a Millennialist Movement." In *Millennialism, Persecution, and Violence: Historical Cases,* edited by Catherine Wessinger, pp. 241–260. Syracuse, N.Y., 2000. Startling analysis of Nazi millennialism as a progressive millennial movement.

Kaplan, Jeffrey. *Radical Religion in America: Millenarian Movements from the Far Right to the Children of Noah.* Syracuse, N.Y., 1997. Study of American millennial movements on the far right: Christian Identity, Odinism and Ásatrú, and B'nai Noah, and the anticult movement and watchdog groups who oppose them.

Lanternari, Vittorio. *The Religions of the Oppressed: A Study of Modern Messianic Cults.* Translated by Lisa Sergio. New York, 1963. Pioneering study of nativist millennial movements as the products of "culture clash" situations.

Lowe, Scott. "Western Millennial Ideology Goes East: The Taiping Revolution and Mao's Great Leap Forward." In *Millennialism, Persecution, and Violence: Historical Cases,* edited by Catherine Wessinger, pp. 220–240. Syracuse, N.Y., 2000. Compares the Taiping Revolution with Mao Ze-dong's Great Leap Forward.

Lucas, Phillip Charles. *The Odyssey of a New Religion: The Holy Order of MANS from New Age to Orthodoxy.* Bloomington, Ind., 1995. In-depth case study of the development of a new religious movement, which provides an excellent example of how a group's millennial views change in response to changes in the social context.

Palmer, Susan J. "Peace, Persecution and Preparations for Yahshua's Return: The Case of the Messianic Communities' Twelve Tribes." In *Christian Millenarianism: From the Early Church to Waco,* edited by Stephen Hunt, pp. 209–223. Bloomington, Ind., 2001. Excellent study of the dynamics of a millennial group's peaceful responses to persecution.

Robbins, Thomas, and Dick Anthony. "Sects and Violence: Factors Enhancing the Volatility of Marginal Religious Movements." In *Armageddon in Waco: Critical Perspectives on the Branch Davidian Conflict,* edited by Stuart A. Wright, pp. 236–259. Chicago, 1995. An important discussion of the factors that promote volatility of millennial groups. Particularly noteworthy is the discussion of the instability of charismatic leadership.

Robbins, Thomas, and Susan J. Palmer, eds. *Millennium, Messiahs, and Mayhem: Contemporary Apocalyptic Movements.* New York, 1997. Collection of excellent articles by experts on diverse contemporary millennial movements.

Rosenfeld, Jean. E. "Pai Marire: Peace and Violence in a New Zealand Millenarian Tradition." *Terrorism and Political Violence* 7, no. 3 (1995): 83–108. Discusses the factors involved in the different phases of the Pai Marire movement among the Maori.

Salter, Richard. "Time, Authority, and Ethics in the Khmer Rouge: Elements of the Millennial Vision in Year Zero." In *Millennialism, Persecution, and Violence: Historical Cases,* edited by Catherine Wessinger, pp. 281–298. Syracuse, N.Y., 2000. Demonstrates continuities of Khmer Rouge Communism with Cambodian Buddhism.

Stein, Stephen J. *The Shaker Experience in America.* New Haven, Conn., 1992. The definitive history of the Shakers.

Stone, Jacqueline. "Japanese *Lotus* Millennialism: From Militant Nationalism to Contemporary Peace Movements." In *Millennialism, Persecution, and Violence: Historical Cases,* edited by Catherine Wessinger, pp. 261–280. Syracuse, N.Y., 2000. Discusses Buddhist millennial contributions to the Japanese war effort in World War II, and the subsequent shift by many to pacifism after the defeat.

Thompson, Damian. "A Peruvian Messiah and the Retreat from Apocalypse." In *Christian Millenarianism: From the Early Church to Waco,* edited by Stephen Hunt, pp. 187–195. Bloomington, Ind., 2001. This study of the Israelites of the New Universal Covenant discusses how their messiah is abandoning predictions of the end of the world as the group is successful in establishing its community.

Van Zandt, David E. "The Children of God." In *America's Alternative Religions,* edited by Timothy Miller, pp. 127–132. Albany, N.Y., 1995. Solid discussion of the controversial millennial religion also known as the Family.

Wallace, Anthony F. C. "Revitalization Movements." *American Anthropologist* 58, no. 2 (1956): 264–281. Classic article introducing the term "revitalization movement" as "a deliberate, organized, conscious effort by members of a society to construct a more satisfying culture" (265). Most of the examples used by Wallace are what have come to be termed "nativist movements" or "nativist millennial movements."

Wessinger, Catherine Lowman. *Annie Besant and Progressive Messianism.* Lewiston, N.Y., 1988. Study of Annie Besant's Theosophical progressive millennialism, which culminated in her creation of a messianic movement centered on J. Krishnamurti.

Wessinger, Catherine. "Millennialism with and without the Mayhem." In *Millennium, Messiahs, and Mayhem: Contemporary Apocalyptic Movements,* edited by Thomas Robbins and Susan J. Palmer, pp. 47–59. New York, 1997. Proposes the categories "catastrophic millennialism" and "progressive millennialism" as being more conducive to promoting the study of millennial phenomena in diverse religious traditions as opposed to the categories applicable only to Christianity, "premillennialism" and post-millennialism.

Wessinger, Catherine, ed. *Millennialism, Persecution, and Violence: Historical Cases.* Syracuse, N.Y., 2000. Cross-cultural study of cases of millennial groups involved in violence, including assaulted millennial groups, fragile millennial groups, and revolutionary millennial movements.

Wessinger, Catherine. *How the Millennium Comes Violently: From Jonestown to Heaven's Gate.* New York, 2000. Compares case studies of Jonestown, Branch Davidians, Aum Shinrikyō, the Montana Freemen, Solar Temple, Heaven's Gate, and Chen Tao, to discern dynamics that involve millennial groups in violence.

Wessinger, Catherine. "New Religious Movements and Conflicts with Law Enforcement." In *New Religious Movements and Religious Liberty in America,* edited by Derek Davis and Barry Hankins, pp. 89–106, 201–204. 2nd ed. Waco, Tex., 2003. Proposes relevant factors and categories for use when evaluating situations involving millennial groups for the potential for volatility, and makes recommendations to law enforcement agents about how best to deal with such cases.

Wojcik, Daniel. *The End of the World as We Know It: Faith, Fatalism, and Apocalypse in America.* New York, 1997. A folklorist's detailed approach to the study of the varieties of millennialism in America. Movements discussed include Christian Dispensationalism, the Bayside apparitions, Punk, and UFO millennialism. Among the book's many insights is that there are currently secular, fatalistic, and nonredemptive apocalyptic expressions, particularly in response to the nuclear age.

Zablocki, Benjamin D. "Exit Cost Analysis: A New Approach to the Scientific Study of Brainwashing." *Nova Religio: The Journal of Alternative and Emergent Religions* 1, no. 2 (1998): 216–249. Introduces the concept of high "exit costs" as being a barrier to people choosing to leave unconventional religious groups in an article seeking to rehabilitate the brainwashing theory.

CATHERINE WESSINGER (2005)

NEW RELIGIOUS MOVEMENTS: NEW RELIGIOUS MOVEMENTS AND VIOLENCE

The study of religion and violence has largely centered on established traditions, given the long history of religiously inspired wars, crusades, witch-hunts, and persecutions around the world. Contemporary cases include, for example, Protestant-Catholic violence in Northern Ireland, Israeli-Palestinian violence in the Middle East, and Hindu-Muslim violence in India. The appearance of a cohort of new religious movements, popularly called *cults*, in the early 1970s triggered renewed scholarly and public policy concern with the religion-violence connection. There were ongoing, largely unfounded allegations of impending violence by new religious groups during the early 1970s. However, it was the 1978 conflict between the Peoples Temple and its opponents, resulting in the deaths of 914 individuals in Jonestown, Guyana, that raised scholarly and public policy concerns about potential violent episodes involving new religions.

The Peoples Temple episode was followed by four incidents during the 1990s: the death of eighty people during the conflict between federal agents and the Branch Davidians at their residence outside of Waco, Texas, in 1993; the murders-suicides of seventy-five members of the Solar Temple in Switzerland and Quebec in 1994, 1996, and 1997; the murders by members of Aum Shinrikyō of thirty-one members and opponents, as well as a dozen other innocent subway passengers in Tokyo in 1995; and the collective suicide of thirty-nine members of Heaven's Gate in California in 1997. There was also a major episode in Uganda in 2000 in which approximately 780 members of the Movement for the Restoration of the Ten Commandments of God were murdered or committed suicide. Relatively little is known about this incident, however, because of its remote location and a lack of systematic investigation. This entry will focus on the three cases of collective violence that have occurred since the 1970s in North America and Europe.

THE VIOLENCE AND NEW RELIGIONS CONNECTION. New religious movements have encountered intense opposition from some established religions (the countercult movement) and family based organizations (the anticult movement). Referred to as *cults* by both sets of oppositional groups, new religions have often been characterized as dangerously unstable and predisposed to violence. This global assertion of a proclivity of new religions for violence, however, has not stood the test of close scrutiny.

One problem in linking new religions to violence is that distinguishing new religious movements from established religions is more complex than it first appears. Most new religions are not entirely novel. Rather, most have borrowed both cultural and organizational elements from established traditions, and many different traditions are represented. For example, the International Society for Krishna Consciousness (Hare Krishnas) is a sectarian Hindu movement; Aum Shinrikyō draws on the Buddhist tradition; the Branch Davidians are one of a myriad of schismatic offshoots of Seventh-day Adventism; the Family (Children of God) grew out of the Jesus People movement; and Heaven's Gate blended the Christian and UFO traditions. This means that far from being a homogeneous set of movements that can be contrasted to established traditions, as conveyed by the term *cults*, new religious movements are diverse in doctrines, practices, and organization.

There have been a few historical cases of violence by religious movements in North America, such as the nineteenth-century attacks by Mormons on pioneers passing through Mountain Meadows, Utah. Contemporary instances would include the 1970s murders during a power struggle by Ervil Le Baron's polygamist Church of the Lamb of God, and the Nation of Islam's murders of leaders of rival Muslim organizations, also in the 1970s. However, these incidents have been rare. The more common occurrence has been violence *against* minority religious groups. The public hanging of Quakers in New England during the 1660s and the 1890 assault on a Lakota Sioux band at Wounded Knee by federal troops are well-documented incidents.

Violence by contemporary new religions also appears to be rare. There are currently over two thousand religious groups now functioning in the United States, and half of these were established since 1960. If all groups that incorporate religious qualities are included, such as many New Age groups, then the numbers are far higher. However, since the 1970s fewer than two dozen groups have been involved in incidents of homicide or suicide resulting in multiple deaths. By contrast, there have been numerous cases in which members of new religious groups have been the targets of abduction, armed attacks, and provocative police actions. In virtually all of these cases, movements have responded by initiating civil and criminal judicial proceedings rather than physical reprisal.

Finally, incidents of violence involving new religions have appeared to be more numerous than they actually are. When individuals affiliated with new religions are involved in violent acts, as either perpetrators or victims, these acts are much more newsworthy and more likely to be connected to their religious tradition than is the case for members of conventional faiths. Further, unsubstantiated rumors of impending violence by new religions receive widespread press coverage, while disconfirmation is rarely reported. Allegations of imminent mass suicide in 1988 by Chen Tao, a Taiwanese millennial group located in Texas at the time, and the Colorado-based Concerned Christians, who were expelled from Israel in 1999, were cases of this kind. The aggregation of all types of violence involving members of new religions, attributions of acts to "cultic" qualities, and the high-profile publicizing of rumors and incidents has created the impression of pervasive violence. It certainly is true that, by contrast, mainline denominations in Western societies currently are not in active resistance to established social institutions. However, many denominations have relatively stormy histories, and fringe elements of these traditions have countenanced or perpetrated violence over such issues as racial integration, abortion, and centralized governmental authority.

EXPLANATIONS OF VIOLENCE INVOLVING NEW RELIGIOUS MOVEMENTS. Given assertions of a proclivity to violence by new religions, the five major episodes of collective violence that occurred between 1993 and 2000 produced an impetus to investigate the relationship between new religions and violence. The result has been theoretical explorations of specific factors thought to be linked to violence, as well as general models that propose sets of factors that, in combination, yield violent outcomes. A central concern in both types of explanation has been the extent to which violent episodes are the product of the internal organization of the religious movements involved, external pressures, and interaction between movements and societal control agencies. There is vigorous ongoing debate over this issue.

Single-factor explanations. Three potentially causal factors have been identified in violent episodes involving new religious groups: ideology, leadership, and organizational structure. It has been hypothesized that groups with millennial/apocalyptic belief systems might be more violence prone because they reject established social institutions, have limited commitment to institutional normative proscriptions, and have dualistic worldviews that expect conflict. However, numerous conservative Christian denominations, such as the Seventh-day Adventists and Jehovah's Witnesses, hold millennial/apocalyptic beliefs, and there is no evidence that such denominations are predisposed to violence. Although millennialism and apocalypticism probably do not predict violence, there is continuing exploration of the possible connection of specific forms of millennialism and violence. Millennial belief systems in which humans are depicted as playing a major role in setting the stage for divine intervention tend to have a gradualist orientation, with decisive events set some time in the future. The result may be less group volatility and a less confrontational stance. By contrast, belief systems that define the existing social order as morally unredeemable and predict its imminent, catastrophic destruction are more likely to produce a polarized relationship between movement and society. Under these conditions, societal control initiatives may be taken as confirmation of societal intractability and a sign of the impending apocalypse.

Two elements of movement organization have been postulated as predictive of violence, charismatic leadership and totalistic organization. Many new movements begin with a charismatic leader and a few dozen followers. (A charismatic leader is one who is believed to have access to an unseen source of authority, such as revelation.) Charismatic leadership has been characterized as problematic because it is a less stable, noninstitutionalized form in which the personal volatility of the prophet or messiah can have a substantial impact on a group. When leaders claim or are granted extraordinary spiritual status, they are likely to have enormous influence over a movement's functioning and development. Therefore, there has been speculation that charismatic leadership predisposes those groups to violence. However, there are numerous highly charismatic religious leaders (e.g., Billy Graham, Martin Luther King, Oral Roberts) who have shown no proclivity to violence.

A more useful approach may be to examine how charismatic leadership is organized. Certain attributes of charismatic leadership may contribute to movement volatility. Many movement leaders withdraw from followers at some point to preserve an aura of mystery that is critical to their power. This can result in isolation and an inability to obtain appropriate feedback from both inside and outside the movement, which can lead to extreme decisions. The overidentification of followers with a leader can lead to a sense of threat throughout the movement if the leader is denounced by outsiders or former members. In such instances, there may well be an escalation of tension. Charismatic leaders may resist the development of more institutionalized forms of movement governance in order to preserve personal power. They may employ a variety of tactics—changing doctrines, increasing demands for personal sacrifice and loyalty, creating crises, suppressing dissent—in order to render followers more dependent on their personal authority. Such tactics can increase instability in movements and create the potential for extreme actions.

While such factors as specific forms of organization and leadership are useful in explaining violence, it is likely that combinations of factors will be more predictive of violent episodes. For that reason, several general models have been developed that attempt to specify sets of factors, and interactions among, them that are associated with the outbreak of violence.

General models of movement-society violence. Three general explanatory models have been proposed to account for violence involving new religious movements. All three are concerned with the combination of factors that produces violent episodes, and with the issue of whether these factors constitute movement or external-control agency precipitation of violence. Marc Galanter's model, developed in *Cults: Faith, Healing, and Coercion* (1999), stresses internal factors; the

John Hall, Philip Schuyler, and Silvaine Trinh model detailed in *Apocalypse Observed: Religious Movements, the Social Order, and Violence in North America, Europe, and Japan* (2000) emphasizes external factors; and David Bromley's model, outlined in *Cults, Religion, and Violence* (2002), allows for a preponderance of either internal or external factors.

Galanter analyzes the Peoples Temple, Branch Davidian, Aum Shinrikyō, and Heaven's Gate cases. He concludes that these episodes contain four conditions in common: group isolation, leader grandiosity and paranoia, absolute dominion, and governmental mismanagement. Isolation can lead to extreme actions because groups reduce the possibility of external feedback to their actions and operate solely on the basis of internally constructed definitions of events. Movements can isolate themselves from conventional society either through geographic separation or constant mobility. Galanter argues that another dynamic in violent episodes is the need of the leader or leaders to maintain absolute control, which can produce paranoid fears that others inside or outside the movement will usurp their power. In order to protect their positions, leaders create a siege mentality within the group in order to maintain solidarity and loyalty. Movements may also exercise centripetal control mechanisms that closely regulate members' lives, leading to absolute domination of the thoughts and behavior of individuals. Finally, governmental mismanagement refers to the failure of government agencies to immediately control illicit activity and to prevent young adults from being enticed into these movements. In the Galanter model, then, all of the factors except governmental mismanagement refer to attributes of movements, and the one external factor specifies government inaction rather than overreaction.

Hall, Schuyler, and Trinh base their analysis on the Peoples Temple, Branch Davidian, Aum Shinrikyō, Solar Temple, and Heaven's Gate cases. They identify a number of movement characteristics that may create a proclivity toward violence: an apocalyptic worldview, charismatic leadership, a high level of internal control, and high internal solidarity or isolation from conventional society. However, it is not these characteristics in themselves that result in conflict, but rather the interaction between the movement and society. According to Hall, Schuyler, and Trinh, conflict is likely to move in one of two directions. A "warring apocalypse of religious conflict" describes a situation in which conflict escalates between a movement and a coalition of movement opponents, governmental agencies, and media representatives. The second type—a "mystical apocalypse of deathly transcendence"—involves flight from external opposition. In this case, the group elects collective suicide and, from the groups' perspective, moves to another realm of existence. The Hall, Schuyler, and Trinh model thus emphasizes movement-societal conflict in which movements respond to external opposition.

In his analysis of the Peoples Temple, Branch Davidian, Aum Shinrikyō, Solar Temple, and Heaven's Gate episodes, Bromley argues that movement-society conflicts develop through three stages: latent tension, nascent conflict, and intensified conflict. Most conflicts do not reach an intensified level because all parties have the option of contestation, accommodation, or retreat. In most cases conflict is resolved at a lower level. At the intensified level, the movement and its opponents engage in heightened mobilization and radicalization; coalitions of allies and opponents form, and parties mutually begin to define one another as dangerous rather than merely troublesome. When conflict reaches the intensified stage, what Bromley terms "dramatic denouements" occur.

Dramatic denouements are climactic moments when the movement, society, or both conclude that the requisite conditions for their existence are being subverted. The parties to the conflict polarize as they engage in threatening actions, symbolic degradation of opponents, and internal radicalization. The conflict relationship destabilizes as a result of secrecy of actions, elimination of mediating third parties, and organizational consolidation or fragmentation. With polarization and conflict destabilization, one or both parties embark on a project of final reckoning that is intended to reestablish appropriate moral order. The most likely projects are either "exodus" (collective withdrawal from the realm in which the conflict is taking place) or "battle," in which the initiating party rejects the prospect of mutual existence and seeks to restore appropriate moral order through coercion. Each of these two responses is thus premised on a position of moral superiority and on a repudiation of continued mutual existence in the same social space. In the Bromley model, violent episodes are clearly interactional, and either the religious movement or societal units may precipitate a dramatic denouement.

CASE STUDIES OF VIOLENT EPISODES. One of the central issues in the study of violent episodes involving new religious movements has been whether these episodes are the product of movement characteristics, external provocation, or the nature of interaction between the movement and control agencies. While there is debate over this issue, there is broad agreement that cases vary on this dimension. Of the major episodes of violence during the 1990s that have been studied in depth, the Branch Davidian case is the most likely to be attributed to external provocation, the Solar Temple case to mixed internal and external factors, and the Heaven's Gate incident to primarily internal dynamics.

The Branch Davidian episode. The Branch Davidians began in 1929 as a schismatic offshoot of Seventh-day Adventism and existed for more than fifty years in relative obscurity before the arrival of David Koresh (1959–1993). The community was in disarray when Koresh assumed leadership; he rebuilt the group's economic and membership bases and enhanced his spiritual authority by pronouncing himself an heir to the biblical King David. His divinely ordained errand was to interpret the seven seals contained in the New Testament *Book of Revelation* and to reveal the sequence of imminent endtime events. Under Koresh's leadership the Branch Davidian community became more tightly organized, communal, and hierarchical (earlier Davidians lived in a community but not communally). There were heightened expectations of an imminent apocalypse, which the Branch Davidians believed would begin with an attack on their group.

While the Branch Davidians were characterized by a high level of charismatic authority, communal organization, and apocalyptic expectation, it was Koresh's "new light" doctrine, proclaimed in 1989, that was pivotal in mobilizing opposition. Koresh taught that he must father children with women in the community to create a new spiritual lineage; the children born of these unions would erect the House of David and ultimately rule the world. Some of the members Koresh selected for his House of David were wives and daughters of members, and some of the daughters were legally minors. The result was a number of defections, as well as legal grounds for external intervention by Texas Child Protective Services. Beginning in 1989 a coalition of Koresh opponents formed, including family members concerned about the children's welfare, some of Koresh's past sexual partners who were hostile to the House of David, and apostate members. This coalition appealed to the media and a number of state and federal agencies, most notably the Texas Child Protective Services, the federal Bureau of Alcohol, Tobacco, and Firearms (ATF), and the Federal Bureau of Investigation (FBI).

There were two sources of tension that escalated the conflict. Koresh's sexual relationships with teenage girls constituted a direct challenge to the child-abuse protection mandate of the Texas Child Protective Services. The agency's frustration mounted when it was unable to document abuse through inspections and investigations. The ATF suspected the Branch Davidians were involved in weapons violations and placed an undercover agent in the group, whose identity was soon discovered. Several factors contributed to the ATF's decision to conduct a raid on the Branch Davidian community at Mount Carmel, near Waco. The bureau was concerned about weapons violations, but it was also seeking high-profile interventions to fend off efforts to reduce its budget and reorganize its structure. Furthermore, the oppositional coalition fed the ATF false information about drug manufacturing at the residence, widespread child abuse, and potential mass suicide.

After the initial AFT raid on February 28, 1993, in which there were both Branch Davidian and AFT casualties, the FBI assumed control of the situation. The conflict was now highly polarized because law enforcement officers had been killed, and because the Branch Davidians interpreted the ATF raid as the beginning of the apocalypse. As the standoff between the Branch Davidians and the FBI continued, tactical units of the FBI gained the upper hand over the negotiating teams and initiated psychological warfare, which included cutting off utilities, surrounding the residence with armored vehicles, and flooding the residence with noise and light around the clock. During the standoff, Koresh led the Branch Davidians in seeking divine instruction on the proper course to follow. Ultimately, federal agents perceived, probably incorrectly, that neither conciliation nor duress would succeed and that continued flouting of legitimate authority could not be tolerated. A CS (tear) gas assault on the residence was launched on April 19; seventy-four residents, including twenty-three children, died in ensuing the fire.

The Solar Temple episode. The Order of the Solar Temple (abbreviated OTS from the French form of the name, Ordre du Temple Solaire) is one of a number of religious movements drawing on Western esotericism, including Rosicrucianism (a mythical, ancient brotherhood) and the Knights Templar movements (groups claiming an association with the Catholic religious order suppressed in the fourteenth century). The Order of the Solar Temple was founded by Joseph Di Mambro (1924–1994), a Swiss jeweler. Di Mambro had previously been involved in a variety of contemporary esoteric groups, such as the Golden Way Foundation, before establishing the Solar Temple in 1981 with Dr. Luc Jouret (1947–1994). The charismatic Jouret added to Di Mambro's esoteric teachings a mix of homeopathic medicine, New Age spirituality, and environmental apocalypticism. His personal charm also attracted large audiences of well-educated and prosperous individuals to his public lectures in Europe, the Caribbean, and Canada. The OTS was a highly secretive organization. Di Mambro and Jouret established two public groups, the Amenta Club and Arcadia Club that served as recruiting organizations for the OTS. Members of the Solar Temple engaged in secret initiations, vows of secrecy, and encounters in hidden ritual chambers with the spiritual manifestations of a mysterious group of ascended "Masters."

Based on its apocalyptic expectations, the OTS began expanding into North America in the mid-1980s. The group established its headquarters and a commune in Quebec, a location deemed to be relatively safe against impending environmental catastrophes. By 1989, OTS had about five hundred members in Europe and North America. In the early 1990s, due to opposition, the group's outlook became increasingly bleak and apocalyptic, and group leaders began discussing a mystical "transit" to another realm of existence. Leadership authority and member commitment were both heightened. For example, leaders assumed authority for arranging "cosmic marriages" that restructured members' existing marital relationships.

The movement's public troubles began early in the 1990s when two members were arrested for purchasing illegal weapons for unknown reasons, a rift developed between Jouret and Di Mambro, and the movement's ability to recruit members plummeted as its apocalyptic message was publicly revealed. Even more threatening were a series of defections by members who threatened to expose financial irregularities by leaders. The technician who orchestrated the electronic special effects used to create the appearances of the Masters left the movement, and revelations that the Masters' appearances had been carefully orchestrated illusions undermined the commitment of members. A wife who had lost her spouse to a cosmic marriage took her complaints to the media and anticult groups. In addition, the police mistakenly connected the OTS to anonymous threats made to the life of the Quebec minister of public security and several parliamentary deputies, resulting in an intensive investigation of the movement. As a result of these developments, the loyalty of members was eroded, the authority of the OTS leaders was undermined, and the financial base was endangered. OTS leaders concluded that the movement was the object of a vast conspiracy and faced the prospect of public disgrace. The group was, therefore, confronting both internal and external sources of destabilization.

Late in 1993 and early in 1994 the final events appear to have begun coalescing. OTS leaders began planning an interstellar "transit" that they believed would be supported and protected by transcendent powers. In early October, many current and past members of the group were invited to meet in Switzerland. Some were aware that the meeting was to be a time of reckoning and initiation of a transit, others were not. On October 4, 1994, police began receiving reports of fires in Cheiry and Granges-sur-Salvan in Switzerland and Morin Heights in Canada. Ultimately, fifty-three members and former members of the OTS were found dead from stabbing, gunshots, poisoning, or suffocation. Opponents and former members who were viewed as traitors appear to have been executed. Some OTS members and leaders took their own lives to initiate the transit, and other members who lacked the courage to take their own lives apparently were "helped" to undertake the transit. The group left messages intended to condemn its critics and defend its own vision of its mission. More than one year later sixteen OTS members decided to join their comrades and ritualistically took their own lives in France; five more did the same in Quebec in 1997.

The Heaven's Gate episode. The movement that came to be known as Heaven's Gate began as a spiritual quest by Marshall Herff Applewhite (1931–1997) and Bonnie Lu Nettles (1924–1985) in 1973. Over the next two years a loosely organized movement emerged. Applewhite and Nettles first began referring to themselves as the "two witnesses" in the *Book of Revelation* who would be martyred and then ascend to heaven in a cloud, which they believed would actually be a space ship. They taught their small group of followers that members of the "Next Level" had created earth as an experiment in evolution. Jesus' mission had been to gather the faithful on earth to ascend to the Next Level, but humans were not yet prepared. However, humans would soon be transported by spacecraft to the kingdom of heaven and live eternally as androgynous beings. Through vigorous proselytizing, the group gradually grew to more than two hundred members by the mid-1970s. Recruitment successes resulted in opposition to the conversions and unflattering media coverage. In response, the group went underground in 1976 and lived a migratory communal existence with a much smaller number of members. Members prepared for life at the Next Level by relinquishing all earthly habits and relationships and acquiring appropriate Next Level attributes.

Because the group lived a secretive lifestyle, it largely escaped conflict with control agencies. Members were apprehensive about their own fate following the conflagration that destroyed the Branch Davidians, and they harbored unsubstantiated suspicions that they were under police surveillance. However, the only reaction by Heaven's Gate to suspected opposition was a largely ineffectual campaign to challenge what it regarded as misinformation and misconceptions about the movement. The developments that moved Heaven's Gate toward a "transit" to the Next Level were primarily internal in nature. In 1985 Nettles died of cancer. Her death brought into question the movement's belief that entry to the Next Level would be achieved with a corporeal body. The group then came to regard the human "vehicle" as simply a "container" that could be jettisoned, a development that made it possible to think about abandoning earthly bodies. The movement's ideology also became more apocalyptic as members proposed the existence of evil space aliens who used religion and sexuality to keep humans in bondage. Indeed, when the group was unsuccessful in eliminating sexual desire, some members arranged their own castrations to resolve the problem. Finally, members progressively replaced earthly social forms with those they understood to be appropriate to the Next Level. They lived their day-to-day lives as an "Away Team" in a replica of the spacecraft environment through which they would be transported to the Next Level. Much of their time was spent attempting to connect with the Next Level and learn the timing of their impending transit.

As the process of distancing from conventional society continued, the movement gradually was left with a small number of long-term members with little connection to outsiders. Applewhite, who was the source of the group's revelations, believed he was suffering from progressively declining health. Increasingly disillusioned with conventional society, the movement initiated one final effort to publicize its message and warn outsiders of the apocalypse that awaited them. When this campaign was met with indifference and ridicule, the group concluded that their preparation for the exit was over. The appearance of the Hale Bopp comet in 1997 was viewed as a sign that the moment for departure had arrived, and members quickly prepared for the exit. Those who made the exit on March 22 to 24, 1997, regarded their act as a demonstration of the power of Heaven's Gate to transcend the apocalypse that awaited those who had chosen not to join them. The members consumed a deadly combination of alcohol and barbiturates, lay down dressed in their Away Team uniforms covered by purple shrouds, and tied plastic bags over their heads. Two more Heaven's Gate members attempted an exit on May 7, 1997; one succeeded and the other was revived. This member, Chuck Humphrey, after distributing informational materials about Heaven's Gate, made his exit in February 1998.

CONCLUSIONS. The series of unrelated violent episodes involving new religious movements during the 1990s propelled violence onto the scholarly and public policy agendas. Widely accepted assertions about a proclivity for violence by new religions have not been supported, however, and the historical evidence indicates that instances of movement-precipitated violence have been rare. Specific characteristics of religious movements—apocalyptic ideology, charismatic leadership, and totalistic organization—are significant in understanding the likelihood of violence, but general models that incorporate an interrelated set of factors are more promising. A major debate continues over what balance of internal and external factors is most useful in understanding violent incidents. There is general agreement that cases vary in their internal-external causation, and that useful models must allow for this diversity. There is also agreement that future episodes will be difficult to anticipate because they tend to involve small, relatively unknown groups rather than more visible groups that are in open conflict with conventional society.

SEE ALSO Anticult Movements; Aum Shinrikyō; Branch Davidians; Deprogramming; Heaven's Gate; Jonestown and Peoples Temple; Koresh, David; Movement for the Restoration of the Ten Commandments of God; Temple Solaire; Violence.

BIBLIOGRAPHY

Bromley, David G., and J. Gordon Melton, eds. *Cults, Religion, and Violence.* Cambridge, U.K., 2002. A collection of essays focused on the major episodes of collective violence involving new religious groups during the 1990s.

Galanter, Marc. *Cults: Faith, Healing, and Coercion.* 2d ed. New York, 1999. A theoretical analysis of a number of charismatic groups that includes a discussion of internal movement factors conducive to collective violence.

Hall, John R. *Gone from the Promised Land: Jonestown in American Cultural History.* New Brunswick, N.J., 1987. A thorough sociological and historical account of the Peoples Temple.

Hall, John R., with Philip Schuyler, and Silvaine Trinh. *Apocalypse Observed: Religious Movements, the Social Order, and Violence in North America, Europe, and Japan.* New York, 2000. A theoretically informed series of case studies of collective violence involving new religious groups that proposes a model for connecting these diverse events.

Lifton, Robert Jay. *Destroying the World to Save It: Aum Shinrikyō, Apocalyptic Violence, and the New Global Terrorism.* New York, 1999. A more psychologically oriented analysis of one of the major episodes of collective violence involving new religious groups during the 1990s.

Reader, Ian. *Religious Violence in Contemporary Japan: The Case of Aum Shinrikyō.* Richmond, U.K., and Honolulu, 2000. An account of the Aum Shinrikyō violence episode that emphasizes internal movement factors as the initial source of violence.

Richardson, James T. "Minority Religions and the Context of Violence: A Conflict/Interactionist Perspective." *Terrorism and Political Violence* 13, no. 1 (2001): 103–133.

Robbins, Thomas, and Susan J. Palmer, eds. *Millennium, Messiahs, and Mayhem: Contemporary Apocalyptic Movements.* New York, 1997. A collection of essays examining apocalypticism in a variety of religious traditions.

Tabor, James D., and Eugene V. Gallagher. *Why Waco? Cults and the Battle for Religious Freedom in America.* Berkeley, 1995. A comprehensive analysis of the history of the Branch Davidians and the dynamics of the confrontation between the movement and federal authorities.

Wessinger, Catherine. "New Religious Movements and Conflicts with Law Enforcement." In *New Religious Movements and Religious Liberty in American,* edited by Derek H. Davis and Barry Hankins, 2d ed., pp. 89–106, 201–204. Waco, Tex., 2002.

Wessinger, Catherine, ed. *How the Millennium Comes Violently: From Jonestown to Heaven's Gate.* New York, 2000. An analysis of Peoples Temple, Branch Davidian, Aum Shinrikyō, Montana Freemen, Solar Temple, and Heaven's Gate violence episodes emphasizing the role of both internal and external factors in precipitating violence.

Wessinger, Catherine, ed. *Millennialism, Persecution, and Violence: Historical Cases.* Syracuse, N.Y., 2000. Includes articles by Michelene Pesantubbee on Wounded Knee, Massimo Introvigne on Solar Temple, Grant Underwood on the Mormons, among others, plus Wessinger's introduction, "The Interacting Dynamics of Millennialism, Persecution, and Violence."

Wright, Stuart, ed. *Armageddon in Waco: Critical Perspectives on the Branch Davidian Conflict.* Chicago, 2000. A collection of essays thoroughly analyzing the Branch Davidian violence episode, including the role of the media, government agencies, experts and consultants, and movement opponents.

DAVID G. BROMLEY (2005)

NEW RELIGIOUS MOVEMENTS: NEW RELIGIOUS MOVEMENTS IN THE UNITED STATES

Shortly after the adoption of the U.S. Constitution in 1788, the new nation ratified a Bill of Rights whose first order of business was freedom of religion. The First Amendment laid down what was then a bold precept: the United States would have no established, or officially endorsed, religion, and it would permit the free exercise of religion. More than two centuries later more religions are being freely exercised than the nation's founders could possibly have anticipated. Every substantial religion in the world has an American manifestation, and many homegrown startups have appeared in the United States. It is safe to say that no place in the world has greater religious diversity than the United States at the dawn of the twenty-first century.

TERMINOLOGY. One small but vital part of that diversity consists of what are variously known by dozens of labels—

sects, cults, new religious movements, alternative religions, marginal religions, and many more. Among scholars specializing in the study of such groups, the prevailing label is *new religious movements* (NRMs), although not all are happy with this term. It has one notable flaw: most of the groups included in the category are not new. Some, in fact, are thousands of years old. But new religious movements has been used more widely than any other nonpejorative term, and it does a good job of conveying the subject to most people.

Sect and *cult* are terms that were once used with a fair degree of academic precision. Classically a sect is a splinter group, a movement that has split from an existing religious body for some reason. Often such groups see themselves as revitalization movements that seek to return to a pristine purity from which, it is believed, the parent group has departed. The Holiness movement, for example, began when some Methodists came to believe that their church had undergone a degree of liberalization that took it unacceptably far from its Wesleyan roots, and the dissenters set up new churches that they saw as restoring pure Methodist doctrine. A cult, on the other hand, is classically a more distinct group—one that does not have clear roots in an existing, well-established tradition. A cult may be a newly created religion, usually one formulated by a founding prophet of some kind, or it may be a religion that is simply unfamiliar (and in that sense "new") in the American context. Some Hindu movements that have come to the United States, for example, have been widely regarded as cults because they are not familiar to Americans, even though they would be part of the religious mainstream in India.

These once-precise terms, however, became pejoratives in the last decades of the twentieth century. The word *cult,* especially in popular usage, is decidedly negative in tone. A cult is regarded as somehow evil or at least misguided. At all costs one should avoid cults, which are popularly understood to be grasping and deceiving, trying to catch newcomers in their webs. The neutral descriptive term of earlier times has changed, just as the word *gay* has evolved, for the most part, from meaning "happy" to meaning "homosexual." The case is less severe with the word sect, at least in the United States, but it too tends to have a pejorative edge. In Europe sect is the equivalent of the American cult—a term that carries strong derogatory implications.

Academic scholars of new religions therefore generally shy away from using both sect and cult. Lacking consensus support for any other term, they generally speak of new religious movements. *Alternative religions* is also used by some, and other terms, such as the adjective *nonmainstream,* have their advocates as well. Although those terms have the advantage of not containing the word *new,* new religious movements is the generally accepted nonpejorative term.

What constitutes a new religious movement? Matters of definition are exceedingly thorny, but this entry seeks to survey a wide range of nonmainstream religions and will cast its net broadly. This entry will presume that there is an American religious mainstream that consists of the major, culturally well-established branches of Christianity and Judaism, including Roman Catholicism, Eastern Orthodoxy, mainline Protestantism, most evangelical Protestantism, and the three major branches of Judaism (Orthodox, Conservative, and Reform). New religious movements are groups outside that mainstream. Admittedly there are many shades of gray in such a definition, but living with ambiguity is essential to any study of religion.

One might argue that groups derived from great world religions, all of which are present in the United States, should not be regarded as NRMs. The point of their inclusion in that category is simply that in the United States they do not have the long histories, cultural dominance, and (usually) large numbers of adherents that the mainstream groups do. These NRMs may be growing substantially and may be in the process of moving into the mainstream, but in the eyes of most Americans they are not yet fully mainstream.

NRMs in American History. NRMs have always been a part of the American religious scene, and controversy has always surrounded them. Some of the earliest European settlers came to what is now the United States precisely because their dissenting forms of religion were not well accepted in their home cultures. These settlers may not have been devoted to religious freedom, however; in many cases they tried to make their own forms of Christianity dominant in their new provinces (the Puritans of New England are a dramatic example). Nevertheless religious dissent cropped up almost as soon as the pioneering settlers stepped off their ships. As early as 1627, when Thomas Morton (c. 1575–1647) erected a maypole for a May Day celebration, he was deported to England for recognizing a pagan holiday. A few years later the Puritan authorities of Boston attacked Samuel Gorton (c. 1592–1677) for "all manner of blasphemies," eventually forcing him from the colony. By the 1650s a new threat confronted the orthodox rulers of Massachusetts with the arrival of the Quakers. Adopting a series of ever more stringent laws, Massachusetts in 1658 made Quakerism a capital crime. Four Quakers were subsequently executed for their faith. The first Mennonites arrived later in the century; they were refugees from Europe, where they were persecuted for such distinctive beliefs as adult baptism, pacifism, and separation of church and state. Throughout the Mennonites' long history in the United States they have attracted controversy; in wartime especially they have been derided, and in some cases assaulted, for their refusal to perform military service.

By the eighteenth century adherents of dissenting religions were arriving on American shores with some regularity, and just as regularly they experienced persecution in a country whose devotion to religious liberty was less than perfect. In 1774 a small group of Shakers arrived under the leadership of Ann Lee (1736–1784), and eventually they opened a communal settlement in upstate New York. A 1780 convert, Valentine Rathbun, soon dropped out of the movement and accused the Shakers of deception and even, perhaps, what some would now call brainwashing. The Shakers received visitors joyfully, Rathbun wrote, feeding and lodging them readily. But after his departure from the group, he claimed it was all a ruse designed to create "absolute dependence" among members. Some years later the Shakers found themselves challenged by an even more formidable opponent, Mary Marshall Dyer (1780–1867), whose opposition to the group she had joined and then left became her life's work. Dyer's anti-Shaker polemics sounded like many anticult diatribes of the late twentieth century; among other things, she accused the movement of using mind control of a sort that amounted to hypnotism. In the twenty-first century the Shakers are best known for their classic furniture and exquisite villages, and the few surviving Shakers in Maine enjoy great admiration and support. Only with time—and perhaps with their steep decline in numbers—has their unusual religion become acceptable.

A similar situation obtained with the arrival of groups of radical German Pietists in the eighteenth and nineteenth centuries. The Pietists' dissent was founded in their critique of the state churches in their homeland, which they considered formal and cold. The dissenters became entangled in disputes with various German authorities and in several cases decided to depart for the New World, where, they thought, they could pursue their chosen way of life in peace. Levels of controversy surrounding them varied. Some Pietists, such as the group that became known as the Amana Society in Iowa, managed to live in relative isolation and to avoid endlessly antagonistic relationships with their neighbors. But others were not so lucky. The Harmony Society, for example, was caught up in the same kinds of disputes that had afflicted the Shakers. Arriving in the United States in 1804, the Harmonists founded communal villages in Pennsylvania and Indiana, where they experienced conflict repeatedly. Their practices of celibacy and community ownership of goods were suspect to the American majority. When a large group of members defected in 1832, they accused the Harmonist leader George Rapp (1757–1847) of being power mad and voraciously greedy. The lawsuits that dogged the Harmonists throughout their history typically made the kinds of charges that "cult" opponents have made more recently—mind control, coercive leadership, and misuse of funds. Although the Harmonist movement withstood the conflicts, it gradually declined after Rapp's death and died quietly in the early twentieth century, leaving behind, as did the Shakers, several charming museum villages.

Another religious movement that arose while the Shakers and Harmonists were flourishing had the dubious distinction of being arguably the most controversial religious group in American history. Founded in 1830, the Latter-day Saints, or Mormons, based their distinctive version of Christianity, which featured an unorthodox account of American history before Christopher Columbus, on revelations that the founder Joseph Smith Jr. (1805–1844) claimed to have received. No religious group in American history has suffered more persecution than the Mormons; for nearly a century they were widely derided as devious outlaws and sexual miscreants. Conflicts with neighbors drove the early Mormons from New York State to Ohio, Missouri, Illinois, and finally to Utah after the lynching of the founder Smith in 1844. Ex-Mormons fanned the flames with stories of dictatorial theocracy, violence, and corruption among the Latter-day Saints. Although their practice of polygamy was not announced publicly until after the migration to Utah, it had been practiced for years. Such early Mormon leaders as Smith and his successor Brigham Young (1801–1877) each had dozens of plural wives. Word about the practice that leaked out provided sensational fuel for the anti-Mormon flames. Only with the passage of time did anti-Mormon agitation diminish. The Mormons, for their part, helped deprive their opponents of rhetorical ammunition by retreating from their most controversial ideas and practices. Polygamy was phased out in the late nineteenth century and early twentieth century, and a teaching that suggested that African Americans were inferior to whites was abandoned in 1978.

The Mormons were not the only religious believers to be attacked for their unconventional marital and sexual practices. The nineteenth century saw a proliferation of movements addressing all kinds of social reforms, and some of the more radical reformers promoted decidedly unconventional sexual arrangements. No group was more famous for its unorthodox marital philosophy than the Oneida Community, a body of Christian Perfectionists who created a long-lasting group marriage involving hundreds of men and women. Prosperous from businesses producing such commodities as animal traps and silverware, the Oneidans flourished from the early 1850s through the 1870s. Although internal tensions contributed to their eventual dissolution, it was vehement persecution by a variety of opponents that finally proved overwhelming. Perhaps the most striking part of the story is that a community publicly engaging in such wildly unconventional sexual arrangements managed to survive as long as it did in the Victorian-era United States.

In the 1830s and 1840s millennial excitement swept the country, especially with the rise of the Adventist movement of William Miller (1782–1849), who predicted that the world would come to an end soon, finally settling on October 22, 1844, as the apocalyptic date. Miller's movement was controversial, and in the wake of the failure of the world-ending events to happen on schedule (October 22, 1844, has ever since been known to the faithful as the "Great Disappointment"), several subsequent millennial groups coalesced. The Seventh-day Adventists began to take shape in the 1850s under Ellen White (1827–1915), who was regarded as a prophet and who had thousands of visionary experiences in her lifetime. The Adventists were distinctive not only for their ongoing anticipation of an imminent millennium but for observing the Jewish Sabbath and for a strong focus on diet and health.

In the 1870s another millennial group, eventually known as Jehovah's Witnesses, developed under the leadership of Charles Taze Russell (1852–1916), who, like Miller, undertook an extensive analysis of the Bible and concluded that he could predict the year of the final culmination—1914. Although Russell's chronology was obviously imprecise, his movement continued to grow long after the appointed date, eventually embracing millions worldwide. Controversy grew apace. The Witnesses' tireless door-to-door evangelism always had its detractors, and their refusal to salute the American flag (on the grounds that the flag salute was tantamount to idolatry) spawned legal cases that twice reached the U.S. Supreme Court (where their right not to salute the flag was upheld). Jehovah's Witnesses have consistently refused military service on grounds that their service must be to God, not to any earthly government. And much controversy has surrounded their refusal to accept blood transfusions, which they regard as a violation of the biblical injunction not to consume blood.

In 1848 two sisters, Kate Fox (c. 1839–1892) and Margaret Fox (c. 1833–1893), began hearing rapping noises that they said conveyed intelligible messages from a mysterious spirit being. Their apparent ability to exchange messages with an otherworldly being quickly attracted a wide following, and soon Spiritualism, as the movement became known, was a nationwide phenomenon with such manifestations as automatic writing, clairvoyance, and trance speaking. Eventually it became clear that many of the spiritual phenomena associated with devotees of the movement were fraudulent, and Spiritualism declined. It has remained a small but steady part of the alternative religious world, however, and new versions of it have emerged and found followings from time to time, as in the case of the *Urantia Book*, a huge tome purportedly dictated by spirit beings to an anonymous scribe in the 1930s. Many forms of Spiritualism are active at the beginning of the twenty-first century, and they remain as controversial as ever.

One form of Spiritualism went on to become a separate cluster of NRMs. Founded in 1875 and based on the teachings of Helena P. Blavatsky (1831–1891), Theosophy combined a belief in psychic communications from "masters" (spiritual adepts living in remote places) with what it called "ancient wisdom," teachings from various alternative Western traditions (such as Neoplatonism) as well as from Asian religions. Like its precursor Spiritualism, Theosophy had its detractors; especially heated were assertions that Blavatsky fabricated her supposed communications from the "masters of the wisdom," notably those that took the form of letters written on paper and appeared mysteriously in certain places. Although the movement splintered after the death of Blavatsky, many branches have survived, and Theosophy has become a well-established fixture in the firmament of NRMs.

At the end of the nineteenth century Hinduism and Buddhism got a boost in public visibility when both were represented by delegates to the World's Parliament of Religions at the Chicago World's Fair of 1893. Vivekananda (1863–1902), a bright young swami from the Ramakrishna order of India, stole the show at the parliament, demolishing stereotypes about Hinduism and offering a religion that was peaceful, tolerant, and charitable. He stayed in the United States for a time after the parliament and laid the groundwork for Vedanta Societies in major cities. It was the first Asian religious movement to have a substantial appeal to a non-Asian constituency in the United States. A few years later another swami, Yogananda (1893–1952), arrived with similarly expansive teachings and started the Self-Realization Fellowship, which became one of the largest Asian-based religions in the country. Several Buddhist teachers, like their Hindu counterparts, also began to attract non-Asian followers. The Asian teachers were decidedly out of the American mainstream, and for that, if nothing else, they had their critics, but their work formed a base for an ongoing Asian religious presence in the United States.

This list of NRMs in American history could be extended almost indefinitely. Inescapably new religions have been a part of the American landscape for hundreds of years. These groups have never been large, but they have constituted a steady minority presence within the realm of American religion, and they have always attracted critics.

AFTER 1965. Changes in the immigration laws that allowed spiritual teachers to enter the United States in much greater numbers than previously are frequently credited with the great surge in NRMs that erupted after 1965. Still the cultural upheaval that shook Western society during the same period had as much to do with the expansion of alternative religiosity as did the arrival of spiritual teachers from abroad. The cultural ferment of the 1960s era (actually the late 1960s and early 1970s) brought to prominence certain NRMs that had previously operated in relative obscurity, and the decade saw many more NRMs start up. New religions since 1965 have been enormously diverse, consisting of groups based in Asian religious traditions, new and unconventional versions of Christianity, movements claiming to restore ancient but forgotten traditions, and a few groups that seem largely unrelated to anything that has come before.

Scientology was on the scene as early as the 1950s, but its main growth took place in the last years of the twentieth century. Founded by the science fiction writer L. Ron Hubbard (1911–1986), Scientology promoted a kind of psychological therapy program in an unconventional religious context. The psychological analysis of practitioners was facilitated using a device known as the e-meter, a type of lie detector. The promises made to practitioners were nothing short of spectacular: one could, with enough work, become an optimal and enormously powerful human being. Whatever the truth of those claims, Scientology has received a great deal of criticism. It has operated largely on a fee-for-services basis (rather than by free-will offerings), and critics have accused the leaders of raking in enormous amounts of money. The authoritarian leadership style of Scientology and its overly vigorous response to its critics have also come under attack. Nevertheless the movement has attracted large numbers of followers, including entertainment and sports celebrities, and Scientology represents a major force among contemporary NRMs.

Another movement active in the United States before 1965, but only coming into prominence after that date, is the Unification Church. Sun Myung Moon (1920–) of Korea started this new religion, which blended elements of Christianity with various Asian religions, including traditional Korean shamanism, in 1954; five years later Moon's followers began to spread the Unification message in the United States. Central to Unification teachings is the precept of the restoration of the true church and of fallen humanity to their proper godliness. Moon himself is understood to play a messianic role in the process of restoration. The early American growth of the Unification Church was slow, but it reached prominence with a series of speaking tours that Moon undertook in the 1970s. As his visibility grew, so did controversy about his movement, which was accused of deceptive recruiting practices and exploitation of its young members. Deprogramming, the practice of forcibly removing an NRM member to a remote location and putting him or her through a deconversion process, was perhaps aimed at "Moonies" more than adherents of any other religious group. Controversy has lingered, although it has become muted as Moon has established ties to American political conservatives and has focused his work increasingly on other parts of the world, especially South America.

A quintessential new religion of the late 1960s counterculture was the International Society for Krishna Consciousness (ISKCON), commonly referred to as the Hare Krishna movement after its mantra (devotional chant). ISKCON's founder, Swami A. C. Bhaktivedanta (1896–1977), known to his followers as Prabhupada, undertook a mission to spread his form of Hinduism in the West and to that end arrived in the United States in 1965. Setting up headquarters in New York, Bhaktivedanta began to draw a variety of spiritual seekers to his work. Soon there were ISKCON temples in several American cities as well as farm communes and businesses supporting the movement and its members. To the public the ISKCON devotees were best known for *sankirtan* (public chanting and dancing in praise of Kṛṣṇa) and for selling books in public places, especially airports. Like Unificationists, they inspired spirited criticism, and some ISKCON members were subjected to deprogramming. After the death of Bhaktivedanta, the movement experienced tumultuous internal upheavals and scandals over problems ranging from venal leadership to child abuse. In the early twenty-first century small numbers of devotees continue to live the disciplined spiritual life that has long been the ISKCON hallmark.

One important component of the 1960s countercultural search for spiritual fulfillment was the rise of the Jesus Movement. The Jesus freaks, as the movement's adherents were popularly known, were young people who espoused evangelical Protestantism but retained the outer trappings (clothing and hairstyles, for example) of hippies. Although some of them were eventually absorbed into relatively conventional churches, others came together in new movements that reflected their cultural style and values. One of the most visible of the new groups, and certainly the most controversial, was the Children of God. Founded in 1967 as a coffeehouse ministry in Los Angeles by David Berg (1919–1994), a former Christian and Missionary Alliance pastor, the Children of God soon developed a distinctive evangelistic style that included wearing biblical robes and carrying signs warning of impending doom. By about 1970 members of the Children of God began to withdraw from contact with the outside world; most left the United States. The group's evangelization continued, however, and one new development was especially controversial—"flirty fishing," or the use of sex to attract new (usually male) converts. In the late 1980s members began to return to the United States and to reestablish a public presence there. Although accusations of misbehavior, including child abuse and sexual misconduct, have continued to be aimed at the Children of God (now known as the Family), over time they have dropped some of their most controversial practices and have moved closer to orthodox evangelical Protestantism. Their relatively liberal sexual attitudes, however, continue to be a major point of controversy.

Another NRM with roots in the Jesus Movement is the federation of Christian communities known as the Twelve Tribes. From enthusiastic beginnings in Chattanooga, Tennessee, in 1972 under the leadership of Elbert Eugene Spriggs (1937–), the movement in the early twenty-first century consisted of nearly three dozen communities, including several in South America, Europe, and Australia. Although spawned in the freewheeling environment of the American 1960s era, the Twelve Tribes has become a strongly disciplined movement with patriarchal leadership and strict child-rearing practices. Twelve Tribes communities are controversial in some locations, but they are becoming well established on the American religious scene.

Another spiritual path that has garnered wide appeal during and since the 1970s is earth-centered religiosity, most frequently known as Neopaganism or simply paganism. Much of the contemporary pagan movement—if it can be called a movement, given its diversity and lack of dominating organization—sees itself as re-creating the pre-Christian religions of Europe, especially northern Europe. Wiccans, or Witches, the best-known of the Neopagans, fall into that category. Other Neopagans look to ancient Egyptian or classical Roman and Greek religions for models. Whatever their specific orientations, most Neopagans incorporate into their beliefs and rituals a strong connection to the earth, fertility, and nature; not incidentally many Neopagans are also environmental activists. In addition they typically emphasize a recovery of feminine power and authority, which they believe was suppressed as male-dominated Christianity spread over most of the Western world. Leadership in Neopagan groups is to a large degree female, and the deities invoked are as likely to be feminine as masculine. Because of popular prejudices against witchcraft and paganism, many practitioners keep their allegiances hidden, but persons who consider themselves at least to some degree pagan are found throughout the United States in greater numbers than many would expect.

Although the 1960s era was a time of great ferment for American religion, other new religions emerged (and became subject to controversy) after that period. One controversial religious movement that rose to prominence is the International Church of Christ, also known as the Boston Movement. The Boston Movement arose from the Churches of Christ, a branch of the Restoration movement of nineteenth-century America whose most prominent descendant in the twenty-first century is the Christian Church (Disciples of Christ). Kip McKean (1954–) became pastor of the local Church of Christ in Lexington, Massachusetts, in 1979 and soon moved it into Boston, renaming it the Boston Church of Christ. By the early 1980s satellite churches were being founded in other American cities, and the movement experienced great growth, all of it accompanied by increasing controversy. The heaviest criticism was aimed at "discipling," a practice in which each member is assigned a spiritual supervisor who oversees much of the member's day-to-day life. Although the strictness of life in the Boston Movement has contributed to a high attrition rate, a steady stream of new converts has assured continued growth.

CONTROVERSY AND CRITICISM. Unconventional religions have always been socially controversial, and the last decades of the twentieth century witnessed seemingly endless contention over what some saw as a growing and threatening presence of dangerous religions in the United States. Those conflicts became particularly prominent in the wake of several spectacular and, in some cases, fatal events. In the United States three such events stand out.

In November 1978 more than nine hundred mostly American members of the Peoples Temple died in a mass murder-suicide at Jonestown, Guyana. The Peoples Temple, led by Jim Jones (1931–1978), was a California-based local congregation of the mainstream Disciples of Christ denomination. The Peoples Temple first received wide attention for its high level of racial integration and extensive social service programs. In 1974 the church established a communal "agricultural mission" in Guyana, South America, and eventually many church members migrated there, in part to escape the increasing conflicts, both internal and external, that plagued the church in California. The murder-suicide took place in the context of a visit by a U.S. congressman seeking to investigate conditions at the colony.

In April 1993 approximately eighty members of the Branch Davidian movement died in a federal raid and subsequent fire that swept their communal center outside Waco, Texas. The original Davidian movement emerged as a Seventh-day Adventist splinter group in 1929; it divided into factions after the death of the founder Victor Houteff (1885–1955). One of the factions, headed by Benjamin Roden, came to be known as the Branch, or Branch Davidians. Vernon Howell (1959–1993) joined that group in 1981 and a few years later became its leader, changing his name to David Koresh. In February 1993 agents of the federal Bureau of Alcohol, Tobacco, and Firearms conducted a raid on the Branch Davidian headquarters in Waco. The raid led to a fifty-one-day siege by the Federal Bureau of Investigation (FBI) and ended with a fire that killed most of the Branch Davidians present, including Koresh.

In March 1997 thirty-nine members of the Heaven's Gate movement committed suicide at Rancho Santa Fe, California. Heaven's Gate took shape in the 1970s as the founders Marshall Herff Applewhite (1931–1997) and Bonnie Lu Nettles (1924–1985) began to develop an evolutionary theology in which a few selected humans would advance to a level above human; a spacecraft would be the vehicle that would take them to the next realm. The appearance of the comet Hale-Bopp was taken as the signal that it was time for believers to abandon their human bodies—hence the suicides.

The Peoples Temple, the Branch Davidians, and Heaven's Gate were dissimilar movements, and the circumstances of their dramatic and fatal ends differed enormously. Nevertheless the massive media coverage that followed the demise of each group tended to cause the three to merge in the public mind, and activism against NRMs was stimulated as a result.

Opposition to new religious movements tends to be of two types, commonly referred to as anticult and countercult. Anticult activists believe that "cults" pose a threat to their members and to society and thus need to be denounced, perhaps abolished, in the interest of the common welfare. Countercult activism, on the other hand, is based in relatively orthodox (usually evangelical Protestant) churches and opposes NRMs as heresies, or false religions, that must be challenged theologically and socially. The two strands have combined to produce wide agreement in American culture that "cults" do exist and the public needs to be aware of their danger. The general image that has developed is that dangerous "cults" are widespread and growing, that they are led by evil or at least power-hungry leaders, that they are highly skilled at accumulating money, and that they pose a threat not only to the individuals who join them but to the larger society as well. Moreover because "cults" tend to appeal to young adults who are sometimes still living with their parents and siblings, such religious groups are destructive of traditional family life.

Perhaps the most contentious debate about the influence of NRMs involves the allegation that they engage in what is often called brainwashing or mind control. Opponents of new and unconventional religiosity contend that "cult" leaders use mental, and sometimes physical, coercion to induce members to do things they would not normally do. Sometimes, it is argued, members operate in trance-like states or behave in previously unthinkable ways. Most scholars who study NRMs hold the opinion that nothing that merits the label of brainwashing or mind control has been shown to have occurred by critics of NRMs. These scholars argue that some people can be influenced to join and become devoted to a particular movement, but the social phenomena of religious conversion and commitment found in NRMs are not essentially different from those seen in mainstream religions.

A related charge is that of totalism, the allegation that movements demand not merely casual participation, such as Sunday churchgoing, but absolute and total involvement on the part of an adherent. However, although some NRMs do ask for high levels of commitment and involvement, no one has shown that such commitment is involuntary or otherwise contrary to the standards of a society that generally allows its members to make their own decisions concerning their lives.

During the 1970s and 1980s, when promoters of the brainwashing and mind control hypothesis enjoyed their highest visibility, some opponents of NRMs (often the parents of young adults who had joined various movements) concluded that coercion had to be met with coercion, and they began to engage in what became known as deprogramming. In the typical scenario an NRM member was abducted forcibly, taken to isolated surroundings, and subjected to intensive argumentation and psychological pressure (and occasionally physical abuse) in an effort to convince the adherent to leave the group in question. Professional deprogrammers charged steep fees for their services, which were not always successful. Eventually the practice fell out of fashion, especially after some deprogrammers were convicted of kidnapping and illegal restraint. Thereafter a less-coercive strategy known as exit counseling was developed by those who sought to convince adherents to leave NRMs.

Closely related to the controversy over brainwashing, mind control, and deprogramming is the issue of leadership in NRMs. Opponents of NRMs often charge that movements are dominated by powerful, charismatic leaders who typically manipulate members for their own ends. Although most religions are indeed founded and led by strong personalities (religions are rarely created by committees), most NRM founders have not proved to be deviant or pathological. It is inevitably true that some leaders of religious movements are greedy and amass substantial assets. Some have also engaged in physical, psychological, or sexual abuse of their followers, and a few (probably very few) have been outright charlatans, fleecing the unwary. However, those patterns clearly do not typify NRM leaders any more than they typify religious or social leaders generally. There is no evidence, for example, that NRM leaders have abused their followers in proportionately larger numbers than some Catholic priests have abused young church members. As for greed, one could argue that the abuses of a small number of NRM leaders pale beside the excesses of some corporate executives. It seems to be inescapable in all areas of life that a few persons will behave unethically, and no one has demonstrated that NRM leadership has a greater propensity for such behavior than leadership in any other phase of human endeavor.

Similarly most religious movements do not end up amassing great wealth. If anything the opposite is true; religions of all kinds typically struggle to make ends meet. The financial circumstances of American religions are difficult to investigate, however, because the U.S. government does not require religious organizations to provide financial disclosure; even when such information is voluntarily provided, it is not usually audited and thus may not accurately reflect the true financial situation of the organization and its leaders. A few NRMs, in particular the Church of Scientology, do appear to have substantial resources. However, it is likely that NRMs in general do not possess greater per capita wealth than do other religious organizations.

Critics of NRMs often say that they are destructive of families. New members are presumed to be typically young adults just setting out in life and moving away from their parents. NRMs, as the conventional picture has it, provide members with highly controlled environments and isolate them from social influences that might undermine their newfound commitments. NRM leaders thus regard contact with parents and siblings as especially dangerous and therefore to be avoided.

This stereotype, like others, has some truth to it, but it can hardly be accurate in every case. Religious conversion does sometimes entail a changing of one's personal frame of reference, and more than a few religions think of themselves as families—spiritual families that may displace members' birth families, partially or entirely. Cutting oneself off from old friends and family members is one long-accepted way to promote one's chosen new spiritual path. Jesus is reported in the Gospels to have demanded that his disciples renounce their parents and siblings (*Lk.* 14:26), and historically persons who have joined monastic orders have sharply reduced their family contacts. Many Shakers broke relations with their families, and some of their movement's spiritual songs denounce family ties, as does one called "Gospel Relation."

> Of all the relation that ever I see
> My old Fleshly kindred are furthest from me,
> So bad and so ugly, so hateful they feel
> To see them and hate them increases my zeal.
> O how ugly they look! How ugly they look! How nasty they feel!

Nevertheless it is not the case that complete separation from one's family is a necessary adjunct of religious conversion. Most religious movements permit members to have as much contact with their families as they like. Various movements have tried to shield members from their families when members are threatened with deprogramming or other overtly hostile activity, and some NRM members have chosen to minimize contact with their families, especially when they perceive family members as hostile to their new faith. However, in most cases contact with one's birth family is permitted.

WOMEN IN NEW RELIGIONS. New religious movements, like other religions, have tended to be defined and dominated by males, but that pattern is not universal. Some movements, especially those rooted in religious traditions that mandate specific gender roles, have restricted the participation of women in various ways. The International Society for Krishna Consciousness, for example, which is rooted in traditional Indian Hindu culture, has always maintained a male-only top leadership and has carefully circumscribed male-female interaction. Many Christian-based NRMs, like the majority of Christian churches historically, have barred women from playing leading roles, especially participation in the clergy. Other movements offer gender equality in theory but not in practice, a tendency that reflects the pattern of many mainstream contemporary religious and social institutions.

However, although NRMs have not as a whole been bastions of egalitarianism, they have offered women opportunities for leadership and participation that have rarely been available in more traditional religions. Many founders and leaders of American new religions have been female. Ann Lee led the early Shakers to the United States, and she presided over their formation as one of America's longest-lived communal religious groups. Mary Baker Eddy (1821–1910) founded and led Christian Science, one of the most influential of America's new religions. Emma Curtis Hopkins (1849–1925) was the most influential of the founders of New Thought, a nineteenth-century movement that espoused human health and happiness, and Myrtle Fillmore (1845–1931) was the visionary leader of Unity, the largest of the many New Thought organizations. Helena P. Blavatsky created and led the Theosophical Society. Spiritualism was the creation of the Fox sisters of upstate New York. The list is a long one; clearly NRMs have provided an opening for the exercise of spiritual and organizational gifts that some extraordinary women have manifested—gifts that might have been stifled in more traditional religions.

Most women and men are not founders or leaders of religions; they are day-to-day adherents. Here the pattern in NRMs is mixed; in some cases women cook, clean, and raise children, whereas men have a wider range of options available to them, but in other NRMs women are freed from limited and subservient roles. In the Oneida Community, the nineteenth-century Perfectionist commune in upstate New York, women worked alongside men in construction and other traditionally male work. Oneida women also modified their clothing and hair for practical reasons, wearing pants (with short skirts over them) and cutting their hair short. Both women and men were allowed, indeed encouraged, to have multiple sexual partners in the Oneida Community's system of "complex marriage." In the Holy Order of MANS, an esoteric Christian group founded in 1968 that emphasized monasticism and human services, women could become priests (until the movement merged into Eastern Orthodoxy in 1988).

ETHNICITY AND NRMS. The ethnic makeup of NRMs varies widely from group to group. Some movements with roots in Asia have appealed heavily to Americans of Asian extraction and thus have ethnic Asian majorities. The International Society for Krishna Consciousness, for example, originally made converts among non-Asian Americans but later found more and more ethnic Indians participating, and in the early twenty-first century the active members of many temples are overwhelmingly Indian. Most NRMs, however, have constituencies that are not ethnically related to the movement's foreign land of origin. Most American Ṣūfīs, for example, are not from the Islamic lands that gave birth to Sufism.

It is a fair guess that African American membership in NRMs is low, but some movements, usually those with black leadership, have developed strong African American followings. One of the most prominent of the predominantly black NRMs was the Peace Mission Movement of Father Divine (1879–1965), which reached its peak in the 1930s. Father Divine was regarded as God in the flesh by his followers, and he addressed his members' material as well as spiritual needs, providing food, housing, and jobs to a predominantly poor membership. Other African American religious movements, such as the United House of Prayer for All People, led by Charles "Sweet Daddy" Grace (1881–1960), followed similar patterns.

Some African American religious leaders have rejected Christianity as a slave religion and have sought freedom in other traditions, notably Judaism and Islam. The first black Jews appeared in the 1890s with the founding of the improbably named Church of God and Saints of Christ by William S. Crowdy (1847–1908). Other similar organizations appeared over the next several decades, drawing on growing currents of black nationalism in the northern cities of the United States. In 1913 the religious focus of such groups began to shift from Judaism to Islam with the founding of the Moorish Science Temple of America by Timothy Drew, known as Noble Drew Ali (1886–1929). Then in 1930 a mysterious peddler commonly referred to as W. D. Fard began to preach a new racialistic version of Islam that grew into the Nation of Islam. Fard disappeared in 1934, but under his successor, Elijah Muhammad (1897–1975), the movement spread nationwide. Muhammad's son and successor, Wallace Muhammad, later known as W. Deen Mohammed (1933–), steered the movement away from black supremacy toward conventional Islam. Traditionalists led by Louis Farrakhan (1933–) subsequently built a reconstituted version of the former Nation of Islam. In the meantime several other African American Muslim groups appeared in the United States.

MILLENNIALISM AND VIOLENCE IN NRMS. Many new religions are characterized by an urgency that is driven by millennial expectations—a sense that the world is headed toward apocalyptic upheaval, or at least a major transformation, in the near future. In addition many NRMs are associated in the public mind with violence, or the potential for violence, although historically NRM members have more frequently been victims than perpetrators of violence.

Some NRMs have optimistic expectations for the millennial future; others are profoundly pessimistic. The expected changes may be violent or peaceful; the world may be destroyed or it may be transformed into something far better than humans have ever seen. Supernatural intervention may cause the dramatic events to happen, or good faith and works by devoted humans may suffice. NRMs embrace the wide range of millennialism found in the religions of the world.

The two principal categories of millennialism may be labeled progressive and catastrophic. The catastrophic variety, which is associated with conservative Protestantism as well as with some NRMs, is the more vivid of the two; it sees the world becoming increasingly degraded, increasingly distant from the divine will and purpose, and headed inevitably toward such events as an ultimate war between the forces of good and the forces of evil, rule of the world by unspeakably evil agents, and a final judgment in which the vast legions of the unfaithful will be cast into eternal torment. Many Christian-based NRMs espouse this kind of scenario. Progressive millennialism, on the other hand, sees the coming transformations in a positive light. Through the efforts of dedicated souls the world will become a better and better place; long-standing evils such as poverty, war, and injustice will gradually disappear, and a perfect human society will be established at last. Some Theosophical and New Thought groups, as well as many mainline Christian denominations, see millennialism in such a fashion.

Although violence is linked to NRMs in the public mind, NRMs have only rarely been notable perpetrators of violence. Perhaps the most vivid image of NRM–related violence is the deadly conflagration that ended the siege of the Branch Davidians at Waco. That siege, however, was initiated by an agency of the federal government, and the FBI's subsequent tank and CS gas assault culminated in a fire, although the actual cause of the fire that killed the group's members remains disputed.

Some NRMs have used violent rhetoric, but their words have rarely led to deeds. The Nation of Islam as it developed under Elijah Muhammad envisioned a millennial race war in which the dominant white race would finally be overthrown. In practice, however, Muhammad's followers were remarkably restrained. A number of groups associated with the Christian Identity movement have been involved in militaristic activities that have sometimes threatened violence against African Americans as well as Jews and other non-Christians, but as with the Black Muslims, Christian Identity rhetoric has been much stronger than the actions of members. The few acts of racial violence that have occurred, including some attacks on Jews and on mixed-race couples, have been perpetrated by loners not acting as sanctioned representatives of any organized Christian Identity group. Satanic groups have been portrayed as purveyors of violence (they have been accused, for example, of the ritual killing of infants), but actual Satanists are few in number, and evidence of murders for ritual purposes has been virtually impossible to locate. Some members of NRMs do own weapons, but no research has shown that NRM members are more likely to own or use them than are other Americans.

Some Christian-based (and occasionally other) movements have espoused strict discipline and corporal punishment of children, and physical abuse of children has taken place in a number of instances. In addition some would regard the withholding of medical treatment, which is practiced by certain NRMs, as child abuse. Most cases of NRM–related violence, however, are perpetrated by individuals who may invoke religious precepts (such as holy war or divine retribution) to justify their aberrant acts. Moreover American NRMs operate in a broader culture that encourages ownership of deadly weapons and generally tolerates a high level of violence. Specific incidents of NRM–related violence tend to arise from the convergence of specific expectations and characteristics of a given group and some kind of external situational trigger, perhaps the response the group has evoked from its neighbors and antagonists or from public authorities. There is nothing inherent to NRMs that makes them more violent than other social institutions, nor is there any reason to suspect that NRMs attract unusually violent persons as members.

MATURATION AND DEVELOPMENT OF NRMS. As recently as the 1960s scholars generally assumed that religions of the "cult" type were heavily centered on strong founder-leaders and that such a group would not long survive the leader's departure. Additional decades of observation of NRMs, however, demonstrate clearly that most do not vanish soon after the deaths of their founders. Although charismatic leadership is frequently key to the early development and spread of an NRM, over time many groups develop more enduring and institutionalized types of management that enable them to survive the deaths of their founders. Such movements as Spiritualism, Theosophy, New Thought, and Mormonism are prospering in their second centuries of existence, long after the passing of their founders.

When a charismatic founder lives a long and full life, he or she typically begins to look toward the future and to set up structures that will carry the movement forward under second-generation leadership. Normally the transition involves a movement toward increased bureaucratization; leadership becomes less concentrated in one person, and the organization comes to be administered through regulations and committees. For example, the leadership of Christian Science became vested in committees operating under rules that Mary Baker Eddy laid down before her death.

In other cases, especially when the founding leader dies or is deposed unexpectedly, a new authoritative figure may step forward to lead a movement that otherwise would suffer from lack of firm guidance. That happened with the Mormons after the founder Joseph Smith Jr. was murdered when he was only thirty-eight years old. Several potential new leaders claimed Smith's mantle, and some of them started their own Mormon-based movements, but the largest group of Mormons fell into line behind Brigham Young, who provided another three decades of charismatic leadership in his own style. Young also oversaw the development of bureaucratic structures that have enabled the church to function effectively ever since.

It is probably impossible for strongly charismatic leadership to continue indefinitely, generation after generation. Charismatic leadership involves a unique interaction between a given leader and his or her followers that has the "chemistry" to sustain deep commitment. No matter how great the ability or attractiveness of a next-generation leader, he or she will differ from the predecessor leader, and the former chemistry will not be present. Although commitment to a common cause may enable the new leader and group members to push ahead for a time, the development of a more-bureaucratic and less-spontaneous leadership style seems inevitable. A later-generation charismatic leader may develop his or her own chemistry with a group of believers; in that case a splinter group typically develops, whereas the main movement continues under bureaucratic leadership.

The move from charismatic leadership to collective administration engenders the development of a leadership cohort whose expertise is certified by appropriate training rather than force of personality. In the United States expertise is typically certified by the completion of academic courses of study. Thus the development of an intelligentsia is a typical step in the maturation of a religious movement. That pattern tends to take shape even in movements that originally disavow formal leadership training in favor of charismatically based qualifications. The Unification Church offers an excellent example of the process: less than two decades after its arrival in the United States, the movement opened a theological seminary that began to train church leaders and ministers, and it sent its best intellectuals to some of the nation's leading graduate schools for advanced study. Ranking Unificationists now have doctorates from such institutions as Harvard, Yale, and Vanderbilt.

Furthermore the spreading of an NRM's message is often conducted through mass media, and expertise in writing and speaking, video production, and Web site development has become a critical tool for the propagation of a group's message. Here again the growth of a class of specialized professionals is essential to a religious movement's growth and prosperity.

THE ACADEMIC STUDY OF NEW RELIGIONS. Scholarly study of NRMs has expanded and changed with the increased visibility of movements after 1965. Before 1900 scholars paid little attention to dissenting religious movements except in judgmental terms: they were considered heresies, departures from the true faith. After 1900 a few pioneers began to take a less-jaundiced view of new religions. The German sociologist Max Weber (1864–1920) remains influential, especially for his observations about the pivotal role of charismatic leadership in the development of new religions. The theologian Ernst Troeltsch (1865–1923), also a German, wrote at length about the differences between church-type and sect-type religions, showing that sectarianism was a social phenomenon that deserved study in and of itself and not merely in terms of its deviation from received truth. H. Richard Niebuhr (1894–1962) provided a distinctly American focus for the scholarly conversation in his examination of sectarian social dynamics.

Several propositions that emerged from early-twentieth-century scholarship have proved less than reliable. Troeltsch and Niebuhr were convinced that sectarianism was a phenomenon that emerged from the lower social classes. Another generally accepted analysis maintained that a group founded by a charismatic leader could not long survive the death of that leader. What is now clear is that generalizations about NRMs can be hazardous. It is now known that people from all levels of society can be attracted to NRMs and that many movements have had their greatest success long after the lifetime of the founder, without, as Niebuhr posited, evolving into completely conventional denominations.

Other scholars studied new religions later in the twentieth century. J. Milton Yinger wrote important sociological analyses of NRMs in the 1950s. During the 1940s and 1950s such observers as Marcus Bach, Elmer T. Clark, and Charles S. Braden surveyed the nonmainstream religious scene and discovered many previously little-noticed religious movements, describing them in terms that did not dismiss them as heretical or diabolical.

The greatly increased visibility of NRMs in American culture after 1965 spawned a new generation of scholarly NRM researchers. One drawing card for many of them was the opportunity to study a religion in its formative stages, as it develops its beliefs and practices, rather than as a fully evolved social institution. In the 1970s and 1980s several major academic organizations, including the Society for the Scientific Study of Religion and the American Academy of Religion, began to provide venues for research in the field, and publishers disseminated new findings.

By and large the new research on NRMs looked at the movements descriptively, tracking their social evolution, their beliefs, and the processes through which new converts joined. Most researchers found that NRMs were not more virtuous or more pathological than other American religions. Many also argued that hostility toward NRMs manifested a fear of the different and a belief that the different is dangerous, a pair of pervasive themes in American society. The scholars' conclusion of benignity, however, ran sharply counter to the public's perception that "evil cults" were proliferating in the land, brainwashing impressionable young people and turning them into subservient lackeys, amassing huge assets (sometimes through deceptive means), and threatening American peace and tranquility. That public perception was fueled by a number of organizations founded specifically to combat what they saw as the menace of "cults" (the Cult Awareness Network became the best-known of them), supported by a minority of scholars. For several years the fulcrum of the dispute was the hotly debated phenomenon of deprogramming, regarded by its advocates as a radical strategy necessitated by the enormity of the misconduct of the "cults" but seen by its opponents as nothing more than kidnapping, assault, and battery. Deprogramming eventually faded as a popular anticult strategy, but the deep division between scholarly consensus and prevailing public perception endures.

A majority of scholars eventually coalesced around what might be called a "freedom of religion" position, an agreement that there was no basis for sweeping condemnation of "cults" as a category but rather that a principle of innocent until proven guilty should apply to NRMs. A minority of scholars demurred, contending that something that could be called brainwashing or mind control did in fact occur and that many NRMs posed real threats to society. These scholars, aligned with the larger anticult and countercult movement, criticized the scholarly majority as naive about the groups they studied and as unwitting accomplices to aberrant "cult" activities. Relations between the two schools of thought continue to be troubled.

Despite the controversies, stereotypes, and allegations of misbehavior directed at NRMs, these new religious groups do, like other religions, reflect the society from which they arise. Their members are not unlike other people who search for meaning and value in ways that suit them best.

SEE ALSO Anticult Movements; Blavatsky, H. P.; Brainwashing (Debate); Branch Davidians; Christian Identity Movement; Christian Science; Cults and Sects; Daddy Grace; Deprogramming; Disciples of Christ; Eddy, Mary Baker; Elijah Muhammad; Family, The; Father Divine; Fillmore, Charles and Myrtle; Heaven's Gate; Holiness Movement; Holy Order of MANS; Hopkins, Emma Curtis; Hubbard, L. Ron; International Society for Krishna Consciousness; Jehovah's Witnesses; Jesus Movement; Jones, Jim; Jonestown and Peoples Temple; Koresh, David; Law and Religion; Lee, Ann; Mennonites; Mormonism; Nation of Islam; Neopaganism; New Thought Movement; Pietism; Prabhupada, A. C. Bhaktivedanta; Puritanism; Quakers; Satanism; Scientology; Seventh-day Adventism; Shakers; Smith, Joseph; Spiritualism; Sufism; Theosophical Society; Twelve Tribes; Unification Church; Unity; White, Ellen Gould; Wicca; Witchcraft, article on Concepts of Witchcraft; World's Parliament of Religions; Yogananda; Young, Brigham.

BIBLIOGRAPHY

Bach, Marcus. *Strange Sects and Curious Cults.* New York, 1961.

Braden, Charles S. *These Also Believe: A Study of Modern American Cults and Minority Religious Movements.* New York, 1949.

Clark, Elmer T. *The Small Sects in America.* Nashville, Tenn., 1937; rev. ed., New York, 1949.

Melton, J. Gordon. *The Encyclopedia of American Religions.* Detroit, Mich., 2003.

Miller, Timothy, ed. *When Prophets Die: The Postcharismatic Fate of New Religious Movements.* Albany, N.Y., 1991.

Miller, Timothy, ed. *America's Alternative Religions.* Albany, N.Y., 1995.

Niebuhr, H. Richard. *The Social Sources of Denominationalism.* New York, 1929.

Palmer, Susan Jean. *Moon Sisters, Krishna Mothers, Rajneesh Lovers: Women's Roles in New Religions.* Syracuse, N.Y., 1994.

Troeltsch, Ernst. *The Social Teaching of the Christian Churches* (1911). Translated by Olive Wyon. New York, 1931.

Weber, Max. *The Protestant Ethic and the Spirit of Capitalism* (1904–1905). Translated by Talcott Parsons. New York, 1930.

Wessinger, Catherine. *How the Millennium Comes Violently: From Jonestown to Heaven's Gate.* New York, 2000.

Wessinger, Catherine, ed. *Women's Leadership in Marginal Religions: Explorations outside the Mainstream.* Urbana, Ill., 1993.

Yinger, J. Milton. *Religion, Society, and the Individual: An Introduction to the Sociology of Religion.* New York, 1957.

Zablocki, Benjamin, and Thomas Robbins, eds. *Misunderstanding Cults: Searching for Objectivity in a Controversial Field.* Toronto, 2001.

TIMOTHY MILLER (2005)

NEW RELIGIOUS MOVEMENTS: NEW RELIGIOUS MOVEMENTS IN EUROPE

The new religious movements (NRMs) with which this article is mainly concerned are those that first appeared, or became noticeable, in Europe during the second half of the twentieth century. Many, indeed most, have their roots in one or more religious tradition, but they are termed *new* because they arose in a new form, with a new facet to their beliefs, or with a new organization or leadership that renounced more orthodox beliefs and/or ways of life. They are, moreover, distinguishable from those religions that are new merely to Europe, having been brought by immigrants, in that the NRMs have consisted, at least initially, of a predominantly first-generation membership of converts. Some of the movements have been denounced by other movements, or have themselves rejected the label "religious." No attempt will be made here to argue what a "real" religion should or should not consist of, beyond stating that the movement/group makes some attempt to address questions of ultimate concern. The term *NRM* is, thus, employed as a general concept that refers to a multitude of groups that others might call cults, sects, spiritual groups, or alternative belief systems.

Already it will be apparent that, faced with such a wide classification, NRMs will differ greatly from each other, and indeed the first generalization that must be made about them is that one cannot generalize. One could in fact say that the only attribute which all the movements have in common is that they have been referred to as new religions. That said, however, some trends and some characteristics are shared by some NRMs.

MILLENNIA-LONG BACKGROUND OF RELIGIOUS DIVERSITY. From the *brochs* of the Shetland Isles in the north to Cape Sounion's Temple of Poseidon in the south, and in literature still taught in some schools, there is abundant evidence of a rich European history of pagan beliefs and practices associated with Greek, Roman, Norse, Celtic, and other indigenous gods. Christianity entered Europe immediately after the death of Jesus, eventually spreading throughout the entire continent—although it was not until the mid-twelfth century that it succeeded in supplanting Paganism in Sweden. In Western Europe, the mushrooming of assorted varieties of Protestants from the fifteenth century to the present day followed the Reformation. Islam has also played an important role in European history: Islamic Spain contained a mostly harmonious multicultural mixture of Muslims, Jews, and Christians for more than six centuries. Under the Ottoman Empire, diversity was controlled through the millet system, in which relatively autonomous religious communities were ruled by their own religious leaders.

While there have always been new religions emerging throughout Europe, there have been periods when these became particularly visible and gave rise to persecution. Early Christian heretics such as the Aryans or Manichaeans were dealt with on an ad hoc basis, but during the Middle Ages more institutionalized methods evolved. For example, Cathars were systematically burned at the stake by the Papal Inquisition. Later sectarian communities (including Hutterians, Mennonites, Doukhobors, and Separatists) emigrated to the New World to escape the persecution they suffered in different parts of Europe.

While the nineteenth and early twentieth centuries saw the emergence of various Christian-based groups such as the Salvation Army, there also surfaced several esoteric groups and/or groups of Eastern origin (including Theosophy, Anthroposophy, Subud, and the Martinus Institute). These spread their gnoses to North America and, when American immigration law was liberalized in 1965, several gurus departed from Europe to find new disciples on the other side of the Atlantic.

IMMEDIATE HISTORICAL SETTING. During the late 1940s and early 1950s, there was a widespread concern to "pick up the pieces" in the aftermath of World War II, which had itself followed a period of economic depression and high unemployment throughout most of the West. By the late 1950s, Western Europe had, generally speaking, made a remarkable recovery. Future prospects seemed hopeful. By the middle 1960s, however, there had grown up a new generation with a new set of hopes and values. The immediate relief of peace and the relative political and economic stability were forgotten as it became increasingly obvious that the rosy expectations of continuing tranquility and prosperity were not being entirely fulfilled. A vociferous group of students in universities throughout Europe, but especially in England, Germany, France, the Netherlands, and Italy, joined the protesters of North America in attacking the Vietnam War, Western imperialism, and bourgeois capitalism. By the end of the 1960s, however, this section of middle-class youth seemed to be giving up hope of changing the structure of society through mobilizing political pressure and organizing demonstrations. They turned instead to an outright rejection of structures and standards, replacing these with the celebration of free love. Although the "flower children" were never as visible in Europe as they were in California, they certainly existed, being most obviously evident among segments of English, Scandinavian, Dutch, and German culture; however, the sunny Mediterranean coasts of Greece, France, and Spain were attracting seekers who intermingled with those who had discovered, often with the help of hallucinogenic drugs, their paths to a new truth or spiritual enlightenment in California and/or along the hippie trails of India, Nepal, and Afghanistan.

Then, during the 1970s, this wave of alternative movements was augmented by a conservative backlash and the establishment of more organized and authoritarian NRMs, which imposed strict rules, order, and offered clear answers in place of the antinomian laxity of the hippies. At the same time, there was the spread of neo-Pentecostal revivalism and charismatic renewal. The search for order and certainty was also apparent in conservative reactions within many traditional churches in opposition to the liberalization of theology and general worldview evidenced, in part, by Vatican II (1962–1965). By the early 1980s, there existed many hundreds of groups competing for souls and, frequently, the total commitment and financial resources of the young, and, in some cases the not so young, throughout most of Western Europe.

There had been a handful of representatives of various NRMs in at least some parts of Eastern Europe during the 1980s and even earlier. These had frequently operated underground (some slipping into Poland, Hungary, and Czechoslovakia from bases in Vienna). When discovered, members might be deported or imprisoned; some, including four members of the International Society for Krishna Consciousness (ISKCON), died in jail in the Soviet Union. But with the arrival of *glasnost* and *perestroika* and the eventual removal of state-imposed secularism, missionaries from NRMs and several older religions swarmed into Eastern Europe. Apart from providing a context within which (and concepts with which) the religiously starved could explore religious ideas and practice spiritual rituals and techniques, the movements brought all manner of secular hand-outs: Unificationists offered visits to the West and English language lessons; Scientologists offered communication and purification courses; posters were pasted on walls and lampposts throughout the region, advertising classes leading to health and wealth and a wide variety of yogic, meditation, and other Eastern practices.

THE RANGE OF MOVEMENTS. Most European countries have produced at least some of their own NRMs. Among these, the Aetherius Society, Emin Foundation, Exegesis,

Findhorn, the Jesus Army, the Process, the School of Economic Science, TOPY, and various esoteric orders associated with Aleister Crowley (1875–1947) and Gerald Gardener (1884–1964) originated in Britain. The Raelians, Aumism, and Roux's L'Église Chrétienne Universelle were founded in France; the Ananda Ashram in Denmark; Damanhur in Italy; Dragon Rouge and Livets Ord in Sweden; the Lou Movement in the Netherlands; and Al-Murabitun in Spain. In Eastern Europe, Vissarion's Church of the Last Testament in Russia, the New Jerusalem in Romania, and Mariya Devi Khristos' White Brotherhood in Ukraine emerged, or, as in the case of Duenov's Brotherhood of Light in Bulgaria, reemerged. Several Neopagan groups and Wicca covens have professed their allegiance to local European gods and goddesses in, for instance, the Caucuses, the Baltic, Volga, Norse, and Celtic regions. Moreover, several movements considered to exhibit sectarian characteristics have arisen within the Roman Catholic Church (Focolare, Communion and Liberation, Neocatechumenate, Poland's Radio Maryja, and, although it was founded in 1928, some would include Opus Dei).

The majority of NRMs are, however, not indigenous to Europe. Many can be traced to the United States (frequently to California), including offshoots of the Jesus Movement (such as the Children of God, later known as the Family); the Way International; International Churches of Christ; the Church Universal and Triumphant (known as Summit Lighthouse in England); and much of the human potential movement (such as *est,* which gave rise to the Landmark Forum, and various practices developed through the Esalen Institute). Several of the movements came from Asia, mainly India (Rajneesh; ISKCON; Brahma Kumaris; Divine Light Mission [later called Élan Vital]; Sathya Sai Baba, Transcendental Meditation; Sahaja Yoga; Ananda Marga; and various practices associated with Tantra, *kuṇḍalinī,* and other types of yoga), but also from Japan (Sōka Gakkai; Risshō Kosei Kai; Agon Shu; Mahikari; Tenrikyō); Korea (the Unification Church); and other parts of Asia (Caodaism from Vietnam; Fo Guang from Taiwan; Falun Gong from China). There are also groups from the Caribbean (Rastafarianism) and Africa (Cherubim and Seraphim; the Brotherhood of the Cross and Star), most of these finding their home among the black populations residing in Europe. Another development has been the growth of a number of Islamic groups (Hizb ut-Tahrir; the Nation of Islam; Al-Muhajiroun; Murabitun).

Not infrequently, movements with roots in the East (such as ISKCON) have been introduced to Europe indirectly, via the United States. It is, however, noteworthy that several of the Eastern religions show the influence of Europeans who had traveled to Asia, carrying with them either the Christian message or, more recently, the language and perspectives of various forms of humanistic psychology and the human potential movement—a movement that has itself been traced both to the East and to seventeenth- and eighteenth-centuries pietism in the West. Thus it is that, although many NRMs may appear alien and/or exotic to Europeans, it is possible to identify a not inconsiderable contribution from Europe that could have "prepared the way" or made the novelties more acceptable to Westerners. There is, moreover, a further twist to this growth of cultural exchange and syncretism: it is sometimes the accretions of American culture, such as a "happy-clappy" enthusiasm, that the new movements bring across the Atlantic that are most strongly objected to by their European critics.

Mention should also be made of what has come to be known by Troeltsch's term, popularized by Colin Campbell (1972): "cultic milieu." Many Europeans who would not consider themselves to have any connection with an NRM do, nonetheless, draw on concepts that owe their origin to Eastern philosophies, often transported through NRMs and the media—concepts such as reincarnation, for example, are accepted (often with the concept of resurrection) by roughly one-quarter of Europeans, and many Christians can be found attending yoga and meditation classes that are based on religious precepts at variance with traditional interpretations of the New Testament.

The Spread of the Movements. All European countries play host to some new religions, with a number of geographical centers such as Glastonbury, Lyons, Turin, St. Petersburg, and Amsterdam attracting particular genres. Rodney Stark (1985) has argued that much of Europe, having experienced more secularization than the United States, is more receptive to NRMs than had been generally assumed, and that the more northern, Protestant countries, in which traditional churches are weakest, are the most receptive to alien religions (cults), whereas the more southern, Catholic countries, in which conventional religion is stronger, are more likely to be receptive to sectarian (revivalist) activity.

Calculating precise statistics for NRMs and their membership is difficult because definitions as to what is and is not an NRM vary; many movements do not advertise their existence and may not be recognized for some time; several movements are secretive about, or grossly exaggerate, their membership numbers; and most NRMs, like traditional religions, have different levels of membership ranging from an inner core to associate members, and each group is liable to use a different criterion for what comprises membership. Moreover, NRMs frequently gloss over their high turnover rates, counting only converts, not defectors.

It is, however, likely that the number of NRMs in Europe is in excess of two thousand, but that most have a relatively small membership (occasionally less than a score, with only a handful having more than a thousand members in any one country at any one time). Britain is certainly not representative of Europe as a whole, but INFORM had collected details about more than 800 different NRMs that were active in the United Kingdom at some point between 1984 and 2004. This number might be doubled if, for example, they included all New Age and pagan groups as separate entities, nineteenth-century religions (such as the Jehovah's Witnesses and Mormons), and Buddhist and Hindu groups considered traditional in their countries of origin. Just under half (373) of the 806 NRMs were recognizably of Christian origin, and by far the largest number of these (171) could most easily be classified as some form of Protestantism, with twenty-seven being related to Catholicism, and twenty to African Independent Churches. There were, unambiguously, sixty-six Buddhist, thirty-eight Hindu, forty Muslim, and twelve Jewish NRMs, and a motley assortment of syncretistic, Shintō, yoga, esoteric, Gnostic, New Age, pagan, shaman, human potential, Satanic, Spiritualist, UFO, and other groups. Altogether INFORM has a record of more than three thousand different organizations, including several that are active elsewhere in Europe. And there are undoubtedly many other groups about which INFORM (and most other people) are ignorant.

REACTIONS TO NRMS. As elsewhere throughout the world, NRMs in Europe have been greeted with suspicion and hostility. Almost without exception, media coverage has been of a sensational and negative nature. Headlines have told of mass suicides and murders; bizarre sexual practices; blasphemous beliefs; brainwashing techniques; kidnapping; deception; broken-hearted parents; political intrigue; exploitation of members; and the vast wealth amassed by leaders.

The intensity and focus of responses to NRMs have varied both between and within the different countries of Europe at different times, each of which started from a different position—while religious freedom was virtually unchallenged in Britain, Scandinavia, and the Netherlands, it was not until 1970 that non-Catholic religions could operate legally in Spain, and there was state-imposed secularism in Eastern Europe until the collapse of communism. In the 1970s, the movement that received the most attention was the Unification Church, its members being popularly referred to as "Moonies." The French displayed concern particularly about the movement's political and financial concerns; the Norwegians about its theological status; the English worried about brainwashing and the break-up of families; the Germans about social security payments and the possible emergence of a new Hitler Youth movement; while the Finns appeared remarkably unaware of the Unificationists in their midst. Another group to be singled out at a relatively early stage was Scientology, which has continued to be met with considerable opposition, especially in Germany and Belgium. Other NRMs that have frequently hit the headlines include ISKCON, the Children of God (later known as the Family), the followers of Bhagwan Shree Rajneesh, and the International Churches of Christ.

Whatever the movement in the news, after 1978 almost all media reports referred to the horrific events in Jonestown; but it was not until after the 1994/5 murders and suicides of members of the Solar Temple in French-speaking Canada and Switzerland and, later, in France itself that "cult-associated atrocities" became widely recognized in the European political scene. Then, in 1995, the release of sarin gas in the Tokyo subway by members of Aum Shinrikyō alerted European governments to dangers not merely to those associated with NRMs, but also to the public at large—a fear that was confirmed and magnified beyond any previously imagined expectation when al-Qāʿidah hijackers flew airplanes into the World Trade Center and the Pentagon on September 11, 2001, with the fear of "sectarian terrorism" in Europe becoming firmly established in 2004 with the railway bombings in Madrid.

By the end of the 1970s, a loose network of groups, whose avowed goal was to expose and curtail the activities of NRMs, had been established throughout most of the continent. Anticult groups were particularly prominent in France, Germany, and Britain, but there were also individuals or small groups actively opposing NRMs in Denmark, the Netherlands, Belgium, Italy, and elsewhere. Some of these, founded in the mid-1970s, such as FAIR (Family Action Information and Rescue—the R being changed to Resource in 1994) in Britain and ADFI (Association de Défense de la Famille et de l'Individu) in France, organized a number of forcible deprogrammings, but by the end of the century these illegal abductions were almost completely stopped in Europe, non-forcible exit counseling having become the preferred option. Nonetheless, the number of cult-watching groups expanded and these were joined by some in Eastern Europe in the 1990s, one of the most active and influential, St. Irinaeus of Lyon Information-Consultation Center, operating under the patronage of the Moscow Patriarchy. In 1994, a network of European anticult groups, FECRIS (Fédération Européene des Centres de Recherche et d'Information sur le Sectarisme), was formed. This network includes among its members AGPF (Aktion für Geistige und Psychische Freiheit) in Germany; FRI (Förening Rädda Individen) in Sweden; the Polish Family Association; GSK (Gesellschaft Gegen Sekten und Kult Gefahren) in Austria; AIS (Asesoramiento e Información sobre Sectas) in Spain; SADK (Schweizerische Arbeitgemeinschaft Destruktive Kulte) in Switzerland; and the Ukrainian National Center of Religious Safety and Help to Victims of Destructive Cults.

There also emerged a number of centers run on more academic lines that were largely the result of scholars reacting to the selective and sometimes inaccurate information being disseminated in the media and elsewhere by both the NRMs and their opponents. Among these were CESNUR in Italy, which has a useful Web site (http://www.cesnur.com); FINYAIR in Sweden; VIK (Center for Information on Religion) in Hungary; RENNER (Research Network on New Religions) in Denmark, REMID (Religionswissenschaftlicher Medien- und Informationsdienst) in Germany; NRTIC (New Religions Research and Information Center) in Lithuania; and INFORM (Information Network Focus on Religious Movements), an information network based at the London School of Economics and supported by the British government and mainstream churches. In Eastern Europe, there had been very little opportunity to study new religions before 1990, but some scholars who had been interested in the subject have been meeting (with one or two Westerners) since 1991, and by 1995 they had founded ISORECEA (International Association for the Study of Religion in Eastern and Central Europe), which holds regular conferences and has published, mainly through the Polish publishing house Nomos, a number of volumes containing papers about NRMs in post-communist Europe.

Official government interest in NRMs in Europe has, unsurprisingly, varied from country to country. There was not much concern until after the Jonestown incident, and even then it was minimal. A number of reports were commissioned: both the Germans (1980 and 1998) and the Dutch (1984) concluded that there was little to worry about that could not be dealt with by the law as it stood; a French report (1985) expressed more anxiety and included the recommendation that judges be allowed to give parents the power to extract their adult children from religious organizations, but little action was taken at the time. In England, the Unification Church lost a six-month libel action against the *Daily Mail* (1981) and pressure was put on the Charity Commissioners to remove the charitable status of two Unification-related organizations, but by 1988 the case had been dropped due to insufficient evidence.

In May 1984, the European Parliament adopted a resolution calling for "a common approach by the Member States of the European Community towards various infringements of the law by new organizations operating under the protection afforded to religious bodies" (PE 90.562:49). The resolution expressed concern about some of the practices of the new religions, and listed a number of "criteria [that should] be applied in investigating, reviewing and assessing the activity of the . . . organizations" (PE 90.562:51). The supporters of the resolution were in favor of instituting a voluntary code of practices to be followed by the movements; several of the movements responded that not only did they follow most of the code's rules anyway, but that any such code ought to apply to all religions, not just to the "new" ones (which were, furthermore, notoriously difficult to define). Further reports for the Council of Europe (1999) and two commissioned by the European Parliament (1992 and 1998) again warned of the need to be alert to the dangers NRMs might pose, but no action was taken.

One of the reasons for government reluctance to introduce special legislation to control NRMs has been a concern to observe Article 9 of the European Convention on Human Rights and Fundamental Freedoms (1950): "Everyone has the right to freedom of thought, conscience and religion; this right includes freedom to change his religion or belief and freedom, either alone or in community with others and in public or private, to manifest his religion or belief, in worship, teaching, practice and observance." After the Solar Temple and Aum Shinrikyō episodes, the Article's second clause, which stated "subject only to such limitations as . . . are necessary . . . for the protection of public order, health or morals, or for the protection of the rights and freedoms of others," has formed a more persuasive basis for advocating control in one form or another in some European countries.

In 1995, a second government-sponsored report was published in France. This contained a list of 173 *sectes* (including Anthroposophy, which later (2000) successfully sued the Rapporteur for defamation). This report resulted in 1998 in the establishment of MILS (Interministerial Mission to Fight the Sects), which was replaced in 2002 by MIVILUDES (Interministerial Mission of Vigilance and Fight against Sectarian Deviances). In 1997, a report commissioned by the Belgian government included a list of 189 movements (including the Quakers and the YWCA, though not the YMCA). This resulted in a law establishing CIAOSN (Information and Advice Centre Concerning Harmful Sectarian Organizations), which has offered its services, including access to a now-substantial library, to the public since 2000. Although neither the French nor the Belgian governments officially incorporated their lists into law, several NRMs have been discriminated against merely because they were on one of the lists. When the Swedish government published a report in 1998, its list included all known religions in Sweden, including both Satanism and the (then-established) Lutheran Church of Sweden.

Other West European governments, including Austria (1998) and the Swiss Canton of Geneva (1997 and 1999), have produced reports and/or passed laws that result directly or indirectly in NRMs either being denied privileges (such as registration) that are available to older traditions, or treated in some way that distinguishes them from more socially acceptable religions.

Appealing to the European Court of Human Rights (ECHR) is a final option available to NRMs that believe their rights have been violated. There are numerous cases in which Jehovah's Witnesses have, on the basis of Article 9, won decisions in their favor from the court on issues such as child custody, conscientious objection to military service, the right to proselytize, the right to gather for worship, and the right to refuse to participate in ceremonies or activities (such as bearing arms) that would violate their conscience. One of the best-known cases is that of Minos Kokkinakis, who had been arrested for proselytism on more than 60 occasions. In 1993, the ECHR ruled in his favor and Greece was ordered to pay both damages and costs. Greece remains, however, the only European Union country that bans proselytism under its constitution, and the police can prosecute religious communities that operate or build places of worship without the permission of both the government and the Greek Orthodox Church. Another case concerned an Austrian court's decision that a mother was "unfit" as a parent because she was one of Jehovah's Witnesses. The ECHR determined that "a distinction based essentially on a difference in religion alone is not acceptable," and custody was returned to the mother.

Despite the euphoria of celebrating religious freedom after the collapse of communism, by the end of the century the majority of Eastern European countries were introducing laws that curbed the activities of NRMs. These laws have frequently been related to registration, which often entails having a minimum number of members and a minimum number of years of residency in the country. In 1997, Russia passed its Law on Freedom of Conscience and Religious Associations, in which one of the requirements for registration is documental proof that the organization "has existed over the course of no less than fifteen years on the relevant territory" (Article 11.5). Those religions that do not succeed in getting registered may be "liquidated." In March 2004, the Moscow Golovinsky District Court issued an order that the local Jehovah's Witness society be closed down, and numerous landlords throughout the country immediately canceled rental agreements with local congregations.

THE AGING OF NRMs. While stressing the importance of not generalizing about NRMs, there might, nonetheless, be certain characteristics that some of them tend to share at all times and all places merely because they are new and religious. One universal fact is that NRMs do not remain new forever. With the passage of time, many disappear; a few, such as the Worldwide Church of God, start to grow then shatter into literally hundreds of schisms. Those that survive exhibit a tendency towards "denominationalization." Enthusiastic young converts mature and have to devote time and money to children who need to be socialized and are quite likely to question the movement's beliefs and practices. Founders die, and their charismatic authority becomes routinized, making the movement more predictable. Dichotomous worldviews with sharp distinctions (godly/satanic, true/false, right/wrong, them/us) become modified and, rather than insisting on how different they are from the rest of society, members begin to stress how normal they are. The host society may become less fearful of the movements, even accepting them as part of the religious scene. In Britain, for example, dropouts and former drug addicts from the hippie scene who decided to become Krishna devotees can be heard representing the Hindu community on the BBC. In most of Eastern Europe, however, ISKCON continues to be treated as a dangerous cult. Some NRMs, whose techniques, such as yoga and meditation, appeal to a wide range of Europeans and have gained sufficient respectability to organize classes under the auspices of local authorities, or to provide courses for large corporations and even government departments.

LONG-TERM SIGNIFICANCE. It is difficult to assess the long-term significance of NRMs in Europe. New new religions continue to emerge, but it must be stressed that only a tiny proportion of those that abandon their commitment to traditional religions avail themselves of the new options. Far more common in Europe is a "soft secularism," which turns to religious institutions only at times of crisis or for formal rites of passage. Others may claim that they enjoy some kind of spirituality in their lives but that this has little or nothing to do with any formal religiosity.

By the start of the third millennium, few, if any, NRMs had succeeded in becoming a major player in the European religious scene. It is, indeed, arguable that reactions to NRMs are more significant than the movements themselves. Taken as a group, new religions have certainly contributed to the growing multiculturalism that is most evidenced in the effects of mass media, migration, and globalization. They are also playing a significant role in testing limits of tolerance and control of minority religions through the legal activities of several countries and the ECHR. What remains to be seen is the role they may yet have to play in a constantly changing Europe, with its expanding economic and political interactions through the pan-European structures that are seen by many to undermine individual identity and the cultural and religious heritage of the 47 or so countries of Europe.

SEE ALSO Anthroposophy; Anticult Movement; Aum Shinrikyō; Church Universal and Triumphant; Crowley, Aleister; Cults and Sects; Falun Gong; Family, The; International Society for Krishna Consciousness; Jehovah's Witnesses; Jonestown and Peoples Temple; Mormonism; Nation of Islam; Neopaganism; New Age Movement; Raëlians; Rajneesh; Rastafarianism; Satanism; Scientology; Sōka Gakkai; Temple Solaire; Tenrikyō; Theosophical Society; Transcendental Meditation; Unification Church; Wicca.

BIBLIOGRAPHY

There are no books dealing systematically with the new religious movements in Europe as a whole. Much of the American literature is, however, applicable to the European scene so far as individual movements are concerned, and there are numerous collections that include articles on European movements, concentrating on particular movements and/or European societies. *New Religious Movements in the Twenty-First Century Legal, Political, and Social Challenges in Global Perspective,* edited by Phillip Charles Lucas and Thomas Robbins. New York and London, 2004. Includes chapters on NRMs in Britain, Denmark, France, Germany, Italy, the Baltic States, Russia, and the Caucasus. Eileen Barker and Margit Warburg, eds. *New Religions and New Religiosity.* Aarhus and Oxford, 1998. Contains further chapters on particular movements and comparisons between the situation in Europe and elsewhere. Robert Towler, ed. *New Religions and the New Europe.* Aarhus, 1995. With chapters on movements in Lithuania, Romania, Belgium. Helle Meldgaard and Johannes Aagaard, eds. *New Religious Movements in Europe.* Aarhus, 1997. With contributions on Greece, Italy, Switzerland, Ireland, Britain, the Netherlands, Germany, Austria, Denmark, and Scandinavia, as well as some more general comparisons. The following countries are featured: Poland, Belarus, Hungary, the Czech Republic, Bulgaria, East Germany. Ukraine and Russia are among the countries that feature in *New Religious Phenomena in Central and Eastern Europe,* edited by Irena Borowik and Grzegorz Babinski. Krakow, 1997. Among the many books on European Paganism, a good starting point is Graham Harvey and Charlotte Hardman's edited volume *Paganism Today: Wiccans, Druids, the Goddess and Ancient Earth Traditions for the Twenty-First Century.* London, 1995. For an overview of the New Age, see Paul Heelas' *The New Age Movement: The Celebration of the*

Self and the Sacralization of Modernity. Oxford, 1996, and Wouter Hanegraaff's *New Age Religion and Western Culture: Esotericism in the Mirror of Secular Thought.* Albany, 1998. A report on the Satanism scare in Britain is to be found in Jean La Fontaine's *Speak of the Devil: Tales of Satanic Abuse in Contemporary England.* Cambridge, 1998. Some of the darker aspects of occult Europe are explored in Nicholas Goodrick-Clarke's *Black Sun: Aryan Cults, Esoteric Nazism and the Politics of Identity.* New York, 2002. Some excellent articles on how Europe has responded to the recently increasing religious diversity (and other aspects of NRMs) can be read in *Challenging Religion,* edited by James A. Beckford and James T. Richardson. London, 2003. Detailed analyses of legal issues surrounding NRMs in Europe (and elsewhere) are included in *Regulating Religion: Case Studies from Around the Globe,* edited by James T. Richardson, New York and Dordrecht, 2004, and in *Facilitating Freedom of Religion and Belief: Perspectives, Impulses and Recommendations from the Oslo Coalition,* edited by Tore Lindholm, Bahia Tahzib-Lie, and W. Cole Durham. Dordrecht, 2004. Numerous references and contact details can be found in Eileen Barker's *New Religious Movements: A Practical Introduction.* London, 1989. Two books by Grace Davie, *Religion in Modern Europe: A Memory Mutates* (Oxford, 2000) and *Europe: The Exceptional Case: Parameters of Faith in the Modern World* (London, 2002), while not focusing specifically on NRMs, discuss the overall context within which the movements operate. Reference was made in the foregoing article to Rodney Stark's ideas in "Europe's Receptivity to Religious Movements," found in pp. 301–344 of *Religious Movements: Genesis, Exodus and Numbers,* which Stark himself edited. New York, 1985. Colin Campbell was largely responsible for popularizing the concept of the cultic milieu through his article "The Cult, the Cultic Milieu and Secularization" in *A Sociological Yearbook of Religion in Britain* 5 (1972): 119–136.

EILEEN BARKER (1987 AND 2005)

NEW RELIGIOUS MOVEMENTS: NEW RELIGIOUS MOVEMENTS IN JAPAN

The modern era has been a prolific period for new religious movements in Japan. In Japan, scholars define a new religion as having most or all of the following attributes:

1. Establishment within the last two centuries, usually characterized by features that suggest a religious response to the crises of modernity;
2. A definite moment of establishment and usually a founder possessing special charisma;
3. An important new, distinctive revelation or realization, expressed through some novel doctrine and usually attributed to supernatural sources;
4. A separate institutional structure;
5. Distinctive rites or practices.

In Japan, "old" new religions, which appeared before the restoration of the Meiji emperor in 1868, are distinguished from "new" new religions, which originated after 1970. Some Japanese new religions since the 1960s have become international religions with converts in other countries, while new religions originating in other countries have made converts in Japan. Japans's new religions are significant in the history of religions in Japan and are an important part of global pluralism.

HISTORICAL BACKGROUND. Japanese new religions generally fall into one of the following categories: (1) early new religions, basically Shintō in style of worship but focusing on one central deity and incorporating various Buddhist ideas, and originating before the Meiji restoration of 1868; (2) Ōmoto, whose founders were influenced by the syncretistic, eschatological, and spiritualistic movement of that name dating from the 1890s and its offspring; and (3) the Nichiren group, a category representing revitalizations of Nichiren Buddhism. But there are all sorts of new religions whose religious sources are diverse, including Buddhism, Shintō, Confucianism, Christianity, and others.

The roots of such movements in Japan lie in the rising popular discontent that marked the Tokugawa shogunate (1600–1868) as it drew to a close. During the entire period mass pilgrimages to the shrine of the sun goddess, Amaterasu, at Ise, countryside shamanism, and religious dance rituals were aspects of popular religion, as were the more decorous movements associated with moral philosophers, such as Ishida Baigan (1685–1744), founder of Shingaku (heart learning), and the "peasant sage" Ninomiya Sontoku (1787–1856). The moralists reinforced the Confucian values of work and obligation that made society function, whereas the syncretic "enthusiasts" gave vent to diverse spiritual impulses within a nominally regimented Confucian order. Both tasks became more urgent as the Tokugawa regime went into decline in the early nineteenth century. In those decades the early new religions, synthesizing elements of both popular exuberance and conventional morality, crystallized out of the spiritual ferment.

Many of the new religions offered stability by making pivotal a single example of each type of religious expression in popular religion. Each featured one god out of the many *kami* and buddhas; one divine teacher and one revelation out of the numerous shamans and visions of the era; one preeminent rite; one religious center and magnet for pilgrimage; one scripture; one institution. At the same time, they interpreted rapid change by explaining it in familiar eschatological language: God is hastening the coming of a new divine age. They helped ordinary people adjust to the ways of the new civilization through their own adaptations of its schools, bureaucracies, and mass media. At the same time by expecting a definite personal commitment of faith (unlike the traditional community Shintō shrines and Buddhist temples), they aided people in meeting the most profound challenge imposed by modernization: taking responsibility for one's own life in a changing and pluralistic world. The influence of the idea of the holy empire gradually dominated the millennialistic imagination during the first half of the twentieth century. Many groups suffered from the strict control of the government because of their deviance from the state system of emperor worship.

After 1945, with the coming of full religious freedom and the discrediting of prewar Shintō and Buddhism in the eyes of many, the new religions grew mightily for several decades. Most were direct or indirect continuations of prewar movements. But they took advantage of the new liberal atmosphere to purify their teaching and practice and drew on Japan's burgeoning affluence to build great temples and even spiritual cities. In the 1970s and 1980s their rate of growth tended to level off, but the new religions remain important aspects of Japanese society; their total membership was estimated somewhere between 10 to 20 percent of the Japanese population in the early twenty-first century.

General Characteristics. Common characteristics of the Japanese new religions include the following:

1. Founding by a charismatic figure whose career often recalls the shamanistic model; that is, supernatural calling, initiatory ordeal, wandering, and oracular deliverances from the spiritual world. As in Japanese shamanism generally, the founder is often female.
2. Tendency toward monotheism or a single, monistic source of spiritual power and value. Against the background of the spiritual pluralism of popular Shintō and Buddhism, the new movements set one deity, one founder, and one revelation as definitive.
3. Syncretism, drawing from several strands of religion and culture. The new religions typically embrace Buddhist doctrine (at least to the extent of inculcating doctrines of *karma* and reincarnation), extol a basically Confucian morality (as well as what is really a neo-Confucian idea of God as supreme principle or unity), and incorporate Shintō styles of worship. At the same time, notions may be borrowed from Western Spiritualism, New Thought (a nineteenth-century movement stressing the power of thought to heal and bring success), or evolutionism. There is also a strong desire to harmonize the religion with "modern science."
4. The centrality of this world, human beings, and body; a definite, this-worldly eschatology or millennialism. The new religions usually teach that rapid change is afoot and a divine new age imminent, and they place an emphasis on healing. Indeed most of the new religions began as spiritual healing movements, only gradually developing a full spectrum of doctrine and practice. Personal experiences by ordinary people are regarded as important, and accounts of religious experiences play central roles in their practices.

The Early New Religions. The "old" new religions, which appeared before the Meiji restoration, served as prototypes and often training grounds for later new religions. They are characterized by a rural background, making an originally Shintō or folk deity into a monotheistic supreme being and, compared to later movements, show little real evidence of Western influence.

Kurozumikyō. The saintly Kurozumi Munetada (1780–1850) founded this movement after a revelation in 1814. Kurozumi believed himself possessed by the Shintō sun goddess Amaterasu, whom he identified as the infinite deity. This small but influential movement emphasizes healthy living, healing, the cultivation of joy, and worship of the indwelling divine spirit.

Tenrikyō. Tenrikyō (religion of heavenly wisdom) originated in 1838, when a farmer's wife, Nakayama Miki (1798–1887), was possessed during a shamanistic rite by a deity who identified himself to her as the true and original God. Subsequently, this deity, now known to followers as God the Parent, imparted through Miki healing gifts and revealed scripture. Tenrikyō features an account of the Creation and the performance of a dance ritual that recalls it.

Konkōkyō. In 1859 a peasant, Kawate Bunjirō (1868–1912), felt himself called by the high god Tenchi Kane no Kami to a ministry of mediation between the divine and humankind. This he did through the Konkōkyō (religion of golden light), a faith that teaches that God is benevolent and that offers a practice called *toritsugi,* in which supplicants receive spiritual counsel from a priest.

The Ōmoto Group. The prolific Ōmoto (great source) new religions, stemming from the late-nineteenth-century Ōmoto faith itself, are characterized by a monotheism combined with a rich vision of a complex spiritual world from which souls descend into matter, a picture somewhat reminiscent of Western Neoplatonism and Gnosticism. They also have a strong affirmation of immediate and continuing divine revelation and an eschatological bent emphasizing an imminent paradisical new age. The influence of Western Spiritualism, Swedenborgianism, and New Thought is apparent.

Ōmoto. In 1892 Deguchi Nao (1837–1918), a peasant woman and member of Konkōkyō who had experienced many personal troubles, began to deliver divine oracles. Although the messages were initially from the Konkōkyō deity, Nao left that faith in 1897 and soon thereafter met Ueda Kisaburō (1871–1948, later Deguchi Onisaburō), a mystic and spiritualist whom she believed to be the great teacher her revelations had predicted would be sent from God. Under him Ōmoto became a well-organized and rapidly expanding religion that emphasized the oneness of God, the existence of a formative spiritual world behind the material, the temporary descent of souls from the spirit realm into the world of matter, the expression of the divine through art, and the coming of a new age heralded by a great teacher. Onisaburō also devised rites of healing, as had Nao in the early years of the movement. The increasingly totalitarian government forced it to disband in 1935. Although it was reorganized in 1946, it has never regained its former strength.

Seichō no Ie. The founder of Seichō no Ie (literally, house of growth), Taniguchi Masaharu (1893–1985), was an avid reader of Western and Eastern philosophy as a young man and participated in Ōmoto for four years. In 1928, by chance, he discovered a book by the American New Thought teacher Fenwicke Holmes. This book helped him crystallize a system of thought that was officially launched as Seichō no Ie in 1930, when Taniguchi began publishing a magazine of that name. Seichō no Ie affirms the perfection and spiritual nature of all things and denies the reality of matter, suffering, or evil—one may escape from them through the affirmative power of mind. It teaches a distinctive form of meditation called *shinsokan* and certain chants.

World Messianity. The founder of World Messianity, Okada Mokichi (1882–1955), was an active worker in the Ōmoto faith until 1934, when he felt called to form his own organization. The present name was adopted in 1950. Emphasizing the coming of a paradise on earth through an accelerating inpouring of divine light, World Messianity seeks to prepare the way through a practice called *jorei,* channeling divine light through a cupped, upraised hand to a body or other object to cleanse it of evil. World Messianity also regards art and beauty, including gardens, as precursors of the earthly paradise.

THE NICHIREN GROUP. The medieval Buddhist prophet Nichiren (1222–1282) started a movement from which most important sectarian developments in Japanese Buddhism have stemmed. Nichiren Buddhism's fundamental conviction is that the *Lotus Sūtra* is the supreme and full doctrine; it is worshiped in the form of a *maṇḍala,* the Gohonzon, by means of a chant called the Daimoku. Nichiren Buddhism claims to be the one true Buddhism. It emphasizes the coming of a spiritual new age and the power of the faith to bring benefits here and now.

Sōka Gakkai. Sōka Gakkai was established in 1937 by Makiguchi Tsunesaburō (1871–1944), an educator and convert to Nichiren Shōshū. He shared the belief of pragmatism that human benefit is of greater importance than truth regarded as an abstract ideal, and he saw a compatible view in Nichiren's emphasis on present attainment of the benefits of practice. Sōka Gakkai was reconstructed after World War II under the dynamic leadership of Toda Jōsei (1900–1958) and became a highly organized promotional arm of Nichiren Shōshū. Whereas its tactics were often criticized, in this period it was hailed as the "fastest growing religion in the world," claiming by 1960 some 750,000 households. After Toda's death, leadership passed to Ikeda Daisaku (b. 1928). Emphasizing the movement's cultural and social significance, Ikeda founded a related political party, the Kōmeitō (Clean Government Party) and otherwise sought to advance the coming of the Third Civilization, when true faith would spread over the world, ushering in an era of peace and plenty.

Reiyūkai. The oldest major modern Nichiren sect, Reiyūkai (spiritual friends association) was founded in 1925 by Kubo Kakutarō (1892–1944) and his sister-in-law Kotani Kimi (1901–1971), both of humble backgrounds. Essentially a lay organization, it depends on informal groups and volunteer teachers. In addition to the usual Nichiren emphases, Reiyūkai stresses the importance of ancestor worship, features quasi-shamanistic faith-healing practices, and has developed an influential kind of group counseling called *hoza* (*dharma* circle). Reiyūkai suffered many difficulties after World War II, but by the 1970s the movement was again an established part of Japanese spiritual life, inculcating conservative social values.

Risshō Kōseikai. Many new Nichiren movements arose out of the decentralized, charismatic matrix of Reiyūkai. By far the most successful was Risshō Kōseikai (society establishing righteousness and harmony), founded in 1938 by Niwano Nikkyō (b. 1906) and a housewife, Naganuma Myōkō (1889–1957), both former members of Reiyūkai. Risshō Kōseikai includes healing and divination practices and *hoza* group counseling; it presents an eclectic form of Nichiren Buddhism. After World War II, Niwano attained international recognition for his activity in worldwide peace and interreligious organizations.

JAPANESE NEW RELIGIONS AROUND THE WORLD. New religions in Japan were eager to propagate themselves among the Japanese immigrants, but they were rarely successful in recruiting foreigners until the 1950s. Exceptions were Tenrikyō in colonial Korea and Ōmoto in Brazil. But after the 1960s many new religions started systematically to influence foreigners and experienced some success. In Brazil and Korea many groups attracted substantial numbers of followers. Seichō no Ie, in particular, claims to have millions of followers in Brazil, most of them non-Japanese. In 2003, Sōka Gakkai claimed more than 1.5 million followers in 186 countries all over the world.

NEW NEW RELIGIONS. After around 1970, most of the existing new religions fell into stagnation. On the other hand, some newly organizing new religions, sometimes called "new new religions," gained recognition. Among the fastest growing were Agonshū, Sūkyō Mahikari, and GLA (God Light Association). Also, other groups, including the Unification Church and Jehovah's Witnesses, that were established in other countries started to grow rapidly in Japan after around 1970.

Although most of the older new religions were stagnant after the 1970s, Shin'nyoen, established in 1936 by Ito Shinjo and his wife Ito Tomoji, was an exception. Their spiritual resources are derived from shamanistic folk religions, modern spiritualism, and Esoteric Buddhism of the older Buddhist sect in Japan. They have their own system of shamanistic or spiritualistic mediumship combined with counseling and the Esoteric Buddhist system. In the 1960s they were already a fairly big organization. They continued to grow in the later decades and became one of the largest new religions in the 1980s.

The 1980s produced a new wave of aggressive movements, including Kofuku no Kagaku, Aum Shinrikyō, and Worldmate. The founders of these new religions were young and sometimes well educated. In the case of Kofuku no Kagaku, the founder graduated from the prestigious University of Tokyo. In the case of Aum Shinrikyō, although the founder, Asahara Shōkō, did not attend any university, the movement attracted many converts who had studied in well-known universities and graduate schools. While most active members of the older new religions were middle-aged housewives, young people are active participants in some new new religions.

One important feature of new new religions is that they are less this-world affirming than older new religions. They tend to emphasize the reality of the other dimensions of the world, and sometimes they segregate themselves from the outer society. The life after death and the eternal existence of the human soul is emphasized. In contrast, ancestors and family are cherished less. The emphasis is on individuality, and ritual settings tend to be less interactive and more theatrical.

Aum Shinrikyō has committed many crimes, including the sarin gas attack in the Tokyo subways in 1995, which injured over five thousand people and killed twelve. The founder, Asahara Shōkō, was sentenced to death in 2004. Asahara, born in 1955, was a member of Agonshū around 1980, but, influenced by Tibetan Buddhism, he practiced Yoga meditation much more intensely. Gradually he became an independent religious leader and claimed to have achieved the last stage of spiritual emancipation. In the late 1980s he started to kill members who wanted to defect and those whom he assumed to be enemies. Then, in the 1990s, he emphasized that Armageddon was coming soon and that to survive Japan and the whole world had to change. After the subway sarin gas attack in 1995, not only Aum Shinrikyō but other new religions were viewed critically as "cults."

New religions in early twenty-first-century Japan are less powerful compared with the latter half of the twentieth century, which is characterized as the period that started with the amazingly rapid growth of new religions and ended with catastrophic trauma for new religions as a whole.

SEE ALSO Aum Shinrikyō; Konkōkyō; Kurozumikyō; Nichirenshū; Ōmotokyō; Reiyūkai Kyōdan; Risshō Kōseikai; Sōka Gakkai; Tenrikyō.

BIBLIOGRAPHY

Several books accessible to the general reader on the new religions of Japan can be recommended, including H. Neill McFarland's *The Rush Hour of the Gods* (New York, 1967), a well researched, sometimes critical overview; Clark B. Offner and Henry van Straelen's *Modern Japanese Religions* (Leiden, 1963), a careful study emphasizing healing practices; and Harry Thomsen's *The New Religions of Japan* (Rutland, Vt., 1963), a lively survey. Among accounts of particular religions are Kenneth J. Dale and Akahoshi Susumu's *Circle of Harmony* (Tokyo, 1975) on the *hoza* (group counseling) procedures of Risshō Kōseikai; James Allen Dator's *Sōka Gakkai, Builders of the Third Civilization* (Seattle, Wash., 1969), a substantial sociological study; Robert S. Ellwood's *Tenrikyo, A Pilgrimage Faith* (Tenri, Japan, 1982); Winston Davis's *Dojo: Magic and Exorcism in Modern Japan* (Stanford, Calif., 1980); Helen Hardacre's *Lay Buddhism in Contemporary Japan, Reiyūkai Kyōdan* (Princeton, N.J., 1984), representing high-level sociological research; and Delwin Byron Schneider's *Konkokyo, A Japanese Religion* (Tokyo, 1962). For a complete bibliography, see H. Byron Earhart's *The New Religions of Japan: A Bibliography of Western-Language Materials*, 2d ed. (Ann Arbor, 1983). Works of detailed study on new religions in Japan include Helen Hardacre's *Kurozumikyō and the New Religions of Japan* (Princeton, N.J., 1986) and H. Byron Earhart's *Gedatsu-Kai and Religion in Contemporary Japan* (Bloomington, Ind., 1989). A detailed description of Aum Shinrikyō in English is in Ian Reader, *Religious Violence in Contemporary Japan: The Case of Aum Shinrikyô* (Richmond, U.K., 2000).

ROBERT S. ELLWOOD (1987)
SHIMAZONO SUSUMU (2005)

NEW RELIGIOUS MOVEMENTS: NEW RELIGIOUS MOVEMENTS IN LATIN AMERICA

Latin American societies have fostered an abundance of religious revitalization movements since the early colonial period. Ongoing religious ferment and innovation in Iberoamerican contexts has often been interpreted as an adaptive response to such conditions as land dispossession, widespread poverty, racialized social systems, acculturative processes, political instability, and the demands of nation-building. Explanations of these movements must also consider the fact that religious systems have long played central roles in constructing and critiquing the social order in Latin America. Since remote antiquity, the indigenous peoples of the Americas have fashioned highly adaptive cultures centered on mystical cosmologies that encompass all aspects of life and natural relationships. The Spanish and Portuguese colonizers, and the later independent states, espoused forms of governance and culture rooted in an almost hermetically Catholic conception of social life. The encounters of these religious influences, in the context of severe social circumstances and frequently shifting political orders, create fertile conditions for symbolic change and religious mobilization.

In his seminal 1956 work on revitalization movements, Anthony Wallace proposed that the process of religious revitalization involves an effort by a segment of a society to resolve incommensurability between existing religious formulations and changing perceived realities. From this perspective, prophets function as diagnosticians who resynthesize religious knowledge and address sociocultural stresses. This article surveys the nature of Latin American revitalization movements through four empirical varieties of movement activity:

(1) Indigenous nativisms and utopias;

(2) Folk-saint movements;

(3) Spiritist cults;

(4) Protestant-related religious movements.

Burgeoning Protestant recruitment since the 1970s accounts for the fastest rate of religious change that Iberoamerica has experienced since the introduction of Catholicism.

INDIGENOUS RELIGIOUS MOVEMENTS. From the Amazon to the deserts of northern Mexico, the impact of European contact and modern state–minority relations have precipitated dramatic religious responses among indigenous peoples. The most common variety of indigenous religious movement is nativism, a belief in the return of an idealized native culture or age, as exemplified in the nineteenth-century Ghost Dance of the Plains Indians. However, the imagined past usually reflects some blending of symbolic elements that results from acculturative processes. Historically, armed rebellions have frequently followed nativistic prophecies and rituals. As one might expect, native movements that involved uprisings produced the richest archival evidence. Such movements generally represent attempts to intensify and defend ethnic boundaries and to symbolically mediate (often through syncretism) between the religion and social-status system of a minority group and those of dominant society. Mexican indigenous societies have produced some of the most famed examples of nativistic movements. Prominent among these are the Chiapanec Mayan cults and rebellions of Cancuc (1712) and Chamula (1867–1870), the Yucatec Mayan Caste War movement of the Talking Cross of the mid-1800s, Yaqui and Mayo millenarian movements of the late nineteenth century, and the Great God Engineer cult of the Oaxacan Chinantec of the 1970s. The Chinantec cult arose in response to the Mexican government's proposal to relocate peasants in order to build a dam for commercial agriculture.

The movement centered on the town of Chamula, in the southern Mexican state of Chiapas, resulted in a revolt known as Cuscat's War, or the War of Saint Rose. It exemplifies the themes of resistance and religious blending of many nativistic movements. The cult was a response to 350 years of domination by regional elites and rising pressures within Mayan communities resulting from Mexico's recently promulgated liberal laws, which aimed at breaking up all land corporations. A Chamulan prophet, Pedro Díaz Cuscat, declared himself to be an Indian priest, and he donned a Catholic priest's garb after three obsidian oracle stones began to speak through his niece. Cuscat established an altar with a deity's image, declaring his niece to be the mother of the god. The movement attracted throngs of Maya, and the cult center became an important marketplace. Cuscat revealed that the Maya should reject worship before any *ladino* (Euro-Mexican) sacred images. He presided over the crucifixion of a Mayan boy on Good Friday of 1868. *Ladino* authorities, worried about a possible Mayan revolt, imprisoned Cuscat for a brief period. The following year, a *mestizo* militarized cult followers and was executed for leading a failed assault on San Cristóbal, the region's seniorial city. Cuscat raided *ladino* properties up until 1870, when he died and the movement faded. Some features of modern-day Chamulan ritual still show the influence of the Cuscat cult. The nativistic search for an ideal age through the creation of an indigenous saint, the indigenous Christ, and an Indian mother of God, sprang from Mayan yearnings for cultural and economic self-determination. Oracular flint cults have ancient roots in Mayan religions. But, as with similar movements, the symbolic solution proposed by the prophet incorporated non-indigenous elements in an effort to exercise control over the Indians' acculturative realities.

Amazonian nativistic movements tend to exhibit definite millenarian traits. Tukanoan, Arawakan, and Tupí-Guaraní peoples of the Amazonian lowlands have an extensive record of nativistic activity. Some movements have led to insurgency under messianic leadership, occasionally by an outsider, as in the Chamulan revolt. Perhaps the best-known millenarian cases from this region are the so-called "Land Without Evil" movements of colonial Brazil. During the sixteenth and seventeenth centuries, Tupí-Guaraní believers migrated great distances across South America, following the revelations of marginal shaman-prophets (*caraís*), men sometimes identified with Catholic supernaturals. The pilgrims' goal was to reach a utopian land where they would find peace, immortality, and safety from the mass die-offs of native peoples caused by European diseases plaguing the Portuguese-dominated coastal regions. Michael Brown's 1991 ethnohistorical study of Amazonian millenarian movements suggests that cultural blending and hierarchical shifts within these movements point to an internal cultural critique, as well as a reaction against external forces. Movement adepts may view their cultural systems as lacking in certain adaptive powers and may attempt, through religious means, to adopt certain aspects of the majority cultural tradition that they regard as more efficacious.

Andean indigenous cosmologies possess a millenarian strain expressed in the notion of the *pachacuti*, a divinely caused upheaval or change in era. Since colonial times, members of Kechwa (Inca) nativistic movements have awaited the return of Inkarri, a mythical Inca ruler executed by the Spanish. Though decaptitated, Inkarri's body continued to grow inside the earth. Andean messianic tradition holds that he will liberate Peru's indigenous peoples by reestablishing the pre-Conquest Inca state and civilization. Perhaps the most renowned movement based on this tradition was that led in 1780 to 1781 by José Gabriel Condorcanqui, or Túpac Amaru II, a descendant of the Inca emperor Huayna Cápac. He led more than 20,000 Kechwa peasants into armed rebellion against Spanish abuses in the Andes. Followers regarded him as a legitimate Inca ruler with a corresponding semi-divine nature. Túpac Amaru rebels were unable to take the ancient Incan capital of Cusco, and the movement waned. The colonial administration executed Túpac Amaru II and members of his family in 1781.

Even when nativistic groups were not engaging in military activities, as in some Amazonian cases, governments often regarded them as politically threatening. A prophet might urge followers to alter their economic behavior or to criticize governmental legitimacy. For instance, in the Venancio Christo movement of the northwest Amazon, from 1857 to 1858, the prophet revealed that his tribal followers should not perform any labor for whites. He also prophesied that whites who did not heed his message would be obliterated. Missionaries were excluded by Venancio's creation of a ministerial corps bearing saints' names to confer the sacraments. Consequently, the Brazilian government vigorously persecuted the movement. Violent state suppression of various kinds of prophetic groups has been common in many Latin American countries.

FOLK-SAINT MOVEMENTS. Since the 1870s, Latin American peasantries have produced several messianic movements and prophetic holy cities based upon a folk-Catholic worldview, folk-saint cults, apocalypticism, and oppositional ideologies. Folk Catholicism is a religious worldview associated primarily with the poor. It focuses on practical solutions and thaumaturgy over other-worldly salvational issues. Folk saints are individuals whom folk-Catholic practitioners, rather than the hegemonic Roman Catholic Church, regard as charged with saintliness in both life and death. The holiness of the folk saint is judged by his or her willingness to suffer vicariously, and by his or her readiness to use divine gifts for miraculous healing, giving counsel, and interpreting mystical signs in order to aid the believer. Folk-saint cults using doctrinal revelation through a medium have shown considerable potential to evolve into sectarian organizations.

The holy city of Joaseiro do Norte, today a large city in the northeast Brazilian state of Ceará, began as a secular hamlet of the same name. In 1889 Father Cícero Romão Batista was distributing Ash Wednesday communion in the town when a host shed blood on the tongue of a young laundress, Maria de Araújo. Thousands of impoverished northeastern Brazilians poured into the town, drawn by the miraculous sign and the saintly reputations of Father Cícero and Maria. Maria revealed that Joaseiro would be the ark of salvation to protect humanity from the punishing hand of God. Father Cícero was suspended by his bishop for preaching his millenarian notion that the shedding of Christ's blood in the latter days at Joaseiro represented a second redemption. The colony's population reached 15,000 by 1910. Even in death, Father Cícero continues to enjoy a reputation as a thaumaturge and national hero.

Joaseiro was preceded by the colony of Império do Belo Monte (Canudos) of the folk saint and prophet Antonio Conselheiro. In the1880s, Conselheiro (or Good Jesus, as his followers called him) preached the condemnation of the new Republican government of Brazil and led revivalistic folk-Catholic services in the impoverished backlands of northeast Brazil. A holy city of perhaps 5,000 followers sprang up in the region. The colony's professed belief that the republic was ungodly and that the monarchy should return prompted a military siege of the city. Conselheiro died during the attacks, most of the male defenders were massacred, and government militias captured a large number of prisoners. Similarly, a millenarian thaumaturge in the mountains of the Dominican Republic, Olivorio Mateo, died leading hundreds of his chiliastic rural followers in their defense against government attacks on their camps around 1916.

Recruitment to the Brazilian colonies was promoted by a long-standing fervent millenarian brand of folk-Catholic belief common among the Sertão region's peasants. The republic at the turn of the century began to encourage the breakdown of patron-client ties between landholders and peasants through the sale of land and contractual labor policies. Severe droughts produced widespread destitution and hunger, along with loss of access to cultivable land and food redistribution. Peasants believed that their protective patron-client ties were divinely ordained. Thus, the sacred order appeared to be in upheaval, requiring an apocalyptic restoration under a new, saintly patron. Historical evidence points to peasant seekers' desire to join the colonies in order to escape banditry, to acquire a livelihood and food, and to find personal religious reform.

A contemporary millenarian colony has existed in Michoacán State, Mexico, since 1973. Nueva Jerusalén originated in a movement centered on millenarian apparitions of the Virgin of the Rosary to a peasant seer, Gabina Romero (d. 1981). The Virgin announced that the world would end before the year 2000, and that the Catholic hierarchy had lost its legitimacy. She requested a special community where she could live in body and soul and save the world. Gabina took the Virgin's message to Father Nabor Cárdenas, a local parish priest whom the Virgin had designated as her "chosen son." Father Nabor, also called "Papá," founded the colony, became a charismatic leader, and renounced the post–Vatican II church. The Virgin gave ongoing messages to Gabina and her successor medium, building up the colony's doctrine and highly stratified social structure. Residents and pilgrims spun miracle stories about seer and prophet over the years. Gabina became the Virgin's chosen handservant, the holiest woman on earth. The Virgin made Father Nabor the acting head of the church and declared that he is incapable of intentionally offending God.

Nueva Jerusalén's population of mostly peasants reached nearly 5,000 in the early 1980s, and currently stands at about 3,100 members. The sect's beliefs are rooted in Father Nabor's interpretation of apocalyptic varieties of the Catholic Traditionalist movement, combined with elements of Mexican folk Catholicism. Traditionalists hold that the post–Vatican II church is in apostasy. As Nueva Jerusalén is believed to be the remnant Catholic Church in the latter days, its bureaucracy replicates various religious orders for priests, monks, and a convent of about 400 nuns. Lay residents are ranked in quasi-monastic groups with an ascetic lifestyle. Ritual participation, penance, and work life are intensive and tightly regulated.

Recruits joined the colony with many of the same motivations as the Brazilian followers. Mexican peasants in the 1970s were under rising pressure due to increasing production costs, poor and inadequate land, and government efforts to connect rural producers to agribusiness. These factors promoted many peasants' availability to migrate to the colony. In addition, ethnographic research on the colony shows a strong pattern of interest in personal reform among men, with women acting as key agents in their sons' and husbands' recruitments. The folk-saint colony functions as a total institution where personal problems are formulated entirely in mythological and ritual terms. The highly structured, world-rejecting lifestyle of the colony's elect strongly supports personal change and discourages recidivism after conversion. Nueva Jerusalén's millenarian teachings do not appear to have played a significant role in most peasants' recruitments, although they do underwrite the colony lifestyle that many recruits found attractive.

El Niño Fidencio is perhaps the most successful folk-saint healer in Latin American history. José Fidencio de Jesús Síntora Constantino, a ranch worker in northern Mexico, received visions of Christ and God the Father instructing him to cure the sick. Between 1925 and his death in 1938, his healing ministry attracted tens of thousands of pilgrims to the desert site of Espinazo, Nuevo León. Fidencio combined spiritualist techniques and beliefs with those of folk-Catholic *curanderismo* (the Mexican folk health-care system). A line of trained mediums, mostly women, have ensured that he could continue to work after his death through spirit possession. Networks of El Niño's devotees are spread throughout Mexico and U.S.-Mexican communities. In July 1993 the Mexican government registered an independent religious association derived from the cult, the Iglesia Fidencista Cristiana. The new church is an unusual example of an institutionalized, officially recognized folk-saint movement, for most of these cults remain diffuse and noncorporate in character. The Fidencista Church employs its own adaptation of the Novus Ordo Catholic mass, containing references to spiritualist beliefs and the supremacy of Fidencio in the spirit world. More than 600 mediums are said to be registered with the church in both Mexico and the United States. Unaffiliated mediums and devotees still constitute the overwhelming majority of followers. Like Fidencio himself, they consider their identity to be simply Catholic.

Another large Mexican folk-saint movement was that of Teresa Urrea, known as the Saint of Cabora, who was active between 1889 and 1906 in the Arizona-Mexico border region. Teresa was famed for her ability to heal miraculously with mixes of dirt, oil, and saliva. "Long live the Saint of Cabora" became a rallying cry in nativistic, millenarian revolts among the Rarámuri and the Mayo in 1891 and 1892. Fearful of her reputation, the regime of Porfirio Díaz banished her to Arizona, where she continued to heal until her death in 1906.

SPIRITIST CULTS. Latin American movements oriented around the mystical provision of health and advice often show strong roots in Kardecist spiritualism. (Kardecist beliefs and practices stem from the teachings of the nineteenth-century French educator, Allan Kardec, regarding human contact with the spirit world.) These therapeutic new religious movements (NRMs) are usually diffuse, have no folk saints, and draw upon folk-Catholic traditions. Spiritualist healing, centered on temples and mediums, witnessed an upswing in popularity in Latin American societies during the early twentieth century. Theosophical spirituality has contributed to the rise of a number of healing movements, such as the Mexican Espiritualismo Trinitario Mariano (Marian Trinitarian Spiritualism). Umbanda is among the most studied of the spiritist movements.

Umbanda (an invented term) is essentially an eclectic audience cult. Men of the business and upper classes in Brazil started the movement in the 1920s by melding Kardecism, aspects of Catholic teaching, and Afro-Brazilian Candomblé, a creolized spirit-possession tradition centered on the worship of Yoruban deities, called *orixás* (orishas). The syncretization became part of an effort to forge a distinctively Brazilian spiritual tradition that could sidestep allegedly backward black ethnic religion and Catholic dogma, both of which were considered inappropriate for modernizing whites and mulattos. Umbanda temples, or *terreiros*, now exist by the thousands in major Brazilian cities. It has been estimated that at least 60 percent of adult Brazilians, most of whom identify as Catholics, consult with Umbanda mediums. The movement has indeed become a national religious tradition.

Umbanda takes a variety of forms that may be arranged along a continuum, from the most Candomblé-like appearance to the most Kardecist. All Umbanda varieties focus on spiritualist notions of charity and spirit consultation as a means of aiding the living. The most Kardecist form is sometimes referred to as Umbanda Pura or Umbanda Branca. Mediums wear white spiritist robes, and African *orishas*, or deities, are shunned. However, the term *orixás* is used generally in Umbanda to denote the spirits. Umbanda's creators introduced spirits of Brazilian political and other historical luminaries, masculine Amazonian Indians (*caboclos*), and wise black slaves (*pretos velhos*). A panoply of spirits has grown over the decades to include people from many walks of life, each with his or her own personal history, known specialties, and favorite ritual offerings. The *terreiro* is headed by a master medium, called a mother of the saint (*mãe de santo*) or a father of the saint (*pãe de santo*). A believer identifies a spirit with whom she or he wishes to consult for a remedy, then approaches a medium in trance. The spirit will often prescribe a ritual involving such features as number symbolism or food offerings to keep trickster spirits (*exús*) at bay. An offering is left for the temple. Head mediums compete for clients in Brazil's libertarian religious environment, making the *terreiro* an unstable enterprise.

The spirit possession cult of María Lionza in Venezuela strongly resembles Umbanda. María Lionza also originated in the early twentieth century as part of an effort to invent a national image rooted partly in imagery of an indigenous past. The principal spirit being, María Lionza, is symbolized under two representations: as a nude Indian girl, Yara, who straddles a tapir, and as María, a girl dressed in the style of the Virgin Mary. Other spirits include Simón Bolívar, the spirit-doctor and folk hero José Gregorio Hernández (now in the process of canonization), and other prominent Venezuelans. Mount Sorte in María Lionza National Park, near Caracas, serves as the focal point for pilgrimages and is believed to be an ancient indigenous sacred site. Clearly, Umbanda and María Lionza originated as symbolic resources for shaping and celebrating emerging national identities.

PROTESTANT RELIGIOUS CHANGE. The spectacular growth of Protestant-related faiths in Latin America is now the subject of a large body of scholarly publications. In the twentieth century such groups as the Jehovah's Witnesses, the Church of Jesus Christ of Latter-day Saints, Baptists, and Presbyterians have become firmly established in every Latin American country, and over half of all Protestant members practice some type of Pentecostal worship. In most cases, U.S. Protestant missionaries helped to establish these groups early on. Later, new churches developed authochtonous leadership and adapted their worship to local cultures. For instance, two Swedish Americans founded the first Pentecostal church in Brazil in 1910, Assambléias de Deus. The church has long since become totally Brazilian in its hierarchy and operation. Migrants to the United States often have imported Pentecostal or other Protestant models for building native churches. In 1914 Romana Valenzuela established the first Mexican Pentecostal church in Chihuahua State, following her contact with William Seymour's Azusa Street Mission. Her Iglesia Apostólica de la Fe en Cristo Jesús had grown to 130 congregations by 1944. Mexico's largest Protestant church is Iglesia de La Luz del Mundo (Light of the World), founded by a prophet from Guadalajara in the 1920s. The church has charismatic leadership and a sectarian colony organizational model, with colonies in various parts of central and eastern Mexico. La Luz del Mundo has expanded into the United States, carried by missionaries and Mexican immigrants.

Pentecostal churches have several features that substantially enhance their appeal among masses of folk Catholics. Pastors require little or no formal education in the ministry, and most possess class and cultural backgrounds similar to those of their working-class congregants. Pentecostal worship is ecstatic, involving a heightened emotional style through the use of *glossolalia* (speaking in tongues), lively music, liturgical dancing, and testimonials. Pentecostal churches are mostly local, independent congregations rooted in oral tradition. Pentecostals see the causes of illness largely in the folk-Catholic terms of negative spiritual forces, such as witchcraft, which only the Holy Spirit can banish. Most Pentecostal converts are attracted by promises of miraculous cures, something of great importance in an impoverished environment. They often remain because they either witness or receive a miraculous healing. Brazil's largest Pentecostal (or neo-Pentecostal) church, Edir Maçedo's Universal Church of the Kingdom of God, specializes in exorcising Umbanda *orishas.* The spirits are believed to cause mental confusion that prevents the nonbeliever from making prudent lifestyle decisions and becoming a prosperous wage-earner or entrepreneur.

The growth of evangelical Protestantism, Mormonism, and the Jehovah's Witnesses as a whole is supported by an ascetic ethic that rejects the male prestige complex of heavy alcohol consumption and sexual conquests, along with secular entertainments in general. Women's interests in domesticating their husbands and sons thus drive much of the expansion. Pentecostal congregations in Brazil and elsewhere draw strong distinctions between the folk-Catholic male domain of the street and the household. Male Pentecostal converts in Brazil are said to change from being "kings of the street" to "masters of the house." Protestant emphases on work, frugality, marital fidelity, and financial security of the family helps converts to maintain personal health and to accumulate assets. Although women do not usually acquire ministerial status within these churches, neither do they escape a patriarchal social system, but they do welcome the investments that a man makes in his household as a result of his conversion. Women also receive treatment as spiritual equals in the churches, because they have the gift of the Spirit, give testimonials, and serve in congregational ministries. In Mesoamerican and Andean indigenous communities, evangelical or Mormon frugality and the rejection of Catholicism enable converts to abandon systems of ritual obligation, such as the fiesta system, that hinder the accumulation of capital. Thus, studies of non-Catholic conversion are contributing ethnographic perspectives towards the critique of Max Weber's thesis linking the the capitalist ethic to the rise of Protestant values.

An interesting counterpoint to Pentecostal recruitment rates is the fact that Pentecostal churches tend to have the highest apostasy rates of all Latin American Protestant churches. The drop-out rate results partly from tension with the broader society and stringent behavioral and commitment norms. Congregants may be expected to attend long, ecstatic evening worship services twice a week, producing burn-out and lack of moral compliance, particularly for males. Thus, most Pentecostal groups rely on constant proselytization for replacement and sustained growth.

Latin American Pentecostalism may be understood as a largely endogenous movement, generated out of a folk-Catholic milieu. Since folk Catholicism is a practical religious variety that places high value on thaumaturgy, Pentecostal claims do not fundamentally break from the dominant religious worldview of the poor. Latin American Pentecostalism entails a redirecting of folk-Catholic belief. Nonetheless, Pentecostal and other non-Catholic groups significantly differ from surrounding society in the formation of corporate structures. Corporateness is marked and reinforced by a sense of spiritual election, signalled by glossolalia and baptism of the Spirit in Pentecostalism. Evangelicals often refer to themselves as *creyentes* or *crentes* (believers), distinguishing themselves from the dominant Catholic milieu. Church structures exert needed social pressure for healing the social illnesses associated with the male prestige complex and maintaining separation from worldliness. Dense internal networks of believers and tithing provide members with security, the faith that their investment in the church will mystically give them a return of health and prosperity. Such features are largely absent in spirit cults and folk Catholicism, whose practitioners do not profess a clear break with worldly behaviors.

Political adaptations of Protestant groups are far from uniform in Latin America. Major denominations have formed political associations at the national level to defend their interests. Unlike the mainline Protestant churches, the majority of Pentecostal congregations are small and marginal and have no bureaucracies to represent them before the state. In Mexico and other countries with histories of hostility towards Protestants, Pentecostals are often vulnerable to persecutions and discrimination by government and the general populace. In Chiapas State, Mexico, Maya traditionalists and folk Catholics have forcibly expelled large numbers of Protestants from Chamula. In recent years, the Mexican government considered a measure, backed by the country's Catholic bishops, that would have excluded any church having less than 1.5 percent of the national population from being recognized officially as a religious association. Obviously, this would rule out most Mexican Pentecostal groups.

In Brazil and Mexico, Pentecostal pastors may seek to forge patron-client ties with powerful political figures, exchanging votes for "God's candidate" for material improvements for their congregants. Bargaining of this sort often leads to public controversy. La Luz del Mundo has courted the Mexican official party, the Partido Revolucionario Institucional (PRI), bringing party officials to their mother colony in Guadalajara. Pentecostal members are likely to hold that divine blessings accrue to the church from working within a system of political patronage. By contrast, progressive Catholic groups, such as the Base Ecclesial Communities, attempt to improve conditions for the poor through direct confrontation and political activism. Pentecostal ideology deemphasizes political activism in part because of a fundamentalist scriptural orientation, supporting the notion that secular authorities are divinely sanctioned. Their viewpoint derives in large measure from their reading of *Romans* 14:1–2.

Pentecostal orientation towards political participation with other Protestants is changing somewhat in response to economic hardship and political crises. In Chiapas, the winner of the gubernatorial election of 2000 was the independent candidate, Pablo Salazar Mendicuchia, a lawyer with a Presbyterian and Nazarene family background. He ran on a platform critical of governmental neglect of indigenous rights and failure to resolve the guerrilla conflict in the state. Salazar was backed by Presbyterians, Nazarenes, Baptists, and the Assemblies of God, as well as the liberal and influential Catholic bishop, Samuel Ruiz. The first Protestant Mexican governor, Salazar has created effective ecumenical committees to resolve long-standing religious conflicts in his state, which has the largest non-Catholic population in Mexico. In recent years, Mexican Pentecostals have begun to discuss the formation of local evangelical political parties.

Protestant ideology and organization are highly adaptive in both rural and urban environments. The Protestant work ethic and its associated asceticism enable followers to gain some upward mobility and to foster a sense of well-being and cooperation. Latin American societies will continue to engender a wide range of spiritual traditions in response to the rapid socioeconomic and cultural changes sweeping the region.

For five centuries, movements of religious change in Latin America have generated remarkably wide-ranging blends of native and exogenous religious influences. The revitalization process has served as a potent means of defending indigenous cultures, advancing political ideologies, restoring health, and bringing hope to the marginalized in the region. Thus, new religious activities among Latin American peoples richly illustrate the dynamic nature of their cultures and identities.

See Also Afro-Brazilian Religions; Kardecism; Pentecostal and Charismatic Christianity; Spiritualism; Yoruba Religion.

Bibliography

Annis, Sheldon. *God and Production in a Guatemalan Town.* Austin, Tex., 1987. A widely cited study of Protestant conversion and its effects on peasant household economics.

Barabas, Alicia M. "Chinantec Messianism: The Mediator of the Divine." In *Western Expansion and Indigenous Peoples: The Heritage of Las Casa,* edited by Elías Sevilla-Casas, pp. 221–254. The Hague, 1977. An in-depth study of the Great God Engineer nativistic movement in Oaxaca, Mexico, a reaction to a development project.

Barabas, Alicia M. *Utopías indias: Movimientos sociorreligiosos en México.* Mexico City, 1989. An excellent ethnohistorical compendium of Mexican indigenous religious movements from the Spanish Conquest to the 1970s.

Bastian, Jean-Pierre. "The Metamorphosis of Latin American Protestant Groups: A Sociohistorical Perspective." *Latin American Research Review* 28 (1993): 33–62.

Bowen, Kurt Derek. *Evangelism and Apostasy: The Evolution and Impact of Evangelicals in Modern Mexico.* Montréal and Buffalo, N.Y., 1996. One of the most complete studies of recruitment and attrition in Latin American Pentecostal environments.

Bricker, Victoria Reifler. *The Indian Christ, the Indian King: The Historical Substrate of Maya Myth and Ritual.* Austin, Tex., 1981. Several Mayan religious movements are explored in this volume, including the War of St. Rose and the Talking Cross cult. A major source on Maya religion and worldview.

Brown, Diana DeG. *Umbanda: Religion and Politics in Urban Brazil.* New York, 1994. A detailed study of the origins, evolution, and structure of Umbanda varieties. Includes a case study of Umbanda practice in Rio de Janeiro.

Brown, Michael F. "Beyond Resistance: A Comparative Study of Utopian Renewal in Amazonia." *Ethnohistory* 38 (1991):

388–413. Provides new insights into the ways in which Amazonian indigenous movements not only express protest, but also critique sociocultural features in tension within their own societies.

Brusco, Elizabeth E. *The Reformation of Machismo: Evangelical Conversion and Gender in Colombia.* Austin, Tex., 1995. A nicely written ethnological case study of Pentecostal, Lutheran, and Presbyterian evangelicals in a Colombian town. One of the first ethnographies of women's issues in Latin American non-Catholic expansion. Complements Finkler's (1985) and Chesnut's (1997) studies of Mexico and Brazil, respectively.

Burdick, John. *Looking for God in Brazil: The Progressive Catholic Church in Urban Brazil's Religious Arena.* Berkeley, Calif., 1993. Burdick introduces the concept of the "religious arena" to analyze the competition and coadaptation that occurs among progressive Catholic (CEB), Pentecostal, and Umbanda groups. Based on fieldwork in the Rio de Janeiro area. A highly influential ethnological study of Brazilian religions.

Chesnut, R. Andrew. *Born Again in Brazil: The Pentecostal Boom and the Pathogens of Poverty.* New Brunswick, N.J., 1997. A well-written ethnographic treatment of the relationship of gender and class backgrounds to Brazilian Pentecostal recruitment and conversion, with a good discussion of folk-Catholic background factors. Focuses on Belém, northeast Brazil, in its discussion of Pentecostal varieties, expansion trends, and national political engagement. An important source.

Clawson, David Leslie. *Religion and Change in a Mexican Village.* Ann Arbor, Mich., 1976. A pioneering study of schism, revitalization, and economic impacts of religious change among indigenous Latter-day Saints (Mormons) in central Mexico.

Crumrine, N. Ross. *The Mayo Indians of Sonora: A People who Refuse to Die.* Tucson, Ariz., 1977. An ethnographic study highlighting Mayo nativism in northwest Mexico.

Deive, Carlos Esteban. "Olivorio: Estudio de un movimiento mesiánico en Santo Domingo." *Actas del XLI Congreso Internacional de Americanistas* 3: 132–142. Mexico City, 1970. Documentation of a neglected but fascinating folk-saint movement among Dominican peasants.

Della Cava, Ralph. *Miracle at Joaseiro.* New York, 1970. A definitive and dramatic account of Father Cícero's Joaseiro movement.

Diacon, Todd A. *Millenarian Vision, Capitalist Reality: Brazil's Contestado Rebellion, 1912–1916.* Durham, N.C., and London, 1991. An ethnohistorical analysis of the political-economic roots of one of the great prophetic new religious movements of Latin America.

Dow, James, and Alan Sandstrom, eds. *Holy Saints and Fiery Preachers: The Anthropology of Protestantism in Mexico and Central America.* Westport, Conn., and London, 2001. An excellent collection of articles exploring the causes of expansion and cultural change associated with Pentecostal and other Evangelical groups in Mesoamerica, primarily in indigenous communities.

Evans, Timothy Edward. *Religious Conversion in Quetzaltenango, Guatemala.* Ann Arbor, Mich., 1990. An insightful ethnographic analysis of recruitment and conversion to Pentecostalism among the highland Maya. Evans examines the roles of the recovery of mysticism and the progressive Catholic clergy's influence in Pentecostal growth.

Finkler, Kaja. *Spiritualist Healers in Mexico: Successes and Failures of Alternative Therapeutics.* South Hadley, Mass., 1985. A highly recommended study of spiritualist history, beliefs, recruitment, curing practices, and reformative effects in central Mexican temple communities. A thorough analysis of gendered differences in recruitment motivations and treatment outcomes.

Fortuny Loret de Mola, Patricia. *El protestantismo y sus implicaciones en la vida política: Un estudio de comunidad en la ciudad de Mérida.* Cuadernos de la Casa Chata 165. Mexico City, 1989. A landmark comparative study of conversion and urban adaptation among Jehovah's Witnesses, Pentecostals, and Latter-day Saints in Mérida, Yucatán.

Fortuny Loret de Mola, Patricia. "Origins, Development and Perspectives of La Luz del Mundo Church." *Religion* 25 (1995): 147–162. Fortuny, an anthropological expert on Protestant religious groups in Mexico, provides an overview of Mexico's largest charismatic-led movement.

Garma Navarro, Carlos. *Protestantismo en una comunidad totonaca de Puebla.* México, 1987. An award-winning (and the first) ethnological study of an authochtonous variety of Pentecostalism in a Latin American indigenous community. Analyzes the impact of Pentecostal membership on local politics, economic behavior, and Totonac ethnic identity.

Garma Navarro, Carlos. "Pentecostal Churches and Their Relationship to the Mexican State and Political Parties." *Journal of Ritual Studies* 15 (2001): 55–65. An update on the changing political views and activities of Pentecostal groups in Mexico.

Gow, Rosalind. "Inkarri and Revolutionary Leadership in the Southern Andes." *Journal of Latin American Lore* 8 (1982): 197–223. Examines the impact of Andean messianism on movements of political change in Peru.

Griffith, James S. *Folk Saints of the Borderlands: Victims, Bandits, and Healers.* Tucson, Ariz., 2003. A welcome synthesis of ethnographic investigations into folk-saint shrines and associated movements in the Mexico–United States borderlands region.

Knowlton, David C. "Mormonism in Latin America: Towards the Twenty-First Century." *Dialogue* 29 (1996): 159–176. Trends in Latter-day Saints' adaptation in Latin American settings, by an ethnologist with extensive fieldwork on Mormonism in Andean societies.

Lagarriga Attias, Isabel. *Espiritualismo Trinitario Mariano: Nuevas perspectivas de análisis.* Xalapa, Mexico, 1975. A major study of this well-known and fascinating Mexican healing sect, which syncretizes theosophy and Catholicism.

Leatham, Miguel C. "Practical Religion and Peasant Recruitment to Non-Catholic Groups in Latin America." *Religion and the Social Order* 6 (1996): 175–190. Compares recruitment themes from several types of rural religious movement in Latin America, and discusses the nature of folk Catholicism.

Leatham, Miguel C. "Rethinking Religious Decision Making in Peasant Millenarianism: The Case of Nueva Jerusalén." *Jour-*

nal of Contemporary Religion 12 (1997): 295–309. An ethnological analysis of peasant recruitment dynamics at the sectarian colony of Nueva Jerusalén, Mexico.

Macklin, Barbara June, and N. Ross Crumrine. "Three North Mexican Folk Saint Movements." *Comparative Studies in Society and History* 15 (1973): 96. Charts and compares the folk-saint careers of Niño Fidencio, Teresa Urrea, and the Mayo prophet San Damián Bohorqui. An important exploration of folk-saint charisma-building.

Martin, David. *Tongues of Fire: The Explosion of Protestantism in Latin America.* Oxford, 1990. A major source on the process of Pentecostal expansion throughout Latin America. Martin also explores Pentecostalism's potential to promote political transformation in the region.

Ossio, Juan M., ed. *Ideología mesiánica del mundo andino.* Lima, Peru, 1973. An important volume of ethnohistorical and ethnographic articles on messianic and millenarian myths in the indigenous Andes.

Pereira de Queiroz, Maria Isaura. *O Mesianismo: No Brazil e no mundo.* São Paulo, Brazil, 1977. An encyclopedic sociological discussion of the histories and dynamics of Brazilian religious movements.

Pessar, Patricia R. "Unmasking the Politics of Religion: The Case of Brazilian Millenarianism." *Journal of Latin American Lore* 7 (1981): 255–277. An ethnohistorical interpretation of nineteenth-century peasant millenarianism in the context of rapid socioeconomic change. Provides perspectives on how the worldview of Brazil's peasantry influenced participation in prophetic movements.

Placido, Barbara. "It's All to Do with Words: An Analysis of Spirit Possession in the Venezuelan Cult of María Lionza." *Man* 7 (2001): 207–224. An ethnographic study of spirit mediums' active shaping of messages during spirit possession in a Venezuelan new religion. A brief historical overview of the cult is provided.

Stoll, David. *Is Latin America Turning Protestant?: The Politics of Evangelical Growth.* Berkeley, Calif., 1990. A somewhat controversial survey of Protestantization trends around Latin America. Stoll focuses on foreign political connections and questions the role of new Evangelical groups in maintaining U.S. hegemony in Latin American countries.

Vanderwood, Paul J. *The Power of God against the Guns of Government: Religious Upheaval in Mexico at the Turn of the Nineteenth Century.* Stanford, Calif., 1998. Examines the role of Teresa Urrea's folk-saint cult in the famed Tomóchic nativistic revolt of the Rarámuri.

Vidaurri, Cynthia L. "Las que Menos Quería el Niño: Women of the Fidencista Movement." In *Chicana Traditions: Continuity and Change,* edited by Norma E. Cantú and Olga Nájera-Ramírez, pp. 133–142. Urbana, Ill. and Chicago, 2002. An ethnographic account of gendered experience among Mexicana mediums in a folk-saint movement.

Wallace, Anthony F. C. "Revitalization Movements: Some Theoretical Considerations for Their Comparative Study." *American Anthropologist* 58 (1956): 264–281. Frequently cited anthropological formulation of the multistage process by which new religious movements form. Highlights the role of prophetic revelators in resolving cultural crises. Illustrates with cases of prophetic movements in tribal settings.

MIGUEL C. LEATHAM (2005)

NEW TESTAMENT SEE BIBLICAL LITERATURE

NEW THOUGHT MOVEMENT.

The New Thought movement is a diverse and loosely affiliated collection of religious communities that share an idealistic theology, an optimistic worldview, and an emphasis on religious rituals that focus on personal well-being, health, and material success. The movement emerged in the United States in the last quarter of the nineteenth century and was well established by the first decade of the twentieth. It is the largest movement in what is often broadly referred to as the "metaphysical" tradition, which also includes Christian Science, Theosophy, and Spiritualism. In theory and practice, New Thought, like Christian Science, is a popular expression of religious idealism, and idealism is the unifying foundation of all forms of New Thought. Emma Curtis Hopkins (1849–1925) is properly cited as the founder of the movement, with its immediate precursors including Mary Baker Eddy (1821–1910) and her Church of Christ, Scientist; Phineas Parkhurst Quimby (1802–1866) and his students; the New England "Mind Cure" movement; and various independent groups and individuals practicing mental healing. Other less significant but notable formative influences can be attributed to Swedenborgianism, spiritualism, New England Transcendentalism, the Hegelian Societies of the late nineteenth century, imported forms of Hinduism (especially Vedānta), and secularization. New Thought is still centered in the United States, although the movement is well represented throughout the world.

The New Thought movement has revealed sustained growth throughout the twentieth century, and since the 1950s it has supplied institutional legitimation and theological support to the alternative healing movement and various beliefs and practices associated with the New Age movement. The impact of New Thought on American culture is revealed in its role as a precursor to and possible precipitating influence on popular psychology and the self-help movement, the ordination of women as ministers in mainstream Protestantism, best-selling popularizations of idealism such as Napoleon Hill's *Think and Grow Rich* (1937) and Norman Vincent Peale's *Power of Positive Thinking* (1952), and the development of prosperity and success teachings in secular culture and mainstream Protestantism.

Despite its longevity and impact on American culture, New Thought and its various subgroups have received little scholarly attention, although publications by Gail M. Harley, Beryl Satter, John K. Simmons, and J. Gordon Melton have offered good insights into certain aspects of its formative period. Encyclopedias and general texts on new religions often have brief sections on New Thought or representative groups (especially Unity), as do textbooks on religion in America. As often as not, however, New Thought is absent in general dictionaries of religion and textbooks on world religions. There are no critical histories of the movement and no significant scholarly treatments of its theology. In this regard, Charles S. Braden's now dated *Spirits in Rebellion* (1963) still offers the only general history of New Thought, and J. Stillson Judah's equally dated *History and Philosophy of the Metaphysical Movements in America* (1967) is the best overview of the movement's theology.

WORLDVIEW, PRACTICES, AND AIMS. As a contemporary manifestation of popular religious idealism, the deepest historical roots of New Thought can be traced to Plato (428–348 BCE), the father of the idealist tradition in philosophy. Other distant forebears include ancient Gnosticism, Neoplatonism, and pre-Nicean forms of Christianity associated with the Alexandrian school and typified by Origen (185–254). Philosophical precursors in the modern period are Rationalists such as René Descartes (1596–1650) and Baruch Spinoza (1632–1677), and Idealists such as Johann Fichte (1763–1814) and G. W. F. Hegel (1770–1831).

New Thought's brand of idealism holds that the ultimate basis of existence is mental (God as Mind) and all material/physical conditions are secondary to and products of human mental states and conditions. What this means for New Thought is that consciousness, ideas, and thoughts are the basis of reality and function as the casual forces behind all material/physical phenomena—from objects, including human bodies, to the events and circumstances of an individual's life. A formal statement of New Thought's foundational idealism is offered in the "Declaration of Principles" of the International New Thought Alliance (INTA), which declares (among other claims): "We affirm God as Mind, Infinite Being, Spirit, Ultimate Reality. . . . [and] that our mental states are carried forward into manifestation and become our experience in daily living" ("Declaration of Principles," 2001, p. 19). In principle, New Thought's idealism is similar to that of Christian Science, yet unlike the earlier movement, New Thought generally interprets matter and physical experiences in a positive light, viewing them as limited (but perfectible) manifestations of Spirit (Divine Mind). In this regard, New Thought groups tend to be world-affirming, harmonial (with respect to ultimate reality and humans), and proponents of human spiritual evolution.

In New Thought the ultimate power (e.g., God, Mind, Divine Mind, Principle, Truth, Intelligence) is understood as supremely good (the Good) and the ground of perfection. The omnipotence of the Good is expressed succinctly in INTA's Declaration of Principles as follows: "We affirm that God, the Good, is supreme, universal and eternal" ("Declaration of Principles," 2001, p. 19). The essence of humanity is divine, and humans are seen as spiritual beings that are linked with Divine Mind through their highest consciousness (e.g., Christ Mind, superconsciousness, Christ within). This relationship of unity is analogous to the relationship of *brahman* (the manifestation of ultimate reality) and *ātman* (the self) in Hinduism, as well as understandings of the human essence found in the Western Esoteric tradition, influenced by Neoplatonism and Gnosticism.

The failure of humans to fully demonstrate their innate spiritual perfection is the result of ignorance and wrong thinking (e.g., "error thought" and "mortal consciousness"). New Thought believes that because human consciousness is causative it is the source for all the experiences and conditions in a person's life—both positive and negative. Negative experiences and conditions (illness, poverty, theft, death, etc.) are the result of negative states in consciousness, and positive experiences and conditions are the result of positive states. The key to eliminating specific negative conditions and creating a tendency to ever more positive experiences is based in the belief that all persons are in essence spiritual beings, and that Divine Mind is accessible to human minds. When Divine Mind is properly engaged by human consciousness, the Good is brought into material/physical manifestation, thus eliminating negative experiences and conditions and replacing them with positive ones. This engagement is believed to occur "scientifically" through precise and systematic religious exercises, such as prayer, "spiritual treatment," "visualization," "affirmations," and, in some cases, "denials."

Through continued practice of these exercises (which are typically quite specific and individualized but may be general and collective) an individual's consciousness becomes increasingly attuned to the "Truth" so that the reality of Divine Mind is more frequently brought into manifestation. As a result, adherents may report improvement in general and specific conditions of their lives. This thoroughgoing idealism forms the basis of New Thought's theology and the foundation for its optimistic worldview. It is the premise upon which the movement's primary myths and rituals are predicated.

In practice, most New Thought rituals are individualistic in focus and aim to bring about improvements in precise areas of a special concern to individuals. The most common areas are the following: physical and emotional health, material prosperity, and personal relationships. Corporate religious activities are less common than individual religious practices, although New Thought congregations routinely engage in group prayer and treatment rituals. The movement as a whole affirms a positive expectancy for humanity and a belief in spiritual evolution, but individual groups are seldom socially active and tend to be silent on political, economic, and legal issues.

Early in its history, New Thought produced two notable theorists, Warren Felt Evans (1817–1889) and Horatio Dresser (1866–1954), but the movement as a whole rejected their scholarly explications of religious idealism in favor of the popular approaches utilized by Emma Curtis Hopkins and her students. As a result, the New Thought movement has never articulated its idealistic cosmology in a formal philosophical context. Rather, it has restricted academic horizons, it lacks a systematic theology, and it has developed no schools of higher learning. Nonetheless, in an era that has seen the devaluation of idealism in the academic community, especially among professional philosophers, it is significant that New Thought has remained firmly committed to its idealistic theology. Equally significant is the sustained growth of the movement in light of the decline of America's other major version of popular religious idealism, Christian Science.

Origins, Development, Leaders. As a unique expression of human religiosity, New Thought is a decidedly American religious phenomenon. From its birth in the 1880s in the Chicago ministry of Emma Curtis Hopkins, New Thought emerged in the context of (and was enriched by) the secularization process. Although the roots of New Thought can be traced to Christian Science, Mind Cure, and the mental healing movement, from its earliest days New Thought offered a unique and comprehensive interpretation of individual existence and humanity as a whole. Mental healing has continued to be a major component in New Thought systems, but as the movement grew the implications of mental healing expanded beyond bodily healing to include all areas of life. This is especially to be noted in the movement's "prosperity" teachings, which began to develop in the late 1880s.

The decisive origin of the movement, per se, can be traced to the writing, teaching, and evangelical ministry of Hopkins, a former student and professional associate of the founder of Christian Science, Mary Baker Eddy. Strong arguments are sometimes advanced for ascribing its origin to Phineas Parkhurst Quimby, a mental healer and former mesmerist who shared his technique with a small circle of his clients. Another reasonable source for New Thought is Christian Science and Eddy herself. Eddy had been a client and student of Quimby and later a teacher of Hopkins. Hopkins's dissatisfaction with Eddy's religion, and possibly a professional misunderstanding between the two women, led to Hopkins's separation from Eddy's work and her development of an independent form of Christian Science in Chicago in the mid-1880s.

Hopkins's Chicago work led to the establishment of a seminary and, beginning in 1889, the ordination of ministers. On the basis of her encouragement, Hopkins's students took the New Thought message to all parts of the United States, chiefly the emerging urban centers of the Midwest and West, in particular San Francisco, Denver, Kansas City, and Saint Louis. Included among the major New Thought leaders who studied with Hopkins were Kate (Mrs. Frank) Bingham, the teacher of Nona Brooks (1861–1945) and a founder of Divine Science; Malinda Cramer (1844–1906), also a founder of Divine Science; Charles Fillmore (1854–1948) and Myrtle Fillmore (1845–1931), co-founders of Unity; Annie Rix Militz (1856–1924), a prominent author in Unity's early years, founder of Homes of Truth, and publisher of *Master Mind* (1911–1931) magazine; Helen Wilmans (1835–1907), the founder of Mental Science; Frances Lord, who carried New Thought to England; H. Emilie Cady (1848–1941), author of New Thought's most widely disseminated text, Unity's *Lessons In Truth*; Ella Wheeler Wilcox (1850–1919), poet and syndicated columnist; and Elizabeth Towne (1865–1960), INTA president (1924–1925) and the publisher of the major New Thought periodical, *The Nautilus* (1898–1954). After her retirement from public teaching and administrative work, Hopkins tutored Ernest S. Holmes (1887–1960), founder of Religious Science. All told, by the time Hopkins left active ministry in 1895, she had ordained more than one hundred persons, and these, together with numerous others who had been exposed to her work, formed the first generation of New Thought leaders. For this reason, Hopkins was referred to as "the teacher of teachers" in the movement.

As Hopkins's version of Christian Science transformed itself into New Thought, the younger movement became clearly distinguished from Eddy's work. Aside from abandoning the term *Christian Science* in its self-references, the three most prominent distinctions pertain to the status of doctrine, the material world, and medicine. In contrast to Christian Science, New Thought and its representative groups have no authoritative doctrines, and even in denominations with distinct and venerated founders (e.g., Unity and Religious Science) the authority of the founder's teachings is minimal at best. New Thought also differs from Christian Science in its generally positive evaluation of the material world. In distinction to Christian Science beliefs, in New Thought, matter is not illusionary and the material world is not antithetical to Spirit (Divine Mind). Instead, New Thought tends to view the material world (including humankind) as an extension or expression of Spirit, which is growing toward perfection. Finally, New Thought is not opposed to the medical resolution of physical illness. In conformity with its generally optimistic and harmonial worldview, New Thought embraces all forms of healing, including traditional Western medicine.

Entering the twentieth century, New Thought's idealistic theology and optimistic worldview allowed it to assume a congenial stance relative to the new realities of American life: secularization, urbanization, industrialization, pluralism, and consumerism. Called "the religion of healthy mindedness" by William James in *The Varieties of Religious Experience* (1902), the movement affirmed a positive vision of humanity and sacralized critical aspects of what was coming to be the American dream: health, wealth, and peace of mind. Its message of happiness and prosperity had particular resonance with members of the expanding urban middle class, which was then reaching majority status and sociocultural self-consciousness. It was this class that first embraced New Thought, and it has remained the primary source for membership in the movement.

From a practical standpoint, and in addition to its idealistic principles and "scientific" optimism, New Thought's early and enduring success is owed to five major factors, probably in this order: (1) confidence of its leaders and movement-building; (2) professional empowerment of women; (3) prosperity teachings; (4) skillful use of mass media; and (5) a general ease with and adaptability to secularization.

The confidence of the early New Thought leaders was intense. Zealous missionaries, they believed in the truth of their message with the evangelical ardor frequently expressed by members of young and dynamic religions. The writings and addresses of Hopkins's and her students reveal the confidence typical of early New Thought leaders, with Hopkins's "Baccalaureate Address" (1891) and *High Mysticism* (1920) serving as representative texts. Following Hopkins's model, many of her students developed distinct movements of their own, establishing ministerial schools, ordaining ministers, and sending them forth to establish religious communities (churches, societies, centers, and temples), then networking these communities together into distinct, though loosely structured, denominations. Examples of this developmental strategy include Hopkins's own movement, Wilmans's Mental Science Association, Militz's Homes of Truth, the Fillmore's Unity School of Christianity, and Cramer's and Brooks's Divine Science. Although many of the early denominations were short-lived, Unity and Divine Science, both founded in the 1880s, have endured, ranking first and third, respectively, in size at the beginning of the twenty-first century.

The majority of Hopkins's students and ministers were women, and the early movement had a distinctly feminist character and public profile. Hopkins appears to have been the first woman in modern times to ordain women as Christian ministers. As a consequence, New Thought had particular appeal to women with professional aspirations who were otherwise often excluded from public life. The professional empowerment of women contributed to the early success of New Thought by not only attracting talented women to the movement, but also reform-minded men and persons of both genders with progressive social visions. The movement has maintained its commitment to female leadership, with women forming the majority of New Thought ministers.

New Thought's growth was also fueled by its promotion of prosperity teachings, whose deepest cultural influences can be traced to the Calvinist notion of the "visible signs" of one's predestination for salvation. Other contributing influences were Benjamin Franklin and Ralph Waldo Emerson, both of whom proposed methods of general self-improvement, which they believed would also lead to economic success. An even more direct influence was the expansion of economic opportunity for members of the middle class in the late nineteenth century, as well as the growing acceptance that material affluence was a cultural ideal if not a moral imperative. New Thought offered the promise that affluence could be achieved; in fact, New Thought affirmed that God wanted all people to be prosperous. Through its prosperity techniques, which were essentially extensions of its mental-healing methods, New Thought introduced itself to America's middle class as a religion that proclaimed the spiritual virtue of affluence and financial success. In this regard, New Thought's prosperity teachings have affinities with Andrew Carnegie's *Gospel of Wealth* (1900) and later Napoleon Hill's *Think and Grow Rich* (1937). Prosperity continues to be a major theme of New Thought literature, with Charles Fillmore's *Prosperity* (1936) and Catherine Ponder's *The Dynamic Laws of Prosperity* (1962) being classics of the genre.

From its earliest days, New Thought leaders were quick to recognize the potential of the mass media. By the early twentieth century, periodicals with a national reach were widely used to disseminate the New Thought message to the general public. They also served to maintain the networks of the developing denominations. Later (and this is especially true of Unity), New Thought leaders made extensive use of radio. Only with the dawning of television did New Thought's aggressive use of advanced media technology begin to decline. In the twenty-first century, New Thought denominations and many individual churches have websites, and worship services of larger churches are aired on radio and cable television in most metropolitan areas. Although both the number and circulation of New Thought publications have been declining since the mid-twentieth century, major New Thought groups continue to publish periodicals, including Unity's *Daily Word*, the United Church of Religious Science's *Science of Mind*, and INTA's *New Thought*. *Daily Word* is the largest of these publications, with over a million subscribers.

Unlike many traditional forms of American religion, New Thought was not and is not antagonistic to the astonishing transformation of culture and society wrought by secularization. Rather than decrying the sins of secularization, New Thought either ignored or actively embraced the widespread cultural change that characterized Western culture in the twentieth century. In doing so, New Thought has proven itself remarkably adaptable to and implicitly (if not explicitly) supportive of pluralism, individualism, racial and gender equality, modifications in traditional gender roles and family structures, globalization, and consumerism. Nonetheless, in harmony with its general apolitical character, the movement has seldom taken public positions advocating social change.

MAJOR COMMUNITIES. The twenty-first-century New Thought movement is comprised of numerous religious communities, most of which are small independent churches, although several can be rightly classified as denominations.

Divine Science. Among these major groups, the oldest is Divine Science. The roots of Divine Science can be traced to the ministry of Malinda E. Cramer in San Francisco in 1888 and, more significantly, to the work of three sisters (Fannie Brooks James, Alethea Brooks, and especially Nona Brooks) in Denver in the 1890s. Cramer's International Divine Science Association (founded in 1892) was the first national organization of New Thought religious communities and arguably the predecessor of INTA. Of the major forms of New Thought, Divine Science has been the least evangelistic and least institutionalized.

In the late 1990s a small number of churches separated from the original Divine Science Federation, forming the United Divine Science Ministries. Central texts of Divine Science are Cramer's *Divine Science and Healing* (1902) and a compilation from the works of Cramer and Fannie Brooks James, *Divine Science: Its Principle and Practice* (1957). The movement's most recognized leader was Emmet Fox (1886–1951), the author of numerous widely popular texts, including *The Sermon on the Mount* (1934) and *Power Through Constructive Thinking* (1940). His pamphlet *The Golden Key* (1937) offers an abbreviated outline of spiritual healing treatment as it is practiced in New Thought, and his idealistic maxim, "life is consciousness," is among the most well-known aphorisms in the movement. Divine Science is the smallest of New Thought's denominations, with a total membership of less than five thousand as of 2004.

Unity is second oldest and most clearly Christian denomination in New Thought. It is the largest and most culturally prominent New Thought group. Unity was cofounded in Kansas City in 1889 by Charles and Myrtle Fillmore, a married couple. From its inception as a prayer and publication ministry, it has experienced relatively sustained growth. Since 1966 it has been represented by two loosely affiliated organizations: Unity School of Christianity and the Association of Unity Churches. Unity School, located at Unity Village in Kansas City, Missouri, is the largest material complex in New Thought. It is the successor of the Fillmores' original organization and directs the denomination's publishing, prayer, and education ministries. The Association manages Unity's ecclesiastical operations, ordains ministers, supervises churches, and directs expansion.

Two other small independent Unity groups emerged in the 1990s: the Unity-Progressive Council and the World Federation for Practical Christianity (formerly the World Federation of Independent Unity Churches [name changed in 2003]). Unity's primary textbook ("together with the Bible") is Cady's *Lessons in Truth*, which was first published as a series of articles in *Unity* magazine beginning in 1894. Unity is New Thought's largest book publisher, and, among its sizable collection of texts, two of the more distinctive are Charles Fillmore's *Christian Healing* (1909) and *The Twelve Powers of Man* (1930). His *Metaphysical Bible Dictionary* (1931) is New Thought's only comprehensive lexicon offering a "metaphysical" (allegorical) interpretation of the names of persons and places found in the Bible. Outside of New Thought, Unity is perhaps best known for its prayer ministry, Silent Unity, which receives about one million contacts annually—a number far in excess of the total number of active Unity participants. There are nearly one thousand ministries and study groups worldwide, with membership probably in the 150,000 range.

Religious Science. The second largest New Thought denomination is Religious Science, founded in Los Angeles in 1927 by Ernest Holmes. Originally established as the Institute of Religious Science and Philosophy, churches were being established by the 1940s, and the movement began to develop a more traditional religious appearance. In 1954, tensions over ecclesiastical structure led to a schism, with a small number of churches separating from what became the United Church of Religious Science and forming what became Religious Science International. Over the years, the two groups have maintained a relatively cordial relationship, with the major differences being organizational rather than doctrinal. In the early 1990s a third Religious Science organization was formed: Global Religious Science Ministries.

Religious Science is notable for its rejection of identification with Christianity. The United Church remains the largest branch of the denomination. All branches of Religious Science recognize Holmes's *Science of Mind* (1926) as their foundational text. Other notable works by Holmes are *This Thing Called Life* (1943) and *What Religious Science Teaches* (1944). Total membership in all branches of Religious Science is around sixty thousand worldwide.

Universal Foundation for Better Living. The youngest New Thought denomination is the Universal Foundation for Better Living (UFBL), founded in Chicago in 1974 by Johnnie Colemon (Johnnie May Colemon Nedd). UFBL is the most successful Unity-derived movement, although there are no formal ties between UFBL and Unity's historical institutions. Prior to the founding of UFBL, Colemon had been a successful minister in the Unity movement, developing a large congregation in Chicago, expanding the reach of New Thought teachings to the African American community, and serving as the President of the Association of Unity Churches (1970). Institutional disagreements led to the founding of UFBL, which was originally founded as Unity Foundation for Better Living but changed by Colemon when authorities in the Unity movement challenged the use of the name "Unity." The current President is Mary Ann Tumpkin, who replaced Johnnie Colemon in 1996.

UFBL bases its beliefs on the traditional teachings of the Unity movement, especially as promulgated in the works of Unity's founders, Myrtle and Charles Fillmore, and H. Emilie Cady's *Lessons In Truth*. The movement is strongly committed to higher learning in the New Thought tradition and has developed a number of unique educational initiatives, most notably a project to establish an accredited New Thought seminary.

The movement is the third largest New Thought denomination, with 27 affiliated religious communities and an estimated 20,000 members. In addition to the USA, UFBL has affiliated groups in Canada, the Bahamas, Jamaica, and Guyana. It publishes a monthly devotional magazine, *Daily Inspiration for Better Living*.

INTA. Properly speaking, the International New Thought Alliance (INTA) is not a denomination but rather an umbrella organization comprised of religious groups, individual churches, and individuals. INTA is the most democratically structured of all the major New Thought groups, with full membership rights extended to laypersons. Its general aims are to promote the New Thought movement as a whole, disseminate New Thought teachings internationally, and facilitate solidarity among all New Thought participants. INTA was founded in 1914, although its roots can be traced to predecessor groups dating to the 1890s. Throughout its history, the success of INTA has largely been contingent on the support of the major New Thought denominations and prominent leaders in the movement. Since the early 1990s the significance of INTA appears to have decreased as individual denominations have grown in size and institutional self-identity. In addition, a leadership struggle in 1996 resulted in a number of influential leaders leaving INTA to form the Association for Global New Thought. The president of INTA in 2004 was Blaine C. Mays, who became president in 1974 and held the office longer than any other INTA president. The Alliance publishes *New Thought*, a quarterly magazine, and its creedlike "Declaration of Principles" embodies the general beliefs of most New Thought adherents.

Seicho-no-Ie. The global scope of New Thought is reflected in its presence on all continents and in more than sixty countries, with a particularly strong presence in sub-Saharan Africa. A related movement, Seicho-no-Ie (Home of Infinite Life, or House of Blessing), was founded by Masaharu Taniguchi (1893–1985) in Japan in 1930. Taniguchi was inspired in part by Religious Science, and the movement's foundational idealism and optimistic worldview suggests a close affinity with traditional New Thought beliefs. Seicho-no-Ie is, however, more broadly syncretistic than other New Thought groups and includes elements of Buddhism and Shintō otherwise not found in the movement. Seicho-no-Ie is also more socially conservative and politically active than traditional New Thought denominations. If included within the movement, Seicho-no-Ie would be by far New Thought's largest denomination, with a worldwide membership of over 1.25 million, including 400,000 to 500,000 members in Brazil.

SEE ALSO Hopkins, Emma Curtis; Unity.

BIBLIOGRAPHY

Anderson, C. Alan. *Contrasting Strains of Metaphysical Idealism Contributing to New Thought.* Santa Barbara, Calif., 1991.

Anderson, C. Alan. *Healing Hypotheses: Horatio W. Dresser and the Philosophy of New Thought.* Boston: Ph.D. Dissertation. Boston University, 1963. New York, 1993.

Anderson, C. Alan. "Quimby as Founder of New Thought." In *Journal of the Society for the Study of Metaphysical Religion* 3, no. 1 (1997): 5–22.

Anderson, Ferne. "Emma Curtis Hopkins: Springboard to New Thought." M.A. thesis, University of Denver, 1981.

Braden, Charles S. *Spirits in Rebellion: The Rise and Development of New Thought.* Dallas, Tex., 1963.

Carpenter, Robert T., and Wade Clark Roof. "The Transplanting of Seicho-no-ie from Japan to Brazil: Moving Beyond the Ethnic Enclave." In *Journal of the Society for the Study of Metaphysical Religion* 2, no. 2 (1996): 117–139.

deChant, Dell. "New Thought and the New Age." In *New Age Encyclopedia*, edited by J. Gordon Melton. Detroit, Mich., 1990.

deChant, Dell. "Myrtle Fillmore and Her Daughters." In *Women's Leadership in Marginal Religions: Explorations Outside the Mainstream*, edited by Catherine Wessinger. Urbana, Ill., and Chicago, 1993.

"Declaration of Principles." *New Thought* 85, No. 3 (2001): 19.

Dresser, Horatio W. *A History of the New Thought Movement.* New York, 1919.

Dresser, Horatio W., ed. *The Quimby Manuscripts.* New York, 1919.

Fuller, Robert C. *Mesmerism and the American Cure of Souls.* Philadelphia, 1982.

Harley, Gail M. *Emma Curtis Hopkins: Forgotten Founder of New Thought.* Syracuse, N.Y., 2002.

Jackson, Carl T. "The New Thought Movement and the Nineteenth Century Discovery of Oriental Philosophy." In *Journal of Popular Culture* 9 (1975): 523–548.

Judah, J. Stillson. *The History and Philosophy of the Metaphysical Movements in America.* Philadelphia, 1967.

Laughlin, Paul. "Re-Turning East: Watering the Withered Oriental Roots of New Thought." *Journal of the Society for the Study of Metaphysical Religion* 3, no. 2 (1997): 113–133.

Melton, J. Gordon, ed. *New Thought: A Reader.* Santa Barbara, Calif., 1990.

Melton, J. Gordon. "Emma Curtis Hopkins: A Feminist of the 1880s and Mother of New Thought." In *Women's Leadership in Marginal Religions: Explorations Outside the Mainstream*, edited by Catherine Wessinger. Urbana, Ill., and Chicago, 1993.

Melton, J. Gordon. "The Case of Edward J. Arens and the Distortion of New Thought History." *Journal of the Society for the Study of Metaphysical Religion* 2, no. 1 (1996): 13–29.

Melton, J. Gordon. "How Divine Science Got to Denver." In *Journal of the Society for the Study of Metaphysical Religion* 7, no. 2 (2001): 103–122.

Parker, Gail T. *Mind Cure in New England: From the Civil War to World War I.* Hanover, N.H., 1973.

Satter, Beryl. *Each Mind a Kingdom: American Women, Sexual Purity, and the New Thought Movement, 1875–1920.* Berkeley, Calif., 1999.

Simmons, John K. "The Ascension of Annie Rix Militz and the Home(s) of Truth: Perfection Meets Paradise in Early Twentieth-Century Los Angeles." Ph.D. diss., University of California, Santa Barbara, 1987.

Simmons, John K. "The Forgotten Contributions of Annie Rix Militz to the Unity School of Christianity." In *Nova Religio: The Journal of Alternative and Emergent Religions* 2, no. 1 (1998): 76–92.

Simmons, John K. "The Eddy-Hopkins Paradigm: A 'Metaphysical Look' at Their Historic Relationship." In *Journal of the Society for the Study of Metaphysical Religion* 8, no. 2 (2002): 129–151.

Szasz, Ferenc. "'New Thought' and the American West." In *Journal of the West* 23, no. 2 (1984): 83–90.

Teener, James W. "Unity School of Christianity." Ph.D. diss., University of Chicago, 1942.

DELL DECHANT (2005)

NEWTON, ISAAC (1642–1727), widely regarded as the greatest scientist of all time. Born prematurely (at Woolsthorpe, Lincolnshire, England), Newton developed into a physically weak, lonely, unhappy child; he was also an indifferent student until an encounter with a school bully roused him to excel. In 1661, he entered Trinity College at Cambridge University, where he showed no distinction until he came under the influence of Isaac Barrow, a professor of mathematics. A man of great insight, Barrow was the first to recognize Newton's genius; in fact, he resigned his professorship so that Newton, at age twenty-six, could be appointed to it.

Shortly after Newton graduated in 1665, the university was closed because of plague, and he had to return to Woolsthorpe. There he spent eighteen months in studies that laid the foundation for much of his later work. He discovered the binomial theorem, differential and integral calculus, the theory of color, several other important theorems in mathematics, and the celebrated law of gravitation—which for nearly 250 years was regarded as the epitome and exemplar of scientific laws of nature.

Newton's interests were both mathematical and experimental. He invented a reflecting telescope to free telescopes from the chromatic aberration of refracting lenses. He presented a small version of his telescope to the Royal Society, which honored him by electing him a fellow when he was only thirty. In 1672, when Newton published his new theory of light and color—including the experiments showing that white light can be separated into its component colors by a prism—the society was bombarded with letters disputing his conclusions. Some of the correspondents were scientists of note, among them Robert Hooke and Christiaan Huygens. The controversy affected Newton greatly and, thereafter, he tended to withdraw from the public eye. Though he had vowed after the controversy not to publish any further discoveries, he did, in fact, continue to publish.

Newton conceived a proprietary interest in every subject he investigated; there was hardly any achievement of his creative scientific life that was unaccompanied by acrimony and quarreling. This was largely owing to a great deal of paranoia and self-doubt in Newton's personality. His ego needed to be continually bolstered by the praise and admiration of others, a trait that may have had its cause in Newton's humble origins—his father was a yeoman, a fact that always made Newton uneasy and that he tried to obscure by inventing grandiose genealogies for himself.

In 1684, Newton received a visit from the astronomer Edmond Halley, who consulted him about some mathematical points concerning gravitational attraction (Halley and Hooke had been working on this problem for some time). To Halley's great surprise, Newton replied that he had already made these calculations many years earlier, but that he could not find the appropriate papers. Halley urged Newton to recalculate, using his original theorems, and to prepare a manuscript for the Royal Society. Halley showed enormous tact and good judgment in not letting Hooke's claim to the inverse-square law of gravitation and the attendant acrimony between Hooke and Newton vitiate the whole project. Financed by moneys from Halley's personal funds, Newton's work was finally published in 1687 under the title *Philosophia naturalis principia mathematica.*

Newton's *Principia*, as it has come to be known, is justifiably regarded as the greatest scientific work ever produced. It integrated into one coherent whole diverse data and mathematical principles concerning the motion of material particles and gravitation. As the publication of Copernicus's *De revolutionibus* in 1543 marked the beginning of the great scientific revolution, the publication of the *Principia* marked its completion and the beginning of the modern scientific age.

Indeed, Newton is often described as the inaugurator of the "age of reason." Alexander Pope hailed him thus:

> Nature and Nature's laws lay hid in night: God said, let Newton be! and all was light.

And many were other accolades from philosophers, theologians, and poets, although few of them ever read the *Principia* or had the mathematical ability to comprehend it, as the philosopher John Locke confessed about himself. For his own and the immediately succeeding generation, Newton epitomized reason, sound judgment, and even saintly goodness. But by the beginning of the nineteenth century, poets like Blake, Wordsworth, Shelley, and Keats had vilified Newton, identifying him—and the science that he had helped create—with the forces of mechanization that were despiritualizing the cosmos. Blake, for example, regarded Newton, along with Locke and Francis Bacon, as a member of an "infernal trinity" that had a satanic influence on "Albion," by which Blake meant unspoiled England, or archetypal man.

In 1693, Newton suffered a sort of nervous breakdown. He had represented the university as a member of Parliament since 1689, and he had devotedly attended to his mother during her final illness, and these responsibilities must have weighed on him. After his recovery, he resumed his life in London, where he became warden and later master of the Royal Mint. In 1703 he became president of the Royal Society, a post he used, often unscrupulously, in his various and many feuds, including one with G. W. Leibniz over the question as to which of them had first discovered differential calculus. He published his *Opticks*, written in a very different style from the *Principia*, in 1704; it was actually read not only by his scientific colleagues but also by other intellectuals. He was knighted in 1705. Shortly before his death, he removed to the country air of the village of Kensington. He died there in 1727, without having requested last rites. He was buried alongside kings and princes in Westminster Abbey.

Throughout his life—and by no means only during his nervous breakdown, as some have maintained—Newton was highly interested in theological, chronological, and alchemical studies. It is estimated that he wrote some two million words on these subjects, a total far surpassing that of his writings in mathematics and physics. Much of this material, particularly that on alchemy, consists of the writings of others that Newton copied for his own use, but he also wrote books of his own on these subjects. It may even be true, as Newton himself seems to have hinted, that his real interest lay in a wide and comprehensive knowledge that he hoped to acquire through alchemy and theology, and that he viewed his scientific studies only as amusing diversions. Since he could not, in general, be accused of excessive humility, we may have to understand in another light a well-known remark he made toward the end of his life: "I do not know what I may appear to the world; but to myself I seem to have been only like a boy, playing on the seashore, and diverting myself in now and then finding a smoother pebble or a prettier shell than ordinary, while the great ocean of Truth lay all undiscovered before me."

Newton certainly believed in the *prisca sapienta*, an ancient wisdom that had existed among priest-scientists such as the Chaldeans in Babylonia, the brahmans in India, and Moses and Pythagoras among the Hebrews and the Greeks. He believed that this wisdom was now largely lost, that he, Newton, was one of an esoteric brotherhood extending back to ancient times, and that he was redisclosing this knowledge in a new form, more mathematical than metaphysical or mythological. "Newton was not the first of the age of reason," the economist John Maynard Keynes concluded after examining Newton's alchemical papers. "He was the last of the magicians, the last of the Babylonians and Sumerians, the last great mind which looked out on the visible and the intellectual world with the same eyes as those who began to build our intellectual inheritance rather less than 10,000 years ago."

Newton was a staunch monotheist and strongly antitrinitarian. Perhaps owing to this, he never took holy orders and could not become the master of Trinity College. His antitrinitarian sentiment, however, was a dreadful secret that Newton tried desperately all his life to conceal. He himself often maintained the philosophical autonomy of nature and revelation, but for himself he certainly regarded his work in natural philosophy to be a gloria and a study of God's works. Future generations, in denigrating religion and exiling God from natural philosophy, were more influenced by the science and its mechanistic implications, a science of which he was the supreme representative and symbol, than by Newton's own example or beliefs. This trend would have horrified Newton, who felt an emotional, personal relationship with God. In fact, Newton himself would have wished to be regarded as a prophet of God.

SEE ALSO Alchemy, article on Renaissance Alchemy; Rosicrucians.

BIBLIOGRAPHY

The standard biography of Newton is Louis Trenchard More's *Isaac Newton: A Biography* (New York, 1934). A short, popular account is given by E. N. Andrade in his *Sir Isaac Newton* (New York, 1954). A more recent, reliable biography is Richard S. Westfall's *Never at Rest: A Biography of Isaac Newton* (Cambridge, 1980). A fascinating study of the psychology of this complex genius is Frank E. Manuel's *A Portrait of Isaac Newton* (Cambridge, 1968). For Newton's chronological, religious, and alchemical interests and studies, the following three books, respectively, are indispensable: *Isaac Newton: Historian* (Cambridge, Mass., 1963) and *The Religion of Isaac Newton* (Oxford, 1974), both by Frank E. Manuel, and *The Foundations of Newton's Alchemy, or "The Hunting of the Greene Lyon"* (Cambridge, 1975) by Betty Jo Teeter Dobbs. A good and representative selection of Newton's writings concerning his philosophy of nature and natural theology is to be found in *Newton's Philosophy of Nature*, edited, arranged, and annotated by H. S. Thayer (New York, 1953).

New Sources

Aughton, Peter. *Newton's Apple: Issac Newton and the English Scientific Renaissance.* London, 2003.

English, John C. "John Hutchinson's Critique of Newtonian Heterodoxy," *Church History* 68/3 (1999): 581–597.

Lincoln, Bruce. "Issac Newton and Oriental Jones on Myth, Ancient History and the Relative Prestige of Peoples," *History of Religions* 42/1 (2002): 1–18.

Newton and Religion. Dordrecht, Netherlands, 1999.

Pfizenmaier, Thomas C. "Was Issac Newton an Arian?" *Journal of the History of Ideas* 58 (1997): 57–80.

RAVI RAVINDRA (1987)
Revised Bibliography

NEW YEAR FESTIVALS.

The concept of year, which is found in all higher cultures (as solar year or lunar year or some combination of the two), is not known in all archaic cultures. Some cultures reckon only in periods of approximately six months; this is especially the case in tropical lands where seedtime and harvest come twice in the course of a single year. Even when the year is regarded as a basic division of time, the calculation is often based not (or not exclusively) on the sun and the moon but on the visibility of certain constellations; in tropical and subtropical areas, it is based with special frequency on the heliacal early rising of the Pleiades. The beginning of the year, or the "New Year," is often not a precise and fixed date that is astronomically determined (e.g., by equinoxes or solstices). Rather, it is a period that is determined by the annual vegetation cycle or, more generally, by climatic processes (passage from the dark period of the year to the bright, from the cold to the warm, from the stormy to the calm, from the dry to the rainy). Such periods are often accompanied by festivities, and when the interval between such festivities is approximately as long as a solar year, one is justified in speaking of New Year festivals.

Even where the year is known as a unit of time, it does not necessarily follow that the years are counted and that a chronology exists. "It is true indeed of most primitive peoples . . . that they are well acquainted with . . . the concrete phenomenon of the year . . . as a single period of the seasonal variation, but do not reckon in years in this sense. That is to say, the year is by them empirically given but not limited in the abstract: above all it is not a calendrical and numerical quantity" (Nilsson, 1920, p. 90). Thus in archaic cultures and in early high cultures the importance of New Year festivals is not, or is only in small measure, found in the fact that they are measures of time; the principal function of such ceremonies is to ensure, during a critical transitional period, a renewal of life and the life force. In fact in many instances they even assume the form of a symbolic new creation out of chaos.

Whereas New Year ceremonies vary widely from culture to culture, their meaning is essentially concerned with the phenomenon of transition or passage in its two aspects of "elimination" and "inauguration." What is old, exhausted, weakened, inferior, and harmful is to be eliminated, and what is new, fresh, powerful, good, and healthy is to be introduced and ensured. The first aspect finds expression in ceremonies of dissociation, purification, destruction, and so on. These involve washing, fasting, putting off or destroying old clothing, and quenching fires as well as the expulsion of sicknesses and evil powers (demons) through cries, noisemaking, and blows or through the dispatch of an animal or human being on which are loaded the sins of the previous period of time. The ceremonies may also reintroduce chaos through the dissolution of the social order and the suspension of taboos in force at other times and, in some cases, through the election of a temporary pseudo-king. The conflict between the old and the new time is also symbolized by ceremonial battles and by masquerades (in which the demons to be expelled or the creative ancestors of the primordial time may be represented). In addition there is often a temporary suspension of the division between the world of the living and the world of the dead, with a return of the latter to the houses of the living, where they receive sacrifices and food but from which they are ceremoniously dismissed at the end of the festal period.

The second and positive aspect of the passage from old to new is seen in the donning of new clothes, the lighting of a new fire, and the drawing of freshwater as well as in green branches and other symbols of life, in initiations (reception of young people into the cult community), and in orgiastic festive joy that leads to many kinds of excesses: immoderate eating, drinking, and dancing and, often, sexual orgies (these are to be regarded not only as a reintroduction of chaotic conditions but also as an attempt at the forcible augmentation of the life forces). In agrarian cultures there is often a suspension of taboos at the new harvest and the renewal of food reserves. Only rarely, however, are all these elements found conjoined. In any case, a purely phenomenological approach is inadequate and can even be misleading, because it presumes a fictitious universality. A phenomenological consideration of the traits common to New Year festivals must therefore be supplemented by a detailed examination of the form they have taken in the context of particular cultures. This kind of detailed analysis is extensively provided in works by Vittorio Lanternari (1959, 1976).

ARCHAIC CULTURES. In most archaic cultures New Year ceremonies are a dramatic representation of occurrences in the primordial time and, more specifically, of the *fondazione degli alimenti* or the establishment of the manner of obtaining food, which is recorded in myths about the primordial time. To this symbolic re-creation of the established order is added the concern with the expulsion of the unfavorable period of the year and the inauguration of the favorable period.

Hunting and food-gathering cultures. In most hunting and food-gathering cultures New Year ceremonies take place at a time when food is beginning to be scarce. In Australia this is usually toward the end of the dry period (in many parts of Australia the rainy season begins in October, in other parts in December). The San of the Kalahari Desert in southern Africa also conduct their New Year ceremonies at the beginning of the rainy season. Among the Selk'nam (in the Tierra del Fuego archipelago) and the Andaman Islanders, the ceremonies focus chiefly on banishing the bad (cold or stormy) season of the year; elsewhere the emphasis is on inaugurating the good season with its abundant food (as in the ceremonies of the Australian Aborigines, which aim at an increase in certain species of animals). In the arctic climate of the Inuit (Eskimo) hunting (which consists chiefly of the slaying of marine mammals) is impossible during the winter months; these months are instead a time of intense ritual activity that reaches its climax at the winter solstice. Among the Inuit, religious exaltation finds expression in shamanistic activity and especially, as with hunters and food collectors generally, in dancing. These dances represent in dramatic form the events of the primordial time, that is, the deeds of the ancestors and culture heroes.

Unrestrained eating and drinking are not found at these feasts of hunters and gatherers, and sexual orgies are rare. Such orgies do occur among some Western Inuit tribes, but their New Year festivals clearly show the influence of the fishing cultures of the American Indians of the Northwest Coast. Among Australian Aborigines, sexual orgies are connected with initiations, but these are not part of New Year festivals. The belief in collective return of the dead from the sea is usually not found except among some few Inuit tribes, and in this case the form of the belief is connected with their manner of life as hunters of marine mammals, a connection found also in the belief systems of the fishing cultures. Finally, among hunting and food-gathering cultures, the sacrifice of firstlings is not part of New Year celebrations (as it is among nomadic herdsmen and cultivators). Where sacrifices of firstlings are customary, they are offered immediately after a successful hunt.

Fishing cultures. The term *fishing cultures* is here used in a broad sense to include those peoples who hunt chiefly marine mammals or even other sea animals, such as tortoises. Because the peoples in question are sedentary inhabitants of islands and coasts, they are also often agriculturalists, where climatic conditions allow. But where the character of experience is determined primarily by the group's relation to the sea, this relation manifests itself in the New Year festival. Thus even the time for the New Year festival is determined by the condition of the sea; the festival may occur at the solemn inauguration of the fishing period (when, for example, certain fish or other marine animals appear in great numbers) or at the close of this period (when fishing becomes impossible for a long time because of storms or excessive cold). Among the American Indians of the Northwest Coast (the Kwakiutl, Tsimshian, and others), the ceremonies take place when the salmon enter the rivers in great schools and the salmon catch begins; during the ceremonies certain parts of the catch are thrown back into the water (the same is done among some Inuit tribes of the Northwest Coast). Similar ceremonies are conducted by the coastal Koriak and coastal Chukchi, Siberian peoples who live chiefly by hunting whales and seals, but these ceremonies are conducted at the end of the hunting season.

An important element in the New Year festivals of fishing cultures is the belief in a collective return of the dead, especially of those drowned at sea; this idea is particularly important among peoples of the Northern Hemisphere, and it has left its mark on European folklore. Where sacrifices of the animals caught are offered (these are to be regarded in part as sacrifices of firstlings), they are addressed either to the sea as such or to the dead; in the former case a belief in a return of the animals to life is also of some importance at times.

Nomadic herding cultures. The special characteristics of New Year festivals among cattle-breeding nomads are most clearly seen in northern Eurasia, where the distinction between the cold and warm seasons of the year is pronounced. These peoples, whether breeders of reindeer (Saami, Samoyeds, Tunguz, Koriak, Chukchi) or breeders of horses, sheep, and cattle (Altai Tatars, Abakan Tatars, Yakuts, Mongols), celebrate their New Year festivals in the spring, when the vegetation revives, the animals produce their young, and milk and milk products are abundant. At this time sacrifices of firstlings are offered to the higher powers and especially to the supreme heavenly being in gratitude for the increase of the flocks; these offerings consist both of young animals and of bloodless victims (milk and milk products, such as koumiss, an alcoholic drink made of mare's milk); often too the rite of bloodless dedication of animals is practiced. Festive joy finds expression also in abundant meals and in sporting competitions that represent in symbolic form the victory of summer over winter.

In tropical regions the shift of seasons often occurs in a less striking way, and animals often produce young throughout the entire year. For this reason New Year festivals of the type found in northern Eurasia are rarely found among the herding peoples of Africa, except for certain festivals that occur before the beginning of the rainy season. But in subtropical regions, for example, in Southwest Asia, springtime festivals are found, or at least traces of them can be seen, as among the Arabs and in the Israelite Pesaḥ.

It can be said of all nomadic herding cultures that they do not have a belief in the regular collective return of the dead. Sexual orgies too are almost unknown among them.

Primitive cultivation cultures. According to Lanternari (1976), three types of agrarian cultures are to be distinguished: (1) primitive cultivators (tuber cultivators) without social stratification; (2) advanced cultivators with improved methods of tilling and a social stratification; and (3) grain growers, who already represent a transition to the high cultures. A vivid example of the New Year festivals of primitive tuber cultivators is the Milamala festival of the Trobriand Islanders of Melanesia, which Bronislaw Malinowski, in particular, described in great detail. It has its foundation in mythology and is celebrated for an entire lunar month, that is, in August–September, when the harvest of yams, which are the principal food, has been completed and there is thus an abundance of food. During the entire month work in the produce gardens is strictly forbidden; the time is spent in singing, dancing, eating copious meals, and engaging in sexual orgies. During this period the spirits of the dead enter the village and are offered food; at the end of the festive period they are ceremonially expelled.

Festivals of a similar character are widespread among the tribal peoples of Melanesia (Solomon Islands, Vanuatu, Fiji, New Britain, New Ireland, New Guinea, New Caledonia), where the cultivation of tuberous plants everywhere provides the staple foods. Typical elements in these festivals are reverence for the earth (as agent of fruitfulness and dwelling place of the dead); the collective return of the dead, to whom sacrifices of firstfruits from the new harvests are offered; and the orgy in its various forms (copious meals, dances, sexual abandon). The collective return of the spirits of the dead and the sacrifice of firstfruits from the harvest are also documented outside Melanesia (in Africa, Indonesia, and elsewhere). In some parts of Melanesia cultic societies (of a more or less secret character) play a role in the New Year festivals. Other Melanesian tribes have special ceremonies not found in the Milamala festival, including, for example, initiatory celebrations, the appearance of masked dancers in dramatic presentations, and the slaying of large numbers of pigs. Moreover the Festival of Pigs frequently takes a form in which the enhancement of social prestige plays a special role. Whereas this particular festival is celebrated not annually but at longer intervals, there are nonetheless many indications that it was originally connected with the New Year festivals.

Sexual orgies are regarded as a means of intensifying the life force and promoting the fertility of plant life. Such celebrations are also found as part of the New Year celebrations among more highly developed agrarian cultures.

Advanced cultivation cultures. The culture of the Polynesians may be taken as a typical example of advanced cultivation cultures. Polynesian culture is based chiefly on the cultivation of the breadfruit tree; on some islands this is supplemented by taro or sweet potatoes, for which irrigation is used. Because of the climate, there is no sharp contrast between the seasons of the years and between periods of abundance and dearth. Surplus agricultural production has made possible the development of a hierarchic social order, often with a sacral or even divinized king at its apex. The upper classes are not directly involved in agricultural production but exercise other functions, particularly ritual ones. For this reason the purpose of the New Year ceremonies (which do not occur at the same time on all the islands) is less to ensure the food needed for life and much more to validate the social order: the first fruits of the harvest are not offered to the returning dead as a whole but to the kings and the chiefs (who then often make a further distribution of them) as well as to the royal ancestors and the gods; the latter are often of an agrarian-solar type. Ceremonial battles take place and at times a symbolic deposition or slaying of the king, followed by his reenthronement. Unrestrained dancing and sexual orgies are often part of the fertility cult, as they are among primitive cultivators. The New Year festival shows comparable forms with a similar content in various cultures that combine cultivation of the soil and cattle breeding and that also have a hierarchic social structure, such as among southeastern Bantu peoples, in West Africa, and in Madagascar.

Grain-growing cultures. The New Year festival in grain-growing cultures has much in common with the festival found in other agrarian cultures; there are, however, distinguishing features that can be seen among rice farmers (ancient Japan, ancient China) and maize growers (North America and Mesoamerica). The contrast between the cold, dark, and unfruitful and the warm, bright, and fertile periods of the year is marked (this opposition accounts, for example, for the great importance of new fire as a symbol of light in the New Year ceremonies—something also found among nonagrarian peoples of the north, such as the Inuit and northern Asiatics). In grain-growing cultures the sun, the influence of which on the growth of cereals is directly visible, is of paramount importance; not so among tuber cultivators, who ascribe fertility directly to the earth and the dead. (The great importance of the solar complex among the Polynesians can be traced back to Asian elements in their culture; a further significant similarity with East Asia is the importance of the sacral ruler for the general prosperity.) A dominant theme in the myths of grain growers is the marriage of heaven (the sun) and earth. In some grain-growing cultures the New Year festivals are connected with the solstices, in others with the revival of the vegetation in the spring or with the conclusion of the harvest.

Cultures of the Ancient Middle East and of the Mediterranean World. The influence of the mythical ideas and corresponding rituals of the grain-growing cultures reaches into the agrarian and urban cultures of the ancient Middle East and of the Mediterranean region. In these cultures, however, the ceremonies are enriched with numerous new elements. First, the vegetative cycle and its accompanying round of agricultural labors determine the demarcations of the year; however, there is also a more refined astronomical observation. Thus the beginning of the year is determined partly by climate and vegetation (therefore the year begins either in the spring or in the autumn), partly by the equinoxes, and more rarely by the solstices (as in Phoenicia and Syria). In Ugarit there seems to have been a cultic year that began in the autumn and a "civic" year that began in the spring. In Mesopotamia the Akitu festival among the Sumerians was originally an autumn festival marking the resumption of fieldwork after the summer drought. The Babylonian New Year festival (Sumerian, Zagmuk; Akkadian, Zagmukku), also called Akitu, which was celebrated in the spring at the beginning of the month Nisan, represented the fusion of two originally distinct festivals, one in the spring, the other in the fall. The Iranian New Year festival (Nowrūz), celebrated at the time of the spring equinox, also replaced an older custom of starting the year in the fall. In pre-Islamic Arabia the year began in the fall; in only a few northern frontier areas was there a shift to a year beginning in the spring. It is not known when the year began in the ancient cultures of southern Arabia; in modern times the year begins sometimes in the spring, sometimes in the fall.

As for the ceremonies of the New Year festivals in the Middle Eastern and Mediterranean cultures, members of the "cult history" school (known also as the "myth and ritual" school) delineated a "pattern" for the urban New Year festival that includes the following elements: "The dramatic representation of the death and resurrection of the god; the recitation or symbolic representation of the myth of the creation; the ritual combat, in which the triumph of the god over his enemies was depicted; the sacred marriage; the triumphal procession, in which the king played the part of the god, followed by a train of lesser gods or visiting deities" (A. M. Johnson in Hooke, 1958, p. 226). Judah B. Segal brings together what is known about New Year ceremonies in ancient Egypt, Greece, Rome, and Babylonia, among the Hittites, and in Syria, Phoenicia, and Arabia to derive components of a general pattern:

> The New Year is fixed by the calendar. In all communities we find a ritual going-forth from the city to the open country. In all are rites of purification, which include fasting and the wearing of new clothes, processions, the exchange of gifts, sacrifices, and feasting. In some communities there is a solemn recital of a myth

of Creation, in several the sacred marriage is enacted. Most include the temporal removal of conventional social restrictions. The New Year appears to be an appropriate time for the dedication of a temple. (Segal, 1963, pp. 125–126)

The Israelite New Year festival is not derived from this urban type, which supposedly split into a spring festival and an autumn festival. One must suppose rather that the Israelite festivals contained independent elements derived from the nomadic period and that in part they were remodeled Canaanite festivals (through which Mesopotamian influences were indirectly at work) that were taken over after the settlement. The Canaanite influence is especially apparent in the New Year festival in the autumn; nomadic traditions, on the other hand, are reflected in the spring festival (Pesaḥ) at the beginning of the year. The very details that give the Pesaḥ ritual its specific character are the ones that do not fit into the general pattern that has been presented by Segal. In Arabia the pre-Islamic (nomadic) spring festival lives on in changed form in the *ʿumrah* of Mecca, whereas the pre-Islamic (agrarian) autumn festival can be seen in the *ḥājj.*

Spring and autumn festivals that mark the beginning of the year (or at least critical turning points during the year) are also to be regarded, in the folklore of North Africa and the southern European countries, as survivals of a common ancient Mediterranean agrarian culture. Among the common features are sexual rituals as a means of promoting fertility (although these have for the most part been reduced to symbolic actions or purely verbal manifestations), masks as representations of the returning dead, and the role played by a temporary sacral "agrarian king."

The Christian feast of Easter is connected with the Israelite Pesaḥ and, as the feast of the resurrection of Christ, has its own specific salvation-historical content. In addition, however, it contains (partly in the official rites of the Roman Catholic and Eastern Churches, partly in popular customs) numerous details that derive from archaic cultures and the cultures of the ancient Middle East; these details symbolize a transition and a new beginning and to this extent make it possible to regard Easter as the real Christian New Year festival.

CONTEMPORARY SOCIETIES. The New Year is usually celebrated at the beginning of the secular year on January 1, though other New Year celebrations are also practiced. These include secular celebrations, such as the beginning of the school or university year, and religious celebrations, including the Jewish, Christian, Islamic, Hindu, and Buddhist New Year celebrations.

Secularized Western Christian celebrations. Many regional and local traditions mark the secular New Year. In Germany firecrackers at midnight (between December 31 and January 1) indicate the end of the old and the beginning of the new year. According to Germanic traditions, loud noise helps hinder bad spirits from entering the new year. In Italy men used to wear red pieces of cloth with their underwear because it was believed that this would bring good luck. In addition special dishes, such as carp and sweetbreads in Germany, are served on New Year's Day. Some Germans smelt lead on New Year's Eve in order to predict the future on the basis of the forms the lead takes after it has warmed up. Chimney sweeps are believed to bring good luck on New Year's Day. Good wishes are often exchanged, orally or in letters and postcards. A specific German New Year's wish is that of a good *Rutsch,* which is a slight deformation of the Yiddish-Hebrew word *Roʾsh,* an abbreviation of Roʾsh ha-Shanah.

Jewish celebrations. Roʾsh ha-Shanah is the Hebrew name for the Jewish New Year in autumn. It is celebrated on the first of the month of Tishri, the seventh month of the Jewish calendar year. The name was unknown in biblical times, where, with reference to *Leviticus* 23:24–25, the sacred day was called the Day of Remembrance (Yom ha-Zikkaron) or Day of Sounding the Shofar (Yom Teruah). It marks the beginning of a ten-day period of spiritual self-examination and repentance that culminates with Yom Kippur, the Day of Atonement. This period of celebration is clearly not mirthful compared with the New Year celebrations that are held at the beginning of the secular year. Rather, Roʾsh ha-Shanah carries strong religious implications of remembering the sins of the past year. The holiday finds its expression when people walk, according to an old tradition, to a source of flowing water, such as a creek or a river, on the afternoon of the first day and empty their pockets into the water, symbolically casting off their sins.

Many Jews, in particular American Jews, use the New Year as a time to plan a better life, making "resolutions" for the year to come. It is in this spirit of renewal that white clothes are recommended and white skullcaps are suggested as symbols of purity. Intensive house cleaning is on the agenda, debts are paid back, and reconciliation is sought in cases of discord. The sounding of the shofar, the ram's horn, is the most characteristic sign marking the New Year. "During the course of the Rosh Hashana service, a total of 100 notes are sounded. Ancient tradition has handed down three distinct shofar notes: a long drawn-out sound (*tekiah*), a broken, plaintive sound (*shevarim*), a series of sharp, staccato sounds (*teruah*)" (Donin, 1972, p. 245). If the New Year falls on a Sabbath, the shofar is not blown. No work is permitted on Roʾsh ha-Shanah. Much of the day is spent in the synagogue. Eating apples dipped in honey is popular on this day, as is sending postcards to wish a happy New Year to relatives and friends.

Christian observances. In all Christian churches and denominations the secular New Year is the designated date for New Year observances, be it the reformed Gregorian calendar date of January 1 or, as in some Orthodox areas, the original Julian date of mid-January. Thus the beginning of the religious year (in Western Christianity the first Sunday of Advent, four weeks before Christmas) has no importance as a Christian New Year. However, many Western Christian churches welcome the secular New Year by ringing the church bells at midnight on New Year's Eve.

Muslim observances. In the Muslim world there are two types of New Year: the lunar Islamic New Year on the first day of Muḥarram, the first month of the lunar calendar, and the solar Nowrūz in March. The lunar calendar is the official Muslim calendar and reminds Muslims of the foundation of the *ummah* in Medina after the prophet Muḥammad's migration from Mecca to Medina in 622 CE. Because the lunar year is eleven days shorter than the solar year, the lunar Islamic New Year moves backward over the seasons and thus can occur in any season. Remembrance of the prophet Muḥammad's migration is central, and this story is recounted in private ceremonies, publicly in mosques, and in the modern Muslim world on radio and television. Some Muslims have also started sending postcards to wish friends and relatives a happy New Year.

There is no official religious service associated with the Muslim lunar New Year. In some areas, in particular those under Persian cultural influence, a fixed date, namely the spring equinox, marks the New Year, which is recognized with a celebration that dates back more than three thousand years. This holiday is celebrated by all Iranians regardless of religious affiliation, including both Zoroastrians and Muslims. People generally clean their houses and themselves before the New Year starts. New clothes mark the event. Rural Iranians construct and light piles of thorn and brushwood, and people jump over the fire on the last Tuesday of the year. It is believed that this act will purify the jumper and help rid him or her of illnesses and misfortunes. Every day of this thirteen-day celebration is marked by a special action, including visiting relatives and friends and exchanging gifts and good wishes. New Year's Day is set aside for the preparation of seven items (*haft sīn*), the names of which all begin with the letter *sīn*: *sīb* (apple), *sīr* (garlic), *sumāḳ* (sumac), *sindjīd* (jujube), *samanū* (a kind of sweetmeat), *sirka* (vinegar), and *sabzī* (greens).

Hindu observances. In Hindu communities the beginning of the New Year is celebrated by the Dīvālī (Diwali) Festival of Lights in November. It is celebrated all over India, although different regions celebrate Dīvālī in different ways. What is common is the lighting of many small earthenware oil lamps, which set homes and gardens aglow with twinkling lights. The origin of the feast is the return of Rāma to his northern kingdom after having been sent away by his mother Bhārat to hinder him from becoming king. Rāma finally returns successfully, thus symbolizing the victory of good over evil. People exchange good wishes and give gifts during the Dīvālī festival; they also buy and wear new clothes, hold family meetings, serve special holiday meals, and decorate doorways and homes with small red and white footprints to symbolize Rāma's happy return. Fireworks and firecrackers are also an important part of the celebration.

Buddhist observances. In Buddhist countries several dates are used to mark the New Year. In Theravāda countries (Thailand, Myanmar, Sri Lanka, Cambodia, and Laos) the New Year is celebrated three days from the first full moon day in April. In Mahāyāna countries the first full moon day in January is considered the New Year. The date of the Buddhist New Year also depends on the country of origin or ethnic background of the people who are celebrating it. For example, Chinese, Koreans, and Vietnamese celebrate the New Year in late January or early February, according to the lunar calendar, whereas Tibetans usually do so about one month later. Water plays an important role in Buddhist New Year celebrations, where it is used for purification of temples, homes, and individuals.

Chinese observances. The Chinese New Year starts with the new moon on the first day of the new secular year and ends on the full moon fifteen days later. The fifteenth day is called the Lantern Festival, which is celebrated at night with lantern displays and children carrying lanterns in parades. New Year's Eve and New Year's Day are celebrated as a family affair. Heaven and earth are honored, as well as the gods of the household and the family ancestors. Rules govern what to eat and what to do on each of the fifteen days. Many families use special New Year's recipes for the holiday foods. It is common to abstain from eating meat on the first day of the new year because this will ensure a long and happy life. People also visit temples to pray for good fortune and health.

Japanese observances. The Japanese New Year (Oshogatsu) lasts for a week, starting on December 28 and running through January 6. Cleaning and cooking are important activities in preparation for the Oshogatsu. Shortly before midnight on New Year's Eve, *toshi-koshi* soba, a type of noodle soup, is served. People then listen to 108 midnight gongs rung at local temples and broadcast throughout Japan. The 108 gongs symbolize each of the 108 desires, listed in Buddhist texts, which hinder people from reaching salvation. On New Year's Day specific traditional meals are served, good wishes cards are delivered, and people gather with their families and visit temples.

SEE ALSO Akitu; Dīvālī; Dragons; Hieros Gamos; Light and Darkness; Nowrūz; Seasonal Ceremonies.

BIBLIOGRAPHY

Caillois, Roger. *Man and the Sacred.* Translated by Meyer Barash. Glencoe, Ill., 1959.

Donin, Hayim Halevy. *To Be a Jew: A Guide to Jewish Observance in Contemporary Life.* New York, 1972.

Eliade, Mircea. *Cosmos and History: The Myth of the Eternal Return.* Translated by Willard R. Trask. New York, 1959.

Henninger, Joseph. "Primitialopfer and Neujahrsfest." In *Anthropica: Gedenkschrift zum 100, Geburtstag von P. Wilhelm Schmidt*, pp. 147–189. Sankt Augustin bei Bonn, Germany, 1968. Includes a critical evaluation of Vittorio Lanternari (1959).

Henninger, Joseph. *Les fêtes de printemps chez les Sémites et la Pâque israélite.* Paris, 1975. Includes a critical evaluation of S. H. Hooke (1958) and Segal (1963).

Henninger, Joseph. "Zur Kulturgeschichte des Neujahrsfestes." *Anthropos* 77 (1982): 579–591. Includes a critical evaluation of Vittorio Lanternari (1976).

Hooke, S. H., ed. *Myth, Ritual, and Kingship: Essays on the Theory and Practice of Kingship in the Ancient Near East and in Israel.* Oxford, U.K., 1958.

Lanternari, Vittorio. *La grande festa: Storia del Capodanno nelle civiltà primitive.* Milan, Italy, 1959.

Lanternari, Vittorio. *La grande festa: Vita rituale e sistemi di produzione nelle società tradizionali.* 2d ed. Bari, Italy, 1976.

Levy, R. "Nawrūz: In the Islamic Heartlands." In *Encyclopaedia of Islam,* new edition, edited by C. E. Bosworth, vol. 7. Leiden, Netherlands, and New York, 1993.

MacCulloch, J. A. "Feasting (Introductory)." In *Encyclopaedia of Religion and Ethics,* edited by James Hastings, vol. 5. Edinburgh, U.K., 1914.

Nilsson, Martin P. *Primitive Time-Reckoning: A Study in the Origins and First Development of the Art of Counting Time among the Primitive and Early Culture Peoples.* Lund, Sweden, 1920.

Segal, Judah B. *The Hebrew Passover from the Earliest Times to* A.D. *70.* New York, 1963.

Servier, Jean. *Les portes de l'année, rites et symboles: L'Algérie dans la tradition méditerranéenne.* Paris, 1962.

Waddell, L. A., et al. "Festivals and Feasts." In *Encyclopaedia of Religion and Ethics,* edited by James Hastings, vol. 5. Edinburgh, 1914.

JOSEPH HENNINGER (1987)
PETER ANTES (2005)

NEZ PERCE (NIIMÍIPUU) RELIGIOUS TRADITIONS.

The Nez Perce people are one of two Sahaptian-speaking groups—the Nez Perce and the Sahaptin—to inhabit the southern Columbia Plateau region of western North America. Aboriginally, the Nez Perce–speaking peoples are ancient occupants of the southern Columbia Plateau whose ancestral lands extend along middle Snake River in Oregon, Washington, and Idaho. The Nez Perce, as well as other Sahaptin groups, report no migration tradition placing them outside their current ancestral homelands; instead, their oral traditions contain imagery of mammoths, ice-age phenomena, and ancient volcanic activity. At the time of contact, the Nez Perce were composed of an estimated forty independent bands and were dispersed along three major tributaries of the Snake River: the Grande Ronde River (Oregon), the Clearwater River (Idaho), and the Salmon River (Idaho). Two dialect variants differentiated the Nez Perce speech community: the Lower River dialect and the Upper River dialect. Like other neighboring Sahaptin groups, the Nez Perce were known principally as a hunting and gathering culture, centered on the annual food quest of fishing, hunting, and gathering roots. As a consequence, the Nez Perce territory covers a diverse geography, each part of which has its own biodiversity. Culturally, the Nez Perce people identify themselves as *Niimíipuu* the Real People; however, it is also quite common for tribal members to use their ancestral band designation as an identity marker. In the historic period, the name *Nez Percé,* a French term meaning pierced nose, was applied to the *Niimíipuu* by French fur traders and through later historic usage the name has come to identify both the *Niimíipuu* language and its people. Today, the majority of the Nez Perce people (a population estimated at 3,000) reside on the Nez Perce Reservation in central Idaho, with several smaller communities of Nez Perce in Oregon and Washington. The Nez Perce language, like many indigenous languages of North America, is endangered and is spoken by sixty to seventy fluent elders, the majority of whom speak the Upper River dialect. Only a handful of elders still speak the Lower River dialect.

The religious traditions of the *Niimíipuu,* the Nez Perce people, trace their origin to the mythic emergence of the *Netíitelwit,* the first human beings to inhabit the earth. The emergence of the *Netíitelwit* brought to an end the existence of powerful mythic beings and signaled the beginning of a world inhabited by ordinary humans. A principal myth celebrates this transformation and is known among the Nez Perce as the climactic episode in a long series of encounters in which *'Itseyéeye* (Coyote) slays a mythic being too powerful and dangerous for the emerging *Netíitelwit.* The dismembered remains of this slain being embody the cultural landscape as *Tim'néepe* (Heart Place), *Sit'éexspe* (Liver Place), and *Qaháspa* (Breast Place) and locate the mythic emergence of the *Netíitelwit* on the Clearwater River of north-central Idaho.

Through the mythic emergence of the *Netíitelwit,* a core Nez Perce cosmology is conceived. The universe is distinctly defined as including the realm of humans and a former world inhabited by supernatural entities. Its structure is mediated by a deep time separation whereby the mythic past remotely precedes the human present. Though rare, this time separation is sometimes breached by accounts of supernatural entities coexisting with and coming into contact with ordinary humans. Nez Perce oral traditions, known as *titwatitnáawit,* reinforce this notion of mythic time as an enduring continuum between two possible worlds. The more immediate social value of *titwatitnáawit,* however, is to impart fundamental knowledge about the world and its living inhabitants in addition to basic human values and beliefs.

THE *WÉEYEKIN* SYSTEM. The Nez Perce, like many cultures throughout the Columbia Plateau, base their belief system upon the *wéeyekin* (spirit guardian), also called the spirit-guardian tradition. The *wéeyekin* system consists of a core set of religious beliefs centering on the existence of transcendent power as well as a set of unifying cultural practices that integrate such beliefs into Nez Perce society. A fundamental notion informing the *wéeyekin* system is the existence of an innate power or force in the universe. Elements of this power can become manifest as superhuman agents or spirit beings who become attached to individual human beings. Once acquired, a *wéeyekin* acts as a lifelong tutelary to its human recipient.

A *wéeyekin* is obtained through a childhood spirit-guardian quest, inheritance, dreams, life crises, or incidental contact. While an individual may acquire a *wéeyekin* at any stage in life, it was more common in aboriginal times to acquire one during a childhood spirit-guardian quest called a *wáay'atin.* The *wáay'atin* involved isolation in a remote geographic location, most often a sacred area where spirit powers were known to be especially potent. For many Nez Perce children, the *wáay'atin* was the culmination of a more general regimen of training that started early in life and extended independently through adulthood.

Individual narrative accounts reveal that the vision experience unfolds as a dialogic encounter. The experience consists of (1) the direct apprehension of a *wéeyekin,* which typically occurs in an altered state of consciousness or dream state; (2) a set of directives in which the *wéeyekin* vocally transmits information about its identity, attributes, and powers; and (3) the transfer of powers from the *wéeyekin* to the human participant. The outcome of such an encounter is characterized as *wéeyexnin'* (to be blessed by a *wéeyekin*). In addition, the human participant is later endowed with a personal spiritual name that identifies the *wéeyekin,* a set of prescriptive ritual behaviors to maintain spiritual empowerment, and a personal spirit song. The full extent of these endowments was usually not realized until the human participant had matured and entered into adult life. Ultimately, however, they provided the key ingredients for individual and group success in the overall survival of the Nez Perce.

The spiritual attainment of *wéeyexnin'* was understood to be a foundational element in the formation of a true autonomous self. Intensified forms of personal awareness were known to emerge over the life of an individual as a consequence of the originating vision experiences. This awareness often culminated in *cúukwenin'* (the supernatural ability to "know spiritually"), and was believed to contribute to a coherent understanding of human experience, life forces, and the basic structure of the world. The alternative was to be *weyexnéey'*—without a *wéeyekin*—and attempts at attaining anything more than a common, mediocre life would be a long and arduous undertaking.

The core beliefs informing the *wéeyekin* system find their greatest elaboration in the annual winter ritual performance known as the *wéeyekweecet* (spirit-guardian dance). The *wéeyekweecet* is primarily structured around the enactment and display of *wéeyekin* powers. It includes the public performance of one's *weeyekwe'nípt* (spirit-guardian song) as well as power exhibitions by mature shamans. The *wéeyekweecet* constitutes a collective communicative process in which information pertaining to one's inner experience is externalized through ritual performance.

The *wéeyekin* tradition is a belief system of great antiquity and the empowering, transformative vision experience upon which it is based is a core feature in recent Nez Perce religious traditions. The visionary realm continues to retain its inherent potency; narrative accounts show, however, that the visionary content upon which the new religious traditions are based appears to be much more universal in orientation. It includes (1) the direct apprehension of the universe, which typically occurs in a death-like altered state of consciousness or dream state; (2) the receipt of a set of directives or laws that transmits information about the existence of an omniscient creator and human life potential; and (3) the transfer of prophetic powers, songs, and rituals to the human participant. The variation and development of these modern religious traditions are not so much about the embodiment of spiritual power as they are a means to bring about changes in the world through collective ritual action.

THE *TUULÍIM* CULT. The earliest documented religious development to emerge among the Nez Perce was the *tuulíim* cult. In contrast to the *wéeyekin* system, the *tuulíim* cult was characterized by the formalization of religious ritual centering on prophecy and revelation. Its most salient feature was the ritual transmission of sacred knowledge that was obtained during a death-like transitory state or vision experience. The revelatory and prophetic structure of this knowledge was derived, in part, from the visionary perception of the cosmos and human existence. Its content and form were later integrated into the everyday world as communicative ritual acts known as *talapóosa* (worship), *we'nípt* (singing), and *waa'láasat* (a sacred form of dancing). Among its most central beliefs were concepts of a hereafter, an omniscient creator (*haniyaw'áat*), human moral conduct, and world renewal.

Based on archaeological and ethnographic evidence, the *tuulíim* cult arose during the protohistoric period (1600–1750) in response to the widespread introduction of non-aboriginal influences into the Columbia Plateau. Their cumulative impact had the unprecedented effect of transforming the physical realms (via material resources and technology), the social realms (in interpersonal and tribal relationships), and the cognitive realms (through psychology and religion) of everyday Nez Perce life. But by far the single most important event to shape the lives of Columbia Plateau peoples was a series of smallpox epidemics that swept through the ancient villages of the Columbia and Snake River areas. As an intellectual and spiritual force, the *tuulíim* cult and its progenitor the Prophet Dance provided a means of mediating the weakened, liminal state of existence by offering to restore vitality in a crisis-ridden world.

THE *'IPNÚUCILILPT* RITUAL. By the post-contact era, the fundamental elements of the *tuulíim* cult were so fully integrated into Nez Perce life that it reemerged as a revitalized form of worship called *'ipnúucililpt* (making oneself turn). In its most basic form, the *'ipnúucililpt* ritual is a modern adaptation of its protohistoric progenitor. Significantly, it continues to be grounded in the transformative power of prophecy and revelation precisely because many of its original prophetic predictions, such as the arrival of whites, the appearance of instruments of writing, and other wondrous technologies, had come to pass. Drawing on the symbolic structure of its predecessor, *'lipnúucililpt* philosophy is distinguished by an adherence to natural laws, ethical codes of respect, religious authority, and ritual order. World renewal rituals such as the First Foods ceremony and children's rites of passage receive greater emphasis, as does the adoption and use of ancient symbolic imagery centering on primal sources of light such as the sun, moon, and stars.

This process of reinterpretation provided the various traditional bands of Nez Perce with a sense of social solidarity and continuity in the face of rapid change. However, the increase in opportunities for religious affiliation also had the effect of reducing the internal diversity of the *'ipnúucililpt* adherents until they became collectively identified as followers of the Wanapam prophet Smohalla, a key historical figure in the native struggle to retain ancestral lands. In the political sphere, adherents of the *'ipnúucililpt* faith eventually became unified to fight U.S. government attempts to extinguish aboriginal title to lands held sacred by the Nez Perce. Ultimately, however, the deep fundamental differences in religion and worldview were too great to prevent the Nez Perce War of 1877 and the division of the Nez Perce people. Today, remnants of the *'ipnúucililpt* religious practices and *wéeyekin* tradition continue in isolation in the life of a small group of traditional Nez Perce.

BIBLIOGRAPHY

Axtell, Horace, and Margo Aragon. *A Little Bit of Wisdom: Conversations with a Nez Perce Elder.* Lewiston, Idaho, 1997.

Coale, George L. "Notes on the Guardian Spirit Concept among the Nez Perce." *International Archives of Ethnography* 47 (1958): 135–148.

Walker, Deward E. *Conflict and Schism in Nez Perce Acculturation.* 2d ed., with an introduction by Robert Hackenberg. Moscow, Idaho, 1985.

Walker, Deward E. "Plateau: Nez Perce." In *Witchcraft and Sorcery of the American Native Peoples,* edited by Walker, pp. 113–140. Moscow, Idaho, 1989.

Walker, Deward E. "Nez Perce." In *Handbook of North American Indians,* vol. 12: *Plateau,* edited by Walker. Washington, D.C., 1998.

PHILLIP CASH CASH (2005)

NGARINYIN RELIGION SEE UNGARINYIN RELIGION

NGUKURR RELIGION.

The Aboriginal township of Ngukurr is located on the remote Roper River in southeastern Arnhem Land in Australia's Northern Territory. Its population, which in the 1970s fluctuated between 350 and 500, consists of the descendants of the Aboriginal tribes of the lower and middle Roper River and the adjacent coast, mainly the Alawa, Mara, Ngalagan, Ngandi, Nunggabuyu, and Wandarang. The people of Ngukurr still retain close spiritual and physical ties to their tribal land.

THE SETTING. The Arnhem Land region has an area of about ninety-five thousand square kilometers. It was set aside in 1931 by the Australian government as a reserve for the Aborigines and remained as such until 1977. Following the passage of the Aboriginal Land Rights (Northern Territory) Act of 1976, the ownership of Arnhem Land was transferred from the Australian government to various Aboriginal bodies.

Arnhem Land, and in particular southeastern Arnhem Land, is physically remote and economically underdeveloped. The only productive enterprises in the area around Ngukurr are beef-cattle raising and fishing. The country to the south and west of Ngukurr is occupied by large cattle stations (ranches), varying in size from one thousand to seven thousand square kilometers.

Prior to 1969 Ngukurr was known as Roper River Mission and was administered by the Church Missionary Society, an evangelical missionary body within the Anglican Church of Australia. The Aborigines were residents of the mission settlement and lived under the control and direction of the mission staff.

The administrative structure and political control of Ngukurr has undergone sweeping changes beginning late in 1968, when Ngukurr became a government settlement run by the Welfare Division of the Northern Territory Administration. The administration of the town of Ngukurr was transferred to a locally elected council in 1975. Government grants finance the town's budget and the major part of the people's incomes with employment and social service payments. Ngukurr has few productive activities and a very high rate of chronic unemployment.

RELIGION AND THE MISSION. The Aboriginal community at Ngukurr operates within two religious universes. One derives from the indigenous traditions of the Aboriginal people who make up the present-day community, and the other from the people's subjugation by Europeans, in particular the Christian missionaries.

Christianity and indigenous religion today have an uneasy relationship within the community. Each tolerates the existence of the other, but they are considered as separate. There is no intellectual cross-fertilization, though to an extent they share practitioners and believers.

The structure of Christianity at Ngukurr in the early 1970s reflects its mission origin. From 1908 until 1968, the Church Missionary Society integrated Christianity and social control: Aboriginal residents were able to gain social preference through participation in church activities and nonparticipation provoked negative sanctions. Participation in the church declined dramatically following the transfer of secular control to the Australian government. By 1970 the active Aboriginal congregation was reduced to less than twenty adults, mostly older men and women who had a long history of residence at the mission.

The main point of contact between the local church and the indigenous religion in 1970 was through the composition of the church's lay council. The adult male members were all active participants in the indigenous religious realm. Some, including two of the lay preachers, were leaders in the organization of indigenous cult performances. These men wore their dual positions lightly. As councillors they participated in the church's decision-making process and occasionally attended services at the church, but they fulfilled their main religious role within the indigenous religion. However, their political positions were maintained through participation in both realms.

The Indigenous Realm. The people of Ngukurr, as Aborigines, see themselves and are seen by others as culturally distinct from the mainstream of Australian society, and this distinctiveness is considered a positive value that encapsulates a traditional conception of society.

The conduct of religious cults is the main arena of social life that appears fully contained by this traditional worldview. The social strictures found in the cults, together with the Ngukurr kinship system, provide the framework for social relations in those areas not yet entirely subordinated to the non-Aboriginal world. Today these manifold relations have two main foci: (1) the right to make decisions about and to participate in the religious cults and (2) the distribution of rights and access to the land.

Aboriginal religion is articulated around the relations between groups of people and the land that their forebears occupied and exploited (and that the Aborigines are again seeking to occupy). The foci of the Aboriginal religious systems are supernatural, totemic beings that may or may not be representations of natural species. The more important totemic powers in the Ngukurr pantheon are the *nagaran* (a supernatural spirit usually represented as a male giant), the plain kangaroo, various species of monitor lizard (goannas), rain and lightning, the *gilyiring-gilyiring* (which takes various forms, though it is most commonly glossed as a woman or a mermaid), and various species of snakes and fish.

At their most innovative, they are world-creative forces that transform an unfeatured landscape into its known social forms. They pass through the country creating places, leaving their paths, establishing ceremonies, and meeting and establishing structured relations with other powers. Different parts of the country are associated with different powers or ensembles of powers.

The totemic powers organize religious life by bonding particular groups of people with particular sites, paths, or tracts of land. They also articulate the relations between groups that are linked to different sites and tracts of land made by a particular totemic power or constellation of powers. This is made more complex by the fact that people are also related through the interconnections between their different totemic powers. There is in Aboriginal religion, therefore, an intricate interweaving of interests that structures and spreads sociality. Ideally this balances the contradictory tendencies of parochial and universalizing interests.

The Development of Ngukurr Religious Practice. In their traditional habitat and across their own countries, people held ceremonies at the sites being celebrated, but when colonists appropriated the land ceremonies had to be held away from these places.

Mission authorities actively discouraged ceremonies within the mission area, though they continued to be held with difficulty. The mission's attitude prevented ceremonies at Ngukurr until mission policy changed in the mid-1950s. Up to the 1950s Ngukurr was only one of a number of population centers (the others being cattle stations) that shared the cult life of the Roper area. This cult life, richer than that now performed at Ngukurr, included four secret male cults, the Yabuduruwa, Gunabibi (called Kunapipi elsewhere), Balgin, and Maddaiin. An elaborate circumcision ritual and secret women's cults were also part of this religious practice.

All the ceremonies organized by Ngukurr men after 1957 were held in the vicinity of Ngukurr. This occurred alongside the decline in the attendance of Ngukurr men at ceremonies elsewhere in the region, the dropping of the Maddaiin and the Balgin cults from the men's repertoire, and the abbreviation of the circumcision rites. Performance of the women's cults had ceased before this time. Between the mid-1950s and the mid-1970s about eight Yabuduruwa ceremonies and six Gunabibi ceremonies were held at Ngukurr. Each was associated with one or two of the nine "estate-group territories" (for an explanation of the term *estate*, see below). It has been described elsewhere (Bern, 1979) the changes that brought about the establishment of a specific Ngukurr society. The changes during the 1950s resulted in the appearance of a ritual life specific to Ngukurr and of a distinct set of Ngukurr religious properties.

The Cults. Indigenous religious practice at Ngukurr centers on the conduct of the two cults of the Yabuduruwa and the Gunabibi. These cults celebrate, with great complexity, the relations between people, between people and the totemic powers, between people and the land, and between the land, people, and the totemic powers. Intergroup relations are specified through the identification of particular kinship-based groups with particular territories. Such groups are called *estate groups*. Relations between people are also specified through sociocentric categories. Thus patrilineal moiety and semi-moiety affiliations are ritualized.

Moieties and semimoieties. At the most inclusive level the organization of the Yabuduruwa and Gunabibi cults is based on the division of society into two patrilineal moieties, within which context people's positions and actions are defined. People who are related through their fathers to the totemic powers represented in a cult are called *mingeringgi*, and they have a certain set of rights and obligations. The people of the opposite moiety, who are related to the powers through their mothers and fathers' mothers, are called *junggaiyi*, and they have a set of rights and obligations complementary to those of the *mingeringgi*.

The *mingeringgi* are the celebrants and the human representation of a cult. They bear the responsibility for any errors or damage to the cult's artifacts or integrity. The *junggaiyi* care for and organize the emblems, paraphernalia, and performances of the cults. The Yabuduruwa cult celebrates the estates and totemic powers of the people of the Yiridja moiety and they are its *mingeringgi*. The Gunabibi cult celebrates the estates and totemic powers of the people of the Dua moiety and they are its *mingeringgi*.

The Yabuduruwa and the Gunabibi are also semimoiety cults. At Ngukurr the semimoieties belonging to the Yiridja moiety are called Budal and Guyal. Those belonging to the Dua moiety are called Mambali and Murungun. The semimoiety division is utilized in a number of ways in the two cults.

The totemic powers and the sites represented in the cults are identified with one or another of the semi-moieties as well as with a particular moiety. The *nagaran* estate-group territories are celebrated in the Yabuduruwa cult. This power is associated with the Yiridja moiety and the Guyal semimoiety. Another Yabuduruwa-cult estate-group territory is the Plain Kangaroo territory, which is also identified with the Yiridja moiety, but which is further identified with the Budal and not the Guyal semimoiety. Similarly, the *gilyiring-gilyiring*, which is celebrated in the Gunabibi cult, is associated with the Dua moiety and the Mambali semimoiety at Ngukurr, while the king brown snake is identified with the Dua moiety and the Murungun semimoiety.

At the moiety level both semimoieties of Dua are *mingeringgi* for the Gunabibi. However, there are times when the semimoieties are structurally separated and only one qualifies as *mingeringgi*. The other semimoiety of the Dua moiety then occupies a position called *dalnyin* (lit., "mother's mother"). The same applies for the Yiridja moiety in the context of the Yabuduruwa. The *dalnyin* have a largely supplementary role and can in certain circumstances act as both *mingeringgi* and *junggaiyi*.

In each of the cults there are important rites in which the two semimoieties of the *mingeringgi* moiety are separated and perform distinct segments. A striking example of this separation occurs in the Yabuduruwa ceremony; in parts of this ceremony, those in the opposite semimoiety (but the same moiety) to that of the ceremony initiators can assume the role of *junggaiyi* in the absence of appropriate senior *junggaiyi*.

The same separation of semimoieties does not occur within the *junggaiyi* category. Two of the most important reasons for this are the composition of the estate group, which includes *junggaiyi* from both semi-moieties, and the importance of individual kinship ties. Ego-centered kinship relations are activated in the organization and conduct of the cults. For example, in the preparation of individual male performers particular tasks can be performed only by cross-cousins and others only by a mother's brother. One's cross-cousins and mother's brothers would normally be found in different semimoieties of the opposite moiety.

The estates. The cults also have a narrower perspective in the celebration and reinforcement of social relations. The social features of the landscape are established by the movements of the totemic powers and the sites that they created. Particular groups have special attachment to and responsibility for parts of the landscape associated with a particular power or ensemble of powers. These are the ritual "estates." The groups associated with each estate have a complex structure.

The core of the "estate group" is composed of people who are related to the estate through their fathers. Individual members of the core group have names that are taken from the names of features in the estate, and collectively the core is known by the name of the estate. Other members of the estate group are people who trace their relationship to the estate through their mothers, their fathers' mothers, or their mothers' mothers. In the context of the estate, the ones who trace their relationship through their fathers are the estate's *mingeringgi;* those whose relationship is through their mothers or fathers' mothers are the *junggaiyi;* and those people related through their mothers' mothers are the *dalnyin*.

A major emphasis in both the Yabuduruwa and the Gunabibi cults is the celebration of particular estates and their totemic powers, in ceremonies initiated by the senior men. The occasion is often to commemorate a recently deceased senior core-member (no less than two years and preferably no more than ten years deceased). However, the reason may simply be that this group has not had a ceremony for its own estate for a long time. Their ownership is acknowledged by the initiated core members, who take the lead in most of the performances of the ceremony, and by the organizers of the ceremony, who are the estate's senior *junggaiyi*. The main dance ground and associated structures are built to dimensions that are specific to the estate.

Estates are specifically celebrated in certain rites held in both cults. Within these rites *mingeringgi* perform individual dances, wearing designs that represent a totemic power and site from their estate. The dances, designs, and paraphernalia worn by the performers, as well as songs and myths that particularly concern the estate, are part of the estate's *gulinga*, a Ngukurr term which encompasses all aspects of an estate's religious property. A group without a *gulinga* has no ceremony, though they may still have an estate.

Control and participation. Both the Yabuduruwa and the Gunabibi are cults of initiated men; the most important parts of a Yabuduruwa or Gunabibi ceremony's performance, its paraphernalia, and the knowledge it conveys are kept secret from the women, novices, and children of the community (as well as all other uninitiated people). The men also control the organization and most aspects of the conduct of the ceremonies, and perform most of the cult's rites.

Women, however, play an indispensable, though subordinate, part in both the organization and the conduct of the cults. They prepare food on behalf of the male participants, and they have responsibility for the public part of the ceremonial precinct, which is a cleared area within the total ceremonial precinct and which is located about half a kilometer from the main ceremonial ground. In the Yabuduruwa cult they also have the care of the novices, who remain at the public precinct before they are taken to the main performing ground to observe the men's performance. Women also participate as actors in some of the central rites in both ceremonies.

While the two cults together impart symmetry to Ngukurr's religious practice, there are significant differences between them. Unlike the Yabuduruwa, the Gunabibi includes song cycles in its performance. The training of novices is more thoroughly pursued in the Gunabibi than it is in the Yabuduruwa. In the former, dogma prescribes that novices are withdrawn from the community for the duration of the ceremony and put in the charge of initiated young men. However, at Ngukurr, this is usually modified to the extent that novices remain within the male area of the ceremonial precinct for the duration of a session, which usually covers a weekend of performances. In the Yabuduruwa cult, by contrast, the novices remain within the community and are only obliged to attend the ceremony for the duration of each performance. Even then they are kept at the women's area during the period of preparation for a performance.

The Gunabibi cult emphasizes social control of the emerging generation of males through the separation of novices from the secular world and their subjection to adult male discipline, while the Yabuduruwa cult lays less emphasis on such a *rite de passage*. The Yabuduruwa's central concern is with the dramatization of exclusion and of the hierarchical order of society. The former has its highlight in the Goanna Tail rite, in which women, the main actors, are led to the men's secret dance ground at night. They keep their heads bowed. They approach a fire on the ground and light rolls of paperbark and then return to the women's precinct. (The rolls of paperbark symbolize the tails of goannas, which are a central motif of the Yabuduruwa. The goanna tails are an important phallic representation and are also the most desired part of the goanna for eating.) If they were to raise their heads during their trip to the men's secret dance ground, the women could see the sacralia of the men. Kenneth Maddock offers a convincing interpretation of this rite as a dramatization of the exclusion of women from the cult's innermost secrets (1982, pp. 133–134).

The issue of hierarchy is encapsulated in the final rite of the Ngukurr Yabuduruwa cult, performed after the ceremony has been officially concluded. The senior men return to the main ceremony ground, taking with them some specially chosen younger initiated men. They give as the reason for their return the need to clean up the ceremony ground. However, a rite is performed there by the two most senior *mingeringgi*, which is witnessed only by this select group. During the preparation for this rite the men discuss any infractions that have occurred during the course of the ceremony and decide what, if anything, they will do about such infractions.

Religion and the Community. The continuity of Ngukurr religion, in the form outlined here, is not certain. The influences at work have contradictory effects. The rapid changes of recent years have not yet been fully worked out and externally imposed changes are still taking place. One hope, that European authority would be replaced by one based on traditional values, has not eventuated. For a while the Gunabibi cult was seen as a possible vehicle of social control, especially of the teenage males. This hope has not been realized and even the rhetoric of this movement had disappeared by the mid-1970s.

People continue to believe in the bond between themselves and their land, and the myth and structures represented in the cults still mediate these beliefs. The legislation on land rights has given this recent material support, and this, at least, can be seen as supportive of the indigenous religion.

See Also Australian Indigenous Religions; Dreaming, The.

Bibliography

Bern, John. "Politics in the Conduct of a Secret Male Ceremony," *Journal of Anthropological Research* 35 (Spring 1979): 47–60. In this article I deal with the political dimensions of the organization of a Yabuduruwa ceremony held at Ngukurr in 1970. The article also contains a description of the cult.

Berndt, Ronald M. *The Kunapipi.* Melbourne, 1951. Berndt describes the organization of a Gunabibi ceremony held in northeastern Arnhem Land in the late 1940s. This ceremony was largely organized by men from east and south Arnhem Land who had connections with the Ngukurr people.

Capell, Arthur. "The Wandarang and Other Tribal Myths of the Yabuduruwa Ritual." *Oceania* 30 (March 1960): 206–224. Capell presents and translates myths from the Ngukurr Yabuduruwa that he collected in the 1950s. There are versions of both the *nagaran* and goanna myths.

Elkin, A. P. *Two Rituals in South and Central Arnhem Land.* Sydney, 1972. This is a collection of Elkin's articles describing Yabuduruwa and Maddaiin ceremonies from different parts of Arnhem Land. The most pertinent is an account of a Yabuduruwa ceremony held at Ngukurr in 1966. Elkin's account is based on a film of the event made by the Australian Institute of Aboriginal Studies.

Hiatt, L. R., ed. *Aboriginal Landowners: Contemporary Issues in the Determination of Traditional Aboriginal Land Ownership.* Sydney, 1984. The main theme of this collection of articles is the examination of the structure of traditional rights in land in the context of the current Australian government legislation concerning the granting of title in land to Aborigines. The articles by myself and Robert Layton and by Frances Morphy and Howard Morphy deal with land claims in the Roper River area.

Maddock, Kenneth. *The Australian Aborigines: A Portrait of Their Society.* Rev. ed. Ringwood, Victoria, 1982. Maddock's study is an important introduction to Aboriginal society written from a structuralist viewpoint. His discussion of Aboriginal religion is comprehensive. He uses descriptions of parts of both the Yabuduruwa and Gunabibi cults in his analysis. His description of these is largely based on his own research in southwestern Arnhem Land.

Stanner, W. E. H. *On Aboriginal Religion.* Sydney, 1964. Stanner's study is the definitive work on Aboriginal religion. While it is primarily an analysis of religious practice of the western part of the Northern Territory, it addresses general theoretical issues. One of the cults discussed by Stanner is the Karwadi, which is cognate to the Gunabibi.

JOHN BERN (1987)

NIANFO. The Chinese term *nianfo* (Jpn., *nembutsu*) is a translation of the Sanskrit word *buddhānusmṛti. Anusmṛti* is a feminine noun derived from *smṛ-*, a verbal root, with the prefix *anu-* meaning following, toward, or along. English translations of *anusmṛti* include holding in one's mind, remembering, thinking of [upon], contemplating, and reciting. Most of the definitions refer to aspects of meditation, whereas the last definition, reciting, means the repeated oral recitation (of a particular formulaic utterance), or the mental recitation of this same formula. This usage gave rise to the recitative *nianfo* that became an important practice in East Asian Buddhism from about the fifth century CE.

PRIMITIVE *NIANFO*. In its earliest form, *nianfo* referred to *buddhānusmṛti*, a simple remembrance or thinking about Śākyamuni Buddha, as in reverence to a teacher. First mention of *nianfo* is found in the initiation ceremony of the Buddhist order held while Śākyamuni Buddha was still alive. This simple profession of faith in the Three Treasures—the Buddha, the Dharma, and the Saṅgha (the Buddhist order)—encouraged members of the order to put trust in, worship, and adore Śākyamuni Buddha as a teacher. This type of *nianfo* gradually became practiced by believers even far removed from Śākyamuni in time or place as a means of asking for his protection in times of crisis. From this, the ten titles of Śākyamuni, the ten faculties of the Buddha, and the thirty-two features of the Buddha came to be regarded as the object of remembrance. By the constant and incessant *anusmṛti* the early disciples of Śākyamuni Buddha thus kept alive the memory of their master.

MEDITATIVE *NIANFO*. The simple practice of remembrance, adoration, and trust in Śākyamuni Buddha gradually developed into an actual visualization of his features and virtues. Such meditation was directed not only toward Śākyamuni but also toward such Buddhas as Amitābha (Jpn., Amida), Bhaiṣajyaguru, and Mahāvairocana, and such *bodhisattvas* as Avalokiteśvara and Maitreya. One of the earliest sūtras to advocate such a practice was the *Pratyutpannasamādhi Sūtra* (Chin., *Banzhou sanmei jing*). In this sūtra (as well as in many other scriptures) the subject of *nianfo* came to be Amitābha and other Buddhas rather than Śākyamuni, and birth in Amitābha's Pure Land rather than in the various Buddhist heavens. The practice of *nianfo* directed toward Amitābha Buddha is also emphasized in the *Larger Sukhāvatīvyūha Sūtra* (Chin., *Wuliangshou jing;* Sūtra on the Buddha of infinite Life), the *Amitāyurdhyāna Sūtra* (Chin., *Guan wuliangshou jing,* or Meditation sūtra on the Buddha of immeasurable life), and the *Smaller Sukhāvatīvyūha Sūtra* (Chin., *Emituo jing,* Sūtra on the Buddha Amitābha). These three scriptures are known in Japan as the Triple Sūtra of the Pure Land.

The *Pratyutpannasamādhi Sūtra* preaches the practice of *nianfo* for the laity and the doctrine of emptiness (*śūnyatā*) for monks. It teaches that one can see the Buddhas of the ten directions by attaining the meditational consciousness of emptiness. This is accomplished by keeping the precepts and meditating on the Buddha Amitābha for a period of from one to seven days and nights. The sūtra also declares that it is possible to be born in the Pure Land of the Buddha Amitābha by wholeheartedly meditating on his name for a period of from one to seven days.

Within the Pure Land tradition, a number of different types of meditative *nianfo* were introduced. These included *nianfo* with a concentrated mind for those of advanced capacities, *nianfo* with a distracted mind for people of lower spiritual capacities, *nianfo* of formless principle, *nianfo* of a Buddha's form, single-hearted *nianfo* on Amitābha alone, *nianfo* on other Buddhas, *nianfo* through self-power, and *nianfo* through other-power.

The *Smaller Sukhāvatīvyūha Sūtra* states that a person who single-heartedly bears the name of Amitābha in mind from one to seven days will see Amitābha at his deathbed and obtain birth in his Pure Land. This thought is presumed to derive from the *nianfo* of the *Pratyutpannasamādhi Sūtra.* The characteristic point of the *Smaller Sukhāvatīvyūha Sūtra* is that birth in the Pure Land takes place at the moment of death, not while visualizing the Buddha in one's daily life. Moreover, what is borne in mind here is the Buddha's name, not his figure or characteristics as was the case in meditative *nianfo* of the *Pratyutpannasamādhi Sūtra.*

Traditionally, the *Larger Sukhāvatīvyūha Sūtra* has been considered the basic *text* of Pure Land teachings. The most important section of the sūtra is the description of Amitābha's vows, in which Amitābha sets forth the conditions that he shall fulfill before achieving final enlightenment. In the Wei dynasty translation of this sūtra (252 CE), the all-important eighteenth of Amitābha's forty-eight vows states: "If, when I shall attain Buddhahood, sentient beings in the ten quarters who have sincere mind, serene faith, and desire to be born in my country should not be born there even after (directing) ten thoughts (to me), may I not attain Perfect Enlightenment." Various interpretations of the precise meaning of the term *ten thoughts* have been given. Basically, the words may be taken to refer to the continuity, for a certain period of time, of sincere mind, serene faith, and desire for birth in the Pure Land.

The *Amitāyurdhyāna Sūtra* teaches thirteen methods of meditation on the features of Amitābha and his Pure Land.

Through the successful accomplishment of this meditative *nianfo* the aspirant may be born in the Pure Land and see all the Buddhas of the ten directions. In addition to these thirteen meditations, in the latter portion of the text another way of birth into the Pure Land is expounded for those with distracted minds. This section of the sūtra teaches that even the lowliest beings, those who have committed such misdeeds as the Five Grave Sins or slander of the Dharma, can be born in the Pure Land by uttering the Buddha's name ten times at the last moment of life. For Pure Land Buddhists, the importance of this sūtra lies in the teaching that birth in the Pure Land by means of ten recitations of the name is assured even to beings of diminished spiritual capacities. This concept is pivotal in the historical development of *nianfo* thought. Thus, all three Pure Land sūtras played a decisive role in the transformation of the concept of *nianfo* from meditation to simple recitation of the name of Amitābha.

RECITATIVE *NIANFO.* Although early *nianfo* practice was primarily meditative, oral recitation of the Buddha's name was often used concurrently as an aid to concentration. Thus, two types of *nianfo,* meditative and recitative, began to be used in all schools. It was generally believed that recitative *nianfo* was easier, though inferior, to meditative *nianfo*: the former was regarded as a mere accommodation to those not qualified to practice meditation or other forms of mental cultivation. The practice of recitative *nianfo* as an independent and self-sufficient discipline, however, was developed later, in the thought of several important Buddhist thinkers: Nāgārjuna (c. 150–250) and Vasubandhu (c. 320–400) in India; Tanluan (476–542?), Daochuo (562–644), and Shandao (613–681) in China, and Genshin (942–1017), Hōnen (1133–1212), and Shinran (1173–1262) in Japan.

Nāgārjuna divided the Buddha's teachings into difficult and easy practices for the attainment of enlightenment. This latter path, better suited to beings born in an age of the five corruptions, requires only that one hear the name of Amitābha and utter it with sincerity in order for the devotee to achieve a state of spiritual nonretrogression in the Pure Land and thereafter attain enlightenment. Vasubandhu taught that the practice of the *wunian men* (five devotional gates: worship, praise, aspiration, perception, and the transfer of merit) would bring about birth in the Pure Land. The disciplines set forth under the Five Devotional Gates, however, were intended more for the sake of sages (i.e., the spiritually advanced) than for the ordinary person, as they were difficult to accomplish in the proper manner.

Tanluan interpreted Vasubandhu's teachings to mean that even the most sinful person could practice the Five Devotional Gates insofar as the power to perform these practices originates in Amitābha's sacred vow to save all sentient beings, not in the devotee himself. Tanluan asserted that birth in the Pure Land is ensured by means of ten utterances of the name.

A major concept contributing to the transformation of *nianfo* practice from that of meditation to recitation was consciousness of the historical degeneration of the Buddha's teachings. Traditionally, Buddhism has postulated three periods of the Buddha's Law. These are known in Chinese as *chengfa* (the era of the righteous law), *xiangfa* (the era of the counterfeit law), and *mofa* (Jpn., *mappō*; the latter days of the law). It was held that the Era of the Righteous Law was a five-hundred-year period following the decease of Śākyamuni during which the Buddha's teaching, the aspirants' religious discipline, and their enlightenment all flourished. The Era of the Counterfeit Law is a period in which the teaching and practice remain, but none actually attains enlightenment. During the third period, the Latter Days of the Law, there is neither practice nor enlightenment. Only the Buddha's teachings remain.

Concerning the duration of the three periods, Daochuo writes in his *Anluo ji* (A collection of lines concerning the country of peace and happiness) that the Righteous Law taught during Śākyamuni's lifetime had lasted for five hundred years, the Counterfeit Law would prevail for one thousand years, and the Latter Days of the Law for ten thousand years. Daochuo lived during a period in which people were highly conscious of how the religious climate of their own age differed from the one in which the influence and the personality of Śākyamuni were directly felt by the *saṃgha.* In particular, the Chinese of the seventh century were vexed by the perceived depravity of the Buddhist world, the episodic oppression of Buddhism by the secular authorities, and the inferior capacity of contemporary members of the Buddhist order with regard to the practice of monastic discipline.

Daochuo complemented Tanluan's teachings by emphasizing that a lifelong sinner could be born in the Pure Land by means of the infinite compassion of Amitābha. This concept took into account the fact that people of the latter two stages of the Law's degeneration were less capable of undertaking strict meditative practice than those living in the Era of the Righteous Law. Shandao, the third Chinese Pure Land patriarch, emphasized a further point, that an ordinary person could be born in Amitābha's true Pure Land rather than a provisional Pure Land where additional practice would be necessary before supreme enlightenment is attained. He also stressed that the recitation of the name itself is the true cause of entering *nirvāṇa.* But this overall concept of the primacy of the recitative *nianfo* did not take permanent root in China, as evidenced by the fact that after the middle of the Tang dynasty the Pure Land tradition gradually embraced a combined regiment of meditation, discipline, and recitation of the name.

In Japan, however, the doctrine of recitative *nembutsu* flowered through the teachings of Genshin and Hōnen. Genshin stressed the belief that of all the teachings of Śākyamuni, the most important for people of the Latter Days of the Law, was recitation of the name. He taught that the ordinary person, eyes blinded by passion, was constantly enveloped by the infinite compassion of Amida Buddha, thereby assuring his or her salvation, Hōnen reemphasized the point that for the defiled person the only way to attain enlightenment was to recite the name. At the same time, he insisted that mere recitation of the name would not assure birth in the Pure Land unless supported by sincere faith in Amida. Shinran took Hōnen's teachings a step further by maintaining that more important than recitation of the Buddha's name was the true and real faith underlying the recitation. He taught that true faith could only be an endowment from Amida Buddha.

In the history of the recitative *nianfo* many special forms of practice emerged. For example, the *wuhui nianfo* (Jpn., *goe*, five-toned, *nembutsu*) was introduced into Japan from China by the Tiantai monk Ennin (749–864). This form of *nianfo* later developed in Japan into *fudan nembutsu* (incessant recitation of the name) and *inzei nembutsu* (chanting of the name with a prolonged voice). There also appeared such *nembutsu* forms as *yūzū nembutsu* (*nembutsu* of the interpenetration of all beings), *kan nembutsu* (midwinter *nembutsu*), *uta nembutsu* (chanting the name in song), and *odori nembutsu* (dancing *nembutsu*).

Today, Pure Land devotees comprise the largest single Japanese Buddhist group. Daily worship of Amida Buddha before the family altar, including recitation of his name and the chanting of Pure Land scriptures, is a widespread practice. Recitation of the name is heard during funerals and worship services and on radio and television programs. The same recitation is heard coming from the lips of devout believers when they are walking, working, and resting. Through the recitative *nianfo*, Amida Buddha is as close to the believer as the movement of the lips.

See Also Amitābha; Jingtu; Jōdo Shinshū; Jōdoshu; Mappō; Pure and Impure Lands.

Bibliography

Andrews, Allan A. *The Teachings Essential for Rebirth: A Study of Genshin's Ōjōyōshū.* Tokyo, 1973. This translation and study of Genshin's text provides detailed information on the *nembutsu* teachings of the Japanese Tendai sect.

Fujiwara Ryōsetsu. *Nembutsu shisō no kenkyū.* Kyoto, 1957. A comprehensive study of the historical development of the concept of *nembutsu.*

Fujiwara Ryōsetsu. *Ōjō raisan gaisetsu.* Kyoto, 1962.

Izumi Hokei. *Bombun Muryōjukyō no kenkyū.* Kyoto, 1939. English and Japanese translations of the *Larger Sukhāvatīvyūha Sūtra.*

Mochizuki Shinkō. *Bukkyō kyōten seiritsushi ron.* Kyoto, 1946.

Robinson, Richard H., trans. *Chinese Buddhist Verse.* London, 1954. Contains translations of two short Pure Land works attributed to Nāgārjuna.

Takakusu Junjirō, trans. *"Amitâyur-dhyâna Sûtra."* In "Sacred Books of the East," vol. 49. Oxford, 1894. Reprinted in *Buddhist Mahâyâna Texts* (New York, 1969).

Tsujimoto Tetsuo. *Genshi Bukkyō ni okeru shōten shisō no kenkyū.* Kyoto, 1936. Includes an excellent discussion of the differences in the Buddhist understanding of rebirth in heaven and in the Pure Land.

New Sources

Bloom, A., K.K.i. Tanaka, and E. Nasu. *Engaged Pure Land Buddhism: Challenges Facing Jodo Shinshu in the Contemporary World: Studies in Honor of Professor Alfred Bloom.* Berkeley, 1998.

Carter, J. R. *The Religious Heritage of Japan: Foundations for Cross-Cultural Understanding in a Religiously Plural World.* Portland, Ore, 1999.

Hōnen and Senchakushu English Translation Project. *Hōnen's Senchakushu: Passages on the Selection of the Nembutsu in the Original Vow.* Honolulu, 1998.

Tanabe, G. J. *Religions of Japan in Practice.* Princeton, 1999.

Wright, Dale S. "Koan History: Transformative Language in Chinese Buddhist Thought." In *Koan: Texts and Concepts in Zen Buddhism,* edited by Steven Heine and Dale S. Wright, pp. 200–212. New York, 2000.

Fujiwara Ryōsetsu (1987)
Revised Bibliography

NICAEA, COUNCIL OF See COUNCILS, *ARTICLE ON* CHRISTIAN COUNCILS

NICEPHOROS See NIKEPHOROS

NICEPHOROS CALLISTUS See NIKEPHOROS KALLISTOS

NICHIREN (1222–1282) was a Japanese Buddhist monk of the Kamakura period (1192–1282) and eponymous founder of the Nichirenshu (Nichiren sect). In his radical insistence on the priority of the *Lotus Sūtra* (Skt., *Saddharmapuṇḍarīka Sūtra; Jpn., Myōhōrengekyō;* also known by its abbreviated title, *Hokekyō*) over all other teachings and forms of Buddhism, Nichiren established himself as one of the major figures in the history of Japanese Buddhism. His influence persists to this day through the various schools and movements that look to Nichiren as their founder.

Life. Nichiren was born in the village of Kominato in Awa Province (Chibaken), the son of a fisherman and minor manorial functionary. His talents as a youth brought him to the attention of the lord of the manor, who had him enter the Tendai monastery Kiyosumidera (Seichōji) in 1233 in order to begin his formal education. In 1237 he became a monk and adopted the religious name Renchō. Later, Nichiren left the Kiyosumidera for Kamakura, the seat of the military government, where he studied Pure Land Buddhism and Zen. The year 1242 found Nichiren on Mount Hiei, the center of the flourishing Tendai sect, and thereafter he studied on Mount Kōya, the center of the Shingon (Esoteric) school, and in the ancient capital of Nara. Convinced of the inadequacy of the Buddhism of his times, Nichiren returned to the Kiyosumidera in 1253 and began his self-appointed mission to bring what he believed to be true Buddhism to the Japanese. On April 28 of that year he publicly denounced all other forms of Buddhism as incomplete and ultimately false, and advocated a wholehearted faith in the teachings of the *Lotus.* It was at this time that he adopted the name Nichiren.

The remainder of Nichiren's life was marked by his conflicts with the government and the leaders of the established Buddhist sects. The year 1253 found Nichiren expelled from Kiyosumidera and disseminating his teachings in Kamakura, where he became deeply concerned about the social and political disorder of the times. In 1260 he presented his treatise *Risshō ankokuron* (Establish the right law and save our country) to the government. In it he ascribed the increase in floods, pestilence, famines, political strife, and conspiracies to the government's refusal to accept the Buddha's true teachings as found in the Lotus and their tolerance of the false doctrines of "heterodox" schools. He admonished the Hōjō rulers (military regents from 1213 to 1333) to abandon these expedient teachings and warned of the inevitability of rebellions and foreign invasions that would result from failure to embrace the true Buddhism. His criticism of the Hōjō family provoked the eldest member, Hōjō Shigetoki, a fervent Nembutsu (i.e., Pure Land) practitioner and a patron of Ryokan, the chief priest of the Shingon-Ritsu temple in Kamakura and one of Nichiren's foremost rivals. It is highly probable that Nichiren's hermitage in Kamakura was destroyed in 1260 by outlaws hired by Shigetoki. In 1261 the government exiled Nichiren to the province of Izu (Shizuoka-ken), only to pardon him in 1263. While visiting his home province in 1264, his old enemy Tōjō Kagenobu, a Nembutsu follower, planned an ambush from which Nichiren narrowly escaped.

In 1268 a Korean envoy arrived in Japan demanding the payment of tribute to the Mongolian ruler, Khubilai Khan. Nichiren submitted a proposal to the government reminding the Hōjō rulers that he had foretold such foreign invasions in his *Risshō ankokuron* and claiming that only he and, of course, faith in the *Lotus,* could save the country. Although the government ignored both the request of the envoy and Nichiren's warning, the masses, fearing the threat of invasion by Mongolian troops, turned in greater numbers to Nichiren's school. Concerned over Nichiren's growing popularity, the monks of several established Buddhist sects in Kamakura brought formal charges against Nichiren. These resulted in his arrest and, in 1271, his exile to Sado Island. After more than two years, in 1274, he was pardoned and returned to Kamakura. Soon after, Nichiren retired from public life and secluded himself in a mountain retreat in Minobu (Yamanashi-ken). There he became ill; in 1276 he moved to Ikegami in Musahi Province (Tokyo), where he died in 1282.

THOUGHT AND WORKS. Although Nichiren remained fundamentally within the Tendai tradition, he is known as a reformer, if not a radical, who departed from many of the teachings of Saichō, the founder of that sect. Indeed, he virtually reduced Tendai doctrines to the sole practice of chanting the Daimoku ("sacred title") of the *Lotus Sūtra,* that is, the recitation of the formula "Namu *Myōhōrengekyō*" ("Adoration be to the Lotus of Perfect Law"). The Daimoku, according to Nichiren, contains the entire universe and symbolizes absolute truth or, in other words, Śākyamuni Buddha. In his *Kanjin honzonshō* (The object of worship revealed by the introspection of our minds), written while exiled on Sado Island, Nichiren established Śākyamuni as the true object of worship and the Daimoku as the practice for revealing the absolute truth.

An integral aspect of his method of conversion (*shakubuku*) was the condemnation of the popular sects of Buddhism. Nichiren held that by deliberately provoking people and raising their anger he would cause them to evaluate their beliefs. Anger and hatred, in Nichiren's system, were productive and creative emotional states. While at Kiyosumidera Nichiren's denunciations were focused primarily on the proponents of Nembutsu and Zen practices. He criticized Pure Land for engaging in expedient practices that would lead (he claimed) to rebirth in the lowest of hells and for emphasizing the notion of a Western Paradise, a belief, Nichiren held, that discourages people from establishing peace in their present lives. He criticized Zen for stressing a transmission outside scripture and for their belief in the efficacy of "no-words." Nichiren argued that without *sūtras* and words the teachings of the Buddha could not be transmitted at all. Later, Nichiren added Ritsu (Vinaya), Shingon, and the esoteric subsects of Tendai to his list of heterodox schools.

Nichiren's exile on Sado Island proved to be a period of great creativity. Among the essays and treatises he wrote during this period was the *Kaimokushō* (Liberation from blindness). Here he departs from traditional Tendai notions of spiritual filiation by claiming that he is the successor to and reincarnation of the Viśiṣṭacāritra Bodhisattva (Jpn., Jōgyō Bosatsu), to whom Śākyamuni is said to have entrusted the *Lotus Sūtra* and whose reappearance is prophesied in that text. Another work, the *Daimandara* (Great maṇḍala) reiterates this theme. The *maṇḍala* itself, inspirationally revealed to Nichiren, represents all living beings in the Buddha world expressed in the *Lotus Sūtra.* It depicts the Daimoku surrounded by the names of Śākyamuni, various *bodhisattvas* led by Viśiṣṭacāritra, *śrāvakas,* Japanese gods (*kami*), and Tendai masters arranged on levels in descending order. The image of Śākyamuni and the Daimandara became the chief objects of worship in Nichiren's thought. Other of Nichiren's writings include 434 essays and epistles and a commentary on the *Lotus Sūtra.* The original of this commentary, which is still extant, is written on the back pages of a copy of the *Triple Lotus Sūtra,* a set of three *sūtras* including the *Myōhōrengekyo* (*Lotus Sūtra*); the *Muryōgikyō,* regarded as an introduction to the *Lotus;* and the *Kan Fugen bosatsu gyōhōkyō,* an epilogue to the *Lotus.* Aside from the *Risshō an-*

kokuron, the most significant of Nichiren's essays include *Kaimokushō, Kanjin honzonshō, Senjishō* (Selection of the Proper Time), and *Hōonshō* (Requitment of Favors).

SEE ALSO Nichirenshū.

BIBLIOGRAPHY

Primary Sources

The collected works of Nichiren are available in the *Shōwa teihon Nichiren Shōnin ibun,* 4 vols., compiled by Minobusan Kuonji (Yamanashi, 1952–1959). Some of these works have been published in English. These include *The Awakening to the Truth; or Kaimokushō,* translated by Ehara Ryozui (Tokyo, 1941); *Risshō ankokuron; or Establish the Right Law and Save Our Country,* translated by Murano Senchu (Tokyo, 1977); and *Nyorai metsugo go gohyakusaishi kanjin honzonshō; or, The True Object of Worship Revealed for the First Time in the Fifth of Five Century Periods after the Great Decease of the Tathagata,* translated by Murano Senchu (Tokyo, 1954).

Another collection of Nichiren's works is the *Nichiren Daishōnin gosho zenshū* (Tokyo, 1952). Portions of this work are now being published in English under the title *The Major Writings of Nichiren Daishōnin,* edited and translated by the Seikyo Times (Tokyo, 1979).

Secondary Sources

Anesaki Masaharu. *Nichiren, the Buddhist Prophet* (1916). Gloucester, Mass., 1966.

Anesaki Masaharu. *Hokekyō no gyōja Nichiren.* Tokyo, 1933.

Masutani Fumio. *Nichiren.* Tokyo, 1967.

Matsunaga, Alicia, and Daigan Matsunaga. *Foundations of Japanese Buddhism,* vol. 2, *The Mass Movement (Kamakura and Muromachi Periods).* Los Angeles and Tokyo, 1976. See chapter 3.

Mochizuki Kankō. *The Nichiren Sect.* Translated by Murano Senchu. Tokyo, 1958.

Motai Kyōkō. *Kanjin honzonshō kenkyū josetsu.* Tokyo, 1964.

Nichiren Shōnin ibun jiten. Edited by Risshō Daigaku Nichiren Kyōgaku Kenkyūsho. Yamanashi, 1985.

Nichirenshū jiten. Published by the Nichiren Sect Headquarters. Tokyo, 1981.

Ōno Tatsunosuke. *Nichiren.* Tokyo, 1958.

Renondeau, Gaston. *La doctrine de Nichiren.* Paris, 1958.

Satomi, Kishio. *Japanese Civilization: Its Significance and Realization, Nichirenism and the Japanese National Principles.* London, 1933.

Takagi Yutaka. *Nichiren.* Tokyo, 1970.

Watanabe Hōyō. *Nichirenshū shingyōron no kenkyū.* Kyoto, 1979.

Yamakawa Chiō. *Hokke shisōshijō no Nichiren Shōnin.* Tokyo, 1934.

New Sources

Christensen, J. A. *Nichiren: Leader of Buddhist Reformation in Japan.* Fremont, Calif., 2001.

Hurst, Jane D. *Nichiren Shoshu Buddhism and the Soku Gakkai in America: The Ethos of a New Religious Movement.* New York, 1992.

Montgomery, Daniel B. *Fire in the Lotus: The Dynamic Buddhism of Nichiren.* New York, 1991.

Osumi Kazuo. "Buddhism in the Kamakura Period." In *The Cambridge History of Japan,* vol. 3: *Medieval Japan.* New York, 1990.

Snow, David A. *Shakubuku: A Study of the Nichiren Shoshu Buddhist Movement in America.* New York, 1993.

WATANABE HŌYŌ (1987)
Revised Bibliography

NICHIRENSHŪ broadly refers to all religious bodies claiming derivation from the Japanese Buddhist teacher Nichiren (1222–1282), including traditional temple denominations as well as lay associations and new religious movements. While *Nichirenshū* is also the official name of a specific Nichiren Buddhist denomination, this entry will address the larger Nichiren tradition. Nichiren Buddhism is based on faith in the *Lotus Sūtra* (in Japanese, *Myōhō-renge-kyō;* sometimes shortened to *Hōkekyō),* a Mahāyāna scripture revered throughout East Asia for its promise that all shall attain buddhahood. The central practice of Nichiren Buddhism is chanting the *daimoku* or title of the *Lotus* in the formula *Namu Myōhō-renge-kyō* (literally, "Homage to the sūtra of the lotus blossom of the wonderful *dharma*"), said to embody all the Buddha's practices and resulting virtues as well as the essence of all Buddhist teachings.

THE FOUNDER NICHIREN. Nichiren is regarded as one of the founders of the new Buddhist movements of the Kamakura period (1185–1333) and numbers among Japan's most compelling religious figures. Ordained at age sixteen at the temple Kiyosumidera (or Seichōji) in Awa province (modern Chiba prefecture), as a young man he traveled extensively for study. He was versed especially in Tendai Buddhist teachings and also in Esoteric Buddhism. Eventually he based himself in Kamakura, center of the recently established shogunate or military government, where he won followers among the warriors of the eastern provinces. Nichiren is known for his teaching of exclusive devotion to the *Lotus Sūtra,* regarded especially in the Tendai tradition as embodying the Buddha's ultimate teaching. Like many of his contemporaries, Nichiren believed his own time to be that of the Final *Dharma* age *(mappō);* in this degenerate era, he asserted that only faith in the *Lotus Sūtra* leads to liberation, and he advocated chanting its *daimoku* as a universal practice. In chanting the *daimoku* with faith, Nichiren taught, the practitioner becomes one with the eternal, original Buddha revealed in the *Lotus Sūtra.* He also devised a calligraphic *maṇḍala* written chiefly in Chinese characters with the *daimoku* inscribed down the center, surrounded by the buddhas, *bodhisattvas,* deities, and other members of the *Lotus Sūtra* assembly. Nichiren made numerous individual copies of this *maṇḍala* as a personal object of worship for his followers.

Drawing on Tendai teachings concerning the unity of mind and all phenomena, and of individuals and their objective world, Nichiren attributed the disasters of his day—including famine, epidemics, natural disasters, and the threat of Mongol invasion—to widespread rejection of the *Lotus Sūtra* in favor of "inferior" teachings, such as those of Pure Land Buddhism and Zen. Conversely, he held that the spread of exclusive faith in the *Lotus* would transform the present world into a buddha land. Nichiren maintained this conviction throughout his life, but its most famous statement occurs in his admonitory treatise *Risshō ankoku ron* (On establishing the true *dharma* and bringing peace to the land), submitted in 1260 to Hōjō Tokiyori, the most powerful figure in the Kamakura government.

Nichiren's growing conviction that only faith in the *Lotus Sūtra* could save the country from disaster led him to adopt *shakubuku*, a confrontational method of teaching the *dharma* by directly rebuking attachment to mistaken views. His criticisms of other forms of Buddhism, and of high officials for supporting them, provoked the anger of the authorities. He himself was arrested and exiled twice, while a number of his followers were imprisoned, stripped of their land holdings, and in a few cases executed. For Nichiren, however, loyalty to the *Lotus Sūtra* superseded obedience to worldly rule. His writings assert the need to admonish "slander of the *dharma*" as an act of compassion, even at the risk of one's life, and express confidence that enduring harsh trials for the sake of the *Lotus Sūtra* will eradicate the practitioner's past sins and guarantee his or her future buddhahood. Nichiren's ideal of realizing the buddha land in the present world, and his example in defying worldly authority for the sake of his faith, have inspired followers and sympathizers down to the present. At the same time, his exclusive truth claim has generated considerable controversy.

The Medieval Hokkeshū. Shortly before his death, Nichiren designated six senior disciples to assume leadership of his community: Renge Ajari Nichiji (1250–?), Iyokō Nitchō (1252–1317), Sadokō Nikō (1253–1314), Byakuren Ajari Nikkō (1246–1333), Daikoku Ajari Nichirō (1245–1320), and Ben Ajari Nisshō (1221–1323). Nichiji is said to have embarked in 1295 on a journey to northern China to spread Nichiren's teachings abroad; the others proselytized chiefly in eastern Japan. Congregations formed around them and their successors, giving rise to the first lineages of the Hokkeshū (Hokke or Lotus sect), as Nichiren's followers would be known in medieval times. Mount Minobu in Kai province (Yamanashi prefecture), where Nichiren had spent his last years, held special significance for the sect as a whole; in addition, each lineage established its own major temple or temples, which served as centers of propagation and monastic education. Branch temple networks formed as new temples were built or converted. Within a half century of his death, Nichiren's teachings had spread throughout Japan.

Early on, Nikkō's Fuji lineage broke away from the others. Nikkō's successors would claim retrospectively that he alone had been Nichiren's true *dharma* heir. This first schism was a decisive one; to this day, Nichiren Shōshū—the chief modern successor of the Fuji school—maintains its own distinctive interpretations. Further schisms and new lineage formation would occur during the fourteenth through sixteen centuries due to geographic separation, institutional rivalry, and differences of interpretation.

After 1333, when the Kamakura shogunate was overthrown and the locus of political power shifted back to the imperial capital in Kyoto, Hokke monks began to proselytize there. Nichirō's disciples took the lead in this endeavor: Nichizō (1269–1342) established the Shijō lineage, and Nichijō (1298–1369) the Rokujō lineage, followed by representatives of other Hokkeshū branches. In the predominantly rural east, Hokke temples were supported chiefly by the patronage of provincial warriors or other local landholders. In the western cities of Kyoto and Sakai, however, while attracting some warrior and even aristocratic followers, the Hokkeshū drew its major support from the emerging urban mercantile class (*machishū*), whose wealth enabled the sect to prosper. By the mid-fifteenth century, there were twenty-one Hokke temples in Kyoto, and about half the city's population, it is said, were Nichiren followers.

Despite institutional friction and differences of interpretation, the Hokkeshū shared doctrinal foundations with Tendai, and Hokke monks often studied at major Tendai centers, such as Enryakuji on Mount Hiei near Kyoto or Tendai seminaries in the east. Nonetheless, they upheld a strong sense of independent Hokkeshū identity and actively practiced *shakubuku* by preaching, writing, and debate. From time to time, temple abbots and lineage heads followed Nichiren's example of "admonishing the state" by submitting letters of remonstration to local or shogunal officials or occasionally, to the shogun or emperor himself, urging a policy of exclusive devotion to the *Lotus Sūtra* for the country's peace and prosperity. Repeated remonstrations sometimes provoked official wrath, and the sect's hagiographical tradition celebrates those monks who, like Nichiren, endured persecution from the authorities in the course of their proselytizing efforts.

Tensions and Controversies. Like other medieval Japanese Buddhist traditions, the Hokkeshū was characterized by the development of rival lineages, each stressing the authority of its own interpretations in both doctrinal and ritual matters. Often these interpretations took the form of "secret transmissions" said to derive from Nichiren himself or from his immediate disciples. One focus of ongoing doctrinal dispute involved the two parts into which traditional Tendai exegesis divides the *Lotus Sūtra*—the "trace teaching" (*shakumon*), or first fourteen chapters, which present Śākyamuni Buddha as a "trace" or historical manifestation, and the "origin teaching" (*honmon*), or latter fourteen chapters, which identify him as the eternal, original Buddha. Nichiren had based his thought on the origin teaching, but his successors debated the precise relationship between trace and origin teachings. The so-called *itchi* (unity) faction held them to be ultimately one and inseparable, while the *shōretsu* (superior-inferior) faction held the origin teaching to be distinct and superior. Both positions were variously elaborated. While this debate probably held little relevance for most lay believers, it afforded scholar-monks a vehicle to display their erudition and was central to the self-definition of their particular Hokke lineages.

Other controversies involved matters of practice, such as whether Nichiren had ultimately intended the "Buddha" or the "*dharma*" as the true object of worship, along with the related issue of whether or not the icon employed in actual practice should be an image of the eternal Śākyamuni Buddha or Nichiren's calligraphic *maṇḍala*. Differences concerning the object of worship continue to this day. Still other controversies involved the ongoing issue of how rigorously Nichiren's *Lotus* exclusivism should be maintained, and what concessions might legitimately be made to the larger religious culture. An example was the propriety of venerating the *kami*, or local Japanese deities. Since shrines to the *kami* were often affiliated with other Buddhist schools, some Hokke monks argued that making offerings at such shrines was tantamount to supporting "*dharma* slanderers." In the fourteenth century, many Hokke temples began to incorporate their own mode of *kami* veneration in the form of a cult of thirty protector deities (*sanjūbanjin*), one for each day of the month, and scholars of the sect produced distinctive theories of Hokke Shintō, a subset of a larger medieval discourse incorporating *kami* into a Buddhist framework. Nonetheless, a minority opinion within the Hokkeshū opposed venerating *kami* altogether.

ASCENDANCY, SUPPRESSION, AND ACCOMMODATION. As shogunal power declined following the Ōnin War (1467–1477), townspeople in Kyoto had to mount their own defenses against incursions from provincial warlords and armed peasant leagues. In an era when religious institutions were also economic, political, and even military powers in their own right, the townspeople's district organizations for self-government and self-protection were closely tied to their Hokke temples. The sect's exclusivist orientation served as a basis for *machishū* solidarity vis-à-vis traditional overlords, who included not only aristocrats and warriors but also powerful shrines and temples. In 1532, having united with warrior allies to repel peasant forces organized by the Jōdo Shin, or True Pure Land sect, the Hokke-based *machishū* set up a virtually autonomous government in Kyoto, carrying out police and judicial functions and refusing to pay various taxes and rents. The reign of the Lotus League (*Hokke ikki*) lasted until 1536, when monks of Mount Hiei, joined by other traditional elites who resented the erosion of their authority in the capital, attacked and burned every Hokke temple in Kyoto.

While eventually able to rebuild, the Hokkeshū never regained its original strength in the capital. It was further weakened by the religious policies of successive warlords—Oda Nobunaga, Toyotomi Hideyoshi, and Tokugawa Ieyasu—who suppressed the power of Buddhist sects and temples in their efforts to extend their rule. In 1595, when Hideyoshi demanded the participation of a hundred monks from each sect in monthly memorial services for his deceased relatives, most Hokke leaders saw no choice but to comply, although joining in intersectarian rites and receiving offerings from Hideyoshi, a nonbeliever, violated strict *Lotus* exclusivism. However, the monk Busshōin Nichiō (1565–1630) initiated a dissident movement known as *fuju fuse* (neither receiving nor giving), meaning a refusal to accept offerings from those who do not embrace the *Lotus Sūtra* or to provide them with ritual services. Nichiō insisted that believers should defy even the ruler to uphold the purity of Nichiren's teaching, even at the cost of their lives. His position eventually gained support, dividing the Hokkeshū between *fuju fuse* proponents and those favoring a more accommodating stance. The new Tokugawa shogunate, established in Edo (modern Tokyo) in 1603, saw in the *fuju fuse* movement a threat to its authority and policy of religious control and suppressed it repeatedly, sometimes with the cooperation of conciliatory factions within the Hokkeshū itself. *Fuju fuse* leaders were killed or exiled and their followers driven underground. Like the Japanese Christianity of the same period, which was similarly persecuted, the *fuju fuse* movement stands as a striking example of religiously based defiance of ruling power.

Under the new government, Buddhist temples of all sects were integrated into the state apparatus of census taking and social control; temple registration became mandatory for all families, and changing sectarian affiliation was forbidden. Traditional *shakubuku* and intersectarian debates were no longer possible. Like other sects, the Hokkeshū (or Nichirenshū, as the sect was by now alternatively called) turned its energies toward doctrinal study, an effort that flourished in the context of an emergent print culture. New Nichiren Buddhist seminaries were established throughout the country; compilations of Nichiren's writings were edited and published; and sectarian doctrine was codified. Accounts of Nichiren's life were also published, sometimes with illustrations and in vernacular Japanese. These hagiographies both reflected and encouraged a trend toward founder veneration, expressed in pilgrimages to sacred sites, festivals marking events in Nichiren's life, and the traveling display of statues, *maṇḍalas*, or other sacred objects held by noted temples. Such activities were supported by the many associations of lay followers (*kō* or *kōchū*) that flourished especially in the eighteenth and nineteenth centuries, often under lay leadership. Images of Nichiren as a religious hero also circulated in the wider society, events in his life being dramatized in kabuki performances, the puppet theater, and also popular storytelling.

MODERN DEVELOPMENTS AND INTERPRETATIONS. After the fall of the Tokugawa shogunate and the Meiji restoration (1868), the Nichiren Hokkeshū was reorganized. In 1876 the *itchi* lineages united as one denomination under the name Nichirenshū, while the major *shōretsu* lineages each took independent names; the *fuju fuse* faction also resurfaced and gained legal recognition. The most striking feature of modern Nichiren Buddhism, however, is its vigorous lay movements, often independent of traditional temples—a phenomenon unparalleled in other Japanese Buddhist sects. Some lay Nichiren Buddhist organizations have roots in early modern lay associations such as the Butsuryūkō, founded in 1857. Others emerged after the Meiji restoration. The influential Kokuchūkai (Pillar of the nation society), founded by Tanaka Chigaku (1861–1939), promoted what he called *Nichiren-shugi* (Nichirenism), a lay-oriented reading of Nichiren Buddhism welded to concerns of nationalism and modernization. (This term, *Nichiren-shugi*, has also come to be used in a broader sense to encompass all forms of Nichiren-Buddhist influenced thought.) Other Nichiren- or *Lotus Sūtra*-based lay groups have often been categorized as "new religions" and include Reiyūkai, Risshō Kōseikai, and Sōka Gakkai. Such groups frequently engage in active proselytizing and stress personal benefits, character development, and social transformation through faith. Nichiren himself has continued to be celebrated as a Japanese cultural figure; in the twentieth century alone, more than a hundred literary works about him appeared, including novels, plays, and biographies.

During Japan's modern imperial period (1895–1945), Nichiren's mandate to spread faith in the *Lotus Sūtra* was widely interpreted in terms of Japanese national destiny and the armed expansion of empire. Tanaka Chigaku and Honda Nisshō (1867–1931), head of the Nichiren denomination Kenpon Hokkeshū, were especially influential in promulgating nationalistic Nichirenist ideology and won support from military officers, government officials, and intellectuals. Tanaka's Japan-centered reading of Nichiren doctrine, which equated the *Lotus Sūtra* with the Japanese national polity (*kokutai*), inspired such figures as the right-wing nationalist author Kita Ikki (1883–1937) and army officer Ishiwara Kanji (1889–1949), who was instrumental in Japan's 1931 armed takeover of Manchuria. Among Nichirenshū clerics as well, some extremist ideologues aligned themselves with state Shintō and asserted the emperor to be the object of worship.

Nonetheless, one finds significant exceptions to these imperialistic readings. The Christian leader Uchimura Kanzō (1861–1930) admired Nichiren for his devotion to scripture and the courage of his religious commitment. The leftist writer Seno'o Girō (1890–1961), imprisoned for his socialist activities, looked to Nichiren as a figure of resistance. Some writers originally drawn to Tanaka's *Nichiren-shugi* also came to reject his nationalistic interpretation: The literary critic and novelist Takayama Chōgyū (1871–1902) saw Nichiren as a heroic "Nietzschian" individual who valued truth above nation, while the poet Miyazawa Kenji (1896–1933) depicted the plight of impoverished farmers from the perspective of his *Lotus Sūtra* faith.

During the Fifteen Years' War (1931–1945), under a government religious policy dominated by state Shintō, some Nichiren believers met persecution for their beliefs. In the 1930s and 1940s, government ministries repeatedly demanded that sectarian officials delete from Nichiren's works passages deemed disrespectful to Japanese deities or emperors. Sōka Gakkai founder Makiguchi Tsunesaburō (1871–1944) refused to have his followers accept the talismans of the imperial Ise Shrine and was imprisoned with other leaders of his society on charges of violating the Peace Preservation Law; leaders within the denomination Hokke Honmonshū were also indicted for asserting doctrinal positions contrary to the imperial cult.

Since Japan's defeat in 1945, Nichiren Buddhist followers have widely adopted the causes of peace and opposition to nuclear weapons. The small monastic order Nipponzan Myōhōji has embraced a stance of absolute nonviolence and practices peaceful civil disobedience on the Gandhian model, while lay organizations such as Sōka Gakkai and Risshō Kōseikai are NGO members of the United Nations and support various forms of relief work, peace education, and other humanitarian causes. The assimilation of Nichiren's ideal of establishing the buddha land in the present world to a range of social and political agendas—from militant nationalism to postwar pacifism—is a noteworthy development within modern Nichiren Buddhism.

ORGANIZATION AND OBSERVANCES. At the turn of the twenty-first century, there are some forty legally recognized Nichiren Buddhist religious bodies. Despite a forced merger of some of the smaller Nichiren sects under the wartime government's policy of religious control, most of the denominational divisions established in the 1870s were reasserted after the war ended. The largest Nichiren Buddhist temple denomination takes Nichirenshū as its legal name and has Kuonji at Mount Minobu in Yamanashi prefecture as its head temple. Risshō University, which is affiliated with Nichirenshū, is home to Japan's leading research institute for the study of Nichiren Buddhist doctrine and history. The other major Nichiren Buddhist denominations include Hokkeshū Honmon-ryū, Hokkeshū Jinmon-ryū, Hokkeshū Shinmon-ryū, Honmon Butsuryūshū, Honmon Hokkeshū, Kenpon Hokkeshū, Nichiren Honshū, Nichiren Kōmonshū, Nichiren Shōshū, and Nichirenshū Fuju Fuseha. The numerical strength of contemporary Nichiren Buddhism, however, lies in its lay movements. Sōka Gakkai and Risshō Kōseikai in particular claim membership figures in the millions, including substantial followings outside Japan.

Despite considerable differences of interpretation and ritual observance among Nichiren Buddhist groups, one also finds points of commonality. Reciting portions of the *Lotus Sūtra* and chanting the *daimoku* constitute the basic daily practice of both clergy and laity and are also performed at formal ceremonies. In addition to annual rites conducted by temples of all Japanese Buddhist sects, such as New Year's observances and memorial services for the dead at the equinoxes and during the summer Obon festival, Nichiren Buddhist temples and lay organizations hold festivals and ritual observances on dates sacred to their tradition, usually transposed from the lunar to the Western calendar. These include Nichiren's birthday (celebrated February 16); his first sermon, said to mark the founding of the Nichiren sect (April 28); commemorations of various persecutions that Nichiren encountered in spreading his teachings; and the Oeshiki observances commemorating the anniversary of his death (October 13).

SEE ALSO New Religious Movements, article on New Religious Movements in Japan; Nichiren; Nikkō; Reiyūkai Kyōdan; Risshō Kōseikai; Sōka Gakkai.

BIBLIOGRAPHY

Primary Sources

Nichiren's works: The critical edition of Nichiren's works is the four-volume *Shōwa teihon Nichiren Shōnin ibun* published by Minobusan Kuonji (Yamanashi, Japan, 1952–1959; rev. ed., 1988), head temple of Nichirenshū. This edition forms the basis of the *Writings of Nichiren Shōnin*, two volumes of English translations done by Kyōtsū Hori and others of the Nichirenshū Overseas Propagation Promotion Association (Tokyo, 2002 and 2003). A one-volume edition of Nichiren's works, with those originally written in Sino-Japanese (*kanbun*) rendered into Japanese, is the *Nichiren Daishōnin zenshū*, published by Sōka Gakkai (Tokyo, 1952). The *Selected Writings of Nichiren* (New York, 1990) and *Letters of Nichiren* (1996), edited by Philip B. Yampolsky and translated by Burton Watson and others, are based on this edition. These translations represent revisions of those contained in Sōka Gakkai's *The Major Writings of Nichiren Daishonin* (7 vols., Tokyo, 1979–1994) and reissued in the one-volume *Writings of Nichiren Daishonin* (Tokyo, 1999). In addition to Nichiren's writings, there are the critical edition of Nichiren's personally annotated copy of the *Lotus Sūtra* (*Teihon Chū Hokekyō*, 2 vols., Kyoto, 1980) and collection of photographic reproductions, with notes, of his extant holographic *maṇḍalas* (*Nichiren Shōnin shinseki no sekai*, vol. 1, Tokyo, 1992), both edited by Yamanaka Kihachi.

The later tradition: The 23-volume *Nichirenshū shūgaku zensho*, edited by the Risshō Daigaku Nichirenshū Kyōgaku Kenkyūjo (Tokyo, 1959–1962), contains historical records and other writings from the major Nichiren lineages. The eight-volume *Nichirenshū zensho* (Tokyo, 1910–1916; rev. ed., Kyoto, 1973–1978) contains late medieval and early modern commentaries on Nichiren's works, as well as biographies of Nichiren and later figures in the tradition. There are also collections of the works of individual figures or records of particular lineages in the Nichiren tradition, as well as the *Honzon shiryō* (rev. ed., Kyoto, 1998), a collection of medieval transmissions concerning Nichiren's *maṇḍala*. As yet one finds little secondary scholarship on Nichiren Buddhism in Western languages, but numerous studies and reference works exist in Japanese, a few of which are cited below.

Secondary Sources

Allam, Cheryl M. "The Nichiren and Catholic Confrontation with Japanese Nationalism." *Buddhist-Christian Studies* 10 (1990): 35–84.

Dolce, Lucia. "Esoteric Patterns in Nichiren's Interpretation of the Lotus Sutra." Ph.D. diss., University of Leiden, Netherlands, 2002.

Dolce, Lucia. "Hokke Shinto: Kami in the Nichiren Tradition." In *Buddhas and Kami in Japan: Honji Suijaku as a Combinatory Paradigm*, edited by Mark Teeuwen and Fabio Rambelli, pp. 222–254. London and New York, 2003.

Fujii Manabu. *Hokke bunka no tenkai.* Kyoto, 2002. Collected historical essays on medieval and early modern Hokke Buddhist culture in Kyoto and other localities, prominent figures within the sect, and its relations with the state.

Habito, Ruben L. F. "Lotus Buddhism and its Liberational Thrust: A Re-reading of the *Lotus Sutra* by Way of Nichiren." *Ching Feng* 35, no. 2 (1992): 85–111.

Habito, Ruben L. F., and Jacqueline I. Stone, eds. *Revisiting Nichiren. Japanese Journal of Religious Studies* 26, nos. 3–4 (1999). A special issue focused on Nichiren in his historical context and including a select bibliography of Western-language studies of the Nichiren tradition.

Hunter, Jeffrey. "The *Fuju Fuse* Controversy in Nichiren Buddhism: The Debate between Busshōin Nichiō and Jakushōin Nichiken." Ph.D. diss., University of Wisconsin-Madison, 1989.

Imatani Akira. *Tenbun Hokke no ran: Busō suru machishū.* Tokyo, 1989. A study of the rise and decline of the Hokkeshū in medieval Kyoto.

Kageyama Gyōō. *Nichiren kyōdanshi gaisetsu.* Kyoto, 1959. An overview of Nichirenshū history through the 1950s.

Kitamura Gyōon. *Kinsei kaichō no kenkyū.* Tokyo, 1989. A study of the activities of early modern Nichiren Buddhist temples and lay societies, focusing on the practice of *kaichō*, the ritualized display of *maṇḍalas*, images, or temple treasures not usually on view.

Matsumura Jugon. *Nichirenshū gireishi no kenkyū.* Kyoto, 2001. A study of the history of Nichiren Buddhist ritual practices, including liturgies, funerals, and memorial rites.

Miyazaki Eishū. *Fuju Fuse-ha no genryū to tenkai.* Kyoto, 1969. A classic study of the *fuju fuse* movement and its persecution, with attention to doctrinal roots, social context, and historical development.

Miyazaki Eishū, ed. *Nichiren jiten.* Tokyo, 1978. A basic dictionary of the Nichiren tradition.

Mochizuki Shinchō. *Kinsei Nichirenshū no soshi shinkō to shugojin shinkō.* Kyoto, 2002. A study of founder veneration, sacred sites, pilgrimage, and cults of protective deities in early modern Nichiren Buddhism.

Nakano Kyōtoku, ed. *Kindai Nichiren kyōdan no shisōka.* Tokyo, 1977. Includes studies of eight leading figures in nineteenth- and twentieth-century Nichiren Buddhism.

Nakao Takashi. *Nichiren shinkō no keifu to girei.* Tokyo, 1999. A historical study of the development of founder veneration and related practices in Nichiren Buddhism.

Nichirenshū Jiten Kankō Iinkai, ed. *Nichirenshū jiten.* Tokyo, 1981. A comprehensive dictionary of the history of Nichiren Buddhism, indispensable for scholarly study.

Ōtani Eiichi. *Kindai Nihon no Nichiren-shugi undō.* Kyoto, 2001. A detailed study of the nationalistic Nichirenist movements of Tanaka Chigaku and Honda Nisshō.

Risshō Daigaku Nichirenshū Kyōgaku Kenkyūjo, ed. *Nichiren kyōdan zenshi*, vol. 1. Kyoto, 1984. The first in a projected two-volume history of the Nichiren sect, based on primary sources. This volume covers up to the early seventeenth century.

Shigyō Kaishū. *Nichirenshū kyōgakushi.* Kyoto, 1952. A history of Nichiren Buddhist doctrinal studies, organized by lineage, up through the mid-nineteenth century.

Stone, Jacqueline. "Rebuking the Enemies of the *Lotus*: Nichirenist Exclusivism in Historical Perspective." *Japanese Journal of Religious Studies* 21, nos. 2–3 (1994): 231–259.

Stone, Jacqueline I. *Original Enlightenment and the Transformation of Medieval Japanese Buddhism.* Honolulu, 1999. Chapters six and seven deal respectively with Nichiren and his medieval successors, with attention to their interactions with Tendai Buddhism.

Takagi Yutaka. *Nichiren to sono montei.* Tokyo, 1965. A classic study of Nichiren and his early community of followers in their medieval social context.

Tamura Yoshirō and Miyazaki Eishū, eds. *Kōza Nichiren* 3: *Nichiren shinkō no rekishi.* Tokyo, 1972. A collection of essays on the history of Nichiren Buddhism.

Tamura Yoshirō and Miyazaki Eishū, eds. *Kōza Nichiren* 4: *Nihon kindai to Nichiren-shugi.* Tokyo, 1972. Collected essays on aspects of modern Nichirenism, including nationalism, images of Nichiren, and new religious movements.

Tanabe, George J., Jr. "Tanaka Chigaku: The *Lotus Sutra* and the Body Politic." In *The Lotus Sutra in Japanese Culture,* edited by George J. Tanabe Jr. and Willa Jane Tanabe, pp. 191–208. Honolulu, 1989.

Tokoro Shigemoto. *Kindai shakai to Nichiren-shugi.* Tokyo, 1972. An overview of Nichirenist thought, figures, and movements from the late nineteenth century up to the 1970s.

Watanabe Hōyō. *Nichirenshū shingyōron no kenkyū.* Kyoto, 1976. A study of medieval and early modern Nichirenshū discourses of faith and practice.

JACQUELINE I. STONE (2005)

NICHOLAS OF CUSA (1401–1464), German canonist, Christian theologian, and philosopher. Nicholas was born at Kues (present-day Bernkastel-Kues) on the Moselle, and studied at Heidelberg, Padua, and Cologne. At the Council of Basel, with his treatise *De concordantia catholica* (1434), he defended conciliar authority over the pope and proposed extensive reforms consistent with this position. He later converted to the cause of the papacy. As papal legate he traveled to Constantinople to promote Christian reunification (1437), and as cardinal and bishop of Brixen, he worked throughout Germany and Bohemia on behalf of papal authority and ecclesiastical reform. During his last years in Rome, Nicholas lived simply, having used much of his income to establish the Saint Nikolas Hospital in Kues, which still contains his large personal library.

Amid this active life Nicholas wrote numerous speculative works, beginning with *De docta ignorantia* (Learned Ignorance; 1440). He accords intellect a central role in the religious life, and emphasizes the desire to know God. All inquiry requires a "proportion" between the known and the as yet unknown, but there is no proportion between the infinity of God and the finite human intellect. Knowledge of God therefore becomes "learned ignorance," that is, the knowledge that one cannot know God precisely in the divine nature, but only symbolically through God's self-revelation in the universe and in Christ, who unites finite humanity and divine infinity. Nicholas correlates learned ignorance with "conjecture" (*De coniecturis,* 1442–1443). More than mere guesswork, conjecture approximates truth in limited, indirect ways. Nicholas's conjectures include many metaphors, mathematical symbols, and attempts to name God (e.g., as Absolute Maximum; as *Possest,* or the union of possibility and actual being; and as Not-other). Nicholas uses a distinctive logic, the "coincidence of opposites," which points beyond the contrasts of finite reason toward the infinite unity of God. The ability to formulate this logic indicates that the mind, while finite, nevertheless conceives of divine infinity and approaches it without limit. In *Idiota de mente* (The Layman: About Mind; 1450) Nicholas claims that the mind is a living image of God that "has the power of corresponding more and more without limit to its unreachable original." Participating in God's creative activity, humanity also creates a cultural world. This human world provides examples for Nicholas's art of conjecture, for example in his *De ludo globi* (1463), in which a ball game becomes the focus for theological speculation.

Nicholas's tolerance of religious diversity emerges in two works written in response to the Turkish conquest of Constantinople. *De pace fidei* (The Peace of Faith; 1453) recognizes the conjectural truth of all religions, yet sees their fulfillment in Christianity. *Cribratio Alcoran* (Sifting the Qurʾān; 1461) is perhaps the most tolerant examination of Islam in the late medieval West.

In controversies over conciliarism, theology, and Islam, Nicholas of Cusa is an original, even idiosyncratic, thinker. The roots of his thought run deep in the medieval world, particularly in the Christian Neoplatonic tradition. His works were widely circulated in four early printed editions. He influenced Giordano Bruno, through whom Leibniz and other German thinkers encountered Nicholas's ideas. Commentators like Ernst Cassirer have viewed Nicholas as the first modern philosopher because of his novel epistemology and cosmology. While claims for Nicholas's modernity should be tempered, his learned ignorance, conjectural theology, and religious tolerance do address persistent problems of religious knowledge and practice.

BIBLIOGRAPHY

The critical edition of Nicholas of Cusa's *Opera omnia* (Leipzig and Hamburg, 1932–) is in progress under the direction of the Heidelberg Academy. There is also a more accessible edition of the Latin text, with German translation: *Philosophische-Theologische Schriften* (Vienna, 1964–1967; 3d edition, 1989). English translations include Paul E. Sigmund's *The*

Catholic Concordance (Cambridge, 1991), H. Lawrence Bond's *Nicholas of Cusa: Selected Spiritual Writings* (New York, 1997), and Jasper Hopkins's *Complete Philosophical and Theological Treatises of Nicholas Cusa,* 2 vols. (Minneapolis, Minn., 2001). Perceptive studies are Paline M. Watt's *Nicolaus Cusanus: A Fifteenth-century Vision of Man* (Leiden, 1982), James E. Biechler's *The Religious Language of Nicholas of Cusa* (Missoula, Mont., 1975), Clyde Lee Miller's *Reading Cusanus* (Washington, D. C., 2003), and the essays edited by Gerald Christianson and Thomas M. Izbicki in *Nicholas of Cusa on Christ and the Church* (Leiden, 1996).

DONALD F. DUCLOW (1987 AND 2005)

NIEBUHR, REINHOLD (1892–1971), American theologian, ethicist, and political philosopher. Niebuhr was born in Wright City, Missouri, on January 21, 1892. His mother was a second-generation German-American; his father, a German immigrant, was a pastor in the Evangelical Synod of North America, the offspring of the Prussian Union Church, which was predominantly Lutheran with a strain of Calvinism. At the age of ten Niebuhr declared that he wanted to become a minister because his father was the most interesting man in town.

After studies at the denominational schools Elmhurst College and Eden Theological Seminary, Niebuhr entered Yale Divinity School, where he earned B.D. (1914) and M.A. (1915) degrees. He later enjoyed recalling that he was admitted to the M.A. program on probation because he had received his earlier education at unaccredited schools. Rather than embark on a program of doctoral studies, he accepted assignment to a pastorate in Detroit, partly for family financial reasons (his father had died in 1913), partly out of obligation to his denomination, and partly because he "desired relevance rather than scholarship."

During the thirteen years that Niebuhr served as pastor of Bethel Church, its membership grew from 65 to 650. The congregation reflected a broad spectrum of the American population, from automobile workers to two millionaires; during his pastorate Niebuhr drew a few black families into some activities of the church. The Detroit ministry plunged the young pastor into the problems of urban, industrial America. Niebuhr vociferously objected to the inhumanity of the automotive assembly lines, the forced unemployment during retooling, and the abject dependence of workers upon corporations that resisted unions. After a period of racial conflict, he chaired the mayor's Race Committee. Meanwhile he won a reputation as a lecturer and preacher, especially in colleges, and as a contributor to periodicals.

Niebuhr supported World War I with mixed feelings, opposing the mixture of German loyalty and quasi-pacifism common in his denomination. A visit to Germany in 1923 added to his increasing disillusionment with war and confirmed his growing pacifism.

In 1928 Niebuhr joined the faculty of Union Theological Seminary in New York. Although in point of fact there was no faculty opening, President Henry Sloane Coffin was interested in Niebuhr, and Sherwood Eddy, a leader in many Christian causes, located funds to support the appointment initially. The move enabled Niebuhr to expand his scholarly and organizational activities. Later he also joined the graduate faculty of Columbia University. He continued to preach almost every weekend in pulpits within and outside the city. He founded the Fellowship of Socialist Christians (1930) and its quarterly, *Radical Religion* (1935), later renamed *Christianity and Society.* He ran as a Socialist for the New York State Senate (1930) and for Congress (1932), but assured Coffin that he had no chance of winning and would continue his teaching without interruption.

In 1931 Niebuhr married Ursula Keppel-Compton, an English fellow at Union. They were a devoted pair and soon became parents. For many years students and friends, some famous and some unknown, crowded the Niebuhrs' apartment at their frequent "at-homes."

Niebuhr was active in countless organizations involving labor unions, tenant farmers, and liberal or left-wing causes. In a period of great political tensions, he struggled with conflicts between pacifists and those concerned about the menace of Hitlerism, as well as conflicts between conservatives, liberals, and communists. In 1933 he resigned from the executive committee of the pacifist Fellowship of Reconciliation, of which he had been national chairman since 1931. In 1940 he resigned from the Socialist Party, and the next year he founded the biweekly *Christianity and Crisis* as an organ for relating theology to liberal anti-Nazi political policies. In 1941 he was a chief organizer, and then national chairman, of the liberal anticommunist Union for Democratic Action. In 1944 he helped found the Liberal Party in New York and became a state party vice-chairman.

Meanwhile, Niebuhr's eminence as a theologian was increasing. *Moral Man and Immoral Society* (New York, 1932) was an epoch-making contribution to social ethics. Niebuhr's international reputation flourished with his participation in the Oxford Conference on Life and Work (1937) and his delivery of the Gifford Lectures at the University of Edinburgh (1939).

When World War II broke out, Niebuhr advocated American support of Britain and France, short of armed intervention. After the attack on Pearl Harbor, he supported the war but criticized mass bombings of German and Japanese cities. After the war, Niebuhr became an adviser to the State Department's Policy and Planning staff, headed by George Kennan. Although a strenuous critic of Soviet power, he emphasized the necessity, in a nuclear age, of international policies that would build "mutual trust and tissues of community." He was a frequent visitor to Europe on religious, scholarly, and governmental missions, and served as a major speaker at the first assembly of the World Council of Churches in Amsterdam in 1948. In 1949 he cochaired the founding conference of Americans for Democratic Action, an organization of the liberal left. The postwar years saw a stream of major lectureships and books.

In 1952, Niebuhr suffered the first of a series of strokes that sapped his strength for the rest of his life; from this point on, periods of severe illness alternated with periods of active life. In 1955 he became vice president of Union Theological Seminary; in 1958 he was a visiting fellow at the Institute for Advanced Studies in Princeton. After retirement from Union in 1960 he spent one year at Harvard. He made his home in New York, but later moved to Stockbridge, Massachusetts. In 1964 he was awarded the President's Medal for Freedom by Lyndon Johnson. In his final years he suffered great pain and disability, but a steady stream of visitors and correspondents helped him maintain ties with theological scholarship and public affairs. Death came on June 1, 1971.

DEVELOPMENT OF NIEBUHR'S THOUGHT. Niebuhr was a man in motion, often (as he liked to say) tilting at windmills he himself had built earlier. His thought was an ongoing dialectical process: usually the new idea was both a criticism and a transformation of the old.

His earliest writings—posthumously published in *Young Reinhold Niebuhr,* edited by William G. Chrystal (Saint Louis, 1977)—reveal a seminarian in the pietistic evangelical tradition, objecting to the politicization of religion and urging that the way to improve the world is "to make more men Christians and all Christians truer" (p. 42). At Yale Divinity School he imbibed liberal theology. The Detroit pastorate moved him to the left wing of the Social Gospel movement while intensifying his pastoral concern in ministry to the sick and the dying. His adoption of socialism was a pragmatic one, and indeed was initially almost innocent of Marxism.

Moral Man and Immoral Society (New York, 1932) established Niebuhr's reputation as a major thinker. The title, which Niebuhr admitted was an exaggeration for pedagogic reasons, expressed the book's theme: the gap between the behavior of individuals in their personal relations and in their human collectivities (nations, classes, corporations, and so on). The book was an assault on liberal hopes for the effecting of social improvement through rationality and religion. Rationality and religion, said Niebuhr, are more often instruments of power than correctives of it.

Two years later, Niebuhr described himself as moving to the left politically and to the right theologically. As he sometimes said, he was trying to relate Christian religion (which was politically deficient) to Marxist political realism (which was religiously false). The theological movement was guided above all by Augustine's conceptions of human nature and history. In the Gifford Lectures, published as *The Nature and Destiny of Man* (New York, 1941 and 1943), he added Kierkegaard's insights to those of Augustine, and he became more critical of Marx.

For his attacks on "liberalism," Niebuhr was often called "neoorthodox," a term that he disliked. He offended the orthodox by treating their fondest beliefs as "myths," and he offended liberals by taking those myths "seriously, but not literally." He provided fresh interpretations of Christian beliefs about the creation of humankind in God's image, the Fall, original sin, justification by faith, and the coming kingdom of God. Whereas he criticized liberalism for its optimism, its inattention to conflicts of power, and its utopianism, he was liberal in his acceptance of critical scholarship and his eagerness to relate Christian faith to the whole range of human knowledge. If university faculties saw Niebuhr as a critic of liberalism, average Americans regarded him as plainly liberal—as he discovered when a flood of "hate mail" poured in after his public criticism of Billy Graham.

Although the Gifford Lectures stand as Niebuhr's greatest intellectual monument, they do not record his final position. In the years following the lectures, his pragmatic tendencies, significant from his Yale days onward, became more conspicuous as he criticized doctrinaire theology and political thought, including his own. The concept of grace, always important to his thought but often subordinated in discussions to the doctrine of sin, now became a major theme. Partly under the influence of his friend Erik Erikson, the psychologist, Niebuhr became more appreciative of self-affirmation. From the works of the eighteenth-century English statesman Edmund Burke he learned to consider the continuities and the organic characteristics of history as well as the historical conflicts and cataclysms that had always impressed him. But to the end the polemical fires still flared, particularly against idolatries of race, wealth, and political power.

PRINCIPAL IDEAS. Niebuhr frequently denied that he was a theologian. He sometimes described himself as a circuit-riding preacher with an interest in ethics. He had little interest in the niceties of doctrine. However, his chief insights have reverberated through the whole of theology.

To find definitive statements of his main positions is difficult. Niebuhr often wrote in polemical situations. If some extravagant statement he had made was quoted back to him later, he was likely to reply with a laugh, "That's one of the many foolish things I've said." He was too impatient to revise his own writings. Yet on many themes he was scholarly, subtle, and persistent. For the truest account of his opinions on a subject, one must look at his extended statements on it, then dig out the scattered self-corrections made over subsequent years.

Echoing Pascal, Niebuhr loved to speak of the grandeur and frailty of the human being. He saw the essence of selfhood as freedom, which included qualities of imagination, rationality, and foresight—all captured in the biblical phrase "the image of God." Freedom brings anxiety: the awareness of insecurity and of the inevitability of death. Faith, in turn, can channel anxiety into creativity; without faith the creature strains for false security (the classical sin of pride) or tries to avoid risk in a less-than-human existence (sloth). Of these two, Niebuhr wrote far more about pride—perhaps, as it is often said, because sloth was no temptation for him. Pride overcomes individuals as well as groups; in the latter it may appear as nationalism, economic domination, racism, or claims of gender superiority. Attempts to subdue pride by moral accomplishments usually reinforce it instead; the only answer is the intervention of divine grace, both the common grace known in many human experiences and the special grace known in Christ.

Niebuhr's doctrine of history began with the Old Testament prophetic faith in history as showing marks of divine judgment and grace. He qualified this with the New Testament belief that history finds its fulfillment only in the kingdom of God that is yet to come. Any effort to find the meaning of history within history—say, in the triumph of a nation or a religion or a social class or even the best of projected societies—is error and idolatry.

Niebuhr affirmed the biblical idea of a linear, rather than cyclical, history. But he rejected the "heresy," nourished in the Renaissance and the Enlightenment, that transmutes the directedness of history into faith in progress. There are obvious evidences in history of progress in technique, in some kinds of rationality, and in social organization, but history as a whole is not a progressive story, and its achievements never eliminate the lurking threat and presence of sin. Thus Niebuhr became a constant critic of utopianism. Despite his excoriation of nationalistic idolatries, he objected to proposals for world government. World government represented to him either a "soft" utopia (relying on reason and goodwill, without attention to the painful realities of power) or a "hard" utopia (imperialistic conquest resulting in one power's hegemony over the world). Instead, he advocated the difficult effort to negotiate limited agreements among nations with attention to both morality and power.

Niebuhr's critics charge that anti-utopianism cuts the nerve of action. In fact, Niebuhr himself said the same in his earlier writings, but later he renounced that position. He affirmed that there are "indeterminate" possibilities for social improvement, but he held that those who neglect the persistent power of sin are most likely to misconstrue its workings in themselves and in history.

For Niebuhr the ultimate ethical possibility is love, which in mutuality enhances life and society, but which sometimes requires sacrifice, as represented in the cross of Christ. However, love is sentimental unless it finds realization in justice. Justice is the attempt to embody something of the responsibility of love in human institutions. Yet justice, with its legal and juridical forms, is at best an incomplete embodiment of love. And because justice requires enforcement, it readily becomes a contradiction to the free and voluntary nature of love. Whereas love gives freely, justice imposes and enforces obligations.

Thus love and justice interact in a continuous dialectic. They need each other: love that does not seek justice is unreal love, and justice without love is a graceless legalism that is not really just. Yet the two live together in tension, and no formula can relate them perfectly.

Faith and political activity meet in a comparable dialectical relation. Serious faith has implications for political life. Pretenses to the contrary, especially in a modern democratic society, are an evasion of responsibility and usually a tacit support of an unjust status quo. But faith (or religious beliefs) can never be embodied fully in politics. And the ultimate loyalties of faith relate only uneasily to the negotiations, the maneuverings, and the exercises of power that characterize politics. Niebuhr criticized those who try to keep faith uncontaminated by politics as well as those who give their political opinions divine sanction. As with love and justice, there is no easy way to combine faith with politics.

INFLUENCE. During Niebuhr's lifetime he was a powerful figure, an intimidating force in polemics, yet a friendly person known to many as "Reinie" (except to his wife, who called him Reinhold). The South African novelist Alan Paton in his autobiography, *Towards the Mountain* (New York, 1980), described Niebuhr as "the most enthralling speaker" he had ever heard. Niebuhr's style, despite many awkward sentences, was impetuous, biting, witty, reverent, and serene, often in the course of a single speech or sermon. His writings have been translated into many European and Asian languages. During his lifetime he set so many agendas that his critics, no less than his supporters, often acted on issues he enunciated.

Niebuhr advocated an ethical "realism" that searched out the moral issues in every controversy yet never imposed moral answers without giving due attention to the realities of power. The famous political scientist Hans Morgenthau in 1961 called Niebuhr "the greatest living political philosopher of America" (Landon, 1962, p. 109). Through friendships with Eleanor Roosevelt, George Kennan, Arthur Schlesinger, Jr., and Hubert Humphrey, as well as with several labor leaders and journalists, he exercised some influence on public policy—although he rebuked Vice President Humphrey for supporting the war in Vietnam.

Who continues Niebuhr's heritage? The question is a controversial one. In 1981 a bemused Senate committee heard tedious arguments on just this issue. Neoconservatives, pointing to his Burkean strain and his anti-utopianism, sometimes claim him as part of their heritage. On the other hand, he always regarded himself as left of center; and his final writings, produced in the years of pain and illness, were furious attacks against abuses of presidential power.

Niebuhr's influence is least among those who isolate their religious faith from political action and those who maintain any dogmatic religious and political position, whether reactionary or revolutionary. But where people struggle to relate faith to justice in a perplexing world, Niebuhr remains an important figure in the conversation.

BIBLIOGRAPHY

Works by Niebuhr

Niebuhr's published books, articles, reviews, editorials, sermons, and prayers number about a thousand. An identification of all is impossible, because some were unsigned editorials. A diligent listing in 268 pages, including some publications about Neibuhr, is that of D. B. Robertson, *Reinhold Niebuhr's Works: A Bibliography* (Lanham, Md., 1983). What follows is a selective list of books that provide sustained expositions of his major ideas.

Moral Man and Immoral Society. New York, 1932. The innovative book that established Neibuhr's national and international reputation.

The Nature and Destiny of Man. Vol. 1, *Human Nature,* 1941. Vol. 2, *Human Destiny,* 1943. Reprint in one volume, New York, 1951. The Gifford Lectures and the most extensive exposition of Niebuhr's thought.

The Children of Light and the Children of Darkness: A Vindication of Democracy and a Critique of Its Traditional Defense. New York, 1944. A discussion of political and economic issues grounded in Niebuhr's understanding of human nature.

Faith and History: A Comparison of Christian and Modern Views of History. New York, 1949.

The Irony of American History. New York, 1952. A study of the ways in which American experience exhibits an inner logic, often contrary to its declared intentions.

The Structure of Nations and Empires: A Study of the Recurring Patterns and Problems of the Political Order in Relation to the Unique Problems of the Nuclear Age. New York, 1959.

Man's Nature and His Communities: Essays on the Dynamics and Enigmas of Man's Personal and Social Existence. New York, 1965. Niebuhr's last revision—although brief and written under great handicaps of illness—of the themes for which he was famous.

Works about Niebuhr

The two most personal books about Niebuhr, both rich in anecdotal memories, are: June Bingham, *Courage to Change: An Introduction to the Life and Thought of Reinhold Niebuhr* (New York, 1961, 1972) and Ursula Niebuhr, ed., *Remembering Reinhold Niebuhr: Letters of Reinhold and Ursula M. Niebuhr* (San Francisco, 1991). The two most exhaustive biographies, written from clashing perspectives, are: Richard Wightman Fox, *Reinhold Niebuhr: A Biography* (2d edition, Ithaca, N. Y., 1996) and Charles C. Brown, *Niebuhr and His Age: Reinhold Niebuhr's Prophetic Role and Legacy,* New Edition with Foreword by Arthur M. Schlesinger, Jr. (Harrisburg, Penn., 2002). *Reinhold Niebuhr: His Religious Social, and Political Thought,* edited by Charles W. Kegley and Robert W. Bretall (New York, 1956), includes twenty critical essays about Niebuhr, along with Niebuhr's short "Intellectual Autobiography" and his response to the critics. A later edition (New York, 1982) includes an essay by John C. Bennett on Niebuhr's social thought in his later years. *Reinhold Niebuhr: A Prophetic Voice in Our Time,* edited by Harold R. Landon (Greenwich, Conn., 1962), contains essays by Paul Tillich, John C. Bennett, and Hans Morgenthau, together with Niebuhr's response. Of the many books about Niebuhr, there are three impressive treatments of different aspects of his mature thought and activity: Ronald M. Stone, *Professor Reinhold Niebuhr: A Mentor to the Twentieth Century* (Louisville, Ky., 1992); Robin W. Lovin, *Reinhold Niebuhr and Christian Realism* (Cambridge, U.K., 1995); and Langdon Gilkey, *On Niebuhr: A Theological Study* (Chicago, 2001). Other books are in process of publication.

ROGER LINCOLN SHINN (1987 AND 2005)

NIEN-FO SEE NIANFO

NIETZSCHE, FRIEDRICH (1844–1900), German philosopher and social, cultural, and religious critic.

Friedrich Nietzsche is one of the most remarkable, controversial, original, and important figures in modern philosophical and intellectual history. In his short productive life (which ended with his collapse in 1889, although he lived on until 1900), he published an astonishing number and variety of works, and wrote a great deal more. His writings attracted relatively little attention prior to his collapse; but the subsequent impact of his thought was and continues to be both great and diverse.

LIFE AND WORK. Nietzsche was born on October 15, 1844, in Röcken, Saxony (in Prussia). The son of a Lutheran pastor (who died when he was six), he entered a boarding school in Pforta in 1858, excelling in his studies of religion and classical and German literature. In 1864 he entered the University of Bonn, intending to study theology and classical philosophy; but after only one year he transferred to the University of Leipzig, where he concentrated on philosophy. While there he discovered Arthur Schopenhauer's *The World as Will and Representation,* which profoundly influenced him. It was as a classical philologist, however, that he received a call from the University of Basel at the astonishingly early age of twenty-four.

Nietzsche taught at Basel from 1869 until 1879, when he retired owing to the deterioration of his health (which resulted from illnesses he contracted in 1870 as a volunteer medical orderly in the Franco-Prussian War). During this period he formed a close association with Richard Wagner, his early fascination with whom is reflected in his first book, *The Birth of Tragedy* (1872). His later break with Wagner, culminating in his polemic *The Case of Wagner* (1888), was both profound and painful to him. At first regarding Wagner as showing the way to a cultural and spiritual renewal, Nietzsche came to see him as epitomizing and fostering decadent and dangerous tendencies.

These concerns with the direction and health of contemporary cultural and intellectual life were the real focus of most of Nietzsche's early writings. As he developed his own quite distinctive philosophical idiom and method, he drew strongly upon the idea and practice of interpretation associated with his discipline of classical philology. He departed increasingly from the conventional limits and norms of that discipline, however, and the unorthodox character of his published work during his tenure at Basel—beginning with *The Birth of Tragedy* and becoming more pronounced in his

Untimely Meditations (1873–1876) and *Human, All-Too-Human* (1878)—effectively divorced him from it. This rendered his retirement in 1879 merely the ratification of an accomplished fact.

The following decade, most of which Nietzsche spent alternating between residences in Switzerland and northern Italy, was phenomenally productive. *The Dawn* (1881) and the first four books of *The Gay Science* (1882) were followed by the four-part *Thus Spoke Zarathustra* (1883–1885). The next four years saw the appearance of *Beyond Good and Evil* (1886), the fifth book of *The Gay Science* and *The Genealogy of Morals* (1887), *The Case of Wagner* (1888), and *Twilight of the Idols* (1889) as well as the completion of several other works that were published some years later: *The Antichrist* (1895) and *Ecce Homo* (1908). During this period he also amassed a great deal of material in notebooks. (A substantial selection of this material, the significance of which is a matter of considerable controversy, was arranged and published posthumously under the title *The Will to Power.*)

Having written the last four of these works in the single year of 1888, Nietzsche suffered a complete mental and physical breakdown in early January of 1889, in Turin. His illness probably was the consequence of his having contracted syphilis many years earlier. He remained a partially paralyzed invalid, never regaining his health and sanity. During the remaining years of his life he was cared for by his sister, Elizabeth Förster-Nietzsche. She obtained control of his writings, sought to enhance and exploit his reputation, and was partly responsible for the misrepresentation of his thought that culminated in the travesty of his work being presented as the philosophical inspiration of National Socialism. This seriously damaged his reputation and long obstructed a just assessment of his work.

Nietzsche's style and manner of writing have affected his reception as well. Unlike most philosophers, he generally did not set out his views systematically, in clearly discernible lines of argument cast in dry and measured prose. His works, for the most part, consist of series of short paragraphs and sets of aphorisms, often only loosely (if at all) connected. Many deal with philosophical topics, but in very unconventional ways. His language, moreover, is by turns coolly analytical, heatedly polemical, and highly metaphorical. It is not surprising, therefore, that many philosophers have found it difficult to know what to make of him or whether to take him seriously, and that they have interpreted his work in many different ways.

THOUGHT. The early Nietzsche was greatly concerned with basic problems he discerned in contemporary Western culture and society, for which he considered it imperative to seek new solutions. He was further convinced that Schopenhauer's bleak picture of the world and the human condition was fundamentally sound, and yet he was determined to discover some way of avoiding Schopenhauer's pessimistic conclusions. In *The Birth of Tragedy* he looked to the ancient Greeks for clues and to Wagner for inspiration, believing that their art held the key to human flourishing in a Schopenhauerian world. In his subsequent series of four essays collectively titled *Untimely Meditations,* he expanded upon the need to reorient human thought and endeavor in a manner more conducive to the creativity and vitality of human life.

These essays were followed by a number of aphoristic books in which Nietzsche refined and extended his assessment of various human tendencies and social and cultural phenomena. During this period his thinking became much more sophisticated, and he developed the philosophical style and outlook that found mature expression in his writings of the 1880s. He prophesied the advent of a period of nihilism as traditional modes of interpretation and valuation collapsed in conjunction with the "death of God," the demise of metaphysics, and the discovery of science's inability to yield anything like absolute knowledge. However, the prospect of this forthcoming crisis deeply disturbed him. He took the basic challenge of philosophy to be that of overcoming not only traditional metaphysics and scientific rationalism but also the nihilism resulting from their abandonment. In the early 1880s, when he conceived and wrote *Thus Spoke Zarathustra,* he arrived at a conception of human life and possibility—and with it, of value and meaning—that he believed could serve to fill the void left by the bankruptcy of traditional philosophy and religion and the poverty of science.

What Nietzsche called the "death of God" was both a cultural event—the waning of the "Christian-moral" interpretation of life and the world—and a philosophical development: the dismissal of the idea of God as a concept deserving serious philosophical attention. As a cultural event it was a phenomenon to be reckoned with, and a source of profound concern. As a philosophical development, on the other hand, it was his point of departure, demanding a radical reconsideration of the nature of life and the world, human existence, knowledge, value, and morality. Thus the "de-deification of nature," the "translation of man back into nature," the development of a "naturalistic" value-theory and its application to a "revaluation of values," and the tracing of the "genealogy of morals" and their critique were among the main tasks he set for himself.

Nietzsche emphatically rejected not only the "God-hypothesis" but also any metaphysical postulation of a "true world of 'being'" transcending the world of life and experience, and likewise deemed the "soul" and "things-in-themselves" to be ontological fictions. He conceived of all existence in terms of an interplay of forces without any inherent structure or final end; these forces ceaselessly refigure themselves as the fundamental disposition he called "will to power" gives rise to successive arrays of power relationships among them. His idea of the "eternal recurrence" underscores this conception of the world, in which things ever happen in this same manner. He thus construed human nature and existence naturalistically: "The soul is only a word for something about the body," he wrote; and the body is fundamentally an arrangement of natural forces and processes manifesting the "will to power." At the same time, however, he stressed the importance of social institutions and interactions in human development. He also insisted upon the possibility of the emergence of exceptional human beings ("higher men") capable of an independence and creativity elevating them above the general human level ("the herd"), and he proclaimed the "overman" (*Übermensch*) to be "the meaning of the earth," representing the overcoming of the "all-too-human" and the attainment of the fullest possible "enhancement of life."

Thus, far from seeking to diminish one's humanity by stressing animality, Nietzsche sought to direct one's attention and efforts to the emergence of a "higher humanity" capable of endowing existence with a redemptive human justification. He espoused a "Dionysian value-standard" based upon an affirmation of the "will to power" as the creative transformation of existence; and he accordingly made the "enhancement of life" and creativity the central themes of his "revaluation of values" and value-theory.

Insisting that moralities ought to be understood and assessed "in the perspective of life," Nietzsche argued that most of them were obstructive rather than conducive to the enhancement of life, reflecting all-too-human needs, weaknesses, and fears. Distinguishing between "master" and "slave" moralities, he found the latter to have eclipsed the former, issuing in a dominant "herd-animal morality" well-suited to the mediocre who are the human rule but stultifying and detrimental to potential exceptions. Therefore he advocated a "higher morality" for the latter, one that would be "beyond good and evil" and better attuned to their attainment of an enhanced, creative form of life. This reflects the linkage of his notions of such a "higher humanity" and the associated "higher morality" to his conception of art. Art, involving the creative transformation, in restricted contexts, of the world as humans find it, anticipates the kind of life that might be lived more fully in this manner and constitutes a step toward its emergence.

INFLUENCE. In the decades following Nietzsche's collapse, a veritable Nietzsche cult developed in central Europe, as self-styled followers produced a variety of influential but simplistic and distorted interpretations of his thought. Thus he was depicted by turns as a latter-day Romantic, an iconoclastic nihilist, a social Darwinist, and a racist and protofascist. He also attracted a substantial following in artistic and literary circles beyond as well as within central Europe. It was only slowly, however, that he began to be taken seriously by philosophers, and even then he was, and continues to be, interpreted in ways lending themselves to diverse philosophical purposes that often stand in a rather problematical relation to his own.

The common association of Nietzsche with existential philosophy, for example, is owing to his appropriation (in different ways) first by such German existential philosophers as Heidegger and Jaspers and then by French existentialists, notably Sartre and Camus. For others, he was a leading representative of *Lebensphilosophie;* as such he influenced the philosophical-anthropological movement that developed out of this school in central Europe. He was also one of the sources upon which members of the Frankfurt School drew in their attempts to develop a critical theory of society and culture. More recently still, he has been warmly embraced by post-structuralist French philosophers, who derive much of their inspiration from their reading of him. Certain recent Anglo-American analytical philosophers have discovered in him a kindred spirit as well.

NIETZSCHE AND RELIGION. Unlike most philosophers of importance before him, Nietzsche was openly and profoundly hostile to most forms of religious thought (with the notable exception of that of the early Greeks). He declared "war" upon the major world religions and their theologies, contending not only that they perpetuate superstitions and errors for which there is no longer any excuse but also that they are deeply objectionable owing to their detrimental impact upon human life. It was above all their purported "crimes against life" for which he attacked them, arguing that they have fed upon and fostered weakness, sickliness, life-weariness, and *ressentiment,* and that they have poisoned the wellsprings of human health, strength, and vitality by "devaluing" all "naturalistic values."

Thus Nietzsche undertook to "revalue" religious values, to expose the "all-too-human" origins and motivations of religious ways of thinking, and to undermine all otherworldly theologies, seeking to deprive them of any appearance of legitimacy they might still retain. He intended both to make their emergence and continuing acceptance understandable as human phenomena and at the same time to render them unacceptable to those capable of doing without them and of thinking clearly and honestly. He had some respect for a religion like Christianity as a form of life answering to a certain (interesting but flawed) configuration of human traits, and associated Jesus with this human possibility, but he contended that historical Christianity represented a perversion of it, fostering life-endangering attitudes and seducing potentially healthier human types into stunted or self-destructive forms of existence.

Although Nietzsche may have done religion in general and Christianity in particular a considerable injustice, he compelled their advocates to consider whether and how various forms of religion could be exonerated of his charges against them. He also gave strong impetus to attempts to develop new theologies that dispensed with traditional conceptions of God and the soul in favor of alternative ways of conceiving of the divine and the spiritual nature of mankind. In other quarters, his attack upon traditional religious ways of thinking prompted their defiant defense, thereby contributing indirectly to the resurgence of neo-orthodoxy in opposition to the liberal-theological and naturalistic secular currents of modern thought. Finally, Nietzsche helped to stimulate a reconsideration of the relation between religion and theology. The idea that the most important thing about a religion is the difference it makes in the lives of those who embrace it, rather than the belief system it elaborates, owes much to him, even though most religious thinkers who have followed him in this have tended to assess the effects of religion on the lives of believers very differently than he did.

Nietzsche may not have subverted religion as decisively as he desired and claimed to have done, for his criticisms do not leave all its forms without any means of defense. His critique cannot be lightly dismissed, however, and if it is accorded the serious consideration by religious thinkers it deserves, then the religious issue of this confrontation will be arguably more deserving of respect than most of religion as he knew and conceived it. In any case, anyone well disposed toward religion would do well to make the experiment of attempting to view it through Nietzsche's eyes. This may not lead one to abandon religion, but it is almost certain to alter one's view of it to good effect.

BIBLIOGRAPHY

Works by Nietzsche

The definitive new German edition of Nietzsche's writings is the thirty-volume *Werke: Kritische Gesamtausgabe,* edited by Giorgio Colli and Mazzino Montinari (Berlin, 1967–1978). The best English translations of most of his writings have been made by Walter Kaufmann and R. J. Hollingdale (sometimes in collaboration). These include *The Birth of Tragedy* and *The Case of Wagner* (New York, 1967); *The Gay Science* (New York, 1974); *Beyond Good and Evil* (New York, 1966; Harmondsworth, 1973); *On the Genealogy of Morals* and *Ecce Homo* (New York, 1968); *The Will to Power* (New York, 1967); *Thus Spoke Zarathustra* (Harmondsworth, 1961); and *Twilight of the Idols* and *The Antichrist* (Harmondsworth, 1968). The last three, with *Nietzsche Contra Wagner,* are also contained in *The Portable Nietzsche* (New York, 1954). See also *A Nietzsche Reader* (Harmondsworth, 1977).

Works on Nietzsche

Danto, Arthur. *Nietzsche as Philosopher.* New York, 1965.

Hayman, Ronald. *Nietzsche: A Critical Life.* Oxford, 1980.

Hollingdale, R. J. *Nietzsche.* London, 1973.

Kaufmann, Walter. *Nietzsche: Philosopher, Psychologist, Antichrist.* 4th ed. Princeton, 1974.

Magnus, Bernd. *Nietzsche's Existential Imperative.* Bloomington, Ind., 1978.

Morgan, George A. *What Nietzsche Means.* Cambridge, Mass., 1941.

Schacht, Richard. *Nietzsche.* London, 1983.

Wilcox, John T. *Truth and Value in Nietzsche.* Ann Arbor, 1974.

RICHARD SCHACHT (1987)

NIGHTINGALE, FLORENCE

NIGHTINGALE, FLORENCE (1820–1910), is remembered as a nurse, yet she wrote in her seventies that, when planning her future as a young woman, her one idea was not to organize a hospital but to organize a religion. Nursing researchers, sociologists, and scholars of religion, who are now examining Nightingale's voluminous but previously unpublished ideological and religious writings, are discovering the truth of these words.

NIGHTINGALE'S LIFE. Nightingale was born on May 12, 1820, the second daughter of William and Frances Nightingale, members of the upper class from Derbyshire, England. Although Florence Nightingale was raised in the Church of England, her Cambridge-educated father instilled in her his Unitarian heritage while tutoring her in many languages, history, science, and philosophy. The young Nightingale disdained her privileged life, preferring to help the village poor. At age seventeen she received a call to serve God. Encountering family resistance, she bided her time, studying hospital reports and documents on social reform. Trips to Europe exposed her to emerging political, religious, and social thought. She visited convents, observed their work, and adopted their spiritual exercises even though her religious ideas prevented her from joining a Catholic religious order. While in Egypt at age thirty, Nightingale received a second call to serve the poor and made a private vow to God. She visited a Protestant deaconess order serving the poor in Kaiserswerth, Germany, in 1850 and 1851, but further plans were sabotaged by her family. Nightingale channeled her rage into *Cassandra* (1852), an autobiographical fiction about powerless Victorian women that foreshadowed later feminist arguments. After receiving another call to serve England's poor, she began a theological treatise, *Suggestions for Thought to the Searchers after Truth among the Artizans of England* (1852).

Leaving home in 1853, Nightingale became superintendent of a home for destitute governesses. The following year Lord Sidney Herbert, the secretary of war, sent her to the Crimea to care for wounded British soldiers. After sixteen months Nightingale returned a heroine but refused to start a nursing school with the Nightingale Fund established in her honor, focusing instead on reform of the army and its medical services. She wrote a lengthy report on army health; helped launch royal commissions on Britain's army in England and India; analyzed her Crimean medical statistics; wrote *Notes on Hospitals* (1859) and *Notes on Nursing* (1860), and declared herself an invalid. She retired to her home, where prominent politicians came to consult with her. The Nightingale Training School for Nurses was established at Saint Thomas's Hospital in London in 1860. While Nightingale submitted proposals, her first visit to the school did not occur until many years later. Nightingale lived for many years as an invalid in seclusion while pursuing her many reforms. She died on August 13, 1910, and is buried in East Wellow, Hampshire, England.

THEOLOGICAL IDEAS AND ACTIVITIES. Nightingale's religious vocation was central to her life, and her work lies within this vocation. Each year she reviewed her spiritual progress, and later she celebrated the jubilee of her first call. She read and translated medieval mystics in preparation for writing a book. Her invalidism has been attributed to chronic illness, post-traumatic stress, and a desire to escape from family demands, yet it also created a monastic existence in lieu of a religious or secular order. In 1860 Nightingale expanded *Suggestions for Thought*, sending drafts to six scholars, including Benjamin Jowett of Balliol College, Oxford, and the reformer John Stuart Mill. The manuscript addressed the same issues as *Essays and Reviews* (1860), a Church of England Broad Church Movement publication that resulted in heresy trials. While *Essays and Reviews* critiqued the church, Nightingale's *Suggestions for Thought* offered the working class a reasonable religion that rejected the prevailing teaching that poverty was God's will. Nightingale's topics included God, universal law, God's will, human will, sin, evil, family life, women, spirituality, and life after death. Mill quoted her in his parliamentary speech on women's rights, and Jowett acknowledged the qualities of her mind, beginning a thirty-year intimate friendship with Nightingale.

Nightingale's theology prefigured twentieth-century liberation theology, which begins not with traditional doctrines and ancient texts but with the experience of the oppressed, as does feminist theology. Nightingale suggested that oppressive social systems were human constructions held in place by the powerful, whether government or church, not God's will. A liberating religion should not ask people to passively believe and accept their lot but make rational sense to everyone. Since God's spirit was in all people, rich or poor, all could participate in God's new society by learning, through observation, education, and statistical analysis, God's will written in the universe. Nightingale called statistics a "sacred science" because it transcended individual experiences to uncover God's larger thoughts, as her Crimean statistics demonstrated.

Prefiguring another contemporary debate, Nightingale argued that the concept of God evolved through history and was still evolving. While primal people propitiated an all-powerful God with sacrifice, worship, and prayer, believing suffering reflected divine displeasure, an arbitrary God intervening at will was not viable for a scientific age. A moratorium on God language was necessary until divine metaphors were reshaped. For Nightingale, God was embodied (incarnated) in the universe. Humans, as part of the universe, participated in this divinity, being drawn into mystic union with God through learning divine universal laws more reliable than claims of special revelation delivered in culturally bound language through selected interpreters. Good health and social conditions did not come by divine intervention but through human observation and application of divine laws.

Incarnation, Trinity, and theories localizing God in one incarnation and one day of suffering, while ignoring God's suffering, work, and passion through eternity, needed rethinking. Medieval atonement ideas of God's Son sacrificed because of divine offense at human sin were culturally bound explanations from an era demanding judgment and punishment, not reform. Instead, Nightingale's Trinity comprised: (1) God as thought, purpose, and will-engendering development; (2) Son as divine manifestation in all humanity developing according to God's will, Jesus being the perfect example and greatest teacher; and (3) Spirit as the divine in each, through which God as thought communicates. Life was about progressive learning from errors with the Spirit's help, as well as help from many human saviors, like Nightingale, to lead to truth, both in this world and other reincarnations.

WOMEN'S ISSUES. Nightingale challenged a divine order of creation automatically placing men over women; she believed that women were also called to serve God as handmaids of the Lord. She advocated a secular order of trained, salaried single women across all classes to serve the poor while also gaining economic independence—her nursing model. Her parliamentary efforts changed laws restricting women's rights to children, property, and divorce. She did not work for women's suffrage in the 1860s because she was busy with army reform and knew that, because not all men could vote, any women's votes would go to a privileged few. The Adam and Eve story justifying male headship was tightly woven into Britain's religion, class, and family systems and needed challenging before women could vote.

When Nightingale died at age ninety, she left a formidable literary legacy. Her writings in the British Library form one of its largest single collections. Since women of her era could not obtain university degrees, her scholarly writings remained largely unpublished and unheeded until the late twentieth century, yet her religious ideas parallel contemporary process and relational theology and prefigure by one hundred years liberation and feminist theology.

SEE ALSO Feminist Theology, article on Christian Feminist Theology; God, article on God in Postbiblical Christianity; Liberation Theology.

BIBLIOGRAPHY

Calabria, Michael D., and Janet A. Macrae, eds. *Suggestions for Thought: Selections and Commentaries.* Philadelphia, 1994. Seminal analysis of extracts of Nightingale's unpublished manuscript.

Cook, Sir Edward T. *The Life of Florence Nightingale.* 2 vols. London, 1913. Nightingale's authorized biography published three years after her death.

Dossey, Barbara Montgomery. *Florence Nightingale: Mystic, Visionary, Healer.* Springhouse, Pa., 2000. A comprehensive study of Nightingale and her context, including her social activism and mysticism.

Jowett, Benjamin. *Dear Miss Nightingale.* Edited by Vincent Quinn and John Prest. Oxford, 1987. Thirty years of letters from Benjamin Jowett to Nightingale.

McDonald, Lynn, ed. *Florence Nightingale: An Introduction to Her Life and Family.* Collected Works of Florence Nightingale, vol. 1. Waterloo, Ontario, 2002. A proposed 16 vols. of Nightingale's known writings, with analysis, is planned. The sheer volume of this project indicates the wide range of Nightingale's creativity in the areas of social and philosophical thought, religion, spirituality, and mysticism.

McDonald, Lynn, ed. *Florence Nightingale's Spiritual Journey: Biblical Annotations, Sermons, and Journal Notes.* Collected Works of Florence Nightingale, vol. 2. Waterloo, Ontario, 2002.

McDonald, Lynn, ed. *Florence Nightingale's Theology: Essays, Letters, and Journal Notes.* Collected Works of Florence Nightingale, vol. 3. Waterloo, Ontario, 2002.

McDonald, Lynn, ed. *Florence Nightingale on Society and Politics, Philosophy, Science, Education, and Literature.* Collected Works of Florence Nightingale, vol. 5. Waterloo, Ontario, 2003.

McDonald, Lynn, ed. *Florence Nightingale on Public Health Care.* Collected Works of Florence Nightingale, vol. 6. Waterloo, Ontario, 2004.

Sullivan, Mary C., ed. *The Friendship of Florence Nightingale and Mary Clare Moore.* Philadelphia, 1999. Twenty years of correspondence between Nightingale and Mother Mary Clare Moore of the Sisters of Mercy, who was with Nightingale in the Crimea.

Vallée, Gérard, ed. *Florence Nightingale on Mysticism and Eastern Religions.* Collected Works of Florence Nightingale, vol. 4. Waterloo, Ontario, 2003.

Webb, Val. *Florence Nightingale: The Making of a Radical Theologian.* St. Louis, Mo., 2002. An analysis of Nightingale's lifelong religious vocation and her radical theology for England's poor that provides ample evidence that her theological thought resonates more with contemporary feminist, liberation, and process theology than with dominant Victorian ideas of her own day.

Woodham Smith, Cecil Blanche Fitz Gerald. *Florence Nightingale, 1820–1910.* London, 1950. A biography including material not available for Sir Edward Cook's 1913 biography.

VAL WEBB (2005)

NIHILISM

SEE DOUBT AND BELIEF; NIETZSCHE, FRIEDRICH

NIITSITAPPI RELIGION

SEE BLACKFEET RELIGIOUS TRADITIONS

NIKEPHOROS

NIKEPHOROS (758–828), patriarch of Constantinople. Nikephoros lived during the Iconoclastic Controversy (726–843), a crisis that involved all levels of Byzantine society in a desperate struggle. The reality of Christ became the theological justification for the veneration of icons, which was tested and fought for in the arenas of imperial and ecclesiastical authority. The iconophiles, who supported the use of icons in the church, perceived the challenge of their iconoclast rulers as an attack against the person of Jesus Christ.

Nikephoros's birth in Constantinople coincided with a brewing storm of persecution initiated by Emperor Constantine V (741–775), which was also directed against Nikephoros's father. Attached to the service of the empire as secretary and director of the largest poorhouse in the capital, Nikephoros also served as the imperial spokesman at the Second Council of Nicaea (787). This experience was to serve him well during his tenure as patriarch (806–815), during which he witnessed the political vicissitudes of three imperial masters.

Like his predecessors Germanos and Tarasios, the patriarch was an advocate of a moderate policy through which concessions were made to extremists of both the imperial and ecclesiastical factions. Nikephoros remained resolute when the orthodox faith was at stake, as is proved by his long exile under Leo V from 815 until his death.

Scholars have increasingly recognized that Nikephoros's role in the controversy was more important during this period of exile, when he turned to a literary refutation of the heterodoxy of Constantine V and the iconoclastic Synod of Hagia Sophia (815), than it was during the preceding period, when he was a hierarch actively in office.

Dogmatically sophisticated, Nikephoros displayed extraordinary skill as he worked within the larger context of theological concerns, which he presented in such a way as to support the veneration of icons. Moreover, as a direct descendant of the apostolic tradition and Cappadocian synthesis, he worked out the problems faced by both John of Damascus and Theodore of Studios by elucidating the dogmatic and philosophical relation between an image and its archetype, the difference between art and circumscription, and the continuity of tradition as exemplified in the church's kerygma and witness concerning the icons. His subtle argumentation is a unique addition to the iconophiles' arsenal supporting Christ's iconographic depiction. Nikephoros's singular achievement was to sever the teaching on icons from an iconoclastic theology—traceable back to monophysitism with its Origenistic, Neoplatonic spiritualism—and to identify this teaching as an uninterrupted continuation of Chalcedonian Christology, with its reaffirmation of the historical facts of the New Testament.

As the last well-known iconophile theologian, Nikephoros may have wanted to be remembered primarily as the author whose work could have served as the basis for a future orthodox synod. But his generation overlooked, perhaps not intentionally, his theological efforts and praised the sanctity of his life. The patriarch in exile became the symbol of unity for both clergy in the world and monastics and a reconciler between iconophiles and iconoclasts in the strife that lasted for two more decades. Not until the restoration of the icons (March 11, 843) could his followers transfer his holy relics back to Constantinople and honor their prelate as a saint-confessor of Orthodox Christianity.

BIBLIOGRAPHY

The published works of Nikephoros can be found in *Spicilegium Romanum,* edited by Angelo Mai, vol. 10 (Rome, 1844), pp. 152–156; *Patrologia Graeca,* edited by J.-P. Migne, vol. 100 (Paris, 1860); and *Spicilegium Solesmense complectens sanctorum patrum scriptorumque ecclesiasticorum anecdota hactenus opera,* 4 vols., edited by Jean-Baptiste Pitra (Paris, 1852–1858), vol. 1, pp. 302–503, and vol. 4, pp. 233–380.

The most comprehensive book on the historical period, with an excellent bibliography and a summary of the patriarch's unpublished *Refutation,* remains Paul J. Alexander's *The Patriarch Nicephorus of Constantinople: Ecclesiastical Policy and Image Worship in the Byzantine Empire* (Oxford, 1958). For a systematic description of the patriarch's theology, see my book *In Defense of the Faith: The Theology of Patriarch Nikephoros of Constantinople* (Brookline, Mass., 1984).

JOHN TRAVIS (1987)

NIKEPHOROS KALLISTOS (c. 1256–1335), more fully Nikephoros Kallistos Xanthopoulos; Byzantine theologian and church historian. Most probably Nikephoros was a native of Constantinople and had served as a priest on the staff of the Hagia Sophia cathedral. Of the very little that we know about his life, it seems certain that, during the reign of Emperor Andronikos the Elder (r. 1282–1328), Nikephoros was active in ecclesiastical affairs and sided with those who opposed union with Rome.

Nikephoros wrote several works. His eighteen-book *Ecclesiastical History* covers the period from the birth of Christ to 610 and is important because it provides information on hagiology and on the theological and Christological controversies of the early centuries. A summary of five more books at the end of his introduction to the *History* has been accepted as an indication that he intended to continue the narrative to 912. There is no evidence that Nikephoros intended to write a general ecclesiastical history from the church's inception to his own time. Though the earliest books depend heavily on the church historians of the fourth, fifth, and sixth centuries, such as Eusebius of Caesarea, Socrates, Sozomenos, Theodoretos, Evagrios Scholastikos, and Theodore the Lector, Krumbacher (1897) has rightly observed that "in matters and topics dear to him, [Nikephoros] was an original and worthy author."

Of his other writings, Nikephoros's didactic poems became very popular and have survived in many manuscripts. He also wrote several liturgical, exegetical, and hagiographical works, including a synopsis of the holy scripture in iambics, the *Siege of Jerusalem,* the life and miracles of Nicholas of Myra, seven hymns to the *theotokos,* and several short hymns for the Akathistos Hymn. He wrote homilies on and commentaries to *Psalms* and homilies on Gregory of Nazianzus.

BIBLIOGRAPHY

Works by Nikephoros Kallistos

The writings of Nikephoros Kallistos can be found in volumes 145, 146, and 147 of *Patrologia Graeca,* edited by J.-P. Migne (Paris, 1865).

Works about Nikephoros Kallistos

Beck, Hans Georg. *Kirche und theologische Literatur in Byzantinischen Reich.* Munich, 1959. See pages 705–706.

Krumbacher, Karl. *Geschichte der byzantinischen Literatur von Justinian bis zum Ende des oströmischen Reiches, 527–1453.* 2d ed. Munich, 1897. See pages 291–293.

Papadopoulos-Kerameus, A. "Nikephoros Kallistos Xanthopoulos." *Byzantinische Zeitschrift* 11 (1902): 38–49.

Politēs, Linos. "Agnōsto ergo tou Nikephorou Kallistou Xanthopoulou." *Klēronomia* 3 (1971): 69–84.

DEMETRIOS J. CONSTANTELOS (1987)

NIKKŌ (1246–1333), Japanese Buddhist priest and one of the chief disciples of Nichiren (d. 1282). Although Nichiren did not designate a particular successor, on his deathbed he selected six of his senior disciples, Nisshō (1221–1323), Nichirō (1245–1320), Nikō (1253–1341), Nitchō (1252–1317), Nichiji (1250–?), and Nikkō, to carry on his work. Following the death of Nichiren, these six decided among themselves to assume care on a rotating basis of the temple named Kuonji that had been founded at Mount Minobu by Nichiren in 1281. Under this agreement, the priests, assisted by disciples living in the area, resolved to take up residence at the temple in one-month shifts. Political circumstances, however, intervened to frustrate their plans. Nikkō and Nichiji, who were living near Minobusan, faced little difficulty in fulfilling their obligations, but the other priests came under considerable pressure from Nagasaki Yoritsuna, minister of war and a powerful foe of the Nichiren group, and thus were unable to leave the capital city of Kamakura. In 1285, Nikkō agreed to a request by Nambu Sanenaga, a patron of the temple, and the other five senior disciples that he take up permanent residence on Minobusan. By 1288, Nikō was able to join Nikkō there following the relaxation of Yoritsuna's efforts to suppress the order.

Later, Nambu Sanenaga made an image of Śākyamuni Buddha and worshiped it. Nikkō contended that the image of the Buddha should be accompanied by companion images of the four disciples of the "original" Śākyamuni in order to distinguish it from that of the "historical" Śākyamuni. Nikō, on the other hand, was inclined to permit worship of the icon unflanked by images of the four disciples. When Nambu Sanenaga sided with Nikō, Nikkō left Minobusan and in 1288 founded the Kōmon-ha subsect. In 1290 he established his own temple, the Taisekiji, at Ōishi-ga-hara in Suruga province (Shizuoka-ken), and the following year moved to a new hermitage at Kitayama, two miles north of the Taisekiji. In 1298 the hermitage was remodeled into a full-fledged temple and renamed the Honmonji. Nikkō served as abbot of both temples until his death in 1333.

Although Nikkō is not responsible for the formulation of any independent doctrine, he is historically significant for his role in creating the first split in the Nichiren school. Later generations of Kōmon-ha adherents, notably Nichiu (1409–

1482), the ninth abbot of the Taisekiji, advocated an identification of Nichiren with the "original" Buddha and prohibited the worship of images, but these doctrines cannot be traced back to the influence of Nikkō.

BIBLIOGRAPHY

Works on the life of Nikkō include Hori Nichikō's *Fuji Nikkō Shōnin shōden* (Tokyo, 1974) and Kawai Hajime's *Nikkō Shōnin den* (Tokyo, 1976).

MURANO SENCHU (1987)

NIKODIMOS OF THE HOLY MOUNTAIN

(c. 1749–1809), known also as the Hagiorite, Greek Orthodox spiritual father and writer. Nikodimos was born on the Greek island of Naxos and studied in Smyrna, where he was taught Latin, Italian, and French. His teacher was the famous monk Chrysanthos Aitolos (d. 1785). Nikodimos was influenced by the hesychast tradition, which stressed mental prayer, and by the Kollyvades movement, which emphasized strict adherence to the doctrinal and liturgical traditions of the church. At the age of twenty-six Nikodimos went to Mount Athos. Two years later, in 1777, Makarios of Corinth arrived there, and a fruitful collaboration between him and Nikodimos began. Together, they published the *Philokalia*, a collection of the writings and sayings of the great ascetic Fathers of the church. Nikodimos also published *Concerning Continual Communion*, in which he made the unusual recommendation to the Orthodox that they receive Holy Communion frequently, in accordance with the ancient Christian practice. In his *Handbook of Counsel* Nikodimos developed the practice of mental prayer. In the *Pedalion* (The Rudder) he collected and paraphrased the canons of the church. Finally, in addition to editing hymns and publishing exegetical works and lives of the saints, Nikodimos translated into Greek an Italian work by the Jesuit Giovanni P. Pinamonti (1632–1703) that was probably based on the *Spiritual Exercises* of Ignatius of Loyola. He also translated *Spiritual Combat* by Lorenzo Scupoli (c. 1530–1610) into Greek, calling it *Unseen Warfare*.

In 1955 the ecumenical patriarchate of Constantinople officially proclaimed Nikodimos a saint of the church, and his memory is commemorated on July 14. As a prolific writer, splendid theologian, and practitioner of the prayer of the heart, Nikodimos contributed greatly to the awakening of the Greek Orthodox people during the difficult years of the Ottoman conquest.

BIBLIOGRAPHY

Several works by Nikodimos have been translated into English. These include Eugènie Kadloubovsky and G. E. H. Palmer's *Early Fathers from the Philokalia* (London, 1954) and the complete text of *The Philokalia*, translated and edited by G. E. H. Palmer, Philip Sherrard, and Kallistos Ware, 3 vols. to date (Boston, 1979–); and *The Rudder*, translated by Denver Cummings (Chicago, 1957). Two books about Nikodimos are Constantine Cavarnos's *St. Nicodemos the Hagiorite*, "Modern Orthodox Saints," no. 3 (Belmont, Mass., 1974), and my "St. Nicodemos the Hagiorite," in *Post-Byzantine Ecclesiastical Personalities*, edited by Nomikos Michael Vaporis (Brookline, Mass., 1978).

GEORGE S. BEBIS (1987)

NIKON

(1605–1681), patriarch of Moscow, Russian Orthodox church reformer. Nikon briefly dominated the Russian political and ecclesiastical scene in the mid-seventeenth century. Not least of his achievements was that he rose from utter obscurity to do so. He served a Moscow parish for ten years but turned his back on the capital in the early 1630s when his three children all died suddenly. Both he and his wife decided to become monastics. Much of the time Nikon lived as a solitary (1634–1643). He was, however, elected abbot of the Kozheezero hermitage and by 1646 was abbot of an important monastery in Moscow. There he was befriended by the tsar. Hardly three years later he was appointed metropolitan (archbishop) of Novgorod and by 1652 was in line for election to the patriarchal throne itself.

By this time Nikon was clearly aligned with the reformers of the Russian church, the "God-seekers." They had encouraged a notable revival in the moral and liturgical life of the Russian people. At the time of his election Nikon had elicited an unusual promise of obedience from the tsar and boyars of the realm. He was now to implement it in an unprecedented fashion. He proceeded at an accelerated pace—and at his own initiative—with new liturgical reforms. The principle on which he based these reforms was that Orthodoxy was universal rather than merely Muscovite; that Russia gained its Orthodoxy from the Greeks; and that Greek models should be followed wherever any discrepancy could be detected between Greek and Russian practice. Nikon did not pause to consider that such discrepancies could well be legitimate and that seventeenth-century Greek practice might not be any more "authentic" than Russian.

Popular piety was outraged by some of Nikon's earliest reforms, not least because they involved the use of three fingers instead of two for the frequently used sign of the cross. In any case, Russians had long been used to thinking of Muscovite faith and practice as normative. Within a few years a schism developed. Whereas Nikon's own commitment to his reforms seems to have wavered within a few years, Old Ritualists (otherwise known as Old Believers) consistently accepted persecution rather than tolerate the new ways.

Paradoxically, the Russian church councils of 1666 and 1667, which accepted the Nikonian reforms and excommunicated the conservative Old Ritualists, also sat in judgment on Nikon himself. Their hidden agenda was the question of authority. Nikon was seen by the councils as having too readily accepted papal standards of authority. For example, he had published in Russian the spurious *Donation of Constantine* (a ninth-century document fabricated to strengthen the power of the Roman see), and he advocated the medieval formulation of the "two swords," which was held to justify the pope's authority over church and state alike. He insisted that the priesthood possessed primacy vis-à-vis the ruler and resisted any secular challenge to church prerogatives or ownership of land. All this caused resentment among the boyars and eventually also in the tsar. It was Tsar Aleksei himself who saw to it in 1666 that the church council depose his former friend Nikon. He thus paved the way for the 1720 reforms of Peter the Great, which involved the absolute (administrative) subjugation of church to state.

Nikon was subsequently exiled to the north and his status reduced to that of a simple monk. When the new tsar, Fedor, permitted him to return to Moscow (1681) it was already too late: Nikon died on the journey south at Yaroslavl. Nonetheless, his burial was that of a patriarch.

Bibliography

A wide range of contemporary documents relating to Nikon (some of them from his own hand) were translated by William Palmer as *The Patriarch and the Tsar*, 6 vols. (London, 1871–1876). A number of these have yet to appear in the original. An important study of Nikon's ideas is provided in M. V. Zyzykin's *Patriarkh Nikon: Ego gosudarstvennye i kanonicheskie idei* (Warsaw, 1931–1938). A vivid and authoritative picture of the age is provided by Pierre Pascal in *Avvakum et les débuts du Raskol: La crise religieuse au dix-septième siècle en Russie*, 2d ed. (Paris, 1963).

Sergei Hackel (1987)

NILSSON, MARTIN P.

NILSSON, MARTIN P. (1874–1967), Swedish classicist. Martin Persson Nilsson enrolled as a student in classical studies at the University of Lund in 1892, where in 1900 he earned his Ph.D. degree with a dissertation on the Attic festivals of Dionysos. He became instructor of Greek language and literature at the same university, and also taught archaeology; under the university's auspices he participated in the Danish excavations at Lindos, Rhodes, between 1905 and 1907. In 1909 he was appointed to the new chair of classical archaeology and ancient history at Lund, which he occupied until his retirement in 1939. Among the numerous recognitions he received were his appointment as member to the Society of Letters (in Lund), membership in the Royal Academy of Letters, History, and Antiquities (in Stockholm), and membership in the Royal Danish Academy. In 1939–1940 he taught at the University of California at Berkeley and lectured at various places in the United States under the auspices of the American Council of Learned Societies and the Norton Lectureship of the Archaeological Institute of America.

In his early years, Nilsson was greatly interested in primitive religion and in anthropology, interests that resulted in publications on primitive culture and religion. Although he himself dated the beginnings of his extensive work on Greek religion to the early 1920s, James G. Frazer wrote as early as 1924 that Nilsson had "long been known to scholars as one of the most learned and sagacious exponents of ancient Greek life and thought," in his introduction to Nilsson's *A History of Greek Religion* (1925). Among Nilsson's other studies on Greek and Roman religions in general, the most widely known are "Die Griechen," a chapter in P. D. Chantepie de la Saussaye's edition of *Lehrbuch der Religionsgeschichte* (1925), and especially his major work, *Geschichte der griechischen Religion* (1941–1950). He dealt specifically with Greek folk religion and piety in *Greek Popular Religion* (1940) and *Grekisk religiostet* (1946). By his careful analysis of the impact and influence of the Minoan-Mycenaean religion and culture upon ancient Greek religion, Nilsson has undoubtedly made his most widely recognized contribution to the field. In all his major studies on Greek religion Nilsson discussed this subject, and a number of his publications specifically deal with it, especially *The Minoan-Mycenaean Religion and Its Survival in Greek Religion* (1927).

Among his numerous other publications, several deal with festivals, calendars, and time reckoning, primarily (but not exclusively) using data from the Greek world. Bordering the field of New Testament studies is his *The Historical Hellenistic Background of the New Testament* (1941), while some of his other essays treat the wider fields of religious studies in general and the history and comparative study of religions. At points, his work touches on some methodological issues. In his writings Nilsson often offers valuable surveys and critical assessments of existing literature. For example, he rejects Erwin Rohde's thesis of the Thracian-Dionysian origin of the belief in immortality; he objects strongly to all antievolutionists and to every approach that he brands "ahistorical" (including that of Walter F. Otto); and he speaks sarcastically about Geo Widengren and other "adherents of the High God Belief." For the context of this last criticism, see his article "Letter to Professor Arthur D. Nock on Some Fundamental Concepts in the Science of Religion" (*Harvard Theological Review* 42, 1949, p. 105).

Nilsson's own understanding of primitive religion included a modified notion of *mana*, or sacred power. He opted, with Gerardus van der Leeuw, for the term *dynamism* to describe the religions of primitive peoples, but he stressed that "power appears to consciousness only in separate phenomena or cases" and that "one cannot speak of a concept of power" (ibid., p. 91). This integral aspect of Nilsson's work, along with his self-confessed evolutionism (not in the sense of historical development but as a conceptual, logical series) are some of the points on which Nilsson has been most severely criticized. Specifically, the impact of his idea of *mana* on his interpretation of the Greek concept of the *daimon* as "impersonal power" has been sharply attacked.

Bibliography

Many of Nilsson's numerous publications are available in English translation. A helpful bibliography of Nilsson's major works appears in Jacques Waardenburg's *Classical Approaches to the*

Study of Religion, vol. 2 (The Hague, 1974). Other bibliographical resources include Erik J. Khudtzon's "Beiträge zu einer Bibliographie M. P. Nilsson, 1907–1939," in *Dragma: Martin P. Nilsson* (Lund, 1939), pp. 569–656; and Christian Callmer's article, "The Published Writings of Professor Martin P. Nilsson, 1939–1967," *Scripta Minora Regiae Societatis Humaniorum Litterarum Lundensia* 1 (1967–1968): 117–139. For biographical data, see Carl-Martin Edsman's article, "Martin P. Nilsson, 1874–1967," *Temenos* 3 (1968): 173–178.

New Sources

Bierl, Anton, and William M. Calder III. "Instinct against Proof: the Correspondence between Ulrich v. Wilamowitz Moellendorff and Martin P. Nilsson on Religionsgeschichte (1920–1930)." *Eranos* 89 (1991): 73–99.

Gjerstad, Einar, Erik J. Kundtzon, and Christian Callmer. *Martin P. Nilsson.* Lund, 1968.

Mejer, Jørgen. "Martin P. Nilsson." In *Classical Scholarship. A Biographical Encyclopedia,* edited by W. Ward Briggs and William M. Calder III, pp. 335–340. New York and London 1990.

Pasquali, Giorgio. "Martin Nilsson." *Atene e Roma* 34 (1989): 655–673.

Rüpke, Jörg. *Römische Religion bei E. Norden: die "Altrömischen Priesterbücher" im wissenschaftlichen Kontext der dreissig Jahre. Im Anhang Briefe von E. Norden an M.P. Nilsson (1920–1939).* Marburg, 1993.

WILLEM A. BIJLEFELD (1987)
Revised Bibliography

NIMBĀRKA (fl. mid-fourteenth century?), a Telugu brahman, also called Mimbāditya or Niyamānanda. It is believed that Nimbārka came from Nimba or Nimbapura in the Bellary district (Mysore state), but tradition associates him mostly with Mathurā, the center of the Vaiṣṇava faith in North India. His date has been a matter of controversy among scholars. Since he refers to Rāmānuja's view in his commentary on the *Brahma Sūtra,* he must have lived shortly after Rāmānuja (R. G. Bhandarkar's conjecture). But Surendranath Dasgupta (1940) dates him roughly around the middle of the fourteenth century CE. Dasgupta's argument seems convincing, for this date fits well with the tentative chronology of the four Vaiṣṇava Vedānta schools—those that opposed the Advaita Vedānta school of Śaṅkara. Nimbārka was the founder of one of the four traditionally recognized Vaiṣṇava sects or *sampradāyas.* These sects are known as Śrī Sampradāya (followers of Rāmānuja), Brahma Sampradāya (followers of Madhva), Rudra Sampradāya (followers of Vallabhacarya), and Sanakādi Sampradāya (followers of Nimbārka).

Of the approximately nine works attributed to Nimbārka, the most notable are his commentaries on the *Brahma Sūtra* and on the *Vedāntapārijātasaurabha,* and an independent work, the *Daśaślokī.* Some of the others are neither available in print nor completely preserved, even in their manuscript forms.

Nimbārka's philosophy is usually called *dvaitādvaita-vāda,* "the theory of dualism and nondualism." This description is based upon the main question raised by all the Vedāntins: what is the relation between *brahman* and the world, or between *brahman* and man? Is this an absolute nondifference (Śaṅkara) or absolute difference, or both? Unlike Śaṅkara, all the Vaiṣṇava Vedān tins argued that the world is real. Rāmānuja was the first to take the lead in attacking Advaita. But while Rāmānuja called his view "qualified nondualism" Nimbārka called it "both dualism and nondualism." Madh-va asserted the view of "dualism" while Vallabha leaned toward "nondualism." For Nimbārka, *brahman* was not an impersonal entity, but was identified as a personal, omnipotent God. Unlike Śaṅkara, all of the Vaiṣṇavas talked about a personal god (=*brahman* =Kṛṣṇa=Hariisnu=Viṣṇu) and supported the cultivation of *bhakti* ("devotional attachment") toward such a godhead. Nimbārka's Vedānta is very similar to Rāmānuja's in this regard.

According to Nimbārka, the *brahman* is Śrī Kṛṣṇa, who is omniscient, omnipotent, and the ultimate cause. He is all-pervading. He has transformed himself into the material constituents of the world and *jīvas* ("sentient beings"). Two analogies are cited to emphasize that in spite of this essential nondifference (one interpretation of "transformation") between cause and effects, *brahman* maintains his independence or difference. Just as the *prāṅa* ("life force") manifests itself into various activities of the senses and the mind, but still retains its independence and individuality, and just as a spider spins out of its own body the web and yet remains independent, *brahman* creates sentient beings and the material world out of himself but still remains pure and full and undiminished in his glory and power.

Nimbārka used his dialectical skill in refuting the views of Śaṅkara and other rivals. In spite of the fact that his theory was very similar to that of Rāmānuja, his skill in argumentation and his novelty in presentation earned him a permanent and independent place in the Vaiṣṇava Vedānta tradition. His explanation of the *līlā* theory (that creation is only a spontaneous sport of the ever-perfect, ever-blissful Hari) had a freshness that captured the imagination of many *bhaktas* or devotees. His immediate pupil, Śrīnivāsa, wrote a commentary called *Vedānta-kaustubha* on his *Vedānta-pārijāta-sau-rabha.* Many other scholars followed Śrīnivāsa. Among them were Keśava Kāśmīrī Bhaṭṭa, Puruṣottama Prasāda, Mukunda, and Vanamāli Miśra, who kept alive the Nimbārka substream of Vaiṣṇava Vedānta.

SEE ALSO Madhva; Rāmānuja; Śaṅkara; Vallabha.

BIBLIOGRAPHY

Bhandarkar, R. G. *Vaiṣṇavism, Śaivism and Minor Religious Systems.* Varanasi, 1965.

Bose (Chaudhuri), Roma. *Vedānta-Pārijāta-Saurabha of Nimbārka and Vedānta-Kaustubha of Śrīnivāsa.* 3 vols. Calcutta, 1940–1943.

Dasgupta, Surendranath. *A History of Indian Philosophy*, vol. 3. London, 1940.

BIMAL KRISHNA MATILAL (1987)

NIMBUS. The nimbus, or halo, usually pictured as a luminous figure around the head of a god or holy person, is clearly related in some instances to the sun and solar divinities. Among the native civilizations of Central America, agrarian gods are often pictured with golden crowns or nimbuses. The Inca deity Viracocha wears a tiara that is also the sun. Combining the natures of a sun god and a storm god, Viracocha participates in the character of the highest universal beings, such as Yahveh/El, Zeus, and the Buddha, who in some representations both wields a thunderbolt and wears a nimbus. The nimbus can also be traced, however, to the idea of an external expression of an internal supernatural force, and hence partakes of the full range of light symbolism from both Western and Eastern traditions; in particular, its light signifies intellect or mystical knowledge.

The Iranians pictured what the Avesta terms the *khvarenah* as a sort of supernatural fire, a nimbus, or an aureole, which is like the nimbus but encircles the whole person. It belonged primarily to the gods but could be given to royalty by the grace of the chief divinity, Ahura Mazdā. In Vajrayāna Buddhism in Tibet, the Vidyārajas represent the wrathful side of the absolute wisdom of Vairocana as the *bodhisattvas* represent the calm side. Encircling the supreme being, they wear aureoles of blazing flames and direct them against the darkness of *avidyā* (ignorance), which prevents aspirants from gaining emancipation.

More commonly, the nimbus expresses holiness or sacred character rather than action: two early texts of Mahāyāna Buddhism describe the *bodhisattva* as having a halo studded with five hundred Buddhas, each of which is, in turn, attended by numberless gods. As a way of picturing the wholly transcendent nature of the Buddha, some portraits show his head and halo as a wheel.

In Greece and Rome, the nimbus was often shown around the heads of gods and those in special relationships with them. It acquired fine distinctions in Christian art: the rectangular nimbus, for example, belonged to someone still living at the time the picture was made, whereas a nimbus with three rays or groups of rays was one of several forms that could be given only to the members of the Trinity, usually to the Son.

Between the sixth and twelfth centuries CE, the nimbus was depicted as luminous and transparent. Later representations were more stylized. Sometimes it was opaque, and between 1300 and 1500 the name or initials of a saint were often decoratively inscribed on the nimbus itself. During this same period, the nimbus sometimes appeared around animals when they symbolized divinities or holy persons. In depictions of Jesus Christ or the Virgin Mary with the child Jesus, the aureole was sometimes used.

Another, possibly related, version of the aureole occurs in Islamic representations of a person inside a pearl: here the pearl represents Paradise, where those who are blessed go after death.

SEE ALSO Iconography.

BIBLIOGRAPHY

The nimbus as a Christian symbol has been described in detail in many books on Christian symbolism in art. Typical of these is George W. Ferguson's *Signs and Symbols in Christian Art* (Oxford, 1954). Most of the time these discussions are general and have little or no explanation of deeper meanings. The Mahāyāna texts in which the nimbus of the *bodhisattva* is described are the *Amitāyurdhyāna Sūtra* and the *Vajracchedika Sūtra.*

New Sources

Hagstrom, Aurelie A. "The Symbol of the Mandorla in Christian Art: Recovery of a Feminine Archetype." *Arts* 10 (1998): 25–29.

ELAINE MAGALIS (1987)
Revised Bibliography

NINHURSAGA ("lady of the mountain") was the name given by Ninurta after his victory over the Kur to his mother Ninlil, who gave birth to him from his father Enlil, the powerful god of Nippur. Under the name Ninhursaga, she created the "black heads" (as the Sumerians called themselves) along with An and Enlil. She also took part in the council of the major gods—An, Enlil, Enki, and Ninhursaga—when they decided to inflict the universal flood upon the earth. In the myth of Enki and Ninhursaga she instead appears as the wife of Enki, here with the name Nintu. After intercourse with Enki she gives birth to Ninsar, "the lady of vegetation." In the underworld myths Ninhursaga receives gifts from Gilgamesh.

Under the name Ninhursaga, she plays an important part in Sumerian texts of the pre-Sargonic period. She is directly linked to the institution of the divine kingship: she "breastfeeds with delicious milk" the future sovereign at the moment of his birth (Eannatum of Lagash and Lugalzaggesi of Uruk), while Mesalim styles himself the "beloved son of Ninhursaga." Ninhursaga also appears with the great gods who guarantee the treaty between Lagash and Umma in the list of curses on the Vulture Stele, where she is given the second rank in the company of Enlil, Enki, Utu, and Ninki. The pre-Sargonic royal texts of Lagash record that their sovereigns erected the Gigunu of Tirku for her, whereas in texts from Ur one learns that A'annepada of Ur built her a temple.

The text of the Barton cylinder, which Jan van Dijk says is a copy of a much older story predating the neo-Sumerian period, mentions Ninhursaga by her epithet "mighty sister of Enlil." The text may be subdivided into two sections: the first is an etiological description of the outbreak of the mythical storm, which takes place in "a day, a night, a year," near the sanctuary of Nippur, the historical abode of the poliad god Enlil, and which causes the sky and the earth to touch. The second part describes a sacred marriage between An and Ninhursaga, the mighty sister of Enlil. The appearance of a dragon, with whom the earth talks, introduces the mythical serpent into the story.

The myth of "Enki and Ninhursaga," as recognized by Thorkild Jacobsen, is actually a conflation of two stories that must have been transmitted separately. This can be clearly seen from the name of Enki's wife, who is called Ninsikil in the first story and Nintu-Ninhursaga in the second. There are various perplexing difficulties with the text, so that, for example, Ninsikil is first the wife of Enki, whereas later Ninhursaga gives birth to her.

With this caveat in mind, here is the structure of the myth as it survives. It starts with a description setting the scene where events take place—Dilmun, which is still in pristine condition but needs to be provided with water. When Ninsikil complains about the lack of this essential commodity; Enki promises that the god Utu will not only provide Dilmun with water but will grant it a host of good things from other countries. This is virtually the entire first story.

The theme of the second story consists of accounts of sexual intercourse between Enki and his wife, then with successive daughters, who are in turn produced incestuously: Enki and Nintu beget Ninsar, who begets Ninkurra, who begets Ninimma, who begets Uttu. After Enki has tricked Uttu into having intercourse with him, Ninhursaga intervenes and makes eight plants grow to protect Uttu's daughter, but these are eaten by Enki, who as a result becomes afflicted with eight illnesses. At this point Ninhursaga curses Enki and goes off to hide so she will not see her hated husband any longer. However, the death of Enki, the god of wisdom, would have broken the balance of the universe, so Enlil (with the help of a fox) manages to bring Ninhursaga back to Nippur, where she is finally ready to forgive her husband. Ninhursaga now gives birth to eight gods who will cure Enki of the eight illnesses that have attacked and weakened his body, and she gives these gods eternal life.

Jacobsen suggested that the goddess Nintu, whose name means "lady of childbirth," may be simply a secondary name for Ninhursaga, a theory upon which Marcos Such-Gutierrez (2003) has cast doubt. In favor of Jacobsen's theory is the fact that the sign *TU* in the name *Nintu* ends with the consonant *r*, though it should end with the consonant *d*. Furthermore it has been demonstrated that during the second dynasty of Lagash and the third dynasty of Ur, Ninhursaga is considered the wife of Enlil and is therefore synonymous with Ninlil. This last assertion is confirmed by the myth an-gim-dím-ma, in which Ninurta has Enlil as his father and Nintu as his mother.

Along with the identification of Ninlil with Ninhursaga, documented in the myth of "Ninurta from Lugal-e," the mythological texts suggest other interesting identifications. In the document "Ninurta, Enki, and the Turtle" one finds that Ninurta's mother is Ninmena, "lady of the tiara," whereas in the Akkadian myth "Ninurta and Anzu" the hero's mother is Mami, which suggests that the term had a generic value and meant "mother-goddess." In almost all the myths analyzed, the role of "mother" of the heavenly gods is played by Ninhursaga, who is mentioned under various names, including Mami, as in the last myth, and Nintu, as in the story of "Enki and Ninhursaga," as well as Dingirmah and Ninmah.

Ninhursaga also had the epithets Ninzizna (mistress of the embryo), Nindim (mistress fashioner), and Nagarshaga (carpenter of the womb). She is a very early goddess, with roots in European and Anatolian Neolithic cultures. A plaque dating from Old Babylonian times pictures her nursing an infant and with babies' heads protruding from her shoulders. On either side of her hangs on pegs her omega-shaped symbol, a representation of the uterus of a cow, and on the ground squat two emaciated figures supporting their chins in their hands. They represent embryos, possibly prematurely born fetuses, for which a Sumerian term was *shusagaduga* ([with] the hands put to the head). Such figures have been found with images of a birth goddess in Romania and Moldavia dating from the fifth millennium BCE.

It is certainly surprising that Ninhursaga is mentioned in the myth "Death of Gilgamesh," where she is listed among the gods of the underworld who receive Gilgamesh, who has just arrived in the Land of No Return. The goddess Ninhursaga is mainly active in heaven or on earth in the role of a nurse for those destined to be king, as in the case of Eannatum and others.

Ninhursaga has been connected with the theory of primitive matriarchy by some scholars. However, most contemporary historians of religion accept the anthropological view that a stage of matriarchy never existed, although a few eminent scholars continue to support the idea of an age of "mother right" that preceded patriarchy. They insist that this has been confirmed by archaeological evidence. Although most feminist scholars of the early twenty-first century agree with the anthropological position, there remain a few articulate feminist authors who continue to perpetuate the idea of an original matriarchal stage.

SEE ALSO Goddess Worship, overview article; Mesopotamian Religions, overview articles; Patriarchy and Matriarchy.

BIBLIOGRAPHY

Attinger, Pascal. "Enki et Ninhursaga." *Zeitschrift für Assyriologie* 74 (1984): 1–52.

Braun-Holzinger, Eva. "Ninhursaga B. Archäologie." *Reallexikon der Assyriologie* 9 (1998–2001): 381–383.

Deimel, Anton. *Pantheon Babylonicum: Nomina deorum textibus cuneiformibus excerpta et ordine alphabetico distributa.* Rome, 1914. See pages 208–209.

Edzard, Dietz Otto "Mesopotamien: Die Mythologie der Sumerer und der Akkader." In *Wörterbuch der Mythologie*, vol. 1: *Göt-*

ter und Mythen im Vorderen Orient, edited by H. W. Haussig, pp. 104–105. Stuttgart, Germany, 1965.

Frymer-Kensky, Tikva Simone. *In the Wake of the Goddesses: Women, Culture, and the Biblical Transformation of Pagan Myth.* New York, 1992.

Gimbutas, Marija. *The Language of the Goddess: Unearthing the Hidden Symbols of Western Civilization.* London, 1989.

Heimpel, Wolfgang. "Ninhursaga A." *Reallexikon der Assyriologie* 9 (1998–2001): 378–381.

Jacobsen, Thorkild. "Notes on Nintur." *Orientalia* 42 (1973): 274–298.

Krebernik, Manfred. "Muttergöttin A. I. in Mesopotamien." *Reallexikon der Assyriologie* 8 (1993–1998): 502–516.

Merlin, Stone. *When God Was a Woman.* New York, 1976.

Selz, Gebhart. *Untersuchungen zur Götterwelt der altsumerischen Stadtstaates von Lagaš.* Philadelphia, 1995. See pages 252–255.

Such-Gutierrez, Marcos. *Beiträge zum Pantheon von Nippur im 3. Jahrtausend.* Rome, 2003. See pages 274–279.

Tallqvist, Knut. *Akkadische Götterepitheta.* Studia Orientalia 7. Helsinki, 1938. See pages 407–408.

THORKILD JACOBSEN (1987)
GIOVANNI PETTINATO (2005)
Translated from Italian by Paul Ellis

NINURTA. A divinity of Nippur, Ninurta was the son of Enlil and Ninlil. Ninurta's epithets include Uta'ulu, "Sun of the South," as well as "conqueror of the Kur" and "upright diadem of Ashnan." He is said to have "sprung from Ekur," the main temple of Nippur and home of the divine couple Enlil and Ninlil. In Sumerian mythology his greatest feat is the epic war against the Kur, specifically against Asag, the fiendish monster begotten by An and given birth to by Earth, who wanted to oppose his supremacy. Ninurta not only kills him but lays the foundations of agriculture, the life-giving, essential activity of the land.

THE NINURTA STORY. The myth begins with a hymn to the god Ninurta and the background of the story. While he is sitting with all the other gods, Ninurta orders his weapon Sharur to keep watch on the Kur. The response he receives is far from reassuring. The Kur are in revolt, on this occasion provoked by an alliance formed between Asag and the coalition of stones, and what is more the rebels have actually triumphed. Ninurta wants to suppress the revolt immediately and rushes against the Kur, armed with all his divine weapons, unleashing a fiery tempest. But the weapon Sharur says that the attitude of the Kur is not completely hostile. Sharur, believing that the monster is no less powerful than the god, is afraid of a straight fight between Ninurta and Asag and advises Ninurta not to attack. Ninurta is not inclined to listen to reason, however, and wants the fight to take place in the open. So the two heroic figures fight a duel, and Ninurta indeed comes off the worse. All the gods get wind of the hero's difficulties, and the mood of the assembly of the gods is not pleased. Sharur returns to Enlil, Ninurta's father, asking him to intervene on behalf of his son, who is in difficulty. Enlil agrees and rallies his son, who launches a new, deadly onslaught and manages to defeat and kill the monster. The first part of the myth concludes with the cursing of Asag and the blessing of the weapon Sharur.

The second part of the story begins with a description of the organizing influence of the god. Up to this point the work has been undertaken entirely by the gods, and the mountain full of ice has required an enormous effort. Ninurta now melts the snows, channels the water along the bed of the Tigris, and creates dikes and canals for irrigation of the fields. In effect he invents agriculture.

After an interlude in which Ninurta's mother Ninlil is given the new title "lady of the mountain" to commemorate Ninurta's victory, this part of the myth is wholly concerned with the fate of the stones that had taken part in the war. The hostile stones are cursed, whereas the stones that surrendered meet with a more favorable fate.

OTHER DOCUMENTS. The myth *an-gim dím-ma* is directly linked to the preceding tale and describes the triumphant return of Ninurta from his victorious campaign against the Kur. On this occasion the writers, just in case some doubt still remains, emphasize the extraordinary feat the hero achieved. The mere list of the trophies brought back from the Kur makes one realize that Ninurta engaged in combat with truly superhuman creatures.

This story begins with a hymn to the hero, who resumes his position in the Sumerian pantheon, and his exploits in the Kur. It tells how he plundered the six-headed wild ram, the warrior dragon, the Magilum of the deep sea, the buffalo Kulianna, the chalk, the strong copper, the eagle Anzu, and the seven-headed serpent. The son of Enlil loads these goods aboard his boat, lays them all out decoratively, and sets sail for Nippur. But the voyage is described as fraught with problems. A messenger from Enlil rushes to Ninurta and asks him not to frighten the gods with his powerful splendor. The hero understands the reluctance of the gods, because he has seen the fear of the divine world regarding the Kur already. After a detailed list of the wonderful weapons that helped him in his fight, he asks humbly to reenter the city of his birth. There follows a eulogy of self-praise, so Ninkarnunna, on behalf of Enlil, accepts his good intentions and invites Ninurta to enter the temple dedicated to him and his wife Ninnibru. The myth concludes with a hymn of praise for the hero, who has indeed shown his heroism.

Ninurta goes to Eridu to the house of Enki twice, once with hostile intent—that is, to steal the powers of Kur and the tablets of destiny from the god Enki. One journey finishes disastrously, but the second has a positive outcome as the hero pays a polite visit to the king of the underworld.

The first story begins with a meeting between Ninurta and the eagle Anzu, which the hero had caused to lose the "divine powers." After the defeat these powers returned to

Eridu, to the house of the god Enki, the keeper and guardian of these symbols. Anzu bemoans the loss of the divine powers and tells Ninurta to go to Eridu to recover them. Ninurta goes to Eridu and is welcomed joyfully by Enki. But the visitor remains cold in the face of the happiness displayed by his host because he is not really coming for a polite visit but to carry out a theft. The god of wisdom knows the secret thoughts of the hero and considers his response. He creates a turtle that begins to dig a pit in the underworld. When Ninurta, unaware of the trap, finally leaves Enki's house and follows the turtle, the turtle grabs Ninurta by the ankles and drags him into the pit, from which the hero cannot escape. When Ninurta expresses surprise, Enki answers that he had been goaded into doing this by the arrogance of the conqueror of Kur. The myth concludes with an invocation by Ninurta's mother, Ninmenna, who, weeping, wonders what she can do to save her son.

In the above myth, Ninurta disgraces himself with Enki specifically because he is dishonest when he meets with his host, who punishes him by mocking him. On this second journey, which is to sanction the cosmic supremacy of Ninurta, matters turn out differently, in particular because everything happens with the complete consent of his father Enlil, who has now appointed him as his successor. After the introduction of the god, in which it is emphasized that he originates from Ekur, the reason behind the journey to Eridu is given, namely to ensure blessings and justice for the land of Sumer. Ninurta reaches the underworld of Enki, who greets him joyfully and agrees to his proper requests. The next part deals with the glorification of Ninurta, the rightful heir of Enlil. The epithets given to him rival those of the greatest gods in the pantheon. Following his war with the Kur, Ninurta has been duly awarded a preeminent place in the divine world. This document can be considered as the second part of the deeds of the god Ninurta, which are recorded in the myth *Lugal-e.*

Ninurta, the hero of the myth "Ninurta and Anzu," already paralleled in Sumerian mythology, also exists in Assyro-Babylonian mythology in the same "Ninurta and Anzu" but always as the savior of the cosmic order. In the Sumerian cosmos he actively suppresses the revolt of the Kur, the cosmic mountain, killing the monster Asag and showing complete mastery of the stones that rushed to help Asag. In the Assyro-Babylonian myth, Ninurta has to fight the lion-headed eagle Anzu, and he is responsible for a serious theft when he meets with his father Enlil.

It is a great pity that the Old Babylonian version is not complete, because the final outcome of the myth preserved in that version remains unclear. In contrast to the Sumerian myths, in the Old Babylonian version Ninurta is portrayed as disrespectful and rebellious. Instead of giving back the symbols stolen from Anzu, he refuses to return them to their rightful owner, thus causing disorder in the cosmos.

This myth is set down in three tablets. It unfolds with a hymn to the god Ninurta, called Ningirsu in the earliest version, in which his wonderful qualities are elaborated. After recalling the original drought, it continues with the story of the birth of Anzu, news of which is brought to Enlil. The god Ea advises his brother to take on the new being as his bodyguard, and Enlil does so. Anzu thus receives the task of helping the god in his private chambers. In this role he sees the god washing and getting dressed every day and also at times remaining completely naked. At this point he conceives of an evil plan to steal the symbols of power. Once he has stolen them, Anzu flees to the mountain, leaving the divine world in a state of near-complete despair. Champions are chosen to kill Anzu and bring back the stolen property. First Adad is sent, but his attempt is unsuccessful. Then Girru and Shara are chosen, with the same results. The god Ea next suggests calling upon Mami to ask her to send her son Ninurta. The mother goddess agrees to the request, calls her son, and instructs him regarding the battle. Ninurta, in full armor, goes to fight Anzu. The battle is bloody, but the divine hero does not prevail and is thus obliged to send his powerful weapon Sharur to Ea to ask for help. The god Ea understands the reason for the initial failure and suggests wearing out Anzu until he can no longer flap his wings. Sharur returns with Ea's advice, and by putting it into action Ninurta manages to kill Anzu and take from him the divine symbols of his father and the tablets of destiny.

Enlil, who is called Dagan at this point, learns of his son's victory and announces it to all the gods, who invite Ninurta to return. Ea suggests sending a messenger to his son to bring back the tablet of destiny, and Enlil sends Birdu. But Ninurta refuses to hand over the symbols of power, reacting as Anzu had previously. When the surviving text resumes, it deals with a long votive offering to the gods and a hymn of praise for Ninurta. The fragmentary nature of the final part of the third tablet prevents a full understanding of the significance of the long list of titles attributed to Ninurta and in particular syncretism with the other polyadic gods of the numerous cities of Mesopotamia and the surrounding region, which suggests an attempted and unfinished religious revolution.

As the god of war, Ninurta achieved special prominence in the militaristic Middle Assyrian and neo-Assyrian periods. Ninurta was also god of the hunt. Tiglath-pileser I (ruled c. 1115–1077 BCE) recorded that at Ninurta's command, during a certain hunt, he slew numerous "extraordinary wild virile bulls," ten strong bull elephants, hundreds of lions, and every kind of wild beast and winged bird of the heavens.

SEE ALSO Herakles; Mesopotamian Religions, overview article.

BIBLIOGRAPHY

Alster, Bendt. "Ninurta and the Turtle, UET 6/1 2." *Journal of Cuneiform Studies* 24 (1972): 120–125.

Annus, Amar. *The Standard Babylonian Epic of Anzu.* Helsinki, Finland, 2001.

Burkert, Walter. *The Orientalizing Revolution.* Cambridge, Mass., 1992.

Dijk, J. J. A. van. *Lugal ud me-lam-bi nir-gal: Le récit épique et didactique des Travaux de Ninurta, du Déluge et de la Nouvelle Création,* vols. 1–2. Leiden, 1983.

Hallo, William W., and William L. Moran. "The First Tablet of the SB Recension of the Anzu-Myth." *Journal of Cuneiform Studies* 31 (1979): 65–115.

Hruška, Blahoslav. *Der Mythenadler Anzu in Literatur und Vorstellung des alten Mesopotamien.* Budapest, 1975.

Jacobsen, Thorkild. *The Treasures of Darkness: A History of Mesopotamian Religion.* New Haven, Conn., 1976. See pp. 127–134.

Pettinato, Giovanni, ed. *Mitologia Sumerica.* Turin, Italy, 2001.

Saggs, X. W. F. "Additions to Anzu." *Archiv für Orientforschung* 33 (1986): 1–29.

Seminara, S. "Gli dei Enlil e Ninurta nel mito sumerico *Lugal-e*: Politiche religiose, dibattito teologico e 'riscrittura' dei 'testi sacri' nell' antica Mesopotamia." *Rendiconti dell'Accademia Nazionale dei Lincei* 9–11, no. 3 (2000): 443–468.

Such-Gutièrrez, Marcos. *Beiträge zum Pantheon von Nippur im 3. Jahrtausend.* Rome, 2003. See pp. 143–172.

West, Martin L. *The East Face of Helicon.* Oxford, 1997.

GIOVANNI PETTINATO (2005)
Translated from Italian by Paul Ellis

NIRVĀṆA

NIRVĀṆA. About twenty-five centuries ago in northern India, Siddhārtha Gautama achieved *nirvāṇa.* That event ultimately changed the spiritual character of much of Asia and, more recently, some of the West. That something indeed happened is an indisputable fact. Exactly what happened has been an object of speculation, analysis, and debate up to the present day.

Nirvāṇa is both a term and an ideal. As a Sanskrit word (*nibbāna* in Pali), it has been used by various religious groups in India, but it primarily refers to the spiritual goal in the Buddhist way of life. In the broadest sense, the word *nirvāṇa* is used in much the same way as the now standard English word *enlightenment,* a generic word literally translating no particular Asian technical term but used to designate any Buddhist notion of the highest spiritual experience. Of course, Buddhism comprehends a diverse set of religious phenomena, a tradition with sacred texts in four principal canonical languages (Pali, Sanskrit, Tibetan, and Chinese), and a spiritual following throughout the world. Not surprisingly, then, when referring to the ultimate spiritual ideal many Buddhist groups prefer to emphasize their own distinctive terms instead of *nirvāṇa.*

NIRVĀṆA IN THE EARLY BUDDHIST AND ABHIDHARMA TRADITIONS. In the Pali *nikāyas* and Chinese *āgamas,* works first written down or composed two or three centuries after the death of the Buddha, there is little philosophical discussion about the nature of *nirvāṇa.* Indeed, on technical points such as the enlightened person's status after death, the sūtras admonish that such metaphysical speculation is only an obstacle to achieving the ultimate goal. In a famous story found in the *Majjhima Nikāya,* for example, Māluṅkyāputta asked the Buddha several metaphysical questions, including whether the Buddha continues to exist after death. The Buddha responded that such questioning is beside the point; it would be comparable to a man struck by a poison arrow who worried about the origin and nature of the arrow rather than pulling it out.

> Whether there is the view that the Tathāgata both is and is not after dying, or whether, Māluṅkyāputta, there is the view that the Tathāgata neither is nor is not after dying, there *is* birth, there is ageing, there is dying, there are grief, sorrow, suffering, lamentation and despair, the suppression of which I lay down here and now. (Horner, 1954–1959, vol. 2, pp. 100–101)

In short, the early Buddhist texts primarily approached *nirvāṇa* as a practical solution to the existential problem of human anguish. Specifically, they maintained that by undertaking a disciplined praxis the Buddhist practitioner can achieve a nondiscursive awakening *(bodhi)* to the interdependent nonsubstantiality of reality, especially of the self. With that insight, it was believed, one could be released from the grips of insatiable craving and its resultant suffering.

In most cases *nirvāṇa* is described in negative terms such as "cessation" (*nirodha*), "the absence of craving" (*tṛṣṇākṣaya*), "detachment," "the absence of delusion," and "the unconditioned" (*asaṃskṛta*). Although in the *nikāyas* and subsequent Abhidharma school commentaries there are scattered positive references to, for instance, "happiness" (*sukha*), "peace," and "bliss," and to such metaphors of transcendence as "the farther shore," the negative images predominate. Indeed, the word *nirvāṇa* itself means "extinction," and other words used synonymously with it, such as *mokṣa* and *mukti,* refer to emancipation. One difficulty with the early texts, however, is that they were not always clear or unequivocal about *what* was extinguished and *from what* one was emancipated. One prominent tendency was to understand *nirvāṇa* as a release from *saṃsāra,* the painful world of birth and death powered by passion, hatred, and ignorance. According to the early texts, the Eightfold Path leading to *nirvāṇa* is the only way to break free of this cycle and to eliminate the insatiable craving at its root. The Path is not merely a set of moral exhortations, but rather, a program of spiritual reconditioning that liberates one from the pain of *saṃsāra.*

The Buddhist view of *saṃsāra* developed as the notion of rebirth was taking root in ancient India. So enlightenment came to be understood as the extinction (*nirvāṇa*) of what can be reborn, that is, as the dissolution of any continuing personal identity after death. This led to the need to distinguish between (1) the enlightenment of the person who has transcended in this world the suffering caused by craving, and (2) the perfect *nirvāṇa* achieved only when that person dies and is fully released from *saṃsāra,* the cycle of birth, death, and rebirth. The Pali texts, therefore, distinguished "*nirvāṇa* with remainder" (*saupādisesa nibbāna*) from "*nirvāṇa* without remainder" (*anupādisesa nibbāna*), or even more simply, enlightenment (*nibbāna*) from *complete* enlightenment (*parinibbāna;* Skt., *parinirvāṇa*).

The Abhidharma traditions interpreted the distinction in the following way. After many lifetimes of effort and an overall improvement in the circumstances of rebirth, the person undertaking the Path finally reaches the stage at which craving and its attendant negative effects are no longer generated. This is the state of "*nirvāṇa* with remainder" because the residue of negative karmic effects from previous actions continues. The enlightened person still experiences physical pain, for example, as a consequence of the mere fact of corporeality, itself a karmic "fruit." Once these residues are burned off, as it were, the person will die and achieve the perfect "*nirvāṇa* without remainder."

An ambiguity in the distinction between *saṃsāra* and *nirvāṇa* is whether the contrasted terms refer to psychological or ontological states. That is, are *saṃsāra* and *nirvāṇa* states of mind or kinds of existence? If *saṃsāra* refers to the psychological worldview conducive to suffering, then the transition from *saṃsāra* to *nirvāṇa* is simply a profound change in attitude, perspective, and motivation. If, on the other hand, *saṃsāra* refers to this pain-stricken world itself, then *nirvāṇa* must be somewhere else. Here the ancient metaphor of *nirvāṇa* as "the farther shore" could assume a metaphysical status. In effect, *nirvāṇa* could be understood as a permanent state of bliss beyond the world of birth, death, and rebirth. The reaction against such an interpretation influenced the Mahāyāna Buddhist views of enlightenment.

NIRVĀṆA IN THE INDIAN MAHĀYĀNA BUDDHIST TRADITIONS. Indian Mahāyāna Buddhists minimized the opposition between *nirvāṇa* and *saṃsāra,* renouncing the suggestion that *nirvāṇa* was an escape from the world of suffering. Instead, they thought of enlightenment as a wise and compassionate way of living in that world. The adherents of the two major Indian branches of Mahāyāna philosophy, Mādhyamika and Yogācāra, each developed their own way of rejecting the escapism to which, it was thought, the Abhidharma interpretation led.

The Perfection of Wisdom and Mādhyamika traditions. One Mahāyāna strategy was to undercut the epistemological and logical bases for the sharp distinction between the concepts of *nirvāṇa* and *saṃsāra.* Without *nirvāṇa* there is no *saṃsāra,* and vice versa. How then could one be absolute and the other relative? This question was most clearly raised by the Perfection of Wisdom (Prajñāpāramitā) literature and philosophically analyzed in the Mādhyamika school founded by Nāgārjuna (c. 150–250 CE).

In effect, Mādhyamika thought radicalized the Buddha's original silence on this critical issue by trying to demonstrate that any philosophical attempt to characterize reality is limited by the logical interdependence of words or concepts. Assuming an isomorphic relationship between words and nonlinguistic referents, Nāgārjuna reasoned that the interdependent character of words precludes their referring to any absolute, nondependent realities. To the very extent one can talk or reason about *nirvāṇa* and *saṃsāra,* therefore, they must depend on each other. Neither can be absolute in itself.

For the Mādhyamikas, the real cause of human turmoil is that through naming and analyzing one tries to grasp and hold onto what exists only through the distinctions imposed by the conventions of language. From this perspective, Buddhist practice frees one from this attachment to concepts by cultivating *prajñā,* a nondiscursive, direct insight into the way things are. Once one recognizes that the substantialized sense of ego is based on a linguistic distinction having no ultimate basis, an enlightened attitude develops in which one actively shares in the suffering of all other sentient beings. In this way, the wisdom of *prajñā* can also be considered a universal form of compassion, *karuna.* This *prajñā-karuna* ideal eventually became a major paradigm of enlightenment within the entire Mahāyāna tradition in India, Tibet, and East Asia.

***Nirvāṇa* in the idealistic and yogācāra traditions.** The typical approach of such idealistic texts as the *Laṅkāvatāra Sūtra* and of its related philosophical school, Yogācāra, was to assert that *nirvāṇa* and *saṃsāra* had a common ground, namely, the activity of the mind. The terminology varied from text to text and thinker to thinker, but the thrust of this branch of Mahāyāna Buddhism was that the mind was the basis of both delusion (understood as *saṃsāra*) and enlightenment (understood as *nirvāṇa*). For many in this tradition, this implied that there is in each person an inherent core of Buddhahood covered over with a shell of delusional fixations. Sometimes this core was called the *tathāgata-garbha* ("Buddha womb, Buddha embryo," or "Buddha matrix"); in other cases it was considered to be part of a store-consciousness (*ālaya-vijñāna*) containing seeds (*bīja*) that could sprout either delusional or enlightened experience. In either case, Buddhist practice was seen as a technique for clarifying or making manifest the Buddha mind or Buddha nature within the individual. This notion of mind and its relation to Buddhist practice influenced the later development of Mahāyāna Buddhism, even the schools that first flourished in East Asia, such as Tiantai, Huayan, and Chan (Zen).

A problem raised by this more psychological approach to enlightenment was the issue of universality. Is the inherent core of enlightenment in one person the same as in another? Is it equally present in everyone? With such questions, the difficulty of the ontological status of enlightenment once again emerged. That is, if both *nirvāṇa* and *saṃsāra* are dependent on the mind in some sense, the problem for the Yogācāra philosophers was to explain the objective ground for *nirvāṇa.* Otherwise, truth would be merely subjective. Yogācāra thinkers such as Asaṅga (fourth century CE) and his brother, Vasubandhu, approached this problem by asserting a transindividual, mental ground for all experience called *ālaya-vijñāna.* Other Yogācāra thinkers such as Dignāga, however, rejected the existence of such a store-consciousness and tried to establish the necessary ground for objectivity within mental cognition itself, while denying the substantial reality of any object outside cognition. In general, the former approach persevered in the transmission of Yogācāra's philosophy into East Asia, where the idea of the ground of enlightenment or of the Buddha nature would become a major theme.

Buddhahood in devotional Mahāyāna Buddhism. *Nirvāṇa*'s ontological or metaphysical nature was also a theme in Mahāyāna religious practices quite outside the formal considerations of the philosophers. This development was associated with the rise of the notion that the historical Buddha who had died in the fifth century BCE was actually only an earthly manifestation of an eternal Buddha or of Buddhahood itself. This line of thought developed into the construction of a rich pantheon of Buddhas and *bodhisattvas* living in various heavenly realms and interacting with human beings in supportive ways. These heavenly figures became the objects of meditation, emulation, reverence, and supplication.

The evolution of the Buddhist pantheon was consistent with the general Mahāyāna principle that a necessary component of enlightenment is compassion. The Buddha, it was believed, would not desert those who had not yet achieved *nirvāṇa* and were still in a state of anguish. Whereas the physical person of the Buddha was extinguished, the compassion of his Buddhahood would seem to endure. Following this line of reasoning, the historical Buddha was taken to be only a physical manifestation of enlightened being itself. This interpretation made moot the question of *nirvāṇa* as the release from the cycle of birth, death, and rebirth. If Buddhahood continues even after the physical disappearance of the enlightened person, enlightenment must be more *manifested* than achieved. This way of thinking was conducive to Mahāyāna Buddhism's transmission into East Asia.

***NIRVĀṆA* IN EAST ASIAN BUDDHIST TRADITIONS.** The Mahāyānists were generally more interested in the truth to which enlightenment was an awakening than the pain from which it was a release. This emphasis on the positive aspect of enlightenment also caused to be diminished the importance of *nirvāṇa* as the release from rebirth. This perspective was well suited to Chinese thought. Because the Chinese had no indigenous idea of the cycle of rebirth, release from that cycle was not the existential issue in China it had been in India.

A second Mahāyānist idea readily accepted by the Chinese was that enlightenment is available to anyone in this very lifetime. The Abhidharma traditions generally assumed the path to enlightenment would take eons, and that the last rebirth in this progression of lifetimes would be that of a monk blessed with the circumstances most conducive to concentrating on the final stages of the Path. This view led to a distinction between the spiritual development of monastics and laypersons: Laypersons were to support monastics in their religious quest; such support would, in return, give the laypersons meritorious *karman* leading to successively better rebirths until they too were born into circumstances allowing them to reach the final stages of the Path.

The Mahāyāna ideal, on the other hand, was that of the *bodhisattva,* the enlightened (or, more technically, almost enlightened) being who chooses to be actively involved in alleviating the suffering of others by leading them to enlightenment. In other words, the *bodhisattva* subordinates personal enlightenment to that of others. Both Abhidharma and Mahāyāna Buddhism aim for the enlightenment of everyone, but whereas in the Abhidharma view enlightenment is achieved by one person at a time and the group as a whole pushes upward in a pyramid effect, supporting most the spiritual progress of those at the top, in Mahāyāna Buddhism the *bodhisattvas* at the top turn back to pull up those behind them until everyone is ready to achieve enlightenment simultaneously. Ultimately, the Mahāyāna model dominated in East Asia, partly because the collectivist viewpoint was more consistent with indigenous Chinese ideas predating the introduction of Buddhism.

When Buddhism entered China around the beginning of the common era, Confucianism and Daoism were already well established. Confucianism placed its primary emphasis on the cultivation of virtuous human relationships for the harmonious functioning of society. This emphasis on social responsibility and collective virtue blended well with the Mahāyāna vision of enlightenment.

Compared to Confucianism, Daoism was relatively ascetic, mystical, and otherworldly. Yet its mysticism was strongly naturalistic in that the Daoist sage sought unity with the Dao by being in harmony with nature. In Daoism, as in Mahāyāna Buddhism, the absolute principle was completely immanent in this world, accessible to all who attune themselves to it by undertaking the proper form of meditation and self-discipline. Because one of the root meanings of the term *dao* is "path," the Chinese found parallels between the Buddhist sense of the Path and the Daoist understanding of achieving oneness with the Dao.

***Nirvāṇa* in the Tiantai and Huayan schools.** Eventually there arose new forms of Mahāyāna Buddhism distinctive to East Asia, schools either unknown or only incipient in India. The term *nirvāṇa,* possibly because it carried connotations of a foreign worldview replete with such ideas as rebirth and the inherent unsatisfactoriness (*duḥkha*) of existence, tended to lose its privileged status in favor of such terms as "awakening" (*chüeh*) and "realization" (*wu*).

The Chinese Tiantai and Huayan traditions formulated their own sophisticated philosophical worldviews out of ideas suggested by Indian sūtras. Both schools emphasized the interpenetration of all things. In Tiantai terminology as developed by such philosophers as Zhiyi (538–597), all the "three thousand worlds" are reflected in a single instant of thought. Reality's underlying, unifying factor was understood to be mind. For Tiantai followers the fundamental mind is itself always pure and does not contain, as most Indian Yogācārins held, both delusional and enlightened seeds.

The Tiantai assumption of an underlying, inherently pure, mind had two important consequences. First, the goal of its primary contemplative practice, known as "cessation and discernment" (*zhiguan*), was explained as immersion into, rather than the purification of, mind. By ceasing to focus on the surface flow of ordinary phenomena, one can discern the underlying single mind at the source of all things. Second, because the underlying mind is pure or enlightened, it follows that all things, even inanimate ones, are endowed with Buddha nature. This corollary was first proposed by the ninth patriarch of the tradition, Zhanran (711–782), who clearly articulated the view that the entire world, as it is, is already somehow enlightened. The goal, then, is to realize, awaken to, or manifest that enlightenment in one's own life. The relationship between inherent and acquired enlightenment became a central problematic in the Tiantai tradition and a major theme behind the development of the various schools of Japanese Buddhism in the Kamakura period (1185–1333) as well.

Chinese Huayan Buddhism also affirmed the interdependence among, and harmony within, all things. Unlike the adherents of Tiantai, however, the Huayan philosophers did not think of mind as the underlying, unifying entity. Fazang (643–712), for example, preferred to deny any single unifying factor and used the phrase "the nonobstruction between thing and thing" *(shishi wu'ai)*. In other words, each phenomenon itself was thought to reflect every other phenomenon. Zongmi (780–841), on the other hand, favored the phrase "the nonobstruction between absolute principle and thing" *(lishi wu'ai)*. Thus, he regarded principle *(li)* as the fundamental unifying substrate, even the creative source, of reality.

In all these Tiantai and Huayan theories is found a recurrent, distinctively East Asian, interpretation of *nirvāṇa*. Just as the Confucians sought harmony within the social order and the Daoists harmony within the natural order, the Tiantai and Huayan Buddhists understood enlightenment in terms of harmony. Rather than emphasizing the painful aspect of the world and the means to emancipation from it, the Tiantai and Huayan Buddhists focused on recognizing the intrinsic harmony of the universe and feeling intimately a part of it.

***Nirvāṇa* in the Chan (Zen) school.** Chan (Kor., Son; Jpn., Zen) is another school with roots in India, but it developed into a full-fledged tradition only in East Asia. It is distinctive in its de-emphasis of the role of formal doctrine and religious texts in favor of a direct "transmission of mind" from master to disciple. Chan focused most on the interpersonal aspect of the enlightenment experience. Enlightenment was considered a stamp embodied in a particular lineage of enlightened people going back to the historical Buddha, and the personal encounters of great masters and disciples were recorded in order to serve as the object of meditation for future generations.

One topic of debate about enlightenment in the Chan school concerned the issue of whether enlightenment was "sudden" or "gradual." The Northern school emphasized the inherent purity of the mind and, therefore, advocated a practice intended to remove delusional thoughts covering over that intrinsically undefiled core. Then, it was assumed, the inherent enlightenment of the mind could shine forth ever more brilliantly. According to the *Platform Sūtra,* a text of the Southern school, this position was expressed in a poem by Shenxiu (606–706) as follows:

> The body is the Bodhi tree,
> The mind is like a clear mirror.
> At all times we must strive to polish it,
> And must not let the dust collect. (Yampolsky, 1967, p. 130)

The members of the Southern school, on the other hand, accused their Northern school counterparts of reifying enlightenment into an independently existing thing. In the expression of Huineng (638–713) also recorded in the *Platform Sūtra*:

> Bodhi originally has no tree,
> The mirror also has no stand.
> Buddha nature is always clear and pure;
> Where is there room for dust? (ibid., p. 132)

In other words, enlightenment should be manifest at all times in all one's activities. It is not a separate state or seed to be nurtured or cared for. The goal for the Southern school, therefore, was to make enlightenment manifest while going about one's daily affairs. This viewpoint eventually led some Southern masters, especially those in the lineage of Mazu (709–788), to de-emphasize simple meditation in favor of the shock tactics of shouting, striking, and using the *gongan* (Jpn., *kōan*). These special techniques were all ways of making the disciple realize and manifest Buddha nature in a sudden manner.

Another approach to the sudden/gradual issue was originally taken by the previously mentioned Huayan (and Chan) master Zongmi, and later developed extensively by the great Korean Sŏn master, Chinul (1158–1210). Their view was that the Southern school (which eventually dominated for political as much as religious or philosophical reasons) was correct in maintaining that enlightenment, the awakening to one's own Buddha nature, had to be a sudden realization. Yet Zongmi and Chinul also maintained that realization had to be gradually integrated into one's life through a continuously deepening practice of spiritual cultivation. Thus, their position is known as "sudden awakening/gradual cultivation," rather than "sudden awakening/ sudden cultivation." This distinction exemplifies the importance Chan philosophers accorded the need to define as precisely as possible the relationship between practice and enlightenment. Dōgen

(1200–1253), the founder of the Japanese Sōtō Zen tradition, addressed the problem of how enlightenment could be inherent and yet practice still necessary. That is, if people are already primordially enlightened why should anyone bother to sit in meditation? Dōgen understood practice to be enlightened activity itself: one does not sit in meditation in order to achieve enlightenment, but rather, one's enlightenment is expressed as one's sitting in meditation.

For virtually all the Chan (and Sŏn and Zen) traditions, enlightenment is more than an insight or even a sense of harmony. It is also a mode of *behavior* to be continuously enacted and tested in everyday life. Much of the interpersonal dynamics between master and disciple is designed to challenge the person to make *nirvāṇa* manifest in such ordinary activities as talking, working, eating, and washing, as well as meditating.

***Nirvāṇa* in the Pure Land traditions.** All forms of Buddhism discussed up to now have assumed that one can only achieve *nirvāṇa* through years (or even lifetimes) of concentrated practice. The Pure Land tradition, especially as developed by Shinran (1173–1262) in Japan, radically reinterpreted the notion of Buddhist practice, however.

Pure Land Buddhism is another Mahāyāna tradition that had its basis in Indian sūtras but that only fully blossomed in East Asia. It began with a rather otherworldly orientation: The present period of history was considered so degenerate that it was thought to be no longer possible for human beings to practice genuine Buddhism and to achieve *nirvāṇa*. A *bodhisattva* named Dharmākara (Hōzō in Japanese), however, vowed not to allow himself to achieve full Buddhahood if people who called on his name with faith were not reborn in a Pure Land, a place ideally suited for Buddhist practice. In that Pure Land, people could attain enlightenment and even come back into the world as *bodhisattvas* to aid in the spiritual progress of others. The Pure Land sūtras go on to explain that Dharmākara became the Buddha Amitābha/Amitāyus (Jpn., Amida). Therefore, he must have fulfilled his vow, and thus if people can call on that Buddha's name with complete faith in his compassion and power to help they will be guaranteed rebirth in the Pure Land.

The major lesson in this account for Pure Land Buddhists like Shinran was that human beings today cannot achieve *nirvāṇa* by their "own power" (*jiriki*). Rather than help themselves through the practice of calculated, self-conscious actions (*hakarai*), people should simply resign themselves completely to the "power of another" (*tariki*), that is, the power of Amida's compassionate vow. Even this act of the "entrusting heart and mind" (*shinjin*) must itself be an expression of Amida's vow and not an effort on one's own part. In this way, Shinran maintained that enlightenment could ultimately only be achieved by first releasing oneself to the spontaneousness "naturalness" (*jinen hōni*), the active grace of Amida's compassion as this world itself. "Amida Buddha is the medium through which we are made to realize *jinen*" (Ueda, 1978, pp. 29–30). By subordinating even Amida and his vow to the principle of spontaneous naturalness in this way, Shinran removed the otherworldly traces in Pure Land teaching, making it more suitable to its East Asian, particularly Japanese, context.

***Nirvāṇa* in the Esoteric traditions.** The Esoteric, Vajrayāna, or Tantric forms of Buddhism can be generally viewed as extensions of Mahāyāna. In general, however, Esoteric Buddhism was most permanently influential in Tibet (including the Mongolian extensions of Tibetan Buddhism) and in Japan. In both cases, Esotericism merged its practices and doctrines with the indigenous shamanistic, archaic religions of, respectively, Bon and Shintō.

In terms of their understanding of *nirvāṇa* the Esoteric traditions added an important dimension to their otherwise generally Mahāyānistic outlook, namely, that enlightenment should be understood as participation in the enlightenment of the Buddha-as-reality (the *dharmakāya*). From this viewpoint, sacred speech (mantras), sacred gestures (*mudrās*), and sacred envisioning (*maṇḍalas*) constitute a Buddhist ritualistic practice having an almost sacramental character. That is, in performing the rituals outlined in the Tantras, the Esoteric Buddhist believes that one's own speech, action, and thought become the concrete expression of the cosmic Buddha's own enlightenment.

This notion found a particularly clear formulation in the Japanese Shingon Buddhism established by Kūkai (774–835). According to Kūkai, the fundamental principle of Shingon practice and philosophy is that of *hosshin seppō*, "the Buddha-as-reality [*dharmakāya*] preaches the true teaching [*dharma*]." In making this claim, Kūkai rejected the exoteric Buddhist notion that only a historical Buddha (*nirmāṇakāya*) or a heavenly Buddha (*saṃbhogakāya*) can preach. All of reality in itself, according to Kūkai, is the symbolic expression of the *dharmakāya* Buddha's enlightened activity and, as such, is the direct manifestation of truth. The way to grasp this symbolic expression is not to be an audience to it, but rather to take part in it directly through Esoteric rituals. The individual's own enlightenment was considered an aspect of the cosmic Buddha's enlightened activity. Kūkai identified the Buddha-as-reality or the cosmic Buddha as the Great Sun Buddha, Dainichi Nyorai (Skt., Mahāvairocana).

Kūkai's view of enlightenment was, therefore, summarized in the phrase "attaining Buddha in and through this very body" (*sokushin jōbutsu*). Through the ritualized, physical participation in the world, the person could become a concrete expression of Dainichi Buddha's enlightened action. Kūkai expressed this intimacy between the individual and Dainichi Buddha as "the Buddha enters the self and the self enters the Buddha" (*nyūga ganyū*). In effect, the Mahāyāna Buddhist's identification of *nirvāṇa* with the world was taken to its most radical conclusion. That is, from the Shingon perspective, this very world *is* the Buddha Dainichi. This means that enlightenment is not inherent in the world, but rather, the world itself is the experience of enlightenment.

CONCLUSION. As this article has shown, there is no single Buddhist view of *nirvāṇa.* The Buddhist ideal varies with the culture, the historical period, the language, the school, and even the individual. Still, one does find in the Buddhist notions of *nirvāṇa* what Ludwig Wittgenstein would have called a "family resemblance," that is, a group of characteristics that no single family member entirely possesses but that all members share to such an extent that the members of one family are distinguishable from the members of another. In this case, the Buddhist conceptions of *nirvāṇa* share a set of qualities that can be summarized as follows.

1. *Nirvāṇa* is the release from ignorance about the way the world is. Because one does not understand the nature of human existence and the laws affecting human life, one lives in either a state of outright suffering or in a state of disharmony. *Nirvāṇa* is ultimately acknowledging and living by the truths of the world. In that respect, its orientation is this-worldly.

2. The knowledge achieved by *nirvāṇa* is not merely intellectual or spiritual. *Nirvāṇa* is achieved through a process of psychological and physical conditioning aimed at reorienting and reversing ego-centered forms of thinking and behaving. *Nirvāṇa* is achieved through and with the body, not despite the body.

3. One is not alone on the Path. There is support from texts, philosophical teachings, religious practices, the Buddhist community, the examples of masters, and even the rocks and trees. Most of all, there is the power of compassion that one receives from others and that grows stronger the more it is offered to others.

4. *Nirvāṇa* is achieved by penetrating and dissolving the slashes or virgules separating humanity/nature, self/other, subject/object, and even *nirvāṇa/saṃsāra.* The particular pairs of opposition vary from place to place and time to time as Buddhism attacks the special dichotomies most destructive in a given culture during a specific period. *Nirvāṇa* entails a recognition of the inherent harmony and equality of all things.

5. *Nirvāṇa* has an intrinsically moral aspect. By eliminating all egocentric ideas, emotions, and actions, the enlightened person approaches others with either complete equanimity (wherein self and others are treated exactly the same) or with a compassionate involvement in alleviating the suffering of others (wherein self is subordinated to the needs of those less fortunate). Morality can be considered the alpha and omega of *nirvāṇa.* That is, the Path begins with accepting various rules and precepts of behavior, whereas *nirvāṇa* culminates in the open, moral treatment of other people and things.

6. Although in any given context, one viewpoint is emphasized over the other, generally speaking, *nirvāṇa* can be understood from either a psychological or ontological perspective. Psychologically viewed, *nirvāṇa* is a radical change in attitude such that one no longer experiences the negative influence of egocentric thinking. If this perspective is misunderstood and overemphasized, however, it leads to a psychologism that holds that truth is simply in the mind without any connection to an external reality. The remedy for this distortion is to assert the ontological aspect of *nirvāṇa.*

Ontologically speaking, *nirvāṇa* is the affirmation of the inherent goodness of the world and even of human nature. In this sense, *nirvāṇa* is not merely a kind of experience (as depicted by the psychological view) but is also the content or even *ground* of an experience. If this ontological viewpoint is overemphasized, on the other hand, it can lead to the distorted idea that diligence and practice are arbitrary or even unnecessary. The remedy is, conversely, to neutralize that distortion with more emphasis on the psychological side of *nirvāṇa.*

In short, both the psychological and ontological views contain truths about the nature of *nirvāṇa,* but if either position is developed in such a way as to exclude the other, the result is a distortion of the Buddhist Path. For this reason, the two views coexist throughout Buddhist history, one view always complementing the other and checking any distortions that might arise out of a one-sided perspective.

SEE ALSO Ālaya-vijñāna; Amitābha; Asaṅga; Bodhisattva Path; Buddhism, Schools of, article on Esoteric Buddhism; Buddhist Ethics; Buddhist Books and Texts, article on Exegesis and Hermeneutics; Buddhist Philosophy; Celestial Buddhas and Bodhisattvas; Chan; Chinul; Confucianism; Daoism, overview article; Dignāga; Dōgen; Eightfold Path; Fazang; Huayan; Huineng; Karuṇā; Language, article on Buddhist Views of Language; Mādhyamika; Mahāvairocana; Nāgārjuna; Prajñā; Shingonshū; Shinran; Soteriology; Tathāgatha-garbha; Tiantai; Vasubandhu; Yogācāra; Zen; Zhenyan; Zhiyi; Zongmi.

BIBLIOGRAPHY

As the fundamental ideal of Buddhism, *nirvāṇa* is discussed in a wide variety of works: sūtras, commentaries, and secondary critical works by scholars of various traditions. Any bibliography must be, therefore, incomplete and, at best, highly selective. The following works have been chosen for their particular relevance to the issues discussed in the foregoing article.

Nirvāṇa in the Indian Buddhist Traditions

Of the many references to *nirvāṇa* in the early Indian texts, certain passages have traditionally received the most attention. For example, in the Pali scriptures, the status of the Buddha after death (*parinibbāna*) is handled in various ways. Most prominent, undoubtedly, is the traditional account of the Buddha's passing away described in chapter 6 of the *Mahāparinibbāna Suttanta.* A translation of this text by T. W. Rhys Davids is readily available as *Buddhist Suttas,* volume 11 of "The Sacred Books of the East," edited by F. Max Müller (1881; reprint, New York, 1969). An interesting feature of this account is its clear distinction between the Buddha's *nirvāṇa* and his meditative capacity to cause the complete cessation (*nirodha*) of perceptions, thoughts, and feelings. This passage is often quoted, therefore, against any claim that the early Buddhist view was simply nihilistic and world-renouncing.

Notably absent in this text, however, is any detailed treatment of the classic distinction between *nirvāṇa* with remainder and *nirvāṇa* without remainder. That distinction is more clearly presented in *Itivuttaka,* edited by Ernst Windisch (London, 1889), esp. pp. 38–39. An English translation by F. L. Woodward is in the second volume of *Minor Anthologies of the Pali Canon,* edited by C. A. F. Rhys Davids (London, 1935).

Another commonly analyzed theme is the Buddha's own reticence to describe the status of the enlightened person after death. On this point, there are two particularly provocative textual references. One is the above-mentioned story about Māluṅkyāputta in *Majjhima-Nikāya,* 4 vols., edited by Vilhelm Trenckner, Robert Chalmers, and C. A. F. Rhys Davids (London, 1887–1925), *suttas* 63–64; the other is in *The Saṃyutta-Nikāya of the Sutta Pitaka,* 6 vols., edited by Léon Freer (London, 1884–1904), vol. 3, p. 118. English translations of these two complete collections are, respectively, *The Collection of the Middle Length Sayings,* 3 vols., translated by I. B. Horner (London, 1954–1959), and *The Book of Kindred Sayings,* 5 vols., translated by C. A. F. Rhys Davids and F. L. Woodward (London, 1917–1930).

As already mentioned, descriptions of *nirvāṇa* are for the most part posed in negative terms; the interested reader can find a multitude of examples by consulting, for example, the excellent indexes in the collections of early Pali texts cited above. One particularly striking exception to this rule, however, is found in *The Saṃyutta-Nikāya,* vol. 4, p. 373. This passage gives a rather lengthy string of mostly positive equivalents to *nirvāṇa,* including terms that mean "truth," "the farther shore," "the stable," "peace," "security," "purity," and so forth. Such positive characterizations of *nirvāṇa* are found elsewhere, but never in quite so concentrated a list.

On the issue of the transcendent, mystical, or metaphysical aspect of *nirvāṇa* in the early Buddhist tradition, a pivotal textual reference is in *Udāna,* edited by Paul Steinthal (London, 1948). An English translation also occurs in volume 2 of Woodward's *Minor Anthologies,* cited above. On pages 80–81 of *Udāna,* there is found an indubitable reference to a state of mind or a place beyond birth and death, beyond all discrimination and ordinary perceptions. Controversy still continues over the proper interpretation of the passage. In Rune E. A. Johansson's *Psychology of Nirvāṇa* (London, 1969), for example, there is a sustained discussion of the enlightened state of mind as being a mystical, transempirical, nondifferentiated state of consciousness. The passage from *Udāna* naturally figures prominently in Johansson's argument. On the other hand, this viewpoint is severely criticized in David J. Kalupahana's *Buddhist Philosophy: A Historical Analysis* (Honolulu, 1976), chap. 7. By interpreting this passage as referring to the state of cessation (*nirodha*) just prior to the Buddha's death but not to ordinary *nirvāṇa* in this world, Kalupahana argues that early Buddhism consistently maintained that the achievement of *nirvāṇa* does not require, or entail, any transempirical form of perception. In this regard, Kalupahana is expanding on the theory that early Buddhism was primarily empirical in outlook, an interpretation first fully developed in Kulitassa Nanda Jayatilleke's *Early Buddhist Theory of Knowledge* (London, 1963).

Another controversial issue among modern scholars is the relationship between early Buddhism and the contemporary form of Hinduism. Whereas Kalupahana's approach sharply distinguishes the early Buddhist view of *nirvāṇa* from the contemporary Hindu ideal of the unity of *ātman* with *brahman,* Johansson tends to see a common mystical element in the two. A generally more balanced and convincing position on this point can be found in the thorough discussion of Kashi Nath Upadhyaya's *Early Buddhism and the Bhagavadgītā* (Delhi, 1971).

A good introduction to the modern view of *nirvāṇa* from the standpoint of the only living tradition of Abhidharma, the Theravāda, is Walpola Rahula's *What the Buddha Taught,* rev. ed. (Bedford, U.K., 1967), chap. 4. This small work is highly regarded for its ability to explain the gist of centuries of Abhidharmic analysis in a straightforward, accurate, and yet nontechnical manner. On the way *nirvāṇa* actually functions today as an ethical ideal in Theravāda daily life, see Winston L. King's *In the Hope of Nibbana: An Essay of Theravada Buddhist Ethics* (La Salle, Ill., 1964). For a more historical and specialized approach to the development of the early Abhidharma views of *nirvāṇa,* see Edward Conze's *Buddhist Thought in India* (1962; reprint, Ann Arbor, Mich., 1970), esp. sections 1.5 and 2.3. Although this book is poorly written and organized, it still contains some information not readily available in English elsewhere.

For Nāgārjuna and the Mādhyamika school, the *locus classicus* is Nāgārjuna's discussion in chapter 25 of his *Mūlamadhyamakakārikā.* The complete Sanskrit original and English translation of this work with extensive commentary is found in David J. Kalupahana's *Nagarjuna: The Philosophy of the Middle Way* (Albany, N.Y., 1985). A good discussion of Nāgārjuna's basic position with respect to *nirvāṇa* also appears in Frederick J. Streng's *Emptiness: A Study in Religious Meaning* (New York, 1967), pp. 69–81.

For studying the Yogācāra and idealist position, the reader may wish to consult *The Laṅkāvatāra Sūtra,* translated by D. T. Suzuki (1932; reprint, Boulder, Colo., 1978). The identifications of *nirvāṇa* with the pure *ālaya-vijñāna* or the *tathāgata-garbha,* as well as with the mind released from delusional discriminations are particularly discussed in sections 18, 38, 63, 74, 77, and 82. For the more systematically philosophical developments of the Yogācāra tradition, the reader may refer to the following works. Asaṅga's *Mahāyānasaṃgraha* has been translated and edited by Étienne Lamotte in *La somme du Grand Véhicule d'Asaṅga,* vol. 2 (Louvain, 1939). Translations of Vasubandhu's *Viṃśatikā* and *Triṃśikā* by Clarence H. Hamilton and Wing-tsit Chan, respectively, can be found in *A Source Book in Indian Philosophy,* edited by Sarvepalli Radhakrishnan and Charles A. Moore (Princeton, N. J., 1957). Sylvain Lévi's *Matériaux pour l'étude du système Vijñaptimātra* (Paris, 1932) remains the definitive discussion on Vasubandhu's writings. For an analysis of Dignāga's thought, see Hattori Masaaki's *Dignāga, on Perception* (Cambridge, Mass., 1968).

For a straightforward and detailed discussion of Indian Buddhist theories of *nirvāṇa,* see Nalinaksha Dutt's *Mahāyāna Buddhism* (rev. ed., Delhi, 1978), chap. 7. Although sometimes biased against the Abhidharma traditions, his account of the differences among the Indian Buddhist schools is very good. For a thorough and fascinating discussion of the attempts of Western scholars to interpret the idea of *nirvāṇa* as found primarily in the Pali texts, see Guy R. Welbon's *The Buddhist Nirvāṇa and Its Western Interpreters* (Chicago, 1968). Welbon includes a good bibliography of works in Western languages. His book culminates in the famous debate between Louis de La Vallée Poussin (1869–1938) and Theodore Stcherbatsky (Fedor Shcherbatskii, 1866–1942). Both were noted as first-rate commentators on Mahāyāna Buddhism, but their own personalities and temperaments led them to take distinctively different views of Buddhism and its intent. Thus, in examining the same early Buddhist texts, the former emphasized the yogic and religious aspects whereas the latter favored the philosophical. Despite their limitations, however, La Vallée Poussin's *Nirvāṇa* (Paris, 1925) and Stcherbatsky's *The Conception of Buddhist Nirvāṇa* (Leningrad, 1927) remain classic works on this subject.

East Asian Traditions

For the reasons given in the essay, the idea of *nirvāṇa* is not discussed as explicitly in the East Asian as the South Asian traditions. When *nirvāṇa* is analyzed by East Asian Buddhists, the sharply etched distinctions among the various Indian Mahāyāna schools are softened. A clear example of this is D. T. Suzuki's *Outlines of Mahayana Buddhism* (New York, 1963), chap. 13. In this chapter, and indeed throughout the book, Suzuki approaches the ideas of Mahāyāna Buddhists as coming from discrete traditions but involving an underlying common spirit.

For the view of the Tiantai school as developed by Zhiyi, the most thorough discussion in English is Leon N. Hurvitz's *Zhiyi (538–597); An Introduction to the Life and Ideas of a Chinese Buddhist Monk* (Brussels, 1962). For the impact of the Tiantai idea of inherent enlightenment on Japanese Buddhism in the Kamakura period, see the comprehensive study in Tamura Yoshirō's *Kamakura shinbukkyō shisō no kenkyū* (Tokyo, 1965).

Like Tiantai, the Huayan tradition has not yet been comprehensively studied in Western works. One of the better philosophical overviews of Huayan theory in relation to enlightenment is the discussion about Fazang in Fung Youlan's *A History of Chinese Philosophy,* translated by Derk Bodde (Princeton, N. J., 1953), vol. 2, chap. 8. Fazang is also central to the analysis in Francis D. Cook's *Huayan Buddhism: The Jewel Net of Indra* (University Park, Pa., 1977). Essays on the history of Huayan practice are included in *Studies in Chan and Huayan,* edited by Robert M. Gimello and Peter N. Gregory (Honolulu, 1984).

On the theory of the four realms of reality (*fajie*), the culmination of which is the "nonobstruction between thing and things," a key text is Chengguan's *Huayan fajie xüanjing,* a translation of which is found in Thomas Cleary's *Entry into the Inconceivable* (Honolulu, 1983). One noteworthy point about the translation, however, is that it translates *li* as "noumenon" and *shi* as "phenomenon," a rendering popular in earlier English translations, but now usually replaced by terms less speculative and philosophically misleading, such as, respectively, "principle" and "event" (or "principle" and "thing").

On the Chan distinction between sudden and gradual enlightenment, the exchange of poems by Shenxiu and Huineng is recorded in the first ten sections of the *Liuzu tanjing,* a good translation of which is Philip B. Yampolsky's *The Platform Sutra of the Sixth Patriarch* (New York, 1967). For Zongmi's view of sudden enlightenment and gradual cultivation, as well as Chinul's elaboration on this point, see the discussion in *The Korean Approach to Zen,* translated by Robert E. Buswell, Jr. (Honolulu, 1983). For Dōgen's view of the oneness of cultivation and enlightenment, see Hee-Jin Kim's *Dōgen Kigen: Mystical Realist* (Tucson, 1975), chap. 3, and my *Zen Action/Zen Person* (Honolulu, 1981), chaps. 6–7.

For an overview of the Pure Land tradition and, in particular, Shinran's view that enlightenment is unattainable through any efforts of one's own, see Alfred Bloom's *Shinran's Gospel of Pure Grace* (Tucson, 1965), still the only major objective study of Shinran in English. There are two good translation series of Shinran's works: the "Ryūkoku Translation Series" and the "Shin Buddhism Translation Series," both of Kyoto, Japan. Neither series is complete but, between the two, most of Shinran's works have been adequately translated. The quotation in the foregoing essay is from the first volume of the latter series, namely, *The Letters of Shinran: A Translation of Mattōshō,* edited and translated by Ueda Yoshifumi (Kyoto, 1978).

For Kūkai's view on the distinctiveness of Esoteric Buddhism, a key text is *Benkenmitsu nikyo ron* (On distinguishing the two teachings—Exoteric and Esoteric). On the role of ritual in enlightenment, see his *Sokushin jōbutsu gi* (On achieving buddhahood with this very body) and *Shōji jissō gi* (On sound-word-reality). English translations of these works and others can be conveniently found in Yoshito S. Hakeda's *Kūkai: Major Works* (New York, 1972).

New Sources

Collins, S. *Nirvāṇa and Other Buddhist Felicities: Utopias of the Pali Imaginaire.* New York, 1998.

Gombrich, R. F. *Kindness and Compassion as Means to Nirvāṇa.* Amsterdam, 1998.

Kasulis, Thomas P. "Nirvāṇa." In *Buddhism and Asian History,* edited by Joseph Mitsuo Kitagawa and Mark D. Cummings, pp. 395–408. New York, 1989.

Obermiller, E., and H. S. Sobati. *Nirvāṇa in Tibetan Buddhism.* Delhi, 1988.

Sukla, K. *Nagarjuna Bauddha Pratisthanam, Nature of Bondage and Liberation in Buddhist Systems: Proceedings of Seminar Held in 1984.* Gorakhpur, India, 1988.

Swaris, N. *The Buddha's Way to Human Liberation: A Socio-Historical Approach.* Dehiwala, Sri Lanka, 1999.

Thomas, E. J. *The Road to Nirvāṇa: A Selection of the Buddhist Scriptures Translated from the Pali.* Rutland, Vt., 1992.

Tilakaratne, A., and the University of Kelaniya. *Nirvāṇa and Ineffability: A Study of the Buddhist Theory of Reality and Language.* Sri Lanka, 1993.

THOMAS P. KASULIS (1987)
Revised Bibliography

NISHIDA KITARŌ (1870–1945) is generally considered the most original modern Japanese philosopher and the galvanizing force behind the creation of the Kyoto school of philosophy. Nishida, who incorporated Mahāyāna Buddhist spirituality and its worldview into his philosophical system, made his debut in Japanese philosophical circles in 1907, while he was a professor of psychology and logic at the Fourth Higher School in Kanazawa. After a year of teaching at Gakushūin, the Peers School, in Tokyo, he became, in 1910, a professor at the Imperial University of Kyoto, where his career flourished. Nishida's personal life during this period, however, was plagued by a series of illnesses and the deaths of several members of his family, causing him to call the source of philosophy the "pathos of life" rather than the "wonder." His retirement from the university in 1928 marked the beginning of a productive period of philosophizing. He died on June 7, 1945, two months before the bombing of Hiroshima and Nagasaki. During his lifetime, Nishida was widely recognized in Japan as a leading intellectual and a voice of conscience. His writings, lectures, and correspondence are compiled in nineteen volumes titled *Nishida Kitarō Zenshū* (*Collected Works of Nishida Kitarō*, 4th edition, 1987–1989).

Beginning in his midtwenties, Nishida underwent Rinzai Zen Buddhist practice for a decade, and this imparted a unique flavor to his philosophical thinking. *Zazen*, or the practice of seated meditation, requires the full engagement of the mind and body. The questions, or *kōan*, given by the master, carry the practitioner beyond the ordinary mental habits characterized by the subject-object dichotomy. Zen practice was a personally self-transforming experience for Nishida, and it opened up the vital reality that preceded mental analysis. Nishida incorporated epistemological principles of unity (of mind and body, of subject and object) into his philosophical vocabulary, and he advanced such ideas as pure experience, absolute nothingness, and action-intuition. The Zen tenet that each individual possesses the Buddha nature also underscored Nishida's philosophical vision.

NISHIDA'S THOUGHT. In 1939 Nishida reflected on his philosophical path and noted that his aim had been "to approach things from the most immediate and most fundamental standpoint from which everything emerges and to which everything returns" (*Collected Works* 9, p. 3). Indeed, while he was still a higher school student, he was convinced that reality (*jitsuzai*), as it is, is absolute (*genjitsu sono mama*) (*Collected Works* 1, p. 7). In his first book, *Zen no kenkyū* (An inquiry into the good, 1911), he unfolded his view of the ontological primacy of experience over an individual self—experiences make up a person rather than a person "having" experiences. By taking pure experience (*junsui keiken*)—the primary mode of experience before its bifurcation into subject and object—as the unifying principle, Nishida attempted to analyze the objective world. In this study he was indebted to the philosophical language of William James (1842–1910) and Henri Bergson (1859–1941). Dissatisfied with the psychological aspects of this approach, however, Nishida proceeded to question the nature of intuition and logical reasoning. He put these under scrutiny by engaging in a dialogue with modern mathematical theories, as well as with German neo-Kantianism and Husserlian phenomenology.

This series of philosophical investigations resulted in Nishida's second book, *Jikaku ni okeru chokkan to hansei* (Intuition and reflection in self-consciousness, 1917). Therein he made a detailed analysis of self-consciousness (*jikaku*); that is, consciousness that gives rise to self-awareness as the all-encompassing system of which intuition and cognition are two aspects. Through this investigation, he arrived at the primacy of free will, which transcends cognition and on account of which experiences are repeatable. Furthermore, he saw at the ground of free will ("that which acts") a field of consciousness ("that which sees"), which he developed in his essay, "*Basho*" ("Topos" or "Field," 1926). *Basho* is the matrix wherein all things come into being and from which they disappear. Nishida called *basho* "absolute nothingness" (*zettai mu*) because in itself it is an unobjectifiable reality transcending both being (*u*) and nonbeing (*mu*). His reflections on the nature of time explain "absolute nothingness" as a moment that comes into being at one "present" and disappears in the next. If the present moment were some kind of being that could be grasped, there would be no time; if the present were simply nonbeing, there would also be no time. Time, then, should be considered the coincidence of absolutely nothing and being. The present moment (i.e., absolute nothingness) is where being and nonbeing come together (*Collected Works* 14, pp. 140–141). Furthermore, Nishida saw time as the continuation of discrete or discontinuous moments, and as such time has a spatial extension, inasmuch as space has a temporal direction. Nishida came to call these contradictory features inherent in the very mode of reality "dialectical."

Nishida's basic assertion was that cognition is a phenomenon of consciousness. Taking a hint from Aristotle's definition of *hypokeimenon* (substance), Nishida proposed a "logic of *basho*" (*basho no ronri*) that includes the very act of judgment within itself. If Aristotle's logic is a logic that focuses on the subject-term of the proposition, as the observer studies and classifies the subject under discussion, Nishida attempted to account for how such an observer is actually included in making logical pronouncements. Nishida considered predicates to be already contained in the field of consciousness in which the observer is embedded. The one who judges emerges from the field of consciousness at the moment of intellectual reflection and submerges back into it at the moment of volition and experience.

Nishida sometimes developed his thought in response to specific challenges and issues of his day. By the end of the 1920s, Marxism had become an intellectual fashion among Japanese thinkers. Although Nishida did not personally embrace it, Marxism challenged him to add social and historical dimensions to his thought. The rise to power of the Nazis in Germany in the 1930s drew his attention to world affairs and led him to reflect on the meaning of history and race, and on the nature and role of the state.

As Nishida's perspective grew progressively global and more concrete, he moved away from the language of self-consciousness, and in its stead he developed his dialectics. In his *"Benshōhōteki ippansha to shite no sekai"* (The world as the dialectical universal, 1934), he described the individual self as "none other than an individual determination of the self-determining world" (*Collected Works* 7, p. 203). This is not to belittle the significance of the individual self but rather to emphasize the universal dimension of each individual. Human existence, obtained as the self-determination of the world, is by definition rife with self-contradictions. Precisely by knowing the profound contradictions that lie at the base of our self-existence, Nishida suggested that we undergo absolute negation and arrive at absolute affirmation, which is a step beyond the philosophy of anxiety or *Angst*, the trend that dominated the European philosophical scene.

In his 1935 essay, "*Kōiteki chokkan no tachiba*" (The standpoint of action-intuition), Nishida elaborated on the idea of action-intuition (*kōiteki chokkan*) and the role of "things" (*mono*). A thing is not just an item over there, it exists in vital relation to us and incites our action: "We see things by our action, and things determine us, just as we determine them" (*Collected Works* 8, p. 131). Further, he came to describe the authentic mode of action in terms of our "becoming a thing," that is, for us to embody the full objective reality of our physical existence. Nishida wrote the following: "Just as the body of an artist is the organ of art, so the body of a scholar is an organ of scholarship; the life of an artist lies in beauty and that of a scholar in truth. The operation of our cognition does not exist separate from our body" (*Collected Works* 8, p. 174). Our body is established as the self-determination of the historical world, and as such is a "historical body" (*Collected Works* 8, p. 180).

For Nishida, the essence of the self lies in one's creativity and expressive operations. This emphasis on creativity (*poiesis*, artistic and otherwise) is central to his definition of the person. We are born into this world as "that which is created" (*tsukurareta mono*), but we in turn become "that which creates" (*tsukuru mono*). Accordingly, a society that does not allow individual freedom to be creative is doomed—this was his bone of contention with totalitarian societies.

In "*Ronri to seimei*" (Logic and life, 1936), Nishida examined his thesis that logic is closely tied with the expressive self-formation of historical life. In "*Shu no seisei hatten no mondai*" (The problem of generation and development of species, 1937), he emphasized the radical irreducibility of the individual—"An individual is an individual only in standing against another individual" (*Collected Works* 8, p. 523)—as he meditated on "freedom" and "necessity" for individuals who exist in the historical world. In his 1939 essay "*Zettai mujunteki jiko dōitsu*" (Absolutely contradictory self-identity), he fully developed his dialectical logic, in which the individual, like a monad, assumes a double structure: that which reflects the world and that which is simultaneously a focal point of the world. Differing from Leibnizian monads, however, Nishida considered individuals as "self-fashioning," creative, and dynamic; each individual is a living history in that each, being creative, contributes to the formation of history (*Collected Works* 9, p. 155 and pp. 169–173).

For the rest of his life, Nishida continued to develop his dialectics in terms of the contradictory self-identity of the self and the world as two vantage points, and the one and the many as the modality. His final essay, "*Bashoteki ronri to shūkyōteki sekaikan*" (The logic of *basho* and the religious worldview), completed two months before his death, dealt with the religious consciousness of the person explained in terms of the "logic of *basho*."

NISHIDA'S POLITICAL LIFE. Born in 1870, the third year of the Meiji era, Nishida witnessed the dynamic period when Japan began to interact with the wider world after two centuries of self-imposed isolation. There was a prevailing sense of freedom and optimism among the young generation of that time, and Nishida was no exception. He supported the idea of a constitution and felt personal respect for Emperor Meiji as the head of the modern state. But he was against any ultranationalistic movements that deified the emperor to justify Japan's colonial aggression as staged by the military. Nishida took no part in promoting the cult of Shintō as a national rite, and he was critical of the government's indoctrination of youth.

Through his connection with the Peers School, Nishida came to know Konoe Ayamaro (or Fumimaro) and Kido Kōichi, who were prominent members of the "court group" that closely assisted Emperor Hirohito through 1945. But Nishida's opinions concerning politics and education were deemed overly idealistic to those engulfed in politics.

Nishida's political life came under criticism by Western scholars from the 1980s through the mid-1990s, partly in association with the German philosopher Martin Heidegger (1889–1976). The argument was made that if Heidegger was connected with Nazism, Nishida could have been similarly connected with Japanese fascism. Remarks by Nishida were taken out of context and used to depict him as an ultranationalist, and his philosophy as "intrinsically nationalistic" by implication. A clear distinction between regionalism and nationalism could have clarified the confusion: celebration of one's cultural heritage (regionalism) does not necessarily make a person nationalistic. The perspective of cultural pluralism can shed light on what Nishida was attempting to achieve by ideas such as "Oriental nothingness." Nishida was depicted as a nationalist by Western scholars who relied on the views of a small number of ideological Japanese scholars. The debate began to subside as scholars recognized the need for returning to and reevaluating Nishida's philosophical texts, essays, and letters.

BIBLIOGRAPHY

Nishida's works are cited above according to the volume and page number(s) of Nishida Kitarō, *Nishida Kitarō Zenshū* (*Collected Works of Nishida Kitarō*), 19 vols., 4th ed. (Tokyo, 1987–

1989). For an intellectual biography of Nishida see Michiko Yusa, *Zen and Philosophy: An Intellectual Biography of Nishida Kitarō* (Honolulu:, 2002), which includes English translations of ten essays by Nishida. For a Japanese biography see Michiko Yusa, *Denki Nishida Kitarō* (A biography of Nishida Kitarō), supp. vol. 1 of *Nishida Tetsugaku Senshū* (Selected works of Nishidan philosophy; Kyoto, Japan, 1998). Invaluable biographical information can be found in Keiji Nishitani, *Nishida Kitarō*, translated by Seisaku Yamamoto and James Heisig (Berkeley and Los Angeles, 1991).

For translations of Nishida's works, see *An Inquiry into the Good*, translated by Masao Abe and Christopher Ives (London and New Haven, Conn., 1990); *A Study of Good*, translated by Valdo Viglielmo (Tokyo, 1960); *Intuition and Reflection in Self-Consciousness*, translated by Valdo Viglielmo, Yoshinori Takeuchi, and Joseph O'Leary (Albany, N.Y., 1987); *Art and Morality*, translated by David Dilworth and Valdo Viglielmo (Honolulu:, 1973); *L'Io e il Tu*, translated by Renato Andolfato (Padova, Italy, 1996); *Fundamental Problems of Philosophy: The World of Action and the Dialectical World*, translated by David Dilworth (Tokyo, 1970); *Intelligibility and the Philosophy of Nothingness*, translated by Robert Schinzinger (Tokyo, 1958; reprint, Westport, Conn., 1973); *Logik des Ortes: Der Anfang der modernen Philosophie in Japan*, translated by Rolf Elberfeld (Darmstadt, Germany, 1999); *Last Writings: Nothingness and the Religious Worldview*, translated by David Dilworth (Honolulu:, 1987); and Michiko Yusa, "The Logic of *Topos* and the Religious Worldview," *Eastern Buddhist* 19, no. 2 (1986): 1–29 and *Eastern Buddhist* 20, no. 1 (1987): 81–119.

Other translations of Nishida's essays include "On the Doubt of Our Heart," translated by Jeff Shore and Fusako Nagasawa, *Eastern Buddhist* 17, no. 2 (1984): 7–11; "An Explanation of Beauty," translated by Steve Odin, *Monumenta Nipponica* 42, no. 2 (1987): 215–217; "Gutoku Shinran," translated by Dennis Hirota, *Eastern Buddhist* 28, no. 2 (1995): 242–244; and "The Principle of the New World Order," translated by Yoko Arisaka, *Monumenta Nipponica* 51, no. 1 (1996): 100–105. For a more complete listing, see Wayne Yokoyama, "Nishida Kitarō in Translation: Primary Sources in Western Languages," *Eastern Buddhist* 28, no. 2 (1995): 297–302.

For critical works on Nishida and the Kyoto School, see James Heisig, *Philosophers of Nothingness: An Essay on the Kyoto School* (Honolulu, 2001); James Heisig and John Maraldo, eds., *Rude Awakenings: Zen, the Kyoto School, and the Question of Nationalism* (Honolulu, 1994); Michiko Yusa, "Nishida and the Question of Nationalism," *Monumenta Nipponica* 46, no. 2 (1991): 203–209; Michiko Yusa, "Correspondence," *Monumenta Nipponica* 49, no. 4 (1994): 524–527; Michiko Yusa, "Reflections on Nishida Studies," *Eastern Buddhist* 28, no. 2 (1995): 287–296; Yoko Arisaka, "The Nishida Enigma," *Monumenta Nipponica* 51, no. 1 (1996): 81–99; and Graham Parkes, "The Putative Fascism of the Kyoto School and the Political Correctness of the Modern Academy," *Philosophy East and West* 47, no. 3 (1997): 305–336. On select philosophical concepts of Nishida and his successors, see Michiko Yusa, "Contemporary Buddhist Philosophy," in Eliot Deutsch and Ron Bontekoe, eds., *A Companion to World Philosophies* (Oxford, 1997), pp. 564–572. For Nishida's students and European thinkers, see Michiko Yusa, "Philosophy and Inflation: Miki Kiyoshi in Weimar Germany, 1922–1924," *Monumenta Nipponica* 53, no. 1 (1998): 45–71.

MICHIKO YUSA (2005)

NIẒĀM AL-DĪN AWLIYĀʾ

NIẒĀM AL-DĪN AWLIYĀʾ (AH 636–725/1238–1325 CE) was a major Ṣūfī saint of the Chishtī order. Under his leadership, the order expanded into a mass movement across India. Great men of letters from Amīr Khusraw (d. 1325) to Muḥammad Iqbāl (d. 1938) have eulogized his religious charisma and sought solace in prayers at his grave. Muḥammad Tughluq (r. 1324–1351) was a pallbearer at his funeral and built the mausoleum over his grave. It is a measure of Niẓām al-Dīn's authority with the people that Bābur (r. 1526–1530), founder of the Mughal dynasty, felt it necessary, during his conquest of Delhi, to pay his respects at the shrine. It remains a major site of pilgrimage for non-Muslims as well as Muslims.

Niẓām al-Dīn's paternal and maternal grandparents were refugees from Bukhara, two of many distinguished families who fled the depredations of the Mongols in Central Asia. They eventually settled in Badaon, a city to the east of Delhi, where Niẓām al-Dīn was born. When he was perhaps five, his father died. His religious temperament was forged during the years of privation that followed. His mother, Zulaykhah, faced extreme hardship with a serene reliance on the compassion of God that proved a decisive, lasting influence. She recognized in her son an instinct for learning and devotion and encouraged it. His intellectual talents recommended him to the best of Badaon's teachers, and he excelled in all branches of the Islamic sciences.

At sixteen, knowing he could get no further as a scholar in Badaon, he asked permission to go to Delhi. His mother consented, and the family moved to even deeper penury in the capital. In later life, Niẓām al-Dīn recollected with pleasure how often his mother would say, as if announcing an honor, "Today we are the guests of God," meaning that there was no food in the house. He soon established a reputation as a devout scholar with formidable debating skills. He considered a career as a *qāḍī*, intending to help the people by dispensing justice. But instinctive asceticism and mystical yearning, deepened by the example of his teachers (in Badaon, Shādī Muqrī and ʿAlāʾal-Dīn Uṣūlī, and in Delhi, Khawājah Shams al-Dīn and Kamāl al-Dīn Zāhid), had marked him for a different vocation. Accounts he heard of the sanctity of Bābā Farīd al-Dīn Ganj-i Shakar, then head of the Chishtī order, stirred his heart. He visited the venerable *shaykh* in Ajodhan (now Pak Pattan) in northwest Punjab, and there enrolled as his disciple.

According to traditional accounts of Niẓām al-Dīn's life, Bābā Farīd perfected his moral character, erasing from it traces of pride in academic reputation. When Niẓām al-Dīn was only twenty-three, Bābā Farīd appointed him as his successor, ordering him to found a *khānqāh* (lodge) in

Delhi and to "take the spiritual kingdom of Hindustan." Niẓām al-Dīn settled in Ghiyathpur, a village beside the river Jumna, a little way outside the capital. Originally a straw hut, the *khānqāh* of Niẓām al-Dīn became the largest of its kind in India. His reputation grew, as did the *futūḥ* or unsolicited gifts upon which the *khānqāh* depended. People from all classes, including the social and political elite, sought his counsel; many submitted to the rigors of *khānqāh* life to become disciples. His famous disciples included Nāṣir al-Dīn Chirāgh in Delhi, Quṭb al-Dīn Munawwar in the Punjab, Burhān al-Dīn Gharīb in the Deccan, the famous poet Amīr Khusraw, the historian Ẓiyā᾽ al-Dīn Baranī, and the noted scholar Fakhr al-Dīn Zarrādī.

Niẓām al-Dīn never turned anyone away, whatever their initial motives for calling on him, and he did his utmost to satisfy them. He is said to have had achieved such self-transcendence that he lived the problems of others as his own and attended to them with unfailing compassion. He taught through parables (typically presented as anecdotes from the life of holy men) with implicit relevance for the questioner's situation. The latter then had to engage his own resources to work out the course of action appropriate for him, and was thereby relieved of the psychological burden of having felt helpless.

The people's trust in Niẓām al-Dīn also rested on the moral reputation of the *khānqāh*. Following the traditions of the order, any association with political power was rejected; government employment was forbidden to senior disciples; gifts with conditions attached or gifts (like grants of property or land) offering a regular income were refused. Poverty was allowed to alternate with plenty in the resources of the *khānqāh*. Income from *futūḥ* was distributed to the poor as soon as received, or expended in the form of food prepared and served in the *khānqāh*. All who entered the discipline of the *khānqāh*, whatever their eminence outside, were expected to and did serve the poor at table. Such service was essential training for, and the primary expression of, service of God. Niẓām al-Dīn encouraged Islamic scholarship and insisted on the normal rites and other demands of the *sharī῾ah*. The goal of his efforts was a deeper relationship with God, and his Islam was vigorously tolerant and inclusive. Non-Muslims as well as Muslims were drawn to the *khānqāh* as a haven of gentleness and spiritual serenity.

The formative years of the Delhi *khānqāh* coincided with the expansion and consolidation of the Delhi sultanate during the reign of ῾Ala᾽ al-Dīn Khaljī (r. 1296–1316). The sultan's invitations to the saint were always refused, but the sultan neither resented nor feared the other's popularity: ambitious himself, he recognized the absence of worldly ambition in the saint, and exempted his *khānqāh* from the intrusive control he favored for all aspects of political and economic life in his dominions. Later Niẓām al-Dīn again became the object of court intrigue focused on his sanctioning of music as an aid to religious rapture, which the court scholars disapproved. But these machinations, though a nuisance, did not impede Niẓām al-Dīn in his calling: the order continued to expand, and people still flocked to him for guidance and blessing.

A lifetime of vigils and fasting weakened the health of Niẓām al-Dīn. He continually suffered ailments of the stomach and bowels. He died on April 3, 1325, and was buried in the garden of the *khānqāh*. He left no written works. Niẓām al-Dīn's legacy was a lived example, cherished and relived through the centuries by his followers. They remember his example of spiritual wakefulness expressed as service to humanity and his teachings that emphasized that divine compassion was ever present, without discrimination of class or creed: the role of those who loved God was, accordingly, to mirror his compassion and relieve the human distress that arises from physical and spiritual poverty.

BIBLIOGRAPHY

The most important collections of Niẓām al-Dīn's teachings and anecdotes (*malfūẓāt*) are the *Fawā᾽id al-fu᾽ād* by Ḥasan Sijzī (Lucknow, India, 1884) and *Durar-i Niẓāmī* by ῾Alī Jāndār (Hyderabad, India, n.d.). *Fawā᾽id al-fu᾽ād* has been translated by Bruce B. Lawrence as *Niẓām ad-Dīn Awliyā: Morals for the Heart* (New York, 1992). Useful biographical accounts are available in Jamāl Qiwām al-Dīn, *Qiwām al-῾aqā᾽id* (Hyderabad, India, n.d.), and Mīr Khurd, *Siyar al-awlīyā᾽* (Delhi, 1885). The best contemporary chronicle of the Delhi sultanate is Ẓiyā᾽ al-Dīn Baranī, *Tārīkh-i Fīrūz Shāhī* (Calcutta, 1860). In English a popular biography of the saint is Khaliq A. Nizami, *The Life and Times of Shaikh Nizam-u'd-din Auliya* (Delhi, 1991). For a history of the period, see Mohammad Habib and Khaliq A. Nizami, eds., *A Comprehensive History of India*, reprint ed. (Delhi, 1982). For an excellent historical account and evaluation of the Chishtī order, see Khaliq A. Nizami, *Religion and Politics in India during the Thirteenth Century* (Oxford, 2002).

AZRA ALAVI (2005)

NIẒĀM AL-MULK (AH 408–485/1018–1092 CE) was a celebrated Persian vizier. Abū ῾Alī al-Ḥasan ibn ῾Alī ibn Isḥāq al-Ṭūsī was born in Nawqān, a village near Ṭus in Khurāsān. He served two Saljūq sultans, Ālp Arsalān (r. 1063–1073) and his son Malikshāh ibn Ālp Arsalān (r. 1073–1092), and held the honorifics Niẓām al-Mulk (administrator of the realm), Qawām al-Dīn (upholder of religion), and Ghiyâth al-Dawla (mainstay of government). Niẓām al-Mulk was a Shāfi῾ī in law and an Ash῾arī in theology. He befriended Ṣūfīs and built numerous educational institutions, known as *madrasahs*. He was assassinated in 1092 in a small village outside of Iṣfahān. In his seventy-four years, Niẓām al-Mulk rose from being a member of the bureaucracy of the provincial governor of Balkh (in present-day Afghanistan) to the de facto ruler of a vast empire, with a final apotheosis as the archetypal good vizier in the world of Islam.

Modern appraisals of Niẓām al-Mulk, often based on an uncritical distillation of medieval sources, tend to cast him in the mold of later reformist but absolutist rulers, who promoted religious orthodoxy, particularly through the founding of religious institutions, to counter latent forces of anarchy inherent in a world of steadily disintegrating spiritual authority and ever increasing tribal incursions and political conflicts. But a reading of the same sources, shorn of these underlying assumptions, reveals other traits and priorities. The ideal medieval statesman emerging from the scattered references to Niẓām al-Mulk in chronicles, biographies of viziers, manuals of conduct, panegyrics of court poets, and other sources is not the homogenized single icon of a bureaucratic state-builder, but the emblematic site where seemingly discordant civic and personal virtues can be fused together in a concatenated bio/hagiographical account of a life depicted in distinct stages. Thus, as in the biographies of many an outstanding spiritual figure before and after him (including, for example, the Prophet himself or the great poet and mystic Jalāl al-Dīn Rūmī), his precocious gifts are at once spotted and remarked upon, and so in a sense authenticated, by an outstanding contemporary luminary, in his case the great Ṣūfī master Shaykh Abū al-Saʿīd Abū al-Khayr (d. 1049). Later we see Niẓām al-Mulk climb up rapidly on the slippery bureaucratic ladder, stepping on his rivals' toes whenever necessary.

Although biographical information in the medieval Islamic sources on Niẓām al-Mulk is sketchy and the sources often contradict each other, almost all concur on his arduous early years, fraught with financial and political difficulties, before he became a vizier. Although born to a *dihqān* (landed aristocracy dating back to pre-Islamic Iran) family, Niẓām al-Mulk (or his father, for here sources vary) witnessed several injustices in his youth, and the family possessions were confiscated several times when he (or his father) served Ghaznavid (r. 977–1186) officials in Khurāsān. But Niẓām al-Mulk's fortune changed when the Saljūqs entered Khurāsān in 1038. He was recommended to the new sultan either by the provincial governor of Balkh or by the *imām* al-Muwaffaq (d. 1048), the respected leader of the Shāfiʿī faction of Nīshāpūr, again depending on the source one uses. In so doing, al-Muwaffaq bypassed another student of his, the ʿamīd al-Mulk al-Kundurī. Although al-Muwaffaq recommended Niẓām al-Mulk, al-Kundurī also entered into Saljūq service, serving the governor of Khurāsān, who was the brother of the reigning sultan.

In 1063, when Ālp Arsalān succeeded his father and uncle as the sole ruler of the Saljūq Empire, he kept al-Kundurī in office, as recommended by his father. Although initially a Shāfiʿī and Ashʿarī himself, al-Kundurī initiated the public cursing of Shīʿah and Ashāʿirah from the pulpits in Khurāsān in 1062, in retaliation for the *imām* al-Muwaffaq's support of his rival. Several eminent Ashʿarī/Shāfiʿī figures, among them the *imām* al-Ḥaramayn al-Juwaynī (d. 1085) and the Ṣūfī master Abū Qāsim al-Qushayrī (d. 1072), left for Mecca in protest. They did not return until Niẓām al-Mulk reversed these divisive policies and brought the downfall of his rival. Even in the most sympathetic accounts of the life of Niẓām al-Mulk, he is held responsible for the execution of al-Kundurī in 1064, whose office he inherited. The dramatic aspect of the episode is enhanced in a number of sources by inserting al-Kundurī's oracular last words, addressed to Niẓām al-Mulk: "You have taught these Turks the practice of killing their viziers."

The long years of Niẓām al-Mulk's administrative reign are regarded as the halcyon days of the dynasty he served, with his own personal retinue reflecting the opulence of the realm he managed. Al-Subkī's (d. 1369/70) entry on Niẓām al-Mulk in his *Ṭabaqāt al-Shāfiʿīyah al-kubrá* suggests that he had a personal army of Turkic slaves numbering over eighty thousand men, that he was one of the richest men in the Islamic lands, and that he conducted the affairs of the vast empire with effortless ease. But worldly riches are nicely balanced in the sources by unworldly concerns, and many anecdotes depict him identifying himself with Ṣūfīs and their spiritual interests and taking an active part in religious debates of his time. In his *Ghiyāth al-'umam fī iltiyāth al-ẓulam,* written between 1072 and 1085, the *imām* al-Ḥaramayn al-Juwaynī alludes to Niẓām al-Mulk as the most qualified and capable administrator of his time, clearly surpassing the reigning Abbasid caliph in both real power and spiritual legitimacy, a significant compliment, coming as it does from one of the leading jurists of the eleventh century.

Niẓām al-Mulk's downfall also bears the teleological stamp of the didactic and polemical reading of history inherent in the sources. In spite of his long years in power, Niẓām al-Mulk finally fell victim to the arbitrary nature of medieval kingship, like so many of his predecessors and successors. Spearheaded by the sultan Malikshāh's favorite wife, Turkān Khātūn (d. 1094), and exploiting a succession dispute, his enemies at the Saljūq court succeeded in convincing the sultan that the old vizier harbored ambitions to rule the empire. The history of the demise of Niẓām al-Mulk is cast in the familiar medieval mold of heresy, the stealthy intervention of women in politics, and conspiracy at court. Turkān Khātūn, allied with the Ismāʿīlīs and others accused of being enemies of Islam, persuaded Malikshāh to charge Niẓām al-Mulk with nepotism and treachery. The vizier wrote back, reminding the sultan that his fate was intertwined with Niẓām al-Mulk's fate, and that God, who had given one the turban, had given the other the crown. Malikshāh replaced him with one of his wife's allies, the Shīʿī Tāj al-Mulk (d. 1093), a person of unsound religious views, according to the sources. A year later, Niẓām al-Mulk was assassinated, allegedly by adherents of another unorthodox creed, the Ismāʿīlīs. On that oft-evoked complicity, too, there is much disagreement in the sources, as some hold Malikshāh responsible for his vizier's death and some even claim that Malikshāh himself had, at the instigation of his wife, converted to Ismāʿīlism and was thus manipulated into arranging for the murder of his own vizier, the upholder of orthodox religion. Perhaps the only flicker of truth in this fog of conspiracy was the charge of nepotism, for the Vizier did, after all, secure the continuation of his policies by installing a number of his relatives in prominent positions. Five of his sons, two of his grandsons, and one great-grandson held the office of vizier to one or another of the rulers after him, though none could reach his eminence, as recounted succinctly in Ibn Funduq's (d. 1170) *Tā rīkh-i Bayhaq*, a rich source on the rise and lingering influence of Niẓām al-Mulk's family in the Saljūq empire.

The more general attribution that he lived and died a stalwart of orthodoxy, tacitly accepted by many modern scholars of medieval Islam, should be reconsidered. Nearly contemporary Shīʿī sources, such as ʿAbd al-Jalīl al-Qazvīnī (d. after 1189) in his *Kitāb al-naqd* (1164/65), and the poet Ibn al-Habbārīyah (d. 1115) in his anthology, have praised Niẓām al-Mulk for his evenhandedness, and it should be borne in mind that one of the vizier's daughters was married to the son of the prominent Shīʿī leader, Sayyid Murtaḍā al-Qummī. There is praise for his tolerance from opposing sides. In the annals of the year 1077 in his *Al-Muntaẓam*, the Ḥanbalī historian Ibn al-Jawzī (d. 1200) has preserved a letter from Niẓām al-Mulk to Shaykh Abū Isḥāq al-Shīrāzī (d. 1083), whom he had appointed to teach at the Niẓāmīyah in Baghdad. It concerns a series of riots by the Ḥanbalīs of Baghdad following fiery sermons by the Shāfiʿī professor at the Niẓāmīyah. Niẓām al-Mulk advises the professor to be prudent in his sermons, especially as many Ḥanbalīs lived in Baghdad, and the *imām* Aḥmad ibn Ḥanbal (d. 855), the founder of the legal and theological school that bore Niẓām al-Mulk's name, was among the most venerated figures of Islam. Niẓām al-Mulk also informed the shaykh that the Niẓāmīyah, in line with his overall policy, was conceived to facilitate learning, to protect the learned, and to discourage sectarian strife. Should the *madrasahs* fall short of this objective, he would have no alternative but to shut them down. This last cautionary statement is significant in the context of the persisting misapprehension that clouds modern scholarship on the *madrasah*s sponsored by Niẓām al-Mulk. The Niẓāmīyah were not generally perceived as instruments of government policy by medieval Muslim historians, nor did they succeed in transforming the highly personal structure of Islamic education. In fact, medieval histories preserve little to document a long-lasting effect of the Niẓāmīyahs, beyond their founder's lifetime, on the educational infrastructure of Islamic society.

Similarly, and contrary to the tone of most modern studies on Niẓām al-Mulk, his authorship of a treatise on political and courtly decorum, the *Siyar al-Mulūk*, does not loom large in the medieval accounts. The *Siyar al-Mulūk*, rather than a treatise on political thought in the modern sense of the term, is essentially an ethical treatise, which bears more of a resemblance to the ninth-century pseudo-Aristotelian *Secretum Secretorum* than to Machiavelli's *The Prince*.

BIBLIOGRAPHY
For a general introduction to the life of Niẓām al-Mulk, see Neguin Yavari, "Niẓām al-Mulk Remembered: A Study in Historical Representation," Ph.D.diss., Columbia University, 1992. For sectarian strife, see Richard W. Bulliet, *Patricians of Nishapur: A Study in Medieval Islamic Social History* (Cambridge, Mass., 1972). For a critique of the Sunnī revivalist project, see Roy Mottahedeh, "The Transmission of Learning: The Role of the Islamic Northeast" in *Madrasa: La transmission du savoir dans le monde musulman*, edited by Nicole Grandin and Marc Gaborieau (Paris, 1997); see especially pages 65 and following. For the *madrasas*, see Daphna Ephrat, *A Learned Society in a Period of Transition: The Sunni ʿUlama' of Eleventh-Century Baghdad* (Albany, N.Y., 2000). For the *Siyar al-Mulûk*, see Hubert Darke's "Introduction" in Niẓām al-Mulk, *The Book of Government or Rules for Kings*, translated and edited by Darke (London, 2d ed., 1978); and Charles-Henri de Fouchécour, *Moralia: Les notions morales dans la littérature persane du 3e/9e au 7e/13e siècle* (Paris, 1986).

NEGUIN YAVARI (2005)

NJORÐR (Njord) is the most outstanding of the group of Germanic gods known as the Vanir. Their war with the Æsir (the primary group of gods) and the move of Njǫrðr, his son Freyr, and his daughter Freyja to the Æsir's citadel, Ásgarðr, as hostages has been seen as a reflection of an actual religious war or the replacement of one cult with another, but it has also been taken as a symbolic explanation of the existence of different aspects of divinity. According to Snorri Sturluson (1179–1241), Njǫrðr is extremely wealthy and prosperous and can grant land and movables to those who call on him. The protector of seafarers and fishermen, he sends favorable winds and calm seas. His dwelling in Ásgarðr is called Nóatún (Harbor), a name that points to his association with sailing. But Njǫrðr does not stay with the Æsir forever; according to the eddic poem *Vafþrúðnismál* (st. 39), after their last battle against the giants and monsters at Ragnarǫk, Njǫrðr will return to the land of the Vanir.

The mythology about Njǫrðr is dominated by his move to Ásgarðr. The incestuous relations allowed among the Vanir were alien to the Æsir, and in the eddic poem *Lokasenna* (st. 36), Loki reproaches Njǫrðr with having begotten his children with his own sister. Njǫrðr enters into a marriage that serves the Æsir but turns out to be a disaster of temperamental incompatibility for both spouses. The legitimacy of Freyr and Freyja was evidently a problem for Snorri, who implies they were the offspring of Njǫrðr and his new wife. The story of this marriage is an intertwining of *Märchenmotive* (folktale motifs) and fertility rites. Through Loki's deceit, the giant Þjazi was killed by the Æsir, and when his daughter Skaði came to Ásgarðr to claim compensation, she was offered her choice of a husband from among the Æsir, provided that she look only at their feet. She expected her choice to be the handsome Baldr, but she had picked Njǫrðr, whose feet were evidently washed clean by his watery domain. Skaði had accepted this arrangement only on condition that the gods would make her laugh; Loki was able to do so by tying one end of a string to his scrotum and the other to a goat's beard; when both pulled, there was a lot of shouting and howling until Loki fell on his knees in front of Skaði, who burst out laughing. Unfortunately, Skaði and Njǫrðr turned out to be incompatible; they alternated living at Nóatún and at Þrymheimr, but she hated living by the sea, and he hated living in the mountains. Snorri mentions that she left her husband, so there was probably a myth recounting her return to her father's estate.

Despite the scanty information about Njǫrðr in Old Norse literature, his cult was important in Germanic antiquity. This is confirmed by the considerable number of cult place-names, which occur particularly in eastern Sweden and western Norway, but in Denmark and Iceland as well. Whereas the Norwegian and Icelandic place-names are always found near the coast, as would be expected for a seafaring god, the Swedish place-names are always found in inland agricultural areas, suggesting that Njǫrðr was worshiped as a fertility god in those areas. A number of the Swedish place-names go back to an original *Njarðarvé* (Njǫrðr's temple) and show that he was publically worshiped at an early period. Worship at a later period is implied by the place-names in southeastern Norway going back to *Njarðarhof*, where *hof* is a newer word that also means temple. Another indication of his importance in the pagan religion is found in the extant remnant of the pagan law code of Iceland, where it is laid down that a person performing legal business should swear an oath on the holy ring, saying "so help me Freyr and Njǫrðr and the all-powerful god."

A major problem in discussing Njǫrðr is his relation to the mother goddess of the Inguaeonic tribes, Nerthus, whom the first-century CE Tacitus (*Germania*, ch. 40) says was worshiped on an island in the Baltic; he equates her with *Terra mater* (Mother Earth). *Njǫrðr* and the Latino-Germanic *Nerthus* reflect the proto-Germanic **nerþuz*, but why is the earlier deity a goddess and the later one a god? The change has been ascribed to the "masculinization" of agriculture that occurred between Roman times and the Viking Age, for according to Tacitus, the early Germanic tribes left the cultivation of the land to women, the elderly, and the weaker members of the extended family (*Germania*, ch. 14), whereas farming in the Viking period was carried out by men. According to Jan de Vries in *Altgermanische Religiongeschichte* (1967), such an explanation is not wholly convincing, as it does not account for the shift of the deity's main domain from fertility to the sea and navigation. Modern research tends to emphasize the fact that Njǫrðr has always been a "man of the sea," and the change of sex is explained by postulating a hermaphroditic deity or supposing that Njǫrðr and Nerthus were brother and sister.

The significance of Njǫrðr is also reflected in his role in medieval euhemeristic tales describing the legendary early history of Scandinavia, in which he is said to have assumed the throne of Sweden after "King Óðinn" passed away. Such peace and plenteous harvests followed that the Swedes believed he controlled the crops and the well-being of humankind.

SEE ALSO Germanic Religion; Loki; Óðinn.

BIBLIOGRAPHY

Clunies Ross, Margaret. *Prolonged Echoes: Old Norse Myths in Medieval Northern Society*, vol. 1, *The Myths*. Odense, Denmark, 1994.

Dumézil, Georges. *From Myth to Fiction: The Saga of Hadingus*. Translated by Derek Coltman. Chicago, 1973.

Lindow, John. *Scandinavian Mythology: An Annotated Bibliography*. New York, 1988.

Turville-Petre, Gabriel. *Myth and Religion of the North: The Religion of Ancient Scandinavia*. London, 1964.

Vries, Jan de. *Altgermanische Religionsgeschichte*, vol. 2. 2d rev. ed. Berlin, 1967.

EDGAR C. POLOMÉ (1987)
ELIZABETH ASHMAN ROWE (2005)

NOAH, son of Lamech and father of Shem, Ham, and Japheth, according to the Hebrew scriptures (*Gn.* 5:29–30, 6:10); chosen by God to be saved from the universal flood that destroyed the earth. Plausibly, this story has ancient Mesopotamian roots, as do many other features of the biblical flood traditions. But while ancient Sumerian tradition and its reflexes refer to a hero who attained immortality after the flood, biblical tradition speaks of the mortality of Noah.

As one born in the tenth generation after Adam, Noah is clearly linked to Adam. Indeed, his position as an Adam *redivivus* is more expressly indicated in the popular etymology of his name in *Genesis* 5:29, which regards him as the one who "will comfort us from our labor and the travail of our hands, out of the earth which Yahveh has cursed," a thematic and verbal allusion (and, indeed, a hoped-for end) to the divine curses announced in *Genesis* 3:17. Moreover, after the flood Noah and his sons are given the same blessing and earthly stewardship as was Adam, with the singular exception that now flesh is permitted as food, whereas Adam was a vegetarian (*Gn.* 9:1–7, 1:28–30). In the postdiluvian world, Noah also goes beyond his ancestor Adam insofar as he is considered a man of domesticated labor—a vintner (*Gn.* 9:19). Later biblical tradition remembered Noah as the hero of the flood (*Is.* 54:9) and as one of the three most "righteous" men of antiquity (*Ez.* 14:14, 14:20). In this latter attribution, there is an obvious link to the statement in *Genesis* 6:9 that "Noah was a righteous man; perfect in his generation."

In the Midrash and *aggadah*, rabbis developed the traditions of Noah's righteousness, emphasizing, on the one hand, both his fellow feelings and his concern that his generation repent of their sins (a tradition also found in the church fathers) and, on the other hand, his concern for all animals and species of life. A more jaundiced note is sounded by both the rabbinic view that Noah merely excelled in his own generation, which was very evil, but was not himself of exemplary righteousness (*Gn. Rab.* 30.9) and the later Hasidic comment of Yaʿaqov Yosef of Polonnoye that Noah was a self-centered *tsaddiq*, or righteous leader, since he did not seek the spiritual-social transformation of the entire people.

In Christianity, Noah served as one of the most important typological figures insofar as he symbolized the just person who, in a sinful world, submitted in faith to God (cf. *Heb.* 11:7, *Lk.* 17:26, *1 Pt.* 3:20, *2 Pt.* 2:5). The flood, ark, and dove prominent in the biblical story also serve as Christian prefigurations, for just as Noah rises above death by water, so Jesus and the Christians defeat Satan and death by the waters of baptism (*1 Pt.* 3:18–21). In other traditions, Noah prefigures Jesus as one who announces judgment and saves humanity from complete destruction, and his ark symbolizes the church. The dove sent forth by Noah comes to symbolize the Holy Spirit of peace and divine reconciliation moving over the baptismal waters. In Muslim tradition, Noah (Arab., Nuh) also plays a strong role: an entire *sūrah* of the Qurʾān (17) is devoted to him, and Muḥammed considered Noah's life as prototypical of his own.

Bibliography

Allen, D. C. *Legend of Noah: Renaissance Rationalism.* Urbana, Ill., 1949.

Ginzberg, Louis. *The Legends of the Jews* (1909–1938). 7 vols. Translated by Henrietta Szold et al. Reprint, Philadelphia, 1937–1966. See the index, s.v. *Noah.*

Sarna, Nahum M. *Understanding Genesis.* New York, 1972.

Speiser, E. A. *Genesis.* Anchor Bible, vol. 1. Garden City, N.Y., 1964.

New Sources

Bailey, Lloyd R. *Noah: The Person and the Story in History and Tradition.* Studies on Personalities of the Old Testament. Columbia, S.C., 1989.

Ochs, Carol. *The Noah Paradox: Time as Burden, Time as Blessing.* Notre Dame, Ind., 1991.

Pleins, J. David. *When the Great Abyss Opened: Classic and Contemporary Readings of Noah's Flood.* Oxford and New York, 2003.

MICHAEL FISHBANE (1987)
Revised Bibliography

NOCK, ARTHUR DARBY (1902–1963), Anglo-American historian of religions. Nock, who was born in Portsmouth, England, and died in Cambridge, Massachusetts, showed early promise of becoming what Martin P. Nilsson was to call him: "the world's leading authority on the religion of later antiquity." His *Sallus-tius: Concerning the Gods and the Universe* (Cambridge, England, 1926), a model edition of an allegorical treatise from late antiquity, is notable for its essay on the treatise in its fourth-century setting.

A fellow of Clare College, Cambridge, Nock shared some of the interests, if not all the beliefs, of a group of learned Anglo-Catholics who were producing a set of essays on the Trinity and the Incarnation. He maintained his independence and objectivity while preparing an enduringly valuable essay entitled "Early Gentile Christianity and Its Hellenistic Background," in which he anticipated much of his later work on both subjects. Quite soon Nock was invited to Harvard University, where he became Frothingham Professor of the History of Religion in 1930. His Lowell Lectures were published as *Conversion: The Old and the New in Religion from Alexander the Great to Augustine of Hippo* (Oxford, 1933).

Nock's scholarly range was immense, his depth and intensity remarkable. His shorter papers reflect great energy governed by a strong mind. Legend has it that he had spent his earlier years reading all the Teubner texts before going on to all the secondary literature. For many years he worked with A.-J. Festugière, O.P., on an edition of the theosophical *Corpus Hermeticum* (Paris, 1945), freeing the text from needless emendations and setting the whole in its Middle Platonic environment. To clarify historical context was always his goal. As he wrote in the preface to *Conversion,* "We shall seek to see as a pagan might the Christian Church and the Christian creed. The evidence at our disposal does not admit of complete success in this quest; we can but hope to have a reasonable approximation to the truth and, in the Swedish proverb, 'to put the church in the middle of the village.'"

Publication of Nock's Gifford Lectures, delivered in 1939 and 1946, was delayed by World War II and was finally nullified by his perfectionism. He was too busy to look back. He had already produced a masterly chapter on late Roman religion, "The Development of Paganism in the Roman Empire," making full use of the coins, for the *Cambridge Ancient History,* vol. 12 (Cambridge, 1939), and he was responsible for editing the *Harvard Theological Review*—which he continued to do for thirty-three years—as a journal for ancient religion, chiefly Greek and Roman.

Nock was opposed to the proliferation of hypotheses and to the building of theory upon theory. Reluctant to generalize, he spoke of the sacredness of fact, although he valued facts not for their own sake but as the foundation stones of knowledge. Revered by his students and colleagues for his knowledge and judgment, he helped many to resist speculation, thus pointing the way to a truly collaborative study of religion.

Bibliography

Particularly notable, along with the works mentioned above, is Nock's *Early Gentile Christianity and Its Hellenistic Background* (New York, 1964), which includes the essay by that title as well as two other papers. Among Nock's many articles, it is difficult to select the most important, although certainly his "Sarcophagi and Symbolism," "Hellenistic Mysteries and Christian Sacraments," and "The Roman Army and the Religious Year" deserve attention. Nock's 415 publications are listed—and 59 of them are reprinted—in his *Essays on Religion and the Ancient World*, 2 vols., edited by Zeph Stewart (Oxford, 1972).

New Sources

As far as secondary literature is concerned, besides the obituaries written by André-Jean Festugière, *Revue Archéologique* 1 (1963): 203–205; Martin P. Nilsson, *Gnomon* 15 (1963): 318–319; Henry Chadwick and Eric Robertson Dodds, *Journal of Roman Studies* 53 (1963): 168–169, and other ones, see, more recently, William M. Calder III, "Harvard classics 1950–1956." *Eikasmos* 4 (1993): 39–49. The same author has devoted some pages to Nock in his *Men in Their Books: Studies in the Modern History of Classical Scholarship*, edited by John P. Harris and R. Scott Smith (Hildesheim, 1998). Nock's scientific legacy is well outlined in Mario Mazza's valuable introductory essay premitted to the Italian translation of *Conversion* (Bari, 1974), pp. i–xlvi.

ROBERT M. GRANT (1987)
Revised Bibliography

NOISE SEE PERCUSSION AND NOISE

NOMINALISM. The philosophical view of nominalists is based on the conviction that in human discourse only names (*nomina*), nouns, or words are "universal," not things, common natures, or ideas, as claimed by the realists. The problem of universals, first raised in logic, concerned the status of terms that are predicable of many subject-terms. The problem raised other questions that had to be answered in psychology or epistemology, with serious ramifications in theology. The logical problem of universals was heatedly debated in the eleventh and twelfth centuries in response to Abelard; the larger problem was debated even more heatedly in the fourteenth and fifteenth centuries in response to Ockham and his followers.

In the early Middle Ages logicians encountered the problem of universals in teaching Aristotle's *Categories* and Porphyry's *Isagoge* (Introduction). In the *Categories* Aristotle listed ten classes of terms that are predicable of subject-terms in discourse (substance and the nine accidental characteristics). Porphyry grouped these into five types of univocal predicability called "universals" (*uni-versus-alia*), namely, genus, species, difference, property, and accident. Concerning their status Porphyry raised three questions: namely, whether they exist substantially or only in the mind; if the former, whether they are corporeal or incorporeal; and, third, whether they exist separately from objects of sense or only in them. Porphyry gave no answer but implied a Platonic solution. Boethius (c. 475–c. 525), in his commentary, further asks whether these universals are "things," as the Platonists hold, or only "names" as Aristotle seems to hold.

Early teachers such as John Scottus Eriugena (fl. 847–877), Anselm (c. 1033–1109), and William of Champeaux (c. 1070–1121), largely influenced by the Platonic realism of the early church fathers, maintained that predicable terms immediately reflect common natures in creatures and mediately reflect ideas in the mind of God. The earliest opponent of such realism was the French teacher Roscelin (fl. 1080–1125), who taught Peter Abelard (1079–1142). Arguing that things as such exist only as individuals and cannot be predicated universally, Roscelin attributed universality solely to vocal utterances. Modifying the extreme view of Roscelin, Abelard held that in predication it is simply names that are predicated of subject-terms, and the main function of names is to signify whatever is agreed upon by men. The meaning of the term *rose* being agreed upon, the name of the rose and its signification remain even when there are no more roses. Signification, for Abelard, exists only in the mind, not in individual things existing outside the mind. Abelard, however, did not raise the more serious questions of psychology or epistemology, since he did not know the rest of Aristotle's philosophy.

Logicians after Abelard distinguished between the meaning (*significatio*) of names and their intended use (*suppositio*) in sentences. Three kinds of supposition were noted: "simple," as in the simple meaning of a name; "material," as in the sounds or letters with which it is composed; and "personal," as in the proper subject possessing the attribute. In the thirteenth century wider issues were also discussed, such as the psychology of knowledge and the epistemological foundations of all knowledge. Moderate realists explained universal concepts in terms of "abstraction" by the human intellect from sense knowledge directly perceiving existing individuals.

Early in the fourteenth century William of Ockham (c. 1285–1349) rejected every shade of universality in things outside the mind, even fundamentally and potentially: "All those whom I have seen agree that there is really in the individual a nature that is in some way universal, at least potentially and incompletely" (*Sentences* 1.2.7). Ockham's unique nominalism rests on three crucial positions. First, in logic he substituted a new meaning for "simple" supposition: namely, when a term used stands for a mental intuition (*intentio animae*), but without that meaning, that is, without signifying something mental. As a consequence "personal" supposition became the concrete individual indicated by the name (*Sum of Logic* 1.64). Second, in psychology Ockham eliminated all distinctions between the soul and its faculties, among the faculties themselves, and between intellectual and sense knowledge. For Ockham, the intellect directly perceives the concrete individual by "intuitive" knowledge. Third, as for existing realities, only "absolute things" (*res absolutae*) can exist, namely, individual substances (matter or form) and sensible qualities: "Apart from absolute things, viz. substances and qualities, nothing can be imagined [to exist] either actually or potentially" (ibid., 1.49). Thus the other Aristotelian categories, such as quantity, relation, and the like, were reduced to mental intuitions (*intentiones animae*) that referred to individual "absolute things" variously perceived.

Ockham's nominalism eliminated much of what was traditionally considered "real" in philosophy and theology. Thus the name "motion" in any variation did not refer to a reality other than the body itself in motion; it signified a body (personal supposition) considered as being in one place after another without interruption (in simple supposition). Since "without interruption" is a negation, it cannot exist outside the mind in order to be distinct from the body in motion. Similarly, "grace" signifies a sinner acceptable to God as pleasing to him, not a reality in man distinct from the sinner. This simplification of names appealed to many philosophers and theologians after Ockham.

Many of the leading theologians in the fifteenth century—Gabriel Biel, Pierre d'Ailly, and Peter of Candia (the antipope Alexander V), for example—were nominalists. Moreover, most universities of Europe in the sixteenth century considered nominalism a mark of Catholic orthodoxy.

SEE ALSO William of Ockham.

BIBLIOGRAPHY

Carré, Meyrick H. *Realists and Nominalists.* Oxford, 1946.

Oberman, Heiko A. *The Harvest of Medieval Theology: Gabriel Biel and Late Medieval Nominalism.* 2d ed. Grand Rapids, Mich., 1967.

Reiners, Joseph. *Der Nominalismus in der Frühscholastik. Beiträge zur Geschichte der Philosophie des Mittelalters,* vol. 8, no. 5. Münster, 1910.

Vignaux, Paul. "Nominalisme." In *Dictionnaire de théologie catholique,* vol. 11. Paris, 1931.

Vignaux, Paul. *Nominalisme au quatorzième siècle.* Montreal, 1948.

New Sources

Dupré, Louis. *Passage to Modernity: An Essay on the Hermeneutics of Nature and Culture.* New Haven, 1993.

Langer, Ulrich. *Divine and Poetic Freedom in the Renaissance: Nominalist Theology and Literature in France and Italy.* Princeton, N.J., 1990.

Tooley, Michael, ed. *The Nature of Properties: Nominalism, Realism, and Trope Theory.* New York, 1999.

JAMES A. WEISHEIPL (1987)
Revised Bibliography

NONVIOLENCE.

Virtually every religious tradition contains some sort of injunction against taking human life. The biblical instruction "Thou shalt not kill" (*Ex.* 20:13, *Dt.* 5:17), considered normative for both Jewish and Christian traditions, is echoed in the New Testament (*Mt.* 5:21) and also in the Qurʾān: "Slay not the life that God has made sacred" (6:152). In the Buddhist tradition, the first of the Five Precepts mandated as part of the Eightfold Path of righteous living is the requirement not to kill. A Jain text claims that "if someone kills living things . . . his sin increases" (*Sūtrakṛtāṅga* 1.1), a sentiment that is also found in Hinduism: "The killing of living beings is not conducive to heaven" (*Manusmṛti* 5.48).

Despite the general agreement over the immorality of killing, however, there is a great deal of disagreement within and among religious traditions over such crucial matters as (1) how the rule against killing is justified; (2) when the rule may be abrogated; (3) whether it applies to all animate life; (4) whether it includes a prohibition against forms of harm other than physical; and (5) how central it is to each tradition.

A comparative survey of the concept of nonviolence is also complicated by the fact that the terms used for nonviolent acts and attitudes differ widely from culture to culture and from one century to the next. The words *pacifism* and *nonviolence,* for instance, are relatively new inventions in the English language. *Nonviolence,* a translation of the Sanskrit term *ahiṃsā* (lit., "no harm"), came into common English usage only in the twentieth century through its association with Mohandas Gandhi and his approach to conflict. While the term has parallels in religious traditions throughout the world, the idea is central primarily in the religious traditions found in India.

In the following survey of nonviolence in the world religious traditions, the concept can be seen as conceived in three basic ways:

1. *As an inner state or attitude of nondestructiveness and reverence for life.* This idea is expressed primarily in the Jain, Buddhist, and Hindu traditions through the notion of *ahiṃsā.* It is also found in certain African and Native American tribal societies and in some Christian communities, including the Quakers.
2. *As an ideal of social harmony and peaceful living.* This concept, associated with the Hebrew term *shalom* and the Islamic term *salām,* is also found in ancient Greek religion, where gods such as Demeter and Apollo incarnated the virtues of peace. It is linked with visions of a perfect future found in Christianity and in various tribal religions.
3. *As a response to conflict.* A nonviolent approach to confrontation, even in oppressive situations, has been the hallmark of the Christian notion of sacrificial love, the Jewish concept of martyrdom, and the Gandhian strategy of nonviolent conflict.

ANCIENT INDIA. During the Vedic period (c. 1500–500 BCE), the concept of nonviolence was virtually unknown. The culture of the time was permeated with the values of a military society, and animals were widely used for food and sacrifice. The mythological accounts of Vedic gods are filled with acts of violence, vengeance, and warfare—activities in which the gods of the great epics also participated.

The first mention of nonviolence as a moral virtue is found in the *Chāndogya Upaniṣad* (3.17.4), where the word *ahiṃsā* implies self-sacrifice and restraint. The *Yoga Sūtra* later requires it as a vow for those undertaking yogic practices. The further evolution of the concept, however, is linked with another notion that arises in the Upaniṣads, the belief in *karman,* that is, that one's attitudes and deeds in this life will influence one's status in the next. Acts and attitudes destructive to life are considered to have an especially bad influence. The concept of *ahiṃsā,* thus elevated, came into a central position in the teachings of the heterodox masters of the sixth century BCE, notably Mahāvīra, the prominent figure in the Jain tradition, and Siddhārtha Gautama, the Buddha.

JAIN TEACHINGS. The importance of nonviolence in Jainism is due to the tradition's stark view of the law of *karman:* any association with killing, even an accidental one, is a serious obstacle on the path of karmic purity. For that reason, pious Jains wear masks over their faces to avoid breathing in (and thereby destroying) tiny insects, and they sweep the ground before them in order to avoid stepping on anything living as they walk. In addition, all Jains adhere to a vegetarian diet. Vegetables are also living things, of course, but certain vegetables are thought to carry a greater karmic weight, and these the Jains try to avoid. Jain monks, whose code is even stricter than that of the laity, hold as an ideal the logical conclusion of an extreme form of *ahiṃsā:* the completion of one's life by starving to death.

BUDDHISM. The Buddhist ideal of *ahiṃsā,* even as practiced by Buddhist monks, is not as strict as that of the Jains. Buddhists emphasize motivation as well as action, and traditional Buddhist teachings require five conditions, all of which must be present before one can be considered culpable of an act of killing: (1) something must first have been living; (2) the killer must have known that it was alive; (3) he or she must have intended to kill it; (4) there must have been an act of killing; and (5) it must, in fact, have died.

It is the absence of the third of these conditions that typically allows for some mitigation of the rule of total nonviolence in the Buddhist case. For instance, many Buddhists will eat meat as long as they have not themselves intended that the animal be slaughtered or been involved in the act of slaughtering. Armed defense—even warfare—has been justified on the grounds that such violence has been in the nature of response, not intent. To use violence nondefensively, however, for the purpose of political expansion, appears to be prohibited under the Buddhist rule.

Perhaps for this reason, the great Buddhist emperor Aśoka came to accept the principle of nonviolence only after his bloody wars of expansion. From his headquarters in what is now the North Indian state of Bihar, Asoka conquered a goodly portion of the South Asian subcontinent in the third century BCE. Once in power, however, he instituted the rule of nonviolence as state policy.

Even in modern Buddhist societies such as Thailand, where kingship is a religious as well as a political role, there is a tension between the obligations of political authority and the adherence to the rule of nonviolence. In countries such as China and Japan, where Buddhism is intertwined with other religious traditions, the stringent Buddhist standards are maintained only by monks, while those in political authority rely on other religious traditions, such as Confucianism and Shinto, to justify political force.

Chinese culture has been receptive to Buddhist ideas on nonviolence, however, due to the existence of similar notions in traditional Chinese thought. The Daoist concept of *wuwei* ("nonstriving") connotes an ideal of peaceful living and the absence of aggression much like that conveyed by the concept of *ahiṃsā.*

MEDIEVAL AND MODERN HINDU ATTITUDES. Sometime after the rise of Buddhism, and perhaps because of its influence, the idea of nonviolence gained popularity throughout India and became linked with two other notions, vegetarianism and respect for the cow. Some scholars regard cow worship as a vestige of an earlier nature-goddess religion in India, but in its later, Hindu interpretation, veneration of the cow became a symbol of respect for all living beings, and by extension, a symbol of nonviolence. Despite the popularity of the concept, however, the political history of India has been dominated by military rulers, often members of the warrior caste (*kṣatriya*) whose moral obligation (*dharma*) includes leadership in battle.

It was Mohandas Gandhi (1869–1948) who brought the concept of nonviolence into the political sphere. By combining the notion of nonviolence with a traditional means of protest—*dharṇā* (a general strike)—Gandhi made movements of nonviolent noncooperation into instruments of significant political power. By employing nonviolence as an essential element of the consensus style of decision making traditionally practiced by India's village councils (*pañchāyat*), Gandhi developed a novel method of conflict resolution he called *satyāgraha* ("truth force"). He applied this term both to his campaigns for India's independence and to his way of dealing with differences of opinion in everyday life.

Although Gandhi insisted on nonviolence as a general rule, he allowed for several significant exceptions. He condoned the violence required to stop snipers or rapists as they attacked, and permitted the killing of pests and wild animals that threatened his rural commune. He claimed that he preferred violence over cowardice, and he placed the battle for truth on a higher plane than the strict observance of nonviolence. Yet Gandhi also regarded nonviolence as the litmus test that would reveal where truth was to be found. In Gandhi's view, any form of coercion or intimidation was violent and to be abhorred.

HINDU AND SIKH MILITANTS. The persistence of violence in India's public life is ample testimony that Gandhi's approach was not unanimously accepted even in his own land. The movement for national independence that Gandhi led was marred by violence, including that perpetrated by Bengali nationalists inspired by Durga, a goddess to whom great destructive powers were ascribed. At the time of independence, Hindu militants led violent assaults against their old Muslim foes and, in 1948, one of them led the fatal assault on Gandhi's life as well.

The assassination in 1984 of Prime Minister Indira Gandhi of India was also motivated by religious concerns. Mrs. Gandhi was killed by a member of the Sikh community in retaliation for her part in ordering a military assault on the Sikh Golden Temple. The fundamental teachings of the Sikhs are not, however, violent: the fifteenth- and sixteenth-century spiritual masters who are regarded as founders of the faith are portrayed as such gentle souls that Gandhi himself claimed to have been inspired by them. But over the years the ranks of the Sikh movement swelled with members of a militant tribal group, the Jats, and Sikhs were involved in violent clashes with the Mughals, the British, and other Indian rulers. The core of the Sikh community is known as "the army of the faithful," and their symbol is a double-edged sword.

BIBLICAL JUDAISM. Western religious traditions are no less inclined than their Eastern counterparts to combine violent and peaceful images of the divine. And, as in the Hindu tradition, some of the earliest images are the most violent. "The Lord is a warrior," proclaims *Exodus* 15:3. The utter desolation with which God destroyed his enemies indicated just how fierce a warrior he could be.

Later sections of the Hebrew scriptures temper this image with an attitude of compassion, and some even show a disdain of things military (see *Ps.* 20, 30, 33, 147; *Is.* 30). David, for instance, was not allowed to build the Temple because he had shed blood (*1 Chr.* 28:2–3), and the prophetic vision that nations will "beat their swords into plowshares" and "never again be trained for war" (*Is.* 2:4, *Mi.* 4:3) is one of the most vivid images of pacifism in any religious scripture.

An even more positive approach is indicated by the growing prominence of the biblical term for "peace," *shalom*, which appears often in the prophetic books of the Hebrew scriptures, especially *Jeremiah* and *Isaiah*. The term signifies not only an absence of warfare, but the presence of a spirit of well-being and harmony. In this respect, *shalom* is the Hebrew equivalent for the positive aspects of *ahiṃsā*, especially the absence of the desire to harm.

RABBINIC AND MODERN JUDAISM. Writings in the Babylonian Talmud continue this Jewish emphasis on *shalom* and further elaborate a series of ethical restrictions on using violence. On an interpersonal level, the absence of violence is applauded even in the face of provocation. If one is attacked, a fourth-century rabbi advised, "let him kill you; do you commit no murder" (*Pes.* 25b). At the level of statecraft, the rabbis did sanction warfare, but they distinguished between "religious" war and "optional" war. The former they required as a moral or spiritual obligation—to protect the faith or defeat enemies of the Lord. These contrasted with wars that are waged for reasons of political expansion and power; such optional wars are justified only if they are initiated for virtuous reasons.

During the rabbinic period, the Jewish community was also beginning to develop nonviolent forms of self-defense and resistance, both as individual and as communal actions. The confrontations with the occupying Roman government included not only militant clashes, such as the Maccabean Revolt (166–164 BCE), but also nonviolent encounters, as when the Jewish community resisted Caligula's attempt to establish a statue of himself as Zeus in the Temple at Jerusalem in 40 CE. The revolt at Masada in 73 CE, although violent, involved a show of religious solidarity that culminated in mass suicide, and the rebellion led by Bar Kokhba (c. 132–135 CE) involved a kind of passive resistance that resulted in martyrdom.

The concept of martyrdom, *kiddush ha-Shem* ("sanctification of the divine name"), is central to the Jewish tradition of nonviolent resistance. The term implies that those who revere the divine order must be unflagging in their witness to it, even at the cost of their lives. A rabbinical council in the second century CE narrowed to three the number of offenses that one should refuse to commit even under the threat of death: idolatry, unchastity, and murder. By extension, however, martyrdom was expected in any situation where one was forced to deny the basic tenets of the faith.

In times of political oppression, the ideal of *kiddush ha-Shem* has served to inspire Jewish resisters to acts of courage and faithfulness even at the risk of their lives. This ideal was tested in the fifteenth century when, during the Spanish Inquisition, many Jews were persecuted for adopting a technique that amounted to passive resistance: they claimed to be Christian converts when in fact they were secretly observing the Jewish faith. In the twentieth century, faced with massive Nazi attempts at genocide, the European Jewish community adopted both violent and nonviolent forms of resistance. One of the most common responses to the Nazis, especially among the Orthodox, was based on the traditional notion of *kiddush ha-Shem*: they faced their opponents with dignity and faithfulness, rather than adopting any aspect of the enemy's behavior, even if it meant risking death.

EARLY CHRISTIANITY. Martyrdom was an important feature of early Christianity as well, partly because it seemed an imitation of the sacrifice of Jesus, but there has been disagreement among Christians from that time to the present over whether Jesus' example of selfless love (agape) was meant to be followed to similar extremes by other members of the Christian community. Those who thought so expected that the peaceable kingdom of God that is often depicted in the Gospels would be realized in this world, and they took literally Jesus' advocacy of a nonviolent approach to conflict: "Love your enemies and pray for those who persecute you" (*Mt.* 5:44).

The early church fathers, including Tertullian and Origen, affirmed that Christians were constrained from taking human life, a principle that prevented them from participating in the Roman army. The fact that soldiers in the army were required to swear allegiance to the emperor's god was also a deterrent, since it would have forced Christians into what they regarded as idolatry.

The adoption of Christianity as the state religion by Constantine in the fourth century CE brought about a major reversal in Christian attitudes toward pacifism and led to the formulation of the doctrine of just war. This idea, based on a concept stated by Cicero and developed by Ambrose and Augustine, has had a significant influence on Christian social thought. The abuse of the concept in justifying military adventures and violent persecutions of heretical and minority groups led Thomas Aquinas, in the thirteenth century, to reaffirm that war is always sinful, even if it is occasionally waged for a just cause.

Pacifist Christian Movements. The late medieval period witnessed the rise of a series of movements dedicated to pacifism and the ethic of love that Jesus had advocated in his Sermon on the Mount. One of the first of such groups was the Waldensian community based in France and North Italy; this was founded by Pierre Valdès, who in 1170 had committed himself to a life of poverty and simplicity, and who refused to bear arms. Although Valdès was excommunicated from the church, he is said to have influenced the young Francis of Assisi, whose religious order later adopted many of Valdès's principles. Similar pacifist teachings were advocated by John Wyclif and his Lollard followers in fourteenth-century England, and in the same century the Hussite and Taborite movements in Czechoslovakia rejected all forms of violence, as did their successors, the Moravians.

The Protestant Reformation provided a new stimulus for groups that rejected the church's compromise with what it often regarded as the political necessity of military force. In the first decades of the sixteenth century, the Anabaptists broke away from Ulrich Zwingli's branch of the Swiss Reformation over the issues of voluntary baptism and absolute pacifism—teachings the Anabaptists affirmed and that, later in the same century, were adopted by Menno Simons and his Mennonite followers in Holland. In a tragic and ironic twist of fate, many of these pacifists were persecuted by fellow Protestants as heretics, and were burned at the stake.

Perhaps the best-known Protestant pacifist movement is the Society of Friends, commonly known as the Quakers, which was established by George Fox in England in 1649. The nonviolent ethic of this radical Puritan movement was based on the notion that a spark of the divine exists in every person, making every life sacred. With this in mind, the Quaker colonialist William Penn refused to bear arms in his conflict with the American Indians, with whom he eventually negotiated a peace settlement.

Many pacifist Christian movements in the nineteenth and twentieth centuries, such as the Jehovah's Witnesses, owe a substantial debt to Christian predecessors such as those mentioned above. Others have been influenced by Western humanist and Asian pacifist thought, especially, in the twentieth century, by the ideas of Mohandas Gandhi. Gandhi, in turn, was influenced by Christian pacifists, including the Russian novelist and visionary Lev Tolstoi and the American Christian social activists Kirby Page, Clarence Marsh Case, and A. J. Muste. The largest Christian pacifist organization of modern times, the Fellowship of Reconciliation, was founded in England in 1914; and a number of statements urging nonviolence have been issued from the Vatican and from the World Council of Churches in response to the two world wars of this century. In the United States during the mid-twentieth century, Christian pacifist ideas played a significant role in Martin Luther King, Jr.'s nonviolent movement for racial justice, the movement against the American involvement in the Vietnam War, and in movements against the proliferation of nuclear weapons. Some Christian "nuclear pacifists," however, restrict their advocacy of nonviolence to nuclear arms, whose massively destructive power, they feel, vitiates the traditional Christian defense of weaponry in a "just war."

Islam. The concept of nonviolence is not so thoroughly developed in Islam as it is in many other religious traditions, but certain parallels do exist. The Islamic concept of peace, for instance—*salām*—is as central to Islam as *shalom* is to Judaism, and plays a similar role in providing a vision of social harmony. To that end, Islamic communities have placed great emphasis on arbitration and mediation so that intra-communal conflicts will not erupt into violent confrontations.

Yet there are times when recourse to violence is permitted in Islamic law: inside Islam, it is justified as a means of punishment, and beyond Islam, as a tool to subdue an enemy of the faith. The latter situation is known as *jihād*, a word that literally means "striving" and is often translated as "holy war." This concept has been used to justify the expansion of territorial control by Muslim leaders into non-Islamic areas. But Muslim law does not allow it to be used to justify forcible conversion to Islam; the only conversions regarded as valid are those that come about nonviolently, through rational persuasion and change of heart. For that reason, non-Islamic groups have traditionally been tolerated in Islamic societies, and the Jews in Moorish Spain are often said to have been treated less harshly under their Muslim rulers than under subsequent Christian ones.

Muslim mystics, known as Ṣūfīs, have on occasion rejected the common notion of *jihād* by redefining it so that it refers primarily to an inner struggle, which they consider "the greater *jihād*": the conflict of truth and evil within every person. In addition, there have been overtly pacifist sects in Islam, such as the Māziyārīyah and Aḥmadīyah movements. The twentieth-century Muslim Pathans in North India, influenced by Gandhi and led by Abdul Ghaffir Khan, conducted an extensive nonviolent campaign for independence from the British. In other cases, Muslims have responded to oppressive regimes by noncooperation and witnessing to the faith even at peril of death—a form of martyrdom much like that found in the Jewish and Christian traditions.

See Also Ahiṃsā; Gandhi, Mohandas; Peace.

BIBLIOGRAPHY

A general overview of concepts of nonviolence in the major religious traditions is to be found in John Ferguson's *War and Peace in the World's Religions* (New York, 1977), and a description of the various ways religious traditions have put nonviolence into practice in conflict situations is provided in Richard B. Gregg's *The Power of Non-Violence* (Philadelphia, 1934); in *The Quiet Battle: Writings on the Theory and Practice of Nonviolence*, edited by Mulford Q. Sibley (Chicago, 1963); and in Gene Sharp's *The Politics of Nonviolent Action*, 3 vols. (Boston, 1973–1980).

Other works are specific to particular religious traditions. For the concept of *ahiṃsā* in ancient India, see W. Norman Brown's *Man in the Universe: Some Continuities in Indian Thought* (Berkeley, 1966); for early Buddhism, see David S. Ruegg's "Ahiṃsā and Vegetarianism in the History of Buddhism," in *Buddhist Studies in Honour of Walpola Rahula*, edited by Somaratna Balasooriya et al. (London, 1980); and for the Jain tradition, see Padmanabh S. Jaini's *The Jaina Path of Purification* (Berkeley, 1979). Later developments of the idea in Buddhism are explored in Winston L. King's *In the Hope of Nibbana: An Essay on Theravada Buddhist Ethics* (LaSalle, Ill., 1964) and Stanley J. Tambiah's *World Conqueror and World Renouncer: A Study of Buddhism and Polity in Thailand against a Historical Background* (Cambridge, 1976). The Gandhian approach is described in Joan Bondurant's *Conquest of Violence: The Gandhian Philosophy of Conflict* (Princeton, 1958) and in my *Ghandi's Way: A Handbook of Conflict Resolution* (Berkeley, Calif., 2003).

With regard to the Jewish tradition, biblical attitudes are examined in D. Martin Dakin's *Peace and Brotherhood in the Old Testament* (London, 1956), and a number of works explore the rabbinic views, including Nahum N. Glatzer's "The Concept of Peace in Classical Judaism," in his *Essays in Jewish Thought* (University, Ala., 1978), and André Neher's "Rabbinic Adumbrations of Non-Violence," in *Rationalism, Judaism, and Universalism*, edited by Raphael Loewe (London, 1966). For one of the Jewish responses to Gandhi during World War II, see Judah L. Magnes's "A Letter to Gandhi," in *Modern Jewish Thought: A Source Reader*, edited by Nahum N. Glatzer (New York, 1977).

A useful sourcebook of Christian writings on nonviolence is *War and the Christian Conscience: From Augustine to Martin Luther King, Jr.*, edited by Albert Marrin (Chicago, 1971), and an excellent discussion of the historical development of the idea is to be found in the brief essays by Geoffrey Nuttal in his *Christian Pacifism in History* (Oxford, 1958). Good examples of the current discussion of nonviolence in the field of Christian ethics are James F. Childress's *Moral Responsibility in Conflicts* (Baton Rouge, 1982) and William Robert Miller's *Nonviolence: A Christian Interpretation* (London, 1964). The Islamic point of view is presented in Majid Khadduri's *War and Peace in the Law of Islam* (Baltimore, 1955), and comments of Muslim writers on the subject of peace and nonviolence can be found in Eric Schroeder's *Muhammad's People* (Portland, Maine, 1955).

MARK JUERGENSMEYER (1987 AND 2005)

NORITO are religious statements addressed to the deities (*kami*) in Shintō rituals. They usually follow upon a one- to three-day purification rite, at the conclusion of which the *kami* are invited by the Shintō priests to be present at the ceremony. A *norito* generally contains the following elements: (1) words of praise to the *kami*, (2) an explanation of the origin of, or reasons for, this particular ritual or festival, (3) entertainment for the *kami*, (4) expressions of gratitude for protection and favor given, and (5) prayers for the successful completion of the matter at hand. *Norito* are composed in the classical language, and contain expressions of great beauty; they are usually written exclusively in Chinese characters, some of which have merely a phonetic function. The rhythm produced by the peculiar word arrangement, which involves many pairs of expressions and sets of words to modify the same object, is intended to pacify both the *kami* and the participants and instill in them a feeling of unity.

Although there are many etymological theories regarding *norito*, examples drawn from the classics and Shintō history suggest that they were words of blessing spoken to all the *kami* and to the people by the emperor, the descendant of the sun goddess Amaterasu and the "great life-giving" *kami* Takamimusubi. *Norito*, therefore, were originally regarded as able to produce a beneficial response from heavenly *kami*. Later, however, two families, the Nakatomi and the Imbe, were given the exclusive right to recite *norito* on prescribed occasions to all enshrined *kami*.

The oldest known *norito* are a collection of twenty-four such documents edited in 820 CE, during the reign of Emperor Saga, as part of detailed legal regulations that were eventually compiled in the *Engishiki* in 927. The most important *norito* are entitled "Grain-Petitioning Festival," "Festival of the Sixth Month," "Festival of the First-Fruits Banquet," and "Great Exorcism of the Last Day of the Sixth Month." All of these begin with the expression "By the command of the sovereign ancestral male *kami* and the female *kami* who remain in the High Celestial Plain." The first three are concerned with ensuring a bountiful rice harvest so that the country may be stable and prosperous. The last is a purification ritual for the land and people, and is especially valuable for its precise description of both heavenly and earthly sin, in the Shintō sense.

A second group of six important *norito* in the *Engishiki* collection is dedicated to the personal safety and repose of the emperor. Among them, the "Ritual for the Tranquillity of the Imperial Spirit" is recited to lay to rest the emperor's spirit in the Office of Rites sanctuary. The next three, "Blessing of the Great Palace," "Festival of the Gates," and "Fire-Pacifying Festival," are dedicated to the protection of the emperor from external danger. Although the remaining two are not regular or seasonal, they too have the same basic function, protecting the emperor from evil spirits. It should also be mentioned that the formula "the heavenly ritual, the solemn ritual words" is used only in *norito* connected with pacification of evil spirits. This unusual phrase is believed to refer to a special magic formula that was transmitted to the Nakatomi family from the deities but that has been lost over time.

Most of the remaining *norito* are for rituals observed at the Grand Shrine at Ise. Of special significance is the *norito* called "Divine Congratulatory Words of the Kuni no Miyatsuko of Izumo," which indicates through its title that in ancient times the chief priest of Izumo Shrine, who was also the ruler of that area, represented other local leaders in the ritual presentation of local land-spirits to the emperor.

With the decline of imperial power in the late twelfth century, a new type of *norito* emerged, a type deeply influenced by Buddhism and concerned especially with ritual purification. After the eighteenth century a movement to revive Shintō arose, but no attempt was made to standardize *norito* until the beginning of the Meiji era (1868–1912). In 1875, and later in 1914, the government ordered that the shrine rites and rituals as well as official *norito* be standardized, but today there is a tendency to use contemporary expressions in order to adjust to the demands of a changing society.

BIBLIOGRAPHY

Kamo no Mabuchi's treatise of 1768, *Noritokō*, in *Kamo Mabuchi zenshū*, vol. 7 (Tokyo, 1984), and Motoori Norinaga's commentary of 1795, *Oharae kotoba kōshaku*, in *Motoori Norinaga zenshū*, vol. 7 (Tokyo, 1971), remain classic introductions to the topic. For more modern studies, see the following works.

Orikuchi Shinobu. "Norito." In *Orikuchi Shinobu zenshū, nōto-hen*, vol. 9. Tokyo, 1971.

Philippi, Donald L., trans. *Norito: A New Translation of the Ancient Japanese Ritual.* Tokyo, 1959.

Tsuita Jun. *Norito shinkō.* Tokyo, 1927.

Ueda Kenji. "Shiki noritoko." In *Shintō shisoshi kenkyu.* Tokyo, 1983.

UEDA KENJI (1987)

NORSE RELIGION SEE GERMANIC RELIGION

NORTH AMERICAN INDIAN RELIGIONS

This entry consists of the following articles:

AN OVERVIEW
MYTHIC THEMES
NEW RELIGIOUS MOVEMENTS
HISTORY OF STUDY

NORTH AMERICAN [INDIAN] RELIGIONS: AN OVERVIEW

Because of the isolation of the New World from the high civilizations of Europe, Asia, and Africa and from the communicative network between them, North America had preserved, until the end of the last century, cultures and religions of archaic types. Local historical traditions, intertribal diffusion, social structure and environmental pressure combined to form among the North American Indian tribes a series of religions that were only secondarily influenced by elements from outside the continent. North American religions have become known as varied, colorful, and spiritual. In the religio-scientific debate among anthropologists and historians of religion, such concepts as power and supreme being, guardian spirits and totems, fasting visions and shamanism, myth telling and ritualism, have drawn on North American ideas and religious experiences.

Soon after the arrival of the white man in the 1500s the first information concerning Indian religious worship reached the Europeans. Through Jesuit documents and other reports the religious development of the Iroquoian and eastern Algonquian groups can be followed continuously from 1613 onward. Spanish sources from the same time illuminate at least some aspects of Southwest Indian religious history. In the eighteenth century travel records and other documents throw light on the Indians of the Southeast Woodlands, of the mid-Atlantic region, and of the Prairies and on their religions. It was, however, only at the end of the eighteenth century and in the course of the nineteenth century that knowledge spread of the Plains, Basin, California, Plateau, Northwest Coast, western Canadian, and Alaskan Indian religions.

MAIN RELIGIOUS FEATURES. North America is a continent with many diverse cultures, and it is therefore meaningless to speak about North American religion as a unified aggregate of beliefs, myths, and rituals. Still, there are several religious traits that are basically common to all the Indians but variously formalized and interpreted among different peoples. These traits are also found in the religions of other continents and areas, particularly among the so-called primitive or primal peoples. Two characteristics are, however, typically Amerindian: the dependence on visions and dreams, which can modify old traditional rituals, and an intricate and time-consuming ceremonialism that sometimes almost conceals the cognitive message of rituals.

Spirit World. To these common elements belongs the idea of another dimension of existence that permeates life and yet is different from normal, everyday existence. Concepts such as the Lakota *wakan* and the Algonquian *manitou* refer to this consciousness of another world, the world of spirits, gods, and wonders. This supernatural or supranormal world is sometimes manifest in nature, which then receives a sacred import. Often the campsite or the village is arranged in a pattern that establishes a ritual identity with the supernatural world. In twentieth-century pan-Indian religion the connection between terrestrial phenomena and the other world is extremely important.

Supreme being. The supernatural world is primarily expressed through the spiritual powers residing in a host of gods, spirits, and ghosts. In many American tribes prayers are directed to a collectivity of divine or spiritual beings, as in the pipe ceremony. Foremost among these divinities is, in most tribes, a sky god who represents all other supernatural beings or stands as their superior and the ruler of the universe. The Pawnee Indians in Nebraska, for instance, know a hierarchy of star gods and spirits, all of them subservient to the high god in the sky, Tirawa. It could be argued that their idea of a high god is formed after Mexican conceptual patterns, since the Caddoan-speaking peoples to whom the Pawnee belong were much inspired by the Mexican-derived prehistoric Mississippian culture. However, there are clear examples of a supreme being among many North American peoples, and scholarly attempts to trace these figures to Christian influence have so far failed. In most cases the supreme being is vaguely conceived as the ulterior religious force in situations of need and frustration.

The supreme being is closely associated with the *axis mundi*, or world pillar. The Delaware Indians say that he grasps the pole that holds up the sky and is the center of the world. In ceremonial life the world pole, or world tree, is the central cultic symbol in the great annual rites of peoples of the Eastern Woodlands, the Plains, the Basin, and the Plateau. At this annual celebration the Indians thank the supreme being for the year that has been (the ceremony takes place in the spring in most cases) and dance in order to secure the support of the Great Spirit and all the powers for the year to come: the Plains Sun Dance is a good example.

In California, a region of frequent earthquakes, similar world renewal rituals have as their main aim the stabilizing of the universe. In the east, the Delaware Big House ceremony is an adaptation of the hunters' annual ceremony to the cultural world of more settled maize-growing peoples: the sacred pillar is here built into a ceremonial house. In many places throughout North America myths testify that the annual ceremony is a repetition or commemoration of the cosmic creation at the beginning of time. This connection is, however, not present everywhere, and many Sun Dance rituals have origin myths of quite a different character.

The culture hero. The connection of the supreme being with creation is often concealed by the fact that in mythology another supernatural being, the culture hero, is invested with creative powers. His true mission is to deliver cultural institutions, including religious ceremonies, to the first human beings, but he is sometimes an assistant creator as well. In this quality he competes with the Great Spirit and appears as a ludicrous figure, a trickster, or an antagonist of the Great Spirit, an emergent "devil." (It should be observed that all this takes place only on a mythological level, for the culture hero disappears after his work has been completed and in many quarters becomes a star.)

Trickster tales occupy a major part of American Indian mythologies and have attracted all kinds of comic folktale motifs. The tales usually portray the culture hero/trickster as a zoomorphic being: a white hare in the Northeast; a coyote on the western Plains, in the Basin, the Plateau, and California; and a raven in the Northwest.

Spirits and ghosts. The other beings of the supernatural world—and they are innumerable, varying from tribe to tribe—may be partly distinguished according to their physical location:

1. *Sky beings*, including star gods, Sun (usually a manifestation of the supreme being), and Moon (who sometimes represents the vegetation goddess). The Milky Way is thought of as the road of the dead in some places, and the northern lights as the dead at play.
2. *Atmospheric spirits*, which usually comprise the Four Winds (they emanate from caves situated in the four cardinal directions), Whirlwind (often thought of as a ghost), the rain spirits, and Thunderbird. This last spirit, of which a parallel conception is also found in Siberia, is a giant eaglelike bird; according to many informants his blinking eyes make the lightning, while his flapping wings cause the thunder.
3. *Spirits of the biosphere*, many of them rulers, or owners, of animal species or plant species (Buffalo Spirit, Caribou Spirit, Maize Spirit), others connected with natural places like mountains, stones, deserts, swamps, waters, and so on. Human beings (medicine-men, for example) may also manifest supernatural powers.
4. *Powers of the underworld*, such as Mother Earth, underwater monsters (snakes or panthers), and the ruler of the underground dead, who is usually identical with the first ancestor or is a brother of the culture hero.

However, there are powers that do not fit into this scheme. Such powers are the dead, who operate in different places in different types of cultures. Hunters believe the dead are in the sky or somewhere beyond the horizon—beyond the western mountains, beyond the sea where the sun sets. Horticulturists may believe that the dead are in the ground, returning to Our Mother's bosom, or at the place of emergence of mankind; and in stratified agricultural societies like those of the Mississippian culture there are different abodes for different social categories of dead. At the same time there is everywhere a belief in ghosts on earth, who are often heard whistling in the night. Independent of these beliefs is a ubiquitous idea of reincarnation or transmigration into animals.

Guardian spirits and vision quests. Other spirits are the guardian spirits acquired in fasting visions by youths of the Plateau and the Northeast Woodlands and by both boys and men of the Plains and the Basin. These spirits are mostly zoomorphic. They may be animal spirits or spirits that show themselves in animal disguise. Everywhere except among the pueblo-dwelling peoples of the Southwest it has been the individual hunter's ambition to acquire one or several of these guardian spirits. They usually appear to the person after a vision quest during which he has spent several days and nights in fasting and isolation at some lonely spot in the wilderness. The spirit endows his client with a particular "medicine," that is, supernatural power (to hunt, to run, to make love, to cure), gives him a sacred song, and instructs him to make a pouch or medicine bag in which he is to keep the sacred paraphernalia associated with his vision. The vision quest is basic to most American Indian hunting religions.

In some places special societies were established for young spirit seekers who expected to meet the same spirit. This was, for instance, the case among the Kwa-kiutl of Vancouver Island and vicinity. The vision itself was no longer central here, the neophyte being abducted by masked men to the woods and told there the secrets of his patron, Cannibal Spirit, whose frenzied behavior he imitates in a ceremony on his return.

There seems to be a direct relationship between the individual's guardian spirit and the complex of totemism. If totemism is defined as the mysterious relationship between a segment of a tribe, usually a clan or other unilineal kinship group, and a particular animal species that is its congener and patron, then totemism exists in many places where unilineal societies exist. Several American cases suggest that the totem is the original guardian spirit of an individual that has then been inherited by this person's descendants as their common supernatural partner.

In some more complex societies the medicine bags, or sacred bundles, have become inherited treasures within the vision seekers' families; in other societies they can even be purchased. Where a powerful object has been handed down in a family it is often made a symbol for a larger community, and its uncovering is surrounded by rituals and recitations of its origin myth. A typical example is the sacred bundle of the Arapaho, which contains a flatpipe.

Medicine men and medicine societies. The medicine man is a visionary who has succeeded in receiving power to cure people. However, visionaries with other extraordinary powers, such as the capacity to find lost things or divine the future, have also been labeled "medicine men." In very many cases a bear spirit is the medicine man's patron, so he dresses in a bearskin and mimics a bear's movements and sounds when doctoring people. Diseases may be ascribed to any of several causes, such as witchcraft or the breaking of a taboo. They manifest themselves mainly in two ways: a spirit or disease object is supposed to have intruded into the body (or even, on the Northwest Coast, to possess the person in a psychological sense); or the sick man's soul—in some cases, his power—has been stolen. In the former case it is the medicine man's task to frighten the spirit away or to remove it from the body by sucking, fanning, or drawing it out; in the latter case he has to catch the lost soul, which can be done in an imitative séance. Alternatively, the medicine man may sink into a trance, release his own soul, and send it out after the runaway or stolen soul. The medicine man who becomes entranced in this way may be characterized as a shaman.

In cultures with more complicated social organizations, medicine men may join together, exchanging experiences and working out a common, secret ideology, or they may form medicine societies into which persons are accepted after passing through a series of ritual events. An example of this is the Midewiwin, or Great Medicine society, of the Ojibwa, which is organized like a secret order society and has four or eight hierarchical grades.

In some cultures in the Southwest where collectivism is part of the cultural pattern—as, for instance, among the agricultural Pueblo—the medicine man is replaced by an organization of professional healers, and rituals are performed to aid individuals. Among the Navajo, the old medicine man lives on as a diagnostician ("hand trembler") whereas the curing itself is performed by a ritually skilled singer. The regaining of the patient's health means that harmony has been restored between man and the world of the gods and spirits.

Ritual acts. Harmony or spiritual balance is what North American Indians want to achieve in their relations with the supernatural powers. A harmonious balance can be reached through prayers and offerings or through imitative representation of supernatural events.

Prayers and offerings. Prayers range from a few words at meal offerings to detailed ritual prayers, from casual petitions of blessing to deeply emotional cries for help and sustenance. Indeed, Navajo prayer has been characterized by one researcher as "compulsive words," by another as "creative words." There is often beauty in Indian prayers, the usual eloquence of the Indians giving moving expression to their religious experience.

There are many kinds of offerings. A simple form is throwing tobacco or food into the fire or onto the ground at mealtimes. Another example is the placing of tobacco pouches on the ground at the beginning of dangerous passages, such as crossing a lake or walking over a mountain ridge.

Tobacco has been intimately related to American Indian religious practice. Even today no Indian conventions or powwows are undertaken without a preliminary pipe ceremony, an invocation of the powers that grant harmony between men and between gods or spirits and men.

When hunters killed game they usually performed rites over the body. For instance, after the animal was eaten, the bones might be given a ritual burial; they were reassembled in anatomical order, and the skull of the animal was elevated on a pole or a tree. These rituals were especially important in the case of the bear. This so-called animal ceremonialism was often intended to appease a particular spirit, the master of the game, but the primary purpose of such burials was to ensure the return of the game by showing proper respect for the animals. True sacrifices were not common, but did occur in the Northeast Woodlands, where white dogs were sacrificed to the powers. In many places the skins of animals (and, later, pieces of cloth as well) served as offerings. There was religious cannibalism in the East, even endocannibalism (the eating of one's family dead) in ancient times. Mutilations of fingers and other cases of self-mutilation as offerings occurred in the Sun Dance of the Lakota and in the closely related Mandan Okipa ceremony.

Ritual representations. Harmonious relations with the supernatural world could be restored by the dramatic imitation of the creation, often in an annual rite, as, for instance, the Sun Dance. The performance of such rituals often had the character of dancing, and most observers have therefore described American Indian ceremonies as dances. In the enactment of mythical drama, performers assumed the roles of supernatural beings, as in the representation of the kachina, cloud and rain spirits, and spirits of the dead in the Pueblo Indian Kachina Dances. In the Pawnee sacrifice to Morning Star, a young captive girl was tied to a frame and shot with arrows; she was supposed to represent Evening Star, a personification of the vegetation whose death promotes the growth of plants. Even today a Navajo patient is cured through a process of ritual identification with the universe and its powers: the patient sits in the middle of a sand painting symbolizing the cosmos and its powers while the practitioner pours colored sand over him.

HISTORICAL SURVEY. Most North American religions express the worldview typical of hunters and gatherers. This is natural, since the first immigrants who arrived perhaps forty to sixty thousands years ago were Paleolithic hunters who came by way of the Bering Strait. At that time the sound between Asia and North America was dry, due to the absorption of oceanic waters into the glaciers of the Great Ice Age. A narrow corridor stretched between the ice fields, allowing the migration of North Asiatic proto-Mongoloid groups into Alaska. The migration probably involved small groups who traveled independently, perhaps at a rate of four miles a year. Since ecological conditions were similar on both sides of the Bering Sea, the migration did not entail any break in historical and cultural traditions.

The Arctic substratum. This origin in northern Asia explains why so much of American Indian religion bears an Arctic or sub-Arctic stamp, and why so many features even in more temperate areas seem to be derived from northern cultures. Of course, particularly in the extreme north, we find native religions that are direct counterparts to the circumpolar religions of northern Eurasia. Both ecological and historical factors account for this uniformity. We may pinpoint such common religious elements as belief in a high god, Thunderbird, and Mother Earth; practices such as the bear ritual, hunting taboos, the sweat bath for ritual cleaning, and shamanic rituals; and a good many myths and tales. All these circumpolar traits represent Arctic or sub-Arctic forms of the ancient Paleolithic hunting culture in Eurasia.

There are some problems in establishing American connections with the Old World circumpolar culture, however. The weaker cultural links in eastern Siberia may be correlated with the influx into this area of Tunguz and Turkic tribes from the south during the last millennia. Perhaps under the influence of Lamaism and other forms of Buddhism, there evolved in Siberia an intense form of shamanism, with emphasis on deep ecstasy and possession by spirits. This specialized form of shamanism, so typical of parts of Siberia, finally spread to North America, where it influenced the Northwest Coast Indians and the Inuit (Eskimo). Other shamanic rituals in North America, such as the so-called Shaking Tent (the tent is shaking when spirits enter at the request of the shaman, who is fettered in the dark), found among Inuit groups, and Algonquian- and Salish-speaking tribes of the Plateau, also have their close counterparts in Siberia. But these other rituals derive from a more general form of shamanism that is also present in South America and Southeast Asia and is certainly a heritage from very ancient times.

The languages of the North American Indians are enormously diverse, and with the exception of the relatively lately arrived Athapascan groups none seem related to known Old World languages. The common factor joining them all is their polysynthetic structure, whereby many sentence elements are included in a single word by compounding and adding prefixes and suffixes. Paul Radin suggested many years ago that there may be a genetic relationship between most of these languages, except those of the Aleut and Inuit, who differ from the mainstream of American aborigines in race, culture, and religion.

Development of hunting religions. The early hunters brought with them a legacy of ideas and rituals developed in the Old World. These were adapted to the changing habitats in the New World. We can follow the major trends in cultural differentiation after about 10,000 BCE, and we can draw some conclusions also about probable religious orientations.

Thus, the Paleo-Indians of eastern North America were big-game hunters, concentrating on animals like the mammoth, the giant bison, the three-toed horse, and the camel. In all likelihood the inherited concepts of animal ceremonialism and the master of the animals were applied to these animals. The big game died out, because of climatic changes or human overkilling, during the period from 8000 to 4000 BCE. Only one big animal—the bear—survived and continued to be the focus of special rites. The ritual around the slaying of the bear, distributed from the Saami (Lapps) of Scandinavia to the Ainu of northern Japan, and, in North America, from the Inuit and Athapascans in the north and west to the Delaware in the east and the Pueblo Indians in the south, seem to be a leftover from these Paleolithic and Mesolithic days.

It is difficult to say whether Asian ideas still streamed into North America at this time, but it seems probable. We know that many myths disseminated from Asia are mostly found south of the sub-Arctic area in North America. To this category belongs the myth of the earth diver, a primeval divine hero who fetches mud from the bottom of the sea, thereby creating the ground on which men live. It is important because it includes not only the flood myth, or the myth of the primeval sea, but also the idea of twin creators, one good and one less good or even bad, or one the main creator and the other his assistant (the culture hero). Another important myth that scholars have traced to Asia is the Orpheus myth, but proofs of its dissemination are inconclusive. Several mythic motifs have, however, definitely spread from the Old World, such as the magical flight and the Symplegades (clashing rocks), or the motif of the celestial vault that moves up and down.

The old hunting culture slowly disintegrated into a series of more specialized regional cultures about 7000–5000 BCE, and there are reasons to presume that the religious structures changed accordingly. In fact, it seems that the native hunting, fishing, and gathering cultures and religions that persisted into the historical period began to take form at this time, the changes stimulated to a major extent by ecological and climatic shifts.

An exceptional development took place in the south. In the increasingly arid regions of the Great Basin, the Southwest, and parts of California a so-called desert tradition was established, with heavy dependence on wild plants, seeds, and nuts. The corresponding religious system survived in late Great Basin religions, and part of it was also preserved in many Californian Indian religions. In the Southwest, the Basket Making culture, while an example of the desert tradition, also served as a link to horticultural development.

There is some evidence that psychotropic or hallucinogenic drugs were used primarily in plant-collecting areas. Within the region covered by the desert tradition jimsonweed, peyote (in northern Mexico), pulque, and, of course, tobacco were all employed.

Growth of agricultural religions. It seems fairly certain that the cultivation of tobacco spread from Mexico into North America with maize, for maize and tobacco cultivation share the same general distribution within the eastern regions of North America. In the Southwest, however, while maize was cultivated, tobacco was gathered wild.

The introduction of maize, or Indian corn, had basic consequences for aboriginal religions, for it changed the whole outlook on life, the religious pattern, and the character of supernatural powers. There were many incentives for this change: the concentration of the population in more or less settled villages; the preoccupation with sowing, planting, and harvesting; the enhanced position of women (from that of seed collectors to that of seed producers); and the new forms of social organization (matrilineage, or, among the Iroquois, even some sort of matriarchy). Typical of these agricultural religions were concern for crops and fertility, the rise of priestly organizations, the creation of temples and shrines, and the appearance of deities, often of the female sex (or even androgynes), who impersonate the plants or lend fertility. Rituals, in turn, grew more complex, incorporating greater numbers of discrete actions, and sacrifices of a bloody kind (including human sacrifice) became more widespread. Nowhere, however, did agriculture entirely supplant hunting, particularly not in the east, where the rituals for encouraging the growth of maize, beans, and squash are basically the same as the rituals for slain animals. Of course, the death-and-revival pattern is fundamental to both animal and vegetational ceremonialism.

Appearance of maize religion in the Southwest. The introduction of maize into North America occurred in two places, the Southwest and the Southeast. From all appearances it was known earlier in the Southwest, where it is recorded from 3000 to 2000 BCE in the wooded highland valleys of New Mexico. Village agriculture was firmly established at the beginning of the Common Era and was effective after 500 CE.

Some of the religious innovations surrounding the maize complex and accompanying it on its diffusion from Mexico have been revealed through archaeology. The best illustrations are provided by the so-called Hohokam culture in southern Arizona. It was deeply influenced by Mesoamerica from about 500 to 1200 CE, when it suddenly declined, probably as a consequence of the fall of its model, the Toltec empire in Mexico. The most important evidence of the cultural influence from the south is the architectural planning of the towns: irrigation canals, oval ball courts for ritual games, and platform mounds of earth or adobe serving as substructures for temples with hearths and altars.

The Mexican influence on religion can also be seen in the neighboring Anasazi or Pueblo cultures down to our own time. Mesoamerican symbols appear in the bird designs that decorate Hopi pottery. Some of the religious fraternities that meet in the semisubterranean ceremonial chambers probably have Mexican prototypes, for instance, the kachina societies that are reminiscent of the cult organizations that surrounded the Mexican rain god Tlaloc.

Appearance of maize religion in the Southeast. The maize complex entered the Southeast slightly later than the Southwest, perhaps sometime after 1000 BCE; there is, however, no certain proof of agriculture there until the birth of Christ. It seems that influences from Mesoamerica were responsible for the so-called Burial Mound cultures, 1000 BCE to 700 CE, with their earthworks, including mortuary mounds, and for their ceramic figurines. At least the latest of these cultures, the Hopewell, was acquainted with maize ceremonialism.

A major change took place with the introduction of the so-called Mississippian tradition about 700 CE. Large rectangular and flat-topped mounds of unprecedented size were arranged around rectangular plazas. The mounds served as foundations of temples, whence the name Temple Mound, also used to designate these cultures. Intensive agriculture belonged to this new tradition, which flourished in the lower and middle Mississippi Valley but was particularly anchored in the Southeast. Its last representatives were the historical Natchez Indians of the lower Mississippi, known for their hierarchical class system with a sacred king, called the Great Sun, at its apex, for their sacred center, including temple and burial mounds, and for an elaborate ceremonial complex.

The agricultural religions rarely reached such an advanced stage of development in eastern North America, but they spread from the Southeastern hearth in different directions. Mississippian traits mingled with older Woodland traits in the Iroquois culture in the north and, after 1000 CE, with Plains hunting religions in the river valleys to the west.

A Regional Survey. The religions of the indigenous peoples in North America have developed on the foundations that have just been described. However, factors other than historical have contributed to the differentiation in religious profiles that occurs in every region, and especially in the Pacific Northwest, the Southwest, and the Plains. Such factors include local geographic conditions and the ecological adaptations of individual cultures. Religious differentiation is closely related to cultural diversity, for geographical and ecological factors act first of all on a group's cultural and social structure, and then through these structures on religion.

Roughly speaking, North America can be divided geographically into two main parts, the mountainous regions in the west, or the Rocky Mountains system, and the large plain and woodland country to the east. We find a relatively greater number of tribes and tribelets, often in great isolation from each other, in the mountainous West. The cultural variation there is therefore considerable. The vast eastern country, on the other hand, is populated by widely dispersed, large tribes in close contact with each other. Culturally, it can be seen as one large, relatively uniform area, in which the regional variants are relatively undifferentiated.

As Clark Wissler and others have noted, the geographic regions and the cultural areas correspond closely to each other. Since geographical and ecological factors have influenced religious forms, each region reveals unique features.

Arctic. The barren country around the Arctic coasts is sparsely inhabited by the Inuit and, on the Aleutian Islands, their kinsmen the Aleut. Inuit religion carries all marks of a hunting religion, concentrating on beliefs and rituals related to animals and on shamanism. The hunting rituals are rather intricate, in particular in Alaska where they focus on the whale (whale feasts are also found among the Nootka of the Northwest Coast and the Chukchi and Koriak of Siberia). A great role is played by the mistress of the sea animals, called Sedna among the Central Inuit. She figures in shamanic rites: when taboos have been transgressed her hair gets filthy, and in rage she holds back the animals; it is the shaman's task in a séance to descend to her home at the bottom of the sea and clean her hair so that she will free the animals again.

Sub-Arctic. A vast region of the coniferous forests, lakes, and swamps in interior Alaska and Canada, the sub-Arctic is sparsely inhabited by Athapascan-speaking Indians in its western half and Algonquian-speaking Indians in its eastern half. The Athapascans are latecomers from Siberia, arriving perhaps around 9000 BCE; their linguistic affiliations are with the Sino-Tibetan tongues. The Algonquian tribes conserve religious traits that associate them closely with the circumpolar culture.

The region is inhabited by hunting cultures, with inland game, in particular the caribou and the moose, as food resources. People are organized in loose bands or, since the introduction by Europeans of the hunting of fur-bearing animals, in family groups who have hunting grounds reserved for their exclusive use.

Religion is dominated by hunting ceremonialism and, to a certain extent, by shamanism. Bear ceremonialism is widespread, and hunting taboos are very common. Sweat baths grant their practitioners ritual purity before hunting or important ceremonies. The vision and guardian-spirit quest is fairly common. Shamanism is characterized by shaking tent ceremonies, usually performed for divination, and by scapulimancy (foretelling the future by inspecting the shoulder blades of animals). Athapascan and Algonquian groups show separate development: the former hold girls' puberty rites and fear their dead; the latter are known for a strong high-god belief, a consistent system of masters of the animals (in which each species has its own master), and an intense dread of cannibal monsters, which are called *windigo*.

Northeast woodlands. Formerly covered by mixed coniferous and deciduous trees, the Northeast woodlands held a large population of Algonquian-, Iroquoian-, and Siouan-speaking tribes. In historical and protohistorical times both agriculture and hunting were practiced, particularly by the Iroquoian groups; the Algonquian tribes were hunters with only limited horticulture. The social systems of these groups were often complicated, with unilineal kinship groups, clan organization, and chieftaincy.

The double economic heritage is to some extent mirrored in the religious pattern. The hunters concentrate on hunting rituals and vision quests, the planters on rituals and beliefs surrounding the crops. The Iroquois, for instance, have a series of calendar rites celebrating the planting, ripening, and harvesting of the "three sisters": maize, squash, and beans. The midwinter ceremony, formerly a new year ceremony with the kindling of new fire and the sacrifice of a white dog, is the main ritual event. As in many other rituals of agricultural peoples, great attention is paid to the dead, in whose honor feasts are arranged.

Southeast woodlands. In the southern deciduous forests, with their savannas and swamps, the tribes of Muskogean stock, interspersed with Siouan groups and the Iroquoian-speaking Cherokee, kept up a peripheral high culture, the last vestiges of the prehistoric Mississippian culture. The Southeastern Indians were, at least at the beginning of the historical era, predominantly engaged in agriculture, and their sociopolitical organization was adjusted to this fact. Thus, the Creek had a maternal clan system, with clans subordinated to both phratries and moieties. The latter had ceremonial functions, often carried out in ball games.

Characteristic of Creek religion is the emphasis laid on ceremonialism and priestly functions. The priests, who were instructed in secrecy in the woods, along lines reminiscent of the vision quest, were divided into several classes: one was in charge of the sacred cult objects, another divined hidden things (such as the causes of diseases), and still another cured people from diseases. Even today, a major part of the curing ceremonies is the recitation of sacred formulas.

The main religious ceremony is the maize harvest ceremony, called the Busk. It is also a New Year ritual, in which old fires are extinguished and a new fire is kindled and people ritually cleanse themselves through washing and the drinking of an emetic.

Prairies and plains. The tall-grass area (with some parkland and river-bottom woodland) between the woodlands in the east and the high Plains in the west is known as the Prairies. The Plains are the short-grass steppe country, too dry for agriculture, that stretches toward the mountains and semideserts in the far West. (In Canada, the Great Plains are sometimes referred to as the Prairies.)

The historical cultures were formed during the seventeenth and eighteenth centuries when the acquisition of horses made the wide-open spaces easily accessible to surrounding tribes and white expansion forced woodland Indians to leave their home country for the dry, treeless areas. Algonquian and Siouan tribes immigrated from the east and northeast, Caddoan tribes from the south. Several groups ceased practicing horticulture (the Crow and Cheyenne) and turned into buffalo hunters, but they kept parts of their old social and political organization. In the west, Shoshonean groups held the ground they had traditionally occupied, and groups of Athapascans—for example, the Apache—forced their way to the southern parts of the region.

Whereas the Prairies could be regarded as a periphery of the Eastern Woodlands, the Plains region offers a late cultural and religious complex of its own. The religion is a mixture of derived agricultural ceremonialism and hunters' belief systems. The major New Year ceremony is the Sun Dance, during which asceticism, dancing, praying, and curing take place. Other forms of ritualism center around tribal and clan bundles, and the sacred ritual known as the Calumet Dance, or Pipe Dance. There is much cosmological speculation and an advanced concept of the godhead. The vision and guardian spirit complex is well developed. The Plains religious pattern has become among modern Indians the model for a pan-Indian religion, transcending old tribal and cultural boundaries.

Northwest Coast. The broken coastline, high mountains, and deep fjords of the Northwest Coast were the home of the Tlingit, Haida, Tsimshian, and Wakashan tribes and some Coast Salish and Chinookan groups in the south. With their totem poles, their plank houses and canoes, and their headgear reminiscent of East Asian conic hats, these Indians make an un-American impression, an impression that is strengthened by their social organization with its give-away feasts (pot-latches) intended to "shame" invited guests and thus increase the host's prestige. There have apparently been contacts with both northern and eastern Asian cultures, although the nature of this exchange is little understood. The basic substratum seems to be a fishing culture that developed on both sides of the North Pacific and gave rise to both Inuit and Northwest Coast cultures. The abundant animal and fish life along the coast, together with the rich herbal and animal life of the dense woods, provided a living standard that sometimes excelled that of the agriculturists. It is perhaps not surprising that rank differentiation, based partly on wealth, and slavery appeared here.

The religion is characterized partly by its association with the activities of hunters and fishermen, partly by its secret societies adapted to the complicated social structure. The animal ceremonialism is focused on the sea fauna, and there are many sea spirits in animal forms. The dead have their realm, or one of their realms, at the bottom of the sea. The secret societies recruited individuals who had an inherited right to make contact with a certain kind of guardian spirit. Famous societies are the Wolf society of the Nootka and the Cannibal society of the Kwakiutl. Possession by spirits also occurred in shamanism, which here reached a high point of development in America.

Plateau. The Intermountain area, which includes both the Columbia and the Fraser river drainages, is known as the Plateau; it was inhabited by Salish and Shahaptin tribes that lived on fish and, secondarily, on land animals and roots. The area is partly wooded, partly a bunchgrass steppe. The culture area is an offshoot of the sub-Arctic hunting culture, tempered by influences from the Northwest Coast and the Plains. The sociopolitical group consisted of the village, under the formal control of a hereditary chief.

In their religion the Plateau Indians stressed the visionary complex and food ceremonies. The vision quests were undertaken at puberty by both sexes. The relation between the guardian spirit and his client was displayed in the Winter Dance, or Spirit Dance, a ceremony, under the supervision of a medicine man, in which the spirit was impersonated. Important celebrations were firstling rites, first-fruits rites, and the First-Salmon rite. In this last rite, which was guided by a so-called salmon chief (who had the salmon as one of his guardian spirits), the first salmon was greeted and its "leader" hailed with special ceremonies.

Great Basin. A dry region of sands and semideserts, the Great Basin was inhabited by Shoshonean (Numic) groups, some of them, like the Gosiute, the most impoverished of North American groups. Seeds, nuts, and rodents provided the principal food. The social organization was often atomistic. The cultural profile represented a remnant of the old desert tradition.

The religious pattern was closely adapted to a lifestyle based on the bare necessities. Hunters had to be blessed by spirits in visions in order to be successful, but there was little elaboration of guardian-spirit beliefs. Medicine men had specialized powers; for instance, the antelope medicine man attracted the antelopes by singing. Harvest ceremonies were round dances at which thanks were given to the supreme being.

California. Whereas the northern, eastern, and southern parts of California were peripheral to the Northwest Coast, Great Basin, and Southwest cultural areas, respectively, the central valleys and coastland constituted a separate cultural area, known as the California region, densely populated by Penutian, Hokan, and Numic groups. These natives, living in a mild climate, dedicated themselves to collecting, hunting, and fishing. Their staple food consisted of wild plants and their fruits, in particular acorns, all of which were found in abundance. The political unit was usually the village (under the leadership of a headman), but was sometimes a lineage.

In this diversified culture area religious expressions were most varied. North-central California is known for its lofty concept of a supreme being and for its initiation of youths into religious societies, such as the Kuksu, Ghost, and Hesi societies. Guardian spirit quests were rare, and medicine men received unsought visions. In the southern part of the area, initiation ceremonies were accompanied by the drinking of drugs prepared from jimsonweed and by various symbolic acts referring to death and rebirth. In some places there were great commemorative ceremonies for the dead.

The Southwest. A magnificent desert country with some oases, particularly along the Rio Grande, the Southwest was populated by hunting and farming groups of Piman and Yuman descent, by former hunters like the Athapascan Apache and Navajo—who did not arrive here until about 1500 CE—and by the Pueblo peoples, intensive agriculturists mostly belonging to the Tanoan and Keresan linguistic families. I shall here concentrate on the Pueblo groups, the descendants of the prehistoric Anasazi culture. Their culture is famous for its big community houses on the mesas, its intensive horticulture (with irrigation in the Rio Grande region), and its complex and beautiful ceremonialism. Each Pueblo town is an independent unit governed by the heads of the religious societies.

Religion penetrates all aspects of Pueblo life. A rich set of ceremonies that mark the divisions of the year are conducted by different religious societies. Their overall aim is to create harmony with the powers of rain and fertility, symbolized by the ancestors, the rain and cloud spirits, and the Sun. Each society has its priesthood, its attendants, its sacred bundles, and its ceremonial cycle. There are also medicine societies for the curing of diseases—the inspired, visionary medicine man has no place in this collectivistic, priestly culture.

No other American Indian societies lay so much stress on ceremonialism as do the Pueblo. Their supernatural beings are almost unthinkable without the rituals through which they are manifested.

SEE ALSO Cosmogony; Inuit Religious Traditions; Sedna; Tobacco.

BIBLIOGRAPHY

For discussion of sources and research the reader is referred to my work *The Study of American Indian Religions* (Chico, Calif., 1983) and Harold W. Turner's *North America*, vol. 2 of his *Bibliography of New Religious Movements in Primal Societies* (Boston, 1978).

On the topic of North American Indian religions, several surveys and introductions are available. In chronological order there is first Werner Müller's "Die Religionen der Indianervölker Nordamerikas," in *Die Religionen des alten Amerika*, edited by Walter Krickeberg (Stuttgart, 1961), a thoughtful presentation of native religious structures. Ruth M. Underhill's *Red Man's Religion* (Chicago, 1965) describes religious beliefs and practices in their cultural interaction. Two later syntheses are my *The Religions of the American Indians* (Berkeley, 1979), which concentrates on religious ideas in historical perspectives, and Sam D. Gill's *Native American Religions* (Belmont, Calif., 1982), which emphasizes some major features of Indian religious life. A detailed, provocative investigation of the religions east of the Rocky Mountains will be found in Werner Müller's *Die Religionen der Waldlandindianer Nordamerikas* (Berlin, 1956).

A number of scholars in the field have issued collections of their articles on North American native religions. Here could be mentioned Müller's *Neue Sonne—Neues Licht*, edited by Rolf Gehlen and Bernd Wolf (Berlin, 1981), a representative selection of this author's most engaging articles; my *Belief and Worship in Native North America* (Syracuse, N. Y., 1981), which among other things discusses belief patterns, ecology, and religious change; and Joseph Epes Brown's *The Spiritual Legacy of the American Indian* (New York, 1982), a book that beautifully outlines the deeper meaning of Indian philosophy and ceremonialism. An older publication in the same genre is the philosopher Hartley Burr Alexander's posthumous work, *The World's Rim: Great Mysteries of the North American Indians* (Lincoln, Nebr., 1953). Anthologies by several authors are *Seeing with a Native Eye*, edited by Walter Holden Capps (New York, 1976), and *Teachings from the American Earth*, edited by Dennis Tedlock and Barbara Tedlock (New York, 1975). The former contains articles by scholars of religion; the latter, articles by anthropologists.

Among general comparative works, a classic in the field is Ruth Fulton Benedict's *The Concept of the Guardian Spirit in North America* (Menasha, Wis., 1923). Shamanism in North America is the object of a study by Marcelle Bouteiller, *Chamanisme et guérison magique* (Paris, 1950). The patterns of soul and spirit beliefs are analyzed in my work *Conceptions of the Soul among North American Indians* (Stockholm, 1953). The corpus of American Indian myths and legends is carefully annotated in *Tales of the North American Indians*, edited by Stith Thompson (Cambridge, Mass., 1929). My study *The North American Indian Orpheus Tradition* (Stockholm, 1957) is an extensive treatment of the Orpheus myth and its religious prerequisites. One mythological character, the culture hero and trickster, is the subject of Arie van Deursen's detailed research work *Der Heilbringer* (Groningen, 1931). Secret societies and men's societies are penetratingly discussed in Wolfgang Lindig's *Geheimbünde und Männerbünde der Prärie- und der Waldlandindianer Nordamerikas* (Wiesbaden, 1970). Among comparative works on rituals and ritualism three interesting studies are Ruth Underhill's well-known *Ceremonial Patterns in the Greater Southwest* (New York, 1948), John Witthoft's illuminating *Green Corn Ceremonialism in the Eastern Woodlands* (Ann Arbor, 1949), and William N. Fenton's detailed ethnohistorical study *The Iroquois Eagle Dance: An Offshoot of the Calumet Dance* (Washington, D. C., 1953).

An Indian's own view of native American religions in their relations to Christianity and to whites is presented, somewhat polemically, in Vine Deloria Jr.'s *God Is Red* (New York, 1973).

ÅKE HULTKRANTZ (1987)

NORTH AMERICAN INDIAN RELIGIONS: MYTHIC THEMES

The very broad subject of mythology among traditional peoples is often juxtaposed with "history" in the modern, Western sense. However, this confluence presents problems for both traditional indigenous communities and Western modernity. There is a dichotomy between these subjects that generally rests on the issue of veracity, so that the broad class of narrative known as myth, along with such subgenera as legend, folktale, fable, and the like, is easily subsumed into one broad "false but relevant" classification with semiotic significance to the narrative's home culture.

However, it is also possible to view aspects of "historic" events and their retelling from one generation to the next through the same lens with which we view myth. In this approach, the mythic narratives of a culture have many levels of significance, both for their culture of origin and for those who analyze them. It is assumed here that both of these positions are valid. However, the Western terms *myth, tale,* and *legend* will be employed at times as this designates the esoteric nature of certain aspects of these sacred histories.

In the case of American Indian sacred narrative, those communities for whom the stories are culturally relevant view these tales in ways which cross, and often transcend, the Western category of history. These "sacred histories" serve to orient their communities in time and space in ways that operate within the logic of the universe they inhabit, and in turn provide outsiders with insight into the ethos and worldview of their home cultures.

Western historical narratives tend to rely upon a linear pattern in which one event transpires after, and sometimes due to, the one preceding it, which also makes specific dates and actors the key issues in these tales. American Indian sacred narratives operate in a different way, developing within the specifics of the producing culture based on the logic of their universe. This logic is often cyclical, or rhythmic, in nature, and the focus is not on linearity but on the maintenance of ongoing natural rhythms.

There usually exists, in each Native American community, various categories of story, each with a specific purpose and appropriate use. The Hopi, for example, distinguish between four types of narrative: *navoiti,* or knowledge to which the speaker has a direct link, even if that link is from a very distant past; *tutavo,* or stories about the Sacred; *wuknavoti,* which is usually translated as "prophesy" but includes all sorts of prognosticative stories; and *tuuwutisi,* the term most often translated as "myth" but also considered a historic accounting of events that occurred in sacred time. This is distinguished from *navoiti* in that the connections to the events and actors in the story are secondhand or happened in the esoteric realm of the before-time.

There is a Chumash term, *timoloquinas,* often translated as "stories generally thought to be true," that also describes this category of tale, where "truth" is a very slippery concept and relative to the overall meaning of the tale to its intended audience. It is via these orally transmitted tales that the entirety of a people's history is conveyed—spiritual, economic, and political. These tales represent a body of knowledge the continuity of which is only recently beginning to become apparent to non-Indian minds.

This knowledge is passed from generation to generation through oral narratives that encode both pertinent and proper behaviors for the edification of future generations. In the telling of these tales, both the narrator and the audience have active roles: the teller of the tale is expected to maintain the story's integrity from telling to telling, and the audience holds the storyteller to task with their own memories of the stories. These tales are told at events bound by communal dictates, which must be supported by the audience. The young people learn the importance of these events and come to give them the kind of attention and respect that facilitates those dictates. The telling of stories, then, provides opportunities for the truths contained in them to be practiced as well as learned.

Stories about the community's sacred history also allow the people to examine specific ideas that the community considers important. Some narratives relay information about the origins of a particular Native American people, as well as their indelible links to their sacred past. Others revolve around pertinent political, economic, and social issues or explore themes of community membership and identity.

Prior to the devastating effects of colonialism, these stories were the key link between members of particular tribal groups, as well as that group's link to their land. Elders serve as repositories of the knowledge and wisdom that makes the people a people, transferring moral precepts and appropriate community parameters to the next generation. When the U.S. government attempted to assimilate Indian children, they did so by taking them away from their families and placing them in boarding schools, in hopes that separating them from their elders and storytellers would destroy their cultural identity.

Fortunately, much of the imagery, humor, pathos, and personality of the tales was nevertheless passed along to the boarding-school generation, and the translation of the stories into English, especially due to the rising discipline of ethnography around the turn of the last century, guaranteed that most of these tales, and the cultures that they encode, would not be lost. Though these are properly oral traditions, many tales have been transcribed by non–Native Americans and, more recently, written down by American Indians themselves. The shift to written form should, however, be seen as archival in nature, as the pressures of modernity make the regular telling of these tales difficult for some Native American communities. This is not, therefore, a shift away from the oral tradition, but a response to the challenges presented by current conditions.

Given the cultural continuity and thematic integrity that these tales have displayed, it is somewhat counterintuitive to say that they remain dynamic tales for which there is rarely a definitive version. However, the changes in the narrative flow or differences in details are often due to the shifting needs of the audience, rather than omissions or transformations designed by the narrator. For example, in the Ojibwe tales of Nanabush, the trickster/creator and cultural hero reacts to European invasion by moving west, and sleeps as a large promontory at Thunder Bay. Nanabush sleeps there still, waiting for the time when the Ojibwe can bring about a resurgence of Ojibwe culture and religion. Some contemporary Ojibwe speak of a recent stirring in Nanabush, as his people are working to realize this resurgence.

There are also smaller, subtler changes in the tales, such as when Nanabush gets tangled up in telephone wires, in contrast to the ropes found in older versions. This dynamic quality reinforces the ability of Native American myth to remain relevant and meaningful throughout the whole of the community's experience. And it illustrates the fact that American Indians, while they remember the sacred stories from many generations past, are not themselves mythic figures trapped in antiquity.

For the American Indian communities, the world is populated not only by humans, but by other beings as well. These beings include the natural world and all that is in it, as well as spiritual or other-worldly beings who have the ability to communicate with, to do harm and good to, and generally act within the human realm. The most important aspect of this arrangement is the other-than-human beings' ability to form relationships, with each other as well as with the people. It is important to stress that these beings are not simply natural forces or unknown events that have become personified, but fellow inhabitants of the world—neighbors and relatives—who require respectful attention of one kind or another. The other-than-human realm interacts with its human cousins and neighbors in Native American sacred histories in many different ways, sometimes benevolently, sometimes malevolently, all due to the fact that they are nearly always more powerful and erudite than humans.

This system of sacred narrative and the actors, events, and lessons contained therein can be divided into tales of creation, theories about the natural world, and stories that place the people within their tribal sacred history. The following sections will look at some examples of these myths.

CREATION. Creation stories not only tell the people how the universe came to be, but also set in motion the logic within which it operates. Origin myths, those that draw upon the creation of all things (as opposed to the post-creation establishment of a feature of the landscape or a ritual complex), effectively frame the ways in which all that comes after is possible. Like the origin myth found in the first part of the book of Genesis, the world subsequently responds in ways that are in keeping with its initial creation, such as the dynamics of male–female or human–animal relationships or the hierarchical theme found in subsequent Hebrew and Christian mythologies.

The Navajo origin myth. The Dinée (Navajo) origin story is an example of a creation story from Native America. In this tale, the present world of the Dinée comes about only after three preceding worlds have emerged, one from another, on the surface of the earth. First Man ('Altsé Hastiin) and First Woman ('Altsé 'Asdzáá) were two of the beings from the First, or Black, World. First Man was made in the east from the meeting of the white and black clouds. First Woman was made in the west from the joining of the yellow and blue clouds. Spider Woman (Na ashje'ii 'Asdzáá), who taught Navajo women how to weave, was also from the First World, as was Begochiddy, a creator figure who made and ordered all that was in the First World. The Black World produced many creatures, and it became a crowded place of quarrelling and strife, necessitating the move into the Second, or Blue, World. In some variations of the tale, this movement was facilitated by a reed which allowed some of the First People to climb into the Blue World, bringing with them all that Begochiddy had made.

There were creatures already inhabiting the Second World, and as Begochiddy continued the task of creation, those beings hampered the process, and strife, fighting, and killing made the Second World an undesirable place. So some of the inhabitants climbed upward into the Third World. The Third, or Yellow, World was where sexual desire was created. The essences of maleness and femaleness had been part of the creative endeavor, and Begochiddy created a class of people, not yet the Dinée, who were male and female. Tensions arose between them that were ultimately resolved by bringing about an inexorable connection between them. Problems within the Yellow World, of different types and origins depending upon the telling, necessitated the move into this, the Fourth, or Glittering, World. This is when the Dinée were created, along with the original Hogan. The Hogan, the archetypal house and sacred space for the Dinée, held the first Beauty Way, the girls' puberty ceremony. This first Beauty Way was for Changing Woman, the ultimate creatrix of the Dinée and scion of feminine creativity. Young Dinée women undergo a ritual transformation into Changing Woman in the course of their initiation, and it is during this ceremony that the Dinée creation story is told in its entirety, culminating in the ritual reenactment of the first Beauty Way.

The Dinée origin narrative contains the deeply held existential truths of Dinée culture. Changing Woman creates the Dinée using elements found in the Glittering World along with flakes of her own skin; thus their very bodies are made up of the place the Dinée call home. Nothing in the logic of Dinée culture derives from outside the place of their emergence.

The balance that in all three subsequent worlds was upset by human foibles must be maintained in this world, lest the Dinée bring about their own destruction. The creation story, then, also serves as a cautionary tale, and with it is passed along the traditional wisdom that, when dutifully employed, helps the Dinée maintain that balance. This includes the elements of the story that speak of the importance of corn, which, in addition to being an important food staple, is also a symbol for what is truly important for the universe and how one is to behave in it.

Pueblo cultures. The Hopi, Zuni, Tewa, Keres, Tiwa, and Jemes, have a similar creation epic in which the world known to the Pueblos is created after they have migrated upward through a succession of worlds, usually three, before arriving in the fourth world, which is the world of today. As in the Dinée tale, the people in each of the worlds were typically compelled to move on because various transgressions against the order of things led to imbalance and conflict. In the Pueblo tales, however, individuals often caused the conflict by directly violating the sacred order, and were subsequently left behind for their behavior. The rest of the people would be assisted in their journey to the next world by sacred beings, often in the form of animals.

The animals who lend their support not only play a logistical role in the people's migration, but also teach the people valuable lessons about how the world works and what their responsibilities are in it. These responsibilities include both an understanding of the world and gaining knowledge of important rituals and ceremonies. Among the Hopi and Zuni, for example, the people acquire the knowledge necessary for summoning the rain. Among the Hopi, the tale begins in Tokpela (Endless Space). Tokpela was shapeless until Taiowa, the Sun and Creator, made his nephew, Sótuknang, the god of the universe and creator of all ceremonies. On this world was placed a helper, Spider Woman, who also possessed creative power and used her abilities to make the world ready for human habitation. In addition to creating the necessary elements of the world such as plants and animals, Spider Woman made a pair of hero twins who would protect the people from harm. While they were in Tokpela, however, the people's numbers increased and they began to drift apart, and illness came to be.

The people then moved on to the next world, Tokpa (Dark Midnight), where they built villages, stored food, and traded among themselves. Consequently, the people became greedy for material possessions, and strife again ensued. Next the people emerged into the Third World, Kuskurza, a name whose meaning remains unknown. Again the people increased, expanding into larger and more complex villages. Again corruption, greed and infighting led to imbalance, and Kuskurza was flooded. Only a few emerged into the Fourth World, Túwaqachi (World Complete), via a hollow reed. Like the Dinée, it is up to them to maintain the balance of this world.

The Zuni creation is very similar, but the Sun brings about the movement from one world to the next after the people fail to adequately make prayer offerings. In the Third World, hero twins come to bring the Zuni into this, the Fourth World. In both Zuni and Hopi creation tales, the emergence into the Fourth World requires that each clan find its place, and the tales describe the Pueblo people's divisions and establishe the territories assigned to each.

What finally emerges out of this epic narrative is a worldview characterized by six directions, which are inhabited by a pantheon of sacred beings. For the Zuni, each of the four cardinal directions contains an ocean, and in these four oceans are four mountains, each symbolized by a different color. For the Dinée, both the orientation to the landscape and the ethos of the people derive from the creation story. Therefore, Pueblo mythology is locatable in the surrounding landscape, and pertinent to everyday life.

Orientation. Elements of a culture's sense of itself and what it is supposed to be about in the world often have their roots in the creation narrative. For hunting and wild-horticulture groups, animals and plants play heavily in the creation story. The Ojibwe, for whom the Great Lakes region is home, are among the cultures with earth-diver elements to their tale. The earth-diver is a familiar animal—Muskrat, in the case of the Ojibwe—who dives to the bottom of a vast body of water to retrieve a small bit of earth that becomes the world.

Many Native American communities in the Eastern Woodlands and Great Lakes area share the Pueblo and Navajo idea that the present earth has been remade from a world salvaged after the destruction of a previous one. The earth-diver in these tales must dive to the bottom of the waters that have flooded the old world to retrieve earth with which a new world can be made. In the Ojibwe versions, characters sometimes shift, and regional variations may occur, but the core narrative line always includes a friendship or kinship between Nanabush, the Ojibwe trickster and creator, and a wolf. The wolf, usually because he is capricious or unwary, falls through thin ice into a lake and is killed by underwater spirits, the manitous, led by their chief, Mishebeshu. Mishebeshu is a very powerful manitou who owns the water world and appears as a horned serpent or dragon. Mishebeshu means "Great Lynx," and he is so powerful that his name is only to be mentioned in winter when he is safely under the ice. Mishebeshu is not evil, but neither is he a friend to humans.

It is always best in Ojibwe culture to treat the other-than-human realm with enormous amounts of respect, which the wolf fails to do when he ignores the melting spring ice. Devastated by the loss of Wolf, Nanabush exacts revenge by traveling to Mishebeshu's home and killing him. Since Mishebeshu is a powerful manitou, he either regenerates himself or his many other selves multiply to flood the world. Nanabush takes refuge on a turtle's back and calls the diving animals to him to ask them to retrieve a bit of earth from below the waters. It is usually the least among these, Muskrat, who succeeds, and the earth is regenerated. Nanabush, or in some variations Kitche, or Great Manitou, creates humans and readies the earth for them with the help of the plant and animal people.

This, like most creation tales, is replete with lessons about the fragility of the earth, the need to respect the boundaries set out by the manitous, and the ultimate cost of revenge.

The people. Another key feature of many creation tales is the role that the animal and plant kingdoms play in human life. They are seen as elder siblings, here before the people and wiser because of that. Often plants, animals, water beings, wind, and rocks play an important role in the creation of the people.

The Chumash of the central California coast tell of their creation by a committee of animals that includes Coyote, Lizard, Hawk, and others, who debate the various features that the humans will possess. Coyote and Lizard enter into a debate about what kind of hands the new creatures will have, and the other animal beings take sides. In the end Coyote wins out, and he prepares to press his hand into the surface of a fine-grained stone and create the model for human hands. But, at the last second, Lizard sneaks up and places his hand into the stone, deciding the form of the human hand.

In addition, the group debates human mortality. The Jerusalem Cricket argues that human beings should eventually die, while Coyote argues for immortality in the form of a lake where humans can immerse their dead and bring them back to life. Cricket wins the debate, sealing his fate as an omen of bad luck for the Chumash people. In both stories, the roles of animals, the vicissitudes of life, and the need for proper behavior are all established along with the creation of human beings, forging a strong link between the way the world works and how the people are to behave in it. In creation tales, the universe, created with a working logic in place that represents balance and attention to the rhythms of nature, is established for all creatures. And all creatures have some responsibility for and to that creation in order that it continue on in balance.

NATURE. The operation of the universe can be seen as a sort of dependent variable, in that things must be done by those who have been created in order to keep creation balanced, but creation itself effects the possible choices of those creatures. Therefore, many American Indian narratives contain explanatory elements as well as evidence of what happens when the creatures do or do not complete the tasks for which they are responsible.

In these stories, the way in which creation looks and acts is explained, but in a multilayered way that allows these stories to remain relevant throughout the life of the listener. Children delight in the stories while gaining important information about the world, and adults perceive nuanced aspects appropriate to their lives as well. For example, the Seneca tell of Old Man Winter and his companion North Wind being defeated by Spring, which gives children imagery with which they can envision the changing seasons, but the story can also be told in a way that allows adults to ponder the need to allow old feelings to melt away like Old Man Winter does in the tale, to make room for a renewal in their hearts and minds that mirrors the coming of Spring.

The Cherokee explain the origin of the deer's curly tail in a story about Wild Boy and his brother, who make a game of allowing all of the animals to escape, thus causing the need for hunting. In this story, we discover not only why the deer's tail is curly and why people must hunt game to eat, but also that there is potential harm in not attending to one's duties, and that there can be no doubt as to what a good person must do when faced with opportunities for impetuous and facetious behavior.

Trickster tales. Another type of story that falls into this category is the so-called trickster tale, an extensive and largely misunderstood genre of traditional storytelling. It is the trickster—usually in the form of an animal known to the people, such as Raven, Coyote, or Hare, and almost always a male—who tends to represent both the best and the worst that a person can be. At times, the trickster is a creator, bringing about aspects of the world, such as fire, that make life much more pleasant. At other times, the trickster behaves badly, usually in the realms of gluttony or lust, bringing about negative aspects of the world or merely providing an entertaining way to point out the consequences of bad behavior.

One fine example of the latter is the tale told by the Yokuts of California about Coyote tricking Cricket into believing that she is the most beautiful of all insects. He uses her to demand tribute from the rest of the animals as their chief. Eventually, the Animal People grow tired of Coyote and Cricket and their demands, and Coyote impersonates the Creator in order to exact tribute. For this he is punished and sent to live in the North Star, and Cricket, for her vanity, must forever visit her lover Coyote during the day only, returning to Earth at night to play her sad song.

Another California tale, from the Karuk, shows the trickster in his creator aspect, as Coyote obtains fire from the stingy yellow jackets. Through a sort of relay race that sends the burning ember from animal to animal until it eventually falls into a softwood tree, Coyote shows the animals, and thus the people, how to extract fire from the wood, bringing the warmth and utility of fire to the world. A similar tale from around the Indian communities of the Pacific Northwest has Raven, their trickster, retrieving the sun from a selfish chief and placing it in the sky for the benefit of all.

The key issue with regard to these trickster tales is that the term *trickster* cannot adequately convey all of the nuances in the tales to which it is assigned. This glossing over of an important theme in American Indian sacred narrative, therefore, must be used with caution. The negative connotations usually associated with the word *trick* creates a view of these tales that is somewhat skewed. In the sense that it denotes clown-like and regrettable behavior, the term *trickster* places this important Native American cultural theme into roughly the same category as Brer Rabbit, Wile E. Coyote, and the Three Stooges. When this term is applied to characters who may be heroes, creative deities, and powerful advocates of humans, these cultural icons are denigrated. American Indian thinkers such as Gerald Vizenor stress that *trickster,* as a term, should not be understood as an anthropological or folkloric category, but rather as a metaphorical idea or a consciousness within the stories that explains to the people who they are, where they are from, and how it is that they should live.

SACRED HISTORY. All of the above tales can be considered aspects of sacred history, and important mythic themes connect Native American people to their traditions through their direct relationships with the actors in the tales. While characters like Coyote or the animal and plant beings may not qualify as relatives in the sense that Western biological or historic realities dictate, the realities of Native American communities render a much different accounting of the family tree.

For the Lakota of the Great Plains, the story of White Buffalo Woman's visit to the people to bring them their seven central ceremonies and the sacred pipe affirms the already established, but perhaps neglected, familial relationship between the Lakota and the bison. The story tells of a time when the Lakota were experiencing famine, due in part to the reluctance of the Buffalo Nation to appear and be hunted. The people had forgotten the way to behave, and became more angry and confused as the consequences visited themselves upon them.

Then it happened that two young men were travelling in search of game when they spied a white mist, from which a beautiful young woman emerged. As she neared them, the men could see that she was naked. One young man averted his eyes and maintained decent thoughts, while the other approached her with evil intentions. The latter was swallowed up by a mist which left him nothing more than a skeleton. The other young man humbled himself, still covering his eyes, and the woman told him to go back to his people and have them make ready for her arrival, preparing a lodge where the women would attend her while the men averted their gazes until the appropriate time.

It came to pass as she instructed, and the woman made her way into the camp carrying a bundle. After she was bathed and dressed, she called all of the people together and taught them the ceremonies that would keep their minds and hearts attentive to their responsibilities to the world. She taught them to pray with the pipe, presenting a pipe to them and instructing them as to how subsequent pipes were to be made. As she left them, she rolled in the dust four times, each time turning into a buffalo of a different color. The last was a white buffalo, and then she was gone.

This tale is seen as a history of the religious use of the pipe among the Lakota, and the pipe that White Buffalo Woman gave to the people is still in existence, in the care of descendants of the first recipient. The tale, along with the ceremonies the people learn in the course of it, reoriented fallen ones to their sacred responsibilities to the world, especially to their relatives, the Buffalo Nation. In the Lakota creation narrative, the people and the buffalo emerge together from the Black Hills with common ancestors who can now be traced as easily as one traces their biological family tree. In addition to these important aspects of Lakota life, the story teaches humility and the proper treatment of women, as well as providing an inexorable link between the Lakota, their ritual cycle, and the land that produced them both.

In a similar way, the Chumash tell of their movement to the mainland of what is now California from the Channel Islands via a rainbow bridge placed by Hutash, the earth and fertility goddess. Hutash wanted to move some of her people from the islands to the mainland, so she provided a bridge. There was only one caveat: do not look down as you cross. Some of the people did look down, and fell into the ocean below. Several of the beings from Chumash mythology asked Hutash to do something for the people, as they would surely die as a result of the mishap. So Hutash turned them into dolphins as they fell, and they safely lived out their lives in that form. Thus the Chumash see themselves as related to the dolphins that inhabit the waters off the coast, and also remember to heed the lesson learned and remain mindful of the rules set out by Hutash.

In a Haida tale (one with many variations), a child discovers a bit of mold on the fish he is about to eat and complains about it, ultimately refusing the fish entirely. The people warn him that if he continues to speak disrespectfully, the Fish People will see to it that he learns a difficult lesson. Sure enough, as the child is playing by the shore he is taken into the sea by the Salmon, who change him into one of their own. The story contains many vignettes about the boy's travels as a salmon, and he eventually returns to the shore from which he was abducted. His mother catches him and starts to prepare him for drying when she notices that the salmon has a small charm around his neck. The village priest is called, and he sees that the fish is her long-lost son. The woman is to lay the salmon on the roof of her house, and when it rains, the fish will be transformed back into her son. This does indeed come to pass, and the boy grows to become a powerful priest and healer in his own right. This multilayered tale contains lessons about respect and propriety, and also establishes traceable links between the human world and the other-than-human world. The boy who becomes a priest is invariably referred to by people as a relative, and this relative was himself a salmon, if only for a while.

The Ojibwe have a series of tales about the Thunderers, sometimes called the Thunder Birds or Thunder Beings, who continue to interact with the people. There are tales in historic times of the Thunderers coming to people's aid in dire circumstances. The Thunderers provide a connection between the people and their sacred history, as these powerful beings appear in stories of long, long ago as well. The Thunderers are seen by the Ojibwe as grandparents, powerful manitous who assist those humans who know enough to respect them. They bring rain, they signal changes in the seasons, and they speak to humans and protect them from the threats of Mishebeshu and his kin.

In one story, Nanabush creates the Thunderers in order to keep the people, whom he has made, from disappearing. The Thunderers are instructed to watch over the humans and to strike against Mishebeshu. To continue to interact with these beings in contemporary circumstances brings the Ojibwe mythic cycle deeper relevance. The stories are taken as a nexus of events, and when one person evokes the sacred narrative through a personal experience of an other-than-human nature, it validates the entire corpus. Such hero figures, often the focus of ethnographic or folkloric analyses of American Indian mythic narratives, also fall into the category of sacred history in that they are often the originators of specific families or clans. Many Native American communities are organized along clan lines, with the clans originating in mythic times.

Another common theme in the hero tales is that of human heroes who provide edification or resolve via their behavior, as in the Coeur d'Alene accounts of a boy who, in the face of intimidation by a camp bully or certain defeat at the hands of an enemy, uses his courage and tenacity to overcome his adversary. Such a tale is that of Four Smokes, which tells of a group of men who are surrounded by enemies while hunting in Crow country. A young boy is asked to divert the warriors away from the camp while the rest of his family escapes. Out of concern for his family, the young boy reluctantly agrees. At each of four enemy charges the young boy gives a war cry and, with bullets flying about him, runs to a nearby bush. On each occasion he makes it to safety, and the Crow warriors, convinced that the boy has special powers, retreat. That evening the elders give the young boy the name Four Smokes in honor of the four times the Crow rifles discharged gun smoke but failed to hit the boy. The modern weaponry of the Crow party proves that Four Smokes is a historic character; one who can be seen as a close relative of the contemporary Coeur d'Alene and an exemplar of familial fidelity and courage in the face of adversity.

Themes that make up American Indian sacred narrative are governed by several key factors. First is the logical working of the universe as each specific tribal culture sees it. The creation stories set the parameters of the possible and the necessary, giving the people a guide by which decisions can be made, relationships understood, and success measured. Second, the narratives emphasize the way the actual day-to-day world works, which is similar to the first concept, but different in scope.

Whereas each tribal tradition can be seen as a philosophical system, the stories about the earth and how it operates can be seen as a science of sorts, a method for working within the rules set out in the creation narratives that will bring about expected results while avoiding the pitfalls that occur when one does things incorrectly. Often, tribal traditions make it clear that things must be done in a good way, which generally translates into a protocol within which propriety can be maintained, needs met, and problems assuaged. Finally, these are histories, stories of the people—where they came from and where they are going. Actors in these tales are often beings that one could encounter at any time, and one does encounter them, thus providing the impetus to maintain these traditions in perpetuity.

Modernity, in many ways, is anti-traditional, favoring the new, the innovative, and the topical. Sacred histories allow traditional cultures to exist in the modern world and yet maintain their link to the past, keeping their stories of the before-time, powerful other-than-human beings, and plant, animal, and elemental relatives because they are old. Wisdom comes with age, and American Indian stories have the power to bring ancient wisdom to bear on current topics. Contemporary indigenous communities the world over remain faithful to their own stories and legacy, rather than the sometimes more popular myths of modernity.

SEE ALSO Fiction, article on Native American Fiction and Religion; Lakota Religious Traditions; Poetry, article on Native American Poetry and Religion; Sedna; Tricksters, overview article and article on North American Tricksters.

BIBLIOGRAPHY

Aoki, Haruo. "Nez Perce Texts." *University of California Publications in Linguistics* 90 (1979).

Basso, Keith H. *Wisdom Sits in Places: Landscape and Language among the Western Apache.* Albuquerque, 1996.

Bunzel, Ruth L. *Zuni Ceremonialism.* Albuquerque, 1992.

Courlander, Harold. *The Fourth World of the Hopis: The Epic Story of the Hopi Indians as Preserved in Their Legends and Traditions.* Albuquerque, 1987.

Cruikshank, Julie. *The Social Life of Stories: Narrative and Knowledge in the Yukon Territory.* Lincoln, Neb., 1998.

Deloria, Vine. *Red Earth, White Lies: Native Americans and the Myth of Scientific Fact.* New York, 1995. See pages 37–61, 81–107.

Dongoske, Kurt, Leigh Jenkins, and T. J. Ferguson. "Understanding the Past through Hopi Oral Tradition." *Native Peoples Magazine* 6, no. 2 (1993): 24–31.

Dozier, Edward P. *The Pueblo Indians of North America.* New York, 1970.

Ferguson, T. J., Kurt Dongoske, Mike Yeatts, and Leigh Kuwanwisiwma. "Hopi Oral History and Archaeology." In *Working Together: Native Americans and Archaeologists,* edited by Kurt E. Dongoske, Mark Aldenderfer, and Karen Doehner, pp. 45–60.Washington, D.C., 2000.

Frey, Rodney. *Landscape Traveled by Crane and Coyote: The World of the Schitsu'umsh (Coeur d'Alene).* Seattle, 2001.

Kawagley, A. Oscar. *A Yupiaq Worldview: A Pathway to Ecology and Spirit.* Prospect Heights, Ill., 1995.

Kidwell, Clara Sue, Homer Noley, and George E. "Tink" Tinker. *A Native American Theology.* Maryknoll, N.Y., 2001.

McPherson, Robert S. *Sacred Land, Sacred View: Navajo Perceptions of the Four Corners Region.* Salt Lake City, 1992.

Nequatewa, Edmund. *Truth of a Hopi: Stories Relating to the Origin, Myths, and Clan Histories of the Hopi.* Flagstaff, Ariz., 1990.

Ortiz, Alfonso, ed. *Handbook of North American Indians,* vol. 9, *Southwest.* Washington, D.C., 1979.

Parkhill, Thomas C. *Weaving Ourselves into the Land: Charles Godfrey Leland, "Indians," and the Study of Native American Religions.* Albany, N.Y., 1997.

Vizenor, Gerald "Trickster Discourse." *American Indian Quarterly* 14 (1990) 277–288.

Walker, James R. "James R. Walker: His Life and Work." In *Lakota Belief and Ritual,* edited by Raymond J. DeMallie and Elaine A. Jahner, pp. 3–61. Lincoln, Neb., 1980.

DENNIS F. KELLEY (2005)

NORTH AMERICAN INDIAN RELIGIONS: NEW RELIGIOUS MOVEMENTS

From the time of their earliest contact with European settlers and explorers, Native Americans have defended their lands, cultures, religions, and political rights. Often, Native American efforts to preserve their communities and cultures take the form of religious, military, political, and cultural movements. The ways that Native nations have sought to preserve their cultures and territories have varied considerably throughout colonial history and in the contemporary world. There were wars, battles, and strategic political alliances during the colonial period before and after the establishment of the United States. Religious movements, or revitalization movements, characterize Native responses to colonialism as American Indian peoples sought cultural solutions to drastically changing economic, political, and cultural situations.

Many Native American traditions, religions, and revitalized cultures continue into the present day as living communities. During the last quarter of the twentieth century, Native peoples openly practiced, reclaimed, and maintained their religious beliefs and understandings. If there is one generalization about Native American communities over the past five hundred years of colonial contact, it might be that Native nations have sought to preserve their cultures, communities, political rights, and territories. Social and religious movements have been among the ways in which Native people have sought to preserve core aspects of their cultures while accommodating changing political, economic, and cultural relations in an increasingly globalized world.

MILITARY AND DIPLOMATIC MOVEMENTS. Eastern North America was colonized by an assortment of colonial powers, including the English, French, Spanish, Dutch, and Swedes. As the competitive and warring nation states of Europe transferred their disputes to the colonies, diplomatic and economic rivalries were played out as part of the policies of the mother countries. The hunt for gold was an early motivating factor for the colonizers, but they soon turned their attention to the export of furs and skins. Native people were willing to trade furs for European manufactured goods such as ironware, rifles, traps, cloth, and pots and pans. Native trappers and hunters became sources of labor in complex intercontinental markets extending back to the European capitals.

Native communities soon became dependent on trade with Europeans for manufactured products they could not produce themselves. Economic dependence required a European trading partner, and the eastern Native nations soon found themselves forced to ally with one or another European colony for trade and military protection. Trade allies became military allies during times of war, and the Native nations were soon swept into a series of conflicts that were often initiated to serve European interests far away from North America. Warfare became more frequent, involved more combatants, marshaled greater firepower, and was far more deadly than traditional Native American conflicts.

Working according to the dictates of the European market, European traders demanded more and more furs from Native American hunters and trappers, coercing them to trap more by reducing the value of furs relative to trade items; thus more furs were required to trade for necessities. Traders used alcohol as an inducement to bring in more furs or a distraction leading to poor trades, requiring additional hunting. Market demands for furs led to Native hunters overhunting local animal resources, and often forced tribes like the Delaware and Munsee to fall back into the interior to follow the disappearing hunting grounds. Movement into the interior, however, often led to conflict with other nations who had already claimed the hunting grounds.

By the 1640s the Iroquois (Haudenosaunee) saw their local beaver and deer supplies shrink to levels that could not sustain trade with the Dutch colony of New Amsterdam. Consequently, the Iroquois sought trade agreements with the Native nations of the interior, but were rebuffed because the interior nations had their trade and diplomatic alliances with the French. With Dutch support, the Iroquois initiated a series of battles and wars in the middle 1640s that lasted until about 1700, known as the Beaver Wars. From the 1640s until 1820 in eastern North America there was nearly continuos warfare and economic and diplomatic competition that ended only with the emergence of the United States and the extension of its control over the region.

The trade and diplomatic ties of the Native nations to European colonies not only involved them in the European wars but intensified military and economic interactions among the Native nations. The Iroquois, supported by Dutch and later English alliances and weapons, pushed out or dispersed many of the Native nations of the lower Great Lakes, and forced the Ojibwa, Potawatomi, Odawa, Sac and Fox, Wyandot, and others farther west. In turn, the migrating Native nations, often better supplied with weapons, pushed others like the Lakota, Dakota, Nakota, Gros Ventre, and Cheyenne farther to the west and onto the plains.

The intensification of diplomatic, military, and trade relations greatly affected the ability of many Native nations to maintain their territorial and economic integrity. Most nations in eastern North America were forced into a trade, military, or diplomatic alliance with one or another European colony. Many coastal nations were quickly subjugated by the English colonies. The Pamunkey Algonquins under Powhatan (c. 1550–1618) were early subject to English land encroachments, taxes, and pressures to convert to Christianity that resulted in several conflicts, ending with the social, political, and cultural marginalization of the Virginia nations by 1675.

At about the same time, the Native nations of New England were increasingly forced to cede land and political autonomy to the English. The Wampanoags did not believe they could live under English rule, and the economic and cultural changes were corrupting their way of life. The defeat of the Wampanoags and allied New England nations in King Philip's War (1675–1676) led to their relegation to small tracts of land and communities often called Indian Praying Towns. The New England nations adopted town-government democracy and Christian Protestant religions, although they have maintained a sense of Native identity to the present day.

While most Native nations in the thirteen original U.S. colonies were eventually brought under colonial control, the nations farther to the west continued to engage in trade, diplomatic, and military relations with the rival European colonial powers. By 1700 some of them began to realize that the expansionist goals of the English colonists were a threat to their sovereignty and traditional territories. The Iroquois and Creek confederacies began to form alliances of Native nations in order to manage relations with the Europeans more effectively. During the early 1700s the Iroquois often boasted that they had a military alliance with fifty Native nations, although most likely this claim was a bargaining ploy for negotiating with the Europeans.

The Iroquois Confederacy held together an alliance of Native nations based on economic treaties that allowed the Iroquois access to western hunting grounds, and in exchange they gave the western nations access to British trade goods at Albany in the New York colony. The Iroquois managed this alliance for their own and English trade and diplomatic interests, but it unraveled after the 1750s as trade moved farther west and Pennsylvania traders moved into the Ohio region. The alliance was increasingly taken over by Shawnee and Delaware leadership.

During the early 1760s, Pontiac (c. 1720–1769) assembled many groups from the northern confederacy to attack British forts in the Great Lakes region. This same confederacy was united to oppose U.S. expansion during Little Turtle's War in the 1790s, and in 1812 Tecumseh (1768–1813) was appointed warrior head of the confederacy that fought with the British against the United States in the War of 1812. After the War of 1812 the northern alliance was left depleted and in disarray.

The Creek nation also tried to strengthen its trade and diplomatic position by inviting coastal groups and other nations or villages to join the Creek Confederacy. The Creek leadership tried to manage relations among the English, French, and Spanish colonies of the south in order to gain diplomatic and trade advantages. The Creek were relatively successful with these methods during the second half of the 1700s. During the early 1760s the southern tribes, including the Creek, rejected overtures by the Shawnee and Delaware to join with the northern confederacy against the British. And in 1811 the southern Native nations generally declined to ally with the northern confederacy by refusing to join Tecumseh to oppose the expansion of the United States into Native lands.

Many Native nations during the late 1700s and 1800s engaged the U. S. government in warfare. Most were defending territory and their way of life, or moving to preserve an economic resource like the buffalo. Native military alliances were usually loose coalitions of friendship, and often seasonally deployed. In general, they were hard to sustain in the field, could not manufacture their own rifles and ammunition, and depended on the backing of a strong European colonial ally who was willing to provide military supplies and, hopefully, armed forces. After the War of 1812 and the sale of Florida and West Florida (present-day Alabama and Mississippi) by Spain to the United States, the eastern Native nations were left without effective allies and were forced to recognize U.S. authority in the region.

Movements of Religious Fundamentalism and Reform. As eastern North America became increasingly engaged in trade, diplomacy, and the economic markets, the encroachments of colonial power led to the dispersion and social and economic degradation of Native life and culture. Native communities were forced to migrate farther west, game disappeared, colonists took over land and made farms, disease greatly reduced the numbers and life expectancy of Native peoples, and economic and political dependencies required interaction and compliance with colonial authorities and traders. European trade goods, access to alcohol, overspecialization in the fur-trade economy, and new Christian religious ideas and concepts were changing and modifying everyday life. Native social and living conditions deteriorated noticeably, and the colonial expansion westward was increasing.

Under these conditions many Native American leaders and spiritual guides began to lament the declining conditions of the Native nations and sought answers. While military action was one option, many leaders hoped to understand the spiritual and religious significance of the changes that were occurring and sought remedies through spiritual means. There are reports of spiritual preaching among the Iroquois as early as the 1720s, but not to the extent of becoming a full-fledged movement. There may have been many spiritual leaders who discussed the issues of the day in spiritual terms but did not lead recognizable movements, or who have been lost in history.

Among the Delaware in the 1740s, there appears to have been much distress because of migrations and declining conditions, and there are hints of spiritual unrest. Several prophets appeared among the Delaware in the late 1750s and early 1760s. The British had just won the French and Indian War, and many tribes in the northern alliance, including the Delaware and Odawa, who were both allied with the French, were highly suspicious of British motivations. The British now controlled trade and gained control of the military forts in the Great Lakes region. The Native nations in the region expected British retaliation and were unhappy under British administration. Under these conditions two religious movements emerged among the Delaware. One led to the unified national Delaware Big House religion, and the other to the militant teachings that the Odawa Pontiac endorsed and used to collect a military coalition to try to force the British out the Great Lakes region.

The militant prophet's teachings combined elements of Christianity with selected Native teachings. The prophet Neolin (the Delaware Prophet) had a near death experience and dreamed he went to heaven and received instruction directly from god. In general, his teachings suggested that the Native people had abandoned the religious teachings and lifeways of their forebears and had adopted too many European ways, including their clothing, trade, alcohol, and Christianity. These changes had corrupted Native life, and the solution was to return to the beliefs and life of their ancestors, which would help restore the Native American nations to their former health and prosperity. The Europeans would have to be pushed off the continent through warfare, and no warrior could reach the next world if he did not believe in the prophet's teachings and do his bidding. Pontiac and the militant Delaware prophet used these teachings to organize the northern confederacy against the British, but after losing a brief war, called Pontiac's War, the teachings were lost or went underground. This movement, which emphasizes spiritual solutions to colonial situations and a return to the culture and religion of the ancestors, we can call fundamentalist.

The second Delaware religious movement during the early 1760s led to the political, social, and religious reform of Delaware society. This prophet synthesized elements of traditional Delaware religious views, brought them together into a common ceremonial structure, the Big House, unified three phratries of a dozen clans each into a common religious-kinship structure, and established unified chief and leadership positions for all three phratries. The phratries are known to us as the Wolf, Turkey, and Turtle divisions, or perhaps more generally as four-leggeds, two-leggeds, and those that walk on land and water.

The newly established chief of the Turtle division was the first leader of the newly reformed Delaware nation. The reformed Delaware religion-society helped centralize and unify Delaware political and religious relations, and helped the Delaware more effectively manage relations with other tribes and Europeans. The Delaware Big House religion was practiced until at least the 1920s. This movement can be called a reform movement because it led to long term and durable institutional change in Delaware society. Its purpose was religious, moral, social, and political reform.

The fundamentalist movements. The Native religious landscape had numerous fundamentalist and reform movements. The fundamentalist movements have generally been more historically colorful and often gained considerable attention. They include the Pueblo Revolt (1680s), the Shawnee Prophet movement (1805–1811), the Cherokee Prophet movement (1811–1813), the Red Stick War (1813–1814), White Path's Rebellion (1826), the Winnebago Prophet movement (1830–1832), the first Ghost Dance (1869–1870) and the second Ghost Dance (1889–1890), and the Snake movements among the Cherokee, Choctaw, and Creek during the 1890s. These generally fundamentalist movements favored a return to traditional ways and rejected the social, cultural, and economic changes brought by the colonies or the United States.

Many of these movements adopted elements of Christianity, such as the idea of a second coming or the concepts of heaven and a single anthropomorphic God, but their solution to the economic, demographic, and political decline of the Native communities was to seek a solution through spiritual intervention and a restoration of the way of life that existed before the Europeans arrived. The second Ghost Dance asked the faithful to dance at regular intervals in a circle to induce dreams and communication with the ancestors in order to learn about the ancestors' immanent return and restoration of the Native way of life. The Cherokee Prophet, in 1811–1813, taught that the changes in Cherokee society were corrosive and that the community would be destroyed in a hailstorm of fiery rocks. Only those who went to Lookout Mountain would be saved. The first Ghost Dance taught that the people would be saved by trainloads of manufactured goods that would arrive only for the Native people. This movement is reminiscent of the cargo cults in the Pacific.

The Winnebago Prophet taught that by resisting the Americans militarily, the Winnebago and Sac and Fox would regain their traditional lands when a group of spiritual warriors appeared to defeat the U.S. Army. The Creek Red Sticks opposed economic and political change introduced by U.S. Indian agents, and they started a civil war for cultural reasons, which later developed into the Creek War (1812–1813). The Pueblo Revolt was strongly influenced by a rejection of Christianity and Spanish political domination, and it earned the Pueblo the right to practice their own religion, although most Pueblo people were returned to Spanish control in the 1690s. The Cherokee, Choctaw, and Creek Snake movements were ways to mobilize a political organization to oppose the abolishment of the tribal governments and force their inclusion in the state of Oklahoma. The members of the Snake movements were the most culturally conservative members of the Cherokee, Choctaw, and Creek nations.

The fundamentalist movements, generally, have been strongly resistant to cultural and political change, favoring military or spiritual solutions to the degradation of life under colonial domination. Some of the movements have relied on a cataclysmic spiritual event to intervene and restore the old order and tradition. If the significant spiritual event does not occur, however, then most people lose faith in the movement and the movement disintegrates, though sometimes small groups of adherents remain and carry on the beliefs, often in secret.

The reform movements. Reform religious movements are aimed at changing or supporting community social and cultural values to accommodate fluctuating political, cultural, and political conditions. Native American reform movements include the Yaqui religion (1500–present), the Handsome Lake movement (1797–present), the Munsee Prophetess movement (1804–1805), the Kickapoo Prophet movement (1815–present), the Cherokee Keetoowah Society (1858–present), the Washat Dreamers religion (1850–present), the Indian Shakers (1881–present), the Native American Church (1800s–present), the Shoshoni Sun Dance (1890–present), and perhaps the New Tidings religion of the Canadian Sioux (1900–present) and Ojibwe Drummer movement (contemporary). Most of these religions adopt some concepts from Christianity but have a predominantly Native cultural and philosophical focus that would not be generally recognized as Christian.

The most characteristic of the religious reform movements is the Handsome Lake movement among the Seneca and Iroquois. Handsome Lake, after having a near-death experience, brought back a message of reform to the Seneca from god. Elements of Catholicism and Quakerism are integrated with selected features of traditional religion and ceremony to create a reform message. Handsome Lake's movement emerged as the Iroquois were relegated to small reservations. He advocated no gambling or drinking and legitimized the role of men in farming, which previously was women's work, by suggesting that males take up the horse and plow while women focused on horticulture using hand implements. The prophet advocated social and culture reform as a means of helping the community adapt to life on small reservations. Strong emphasis is given to moral issues and individual responsibility, and Christian concepts of heaven and hell and punishment in the afterlife are emphasized for those who would break the new moral code. Handsome Lake is given credit for introducing significant social reform into Iroquois society. His followers established a church about fifteen years after his death.

The Kickapoo Prophet, Native American Church, and Indian Shaker movements follow analogous patterns of moral and community reform and continue as contemporary religious movements. The Yaqui religion is an example of the formation of a reformed religion, borrowing significantly from Christian Catholic teachings but recreated and relocated within Yaqui tradition and history. Some movements are less influenced by social or cultural change and instead emphasize and support the continuity of community and tradition. Such movements are the Munsee Prophetess movement, the New Tidings religion, and the Ojibwa Drummer movement.

The religious reform movements are generally responses to radically changing social, cultural, political, and economic conditions experienced by many Native communities over the past two centuries. Traditional religions seemed ill equipped to interpret and give guidance under radically changing colonial conditions, and some people have looked for new ways to understand the world and make accommodations to it. Some Native Americans have adopted Christianity, but often continue to engage with the Native community and beliefs. Native American Christian churches, such as the Cherokee, Seminole, Choctaw, and Creek, are based on Native languages and social and cultural organizations. Native religious reform movements often provide syncretic religious solutions to a community undergoing rapid change, as well as provide a new set of moral values, beliefs, ceremonies, and sometimes community organization to help people endure and live under the new conditions. The reform movements usually retain many central Native concepts and philosophies.

CONTEMPORARY SOCIAL MOVEMENTS. Current Native American social movements take many forms. Native peoples are actively engaged in many activities in the area of land claims, education, Native rights, international rights, and many others. The focus here will be on the movements that are related to religious issues.

During the 1970s the Red Power movement's activities ranged from the occupation of Alcatraz Island to the second Long Walk in 1978. Contemporary Red Power activities have been less visible, but have taken the form of occasional protests, especially over nuclear waste sites on or near reservation land, as well as sacred walks or sacred runs. American Indian Movement (AIM) chapters are still active, meet in national meetings, and are engaged in community issues and cultural events. Native American students at colleges and universities are engaged in Native American issues, recruitment, cultural events, and community activities.

One major outgrowth of the Red Power movement was the open revival of Native traditions in many Native American communities. Activism in the 1970s started in urban areas but soon moved to the reservation communities, where young Native Americans sought greater knowledge and understanding of traditional culture. These events encouraged many spiritual leaders and traditionalists to bring Native ceremonies, dances, and stories out into public view, when they had been hidden away for many years. Elders and traditionalists gained more respect, and they became more active and visible in Native American communities. Tribal community colleges and universities started teaching Native languages and culture.

Native religious freedom issues were defended in the courts to preserve the right to smoke sacred peyote in ceremonies. Twice Congressional bills were written to preserve Native American religious rights through the American Indian Religious Freedom Acts. Native Americans moved to protect sacred sites and places of worship, both on and off the reservations. Native religion and traditional knowledge became more highly regarded within Native American communities. Contemporary Native peoples are actively engaged in the world through a variety of social, religious, political, educational, and cultural movements aimed at preserving their communities, identities, religions, and political autonomy.

See Also Ghost Dance; Handsome Lake; Neolin; North American Indians, article on Indians of the Plains; Sun Dance; Tecumseh; Wovoka.

Bibliography

Aberle, David F. *The Peyote Religion among the Navajo.* Norman, Okla., 1991.

Brown, Joseph Epes. *The Spiritual Legacy of the American Indian.* New York, 1995.

Champagne, Duane. "The Delaware Revitalization Movement of the Early 1760s: A Suggested Reinterpretation." *American Indian Quarterly* 12:2(1988):107–126.

Eby, Cecil. *That Disgraceful Affair, The Black Hawk War.* New York, 1973.

Edmunds, R. David. *The Shawnee Prophet.* Lincoln, Neb., 1983.

Hendrix, Jane B. "Redbird Smith and the Nighthawk Keetoowahs." *Journal of Cherokee Studies* 8 (1983): 73–86.

Herring, Joseph B. *Kenekuk: The Kickapoo Prophet.* Lawrence, Kans., 1988.

Hittman, Michael. *Wovoka and the Ghost Dance.* Yervington, Nev., 1990.

Johnson, Troy, Joane Nagel, and Duane Champagne. *American Indian Activism: Alcatraz to the Longest Walk.* Urbana, Ill., 1997.

Jorgensen, Joseph G. *The Sun Dance Religion: Power for the Powerless.* Chicago, 1972.

Knaut, Andrew L. *The Pueblo Revolt of 1680: Conquest and Resistance in Seventeenth-Century New Mexico.* Norman, Okla., 1995.

Lassiter, Luke E. "Southwestern Oklahoma, the Gourd Dance, and 'Charlie Brown.'" In *Contemporary Native American Cultural Issues,* edited by Duane Champagne, pp. 145–166. Walnut Creek, Calif., 1999.

McLoughlin, William. *The Cherokee Ghost Dance.* Mercer, Ga., 1984.

Mooney, James. *The Ghost Dance Religion and Wounded Knee.* Mineola, N.Y., 1973.

Newcombe, William W., Jr. *The Culture and Acculturation of the Delaware Indians.* Ann Arbor, Mich., 1956.

Parker, Arthur C. *Parker on the Iroquois.* Syracuse, N.Y., 1968.

Pflug, Melissa. *Ritual and Myth in Odawa Revitalization: Reclaiming a Sovereign Place.* Norman, Okla., 1998.

Ruby, Robert H., and John A. Brown. *John Slocum and the Indian Shaker Church.* Norman, Okla., 1996.

Shultz, Jack M. *The Seminole Baptist Churches of Oklahoma: Maintaining a Traditional Community.* Norman, Okla., 1999.

Smith, Huston, and Rueben Snake, eds. *One Nation under God: The Triumph of the Native American Church.* Santa Fe, N.Mex., 1996.

Speck, Frank. *A Study of the Delaware Indian Big House Ceremony.* Harrisburg, Pa., 1931.

Spier, Leslie. *The Prophet Dance of the Northwest and Its Derivatives: The Source of the Ghost Dance.* Menasah, Wisc., 1935.

Stevens, Frank. *The Black Hawk War.* Chicago, 1903.

Stewart, Omer C. *Peyote Religion: A History.* Norman, Okla., 1987.

Trafzer, Cliff E., and M. A. Beach. "Smohalla, the Washani, and Religion as a Factor in Northwestern Indian History." In *American Indian Prophets,* edited by Cliff E. Trafzer, pp. 71–86. Sacramento, Calif., 1986.

Wallace, Anthony F. C. "New Religious Beliefs among the Delaware Indians, 1600–1900." *Southwest Journal of Anthropology* 12 (1956): 1–21.

Wallace, Anthony F. C. *The Death and Rebirth of the Seneca.* New York, 1972.

Duane Champagne (2005)

NORTH AMERICAN [INDIAN] RELIGIONS: HISTORY OF STUDY

The religions of North American Indians manifest considerable complexity and diversity. In 1492 several hundred cultural groups practiced distinctive forms of religion. While we customarily begin the documentary record at the time of initial European contact, discoveries in archaeology have extended religious perspectives far back into prehistory. Burial mounds in the Midwest, Southeastern ceremonial sites, abandoned *kivas* in the Southwest, stone medicine wheels on the Plains, California petroglyphs, and other remains all evoke the antiquity of North American religions.

Despite its intrinsic value for comparative religion, the field of indigenous North American religions has been undercultivated by religious scholars. Too often dismissed as "primitive," these religions have been generally relegated to an undifferentiated residual category shared with other religions of primal peoples around the world. Interest in these religions has been limited to their supposed evolutionary position as stages logically antecedent to what are commonly called the "great religions," which command the allegiance of the majority of the world's population. Rarely, until recently, have North American Indian religions been studied as valid subjects in their own right. Nevertheless, research has revealed intricately structured rituals and ceremonies, myths densely packed with symbolic meanings, cosmologies that embrace subtle relations with nature, and highly elaborated varieties of individual religious experience.

One difficulty in studying native North American religions is that their institutions tend to be much less obviously compartmentalized than those of the so-called great religions. Their religious beliefs and practices pervade many spheres of practical activity; for example, among the Nootka constructing a canoe is considered a religious act, as is Hopi horticulture, the rabbit drive of the Rappahanock, the Paiute piñon gathering, and so on.

A second problem confronting students of North American Indian religions is the absence of literacy in traditional native societies. Lacking bodies of orthodox written doctrine, they have depended on oral and visual transmission of religious tradition. Such modes place a premium on mnemonic devices, rhetorical skills, and tacit understandings gained through participation. The absence of written texts has in the past allowed considerable flexibility in adapting to change and permitted considerable latitude for idiosyncratic interpretation.

A third difficulty is that the religions of North American Indians are typically dynamic. Efforts to depict or reconstruct these religions as timeless, fully integrated systems of belief and action are usually doomed to failure. Religious movements are recurrent features in North American history and prehistory. These movements, usually inspired by prophecy, originated within particular tribes but often spread beyond tribal boundaries. Deeply embedded in many of these religions are many reintegrated traits that ultimately derive from early contacts with Christianity.

Early Observers. The study of North American religions begins with the early European explorers. Many explorers carried with them strong Christian theocentric biases that denied the existence of religion in aboriginal societies. People who went naked and lived communally, who practiced polygamy, anthropophagy, and human sacrifice were sometimes judged as less than human. What served as religion to the Indian was disdainfully dismissed by the European newcomer as devil worship, idolatry, or irrational superstition. However, since part of the European mission to explore and settle the New World was religiously motivated, earnest efforts were made to convert the heathens to the "true faith" through both coercion and persuasion.

Later explorers of the interior regions were scarcely more perspicacious than their predecessors concerning native religions. Older stereotypes persisted: Indians were said to be haunted by demons, their religious practitioners were derided as conjurors, jugglers, and imposters, and their rites were regarded as ridiculous and absurd. On matters of religion, the accounts of the explorers replay their presuppositions with monotonous regularity.

Nevertheless, in the performance of their evangelical tasks, missionaries sometimes mastered native languages and were able to penetrate the belief structures of their potential converts. The Recollet and Jesuit fathers bequeathed an unprecedented record of seventeenth- and eighteenth-century religious customs among Algonquian- and Iroquoian-speaking groups in the Northeast. Not only does the seventy-three-volume *The Jesuit Relations and Allied Documents* (compiled 1610–1791; first published in 1896–1901; reprint in 39 vols., New York, 1959) contain accurate first-hand observations, but the scholarly training of these priests enabled them to engage in speculative comparative ethnology. The high point of Jesuit anthropology was reached by the priest Joseph François Lafitau in his two-volume *Moeurs des sauvages ameriquains comparées aux moeurs des premiers* (1724; translated by William N. Fenton and Elizabeth L. Moore as *Customs of the American Savages, compared with the Customs of Primitive Times*, Toronto, 1977). Lafitau offered a detailed overview of religious customs based on the works of his Jesuit predecessors and supplemented by his own inquiries. He systematically compared Indian religious practices with those of classical antiquity. Convinced that the Indians had emigrated from Asia, Lafitau argued for the unity of the human race, all of whom had in the remote past, he believed, shared a common God-given religion. Lafitau maintained that through migrations, local adaptations, and forgetfulness, primal beliefs and practices degenerated; yet vestiges of this original condition could still be discerned in the customs of contemporary savages, which presented clues for unraveling unwritten history. Lafitau's ideas were not unique, but the reliability of his documentation and his attempts at systematic comparison place him in advance of his times.

Spanish and English missionaries, with rare exceptions, fell far short of the high standards set by the French. The rigid religious orthodoxy of the Spanish and the notorious ethnocentrism of the English seemed to conspire in precluding sympathetic tolerance for native beliefs. Only in the late eighteenth century do missionary accounts of native religions begin to possess substantive worth.

Along with the records of enlightened missionaries, the reports of early travelers and traders offer valuable material on North American Indians. Travelers, by virtue of their experiences with a series of different groups, frequently were sensitive to religious variations. Lack of sustained observation tended to diminish the reliability of these reports, but this deficiency was overcome by exceptional traders and administrators who resided for long periods in Indian communities, learned Indian languages, and often married Indian women. For example, the trader John Long in his account of the Ojibwa (*Voyages and Travels of an Indian Interpreter and Trader*, 1791) is the first to refer to the concept of totem, which he describes as an association established with a guardian spirit during a vision quest. Later scholars misappropriated and universalized the term to denote names for descent groups and elementary forms of religion.

Much knowledge about traditional religion among Indians of the Southeast Woodlands derives from James Adair's *The History of the American Indian* (1775). Adair, who lived for forty years among the Cherokee and Chickasaw, believed that the Indians were descended from the lost tribes of Israel. To sustain his argument, he established twenty-three points of specific convergence between Indian and Israelite customs. Despite his erroneous thesis, Adair's mode of analysis forced him to ask questions and record important religious information that might otherwise have been ignored.

EMERGENCE OF A FIELD OF STUDY. Early theories about the indigenous people of North America revolved around questions of origin. Who were they? Whence did they come? Few theorists subscribed to an autochthonous origin; some, influenced by the foreshortened biblical chronology, attempted to link them with historically known Old World peoples. Such speculations encouraged the collection and analysis of ethnological materials, among which religious information was considered critical. Simple connections proved untenable, and the origins of North American Indians were pushed farther into the past. Many European and colonial philosophers and universal historians equated indigenous peoples with early stages of human development, as epitomized in Locke's famous phrase, "in the beginning all the World was America." Themes of native degeneracy and inherent inferiority were countered by the philosophical and literary image of the "Noble Savage," a convention that attained popularity in the mid-eighteenth century more as a critique of Western morality than as a serious effort accurately to portray Native Americans.

The post-Revolutionary consolidation of a national identity on the part of Americans provided another stimulus to the study of North American Indians. Intellectuals of the new republic sought to advance evidence proving that their continent was not inferior to the Old World and could support civilization. Under the influence of such leaders as Thomas Jefferson, Benjamin Barton, Peter DuPonceau, Lewis Cass, and Albert Gallatin, coordinated efforts were undertaken not only to "civilize" the Indians but also to preserve for posterity a record of their traditional cultures.

The career of Henry Rowe Schoolcraft (1793–1864) exemplifies the transition from amateur observer to professional ethnologist. Schoolcraft's younger years were spent on the frontier as a geological explorer and Indian trader. After taking up residence among the Chippewa of Sault Sainte Marie, he married an Indian woman, learned Chippewa, and became a governmental agent. In 1839 he published his influential *Algic Researches*, (New York, 1839) in which he sought to reveal the deeper levels of Indian mentality through the collection of myths and folklore and the analysis of subtleties in Algonquian linguistics. His scholarly reputation thus established, Schoolcraft deserted the frontier to promote the fledgling science of ethnology. He secured federal support and was responsible for compiling the mammoth, six-volume *Historical and Statistical Information Respecting the History, Condition and Prospects of the Indian Tribes of the United States* (Philadelphia, 1851–1860). This work is laced with important data from missionaries and Indian agents, but its cumbersome and disorganized format limits its utility.

ADVANCES UNDER THE BUREAU OF ETHNOLOGY. The founding of the Bureau of Ethnology in 1879 auspiciously launched formal government anthropology in the United States. The bureau's mission was primarily salvage ethnology and scientific systematization of knowledge about America's original inhabitants. Under the inspired directorship of John Wesley Powell, a dedicated group of scholars was assembled who left enduring contributions to the understanding of Indian religions.

The Southwest became an important area of investigation, since Apachean-speaking and Pueblo groups retained viable neoaboriginal religious systems. Such bureau-sponsored researchers as James Stevenson and Matilda Stevenson, J. W. Fewkes, Washington Matthews, J. G. Bourke, and Frank Hamilton Cushing produced papers and monographs on Southwestern ceremonialism that attracted international attention.

Other areas as well were attended to by the bureau. Clay MacCauley, James Mooney, and, later, John R. Swanton studied Southeast Woodlands religions. Research on Iroquois religion persisted through the works of Lewis Henry Morgan and Horatio Hale, whose *The Iroquois Book of Rites* (Philadelphia, 1883) represents the first modern monographic treatment of North American Indian ceremonialism. Such bureau scholars as Erminnie Smith and J. N. B. Hewitt contributed significant studies on Iroquoian myths and cosmology. Other aspects of Eastern Woodlands religion were documented by W. J. Hoffman's works on the Ojibwa and Menomini and later by Truman Michaelson's impressive corpus on the Fox.

The heyday of Plains culture still survived within living memory when bureau ethnologists entered the field. J. Owen Dorsey collected valuable information on Siouan religions; James Mooney reported on the Kiowa and Cheyenne; Alice Fletcher, in collaboration with native intellectuals Francis La Flesche and James Murie, produced classic monographs on Omaha and Pawnee religion. Mooney's brilliant description and analysis of the contemporary Ghost Dance remains a recognized masterpiece of religious ethnology. Very little bureau work was undertaken among tribes west of the Rocky Mountains until the twentieth century.

RISE OF UNIVERSITY SPECIALIZATIONS. By 1900 the center of American anthropology began to shift from museums and government agencies to universities. As gifted and resourceful as the early researchers of the Bureau of Ethnology were, none had received formal academic training in anthropology. The central figure in the movement toward professionalization was Franz Boas, a European-trained scholar, who exerted a dominant influence on American anthropology for the next half century. Boas developed the modern concept of culture, set new standards for fieldwork, and trained several generations of students destined to make decisive contributions to the study of Indian religions. Boas's own works on the Northwest Coast demonstrated a meticulous concern for ethnographic particularism aimed toward problems of cultural-historical reconstruction. Later he moved from an emphasis on trait analysis and diffusion toward interpretation of the dynamics of cultural integration. Reluctant to generalize and distrustful of grand theory, Boas assiduously collected native-language texts, many of which involve religious topics. Some have argued that Boas's strong positivistic empiricism inhibited theoretical development in North American anthropology; however, his insistence on obtaining the native viewpoint through texts provides a tangible legacy for modern anthropology.

Regardless of how one evaluates Boas's direct contributions to religious ethnology, his students and collaborators succeeded in filling out in fine descriptive detail the major lineaments of indigenous North American religions. Substantive works by such field-workers as Ruth Benedict, Ruth L. Bunzel, Roland B. Dixon, Alexander A. Goldenweiser, Esther Goldfrank, Erna Gunther, Herman Haeberlin, George L. Hunt, Melville Jacobs, A. L. Kroeber, Robert H. Lowie, Elsie Clews Parsons, Paul Radin, Gladys A. Reichard, Edward Sapir, Frank G. Speck, Leslie Spier, John R. Swanton, James A. Teit, Ruth M. Underhill, and Clark Wissler cannot be reviewed here. However, some brief comments on emergent trends can be mentioned. Increasingly, one finds concern with the nature of religious experience and religious meaning for the individual. Stylistic and literary features of myths and tales are given serious attention. Interest in culturally constituted worldviews becomes more apparent. Finally, there emerges an implicitly functional approach that relates religion to other aspects of culture, society, and the individual. Many of these scholars reached beyond ethnographic particularities to address problems of general theory and to impart the facts of native North American religions to a wider audience.

From the beginning, religious materials from North American Indian sources served as ammunition for the heavy artillery of European "armchair" theorists. These materials were employed in hit-or-miss fashion to support the global theories of such commanding figures as E. B. Tylor, James G. Frazer, Andrew Lang, R. R. Marett, W. J. Perry, Émile Durkheim, Marcel Mauss, Lucien Lévy-Bruhl, Wilhelm Schmidt, and Adolf E. Jensen. American reaction to these theories has typically been defensive and critical. It must be admitted that, with few exceptions, these theorists and subsequent European ethnologists, comparativists, and religious historians lacked direct American field experience. Yet they have contributed significantly by viewing the American data from the broader perspective of world religions, by constructing typologies with which the American evidence can be analyzed and compared, and by probing deeply into the philosophical implications of these materials. Recent European scholars whose work deserves greater recognition by their American colleagues include Kaj Birket-Smith, Josef Haekel, Rolf Krusche, Werner Müller, Raffaele Pettazzoni, and Anna Burgitta Rooth. The prolific and more accessible works of Åke Hultkrantz, a Swedish scholar, deserve special comment. Hultkrantz conducted field research among the Shoshoni and Arapaho, but his principal eminence derives from his unparalleled grasp of the published literature on native North American religions, displayed in several comprehensive comparative monographs and in numerous topical essays.

RECENT TOPICS OF STUDY. The post-Boasian period from World War II to the present has witnessed an accelerating interest in the indigenous religions of North America, and many profitable approaches have been taken. Psychological anthropology, for example, has brought new insights into the nature of religious experience through the study of alternate states of consciousness induced through ritual use of hallucinogens and other means. Weston La Barre's *The Ghost Dance* (Garden City, N. Y., 1970) is particularly notable for its profound psychological interpretation of Native American religions.

Another approach is through environmental issues, which have stimulated considerations of the effects of religious ideology on ecological adaptation. Calvin Martin's *Keepers of the Game* (Berkeley, 1978), a historical account of Indian participation in the fur trade, has evoked a wide variety of responses on the role of religious motivation in hunting activities. Probably the most solidly crafted study to address this problem is Adrian Tanner's monograph on the Cree, *Bringing Home Animals* (New York, 1979).

The study of religious movements, too, commands much attention. Anthony F. C. Wallace's *The Death and Rebirth of Seneca* (New York, 1969), an eloquent account of the Handsome Lake religion, is a modern classic. Considerable study has been devoted to variations of the peyote religion. La Barre's enlarged edition of *The Peyote Cult* (New York, 1969) offers the best general overview of the subject, while David F. Aberle's *The Peyote Religion among the Navaho* (Chicago, 1982) and J. S. Slotkin's several publications on Menomini peyotism provide excellent accounts of specific manifestations. Homer Barnett's monograph *Indian Shakers* (Carbondale, Ill., 1957) stands as a definitive treatment of its subject.

The structuralism of Claude Lévi-Strauss has opened new vistas for the reinterpretation of North American totemism, art, myths, rituals, and the witchcraft-sorcery complex. Lévi-Strauss himself has utilized North American materials extensively in his provocative publications. Structuralism has inspired a whole generation of primarily younger scholars to think about previously collected data in interesting new ways.

Several noteworthy reworkings of important manuscript collections have recently appeared. Irving Goldman, synthesizing Boas's notes and scattered publications, has accomplished what Boas was never able to do—produce a coherent, theoretically informed account of Kwakiutl religion. Goldman's *The Mouth of Heaven* (New York, 1975) is complemented by Stanley Walens's symbolic analysis of Kwakiutl art and ritual, *Feasting with Cannibals* (Princeton, 1981). Raymond J. DeMallie and Elaine A. Jahner have made available the rich previously unpublished Lakota materials that were collected early in the century by James R. Walker (*Lakota Belief and Ritual*, Lincoln, Nebr., 1980; *Lakota Society*, Lincoln, Nebr., 1982; and *Lakota Myths*, Lincoln, Nebr., 1983). DeMallie has also assembled primary materials relating to the renowned Lakota medicine man Black Elk (*The Sixth Grandfather: Black Elk's Teachings Given to John G. Neihardt*, Lincoln, Nebr., 1984). William Power's *Oglala Religion* (Lincoln, Nebr., 1977) and his excellent descriptions of an Oglala curing ritual in *Yuwipi* (Lincoln, Nebr., 1982) amplify our understanding of Lakota religion. James R. Murie's account of Pawnee ceremonialism has been edited by Douglas Parks and published as *Ceremonies of the Pawnee* (Washington, D.C., 1981). Another important contribution to Plains research is Peter J. Powell's masterful, two-volume opus on Cheyenne religion, *Sweet Medicine* (Norman, Okla., 1969). Elisabeth Tooker has combed *The Jesuit Relations* to reconstruct Huron religion in her *An Ethnography of the Huron Indians, 1615–1649* (Washington, D.C., 1964), and she has also published a useful study entitled *The Iroquois Ceremonial of Midwinter* (Syracuse, N.Y., 1970). William N. Fenton has contributed mightily to Iroquois studies with his superb monograph on the Eagle Dance (*The Iroquois Eagle Dance*, Washington, D.C., 1953) and a continuing stream of research on Longhouse rituals. Information on several extinct Californian religions have been resurrected from the field notes of the remarkable J. P. Harrington and published in various books and articles.

The Ojibwa and the Winnebago remain two of the best-documented American religious traditions. The works of Alanson Skinner, John Cooper, A. Irving Hallowell, and Paul Radin have provided sturdy scaffolding for subsequent research. Ruth Landes's *Ojibwa Religion and the Midewiwin* (Madison, Wis., 1968) and recent historically oriented works on the Ojibwa by Christopher Vecsey (*Traditional Ojibwa Religion and its Historical Changes*, Philadelphia, 1983) and John A. Grim (*The Shaman: Patterns of Siberian and Ojibwa Healing*, Norman, Okla., 1983) illustrate this continuity. Landes's monograph on *The Prairie Potawatomi* (Madison, Wis., 1970) and James H. Howard's summary of Shawnee ceremonialism (*Shawnee: The Ceremonialism of a Native Indian Tribe and Its Cultural Background*, Athens, Ohio, 1981) enlarge our picture of Algonquian religions.

The Southwest continues as a focus of important research on religion. The complexities of Navajo religion, in particular, have been elucidated in the ethnographic and textual works of David F. Aberle, Leland C. Wyman, Berard Haile, David P. McAllester, Charlotte J. Frisbie, Louise Lamphere, and Gary Witherspoon, as well as in useful work by Sam D. Gill and Karl W. Luckert, both skilled historians of religion. Elsewhere in the Southwest, Alfonso Ortiz, a leading Tewa anthropologist, has written a sensitively informed account of Pueblo religion (*The Tewa World: Space, Time, Being and Becoming in a Pueblo Society*, Chicago, 1969), and Carobeth Laird, an affinal Chemehuevi, has recorded religious materials based on a lifetime of observation in her richly textured *The Chemehuevis* (Banning, Calif., 1976).

Knowledge of Southeast Woodlands Indian religion has been enriched by studies of religious continuities in modern Oklahoma (to which many Southeast Woodlands tribes were forcibly removed in the mid-nineteenth century); William L. Ballard's elegant analysis, entitled *The Yuchi Green Corn Ceremonial* (Los Angeles, 1978), and James G. Howard's *Oklahoma Seminoles: Medicine, Magic, and Religion* (Norman, Okla., 1984) are notable in this regard. Howard also provocatively analyzed the ceremonial complex of the prehistoric Southeast Woodlands Indians in *The Southeastern Ceremonial Complex* (Columbia, Mo., 1968), in which he gains insights from surviving beliefs and practices. A collection of papers edited by Charles M. Hudson, *The Black Drink* (Athens, Ga., 1979), represents another effort to link prehistoric and ethnographic horizons.

The present surge in attention to native religions of North America derives from many sources. Most important is the growing recognition by Indians and non-Indians alike that religion constitutes a viable aspect of past, present, and future North American Indian societies, a point made in Vine Deloria's vigorous manifesto *God is Red* (New York, 1973). Not only have areas such as the Southwest enjoyed unbroken religious continuity, but elsewhere, once-moribund ceremonies—such as the potlatch in the Northwest, the Spirit Dance among the Salish, and the Sun Dance in the Plains—have been revivified. Syncretic and ecumenical native religions are achieving legitimacy, and in many areas Christianity has assumed a distinctively native flavor. These trends reflect changes in the political atmosphere toward native self-determination. Among other developments, passage of the Religious Freedom Act in 1978 has had far-reaching consequences in preserving sacred sites.

Academic concern with indigenous North American religions has grown dramatically in recent years. The establishment of special programs of study in many universities, the increased number of religion scholars of Native American descent, and the seriousness with which indigenous religions are now treated in many theological centers all testify to a new enlightenment. Yet despite the enhanced academic and popular visibility of Native American religions and the proliferation of publications in the field, much groundbreaking work remains. Only the surface has been scratched.

BIBLIOGRAPHY

Åke Hultkrantz's *The Study of American Indian Religions* (New York, 1983) has proved indispensable in preparing this entry. The same author's *The Religions of the American Indian* (Berkeley, 1979) and *Belief and Worship in Native North America* (Syracuse, N. Y., 1981) are valuable sources on native North American religions. A slightly older synthesis, Ruth M. Underhill's *Red Man's Religion* (Chicago, 1965), remains a useful introductory survey. A pair of works by Sam D. Gill, *Native American Religions: An Introduction* (Belmont, Calif., 1981) and *Native American Traditions: Sources and Interpretations* (Belmont, Calif., 1983), offer a lively introduction to the subject. Three anthologies with diverse contents are *Teachings from the American Earth*, edited by Dennis Tedlock and Barbara Tedlock (New York, 1975); *Seeing with a Native Eye*, edited by Walter H. Capps (New York, 1976); and *Native Religious Traditions*, edited by Earle H. Waugh and K. Dad Prithipaul (Waterloo, Ont., 1979). A carefully annotated areal selection of native texts is presented in Elisabeth Tooker's *Native North American Spirituality of the Eastern Woodlands* (New York, 1979). Other areal guides can be found in the available volumes of the new Smithsonian *Handbook of North American Indians* (Washington, D.C., 1978–). *Systems of North American Witchcraft and Sorcery*, edited by Deward E. Walker (Moscow, Idaho, 1970), and Virgil Vogel's *American Indian Medicine* (Norman, Okla., 1970) are useful sources. Harold W. Turner's *Bibliography of New Religious Movements in Primal Societies*, vol. 2, *North America* (Boston, 1978), is a major resource.

RAYMOND D. FOGELSON (1987)

NORTH AMERICAN INDIANS

This entry consists of the following articles:

NORTH AMERICAN INDIANS: INDIANS OF THE FAR NORTH

The North American sub-Arctic, home to the indigenous cultures of the far north and the largest region in North America, stretches from Labrador to Alaska and features several ecological zones. Wide swathes of upland and lowland tundra in the coastal areas reflect the former weight of the Laurentide Ice Sheet from the late Pleistocene era. Throughout these sub-Artic tundra areas in both Alaska and Canada, drumlins, glacial moraines, swamps, and post-glacial hummocks provide continuous variation in landforms. In some cases the treeless taiga reaches hundreds of miles longitudinally and latitudinally, into the interior of both Canada and northern and western Alaska. The low-growing sedges, mosses, and lichens provide food and shelter for a plethora of small mammals, indigenous and migratory waterfowl, many species of flies and mosquitoes, and occasional large mammals. The octagonal shapes of post-glacial flora seem flat from a distance, but in actuality are dense with vegetation and hillocks just tall enough to hide the approach of predators for long distances. According to oral traditions, native North Americans have long harvested tundra berries and many species of plants for nutritional and medicinal purposes.

The tundra regions give way to taller shrubs and sedges, and in the interior areas boreal forests provide wood for housing, transportation, and other forms of hunting around the Great Slave Lake, Lake Athabasca in Canada, and the Yukon Flats region in Alaska. Both coniferous and deciduous trees (spruce, cottonwood, alder, birch, tamarack, and poplar) cover this region. In both the eastern and western regions of the southern extension of the sub-Arctic, the boreal forests surround prairies and the northern rain forests of the Pacific.

ADAPTATION TO CLIMATE. The harsh extremes of the climates in the region, including six to eight months of severe winters and correspondingly short summers, set some of the cultural limits of the indigenous peoples. One common feature crossing all cultural boundaries and surviving the passage of time has been the small size of communities. In the past, most sub-Arctic communities were comprised of two or more nuclear families ranging in population from twenty to fifty individuals. The small group sizes reflected the nature of continuous travel with children, and the need to keep noise to a minimum for safety and hunting success. In the present day sub-Arctic communities are inhabited year-round and range in population from a few dozen people to several thousand.

Another dominating feature of pre-colonial social life in the sub-Arctic was reliance on partners. Men and women usually had "same gender" partners among neighboring communities. Partners of this sort depended on each other for protection while in the partner's territory, for temporary housing, and for lifelong friendship. They vouched for each other's credibility and found marriage partners for each other's children. Within their own communities, men and women formed lifelong partnerships among those with whom they hunted, sharing household tasks, family responsibilities, medical and other emergency needs, and company.

Although contemporary societies make desultory attempts at agriculture, none of the indigenous sub-Artic inhabitants appeared to make consistent use of horticulture. Humans depended on hunting and fishing and moss, frond and berry picking. Most of them engaged in seasonal travel between camps, depending on hunting resources such as muskrats in early spring, followed in some areas by caribou and moose hunting in late spring; fishing in lakes and streams during the summer; and early fall hunts for large deer such as caribou and moose. Mid-winter often kept people captive in their dwellings during blizzards, long freezing spells, or heavy snow. They relied during winter on stored food such as dried or smoked meat, fish, berries, and plants. Sometimes their attempts to harvest and successfully prepare food for winter were inadequate. Themes of starvation figure prominently in oral traditions of most of the sub-Arctic nations. Hunting tools included the bola, spears, bows with arrows, and snares designed for most land species from mink to caribou. Weirs, nets, spears, and occasionally hooks served most regions for fishing.

Housing designs varied depending on region, materials available, and traditions. In most areas, dome-shaped structures were made from elaborately woven willows covered with deer hide in the more northerly regions, and bark or straw served as convenient winter structures in the south. The willow housing structure was often made in such a way that it could be transported by sled or boat to the next seasonal camp and covered anew in little time. In Alaska, the Athabascans near the coastal Yup'ik and Inupiat peoples made use of semi-subterranean sod houses for winter. Summer shelters varied significantly by region and culture. Today these structures have given way to year-round framed wooden houses, often subsidized by governmental funding.

Cool, rainy summers in the sub-Arctic can pose a challenge, preventing the collection of adequate dry tinder and wood for smudge fires by which meat and fish can be prepared for winter usage. Additionally, the sub-Arctic is frequently visited by random spring and summer snowfalls, yet another environmental calamity that can prevent families from processing their seasonal catches in time or at all. Hordes of mosquitoes, bot flies, horse flies, and numerous other flying insects often prevent humans (and other animals) from accomplishing planned harvests in a timely manner. The final impact of such disasters occurs in midwinter when supplies dwindle and travel to the nearest human community to get help may prove difficult due to inclement weather.

INDIANS OF THE SUB-ARTIC. European and Asian explorers from the east and west encountered sub-Arctic nations belonging to three linguistic families: the Eskimo-Aleut along the Arctic Ocean; the more than twenty-five Athabascan nations in Alaska and northern Canada; and the fourteen Algonquian nations in eastern Canada, including the Naskapis, Ojibways, Innu (formerly known as Montagnais), and Crees. Among the Algonquian are also included the Abnaki of New Brunswick and Maine (Mi'kmaq, Maleseet, Passamaquoddy, Penobscot, and Abnaki), who have preserved vestiges of their sub-Arctic way of life up to the present. The non-Indian Inuit will not be treated here, as they are the subject of a separate article.

The Algonkians. The three largest Algonkian nations are the Crees, the Naskapis, and the Innus. The Innus of eastern and northern Quebec refer to themselves as Innuat, or human beings. The French explorers early on named them for their mountainous environment, hence Montagnais. Like many First Nations peoples in Canada and the United States, they have reclaimed their indigenous name for themselves. The Innu dwell among heavily forested mountains and river drainages. Like most people of the pre-colonial and colonial sub-Arctic, the Innus spent their time making seasonal trips in quest of subsistence game animals and fish. Among the animals they sought were beaver, about which there are numerous stories that match the large technology that attends hunting and processing both fur and meat from the catch. Besides beaver, the Innu are known for their skill in hunting birds with arrows and darts. Innu fishing technology is similar to that of their Algonkian neighbors as well as most Athabascans to the north. The Innus also used stone fences to guide fish into weirs.

Besides fish, caribou and other large deer used to dominate the Algonkian landscape. Like the Athabascans in Alaska and northern Canada, Algonkian hunters developed skills in organizing annual caribou hunts in which corrals made of stone, willow, sinew, and natural formations of cliff sides, rivers, and lakes formed boundaries to trap caribou. Some of the corrals were open-ended but with a tightened funnel shape through which many deer were expected to escape. The purpose of such corrals was to cull specifically sized deer from the rest of the herd for limited harvests. In such a corral, the hunters, including women as well as men, would fashion snares of varying sizes and set them at appropriate heights for the desired size, gender, and rank of the deer taken. Stone mannikins or inuksuks, found throughout Canada nowadays as decorations or roadside sculptures, were used, in the way farmers use scarecrows, to deceive the caribou into thinking the stones were humans, thus leading them away from freedom toward the corrals.

As might be expected when winter temperatures can reach fifty degrees below zero Celsius (eighty degrees below zero Fahrenheit), survival is a constant theme of human existence in the sub-Arctic. Surprisingly, the freezing temperatures and strong winds pose less of a threat in the sub-Arctic than does starvation. Each of the cultural areas developed and have shared with each other their techniques for clothing construction and the best materials to use for each environmental challenge. Where the appropriate fur-bearing creature cannot be trapped or hunted, trading provides a welcome reason for travel to trade in late winter (February through March), when the still-frozen rivers provide convenient sled or snowshoeing avenues for the entire family.

The Athabascans. Occupying the greatest portion of the sub-Arctic are the Athabascan-speaking nations, of which eleven inhabit Alaska and fourteen or more occupy Canada. Linguistically, the Athabascans speak languages that are closely related to Apache, Navajo, and a number of Pacific coast peoples in northern California and southern Oregon. Culturally there are many aspects of material culture held in common between the Athabascans and the Algonkians. One of the most well known and used by men, women, and children alike are snowshoes. Archeologists conjecture that Athabascans began dog sledding around fifteen hundred years ago in Alaska. Davidson (1937) considers that open-frame snowshoes may have originated with Athabascans. In Davidson's view, the style of snowshoe featuring two pieces of willow or alder bound at toe and heel with babiche and held together with layouts based on a mesh of nested triangles, a distinctively Athabacan design, may be the oldest style of snowshoe. A frequent character appearing in Athabascan narratives is He-Who-Faces-Ahead-and-Behind. Often a villain, He-Who-Faces-Ahead-and-Behind provides mystery and tension, much as the tracks of Athabascan snowshoes, pointed at both ends, bewilder the person who happens upon them as to the direction the snowshoer may have taken.

Athabascan values are centered on self-sufficiency, hard work, and family. In-born in Athabascan cultures is the tension between individual autonomy and expectations that one's extended family is more important that any given individual. All Athabascan stories and ritual activities engage in explorations of this core area of trouble and offer three modes of resolution: humor, generosity, and respect. Stories reflect the terrors befalling people who fail to meet any of those standards, and life cycle potlatches, particularly memorial potlatches, provide ritualized opportunities for elders and others who have established their authority in the community to remind the others of their obligations to share with each other, cooperate with each other, and to follow relatively informal rules of protocol in social areas. The most rigidly enforced rule of behavior is silence and waiting before speaking. Long pauses, by American or European standards, between the end of one person's speech and the next fill every notion of respect for reciprocal relations between humans, the spirit world, and the rest of the natural world.

The sub-Arctic methodologies for survival reflect ingenious adaptation to their inland environments, and therefore make a strong contrast with the material cultures of the Inuit along the Arctic coast, who have a complex toolkit specialized for maritime hunting and weather. Another distinctive contrast between Inuit peoples and their interior counterparts is the abundance of subsistence resources. Cold and ice-jammed as the coastlines in the Arctic may be, they provide larger game animals in greater frequency than can be found in the sub-Arctic. The Algonkian and Athabascan peoples have designed a wide array of tools and methods of processing food to meet the ever-constant threat of uneven harvests throughout the year. Algonkian and Athabascan religious traditions all reflect the domination of the climate, the need for reliable means of providing food to growing families on a daily basis, and the dangers represented by animals that are larger, more aggressive, and better suited biologically to hunt, survive, and defend themselves from their enemies. Constant awareness of the need to survive these elements of life in the sub-Arctic serves as a common denominator of the human experience, which is awareness of human vulnerability in a world that treats human beings as subsistence resources rather than as predators and dominators of the world.

MYTHOLOGY. As Nelson (1983) observed about the Koyukon of the Yukon and Koyukuk Rivers in Alaska, the Athabascan world is alive and always watching its human inhabitants. Even thoughts become apparent to the animals, plants, and other environmental factors such as wind, mountains, rivers, and air that pass judgment on the struggling sub-Arctic hunters. Epistemological tenets in the sub-Arctic religious traditions inform humans that their hierarchical position in the combined worlds is low, that all other creatures in the natural and spiritual worlds have powers that can harm human beings and interfere with human efforts. Failure to be respectful, generous, loving, or loyal to one's human companions as well as all creatures in the environment can result in the "withholding" of hunting success or good food processing conditions from people whose central theme is survival. Mythological figures fit imagery complying with the omniscience of the physical and spiritual worlds.

Four genres of myth are common in Algonkian and Athabascan oral traditions. The first genre consists of ontological stories designed to enculturate youth about the key forces in the natural, social, and spiritual worlds. The second involves voyager stories in which one and sometimes two characters travel to new places, either populating the world as the first of any given species or performing key actions or behaviors for the first time. Petitot (1886) argued that these stories make up a large pantheon of tales that fit into a large opus of narrative similar to the Iroquoian creation stories. The third genre is made up of morality stories featuring a frightening being of indeterminate ontology who lurks in the forests causing trouble, abducting children, or simply frightening people.

The Gwich'in Athabascans of both Alaska and Canada refer to such entities as *nain,* and in Koyukon they are called *nicolina.* Algonkian stories are rife with a similar entity known as Windigo, varying from story to story as a tall man or as a tree. The fourth genre consists of raven stories in Alaska and parts of Canada that serve to explain family relations, in which the raven plays the part of the relation one must regard with simultaneous suspicion and respect.

As nineteenth-century writers like Petitot discovered, Canadian mythologies reveal a chronological, environmental, and social order that complies with social norms of both Athabascan and Algonkian cultures. Mythological tradition is structured by epochal events beginning with a time in which all beings spoke the same language and understood each other's social needs. Petitot wrote of two Dene (Athabascan) first people, a mythological woman who wore dentallium shells and her husband, Ko'ehdan (The Man without Fire), who named her Ch'atthan Vee (Dentallium Shell Woman) in eastern Gwich'in and Latpatsandia (Prize

Woman) in western Gwich'in after he rescued her from her Inuit abductors. The term *Ch'atthan* calls to mind the White Shell Woman in the Apache and Navajo (southern Athabascan language speakers) creation stories, although in fact it carries a direct reference to the Tlingit traders of the Pacific Coast, as dentallium shells were once highly prized trade goods the Athabascans sought from the Northwest Coast. Ko'ehdan by turns reveals his shamanic powers in many adventures, including his blindness and subsequent recovery of his vision. The couple had two sons: the younger is mischievous and the elder is heroic. The brothers engage in adventures that give rise to the voyager or traveler stories known throughout the sub-Arctic. Among the Gwich'in Athabascans, the older brother is known as Vasaagihdzak. The pair of brothers figure together and separately in a number of stories.

EPOCHS OF THE WORLD. Generally speaking, the sub-Arctic oral traditions fall into three eras or stages (see Jetté, 1907; Osgood, 1932; and Goddard, 1917). In the earliest period there were no divisions between living creatures; each could assume any animal's form and discard it again at will. All moving creatures spoke a single language; no barriers stood in the way of understanding. A second period began with the birth of a culture hero (woman or man) whose identity changes by region, language and culture. The culture hero is a great teacher and leader. Material and spiritual knowledge derived from the culture hero. The house, tent, snowshoe, sled, bark canoe, bow, arrow, lance, and knife—in short, all material cultural objects—stem from the culture hero, as does knowledge of the land of the dead, the stars and constellations, the sun, the moon, and the calendar months. In an Algonkian version, a male culture hero ordered the muskrat to dive into the water to begin creation of the world from the mud that was brought up. This story is patterned along lines similar to Iroquoian, Mayan, Aztecan, and other more southern Native American mythologies. The third epoch is the present time, and genealogy plays an important role in explaining one's role in society. Culture heroes are shamans who continue to mediate between the spirit world and the physical world. Oral traditions in the third era are located in the family and the region, and reveal historical specificity.

Cultural differences prevail, emphasizing differing ontological realities. For example, among the Koyukon, the northwestern-most Athabascan nation in Alaska, oral traditions address five world periods: the hazy time before there was light on the earth; the epoch when man could change into animals and animals could change into men; the time when the traveler created the present state; the past time of legends; and the present as far back as memory reaches (Clark, 1981, p. 595).

UNITY BETWEEN REALMS. The mythologies of each region in the sub-Arctic represent worldviews, ontologies, and epistemologies that organized the unity of life for each human being within the province of the tale. Such worldviews persist today in traditional beliefs and customs recalling events or conditions revealed in each epoch. Especially important are the earliest periods in which boundaries between human, natural, and spiritual worlds are permeated, inhabited, and fully understandable as such. An important theme contained in the mediation between realms is unity, harmony, and peace throughout the known world of each nation occupying the sub-Arctic. By the ontological rules represented in their oral traditions, the Gwich'in (formerly known as Kutchin), a northern Athabascan nation inhabiting the region between the Mackenzie River delta and the upper Yukon in both Alaska and Canada, possess a special relationship with the caribou. Ontologically, every Gwich'in human being carries a small piece of caribou heart, and likewise, every caribou holds a portion of human heart. Hence, each of these partners knows what the other feels and thinks (Slobodin, 1981, p. 526). The Sekani of British Columbia believe that a mystical bond links human beings and other animals (Denniston, 1981, p. 439). The Koyukon call the bear "Grandfather" and the wolf "Brother" (Clark, 1981, p. 593). The Chipewyan, an Athabascan nation west of Hudson Bay, identify with the wolf (Smith, 1981, p. 279). The names of certain Athabascan nations—Dunne-Za (formerly known as Beaver), Dogrib, Hare—point to familial ties with certain animals. In all of these examples we hear an echo of the earliest epoch, when a common language prevailed and all creatures had the ability to transform themselves and thus to overcome every barrier between them.

THE CULTURE HERO. Legends about culture heroes continue to be popular in the sub-Arctic literary canon. Athabascans nickname their sons Ko'ehdan after The Man without Fire, and many eastern Athabascan storytellers recount episodes of his mythic life. The figure of the hero is well developed by Algonquians of the Atlantic coast. The Mi'kmaq of Cape Breton Island, for example, call the teacher of mankind Kuloscap ("liar" or "deceiver") because he always does the opposite of what he says he will do. Oral traditions of the Maliseet of New Brunswick hold forth Gluscap, a culture hero whose adventures are remarkably akin to those of the Mi'kmaq and the Passamaquody. The settings and events of Kuloscap's life still can be seen in the natural features of the maritime sea and landscapes. Cape Breton Island abounds in references to the hero. Every large rock, every river, every waterfall, testifies to his deeds.

All the sub-Arctic Indians have a similar mythical geography. West of the Mi'kmaq and Maliseet, other names for the culture hero emerge. In Labrador the Montagnais-Naskapi call their culture hero *Little Man* or *Perfect Man.* The Cree on either side of James Bay refer to the *One Set in Flames* or the *Burning One.* Among the Chipewyan Athabascans, he is called *Raised by His Grandmother.* Among the Dunne-Za Athabascans, he is called *He Goes along the Shore.*

Northern Athabascan mythological names exploit their various culture heroes' wanderlust. In the Canadian northern lake regions, the Gwich'in, Koyukon, and Kolchan names for their traveler have been translated as the Wanderer, Ferryman, Celestial Traveler, He Paddled the Wrong Way, He Who Went Off Visiting by Canoe, or One Who Is Paddling Around, designations that refer to a particular task of the hero. He is said to labor continuously to combat giants, cannibals, and monsters for the benefit of mankind. The mass of fantasy figures in whose deeds the mythologies abound—such minor heroes as Moon Boy, Moon Dweller, Shrew, Moss Child, Wonder Child, White Horizon, the Hero with the Magic Wand—follow the same path as the tireless figure of the Wanderer. The designation *First Brother* reveals that pairs of brothers also appear among these parallels to the great culture hero.

Robin Ridington's 1978 account of the religious culture of the Dunne-Za Athabascans of Alberta is the most vivid report we have about an Athabascan people. The emergence of a genuinely sub-Arctic world genesis is remarkable in itself, but of equal importance is the picture of the culture hero, Saya (Swan), that Ridington brings to light. The Dunne-Za view this figure as a paradigm of their most important cultural values. Saya illustrates the means by which young men acquire spirit guides and a song bearing his medicine power. In the myths, Saya eliminates the hostile monsters and teaches humans (both male and female) to hunt and to avoid being caught unprepared for unexpected danger. Daily life mirrors the epistemological expectations presented in Athabascan oral traditions about their culture heroes.

In winter, people of the sub-Arctic abide in their winter dwellings rather than attempt to hunt for animals that are either emaciated themselves or hidden in hibernation. During this time of year, people tell stories to while away long periods of inactivity. Rituals, such as the Athabascan funeral and memorial potlatches, occur irregularly, but some activities have become routinely attached to a time of year. For example, many Athabascan nations in Alaska and Canada engage in riddling contests. Such contests, like the Messenger Feasts of the Inuit, are planned events in which one community invites another community to feast with them. Gifts are mandatory, but the decision about which community provides the gifts depends on which is unsuccessful in solving a riddle posed by the other group. Riddling feasts usually happen in winter.

In spring, the return of specific species and the emergence of new plant life are celebrated in ritual. The national holiday of the Mi'kmaq, Saint Anne's Day (26 July), is a blend of Christian and Indian traditions and celebrated with games, dances, singing and feasting. The Koyukon, for example, celebrate the winter solstice, a time at which they also honor their dead. It is the time "when the long and short days meet" (Clark, 1981, p. 593). Implicit in that phrase is precise knowledge of the movements of the sun, moon, and stars, all part of the hunters' knowledge base for finding his or her way to and from homesites.

SUB-ARTIC INDIANS AND A SUPREME BEING. Early explorers sought terms among indigenous peoples of the sub-Arctic regarding a supreme being, but instead they encountered numerous terms for indeterminate powers dominating the lives of all creatures. The Gwich'in Athabascans of Canada and Alaska refer to them by two terms, K'eegwaadhat and Vit'eegw__hchy'aa. K'eegwaadhat means both *heat* and *that which gives orders.* Vit'eegw__hchy'aa means *that upon which we depend.* Both terms refer to something powerful and ubiquitous with no identifiable physical construction. In common with other cultures of the sub-Arctic, Gwich'in leaders had to demonstrate prowess in communication with the sacred for hunting, war, trading, and healing to gain the respect of their communities. Much of this activity was related to dreams that contained prophetic data. Leadership in the sub-Arctic reflects standards of life in an unmerciful environment as well as continental attitudes toward the nature of power. In the sub-Arctic, a crucial aspect of the ineffable quality of the numinous has been its lack of interest in any being, humans included.

Life in the harsh sub-Arctic environment has led to religious and social theories that expect no special treatment from either the natural or spiritual realms, but expect punishment for egocentric behavior. Leaders are thus faced with a dilemma, which is to remain self-effacing while giving orders, making hard decisions, and pulling together human resources to perform community efforts together. Motivational factors stem from demonstrations of shamanic power, thus displacing cause from the personal motives of the leader to the numinous. Like ordinary hunters (both women and men), who act upon dreams or other signals from the numinous, leaders are expected to receive ideas or corroboration for their decisions directly from the unseen forces of the universe. The disparity between these two opposing issues finds resolution through the union of two concepts of strength: vat'aii (personal strength) and dat'aii (public strength). In this sense, the Gwich'in are metaphorically reminded that these two realms of behavior are supposed to co-exist harmoniously. The net effect is that Gwich'in leaders come and go, but individual projects succeed through communal action and need.

SHAMANISM. Central to all hunting, medical, and life cycle events is the development of shamanic skills. Every hunter is expected to develop his or her shamanic skills to the greatest extent possible. While both men and women are viewed as equally capable of such power, shamanic power is generally thought of as weaker than the power of women to create life. As a consequence, most sub-Arctic cultures include numerous prohibitions against contact between men or men's hunting tools and women engaged in their creative powers, meaning menses, pregnancy, or nursing.

Common to all Arctic and sub-Arctic peoples are principles of mutual interdependence and individual autonomy in the face of imminent danger and starvation. Thus, adherence to such cultural norms follows lines of cultural logic that are substantiated time and again through oral traditions. Sub-Arctic shamans are reputed to engage in a number of feats, including healing through surgery and herbs, levitation and transportation. All such abilities reflect cultural epistemologies about reciprocal relationships between humans, animals, plants, and entities of the spirit world. The most common ability, Dreaming, makes prophecies about the specific location and markings of wildlife. The many who have researched sub-Arctic dreaming customs include Hugh Brody (1981) in northeastern British Columbia and Jean-Guy A. Goulet (1994) among the Dénés Tha (formerly known as Slavey Athabascans). Marie-Françoise Guédon (1994), in a comparison of the Ahtna of Alaska and the Nabesna of British Columbia, describes a revitalization of shamanic dreaming in both regions. In addition, Ronald Niezen (1998) describes a similar investment in reciprocal relationships between humans, nature, and the spiritual world among the James Bay Cree.

The word *shaman* derives from Tunguz and is thus a foreign term in Indian languages. Indigenous names, equivalents of *clairvoyant, dream doctor, singer, and dreamer* (DeLaguna and McClellan, 1981, pp. 660 ff.), or *shadow man, arrogant one, and head full of songs* (Petitot, 1876, p. 224), are translations of concepts far removed from European comparables such as *medicine man, sorcerer,* and *magician.*

The shaman's important and essential characteristics are attained through dreams. The visions befall selected candidates. The chosen must have a "peculiar aptitude" (Snow, 1981, p. 607), but family inheritance can also play a role. The strength of a shaman depends on spirit helpers that are either acquired through dreams or inherited from his father or his maternal uncle. Every hunter has one such helper, acquired in the years of childhood through *dream-fasting,* but the shaman has at least half a dozen. The spirits manifest themselves in the form of animals, in natural phenomena such as the sun and the moon, or in the souls of deceased shamans (Lane, 1981, p. 409).

CONCLUSION. The sub-Arctic is a large region with relatively few human occupants. Life for humans in pre-colonial eras was fraught with constant fear of unpredictable catastrophic events; tension arising from requirements to be self-sufficient while supporting the rest of one's family and self-effacing while demonstrating amazing shamanic gifts; and emotional upheaval when family members died or became disabled. Religious traditions in the sub-Arctic reflect cultural efforts to resolve these frequent situations and constant fears through development of ritual behaviors to express pain, grief, anger, and fear. Mythologies of this region also educate the young about matters of great technological and environmental importance, and likewise offer a means to communicate personal and cultural histories through one of the few methods of community entertainment, storytelling. Oral traditions also enculturate youth into awareness of moral behaviors, such as the need for men to avoid sexual feelings toward their mothers and sisters, and women in menses and pregnancy to avoid contact with men and their equipment. Each of these prohibitions fits into a holistic union of social and spiritual harmony that honors two forms of spiritual power: the power to predict weather, warfare and subsistence resources and the power to create new life. Men and women of the sub-Arctic are expected to be equals in terms of providing food and shelter for each other, but different in terms of life cycle events and usage of spiritual powers.

SEE ALSO Dreaming, The; Inuit Religious Traditions; Sun Dance.

BIBLIOGRAPHY

Abel, Kerry. *Drum Songs: Glimpses of Dene History.* Montreal, 1993.

Bonvillain, Nancy. *Native Nations: Cultures and Histories of Native North America.* Upper Saddle River, N.J., 2001.

Brody, Hugh. *Maps and Dreams: A Journey into the Lives and Lands of the Beaver Indians of Northwest Canada.* Vancouver, 1981.

Cruikshank, Julie. "Legend and Landscape: convergence of oral and scientific traditions in the Yukon Territory." *Arctic Anthropology* 8, no. 2 (1981): 67–93.

Davidson, Daniel Sutherland. "Snowshoes." Philadelphia, 1937.

Goddard, Pliny Earle. "The Beaver Indians." *Anthropological Papers of the American Museum of Natural History,* 10, no. 4 (1917a): 201–293.

Goddard, Pliny Earle. "Beaver Texts." *Anthropological Papers of the American Museum of Natural History,* 10, no. 5 (1917b): 295–397.

Goulet, Jean-Guy. "Récit de rêves et de vision chez les Dénés Tha contemporains. Vision du monde et principes épistémologiques sous-jacents." *Anthropologie et Sociétés,* 18, no. 2 (1994): 59–74.

Guédon, Marie-Françoise. "La pratique du rêve chez les Dénés Septentrionaux." *Anthropologie et Sociétés* 18, no. 2 (1994): 75–89.

Hara, Hiroko Sue. *The Hare Indians and Their World.* Ottawa, 1980.

Jetté, Julius. "On the Medicine-Men of the Ten'a." *Journal of the Royal Anthropological Institute of Great Britain and Ireland* 37 (1907): 157–188.

Kan, Sergei. *Symbolic Immortality: The Tlingit Potlatch of the Nineteenth Century.* Washington, D.C., 1989.

Martin, Calvin. *Keepers of the Game: Indian-Animal Relationships and the Fur Trade.* Berkeley, Calif., 1978.

McKennan, Robert A. *The Upper Tanana Indians.* New Haven, Conn., 1959.

McKennan, Robert A. *The Chandalar Kutchin.* Montreal, 1965.

Moore, John H. "Truth and Tolerance in Native American Epistemology." In *Studying Native America: Problems and Prospects,* edited by Russell Thornton, pp. 271–305. Madison, Wis., 1998.

Napoleon, Harold. *Yuuyaraq: The Way of the Human Being. With Commentary.* Edited by Eric Madsen. Fairbanks, 1991.

Nelson, Richard K. *Make Prayers to the Raven: A Koyukon View of the Northern Forest.* Chicago, 1983.

Niezen, Ronald. "Healing and Conversion: Medical Evangelism in James Bay Cree Society." *Ethnohistory* 44, no. 3 (1997): 463–491.

Niezen, Ronald *Defending the Land: Sovereignty and Forest Life in James Bay Cree Society.* Boston, 1998.

Niezen, Ronald. *Spirit Wars: Native North American Religions in the Age of Nation Building.* Berkeley, Calif., 2000.

Osgood, Cornelius. *Contributions to the Ethnography of the Kutchin.* New Haven, Conn., 1936.

Osgood, Cornelius. *Ingalik Social Culture.* New Haven, Conn., 1958.

Osgood, Cornelius. *Ingalik Mental Culture.* New Haven, Conn., 1959.

Osgood, Cornelius. *The Ethnography of the Tanaina.* New Haven, Conn., 1966.

Osgood, Cornelius. *The Han Indians: A Compilation of Ethnographic and Historical Data on the Alaska-Yukon Boundary Area.* New Haven, Conn., 1971.

Paul, Daniel N. *We Were Not the Savages: a Mi'kmaq Perspective on the Collision between European and Native American Civilizations.* Halifax, Nova Scotia, 2000.

Petitot, Emile. *Traditions indiennes du Canada nord-ouest.* Paris, 1886.

Petitot, Emile. *The Book of Dene: Containing the Traditions and Beliefs of Chipewyan, Dogrib, Slavey, and Loucheux Peoples.* Translated from French and compared with versions in the original tongues. Yellowknife, Northwestern Territory, 1976.

Petitot, Emile, and Joseph Stanislas. *Quinze ans sous le Cercle Polair.* Paris, 1889.

Ridington, Robin. "Beaver Dreaming and Singing." *Anthropologica,* 13 no. 1 (1971): 115–128.

Ridington, Robin. "Wechuge and Windigo: A Comparison of Cannibal Belief among Boreal Forest Athapaskans and Algonkians." *Anthropologica* 18, no. 2 (1976): 107–129.

Ridington, Robin. *Swan People: A Study of the Dunne-za Prophet Dance.* Ottawa, 1978.

Ridington, Robin. "From Hunt Chief to Prophet: Beaver Indian Dreamers and Christianity." *Arctic Anthropology* 24, no. 1 (1987): 8–18.

Ridington, Robin. *Trail to Heaven: Knowledge and Narrative in a Northern Native Community.* Iowa City, 1988.

Ridington, Robin. *Little Bit Know Something: Stories in a Language of Anthropology.* Iowa City, 1990.

Ridington, Robin. "Voice, Representation, and Dialogue." In *Native American Spirituality: A Critical Reader,* edited by Lee Irwin, pp. 97–120. Lincoln, Neb., 2000.

Ridington, Robin, and Tania Ridington. "The Inner Eye of Shamanism and Totems." *History of Religions,* 10 (1970): 49–61.

Sharp, Henry S. "Shared Experience and Magical Death: Chipewyan Explanations of a Prophet's Decline." *Ethnology* 25 no. 4 (1986): 257–270.

Simeone, William E. *Rifles, Blankets, and Beads: Identity, History, and the Northern Athapaskan Potlatch.* Norman, Okla., 1995.

Slobodin, Richard. "Kutchin Concepts of Reincarnation." *Western Canadian Journal of Anthropology* 2, no. 1 (1970): 67–79.

Smith, David Merrill. *INKONZE: Magico-Religious Beliefs of Contact-Traditional Chipewyan Trading at Fort Resolution, NWT, Canada.* Ottawa, 1973.

Sturtevant, William C., and June Helm, eds. *Handbook of North American Indians,* vol. 6, *The Subarctic.* Washington, D.C., 1981.

WERNER MULLER (1987)
PHYLLIS ANN FAST (2005)

NORTH AMERICAN INDIANS: INDIANS OF THE NORTHEAST WOODLANDS

The Northeast Woodlands peoples occupy an area within 90° to 70° west longitude and 35° to 47° north latitude. The region can be divided into three smaller geographical areas: (1) the upper Great Lakes and Ohio River Valley region, (2) the lower Great Lakes, and (3) the coastal region. Their settlement patterns varied from the northern nomadic hunting groups of extended families through combined bands in semisedentary villages to relatively permanent agricultural settlements. The organization of lineage descent was matrilineal among the Iroquoian-speaking peoples, matrilineal or bilateral among the coastal Algonquian-speaking peoples, patrilineal or bilateral among the upper Great Lakes and Ohio River Algonquian- and Siouan-speaking peoples. Population density in the Northeast varied. At the time of first contact with Europeans the number of persons per hundred square kilometers was ten to twenty-five in the upper Great Lakes and Ohio River areas; twenty-five to sixty in the lower Great Lakes region; and among the coastal Algonquian from three hundred in the Virginia-North Carolina area and decreasing northerly to fewer than twenty-five in the more northern regions of New England (Driver, 1969). These conservative estimates have been extensively challenged causing revisions that suggest significantly higher populations in these areas (Dobyns, 1983 and Thornton, 1987).

The most prominent tribes, divided according to language group, are (1) Algonquian-speaking (Southern Ojibwa, Ottawa, Potawatomi, Menomini, Sauk, Fox, Kickapoo, Miami, Illinois, Shawnee, Narraganset, Mohican, Delaware, Nanticoke, and Powhatan), (2) Iroquoian-speaking (Huron, Erie, Neutral, Petun, Seneca, Oneida, Onondaga, Cayuga, Mohawk, and Tuscarora), and (3) Siouan-speaking (Winnebago, Tutelo).

The oldest ethnographic material that scholars now rely on deals with these people as they were originally situated. However, significant materials have been gathered subsequently as different tribes either migrated or reorganized on reservations.

These Indian peoples began a period of intense movement in the seventeenth century or earlier, which has continued for many tribes into the present century. Although discussion of these movements will not be undertaken here, no treatment of the religious life of these people can be attempted without acknowledging the intensely disruptive experiences of the past four centuries. The severing of cultural and religious ties to specific geographical locations has been seen by some Native American religious leaders not simply as a loss of natural resources but as a sacrificial or holocaust event with profound consequences for the survival of individual tribes and their religious practices. In particular, the loss of ancient ancestral sites has disrupted the linkage between the North American Indian peoples and the land through which the insights, power and meaning of their religious culture manifested itself.

Cosmological Beliefs. The cosmological beliefs of the Northeast Woodlands peoples involve the concept of power as manifested in the land, in the dialectic of the sacred and the profane, and in patterns of space and time. According to the mythic thought of these peoples, power is that transformative presence most clearly seen in the cycles of the day and the seasons, in the fecund earth, and in the visions and deeds of spirits, ancestors, and living people. This numinous power is so manifestly present that no verbal explanation of it is adequate; rather it is itself the explanation of all transformations in life. While generally regarded as neutral, power may be used for good or ill by individuals.

Power. This all-pervasive power is expressed among Algonquian-speaking tribes by the word *manitou* or one of its linguistic variants. *Manitou* is a personal revelatory experience usually manifested in dreams or in visions of a spirit who is capable of transformation into a specific human or animal form. The efficacy of power is symbolized as "medicine," either as a tangible object reverently kept in a bundle or as an intangible "charm" possessed internally. The term *manitou* is used here to indicate both the singular form of power as the binding concept throughout the highly individual Algonquian belief systems and as the plural form of tutelary spirits who embody such binding force. *Manitou*, in its various contexts, has both noun forms that indicate entities that empower and verb forms that indicate a moral responsibility to cultivate power. While individually experienced, these plural forms of power manifestation reached their highest religious expresion in actions undertaken for the benefit of the community as a whole.

The belief in *manitou* can be found among the coastal Algonquians from New England to North Carolina. Similarities may be seen in the name for the Great Manitou: for the Narraganset he was Kautantowwit and for the Penobscot, Ktahandowit. The Delaware worshiped as Great Manitou a spirit called Keetan'to-wit, who had eleven assistants (*manitowuks*), each having control over one of eleven hierarchically organized "heavens." The most ancient of the *manitou* was Our Grandfather, the great tortoise who carries the earth on his back. The Virginia Algonquians called those *manitou* who were benevolent *quiyoughcosuck*; this was also the name given to their priests. The evil *manitou* were called *tagkanysough*. Southeast Woodlands influences led to the depiction of *manitou* in carvings and statues, usually found in the sacred architecture of the North Carolina and Virginia Algonquians.

The Huron concept of *oki* referred both to a superabundance of power or ability and to spirit-forces of the cosmos, or guardian spirits. An *oki* could be either benevolent or malevolent. The supreme *oki*, Iouskeha, dwelt in the sky, watched over the seasons and the affairs of humans, witnessed to vows, made crops grow, and owned the animals. He had an evil brother, Tawiskaron.

The Iroquois *orenda*, a magico-religious force, was exercised by spirit-forces called Otkon and Oyaron; it was present in humans, animals, or objects that displayed excessive power, great ability, or large size. The Iroquois had a dualistic system whereby all of the spirit-forces deemed good were associated with the Good Twin and all of those deemed evil with his brother the Evil Twin.

The land. In many of the mythologies of the peoples of the Northeast Woodlands this cosmic power was intimately connected with the land. In their origin myth, the Menomini relate that they came into existence near the mouth of the Menominee River in Wisconsin; here two bears emerged from the earth and became the first man and woman. Near Fond du Lac, where a prominent rock ledge projects into Lake Winnebago, three thunderbirds descended and also became humans. Thus the Menomini use sacred stories associated with the local landscape to mark their origin as well as to relate the division of the tribe into earth and sky clans. The interweaving of tribal myth and sacred geography serves to integrate the community into both personal and cosmic levels of meaning. The intimate relationship of these Algonquian speakers with the land was reflected in their image of the land as Nokomis ("grandmother earth"), who nurtured her grandchildren.

A Seneca myth derives the presence and power of the land from twin sources: the mud brought up by Muskrat, the earth-diver, from the deep waters and deposited onto the back of Great Turtle; and the soil and seeds grasped from the sky world by Mature Flowers as she fell through a hole in the sky and was lowered by fowl onto the back of Great Turtle.

This intimacy of kinship with the earth was also part of an elaborate hierarchical perspective that located the earth within a vast schema of layers of power in the cosmos. These plural expressions have been labeled pantheism but this term stresses an abstract and conceptual sense of divinity rather than the place-based, ecological, and communitarian ideals evident in Algonkian religious thought. Both the Algonquian speakers and the Siouan-speaking Winnebago developed cosmologies in which the heavens above and the earth regions below were seen as layered in hierarchies of beneficial and harmful spirits. The highest power was the supreme being called Great Spirit by the Potawatomi, Ottawa, Miami, and Ojibwa; Master of Life by the Menomini, Sauk, and Fox; Finisher by the Shawnee and Kickapoo; and Earthmaker by the Winnebago. Among the Iroqouian peoples, the highest power was known by several names: the Master of Life, Sky-Holder, the Good-Minded Twin and Creator. This "great mysterious" presence maintained a unique relationship with the last and weakest members of creation, namely, human beings.

Spirit-forces. Power and guidance entered human existence from the cosmic spirit-forces, from the guardian spirits of individuals and medicine societies, and from spirits of charms, bundles, and masks. Dreams, in particular, were a vehicle for contacting power and thus gaining guidance for political and military decisions. New songs, dances, and customs were often received by the dreamer and were used to energize and reorder cultural life; dreams channeled power as consolation and hope during times of crisis, and often initiated contact between visionary power and the shamans. One means of describing the human experience of this cosmic power is through the dialectic of the sacred and the profane.

This dialectic is useful even though the Northeast Woodlands peoples did not draw a sharp distinction between the sacred and profane. The dialectic refers to the inner logic of the manifestation of numinous power through certain symbols. Profane objects, events, or persons might become embodiments of the sacred in moments of hierophany. This manifestation of the sacred in and through the profane frequently became the inspiration for sacred stories and mythologies that narrated the tribal lore. Among the Winnebago and other Northeast Woodlands peoples, narrative stories were distinguished as *worak* ("what is recounted") and *waika* ("what is sacred"). Telling the *worak* stories of heroes, human tragedy, and memorable events was a profane event, whereas narrating the *waika* stories evoked the spirits and was therefore a sacred ritual. Thus the ordinary act of speaking could become the hierophany that manifests power. Not only narrative but also the interweaving of sacred space and time gave real dimensions to cosmic power.

Sacred space. A place of orientation that provides individuals or groups with a sense of both an integrating center and a cosmic boundary is called "sacred space." This concept is exemplified by the Medicine society's rite, which originated among the Ojibwa and was transmitted throughout the eighteenth century to the other tribes of the upper Great Lakes. For this Medicine rite a special lodge was constructed of arched trees, covering an earthen floor with a rock and an elaborate pole in the center. These items varied slightly throughout the area of the ritual's diffusion, but in every instance they were used to delineate sacred space and to symbolize the cosmos. For the Winnebago, the arched trees of the lodge symbolized the water spirits (snakes who occupied the four cardinal directions). For the Potawatomi the earthen floor was Nokomis ("grandmother earth"). Among the Sauk the central stone in the lodge indicated the abiding presence of power. For the Ojibwa, originators of this ceremony, which they called Midewiwin ("mystic doings"), the pole symbolized the cosmic tree that penetrated the multilayered universe and united all the assembled *manitou.*

Iroquoian and coastal Algonquian peoples lived in rectangular "longhouses" or "big houses," in groups comprised of several matrilineally connected families. That the longhouses and big houses were seen as microcosms is most clearly reflected in the symbolism of the Delaware big house. The floor and ceiling represented the earth and sky, respectively. There was a door where the sun rose and a door where the sun set, and these doors were connected by the ceremonial Good White Path, symbolizing the journey human beings make from birth toward death. The fact that there was a door, an opening toward the west, and the fact that the dances eventually circled back, point to the Delaware hope in an afterlife and, for some, a rebirth. Ritual movement in relation to the sacred architecture suggests a concern for the flow of relational meaning and identity rather than fixed or hieratic devotional presences. In the center of the big house stood a post with a carved face that was made from a tree and that symbolized the *axis mundi*; from its base the post was believed to run upward through the twelve cosmic levels, the last being the place of the Great Manitou. This post was the staff of the Great Manitou, whose power filled all creation. Power manifested in the spirits was symbolized by the faces carved into low posts situated around the inside of the big house.

Sacred time. The period of contact with sustaining power is "sacred time." Such contact was believed to occur in the movement of the seasons, the fecundity of nature, and the personal life cycle. Among the native peoples of the upper Great Lakes, time was also sacralized in the narratives and rituals that reconstituted the mythic time of *manitou* revelation. During the Menomini Mitawin, or Medicine rite, while the origin myth of the ceremony itself was narrated, the society members imagistically participated in the original assembly of the *manitou* who began the ceremony in mythic time. Such an evocation of relationship with cosmic powers and identification with them in the oral narratives structured an experience of sacred time.

The Delaware Big House ceremony evoked powers that made possible the transition from the old year of chaos to the new year of cosmos. The origin myth narrated during that ceremony set the context for a renewal of the earth and of the tribe's binding relationships with the spirit-forces. The myth related that long ago the very foundation of life itself, the earth, was split open by a devastating quake. The forces of evil and chaos erupted from the underworld in the form of dust, smoke, and a black liquid: all creatures were struck with fear at these events. The humans then met in council and concluded that the disruptions had occurred because they had neglected their proper relationship with the Great Manitou. They prayed for power and guidance. The *manitou* spoke to them in dreams, telling them how to build a house that would recreate the cosmos and how to conduct a ceremony that would evoke the power to sustain it. This ceremony would establish their moral relationship with the *manitou,* and by the carvings of their *mesingw* ("faces") on the posts an identification with each of these cosmic forces would occur as one moved ritually along the Good White Path.

Furthermore, the recitation of puberty dream-visions would renew and revivify the individual's relationship with his or her personal *manitou.* The old time was one of impurity, symbolized by dirt and smoke. To make the transition into sacred time everyone and everything had to be purified, including attendants, reciters of dreams, and the big house itself. Purifying fires burned on either side of the center post. Power objects or persons from different religious contexts such as menstruating women were considered inappropriate to enter the Big House at this time.

The Iroquois Midwinter ceremony renews life at the turning of the year. Ashes are stirred, prior dreams and cures renewed, stories are told and ceremonies performed. At the center is the Tobacco Invocation which begs all the spirit-powers of the universe to perform their duties as assigned by the Creator in the coming year. And as the seasons and subsistence activities unfold during the year, the Thanksgiving Address, which opens each of a sequence of celebratory ceremonies, gives thanks to the Creator and all spirit-powers for responding to the Midwinter prayers of the people.

CEREMONIAL PRACTICES. Some understanding of the rich and complex ritual life of the Northeast Woodlands peoples can be obtained by considering selected ceremonies concerned with subsistence, life cycles, and personal, clan, and society visions.

Subsistence. Through subsistence rituals, tribes contacted power to ensure the success of hunting, fishing, or trapping; gathering of herbs, fruits, or root crops; and agricultural endeavors. Among the Sauk and Menomini there were both private and public ceremonials for hunting that focused on sacred objects now generically labeled "medicine" in English. The large public medicine-bundles of three types were believed to have been obtained by the trickster-culture hero Manabus from the Grandfathers, or *manitou* spirits. The first hunting bundle, called Misasakiwis, helped to defeat the malicious medicine people who tried to foil the hunter's success. Both the second bundle, Kitagasa Muskiki (made of a fawn's skin), and the third (a bundle with deer, wolf, and owl skins), fostered hunting success. Each bundle might contain a variety of power objects such as animal skins, miniature hunting implements, wooden figures, herbal preparations, and often an actual scent to lure animals. The bundle's owner obtained the right to assemble or purchase such a bundle from a personal vision. Songs, especially, evoked the powers of the bundle; these songs often recalled the agreement between the visionary and the *manitou* as well as the prohibitions and obligations that impinged upon the owner of a bundle. In this way the bundle owner, and the hunters he aided, thwarted the evil ones and contacted the *manitou* masters of the hunted animals. Thus power objects from the environment, along with the empowered hunters, chanting, and the ritually imaged *manitou*-spirits, functioned together to bring sustenance to the people.

Although the growing season varied within the Northeast, most of these peoples practiced some form of agriculture. With the introduction of agriculture new symbol complexes developed, giving meaning and power to this new subsistence activity and integrating it into the larger cosmic order. The northern Iroquois, for example, linked together woman, earth, moon, and the cycles of birth and death.

According to northern Iroquois mythology, agricultural products first emerged from the dead body of the Creator's mother. Out of her breasts grew two corn- stalks, and from her arms and body came beans and squash. Her death had been caused by the Creator's evil-minded brother, who was frequently associated with winter and ice. In giving birth to winter the Earth Mother "dies," but she brings forth life in the spring. The gathering of plants and the planting of crops were also the practical tasks of Iroquois women. Consequently, these women played a key role in scheduling and celebrating the ceremonies marking the yearly cycle of life: the Our-Life-Supporters Dances, the Bush Dance, and the Maple, Seed Planting, Strawberry, Raspberry, Green Bean, Little Corn, Green Corn, and Harvest rituals.

The spirit of the Earth Mother was also made into the Moon by her son, the Creator (or Master) of Life. Grandmother Moon was connected with life, as it was her duty to watch over all living things during the night. The monthly cycle of the moon and the yearly cycle of vegetation were associated with the mystery of life, death, and rebirth; women and the earth were seen as connected because they both have the power to bring forth and nourish life.

The domestic ceremony of apology for taking life is also found among all these Northeast Woodlands people. This profound yet often simple ceremony illustrates the moral character of the force that was believed to bind the cosmos together. The ceremony consisted of a spoken apology and a gift of sacred tobacco for the disturbance caused to the web of life by taking animal life, cutting trees, gathering plants, or taking minerals. For example, William Jones, in his *Ethnography of the Fox Indians* (1939), quotes a Fox tribesman as saying: "We do not like to harm trees. Whenever we can, we always make an offering of tobacco to the trees before we cut them down. If we did not think of their feelings . . . before cutting them down, all the other trees in the forest would weep, and that would make our hearts sad, too" (p. 21). This ceremony is both a thanksgiving for the blessing of a material boon and an acknowledgment of the environmental ethics that binds the human and natural worlds.

Life cycles. Life-cycle rites of passage are illuminating examples of these peoples' recognition that the passage through life's stages required a structured encounter with power. These ceremonies included private actions that invoked power at liminal moments such as menstruation, marriage, and birth. For example, menstruating women withdrew to specially constructed lodges, and the marriage ceremony was generally validated by an extensive exchange of gifts between families. Similarly, conception was ensured by protective fetal spirits, and new birth required a period of seclusion for purification of the mother and cradle-amulets for the child. Although there were taboos surrounding pregnancy and delivery, there were no elaborate birth rituals among the northern Iroquois or coastal Algonquians. Other life-cycle ceremonials, however, were marked by elaborate ritual activities, such as naming, puberty, and death ceremonies.

Birth and early childhood. Naming ceremonies arise both from the belief that humans are born weak and require power for growth and survival as well as a belief that new life should be introduced into the cosmos. Generally, two types of naming ceremonies have been found. Among the Southeast Woodlands tribes a child was given an ancestral clan name. This situated that child in the clan lineage and empowered the child by directly connecting him or her to the ancestral vision embodied in the clan medicine bundles. Another ceremony associated with the Menomini, Potawatomi, Ojibwa, and Ottawa, but occasionally practiced by the other groups, involved naming by virtue of a dream vision. In this ritual a person was chosen by the parents to undergo a fast or a sweat lodge purification so that they might receive a name for the child from the *manitou.*

Among the Iroquois and Delaware the naming ceremony, which was conducted in the longhouse, was the most significant ritual of early childhood. Delaware parents were attentive to their dreams for a revelation of the name. They would give their child to an elder in the big house who would announce the child's name and offer prayers of blessing for it. A similar ceremony would be conducted for an adult who decided to change his or her name due to a significant deed or because the first name no longer seemed appropriate. The Huron pierced the ears of the child and named it shortly after birth; the child's name then belonged to the clan and could not be used by another member of the tribe. The Iroquois named their children either at the Green Corn ceremony in the summer or before the Midwinter ceremonies. A child who resembled a dead ancestor might be given his or her name since it was believed that the name might have some of the ancestor's personality. The name remained the child's exclusive privilege and the focus of his or her early spiritual formation until the puberty ceremonials.

Puberty. It is uncertain whether the puberty rites of the Algonquians of Virginia and North Carolina involved a vision quest. However, the vision quest was part of the puberty rites of all of the upper Great Lakes peoples with variations according to the tribe. Some southern Ohio River groups such as the Shawnee emphasized less ecstatic experiences such as a boy's first kill. Among the Potawatomi, however, on specially designated mornings the parents or grandparents would offer a youth in his or her early teens a choice of food or charcoal. Encouraged to choose the charcoal and to blacken their faces, the youngsters were taken to an isolated place, often to perch in the limbs of a tree. There, alone, they fasted for dream visions. Although boys and girls might undertake vision quests, many tribes in this area had special ceremonies for girls.

The northern Iroquois, the Delaware, and the coastal Algonquians secluded girls in huts during their first menstruation. Among the Delaware the girls observed strict rules regarding food, drink, and bodily care; while in seclusion they wore blankets over their heads, and they were not permitted to leave the huts until their second menstrual period. This rite signified a girl's eligibility for marriage. There is evidence that some northern Iroquoians did not seclude their women during menstruation, although certain taboos had to be observed.

Among the Kickapoo a young girl was isolated from the village in a small hut during her first menses. Tended by her female kin, the girl followed strict prohibitions. Her dreams, like those of the isolated youth in the forest, were of special importance. Accounts of these momentous visions and dreams speak of encounters with tutelary *manitou* who bestowed blessings. Visions of such entities as wind, trees, fire, or birds, were all considered symbolic indications of the young person's future life. A successful dreamer might narrate part or all of his or her dream to an elderly family member or a shaman empowered to interpret dreams. This dream-vision was a means of acquiring psychic integration and spiritual strength so as to meet the challenges of life and death.

One of the most striking puberty rites was the Huskanawe of the Algonquians of Virginia. This rite was undergone by boys selected to be future chiefs and priests, positions of great importance in a highly stratified society. The ceremony began with the ritual tearing away of the children from their mothers and fathers, who had to accept them thenceforth as "dead." The boys were taken into the forest and were sequestered together in a small hut. For months they were given little to eat and were made to drink intoxicating potions and take emetics. At the end of this period of mental and emotional disorientation, they completely forgot who they were, and they were unable to understand or speak the language they had known. When the initiators were sure that the boys had been deconditioned, they took them back to the village. Under close supervision from their guides, the boys formed a new identity; they relearned how to speak and were taught what to wear and the intricacies of the new roles now assigned to them. As rulers or priests they had to be free from all attachments to family and friends. Their minds had been cleansed and reshaped so that they might see clearly and act wisely. Their claim to authority and their power to lead others rested on their successful ritual transition to a sacred condition.

Death. The form of death rites varied widely among the Northeast Woodlands peoples. In the tribes of the upper Great Lakes area, bodies were usually disposed of according to the individual's wishes or clan prerogatives for scaffold exposure, ground burial, or cremation. Among the Fox, death was a highly ritualized event announced to the village by a crier. The members of the deceased's clan gathered for a night of mourning. The clan leader addressed the corpse, advising it not to look back with envy on those still alive but to persevere in its journey to the ancestors in the west. After burial there were the rituals of building a grave shed and installing a clan post as a marker. A six-month period of mourning then followed, during which time a tribesperson was ceremoniously adopted to substitute for the deceased person, especially at memorial feasts.

Burial practices differed among the peoples of the lower Great Lakes and coastal region. The Algonquians of Carolina buried common people individually in shallow graves. The Algonquians of Virginia wrapped the bodies of common people in skins and placed them on scaffolds; after the decay of the flesh was complete, the bones were buried. The rulers of both peoples, however, were treated differently. After death their bodies were disemboweled and the flesh was removed, but the sinews were left attached to the bones. The skin was then sewn back on to the skeleton, after being packed with white sand or occasionally ornaments. Oil kept the body's oils from drying. The corpses were placed on a platform at the western end of the temple and attended by priests.

The Nanticoke and other tribes of the southern Maryland and Delaware peninsula area practiced a second ossuary interment, in some cases preceded by an inhumation and in others by scaffold burials. The rulers of most of these tribes were treated like those of the Algonquians of Virginia and North Carolina. Some of the southern Delaware also had a second ossuary burial, but the main tribal group had one inhumation only; no special treatment for chiefs was noted.

The Huron and some Algonquian groups had two inhumations, the second one in an ossuary. Their Feast of the Dead was conducted at periodic intervals of ten to twelve years. At that time all of the bodies buried during the preceding decade were disinterred, their remaining flesh was removed, and after a ten-day ceremony the skeletons were reburied. Village bands solidified alliances in these ceremonies in which the bones were deliberately mixed. This was a symbol of the unity that should exist among the living. The Petun followed the Huron, while the Neutral and Wenro had a scaffold burial followed later by burial in an ossuary. The Wyandot and Iroquois had only one inhumation but had an annual or semiannual feast for the dead. Eastern New York State, including Long Island, may mark the northern coastal border of secondary burials.

These life-cycle ceremonials were an integral part of every tribesperson's passage through life. Indeed, in the Winnebago Medicine rite the image of human aging in four steps is presented as a paradigm of all life. However, such ceremonial rites of passage can be distinguished from certain personal, clan, and group rituals.

Individual, clan, and group. Power objects given by the *manitou,* such as medicine bundles, charms, and face-paintings, became the focus of personal rituals, songs, and dances. An individual evoked his or her spirit and identified with it by means of rhythmic singing, drumming, rattling, or chanting; one would then channel the power brought by the spirit to a specific need such as hunting, the healing of sick people, or, in some cases, toward more selfish ends.

The Huron owned power charms (*aaskouandy*). Many of these were found in the entrails of game animals, especially those who were difficult to kill. Charms could be small stones, tufts of hair, and so on. One of the abilities of a power charm was to change its own shape, so that a stone, for example, might become a bean or a bird's beak. *Aaskouandy* were of two types: (1) those that brought general good luck and (2) those that were good for one particular task. The particular use of a charm would be revealed to its owner in a dream.

An individual or family might collect a number of charms and keep them in a bundle consisting of, for example, tufts of hair, bones or claws of animals, stones, and miniature masks. The owner was periodically obliged to offer a feast to his charms, during which he and his friends would sing to the charms and show them honor. The owner usually established a relationship to the charm spirit, similar to that between an individual and a guardian spirit, although charm spirits were known to be more unpredictable and dangerous than guardian spirits. An individual or family who wished to get rid of a charm had to conduct a ritual and bury it; even then uneasiness surrounded the event.

Among the Huron and Iroquois, there were masks that had to be cared for in addition to a charm or bundle. A person acquired a mask through dreaming of it or having it prescribed by a shaman. A carver would go into the forest and search for a living tree; basswood, cucumber, and willow were the preferred woods. While burning tobacco, he recited prayers to the tree spirit and the False Face spirits. The mask was carved into the tree and then removed in one piece. The finishing touches, including the eye-holes (which were surrounded with metal) and the mouth hole, were added later. If the tree had been found in the morning, the mask would be painted red; if in the afternoon, black. The hair attached to the mask was horsetail.

Because the mask was considered sacred and full of power the owner had to treat it correctly. He would keep it in a cloth carrier with a turtle rattle placed in the hollow side. If a mask was hung on a wall, it had to face the wall, lest some unsuspecting person be possessed by it. Periodically the mask would be fed mush and anointed with sunflower oil. If a mask fell or if a person dreamed of his mask, he would burn tobacco to it. One or two small bundles of tobacco were also hung inside the mask. The owner of a mask belonged to the False Face society and engaged in its curing rituals. The mask not only brought the owner power and protection but also the ability to heal the sick.

Personal power could overwhelm individuals, causing them to seek only self-aggrandizement. The Shawnee have myths that relate the origin of witchcraft to that mythic time when a crocodile's heart, which was the embodiment of evil, was cut out and carried home to the village by unwitting tribespeople. While the tribes of the Northeast fostered belief in contact with power, they also condemned the misuse of such power in sorcery. They tried to control their exceptional personalities by threatening the return of all evil machinations to the perpetrator. Nonetheless, witch societies have been prominent in Menomini history. Even though these destructive medicine practices may at times have been widespread among the Northeast Woodlands tribes, their many religious societies never completely abandoned the constructive use of power.

These religious societies could be either temporary or permanent. Participants were usually selected according to criteria based on clan membership, on blessing from the same tutelary spirit, or on personal conduct and achievement. Their ceremonial activities, including narrative rituals, feasts, dances, and games, all had sacred meaning because they were performed to honor clan ancestors, guardian spirits, or departed society members. The Miami and Winnebago each had religious societies formed around clan war-bundles. The Kickapoo still have clan societies that hold spring renewals centered on their ancestral bundles. Vision societies also developed among individual Winnebago, Sauk, Fox, Kickapoo, Illinois, Miami, and Shawnee people who had received vision revelations from the same *manitou* spirit. Throughout this region societies also formed around those warriors or braves whose heroic acts in battle were seen as special signs of personal power. So also the Potawatomi Southern Dance temporarily brought together tribespeople who still grieved for deceased relatives. The medicine societies and other groups, such as the Dream Dance (or Drum Dance) and the Native American Church (Peyote), admitted tribespeople who felt called to these societies and were willing to submit to the societies' ethics.

At present the primary medicine society among the Iroquois is the Society of Medicine Men (also known as Shake the Pumpkin) to which most members of other societies belong. This society is dedicated to the medicine animals who long ago promised to heal humans in exchange for ceremonies and feasts.

The Society of Mystic Animals includes the Bear, Buffalo, Otter, and Eagle societies; members of each group take its tutelary spirit as their own when they are healed by it. The Little Water Medicine society guards and cures with the most potent of Iroquois medicines, which come from parts of animals, birds, and plants. Rituals to renew the power of this medicine are held several times a year. The Little People society (also known as Dark Dance) receives power from its relationship with the "little people" who live in stream banks, forests, and underground.

The False Face society is one of the most popular Iroquois societies. As described above, the wooden faces represent spirits of the forest who appear to people in dreams. The society has its own curing ceremonies, but it also participates in the Midwinter ceremony. The Husk Faces are agricultural correlates of the False Faces; they are dedicated to the spirits of maize, beans, and squash. Besides having private curing ceremonies, members of the Husk Face society are doorkeepers at the longhouse when the False Faces perform and also function as police during Longhouse ceremonies.

Religious Personalities. The shaman is the most important religious figure among the upper Great Lakes and Ohio River native peoples. Primarily a healer and diviner, the shaman contacts power by means of a trance and channels that power to specific needs. Shamans are known by a variety of names derived from the calls to their vocation they have received by way of visions, as well as from their particular healing functions. Generally, four shamanic vocations are found among the northeastern Algonquian peoples. There are also a number of shamanic techniques. Both the shamanic vocations and techniques are documented from the seventeenth century.

The most celebrated shamanic figure among the Algonquian peoples is the shaking-tent diviner and healer, whom the Ojibwa call *tcisaki*, the Menomini *tcisakos* and the Potawatomi *tcisakked*. Among the Ojibwa, this shamanic figure received the vocation after a dream "call" from the *manitou* called Mistabeo had occurred four times. The *tcisaki*'s technique was to enter a special lodge that swayed when the *manitou* arrived. The *tcisaki* then mediated between the spirits and the audience during a question-and-answer session in which the location of a lost object or the cause of an illness was sought. In the case of illness, the diviner might determine the cause of the sickness while inside the shaking tent and then come out to perform a sucking cure.

Another ancient shamanic profession is that of the tube-sucking curer whom the Ojibwa called *nanandawi*. Several *manitou* could give this healing vocation, but the Thunderer was especially favored. The sucking curer often used the bones of raptorial birds to suck the affected area and to remove objects believed to have been shot into a person by malicious witches. The curer would partially swallow as many as seven bones down his esophagus; he would apply the bones, which projected out of his mouth, to the area of the patient's body that was being treated.

The manipulation of fire for healing purposes is also an ancient shamanic vocation; the Ojibwa call this healer *wabeno*, the Menomini called him *wapanows*, and the Potawatomi, *wapno*. The traditional call to this vocation came from Morning Star, who was imaged as a *manitou* with horns. The *wabeno*, working individually or in a group, healed by using the heat of burning embers to massage and fascinate his patients.

An initiated shamanic personality resulted from membership in one of the medicine societies. For example, the Ojibwa Mide, or Medicine society, is composed of the tribe's recognized shamans and candidates initiated into the society as well as healed patients. Thus the healing shamans and ritually initiated members perform together with the healed patients during the ritual. There is a basic difference in technique between the members of these shamanic societies and the individual shamanic healers previously discussed. Among individual healers, healing through spontaneous trance is central, whereas within shamanic societies, transmission of sacred knowledge is primary and trance states are more formally structured and ritually transmitted. Thus the role of the religious leader in the medicine societies may be more accurately described as that of a shaman-priest.

Shamanism among the Huron and the Iroquois of the seventeenth century was primarily an individual enterprise, although societies did exist. In subsequent centuries the Iroquois channeled shamanistic powers and skills into the growing number of medicine societies. The central concern of the Huron shamans was the curing of illness. Illness was caused by either (1) natural events, (2) witchcraft, or (3) desires of the soul. The first could be handled by an herbalist or other practitioner. The second and third required the diagnostic and healing abilities of a shaman (*arendiwane*), including divining, interpreting dreams, sucking, blowing ashes, and juggling hot coals.

The *ocata* was a shaman skilled in diagnosis. In the case of a hidden desire of the soul whose frustration was causing illness he would seek to have a vision of what was desired. To do this he might gaze into a basin of water until the object appeared or enter into a trancelike state to see the object or lie down in a small dark tent to contact his spiritual allies to assist him.

A personal spirit relationship (*oki*) was won after a long fast and isolation in the forest; it could take the form of a human, an animal, or a bird such as a raven or eagle. Sometimes the power and skill needed to cure would come through a dream. There were shamanic specialists who handled hot coals or plunged their arms into boiling water without injury; frequently a power song, which allowed the person to accomplish this, was sung. Other shamans cured by blowing hot ashes over a person or by rubbing the person's skin with ashes.

Witchcraft was combatted by the *aretsan*; usually the *aretsan* would suck out the evil spell that the witch had magically injected into his victim. Divining shamans could see things at a distance, cause rain, persuade animal guardian spirits to release game, or give advice on military or political matters.

Outside of these established vocations, certain shamanic techniques were available to all lay people among the tribes of the Northeast. These included tattooing, naming, divining, bloodletting, induced vomiting as a cure, weather control, and herbal healing. However, at times individual shamans or shamanic societies were so strong that they absorbed these and other curing practices as their exclusive prerogative.

Other outstanding religious personalities included the war chiefs, who led war bundle ceremonies and war parties, and the peace chiefs, who did not go to fight but who acted as mediators, working for peace within the tribe as well as between separate tribes. The Menomini chose hereditary war chiefs from the Bear clan and peace chiefs from the Thunderer clan. All Northeast Woodlands tribes used a war and peace chief system, but the clan totems from which these leaders were selected often differed from band to band.

Occasionally singular religious figures appear in the ethnohistory of the Northeast Woodlands peoples. The Winnebago have had sacred clowns and "contraries" who performed ritual actions backward or in a humorous manner to accentuate the ambiguity of life. Transvestite visionaries such as the Miami "whitefaces" wore women's clothes and did women's work; occasionally they gained reputations as healers or diviners because of their unusual call and personal abilities. Among other exceptional personalities were the ecstatic visionaries often called "prophets." The Delaware prophet Neolin called for a rejection of white influences and a return to the old ways and inspired many to join Pontiac's uprising in the 1760s. The famous Shawnee prophet, Tenkswatawa, brother to Tecumseh initiated a nativistic movement uniting many woodland peoples against American expansion in the late eighteenth and early nineteenth centuries. Handsome Lake, of the Seneca, inspired a reformed way of life for the Iroquois in the early nineteenth century. During the same period the Kickapoo prophet Kenekuk led a religious movement that fostered his people's accomodation to some American cultural influences. The Winnebago prophet Wabokieshiek began a short-lived revitalization of traditional values during Black Hawk's War in the 1830s. These and other minor prophets received revelations concerning the need to transform specific historical situations. They represented a shift in religious thought among these native peoples from the predominantly individual concern and responsibility for harmony with cosmic powers in nature to a more structured ethics based on an interior religious imperative.

Northeast Woodlands peoples have struggled to maintain their traditions into the present period. Not only have they endured the cultural inroads of a variety of Christian missionaries, but these native traditions have also persisted in the face of tribal fragmentation and degradation. This struggle was reflected in the life of the Seneca leader Handsome Lake; he was able to give focus to his people's plight by drawing on the spiritual power of dreams that came to him during an illness brought on by drunkenness and despair in the face of the pervasive oppression of his cultural way of life. The traditional sanction of dreams and visions in native Northeast Woodlands religions continues into the present revitalization of the sweat lodge, the vision quest, and medicine-wheel gatherings. The relevance of these traditional ceremonies to contemporary needs is highlighted by the growing participation of non-Indians in these meditative rituals. In summary it is evident that the spiritual life of the Indians of the Northeast Woodlands resists any attempt to simply objectify and list representative paractices or beliefs. Even the term religion may not be as helpful for understanding these complex lifeways that activate visionary experiences, the sovereignty of the community of life, ecological affectivity, and cosmological centeredness.

SEE ALSO Handsome Lake; Iroquois Religious Traditions; Neolin; Shamanism, article on North American Shamanism; Tecumseh.

BIBLIOGRAPHY

Anthropological Papers. New York, 1907–. These volumes, published by the American Museum of Natural History, contain extensive materials on the religious beliefs and practices of Northeast Woodlands peoples as, for example, in Alanson Skinner's *Social Life and Ceremonial Bundles of the Menomini Indians* and *Folklore of the Menomini Indians,* in volume 13, parts 1 and 3 (New York, 1915).

Beverley, Robert. *The History and Present State of Virginia* (1705). Edited by Louis B. Wright. Chapel Hill, N. C., 1947. A primary document on the Virginia Algonquians drawing on the author's own observations and those of earlier sources, written and verbal. More sensitive than most works of the period regarding both the native peoples and the natural environment.

Black, Mary. "Ojibwa Power Belief-Systems." In *The Anthropology of Power,* edited by Raymond Fogelson and Richard Adams, pp. 141–151. New York, 1977. A seminal study of the concept of power in the religious belief systems of the Ojibwa peoples.

Blair, Emma, ed. and trans. *The Indian Tribes of the Upper Mississippi Valley and the Region of the Great Lakes* (1911). 2 vols. New York, 1969. A fine collection of primary documents describing the upper Great Lakes and Ohio River native peoples during the seventeenth and eighteenth centuries.

Bureau of American Ethnology. *Annual Reports* and "Bulletins." Washington, D.C., 1888–. These reports and bulletins present materials on native peoples' beliefs and religious practices which, however, often need further interpretation. Special mention can be made here of the following monographs published as "Bulletins of the Bureau of American Ethnology": *The Midewiwin or 'Grand Medicine Society' of the Ojibwa,* no. 7 (1885–1886), and *The Menomini Indians* no. 14, (1892–1893), both by Walter J. Hoffman; *Ethnography of the Fox Indians,* no. 125 (1939), by William Jones; *Contributions to Fox Ethnology,* 2 vols., nos. 85 (1927) and 95 (1930), and *The Owl Sacred Pack of the Fox Indians,* no. 72 (1921), by Trumen Michelson; and *The Winnebago Tribe,* no. 37 (1915–1916), by Paul Radin.

Callicott, J. Baird, and Michael Nelson. *American Indian Environmental Ethics: An Ojibwa Case Study.* Upper Saddle River, N.J., 2004. A study of stories from the Ojibwa that demonstrates how their cultural worldview supports specific principle and practices related to an environmental ethics.

Dobyns, Henry. *Their Numbers Became Thinned: Native Population Dynamics in Eastern North America.* Knoxville, Tenn., 1983. This study proposes a major revision of population estimates of Native American population for the New England region based on early death records of native villages.

Driver, Harold E. *Indians of North America.* 2d ed., rev. Chicago, 1969. Somewhat dated in parts but overall good statistical information on all Native American tribes, including those of the Northeast.

Flannery, Regina. "An Analysis of Coastal Algonquian Culture." Ph.D. diss., Catholic University, 1939. A detailed classification of cultural topics and documentation for all areas of coastal Algonquian life, drawn mostly from sixteenth- and seventeenth-century documents.

Greeman, Emerson F. *The Wolf and Furton Sites.* Occasional Contributions, Museum of Anthropology, University of Michigan, no. 8. Ann Arbor, 1939. Study of a woodland archaeological site of proto-historical period.

Grim, John A. *The Shaman: Patterns of Siberian and Ojibway Healing.* Norman, Okla., 1983. A study of the Ojibwa shaman that, in addition, traces broad patterns of shamanic expression. Includes an extensive bibliography on the religious figure of the shaman.

Hallowell, A. Irving. "Ojibwa Ontology, Behavior, and World View." In *Culture in History: Essays in Honor of Paul Radin,* edited by Stanley Diamond, pp. 19–52. New York, 1960. An important analysis of the categories and orientations of Ojibwa ethnometaphysics that is helpful in interpreting the religious practices of these woodland peoples.

Harrington, Mark R. *Religion and Ceremonies of the Lenape.* New York, 1921. The first and still the best work on the religion of the Delaware in the late nineteenth and early twentieth centuries.

Hewitt, J. N. B., ed. "Iroquois Cosmology," part 1. In *Bureau of American Ethnology Twenty-first Annual Report,* pp. 127–339. Washington, D.C., 1899–1900.

Hewitt, J. N. B., ed. "Iroquoian Cosmology," part 2. In *Bureau of American Ethnology Forty-third Annual Report,* pp. 449–819. Washington, D.C., 1925–1926. The best collection of Iroquois cosmogonic myths available.

Kinietz, W. Vernon. *The Indians of the Western Great Lakes, 1615–1760.* Occasional Contributions, Museum of Anthropology, University of Michigan, no. 10. Ann Arbor, 1940.

Landes, Ruth. *Ojibwa Religion and the Midewiwin.* Madison, Wis., 1968.

Landes, Ruth. *The Prairie Potawatomi.* Madison, Wis., 1970. Both of Landes's works explore, from an anthropological perspective, selected myths and rituals associated with the presence of religious power.

McNally, Michael. *Ojibwe Singers: Hymns, Grief, and a Native Culture in Motion.* New York, 2000. A study of the changing religiosity among Anishinabe Great Lakes peoples.

Parker, Arthur C. *Parker on the Iroquoi.* Edited by William N. Fenton. Syracuse, 1968. Contains important documents such as "The Code of Handsome Lake, Seneca Prophet," and "The Constitution of the Five Nations."

Radin, Paul, ed. *The Road of Life and Death.* New York, 1945. Contains the text of the Winnebago Medicine rite with some commentary by Radin on the circumstances that prompted Crashing Thunder (Jasper Blowsnake) to narrate this esoteric lore. This book also includes Big Winnebago's autobiography, as edited by Paul Radin.

Shimony, Annemarie Anrod. *Conservatism among the Iroquois at the Six Nations Reserve.* Syracuse, 1994. Essential reading for an understanding of contemporary Iroquois religion and the struggle to assure its continuation.

Speck, Frank G. *A Study of the Delaware Indian Big House Ceremony.* Harrisburg, Pa., 1931. The foremost study of the Big House ceremony among the Delaware of Oklahoma.

Sturtevant, William C., and Bruce Trigger, eds. *Handbook of North American Indians.* Rev. ed. Washington, D.C., 1981. An excellent overview of the specific tribal groups in this area with a brief treatment of religious beliefs and practices.

Thornton, Russell. *American Indian Holocaust and Survival: A Population History Since 1492.* Norman, Okla., 1987. A significant study of early records to reassess native populations and the deaths by pandemic diseases to which native populations had little or no resistance.

Thwaites, Reuben Gold, ed. *The Jesuit Relations and Allied Documents..., 1610–1791* (1896–1901). 73 vols. in 39. Reprint, New York, 1959. An indispensable work especially on the tribes of "Huronia" and "Iroquoia" as related by Jesuit missionaries.

Tooker, Elisabeth. *Native North American Spirituality of the Eastern Woodlands.* New York, 1979. Ethnographic selections from the religious rituals of various Northeast Woodlands peoples with some general interpretative sections.

Trigger, Bruce G. *The Children of Aataentsic: A History of the Huron People to 1660.* 2 vols. Montreal, 1976. Excellent reconstruction of the history, culture, and religion of the Hurons, relying on the earliest documents available.

Trowbridge, C. C. *Meearmar Traditions.* Occasional Contributions, Museum of Anthropology, University of Michigan, no. 7. Ann Arbor, 1938. A study of the Miami people.

Trowbridge, C. C. *Shawnese Traditions.* Edited by W. Vernon Kinietz. Occasional Contributions, Museum of Anthropology, University of Michigan, no. 9. Ann Arbor, 1939.

Williams, Roger. *The Complete Writings of Roger Williams* (1643). 7 vols. Edited by Reuben A. Guild et al. New York, 1963. Especially valuable for information on the Narraganset is "The Key into the Language of America" found in volume 1.

JOHN A. GRIM (1987 AND 2005)
DONALD P. ST. JOHN (1987 AND 2005)

NORTH AMERICAN INDIANS: INDIANS OF THE SOUTHEAST WOODLANDS

Culturally and linguistically diverse Native American communities of various sizes recognize the area now known as the southeastern region of the United States as their ancestral homeland. At the beginning of the twenty-first century, several are federally recognized groups, while other communities continue to press for state and federal recognition. While those that have governmental recognition are officially identified as "American Indian tribes" or "bands," members of these groups self-identify in a number of ways, but most often by means of group names, which are either indigenous or commonly accepted English terms. Depending on personal preference, individuals also may employ such terms as First Nations, First Peoples, Indigenous Nations, Native Americans, or Indians. Certain of these First Peoples of the Southeast count as many as tens of thousands of members, while many more individuals living in the region claim some measure of Native American heritage.

Historically, the Native American religious traditions of this region included a variety of ritual practices, beliefs, and narrative traditions, and this is still the case today. Individual communities each have distinct religious systems, and there continues to be diversity within communities as well. A variety of Christian denominations flourish, in addition to contingents of people who maintain indigenous religious systems. There also are people who draw comfortably from both types of systems throughout their lives.

Research suggests that there are some elements of religious systems that are, and have been, common to most southeastern groups. Certain ritual activities, cultural narratives ("myths"), and beliefs that reflect recurrent themes are discernable, and oral transmission of knowledge continues in many communities. However, what the anthropologist John R. Swanton observed in the 1940s is still the case today: while "the background of the religious beliefs of these tribes and their medical practices. . .[are] similar, . . . the religious attitude seems to . . . [vary] considerably from one tribe to another and the ceremonial patterns . . . [are] often markedly distinct" (Swanton, 1946, p. 805).

THE "SOUTHEAST WOODLANDS" AND FIRST PEOPLES. It is difficult to speak about groups and precise land area when discussing First Peoples of the region, past and present, and benchmark surveys do not always agree. Generally speaking, scholars have identified the Southeast as that sector of North America bounded by the Atlantic Ocean and Gulf of Mexico at the east and south, by the longitude 95° west, and by a latitude between 35° and 40° north. Historically as many as 170 tribes are thought to have made the Southeast their home, with the following language families represented: Algonquian, Caddoan, Iroquoian, Muskogean, Siouan, Tunican, and Yuchean. Today, depending on criteria, estimates of communities in this large area range from the mid-twenties to fifty.

The process of colonization had manifold effects on the First Peoples of this region. In certain cases, distinct indigenous linguistic and cultural social units joined together as nations to meet the challenges posed by European colonists. Other politically and ceremonially autonomous groups linked by such factors as language and geography coalesced in a like manner. Most groups were organized by means of matrilineal clans, which provided a ready-made organizational structure for such amalgamations as the Cherokee, Creek, Chickasaw, Seminole, and Choctaw. For example, the Cherokee, or *Tsa:la:gi* nation was formed from many towns or villages of people who referred to themselves as *Ani:Yunwiya* (the Principal People) and spoke three dialects of what is now called the Cherokee language. The term *Cherokee* is of uncertain origin, and all three terms are still in use today, though *Cherokee* and its Cherokee translation, *Tsalag* or *Anitsalagi,* predominate.

A different model is presented by the towns, or *talwa (tvlwv)* of distinct peoples who, in order to repel outside threats, formed what became known as the Creek Confederacy. These included communities speaking the Muskogean linguistic family languages—Mvskoke (Muskogee), Alabama, Koasati, Apalachee, Hitchitee, and Mikasuki, in addition to, at some point in time, members of Yuchi, Shawnee, Natchez, Guale, Yamasee, Cusabo, and Tawaso groups (Lewis and Jordan, 2002, p. 5). The terms *Mvskoke, Muskogee,* and *Creek* can refer to the people, the language, or both.

Some of these amalgamations were decimated by warfare and disease, as were many autonomous communities before them. Others were torn asunder by the U.S. government policy of forced removal during the 1830s. Consequently, until that time the contemporary South was populated by groups that for the most part now have larger populations in Oklahoma. Because indigenous peoples that now have communities in the Southeast as well as in Oklahoma once belonged to the same cultural units, they have shared common elements of religious systems, although time and place have created differences. In Oklahoma, close proximity to other groups from the Southeast created further augmentations of belief and ritual. During the twentieth century, particularly the second half of the century, many eastern and western communities increased efforts to strengthen their ties.

Despite adversity, contingents of certain nations were able to maintain a presence on some portion of their ancestral lands, and over time solidify this presence. Currently, many indigenous religious systems are undergoing revivals as part of wider cultural revitalizations. The Eastern Band of Cherokee Indians (North Carolina), the Poarch Band of Creeks (Alabama), the Seminole Tribe and Miccosuke Tribe (both in Florida), the Mississippi Band of Choctaw Indians, and the Alabama-Coushatta Tribe of Texas, as well as the Coushatta, Chitimacha, and Tunica-Biloxi Tribes (all in Louisiana), are testaments to the resolve of indigenous southeastern nations to retain their religious, social, and political identities while undergoing cultural change.

Lengthy legal or legislative actions often were required to guarantee and insure the rights associated with such group identity, and circumstances could and did change. To give one example, the Catawba people of South Carolina banded together for survival with several North and South Carolina peoples in the first half of the eighteenth century. The Catawba Indian Nation was terminated as a federally recognized tribe in 1962, recognized by the federal government again in 1993, and received a monetary settlement to resolve a land dispute that began in 1840.

Other communities have worked for full recognition of their collective identities as well. At the start of the twenty-first century, North Carolina groups such as the Lumbee (who list approximately fifty thousand members), Haliwa-Saponi, Waccamaw, and Coharie, as well as the Pamunkey and Mattaponi of Virginia, are recognized by their respective states even as they continue to seek federal recognition. The fact that they are not always supported in their efforts by federally recognized Native American communities speaks to the complexity of identity issues in the United States; the ongoing efforts of such groups also highlight the complex and often contradictory systems of classification by which federal and state agencies determine Native American identity.

OVERVIEW OF ARCHAEOLOGICAL AND HISTORICAL DATA: CONTACT, COLONIZATION, AND CULTURAL NEGOTIATION. Standard archaeological timelines, often constructed with a strong teleological component assuming Western civilization as the goal, have traced the history of religious traditions in the Southeast by means of a developmental societal pattern, with the religious systems reflecting changes in other social spheres as societies "progress" toward "civilization" in terms of complexity and technology. Typically, five periods of human occupation are delineated in the region: Paleo-Indian (c. 9000–7000 BCE), Archaic (c. 7000–1000 BCE), Woodland (c. 1000 BCE–700 CE), Mississippian (c. 700–1500 CE), and Historic (c.1500 CE–present). Generally speaking, scholars have linked the religious behavior of communities in the region to subsistence activities in each of these periods.

Because of the archaeological evidence that led to such a timeline, the concept of a "Southeastern Ceremonial Complex" or "Southern Cult" was popular in the field of archaeology for many years. As originally conceived, the theory—based on archaeological evidence from "late prehistoric sites"—was that during the Mississippian and early historic periods the societies in what is now the southeastern United States shared many similar material characteristics, suggesting broader religious and political affinities (Muller, 1989, pp. 11, 19). Common religious features included the development of a chiefly/priestly social class, veneration of and tribute to a sun deity tied to corn production, and ritualized burial techniques. In addition, shell gorgets and other items from these periods bear common artistic motifs such as spirals, circles, and spiders, which scholars speculate have spiritual significance. The theory still has its adherents, but contemporary scholarship has greatly abridged its explanatory capacity. While there were iconographic similarities across the region during the Mississippian period, it remains unclear to what extent ritual activities and beliefs can be interpolated from archaeological data.

Although Spanish political influence was temporary in most areas of the present-day Southeast other than Florida, the travels of the Spanish explorer Hernando de Soto throughout the region in the 1540s would prove to have more lasting consequences. As other expeditions followed in his wake, the ensuing combination of warfare and epidemics devastated numerous groups. In the seventeenth century certain southeastern peoples were decimated (Yamasee, Timicua) while others were forced to emigrate and reside with confederacies of nations or emerging nation-states (Tuscarora, Yuchi). Within societies that avoided these two fates, in addition to the obvious effects of such upheaval and depopulation, in some cases the transmission of religious knowledge to younger generations was interrupted.

Religious-studies scholar Joel W. Martin argued in the late 1990s that such factors led to the fourth in a series of religious revolutions, the first three of which coincided with the transitions from the Archaic period to the historic period. According to Martin this resulted in the seventeenth- and eighteenth-century "postholocaust, village-based religions" of such groups as the Cherokee, Choctaw, Chickasaw, and Muskogee (1997, p. 156). This theory is suggestive and situates postcolonial history in the much longer time span of human occupation of the region; further questions remain, however, as to the extent of regional homogeneity (as discussed above).

British, French, and Spanish forces arriving in the Southeast encountered diverse sociopolitical entities with longstanding ties to the land. Yet the peoples of the region were not passive observers; among indigenous groups, there was a gradual shift in power relations that initially favored those groups able to manipulate European governments and pit them against each other. Indigenous communities also had longstanding alliances or disputes in the region, which colonists were able to exploit to their advantage. This was the case especially once the British gained control of the region in 1760s after the war against the French and their Native American allies. All the while, people were on the move and new alliances were being formed. For example, Muskogee people immigrated to Florida in the eighteenth century, incorporated (in some cases forcibly) people from Yamasee, Apalachee, and other communities, including Africans, and became known as *Seminoles.*

In the early nineteenth century, increasingly encroaching colonial settlements and government designs on natural resources such as farmland and gold resulted in land loss for many groups who had survived earlier hardships. This period coincided with sustained Christian missionary efforts among groups throughout the Southeast. The prevalent ideology of the times inextricably linked Christianization and "civilization," and students in missionary schools were taught all aspects of "civilized" social behavior. European American observers dubbed the Cherokee, Choctaw, Muskogee, Chickasaw, and Seminole nations the "Five Civilized Tribes," because they felt that these groups best approached the appropriate level of cultural development.

Even these nations eventually were targets for forced removal. Although many missionaries saw this as the only solution, a small number were actively involved in the efforts of nations to retain their homelands. In the 1830s the majority of the Cherokee, Choctaw, Muskogee, and Chickasaw nations, who had for the most part preserved their homelands and remained relatively autonomous until that time, were forcibly marched to territories in Oklahoma. These involuntary emigrations resulted in great loss of life, and each has become known as a Trail of Tears, though frequently history texts focus only on the Cherokee Removal. The Seminole nation resisted such efforts, and the U.S. military ultimately succeeded only partially in removing them.

The cultural impacts of Christianity upon southeastern communities have been complicated and multiple. The focus on acculturation created conflicts, and in the eighteenth, nineteenth, and early to mid-twentieth centuries, the result in sectors of many communities was a de-emphasis on traditional beliefs and practices in favor of Christianity. However, there were individuals and contingents throughout the Southeast who steadfastly maintained indigenous religious systems, though they often did so away from the gaze of observers, scholarly and otherwise. On the other hand, in some cases (as with the Choctaw and Cherokee) Christian churches actually have worked to preserve cultural and group identity by incorporating local languages into services or by being a focal point for communities (see, for example, Pesantubbee, 1999).

CONTEMPORARY LANDSCAPE. The Mississippi Choctaw reservation is about seventy miles northeast of Jackson, mostly in Neshoba County. Of the approximately 9,000 Choctaw people living there, the majority identify themselves as Christian. While there is a range of denominations, Baptist, Catholic, and Pentecostal denominations dominate. However, people in certain communities, such as the Bogue Chitto, have steadfastly maintained their traditions, and refused to accept Christianity (Mould, 2003, p. xxiv). Additionally, since the 1970s there has been a resurgence of interest in "distinctly Choctaw" culture in Mississippi, where in addition to all-night sings at churches and other community-based events, an annual Choctaw Labor Day Festival features social dancing, traditional crafts, food, and stickball alongside country music and other standard attractions (Lambert, 2001, p. 317). Other activities such as sweat lodges also are gaining in popularity, though opinions are mixed as to whether or not this affects the uniqueness of Choctaw traditions (Mould, 2003, p. 204).

Similar events also take place on the Qualla Boundary in western North Carolina, in Swain and Jackson counties (about sixty miles west of Asheville), where approximately 7,000 members of the Eastern Band of Cherokee Indians (of a total membership of 13,000) support at least twenty-two churches. Baptist churches are the most numerous, and there are several different Holiness tradition churches, as well as those of other denominations. Since the late twentieth century, certain townships (though members of all townships are involved) have been at the forefront of efforts to revive or preserve particular cultural elements such as traditional dancing, the Green Corn Ceremony, and the Cherokee language. As they have for centuries, religio-medicinal specialists continue to work and pass on traditions to younger generations; in a like manner traditions such as *anetso*, the Cherokee ball game, and its associated ceremonial cycle continue to be maintained in some townships.

In Alabama, approximately 1,500 Mvskoke people (of approximately 2,200 members) predominantly associate with Protestant denominations, including Baptist, Holiness, and Episcopal churches. They reside near Poarch, Alabama, in Escambia County, fifty-seven miles east of Mobile. In recent decades specialists from Oklahoma have been retained to revive various cultural activities, including the Mvskoke language and sweat bath activities. Religio-medicinal specialists have continued to work in this community as well (see below).

At the beginning of the twenty-first century, approximately 1,200 to 1,500 Seminole and Miccosukee (Mikasuki) people live in Florida, many on three reservations: Brighton (northwest of Lake Okeechobee), Big Cypress (the northeast edge of Big Cypress Swamp), and Dania, or Hollywood (outside Hollywood, Fla.). Perhaps between 15 and 20 percent do not officially affiliate with either tribal entity; according to one source, approximately 60 percent of the Seminole people in Florida are non-Christian (Beck et. al, 1996, p. 245). Today, they are known as the Seminole Tribe. Though initially considered by the federal government as just a splinter Seminole group, the Miccosuke Tribe of Florida gained a corporate charter and drafted a constitution in 1961, and they established separately in 1965 along the Tamiami Trail highway. The Miccosuke people distinguish themselves from Seminoles culturally; their Hitchiti language, *ilaponki,* is spoken by about two thirds of the larger group, with the rest speaking Mvskoke.

SUPERNATURAL OR "OTHER-THAN-HUMAN" BEINGS. Many First Peoples of the Southeast reference a "supreme being," but often the term connotes a more abstracted power, force, or perpetuity. These beings or entities can be beseeched for assistance and are considered important forces in many peoples' lives. Though different terms can be used to refer to them, a select few are the Cherokee term *une:hlanv':hi* (translated as "Provider," from the verb "to provide"; also translated "Creator") and the Mvskoke terms *Hesaketvmesē* (translated as "Breath Holder," "Master of Breath," or "Breath") and *Ibofanga* (translated as "the existence of all things and energy within all things," or "the one above us" (Kilpatrick, 1991, p. 58; Fixico, 2003, p. 3; Swanton, [1928] 2000, p. 481).

The Choctaw term for this entity most often cited is *hvshtahli* [*hvsh-táh-li*] and is translated as "Great Spirit," with the caveat that this term was a pre-Christian concept (Haag and Willis, 2001, p. 334). According to one source, it also can be translated as "governor of the world, whose eye is the sun"; both this term and the term for sun—*nanapisa* (the one who sees)—express the distinction that the sun was an aspect of a more abstract force and not in and of itself a deity or focus of worship (O'Brien, 2002, p. 3). Similarly, the Chickasaw term for this supernatural being, Luak Ishto Holo Åba, is translated as "the great holy fire above," and the Natchez term, *Uwa'shīl,* as "Big fire" (Swanton, [1928] 2000, p. 482).

Cultural narratives often are populated by a variety of other beings that may be more regularly involved with humans or beseeched for assistance. They are not worshipped, but are respected for their power and abilities, both positive and negative. Defying characterization as "good" or "evil," they have the capacity to help as well as harm humans, especially if they are not treated with proper respect.

These can be natural elements, "archetypal forms" of animals or human-like beings such as Corn Woman (see below). Depending on the religious system, natural phenomena including the sun, thunders, and running bodies of water such as rivers and streams are considered sentient beings (Cherokee, Choctaw, Natchez, Mvskoke). All of these beings can be understood as "other-than-human persons," to use A. Irving Hallowell's term from his seminal article on Ojibwe traditions ([1960] 1975, p. 145).

NARRATIVE TRADITIONS AND COSMOLOGY. Southeastern communities traditionally have transmitted a variety of historical accounts, cultural narratives, and items of religious knowledge orally. Though the proliferation of scholarship has made written accounts readily available over the last century and a half, in many cases the preferred mode of transmission continues to be oral. The term "cultural narratives" is used in the context of this article to refer to what are commonly called "myths"; this term implies cultural significance without assigning a truth-value. While there are a variety of such cultural narratives, several southeastern communities share certain narratives in common, though individual details differ.

Certain of these narratives are of a sacred character, and are equal in significance to narratives contained in the holy books of other cultures. As is the case in any religious community, individuals in southeastern groups interpret these narratives in a variety of ways, both literally and metaphorically, and incorporate other information in their assessments. These narratives can be used to explain current circumstances, for instance how a people came to live where they do, and why they perform certain activities, be they subsistence-related or ceremonial. Other narratives, which sometimes are humorous, allegorically highlight human foibles or are etiological.

Both Cherokee and Mvskoke cultural narratives present cosmologies that recognize different worlds, or planes, including the world humans now inhabit, an underworld, and a world above the sky. The middle world is conceived as being a flat surface surrounded by water, over which a stone sky vault arches and tilts daily to allow beings and forces to pass between worlds. Other groups of human-like beings also inhabit the middle world, including the Little People (Cherokee, *Yun:wi Tsun:sdi'*), recognized by many groups. Mostly keeping to themselves, they are sometimes mischievous; on occasion their presence is more dangerous.

Cherokee cosmology posits a tiered series of planes culminating in the seventh height, or *galv':ladí* (*galunlati*), which translates as "above" or "above everything," located above the sky vault; this is home to various forces such as thunder and the sun, as well as for archetypal animals (Kilpatrick, 1991, p. 58; Irwin, 1992, p. 240). Typically, the underworld does not have a negative moral value. Certain beings such as large horned snakes and panthers make their home in the underworld, accessed through rivers, streams, and waterfalls. However, even such dangerous beings possess ambiguous attributes; the large horned snake (Cherokee, *uk:-tena*), for example, has a jewel-like crest on its forehead that is prized for its powers. The Mvskoke narrative tradition speaks of the tie snake as another such being.

Creation of the World and the Appearance of Humans. According to one Cherokee cultural narrative, the world of human habitation was created when animals living in *galv':ladí* felt crowded and sent a water beetle to search for a place to live below the sky vault, where all was water. The water beetle retrieved mud from the bottom of the water, and this mud was fastened to the sky vault with four cords, one at each cardinal direction. Individual Mvskoke narratives differ somewhat in describing the creation of the world, but several examples revolve around an animal or bird (e.g., crawfish, dove, pigeons) procuring the dirt or blade of grass that would be used to create the earth. The Seminole oral tradition describes the creation of the earth from the back of the Great Turtle, who emerged from the sea. His shell cracked and four giant ant brothers put it back together; though the turtle perished, he decreed that Earth Children should walk over it. They emerged from beneath an earth mound that had formed on this surface. There are Alabama, Chitimacha, Natchez, and Yuchi versions of this "earth diver" narrative form as well.

Cultural narratives also locate inhabitants in the southeastern region. While some narratives describe migration from elsewhere at a distant time in the past (Mvskoke, Cherokee, Choctaw, Chickasaw), others state that present-day southeastern locales are in fact ancestral homelands (Mvskoke, Cherokee, Choctaw). Thus, in several cases, emergence from the earth is either stated (Mvskoke, Choctaw) or implied (Cherokee). The existence of different narratives about single events within religious systems should not be misconstrued as problematic, nor considered as logical flaws in the system. For example, the presence of two different creation stories as well as two flood narratives woven together in the *Book of Genesis* does not typically result in such conclusions about Judaism and Christianity; nor does the existence of Four Gospels do so for the latter.

In these southeastern narrative traditions, animals existed on the earth before humans, and engaged in a variety of activities that humans would as well, including conducting councils, staging dances, and engaging in athletic contests. Humans arrived on the earth soon after, and quickly began to wear out their welcome by killing animals, competing with them for resources, and driving them from their homes. Many of the animals played a role in alterations to both the landscape and the way of life in the world of human inhabitation.

According to a Cherokee narrative, the animals, meeting in emergency council, determined to thin out the human population by devising individual diseases. Hearing of the animals' plans, the plants decided to come to the aid of the humans by providing themselves as medicines to cure the various diseases. Thus humans gained a valuable ally. At least one Mvskoke cultural narrative relates how plants made a pact with a "Holy Man," or *Mēkko-hoyvnēcv* (King passing through) to cure people together (Lewis and Jordan, 2000, pp. 74–76).

Narratives Concerning the Corn Woman. In most southeastern traditions, a significant narrative recounts the selfless, ultimately sacrificial act of a Corn Woman who in life provided food from her body and in her death the plants for cultivation to sustain her people (Cherokee, Mvskoke, Natchez). Though it varies somewhat within and between communities, the basic storyline is that one or two sons (in one Natchez version it is twin girls, in another it is a single boy) spied on their mother or grandmother as she privately rubbed her body to produce corn (and sometimes beans as well). They were shocked as they saw the food emanate from between her legs (in at least one Cherokee version it is said to have come from her vagina; in Mvskoke versions it came from either between her legs as she scratched her thighs, or from her feet; and in a Natchez version it issued from her anus). Fearing this trusted woman was a witch, they refused to eat the food, and then either she offered herself to them as a sacrifice (Natchez, Mvskoke, Cherokee), she did so after they resolved to kill her (Cherokee), or she sent them off to live elsewhere for a time (Mvskoke).

One further version of the narrative, from the Koasati people (of present-day Alabama), tells of an old woman who provided food for orphans, though she had been shunned because of sores and uncleanliness. Choctaw narratives attribute the origin of corn to the daughter of a Choctaw sacred being who, after being fed by two hunters, instructed them to return to their meeting place at the next midsummer moon. When they did they discovered a corn plant, which they cultivated.

In Cherokee and Mvskoke versions of the Corn Woman narrative, there appears to be a link between the production of corn and menstruation. Interestingly, both Cherokee and Shawnee narratives feature menstruating women defeating malevolent beings (such as a stone-covered cannibal or great horned serpent). It seems clear that these are expressions of women's power—although scholars continue to debate the narratives' perspectives on this power (i.e., whether or not it is portrayed positively or negatively). Either way, women play key roles in these foundational narratives; in the former cases the women provide a staple crop for the benefit of future generations, and in the latter they defeat enemies threatening their communities.

Medico-Religious Specialists and Medicinal Traditions. Generally speaking, ritual specialists seek the intercession of supernatural beings in the affairs of humans; they can offer prayers, divine information, and administer medicinal substances. Such specialists can be either male or female. These activities and the forces and beings they involve are part of religious systems that encompass both positive and negative elements. Due in part to the common English translation of these activities as "conjuring," and an unfortunate focus upon its negative aspects, many observers have mislabeled the activity "witchcraft." Such beliefs are still strong among some circles in southeastern communities, though they are rejected as superstition by others in the same communities. Many people find traditional and Christian activities complementary, and certain contemporary practitioners report that Christian beliefs power their abilities.

Such Cherokee practitioners often are known in English as "conjurers" or those who "doctor"; they are identified by terms that designate their particular abilities and specialties. For example, religious studies scholar Lee Irwin culled terms from several works, including *ada'nunwisgi* (healers or curers); *amayi didadzun:stisgi* (the one who "takes them to water"—interpreted as "priest"); and *dida'nunwiski* (sing., well-known and mature healer) (Irwin, 1992, pp. 244–245). This final term was translated by Cherokee studies scholar Alan Kilpatrick as "knowledgeable shaman" (1991, p. 50). Some specialists focus primarily on divination, which can include locating lost objects, diagnosing disease, or predicting the date of an individual's death.

Formulaic utterances, or *idi:gawé:sdi* (often called "songs" or "formulas"), are integral to any healing activity, as well as to other pursuits such as hunting or warfare. They are standardized speech acts that incorporate elements of prayer, entreaty, and instruction on producing desired effects, as well as directions for preparation and usage of medicines. Through the use of formulas, ritual specialists can seek the intercession of supernatural beings and effect circumstances in the course of human events. With the creation of the Cherokee syllabary by Sequoyah in 1821, many specialists began writing these formulas in notebooks.

In Mvskoke culture, *Heleswv* (medicine) is utilized in individual cases of illness, as well as for activities such as ball games. Tools include specially prepared sticks, crystals *(sabiā),* and horns made from pieces of a special horned snake—the latter are used to extract negative substances from ill patients. These crystals were once in use among several groups in the region, including the Cherokee, Mvskoke, Alabama, and Natchez.

For Mvskoke people, the ideal of *hecvs,* or "seeing," involves the simultaneous recognition of the presence of a variety of beings and forces, both physical and metaphysical, and of the "totality of *Ibofanga* ['the one above us']" (Fixico, 2003, pp. 7, 11). Religio-medicinal specialists are divided into three categories, though the first, the *heles-hayv* (medicine maker), can possess the abilities of all three. The other two specialists are the "*owalv* (prophet or seer)" and the "*kerrv* (one who knows)," or *Kerrata* (key-tha) (Lewis and Jordan, 2002, p. 39; Fixico, 2003, p. 3). These individuals can be male or female. Unlike the Cherokee tradition, written books with songs and words ("formulas") are considered a sign of weakness.

Choctaw terms applied to human beings, such as *ishtahullo* ("being endowed with occult power"; see also *stahullo,* "witch," below), also refer to the power of natural forces such as thunder, or to the power provided by dreams. The word *ishtahullo* can be applied to all women generally, as well as to particular men and women of distinction, including at least one Jesuit missionary (O'Brien, 2002, pp. 3, 4, 7, 8). Its roots refer to generative principles and the genitalia associated with them (*hullo,* menstruation, and *hasi,* penis or vagina) (O'Brien, 2002, p. 5). At one time a number of medicinal and ritual specialists were active in Choctaw society; though the designations have differed, many sources agree on three groups rendered in Choctaw and English by one scholar as "*alikchi* (physician), *apoluma* (conjurer), and *stahullo* (witch)" (Noley, in Mould, 2003, p. 121). According to one Choctaw source, contact produced a kind of assimilation of all three functions into single individuals, though today most such individuals are gone (Denson in Mould, pp. 121, 122). Some medicine men and women do continue to practice, however; and at present according to one scholar, the term *hopaii,* which once meant "prophet," now means "witch," someone who harms others by means of supernatural powers (Mould, 2003, pp. 121, 126).

In all southeastern communities where such individuals are still active, their presence often goes unnoticed by researchers and other visitors, because most of these specialists do not seek publicity. While some do publicize themselves, often the most powerful and respected individuals go out of their way not to draw attention to themselves. This unobtrusiveness in many cases shields them from the nuisance of curious visitors and allows them to concentrate all their energy on the important tasks they are called upon to perform. Those entrusted with transmission of cultural narratives also may adopt this strategy, in part out of a sense of propriety. Historically, incorrect conclusions about the survival of cultural traditions have resulted from long-standing precepts regarding appropriate times and places to discuss such information as well as people with whom it should be shared. These attitudes continue to impact both ethnographic and missionary enterprises in indigenous communities.

RITUAL ACTIVITIES. There are several activities that southeastern communities practice in common. One key activity is ritual immersion or laving in naturally running water (Cherokee, *amó:hi atsv':sdi,* "going to water"), which can be performed daily by solitary individuals in order to maintain health and well-being. People also can enjoin ritual specialists to accompany them in order to diagnose conditions, administer medicinal treatments, and beseech other-than-human persons for assistance. On ceremonial occasions such as green corn ceremonies, entire families might join together in this activity, as would groups on the occasions of births, marriages, and deaths. In the past, on particular occasions people took sweat baths in special structures before the ritual immersion (Cherokee, *osi*), and this latter practice has been revived lately among some groups, but, as discussed above, not without controversy.

For a range of conditions, psychological as well as physical, medicines prepared from plant substances are either ingested or applied externally to those in need by ritual specialists, and this practice almost always is accompanied by the recitation of formulas. Scarification or scratching is another activity that has been used in medicinal and religious contexts to aid in general healing or in specific treatment routines. It is usually performed with comb-like instruments and accompanied by the application of medicine on the scratches. Community dances, once weekly events lasting through the night, typically have incorporated expressions of thanksgiving, celebrations of human achievement, and ribald social commentaries, in addition to specific dances of a social nature in which dancers imitate particular animal movements. Finally, though there is a paucity of research in this area, scholarship suggests that women in most southeastern groups made use of menstrual huts, and that these structures were places of instruction and communion.

GREEN CORN CEREMONIALISM. Ceremonial activities tied to the first harvest and consumption of green corn once were widespread religious events throughout the Southeast, although as noted above by Swanton, particularities of meaning and performance often have differed. Dances and several other activities marked the yearly occasions. These harvest thanksgiving ceremonies, such as the Mvskoke *posketv,* are commonly known as "green corn ceremonies" or just "green corn"; in some communities these events also initiate the new year. These names refer to the central activity of the celebration, the preparation and consumption of boiled or roasted green corn, symbolic of the first fruits of the harvest.

A key ceremony was the kindling of new fires from a central, consecrated fire, after all old fires had been extinguished. Other activities have included dancing, singing, and ritual cleaning of homes. An emetic (often containing *Ilex vomitoria*) was at one time utilized to cleanse male individuals, both physically and spiritually, during this ceremony. Interestingly, one Oklahoma Mvskoke individual has suggested that at least in cases with which he was familiar, the substance was not an emetic and the vomiting was "a *cultural,* not a *biological* act" (Howard and Lena, 1984, p. 43). In addition, drinking a green corn medicine was at one time a common requirement before tasting the corn.

The *posketv* (mistransliterated as "Busk" by some observers) or Green Corn Ceremony is the most visible of the Mvskoke stomp dances, and is held in July. Still actively observed in many Mvskoke dance grounds in Oklahoma, and increasingly in Alabama communities of the Poarch Creek band, the ceremony includes activities such as dancing, fasting, stickball, and the ingestion of the *vsse* medicine. This substance, mistakenly referred to by many observers as the "black drink," is made from a red root and is more the color and consistency of a brackish tea; it is actually commonly known within communities as the "the white drink" (Swan, in Swanton, [1928] 2000, p. 548). While several observers have attributed this name to the substance's properties of "purification," it might be more accurate to think of it in terms of the regulation of interpersonal and therefore societal harmony (Martin, 2000, p. 95)

For Seminole and Miccosuke people in Florida, the Green Corn Dance continues as a time for renewal of both humans and certain medico-religious tools. These ceremonies have continued to be public occasions in Florida. Over the course of four days (including the weekend) at the time of the new moon either in late June or early July, elders meet in council, and men fast, participate in sweat baths, and ingest an emetic. Both adults and children are "scratched" or undergo scarification, to revitalize the blood, though in more recent times women and girls have not participated. Boys and girls are honored for growing into new phases of their lives, and two kinds of ball games are played during the weekends: a more lighthearted single-pole game between men and women, and a rougher game between teams of men who compete to score goals at either end of a playing field.

As one source noted, each stomp ground does things a bit differently, and these variations can be likened to those between denominations (Beck et. al, [1977] 1996, p. 254). At the end of the Dance, a medicinal specialist gives a summation of the proceedings as he offers prayers of thanks to the corn and the "The Mighty One" (Beck et. al, [1977] 1996, p. 256). The medicine bundle—containing all substances necessary for success in a wide range of endeavors and for the general health of all community members—also is renewed with blessings before sunrise on the final day of the Dance. The same source reported that only two medicine men were still knowledgeable about the medicine bundles and their renewal during the Green Corn Dance (Beck et. al, [1977] 1996, pp. 250, 245).

CURRENT SCHOLARSHIP ON RELIGIOUS TRADITIONS OF THE SOUTHEAST WOODLANDS. Though elements of several religious systems are isolated and categorized above in this article, each community combines them into internally logical systems that provide meaning as well as help to define individuals, groups, and the relationships of existence. Providing important counter-perspective to existing and ongoing scholarship, many of the significant recent works on the religious systems of southeastern groups have been authored or coauthored by indigenous scholars or elders who write about their own cultures and who elucidate indigenous epistemologies. In addition, a lively debate has developed regarding the 1976 book *The Southeastern Indians,* by the historian Charles M. Hudson. As the historian James T. Carson noted of this text, "Hudson crafted what has become the orthodox interpretation of not just Creek religion but southeastern cosmology as a whole by combining Swanton's work on Creek religion with his colleague James Mooney's observations of the faith of Eastern Cherokees" (Carson in Swanton, [1928] 2000, p. vi).

Hudson, it should be noted, made no such claims about his book. He did rely heavily on Cherokee materials, and less so on Mvskoke materials, in the chapters "The Belief System" and "Ceremony"; elsewhere in the book he provided ample individual examples from many southeastern nations (see Hudson, 1976, pp. 120–183; 317–375). Mary Churchill, a religious studies and women's studies scholar, published an interesting 1996 article critiquing Hudson's work, focusing upon notions of "purity" and "pollution" in the Cherokee universe, to which Hudson responded with an article of his own (see bibliography). The increase in area scholarship that began in the 1980s continues to produce more varied studies and highlight additional perspectives, ensuring continued scholarly interest and theoretical development while complementing the large body of valuable existing work.

See Also Cherokee Religious Traditions; North American [Indian] Religions, article on History of Study.

Bibliography

Beck, Peggy V., Anna Lee Walters, and Nia Francisco. "Sacred and Secular: Seminole Tradition in the Midst of Change." In their *The Sacred: Ways of Knowledge, Sources of Life*, rev. ed., pp. 245–264. Tsaile, Ariz., 1996.

Carson, James T. "Introduction to the Bison Books Edition." In John R. Swanton's *Creek Religion and Medicine*. Lincoln, Nebr., 2000. Originally published as *Religious Beliefs and Medicinal Practices of the Creek Indians*, Forty-Second Annual Report of the Smithsonian Institution Bureau of American Ethnology, 1924/1925, (Washington, D.C., 1928).

Churchill, Mary C. "Purity and Pollution: Unearthing an Oppositional Paradigm in the Study of Cherokee Religious Traditions." In *Native American Spirituality*, edited by Lee Irwin, pp. 205–235. Lincoln, Nebr., 2000. First published as "The Oppositional Paradigm of Purity versus Pollution in Charles Hudson's *The Southeastern Indians*," *American Indian Quarterly* 20 (June 1996): 563–593.

Eastern Band of the Cherokee Indians website. http://www.cherokee-nc.com.

Fixico, Donald L. *The American Indian Mind in a Linear World: American Indian Studies and Traditional Knowledge*. New York, 2003.

Fogelson, Raymond D. "An Analysis of Cherokee Sorcery and Witchcraft." In *Four Centuries of Southern Indians*, edited by Charles M. Hudson, pp. 113–131. Athens, Ga., 1975.

Fogelson, Raymond D. "Cherokee Notions of Power." In *The Anthropology of Power: Ethnographic Studies from Asia, Oceania, and the New World*, edited by Raymond D. Fogelson and Richard M. Adams, pp. 185–194. New York, 1977.

Haag, Marcia, and Henry Willis. "Choctaw-English Glossary." In their *Choctaw Language and Culture: Chahta Anumpa*. Foreword by Grayson Noley. Norman, Okla., 2001.

Hallowell, A. Irving. "Ojibwa Ontology, Behavior, and World View." In *Teachings from the American Earth: Indian Religion and Philosophy*, edited by Dennis Tedlock and Barbara Tedlock, pp. 141–178. New York, 1975. First published in *Culture in History: Essays in Honor of Paul Radin*, edited by Stanley Diamond (New York, 1960).

Howard, James H., in collaboration with Willie Lena. *Oklahoma Seminoles: Medicines, Magic, and Religion*. Norman, Okla., 1984.

Hudson, Charles. *The Southeastern Indians*. Knoxville, Tenn., 1976.

Hudson, Charles. "Reply to Mary Churchill." *American Indian Quarterly* 24, no. 3 (Summer 2000): 494–502.

Irwin, Lee. "Cherokee Healing: Myth, Dreams, and Medicine." *American Indian Quarterly* 16 (Spring 1992): 237–257.

Kilpatrick, Alan Edwin. "Going to the Water: A Structural Analysis of Cherokee Purification Rituals." *American Indian Culture and Research Journal* 15, no. 4 (1991): 49–58.

Lambert, Valerie Long. "Contemporary Ritual Life." In *Choctaw Language and Culture: Chahta Anumpa*, edited and written by Marcia Haag and Henry Willis. Foreword by Grayson Noley. Norman, Okla., 2001.

Lewis, Jr., David, and Ann T. Jordan. *Creek Indian Medicine Ways: The Enduring Power of Mvskoke Religion*. Albuquerque, 2002.

Martin, Joel W. *Sacred Revolt: The Muskogees' Struggle for a New World*. Boston, 1991.

Martin, Joel W. "Indians, Contact, and Colonialism in the Deep South: Themes for a Postcolonial History of American Religion." In *Retelling U.S. Religious History*, edited by Thomas A. Tweed, pp. 149–180. Berkeley, Calif., 1997.

Martin, Joel W. "Rebalancing the World in the Contradictions of History: Creek/Muskogee." In *Native Religions and Cultures of North America*, edited by Lawrence E. Sullivan, pp. 85–103. New York, 2000.

Mississippi Band of Choctaw Indians website. http://www.choctaw.org.

Mooney, James. *Myths of the Cherokee and Sacred Formulas of the Cherokees*. Nashville, Tenn., 1982. "Myths of the Cherokee" first published as the *Nineteenth Annual Report of the Bureau of American Ethnology, 1897–1898* (Washington, D.C., 1900); "Sacred Formulas of the Cherokees" first published in the *Seventh Annual Report of the Bureau of American Ethnology, 1885–1886*, pp.301–397 (Washington, D.C., 1891).

Mould, Tom. *Choctaw Prophecy: A Legacy of the Future*. Tuscaloosa, Ala., 2003.

Muller, Jon. "The Southern Cult." In *The Southeastern Ceremonial Complex: Artifacts and Analysis*, edited by Patricia Galloway, pp. 11–26. Lincoln, Nebr., 1989.

O'Brien, Greg. *Choctaws in a Revolutionary Age, 1750–1830*. Lincoln, Nebr., 2002.

Pesantubbee, Michelene. "Beyond Domesticity: Choctaw Women Negotiating the Tension between Choctaw Culture and Protestantism," *Journal of American Academy of Religion*, 67/2 (June 1999): 387-409.

Seminole Tribe of Florida website. http://www.seminole-tribe-florida.com.

Sider, Gerald M. *Lumbee Indian Histories: Race, Ethnicity, and Indian Identity in the Southern United States*. New York, 1993.

Swanton, John R. *Creek Religion and Medicine*. Lincoln, Nebr., 2000. Originally published as *Religious Beliefs and Medicinal Practices of the Creek Indians*, Forty-Second Annual Report of the Smithsonian Institution Bureau of American Ethnology, 1924/1925 (Washington, D.C., 1928).

Swanton, John R. *The Indians of the Southeastern United States.* Washington, D.C., 1979. Originally published as the Smithsonian Institution Bureau of American Ethnology Bulletin 137 (Washington, D.C., 1946).

Witthoft, John. *Green Corn Ceremonialism in the Eastern Woodlands.* Occasional Paper from the Museum of Anthropology of the University of Michigan 13. Ann Arbor, Mich., 1949.

MICHAEL J. ZOGRY (2005)

NORTH AMERICAN INDIANS: INDIANS OF THE PLAINS

The Plains region, an area delineated by the Rocky Mountains on the west; the Canadian provinces of Alberta, Saskatchewan, and Manitoba on the north; the Mississippi River on the east; and the Gulf of Mexico on the south, is home to philosophies, traditions, and ways of life that are some of the most varied and complex in the United States. The Great Plains measure 1,125,000 square miles, roughly equal to one-third the landmass of the United States, and serves as home for more than fifty American Indian nations, sometimes referred to as bands, tribes, and confederacies, representing significant linguistic, cultural, and traditional diversity. This complexity also is reflected in the extensive geo-ecological diversity and biodiversity of the region.

Some American Indian groups who currently occupy areas of the Plains do not consider this region their ancestral homeland as bestowed by the Creator. Over thirty American Indian groups were removed to the Oklahoma Territory as part of the Indian Removal Act of 1830, signed into law by Andrew Jackson. Removal was enforced first for Indian communities east of the Mississippi in the southeastern portion of the United States, including Creek, Choctaw, Cherokee, and Chickasaw. Later, groups in the Plains region also were subject to removal, including the Pawnee, Cheyenne, Arapaho, and Comanche. Between 1830 and 1843 more than 100,000 Native Americans were relocated to the Oklahoma Territory. During the long march to Oklahoma, which was enforced by the U.S. military, many thousands died, including over a third of the Cherokee people who were removed. This horrific event is often referred to as the Cherokee "Trail of Tears," but all of the Native Nations removed remember this time with great sadness.

LANGUAGE DIVERSITY. Today, the Plains region is one of the most linguistically diverse areas in the United States as far as American Indian languages are concerned. It is the ancestral homeland of linguistic groups that include speakers of Algonquian, Athapascan, Caddoan, Kiowa-Tanoan, Salish, Siouan, and Uto-Aztecan languages, whose languages reflect cultures and traditions associated with the natural world. Because of forced removal, some American Indian languages are represented in Oklahoma that historically were not found in the Plains region, such as Muskogean and Euchee. In all communities, stories and narratives in the language of the Peoples, often referred to as "Heritage Language," provides the context for cultural and traditional knowledge.

The American Indian Languages Act of 1994 was intended to provide Native students with the opportunity to study and learn their heritage language. Elders who speak these languages have much information to impart, not only about vocabulary and grammar, but also about kinds of knowledge, worldviews, and the ways in which utterances construct their lives. Intensive efforts to document conversations among fluent speakers are underway in many tribal communities, at tribal colleges, and at four-year institutions in an effort to preserve the heritage languages. In most cases, the urgency of these linguistic efforts is pressing because many heritage language speakers are elderly, and with each successive generation fewer people are learning the languages. This is one of the devastating results of forced schooling, missionization, and assimilation measures. Although language education is working to increase the number of fluent speakers, currently the number of heritage language speakers in all groups remains small. Of twenty-seven Native American languages spoken in Oklahoma today, only four are learned from childhood.

Linguists identify more than ten different language families and language isolates in the Plains region. These include:

1. *Algonquian,* largely spoken by groups along the Atlantic Coast, but also spoken by woodlands and northern Plains groups such as Cree, Ojibwe (or Ojibwa), Anishinaabeg, Chippewa, and Ottowa in Wisconsin, Michigan, and the northern Great Lakes region. Algonquian-language-speaking groups include Northern Arapaho of Wyoming and Southern Arapaho of Oklahoma; Atsina or Gros Ventre of the Prairies; the Blackfeet Confederacy, comprising Siksika, Kainah (Blood), and Piegan; Northern Cheyenne (in Montana) and Southern Cheyenne (in Oklahoma); Menominee (in Michigan and Wisconsin); Potawatami and Sauk and Fox (originally from Michigan, now also in Wisconsin, Iowa, Oklahoma, and Kansas); and Blackfoot (in the northern Plains and Alberta).
2. The *Athapascan-Apachean* branch, represented by Lipan Apache (whose original homeland is part of what is now southwestern Texas); Kiowa Apache in Oklahoma; and Mescalero, Chiricahua, and Jicarillo Apache in Arizona and New Mexico.
3. *Caddoan,* represented by Arikara (in North and South Dakota); Caddo (originally in Louisiana, Arkansas and Texas, but removed to Oklahoma); Pawnee (originally in Nebraska, but removed to Oklahoma); and Wichitas (in Kansas and Oklahoma).
4. *Kiowa-Tanoan,* represented on the Plains by only one tribe, the Kiowa, who now live in Oklahoma. This language family is also represented in New Mexico and Arizona by Pueblo peoples who are speakers of the Tewa, Tiwa, and Towa languages.
5. *Muskogean,* represented by Choctaw and Chickasaw peoples (originally in Mississippi, Louisiana, Kentucky,

and Tennessee; after forced removal also in Oklahoma); Creek (Muskogee), including Seminole (originally in Alabama, Georgia, and Florida; after forced removal also in Oklahoma).

6. *Salish,* represented in the northwestern Plains region by Salish-Kootenai, Spokane-Kalispel-Flathead, and Coeur d'Alene, whose ancestral homeland includes Idaho, Montana, and Washington, as well as parts of what is now southern Canada.
7. *Siouan,* by far the largest group on the Plains, represented by Assiniboine, also known in Canada as Stoney; Crow (Absaroka) in Montana; a subdivision of the Siouan family known as Deghiha, comprising Kansa (Kaw), Omaha, Osage, Ponca, and Quapaw, all of whom live in Oklahoma; Hidatsa (Gros Ventre); Iowa, Oto, and Missouri, who form a linguistic subdivision called Chiwere and who reside in Oklahoma; Mandan, who share a reservation with Arikara and Hidatsa in North Dakota; Hochunk (Winnebago); Dakota (Santee) in Minnesota, Nebraska, and parts of the Dakotas; Lakota, primarily in the western Dakotas; and Nakota or Yankton, primarily in the eastern Dakotas. The Mandan, Arikara, and Hidatsa are referred to as the Three Affiliated Tribes. The Dakota, Lakota, and Nakota are conventionally know as the "Sioux," a pejorative term loosely translated as "snakes in the grass," continues to be employed in the literature and in everyday speech.
8. *Tonkawan,* represented exclusively by Tonkawa in Oklahoma.
9. *Uto-Aztecan,* the speakers of which are found in a wide area of western North America and northwest Mexico. Currently represented in the Plains by Comanche originally from the southern Plains and now in Oklahoma; Shoshoni (in Idaho, Wyoming, Nevada, and Utah); and Ute-Southern Paiute (in Utah, Colorado, California, and Nevada).
10. *Euchee (Yuchi),* a language isolate, spoken by only a few remaining elders. Euchee people were moved from their homeland in Georgia to Oklahoma during the period of forced removal.

In addition to these spoken languages, Plains tribes used sign language, which facilitated trade by permitting people speaking diverse languages to communicate with each other.

CULTURAL DIVERSITY. Plains Indian nations present cultural diversity and complexity as well as linguistic diversity, and display significant cultural variation and resiliency—yet similarities exist. Philosophy and values acknowledge a holistic view of life that is cyclic in nature, representing unity and equality for all members. Concepts are interconnected and unified throughout all aspects of life including art, literature, music, language, social organization, religious traditions, law, and the environment. This integrated approach is thought to make life more satisfying and fulfilling.

Plains Indian communities document continuous habitation of the region for thousands of years through their histories and "stories of the people," and archaeologists as well have found evidence that supports human habitation for more than twelve thousand years. With the introduction and diffusion of the horse in the seventeenth century, the number of equestrian groups whose economy was based on buffalo hunting increased. Those most recognized as nomadic include, among northern peoples, the Absaroka, Assiniboine, Cheyenne, Gros Ventre, and Lakota; and, among southern peoples, the Arapaho, Comanche, and Kiowa. Some river valley and northern woodlands peoples maintain aspects of their traditional horticultural way of life. For example, Mandan, Hidatsa, and Arikara on the northern high Plains, and Pawnee, Cree, Iowa, and Deghiha speakers on the southern Plains, as well as Shoshone and Ute in the western mountains, established traditions and worldviews significantly different from those of the more nomadic peoples. In the past, river valley and woodlands peoples lived in earth lodges, tilled the soil near their homes, and maintained agriculturalist and agrarian lifestyles. The more nomadic peoples lived most of the year in more portable housing, such as tipis, and transportation was by horse and dog travois over land and by round-shaped bullboats over water.

The most common forms of burial on the Plains were scaffold and tree burials. The deceased were dressed in fine clothing and wrapped in a buffalo hide, then placed on a scaffold or tree and secured tightly. During the burial, close relatives prepared foods for the spirit's journey to the hereafter and placed necessary implements and objects for the spirit near the burial site. The Cree and Ojibwa, unlike some of the other Plains peoples, buried their dead in the ground and conducted an annual Feast of the Dead. As in times past, most Native peoples today are respectful of the spirit of the deceased, so burial grounds are considered sacred. Although some of the above-ground burial practices have changed, the traditional respect for the spirit and the practice of helping the spirit prepare for its journey remain.

Extensive contact, trading, sharing of resources, and competition among and between groups took place prior to white encroachment, and sharing and crossover of traditions likely occurred. This blending of traditions was accelerated, paradoxically, by various U.S. government measures, such as the Removal Act of 1830, which through forced relocation put previously separated groups into contact with one another. For many groups and contributed to a crossover of traditions. Even more destructive to the survival of Native cultures was a series of U.S. government measures aimed at assimilation and acculturation, or the outright theft of their land, most notably the Dawes Act (1887), the Curtis Act (1989), the Indian Reorganization Act (1934), the Relocation Program (1952), the Termination Act (1953), and the Indian Self-Determination and Education Assistance Act (1975). However, with the civil rights and Red Power movements of the 1960s and 1970s, many American Indian nations increased cultural preservation efforts and began reviving and recovering their languages, traditions, and ceremonies, each culturally unique and significant.

Religious Diversity. Christian missionaries who proselytized throughout the Plains region were particularly Eurocentric in their response to Native religious beliefs, holding that Christianity provided a more bona fide religion than Native traditions and that conversion to Christianity was necessary to help the peoples become assimilated and acculturated. Many actively sought government sanctions and laws against the practice of Native traditions, and worked assiduously to eradicate Native beliefs. They also believed that Native religious practices were primitive and that the self-mortification practiced by some of the tribes was immoral. The U.S. government banned most religious traditions and ceremonies, including the Sun Dance, during the 1880s and specifically in 1894 through an act of Congress. On the northern Plains, however, the Sun Dance went underground and was maintained by medicine men and holy interpreters. This ceremony cautiously emerged into public view again only in 1934. Many Indian religious practices, however, remained underground or were lost during this time period until the Native American Religious Freedom Act of 1978. Although missionaries and Christian religions in general became more accepting of Native beliefs over time, many of the attitudes of the past persist, as evidenced by continuing missionary proselytizing and conversion efforts.

For most Indian nations, the terminology and constructs used to describe religion, religious practices, and ideas of the sacred do not translate from the Native language with the same meanings and connotations as in English and Western religious thought. For example, spirituality and a relationship to the sacred permeate daily life, and most Indian languages do not have specific terms for the word *religion;* likewise, the English word *religion* does not accurately encompass Native ways of life, beliefs, traditions, and ceremonies. Furthermore, the term *sacred* encompasses both individual and collective revitalization, as well as the knowledge gained through visionary experiences. Therefore, the descriptions of various aspects of Native religion presented below should serve only as illustrations of general concepts, and should not be understood as exact replications in English of Native meanings.

Prevalent Traditions. This category encompasses beliefs, practices, and roles that are characteristic of a number of Plains peoples, yet have elements that are particular to each group. It includes symbols such as the pipe, tobacco, the eagle, and a spirit known as the trickster; the role of spiritual leaders or interpreters, who often consider themselves "common men" with a gift, but not holy (referred to as medicine men, shamans, or ritual practitioners in anthropological literature); and primary religious practices and ceremonies such as the Sun Dance, the vision quest, and the sweat lodge.

The pipe or calumet. A symbol of Plains Indian communities, the long-stemmed pipe or calumet, is a medium for prayer. When people pray with the pipe, the smoke rising from the pipe carries their message to the Creator. In many communities, smoking the pipe is also a prelude to various other ceremonies and activities. The pipe is smoked as a means of communicating with the spirits, as preparation for making a good decision, for thoughtfully considering one's actions, and while deliberating on important topics of concern. Pipes can be made from a number of substances. Those made with a bowl fashioned from catlinite, a red stone found in Pipestone, Minnesota, are valued and distributed throughout the Plains. Because the pipe is a gift from the spirits and considered sacred and powerful, it is treated with respect. The bowl is made separately from the pipe stem, which is wood or, in some cases, pipestone. Some tribes consider it disrespectful to store the pipe with the bowl attached to the stem; consequently the two parts are separated when not in use. People are careful of the language they use around the pipe, and individuals who act as "pipe carriers" assume a great responsibility for acting on behalf of the community. Children are taught respect for the pipe from an early age. Showing disrespect to the pipe by stepping over it or dropping it is avoided. If such an incident occurs, prayers and cleansing ceremonies directed by someone identified as knowledgeable in this area are employed.

Tobacco. Several types of Indian tobacco are smoked in the pipe. Tobacco is considered sacred and is spoken to as a spirit that is alive. It is sometimes wrapped in small pieces of cloth, called "prayer or tobacco ties," and used as offerings for honoring the spirits. Among the Crow (Absaroka), various types of tobacco historically were cultivated and traded with both European and Indians alike. Crow people consider tobacco important to their welfare and developed "tobacco societies" inspired by the visions and dreams of individuals. Members are given the task of overseeing the planting and harvesting of the crops. In times past, both men and women belonged. Specific songs, dances, and ceremonies are associated with tobacco societies, most of which are known only to members. For the Crow as well as other Plains nations, tobacco is viewed as medicine, bestowed by the spirits that brings the gift of power.

The eagle. The eagle is regarded as the most significant of all birds because of its great strength, prowess, hunting ability, and capacity to see. This bird is believed to be a messenger to and from the Creator or Great Spirit, and it assists humans in communicating with the spirits. Through the smoke that is emitted from the pipe, the eagle carries the smoke—that is, the prayers and supplications of humans—to the Great Spirit. Eagle feathers are prized for ceremonial purposes because of the bird's qualities and powers. They are bestowed on individuals deemed worthy on the basis of some act or supplication, or as a marker when an individual is moving through a life transition.

The Hidatsa are known for their ability to trap eagles. Eagle trapping is regarded as both a sacred and a dangerous event. In the past, late in the fall, eagle trappers would build a camp a mile or so from the village. High atop the hills each trapper dug a pit about three feet deep and covered it with grass and twigs to form a blind. Using a rabbit or small fox for bait, the trapper climbs into the pit and waits for an eagle to soar overhead and spot the bait. When the eagle lands on top of the pit, the trapper thrusts his hands upward and grabs the eagle by its legs, pulling it down into the pit and strangling it. After the feathers are secured, there is a ceremony in which the eagle's body is buried and offerings are made in thanks to its spirit.

The trickster. The trickster image figures prominently in Plains oral traditions as a humorous comic spirit, mediator between the spirits and humankind, and significant part of cultural identity. The trickster is admired for taking risks, and for transforming and breaking rules, yet also is held up as an example of what not to do. The trickster goes by a number of names, such as *Iktomi* (spider) among the Lakota; *Manabozho* (the compassionate trickster) among the Anishinaabeg; Great White Hare among the Algonquian speakers; Rabbit among the Seminole; and Old Man or Coyote among the Crow. In creation stories, the trickster teaches humans about culture after the establishment of the earth. He also is the principal character in a cycle of morality stories in which positive values are taught through negative example—that is, the hero always makes mistakes and demonstrates poor judgment. Children are told the stories to ensure that they grow up to be good people and do not behave like the trickster.

Spiritual leaders or interpreters. Most Plains traditions include community members who are spiritual leaders or interpreters for the spirits. Each leader or interpreter is well known in the community for his or her specialization in healing, prayer, or communication with the spirits, and this role is considered a gift from the spirits that is demanding, requiring many hours of service. Acceptance of responsibility for using the gift to the best of their ability is critical to the lives of spiritual leaders and to the lives of people in the community. For many Plains groups, the spiritual leader may be someone who the spirits have given the power to act as an interpreter. Sometimes, they are given the power to cure illness with the help of spirits or by ritual means, such as singing, dancing, or praying. Other times, they act as specialists in herbal curing.

Spiritual leaders differ according to the specific type of knowledge they have gained from the spirits and through visions. Although *shaman* and *medicine man* are general terms applied by scholars and others to a range of spiritual leaders, in each Native language specific and discrete terms are used to identify these individuals. For example, in Lakota, some of these leaders are known as *wocekiya wicasa* or *wapiya wicasa,* men of prayer, intercessors to the spirits, or "one who fixes." Public and private ceremonies directed by spiritual leaders take many forms, since they are conducted and performed according to the instructions received by the interpreter. The spiritual leader is usually paid for his services in food, money, or other necessities, although most indicate that payment is not required.

Spiritual leaders and interpreters are consulted in a variety of circumstances and involved in a range of activities, such as healing the sick, advising in family matters, naming children, conducting ceremonies, praying for an individual's welfare, and interpreting visions. In formal ceremonies such as the Sun Dance, the interpreter serves as an intermediary between the people and the spirits, and as someone who provides exclusive and extensive knowledge of the cosmological mysteries. Often, this knowledge is reflected in the use of a sacred language, one that is only understood by the spirits and other interpreters or medicine men.

The Plains Cree and Ojibwe brought a number of ceremonies from their Great Lakes homeland. One ceremony, probably related to the ceremonies of the Midewiwin or "Great Medicine society" in the Great Lakes, includes a practitioner (or leader) who is bound hand and foot and placed in a tipi. During the ceremony, spirits enter the tipi, untie the practitioner, and teach him how to cure the sick and find lost articles. Sometimes the tipi shakes while the practitioner is being untied. On the northern Plains among the Arapaho, Cheyenne, Lakota, and others a similar tradition exits. For Lakota, *Yuwipi* is the term for a curing ceremony held in a darkened room with a *yuwipi* man who is completely wrapped in a blanket and securely tied with ropes. At the end of the ceremony, the spirits have healed the individual and untied the *yuwipi* man.

The Sun Dance. An important religious ceremony of the Plains is the Sun Dance, often participated in to offer one's suffering as sacrifice so that others may not suffer. Each participant makes a commitment that necessitates humility, respect, and supplication. The ceremony is usually performed during the summer months. Men and women make vows to participate in the ceremony throughout the year (or during previous years; commitments can be for four consecutive years). They dance for several days (the number of which varies according to the tradition) gazing at the sun, or more precisely, in the direction of the sun. It is useful to note that the Sun Dance is held also in cloudy and even rainy weather, and may be performed at night during the time of a full moon. In fact, in Lakota there is no distinction between the words for sun and moon; both are called *wi,* and the only way to differentiate between them is by the use of a qualifier: the sun is known as "day *wi*" and the moon as "night *wi.*" Thus a phrase translated as "to gaze at the sun" cannot necessarily be linguistically differentiated from "to gaze at the moon," although conventionally the current translation always refers to the sun.

The Mandan Sun Dance, called *Okipa,* traditionally was held indoors in the tribe's medicine lodge, and typically lasted four days. During this time, the dancers are suspended from the lodge rafters. In other tribes, the Sun Dance is held outdoors within a defined sacred space at the center of a large circular arena that is surrounded by a shade arbor. The medicine man uses skewers or eagle claws to pierce the chest or back muscles of the male dancers who are prepared and in "the right frame of mind" for participation. Then, the skewers are attached to rawhide thong ropes that are tied to a sacred center pole. The dancers pull backward until they break free, thus releasing themselves from the thongs. According to Lakota philosophy, the only thing that one can offer to the Great Spirit is one's own body, because it is the only thing that a human being really owns. The Sun Dance allows such an offering to be made, and its ritual of suffering and release from suffering is offered as a service to the people.

The Blackfeet Sun Dance differs inasmuch as a woman, known for her industry, leads the dancers and bears the title "medicine woman." Although she does not go through the physical practices that her male counterparts do, she participates in a number of ceremonies that precede the actual dance. She presides over two important ceremonies: the Buffalo Tongues ceremony and the sweat lodge ceremony. Before the Sun Dance, people are asked to bring buffalo tongues to a certain lodge erected for this purpose. The tongues are ceremoniously skinned, cleaned, boiled, and then distributed. A sweat lodge is constructed from one hundred willow saplings that are placed in the ground and tied together at the top. The dancers fast and join in the sweat lodge before dancing.

The vision quest. The vision quest, or "dream seeking," is an essential part of Plains Indian conceptual and linguistic worldview, which is very much focused on dreaming and dream experiences. The ideas behind the vision quest are based in experiential processes that are broadly similar for many Native peoples, but that vary in specific detail depending on the tradition. Dream seeking is considered a mythic discourse incorporated into an intentional structure and regarded as a primary source of knowledge and power. The context of the vision, the knowledge that is gained, and the type of vision are unique to each individual. Some have described the experience as a merging of the dreaming and waking state that provides the seeker with knowledge and awareness. It is an intentional act, a search for power and explicit contact with the sacred.

During the vision quest, a person, usually male, seeks to find their purpose within their community. The dreamer embarks upon an ordeal in isolation from the community. Under the direction of a medicine man, each dreamer is led to a hill or other secluded spot, where they stay for an agreed-upon number of days in constant prayer and fasting in an effort to receive a vision that will be useful for their life and the lives of community members. The Lakota notion of *wacinksapa* or "respectful attention" characterizes the dreamer's attitude, concentration, and state of mind before, during, and after the ceremony. If a vision occurs, the dreamer may receive knowledge presented in experiential and imagistic forms; visions can be a vivid communication visualized as an animate form, an inanimate object, an idea, or a sensory experience. These communications from the spirits are treated with great care. The seeker may be instructed on how to maintain a connection to or awareness of the vision in order to remain cognizant of the gift that has been given. These manifestations of the spirits and the sacred may be used in times of need as important knowledge given to the seeker for a specific purpose. Sometimes these manifestations are evidenced in the creation of a painting, with attention given to specific colors and shapes that signify the vision. Power and knowledge gained through a vision also can be recalled through an object used in a medicine bundle, or through prayers and songs acquired and learned during the vision. The seeker also might acquire a new name, receive a calling to act in service to the people or be given a task to perform or goal to be pursued. Guardians, helpers, or spirits may present themselves and provide the seeker with guidance. Interpretation of the vision may come soon after the experience in conversation with the medicine man or may not become available to the seeker until some time after the experience. In all cases, the purpose of the quest is to receive instructions about important actions, events, or opportunities that will affect the seeker's life and, often, the life of the community.

The sweat lodge. The sweat lodge is regarded as a means of purifying individuals both physically and spiritually. Participation provides an opportunity to contemplate, pray for those in need, and enter into a sacred space. A small number of participants join together with a medicine man in a dome-shaped lodge constructed of saplings and covered with hides and blankets to make it airtight and dark. Some preparations are necessary prior to the ceremony. The lodge must be maintained, kept clean and ready for use, with rocks and wood collected. A fire for heating the stones is started and tended for a number of hours prior to the ceremony, and individuals who know the songs and can participate in the singing must be on hand. In the center of the lodge floor, a hole is dug into which the heated stones are ladled by the fire tender. The hides are secured firmly over the lodge and, closing the door flap, the medicine man sprinkles water over the heated stones, causing steam to fill the lodge. The participants perspire as they sing and pray together, asking for help from the spirits who come into the lodge and praying for the welfare of the people. Frequently, a sweat lodge is conducted as a prefatory or cleansing ritual, or before undertaking a vision quest or other religious ceremony. Sometimes the focus of prayers is for the healing of specific individuals who suffer from mental, physical, or spiritual illness.

INTERTRIBAL AND DIFFUSED TRADITIONS. The Ghost Dance and the Native American Church provide examples of beliefs and rituals that are acknowledged as intertribal and diffused traditions, and that are not limited specifically to Plains peoples.

The Ghost Dance. Between 1869 and the 1890 massacre at Wounded Knee, a pacifistic movement called the Ghost Dance spread throughout the Plains. Participants in the dance sought to fight against white domination and sing the spirits of the ancestors back to life. It is often associated with the Earth Lodge Cult, begun around the same time, which called for the destruction of whites in a cataclysmic event. The Ghost Dance began when Wovoka, a Paiute prophet, had a vision in which he was instructed that if Native peoples retained their ways, danced, and prayed for a further vision, then the whites would disappear and all the relatives who had died, including the four-legged ones such as the buffalo, would return. In his vision, Wovoka said he visited with the spirits of the deceased, and they taught him a dance that would bring about these events. Talk of the vision spread across the Plains and prompted people to participate in an effort to restore lost relatives and the traditional way of life. The dancers performed for long periods of time until they fell to the ground. When they awoke, they talked and sang of meetings with their dead relatives and of how happy they were that the old way of life would soon return.

The prophet's vision and the Ghost Dance emerged out of a time of desperation, intense suffering, starvation, death, and loss of a way of life for Native peoples. The return of relatives did not come during Wovoka's time or at the height of the movement. Instead, the federal government, fearing that the dance would serve to engender hostilities, ordered all dancing stopped. On December 29, 1890, a band of peaceful peoples fleeing persecution were surrounded at Wounded Knee Creek on the Pine Ridge Reservation. For allegedly participating in the dance, and out of fear of Indian community revitalization, over three hundred disarmed Lakota men, women, and children from Chief Big Foot's Mnicoujou band were massacred. This event has served as a marker for the end of the Ghost Dance movement and the Plains Indian wars. However, Native American scholars acknowledge that the principles behind the Ghost Dance movement continue to be evidenced today in Native communities through the recognition of the importance of the past, assessments of current conditions in Indian communities, personal commitments to taking action against existing conditions, and visions of a better life in the future. Furthermore, some Native scholars believe that the prayers of the Ghost Dancers are coming true today because the white man is leaving the Great Plains and the buffalo are coming back. In this, the buffalo are considered to be an agent in the restoration of their way of life.

The Native American Church. An intertribal religion established well over 7,000 years ago that spread across the Plains at the turn of the twentieth century is the Native American Church, also known as the "Peyote Road." Long before Columbus arrived in the New World, the Native peoples of Mexico were using a plant from the cactus family in their religious ceremonies. The Aztecs called it *peyotl,* a term that refers to a number of plants with elements that produce hallucinatory sensations when ingested in a green or dry state or in a tea. The Huichols of Mexico established a complex cultural life in relation to the use of peyote that includes a long history, dating back to before 200 CE, of pilgrimages to gather peyote and care for the peyote fields. They believe peyote to be the heart, soul, and memory of the Creator, given to them so that they could learn about relationships and respect. Likewise, peyote *(Lophophora williamsii LeMaire)* is regarded by members of the Native American Church as a sacred plant, a sacrament, and a gift from the Great Spirit that may be consumed for the welfare of the people during prayer meetings.

The peyote plant, whose "buttons" contain the hallucinogen mescaline, is found in Mexico and Texas on both banks of the Rio Grande. From the tribes of Mexico, the plant itself and certain ceremonies associated with it diffused northward to the Comanche, Apache, Tonkawa, Kiowa, Cheyenne, and Arapaho, and ultimately to other surrounding tribes. Some credit Quanah Parker, a Comanche leader, with bringing Half Moon–style peyote meetings to the southern Plains. After being injured while traveling south, he was cured by a Lipan Apache *curandera* who practiced the sacred use of peyote.

The Peyote Road or Road of Life has been influenced by Christianity as well as individual tribal beliefs; thus there are minor differences in the ceremonies from one church meeting to another. There are two major divisions, analogous to denominations: the Half Moon, by far the most popular and freer of Christian influences, and the Big Moon (also known as Cross Fire). The rituals of the two divisions differ somewhat, the greatest ideological difference being that Big Moon uses the Bible in its ceremonies and does not always employ tobacco as a catalyst for prayer. Members of both divisions pray to Jesus Christ, equate the consumption of the peyote button with the sacrament of Holy Communion, and espouse basic tenets of Christian churches in their prayers and songs. If all members attending a meeting are from the same tribe, it is likely that one Native language will be used. If members from several tribes gather together, often English is used, and the songs are sung in a variety of Native languages, many in Diné (Navajo) and Lakota. The content and form of meetings are decided by "the peyote roadman," and despite variations, there are some features, customs, and practices that are common to all.

Peyote meetings are held on Saturday nights, usually from sundown to sunup on Sunday. They take place in traditionally shaped tipis made from canvas, which are conscientiously erected for the occasion and dismantled after a meeting is concluded. To insure the proper attitude of respect, great care and attention is paid to all details including beadwork, paintings, and the creation of the altar. The doorway of the tipi faces east, and in the center of the tipi a fireplace is built, behind which is a crescent-shaped earthen altar. On top of the altar is placed a large peyote button called Father, or Chief, Peyote. Between the fire and the altar is another crescent made from ashes. Between the fireplace and the doorway of the tipi are placed food and water that later will be ceremonially consumed.

The principal leaders of the meeting are assigned special seats inside the tipi. The peyote "roadman," or "road chief," sits directly opposite the doorway, in what is for most Plains tribes the traditional seat of honor. To his left sits the cedar chief, and next to the doorway sits the fire boy. To the right of the roadman sits the drum chief, the keeper of the special drum used in the ceremony. The drum chief is entrusted with keeping a commercially made three-legged brass kettle over which he stretches a hide. The kettle is partially filled with water to regulate the tone, and the hide is tied to the kettle by a rope in such a manner that when the tying is complete the rope forms an outline of a six-pointed star, called the "morning star," on the underside of the drum. Each person has his own drumstick, usually carved out of the same wood as the staff and gourd handle also used in the ceremony. The rest of the congregation is interspersed between the ritual leaders around the perimeter of the tipi. If a Bible is used it is placed between the earth altar and the roadman.

Each member has their own ritual belongings that are stored in a "feather box," typically rectangular and made of wood and often decorated with inlaid silver or with painted designs, including representations of the crescent moon, the tipi, a stylized version of a water turkey *(Anhinga anhinga),* a star, and utensils used in the ceremony. The box usually contains a "loose fan," so called because the feathers are not set rigidly into the handle; a large Father Peyote; a staff—constructed in three sections from a rare wood such as ebony (in Christian-influenced meetings this is often called the "staff of life")—and sometimes a gourd rattle; and an arrow with a blunt head; all (except for the peyote itself) are symbols of peace. Most peyotists wear a blanket made of red and blue material, usually a copy of old-time wool cloth received from traders. The red is symbolic of day, the blue of night.

Peyote meetings are generally held to pray for the welfare of the people. They also may be conducted for special purposes such as curing ceremonies, birthday celebrations, funerals, or memorial services, or when people leave the community to travel great distances or return from the armed services. Someone wishing to initiate and participate in the ceremony formally asks for a meeting to be conducted and offers tobacco to a roadman. When a meeting is scheduled, participants arrive at the home of the sponsor, who provides all the peyote buttons for consumption during the meeting, as well as the food that will be shared by the participants at the conclusion of the ceremony. At dusk the roadman asks all who wish to pray for a good life for their families and others to follow him into the tipi. The roadman places Father Peyote upon the altar and the cedar chief sprinkles needles on the fire. Often, cigarettes made from cornhusks and tobacco are rolled and passed around the circle of participants. When the ritual smoking has ended, the ashes of the cigarettes are collected and placed near the altar. Sage is passed around and each member rubs sage on his hands, arms, and face, or chews pieces of it. Next the peyote buttons are passed around and each member takes four of them. At this point the singing begins.

The peyote chief takes some sage, the staff, and the gourd rattle and tells the drum chief to begin. As the drum resounds, the peyote chief sings the opening song of the ceremony. This is sung four times, and when he finishes, each member in turn eats some of the peyote buttons and sings four songs. The man to the right of the singer plays the drum while the singer shakes the gourd rattle. In this manner the ritual of eating and singing progresses around the tipi clockwise. Concurrent with the visionary experience, during meetings there is a feeling of closeness with God. The praying, eating of peyote, and singing continue until midnight, when the fire boy informs the peyote roadman of the time and leaves the tipi to get a bucket of water. He returns with the water for the roadman, who dips a feather into the bucket and splashes water on the people. After smoking and praying, the water is passed around to the members so that each may drink. During this part of the meeting another standard song is sung. After the water drinking, the bucket is removed and the singing and drumming continue.

Before each major segment of the meeting, the cedar chief burns incense and the members purify themselves and their belongings in the smoke. The ceremony lasts until dawn, when the morning-water woman is called into the lodge bearing another bucket of water. She is usually a relative of the peyote chief, who now sings the dawn song. The roadman smokes and prays and may doctor those who are ill or pray for the welfare of the people. After the ceremonial water drinking, the woman retrieves the bucket and leaves the tipi. The peyote chief then sings the "quittin' song" while the morning-water woman prepares the traditional breakfast consisting of water, corn, fruit, and meat.

Many missionaries frown on participation and membership in the Native American Church, despite its Christian aspects. Yet, it has become increasingly popular among many tribes, currently having approximately 300,000 members. In 1965 the Federal Drug Administration classified peyote as a controlled substance, and there has been a great deal of controversy over Indians' use of the plant in their religious meetings. Yet neither the legal issues nor the implication of immorality on the part of whites has prevented the Native American Church from becoming an important religious movement in the United States and Canada. The American Indian Religious Freedom Act (1978) guaranteed protection of religious rights for Native Americans, including the right to use peyote. However, church members were still liable to prosecution for possession. It was not until the Religious Freedom Restoration Act (1993) and, a U.S. Supreme Court ruling regarding the transportatin of peyote in 1994 (see Smith and Snake) that members of the Native American Church were guaranteed the right to both use peyote during ceremonies and transport it from the gathering fields across state lines.

ADDITIONAL PHILOSOPHY. Ideas of the sacred, as well as proscriptions against what is forbidden or profane, are unique to each nation and community. Many Native peoples describe their histories and the contexts of their ceremonies as particular to time and place and originating from specific events or through the mentorship of a prophet or holy person, someone who brings the ceremonies to the people for their continued well-being. Both states, the sacred and profane, may be changed through the intercession of the spirits and the mediation of prayer, song, and dance to strengthen the community by contact with the spirits. Aspects of the sacred and profane can be changed through this intercession. The idea of the holy is often expressed in Native terms such as *Wakan* (Lakota), Algonquian variants of *Manitu, Xube* (Ponca), *Wakonda* (Omaha), and *Puha* (Comanche). All animate and inanimate objects serve as evidence of the sacred. The rituals employed to transform persons or objects from a profane state to a sacred one have frequently, but erroneously, been called "medicine," or "making medicine"; likewise, the source of a medicine man's personal power is kept in a "medicine bundle." Medicine, however, is a term encompassing sacred power in all its revelations.

The supernatural. In each Native language, power and sacredness are distinguished from each other. Certain English-language renderings of Native terms, such as *Great Mystery* and *Great Spirit,* seem to refer to a single creator or prime mover, and this led Christians to falsely ascribe to Native Americans a belief in a monotheistic god prior to European contact. However, there is no empirical evidence for this belief, and today terms such as *Supreme Being* or *Mysterious Being* are usually acknowledged as designating the totality of all supernatural beings and powers, as well as "a Power" greater than the individual. Various terms in Native languages reference the idea of the "great holy," including *Behä'tixtch,* "the Leader of All" (Gros Ventre); *Wakantanka,* most often translated as "Great Mystery" or "Great Spirit" (Lakota); and *Mahópini,* "inexplicable power" (Mandan). Often symbols are used to designate important spirits associated with star phenomena, and the Great Mystery may be addressed as the Sun or Morning Star, or as a terrestrial counterpart, Mother Earth. These references are significant since Plains peoples are avid and accurate astronomers and geographers who carefully note the cyclic nature of the stars and planets.

Often, prohibitions associated with intercourse, menstruation, and food—prominent on the Plains as in a number of traditions and cultures—have been misinterpreted and misconstrued. For example, previously in the anthropological literature, restrictions on menstruating women were interpreted as degrading toward women. It is more accurate, however, to see women's isolation and separation as related to issues of power and access to power. Women are seen as powerful particularly during times of fertility because of their ability to create life. (From the time a woman begins to menstruate she is seen as having the power to create life, regardless of the time of her specific cycle.) Men protect their power by not associating with women during this time in a woman's cycle, and rather than originating in a view of menstruation as "taboo," the proscriptions associated with avoidance of menstruating women reflect reverence for power inherent in women and the sacred nature of life.

The hereafter. A belief that each person has more than one "spirit," often equated with the Christian notion of "soul"—one that inheres in the living until death, another that corresponds to the notion of a ghost, as well as to other concepts—is common among Plains peoples. When someone dies, they travel along the path of the dead, associated with the Milky Way, toward their final destination located in the Southern Hemisphere. Death is respected as part of the path of life, and throughout one's life there is meaning, purpose, and responsibility. Mourners may stay near a relative's body for several days after death, and during funeral proceedings the deceased as well as the mourners are addressed. Women and men may show respect for those who have died by cutting their hair short or by acts of physical sacrifice that may include an attitude of mourning for a period of time. It also is customary for relatives to give away all of the deceased's belongings. The Lakota mourn their dead for one year, sometimes through a special ceremony called Ghost Keeping in which a close relative keeps a lock of the deceased's hair in a special bundle for one year. Each day during the year, the ghost (that is, the deceased's spirit) is fed by the relative keeping the ghost. At the end of the year a farewell ceremony is held on the ghost's behalf, relatives assemble for the last time, and the spirit is freed.

Belief in spirits is common among Plains Indians, and it is accepted that spirits are capable of advising humans about the welfare of the tribe. Medicine men may ask the advice of spirits on how to cure people, and spirits may predict certain events in the lives of the living. Spirits also are capable of finding lost or stolen articles, and in some cases of taking another life. It is commonly believed that when a person dies, the spirit may attempt to entice a close relative to join it in death. Spirits herald their presence in numerous ways, and some believe that the sound of a baby crying outside in the night, or of a wolf howling or rooster crowing, means a spirit is calling someone to die. Family members may fire guns to frighten away the spirit, or medicine men may burn incense with an aroma that is displeasing to spirits.

Creation stories. Plains peoples have developed comprehensive philosophies, religious systems, and sacred ways based on oral tradition and knowledge. Their origin or creation stories express complex truths about the histories of Native peoples, and the stories are used to educate children and to document the history of each nation.

Among Plains nations, the Pawnee provide an example of religious innovation, having established a comprehensive religious philosophy. Pawnee creation stories describe the creation of the world; the origin of animals, humans, and all other living things; and the power of the spirits. The Pawnee creation story tells of Tirawa, the Supreme Being, who was married to the "Vault of Heaven." Purely spiritual beings with no physical shape, these two reigned somewhere in the heavens beyond the clouds. Tirawa sent his commands to humans through a number of spirits and messengers who manifested themselves to the Pawnees. Tcuperika (Evening

Star) is personified as a young maiden and is keeper of a garden in the West, the source of all food. She has four assistants, Wind, Cloud, Lightning, and Thunder, and is married to Oprikata (Morning Star), a strong warrior. From Tcuperika and Oprikata, the first human on earth was born. Other spirits include the four directions, the northeast, southeast, southwest, and northwest, and the three spirits of the north: "North Star," chief of all stars; "North Wind," who gave the buffalo to humans; and Hikus (Breath), who gave life itself to the People. "Sun" and "Moon" were married and produced the second person on earth, whose marriage to the offspring of "Morning Star" and "Evening Star" gave rise to the human race. At the southern end of the Milky Way stood "Star of the South," and the campfires of the departed that received the spirits of the dead. Another star named Skiritiuhuts (Fool Wolf) became offended at one of the councils of star people and in revenge introduced death to the world of humans.

The Hako. Pawnee ceremonies include those dedicated to "Thunder," to "Morning Star," and to "Evening Star," practiced in connection to the planting and harvesting of Mother Corn as well as for the general welfare of the people. The Hako is performed to acknowledge relationships and a sense of responsibility between community members, and to ensure that community members enjoy long life, happiness, and peace. The *Ku'rahus* (elder, or "Man of Years"), who is venerated for his knowledge and experience, conducts the Hako. To him is entrusted the supervision of the songs and prayers, which must be performed precisely in the same order each time. The Hako is usually performed in the spring when birds are nesting or in the fall when they are flocking. Performers pray for the life, strength, and growth of the people.

Those taking part in the ceremony are divided into two groups: the fathers who sponsor the ceremony and the children who receive the focused intentions, prayers, and gifts from the fathers. The head of the fathers' group, called Father, is responsible for employing the *Ku'rahus.* The head of the children's group, called Son, acts on behalf of the other children. The most important objects used in the Hako are the sacred feathered wands resembling pipe stems without the bowls attached. In the past the ceremony took three days and three nights, during which time twenty-seven rituals were performed, each ritual and song unveiling sacred history and stories and cementing the relationships of fathers and children. At the end of the ceremony the wands are waved over the children, sealing the bond between fathers and children. Most of the ritual objects are discarded, with the exception of the feathered wands, which are given to one of the children for keeping. At a later date the children assume the fathers' role and offer prayers to another group of children, thus perpetuating the tradition and solidarity of the Pawnee. The children may also take the wands to other tribes as an offering of peace.

Sacred Arrow Renewal. The Sacred Arrow Renewal ceremony is an important one for the "People Like Us," referred to in English as the Cheyenne. The Cheyenne are closely related to "Our Own Kind of People," known as the Arapaho, and the creation story of both groups is closely guarded and considered sacred. The Cheyenne believe that long ago Maiyun, the Supreme Being, gave four sacred (medicine) arrows to their prophet, Sweet Medicine, in a cave located in the Black Hills of South Dakota. When Sweet Medicine gave the arrows to the People, one person was appointed Keeper of the Sacred Arrows. In 1833, according to Cheyenne histories, the Pawnee captured the Sacred Arrows and, as a result, difficulties befell the People. Although two of the arrows were returned, two substitutes remain in place of two other arrows that are still missing.

Maiyun instructed Sweet Medicine in the proper care of the arrows and the sacred ceremonies associated with them. Sweet Medicine was given the responsibility of teaching the Cheyenne about the powers of the arrows and their importance for the survival of the People. Sweet Medicine lived with the People for 446 years and provided them with instructions on ways to live; among other things he counseled them to form a representative government in which spiritual and medicine people are vested with the highest authority. He prophesized the coming of the white people, and of the misfortune, illness, death, and devastation that would befall the People with their arrival. Another prophecy described a prophet the People would meet named *So'taaeo'o* (Erect Horns), who later taught them the Sun Dance and other sacred traditions distinctive to the Cheyenne.

The Sacred Arrow Renewal ceremony traditionally takes four days to perform and occurs every other year. After the site has been chosen by a group of individuals (usually men held in high esteem), a special lodge is prepared on the first day. New poles are cut and the lodge covering is borrowed from families of good reputation. Inside the lodge the medicine people of the tribe sit on beds of sage. As part of the preparations, each Cheyenne family provides a special counting stick to the leader of the ceremony that symbolically represents each member of the tribe. An individual pledges to sponsor a Sacred Arrow Renewal ceremony, and the arrows are unwrapped and displayed. The man making the pledge does so to fulfill a vow. Although only one person makes the pledge, the ceremony is given on behalf of all Cheyenne, to protect against famine and annihilation and to ensure a long and prosperous life for all.

On the second day the sacred arrows are obtained from the keeper and the bundle is opened and examined. If the flight feathers of the arrows are in any way damaged, a man known for his bravery is chosen to replace the feathers. On the third day the arrows are renewed and each of the counting sticks is blessed on behalf of all the families in the tribe. On the last day the arrows are exhibited to the male members of the tribe. The Cheyenne say that it is difficult to look directly at the arrows because they give off a blinding light. To conclude the ceremony, the medicine people make predictions about the future of the People. With the conclusion of a sweat lodge ceremony, the Sacred Arrow Renewal ritual is officially over, and the Cheyenne symbolically began life anew.

See Also Blackfeet Religious Traditions; Ghost Dance; Lakota Religious Traditions; Sun Dance; Tobacco; Wovoka.

Bibliography

Beck, Peggy V., Anna Lee Walters, and Nia Francisco. *The Sacred: Ways of Knowledge, Sources of Life.* Tsaile, Ariz., 1977. Good overview reference and study of concepts and ways for thinking about the traditional practices, beliefs, and sacred ways of Native North America.

Bowers, Alfred W. *Mandan Social and Ceremonial Organization.* Chicago, 1950. This book, written by a ethnographer, includes a detailed description of the Okipa, the Mandan Sun Dance.

Catlin, George. *O-kee-pa: A Religious Ceremony and Other Customs of the Mandan.* Rev. ed. Edited and with preface by John C. Ewers. New Haven, Conn., 1967. This edition of Catlin's 1867 work contains the controversial "Folium Reservatum," not included in the original edition because of its discussion of sexual symbolism in the ceremony.

Fletcher, Alice C., and Francis La Flesche. *The Omaha Tribe.* Washington, D.C., 1911; reprint, Lincoln, Nebr., 1972. Includes important information on Omaha religion compiled by one of the earliest female ethnographers in collaboration with a member of the Omaha tribe.

Grinnell, George Bird. *The Cheyenne Indians: Their History and Ways of Life.* 2 vols. New Haven, Conn., 1923; reprint, Lincoln, Nebr., 1972. Volume 2 contains information on the medicine lodge, Sweet Medicine, and the Massaum ceremony, and is a classic cultural history of the Cheyenne.

Hultkrantz, Åke. *Religions of the American Indians.* Translated by Monica Setterwall. Los Angeles, 1979. Written by a leading historian of comparative religions who specializes in American Indian religion. It contains a great deal of comparative material on Plains Indians.

Hinton, Leanne. *Flutes of Fire: Essays on California Indian Languages.* Berkeley, Calif., 1994. Exceptional text from a foremost scholar of California Native languages, with information on language families and histories and on efforts to keep various languages alive.

Irwin, Lee. *The Dream Seekers: Native American Visionary Traditions of the Great Plains.* Norman, Okla., 1994. The most comprehensive and scholarly treatment of an important subject, that reaches into the substance of visionary experiences.

Lowie, Robert H. *The Crow Indians.* New York, 1935; reprint, 1956. The religious life of the Crow Indians is related to their workaday world in one of the classics of anthropology.

Mann, Henrietta. *Cheyenne-Arapaho Education, 1871–1892.* Niwot, Colo., 1997. Significant text documenting the educational history of Cheyenne and Arapaho peoples and their relationship with the U.S. educational system during this time period.

Mooney, James. *The Ghost Dance Religion and the Sioux Outbreak of 1890.* Introduction by Anthony F. C. Wallace. Chicago, 1965. Abridgement of study originally published in the *U.S. Bureau of Ethnology Annual Report* 14, pt. 2 (1896): 641–1136. Mooney interviewed participants of the Ghost Dance at the time it was being performed. The book provides comparative materials on the Arapaho, Caddo, Cheyenne, Comanche, Kiowa, Kiowa Apache, and Lakota, and on some non-Plains tribes.

Powers, William K. *Indians of the Northern Plains.* New York, 1969. A survey of the principal tribes of the northern Plains with a separate chapter on religion.

Powers, William K. *Indians of the Southern Plains.* New York, 1971. A survey of the principal tribes of the southern Plains with separate chapters on traditional religion and on the Native American Church.

Powers, William K. *Yuwipi: Vision and Experience in Oglala Ritual.* Lincoln, Neb., 1982. A translation of an entire shamanic curing ceremony conducted on the Pine Ridge reservation in 1966, showing the relationship among Yuwipi, the vision quest, and the sweat lodge ceremony.

Ryan, Allan J. *The Trickster Shift: Humour and Irony in Contemporary Native Art.* Seattle, Wash., 1999. Excellent text for explicating the trickster's cultural importance, particularly as a humorous spirit reflective of Native identity.

Silver, Shirley, and Wick R. Miller. *American Indian Languages: Cultural and Social Contexts.* Tucson, Ariz., 1997. Comprehensive survey of indigenous languages in the Americas that introduces readers to the diversity of Native languages.

Smith, Huston, and Reuben Snake, eds. *One Nation under God: The Triumph of the Native American Church.* Santa Fe, N. Mex., 1996. Excellent source of information on the Native American Church and U.S. government actions and court decisions regarding it.

Underhill, Ruth M. *Red Man's Religion: Beliefs and Practices of the Indians North of Mexico.* Chicago, 1965. A classic survey of American Indian religions and ethnology. The language is somewhat dated but the book nonetheless provides a wealth of information.

Weaver, Jace, ed. *Native American Religious Identity: Unforgotten Gods.* Maryknoll, N.Y., 1998. Well-edited volume of topics of interest in the discussion of Native religious identity.

White, Phillip M. *Peyotism and the Native American Church: An Annotated Bibliography.* Westport, Conn., 2000. Excellent compilation of references concerning the Native American Church.

Wood, W. Raymond, and Margot Liberty, eds. *Anthropology on the Great Plains.* Lincoln, Neb., 1980. Anthropological research on Plains Indians with separate chapters on the Sun Dance, the Ghost Dance, and the Native American Church.

William K. Powers (1987)
Kathleen J. Martin (2005)

NORTH AMERICAN INDIANS: INDIANS OF THE NORTHWEST COAST [FIRST EDITION]

The peoples of the Pacific Northwest Coast of North America live along a narrow strip of land that extends from the mouth of the Columbia River north to Yakutat Bay in Alaska. Cut off, for the most part, from the tribes around them by the rugged, impenetrably forested mountains that rise from the sea, and relatively isolated from one another by the scarcity of habitable beach sites, they developed a variety of distinct but intertwined local traditions.

For the sake of convenience, the Northwest Coast culture area has been divided into three subareas: the northern area is inhabited by the Tlingit, Haida, and Tsimshian peoples; the central by the Bella Coola, Nootka, and Kwakiutl groups; and the southern by the Coast Salish and Chinookan tribes of the Washington and Oregon coasts. While the cultures within each sub-area share some basic traits that distinguished them from one another, the bewildering variety of linguistic, social, political, and ideological variations within each area implied numerous migrations, acculutrations, and cultural borrowings that make any retrospective synthesis of Northwest Coast culture a formidable task.

Adding complexity are the effects of contact with white culture, which did not begin until the late eighteenth century. The vast wealth introduced into the area by the sea-otter fur trade altered the balance of wealth and power that had existed in the aboriginal period. During the nineteenth century (usually referred to as the "historical" period, and the time frame for this essay) the peoples of the Northwest Coast underwent dramatic social change, including cultural efflorescence, drastic population decline, wholesale abandonment of ancestral villages, the formation of new composite villages, increased trade, and intermarriage between all of which contributed to the tribes, diffussion of religious traditions at a vastly accelerated rate. The indigenous peoples eventually, came under heavy governmental and missionary pressure to abandon all native customs.

Material Culture. The lives of the Northwest Coast Indians were entirely oriented toward the sea, on whose bounty they depended. The staple food of the area was salmon; varieties of salmon were smoked and stockpiled in immense quantities. However, many other types of fish, sea mammals, large land mammals, water birds, shellfish, and varieties of wild plants were also collected. Though food was plentiful, the rugged topography of the land limited access to food-collecting sites. Access to these sites was also controlled by an oligarchy of hereditary nobles (called "chiefs") who maintained their power primarily through ritual performances that legitimized their claims.

Northwest Coast technology was based on a complex of wood and animal products. Wood and tree bark, especially from cedars, were the fundamental materials and were used ubiquitously. Humans lived in houses, traveled in canoes, caught fish with hooks, trapped salmon in weirs, stored their belongings and were themselves interred in boxes, and wore clothing and ceremonial costumes all made from wood products. A system of symbolic correspondences between objects underlay the entire ceremonial system. Skins, flesh, and bones from animals were also used and played a critical symbolic role in religious activities.

Social Organization. The basic principles of Northwest Coast social organization have been the object of much theoretical controversy. Traditional tribal appellations may lump together groups with similar languages but very different customs, and vice versa. Essentially the basic unit of social and political organization was the independent extended local family, defined by some degree of lineal descent and by coresidence in a single communal household in a single winter ceremonial village. (Winter was the season in which virtually all ceremonies were held.) Group membership was defined less by kinship than by concerted economic and ceremonial activity, though in the northern subarea suprafamilial kin groups played a role in setting the boundaries of a group. The head of each household was its political and spiritual leader, the inheritor and custodian of the house's aristocratic titles, and its ambassador to both human and supernatural worlds. All aristocratic titles in each area were ranked hierarchically for all ceremonial activities. Whether or not the hierarchical system created a class structure as well as a rank structure is a controversial theoretical question. While there was some social mobility, social position was primarily ascribed and inherited. However, all succession to rank had to be validated by the giving of a potlatch at which the heir recounted or reenacted in dance drama the family myths that proved the legitimacy of his claim; the potlatch also proved his personal power and spiritual worthiness by the heir's distribution of wealth to other chiefs. The potlatch was a major mechanism for promoting group solidarity, organizing labor, and maintaining the structure of the hierarchical system. As one goes north within the area, hierarchical systems seem to increase in importance and are firmly embedded in a religious matrix. The peoples of the southern subarea seemed to put little emphasis on hierarchy and exhibited a social structure and religious ideology with more similarities to peoples of the Plateau and California areas than to the coastal peoples to their north.

Belief and Ritual. There was little synthesis of religious ideas and institutions on the Northwest Coast. Rituals and myths developed into a multiplicity of local traditions that directly integrated local history and geographical features with the more universal elements of creation. Different families and different individuals within families might have conflicting accounts of family history and its mythic events, giving the religious traditions an atomistic quality that permitted a continual restructuring of ceremonies and renegotiating of meanings. However, much of the cognitive conflict that might arise from such discrepancies was mitigated by the fact that although there was an extraordinary amount of public ceremony most rituals were performed in secret and were known only to the rankholder and his heir.

Like the religious traditions of other native North American peoples, the beliefs of the Northwest Coast Indians focused on the critical relationship of hunter to prey and on the set of moral principles that permitted that relationship to continue. Humans were thought to be essentially inferior to the rest of the world's inhabitants and were dependent on other creatures' good will for survival. Humans were important as mediators between different spirit realms because supernatural beings had granted them gifts of knowledge and insight about how the world operates and how they fit into the world. The features unique to Northwest Coast religion centered on the private possession and inherited control of the religious institutions by titled aristocrats. Access to the supernatural beings (called "spirits" by anthropologists because of their essential rather than corporeal nature) and their power was strictly under the control of chiefs, as was access to food.

Spirits. The origin of all power—both the power to control and, more importantly, the power to become aware—was in the spirit world, and the actions of spirit power, which gave form and purpose to everything, were visible everywhere. All objects, ideas, forces, and beings were believed to have inherent power that could be released and directed into human affairs, if correctly integrated into ritual action. The world was seen as filled with spirit power that could be reified in human rituals. Spirits, the personified categories of power, were less characters than ineffable forces. As a salmon could be brought into the human world when caught in a properly constructed net, so could spirit power be brought into the human world when caught in a net of properly constructed ritual action. Humans could never perceive the true nature of spirits, but they could see that the costumes—created as coverings for the spirits—became animated when the spirits covered themselves with them and danced.

An example may better explicate the idea of spirits as essences: the *sisiutl*, visible to humans in its manifestation as a huge double-headed serpent, was one of the most powerful spirits in Kwakiutl ceremony. It was the reification of all the inherent qualities and power of that which is wet and fluid—ocean, rain, blood, tears, and so on—and by extension all that is uncontainable and transitory and all that is insignificant in small quantities, life-sustaining in proper amounts, and dangerous in excess. The *sisiutl* thus provides a metaphor for a key ideological tenet of Kwakiutl thought: that the world is in motion and can be stopped (and thus perceived as a material entity) only temporarily; that human life, ritual, understanding, wealth, and power will come to pass but will flow away like water. The *sisiutl* was only one among hundreds of creatures depicted in Northwest Coast myth and ritual—each a vision, a realization, of the processual nature of the universe, and each a metaphorical statement of a fundamental philosophical idea.

The peoples of the Northwest Coast saw their world as one in which myriad personified forces were at work, competing for a limited supply of food and souls. Every human, every group, every species, and every spirit-being had its own needs, its own specialized niche in the food chain. All of their conflicting demands and needs had to be balanced against one another, and this could be achieved only through ritual, which was seen as a method of mediation between the various creatures of the universe. The world was filled with a seemingly endless variety of raptorial creatures who feed on human flesh and souls just as humans feed on salmon flesh. Man-eating birds and other animals, ogres, dwarves, giants, and monsters were believed to prey upon humans as raptorial birds prey upon mice (a frequent image in Northwest Coast myths).

Animals, which were seen as the material representations of spiritual beings, sacrificed themselves for the benefit of human survival because humans had agreed to sacrifice themselves for the benefit of the spirits. The metaphors of Northwest Coast ritual continually repeat the image of the responsibility of humans to support the spirit world. Humans and spirits, living off each other's dead, were intertwined in a reincarnational web. By eating the substance of each other's bodies, they freed the souls and permitted their reincarnation. If any link in the ritual chain was lost, the entire system of reincarnation broke down.

Food. Food was thus a sacramental substance, and meals were inherently ceremonial occasions. Northwest Coast religosity placed a heavy emphasis on the control of food-related behavior, on the denial of hunger (which was thought to be a polluting desire), and on the ritual distribution of food and other material substances. The rules, taboos, and rituals associated with food are ubiquitous and enormous in number.

Of all the ceremonies directed toward the propitiation of the animals on which humans feed, those known collectively as the first-salmon ceremonies were the most widespread. These were sets of rituals performed every year in each area over the first part of the salmon catch of each species. Similar ceremonies existed for other species as well. The fish were addressed as if they were chiefs of high rank and were killed, prepared, and served in a ceremonious manner. Their released souls returned to the land of their compatriots to inform them of the proper treatment that they had been accorded. Like most other Northwest Coast rituals, these ceremonies were the property of individual chiefs, who performed them for the benefit of all of the people. All hunting was imbued with ceremony, since success in the hunt was strictly a matter of the proper ritual relationship to the hunted animal. The ceremonies associated with hunting were an important part of a family's inheritance.

Guardian spirits. In theory, a person could obtain a guardian spirit by dedication to a regimen of self-mortification, abstinence, fasting, prayer, and ritual bathing. However, the most powerful contracts with the spirits were obtained in mythic times through the group's ancestors, and these contracts formed the basis of the rank system. Every ranked position was actually an embodiment of a spiritual contract—a covenant between the rankholder and the spirit world. The relationship between the ancestor and the spirit was the primary element of a family's patrimony and was constantly reaffirmed in ritual. As the living representative of the ancestor, the rankholder acted as an intermediary to the spirits on secular occasions and as an impersonator or embodiment of a spirit on sacred occasions.

The relationships between particular aristocrats and particular spirits were manifested in a system of "crests," which were images of spirits that have become allied with individual families. The right to depict the image of a spirit, or in some cases even to pronounce its name in public, was a fiercely guarded possession. All objects of spiritual importance were decorated with images of a person's guardian spirits. This gave the objects a name, an identity, and the ability to act as a conduit through which spirit power could be directed. While crest images acted on one level as emblems of a group's status, they were more than mere coats of arms—they were ritual objects of causal power. Most crest images presented representations of transformation, a key idea in Northwest Coast thought, which expressed the interlocked identities and destinies of humans and spirits. Through the crest, the identity of the aristocrat was connected to that of the spirit being, and through this connection the aristocrat's self expanded to a more cosmic identity. The widespread use of crest objects was graphic proof of the extent to which religious ideas permeated the entire fabric of Northwest Coast culture.

In addition to having shared destinies, humans and spirits were interrelated in that all creatures were considered to be human and to possess human souls. Each lived in its own place in one of the levels of the universe, where it inhabited a house, performed ceremonies, and otherwise acted like a human being. At the proper season, the spirits donned costumes and visited the world of humans, where they appeared in their transformed identity. Similarly, humans who appeared to themselves as humans put on costumes and appeared to the spirits as spirits.

With the exception of Frederica De Laguna's account of Tlingit culture (1972), Northwest Coast Indian ideas of the self, its components, and its relationship to the spirits are not well documented. It is clear that the soul was believed to have several material manifestations as well as several incorporeal components. A person was viewed as a combination of life forces and parts from different planes of existence, and therefore as having spiritual connections in many directions. Whatever their component parts, souls were thought to exist in only limited numbers, to undergo metempsychosis, to be transferred from one species to another, and to be reincarnated alternately in first a human and then either a spirit or animal being. A human death freed a soul for an animal or spirit, and vice versa, linking humans, animals, and spirits in a cycle of mutual dependency. Ideas about the soul and its nature seem to have been better codified among the Northern peoples, though this impression may be an artifact of the high quality of De Laguna's ethnography.

Shamanism. Connections to the spirit world could be made through inheritance or by acquiring, through a vision, the power to cure disease. All illnesses and death were considered a sickness of the spirit that was caused either by the magical intrusion of a foreign substance into the body or by the wandering or the loss of the soul. When methods for reestablishing one's spiritual purity failed to alleviate the symptoms, a curer (or "shaman") was called in. A shaman cured an illness by going into a trance during which his guardian spirits would fight with the soul of the disease or of the witch who had sent the disease. When the shaman came out of his trance, he was able to display a small object that symbolically represented the empty husk of the diseased spirit body. Shamanic paraphernalia, like other ritual objects, were formed and moved so as to direct the spirit power in the proper ways to effect a cure. Shamanic performances were dramatic events, with much stage illusion as well as singing, dancing, and praying.

Shamans acted as intermediaries between humans and the forces of nature and the supernatural, and were thought to be able to foretell the future, control the weather, bring success in war or in hunting, communicate with other shamans at a distance, and, most importantly, cure illnesses and restore souls stolen by witches or maleficent spirits. The shaman was believed both to control and to be inspired by the spirits with whom he was connected. Among the Tlingit, shamanic rituals were usually inherited, but among the central tribes they were obtained through visions. Shamans had to undergo strict regimens if they were to retain their powers; shamanism was a route to prestige but not to title, nor was it a lucrative profession. It was believed that the shaman received his calling involuntarily, but that, having been chosen, it was his responsibility to accept wholeheartedly the burdens of his profession.

Witches. Northwest Coast Indian beliefs about shamans were complemented by their beliefs about witchcraft, an introduced concept. Witches were thought to be motivated by envy and jealousy, either conscious or unconscious, and there was no act, no matter how terrible, of which they were thought incapable. Patterns of witchcraft among the Northwest Coast Indians were parallel to those of other North American groups: it seems likely that few if any people practiced witchcraft, but accusations of witchcraft were an important means of articulating rivalry and competition. Among the central tribes, witches were generally thought to be shamans from enemy tribes; among the northern groups, where fear of witches was more prevalent, witches were thought to belong to the same kin group as their victims. Witches were thought to be under the compulsion of a possessive spirit, from whose influence the witch could be freed by torture. Occasionally witches died under torture or were executed despite their confession. The best protection against witches was to maintain spiritual purity through fasting and the correct performance of ceremonies. As long as the ceremonies were performed, the world existed in the proper balance, and witches could not do harm.

The causal principle underlying the ideas of the Northwest Coast Indians on the effectiveness of ritual lay in the idea that under the proper analogical conditions, the patterned motions or words of human beings have an inherent ability to coerce the spirits into parallel actions. Thus a human action could be magnified and intensified into a power that alters the state of the world. Human beings were conduits for supernatural power: although they possess no powers themselves, humans could become the vehicles of supernatural power if they observed the proper ritual actions. In creating analogies between themselves and the spirits, humans gained the ability to influence the actions of those more powerful than themselves.

Creation. Supporting the social and ritual systems was an extensive and varied body of myths and tales (which, except in the work of Claude Lévi-Strauss, have been little analyzed). There were few myths about the creation of the world as such, since the world was seen as a place of innumerable eternal forces and essences. Like other North American groups, the Indians of the Northwest Coast were less interested in how the world was created as material substance than in how it was made moral or how the inherent powers of the universe could be controlled for the benefit of its inhabitants. The creation of material phenomena—the sun and moon, human beings, animal species—is always secondary to the moral dilemmas presented in the myths and the resolution (or lack thereof) of those dilemmas. For example, though there are no myths about the sun being created out of nothing, there are many myths about the sun being placed in the sky, in order to fulfill its proper role by enabling people to see—reminding them of the continual motion and flux of the world and of the balance of light and darkness.

Transformers. Although there are few myths about a creator spirit (and those possibly developed after contact with whites), there are cycles of myths about a transformer or trickster figure who through his actions places the forces of the world in balance. The most detailed and integral of these is the Raven cycle found among the Tlingit (though each tribe had some form of trickster or transformer cycle, not always associated with Raven). Raven is a creature of uncontrollable desires and excesses, and in the act of trying to satisfy his desires, he inadvertently creates moral order and constraint. Incidental to each act of moral creation is the creation of some physical attribute of the world—a mountain or other geographical feature, or the color of a mallard's head or an ermine's tail—that serves to remind people of the myth and its moral import. Thus the world is made up of signs and images of mythic significance for those who know the stories behind them.

In general, the trickster cycles of the Northwest Coast parallel those of other areas in their nature and social function, although imagistically the Northwest Coast trickster stories more strongly emphasize the maintenance of the flow of wealth as representation of the correct motion of the universe. This image of flow—the release of wealth from its temporary container, whether it be the material wealth of a chief or the spiritual soul that is released from the body of a dead person when ravens begin to tear it apart—runs throughout the Northwest Coast mythology. However, not all Northwest Coast transformers are trickster figures: the Kwakiutl culture hero is one of a set of rather solemn mythic beings.

Myths of origin. Every feature of the geographic, social, and ceremonial world had an origin myth that encapsulated it into the basic structure of power and ideology, and these myths formed the basic material for Northwest Coast religion and ceremony. No public ceremony occurred without the retelling—either in recital or a dance reenactment—of the origin myths of the people involved, which is to say that no ceremony took place without the reenergizing of the connection between humans and spirits. Clan and family myths were integrated individually into the larger corpus of hero mythology, so that every family and person of title was in some specific way linked to the events and forces of the universe. Myth is a depiction of the interaction of universal forces, and the retelling of the myth reactivates and redirects those forces.

Northwest Coast rituals, like myths, developed into a multiplicity of local traditions, resulting in the direct linking of local history to the more cosmic elements of creation. Ceremonies were always changing as new rituals were acquired through war, marriage, new visions, or the emigration of families. There was a constant renegotiation of the meanings and structure of all rituals and stories, as traditions coalesced, melded, or broke apart; conflicting versions of stories were constantly being reworked.

Winter ceremonials. Spirit power was an essential part of the success of any task; thus there was ceremony in all human endeavor. Even so, there was a clear division of the year into secular (summer) and sacred (winter) seasons. Large-scale ceremonial performances were given in the winter. These were most important among the Kwakiutl and Nootka. Among the southern tribes there was a ceremony of spirit-possession and occasional rituals of world renewal similar to those of the peoples of northern California. Some scholars feel that the spirit-possession ceremony was more widespread until the beginning of the nineteenth century, when cultural change promoted the rapid efflorescence and diffusion of northern and central ceremonial forms, but the evidence for such a historical change is contradictory.

The narrative structure of the Kwakiutl winter ceremonials, like that of the family origin myths, was based on a simple set of images that were endlessly elaborated: a hero cuts himself off from the material world of humans, seeks or is kidnapped by spirits who take him to their home, learns the rituals of the spirits, obtains some of the spirits' power, and then brings the rituals back to the human world. He becomes frenzied as his frail human form attempts to contain the potency of the spirit power. During the ceremony the hero's fellow humans gradually came to control the power that threatened to destroy them, and it was they who "tamed" him. These rituals were performed in the most sensationalistic fashion, with elaborate stage effects and illusions, masked performances, complicated props, and stunning displays of strength and athletic agility.

The winter ceremonials were complex and changing ceremonies. All performances were carefully integrated into a larger dramatic structure with important ritual implications, depending on the number and type of dances being given, the guests' status, the time of the season, and a number of other factors. Each type of dance, of which there were hundreds, was a metaphorical connection to the spiritual universe. Just as the world is made up of people separate but interdependent, so were Northwest Coast rituals structured so as to place individuals in a web of mutual reinforcement. The agenda of dances was ordered so that each individual dance would contribute to their combined effect. One dance would act as contrast or catalyst for the next, giving added power to their combined performance. Feasts were carefully interspersed so as to distribute, in the form of food and wealth, the powers that had been brought into the human world through the preceding dances.

The rituals of the winter ceremonials were under the jurisdiction of groups called "dance societies" or "secret societies." Membership in these groups was inherited and strictly limited. A new member could be invested only upon the retirement of his predecessor, but there were many stages of initiation and many years of preparation before complete initiation. Most of the ceremonies of the dance societies were performed away from public scrutiny, to maintain private ownership of the rituals and to prevent the uninitiated from being harmed by the presence of immense spirit power. A small proportion of the ceremonies were performed only for members of the dance society or for a small group of aristocrats, and a very few were performed for the entire village. Yet even this small proportion of rituals went on for hours every day over a period of four or five months. In essence, then, the entire winter period was given over to ceremony—a fact that belies the usual claim by anthropologists that the peoples of the Northwest Coast were primarily interested in status.

Of all the winter-ceremonial performances, the most famous and widely discussed is the Hamatsa dance, which the Kwakiutl considered to be their most powerful ceremony. The Hamatsa dance seems to best encapsulate the ethos of Northwest Coast religious ideology. The *hamatsa* was a human who had been carried away by those supernatural creatures who preyed on the flesh and substance of human beings; while living with these supernatural creatures in their ceremonial house, the *hamatsa* took on their spiritual qualities (especially their affinity with death and killing); and when he returned to the land of human beings, he was possessed with the wild desire to eat human flesh. In a long series of rites, the members of the tribe gradually tamed his wildness through a series of pledges to sacrifice their wealth and (when they eventually died) their souls, to feed the spirits so that the world would remain in equilibrium. The violence and energy with which the *hamatsa* acted was a potent representation of the intensity of the struggle or task that humans had to accept if the world were to be kept moral. The burden of spiritual power demanded not a quiet acceptance but energetic activity, a ferocity for right action.

CONCLUSION. Although founded on the same basic philosophical principles as that of other native North American religious traditions, Northwest Coast religion developed those ideas into a distinct set of social and religious institutions that were adaptable to the changing fortunes and histories of each village and its individual members. It was a system in which atomistic elements could be separated from their original relationships with each other and reformed in new combinations dealing in a powerful, cohesive, creative, and poetic way with the purposes and dilemmas of human existence.

Unfortunately, much of Northwest Coast culture was irrevocably altered or destroyed in the course of the nineteenth and early twentieth centuries. All Northwest Coast religion was illegal in Canada from 1876 to 1951, though enforcement of applicable laws was uneven, and some ceremonial life persisted. In the last several decades, there has been a new emphasis on the traditional rituals, but how much they retain of their original character and the place they hold in the lives of the people today are questions that remain to be answered. As North American Indians and concerned scholars both reexamine the historical record to determine the significance of the Northwest Coast for the present, it can only be hoped that there will be new interpretations and understandings of what is unquestionably one of the most vibrant and fascinating of the world's tribal ceremonial complex.

SEE ALSO Potlatch.

BIBLIOGRAPHY

Traditional trait-oriented surveys of Northwest Coast culture can be found in Philip Drucker's *Cultures of the North Pacific Coast* (New York, 1965) and in the excellently illustrated *People of the Totem* by Norman Bancroft-Hunt, with photographs by Werner Forman (New York, 1979). No synthesized scholarly accounts of Northwest Coast religion exist. The best ethnographic accounts of the beliefs of specific tribes are the many volumes by Franz Boas on the Kwakiutl, Philip Drucker's *The Northern and Central Nootkan Tribes* (Washington, D.C., 1951), and Frederica De Laguna's *Under Mount Saint Elias* (Washington, D.C., 1972). Irving Goldman's *The Mouth of Heaven* (New York, 1975) and my *Feasting with Cannibals* (Princeton, 1981) both reanalyze Boas's materials and emphasize the critical role of religious thought in Kwakiutl life. Pamela Amoss's *Coast Salish Spirit Dancing* (Seattle, 1978) is the best account of contemporary Northwest Coast religious activity.

STANLEY WALENS (1987)

NORTH AMERICAN INDIANS: INDIANS OF THE NORTHWEST COAST [FURTHER CONSIDERATIONS]

The principal legislative developments in the United States are the passing of the American Indian Religious Freedom Act (AIRFA) of 1978 and the Native American Graves Protection and Repatriation Act (NAGPRA) of 1990. Taken together the two pieces of legislation were intended to redress past wrongs relative to the systematic eradication of Native American religious practices. Despite their intention the two acts led to unexpected complexities and dilemmas. Canada has also responded to repatriation requests and is negotiating with Aboriginal First Nations to determine the terms of self-governance. The significance of these developments is in the diverse ways that the varied Northwest Coast peoples have approached the repatriation of their material and cultural property. Underlying these efforts is the repatriation of the sacred, be it objects and burial remains or intangible properties such as religious practices and sacred or esoteric knowledge.

The main body of this article succinctly sketches out the complexity of the Northwest Coast cultural phenomenon. To do so, it divides its topics by linking them to themes such as kinship, social organization, ceremonies, and so on. The process of repatriation does the opposite. Through the various repatriation claims the objects that are being repatriated are not merely returning to their respective communities. They are also being reintegrated into their particular worldviews. For example, the Kwakiutls were forced to relinquish their potlatch regalia when their potlatch was raided by Canadian authorities in December of 1921. In the intervening years the Kwakiutl communities have endured the loss of their cultural property as well continual challenges to their lifeways. When they were able to repatriate the potlatch regalia, not only was the material returned, but prestige was returned to the community as well. This is clearly expressed in their new Kwakwaka'wakw First Nation museum. Similarly, the Haidas have been repatriating sacred objects and burial remains. When smallpox epidemics decimated the Haida population in the early nineteenth century, collectors "acquired" much treasured material from the Haida communities. Today, the Haidas are actively pursuing the repatriation of those objects. As in the Kwakwaka'wakw case, the Haidas are also celebrating through traditional ceremonies the return of not only the objects but also the honor, prestige, and spirituality inherent in the objects. In both cases, as happened with many other Northwest Coast peoples, the collected objects had become objects of curiosity and national treasures bereft of their sacred and social significance. Their successful repatriation is also the successful repatriation and revitalization—better yet, the re-vindication—of Northwest Coast cultural beliefs and practices.

As stated above the U.S. government has made attempts to recognize the integrity of Native American religious practices through the passage of AIRFA and NAGPRA. Taken together these two pieces of legislation not only began to address the return of burial remains and sacred objects to Native American communities but also the protection of those communities' religious practices. However, as Native American communities sought to claim their rights to religious practices and the return of burial remains and sacred objects, it became apparent that they faced much resistance. For example, the right to use sacred landscapes for religious practice and observance was constantly challenged by logging or recreational interests. The lower courts frequently recognized that specific Native American religious practice were protected by AIRFA, but all too often the higher courts would overturn the lower courts' rulings. Similarly, Native claims to burial remains and sacred objects would often require mediation over the definition of "sacred" and discussion of whether particular objects did or did not fit the definition. In the case of the Northwest, the Kennewick Man controversy in Washington State has fueled contentious debate, most notably revolving around tensions between Native American religious practices and the physical anthropological sciences. On the northwest coast of Washington, an archaeological excavation begun in 1970 and completed in 1981 produced yet another controversy regarding repatriation efforts. The Makah site of Ozette has revealed a well-preserved Makah village dated to around the 1490s. Archaeologists have been collaborating with the Makahs in the excavation project. But when the Makahs attempted to repatriate objects in museum holdings the process became more difficult. NAGPRA did not recognize individual ownership of sacred objects, whereas the Makahs traditionally regarded many of the sacred objects as individually owned. As NAGPRA was being negotiated, no one had thought to consult the Makah Nation. Despite this oversight, the Makah people are repatriating many sacred objects. Through traditional ceremonies these objects have been reintegrated into personal and social Makah networks.

Farther to the north in Alaska, the Tlingits are engaged in their own repatriation projects. As with the above examples, the properties being repatriated are not only tangible properties (material objects) but also intangible properties, such as language, clan totems, stories, and law. One such project involves the recognition of the sacred aspects of the landscape of the Tlingit region. This landscape is not only a resource to be exploited for subsistence but is also a sacred place. It is through the sacred that the resources are there for the peoples' benefit. But the resources must be honored and protected. The landscape is a sacred map, to which Tlingit clan names, histories, and stories are tied. Taken together the landscape is a cosmological reminder of Tlingit connection to place. This kind of project is a repatriation of intangible properties like cosmology, kinship, history, and language but most important of all, it is the repatriation of Tlingit identity.

All the above repatriation projects could be viewed as various forms of retrieval or revitalization of cultural lifeways—but that would only belittle the process. Rather, repatriation is on ongoing form of a process that Northwest Coast peoples have practiced all along. It is their attempt to continue to live as Tlingits, Haidas, Kwakwaka'wakws, Makahs, or any other Northwest Coast peoples, and to live on their own terms. Repatriation is merely a formal process for returning items that were wrongfully taken from the Northwest Coast peoples. In effect, repatriation is the Canadian and United States Governments' belated show of respect for the integrity and the vitality of the Northwest Coast peoples.

Bibliography

The *Handbook of American Indian Religious Freedom,* edited by Christopher Vecsey (New York, 1991), provides good commentary on the practice and politics of AIRFA by providing analyses of several case studies. Some of the issues served as the legal and ideological background for NAGPRA. Repatriation became a hotly contested subject and many of the issues are discussed in Devon A. Mihesuah's [ed.] *Repatriation Reader: Who Owns American Indian Remains?* (Lincoln, Neb., 2000). The cases and positions provide a good introduction to the theory and practice of repatriating tangible property. However, for the theory, law, and practice of repatriating intangible properties, Phyllis Mauch Messenger's [ed.] *The Ethics of Collecting Cultural Property: Whose Culture? Whose Property?* [foreword by Brian Fagan, 2nd ed., updated and enl.] (Albuquerque, 1999) provides valuable critical essays of cases and issues. More general discussions of property rights and intangible property can be found in *Borrowed Power: Essays on Cultural Appropriation* [edited by Bruce Ziff and Pratima V. Rao] (New Brunswick, N.J., 1997). The above discussions provide the necessary background to understand the religious importance of the repatriation of sacred objects among the Kwakwaka'wakw and Haida. A good general discussion of the potlatch can be found in *An Iron Hand upon the People: The Law against the Potlatch on the Northwest Coast,* by Douglas Cole and Ira Chaikin (Vancouver, Canada, and Seattle, Wash., 1990) and *The Potlatch Papers: A Colonial Case History* by Christopher Bracken (Chicago, 1997). However, two articles—"Contested Ethnie in Two Kwakwaka'wakw Museums" by Ian Fowler and "Art, Argument and Anger on the Northwest Coast" by Barbara Saunders—in *Contesting Art: Art, Politics and Identity in the Modern World,* edited by Jeremy MacClancy (Oxford and New York, 1997), illustrate the complexities of the repatriation issues for Northwest Coast communities; and Mary Lee Stearns's *Haida Culture in Custody: The Masset Band* (Seattle, 1981) is an excellent discussion of the history of dispossession and subsequent social revitalization among the Haida of the Masset Band. In the United States, the Makah have been involved in repatriation projects and two excellent sources for information are *Voices of a Thousand People: The Makah Cultural and Research Center* by Patricia Pierce Erikson with Helma Ward and Kirk Wachendorf [foreword by Janine Bowechop] (Lincoln, Neb., 2002) and *Drawing Back Culture: The Makah Struggle for Repatriation* by Ann M. Tweedie [foreword by Janine Bowechop] (Seattle, 2002). Also in Washington, the Kennewick Man debate has been a focal point for challenging and/or protecting NAGPRA legislation. For a general overview of the debate and the implications for all interested parties see David Hurst Thomas' *Skull Wars: Kennewick Man, Archaeology, and the Battle for Native American Identity* (New York, 2000). The Tlingit cultural revitalization project and their reappraisal of their connectedness to the landscape can be found in their *Will the Time Ever Come? A Tlingit Source Book* [as edited by Andrew Hope III and Thomas F. Thornton] (Fairbanks, 2000).

Bernard C. Perley (2005)

NORTH AMERICAN INDIANS: INDIANS OF CALIFORNIA AND THE INTERMOUNTAIN REGION

The Intermountain Region of North America is framed on the east by the Rocky Mountains of Canada and the United States and on the west by the Cascade and the Sierra Nevada ranges. Ethnographers customarily divide this region into two indigenous "culture areas," the Plateau and the Great Basin. The Plateau is bounded on the north by the boreal forests beyond the Fraser Plateau of British Columbia and on the south by the Bitterroot Mountains of Idaho and the arid highlands of southern Oregon and northwestern Montana. It includes the Columbia River's plateau and drainage in Washington, Oregon, and a small portion of northern California. The Great Basin is the area of steppe-desert lying primarily in Nevada and Utah but including parts of southern Idaho, western Wyoming, and western Colorado. It runs south from the Salmon and Snake rivers of Idaho to the Colorado Plateau, is bounded by the Colorado River on the south, and includes the interior deserts of southwestern California. "California," as an indigenous culture area, thus comprises the lands west of the Sierra Nevada crest to the Pacific Ocean, most of southern California and northern Baja California, and most lands north from there to the present Oregon border.

California and the Plateau have supported large and varied native populations. The Great Basin, with its exceedingly restrictive ecology, has always been less heavily populated and more culturally uniform than either California or the Plateau. Nonetheless, even in the Basin, sweeping areal generalizations can serve only as starting points in investigating both intra- and inter-areal diversity among native peoples, for the three areas are foci of cultural adaptation, expression, and influence, rather than impermeably bounded cultural or historical isolates.

Although the indigenous peoples of the Basin were all speakers of closely related Numic languages, the languages of the Plateau were more varied, and those of California had a truly extraordinary diversity. Broadly speaking, cultural and linguistic diversity were correlated in the three areas. In terms of religious practice, the greatest diversity was in California and the least in the Basin, with the Plateau falling somewhere between.

General Themes. The pervasiveness of religious concerns and behavior in the daily lives of all of these peoples is suggested by the range of religious themes that are common to the three areas, despite the diverse, area-specific expressions given them.

Power. Significant contacts with European influences occurred in the three areas beginning in the eighteenth century and had achieved devastating impact by the mid-nineteenth century. As will be seen, European influence tended to elevate concepts of anthropomorphic creator figures to new eminence. Before contact, however, a widespread perception of a diffuse, generalized, and impersonal cosmic force, often referred to today as "power," was far more significant. This energic field of all potentials is a neutral, amoral, and generative presence that produces all things.

Mythology. In some cases, power was first manifested by a world creator who, through it, brought the world into its present form. Such creators might be culture heroes and transformers, such as Komokums among the Modoc, a people interstitial between California and the Plateau. Komokums and many others like him acted in conjunction with earth divers to form the earth from a bit of soil raised from the depths of a primordial sea. In other cases, especially in north-central California, world creators are likely to be true creator gods, thinking the world into existence or bringing it forth with a word. In southern California we find creation myths of great metaphysical complexity and subtlety, such as those of the Luiseño, for whom creation arose by steps, out of an absolute void. Even here, however, we find a transformer, Wiyot, shaping the present world from an earth that preceded his existence, and this seems the more typical pattern. Such gods and heroes tend to become otiose after their work is accomplished, rather than lingering on as moral overseers.

Unlike the Californians, neither the peoples of the Basin nor those of the Plateau seem to have been much concerned with world origins. Yet they shared with Californians a profound concern for a variety of prehuman spirits—usually animals, but also celestial beings, monsters, and others—who aided in bringing the world to its present shape and in establishing culture. Thus, throughout the region one finds arrays of such prehuman beings, each exercising power for good or ill according to its innate proclivities. The actions of each are recounted in a broad spectrum of myths and stories. Commonly, one or more of these beings, most often Coyote but others as well, emerge as a trickster, undoing the good works of the heroes and creators through a peculiar blend of innocence, greed, and stupidity. Such tricksters may be creatively helpful as well as negatively influential, and sometimes creators and tricksters are one and the same, which accounts for the multivocality of existence. Often the trickster is the sibling of a culture hero, as Coyote ("little wolf") is of Wolf among the Shoshoni, Short-tailed Weasel is of Long-tailed Weasel among the Washo of the eastern Sierras, and Frog Woman is of Wiyot among the Luiseño.

Spirits and personal power. Many animal spirits, including tricksters, remained in the world as sources of specialized powers for human beings. Other unique power potentials might reside in celestial and landscape features and in common, manufactured objects. People might encounter such spirits, usually in their anthropomorphic forms, in visions or in dreams. Through such encounters individuals gained spirit-helpers, enhancing the power innate in themselves and gaining particular powers that, through volitional control, brought success in specific endeavors. Vision quests in many different forms are found throughout the three areas.

Seeking increased, specialized power and protection through intentional encounters with spirit-beings was a primary concern of the religions of the Plateau. In the Basin, visions and personal powers tended to come to individuals spontaneously, at the spirits' will, and were not often sought through formal quests. In California, spirit encounters sometimes resulted from stringent austerities and Plateau-style questing, as among the Achomawi and Atsugewi in the northeast. Often they were sought through participation in initiatory "schools" of pubescent boys seeking power collectively under the tutelage of older initiates. Such schools were central to the visionary religions of the south and the elaborate dance and healing societies of northern California.

In many such California initiation schools, sodalities—secret, mythically chartered societies—were at the forefront. Membership in such sodalities was often restricted; males alone were accepted, and sometimes only those representative of elite kin groups. In parts of the Plateau, especially among the Nez Perce and the Tenino, specific guardian spirits might be transmitted through inheritance. In the notably egalitarian Plateau, however, this did not have the effect of centralizing both spiritual and social ascendency in elites, as did sodality membership in the more stratified of California groups.

More generally, both males and females had access to the spirits and, thus, to personal power. In the Plateau, young boys and girls alike often sought visions, although boys did so more frequently than girls. In the Basin, both males and females could receive spirit powers at any time during their lives, although it appears that men were more often so favored. The situation in California was more complex. In each of three major subareas, women were initiated into some groups but not into others and, among these groups, there were often varying, ranked degrees of male and female spirit acquisition and initiation.

Throughout the three culture areas, the specific spirits that one might encounter and the powers that they enabled were varied. Hunting or fishing skill, the ability to cure and to injure, success in courting and in fighting, finesse in crafts and in song making, gambling luck, wealth, wisdom, and many other potentials might be realized.

Although increased and specialized powers could be acquired and maximized through contacts with spirits, they could also be lost by offending those spirits through failure to adhere to taboos imposed in vision or dream; through misuse of songs, rituals, or power objects; through more general breach of custom, or simply through baffling happenstance. Every increase in an individual's power had its price.

Shamans. The shamans were the most powerful of people, the most respected for their spirit contacts, and the most feared. It was they who paid the highest price for their acumen. (*Shaman* here means a healer who obtains and exercises his powers through direct contact with spiritual beings.) In the Plateau, special effort was not usually exerted to obtain the guardian spirits that brought shamanic powers. Here, as in the Basin, both men and women could receive shamanic powers, although male shamans predominated. The same was largely true of Californians, although shamans among Shoshoni, Salinan, and some Yokuts groups were exclusively male, whereas in northwestern California female shamans vastly predominated, those who were the daughters and granddaughters of shamans having the greatest proclivity toward acquiring such powers.

Throughout the three areas, initial encounters with spirits capable of bestowing shamanic powers (sometimes volitionally sought in California and, to a lesser extent, in the Basin) were followed by intensive and often longterm training in the control of the spirit-power and an apprenticeship in its use under a recognized shaman. Such training might include initiation in the secrets of legerdemain, fire handling, and ventriloquism, on which shamanic performances often depended for their dramatic impact. Yet although shamans everywhere were expected to display their powers in such feats, and occasionally to best other shamans in public power contests, their primary function was as curative specialists, and the tricks of the trade were subordinate to success in this important function.

Theories of disease were fairly uniform. Illness came through magical objects projected into the sufferer's body by human sorcery or witchcraft. Again, ghosts or spirits whose rules for conduct had been ignored or whose special places had been defiled might make people ill. The spiritual essence of the patient could be called away by unseen beings or injured by a sorcerer or witch. Finally, one could be poisoned by a witch, either psychically or physically. In the Plateau all such power-related disease was distinguished from natural, physical illness; shamans treated only the former, whereas the latter were treated through exoteric remedies, often by lay specialists. Among the Washo of the Basin, however, all death was attributed to sorcerers.

As theories of spiritually induced disease were quite uniform, so were therapeutic measures. Shamans diagnosed the illness and then entered a trance through singing, dancing, and, occasionally, the ingestion of powerful substances. The shaman then sucked out the introjected objects and disposed of them or used his breath to blow off the "shadows" of offended spirits that had lodged in the patient's body. He might also heal through various forms of massage. Many shamans specialized in one or another approach to particular sorts of illnesses. Some, especially in the Plateau, traveled out of their bodies to find and retrieve the lost souls of patients or to regain these in other ways. Illnesses might be caused by the misdeeds of members of the community other than the patient himself, and both public confessions and the identification of sorcerers were common features of performances.

Shamans in most groups acquired other, noncurative powers and specialties as well. In the Great Basin, in southern California, and north through the central California subarea, rattlesnake handling was practiced by shamans specially related to this powerful creature and capable of curing its bites. Weather shamans who both caused and stopped rains were found in these areas as well. In the Basin, shamans served as hunt leaders, dreaming of quarry such as antelope, leading drives, and charming the game into enclosures. Other specialties abounded. Paiute shamans in the Basin and many in central and northern California became "bear doctors," imitating these animals and using their powers for both benign and malign ends. Others might gain the power to find lost objects, to predict the future, or to conjure, as among the Colville and the Kutenai of the Plateau, whose rites were similar to the shaking tent rites more common far to the east. Virtually everywhere, even among the Plateau and Basin groups whose shamans first obtained their powers without special questing, such practitioners often sought to augment their acumen through gaining additional spirit helpers, often seeking these in special places.

Power itself is neutral, its potential for good and ill being manifested at the discretion (or indiscretion) of those spirits, ghosts, or human beings who have more than usual control of it. Thus shamans were universally feared for their potential to use power in malign ways, as sorcerers. In the Basin and in much of California shamans were viewed with great suspicion; they were thought to induce or prolong illness in order to collect higher fees and to kill outright for a fee from an aggrieved party. Among the Mohave and other River Yuman groups in southeastern California, the killing of a shaman, on whatever grounds, was not considered reprehensible. Elsewhere shamans were killed only in the event of their patient's death. In northwestern California, shamans simply returned their fee should the patient die, greed being more commonly attributed to them than sorcery. The shaman's position was not always enviable, and, particularly in the Great Basin and Plateau, people tended to become shamans only at the behest of a spirit who could not be refused, or they refused to accept shamanic powers when opportunities to acquire them arose.

First-fruits rites. First-fruits rites, celebrated for a variety of resources throughout the region, were often conducted by shamans. This was true, for example, of the small, local first-salmon rites that were common along many of the rivers and streams of the Plateau, along the northern California coast south to San Francisco Bay, and among the Pyramid Lake Paviosto, the Lemhi Shoshoni, and some other groups in the northern Great Basin. In some cases, however, first-salmon and other first-fruits rites were incorporated into larger-scale renewal ceremonies, as in northwestern California, and were directed by specialized priests—intermediaries between the human and nonhuman worlds who, as holders of inherited and appointed offices, recited codified liturgies.

Girls' puberty and menstrual seclusion. The ritual initiation of females into adulthood at menarche and, often, the public celebration of this event constitute a second widespread ritual element in the religions of the three culture areas. In general, throughout the region women were isolated at menarche and placed under a variety of restrictions, their conduct during the time being thought to presage their future. Emphasis on girls' puberty tended to be greater among peoples more dependent on hunting than on gathering. Thus, periods of training might be as short as five days, as among the peoples of the western Basin, or extended as long as four years, as among the Carrier Indians of the northern Plateau. In coastal southern California, puberty was a community concern, and all young women reaching menarche during a given year were secluded and instructed together, sometimes being "cooked" in heated pits in a way reminiscent of the training of novice shamans to the north in California. Indeed, it can be argued that puberty rites in many groups represent a female equivalent of male spirit quests and sodality initiations. Such "cooking" of pubescent girls is found elsewhere, as among the Gosiute of the Basin. Communal rites are paralleled in the Plateau, where the Chilcotin, the Southern Okanogen, the Tenino, and the Nez Perce utilized communal seclusion huts for the initiation of young girls.

There were, however, no elaborate public female puberty celebrations in the southern Plateau, where girls' puberty was marked by simple elaborations of more general menstrual customs. Public ceremonies did occur, usually at the discretion of the girl's family, in the Great Basin—as among the Washo and others. Here, girls' puberty might be celebrated in conjunction with a Big Time, an intergroup gathering for shared subsistence enterprises, ritual, feasting, trading, dancing, gambling, and games. In California, girls' puberty dances were held by many northern groups as the year's ritual highlight—again, often in conjunction with Big Times. Occasionally, and especially among the Athapascan-speaking groups of the northwest, such dances were the prerogative of elite Californian families.

The prevalence of concern for female puberty in the three areas is clearly related to a concern for menstruation in general. Menstrual blood was viewed as among the most powerful of substances, highly dangerous if not properly controlled and, although often of positive virture to the woman herself, inimical to the welfare of others, especially males. The isolation and restriction of girls at menarche was thus widely repeated—although with far less elaboration—at each menses. Communal menstrual shelters were found in some Plateau communities and perhaps in parts of California. Elsewhere, a small hut for the individual menstruant was constructed, as in much of the Basin, or her movements were restricted to the family's dwelling, as among the River Yuman groups. Menstrual seclusion and dietary and other restrictions varied in duration from the time of the flow up to ten or twelve days, as in northwestern California.

Sudatories. Male concern for menstrual pollution and for other pollutants that might hinder the exercise or acquisition of power, or "luck," was certainly related to the prevalence of male sweating, carried out in a variety of sudatories in all three areas. Such sudatories might be small and temporary or large and permanent structures. In northwestern California, for example, "sweat houses" were sizeable, semisubterranean houses, men's clubs where all adult males slept, worked, and practiced rituals, as well as sweated. Among the Nomlaki substantial men's sweat houses were the domain of a male sodality, the *huta.* The religious nature of purification through regular sweating is evident in the veneration with which the sudatory was regarded. Among certain Plateau groups, such as the Sanpoil, the sweat house itself was the mundane manifestation of a powerful sweat-house god.

MAJOR RELIGIOUS SYSTEMS. In each area, and often in specifiable subareas, the general themes outlined above were manifested within the context of—and were given particular ideological inflections by—area-specific religious systems.

Among the peoples of the Great Basin, environmental conditions demanded small populations divided into highly mobile bands, reduced at times to the extended nuclear family, and expanding at more abundant times to small bands of such families. There was little need for social or political organization on a wider scale that would ensure the privileges of more complex kin groups or the territorial autonomy of a large political unit. By the same token, dispersed resources could not be collected in sufficient quantities to provide for the needs of frequent, large gatherings. Complex ritual systems depending on cyclic collective action did not develop in the Basin as they did in both California and the Plateau. By contrast, in these latter areas more sedentary peoples, enjoying richer resource bases and enacting more complex and farther-reaching kinship and political organizations, created religious systems through which large numbers of people were regularly assembled for collective ritual experience.

The Great Basin. Basin religion was largely an individual or small-band concern, and shamans provided spiritual leadership sufficient to the needs of most bands. Rituals, such as girls' puberty celebrations, that in other areas served as foci for large gatherings here tended to be small, family affairs. The healing performances of shamans might provide occasions for shared ritual participation, but such gatherings, too, were small, limited to band members, and not held according to a fixed schedule.

Large-scale Big Times did occur with some regularity among the Washo and Paiute of the western Great Basin, several bands gathering together for harvest of the more abundant wild crops (such as piñon nuts) for ritual, and for recreation. The Paiute reciprocated such Big Times with the Mono and Miwok of California. Interband antelope drives, sometimes in conjunction with Big Times, were ritually prepared and imbued with religious significance, as suggested by the many Basin rocks displaying petroglyphs and pictographs that date from the remote past through the nineteenth century.

The Big Times of the western Great Basin and California were supplanted in the eastern portion of the Basin area by other sorts of events. Ute and Shoshoni bands convened several times a year for "round dances." Among the Ute, a more ritually focused Bear Dance, marking the return of bears from hibernation and thus the renewal of the world in spring, was performed annually in late winter.

The Plateau. In the Plateau the common western theme of personal spirit-power was honed to its greatest refinement and served as the basis for an areal religious system keynoted by collective "winter spirit-dances." Although there were a great many variations in the specifics of individual guardian-spirit quests and of winter dances among Plateau tribes, a generalized account may be offered as an introduction.

Among the Sanpoil-Nespelem and most other Salish groups, boys and many young girls began spirit questing at or before puberty, often when they were as young as six or eight. (Sahaptin groups placed less emphasis on spirit quests, and others, such as the Carrier, restricted them to certain males.) The child was sent out to fast, scour himself with rough foliage, bathe in cold pools, and keep vigils in isolated places. In dreams, as among the Carrier, or in visions, the supplicant was visited by an animal spirit or the spirit of an object or place. The spirit instructed the person in a song that often had an associated dance step, and sometimes revealed power objects. In many groups, the supplicant, on returning from a successful quest, "forgot" both encounter and song. (The Kutenai, whose youths sought only a single, immediately effective spirit, present an exception.) Among the Salish, when the individual reached full adulthood, usually about age twenty-five for men, the spirit returned, often causing illness. With the aid of a shaman, the individual "remembered" the song and spirit. Once fully accepted, one's spirit became an intrinsic aspect of one's being, like a soul, a "partner" whose loss was life-threatening. Throughout their lives, people might seek different, additional spirits with associated powers and specialties.

During a two-month period in the winter, anyone who had a guardian spirit—a shaman or a layman—might sponsor a spirit dance. The dances, held in a winter lodge, lasted two or three nights and were scheduled so that people of a given locale might attend several in a winter. Under the supervision of shamans, dancers imitated their own guardian spirits, singing their songs and performing their dance steps. New initiates to whom spirits had recently returned used the occasion to legitimize their relationships with their spirits. Other components of the dances included feasting and the giving of gifts to visitors, the offering of gifts to spirits at a center pole, and shamans' displays and contests. The conduct of the audience was rigidly controlled during the dances, and in some groups their behavior was policed by officiants.

Among the Sanpoil, Colville, Kutenai, Kalispel, Spokan, Coeur d'Alene, and Flathead, a society of men possessing Bluejay as guardian spirit served this policing function. These "Bluejay shamans" identified entirely with Bluejay during the winter dance period, painting their faces black, keeping to themselves, and scavenging food. The Bluejay shamans perched in the rafters of dance houses during performances, swooping down on those who broke the rules of conduct. They also performed services as finders of lost objects and as curers, and were ritually returned to a normal state at the end of the dance period. Although the Bluejay shamans suggest an at least latent sodality structure in the southeastern Plateau, such sodalities were fully developed only in California.

California. There were four major subareal ritual complexes in aboriginal California. Beyond serving as vehicles for religious expression, such complexes served important functions in social, economic, and ecological regulation, in ethnic maintenance, and, through creating unifying networks, in political organization.

Toloache. From the Yuman tribes of the south, north through the Yokuts and, in diminished forms, to the Miwok, the use of *Datura stramonium*—jimsonweed, or *toloache* (from the Nahuatl and Spanish)—was a common and central feature of religious practice. A psychotropic decoction was made from the root of this highly toxic plant and carefully administered to initiates by shamans or by specialized priests. After a period of unconsciousness the initiates awoke to a trancelike state of long duration during which, guided by adepts, they acquired animal or celestial spirit-helpers. Such collective, drug-induced vision questing was often undertaken by males at puberty and in the context of an extended "school," as among the Luiseño-Juaneño, the Cahuilla, the Ipai-Tipai, the Cupeño, and the Gabrielino. Schooling included severe physical ordeals, instruction in mythic cosmology carried out through dry painting, and in some cases the creation of rock art. In such groups as the Chumash and the Serrano, training was restricted to the sons of an elite. In all cases, the group of initiated men, and—among the Monache and the Yokuts—women, formed a sodality that bore defined religious, economic, and political responsibilities. Among the Chumash, such an organization provided the basis for a highly complex, elite socioreligious guild, *Iantap*, led by priest-astronomers. Throughout the subarea, shamans made use of *toloache* in achieving curing trances.

In the extreme southeast, among the Mohave, the role of *toloache* was secondary to that of dreaming. Men learned clan myths through intentional dreaming and chanted these in long, collective "sings." Kin group solidarity was important to religious practice among other southern California groups as well, many keeping sib medicine bundles that were revealed only to *toloache* adepts.

Mourning anniversaries. With their stress on ritual death and rebirth, the *toloache* religions of southern and central California reflected an overriding concern with personal and cosmic death and renewal. A second feature, the "mourning anniversary," accompanied the *toloache* complex. In broad outline, mourning anniversaries were large public gatherings in which effigies of the year's dead, together with large quantities of property, were burned on poles erected in circular brush shelters, the assembled audience mourning its collective losses. The occasion often served as a vehicle for girls' puberty celebrations, for the giving of new names, for honoring chiefs, and for expressing reciprocity between kin groups. Often an Eagle (or Condor) Dance, in which shamans displayed their power by slowly killing a sacrificial bird, formed an important part of the event.

The mourning anniversary, with many local variations, was practiced by the Basin peoples of the southern portion of contemporary California—the Cheme-huevi, the Panamint, the Kawaiisu, and the Tubatulabal —as well as by virtually all groups in the southern California culture area. The practice extended northward through the *toloache*-using groups and beyond, being performed by the Maidu and Nisenan of northern California in conjunction with another religious complex, the Kuksu cult.

Kuksu. In northern California the *toloache* complex gave way to a second great ritual system, the Kuksu cult. The term *Kuksu* derives from the Pomo name for a creator-hero who is impersonated by masked dancers in the periodic performances that are the focus of the religious system. A parallel figure, Hesi, was prominent in the performances of groups in the Sacramento Valley and the Sierra Nevada foothills. The Hill Maidu expression of the complex featured a third such figure, Aki, who is found together with Hesi among the Northwestern Maidu. Kuksu and Hesi are sometimes found together among other groups.

Masked and costumed dancers impersonated these and other spirits and mythic figures in elaborate ceremonials performed in dance houses before large audiences during gatherings that lasted several days. Dances at various ceremonial centers were reciprocally supported. As with *toloache* religions, the various Kuksu religions provided collective "schools" for pubescent initiates who were, through cultic indoctrination and participation, conducted into secret, often ranked sodalities. Such sodalities could exercise great political and economic influence, as well as spiritual power. The Kuksu dances themselves returned the world to its pristine, mythic condition and often included first-fruits and curing elements in their scope. Intergroup trading, gambling, shamans' contests, and recreation were features of the Big Times that usually followed Kuksu performances.

Among groups that had both Kuksu and Hesi sodalities, as well as some others, participation was open to young men and also to some young women, as among the Cahto and the Yuki. More commonly, membership in such sodalities was restricted to males. In some groups, membership was further restricted to elite cadres who worked their way up through the sodality's ranked levels, as among the Pomo-speaking groups. In such groups a second sodality, the Ghost society, was open to all young men, as among the Patwin, and sometimes to women as well, as among the Eastern Pomo. These less prestigious sodalities presented masked dances that paralleled those of the Kuksu type and emphasized the honoring of the departed, the curing of ghostdisease, and the continuity of generations. Such themes were present in the mourning anniversaries prevalent to the south. Thus, the Ghost society was not found among groups in the Kuksu subarea (such as the Maidu and the Nisenan) that practiced mourning anniversaries.

World renewal. Mythic reenactment, collective mourning, generational continuity, and world renewal are all motives present in the Kuksu religion that found other expressions in northwestern California, where a fourth areal ritual complex, the World Renewal cult, flourished. This complex featured cyclic ten-day ceremonials within more extended periods of ritual activity performed by specialized officiants. The various dances were given reciprocally at two- to three-year intervals at perhaps thirteen ceremonial centers in Yurok, Karok, and Hupa territories. Close equivalents of these World Renewal dances were held by Tolowa-Tututni, Wiyot, Chilula, and Shasta groups as well. The focal occasions were religious festivals, extended periods of public and private ritual, dancing, feasting, and communality that at times attracted several thousand participants. World Renewal festivals thus replaced both Big Times and mourning anniversaries in the northwestern subarea. However, the primary purpose of these large gatherings was the prevention of world disorder and the reaffirmation of interdependency. The world, potentially imbalanced by the weight of human misconduct, was "fixed" or "balanced" through the Jump Dance, the interdependence and abundance of all life reaffirmed and ensured through the Deerskin Dance. In both, teams of dancers displayed finery and power objects emblematic of the spiritual ascendency of their sponsors, and it was in this sense that such costumes and objects were considered "wealth."

The World Renewal religion was given different inflections by the different participating groups: the Yurok incorporated first-salmon rites and collective fishing as well as the rebuilding of a sacred structure; the Karok included "new fire" (new year) elements, as well as a first-salmon rite; and the Hupa celebrated a first-acorn rite, the rebuilding of a cosmographic structure, and so on. All stressed the reenactment, by priests, of the origins of the dances and their attendant rituals. The recitation of long, codified mythic scenarios was a central feature. School-like organizations of "helpers" were instructed by the priests. These organizations were similar to the initiatory sodalities of south and central California and included both men and women. Neither priests and their assistants nor dancers impersonated spirit beings, however, as was done in Kuksu performances or the spirit dances of the Plateau.

The sketches given here do not exhaust the aboriginal ritual inventories in any of the areas and subareas dealt with. There were many less prominent but no less meaningful ritual activities, both private and public. Throughout these areas religious knowledge and practice were fully integrated with social action. The European invasion of the American West, in disrupting ecological, social, and political systems, also disrupted religious systems.

POSTCONTACT RELIGIOUS CHANGE. The religions of California, the Great Basin, and the Plateau have undergone thousands of years of slow change and development. They were probably changed most suddenly and drastically by the direct and indirect influences of Europeans and Euro-Americans that began in the eighteenth century.

The Roman Catholic missionization of California, beginning in 1769, had largely disastrous effects on the native populations of the area. Voluntary conversions took place, but forced baptism and forced residence in mission communities were more common. Ultimately, the successes of Catholic missionization north to San Francisco Bay were negated by the fearsome toll exacted by the diseases fostered by overcrowded missions and forced labor under the Spanish *encomienda* system. Success measured in lasting conversions was modest, and negative in terms of human welfare, but the missionaries contributed to native religious revitalization. For example, Catholicism seems to have provided the basis for a new high god, Chingichngish, in the *toloache* religions of the south. This moralistic, omniscient creator, which originated among the Gabrielino, also supplemented the mythic pantheons of the Luiseño-Juaneño, the Ipai-Tipai, the Chumash, and the Yokuts.

Other missionaries, primarily Protestant and Mormon, also made extended efforts in the nineteenth century in California, the Basin, and the Plateau. Yet the effects of later missionization were broadly similar: rather than supplanting native religions, Christianity provided symbolic means through which native religions found new forms to cope with the radically changing circumstances of life.

However, the effects of conquest were not limited to innovations informed by Christian ideology. The introduction of the horse onto the Plains and thence into the Plateau and the northwestern Basin in the early eighteenth century had an important impact on the peoples of these areas. Together with the horse came other Plains influences. Military sodalities were integrated into the religions of the Kutenai and the Flathead, as was the Sun Dance. The Sun Dance also spread to the Great Basin, where it was taken up by the Wind River Shoshoni and the Bannock and was introduced to the Utes by the Kiowa as late as 1890.

The preponderant contact phenomena evidenced in the religious life of all three areas, however, were the millenarian crisis cults inspired by a variety of "prophets" whose visions had been shaped by Christian influences. Typically, such visions occurred in deathlike states in which prophets met God or his emissary and received word of the coming millennium and the practices and moral codes that would ensure Indians' survival of it. Perhaps the best known of such crisis cults are the Paiute Ghost Dances of 1870 and 1890.

The first of these, initiated by the prophet Wodziwob in 1870, moved through the Basin and into central California. It was taken up by a number of California groups and moved north to the Shasta. The Ghost Dance doctrine stressed the destruction of the whites by the Creator, the return of the Indian dead, and the restoration of the earth to its pristine, precontact condition. It inspired a number of variants in the years following 1870. Most of these represented fusions of Kuksu-type and Ghost society dances with the new millenarianism. Such cults included the Earth Lodge religion practiced by many central and northern California peoples. Adherents awaited the millennium in large, semi-subterranean dance houses. Other cults inspired by the 1870 Ghost Dance included the Big Head and Bole-Maru cults of the Hill Patwin, the Maidu, and the Pomo-speaking groups, and a succession of other local cults led by various "dreamers."

The 1890 Ghost Dance, initiated in 1889 by the Paiute prophet Wovoka, again spread through the Basin, this time moving east onto the Plains. It directly affected neither California nor the Plateau.

The two Ghost Dances are but the better known of a large number of similar efforts toward religious revitalization that flourished, particularly in the Plateau area, in the nineteenth century. In the 1830s, many prophets, not acting in concert, spread the Prophet Dance through the central and southern Plateau. This round dance, always performed on Sundays and reflecting belief in a high god, showed Christian influence, although some have argued that it had aboriginal precedents as well. The dance took many forms under the guidance of many prophets and dreamers, of whom the best known is perhaps Smohalla, a Sahaptin dreamer who revived the Prophet Dance in the 1870s in a form that spread widely.

In 1881 a Salish Indian from Puget Sound named John Slocum underwent what was by that time the established visionary experience of a prophet. Together with his wife Mary he inaugurated the Indian Shaker church, a Christian church in which the presence of God's power, signified by physical trembling ("the shake"), was used by congregants to cure the sick. This mixture of Christian and native shamanistic elements proved highly appealing, and the Indian Shaker church spread into the Plateau, where it was accepted by Yakima, Umatilla, Wasco-Tenino, Klamath, and, to a lesser extent, Nez Perce Indians. In northwestern California in 1926, churches were built by Yurok, Tolowa, and Hupa congregations. The Shakers' popularity in California began to wane in the 1950s, the result of internal schism, competition with evangelical Christian churches, and increasing stress on "Indianness" and the accompanying return to old ways.

These two apparently conflicting ideologies, based on the salvific powers of Jesus Christ, on the one hand, and on an Indian identity perceived as traditional, on the other, seem to have reached mutual accommodation in peyotism and its institutionalized expression, the Native American Church. The Peyote Way has been accepted by a large number of Basin Indians, spreading among the Ute, Paiute, Gosiute, and Shoshoni in the early twentieth century, its acceptance perhaps facilitated by the collapse of the 1890 Ghost Dance. The Washo received peyote from Ute believers in 1936.

Peyotism spread through the Basin despite the resistance of many traditionalists, becoming itself the basis for a new traditionalism. It was not, however, established in California, although Indians from such cities as San Francisco make frequent trips to take part in peyote meetings sponsored by the Washo and others in Nevada.

Many other postcontact religious systems, including the Sun Dance, continue to be enacted. Chingichngish remains central to religious life on the Rincon and Pauma reservations in southern California; Smohalla's Prophet Dance is still practiced as the basis of the Pom Pom religion of the Yakima and Warm Springs Indians; and Bole-Maru and other postcontact transformations of Kuksu religions are viable among Pomo and other central Californian groups. The Indian Shaker church survives in many communities.

Since the 1960s Indians of all three culture areas have made concerted efforts to reassert religious, as well as political, autonomy; indeed, the two realms continue to be closely intertwined. Traditional religious specialists and, in many cases, collective ritual activities have survived both conquest and christianization. Younger Indians are increasingly turning to elderly specialists and investing themselves in old ritual practices. Annual mourning ceremonies are still prominent in parts of southern California; northwestern Californians continue to dance in World Renewal rituals; and shamanism survives in the Basin, as does spirit questing on the Plateau. A myriad of other native ritual events and private practices continue throughout the region. Such state agencies as California's Native American Heritage Commission, as well as federal legislation such as the 1978 American Indian Religious Freedom Act, support these efforts to a degree. Withal, one can see the durability of the ancient ways, their persistence, and their ability to continue through modern transformations.

See Also Ghost Dance; Psychedelic Drugs; Sun Dance.

Bibliography

The most valuable sources in the beginning study of the religions of California, the Great Basin, and the Plateau are the pertinent volumes of the *Handbook of North American Indians*, 20 vols. (Washington, D.C., 1978–). Volume 8, *California*, edited by Robert F. Heizer, was issued in 1978. Heizer's *California* volume to an extent supplants A. L. Kroeber's *Handbook of the Indians of California* (1925; reprint, New York, 1976), although this earlier work remains of interest.

Useful bibliographies can be found in the volumes of the new *Handbook* and in several other important sources: *Ethnographic Bibliography of North America*, 4th ed., 5 vols., edited by George Peter Murdock and Timothy J. O'Leary (New Haven, 1975); Robert F. Heizer, *The Indians of California: A Critical Bibliography* (Bloomington, Ind., 1976); Joseph P. Jorgensen, *Western Indians* (San Francisco, 1980); and Omer C. Stewart, *Indians of the Great Basin* (Bloomington, Ind., 1982).

Jorgensen's *Western Indians* is a computer-assisted distributional study with chapters on a number of pertinent topics, placing religious practices in ecological and political context. As such, it is a sophisticated continuation of earlier culture-element distribution surveys. One such study by Harold E. Driver, "Girls' Puberty Rites in Western North America," *University of California Publications in Anthropological Records* 6 (1941/42): 21–90, provides a comprehensive overview of its topic, an important one in all three culture areas under consideration here. Other such Western themes are explored in Willard Z. Park's *Shamanism in Western North America* (1938; reprint, New York, 1975) and in Erna Gunther's two analyses of first-salmon ceremonies in the *American Anthropologist* 28 (1926): 605–617, and in *Washington University Publications in Anthropology* 2 (1928): 129–173. Park's *Shamanism* contains a detailed account of Northern Paiute (Paviosto) shamanism and thus serves to introduce specific aspects of Great Basin religion, while Verne F. Ray's *Cultural Relations in the Plateau of North America* (Los Angeles, 1939) surveys the complexities of that area's religious life in a way that remains important.

There are various sources on the major religious systems of California. A. L. Kroeber and E. W. Gifford's "World Renewal: A Cult System of Native Northwestern California," *University of California Publications in Anthropological Records* 13 (1949): 1–56, gives good descriptive materials, although its interpretations are rather narrow. Edwin M. Loeb's "The Western Kuksu Cult" and "The Eastern Kuksu Cult," *University of California Publications in American Archaeology and Ethnology* 33 (1932/33): 1–138, 139–232, are comparable, Kroeberian works. More recent studies include *ʔAntap: Californian Indian Political and Economic Organization*, edited by Lowell John Bean and Thomas F. King (Ramona, Calif., 1974), and Raymond C. White's "The Luiseño Theory of 'Knowledge,'" *American Anthropologist* 59 (1957): 1–19. The two, together, provide entrée into the study of southern Californian religions. White's essay is also included in a volume of largely theoretical papers, *Native Californians: A Theoretical Retrospective*, edited by Lowell John Bean and Thomas C. Blackburn (Socorro, N. Mex., 1976), which provides a number of stimulating interpretations of aboriginal California religious systems.

Finally, the *Journal of California and Great Basin Anthropology* (Banning, Calif., 1979–), succeeding the *Journal of California Anthropology* (1974–1979), publishes current explorations in the religions of California and the Great Basin fairly regularly.

Thomas Buckley (1987)

NORTH AMERICAN INDIANS: INDIANS OF THE SOUTHWEST

From the southern end of the Rocky Mountains in Colorado, the Southwest culture area extends southward through the mountains, high sandstone mesas, and deep canyons of northern New Mexico and Arizona, and dips over the Mogollon Rim—the southern edge of the Colorado Plateau—into the arid, flat, and sparsely vegetated, low-lying deserts of southern New Mexico and Arizona and northwestern Mexico, to the warm shores of the Gulf of California. It is interspersed throughout with mountain ranges, some bearing dense forests and large game animals. Major rivers are few: the Colorado, its tributaries, and the Rio Grande are the primary sources of water for large sectors of the southwestern ecosystem.

Given the variegation in topography, vegetation, and climate, it is not surprising that the Southwest should contain an equal cultural variety. Four major language families (Uto-Aztecan, Hokan, Athapascan, Tanoan) are represented by a large number of peoples, and two other languages (Zuni and Keres) comprise language isolates. But it should not be thought that language boundaries are a guide to cultural boundaries. The thirty-one pueblos of New Mexico and Arizona include speakers of six mutually unintelligible languages from four language groups. Yet they share numerous cultural, and specifically religious, features. On the other hand, among the groups speaking Uto-Aztecan languages are found sociocultural forms as disparate as the hunter-gatherer bands of Shoshoneans in the north and the great Aztec state to the south of the Southwest culture area.

ECONOMIC PATTERNS. General typologies of Southwest cultures inevitably simplify such diversity. Despite such shortcomings, they may provide a framework within which to make some systematic generalizations. Edward Spicer (1962) has suggested four major divisions according to distinctive economic types at the time of European contact: rancheria peoples, village peoples, band peoples, and nonagricultural bands. The rancheria peoples all traditionally practiced agriculture based on the North American crop triumvirate of maize, beans, and squash. They lived in scattered settlements with households, or "small ranches," separated by some distance from each other. This general economic pattern was followed by groups as disparate as the Tarahumara and Concho in the Sierra Madre of Chihuahua, the Pima and Papago of southern Arizona, the Yaqui and the Mayo concentrated in the river deltas along the Sonoran coast of the Gulf of California, and the riverine and upland Yuman groups. Considerable differences of settlement pattern, including greater population concentrations among Pimans and seasonal movements from ridges into valleys for the Tarahumara and Concho, obtain from people to people. Still, the designation *rancheria* is helpful as a general characterization of Southwest agricultural economies that do not support densely populated, permanently sedentary communities.

The village peoples of Spicer's classification are, by contrast, sedentary communities with tightly integrated populations in permanent villages of stone and adobe construction. These are the Pueblo peoples, who have come to be regarded as the archetypical indigenous agriculturalists of the Southwest. The Tanoan Pueblos include the Tiwa, Tewa, and Towa, whose villages stretch up and down the upper portion of the Rio Grande in New Mexico. Also living for the most part along the Rio Grande or its tributaries are several Keresan Pueblos, with linguistically close Laguna and Acoma a little farther west, on the San Jose River. Moving west across the Continental Divide lies the pueblo of Zuni on a tributary of the Little Colorado River. At the western edge of Pueblo country, on the fingerlike mesas that extend southwestward from Black Mesa of the Colorado Plateau, are the eleven Hopi villages, whose inhabitants speak Hopi, a Uto-Aztecan language. Also located in this vicinity is one Tewa village, Hano, settled by refugees from the Rio Grande valley after the Great Pueblo Revolt of 1680.

The Pueblos are intensive agriculturalists. Among the Eastern Pueblos (those occupying the Rio Grande area) and in Acoma, Laguna, and Zuni (which with the Hopi constitute the Western Pueblos), agriculture is based on a variety of irrigation techniques. Hopi country has no permanent watercourses, and agriculture there is practiced by dry farming. Their sedentariness is a striking feature of the village peoples: Acoma and the Hopi village of Oraibi vie for the status of oldest continuously inhabited community in North America, with ceramic and tree-ring dates suggesting occupation from at least as far back as the twelfth century CE.

Spicer's third subtype is that of the band peoples, all Athapascan speakers. These consist of the Navajo and the several Apache peoples. These Athapascans migrated into the Southwest, probably via the Plains, from northwestern Canada not long before the arrival of Spanish colonists at the turn of the sixteenth century. They variously modified a traditional hunting and gathering economy with the addition of agriculture from the Pueblos (Navajo and Western Apache) and of sheep (Navajo) and horses (all groups) from the Spanish. The means of acquisition of these economic increments—through raiding of the pueblos and Spanish settlements—points up another important feature of Apache economies.

The fourth economic subtype Spicer refers to as nonagricultural bands. The Seri of the northwestern coastline of the Mexican State of Sonora are the primary representatives of this subtype. Traditionally, they hunted small game, fished and caught sea turtles, and gathered wild plant resources along the desert coast of the Gulf of California.

Variations in economy do not, of course, suggest variations in religious structure and orientation *tout court.* Still, modes of environmental adaptation do, within certain bounds, constrain the possibilities of social complexity. Southwest Indian religious patterns frequently do reflect forms of environmental adaptation because of a prevailing notion of social rootedness within a local environmental setting. Since many of the religious concerns of Southwest peoples pertain to man's relationship with environmental forces, the interplay between economic and religious spheres is fundamental.

RELIGIOUS PATTERNS. Among the panoply of indigenous Southwestern cultures, two general patterns of religious action are evident: that focusing on the curing of sickness and that celebrating, reaffirming, and sanctifying man's relationship with the cyclical forces of nature. Religious actions of the former type are usually shamanic performances whose participants include an individual patient and an individual ritual specialist (or a small group of specialists). The latter type includes communal rituals involving large groups of participants under the direction of cadres of hereditary priests. These two general forms are present in the Southwest in a variety of combinations and permutations. Among the Yumans, the Tarahumara, and the Apache, shamanistic curing is the prevalent religious form, and little emphasis is placed on communal agricultural rituals. (The Havasupai, who until the turn of the century held masked ceremonial performances at stages of the agricultural cycle—a practice probably borrowed from their near neighbors, the Hopi—provide a partial exception.) Historically the Pima and Papago peoples held communal agricultural rituals as well as shamanic performances, but with sociocultural change the former have passed from existence while the latter, by themselves, have come to represent traditional religion. At the other end of the continuum, the Pueblos devote most religious attention to the calendrical cycle and have even communalized their curing ceremonies by creating medicine societies to fill the role played in less communally oriented societies by the individual shaman. (The Hopi are an exception, in that they still recognize individual medicine men and women.)

In general, the religious activities oriented around shamanic curing and the acquisition of personal power through individual control over supernatural resources occur in those societies with less (or no) emphasis on agriculture and without concentrated settlement patterns. Communal ceremonies interwoven with the seasonal cycle predominate in agriculture-dependent societies, which have developed highly elaborate and complex ritual systems; as Åke Hultkranz states, "No other Amerindian societies lay so much stress on ceremonialism" as do the Pueblos.

SEVERAL CAVEATS TO STUDENTS OF SOUTHWEST RELIGIONS. A key problem facing the student of Southwest Indian religions is sociocultural change. The Spanish conquest and colonization of the sixteenth and seventeenth centuries affected all Southwest cultures, though individual peoples were treated differently. Our knowledge of indigenous religious beliefs and practices is in some cases (for example, the Seri) severely limited by the wholesale abandonment of indigenous beliefs and their replacement with Christian concepts. Syncretism of traditional and introduced forms is, as among the Yaqui and Mayo, so historically entrenched that it is impossible to isolate the threads of precontact religious life. The traditional Yaqui and Mayo system of three religious sodalities fused in the seventeenth century with Jesuit beliefs and came to embody largely Christian notions, but these peoples' version of Christian ceremonies, such as the rituals recapitulating the Passion of Christ, incorporate traditional figures with clear similarities to the *kachinas* and clowns of the Pueblos. Since such syncretic processes began long before careful ethnographic records were made of indigenous belief and practice, the "pure forms" are simply irretrievable.

The Pueblos, the Navajo, and the Apache have maintained more of their traditional religious systems intact than other Southwest peoples. Of these groups, the Pueblos have the most complex religious systems, which in many instances preserve indigenous forms intact and distinct from religious elements introduced by Europeans. Hence I shall focus upon the Pueblos in this essay. The persistence of Pueblo religious patterns, despite almost four hundred years of colonial domination, is remarkable. The presence of Puebloan peoples in the Southwest, and of the earlier so-called Basket Makers, with whom there is a clear cultural continuity in the archaeological record, reaches far back into antiquity. The remains found in New Mexico's Chaco Canyon and Colorado's Mesa Verde of the civilization of the Anasazi are simply the better-known evidences of this socially complex and culturally sophisticated people, the direct ancestors of the historical Pueblos. The height of Anasazi culture (twelfth and thirteenth centuries CE) is represented by monumental architecture and elaborately constellated settlement patterns that suggest extensive social networks over large regions. For reasons we can only guess at—perhaps drought, war, disease, population pressure, internal social strife, or all of these in concert—the larger Anasazi pueblos had given way to the smaller pueblos by the time of the earliest historical records (c. 1540).

How much change and persistence have occurred in religion is an unfathomable problem. Nevertheless, the religious conservatism of the modern Pueblos, as well as archaeological indications (such as certain petroglyphs) suggest that more than a few Pueblo religious practices have persisted for a very long time. These two factors—the conservatism and antiquity of Pueblo religious practices—reflect another prominent characteristic: that the more important Pueblo beliefs and ritual practices are deliberately and rigorously preserved by an all-encompassing cloak of secrecy. The Pueblos have been and remain today extremely reluctant to reveal anything beyond the superficial aspects of their religious life. No anthropologists, apart from native Pueblo individuals, have been allowed to conduct extended resident field research by any of the Eastern Pueblos. Questions about religion meet with evasion or a purposive silence. Often information obtained by outsiders has been gathered in unusual ways, such as by interviewing individuals in hotel rooms distant from their pueblos. Only limited aspects of Pueblo religious performances are public; no non-Indian outsider has been permitted to witness a *kachina* performance in any of the Rio Grande pueblos since the seventeenth century.

Secrecy is pervasive not simply to preserve the integrity of traditional religion from the corrupting influences of the outside world, but also to protect the religious practices' integrity within the pueblos themselves. Initiates into religious societies are inculcated with the idea that their disclosure of secret, ritually imparted knowledge will have dire supernatural (their own or their relatives' deaths) and social (their ostracism from the pueblo) consequences. The result is that knowledge of Pueblo religion is fragmentary, flimsy, and in some cases inaccurate. We do know something of the surface contours of Pueblo religion, and these are discussed below. In deference to the Pueblos' rights to maintain their religions as they see fit, perhaps this surface level is as far as we may conscionably prosecute our inquiries.

The Pueblo Cosmos. In Pueblo thought generally, there is no absolute origin of life or of human beings. Although there have been a number of transformations since the earliest times, the earth and the people have always existed. Accordingly, there is less concern with primordial origins than with the process through which human beings were transformed into their present state of being from previous states.

Southwest peoples in general envision a multilayered cosmos whose structure is basically tripartite: "below," "this level," and "above." Each level has subdivisions, but the number and character of the subdivisions vary from culture to culture. All the Pueblos believe themselves to have originated beneath the present earth's surface. The layer below is characterized as a previous world, or as several previous worlds (or "wombs") stacked one atop another. The Zuni and the Keresans conceive of four previous worlds, the Hopi of three, and the Tewa only one. The last world "below" lies under a lake or under the earth's surface. At the beginning of the present age, the people were impelled—by supernatural signs in some versions of the Emergence story, by the need to flee evil in other versions—to seek a new life in the world above. By methods that vary from story to story (in some versions by climbing a tree, in others a giant reed), the people ascended to this level. The earth's condition was soft, and it required hardening. This was accomplished with the supernatural aid of the War Twins, who are found among all the Pueblo groups, or it was done by a human being with special powers—for example by the Winter Chief, who in the Tewa story hardened the ground with cold.

Accounts differ with regard to the creation of the Sun, Moon, and stars and to the origin of cultigens. For the Eastern Pueblos, the Sun was a beckoning force encouraging the people's ascent into this world. In Hopi tradition, by contrast, the ritual leaders had to create the Sun and Moon by flinging disks of buckskin or cotton into the sky. After the Emergence, the Hopi met with a quasi-anthropomorphous supernatural, Maasawu, who introduced them to maize, beans, and squash. The stars were formed, the Hopi recount, by Coyote's negligence. Coyote had been instructed to carry a sealed pot toward the eastern house of the Sun, but before he reached his destination he grew weary and decided, against instructions, to lift the lid off the pot. All the stars flew out and formed the Milky Way. In Zuni tradition, a supernatural slayer of monsters cut up one monster's body parts and threw them into the sky, where they became the stars.

The timing and methods of the creation of natural phenomena vary, but the trajectory of human progress is the same throughout the various Pueblo traditions. After their emergence onto the earth's surface through an opening referred to as an "earth navel," the people migrated over the earth, stopping at locations that are identified by oral tradition with the numerous ruins throughout the Southwest, before reaching their final destination in the present-day villages. Variant migration patterns reflect differing forms of social organization: the matrilineal clans of the Hopi migrated independently and arrived at the present Hopi towns as separate units, whereas the two moieties of the Tewa— Winter and Summer—migrated down opposite banks of the Rio Grande from their Emergence point in the north.

Hence Pueblo origin myths emphasize the process of becoming the Pueblo peoples of the present. Each pueblo is highly independent, and, but for exceptional occasions requiring dire responses (such as in the Pueblo Revolt of 1680 or during severe famines), there is no political unity among pueblos whatsoever. Such independence is reflected in Pueblo worldview: each pueblo regards itself as the center of the bounded universe. Forces radiate both centripetally from the outer limits and centrifugally from a shrine at the pueblo's center, which is represented as the heart of the cosmos. Thus the Zuni are "the people of the middle place," the Hopi of Second Mesa live at the universe center, and each of the various Tewa villages lies about its "earth-mother earth-navel middle place" (Ortiz, 1969, p. 21). The outer limits of the world are marked variously. Among the Eastern Pueblos and the Acoma and Laguna, the world is a rectangular flat surface (although of course broken by topography) bounded by sacred mountains in the cardinal directions. For the Zuni, the surface is circular and is surrounded by oceans that are connected by underworld rivers. The Hopi world is more abstractly bounded, although sacred mountains and rivers act as circumscribing features.

All Pueblo worlds are rigorously aligned by six cardinal directions, four of which correspond to our north, west, south, and east (or, in the Hopi case, sunrise and sunset points on the horizon at the solstices—roughly northwest, southwest, southeast, and northeast) and the zenith and nadir. From the viewpoint of its inhabitants, each pueblo lies at the center formed by the intersection of the axes of opposed directions. The directions are symbolized by numerous devices: colors, mammals, birds, snakes, trees, shells, sacred lakes, deity houses, and so forth.

The Zuni and the Tewa seem to have elaborated the axial schema to the greatest extent. For the Zuni, the six directions serve as a multipurpose organizational model for society—in terms of matrilineal clan groupings, priesthood sodalities, *kiva* (ceremonial chamber) groupings—and for nature, in that the taxonomy of species is directionally framed. The fourfold plan (i.e., excluding the vertical axis) of the earth's surface is represented by the Tewa as a series of concentric tetrads, which are marked by four mountains at their extremities and by four flat-topped hills, four directional shrines, and four village plazas as the center is approached. Neither is this a static abstraction in Tewa belief: ritual dancers in the plazas must face the four directions; songs have four parts; and so forth. Each of the physical features marking the corners of the concentric boundaries (the four mountains, hills, shrines, and plazas) is a place of power. Each contains an "earth navel" that connects the three levels of the cosmos and that is presided over by particular supernaturals.

THE PUEBLO PANTHEON. Associated with the levels and sectors of the Pueblo world is a panoply of supernatural beings. Elsie C. Parsons (1939) divides these beings into collective and individualized categories.

Collective supernaturals. The collective category signally includes clouds, the dead, and the *kachinas*. Clouds and the dead have an explicit association: the specific destiny of the deceased person depends upon the role he played during life, but in general the dead become clouds. The cloud beings are classified according to the directions and, accordingly, associated with colors. *Kachina* is a fluid spiritual concept that refers both to supernatural beings and to their masked impersonators at Pueblo ceremonies. *Kachinas* appear in numerous guises and represent many features of the natural and supernatural worlds. They are dramatized in masked impersonation and in stories, where they appear in the forms of animals, plants, birds, the sun, and stars and as spirits such as the War Twins, sky deities, culture heroes, and so on. Some *kachinas* also represent game animals, and *kachinas* associated with the directions are also linked with hunting. *Kachinas* dwell in locations on the edges of the bounded world: in mountains, for instance, or in lakes or other sites associated with the powers of moisture. The three concepts of the dead, the clouds, and the *kachinas* overlap: the dead may become *kachinas*, and *kachinas* may manifest themselves as clouds. The interrelation among clouds, the dead, and *kachinas* points up a significant concern of Pueblo beliefs and ritual practices: the importance of rainfall in this largely arid environment is paramount, and the *kachinas*, as rain spirits, have the power to bring rain to nourish the crops—the central link in the Pueblo chain of being.

Individualized supernaturals. In some respects, individualized supernaturals reflect the arrangement of the cosmos into levels. Thus among the Hopi, Sootukw-nangw ("star-cumulus cloud"), the zenith deity, is associated with lightning and powerful rain; Muyingwu, an earth deity associated with the nadir, is the spirit of maize, germination, and vegetation; and Maasawu is the guardian of this level, the surface of the earth. But each of these figures has multiple aspects and cannot be neatly slotted into an abstract cosmic layer. Through his power to shoot lightning like arrows, Sootukw-nangw is also an important war deity, and Maasawu, especially, has a cluster of characteristics. He is associated with fire, war, death, and the night, and he looks and behaves in a more manlike fashion than do the deities of above and below. Supernaturals associated with cosmic features also embody moral principles (Maasawu represents humility, conservatism, lack of avarice, serious commitment to the duties of life, and the terrifying consequences of excessive individualism) and biological principles (Sootukwnangw's lightning arrows are associated with male fertilization). Further, there is a plethora of other supernaturals who are not arranged hierarchically but who crystallize a number of religious concerns. The Pueblo pantheon lacks systematization: supernaturals often overlap in meaning and function, and this is further evident in the pattern of religious organization. Discrete segments of Pueblo society often focus exclusively upon the sets of supernaturals under their control; individuals not in a particular social segment do not have rights of appeal to its set of deities, and they risk severe social repercussions for unauthorized attempts at intercourse with such deities.

The sun, regarded everywhere as male, is a powerful fertilizing force, the father in relation to the earth, who is the mother. Traditionally, every individual was expected to offer cornmeal and to say a prayer to the sun at dawn, when the sun leaves his house (or *kiva*) at the eastern edge of the world and begins his journey to his western house. Prayers to the sun refer to the desire for a long and untroubled path of life for each individual. After a period of seclusion in darkness, the newborn Pueblo infant is taken out and shown to the sun to request a long and happy life and the sun's beneficent attention. As Father, the sun is equated with the care and spiritual nurturance of his children. Songs are addressed to him to ask for his life-giving powers of light and warmth, kept in balance so as not to burn the crops or dry them out. Sun is also a deity of hunting and war; the Keresans, Tiwa, and Hopi seek his assistance in these endeavors.

Other celestial deities. Less significant by comparison, other celestial deities include, first, the moon, who is variously female (Zuni, where Moonlight-Giving Mother is the sun's wife) and male (Tewa, Towa, Tiwa). Moon is rarely addressed in prayer or song. In association with the sun and some constellations, however, the moon's movements and phases are utilized to plan the calendrical cycle of ceremonies. The antiquity of such practices is suggested by the numerous lunar and solar marking devices found in prehistoric Puebloan sites, such as the well-known Sun-Dagger petroglyphs in Chaco Canyon.

The morning star and the constellations Orion and the Pleiades have associations with war and with the timing of ceremonies. The movement of celestial phenomena is critically linked to the seasonal passage of the year. The ceremonial moiety division of the Tewa into Winter and Summer people, each of which has ritual and political charge of half the year, is an indication of the thoroughgoing nature of seasonal principles. The Hopi and Zuni divide their seasons by the solstices, the Tewa by the equinoxes, but the pattern of opposed dual principles is pervasive.

Dawn is deified in the form of Dawn Youths (Tewa), Dawn Mothers (Zuni), and Dawn Woman (Hopi). At Hopi, Dawn Woman is linked with another female deity, Huruingwuuti ("hard substances woman"), who has a formative role in the cosmogonic process. In the Keresan pueblos, she seems to have a counterpart in Thought Woman, whose every thought became manifest into substance. Thought Woman mythologically precedes Iyatiku, a chthonic being who is the mother of people, *kachinas*, game, and maize and who occupies the most prominent role in the Keresan pantheon. Iyatiku is in some respects parallel to Muyingwu, the Hopi maize and germination deity of the below. The principle of human and animal fertility is represented at Hopi by Tiikuywuuti ("child-water woman"), who is Muyin-gwu's sister.

Other common supernaturals. This group includes the War Twins, who are war gods, culture heroes, and patrons of gamblers; the maternal spirit animating the earth (whose body parts may be represented by vegetation, hills, and canyons); the Feathered and Horned Serpent, who lives in the water forms of the earth—springs, pools, rivers, the oceans—and who is a dangerous, powerful water deity responsible for floods and earthquakes; Spider Grandmother, a cosmogonic creator whom the Hopi consider grandmother of the War Twins; Salt Woman or Salt Man, deities of salt lakes and other salt sources; Fire Old Woman, Ash Man, and Ash Boy, with obvious associations; a giant eagle, or Knife Wing (Zuni), one of several war deities; Poseyemu, generally father of the curing societies, a miracle worker, and a possible syncretic counterpart of Christ; the master spirits of particular animals, such as Bear, Badger, Mountain Lion, Wolf, and Coyote, who are patrons of specific curing societies; the sun's children, patrons of the clown societies; and many others.

Each of these supernatural entities embodies a different form of power. They are, however, discrete forms and not subsumable under a concept of pervasive supernatural power such as *mana* or *orenda.* They may be harnessed by human beings and used to transform events and states in the world. Access to power is, however, strictly limited in these societies and is based upon initiation into a religious sodality and, especially, a priestly office. There is no vision quest whereby power (at least for males) is democratically accessible.

Religious Organization and Ritual Practice. The basic form of religious organization in the pueblos consists of ritual societies, which serve a variety of purposes. Pueblo religion focuses on a number of issues: agricultural fertility and productivity, human fertility, fertility and productivity of game animals, war, and curing. These major issues are further divisible into aspects. Thus agricultural concerns are trained on the attainment of adequate—but not excessive—moisture, adequate heat and light, and the effective prevention of many crop pests and of excessive wind and cold. Rituals concerning game animals and hunting may be divided according to the species pursued. War society rituals are prophylactic, ensuring strength and success, as well as being celebrations of victory and rituals of purifying and sacralizing scalps taken in battle. Curing societies are organized according to the types of sicknesses they cure. "Bear medicine," "Badger medicine," and so forth are sympathetically and contagiously associated with particular ailments and are used by societies of the same names to produce cures. Typically, societies are composed of small numbers of priests and some lay members, and each society follows an annual cycle of ritual undertakings. In their most spectacular forms, such undertakings climax in dramatic public performances at specified times of the calendrical cycle.

Hopi religious societies. An examination of Hopi religious societies provides insight into the structure of such societies in Pueblo cultures generally. In Hopi thought, the religious societies have different degrees of importance and confer different degrees of power on the initiated. A ranking of the societies into three orders of ascending importance may be constructed as follows (translations are given where Hopi names are translatable): *Kachina* and Powamuy are third-order societies; Blue Flute, Gray Flute, Snake, Antelope, Lakon, and Owaqöl are second-order societies; and Wuwtsim, One Horn, Two Horn, Singers, Soyalangw, and Maraw are first-order societies.

Each of these societies focuses upon a different set of supernatural beings and a different set of specific concerns. The ranking into three orders parallels the age requirements for initiation into particular societies. All children aged six to ten (male and female) are initiated into either (the choice is their parents') the *Kachina* or the Powamuy society. After this initiation, they are eligible to join second-order societies, although not all individuals will actually join. (Second-order societies are distinguished by sex: Lakon and Owaqöl are female; the rest male.) At about age sixteen, all males (traditionally) are initiated into one of the four manhood societies (Wuwtsim, One-Horn, Two-Horn, Singers) and females into the Maraw (womanhood) society. Initiation into one of the manhood societies, together with birthright, is prerequisite to participation in the Soyalangw society; since this society carries no formal initiation, it can be regarded as a more exclusive extension of the manhood societies.

The ceremonial cycle. The public dimension of each society's activities is concentrated at particular points in an annual liturgy. The beginning of the year, which is reckoned in lunar months, falls from late October to late November and is marked by the manhood society ceremonies. Following an eight-day retreat in the *kivas* (semisubterranean ceremonial chambers), which involves private rituals, two of the societies (the Wuwtsim and the Singers) process slowly around the village in two facing columns. (Members of both societies are in each column.) The columns are "guarded" at both ends by some members of the Two-Horn society. The Wuwtsim and Singers sing songs composed for the occasion, some of which poke fun at the sexual proclivities of the Maraw society (the women's counterpart to the Wuwtsim society). The remaining members of the Two-Horn society and all the One-Horns are meanwhile continuing with private rituals in their respective *kivas*. After the final circuit of the Wuwtsim and Singers, all the Two-Horn and One-Horn members, in two separate processions (which are dramatic although unaccompanied by song) visit a series of shrines around the village and deposit offerings. Each manhood society is regarded as complementary to the other three, and each is associated with a particular religious concern: the Wuwtsim and Singers with fertility, the Two-Horns with hunting and game animals, and the One-Horns with the dead and with supernatural protection of the village.

A month later, at the time of the winter solstice, the Soyalangw ceremony occurs. This is one of the most complex Hopi ceremonies and involves the participation of the most important priests in the village. They ritually plan the events of the coming year and perform a variety of ritual activities concerned with reversing the northward movement of the sun and with the regeneration of human, floral (both wild and cultivated), faunal (wild and domestic), and meteorological harmony. Several key themes of Hopi religious concern are sounded in this winter solstice ceremony, which renews and reorients the world and man's position within it. After Soyalangw, game animal dances are held (nowadays particularly Buffalo Dances). These are regarded as "social" dances, as are a group of dances performed in September, which include, among others, Butterfly Dances and "Navajo Dances." The distinction between social dances and sacred performances is not completely clear; songs sung at social dances frequently express desires for beneficial climatic conditions, and in general the social dances evince continuity with the religious concerns of the sacred performances. Clearly, however, the social dances are regarded with less solemnity, and there are only minor religious proscriptions on the performers.

The Soyalangw ceremony opens the *kachina* "season." *Kachinas* are impersonated in repeated public performances from January to July. As has been noted, the *kachina* concept is multiple. The *kachina* costume worn by impersonator-performers includes a mask (there are more than three hundred kinds) and specific garments and body paints. The Hopi regard the masked representations of *kachinas* to be fully efficacious manifestations of the *kachina* spirits; when speaking English, they avoid the term *mask* because of the implication that "masking" is somehow less than real. Many *kachinas* have distinct emblematic calls and stylized body movements. *Kachina* performers represent a great variety of spirits, including those of plant and animal species, deities, and mythological figures of both benign (e.g., the "mudheads") and severe (e.g., the cannibal ogres) countenance. Positive and negative social values are sometimes fused in the same *kachina*. Often a *kachina* represents many elements and practices simultaneously and contains a thick condensation of symbolic devices. Some *kachinas* ("chief *kachinas*") are more important than others and are "owned" by particular clans and regarded as significant clan deities. Usually from January through March *kachinas* appear in groups to dance at night in the *kivas*; for the remainder of the *kachina* season, they appear during the day to dance in the village plaza. During daytime performances, the *kachinas* may be accompanied by a group of unmasked sacred clowns, who conduct a ceremony in parallel to the *kachina* performance. Clowns are given broad license and are social commentators *par excellence*. They expose numerous social aberrancies on the part of village members and poke fun at everything from sacred ceremonial actions to current events.

The two most important *kachina* ceremonies occur in February (Powamuy, "the bean dance") and in July (Niman, "the home dance"). At Powamuy, children may be initiated into either the *Kachina* or Powamuy society in an evening ceremony inside a *kiva*. During the day a large and multifarious assemblage of *kachinas* proceeds in ceremonial circuits around the village. This facinating and beautiful pageant features a series of minipageants occurring in different parts of the village simultaneously. Powamuy purifies the earth and also prefigures the planting season. Beans are germinated in soil boxes in the *kivas* by the artificial warmth of constant fires. During the day of the public pageant, the bean plants are distributed by *kachinas* to each household, where they are cooked in a stew. At the same time the *kachinas* distribute painted wooden *kachina* dolls and basketry plaques to girls and painted bows and arrows to boys, ensuring their futures as fertile mothers and brave warrior-hunters.

The Niman ("homegoing") ceremony, marks the last *kachina* performance of the year. At the close of Niman, the *kachinas* are formally "sent" by several priests back to their mountainous homes in the San Francisco Peaks and elsewhere. They are requested to take the prayers of the people back with them and to present them to the community of *kachina* spirits.

The *kachina* season is followed by the season of "unmasked" ceremonies. In August occur the Snake-Antelope ceremonies or the Flute ceremonies, the performance of which alternates from year to year. In either case, the two societies from which the ceremonies take their names come together at this time to perform complex rituals that last nine days. The Snake-Antelope rites include a public performance in which the Snake men slowly dance in pairs around the plaza while the Antelope men form a horseshoe-shaped line around them and intone chants. The Snake-Antelope and the Flute ceremonies are densely expressive. Both include a magical attempt to bring clouds over the fields to give rain to the crops; both mark the sun's passage; and both dramatize the mythological entrance of particular clans into the village.

Following these ceremonies in the annual liturgy come the ceremonies of the women's societies. The Lakon and Owaqöl, both referred to in English as Basket Dances, feature a circular dance in the plaza. Selected society members run in and out of the circle throwing gifts to the men, who throng the edges of the circle and dispute over the gifts. Both Lakon and Owaqöl women hold basketry plaques in front of them while they sing. The Maraw society's ceremony features a similar circle in which women hold long prayer-sticks. A number of other rites occur during the nine-day Maraw, including burlesques of male ceremonial activities. Maraw rites relate to war and fertility; Lakon and Owaqöl rites stress fertility and the celebration of the harvest.

This bare outline of the Hopi ceremonial cycle reveals some basic concerns of Pueblo religion. The timing of ceremonies is intimately connected with the annual progress of nature. The *kachina* performances are especially related to the life cycle of cultivated plants, and they occur at critical points in this cycle. The first ceremonies of the year prefigure the planting and successful fruition of crops; they are designed to bring snow and rain to saturate the earth with moisture, which will remain there until planting occurs in April. The daytime *kachina* performances likewise seek rainfall to help the crops grow. Niman, the Homegoing, signals the end of the early phases of crop maturation; the *kachinas*' departure suggests that the spirits of the crops are sufficiently mature no longer to require the *kachinas*' nurturance. The Snake-Antelope and Flute ceremonies complete the course of metaphysical encouragement and nourishment of the crops. Coming at the hottest, driest time of the year, they invoke powerful forces to bring one last bout of rain to ensure the full maturing of the crops and to prevent the sun's fierce gaze from withering them. The women's society Basket Dances celebrate the success of the harvest by the joyful distribution of basketry plaques and household goods.

Private rituals. All ceremonies include private rituals in *kivas* prior to the public performance. Typically such private rituals include the construction of an altar, which consists of a rectangular sand painting in front of a vertical assemblage of painted and carved wooden pieces that incorporate symbolic designs of birds, animals, and supernaturals. The sand painting also incorporates many symbolic elements. Long songs are incanted over the altar, and tobacco is ceremonially smoked and blown to portray clouds. (Smoking binds together the hearts of the priests as they pass the pipe around a circle and gives them a collective power to express their prayers more forcefully.) The *kiva* itself is a multiplex symbol: it is axially oriented by the directions, and at its center is a hole representing the *sipapu*, the place of emergence from the world below. The *kiva*'s four levels, from the underfloor to the roof, are identified with the worlds through which man has ascended; the passage into this world is portrayed by the *sipapu* and the *kiva* ladder that leads to the roof.

Maize Symbolism and Ritual. Maize is the dominant, pervasive symbol of Hopi religious life. Maize is regarded as the mother of people, since it is the primary sustainer of human life. "Corn *is* life," the Hopi say. Two perfect ears of white maize are given to a newborn child as its "mothers"; when a person dies, ears of blue maize similarly accompany him on his journey beyond life. Maize seeds, ears, tassels, milk, pollen, and meal all serve as sacramental elements in differing contexts. Moreover, other important symbols are related to the maize cycle. Clouds, rains, lightning, feathered serpents, and various species associated with water, such as frogs, ducks, reeds, and so forth, all underline a paramount interest in securing water for maize.

Two devices, above all others, serve as mechanisms for establishing holiness or for communicating with supernatural forces: cornmeal and prayer feathers. Corn-meal is an all-purpose sanctifying substance; it is sprinkled on *kachina* dancers, used to form spiritual paths for *kachinas* and the dead, offered to the sun and to one's own field of growing maize plants, and accompanies all forms of private and public prayer. The act of making a prayer to various supernatural forms with the sprinkled offering of cornmeal may be considered the most fundamental religious act for the Hopi as for all the Pueblos.

Feathers of many different bird species are used in innumerable ways in Hopi ritual; they are worn in the hair and around arms and ankles, and they decorate *kachina* masks, altars, and religious society emblems. Prayer sticks and prayer feathers are the two basic forms of feather offerings. Prayer sticks, carved in human or supernatural forms, are living manifestations of prayer and are simultaneously petitions for aid. Feathers are regarded as particularly effective vehicles for conveying messages to supernaturals: they "carry" the prayers of people with them.

Comparisons. It is evident from the Hopi situation that religious action is multiple. There is no single set of activities we can demarcate as "Hopi religion" as distinct from Hopi agriculture or even Hopi politics, since political activity goes on even within the context of private ceremonial gatherings. Also, the exclusiveness of religious societies above the third order suggests a socially fragmented pattern of religious belief and practice. Religious knowledge is highly valued and tightly guarded, and it serves as the primary means of making status distinctions in Hopi society. Hopi explanations of the diversity of their religious activities point to historical circumstances: each cult is identified with a particular clan that introduced it when the clan negotiated admission to the village in the distant past. Although lay cult members may be from any clan, the chief priests should always be of the clan which "owns" the ceremony. In part, then, ceremonial performances celebrate separate clan identities and mark off particular ritual activities as the exclusive prerogative of particular clans. This pattern of closed ceremonial societies with exclusive rights in certain forms of religious action is a fundamental characteristic of Pueblo religion.

The Zuni cult system. Other Pueblo groups depart significantly from the Hopi scheme yet still exhibit similarities that suggest some common patterns of belief and practice. Ethnologists have identified six major types of cults or societies among the Zuni.

1. *The Sun cult.* Responsibility for the important religiopolitical officer called the *pekwin* (Sun priest) belongs to the Sun cult. Membership is restricted to males, and the sodality conducts its ceremonies at the solstices.
2. *The Uwanami ("rainmakers") cult.* This cult is composed of twelve distinct priesthoods of from two to six members each. Membership is hereditary within certain matrilineal families. Each priesthood holds retreats (but no public ceremonies) during the summer months from July through September.
3. *The Kachina cult.* Unlike the Hopi *Kachina* society, membership in the Zuni *Kachina* society is not open to females. The cult has six divisions, which are associated with the six directions and are accordingly headquartered in six *kiva*s. Each *kiva* group dances at least three times per year: in summer, in winter following the solstice, and following the Shalako ceremony in late November or early December.
4. *The cult of the kachina priests.* Whereas the *Kachina* society is primarily concerned with rain and moisture, the cult of the *kachina* priests focuses on fecundity—of human beings and game animals. The *kachina* priests are responsible for the six Shalako *kachina*s, the ten-foot-tall, birdlike figures whose appearance marks the most spectacular of Zuni religious dramas, and for the koyemsi ("mudhead") *kachina*s, who are at once dangerously powerful beings and foolish clowns. Other *kachina*s under the charge of the *kachina* priests appear at solstice ceremonies, at the Shalako ceremonies, and every fourth year at the time when newcomers are initiated into the general *Kachina* cult.
5. *The War Gods cult.* The Bow priesthood, which is exclusively male, controls the War Gods cult. Traditionally, initiation required the taking of an enemy's scalp. The Bow priests are leaders in war and protectors of the village, and they serve as the executive arm of the religiopolitical hierarchy, in which role they prosecute witches. (The extinct Momtsit society may have been the Hopi counterpart of the Bow priests.)
6. *The Beast Gods cult.* The cult is overseen by twelve curing societies, and membership is open to both men and women. Each society focuses on a particular source of supernatural power, which is embodied in the bear, mountain lion, or another predatory animal. The individual societies practice general medicine, but each also specializes in healing specific afflictions. The collective ceremonies of the societies are held in the fall and winter.

The division of Zuni religious practice into cults is underpinned by an extremely complex ceremonial calendar that coordinates and interrelates ritual activities throughout the year. Each cult has a cycle that includes private and public ritual actions and that begins and ends with the winter solstice. As among the Hopi, the year is divided by the solstices. From winter to summer solstice, the main focuses of ceremonial action are medicine, war, and human and game-animal fertility. Throughout the summer, ceremonial emphasis is upon rain and the maturation of the crops. At the solstices, all major religious interests converge. Thus at Zuni, religious organization shows significant differences of emphasis, formally and functionally, though these appear as nuances rather than radical divergences. Overall, there appears to be greater emphasis on curing and less on agriculture than at Hopi, a difference of emphasis that intensifies as one moves on to Pueblo groups further east.

Keresan Pueblo religious practice. Among the Keresan Pueblos—Acoma and Laguna to the west, Santo Domingo, Cochiti, San Felipe, Santa Ana, and Zia to the east on the Río Grande and its tributaries—the chief religious organizations are referred to as "medicine societies." With variations from pueblo to pueblo, the basic pattern consists of four major medicine societies—Flint, Cikame (an untranslatable Keresan word), Giant, and Fire—and a number of minor societies, including Ant, Bear, Eagle, and Lizard. The medicine societies conduct a communal curing ceremony in the spring, echoing a theme of the Hopi Bean Dance, and they hold performances throughout the year to effect the cure of individual patients. The societies also have rainmaking functions, which they fulfill at private ritual retreats during the summer months. Reportedly, these societies erect altars and construct sand paintings similar to those described for the Hopi and the Zuni. The same major sacramental elements—prayer sticks and cornmeal—are central vehicles for religious action, and extensive songs and prayers designed to make unseen power manifest in the world are a key part of ceremonial content. The medicine societies also have important roles in solstitial ceremonies aimed at reversing the course of the sun.

Other important Keresan societies include a paired group: the Koshare, which is a clown society parallel in many ways to Hopi clown societies, and the Kwirena, which is primarily associated with weather control. A Hunters society, with a permanently installed "hunt chief," and a Warriors society, composed of scalp-takers, are other important societies that traditionally held ceremonies during the winter. A village-wide *Kachina* society is divided into two ceremonial moieties, Turquoise and Squash, associated with the two *kiva*s in the village. *Kachina* performances by both moieties occur during fall and winter, but especially during the summer immediately following the rainmaking retreats of the medicine societies. These retreats include a supernatural journey to the *sipapu*, from which the *kachina*s are brought back to the village. As among other Pueblo groups, ritual activities among the Keresans are dominated by males; although both sexes may join medicine societies, women serve as secondary assistants, and only men may perform as *kachina*s.

The climatic and ecological situation of the Keresan Pueblos is of much greater reliability than that of the Hopi. The Keresans' religious concern with the agricultural cycle is evident, but, since the Keresans have irrigation and more plentiful precipitation, they put less emphasis on the agricultural and more on the curing functions of religious societies. A primary function of the more important medicine societies is to combat witchcraft by evil-hearted human beings and evil supernaturals, which is believed to be the cause of illness. Witchcraft is, and has been historically, a profound concern of Hopi and Zuni also, although at Hopi the concern receives less concerted attention from the major religious societies.

The theme of dualism, which appears at Hopi and Zuni in the form of the solstitial switching of ritual emphases, is manifested at the Keresan Pueblos with the division of the ceremonial organization into moieties centered in two *kivas*.

Tewa, Tiwa, and Towa religious systems. The theme of dualism in Southwest religion achieves perhaps its maximum expression in the religious life of the six Tewa pueblos: San Juan, Santa Clara, San Ildefonso, Tesuque, Nambe, and Pojoaque. The division of people into Winter and Summer ceremonial moieties is part of a thoroughgoing dual scheme phrased in terms of seasonal opposition. The division of significance among the Tewa is by equinoxes; the seasonal transfer ceremony that is held (roughly) at each equinox places one or the other of the ceremonial moieties in charge of the village for the following season. Hence there are two overarching religious leaders, or caciques, each the head of a moiety. The calendar of religious activities is planned in accordance with the division into summer (agricultural activities) and winter (nonagricultural activities).

Typically, each Tewa pueblo has two *kivas* in which the ceremonial moieties are headquartered. There are eight religious societies in all: the Winter and Summer moiety societies, each headed by a moiety priest; the Bear Medicine society; the Kwirena ("cold clowns") and Kossa ("warm clowns") societies; the Hunt society; the Scalp society; and the Women's society. The most intensive ritual activity occurs between the autumnal and vernal equinoxes. This contrasts with the Hopi model, in which the most active part of the cycle occurs from the winter to the summer solstice (and just thereafter). Parallel elements are otherwise clear: religious-society organization among the Tewa is reminiscent of the nearby Keresans. Religious concerns, too, are similar between the Tewa and Keresan Pueblos, though the Tewa Pueblos place less emphasis on curing. The main sacraments are the same; the *kachina* performance is a fundamental religious practice, though more restricted here than among the Hopi, Zuni, and western Keresans.

The traditional religious practices of the Tiwa pueblos—Taos and Picuris in the north and Sandia and Isleta in the south—are the least well known. Taos, in particular, has been most effective in protecting matters it regards as not appropriate for public consumption. At Taos, each of the six *kivas* (which are divided into three on the "north side" and three on the "south side" of the pueblo) houses a religious society. *Kiva* society initiation involves a set of rituals prolonged over a number of years and is restricted by inheritance to a select group. The *kiva* organization at Taos seems to serve the same purpose as religious societies at other pueblos. At Taos, there is greater ritual emphasis upon game animals and hunting, in line with the pueblo's close cultural ties with Plains peoples, than there is upon the agricultural cycle. Taos may be the only pueblo in which *kachinas* are not represented in masked performances. Picuris seems traditionally to have done so, and it otherwise exhibits more religious similarity with the Tewa pueblos than it does with Taos, its close linguistic neighbor. *Kachinas* do occur, however, in Taos myths.

The southern Tiwa in Isleta pueblo have a system of ceremonial moieties divided into Winter (Black Eyes) and Summer (Red Eyes), each with its "moiety house" (which is equivalent to a *kiva*). In addition, Isleta Pueblo's five Corn groups, associated with directions and colors, seem to parallel *kiva* organizations at Taos. The moieties conduct seasonal transfer ceremonies similar to those at Tewa pueblos, and likewise each moiety controls the ritual activities for the season over which it presides. The ceremonial cycle is attenuated in comparison with that at other pueblos; there is a Land Turtle Dance in the spring and a Water Turtle Dance in the fall. Although unverified, it has been reported that *kachina* performances are conducted by a colony of Laguna Pueblo people who have lived in Isleta since the late nineteenth century.

Jemez, the only modern representative of the Towa Pueblos, exhibits an extraordinarily complex ceremonial organization, with twenty-three religious societies and two *kiva* moieties. Every Jemez male is initiated into either the Eagle society or the Arrow society; other societies are more exclusive. Societies can be classified according to function: curing, rainmaking and weather control, fertility, war and protection, and hunting. The Jemez ceremonial cycle includes a series of retreats by the different religious societies. In the summer, these celebrate agricultural growth; in the fall the ripening of crops; in the winter war, rain, ice, snow, and game animals; and in the spring the renewal of the forces of life. The two ceremonial *kiva* moieties are Turquoise and Squash, the same as among the eastern Keresans, and although the principle of dualism is in evidence it is not so pronounced as among the Tewa.

Life, Death, and Beyond. The Pueblos hold that an individual's life follows a path, or plan, that is present in his fate from birth. A long, good life and a peaceful death in old age are the main requests contained in prayers delivered at the birth of a new person. Through the course of maturation, the person becomes increasingly incorporated, in a ritual sense, into the world. So the Tewa, for example, perform a series of childhood baptismal rites—"name giving," "water giving," "water pouring," and "finishing"—that progressively fix and identify the individual in relation to the forces of society and the cosmos. Religious society initiations and marriage mark further passages in the individual's path of life.

Beliefs about and rituals surrounding death reveal some of the most essential features of Pueblo conceptions of the nature of existence. I have noted above the association between the dead, clouds, and *kachina* spirits. In general, Pueblos believe that when a person dies, the spirit, or breath, returns to the place of the Emergence and becomes transformed into cloud. Cloud spirits have myriad conceptual associations, and the dead (or certain of them) may likewise be given special associations. So, although clouds are generally regarded as the spirits of all the ancestral dead, distinctions are also made between different afterlife destinations, which vary according to the status the deceased person held while alive.

All the Pueblos distinguish between two kinds of people: those who hold important religious offices (or who are initiated members of religious societies) and everyone else. The former are regarded as supernaturally and socially powerful, ritually significant people; the latter are commoners. For the Tewa, the distinction is between "made," or "completed," people and "dry food" people; for the Zuni, the distinction is between valuable and ceremonially poor, or unvaluable, people; among the Keresans the term *sishti* ("commoners") denotes those without ceremonial affiliation; and for the Hopi, the distinction is between *pavansinom* ("powerful" or "completed" people) and *sukavungsinom* (common people).

The afterlife fate of these different categories may vary from one Pueblo group to another. Deceased members of the Hopi Two-Horn and One-Horn societies judge the newly dead at the house of the dead. Witches, suffering a different fate from that enjoyed by the righteous, may be transformed into stinkbugs! Zuni rain priests join the *uwanami* spirits who live in the waters, whereas Zuni Bow priests join their spiritual counterparts in the world above as makers of lightning. Other religious society members return to the place of the Emergence, but Zuni commoners go to "*kachina* village," the home of the *kachinas*, which is at a distance of two days' walk to the west of Zuni. In short, the social and religious organization in life is replicated in the organization of the dead.

SYNCRETISM AND CHANGE. The Pueblos were first exposed to Christian practices through the Franciscan friars who accompanied Francisco Vasquez de Coronado during his exploration of the Southwest (1540–1542). When the Province of New Mexico was made a colony of Spain in 1598, the Franciscan order was given special jurisdiction over the souls of the Indians. Missions were built in most of the pueblos; tributes were exacted; strenuous discipline was enforced; and extremely brutal punishments were levied for infractions of the total ban on indigenous religious practices. In reaction to this colonial domination, and especially to the religious oppression, all the pueblos united in an uprising in 1680, under the leadership of Popé, a Tewa priest. Many Spanish priests and colonists were killed, and the rest were forced to withdraw from New Mexico. Most of the pueblos immediately dismantled their missions. The Oraibi Hopi record that in the Great Pueblo Revolt the Roman Catholic priests were actually killed by warrior *kachinas*, symbolically demonstrating the spiritual rectitude of the action and the greater power of the indigenous religion.

Removed from the mainstream of Spanish settlements, the Hopi never allowed Spanish missions to be built among them again, and their religious practices remained free of Franciscan influence. The other Pueblos all suffered the reestablishment of missions after the Spanish reconquest of the 1690s. The influence of the missions depended upon the regularity and zeal with which they were staffed. At Zuni, a desultory missionary presence seems to have had little impact on traditional religious forms. The Rio Grande pueblos, on the other hand, came under a great deal of Franciscan influence. These pueblos are all nominally Catholic and observe many ceremonies of the Christian calendar. Each town has a patron saint and holds a large dance—called a Corn Dance or Tablita Dance—to celebrate the saint's day. The dance is thoroughly indigenous in character; however, a Christian shrine honoring the saint stands at one side of the plaza during the dance. At the conclusion of the dance, all the participants enter the church and offer prayers and thanks in a Christian fashion. Thus the two traditions coexist in a "compartmentalized" fashion. In some areas, such as rites of passage, Christian practices have supplanted indigenous Pueblo forms, especially in those pueblos that have become increasingly acculturated during the twentieth century (Pojoaque, Isleta, Picuris, and Laguna are examples). Many Eastern Pueblos have also taken over Spanish and Mexican religious dramas, such as the Matachine performances, which are also practiced among the Yaqui, Mayo, and Tarahumara.

Protestant churches have been attempting to proselytize the Pueblos since the latter nineteenth century, though in general without much success. Despite sustained longterm efforts by the Mennonites, Baptists, Methodists, Roman Catholics, Mormons, and Jehovah's Witnesses among the Hopi, their rate of conversion to Christianity has remained below 10 percent. On the other hand, major Christian holidays such as Christmas and Easter are popular occasions and may be having some impact on traditional religion. A *kachina* dance is regularly scheduled for Easter weekend nowadays, and among the array of presents they bring the *kachinas* include baskets of colored eggs. Regarding other nontraditional religions, only at Taos has peyotism to some extent been adopted, and even there its practice is evidently kept compartmentalized and apart from both indigenous religious practice and Catholicism.

CONCLUSION. The religious traditions of other Indians of the Southwest contain their own conceptual and historical complexities. I have chosen to focus upon the Pueblos here because of the richness of their extant religious practices and because of the separate treatment that the Apache and the Navajo receive in this encyclopedia. This does not imply that Pueblo religions are somehow representative of the religions of other native Southwest peoples, though certain Pueblo themes are echoed in different ways among non-Pueblo peoples. Sodalities and clown societies exist among the Yaqui and Mayo; sand painting is practiced by the Navajo, Pima, and Papago; and masked impersonators of supernatural beings perform rainmaking dances among the Havasupai, Yavapai, Pima, and Papago: but these common threads occur in cloths of quite different weaves. Let me emphasize at the last that the indigenous Southwest is enormously diverse. The sheer complexity of its religious practices belies any attempt to standardize these into a meaningful common pattern.

See Also Apache Religious Traditions; Clowns; Navajo Religious Traditions; Power.

Bibliography

On account of their richness and complexity, Southwest Indian religions have proven irresistible to generations of scholars. As the cradle of American anthropology, the indigenous Southwest has produced perhaps a greater volume of ethnographic studies than any other comparably populated area in the world. W. David Laird's *Hopi Bibliography: Comprehensive and Annotated* (Tucson, 1977), for example, contains listings for about three thousand items on this people alone. The contemporary *sine qua non* of Southwest ethnographic material is the *Handbook of North American Indians*, vols. 9 and 10, The Southwest, edited by Alfonso Ortiz (Washington, D.C., 1979, 1983). Encyclopedic in scope, these volumes treat Pueblo (vol. 9) and non-Pueblo (vol. 10) cultures; particularly pertinent synthetic articles include Dennis Tedlock's "Zuni Religion and World-View" (vol. 9, pp. 499–508), Arlette Frigout's "Hopi Ceremonial Organization" (vol. 9, pp. 564–576), Louis A. Hieb's "Hopi World View" (vol. 9, pp. 577–580), and Louise Lamphere's "Southwestern Ceremonialism" (vol. 10, pp. 743–763). Complex and detailed statements on specific religious practices may be found in the numerous writings of Jesse Walter Fewkes, H. R. Voth, and A. M. Stephen for the Hopi (see the Laird bibliography mentioned above); Frank H. Cushing for the Zuni; Matilda Coxe Stevenson for the Zuni and Zia; Leslie White for the individual Keresan pueblos; and Elsie C. Parsons for many Pueblo groups (the bibliography in volume 9 of the *Handbook* should be used for specific references).

I recommend a number of works (presented here in order of publication) that either focus specifically on religious practice or devote significant attention to it. H. K. Haeberlin's *The Idea of Fertilization in the Culture of the Pueblo Indians* (Lancaster, Pa., 1916) is an early synthesis that has yet to be superseded. Ruth L. Bunzel's "Introduction to Zuni Ceremonialism," in the *Forty-seventh Annual Report of the Bureau of American Ethnology* (Washington, D.C., 1932), and her other articles in the same volume are excellent windows not only into Zuni religion but into Pueblo religion more generally. The classic, comprehensive (albeit fragmentary) source is Elsie C. Parsons's *Pueblo Indian Religion*, 2 vols. (Chicago, 1939). Mischa Titiev's *Old Oraibi: A Study of the Hopi Indians of the Third Mesa* (Cambridge, Mass., 1944) is perhaps the best single account of the Hopi, although the second volume of R. Maitland Bradfield's *A Natural History of Associations: A Study in the Meaning of Community*, 2 vols. (London, 1973), brings together an enormous amount of earlier material on Hopi religion for a novel synthesis. Alfonso Ortiz's *The Tewa World* (Chicago, 1969) is the most sophisticated and best-written account of any of the Pueblos, and it stands as the single most essential monograph on one Pueblo people. Edward P. Dozier's *The Pueblo Indians of North America* (New York, 1970) is a complete, concise summary concerning all the Pueblos. *New Perspectives on the Pueblos*, edited by Alfonso Ortiz (Albuquerque, 1972), contains several articles on religious practices and beliefs. Although somewhat difficult of access for readers of English, two exceptionally good interpretations of Pueblo ritual and myth have appeared in French: Jean Cazeneuve's *Les dieux dansent à Cibola* (Paris, 1957) and Lucien Sebag's *L'invention du monde chez les Indiens pueblos* (Paris, 1971).

Beyond the Pueblos, and excluding the Navajo and the Apache, little of comparable depth exists. Ruth M. Underhill's *Papago Indian Religion* (New York, 1946) and *Singing for Power* (Berkeley, 1938) are notable exceptions, and her *Ceremonial Patterns in the Greater Southwest* (New York, 1948) is another historic synthesis. For sources on other Southwestern cultures, volume 10 of the *Handbook* is the best guide. Edward H. Spicer's *Cycles of Conquest: The Impact of Spain, Mexico, and the United States on the Indians of the Southwest, 1533–1960* (Tucson, 1962), cited above, is a thorough historical study of all indigenous Southwestern peoples.

Peter M. Whiteley (1987)

NOWRŪZ (lit., "new day"), the Iranian national festival that celebrates the arrival of spring. A festival of renewal, hope, and happiness, Nowrūz begins on the first day of Farvardīn, the first month of the Iranian solar calendar, at the spring equinox, and continues for twelve days. It is the most widely celebrated, the longest, and the most colorful of Iranian festivals, and though inherited from Zoroastrian Persia, it is the only festival that is not confined to a single religious group.

The origins of Nowrūz are obscure. In popular legend its institution is associated mostly with Jamshēd, the mythical Iranian king. In Firdawsi's epic, the *Shāh-nā mah* (completed about 1000 CE), it is said that the feast commemorates Jamshēd's ascent into the skies in a chariot built by the demons whom he had subdued and forced into the service of mortals. Nowrūz appears, however, to have been originally a pagan pastoral festival that marked the transition from winter to summer: rites of fertility and renovation can be easily recognized in some of its customs.

Zarathushtra (Zoroaster), the ancient prophet of Iran, probably reconsecrated Nowrūz to his religion. In any event, like Mihragan, the festival that marked the end of summer, Nowrūz continued to be observed in Zoroastrian Iran with full vigor; the two celebrations formed the festive poles of the Iranian calendar year. Nowrūz was immediately preceded by Hamaspathmaēdaya, a major religious feast that fell on the thirtieth day of the last month of the year (March 20) and was dedicated to the spirits of the departed, the *fravashis*. These spirits were thought to come down to the earth during this period to visit their abodes and to dwell with their families. In anticipation of the *fravashis*'s arrival, houses were cleaned, and food and drink were laid out for them. Nowrūz thus had a sober and commemorative prelude, informed by the remembrance of the departed family members, ancestors, and pious believers. Among the Zoroastrians the two festivals eventually merged, and the Farvardigan holidays came to comprise both.

In Zoroastrian Iran, Nowrūz proper began at dawn as the *fravashis* withdrew and the old year faded away. For the Zorastrians the festival also celebrated the creation of fire and its celestial guardian, Artavahisht. On the first day of spring, prayers were offered to Rapithwan, a helper of the powerful deity Mehr (Avestan, Mithra). Rapithwan, who personified noon, the ideal time, would withdraw underground during the winter months to protect the roots of plants and springs of water from frost, a creation of the demons. At Nowrūz, he would appear above ground to usher in the summer season.

The Achaemenid kings (559–330 BCE) celebrated Nowrūz above all at Persepolis, their capital, and some scholars have hypothesized that the parade of gift-bearers from various nations depicted in the bas-reliefs of the palace walls represent Nowrūz ceremonies. Under the Sassanids (226–652 CE), Nowrūz, together with Mihragān, was to some extent secularized. People cleaned their houses, put on new clothes, visited relatives and friends, exchanged gifts, and engaged in merrymaking with wine, music, and songs, especially the melodies composed for the occasion. Newly enthroned kings celebrated their official coronation on Nowrūz, and monarchs in general held court and at times remitted taxes. It is even recorded that kings were obliged to hold public court and answer any complaint against or addressed to them. Contemporary accounts as well as reports in early Islamic sources attest to the Sassanid kings' lavish celebration of Nowrūz and its colorful ceremonies and customs. Some of these tended to observe the number seven: for instance, seven kinds of seeds were grown in small containers as part of the festival rites and decoration, a custom still observed in the few remaining Zoroastrian villages in Iran. Furthermore, it is said that at Nowrūz seven kinds of grain, twigs from seven different trees, and seven silver coins were placed before the king. In the early twenty-first century, an essential and cherished decoration of Nowrūz is a collection of seven items whose names begin with the letter *s* in Persian (*haft sīn*). Of ambiguous or obscure origin, these are most often apple, seeds of wild rue, samanu (a paste prepared by slowly cooking the sap of ground germinating wheat in water, oils, and flour), vinegar, sumac, garlic, silver coins, sorbapple, and fresh grass.

Stripped of its Zoroastrian connotations, Nowrūz survived the advent of Islam and continued as the Iranian national festival. The Abbasid caliphs celebrated with banquets of wine, song, music, and exhange of gifts. The Shīʿī Muslims of Iran, however, came to associate important religious events with Nowrūz. Muḥammad Bāqir Majlisī quotes a number of traditions from the Shīʿī imams (in *Biḥar al-anwār,* volume 14, the section on *nayrīz*), who report that it was on Nowrūz that Adam was created, that God made a covenant with humankind, that Abraham destroyed the pagan idols, that the prophet Muḥammad took his young son-in-law ʿĀli on his shoulders to smash the idols in Mecca, and, most important of all, that he chose ʿĀli as his rightful successor. The Muslim rulers of Iran, continuing the Sassanid tradition, celebrated Nowrūz with pomp and circumstance. The ceremonies generally included the recitation of congratulatory panegyrics, feasting, the reception of dignitaries, music and dance, and the exchange of gifts. From about the middle of the sixteenth century, when Iran came into the possession of firearms, the onset of Nowrūz was announced in larger cities by the firing of cannon.

As a religious feast, Nowrūz apparently began as a one-day celebration, but calendar reforms, combined with the popular tendency of observing the festivals according to the old calendar, seem to have stretched it first to six days, with its division in Sassanid times into Lesser Nowrūz (the first day) and Greater Nowrūz (the sixth day), and eventually to its present length. In or about the year 1006, the first of Farvardīn fell on the first day of spring, and in 1079 a calendar reform, in which the poet ʿUmar (Omar) Khayyām participated, fixed the date of the feast on the first of Farvardīn and arranged for keeping it constant by intercalating one day before the New Year festival every four years.

Preparations for Nowrūz begin well in advance of the holiday. Although there are local variations, some practices are fairly general. A week or two before the New Year, grains of wheat or lentils are soaked in water and, after they germinate, are spread over a dish to grow. The resulting fresh mass of green blades (*sabzeh*) is an essential and symbolic decoration of the festival. In addition to the *sabzeh* and the *haft-sīn,* the Nowrūz table is adorned with a mirror, a copy of the holy book of the household's faith, a bowl of water in which green leaves or flower petals may float, and colored eggs, as well as fruits, fresh herbs, cakes, and candies. The "turn" of the year is awaited with eagerness and excitement, particularly by the young. A few moments before the solemn announcement of Nowrūz, the members of the family, by this time all bathed and clad in new or clean clothes, gather around the table, ready to embrace and exchange greetings and gifts. The visiting of relatives and friends is a common Nowrūz activity. In villages young men often engage in wrestling and other athletic games.

On the thirteenth day of Nowrūz, the ceremonies are brought to an end with a picnic in the countryside. The *sabzeh* must now be taken out and thrown into running water, which is thought to take away with it any bad luck of the previous year. Wishes are made, especially by young girls, for a happy future. The Parsis of India, who left Iran in the tenth century in order to preserve their Zoroastrian faith, also continue to celebrate Nowrūz (*jamshedī Navroz*) as a major feast.

Bibliography

For Nowrūz in ancient Iran and its religious significance see Mary Boyce's accounts in the *Cambridge History of Iran,* vol. 3, pt. 2, edited by me (Cambridge, 1983), pp. 792–815 (esp. pp. 792–800) and the bibliographical section; for Nowrūz in Islamic sources and bibliography see Nadir Karimiyan Sardashti and 'Alireza 'Askari Chavardi, *Kitabshenasi-e Nowrūz* (Bibliography of Nowrūz) (Tehran, 2000). Descriptions of current Nowrūz ceremonies with bibliography will be found in my "Now Ruz: The New Year Celebrations in Persia," *Iran Review* 4 (March 1959): 12–15; Henri Massé, *Croyances et coutumes persanes suivi de contes et chansons populaires* (Paris, 1938), pp. 145–162; Abollah Mostofi, *The Administrative and Social History of the Qajar Period [The Story of My Life],* translated by Nayer Mostofi Glenn, 3 vols. (Costa Mesa, Calif., 1997), vol. 1, pp. 200–205; A. Shapur Shahbazi, "Haft sin," in E. Yarshater, ed., *Encyclopaedia Iranca* IX, 2002, pp. 524–526; and Shabazi's "Nowrūz," available at www. Iranica.com. Jivanji Jamshedji Modi gives an account of the rites and ceremonies of the Farvardīgān, the holidays for the remembrance of the dead, among the Parsis (Zoroastrians) of India in his *Religious Ceremonies and Customs of the Parsees,* 2d ed. (Bombay, 1937). On the historical development and religious purport of Nowrūz in general, with comparative data, see Josef Marquart's "Das Nawrūz, seine Gechichte und seine Bedeutung," in *Dr. Modi Memorial Volume* (Bombay, 1930), pp. 709–765, translated by Manilel Patel as "The Navraz: Its History and Its Significance," *Journal of K. R. Cama Oriental Institute* (Bombay) 31 (1937): 1–51; Konstantin Inostrantsev (Inostrancev), *Sasanidskie etiudy* (St. Petersburg, 1909), pp. 82–109; Arthur Christensen's *Les types du premier homme et du premier roi dans l'histoire légendaire des Iraniens* (Leiden, 1934), pp. 85ff., 138–160, and Mary Boyce, above. For calendrical aspects of Nowrūz, see S. H. Taqīzādah's *Gāhshumārī dar Īrān-i qadīm* (Tehran, 1937), pp. 53ff., 115ff., 154–157, and 191.

Ehsan Yarshater (1987 and 2005)

NOYES, JOHN HUMPHREY

NOYES, JOHN HUMPHREY (1811–1886), American religious reformer and founder of the Oneida Community. Born to a prominent family in Brattleboro, Vermont, John Humphrey Noyes graduated from Dartmouth College and attended Andover and Yale theological seminaries, studying under Nathaniel W. Taylor. Because of his unorthodox "perfectionist" beliefs, Noyes soon lost his ministerial license and became the focus of opprobrium and ridicule. He argued that Christ's second coming and the end of the Jewish dispensation had occurred in 70 CE, when the Temple was destroyed in Jerusalem. Henceforth, "perfect holiness," a right attitude that would lead to right works, was literally possible on earth as part of the establishment of the kingdom of God.

These beliefs, which Noyes attempted to propagate throughout New York State and New England, attracted little support. In 1836 Noyes returned to his family estate in Putney, Vermont, and started a Bible school, which became the Putney Community. By 1845 the group had moved toward full communal ownership of property, inspired by the Christian communism of Acts 2:44–45. An effort in 1846 to introduce a form of group marriage led to expulsion from Putney in 1847 and the establishment of the Oneida Community in central New York State in 1848.

At Oneida, and at the smaller related community established in 1851 at Wallingford, Connecticut, the practices that had originated at Putney became fully institutionalized. Central to these was "complex marriage." Oneida Community members, who eventually numbered more than two hundred adults, all considered themselves married to each other in an "enlarged family." Men and women exchanged sexual partners frequently, and exclusive romantic attachments were broken up as threats to group stability. Members lived, ate, and worked together, had a system of communal child rearing, and held all but the most basic property in common. Government was achieved through a daily religious and business meeting, a method of group feedback and control called "mutual criticism," and an informal hierarchy known as "ascending and descending fellowship." A system of birth control called "male continence," technically *coitus reservatus,* was used exclusively until the final decade of the community's existence, when a "stirpiculture," or eugenics, experiment was inaugurated among some members. At Oneida there was far less sex-role stereotyping than in comparable American groups. Men and women worked alongside each other, and women served in positions of authority over men in certain jobs.

Complex marriage existed at Oneida from 1848 until 1879, when it was renounced because of internal dissatisfactions and external pressure. Noyes, with a few of his followers, had meanwhile fled to Canada, where he lived until his death in 1886. In 1881 the group also gave up its communistic system of economic organization, reorganized as a joint-stock corporation, and went on to become a successful business, best known for its silverware. Throughout his career, Noyes was primarily concerned with disseminating his religious ideas through the newspapers that he and his associates published. Subsequent scholars and popular writers, however, have been most fascinated by his unorthodox sexual ideas and practices, which sometimes have been held up as a prototype for the future.

Bibliography

The only comprehensive biography that captures the spirit of John Humphrey Noyes and his communal efforts is Robert Allerton Parker's *A Yankee Saint: John Humphrey Noyes and the Oneida Community* (New York, 1935). The most accessible primary materials are found in George Wallingford Noyes's two edited documentary volumes, *The Religious Experience of John Humphrey Noyes* (New York, 1923) and *John Humphrey*

Noyes: The Putney Community (Oneida, N. Y., 1931), and in *Free Love in Utopia: John Humphrey Noyes and the Origin of the Oneida Community* (Urbana, Ill., 2001), compiled by George Wallingford Noyes and edited by Lawrence Foster. Two classic and complementary nineteenth-century studies that analyze the Oneida Community within the context of the communitarian movement of which it was a part are John Humphrey Noyes's *History of American Socialisms* (Philadelphia, 1870) and Charles Nordhoff's *The Communistic Societies of the United States* (New York, 1875). For the most important primary source material on Noyes and his various communal ventures, serious scholars must consult the periodicals that he and his associates published between 1834 and 1879. These went by many different titles, including *The Circular* (Brooklyn and Oneida, N. Y., and Wallingford, Conn., 1851–1864), and are available through University Microfilms, Ann Arbor, Mich., or the Syracuse University Library, the official repository of Oneida materials.

LAWRENCE FOSTER (1987 AND 2005)

NUBŪWAH, communicating with supernatural beings or realms, is a major element in religious life. It is usually accomplished by persons acting as direct or indirect intermediaries, be they human, divine, or part human and part divine. Shamans, mystics, and soothsayers are examples of direct intermediaries. Unlike them, indirect intermediaries do not communicate with the divine except through a text that they presume to interpret in order to uncover the sacred message embedded within it. Someone who deciphers entrails, casts horoscopes, reads magical numbers, or performs charismatic exegesis is an indirect intermediary. Some individuals can be direct as well as indirect intermediaries, and they may also intermediate on special occasions rather than regularly or predictably.

Important intermediaries are referred to in English by such terms as *prophet* and *apostle,* in Greek by *prophētēs* and *promantis,* in Hebrew by *navi',* in Arabic by *nabī* or *rasūl,* and in Persian and Turkish by *payghambar* or *peygamber.* Since each label has connotations associated with the religious outlook of a particular culture, generic terms are needed to facilitate comparative discussions. All of these terms refer to some kind of "commissioned communicator"—a human being who feels called upon to speak on behalf of a force perceived to be beyond his or her control. Within monotheistic communities, commissioned communication took on the form of messengership; it involved delivering intelligible messages to other human beings from the Unseen that reinterpreted, and often challenged, the status quo.

This minimal definition distinguishes messengers from such commissioned communicators as shamans or soothsayers—spirit helpers whose primary function is not to deliver intelligible messages but to invoke friendly spirits during trance. It also excludes a phenomenon sometimes called prophecy, one in which the "messages" take the unintelligible form of speaking in tongues. However, there have been prophets, such as the African Isaiah Shembe, who delivered intelligible and unintelligible messages alternately. Since the "mystery letters" that begin certain chapters in the Qurʾān have remained unintelligible, albeit subject to intense scrutiny and multiple interpretations, it can be said that messengers must deliver intelligible messages as a primary task but may also deliver unintelligible ones. In Islamic exegesis of the Qurʾān, this distinction is observed through two key words provided in *sūrah* 3:7: *muhkamat,* referring to passages that form a firm or categorical basis for gauging the divine will, and *mutashabihat,* referring to metaphoric or allegorical passages and also to the mystery letters at the outset of some Qurʾanic chapters.

Within these parameters, the social roles of commissioned communicators vary significantly. Some "publish" their message in response to the request of other human beings; others, only in response to an inner urging interpreted as having a supernatural source. Biblical prophets did both; the human channels for the Greek oracles, only the former; and Muḥammad, only the latter. Although the sense that they have been called usually precludes social and political passivity as a response, there is no mandate that such figures mobilize and lead others. Sometimes their messages are random and disorganized; they may also have only local significance. At other times, they are canonized into a book with decisive moral guidelines that are deemed to have universal applicability.

Beyond functional similarities, there are historical reasons to argue that messengers can be grouped for purposes of cross-cultural study; few roles have such strong diachronic commonalities as messengership. Monotheistic messengership grew out of an ancient tradition of direct mediation between the divine and the human, prevalent throughout the Mediterranean and the Nile-to-Oxus regions. After it emerged—first in Judaism, then in Christianity, Zoroastrianism, and Islam—the role was conveyed to various societies not only through scriptures but also through a shared folklore. To the present day, these common symbols, figures, and stories have continued to supply standards against which claimants to the role can be evaluated. Near-contemporary messenger figures, such as Tenskwatwa, Joseph Smith, Bahāʾ Allāh, and Isaiah Shembe, were culturally unconnected yet they shared the inheritance of messengership. Their temporal convergence underscores the extent to which messengership is a central religious phenomenon, at once diffuse and pervasive. Yet scholarly labor has remained narrowly focused on only a fraction of the relevant data, with Old Testament prophethood remaining the norm for most comparative generalizations. If few comparativists have paid attention to Islam, a religious tradition in which messengers and messengership are central, Islamicists, for their part, have continued to neglect the cross-creedal, comparative dimensions of *nubūwah.*

THE QURʾANIC MESSENGER FIGURE. The Qurʾān, the foundational text of Islam, uses two Arabic nouns for messenger figures: *nabī* and *rasūl.* The latter frequently appears in the phrase *rasūl Allāh* (messenger of God), which became the preferred term for Muḥammad and a key element in the *shahādah,* or profession of faith, as central to Islam as baptism is to Christianity. A common Persian equivalent, *payghambar,* literally means "messenger," as does *rasūl.* The noun for the role or office of *nabī* is *nubūwah,* just as *risālah* is sometimes used to denote the mission or message of a *rasūl.*

Much has been made of the Qurʾanic use of two terms for such figures. Both Muslim and non-Muslim scholars have tried to clarify the presumed distinctions between the two. Some have concluded that the words are interchangeable; others have identified *nabī* as a word for figures who are called to receive revelation, and reserved *rasūl* for those who not only receive revelation but also are sent on a mission to a particular community. Some have linked *nabī* to ordinary messengers, while marking as *rasūl* only seven prophets, those deemed to be the greatest: Adam, Noah, Abraham, Moses, David, Jesus and Muḥammad. A less common interpretation links *nabī* with messengers who were descended from Abraham and therefore specially gifted with *nubūwah,* while *rasūl* is said to connote a messenger sent to bring his own community to God. Further complicating the picture is that angels can be denoted as *rusūl* (*sūrah* 35:1), but never as *nabiyūn.*

While the full significance of this etymological complexity remains unclear, its very existence calls attention to the fact that in the Qurʾān *nubūwah* is a rich, vital and evocative topic. *Nubūwah* has been the primary vehicle by which the divine communicates with humankind. It involves a long and continuous chain of revelation-bearers who were related both functionally and genealogically. They were sent to help God communicate to humankind his desire for their surrender *(islām)* to his will. They were therefore all given the same message, except that certain ones were sent to fulfill very specific leadership missions within their own communities. The chain stretched from the very first human, Adam, to the deliverer of the Qurʾān, Muḥammad. It included figures considered prophets by Jews and Christians (Abraham, Jacob, Moses), along with others familiar to them but not classed by them as prophets (Joseph, David, Jesus). It included still others entirely unfamiliar to any but Arabs (Hūd, Ṣāliḥ, Shuʾayb). Joseph is the subject of the longest Qurʾanic narrative (*sūrah* 12).

All these prophets share Abrahamic descent. Abraham was the patriarch of a single family whose lineages, for Israelites and Arabs respectively, stemmed from Isaac or Isḥāq and Ishmael or Ismāʾīl. In accepting *islām* or submission, in surrendering to God's absolute authority, and in putting themselves in the only right relationship with him, Arabs contemporaneous with Muḥammad not only acknowledged their own forefathers as divine messengers, they also saw themselves as returning to their original religion, and also to the original religion of all humankind. Mecca was the natural center of this reclaimed trust that now became the new religion of Islam. Before it became the birthplace of Muḥammad, Mecca had been the site of Abraham's house of God, at its center the Kaʿbah or sacred mosque, and within the Kaʿbah the Black Stone vouchsafed to Ismāʾīl as a divine bequest.

Muḥammad is Abraham's legatee and more. As *rasūl Allāh,* messenger of God, Muḥammad becomes the composite of all the major messengers who preceded him—a radical monotheist like Abraham, a lawgiver and warrior like Moses, and a friend of God like Jesus. What others received partially Muḥammad received in full. He is given a perfect form of the revealed truth that God has sent through every messenger since the beginning of humankind. Functionally Muḥammad resembles his predecessors and becomes who he is by comparison with them:

- He is chosen by God from among his own people, neither seeking to be chosen, nor showing enthusiasm for the task. He is guided by God, whose guidance is parceled out as needed. He is distinct from the angels, who are neither human nor divine. He is mortal and subject to death.
- He polarizes his audience: he is believed by some and opposed by many, including Satan, partly because he rejects polytheistic ancestral custom in favor of *tawḥīd,* that is, the declaration of God's unequivocal and unqualified oneness. Those who oppose him call him a liar. They harm his person and expel him from his hometown. Yet they are marked in turn by God through the term *kufr.* A *kafir* (unbeliever) exhibits *kufr:* one who is both unfaithful and ungrateful displays infidelity and ingratitude to the Almighty. *Kufr* becomes one of the strongest terms of opprobrium in the Qurʾān, and the status of *kafir* amounts to a sentence of spiritual and social exile for Muslims.
- He has two major functions related to the Day of Judgment: to bring good tidings of the possibility of salvation, and to warn of punishment for wrongdoers and naysayers (the *kuffar,* plural of *kafir*). Both functions are announced and supported in the noble book, the holy Qurʾān, which God reveals to humankind through the agency of Muḥammad.
- He possesses a constellation of exemplary personal characteristics: patience, unswerving devotion, compassion, trust in God, and a pure faith that is the absolute opposite of *shirk.* A *mushrik* performs *shirk:* one who professes loyalty to others along with God (an idolator or polytheist) denies God's oneness *(tawḥīd)* and replaces it with diluted loyalty *(shirk).*
- Obeying God extends to honoring his prophet and upholding his community. Obedience means belief in God's book, the angels, and the last day, but it also means esteeming the prophet and his companions, and then helping to establish an *ummah,* that is, a community based on God's revelation and committed to establishing the rules necessary for its survival and expansion.

The special significance of *nabī/rasūl* is further underscored by the Qurʾanic insistence on distinguishing this from other roles that presumed divine-human mediation in seventh-century Arabia. The major competitive roles were *kāhin* (diviner, shaman, seer) and *shāʿir* (poet). Both recur in the Qurʾān but with different valuations. Divination is never explicitly condemned; prophecy, in one sense, is a perfected form of divination. Poetry, however, is condemned, largely because the poet's inspiration is seen to be his own and not divine. Muḥammad's task was not unlike the biblical *nevi'im,* who had to distinguish themselves from figures claiming direct mediation with the divine while lacking the historical and moral significance reserved for prophets.

Notably absent from the Qurʾān's picture of *nubūwah* is the element of futurism, or prophecy as prediction, that dominates many Christian understandings of Old Testament prophetic action. Although many of Muḥammad's messages are future-oriented in an apocalyptic sense, prediction of specific historical events is virtually absent. (*Sūrah* 105 is an exception. It predicts the destruction of a Yemeni Christian army intent on invading Mecca. But even that is a prediction given after the fact, since the failed invasion took place in the year of Muḥammad's birth.) Miraculous acts are also absent; Muḥammad's message is seen as an encompassing and ongoing miracle. The giving of the Qurʾān validates Muḥammad as messenger without the need for ancillary proof from the redirection of nature. One future event is predicted, the end of time, also known as the Day of Judgment. Neither specified nor left open to debate, the Day of Judgment will be knowable from clear signs, vividly described in *sūrah* 82.

THE SEALING OF PROPHECY. Shortly after Muḥammad's death, the core of his supporters articulated and enforced a particular understanding of the Qurʾanic reference to Muḥammad as *khatm al-anbiyāʾ* or "seal of the *nabīs*" (*sūrah* 33:40). Muḥammad was said to be the culmination and termination of that long process of direct revelation that God had begun with Adam. The decision to view Muḥammad in this way was necessitated by competing claims to revelation of other Arab tribal leaders. Although it invalidated them and made Muḥammad unique, it did not demote previous messengers. Rather, accepting the finality of Muḥammad's messengership became an essential part of being a Muslim; it redefined Muslims as Abrahamic loyalists who embraced but also fulfilled prophecies given earlier to Jews, Christians and Zoroastrians. Although the decision did not entirely prevent later Muslims from using the labels *nabī* and *rasūl* or even claiming to bring a new Qurʾān, it did restrict such activity: claimants were compelled to make implicit rather than explicit claims to be "like" Muḥammad.

It is difficult to overestimate the historical impact of the concept of *nubūwah* as exemplified in Muḥammad's life and clarified after his death. It expanded previous Perso-Semitic notions of prophetic action, and stretched them to new limits. Not only did it direct the course of leadership patterns within Islamic societies, but it also affected almost all subsequent non-Muslim conceptualizations of prophecy and prophets.

LITERARY DEVELOPMENTS. Muslims enlarged previous notions of *nubūwah* simply by putting all messengers into a class that ended with Muḥammad. Just as Muḥammad had to be shown to be like them, they had to be shown to be like Muḥammad. This "leveling" is particularly evident in three literary genres, *ḥadīth, sīrah,* and *qiṣaṣ al-anbiyāʾ*.

The *ḥadīth* comprise an expansive and contested corpus of reports that convey Muḥammad's *sunnah*—his exemplary words, deeds, and silent approval. Their content varies enormously within Sunnī and Shīʿī branches of Islam, but common to all *ḥadīth* compilations is the notion that the *nabī* became a personal exemplar of unprecedented and unparalleled authority. The wide circulation of *ḥadīth* about other *nabīs,* especially Moses, Joseph, Abraham, and Jesus, made them exemplary as well. Later Muslim scholars explored the possibility of extrascriptural revelation to prophets, especially in a subclass of *ḥadīth* known as *ḥadīth qudsī,* which quote direct speech from God to Muḥammad that does not appear in Qurʾān but remains authoritative beyond "ordinary" *ḥadīth.*

The chain of Muslim messengers grew so large that by some counts it was said to number 124,000. It also included figures not considered prophets by non-Muslims, principal among them Jesus. Muslims viewed Jesus as a major *rasūl,* a completely human emissary whom God saved from dying by substituting another on the cross. Thus they preserved, in reworked form, an early Judeo-Christian view of Jesus that had fallen into disuse with the rise of Gentile Christianity and the conciliar decrees of the Roman church.

Using the *ḥadīth* as an important source, a genre known as *sīrah* presented the life of Muḥammad specifically as the life of a messenger of God. Most early *sīrahs* were written in the crosscultural, multicreedal environment of the empire's central cities; some, such as the *Sīrat Rasūl Allāh* of Ibn Isḥāq (d. 768), were produced by converts to Islam. They sought to establish Muḥammad's legitimacy with regard to previous messengers and, by extension, the right of Muslims to rule over Jewish and Christian subjects. They viewed Muḥammad's particular blend of social, military, and political leadership, as well as his revelatory utterances, spiritual guidance, and lawgiving, as a standard against which others could be measured. Perso-Semitic concepts of prophetic leadership became institutionalized and idealized for the first time in history: Muḥammad not only brought a book but also constructed, on the basis of that book, a lasting, divinely guided community. Gradually, a Muslim vision of world history crystallized: Muḥammad's creation of a divinely guided community culminated earlier epochs marked by divine-human mediation, at the same time that its own initial epoch, the so-called period of the first three generations, projected an ever present ideal for leading the good Muslim life. While Muḥammad was preeminent among messengers, a small number of others, most notably Abraham, Moses, and Jesus, were also held in high esteem as major messengers. Jews and Christians had been sent "Muslim" messengers but had misconstrued or diluted their messages. As a consequence, with the advent of Islam they had yet another option to become Muslim, but if they chose to remain as People of the Book, that is, scriptuaries like Muslims but not fully Muslim in their outlook, they could remain protected minorities *(dhimmīs)* under Islamic rule.

The *sīrah* of Ibn Isḥāq also established a paradigm for the career of the messenger of God that many Muslim leaders tried to emulate, even when they were not claiming *nubūwah* for themselves. It described a birth and infancy filled with propitious occurrences and omens; a youth of involvement with conventional religious practices accompanied by spiritual searching and confusion; a sudden call at age forty, resisted three times; acceptance by a few and rejection by most; emigration (*hijrah*); and consolidation of power in an adopted home and a triumphal return to the original home. Gradually legists and theologians elaborated other *dalāʾil al-nubūwah* (signs of prophethood), such as a mark between the shoulders, innocence of youth, and paranormal experiences. They went on to develop, by the thirteenth century, the doctrine of *ʿiṣmah* (protection from sin and error), which was applied broadly to Muḥammad and selectively to previous messengers. Thereafter, insulting Muḥammad became a serious misdeed, and Mecca and Medina were closed to non-Muslims. Eventually the scholars added an eschatological role: Muḥammad would lead his community into Paradise, and there intercede for those whom God had excluded.

The comparability of Muḥammad with all previous messengers, and vice versa, came to be demonstrated in another literary form, *qiṣaṣ al-anbiyāʾ* ("tales of the *nabīs*"). By the time al-Kisāʾī (fl. 1200) composed one of its most famous works, the genre had become comprehensive, dramatic, and influential. Because its authors believed in prophetic continuity, they could rework non-Muslim tales about the prophets into an Islamic vision of the religious history of the world. When the predictive, miracle-working facets of Jewish and Christian prophecy resurfaced here, they did so in "islamized" fashion. The preempting of pre-Islamic messengers and the exalting of Muḥammad assumed architectural form in the Dome of the Rock in Jerusalem. A late seventh-century monument constructed by the Umayyad Caliph ʿAbd al-Malik, it hallows the memory of the Prophet's night journey *(israʾ)* and his subsequent ascent *(Miʾrāj)* to the highest heaven, alluded to in the Qurʾān (*sūrah* 12) but more fully elaborated in *ḥadīth.*

SUFISM AND PHILOSOPHY. Another kind of reinterpretation, consolidation, and expansion of the concept of *nubūwah* occurred when Ṣūfī thinkers gave these stories an esoteric, interiorized meaning. Messengers became prototypes for individual spiritual development, illustrating the ability of human beings to receive divine inspiration. In well-known early modern examples of the genre, *Taʾwīl al-aḥādīth* and *al-Fauz al-Kabir* of the Indian Ṣūfī theologian Shāh Walī Allāh (d.1762), numerous messengers exhibit one or more aspects of the Ṣūfī search for truth, even as they exemplify humanity's complete dependence on God. They are quintessential servants and friends of God who serve as instruments in God's plan as they strive for human perfection in their devotion, self-control, and discipline. For example, Adam is a microcosm of all the realities of the universe, physical and spiritual. His fall was designed by God to ensure his becoming an earthly delegate: the prohibitions against eating from the tree were revealed in a dream; the violation of the prohibitions were brought about by satanic action. Noah is the first messenger to lead a community forcibly to God's will, bringing law in order to subordinate animal to spiritual impulses. Abraham exemplifies utter devotion to God and the unstinting pursuit of the true religion. Joseph triumphs over affliction by his constancy. For many Ṣūfīs, Muḥammad is *insān al-kāmil,* the perfect or universal human being who epitomizes union with God.

Muslim philosophers found it more difficult to appreciate Muḥammad's mission as messenger. At the least, they distinguished prophetic truth—which is communicated in easily comprehensible everyday language and expressed in stories and analogies that appeal to the common people in particular communities—from philosophical truth, which is universal, esoteric, abstract, and rational. Some, such as al-Kindī (d. after 870), saw prophetic and philosophical truth as two sides of the same coin, the former a parable for the latter. Others, however, publicly stated that the two truths should not contradict each other but privately thought of revelation as a vulgar form of higher truth. For example, al-Fārābī (c. 870–950) implied that prophetic knowledge was inferior to philosophical knowledge by demonstrating that the true knower—the philosopher-king—had to do what the prophets had done, and more. According to Ibn Ṭufayl (d. 1185), ultimate truth could be gained without recourse to divine revelation. It was available to reflective, reasoning human beings like the island-dwelling protagonist of his philosophical story *Ḥayy ibn Yaqẓān* (Living, son of the wakeful), its very title a play on one of the 99 divine names (al-Ḥayy) attributed to God. Despite such condescension, many philosophers did value Muḥammad's lawgiving role since it fostered the ordering of society that they too cherished and pursued.

LEADERSHIP AND LEGITIMACY. In the Islamic faith, as in other religious traditions, the death of the final messenger and the cessation of new revelation tended to enhance the importance of other forms of leadership based on divine guidance and inspiration. Simultaneously, the maintenance of the stability grounded in revelation had to coexist, as in other traditions, with the pursuit of the spontaneity that had characterized the faith in its origins. The growth of a multivalent conception of *nubūwah* provided numerous ways in which its legitimacy could be emulated without being imitated, in stability and spontaneity alike.

When *nubūwah* was sealed, its authority had to flow into other leadership roles if the ummah was to survive. However, because none of them could duplicate the legitimacy of *nubūwah,* each had to establish a particular identity that could never compete successfully with *nubūwah.* Out of this paradox was born one of the great problems of Islamic civilization—the inimitability of the ideal leader.

Among Sunnī Muslims, the ending of *nubūwah* eventuated in a relationship of mutual dependence between the *khalīfahs* (caliphs), whose temporal authority protected and defended the unity of the *ummah,* and the *ʿulamāʾ* (religious scholars), whose acquisition of authentic religious knowledge enabled them to define the proper Muslim life. These men, like rabbis, acted as indirect intermediaries, teasing out the legal and moral implications of God's direct revelations and shaping them into a system of rules: the *sharīʿah.* Thus were preserved the spiritual guidance and earthly power of the prophetic experience, if not its immediacy. Although neither *ʿulamāʾ* nor *khalīfahs* could claim Muḥammad's full authority, both derived their legitimacy from him, and jointly they possessed the two powers he had combined.

The leadership model preferred by Shīʿī Muslims, *imāmah,* overcame this bifurcation with paradoxical consequences: it both greatly extended and radically contained charismatic authority; its successful combination of spiritual and temporal power was bought at the price of never exercising the latter; and by virtue of its having to remain distinct from *nubūwah, imāmah* eventually became the superior of the two. The *imāms* of the major Shīʿah group (the Ithna *ʿasharīya* or Twelvers) were twelve descendants of Muḥammad believed to have inherited his blood and physical traits and were inspired by god to interpret the meaning of revealed truth without altering it, a belief also common to the Ismāʾīlīyyah, the other major group of Shīʿah. They were conceived in God's mind as the principle of absolute good, which was transmitted into the loins of the *nabīs* and the wombs of holy women as entities of light and made concrete after Muḥammad's death. Together with the messengers, the *imāms* are the proofs of God, and while the earth has been without a messenger since the death of Muḥammad, it is never without an *imām.* The *imāms* become the "speaking Qurʾān," guarding the true meaning of the "silent Qurʾān" and interpreting it as alive and fresh in their time.

In one Shīʿī view, these special qualities and esoteric knowledge are *wilāyat Allāh,* the custodianship of God. The wilayat Allāh was entrusted to the angel Gabriel from the creation of the world. Gabriel gave it to all the prophets and finally to Muḥammad, who passed it on to his cousin and son-in-law ʿAlī, who in turn passed it on to Muḥammad's grandsons and through them to the rest of the *imāms.* Thus the *imāms* became the only individuals capable of bringing divine guidance to the world after Muḥammad sealed *nubūwah.* Though they were the only rightful spiritual and temporal authorities after Muḥammad, a series of erroneous decisions by the Muslim majority postponed their actual exercise of temporal power until the return of their last member, the Mahdī (messiah).

Despite the overlap of *nubūwah* and *imāmah,* all but the very extremist Shīʿah refused to call the *imāms nabī,* insisting on one fundamental distinction: the *imāms,* unlike Muḥammad, did not bring a new revelation or a new law. However, since they possessed all the other qualities of the messenger as well as the distinct, inimitable, and infallible characteristics of the *imām,* it was easy for their devoted followers to view them as preeminent. Indeed, the very absence of new revelation further enhanced the authority of *imāms*: they and they alone knew the message of the Qurʾān due to their error-free *(maʿṣūm)* abilities in charismatic exegesis.

In Shiʿi popular devotion *nubūwah* and *imāmah* were inextricably conflated. All the messengers of God came to be thought of as having participated in the suffering of the holy family. The *ahl al-bayt,* or people of the household (of Muḥammad), included ʿAlī, Muḥammad's cousin, Alī's wife, who was also Muḥammad's daughter, Fāṭimah, and their sons Ḥasan and Ḥusayn. They endured what earlier prophets had anticipated, themselves tasting a little of the fate of Muḥammad's family through their own persecution. Shiʿi devotional poetry expanded the tales of the prophets in new ways by likening them to the experiences of the holy family and the *imāms*; at the same time, their mournful verses elevated the *imāms* above all antecedent figures except Muḥammad. Thus *imāmah* completed *nubūwah* in such a perfect pattern of divine logic that the latter came to be, in the eyes of many of the Shiʿah, merely a precursor to the former.

Among both Sunnīs and the Shīʿah, other roles reflected the impact of the sealing of *nubūwah.* The Ṣūfī *shaykh* identified with the spiritual, if not genealogical, legacy of the *nabī* because he could receive individual divine inspiration and achieve intimacy with God. In so doing, such figures reclaimed the immediacy of the *nabī*'s experience; sometimes they also emulated his political and social activism, as did Sayyid Idrīs (1890–1983), the Libyan nationalist leader of the Sanusiyah.

Perhaps even more important are the myriad apocalyptic, millenarian, and reformist figures, Sunnī and Shīʿī alike, who have adopted labels such as *mujaddid* (centennial renewer), *mahdī* (divinely guided one, the messiah), or *mujāhid/jihādī* (leader of a *jihād).* Often these figures have emerged in circumstances perceived to be like those of Muḥammad, for example, in an area where Islam was imperfectly established or not established at all. Although a few, such as the Almohad *mahdī* Ibn Tūmart (c. 1082–1130), may have claimed to bring new revelation, most managed to emulate Muḥammad's activist, reformist leadership without making dangerously explicit claims to his most distinguishing characteristic. By reintroducing Muḥammad's spiritual spontaneity and social renewal, and by emulating aspects of his *sunnah* and *sīrah,* they have evoked *nubūwah* without claiming it. Such was the case with the Indian Ṣūfī reformer, Ahmad Sirhindi (d. 1624), who viewed his own time on the cusp of a new millennium in the Islamic calendar (AH 1000= 1592 CE) as a moment of degeneracy and decay not unlike that facing Muḥammad in his day. The Day of Judgment was imminent, the process of decay could only be reversed by a renewer, in this case, a millennial renewer *(mujaddid-i alf-i thani),* on whom God entrusted prophetic perfections. Neither Sirhindi's claim nor that of later renewers, such as the Yemeni jurist Muḥammad al-Shawkani (d. 1834), has gone unchallenged, but their claims do expand the notion of prophetic charisma even while upholding the finality of Muḥammad as a law-giving prophet.

EXCHANGES WITH NON-MUSLIMS. The impact of the concept of *nubūwah* extended beyond the Muslim community, too. While developing it, Muslims were beginning to interact with their empire's subject population of Jews, Christians, and Zoroastrians. In the course of the ensuing polemic, each group had to adjust its understanding of the history of messengership so as to remain distinct from the others. Post-Islamic Zoroastrian biographies of Zarathushtra viewed him as an Islamic-type *payghambar,* a messenger sent with a book to a particular community. Some went on to exalt him above all other messengers, just as Muslims exalted Muḥammad. Arab Christian reactions were diametrically opposite: they defined genuine prophets as everything they argued Muḥammad was not—devoid of earthly motives, noncommercial, nonmilitant, and miracle working. This familiar picture of prophethood, somewhat awkward from the point of view of the Old Testament, eventually found its way into Western Christian medieval polemic as well. Muslims accommodated themselves to Christian polemic by clarifying the doctrine of *iʿjāz al-Qurʾān* (the miracle of the Qurʾān): the inimitability of the Qurʾān, combined with Muḥammad's illiteracy, constituted the greatest miracle. It was God-given and it needed no lesser demonstrations of divine agency to confirm Muḥammad's unique status among messengers.

Miracle working also found other routes into Islamic views of Muḥammad. In popular literature, as well as in genres like *qiṣaṣ al-anbiyā,'* the mountain began to come to him as his life story filled with a plethora of extracanonical prodigies. Such glorification appears, for example, in one of the most lastingly popular poems used to celebrate Muḥammad's birthday, or *mawlid.* Though a companion of the Prophet, Ka'b ibn Zuhayr (d. c. 630), composed the earliest panegyric of Muḥammad, the *Burdah* or *Mantle Poem* of al-Būṣīrī (d. 1298), which was composed in Egypt during the Crusades, has become the most famous. It warns against succumbing to temptations of the flesh and then develops a depiction of Muḥammad as above all a high-minded helper from heaven attentive to all who call his name. In popular practice, Muḥammad's tomb became a place to seek his earthly intercession.

Modern Muslim thinkers have continued to enlarge the concept of *nubūwah* by emphasizing particular dimensions of Muḥammad's *sunnah;* because the *ḥadīth* document the *sunnah,* they have become more important than ever. In modernist thought, the messenger's mission is often likened to that of the modern social reformer; his ability to serve as a moral exemplar and rehabilitator in a time of decay is stressed. According to such interpretations, Muḥammad's teachings demonstrated the primacy of the social in humankind's goals and encouraged the use of consultation and cooperation, indeed flexibility. His ability to relate eternal truth to his own special circumstances was a model of and justification for applying Islamic principles according to circumstances.

Despite such updating, one aspect of *nubūwah,* its having come to an end with Muḥammad, remains nonnegotiable. In the last century, a group of former Shīʿī Muslims accepted the possibility of new revelation and new messengers. The explicit claims of their messenger, Bahāʾ Allāh (1817–1892), led inevitably to the founding of a separate religious tradition, just as it did within Christianity for the Mormon followers of his American near-contemporary Joseph Smith (1805–1844). Even more explosive within the arc of Islamic cultural politics has been the attempt of Ahmadis to redefine prophecy after Muḥammad. The Ahmadis ascribed to their eponym, the South Asian reformer Mirza Ghulam Ahmad (d. 1908), the qualities of a renewer who is also the *mahdī* and the *masīḥ* (or messiah). They defined themselves in the tradition of Ṣūfī reformers like Ahmad Sirhindi and Shāh Walī Allāh, and enjoyed enormous success worldwide as a missionary movement within Islam. Yet their adversaries saw them as *kuffar,* those who denied the finality of Muḥammad's claim to *nubūwah* and were therefore outside the pale of Islam. The Ahmadi movement ignited a fierce controversy in British South Asia and then after 1948, in Pakistan. It did not subside even when the National Assembly of Pakistan amended the 1973 constitution to declare the Ahmadis a non-Muslim minority. A subsequent 1984 presidential decree attempted to criminalize the entire Ahmadi community. In South Asia and elsewhere *nubūwah* clearly remains as critical an issue today as it was at Islam's inception.

SEE ALSO Imamate; Prophecy; Walāyah.

BIBLIOGRAPHY

There is no single comprehensive study of *nubūwah,* but the issue has been addressed within a number of broader investigations. Tor Andrae's classic work, *Die person Muhammeds in lehre und glauben seiner gemeinde* (Stockholm, 1918), offers valuable insights into the process by which the figure of Muḥammad and his mission as messenger of God expanded and deepened through centuries of devotion. A thorough survey and synthesis of previous views on the Qurʾanic distinction between *nabī* and *rasūl* can be found in Willem A. Bijlefeld's "A Prophet and More Than a Prophet?" *Muslim World 59* (January 1969): 1–28, which also suggests a new and less dichotomous interpretation.

William A. Graham's *Divine Word and Prophetic Word in Early Islam* (The Hague, 1977), especially part 1, "Revelation in

Early Islam," provides an imaginative description of how two separate sacred messages, scripture and prophetic example, crystallized out of the unitary prophetic experience; the bibliography includes many major European works on Muḥammad. On the Shīʿī tradition in particular, Mahmoud M. Ayoub's *Redemptive Suffering in Islam: A Study of the Devotional Aspects of ʿAshurā' in Twelver Shīʿism* (The Hague, 1978) presents extensive materials on the history of the prophets as it was incorporated into the history of Shīʿī martyrdom, while Abdulaziz Abdulhussein Sachedina's *Islamic Messianism: The Idea of Mahdī in Twelver Shʿism* (Albany, 1981) offers a clear and effective historical account that includes an examination of the relationship between *imām* and *nabī* in Shīʿī thought. One unusual effort to explain the appearance and displacement of Muḥammad's competitors in the claim to divine messengership is Dale F. Eickelman's "Musaylima: An Approach to the Social Anthropology of Seventh Century Arabia," *Journal of the Social and Economic History of the Orient* 10 (1967): 17–52. The impact of early Muslim-Christian polemic on evolving notions of revelation and prophetic mission in both communities, a topic that has not garnered much attention, receives enlightening treatment in two articles by Sidney H. Griffith, "Comparative Religion in the Apologetics of the First Christian Arabian Theologians," in *Proceedings of the PMR Conference* (annual publication of the Patristic, Mediaeval and Renaissance Conference) 4 (1979), pp. 63–87, and "The Prophet Muḥammad: His Scripture and His Message according to the Christian Apologies in Arabic and Syriac from the First Abbasid Century," in *La vie du prophète Mahomet: Colloque de Strasbourg,* 1980 (Paris, 1983), pp. 99–146.

Another perspective can be gleaned from Sven S. Hartman's, "Secrets for Muslims in Parse Scriptures," in *Islam and Its Cultural Divergence,* edited by Girdhari L. Tikku (Urbana, Ill., 1971), pp. 67–75, which traces the impact of *nubūwah* on post-Islamic Zoroastrian conceptualizations of Zarathushtra. For a look at the impact of Muḥammad's biographical representation on the careers of nineteenth-century West African Muslim reformers and the complementary effect of the reformers' own lives on their representations of Muḥammad's career, see Marilyn R. Waldman, "The Popular Appeal of the Prophetic Paradigm in West Africa," *Contributions to Asian Studies* 17 (1982): 110–114. In the twentieth-century context, an Egyptian study of the Prophet's life is analyzed by Antoine Wessels in *A Modern Arabic Biography of Muḥammad: A Critical Study of Muḥammad Ḥusayn Haykal's Ḥayat Muḥammad* (Leiden, 1972). Study of the controversial Ahmadi movement has been enhanced by Yohanan Friedmann's *Prophecy Continuous: Aspects of Ahmadi Religious Thought and Its Medieval Background* (Berkeley, 1989), while the status of renewal among Sunnī jurists has been highlighted through Bernard Haykel's *Revival and Reform in Islam: The Legacy of Muḥammad al-Shawkani* (Cambridge, 2003).

In addition to these critical studies, a number of primary sources, reflecting various genres and time periods, are available in English translation. *The Life of Muḥammad: A Translation of [Ibn] Isḥāq's Sīrat Rasūl Allāh,* translated by Alfred Guillaume (1955; reprint, Lahore, 1967), is the well-known eighth-century biography that sought to establish the Prophet's legitimacy in regard to Judeo-Christian messenger figures. It, along with other early sources, has now been subjected to critical review and speculative revaluation by a host of scholars drawn to the question of Islamic origins. For the most comprehensive overview of this debate, and also the variant stances of its protagonists, see Herbert Berg, ed. *Method and Theory in the Study of Islamic Origins* (Leiden, 2003). A tenth-century example of a philosophical middle position on the relationship between philosophical and revealed truth, and between the philosopher-king and the messenger of God, can be found in Alfarabi's *Philosophy of Plato and Aristotle,* translated by Muhsin Mahdī (New York, 1962), part 1, "The Attainment of Happiness," while Ibn Ṭufayl's *Hayy Ibn Yaqẓān* can be enjoyed, along with a spirited commentary, in Lenn Evan Goodman's book of the same title (Los Angeles, 1983). *The Tales of the Prophets of al-Kisāʾī,* translated by Wheeler M. Thackston, Jr. (Boston, 1978), reflects the important genre of *qiṣaṣ al-anbiyāʾ* in which extracanonical Jewish and Christian tales are adduced in an Islamic context. "The Mantle Poem of al-Buṣīrī" also exists in translation, in *A Reader on Islam,* edited by Arthur Jeffery (The Hague, 1962), pp. 605–620; it presents another form of popular literature, the devotional poem that commemorates the Prophet's birthday and stresses the miraculous dimension of his life. *A Mystical Interpretation of Prophetic Tales by an Indian Muslim, Shāh Walī Allāh's Taʾwīl al-Aḥādīth,* has been translated by J. M. S. Baljon (Leiden, 1973), and despite some flaws, it offers an example of Ṣūfī esoteric interpretation by a major eighteenth-century Indian mystic and theologian, whose own legacy and stature as a renewer have become better known through the translation of his magnum opus, *The Conclusive Argument from God: Shāh Walī Allāh of Delhi's Hujjat Allāh al-Baligha,* translated by Marcia K. Hermansen (Leiden, 1996).

MARILYN ROBINSON WALDMAN (1987)
BRUCE B. LAWRENCE (2005)

NUDITY. People are nude in the most innocent moments as children and later at times of profound vulnerability—during sex and orgasm, while bathing, in sickness, and under the care of medical personnel. Much later, bodies may be exposed to adult children and other caregivers. And finally, one is exposed again in death, when one's body is prepared by morticians and other specialists in the ritual care of the dead. And yet it would be naive—too innocent of gender and sexuality and their capacity to mark human interactions with the signs of dominance and submission—to equate nudity only with innocent vulnerability. The man who wears a raincoat to the park and displays himself to hapless observers is not innocent in his vulnerability but is driven by the awareness that exposing one's sexual organs can strike fear in the beholder.

From the female figures exposing their labia to protect cathedrals built in the Christian West to the ithyphallic and sexually gymnastic figures decorating supporting struts and exterior walls of temples in South Asia (said to prevent damage caused by lightening strikes), examples of the naked body striking an aggressive, "keep your distance" pose abound in the history of religions. Apotropaic rituals often utilize nudity. Images of nude humans, animals, deities, demons, and monstrous hybrids can be found in (and on the borders of) many configurations of sacred space.

NUDITY AND SEXUALITY. To display one's naked body in an inappropriate context can certainly engender powerful emotions in those who observe the spectacle. Why are social conventions being flouted? Is this person crazy, or worse—a menace, a pervert, an evildoer? Religious discourses often provide contexts for making such judgments. Sociobiological theory pertaining to sex and the capacity of the human body to organize social life by means of sexuality provides a framework for exploring these religious discourses. Although feminists and queer theorists regard Desmond Morris's work warily, the patriarchal, hetero-normative assumptions behind the story of human evolution that Morris imaginatively reconstructs in his magnum opus, *The Naked Ape,* help link the patriarchal norms of many religious strictures around nudity to a sociobiological vision of how sexuality organizes human social life. Despite his ostensibly secular, agnostic stance, Morris tells a story of the human past that resonates nicely with patriarchal religious codes and the myths of origin in which many such codes are grounded.

Sociobiologists like Morris say that humans are naked apes: highly evolved animals who have found it evolutionarily adaptive to maintain stable monogamous pair-bonds through the constant receptivity to sexual arousal that humans, with relatively hairless bodies, enjoy. Humans are unique among mammals in the unprotected, furless condition. Humans have replaced shaggy coats of fur with clothing, keeping only vestigial fur patches around the scent organs that send aromatic messages to mates. Human females need not wait for their estrus cycles to connect them to the rewards of sexual intimacy with their mates; the female of the species is bound to her mate largely by the constant possibility of sexual pleasure.

According to Morris, the heterosexual pair-bond developed at the beginning of human evolution and provides the key to the survival and success of Homo sapiens. Humans are sapient because we form strong familial bonds that yield more brainpower in offspring. The sexual fidelity of the heterosexual couple allows human infants to develop slowly, cared for by a stable set of parents, which allows for maximal cognitive development and minimal instinctual "hardwiring." The young, swaddled in clothing, are still nursing when the offspring of other species are already engaging in acts of sexual reproduction and parenting their own young. That is surely innocence but of a special sort. Human young remain "in the nest" long after sexual awareness has dawned in them. Without constant restraint of sexual urges, the primal pair-bond between parents would be threatened by the intrusion of incestuous sexual activity in the family.

Obviously the disciplined observation of sexual impulses and the policing of sexual expression are spheres where religious discourse about purity and impurity, proper and improper, dignity and shame, right and wrong can be helpful, as the work of Georges Bataille and Michel Foucault makes abundantly clear. To be on the wrong side of these polarities moves one into the realm of sinister forces, of monstrosity and excess. Nudity in this context acts with the force of the *ganz anderer,* a terrifying absence of familiar contexts, an overwheling disruption of the familiar order.

With rare exceptions, public nudity is a category mistake. Aside from cases of social abjection (such as corporal punishment in which the criminal's transgression against society is publically inscribed through the savaging of the criminal's body), most of the contexts in which one undresses before another are private affairs, affairs in which one's body is under the gaze of selected others, invited and authorized to observe one's naked body. Even in climates where clothes can detract from comfort, primary (and often secondary) sexual characteristics are rarely displayed for all to see. Unless one has joined a colony of nudists, public nudity cannot help but engender powerful emotions. Hence the apotropaic function of public nudity: the naked flesh wards off harm by its manifest refusal to follow the rules, to know its place.

RITUALS OF PASSAGE. Indeed as a symbol of category violation and liminal moments in transition between categories, nudity figures prominently in any number of ritually conferred changes of state: in the initiation of children into adulthood, in mortuary rites that send off the dead, in mourning practices that reconfigure the social world of the living, and in fertility rites that annually renew nature's infancy and potency after the senescence of winter. The works of Mircea Eliade and Victor Turner amply illustrate the utility of the symbol of the naked body in mediating such transitions between states. Baptism (at least for Paul and Christians influenced by him) entails an *imitatio Christi* whereby the neophyte suffers a symbolic death and rises again, transformed. Conversion to Judaism originally involved nudity and played on a wide symbolic range of religious symbols of rebirth and purity. The *Brit Milah* or ceremony of circumcision that Jewish males undergo as a mark of the covenant entails a change of state inscribed in the alteration of the exposed sexual organ. In many Islamic countries, boys become men through the exposure of their genitals in rites of mass circumcision.

HOLY SHAMELESSNESS. For those ascetics whose social death frees them (at least in theory) from all social labels, nudity can signify the refusal to occupy a fixed social status, as among the Digambara ("sky clad") Jain mendicants of India. Narratives about the conversion of high-status Christian men such as Saint Anthony also suggest a divestiture of social privilege and status symbolized by public disrobing. But for a woman, sartorial divestiture can be a double-edged sword. What for a man clearly signals the opting out of the social world can sometimes for a woman suggest a promiscuous freedom within that world or at least within the demimonde where "loose" women circulate. Mahādevī of Karṇāṭaka, a twelfth-century South Indian poet-saint, reportedly left her Jain husband (who refused her the right to worship the

Hindu god Śiva) and wandered naked as a mendicant. Although in medieval India the practice of nudity as a sign of having renounced all possessions and all attachments to self-image was common in male monastic communities (as it still is in the early twenty-first century in both Jain and Hindu ascetic circles), it was highly unusual for a woman to go uncovered. The threat of rape, concerns about provoking sexual desire, and aversion to the sight of menstrual blood are cited in Jain texts translated by P. S. Jaini in *Gender and Salvation: Jaina Debates on the Spiritual Liberation of Women* as reasons why women should not attempt the practice of nudity. But in the community of Liṅgāyat Śaiva Hindu saints that Mahādevī joined after leaving her husband, she was not only supported in her practice of nudity but was encouraged to completely eradicate shame from her consciousness. It is said that when Mahādevī sought admission into the community of saints, she was asked to explain why, having abandoned her clothes, she arranged her hair so that it covered her breasts. Only after explaining that she did this as a concession to human weakness and not out of shame was she accepted as a member of the community.

But Mahādevī eventually left the community of saints and took up a life of solitary wandering. And her poems indicate that she attracted a great deal of unsolicited attention in her wanderings and was often accosted. Justifying her nakedness by reference to a monistic worldview that renders shame ludicrous, Mahādevī's recorded sayings suggest that she responded with an attitude of holy shamelessness:

> People, male and female, blush when a covering comes loose. When the lord of lives drowned without a face in the world, how can you be modest? When all the world is the eye of the lord, onlooking everywhere, what can you cover and conceal? (Ramanujan, 1973, p. 131)

When one recognizes Śiva as the unmanifest reality behind every phenomenal appearance, there is nothing of which one should be ashamed. It is all God, whether breasts or buttocks or eyes which behold them. Such responses to interlocutors suggest that this poet-saint challenged cultural expectations about proper female self-presentation without conceding any ideological ground to those who found her behavior shameful.

HOLY SHAME. In these cases of ascetic nudity, as in the ritualized passage from one social status to another, nudity can instantiate the innocence and vulnerability of the infant as well as the knowing stance of the exhibitionist. When God is omniscient, Mahādevī suggests, there's no point in covering one's genitals. To cover them only shows one's ignorance of divine omnipresence and omniscience; exposing oneself shamelessly displays one's understanding of the nature of reality. The naked neophyte also dispenses with shame in the knowledge that his or her ritualized state of nudity will lead to a properly exalted status in which propriety in dress will be observed.

In the narrative of the Garden of Eden and the first humans' transition from innocence to the knowledge of good and evil (told in the Hebrew Bible's second creation account), self-awareness leads the primordial human couple to cover their nakedness. Adam and Eve's awareness of their transgression against God's command is heralded by a sudden desire to cover themselves. The fruit that the serpent had promised would make them wise also opened their eyes to their own nakedness, and they sewed together fig leaves to cover their genitals. Here wisdom is not shameless. Indeed to have shame, to be modest in covering one's sexual organs, is to show an understanding of one's place in the divinely created order.

This order is reflected, if Elaine Scarry is correct, in the emphatic embodiment of inferiors and the relative disembodiment of superiors (such as deities, kings, patriarchs, and other powerful persons) in the ancient Near East that Scarry describes in *The Body in Pain.* Thus while Morris might regard the shame surrounding the patriarch Noah's nakedness (*Gn.* 9:20–27) as having to do with worries about incest, Scarry would suggest that it would demean a patriarch to be exposed involuntarily to the gaze of his children. Noah's sons must walk backward into his tent to cover the old man's naked body when the drunken patriarch involuntarily exposes himself. The lineage of the son who looked at Noah's nakedness (the Canaanites) is cursed, whereas the lines of those who cover his nakedness (Shem and Japeth) are blessed.

Social inferiors are not to see the genitals of their superiors on pain of death in many cases. In his introduction to *People of the Body: Jews and Judaism from an Embodied Perspective,* Howard Eilberg-Schwartz provides support for Scarry's linkage between the relative disembodiment of deities and that of powerful humans in the ancient Near East when he notes that the same author (the J source) who tells the story of Noah's nakedness also recounts that, when Moses asked to see God, God allowed Moses only to see his backside (*Ex.* 33:23). Eilberg-Schwartz suggests in his introduction that Israelite literary sources are "extremely reticent about describing the divine body" and that even those sources that insist that the body of God is visible to certain humans avoid describing that body above the feet (Eilberg-Schwartz, 1992, p. 31). When this God of the Hebrew Bible manifests himself, he is as likely to take the form of fire or light as to take the form of flesh. When God permits himself to be materialized in the tabernacle (as described at the end of *Exodus*), he provides instructions for multiple layers of curtains, skins, and bronze gratings. The result, Scarry asserts in *The Body in Pain,* is that God materializes in veiled form, coming before people as "the veil, the materialization of the refusal to be materialized, the incarnation of absence. It is a realm of exclusion, entered only by the priests (whose bodies are, like the altar that is the symbolic representation of the human body, themselves surrounded by layers and layers of woven garments)" (Scarry, 1985, p. 211).

Seen in this light, the modesty shown by Adam and Eve after eating the fruit seems to exalt them above the condition of animals and the lower orders of creation. The first humans showed wisdom in their refusal to be seen in the nude. Of course as punishment for their disobedience the primal couple suffered the wages of embodiment: death, pain in childbirth, and the sweat of labor. It took the profound embodiment of God enfleshing himself in Jesus and suffering the ultimate humiliation of corporal punishment to restore humans to their rightful place, according to Christians.

In the Hebrew Bible, the covenant between Yahweh and his people is marked on the exposed flesh of male Israelites. The incarnation of Jesus, Scarry suggests, changes that dynamic of a vocal but invisible God underscoring the embodiment of his people through the cutting of flesh. Now God not only shows himself but also turns the knife on himself, as it were, incarnating as a low-status human who would be exposed, humiliated, and tortured in a public execution. The willingness of Jesus (and through him God) to be mocked and exposed before the public is replicated again and again in the actions of Christian martyrs prior to the conversion of Constantine.

For women martyrs the stakes were especially high, as Margaret Miles, Virginia Burris, Elizabeth Castelli, and others have shown. In Christian accounts of women's martyrdom, the unclothed female body often stands out as a powerful symbol. One can find in many accounts a discrepancy between the prurient interest of the audience and the unashamed innocence of the martyr. Flying in the face of cultural expectations that their appearance is immodest and degrading, many women martyrs do not regard themselves as debased. In their visions, Perpetua, a twenty-two-year-old Carthaginian, and Febronia, the twenty-year-old Syrian martyr, regender themselves and see themselves as muscle-bound gladiators, stripped naked for athletic struggle with Satan's minions, as Margaret Miles recounts in *Carnal Knowing: Female Nakedness and Religious Meaning in the Christian West.* What could be a moment of acute humiliation becomes an opportunity for righteous aggression whereby opponents of Christianity are put to shame. The Syrian martyr Mahya tells the ruler who had ordered her stripped naked, "It is to your shame . . . that you have done this; I am not ashamed myself" (Miles, 1989, p. 58). Being stripped of clothing can thus serve to highlight a devout woman's subjectivity and agency in two ways. Nakedness can serve as a means of resistance against culturally determined understandings of the body for someone whose values are counter to those prevailing in the culture, and nakedness can also serve as a means of shaming those who look, turning passivity into agency and victimization into victory.

Nudity and the intended shame that it was meant to incite ricochets back on the oppressor in a much-anthologized modern retelling of the Hindu epic heroine Draupadī's story by the Bengali writer and activist Mahasveta Devi. In Devi's short story "Draupadi," known to English readers through Gayatri Spivak's 1990 translation, Draupadī is called Dopdi, a tribal version of the name Draupadī. The narrative is set in the time of the Naxalite peasant uprisings in twentieth-century Bengal. Dopdi is a communist revolutionary who is captured, stripped, and gang-raped. Although her captors believe that this form of torture will force her to name her comrades, Dopdi does not do so. In the morning the guards bring her a pot of water so she can clean the blood off her body and dress in preparation for a visit to the quarters of Senanayak, the commanding officer. At this point Dopdi causes a commotion that sends shock waves through the camp. She knocks the water pot to the ground, then tears the garment they have given her and walks out into the sunlight naked with her head held high. Gaining advantage from what might otherwise be a shameful situation, Dopdi uses her ravaged body to shame Senanayak. Spivak's translation of Mahasveta Devi's text is terse and powerful at this climactic point in the narrative:

> Draupadi stands before him, naked. Thigh and pubic hair matted with dried blood. Two breasts, two wounds. "What is this?" He is about to bark. Draupadi comes closer. Stands with her hand on her hip, laughs and says, "The object of your search, Dopdi Mejhen. You asked them to make me up; don't you want to see how they made me?" "Where are her clothes?" "Won't put them on, sir. Tearing them." Draupadi's black body comes even closer. Draupadi shakes with an indomitable laughter that Senanayak simply cannot understand. Her ravaged lips bleed as she begins laughing. Draupadi wipes the blood on her palm and says in a voice that is terrifying, sky-splitting, "What's the use of clothes? You can strip me, but how can you clothe me again? Are you a man?" She looks around and chooses the front of Senanayak's white shirt to spit a bloody gob at and says, "There isn't a man here that I should be ashamed. I will not let you put my cloth on me. What more can you do? Come on, counter me, counter me. . . ." Draupadi pushes Senanayak with her two mangled breasts and for the first time Senanayak is afraid to stand before an unarmed target, terribly afraid. (Devi, 1990, p. 104)

Refusing to cover herself, this heroine uses her ravaged body as a weapon by which to censure the man who has sanctioned the use of gang rape as a weapon against her.

For all her righteous shamelessness, however, Draupadi-Dopdi never challenges the presupposition that it is shameful for a woman's body to be exposed to the gaze of men as Mahādevī does. The way that Dopdi shames Senanayak is by saying, "There isn't a man here that I should be ashamed." This statement suggests that if he were a man by virtue of his just conduct and unquestionable virtue as an officer, she would cover her naked body out of deference to his position. But since he is not a man, she need not acknowledge that she is a woman. Thus she is able to shame him by treating him as a junior male, a male before whom a woman can expose more of her body than in the presence of other men without violating the rules of deferential distance.

Dopdi's stance echoes the situation of the epic heroine Draupadī, for the man who claims ownership over Draupadī and orders her stripped of her sari is a villain, a cheater who wins her in a crooked dice game. Draupadī uses her considerable intelligence and quick tongue to try to prevent exposure, telling the villain that she is menstruating. But in the end she is forced before the assembly of men and her sari rudely pulled away from her body. But the force of Draupadī's virtue counters that of Dushasana's wickedness. As the garment is pulled away, another one appears underneath it. And when that one is removed, another appears. Dushasana pulls yards and yards of fabric until finally he is overtaken by exhaustion. (According to some versions of the tale, it is the god Kṛṣṇa who causes Draupadī's garment to miraculously lengthen—a surprising turn of events, given that this same god is represented in other contexts as a practical joker who steals women's clothing while they are bathing.)

The phenomenological situation of nudity includes not only a naked body observed by other people but also the state of mind and self-concept of the subject who is exposed as the object of vision. Thus to understand any one instance in which public exposure of the naked body occurs in a religious context, the subjective as well as the objective dimensions of the disrobing must be understood. Who objectively dominates whom? What does nudity mean subjectively for the person exposed? What does it mean for the observers? Is there a moral victory to be won, perhaps separate from the scorecard of social dominance and submission? Who, in the end, is the victim and who the victor? If humans are indeed naked apes, the possibility of sexual interaction marks every human situation with the signs of sexual fidelity or infidelity, familial protection or abandonment, submission or dominance, shame or shamelessness. The sentience of these various possibilities and their subversion generates a wide range of meanings whenever a body is publicly exposed.

SEE ALSO Human Body, article on Human Bodies, Religion, and Art, and article on Myths and Symbolism.

BIBLIOGRAPHY

Bataille, Georges. *The Tears of Eros.* Translated by Peter Connor. San Francisco, 1989.

Burris, Virginia. "Reading Agnes: The Rhetoric of Gender in Ambrose and Prudentius." *Journal of Early Christian Studies* 3 (1995).

Castelli, Elizabeth. "Visions and Voyeurism: Holy Women and the Politics of Sight in Early Christianity." In *Colloquium Proceedings.* Berkeley, Calif., 1994.

Devi, Mahasveta. "Draupadi." In *The Inner Courtyard: Stories by Indian Women,* edited by Lakshmi Holmstrom. London, 1990.

Eilberg-Schwartz, Howard. *The Savage in Judaism: An Anthropology of Israelite Religion and Ancient Judaism.* Bloomington, Ind., 1990.

Eilberg-Schwartz, Howard. *People of the Body: Jews and Judaism from an Embodied Perspective.* Albany, N.Y., 1992.

Eliade, Mircea. *Birth and Rebirth: The Religious Meanings of Initiation in Human Culture.* London, 1958.

Foucault, Michel. *Histoire de la sexualité.* 2 vols. Paris, 1976.

Foucault, Michel. "Excess." In *Readings: Acts of Close Reading in Literary Theory,* edited by Julian Wolfreys. Edinburgh, 2000.

Jaini, Padmanabh S. *Gender and Salvation: Jaina Debates on the Spiritual Liberation of Women.* Berkeley, Calif., 1990.

Lévi-Strauss, Claude. *The Naked Man.* Translated by John and Doreen Weightman. New York, 1981.

Miles, Margaret. *Carnal Knowing: Female Nakedness and Religious Meaning in the Christian West.* Boston, 1989.

Morris, Desmond. *The Naked Ape: A Zoologist's Study of the Human Animal.* London, 1967.

Ramanujan, A. K. *Speaking of Shiva.* Baltimore, 1973.

Scarry, Elaine. *The Body in Pain: The Making and Unmaking of the World.* New York, 1985.

Smith, Jonathan Z. "The Garments of Shame." *History of Religions* 5 (Winter 1966): 217–238.

Turner, Victor. *The Ritual Process: Structure and Anti-Structure.* Chicago, 1969.

LIZ WILSON (2005)

NUER AND DINKA RELIGION. The Nuer and Dinka peoples belong to the Nilotic group of the Nilo-Saharan language family and inhabit the savanna and sudd region of the upper Nile in the southern part of the Republic of the Sudan. The Nuer number some 300,000 and the Dinka about 1 million; the figures are approxiamte, partly because some sections of each group have intermingled. It has been argued that they should be considered a single people, but cultural and political differences are marked enough to distinguish them, and each considers itself to be distinct from the other. Their religious systems should also be differentiated, although perhaps as variants of a common system.

Both Nuer and Dinka are cattle herders on the vast savannas of the region. The Nuer are fully transhumant; the Dinka less so as their environment is less harsh and better watered, consisting of orchard savanna rather than the treeless plains of Nuerland. Relations between local groups based on patrilineal clans and lineages take place largely through exchanges of cattle at marriages and, in times of hostility, through cattle raiding; cattle also have a central religious importance, with a strong sense of spiritual identification between humans and cattle. The Nuer lack any form of traditional political authority other than the rudimentary (and essentially religious) authority of Leopard-skin priests and prophetic leaders. The Dinka leaders, the Masters of the Fishing Spear, exercise more consistent authority over more clearly defined groupings. The traditional patterns changed considerably due to colonial rule and, later, to political independence. Both peoples are characterized by their fierce sense of independence, seeing themselves alone in a world that is hostile to them both environmentally and politically. Observers have all stressed the importance of religion to them in their everyday affairs.

DIVINITIES AND SPIRITS. In both religions the world is said to have been created by a high god. The Nuer refer to this

God as Kwoth (a word that also means "spirit," or "breath"), or as Kwoth Nhial; among the Dinka the supreme being is known as Nhialic, which might be translated as "sky." Even though the two concepts may not be identical it is convenient to use the term *Deity* here for both. The source both of life and of its paradoxes, the Deity is omnipotent, ubiquitous, everlasting, and beyond the comprehension and the control of ordinary living people. Although now remote from human beings (in both religions there are myths of the separation of people from the sky), the Deity remains ultimately concerned with the world and liable to interfere in its everyday affairs at any time. Prayers and offerings are made continually and informally to the Deity, never far from the thoughts of the living.

In terms of everyday behavior the mystical or spiritual forces that are in most constant watch over people and in communication with them are the many kinds of spirits, or lesser deities, that are nearer to the mundane world. The natures, identities, and motives of these lesser deities are many. They represent, on a mystical plane, the countless and always changing aspects of the human experience of the world, of the acts of the Deity, and of themselves; any attempted classification of them except in general terms can only be uncertain and ever shifting. In both religions a somewhat similar pattern is discernible, but similarities should not be pushed too far.

The Nuer divide the lesser deities into spirits of the air (or of the above) and spirits of the below. The former are more powerful, more wide ranging, and more dangerous. Most are thought of as alien, originating from the Dinka. They are distinct from the Deity, even though both they and the Deity are known as *kwoth*. There is only one Deity, and it is original to the Nuer; the spirits of the above are many and may come from other peoples (although the *colwic*, spirits of people killed by lightning, appear to be older and not of alien origin). The Deity is seen as a benevolent father and friend, whereas the spirits are less benevolent and more immediately demanding. They possess people by sickness to signal that the latter have committed sins, and the relationship thus established between spirit and person may be inherited. Sacrifice is made to remove the sin from the possessed person, who is thereby cured, and the spirit is sent back to its proper place in the outside world. And it is the spirits of the above who possess certain people who thereby become prophets.

The spirits of the below are nearer to people. They include totemic spirits, attached to local groups; totemistic spirits, attached to individuals; and various nature and other spirits. They are all of less importance than the spirits of the above and not held in great esteem. But being more closely attached to individuals they may partake of ordinary human spite and hatred and so be demanding and unpleasant.

The Dinka distinguish what they call the sky divinities or free divinities, the more important, from the clan divinities that are attached to local groups, lesser divinities, and ancestors. The main distinction in everyday life is that a clan divinity, associated with an animal species or a class of objects, is the concern of all the members of a particular clan, whereas the sky divinities force themselves upon the living by possession and so create a permanent relationship with them individually and irrespective of clan affiliation. They are more difficult to understand and predict and thus more powerful and more dangerous. A divinity that possesses an individual is identified by divination so it can be separated from the possessed person by sacrifice. Sky divinities are regarded as external realities that represent inner psychological states and so are linked with situations of social and moral ambiguity, confusion, and sin.

PRIESTS AND SACRIFICE. Each society has ritual experts who are thought to cope with the spiritual powers and to protect ordinary people from them. Among the Nuer they are the Leopard-skin priests, members of particular lineages who possess powers, the principal of which is to purify those who have been placed, through their own or others' deeds, in a state of pollution and spiritual danger. Among the Dinka they are known as Masters of the Fishing Spear, the heads of priestly lineages. They are said to be "the lamps of the Dinka" as they "carry life" and guide their people through the darkened ways of the everyday world. They have a life-giving power given to them by the divinity Ring ("flesh"). Oral traditions state that the first Master of the Fishing Spear was Aiwel Longar, whose prayers were powerful and truthful enough to maintain the fertility of people, livestock, and land. Longar's spears were accurate and deadly when used to kill sacrificial oxen, and so are those of the present-day masters; the spiritual power resides in the spears, used for sacrificial killing and thereby also to preserve life. The invocation and the immolation of the victim is a repetition of Longar's original ritual action. The sacrificial animal is symbolically identified with the person on whose behalf the rite is performed. Guilt and sickness are placed "on the back" of the sacrificial victim and carried away at its death: its death expels sin and sickness from the group and releases the individual concerned from them.

Masters of the Fishing Spear bring and retain the "life" of their people. They may not die a normal death and so are buried alive at their own request. Since the master's life is not lost (it remains among the living to strengthen them), the people do not mourn him and feel only joy.

PROPHETS. The Nuer and Dinka have long had to face the radical (and seemingly both destructive and irrational) effects of outside interference and to make some satisfying response to them. Besides such natural disasters as famines and epidemics, the most serious cases in recent centuries have been Arab slavers, British colonial rule and "pacification," and then overrule under the Republic of the Sudan.

Little is known about their earliest responses, but during the late nineteenth and early twentieth centuries both the Nuer and Dinka produced religious movements led by prophets. Nuer prophets organized large groups of people to raid the Dinka, introduced new rites to stop new epidemics, and led the resistance against slavers. Toward the end of the last century there appeared a prophet called Ngundeng, a member of a Leopard-skin priest lineage and perhaps of foreign (Dinka) origin. He acquired a reputation for healing, announced that his powers came from a Dinka sky divinity called Deng and went into ritual seclusion and fasting, which marked his acquisition of a new and prophetic role. He had a wide following, and his supporters spent two years building a pyramid of earth and ashes, a "house of spirit" in honor of his sky divinity. After his death in 1906 his powers passed to his son Gwek. A deformed and ugly man known for his healing powers, Gwek appeared regularly at the top of the pyramid in a state of extreme possession, uttering prophecies. Like his father, he periodically fasted in solitude and wore long and unkempt hair, signs of being imbued with divine power. He headed the resistance to the British administration and was killed by government forces. Many other Nuer prophets have had generally similar attributes.

Dinka prophets were also important and numerous. The most famous was Arianhdit, who was at his height during World War I and lived until 1948. Dinka prophets were Masters of the Fishing Spear who, by acquiring additional powers directly from the Deity, also became Men of Divinity. They were thus more directly involved with traditional authority and social organization than were the Nuer prophets. They led many risings and movements of political significance in the early years of this century.

Christian missionaries have been active among both peoples. They have had little success among the Nuer and rather more among the Dinka, perhaps because the Dinka, as the largest group in the southern Sudan, give greater importance to Western forms of education and to their political ambitions in the modern world.

BIBLIOGRAPHY

The principal sources for the religions of the Nuer and Dinka are E. E. Evans-Pritchard's *Nuer Religion* (Oxford, 1956) and Godfrey Lienhardt's *Divinity and Experience: The Religion of the Dinka* (Oxford, 1961). Both are based on meticulous and rich ethnographic research and on intensive understanding of the theoretical and comparative problems in studies of alien religious beliefs and rites. Both are outstanding studies of highly complex matters. Evans-Pritchard also published scores of articles on various aspects of Nuer religion, which are listed in *A Bibliography of the Writings of E. E. Evans-Pritchard,* compiled by himself and edited by T. O. Beidelman (London, 1974). Other works include J. Pasquale Crazzolara's *Zur Gesellschaft und Religion des Nueer* (Mödling bei Wien, 1933), by a Catholic missionary with long experience of the Sudan, and F. M. Deng's *The Dinka of the Sudan* (New York, 1972), by a distinguished Dinka scholar.

JOHN MIDDLETON (1987)

NUM is the highest god of the Nentsy, a Samoyed people of western Siberia. He is the creator of the world but remains relatively remote from humans, both during life and after death (when humans descend to the underworld). Contact with Num is established only exceptionally, through spirits and through shamans and their assistant spirits. In the Nenets religion Num is the father of Nga, the god of evil and of death, and is therefore his antipode. (Among the Selkup, Nom is the highest god but does not participate in a polar opposition; in Selkup *nga* means simply "god.") The sacrifices offered to Num on specified occasions are in the form of animals, food, clothing, and money. In the terminology of syncretic Samoyed Christianity, "Num bread" refers to the eucharistic wafer, the Host.

Literally, *num* means not only "the highest god who resides in the heavens" but also "sky, firmament." The term is found in all Samoyed languages and can be reconstructed for proto-Samoyed religion with the meanings "heaven above" and "highest god." However, because the obviously cognate forms *nu-* and *num* with the meanings "up, above, top" and "sky" are also found in Khanty and Mansi (two Finno-Ugric languages related to Samoyed and spoken to the west and south of the Samoyed area), it is likely that *num* is a cultic word that in the course of time has migrated over western Siberia. Attempts to connect *num* with the root *jum(a)* found in the Finnish word for "god," *jumala* (*-la* is a local suffix), must be rejected on phonological grounds in favor of the assumption that *jumala* and related terms in some other Finno-Ugric languages are borrowed from Indic (cf. the Sanskrit *dyumān,* "bright, shining," which refers to an attribute of Indra).

BIBLIOGRAPHY

There are no works specifically devoted to Num. The interested reader may, however, profitably consult *The Samoyed Peoples and Languages* (Bloomington, Ind., 1963) by Péter Hajdú and *The Mythology of All Races,* vol. 4, *Finno-Ugric, Siberian* (Boston, 1927) by Uno Holmberg.

ROBERT AUSTERLITZ (1987)

NUMBERS

This entry consists of the following articles:

AN OVERVIEW
BINARY SYMBOLISM

NUMBERS: AN OVERVIEW

Numbers, in which the power and sanctity of both time and space are experienced in visible form, have fascinated humankind since early days, although methods of counting and systems of expressing numerals have differed considerably from culture to culture. The highest achievements in this field are the Maya system and the "Arabic" (originally Indian) numbers that were introduced in the West in the twelfth century. The presence of zero in them facilitated mathematical operations.

THE MATHEMATICAL SPIRIT. Augustine found numbers in the scriptures to be both sacred and mysterious, and people today still react positively or negatively to numbers such as seven and thirteen, for the mathematical spirit is innate in humankind and manifests itself wherever human beings live, beginning with simple geometrical ornaments. Observation of the rhythm of days and nights and the phases of the moon seem to have led to early human occupation with numbers, and the Sumerian-Babylonian astral system lies behind much of the later development. Numbers have sometimes been given divine qualities: In India, the number is called "of the kind of Brahmā," and the name of Sāṃkhya philosophy alludes to the system's reliance on numbers, for it literally means "count."

But the first religio-philosophical interest in numbers appeared in Greece with the Pythagoreans, who regarded numbers as metaphysical potencies and the cosmos as isomorphic with pure mathematics (Bell, 1933, p. 140). They defined geometrical theorems, tried to develop objective standards of beauty (the Golden Section), and found the relations between numbers and music. (In the sixteenth century, Kepler's work was still permeated by the idea of the *harmonia mundi.*) Pythagorean thought remained basic for later numerology and arithmology, all of which lays particular stress on the first ten integers, in which, as it were, the fullness of the world is contained. The classification of odd numbers as masculine and lucky and even numbers as feminine and unlucky stems from the Pythagorean system. "Lucky" odd numbers have therefore been preferred for use in magic spells, in religious repetitive formulas, and in rites of healing.

Speculations on the properties of numbers were continued in the works of Iamblichus and Philo Judaeus, and arithmology as the philosophy of the powers and virtues of particular integers was further elaborated by Nikomachos of Gerasa, Capella, Boethius, and others. It played an important role in Augustine's hermeneutics, offering him and numerous medieval Christian authors (among them particularly Hugh of Saint-Victor) a clue to biblical allegories. In the early seventeenth century, Peter Bongo (Bungus), in *De numerorum mysteria* (1618), was still trying to prove that numerology alone enables an understanding of the world.

Similar numerical allegory is found, in its most developed form, in Jewish Qabbalah; it is also incorporated into Islamic mystical thought, as in the philosophy of the Ikhwān al-Ṣafāʾ and the Ḥurūfī tradition. In both Jewish and Islamic works (as in ancient Greek) the interchangeability of letters and numerals was central for the mystico-magical interpretation of texts (i.e., in *gematriah* and *jafr*). The qualities of numbers as they appear in the biblical tradition became significant for the Christian liturgy and visible in Christian architecture; they permeate the structure and imagery of medieval and Renaissance literature. Proverbial and folkloristic usage of certain numbers, such as three or seven, reveals the general feeling toward these integers, and both religious and popular literature use the device of ascending numbers, or descending numbers (as in the *Aṅguttara Nikāya*), for counting purposes. The widespread use of magic squares is only one example of the faith in certain numbers.

Interpretation of Numbers. Although the numbers have been interpreted in various ways, it can be seen that these are generally rather similar.

1. One, according to the Pythagoreans, is both odd and even. Not a number in the normal meaning of the word, it points to the all-embracing unity that incorporates the possibility of multiplicity. "God is an odd number and loves odd numbers," says a Muslim tradition derived from classical antiquity (see Vergil's *Numero deus impare gaudet*). Geometrically, one is represented by the dot, out of which forms and figures are developed.

2. Unity breaks up into duality. Two is the number of duality, of contrast and tension: The German *zwei* ("two") in *Zwietracht* ("discord") expresses this relation, as do compounds formed with the prefix *dis.* Two signifies the tension between the positive and negative current, between systole and diastole, inhaling and exhaling, between male and female; in short, it signifies the tension that generates the continuous flow of life, for the world is composed of pairs of opposites.

"Whatever comes from the tree of knowledge has duality," says a qabbalistic text. This principle is well expressed in the Chinese figuration of *yang* and *yin.* Zoroastrian religion postulates the constant strife between the principle of darkness and that of light, which in gnostic religions develops into the strife between material evil and spiritual good. Islam sees the manifestation in time and space of the peerless, numinous One in two aspects: *jamāl* ("beauty") and *jalāl* ("majesty"). Two is further valorized in the creative word *kun* ("Be!"), which consists of the two letters *k* and *n,* and in the letter *b* (whose numerical value is two) of the Basmalah ("In the name of God . . .") at the beginning of the Qurʾān, similar to the *b* at the beginning of the Torah. In the biblical tradition, the two stone tablets of Old Testament law, like the two testaments themselves, the Old and the New, are complementary, as are the two types of life, the active and the contemplative, personified in Leah and Rachel and in Martha and Mary. Geometrically, two corresponds to the line. The presence of the dual in many languages shows how the I and Thou are juxtaposed against the multiplicity of beings.

3. Three "heals what two has split." As the first number that has a beginning, a middle, and an end, it is the first real number, "the eldest of odds, God's number properly," as Joshua Sylvester (after du Bartas) calls it. It is the first and basic synthesis, represented in the first geometrical figure, the triangle, and in the triadic rhythm of thesis, antithesis, and synthesis. As the first number beyond I and Thou, it is the first to mean "multitude" and therefore implies the superlative.

Numerous are the divine triads that can be named, from the Sumerian An, Enlil, and Enki and the Babylonian Shamash, Sin, and Ishtar to the Hindu triad of Viṣṇu, Śiva, and Brahmā and to the Christian Trinity. Concerning the last-named group, it has been pointed out that

> the paramount doctrinal weakness of Christianity, as the Arian heresy testifies, was the duality of the God-head (Father and Son). . . . That the Father and Son were one was questionable on numerical as well as philosophical ground. But Father, Son and Holy Spirit were unquestionably One by very virtue of being Three. (Hopper, 1938, p. 73)

Lesser divine or semidivine beings also appear in groups of three: The Greek Moira, the Nordic Norns, and the Roman Maters, and tricephalic deities are found in many traditions, from the Celtic to the Hindu. Even Islamic monotheism knows groupings of three, such as, among the Shīʿah, Allāh, Muḥammad, and ʿAlī.

"All good things come in threes," it is said, and everything seems to fall in triparte units: heaven-earth-water, or, as in China, heaven-earth-humanity, hence the concept of three worlds. The *Ṛgveda* knows Viṣṇu's three strides (connected with the position of the sun during the day), and three is the number of the twice-born social classes in Vedic religious anthropology. Three is also an important liturgical number, as the tripartition of places of public worship shows. Threefold invocation of the deity is common to most traditions, be it the Trisagion of Christian liturgy, the threefold repetition of *śāntiḥ* ("peace") at the end of recitation of Hindu Scriptures, or the threefold blowing of the shofar on Jewish holy days.

Metaphysical concepts often occur in groups of three: *sat-cit-ānanda* ("being, knowledge, bliss") is a common triad in Indian thought; wisdom, reason, and gnosis were manifested, according to the *Zohar,* in Abraham, Isaac, and Jacob. Buddhism conceives of *triloka* ("three worlds") and *trikāya* ("three bodies" of the Buddha), and Islam disginguishes between *islām* ("surrender"), *īmān* ("faith"), and *iḥsān* (acting perfectly beautifully). The spiritual path is usually divided into three, as, for example, *via purgativa, via illuminativa,* and *via unitiva* or as *sharīʿah* ("law"), *ṭarīqah* ("the path"), and *ḥaqīdah* ("truth"). Three plays a role in anthropological concepts, too: The spiritual powers can be divided into intellect, will, and mind, or, in Islam, into *nafs ammārah* ("inciting to evil"), *lawwāmah* ("blaming"), and *muṭmaʾinnah* ("at peace"). In indian thought, one finds the *triguṇa,* the "three strands" of matter: *tamas* ("heaviness, dullness"), *rajas* ("acitvity, change"), and *sattva* ("brilliance, perfect equanimity").

Time is commonly periodicized in three, as past, present, and future, and the Christian church knows the kindgom of the Father, the Son, and the Holy Spirit. The latter concept is important in millenarian prophecies such as that preached in the thirteenth century by Joachim of Fiore. In the more recent past, with the Third Reich (which was, historically speaking, at least the fourth German state), myth overcame history.

Three is cumulative; whatever happens thrice is law. It often simply denotes the plural, or "everything." Therefore it is used in folk tales and legends as a statistical number: Joseph was three days in the well, Jonah three days in the belly of the whale. The three Magi are as well known as groups of three brothers or sisters; three roses, three ravens, three wishes, and three guesses are frequent in folk songs, fairy-tales, and legends. One also finds the action triangle in practice (*ménage à trois*) and in drama, and the number of titles of fiction and nonfiction works that group persons or events into three is legion.

4. Four "brings order into the chaos." It is a material and cosmic number. The four phases of the moon and the four cardinal points of the earth (pre-formed in the name *Adam*) offer such ordering; so do the four elements and the four humors, and on the mythical plane, in Islam, the four rivers in Paradise and, in the Vedic tradition, the four milk streams that flow from the udder of the heavenly cow. The Pythagoreans considered four the number of justice, and their geometry discovered the four perfect solids. The term *square* still points to right, orderly, and ordering structure. As a number of cosmic order, four often divides the time: the four seasons, Hesiod's four ages of humanity, the Hindu concept of four world epochs (*yugas*), and the Zoroastrian idea of four periods. Chinese religion and Islam know four sacred scriptures, as Christianity accepts only four gospels as authoritative. For the Christian, the cross, with its four right angles, is "the rightest figure of all," extending over the four corners of the world, while the Jewish tradition emphasizes the mystery of the tetragrammaton, *YHVH.* Quaternity as an ancient symbol of perfection was reevaluated by C. G. Jung as an antidote to the unstructured, "Wotanic" spirit of his time.

5. Five is the number of natural humanity, the first number mixed of even and odd. It does not constitute an ordering number in crystals, but it occurs frequently in botanical forms, in petals and leaves (see Sir Thomas Browne's *Garden of Cyrus,* 1658), and it has therefore been considered by some as a "revolutionary" number. In antiquity, five was the number of Ishtar and Venus and is thus connected with sexual life and marriage, as in the parable of the five foolish virgins and the five wise virgins in *Matthew* 25. The pentagram, which can be derived from the zodiacal stations of Venus, is endowed with apotropaic and magic powers, while in alchemy the *quinta essentia* contains the rejuvenating force of life.

In China, five has traditionally been a lucky number; in the Western tradition one usually thinks of the five senses. Manichaeism knows five archons and the five corresponding aeons of darkness, while Islam, it is said, is "founded on five," for there are no more than five unconnected letters at the beginning of any Qurʾanic surah, and there are five Pillars of Faith, five daily prayers, and five lawgiving prophets. In Shīʿī Islam the *panjtan* (Muḥammad, Fāṭimah, ʿAlī, Ḥasan, and Ḥusayn) appears as a protective unit, popularly connected with the "hand of Fāṭimah." The human hand with its five fingers is a basis of some numeral systems, and its image has been frequently used in magic. The number of philosophical pentads ranges from the five Platonic bodies to Islamic Neoplatonic formulations.

6. Six is the macrocosmic number: The hexagon, consisting of two triangles, expresses the combination of the spiritual and the material world, hence the idea that "what is there is here." Six is a perfect number, formed from both the sum and the product of one, two, and three (1 + 2 + 3 and 1 × 2 × 3). Therefore, according to both Philo and Augustine, the world had to be created in six days. In Islam, six is used to symbolize the phenomenal world, which appears like a six-sided solid, that is, a cube.

7. Seven is a sacred number in many traditions. Because it is, according to Hippocrates of Chios, related to the lunar phases, seven influences all sublunar things. It appears in the periodicity of chemical elements and of music, and it has generally been connected with the phases of human development to a Grand Climacterium of sixty-three (7 × 9). Seven is the first prime number of symbolic meaning; it is "virgin," because it does not generate by multiplication any number under ten, and it is the only integer of the first decade that is not a divisor of 360. Consisting of the spiritual ternary and the practical quarternary (3 + 4), seven embraces everything created.

Whether the sanctitude of seven was derived by the Sumerians from the seven planets (the five visible planets plus sun and moon) or whether, conversely, they looked for seven planets to match their idea of the perfect number is a matter of dispute. The number of planets in turn determined the number of days in a week. (Niẓāmī's Persian epic *Haft paikar* expresses this belief poetically.) In Babylon every seventh day was considered dangerous, and it was thought that nothing should be undertaken; the seventh day was then sanctified in Judaism as Sabbath, the day on which God rested after creation.

The demonic qualities of seven are preserved in heptads of devils, witches, magic knots, and so on, but its sacred qualities are perhaps more numerous. Some traditions speak of seven worlds, or, in accordance with the "planets," seven spheres; therefore, the ascension of the soul usually leads through seven gates, steps, valleys, or veils (thus from the Mithraic mysteries to ʿAṭṭār, Ruusbroec, and Teresa of Ávila). In extension, Islam knows seventy thousand veils between the soul and God. Seven appears also in connection with deities of other religions; it is Apollo's number, and, in India, it is especially prominent in connection with Agni. In Iran, the heptad of the Amesha Spentas consists of six plus the all-embracing Ahura Mazdā.

But the number seven gained its greatest importance in the Judaic tradition, whence it extends into Christianity and Islam. From the seven days of creation to the seven pillars of wisdom, the Hebrew scriptures contain "unnumbered heptads." The *menorah* with its seven candles points to some of the secrets of seven. Numerous biblical stories use seven as a statistical number (Pharaoh's dream of seven fat cows and seven thin cows; Jacob's seven years of service, and then seven more). Blood should be avenged seven times, or seventy-seven times (*Gn.* 4:24), but seventy times seven should be the times of forgiving (*Mt.* 18:22). The *Book of Revelation* is filled with heptads, too, leading John of Salisbury in the twelfth century to write his treatise *De septem septenis.* Both the Lord's Prayer and the Qurʾanic Fātiḥa consist of seven sentences. Catholic churches speak of seven major sins and seven virtues, seven sacraments, and seven gifts of the Holy Spirit, and the Mass consists of seven parts.

The sevenfold repetition of religious acts is common in Islam; thus the sevenfold run between Ṣafah and Marwah and the three times seven stones cast at the devil during the pilgrimage. Sufism knows seven *laṭāʾif,* subtle centers of the body, connected in meditation with the seven essential attributes of God and the seven great prophets. A *ḥadīth* speaks of seven layers of Qurʾanic interpretation, which has been practiced especially by the Ismāʿīlīyah, whose basis is the seventh imam of the Shīʿah. They know seven cyclical periods with seven imams; the seven great prophets correspond to the seven spheres, the imams to the seven earths.

In folk tales and legends, seven is a round number: To do anything seven times is especially effective. Christian and Islamic legends know groups of seven feminine or masculine saints, most prominently the Seven Sleepers. The continuing preference for the number seven is reflected today even in the designation of airplanes as Boeing 707, 747, and so on.

8. Eight, the double four, is associated with good fortune. In Judaism the eighth day is singled out for circumcision. Christian tradition sees in the eighth day (the day after Sabbath) the resurrection of Christ; hence eight points to eternity. The eight paradises in Islam and the eight pillars of heaven in Chinese religion belong to the same concept; the eight blessings in the Sermon on the Mount as well as the Eightfold Path of the Buddha are equally connected with eternal bliss. Therefore, the traditional shape of a Christian baptistery is octagonal.

9. Nine, as three times three, is the number of completion. Only rarely in Christian theology is it considered incomplete, as ten minus one. Christianity speaks of the nine orders of angels, and Dante thus saw Beatrice as the embodiment of nine. But the number is more widely connected with Germanic, Celtic, and Inner Asian peoples. The traditions about King Arthur as well as the songs of the Nordic *Vǫluspá* show an abundance of nines, from the nine days that Óðinn (Odin) was hanging on the tree to the number of Valkyries, from ninefold sacrifices to rituals in which nine or a ninefold number of persons had to participate. This predilection for nine has been attributed to the nine months of winter in the northern areas of Eurasia, although nine occurs frequently in the more southerly lore of the ancient Greeks as well.

Such expressions as "to the nines," meaning "perfect," and "to be on cloud nine" show the old Germanic esteem for nine. The number frequently appears in Germanic popular tales, although it has often been replaced by seven under Christian influence. Its role in folklore among Germanic peoples is important, and it often occurs in connection with witchcraft (a cat, which has nine lives, can turn into a witch at the age of nine). Among the Chinese and Turco-Mongolian peoples, everything valuable has traditionally had to be ninefold: A prince has owned nine yak-tail standards; ninefold prostration has been required; and gifts have been offered in groups of nine, so that the word *tōqūz* ("nine") often means simply "present." In China a nine-storied pagoda represents the nine spheres, which are also known in the eastern Islamic tradition. The eight roads that lead to the central palace in Beijing reflect the ninefold structure of the universe.

10. Ten, the number of human fingers, and thus a basis of the decimal system, is connected with completion. In the decade, multiplicity returns again to unity, and the system is closed. The Pythagoreans regarded ten as the perfect number, because it is the sum of the first four integers (1 + 2 + 3 + 4) and is represented in the perfect triangle seen in figure 1.

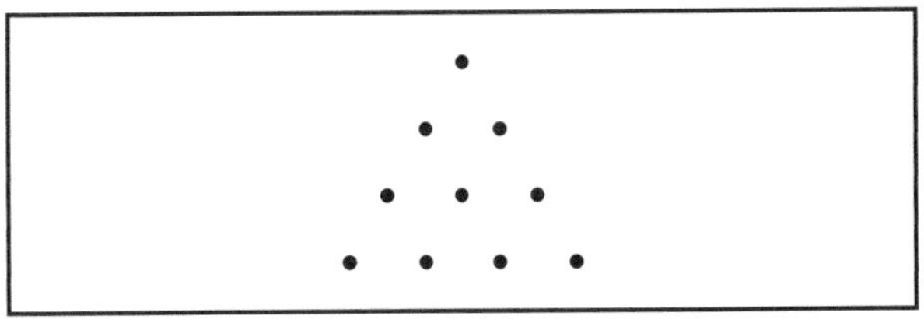

FIGURE 1.

Both the Hebrew and the Buddhist scriptures teach a decalogue, and sets of ten principles are known for the Ṣūfī novice. Likewise, Aristotle's ten categories show "completeness." In early Christianity, the three persons of the Trinity and the seven elements of created beings were thought to be represented by ten; but already the Torah had provided the ten words of creation that became the basis of "practical" (i.e., magical) Qabbalah, with its concept of *sefirot* ("numbers"). These ten *sefirot,* along with the twenty-two letters of the Hebrew alphabet, point to the thirty-two ways of salvation. Ten were the best companions of Muḥammad, and of several Ṣūfī masters, while the Ismāʿīlī system knows the ten higher orders of the *ḥudūd,* consisting of groups of three and seven.

11. Eleven is normally explained as a number of transgression, being beyond the perfect ten, or as incomplete, being beneath the equally perfect twelve; it is therefore an unfortunate, "mute" number.

12. Twelve (3 × 4; 5 + 7) is the great cosmic number. From Sumer and ancient China onward, it is the number of the signs of the zodiac and the basis of the sexagesimal system. In many cultures, day and night were divided into twelve hours, the year into twelve months, and gnostic religions speak of twelve aeons. The "great period" in Babylon was twelve times twelve thousand days, and multiples of twelve appear frequently in later mythology. The meaning of completion is as evident in the twelve tribes of Israel as in the twelve disciples of Christ and the twelve gates of the heavenly Jerusalem, where twelve times twelve blessed will adore the Lamb of God. The minor prophets of Israel, the Greek sibyls, and the imams of the Twelver Shīʿah number twelve. For medieval Christian exegetes, twelve meant faith in the Trinity that had to be diffused to the four corners of the earth. In popular traditions and sayings, it is, again, a round number, manifest in periods of twelve days or years, in twelve endangered heroes, and so forth.

13. Thirteen (12 + 1) disrupts the perfection of the duodecimal system and, being connected with the intercalary month, was considered unlucky in Babylon, a superstition that continues to the present day. In fairytale, Death becomes the godfather of a thirteenth child. But one can see thirteen also as a combination of one leader and twelve followers, of twelve members of a jury and a judge, of twelve open rooms and a closed one, of a father and twelve sons, and so on. Thirteen therefore sometimes alternates with twelve. In ancient Israel, thirteen was sacred, for thirteen items were necessary for the tabernacle. It also corresponds to the numerical value of *aḥad* ("one"); thus, thirteen rivers of balsam await the believer in paradise. The superstition that thirteen people should not sit at one table (based on the Last Supper) is comparatively recent.

14. Fourteen (2 × 7) is a lucky number, manifested in the fourteen helping saints (*Nothelfer*) of Christianity and the fourteen innocent martyrs of Shīʿah Islam. It is the number of the full moon and is, therefore, the ideal age of the moonlike beloved of which Persian poets sing. In Islam, it is further connected with the so-called sun- and moon-letters and with the unconnected letters at the beginning of certain surahs, both of which sum up to fourteen, half of the twenty-eight letters of the Arabic alphabet. The Ḥurūfīyah emphasize that the Arabic words *yad* ("hand") and *wajh* ("face") both have the numerical value of fourteen, twice the sacred seven.

15. Fifteen is the key number in the Daoist liturgical dance known as the Pace of Yu; the nine stations, or "gates," of the dance follow the sequence of a magic square whose rows, columns, and diagonals all add to fifteen.

16. Sixteen (4 × 4), in the Indian tradition, expresses completeness, in ornaments, features, meters, and poetry.

17. Seventeen, nowadays barely popular, appears in antique music and poetry (9:8 = simple interval) and in the seventeen consonants of the Greek alphabet. In Christianity it signifies the Ten Commandments plus the seven gifts of the Holy Spirit, and it figures in calculations of the number of the fishes mentioned in *John* 21:11 (9 × 17 = 153; 1 + [Product][Product][Product] + 17 = 153). Seventeen appears in Islamic alchemy (e.g., in the writings of Jābir ibn Ḥayyān), in the Shīʿah tradition, and in Turkish epics. There are seventeen *rakʿah*s (sequences of prostration) in the ritual prayers of one day, and God's Greatest Name is thought to consist of seventeen letters.

18. Eighteen (2 × 9; 3 (6) is sacred in Qabbalah, as it is the numerical value of the Hebrew word *ḥay* ("living"). In Islam, it is the number of the letters of the Basmalah, and it is highly respected among the Mevlevi order of dervishes, inasmuch as the introductory verses of Rūmī's *Mathnavī* number eighteen. By extension, the number of the worlds is eighteen thousand. The perfection of eighteen can also be understood from the fact that the Buddha had eighteen principal *arhat*s.

19. Nineteen, with the numerical value of *wāḥid* ("one"), is the sacred number of the Bahāʾīs, who count a year of nineteen months with nineteen days each.

20–29. Among the lower twenties, twenty-two is the number of letters of the Hebrew alphabet and the number of the great arcana of Tarot. Augustine divided *De civitate Dei* into twenty-two chapters, ten (2 × 5) devoted to refutation (ten negative commandments) and twelve (3 x 4) to positive teachings. Twenty-four can be numerically interpreted in several religiously significant ways (3 × 8; 4 × 6; 12 × 2), and medieval Christian interpreters used whichever combination fit with what they sought to prove. Among the higher twenties, twenty-five is the Jubilee number, and twenty-eight is the lunar number, central to the whole heptadic system.

30–39. Among the thirties, thirty-three means perfection, as a multiple of three, and as the years of Christ's earthly life. For Muslims as for Christians, it is also the age of the blessed in Paradise. Thirty-six, four times the perfect number nine, was in early China the number of the provinces and the foreign peoples beyond the borders.

40. The most important higher number is forty. As the number of days that the Pleiades disappeared (i.e., were not visible), in Babylon forty came to signify a fateful period, connected with expectation and patience. Human pregnancy lasts seven times forty days. Purifications and rites connected with death were measured according to forty in ancient Israel, as they are in Islam. The times of affliction of Israel were counted by forty: The Flood lasted forty days, the wandering in the desert forty years. Moses, Elijah, and Jesus each spent forty days in the wilderness, and Jesus remained forty hours in the grave. Forty is the span of days between the resurrection and ascension of Jesus, and it is the time of preparation for the dervish, who spends forty days in retirement (*chilla*), poetically interpreted in ʿAṭṭār's *Muṣībatnāma.* At forty years one becomes wise; the Prophet of Islam was called to preach at this age. In the Pythagorean system, forty is the perfected tetractys (4 × 10).

Forty often appears in Islamic lore as a coterminus with "very many," such as Ali Baba's forty thieves; groups of forty dervishes, forty saints, or forty Christian martyrs; and the customary selection of forty *ḥadīth,* representing the fullness of the tradition. In the Persian and Turkish tradition, women miraculously give birth to forty children. As forty in the Old Testament means "one generation," it is a temporal measure. In Turkey, where the number forty is extremely popular, great events and feasts last forty days and forty nights; to see someone "once in forty years" means "rarely." In many areas, weather predictions are made for forty days.

50. Fifty (7 × 7 + 1) is the number of the *jobel* year, a year of peace, the divine eternal rest. In connection with Psalm 50, it can point to repentance and forgiveness. A predilection for 50 and 150 is apparent in Irish folk tales.

60. Among the higher numbers, many are endowed with qualities similar to those of the bases in the first decade. Sixty is especially important as the basis for the Babylonian sexagesimal system, in which it forms the higher unit after ten; from these units, sixty and ten, result the multiples that are associated with cosmic time. According to Plato, the "cosmic day" and the "cosmic year" are reckoned by sixties. Because sixty can be easily divided, it still rules in the temporal system. The Chinese, who reckon time in cycles of sixty years, have traditionally considered that number as the full complement of a person's life. The Talmud knows fragments of sixtieths: Dream is one-sixtieth of prophecy, fire one-sixtieth of hell, and so on.

70–79. Seventy participates in the qualities of seven, and the numbers seventy to seventy-three are often interchanged in the Semitic tradition. Among them, seventy-two is most important; it is one-fifth of the circumference of the circle as well as the product of eight and nine. It usually designates great diversity: from the seventy-two disciples of Christ who were sent into the world to the seventy-two martyrs of Karbala and the seventy-two sects of Islam. Abulafia speaks of the seventy-two letters of the name of the Lord.

Higher numbers. Ninety-nine, the heightened angelic perfection of nine, is the number of the Most Beautiful Names of God in Islam, while one hundred as the new basis of the decimal system, is another complete number. Higher than that is 108 (12 × 9), the number of beads in the Buddhist rosary, the number of books of the Tibetan Kanjur, and the number of beautiful *gopīs* who danced with Lord Kṛṣṇa. Higher still are 360 and 365, which are connected with the annual cycle, and 666, the "number of the beast" (*Rv.* 13), which has been interpreted ever since antiquity as the name of a man particularly detested at various times, be it Nero, Pope Leo X, Luther, Napoleon, or some other. Symbolically, one thousand and ten thousand are both endless; 1,001 thus transgresses the largest imaginable number, while ten thousand means immortality in the Chinese tradition. The enormous numbers of Hindu and Buddhist cosmology form a theme in themselves.

CONCLUDING REMARK. The interest in numbers and their specifications continues in spite of the modern scientific worldview, especially among those who seek for a meaningful structure of the world. As Le Corbusier once wrote: "Behind the wall, the gods play; they play with numbers, of which the universe is made up."

SEE ALSO Dualism; Quaternity; Triads.

BIBLIOGRAPHY

The literature on numbers cannot be numbered; many highly specialized works have been written, especially in German, and a vast literature on modern numerology exists in German, French, and English. As a basic source, the article "Numbers" in the *Encyclopaedia of Religion and Ethics,* vol. 9, edited by James Hastings (Edinburgh, 1917), is still useful. On the development of counting systems, see Karl Menninger's *Number Words and Number Symbols,* translated by Paul Broneer (Cambridge, Mass., 1969). *Numerology* (Baltimore, 1933), a study by Eric T. Bell and others, sharply criticizes numerology from the vantage point of a mathematician. A good survey by Franz C. Endres, *Mystik und Magie der Zahlen,* 3d ed. (Zurich, 1951), has now been updated by my enlarged version of his work, *Das Mysterium der Zahl: Zahlensymbolik im Kultur-Vergleich* (Cologne, 1984). *Number Symbolism* (London, 1970) by Christopher Butler is a useful introduction. Vincent Foster Hopper's *Medieval Number Symbolism* (1938; reprint, Ann Arbor, 1966), an excellent introductory study, has in a certain way been continued by Heinz Meyer's *Die Zahlenallegorese im Mittelalter* (Munich, 1975). For a Jungian approach, see Ludwig Paneth's *Zahlensymbolik im Unbewussten* (Zurich, 1952).

Numerous studies have been devoted to single numbers, primarily three, seven, nine, and thirteen; among them, Desmond Varley's *Seven: The Number of Creation* (London, 1976) stands out not only for its quantity of information but also for its daring hypotheses. Articles on Germanic lore by Karl Weinhold and on classical antiquity by W. H. Roscher, both of whom wrote at the turn of the century, are still fundamental. On the number forty in the Islamic-Turkic tradition, see Abdul Kadir Karahan's "Aperçu général sur les ʿQuarante Hadiths' dans la littérature islamique," *Studia Islamica* 4 (1955): 39–55.

New Sources

Abas, Syed. *Symmetries of Islamic Geometrical Patterns.* Singapore, 1995.

Abellio, Raymond, and Charles Hirsch. *Introduction à une théorie des nombres bibliques.* Paris, 1984.

Begey, Roger. *Géometrie sacrée, ou la magie des formes.* Paris, 1995.

Emmer, Michele. *The Visual Mind: Art and Mathematics.* Cambridge, Mass., 1993.

Harvey, H. R., and B. J. Williams. "Aztec Arithmetic: Positional Notation and Area Calculation." *Science* 210 (1980): 499–505.

Lawlor, Robert. *Sacred Geometry.* New York, 1982.

Mandelbrot, Benoit. *The Fractal Geometry of Nature.* San Francisco, 1982.

Nielsen, Bent. *Companion to Yi jing Numerology and Cosmology: Chinese Studies of Images and Numbers from Han (202 BCE–220 CE) to Song (960–1279 CE).* London, 2003.

ANNEMARIE SCHIMMEL (1987)
Revised Bibliography

FIGURE 1. Leibniz's Symbol.

NUMBERS: BINARY SYMBOLISM

Binary numbers are a system of counting and computing using two digits, 1 and 0. This system is known today as the principle of the digital computer that represents numbers through the presence (1) and absence (0) of electrical current. The first electronic digital circuit was created in 1919. As early as 1932 binary numeration was used in electronic counting circuits. However, the first binary calculator was designed in 1679 by the great German mathematician and philosopher Gottfried Wilhelm Leibniz (1646–1716), who invented the binary number system. His plan called for using moving balls to represent binary digits. The first completed statement of the number system and its operations was made eighteen years later in a New Year's greeting Leibniz sent to Duke Rudolph Augustus of Brunswick on January 2, 1697. The letter provided a detailed description of a design that Leibniz hoped the duke would strike in the form of a silver medallion. The image reproduced here (see figure 1) was created in 1734 by Rudolph August Nolte following Leibniz's instructions.

The symbol contains three of the chief number systems: the Roman, the decimal (base 10), and the binary (base 2). Roman numerals provide the date (1697) of the greeting to the duke, no doubt to "copyright" the system for Leibniz. In the table in the center are the binary numbers up to 10001 and their decimal analogs up to 17. At the sides of the table are examples of binary addition and multiplication. The system was an *imago creationis* ("image of creation"), as Leibniz explained to the duke, because it showed how God, the Almighty One, created the world out of nothing, the zero. Thus the caption over the design reads: "2, 3, 4, 5, etc. / For everything to be drawn out of nothing, the one suffices."

Leibniz claimed that the binary system practically proved the Christian doctrine of creation *ex nihilo,* (the creation of the universe out of nothing, through God's omnipotence) by showing the origin of numbers through the use of one and zero. He decorated the symbol with imagery from the creation myth that appears at the beginning of the *Book of Genesis.* The rays at the top of the design represent the breath of God, the "almighty one," hovering over the waters, the "nothingness and void," in the moment before creation begins. The system also demonstrated the goodness of creation alluded to several times in *Genesis.* Binary numbers revealed the innate order of numerical relations hidden by decimal numbers. For example, the relation between 2, 4, 8, 16, (2, 2^2, 2^3, 2^4), is obviously the same as that between 10, 100, 1000, 10000; hence the asterisks.

Leibniz's cosmogonic symbol documents the great themes of science and religion in the seventeenth century and their secularizing and syncretistic aspects. The conviction that the universe was a mathematical artifact was almost unanimous among seventeenth-century scientists and philosophers. But this notion did not have a traditional source; scripture provides scant references to God creating with numbers. Instead, it represents the legacy of the Pythagoreans (sixth century BCE), which haunted the Western philosophic tradition for millennia. According to Pythagoras, numbers were the origins of things, proceeding from the relation of the one (limit) and the void (unlimited). The mathematical structure of physical phenomena had been so well realized in the seventeenth century that Leibniz took the equation of numbers and the universe for granted. It was the religious doctrine of creation *ex nihilo* that needed justification. In the letter Leibniz states that the doctrine was one of the main points of Christianity" that have met with the least acceptance on the part of the worldly wise and are not easily imparted to the heathen," taking a distinction Paul reserved for the doctrine of the son of God crucified (*1 Cor.* 1:24–25). But in the seventeenth century the Incarnation was no longer the primary manifestation of God. Instead people read of God's activities in the sacred book of nature. Science provided the means to read nature, mathematics, and with it demonstrated the power and wisdom of God in his creation. Leibniz was so convinced of his system's success in making God's creative act transparent that he sent his invention to the Jesuit mathematical tribunal in China. He wrote Duke Rudolph that the emperor of China might now see for himself the mystery of creation and the excellency of the Christian faith. It seems clear that mystery here means a logical conundrum and excellency, rationality. The secularizing of the tradition is confirmed by Leibniz's remark in the letter that he added the imagery from *Genesis,* the breath of God over the waters, "so that something more pleasing than number be on the design." The mythical imagery only ornamented the now reasonable doctrine of creation out of nothing.

Leibniz's symbol is more than a brilliant reflection of seventeenth-century science and religion. It also documents a historical process made possible by the nature of symbolism itself. By making relations between different realms of meaning and experience specific, transparent, and concrete, symbols can remain of continuing relevance beyond their original cultural manifestations, as the rich histories of the one and the zero demonstrate.

Leibniz's ease in combining the Pythagorean doctrine and the Jewish and Christian teaching on creation was made possible by the sacrality of the one. The paradigmatic command of the religion of Israel demanded: "Hear, O Israel: the Lord our God, the Lord is one" (*Dt.* 6:4). In the Hebrew and Arabic languages counting began with two, one being reserved for God alone. Likewise the Pythagoreans did not consider one a number because it generated all numbers—a consideration held by Aristotle and repeated up through the Middle Ages. Leibniz was certainly aware of some of these aspects of the symbolism of the one, but there is no evidence he was aware of the religious associations in the history of the zero. However, Leibniz's appropriation of the zero from the decimal system in his binary number system was just one development in a long process of religious and mathematical creativity.

Place value notation is often hailed as one of humanity's great inventions. In numerical place value the position a number symbol occupies determines its value. As a result a minimum of symbols can convey a maximum of numbers. The success of this mode of numbering depends upon the zero, the symbol of the empty place in a number that preserves the value of the position. As the uncounted counter it makes rapid calculation possible. Though possibly invented independently in several civilizations, the Babylonian and Indian inventions of place value notation were the ones that influenced Leibniz's system.

By 1600 BCE the Babylonian sexagesimal number system (base 60) employed a marker for the empty place. A functional place value symbol was employed in astronomical observations recorded in sexagesimal numbers by 300 BCE. These observations became available to the Greeks, who then used an empty circle for the place value. The sexagesimal number system is still employed in astronomy and in calculations involving circles (degrees, minutes, seconds). The earliest Indian translations of Greek astronomical texts (c. 150 CE) use the Sanskrit words *kha* ("sky") and *bindu* ("dot") for the sexagesimal place value. At the same time, the Indian decimal system was so well developed and widely known that a Buddhist text used place value, the marker of the empty position, to explain how *dharmas* ("elements") exist in time. This was at the time when Nāgārjuna, the founder of Mādhyamika Buddhism, described the reality of *dharmas* by *śūnyatā* ("emptiness"). *Śūnya,* from the Sanskrit root *śvi* (to "swell" and hence "hollow out"), had been used since Vedic times (c. 1000 BCE) as a synonym for words describing the sky or celestial vault, for example, *kha* and *ākāśa* ("ether"). But these words along with *bindu,* were used to name the place value symbol. The subsequent evidence suggests a gradual process of syncretic symbolization. By the third century CE the *bindu* had been used as the decimal place value notation in an Indian astronomical text. In the sixth century *śūnyabindu* was used to name the zero in a metaphor about the stars being ciphers scattered in the sky. *Śūnya* is thereafter found with increasing frequency as the name for the zero. The *bindu* (the dot) was incorporated into the typical Buddhist shrine, the *stūpa*. As the summit it symbolized the point where *śūnyatā* and *dharmadhātu* (the realm of element), were unified as *ākāśa,* the all-pervading ether. Emptiness and plenum were one. It was the realization of the idea of enlightenment.

It remains difficult to specify the exact relation between the religious symbolism of emptiness and the mathematical zero. The mathematical symbol of an emptiness that bears a value seemed an obvious representation of the Buddhist insight into phenomenal and conceptual reality. Interestingly enough, Leibniz's use of the zero in his binary number design gives to it a meaning not altogether different from the Buddhist value and thus helps to clarify what is centrally important. The place value suggested how conditioned or created being was absolutely distinguished from what is ultimately real, yet inseparable from it.

Leibniz took the zero from the decimal system brought to the West from India by the Muslims in the twelfth century. *Zero* and *cipher* both come from Latin transliterations of the Arabic *ṣifr* ("empty"), a straightforward translation of *śūnya.* Its symbols were the dot and the empty circle. Dots are still used today in the ellipsis, to indicate omission.

Knowingly or not, Leibniz drew upon ancient religious and mathematical expressions, the achievements of the cultures of Babylon, Greece, Israel, Arabia, and India, to fashion a number system of unforeseen usefulness. The history of the system manifests the processes of secularization, syncretism, and symbolization, as well as the processes of mathematical invention and discovery. It is a useful reminder of the global nature of the relations of the religions and the sciences. Few today may see the image of creation in their video display terminals, but the changes wrought by the technology employing the binary number system testify to the cosmogonic effectiveness of Leibniz's system.

Bibliography

The complete text of Leibniz's letter describing his invention is found in his *Deutsche Schriften,* edited by G. E. Guhrauer, vol. 1 (Berlin, 1838), pp. 394–407. An English translation of part of the letter is provided in Florian Cajori's "Leibniz's 'Image of Creation,'" *The Monist* 26 (October 1916): 557–565. It is accompanied by a patronizing discussion of its religious significance. He mentions how Leibniz's system caused the Jesuits in China to interpret the figures of the *Yi jing* as a binary number system and thus the invention of the zero and binary numbers was attributed to the Chinese. A great part of Leibniz's letter is translated in Anton Glaser's *History of Binary and Other Nondecimal Numeration* rev. ed. (Los Angeles, 1981), pp. 31–35, but he refrains from including two paragraphs where the references to *Genesis* are quite explicit. He also discusses the history of the *Yi jing* as a binary system. The book includes a chapter on seventeenth-century experimentation with number systems and an account of the application of binary numbers to electronic computation. The best introduction to the problems inherent in discussing the origin of the zero is Carl B. Boyer's "Zero: The Symbol, the Concept, the Number," *National Mathematics Magazine* 18 (May 1944): 323–330. For a summation of the controversy over the Indian origin of the zero with bibliographic references, see Walter Eugene Clark's "Hindu-Arabic Numerals," in *Indian Studies in Honor of Charles Rockwell Lanman* (Cambridge, Mass., 1929), pp. 217–236. David S. Reugg's "Mathematical and Linguistic Models in Indian Thought: The Case of the Zero and *Śūnyatā,*" *Wiener Zeitschrift für die Kunde Südasiens und Archiv für Indische Philosophie* 22 (1978): 171–181, examines new information concerning the history of place value in India and its connection to Buddhism, though he declines to specify any relationship between the mathematical zero and Buddhist doctrines of "emptiness." The symbolism of *bindu* in Buddhist architecture is discussed in Lama Anagarika Govinda's *Psycho-Cosmic Symbolism of the Buddhist Stūpa* (Emeryville, Calif., 1976), esp. pp. 92–98.

New Sources

Blazek, Václav. *Numerals: Comparative-Etymological Analyses of Numeral Systems and Their Implications.* Brno, 1999.

Diller, Anthony. "Sriwijaya and the First Zeros." *Journal of the Malaysian Branch of the Royal Asiatic Society* 68, no. 1 (1995): 53–66.

Ifrah, Georges. *From One to Zero: A Universal History of Numbers.* Translated by Lowell Blair. New York, 1985.

Ifrah, Georges. *The Universal History of Numbers.* Tranlsated by David Bellos, E. F. Harding, Sophie Wood, and Ian Monk. New York, 1998.

Van Nooten, B. "Binary Numbers in Indian Antiquity." *Journal of Indian Philosophy* 21 (1993): 31–50

Michael A. Kerze (1987)
Revised Bibliography

NUMEN. The word *numen* is a neuter form ending in *-men* and derived from **nuere* (found in the composite verbs *adnuere,* "agree with a nod of the head," and *abnuere,* "refuse with a nod of the head"). The formation is Latin, even though it is based on an Indo-European root, **neu-,* which produced a parallel word of the same meaning in Greek, *neuma. Numen* is semantically related to *nutus* ("nod of the head"), as correctly pointed out by Varro: "numen . . . dictum ab nutu" (*De lingua Latina* 7.85). It signifies the manifestation, will, or power of a divinity. Because this is its characteristic meaning until the end of the republic (including Cicero), *numen* never appears unless accompanied by the genitive form of the divinity's name. The most ancient example is in a text of Accius cited by Varro: "Alia hic sanctitudo est aliud nomen et numen Iouis" ("Here, the holiness of Jupiter is one thing, the name and power of Jupiter another"; *De lingua Latina* 7.85).

This usage is also reflected in the balanced definition of Festus: "The numen is, as it were, the nod or power of a god" (Festus, ed. Lindsay, 1913, p. 178 L.). Even when the poets of the Augustan period began to substitute at times *numina* for *dei,* by way of simplication and, often, metric accommodation, the ancient usage still made itself felt. Theodor Birt has shown that Vergil was able to maintain the original sense of the word in a phrase from the opening verses of the *Aeneid* (1.8), "quo numine laeso," which here refers to the queen of the gods and can only mean "in consequence of the violation of her [Juno's] will."

Certain scholars, in search of "primitive culture," have tried to give a completely different orientation to the Latin term by identifying *numen* with a Melanesian word, *mana.* In his book *The Melanesians,* R. H. Codrington in 1891 advanced the latter term, as meaning an "autonomous, impersonal force." This assimilation of *numen* to "an impersonal active power" led Hendrik Wagenvoort to pass over the constant usage of the republican period and to postulate a pre-deist world that in Rome would have preceded the advent of personal divinities. He reached the point of questioning the antiquity of the expression *di novensiles.* He preferred to shorten it simply to *novensiles.* Interpreted in his own way, novensiles would mean, with reference to *numen* (**nou-men*), "filled with motive power." This etymological lucubration would be no more than a venial fault if at the same time it did not betray a serious error of perspective. Indeed, the attempt to abolish every individual and personal divinity at the origins of Rome results in misunderstanding the universality of an Indo-European fact: the presence of the term **deiwos* for the idea of divinity, represented at the eastern and western extremes of the Indo-European domain. *Numen,* from the ancient times until Vergil, only expresses the manifestation of a **deiwos* become *deus* in Latin.

Bibliography

Dumézil, Georges. *Archaic Roman Religion.* 2 vols. Translated by Philip Krapp. Chicago, 1970.

Meillet, Antoine. "La religion indo-européenne." In *Linguistique historique et linguistique générale.* Paris, 1948. See pages 323–334 and, above all, page 326 on **deiwos.*

Pfister, Friedrich. "Numen." In *Paulys Real-encyclopädie,* vol. 17. Stuttgart, 1937. See especially pages 1273–1274, a fact list of the republican epoch.

Rose, H. J. *Primitive Culture in Italy.* 1926.

Wagenvoort, Hendrick. *Roman Dynamism.* Oxford, 1947. See pages 73–103 and, in particular, pages 75 and 83–85, which provide an exegesis of *novensilis.*

New Sources

Cels-Saint-Hilaire, Janine. "Numen Augusti et Diane de l'Aventin. Le témoignage de l'ara Narbonensis." In *Les grandes figures religieuses. Fonctionnement pratique et symbolique dans l'Antiquité, Besançon 25–26 avril 1984,* pp. 455–502. Paris, 1986.

Fishwick, Duncan. "Genius and numen." *Harvard Theological Review* 62 (1969): 76–91.

Fishwick, Duncan. "Sanctissimum numen: Emperor or God?" *Zeitschrift für Papyrologie und Epigraphik* 89 (1991): 196–200.

Fishwick, Duncan. "Numinibus Aug(ustorum)." *Britannia* 25 (1994): 127–142.

Henig, Martin. "Ita intellexit numine inductus tuo: Some Personal Interpretations of Deity in Roman Religion." In *Pagan Gods and Shrines of the Roman Empire,* edited by Martin Henig and Anthony King, pp. 159–169. Oxford, 1986.

Pötscher, Walter. "Numen und numen Augusti." In *Aufsteg und Niedergand der Römischen Welt* 2.16.1, pp. 355–392. Berlin and New York, 1982.

ROBERT SCHILLING (1987)
Translated from French by Paul C. Duggan
Revised Bibliography

NUMINOUS, THE

SEE HOLY, IDEA OF THE; NUMEN; OTTO, RUDOLF; SACRED AND THE PROFANE, THE

NUM-TŪREM.

The Khanty (Ostiaks) and the Mansi (Voguls) live in an area in northwestern Siberia bordered on the west by the Ural Mountains. For the most part, they are settled on the banks of the rivers there, with the Ob River flowing through the middle of their territory. As speakers of Ugric languages, they are thus known as the Ob-Ugrians. Fishing and hunting are their most important means of subsistence, although some of these peoples tend reindeer and others, especially in the southern part of the area, farm and keep livestock. Their widely differing languages belong to the Finno-Ugric family. Similar living conditions and a neighborly relationship have produced similarities in both material and spiritual culture, but the obvious variations that are nonetheless found lead scholars to distinguish between different cultural areas. The boundaries between these are fluid, however, so that certain phenomena—in this case the god of the heavens—may be treated as common to all of them.

The Ob-Ugrians, like other peoples of northern Siberia, consider that the universe consists of several worlds: earth, an upper world, and a netherworld. Popular tradition divides the upper world into a number of spheres—certain stories speak of three, others of seven—and each world is ruled by its own deity.

Prayers and the stereotyped formulae that accompany sacrificial rites address a god of the heavens as Num-Tūrem (Khanty) or Numi-Tārem (Mansi). *Tūrem* or *tārem* is interpreted as "up there" or "the high god." *Num* or *numi* denotes the visible sky, while *tūrem* or *tārem* expresses "weather, air, sky, heavens, world," "higher being, lord of the heavens," and "lord of the universe"; it may therefore be a general expression for "god." According to K. F. Karjalainen, the word also means "time" or "period of time"—for instance, "lifetime"—as well as "situation" or "state"—"state of dreaming," for example. There are different theories as to its etymology. Attempts have been made to link it to the Saami (Lapp) *Tiermes,* the name of a god of the air and heavens, or to the Turco-Tatar *tengri,* meaning "heavens."

However, the sky god has many other names in which the adjectival epithet indicates its nature; he is "great," "radiant," "bright," "lustrous as gold," and "white" as well as "Lord" and "Father." These epithets are important; some of them have become detached from their head-words to serve as proper names. Thus the name of the Khanty god of the heavens is Sängke-Tūrem, "the radiant or bright Tūrem," or quite simply Sängke, ("light"), which indicates the god's connection with the sun or the sky in daylight.

Num-Tūrem is a powerful being in folk poetry; he takes part in the creation of both the world and humankind, and as such he is also a god of fate worshiped in various ways by the two peoples. He is never portrayed in pictures, however, although in mythical accounts he is personified. In the Khanty myths he is enthroned as an anthropomorphic (male) deity in one of the upper worlds, where he lives with his family and a large retinue (like that of a prince). From there he supervises the entire creation: His ears "great as the Ob" hear everything, his eyes "large as lakes" see all, and he is all-powerful. Because nothing is hidden from him, he is also regarded as the guard of morals and justice. Many scholars, however, hold that this omnipotence bears traces of foreign influence from Islam, Orthodox Christianity, and Turco-Tatar myths concerning their major deities. It is known from historical sources that the Mansi heard Christian sermons as early as the fifteenth century and that the Tatars acquired a certain influence in the Khanty area, thus spreading both their own popular beliefs and Muslim doctrine.

Although Num-Tūrem is the Ob-Ugric god about whom the most numerous and most detailed stories have been told, he nevertheless does not seem to be worshiped by all the different groups with a special cult dedicated to him alone, nor does he have a specific field of activity. He is revered and asked to bring good health, prosperity, and good hunting, the same favors that are requested of other divinities such as the god of the forest, the Old Man of the Urals, the Great Goddess of Kazym, called Vut-imi, and Jalpus, the guardian spirit of the Khanty. Compared with other deities Num-Tūrem is more of an abstraction.

Although the narrative tradition centering on Num-Tūrem is richer among the Mansi, it is the Khanty of the southeast who perform the most elaborate sacrifices to him. These offerings, in which a white horse is the most important sacrificial animal, are addressed directly to him. This southeastern group of Khanty are small-scale farmers, and it is believed that they may have acquired these horse sacrifices from the nomadic Tatar horsemen and more generally from the large-scale stock breeders of Central Asia, because the horse does not belong to the biotope of this northern area. Extensive sacrifices to different deities were still being performed as recently as the 1930s. Similarly, the fact that the god of the heavens is ranked as the supreme being and father is ascribed to Muslim and Christian influence. In other areas, among the other Ob-Ugric hunters and reindeer breeders, sacrifices are much less prominent in the worship of the god, although he is the focus of an elaborate myth.

According to K. F. Karjalainen and others, the Ob-Ugric god of the heavens was regarded originally as a personal being "in the upper world nearest the earth," that is, in the visible sky. He was a *deus otiosus,* high above and far away from everyday human life, mostly responsible for such atmospheric phenomena as storms, the wind, thunder, rain, and so on. He was Num-Tūrem, the "god on high," but Islamic and Christian influences brought him nearer to humanity and the old sacrificial custom was invested with a new conceptual framework.

Judging from the fragments at scholars' disposal, the god of thunder known by the eastern Saami as Diermes or Tiermes also has uranian features. The etymology of the word is unknown, but *Tiermes* and *Tūrem* probably have a common origin. The name occurs very rarely in source materials, however. This and the fact that his function is only vaguely indicated make him a very elusive being.

See Also Khanty and Mansi Religion; Sky, article on The Heavens as Hierophany; Tengri.

Bibliography

Russian chroniclers mention Ob-Ugric religion as early as the twelfth century. K. F. Karjalainen has compiled available information in the first part of a detailed survey, *Die Religion der Jugra-Völker,* 3 vols., "Folklore Fellow Communications," nos. 41, 44, and 63 (Helsinki, 1921, 1922, 1927). Much earlier, in *Die Weltgottheiten der wogulischen Mythologie,* vol. 3, "Keleti Szemle," no. 9 (Budapest, 1908), Bernhard Munkàcsi wrote about the Mansi supreme deity, giving him thoroughly Christian features. Munckàcsi's very worthwhile work contains both prayers and mythological narratives. An important treatment of mythology is Artturi Kannisto's *Materialien zur Mythologie der Wogulen,* edited by E. A. Virtanen and Matti Liimola (Helsinki, 1958). Other valuable information can be found in A. F. Anisimov's "Cosmological Concepts of the Peoples of the North," in *Studies in Siberian Shamanism,* edited by Henry N. Michael (Toronto, 1963), pp. 157–229; this work is number 4 in the series "Anthropology of the North: Translations from Russian Sources," issued by the Arctic Institute of North America. The Russian ethnographer Zoia Sokolova is an expert on the Ob-Ugrians and has described the people and their traditions in *Das Land Jugorien* (Moscow and Leipzig, 1982), where she notes that their tenacious religious beliefs and superstitions live on in their contemporary religious practices.

New Sources

Hoppál, Mihály, and Juha Pentikäinen. *Northern Religions and Shamanism.* Budapest, 1992.

Louise Bäckman (1987)
Revised Bibliography

NUNS

This entry consists of the following articles:

AN OVERVIEW
BUDDHIST NUNS
CHRISTIAN NUNS AND SISTERS

NUNS: AN OVERVIEW

Although the word *nun* carries a specific, historically circumscribed meaning, especially in Catholic Christianity, it is also widely used to refer more generally to women ascetics and monastics in different religious traditions. In this overview, nuns are mainly considered phenomenologically as a specific group of religious persons who share certain characteristics across different religious traditions, cultures, and historical periods.

MEANING OF THE WORD *NUN*. In its original Christian context, the term *nun* refers to a member of a religious order or a congregation of women living under the vows of poverty, chastity, and obedience. In Roman Catholic Canon Law, only those women living under so-called solemn vows are truly "nuns" (*moniales*) in a full sense, whereas those under "simple vows" are called "sisters" (*sorores*). However, this strict legal and linguistic distinction is little observed; the popular usage of the term *nun* has been widened to include both Christian women living in enclosed convents, as well as countless sisters devoted to charitable services, such as tending the sick, dying, poor, and imprisoned, in addition to providing education and helping others in many ways. From its more inclusive use in an originally Christian context, the meaning of *nun* has been further extended to religious traditions other than Christianity. The word is now loosely applied comparatively and cross-culturally to describe a wide range of diverse phenomena relating to women's pursuit of the religious life, indicating a path of renunciation and asceticism. The word *nun* can thus refer to different groups of religious women living under vows—either together in community—or as individual women ascetics and renunciates (*sādhvīs*), as for example in Hinduism and Jainism.

MONASTICISM AND GENDER. The story of women's asceticism and monasticism represents an important part of the global history of religions, and of the larger story of women in religion, replete with numerous examples of heroic female choices and spiritual attainments. Until the recent arrival of women's and gender history, this story has been largely neglected or silently subsumed under the general history of monasticism, and for the most part described without specific attention to gender differences. It has also been tied up with male concepts of female spirituality, often defined in relation to the traditionally dominant gender roles that women, through becoming nuns, chose to resist or considerably modify. A growing number of detailed historical, textual, and tradition-specific studies of particular religious women or whole female religious communities is slowly building up a cumulative record of women ascetics and nuns. More research is needed, however, to complete the rich and diverse picture of women's active involvement in—and experience of—asceticism and monasticism. The significant contribution of nuns to different religious communities, stretching over many centuries, has been minimally recovered so far. *Sisters in Arms: Catholic Nuns through Two Millennia*, by Jo Ann Kay McNamara (1996), is a comprehensive study of Christian nuns, but no comparable overview exists for Buddhist, Jaina, Hindu or Daoist nuns.

MOTIVATION, GOAL, AND SHARED CHARACTERISTICS OF NUNS. What is the attraction to the religious life of a nun or ascetic? In each religious tradition there exist maximalist and minimalist approaches to conform human life to a spiritual ideal and to put it into practice, both by the individual and by the community. Those who are attracted to ascetic ideals—whether women or men—follow a strict understanding of their religious teachings, rites, and observances. Through voluntary choice, they pursue the embodiment of this spiritual ideal with great seriousness, sometimes with such rigor that it can lead to extremes and incite tensions, criticism and resistance. Thus all followers of a religious tradition fall into different categories, from the merely lax to the utterly committed, from laypeople to institutionalized office bearers to inspiring charismatics, who in turn may become critics and reformers.

Through the centuries women, like men, have experienced a strong calling to follow single-mindedly a more dedicated religious path in search of liberation (or *moksha*), holiness, and perfection. They have also chosen selfless service to others through renunciation, meditation, prayer, fasting, and other ascetic practices. The purpose of following an ascetic life and becoming a nun is ultimately an other-worldly, transcendent goal, reachable only through profound personal transformation. The pursuit of such an arduous goal is difficult for all people, but it is doubly difficult for women because of their traditional family roles, the reproductive duties expected of them, and their subjection to male authority in patriarchal society. Because of the widely accepted division of gender roles and the assumed equation of mind and spirit with the male sphere—and that of body and sexuality with the female sphere—women often had a great struggle to free themselves from traditional gender assumptions in order to pursue a religious path. The history of nuns in Hinduism, Buddhism, and Christianity provides plenty of evidence for this.

The motivations for pursuing such an unconventional path—one that requires a struggle against much social resistance—might be mixed. One motivation could be a genuine attraction to a spiritual ideal; another could be the alternative of trying to escape from the burden of marriage and sexuality, child-bearing, and family bonds for a young woman. For an older woman—a widow, for example—it could be the choice of joining a like-minded religious community in order to complete her life in dedication to a religious ideal. Such mixed motivations are clearly evident from the study of women renunciates (Khandelwal, 2004), and nowhere are the mixed motives in the struggle for liberation more clearly expressed than in the famous songs of the Buddhist Therīgātha (Blackstone, 1998).

WOMEN AND ASCETICISM. A woman ascetic or nun—the terms are often used interchangeably—can be characterized as an ideal type of religious figure that exists in numerous variations and a wide variety of historical configurations. In terms of the shared characteristics of nuns, one can examine the similarity or dissimilarity of their vows across time and traditions, as well as whether such vows are the same in number and kind as those of men in the same religious tradition, or, on the contrary, whether they are considerably more numerous and different, as is the case in Buddhism. A person can look at the patterns and rhythms of the nuns' religious practices, their clothing, and and their food habits—especially in terms of the use and renunciation of food—all of which imply different degrees of self-denial and widely varying attitudes towards the human body.

In the first volume of the *Encyclopedia of Religion*, Walter Kaelber defined asceticism as "a voluntary, sustained, and at least partially systematic program of self-discipline and self-denial in which immediate, sensual, or profane gratifications are renounced in order to attain a higher spiritual state or a more thorough absorption in the sacred" (1987, p. 1:441). However, this definition does not articulate the multi-dimensional aspects of asceticism nor its gender variations. Many women ascetics, like men, practice what has been called a "heroic asceticism," a term which groups together several practices of physical deprivation, such as bodily injuries and laceration of the flesh, sleep deprivation, fasting, and starvation. These practices can lead, in certain cases, to altered states of consciousness, ecstatic, mystical, and possession experiences. In the discussion of asceticism, however, most attention has been given to sexual renunciation, chastity, and virginity, especially in studies of Christian asceticism (Brown, 1988; Castelli, 1986). A "virginal asceticism" developed in the early Christian church before the organization of a more specialized monasticism, but it was often tied to a marked misogynism (Ruether, 1974).

Because women's bodies are considered impure in many religions, the ascetic ideal of controlling sexual and other physical needs was particularly attractive to women who sought sainthood and perfection. In withdrawing from the world by renouncing property, marriage, family bonds, and household responsibilities, women could assert their autonomy by removing themselves—to some extent—from the patriarchal control of men (although most religious traditions rank monks above nuns who in status, attainment, and authority, usually remain subordinate to male renouncers). Through the renunciation of sexual activity, women also obtained control over their bodies and transcended traditional femaleness, becoming, so to speak, "honorary males." Because they were no longer valued for their reproductive sexuality and social function, these women gained a new, spiritual authority and power that was widely recognized among ascetics and mystics of different religious traditions.

In the Western tradition, the figure of the "virgin-ascetic" goes back to at least Roman antiquity (Brown, 1988; Cooper, 1996), whereas the Greek tradition is without a parallel notion of asceticism. The early Christian ascetics soon developed the monastic ideal. Originally intended as a solitary life pursued by the individual (*monos* = alone), this ideal soon took on a corporate character. Teachings, rules, leaders, and women's asceticism and monasticism developed along with, or even before, that of men. When the great monastic orders were later founded by men, a number of women's orders grew as well, maintaining a close connection with—and dependence upon—the male orders. This occurred because the nuns were affiliated to the same rules and monastic constitutions, without separate developments of their own.

Strictly speaking, nuns are the cloistered women monastics of these ancient orders. But in post-Reformation Europe, from the sixteenth century onwards, a great number of entirely new, unenclosed female religious congregations and sisterhoods developed that were entirely independent from any existing order of men. These congregations and sisterhoods owed their foundation to original ideas and unusual, strong women dedicated to new spiritual, social, and educational ideals. Today these Christian sisters, whose many congregations were largely founded during the nineteenth century, are also referred to as nuns.

NUNS IN DIFFERENT RELIGIONS. In terms of origin, the earliest groups of nuns are perhaps found in Jainism, which knows of women renouncers since about the time of Mahāvīra (c. 490–410 BCE) around the fifth century BCE, followed closely afterwards by Buddhist nuns. Although there seems to have been less reluctance among Jainas than on the Buddha's part to admit women on an equal basis from the start, Jaina nuns share with Buddhist nuns the requirement that they must follow additional and stricter rules than monks. The two major Jaina groups, the Śvetāmbaras and Digambaras, as well as several subsects, all possess distinct groups of nuns; in fact, among the Śvetāmbaras, nuns far outnumber the monks. In spite of more detailed recent case studies (Vallely, 2002; Shanta, 1985), much further research is needed to make the nuns' contribution to Jainism better known and understood.

More information, though far from sufficient, is available on Buddhist nuns, where there exist a great variety of monastic groups across the Buddhist world. Usually, but not always, the number of nuns is less than that of Buddhist monks, although this varies from country to country. In Taiwan, for example, there are two-thirds more nuns than monks. Korea also knows a large number of nuns whose work, like that of other nuns, has been little recorded in Buddhist texts, nor has it been much investigated by scholars. This is changing, however, because Buddhist women have organized themselves into a global network in order to promote closer collaboration and study of their own history and activities.

In Hinduism, the ancient Vedas know of some solitary women seekers and ascetics, and the Sanskrit language possesses a female equivalent to the male renouncer: there is the *sādhvī* as well as the *sādhu,* the *saṃnyāsin* as well as the *saṃnyāsīs.* But due to the prohibition on women and non-Brahmans to study Vedic texts or perform Vedic rites, women were effectively barred from taking vows to pursue renunciation (*saṃnyāsa*), except as members of unorthodox sects. Thus there are no female Hindu monastic orders until the modern foundation of the Śrī Śāradā Maṭha in 1954 as a parallel to the Ramakrishna Order (Sinclair-Brull, 1997). In the past, individual male *saṃnyāsins* may occasionally have accepted female monastic disciples, and individual women ascetics may sometimes have become gurus, but these remained exceptions, whereas women gurus have grown much more prominent during the twentieth century. Past female ascetics usually did not take monastic vows but lived away from home, in holy cities such as Vārāṇasī, either alone or in groups, retaining lay status so that no organized order of Hindu women nuns existed in earlier times (Ohja, 1981, 1984). However, in spite of the growing interest in the comparative study of female ascetics and nuns, the phenomenon of women renouncers in the Hindu tradition remains too little researched; only a few studies of the varieties of contemporary Hindu female ascetics exist (Khandelwal, 2004; Denton, 1991).

Less information is available on Daoist nuns, whose study is also in its initial stages. Although women have had a notable presence in Daoism, it was originally not a monastic religion, and nuns only appeared during the seventh to ninth centuries CE, when some women from the Chinese court chose the path of renunciation. Women's religious establishments flourished during medieval times, whereas few women's monasteries exist in China today. In some cases, however, nuns are known to hold positions of authority (Levering, 1990; Cahill, 1993).

More is known about Christian nuns than nuns of any other religion. In the contemporary world, Christian nuns far outnumber monks and priests (some years ago the ratio was three to one). Although long neglected in historiographical accounts and studies of Christian monasticism, in the late twentieth century many sources about women ascetics, individual nuns, and whole communities of sisterhoods—whether in early Christianity, the medieval church, or the post-Reformation church—were discovered and closely studied. From what is known so far, earlier groups of Christian nuns possessed several characteristics not found elsewhere, and with few equivalents in contemporary Christianity. There existed the cultivation of a close spiritual companionship between male and female ascetics (known as *syneisactism*), which was not based on sexual or family ties. It was based, rather, on the common pursuit of a spiritual goal, the use of family language and familial metaphors for the monastic community of women and men (Krawiec, 2002), and, for many centuries, the presence of double monasteries where communities of nuns and monks lived together—though in separate groups—and where the overall authority for the entire monastery was sometimes given to a woman abbess.

CONCLUSION. The comparative phenomenological study of nuns remains relatively undeveloped. Yet it offers a large field for scholarly investigation that can yield exceptionally rich historical and empirical data for more nuanced theoretical reflections on questions of spiritual authority, autonomy, power, monastic lineage, hierarchy, equality, and community in the growing area of gender studies in religion. It is up to younger scholars to perceive this great research potential and seize the opportunity to obtain a more detailed picture about the global history of women ascetics and nuns.

SEE ALSO Asceticism; Gender and Religion, articles on Gender and Hinduism, Gender and Jainism; Guru; Human Body, article on Human Bodies, Religion, and Gender; Menstruation; Monasticism, articles on Buddhist Monasticism, Christian Monasticism; Mysticism; Prayer; Sādhus and Sādhvīs; Spirit Possession, article on Women and Possession; Virginity.

BIBLIOGRAPHY

Blackstone, Kathryn R. *Women in the Footsteps of the Buddha. Struggle for Liberation in the Therīgātha.* Richmond, U.K., 1998. A detailed study of the songs of the early Buddhist nuns that vividly express their motivation in seeking renunciation, and the obstacles in obtaining it.

Brown, Peter. *The Body and Society: Men, Women, and Sexual Renunciation in Early Christianity.* New York and Chichester, U.K., 1988. A classic study by now, this magisterial survey closely examines the understanding of sexuality and sexual renunciation in early Christianity among both men and women.

Cahill, Suzanne E. *Transcendence and Divine Passion: The Queen Mother of the West in Medieval China.* Stanford, Calif., 1993. Provides information on the development of Daoist nuns in medieval China.

Castelli, Elizabeth. "Virginity and Its Meaning for Women in Early Christianity." *Journal of Feminist Studies in Religion* 2, no. 1 (1986): 61–88. An informative and extensively referenced article on the roots of asceticism and the idea of virginity in the early Christian church.

Cooper, Kate. *The Virgin and the Bride: Idealized Womanhood in Late Antiquity.* Cambridge, Mass. and London, 1996. In discussing the options available to women in late antiquity, this book investigates the tensions that existed between the Christian ideals of virginity and marriage during the rise of asceticism.

Denton, Lynn Teskey. "Varieties of Hindu Female Asceticism." In *Roles and Rituals for Hindu Women,* edited by Julia Leslie. London, 1991. Compares the values of the woman-as-householder with those of the ascetic, and discusses different forms of Hindu asceticism open to women.

Kaelber, Walter O. "Asceticism." In *Encyclopedia of Religion,* vol. 1, edited by Mircea Eliade, pp. 441–445. New York, 1987.

Khandlewal, Meena. *Women in Ochre Robes: Gendering Hindu Renunciation.* Albany, N.Y., 2004. A fascinating account of the lives of contemporary *saṃnyāsīs* describing their daily lives in ashrams, their dress, food, conversation, service, ritual, and devotion. Contrary to the assumption that renunciation transcends gender, arguments are provided that renunciation can underscore the importance of gender.

Krawiec, Rebecca. *Shenoute and the Women of the White Monastery: Egyptian Monasticism in Late Antiquity.* Oxford, 2002. Using Coptic sources, this fascinating study of one of the most important Egyptian monasteries of the fourth and fifth century with several thousand monks and nuns shows how a community of vibrant ascetic women was chafing under the leadership of a stern and irascible man, the abbot Shenoute. Negotiations over food, clothing, and other everyday matters within a large, mixed community reveal important issues of monastic authority, of the intersection of power and gender, and of women's role in the monastic family.

Levering, Miriam. "Women, Religion and the State in the People's Republic of China." In *Today's Woman in World Religions,* edited by Arvind Sharma. Albany, N.Y., 1994. Contains information on Daoist women practitioners in contemporary China.

McNamara, Jo Ann Kay. *Sisters in Arms: Catholic Nuns through Two Millennia.* Cambridge, Mass., and London, 1996. Hailed as a groundbreaking work, this history of Christian nuns shows the great variety of women religious, including scholars, mystics, artists, political activists, teachers, and healers. Although women had to struggle against the male church hierarchy and larger forces of social and cultural change, the book provides rich evidence that monastic communities gave women a space that allowed them to evolve spiritually, intellectually, and emotionally.

Ojha, Catherine. "Female Asceticism in Hinduism: Its Tradition and Present Condition." *Man in India* 61, no. 3 (1981): 254–285. An early study of Hindu female ascetics, with some discussion of their past history and present situation, in contrast to the life and duties of most Hindu women.

Ojha, Catherine. "Condition féminine et renoncement au monde dans l'Hindouisme. Les communautés monastiques de femmes à Benares." *Bulletin de l'École Française d'Extrême-Orient* 73 (1984): 197–221. A further development of Ojha's 1981 essay on female renunciation cited above, this article mentions about one hundred women ascetics (as compared to 1,200 men) in Benares, living either alone or in a monastic community, of which three are closely examined here.

Ruether, Rosemary Radford. "Misogynism and Virginal Feminism in the Fathers of the Church." In *Religion and Sexism: Images of Woman in the Jewish and Christian Tradition,* edited by Rosemary Radford Ruether. New York, 1974. Discusses early Christian attitudes towards virginity and women's asceticism.

Shanta, N. *La voie Jaina: Histoire, spiritualité, vie des ascètes pèlerines de l'Inde.* Paris, 1985. Translated by Mary Rogers as *The Unknown Pilgrims: The Voice of the Sadhvis: The History, Spirituality and Life of the Jaina Women Ascetics.* Delhi, India, 1997. A wide-ranging, pioneering study of women ascetics in Jainism based on classical texts and contemporary fieldwork.

Sinclair-Brull, Wendy. *Female Ascetics. Hierarchy and Purity in an Indian Religious Movement.* Richmond, U.K., 1997. Discusses the nature of Hindu asceticism with reference to the modern foundation of a monastic order for women, the Śrī Śāradā Maṭha, parallel to the Ramakrishna Order. Based on fieldwork at a branch of the Śrī Śāradā Maṭha in Kerala, the author focuses especially on the dynamics of purity and hierarchy operating among the *saṃnyāsinis,* and between them and the surrounding village communities.

Vallely, Anne. *Guardians of the Transcendent: An Ethnography of a Jain Ascetic Community.* Toronto, Canada, 2002. Based on fieldwork in Rajasthan, this study provides many insights into the lives of the women ascetics of a particular Jaina sect, the Terāpanthī.

URSULA KING (2005)

NUNS: BUDDHIST NUNS

Buddhism has evolved during more than 2,000 years in many different Asian countries (including India, Sri Lanka, Thailand, Myanmar, China, Korea, Japan, and Tibet). At times Buddhist nuns had a prominent and respected role and at other times they vanished into obscurity. This article will endeavor to explain why there exist such diverse types of Buddhist nuns with different status, robes, and cultures.

Two thousand five hundred years ago in India, Buddhist women shaved their heads, donned saffron robes, and became celibate nuns. They aspired to awakening, meditated, and taught lay followers. Their precepts forbade them to touch money, and thus they depended on alms for their support. The nuns' accomplishments and awakening experiences are recounted in the *Therīgāthā* (*Psalms of the Sisters*), seventy-three poems expressing the spiritual search and struggles of the first Buddhist nuns, which had been orally transmitted until they were written down six hundred years later, and the *Apadāna* (collection of moral biographies) composed in the second and first century BCE, which contains forty biographies of eminent early nuns.

The order of Buddhist nuns (*bhikṣuṇī*) began later than the monks' order (*bhikṣu*). As tradition has it, the Buddha at first seemed reluctant to give ordination to his female followers. His attendant, Ananda, pointed out that because the Buddha agreed that men and women were equal in their capacities for spiritual attainment, it seemed only equitable to let women enter his order of mendicants. Ananda was moved by the distress and spiritual aspiration of the Buddha's foster mother and aunt, Mahāpajāpatī, and of the many women in her entourage. They became the first Buddhist nuns.

Nonetheless, according to tradition, the Buddha gave eight extra rules to the nuns for entering the homeless life:

> A nun who has been ordained for a century must bow to a monk who has been ordained for a day.
>
> A nun must not spend the meditation season (*vassa,* i.e., the monsoon period) in a place where there are no monks.
>
> Every fifteen days, the nuns must ask the monks for the date of the observance day, and must ask them to give the nuns a teaching.

> After the meditation season a nun must tell her faults to both the order of monks and the order of nuns.
>
> If a nun commits a grave error she must submit herself to the scrutiny of both orders for fifteen days.
>
> A nun can obtain full ordination from both orders only after she has observed the six precepts during two years as a postulant.
>
> A nun must never scold a monk.
>
> The nuns cannot teach the monks, but the monks can teach the nuns.

As with the monks' order, a vinaya (rule of discipline) was developed for the Buddhist nuns' order in which their precepts were collected. After the death of the Buddha, different schools developed their own vinayas. Today, the Theravāda Vinaya, which contains 227 precepts for monks and 311 for nuns, is followed by the monastics in Southeast Asia (Thailand, Sri Lanka, and Burma [now Myanmar]); the Dharmagupta Vinaya, which contains 250 precepts for monks and 348 for nuns, by those in Northeast Asia (China, Korea, and Vietnam); and the Mūla-Sarvāstivāda Vinaya, with 253 precepts for monks and 364 for nuns, by those following the Tibetan tradition. Some scholars account for the greater number of precepts for nuns by the fact that the relevant monks' precepts were the starting point for the nuns' list. Specific rules relating to the nuns' situation were then added.

THERAVĀDA NUNS. At the time of the Buddha, women were required to observe six precepts for two years before receiving higher ordination. Over time this situation changed for Buddhist nuns as they encountered different historical and cultural conditions. As Buddhism spread in the Indian subcontinent after the death of the Buddha, the nuns' order reached Sri Lanka in the third century BCE, and many nunneries were established. But the female order died out in Sri Lanka in the tenth century CE and was never reconstituted. It did not seem to reach Thailand or survive in Myanmar, and died out totally in India.

At the end of the nineteenth century some Sri Lankan laywomen were attracted to the religious life and decided to take ten precepts. They shaved their heads and started to wear white and saffron clothes—white being the color for the Buddhist lay followers, and saffron the color of the monks' robes in most Theravāda countries. Eventually most of them started to wear saffron only. They were called *dasasil mātās* (ten-precept women). They created an in-between status role for Buddhist women. Some lived by themselves; others gathered in nunneries. Today most of them serve their communities by counseling, teaching, and performing religious ceremonies for laypeople; some devote themselves to meditation.

Until recently it was thought to be impossible to revive the higher ordination for nuns. Because the order had died out, the necessary quorum of ten nuns *(bhikṣuṇī)* to ordain others did not exist. In the mid-1980s, various attempts were made to restore the higher ordination in Sri Lanka, but there was great opposition from the conservative elements in the male hierarchy. Finally, thirty Sri Lankan nuns were fully ordained in February 1998 in Bodh Gayā, India, at an international ordination for both men and women, organized by Chinese monks and nuns from Taiwan. Several higher ordinations followed in Sri Lanka in the Dambullah Temple, whose monks are supportive of the nuns' movement. In 2004, there were about 400 fully ordained nuns *(bhikṣuṇī)* and 2,100 *dasasil mātās* in Sri Lanka.

There were about 30,000 nuns in Myanmar in 2004. They take eight or ten precepts but are not considered novices *(śrāmaṇerikā),* but *tila shin* (possessors of morality). The nuns wear pink robes, and the monks wear the original saffron. Many are great meditators and do in-depth study of Buddhism. They are less well-supported financially than the monks.

The lowest position for Buddhist nuns must be in Thailand, where it is forbidden by a Buddhist law promulgated by a supreme patriarch in 1928 that a Thai *bhikṣu* give any ordination to women. So women with a religious vocation take five or eight precepts and are called *maeji* (mother ascetic) and wear white. There were 10,000 *maejis* and 850 nunneries in 2004. Since creating the Thai Nuns' Institute in 1969, nuns have started to organize themselves and to develop opportunities for studies and meditation, which have led to greater respect and support from the Buddhist lay followers.

In 1956 Voramai Kabilsingh received her first ordination from Pra Prommuni, the deputy abbot of Wat Bavorn in Bangkok, and in 1971 she received full ordination in Taiwan. She started to wear light yellow robes and was criticized by the monastic hierarchy for doing so. Her daughter, Chatsumarn Kabilsingh, followed in her footsteps by receiving the lower ordination in Sri Lanka in 2001 and higher ordination in 2003 from the newly formed *bhikṣuṇī* order there. She wears brown robes. Her actions have stirred great debate at all levels of Thai society (government, Buddhist hierarchy, media). However, not all five-, eight-, or ten-precept nuns want to become *bhikṣuṇīi.* Some foresee difficulties in trying to maintain 348 precepts, some of which are outmoded and hard to follow. They are very aware that they would be scrutinized even more closely than the monks. Many nuns actually enjoy their freer status and also the fact that they are not controlled by the male hierarchy. In England, Western monks trained in the Thai tradition asked for a derogation and in 1994 were able to ordain Western nuns, who wear brown habits and follow ten precepts, in Amaravati Temple near London.

CHINESE, TAIWANESE, KOREAN, AND JAPANESE NUNS. In the fifth century CE, Sri Lankan nuns traveled to China by sea and founded an order of *bhikṣuṇī* that has been preserved to this day and that also spread to Korea and Vietnam. The lives of these early Chinese nuns are recorded in the *Biqiuni zhuan,* a collection of biographies of sixty-five eminent Chinese Buddhist nuns from the fourth to the sixth centuries.

These nuns were great scholars, teachers, meditators, and ascetics. On the basis of statistical research, some Western scholars have claimed that at the beginning of the twentieth century there were three million monks and nuns in China. Monks and nuns suffered greatly, but some survived the Cultural Revolution (1966–1976), and at the beginning of the twenty-first century one could find a few Buddhist nunneries in mainland China. The nuns perform religious services, study, and meditate, but many of them are quite old, though a few younger ones are starting to enter the homeless life. Of the thousands of nuns living in Vietnam, Cambodia, and Laos before 1962, many died or had to disrobe because of wars and the Communist takeover. Since then, however, women in these countries have regained an interest in the ordained life.

After 1949, mainland Chinese Buddhist nuns went to Taiwan and Hong Kong and strengthened Buddhism there. In Taiwan in 2004, Buddhist nuns number about 7,000—two-thirds more than the number of monks—and half of them are young women, newly ordained. They receive a good Buddhist education and are very active and involved with society. Bhikṣuṇī Zhengyan (b. 1937, ordained in 1963, she has been called China's Mother Theresa) was able to develop the Ciji Foundation, which builds hospitals and medical schools in Taiwan and provides disaster relief all over the world by encouraging her followers to create financial surplus to help others. Bhikṣuṇī Hiu-wan created Hua Fan University near Taipei, founded a nun seminary, and is also a renowned scholar and painter.

Buddhism came to Korea in the fourth century CE and developed until the thirteenth century; thereafter, it was repressed until the turn of the twentieth century by the Confucian state. But the nuns' order managed to survive intact, and at the turn of the twenty-first century Korea was a vibrant place for nuns, who number about 8,000. Their status is fairly equal to that of the monks and they live separately from them. Over time in China and Korea, the eight extra rules given by the Buddha to his aunt diminished in importance. In modern Korea, there are many nunneries set far away from monasteries, the monks and the nuns bow equally to each other, and the nuns have total control of their own affairs. Following the devastation of the Korean War in the 1950s, nuns even rebuilt some monasteries and transformed them into nunneries. One such is Unmun Temple, a leading seminary with 300 young nuns under the direction of scholar and abbess, Bhikṣuṇī Myŏngsŏng.

Korean women can become nuns after high school graduation. They begin by being postulants for a year to learn about the celibate life and to decide if it is their vocation. After a year they become novices *(śrāmaṇerikā)* with ten precepts. After another three to five years they can then receive the full ordination of a *bhikṣuṇī*, first given by a panel of ten nuns and secondly by a panel of ten monks. The novices study Buddhist texts for three years, then join a meditation hall for the biannual three-month meditation retreats. They will meditate for at least ten hours a day with ten to fifty other nuns. Upon reaching middle age, they might take a position such as a manager or abbess in their home nunnery, or a professor at a seminary or a university. Some have become artists. Others serve laypeople in towns or villages or create charitable organizations; Bhikṣuṇī Myohi, for example, built a retirement home for old nuns and women without support.

In Japan, the full ordination for monks and nuns lasted only briefly after the introduction of Buddhism in the sixth century CE. Over time, different sets of precepts were adopted, such as the fifty-eight or the sixteen *bodhisattva* precepts. At the end of the nineteenth century the Meiji government put an end to celibacy for all Buddhist monks and it became a matter of choice whether to be celibate or not. (It has been suggested that Japanese married monks should be called priests.) Most Japanese monks are married, and most Japanese nuns are celibate, though Western female priests from Japanese Buddhist traditions who teach in the United States and Europe are often married.

There were relatively few nuns in Japan in 2004: the number 2,000 nuns in 1,500 temples has been reported. There are three training centers for nuns in the Soto tradition and one in the Pure Land tradition. The biggest such center is Aichi Semmon Nisodo (Sōtō Zen) in Nagoya, founded in 1903, whose abbess, Aoyama Sensei (a celibate nun), is remarkable in her practice and her scholarship. Most Japanese nuns live on their own in small temples where they perform religious services for laypeople and support themselves by teaching arts such as tea ceremony and flower arrangement.

TIBETAN NUNS. When Buddhism came to Tibet in the seventh century CE the higher ordination for nuns was not transmitted: women were only able to receive ten precepts from fully ordained monks and become novices. Tibetan nuns still take ten precepts, which are subdivided into thirty-six. In 1959 there were 618 nunneries with 12,398 nuns in Tibet, but they suffered greatly during the Chinese Communist takeover and Cultural Revolution. A few nunneries can still be found in Tibet, and some nuns still practice as hermits in caves, but their circumstances are very difficult. There are nunneries in the border regions of Tibet (Ladakh, Nepal, Sikkim, Bhutan), but the social position of nuns is often quite low and sometimes they have to serve menially the monks or even their own families. To remedy this situation, training nunneries have been built in Dharamsala, the residence-in-exile of the Dalai Lama, and other places in northern India. For example, the English nun Tenzin Palmo, who was a hermit in the Himalayas for ten years, has started a nunnery for women from the Indian border regions to train, study, and practice like the monks. In the West there are an increasing number of Western nuns (more than 300) in the Tibetan tradition, but there are very few places where they can train together. One exception is Dhagpo Kundrel Ling, a Tibetan Buddhist training center in France, dedicated to three years' retreats and monastic life. In November

2004 ten of the fifty women who became nuns for the duration of the traditional three years' retreat joined thirty other nuns living in a hermitage for nuns with a life-long commitment. These nuns follow a rigorous training but also participate in the life of the center and teach worldwide.

INTERNATIONAL OUTREACH. The first International Conference on Buddhist Nuns took place in 1987 in Bodh Gayā, India. At the end of this conference, the international Buddhist women's association Sakyadhita (Daughters of the Buddha) was created. Its objectives were to create a network for Buddhist women around the world, to educate women as teachers of Buddhism, to conduct research on women and Buddhism, and to work for the establishment of the *bhikṣuṇī saṃgha* where it does not currently exist. Sakyadhita has been instrumental in the reestablishment of the higher ordination in Sri Lanka. Since 1991, Sakyadhita has organized international conferences on Buddhist women every two years in various Asian countries (Thailand, Sri Lanka, India, Cambodia, Nepal). There has also been one North American conference. Most of the conferences are situated in Asia to enable Asian women and nuns to participate in greater numbers and to support Buddhist nuns by bringing highly educated and respected *bhikṣuṇī* to countries where the position of nuns is low. Often these conferences have stimulated improvements for the nuns in the places visited. They have also helped nuns in isolated situations to make contact and gain support from nuns and women from all over the world. At the conference in Ladakh in 1995, 108 delegates came to this remote part of northern India and met with many Buddhist women from the Himalayan border regions for a conference titled "Women and the Power of Compassion: Survival in the Twenty-First Century."

There is no doubt that the topic of Buddhist nuns has been an underresearched area, but this is slowly changing as contemporary scholars begin to delve into historical and archival materials in Sanskrit, Chinese, and Korean to seek the traces left by Buddhist nuns. It is a search rendered difficult by a patriarchal cultural and religious bias, which have resulted in Buddhist nuns having nearly no place in the lineage, little authority, and no part in the formal hierarchy. Thus they have tended to be omitted in official records. Most of the inscriptions with reference to nuns show them as donors or sponsors of religious festivals.

Because Buddhism is a decentralized religion which has found diverse expressions throughout Asia, Buddhist nuns have been unable to speak in a single voice and with a formalized authority. With the founding of Sakyadhita, Buddhist nuns and women have been able for the first time to meet and support each other and to develop the basis for a nondogmatic authority where diversity is encouraged and Buddhist women and nuns are able to establish their own authority both as individuals and as part of a larger tradition.

SEE ALSO Gender and Religion, article on Gender and Buddhism, Jainism; Monasticism, article on Buddhist Monasticism.

BIBLIOGRAPHY

Aoyama Shundo. *Zen Seeds: Reflections of a Female Priest.* Tokyo, 1990. In this collection of essays, Shundo Aoyama, a prominent Japanese Buddhist nun, presents her understanding of Buddhist practice and philosophy.

Barnes, Nancy J. "Buddhist Women and the Nuns' Order in Asia." In *Engaged Buddhism,* edited by Christopher S. Queen and Sallie B. King, pp. 259–293. Albany, N.Y., 1996. Presentation of Buddhist nuns in modern times and exploration of the controversial issue of the reestablishment of the *bhikṣuṇī saṃgha.*

Batchelor, Martine. *Women on the Buddhist Path.* London, 2002. The diversity of expression of female spirituality in Buddhism is shown through the lives and practices of eighteen Buddhist women and nuns in the East and West.

Blackstone, Kathryn R. *Women in the Footsteps of the Buddha: Struggle for Liberation in the Therīgāthā.* Richmond, U.K., 1998. Detailed textual study of the theme of liberation among early *bhikṣuṇīs,* which reveals rich symbolism, but also the inherent attitudes, assumptions, and images relating to women renouncers in this important early text.

Findly, Ellison Banks, ed. *Women's Buddhism, Buddhism's Women: Tradition, Revision, Renewal.* Somerville, Mass., 2000. Exploration of how Buddhist women and nuns have sustained a vital place for themselves within the tradition, and are bringing changes in the forms, practices, and institutions of Buddhism.

Kabilsingh, Chatsumarn. *A Comparative Study of Bhikkhuni Patimokkha.* Varanasi, India, 1984. Comprehensive study of the monastic rules for Buddhist nuns based on Pali, Thai, English, and Chinese sources.

Murcott, Susan. *The First Buddhist Women: Translation and Commentary on the Therīgāthā.* Berkeley, Calif., 1991. Translation and commentary on the spiritual verses of the first female disciples of the Buddha.

Pra Maha Narin. "Problems of Bhikhuni Ordination and Solutions." *Yasodhara—Newsletter on International Buddhist Women's Activities* 17/39, no. 67 (April–June 2001): 3–4. Article about the *bhikṣuṇī saṃgha* in Thailand.

Tsai, Kathryn Ann, trans. *Lives of the Nuns: Biographies of Chinese Buddhist Nuns from the Fourth to Sixth Centuries.* Honolulu, 1994. Sixty-five biographies of Buddhist nuns showing women's participation in Buddhist monastic practice in premodern China.

Tsomo, Karma Lekshe, ed. *Sakyadhita: Daughters of the Buddha.* Ithaca, N.Y., 1988. Collection of essays from the first international conference of Buddhist nuns, looking at their problems and their future in the modern world.

Tsomo, Karma Lekshe, ed. *Buddhist Women across Cultures: Realizations.* Albany, N.Y., 1999. Cross-cultural analysis of the Buddhist women's movement and exploration of the "feminization of Buddhism."

Tsomo, Karma Lekshe, ed. *Innovative Buddhist Women: Swimming against the Stream.* Richmond, U.K., 2000. A unique set of essays analyzing Buddhist women's historical and contemporary experience in different Buddhist cultures, including the widely varying experience of Buddhist nuns. Discussions include issues of ordination, authority, gender, ethnicity, and debates about social action.

Ven. Dhammananda. "Three Waves of Bhikkhuni Sangha in Thailand." *Yasodhara—Newsletter on International Buddhist Women's Activities* 19/4, no. 76 (July–September 2003): 5–7. Article on the problems of *bhikṣuṇī* ordination.

Walters, Jonathan S. "Gotamī's Story." In *Buddhism in Practice,* edited by Donald S. Lopez, Jr., pp. 113–138. Princeton, N.J., 1995. Translation from the *Apadāna* of the story of Buddha's maternal aunt and foster mother, the first Buddhist nun.

MARTINE BATCHELOR (2005)

NUNS: CHRISTIAN NUNS AND SISTERS

The earliest Christian women's communities date to the third and fourth centuries and emerged out of a movement of thousands of individuals who had fled to the desert regions of Egypt, Palestine, and Syria to lead lives of strict prayer and ascetic discipline. Surviving sources, all composed by men, suggest there were far fewer female than male desert dwellers. Many ascetics lived as solitaries, but others spontaneously adopted a communal lifestyle, a shift possibly spearheaded by women since community life offered them important protections.

Women associated with this movement include the desert mother Syncletica, who appears to be addressing a community of women in sayings attributed to her; Paula, who cofounded a monastery in 386 in Bethlehem with Jerome (c. 342–420); and the Roman patrician Melania the Elder, who led some fifty women in a monastery she established on the Mount of Olives. A pivotal figure outside the desert movement is the spiritual teacher Macrina the Younger (c. 327–380), known as the Mother of Eastern Monasticism, who cofounded a monastery with her mother on the family estate.

By the fifth century, monasteries in the West emerged as independent houses, following a variety of religious rules. The first known rule intended specifically for nuns was written by Caesarius of Arles (d. 542), who incorporated changes based on the nuns' own experience. The nuns daily recited the Divine Office, did manual labor such as weaving, and practiced a variety of austerities. They lived within a defined precinct of the monastery building or buildings known as an enclosure or cloister, and were allowed to leave it only under exceptional circumstances. In various times and places, enclosure was more or less rigorously enforced. The monastic lands surrounding the enclosure were in essence a feudal estate, worked by peasants for the support of the mostly upper-class nuns. Aristocratic families considered monastic life a socially acceptable state of life for unmarried women, widows, and wives released from their marital responsibilities, and were often the donors of monastic properties. Nuns' dowries and family connections could be quite influential in determining a monastery's success. Monastic life often allowed women access to education, power, and other opportunities unavailable even to other privileged women. Some abbesses were exceptionally erudite and powerful, exercising quasi-episcopal authority and settling political and religious disputes. Some ruled over women and men in linked female and male "double monasteries." Influential early medieval abbesses include Brigid of Kildare (c. 524/25) in Ireland; Hilda of Whitby, who hosted the English church's Synod of Whitby (663); and the Anglo-Saxon Lioba (d. 754), who, with Boniface, was a missionary to German lands, where she founded monasteries. By the ninth or tenth centuries, most monasteries followed some version of the *Rule of Benedict.*

Religious life responded to the increasing social complexity of the central Middle Ages through diversification. Often from the lower classes, female hermits, in contrast to nuns, existed throughout the medieval period and multiplied in the tenth century. New male monastic foundations, such as the eleventh-century Cistercians, who adopted a simpler liturgy, more manual labor, and greater corporate poverty, inspired similar female foundations. The twelfth-century Gilbertines of England, who began with female hermits organized by Gilbert of Sempringham, altered monastic life by admitting lay sisters from humble social strata who worked for the nuns, yet also took vows and participated in the liturgy. The monastery of Fontevrault in the Loire Valley, organized by Robert of Arbrissel (d. 1116), accepted social outcasts, although some, such as repentant prostitutes, were housed separately. Male religious, admitted to serve the nuns as priests or laborers, were entirely obedient to the abbess. By the twelfth century, women's monasteries existed in places such as Hungary, Bohemia, Norway, and Iceland.

Enclosure was often legislated vigorously for women, variously for reasons of safety, sexual decorum, and social control, but it was not always observed. Nuns served their societies not only through prayer, but also by copying and illuminating manuscripts, providing hospitality to travelers, making vestments, and educating children, especially girls. Some also cared for the poor and sick, as did the few women who joined military orders such as the Templars and Hospitallers, founded in the Holy Land during the Crusades.

In the eleventh century, people from many classes began to emulate the "life of the apostles" by living materially poor lives of active service, among people, especially in the new urban milieus. Men could join the new mendicant orders such as the Franciscans or Dominicans, but similar groups for women were never sanctioned. Thus an array of lay women's movements flourished, including the Sisters (and Brothers) of Penance, the Beguines, and female (and male) single and married tertiaries who were loosely associated with the mendicant orders.

Women in general lost authority in the later Middle Ages. Unregulated lay religious women, especially as their numbers grew, attracted suspicion and were gradually forced to accept clerical supervision. Many Beguines were pronounced heretical or pressured to live in communal beguinages, likening them more to nuns. Many tertiaries were similarly regulated. The church attempted to enforce strict enclosure on nuns, and men's orders limited or severed ties with them.

The sixteenth-century Protestant Reformation led to the suppression of monastic life in many countries. While the Catholic Church was rapidly sanctioning a host of new male "apostolic religious orders" dedicated to specific services in the world, such as the Jesuits, it was attempting to curtail the same impulse among women. It imposed strict cloister on nuns after the Council of Trent (1545–1563) and welcomed observant and cloistered reform orders such as the Discalced Carmelites, founded by Teresa of Ávila (d. 1582).

Women struggled throughout the sixteenth to eighteenth centuries to establish apostolic communities dedicated to specific works. Angela Merici's Company of St. Ursula (1535), committed to educating girls, escaped cloister by wearing secular clothes and living in their own homes. After Merici's death in 1540, however, the women were urged to accept episcopal control, common life, and distinctive garb. By the seventeenth century, virtually all Ursulines had become fully enclosed and educated girls only within the cloister walls. In England, Mary Ward modeled her Institute of the Blessed Virgin Mary after the Jesuits, with the goal of educating young women. Derided as "Jesuitesses" and "galloping gals," the group was suppressed in 1631 after Ward had spent a year in prison as a "heretic." The women were reclassified as ecclesiastical persons and forced to modify their work. The Catholic Church sharply distinguished nuns, the "true religious," from pious secular people who remained in the world and took simple vows.

Others, including some bishops who valued women's ministries, devised strategies to satisfy church laws. Communities were cleverly termed congregations, societies, or institutes instead of religious orders. Some women gave up pronouncing the vows they lived by. Vincent de Paul and Louise de Marillac, founders of the Daughters of Charity (1633) in Paris, chose the lesser designation secular daughters over religious so the women could run soup kitchens and care for the poor and socially marginalized. De Paul famously remarked, "Your convent will be the house of the sick, your cell a hired room, your chapel the parish church, your cloister the city streets or the hospital wards, your enclosure obedience, your grille the fear of God, your veil modesty." Most people admired such women and increasingly viewed them as genuine religious. In France, they were called *congréganistes* instead of *religieuses,* the term for monastic women. Today, the words *sisters* and *nuns* are used to make the same distinction.

The French church, which had been the spiritual center of Europe in the seventeenth century, dramatically declined in the eighteenth century. Enlightenment ideas undermined belief, and the vast economic wealth and privileges of monasteries and the male hierarchy fueled disaffection. Between the 1740s and 1780s, recruitment into women's orders fell by about forty-five percent. Leaders of the French Revolution then ended monastic life and confiscated properties, but spared some lay sisters in apostolic communities since they served society.

The restoration of the Bourbon Dynasty in 1815 launched the "golden age" of women's religious life, centered in France. Between 1800 and 1880, almost four hundred new women's orders were founded, attracting some 200,000 women, mostly to apostolic congregations. Only one-fifth as numerous as monastic women on the eve of the French Revolution, they made up over four-fifths of women dedicated to religion some ninety years later in 1880. Women for the first time outnumbered male clergy and religious combined, a trend that has continued into the twenty-first century. Paralleling changes in social and political life, religious life throughout Europe was becoming more democratized, with women from middle and lower classes now outnumbering those from upper classes and assuming positions of leadership.

The papacy belatedly recognized a woman's apostolic congregation for the first time in 1841 when it approved the Sisters of Mercy, who eventually spread beyond Ireland to become the largest women's order in the English-speaking world. Apostolic congregations were finally recognized as "true religious life" in the 1917 Code of Canon Law, which also, however, sapped spontaneity and zeal from these orders by requiring them to accept many uniform requirements.

The dramatic rise in numbers of religious women allowed many congregations to become centralized, mobile, international organizations. The French Society of the Sacred Heart, founded in 1800 by Madeleine Sophie Barat and renowned for the education it offered upper-class girls in particular, spread quickly to other European countries, the Americas, and elsewhere by following invitations from bishops and lay people. Outside Europe, religious women worked among European immigrants and among native populations. By 1750, the Ursulines of New Orleans, who educated French, Amerindian, and enslaved African girls and women, had helped raise women's literacy rate to above seventy percent, which was higher than men's rate, and far better than that of women elsewhere in the colonies. Women missionaries, who had been few prior to the nineteenth century, established numerous schools, dispensaries, and other social services among native populations in the Americas, Asia, Africa, and Oceania, settling especially in places colonized by Europeans. Some orders were founded specifically as missionary orders.

Many women religious were kind to indigenous people and defended their rights, but they frequently evinced colonial and racist attitudes. For example, nuns and sisters who educated Amerindians, mestizos, black Africans, and mulattoes on the American frontier typically segregated them from children of European descent and taught them manual skills instead of more academic or refined subjects. Civilizing "savages" and other people of color often involved suppressing their own customs. White European orders and orders of European descent, whether male or female, were slow to accept vocations from people of color. The Oblate Sisters of Providence (1831) were exceptional in being founded specifically for African American and mulatto women who ministered to people of color. Only in the latter half of the twentieth century did most orders in Latin America, Asia, Africa, and Oceania cede significant authority to indigenous women and thereby cease to be "missionary" orders.

There were few Protestant religious women prior to the nineteenth-century. The Oxford movement, which attempted to renew the Church of England by reincorporating Catholic rituals and teachings, led to the foundation in Great Britain and Ireland after 1848 of over one hundred communities of women, most committed to teaching or works of charity. By the beginning of the twenty-first century, these orders had declined in Great Britain and Ireland, but grown elsewhere, with over 1550 women in communities around the world. Protestant women belong to a range of other foundations, including the Evangelical Marian Sisterhood of Germany, the ecumenical communities of Grandchamp, Switzerland, and the St. Brigid of Kildare Methodist Monastery of Minnesota founded in 2001.

The Second Vatican Council (1962–1965), which aimed to renew the Catholic Church in light of the exigencies of the modern world, was the great twentieth-century turning point for Christian nuns and sisters. The Council advocated greater collegiality and shared decision-making and directed all religious orders to revise their mission in light of the world's pressing needs. Women religious, who had made significant advances theologically and educationally just prior to the Council in places such as the United States and Europe, were generally well-prepared to embrace the radical changes inspired by the Council. Influenced also by the women's movement, nuns and sisters revamped outmoded authority structures within their own orders, and vigorously challenged them within the overwhelmingly male-dominated Catholic Church. Many religious, "to be in the world for the world," rejected cloister and semi-cloister, distinctive dress, institutional living, and the spiritual elitism these fostered, and adopted instead secular clothing and simple community life in small homes inserted among lay society. They refocused many of their charitable works—or in the case of monastic nuns, their prayer—toward dismantling the unjust structures that make charitable work necessary in the first place. A visible minority of sisters became involved in political activism. Sisters contributed importantly to many twentieth-century liberation movements in places such as Latin America.

These changes were accompanied by others just as dramatic, whose meaning is still debated. Between 1950 and 2000, numbers of religious women declined in Europe (31 percent) and North America (51 percent). After the Second Vatican Council, many women in the richer industrialized nations left religious life because they were disillusioned by the changes or dissatisfied with their pace. New membership slowed dramatically and by 2000 had virtually ceased in many orders. In the same period, however, religious women increased in Latin America (ninety-four percent), Asia (551 percent), and Africa (1503 percent). Religious women in the richer northern industrialized lands still comprise the majority of women religious, but they are generally elderly in contrast to the youthful and burgeoning group of religious women in the poorer developing and mostly Southern Hemisphere lands. Most of these women belong to apostolic congregations that staff schools, medical facilities, and provide other social services. Their greater numbers reflect the shift in the Catholic Church's center of gravity away from Europe and the industrialized world and toward the Southern Hemisphere, where Catholics are increasing even more rapidly than nuns and sisters. For example, Catholics in Africa, who grew by almost four thousand percent between 1950 and 2000, far outpaced the growth of religious women (1503 percent).

In 2000, when women religious around the world were counted with male Catholic Church personnel consisting of religious, diocesan priests, and deacons, they constituted almost two-thirds of the total. In the early years of the twenty-first century, nuns and sisters around the world continue to make major contributions to the Catholic Church and to the societies where they live and work.

See Also Benedict of Nursia; Feminist Theology, article on Christian Feminist Theology; Gender and Religion, article on Gender and Christianity; Monasticism, article on Christian Monasticism; Teresa of Ávila; Ward, Mary.

Bibliography

Burke, Joan F. *These Catholic Sisters Are All "Mamas"! Towards the Inculturation of the Sisterhood in Africa, an Ethnographic Study.* Leiden, 2001.

Coburn, Carol K., and Martha Smith. *Spirited Lives: How Nuns Shaped Catholic Culture and American Life, 1836–1920.* Chapel Hill, N.C., and London, 1999.

Gilchrist, Roberta. *Gender and Material Culture: The Archaeology of Religious Women.* London and New York, 1994.

Langlois, Claude. *Le catholicisme au féminin: Les congrégations françaises à supérieure générale au XIXe siècle.* Paris, 1984.

Magray, Mary Peckham. *The Transforming Power of the Nuns: Women, Religion, and Cultural Change in Ireland, 1750–1900.* New York, 1998.

McNamara, Jo Ann Kay. *Sisters in Arms: Catholic Nuns through Two Millennia.* Cambridge, Mass., 1996. A broad survey.

Ranft, Patricia. *Women and the Religious Life in Premodern Europe.* New York, 1996. A brief, but very solid introduction.

Rapley, Elizabeth. *The Dévotes: Women and Church in Seventeenth-Century France.* Montreal, Canada, and Buffalo, N.Y., 1990.

Simons, Walter. *Cities of Ladies: Beguine Communities in the Medieval Low Countries, 1200–1565.* Philadelphia, 2001.

Talbot, Alice-Mary. *Women and Religious Life in Byzantium.* Aldershot, U.K., and Burlington, Vt., 2001.

Catherine M. Mooney (2005)

NŪR MUḤAMMAD ("light of Muḥammad") or *Nūr Muḥammadi* ("Muḥammadan light") is a term central to later Ṣūfī and Shīʿī speculation. Although the Qurʾān repeatedly states that Muḥammad is only human, a messenger entrusted with the guidance of the people (see surahs 6:50, 25:8, 25:22), later currents in Islam transformed him increasingly into a spiritual, luminous being. The historical Muḥammad was thus metamorphosed into a transcendent light, like the sun, around which everything created revolves. This idea has colored later mystical Islam on both the elite and folk levels.

The basis for such speculations, however, was found in the Qurʾān, where Muḥammad is called "a shining lamp" (*sirāj munīr,* 33:45) and where it is said, "There came to you from God a light and a clear book" (5:15). Ḥāssan ibn Thābit, the Medinese poet who eulogized Muḥammad, reflects these ideas in his verse; he is the first in a long series of writers to compare the face of the Prophet to the full moon at night, a comparison that plays on the words *badr* ("full moon") and *Badr,* the name of the site of the Muslims' first victorious battle in 624.

Such poetical expressions, however, still lacked a theological basis. It was left to the theologian Muqātil (d. 767?) to interpret the famous "light verse" of the Qurʾān (24:35) as a reference to the Prophet:

> God is the light of the heavens and the earth; the likeness of his light is as a niche wherein there is a lamp, the lamp in a glass, the glass as it were a glittering star, kindled from a blessed tree, an olive tree neither of the East nor of the West, whose oil wellnigh would shine, even if no fire touched it. Light upon light. God guides to his light whom he will. And God strikes similitudes for man, and God has knowledge of everything.

It is the lamp, *miṣbāh,* that Muqatil sees as a fitting symbol for Muḥammad; through him the divine light shines upon the world, and through him humanity is guided to the origin of this light. The formula "neither of the East nor of the West" could then be taken as a reference to Muḥammad's comprehensive nature, which is not restricted to one specific people or race and which transcends the boundaries of time and space.

Up to the present day one of the most common epithets used for the Prophet is *nūr al-hudā* ("the light of right guidance"), and allusions to his luminous nature are found even in the titles of *ḥadīth* collections, such as *Mashāriq al-anwār* (The Rising Points of Lights), *Ma-ṣābīḥ al-sunnah* (The Lamps of the *Sunnah*), or *Mishkāt al-maṣābīḥ* (The Niche for Lamps). Likewise, through the centuries one of the most famous prayers attributed to Muḥammad is the prayer for light:

> O God, place light in my heart, light in my soul, light upon my tongue, light in my eyes, and light in my ears; place light at my right, light at my left, light behind me, and light before me, light above me, and light beneath me. Place light in my nerves, and light in my flesh, light in my blood, light in my hair and light in my skin. Give me light, increase my light, make me light.

Theories about Muḥammad's luminous nature began to develop, on the basis of Muqātil's exegesis, in the second half of the ninth century. The Iraqi Ṣūfī Sahl al-Tustarī (d. 896) was the first to express the whole *Heilsgeschichte* in the terminology of the light of Muḥammad as suggested in the light verse. The inaccessible divine mystery of light articulates itself in the pre-eternal manifestation of "the likeness of his light." The origin of the *nūr Muḥammad* in pre-eternity is depicted as "a luminous mass of primordial adoration in the presence of God, which takes the shape of a transparent column of divine light and constitutes Muḥammad as the primal creation of God" (Böwering, 1980). When this light reached "the veil of majesty," it prostrated itself before God, and from its prostration God formed a mighty column, one both outwardly and inwardly translucent. Sahl even interpreted surah 53:13, "And he saw [God] still another time," as pertaining to the beginning of time, when this luminous column was standing before God in worship "with the disposition of faith, and [to him] was unveiled the mystery of the mystery itself 'at the Lote-tree of the Boundary.'" Then, when the actual creation began, God created Adam, and finally all else that exists, from the light of Muḥammad. The light is thus seen as the primordial material out of which everything is formed; it becomes the ultimate source of existence, and through Muḥammad, the historical form of this light, beings become illuminated, thus participating in the divine light as embodied in the actual Prophet.

Sahl's high-soaring speculations were elaborated more poetically by his disciple al-Ḥallāj (d. 922), who devoted the first chapter of his *Kitāb al-ṭawāsīn* to Muḥammad, calling it *Ṭāsīn al-sirāj* (The *Ṭāsīn* of the Lamp, alluding to the Arabic letters *ṭā* and *sīn* found at the head of surah 27):

> He was a lamp from the light of the invisible . . . a moon radiating among the moons, whose mansion is in the sphere of mysteries. . . . The lights of prophethood—from his light did they spring forth, and their lights appeared from his light, and there is no light among the lights more luminous and more visible and previous to preexistence than the light of this noble one.

As preceding preexistence, Muḥammad is seen as absolutely eternal, mentioned "before the Before and after the After."

Al-Ḥallāj's rhyming prose was written less than three centuries after Muḥammad's death. During those years there appeared several *ḥadīth* pointing to the mystery of the *nūr Muḥammad:* "The first thing God created was my light," says the Prophet, and his remark, "My companions are like stars," fits well with his role as the central sun or the full moon of the world.

The Ṣūfīs lovingly interpreted this idea. Al-Thaʿlabī (d. 1038), in his *ʿAraʾis al-bayan,* written shortly after the year 1000, cites a colorful myth in which the light appears as a radiant pearl. Najm Dāyā Rāzī, in the early thirteenth century, offers an elaborate story of creation using similar imagery; the pearling drops of sweat that emerge from the primordial *Nūr Muḥammad* are the substance out of which the 124,000 prophets sent before Muḥammad were created. ʿAbd al-Karīm al-Jīlī (d. 1408?) elaborates on this idea by comparing the *nūr Muḥammad*—also interpreted as the *ḥaqīqah muḥammadīyah,* the archetypal "Muḥammadan reality"—to a luminous pearl, or a white chrysolith, which grows embarrassed when God looks at it lovingly and thus begins to perspire, finally dissolving into waves and other watery substances out of which the created world emerges.

This image has inspired hundreds of poets in the Islamic world. In the sixteenth century, for example, a Turkish poet, Khaqani, speaks in his *ḥilyah* (the poetical description of the Prophet's noble features and qualities) of this event: "God loved this light and said 'My beloved friend!' and became enamored of this light." Overwhelmed by this divine love, the primordial Muḥammadan light produced drops of perspiration from bashfulness, and from them the world emerged in descending degrees. The same idea is found in Bengali mystical folk poetry of the fifteenth and sixteenth centuries, especially in the work of Shaykh Chānd.

Sahl's ideas of the column of light seem to have been quite well known in mystical circles even before their systematization by Ibn al-ʿArabī (d. 1240) in the first half of the thirteenth century. Few passages in medieval Persian poetry prior to Ibn al-ʿArabī reflect this idea more eloquently than those of Farid al-Dīn ʿAṭṭār (d. 1220). In the introduction of his epic *Manṭiq al-ṭayr* (The Conversation of the Birds), ʿAṭṭār speaks of how, from this Muḥammadan light, the divine Throne, Footstool, Pen, and Tablet appeared, and how the great light then prostrated itself before the Lord and remained for ages in prostration, genuflection, and standing, thus prefiguring the movements of Muslim ritual prayer. The Turkish mystical poet Yunus Emre (d. 1321) puts in God's mouth the words

> I created him from my own light
> And I love him yesterday and today.
> What would I do with the world without him?
> My Muḥammad, my Ahmad of light!

In the same period, a Ṣūfī in India claimed that the light of Muḥammad became embodied in the Prophet's person "just as the light of the moon is taken from the sun." For the faithful, the participation in the light of Muḥammad is the goal of life, for whosoever is surrounded by this uncreated light will not be touched by the created fire of Hell.

That the idea of the Muhammadan light was popular even before Ibn al-ʿArabī is clear from the very title of al-Ghazālī's (d. 1111) booklet *Mishkāt al-anwār* (The Niche for Lights), which contains his prophetology, in which Muḥammad appears as the *muṭāʿ* ("one who is obeyed"). This attribution also occurs quite frequently in poetry at later periods; there, however, it does not assume the mysterious role as a kind of demiurge, a being between the undifferentiated One and the phenomenal world, as described by al-Ghazālī. For him, this primordial "light of lights" illuminates the darkness, and, even more, it brings all things into manifestation out of "not-being."

These theories on the *nūr Muḥammad* were, like so many early trends in Sufism, elaborated and systematized by Ibn al-ʿArabī, who states in his probably spurious profession of faith that "the first light appears out of the veil of the Unseen and from knowledge to concrete existence and is the light of our prophet Muḥammad." He then goes on to compare Muḥammad, the *sirāj munīr,* to the sun and infers that the heavenly intelligences, the spirits, the intuitions, and the essences are nourished by the luminous essence of (Muḥammad) Muṣṭafā the Elect, "who is the sun of existence." In philosophical terms, with Muḥammad, the first self-determination of the Absolute, the Divine begins to manifest itself gradually to the world, and the primordial light, which has permeated all prophets from the beginning, reaches its full development in the Perfect Man, the historical prophet Muḥammad.

As such, Muḥammad is praised in ever new images. It is no accident that the literature dealing with his miraculous birth always points to the light that shone from his father's forehead and was carried in Amīnah's womb; following the Prophet's birth, this light illuminated the world to the castles of Bosra in Syria. Muḥammad is the *shamʿ-i maḥfil,* the "candle of the assembly," which illuminates the night of this world as medieval Persian poets wrote; and it is "the light of his name" by which the Muslims should bring light into the darkness of this time, as Muhammad Iqbal (d. 1938), the Indo-Pakistani modernist poet, says in his Urdu poem *Answer to [Man's] Complaint* (1912). The mystics and poets were happy to interpret the beginning of surah 93 ("By the morning light!") as pertaining to Muḥammad's radiant face, which represents at the same time the radiance of faith—an image probably coined by Sanāʾī of Ghaznah (d. 1131?) and lovingly repeated through the centuries by poets in all parts of the Muslim world.

One can say without exaggeration that, in eulogies composed for Muḥammad, his luminous character is among those features most frequently noted. One finds, for example, mention of the Prophet as "the light of all lights" and the beliefs that he did not cast a shadow and that his light was visible in the dark night. Following these ideas, calligraphers writing in Arabic found it logical that none of the Prophet's original names—Muḥammad, Aḥmad, Ḥāmīd, and Maḥmūd—nor his epithet—*rasūl Allāh* ("messenger of God")—was written with diacritical marks. One even finds attempts to write eulogies for him in which all diacritical marks are left out as a way of stressing his luminous purity.

The origin and early development of the theory of the light of Muḥammad are difficult to trace. One source of this mysticism of light might have been Hellenistic gnostic speculations. Shīʿī theories about the light of the imams also may have strongly contributed to the development of these ideas. Ibn al-ʿArabī associated this concept with the tradition (*ḥadīth qudsī*) in which God says, "I was a hidden treasure and wanted to be known; therefore I created the world." Following Ibn al-ʿArabi's lead, Jami (d. 1492) addressed the Prophet in this manner:

> From "I was a treasure" your true nature has become clear: Your person is the mirror of the unqualified light.

According to Ibn al-ʿArabī and his followers, the *nūr Muḥammad* appears in all prophets, each of them bearing a certain particle of this light, as well as those mystics who tried to reach union with the *ḥaqīqah muḥammadīyah.* These individuals sometimes claimed that they were in the heights with the light of Muḥammad long before Adam was created. The historical Muḥammad is thus endowed with the "totalizing nature" comprising all the divine names and forming the principle in which the divine light can reflect its glory in order to be known and loved. His relation to the inaccessible essence of light is like that of the sunlight in relation to the sun.

On the basis of these ideas later writers compared Muḥammad to the dawn that appears at the border between night and day, between human contingent existence and divine reality. The *nūr Muḥammad* thus becomes a central concept that appears in varied expressions in the Islamic world, and although the emphasis in prophetology has tended to shift from the mythical Muḥammad to the historical man Muḥammad, the "light of guidance" is still admired and praised in the verses of mystically minded poets.

BIBLIOGRAPHY

For more on the *Nūr Muḥammad,* see William H. T. Gairdner's translation, *Al-Ghazzālī's Mishkāt al-anwār* (*The Niche for Lights*) (1924; reprint, Lahore, 1952). A better translation of the *Mishkāt* is Roger Deladrière's *Le tabernacle des Lumières* (Paris, 1981). Indispensable for the study of the *nūr Muḥammad* is Tor Andrae's important work *Die person Muhammeds in lehre und glauben seiner gemeinde* (Stockholm, 1918). Andrae deals especially with the transformation of the image of Muḥammad as reflected in Islamic mysticism and theology. My own *And Muhammad Is His Messenger* (Chapel Hill, 1985) is a survey of the veneration of Muḥammad in mystical and popular traditions. See also Louis Massignon's classic study *The Passion of al-Hallaj: Mystic and Martyr of Islam,* 4 vols., translated by Herbert Mason (Princeton, 1982), and Gerhard Böwering's *The Mystical Vision of Existence in Classical Islam: The Qur'anic Hermeneutics of the Ṣūfī Sahl al-Tustarī (d. 283/896)* (Berlin and New York, 1980). Robert C. Zaehner's *Hindu and Muslim Mysticism* (New York, 1969) is an original work that compares Sufism and Hindu mysticism and contains some interesting observations on the *nūr Muḥammad.*

ANNEMARIE SCHIMMEL (1987)

NUṢAYRĪYAH SEE ʿALAWĪYŪN

NUWAUBIANS.

The term *Nuwaubian* refers to an African American religious communal group that has existed and continues to exist under a variety of names. Founded as the Ansaar Pure Sufi in 1967, it was subsequently known as the Nubian Islaamic Hebrew Mission, the Ansaaru Allah Community and more recently as the Ancient Mystic Order of Melchizedek, the Holy Tabernacle Ministries, the Yamassee Native American Tribe, and the Nuwaubian Nation of Moors. Founder Michael York (b. June 26, 1945) has also assumed different names over the years beginning in 1969, including Amunnubi Rooakhptah, and later, at various times, As Siddid Al Imaan Isa Al Haahi Al Madhi, Chief Black Eagle, Nayya Malachizodoq-El, and Malachi Z. York. The changing image of the group and the shifting persona of its leader has often been a source of confusion and an additional rationale for disparaging remarks by critics.

York emerged in the African American community in Brooklyn, New York at the late 1960s, a time during which Black Nationalism represented by the Moorish Science Temple of America and the Nation of Islam and its various splinter groups was enjoying a revival. As had many of his contemporaries, during the 1960s York had served time for a variety of minor offenses from assault to possession of a deadly weapon. However, in 1967, he decided that his career was as a teacher, and he assumed the religious name Amunnubi Roakhptah and established the Ansaar Pure Sufi organization out of his apartment. Those attracted to his teachings donned black tunics as a sign of their membership. The group changed several times over the next few years, each change accompanied by the members' assuming a new dress and York taking a new name.

An important step was taken in 1970 when York renamed his following the Nubian Islaamic Mission. At that time, the members agreed to live communally. They moved into a house in Brooklyn and opened a bookstore and meeting hall. Growth of the group, along with larger crowds being attracted to its meetings, necessitated several moves over the next two years.

In 1972 York traveled to Sudan where he developed an identification with the legendary Sudanese military and religious leader Muḥammad Ahmed Ibn Abdullāh (1845–1885), best remembered for organizing a revolt against British rule and defeating them at Khartoum in 1885. Following his return, York called himself As Siddid Al Imaan Isa Al Haahi Al Madhi, and claimed descent from Muḥammad Abdullāh. Abdullāh is commonly referred to as al-Madhi and York identified him as the True Madhi, the predicted successor to the Prophet Muḥammad.

Following his return from Sudan, York made a second important change in the group. He separated the more dedicated believers who wanted to build a new nation from the more nominal members who loosely identified with the Islamic and African themes York preached. He now centered his attention only on those committed to the program he was developing.

Through the 1980s, the group was primarily known as the Ansaaru Allah Community and became a visible presence in the many American cities along the East Coast. They also began centers in the Caribbean—Jamaica, Trinidad and Tobago, Puerto Rico, and Guyana. The young adult members of the group, dressed in white, moved about the streets in the black community selling York's books and otherwise spreading his message. York has been a prolific writer, authoring over 400 books and booklets (many transcripts of his talks) covering a wide range of topics from UFOs to personal hygiene.

TEACHINGS. The teachings of the Nuwaubians were built around the development of a new understanding of African American people (a project not unlike that undertaken of the Moorish Science Temple and the Nation of Islam previously). York drew upon the Christian Bible and the Holy Qur'ān for an initial affirmation of Allah as Alone in His Power, the All, the Oneness. Jesus is seen as the Messiah. York taught that Muḥammad, the last of the prophets in the lineage of Adam, passed his lineage to his daughter Fatima (610–633 CE) and son-in-law Ali (599–661 CE).

Adam and Eve (or Hawwah) were Nubian (black people). Problems developed for Adam's descendents in Noah's (or Nuwh) time. One of Noah's sons, Ham, desired to commit sodomy after having come upon his father in an unclothed condition. For his sin, his fourth son, Canaan, was stricken with leprosy, thus acquiring a pale skin. The light-skinned races are descendants of Canaan. An additional important step in human development came with Noah's descendent Abraham. From his son, Isaac and grandson Jacob, came the Israelites. They were enslaved for 420 years in Egypt. From his son Ismael came the Ismaelites, or Nubians. The Nubians include the black people of the United States, the West Indies, and other parts of the globe. York asserted that it was predicted that they would be in slavery for about 400 years at some point. Because of their descent from Abraham, they are rightfully also called Hebrews, just as the modern Jews.

Defining the belief structure of the Nuwaubians in detail has been made all the more difficult by its fluid nature, the constant changes to which it has been subjected, and the seeming esoteric elements not available to outside scrutiny.

CONTINUED EVOLUTION. In 1993 the group began still another transition. York officially changed his name to Malachi York. The next year, approximately 400 members of the group, most from Brooklyn, purchased some 476 acres near Eatonton, Georgia. At this time they became known by their four current designations: The United Nuwaubian Nation of Moors, the Yamassee Native American Tribe, the Ancient Mystic Order of Melchizedek, and the Holy Tabernacle Ministries. It is as the leader of these four entities that York assumes his varied names: Chief Black Eagle, Nayya Malachizodoq-El, and Malachi Z. York.

As conceived by the group, the United Nuwaubian Nation of Moors identifies with its Middle Eastern Sudanese and Abrahamic past. As the Yamassee Native American Tribe, the group claims a relationship to a Native-American people, the Yamassee, who resided in Georgia. The Nuwaubians have asserted their belief that the Yamassee were the original residents of Georgia who came to North America from the Nile Valley prior to the separation of the continents via continental drift.

Through their identification with the Yamassee, who signed over their lands to the United States in 1829, the Nuwaubians have attempted to establish their claim to be a separate nation. They have asserted their claim as an indigenous people who should be seen as an indigenous nation (following United Nations definitions) in pursuit of autonomy. As such, they do not recognize the jurisdiction of the United States and its laws over them, and have created their own constitution and legal code. The Ancient Mystical Order of Melchizedek is a lodge in the Masonic tradition. People who are considered Nubians but who are not presently members of the United Nuwaubian Nation of Moors may join the lodge. The lodge dues are received as income by the Nuwaubians.

The Holy Tabernacle Ministries is an umbrella organization that holds the other three groups together, and through which the group interacts with the outside world. It also distributes the group's books and literature. The ministries manage a group of bookstores located in various cities which have been an additional source of income for the group.

Prior to its movement to Georgia in the early 1990s, the Ansaaru Allah Community was somewhat lost in the larger Islamic world and overshadowed by the better-known Nation of Islam. Occasionally a reporter learned of its existence and a few scholars began to monitor it.

However, once they moved to Georgia in the early 1990s, controversy placed the Nuwaubians on the front page. The initial issues raised by the group were relatively local and minor. Neighbors were disturbed by the influx of so many people to their Georgia center and their slowness to bring buildings up to legal codes. The controversy was heightened by the group's separatism. These problems likely would have been overcome in time had not the revelations of secret illicit behavior on the part of York and several close associates come to light.

The situation locally became focused on the group's erection of a set of highly decorated buildings and statues modeled on ancient Egypt. To the group, these buildings made their identification with the ancient Egyptians visible and immediately drew the attention of both African Americans and Native Americans. Local white residents found the buildings out of place, and legal authorities called attention to building-code violations in the construction and maintenance of them.

The various controversies surrounding the Nuwaubians were put aside, however, when in 2002 York was arrested on numerous charges of child molestation and a variety of additional associated charges stemming from his use of children for sexual purposes. The investigation by federal authorities had been going on for four years. Other members of the group were arrested for their roles in facilitating York's predatory activity. York was convicted in federal court in January 2004 on charges involving racketeering and transporting children across state lines for sexual purposes. He had previously confessed to a number of the child molestation charges. As of 2004, the appeals process in York's case continues. There is every reason to believe that the Nuwaubians may face a series of civil cases once the criminal issues are resolved.

The Nuwaubian Nation of Moors is one of a spectrum of religious groups that became involved in major illegal activity and faced the incarcerations of their founders. Amid public outrage over York's behavior, some members of the group have remained loyal to his teachings and the organizations he created. They have viewed York as a target of religious persecution, and in the years prior to his arrest, a variety of African American leaders came to the group's defense. In light of York's conviction and the revelation of the many charges against him, the continuance of the group has been called into question. However, other groups have survived during and after the incarcerations of their founders (e.g., Israelite House of David, Alamo Christian Foundation, Unification Movement). Given various scenarios that may or may not occur, the future of the Nuwaubians remains unpredictable.

See Also Nation of Islam.

Bibliography

The several scholarly accounts of the Nuwaubians were written prior to the revelations about York's sexual life, and the current account of the group must be created from the many items of newspaper coverage scattered on the internet.

Haddad, Yvonne Yazbeck, and Jane Idleman Smith. *Mission to America: Five Islamic Sectarian Communities in North America.* Gainesville, Fla., 1993. Includes a brief chapter on the Nuwaubians focusing on their Islamic phase.

Ahmad, Muhammad [pseudo. Michael York]. *The Only True Madhi!.* Brooklyn, N.Y., 1984. An early account of York's assertion of his unique leadership role.

Palmer, Susan J. and Steve Luxton. "The Ansaaru Allah Community: Postmodernist Narration and the Black Jeremiad." In *New Trends and Developments in the World of Islam,* edited by Peter B. Clarke, pp. 353–370. London, 1998. Possibly the most complete secondary source on the Nuwabians written prior to York's arrest.

Philips, Abu Ameenah Bilal. *The Ansaar Cult in America.* Riyadh, Saudi Arabia, 1998. A polemic attack on Nuwabian teachings from an Orthodox Islamic perspective.

J. Gordon Melton (2005)

NYAKYUSA RELIGION. The traditional religion of the Nyakyusa-speaking people and of the neighboring Ngonde (who speak a dialect of the same language) was closely observed from 1934 to 1938 and again in 1955. The Nyakyusa occupied the fertile Rungwe Valley of what is now Tanzania, 9° south longitude, 34° east latitude; the Ngonde occupied the adjoining plain in what is now Malawi. Together they numbered perhaps half a million. They were settled cultivators and herdsmen, rotating crops and sustaining banana groves with manure from the byres. Groups of thirty to fifty age mates, with their wives and young children, lived together in villages. The religion of this distinctive people was expressed in two cycles of rituals, one concerning families, the other chiefdoms and groups of chiefdoms. Celebration of these rituals involved acting out dramas that expressed the proper relationships among humans and between humanity and divinity; in essence, they were intended to both regulate human behavior and to mediate between human and divine realms.

There was little elaboration of dogma, though the family rituals were shaped by a conviction that kinsmen, living and dead, were inextricably bound together, by the definition of kinship and by marriage law. Communal rituals were shaped by a mythological charter concerning the coming of certain chiefly lineages which had brought fire, iron, and cattle to a people who had no chiefs, no iron, and no cattle, and who ate their food raw. Theological speculation was expressed through a general awareness of symbolism—a "common symbolic language" of which poets speak. Fire was recognized as representing "lordship" and authority; "eating food raw" was the mark both of a witch and of a person without culture. A detailed interpretation of symbolism was provided by specialists—priests and doctors (both men and women) and by elderly people in general. The associations given here are not the product of guesswork, but rest on the statements given by participants in the rituals. In a rapidly changing and diverse society much of ancient symbolism may become a forgotten language.

The occasions for celebration of family rituals were death and birth, especially abnormal birth; maturity and marriage; and misfortune. The essence of each ritual was a purification, the participants washing and shaving with medicines; a "speaking out," for any individuals who came to the ritual with "anger in the heart" must admit that anger openly and cease to nurse any grudge against those with whom they celebrated; and a communion feast in which living and dead kin shared beer, the staple foods (which varied with altitude), and, at a funeral, beef. Each ritual implied a change in status for the chief participants: spouse, parent, sibling, and child, at a funeral; parents if twins were born, or the mother alone at an ordinary birth; a girl at first menstruation; and her groom as she moved from the confinement at puberty to marriage. But kinsmen also celebrated and were obliged to do so, the range being further in the father's than in the mother's line and varying with the type of ritual. The explicit reason given for celebrating was that the chief mourners, parents of twins, or nubile girl would go mad should the ritual be neglected, and indeed the "actions of a madman" were mimed in the death ritual—mimed and rejected—for the ritual was directed at ensuring acceptance of a new life, a new place in society for a distraught widow, a girl who had grown up, a young mother, or a man bereaved, married, or fearful as the father of twins. In every ritual the chief participants symbolically died and were reborn, and while in the world of the dead they were "brooded over" by the shades. This was something terrible, for the shades, though kinsmen, were numinous, and the awfulness of divinity oppressed humans, who sought to separate themselves from it.

Celebrations for a chiefdom were of various sorts. The first was the coronation ritual during which two heirs (for a chiefdom should split each generation) were secluded with the commoners chosen by the older generation to be their village headmen, instructed in their future duties, and treated with medicines to make them respected—men of authority. At a given signal the young men burst out of the seclusion hut and rushed out to the pasturage, where each chief and his senior headman made fire by friction. All fires throughout the country had been extinguished, and each new fire had to be lit from that of the chief. Each of the heirs established authority in one half of the country and planted two trees and a stone commemorating his coronation and royal marriage. Land in the chiefdom was reallocated, with the older generation moving aside to make way for the younger. The old chief was expected to "die soon," for fertility in people, land, and cattle was believed to be dependent upon the vitality of the chief, and an old, ailing chief was unacceptable. He was smothered and buried beside the trees planted at his coronation.

The second sort of celebration for a chiefdom involved the slaughter of a cow and prayers offered to a former ruler in the sacred grove that had sprung up around his burial place. There no one might chop wood or cultivate, and, as a result, the vegetation in such a sacred place would eventually grow into a forest.

Third, a general purification was held at the break of the rains after the dry season or in national emergency. All the old ashes from homestead fires were thrown out, and grudges between people were openly admitted.

Regional celebrations concerning a group of chiefdoms were directed to a founding hero in his grove. Prayers for rain, fertility, and health for the whole region were then offered. The two greatest of the heroes, Lwembe and Kyungu, had living representatives who were thought to exercise power over rain and fertility, and they too were honored. Lwembe's grove contained a great python (a creature held to represent the hero) that was believed to lick Lwembe's priest, who spent a night alone in the grove, protected by a wicker cage.

The name of one founding hero, Kyala, to whom offerings were made in a cave, was used not only for the hero but also in the sense of "the lord," and it was used by the first missionaries (in 1891) to translate the Christian conception of God. As traditional Nyakyusa religion interacted with Christianity, the idea of a god wholly distinct from the heroes became more and more clear: In 1934 old men still spoke of Kyala "beneath" with the shades, but to most young men—traditional as well as Christian—he was "above" (*kumwanya*), and "above" implied then "in the sky" rather than "on earth" (as opposed to beneath the earth).

The celebrations for Lwembe crossed language as well as political boundaries. Priests brought iron hoes and salt, commodities from the mountains to the east, as gifts to the shrine. People in the rich Rungwe Valley traded grain, pulses, and bananas for these commodities. Kyungu was sent iron hoes and ivory from the mountains surrounding the Ngonde Plain, and unlike Lwembe, he gradually developed secular power and became a chief with subordinate chiefs under him.

Besides celebrations for the shades of a family, chiefdom, or region, Nyakyusa speakers had a lively belief in witchcraft, a mystical power thought to be exercised by certain persons (for selfish purposes) to injure others. Witches were spoken of as greedy, envious, and as consumed with jealousy and anger against their neighbors. They killed men and cattle and caused grain to diminish and cows to dry up by reason of a "python in the belly" that worked evil. So real was this python in imagination that it was sought in autopsies, which were performed both to discover the mystical cause of death and to prove whether the dead person had been a witch.

Witchcraft was wholly evil, but a power akin to it was thought to be properly exercised by village headmen and others to protect a village against the attacks of witches. People known as *abamanga* ("the strong ones") were said to fight witches in dreams. Commoners—the ordinary people—were thought to punish an inhospitable chief or one who had given an unjust judgment in court, or any member of their village who was mean, inhospitable, too conspicuously successful, or who committed some breach of customary obligation such as neglecting a ward or insulting a father. The "breath of men"—murmurs of outraged public opinion—was believed to fall on the miscreant and cause him or her to fall ill of a fever, pine away, or become paralyzed.

There were also "medicines" (*imiti*), chiefly vegetable substances thought to be used for both good and evil ends: to kill or cure, to destroy or promote crops, to murder or to maintain constituted authority.

The moral aspect of religion was constantly stressed: A man who was good was protected by his shades, and his family, stock, and crops increased; a chief who loved and cherished his subjects and ancestors attracted followers; if the founding hero and his living representative were duly honored, the region would be blessed with gentle rain. The good person gave no cause for offense and hoped never to arouse the anger of a neighbor who was a witch or sorcerer. Evil was personified in witchcraft, but any sort of power might be misused. A father who cursed his son or daughter so that the child became sterile should forgive and bless the child when he or she begged pardon with an appropriate gift, even if the anger was justified. The angered father might say, "I forgive you now" and spit on the ground, and all the anger that was in him would come out like spit. Rituals had to be celebrated, correct in every detail, but if participants nursed anger in the heart no ritual could be efficacious. Anger was the root of misfortune.

Like other societies, Nyakyusa society has never been static. The coronation rituals and offerings on behalf of chiefs and regions explicitly celebrated a change that had once occurred: the coming of heroes who brought fire, iron, cattle, and the institution of chieftainship. This was pictured as a single event that had occurred ten generations back. Archaeologists are now tracing the spread of iron and of cattle in Africa, and the first hearths are being sought. Chieftainship, including the secular power of the Kyungu, is known to have spread within historical times. The myths therefore recall real events, but they telescope time. Events such as the domestication of fire and first forging of iron, separated perhaps by a million years, are fused with the coming of cattle and the institution of chieftainship as symbols of the beginning of civilized life.

From 1891 onward, with the coming of Christian missions, trade, and colonial rule, the pace of change accelerated greatly. By 1938, 16 percent of the population in the Rungwe Valley and more on the Ngonde Plain were professing Christians and had largely abandoned traditional rituals; by 1955 even those who did not profess Christianity had curtailed or abandoned some of the rituals, notably that on the birth of twins; and after the independence of Tanganyika in 1961 the institution of chieftainship was abolished in Rungwe Valley and coronation rituals lapsed.

Two trends are clear: first, a growing importance to most people of the idea of God (Kyala) distinct from shades and heroes, and of prayer and worship directed to him; second, a lessening of fear of contamination in death and birth. A sense of the awfulness of divinity and of biological processes in which divinity was manifest have decreased.

Celebration of rituals may be observed and accounts of dogma and myth recorded, but evidence of religious experience is difficult to document. Many people spoke of a sense of presence of the shades in dreams and waking moments, and if a wife or child were ill a man might go to his banana grove with his calabash cup at dusk and blow out water, expressing himself in love and charity with all, living and dead, and calling upon his shades for blessing; but repeated dreams of the dead were feared as an omen of death, and the period of seclusion during a ritual, when the participant dwelt with the shades, was felt to be deeply distasteful. Christian converts, familiar with the traditional patterns, asserted that they valued a sense of presence and communion with God in a different manner from any traditional communion with divinity. All were aware of the destructive power of evil within humans and sought to purge themselves and others of it.

BIBLIOGRAPHY

Park, George K. "Kinga Priests: The Politics of Pestilence." In *Political Anthropology,* edited by Marc J. Swartz, Victor Turner, and Arthur Tuden, pp. 229–237. Chicago, 1966. Compares Kinga with Nyakyusa priesthood.

Wilson, Monica. *Good Company: A Study of Nyakyusa Age-Villages.* London, 1951. An account of Nyakyusa and Ngonde people, particularly of age-villages and accusations of witchcraft.

Wilson, Monica. *Rituals of Kinship among the Nyakyusa.* London, 1957.

Wilson, Monica. *Communal Rituals of the Nyakyusa.* London, 1959. Descriptions of rituals and interpretations of their symbolism based on associations made by participants.

Wilson, Monica. *For Men and Elders.* London, 1977. Change among the Nyakyusa and Ngonde from 1875 to 1971, with particular reference to marriage and relationships between generations.

MONICA WILSON (1987)

NYĀYA. Nyāya is an orthodox, classical Indian school of logic and epistemology established in the second century CE with the writing of the Nyāyasūtras by Gautama (Akṣapāda Gautama). It is described as concerned with the science of argumentation *(ānvīkṣiki)* and as the measure of all other sciences *(pramāṇaśāstra).* Unlike modern Western logic, which is mainly formal and is complemented by an epistemology that presupposes the separateness of the study of epistemology, ethics, and metaphysics and religion, Nyāya defines its method as one of considering the science of argumentation as an instrument for the knowledge of reality that must lead to the attainment of the Highest Good—namely freedom from suffering. The very first aphorism of the Nyāyasūtras thus defines its purpose and content in the following manner:

> It is the knowledge of the real essence of the following sixteen categories that leads to the attainment of the Highest Good: 1. the means of right cognition, 2. the objects of right cognition, 3. doubt, 4. motive, 5. example, 6. theory, 7. factors of inference, 8. cogitation/ decision, 9. demonstrated truth, 10. discussion 11. disputation, 12. wrangling, 13. fallacious reasons, 14. casuistry, 15. futile rejoinders and 16. clinchers. (Gautama, *Nyāyasūtras,* tr. Ganganatha Jha, 1939, p. 3)

Nyāya is traditionally paired with the Vaiśeṣika school, because the two focus respectively on the subject and object of knowledge, with the former therefore being more dominantly epistemological and the latter ontological in nature.

Modern scholarship on Nyāya can largely be divided into two camps. The first provides an apologetic for its metaphysical orientation and prefers to emphasize the technical detail of logic in an attempt to relocate Nyāya within a positivist framework. The historian of Indian philosophy S. N. Dasgupta and more recently Bimal Krishna Matilal belong to this category. The second approach is represented by those like Dharmendra Nath Shastri, Jitendranath Mohanty, and Karl Potter, who argue that the relation to metaphysics is not "added on" but intrinsic to the discourse of Nyāya. This difference in approach has not, however, affected the selection of topics or emphases among authors from either group, as the focus in both cases remains mainly on exegesis with occasional critical analysis. A sustained, conscious, and systematic consideration of Nyāya's method, which consists in the nondualism of fact and value and theory and practice, presupposing a belief in the unity of epistemology (science), ethics, and metaphysics (or religion), has yet to be made. This is one of the major difficulties that hinders understanding of the exact nature of the orientation and development of thought within Nyāya, both internally and in relation to Buddhism and the Mīmāṃsā school and, more significantly, modern Western analytic thought.

Though empiricist and realist in orientation, Nyāya's definition and theory of perception and the object thereof reveals a consistent and systematic attempt to establish the conditions for the possibility of a nondualist science. Nyāya lists four instruments of cognition—perception, inference, analogy, and testimony. Perception is basic and necessary for the other three, and execution, that is, successful effort or action in acquiring or rejecting the object of cognition, is either the consequence of true cognition or its very nature. The object of cognition cannot be known merely through the perception of qualities such as shape, size, color, and weight; rather, it is truly known only when it is also possible to classify it as soul or not-soul, as that which is to be acquired or rejected in light of its being a source of pleasure or pain, in the quest for freedom. To this a caveat is of course added, pointing out that ultimately all pleasure and sources of pleasure are sources of pain from which one must attain detachment. Perception is defined as that cognition that arises from the contact of sense organ and object, which is not designated or expressed in speech, without error, and determinate. This definition includes within its range both sensation and direct experience of the "nameless" One (yogic perception).

Vātsāyana's early-fifth-century commentary on the Nyāyasūtras points out that "contact" with the mind and soul are not mentioned in perception's definition only because they are not unique to this instrument of cognition and are necessary to the other instruments as well. In fact it is the soul that makes it possible to see the object as pain or pleasure or as a source of the same. Finally, the scientific treatise is described as that which deals with the means of destroying pain. The cognizer is one who is stimulated to act in and through his or her calling, personal and professional, by the desire to reject pain and acquire pleasure, with the ultimate aim of renouncing all activity. Thus the co-ordinates of theory and practice, and of fact and value, establish true knowledge.

Nyāya argues that proof of the truth of unseen things spoken of in the Upaniṣads is established by the truth and efficacy of scientific treatises on things seen. The example then is of great importance in Nyāya. It is defined as that which can be directly perceived by both ordinary people and expert or trained investigators and is an essential factor both in establishing the truth of one's position and in disproving that of the opponent. Neither inference nor testimony can stand without the proof of such an example.

Nyāya's main disagreement over the nature of reality is with Buddhist idealism. The period from the fifth to eleventh centuries CE was one of great creative engagement between the two schools. The assumption of the reality of the external world comprising indivisible atomic reals is central to Nyāya. Knowledge of the true nature of an object enables one to attain detachment from it and overcome suffering in this world. Buddhists, on the other hand, characterize reality itself as suffering. Suffering arises from believing the external world to be real and permanent. In fact the reality and permanence of the external world is merely an illusion created when the mind projects unity and continuity onto the causal chain of momentary conceptions *(vikalpa)* that arise and are destroyed in succession, with each moment being the cause of the proceeding one. A realization of the momentariness of existence dissolves the object of desire, as it were, and suffering is overcome. Thus everything that the Naiyāyika (practitioner of Nyāya) depends on—the object, knowledge of the object, and proof through example and tradition—is untenable in Buddhism, which presupposes knowledge of the external world's impermanence, the path shown by the buddha or gurū, and membership of the congregation to overcome this impermanence, rather than the authority of Scripture.

Though an orthodox school, Nyāya presupposes a critical attitude even with respect to the Vedas. This becomes evident in its disagreement with Mīmāṃsā on the issue of *prāmāṇya* (the criterion of truth). Nyāya holds that the criterion of the truth of a statement rests in factors external to the statement itself, whereas for Mīmāṃsā the criterion of truth is intrinsic to the statement, which can only be falsified by external factors. The real issue here is the possibility of having a single theory of truth that will cover both Vedic and ordinary statements without on the one hand laying the truth of Scripture open to faithless doubt and on the other hand making Scripture so rigid that it becomes unavailable to usage and custom. Thus Nyāya advocates the use of *paratahaprāmāṇya* (extrinsic criterion of truth) but articulates clear criteria to identify and establish one who is witness to the truth *(āpta)*. Mīmāṃsā advocates *svatahaprāmāṇya* (intrinsic criterion of truth) but broadens the limits of interpretation through a theory of meaning that holds that the word does not refer to the individual/particular but to the universal *(jāti)*. Contemporary analyses have, however, confined themselves to a narrow interpretation of *prāmāṇya,* and some, like Mohanty, go further and argue that the problem relates to empirical *(vyavahārika)* statements only.

Among the orthodox schools, the Nyāya tradition has perhaps been most alive with original commentaries written by Udyoktara (635 CE) and Vācaspati Miśra (840 CE) and treatises by Jayanta Bhatta (880 CE) and Udayana (984 CE). Around 1200 CE, the Navya-Nyāya, or new school of Nyāya, began with the *Tattvacintāmaṇi* of Gañgeśa (Gañgeśa Upadhyaya). This new school is considered by most to represent a move away from metaphysics. There are difficulties with such a characterization, however, because despite a shift in emphasis toward epistemological issues, there is no philosophical attempt to reject metaphysics. Conversely, one could argue that Navya Nyāya responded to arguments that tended to dichotomize metaphysics and epistemology. For instance, Gadhādhara (fl. c. 1650) defines objecthood as a relation constituted by the very nature of its terms—the self /subject of cognition and the object. Thus, he argues against the view that objecthood is an independent entity and also against the view that it is determined by the nature of the object alone and the view that it is determined by the nature of the cognition/cognizing self. In doing so Gadhādhara is arguing for a definition of objecthood that establishes it as a sign of the relation between the object and the self and not as determined by one or the other. Knowledge of this sign can reveal as much about the self as about the object to which it refers.

Nyāya's presuppositions about the necessary relation between the knowledge of objects and the attainment of freedom, about the unity of ideal and ordinary languages, and about the importance of the example present a structure and method of analytic philosophy at odds with the modern positivist tradition. With Gadhādara's formulation of the issue of objecthood one is further compelled toward the position that Nyāya lays the foundation for a science of semiotics that includes within the purview of a single theory of logic, language, and epistemology, the study of sign, symptom, and symbol.

See Also Indian Philosophies; Vaiśeṣika.

Bibliography

Gadhādhara. *Theory of Objectivity [Viśayatāvāda].* Translated and annotated by Sibajiban Bhattacharya. Delhi, 1990. A technically competent translation, with detailed exegesis and discussion by the translator.

Gañgeśa. *Theory of Truth [Prāmāṇya (jñāpti) vāda].* Translated and annotated by Jitendranath Mohanty. Santiniketan, India, 1966. Contains a long and lucid introduction to issues concerning the Nyāya-Mīmāṃsā debates.

Gautama. *Nyāyasūtras.* Translated by Ganganatha Jha. Pune, India, 1939.

Matilal, Bimal Krishna. *Perception: An Essay on Classical Indian Theories of Knowledge.* Oxford, 1986.

Shastri, Dharmendra Nath. *The Philosophy of* Nyāya-*Vaiśeṣika and Its Conflict with the Buddhist Dignāga School: Critique of Indian Realism.* Delhi, 1964.

Anuradha Veeravalli (2005)

NYBERG, H. S.

NYBERG, H. S. (1889–1974), was a Swedish Orientalist and historian of religions. Born in Söderbärke in Dalecarlia, Henrik Samuel Nyberg received his early education at home and at the senior high school in Västeras. In 1908 he entered the university at Uppsala, and there he stayed, working in various positions, for the rest of his life. He earned his Ph.D. in 1919 and was professor of Semitic languages from 1931 to 1956. Concentrating from the beginning on comparative Semitic philology, Arabic, Hebrew, Aramaic, and Ethiopic, Nyberg became an inspiring teacher and one of the most brilliant representatives of the humanities Sweden has ever had, exerting a great influence on the cultural life of his country. His doctoral thesis, "Kleinere Schriften des Ibn al-ʿArabī," already showed the admirable scope that was to characterize his later studies. It is an edition of three minor writings of the great mystic, with an introduction that investigates the origin of Islamic mysticism and attempts to understand the system of Ibn al-ʿArabī as a phenomenon of syncretism.

In 1924–1925 Nyberg sojourned in Egypt for practical studies of Arabic. The most remarkable result of the trip was his discovery of the manuscript of *Kitāb al-Intiṣār* by the Muʿtazilī al-Khayyāṭ (ninth century). Nyberg published the text in Cairo in 1925 with an important commentary in Arabic: *Le livre du triomphe et de la réfutation d'Ibn er-Rawendi/ Ibn Mohammed/l'hérétique par Abou l-Hosein Abderrahim/Ibn Mohammed ibn Osman el-Khayyat.* His deep penetration into the earlier polemic literature of Islam later enabled him to write his famous article, "Muʿtazila," for *The Encyclopaedia of Islam* (1934).

Nyberg's interest in the dialectology of Aramaic led him to the investigation of some documents from Avroman in Kurdistan. The Aramaic script of the documents appeared to contain a Middle Iranian dialect, and in 1923 he published his pioneering study "The Pahlavi Documents from Avroman" (*Monde oriental* 17). Thenceforth he was to devote much of his time to the study of Pahlavi; he eventually created the first scientific handbook of this language and was responsible for introducing Iranian studies as an academic discipline in Uppsala.

Influenced by Nathan Söderblom (1866–1931) and by his friend Tor Andrae (1885–1946), Nyberg now began his investigations of the Avesta, especially the *Gāthās.* In this field he made his most important contribution to the study of Iranian religious history, collected in the monumental book *Irans forntida religioner* (1937). One of the most remarkable traits of this work is the revaluation of the historical impact of Zarathushtra (Zoroaster), considered by Nyberg as a conservative champion of the religion of his own tribe. The consciousness of Zarathushtra's vocation was, according to Nyberg, conditioned by a type of Central Asian shamanism. Highly contested on many points, Nyberg's view in this work has nevertheless exerted a strong influence on scientific discussion in this field.

Familiar with the world of the Bible, Nyberg also worked from time to time in Hebrew. In his much debated *Studien zum Hoseabuche* (1935), he strongly emphasizes the importance of the oral tradition for the historical understanding of the textual form of the Hebrew scriptures, deliberately practicing a conservative textual criticism and eschewing the predilection for emendations common among many Old Testament scholars.

BIBLIOGRAPHY

Nyberg's monumental study *Irans forntida religioner* (Stockholm, 1937) was translated into German as *Die Religionen des alten Iran* (Leipzig, 1938) by H. H. Schaeder. It was reprinted in 1966 with a *Begleitwort* by Nyberg. Obituary notices and a complete bibliography of Nyberg's works can be found in the *Monumentum H. S. Nyberg*, 4 vols., "Acta Iranica," vols. 1–4 (Leiden, 1975).

New Sources

Kahle, Sigrid. *H. S. Nyberg: En vetenskapsmans biografi.* Stockholm, 1991.

Utas, Bo., ed. *Frahang ī Pahlavīk.* Wiesbaden, 1988.

FRITHIOF RUNDGREN (1987)
Revised Bibliography

O

OATHS SEE VOWS AND OATHS

OBEDIENCE consists in the act of voluntary submission to an authority. Religious obedience, the subject of this article, is therefore the voluntary submission to a specifically religious authority, and its different forms correspond to differences in the types and levels of such authority. In many world religions, authority rests with a single principle, being, or god, and religious obedience is accordingly due to an all-embracing law or to the divine will. But even in these cases, where there is clearly a single and absolute source of authority, the obligation of obedience may be expressed on a variety of levels. Thus in Hinduism, for instance, obedience to the *Laws of Manu* is enjoined upon all, but at the individual level a disciple's obedience to his *guru*, or, at a corporate level, to the rules of his sect, religious establishment, or *maṭha* may be equally or even more important.

Obedience in Christianity can similarly be seen as extending from the general principles of the Decalogue, through the observance of the rules of the church or monastery, to the individual's obedience of his own immediate ecclesiastical superior. In Islam, obedience may extend from the observance of the *sharī'ah*, to the rules of one's *ṭarīqah*, and finally to obeying one's spiritual mentor or *pīr*. Likewise in Buddhism, apart from the moral precepts, the corporate rules of the *saṃgha* are to be observed by the monks and nuns, and even though Buddhism generally places less emphasis on the unique master-disciple relationship common in Hinduism, even here each novitiate is assigned initially to an individual elder.

Differences in the forms of religious association will also result in different forms of obedience. In religions that continue to be organized along the lines of natural kinship

CLOCKWISE FROM TOP LEFT CORNER. Osiris, the Egyptian god of death and resurrection, in a painting from the tomb of Sennutem in the cemetery of Deir el-Medina, Egypt. *[©Erich Lessing/Art Resource, N.Y.]*; Orpheus playing the lyre among the Thracians on a red-figure krater from ancient Greece, 480–330 BCE. Antikensammlung, Staatliche Museen zu Berlin. *[©Bildarchiv Preussischer Kulturbesitz/Art Resource, N.Y.]*; Eighteenth-century wood sculpture of a Maori couple in an embrace that can be broken only by the intervention of Tane, god of the forests. Otago Museum, Dunedin. *[©Werner Forman/Art Resource, N.Y.]* ; Pre-Columbian Olmec stone head. Anthropology Museum, Veracruz, Mexico. *[©Werner Forman/Art Resource, N.Y.]*; Detail from a marble relief of Dionysus discovering Ariadne, from the Greek island of Naxos. Musée du Louvre, Paris. *[The Art Archive/Musée du Louvre Paris/Dagli Orti]* .

groups, religious obedience will often be a simple extension of one's normal obligations to one's family. Thus in Confucianism the filial relationship becomes paradigmatic for obedience of all kinds. But even when natural forms of association are left behind, obedience may continue to be understood metaphorically in terms of spiritual parentage. In the mystical traditions of several religions, including Christianity, the spiritual mentor is often compared to a father. Each individual, or even the religious community as a whole, may be visualized as undergoing a period of religious tutelage that requires the unquestioning obedience of a child. In many cases, the rite of religious initiation closely parallels that of birth and is often considered a kind of rebirth. Just as children are not supposed to disobey, so the neophytes undergoing initiation or puberty rites must behave humbly, obeying their instructors and accepting arbitrary punishment without complaint. Here one thinks of the obedience that Zen monks owe to their *rōshi.*

With the spiritual coming-of-age of an individual or a community, as in the biological parallel of growth during adolescence, obedience becomes more problematic, and at times even self-defeating. One encounters both the problem of disobedience and the more subtle problem of the conflict between the "spirit" and the "letter." The latter problem is illustrated by the Christian attitude toward Jewish law and by the Buddhist rejection of the cumbersome Hindu codes of conduct. More enlightened approaches emerge at the individual level in which disobedience becomes a higher form of obedience. Thus the Hindu religious leader Rāmānuja (eleventh century CE) disobeyed his master by making public formerly esoteric doctrines of salvation in order that all might be saved. Such "disobedient" transcendence of the conventional letter of the law is will illustrated by a Zen master's response to his disciple, who one evening questioned the propriety of his master's carrying a lady across a flooded rivulet that morning because it infringed the Vinaya rule against touching women: "I left her on the bank in the morning," he replied, "and you are still carrying her!" Similarly the Chinese sage Mengzi (Mencius) held that a man who would not pull his drowning sister-in-law out of a river, for fear of disobeying the rule that she not be touched, is no better than a wolf.

The appropriateness of obedience, or indeed the very question of what constitutes obedience in a given situation, cannot always be mechanically ascertained. Nevertheless, the consequences of disobedience cannot simply be dismissed. According to the Tibetan tradition, Mi la ras pa (Milarepa) had to suffer the consequences of disobeying his master's orders to the full, which were designed to wear out his *karman.* Thus although theoretically and retrospectively one may speak of enlightened disobedience, it presents difficulties in practical terms.

Another important issue in relation to obedience pertains to the conflict of different laws or values within a single tradition. This conflict was clearly recognized by the Hindu tradition, which sought to deal with it by relegating such conflicting norms to different historical epochs. The *dharma* appropriate to one age, it was held, may not be appropriate to another. But even without introducing this historical dimension, such conflict may be recognized as part of the essential tension present within a tradition at any given time, the tension, once again, between the "spirit" and the "letter." The recognition of this tension is exemplified by Confucius's remark to the duke, who had praised the rectitude of a son in testifying against his father in a case of theft: "The honest men of my country are different from this. The father covers up for his son, the son covers up for his father—and there is honesty in that too." The case is similar with Islam, which requires unquestioning obedience to the Qur'ān, but at the same time provides for *ittiḥād.*

A closely related issue is that of law and freedom; how much freedom is to be allowed in the interpretation of the law? Is obedience to the law compatible with a relative freedom in its interpretation? Or does true obedience require a "rigorist" reading of the letter of the law, with the interpreter being allowed only the absolute minimum of freedom? This issue has been particularly important in the Christian tradition, where a broad range of positions has been defined.

The importance of obedience in religious life is undoubtedly due in part to its importance for the successful operation of family, society, and polity in general. However, obedience also functions as a specifically religious virtue. The triple vows of poverty, chastity, and cenobitic obedience in the context of Christian monasticism offer a possible example of such specifically religious obedience. However, all forms of cenobitic monasticism, as distinguished from the eremitic, involve rules necessary to the maintenance of a community and may therefore merely reflect the need for the maintenance of order. No such reductionistic explanation is possible, however, in the practice of spiritual and ascetic disciplines. Here obedience has an exclusively religious goal, as an essential precondition of spiritual knowledge. Thus when a Greek king wished to learn the wisdom of India from the gymnosophists, the first thing required of him was obedience: "No one coming in the drapery of European clothes—cavalry cloak and broad-brimmed hat and top-boots, such as Macedonians wore—could learn their wisdom. To do that he must strip naked and learn to sit on the hot stones beside them." Obedience may however play a role at the end of the path as well, if it is understood spiritually as surrender. In this sense it constitutes the annihilation of the individual ego which constitutes the last obstacle to the plenary experience. According to the modern Hindu mystic, Ramaṇa Maharshi (1879–1950): "The disciple surrenders himself to the master. That means there is no vestige of individuality retained by the discipline. If the surrender is complete all sense of individuality is lost and there is thus no cause for misery. The eternal being is only happiness, that is revealed" (*Talks with Sri Ramaṇa Maharshi,* 1984, p. 318). Thus while obedience is the necessary prerequisite for entry upon the spiritual path, it is also in a sense the goal. This is particularly clear in the case of Islam, which literally means "surrender." Here man is viewed as having his final end outside himself, in the transcendence of the divine. True peace is accordingly to be found only in surrender, in true and total obedience to the divine will.

See Also Authority; Casuistry; Monasticism; Spiritual Guide.

Bibliography

Majumdar, R. C., ed., *The Age of Imperial Unity.* Bombay, 1951.

Schuon, Frithjof. *Islam and the Perennial Philosophy.* Translated by J. Peter Hobson. London, 1976.

Smith, Huston. *The Religions of Man.* New York, 1958.

Talks with Sri Ramaṇa Maharshi. 7th ed. Tiruvannamalai, India, 1984.

Turner, Victor. *The Ritual Process: Structure and Anti-Structure.* Chicago, 1969.

Zaehner, R.C., ed. *The Concise Encyclopedia of Living Faiths.* 2d ed. New York, 1971.

Arvind Sharma (1987 and 2005)

OB-UGRIANS See FINNO-UGRIC RELIGIONS; KHANTY AND MANSI RELIGION

OCCAM, WILLIAM OF See WILLIAM OF OCKHAM

OCCASIONALISM.

[*This entry deals specifically with Islamic occasionalism.*]

The adjective *occasional,* as applied to causes or events, is used by medieval European theologians such as Thomas Aquinas to mean an "indirect cause which determines any disposition to any effect" (*Summa theologiae* 1.114.3, 2.1.88.3, 2.1.98.1–2, 2.1.113.7, *et passim*). In modern philosophy, the term *occasional* and its derivatives are used by Cartesians such as Malebranche (d. 1715), Guelincks (d. 1669), and Cordemoy (d. 1685) to refer to the relations between the modifications of mind and those of body, as well as to natural occurrences in general. Malebranche in particular denies any necessary connection between those two classes of modifications and refers all natural occurrences, human actions, and other events to God's direct intervention, of which the manifest or natural causes are nothing but the "occasions" (*Entretien sur la métaphysique* 7.11, 7.13).

In the history of Islamic theology (*kalām*), an "occasionalist" tendency is clearly discernible from the eighth century on. The earliest writers on theological questions, such as al-Ashʿarīand his followers, were overwhelmed with the Qurʾanic concept of God "who is unlike anything else" (surah 42:11) and whose decrees are irreversible and inscrutable. Accordingly, they attempted to formulate a cosmological view that would justify the referral of all activity or development in the world to this God, whom they called the "Lord of the worlds" and the "Lord of the heavens and the earth."

By the eighth century the Muslim theologians (*mutakallimūn*) realized that Aristotelian physics, which presupposes a necessary connection between natural events or entities, is incompatible with the concept of God's lordship or sovereignty in the world. In its place they proposed a more theologically acceptable metaphysics of atoms and accidents in which every entity or event comes into being and passes away at the behest of God. According to this metaphysics, probably derived from Greek (Democritean) sources with certain Indian modifications, everything in the world is made up of substance and accident. The majority of the *mutakallimūn* define substance (*jawhar*) as that which bears the accidents, although some argue that this is the specific characteristic of body. Substance and accident, however, always exist in conjunction. Some accidents are more primary than others and include the "modes" or original properties of unity, motion, rest, composition, and location. A body can never be divested of these accidents, although it can be divested of the other "secondary" accidents, such as weight and shape. Most of the later *mutakallimūn* appear to have held that no substance can be divested of the accident of color, so that they define substance as "anything endowed with color."

The most characteristic feature of substance is its indivisibility; hence the majority of the *mutakallimun* identify substance with the atom (*juzʾ*) and dwell on its relation to the primary and secondary accidents. Thirty positive accidents, or their opposites, are said to inhere in each substance. When God wishes to create an entity, by "commanding" it to be (as the Qurʾān has put it), he first creates the atoms, then the accidents making up its physical or biological nature or character. But since accidents cannot endure for two moments of time, as a leading Ashʿarī theologian of the tenth century, al-Bāqillānī, put it, this entity will not continue to exist unless God constantly recreates the atoms and accidents it is made of. This theory of "continuous recreation" (Macdonald, 1927) constitutes the basis of Islamic cosmology and moral theology, especially in its Ashʿarī form. It presupposes, in addition to the duality of atom and accident, the atomic composition of time and that of the soul. Should God decide to put an end to the existence of a particular entity, the theory requires that he either cease to recreate the "accident of duration" in it (the Muʿtazilī view) or simply stop recreating the stream of atoms and accidents making it up (the Ashʿarī view), whereupon the particular entity would cease to exist at all.

This theory had its critics in subsequent centuries, the most important and vocal of whom was probably the great Aristotelian commentator, Ibn Rushd (Averroës) of Cordova

(d. 1198). In general it might be said that the theologians were sympathetic to the occasionalist view of the universe or some aspects of it, whereas the philosophers as a rule were either hostile or critical.

SEE ALSO Descartes, René; Scholasticism.

BIBLIOGRAPHY

One of the earlier studies of Islamic occasionalism and its theological implications is D. B. Macdonald's "Continuous Recreation and Atomic Time in Muslim Scholastic Theology," *Isis* 9 (1927): 326–344. The standard work on Islamic atomism continues to be Salomon Pines's *Beiträge zur Islamischen Atomenlehre* (Berlin, 1936). My *Islamic Occasionalism and Its Critique by Averroës and Aquinas* (London, 1958) deals in a preliminary way with the implications of occasionalism for the struggle between the theologians and the philosophers. Max Horten's *Die philosophischen Systeme der spekulativen Theologen im Islam* (Bonn, 1912) includes a discussion of Islamic occasionalism and atomic theory. Moses Maimonides' summary in the *Guide of the Perplexed,* translated by Salomon Pines (Chicago, 1963), should also be consulted for the major propositions of *kalām* and their occasionalist significance.

MAJID FAKHRY (1987)

OCCULTISM.

OCCULTISM. Occult and occultism have taken on several meanings. Occultism has been the object of a variety of definitions, which for the most part are related to the notion of esotericism. In academic usage, occultism tends to refer to one modern Western esoteric current, that which flourished from the second half of the nineteenth to the first half of the twentieth centuries.

THE TERMS OCCULT AND OCCULTISM. A distinction must be made between the original adjective *occult* and the substantive *occultism* which first appeared in the nineteenth century. *Occult* has a long history. For example, in the Renaissance it was often used in the expression occult properties, as in Marsilio Ficino's *De Vita coelitus comparanda* (1486, III, ch. 12), when he described how certain stones can attract celestial influences. Likewise, Cornelius Agrippa, in *De Occulta Philosophia* (1533, I, 10), explains that they "are called occult properties because their causes lie hidden, so that man's intellect cannot in any way reach and find them out; wherefore philosophers have attained to the greatest part of them by long experience rather than by the search of reason."

Such a belief remained widespread at the time that saw the rise of experimental science (in the period following the Renaissance). The notion of occult forces, and ultimately of one occult force, was used at the time of the Enlightenment, particularly in mesmerism and animal magnetism, against the mechanistic and materialist positions of the new mainstream science. In the nineteenth century and beyond, notions such as ether and/or Od force (of Karl von Reichenbach) came to a head in Helena Petrovna Blavatsky's "Fohat," by which she meant a vital fluid permeating the universe. Alongside such notions, that of occult philosophy (later called occult science[s]) came into use in the Renaissance, meaning a synthesizing religious project of a philosophical and cosmological nature, on which occult practices proper were supposed to be founded. As for the substantive *occultism* (*l'occultisme*), it seems to have appeared for the first time in Jean-Baptiste Richard de Randonvilliers' *Enrichissement de la langue française-Dictionnaire des mots nouveaux.* Shortly after, Éliphas Lévi (1810–1875; pen name of Alphonse Louis Constant) used it in the "Discours préliminaire" of his *Dogme et rituel de la haute magie* (1856), and henceforth it was widely circulated. In English, it appeared probably for the first time in 1875, in Blavatsky's article "A Few Questions to 'Hiraf,'" published in *Spiritual Scientist.*

THE VARIOUS DEFINITIONS OF OCCULTISM. In some of his ground-breaking writings devoted to methodological issues, Marco Pasi has cogently submitted that, historically, the relationship between esotericism and occultism has been the object of five distinct approaches:

1. Occultism is a synonym of esotericism. This was the position of many occultists (i.e., of those who stood within the so-called occultist current). They considered occultism as a very ancient tradition (be it Western or universal) to which they took themselves to be the heirs. Some scholars also, like Pierre Riffard, occasionally use both terms indifferently and in a universal sense. Wouter J. Hanegraaff, who does not stand for this definition, has discussed the term *the occult,* used as a substantivized adjective. He mentioned in this respect Colin Wilson's 1971 bestseller *The Occult* as having exerted a major influence on the popular currency of this term which, in this context, is more or less used as the equivalent of esotericism, in particular among journalists and some sociologists. Indeed, occultism still serves as a catch-all word to designate a variety of currents (e.g., Oriental mysticism), practices (e.g., channeling, parapsychological experiments), and beliefs (e.g., fairies, spirits, UFO-abductions, vampire legends) which do not easily fall under the heading science and religion. Be that as it may, neither in that considerably extended meaning, which often tends to indiscriminately designate an overall form of rejected knowledge, nor in the aforementioned one generally adopted by the occultists should it be confused, as noted by Hanegraaff, with what the now-classical modern academic usage intends under Western esotericism. As remarked by Jean-Pierre Laurant, although born at approximately the same time, the terms *esotericism* and *occultism* are not identical twins, but rather fraternal ones.

2. Occultism is a drift from esotericism and/or a degeneration of it. This is, for example, the so-called traditionalist position as represented by René Guénon. He and his followers have opposed occultism (understood pejoratively) against their own concept of esoteric metaphys-

ics. This distinction was adopted by Serge Hutin in his famous article "Esotérisme."

3. Occultism is the practical dimension of esotericism. This definition often overlaps the second one. It may be due to the existence of the expression occult sciences, usually comprised mainly of magic, astrology, alchemy, and *magia naturalis* (natural magic), which are often interrelated. It can be traced already in *Le Christianisme césarien* of the Abbot Alta (pen name of Calixte Mélinge): "Occultism came later [than esotericism] in order to represent . . . material but dangerous things that wisdom forbade to display to everyone. Occultism was concerned with material things: natural forces, like electricity, magnetism [, whereas] the object of esotericism is the supernatural forces—those of higher Nature, that is, the invisible, spiritual, divine things" (as quoted by Laurant, 1992, p. 174). Much later, in the 1970s, a similar distinction can be traced in the so-called sociology of the occult, under the pen of scholars like Edward A. Tiryakian and Marcello Truzzi—the first to use the term. The former wrote: "By 'occult' I understand intentional practices, techniques, or procedures which (a) draw upon hidden or concealed forces . . . , and (b) which have as their desired or intended consequences empirical results . . . . By 'esoteric'; I refer to those religio-philosophic belief systems which underlie occult techniques and practices. . . . By way of analogy, esoteric knowledge is to occult practices as the corpus of theoretical physics is to engineering applications" (Tiryakian, 1972, pp. 498–499). Tiryakian's distinction was endorsed in the 1980s by a number of scholars, including Mircea Eliade (1907–1986) and Antoine Faivre. It has been more or less discarded since, although Bettina Gruber took it over again in 1980. Be that as it may, Pasi considers it—and rightly, so it seems—to be superfluous, and notes that it has been cogently criticized by other scholars like Robert Galbreath, whose position he endorses—"the notion of a purely abstract knowledge divorced from personal development and personal participation is alien to ['occultists' and 'esotericists' alike]. It is a nonexistent distinction" (Galbreath, 1983, p. 18).
4. Occultism is only one specific historical current among those of which modern Western esotericism is comprised. Indeed, since the 1970s, in academic parlance occultism has tended to be used mostly as referring specifically, and in a descriptive sense, to the esoteric current which began to flourish from the time of Lévi in the middle of the nineteenth century and well into the first half of the twentieth. This position has been the current one adopted by scholars since the beginning of the 1990s, including by Jean-Pierre Laurant, Antoine Faivre, and Joscelyn Godwin.
5. Occultism is a modification of esotericism under the impact of secularization. This fifth sense (in Pasi's list) of occultism has been introduced and defended by Hanegraaff and should not be confused with the fourth definition. Indeed, Hanegraaff prefers not to intend occultism as a historical current but rather as a category, among others, in the study of Western religions. Here it refers, in an analytic and typological sense, to the type of esotericism which characterizes various forms of esotericism from the second half of the nineteenth up to the first half of the twentieth centuries. Hanegraaff submits that it is comprised by "all attempts by esotericists to come to terms with a disenchanted world or, alternatively, by people in general to make sense of esotericism from the perspective of a disenchanted secular world" (Hanegraaff, 1996, p. 422; see also 1995, pp. 119–121). In other words, occultism is the form that traditional esotericism has taken on under the impact of secularization, in particular since the end of the eighteenth century. Hanegraaff speaks of a "transformation of esotericism into occultism" (Hanegraaff, 1996, p. 409), and uses this latter term to designate a range of various theories and practices: not only occultism as defined above in point four, but also such others as animal magnetism, spiritualism, up to some aspects of the New Age movement. Such an approach is congenial to the theoretical thesis which underlies his book *New Age Religion and Western Culture* (1996), according to which the process of secularization of Western esotericism has brought about considerable changes within the physiognomy of the Western esoteric landscape. By way of consequence, and in terms of vocabulary, he has found it appropriate to replace esotericism by occultism when dealing with the various forms of esotericism of the nineteenth and twentieth centuries.

   While Hanegraaff was certainly right in stressing the importance of secularization (he was the first to do so in such a cogent and convincing manner), the problem is that endorsing his thesis does not necessarily entail accepting his terminological choice. As a matter of fact, the latter has been called into question not only by Pasi but also by a number of scholars, such as Olaf Hammer who prefers to speak of "post-Enlightenment esotericism." Indeed, the occultist current considered as one among other esoteric ones is endowed with a sufficiently precise specificity that it does not seem to be necessary to assimilate it with a range of other contemporary phenomena, like spiritualism.

Characteristics and Historical Survey of the Occultist Current. The so-called occultist current which flourished from the second half of the nineteenth to the first half of the twentieth centuries seems to display five characteristics which mark its originality within the context of the other Western esoteric currents:

1. A new attempt at synthesizing the so-called esoteric tradition as the occultists of that time from the middle of the nineteenth up to the first half of the twentieth cen-

turies saw it. It was a matter of integrating—more than had been hitherto the case—a variety of new elements, like the tarot and Eastern (mostly Indian) forms of religious wisdom.

2. A strong emphasis on the importance and the practice of the so-called occult sciences, namely alchemy, astrology, Qabbalah, and in particular "magic" (understood mostly within the context of Western magical traditions).
3. An attempt at legitimizing its positions in establishing a dialectical relationship of acceptance and refusal with mainstream science and/or the positivistic culture of the time. Indeed, this current presented itself as an alternative to the triumph of scientism. Generally, occultists did not condemn scientific progress or modernity. Rather, they tried to integrate them within a global vision likely to make the vacuousness of materialism more apparent. In this an echo of the program of the *Naturphilosophie* of the end of the eighteenth and of the first half of the nineteenth centuries can be recognized but the new orientation differed, in particular because of its marked penchant for uncommon phenomena and scientific or pseudo-scientific experimentations.
4. An increasing emancipation from Christianity (contrary to the esoteric currents of the earlier periods, which for the most part were still very Christian in character).
5. A tendency to demarcate itself from a number of contemporary trends, like animal magnetism, spiritualism, and parapsychology, although this tendency became less and less marked in the latest decades of the period. Indeed, occultism forged its identity in confronting itself with them. (Similarly, Guenonian traditionalism has forged its own identity by way of a polemical confrontation with occultism.) Whereas spiritualism dealt with the spirits of the deceased, occultism was more interested in elementals (in the Paracelsian tradition), angels, and in particular in the so-called disincarnated Masters. These latter were supposed to dwell in exotic, far-off places (generally in Tibet), and to be able to communicate with their Western disciples. Furthermore, many occultists considered that the practices of spiritualism were not only passive in character, failing to stress the powers of the human will, but dangerous also, in view of the dubious nature of the entities conjured up in séances. They ascribed these shortcomings to the absence of an overall metaphysical worldview.

However useful these five characteristics may be, it still remains (as Pasi himself admits) that they are a mere academic construct. In reality, their borders are often blurred.

The Occultist Current in Context, and Some of Its Main Representatives. The industrial revolution had given rise to an increasingly marked interest in the "miracles" of science. It had promoted the invasion of daily life by utilitarian and socioeconomic preoccupations of all kinds. In the middle of the nineteenth century, along with smoking factory chimneys, both the fantastic as a new literary genre and the phenomenon of spiritualism (since the 1840s) came into existence. These two possess a common characteristic: each takes the real world in its most concrete form as its point of departure and then postulates the existence of another, supernatural world, separated from the first by a more or less impermeable partition. Fantastic literature then plays upon the effect of surprise that is provided by the irruption of the supernatural into the daily life, which it describes in a realistic fashion. Spiritualism, considered as both a quasi-religion and a practice, follows the inverse procedure, teaching how to pass from this world of the living to the world of the dead, through séances of spirit rappings and table tippings, the table playing a role analogous to that of the traditional magic circle. It is telling that the occultist current appeared at the same time as fantastic literature and spiritualism. Not unlike them, it displayed a marked interest in supernatural phenomena, that is to say, in the diverse modes of passage from one world to the other.

Almost at the same time as Lévi's first important publication, Jean-Marie Ragon's *Orthodoxie Maçonnique* and *Maçonnerie occulte* (1853), and Henri Delaage's *Le monde occulte* (1851) appeared. Though both men paved the way for the beginnings of the occultist current proper, Lévi may be considered the first main exponent of the latter, with his *Dogme et rituel de la haute magie* (1854–1856), *Histoire de la magie* (1860), and *La clef des grands mystères* (1861).

Some other strong personalities dominated a rather heteroclite crowd. Again in France, Papus (1865–1915; pen name of Dr. Gérard Encausse), nicknamed the "Balzac of occultism" because of his numerous and voluminous works, authored among other books a *Traité de science occulte,* which came out the same year (1888) as the first issue of his journal *L'Initiation.* Papus, with his friend from Lyons, L. N. A. Philippe, otherwise called Maître Philippe (1849–1905), went several times to St. Petersburg at the request of Nicholas II whom they initiated into the Martinist Order (created by Papus). Among these French occultists, other prominent individuals include Stanislas de Guaïta (1861–1898; *Au seuil du mystère,* 1886; *Le serpent de la Genèse,* 1891–1897), Joséphin Péladan (1858–1918), Albert de Rochas (1837–1914), François-Charles Barlet (pen name of Albert Faucheux, 1838–1921), and Albert Jounet (pen name of Dr. Emmanuel Lalande, 1868–1929). In Germany, Franz Hartmann (1838–1912) was a noted occultist, while at that time in Russia, P. D. Ouspensky (1878–1947) had already written almost all his work, including *Tertium Organon* (1911). Especially in Anglo-Saxon countries, occultist/esoteric erudition characterizes many noteworthy occultists. Among these, at least three names stand out prominently: G. R. S. Mead (1853–1933), William W. Westcott (1848–1925), and Arthur Edward Waite (1857–1942).

Not unlike the last decades of the eighteenth century, those of the nineteenth saw a proliferation of new initiatory societies which were instrumental in the development and dissemination of the occultist current, although they also contained elements pertaining to other, more generally esoteric ones. Many such societies belonged to the so-called fringe-Masonry, which for its most part is comprised of rites with higher degrees (i.e., above the three traditional degrees of freemasonry proper). Here are a few examples of those initiatory societies with a markedly occultist orientation: The Fraternitas Rosae Crucis was founded in 1868 by Paschal Beverly Randolph (1825–1875). Twenty years later in France, Guaïta and Péladan founded the Order of the Rose-Croix Kabbalistique, which was to go through many an explosion and fragmentation. In 1891, Papus established an Ordre Martiniste. In 1888, in England, Westcott established the Order of the Golden Dawn (OGD), whose founders were important members of the Societas Rosicruciana in Anglia (SRIA), created in London in 1867. The SRIA also was an occultist group, Christian in character and less oriented towards magical practices than the OGD. Between 1906 and 1912, Theodor Reuss (1855–1923) established a secret science research lodge, the Ordo Templi Orientis, whose program was similar to that of the OGD and in which the famous magician Aleister Crowley (1875–1947) held one of the leadership roles. Outside the pale of these fringe-Masonic orders, the Theosophical Society, which Blavatsky cofounded in New York in 1875, was to become the most influential and disseminated esoteric organization until the present time. It has some linkage to the occultist current, insofar as one of its official goals is to study the law of nature as well as the psychic and spiritual powers of the human being.

See Also Esotericism.

Bibliography

Blavatsky, Helena Petrovna. "A Few Questions to 'Hiraf.'" In *Spiritual Scientist* (July 15, 1875): 217.

Blum, P. R. "Qualitas Occulta." In *Historisches Wörterbuch der Philosophie,* edited by Joachim Ritter and Karlfried Gründer, vol. 7. Darmstadt, Germany, 1989.

Eamon, William. *Science and the Secrets of Nature: Books of Secrets in Medieval and Early Modern Culture.* Princeton, N.J., 1994.

Eliade, Mircea. *Occultism, Witchcraft, and Cultural Fashions.* Chicago and London, 1976.

Faivre, Antoine. "Questions of Terminology Proper to Study of Esoteric Currents in Modern and Contemporary Europe." In *Western Esotericism and the Science of Religion,* edited by Antoine Faivre and Wouter J. Hanegraaff, pp. 1–10. Louvain, 1998.

Faivre, Antoine. "Conférences de la première heure." In *Annuaire, Résumé des conférences et travaux de l'Ecole Pratique des Hautes Etudes, Sciences Religieuses,* vol. 110 (2001–2002) pp. 405–409. Paris, 2003.

Galbreath, Robert. "Explaining Modern Occultism." In *The Occult in America: New Historical Perspectives,* edited by Howard Kerr and Charles L. Crow, pp. 11–37. Urbana, Ill., 1983.

Godwin, Joscelyn. *The Theosophical Enlightenment.* Albany, N.Y., 1994.

Gruber, Bettina. "Mystik, Esoterik, Okkultismus: Überlegungen zu einer Begriffs-diskussion." In *Mystique, mysticisme et modernité en Allemagne autour de 1900,* edited by Moritz Bassler and Hildegard Châtellier, pp. 27–39. Strasbourg, France, 1998.

Hanegraaff, Wouter J. "Empirical Method in the Study of Esotericism." *Method and Theory in the Study of Religion* 7, no. 2 (1995): 99–129.

Hanegraaff, Wouter J. *New Age Religion and Western Culture: Esotericism in the Mirror of Secular Thought.* Leiden, 1996.

Hanegraaff, Wouter J. "The Study of Western Esotericism: New Approaches to Christian and Secular Culture." In *New Approaches to the Study of Religion (Religion and Reason),* edited by Peter Antes, Armin W. Geertz, and Randi Warne. Berlin and New York, 2004.

Hutin, Serge. "Esotérisme." In *Encyclopedia Universalis.* Paris, 1972.

Laurant, Jean-Pierre. *L'ésotérisme chrétien en France au XIXe siècle.* Lausanne, Switzerland, 1992.

Laurant, Jean-Pierre. *L'Esotérisme.* Paris, 1993.

Pasi, Marco. "La notion de magie." In *Annuaire, Résumé des conférences et travaux de l'Ecole Pratique des Hautes Etudes, Sciences Religieuses,* vol. 110 (2001–2002), pp. 420–422. Paris, 2003.

Pasi, Marco. *La notion de magie dans le courant occultiste en Angleterre (1875–1947).* Ph.D. diss., Ecole Pratique des Hautes Etudes, Sciences Religieuses, Paris, 2004.

Riffard, Pierre. *L'Occultisme.* Paris, 1981.

Riffard, Pierre. *L'Esotérisme.* Paris, 1990.

Secret, François. "Du *De Occulta Philosophia* à l'occultisme du XIXème siècle." *Charis: Archives de l'Unicorne* 1 (1988): 5–30 (originally published in 1973).

Tiryakian, Edward A. "Toward the Sociology of Esoteric Culture." In *On the Margin of the Visible: Sociology, the Esoteric, and the Occult,* edited by Edward A. Tiryakian, pp. 257–280. New York, 1974 (first published in *American Journal of Sociology,* 1972).

Truzzi, Marcello. "Definition and Dimensions of the Occult: Towards a Sociological Perspective." In *On the Margin of the Visible: Sociology, the Esoteric, and the Occult,* edited by Edward A. Tiryakian, pp. 253–255. New York, 1974.

Webb, James. *The Occult Underground.* LaSalle, Ill., 1974.

Yates, Frances A. *The Occult Philosophy in the Elizabethan Age.* London, 1979.

Antoine Faivre (1987 and 2005)

OCEANIC RELIGIONS

This entry consists of the following articles:

OCEANIC RELIGIONS: AN OVERVIEW

The Pacific Islands are dispersed over the widest expanse of sea in the world. They consist of semi-continents (such as New Guinea), strings of large mountainous islands (along the curve of the Melanesian chain), and groups of larger and smaller islands further east, which are arranged as isolated atolls, or, more rarely, organized into whole archipelagoes, such as the Tuamotus and the Carolines. The classic view is that one should distinguish between three large cultural areas: Micronesia in the northwest, Melanesia in the south, and Polynesia in the east. The reality is that whereas Micronesia is somewhat distinct in that its cultures display the influences of constant Asian contacts, Melanesia and Polynesia are artificial concepts created by Western powers. The Europeans overran and Christianized Tahiti and eastern Polynesia, using the peoples of these islands to contact and control islands further west—as soldiers, Christian teachers, and petty civil servants who were accorded a status slightly higher than that of the supposedly "cruel" Melanesian "savages." In Polynesia the islanders resisted European settlement by force, and land transfers to the newcomers were often obtained through marriages with local women of high rank: these practices provided support for the inaccurate conception that the islanders of the east were closer to their colonizers in terms of civilization, whereas those of the west were uncouth and dangerous.

The islands are in fact very similar, showing the same range of variations along their coasts. All the atolls are alike, with their peaceful lagoons ringed by white beaches crowned by endless rows of coconut trees and ironwood trees, their dazzling sun, their fragility in time of hurricane, their lack of fresh water, and the many hardships of life and the precarious food supply if no rain comes. Power and authority are exercised with a streak of what is called "bigmanship"—that is, the use of cajolery and intrigue, as well as good husbandry and economic sense, to further one's ambitions. Hereditary chieftainships exist, throughout Melanesia as well as in Polynesia, and chiefs are often surrounded by such formal behavior and etiquette that Westerners gave the title of "king" to all such titular heads of extended descent groups without checking to see if these "kings" in fact had kingdoms. The view that chieftainships are found only in Polynesia and that Melanesia only knows "big men" is not supported by facts. Complex systems of chieftainship exist in both cultural areas, as well as in the Solomon Islands, Vanuatu, New Caledonia, the Loyalty Islands, and Fiji, Tonga, and Samoa.

The foundations of Oceanic religions are locality and the cult of the dead. (This article will avoid the commonly used word "spirits," as it is quite imprecise.)

The Cult of the Dead. Corpses in Oceania receive all sorts of ritual treatment. They may be laid in a grave or buried fetus-like in the ground, with the head sticking out; the head might later be removed for use in special mortuary rites. In southern Malekula the corpse is put on a platform and a small fire is kindled underneath to accelerate the putrefaction process. When this is accomplished, the villagers remove the head and place it in an ant's nest for thorough cleaning, after which the face is rebuilt with vegetable paste before being fixed to the top of a life-size puppet, the *rambaramb,* which bears marks indicating the dead man's rank. This puppet is present, six months after a man's death, at the deceased's last funerary ceremony and dance. After this the widow is allowed to remarry, usually with the dead man's younger brother, to whom she was in many cases forbidden to speak during her husband's lifetime. The skull is then put in a special place—in a rocky area, for example, or on the edge of a sacred grove, or on the flat stones at the back of the men's house—where it remains, and where it may be offered prayers. Mortuary techniques vary from place to place, and change according to fashion. For instance, the custom of rubbing newborn children with the dead person's fat and of eating parts of the dead body, particularly the brain—a practice that was the origin of the famed *kuru* sickness—was introduced into the Fore area of the New Guinea Highlands only six generations ago. Corpses kept whole can be burnt (North Solomon Islands and inland New Guinea); laid on the ground, with stones all round (South New Caledonia); left inside the deceased's house; put inside clefts of a raised cliff and laid on an old carving (central New Caledonia) or a piece of a broken canoe (Loyalty Islands); or thrown into the sea where a guardian shark will deal with it (Tanna and Efate in Vanuatu). The bones can be made into parcels and kept in a sacred grove or cave.

Throughout much of Oceania, a special rite often occurs ten days after death, during which the deceased person is reverentially asked to depart his lifelong place of residence and join the other dead in their abode, where he now belongs. One day each year, in Vanuatu and elsewhere, food is displayed for the benefit of the dead, who are invited, often through calls on conch shells, to come and partake of it. The next day, toward dusk, the dead are sent home by the same means. This practice does not prohibit the dead from being called for at any time in the year, as when the sickness of a close kinsman or one's own child warrants their help.

The dead who are prayed to are always those related to and from the locality of the descent group. Foreign ghosts are feared, the most so when the unwelcome visit is thought to be from the ghost of an unburied man, or *temes bal* (North Vanuatu), murdered on some path and craving revenge on anybody around. Such ghosts can enter the food produced ceremonially and make people sick—so doors may be shut to prevent this from happening. Any object pertaining to the white man may be put out of the house at this particular time for this very reason, its presence being thought of as introducing the *temes bal.* Food cooked inside the stone oven will be cut and shared with a bamboo knife, metal tools being left on the side for the same reason.

In some places, the dead are thought to have their own island (Bulotu in central Polynesia, Buloma at the eastern tip of New Guinea), which can fade into the skyline the more a canoeist strives to get there. Elsewhere, the land of the dead is aerial (Banks Islands), submarine, or under the face of the earth (New Caledonia). It can be inside a cave (North Malekula, Vanuatu) or inside the crater of a live volcano (East Malekula, Ambrym, and Tanna, Vanuatu).

The deceased traveling to the land of the dead follow a route—beginning along an open road, then continuing down subterranean paths—that links together neighboring districts (northern Viti Levu, Fiji) or neighboring islands (Lifou and Ouvea in the Loyalty Islands, East Malekula and Ambrym in Vanuatu). Members of specific lineages who live along the aboveground part of these routes hold the power to send back those among the deceased who are not yet ready to travel to the land of the dead. As they travel, the dead are armed with objects that have been placed in their graves, such as a rope—usually tied to a pig's foot, symbolizing the tusker pig that must be offered to the godly warden on the road to gain his permission to proceed further—or a model canoe, which allows the incorporeal dead to cross the sea.

Live humans have been known to follow these routes and survive, if they manage to keep looking only in front of them and resist the enticements of the fair-haired maidens (called *konghoc* in Ouvea, where they are believed to be the daughters of the godly pair Walewe and Hida) who appear on the side of he road. Eventually, they are confronted by a stem god or goddess, with arms ending in crab pincers, who will either ask a question; draw a design on the sand, then rub out half of it (the person is then expected to complete it); or closely examine the lobe of the person's ear and pierce it if it is lacking a hole.

Some men and women are said to be in the habit of going to the land of the dead to carry on an affair with a man or woman there; when they return, they bring back presents for their family: new knowledge, new songs, and new dance music. They might even bring back an invisible spouse, powerful in ritual matters pertaining to agriculture, thus bringing to the living part of the couple great crops of yams, or the techniques of making "sweet" dishes. But the goddesses who come back to live with a human male are made jealous and go back with the human's child if the husband starts an affair on the side with a living woman.

At the start of the twenty-first century, the cult of the dead is still flourishing in Oceania, though some elements have disappeared and beliefs tend to be intellectualized in towns, where the traditional spatial references are lacking. The cult's existence, however, is strongly hidden from Western onlookers.

GODS. The land of the dead is governed by gods and goddesses, who have always been in existence and, in the words of Robert H. Codrington, have never been either dead or alive as humans. Thus there is always a chief of this land, as well as a guardian of the entrance, a master of the dance of the dead, and a messenger—often a bird—who serves as a go-between, and is often seen fluttering near chiefly houses as well as flying away to join the other gods.

In many parts of Oceania one finds a belief in a sky world, which can be reached from the world of the living in various ways: via a path made of arrows, through the swinging of a club that, with the help of the South Wind, can break open the sky, or by means of a rope that the people in the sky let down.

Another link to the sky world is provided by winged maidens (the *tuarere* of central and northern Vanuatu) who meet at night on reefs to bathe and fish. Men can sneak up on them and hide one of their pairs of wings, then claim as a wife the young woman who is bereft of her wings, and thus powerless to go back to her people. It is said that one of these maidens taught the men how to make love in the right fashion, cutting a too-long penis with a shell knife until it was the right length. Another *tuarere,* having born two children to her human husband, was so incensed that he had talked badly of her to her children that, having found her well-hidden wings, she flew away, coming back ten days later with her sisters, who killed and ate the man bit by bit, only leaving the hairs and bones for the children to bury.

Another story tells of a man who, either in a canoe or carried by the *tuarere* over the seas, landed on an island (Merig of the Banks Islands) that was inhabited only by women, whose spouses were flying foxes that came to visit them at night, landing on the protruding bamboo roofs of each house. He laughed at the women and taught them about true love—and how to cook and eat their former husbands. This island is still peopled by women who are in effect the owners of the land, their brothers and sisters having all married elsewhere, and they themselves having married older men who had agreed to come and live on this small island, which is beautiful but very remote.

There are also stories that involve just-married men or women who have lost their spouse, either through an accident or because the spouse has been killed by a jealous local chief. The living spouse follows the road going to the land of the dead and negotiates with the warden at the entrance the way by which they can bring back to life their loved one. In some sadder versions of this story the return is deemed impossible and the couple must part; each tells the other how to know if they are close by, inside a rainbow or in the mist climbing down a mountain in the morning (Northwest New Caledonia).

Specific godly beings are the masters of a particular part of the universe: the sun, the moon (the woman in the moon is called Siva, or Hiva in Polynesia), the rain, each of the winds, the hurricane, fish in the high seas, forests and their inhabitants, the tilled land and its food crops. All these beings are said to be powerful, which means they each can bring to life what they control, or what they are said to be themselves, to work either for the benefit of man or against him.

POWER. Any power, mythical or magical, works both ways, for the good or for the bad. Prayers and offerings are used to summon both kinds of powers. Prayers can be spoken or silent and may be public or private depending on who the supplicant is: an ordinary individual, who may choose to speak out in the open if the matter is of interest to others, or a priest, who always acts alone in a secluded spot. Offerings are of all sorts: flowers, grasses, and leaves fastened to an ironwood pole; a yam tuber (or a white rooster with legs fastened) deposited on a stone in a sacred spot; great quantities of food that are shown to the dead and the gods, and then eaten by the men in their special club house (in the second half of November, after the rise of the *palolo* in Vanuatu, Fiji, West Polynesia, or after the flowering of the erythrina tree in New Caledonia); or shell money, which is either inserted inside holes in underwater rocks, in rivers or out at sea, or opened up on a sacred stone at a distance from any house, while an ancient chant in an archaic language is sung, asking for rain to come (New Caledonia) or for the crop to be abundant. Prayers are not complex poetical texts, being usually made up of a list of the gods and dead ancestors who are being called upon, to which is added only a very few sentences, some explaining the supplicant's wish in a precise and straightforward way, others offering a symbolic expression of the same wish.

Complex cosmogonies in Oceania are found only in East Polynesian cultures, and are the product of a caste of priests. Pacific Islands societies have tended to resist the formation of colleges of priests, which traditionally were only found in Tahiti and Hawai'i. Chiefs did not usually cherish the idea of sharing what power they had—it was *never* absolute—with a community of priests living by their own rules. Whereas in New Zealand a youth could be trained to become both *ariki* and *tohunga,* chief and priest, in Melanesia, Fiji, and West Polynesia power was shared through a system of linked social actors. One principal chief dealt with earthly matters, while another served as the orator, or talking chief *(matapule),* who was responsible for knowledge of the oral tradition and for protecting the principal chief from dangers originating in the outer world beyond the village. There are examples of this special dignitary being killed and buried with the principal chief, along with the latter's wives. His corpse was then placed just under the chief's head, the wives being laid out on the three other sides (South Central Vanuatu).

One specialized function of the *matapule* was to stand between two chiefs as they drank *kava,* so that the *mana* of one chief did not interfere with the *mana* of the other and so cause sickness. This precaution was general in Polynesia, but could be found also in Melanesia among *kava*-drinking peoples (North Malekula, Vanuatu).

This brings us to the concept of *mana* (or *men*), which is not strictly Polynesian, as thought by many modern scholars, but was first found by Codrington in the Banks Islands, among Melanesian language–speaking people. *Mana* is the power held by an individual through their particular relation with the world of the dead, that is, through the rank of the forebears protecting them. *Mana* can grow or diminish according to the way each person deals with the power they have inherited at birth. Losing a war and being taken prisoner diminishes one's *mana,* the more so if one is sent to the kitchen as a servant working with the women. Only blood spilt through a massacre can restore the former level of *mana* in such extreme cases. *Utu,* the necessity for revenge, or "payback," as they say in New Guinea, is justified by the need to reclaim lost *mana.* When this is not feasible, a suicide will do. In New Zealand, wives of high rank have been known to leave their lesser-ranked husband to stop their personal *mana* from being overcome by the renown earned in battle by their warrior spouse.

Mana is linked to *tapu* (*kap, kep,* etc.), which, from the perspective of a particular possessor of *mana,* is a power held by others that threatens *mana.* The back and back of the head are the most *tapu* parts of the body and are not to be touched. The gravity of this *tapu* depends on the rank of the person. Thus one will go a long way round so as not to pass close to the back not only of a chief, but also of his, or his wife's, relatives. A person's *tapu* grows or diminishes with the amount of their *mana.* The greatest *tapu* was that of several Hawaiian princesses who married their own brother; being older, they outranked their brother/husband and could only go out at night. Any person who saw their faces had to be killed on the spot. So the women stayed secluded in the day, and at night had special servants walking in front of them, warning people to look the other way.

Similar procedures involving *tapu* were played out on the battlefield. No real or classificatory kin of a warrior's wife could be hurt in any way—which explains why, as a rule, war in the islands led to few deaths. (It should be understood that marriage is regularly practiced between antagonistic descent lines, notwithstanding the fact that they are in a competition for prestige with one another.) The very strong *tapu* associated with eating, drinking, or smoking inside a communal Maori house still under construction can only be broken by a Maori first-born girl of high rank cooking and then eating a roast *kumara* (sweet potato) inside the house. Then only can other women and children enter the house, and can everybody eat inside. This *tapu* is still respected today, and horror stories are told of newly Christianized carvers and carpenters falling sick and dying after eating inside a house under construction.

Another system of multiple authorities, encompassing both opposition and complementary functions, involves the chief and the master of the land (*mata ni vanua* in Fiji). This situation displays a great number of variations. The masters of the land can have been chased away, in order that their former territories be taken over, and thus not be present at all. They can live next door to the chief, under new names forced upon them so as to cut their former privileged link to the land. They can be just there and occasionally honored ceremonially without being recognized for any specific function (the *üay* in Ouvéa). They can have retained a strong link to the non-human world, by being the only priests (*ten adro:* "who is on the land," or *alalu:* "who goes two by two") able to communicate with the different godly beings, and thus appear too dangerous to be accepted inside the chiefly court, where they are represented by special secondary chiefs (or *atresi,* for *atre sine haze,* "on the side of gods," in Lifou). These secondary chiefs are treated in ceremonial contexts as if they control the gods *(haze)* the *ten adro* serve. In fact the *atresi* have no power as such, but must go through the specific *ten adro* priest who can refuse to act as wished.

The island societies of Oceania revolve around interlocking systems of social status, which function as part of fragile balancing acts, by which individual heads of families, or lineages, strive constantly to protect as much as is feasible of their autonomy of action. They are not constantly consensus-seeking, as is so often said, but, to the contrary, use what consensus they can build, or help bring about, to further their real aim, which is to gain a modicum of prestige at the expense of others. In most cases, every man of some rank is embroiled in a prestige competition with another man of equivalent rank, as happened with both their fathers before them. Competition between chiefs is so extensive that the real institution appears to be the competition itself, rather than the competing chiefdoms. Each side appeals to its part of the outer world, which means that the invisible land of gods and ancestors is divided into the same competing camps found in the world of humans.

When soccer was introduced in the islands, young people consulted with the local traditional priests in order to win matches, feeling that the Christian god, being for everybody, could not be expected to help them in particular. Political decisions rested on the words of seers, or diviners, who could be either men or women. Would-be rebels against colonial authority had to have their plans approved through divination. As a result, colonial police had trouble predicting when and where problems would arise.

During the nineteenth century, a new belief developed about a kind of power—always deemed negative—associated with so-called witchcraft parcels. Carried from man to man and not inherited, these parcels had the power to kill the person who was in the direction they were pointed. Known as *doki, doghi,* or *narëk,* they appear to have first arrived in Oceania during the seventeenth century, aboard ships bringing missionaries and their families to Melanesia. They were in the possession of *lascar* sailors who brought them all the way from the Portuguese Congo, which they had fled following a campaign against witches initiated by Portuguese Jesuits.

The god hidden inside the parcels is said to have a sex organ made of fire, and to "eat" his successive owners if he is not given enough victims. This belief grew strongly as the Melanesian population began to dramatically decrease, due to the prevalence of gonorrhea. Belief in the power of witchcraft parcels faded, however, following two World Health Organization campaigns (in 1960 and 1962) that largely eradicated gonorrhea in Vanuatu. Today witchcraft is rarely discussed in Melanesia, except in towns, where it is a subject that fascinates many in white and half-caste communities. Aboriginal islanders expound upon it for the sake of white people, because they know Westerners love horror stories.

Missionary as well as lay European authors tend to believe that witchcraft is a fundamental aspect of Oceanic culture. This is nothing more than a case of attributing to the islanders what was part of our own culture. What can be found everywhere in the area are healers and seers, and an involved system of blessings and curses—but it would be a mistake to equate this with Western sorcery and witchcraft, as the belief systems underlying Oceanic practices are quite different.

MYTHOLOGY. Authentic textual records of Oceanic oral traditions are today, happily, replacing the older adaptations of European authors. The latter collections often shortened stories, or even mixed different versions together; their authors deleted parts of stories that were not of interest to them, and sometimes emphasized story elements artificially on the basis of a quite unscientific rule of thumb: the more a theme is manifested, the more authentic it is. This kind of majoritarian system overlooked the fact that each lineage insists on its own version of any particular story, and that each version is as authentic as the next. Authenticity is a concept introduced by Christian churches. It has no value within a tradition based on multiple perspectives.

Oceanic oral tradition consists of broad themes expressed in a poetical or literary way, with each variant conveying a wealth of information about particular traditions through the use of specific names: names of living creatures, or of the different heroes or godly beings, ancestors' names, and place names indicating the limits and details of the social group's territory.

No synthesis is sought of all these versions. Each one is made to order so as to add to the prestige of the myth-owning descent group. Contradictions between differing versions have no other meaning than as markers of difference and serve to establish each lineage's relative autonomy and prestige.

For the scholar, the methodological problem is to map every bit of information found in the textual record. One must first obtain a complete version of a story, in the vernacular. Through comparisons of different versions (dealing with the same geographical area), one may begin to see what part of the story is explicit, and what part is implicit—that is, accessible to any knowledgeable aboriginal listener, but not easy for a Westerner to grasp. These texts can thus be read on at least two different levels. Taking them at their face value is a currently common mistake. The problem is to learn the meaning of each word, the significance of a sequence of words, and the social symbolism of each name. Names can indicate to the knowledgeable listener that a particular location is a sacred place, an important or insignificant stretch of territory, a place where offerings should be brought (a piece of a brightly colored shrub or a stone put on a heap), a plot of land that is under a curse and cannot be tilled, a spot where a child or a woman with child should not go, and so on.

Paths are individually owned when they only lead to one person's field, but are controlled by a lineage if they penetrate inside its territory, and by the entire social group if they link villages together. The pairing of two names within a story delimits and defines a path or road, and in this way implies the descent group or individual associated with that path or road.

Principal gods are often unnamed except through oblique references, or a very general descriptive name (i.e., "the great god"), or, as in Polynesia, their names can be altered through additions, so that each social group employs a variant of the god's name, allowing them to put him at the start of their descent line without hurting the feelings of the neighboring descent group. There is in theory a single god of the sky and of the forest in Polynesia, known as Tane—but there may in fact be as many Tanes as there are descent groups on a given island, each different Tane being the first name cited in a particular group's genealogy.

The existence of all things present on earth (social, biological, or material) is attributed either to the actions of the dead (who are believed to hold, collectively or individually, enormous power), or to the actions of the so-called culture heroes of the cosmogonic or semi-cosmogonic myths. The origin of culture is often attributed to one of these heroes or to two brothers. In the Madang district of northern New Guinea, these brothers are Kilibob, the inventor of all useful arts, and Manup, the brother responsible for love, magic, sorcery, and warfare. It is believed that both brothers will return: Kilibob's return will be announced by the arrival on the sea of a wooden plate carved in the Siasi Islands, and Manup's by the arrival of a canoe from the north. The so-called cargo cults have integrated this myth into their own system. Often, white explorers were initially taken for the dead coming back to give their riches to their descendants. The extraordinary mobilizing power of such myths has been demonstrated by the messianic cults that have sprouted all over the Pacific, from the early Mamaia cult in Tahiti to the more recent cargo cults in New Guinea and Melanesia. It appears that such prophetic or messianic cults have existed in the area since ancient times: one case (the Roy Mata story, from central Vanuatu) has been archaeologically dated to around 1300 BCE. However, religious concepts are usually a means of justifying the way in which a society and culture function, and thus generally support institutionalization and not change. Autochthonous Oceanic beliefs are responsible, even now, for stability in the societies of this area. Experience over recent decades has shown that aboriginal religious beliefs and concepts are far from dead in the Pacific Islands, although the whole area is nominally Christian. Prayers are still offered to ancestors and to symbolic beings whose invisible presence is still felt.

One case in point is the continued existence, more or less everywhere, of a traditional belief in ogres or ogresses. This should not be understood as a reference to the former practice of cannibalism, as some authors have thought. Examining the range of types referred to by the same names, one finds ogres that are completely benevolent, and never eat anybody, and others that behave as ogres are generally expected to behave. Each is associated with a sacred place, where offerings are made at the time of the first-fruit ceremony. Ogres are distinguished between by referring to their sacred spot, and a mention of the name of a particular spot is by itself enough to indicate a specific ogre to a knowledgeable listener.

The same is valid for any godly being. Local gods or goddesses who send the rain, thunderstorms, and floods are recognized as benevolent or malevolent according to the place with which they are associated—in their case thought to be their home. Knowledgeable islanders thus learn to remember thousands of specific names, which, put together, crisscross the island, thus placing on the map all the descent groups with which such names are associated.

In Oceania, people's ambitions are realized through control of some power over the world around them. Every descent group has its own way of playing a role inside a symbolic representation of the universe. Edible plants, fish, octopuses, sharks, whales, birds, mammals, dangerous beasts, clouds, thunder, rain, hurricanes, volcanoes, the sun—each is owned by a "master" who, in the name of his descent group, assumes responsibility for the necessary ritual that causes the plants to grow, the sun to shine, and the rain to come when needed, or that prevent catastrophes (hurricanes, tidal waves, volcanic eruptions). Each "master" thus plays a role in a universal concert, and does their part for the survival of all. Those who master the sun and the rain are considered powerful people. This system was called totemism by early researchers, who linked it with systems found elsewhere, as they believed in the existence of a universal institution. The facts do not fit this hypothesis. Systems by which people control the universe around them are very varied, and should not artificially be made to fit one pattern. Closer study of the Oceanic system reveals that animals, plants, and meteorological phenomena are considered to be one of the forms the dead of a descent group can take. They assume these forms in order to appear before their descendants when these descendants are attempting to control the particular aspect of the world with which they are associated.

COSMOLOGIES. Pacific Islanders see the world they live in as a dynamic space, in which various forces (of *mana,* amongst other things) unfold along a path that is conceived of as a spiral—according to the politician and poet John Kasaipwalova, from Kiriwina (in the Trobriand Islands), the spiral path is the route any power must take in order to grow endlessly. This explains why dances on the islands making up the Melanesian arch go round, apparently in circles—they are in fact representing the launching of a spiral from a central point, which can be a pole, or only be implicit. Dancers usually move from right to left, but reverse directions if the dance is meant to mark a recent death. This explains also the ubiquitous presence of spirals and concentric circles engraved on rocks.

Another dancing tradition (seen in Tanna, among other places) involves hundreds of male dancers who go from one end to the other of the dancing ground, seemingly showing a preference for a longitudinal axis. But if one observes the dance all night long, one notices that the mass of dancers slightly change the angle of their dancing each time they traverse the dancing ground. Over time, they are slowly and powerfully swirling, and in this way they express the spiraling model.

The spiral is the means by which the land of the dead and the world of humans can be linked. When the living dance, the dead and ghosts are dancing the same dance at the same time, to the same tunes. Parallel worlds thus act in harmony during the nights when hundreds of people come and dance at the same time. These worlds become separate again in the daytime, when the dead and the gods retreat to look on from afar—though they are always present close by if needed.

Families can be brought together not only through intermarriage, but also by visitations from the dead. If a person sees a white ghostly figure coming towards them on the road, they know there has been a death on the other side of the island and set out through mountain passes to be present at the mourning ceremonies.

One must go to Eastern Polynesia—except Easter Island, where things are not exactly clear on this point—to find a view of the universe in which the dead and the gods are separate. Here, the general and, in a way, official gods—responsible for great swathes of the human world (the sea, the air, the forests, tilled land)—are in the skies, leading their own lives there after having started out on Earth, where they established the basis of human society as it was before the coming of the white man. The dead are thought to live inside an underground kingdom of their own. The gods and heroes of Eastern Polynesia were worshipped inside roofless temples. This cosmology has had great appeal for Western scholars, who have focused on what seemed familiar to them.

Many early Western observers were convinced that human sacrifices were a part of the religion of Eastern Polynesia. We know for sure that two levels of sanctions for religious and social transgressions were found on all the Pacific Islands. One obliged the culprit to go into exile, usually where they could find kin of their own; the other required that they be dispatched by an executioner under the orders of a chief. The condemned was killed by a surprise blow on the nape of the neck with a short, often curved, stone club. Parts of the body—the eyes or the heart—could then be offered to a god. But there is no proof of human sacrifices of the sort imagined by missionaries and the first European witnesses.

Outside of Eastern Polynesia most gods lived close by humans, looking after their crops, their fishing, or their hunting. All over Melanesia, certain gods were enshrined yearly inside stone figures placed in the ground. These gods did not live in the skies, and were not dealt with during the great ceremonial gatherings—which in any case had more to do with competition between chiefs than with strongly held beliefs.

Throughout Oceania a carved figure can be the repository of a godly presence, but the god has no obligation whatsoever to choose this particular abode. Gods can be incarnated at will in stones, trees, stone outcrops, whales, sharks, mats, and in carefully wrapped sennit bundles (which in Tahiti bear indications of facial features) or more deliberately constructed figures (which have an abundance of shell pendants). Or gods may take up residence in carved wooden human faces, called "heads of the shell money," which are linked in New Caledonia with Urupwe, one of the names of the god who reigns supreme over the land of the dead. Monumental carvings are rarely thought of as possible repositories for godly presences, with the exception of the Hawaiian wickerwork figures covered with parrot feathers that were carried into battle as representations of Ku-ka'ili-moku, the god of war—but which really represent a particular set of descent groups linked together by their allegiance to the same chieftainship. In the same part of Hawai'i, if the presence of a god was called for inside a dwelling, a large empty space would be shrouded all round with a tapa curtain.

SEE ALSO Cargo Cults; Mana; Melanesian Religions, overview article; Micronesian Religions, overview article; Polynesian Religions, overview article; Power; Taboo.

BIBLIOGRAPHY

Baal, Jan van, with Jan Verschueren. *Dema: Description and Analysis of Marind-Anim Culture.* The Hague, 1966.

Bateson, Gregory. *Naven: A Survey of the Problems Suggested by a Composite Picture of a New Guinea Tribe.* Cambridge, U.K., 1936.

Bernart, Luelen. *The Book of Luelen.* Edited and translated by John L. Fischer, Saul H. Riesenberg, and Marjorie G. Whiting. Pacific History series, no. 8. Canberra, 1977.

Best, Elsdon. *Maori Religion and Mythology: Being an Account of the Cosmogony, Anthropogeny, Religious Beliefs, and Rites, Magic, and Folk Lore of the Maori Folk of New Zealand.* Dominion Museum Bulletin no. 10. Wellington, New Zealand, 1924–1982.

Codrington, Robert H. *The Melanesians: Studies in Their Anthropology and Folk-Lore.* Oxford, 1891.

Deacon, Arthur Bernard. *Malekula: A Vanishing People in the New Hebrides.* Edited by Camilla Wedgwood. London, 1934.

Dubois, Marie-Joseph. *Les Eletok de Maré: Géographie mythique et traditionnelle de l'île de Maré.* Publications de la Société des Océanistes no. 35. Paris, 1970.

Ellis, William. *Polynesian Researches, during a Residence of Nearly Eight Years in the Society and Sandwich Islands.* 4 vols. London, 1832–1836.

Firth, Raymond. *The Work of the Gods in Tikopia.* London, 1940.

Fortune, Reo. *Manus Religion: An Ethnological Study of the Manus Natives of the Admiralty Islands.* Memoirs of the American Philosophical Society, vol. 3. Philadelphia, 1935.

Fox, Charles Elliot. *The Threshold of the Pacific: An Account of the Social Organization, Magic, and Religion of the People of San Cristoval in the Solomon Islands.* London, 1924.

Gagnère, R. P. M. *Étude éthnologique sur la religion des Néo-Calédoniens.* Saint-Louis, France, 1905.

Guiart, Jean. *Un siècle et demi de contacts culturels à Tanna, Nouvelles-Hébrides.* Paris, 1956.

Guiart, Jean. *Mythologie du masque en Nouvelle-Calédonie.* Paris, 1966. Completely rewritten as *Et le masque sortit de la mer: Les pays canaques anciens de Hienghène à Témala, Gomèn, et Koumac* (Le Rocher-à-la-Voile, New Caledonia, 2002).

Guidieri, Remo. *La route des morts.* Paris, 1980.

Haddon, Alfred C., et al, eds. *Reports of the Cambridge Anthropological Expedition to Torres Straits.* Volume 6: *Sociology, Magic, and Religion of the Eastern Islanders,* edited by Alfred C. Haddon. Cambridge, U.K., 1908.

Kamakau, Samuel Manaiakalani. *Ka Po'e Kahiko: The People of Old.* Honolulu, 1964.

Kaniku, John Wills Teloti. *The Epic of Tauhau.* Port Moresby, Papua New Guinea, 1975.

Keesing, Roger M., and Peter Corris. *Lightning Meets the West Wind: The Malaita Massacre.* Oxford, Wellington, and New York, 1980.

King, Michael, ed. *Tihe Mauri Ora: Aspects of Maoritanga.* Wellington, New Zealand, 1978. Collected essays by Maori authors.

Lawrence, Peter, and M. J. Meggitt, eds. *Gods, Ghosts, and Men in Melanesia: Some Religions of Australian New Guinea and the New Hebrides.* Melbourne, Australia, 1964.

Leenhardt, Maurice. *Do Kamo: Person and Myth in the Melanesian World.* Translated by Basia Miller Gulati. Chicago, 1979.

Malinowski, Bronislaw. *Magic, Science, and Religion.* Garden City, New York, 1954.

Malnic, Jutta, with John Kasaipwalova. *Kula: Myth and Magic in the Trobriand Islands.* Wahroonga, Australia, 1998.

Métraux, Alfred. *Ethnology of Easter Island.* Bernice Pauahi Bishop Museum Bulletin, no. 160. Honolulu, Hawai'i, 1940.

Monberg, Torben. *Bellona Island Beliefs and Rituals.* Honolulu, 1991.

Ngata, Apirana Turupa. *The Songs: Scattered Pieces from Many Canoe Areas.* Revised and edited by Pei Te Hurinui Jones. 3 vols. Wellington, New Zealand, 1961.

Sterling, Eruera. *The Teachings of a Maori Elder, as Told to Anne Salmond.* Wellington, New Zealand, 1980.

Telban, Borut. *Dancing through Time: A Sepik Cosmology.* Oxford, 1998.

Trompf, G. W. *Melanesian Religion.* New York, Melbourne, and Sydney, 1991.

Young, Michael. *Magicians of Manumanua: Living Myth in Kalauna.* Los Angeles, Berkeley, Calif., and London, 1983.

JEAN GUIART (2005)

OCEANIC RELIGIONS: MISSIONARY MOVEMENTS

Although nearly all Pacific Islanders are Christians—with the exception of the inhabitants of inland New Guinea, where Christianity has made only some inroads—a few villages, families, and individuals maintain a "heathen" religious status. Although Christianity is deeply entrenched in the Pacific, it is only one of the several cosmological planes on which the islanders simultaneously exist without feeling a sense of contradiction. Families still decide which son will be trained to be a chief; which will receive a European education in order to become a civil servant, Protestant pastor, or Catholic priest or cathechist; and which will stay in the village to learn the traditional religious lore to keep open the old paths to the invisible world.

The Christianity of Pacific Islanders has a predominantly mythical quality. Maurice Leenhardt (1922) captured the essence of Pacific Islanders' understanding of Christianity in his account of Melanesian soldiers passing through the Suez Canal in 1915. These soldiers were astonished to learn that they were near the lands of the Bible. They wrote home to express their surprise: they had never thought that the places mentioned in the Bible actually existed. Even today many islanders do not recognize the historical and even geographical value of the biblical narrative; for them it is merely a story, and Jerusalem and other holy places have only a symbolic existence. However, they rarely say this to a white person. The testimony of the few islanders who have been to Israel carries little weight with the rest.

HISTORY OF CHRISTIAN MISSIONS IN THE PACIFIC. There are both Protestant and Catholic communities on most of the Pacific Islands, with adherents of Protestantism usually being in the majority. The most recent missions have been those of the Seventh-day Adventists, Assemblies of God, Jehovah's Witnesses, Latter-day Saints (Mormons), and Baha'i. Among these groups only the Seventh-day Adventists and the Mormons have had substantial success. In Hawai'i, Tahiti, and the Tuamotus, and more recently in Fiji, Mormon missionary activity has given rise to a breakaway church, the Kanito (or Sanito) movement.

In earlier times, Protestant churches carefully divided the Pacific area into regions in which the different missionary groups would carry out their activities. In 1795 the newly formed London Missionary Society chose Tahiti as its first field for missionary work. After many difficulties it expanded its operations to the Austral Islands, the Cook Islands, Samoa, the Loyalty Islands, western and eastern Papua (southeastern New Guinea), and the Torres Islands. The Wesleyan Missionary Society, which was founded in London in 1814, did its first work on Tonga, Fiji, the Solomon Islands, and New Zealand. The Anglican Church, represented by the Melanesian Mission based in Auckland, New Zealand, was active in northern Vanuatu (formerly the New Hebrides Islands and Banks Islands) and the eastern Solomon Islands. The South Seas Evangelical Mission, based in

Queensland, Australia, and theoretically nondenominational though predominantly Baptist, worked in the central Solomons. The American Board of Commissioners for Foreign Missions, founded in Boston in 1820, was active in Hawai'i and the parts of Micronesia that had not been converted to Catholicism after the time of the explorer Ferdinand Magellan (the Gilbert Islands, now known as Kiribati). The Scottish Presbyterians converted the inhabitants of southern and central Vanuatu. New Zealand was shared among the Church Missionary Society (founded in London in 1799), the Wesleyan Mission, and the Anglican Church. In New Guinea the authorities tried to organize mission work by allocating specific areas to different groups, but before 1914 the northern part of the country had been under the control of Germany, which allowed the Lutheran Church and the Catholic orders to conduct missionary activities in that area. After about half a century the Methodist and Presbyterian churches of New Zealand and Australia took over responsibility in those islands from the churches in the mother countries; the Presbyterians would assign the west coast to Australian missions and the east coast to New Zealand missions.

Roman Catholic missions were rarely the first to arrive in any part of Oceania, and this explains why Catholics are in the minority on most of the islands. The Marist Fathers (Société de Marie) founded in Lyons in 1818, missionized the Solomon Islands, Vanuatu, Fiji, Tonga, Samoa, New Zealand, Bougainville, the Wallis and Futuna Islands, and New Caledonia; in the last three places Catholics today constitute a majority of the population. The Fathers of the Sacred Hearts of Jesus and Mary, based in Paris, have been active in Hawai'i, Tahiti, and the Marquesas Islands. The Fathers of the Sacred Heart of Jesus, originally of Issoudun, France, worked first among the natives of Papua and later in New Britain, the Admiralty Islands, the Gilbert Islands, and Nauru. Other Catholic orders have been successful elsewhere in the area. Catholic Marists who became martyrs include Monseigneur Epalle in the Solomons in 1845 and Father (Saint) Pierre Chanel in Futuna in 1841. The murder of Brother Blaise Mamoiton in Balade, New Caledonia, in 1845 is explained by the people there as resulting from his assignment to look after the mission's food supplies with the assistance of a large dog he had trained to run after and bite the Kanak. There was a famine, and the Marist Fathers refused to share their provisions with the local people. The Kanak killed both the dog and the brother to take food in a time of need.

The history of Christianization shows some regularities, inasmuch as all the Protestant and Catholic missionary bodies used the same technique. Mass conversions were precipitated through the conversion of members of the local aristocracy. Before direct colonial administration was instituted, native leaders often became Christians to obtain official recognition from European powers. Thereafter, they asked for and were sold firearms, which they used to overcome local enemies and establish dominant dynasties. Rival chiefs adopted different faiths, and there were religious wars in Samoa, Tonga, the Wallis Island, Fiji, and Ouvéa and Maré in the Loyalty Islands between Catholic and Protestant converts. The Seventh-day Adventists, to the discomfort of the well-established churches, thrived by converting groups whose politics did not agree with those of the majority church. The Assemblies of God, the Jehovah's Witnesses, and to a lesser extent the Mormons have made gains in a similar fashion.

Christian missions in the Pacific have frequently become involved in local disputes over land and social status. Missionaries were often used by one party to thwart the ambitions of another. There were examples of this in western Tanna in Vanuatu, where the Presbyterian mission was involved in the city of Lenakel, and in Wagap in New Caledonia, where the Marist Fathers were used by a party in a land squabble. The Marists panicked when they were caught in a row with dancing armed Kanaks and called for military reinforcements. The officer in charge decided to shoot a group of chiefs who had been called in to negotitate. The Wagap mission had to be closed because of the bloodshed. Scottish missionary John G. Paton left Port Resolution in the night to save himself from would-be murderers, who actually had resorted to theatricals to end his interference in their daily lives. Paton came back with a British man-of-war and had the village shelled, with the loss of only a few pigs and coconut trees. That overreaction blocked the Christianization of the area for half a century. There have been a number of similar cases, the best documented having occurred on Samoa.

To consolidate the effects of sometimes hurried conversions, missionaries established programs to educate native youths as future leaders in the movement to spread the Christian faith. All the missions set up boarding schools, to which children were brought at an early age; these children were separated from their parents for many years and were taught by often untrained and sometimes self-appointed teachers. When the children grew up, the missionaries would arrange Christian marriages for them.

This system of conversion and indoctrination was employed first by the London Missionary Society, after initial difficulties in Tahiti, with a view toward using Christian couples from one island to establish the mission's influence on other islands. After this period Europeans were introduced as missionaries only in areas where their safety was assured. Thus, except for the Reverend John Williams, who was killed on Eromanga in Vanuatu in 1839, and the Reverend G. N. Gordon, who was killed in the same place in 1861, most of the Christian martyrs in New Caledonia and Vanuatu were Polynesians or, later, Melanesian teachers from the Loyalty Islands in New Caledonia proper; those teachers later worked in Papua and the Torrès Islands.

There were few martyrs. It was Polynesian evangelists who began the public burning of wooden "idols," and in general these native missionaries used highly militant and sometimes violent tactics to gain converts. The best-documented cases of violent conversion occurred in Tahiti, the Cook Islands, Fiji, and southern Vanuatu. However, these incidents occurred only because the missionaries who perpetrated them had wide popular support; rapid mass conversion was seen either as a means of obtaining recognition from European powers or as a way of discouraging European encroachments, which could be shown to be breaches of Christian ethics.

IMPACT OF CHRISTIAN MISSIONS. Protestant missions tended to build village parishes around nuclei of adult communicant members, deacons, and native teachers or, much later, pastors. These teachers and their wives had been trained in centralized institutions, and they often replaced the European missionaries who had performed the initial conversions. The desire to have a resident white man who could provide protection against all others, and the prestige derived from that man's presence, resulted in a type of long-lasting collective sorrow when a white missionary left and was replaced by a native teacher, as occurred on the island of Futuna in South Vanuatu when Dr. Gunn departed, and on the island of Mota in the Banks Islands when the Anglican Theological College's staff and students were sent to the Solomon Islands. The London Missionary Society and the Anglican Church added strong Bible study groups and women's associations to this structure. Catholic missionaries usually were content with installing a catechist in each village to promote further conversions. The first Kanak priest, Robert Sarawia, was consecrated by the Melanesian Mission in 1874; other missions waited the better part of a century before following suit.

Missions eventually became involved in promoting trade between Europe and the islands. The impetus for that trade came in part from the newly converted natives, who from the outset wanted access to European money and goods. The London Missionary Society, the Anglicans, and the Church Missionary Society bought or leased ships to supply food to their widely dispersed converts and established chains of local trading stations. Those well-organized local mission stations prospered and also acted as a means of bringing native produce to European markets. Eventually, the missions also acquired plantations.

At first the missionaries claimed that this was done to prevent Europeans from staking claims to large tracts of land. Eventually, however, missions began to obtain lands for their commercial potential and to support their work, and the native inhabitants suffered economically. In some cases, disputes over land acquired by the missions still have not been resolved. Those missions became a source of controversy for the churches, and sometimes the land was taken back by the local inhabitants at the time of independence. Mission general stores were intended to provide native converts with access to European goods at a reasonable price. On islands that came under colonial rule, these stores were denounced by European settlers, most of whom wanted to garner quick profits from trade with the natives and establish themselves as agricultural barons. The resulting bad relations between the missions and the local Europeans continued until the time of independence.

Nuns and missionaries' wives trained women and girls in new ways of dressing, sewing, and cooking, as well as new methods of child care and general hygiene. This explains the early popularity of portable sewing machines among women over all the islands. They also taught the women to read and write in their own languages, while their husbands taught the same skills to the native men. The acquisition of literacy was welcomed by the islanders and helped them deal with the pressures introduced by the whites.

There were as many Catholic nuns involved in mission work as Catholic priests and brothers. The nuns attended to the daily needs of the priests, ran mission schools, and sometimes did medical work. Local orders, which recruited native women, were often founded on the islands.

It was in the area of intellectual life that missionaries had their greatest impact on Pacific Island societies. The London Missionary Society commissioned the German philologist F. Max Müller to design a system of writing for the Oceanic languages, and Protestant clergymen devoted much of their time to learning native languages and translating the Bible into them. Newly literate islanders were proud to acquire Bibles and other religious publications, such as John Bunyan's *Pilgrim's Progress.* Since the content of the Bible was familiar to nineteenth-century Europeans, it could serve as common conceptual ground and a medium of communication between native inhabitants and Europeans.

The islanders adopted biblical patterns of speech and behavior to make themselves acceptable to Europeans. They also put forth the biblical kings David and Solomon as models of Christian statesmanship in an attempt to deter Europeans from establishing colonial control over the islands. However, the Kingdom of Tonga (which managed to evade any sort of colonial system) and Western Samoa have managed to maintain a rather carefully drawn line between European ideas and traditional patterns of political behavior.

The curricula of the missionary schools in the mid-nineteenth century were strikingly modern. In the lower grades, classes were taught exclusively in the vernacular. In the upper grades instruction in the native language was supplemented by education in English or French for the most promising students. Eventually parents demanded a thoroughly European education for their children. In the 1930s, the Seventh-day Adventists were the first to open schools with curricula modeled on the European system and taught completely in European languages; other Christian groups quickly followed suit. However, these schools have been returning (in some cases) to the original system of classes taught in the native tongues with English or French as a second language, particularly as islanders have begun to work for the preservation of their languages and cultures.

The medical work of the missions was difficult in the early years. Western medicine had few remedies for tropical diseases and was not much more successful at curing illnesses such as smallpox, measles, influenza, tuberculosis, and venereal diseases, all of which had been brought to the islands by Europeans. The natives died in large numbers while the missionaries preached. Gonorrhea was an enduring scourge that rendered women unable to bear children and kept the islands' populations low for two centuries. Syphilis was rare, however, because of its cross-immunity with yaws. Eventually missionary organizations added trained doctors to their staffs and set up the first modern hospitals in the islands.

Much has been written about the connections between the French and British governments and their national missionary bodies, and missionaries often called upon their nations' naval vessels to provide them with protection. However, those warships also proved to be an effective means of controlling the activities of unscrupulous traders, land hunters, and labor recruiters for Queensland plantations. Thus, conditions might have been worse for the natives without the French and British naval presence.

One aspect of nineteenth-century mission activity in this area that has received comparatively little attention is the churches' resistance to colonial annexation of the islands by European powers. Missionary organizations wanted their governments' sanction and protection against the encroachment of rival missions, but they only slowly became reconciled to the establishment of direct colonial rule. In this way missionaries protected the cultures of the island peoples. Overall, except in Hawai'i and Tahiti, the early arrival of missionaries helped preserve indigenous ways of life from destruction at the hands of the settlers who arrived later. Contemporary independent island nations owe much to the isolated and stubborn missionaries who refused to recognize any authority other than that of their god, and in some cases most of the islander politicians who control these newly independent countries were trained by the Christian missions. Much of what has been preserved of the native cultures was kept underground, without the missionaries knowing, and even the native staff maintained silence on the subject.

By the 1980s, missions in the Pacific had become a thing of the past, albeit of the very recent past. Most missionary stations disappeared as such, although schools and hospitals remained. European staff remained in technical positions under the authority of the local church. The more important missions gave birth to independent Presbyterian (French and Scottish), Methodist, and Anglican churches. Evangelical churches, mostly American, maintained their former missionary structure in New Guinea, centering on smallish mountain airports where their planes provided the only link with the outside world. Mostly in the towns they took over, they continued the fight against alcohol and tobacco that the majority churches had essentially abandoned. People wanting to relinquish drink flocked to these churches with their families. Local governments viewed this development with some anxiety in the case of millenarian churches such as Jehovah's Witnesses. The autonomous government of Tahiti, however, was much more tolerant of the presence of Mormons than the French colonial government had been.

Both Catholic and Protestant churches centered their theological studies in central schools established in Fiji that worked cooperatively with the University of the South Pacific in Suva. These schools produced many independence-minded native scholars. The criteria of academic success in these schools eventually reached international standards. Dropouts became more numerous, although with a higher intellectual level, and sometimes caused trouble when they returned to their churches of birth. Two of them, one Catholic and one Protestant, were implicated in the events in Ouvéa and the murder of Jean-Marie Tjibaou.

In Tahiti the activities of the Catholic charismatic movement, using the methods of the American evangelical churches, had an unforeseen consequence through an uncontrolled offshoot of the movement on the island of Fa'aite in the Tuamotu Islands, where fathers and mothers were burned at the stake by their own children, who believed that the Devil had gotten inside them.

The islanders' attachment to Christianity has remained strong. Ratu Sir Kamisese Mara, the prime minister of Fiji, remarked in the 1970s that Pacific Islanders were the only ones to still take the Sermon on the Mount seriously. The islanders feel that Christianity, having been abandoned by the white men who brought it, now belongs to them.

Methodological Problems. In regard to the methodological problem of studying the growth of Christian churches in Oceania, much of what has been published deals with the history of missions and missionaries, missionary methods, and missionary influence. There have been few studies of indigenous evangelists. Usually, the foreign missionaries did not really know the people they converted. Even if they worked with islanders for years, the details of their status within their own society remained unknown to the missionaries. The missionaries' correspondence and memoirs list the Christian names of their helpers and little else. Most historians have not had the time or the means to find out who really was behind these Westernized designations.

The missionaries were taking charge of a society about which they knew very little. The islanders who were Christianized ended up knowing more about the missionaries than the missionaries knew about them. Documented cases in which the white clerical staff was manipulated by the converts, often for generation after generation, are appearing more often. The Pacific Islanders were never passive and often played tricks on their self-appointed white masters. The story of how Christianity gained ground on the islands has not been written from the viewpoint of the islanders, and the psychological and sociological complexities of conversion have seldom been examined. Maurice Leenhardt was one of the only missionaries to show an interest in this line of research.

Another issue is the rise of prophetic movements after World War II. The question here is not what type of missionary behavior led to these movements but why some groups, such as the Anglican Melanesian Mission, never had to deal with them. This points to the infrequently applied methodological technique of studying within a society not only the areas where a specific institution exists, but also the areas where it is absent.

SEE ALSO Christianity, article on Christianity in the Pacific Islands.

BIBLIOGRAPHY

Armstrong, E. S. *The History of the Melanesian Mission.* London, 1900.

Clifford, James. *Person and Myth: Maurice Leenhardt in the Melanesian World.* Berkeley, Calif., 1982.

Conférence sur la loi naturelle. Comptes-rendus des conferences ecclésiastiques du Vicariat Apostolique de la Nouvelle-Calédonie, vol. 5. Saint-Louis, New Caledonia, 1900.

Crocombe, Marjorie Tuainekoro, ed. *Cannibals and Converts: Radical Change in the Cook Islands.* Suva, Fiji, 1983.

Crocombe, Ron G., and Marjorie Crocombe. *The Works of Ta'unga: Records of a Polynesian Traveller in the South Seas 1833–1896.* Canberra, Australia, 1968.

Crocombe, Ron G., and Marjorie Crocombe. *Polynesian Missions in Melanesia, from Samoa, Cook Islands and Tonga to Papua New Guinea and New Caledonia.* Suva, Fiji, 1982.

Don, Alexander. *Peter Milne, 1834–1924: Missionary to Nguna, New Hebrides, 1870 to 1924.* Dunedin, New Zealand, 1927.

Douceré, Monseigneur Victor. *La mission catholique aux Nouvelles-Hébrides.* Lyons, France, 1934.

Ernst, Manfred. *Winds of Change: Rapidly Growing Religious Groups in the Pacific Islands.* Suva, Fiji, 1994.

Forman, Charles W. *The Island Churches of the South Pacific: Emergence in the Twentieth Century.* Maryknoll, N.Y., 1982.

Garrett, John. *To Live among the Stars: Christian Origins in Oceania.* Geneva and Suva, Fiji, 1982.

Garrett, John. *Footsteps in the Sea: Christianity in Oceania to World War II.* Suva, Fiji, 1992.

Guiart, Jean. "The Millenarian Aspect of Conversion to Christianity in the South Pacific." In *Millennial Dreams in Action: Comparative Studies in Society and History,* edited by Sylvia Thrupp, suppl. 2, pp. 122–138. New York, 1962. (Reissued in *Cultures of the Pacific: Selected Readings,* edited by Thomas G. Harding and Ben J. Wallace, pp. 397–411. New York and London, 1970.)

Gunson, Niel. *Messengers of Grace: Evangelical Missionaries in the South Seas, 1797–1860.* Oxford, Wellington, and New York, 1978.

Hodée, Paul. *Tahiti 1834–1984, 150 ans de vie Chrétienne en Eglise.* Paris and Fribourg, Switzerland, 1983.

Howe, K. R. *Where the Waves Fall: A New South Sea Islands History from First Settlement to Colonial Rule.* Sydney and London, 1984.

Izoulet, Jacques. *Meketepoun: Histoire de la mission catholique dans l'île de Lifou au XIXe siècle.* Paris, 1996.

Leenhardt, Maurice. *La grande terre: Mission de Nouvelle-Calédonie.* Paris, 1922.

Leenhardt, Maurice, and Jean Guiart. "Notes de sociologie religieuse sur la région de Canala (Nouvelle-Calédonie)." *Cahiers Internationaux de Sociologie* 34 (1958): 18–33.

Leenhardt, Raymond. *Au vent de la Grande Terre: Histoire des Îles Loyalty de 1840 à 1895.* Paris, 1957.

Miller, R. S. *Misi Gete: John Geddie, Pioneer Missionary to the New Hebrides.* Launceston, Australia, 1975.

Murray, Archibald Wright. *Wonders of the Western Isles, Being a Narrative of the Commencement and Progress of Mission Work in Western Polynesia.* London, 1874.

Newbury, Colin. *Tahiti Nui: Change and Survival in French Polynesia, 1767–1930.* Canberra, Australia, 1976.

Nicole, Jacques. *Au pied de l'écriture: Histoire de la traduction de la Bible en Tahitien.* Papeete, Tahiti, 1988.

O'Reilly, Patrick, and Jean-Marie Sedes. *Jaunes, Noirs et Blancs: Trois années de guerre aux Îles Salomon.* Paris, 1949.

Ramsden, Eric. *Marsden and the Missions: Prelude to Waitangi.* Sydney, Australia, 1936.

Salinis, R. P. de, SJ. *Marins et Missionnaires: Conquête de la Nouvelle-Calédonie, 1843–1853.* Paris, 1927.

Saura, Bruno. *Les bûchers de Fa'aite: Paganisme ancestral ou dérapage chrétien en Polynésie.* Papeete, Tahiti, 1990.

Trompf, G. W. *Melanesian Religion.* New York, Melbourne, and Sydney, 1991.

Williams, John. *A Narrative of Missionary Enterprises in the South Sea Islands.* London, 1838.

Williams, Thomas, and James Calvert. *Fiji and the Fijians: The Islands and Their Inhabitants: Mission History.* 2 vols. London, 1858.

JEAN GUIART (1987 AND 2005)

OCEANIC RELIGIONS: NEW RELIGIOUS MOVEMENTS

Oceania comprises a "sea of islands" within 181 million square kilometers of the Pacific Ocean (approximately one third of the earth's surface). At the beginning of the third millennium, the Pacific Islands, New Zealand, and Australia had a total population of thirty million people, which is only half of one percent of the world population. Yet there are almost one thousand distinct languages spoken in Oceania, or about a quarter of the world's languages. Language diversity is indicative of the cultural, social, and historical diversity of the region. Oceania is commonly divided into three main cultural groupings: Micronesia, Melanesia, and Polynesia. New Zealand is included in Polynesia. While the Australian subcontinent geographically lies outside Oceania, indigenous Australians (1.5% of the Australian population), have cultural ties with Oceania. Formerly, traditional religions predominated; today, however, over 90 percent of the people of Oceania profess to be Christian.

The first inhabitants of Melanesia and Australia are thought to have arrived about 50,000 BCE during the Ice Age of the Pleistocene era. Some five thousand years ago Austronesian-speaking people began voyages to the islands of Oceania, finally reaching Aotearoa–New Zealand about one thousand years ago. Ferdinand Magellan from Portugal was the first European to sail into the Pacific by way of South America's southern tip, reaching Guam in Micronesia in 1521. European influence continued into the colonial period, accompanied by Christian missionary efforts. Many Pacific states achieved independence only in the later half of the twentieth century. New religious movements have emerged within this sociohistorical context.

RELIGIOUS MOVEMENTS NEW AND OLD. Despite the term *new* applied to Oceanic religious movements, scholars claim that there were religious movements in the traditional culture prior to Western contact. Ronald Berndt (1952–1953) and Richard Salisbury (1958) have documented religious movements in New Guinea prior to European colonization or missionary evangelization. Garry Trompf (Swain and Trompf, 1995, p. 168) points out how the giant statues on Rapanui (Easter Island) reflect an extraordinary burst of cultic energy—this being followed by the "Birdman Cult," which was still active into the mid-1860s. Other scholars refer to traditions of ritual innovation in precontact culture. Chris Ballard (2003, p. 24) points out how in the Papua New Guinea highlands, the foreign was anticipated in a tradition of ritual innovation, so that when Westerners did appear, they were seen as having been prefigured in Melanesian cosmologies. What are often referred to as "cults" may well be examples of innovative indigenous tradition, rather than a response to contact with the West.

Whether new or old, religious movements have been documented throughout Oceania right from the time of early Western contact. These movements combine social, political, and religious elements. In New Zealand, for example, religious movements appeared among the Maori at a time when the population was in decline and the indigenous people were being alienated from the land. In 1863 most of the Taranaki region was proclaimed a confiscated area. In response, Maori prophet Te Whiti-o-Rongomai began teaching about the day of *takahanga*, or freedom from Pakeha (European) authority. He and the people of the Parihaka community tried to assert ownership over the land while at the same time avoiding armed warfare. He sent out men to plough and to build fences across the roads built by the colonial government. The ploughmen were arrested but considered martyrs by Te Whiti and his followers. They were empowered by a millennial vision of *aranga*, or day of reckoning, when the results of their struggle would be harvested in communal prosperity.

Cultural factors and the colonial and postcolonial experience of people in Oceania have continued to influence religious movements. Some movements are strongly influenced by indigenous cultural forms. Others manifest clear links with Judeo-Christianity. They have been labeled variously as movements, cults, and independent churches. While many individual movements have been studied and documented, the bewildering variety of these movements both fascinates and frustrates scholarly attempts to grasp their causes and to understand the phenomenon as a whole.

CONNECTION TO INDIGENOUS FORMS. Indigenous cultural forms, ranging from traditional religious elements to the influence of political and social structure, exert a strong influence on religious movements in Oceania. The Siovili movement appeared in Samoa in the 1830s. Siovili's prophetic activity was a mixture of the traditional *taula aitu* activity (spirit possession) and preaching influenced by Christianity. Religious experiences such as *taula aitu* were familiar to Samoans. Thus, many phenomena associated with the movement, such as being under the power of a spirit and speaking in tongues, were ritual activities familiar to the people.

Political and social influences on the Siovili movement become apparent if one compares it with the Mamaia movement that arose in Tahiti in 1826. In Samoa, traditional religious forms were closely associated with tutelary deities worshiped at the family level. By contrast, in Tahiti, religion was the basis for overall political authority. Thus, in Tahiti, when the Mamaia movement began, it spread quickly by means of traditional political alliances. As with Samoa, prophetic figures possessed by spirits were nothing new in the Society Islands. Thus it was not novel when Teau, the leader of the Mamaia movement, prophesied that he was inspired by the spirit of God to proclaim that the millennium had commenced and that he and his followers could communicate with God without the Tahitian Bible provided by the missionaries. However, the movement was also strongly influenced by local political forces. Mamaia found its greatest support in Taiarapu, where there had traditionally been an atmosphere of revolt against both the Pomare dynasty and the Europeans. According to Jukka Siikala (1982, pp. 248–249), the Mamaia movement can be interpreted as the attempt of the Taiarapu chiefs to manifest *mana* (respect deriving from authority and control) superior to that of Pomare and the chief judges supported by the missionaries.

Even in the 1990s, Christian Pentecostal and revival movements, though outwardly against traditional culture, often showed evidence of indigenous forms in healing, glossolalia, prophetic dreaming, possession, and the like. Franco Zocca (1995, p.181) points out how the millennial and magical components in many new religious movements and in Pentecostal churches fit into the pattern of traditional Melanesian religious experience.

INFLUENCE OF JUDEO-CHRISTIANITY ON NEW RELIGIOUS MOVEMENTS. Mission influence spread swiftly throughout Oceania, and today the majority of people in the region profess to be Christian. Some religious movements arose in opposition to Christianity. The so-called nativistic movements offered an alternative to the Christian denominations and even to the traditional religion. Later movements have tended to develop as offshoots of Christian churches.

Leaders in many movements see parallels between their situation and that of the Israelites in the Old Testament. Te

Ua, the leader of the Pai Marire movement in New Zealand in the 1850s, referred to New Zealand as Kenana, the "land of Canaan." Aotearoa-New Zealand was seen as an island in two halves that needed to be restored (as a new Israel). Just as God had promised the land of Canaan to Abraham, God would restore Aotearoa to the Maori. Thus, Te Ua created a myth-history that linked Maori followers to the Israelites, as well as to their Polynesian ancestors. Dancing around special poles and repeating Pai Marire prayers, people entered into a trance, uttered prophecies, and spoke in tongues.

More than a century later, in Guadalcanal in the Solomon Islands, the Moro movement promotes traditional values and the chieftainship system against the incursion of the West. Members of the movement say that the Bible is for whites and that tradition contains the same truths for islanders. Moses and Jesus, for example, have parallel figures in Guadalcanal legend. During the violent political crisis in the Solomon Islands in 2001, many of the Guadalcanal fighters wore emblems from the Moro movement, which they believed would protect them against the superior firepower of the Malaita Eagle Force, a militant group that undertook armed action on Guadalcanal. Together with disaffected police officers the Malaita Eagle Force seized control of key installations in Honiara and took Prime Minister Ulufa'alu hostage and forced him to resign.

The Christian Fellowship Church, also in the Solomon Islands, broke away from the Methodist Church in 1960. The founder, Silas Eto (sometimes known as "Holy Mama") believed that the Holy Spirit had visited his people as manifested in the *taturu* phenomenon of mass enthusiasm involving drumming, crying out, and involuntary movements during church services. Their theology is basically Methodist, though Eto would read scripture in the light of the *taturu* phenomenon. Eto has since died, but he continues to influence the church by appearing to members in visions. The 1999 census in the Solomon Islands recorded almost ten thousand people claiming to be members of this charismatic independent church.

Scholars debate the degree to which Christian revival movements, common throughout the region in the latter years of the twentieth century, are indeed movements building on indigenous forms or the rejection of those forms. In the revival movements, people seek to purify their Christian lives by setting aside inherited traditions and earlier religious practices. Yet, at a deeper level, traditional understandings often continue to provide the structure by which a new syncretism of Christian beliefs is organized.

INFLUENCE OF THE COLONIAL EXPERIENCE ON THE DEVELOPMENT OF RELIGIOUS MOVEMENTS. Having had to deal with a number of colonial powers—Spanish, American, Dutch, British, German, Australian, and New Zealand—many countries in the Pacific are now independent states. However, even today Niue and the Cook Islands are not fully independent, having free association with New Zealand. France continues to maintain territories in the Pacific with French Polynesia, Wallis and Futuna, and New Caledonia regarded as French overseas territories. In Micronesia the peoples of the Mariana Islands, the Carolines, the Marshalls, and Palau ratified constitutions in 1980 and chose either commonwealth status, free association, or republicanism, all of which guarantee a continued aid package from the United States. The Marianas became a commonwealth in political union with the United States in 1986 (with the exception of Guam, which is an unincorporated territory of the United States). The Caroline Islands divided into two separate entities: Palau and the Federated States of Micronesia. Palau became an independent nation with free association with the United States in 1994. With the termination of the Trust Territory of the Pacific in 1986, the Federated States of Micronesia and Marshall Islands gained independence and free-association status with the United States.

During the colonial experience, Pacific Islanders were adept at making their own adjustments, and religious movements were sometimes part of this. When competing for local resources the Europeans were resisted, but as a new resource they were utilized. Exploitation of European's fighting skills and equipment was a common phenomenon throughout Polynesia. Missionaries too often found themselves pawns in local power politics.

While most islanders (with the exception of Tonga) lost their political independence at some stage, there were other important issues, such as language, cultural integrity, the priority of local custom, and the persistence of practices of kinship and exchange. New religious movements offered alternative values to help the local people deal with such issues.

The Tuka movement appeared in the late nineteenth century in Fiji (*tuka* meaning life or immortality). It has been seen variously as an anticolonial resistance movement and a millenarian movement; however Martha Kaplan has sought to reinterpret it as a movement of "people of the land" (*itaukei*) trying to assert their ownership of the land through ritual and political means. Navosavakaua, the leader of the movement, and his people were opposing the encroachment of coastal chiefs and of Westerners with their Christian God and their colonial powers. He challenged the coastal chiefs and colonial authority, proclaiming that the world would shortly be turned upside down and that the existing state of affairs would be reversed so that whites would serve the Fijians and chiefs would become commoners. Kaplan rereads the Tuka movement as an elaborated version of an important Fijian invulnerability ritual known as *kalou rere* (Kaplan, 1990, p. 10).

Vailala Madness is the name given to an early millenarian movement beginning at Orokolo station in 1917 and spreading throughout the Toaripi region of the Papuan Gulf. During collective trance states people destroyed traditional ceremonial items. The leader, Evara, claimed to be contacting the dead through an artificial wireless antenna, with hopes that a ship crewed by the ancestors would come over the horizon. The body movement and curious sounds convinced government anthropologist Francis Williams that the situation was pathological. Later studies of the movement are less condemnatory, though many agree that the movement arose in response to the collision between traditional cultures and the colonial order (Trompf, 1991, p. 191). Movements of this type have been called *cargo cults* because of the people's expectation of the arrival of large quantities of European items, from food to firearms to refrigerators. The term *cargo cult* is unfortunate in that it tends to reduce a complex matter to just one exotic dimension.

There are many occurrences of anticolonial movements throughout the region, including the Modekngei movement, which appeared on Palau in 1906 in protest at German colonial government reforms. The movement continued into the 1960s and 1970s as a religio-political movement, affirming Palauan identity and independence.

In Malaita in the Solomon Islands following World War II, a movement known as the Maasina (Marching Rule) developed as an expression of both self-determination and spiritual independence. In the postwar period in nearby Vanuatu, on the island of Tanna, many people believed that a mythical figure named John Frum would come from the United States bringing gifts for his devotees. Also in Vanuatu, the Nagriamel Federation Independent United Royal Church appeared as an offshoot from a land reform association movement on the island of Espiritu Santu. The movement sought to reclaim indigenous land in the 1960s, sought national sovereignty in the 1970s, and proclaimed successionist independence in 1980. Nagriamel is decidedly political, but its cultural and religious dimensions are also important. One of the leaders of the movement, Jimmy Stephens, claimed to be Moses leading his people to the promised land. The movement has been in decline since Stephens was arrested by Papua New Guinean forces in 1980.

DEVELOPMENTS WITH POLITICAL INDEPENDENCE OF PACIFIC NATIONS. Church leaders have made a considerable contribution to political leadership in the region. In Vanuatu, Walter Lini, an Anglican priest, was the first and longest-serving prime minister, while the first leader of the opposition was a Catholic priest, Gerard Laymang. In Papua New Guinea, priests, former priests, seminarians, and Protestant ministers have held prominent political roles. Other church leaders, like Bishop Patelesio Finau of Tonga, have been politically active without taking a formal political post.

Associated with political independence, some established churches have become independent. For example, the Presbyterian Church in Vanuatu has been declared an independent New Hebridean church. In 1968 in Papua New Guinea and the Solomon Islands, the Methodist, Wesleyan, and Papua Ecclesia churches joined to form the indigenous independent United Church. In 1975 the Anglican Diocese of Melanesia (encompassing Vanuatu and the Solomon Islands) was officially localized, separating from the New Zealand church to become a province of its own.

Recent writings on cults and movements in the Pacific have focused on the role these movements play in the interpretation of changing colonial and postcolonial relations. An intriguing example is that of Matias Yaliwan and the Peli Association in the Sepik region of Papua New Guinea. Through traditional religious means, such as dreams, Yaliwan came to perceive the survey marker on Mount Hurun as symbolic of European trespass and invasion of traditional lands and life. At Christmas 1969, he and his followers removed the survey marker from the top of the mountain. In the 1970s, as Papua New Guinea prepared for independence, the movement developed into a prosperity cult known as the Peli Association. After national independence in the late 1970s the movement combined with the New Apostolic Church, a millennial Christian group offering 144,000 "firstlings" an opportunity to become citizens of a "new heaven and new earth" (Rosco, 1993, p. 292). Paul Roscoe points out how people were following Yaliwan not just as a traditional leader or "bigman" who could manipulate tangible commodities such as pigs and shell wealth, but one who could produce and manipulate knowledge and ideas. The explanatory schemes with which the Peli Association leaders attracted followers were a series of eschatologically colorful scenarios involving military-style marching, the actual election of Yaliwan to the Provincial Assembly, and his rumored crucifixion and resurrection as the Black Jesus. Canadian missionaries of the New Apostolic Church helped provide legitimacy to this scenario.

Since the 1990s on the island of Bougainville in the North Solomons province of Papua New Guinea, successionist leader Francis Ona has been promoting his idea of *Mekamui* (sacred land)—a state independent of Papua New Guinea. *Mekamui* also has strong links with the Tomo cult, which is a mixture of Christianity and traditional forms. The term *tomo* refers to ashes, which have particular significance in a culture that practiced cremation of the dead.

In the post-independence period, politicians in the Pacific invoke the political support of churches. Responses vary, with leaders of established churches wary of political control, often taking a critical stance, and leaders of newer church groups, particularly those with a conservative fundamentalist theology, willing to cooperate in exchange for legitimacy and material benefits.

INDEPENDENT CHURCHES. Aside from the examples given above of established churches becoming independent, there are also "independent churches" that take a separatist stance towards the churches introduced by the missions. For example, in New Zealand there are several independent Maori churches, the best known being that started by Tahupotiki Wiremu Ratana in 1928. Ratana's healing ministry and his warnings about some aspects of Maori ancestral beliefs were welcomed at first. However, when the Anglican Church condemned him as a false prophet, his followers convinced him to start his own church, which exists today. The independent Ratana Church has been influential in both ecclesial and secular politics, motivating the formation of a Maori bishopric in the Anglican Church of Aotearoa-New Zealand and promoting four Maori seats in the New Zealand parliament.

Since the 1970s, revival movements have flourished throughout Oceania. These movements tend to be Pentecostal in character and generally opposed to traditional religious systems (Tuzin, 1997; Robbins, 2001). Influenced by revival, people tend to condemn their traditional religion, destroying their former sacred places and the paraphernalia used in traditional rituals. They seek to purify their Christian lives by setting aside inherited traditions and what they perceive as forms of syncretism. Paradoxically, although the focus of these revival movements is the rejection of tradition, the parallels with tradition—legalism, fear, and a dualistic worldview labeling everything as belonging either to God or Satan—make it easier for people to accept their teaching. Revival often begins within an established church, but in many cases their beliefs and practices go beyond what is considered acceptable by the church leadership and the movement develops into an independent "local" church, as has happened in a number of cases in Papua New Guinea with groups breaking away from the Lutheran, United, and established Pentecostal churches to form indigenized local variants of Christianity.

In the 1990s and in the lead-up to 2000, many revival movements that had been characterized by such Pentecostal elements as shaking, possession, and glossolalia took a more apocalyptic turn, with frequent reference to the number 666 from the *Book of Revelation* (e.g., those possessing the 666 will have access to wealth), the sinister meaning of bar codes, spiritual warfare, and the antichrist. Besides addressing the question of what might happen at the end of the millennium, these apocalyptic-oriented movements provide an outlet for people struggling to deal with escalating violence and socioeconomic insecurity. Established churches are condemned along with traditional culture as being retrograde and idolatrous. There is often a global dimension to these local churches, for as Ernest Olson (2001, p. 24) notes, people in an all-night Pentecostal prayer vigil in Tonga would share more in common with Pentecostals in Mount Hagen, Papua New Guinea, than the Tongan all-night kava drinking sessions just down the street.

TYPOLOGY OF THE MOVEMENTS. Attempts to develop a typology of religious movements in Oceania tend to fall short in oversimplification, or to founder in the complexity of the phenomena under study. Anthony Wallace used the term *revitalisation movements,* by which he meant the "deliberate, organized, conscious effort by members of a society to construct a more satisfying culture" (Wallace, 1956, p. 265). He differentiated between "nativist," "millenarian," and "messianic" movements. Subsequently, many alternative interpretations have been offered. Harold Turner's spectrum from "primal revival," through "syncretist," to "church revival" (1978, pp. 7ff.) is one of the more promising attempts at classification.

Some scholars see the movements as examples of irrational human behavior (Williams, 1976). Others see them as the product of tensions arising from collisions between traditional culture and the colonial order (Worsley, 1968). Alternatively, they have been viewed as specific Melanesian expressions of indigenous spirituality and value systems (Burridge, 1960; Lawrence, 1964). The weakness of many such interpretations is their tendency to reduce these phenomena to just a few of their respective aspects, or to lump together ideas and practices that may have little in common. Attempted classifications may reveal more about Western rationalism than about the Melanesian ideas and practices to which the classification systems are meant to refer in the first place.

For example, the frequently used term *cult* denotes religious activity but carries with it negative overtones. Moreover, it does not reflect the fact that the sacred and secular are generally distinguished but not separated in Oceanic cultures. Kaplan argues that cults are often created and analyzed in Western terms, serving the purpose of colonizers responding to obstacles to their attempts at "development." Many movements are only truly irrational in the context of Western discourse.

Mircea Eliade (1954) detects a pervasive form of millennialism belonging to an ancient complex spread throughout the Pacific region during the migrations of Austronesian-speaking people. He identifies a theme involving the renewal of the cosmos through the destruction of all existing forms, a regression to chaos, followed by a new creation. Thus, millennial movements are not only a postcontact, post-Christian phenomenon. There were traditions that entailed expectation of a new era and the beginning of a time of well-being. However, for many people of the Pacific, confronted by the encroaching Western powers, their world was ending. Not only were people becoming alienated from their ancient traditions, but their leaders appeared impotent, and in some places their land was being divided and sold. The power of chiefs and ritual experts to mediate between the people and the gods declined. In this context Christian millennialism may have a special appeal for Pacific Islanders, because it has features in common with traditional myths of return.

CONCLUSION. Religious movements have been a constant part of the experience of people in Oceania. However, since the arrival of Europeans and colonial rule, new elements entered into that experience. These movements are a way indigenous people try to deal with change within a world that does not separate religion from the rest of life. In general, the new religious movements arise in the context of social and cultural conditions characterized by disharmonies of opportunity, status, and political and socioeconomic stress generated when a traditional culture is faced with modernization. Which factors are relatively more important is a mater of debate.

From a rational, secular viewpoint the movements appear to be examples of delusion and aberrant behavior. However, from the perspective of indigenous hermeneutics, they may be perceived as the work of visionaries trying to make sense of a changing world in religious terms.

Some new religious movements continue into the twenty-first century, often transformed into local churches and even political parties. In addition, millenarian beliefs continue to animate religious movements in the form of Holy Spirit and Christian revival and apocalyptic movements. Some even become tourist attractions, with cargo cult websites—including a John Frum homepage.

BIBLIOGRAPHY

Ballard, Chris. "Provisional Cosmologies: 'Cargo Cults' and the History of Ritual in the New Guinea Highlands." Unpublished paper presented at the Volkswagen-Stiftung Workshop on Cargo and Culture Critique. Åarhus, Denmark, November 25–28, 1991.

Berndt, Ronald M. "A Cargo Movement in the East-Central Highlands of New Guinea." *Oceania* 23 (1952–1953): 40–65, 137–158, 202–234.

Burridge, Kennelm. *Mambu: A Melanesian Millennium.* London, 1960; reprint, Princeton, N.J., 1995.

Eliade, Mircea. *The Myth of the Eternal Return: Or, Cosmos and History.* Translated by Willard Trask. Princeton, N.J., 1954.

Ernst, Manfred. *Winds of Change: Rapidly Growing Religious Groups in the Pacific Islands.* Suva, Fiji, 1994.

Flannery, Wendy, ed. *Religious Movements in Melanesian Today.* Goroka, Papua New Guinea, 1983–1984.

Kaplan, Martha, "Meaning, Agency, and Colonial History: Navosavakadua and the *Tuka* Movement in Fiji." *American Ethnologist* 17 (1990): 3–22.

Lawrence, Peter. *Road Belong Cargo: A Study of the Cargo Movement in the Southern Madang District, New Guinea.* Manchester, U.K., 1964.

Loeliger, Carl, and Garry Trompf, eds. *New Religious Movements in Melanesia.* Suva, Fiji, 1985.

Olson, Ernest. "Signs of Conversion, Spirit of Commitment: The Pentecostal Church in the Kingdom of Tonga." *Ritual Studies* 15 (2001): 13–26.

Robbins, Joel. "Whatever Became of Revival? From Charismatic Movement to Charismatic Church in a Papua New Guinea Society." *Ritual Studies* 15 (2001): 79–90.

Roscoe, Paul. "The Brokers of the Lord: The Ministration of a Christian Faith in the Sepik Basin of Papua New Guinea." In *Contemporary Pacific Societies: Studies in Development and Change,* edited by Victoria S. Lockwood, Thomas G. Harding, and Ben J. Wallace, pp. 289–303. Englewood Cliffs, N.J., 1993.

Salisbury, Richard F. "An 'Indigenous' New Guinea Cult." *Kroeber Anthropological Society Papers* 18 (1958): 67–78.

Siikala, Jukka. *Cult and Conflict in Tropical Polynesia: A Study of Traditional Religion, Christianity and Nativistic Movements.* Helsinki, 1982.

Swain, Tony, and Garry Trompf. *The Religions of Oceania.* London, 1995.

Trompf, Garry. *Melanesian Religion.* Cambridge, U.K., 1991.

Turner, Harold. "Old and New Religions in Melanesia." *Point* 2 (1978): 5–29.

Turner, Harold. *Bibliography of New Religious Movements in Primal Societies,* vol. 3, *Oceania.* Boston, 1990.

Tuzin, Donald. *The Cassowary's Revenge: The Life and Death of Masculinity in a New Guinea Society.* Chicago, 1997.

Wallace, Anthony, F. C. "Revitalization Movements." *American Anthropologist* 58 (1956): 264–281.

Williams, Francis E. *"The Vailala Madness" and Other Essays.* Edited by Erik Schwimmer. Brisbane, Australia, 1976.

Worsley, Peter. *The Trumpet Shall Sound: A Study of "Cargo" Cults in Melanesia.* London, 1957; 2d ed., 1968.

Zocca, Franco. "'Winds of Change' also in PNG?" *Catalyst* 25 (1995): 174–187.

PHILIP GIBBS (2005)

OCEANIC RELIGIONS: HISTORY OF STUDY [FIRST EDITION]

Oceania is conventionally defined in terms of the three major cultural divisions of the Pacific islanders: Polynesia, Micronesia, and Melanesia. The earliest European knowledge of Oceanic peoples is contained in the journals of Magellan's chronicler, Antonio Pigafetta, who in 1521 provides an account of the initial encounter with the inhabitants of an island that he called Los Ladrones, now identified as Guam. As with most contact narratives, the tale dwells upon visible details and practical difficulties, but it offers little insight into local life. And, as Andrew Sharp writes in his *The Discovery of the Pacific Islands* (2d ed., Oxford, 1962), much the same may be said of the journals of subsequent explorers such as Alvaro de Mendaña de Neira, Francis Drake, William Dampier, and Louis-Antoine de Bougainville. It is only toward the end of the eighteenth century that fuller accounts of Oceanic cultures become available with James Cook's journals on Tahiti and Hawaii, published as *The Journals of Captain James Cook on His Voyages of Discovery* (3 vols., Cambridge, 1957–1967) and with the narratives of castaways and beachcombers in, for example, George Keate's *An Account of the Pelew Islands* (London, 1788), *The Marquesan Journal of Edward Robarts, 1797–1824,* edited by Greg Dening (Honolulu, 1974), and *The Journal of William Lockerby,* edited by Everard Im Thurn and Leonard C. Wharton (London, 1925). The best nineteenth-century sources are largely the works of administrators and other longterm residents, such as Abraham Fornander's *An Account of the Polynesian Race* (1878–1885; reprint, Rutland, Vt., 1969) and George Grey's *Polynesian Mythology and Ancient Traditional History of the Maori as Told by Their Priests and Chiefs* (1855; reprint, New York, 1970).

Despite this growing wealth of information about Oceanic cultures, the systematic study of Oceanic religions remained largely undeveloped before the advent of anthropology in the latter part of the nineteenth century. Unlike the "high" religions such as Christianity, Islam, Buddhism, and so forth, the traditional religions of Oceania were not proselytizing creeds embodied in written texts but were instead embedded in the specifics of the societies in which they were found. Although priesthoods were characteristic of a number of Polynesian societies (e.g., Maori, Hawaiian, Samoan, etc.), these soon collapsed under European pressure. For the remainder of the region religious institutions tended to be diffused throughout the social structure, so that an understanding of them hinged upon an understanding of their social setting. Precisely because of relative hospitality to outsiders, European impact on traditional society was strongest in Polynesia and Micronesia, whereas Melanesia was largely left alone. For these reasons Melanesia has predominated in research on traditional religions in Oceania.

A major goal of early anthropology was the creation of typological schemes to lay the basis for the reconstruction of evolutionary stages from savagery to civilization. Given the nineteenth century's intoxication with progress, human history was viewed as the intellectual movement from magic and religion to the scientific rationalism held to epitomize civilization. For this reason religion played a central role in the theoretical frameworks of writers such as E. B. Tylor and James G. Frazer, whose perspective took exotic religions as indicative of modes of thought. In the process, they identified cultural forms with cognitive capacities in the invidious comparison of savagery with civilization.

Such schemes required generalized concepts to identify characteristic features of "savage" thought, and this was the context in which some of the earliest accounts of Oceanic religions entered into scholarly discussions. Two concepts of particular importance to early theories of religion are those of *mana* and of taboo, both of which arose from ethnographic studies in the Pacific. The notion of *mana* stems from the work of R. H. Codrington, a missionary anthropologist working in eastern Melanesia in the late nineteenth century. In *The Melanesians* (1891; reprint, New Haven, 1957) Codrington identified belief in *mana* as a central tenet of Melanesian religions and defined it as a supernatural power immanent in the cosmos and capable of influencing events for good or ill. *Mana* characterized outstanding success in all enterprises as both sign and source of efficacy, was intimately tied to personal prestige, and served to mark off the singular in experience. Codrington saw all Melanesian religion as an attempt to acquire *mana* for one's own uses. Understood on analogy with electricity, *mana* gave a name to what had long been postulated as a premise of magical thought, that is, the idea that unseen and impersonal powers in the world could be tapped, accumulated, and directed toward human ends. Subsequent work in Oceania found closely analogous concepts, and the notion of *mana* was soon generalized to cover a wide range of cases. More recent ethnographers have shown Codrington's original formulation to be based on a fundamental semantic misunderstanding (see, for example, Roger M. Keesing's "Rethinking Mana," *Journal of Anthropological Research* 40, 1984, pp. 137–156). Nevertheless, the concept gained wide currency in comparative studies as a key analytic category. In a similar vein, the concept of taboo became part of the vocabulary of the anthropology of religion through early analyses of the Polynesian notion of *tapu* (see, for example, E. S. Craighill Handy's *Polynesian Religion*, Honolulu, 1927).

Early treatments of Oceanic religions were attempts simply to record religious practices and beliefs in such a way that they became intelligible to European audiences, and to the extent that larger issues came into play the concern was to isolate particular features that meshed with current theories of social evolution and culture history. One consequence of this essentially typological orientation was that apparent commonalities tended to be stressed at the expense of the distinctive features of particular religious systems, fostering a spurious sense of uniformity. A second consequence was a tendency to view Oceanic religions in atomistic terms, as a series of intellectual categories divorced from the contexts of social life. A decisive shift awaited the emergence of new canons of ethnography associated with Bronislaw Malinowski's fieldwork among the Trobriand Islanders off the east coast of New Guinea.

Prior to World War I, fieldwork in Oceania was largely of two kinds. Often information was obtained by men whose familiarity with an area was grounded in missionary or administrative work. One advantage such workers had was a longterm involvement with local people, but their ethnographic work was secondary to their other duties, which were often at cross-purposes with research interests. Professional anthropologists, on the other hand, tended to pursue their researches by conducting surveys from government verandas or the decks of itinerant vessels calling in at various islands. Here systematic coverage was possible, but it came at the expense of detailed knowledge of life in any particular locale. Malinowski's contribution was the development of longterm fieldwork whose aim was to construct a comprehensive portrait of social life in immediate and concrete terms. Not surprisingly, this work produced very different results from that done by his predecessors.

Inspired by the theories of Émile Durkheim and steeped in the details of Trobriand life, Malinowski in his *Magic, Science and Religion* (New York, 1948), insisted that it was only possible to understand Trobriand religion as an aspect of Trobriand culture in general. Taking issue with those who saw religion as a thing in itself, his style of interpretation ("functionalism") stressed the social dimensions of religious beliefs and the uses to which they could be put: myths of ancestral emergence were charters for territorial claims; beliefs in ancestral spirits and reincarnation reinforced the ties of clanship fundamental to the structure of the society; garden magic coordinated the productive efforts of entire communities, while fishing magic lent the confidence necessary to perilous undertakings. For Malinowski, the interpretation of religion was less a matter of locating general categories or apprehending a particular mode of thought than discovering a pragmatic rationality in what people said and did in the context of a specific social system.

Malinowski's influence upon anthropology was enormous: his style of fieldwork became the hallmark of serious anthropology, while his version of functional analysis became basic to the anthropological tool kit. The period between the wars was marked by a number of fine-grained field studies, in which the works of Gregory Bateson, Reo F. Fortune, Maurice Leenhardt, and F. E. Williams stand out.

Fortune is best known for his *Sorcerers of Dobu* (1932; rev. ed., New York, 1963), but a far more significant work is his *Manus Religion* (Philadelphia, 1935) Enmeshed in a dense network of obligations, Manus Islanders depended on the ghosts of their fathers to punish moral breaches through illness, and when illness struck divination sought out the sufferer's lapses in confession and expiation. Fortune showed how such beliefs occasioned assessment and reparation of personal relationships while seeking to regain the sufferer's health. In the process ghost beliefs were rescued from the dead category of "ancestor worship" by examining their role in the dynamics of village life.

Bateson's *Naven* (1938; 2d ed., Stanford, Calif., 1958) was an ambitious attempt to interpret a central ritual of the Iatmul people of the Sepik River of New Guinea. In the Naven ritual, significant events in an individual's life were marked by a ceremonial inversion of sex roles, and Bateson took the problems posed by this rite as the foundation for a sophisticated development of the concept of structure in cultural analysis. In this way ritual became a lens for understanding the formal underpinnings of psychological attitudes, cosmological principles, intergroup relations, and social roles in Iatmul culture.

F. E. Williams, the Government Anthropologist for Papua until his death in World War II, conducted a number of field studies touching upon traditional religions, but his most significant contribution was his account of the so-called Vailala Madness among the peoples of the Papuan Gulf, published in his *The Vailala Madness and Other Essays* (London, 1976). An early instance of what were later to become familiar as cargo cults, the Vailala Madness was a dramatic cultural transformation in which traditional rites were abandoned wholesale as local people strove to embark on a new mode of life in the face of European contact. The movement was directed through tranced prophets, and key themes were the establishment of contact with ancestors (identified with Europeans), a transcendence of traditional divisions between the sexes, and access to European goods through ritual. Williams's reaction to the movement was ambivalent, but he drew attention to the creative dynamism latent in the interplay of skepticism and openness that marked religious belief for Papuan peoples. This observation was pregnant with implications for prevailing views postulating a relatively static integration of religion and culture.

A missionary anthropologist working in New Caledonia, Maurice Leenhardt, in his *Do Kamo: Person and Myth in the Melanesian World* (Chicago, 1979), developed a novel approach that grew out of his practical and intellectual concern with the relation between traditional religion and Christianity (see James Clifford's *Person and Myth: Maurice Leenhardt in the Melanesian World*, Berkeley, 1982). Seizing upon religious ideas (especially as embodied in myth and in linguistic categories) as a frame for experience, he analyzed New Caledonian concepts of identity in terms of time, space, and personal relationships. This phenomenological undertaking served to clarify the differences between New Caledonian and Western notions of the individual, and this analysis in turn helped to situate his understanding of the process of conversion to Christianity in terms of the transformation of the self.

Prior to World War II, most anthropological work followed Malinowski's program with general ethnographic coverage as the goal. The war itself brought about a total halt in fieldwork and it was not until the 1950s that Pacific anthropology once again became active. When it did so there were several noteworthy differences. Most significant of these was a reorientation influenced by A. R. Radcliffe-Brown and his students. Within this perspective most aspects of culture were seen as epiphenomena to be accounted for in terms of their contribution to the maintenance of the social order as defined by systems of groups such as clans, lineages, and so on. Religious beliefs and practices were accorded a decidedly secondary role and entered into analysis only insofar as they could be shown to reinforce a system of social relations.

One result of these developments was that the study of traditional religions remained to all intents and purposes moribund as analyses of social structure dominated the field until the latter part of the 1960s. The major exception to this trend was afforded by the study of cargo cults. Though widespread throughout the Pacific, cargo cults were neglected before the publication of Kenelm Burridge's *Mambu, a Melanesian Millennium* (London, 1960), despite the availability of Williams's prewar work. Popularly associated with bizarre rites aimed at the acquisition of Western manufactured goods, cargo cults burgeoned in the wake of the massive military operations of World War II.

Burridge's work in the Madang region of New Guinea showed that the notion of "cargo" comprised not only European goods but the ensemble of moral dilemmas embodied in local relations with Europeans and the cash economy. Radically different from traditional forms of exchange, cash transactions entailed no reciprocal obligation and conferred no moral standing and thus called into question traditional measures of man. Through a dialectic of myth, dream, aspiration, and moral critique, cargo movements constituted attempts to formulate an image of a new life and a new morality, made concrete in the figure of the charismatic cargo prophet. An overall concern was to reestablish the moral equivalence basic to Melanesian societies in a Europeanized environment by transcending the limitations symbolized in the notion of cargo. Burridge's study was soon augmented by Peter Lawrence's historical account of Madang cargo movements, *Road Belong Cargo* (Manchester, England, 1964). Lawrence analyzed the career of Yali, a cargo prophet, in the context of native relations with Europeans. An important point made in both of these studies was the extent to which traditional epistemologies based upon mythology and revelatory experiences served to enable historical transformations in Madang societies. These analyses were complemented by Peter Worsley's comparative study, *The Trumpet Shall Sound* (London, 1957), which argued that cargo movements were nascent anticolonial political movements. Each of these works implied a critique of contemporary views of religion as the static appendage of social structure by underscoring the dynamic role of religion in cultural change.

In the mid-1960s, Lawrence and M. J. Meggitt edited *Gods, Ghosts, and Men in Melanesia* (Melbourne, 1965), which is a compilation of a number of detailed accounts of Melanesian religions. Yet with the noteworthy exception of Jan van Baal's *Dema* (The Hague, 1966), most other anthropological treatments of traditional religions remained fixated on social structure as the guiding interpretive frame. One innovative departure was Roy A. Rappaport's *Pigs for the Ancestors* (New Haven, 1968), which viewed the ritual cycle of pig sacrifices among the Maring as a homeostatic mechanism for maintaining ecological relationships between local populations and their environment. Even here, however, the emphasis remained upon the role of religious institutions in underwriting some form of status quo, whether sociological or ecological, portraying them as essentially parasitic upon other features of the social system.

A dramatic shift in the analysis of religious phenomena took place with the publication of Burridge's *Tangu Traditions* (Oxford, 1969) and Roy Wagner's *Habu: The Innovation of Meaning in Daribi Religion* (Chicago, 1972). In a painstaking analysis of Tangu narrative, Burridge extended the thesis adumbrated in his previous work by teasing out the ways in which, through recourse to myth, the Tangu apprehended the singular and numinous in experience. Finding more in myth than a Malinowskian charter for particular social arrangements, Burridge argued that it provided a tool for the exploration of unrealized possibilities, and he demonstrated how mythic content in turn became reformulated in the light of novel experience. In *Habu* Wagner pursued a different line of thought with similar implications. Focusing upon traditional Daribi religion, he developed a theory of innovation upon cultural ideologies that took the process of metaphorization as its key concept. Covering a range of material incuding naming, dream interpretation, the form of magical spells and the patterning of ritual, he argued for a view of cultural meaning stressing a dialectical tension between different realms of experience that afforded scope for creativity in the innovative extension of metaphors across conventional categories of signification. An essential part of Wagner's theory is that these processes be understood as normal properties of all cultural systems. Both of these works locate sources of cultural dynamism in the realm of religious phenomena and emphasize the reflective interplay of image and experience. They thus offer essentially open-ended accounts in which symbols are apprehended less as static structures than as participants in a dialectic that Williams might well have termed "culture on the move" (1976, p. 395).

Anthropology from the mid-1970s forward witnessed a growing interest in processes of symbolization, and this development, coupled with the impact of previous work, prompted a number of detailed studies placing religion once again at the heart of anthropology in the Pacific. Several provocative analyses of ritual emerged, addressing a wide range of theoretical problems.

Wagner extended the logic of his previous analysis in *Lethal Speech* (Ithaca, N. Y., 1978), a study of different genres of Daribi myth. Developing a line congenial to Wagner's work, Edward L. Schieffelin, in his *The Sorrow of the Lonely and the Burning of the Dancers* (New York, 1976), recounts the metaphorically rich *gisaro* ceremony and makes use of the concepts of opposition and reciprocity to situate an overall understanding of the Kaluli worldview. In his *Karavar: Masks and Power in Melanesian Ritual* (Ithaca, N. Y., 1974), Frederick K. Errington showed how rites involving masked dancers articulated a collective image of order against the backdrop of cultural assumptions postulating a chaotic human nature.

Male initiation rites became a focus of attention in, for example, Gilbert H. Herdt's *Guardians of the Flutes* (New York, 1981), a study of the psychological dimensions of sexual identity; Fredrik Barth's *Ritual and Knowledge among the Baktaman of New Guinea* (New Haven, 1975), an examination of the relation between ritual and knowledge; and Gilbert Lewis's *Day of Shining Red* (Cambridge, 1980), a study of hermeneutic problems. One of the most impressive contributions was Alfred Gell's *Metamorphosis of the Cassowaries* (London, 1975), in which a complex and refractory dialectic of succession and renewal became intelligible through a symbolic analysis utilizing structuralist techniques of interpretation. Structuralist principles also contributed strongly to F. Allan Hanson and Louise Hanson's *Counterpoint in Maori Culture* (London, 1983), a sophisticated analysis of complementarity and symmetry in Maori religion and culture, while Marshall D. Sahlin's account of transformations in Hawaiian culture in his *Historical Metaphors and Mythical Realities* (Ann Arbor, 1981) and *Islands of History* (Chicago, 1985) deployed similar techniques to show how metaphorical extensions of religious premises influenced the direction of historical change.

Two of the most significant recent trends in the study of Oceanic religions are the incorporation of a view that accords to symbols an active role in transforming experience and a concern to come to grips with the dynamism of religious life. These orientations grow out of general anthropological preoccupations and at the same time reflect the necessity of coming to terms with history. Pacific pagans are now few and far between, and the last century has seen the emergence of Christianity as the dominant religious form in Oceania. For examples of these trends at work, see *Mission, Church, and Sect in Oceania*, edited by James A. Boutilier et al. (Ann Arbor, 1978); Raymond Firth's *Rank and Religion in Tikopia* (London, 1970); and John Garrett's *To Live among the Stars* (Suva, Fiji Islands, 1982). If the study of Oceanic religions is to retain contemporary relevance it must take as its task an understanding of religious life harking back to Leenhardt's central problem: the retention of authenticity in the face of the christianization of the Pacific.

SEE ALSO Codrington, R. H.; Leenhardt, Maurice; Malinowski, Bronislaw.

DAN W. JORGENSEN (1987)

OCEANIC RELIGIONS: HISTORY OF STUDY [FURTHER CONSIDERATIONS]

During the 1980s, general ethnologies of Pacific cultures had become a decidedly less popular enterprise, and *fin-de-siècle* crisis of identity among anthropologists (who were affected especially by critical theory and post-modernist trends) altered the profile of writings on Oceania's religious life. Doubts that the whole fabric of any society could ever be summarized reached an extreme, and it became almost a given methodologically that one ought to approach a culture through one or two "windows." For example, an unusual feature of Oceanian social life might call for an explanation, and meeting the challenge to explain this feature could thereby open a vista onto the cultural whole through a justifiable special point of entry. One of these entry points might be religion—or specific aspects thereof. An intriguing traditional cult could beckon an account—one involving homosexual rites, for example; or perhaps a cyclopean devouring spirit being occupying a dominant *haus tambaran* (spirit house) as exhibited by Donald Tuzin on the Ilhaita Arapesh in hinterland New Guinea; or cults in which mysterious disclosures of fauna marked various grades of initiation (see Fredrik Barth on the Baktaman, highland New Guinea, and Harvey Whitehouse on Melanesia more generally). Thus, specific features of traditional religion have been scrutinzed in depth, as in the following four key examples: sorcery, by Michele Stephen and Bruce Knauft on the Papuan Mekeo and Gebusi respectively; medical lore, by Stephen Frankel on the Southern Papua New Guinea Highlands Huli; the poetics of space, by Gillian Gillison and James Weiner on other highland cases; and sacrifice, by Valerio Valeri on Hawai'an kingship and sacrifice. Discrete traditional religions have also been described in separate studies, as with Roger Keesing's *Kwaio Religion* (1982, about a Malaitan people in the Solomon Islands), or Mary MacDonald's *Mararoko: A Study in Melanesian Religion* (1991, on the Southern Highland Kewa, Papua New Guinea), and Ward Goodenough's *Under Heaven's Brow: Pre-Christian Religious Tradition in Chuuk* (2002, on a Micronesian case). These shifts in approach have encouraged scholars to take one major topic and explore it across a regional board, whether in symposia or monographs, as in *The Religious Imagination in New Guinea*, edited by Herdt and Stephen (1989) on the imaginal, *Payback: The Logic of Retribution in Melanesian Cultures* by Garry Trompf (1994) on retributive logic in Melanesian religions, and *Handbook of Polynesian Mythology* by Robert Craig (2004) on recurring mythic themes. In a collection inspired by Henri Dumont's *Homo Hierarchicus* (1966) the French duo Daniel de Coppet and André Iteanu (1995) garnished an impressive range of contributions on the relation between cosmological ideas and social structure across the South Pacific. Continental anthropology, indeed, showed increasing sensitivity to the details of traditional religious insights and their relation to ritual organization. The region along and around the Sepik River has received much recent attention (thus Brigitta Hauser-Schäublin on the societal function and symbolism of cult houses; Jürg Wassmann on outer and esoteric knowledge among the Iatmul; and Bernard Juillerat—in a neo-Freudian vein—showing how Yafar myths express traditional views of sexual difference). The most intense feminist reappraisal of anthropological findings was Continental, the Melanesia-wide study of magic and sorcery by Susanne Schröter (1994) being noteworthy, with her worries about prior researchers' non-committal over violence against women in traditional cultures.

Whereas the huge number of traditional religions in Oceania continued to beckon investigation, religious change has come to be placed higher on the research agenda. Adjustment movements in the wake of the early mission impact in Polynesia were skillfully reconstructed by Jukka Siikala in his *Cult and Conflict in Central Polynesia* (1982), which explained, for instance, how the sacral kingship of present-day Tonga arose. Melanesian cargo cults also remain objects of concern, with the most detailed accounts of single cults being undertaken by Patrick Gesch (on the Peli Association in and around the Negrie-Yangoru culture complex, hinterland New Guinea), Elfriede Hermann on the aftermath of the Yali movement of the Madang area famously documented in Peter Lawrence's *Road Belong Cargo*, Andrew Lattas (on the "bush" Kaliai), and Dorothy Billings (on the pro-American Johnson movement, New Hanover). Both of these cases are from the New Guinea Islands.

Building on his research on Tanna Island, Vanuatu, Lamont Lindstrom produced the only general monograph on the subject in the last quarter of the twentieth century with *Cargo Cult: Strange Stories of Desire from Melanesia and Beyond* (1993). Trompf, while editing a collection on cargo cults and millenarian movements that included Pacific materials, also opened up the study of independent churches in Oceania by taking his cue from Bengt Sundkler's pioneering research in Africa. The presence of "spiritistic tendencies" in Melanesian responses to Christianity—altered states such as glossolalia, group experience of a spirit wind, ecstatic prayer, and prophesying—was spotted by John Barr and interpreted as culturally appropriate *rites de passage* into a new religious order. Manfred Ernst, in his *Winds of Change* (1994), went on to explain that the appeal of Christian Pentecostalism still burgeoning across the Pacific partly reflected cultural predispositions.

Religious change in itself increasingly dictated the anthropological agenda. Symptomatic was Ton Otto and Ad Borsboom's edited *Cultural Dynamics of Religious Change in Melanesia* (1997); but one also notes a spate of publications on women's movements and changing gender roles (by Lorraine Sexton, Deborah Gewertz, and Elizabeth Jolly) which introduced religious values being invoked by women to counter male maladjustments to modernity (alcoholism, promiscuity, domestic violence, and so on).

With over ninety percent of Pacific Islanders adopting Christianity it was inevitable that studies of mission would have to be complemented by assessments of indigenous Christianities. Friedegard Tomasetti was first to argue that the time had arrived when anthropologists would often have to begin research within Christian congregations and then work back to tradition. In her *Traditionen und Christentum* (1976), Tomasetti grasped how Melanesians carried with them two basic readings of the world—one applying to the Old Time and the other to the New—with highly varied attempts to integrate the dichotomy. At a later stage, John Barker championed the need for a special research area concerning Pacific Christianity, editing *Christianity in Oceania* (1990). Bronwyn Douglas later advised fieldworkers that they should no longer treat Christians as "invisible," let alone as some kind of "Gothic theater." Joel Robbins, already interested in grassroots eschatological expectations at the turn of the twenty-first century, was one anthropologist who had no trouble adjusting to the pressure, and in his work *Becoming Sinners* (2004) analyzed the moral torment among the New Guinea highland Urapmin and this people's difficulties in transferring from one moral system to another.

Meanwhile, the concern of the documentation and evaluation of the role of missions did not abate. Charles Forman studied the making of islander churches, as can be seen in *The Island Churches of the South Pacific* (1982). A trilogy of books by John Garrett on Pacific mission history from 1668 to the present (1982–1997) was published, and Francis Hezel's contact history of the Caroline and Marshall Islands, *The First Taint of Civilization* (1983) considered the difficulties for early mission work posed by misbehaving seafarers at favorite ports of call as well as the scattered nature of atoll existence.

In his recently republished part of the *Oxford History of the Christian Church*, Ian Breward's *History of the Churches in Australasia* (2004) deals ably with New Zealand and the Pacific Islands, not just the Australian scene. Missionary anthropology was always strong in Irian Jaya (West Papua) and explorations of acculturation and Christianization attained highpoints in Freek Kamma's two-volume *"Dit wonderlijke werk"* (1977 on northern areas) and Jan Boelaar's three-volume *Met Papoea's samen op Weg* (ch 1992-7, on the south). Eminent missiologists applied themselves especially to Melanesia, Theodor Ahrens following up various publications in German, such as *Unterwegs nach der verlorenen Heimat* (1986), with his important *Grace and Reciprocity* (2002) (on Christian reinforcement of the positive side of "payback" in Melanesian religions), and likewise John D'Arcy May adding to his *Christus Initiator* (1990, in German) a study of *Transcendence and Violence* (2003) (an attempt to sort out ambigious relationships between Christian monotheism and negative "payback," with the Melanesian situation to the fore). *Catalyst* and *Point*, issuing from the Melanesian Institute of Pastoral and Socio-Economic Service, have consolidated as the most prestigious serials in missiologically-oriented anthropology in the region, but *Irian* on Indonesia's side of the great New Guinea Island is hardly far behind. The *Micronesian Counselor*, founded by Hezel, favors applied research to solve socio-religious problems in the most isolated places on earth.

The tertiary study of religion and theology within Oceania itself provided better opportunities for broader overviews of regional religious life by expatriate scholars who were able to operate at length from institutions relatively close to their research areas, as well as for projects to be taken up by emergent indigenous intellectuals trained in those institutions. Among work with this wide compass was that of researchers with missiological interests, such as Ennio Mantovani (of the Melanesian Institute) and Theo Aerts (Bomana Regional Catholic Seminary; and Religious Studies, University of Papua New Guinea). Beginning as a foundation Lecturer in Religious Studies at the University of Papua New Guinea, Garry Trompf went on to treat Pacific religion in all its aspects (traditional, transitional, ecclesial, and theological) in *Melanesian Religion* (1991) and, with Tony Swain, on Aboriginal Australia in *The Religions of Oceania* (1995).

As for islander researchers, whereas a few of them studied traditional religions well away from their home islands—Tongan Epeli Hau'ofa, investigator of the Papuan Mekeo (1981) preeminent among them—most were diffident about "spying out" the habits and beliefs of other nearby peoples, even if some were willing to comment on their traditions. Some penetrating islander analyses of new religious movements have been made, with West Papuan/Irianese Benny Giay on Wissel Lakes prophet Zakheus Pakage (1995) and Solomonese Esau Tuza on the Christian Fellowship Church of New Georgia being the best known. In the mainstream scholarship, high indigenous achievements have been in the domain of contextual theology, relating the claims of the Christian Gospel to autochthonous values. An example of this is the recent impressive work by Sevati Tuwere, *Vanua: Towards a Fijian Theology of Place* (2002), on land, worship, and ruling authority in biblical and Fijian understandings. Most islander religious writing is in the Pacific region's theological journals, or in theological collections, or in the form of creative literature.

BIBLIOGRAPHY

Barker, John, ed. *Christianity in Oceania: Ethnographic Perspectives.* Lanham, Md., 1990.

Billings, Dorothy. *Cargo Cult as Theater: Political Performance in the Pacific.* Lanham, Md., 2002.

Ernst, Manfred. *Winds of Change: Rapidly Growing Religious Groups in the Pacific Islands.* Suva, Fiji Islands, 1984.

Forman, Charles H. *The Island Churches of the South Pacific.* Maryknoll, N.Y., 1982.

Garrett, John. *Footsteps in the Sea: Christianity in Oceania to World War II,* and *Where Nets Were Cast: Christianity in Oceania since World War II.* Geneva, 1992–1997.

Giay, Benny. *Zakheus Pakage and his Communities: Indigenous Religious Discourse, Socio-Political Resistance, and Ethnohistory of the Me of Irian Jaya.* Amsterdam, 1995.

Goodenough, Ward H. *Under Heaven's Brow: Pre-Christian Religious Tradition in Chuuk.* Philadelphia, 2002.

Hau'ofa, Epeli. *Mekeo: Inequality and Ambivalence in a Village Society.* Canberra, 1981.

Herdt, Gilbert H., ed. *Ritual Homosexuality in Melanesia.* Berkeley, Calif., 1982.

Herdt, Gilbert H., and Michele Stephen, eds. *The Religious Imagination in New Guinea.* Piscataway, N.J., 1989.

Hezel, Francis. *The First Taint of Civilization: A History of the Caroline and Marshall Islands in Pre-Colonial Days, 1521–1885.* Pacific Islands Monograph Series. Honolulu, 1983.

Keesing, Roger M. *Kwaio Religion.* New York, 1982.

Lattas, Andrew. *Cultures of Secrecy: Reinventing Race in Bush Kaliai Cargo Cults.* New Directions in Anthropological Writing. Madison, Wisc., 1998.

Lindstrom, Lamont. *Cargo Cult: Strange Stories of Desire from Melanesia and Beyond.* Honolulu, 1993.

MacDonald, Mary N. *Mararoko: A Study in Melanesian Religion.* American University Studies, Ser. XI, 45. New York, 1991.

Mageo, Jeanette M., and Alan Howard, eds. *Spirits in Culture, History, and Mind.* New York, 1996.

Meigs, Anna. *Food, Sex, and Pollution: A New Guinea Religion.* New Brunswick, N.J., 1984.

Robbins, Joel. *Becoming Sinners: Christianity and Moral Torment in Papua New Guinea Society.* Berkeley, Calif., 2004.

Swain, Tony, and Garry Trompf. *The Religions of Oceania.* New York, 1995.

Trompf, Garry. *Melanesian Religion.* Cambridge, U.K., 1991.

Trompf, Garry. *Payback: The Logic of Retribution in Melanesian Cultures.* Cambridge, U.K., 1994.

Trompf, Garry and Friedegard Tomasetti. *Religions of Melanesia: A Bibliographic Survey.* Greenport, Conn., 2005.

Tuwere, Sevati. *Vanua: Towards a Fijian Theology of Place.* Auckland, New Zealand, 2002.

Tuzin, Donald. *The Voice of the Tambaran: Truth and Illusion in Ilahita Arapesh Religion.* Berkeley, Calif., 1980.

Whitehouse, Harvey. *Arguments and Icons: Divergent Modes of Religiosity.* Oxford, 2000.

GARRY W. TROMPF (2005)

OCEANS. It is natural to begin a survey of the mythology of oceans with their eponymous deity, the Greek god Okeanos (etymology unknown). All evidence testifies that Okeanos was originally conceived as a river god, rather than a god of the salt sea. This illustrates a characteristic difficulty: To treat rivers, springs, and fountains, or the symbolic and religious associations of water in general, exceeds the compass of this article, but such distinctions are not always rigorous in the mythological traditions.

In the pantheon defined by Hesiod's *Theogony,* Okeanos is the offspring of Ouranos (Sky) and Gaia (Earth), and thus of the race of Titans that included Kronos, the father of Zeus. With his sister Tethys as consort, Okeanos produced the vast brood of Okeanids, spirits of rivers and streams. Parallel to Okeanos is Pontos (Sea): Born of Gaia alone, he unites with her to engender Nereus, whence the Nereids, a species of sea nymphs corresponding to the Okeanids. While Pontos remains a bare abstraction, Okeanos is imagined as dwelling with Tethys at the edge of the world, which he encircles. In descriptions of the shields of Achilles (Homer) and Herakles (attributed to Hesiod), Okeanos occupies the rim.

References in Homer (*Iliad* 14.200f., 244ff., 301f.), as well as in Plato, Vergil, Orphic texts, and elsewhere, identify Okeanos and Tethys as the source (*genesis*) of gods or of the universe. Details of this cosmogony are obscure; according to one version, the primordial waters brought forth an egg that initiated the process of creation (Orphic fragments 54, 57). Okeanos was related to underworld rivers such as the Styx, which was his daughter, according to Hesiod (*Theogony* 361; cf. Plato, *Phaedo* 112e). The Isle of the Blessed, where souls of heroes dwelled, was in Okeanos's waters (*Odyssey* 4.562–568). The relationship between the cosmogonic role of Okeanos and water as the fundamental element in Thales's philosophy is moot.

Okeanos was occasionally represented in sculptures and sarcophagus reliefs, but does not appear to have had a specific cult. The sea was worshiped and appeased in the name of Poseidon, later identified with the Roman Neptune. The primitive evolution of Poseidon is obscure (he is conspicuously associated with the horse). In the Olympian scheme, Poseidon received the waters as his province from Zeus. He was responsible for maritime calm and turbulence, and for earthquakes. As consort of the Okeanid (or Nereid) Amphitrite, he was father of the gigantic Triton, whose torso terminated in a serpent's tail. Various pre-Olympian deities abided in the sea, notably Proteus, who shared with Nereus and with the Nereid Thetis (mother of Achilles) the power to metamorphose and to foretell the future.

The idea of encompassing waters survived into medieval geography, as in the map attached to Ibn Khaldūn's *Muqaddimah* (the name Ūqyānūs in one manuscript renders "Okeanos"). The earth is said by Islamic writers to float on the sea like a grape or an egg.

In the cultures of the ancient Near East, oceanic waters figured largely in cosmogonic myths. According to Sumerian tradition, in the beginning was Nammu (Sea), whence arose a mountain representing heaven and earth, later separated by the air god Enlil. In the Babylonian creation story, recited at the New Year, the primordial gods are two: the masculine Apsu, representing sweet waters, and the feminine Tiamat, the salt-water ocean, from whose union come the gods. Apsu is vanquished by younger gods, but Tiamat continues the battle with the help of Kingu and other monstrous offspring; she is defeated by the storm god Marduk and divided in two, one part of her being raised to contain the upper waters. From the *Epic of Gilgamesh,* it appears that the land of the dead was reached by crossing a body of water. The same narrative incorporates the Sumerian tradition of a great flood, perhaps representing a return to the primordial state.

In Canaanite myth, the senior deity El favors Yam (Sea) against his own son, Baal (associated with fertility and rain). Yam surrenders to Baal and is spared; also vanquished is the serpent Lotan, related to the Hebrew Leviathan (cf. also the defeats of Rahab and Tannin: *Ps.* 74:13, 89:11; *Is.* 51:9; etc.). The biblical sea waters seem to retain a threatening aspect, as though not entirely submissive to creation; certain passages indicate the sea as the site of God's throne (e.g., *Ps.* 104:3; *Ez.* 28:2).

In Egyptian sources, the waters of Nun, on which the earth rests, are sometimes identified as the origin of life. At the parting of the waters appears the primal hill. Nun was also conceived as surrounding the earth (like Okeanos), so that the sun emerged each day from his waters in the east. The route to the afterworld is the river Nile, host also to aquatic deities such as the crocodile, but because the Nile was believed to have its source in the netherworld (Pyramid Texts 1551a, 1557b), the distinction between river and primal waters is not absolute.

The *Ṛgveda* (10.121) alludes to a cosmic egg (Prajāpati) that emerged from water, an idea elaborated in later commentaries (*Śatapatha Brāhmaṇa* 11.1.6) that also record a flood. The identification of Varuṇa as god of the sea is post-Vedic. The ocean is the source of *amṛta,* the liquor of immortality (analogously, the Greek ambrosia is sometimes connected with the ocean). In Hindu mythology, the cobra-like sea demons called *nāgas* (feminine dragons are called *nāginis*) have their kingdom in the west or alternatively are imagined as dwelling in the underworld. In Cambodia, the first Khmer dynasty is said to have sprung from the union of the daughter of a *nāga* king with a Hindu prince.

In Chinese myth, where nature deities play a relatively unimportant part, the four seas that surround the earth are associated each with a dragon king. In one legend the king of all the dragons arose from the sea and prevented the first emperor of Qin from voyaging to the islands of the immortals. The antiquity of such stories is in doubt, as they appear to have been influenced by Hindu myth. Undeniably ancient (dating from the Zhou dynasty) is the story of the flood, which was dammed, channeled, and drained by the god Yu with the help of a dragon, Yu then became the founder of China's first dynasty.

The Ainu (the aborigines of Japan) tell of a small bird that dispersed the primal waters by the motion of its wings. In the *Kojiki,* the main compendium of ancient Japanese myth, the original chaos is compared to oily water, but the sea's major role appears in the tale of the sons of Ninigi, the divine ancestor of Japan's emperors. The younger son, Po-wori, a hunter, borrows and loses the fishhook of his brother Po-deri. A sea deity constructs a boat and advises Po-wori to sail to the palace of Watatsumi, god of the sea, and his daughter Tōyōtama. Po-wori marries Tōyōtama but later desires to return home. Watatsumi recovers the lost hook and gives his son-in-law two jewels to control the tides. Coming home on a crocodile, Po-wori subdues his elder brother. Tōyōtama, assuming the form of a crocodile, bears her husband a child and then returns to the sea, ashamed that he has observed her thus. Her younger sister tends and marries the son, and from this union is born the first Japanese emperor. Shrines are devoted to Watatsumi and other sea divinities.

Meander patterns on Paleolithic vessels of Europe, often in association with maternal figures, eggs, snakes, and waterfowl, suggest water as a fertility symbol. In the Finnish epic *Kalevala* (old version), which preserves Finno-Ugric traditions, the world is created out of eggs laid by an eagle on the knee that the hero Väinämöinen lifts from the sea (Väinä means "still water"). Väinämöinen subsequently sails to death's domain and escapes meshes laid to trap him by metamorphosing into various forms. The Saami (Lapp) god Cacce Olmai (Water Man), a deity of fishing, is said to assume various shapes; also reported is a mermaidlike creature called Akkruva, similar to the Inuit (Eskimo) Inue, a kind of merman.

In Celtic myths, there is a paradisiacal island called Brittia located in the ocean. This ancient account is transmitted by the Byzantine historian Procopius (cf. the Arthurian Avalon, the Irish Tir-na-nogue). Islands are the object of voyages by various heroes or demigods. Bran, a sea giant, encounters an isle of women, an isle of laughter and joy, and other fantastical places on his journey. Similarly, Brendan, in search of the Land of Promise, encounters enchanted islands and monsters; one island proves to be the back of a gigantic sea creature (cf. Sindbad's first voyage). The Roman general Sertorius is said by Plutarch to have attempted such a journey from Spain, which suggests a possible syncretism of Greek and Iberian traditions. The inspiration of Brendan's legend is evident in Dante's version of Odysseus's last voyage.

The province of the sea fell on the Celtic god or hero Ler, and more especially to his son, Manannán mac Lir, patron of sailors and merchants and the eponymous deity of the Isle of Man. Manannán rode the steed Enbarr, which could traverse water as easily as land (cf. the kelpie or sea horse in Scottish folklore).

In the Eddas, the god of the sea is Ægir (cognate with *aqua*), a member of the race of giants who is friendly to the gods. His wife is Ran, and a kenning (metaphorical phrase) speaks of the waves of Ægir's daughters. Ægir is the gods' ale-brewer and a giver of banquets. Norse myth tells of various sea monsters such as the huge fishlike creature called the kraken, as well as mermen and mermaids (see the thirteenth-century *King's Mirror*), the belief in which has persisted into modern times among fishermen of New England and elsewhere.

In the Americas, the creation myths of the Chorti, Maya Indians of Guatemala, mention four seas that are distinguished by color surrounding and beneath the world, with monstrous creatures (angels in Christianized versions) beyond the waters. Among the people of Santa Elena, there is a story of a race of giants who came from across the sea. There is a hint of a primal sea in the *Popol Vuh,* the sacred book of the Quiché Maya of Guatemala.

A widespread North American variant involves the creation of land upon the primordial ocean by means of a diver, whether divine, human, or animal, who brings mud or earth up from the sea bottom. In the Salinan version (California), a dove fetches the substance after a flood produced by the Old Woman of the Sea; a turtle is the agent in Maidu (California) and Blackfeet myth. In a Huron creation account, a toad is successful; in a Mandan (North Dakota) version, it is a duck, while other stories feature the muskrat (Assiniboine, Great Plains), the water beetle (Cherokee), and the crawfish (Yuchi). There are also versions in which the waters simply recede. The Navajo emergence myth, which like the Hopi myth describes four worlds associated with four directions and four colors, has four seas as well. The Winnebago Indians (Great Plains) distinguish two classes of water powers; streams are masculine, while the subterranean waters that uphold the earth are feminine.

Altaic myth (Siberia) also exhibits versions of the diver tale, with the diver as swallow, loon, goose, or other waterfowl. Elsewhere the diver is a man or devil, often in the guise of a bird; a Christian Romanian version casts Satan as the diver. In a Samoyed flood story, a bird discovers land in a manner reminiscent of the bird in the narrative of Noah's ark. The theme of the ark occurs also in Buriat myth. Mention may also be made of a Khanty (Yenisei River) creation story, according to which the earth rests on three great fish, the sinking of which generates floods.

In a Polynesian account, Māui or another deity brings land up from the sea bottom. A Maori tale tells of a conflict between Ta-whiri-ma-tea, the god of storms or winds, and his brother Tangaroa, here the father creator of the world. Ta-whiri-ma-tea attacks Tangaroa, who takes refuge in the ocean. One of Tangaroa's two children, representing fish, retreats to the water. The other child, representing reptiles, hides in the forest, whence the antagonism between the sea and humans, who are descended from the forest deity. The Polynesian practice of burying the dead in canoe-shaped dugouts may reflect a custom of setting bodies adrift to reach the ancestral home or land of the dead. It was believed that souls were carried to Bulotu, the Tongan land of the dead, in an invisible canoe presided over by Hikuleo, the Tongan god of the dead and half-brother of Tangaroa. Near his house, in one account, were the waters of life that could confer immortality. The land of the dead, usually located to the west, was the special destination of chiefs and other notables. Legends tell of parties sailing, usually by mistake, to Bulotu.

Marine myths are not widespread in Africa, but mention may be made of a Yao (Mozambique) story in which human beings are fished out of the sea by a chameleon.

From the foregoing survey, certain broad themes may be identified. The ocean is often conceived as the primordial element, from which land and sometimes living creatures emerge. It surrounds the earth and lies under it, and beyond its waters reside the departed or the blessed, who are sometimes visited by the intrepid voyager. Now and then flood waters challenge creation. The ocean is inhabited by various monsters, often serpentine and capable of metamorphosis. Marine deities are sometimes the ancestors of imperial dynasties. Finally, in some accounts the waters of the deep are life-giving, or the source of life-giving brews.

See Also Water.

Bibliography

On the Greek Okeanos, the best study is Jean Rudhardt's *Le thème de l'eau primordiale dans la mythologie grecque* (Bern, 1971). For the Old Testament, there is a useful survey of oceanic themes in Phillipe Reymond's *L'eau, sa vie, et sa signification dans l'ancien testament* (Leiden, 1958). The ancient Near Eastern materials may be consulted in the collection edited by J. B. Pritchard, *Ancient Near Eastern Texts relating to the Old Testament,* 3d ed. (Princeton, N.J., 1969). A good sampling of creation myths, in which primordial waters play a prominent role, is Barbara C. Sproul's *Primal Myths: Creating the World* (San Francisco, 1979). The encyclopedic *Mythology of All Races,* 13 vols., edited by Louis H. Gray and George Foot Moore (Boston, 1916–1932), is uneven and often out of date in method and content, but it contains much firsthand material and is the most extensive compendium. Robert W. Williamson's *Religious and Cosmic Beliefs of Central Polynesia,* 2 vols. (1933; New York, 1977), presents the numerous variant versions. The volume *Asiatic Mythology,* edited by Joseph Hackin et al. (New York, 1932), is especially good on modern myths, as in the contribution on China by Henri Maspero.

The Japanese *Kojiki* is available in a new translation by Donald L. Philippi (Tokyo and Princeton, N.J., 1969). Sources of Celtic mythology are widely scattered, but there is a readable summary by Charles Squire, *The Mythology of the British Islands: Celtic Myth and Legend, Poetry and Romance* (1909; Fulcroft, Pa., 1975), though it is inconsistent in citing sources and not always reliable in interpretation; see also Marie-Louise Sjoestedt's *Gods and Heroes of the Celts* (London, 1949). There is some information relevant to oceans in Martin Ninck's *Die Bedeutung des Wassers im Kult und Leben der Alten: Eine symbolgeschichtliche Untersuchung* (Leipzig, 1921), along with rich if speculative interpretative suggestions. For works cited in the text, see *The King's Mirror,* translated by Laurence Marcellus Larson (New York, 1917); *The Old Kalevala* of Elias Lönnrot, translated by Francis Peabody Magoun, Jr. (Cambridge, Mass., 1969); and *Pyramid Texts,* edited by Samuel A. B. Mercer (New York, 1952), in which excursuses 14 and 15 are particularly relevant. For Ibn Khaldun, see Franz Rosenthal's translation of the *Muqaddimah,* 3 vols., 2d ed. (Princeton, N.J., 1967); the map is the frontispiece to volume 1. A readable book on modern folklore is Horace Beck's *Folklore and the Sea* (Middletown, Conn., 1973). For Maya traditions, see John G. Foughts *Chorti (Mayan) Texts* (Philadelphia, 1972).

New Sources

Cabartous, Alain. *Le ciel dans la Mer: christianisme et civilisation maritime.* Paris, 1990.

Costa, Giancarlo. *Misteri e leggende del mare.* Milan, 1994.

Fuson, Robert. *Legendary Islands of the Ocean Seas.* Sarasota, Fla., 1998.

Merrien, Jean. *La légendaire de la mer.* Rennes, France, 2003.

Oliver, J. G., ed. *The Sea in Antiquity.* Oxford, 2000.

DAVID KONSTAN (1987)
Revised Bibliography

OCKHAM, WILLIAM SEE WILLIAM OF OCKHAM

ÓÐINN

ÓÐINN (Odin, Wōden, Wuotan) is the chief god of Germanic mythology. His name, meaning "inspired or intoxicated one," developed from the Proto-Germanic. **Wōþanaz,* which is related to IE **wātós,* the source of the Old Norse noun *óðr* (inspired mental activity, intelligence). Non-Germanic cognates are Latin *vātēs* and Old Irish *fáith,* both meaning "seer." Described as the best and the oldest of all the gods by Snorri Sturluson (1179–1241), Óðinn is a complex figure whose many names point to the diversity of his functions (Lorenz, 1984, pp. 91–95, 290–304). He is the father of the Æsir (the dominant group of gods), a great magician and seeker of wisdom, the master of runes, the patron of poets, the lord of battles, the god of the dead, and a betrayer of his human devotees.The brothers Óðinn, Vili, and Vé are the first Æsir, the sons of Borr and the giantess Bestla. They initiate the Æsir hostility against giants, killing their oldest maternal ancestor Ymir to create the world from his body and later repudiating three giantesses who seem to be hoping for husbands. Óðinn often appears in triads of gods and is even called Þriði (Third), leading some to compare Óðinn, Vili, and Vé with the Christian Trinity (Lorenz, p. 146). Like genealogies of Anglo-Saxon kings tracing their ancestry to Wōden, euhemeristic tales describing the legendary history of Scandinavia claim Óðinn as the father of the medieval royal dynasties. In addition, some of his names suggest that various peoples who originally had some other chief god had come to identify that god with Óðinn. For example, Óðinn's name *Gautr* originally may have been the name of the eponymous father of the people of Gautland. His name *Skilfingr* may have been the name of the founding ancestor of the Ynglings of Sweden, whom the Old English poem *Beowulf* instead calls the *Scylfingas.*

From his high seat in the citadel Ásgarðr, Óðinn can look over the nine worlds of the Norse cosmos. His ravens, Huginn (Thought) and Muninn (Memory), bring him news every morning. Óðinn lacks an eye, and he often wears a hat and a cloak. His weapon is the dwarf-made spear Gungnir, and his gold arm-ring Draupnir drips eight equally heavy arm-rings every nine days. His horse is the eight-legged Sleipnir. Despite his power, Óðinn cannot prevent the death of his son Baldr, which leads to the destruction of the Æsir at Ragnarǫk by giants and other monsters (who are also destroyed in this final battle between these forces). Each god has his own opponent in this final conflict, and Óðinn is killed by the wolf Fenrir.

Óðinn is called Alfaðir (All-father), perhaps under Christian influence, as he is not the father of all the gods. Þórr is the illegitimate child of Óðinn's giant mistress, Jörð, and Baldr is the legitimate son of Óðinn and his wife (the goddess Frigg), but the Vanir deities (the second group of gods) are unrelated. Óðinn embarks upon short-term sexual liaisons, usually as a means to some other end, and in a few cases children result. The eddic poem *Hárbarðsljóð* portrays Óðinn boasting about his affairs. In one Norse tradition, he is the creator of human beings: the eddic poem *Vǫluspá* says that Óðinn and two companions shaped the first man and woman from two logs.

WISDOM AND KNOWLEDGE. Most of Óðinn's activities involve his search for wisdom. He asks tidings of the dead and embarks upon journeys during which he gains knowledge through confrontation with supernatural beings. Óðinn's knowledge and the supernatural sharpness of his one eye are his reward for exchanging the other eye for a drink from wise Mímir's well. He also converses with Mímir's head, cut off by the Vanir but magically preserved by the Æsir. Several myths portray Óðinn proving his immense knowledge, as in the eddic poem *Grímnismál.* King Geirrǫðr mistakes Óðinn (traveling under the name Grímnir) for a malicious magician and chains him between two fires. After eight nights, Geirrǫðr's son brings the stranger a drink and is rewarded with a recitation of mythological lore, ending with fifty names for Óðinn that reveal Grímnir's true identity. Óðinn's torture and recitation have been interpreted as a shamanistic performance or the ritual education of a royal heir, but it is more likely an abstract reflection of Scandinavian concepts of sovereignty, for it is Óðinn's mastery of sacred knowledge that justifies his lordship. In the eddic poem *Vafþrúðnismál,* Óðinn challenges the giant Vafþrúðnir to a riddle contest to see who knows the most mythological lore. Defeat means death for the vanquished, and Óðinn is the victor. Paradoxically, Óðinn can demonstrate his superiority in lore over the giants, but some myths show that he needs knowledge about the fate of the world and the gods that they possess but he does not.

Snorri describes Óðinn as a great worker of magic, and Georges Dumézil considers Óðinn to be the Germanic representative of the Indo-European divine king-magician. He knows magic charms and songs, and in unmanly fashion he employs the women's sorcery he learned from Freyja. Although others are experts in the use of runes, Óðinn possesses the most extensive knowledge of their magic. The eddic poems *Hávamál* (sts. 138–139) and *Sigrdrífumál* (st. 3) call Óðinn the inventor of the runes, and the inscription on the Noleby Stone in Sweden (c. 600 CE) says that the runes come from the gods. *Hávamál* describes how Óðinn gained the secrets of runes by hanging from the World Tree for nine nights, wounded with a spear, a sacrifice of himself to himself. All the elements of this myth have parallels in Norse tradition, and it was probably not influenced by the Christian crucifixion. *Hávamál* also enumerates many of the spells Óðinn can cast, such as curing illness, stopping missiles in midair, dispelling witches, and inspiring irresistible love.

INSPIRER, INCITER, AND DECEIVER. Óðinn's patronage of poetry is implicit in his name. The meaning "inspired mental activity" for the Old Norse word *óðr* is confirmed by its use in court verse in the sense of the word *poetry*, the poet being "a smith of inspired thought" (*óðar smiðr*). Óðinn spoke in verse, and he granted his protégé Starkaðr the ability to compose poetry as fast as he could talk. Óðinn's most concrete link with poetry is his acquisition of the mead of poetry. Brewed by the dwarfs, who had to relinquish it to the giants, Óðinn obtains it by seducing its giantess guardian, swallowing it all, changing into an eagle, flying to Ásgarðr, and spewing it out into three crocks the Æsir had ready.

As the god of battle, Óðinn opened the hostilities between the Æsir and Vanir by hurling his spear into the enemy camp. This gesture became a ritual beginning for other battles; it consecrates the dead and captured foes to Óðinn, who houses the ever-growing host of dead warriors in Valhalla for eventual use as his army at Ragnarǫk. Indeed, in order to obtain enough fighters, Óðinn time and again instigates the argument that leads to war. As a protector of warriors, Óðinn teaches his chosen heroes tactics that ensure their victory in combat; for example, he instructs Harald Wartooth to deploy his forces in the field in the shape of a wedge to break the opponents' line (Turville-Petre, pp. 212, 215). Óðinn is also the patron of the turbulent and powerful *berserkir* (bear shirts) and *ulfheðnar* (wolf skins), fighters who attack with frenzied fury. Writing around 1070, Adam of Bremen comments: "Óðinn, that is, 'frenzy,' wages war and provides man with courage against foes" (*Gesta Hammaburgensis,* 4: 26: "woðan, id est furor, bella gerit hominique ministrat virtutem contra inimicos").

Óðinn has qualities that would be valued negatively if they belonged to a member of a subordinate group, but as a member of the dominant class, he can ignore such attributes as the unmanliness associated with Freyja's magic. In the eddic poem *Lokasenna* (st. 22), he is accused of unfairness in granting victory, but if he acknowledges that he let the less deserving win, he justifies himself elsewhere by claiming he needed heroes to help him face Fenrir at Ragnarǫk. However, he clearly relishes inciting conflicts, preventing peace, and deceiving those who serve him. For example, when Starkaðr pronounces the ominous formula "Now I give thee to Óðinn!" after tying a noose of calf gut around his lord's neck as he hits him with a reed, Óðinn changes the weak entrail into a sturdy rope and the reed into a spear, transforming the sham sacrifice into a regicide (*Gautreks saga,* ch. 7; see Turville-Petre, 1964, p. 45). Óðinn betrays his worshiper Harald Wartooth, battering him to death personally (*Gesta Danorum,* 8.220), and he does not hesitate to perjure himself (*Hávamál,* st. 108–109). No wonder that the human Dagr in the eddic poem *Helgakviða Hundingsbana* (II, st. 34), after observing that the god has stirred up strife between siblings, passionately declares that Óðinn is responsible for all evil.

THE ÓÐINN CULT. Óðinn is also called the God of the Hanged, and his cult apparently did involve human sacrifice, as suggested by the story of Starkaðr's unintended killing of Víkarr. Human sacrifice to Óðinn seems to be depicted on the Gotland picture stone of Stora Hammars, and Tacitus (*Germania,* ch. 9) says that Mercury (i.e., Óðinn) was the only god to whom the tribes sacrificed men. A number of shamanistic elements (intoxicants, self-sacrifice, torture, raven messengers, shape changing, passive receptivity to the spirit world of sorcery) are associated with Óðinn, but most though not all scholars see among the Germanic peoples no evidence of shamanistic practices such as drumming and dancing to induce a trance state.

Place-names commemorating Óðinn make up less than ten percent of theophorous place-names (those bearing the name of a deity) in mainland Scandinavia. They are most frequent in southern Sweden and Denmark, are infrequent in southern Norway, and are not found in Iceland at all. However, the place-names based on *-vin* (pasture-land) and *-akr* (acre, field) are ancient, and their existence contradicts the theory that his cult was a new one that displaced the older worship of Týr. Týr is the Germanic development of an Indo-European god, so he probably predates Óðinn in absolute terms, but evidently his religious importance diminished over time, whereas that of Óðinn did not.

Other evidence for the age of the cult of Óðinn comes from the weekday names in Germanic. The standard translation of the Latin *dies Mercurii* was "Wōdan's day" (e.g., Dan. *Onsdag,* Eng. *Wednesday*), and as the translation of the names of the days of the week took place in the fourth century CE, veneration of Óðinn must have been widespread in all of the western and, probably, northern Germanic regions at this time. Depictions of Óðinn may date back to the Bronze Age, if the large spear-bearing god figures on some southern Swedish rock carvings represent him. Fifth-century gold bracteates showing a god accompanied by birds may also represent Óðinn. (Bracteates are Germanic medallions, probably inspired by Roman coins, that depict figures and scenes that are still not fully understood.) The earliest definite representations of Óðinn are sixth- and seventh-century Swedish helmet decorations with Odinic cult scenes. Óðinn is repeatedly depicted on ninth-century picture stones, at times accompanied by birds, more commonly riding his eight-legged horse. In the next century, pagan Norwegian court poets honored their patrons by depicting them as warriors whom Óðinn welcomes to Valhalla, as in the eulogies for Eiríkr Blood-axe (d. 954) and Hákon the Good (d. c. 960). Adam of Bremen, who used eyewitness accounts, says that Óðinn was worshiped in the temple at Uppsala, which was still pagan then.

Theologically, Óðinn is related to the Indian god Varuṇa. Both have the knowledge of sorcery, the gift of changing shape, and control of the fortunes of battle. Both are the gods of rulers and poets, and both receive human sacrifice. Óðinn also has parallels with the Indian god Indra, who has an encounter with the monster Mada (Drunkenness) and who is also the recipient of *soma*, the intoxicating sacrificial liquor that gives poetic ability, immortality, and knowledge of the divine. As with the mead of poetic inspiration, *soma* was brought to the gods by an eagle, or possibly Indra in the form of an eagle.

See Also Berserkers; Eddas; Germanic Religion; Jötnar; Njǫrðr; Snorri Sturluson.

Bibliography

Clunies Ross, Margaret. *Prolonged Echoes: Old Norse Myths in Medieval Northern Society*, vol. 1, *The Myths*. Odense, Denmark, 1994.

Dillmann, François-Xavier. "Georges Dumézil et la religion germanique: L'interprétation du dieu Odhinn." In *Georges Dumézil à la découverte des Indo-Européens*, edited by Jean-Claude Rivière, pp. 157–186. Paris, 1979.

Dumézil, Georges. *Gods of the Ancient Northmen*. Berkeley, Calif., 1973.

Falk, Hjalmar. *Odensheite*. Oslo, 1924.

Helm, Karl. *Woðan: Ausbreitung und Wanderung seines Kultes*. Giessen, Germany, 1946.

Lindow, John. *Scandinavian Mythology: An Annotated Bibliography*. New York, 1988.

Lindow, John. *Handbook of Norse Mythology*. Santa Barbara, Calif., 2001.

Lorenz, Gottfried. *Gylfaginning/Snorri Sturluson*. Darmstadt, Germany, 1984.

Polomé, Edgar C. "The Indo-European Heritage in Germanic Religion: The Sovereign Gods." In *Athlon: Satura Grammatica in honorem Francisci R. Adrados*, edited by A. Bernabé et al., vol. 1, pp. 401–411. Madrid, 1984.

Starkey, Kathryn. "Imagining an Early Odin: Gold Bracteates as Visual Evidence?" *Scandinavian Studies* 71 (1999): 373–391.

Turville-Petre, Gabriel. *Myth and Religion of the North: The Religion of Ancient Scandinavia*. New York, 1964.

Vries, Jan de. *Altgermanische Religionsgeschichte*, vol. 2. 2d rev. ed. Berlin, 1967.

Elizabeth Ashman Rowe (2005)

OFFERINGS See ALMSGIVING; SACRIFICE; TITHES

OGYŪ SORAI

OGYŪ SORAI (1666–1728), Japanese Confucian of the Ancient Learning school (Kogaku). Sorai was born in Edo (modern-day Tokyo), the son of Ogyū Hōan (1626–1705), personal physician to Tokugawa Tsunayoshi (1646–1709), lord of the Tatebayashi domain and later the fifth Tokugawa shogun. As a child Sorai began studying classical Chinese and at the age of seven entered the academy headed by Hayashi Gahō (1618–1680), the son of the academy's founder, Hayashi Razan (1583–1657). He progressed quickly in his studies and by the age of nine was able to write simple compositions; he even kept a diary in classical Chinese.

Sorai's otherwise conventional education and upbringing were disturbed in 1679, when he was thirteen. For reasons that are not clear, in that year Tsunayoshi banished Sorai's father to the village of Honnō in Kazusa, sixty miles from Edo. The exile was understandably difficult, as the family was denied the amenities of urban life and the company of its social equals. While these unfavorable conditions forced the adolescent Sorai to study on his own, it also gave him firsthand knowledge of rural life. In 1690 his father was pardoned and the family returned to Edo, where Hōan once again served as Tsunayoshi's physician. Sorai established an academy in Shiba, near the Zōjōji, the imposing Pure Land temple. Here he attracted the attention of the temple's abbot, Ryōya, who helped him secure a position in the house of Yanagisawa Yoshiyasu (1658–1714), the shogun's chamberlain and confidante. Sorai served Yoshiyasu for fourteen years and performed a variety of tasks: he lectured on the Confucian classics, wrote formal Chinese-style histories, punctuated and annotated Chinese texts, and taught Yoshiyasu's retainers. In 1709 he resigned his position and in 1710 opened a school called the Ken'enjuku (Miscanthus Patch Academy) in Kayabachō, not far from Nihonbashi.

Sorai's personal life was rather tragic. In 1696 he married a woman named Kyūshi who bore him five children. She died in 1705, and in time all of their offspring died as well. In 1715 Sorai married the daughter of the Mito Confucian, Sasa Rikkei (1639–1698?), but she too died, sometime between 1717 and 1718, without bearing any children. The deaths of his wives and children, together with his own repeated bouts with tuberculosis, among other personal tragedies, made Sorai deeply religious. He came to believe that his survival was the work of an omniscient and omnipotent Heaven. He also attributed his scholarly successes to Heaven and believed that Heaven had chosen him to reveal to the world the long-obscured meaning of the Chinese classics. Although modern scholars have seen Sorai's belief in a sentient Heaven as a reaction to the neo-Confucians' more rationalistic view of Heaven, there seems little doubt that his beliefs had much to do with the unhappy circumstances of his personal life.

Sorai is best known for his dictum, "return to the past." The first manifestations of this neoclassicism in his work were literary. Inspired by the work of the Ming dynasty (1368–1644) literary critics Li P'an-lung (1514–1570) and Wang Shih-chen (1526–1590), he distinguished "ancient" and "modern" Chinese literary styles and urged his contemporaries to model their poetic and prose compositions on the former.

After his retirement and the opening of his school in 1710, Sorai turned from literary matters to the more conventional Confucian issues of self-cultivation and statecraft. He became a staunch critic of neo-Confucianism: in *Bendō* (Distinguishing the way) and *Benmei* (Distinguishing names) Sorai recommended that his contemporaries abandon the commentaries written by Zhu Xi (1130–1200) and his followers and instead study classical literary styles, etiquette, ceremonial practices, and forms of dress.

In 1721, Sorai was asked to advise the shogun, Tokugawa Yoshimune (1684–1751), and in this capacity he proposed countless institutional reforms, most of which survive in his *Seidan* (A discourse on government) and *Taiheisaku* (A proposal for a great peace). His most ambitious recommendation was his plan for the rustication of the warrior population of the cities and castle towns, which was designed to liberate warriors from the urban commercial economy and thus from the cycle of consumption, indebtedness, and poverty. His aim here was not to return the country to a natural economy, as is often thought, but to make warriors self-sufficient. He believed that classical Chinese institutions could solve the problems of his day, and so he recommended the adoption of the well-field, rank-in-merit, Six Office, and Six Ministry systems. He also suggested the introduction of supplementary salaries to allow talented individuals of low rank to serve in high positions, and the use of copper cash as a standard for determining the value of gold and silver.

Although Sorai's ideas and proposals seem to be the product of his profound sinophilia, they had more complex and diverse sources: first, his deep, personal belief in Heaven and its agents, the sages and early kings; second, his confidence that the culture and institutions created by the sages and early kings of Chinese antiquity were sufficiently universal to occasion their adoption in his time; third, his belief that social and cultural conditioning would eventually counteract the strangeness of Chinese culture and institutions; and finally, his belief in the value, even superiority, of classical Chinese civilization.

SEE ALSO Confucianism in Japan.

BIBLIOGRAPHY

de Bary, Wm. Theodore. "Sagehood as a Secular and Spiritual Ideal in Tokugawa Neo-Confucianism." In *Principle and Practicality: Essays in Neo-Confucianism and Practical Learning,* edited by Wm. Theodore de Bary and Irene Bloom, pp. 127–188. New York, 1979. An important revision of Maruyama Masao's interpretation that considers Ogyū Sorai's thought in the larger context of neo-Confucianism.

Lindin, Olof G. *The Life of Ogyū Sorai, a Tokugawa Confucian Philosopher.* Lund, 1973. The only biography of Sorai in English.

Maruyama Masao. *Studies in the Intellectual History of Tokugawa Japan.* Translated by Mikiso Hane. Princeton, 1974. A classic study of Tokugawa intellectual history that focuses on Sorai.

Yamashita, Samuel Hideo. "Nature and Artifice in the Writings of Ogyū Sorai, 1666–1728." In *Confucianism and Tokugawa Culture,* edited by Peter Nosco, pp. 65–138. Princeton, 1984. This essay represents current thinking on Sorai's thought.

Yoshikawa Kōjirō. *Jinsai, Sorai, Norinaga.* Tokyo, 1975. An important and highly regarded study of Sorai and two other seminal Tokugawa thinkers by a leading Japanese Sinologist. Translated into English by Kikuchi Yuji as *Jinsai, Sorai, Norinaga: Three Classical Philosophers of Mid-Tokugawa Japan* (Tokyo, 1983).

SAMUEL HIDEO YAMASHITA (1987)

ŌHRMAZD SEE AHURA MAZDĀ AND ANGRA MAINYU

OJIBWE (OJIBWA, OJIBWAY) RELIGIOUS TRADITIONS SEE ANISHINAABE RELIGIOUS TRADITIONS

OKINAWAN RELIGION.

Okinawa, one of the prefectures in Japan, was once an independent kingdom called Ryukyu. When it comes to Okinawan religion, it is usually assumed the whole religious tradition of the Ryukyu archipelago was governed by the Ryukyu dynasty. This archipelago is geographically a part of the subtropical islands extending from Kyushu to Taiwan. This area can be divided into four regions: Amami, Okinawa, Miyako, and Yaeyama. While there are some regional differences, they share a common religious tradition formed during the age of the Ryukyu kingdom (1429–1879). Therefore, the description of Okinawan religion here will combine the greater Ryukyuan cultural area with Amami, notwithstanding Amami has belonged to the Kyushu prefecture since the Meiji era and sometimes is not included in Okinawa.

Okinawan history after the fifteenth century is rather well known from the information gleaned from historical documents of China and Japan as well as the chronicle compiled by the Ryukyuan dynasty; its pre-fourteenth-century history, however, is still wrapped in relative obscurity. Archeological researches, with their continuing new discoveries, report that a foraging culture in Okinawa continued until the eleventh century. Agrarian communities started to emerge in about the twelfth century, and based upon increased productivity with iron a local clan arose in each region. Clan chieftains came to establish polities centered around the fortress called the *gusuku*. By the early fourteenth century, three kingdoms—the Northern (Hokuzan), Central (Chūzan), and Southern (Nanzan)—were consolidated. In 1429 Chūzan unified the others and founded the Ryukyu kingdom with *Shuri gusuku,* which is now a World Heritage Site. Being a tributary state, Ryukyu conducted a flourishing trade with China, and many Chinese cultural and religious traditions were introduced: the annual cycle of festivals, the lunar calendar, ancestral ceremonies and rites, *feng-shui* (geomancy), and Confucian thought. While trading with China, Ryukyu came to be a tributary state of Japan as well. In 1609 the Satsuma clan of Kyushu conquered Okinawa and brought a great deal of Japanese culture to Okinawa. In 1879 Ryukyu was annexed to Japan as the Okinawa prefecture. After experiencing the war and being occupied by the United States from 1945 to 1972, Okinawa came to belong to Japan.

There is no doubt that Okinawan religious culture is deeply linked to Japanese culture in light of the archeological data and the fact that Ryukyuan and Japanese have the same linguistic origin and share similar folk beliefs and practices. And since many have assumed that Okinawan culture has archaic cultural patterns of Japan, some scholars tended to see Okinawan religion and culture as an archive or museum of the archaic age of Japan. Religion and culture in Okinawa, however, should be understood in their own right, for Okinawan people have created their own unique tradition under given geographical and historical circumstances, arranging outside cultural influences such as those from China and Japan. Today many Japanese recognize the uniqueness of Okinawan culture, and the Okinawan people maintain a strong sense of identity derived from this uniqueness.

One of the most salient features of Okinawan religion can be seen in the modality of the village space. It is commonly accepted that a prototype of Okinawa's traditional village form is found in villages settled around agricultural society in around the twelfth century. A village modeled after such a typical traditional form usually has a sacred place called *utaki* (the name differs regionally: *uganju, mui, wan*). The *utaki* is typically located in the sacred grove in a mountain that is behind or near the village, and the core of this sanctuary is the natural stones, rocks, or trees that constitute a primordial altar. It is an important place where a large number of ceremonies and rites are performed. This *utaki* as a ceremonial center provides an orientation for village space, in some cases with the help of the *feng-shui* technique. The *utaki* is a place for *kami* (divine beings) to descend from the sky or the channel to communicate with diverse *kami,* including the ancestral god of their community and the god of *nirai-kanai* (the paradise over the ocean). The *utaki* also has a historically important role. It functioned as a ceremonial center of the polities in the *gusuku* era. Furthermore, located in *Shuri gusuku* (castle), it had become the ceremonial center of the city-state of the Ryukyu dynasty. The *utaki* has been functioning as the center of the space that continuously expands in its historical process.

Another prominent feature of Okinawan religion is the religious primacy of females. The family of the village founder lives nearest to the *utaki,* and this household plays an important role in a clan's religious activity. A female of that household attends the *utaki* and become a priestess to perform ceremonies and rites. This priestess is called *nī-gan* (literally, root *kami*). A male of that household called *nī-chu* ("root person"), who is the brother of the priestess and deals with the community's political affairs. Along with other priestesses, constituted by females of the village, the *nī-gan* priestess performs rituals for fertility in crops, rice, and fish as well as for their thanksgiving. Generally in Okinawa the religious activities of the village community are led by females; males, on the other hand, help females, handle mainly secular things, and do not engage in the main activity of communicating with the divine. Males were once forbidden to enter the *utaki.*

As just described, the female has a primacy in Okinawa's religious context. This primacy is also represented in the *onari-gami* (sister-*kami*) belief that sisters as *kami* protect and help their brothers with spiritual power. *Onari-gami* belief is found in the relationship between brothers and sisters; in other words, a female is not a *kami* for everyone. This belief in the spiritual power of sisters was adapted by the Ryukyu kingdom for its unique hierarchical system in the sixteenth century. In this system the king governed in the political realm while the king's sister (sometimes a female relative of king) called *chifijin* (*kikoeōkimi*) administered the kingdom religiously as she dispatched the state priestesses called *nuru* (*noro*) to each region. Under *chifijin,* the *nuru* led the local priestesses such as *nī-gan* and performed rites to glorify and protect the king and prayed for the prosperity of the kingdom.

Rituals at *utaki,* the sacred space of the villages, are mainly conducted with sacred songs, which are known as *kami-uta,* and also with praying verses. The contents of these songs and verses are diverse, ranging from a cosmogonic myth and legends regarding the founding of villages to prospective ritual songs, that is, songs to illustrate various production processes including farming, weaving, and house building. The ritual songs for the various productions in the community tend to sacralize them, many of which are related to mythic events. Priestesses in this prayer are mediators between the divine and human beings, conveying the divine revelation as perfomative through the sacred songs and verses. The priestesses in the Ryukyu dynasty conducted the rituals with sacred songs that were compiled in Omoro-sōshi. Ritual songs of Omoro-sōshi were collected songs of regions around the Okinawa and Amami islands (not including the Miyako and Yaeyama regions) from about the seventeenth to twentieth century. The Miyako and Yaeyama regions have many of their own *kami-uta* that have been passed down to priestesses by oral tradition.

The veneration of ancestral spirits is also a notable feature of religious tradition of Okinawan. It is said that this belief plays an important role in constructing the self-identity of the people in a kinship and lineage. Almost all the households have altars to revere their ancestors. Traditionally there is a belief in Okinawa that ancestral spirits are the beings that protect the descendant but at the same time bring misfortune if the people fail to revere them. This belief can be seen in ceremonies at the altar of the ancestor. The altar generally consists of three shelves. The upper shelf holds the memorial tablet (*tōtōmē*) with the name of ancestors, the middle shelf holds a censer, and the lower shelf is for the offerings. The tablet is treated as the place in which ancestral spirits reside. The oldest female attends this altar and prays to the ancestor for her family's fortune. The succession of the tablet between generations in the family should be carefully conducted with some strict rules and taboos. For example, the successor has to be the eldest son; a daughter may not be the successor.

The ceremonial formation of Okinawan ancestral belief was to some extent influenced by Buddhism, which was introduced from Japan and was further affected by Confucian thought from China. It is said that from the late seventeenth century to the mid-eighteenth century, Confucian ethics had a great impact on Okinawa, establishing the class system, the accession system, the ancestor tablet, the clan tomb, and various ceremonies, all of which are based on the patrilineal principle. And soon these cultural influences permeated the lower class of society. Despite these influences, some scholars argue that ancestral belief is based on an indigenous pattern in which people revere ancestral spirits as divine beings.

There is yet another altar in the household in Okinawa. Usually this altar consists of three stones and a censor and sits next to the hearth in the kitchen. This is called *hinukan* (or *finukan,* literally, hearth deity) and is also handled by the female. It is said that the *hinukan* altar was originally the hearth itself. The woman in a house prays to the *hinukan* deity for fortune and protection of all its inhabitants. To protect them, the deity needs to know important changes in the household, including birth, marriage, and death. Therefore, such changes in the family are recited every time and on a regular basis. Scholars also point out that the *hinukan* is also a duplicated ceremonial center or a channel to communicate with other deities.

In Okinawa, there are shamanic individuals called *yuta* (or *kankaryā* in Miyako, *nigēbī* in Yaeyama). Most shamans are female and male shamans are very few. Priestesses such as *nuru, nīgan,* and other lower priestesses are in charge of meeting the religious needs of their community. *Yutas,* on the other hand, are concerned with individual problems, telling a client's fortune and praying to cure an individual or his or her family's chronic disease through divine revelation or auguring. A person who is able to become a *yuta* tends to have a strong, innate spiritual power (*siji* or *seji*). Physical and mental anguish as well as auditory hallucination is a part of the initiation (called *kamidārī*) to become a *yuta.* From the Ryukyu dynasty era to the Meiji era, *yutas* were vigorously suppressed; nonetheless, they did not fade away, and even now many *yutas* are meeting individuals' religious needs. There have been cases in which a *yuta* with believers forms a religious group or founds a new religion.

Non-native religions in Okinawa, outside of Confucianism, *feng-shui,* and Buddhism from China and Japan, in the Ryukyu dynasty era include Christianity and Japanese new religions. Christianity was introduced in the Meiji era and was promulgated by missionaries who entered Okinawa after World War II. It is noted that the number of Christians in Okinawa is twice that of mainland Japan. New religions of mainland Japan have also been introduced to Okinawa and are firmly in place.

There is no doubt that so-called traditional ceremonies of the village communities in Okinawa have increasingly declined because of the decrease of successors resulting from changes in ways of life and the modernization of society. Rites and ceremonies have been simplified and in some cases have vanished. This does not mean, however, that Okinawan religion will disappear in the future, for it is clear that there remains a strong tendency and intention for Okinawan people to identify themselves in their culture derived from religious traditions and to revitalize the festival of each community.

SEE ALSO Japanese Religions, overview article; Kami.

BIBLIOGRAPHY

Hosei University. *Okinawa bunnka no kosou wo kangaeru* (*The Substratum of Okinawan Culture*). Tokyo, 1986.

Iha Fuyū. *Onarigami no shima* (*The Island of Onarigami*). Tokyo, 1926.

Ikegami Yoshimasa. "Okinawan Shamanism and Charismatic Christianity." *The Japan Christian Review* 59 (1993): 69–78.

Lebra, William P. *Okinawan Religion: Belief, Ritual, and Social Structure.* Honolulu, Hawaii, 1966.

Pearson, Richard. "The Place of Okinawa in Japanese Historical Identity." In *Multicultural Japan,* edited by Donald Denoon, Mark Hudson, Gavan McCormack, and Tessa Morris-Suzuki, pp. 95–116. New York, 1996.

Reichl, Christopher A. "The Okinawan New Religion Ijun: Innovation and Diversity in the Gender of the Ritual Specialist." *Japanese Journal of Religious Studies* 20, no. 4 (1994): 311–330.

Sakurai Tokutaro. *Okinawa no shamanism* (*Okinawan Shamanism*). Tokyo, 1973.

Sered, Susan. *Women of the Sacred Groves: Divine Priestesses of Okinawa.* New York, 1999.

Tanigawa Kenichi, ed. *Okinawa gaku no kadai* (*The Challenges of Okinawan Studies*). Tokyo, 1972.

Torigoe Kenzaburo. *Ryukyu shukyoshi no kenkyu* (*Study of the History of Ryukyuan Religion*). Tokyo, 1965.

Wacker, Monika. "Onarigami: Holy Women in the Twentieth Century." *Japanese Journal of Religious Studies* 30, nos. 3–4 (2003): 339–359.

CHARLES H. HAMBRICK (1987)
SUNAO TAIRA (2005)

ŌKUNINUSHI NO MIKOTO,

ŌKUNINUSHI NO MIKOTO, also known as Ōkuni or Ōnamuchi, is one of the major deities, or *kami,* in Japanese mythology. The earliest chronicle of Japan, the *Kojiki* (712 CE), refers to him as "the *kami* of the Great Land." According to legend, Ōkuni came to the land of Inaba with his brothers to court a Yakami beauty. Because his brothers made him carry their heavy bundle, he reached the shore of Inaba long after they did. On the beach Ōkuni found a white hare crying, and he asked the reason for the animal's distress. The hare replied that he had been bitten by a shark and that Ōkuni's brothers had advised him to bathe his wounds in salt water, but the treatment had only aggravated his pain. Ōkuni told him to use fresh water and apply sedge pollen to the wound. The hare was cured and in gratitude promised that the beautiful maiden of Yakami would marry none but Ōkuni.

Rebuffed by the Yakami maiden, Ōkuni's brothers learned of the hare's promise, and tried to kill Ōkuni. Twice he was crushed to death, first by a rolling boulder and later by a falling tree, but on both occasions his mother, Kamimusubi, came to his rescue and restored him to life.

Ōkuni then decided to leave Inaba and go to Izumo, where he met Suseri, daughter of the Sun Goddess's brother Susano-o. Suseri fell in love with Ōkuni, but to gain her hand he had to submit to many tests. After successfully passing all the ordeals, he was admitted to Susano-o's house and waited there for a chance to steal away with Susano-o's possessions. An opportunity came when Susano-o was lulled to sleep as Ōkuni picked lice from his hair. Ōkuni stole Susano-o's weapons and his koto (a zitherlike musical instrument that was sometimes used for sorcery) and carried Suseri away on his back.

Ōkuni married Suseri, but he had a roving eye and courted beautiful maidens from lands as far away as Koshi and Yamato. Although Suseri was jealous, she could do nothing about his liaison with other women, many of whom helped him to attain power and wealth.

Ōkuni allied himself with Sukunahikona, a dwarf god who had crossed the sea to Izumo in a bean-pod boat. Shortly thereafter the forces of Amaterasu reached Izumo's frontiers, and a power struggle ensued. After long negotiations Ōkuni renounced his political power and retired to Kizuki Shrine (later known as Izumo Shrine). He did, however, retain spiritual power over Izumo.

Ever since these legends were incorporated into the *Kojiki,* the high priest (*kuni no miyatsuko*) of Izumo Shrine has enjoyed the privilege of presenting congratulatory prayers upon the accession of each sovereign. Legend has it that Ōkuni meets with other deities from all over Japan once per year in Izumo during the tenth lunar month, usually the season of the first crop-tasting festivals. He is revered as the guardian of good marriages and god of agricultural fertility, and is the principal deity of Izumo Taishakyo, a Shintō sect whose headquarters are located in the town of Kizuki, Shimane Prefecture.

SEE ALSO Japanese Religions, article on The Study of Myths.

BIBLIOGRAPHY

Aoki, Michiko Yamaguchi. *Ancient Myths and Early History of Japan.* New York, 1974. A comprehensive cultural and anthropological study from the dawn of Japanese civilization (c. 300 BCE) to the rise of the civil government (700 CE). Ōkuninushi is identified here as Ashihara no Shikowo ("ugly man of the reed field").

Izumo fukoki. Translated and with an introduction by Michiko Yamaguchi Aoki. Tokyo, 1971. Ōkuninushi's role in the Izumo mythic cycle is related here.

MICHIKO YAMAGUCHI AOKI (1987)

OLAF THE HOLY

OLAF THE HOLY (r. 1015–1030), ruler of Norway and Scandinavia's first saint. A missionary king who strove to impose religious unity on Norway, Olaf had great influence on the practice of traditional religion in Norway and Iceland. Olaf (also called Olaf the Stout and Saint Olaf) was a descendant of Harald I (known as Fairhair). He became a Viking at a young age, harrying ships in the Baltic and then off the coast of England. Later he fought for the duke of Normandy. Spurred by a prophetic dream, Olaf began his return to Norway to become king, stopping on the way to spend the winter of 1013–1014 in Rouen, where he was baptized.

In 1028 Olaf was forced to flee Norway because of conflicts with powerful Norwegian chieftains who were allied with the Danish king, Knut. While in exile he had another dream: that it was God's will that he reconquer Norway. Accordingly, he returned—with Swedish help—only to meet defeat and lose his life at the Battle of Stiklastaðir in 1030. Soon after his death Olaf was sanctified. His former enemies in Norway rapidly became disenchanted with the new Danish rulers, ousting them and declaring Olaf's son Magnus king.

The question of why Olaf expended so much effort to bring Christianity to Norway is an interesting one, especially since his mission eventually destroyed him. Monarchy was vital for Christian ideology at that time. The throne represented justice and peace. In becoming a Christian, Olaf became joined to a more enlightened world—materially richer and with higher ideals—than Scandinavia then was. He sought to create peace, and for this he needed the support of the great leaders. Approaching his goal with missionary zeal, Olaf converted his countrymen ruthlessly and confiscated the property of those who refused to convert.

The key to Olaf's success lay in his effectiveness at destroying the old religion, which he accomplished in part by exposing it to ridicule. On one occasion, reports reached the king that during the winter the farmers of Hálogaland were holding great feasts to appease the Æsir, who had become angry because the farmers had let themselves be baptized by Olaf. In this feast of propitiation cattle and horses were slaughtered and their blood spread on pedestals for the purpose of improving harvests. When Olaf summoned the farmers to account for their acts, however, they would admit only to communal drinking.

In a similar incident, the farmers of Mærin denied having included sacrifices to the Germanic gods in their Yule feasts. Olaf continued forcing the inland Norwegians to convert until Dala-Gudbrand called up a large force of farmers to oppose the king and proposed this plan of action: "If we bear Thor [Þórr] out from our temple, where he stands here in this farm and has always helped us, and if he sees Olaf and his men, they will melt away, and he and his men become as nothing" (Snorri Sturluson, *Heimskringla* 8–11). This plan was accepted. And when Olaf arrived he learned that the farmers had a god who was visibly present, everyday, made up in the image of Þórr: "He has a hammer in his hand and is of great size and hollow inside, and he stands on a pedestal. . . . He receives four loaves of bread every day and also fresh meat" (*Heimskringla* 13–16). The following morning the farmers carried out the huge statue of Þórr, and Dala-Gudbrand challenged Olaf, asking him where his god was. Olaf instructed a follower to strike the idol with a club if the farmers were to look away. Then he instructed the farmers to look to the east if they wanted to see the Christian god—just as the sun came over the horizon. At this moment Olaf's follower struck the idol, and as it fell to pieces, out sprang adders and other snakes and mice as big as cats. When the frightened farmers tried to flee, Olaf offered two alternatives, do battle or accept Christianity, whereupon they all accepted the new faith.

BIBLIOGRAPHY

Fully one-third of Snorri Sturluson's *Heimskringla* is taken up by the saga of Olaf the Holy. It has been ably translated by Lee M. Hollander in *Heimskringla: History of the Kings of Norway by Snorri Sturluson,* with introduction and notes (Austin, 1964). Marlene Ciklamini has one chapter on Olaf in her *Snorri Sturluson* (Boston, 1978), and Jan de Vries's *Altnordische Literaturgeschichte,* 2 vols., 2d ed. (Berlin, 1964–1967) contains useful information on the literary traditions on Olaf. For historical details of Olaf's life and reign, see Erik Gunnes's *Riks-samling og Kristning* 800–1177 (Oslo, 1976), volume 2 of the series "Norges Historie," edited by Knut Mykland.

JOHN WEINSTOCK (1987)

OLCOTT, HENRY STEEL. Colonel Henry Steel Olcott (1832–1907) was the first American to formally convert to Buddhism and a major contributor to the Sinhalese Buddhist revival in nineteenth-century Ceylon (now Sri Lanka). He was also a founder and president of the Theosophical Society, the first American organization devoted to promoting Asian religions in the West.

Born into a Presbyterian household in Orange, New Jersey, in 1832, Olcott first made a name for himself in agriculture, establishing a farm school and delivering a series of agricultural lectures at Yale University. He then moved on to careers in journalism and law. During the American Civil War he investigated fraud in the military, then served on the three-person team investigating Abraham Lincoln's assassination.

The life of this self-described "radical anti-Tammany Republican" took a fateful turn when the *New York Sun* dispatched him to write about spirit communications that mediums were receiving in a farmhouse in Chittenden, Vermont. There he met the Russian-born occultist Helena Petrovna Blavatsky, who impressed him with her Bohemian bearing, boundless charisma, and alleged connections with occult "Masters," members of an esoteric brotherhood in the East.

Now devoted to spiritual matters, Olcott joined forces with Blavatsky in New York City in 1875 to establish the Theosophical Society. He was the organization's president and she its corresponding secretary, but more importantly Blavatsky was the charismatic force propelling the society forward, while Olcott's job was to prevent it from spinning out of control. Initially, the "Theosophical Twins," as they were known, focused on reforming Spiritualism. But guided by Blavatsky's "Masters," they quickly reset their sights, transforming their society into the first American organization devoted to spreading the ancient wisdom of the East.

Unfortunately for Olcott and Blavatsky, there was not much of an American audience for their eclectic theology. So in the winter of 1878 to 1879, they took their society to India, first to Bombay (now Mumbai) and later to Adyar, a suburb of Madras (Chennai), where the society is still located. There Olcott edited the *Theosophist,* which offered its readers a heady mix of comparative religion, anti-missionary agitation, free thought, and esotericism. He and Blavatsky also promulgated for the first time the "three objects" of their organization: (1) to form the nucleus of the Universal Brotherhood of Humanity, without distinction of race, creed, sex, caste or color; (2) to encourage the study of comparative religion, philosophy, and science; (3) and to investigate the unexplained laws of nature and the powers latent in man.

In 1880 Olcott sailed with Blavatsky to Ceylon, and in Galle they formally converted to Buddhism. The Buddhism they embraced, however, was confessedly idiosyncratic. "If Buddhism contained a single dogma that we were compelled to accept, we would not have. . .remained Buddhists ten minutes," Olcott explained in his six-volume *Old Diary Leaves* (1895–1935). "Our Buddhism was that of the Master-Adept Gautama Buddha, which was identically the Wisdom Religion of the Aryan Upanishads, and the soul of all the ancient world-faiths."

Given his status as a new convert, Olcott might have spent time sitting at the feet of Buddhist monks, correcting his misapprehensions. Instead he got about the business of converting the island's inhabitants to his understanding of what he called "pure, primitive Buddhism." Soon he was founding Buddhist schools, establishing Young Men's Buddhist Associations, and writing a popular *Buddhist Catechism* (1881), which was published in more than forty editions and at least twenty languages. In the process, he helped to spread, especially among the English-speaking middle-class, a form of Buddhism that borrowed heavily from the liberal Protestantism of his youth. Activistic, optimistic, didactic, progressive, and adaptive, this creole tradition is now widely described as "Protestant Buddhism."

While Olcott upset some monks, he was lionized by the populace, who thronged to hear "the White Buddhist" lecture on the vices of Christian missions and the virtues of Buddhist thought. In his lectures Olcott rejected stereotypes of Buddhism as "a grossly materialistic, nihilistic, a negative, a vile-breeding religion," describing the tradition instead as a philosophy (not a religion) rooted in the ancient teachings of the Buddha and confirmed by experience (rather than faith).

Olcott devoted his last years to intra-Buddhist ecumenism. In the late 1880s and early 1890s, he traveled to Burma and Japan in an effort to enlist all the world's Buddhists into one International Buddhist League. He also helped to design a six-colored Buddhist flag, which was adopted in 1950 as an international Buddhist symbol by the World Fellowship of Buddhists and now hangs in Buddhist centers worldwide.

Back in India, Olcott also made important contributions to the Indian Renaissance, founding schools for Dalits (formerly known as "untouchables"), promoting a Sanskrit revival, and establishing Hindu boys' associations. Olcott's work reverberated most powerfully, however, outside of his adopted homeland, especially in the United States, where his Theosophical activities helped to popularize Asian religions and New Age thought, and in Sri Lanka, where upon his death in 1907 over twenty thousand students were attending 183 grant-in-aid Buddhist schools.

Olcott died in India in 1907, and his cremated remains were scattered in the Ganges and the Indian Ocean. Though largely forgotten in the country of his birth (where the *New York Times* once denounced him as "a man bereft of reason"), Olcott is something of a folk hero in Sri Lanka, immortalized on a postage stamp and remembered each year on Olcott Day. Olcott is also admired in the Theosophical Society, which now maintains hundreds of branches on five continents and continues to preach the essential unity of all religions.

SEE ALSO Blavatsky, H. P.; Theosophical Society.

BIBLIOGRAPHY

Campbell, Bruce F. *Ancient Wisdom Revived: A History of the Theosophical Movement.* Berkeley, Calif., 1980.

Olcott, Henry Steel. *A Buddhist Catechism.* Colombo, Ceylon, 1881.

Olcott, Henry Steel. *Old Diary Leaves: The History of the Theosophical Society.* 6 vols. Adyar, India, 1974–1975.

Prothero, Stephen R. *The White Buddhist: The Asian Odyssey of Henry Steel Olcott.* Bloomington, Ind., 1996.

STEPHEN PROTHERO (2005)

OLDENBERG, HERMANN (1854–1920), German Sanskritist, Buddhologist, and historian of religions. Born in Hamburg on October 31, 1854, the son of a Protestant clergyman, Hermann Oldenberg completed doctoral studies in classical and Indic philology in 1875 at the University of Berlin with a dissertation on the Arval Brothers, an ancient Roman cult fraternity. He submitted his habilitation thesis at Berlin in Sanskrit philology in 1878, going on to become professor at the University of Kiel in 1889, and then at Göttingen from 1908 until his death on March 18, 1920.

Publishing an edition and translation of the *Śāṅkhayana Gṛhyasūtra* in 1878, the young Oldenberg then turned his attention to the Pali Buddhist texts; and it is due to him as much as to any single scholar that serious inquiry into these materials was begun. Previous decades of nineteenth-century European Buddhist research had focused on Mahāyāna Sanskrit (and Tibetan) texts, through which the historical Buddha and the early history of Buddhism were only dimly apparent. Oldenberg edited and translated into English the important Pali chronicle, the *Dīpavaṁsa,* in 1879; he also edited the *Vinaya Piṭaka* ("discipline basket") of the Pali Tipiṭaka (1879–1883), then published English translations of these texts (1881–1885) with T. W. Rhys Davids, founder of the Pali Text Society. The signal publication of this period of intense research on Buddhism is his *Buddha: Sein Leben, seine Lehre, seine Gemeinde* (1881), written when he was only twenty-six, and "perhaps the most famous book ever written on Buddhism" (J. W. de Jong, *Indo-Iranian Journal* 12, 1970, p. 224).

While Oldenberg's active interest in Buddhist studies never flagged, Buddhism was for him one dimension of what was to be his Lebenswerk: nothing less than the systematic examination of India's earliest religious history. Indeed, his achievements in Vedic studies are—if this is possible—even more consequential than his contributions to Buddhist studies. Taken together, his *Die Hymnen des Rigveda* (1888), *Die Religion des Veda* (1894), and *Ṛgveda: Textkritische and exegetische Noten* (1909–1912) constitute a triptych of enormous and continuing importance for research on the form, meters, and textual history of the *Ṛgveda Saṃhitā*. Further, his translations of several Vedic Gṛhyasūtras (*sutras* on domestic religious ceremonies), his book-length studies on the Brāhmaṇas and the Upaniṣads, and his numerous articles on Vedic topics complete an imposing legacy of meticulous scholarship.

Through Hermann Oldenberg's efforts, the sustained historical and literary inquiry into Vedic and Buddhist religions attained maturity. His concern to penetrate to the historical foundations of Buddhism and Vedism, which was representative of contemporary trends of German historical scholarship in the late nineteenth and early twentieth centuries, may seem somewhat naive to scholars today. Oldenberg died little more than a year before the first productive season of archaeological investigations in the Indus Valley, work destined to alter decisively many then-prevailing conceptions of the earliest stages of Indian civilization and religion. One can only conjecture how he would have responded to these discoveries. It seems altogether certain, however, that he would have dealt with them in that same clear-sighted, unsentimental, and critical fashion that characterized all his scholarly work. His persisting efforts to unveil the earliest stages of India's religious thought and history, his rigorous philological method, and the degree to which he integrated insights from other disciplines, stand as important monuments that will continue to inform and guide research.

BIBLIOGRAPHY

Unhappily, the direct impact of Oldenberg's scholarship on investigations in the English-speaking world has been limited by the paucity of translations. English editions of Oldenberg's works include William Hoey's translation of *Buddha: Sein Leben, seine Lehre, seine Gemeinde as The Buddha: His Life, His Doctrine, His Order* (London, 1882), which should be consulted alongside the thirteenth German edition, annotated by Helmuth von Glasenapp, as well as the following books, each of which is accompanied by a valuable introduction: *The Dīpavaṃsa* (London, 1879); *Vinaya Texts* (Oxford, 1881–1885); *The Gṛhyasūtras: Rules of Vedic Domestic Ceremonies*, 2 vols. (Oxford, 1886–1892); and part 2 ("Hymns to Agni") of *Vedic Hymns* (Oxford, 1897). Also, three of his general essays have been published together as *Ancient India* (Chicago, 1898). Of inestimable value is Klaus Janert's careful two-volume edition of *Oldenberg's Kleine Schriften* (Wiesbaden, 1967), which includes not only full texts of more than one hundred articles but also an exhaustive bibliography.

G. R. WELBON (1987 AND 2005)

OLD TESTAMENT SEE BIBLICAL LITERATURE, *ARTICLE ON* HEBREW SCRIPTURES

OLMEC RELIGION.

The Olmec occupied southern Mexico's tropical lowlands in southeastern Veracruz and western Tabasco between 1200 and 600 BCE. Like other Mesoamerican peoples of the period, they lived in villages, practiced agriculture based on maize cultivation, and produced pottery. However, they differed from their contemporaries in their more complex social and political institutions, in the construction of large centers with temples and other specialized buildings, and in their development of a distinctive style of art expressed in monumental stone sculptures and exquisite small portable objects. If they had a writing system, none of their texts has survived; everything known about the Olmec is based upon archaeological excavations at San Lorenzo, La Venta, Laguna de los Cerros, Tres Zapotes, and other major centers. Although religion is a most difficult aspect of prehistoric life for archaeologists to reconstruct, Olmec architecture, sculpture, and artifacts provide many useful insights into their religious beliefs and practices.

STUDY OF OLMEC RELIGION. Archaeological, historical, and ethnographic information provides the basic data for reconstructing ancient Mesoamerican religions. Archaeological data on prehistoric cultures must be interpreted in light of information about later, better documented cultures or studies of modern groups on approximately similar levels of development. For the Olmec, the archaeological data consist of sculptures, architecture, and artifacts. Researchers interpret these in terms of Spanish accounts of Aztec and Maya religions dating from the sixteenth century CE and of contemporary ethnographic studies of religious practices among modern Mesoamerican Indians and tropical forest groups living elsewhere in Latin America. The basic assumption underlying this approach is summarized in the assertion that ". . . there is a basic religious system common to all Mesoamerican peoples. This system took shape long before it was given monumental expression in Olmec art and survived long after the Spanish conquered the New World's major political and religious centers" (Joralemon, 1976, pp. 58–59).

Studies of Olmec religion rely heavily on iconographic analyses of the Olmec art style as expressed in over two hundred known stone monuments and hundreds of small portable objects. These studies have particularly emphasized the identification of deities while neglecting ritual and many other topics. Scholars tend to accept Joralemon's premise of continuity despite legitimate criticisms. And while this historical-ethnographic approach has been quite productive, it does have some serious weaknesses. For example, it cannot automatically be assumed that symbols and motifs retained the same basic meanings over several millennia and over long geographical distances. Furthermore, the much later Aztec religion, which is the primary model for comparison, may be an inappropriate model for the Olmec. The Aztec numbered in the millions whereas Olmec polities contained only a few thousand people at most. The tremendous disparity in social complexity implied by these differences may also indicate fundamental differences in their religious institutions and beliefs. Nevertheless, until archaeologists find ways to replace historical and ethnographic analogy as their primary interpretive tool, researchers will be forced to depend on such comparisons, and must try to employ them as judiciously as possible.

CHARACTERISTICS OF OLMEC RELIGION. The fundamental pattern of Olmec belief seems to have centered on the worship of numerous high gods or supernatural forces that controlled the universe and sanctioned the human sociopolitical structure. Human interaction with them required complex rituals in temples and other sanctified places, and could be achieved only by religious specialists whose personal qualifications or social position qualified them for the task. The belief system they served included a pantheon, a cosmology that explained and structured the universe, and a set of ritual activities that expressed the cosmology.

The pantheon. The nature of the Olmec pantheon is a topic of some controversy. Some scholars argue that Olmec supernaturals were not gods in the Western sense of recognizably distinct personalities, while others accept the existence of deities but disagree on their identifications. For example, what in this article is called the Olmec Dragon has been variously identified as a were-jaguar combining human and feline traits, a caiman, a toad, or a manatee! The reason for the confusion is that researchers have difficulty comprehending the subject matter of Olmec art. The beings portrayed are frequently "creatures that are biologically impossible," things that "exist in the mind of man, not in the world of nature" (Joralemon, 1976, p. 33).

The most thorough research on the Olmec pantheon has been done by Peter D. Joralemon, who originally defined ten Olmec deities (Gods I–X) but later reduced these to six, conforming to three basic dyads (Joralemon, 1971, 1976). Olmec art portrays the deities as creatures combining an endless and bewildering array of human, reptilian, avian, and feline attributes. The most commonly depicted pair are the Olmec Dragon (God I) and the Olmec Bird Monster (God III). The Olmec Dragon, believed to be a crocodilian with eagle, jaguar, human, and serpent attributes, appears to signify earth, water, fire, and agricultural fertility, and may have served as the patron deity of the elite. The Olmec Bird Monster is a raptorial bird, tentatively identified as a harpy eagle, with mammalian and reptilian features. Joralemon associates it with maize, agricultural fertility, the heavens, and mind-altering psychotrophic substances.

Joralemon suggests that the Olmec Dragon was a predecessor of numerous later deities, specifically the Aztec gods Cipactli, Xiuhtecuhtli, Huehueteotl, Tonacatecuhtli, and Quetzalcoatl and the Maya god Itzamná. Some authorities dispute these proposed linkages with later deities, but unfortunately there is a lack of a coherent methodology for resolving the issues of continuity and change in deity concepts through time.

Gods II and IV form an agricultural-fertility complex. God II has maize cobs sprouting from a cleft in the top of its head, and may be an ancestor of later Aztec maize deities such as Centeotl. God IV is an infant or dwarf, probably associated with rain, whom Joralemon sees as an early form of later rain deities, such as the central Mexican *tlalocs* and Maya *chacs.*

The final Olmec dyad consists of Gods VI and VIII. God VI is a deity of springtime and renewal who symbolizes reborn vegetation, and is thought to be an analog to Xipe Totec, the Aztec god whose priests wore human skin, flayed from sacrificial victims, as a sign of rebirth. God VIII is the death god, called Mictlantecuhtli by the Aztec, and symbolized by a fleshless human jaw.

Although much remains to be learned about the Olmec pantheon, the importance of agricultural and fertility deities is evident. This is not surprising in view of the fact that farming was the most important subsistence activity among the Olmec, but it does mark the earliest clear formulation of such deity concepts in Mesoamerica and represents a major Olmec contribution to Mesoamerican culture.

Religious specialists. There is no evidence in Olmec society of an elaborate religious bureaucracy comparable to that reported for the Aztec. The small size of Olmec groups probably precluded this development. Some scholars have called Olmec society a theocracy, but there is no evidence to warrant such a conclusion, although priests were undoubtedly members of the elite. Peter T. Furst has persuasively argued that certain Olmec art objects portray the theme of a "jaguar-shaman transformation complex" in which human shamans assumed the guise of their jaguar alter egos (see Furst's article "The Olmec Were-Jaguar Motif in the Light of Ethnographic Reality," in *Dumbarton Oaks Conference on the Olmec,* edited by Elizabeth P. Benson, Washington, D.C., 1968, pp. 79–110). It is not clear whether Olmec shamans were also elite priests, but it does seem likely.

Cosmology. Although the lack of written accounts makes it difficult to reconstruct Olmec cosmology, the archaeological record contains some interesting clues. Two sculptured monuments from the San Lorenzo area form the basis of the so-called Stirling hypothesis, named after its formulator, Matthew W. Stirling. Stirling maintained that each monument shows a jaguar having sexual intercourse with a woman and that they portray the mythic origin of the were-jaguars so common in Olmec art. Unfortunately, both monuments were badly mutilated in antiquity, and their subject matter is not at all clear.

Another important insight into Olmec cosmology may be contained in depictions of caves. Sculptured scenes of people seated in caves or emerging from cavelike niches suggest an early occurrence of the pan-Mesoamerican belief that ethnic groups and deities emerged on to the surface world through caves, which served as doorways to and from the supernatural realm inside the earth. In some cases the Olmec depictions clearly represent the mouth of the Olmec Dragon. Well-preserved Olmec-style paintings deep within caves in the states of Guerrero and Morelos far from the Olmec Gulf Coast homeland reinforce this interpretation.

Ritual. One of the least understood aspects of Olmec religion is ritual. Research has yielded some knowledge about the architectural settings in which rituals were held and about the nonperishable objects that are assumed to have been used in ritual contexts, but Olmec dances, prayers, chants, feasts, and other behaviors are lost forever.

Pole-and-thatch temples on the summits of earth mounds are widely regarded as having been a focal point for elite rituals. These small structures most likely housed the most important cult images and served as sanctuaries where the priests and leaders gathered in seclusion to conduct the esoteric rites to which only they were privy. The open courtyards and plazas surrounding the mounds were well suited for more public celebrations attended by the general populace.

Archaeological excavations have revealed numerous unusual architectural features that were either used in ritual or had some specific sacred meaning. For example, the gigantic artificial ridges built onto the sides of the San Lorenzo plateau may represent an attempt to transform the entire community into a bird effigy similar to the much smaller effigy mounds constructed by later Indian cultures in what is now the midwestern United States. The twenty or so deep depressions in the surface of San Lorenzo probably originated as sources of soil for mound construction but were later converted into sacred water reservoirs by lining them with special materials. Flooding was prevented by elaborate drain systems constructed of hundreds of U-shaped stone troughs. These reservoirs may have provided water for domestic use, but the year-round availability of fresh water from nearby springs, the substantial labor invested in constructing the drain systems, and the water-deity symbolism on several associated monuments all suggest a ritual function. Two potential uses have been suggested: One is that they served as ritual bathing stations for priests, the other that they were holding tanks for sacred animals such as caimans or manatees.

The Olmec probably played a ritual ball game similar to those popular in later times, as evidenced by clay figurines depicting males dressed in ballplayer garb and who at times hold what appears to be a ball. A rectangular group of four mounds at San Lorenzo has been interpreted as a formal ball court; and although it lacks the rings and benches of later courts, residue of a rubber-like substance found at this site may be the remnants of a ball. Some authorities have suggested that the numerous colossal heads found at several Olmec sites depict ballplayers wearing helmets, but the most recent consensus is that these remarkable basalt human portraits represent individual Olmec rulers. The ball game played by later Mesoamericans did have secular aspects, but it is generally regarded as a primarily religious observance in which players represented supernaturals.

Evidence of a common yet perplexing aspect of Olmec ritual centered around the burial of precious objects in caches and offerings has been found at La Venta. Some caches contain only one or a few objects while others include enormous amounts of material. The small offerings include stone figurines and celts, pottery vessels, and a variety of personal ornaments, even though these are generally not associated with burials. Some offerings display ideologically significant patterns in the placement of objects, such as celts arranged in geometric patterns or stylized deity faces. One particularly interesting cache from La Venta contains jadeite human figurines placed to show a procession scene with four individuals filing past what appears to be an Olmec ruler and his retinue.

The most unusual buried features are the so-called Massive Offerings at La Venta. Huge steep-sided pits were dug into the subsoil and immediately filled with thousands of serpentine blocks laid in clay and topped with a mosaic of finely worked blocks forming a gigantic mask of the Olmec Dragon. Four Massive Offerings have been discovered at La Venta, and like many architectural features at the site they occur in bilaterally symmetrical positions vis-à-vis the site's centerline. It is possible that all the subsurface offerings at La Venta form a colossal pattern of unknown ritual significance, but enough pieces of the puzzle to be able to identify the pattern have not yet been found.

Just as Olmec constructions provide insights into the settings for ritual, their art objects and other artifacts alert scholars to the nature of some of the rituals. Museums and private collections contain hundreds of exotic objects to which can be reasonably assigned a ritual function even though their specific uses are not known. Anthropomorphic and zoomorphic figurines, masks, celts, "spoons," "stilettos," and a host of miscellaneous objects, frequently decorated with religious designs and symbols, indicate a well-developed set of ritual paraphernalia. The objects are often made from jadeite, serpentine, and other blue-green stones whose color obviously had some special significance. In most cases the functions of these objects are not known, but the stilettos may have served as bloodletters used in ritual autosacrifice and the "spoons" may have been used for the administration of hallucinogenic substances. Evidence for the use of mind-altering substances by the Olmecs is weak, but most scholars assume such practices were part of Olmec ritual.

Other ritual accoutrements include iron-ore mirrors, which are masterpieces of pre-Columbian lapidary work. Made from large rectangular pieces of magnetite, ilmenite, and hematite, the polished concave surfaces of these mirrors have such fine optical qualities that they can be used to ignite fires and project camera-lucida images on flat surfaces. An enigmatic grooved rectangular bar of magnetic hematite found at San Lorenzo has been shown to be a compass needle, probably used in geomantic ritual rather than as a utilitarian device.

SEE ALSO Caves; Iconography, article on Mesoamerican Iconography.

Bibliography

Anthony F. C. Wallace's *Religion: An Anthropological View* (New York, 1966) provides the framework in which this article has been written. The most recent and thorough synthesis of Olmec culture is Jacques Soustelle's *The Olmecs: The Oldest Civilization in Mexico,* translated by Helen R. Lane (Garden City, N.Y., 1984). Older but still useful books include Michael D. Coe's *America's First Civilization: Discovering the Olmec* (New York, 1968), and Ignacio Bernal's *The Olmec World,* translated by Doris Heyden and Fernando Horcasitas (Berkeley, 1969). Michael D. Coe and my *In the Land of the Olmec,* 2 vols. (Austin, Tex., 1980) is the basic source of information on San Lorenzo. The basic data on La Venta are scattered through many works; the two most important are Philip Drucker's *La Venta, Tabasco: A Study of Olmec Ceramics and Art* (Washington, D.C., 1952), and Philip Drucker, Robert F. Heizer, and Robert J. Squier's *Excavations at La Venta, Tabasco, 1955* (Washington, D.C., 1959). Karl W. Luckert's *Olmec Religion: A Key to Middle America and Beyond* (Norman, Okla., 1976) is the only book devoted exclusively to this topic, but its unorthodox methodology and assumptions lead to conclusions not supported by the data. Peter D. Joralemon's *A Study of Olmec Iconography* (Washington, D.C., 1971) contains his initial attempt to delineate the Olmec pantheon. *Origins of Religious Art and Iconography in Preclassic Mesoamerica,* edited by H. B. Nicholson (Los Angeles, 1976) contains Joralemon's definitive study of the Olmec Dragon and the Olmec Bird Monster in addition to many other useful articles. Elizabeth P. Benson's *The Olmecs and Their Neighbors: Essays in Memory of Matthew W. Stirling* (Washington, D.C., 1981) contains articles dealing with many aspects of Olmec culture, and a useful bibliography.

New Sources

Coe, Michael D., and Richard A. Diehl, eds. *The Olmec World: Ritual and Rulership.* Princeton, N.J., 1995.

Grove, David C. "Olmec Archaeology: A Half Century of Research and Its Accomplishments." *Journal of World Prehistory* 11, no. 1 (1997): 151–201.

Miller, Mary Ellen. *The Art of Mesoamerica: From Olmec to Aztec.* 3d ed. London, 2001.

Sharer, Robert J., and David C. Grove, eds. *Regional Perspectives on the Olmec.* Cambridge, U.K., 1989.

Soustelle, Jacques. *The Olmecs: The Oldest Civilization in Mexico.* Norman, Okla., 1985.

Stocker, Terry, Sarah Meltzoff, and Steve Armsey. "Crocodilians and Olmecs." *American Antiquity* 45 (1980): 740–758.

Stone, Andrea, ed. *Heart of Creation: The Mesoamerican World and the Legacy of Linda Schele.* Tuscaloosa, Ala., 2002.

Richard A. Diehl (1987)
Revised Bibliography

OṂ, a contraction of the sounds /a/, /u/, and /m/, is considered in the Hindu tradition to be the most sacred of Sanskrit syllables. In a religious setting that reveres the intrinsic power of sound as a direct manifestation of the divine, a setting in which the hierarchy of scripture is headed by the *śruti* ("heard") texts and in which oral tradition has preserved the religious language unchanged over millennia, *oṃ* is the articulated syllable par excellence, the eternally creative divine word. Indeed, the Sanskrit word denoting "syllable" (*akṣara,* literally "the imperishable") commonly serves as an epithet for *oṃ.* Its other epithets include *ekakṣara* ("the one syllable" but also "the sole imperishable thing") and *pranava* (from *praṇu,* "to utter a droning"); the latter term refers to the practice of initiating any sacred recitation with a nasalized syllable. The syllable *oṃ* itself has been associated with the Sanskrit root *av* ("to drive, impel, animate"; *Uṇadi Sūtra* 1.141). It is represented graphically by a familiar mystical symbol combining the syllable's three components.

Articulated at the beginning and end of recitations and prayers, *oṃ* is a particle of auspicious salutation, expressing acknowledgment of the divine or solemn affirmation, in which latter sense it is compared with *amen* ("verily, this syllable is assent"; *Chāndogya Upaniṣad* 1.1.8). Evidence of its use as an invocation occurs in the *Ṛgveda;* though it appears in a relatively late section (1.164.39), this note dates the practice to at least 1200 BCE.

From the sixth century BCE, the Upaniṣads make direct mention of *oṃ.* One of the oldest Upaniṣads, the *Chāndogya,* discusses the syllable at length in setting forth rules for the chanters of the *Sāmaveda* and states that "one has to know that *oṃ* is the imperishable" (1.3.4). By sounding *oṃ,* one intones the Udgītā, the essential canto of the Vedic sacrifice (1.1.5).

In the *Kaṭha Upaniṣad,* the figure Death defines *oṃ* as the goal propounded by the Vedas, and proclaims that anyone who meditates on the syllable *oṃ* can attain *brahman* (1.2.15–16). A later Upaniṣad, the *Taittirīya,* indicates that *oṃ* is both *brahman* and the cosmos (1.8.1–2): The sound symbol is identical to what it represents.

The first chapter of the *Māṇḍukya,* one of the latest of the Vedic Upaniṣads, is devoted to the elucidation of *oṃ.* The sacred syllable is divided into its four phonetic components, representing the four states of mind, or consciousness: /a/ is related to the awakened state, /u/ to the dream state, /m/ to dreamless sleep, and the syllable as a whole to the fourth state, *turīya,* which is beyond words and is itself the One, the Ultimate, the *brahman.* "One should know *oṃ* to be God seated in the hearts of all" (1.28).

The sixth chapter of the *Maitrāyaṇīya,* possibly the latest of the Vedic Upaniṣads, is devoted entirely to the discussion of the sacred syllable, referred to as the "primary sound" (6.22). The devotee is enjoined to meditate on the Self as *oṃ* (6.3). When *oṃ* is articulated, the sound "rises upward." The chapter closes with the invocation "Hail *oṃ*! Hail *brahman*!"

When the *Bhagavadgītā*—a fragment of the *Mahābhārata,* perhaps contemporary with the latest of the Vedic Upaniṣads—proclaims that "the imperishable is *brahman,*" it plays on the term *akṣara,* which may be read either as an adjective ("*brahman* is imperishable") or as a substantive ("*brahman* is the Imperishable [i.e., *oṃ*]").

Manu (*Manusmṛti* 2.74) echoes the assertion made in the *Chāndogya* regarding the articulation of *oṃ* preceding any sacred recitation, and prescribes that it be repeated not only at the beginning but also at the end of the daily recitation of the Veda, under penalty of losing the merit attached to such an exercise. He adds that Prakjāpati, the creator, extracted the milk of three cows (i.e., the three primary Vedas) in order to draw the three phonetic components that make up the syllable.

Through imagery borrowed from archery, the *Muṇḍaka Upaniṣad* indicates how the articulation of *oṃ* was integrated into the practice of meditation according to Indian thought: The syllable *oṃ* is the bow, the *ātman* (the self) is the arrow, and *brahman* is the target (2.2.3–4). One must bend toward the target without diverting the mind; one must make oneself identical to the arrow. (The same image is found in the *Bhāgavata Purāṇa.*) The *Yoga Sūtra* of Patañjali mentions that the various yoga systems all insist on the importance of *oṃ* as a symbol of the devotee's attempt to unite with the Absolute, a goal that is itself the prerequisite to any practice of meditation.

In later times *oṃ* stands for the union of the three gods of the Hindu triad, Brahmā (the creative force, or /a/), Viṣṇu (the sustaining force, or /u/), and Śiva (the dissolving force, or /m/).

As the primary sound symbol for an Indian tradition maintained continuously from the age of the Vedas into modern times, the syllable *oṃ* stands charged with an unquestionable religious energy. Its use as a mantra for profound meditation reflects the Vedic teaching that the devotee is one with the sacred sound and all it represents. Through its constant repetition in recitations, prayers, and even recently composed sacred texts it acts as a pitch that tunes the worshiper to the heart of the prayer.

SEE ALSO Music, article on Music and Religion in India.

BIBLIOGRAPHY

In the absence of monographical studies on the subject the reader would do well to consult André Padoux's *Recherches sur la symbolique et l'énergie de la parole dans certains textes tantriques,* "Publications de l'Institut de civilization indiennes," no. 21 (Paris, 1963).

New Sources

Beck, Guy L. *Sonic Theology: Hinduism and Sacred Sound.* Columbia, S.C., 1993.

A. M. ESNOUL (1987)
Revised Bibliography

OMENS SEE PORTENTS AND PRODIGIES

OMOPHAGIA

OMOPHAGIA is an ancient Greek term (*ōmophagia,* "eating raw [flesh]") for a ritual in the ecstatic worship of Dionysos.

THE RAW AND THE COOKED. All human groups, including the so-called primitives, are aware of their cultural identity by contrast to other, "uncivilized" forms of life. That the opposition of civilization to nature, of human to animal, is most drastically experienced in the dietary code, in the use of cooked food as against "raw-eating" animals, has become popular knowledge in the wake of *The Raw and the Cooked* (1969), the seminal first volume of Claude Lévi-Strauss's *Mythologiques.* This presupposes the conquest of fire, which has been decisive in the evolution of humankind and which still looms large in mythology; knowledge of fire goes together with the special importance of the hunt in early and primitive societies. A constant point of reference in human and even prehuman experience are the big carnivores, especially the leopard and the wolf, that are abhorred as well as imitated. Model hunters, at the same time dreadfully dangerous and admirably powerful, the carnivores are the paradigmatic "raw-eaters." They are human-eaters, too: When the problems of civilization and dietary codes are articulated in ritual or myth, the motif of cannibalism usually makes its appearance.

The category of "raw-eating" most generally finds two applications. In mythology, it designates various demons who naturally take the traits of predators—enemies of the gods or even certain uncanny and dangerous gods. On a more realistic level, ethnocentrism and xenophobia combine to mark certain foreign tribes as "raw-eaters," be they neighbors or faraway people known from hearsay. In Western tradition, this cliché has remained attached to Huns and Tatars. As a variant or for reinforcement, the motif of cannibalism easily comes in. It is notable that the concept of "raw-eaters" goes back to Indo-European strata, that is, to the early third millennium BCE, as shown by the correspondence of the Sanskrit *āmād* with the Greek *ōmēs-tēs;* in the same vein, a Scythian tribe was known as Āmādokoi. Tribalism also admits of mythical transformations: For the Greeks, the centaurs, hybrids of man and horse, living in the woods but sometimes visiting humans to wreak havoc, were not only hunters but "raw-eaters."

In a more complex way the opposition of "raw-eating" to civilized may appear within one ethnic unity: One special group is set apart by this very characterization. The imitation of carnivores is most evident in secret societies of leopard men as attested in Africa, or the folklore of werewolves in Europe, including ancient Greece. They are expected to kill and eat in a beastlike fashion and especially to practice cannibalism. The oldest evidence for leopard men comes from wall paintings of Çatal Hüyük in Neolithic Anatolia about 6000 BCE; details about their function or practice cannot be known, except for their imitating predators through masquerade in the context of hunting.

In more modern times two groups, "raw-eaters" versus eaters of cooked meat, are attested among the Mansi, an Ugric tribe of Siberia, and Andreas Alföldi (1974) has used this attestation to illustrate a similar opposition between two groups of Luperci who performed the ancient festival of Lupercalia at Rome; in both cases it is the group of "raw-eaters" who enjoy the higher reputation as being the swifter, the more vigilant, the more powerful. It seems that in ancient civilizations the opposition of raw versus cooked has sometimes been replaced by that of roasted versus boiled meat, where roasting is more primitive, more hunterlike, more heroic. Thus in a non-Yahvistic ritual mentioned in the *First Book of Samuel* (2:11–17) the priests require raw flesh for roasting while the sacrificial community feasts on boiled meat.

A similar opposition may be enacted not through the institution of permanent groups but in the dimension of time: "raw-eating" as a transitional stage leading back to normal food, that is, to civilization reconfirmed through its opposite in the dietary code. Thus in initiations that involve a marginal status and make the initiates outcasts for a while, disuse of fire and raw-eating has a place. In Greek myth this is reflected in the figure of Achilles, who as a boy is taken from his parents to the "raw-eating" centaurs and gets his unique heroic strength by feeding on the entrails of the most savage beasts (Apollodorus, *Bibliothēkē* 3.13.6).

There are communal festivals too that bring about a temporary reversal, an atavistic return to ancient ways of life that sometimes includes the interdiction of fire and thus enforces a diet of uncooked food. In ancient Greece this is attested for a festival on the island of Lemnos and also for some forms of the Thesmophoria, the festival of Demeter. Accompanying myths tell stories about an insurrection of women against men that, however, had to give way to normality again. Of course, initiations, secret societies, and public festivals may be functionally interrelated in various ways; by themselves or in combination they keep alive the consciousness of alternatives to what is considered normal and thus in fact help to ensure continuity.

DIONYSIAN OMOPHAGIA. Dionysos, the ancient Greek god of wine and ecstasy, is experienced by his followers most deeply and directly in a state known simply as "madness" (*mania*). Hence his female adherents are called Maenads (*mainades*); Bacchants *(bakchoi)* and Bacchantes *(bakchai)*, masculine and feminine, respectively, are about equivalent. High points of bacchantic activity are tearing apart a victim and eating it raw. From a pragmatic perspective, the two activities of tearing apart (*sparagmos*) and eating raw (*ōmophagia*) need not entail each other, but in the Dionysian tradition both combine to form an image of what is both subhuman and superhuman, both beastlike and godlike, at the same time.

The most influential literary text to describe Dionysian phenomena is Euripides' tragedy *The Bacchae* (405 BCE). When the Maenads, who are celebrating their dances in the wilderness, are disturbed by herdsmen, they jump at the herds and tear calves and even bulls asunder "swifter than you could shut your eyes" (ll. 735–747); later on they murder Pentheus in a similar way. Eating is not dwelt upon in this context, except as a horrible prospect (l. 1184); but in the introductory song of the play the god himself, leader of the dances, is presented as "hunting for blood by killing a he-goat, the lust of raw-eating" (ll. 137–139), and the Bacchantes are ready to identify with their leader.

In the Dionysian circle, the imagery of carnivores is ready at hand. Preference is given to the leopard, partly through an overlap with the symbolism of the Anatolian mother goddess, whose distant avatar seems to be the goddess of Çatal Hüyük. *Bassarai* (Foxes) was the title of a lost play by Aeschylus; it was a name for the Maenads who destroyed Lykurgos, another enemy of the god. Classical vase paintings (fifth to fourth century BCE) show dancing Maenads holding parts of a torn animal—a fawn, a goat—in their hands; eating, though, is hardly depicted.

Such restraint is absent from the picture drawn by Christian writers of pagan cult. "You leave behind your breast's sanity, you crown yourselves with vipers, and in order to prove that you are filled with the power of god, with bloody mouths you tear asunder the entrails of goats crying out in protest"—thus said Arnobius in *Against the Pagans* (5.19), following in part Clement of Alexandria's *Protrepticus* (chap. 12). In this view omophagia is the extreme of the pagans' folly.

A most serious problem is to decide how much of the picture evoked by Hellenic poetry on the one side and Christian polemics on the other is to be regarded as cultic reality in the context of Greek civilization of the historical period. There are many convergent testimonies, but few to convince a skeptic. A very ancient epithet of the god is Dionysos Ōmēstēs ("eating raw"), attested by the poet Alcaeus about 600 BCE. Dionysos Ōmadios, mentioned a few times in connection with human sacrifice, is often considered equivalent; linguistically, though, this epithet should rather belong to *ōmadon* ("by the shoulder"), which still refers to "tearing apart" in *sparagmos.* Firmicus Maternus, writing Christian polemics but drawing on some Hellenistic source, asserts that in a Dionysian festival "the Cretans tear apart a living bull with their teeth" (*On the Error of Pagan Religions,* chap. 6; about 350 CE)—which doubtless includes elements of fantasy. In a poem titled *Bassarika,* a certain Dionysios has a human victim, clad in a deer's skin, torn to pieces and devoured by Indians on the command of Dionysos; the remains are to be assembled in baskets before sunrise. The mystic baskets are well known from ritual, but the story with its barbarian setting is a ghastly exaggeration. A more reliable witness is Plutarch, who combines the epithet *ōmēstēs* with another, *agriōnios,* and thus refers to a well-attested festival, Agriōnia. This in turn is connected with a group of myths that tell about the women of a city growing mad, leaving the town, kidnapping their own children in order to kill and even eat them; the Pentheus myth of Euripides' *Bacchae* is in fact one exemplar of the pattern. But to bring imagination back to facts of ritual, scholars have nothing but the too short statement of Plutarch that there are indeed in Greek cults

PORTRAITS

Portraits have the singular advantage of presenting to the votive eye the person whose personality, office, stature, or authority shape a relationship that often goes to the heart of religious belief. Ancestors, teachers, saints, heroes, and deities are made available in their portraits for veneration and petition. The devotional relation that portraiture enables with these venerable figures is perhaps most observable in icons, which are a visual device found in many religious traditions. The term is most closely associated with Orthodox Christianity, which makes extensive liturgical use of icons in its formal worship and devotion. The power of icons consists in their ability to act as apertures or windows through which the devout gaze. Rather than opaque surfaces, icons are experienced as openings in the fabric of the present that enable access to sacred realities such as persons and events. These avenues or conduits conduct devotion and petition from the believer to the venerated person and often act as the route of return to deliver blessing, guidance, or comfort. Although the idea of the Christian icon should not be applied normatively to forms of portraiture in other religions, the icon is a visual category that is not exclusive to Christianity. Fundamental to the sacred portrait is the presumption that faces are the signature of personality, the most reliable and communicative register of the human soul. To see the face is to see the person, to remember him as he actually was, or to see her as she is now in the next world as saint or ancestor. Faces are relics, the enduring countenance of spiritual power, the place to which the devout go to see the sacred looking back at them in the cherished guise of someone they know and trust.

The link between faces and relics is tangible in masks as diverse as Melanesian ritual imagery (**a** and **b**) and the death masks made in

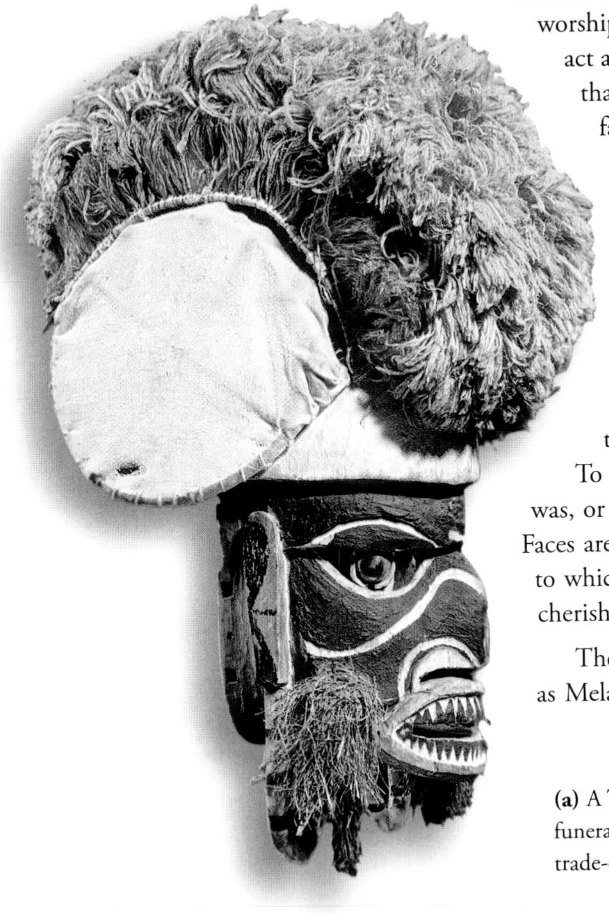

(a) A Tatanua mask for inhabitation by the soul of the deceased in Malagan funerary rites. New Ireland, Papua New Guinea, wood, fiber, shell, lime, and trade-cloth. *[©Galerie Meyer-Oceanic Art, Paris; photograph by M. Gurfinkel, Paris]*

Europe **(c)**. In the case of Melanesian ceremonies, masks were sometimes made from the skulls and hair of the recently deceased, serving to establish their presence as ancestors in nocturnal dances of secret medicine societies on the island of New Britain. Although the mask is not an imitative portrait (its sculpted and painted features are similar to other masks), its actual constituents create its link to the ancestor. So it is a "portrait" in an ontological sense. Yet another manner of "portrait" is the New Ireland *uli* figure **(b)**, which serves as the residence of an ancestor spirit. After a village leader died, an *uli* was invested with the spirit of the leader by a shaman. The image was then able to provide assistance to the new chief and village. Although the figure bore no visual similarity to the deceased leader, it contained his spirit and therefore acted as the means of access to him and his blessing.

(b) ABOVE. A memorial ceremony figure (*uli*) of a deceased leader, made of wood, shell, fiber, and pigment, collected in the early twentieth century in New Ireland, Papua New Guinea. *[©Christie's Images/Corbis]* **(c)** RIGHT. *Togato Barbarini*, a life-sized marble sculpture of the Roman patrician, with busts of his ancestors, late first century BCE or early first century CE. *[©Araldo de Luca/Corbis]*

The marble sculpture of a Roman patrician with the busts of his ancestors **(c)** recalls the importance of portrait relics among later Europeans. Patricians in ancient Republican and Imperial Rome installed their ancestors in a practice of veneration that focused on wax effigies made from the face of a patriarch at death. These images were carried in funeral processions and kept by the family for some time. The marble figure transposes two masks, as well as the proud display of them by a living head of a family. The masks vouched for the pedigree of aristocratic Roman families. The right to use them was guaranteed by law for aristocrats alone. Wax masks of ancestors were kept in the atriums of patrician families and were worn by actors during funerals to perform the parts of ancestors. As Romans established aristocratic practices of collecting and displaying works of art in their homes near the end of the Republican period, the wax masks were replaced by marble sculptures like the image reproduced here.

The use of death masks was common in modern Europe as a way of remembering the appearance of writers and leaders, and the masks were commonly consulted by artists who wished to produce "authentic" portrait paintings or sculptures of the famous person. In the twentieth century the American revivalist preacher Billy Sunday had photographs of himself posed in dramatic preaching gestures made into postcards **(d)**, which were distributed at his massive urban revival meetings across the United States. But carefully rendered, faithful portraits of teachers, philosophers, and religious figures are hardly modern or Western in origin. Naturalistic techniques were used by Chinese and Japanese artists to depict Daoist and

(d) A 1908 postcard of American revivalist preacher Billy Sunday. *[Courtesy of the Billy Graham Center Museum, Wheaton, Ill.]*

Buddhist historical figures, though in each case naturalistic technique served a larger purpose. In the case of the Daoist immortal, Zhongli Quan **(e)**, the painter infused the portrait with an intensity that conveyed the spiritual attainments of this figure who had been a general during the Han dynasty, but abandoned his military career when he encountered a Daoist sage and then a zhenren, or perfected being, who disclosed to him the great secrets of Daoism. He appears here walking over the ocean. When the Buddhist Chan master, Wuzhun, from Szechwan province was invited to the imperial court of the Song dynasty to present a discourse to the emperor, he was named abbot of a monastery and given an official title. The occasion was marked by an official portrait that shows Wuzhun invested with imperial recognition that

(e) Late-fifteenth-century hanging scroll of *The Immortal Zhongli Quan*, attributed to Zhao Qi. *[The Cleveland Museum of Art; purchase from the J. H. Wade Fund, 1976.13]*

extended to Chan Buddhism an official recognition and status, which was identified with the person of Wuzhun. The cultural work of portraits can have much to do with the presentation of the person as more than individual. The dress and gesture in Wuzhun's portrait signal the office of the sitter and construct a likeness suitable to his official function and stature.

Portraits often present sitters performing their official deeds and exercising characteristic duties for which they are remembered or sought out by those who venerate their images. Portraits of a Mouride caliph and of a scholar (**f1** and **f2**) depict each man with the accoutrements of piety, ethnicity, and authority, including prayer beads, text, and costume. Many portraits seek to authorize the religious legitimacy of those they portray. The Egyptian

(f1) ABOVE. Assane Dione, *Serigne Bassirou Mbacke*, 2002, acrylic on canvas, Senegal. *[UCLA Fowler Museum of Cultural History; photograph by Don Cole]* **(f2)** LEFT. Assane Dione, *Serigne Mouhadou Fadel Mbacke*, 2002, acrylic on canvas, Senegal. *[UCLA Fowler Museum of Cultural History; photograph by Don Cole]*

relief carving **(g)** of the pharaoh Akhenaton and his queen, Nefertiti, displays the two controversial promoters of a new monotheistic cult in ancient polytheistic Egypt receiving divine approbation in the form of solar rays descending from Aton and delivering the virtues and powers of authority. Similarly, a German Protestant painter vindicated the cause of the Reformation in an altar painting of the crucifixion (not pictured) by placing Martin Luther at the foot of the cross, pointing to scripture in a gesture that corresponds to John the Baptist's pointing to the savior on the cross.

In another use of portraiture to establish lineage and authority, African American clergy of the African Methodist Episcopal Church **(h)** were celebrated in 1876, the national centennial, in a commemorative print that links them to the cultural achievements of the church in its sixty years of existence (it was founded in Philadelphia in 1816). Their portraits are surrounded by the church's

(g) LEFT. Stone relief of the Egyptian god Aton offering life and gifts to the pharaoh Akhenaton and his queen Nefertiti, c. 1353–1335 BCE, Tell el-'Amarna, Egypt. *[©Archivo Iconografico, S.A./Corbis]* **(h)** BELOW. A commemorative print depicting bishops of the African Methodist Episcopal Church, 1876. *[Courtesy of the American Antiquarian Society]*

cultural institutions and projects, which were established and undertaken by many of the clergy pictured in the image. A print manufactured in India inverts this motif by gathering ten Sikh *gurūs* in commemorative portraits around a scriptural collection of poems and hymns **(i)**. The text, cradled in a throne, is itself known as the *Gurū Granth Sāhib* (Great Reverend Teacher) and is regarded by Sikhs as the sacred embodiment of the *gurūs'* wisdom and spiritual authority. The *gurū* portraits and the holy text are presented by the print as versions of one another.

The Sangye Yarjon, the abbot of an important Tibetan monastery not far from Lhasa, is shown in a painting **(j)** that visually presents his lineage extending back all the way to the historical Buddha himself (seen in the upper left in his easily recognizable pose). Several important Indian and Tibetan teachers and *bodhisattvas* appear as part of the descent to the main figure of the abbot, who occupies the center of the image. Sangye Yarjon shares the

(i) ABOVE. *The Ten Gurūs*, a print by an unknown artist purchased at a Punjabi bazaar in 1965 by W. H. McLeod. ***[Reproduced by permission of Oxford University Press India, New Delhi; W. H. Mcleod, Popular Sikh Art (1991)]*** **(j) LEFT.** Thirteenth-century lineage painting of Sangye Yarjon, the abbot of Taklung Monastery in Central Tibet, pigment and gold on cotton. ***[The Walters Art Museum, promised gift of John and Berthe Ford]***

(k) A Jain worshiper prays before a monumental stone sculpture of Lord Bāhubali in Karkal, India. *[©Chris Lisle/Corbis]*

gesture and established iconography of Buddhism, as well as the markings of the enlightened teacher, suggesting that this is as much a portrayal of the individual in his particularity as the office of a revered teacher and abbot. An even greater reliance on stylization occurs in the Jain statue of Lord Bāhubali **(k)**, one of the twenty-four Jina, located at the most holy of Jain shrines in southern India. This colossal sculpture clearly recalls the Buddhist portrayal of the Buddha and Hindu depictions of Viṣṇu, but the nudity is unmistakably Jain, indicating that the Jina has moved beyond all desire and the stain of karmic bondage and is therefore free of rebirth.

Bibliography

Brilliant, Richard. *Portraiture.* London, 1991.

Brown, Kerry, ed. *Sikh Art and Literature.* London, 1999.

Cormack, Robin. *Painting the Soul: Icons, Death Masks, and Shrouds.* London, 1997.

Strong, Donald. *Roman Art.* 2d ed. Edited by Roger Ling. London, 1988.

Walker, Susan, ed. *Ancient Faces: Mummy Portraits from Roman Egypt.* 2d ed. New York, 2000.

Wardwell, Allen. *Island Ancestors: Oceanic Art from the Masco Collection.* Seattle and Detroit, 1994.

David Morgan (2005)

"unlucky and dreary days in which omophagia and tearing-apart have their place" (*On the Decline of Oracles,* 417c).

Modern scholarship has often connected Dionysian omophagia with the apocryphal Orphic myth that tells how Dionysos himself when still a child was slain, cut to pieces, and tasted by the Titans—in consequence of which, the Titans were burned by the lightning of Zeus, and from their smoke humankind arose. This seemed to place the ritual in the context of a marginal Orphic sect. But it has long been seen that this myth explicitly contradicts a strict understanding of the meaning of *ōmophagia:* The Titans use a knife, and they both cook and roast the remains of their victim. This seems to mirror more complex divisions of marginal groups, Dionysian or Orphic, with differing dietary codes and ideology, as shown especially by Marcel Detienne (1977).

A most interesting text comes from a lost tragedy of Euripides, *The Cretans* (frag. 472 in August Nauck, *Tragicorum Graecorum Fragmenta,* Leipzig, 1889), preserved by Porphyry (*On Abstinence* 4.19): The chorus of Cretans introduce themselves as "initiates of Idaean Zeus"; they have achieved this status "by performing the thunder of night-swarming Zagreus and the raw-eating dinners, and by holding up the torches for the Mother of the mountains." This is a literary elaboration; one might surmise that the poet was not too well informed about the details of Idaean mysteries and liberally added colors from the Dionysian sphere. But he succeeds in giving a meaningful setting to the rite of raw-eating, as a transient phase in initiation to be followed by strict vegetarianism, as the initiates emerge in white clothes from a temple smeared with bull's blood; this is a grim and revolting antidote through which a status of purity is achieved. *Zagreus* is an epithet of Dionysos, especially in the context of *sparagmos.*

There remains one nonliterary, realistic testimony for cult practice, a sacred law from Miletus, dated 276/275 BCE, regulating the privileges of a priestess with regard to the city as well as to private Dionysian mysteries: "It shall not be allowed to anyone to throw in an *ōmophagion* before the priestess throws in one on behalf of the city, nor to bring together the group of revelers (*thiasoi*) before the public one." This clearly is to ensure some prerogative of the city as against private organizations. Unfortunately *ōmophagion,* "something related to raw-eating," is a term that occurs only here, and no agreement has been reached among interpreters as to what exactly it should mean in this context. Is a victim (e.g., a goat) being thrown down at a crowd of ecstatic Bacchants assembled in expectation? (This is the most vivid picture, drawn by, among others, E. R. Dodds, 1951.) Or is a victim being thrown down into a chasm, as attested in the Demeter festival Thesmophoria? Or is some kind of symbolic substitute (perhaps only a mere contribution in money) being "thrown into" some box? In the absence of further evidence there will be no final decision. One may still claim that in such a context ideology is more important than reality. One finds, in a major Greek city close to the classical age, the designation of "raw-eating" in a ritual that is meant to ensure the favor of Dionysos on behalf of the city and that takes precedence in the procession. There were points of reference in cult even to the more exuberant Dionysian mythology.

COMPARATIVE EVIDENCE. A vivid description of pre-Islamic bedouin is contained in a Christian novel from the fifth century CE, *The Story of Nilus,* now finally available in a critical edition: Nilus of Ancyra, *Narratio,* edited by Fabricius Conca (Leipzig, 1983). These barbarians, the text says, delight in sacrificing boys to the morning star; sometimes "they take a camel of white color and otherwise faultless, they bend it down upon its knees, and go circling round it three times"; the leader,

> after the third circuit, before the crowd has finished the song, while the last words of the refrain are still on their lips, draws his sword and forcefully smites the neck of the camel, and he is the first to taste eagerly of its blood. And thus the rest of them run up and with their knives some cut off a small bit of the hide with its hair upon it, others hack at any chance bit of flesh and snatch it away, others go on to the entrails and inwards, and they leave no scrap of the victim unwrought that might be seen by the sun at its rising. (3.3, pp. 12f.)

The importance of the text as a description of a very primitive form of sacrifice was seen by W. Robertson Smith (1889), and explicit comparison with Dionysian phenomena was made by Jane E. Harrison (1903); there is no mention of divine possession, but the narrator seems to consider the bedouin madmen anyhow. It is not to be forgotten, however, that this is a novel, and that horror stories belong to the genre; this fact seriously impairs the authenticity of the report.

A more striking parallel has been adduced from eyewitness reports of modern Morocco, collected especially by Raoul Brunel (1926). The Aissaoua form a kind of secret society consisting of several clans, each of which is named after an animal, and the members, in their initiation rites, are made to imitate their emblem. Clans of jackals, cats, dogs, leopards, and lions specialize in tearing apart animals and devouring them raw on the spot; in the words of an informant quoted by E. R. Dodds (1951), "after the usual beating of tom-toms, screaming of the pipes and monotonous dancing, a sheep is thrown into the middle of the square, upon which all the devotees come to life and tear the animal limb from limb and eat it raw." It is said that the flocks of those who voluntarily offer an animal to the sect will not suffer damage from real predators. Thus a marginal existence is provided with a charismatic status. This seems to be the closest analogy to Dionysian omophagia, though the social setting evidently is fundamentally different.

INTERPRETATIONS. The most common interpretation of ritual "raw-eating" has been based on what James G. Frazer called "the homeopathic effects of a flesh diet": taking in life and strength from a living being in the most direct way. In Hebrew, raw flesh is called "living" flesh. The hypothesis has been added that originally the victim was identical with the god, who is thus appropriated by the worshipers in sacramental communion. A central support of this construct is seen to collapse if omophagia is not directly related to the myth of Dionysos slain. Nor does the hypothesis explain the characteristics of the abnormal usually attached to omophagia, be it a state of madness or a realm of strangers and monsters. Thus it seems preferable to see the rituals in the more general context of precarious civilization struggling with the antinomies of nature, while accepting those antinomies and trying to interpret them within the pertinent cultural systems as a breakthrough to otherness that remains bound to its opposite.

SEE ALSO Cannibalism; Dionysos; Frenzy.

BIBLIOGRAPHY

Alföldi, Andreas. *Die Struktur des voretruskischen Römerstaates.* Heidelberg, 1974. An attempt to trace Eurasian pastoral traditions behind Roman institutions. See pages 141–150 for a discussion of "the raw and the cooked."

Brunel, Raoul. *Essai sur la confrérie religieuse des Aissâoûa au Maroc.* Paris, 1926. An account that has played some role in interpreting Dionysian omophagia.

Burkert, Walter. *Homo Necans: The Anthropology of Ancient Greek Sacrificial Ritual and Myth.* Berkeley, Calif., 1983. An essay on patterns of myth and ritual, including the Dionysian, as formed by prehistoric hunters' traditions.

Detienne, Marcel. *Dionysus Slain.* Baltimore, 1979. A structural study on dietary codes of protest groups.

Dodds, E. R. *The Greeks and the Irrational.* Berkeley, Calif., 1951. A readable and well-documented classic. For a discussion of the Maenads, see pages 270–282.

Frazer, James G. *The Golden Bough* (1890). 12 vols. 3d ed. London, 1911–1915. An indispensable collection of materials, though criticized today for lack of theory and method.

Harrison, Jane E. *Prolegomena to the Study of Greek Religion* (1903). Atlantic Highlands, N.J., 1981. A seminal study on the primitive foundations of Greek religion. Pages 478–500 offer a discussion of omophagia.

Henrichs, Albert. "Greek Maenadism from Olympias to Messalina." *Harvard Studies in Classical Philology* 82 (1978): 121–160.

Lévi-Strauss, Claude. *The Raw and the Cooked.* New York, 1969. A basic book of French structuralism, treating Amerindian myths as a system of nature-culture antithesis.

Nilsson, Martin P. *The Dionysiac Mysteries of the Hellenistic and Roman Age* (1957). New York, 1975. A reliable account of the evidence.

Smith, W. Robertson. *Lectures on the Religion of the Semites* (1889). New York, 1969. A fundamental study on animal sacrifice from a functional perspective.

New Sources

Astour, Michael C. "Sparagmos, Omophagia, and Ecstatic Prophecy at Mari." *Ugarit-Forschungen* 24 (1993): 1–2.

Burkert, Walter. *Ancient Mystery Cults.* Cambridge, Mass., 1987.

Burkert, Walter. *Creation of the Sacred: Tracks of Biology in Early Religions.* Cambridge, Mass., 1996.

Evans, Arthur. *The God of Ecstasy.* New York, 1988.

Godwin, Joscelyn. *Mystery Religions in the Ancient World.* San Francisco, 1981.

Hamerton-Kelly, Robert G., ed. *Violent Origins: Walter Burkert, René Girard and Jonathan Z. Smith on Ritual Killing and Cultural Formation.* Stanford, Calif., 1987.

WALTER BURKERT (1987)
Revised Bibliography

ŌMOTOKYŌ

ŌMOTOKYŌ. Founded at Ayabe, Kyoto prefecture, in 1892, Ōmotokyō constitutes a typical Japanese new religion under the modern emperor system. Ōmotokyō, absorbing folk religious traditions, Kokugaku (National Studies) teachings, and ideas from various modern thoughts, created a distinctive syncretic Shintō doctrine.

The founder of Ōmotokyō, Deguchi Nao (1837–1918), was the widow of a poor carpenter. On the lunar New Year, 1892, at the age of fifty-six, she was by her own account possessed by the *kami* (deity) Konjin. In this early religious experience, Nao, influenced by the teachings of Konkōkyō (an earlier new religion), conceived a powerful faith in the benevolent nature of the *kami* Konjin, a belief that contrasted with established notions of that deity's malevolence. The following year, however, Nao was confined to a room as insane. There, under the command of the *kami,* she began writing her *Ofudesaki* (The tip of the divine writing brush), which became a scripture of Ōmotokyō. Thereafter, Nao's healing powers began to win converts to Konjin, and she eventually left Konkōkyō to promulgate her own teachings.

Nao criticized the new materialistic society that caused suffering for poorer people, calling for a utopian age of peace and compassion. In *Ofudesaki* she proclaimed an eschatological viewpoint of world renewal (*yonaoshi*), urging the realization of the ideal world of Miroku's (Bodhisattva Maitreya's) age and the salvation of the people.

Later, Nao's small following welcomed Ueda Kisaburō (later, Deguchi Onisaburō, 1871–1948), a religious practitioner, and together they created the Kimmei Reigakkai (Association of Konjin Believers and Spiritual Researchers).

Onisaburō was the son of a poor farmer in the suburbs of Kameoka in Kyoto prefecture. As a result of his many religious experiences, he was able to heal the sick and had mastered syncretistic Shintō teachings and shamanistic practices. Together, Nao and Onisaburō worked to systematize their religious insights.

Ōmotokyō proposed a myth of the withdrawal of the nation's founders. This myth emphasized faith in the two *kami* Kunitokodachi no Mikoto and Susano-o no Mikoto, holding that these founding *kami,* who were the original rulers of Japan, had been expelled by evil *kami,* causing chaos in the world. According to Ōmotokyō belief, however, the time will arrive when a legitimate government of the *kami* will be realized. This notion could be perceived as a challenge to the national myth that regards Amaterasu Ōmikami as the divine ancestor of the imperial line, thus denying the divine status of the emperor and the legitimacy of his reign.

In its early years, however, Ōmotokyō was beset by difficulties and dissention. The proselytizing activities of Ōmotokyō's leaders increasingly suffered from police interference and suppression, and by the beginning of the twentieth century the number of believers had dwindled. Internal strife broke out, and as a result of opposition to Nao and the old leaders, Onisaburō left Ayabe for Kyoto, where he became a Shintō priest.

In 1908, having broadened his viewpoint, Onisaburō returned to Ayabe with plans for the expansion of Ōmotokyō. Despite police oppression, the Kimmei Reigakkai grew into the Dainihon Shūsaikai (the Japanese Purification Society) and then the Kōdō Ōmoto (Great Foundation of the Imperial Way). With the beginning of World War I, Ōmotokyō leadership found the time ripe for a reorganization of the world and began intensive campaigns in the streets of Tokyo, Kyoto, and Osaka. The economic and social instability of the age made Ōmotokyō, with its opposition to capitalists, landlords, and the war, an attractive ideology to intellectuals, but prominent military and business figures also became followers.

Kōdō Ōmoto, in accordance with government policy, followed a Shintō-based doctrine that emphasized patriotism. Its members held strong eschatological views and preached rites of possession called *Chinkon Kishin.* The movement advocated a restoration of proper government by the *kami* during the Taishō era. This "Taishō restoration" would take place, the leaders prophesied, when Ayabe became the capital of the government they had envisioned.

Onisaburō was ambiguous about whether he should be the supreme leader, who is the Buddhist savior Miroku or the Japanese emperor (*Ten'no*) would be the savior. But he clearly advocated a wholesale restructuring of society and Japan's supreme leadership in the coming world. In 1921 the Kyoto prefectural police raided the Ōmotokyō headquarters in Ayabe, and the leaders of the movement were arrested on charges of *lèse majesté.* The central sanctuary, a Miroku hall built the previous year, was destroyed, and Nao's tomb was ordered reconstructed because it resembled that of an emperor. The charges against the religion were later dismissed in the amnesty at the time of the funeral of the Taishō emperor.

After surviving its first persecution, Ōmotokyō entered a new stage of development, expanding its activities both within and outside the country. Onisaburō dictated the large scripture *Reikai Monogatari* (Tale of the spirit world; 1922) and while out on bail secretly traveled to Mongolia, where he unsuccessfully attempted to create a separate state by calling himself a living buddha. Ōmotokyō, in consonance with post–World War I international humanist thought, urged the adoption of Esperanto and advanced the notions that all religions have the same origin and that all men are brothers. It cooperated in the Chinese charitable religious organization Dao-yüan (*Doin*), developing the Federated Association of World Religions at Beijing. Within Japan it formed the Jinrui Aizenkai (Association of Benevolence for Mankind).

In 1934 Ōmotokyō formed the Shōwa Shinseikai (Shōwa Sanctity Society), and under the leader Onisaburō it proceeded to the practical implementation of political reform. Taking right-wing politicians as advisers, they called for an end to parliamentary government and urged reconstruction of the state under the supremacy of the emperor. These political views were understandably alarming to the government, which was simultaneously confronted by a series of plots by rightists and young army officers. On December 8, 1935, armed special police made surprise attacks on Ōmotokyō's headquarters at Kameoka and Ayabe, arresting 210 administrators. A nationwide search also was conducted by the commander of the Police Bureau of the Home Affairs Ministry. In the following year sixty-two officials of Ōmotokyō were indicted for the crime of *lèse majesté* and for violation of the Peace Preservation Law; the Ministry of Home Affairs immediately proscribed Ōmotokyō. In the aftermath of this action the government ordered the destruction of Ōmotokyō facilities.

In 1942, after a long court battle and more than six years in jail, the officials were released on bail. Bitterly resentful of the violent oppression by the authorities and convinced of the inevitability of Japan's defeat, Onisaburō criticized the war and preached a faith to the believers who secretly visited him, revealing that his failure to participate in the war effort was a manifestation of divine will. Following the war, Ōmotokyō was reconstructed as Aizen'en and took as its historical mission the establishment of world peace. It was for the foundation of this new world, Onisaburō claimed, that the *kami* had allowed Ōmotokyō to survive the war. Onisaburō died in 1948, and the group returned to its former name Ōmoto in 1952.

In 1949 Ōmoto joined the World Federation movement, and the peace campaign became an important part of its activities. Ōmoto played a major role in the protest movement against the nuclear weapons experiments in the 1950s and the early 1960s. Ōmoto continues to be active in the World Federation movement, but its emphasis on peace has weakened. In the 1990s Ōmoto announced its official view on bioethics. It is critical of the notion of brain death and of research using human embryos. Ōmoto's importance in the religious history of modern Japan is emphasized by the fact that many new religions, including Seichō no Ie and World Messianity, were heavily influenced by Ōmoto. In 2002 Ōmoto's official membership within Japan was 172,000 persons.

SEE ALSO New Religious Movements, article on New Religious Movements in Japan.

BIBLIOGRAPHY

Deguchi Nao. *Ofudesaki, the Holy Scriptures of Oomoto.* Translated by Hino Iwao. Tokyo, 1979.

Iwao, Hino. *The Outline of Oomoto.* Kameoka, Japan, 1968.

Murakami Shigeyoshi. *Japanese Religion in the Modern Century.* Translated by H. Byron Earhart. Tokyo, 1980. Originally published as *Kindai hyakunen no shukyo.*

Oomoto and Universal Love and Brotherhood Association. *Oomoto.* (1956–). An English-language periodical, issued bimonthly.

Ooms, Emily Groszos. *Women and Millenarian Protest in Meiji Japan.* Ithaca, N.Y., 1993.

Yasumaru Yoshio. *Deguchi Nao.* Tokyo, 1977.

MURAKAMI SHIGEYOSHI (1987)
SHIMAZONO SUSUMU (2005)

OMPHALOS SEE CENTER OF THE WORLD

ONA RELIGION SEE SELK'NAM RELIGION

ONGON. In all Mongolian languages, the term *ongon* is applied to the dwelling-place of a spirit or sacred being. In the traditional shamanistic context it refers to any spirit, together with the object in which that spirit resides. There is a great variety of such dwellings. Some are natural (e.g., lakes, trees, living animals, skinned animals), and hence certain scholars refer to the notion of *ongon* as totemism. Others are artificial (e.g., drawings on rock, wooden or felt figurines, drawings on cloth); for these the collective form *ongot* is reserved. Some are suspended and clearly visible either in or outside the yurt; others are locked away in sacks or caskets.

A ritual act, usually carried out by a shaman, is required for each of these natural or artificial mediums to become an *ongon.* For natural *ongons*, this consists of establishing a relationship with the spirit that animates and is indistinguishable from the natural being; and for artificial ones, the rite is one that introduces the desired spirit into the created receptacle. A spirit must be fastened down so that humans can have contact with him and control him, for on the one hand a wandering spirit may be dangerous, and on the other an empty receptacle is in danger of being filled by an undesirable spirit.

The ritual treatment of all categories of *ongons* is essentially the act of feeding them. Food is given to living animals; meat, butter, or cream is either set down beside the figurines, placed in their mouths, or rubbed on them. Tobacco offerings accompany the food, and the practitioner smokes a ritual pipe. The sanction for failure to feed the *ongon* is sickness or death, which has led certain writers to attribute a primarily medical function to the *ongons*.

The *ongon* cult is based on the conception of a structural similarity between intrahuman relationships on the one hand and relationships that tie humans to nature for sources of the former's subsistence on the latter. Everything that happens in one domain inevitably has consequences in the other. Like humans, the animals are conceived as being organized in clans. Furthermore, relationships between humans and animals are modeled on intrahuman relationships. These relationships are both interclan (involving alliance and vengeance) and intraclan (involving filiation or descent). For humans and animals alike, being excluded from a clan creates frustration and therefore the desire to seek revenge, a cause of trouble for the whole community. Hence, in addition to clan *ongons*, there are also *ongons* representing isolated or unaffiliated spirits, which may receive the cult either from one family or from several clans.

The various modes of access to natural resources are what determine the most significant differences between *ongons*. Situated within the confines of the forest and the steppe, the Mongolian peoples have all made their living by hunting. Only subsequently did they adopt pastoralism to a certain extent. When it is hunting that provides sustenance, the relationship between humans and nature is conceived of as based on the model of a marriage exchange, wherein the hunter is to the spirit dispenser of game, Bayan Khangay ("rich forest"), as a son-in-law is to his father-in-law. The hunter takes game from Bayan Khangay just as a man takes his wife from his father-in-law: He is a taker, proud of his catch, yet guilty for not having given anything in exchange. First, the ritual of the hunt aims to reduce the capture of game to a capture of food. The skeleton and the respiratory organs containing the vital breath of life are disposed of in such a way that the animal is allowed to be reborn. Next, the real compensation for the food (i.e., game taken from nature) is made by feeding *ongons* either small tamed animals (eagles, cygnets, etc.) or figurines or drawings representing animals, skins of animals, or the like. Thus this system of food exchange is similar to the exchange of women in the marriage alliance system: a man accepts his wife from one family, and in return offers his sister or daughter in marriage to another. This feeding of *ongons* is primarily intended to ensure that the hunt will not be hindered by the vengeance of decimated animal clans or the revenge of deceased unlucky hunters. In the event of an unsuccessful hunt, the *ongon* that is considered to have failed to carry out its part of the contract, although correctly fed, is reviled, beaten, destroyed, thrown out, and replaced by a new one.

Pastoralism, on the other hand, switches the nature of human-spirit relationships from one of alliance to one of filiation. The attitude of an exacting contracting party that prevails under the alliance model gives way to an attitude of veneration on the part of the filial descendent. This is because there is a patrimony (herds and grazing rights) to protect and hand down. In addition, sacrifices are made to one's ancestors in order to guarantee pastoral legitimacy. The compensation for the resources taken from the herd is the food given to the *ongon:* living consecrated animals (mature males that are raised within the herd, then slaughtered before growing old and replaced by younger males), zoomorphic representations (accompanied by a human silhouette fashioned in tin, representing a soul) or anthropomorphs (primarily representing women who died without experiencing childbirth, a check to filiation that results in the herd being stricken with epizootic diseases). As early as the thirteenth century Giovanni da Pian del Carpini noted felt dolls suspended from two sides of the yurt, made and honored by the women to protect the herds. In addition, the body of the shaman itself is a medium for spirits during the Buriat shamanic séance called *ongo oruulkha,* "introducing the spirits."

As a result of their primary function of linking the social, economic and religious worlds, the *ongons* and the shamans themselves have been subjected to severe persecution from Lamaism. This persecution dates from the time when Lamaism penetrated into central Mongolia (seventeenth century) and the Buriat Republic (nineteenth century).

SEE ALSO Buriat Religion; Mongol Religions; Shamanism.

BIBLIOGRAPHY

Harva, Uno. *Les representations religieuses des peuples altaïques* (1938). Paris, 1959. A rich and well-documented presentation that suffers from an awkward separation of fact from context.

Heissig, Walther. "Die Religionen der Mongolei." In Giuseppe Tucci and Walther Heissig, *Die Religionen Tibets und der Mongolei.* Stuttgart, 1970. Translated as *The Religions of Mongolia* by Geoffrey Samuel (Berkeley, Calif., 1980). A fine historical presentation that illustrates the struggle of the lamas to suppress shamanism and explains the emergence of a syncretic religious form.

Zelenin, D. K. *Kul't ongonov v Sibiri.* Moscow and Leningrad, 1936. Translated as *Le culte des idoles en Siberie* by G. Welter (Paris, 1952). The only comprehensive work on *ongons,* still valuable because of its abundant documentation and recognition of contractual relationships with the *ongons.* In its evolutionist perspective and insistence on the term *totemism* as a classificatory rubric, however, the work is now outdated.

New Sources

Bawden, C. R. *Confronting the Supernatural: Mongolian Traditional Ways and Means: Collected Papers.* Wiesbaden, 1994.

Birtalan, Á. *Die Mythologie der Mongolischen Volksreligion.* Stuttgart, 2000.

Heissig, Walther. "New Material on East Mongolian Shamanism." *Asian Folklore Studies* 49, no. 2 (1990): 223–233.

Hesse, Klaus. "On the History of Mongolian Shamanism in Anthropological Perspective." *Anthropos* 82, nos. 4–6 (1987): 403–413.

Zhugder, C., and G. Luvsantseren. *Mongold feodalizm togtokh ueiin niigem-uls tur, gun ukhaany setgelgee: ertnees XIV zuun khurtel.* Ulaanbaatar, 2002.

ROBERTE HAMAYON (1987)
Translated from French by Sherri L. Granka
Revised Bibliography

ONMYŌDŌ

ONMYŌDŌ is the collective Japanese name for various methods of divination, originally based on the Chinese theories of yin and yang (Jpn., *onmyō, on'yō,* or *in'yō,* the complementary forces seen in all phenomena), the "five elements" (Chin., *wuxing;* Jpn. *gogyō;* i.e., fire, wood, earth, metal, and water), their cyclical interactions, and the influence thereof in the natural and human spheres. The art of advising individuals and governments in the planning of all manner of activities and projects according to the movements of the sun and moon (representing *yang* and *yin,* respectively) and the stars, and the predicting of auspicious and inauspicious conditions as determined by the shifting relationships of the five elements and the sexagenary cycle (Chin. *shigan shier zhi;* Jpn., *jikkan jūnishi*) were highly developed and extensively documented in China by the beginning of the Han dynasty (206 BCE–220 CE). Some of the major texts, such as the *Yi jing* (Jpn., *Ekikyō*) date from much earlier.

From the time of the introduction of these texts and practices to Japan in the sixth century CE, *onmyōdō* encompassed not only *yinyang* and five-element divination per se but also the related fields of astronomy and astrology, geomancy, meteorology, calendar making (on Chinese models), and chrononomy (chiefly with Chinese water clocks). The word *onmyōdō,* meaning the "way (practice, art) of *yinyang,*" labels these various arts and sciences and the beliefs and practices based on them in a manner similar to the way in which the term *Butsudo* may refer to the whole range of Buddhist ideas and practices; likewise, the term *Shintō* refers broadly to the many organized forms of indigenous Japanese religious tradition (as well as its imported accretions, including some rites and festivals originally associated with *onmyōdō*). Similar nomenclature was also used for specific fields within *onmyōdō,* such as *tenmondō* for astronomy and *rekidō* for calendar studies. The word *uranai* ("augury") is another term used widely for the many forms of divination practiced by *onmyōdō* masters as well as by other types of seers and prognosticators. In early chronicles and works of literature, *onmyōdō* specifically identifies the divining arts as taught and performed in the official Bureau of Divination (Onmyōryō), which was established in the seventh century and which was responsible for providing the court with astronomical observations, astrological forecasts, calendars, accurate timekeeping, and the training of practitioners of these arts. However, *onmyōdō* skills were known and used by many persons outside the bureau, including scholars, physicians, and Buddhist priests, as well as by unschooled fortune-tellers and entertainers. Like many aspects of Japanese religion, *onmyōdō* has both an organized, institutional aspect and a popular, unsystematic aspect as well. Both are present in the history of *onmyōdō* from its beginnings, as is the tendency toward undifferentiated linkage with other religious traditions.

It is likely that some forms of *onmyōdō* thought and practice were known in Japan prior to what is recorded as their formal introduction. It has been observed, for instance, that the emphasis on duality in Japanese cosmogony (as narrated in the *Kojiki,* 712 CE) may reflect the influence of the *yinyang* concept. It would appear that *yinyang* and related elements of Chinese philosophy were fairly compatible with indigenous ideas of creation and causation, as well as with other beliefs. Although its origins were just as "alien," *onmyōdō* certainly did not meet with the kind of organized opposition that confronted the contemporaneous introduction of Buddhism.

According to the *Nihonshoki* (720), it was in 513 that Korean scholars introduced the "five texts"—a group of classic Chinese works, including the *Yi jing*—to the court of the (semihistorical) Emperor Keitai. In 554, Korean *Yi jing* professors (*Eki hakase*) and calendar masters who had been serving at the court of Emperor Kinmei were replaced by new ones. In 602, the Korean Buddhist monk Kanroku presented himself to the court of Empress Suiko, along with up-to-date almanacs and books of astrology, geography and magic. Prince Shōtoku (574–622), Suiko's nephew and regent, is said to have chosen the colors of the caps used in his civil rank system on the basis of *onmyōdō* symbolism. The "Seventeen Article Constitution" attributed to him (although perhaps a later work) has also been said to reflect *onmyōdō* concepts of social order. When the scholars Minabuchi Shōgen and Takamuko Genri returned in 640 from a long period of study in China they introduced the latest in Chinese divining texts and practices. But even at this early stage, Japanese *onmyōdō* was distinguished from its Chinese models by the extent to which it incorporated other arts of divination, natural science, and what were probably native forms of magic. Nor was *onmyōdō* thought of as a discipline entirely separate from Buddhism or the other religions, philosophies, and forms of learning imported at the same time; the *onmyōdō* teacher Kanroku, for example, was also a high-ranking Buddhist monk.

Among the Taika reforms instituted in 645 was the adoption of a system of era names (Chin., *nianhao;* Jpn., *nengō*) consisting of two (or occasionally four) auspicious Chinese ideographs with symbolic significance based on *onmyōdō* teachings. The first era name chosen was *Taika,* literally "great change (or reform)." Eras were renamed at irregular intervals, usually when some especially good omen was reported, such as the discovery of rare metals, albino animals (particularly turtles, the color white and the creature both being deemed auspicious), or the sighting of a very favorable cloud formation. Several of the *nengō* of the late seventh and most of the eighth centuries include ideographs for metals, colors (white and red), "turtle," "cloud," and other auspicious signs. In the Heian period, *nengō* were changed more frequently, often in response to such inauspicious phenomena as solar eclipses, typhoons, droughts, and earthquakes.

Emperor Temmu (r. 672–686) is said to have been adept at the *onmyōdō* arts. An astronomical observatory was built early in his reign, and he probably used its findings in the surveying and construction of his capital at Kiyomihara, in what was believed to be a favorable location in relation to the topography and the deserted capitals of his predecessors. Generally, the north was regarded as a seat of power, while the northeast was viewed as the source of malevolence; the North Star, Polaris (Daigoku) was closely watched. As in China, Japanese capitals, including the permanent capitals Heijō (Nara) and Heian (Kyoto), were all constructed on carefully surveyed north-south axes, and official buildings and residences were placed where they might best receive favorable influences or be protected from evil ones, according to *onmyōdō* geomancy.

The Onmyōryō was organized soon after Temmu took the throne, and its structure remained unchanged for centuries. The chief of the bureau (*onmyō no kami*) was a senior master responsible for reporting the observations of his subordinates to the emperor. The bureau employed six divination masters (*onmyōji*), who performed the real work of observing and forecasting, and one professor of divination (*onmyo hakase*), who supervised ten students (*onmyōshō*). There was also one professor in each of the fields of calendar-making and astrology, each with ten students, as well as two professors of chrononomy. *Onmyōji* were also assigned to various provincial administrative centers. Famous masters of the eighth century include Kibi Makibi (693–775) and Abe Nakamaro (698–770), both of whom studied at length in China. Because divination could easily be used either in the interest of or against the government, efforts were made to limit divination activities to officially trained practitioners. The laws governing the activities of Buddhist monks and nuns (Sōniryō), enacted in 757 as part of the Yōrō Code, included specific punishments for those who falsely reported omens of disaster that might cause the people to lose confidence in the authority of the state.

The chronicles, diaries, and literary works of the Heian period (794–1185) are rich with information on the role of *onmyōdō* at court and in society. It is clear that it was at this time that *onmyōdō* reached the height of its importance. About fifty different *onmyōdō* rites are mentioned as having been observed at court. Among them were the Taizenfukunsai, honoring a Chinese deity who oversees the spirits of the dead; the Dokōsai, for Dokujin, or Tsuchi no Kami, the mischievous earth deity whose seasonal movements were closely watched; the Tensochifusai, performed once in each reign to honor war dead and to ward off disease; and the Shikakushikyōsai, wherein the spirits that cause sickness were placated with offerings in each of the four corners of the ceremonial space and at each of the four borders of the state. The increase in the emphasis on these rites closely paralleled, and was sometimes linked to, the increase in the importance of Esoteric (Vajrayāna) ritual in Heian Buddhism. The monk Ennin (794–864), the third abbot of the Japanese Tendai school and the figure who introduced many Esoteric elements to it after his period of study in China, is also said to have introduced the worship of Taizenfukun.

Several works of the Heian period indicate that the *onmyōdō* masters stressed astronomical portents over other types of signs in their reports and forecasts. This may reflect the interest of two influential *onmyō no kami,* Shigeoka Kawahito (d. 874) and Yuge Koreo (bureau chief in the Kanpyō era, 889–898). Concern with overt astrological influences became obsessive, and plans for every type of public or private activity were first submitted to *onmyōji* for readings of the governing signs. Directional taboos (*kataimi*), dictated by the rising and falling of one's birth sign (i.e., the two signs of the sexagenary cycle that were in convergence at the time of one's birth) and their relationship to others' signs, or by the association of those signs or of certain deities with certain directions, were strictly observed. In 865, Emperor Seiwa was advised that traveling from the crown prince's residence to the palace by a northwest-to-southeast route could have fatal consequences, and he duly altered his course. Such directional changes (*katatagae*) were also made to avoid sectors favored at particular seasons by untrustworthy deities, especially Ten'ichijin, (usually called Nakagami), Dokujin, and Konjin, the "metal god." Nakagami's influences were particularly feared. He was believed to be active first in the northeast for six days, then for five days in the east, six in the southeast, five in the south and so on around the compass. The whole forty-four day period was termed a *futagari* ("obstacle"), because activity was blocked at almost every turn.

Travel to and from the dangerous northeast, called *kimon* ("demon's gateway") was also scrupulously avoided. This direction was believed to be favored by a deity called Daishogun, an active manifestation of the deity Taihakujin, identified in turn with the planet Venus. According to Venus's position, specific days in each sexagenary cycle, and certain hours on certain days, were judged especially unlucky. If an appointment required people to travel in a prohibited direction on a given day they might veer off in a safe direction on the day prior to it; after passing the night, they could proceed toward their destination without fear of adverse effect. Sei Shonagon, the author of *Makura no sōshi* (The pillow book), a journal and miscellany of court life, is among the Heian writers who describe this technique. Hikaru Genji, the hero of the great romance *Genji monogatari,* frequently cites directional taboos as a reason for absence from or neglect of one or another of his many lovers.

Within the Heian bureaucracy, the Onmyōryō became the virtually exclusive domain of the Abe and Kamo clans. For generations beginning in the mid-tenth century, *onmyōdō* practices were divided between the two clans, the Kamo being the masters of the art of the calendar and the Abe controlling astronomical studies. The twenty-fourth volume of *Konjaku monogatari shū* contains a series of stories about the exploits of illustrious members of these clans as well as those of their predecessors and of some anonymous practitioners, including Buddhist monks. The emphasis in these stories is on the use of special insights to perceive life-threatening dangers and the secret techniques used to outwit them. Abe Yasuchika, a particularly accomplished *onmyō no kami,* is said to have relied on three texts—*Konkikyō, Suikyō,* and *Jinsūryōkyō*—which he referred to as "the three *onmyōdō* classics." A Sui dynasty manual, *Wuxing taiyi* (Jpn., *Gogyō taigi*), attributed to Xiao Ji was also used by many masters. In 1210, the *onmyō hakase* Abe Takashige was asked by Retired Emperor Go-Toba to prepare a new manual based on classical texts. The result, a work known as *Onmyōdō hakase Abe Takashige kanjinki,* prescribes divination for the undertaking of construction projects and official excursions, with many examples from Heian practice.

After the twelfth century, as political power passed from the Heian court to a series of military dictators, the heyday of official *onmyōdō* came to an end. Calendar studies fell into decline, while interest shifted to numerology, *sukuyōdō,* a form of astrology strongly influenced by Esoteric Buddhism, and folk astrologies. When the Kamo line of *rekidō* masters died out in about 1400, the Abe clan reclaimed the calendar legacy and, as a reward for helpful predictions, were granted the surname Tsuchimikado and the hereditary *onmyōdō* monopoly by Emperor Gokomatsu. The Tsuchimikado name remains closely linked with the remainder of *onmyōdō* history. Tsuchimikado Shintō, also known as Abe Shintō, is a sect that combines *onmyōdō* elements with Shintō. It traces its origins to Tsuchimikado Yasutomi (1655–1717). When the shogun Tokugawa Yoshimune (1652–1751) wanted to adopt a Western calendar he was defied by Tsuchimikado Yasukuni, who asserted the right of his family—and of the Kyōto establishment over the Edo shogunate—to exercise control of the calendar. He prepared a new one, the Hōreki calendar, which was promulgated in 1754.

Meanwhile, a class of professional conjurers, the *shōmonji,* had appropriated many *onmyōdō* functions, which they combined with sūtra chanting, dancing and theatricals. Although licensed to perform such entertainments, the *shōmonji* were a despised class. The word *onmyōji,* which previously had denoted a learned master, came to refer to itinerant magicians who roamed the country selling charms, almanacs and advice. Eventually, in the Edo period (1603–1867), both *shōmonji* and *onmyōji* were labeled outcasts and were forced to reside in ghettos. In some of these, their descendants still practice the ancient arts of their ancestors. Many modern fortune-tellers and astrologers continue to rely on basic *onmyōdō* methods, while many Japanese still refuse to live in a house with northeastern exposure or to position their beds in a way that might invite the malignant effects that come from that quarter.

SEE ALSO Japanese Religions, article on Popular Religion; Yinyang Wuxing.

BIBLIOGRAPHY

The first major work of modern scholarship on *onmyōdō* was Saitō Tsutomu's *Ōchō jidai no onmyōdō* (Tokyo, 1915). More recently, Murayama Shūichi has devoted much of his career to the study of *onmyōdō*'s history, treating it most comprehensively in his *Nihon onmyōdōshi sōsetsu* (Tokyo, 1981). His work is complemented by that of Yoshino Hiroko, whose *Nihon kodai jujutsu: onmyō gogyō to Nihon genshi shinkō* (Tokyo, 1974) and *Onmyō gogyō shisō kara mita Nihon no matsuri* (Tokyo, 1978) document the role of *onmyōdō* in various early cults and rites, with many diagrams and illustrations. See also *Classical Learning and Daoist Practices in Early Japan: Engishiki,* translated by Felicia G. Bock (Tempe, Ariz., 1985). A helpful table, explaining the various applications of the sexagenary cycle, forms part of the article by Fujita Tomio, "Jikkan jūnishi" (in English), in the *Encyclopedia of Japan* (Tokyo, 1983), vol. 4, pp. 55–57. The most comprehensive history of calendar study in Japan is Satō Masatsugu's *Nihon rekigaku shi* (Tokyo, 1968). On era names, see Takigawa Masajirō's *Nengō kōshō* (Tokyo, 1974). A highly regarded study of directional taboos is Bernard Frank's *Kataimi et katatagae: Étude sur les interdits de direction à l'époque Heian* (Tokyo, 1958). Nakamura Shōhachi has transcribed and edited *Gogyō taigi* (Tokyo, 1973) and has also produced a study, *Gogyō taigi no kisoteki kenkyū* (Tokyo, 1976). A translation of the early legal codes, giving the structure of the Onmyōryō as well as a translation of the Sōniryō, may be found in Sir George Sansom's "Early Japanese Law and Administration," *Transactions of the Asiatic Society of Japan,* 2d ser., 9 (1932): 67–109 and 11 (1935): 117–149. There is extensive material on *shōmonji* and the later *onmyōji* in Hori Ichirō's *Wagakuni minkan shinkōshi no kenkyū,* 2 vols. (Tokyo, 1953–1955), some of which is incorporated in his *Folk Religion in Japan,* edited and translated by Joseph M. Kitagawa and Alan L. Miller (Chicago, 1968).

EDWARD KAMENS (1987)

ONTOLOGY. The word *ontology,* meaning "discourse about, or study of, being," was introduced into the philosophical vocabulary in the early seventeenth century. The term was originally used as an equivalent for "metaphysics," which Aristotle, in *Metaphysics* 4.1, had defined precisely as the science that treats "being insofar as it is being." Thus the enterprise of ontology had a long prehistory.

Plato had considered the question of "being" (*to on, ousia*), which for him meant the "what" of things as a stable object of certain knowledge. Hence he thought that the term *being* was properly employed only of the self-identical, changeless, and hence eternal, realm of Forms—that reality, grasped by intellect alone, which is imaged in, but at the same time contrasted with, the mutable realm of "becoming." It was Aristotle, critical of this outright identification of being with the immutable and transcendent Forms, who insisted that the verb "to be" is universally applicable and then proceeded to ask what it means to be (anything). Because, as he frequently observes, "'being' is said in many senses," he denies in effect that the term is used univocally or that it defines an all-inclusive genus. He nevertheless thinks that its primary or focal use is to denote the *subject,* whether of discourse or of change and action: To be is to be some concrete "thing" (*ousia*)—a changing, individual composite of two correlative principles, form and matter or (in more general terms) actuality and potentiality. The former of these is the active principle of the thing's growth and development (*phusis,* "nature"), the intelligible identity of it which the mind grasps in knowledge and expresses in judgment, while the latter is the substratum of possibility that allows for change.

This analysis of what "being" means was substantively taken over in the metaphysics of Thomas Aquinas (1225–1274). Thomas, however, broadened the application of Aristotle's distinction between actuality and potentiality. It included not merely the distinction between the form and the matter that determines the "what" (*id quod,* "essence") of a thing, but also, and more fundamentally, that between what a thing is and the fact that it is (*id quo,* "existence"). Essence for Thomas is a potentiality that is brought into "act" only through existing; hence the study of being, in considering the question what it means to be this or that (thing), must focus not merely on what gives a thing ("substance") its identity but also on what accounts for its "being there," its actual existence.

In his treatise *First Philosophy or Ontology* (1729), however, Christian Wolff (1679–1754), whose work established the normal modern use of the term, understood ontology as a subdivision of metaphysics: the study of being as a genus ("general metaphysics"), to be distinguished from the subjects of "special metaphysics," that is, theology, psychology, and cosmology. *Being,* then, was for Wolff a univocal term denoting "what is" in its most universal characteristics. Aristotle's (and Thomas's) insistence on the "many senses" in which "to be" is said recedes into the background: For Wolff, the fundamental principles of being are the laws of noncontradiction and of sufficient reason. Reality is composed of imperceptible simple substances each of whose essences is exhausted by a single clear and distinct idea, and whose existence is accounted for by appeal to the principle of sufficient reason.

This science of generic being, abstract and deductive in form, was rejected by Immanuel Kant (1724–1804), for whom *ontology*—a term he used very infrequently—came in effect to be identified with his own transcendental philosophy. This enterprise was concerned not with "things in themselves" but with the subjective preconditions of human knowledge—the forms of sense-perception and the categories of the understanding—through which the "objects" of the empirical world are constituted as such. The propaedeutic study of being thus became, for Kant, an investigation of the ways in which the subject of knowing "objectifies" the content of experience and so constitutes the "beings" of the phenomenal world. Like Kant, G. W. F. Hegel (1770–1831) rejected Wolff's "dogmatic" ontology. For him, the study of being took the form of a logic, which explicated the movement—from simplicity to organic complexity, from "being" to "concept"—by which Mind (*Geist*) appropriates itself through self-objectification.

In more recent philosophy, the project of ontology, long neglected save in theological circles where traditional scholastic philosophy prevailed, reappeared in the work of Edmund Husserl (1859–1938). Husserl's search for a sure basis of human knowledge led him to elaborate a phenomenological method that sought to identify and describe "what is" as the world of the "transcendental ego" or "pure consciousness" (as distinct from the empirical self, which is a member of the object-world of scientific inquiry). It was Husserl's student and critic Martin Heidegger (1889–1976), however, who through his *Being and Time* most explicitly and influentially revived the project of ontology. For Heidegger, "being" ("to be") is radically distinguished from "beings" ("what there is"). The former is the subject of ontological, the latter of merely "ontic," discourse. The clue to the question of being is, for him, the existent human subject (*Dasein*), which *is* precisely in the act of asking what it means "to be." To grasp what it is "to be" is thus to grasp what is presupposed in the human existent's asking about its being. Ontology is thus again, as for Kant, a transcendental analysis—but not, in this case, of the preconditions of human knowing so much as of the preconditions of human "being-in-the-world."

See Also Metaphysics.

Bibliography

Gilson, Étienne. *Being and Some Philosophers.* Toronto, 1949.

Kung, Guido. *Ontology and the Logistic Analysis of Language.* New York, 1967.

Martin, Gottfried. *Kant's Metaphysics and Theory of Science.* Manchester, U.K., 1961.

New Sources

Collier, Andrew. *Critical Realism: An Introduction to Roy Bashkar's Philosophy.* 1985; reprint, London, 1994.

Snyder, Daniel Howard, and Paul Moser. *Divine Hiddenness: New Essays.* Cambridge, U.K., 2002.

Weissman, David. *A Social Ontology.* New Haven, Conn., 2000.

Richard A. Norris (1987)
Revised Bibliography

ORACLES.

The word *oracle* is derived from the Latin word *oraculum,* which referred both to a divine pronouncement or response concerning the future or the unknown as well as to the place where such pronouncements were given. (The Latin verb *orare* means "to speak" or "to request.") In English, *oracle* is also used to designate the human medium through whom such prophetic declarations or oracular sayings are given.

Oracles and Prophecy. In Western civilization the connotations of the word *oracle* (variously rendered in European languages) have been largely determined by traditional perceptions of ancient Greek oracles, particularly the oracle of Apollo at Delphi. The term *prophecy,* on the other hand (from the Greek word *propheteia,* meaning "prophecy" or "oracular response"), has been more closely associated with traditions of divine revelation through human mediums in ancient Israel and early Christianity. One major cause of this state of affairs is that in the Septuagint (the Greek translation of the Hebrew scriptures made during the third and second centuries BCE) Greek words from the *prophēt-* family were used to translate words derived from the biblical Hebrew root *nv'* ("prophet, to prophesy"). Because most oracles in the Greek world were given in response to inquiries, oracles are often regarded as verbal responses by a supernatural being, in contrast to prophecy, which is thought of as unsolicited verbal revelations given through human mediums and often directed toward instigating social change. In actuality, question-and-answer revelatory "séances" were common in ancient Israel, and it was only with the appearance in the eighth century BCE of free prophets such as Amos, Isaiah, and Hosea that unsolicited prophecy became common. Further, the preservation of the prophetic speeches of the classical Israelite prophets in the Hebrew scriptures has served to ensure the dominance of this particular image of Israelite prophets and prophecy. Therefore, modern distinctions between "oracles" and "prophecy" are largely based on the discrete conventions of classical and biblical tradition rather than upon a cross-cultural study of the subject, though the terms themselves are often used and interchanged indiscriminately in modern anthropological studies.

Oracles and Divination. Oracles are but one of several types of divination, which is the art or science of interpreting symbols understood as messages from the gods. Such symbols often require the interpretive expertise of a trained specialist and are frequently based on phenomena of an unpredictable or even trivial nature. The more common types of divination in the Greco-Roman world included the casting of lots (sortilege), the flight and behavior of birds (ornithomancy), the behavior of sacrificial animals and the condition of their vital organs (e.g., hepatoscopy, or liver divination), various omens or sounds (cledonomancy), and dreams (oneiromancy). Chinese civilization made elaborate use of divination, partly as an expression of the Confucian belief in fate. Some of the more popular methods included the use of divining sticks and blocks (the latter called *yin-yang gua*), used together or separately; body divination to predict the character and future behavior of select individuals (palmistry, physiognomy); astrology; the determination of the proper location of buildings and graves in accordance with yin and yang factors and the five elements (geomancy); coin divination; planchette divination or spirit writing; and the use of the *Yi jing* (Book of changes) for divination based on the symbol *bagua,* that is, the eight trigrams constituting the sixty-four hexagrams that provide the basis for the book.

Oracles (or prophecies) themselves are messages from the gods in human language concerning the future or the unknown and are usually received in response to specific inquiries, often through the agency of inspired mediums. Oracles have, in other words, a basic linguistic character not found in other forms of divination. This linguistic character is evident in the sometimes elaborately articulated inquiries made of the deities in either spoken or written form. In addition, oracles themselves exhibit a linguistic character ranging from the symbolized "yes" or "no" response, or "auspicious" or "inauspicious" response, of many lot oracles, to the elaborately crafted replies spoken and/or written by mediums while experiencing possession trance or vision trance, or shortly thereafter. This linguistic character of oracles presupposes an anthropomorphic conception of the supernatural beings concerned.

In actuality, oracles are usually so closely associated with other forms of divination that it is difficult to insist on rigid distinctions. Some commentators have vainly attempted to distinguish between oracles and divination by claiming that *oracle* is used only in connection with a specific deity, one often connected with a particular place. Other forms of divination were in fact used in all the ancient Greek oracle sanctuaries, often as an alternate form of consultation. At the oracle of Delphi, for example, where Apollo was believed to be present only nine months each year, oracular consultations were held in ancient times on only one day each year, the seventh day of the seventh month (seven was Apollo's sacred number), though they became more frequent with the passing centuries. On other auspicious days it has been supposed that the god could be consulted by means of a lot oracle, the exact nature of which is disputed. Questions were formulated to receive a yes or no answer, and oracular personnel may have used some type of lot oracle to answer such inquiries. In China divination was employed in all except Confucian temples; even in temples specializing in spirit mediumship, divinatory techniques such as divining sticks and divining blocks were regularly used.

A distinction between oracles and divination was made by the Roman orator Cicero (106–43 BCE), following Plato (c. 429–347 BCE) and the philosopher Posidonius (c. 135–50 BCE). This distinction was between (1) "technical" or "inductive" divination (Lat., *artificiosa divinatio;* Gr., *technikē mantikē*), based on special training in the interpretation of signs, sacrifices, dreams, prodigies, and the like, and (2) "natural" or "intuitive" divination (Lat., *naturalis divinatio;* Gr., *atechnos* or *adi-daktos mantikē*), based on the direct inspiration of the practitioner through trance or vision (Cicero, *De divinatio* 1.6.12; cf. Plato, *Ion* 534c). The Greek term for all forms of divination is *mantikē,* which, on account of its etymological relation to the term *mania* ("madness, inspired frenzy"), might appear a more appropriate designation for intuitive divination, yet even in the most archaic Greek texts it was not so used. A third category can be added, "interpretive" divination, in which a combination of inspired insight and technical skill is required.

TYPES OF ORACLES. Oracles are usually associated either with a sacred place where they are available in the setting of a public religious institution or with a specially endowed person who acts as a paid functionary or a freelance practitioner.

Oracular places. In the ancient Mediterranean world certain places were thought to enjoy a special sanctity, particularly caves, springs, elevations, and places struck by lightning (especially oak trees). The emphasis on the oracular powers inherent in particular sites is due to the ancient Greek belief that the primal goddess Gaia ("earth") was the source of oracular inspiration. While oracle shrines were rare among the Romans (the lot oracle of Fortuna Primigenia, goddess of fertility, at Praeneste was the most popular), they were very common in the Greek world. Apollo, the primary oracular divinity among the Greeks, had oracles at Delphi, Claros, and Didyma. Zeus had oracles at Dodona, Olympia, and the Oasis of Siwa in Libya (as the Egyptian god Amun); the healing god Asklepios had them at Epidaurus and Rome; and the heroes Amphiaraos and Trophonios had oracular grottoes in Lebadea and Oropus respectively. Each of these oracle shrines required supplicants to fulfill a distinctive set of traditional procedures, and each site had a natural feature connected with its oracular potencies. Springs or pools were closely associated with the oracles of Apollo at Delphi, Claros, and Didyma and in Lycia, with the healing oracle of Demeter at Patrae, with the oracle of Glykon-Asklepios at Abonuteichos, and with the oracle of Amphilochos in Cilicia. Further, the Pythia prepared for oracular consultations by drinking water from the Kassotis spring, and the priest-prophets of Apollo at Colophon and Claros did the same (Iamblichus, *De mysteriis* 3.11; Tacitus, *Annals* 2.54). Caverns or grottoes were associated with the lot oracle of Herakles Buraikos in Achaea, with the oracles of Apollo at Delphi (where the presence of a cave—a widespread ancient opinion—has been disproved by modern archaeology) and at Claros, and with the oracle of Trophonios in Lebadea. An oak tree was a central feature of the cult of Zeus and Dione at Dodona.

In the ancient Mediterranean world three distinctive techniques were used at oracular shrines to secure three kinds of oracles: the lot oracle, the incubation (or dream) oracle, and the inspired oracle.

Lot oracles. The process of random selection that is the basis of all lot oracles is based on the supposition that the result either expresses the will of the gods or occasions insight into the course of events by providing a clue to an aspect of that interrelated chain of events that constitutes the cosmic harmony. Lot oracles used a variety of random techniques to indicate either a positive or a negative response to prepared queries, or to select one of a more elaborate set of prepared responses. Both types of response had a basic linguistic character and for that reason must be regarded as oracular. Questions to the ancient Greek oracles were typically put in such forms as "Shall I, or shall I not, do such and such?" and "Is it better and more beneficial that we do such and such?" The oracle of Zeus at Dodona was primarily a lot oracle in which questions framed by supplicants were inscribed on lead strips and rolled up. Though the exact procedure is not known, cultic personnel probably deposited the inscribed questions in a container and simultaneously drew out a question and an object from another container signifying a positive or negative answer from Zeus. The lot oracle of Herakles Buraikos used a form of divination called astragalomancy, or knucklebone divination. Knucklebones with numbers on their four flat sides were cast; the resultant numbers indicated a prepared oracle engraved on the walls of the sanctuary. One such oracular inscription, with the number of each of five knucklebones on the left and their total in the center, is the following (from G. Kaibel, *Epigrammata Graeca,* Berlin, 1878, p. 455, no. 1038; translated by the author of this article):

> 66633 24 From Pythian Apollo
> Wait and do nothing, but obey the oracles of Phoebus.
> Watch for another opportunity; for the present, leave quietly.
> Shortly all your concerns will find fulfillment.

For centuries the Chinese have used divining sticks and divining blocks as a lot oracle similar in basic structure to the system of astragalomancy just described. Temples commonly have bamboo tubes containing a number of sticks, each marked with a number corresponding to a slip of paper containing written advice (i.e., an oracle) in verse. The kneeling worshiper shakes a stick out the of container, and the priest then reads and explains the response in relation to the inquirer's specific problem. Divining blocks may be thrown to determine whether the correct stick has been shaken out. Like the astragalomancy inscriptions, the advice is suitably vague, but usually it suffices. A typical example is the following:

> Food and clothing are present wherever there is life, and I advise you not to worry excessively; if you will only practice filial piety, brotherliness, loyalty and fidelity, then, when wealth and happiness come to you, no more evil will harm you.

Such oracular responses frequently express Confucian values that are received as expressions of the will of the spirit (*shen*) whose advice is being sought.

Incubation oracles. Incubation oracles in the ancient Mediterranean world were revelatory dreams sought in temples after completion of preliminary ritual requirements. Most incubation oracles were sought in connection with healing. The most popular healing god in antiquity was Asklepios, who had more than two hundred sanctuaries by the beginning of the Christian era. Typically, preparation for a revelatory dream or vision from Asklepios included a ritual bath and a sacrificial offering; fees were paid only if the healing was successful. After the lights in the temple or, in some cases, the incubation building (*abaton*) were extinguished, Asklepios was expected to appear in either a dream or a vision and to perform a medical procedure or surgical operation, to prescribe a particular regimen, or to make some kind of oracular pronouncement, usually of a predictive nature. Another type of incubation oracle in the ancient Greco-Roman world was the oracle of the dead (*psuchomanteion*), a shrine that facilitated consultations with the dead through dream or vision oracles.

One famous ancient oracle, that of Trophonios at Lebadea in Boeotia (central Greece), was described in some detail in the early second century CE by the traveler Pausanias (9.39.5–14). While this was not technically an incubation oracle, worshipers sought and received there a visionary experience of an oracular character. Both the protocol and the mythological features of the consultations strongly suggest that the worshiper was to visit the dead in the underworld so as to receive a revelatory experience. Isolated for several days, consultants abstained from hot baths, bathed only in the river Hercyna, made numerous sacrifices, and on the night before the consultation sacrificed a ram over a pit, following the sacrificial protocol appropriate for earth or chthonic divinities. Next, two young boys called Hermais (after Hermes Psychopompos, conductor of souls to the afterlife) led each supplicant to the river, washed him, and anointed him with oil, as in the preparation of a corpse. Priests then had the worshiper drink from the waters of forgetfulness and memory (in accordance with Greek underworld mythology), and finally they led him to the opening of a chasm, where he had to descend to meet Trophonios. Consultants emerged badly shaken and unable to laugh—a state associated by the Greeks with death.

Inspired oracles. In the Greco-Roman world many of the local oracles of Apollo employed a cult functionary who acted as an intermediary of the god and responded to questions with oracular responses pronounced in the god's name. Such mediums experience the cross-cultural phenomenon of an altered state of consciousness. Bourguignon (1973) has suggested that the two primary patterns of altered conscious states be designated "possession trance" (possession by spirits) and "vision trance" (visions, hallucinations, and out-of-body experiences). Of the more than six hundred Delphic oracles collected by Parke and Wormell (1956), only sixteen are not presented as the direct pronouncements of Apollo himself. Similarly, the *dangji* ("divining youth") of the Chinese spirit medium cults of Singapore and mainland China south of Fukien (the mainland origin of immigrants to Singapore) speaks in the first person of the *shen* who possesses him. Though the evidence is ambiguous, it appears that forms of divination other than oracular pronouncements through mediums were preferred at oracles of gods other than Apollo.

The oracle of Apollo at Delphi was in many ways a unique religious institution that exerted a strong influence on other ancient Greek oracles. At Delphi, Apollo's intermediary was always a woman called the Pythia, a priestess but also a *promantis* ("diviner") and *prophētis* ("spokeswoman"), who occupied a permanent position. There is no evidence to suggest that she was selected for her clairvoyant powers. The attendants at Delphi also included five male *hosioi* ("holy ones") and two male priests called *prophētai* ("spokesmen"). Prior to the sixth century BCE, Apollo could be consulted at Delphi only on the seventh day of the seventh month; thereafter consultations were held more frequently, on the seventh day of each of the nine months when Apollo was believed to be present at Delphi. (According to Delphic legend, he spent the three winter months far to the north among the Hyperboreans.)

On a day of consultation, a goat received a ritual bath in a spring; it was then sacrificed if, by trembling appropriately, it signaled the god's presence. Next, the Pythia took her seat within the *aduton* (inmost sanctuary) of the temple upon a tripod that represented the throne of Apollo. Though ancients believed that the tripod was situated over a fissure or chasm that emitted vapors causing divine inspiration, modern archaeology has disproved this notion. But the Pythia did drink water from the Kassotis spring, and later evidence reports that she chewed laurel leaves. Inquirers were assembled in an outer room and apparently spoke directly to the Pythia, who answered them. (No evidence suggests that their questions were submitted in written form.) The priest-prophets (*prophētai*) probably wrote out responses for inquirers who were represented by envoys.

The traditional view, now discredited, held that the Pythia spoke incomprehensibly and that her utterances were interpreted and reduced to written form (often in verse) by one of the priest-prophets. Ancient and modern beliefs that the Pythia was in a state of hysterical ecstasy manifested in bizarre behavior are belied both by ancient literary evidence and by her calm demeanor in ancient vase paintings. The possession trance experienced by the Pythia appears to have been, in the categories of I. M. Lewis (1971), a state of "controlled possession," in distinction to the uncontrolled possession experienced by those not yet fully adept in managing the onset of possession.

A similar phenomenon is found in Chinese spirit possession cults. The intermediaries (*dangjhi* or *jitong*) are not hereditary professionals; as a rule, they are young men or women, usually under twenty, who have an aptitude for experiencing altered states of consciousness, either involuntarily or through conscious cultivation. They are almost exclusively associated with temple worship where the *shen* who possesses the *dangji* is one that is customarily worshiped, and where the *dangjii* are subordinate to the owners of the temple (the promoters of its religious ceremonies), and usually to the *saigong* (Daoist priests). A consultation is usually planned at a temple for a particular time when the *shen* is called down by invocation. The *dangji* must fast beforehand and avoid sexual intercourse, and no pregnant or menstruating woman can be present at the oracular séance. The worshipers usually number about one dozen, though larger groups are possible. Outside the temple, a flag with the eight-trigram (*bagua*) design indicates the presence of a *dangji.* The *dangji* both begins and ends the possession trance on a ceremonial dragon throne, which probably represents the imperial dragon throne where generations of Chinese emperors sat, representing divine ancestors.

The session begins with drums, gongs, and chants. Gradually, the *dangji* starts to exhibit the characteristics of possession (swaying, rolling of the head, staggering, uttering strange sounds) and often at the same time commits acts of self-injury without experiencing pain (cutting the tongue, extinguishing incense sticks with the tongue, piercing the cheeks with sticks). Consultations follow in which the *dangji* gives advice to worshipers, cures their illnesses, and either speaks incomprehensibly with divine wisdom (requiring the interpretation of colleagues) or addresses his colleagues in a shrill, unnatural voice representing ancient Chinese. Clothing and household items are brought to be stamped with the *dangji's* blood for good luck. When no more business remains, the *dangji* signals that the *shen* is about to return; he then leaps into the air and is caught by assistants who lower him onto the dragon chair. Afterward, he does not remember what took place during the consultation.

Oracular persons. Professional diviners and intermediaries often have no permanent relationship to temples or shrines. They may practice their divinatory and oracular arts in their homes, in the marketplace, or in various places of employment such as army posts or governmental offices. These specialists often practice either possession trance or vision trance, but there are other possibilities as well.

Oracle diviners. During the late Shang dynasty in China (under the eight or nine kings from Wu Ding to Di Xin, c. 1200–1050 BCE), the *wu* (shamans) in the service of kings and nobles employed a type of oracle divination called pyroscapulimancy. More than 107,000 "oracle bones" have been excavated (47,000 inscriptions have now been published); about 80,000 were found during excavations from 1899 to 1928, and the remainder from 1928 to 1937 during excavations by the Academia Sinica. Besides being of great value for understanding Shang religion, they are of incalculable importance for Chinese linguistics. The bones themselves consist of bovid scapulae and turtle plastrons. At the moment of consultation heat was applied to a drilled hollow on the inside or back of the shell or bone, causing a crack shaped like the Chinese character *bu* (meaning "to divine, to foretell") to appear on the other side. Both question and answer were recorded on the bone or shell itself, which then became part of the royal archives. The inscriptions usually consist of several parts: (1) preface (cyclical day, name of diviner, and sometimes the place of divination), (2) injunction (usually put into a positive or negative mode), (3) crack number, (4) crack notation, (5) prognostication (e.g., "The king, reading the cracks, said: 'Auspicious'"), and rarely (6) verification. Though most of the oracle inscriptions focus on the nature and timing of sacrifices (a preoccupation of most oracle questions and responses at ancient Greek oracles), others include announcements made to spirits or concern arrivals and departures, hunting and fishing, wars and expeditions, crops, weather, and sickness and health. The oracle questions used in pyroscapulimancy were directed to the great ancestral spirit and the spirits of the deceased kings, who were expected to send down their advice and commands.

Oracular possession-trance. Two legendary figures of ancient Greece and Rome, the *sibulla* (sibyl) and the less popular *bakchis,* were paradigms of possession-trance. The number of sibyls multiplied in antiquity, and lists of them distinguished by epithets formed of place names are not uncommon (see Varro as quoted in Lactantius, *Divine Institutes* 1.6); by the end of antiquity more than forty sibyls had been distinguished. The sibyls (always female) and the *bakchides* (always male) were believed to belong to the remote past; though connected with specific regions, they were often thought of as having traveled extensively. Their oracles, which were preserved in widely circulated collections, were believed to have been uttered in hexameter without solicitation while in a state of divine inspiration or possession. The inspiring deity was invariably Apollo, with whose oracle shrines the various sibyls tended to be associated. However, the oracular utterances of the sibyls and *bakchides* were never formulated as the first-person speech of Apollo but always referred to him in the third person. The popularity of the sibyl among Jews resulted in the composition and circulation of oracles in Greek hexameter uttered in the person of Yahveh, the God of Israel.

The oracles that circulated in collections under the names of various sibyls and *bakchides* were regarded as enigmatic and in need of interpretation. One collection of sibylline oracles was kept in Rome under the supervision of the *quindecimviri sacris faciundis,* a college of fifteen priests, and was consulted only in time of national emergency, so as to obtain instructions for avoiding the peril. When this collection was accidentally destroyed by fire in 83 BCE, a new collection was made. The last consultation occurred in the fourth century CE. The fourteen books of sibylline oracles now preserved are a mixture of pagan and Jewish materials. The content of the sibylline oracles was originally dominated by matters relating to portents, prodigies, and ritual procedures, but they also came to express political and religious protest, particularly against Hellenistic Greek and then Roman hegemony in the eastern Mediterranean area.

In the Chinese tradition, female *wu* specifically called *wangyi* ("women who raise the spirits of the dead") dominate the practice of necromancy. They are frequently widows and over thirty years of age. In contrast to the *tongjii,* the *wangyi* operate almost exclusively in private company and may charge fees for consultations. When consulted, a *wangyi* requires the name of the deceased and the date of death. Using incense sticks and "good luck papers," the medium invokes a particular *shen* to lead her to the kingdom of the dead. The *shen* takes possession of the medium and describes a tour of the underworld. When the correct soul is located (and it has confirmed the identification by describing, for instance, the circumstances of death), its needs are determined for later offerings and sacrifices. Often the soul (who assumes its former kinship status for the duration) speaks to family members present through the medium, in order of seniority. Rarely are more than two or three souls consulted during a séance. When the consultations are concluded, the *shen* emerges chanting from the gates of the underworld; the medium then stands up and falls back on the chair.

Another type of possession trance found in Chinese tradition is *fu ji,* or spirit writing, in which the medium receives the pronouncements or responses of the possessing *shen* in writing. Consultations may be held in temples, but they occur more often in private homes. The writing stick, or planchette (*ji*), is in the shape of a Y, with the lower writing end often carved in the shape of a dragon's head. The top two handles of the stick are grasped by two bearers, one with mediumistic powers and the other a passive participant. A tray of sand is placed before the altar of the invoked *shen,* and the writing stick begins to move, often with initially violent motions, as if of its own accord. According to de Groot (1892–1910), the *shen* often identifies himself by saying "I am Kwan so-and-so of the Great Han dynasty; I have something to announce to you, people that are now seeking for medicines" (de Groot, vol. 6, 1910, p. 1303). An interpreter with pencil and paper stands ready to interpret the incomprehensible marks in the sand. Requests may be addressed to the inspiring *shen* silently, written on paper that is then burned, or read aloud. The answers or pronouncements are discussed by those present. When the session is to be concluded, the *shen* announces his decision to return. Often automatic writing is used, not to answer specific queries but to compile sacred writings consisting of poems, myths, and histories.

Oracular vision-trance. This altered state of consciousness presupposes Ernst Arbman's widely accepted dualistic distinction between the "free soul," which is passive during consciousness but active during unconsciousness (i.e., during a trance), and the "body soul," which endows the body with life and consciousness. This shamanistic experience, however, is only very rarely connected with oracles or prophecy. The ancient Greeks had legends about those whose souls wandered away during trances—for example, Aristeas of Proconnesus, a devotee of Apollo (Herodotos, 4.13–15), and Hermotimos of Clazomenae in western Asia Minor (Apollonius, *Mirabilia* 3; Pliny, *Natural History* 7.174). Two other Greek shamanistic figures shrouded in legend were Empedocles (c. 493–433 BCE) and his teacher Parmenides of Elea (late sixth to mid-fifth century BCE). A great deal of the revelatory literature from the Greco-Roman world and the ancient Near East uses the literary motif of the vision-trance to secure divine revelation in a literary genre known as the apocalypse.

The magical diviner, a common figure in the ancient Greco-Roman world, used vision-trance to secure oracular revelation for himself and his clients. Though the oracles themselves have not survived, many magical recipe books have been preserved on Egyptian papyri dating from the third through the fifth century CE. Along with love magic, revelatory magic constitutes one of the dominant concerns of the magical papyri. In addition to the many methods of divination attested in the papyri (e.g., lamp divination, saucer divination, dream divination), several types of oracular magic are also in evidence. These include procedures for obtaining such things as visions (*autopsia*), foreknowledge (*prognōsis*), a supernatural assistant (*paredros daimōn*), and oracular responses through a boy medium; there are also forms of bowl divination in which the summoned being would appear in a liquid. Several of these procedures seek to invoke the presence of a supernatural being (usually one of minor status) who will answer questions posed by the diviner regarding the future or the unknown, often on behalf of paying clients. In one example of a personal vision recipe, the diviner says "I am a prophet" and then continues with "Open my ears that you may grant oracles to me concerning the things about which I expect a response. Now, now! Quick, quick! Hurry, hurry! Tell me about those matters about which I asked you" (Karl Preisendanz and Albert Henrichs, *Papyri Graecae Magicae,* Stuttgart, 1974, vol. 2, papyrus 6, lines 323–331; translated by the author of this article).

CHARACTERISTICS OF ORACLES. The linguistic character of oracles does not necessarily render their meaning unambiguous. While lot oracles in a positive or negative mode and oracles dealing with sacrifice and expiation are usually clearly expressed, those dealing with other matters often require the skill of an interpreter. Outside the temple of Apollo at Delphi, freelance *exēgētai* ("expounders") would interpret the meaning of oracles for a fee. Similarly, interpreters are essential in the consultations of the *dangji* and in sessions involving automatic writing. In ancient Greek and Roman literature, the ambiguity of oracles that often find unexpected fulfillment became a common motif. Ambiguity also characterizes the prepared oracular responses in certain lot oracles, which must be phrased so as to apply to many situations. A similar ambiguity is found in the verses and commentaries accompanying each of the sixty-four hexagrams in the *Yi jing* (Book of changes).

The inherent ambiguity of oracles was an important factor leading to the formation of oracle collections. Because their original fulfillment remained in doubt, they could be subject to new interpretations. In the Greco-Roman world, professional oracle collectors and interpreters (*chrēsmologoi*) sold their skills in the marketplace. They possessed oracle collections attributed to various sibyls and *bakchides* as well as to other legendary figures such as Orpheus and Musaeus. The archives of oracle temples often contained such collections, and in the Hellenistic period certain individuals traveled to the more famous oracles and made their own collections, which they published with commentary. Though the origin of the Confucian classic *Yi jing* is shrouded in legend, it too functions as an oracle book.

FUNCTION OF ORACLES. Oracles, like other forms of divination, are means of acquiring critical information regarding the future or the unknown that is unavailable through more conventional or rational channels. The very act of consultation requires that what may have been a vague and amorphous concern or anxiety be articulated in a specific, defined, and delimiting manner. Oracles function in a variety of ways, some of which concern the audience (i.e., the inquirer or recipient of an oracle), while others concern the mediums or specialists who obtain oracles, as well as the institutions with which these persons may be associated. In some instances divinatory techniques are consciously monopolized by the state as a means of both maintaining and legitimating political power, as for instance by the Shang dynasty of China. In other instances respected oracles beyond the control of the state are consulted in an attempt to provide religious legitimation for particular decisions or plans inherently fraught with peril or uncertainty (e.g., the utilization of Delphi by the Greek city-states). Rulers and nobles of states are necessarily concerned above all with matters of corporate interest such as war and peace, colonization, expiation and sacrifice, plagues and drought, crops and weather, coronations and succession, and ratification of laws and constitutions. Private individuals, on the other hand, tend to focus on such matters as sickness and health, travel, business ventures, marriage and childbirth, happiness and wealth, good fortune, and recovery of lost or stolen property. Seeking oracular advice on these and other vital matters helps reduce the risks inherent in human experience.

SEE ALSO Asklepios; Delphi; Descent into the Underworld; Divination; Inspiration; Necromancy; Portents and Prodigies; Prophecy; Sibylline Oracles.

BIBLIOGRAPHY

The only comparative study of oracles and prophecy in the ancient Mediterranean world (including Greco-Roman, Israelite, early Jewish, and early Christian oracular and prophetic traditions) is my *Prophecy in Early Christianity and the Ancient Mediterranean World* (Grand Rapids, Mich., 1983), which has a lengthy, up-to-date bibliography. Two important general cross-cultural studies of possession are Erika Bourguignon's *Religion, Altered States of Consciousness, and Social Change* (Columbus, Ohio, 1973) and I. M. Lewis's *Ecstatic Religion: An Anthropological Study of Spirit Possession and Shamanism* (Harmondsworth, 1971). Still valuable is the older study by Traugott K. Oesterreich, *Possession, Demoniacal and Other* (New York, 1930).

The best book on the oracle of Delphi is Joseph Fontenrose's *The Delphic Oracle: Its Responses and Operations* (Berkeley, Calif., 1978), with a catalog of all known Delphic oracles in English translation classified according to grades of authenticity; it includes an extensive bibliography. The earlier standard work on Delphi, with a complete catalog of oracles in Greek, is H. W. Parke and D. E. W. Wormell's *The Delphic Oracle,* 2 vols. (Oxford, 1956); the more recent book by Fontenrose, however, is far superior.

An important introduction to some non-Apollonian oracles, including a collection in English translation of written oracle questions excavated at Dodona, is H. W. Parke's *The Oracles of Zeus: Dodona, Olympia, Ammon* (Oxford, 1967). Two very readable introductions to Greek oracles are H. W. Parke's *Greek Oracles* (London, 1967) and Robert Flacelière's *Greek Oracles* (London, 1965). An important discussion of the function of oracles in ancient Greek city-states is Martin P. Nilsson's *Cults, Myths, Oracles, and Politics in Ancient Greece* (1951; New York, 1972). An older but still useful comparative study of ancient Mediterranean views of revelation is Edwyn Robert Bevan's *Sibyls and Seers: A Survey of Some Ancient Theories of Revelation and Inspiration* (London, 1928). Though now out of date, the most detailed study of Greek divination, useful for putting oracular divination in proper context, is W. R. Halliday's *Greek Divination: A Study of Its Methods and Principles* (1913; reprint, Chicago, 1967). An English translation of the Greek Magical Papyri, including many procedures for securing oracles, is now available in *The Greek Magical Papyri in Translation,* edited by Hans Dieter Betz (Chicago, 1985).

The most important recent study of the sibylline oracles is John J. Collins's *The Sibylline Oracles of Egyptian Judaism* (Missoula, Mont., 1974). A recent translation of the extant fourteen books of sibylline oracles is available in *The Old Testament Pseudepigrapha,* vol. 1, *Apocalyptic Literature and Testaments,* edited by James H. Charlesworth (Garden City, N.Y., 1983), pp. 317–472.

An older work that is still valuable for its consideration of Israelite and Arab traditions with a wide spectrum of prophetic phenomena including "divinatory prophecy," dreams and visions, ecstasy, and magic is Alfred Guillaume's *Prophecy and Divination among the Hebrews and Other Semites* (London, 1938). A book that includes many texts in English translation but that lacks critical discussion is Violet MacDermot's *The Cult of the Seer in the Ancient Middle East* (London, 1971). More recent is a book that considers Old Testament prophecy in the context of comparative studies of possession phenomena: Robert R. Wilson's *Prophecy and Society in Ancient Israel* (Philadelphia, 1980), which includes an extensive bibliography.

The most important work in English on Chinese religion continues to be the magisterial work by J. J. M. de Groot, *The Religious System of China,* 6 vols. (1892–1910; Taipei, 1967); particularly relevant is part 5 in volume 6, "The Priesthood of Animism," pp. 1187ff. A more up-to-date study is Qingkun Yang's *Religion in Chinese Society: A Study of Contemporary Social Functions of Religion and Some of Their Historical Factors* (Berkeley, Calif., 1961), where aspects of both ancient and modern divination and oracles are considered. Also useful is David Crockett Graham's *Folk Religion in Southwest China* (Washington, D.C., 1961). An excellent anthropological study of modern trance-possession cults among the Chinese of Singapore is Alan J. A. Elliot's *Chinese Spirit-Medium Cults in Singapore* (London, 1955). The most important study of the oracle bones and shells of the Shang period, with an extensive bibliography, is David N. Keightley's *Sources of Shang History: The Oracle-Bone Inscriptions of Bronze Age China* (Berkeley, Calif., 1978). Also useful is a book written by one of the excavators, Dong Zuobin's *Xu jia gu nian biao* (Tokyo, 1967).

New Sources

Among the numerous recent studies on the subject here the most important ones will be recalled. Interesting contributions are offered both by monographs or miscellaneous works. See in particular: *Oracles et mantique en Grèce ancienne* (= Kernos 3 [1990], with contributions by Pierre Bonnechere, Dominique Briquel, Luc Brisson, Gérard Capdeville, Jacqueline Champeaux, Emilio Suárez de la Torre and others); *Oracles et prophéties dans l'antiquité: actes du colloque de Strasbourg, 15–17 juin 1995,* edited by Jean-Georges Heintz (Paris, 1997); *Sibille e linguaggi oracolari. Mito storia tradizione. Atti del convegno Macerata-Norcia, settembre 1994,* edited by Ileana Chirassi Colombo and Tullio Seppilli (Pisa, 1998).

As far as Classical Greece is concerned, the following contributions are particularly valuable: Philipp Vandenberg, *Das Geheimnis der Orakel. Archäologen entschlüsseln das Mysterium antiker Voraussagen* (Munich, 1982); Michael Maass, *Das antike Delphi* (Darmstadt, 1993); Marion Giebel, *Das Orakel von Delphi* (Stuttgart, 2001); Veit Rosenberger, *Griechische Orakel* (Stuttgart, 2001); Pierre Bonnechere, *Trophonios de Lébadée: cultes et mythes d'une cité béotienne au miroir de la mentalité antique* (Leiden, 2003); Jules Labarbe, "Du bon usage de l'oracle de Delphes." *Kernos* 7 (1994): 219–230; Alexandre Avram and François Lefèvre, "Les cultes de Callatis et l'oracle de Delphes." *Revue des Etudes Grecques* 108 (1995): 7–23; Walter Burkert, "Olbia and Apollo of Didyma," in *Apollo: Origins and Influences,* edited by Jon Solomon, pp. 49–60 (Tucson, 1994).

Various oracular inscriptions have been published from different places in Greece and Asia Minor. See the most relevant contributions offered in this ambit by Rheinold Merkelbach and Werner Peek in many issues of *Zeitschrift für Papyrologie und Epigraphik.*

Anastasios-Phoebus Christidis, Soterios Dakaris, and Ioulia Vokotopoulou, "Magic in the Oracular Tablets from Dodona." In *The World of Ancient Magic: Papers from the First International Samson Eitrem Seminar at the Norwegian Institute at Athens, 4–8 May 1997,* edited by David R. Jordan, Hugo Montgomery and Einar Thomassen, pp. 67–72 (Athens-Bergen 1999). Emilio Suárez de la Torre, "Sibylles, mantique inspirée et collections oraculaires," *Kernos* 7 (1994): 179–205.

Hellenistic and late antique prophecies, together with their sycretistic features, are investigated by: Giulia Sfameni Gasparro, *Oracoli, Profeti, Sibille. Rivelazione e salvezza nel mondo antico* (Rome, 2002); Arie Van der Kooij, *The Oracle of Tyre: the Septuagint of Isaiah XXIII as Version and Vision* (Leiden-New York, 1998); Roelof van den Broek, *Apollo in Asia. De orakels van Clarus en Didyma in de tweede en derde eeuw na Chr.* (Leiden, 1981); Santiago Montero, *Trajano y la divinación* (Madrid, 2000); David Potter, *Prophets and Emperors* Cambridge, U.K., 1994.

The relationship between Jewish apocalypticism and oracular patterns are deeply investigated. See for example: Valentin Nikiprowetzky, *La Troisième Sibylle* (Paris, 1970); David S. Potter, *Prophecy and History in the Crisis of the Roman Empire. A Historical Commentary on the Thirteenth Sibylline Oracle* (Oxford, 1990); Herbert W. Parke (edited by B. C. Mc Ging), *Sibyls and Prophecy in Classical Antiquity* (London-New York, 1992); John J. Collins, *Seers, Sibyls and Sages in Hellenistic-Roman Judaism* (Leiden, 1997). Bernard Teyssèdre, "Les représentations de la fin des temps dans le chant V des 'Oracles Sibyllins.'" *Apocrypha* 1 (1990): 147–165.

Particular attention is also devoted to philosophical features, which are well outlined by Paolo Desideri, "Il De defectu oraculorum e la crisi della religione antica in Plutarco," in *Italia sul Baetis: studi di storia romana in memoria di Fernando Gascó,* edited by Emilio Gabba, Paolo Desideri, Sergio Roda, pp. 91–102 (Torino, 1996); Polymnia Athanassiadi, "Philosophers and Oracles," *Byzantion* 62 (1992): 45–62; Pier Franco Beatrice, "Towards a New Edition of Porphyry's Fragments against the Christians," in *Sophies Maietores. Chercheurs de sagesse: hommage à Jean Pépin*, edited by Marie-Odile Goulet-Cazé, Goulven Madec and Denis O'Brien, pp. 347–355 (Paris, 1992); Enrico Livrea, "Sull'iscrizione teosofica di Enoanda," *Zeitschrift für Papirologie und Epigraphik* 122 (1998): 90–96; Salvatore Pricoco, "Un oracolo di Apollo su Dio," *Rivista di Storia e Letteratura Religiosa* 23 (1987): 3–36; Salvatore Pricoco, "Per una storia dell'oracolo nella tarda antichità. Apollo Clario e Didimeo in Lattanzio," *Augustinianum* 29 (1989): 351–374; Michael Stausberg, "Von den Chaldäischen Orakeln zu den Hundert Pforten und darüber hinaus," *Archiv für Religionsgeschichte* 3 (2001): 257–272; Teresa Sardella, "Oracolo pagano e rivelazione cristiana nella Theosophia di Tubinga," in *Le trasformazioni della cultura nella tarda antichità. Atti del Convegno tenuto a Catania 27 settembre–2 ottobre 1982*, pp. 545–573 (Rome, 1985).

This late antique oracular collection is now edited by Pier Franco Beatrice, *Anonymi monophysitae Theosophia. An Attempt at Reconstruction* (Leiden, 2001).

As far as the so-called *Chaldean Oracles* are concerned, see the recent commented edition by Ruth Majercik, *The Chaldean Oracles. Text, Translation, and Commentary* (Leiden, 1989).

A popular collection of oracles dating to the imperial age is now edited by Stewart Randall, *Sortes Astrampsychi* (Munich, 2001).

DAVID E. AUNE (1987)
Revised Bibliography

ORAL TORAH

ORAL TORAH is the most common rendering of the Hebrew term *torah shebeʿal peh*. Rabbinic teachings originating in Galilee between the third and fifth centuries CE, particularly works of scriptural exegesis (e.g., *Sifrʾa* to *Lv.* 26:46 and *Sifre* to *Dn.* 33:10) and the Palestinian Talmud (e.g., *Peʾah* 2:6), refer occasionally to religious teachings (*devarim*, "words") transmitted "orally" or "by memory" (*al peh*) and others transmitted "in writing" (*bikhtav*). The former references denote oral traditions preserved among ancient sages, whereas the latter denotes texts of scriptural revelation. The full expression *oral Torah* is rare in rabbinic tradition of late antiquity and only appears in rabbinic texts completed between the fifth and sixth centuries CE (e.g., *Avot Nat.* A:15/ B:26 and the B.T., *Shab.* 31a, *Yomʾa* 28b, and *Qid.* 66a). In these sources oral Torah refers to a body of unwritten oral tradition revealed to Moses on Sinai and transmitted in rabbinic communities as orally performed texts. This oral tradition originates simultaneously with the written revelations gathered in the Five Books of Moses and the remaining scriptural canon. This canon is referred to as the *written Torah* (*torah shebikhtav*). Together the written Torah and oral Torah constitute the entirety of the covenantal contract between Israel and the creator of the universe.

The rabbinic literature compiled prior to the eighth century CE does not systematically define a canon of literary works containing the oral Torah. It assumes that oral Torah is transmitted not in edited documents but rather as oral teachings. Indeed the word *mishnah* and its Aramaic cognate *matnyta* can refer either to general texts of memorized rabbinic tradition or to the early-third-century CE compilation of rabbinic law known as the Mishnah. Whereas some rabbinic passages do link the aspects of oral revelation specifically to the Mishnah (e.g., P.T., *Peʾah* 2:6, B.T., *Ber.* 5a, *Tan.-Bub.*, to *Ex.* 34:27), it is not entirely certain whether the reference is to the document or to the more amorphous oral tradition of which the Mishnah represents merely one early form.

Since the Middle Ages it has become common to anthologize rabbinic tradition in written compilations. Thus the oral Torah has for at least a millennium been studied from written works such as the Mishnah, the Tosefta, various Midrashic compilations, and paradigmatically the Palestinian and Babylonian Talmuds. Commentaries to these works are likewise regarded as part of the oral Torah. In this sense the oral Torah remains an unclosed canon to which new works can in principle be added. Its "orality" lies more in the confidence in its oral origins rather than in the methods of its current preservation and elaboration.

ANCIENT JEWISH ORAL TRADITION AND RABBINIC ORAL TORAH. Oral Torah appears to be a term of exclusive rabbinic coinage. Ancient Judaism of course preserved a rich oral tradition of law, historical memory, biblical interpretation, and theology beyond its scriptural heritage. Yet there is no clear evidence that Jews of the Second Temple period (from roughly 520 BCE to 70 CE) commonly recognized this oral tradition as part of revelation or equivalent to the Torah in religious authority. Indeed whereas Second Temple Jews produced much literature claiming to be the written remnants of revelations given to biblical prophets, there is no record of Jews claiming the status of revelation for orally transmitted traditions.

Perhaps the most likely Second Temple source of the rabbinic concept of oral Torah emerges from a variety of ideas about religious tradition that have been ascribed in various ancient sources to the Pharisees. They were a prominent political-religious party from Hasmonaean and Roman times. Important first-century CE writings, such as the Gospels (e.g., *Mk.* 7:3: *paradosin ton presbuteron*) and the works of the Jewish historian Josephus (*Ant.* 12:290: *paradoseos ton pateron*), describe the Pharisees as great legal scholars and cultivators of "ancestral traditions" that are taken with great reverence in the conduct of life. But such discussions do not mention the key traits of rabbinic oral Torah—that the traditions are part of the revelation to Moses and that they are transmitted in essentially oral form as an authoritative application of the written Torah.

Only new evidence, not yet on the horizon, can determine the Second Temple genealogy of oral Torah. In the meantime it is important to point out that the rabbinic literature itself shows signs that the idea of oral Torah developed within the emerging rabbinic communities that consolidated themselves in the century or so after the destruction of the Jerusalem Temple in 70 CE. The earliest extant compilations of the emerging rabbinic literary tradition in fact are inconsistent in their appeal to and use of concepts equivalent to oral Torah. The most famous rabbinic source usually cited as an example of the rabbinic use of the term oral Torah is from the first chapter of Mishnah *Avot.* But this text claims only that "Moses received Torah from Sinai and transmitted it to Joshua" (M. *Avot* 1:1). It goes on to describe at length the chain of traditional authorities who "received Torah" from their masters and transmitted it to their disciples until it was received by such famous early rabbinic founders as Rabban Yoḥanan ben Zakk'ai (M. *Avot* 2:8). Moreover in a mid-third-century collection of biblical interpretation known as *Sifr'a* the great rabbinic scholar of the second century CE, Rabbi ʿAqivaʾ, is represented as dismissing the idea that a reference in *Leviticus* 26:46 to "teachings" (*torot*) given by Moses implies that the prophet received two Torahs from Sinai. By contrast, the later expansion of Mishnah *Avot,* called *Avot d'Rabbi Nathan,* quite explicitly ascribes the use of the term oral Torah to Herodian figures such as Hillel the Elder. This suggests that the later text has imported its own concept of oral Torah into the Mishnah's conception of Torah from Sinai.

The development of the idea of oral Torah is intimately bound up with the consolidation of nascent rabbinic institutions of instruction and discipleship. As teachers of wisdom in the Greco-Roman world of late antiquity, the rabbinic sages had to reflect on a problem that was of great interest to other moral educators throughout the Mediterranean world, namely what is the relationship of written books to knowledge and what role does the living teacher play in applying the wisdom of books to the moral formation of disciples? This issue was of deep concern to various religious and philosophical communities—from Neoplatonic philosophers to the rhetoricians of the Second Sophistic and from Gnostic spiritual guides to proponents of Stoicism. Each of these communities came to some conventional agreements within their own institutions regarding the degree to which ultimate wisdom resided in the writing of a great sage or in the person of the teacher who expounded the writing. Similarly each community had to determine the role that memorization of great texts played in the moral formation of students. The development of the idea of oral Torah is the rabbinic refraction of this larger cultural concern. The essential idea is that rabbinic teaching derives its authority not from the person of the sage himself but rather from his assiduous cultivation of a chain of tradition that goes back to Moses. The oral character of this tradition—the fact that it was found not in books but in the living teaching of sages alone—ensured that the tradition could only be accessed through personal discipleship to a rabbinic sage. One could not, that is, become a sage by reading the written Torah in concert with texts of oral Torah. The concept of oral Torah, in this sense, insured that access to Jewish religious tradition would be entirely controlled by sages who alone could mediate covenantal knowledge.

This idea of the sage as the exclusive mediator of traditions that could not be learned entirely from books is expressed both through historical narratives and in the development of technical terms for tradition of various sorts. Representations of the idea of oral Torah in narrative include the famous passage of the Babylonian Talmud (*Eruv.* 54b) that describes Moses teaching the oral tradition to Aaron and other disciples by careful repetition and memorization. Another (B.T., *Tem.* 15b–16a) describes the use of the oral Torah's hermeneutical rules to reconstruct oral traditions forgotten by Israel in the despair following the death of Moses. Several rabbinic stories about events in Second Temple times, such as one about a Hasmonaean king who comes to persecute the Pharisees (B.T., *Qid.* 66a), assume that the oral Torah must have been known to sages at that early date. Others, most famously ascribed to the Second Temple figure Hillel, show Hillel teaching oral Torah to converts (*Avot Nat.* A:15/B:26, B.T., *Shab.* 31a).

The emerging technical language of rabbinic jurisprudence also testifies to the increasing significance of the conception that the tradition taught by rabbinic sages is both oral and part of the Sinaitic moment. The distinction between commandments "found in the Torah" (*mide'or'ait'a*) and those "enacted by the Rabbis" (*miderabbanan*) originates in the earliest layers of rabbinic tradition (e.g., M. *Hag.* 1:8/T. *Hag.* 1:9 and M. *Orl.* 3:9) and is developed broadly in the Talmuds. Moreover a host of synonyms for rabbinic tradition, such as "traditional custom" (*halakhah*), "words of the scribes" (*divrei sofrim*), "tradition from Moses on Sinai" (*halakhah lemosheh misinai*), and "repeated tradition" (*mishnah* and *matnyta*), are increasingly interpreted in rabbinic compilations of the fourth and later centuries CE as references to elements of the oral Torah. Thus by the close of late antiquity the consolidating rabbinic communities of the Byzantine and Sassanian Empires had developed not only a rich oral tradition of jurisprudence, history, and theology but also a rich notion of this entire tradition as part of an oral heritage stemming from Sinai and preserved in the present by the emerging rabbinic elites.

Oral Torah in the History of Jewish Thought. At least some sages—such as the third-century CE Galilean leader Rabbi Yoḥanan bar Nappaḥaʾ—held that written copies of texts of oral Torah should not be used in the training of disciples, just as the written Torah should not be cited from memory during the official synagogue liturgy (B.T., *Git.* 60b/ *Tem.* 14b). But in the classical rabbinic literature the distinction between written and oral sources of Torah is more often assumed than explicitly discussed. The concept of oral Torah did not become a defining element of rabbinic ideology until the ninth century CE, when it began to play a key role in a polemic within Judaism known as the Karaite controversy. The Karaites (scripturalists) were a loosely affiliated collection of Jewish communities, from Iraq to North

Africa, who rejected rabbinic dominance over Jewish life in the expanding Abbasid Empire. Central to Karaite criticism of rabbinic authority was the claim that the oral Torah was a purely human construction, invented by rabbis to legitimate their political authority. According to the Karaite polemicists, the only source of textual authority for Jews was the Mosaic Scripture, what the rabbis called the written Torah.

The most articulate responses to the Karaite critiques were mounted by a series of rabbinic scholars who had been appointed by the Abbasid caliphate to the office of the Gaonate. The Gaonate was charged with promulgating and administering Jewish law among the Jewish communities of the Abbasid Empire. The Geonim traced their own intellectual and religious authority back to the Talmudic sages and from them back to Moses. Mining the classic rabbinic literature for references to the antiquity of oral Torah and buttressing these sources with arguments drawn from scriptural interpretation and philosophy, Geonic leaders from Rabbi Sa'adyah ben Yosef al-Fayyumī (882–942 CE) to Rabbi Sherira ben Hanina (906–1006) composed fierce responses to the Karaites. In these responses the entire corpus of rabbinic compilations from antiquity was defined as part of the canon of oral Torah and their authority in the construction of Jewish law and belief clearly explained. As the Karaite threat to rabbinic authority receded, these polemical writings, defending the centrality of oral Torah to rabbinic authority and linking its antiquity to Sinai, became foundational for Jewish historical thinking about rabbinic tradition.

Whereas the classic Geonic development of the idea of oral Torah originated in Islamic lands in polemics primarily with the anti-rabbinic Karaites, rabbinic Jews living in scattered communities in Latin Christendom were also inspired by contextual factors to develop an ideological self-consciousness about oral Torah. Most important among these, from the eleventh century and onward, were the polemical encounters of Jews with Christian theologians. In staged disputes sponsored by church authorities, held for the edification of Christians and a hoped-for conversion of Jews, rabbinic leaders were required to defend the truth of Judaism against the claims of Christianity. The primary focus of these disputes was the tradition of Christian interpretation of the Old Testament, which viewed the latter as a veiled set of parables foretelling the advent of Christ.

Some of the later rabbinic sources of the Byzantine era had proposed long ago that the Mishnah should be regarded as a "mystery" given by God to Israel to ensure Israel's knowledge of the meaning of Scripture against the claims of the emerging church (e.g., *Pes. Rab.* 14b). These and many other sources were retrieved by the pioneering eleventh-century French commentator Rabbi Shelomoh ben Yitsḥaq ("Rashi," 1040–1105) in his commentaries to both the Talmud and the Bible. He carefully glossed biblical verses with rabbinic passages from the oral Torah, arguing that the "simple" or "contextual" sense of the written Torah was found in the sources of the oral Torah. This method enabled Rashi to engage Christian readings of Scripture on two fronts. Where Christian tradition might see certain biblical verses as parabolic references to Christ, Rashi could point out that the "simple" sense (the *peshat*) was contained in the oral Torah. Similarly where Scripture referred repeatedly to various synonyms for *law* that had been given to Moses, Rashi could cite rabbinic materials that linked such verses to the written and oral Torah. Rashi's methods were employed, with variations and expansions, in the exegetical tradition founded by his students, known as the Tosafists ("supplements to Rashi"). They were influential as well in the thirteenth-century biblical commentaries of Rabbi Mosheh ben Naḥman ("Nahmanides," 1194–1270), who frequently cites Rashi only to disagree with him about details.

While rabbinic scholars of Latin Christendom were weaving the idea of oral Torah into their tapestry of exegesis, a work appeared in the Islamic world that would become crucial to Jews in both Islamic and Christian societies. The twelfth-century Spanish-born sage, Rabbi Mosheh ben Maimon ("Maimonides," 1135–1204), writing in Egypt, introduced his prestigious codification of Jewish law with a historical discussion of the origins and transmission history of the oral Torah. Elsewhere in his brilliant code Maimonides held that belief in the origins of the oral Torah in revelation was a fundamental article of Jewish belief, no less crucial than belief in the existence of God (*Hil. Mam.* 3:1). His views, shaped largely by the Geonic interpretations of Talmudic sources, influenced all Jewish thought—legal, historical, and theological—from the thirteenth century until the dawn of the nineteenth.

The mystical movement of Qabbalah, which spread with equal success in the Islamic and Christian areas of Jewish settlement, commonly linked its own conceptual innovations to the idea of oral Torah. Indeed the most important qabbalistic work, the thirteenth-century *Zohar,* was composed in imitation of the language and form of ancient rabbinic works of oral Torah. As late as the eighteenth century and early nineteenth century, innovative movements of Jewish religious renewal, such as Hasidism, offered creative interpretations of the idea of oral Torah as part of their larger efforts to link themselves to authentic rabbinic lineage. With equal ingenuity, some rabbinic opponents of Jewish modernization demonstrated how the interpretive principles of the oral Torah proved that "the modern is prohibited by the Torah."

Since the beginning of the nineteenth century, however, increasing sectors of world Jewry have come under the influence of the modernizing Western culture in which they have been immersed. Grounded in empiricist and historicist assumptions basic to the cultural revolution of the European Enlightenment, many modern Jewish thinkers have found the concept of "revelation" to be especially vulnerable to criticism on historical grounds. Classically understood as a miraculous event in which a personal God speaks in human language to a prophet, revelation has been commonly recast as a psychological, cultural, or moral event. Revelation, in other words, has left the realm of "objective historical fact" and been confined to the domain of "subjective, interpretive experience." Accordingly among most contemporary adherents of modern Judaism, the idea of oral Torah as a revelation coequal with that of the written Torah is hardly a compelling idea, for the very notion of an objective historical revelation is itself under question.

Not all sectors of contemporary Judaism, however, have been willing to give up the concept of oral Torah. Among Orthodox Jews, who are deeply skeptical of the authority of modern culture, there is also a tendency to insist upon the continued authority of oral Torah as part of the divine revelation that governs the concrete behavior of Jews. Paradoxically, in the last decades of the twentieth century certain Jewish thinkers of a postmodern style began to find new complexity in the concept of oral Torah. These thinkers are critical of modernity's often-facile distinction between "subjectivity" and "objectivity." Whereas they may not accept the absolute authority of the rabbis, they are intensely interested in retrieving the idea of oral Torah as a fundamental element of the overall Judaic response to texts and tradition. Thus even among Jewish thinkers who do not explicitly support exclusive rabbinic authority to define Judaism, the idea of oral Torah as the historical embodiment of Jewish forms of "textual reasoning"—living with, challenging, and transforming the meaning of powerful texts—continues to attract great interest.

SEE ALSO Mishnah and Tosefta; Torah.

BIBLIOGRAPHY

Baumgarten, Albert. "The Pharisaic Paradosis." *Harvard Theological Review* 80 (1987): 63–77. This essay offers an excellent discussion of various Second Temple testimonies about the nature of Pharisaic tradition.

Berger, Michael S. *Rabbinic Authority.* Oxford, U.K., and New York, 1998. This is a comprehensive study of the rhetoric for establishing rabbinic authority from classical times into modernity.

Blidstein, Yaakov. "On the Foundations of the Concept of Oral Torah" (in Hebrew). *Tarbiz* 42 (1973): 496–498. This essay studies early lexical items in rabbinic literature that refer to memorized or oral tradition.

Brody, Robert. *The Geonim of Babylonia and the Shaping of Medieval Jewish Culture.* New Haven, Conn., and London, 1998. A most up-to-date and comprehensive study of the institution of the Gaonate and its religious and cultural achievements.

Dane, Perry. "The Oral Law and the Jurisprudence of a Textless Text." *S'vara: A Journal of Philosophy, Law, and Judaism* 2 (1991): 11–24. This essay mounts a postmodernist inquiry into the nature of rabbinic thought on oral Torah.

Elman, Yaakov. *Authority and Tradition: Toseftan Baraitot in Talmudic Babylonia.* Hoboken, N.J., 1994. This study of the Tosefta, a companion document to the Mishnah, breaks fresh ground in studying the mutual influence of writing and oral transmission in the shaping of early rabbinic traditions.

Elman, Yaakov, and Israel Gershoni, eds. *Transmitting Jewish Traditions: Orality, Textuality, and Cultural Diffusion.* New Haven, Conn., and London, 2000. This collection of essays contains valuable studies by an international group of scholars of Jewish oral tradition from rabbinic to modern times.

Fraade, Steven. *From Tradition to Commentary: Torah and Its Interpretation in the Midrash Sifre to Deuteronomy.* Albany, N.Y., 1991. This is a groundbreaking study of rabbinic ideas of oral Torah and their relationship to the stylistic traits of rabbinic scriptural interpretation.

Gerhardsson, Birger. *Memory and Manuscript: Oral Tradition and Written Transmission in Rabbinic Judaism and Early Christianity, with Tradition and Transmission in Early Christianity.* Grand Rapids, Mich., 1998. This work, written in 1961, sums up a century of scholarship on rabbinic oral tradition and links it to the study of early Christian oral tradition.

Gruber, Meyer. "The Mishnah as Oral Torah: A Reconsideration." *Journal for the Study of Judaism* 15 (1984): 112–122. This essay focuses upon ways in which early rabbinic literature links the Mishnah to the idea of oral Torah.

Harris, Jay. *How Do We Know This? Midrash and the Fragmentation of Modern Judaism.* Albany, N.Y., 1995. This book studies the historical conceptions of rabbinic oral-interpretive tradition from ancient to modern times.

Jaffee, Martin S. *Torah in the Mouth: Writing and Oral Tradition in Palestinian Judaism, 200 BCE–400 CE.* New York, 2001. This book offers a broad theory of rabbinic oral tradition in relation to written sources and a study of the conceptual development of the idea of oral Torah until the fifth century CE.

Kepnes, Steven, ed. *Interpreting Judaism in a Postmodern Age.* New York and London, 1996. This pioneering collection of essays includes many that reflect upon postmodern conceptions of rabbinic tradition and its authority.

Lieberman, Saul. "The Publication of the Mishnah." In *Hellenism in Jewish Palestine*, pp. 83–90. New York, 1950. This is a classic essay describing the oral manner in which the Mishnah was compiled and disseminated for study.

Meskin, Jacob. "Textual Reasoning, Modernity, and the Limits of History." *Cross Currents* (Winter 1999). Available from http://www.findarticles.com/cf_0/m2096/4_49/58621580/p1/article.jhtml. This is a programmatic essay on Jewish "textual reasoning" in a postmodern spirit that pays close attention to modern scholarship on Jewish oral tradition and rabbinic oral Torah.

Neusner, Jacob. "Oral Torah and Oral Tradition: Defining the Problematic." In *Method and Meaning in Ancient Judaism*, pp. 59–75. Missoula, Mont., 1979. This essay highlights the important implications of distinguishing between ancient Jewish oral tradition and rabbinic ideologies of oral Torah stemming from revelation.

Neusner, Jacob. *What, Exactly, Did the Rabbinic Sages Mean by "the Oral Torah?" An Inductive Answer to the Question of Rabbinic Judaism.* Atlanta, 1999. This is a convenient summary of a major scholar's thought on oral Torah.

Safrai, Shmuel. "Oral Tora." In *The Literature of the Sages*, pt. 1: *Oral Tora, Halakha, Mishna, Tosefta, Talmud, External Trac-*

tates, edited by Shmuel Safrai, pp. 35–119. Philadelphia and Assen, Netherlands, 1987. This essay offers a convenient survey of rabbinic sources on oral Torah and a historical interpretation of their significance.

Schäfer, Peter. "Das 'Dogma' von der mündlichen Torah im rabbinischen Judentum." In *Studien zur Geschichte und Theologie des rabbinischen Judentums*, pp. 153–197. Leiden, Netherlands, 1978. This essay offers critical and close readings of the various rabbinic references to oral tradition and highlights the crucial role of the third-century CE Galilean school of Rabbi Yoḥanan in developing the ideology of oral Torah.

Schlütter, Margarete. *Auf welche Weise wurde die Mishna geschrieben?* Tübingen, Germany, 1993. This comprehensive study of Rabbi Sherira's famous letter on the history of the oral Torah includes German translations of both extant manuscript versions and an extensive commentary.

Scholem, Gershom. "The Meaning of the Torah in Jewish Mysticism." In *On the Kabbalah and Its Symbolism*, translated by Ralph Manheim, pp. 32–86. New York, 1969. This essay surveys the various symbolic roles played by the term *Torah* in the qabbalistic tradition.

Scholem, Gershom. "Revelation and Tradition as Religious Categories in Judaism." In *The Messianic Idea in Judaism and Other Essays on Jewish Spirituality*, pp. 282–303. New York, 1971. This essay explores crucial ideological dimensions of Jewish concepts of revelation and interpretation in rabbinic and mystical contexts.

Silber, Michael K. "The Emergence of Ultra-Orthodoxy: The Invention of a Tradition." In *The Uses of Tradition: Jewish Continuity in the Modern Era*, edited by Jack Wertheimer, pp. 23–84. New York and Jerusalem, 1992. This essay traces ways in which the conceptual system of rabbinic oral Torah was marshaled in opposition to modern European culture.

Snyder, H. Gregory. *Teachers and Texts in the Ancient World: Philosophers, Jews, and Christians.* London and New York, 2000. This book surveys the various roles that classic texts and living teachers played in moral education in the Greco-Roman world.

Valantasis, Richard. *Spiritual Guides of the Third Century: A Semiotic Study of the Guide-Disciple Relationship in Christianity, Neoplatonism, Hermetism, and Gnosticism.* Minneapolis, Minn., 1991. This fine study describes the role of texts and teachers in the spiritual formation of diverse intellectual-religious communities in late antiquity.

Zlotnick, Dov. *The Iron Pillar, Mishnah: Redaction, Form, and Intent.* Jerusalem, 1988. This book studies various oral-formulaic aspects of the editing of the Mishnah.

MARTIN S. JAFFEE (2005)

ORAL TRADITION, which operates in all religious institutions, tends to be viewed by literate Western scholars as a defective mechanism for perpetuating tradition. Theologians, secular historians, and sociologists of religion, sharing a dichotomous view of oral and literate intellectual systems, have contrasted the fixity of belief in an immutable truth found in literate religious traditions with the variety and mutability of knowledge typical of oral traditions relying exclusively on memory.

However, recent research on the institutionalization of oral and written communication in different societies tends to undermine the dichotomy between "oral" and "literate" societies. It becomes increasingly clear that in both religious and secular contexts literary and oral methods of learning and teaching coexist and interact. The relative stability of knowledge in a given society depends in large part upon how these different methods are institutionalized as well as upon the educational goals and concepts of knowledge that accompany them.

In general, it seems that knowledge based on memory is not as ephemeral as previously had been thought, nor is written knowledge immutable in the actual conditions of social practice. Thus comparative research into the ways in which written and spoken words are organized and used in different societies at present tends to complicate the picture of what oral tradition is, and of how it is related to the presumed stability of written traditions. Overly simplistic models are giving way to less elegant, but perhaps richer, comparative views, which also offer a more accurate picture of the varieties of religious experience that are embodied in written and spoken words.

The two great questions underlying most of the scholarship on oral tradition in religion are those of historical continuity and communicative effectiveness. Up to the present, these two issues have tended to be addressed by different scholars using different methods. The issue of historical continuity has been prominent in the Western comparative study of religion since the late eighteenth century, when the survival of preliterate belief systems in modern European settings was first recognized.

In the twentieth century, one of the most provocative historical comparativists has been Georges Dumézil. Dumézil has gone back to the early literary sources of Indo-European mythology, history, and legend to reconstruct an ideological complex that, he contends, predates the dispersion of the ancestors of the present Indo-European linguistic groups from an original home in Central Asia into the Indian subcontinent, Asia Minor, and Europe. Dumézil argues that his ideological complex was represented in both the social organization and the cosmology of the preliterate Proto-Indo-Europeans, positing a tripartite division of both human and divine spheres of activity into priest-kings, warriors, and agriculturalist-herdsmen. For Dumézil, it is not tripartism in general (a worldwide phenomenon), but these three particular categories that characterize cultural configurations derived from a Proto-Indo-European antecedent.

Followers of Dumézil have examined more recent folk traditions in Europe, such as folk tales, legends, and sagas. In these orally derived traditions they have found evidence of the pre-Christian Indo-European tripartism, which in some cases underlies such overtly Christian subjects as the lives of the saints. Of course, the awareness of pre-Christian content in European oral tradition and its possible impact on Christian orthodoxy was noticed by the earliest Christian missionaries. Several of the nineteenth-century folklorists were clergymen who identified pre-Christian beliefs and practices among their parishioners. Dumézil and his followers, however, unlike many of their predecessors, have detected not mere isolated remnants of tradition, but a conceptual system that, Dumézil argues, informed Indo-European ideas of social and cosmic organization at diverse levels, with varying degrees of explicitness, from the explicit *varna* theory of the Vedic caste system in India to the cryptic reflections that Dumézil has traced in the legendary history of the Roman republic.

Dumézil's historical-reconstructive approach to the oral heritage in written traditions shares some of the weaknesses of its predecessors. A major problem is the variety of relationships between cosmology and social organization. Dumézil and his followers found the Indo-European triad in some cultures at the cosmological level, in others in the configurations of secular history, in yet others in sacred biography. In some cultures (in India, for instance), Indo-European tripartism can be traced in many contexts on a sacred-secular continuum. But as becomes apparent in the study of living religious rituals and scriptures in their social context (and as is painfully obvious to believers who take their sacred models seriously), the sacred order is often not realized in everyday social interaction, and indeed may even be systematically inverted. Anthropologists of religion such as Victor Turner and Claude Lévi-Strauss have based approaches to the study of ritual and myth on the assumption that inversions between sacred and secular discourse are systematic, and even necessary. Dumézil's style of comparison is exciting more for the possibilities it reveals for discovering the manifestations of a belief system in both sacred and secular contexts than for the particular comparative conclusions it can yield.

Although Dumézil and his followers only implicitly address the problem of oral tradition, the identification of traces of an originally oral ideology in societies where that ideology is no longer overt raises the question of the relative importance of self-consciousness in oral and literate intellectual traditions. Literacy is widely regarded by the literate as a facilitator of analytic reasoning and self-conscious intellection. It is believed to enable one to manipulate series of propositions, to reorder them, compare their implications, and identify inconsistencies that would be obscured if one could only consider them in the serial order and social contexts of their immediate presentations.

In the religious context, the writing down of tenets of belief is held to facilitate the development of orthodoxy and of internally consistent bodies of belief, which in turn may contribute to the centralization of religious institutions and religious power. There are paradoxical aspects to this set of assumptions, however, as will be seen below. In any case, Dumézil's comparative studies imply among other things that the development of complex categorical systems of sacred and secular order is possible even in preliterate societies. The continued unselfconscious operation of such conceptual systems can be traced into the literate era, in both the literate and the oral domains of different communities.

A comparative approach to the diverse manifestations of such inherited patterns leads to the question of how these patterns are transmitted and institutionalized. A second major approach to the problem of oral tradition has focused directly on the forms and processes of oral transmission. This approach was initiated by the Amerian classicist Milman Parry, whose examination of the style and structure of Homeric verse led him and his student Albert B. Lord to the study of a European oral epic tradition that still survives in the sectarian poems of border warfare sung in the Balkans. Through this study, Parry and Lord sought to identify mechanisms of oral composition and remembrance that could generate and perpetuate poems of the scale of the Homeric epics.

Francis P. Magoun and other medievalists then applied the Parry-Lord theory of oral stylistics and compositional techniques to Anglo-Saxon poetry. Soon a debate developed among medievalists and biblical scholars concerning the influence on early literary style of an oral rhetoric that was believed to reflect in various ways the oral composition and transmission processes that had been described by Parry and Lord. Arguments ensued about such questions as the relative debt of the Christian poet Cædmon to either the pre-Christian oral poetics of Anglo-Saxon or to the literary tradition of Latin devotional poetry. The organization of the *Book of Psalms* and the Gospels, among other Old and New Testament writings, was examined for evidence of oral composition in both style and structure. The simultaneous existence of variants, along with the presence of formulaic language, was taken as a hallmark of oral tradition. Stylistic studies that saw in the synoptic Gospels (*Mark, Matthew,* and *Luke*), for instance, a series of variants of an original oral tradition of the life of Christ, raised once again the questions concerning the historical reliability of these texts.

In the case of Islam, by contrast, the oral substrate of the tradition was directly taken into account by the earliest Muslim theologians. The word *qur'ān* literally means "reading," and the sacred book of the Qur'ān was originally received through reading, despite the self-avowed illiteracy of the prophet Muḥammad. The first revelation came to the Prophet in the form of an angelic injunction, "Read!", to which the Prophet replied, "I cannot read." This altercation ended with the celestial voice dictating, "Read: And it is thy Lord the Most Bountiful / Who teacheth by pen, / Teacheth man that which he knew not." The Prophet, waking from a trance, remembered the words "as if inscribed upon his heart." Thus the authoritativeness of written scripture was established by explicit revelation.

The Prophet's oral recitations of subsequent revelations were transcribed by various followers. The great body of Muslim oral tradition supplementary to the Qur'ān itself, embodied in the *sunnah* ("practice, custom") and *ḥadīth* ("traditions, narration") of the Prophet, was codified by literate theologians in the century following the Prophet's death. A primary criterion for authenticity was the soundness of the chain of oral transmission by which each bit of information was preserved prior to being committed to writing. It was important to establish that the chain of oral transmitters (*isnād*, or "attribution") specified in each case was comprised of a series of individuals who were in fact contemporaries in direct communication with each other. Thus Islam, in its earliest period, confronted the issue of the reliability of oral transmission very directly. Spiritual authenticity in Islam has continued to be measured in part by the directness of verbal communication between living exponents of the faith, as for instance in the emphasis that the Ṣūfī orders place on the necessity of a sound spiritual genealogy and on direct communication with spiritual guides.

A serious limitation is imposed on researchers' ability to understand the workings of oral transmission in biblical and other traditions by the fact that the compositional history of existing texts is often undocumented, and information about the traditions upon which they were based is scarce. Arguments for the oral origin of parts of the Bible, like similar arguments concerning devotional and secular medieval literature, proceed mainly on stylistic grounds, whereas the reconstruction of the actual process of oral composition remains inferential. In societies where literacy is the skill of a minority, verbal compositions intended for a general audience must be organized to facilitate aural comprehension, whether or not they are composed orally. Furthermore, in societies where literacy is new, the indigenous verbal aesthetic is by definition oral, and early literature might be expected to emulate it to some degree.

The ethnographic evidence available from contemporary societies, together with the scanty indications of the compositional process gleaned from early literary documents, tends to enforce the idea that different societies distribute oral and literary processes in different ways, that there are a variety of techniques of oral composition and transmission just as there are a variety of techniques of literary composition and dissemination, and that these communicative mechanisms interact in complex ways.

Looking at religious traditions in oral and literate societies today, it becomes clear that virtually all societies develop special languages or communicative styles for religious contexts, and that these are distinguished from everyday written or spoken language. It is perhaps best to regard writing not as more authoritative or powerful per se, but as one of several possible strategies for marking off religious language as particularly powerful. Societies with prophetic traditions embodied in written scriptures may develop popular ideologies that venerate all writing, by extension from the veneration of sacred writ. In folk Islam, for instance, *ta'āwīdh* are written formulas believed to have protective power that are worn as charms on the body. Other written charms may be consumed in dissolved form or inhaled as smoke. Their texts, which are specific to the protective function desired, may be derived from holy scripture, from books of prayers compiled for the purpose of *ta'āwīdh* writing, or from a series of numbers or words arranged in geometric patterns that are considered to be powerful.

This use of written words in charms forms part of a larger continuum of protective magical practices that includes the manipulation of other physical objects (such as strings, bits of cloth, beads, foodstuffs, and fragrant herbs). Thus those who use literacy for protective magical purposes are using but one of several strategies for physically embodying sacred power and directing it to human ends. The sacred power of language is no less likely to be embodied in spoken words, even in highly literate traditions such as Islam and Christianity. The invocations, prayers, and injunctions spoken over a written *ta'āwīdh* at its creation are no less important to its efficacy than is its written text.

Much recent research by folklorists and ethnolinguists favors the view that the meaning and power of sacred language emerges from the actual enactment of words by the living, whether the "texts" that serve as the basis for such enactment are written or oral. The dynamism of such oral enactment can often triumph over the professed fixity of a scriptural tradition and become a source of diversity within the tradition. This can be seen in several examples taken from New World Christian traditions.

Some Pentecostal churches in the United States, for example, while preaching the literal truth of the Christian scriptures, seek personal experiences of possession by the Holy Spirit. One group of such churches puts particular emphasis upon the verses of *Mark* 16:17–18: "And these signs will accompany those that believe: in my name they will cast out demons; they will speak in new tongues; they will pick up serpents, and if they drink any deadly thing, it will not hurt them; they will lay their hands on the sick, and they will recover." To this end, and as part of their devotional services, they handle venomous snakes and drink strychnine in trance states induced by very intense rhythmic vocalization, clapping and dancing during sermons, personal testimony, group prayer, and song. Other Pentecostal groups take no interest in snake handling, but preserve the importance of glossolalia and other forms of vocalization in worship. Glossolalia, or speaking in "new tongues" (*Mk.* 16:17), is accepted as an outward sign of the conversion experience and is considered to be the Holy Spirit speaking through the body of the believer. Such "baptism in the Spirit," with its outward vocal forms, is believed to be necessary for salvation.

A debate arises within some fundamentalist congregations concerning the types of vocalization proper to men and women. The apostle Paul's injunctions (*1 Tm.* 2:11, 2:12; *1 Cor.* 14:34–35) that women should be silent in church are interpreted by some to mean that women should not preach but only give personal testimony, sing, and speak in tongues as the spirit moves them. Women who feel called to preach may frame their sermons more in the style of a personal testimony (or their testimonies more in the style of sermons), or they may defend their right to preach by alluding to points in scripture (e.g., *Acts* and *Joel)* where it is said that women will prophesy in the "last days," which are presumed to be at hand. Thus silence for women receives widely divergent interpretations in different communities. The literalist interpretation of scripture typical of such communities in no way inhibits the development of diversity, especially in the dimension of oral practice.

Diversity is no less apparent in Roman Catholic communities, which were until the 1960s restricted to a uniform Latin liturgy and scripture. Among the Tarascan Indians of Tzintzuntzan, Mexico, an elaborate, nine-day communal ritual of religious processions, feasts, and dances has developed around the single verse of *Luke* 2:7: "And she brought forth her firstborn son, and laid him in a manger, because there was no room in the inn." The theme of no room in the inn has formed the basis for communal processions, called *posadas* ("lodgings"), developed with varying degrees of complexity in many Spanish-American communities. Images of the Virgin are carried through the streets during the last days of Advent, begging for lodging. Although the basis is scriptural, the design and execution of these ceremonies are a matter of emergent oral tradition. In Tzintzuntzan, the ritual has developed into a pancommunal ceremony that entails elaborate cooperation within neighborhoods, performances of songs and recitations, and a complicated cast of male and female actors who carry out the roles of holy pilgrims and inhospitable innkeepers. Stanley Brandes suggests that there are extra-religious reasons for this community's elaboration of this particular detail of sacred biography at this time. In Brandes's view, the ritual reflects changes in relations between members of the community.

A distinction introduced by Gregory Bateson can help to clarify the value of orality in many religious traditions. Bateson distinguished between communicative and "metacommunicative" functions of language. While the communicative dimensions convey information and content, the metacommunicative level conveys a relation between speaker and listener. Bateson further observed that, while the literary mode is conceived as primarily communicative, it is the oral mode that is the dimension of metacommunication. Because a primary goal of religious devotion is precisely to establish or reassert a personal relation between the worshiper and the worshiped, Bateson's distinction helps provide an understanding of why the oral dimension is often critically important in both the embodiment and the propagation of religious belief and experience.

Even within a strictly oral tradition, however, the religious value of orality may be differently assessed, and values normally associated with literacy affirmed. In different traditions, the authenticity of religious utterance may be measured by reference to either an ideal of immutability (whether written or oral), or to an ideal of spontaneity. Wallace L. Chafe, distinguishing stylistically between oral and written English, pointed out that in Seneca, a nonwritten American Indian language, the ritual language of religion and recitations of mythic history achieve many of the same effects of depersonalization and grammatical integration that Chafe identified as markers of literary as opposed to colloquial discourse in English. In Seneca oral tradition, the ideal of ritual recitation is a fixed text, and a highly standardized vocal style and physical mannerisms accompany the recited words. According to Chafe, distinctions between oral and written style in English are thus analogous to distinctions between ritual and colloquial style in exclusively oral Seneca.

By contrast with Seneca religious language, some Christian Pentecostal groups in the American Midwest locate spiritual authenticity in religious utterances that entail possession by the Holy Spirit. A preacher in this tradition would never use any sort of written notes or outline to organize his discourse in advance. And yet this ideal of oral spontaneity in devotional practice in no way alters the conviction that the written scriptures are the verbatim word of God. Furthermore, stylistic analysis reveals a highly consistent structure and high level of formulaic language in such inspired spontaneous utterances, both in sermons and in personal testimonies. Other fundamentalist groups may tolerate or even encourage the use of written outlines by the prayer leader, as well as the use of hymnals, but the spiritual authenticity of the prayer or hymn is measured by the degree to which it is "raised up" by the group from the skeletal, written prototype into an embellished improvisational oral performance.

Similar paradoxical relations between oral and written standards of authenticity can be found in other traditions. William F. Hanks describes a shamanic prayer among Yucatec-Maya of southern Mexico, where the local religion is a complex syncretism of Christianity and pre-Columbian beliefs, largely reliant on oral tradition. In this community, the proper form of prayers is so completely dependent upon the context of oral performance that a shaman is unable to recall or reproduce the text of a prayer outside the setting of the ritual. Hanks persuasively argues that the oral text does not exist in any coherent form outside of the immediate curing rituals, for, as the shaman explains, "[It's] a thing [that] passes by you in your thought." In such an oral tradition, the role of rote learning is minimized (shamans learn how to address spirits primarily through personal dreams and visions), to say nothing of fixed texts in the form of written scripts. Nevertheless, in this same cosmology, there is a guardian spirit whose function it is to record in writing, for divine reference, the individual rituals performed by shamans.

These examples illustrate the diversity of relations between oral and literary traditions in different religious settings, and also the continuing, central importance of the spoken word as religious act. Writing has no doubt provided a mechanism to measure the mutability of ostensibly eternal oral traditions, but when scriptural traditions are examined in particular social contexts, their own mutability is equally apparent, at the level of interpretative enactment. It is in the consciousness and acts (verbal and physical) of living believers that religions manifest their meaning, and in that sense, living tradition is always oral tradition.

SEE ALSO Folk Religion; Memorization; Tradition.

BIBLIOGRAPHY

The departure point for a great deal of work on continuity and analytic functions in oral and literary traditions is the work of the British anthropologist Jack Goody, particularly his *Literacy in Traditional Societies* (Cambridge, U.K., 1968) and *The Domestication of the Savage Mind* (Cambridge, U.K., 1977). The best review and critique of the literature on literacy and its effect on knowledge systems is Brian V. Street's *Literacy in Theory and Practice* (Cambridge, 1984). An introduction to the work of Georges Dumézil is C. Scott Littleton's *The New Comparative Mythology*, 3d ed. (Berkeley, Calif., 1980), which includes references to Dumézil's writings, including recent translations. Victor Turner's ideas on ritual are developed in *The Forest of Symbols* (Ithaca, N.Y., 1967) and many other later articles and books. The best starting place for an understanding of Claude Lévi-Strauss's anthropological theories is his *Structural Anthropology*, 2 vols. (New York, 1963–1976). The key general formulation of the Parry-Lord oral-formulaic theory is Albert B. Lord's *The Singer of Tales* (Cambridge, Mass., 1960). John Miles Foley's *Oral-Formulaic Theory and Research* (New York, 1984), which offers a superb annotated bibliography, provides an encyclopedic review of the scholarship pertinent to the theory in both religious and secular traditions. Two excellent collections of essays on, respectively, the relations between oral and written traditions and the relations between oral and written religious language are *Spoken and Written Language*, edited by Deborah Tannen (Norwood, N.J., 1982), and *Language in Religious Practice*, edited by William J. Samarin (Rowley, Mass., 1976).

M. M. Pickthall's *The Meaning of the Glorious Qur'ān* (1930; New York, 1980) provides a reliable translation of the Qur'ān, together with a historical introduction, from which the quoted traditions about the Prophet's first revelation are taken. Annemarie Schimmel's *Mystical Dimensions of Islam* (Chapel Hill, N.C., 1975) and *As through a Veil: Mystical Poetry in Islam* (New York, 1982) contain much information on folk and orthodox Islam and vocal aspects of Ṣūfī mystical practice. Information on *ta'āwīdh* is from my own ethnographic experience in Afghanistan. There is a burgeoning literature in folklore, linguistics, and anthropology journals on language in religion, from which the short ethnographic examples at the end of this essay are a sampling. Much relevant work has appeared in the *Journal of American Folklore:* Steven M. Kane's "Ritual Possession in a Southern Appalachian Religious Sect," vol. 87 (October–December 1974), pp. 293–302; Stanley Brandes's "The *Posadas* in Tzintzuntzan: Structure and Sentiment in a Mexican Christmas Festival," vol. 96 (July–September 1983), pp. 259–280; Elaine J. Lawless's "Shouting for the Lord: The Power of Women's Speech in Pentecostal Religious Service," vol. 96 (October–December 1983), pp. 434–459; Terry E. Miller's "Voices from the Past: The Singing at Otter Creek Church," vol. 88 (July–September 1975), pp. 266–282; and William F. Hanks's "Sanctification, Structure and Experience in a Yucatec Ritual Event," vol. 97 (April–June 1984), pp. 131–166.

Other studies focusing on particular traditions include Wallace L. Chafe's "Integration and Involvement in Speaking, Writing, and Oral Literature," and Shirley Brice Heath's "Protean Shapes in Literacy Events: Ever-Shifting Oral and Literate Traditions," both in Tannen's *Spoken and Written Language*, cited above. References to Gregory Bateson's ideas are further developed in Tannen's introduction to that volume.

New Sources

Dewey, Joanna, ed. "Orality and Textuality in Early Christian Literature." *Semeia* 65 (1994): 1–216.

Flake, Kathleen. "'Not to Be Riten': The Mormon Temple Rite as Oral Canon." *Journal of Ritual Studies* 9 (Summer 1995): 1–21.

Hauser, Beatrix. "From Oral Tradition to 'Folk Art': Reevaluating Bengali Scroll Paintings." *Asian Folklore Studies* 61, no. 1 (2002): 105–122.

Jaffee, Martin S. "Oral Culture in Scriptural Religion: Some Exploratory Studies." *Religious Studies Review* 24 (July 1998): 223–230.

Jones, Gayl. *Liberating Voices: Oral Tradition in African American Literature.* Cambridge, Mass., 1991.

Lord, Albert Bates. *Epic Singers and Oral Tradition.* Ithaca, N.Y., 1991.

McMahan, David. "Orality, Writing, and Authority in South Asian Buddhism: Visionary Literature and the Struggle for Legitimacy in the Mahayana." *History of Religions* 37 (1998): 249–274.

Niditch, Susan. *Oral World and Written Word.* Louisville, Ky., 1996.

Okpewho, Isidore. *African Oral Literature: Backgrounds, Character, and Continuity.* Bloomington, Ind., 1992.

Silberman, Lou H., ed. "Orality, Aurality and Biblical Narrative." *Semeia,* no. 39 (1987): 1–145.

MARGARET A. MILLS (1987)
Revised Bibliography

ORDEAL is a divinatory practice that has a judiciary function. The word reached the English language from the medieval *ordalium*, the latinized form of the German word *Urteil* ("sentence, judgment"). Two kinds of judiciary ordeals may be distinguished: those prescribed by a judge or judicial body as a form of trial and those that also involve the sentencing and punishment of the accused. Ordeals of the first type are based mostly upon the drawing of lots and the identification of the guilty party among a group of suspects. Except for those that involve the simple drawing of lots, it could be said that every ordeal is designed to prove definitively the guilt or innocence of the accused. For example, a Shoshoni medicine man would take two hairs from the accused and place them in his own tent. If they had disappeared the day after, it was seen as a proof of innocence; if the hairs still remained, it indicated guilt. Ordeals of the second type are those that place the accused in mortal risk. If the accused escapes death, he or she is judged innocent; if he or she dies, the death is considered the due punishment of proven guilt. The most common ordeals of this sort are ordeal by poison, in which the accused is forced to ingest poisonous substances (if innocent, the substances will be vomited up); ordeal by water, in which the accused risks drowning; and ordeal by fire, in which the accused risks burning to death.

Types and Sources of Judiciary Ordeal. The most ancient body of laws that includes judiciary ordeals is the Code of Hammurabi (Babylonia, 1792–1750 BCE), which prescribes the so-called ordeal of the river, in evidence during the Mesopotamian era as early as the twenty-fourth century BCE. In the ordeal of the river (which belongs to the second category of ordeal because it includes sentencing and punishment), a woman accused of witchcraft or adultery was thrown into the river. If she drowned, she was considered to have been guilty, and if she survived, she was absolved. It is interesting to note that those two crimes statistically outnumber all others in the comparative documentation of ordeal and that, in the case of witchcraft, the Code of Hammurabi (stele 5, lines 33–56) seems to have imposed the ordeal (or what today would be called "the burden of proof") on the accuser and not, as one would expect, on the accused. Another application of ordeal as a judiciary instrument dates back to the high Middle Ages. Unlike the Code of Hammurabi, which records the laws of the Mesopotamian civilization, ordeal in medieval times represents an aberrant episode in European legal history that has its foundations in Roman jurisprudence. The appearance of ordeal in European culture can be directly attributed to Roman and Christian adaptation of a Germanic custom. Ordeal was adopted because it had been included in the tribal laws of the various Germanic populations (*Lex Visigothorum, Lex Burgundiorum, Lex Salica,* etc.) and because it had also come to be regarded as a manifestation of divine justice, even to the point of being called "the judgment of God." For an example of the interaction of these two frames of reference, the one civic and the other religious, one can refer to the *Lex Frisonorum,* which prescribed the drawing of lots in the case of a crime for which more than one person was suspected. Three elements enjoined for this ordeal gave it a consecrated character: the prayer to God that he might reveal the guilty party; the request for a priest to officiate at the rite; and the obligation to execute the rite in a church or, at least, in the presence of a reliquary. The religious frame of reference was eliminated because of the negative attitude of the church, which on more than one occasion forbade the clergy to lend itself to the execution of ordeal; gradually, this led to the exclusion of ordeal by judicial institutes as well. Hence its presence in Western culture should be considered episodic and anything but characteristic. The *Lex Salica* called for ordeals in which the accused was tested for resistance to pain and for ordeals that involved the drawing of lots. This judiciary ordeal corresponds to the practice of inflicting torture on the accused to extort confessions. The most common use of torture in trial by pain involved boiling water, but a law of 803 CE speaks of trial by sword. In the form of dueling, trial by sword appears to be the most ancient and most easily verified trial of the Germanic tradition. Recourse to a duel between accuser and accused took place when the accused could not find enough witnesses willing to swear to his innocence (the graver the crime, the more witnesses he had to produce). A refusal to duel by the accuser in itself constituted proof of the innocence of the accused, but a refusal by the accused proved his guilt. According to the *Edictus Rotharii* (643), the accused could be represented by a substitute. He could also refuse to duel, if he submitted to a different kind of trial. One trial by sword that substituted for the duel, called *ad novem vomeres,* was practiced by the Thuringians. In an ordeal that could be called trial both by sword and by pain, the accused was made to walk barefoot over nine flaming plowshares. The symbolism of the plowshares in contrast to the sword is evident: This was more appropriate for farmers than was the duel, the typical ordeal for gentlemen. As an ordeal for gentlemen, the duel endured as a standard feature of chivalric codes and has survived even in modern times as a private solution to disputes, sometimes tolerated and at other times expressly forbidden by law.

Biblical Precedents. The medieval concept of ordeal as "the judgment of God" probably found precedent in the Germanic tradition, but another of its precedents was most certainly found in the Bible. One reads there that judgment came from God through lots (*Prv.* 16:33) and that the drawing of lots resolved conflicts (*Prv.* 18:18). In *Joshua* 7:14–22, the judiciary drawing of lots to discover the violator of a divine interdiction was elaborated: First, the tribe of the guilty party was identified, then his family, then his house, and finally the individual himself. It should be noted, however, that the same procedure, from tribe to individual, was also used for the designation of Saul as the first king (*1 Sm.* 10:17–24), and that Saul himself used it as a judiciary method to discover the violator of a civic and not a divine law (*1 Sm.* 14:40–45). In view of his royal position, which detached him from tribal regulations, Saul put to one side all the tribes of Israel and to the other himself and his son Jonathan. The lots designated him and his son, and as the choice was between them alone, the son was named guilty by the lots. In this phase of the history of Israel, the same ordeal was thus used in identifying a guilty man, whether he had broken civic or divine laws, and in the selection of the first king. This would seem to signify not only that a royal prescription is equal to a divine one but also that the acquisition of royalty is itself tantamount to a violation of divine law. In effect, the Bible describes the arrival of monarchy in Israel as a sinful usurpation of divine authority (*1 Sm.* 8), so God himself is entrusted to designate the usurper as one who has violated divine law. In substance, it was a method that freed the community from the responsibility of decision.

Ordeal and Power. It could be said that recourse to ordeal is always liberating, considering the risk of uncertainty that lies in decision making, though this understanding of ordeal depends on a typically Western concept of responsibility. Ordeal, in the biblical case, reflects a system of interdependence among the divine, the royal, and the judiciary. In abstract terms, this interdependence is seen in the formula of a king who, through divine grace, administers justice in the name of a god, or as if he were a god. But in concrete terms, the royal institution is supported by the heredity of the office, whereby a king becomes king by virtue of being the son of the preceding king. Nor can he substitute for a god as supreme judge, because he is not endowed with divine omniscience and also because he himself could become involved in a judgment as accuser or accused. As in the case of Saul, these contradictions can be resolved.

Ordeal and royalty. As one who has not inherited the throne, the first king is designated by the drawing of lots, or it is believed that he has been so designated. A well-known example of this recourse to ordeal as legendary justification of the title to the throne is that of Romulus, who became the first king of Rome because he saw twice the number of vultures as did his brother Remus. Thothmose III (1504–1450 BCE), one of the greatest of Egyptian pharaohs, prided himself on having been designated for the throne by the oracle of Amun. If a king is involved in a judiciary procedure, he is most likely to figure as the injured party or as the object of betrayal. This crime, treason, required a "judgment from God" in the Middle Ages. It should also be noted that the only ordeal known to have existed in the Inca Empire concerned betrayal: The party accused of treason was held for one day in a cell with dangerous beasts or serpents; if he came out alive, he was absolved. However, most instances of ordeal that involved interdependence between the judicial, the divine, and the royal occurred in Egypt, where this institution had its origin. In the classical model that Egypt presents, the pharaoh takes the place of a god or is a god on earth and, as the beneficiary of divine omniscience, exercises judicial power in concurrence with the divine oracles from whom sentences were often asked. There were moments in Egyptian history—for instance, in the twenty-first dynasty (1085–950 BCE)—when the justice exacted by a divine oracle seems to have prevailed over that administered by the king or his courts; but there are also instances of oracular sentences being challenged, with consequent recourse to the royal tribunal.

Ordeal and divinity. The biblical precedent of the medieval "judgment of God" must be considered not only to explain the adaptation of Roman Christian ethos to Germanic custom but also for the phenomenological problem presented by the relationship between ordeal and divinity. Ordeal is an autonomous and not a cultural ritual. Thus, in some historical contexts, that relationship is considered an accessory, almost a reinforcement of the effectiveness of ordeal as a judicial method. At any rate, numerous cases of ordeals imposed for their own sake, without invocations or evocations of divinity, have been documented. The Mesopotamian river ordeal provides for no divine intervention; in fact, the Code of Hammurabi allows two alternative courses of action—ordeal or divine intervention. For one charge, adultery, the woman accused can demonstrate her innocence either by swearing "to the god" (stele 21, lines 68–76) or by submitting herself to the river ordeal (stele 21, lines 77–82; stele 22, lines 1–6). The judiciary function of swearing "by God," which persists even in the judicial halls of the present time, results from the adaptation of the concept of ordeal to the logic of a polytheistic or monotheistic religion, in which a god who punishes perjurers takes the place of the punishment implicit in the trial by ordeal. The god by whom one swears is, in substance, evoked as the judge; historically, these are usually sun gods or gods of enlightenment and, as such, omniscient. Raffaele Pettazzoni (1955) has called this judiciary role the principal function of an omniscient god. The Mesopotamian sun god Shamash, by whom one swore as proof of one's innocence, was called "lord of judgment" (*bel dini*) and was regarded as the father of Kettu (Justice) and Mesharu (Rectitude). The Bible does not provide evidence of judiciary oaths, but biblical oaths have the quality of a pact, a vow, or a curse. The most severe Hebrew sects forbade even the taking or oaths, as did Christ, according to *Matthew* (5:33–37). Nevertheless, an ordeal was called for in cases of suspected adultery and was carried out as if it were an offering to God (*Nm.* 5:11–31). This is the so-called oblation of jealousy. The oblation to God served to evoke his presence; in front of God, the suspected woman swore to her innocence. The possibility of a lie did not require divine intervention: The punishment could be delegated to humans who administered a potion called "bitter water" that the woman had to ingest; if she was guilty, it would make her dropsical. Oaths were common, however, in Roman law, which never prescribed true ordeal as a judiciary process. The several cases in which the accused himself, outside of legal procedure, requested divine intervention to prove his innocence are considered exceptional. The most famous of such cases is that of Quinta Claudia, a Vestal Virgin accused or suspected of immorality, who submitted herself to the judgment of the Magna Mater (204 BCE). While oaths in a judiciary action may separate divine intervention from ordeal, there are cases in which the opposite is true. Sometimes the ordeal itself is divinized. Among the Sudanese of the interior (Azaude and neighboring peoples), for example, the poison used in an ordeal is personified and assigned divine attributes. Because evidence is scanty, it is not possible to ascertain how much this description of an indigenous custom depends on European interpretation (which tends to give priority to divine figures); but it is a fact that such a process has been found even among the descendants of Africans brought to the Americas as slaves. Ordeal by poison is still common among the so-called Maroons (or "Bush Negroes") of French Guiana and Surinam, the descendants of slaves who rebelled and took refuge in the forest in the seventeenth and eighteenth centuries. This ordeal is, however, associated with an invocation to Odun, the god of justice. The name of this god goes back to the denomination (*odu*) used by the Sudanese of the western African coast (e.g., the Yorulas) to designate the signs of their geomantic prophetic system. This demonstrates the prophetic and autonomous character of ordeal more than it does its substitution for "God's judgment."

Ordeal as Prophetic Battle. This article has considered ordeal as a prophetic form with a judiciary purpose. In this sense it has defined the characteristics of dueling, starting with its Germanic, medieval formulation as trial by sword. In the Germanic tradition also, Tacitus (*Germania* 10) describes a functional inversion of the duel from, not as a prophetic form with a judiciary function, but as a battle with a prophetic function. Before battle, the Germans captured an enemy soldier and forced him to fight against one of their own warriors. The outcome of the fight was taken as an omen regarding the outcome of the upcoming battle. This context seems to broaden the definition of ordeal, but in reality it extends the concept to the point of rendering it meaningless, precisely because of its functional reversal of the judiciary practice. On the other hand, this sort of weakening due to reversals of perspective conveniently brings ordeal into the field of prophecy. Ordeal becomes a judicial process, in whatever form an oracular response is sought. The constant recourse to oath—interpretable as ordeal, as has been noted—seems to provide evidence for such a process. Nor is it necessarily true that, in the Germanic practice of the duel as an ordeal before battle, the prophetic function of the ordeal is predominant at the expense of the judiciary function. In fact, on the level of phenomenology, the battle itself can be regarded as judgment, as the solution to a dispute between two human groups (nations, tribes, clans, etc.). Battle, too, can be seen as an ordeal. The difference between reality and appearance lies not so much in facts as in interpretation. An example is the case of the battle between the Horatii and the Curiatii: It is not worthwhile to ask if it really took place or if it is only legend, because what matters for this article's purposes is the interpretive model it offers. This discussion will begin with the disputes involved in this battle: A routine case of Roman farmers trespassing on Alba Longa territory during the reign of Tullus Hostilius and of Alban farmers encroaching upon Roman territory. The conflict was to be decided by a war. Tullus Hostilius called the gods to witness before the war, meticulously following ritual. The Roman king took great care to characterize this war as "holy" (*pium bellum* is the Latin expression used by Livy), what would today be called a "judgment of God." The war, which one might call a figurative ordeal, was then replaced by a genuine ordeal: The Romans and Albans agreed to make three Roman champions (the Horatii) and three Alban champions (the Curiatii) battle each other, designating the outcome of this battle as the solution to the conflict. The model provided by this event can be used to interpret other situations in which war figures, whether in the search for a common structure in legendary wars such as the Trojan War, or for the purpose of classifying ethnological material pertinent to war. The Trojan War, for instance, was a conflict of which it could be said had a judiciary nature (Menelaus against Paris) and that turned into a war between Greeks and Trojans; it even contains evidence of recourse to a duel (Achilles against Hector). To examine this from the point of view of ordeal, one could speak of a dilatory process (from duel to war) and a reductive process (from war to duel). This pattern of dilation and reduction can be applied theoretically as if the subject of disagreement allowed the two modes indifferently. A purely quantitative distinction between war and duel is possible and in fact fully justified by ethnological documentation of cultures that do not have wars of conquest in the Western sense, but in which every conflict seems to assume the aspect of ordeal. Some of these cultures documented by ethnological research know no type of war but resolve every type of conflict by dueling, even between two groups or tribes. Among the Inuit (Eskimo), an ordeal-duel (by blows) between two champions of opposing sides took the place of war. Similarly, the Colombians resolved all hostilities between individuals, villages, and tribes with an ordeal-duel. This is also true of the natives of North America (e.g., the Tlingit), South America (the Botocudo), Africa (the Ashanti), and Australia. Even when one can speak of war, or an extended ordeal, reduction is always noticeable: It can influence the number of combatants, the arms used, the length of battle, and so forth. Among Northwest Coast Indians war between two villages ceased with the death in battle of one of the chiefs. The equivalence of war and dueling is obvious in these cases, and it is not at all exceptional that the death of the chief signals defeat almost everywhere. Although battle requires a great number of participants, only two people count as far as the ordeal is concerned. The outcome of the ordeal is always binary, because there is a choice between two eventual outcomes that are equally probable before the confrontation takes place, just as in the biblical ordeal, cited above, conducted by successive alternates. This duality is well expressed by the Latin term for war, *bellum,* which derives from *duellum.*

Fighting as ordeal, whether war or duel, reveals its ritual nature through the rules that govern it. On the other hand, ritual fighting is found in religious contexts of various kinds, but perhaps the reduction of fighting to ordeal, even though problematic, can be deduced through recourse to documentary material, as is the case with ritual fighting that precedes tribal initiation ceremonies. Initiation fighting is found in various forms and with various functions: between initiates, between initiates and initiators, between the newly initiated and the women, and so on. But to reach an interpretation that illuminates ordeal, each case should be viewed as proving the ability of the young to be admitted into the adult community. Naturally, there are other ways of testing the battle skills of the young; generally, one would speak of athletics rather than of ritual battle. All athletics, which for the most part have been connected with tribal initiations but which in ancient Greece assumed an independent development, can be looked at for their meaning as ordeal. (The custom of wagering on the winner still attests to the ordeal character of athletics.) A "judgment of God" was derived from the Greek athletic arenas, as from medieval ordeal. Athletic trials pertained to the divine; the verdict, or outcome of the competitions, lent a "divine" prestige to the victorious city. As for the connection with battle, it should be remembered that every competition derives from a form of fighting; it could be said that the athletic arena figuratively substitutes for the duel, just as dueling figuratively takes the place of war. According to the logic of these figurative substitutions, athletic contests and wars were incompatible, in the sense that if the former could figuratively substitute for the latter, it became illogical to hold both athletic events and wars at the same time. Every war between Greek cities was suspended during the celebration of the Olympics, as if the decision that had up to that point been delegated to the armies could be deferred to the games. This "as if" implies a theory that, although belied by the fact that real wars were only delayed and not entirely replaced by the games, permits a glimpse a quality in Greek athletics that is not compatible with today's concept of sports: It could be said that they were more "war" than "sport." Angelo Brelich (1961) has brought to light the initiation-athletic elements of certain traditional Greek wars (between Cretan cities, between Eretria and Chalcis, between the Athenians and the Boeotians, between Argos and Sparta, etc.). More "ordeal" than "game," one may say, remembering that, according to one tradition, the first Olympic competition, a race, was instituted in order to establish the succession to the throne of Elis. For its game-war-ordeal-prophecy connection, a Mexican tradition is emblematic. Moctezuma, the Aztec emperor, lost a Mexican ball game against the king of Texcoco, who had wagered his kingdom against three turkeys. The outcome of the game was to verify, with the defeat of Moctezuma, the truth of the prophecy of the arrival of the Spanish, who would conquer Mexico. On the other hand, every game, when the results are binding (as, for instance, in a game of chance), loses the quality of entertainment and assumes the dramatic aspect of ordeal. For such as interpretive orientation, consider the conclusion of Lucien Lévy-Bruhl, who notes how certain trials by ordeal—understood by him to be among the cleromantic practices—are not too far removed from the spirit of today's "games of chance" (*La mentalité primitive,* Paris, 1925, p. 256).

Ordeal as Initiation Ritual. To return to the probatory, and therefore ordeal-like, function of the ritual battle in tribal initiation contexts, it can be said that, in the abstract, not only these but all the trials to which initiates are subjected are more or less comparable to the various known forms of ordeal. It is not difficult to compare initiation trials of resistance to pain with certain trials by ordeal in which such resistance serves to demonstrate the innocence of the accused. Ordeal is represented also by torture in a judiciary function; among the initiation trials inventoried by ethnologists, genuine torture does indeed appear. Along the same line of interpretation, it is not difficult to move from tribal initiation to initiations into certain cults where trial by ordeal becomes the evidence of a superhuman reality in which the initiate takes part. From another point of view, one can speak of the demonstration of exceptional powers, acquired in the circle of a given religious form. The best known of these powers is the one that allows a person to walk unharmed over burning brands or red-hot stones. This may be called an ordeal by fire, very similar to the ordeal of the nine plowshares of the Thuringians. The diffusion of this trial by fire is remarkable. In ancient Latium Vetus the so-called Hirpi Sorani, cult followers of Apollo Soranus on Mount Soracte, practiced it. Walkers on burning brands or red-hot stones have been observed in ancient Cappadocia, India, China, Japan, the Fiji Islands, Tahiti, Yucatán, and elsewhere. But for edification on the religious level, Mazdaism is highly representative as a religion that simultaneously confers on ordeal, called *varah* in the Avestan tongue, the double value of the judiciary and the initiatory. In the *Denkard* (7.5.4–6), a ninth-century Pahlavi text, can be seen the work of Zarathushtra. The text indicates at least thirty-three ordeals to "determine who will be absolved, and who condemned." In the Avesta, there are constant allusions to the methods and functions of ordeal. From several passages (*Yashts* 12.3; *Afrinaqan* 3.9), it would seem necessary to extract a ritual acknowledgment (by ordeal) from the initiate whom the priest, acting as judge, submits to a trial by fire—perhaps immersion of the hand in boiling oil (more precisely, animal and vegetable fat). Elsewhere (*Vendidad* 4.46), trials of an ethical nature are found. However, for the purpose of religious edification, they are figuratively absorbed in trial by boiling liquid. There are also true judiciary ordeals: The accused "must drink water containing sulphur, water containing gold, which produce the proof of guilt, prove the lie with which he opposes the judge and deceives Mithra" (*Vendidad* 4.54). (This potion used for ordeal is spoken of in *Vendidad* 4.55 as well.) Finally, the judiciary function and initiatory function fuse in an eschatological perspective in which a supreme ordeal is the essential proof and brings about the ensuing sentence of reward or condemnation. In this regard, one reads in one of the five *Gathas* attributed to Zarathushtra that initiates will have to distinguish themselves from sinners (noninitiates) in order to have "the compensation that will be attributed to them by the ordeal of molten metal." In conclusion, ordeal is not an accessory element of Mazdaism; rather it produces, within the boundaries of a rite or ritual, the two main characteristics of this religion: dualism and attention to *asha,* a term that can be translated as both "youth" and "justice" (the "just order"). Mazdean dualism responds to the binary code with which ordeal is expressed. Attention to the *asha* corresponds to the judiciary function that, although not always in equal measure, is found in every ordeal in every context.

See Also Games.

Bibliography

In regard to divination by means of ordeal, one text is indispensable: *La divination: Études recueillies,* 2 vols., edited by André Caquot and Marcel Leibovici (Paris, 1968). On the medieval "judgment of God," see Hermann Nottarp's *Gottesurteilstudien* (Munich, 1956). Also for the Middle Ages and ordeal as war, see Kurt-Georg Cram's *Iudicium belli: Zum Rechtscharakter des Krieges im deutschen Mittelalter* (Münster, 1955). About war as ordeal, see M. R. Davie's, *La guerre dans les sociétés primitives* (Paris, 1931). On the relationship between initiations and wars in Greece, see Angelo Brelich's *Guerre, agoni, e culti nella Grecia arcaica* (Bonn, 1961). For ordeal-oath in connection with divine omniscience, see Raffaele Pettazzoni's *L'onni-scienza di Dio* (Turin, 1955). For the formal connection between games of chance and ordeal, besides the Lévy-Bruhl work cited in the text, see also Johan Huizinga's *Homo Ludens,* translated by R. F. C. Hull (London, 1949).

New Sources

As far as ordeal in classical antiquity is concerned see: Henk S. Versnel, "Pepremenos: The Cnidian Curse Tablets and the Ordeal by Fire." In *Ancient Greek Cult Practice from the Epigraphical Evidence: Proceedings of the Second International Seminar on Ancient Greek Cult, Organized by the Swedish Institute at Athens, 22–24 Nov. 1991,* pp. 145–154 (Stockholm, 1994); Andrea Piras, "Le tre lance del giusto Wiraz e la freccia di Abaris: ordalia e volo estatico tra iranismo ed ellenismo," *Studi Orientali e Linguistici* 7 (2000): 95–109; Peter T. Struck, "The Ordeal of the Divine Sign: Divination and Manliness in Archaic and Classical Greece," in *Andreia. Studies in Manliness and Courage in Classical Antiquity,* ed. by Ralph M. Rosen and Ineke Sluiter, pp. 167–186 (Leiden-Boston, 2003); Karel van der Toorn, "Ordeal Procedures in the Psalms and the Passover Meal." *Vetus Testamentum* 38 (1988): 427–445; and Frank Charles Fensham, "Ordeal by Battle in the Ancient Near East and the Old Testament," in *Studi in onore di Edoardo Volterra,* vol. 6, pp. 127–135 (Milan, 1971).

Robert Bartlett, *Trial by Fire and Water: The Medieval Judicial Ordeal* (Oxford, 1986) represents the most important monograph on the subject. The evolution from medieval judicial praxis to modern times is also investigated from a juridical perspective. Among the most important studies, see: Peter Browe, ed., *De ordaliis,* 2 vols. (Rome, 1932–1933); *La preuve,* 2 vols. (Recueils de ls Société Jean Bodin pour l'histoire comparative des institutions, 17; Brussels, 1965); Wolfgang Schield, *Alte Gerichtsbarkeit. Vom Gottesurteil bis zu Beginn der modernen Rechtssprechung* (Munich, 1980); John Baldwin, "The Intellectual Preparation for the Canon of 1215 against Ordeals," *Speculum* 36 (1961): 613–636; Rebecca Colman, "Reason and Unreason in Early Medieval Law," *Journal of Interdisciplinary History* 4 (1974): 571–591; Colin Morris, "Judicium Dei: The Social and Political Significance of the Ordeal in the Eleventh Century," *Studies in Church History* 12 (1975), pp. 95–111; Oliver Guillot, "La participation au duel judiciaire de témoins de condition serve dans l'Ile-de-France au XIe siècle," in *Droit privé et institutions regionales. Etudes historiques offerts à Jean Yver,* pp. 345–360 (Paris, 1976); Paul Hyams, "Trial by Ordeal: The Key to Proof in the Early Common Law," in *On the Laws and Customs of England. Essays in Honor of Samuel E. Thorne,* ed. by Morris Arnold et al., pp. 90–126 (Chapel Hill, 1981); Winfried Trusen, "Das Verbot der Gottesurteile und der Inquisitionsprozeß. Zum Wandel des Strafverfahrens unter dem Einfluß des gelehrten Rechts im Spätmittelalter," in *Sozialer Wandel im Mittelalter. Wahrnehmungsformen, Erklärungsmuster, Regelungsmechanismen,* ed. by Jürgen Miethke and Klaus Schreiner, pp. 235–247 (Sigmaringen, 1994); Gerhard Köbler, "Welchen Gottes Urteil ist das Gottesurteil des Mittelalters?" in *Vom mittelalterlichen Recht zur neuzeitlichen Rechtswissenschaft. Bedingungen, Wege und Probleme der europäischen Rechtsgeschichte (Festschrift Winifried Trusen),* ed. by Norbert Brieskorn, Paul Mikat, Daniela Müller, Dietmar Willoweit, pp. 89–108 (Paderborn, 1994); Stephen D. White, "Proposing the Ordeal and Avoiding It: Strategy and Power in Western French Litigation, 1050 to 1110," in *Power and Society in the Twelfth Century,* ed. by Thomas N. Bisson, pp. 89–123 (Philadelphia, 1995); Stephen D. White, "Imaginary Justice: The End of the Ordeal and the Survival of the Duel," *Medieval Perspectives* 13 (1998): 32–55.

Magical features in ordeal are well outlined by Keith Thomas, *Religion and the Decline of Magic* (London, 1971); Peter Brown, "Society and the Supernatural. A Medieval Change," *Daedalus* 104 (1975): 133–151 (reprinted in his *Society and the Holy in Late Antiquity* [Berkeley, 1982], pp. 302–332); Charles Radding, "Evolution of Medieval Mentalities: A Cognitive-Structural Approach," *American Historical Review* 83 (1978): 577–597; Charles Radding, "Superstition to Science: Nature, Fortune and the Passing of the Medieval Ordeal," *American Historical Review* 84 (1979): 945–969.

DARIO SABBATUCCI (1987)
Translated from Italian by Miriam Friedman
Revised Bibliography

ORDEMA SEE POWER

ORDER OF THE PREACHERS SEE DOMINICANS

ORDERS, RELIGIOUS SEE RELIGIOUS COMMUNITIES

ORDINATION here refers to the practice in many religions of publicly designating and setting apart certain persons for special religious service and leadership, granting them religious authority and power to be exercised for the welfare of the community. The way each religious community practices ordination depends on that community's worldview and religious beliefs. For example, in traditions that emphasize a direct relationship with the divine being or beings, the ordained person may be thought of primarily as a mediator or priest. Communities that consider human beings to be especially troubled by evil spirits or witchcraft look to shamans or exorcists to counteract the evil influences. In religions that present a goal of inner enlightenment and purified life, the ordained person will be a monk, nun, or spiritual master leading the way toward this goal of enlightenment. And religious communities that place much emphasis on living in accordance with the divinely given law set certain persons apart as religious scholars and judges.

Each religious tradition sets up qualifications that candidates must meet before they can be ordained. Sometimes ordination is based on heredity. In many religions the candidate must be male, although some roles are specified for women; other traditions allow both male and female candidates to be ordained. Since the late twentieth century, a major shift has taken place in some traditions that formerly had restricted ordination to men, such as Judaism, Christianity, and Shintō: A number of groups within these traditions have begun to accept women for ordination. While aptness for the religious role is always a requirement, in some traditions the person must already have demonstrated his or her suitability for that role before being chosen, while in others it is assumed that the office will be learned through a period of training. Every religion presupposes some kind of divine call or inner motivation on the part of the candidate.

An authority and power not possessed by the ordinary people of the community are conferred on the candidate through ordination. The source of that authority and power may be the divine powers, the consent of the community, or those who have already been ordained. Upon ordination, the person receives a new religious title. The English term *priest* can be used in many religious traditions to designate those who have been ordained or set apart, but a variety of other terms is sometimes preferred, such as *shaman, medicine man, monk* or *nun, rabbi, bishop, deacon, minister,* or *imam.*

Ordination in Ancient and Traditional Societies. Numerous ancient and traditional societies have beliefs and practices according to which they set apart certain persons as religious leaders, endowing them with special authority and power for the performance of essential religious services, such as serving the gods and spirits, sacrificing, communicating with spiritual powers, warding off evil powers, healing, and the like. Among the great diversity of roles dealing with spiritual power, some basic types are priests, shamans, and medicine men or women.

The term *priest* generally designates a person ordained with authority to practice the cult of certain divinities or spirits. Since these spiritual powers are believed to direct and influence human existence, they must be worshiped, prayed to, consulted, influenced by sacrifices, and the like, for the continuing welfare of the human community. The priesthood may be hereditary, or priests may be called or chosen by the divinity. After selection or calling, the aspiring priest undergoes a period of purification and training. Among the Ashanti of Africa, the novice trains in private with an older priest for three years, during which time the novice's hair is left uncut. He is taught rituals, rules of priestly life and conduct, how to communicate with the various spirits, and so forth. The final act of ordination takes place at a nighttime festival, with the new priest dressed in a palm-fiber kilt and decorated with all his charms. He kneels before his instructor-priest, who shaves off his hair; any "bad matter" that is found is put in a pot, which is then taken off to the bush. The new priest dances all night to the drums and the singing of the people, and he ends the ordination ritual in the morning by sacrificing a sheep to his god.

Ancient Israelite society had a designated priesthood that served Israel's god by prayer and sacrifice, acting as intermediaries for the people. The description of the investing of Aaron and his sons (*Lv.* 8) may be an idealized account, but it presents many important symbols of ordination. All the congregation assembled for the ceremony, and Moses announced to the assembly that God had commanded this ordination. Aaron and his sons were presented, washed with water, vested with special priestly garments, and anointed with oil. Aaron and his sons laid their hands on the "ram of ordination"; after it was sacrificed, its blood was placed on the tips of their right ears, on the thumbs of their right hands, and on the great toes of their right feet. They ate the sacrificial offerings, and then they stayed in the tent for the seven "days of ordination," after which they were authorized to act as priests on behalf of the people. In ancient Egypt, the king (and thus, the god) appointed the priests to act as ritual specialists for the king. After preparation by fasting and abstinence, shaving their hair, and circumcision, the induction ritual for new priests included purification by washing, anointing of their hands, donning of special linen garments, presentation before the gods in the temple, and reception of special divine knowledge.

While priests are holy persons who have power by virtue of their office, other religious roles in traditional societies are set apart for those who demonstrate the appropriate charisma, for example, shamans and medicine men and women, who are able to maintain communication with the spiritual powers and influence those powers for the benefit of humans.

Shamans (male and female) are commonly thought to be elected directly by tutelary spirits, who in a visionary experience initiate the future shaman. Among Siberian shamans, this initiatory experience involves being sick, being carried to the realm of the spirits, having the body dismembered and reconstituted, and receiving instruction in shamanizing from the god. After this visionary experience of death and resurrection, the future shaman is instructed by an elder shaman, and often there is a ceremony that confirms the initiation by the spirits. For example, the Buriat neophyte, after many years of training following his first ecstatic experiences with the spirits, is consecrated in a public ceremony. First a purification ritual is performed, in which his back is touched with a broom dipped in a goat's blood. In the ordination ceremony, the shamans consecrate the shamanic instruments that the novice will use, and the candidate is anointed with blood from a sacrificial animal on the head, eyes, and ears. The "father shaman" leads the neophyte and other shamans in the ritual of climbing birch trees that have been cut from the burial forest and set up on the sacred ground, after which all fall into ecstasy and shamanize. Finally, meat from the sacrificed animals is prepared, and everyone joins in a banquet celebrating the new shaman.

Although the Burmese are Buddhists, they still have beliefs in a variety of spirits, ghosts, and witches; in particular, the spirits called *nats* are thought to be powerful and capable of affecting humans for good and evil, and these *nats* are propitiated by shamans (most are women, though a small percentage are men) who play the important role of "nat wives." Typically, through a trance or dream, a young woman is possessed or "loved" by one of the *nats*, and any resistance is punished by the *nat* until a "marriage" is arranged. The wedding is a costly affair, performed in a *nat* "palace" where there is a ceremonial chamber. As the *nat*'s dance is performed, the bride changes into the proper costume, pays the marriage fee, and enters the bridal chamber. Two shamans perform a ceremony of putting the bride's soul to sleep, and she does a dance to the music associated with the *nat* husband. The marriage has now been consummated, and she remains secluded for seven days with her *nat* husband, after which she is known as a *nat* wife and practices as a shaman.

Among Australian Aborigines, shamans play an important role in diagnosing and curing illnesses, holding séances with the spirit world and spirits of the dead. The profession can be inherited, the person may experience a call or election, or he may seek out the role—but in any case he must be "made" through an ecstatic experience involving a ritual of initiation. Typically the initiate is taken to the bush, and the ordaining medicine man places against his breast large quartz crystals, which are thought to vanish into his body. In other symbolic rituals, he is led into a hole in the ground to a grave, and snakes are also rubbed against him to give him wisdom. The initiation is completed with a symbolic ascent to heaven to communicate with the high god. Among the Azande of Africa, the ceremony of initiation for a medicine man (or woman) includes a ritual burial following a period of purification. The elders bury the upper part of the novice's body in a hole under a mat with dirt heaped on it, on which the other medicine men dance. After about a half hour he is taken out, and medicine is put in his eyes and nostrils. After swallowing powerful phlegm expectorated by a master doctor, the aspiring novice is taken to a stream source and shown the various herbs and shrubs from which the medicine is derived. After this he takes a new name and is authorized to practice as a medicine man.

Zoroastrian and Hindu Ordination. Among Indo-Europeans the priesthood was an important class, as evidenced in the priesthoods of the ancient Romans, Greeks, Celts, Persians, Aryans, and others. The Zoroastrians and the Hindus have continued this emphasis on a class of priests ordained to perform the important purifications, sacrifices, and other ceremonies for the maintenance of a healthy relationship between humans and the eternal divine order of the universe.

The religion of the ancient Persians, as transformed by the prophet Zarathushtra (Zoroaster) into Zoroastrianism, is practiced in the early twenty-first century by small communities in Iran and India (where they are called Parsis). In Zoroastrianism, the aspirant to the priesthood must be a son of a priestly family who has gone through the childhood religious initiation (Naojot), consisting of investiture with the sacred shirt and girdle or thread. A lengthy period of training in chanting the scriptures and performing the rituals qualifies him for ordination.

According to traditional practice, there are two levels of ordination, of which the first (*nāvar*) qualifies the aspirant as a priest who can perform benedictions, investiture of children, marriages, and the like. During the first level of ordination, the candidate must perform two *bareshnūms*, the highest form of purification ritual, lasting nine days each. Under the open sky a sacred liquid is applied to his whole body many times, and then the candidate makes a nine-day retreat in the fire temple. After the two rituals, the candidate bathes and puts on a new set of white clothes and a white turban. In the sacrifice chamber of the fire temple, he removes his upper garments, makes an ablution, and puts on a mouth veil. One of the priests brings him before the assembled priests and asks permission to initiate him. The silence of the assembly indicates their consent, and the candidate is taken back to the sacrificial chamber to perform the ceremony of chanting the Avestan scriptures and other liturgical rituals. These are repeated for four days, after which the candidate is declared to be qualified as a priest of the *hērbad* level.

In order to perform also the higher liturgical services, the priest must qualify himself by going through the second grade of ordination (*martab*). In this ceremony, the priest again goes through a period of purification, then he conducts the Yasna liturgy for ten days. Now finally the priest is ordained as a *mōbad* priest, and he can fully officiate as the directing priest at all religious ceremonies.

In Hinduism, brahman priests have always played an important role. In ancient Vedic times they were thought to uphold the whole social order through their mediation, by virtue of their mastery of the sacred rituals, sacrifices, and formulas. In the early twenty-first century, especially for people of the high castes, it is important to have a brahman household priest (*purohita*) perform the traditional rituals and chant the Vedic texts properly so that the cosmic order will continue with its health and goodness for each according to his or her place in the total order. Some brahmans prepare to be priests of temple worship, where rituals center on the ceremonial treatment of the images of the gods—although many functions of temple worship can be performed by the people without priestly help. And there is a variety of religious specialists from non-brahman castes that serve village gods and perform ritual functions in Hindu communities.

The traditional view in Hinduism is that a priest must be a male from the brahman caste who has gone through the initiation ceremony (*upanayana*) and received the sacred thread as a twice-born brahman. The brahman boy who aspires to become a household or temple priest studies for many years with a teacher at a Vedic training center and learns the correct way of reciting the Sanskrit Vedic scriptures.

After reaching technical proficiency in recitation of the Vedas and in performing the simpler ceremonies, the novice priest must spend a period of time as assistant to a senior priest. For those priests who are training to be domestic priests, this means accompanying the senior priest on his rounds and assisting him. The senior will formally introduce the junior priest to the assembly of professional priests, while the trainee formally announces his apprenticeship under the senior priest. In conducting the ceremonies, the junior first sits behind the senior priest, helping to recite some *mantras*; as he gains confidence, he is allowed to sit next to the teacher. Gradually the novice priest takes charge of rituals while the senior priest withdraws. In this way, eventually the new priest becomes established and recognized as a full-fledged member of the profession of domestic priesthood. For brahmans entering the public temple priesthood of one of the great gods, such as Viṣṇu or Śiva, the ritual consecration is performed in the temple by priests to admit the new priest to their ranks. In a Śiva temple, for example, the consecration ritual is attended by many priests as well as a large crowd of devotees. The officiating priest performs worship for the candidate in the same way as worshiping a Śiva image, bathing him in a variety of substances, dressing him in new clothes, offering food and waving lamps in front of him, demonstrating that the new priest is a form of Śiva and thus has authority to perform the temple rituals. One additional requirement must also be met for the ordination of domestic and temple priests: Because tradition prohibits an unmarried priest from performing public worship or participating in the rituals of the *saṃskāras*, or life passages, the novice priest must take a wife.

In recent years some groups both in India and in Hindu communities in places such as South Africa and Trinidad have begun ordaining women as priests after training them in reciting the Vedas and performing the various rituals. They argue that the Vedic scriptures support a priestly role for women, and that women priests can fill an important need especially as more men are drawn away from the priesthood to other careers in society.

ORDINATION AMONG JAINS AND BUDDHISTS. Two religions that grew up in India along with Hinduism are Jainism and Buddhism, and in these religious traditions spiritual power is understood to reside especially in the monastic communities, that is, among those monks and nuns who have left ordinary secular life to pursue spiritual perfection through ascetic practices. The monks and nuns are primarily devoted to their own spiritual perfection; yet because they possess great power they can perform religious service for the laypeople, such as chanting scripture, performing funeral rites, and teaching.

Among the Jains of India, the monks and nuns are set apart from the lay population by virtue of having embarked on the path of total renunciation. As *sādhus* and *sādhvīs* (male and female mendicants), they pursue their own goal of reaching the highest state of liberation of the soul from all traces of *karman*. For the laypeople who perform their own religious ceremonies, the mendicants function mainly as models and as teachers.

Prior to ordination, the candidate will have gone through a period of training under a qualified master, involving the formal declaration of intention, fasting, study of basic scriptures, and taking a new name. Ordination occurs through the formal assumption of the five Great Vows (*mahāvrata*) in a public ceremony called *dīkṣā*. The five Great Vows are the vows of nonviolence, abstaining from untruthfulness, abstaining from stealing, chastity, and renouncing all love for any thing or any person. The novice casts off all lay possessions and becomes a new person. Particulars of the ceremony differ somewhat among the different sects. A Digambara monk, fulfilling that order's ideal of nudity, will stand before his teacher and renounce every possession, even his loincloth; he is given a small whisk broom, with which he is to remove insects from his sitting or sleeping place. Among Śvetāmbaras, the aspirant is given three large pieces of cloth for a new wardrobe, and also a whisk broom, a begging bowl, a blanket, a staff, and some volumes of scripture. Monks and nuns of the Sthānakavāsi sect are also given a small strip of cloth to keep tied over the mouth at all times save mealtime, to protect organisms that might be injured by an unimpeded rush of warm air. One significant part of the ritual of ordination is the act of slowly and painfully pulling the hair from one's head in five handfuls, signifying the aspirant's determination to meet the severe demands of the ascetic life.

It is significant that nuns have always been more numerous than monks in Jainism, from the time of the founder Mahāvīra. Because Digambara nuns cannot enter a state of ascetic nudity (as required of monks), they are sometimes considered of lower rank. However, Śvetāmbara and Sthānakavāsi female mendicants take the same vows as do the male mendicants, and so they are considered to have equal ordination status.

The people of the community participate in the ordination ceremony. The *dīkṣā* ceremony is accompanied by great pomp and by the performance of various religious acts by the laypeople. On the next day, when the new mendicant goes out with the begging bowl to receive food for the first time, the householder who provides the food is considered to earn great merit.

Among Buddhists also, men and women ordained as monks and nuns (*bhikkhus* and *bhikkhunīs*) are set apart from the lay population by virtue of having embarked on the path toward extinguishing the sense of self and reaching nirvana. The monks and nuns contribute to the welfare of the general community, not as intermediaries between the people and the gods but as reservoirs of merit and models of spiritual perfection. Typically they perform a variety of services for the laity in chanting scripture for various occasions, performing merit-making rituals, praying for the dead, and teaching.

The Buddha established ordination for both the men's order and the women's order of mendicants, teaching that men and women equally can reach enlightenment. According to the scriptural texts, he prescribed several additional requirements for women's ordination, seemingly making nuns dependent on the order of monks and requiring that a nun be ordained both by an assembly of monks and by an assembly of nuns. Eventually the full ordination of nuns disappeared in Theravada Buddhist societies, and attempts to revive it in modern times have been unsuccessful, since there are no fully ordained Theravada nuns to perform the ordination. Dedicated women continue to become mendicants in Theravada societies such as Thailand, Burma, and Sri Lanka, but they receive only a novice ordination and thus are not considered to have the same spiritual status as monks. The full *bhikkhunī* ordination for women has been maintained in Mahāyāna societies, such as in China and Korea.

In Theravada cultures such as those of Burma and Thailand, it is traditional for boys to be ordained on a temporary basis and spend some time in the monastery as novice monks, as a kind of passage to adulthood. This initiation into monkhood *(pabbajjā)* is technically a monastic ordination; the young men have their heads shaved by the monks and recite the Ten Precepts of monastic life, after which they are given new Buddhist names. The Ten Precepts are the following: not to destroy life; not to steal; not to engage in sexual misconduct; not to lie; not to take alcoholic beverages; not to eat after noon; not to participate in dancing, music, and theater; not to wear garlands, perfumes, and ointments; not to use high or wide beds; and not to accept gold or silver.

Although most of the young men return to secular life after a period of time in the monastery, other men and some women take on the monastic ordination as a more permanent role and become members of the *saṅgha* (Skt., *saṃgha*), the monastic order. The ordination ritual that marks this separation from lay life is called *upasampadā,* or higher ordination, and presupposes some twelve years' experience as a novice after the lower ordination.

The monk or nun is to be essentially a homeless, celibate, ascetic mendicant. Being ordained means dying a civil death, so before the ceremony the candidate divests himself or herself of all possessions and gives up title to inheritable property. He or she brings to the ordination, as gifts from lay sponsors, the only property that a *bhikkhu* or *bhikkhunī* is to possess: the yellow robe, a begging bowl, a girdle, a small razor, a needle and some thread, a water strainer to strain insects from drinking water, and a palm-leaf fan. The laypeople—parents and friends—play an essential role in the ordination, in terms of financial support for the ritual and the postceremonial festivities, sponsorship of the novice's application, and the like. Gifts and support of the ordination bring merit to the donor.

The ordination ceremony takes place in an assembly of *bhikkhus* (and an assembly of *bhikkhunīs*, for women candidates) in the special ordination chamber of the monastery, surrounded by boundary stones beyond which laypeople are not to enter. The candidate, dressed in yellow robes and with head and eyebrows shaven, kneels in front of the assembled monks and affirms in response to questions that he or she is a human being of sound body and mind, of legitimate birth, free of debts, a freeman, at least twenty years old, in possession of robes and a begging bowl, and having parental consent. The candidate formally requests admission to the *saṅgha,* and the presiding monk asks three times if any of his colleagues has any objection to the candidate. Silence is taken as consent, the candidate is pronounced a *bhikkhu* or *bhikkhunī,* and his or her new Buddhist name is conferred. The monastic rule from the Vinaya is read aloud, and the new monk or nun promises to comply with all its rules.

Mahāyāna Buddhist communities have the same basic ordination ceremony, with some special differences. In traditional China, for example, it was customary for the aspiring monk to "leave home" by taking a senior monk as his master and receiving tonsure from him, entering into a period of training as a novice within the tonsure family headed by the "father-master."

Ordination in Chinese Buddhism traditionally involves long and complicated rites with a large number of ordinands. Monks and nuns come to the large ordaining monastery and live there for a time of strict training. After a night of repentance and purification, the ordinands kneel before the masters and witnesses, reciting the Three Refuges and accepting the Ten Vows, receiving their robes and begging bowls. Training resumes for a period of time, and at a second ordination ceremony the ordinands accept the monastic rules and go up to the ordination platform in groups of three to be examined by the ordination masters and accepted as full-fledged monks and nuns. An important ceremony in Mahāyāna ordination rituals is the scarring of the scalp with burns; cones of moxa are placed on the shaven scalp and set afire, burning down into the skin and leaving permanent scars identifying the person as a monk or nun. The ordinands finally receive ordination certificates, and they join their family and friends for a celebration in honor of their new vocation.

ORDINATION OF PRIESTS IN DAOISM AND SHINTŌ. Priests in Chinese Daoism function as ritual and liturgical specialists, but they also act as exorcists and healers, expelling and pacifying demons. There are two main traditions of Daoist priests *(daoshi)* in the early twenty-first century, stemming from movements in the long history of Daoism. The Zhengyi (Orthodox Unity, also called Tianshi, Celestial Masters) sect is a diverse movement made up of male priests who are married and perform a whole range of rituals and liturgies for communities and families. The Quanzhen (Complete Perfection) sect is made up of both male and female priests who are celibate and practice monastic Daoist disciplines primarily for self-cultivation.

The ordination ritual in Daoism is basically the liturgical act of transmitting a canon of scriptures from a recognized master to a disciple. Daoist candidates for the priesthood are often designated on the basis of heredity. Since the ritual of Daoism is esoteric, that is, not directly to be understood and witnessed by the laypeople, usually the aspiring priest will join the entourage of a recognized master who knows the important formulas and hidden aspects of ritual Daoism.

The aspirant's expertise is judged by several criteria. First, it is important to have mastered the external performance of Daoist ritual: writing an artistic talisman to cure illness, exorcising evil spirits with sword and oxhorn trumpet, performing the ritual dance steps and acrobatic tumbling, climbing a blade-side-up sword ladder, and the like. But beyond the ability to perform the external rituals, what really determines the ordination rank given to the new priest is reception of particular scriptures and mastery of the esoteric secrets of the religion, including the meditations and breath-control techniques of internal alchemy. Most important is the ability to recite the registers (*lu*) of spirits who will obey the priest's commands and enable communication with the different spheres of the universe. The master also teaches the aspirant the oral explanation of the register, with the appropriate gestures, formulas, and meditation techniques used in summoning and controlling the spirits.

Traditional rituals of ordination include a time of isolation and purification together with a formal visit to the master to pay homage and request transmission of the scriptures. The ritual of ordination includes transcription of the scriptural texts. The master presides over a festival in honor of the many gods who reside in the temple and the whole Daoist pantheon, who are summoned to participate. The master commends the ordinand to the gods and administers oaths in which the ordinand pledges never to misuse the scriptures or reveal them to outsiders. Rituals of empowerment include the giving of official titles, authority to use the scriptures and perform the appropriate rituals, and the right to use the registers, talismans, and other sacred implements. Support from the local community is necessary for the ordination, partly to pay for the considerable expenses of the festival.

Daoist priests of the Zhengyi sect who serve in temples and perform rituals for the people are called "fire-dwellers," that is, they have a hearth and home, marry, and have families. Among Zhengyi priests in Taiwan, often a distinction is made between "Black-head" priests and "Red-head" priests, depending on the ranking of their ordination. Red-head priests tend to be more shamanistic and perform popular rituals, such as protection for homes, pregnancies, children, and exorcisms of various kinds. Black-head priests are authorized to work more with written liturgies, using formal vestments, performing funerals and requiem services, and conducting high rituals such as the Jiao festival of renewal.

Some Daoists in traditional China pursued the path of individual realization more exclusively by taking up residence in a Daoist monastery (*daoguan*) of the Quanzhen sect. In this case, first the aspirant has to be accepted by a master at a hereditary temple as a novice. After a period of study and practice, the master performs the "rites of crown and cloth," binding the hair into a topknot and crowning the novice. Then the novice enrolls in a public, ordaining monastery for several months to prepare for ordination vows. Monastic training particularly involves meditation in practice of "inner alchemy," breath control, and other exercises aimed at cultivating the vital force. At the beginning of the twenty-first century, monasteries such as the White Cloud Monastery (Baiyun guan) in Beijing provide scholarly training and ordination for both men and women seeking to become Quanzhen Daoist priests.

The main function of Japanese Shintō priests (*shinshoku*) of all ranks is to worship and serve the *kami,* the spiritual beings associated with the powerful forces of nature and the ancestors. The priests, generally referred to as *kannushi,* maintain good relations with the *kami* for the divine protection and welfare of the human community.

Priests often come from families with long and strong traditions of Shintō worship. In ancient times a few priestly families supplied most of the priests, although in modern times the priesthood is open to candidates from nonpriestly families also. Very often the right to be a priest at a particular shrine is passed from father to son or daughter. Though in the past priests were nearly all male, there are now significant numbers of women in the Shintō priesthood. The princess who is high priestess (*saishu*) at the shrine at Ise is the highest rank of all the priests, and in certain other shrines there have traditionally been women priests. Some women became priests as a result of war; when a priest was absent or killed in war, the parishioners would sometimes ask his wife to serve as priest. Priests customarily marry and raise families.

Aspiring priests study for a period of time either in the Kokugakuin University in Tokyo, Kogakkan University in Mie Prefecture, or a regional seminary; occasionally taking an examination can substitute for such study. They are expected to get an academic degree and certificate as *chokkai* (the beginning priestly ordination level), issued by the Association of Shintō Shrines (Jinja Honchō) according to the training and merit of the individual. Continuing training and examinations provide opportunity for priests to advance to higher ranks as structured by the Association of Shintō Shrines. The aspiring priest is appointed by the president of the Association of Shintō Shrines to a shrine responsibility appropriate to his rank. Within the priesthood of a particular shrine, the usual designations of rank, depending on the degree and experience, are those of chief priest *(gūji)* of a shrine, associate chief priest *(gongūji)*, priest *(negi)*, and junior priest *(gonnegi)*. When presiding over rituals, the priests wear colorful and elaborate vestments, depending on the age and rank of the priests as well as the season of the year.

ORDINATION IN JUDAISM. The religion of Judaism after the Babylonian exile and especially after the destruction of the

Temple in the Roman period moved away from a sacrificial temple cult and priesthood and, consequently, the most important religious leaders became those ordained as rabbis. They functioned as judges, scholars, teachers, and expounders of the Torah and Talmud; in modern times, rabbis also function as worship leaders, officiants at marriage and burial ceremonies, and spiritual heads of local communities of Jews.

According to the Hebrew scriptures, Moses ordained his successor Joshua by "placing his hands" (*samakh*) on him, transferring to him a part of his authority (*Nm.* 27:18–23; *Dt.* 34:9); and he also ordained seventy elders to assist him in governing the people (*Nm.* 11:16–25). Jewish tradition holds that there was an unbroken chain of ordination down to the time of the Second Temple. Traditionally the most important role of the rabbi was in giving judgments in both religious and secular matters, as covered by Jewish law. Ordination (*semikhah*) was required for membership in the Sanhedrin and the regular colleges of judges empowered to decide legal cases. The practice of laying on of hands was dropped in later times, and ordination took place simply by proclamation or with a written document. The special ordination formula included the words "Yoreh yoreh. Yadin yadin. Yattir yattir" ("May he give direction? He may give direction. May he judge? He may judge. May he permit? He may permit"). The ordinand wore a special garment, and after the ordination the new rabbi delivered a public discourse as a demonstration of his new role.

Changing times, especially the loss of religious autonomy in the Palestinian and Babylonian Jewish communities by the fourth century CE, led to the discontinuation of the original *semikhah* ordination with the early rabbinic idea of passing down divine authority for judicial powers. Eventually ordination as a rabbi became a matter of setting a person apart to function in a professional role as a rabbi, qualified by virtue of training in the Torah and the Talmud and sanctioned institutionally to render decisions for the community that engaged him. In more recent times, pressure developed in Europe for rabbis to be versed in the vernacular and in secular studies, so new rabbinical seminaries were organized that put less emphasis on the Talmud and Jewish law and more emphasis on studying Jewish history and philosophy, preaching, and pastoral work as spiritual leader of a synagogue. Consequently, in contemporary Judaism there is some difference in the conception of ordination to the rabbinate. Some groups have traditional schools (*yeshivot*) that give the traditional *semikhah* ordination with its emphasis on training in the Talmud and Jewish codes. Other groups have seminaries that see preparation for the rabbinate as including not only knowledge of the Talmud and codes but also professional training to function as a synagogue rabbi within modern society.

In the state of Israel in the early twenty-first century, traditional *yeshivot* predominate, although there are branches of American Reform and Conservative seminaries. The *yeshivot* ordain males only, and the role of the rabbi is generally that of judge and scholar, not that of spiritual leader of a local congregation. In the United States, as in Europe, ordination of rabbis differs somewhat among the main Jewish groups. For example, the Orthodox seminary of Yeshiva University ordains graduates in the traditional fashion after a course of study in the Talmud and codes, and women are excluded from such ordination. Jewish Theological Seminary of America (the center for the Conservative movement) graduates its candidates as rabbis and has begun to ordain women candidates for the Conservative rabbinate. Reform Judaism's Hebrew Union College–Jewish Institute of Religion ordains its graduates as rabbis, and for some time women have been ordained into the Reform rabbinate. Women are also ordained as rabbis in Reconstructionist Judaism. In general, rabbis of all American Jewish groups function as spiritual leaders of local congregations of Jews, although their functions differ according to the needs of the community.

ORDINATION IN CHRISTIANITY. Christians hold that Jesus Christ is the great high priest, the real mediator between God and humans, and that all Christians as members of his body participate in his priesthood. While some Christians conclude that there is no need for specially ordained leaders, most Christian groups have recognized the need for ordained priests or ministers to lead the Christian community.

Although traditionally any male Christian could aspire to become a priest or minister, many Christian denominations have begun to ordain women clergy also, while some denominations, such as the Roman Catholic church and the Eastern Orthodox church, continue to ordain male candidates only while providing other non-priestly roles of religious service for women. Candidates are given a course of study and training in a theological seminary before being certified and presented to the church denominational authorities for ordination.

Those set apart for special service are given many different titles: priest, minister, pastor, deacon, and bishop are the most common among those designating the clergy. In addition, many nonclerical roles are entered into by ceremonies of initiation or consecration: the minor orders, orders of monks and nuns, deaconesses and deacons, special church workers, and the like. The traditional clerical ministry of the church, as it developed in the first centuries, consisted primarily of bishops, presbyters, and deacons. The bishop was the "overseer" of a specific community of Christians, with the full responsibility for the ministry of preaching the word and administering the sacraments of the church. Deacons were ordained to help the bishop by serving in an administrative capacity and by working for the welfare of the people. The presbyter (elder or priest) was ordained to help the bishop as a fellow minister in performing the rites and sacraments of the church.

Ordination in the ancient Christian church was a simple affair, consisting of prayer and the laying on of hands by those authorized to ordain (*Acts* 6:6, *1 Tm.* 4:14, *2 Tm.* 1:6). Texts of ordination manuals from the fourth and fifth centuries CE give sets of ordination prayers and emphasize the laying on of hands as a central ritual. The people, especially in the Greek communities, cried "Axios!" ("He is worthy!"), and the ordinand was given the kiss of peace, after which he preached and conducted the service, presiding over the Eucharist. In the medieval period other rituals were added to the ordination, such as vesting the candidate in the vestments of his order, holding a Bible over him, and giving him the implements and symbols of his new office: paten and chalice, Bible, and, in the case of a bishop, pectoral cross and pastoral staff. Bishops were anointed on the head with oil; both bishops and priests were anointed on the hands.

While ordination ceremonies differ in the various Christian communities, in more recent years the liturgical renewal movement has induced many communions to restore the simple, ancient tradition of ordination. Typically this includes most of the following elements for the ordination of a priest or minister by a bishop. Ordination is done in the presence of the congregation, in the company of other priests or ministers, in the context of a divine service. A priest or layperson presents the candidate to the bishop, with the people declaring that he or she is worthy for the ministry. Lessons from the Bible are read, followed by a homily and the saying of the creed. The bishop examines the ordinand, who vows to be faithful to his or her calling. The bishop says the prayer of ordination, laying both hands on the head of the candidate, while the other priests or ministers lay on their right hands. The new priest is vested and given a Bible, being greeted by the bishop and the other clergy. The newly ordained person then proceeds to function by leading the liturgy for the congregation. Afterward the people and the clergy join in a celebration.

Appointing Spiritual Leaders in Islam. In Islam, every Muslim can perform the religious rites, so there is no class or profession of ordained clergy. Yet there are religious leaders who are recognized for their learning and their ability to lead communities of Muslims in prayer, study, and living according to the teaching of the Qur'ān and Muslim law. These religious leaders belong to the learned group of orthodox Muslim scholars and jurists known as the *'ulamā'* (*'alim* in the singular). They have studied at recognized schools of Islamic learning and have secured appointments as mosque functionaries, teachers, jurisconsults, or judges.

The religious leader who is contracted by a local community of Muslims to lead the community in public worship, preach at the Friday mosque prayer, teach, and give advice on religious matters on the local level is called the imam, belonging to the broad group of *'ulamā'*. It should be noted that the concept of the Sh'ī Muslims that an inspired religious leader is necessary for the correct guidance of the community has placed the recognized religious scholars (*mujtahid* in Iran and Iraq) in a position of important power and authority, necessary for the welfare of the whole community. In certain Islamic communities, popular religious leaders possessing special divine power (*barakah*), known as Ṣūfīs or saints, provide leadership for their people in a variety of ways. Ṣūfī aspirants are trained under a master until they themselves have become recognized as masters.

Thus, despite its lack of an ordained institutional priesthood or clergy in the usual senses, Islam has produced a religious leadership that is recognizable and set apart from the ordinary people by a certain amount of religious authority.

Symbolism of Ordination Rituals. From the cross-cultural survey above, it is possible to see a general structure of meaning in the typical ordination rituals. A recurrent theme is that of death with respect to one's former status and rebirth in the new office or status of religious leader or mediator. This general structure can be analyzed in more specific detail by noting five broad types or levels of rituals associated with ordination, denoting separation, training and testing, empowerment, display of power, and support by the laity.

The rituals first of all enact various dimensions of the separation from ordinary life. Very commonly ordination involves rituals of purification. There may be a period of time during which the candidate purifies himself or herself by abstaining from sexuality, by fasting, and by performing acts of penance; rituals of washing and confessing may be part of the ordination ceremony. The fact that the candidate has been called by the divine power to leave the ordinary life will be established. The physical appearance of the candidate will demonstrate separation from ordinary lay life through special clothing, shaved head, long hair bound up in a special way, or the scalp branded with indelible scars. Symbols of death abound: initiatory sickness, symbolic death and burial, mutilation of the body, or the identification of the candidate with the blood of a priest's sacrifice. The vows taken by the candidate often emphasize separation from the former way of life, such as the vows of celibacy, homelessness, chastity, casting off all lay possessions, and nudity.

Second, the rituals of ordination certify the qualifications of the candidate by emphasizing the training he or she has received and by testing and examining the candidate. The long period of training or apprenticeship itself is often set apart by rituals as a sacred period. Rituals of ordination may include imparting secret knowledge and understanding. The candidate may be tested by questions, and the persons already ordained have to give their approval to the novice. There may be ordeals to demonstrate the candidate's mastery of sacred power, such as climbing a sword ladder, pulling hair from one's own head, or enduring the branding of the scalp.

Third, the investing of the ordinand with new authority and power is the subject of important rituals of ordination. These rituals include laying on of hands on the candidate by those already possessing the spiritual power and authority, handshakes or kisses, vesting with special garments, and handing over symbols and implements of the special office. Anointing the candidate, ritually inserting quartz into the candidate's body, or symbolically replacing his or her organs with new organs shows the rebirth or investing that takes place. Prayers call down divine power on the candidate; rituals such as climbing toward the sky or being married to a divine being fill the ordinand with new power. The masters of the office may impart final, decisive knowledge to the ordinand, such as the source of the medicinal material. The public pronouncement of ordination and the ordination certificate or diploma being handed over, together with the granting of new titles and names, may be considered rituals of empowerment. There may also be a period of seclusion after ordination during which time the new ordinand grows in spiritual power.

Fourth, the ordination rituals often include the initial display of the new power and authority of the ordinand. He or she may officiate in leading worship or celebrating sacrifices or sacraments for the people at the completion of the ordination ritual. He or she may inaugurate the new sacred life by giving a spiritual lecture, going on a first begging tour, making a round of visits to the parishioners, and the like. Often there will be continued training or apprenticeship to provide further growth and empowerment.

Fifth, the ordination typically involves some expression of support and celebration of the new ordinand on the part of the laypeople. One of them may present the candidate, and financial support for the occasion will come from them. There may be points in the ritual of ordination when they show their support and acceptance of the ordinand. Typically the ordination will be followed by a celebration in which the people congratulate the new ordinand, give gifts, and join in a festive meal. These rituals symbolize the basic fact that, ultimately, the ordination is for the benefit of the people.

SEE ALSO Ministry; Monasticism, article on Buddhist Monasticism; Priesthood; Saṃgha.

BIBLIOGRAPHY

A classic cross-cultural study of the role of priests in many religions is E. O. James's *The Nature and Function of Priesthood: A Comparative and Anthropological Study* (London, 1955), although he does not single out ordination as a special topic. An example of the selection and ordination of priests in ancient societies is found in Serge Sauneron, *The Priests of Ancient Egypt* (translated by David Lorton; Ithaca, 2000). For practices of setting apart religious leaders in contemporary traditional societies, Adolphus P. Elkin's *Aboriginal Men of High Degree,* 2d ed. (New York, 1977), is a thorough study of medicine men among the Aborigines of Australia; and Mircea Eliade's *Shamanism: Archaic Techniques of Ecstasy,* rev. & enl. ed. (New York, 1964), surveys the initiation of shamans in various cultures. The training and initiation of African priests and medicine men and women is discussed in Geoffrey Parrinder's *West African Religion: A Study of the Beliefs and Practices of Akan, Ewe, Yoruba, Ibo, and Kindred Peoples,* 2d ed. (London, 1961), and in E. E. Evans-Pritchard's *Witchcraft, Oracles, and Magic among the Azande,* 2d ed. (Oxford, 1950). Melford E. Spiro's *Burmese Supernaturalism,* exp. ed. (Philadelphia, 1978), presents a thorough study of female shamans who become "*nat* wives" in Burmese popular religion. In East Asian societies, Laurel Kendall in *Shamans, Housewives, and Other Restless Spirits: Women in Korean Ritual Life* (Honolulu, 1985) gives examples of the training and initiation of female shamans (*manshin*) in Korea, and Susan Sered in *Women of the Sacred Groves: Divine Priestesses of Okinawa* (Oxford, 1999) describes the process by which Okinawan women become divine priestesses (*kaminchu*).

Rustom Masani's *Zoroastrianism: The Religion of the Good Life* (1938; New York, 1968) and Peter Clark's *Zoroastrianism: An Introduction to an Ancient Faith* (Brighton, U.K., 1998) include information about initiation of Zoroastrian priests. The training and social role of household brahman priests in India today is the subject of K. Subramaniam's *Brahmin Priest of Tamil Nadu* (New York, 1974); and C. J. Fuller, *Servants of the Goddess: The Priests of a South Indian Temple* (Cambridge, 1984), describes the training, initiation, and consecration of temple priests. Along with descriptions of the Jain religion, Padmanabh S. Jaini's *The Jaina Path of Purification* (Berkeley, Calif., 1979) and Paul Dundas's *The Jains* (second edition; London, 2002) provide a close look at the ordination and path of Jain male and female mendicants.

Important studies of the training and ordination of Theravada Buddhist monks and nuns are found in Melford E. Spiro's *Buddhism and Society: A Great Tradition and Its Burmese Vicissitudes,* 2d ed. (Berkeley, Calif., 1982), and Jane Bunnag's *Buddhist Monk, Buddhist Layman: A Study of Urban Monastic Organization in Central Thailand* (Cambridge, 1973). *The Initiation of Novicehood and the Ordination of Monkhood in the Burmese Buddhist Culture* (Rangoon, 1986) provides a detailed look at traditional Buddhist ordination rituals. Chatsumarn Kabilsingh, *Thai Women in Buddhism* (Berkeley, Calif., 1991), describes how, despite the lack of full ordination for nuns in Theravadin societies, many women still are ordained and practice the religious path as novice nuns. An informative study of Mahāyāna Buddhism in pre-Maoist China, including information and photographs of monastic ordinations, is Holmes Welch's *The Practice of Chinese Buddhism, 1900–1950* (Cambridge, Mass., 1967). Robert E. Bushnell, *The Zen Monastic Experience: Buddhist Practice in Contemporary Korea* (Princeton, 1992), describes from personal experience the whole process of training and ordination of Sŏn Buddhist monks and nuns.

Much information about Daoist ordination practices in medieval China is provided by Charles Benn, "Daoist Ordination and *Zhai* Rituals," in *Daoism Handbook,* edited by Livia Kohn (Leiden, 2000), pp. 309–339. The role of Zhengyi priests and their ordination rankings in present-day Taiwan is discussed by Michael Saso in his *Taoist Master Chuang* (Eldorado Springs, Colo., 2d ed., 2000). Yoshitoyo Yoshioka, "Taoist Monastic Life," in *Facets of Taoism: Essays in Chinese Religion,* edited by Holmes Welch and Anna Seidel (New Haven, 1979), pp. 229–252, describes the ordination and life of Daoist priests (which include women and well as men) in the monastic Quanzhen (Complete Perfection) sect. Much important information on the structure of the Shintō priesthood as well as the training and ritual activities of the priests and priestesses is contained in John K. Nelson, *Enduring Identities: The Guise of Shinto in Contemporary Japan* (Honolulu, 2000), and in Michael Ashkenazi, *Matsuri: Festivals of a Japanese Town* (Honolulu, 1993).

A thorough study of the history of Jewish ordination is Julius Newman's *Semikhah: A Study of Its Origin, History, and Function in Rabbinic Literature* (Manchester, 1950); and discussion of training and roles of modern rabbis is found in *The Rabbinate As Calling and Vocation: Models of Rabbinic Leadership*, edited by Basil Herring (Northvale, N.J., 1991), and *The Rabbinate in America: Reshaping an Ancient Calling*, edited by Jacob Neusner (New York, 1993). And Pamela Susan Nadell, *Women Who Would be Rabbis: A History of Women's Ordination, 1889–1985* (Boston, 1998), provides a focus on the ordination of women as rabbis. Of many studies of the Christian ordained ministry, *The Ministry in Historical Perspectives*, edited by H. Richard Niebuhr and Daniel D. Williams (New York, 1956), provides a good historical overview. A wealth of information and interpretation concerning the rites of ordination in many of the Christian traditions is provided in the multi-volumed set, *The Process of Admission to Ordained Ministry: A Comparative Study*, edited by James F. Puglisi, translated by Michael Driscoll and Mary Misrahi (Collegeville, Minn., 1996 [vol. 1], 1998 [vol. 2], 2001 [vol. 3]). On the current discussion and practice concerning ordination of women to the Christian ministry, among many books are *Women's Ordination: Official Statements from Religious Bodies and Ecumenical Organizations*, edited by J. Gordon Melton (Detroit, 1992), and *Religious Institutions and Women's Leadership: New Roles Inside the Mainstream*, edited by Catherine Wessinger (Columbia, S.C., 1996), which explores Jewish as well as Christian traditions. *Scholars, Saints, and Sufis: Muslim Religious Institutions in the Middle East since 1500*, edited by Nikki R. Keddie (Berkeley, Calif., 1972), contains many studies of the religious scholars and saints who form the recognized religious leadership of Islam. Muhammad Qasim Zaman, *The ʿUlamāʾ in Contemporary Islam: Custodians of Change* (Princeton, N.J., 2002), provides a thorough study of the changing roles and training of the *ʿulamāʾ*, the scholarly leaders of Islamic communities. And the special dimensions of religious authority and clerical leadership among Shiʿite Muslims is discussed in *The Most Learned of the Shīʿa: The Institution of the Marjaʿ Tajlid*, edited by Linda S. Walbridge (Oxford, 2001).

THEODORE M. LUDWIG (1987 AND 2005)

ORGY

This entry consists of the following articles:

AN OVERVIEW
ORGY IN THE ANCIENT MEDITERRANEAN WORLD
ORGY IN MEDIEVAL AND MODERN EUROPE
ORGY IN ASIA

ORGY: AN OVERVIEW

Work, progress, and convention are no longer essential requirements. Economists, philosophers, and sociologists all agree that, even within a linear view of history, these structures have had their day. Prometheus is under suspicion.

UNPRODUCTIVE PLAY. There is no point in going back to Prometheus except to find support for a description of what will replace the defunct god. The themes of liberation and energeticism have become questionable. They will doubtless reemerge—their birth and death occurs many times throughout human history—but for the present, as a result of saturation, there is a new dawn and other constants are now being proposed; their outlines remain unclear, but the observer of society cannot remain indifferent to them. Thus the return of what has been repressed: unproductive exertion, in other words orgy, is set to replace energetic progressionism.

It is in this sense that one may say that the body as a means of production or reproduction is giving way to the erotic body. Is this a rebellion in the classical sense of a release mechanism? Not necessarily. Instead, we are faced here with a positive power that is found beneath the surface of all social structures and sometimes asserts itself irresistibly, like an unstoppable groundswell. What was once the privilege of the avant-garde—of artists; of proud, solitary geniuses—flows through the entire body of society. Enjoyment of the present and the idea of carpe diem become colossal, unassailable values. Thus we can understand what Octavio Paz calls "the rapturous joy of orgiastic values," in which the feelings, passions, images and situations of the moment express themselves.

To emphasize the effectiveness of orgy, it is helpful to refer to the concept of ludism, which modern rationalism has demoted to the status of a secondary activity. A detailed analysis of the importance of play is unnecessary, since classical studies, including those of Johan Huizinga and Roger Callois, have already done so competently and comprehensively. Play is the irreducible kernel around which so many institutions are arranged. Economic struggle, financial competition, and political theater exist to remind us that nothing in the world is unaffected by games, that societies are molded by them, and that to take this into account is not aesthetic bias but rather the recognition of a constant that cuts across the whole of human reality.

The antithesis of utilitarianism, the orgy is the clearest possible sign of the will to live and of the persistence of sociality. Mystics, whose message is heeded or disregarded depending on the period, have seen this clearly. For Jacob Boehme, for example, there is a "joy of the eternal act of creation" which allows what exists to continue to do so. Following this route is not irrationalism but rather hyperrationalism as described by Charles Fourier (1772–1837), who includes previously excluded criteria in his social analysis. The imagination, the oneiric, and collective play are these neglected criteria.

LOSS AND LETTING GO. It is such clarity of vision that has returned orgy to its position and perceives in the various festive forms, whatever they may be, an expression of the erotic body, which knows how to escape from the imposition of productivity. Manifestations of this Dionysiac ludism cannot be classified under the rubrics *past* or *future*. With amazing consistency, they express the desire for loss in a world that has a constant tendency to be positive about everything. It is in this context that the unproductive and nonfunctional nature of orgy must be understood.

The rites whose religious—or more precisely, orgiastic—basis is understood consist of fantasy incarnate. The word *incarnate* here carries its full semantic force: it indeed refers to aggressive, caressing, colliding, loving bodies. And before they were sanitized in the familiar political and religious rituals, these rites were truly and intimately a violent or tender confrontation, involving fantasy, exertion, loss—in a word, the unproductive. There are many perfect examples of this process in contemporary society, including rave parties. Each involves losing oneself within the group, pushing to its ultimate conclusion the logic of unproductive exertion. The group expression, used repeatedly by young people, is illuminating in this respect: it is about letting go, getting out of oneself, even if this involves using various ad hoc substances, harking back to a kind of religious ecstasy. It is necessary to connect to the other, to the greater whole that is the group. It is not without significance that one of the products used is called ecstasy, a metaphor if ever there was one for the loss of self in the infinite of collective desire.

THE RATIONALIZATION OF EXISTENCE. What Max Weber called the "generalized rationalization of existence" has come to encompass every aspect of existence—consumption, sex, speech, leisure: everything is liable to be measured. In the name of ever greater security, areas of life that had hitherto avoided restriction have been dealt with by particularly efficient specialized institutions. Such a sterile arrangement of life has a tendency to place everything in an accountable and productive system. To play, to love, to enjoy the sun, to make the most of passing time—the entire existential experience, all this is recorded by a specific structure in a system of moderation, of economy. Yet can one be economical with the irrepressible social desire to live?

Counting and limiting results in denial. To allow no place for the forces of pleasure is to expose oneself to the fierce retort of what is repressed. Letting go is like violence: restraining it results in encouraging its exaggerated expression. The wisdom of the ancient world is of real worth in this regard; it allowed for a certain shadowy part, which it ritualized and thus mastered. The sole objective of the Greek Dionysia was to give free rein to wild passions. Plato, in the *Laws,* expresses this ancient realism clearly. Dealing with the Spartiate, a moralist and boring theoretician, the ancient equivalent of the contemporary technocrat, who is giving a management lecture on how to ensure a sober city, Plato recalls that such a policy is like playing with fire: "Spartan stranger, this is all laudable as long as one retains the strength to resist, but once this is relinquished, then this is disastrous." Repression is laudable in a heavenly city, but in our earthly city we should not forget everything that links us to the dark earth. In the last analysis, calculated moderation always entails an even greater immoderation. And like a sorcerer's apprentice, a society that does not know how to use the *coincidentia oppositorum* leaves itself open to a disastrous eruption of the very element that it denies and is unable to control. The fantasy of productivity, the absolute positivism of rationalism, and unidimensionality all are suits of armor that will cause explosions because they are so rigid.

This is, then, the problem. Faced with the hard-working Prometheus, one must demonstrate that the boisterous Dionysus is also an essential character in human society. The question is no longer how to control life but how to spend and enjoy it. As Max Stirner wrote, "It is no longer a matter of making my true self flourish within me, but of harvesting the vintage and consuming my life". This is an excellent way of looking at things, which provides a good summary of everything that contrasts mere productivity and exertion.

FERTILIZATION AND PRODUCTION. It could be said that postmodern values push the logic of consumption to its limits. Perhaps it would be better to use the term *consuming.* It becomes the point of living. Things are good; they provide the good life. This is not harmful to working life, but complements it, but its complementary nature is only of use if adults do not, for the sake of outdated moral principles, restrain the natural expression of youthful excess. This unproductive aspect of youth recalls the "creative joy" spoken of by the mystic Jacob Boehme.

It might be worthwhile to contrast production and fertilization to reach an understanding of the will to live and the persistence of sociality. If a principle of reality were to deny any pleasure principle, would it not be denying itself?

Orgy exists to demonstrate to us that erotic opportunities are not confined to (re)production. It is an endless interplay of contradictory elements, which as a result of their combination and construction allow us to understand how the fertilization of the world is carried on in a clandestine manner.

MYTHIC ROOTS. The play of the world and the world as play: There is the very heart of the return of mythical figures in the festive contemporary—a celebration of roots, a frantic search for symbols, the desire to join with otherness through prototypes that are not representative but are lived here and now.

There is a particular energy there, energy that is not being spread in the body politic, energy that seeps through the intense banality of everyday life. The collective imagination—one might call it the collective unconscious—draws its power from this orgiastic treasury. Objective reality ensures that, without knowing it, the publicity photo, the choreographed pose, even the obscenity of reality TV, show that which unites with that which cannot be portrayed. Hence the need for analogy, a non-causal link, a description like that of a painting, a mosaic construction, in the search for a way to understand this. These are all things that, linked together, cause a nonprojective, essentially present sense, or meaning, to reemerge.

One can interpret a television series as a production involving mythological figures from the Greek pantheon. Similarly, in techno gatherings or love parades, just as in fashion shows, ancient prototypes may be paroxystically rediscovered. Yet it is a repetition that makes them immanent. In Western transcendence, this is far from theological or political. With the figures under discussion, being is Being-in-the-world. Yet the energy exerted to do this, which is close to the Will of Friedrich Nietzsche (1844–1900), is most concentrated and crystallized.

Being-in-the-world would therefore be, if not an explanation, at least an avenue of approach, in a strict sense, to the modern orgy. There is no backdrop; everything is set at the front of the stage. Yet, that being the case, everything is factual and to the point. This *being* is immediate. It forces us to go beyond the concept of being, which we tend to use with a nominal sense: being a man, a woman, leftwing, rightwing, in short being something with an identity. Whereas the post- and premodern theatrical *being* is an infinitive much more encompassing, more part of a matrix, a form of being in which one shares in an almost magical way. This allows one to understand the feeling of belonging: belonging to a group, to a person, to a place, with particular sporting, religious, musical, or sexual tastes.

Encompassing being: that is, no longer being given legitimacy or rationalized by a supreme being, be that God, the State, the Institution, the Individual—a supreme being which offers meaning, but an encompassing being, which establishes that one is something or someone only to the extent that one shares with others an eponymous figure—a star, a guru, an animal, a place. Strictly speaking, this figure provides a name and thus leads to existence. This is the orgiastic revolution: existence is only in relation with, in communion with, others, and the renewed contribution of mythological figures, of archetypes, of fantastic forms (sorcerers, fairies, mythical heroes), makes this relationship apparent.

Such a dependence, at times shocking to modern thinking which is so used to individuality, is all in all simply another means of approach, which the East has used, stressing the similarities, the common features of all the elements, all the aspects of an undivided life.

TRANSFORMATION. In play involving orgiastic theatrical masks, a process of transformation, even transfiguration, occurs, in which the humble individual self is raised to a generic Self. There is a discursive search here, real rather than verbalized, which forms the basis for developing the large number of groups or tribes that make up the social body.

This should raise questions for the social observer, who all too often is satisfied with results drawn from modern philosophical systems that have epistemological individualism as their sole common denominator. In empirical terms, the individual and individuality are inclined to be lost within the longing for tribalism that becomes more and more delirious. Tribes come into being, they reinforce themselves, they express themselves through aggregative figures. Symbolic figures, which, as Emile Durkheim has shown, have a role in establishing "logical conformism."

By reconsidering the term *Einfühlung* as it is used in art history, one can demonstrate that the defining characteristic of our times is empathy. It is useful to observe and understand, as a phenomenon, the tendency to lose oneself in the other, to exist only commensurate with the other. Subjectivity becomes objective through its relationship with a counterpart, whether that counterpart is an object, an animal, a human being, or an element of nature. These are all characteristic of the pre- and postmodern orgy.

EMPATHY. Religious and political fanaticism, the huge number of fan groups, and in all these spheres the varied social hysteria—even in the possession of everyday objects that people think they own—is made clearer by means of empathy. We need only look at the relationship with the mobile phone or even with the laptop computer to understand that here we have a return to the magical object of premodern civilizations.

This recognition of self via the other is instructive in that it emphasizes a vital emission, a philosophy of life that is symptomatic of cultures at the moment of their birth, before rigid intellectual restrictions develop.

Empathy possesses, then, a certain resourcefulness and open-mindedness, which can be seen in the various forms of generosity, the acts of mutual assistance, the development of charity and benevolence, that run throughout the body social alongside economic dominance. The individual is engrossed in these alternative forms of behavior, arranged more or less wildly, which take shape around symbolic figures, whether political, religious, musical, sporting, or intellectual.

Thus in the orgy, the subject is above all transcendental, that is, collective, but subsequently focuses on individual changes. It is complementary, and not alternative to, transcendental reason, distinguishing the scientific advance that has characterized Western thinking. It is a transcendental fantasy, which is in action in the archetypal figures that are expressed in social life. Such *eros energumene* have their roots in the ancestral power of poetry. Not abstract, disconnected poetry, lived in isolation, but connected directly with the power of the orgiastic life.

MASKS. Without necessarily being aware of it, the figures that typify the daily carnivalesque—the masks the persona assumes in his or her professional or love life, the caricatures of various social fluctuations—demonstrate, in a somewhat exaggerated manner, the illusion of individualism that characterizes historical ideology. On the other hand, these phenomena remind us that what predominates is a virtual shared destiny. Postmodern masks are influenced by figures, by ancestral problems. They serve to translate that impersonal, underground force that comes from far away and sometimes emerges in broad daylight.

In various spheres of life, one pays more and more attention to what lies beneath—to cultural substrata, to the ghosts that stir collective dreams, to the persistence of legendary figures. All this has a long-term effect, but it is nothing if not personal. And this is the thing that is undergoing a revival, expressed in the totems around which the many postmodern tribes gather. These renew the link with premodern paganism, reminding civilized humanity of its archaic animism. Indeed, it is a fundamentally pagan reaction that can be found in phenomena as diverse as deep ecology; the growth of alternative medicine; the influence of clairvoyance, astrology, and the paranormal; and the many New Age systems, not to mention demonism and Goth and techno music.

The common denominator in these varied orgiastic phenomena is a new relationship with natural and social otherness, with an emphasis upon correspondence. Unknowingly, one is linked to the Other and thus shares in a common destiny. In this way, it is possible to understand the astonishing mimicry that is everywhere prevalent. It is no longer distinction but rather indistinction.

Orgy is indeed the union by which we are linked to the common spirit of the tribe, and to the common animal nature of our species.

SEE ALSO Agriculture; Earth; New Year Festivals; Sexuality.

BIBLIOGRAPHY

These themes are developed in my *L'Ombre de Dionysos, contribution à une sociologie de l'orgie* (Paris, 1982), translated into English as *The Shadows of Dionysos: A Contribution to the Sociology of the Orgy* (Albany, N.Y., 1993); and in *Le Temps des Tribus, le déclin de l'individualisme dans les sociétés de masse* (Paris, 1988), translated into English as *The Time of Tribes: Decline of Individualism in Mass Society* (London, 1996).

MICHEL MAFFESOLI (2005)
Translated from French by Paul Ellis

ORGY: ORGY IN THE ANCIENT MEDITERRANEAN WORLD

In ancient Greece and Rome the plural *orgia* was a sacral word that applied to any ceremonies practiced in the worship of various deities, with or without implication of extravagance. *Orgia* became, in addition, the technical term to designate mystery cults and rites connected with festivals in honor of Dionysos that were usually characterized by an ecstatic or frantic attitude and were celebrated with dancing, singing, and drinking. It is probably this latter meaning that gradually led to a derogatory usage (see, for example, Plato, *Laws* 910), which, however, is a modern one. From the eighteenth century onwards, in fact, the term *orgy* has been used to refer to wild or dissolute revels marked by license or debauchery; in this sense it is currently employed in religious studies to refer to collective behavior (comprehensive of indulging in excessive bodily activity by means of rave music, dancing, banquets, promiscuous sexual intercourse, and the infringement of normal order or rules) that sanctions a festive period in order to reinforce the vital energies of the cosmos and human communities.

The Greek word *orgia* is first attested in a Milesian inscription dating back to the fifth century BCE that shows a dedication by a dancers' brotherhood (*Sylloge inscriptionum Graecarum* 57.4). Classical writers, including Plato and the tragedians, variously employed the term to designate sacred rituals (see, still in the first century CE, Plutarch, *Life of Alcibiades* 34, about a rite in honor of Athena). Byzantine lexicographers explain *orgia* as synonymous to "mysteries," with particular reference to Dionysos. The term is also employed by the anonymous author of the *Hymn to Demeter* (ll. 273 and 476), who relates it to the Eleusinian mysteries (see also Herodotos 5.61; Aristophanes, *Frogs* 386 and *Thesmophorians* 948). Sometimes *orgia* is applied to Orphism (Herodotos II.81) and the rites of the Cabeiri (Herodotos 2.51, which does not show orgiastic features, notwithstanding the veneration of a sacred phallus; see, however, Diodorus 5.49, which shows an intermingling with the cult of Cybele and the Corybants). There are other examples of frantic and orgiastic dances, probably of Oriental origin, practiced in honor of the Laconian Artemis (Aristophanes, *Lysistrata* 1312; Vergil, *Georgics* 2.487), where the female dancers are often associated with the maenads. In Latin language and literature the word *orgia* shares the same features as in Greek (mystery cults, Dionysiac rites), but it is interesting to note that the term is once employed by the Christian poet Prudentius in his *Peristephanon* (2.65) to understand Christian rites. A hostile usage of the term appears in Jerome, who wants to attack his Origenist adversaries (*Epist.* 84.3).

Despite the gradual development of such a meaning, the ancient etymology (attested by Clement of Alexandria in *Protrepticus* 2.13.1.2; and Servius, *Commentary on Virgil's Aeneid* 4.302), which relates the term to *orgē* ("anger, wrath, excessive passion"), is erroneous. According to modern scholars the word *orgia* must be connected to the verb *erdō* ("to offer a sacrifice"), whose perfect form is *eorga* (see Chantraine, 1968).

ORGY AND SEASONAL FEASTS. Mircea Eliade established the strict relationship between seasonal feasts (for example, New Year ceremonies) and orgiastic performing of rituals. Following hints enucleated by Wilhelm Mannhardt and James Frazer, Eliade considered how the orgy sets flowing the sacred energy of life, so that moments of crisis or abundance in nature are the privileged occasion for unleashing an orgy. It thus becomes simple to explain the orgies practiced by various ethnic groups, as well as the crystallization of some orgiastic relics in modern European farming ceremonies, in connection with the drama of vegetation and particularly with the ceremonials of agriculture in order that the reproductive powers in earth, animals, and humans can be stimulated by phallic dances followed by orgies, thus involving a sort of rebirth. As far as classical antiquity is concerned, certain feasts of vegetation are abundant in orgiastic elements and collective exaltation, such as the Floralia (celebrated in Rome at the end of April), the Lupercalia, or the festivals performed in honor of Caeres or Tellus.

Such an unbounded sexual frenzy can be likened to a divine hierogamy, because when sacred marriage is reenacted all the forces of the community are supposed to increase to their highest point. The earth is reawakened and the sky aroused so that the great cosmic marriage, symbolized by rain, will take place in the best possible conditions to ensure prosperity and new life (in this sense it is possible to explain also the links between orgies and initiation ceremonies).

Orgies can be found not only in the setting of agrarian ceremonies, although they always remained closely connected with rites of regeneration and fertility. A deeper metaphysical significance and psychological function of orgy clearly emerges when considering it as a way of expressing the life of the community as a whole. Humans lose their individuality in the orgy, combining into a single living unity; they perform a total fusion of emotions in which neither norm nor law is observed so that participants can enter a primal, pre-formal, chaotic state, using the power of imitative magic to assist the merging of the seeds into the one womb of the earth. Among the other functions, the orgy fulfils in the spiritual and psychological economy of a community. The orgy also symbolizes a renewal or regeneration of life. In fact, orgies make it possible for creation to be repeated because they bring back mythical states that existed in earlier times and to which humans hope to return, restored and regenerated.

A notion of a cosmos made up of cycles, which was born of chaos and returns to it through a catastrophe or a great dissolution, together with a thirst for regeneration and renewal, are implied in orgiastic ritual performances, whose aberrant forms represent a degradation of this idea of the rhythm of the universe. Since at a cosmological level the orgy represents chaos—that is, the disappearance of limits and boundaries and the fusion into a single unity—this wish for an abolition of time is particularly evident in orgies that take place, at various degrees, during New Year ceremonies, the seasonal dramas *par excellence.* Together with other patterns that characterize similar events, the symbolic return of primeval chaos indicates the abolition of profane time in order to effect the dissolution of the world and restore the mythical moment of the beginning and the end. This is why such festivals are constantly marked by an attempt at abolishing order and consuetudes; license is let loose, all rules are violated, norms are suspended, and there can be an overthrowing of social conditions or a converging of opposites.

ORGIASTIC PATTERNS IN REVERSAL RITUALS. Besides sexual promiscuousness, which is obviously a means to gain fertility or reinforce vegetation and ransom it from obscure and menacing evils, other elements or states of psychic exaltation can be related to orgiastic contexts. Among these are debauchery, revelry, dance, and especially laughter. Scholars have recorded cases that can be considered semi-orgiastic, including the Latin *fescennine*, which are naughty verses usually sung during wedding ceremonies; triumphal songs called *carmina*, in which the *iocatio* ("joke" or "jest", addressed by the troops to their victorious officers) represented an apotropaic device to cast off the idea of death and help the individual psyche escape from an oppressive realm; and the so-called "ritual of the sardonic laughter," recorded by the Greek historian Timaeus (*Fragmente Griechischer historiker* 566 F 64); according to his explanation, old people were sacrificed and pushed over a cliff by their sons, who made grimaces, probably under the effect of a bitter herb. In fact, orgies possess a ritual function connected with the cult of dead people, as can be inferred from persisting customs in ethnic or folkloric contexts where banquets and orgies occur after funerals. The same attitude was found in antiquity, and is testified by certain Church Fathers (Ambrose, *On the Death of His Brother* 2.12; Augustine, *Sermons* 311, *PL* 38.1415) and by many councils (e.g., Arles, 524; Auxerre, 590; London, 1342; York, 1367) that attempted to forbid these orgiastic practices, especially during the Middle Ages.

Mourning and its anomic features can be considered a liminal situation for the relatives of the deceased or for the entire community during periods of disease, epidemic, and famine; it is possible to show that these marginal situations are marked by a great variety of external patterning and reflect opposition to normal social features. The purpose inherent in such marginal situations is to temporarily remove individuals or groups from their normal social existence. Such typical patterns as role or status reversal in matters of clothing, food (e.g., novices consuming food and drinks that are usually forbidden), communication, and language add up to a sort of legal anarchy and have thus been linked to social instances of ransom or rebellion. Such reversals characterize a number of exceptional festivals, like Carnival or similar ancient equivalents.

Classical antiquity records various festivals during which what was normally forbidden was tolerated, including the Sacaea in Babylon (according to the third-century BCE historian Berossus, in *Fragmente Griechischer historiker* 680 no. 2) or in the Pontus region (according to Strabo 11.8), which were celebrated in the summer in honor of the goddess Ishtar or Anaitis and which involved a servant disguised as a king; Zagmuk, or feast of the lots, which took place in Mesopotamia at the beginning of the year and included sexual license and a symbolic king dethronement; Kronia in Greece; Saturnalia in Rome; and women's festivals such as the Thesmophoria, and the Roman celebration of Bona Dea, which gave women in seclusion an opportunity to indulge in excesses in their own way (some writers, for example the Latin satirist Juvenal, considered these feasts to be nothing more than lascivious orgies). As far as these are concerned, in breaking the fetters of social and marital codes women inevitably return to nature—that is, to the premarital status of the maiden. To control such excesses by limiting them to dedicated periods could have helped safeguard the disjunction of sex and maternity that is typical of many cultures, especially Greece and Rome, and that is evidently jeopardized in the fertility festivals.

Temporary liberation from chains and bondage was the central feature of Kronia and Saturnalia. Moreover, like certain other Roman "interstitial" ceremonies, the Saturnalia festivities also included official cessation of all public services, such as the *mundus patet*, and the Saturnalia can thus be paired with the *iustitium* (public mourning). Saturnalia is counted among the most ancient Roman festivals, since it was already mentioned in Numa's calendar and continued till the end of paganism (see Macrobius's *Saturnalia*). The festival began on December 17 and was celebrated by bareheaded people, according to Greek custom. It was an occasion for all Romans, citizens and slaves, to enjoy a holiday. Satire and derision were given free reign. Reversal patterns involved an interruption of normal political and business activities (not to mention the allowance of gambling and dice-playing, otherwise prohibited in everyday life), but the most important reversal was the exchange of roles between masters and slaves. The assimilation of this reversal to Carnival is, however, erroneous; this aspect of Carnival should be linked to New Year celebrations, Carnival being similar to other spring festivals, such as the Roman *Liberalia*.

DIONYSIAC CULT. In classical antiquity Dionysos was the ecstatic divinity most closely related to orgiastic cult. Among the numerous sources, the writer most responsible for consideration of Dionysiac ritual is the Greek tragedian Euripides. In his *Bacchae* (*Bacchant Women*, posthumously performed in 406 BCE) Euripides described the introduction into Hellas of a new religion with a peculiar attitude towards the sacred, different from anything implied in the cult of the traditional Olympian gods. Among modern exegetes, Friedrich Nietzsche, borrowing from tradition, as well as drawing on his own imagination, made the figure of Dionysos an emblem of disruptive power, whose external marker is the divine *mania* or possession in which the followers of Dionysos are caught. The majority of scholarly interpretations rely on Nietzsche when underlining the irrational and "intoxicated" aspects of the cult. His account of ecstatic rituals in their wildest, most unrestrained forms, was taken as a model by subsequent scholars, mostly because his friend Erwin Rohde made this perspective acceptable to scientific thinking by stressing, along with the eruptive character and psychological nature of the Dionysiac, an irruptive and supposedly historical factor, which led Rohde to set the origins of the new religion outside of Greece. Even though Rohde's perspective was sometimes questioned (especially concerning the Thracian origins of the cult or his theory that Orphism was a "reformed Dionysism" deprived of its wildest aspects), in all modern accounts of the Dionysiac, an explosive hint has remained dominant. It is reflected in many scholars, who bound the core of the Dionysian religion in orgiasm. Such an explanation, however, is not unanimously accepted and has been questioned (by, for example, Karl Kerényi) by noticing that this phenomenon was only marginal to the cult of Dionysos.

Dionysiac religion indeed unveiled a particular kind of religious experience, which allowed participants to attain communion with a god and transformed a human being into a *bacchos* or a *bacchē* (an inspired, frantic person). The *orgia* performed in the honor of Demeter and Dionysos represented, so to speak, an absolute form of sacrifice, which was able to grant an absolute form of salvation, as opposed to a relative one. All this meant a radical change in the human condition and implied going beyond human boundaries and limits, that is, taking part in divine realms. Moreover, for those who don't close their minds against Dionysiac experience (the demand for which is sometimes, at their peril, ignored by humans), such an experience can be a deep source of spiritual power and beatitude. It is possible to hint at a further effect, a merging of the individual consciousness within a group consciousness: the worshipper is at one not only with the god master of life, but with his or her fellow worshippers, as well as with the entirety of life on earth. Recent sociological approaches have employed the idea of Dionysiac orgiasm in order to stress, in contemporary daily life, the strong hedonistic ethic, which expresses only passing feelings, passion, and bonds of shared emotion, so typical of a "tribal" or mass society.

Drinking wine, which breaks inhibitions, acquired an important religious value because the wine permitted people to become *entheoi* (full of god). There were other means to reach this status: the strange *oreibasia* (mountain dancing) described in the *parodos* of the *Bacchae* reflects a ritual practiced by women's societies at Delphi (and also in other places) down to Plutarch's time. This took place in midwinter in alternate years (hence the name *trietēris*, "triennial festival") and has often been explained as a commemorative rite, in imitation of the maenads, who are said to have been associated with the god in the old days. Maenadism is supported by testimonies in epigraphic sources and therefore must not be considered a mere literary device. Some scholars have borrowed from medical language the term *collective hysteria* to designate such a phenomenon or have traced similar attitudes in other cultures: it was a compulsive and obsessive dance, characterized by a particular carriage of the head and tossing back of the hair, in which participants experienced a sense of being possessed by an alien personality. It has been suggested that in Greece the ritual *oreibasia* may have developed out of spontaneous attacks of hysteria and that by channeling this hysteria in an organized rite once every two years the Dionysiac cult kept it within bounds and gave it a relatively harmless outlet. Another obviously primitive feature of the *oreibasia* is snake-handling, for which numerous parallels can be traced in folkloric contexts.

The culminating act of the Dionysiac winter dance was the tearing to pieces (*sparagmos*) and eating raw (*ōmophagia*) of an animal body, an act that in all sources is described as a mixture of supreme exaltation and supreme repulsion. It is at once holy and horrible, fulfillment and uncleanness, sacrament and pollution—the same violent conflict of emotional attitudes that lies at the root of all religion of the Dionysiac type. Later writers explained the *ōmophagia* by supposing it to commemorate the day when the infant Dionysos was himself torn to pieces and devoured. Modern explanations, however, link this custom to psychological causes, because it seems likely that the warm and bleeding victim was felt to embody the vital powers of the god, which by this act were transferred to the worshippers. In this rite, therefore, the god was present in his bestial incarnation (bull, lion, snake) and in that shape was torn and eaten. The resulting effect was to liberate the instinctive life in human beings from the bondage imposed on them by reason and social custom: the worshippers became conscious of a strange, new vitality, which was attributed to the god's presence within them. Some scholars went so far as to surmise cases of human sacrifice, even though there are only scattered indications pointing in this direction. Human sacrifices are, however, sometimes linked to initiation rites, and in classical antiquity charges of ritual murders are often associated with orgiastic practice.

ORGIASTIC ELEMENTS IN MYSTERY RELIGIONS AND FOREIGN CULTS. Over the centuries the original features of Dionysiac cult were brought under state control and tamed, loosing much of their original character. Religion of the orgiastic type nevertheless began to emerge again under other names. At the end of the fifth century Athens was invaded by a multitude of foreign gods, as is clearly shown by many literary references to the eastern and northern "mystery" gods Cybele and Bendis, Attis, Adonis, and Sabazios.

The Phrygian god Sabazios is of special interest in relation to Dionysos because Sabazios was considered a sort of Oriental—or still un-Hellenized—counterpart of Dionysos, who promised his devotees identification with deity. Several of the old ritual elements mentioned in the *parodos* of the *Bacchae* are attested by Demosthenes for the Sabazios cult in a well-known passage from his oration *On the Crown*, delivered against Aeschines. Other ancient sources closely relate Dionysos and Sabazios, whose veneration is largely attested (see, for example Diodorus 4.4.1, and Iohannes Lydus, *de Mensibus* 4.51).

The potentially dangerous implications in Dionysiac cult are displayed in the famous scandal of the Bacchanalia, which took place in Rome in 186 BCE and led to the suppression of the cult. Besides the contemporary allusion in the Plautine comedy *Casina*, a detailed account is reported by the Augustan historian Livy (39.8–19). According to Livy, the rites of initiation, including feasting and drunkenness, were held at night so that darkness could conceal "promiscuous mating of free men and women," as well as occasional murders. It was a classical case of immorality under the guise of religion, and the Roman authorities felt bound to prosecute the worshippers of Bacchus by accusing them of *coniuratio* (conspiracy against the state). Bacchants were also persecuted outside the Roman Republic, as is shown in a famous inscription (*Corpus Inscriptionum Latinarum* I² 2581) from southern Italy, which contains the prohibition decree promulgated by the Roman Senate.

In discussing the case of the Roman repression of the Bacchanalia, scholars have noticed how charges of promiscuous intercourse or, more generally, of immoral behavior were directed against foreign cults as a form of ban or marginalization. Of course many of these cults were genuinely characterized, totally or partially, by orgiastic attitudes. These attitudes gradually diminished, as happened with Dionysism, when those cults came to be considered part of public religion.

Some of the most famous and widespread mystery cults during the Hellenistic age and late antiquity are characterized by collective ecstasy and frantic behavior (even though without sexual licentiousness). Among them was Montanism, a Christian sect, strongly influenced by pagan local cults, that originated in Phrygia in the second century CE and counted among its features prophetism and ecstasy. Malicious slanders about Montanists are, however, recorded by Jerome, who mentions cannibalistic rites and children sacrifices (*Epist.* 41).

The annual rites that commemorated Osiris's death and dismemberment were performed with exaggerated lamentations and with a phallophory, that is, the carrying of a phallus in procession. This detail led Herodotos to pair Dionysos and Osiris, but there are too few elements to accept this perspective, except in the sense of a syncretism between these two gods because of their agrarian features.

The veneration of Cybele (originally an Anatolian and Phrygian mother goddess, who was soon interpreted as Demeter) was widespread throughout Greece, and at the very end of the third century BCE Cybele was introduced into Roman culture. By this time the veneration of Cybele had been deprived of its most barbaric features, including loud ululations, rousing music produced by cymbals, drums, and flutes, and wild dances that incited people to bloody self-flagellation, self-mutilation, and self-castration. Similar practices, which reached their apex in the spring festival commemorative of Attis, were reserved for noncitizen adherents. One of the most relevant literary documents, which presents ecstatic frenzy in its most shocking and bloody aspects, is the epyllium *Attis*, written in the first century BCE by the Latin poet Catullus. This poem shows how orgiastic patterns could seem striking and even repugnant to a civilized audience.

Dea Syria (the title of Atargatis-Derketo in the Greco-Roman world) resembles other mother goddesses and fertility goddesses of Asia Minor, such as Aphrodite-Astarte and Rhea-Cybele. Dea Syria shares much with the cult of both of these: procession to the sea, hydrophory (the act of carrying water), *lavatio* (ritual washing), ecstatic dancing, castration, and phallolatry (an account of her rites and her temple in Hierapolis is offered in a pamphlet written by Lucian). Bellona, who was identified with the Middle Eastern goddess Ma after the Roman general Sulla became acquainted with this goddess in 92 BCE during his campaigns in the East, and whose cult shared many patterns with that of the Magna Mater, belongs to the same sphere as Dea Syria. The Latin writer Apuleius (second century CE offers a totally negative account of the priests of the goddess in the eighth book of his *Metamorphoses* (chaps. 26–30) in order to stress a sharp contrast to the Isiac religion of which he was a worshipper. Apuleius describes the priests of the Syrian goddess as thieves and swindlers; indecent, lascivious, and dishonest, they perform wild dervish dances, engage in self-mutilation, and abandon themselves to aberrant and promiscuous sexual practices.

Orgiastic rituals are elsewhere described in classical novels because of a certain fondness for exotic and unusual details. It is disputed whether the mysteries of Priapus described by Petronius in his *Satyricon* (16–26, 6) really took place or must be considered a literary fiction because of the insistence on Priapic themes throughout the novel, along with a constant attitude of parody. These mysteries were intended as a sort of counterpart of the rites of Bona Dea, and are restricted to women. Organized and directed by a lustful matron, the ceremony turns into a long and far-fetched nocturnal orgy, which involves the male actors of the novel.

The *Phoinikika* (Phoenician Histories), a Greek fragmentary romance preserved in a badly damaged papyrus (*Pap. Col. Inv.* 3328), recently attributed to the Sophist Lollianus of Ephesus (late second century CE), describes the ritual murder of a child, followed by the eating of its heart and then promiscuous intercourse. These episodes were compared by Albert Henrichs, who first edited the papyrus, to the myth of Dionysos-Zagreus, dismembered by the Titans, and to the charges against Christian religion and some late accounts about libertine Gnostics. The text is, however, too fragmentary and corrupt to infer such details and to permit so complex a reading. Much more convincing is a reading provided by J. J. Winkler and S. A. Stephen, who dismantle Henrichs's theory and consider the whole scene analogous to the accounts of *scheintod* (apparent death) traceable in other classic novels.

Christians and Gnostics. Charges of immorality were imputed to Christian communities already at the end of the first century. They were also accused of *coniuratio* (conspiracy against the state), and many similarities have been noted between the suppression of the Bacchanalia and accusations against Christians. During the second century accusations of Thyestean banquets (anthropophagy) and Oedipodean intercourse (incestuous or orgiastic practices) increased and provoked rebuttals from a number of Christian apologists, including Justin (*Apology* I 26.7), Tertullian (*Apologeticum* 39), and Minucius Felix (*Octavius* 9), whose accurate accounts probably reflect a pagan source. According to F. J. Dölger, such accusations were often a pagan misunderstanding of the Christian Eucharist and lacked any factual basis. They show nevertheless an underlying ritual pattern, which linked the alleged crimes of the Christians to similar practices of pagan origin in order to construct a coherent ritual series that included, after an overturning of the lamp so that savageness could be concealed, the murder of a child, the partaking of the victim's blood and inner parts for initiatory purposes, the administering of an oath, and finally, sexual libertinism.

Certain Gnostic rites can be considered one constituent among others equally important that shaped the specific character of anti-Christian accusations in the second century. In fact, Gnostic sects, with their peculiar mythology and ethics, including their disdain for popular religion and morality, were natural targets for accusations of immoral behavior. Along with their predecessors at Corinth, which emerge from the reproaches of the apostle Paul (see *1 Cor.* 6.12 ff.), Justin's first apology is apparently aware of affinities between these or similar Gnostic rites and the crimes that were alleged against the Christians. The accounts of the so-called libertine Gnostics found in Clement's *Stromateis* and, later, in Epiphanius's *Panarion* (fourth century) are major sources for knowledge of such rites.

Clement mentions by name various Gnostic groups (Basilidians [3.1.1.1 ff.], Carpocratians [3.2.5.1 ff.], Antitaktai [3.4.34.3 ff.], and many other unnamed sects [3.4.27.1 ff.]) that held lavish banquets, after which they extinguished the lights and indulged in sexual promiscuity. Their practices are compared to the cult of Aphrodites Pandemos and her supposed "mysteries." Some groups of Gnostics in the second century and the beginning of the third (according to Clement) treated women as common property and in their *agapē* practiced what they preached, interpreting sexual intercourse as a "mystical communion." Already the followers of Simon, according to Hippolytus, advocated promiscuous intercourse, asserting that this was perfect love, which helped participants achieve reciprocal sanctification. The Sethians did the same. Irenaeus offers similar accounts of the Cainites, Sodomites, and Carpocratians. At the time of Epiphanius, the libertine sects had apparently multiplied in Egypt, since he mentions by name the Nicolaites, Stratiotici, Phibionites, Zaccheans, and Barbeliotes. What Epiphanius describes about the Gnostic banquet and the orgy that followed, claiming that he personally met some of these sectarians, is nearly identical to Irenaeus, except that the account of Epiphanius is much richer in piggish ritual details. For example, besides uniting themselves in promiscuous intercourse after rich dinners, they practiced *coitus interruptus* and gathered and ate menstrual blood and sperm. In addition, the sectarians could not beget children and if a woman were to conceive after such an orgy, the fetus would be aborted, pounded in a mortar, seasoned with spices, honey, and oil, and then eaten. This cannibalistic feast was, according to their doctrine, the perfect Passah (*Panarion* 26.5.5).

According to Epiphanius, such details also occupied a definite position in Gnostic theology. By examining heresiologists' accounts, it emerges that it is not possible to dismiss libertine Gnostics as mere sexual deviates, for their aim was to throw into confusion the entire present order of the world, insofar as it is the work of the creator. Libertine Gnostics considered the flesh as perishable because it is the archon's own; for the same reason they believed that procreation should be abolished because it only prolonged the time that the psyche had to spend in this world. Even the disgusted way in which Epiphanius describes their dinner fellowship displays certain liturgical characteristics, which parallel some common patterns, such as the idea of eating together or such liturgical formulas as the prayer of dedication after the act or the closing confession.

It is indeed possible that the communitarian dinner of these sects was considered a characteristic meal in which the basic element was the *unio mystica*, which Christians usually explain as a gathering of believers who become one body by partaking of one bread. In Gnostic conventicles such a union was achieved with the production and spreading of sperm, which is the life-giving, divine element of man, indeed a part of God himself. It was "perfect" love, too, in the sense that it was not directed toward procreation or any other selfish end, but was exclusively for the purpose of being led to God. There was also a sort of antiphrastic celebration of the Eucharist, since the object of the dedicated sacrifice is identified with the body of Christ in a physical sense, insofar as it is the life-substance of man, the sperm. According to modern scholars, such a rite represented a sublimation process of the divine spark wrapped in the human body, shaped on the soul's return to divine realms, after having been exiled on earth. This particular form of "libertinism" should be linked to a more generic anomie so peculiar to Gnostic systems, but much more can be related to similar practices attested in Tantrism or Daoism—a sort of sexual mysticism whose purpose is symbolizing cathartic transformation or allegorical elevation towards the divine.

See Also Dionysos; Mystery Religions.

Bibliography

There is no specific work devoted to orgy in classical antiquity, but there is a seminal discussion in Mircea Eliade, *Patterns in Comparative Religion,* translated by Rosemary Sheed (New York, 1958). Eliade also investigated the close connection between orgiastic patterns and marginal groups in *Occultism, Witchcraft, and Cultural Fashions: Essays in Comparative Religions* (Chicago, 1976), chapters 5 and 6. On extra-European folkloric contexts see Vittorio Lanternari, "Orgia sessuale e riti di recupero nel culto dei morti," *Studi e materiali di storia delle religioni* (*SMSR*) 24–25 (1953–1954): 163–188. See also the monograph by Susanna Foral, *Die Orgie. Vom Kult des Altertums zu Gruppensexe des Gegenwart* (Munich, Germany, 1981).

Reversal rituals in classical antiquity, such as the Thesmophoria and the Saturnalia, are exhaustively investigated by H. S. Versnel in *Inconsistencies in Greek and Roman Religion*; vol. 2: *Transition and Reversal in Myth and Ritual* (Leiden, Netherlands, 1993).

Many studies are devoted to Dionysos and his worship. Euripides' *Bacchae* is edited with an introduction and commentary by Eric R. Dodds (Oxford, 1944). The same scholar offers an interesting discussion on maenadism in the first appendix of his monograph, *The Greeks and the Irrational* (Berkeley, Calif., and Los Angeles, 1951). On the same theme, see Albert Henrichs, "Greek Maenadism from Olympians to Messalina," *Harvard Studies in Classical Philology* 82 (1978): 121–160.

After Friedrich Nietzsche's *Die Geburt der Tragödie oder Griechentum und Pessimismus* (Berlin and New York, 1972) and Erwin Rohde's *Psyche: Seelenkult und Unsterblichkeitsglaube der Griechen,* 2d ed. (Tübingen, Germany, 1898), the idea of Dionysiac orgiastic frenzy was developed by Walter F. Otto, *Dionysos: Mythos und Kultus* (Frankfurt am Main, Germany, 1933), as well as by Henry Jeanmarie, *Dionysos: Histoire de culte de Bacchus* (Paris, 1951). See, however, the different attitudes shown by Karl Kerényi, *Dionysos: Urbild des unzerstörbaren Lebens* (Munich, Germany, and Vienna, Austria, 1976), translated into English by Ralph Manheim as *Dionysos: Archetypal Images of Indestructible Life* (Princeton, N.J., 1976). Dionysiac mysteries and similar cults have received a popularized, but well informed, treatment by Gérard Freyburger, Maire-Laure Freyburger, and Jean-Christian Tautil, *Sectes religieuses en Grèce et à Rome dans l'antiquité païenne* (Paris, 1986). See, also, the proceedings of a conference on orgiastic patterns in ancient Greek Religion, "Actes du III Colloque du C.E.R.G.A. sur l'element orgiastique dans la religion grecque ancienne," in *Kernos* 5 (1992): 13-220.

A sociological interpretation of collective frenzy and orgiastic features in modern societies is provided by Michel Maffesoli, *L'ombre de Dionysos, contribution à une sociologie de l'orgie* (Paris, 1982). On the political and religious value of the *Senatusconsultum de Bacchanalibus,* see Matthias Gelzer, *Die* Unterdrückung *der Bacchanalien bei Livius,* in *Kleine Schriften* III, pp. 256–269 (Wiesbaden, Germany, 1964); Robert Turcan, "Religion et politique dans l'affaire des Bacchanales: A propos d'un livre récent," *Revue Histoire Religions* 180 (1972): 3–28; and Wilfried Nippel, "Orgien, Ritualmored und Verschwrung? Die Bacchanalien Prozesse des 186 v.Chr" in *Grosse Prozesse der römischen Antike,* edited by Ulrich Manthe and Jürgen von Ungern Sternberg, pp. 65-73 (Munich, Germany, 1997).

The charges against Christians and other "marginal" groups in antiquity receive an extensive discussion in Franz Joseph Dölger, "Sacramentum infanticidii," *Antike und Christentum* 4 (1934): 118–200; Albert Henrichs, "Pagan Ritual and the Alleged Crimes of the Early Christians," in *Kyriakon: Festschr Johannes Quasten,* edited by Patrick Granfield and Josef A. Jungmann, pp. 18–35 (Münster, Germany, 1973); Robert M. Grant, "Charges of Immorality against Various Religious Groups in Antiquity," in *Studies in Gnosticism and Hellenistic Religions Presented to Gilles Quispel on the Occasion of his 65th Birthday,* edited by R. van den Broek and M. J. Vermaseren, pp. 161–170 (Leiden, Netherlands, 1981); and Agnes A. Nagy, "Superstitio et coniuratio," *Numen* 49 (2002): 178–192. For classical novels (with particular reference to Lollianos), after the edition provided by Albert Heinrichs, *Die Phoinikika des Lollianos. Fragmente eines neuen griechischen Romans* (Bonn, West Germany, 1972), see *Ancient Greek Novels: The Fragments,* edited by Susan A. Stephens and John J. Winkler, pp. 314 ff. (Princeton, N.J., 1995).

On the so called libertine Gnostics, see Norbert Brox, "Nikolaos und Nikolaiten," *Vigiliae Christianae* 19 (1965): 27–30; Stephen Benko, "The Libertine Gnostic Sect of the Phibionites according to Epiphanius," *Vigiliae Christianae* 21 (1967): 103–119; Michel Tardieu, "Epiphane contre les Gnostiques," *Tel Quel* 88 (1981): 64–91; and Giovanni Casadio, *Vie gnostiche all'immortalità* (Brescia, Italy, 1997).

For terminology, see Pierre Chantraine, *Dictionnaire étymologique de la langue grecque: Histoire des mots,* p. 816 (Paris, 1968).

CHIARA OMBRETTA TOMMASI (2005)

ORGY: ORGY IN MEDIEVAL AND MODERN EUROPE

Leveling charges against various dissenting groups or heretical sects both of holding meetings at which babies were ritually slaughtered and of conducting orgies at which every form of intercourse, including incest, together with the worshiping of odd divinities in the form of animals, was almost a standard procedure in the history of religions. Cannibalism or sexual intercourse between close relatives, which are usually considered against human nature and as such forbidden in almost every society, were the natural imputation against persons who saw themselves as outside the normal customs or rules. Moreover, dissenting factions were labeled "conspiratorial organizations" and often faced charges of conducting ritual murder and cannibalistic feasts. In some cases it is possible to establish with certainty that these charges were no more than a stereotype, as in the case of such activities imputed to the early Christians. Besides allegations of cannibalism and sexual promiscuity, radical groups were sometimes accused also of sacrilegious acts, such as spitting and trampling on the crucifix or adoring Satan in corporeal form in some obscene fashion. Sometimes the nocturnal orgy was imagined as presided over and supervised by a demon.

MEDIEVAL CHRISTENDOM. Already in late antiquity some heterodox sects like the Priscillianists in Spain (fourth century) or, according to isolated testimonies, the Montanists in Africa were accused of unleashing orgies and ritual murders of children, but there is no real basis for such accusations. The same can be affirmed for a large number of Christian groups in the Middle Ages, which showed a polemical—and sometimes even schismatic, by the rejection of some dogmas—attitude toward the Catholic Church and sought a radical restoration of its conduct, which should have been more in conformance with Christ's example, for example, by totally abolishing richness and luxury. Among these the Waldensians (who originated at the end of the twelfth century) first and the Fraticelli (who developed from radical Franciscan spiritualism) can be also counted. In spite of their condemnation in 1184, the Waldensians spread throughout Europe, and it is probably against them that the attacks of the inquisitor Conrad of Marburg in Germany were directed. Also the papal bull *Vox in Rama,* issued in 1233 by Gregory IX, which for the first time gave official character to the trivial charges of nocturnal orgiastic and demonic covens, had the same sect in mind. Even though the archbishop of Mainz, in disagreement with Conrad, minimized the phenomenon (reducing the orgies to mere transgressions by individuals), the stereotype survived in the following centuries and periodically caused a repetition of the prosecutions, until the Waldensians were finally rehabilitated in 1509 and given back their confiscated properties.

A trial in 1466 was the end of the Fraticelli as an organized sect, albeit their renown as devil worshipers and cannibals lasted later. This sect, whose adherents were not indeed numerous and did not possess a unified organization, had originated from a radical wing of the thirteenth-century Franciscans, some of whom left the order and then the church (they were the so-called Spirituals, inspired also by the apocalyptic and prophetic writings by the Calabrian abbot Joachim of Fiore). They professed the opinion that Christ and the apostles lived in total poverty and therefore considered the Roman church as the whore of Babylon, a pattern that recurs elsewhere in millennial groups. The trial of 1466 was the final act of a series of minor proceedings that started at the beginning of the century. Many sources, such as Bernardino of Siena and the historian Flavio Biondo, attest the practice of a ritual infanticide (the practice is called *barilotto,* an Italian word that alludes to the little barrel of wine with the ashes of the dead child), followed by a promiscuous orgy.

Similar accusations were used by the French king Philip the Fair to achieve at the very beginning of the fourteenth century the destruction of the Order of the Knights Templar, whose power was more and more increasing: among the charges, often extorted under torture, there were, as usual, those of impiety, blasphemy, and sodomy. But in all cases modern research, by a reexamination of the evidence, has been able to clear these groups of charges, which to some extent have hung over them for five or six centuries.

There are, however, several perplexing testimonies that should discourage us from dismissing the accusations too summarily. This is the case, for example, of the so-called Brethren of the Free Spirit, another heretical sect that played a more important part than Catharism, since it extended over a vast area in Europe (from Germany to Holland and France, and also to Italy) and had an extraordinary capacity for survival, despite being constantly harassed by persecution. It is possible that some of its adherents from Picardy influenced also the Taborite revolution in Bohemia, and a brief but hectic revival of the "Free Spirit" (whose adherents were known as Ranters) took place in seventeenth-century England during its civil war. Its nature has been much debated by historians, also because of the almost total absence of written sources, including inquisitorial documents, not to mention the difficulty of making out the forerunners of the movement and its effective adherents. For example, it is indeed possible that the Beghards, officially condemned by the Council of Vienna in 1312, or the Beguines shared many patterns with the Brethren of the Free Spirit; so did the Amaurians, the followers of Gerardo Segarelli (d. 1300), Fra Dolcino (d. 1307), Wilhelm Cornelisz from Antwerp, and many other mystics of the thirteenth century, among whom many women can be mentioned too (Hadewych, Willemine of Bohemia, Bloemardine, Marguerite Porete). However, it is possible to affirm that this sect was a sort of gnosis intent upon individual salvation, a system of self-exaltation often amounting to self-deification, which concluded in an aberrant form of mysticism and anarchy. What distinguished the Free Spirit from other medieval sects is total amoralism. The core of the heresy of the Free Spirit (which did not form an organized church) lay in its adherents' attitude toward themselves: they stressed the desire to surpass the human condition and become godlike, and they believed they had attained so absolute a perfection that they were incapable of sin, a conviction that often could lead to antinomianism. It was thus permissible to do whatsoever was commonly regarded as forbidden, and, in particular, such antinomianism commonly took the form of sexual promiscuity. Eroticism, far from springing from a relaxed sensuality, possessed above all a mystic and symbolic value of spiritual emancipation. Adultery too was regarded as a transcendental means of affirmation or liberation. Moreover, for the elect, sexual intercourse could not under any circumstances be sinful, so that they were able to indulge in promiscuity without fear of God or qualms of conscience.

In this perspective the Adam cult, which frequently characterizes the sectarians of the Free Spirit, becomes comprehensible. In this form of worship can be outlined a blend of chiliasm and primitivism that became one of the commoner forms of modern romanticism: in fact, the Adam cult involved a sort of re-creation of the lost Paradise and at the same time an affirmation of the advent of the millennium. The most famous episode took place in Cologne in 1325. It ended in a scandal that led to the execution of the most prominent members of the sect, who were recognized as adherents of the Free Spirit. A suspicious husband, in fact, disguised as a Beghard, had followed his wife to a secret meeting that was held in a subterranean chamber, sumptuously decorated and called Paradise. This gathering was presided over by a man (probably an apostate priest identical with the celebrated heresiarch Walter the Dutchman) and a woman, who claimed to be respectively Christ and the Virgin Mary. After the celebration of some kind of Mass, a naked preacher then exhorted those present to remove their clothes in order to be like the innocent and restore the paradisiacal condition. A banquet followed, with much singing and rejoicing, and everything was concluded by the final orgy. It seems that the allegation of an orgy may have been something more than the standard cliché against dissidents, since the mention of ritual nudity is variously reported, as well as sexual promiscuity. Also, in later centuries the descendants of this heresy claimed to perform sexual acts in the same way as Adam and Eve.

The Free Spirit heresy can be partly compared to the case of the Cathars; their peculiar form of Christianity was largely influenced by some dualistic or Gnosticizing movements in Eastern Europe such as the Bulgarian Bogomils, who in turn derived from the Paulicians, recorded by some Byzantine heresiologists (for example, around 1050, Michael Psellos mentions the Thracian sect of the Messalians—probably identical to the Bogomils—and charges its adherents with the usual accusation of orgy and cannibalism). Scholars have long since outlined, for example, the affinity between the *Interrogatio Iohannis*—a Bogomil text—and Cathar sexual morals. This text emphasizes the view that sexual desire and sexual difference were a Satanic creation, imposed on angelic spirits that were originally bodiless, and it presents a dualist account of sexual difference. Scholars have also suggested that the Catholic redefinition of marriage at the end of the twelfth century, according to which it had to be understood in terms not of sexual consummation but of free choice, was an effort to vindicate marriage in response to the Cathar attack. Whereas some sources included the charge that the Cathars advocated sodomy and incest, other inquisitors, on the contrary, defended the "perfects" from the charge of sexual debauchery and insisted on their denying of marriage: when some preachers emphasized the attack on marriage and childbirth as heretical, they were creating the buds of a Catholic view of "normal" sexuality and marriage. Furthermore, some scholars have also suggested that Catharism influenced the troubadours and their poetic of courtly love, which craves for extraconjugal or adulterous relationships.

Reformed Christianity. The usual criticism brought against the church found, so to say, a land of election in Bohemia, not only because of the enormous wealth of the church but also because of a powerful national sentiment that gave impulse to the so-called Hussite revolution. After the execution of its charismatic leader Jan Hus (in 1415), the unrest increased and led the country into a restless struggle that soon took violent forms, in particular when considering the radical Hussites, known as Taborites, a sect lead by Martin Húska and Petrus Kániš and finally defeated in 1421. In fact, this revolutionary wing—characterized by anarcho-communistic features and thus compared to the late antique African circumcellions—was mainly formed by the harassed proletariat and peasantry, people encompassed by a social as well as religious animosity. Not only did they dismiss prayers and Masses for the dead as vain superstitions, neglect the veneration of the relics, and deny the dogma of purgatory, but they were utterly convinced that the earth had to be cleansed of sinners so Christ could descend from heaven in majesty; thus, it was the inescapable duty of the elect to kill in the name of the Lord. Thus, the usual millennial expectations degenerated into an unheard-of violence, massacre, and terror. The Taborites gathered in completely egalitarian communities, held together by brotherly love alone. The most important was near Usti, on a promontory that served as a natural fortress, and was renamed Tabor, after the mountain where Christ had foretold his Parousia. There were even extremer wings, partly influenced by the doctrine of the Free Spirit, which they practiced on a far larger scale. These people are known by the name Pikarti (which alludes to the refugee from Picardy who introduced the heresy in the Taborite community) or Bohemian Adamites. According to the accounts given by some members, after their defeat and imprisonment they lived in a state of community so unconditional that not only did nobody possess anything of his own but also marriage was regarded as an appalling sin and promiscuity seems to have been obligatory. Moreover, on the ground of Christ's remark about harlots and publicans, the Adamites argued that the chaste were unworthy to enter their messianic kingdom. The alleged ritual dances held by naked people around a fire and accompanied by much singing, together with the custom of spending much time nude, were considered a return to the state of innocence enjoyed by Adam and Eve before the fall. The Adamites have sometimes been paralleled to the libertine Gnostics of the third and fourth century, also because they pretended to have a divine nature even superior to Christ's, whose death was regarded as evidence of his mere human condition.

Also Lutheranism and, more generally, Reformed Christianity had to reckon with dissenting groups, which constituted the radical (or, as it has been labeled, "left") wing of the Reformation and to which some charges of immorality were similarly imputed. The same patterns that have already been sketched out for medieval Christian sectarians (millennial enthusiastic exaltation, agapic spirituality, militant evangelism, sometimes dualism), together with a sort of proto-communism, featured some Anabaptist movements too. As far as sexual promiscuity is concerned, originally the only permitted form was marriage between two Anabaptists, and they generally observed a stricter code of sexual morality than most of their contemporaries. A famous example is, however, provided by the Anabaptist "messianic reign" established in Münster (between 1533 and 1535) by Bernhard Rothmann, Jan Matthys, and Jan Bockelson, also known as Jan von Leyden. The latter, who became the absolute regent of the rebellious city, legalized polygamy in July 1534, an unpopular decision that hastened the end of this singular political experiment, also because refusal to comply with the new law was made a capital offence and some women were executed. In explaining how the biblical precept to "increase and multiply" had to be taken as a divine commandment, and how the polygamy already practiced by the patriarchs of Israel should be restored in the New Jerusalem, Bockelson undertook a path that resembles the one carried out by the Brethren of the Free Spirit and by the Adamites. Even allowing for the exaggeration of hostile accounts (which mention also sumptuous banquets and dissoluteness at Jan's court), it seems certain that sexual behavior in Münster turned from rigorous puritanism to sheer promiscuity, and that polygamy was changed into something not very different from free love. It is interesting to remember that the composer Jacques Meyerbeer echoed these events in his grand opera *Le Prophète* (1849).

Witchcraft. Orgiastic themes are a constant feature in the huge literature that flourished around witches and witchcraft because of the alleged nocturnal gatherings in which at regular intervals witches betook themselves to sacrilegious and orgiastic covens, usually known as "sabbats" (a term taken from the Jewish religion, traditionally considered the essence of anti-Christianity, or indeed a form of devil worship). They were usually held at the summit of some famous mountains, but also in churchyards or crossroads. Sabbats could generally involve only the witches of a neighborhood, but three or four times a year ecumenical sabbats were celebrated, attended by witches from everywhere. It is possible to draw a representative picture of the sabbat, since the various accounts—usually recorded from the Inquisition trials onwards—differ only in minor details. It was the devil, in the shape of a monstrous being, half man and half goat, who presided over the sabbat. The coven began with a reassertion of the devil's mastery over his servants, the witches (usually women, but sometimes also men or even children). They knelt down and adored the demon, also kissing him on his left foot or genitals. A parody of the Eucharist followed, and then a meal usually consisting of revolting substances was served. Finally, the participants took part in a hysterical dance, to the sound of trumpets, drums, and fifes, which would become a frantic and erotic orgy. All things, including sodomy and incest, were permitted, and at the height of the orgy the devil would copulate with every person present.

From the nineteenth century down to present times, the subject has been variously investigated. Whereas some historians have encouraged the belief that there were secret societies of witches—sometimes arguing that they were the most extreme of all heresies or the most nihilistic of all sects—and that the authorities who pursued them were in effect breaking the local organizations of that sect, others have suggested that the notion of an organized sect first developed as a by-product of the campaign of the Inquisition against Catharism or other heresies. They have even dismissed the idea that witch hunting was directed against a real society or an effective cult, adducing psychological or sociological explanations, for example considering the sabbat a fantasy of men's hatred and fear of women, and the great witch hunt a bloody episode in the sex war. Furthermore, in his well-known pamphlet *La sorcière* (Paris, 1862), the French writer Jules Michelet argued that witchcraft was nothing more than a protest by medieval serfs against the oppressive social order, which later turned into a ritualized defiance of Christian religion. His romantic description of the Medea-like priestess of the cult who ritually mates with Satan partially involves the idea of a fertility cult that aimed at securing an abundance of crops. This thesis was largely developed in the 1920s and 1930s by folklorist Margaret Murray, who was deeply influenced by the Frazerian vogue of her age. According to Murray, down to the seventeenth century, there persisted in Europe the relics of a religion centered on the worship of the two-faced horned god Dianus, who represented the cycle of crops and seasons. This agrarian cult was easily confused with devil worshiping and, as such, prosecuted. Though mostly discredited, Murray's thesis has enjoyed a certain influence and was responsible also for the proliferation of modern witch covens. In more recent times, other scholars have reconsidered the linking between fertility magic and witchcraft, or centered their attention on the libidinous aspects of the sabbat, suggesting that ecstatic experiences or trances, often induced by drugs or hallucinogenic herbs, share many patterns with the ancient cult of Dionysus, which also was mainly performed by women. It is indeed possible that the stirrings of feminine discontent may have contributed to the orgiastic elements in witches' revels. Those who plausibly deny the existence of covens and organized sects underline how the spreading of such an idea was the product of a society that strongly insisted on religious conformity, repressed dissent, and did its best to enforce that conformity. Nevertheless, whatever might be the final interpretation, it is important to consider how witchcraft was thought of as a collective fact. Though witches performed spells individually, they were a society bound together by communal rites, and in every respect they were thought to represent a collective inversion of Christianity.

Orgiastic practices in heterodox Judaism. During the Middle Ages and the Renaissance, qabbalistic doctrines were often given a shade of mystical eroticism. Such a development reached its apex in the controversial figure of the Smyrnean Sabbatai Sevi, the pretended messiah and founder (in the Ottoman Empire during the second half of the seventeenth century) of a Jewish sect inspired by qabbalistic teachings and pervaded by millennial expectations, who at the end of his life made an astonishing and unclear conversion to Islam in order to have spared his life from the sultan. Sabbatai's behavior presents a strange mixture of erotic mysticism and inhibitions, which increased as he became master over a large number of enthusiastic followers, culminating in an alternation of semierotic and semiascetic rituals (for example, the singing of psalms, clad in phylacteries and surrounded by women and wine). Accounts of his life include also charges of immorality, which cannot be lightly dismissed as an invention of hostile sources. However, there is little or no evidence of debauchery during the early period, as long as he was a Jewish rabbi, despite fits of manic enthusiasm; on the contrary, all allegations of moral excesses date after his apostasy. There may have been tendencies in Sabbatai that remained suppressed for a long time by his ascetic way of life but that erupted sooner or later, perhaps after his marriage with Sarah, through whom a licentious element entered in his life. According to some contemporary Armenian sources, Sabbatai had relations with women or favorites and was accused by his adversaries of lewdness and debauches. Among the disconcerting conduct he kept up, he was variously said to have taken with him for many days some virgins and then returned them, allegedly without having touched them. There are also documents that testify how Sabbatai prided himself on his ability to have intercourse with virgins without actually deflowering them. Also a favorable source, that is, his disciple Abraham Cuenque's idealized account of Sabbatai's residence (during his imprisonment) at the "Tower of Strength" in Abydos, says that the "messiah" and his wife Sarah were attended by beautiful virgins, the daughters of the most illustrious families, and also that several rabbis submitted to him their queries and difficulties in matters of rabbinic law, a description oddly reminiscent of similar and anything but legendary accounts of "Platonic" arrangements at the court of Jakob Frank.

This account, despite its exaggeration, shares many features with the complaints to the Turkish authorities concerning the unbearable abominations committed at Sabbatai's court. The same sources mention, in addition to this example of erotic perversity, instances of antinomianism, such as treading the phylacteries under foot or tearing up a Torah scroll and trampling upon it, or the ritual consumption of forbidden animal fats, preceded by his blasphemous benediction, "that hast permitted that which is forbidden." It is clear that this was essentially a symbolic expression of the abolition of sexual taboos and prohibitions, or, in other words, a demonstration of antinomian, revolutionary messianism. Sabbatai had planned to abolish the ritualistic Jewish observances and had raised a standard of rebellion against the hallowed traditions of the law, and abrogated its prohibitions, including, by implication, those against incest and fornication. The symbolic overtones of his breaking the alimentary taboos must have been obvious. It has also been supposed that his behavior was influenced by his wife (who, in turn, had led an irregular and eccentric life before marriage) and by his own ideas regarding the messianic liberation of women from the yoke of their husbands.

Sabbatai's influence became widespread in Central Europe too and lasted after his fall in disgrace. Messianic expectations could also offer a sort of viaticum to the prosecutions suffered by Jews during that period, or were meant as a way to improve the social condition of the Jews, also because of the decline of the rabbinical schools. However, having lost its political influence messianism assumed a mystical coloring and was transformed into a secret and sectarian cult; in Turkey a half-Jewish, half-Islamic sect was established, the so-called Dönmeh, while in the Polish region of Podolia numerous groups of Sabbatians were formed. Their adherents, in expectation of the messianic revolution, discarded many dogmas and religious customs; the cult thus included elements of both strict asceticism, including self-torture, and sensuality or licentiousness. Despite the attempt of the Polish rabbis at extirpating it, the Sabbatian heresy survived and was practiced in secret, Masonic-like, circles. The Frankist sect, which was very influential in the eighteenth century, originated from Sabbatian ambits. Its founder, Jakob Frank, came from a Sabbatian family and was himself a devoted adherent to the movement, intimate with the leaders. He began gathering sectarians around 1755 in his native Podolia, asserting that he had been directly instructed by Sabbatai's successors in Salonica. After having been excommunicated by a congress of rabbis because of the scandal stirred up by their assemblies, Frank and his followers tried to gain the support of the Catholic hierarchy by proclaiming their rejection of the Talmud. A huge number of them were also able to receive baptism in 1759, but the insincerity of the Frankists became more and more clear, and also a church tribunal judged Frank as a heretic. Though imprisoned, he was able to win a number of followers to his new religion, a strange mixture of Sabbatianism and Christianity. He was released in 1772 and traveled throughout Europe until his death in 1791.

An important role in the organization of the sect was played by Eve, Frank's beautiful daughter, to whom also a peculiar form of cultic veneration was directed (involving a sort of syncretism with the Virgin in Chentsochov); after the death of her father she became the holy mistress and leader of the sect. Frankism remained prominent also during the Romantic age and the nineteenth century, and in a certain way inspired the Polish nationalism, together with other mystical streams, which were more acceptable because of the lack of antinomianism and sexual scandals. In fact, Frankism consisted—more than Sabbatianism—in a total negation of the traditional bulk of Jewish religion and ethics, conforming to a sort of mythology of nihilism, in which the new messianic law entailed a complete reversal of values and the transformation of the prohibitions of the Torah, including sexual unions and incest, into licit acts. The adherents believed that the descent into evil is a condition of ascent toward good, and, in this way, orgiastic practices were turned into the *via mystica* of the new eon. Also the outward conversion to Christianity was intended as the holy sin that would liberate them from the repressions of Mosaic and Talmudic law.

Among the Jewish sects that derived from Sabbatianism and practiced sexual antinomianism, the Moravians in eighteenth-century London can be noted too. Their leader was Count Ludwig Zinzendorf, himself an amateur qabbalist. According to the theories followed by Zinzendorf, God and the universe are dynamic sexual potencies that interact together to generate orgasmic joy when in perfect equilibrium. Furthermore, contacts between Frankists and Zinzendorfians are well documented, as well as contacts with Masonic milieus. Some contemporaries described the Moravians as a subversive secret society, whose leaders aimed at progressively sapping the energy of civil government and establishing an empire within an empire. Their "clinging together" was a euphemism for communal sex, ritual orgies, and comparable "gnostic obscenities" reserved to the higher initiates. Also, Emanuel Swedenborg, who since youth was trained in heterodox Jewish mysticism and in Sabbatianism too, attended the Moravian lodge during his sojourn in London. His diaries testify to many of the shocking sexual ceremonies of the Moravians, in which he was initially concerned but that later repelled him. However, like the Moravians earlier, the Swedenborgians were vulnerable to becoming objects of public ridicule and scandal. This motley crew who populated the clandestine world of illuminist Freemasonry in pre-Victorian London found a sympathetic enthusiast in William Blake, who maintained a lifelong commitment to radical theories of sexuality, including polygamy.

The Khlysts. Even more puzzling are the accounts reported about the Russian orthodox sect of the so-called "people of God," or Khlysts, and it is difficult to distinguish the real significance of this mystical and totally irrational religious approach, since the concealment of their rites was almost total and the majority of our information derives from hostile sources (missionaries or police). The name Khlysts, as the members were called by detractors, derives either from a distortion of "Christ," because the adherents thought that Christ could become incarnate in every one of them, or (and this seems the most probable interpretation) from the Russian word for "whip," with an allusion to ritual practices of self-flagellation. It seems possible to affirm that this sect was an emanation of the various Russian schismatic movements that began their diffusion during the seventeenth and eighteenth centuries and that taught that Christian faith had been destroyed by an Antichrist, after a long period of splendor and decadence, and should be founded again. Whereas Danil Filippovič, a peasant from the Volga region and alleged founder of the sect, seems to be nothing more than a shadowy and legendary figure, the first important representative was Ivan Timofeevič Suslov. In the eighteenth and the nineteenth centuries the sect spread out and reached also the high society in Saint Petersburg.

Both an emotional revelation and a multiplicity of the divine incarnations lay at the ground of the Khlyst spirituality. In order to allow the death of the old person and the mystical resurrection in Christ, which also meant the presence of a divine spark in the intimate self and possession by the Holy Spirit, fasting, chastity, prayer and self-flagellation were necessary. The culmination of their rites consisted in a nocturnal ceremony, which began with a fanatical dervishlike dance, after a dispersion of holy water: men and women concentrically rotated in opposite directions, until they became exhausted and proffered prophecies. Accounts of self-flagellation and a concluding orgy—after the ritual election of a woman, who was then adored as the Virgin Mary—are also reported; these practices, a sort of hybrid between the cult of the ancient Mother Goddess and the Christian veneration of Mary, were justified by asserting that the satisfaction of carnal desires is the straightest way to redemption and that humans can be saved only passing through a hyperbolic degree of depravation and sin. Sexual intercourse, however, was restrained to this singular rite, while usually a strict chastity was observed. The same kind of frantic, insistent attitude toward asceticism and purity led some members to refuse such transgressive behavior and to commit self-castration at the end of a frantic dance (like their pagan antecedents, the Galli, priests of Cybele who emasculated themselves). The new monastic order was founded in the second half of the eighteenth century by Kondratij Selivanov, who asserted in 1765 at the same time that he was the embodiment of God and of Tsar Peter III. The members took the name Skoptzi (literally "whitened"), alluding to their condition: they also proclaimed the intrinsic oneness of God and man and aimed at restoring the chiliastic reign of God on earth. The Khlysts enjoyed a special renown also because, according to many, the famous monk and political intriguer Rasputin (born c.1864–d. 1916) was a member of the sect, even though not all his biographers credit this information. It is true, however, that he exercised a sort of magnetic fascination over women, and he is reported to having seduced many, despite his strong ascetic outlook.

New Religious Movements in the Eighteenth and Nineteenth Centuries. As it has been seen, sex, magic, and secrecy had long been associated in the Western religious imagination, especially as far as esoteric orders are concerned. It is possible to recall here also the radical illuminist sect of the *frères* ("brethren") at Avignon, who were in contact with Masonic and Swedenborgians circles. In their arcane observance they practiced ritual nudity, communal sex, and worship of the *Shekhinah* (the qabbalistic feminine counterpart of God). Accusations about erotic ceremonies at Avignon, as well as biographic details about their chief, Count Grabianka, suggest that these revolutionary sexual theories were not only preached but also performed.

Of course, different is the practice of polygamy or group marriage variously theorized during the nineteenth century by the proto-Marxian French philosopher Fourier and his well-known doctrine of the falansteries, or in the religious experiences of some North American communities, among which it is worth mentioning the Oneida Community, founded in 1844 by John Humphrey Noyes and some friends of his in New York. Regulated by a communist way of life, Noyes's community was deeply pervaded by millennial feelings and practiced so-called complex marriage, according to which every man and every woman were married to each other and could engage in sexual intercourse but could not be attached to each other as stated earlier. In addition, the male members also practiced a form of birth control where during and after sexual intercourse the man could not ejaculate.

However, the first well-developed system of sexual magic is due to Paschal Beverly Randolph (1825–1875), the foremost American exponent of magical eroticism or Affectional Alchemy. This was a sort of sexual magic to which he claimed to have been initiated by some *fakīrs* during a journey to Jerusalem, who were perhaps adherents to the mystical order of the Nuṣayrīs, a group long persecuted by orthodox Islam because of their alleged Gnostic sexual rituals. Randolph saw in sexual orgasm the critical moment in human consciousness and the key to magical power and personal fulfillment as well as social transformation and regeneration. His doctrines were developed mostly by the esoteric movement known as the *Ordo Templi Orientis* (OTO), inspired by Karl Kellner and Theodor Reuss. The OTO taught that it is the polarity of male and female energies that creates the universe, and it is sexual union that leads to the reunion of the divine ego and to angelhood; it also developed a system of nine initiation degrees, the last three of which focused upon the theory of sex magic and the techniques of auto- and heterosexual magic.

It is worth mentioning here also the enigmatic and controversial figure of Edward Alexander (Aleister) Crowley (1875–1947), himself a member and reformer of the OTO and founder in 1920 of the Abbey of Thelema (from the Greek word for "will") in Sicily, a utopian community in which every desire could be gratified and every impulse expressed through free experimentation in drugs, sex, and physical excess. His impact on the modern revival of paganism, magic, witchcraft, and occultist and esoteric practices has been extremely influential, albeit he has been neglected by academic scholarship until recent times. The reason for this neglect is perhaps to be found, besides his more generally outrageous behavior, in his strong insistence on the practice of "sexual magikc" (according to his spelling). During his life Crowley had been the object of intense media scandal and was apparently delighted in offending contemporary British society, not only by proclaiming himself the "Great Beast 666" but also by explicitly using the most "deviant" sexual acts, including masturbation and homosexuality, as central components in his magical practice (therefore, he expanded to eleven OTO's original nine degrees). Sex was believed to conceal some awesome, even sacred, power, the tremendous liberation of which Crowley tried to effect through his magical practices.

Rejecting the prudish hypocrisy of the Victorian Christian world in which he had grown up, Crowley identified sex as the most powerful force in life and the supreme source of magical power. He has been thus compared to other controversial figures of his day, such as D. H. Lawrence and Oscar Wilde, who aimed at bursting the oppressive values and constricting morality of their society. Yet Crowley took the ideal of transgression to its furthest possible extremes, since he deliberately overthrew every imaginable social, moral and sexual taboo in order to accomplish a radical superhuman freedom, self-affirmation, and even self-deification. With a certain fondness for ostentation and scandal, Crowley himself sensationalized his way of life, and his infamy as the wickedest man alive was due to the emphasis of the popular press, which described Crowley's sexual promiscuity in vivid and exaggerated detail and considered him and his followers as members of a blasphemous sect, whose proceedings contributed to immorality of the most revolting character.

Crowley was also one of the first Western authors interested in the Hatha Yoga, Raja Yoga and, most of all, the Hindu and Buddhist traditions of Tantra, even though he seems to have mediated his knowledge of Tantric doctrines by secondary and often highly distorted sources, which partly reflected the prejudicial bias of European Asian scholars. This complex exoteric body of spiritual teaching often involves explicit forms of ritual transgression, such as consumption of food or sexual intercourse in violation of class laws, in order to awake the tremendous power or *shakti* that flows through all things. However, according to recent scholarship, Tantra is in most cases a conservative tradition, which allows social relations and sexual taboos to be violated only in highly controlled ritual contexts so that the ritual authority and social status of male Brāhmans may be ultimately reasserted, that is, reinforced, outside the boundaries of esoteric ritual. Even though sexual union is a fairly minor part of a global spiritual practice, to a Western audience Tantra appeared nothing else than a popular form of spirituality whose core was healthy sexuality or even a perverse confusion of sexuality and religion (in the Victorian age Tantra doctrines were trivialized by Edward Sellon, himself a pornographic writer, who offered titillating descriptions of the licentious orgies among the votaries and of the disregard for every natural restraint). The Western redefinition of Tantra by its sexual element, its comparison to the orgasm theory of Reich, and the vague equation with "spiritual sex," the goal of which is only heightened orgasm and optimal physical pleasure, owes much to Crowley's interest in this doctrine and to his putting the sexual element, as well as perhaps the antinomian one, at the first place; although Crowley had only a superficial understanding of Tantrism, he became a seminal figure in this transformation and is still today widely cited as the modern pioneer of "Tantric Sex Magick."

It seems that some neo-Gnostic movements were permeated by libertine streams, just like their ancient predecessors; at the same time similar patterns are reported also for modern witchcraft, in the forms developed by Charles A. Lelend or Gerald Brosseau Gardner, although there is no real certainty of an effective practice. Orgies feature also the modern Satanic or Luciferian cults (for example, in organized movements like those inspired by Anton La Vey or Martin Lamers) from the eighteenth-century "Hells of Fires" onwards, even though it is very difficult to distinguish whether they have a religious significance or simply represent a way to vent one's own instincts, usually induced or propitiated also by drugs or hallucinogens.

Contemporary Philosophical and Sociological Interpretations of the Orgy. To sum up, some patterns common to all these religious movements can be outlined. Besides the risks involved in an overstatement of the orgiastic phenomenon, often due to the hostility of the sources (for example, as far as the majority of medieval sects is concerned), it is indeed true that in some cases the practice of sexual promiscuity, accompanied by lavish banquets and frantic dances, is well attested and draws on particular philosophical premises. A more general antinomianism—usually permeated by chiliastic instances and sometimes by dualistic conceptions and communism practices—lies at the foundation. Moving from the statement that the (often stereotypical) acts attributed to these outgroups represented a total inversion of the norms, totally forbidden and thus regarded with horror, psychoanalytic attempts at explaining this kind of phenomenon have also been made. While the charge of cannibalism or ritual murder of children can be explained either in terms of homicide fantasies experienced in infancy or early childhood and then deeply repressed, or—as seems more probable—anxiety for the untimely death of children, so frequent in the past centuries, the theme of erotic orgy is simpler to interpret as reflecting repressed desires, temptations, or even misogyny. Such a notion of unconstrained sexuality was combined with that of a systematic and total inversion of the ordinary cult.

Conversely, the sects that really practiced orgies or experienced sexual promiscuity during their (often secret) rituals show a characteristic blending of self-exaltation or rather self-deification and antinomianism, which took the form of an anarchic eroticism. A motif common to all these groups is the sinless condition of the elects (or, in other terms, "awakened," or "perfects"), which allows them to perform all the acts, including prohibited or impure ones. Such persons lose an experience of sin, understood as mortification or mystical death, deprived sexual intercourse of its impure character, and produced an effect of transformation, which helped to destroy one's own conceit. This was achieved also thanks to a sort of neutralization of the individuals who merged into a cosmic-pantheist unity, since orgies permit the individual constraint of eros to be overthrown.

Moreover, sex, particularly in its transgressive, nonreproductive forms, is intended as a way to unleash the supreme creative power, which can be deployed for a wide range of both spiritual and material ends. Recent interpretations (from Julius Evola onwards) consider orgasm as a means to attain a condition of exhaustion taken to the extreme limit, which can create "breakages of consciousness" and so open the mind to the "supersensual." It is thus possible to compare such practices to what Georges Bataille calls the power of transgression, which is a central aspect of eroticism, religious ritual (such as blood sacrifices, carnivals, etc.), and mystical experience alike. According to Bataille, the various acts of transgression imply deliberate violations and systematic inversions of the moral laws and sexual codes of the larger society, though they cannot be understood as mere hedonistic and unrestrained sexual license; their power lies in the dialectic between taboo and transgression, and the ultimate aim of them is to transgress the very boundaries of the self, that is, to smash the limits of finite human consciousness in order to experience the unlimited continuity of the infinite (in this sense eroticism is intimately linked to death itself). According to Bataille, who echoes some theories already outlined by the Marquis de Sade at the end of the eighteenth century, the prohibition is there to be violated, and the best way of enlarging one's desires is to try to limit them, because it is just this experience that brings the blissful sense of continuity and unity with the Other. Nor are there lacking sociological interpretations of the orgy, like those by Michel Maffesoli and Jean Baudrillard, who argue that the present is a "post-orgy world," after the great social and sexual revolutions have broken every conceivable taboo. The orgy, in fact, is the explosive moment of modernity, that of liberation in all domains, although, as a consequence of it, liberation has left everyone in an undefined and uncertain state, in which one's own definition is put into question.

See Also Sexuality, article on Sexual Rites in Europe.

BIBLIOGRAPHY

The Priscillianist heresy and a certain attitude of the church toward magic and occultism is well outlined by Henry Chadwick, *Priscillian of Avila: The Occult and the Charismatic in the Early Church* (Oxford, 1976).

The dualistic grounds that feature many antinomian religious groups have been investigated, with respect particularly to Eastern Europe, by Josef Leo Seifert, *Die Weltrevolutionäre von Bogomil über Hus zu Lenin* (Wien, 1931); see also Ugo Bianchi, *Selected Essays on Gnosticism, Dualism and Mysteriosophy* (Leiden, 1978), who deals with Gnosticism and medieval sects. Norman Cohn's *The Pursuit of the Millennium: Revolutionary Messianism in Medieval and Reformation Europe and its Bearing on Modern Totalitarian Movements,* 2d ed. (New York, 1961) considers in detail the chiliastic expectations of such movements.

For the various late antique, medieval and Renaissance Christian "heretical" groups or sects suspected of libertinism and orgiastic practices, see the compendia arranged by Georges Welter, *Histoire des sectes chrétiennes* (Paris, 1950) and Martin Erbstosser, *Ketzer im Mittelalter* (Leipzig, Germany,1984).

More detailed investigations are provided by: Romana Guarnieri, *Il movimento del Libero Spirito* (Rome, 1965); R. E. Lerner, *The Heresy of the Free Spirit in the Later Middle Ages* (Berkeley and Los Angeles, 1972); Theodora Buttnwer and Ernst Werner, *Circumcellionen und Adamiten* (Berlin, 1959); Howard Kaminski, *A History of the Hussite Revolution* (Berkeley and Los Angeles, 1967); Alexander Patschovsky, "Chiliasmus und Reformation im ausgehenden Mittelalter," in *Ideologie und Herrschaft im Mittelalter,* edited by Max Kerner, pp. 475–496 (Darmstadt, Germany, 1982).

Denis de Rougemont, *L'amour et l'occident* (Paris, 1939) is an attractive—albeit not strictly scientific—monograph about transgressive and adulterous love during the Middle Ages. On the same theme and, more generally, about the Cathar views on sexuality see also Robert Nelli, *L'érotique des trobadours* (Paris, 1963) and *Le phénomène cathare* (Toulouse, France, 1964).

The great European witch hunt of the fifteenth, sixteenth, and seventeenth centuries has been the subject of numerous inquiries, which have been more and more increasing in the last decades. It is worth remembering here the well-known books by Margaret Murray, *The Witch-Cult in Western Europe* (Oxford, 1921; repr. 1962) and *The God of the Witches* (London, 1933); Arno Runenberg, *Witches, Demons and Fertility Magic* (Helsingfors, Finland, 1947) partially follows Murray's views. Shamanistic features in witchcraft are outlined by Elliot Rose, *A Razor for a Goat* (Toronto, 1962); Emmanuel Le Roy Ladurie, *Les paysans de Languedoc* (Paris, 1966; English transl. Urbana, Ill., 1976) reconsiders the "social" explanation of the phenomenon.

A well-documented inquiry is provided by Jeffrey Burton Russell, *Witchcraft in the Middle Ages* (Ithaca, N.Y., 1972) and Norman Cohn, *Europe's Inner Daemons* (New York, 1975), whose totally "negationist" views have, however, been questioned. See, for example, Carlo Ginzburg, *The Night Battles: Witchcraft and Agrarian Cults in the Sixteenth and Seventeenth Centuries* (New York, 1985); *Ecstasies: Deciphering the Witch's Sabbath* (New York, 1992), who partially reconsiders Murray's and Runenberg's arguments, even though without being convincing; see, for example, Giovanni Busino, "La microhistoire de Carlo Ginzburg," *Bibliothéque d'Humanisme et de Renaissance* 61 (1999): 763–778.

Among recent contributions see also: *Early Modern European Witchcraft: Centres and Peripheries,* edited by Bengt Ankarloo and Gustav Henningsen (Oxford, 1993); Lyndal Roper, *Oedipus and the Devil: Witchcraft, Sexuality and Religion in Early Modern Europe* (London and New York, 1994), which deals particularly with post-Reformation Germany; Stuart Clark, *Thinking with Demons: The Idea of Witchcraft in Early Modern Europe* (Oxford, 1997); and, most of all, Walter Stephens, *Demon Lovers: Witchcraft, Sex, and the Crisis of Belief* (Chicago, 2002).

An excellent monograph about Sabbatai Sevi is Gershom Scholem, *Sabbatai Sevi: The Mystical Messiah, 1626–1676* (Princeton, N.J., 1976); for the Frankist movement see Arthur Mandel, *The Militant Messiah or The Flight from the Ghetto: The Story of Jacob Frank and the Frankist Movement* (Atlantic Highlands, N.J., 1979), and Gershom Scholem, *Du frankisme au jacobinisme* (Paris, 1981). Sexual symbolism in the Qabbalah is well investigated (among others) by Moshe Idel, "Sexual Metaphors and Praxis in the Kabbalah," in *The Jewish Family: Metaphor and Memory,* edited by David Kraemer, pp. 197–224 (New York, 1989); and Franco Michelini Tocci, "Simboli di trasformazione cabalistici ed alchemici nell'Ēš Mesarēf con un excursus sul libertinismo gnostico," *Annali dell'Istituto Orientale di Napoli* 41 (1981): 41–81.

The best inquiry on the Khlysts still remains Karl Grass, *Die Russischen Sekten* (Leipzig, Germany, 1907–1909); see also René Fülöp Miller, *Der heilige Teufel Rasputin und die Frauen* (Berlin, 1927; English transl. New York, 1962), which deals with Rasputin's life.

On the utopian idea of group marriages as developed by Fourier see Frank E. Manuel and Fritzie P. Manuel, *Utopian Thought in the Western World* (Cambridge, Mass., 1979), as well as Roland Barthes, *Sade, Fourier, Loyola* (Paris, 1971; English translation by Richard Miller, New York, 1976); for American communities see Lawrence Foster, *Religion and Sexuality: The Shakers, the Mormons, and the Oneida Community* (Urbana, Ill., 1984); and *Free Love in Utopia: John Humphrey Noyes and the Origin of the Oneida Community* (Urbana, Ill., 2001).

For sexual magic and its developments see: Tim O'Neill, "The Erotic Freemasonry of Count Nicholas von Zinzendorf," in *Secret and Suppressed: Banned Ideas and Hidden History,* edited by Jim Keith, pp. 103–108 (Los Angeles, 1993); Marsha K. Schuchard, "Why Mrs. Blake Cried: Swedenborg, Blake and the Sexual Basis of Spiritual Vision," *Esoterica* 2 (2000): 45–93; John Patrick Deveney, *Paschal Beverly Randolph: A Nineteenth Century American Spiritualist, Rosicrucian and Sex Magician* (Albany, N.Y., 1997); Francis King, ed., *The Secret Rituals of the O.T.O.* (New York, 1973); Ronald Hutton, *Triumph of the Moon: A History of Modern Pagan Witchcraft* (Oxford, 2000); John Symonds, *The King of the Shadow Realm. Aleister Crowley: His Life and Magic* (London, 1989); Francis King, *The Magic World of Aleister Crowley* (London, 1987); Lawrence Sutin, *Do What Thou Wilt: A Life of Aleister Crowley* (New York, 2000). Important for the present subject is Hugh Urban, "Unleashing the Beast: Aleister Crowley,

Tantra and Sex Magic in Late Victorian England," *Esoterica* 5 (2003): 138–192.

Julius Evola, *Metafisica del sesso* (Rome, 1969; new edition with a foreword by Fausto Antonini, Rome, 1984; translated into English as *The Metaphysics of Sex* [New York, 1983]; or as *Eros and the Mysteries of Love* [Rochester, Vt., 1991]) is an interesting forerunner of modern sociological approaches to sexuality and orgiasm, such as those developed by Michel Maffesoli, *L'ombre de Dionysos, contribution à une sociologie de l'orgie* (Paris, 1982); see also Jean Baudrillard, *The Transparency of Evil: Essays on Extreme Phenomena* (New York, 1993). For Bataille's views on transgression, see his *Erotism: Death and Sensuality* (San Francisco, 1986); *Visions of Excess: Selected Writings, 1927–1939* (Minneapolis, Minn., 1985); and *The Unfinished System of Nonknowledge* (Minneapolis, Minn., 2001). See also Michel Foucault, *Histoire de la sexualité,* 3 vols. (Paris, 1976–1984; English transl. New York, 1978–1986).

CHIARA OMBRETTA TOMMASI (2005)

ORGY: ORGY IN ASIA

Western scholarship in the history of religions has taken the orgiastic rituals of the eastern Mediterranean (Dionysos, Cybele) as the ideal type of religious behavior manifesting as reckless bodily movements contributing to states of emotional excess, sometimes with the assistance of intoxicants. In the context of large-scale festivities, the force of these excesses sets aside the normal psychological restraints such that religious exaltation is obtained en masse through all types of sensual pleasure. This view enabled scholars and others to link such pre-Christian rites with transgressive behavior in western European history, especially witchcraft and heresy. Theories of "pagan survivals" were advanced to explain both the presence of pre-Christian elements in festivals of the church year and the periodic outbreaks of heresy and sorcery. The weaknesses of these theories of subterranean survival of paganism require some attention in order to avoid applying errors of method to festival-located orgiastic rituals in Asian cultures.

There is little archeological evidence to support the claim that the orgiastic rites of Cybele, Dionysos, the Maenads, or Priapus were handed down, even in mitigated form, from classical antiquity to the customs of medieval Christian pilgrimage sites. At best the evidence from folklore supports a continuity in which the survival, healing, and fertility concerns of human societies were addressed in festival rites at locations that continued to be venerated across the centuries. Rural customs involving magic, cursing, exorcism, and folk medicine were for many centuries associated with Christian saints and their shrines.

At the shrine of Saints Cosmas and Damian in Isernia, Italy, a supposed "phallic cult" (or "cult of Priapus") was thought to have survived from pagan antiquity, when in reality the rites deemed pre-Christian could just as easily have arisen in the context of medieval popular Catholicism. If anything it was the continuity of the site and its geography that carried forward in time the pre-Christian meaning. Cultural anthropologists have come to similar conclusions about South and Southeast Asian shrine festivals, where the village tradition addresses itself to survival, healing, and fertility in its own ritual idiom, even within the matrix of "great tradition" religiosity.

A CRITICAL EXAMINATION OF THE DEFINITION. In such societies the orgiastic ritual is lived as a positive aspect and not primarily as a way to fulfill instinctual drives. Most cultures indulge forms of transgression and release, such as recreational alcoholic consumption, raucous music, banquets, and prostitution. Orgiastic rituals, however, are not primarily recreational activities; they occupy a precise niche in societal expressions of religious emotion.

Transgressive collective behavior should be understood in terms of forms of conduct that are not done openly or outside particular times and places. The counterpoint to the orgy as unbridled collective transgression may be seen in a text from the Pali canon of early Buddhism. This Buddhist "Genesis" myth asserts that sexual relations arise when human karmic propensities undergo embodiment, density, and passion. The sexual act provokes reactions of revulsion and shame, and so the first cabins are constructed in order to conceal the act of coitus. (*Aggañña Sutta* 27; iii; 88–89.16–17: "Accordingly those who indulged in such immoral practices began to build themselves dwellings so as to indulge under cover.") The sexual act performed in the presence of others, whether active participants or spectators, is understood to be "transgressive" on a deep level of human experience. Lived as part of a larger continuum of human activity, however, the orgy effectively reflects the variegated character of human life itself. Such rites enable humans to transcend moral categories under certain circumstances so as to become protagonists in a cosmic drama. Thus human community, and not the individual or couple alone, can become an intentionally sacred representation of larger cosmic energies that require periodic renewal.

To this end human societies sanction periods of festival. Within the matrix of festival, the orgy has an initiatic character, because those who participate for the first time have to be informed in some way about the boundary between the quotidian or profane and the sacred; even the orgy has a sacred confine that encloses its secrets from the uninitiated or the unprepared. The orgy is not merely a ritual to be enacted at the will of the participants. Because a transgression of conventional norms is involved, there has to be a link between the orgiastic rite and the correct time and place. Festivals are calculated to fall on specific conjunctions of the cosmic markers of time. Only under the circumstances in which the human protagonists in a ritual are joined with the cosmic cycle of time can a rite renew the world by reenacting the creative events of primordial time, at the threshold between timelessness and time. Orgy cannot sanction anything without reference to the rightness of time and place, when the vital energies of the cosmos can be renewed. As a conscious, organized human ritual art form enacted during the time of festival, the orgy makes possible a return to the time of origins in which chaos prevailed. This was the time before the ordering principles of the cosmos began to operate so as to establish the social order, with gender distinctions, hierarchy, caste, and rulership. Both the profane interactions of the social order and the agricultural cycles on which human life depends are subject to decay and disharmony. Therefore a cycle of festivals in the course of the year periodically renews environment and society. Some festivals, though not all, have elements of sexuality, violence, role reversal, use of intoxicants, and frenzy.

In effect the orgy is a rite not of stasis and interiorization but of intensely energetic renewal. Orgiastic practices work with the play of energy in forms associated with dancing and singing gods and goddesses to whom the human protagonists are assimilated. Environments and human communities are reconstituted with particular emphasis on the blessings of sex and fertility. Orgiastic spirituality is in stark contrast to those contemplative practices that emphasize stillness, centeredness, silence, renunciation, solitude, and ascetic discipline. In the orgy extreme excess, ritual sacrifice of human beings, cannibalism, mutilation, transgender mimicry, sexual promiscuity, and even warfare can become forms perceived as vehicles of communal and cosmic renewal. Typically these extreme forms undergo mitigation in substitutionary enactments.

Nevertheless the use of drumming, extremely rhythmic music, dance, raucous songs, intoxicants, banqueting, and sexuality continue to have a place in a large number of festivals around the world, however routinized and mitigated they may have become across the span of time. These festivals engage the human body in the ritual play of infracosmic impulses. Often these forces are linked to the presence of the powerful Mother who embodies the earth as a source of vitality, and are intimately bound up with the experience of community and tradition. A community's capacity to renew itself is measured precisely by its obedience to the demands of instinct, with the understanding that instinct, in both the human body and the social body, has its own set of rules. Times of festival open up an anamnetic channel to primeval chaos that allows for the temporary redress of grievances rooted in inequalities of gender, race, and class. The cosmic antinomianism of the orgiastic festival turns all social relations upside down, exposing and assailing patterns of abuse.

Relationship to the "Great Traditions." The dynamic structure of the festival continues to prevail in South and Southeast Asian societies, where the religious meaning of space and time still retains many elements of archaic sensibility. Significant places are typically associated with holy men and women or supernatural beings of the great traditions. Festivals may be linked to events from Buddhist, Hindu, or Muslim history, legend, and mythology. The social coherence of the festival is, however, local in nature and only tenuously linked to the myth and symbol systems of the "great" formal religious traditions. For the vast majority of the population, Hindu and Buddhist textual and philosophical understandings have only tangential relationships to the lived realities of space, time, and other more immediate matters. Among these in particular are the physical environment within which they live, spatially differentiated in terms of its uses for habitation and agriculture, and the ongoing cycle of the year, also closely tied to the agricultural cycle on which human life, with its own rhythms, depends.

India. It is likely that ideas and practices of an orgiastic type are rooted in archaic sex rites magically associating natural and human fertility. These sex rites contributed widely to the development of religious ideas and to the evolution of human thought. In India archaic elements survived and were given new forms and interpretations over time with the larger evolutionary tendencies of the great traditions.

In general the original Vedic rituals made use of an intoxicant (*soma*), sexuality, and obscenity, as in the ritualized copulation in the *Brhadaranyaka Upaniṣads* account of the horse sacrifice. *Maithuna*, sexual union, is suggestive of the doctrine of nonduality between the human and the divine. In myth and ritual even adulterous love (*parakiya*) in Gauḍīya Vaiṣṇava theology came to symbolize the "illicit" and dangerous character of relations between the human soul (Rādhā) and the divine Lover (Kṛṣṇa). At times the valorization of adulterous and promiscuous union would have been enacted in the Bengali Sahajiya Tantric rituals. *Maithuna* is one of the "five m's" of left-hand path Tantra (*Vāmācāra*) in the Kaula Kapalika cults of Shaivism. Some Tantric groups may have advocated uncontrolled use of *maithuna* in ritual "orgies" as an extreme test of control and detachment. In these sectarian contexts the orgiastic festival is reconstructed along the lines of a transformative spiritual yoga or practice (*sādhana*).

Surviving orgiastic festivals in the village setting become a locus for the expression of feelings otherwise prohibited or formally repressed, above all by the caste system and by gender roles. These outbursts, occurring strictly during festival times, are sanctioned by gods such as Kālī or Kṛṣṇa. Their seasonal festivals, such as Holi, or the celebration of the goddess Bhadrakali's defeat of the demon Darika, allow transgressive behavior to become obligatory. There are strict and unpleasant "rules" involving danger, excess, sexuality, transvestism, use of intoxicants, and acts of violence.

The violent aspects of these manifestations might seem to correspond to the hormonal drives of adolescent males and to the sense of frustration and quotidian resentment on the part of married women. However, there is also a kind of ethical side to the violence: the oppressed and marginal categories of society identify and take a playful vengeance on those who normally have all the privileges and make use of them unjustly. In fact the attacks on ritual purity in these events is precisely a divinely sanctioned transgression meant to undermine, even if only for a day or so, the rules of caste, gender, and rituality, so that the true character of human relations might be revealed and vindicated.

Tibet. The ritual traditions of Tibet reflect an assimilation of Tantric deity cycles from India and China within the preexisting Bon worldview. After the first diffusion of the Indian Vajrayāna in Tibet in the eighth and ninth centuries, a period of experimentation ensued in which the orgiastic elements of the Sahajiyā cults were readily imported by a population eager to obtain the benefits of sorcery. A reaction set in during the early eleventh century, spreading as far as Central Tibet, with a consequent suppression not only of the sorcery cults but even of the strictly controlled sexual yogas of the "Path of Means" (*thabs lam*). Milarepa (c. 1052–1137) criticized these reforms, which had made the Tantric methods suspect. He recovered and taught the Path of Means, including the use of *karmamudra* (sexual yoga), as the best way to attain realization of Voidness. The yogin tradition in Tibet preserved many lineages that recognized in the figure of the *ḍākinīs* and other high-energy goddesses the same gendered transformational power that is encountered in shamanism and mediumism. The orgiastic elements were here, as elsewhere, mitigated in the form of festive ritual cycles or as yogic contemplative practices.

Thailand. The annual ritual cycle in Northeast Thai villages provides an obvious example of mitigated orgiastic rituality in the temporary ordination as Buddhist monks of a group of young men of the village each year during the rainy season retreat. The rite is part of a sequence that is related closely to the fertility of the rice fields on which the village depends. This rite also links closely to human fertility, as the explicitly phallic rockets of the rocket festival following the young men's ordination and the accompanying obscene songs make abundantly clear. In fact the period of temporary ordination is also explicitly seen as a preparation for marriage rather than as a commitment to the path of asceticism.

Central Asia. The typology described here corresponds to those elements of the ancient folk beliefs as they have survived in synthesis with Shīʿī Islamic spirituality. The typical practices of dervish Sufism, dancing (whirling) to produce a state of mind open to Divine Remembrance (*dhikr*) and singing "noisy" (*yahri*) mystical poetry, reflect this cultural synthesis. Dervish orders based on the Malamatiya tradition in Iran, in Kazakhistan, and along the Sino-Turkestan border disseminated the ideal of *qalandariya*, the classic wandering dervish, bearer of heterodox theology, whose nonconformist behavior not only repudiated conventional values but sought to subvert static models of spiritual attainment. The beloved Shams al-Tabrizi, who inspired the poetry of Jalāl al-Dīn Rūmī (1207–1273), was the archetype of *qalandariya*.

The extent to which any of the antinomian forms of Sufism could be considered "orgiastic" is debatable. It is true that homosexual activity, reflecting a concretization of the love poetry that reached its heights in writings of Hafiz in the Persian-Turkish cultural world, came to characterize the excesses of courtly life in Central Asia. This Ṣūfī-related trend penetrated as far as North India, always being characterized as somehow a "decadent" form of the devotional pattern of the *qalandariya* brotherhoods. However, in the case of Hafiz there seems to have been an underlying message that the spectrum from mysticism to the bacchanal can be used by the poet to demand a redress of grievances from society and from history. Specifically this would refer to the Iranian cultural resistance to Arabic dominance: the poetry expresses a humanistic vision in opposition to religious rigorism. Thus to take on the appearance of immorality or even to commit illicit acts such as wine drinking or sexual indulgence is tantamount to warding off the sin of pride in oneself and the exposure of arrogance in the false piety of others.

The literary tradition linked to the festival settings of Shīʿī Islam continued to have a place for such figures as late as the nineteenth century. The well-educated, though marginalized poet who likes to make *mullās* look ridiculous became something of a folk hero. Typically he pays inordinate attention to women and young men. This stock character is found in the folk theater tradition, in which the rogue poet (*rend*) shows himself undaunted by authority figures. Social and political criticism could thus be channeled through such characters of satire, farce, and allegory.

China. Primordial rites and festivals are preserved in the perennial syncretism typical of Chinese religion and rituality. Young women's role as shamanesses is a feature of the recognition of the feminine as a bearer of mysterious power going back to prehistory. Closely associated with their shamanic healing rituals are the phenomena of mediumism and possession. Daoist systems sought to channel these primordial elements into systems of sexual hygiene bearing fruit in bodily immortality. The cult of energy in Daoist healing arts is related to breath and sexual energy sometimes cultivated by union with multiple partners but is not typically expressed orgiastically. The body, its instincts, and the rules of instinctual behavior are seen as part of a cosmic synergy of phenomena.

However, the inevitable lure of uncontrollable energy in a tightly knit society finds a time of festivity in which to surface. The Cheung Chau Festival (Festival of the Bun Hills) begins on the eighth day of the fourth moon and lasts for four days. It is an atypical and at times dangerous celebration. Four days of religious rites, Chinese operas, and the burning of paper clothing as gifts are conducted to placate the spirits. Cities are absorbed in a party atmosphere, with processions and celebrations at every turn. Huge structures, typical of fertility rites elsewhere, are built. These towering mounds are covered with baked buns. The signal is given, and young people scramble up the towers, picking off as many buns, which symbolize good luck, as they can hold.

Japan. The role of shamanism is a background for most Japanese rituality. Shintō ritual preserves the primordial spirituality of Japan typically concerned with fertility. The island nation was originally a peasants' country, and each agricultural community had its own local religious celebrations (*matsuri*). Each festival was organized around the Shintō shrine or the local Buddhist temple in order to honor the deities. Festivals still take place all over the country, especially in summer. These folk events are high-energy manifestations of social cohesion through veneration of natural forces (*kami*).

Typically large teams of male youths play the role of bearers of power in festival processions with deity-palanquins (*mikoshi*), even though in some places priestesses continue to preside over the temple rites. The youths, who are plied liberally with sake, wear *happi*, short kimonos that come down to their waists, usually worn with T-shirts underneath and shorts but sometimes just with white loincloths. With a towel or bandana wrapped around the forehead, this is the perfect outfit for a *mikoshi* bearer or *taiko* drummer sweating in the heat of a summer festival in this unique expression of powerful male bonding. The young men who carry the *mikoshi* are not supposed to provide the *kami* with a smooth, fast ride. Instead, they sway in all directions and push the *mikoshi* up and down, often violently to amuse the *kami*. The movement of a *mikoshi* is considered to be directed by the will of the *kami* beyond the control of those shouldering it. In some *matsuri* festivals *mikoshi* of several shrines are brought together. In some others the *mikoshi* is carried into a river or sea to be washed. In other festivals *mikoshis* are brought into contests of one kind or another, often causing blood to be shed. The *kenka matsuri*, or fighting festival, involves violent ramming between competing *mikoshi* until one or another is destroyed.

Although the ancient "orgiastic" elements have been transformed, it is evident that extreme violence, the use of intoxicants, and the hint of sexuality remain in the *matsuri* tradition. In addition the event can bring about the same kinds of role reversals that allow for the correction of faults seen elsewhere. The symbolism of an entire community being "wrapped" in the embrace of the *kami* and its undulating procession is still in evidence. Moreover there is a sense of breaking out of the reserve that characterizes Japanese social behavior most of the year, so that criticisms that would otherwise remain unspoken can be offered in an endurable manner.

The Interplay between Aberration and Festival. The notion of the orgiastic ritual in Western studies of the history of religions is a function of constructions of East Mediterranean polytheism going back to Roman times. The sexual rites of archaic cultures can be seen as reviving agricultural fertility through the apotropaic magic of festival—most often taking the form of dance, rhythmic song, mime, and sexually referent poetry or gesture. Obscene gestures, erotic dancing, and sexually colored lyrics are part of festival and wedding rites in many places, especially in village and archaic cultures, but it is extremely rare to find group, frenzied sexual intercourse as part of a fertility rite or festival. Most cultures of Central Asia, China, Japan, Southeast Asia, and India find the notion of having sex in front of others to be utterly repugnant—an antisocial aberration. Even in the left-handed practices, the initiatic rite in which the guru has intercourse with a female partner in order to produce the male and female sexual fluids used in the rite of initiation, the practice is restricted and highly controlled. This rite was mitigated throughout the Himalayan cultural zone such that symbolic substances and objects replaced the actual coital act. The sexual practices here are yogic, not frenzied. The sexual yoga (*karmamudra*) of the songs of the *mahāsiddhas* are practiced by the partners in secret.

Maenad-type orgies, themselves literary products of the ancient writers who constructed the women of Thrace as "wild and out of control," should not too easily be read into Tantric rites, village festivals, Shintō processions, Daoist erotic therapies, and shamanic healing rituals. Communities celebrate fertility with songs, dances, gestures, costumes, and symbolic objects rather than with the act of coitus itself in any form.

The Failure of the Orgy. The risk of modern orgiastic conduct in the contemporary East Asian avant-garde is that it is transgression without festival in the full sense of the word and as such goes against the instinctual laws of the body. Even instincts have a certain discipline, as is evident in Tantric practice, in cannibalism, in sacrificial violence, and in warfare. Take away the necessary features of *communitas* and there is no festival at all. Take away the characteristics of festival and there is no sacredness. With the deconstruction of sacredness, all that remains is unbridled violence and malice. Libidinous excess brings on brutal dehumanization, not renewal of human and cosmic energies. In this way modern theatrical attempts at orgiastic ritual tend to be little more than a reflection of the soulless postmodern culture against which they purportedly rebel. The social matrix in which sacred time, space, and tradition could allow mitigated orgiastic rites to effect renewal is now being dismantled by the spread of ideological secularism. Invasive modernity constructs oppositions in the form of class, race, and gender conflict rather than complementarity. Deconstruction suppresses the prophetic voice that calls for redress and reconciliation, which was perhaps the most durable social value of the ancient rites.

See Also Tantrism.

Bibliography

Bataille, Georges. *L'Erotisme.* Paris, 1957. Translated as *Eroticism, Death, and Sensuality,* San Francisco, 1986.

Bhattacharyya, N. N. *History of the Tantric Religion.* 2d ed. New Delhi, 1999.

Caldwell, Sarah. *Oh Terrifying Mother: Sexuality, Violence, and Worship of the Goddess Kali.* Oxford, 1999.

Crawley, Ernest. *The Mystic Rose: A Study of Primitive Marriage and of Primitive Thought in Its Bearing on Marriage.* Revised and enlarged by Theodore Besterman. London, 1965. Much on sexual taboos.

Das Gupta, Shashibhusan. *Obscure Religious Cults.* Calcutta, India, 1976. Sahajiyās both Buddhist and Vaiṣṇava, Ṣūfī relations with the Bauls of Bengal.

Girard, René. *Violence and the Sacred.* Baltimore, 1979.

Kapferer, Bruce. *The Feast of the Sorcerer: Practices of Consciousness and Power.* Chicago, 1997. Analysis of violence, passion, and power in Sri Lanka.

Lewis, Franklin. "Hafez and Rendi." Available from www.iranica.com. A study of the demimonde of Hafez's poetry, weaving between social and religious critique and analyzing the nature of transgression in Ṣūfī sectarianism.

Marriott, McKim. "The Feast of Love." In *Krishna: Myths, Rites, and Attitudes,* edited by Milton B. Singer. Honolulu, 1966. A classic anthropological study of orgiastic behavior in North India during the Holi festival.

Samuel, Geoffrey. "The Religious Meaning of Space and Time: South and Southeast Asia and Modern Paganism." *International Review of Sociology* 11, no. 3 (2001): 395–418. Study of three sites in which ritual festivals have persisting elements of ancient fertility cults within the matrix of Hinduism, Buddhism, and Islam. Excellent insights into the role of festival and community.

Tiso, Francis. "Revisiting Pagan and Christian Syncretism: The Shrine of Saints Cosmas and Damian in Isernia." *Origins: Caiete Silvane* 6, nos. 3–4 (2003): 16–25. A study of the phallic cult at an Italian shrine with methodological observations and links with geography and festival customs.

White, David Gordon. *Kiss of the Yogini: Tantric Sex in Its South Asian Contexts.* Chicago, 2003. A key study of ritual sex and its links with magic in Hindu Tantric traditions.

FRANCIS V. TISO (2005)

ORIENTALISM.

Once associated with the exotic "Eastern" themes and styles of Eugene Delacroix's, James McNeill Whistler's, and John Singer Sargent's paintings; Victor Hugo's *Les Orientales*; and Gustave Flaubert's *Salammbô* (though related representations also can be found in subjects ranging from world fairs to such Hollywood films as *The Thief of Baghdad* and *Lawrence of Arabia*), the term *Orientalism* has come to denote a broader complex of discursive assumptions and institutional (especially academic) practices that regulate the understanding, appreciation, and domination of the West's—more precisely, Europe's—supposed "Other." In the study of religion, both from confessional dogmatic and secular comparatist perspectives, *Orientalism* evokes the tendency to mystify, caricature, homogenize, and petrify Asian and North African cultural systems, whether via idealization or via demonization, viewing them as contrasting to and often opposing such "Western" concepts as privatized and rationalized belief or the separation of church and state. Indeed, the modern definition and application of the concept "religion" as a universal category seems a first large step in the direction of Orientalism, as scholars such as Wilfred Cantwell Smith and Talal Asad have argued.

The work of Edward W. Said (1935–2003), especially his path-breaking *Orientalism* (2003), first published in 1978, initiated this shift in the meaning of the term. His *Orientalism* offers trenchant criticism of "Orientalist" scholarship and calls for a theoretical and interdisciplinary rearrangement of knowledge in relation to questions of power and empire that would seek not a new field of research but more integrated and self-reflective approaches in the scholarly study of the global South and East. Subsequent postcolonial, subaltern, and, more broadly, cultural studies, all of which attempt to shed light on increasingly manifold forms of multicultural identities, have greatly benefited from his work. Said himself, however, retained an allegiance to his early literary training in close reading and philology (a training evident in his scrupulous and detailed analyses), and he was at times, as in *Humanism and Democratic Criticism* (2004), somewhat dismissive of "contemporary critics who prefer what is implicit to what the text actually says" (p. 88).

Said's definition of the term *Orientalism* has multiple facets. In his book *Orientalism* he seeks to present and interpret it "as a historical phenomenon, a way of thought, a contemporary problem, and a material reality" (p. 44). In part, this complexity results from his historical insight into the "Orient" as "that semi-mythical construct which since Napoleon's invasion of Egypt in the late eighteenth century has been made and re-made countless times by power acting through an expedient form of knowledge" (p. xiii); in part, it hinges on his conviction that the "sometimes sympathetic but always dominating scrutiny" (p. 57) directed toward things "oriental" entails, not just an economy and an anthropology, but an entire epistemology and ontology, whose axioms and protracted effects must be uncovered by a patient "genealogy."

Although European characterizations of the Orient date back to the Athenian plays of Aeschylus (*The Persians*) and Euripides (*The Bacchae*), and the exploration and exploitation of its central tropes can already be traced in Herodotus and Alexander the Great, Said dates the fateful, as it were official, beginnings of the hegemonic regulation and objectification of this geographical referent and its accompanying imagry much later. Greece and Rome had conceptions of the "primitive," as Arthur O. Lovejoy and George Boas document in their classic *Primitivism and Related Ideas in Antiquity* (1935 [1997]), but only in the Christian Middle Ages did Orientalism find its first expression as "a field of learned study." In *Orientalism* Said writes: "In the Christian West, Orientalism is considered to have commenced its formal existence with the decision of the Church Council of Vienna in 1312 to establish a series of chairs in 'Arabic, Greek, Hebrew, and Syriac at Paris, Oxford, Bologna, Avignon, and Salamanca'" (pp. 49–50, quoting Southern, *Western Views of Islam in the Middle Ages*). These chairs were not exactly disinterested, given that the suggestion came from Raymond Lull, who recommended the study of Arabic out of zeal to use it as a tool in converting Muslims and refuting Arabic philosophy. But such instrumentalization was always counterbalanced by an ambiguous fascination, so that "between the Middle Ages and the eighteenth century such major authors as Ariosto, Milton, Marlowe, Tasso, Shakespeare, Cervantes, and the authors of the Chanson de Roland and the Poema del Cid drew on the Orient's riches for their productions, in ways that sharpened the outlines of imagery, ideas, and figures populating it" (p. 63). Said cites "the Sphinx, Cleopatra, Eden, Troy, Sodom and Gomorrah, Astarte, Isis and Osiris, Sheba, Babylon, the Genii, the Magi" (p. 63), but other examples of the lure of the "exotic" are legion.

In the central pages of *Orientalism* Said traces the academic establishment of the field from the late eighteenth century onward, focusing especially on the insinuation of power into even the most recondite fields and its imbrication in their constitution. Key representatives in this development are Johann David Michaelis and Friedrich Schlegel in eighteenth- and nineteenth-century Germany, Ernest Renan and Louis Massignon in nineteenth- and twentieth-century France, and C. Snouck Hurgronje in the twentieth-century Netherlands. In their very different approaches to the biblical text, the "wisdom of India," the figure of Jesus, and the mystical elements in Islam, these scholars all seemed to agree on "the linguistic importance of the Orient to Europe," as well as on the "unchanging, uniform, and radically peculiar" nature of the Orient as an "object" whose golden age was steadily projected into a bygone past and whose present was therefore historically tied to a "latent inferiority" (pp. 98, 209).

Preoccupation with the Orient led to the founding of many learned and trading societies, just as perceived interest in safeguarding a seemingly undivided Christian West motivated the establishment of explicitly missionary organizations such as the Society for Promoting Christian Knowledge (founded in 1698), the Society for the Propagation of the Gospel in Foreign Parts (1701), the Baptist Missionary Society (1792), the Church Missionary Society (1799), the British and Foreign Bible Society (1804), and many others. The institutional embedding of "Orientalism" was thus also—if not first and foremost—religiously or theologically-politically inflected. The genealogy of "Orientalism" Said proposes needs to unravel this connection.

Said's analysis is based upon a certain conception of humanism and humanistic studies, however, and therefore on the opposition between "secular criticism" and "religious criticism," a distinction introduced in *Orientalism* and elaborated in his later *The Word, the Text, and the Critic* (1983) and *Humanism and Democratic Criticism* (2003). In the preface to the twenty-fifth-anniversary edition of *Orientalism,* he asserts that there is "a profound difference between the will to understand for purposes of coexistence and humanistic enlargement of horizons, and the will to dominate for the purposes of control and external dominion" (p. xix), a claim juxtaposed to his ambition to "use humanistic critique to open up the fields of struggle" (p. xxii). Can his appeal to "worldly secular discourse" and to the "secular world" as "the world of history as made by human beings" (p. xxix) admit a nuanced assessment of the role of religion in his narrative? An attempt to answer this question yields two conflicting elements.

On the one hand, Said's analysis undoes certain preconceptions in the study of Islam, especially concerning Islam's relation to modern notions of private faith, religious experience, violence, and democracy. Stressing the many communities of interpretation and the need to differentiate between historical periods, geographical locations, and individual thinkers, he insists on the importance of avoiding generalizations and stereotypes, including where "religion" is at issue.

On the other hand, Said's project remains based on an unapologetic "'residual' humanism" (p. 339), which sees in religion, even in its broadest and richest definition, stripped of its narrow Protestant and Enlightenment association with a privately held faith, a limited and far from perennial constituent in the psychic and social dimensions of power and knowledge. As Said notes in *The World, the Text, and the Critic* (1983), religion, in this view, is "an agent of closure, shutting off human investigation, criticism, and effort in deference to the authority of the more-than-human, the supernatural, the other-worldly" (p. 290). One can understand Said's reluctance to give in to the "contemporary Manichean theologizing of the 'Other'" (p. 291), but here, in fact, may lie the greatest weakness of his overall project: the suggestion in *Culture and Imperialism* (1993) that all "'returns' to culture and tradition" go hand in hand with intellectual and moral codes that undercut "such relatively liberal philosophies as multiculturalism" and in decolonized countries lead largely to "varieties of religious and nationalist fundamentalism" (p. xiii). Although he seems aware of the historical, geopolitical, and imaginative role of "public religion" (the expression is from José Casanova in *Public Religions in the Modern World* [1994]) in the transition from secular nationalism to different formations of political Islam, well beyond his general observations in *Orientalism* that "what appears in the West to be the emergence, return to, or resurgence of Islam is in fact a struggle in Islamic societies over the definition of Islam," and that no "one person, authority, or institution has total control over that definition" (p. 332), Said apparently does not count "religion"—or the theologico-political—as a potentially emancipatory or empowering, let alone democratizing and humanizing force per se. The remarkable "return to religion" reinforced and refracted by the complicated economic and cultural processes of globalization and driven by the newest technological media therefore poses an anomaly that his overall historical and cultural analysis has difficulty in assessing. In *Humanism and Democratic Criticism* (2003) he speaks of religion mostly in terms of "religious enthusiasm," which he considers "perhaps the most dangerous of threats to the humanistic enterprise, since it is patently antisecular and antidemocratic in nature, and, in its monotheistic forms as a kind of politics, is by definition about as intolerantly inhumane and downright unarguable as can be" (p. 51). In Said's account, Christian, Jewish, Islamic, and Hindu fundamentalism are not fundamentally different in this respect.

This being said, the premises and arguments of Said's project nonetheless provide a model for analyzing processes of religious conflict and dialogue, missionary expansion and ecumenical cooperation, proselytizing and conversion, apologetics and the self-explication of faith seeking understanding in confrontation with different epochs, locations, and cultures.

In *Orientalism* Said leaves no doubt that the critique of Orientalism should not be confused with "anti-Westernism" (pp. 330, 334). He distances himself from the claim, imputed to Orientalism, that the historical phenomenon of Orientalism is "a synecdoche, or miniature symbol, of the entire West, and indeed ought to be taken to represent the West as whole" (pp. 330–331). On the contrary, Said emphasizes repeatedly that he "has no 'real' Orient to argue for," which is a way of saying that "neither the term *Orient* nor the concept of the West has any ontological stability," each being "made up of human effort, partly affirmation, partly identification of the Other," and also that "words such as 'Orient' and 'Occident' correspond to no stable reality that exists as a natural fact," meaning that "all such geographical designations are an odd combination of the empirical and the imaginative" (p. 331). Ultimately, Orientalism and its related studies thus seek to effect a process of *unlearning* (a term from Raymond Williams, *Culture and Society*, 1780–1950 [New York, 1958]) in which—at least the dominant mode of interpreting—the "Orient" and the "Occident" will be eliminated altogether (p. 28). Yet Said leaves no doubt that in this and similar relationships of opposition, polarity, and mirroring, "the development and maintenance of every culture require the existence of another, different and competing alter ego. The construction of identity . . . involves the construction of opposites and 'others' whose actuality is always subject to the continuous interpretation and reinterpretation of their differences from 'us'" (p. 332).

Indeed, Said writes, "even the primitive community we belong to natally is not immune from the interpretive contest," and the constructed "others" upon which the construction of identity depends may be "outsiders and refugees, or apostates and infidels" (p. 332). All others are not created equal, however. Orientalism and Hellenism are crucially different, for example: "The former is an attempt to describe a whole region of the world as an accompaniment to that region's colonial conquest, the latter is not at all about the direct colonial conquest of Greece in the nineteenth and twentieth centuries; in addition, Orientalism expresses antipathy to Islam, Hellenism sympathy for classical Greece" (p. 342).

Said points out in *Culture and Imperialism*, however, that the relationship between European expansion and the non-West was never merely unilateral: "there was always some form of active resistance [armed or cultural], and in the overwhelming majority of cases, the resistance finally won out" (p. xii). Such a conclusion defies the modern understanding of *identities* and requires, in the historiography of *Orientalism* and *empire*, an approach that is no longer "linear and subsuming," but "contrapuntal and often nomadic," not least because "all cultures are involved in one another; none is single and pure, all are hybrid, heterogenous, extraordinarily differentiated, and unmonolithic" (p. xxv).

Said's work has been taken to task by critics, notably Bernard Lewis in his *Islam and the West*, as lacking in nuance and attacking scholarship that can claim more disinterest than Said allows. Others have pointed out that some Orientalists were themselves active opponents of colonialism and imperialism (and not just in the name of an idealized "Orient"), and that non-Western nationalists were, in turn, inspired by Western "Orientalist" writings or adopted the caricatures of themselves as "Other." Still other critics have decried Said's political engagement, since 1967, in the Palestinian cause for national self-determination (as he himself notes in *Orientalism*, "with full attention paid to the reality of the Jewish people and what they suffered by way of persecution and genocide" [p. xxiii]).

Yet Said views the psychological, ideological, and social complex of "Orientalism" as the counterpart and "secret sharer of Western anti-Semitism" (p. 27). As in the writings of the early Frankfurt School, notably "Elements of Anti-Semitism" in Max Horkheimer and Theodor W. Adorno's classic *Dialectic of Enlightenment*, the analysis of "Orientalism" details a historically and culturally determined structure and comportment of prejudice ultimately based upon a mechanism of projection. Depictions of Islam that start from analogy to Christian premises—namely, that "Mohammed was to Islam as Christ was to Christianity" (p. 60)—then proceed to erroneous and pejorative characterizations of Islam as "Mohammedanism" and of Muḥammed as an "impostor" are just one example of how the imaginary geography of Orientalism transposes a never-ending list of qualifications onto a supposedly amorphous "Other" whose contours and meaning, let alone intentions and self-interpretations, seem all but irrelevant: "the Orient acquired representatives . . . and representations, each one more concrete, more internally congruent with some Western exigency, than the ones that preceded it. It is as if, having once settled on the Orient as a locale suitable for incarnating the infinite in a finite shape, Europe could not stop the practice; the Orient and the Oriental, Arab, Islamic, Indian, Chinese, or whatever, become repetitious pseudo-incarnations of some great original (Christ, Europe, the West), they were supposed to have been imitating" (p. 62).

Although in their accounts of primitive myth, magic, and shamanism the neo-Marxists of the Frankfurt School's first generation continued the Orientalist blind spots Said identifies in Marx's own 1848 *The Eighteenth Brumaire of Louis Bonaparte* and 1853 articles on British rule in India (as did, after them, Jürgen Habermas in adopting Max Weber's acceptance of European exceptionalism vis-à-vis China into

Theory of Communicative Action), one of Horkheimer and Adorno's insights is important here. They knew well that where imitation fails (and it necessarily does), discriminatory judgment and ultimately persecution must result.

By contrast, Said offers a non-Marxist critique of power and knowledge based on the heterodox ideas of Antonio Gramsci's *Prison Notebooks*, notably his concept of "hegemony," and on the concept of "discursive formation" from Michel Foucault's *The Archeology of Knowledge* and *Discipline and Punish*. Although, as discursive formation, Orientalism could be seen as a "system for citing works and authors," Said in *Orientalism* corrects Foucault in order to recognize "the determining imprint of individual writers upon the otherwise collective body of texts" (p. 23), the way they count for something in the constitution of its power.

Since the publication of *Orientalism*, scholars have pursued its line of thought in many different geographical and imaginative contexts. Said's own *Culture and Imperialism* broadens his earlier perspective by including critical studies on "a more general pattern of relationships between the modern metropolitan West and its overseas territories" (p. xi), such as Africa, the Caribbean, and Australia, whereas other scholars have focused on the construction of identity in the Western approach to the "religions of the East," whether on the Indian subcontinent or in Southeast Asia, China, and Japan. Thus, the volume *Orientalism and the Postcolonial Predicament: Perspectives on South Asia* (1993), edited by Carol E. Breckenridge and Peter van der Veer, explores the ways in which colonial administrators constructed knowledge about the society and culture of India and the processes through which that knowledge has shaped past and current perceptions of Indian reality. These and other contributions to "modern cultural theory" would seem to confirm Said's view, expressed in his 1994 afterword to *Orientalism*, that "cultures are hybrid and heterogenous and . . . that cultures and civilizations are so interrelated and interdependent as to beggar any unitary or simply delineated description of their individuality" (p. 347).

More recently, the discussion around Orientalism has been shadowed by a parallel consideration of "Occidentalism," as if to challenge Said's claim that "no one is likely to imagine a field symmetrical to [Orientalism] called Occidentalism" (p. 50). In *Occidentalism* (2004) Ian Buruma and Avishai Margalit describe Occidentalism as the "Orientalist view upside down" (p. 10) and hence as the "dehumanizing picture of the West painted by its enemies," directed at the scientific and secular worldview, global capitalism, sexual liberties, pop culture, and a "cluster of prejudices" whose "historical roots," they argue, lie in Europe and its Enlightenment (p. 5). This "hateful caricature" of Western modernity in terms of a mechanical or "machine civilization" is contrasted by Occidentalists to a (lost) ideal of organic and totalizing spirituality (pp. 6, 7).

In contrast to the hardening of opposites in Occidentalism, the true legacy of the Orientalism discussion will surely lie not only in a far more complex understanding of cultural interrelation but in unsettling the categories of Orient and Occident themselves. French phenomenologist Emmanuel Levinas has likewise come, via a different, philosophical route, to the conclusion that the categories of the West and the non-West should be demythologized, indeed, deontologized. He repeatedly claims that Western metaphysics, which he associates with Greece and especially Athens, has fallen prey to a disorientation (désorientation), a certain forgetfulness or faithlessness with respect to what one might term its *Oriental Other* (or at least one of them): the monotheistic tradition of the Bible and Jerusalem.

Setting Levinas alongside Said highlights a weakness in the former, namely, that an all too abstract conception of the Orient tends to elide precisely the Arab populations Said, in his writings and his life, worked tirelessly to advocate. Yet in Levinas's view Greek thought has rightly destroyed the idolatrous and primitivist yearning for participation in diffuse, irrational totalities (of nature, people, collective sentiment). Moreover, Levinas's recognition of an intrinsic instability in both the truths of philosophical reason and the revelation of religious tradition can give us a new perspective on the significance of Orientalism. In critical opposition to both Lévy-Bruhl's *Primitive Mentality* and Lévi-Strauss's *The Savage Mind*, Levinas insists that Europeanization—the philosophical project of Western modernity—and de-Europeanization, including decolonialization and the critique of imperialism, go hand-in-hand. The deconstruction of Europe's investment in knowing and dominating a constructed Other itself relies on eminently European notions of rational discourse, scriptural learning, and hermeneutic sensibility. But to say that all passes through "the West," Levinas knows, is not the same as to claim that everything originates—or ends—there.

Said's *Orientalism*, informed by its author's commitment to European humanism and his training in the field of comparative literature, with roots in late eighteenth and early nineteenth-century Germany and especially philology, is an excellent example of the de-Europeanization for which Levinas calls. Moreover, Europe's Orient, as Said points out in *Orientalism*, is a reminder that constructions and projections of the Other may not be so distant from the self after all: historically, "the Orient is not only adjacent to Europe," not only its "cultural contestant," but also "the source of its civilizations and languages" (p. 1)—and, we might add, of what historically have been its dominant religions.

Bibliography

The texts by Said discussed are: *Orientalism* (New York, 1978; all page references are to the twenty-fifth-anniversary edition of 2003); *The World, the Text, and the Critic* (Cambridge, Mass., 1984); *Culture and Imperialism* (New York, 1993); and *Humanism and Democratic Criticism* (New York, 2004). A large body of literature has been produced in response to or inspired by *Orientalism*. See especially: Nicholas B. Dirks, ed., *Colonialism and Culture* (Ann Arbor, Mich., 1992);

Carol E. Breckenridge and Peter van der Veer, eds., *Orientalism and the Postcolonial Predicament: Perspectives on South Asia* (Philadelphia, 1993); Dipesh Chakrabarty, *Provincializing Europe* (Princeton, N.J., 2000); and a volume published on the occasion of the twenty-fifth anniversary of the publication of *Orientalism*, Inge E. Boer, ed., *After Orientalism: Critical Entanglements, Productive Looks* (Amsterdam, 2004). On the question of religion, see: Wilfred Cantwell Smith, *The Meaning and End of Religion* (New York, 1962); Talal Asad, *Genealogies of Religion: Discipline and Reasons of Power in Christianity and Islam* (London, 1993); Richard King, *Orientalism and Religion: Postcolonial Theory, India, and the "Mystic East"* (London, 1999); William D. Hart, *Edward Said and the Religious Effects of Culture* (Cambridge, U.K., 2000); and José Casanova, *Public Religions in the Modern World* (Chicago, 1994). For eighteenth- and nineteenth-century examples of Orientalist biblical scholarship, see: Jonathan M. Hess, "Johann David Michaelis and the Colonial Imaginary: Orientalism and the Emergence of Racial Antisemitism in Eighteenth-Century Germany," *Jewish Social Studies* 6, no. 2 (2000): 56–101; and Halvor Moxness, "Renan's Vie de Jesus as Representation of the Orient," in *Jews, Antiquity, and the Nineteenth-Century Imagination*, edited by Hayim Lapin and Dale B. Martin, pp. 85–108 (Bethesda, Md., 2003). On the representation of Islam, see R. W. Southern, *Western Views of Islam in the Middle Ages* (Cambridge, Mass., 1962) and Edmund Burke III, "Orientalism and World History: Representing Middle Eastern Nationalism and Islamism in the Twentieth Century," *Theory and Society* 27, no. 4 (August 1998): 589–607. On what could be called Orientalism's predecessor concept, primitivism, see Arthur O. Lovejoy and George Boas, *Primitivism and Related Ideas in Antiquity*, with supplementary essays by W. F. Albright and P.-E. Dumont (Baltimore, 1935; reprint 1997). On the relationship between Marxism and Orientalism, see Karl August Wittfogel's *Oriental Despotism: A Comparative Study of Total Power* (New York, 1981), which attempted to do for non-Western societies, notably China, what Marx and Engels had done for Europe. Marx had used this terminology in 1853 in his articles on British rule in India. See also Raymond Williams, *Culture and Society 1780–1950* (London, 1958). On Orientalism's parallel concept, "Occidentalism," see Ian Buruma and Avishai Margalit, *Occidentalism: The West in the Eyes of Its Enemies* (New York, 2004) and Xiaomei Chen, *Occidentalism: A Theory of Counter-Discourse in Post-Mao China* (New York, 1995). On Kant and the religious construction of identity and ethnicity, see Hent de Vries, *Religion and Violence: Philosophical Perspectives from Kant to Derrida* (Baltimore, 2002). Emmanuel Levinas's most representative writings on the question of Europe and the West are *Difficile liberté: Essais sur le judaïsme* (Paris, 1976), translated as *Difficult Freedom* (Baltimore, 1990), and *Totalité et infini: Essai sur l'extériorité* (the Hague, 1961), translated as *Totality and Infinity* (Pittsburgh, 1969). On the question of globalization and the technological media, see Hent de Vries and Samuel Weber, eds., *Religion and Media* (Stanford, Calif., 2001).

HENT DE VRIES (2005)

ORIENTATION.

ORIENTATION. Symbols of space and its order most clearly illustrate the religious act of orientation, that is, the fundamental process of situating human life in the world. Orientation is the conscious act of defining and assuming proper position in space. Fixing the human place in existence in a significant way is a religious act when it orients a human being toward the sacred. This fundamental disposition toward the sacred extends its significance from the points of orientation to all individual and social acts, as well as to all cosmic structures. In relation to the sacred, inhabited space and history become apprehensible. Various kinds of human living spaces define their order and meaning in relation to the sacred: the cosmos, the city, the village or residence space, the house, and the individual. They are described together with those manifestations of the sacred toward which they are oriented.

SYMBOLIC FORMS. The technology of calculation and measurement used in orientation would make an interesting and controversial study in the history of science. It would include treatment of geomancy, astronomic calculation, use of the gnomon, the astrolabe, and the plumb line, canons of measure derived from human body measurements, and determinations of magnetic north, among other techniques. However, this article's purpose is limited to the religious meaning of the act of orientation and a description of the sacred nature of the points toward which the human situation is aligned. Because orientation involves relating an entity to a reality other than itself, it always entails a conjunction of beings and, in this sense, creates a center where all realities meet.

According to Latin historians, Romulus founded the city of Rome by drawing a circular furrow around the Palatine hill with a plow. The trench around which the furrow was cut, and toward which it was oriented, was called the *mundus* ("world"), the same name applied to the universe. The *mundus* was a pit, an opening between the earthly world and the underworld. For the living it provided a link not only with the sphere of the dead but also with the celestial sphere, for the outline plan (*limitatio*) of the city, especially its division into four quarters, was based on a model of heavenly origin. The *mundus* itself, being a detailed image of the cosmos, was divided into quadrants. Rome was habitable because the city was built in the image of the cosmos—according to a heavenly model of the universe—around a life-giving center, a navel of the world, which permitted contact with all realms of being.

The universe itself possesses a place where communication among all cosmic realms is possible. It is to this center of the world that all other meaningful structures in the cosmos are directed and from which they derive. For the religious life of Indians in the Qollahuaya region of the central Andes, Mount Kaata is the sacred center of all reality. Everything that is whole, whether it be the microcosm of the human body or the universe itself, may be identified with it. Indeed, all integrity derives from it. An individual's life cycle begins when a person's soul emerges from the highland springs; continues while it descends to its burial place at the mountain's foot; and prepares for recycling as it reascends the interior of the mountain along inner waterways, after death. This contemporary belief continues an older idea found in the Huarochiri manuscript, a sixteenth-century Quechua text that reports that Kuntur Qutu, the Mountain of the Condor, stands at the center of the world and at the center of *tahuantinsuyo,* the four quarters of the Inca world. All significant powers, both cosmic and divine, find their place and carry on their powerful processes on this mountain. The cosmic mountain, marking a center from which all creative life in the universe takes its bearings, is a widespread religious theme found throughout the histories of Europe, Asia, the Near East, Oceania, and the Americas.

For the Ngaju Dayak of southern Borneo the universe is centered on the tree of life, of which the inhabited world is only a small part; for the tree encompasses all existence, the totality of being, and the godhead itself. It also includes every possible period of time. As a result, all ceremonies of transition (birth, marriage, initiation, death) center on the tree of life. This allows the human being to return to the period of divine creativity, so that he or she may issue once again from the tree of life as a new creature.

The temple often extends the same symbolism of the sacred mountain toward which life is oriented. For instance, the Mesopotamian ziggurat was explicitly likened to the cosmic mountain. Its seven levels symbolized the number of heavens. The goddess Ningal promised the divinity Nanna that, when he had filled the rivers with waters and brought life to the fields, forests, and marshes, she would join him in his ziggurat in Ur: "In your house on high . . . in your cedar-perfumed mountain, I will come to live."

All of these images of the center toward which reality is oriented call attention, at one and the same time, to the vertical plane of the universe. In short, the world is oriented not only toward the center on a horizontal plane but to the heights of the heavens. This connecting point of heaven and earth may be envisaged as a sacred ladder, rope, liana, or bridge. In the Northern Hemisphere, the North Star becomes a crucial indicator of the center of heaven. Directly below it is oriented the sacred center of the world, where celestial and terrestrial powers join together. In the Southern Hemisphere, the Milky Way at its zenith often pinpoints the center of heaven. In Mismanay, near Cuzco in Peru, for example, the Milky Way is seen as an immense river of semen that, when it is in its zenith, runs through the center of the sky. Mismanay is sited directly below the center of the heavens. It is bisected by the Vilcanota River, the earthly counterpart of the fertilizing river of stars in the heavens. From the center one is able to determine the four points where the sun rises and sets during the solstices. Using the center of the sky marked by the Milky Way at its zenith, the people of Mismanay are able to situate themselves at the center of an organized space and ordered cycle of time. All spaces and life cycles (of humans, animals, rainbows, and supernatural beings) derive their creativity from and relate to one another through the center.

Two important ways of orienting oneself in space bear close relationship to the act of creation, as it is conceived by a culture to have taken place. In the first instance, the center has prestige as a key position for orientation because it is the first place, the place of origin of life. It is the *omphalos,* or navel, around which life takes shape. A second mode of orientation involves sacrifice to consecrate a sacred place. It draws attention to the fact that, at the beginning of time, a primordial being was sacrificed and dismembered. From its parts derives the ordered integrity of the cosmos. In this sacrificial cosmogony, orientation in the universe derives from the very structure of a primordial body, ritually positioned in space. The universe, then, has the same set of relations among its parts as does the human body when consciously shaped in the deliberate acts of ritual. In either case, the points of orientation draw their prestige from their association with creation.

Taking their cue from the structures of the universe as they were created, other entities are located in space and time with reference to the same manifestations of sacred power; that is, following the cosmic model. The village often becomes a small image of the ordered space of the universe, and the same is true even for a house. The Na-Khi, a Tibeto-Burman people living in the upper reaches of the Yangtze River valley of northwestern Yunnan Province in China, perform most of their important rituals at the center of the universe in their homes, which are purified and transformed into the image of Ngyu-na shi-lo ngyu, the cosmic mountain (Mount Kailāśa), by the installation of sacred ritual objects in the house (Jackson, 1979, pp. 113ff., 209). In order that the ritual objects be effective, they are empowered by means of lengthy chanting of their myths of origin.

Planners of cities aligned them to sacred forces, which filled them and made them habitable. In ancient China, at the moment when a sacred city was founded, the king was beseeched to come and "assume responsibility for the work of God on High and himself serve . . . at the center of the land . . . and from there govern as the central pivot" (Wheatley, 1971, p. 430).

The capital and the king became the points from which direction and sacrality emanated throughout the entire kingdom. The power of creation passed out through the city gates to the four quarters and the cycles of time.

Orientation is also a way in which the individual personality becomes aware of the objective in relation to the self. The Ñandeva, a Guaraní group of southern Brazil, picture the human soul as a carefully oriented spatial entity. The soul is composed of three shadows (*nane'a,* "our shadow") that are all oriented on a vertical plane toward the heavens, the source of light that brings them into existence. All the faculties of human intelligence and action are accounted for by the soul's orientation in space. *Ayvú-kué-poravé* ("the good word that we speak") is the shadow that falls directly in front of or directly behind the personality. This central shadow-soul is of divine origin and returns to its celestial source after death. The second shadow-soul is the *atsy-yguá,* the carnal essence of life, which humans share with animals. It is cast to the left of a person. To the right falls the shadow known as the *ayvú-kué* ("the word that sprouts"), which accompanies and obeys the central *ayvú-kué-poravé* (M. A. Bartolomé, 1979, pp. 111–112). The personality is oriented to the center of the celestial realm, the source of light that brings the shadow elements of the person into existence. It is this orientation to another realm of being that enables a truly human consciousness to come into proper existence.

ORIENTATION AND HUMAN CONSCIOUSNESS. All of the entities in the above illustrations are oriented to and, paradoxically, derive their meaning from modes of being other than their own. The various forms of orientation to sacred reality highlight the human desire to inhabit a sacred world, a world as it was created in the beginning, new and powerful.

The kind of orientation situates human living space in meaningful relation to the beings around it. It requires a grasp of the total human situation, a sense of the whole of existence at all its levels. This fundamental stance toward being constitutes a consciousness able to distinguish and evaluate supernatural modes of being for what they are. Orientation effects what it symbolizes: the proper relation of the human situation to the very ground of being within which human life finds itself. For this reason orientation—taking one's place in the world—is conceived of in many religious traditions as the first act of fully human beings living in habitable space. By symbolically assuming one's proper position in the world, one communicates with significant powers at work in the cosmos and gains a sense of one's unique significance in relation to all else.

SEE ALSO Center of the World; Cities; Geography; Geomancy; Home; Human Body, article on Myths and Symbolism; Mountains; Sacred Space; Trees.

BIBLIOGRAPHY

The constancy of the symbolic complex of the mountain is presented in Joseph W. Bastien's *Mountain of the Condor: Metaphor and Ritual in an Andean Ayllu* (Saint Paul, Minn., 1978). Other studies of orientation in the Andes may be found in R. Tom Zuidema's *The Ceque System of Cuzco: The Social Organization of the Capital of the Inca* (Leiden, 1962) and "The Inca Calendar," in *Native American Astronomy,* edited by Anthony F. Aveni (Austin, Tex. 1977), pp. 219–259, as well as in Gary Urton's *At the Crossroads of the Earth and Sky: An Andean Cosmology* (Austin, Tex., 1981), which discuss the techniques and meanings assigned to orientation in the Andes in both rural and urban settings throughout history. Anthony Jackson's *Na-khi Religion: An Analytical Appraisal of Na-khi Ritual Texts* (The Hague, 1979) illustrates clearly the way in which the house may serve as a point of cosmic orientation when ritually linked to the acts of creation. The orientation of the individual is described in Miguel Alberto Bartolomé's "Shamanism among the Avá-Chiripá," in *Spirits, Shamans, and Stars: Perspectives from South America,* edited by David L. Browman and Ronald A. Schwarz (The Hague, 1979), pp. 95–148. Paul Wheatley's *The Pivot of the Four Quarters: A Preliminary Enquiry into the Origins and Character of the Ancient Chinese City* (Chicago, 1971) is a singularly important work for understanding both the methods and meaning of orientation not only in China but around the world. Also helpful in this respect is I-fu Tuan's *Topophilia: A Study of Environmental Perception, Attitudes, and Values* (Englewood Cliffs, N.J., 1974). Mircea Eliade addresses the question of the religious meaning of orientation in *The Sacred and the Profane: The Nature of Religion* (New York, 1959), esp. pp. 32ff. and 79ff. Heinrich Nissen's *Orientation: Studien zur Geschichte der Religion,* 3 vols. (Berlin, 1906–1910), remains a valuable resource of materials. Still stimulating is Ludwig Deubner's "Mundus," *Hermes* 68 (1933): 276–287. Further bibliography and portrayal of more recent approaches to the question may be found in Joseph Rykwert's *On Adam's House in Paradise: The Idea of the Primitive Hut in Architectural History* (New York, 1972) and *The Idea of a Town: The Anthropology of Urban Form in Rome, Italy and the Ancient World* (Princeton, N.J., 1976).

New Sources

Carmichael, David, ed. *Sacred Sites, Sacred Places.* London, 1994.

Chidester, David, and Edward T. Linenthal, eds. *American Sacred Space.* Bloomington, Ind., 1995.

David, Bruno, and Meredith Wilson, eds. *Inscribed Landscapes: Marking and Making Place.* Honolulu, 2002.

Dodds, George, and Robert Tavernor, eds. *Body and Building: Essays on the Changing Relation of Body and Architecture.* Cambridge, Mass., 2002.

Jacobson-Widding, A., ed. *Body and Space: Symbolic Models of Unity and Division in African Cosmology and Experience.* Uppsala, 1991.

MIRCEA ELIADE (1987)
LAWRENCE E. SULLIVAN (1987)
Revised Bibliography

ORIGEN

ORIGEN (c. 185–c. 254), surnamed Adamantius (the man of steel or diamond), is considered the greatest Christian theologian of the Antenicene period.

LIFE. The main source for Origen's life is the sixth book of Eusebius of Caesarea's *Church History.* His teachings are also described in a panegyric delivered by one of his students, who (despite recent doubts) is still believed to be Gregory Thaumaturgus. Much information about Origen that was contained in Eusebius's lost writings is preserved in the writings of Jerome. It is difficult to date precisely the events of Origen's life, and recent attempts to do so are not completely satisfactory.

Origen was probably born in Alexandria in 185, the first of seven children in a Christian family. His father, Leonides, taught him Greek literature and the Bible. In 202, when he was seventeen, his father was martyred (by beheading) during the persecution of Septimius Severus. To support his family, Origen opened a school of rhetoric, and at the same time Bishop Demetrius of Alexandria assigned to him the task of training catechumens. Some years afterward he left the school in order to devote himself entirely to the teaching of Christian doctrine. He divided his students into two groups; the catechumens were taught by his disciple Heraclas, while Origen instructed the more advanced students. According to Eusebius, he castrated himself (taking literally *Matthew* 19:12), and he assisted some of his students in their martyrdom. He completed his own philosophical studies at the school of Ammonius Saccas, who later was the teacher of Plotinus. To deepen his knowledge of the Bible Origen studied Hebrew, although he never became proficient in the language.

Origen began to write between 215 and 220, encouraged by a wealthy man named Ambrose. Ambrose had been led by his intellectual zeal to adopt the Valentinian heresy, but Origen converted him from that heresy and in turn was provided with stenographers and copyists—virtually a whole publishing house.

During this first Alexandrian period of his life, Origen traveled to Rome, to the Roman province of Arabia (present-day Jordan) at the invitation of the governor, and to Antioch. In Antioch he met the dowager empress Mammaea, who wished to learn about Christian doctrines. Along with all teachers of philosophy in Alexandria, Origen was forced to leave the city in 215. Origen stayed for a short period at Caesarea, in Palestine. Here, because of his great knowledge of scripture, he was permitted by Bishop Theoctistus and his colleague Alexander of Jerusalem to preach, even though he was still a layman; but Bishop Demetrius protested against this innovation and called Origen back to Alexandria. About 231 Origen was invited by the bishops of Achaia (Greece) to debate with heretics in Athens. Passing through Palestine, he was ordained a priest at Caesarea by Theoctistus and Alexander. When he returned to Alexandria, Bishop Demetrius, angry at the ordination performed without his consent, summoned a synod of Egyptian bishops and priests that ordered Origen to leave Egypt, and another synod, composed only of bishops, defrocked him. This sentence, however, was not accepted by the bishops of Palestine and neighboring provinces.

Origen was welcomed to Caesarea by Theoctistus and Alexander, and he opened a school in the city. Among his first students were Gregory Thaumaturgus and Gregory's brother Athenodorus. Ambrose followed Origen to Caesarea, bringing his stenographers and copyists, and Origen continued to compose his great works. Many homilies survive, attesting to his extensive pastoral activity. He acquired a high reputation as a theologian, and he was frequently invited by bishops to defend the faith. He traveled extensively throughout the eastern part of the Roman empire, including the provinces of Achaia, Arabia, and Cappadocia, and the towns of Ephesus and Nicomedia.

During the Decian persecution, Origen was imprisoned and several times tortured in the hope that he would apostatize, but he maintained his faith firmly. Upon the death of Decius he was freed, but his health was broken and he died, probably in 254. Up to the thirteenth century his grave could be seen in the old cathedral of Tyre.

WORKS. A great part of Origen's immense production is now lost, and part of what is left survives only in Latin translations by Rufinus of Aquileia, Jerome, and an unknown translator. Most of Origen's works are directly exegetical. He explained the Bible in three kinds of works: scientific commentaries; homilies preached in the church; and scholia, or short texts in which the meaning of a passage was elucidated. Today it is impossible to distinguish the scholia from the multitude of surviving fragments of Origen's lost commentaries and homilies. It has been demonstrated recently that homilies on *Psalms* once attributed to Jerome are slightly adapted translations from Origen. In all, 279 of Origen's homilies are extant. Jerome's four commentaries on Paul's letters to the Galatians, the Ephesians, Titus, and Philemon are also in great part, as the author himself acknowledges, adaptations of Origen's corresponding commentaries.

While still in Alexandria, Origen began his great bible study, the Hexapla. In this work of six parallel columns, two columns contain the Hebrew text of the Old Testament (one in Hebraic and one in Greek characters), and four columns are devoted to four Greek translations: those by Aquila, Symmachus, and Theodotion, and the Septuagint. For some books of the Old Testament, three other Greek versions are also supplied, called "Quinta," "Sexta," and "Septima." Diacritical marks are used to show what had been added or suppressed in each version. Only numerous fragments of this work have been preserved.

Among the works not directly exegetical (although Origen also discusses scripture extensively in them), the most important is the treatise *On First Principles (Peri archon),* the first great attempt at speculative theology by a Christian. This work was the cause of Origen's posthumous misfortunes. The entire book is preserved only in a much-discussed Latin version by Rufinus, although there are two long Greek fragments from it in the *Philokalia of Origen* by the Cappadocian fathers Basil and Gregory of Nazianzus, and many short extracts are quoted by Jerome, Justinian, and other authors. Another major book still preserved in Greek is *Against Celsus,* the main apologetic work of the Antenicene period. This work is a refutation of the *True Discourse,* an attack on Christianity by the Middle Platonist philosopher Celsus. Other nonexegetical books that survive in the original Greek are the treatise *On Prayer,* which gives one of the first explanations of the Lord's Prayer; *Exhortation to Martyrdom,* written during the persecution of Maximinus the Thracian; and *Dialogue with Heraclides,* found during World War II in Egypt and consisting of a discussion in a local synod with a bishop suspected of modalism, a form of unorthodoxy that sees Father, Son, and Holy Spirit as only one person with these names. Greek fragments survive of the lost works *Stromateis* and *On the Resurrection.* Of Origen's important correspondence, two complete letters and fragments of others have been preserved.

Three groups of sources contain all the surviving fragments of Origen's work. First are the two collections of select pieces: Pamphilus of Caesarea's *Apology for Origen,* the first book of which is preserved only in Rufinus's Latin translation, and the *Philokalia.* Second are the exegetical *Catenae,* collections of exegeses from various chruch fathers, including Origen, in which a given book of scripture is explained verse by verse. Third are subsequent authors' quotations from Origen.

The Exegete. Three aspects are mingled to varying degrees in Origen's entire corpus, as well as in each work: he is at once an exegete, a spiritual and mystical writer, and a speculative theologian. Exegesis and spirituality are always present in his main speculative work, *On First Principles.* Together with Jerome, Origen is one of the two main critical and literal exegetes of Christian antiquity.

For Origen, the literal sense of scripture is the foundation for the spiritual sense, and he explains scripture using philology and all the learning of his time. Spiritual exegesis, or allegorical exegesis (synonymous for Origen), begins with New Testament texts in which Old Testament images and prophesies have their fulfillment in Christ. This form of interpretation had been used by some earlier church fathers, but Origen was its first great exponent, particularly in his theory of the three senses of scriptural meaning—corporal, or literal; psychic, or moral; and spiritual, or mystical. Despite its great complexity (the result of later accretions), the heart of Origen's spiritual exegesis of the Old Testament is the manifestation of Christ as the key to the ancient scriptures. These scriptures are a prophecy of Christ, both in their entirety and in their details. In his spiritual exegesis of the New Testament, Origen applies what is said of Christ to the Christian, thus foreshadowing the things to come in the "last days." This exegesis can be understood only in the context of spiritual life, prayer, and preaching. When Origen suggests the meaning of a text whose spiritual sense is not found in the New Testament, he does not claim to give a definitive answer, but only to provide "occasions for contemplation." Often he invites his reader or hearer to follow a better interpretation if it can be found. Origen's spiritual exegesis does not have the same aim as his literal exegesis (which for modern exegetes, unlike for Origen, refers to the meaning intended by the author). Literal exegesis, for Origen, points out the materiality of an expression independently, if possible, of all interpretation. Spiritual exegesis places the passage in the history of salvation and draws spiritual food from it for the faithful. A pastoral purpose is always present in Origen's exegesis.

The Spiritual Writer. Origen is, after Clement, one of the founders of Christian spirituality and mysticism. His trichotomic conception of man derives much more from Paul and the Bible than from Platonism. The spirit (*pneuma*) is a gift of God, something analogous with the *gratia sanctificans.* The incorporeal soul (*psuche*), the seat of free will and personality, is divided into an upper and a lower part; the upper part is the mind (*nous*), the faculty that receives the spirit, whereas the lower part, the "thought of the flesh" (*phronema tes sarkos*) draws the soul toward the body. The body—earthly for man, ethereal for angels and the risen—is the sign of the human "accidental," creaturely condition, in contrast to the "substantiality" of the Trinity, which alone exists without a body.

Humans were created according to the image of God, that is, according to his Son (*Gn.* 1:26–27). This means much more than the reception of "natural" gifts; it means that a seed and a desire for divinization have been planted in humanity, and this seed must with God's help be developed into the perfect "likeness" of the blessedness. Such is the framework of ascetic and spiritual life, which is further explained in terms of knowledge. But the Alexandrian defines knowledge according to *Genesis* 4:1: "Adam knew Eve, his wife." For Origen's synthetic mind, knowledge is identical with love and union. Knowledge begins with the realities of this world, which, in Platonic terms, are copies of "true" realities, that is, the divine mysteries, toward which knowledge must strive. In other words, the way of knowledge begins in the Old Testament and passes through the historical Jesus—the Incarnate Word that enters the soul and leads it, just as the apostles were led on the Mount of the Transfiguration to see the Word through the man Jesus and thus to hear the words of Wisdom spoken among the perfect. The Transfiguration symbolizes for Origen the highest knowledge humans can have of God upon this earth; it is the prelude to the beatific vision, in which humans will contemplate, face to face, the mysteries contained in the Son of God.

Origen was one of the great creators of the mystical language and spiritual themes employed in later centuries. Before his time, the bride in the *Song of Songs* had been interpreted collectively as the church. Origen added to this interpretation an individual meaning: the bride is the soul of the Christian. The imagery of the dart and the wound of love began with him. He often used the Pauline theme of the birth and growth of Jesus in the soul, as well as the theme of the ascent of the Mount of the Transfiguration to express spiritual ascension. Different aspects of grace and knowledge were represented by light, life, spiritual foods, spiritual wine, and the five spiritual senses. He had a doctrine of the discernment of spirits, and he often spoke of Christ in a highly affective manner that was rare in Christian antiquity. His far-reaching ascetic teachings included treatments of such themes as martyrdom, virginity, marriage, spiritual struggle, virtue, and sin.

The Speculative Theologian. It is difficult to evaluate Origen's theology justly, as is known from his history. His theology "in exercise," which was sensitive to the antithetical aspects of Christianity, lacked definitions and accurate terminology. This is understandable, since Origen wrote before the great trinitarian and christological heresies that in subsequent centuries made it necessary to develop more precise terms. To make a fair assessment, the historian therefore must study all that remains of his work: no single text alone suffices to reveal Origen's thought on any point. Because he was the pioneer of theology, Origen must be examined with a strict historical method, with knowledge of the rule of faith of his time—still lacking precision—and of the heresies he fought. The historian must understand his vocabulary and the persecuted church of the third century, so unlike the triumphant church of his later accusers, who were little interested in understanding him on his own terms. Similarly, the historian must avoid projecting on Origen the heresies of later times.

The fundamental concern of Origen's work, stimulated by the search of the convert Ambrose, was to give a Christian answer to problems (derived in part from Greek philosophy) that troubled his contemporaries. He had to ensure that they did not seek the answer in gnostic doctrines, and he had to supply searching Christians with the intellectual food they needed. His efforts in this direction, for which he had prepared himself by acquiring considerable philosophical erudition, were totally misunderstood by his fourth-century and fifth-century opponents, in spite of the fact that the success of Origen's efforts had played an important part in the conversion of the Roman empire.

The philosophical foundation of Origen's theology was the Middle Platonism of his teacher Ammonius Saccas—an eclectic philosophy based mainly on Platonism and Stoicism and to a lesser degree on Aristotelianism. Origen borrowed from this philosophy both terminology and doctrines, but he used it as a theologian, not as a philosopher, to explain and develop what he found in the Bible and in the rule of faith.

It is impossible to give a detailed account of his theology in a short space. Only one of the erroneous doctrines of which he was later accused can safely be attributed to him: his favorite hypothesis of the preexistence of souls. This idea was essentially Platonic, but Origen used it to a Christian end: to refute the Marcionites, who accused the Creator of wickedness, and to answer the great difficulties raised by the two contemporary Christian solutions to the problem of the origin of souls, traducianism and creationism. According to the rule of faith of his time, Origen's hypothesis could not be described as heretical. The other controverted points—the famous *apocatastasis* (the final restoration of all things), the trinitarian subordinationism, and so on—must be examined in the context of Origen's entire work and intentions. If this is done, these opinions lose most of the scandalous character that they have acquired in his accusers' formulations.

POSTHUMOUS HISTORY. Origen has always been a contradictory figure in the history of the church. In spite of some reservations from his followers, he was the teacher of all the great Christian writers of the fourth century: in the East, of Athanasius, Basil, the two Gregories, and Didymus the Blind; in the West, of Hilary of Poitiers, Ambrose, Rufinus, and Jerome. (Jerome owed much to Origen, both early and late in his career, although in his later years he became a strong opponent of Origen.) The first attacks on Origen were launched at the turn of the fourth century by Methodius of Olympus, Peter of Alexandria, and Eustathius of Antioch; Origen was defended by Pamphilus of Caesarea.

In the second half of the fourth century enthusiastic disciples among the monks of Palestine and Egypt turned the ocean of Origen's thought into a well-dammed river, thus making of him a heretic. This "Origenism" provoked the first Origenist controversy. Origen's opponents included Epiphanius of Salamis, Theophilus of Alexandria, and Jerome; his defenders were John of Jerusalem and Rufinus. In the first half of the sixth century, Origenism—or, more properly, "Evagrianism" (named for one of Origen's enthusiasts, Evagrios of Pontus)—agitated some monasteries of Palestine, and Emperor Justinian condemned Origen in a letter in 543. He referred the question of the Palestinian Origenists, rather than that of Origen himself, to the Second Council of Constantinople (553), but the anathemas against Origenism do not appear in the council's official acts. Whereas the Byzantine church found Origen suspect, he was much read in the medieval Latin West until the thirteenth century, and he held an especially important place in the Cistercian tradition. His influence was eclipsed by the rise of Scholasticism but revived during the Renaissance, particularly through the work of Pico della Mirandola and Erasmus. Today Origen, next to Augustine, is probably the most frequently studied church father.

BIBLIOGRAPHY

A general bibliography is supplied in my *Bibliographie critique d'Origène* (The Hague, 1971), and in its first supplement (1982). Origen's works are available in *Patrologia Graeca,* edited by J.-P. Migne, (Paris, 1857), and in *Die griechischen christlichen Schriftsteller der ersten drei Jahrhunderte* (Leipzig, 1899–1953; Berlin, 1953–). English translations of his works are offered in *The Ante-Nicene Fathers,* vol. 4, edited by Alexander Roberts and James Donaldson (Grand Rapids, Mich., 1965); in *Prayer, Exhortation to Martyrdom* and *The Song of Songs, Commentary and Homilies,* nos. 19 and 26 in "Ancient Christian Writers," edited by Johannes Quasten and Joseph C. Plumbe (Westminster, Md., 1954 and 1956); and in *Homilies on Genesis and Exodus,* vol. 71 of *The Fathers of the Church,* edited by Hermigild Dressler and others (Washington, D. C., 1982). For *On Principles,* see *Origen on First Principles,* translated by G. W. Butterworth (1936; reprint, New York, 1966). For *Against Celsus,* see *Origen: Contra Celsum,* translated by Henry Chadwick (1953; reprint, Cambridge, 1980). A general presentation of Origen's life and thought is available in Jean Daniélou's *Origen* (New York, 1955).

HENRI CROUZEL (1987)

ORPHEUS. In the sixth century BCE, a religious movement that modern historians call Orphism appeared in Greece around the figure of Orpheus, the Thracian enchanter. The features of this movement, and even its existence, have been subjects of debate since the nineteenth century.

A CONCISE SURVEY OF THE SCHOLARSHIP. In 1829 Christian Augustus Lobeck (1781–1890) collected and commented on a huge amount of materials about Orphic literature and religion, in stark opposition to Georg F. Creuzer (1771–1858), whose monumental work *Symbolik und Mythologie der alten Völker* (1810–1812) had produced a great deal of mystification. During the nineteenth and the early twentieth centuries, however, information about the activities of the Orphics in the classical and early Hellenistic periods was scarce. Some scholars tended to fill the information gap by elaborating a religious pattern for Orphism based on concepts that are characteristic of modern religions. Such authors as Jane Ellen Harrison and Albrecht Dieterich were convinced that the Orphics made up a true church and had a great influence over contemporary philosophy. Vittorio Macchioro and Robert Eisler even argued that Christianity was only a kind of derivation of Orphism. Against these excesses, Ulrich von Wilamowitz-Moellendorff began, around 1930, a hypercritical reaction (followed by Ivan M. Linforth and E. R. Dodds, among others), which denied the existence of Orphism before the late Hellenistic period. This line of research was so dominant that until the 1970s it was believed that Orphism was nothing more than an artificial product of a series of interpretations advanced by Herodotus, as well as by Neoplatonic philosophers and modern historians enamored of pagan mysteries. Some scholars, however, including Erwin Rohde, Otto Kern, Arthur D. Nock, Martin P. Nilsson, W. K. C. Guthrie, Pierre Boyancé, and Ugo Bianchi, managed to maintain a more measured point of view.

During the 1970s Orphism became better known as a result of discoveries that definitely established its presence and importance in the earliest of times. In 1962 the remains of an "Orphic book," dating to approximately 330 BCE, were discovered in a tomb at Derveni near Thessaloniki. The text, written around 400 BCE and consequently independent of any Platonic influence, is a philosophical commentary on Orphic theogony and cosmogony. The poem that is discussed dates to about 500 BCE, and the author of the commentary also refers to certain rites performed by *magoi.*

In 1978, Soviet archaeologists announced that they had discovered three small bone tablets in Olbia, a Greek town on the Black Sea. The tablets attested the existence in the fifth century BCE of a group called the Orphics, who had an explicit interest in the god Dionysos.

Beginning in 1974 a series of Orphic gold leaves dating from between 400 and 300 BCE were found in Vibo Valentia in Calabria, in Entella in Sicily, in Pharsalos in Thessaly, and in Pelinna in modern-day Paleoyardíki. The leaves contain brief texts, mainly in hexameters, that describe how the deceased must behave and the words they must speak in the "Other World" in order to achieve perpetual happiness and divine status. Although other gold leaves from Petelia, Crete, and Thurii had been discovered earlier, those found in and after 1974 cast a new light on early Orphism and compelled a reconception of the movement. According to these texts, the religion of Persephone is related to that of the Dionysiac *mystai* (initiated) and *bacchoi* (those that have felt an ecstatic trance), and it seems likely that the gold leaves contain fragments of an Orphic *hieros logos* (sacred discourse) about the travel of the soul in the netherworld. As a result of these discoveries, many scholars came to hold the opinion that for many centuries there existed a religious movement of vague boundaries based on the authority of Orpheus. Its followers believed in the immortality of the soul and in the transmigration of the soul until it reached final liberation.

DIFFICULTIES IN MARKING THE BOUNDARIES OF ORPHISM. Orphism occupies an intermediate position between diverse religious and philosophical movements, and it shares certain features with several of them. The Orphics basically believed in the same gods as followers of the Olympic religion that is reflected by such authors as Homer and Hesiod. But while human beings and gods appear categorically separated in the Olympic worldview, the Orphics believed that it is possible for human souls to reach a divine status. The Orphics were also followers of Dionysos, with whom they shared the *ecstasy* (a state of ecstatic trance, referred to by the verb *baccheuein*) that allowed men and gods to join together. However, the Orphics rejected the bloody rites that were characteristic of Bacchic religiosity. Orphism also received some features from Pythagoreanism; Orphics and Pythagoreans both believed in the dualism of the soul and the body, metempsychosis and puritanism, and the associated taboos. But the Orphic ecstasy is not characteristic of the Pythagoreans, and the Orphics had little interest in politics. In addition, Orphism shares with the Eleusinian religion the myth of Demeter and Persephone, the initiatic rites, and a belief in the salvation of the soul. Eleusis, however, was a stable cult, associated with a sanctuary and controlled by certain families, while Orphism lacked sanctuaries and a stable priesthood. Orphism also coincided with certain ideas about divinity developed by such authors as Aeschylos, Pindar, and Heraclitus; these include the proclamation of Zeus as the origin and end of everything. Finally, Orphic texts include features characteristic of oriental religions, such as statements in the gold leaves similar to statements found in the Egyptian *Book of the Dead.* In addition, the central role of time in Orphic theogonies is reminiscent of Iranian Zurvan. Orphism, however, is a typically Greek movement, and by no means an imported one.

Orphism is contradictory in that its traditional character resulted in the maintenance of its identity for centuries, but since it was a religion without stable communities or ecclesiastic hierarchy, it allowed from the very beginning a great degree of variation among its believers and transmitters. Although Orphism was without dogma or church, it was open to anybody and responded to the need for comfort and salvation, allowing each follower to find in it something different. On the other hand, Orpheus's prestige results in the attribution to him of beliefs that sometimes contradict those properly known as Orphic. It seems that from the beginning there were different ways of feeling and transmitting the Orphic message, including one branch of the movement that offered quick solutions to problems by means of a rite that assured a better destiny. In certain cases there were also practices that were clearly magical. From the days of Euripides until Athanasius's time, *magoi* traded with efficient enchantments, which were attributed to Orpheus for the sake of prestige. Another branch tried to refine the Orphic message by giving it a profound philosophical meaning. Between both branches there were, of course, simple believers who participated in rituals called *teletai,* which they considered effective as preparation for death and which offered them hope for the afterlife.

Orphism, thus, was a complex phenomenon. It embraced a long history, from the sixth century BCE to the Neoplatonic exegeses current in Alexandria at the time of Olympiodorus during the sixth century CE. Furthermore, Orphism involved three relatively autonomous types of religious phenomena. First, there were traditions concerning the birth, life, and descent of Orpheus into the underworld, his singing among the Thracians, and his tragic death (he was said to have been torn to pieces by a band of women). Next, there was a literature that included writings attributed to Orpheus, as well as several theogonic accounts. Finally, the Orphic movement included certain practices and rules of conduct, proscriptions, and requirements to be met by those who chose to live in an Orphic manner.

Despite the growing evidence for an Orphic religious movement, scholars such as Luc Brisson are still skeptical about the existence of a specific religious stream with charasteristic rites. Claude Calame has expressed a more moderate (though still skeptical) view. Many beliefs (e.g., the immortality of the soul, the antecedent sin, metempsychosis, the possibility that the soul recovers its divine status), ritual practices (e.g., *teletai*), and personal attitudes (e.g., vegetarianism, Puritanism) appear to have been intertwined. They are thus better understood as belonging to the same movement, rather than as separate entities or beliefs. While each feature attributed to Orphic religion may appear in other religious spheres, there is no other known religious movement in which they all coincide. For example, if the gold leaves are not Orphic, it would be necessary to reconstruct an unknown movement with all the features of Orphism.

WHO WAS ORPHEUS? A figure believed to be Orpheus, the citharist and enchanter, first appears around 570 BCE on a small black-figured vase. He is shown walking with a determined stride and surrounded by two sirens (great angry birds with the heads of women). A frail silhouette armed with a lyre, he clears a path for himself between these powers and their voice of death, between these hybrids whose sexual identity vacillates between the virginal, the androgynous, and the masculine. But the power of the voice and of song triumphs over the sirens and their fatal spells. Thus, before he becomes the founding hero of a new religion or even the founder of a way of life that will be named after him, Orpheus is a voice—a voice that is like no other. It begins before songs that recite and recount. It precedes the voice of the bards, the citharists who extol the great deeds of men or the privileges of the divine powers. It is a song that stands outside the closed circle of its hearers, a voice that precedes articulate speech. Around it, in abundance and joy, gather trees, rocks, birds, and fish. In this voice—before the song has become a theogony and at the same time an anthropogony—there is the great freedom to embrace all things without being lost in confusion, the freedom to accept each life and everything and to renounce a world inhabited by fragmentation and division.

When representatives of the human race first appear in the presence of Orpheus, they wear faces that are of war and savagery yet seem to be pacified, faces that seem to have turned aside from their outward fury. These humans are Thracian warriors, clad in animal skins and motley colored cloaks, and just as birds leave the sky and fish forsake the sea at the sound of Orpheus's song, so too do the warriors come out of the forests. In the midst of a wild audience, his head crowned with laurel, the enchanter is dressed in Greek fashion; he appears so Apollonian that only the clothing of his Thracian entourage distinguishes him from his father, Apollo the citharist. But it is in full Thracian or oriental dress that the vases of southern Italy depict Orpheus as he descends into the underworld, searches for Eurydice, or makes a daring journey to the heart of the realm of Hades.

Orpheus's followers share in his triumph over death. A large Apulian amphora, published in 1976, pictures Orpheus in the underworld, standing and playing the lyre in the presence of a heroized corpse. That corpse is seated in a pavilion, and in its left hand it clasps a papyrus scroll, without doubt an Orphic book similar to the one unearthed near a tomb at Derveni or to the texts of the gold leaves.

The Altamura amphora presents another powerful image. Orpheus the harpist stands before the Lord of the Underworld, while the daughters of Danaus, damned forever, ceaselessly pour water into a bottomless jar. Only the initiated gain victory over the death that others must suffer, and they alone enjoy the banquet and happiness of the blessed. As a result, they become heroes or even resemble the gods themselves.

THE WRITINGS OF ORPHEUS. In Olbia, at Derveni, and in southern Italy, writing was used to prolong Orpheus's voice: the song became a book. According to all sources, books were the main means of transmission of the texts. In Orphism, written literature took the place of oral communication. A container for scrolls formed a part of the Orphic landscape. On an Etruscan mirror (now in Boston) the container stands at Orpheus's feet, while silent beasts encircle the song. Thus, Orphic religion took on features of a "religion of the book."

There were two basic reasons for poets to attribute poems to Orpheus, denying themselves fame as authors. First, for the Greeks, the older an idea was, the more prestigious it was. Plato often refers to Orpheus's works as an "old discourse," which he considers worthy because it is old. Second, the advocates of this new religious doctrine invoked Orpheus's name because if he had returned from the underworld, he would be a reliable witness of what is revealed in the poems.

The oldest poems attributed to Orpheus (from the sixth century BCE until the Hellenistic age) focus on the origin and destiny of human life. Some of the Orphic writings are theogonies; others describe Orpheus's descent to Hades (*katabasis*) and reveal the fate that awaits souls in the Other World. Some books prescribe a dietary regimen and extend to their readers an invitation to attend unblemished sacrifices and sweet-smelling oblations. Some verses from a book of the latter type, in which a cereal diet is associated with justice, are quoted by Sextus Empiricus. Books of the latter type also include the lost *Thuepolikon* (How to make bloodless offerings), to which Plato alludes directly in the *Republic.* Plato also quotes many times a *hieros* or *palaios logos* (sacred or ancient discourse) as a source of doctrines about the soul.

Orpheus was also said to be the author of magical texts, which is not surprising, since Orpheus himself has features of a wizard. Later, in the Roman age, Orpheus became a prestigious name, and a diverse series of astrological, botanical, and medical poems were attributed to him, including a complete a poem about stones (*Lithica*). From the same period comes a version of *Argonautica,* told in first person by Orpheus himself. The religious content of these later poems was already far removed from ancient Orphism.

ORPHIC WAY OF LIFE. Plato summarized the strict rules of the Orphic way of life in the *Laws*: to abstain from all meat and to offer the gods only cakes or fruit soaked in honey, for it is impious and unclean to eat flesh and to stain with blood the altars of the gods. Since the bloody sacrifice was a basic rite of the state religion, these rules would have placed the Orphics outside of the polis.

Herodotus tells us that the Egyptian taboo prohibiting the wearing of wool parallels Orphic and Bacchic observances. In addition, the ecstasy (*baccheuein*) was an important aspect of the Orphic way of life. This way of life was not easy to follow and, according to Plato, many people failed: "Many are narthex-bearers, but the *bacchoi* are few."

THE *TELETE, ORPHEOTELESTAI,* AND *MYSTAI.* The transmission of the Orphic message as recorded in books was carried out through a rite called the *telete.* This rite was probably accompanied by a performance that dramatized the following myth. Zeus decided to appoint his son Dionysos as his successor when Dionysos was still a child. The Titans lured Dionysos away, killed him, and cut his body into pieces, which they boiled, roasted, and ate. In response, Zeus blasted the Titans with a thunderbolt, and human beings were born from the blood and soot of the Titans. Because of the circumstances of their origin, human beings have a divine and positive component, which comes from Dionysos, but their souls retain a "Titanic nature" and the evilness of their ancestors. Human souls can free themselves from their Titanic element by passing through several reincarnations, thus recovering their divine state. Various scholars have doubted the authenticity and questioned the age of this myth. Nonetheless, there are good arguments supporting its status as an ancient myth. Several sources indicate that it was told in the *teletai,* which would only make sense if this myth was related to the origin and salvation of human beings. (See Bernabé, 2002, for a full discussion of the topic.)

The Orphics believed that these rites, along with the ecstasy and a form of puritanism that consisted in avoiding bloodshed, favored their reintegration with divinity. People taking part in the *telete* acquired a mystic knowledge and became aware of their place in the world order. They thus learn how to save their souls and achieve a better destiny in the Other World once they have freed themselves from the antecedent (inherited) sin (they inherited their sin from their ancestors, the Titans; see Bianchi, 1966).

The *telete* was probably performed in various ways, with different types of people participating. Professional initiators (*orpheotelestai*), who are contemptuously described as poor and ragged and always carrying a stack of books, performed rites that supposedly freed people from sin and promised a better destiny in the Other World. Nobody ordained them, and they were patronized by superstitious and ignorant people. After the drastic measures announced in the *senatusconsultus de Bacchanalibus* (186 BCE) against those that took part in Bacchic rituals (see Livy 34, 8), the itinerant initiation priest seems to have totally disappeared from Bacchic mysteries. There were also many vagabonds and seers, who are quoted by Plato in the *Republic.* They were purifiers who claimed that they could heal epilepsy, and were thus reviled by Hippocrates. In addition, beginning in the fourth century, there were people like the commentator of the Derveni papyrus, who respected Orphic poems because they were old, but found some of their content, such as incest and castration, unacceptable. They solved the contradiction by resorting to allegorical interpretations of the texts. Plato refers to them in *Meno,* and he proposes in *Cratylus* his own allegorical interpretations of the old texts. This method of interpretation, which was continued by Plutarch and Plotinus, survived until the era of Neoplatonism. Finally, ordinary men and women participated in *teletai* as *mystai.* They looked to the rite for comfort and for the promise of a better future life.

The Orphics did not usually form stable communities. As a religion that promised individual salvation, Orphism could have been considered dangerous in Greek society, where religion was a means of social integration in the polis.

But the movement's lack of organization ensured that it would never become an alternative to the status quo. Relatively stable Orphic communities have been documented in only a few locations, including Olbia and perhaps Cumae. A fifth-century BCE inscription found in Cumae prevented those that had not felt an ecstatic trance from being buried in that place. Taking this inscription as a starting point, Turcan (1986) claims that a relatively stable Orphic Community may have existed in Cumae. This is disputed, however, by Pailler (1995, 109–126), though without convincing arguments. A second-century CE inscription from Torre Nova depicts a private Bacchic association organized in a hierarchy, which is more suitable for the Roman world.

But who were these people who were interred with a papyrus scroll in their hands, who abhorred blood, wrote cosmogonies, and dreamt strange tales about the birth of the gods? What did they want with Orpheus and his silent incantations? Actually, they sought one goal: health. They wished to heal themselves and sought to do so by fleeing from the world. The Orphics were renunciants who strove for saintliness. They devoted themselves to techniques of purification in order to separate themselves from others, to cut themselves off from the world and from all who are subject to death and defilement.

By returning to a golden age, to the time of the beginning, the Orphics renounced the blood on altars and rejected the eating of any flesh, and in doing so they rejected the values of the Greek state and that state's religious system, including its discrete divine powers, its differentiated gods, and the sharp distinction that it inevitably drew between the divine and the human. The Orphic way of life implied an uncompromising renunciation that is expressed by the condemnation both of sanguinary food and of the social bond that is established within the state when an animal is sacrificed on the altar and its flesh shared in a common feast.

In contrast with the way of life and patterns of thought associated with the followers of Pythagoras, a similar form of mysticism, the Orphics never attempted political reform or envisaged an alternative state with an alternative political cult. For the devotees of Orpheus, who chose writing and books as an effective symbol of their otherness, renouncing the worldliness of the state meant not only finding in vegetarianism a foretaste of life among the gods—that is, life among the gods who precede this world, with its bloody altars—it also meant recasting, with a great deal of effort, the genesis of the world, and rewriting the entire history of the gods. Like the sacrifice, the gods constituted a single structure in which politics, society, and religion were in perfect balance. When the Orphics renounced the gods of other Greeks, they called into question the whole fabric of social life, including polytheism, to the extent that polytheism pervaded society and played an integral role in politics.

But although Orphism distrusted the polytheism of others, it did not reject it entirely. If it had, it would have been in danger of cutting itself off from all communication with those who were at the point of being healed. The plurality of the gods was unavoidable. The Orphics therefore had to reconceive the divine, to transform the order of the divine forces, and to work out an alternative genealogy of powers.

ORPHIC COSMOGONIES AND THEOGONIES. The evolution of the gods is recounted in a series of poems whose refined styles become evident as they are deciphered from new palimpsests.

The Neoplatonic philosopher Damascius (fifth to sixth century CE) refers to the existence of several Orphic theogonies. These include (1) what he calls "current Orphic rhapsodies," which seems to be the only Orphic theogony directly known by the Neoplatonic school—it is also the longest and seems to be a conflation of several older poems; (2) a theogony transmitted by Hieronymus and Hellanicus; and (3) a theogony recorded in the Peripatetic Eudemus as being of Orpheus, which seems to be the same as, or similar to, that of Derveni. The parodic cosmogony in Aristophanes' play *Birds* (414 BCE) may also echo an ancient Orphic theogony.

The Orphic gods are bizarre. The firstborn (Greek, *protogonos*), the primal generator and generatrix described in the *Rhapsodies*, is called variously Protogonos, Phanes, Metis, and Erikepaios. Descriptions of this deity offer repeated affronts to the form of the human body: it has two pairs of eyes, golden wings, the voice of a lion and of a bull, and organs of both sexes, one of which adorns the upper part of the buttocks. There is also the Zeus who rules over the fifth generation of gods and who will transfer his power to his son. Instead of being assured of ruling over the gods forever, this Zeus, on the advice of Night, sends the Firstborn straight to the pit of his belly. Thus he becomes a womb, as it were, the shell of an egg whose dimensions are those of the All. In other tales this god cuts an even poorer figure. He marries his mother (Demeter), and as a result of this incestuous union a daughter (Persephone) is born. Zeus then impregnates Persephone, who is both his daughter and his half sister. The church fathers, who assiduously observed so many couplings, turned from crimson to green.

The Orphic cosmogony/theogony contains a virtual orgy of baroque deities and polymorphic monsters, but the profusion of these multifarious gods is neither gratuitous nor insignificant. It gives meaning to their development. In the beginning was the totality, the oneness of the All, the completeness of Phanes within the perfect sphere of primordial Night. In the course of five successive reigns, the ideal unity undergoes the trials of separation and division on its road to differentiation. The succession of rulers passes from Phanes—via Night, so close to Phanes—to Ouranos and Gaia, Kronos and Rhea, and finally to Zeus. Zeus, born of Rhea (Demeter or Deo), marries her, and later he becomes the husband of Kore (Persephone), his daughter, who will give birth to Dionysos. Dionysos, who was actually already present in the Firstborn, will institute the sixth and final generation of the gods.

What is the motivating force behind this genealogical descent? Differentiation takes place first through sexual activity, then through marriage, which works toward the separation of the divine powers. To be more specific, the first conjugal union in the world of the gods appears in the third generation: there is no *gamos* (marriage) before that of Ouranos and Gaia. Nevertheless, Phanes takes from Night—the second Night, said to be his daughter—the flower of her virginity. This act represents the first appearance of sexuality, but there is not yet any marriage. As Proclus, a good interpreter of Orpheus, writes: "For those who are most united there is no union in marriage."

Sexuality initiates difference; marriage establishes and grounds it by bringing to completion the separation that is in full force until the reign of Zeus in the fifth generation. The Zeus of the fifth generation (in contrast to the Zeus of the fourth) displays two faces; one is the face of degeneracy—his doubly incestuous marriage: the son with his mother, and the father with his daughter—the other is the face of regeneration. Hearkening to Night, he engulfs the Firstborn in his entrails and ushers in the second creation of the world. This Zeus is the pregnant god who realizes within himself both the unity of all things and the distinctiveness of each.

The commentator of the Derveni papyrus confirms this process of differentiation, now in the origin of words and of things, for it deals with the assignation of multiple names to a single god. The vocabulary is philosophical, the vocabulary of Anaxagoras, the vocabulary of separation (*diakrisis*). In particular, column twenty-one states that all things already existed in advance, but they received their names only when they were separated. Thus, naming replicates—on the level of words—the separation and distinctions brought about through sexual activity, in this case the activity of Aphrodite and her father, Zeus. The commentary in the Derveni papyrus attempts to display the truth of Orpheus's words: the linguistic discussion appears as an additional means of conceiving the unity that subsists within the interplay of the figures of separation, a means that is available as a result of the appropriateness of the names bestowed by Orpheus.

In recasting the gods of others, Orphism gives a special meaning to the complicity of two rival powers: Dionysos and Apollo, the two gods who sum up the whole of Greek polytheism. In the various theogonic accounts—the great dramas in which Dionysos is assuredly the protagonist—Apollo plays the role of a tutelary power. He embodies genuine oracular knowledge in the Delphic landscape that he shares with Night, the daughter of Phanes. He collects and pieces together the scattered limbs of Dionysos and then lays the remains of the executed god to rest in his sanctuary at the foot of Mount Parnassus. Finally, he is identified with another great god, the Sun, who inspires Orpheus to sing his theogonic song.

But Dionysos and Apollo also meet and confront each other in the tragic biography of Orpheus and, in particular, in the indirect manner in which Orpheus is slain. In his first tetralogy based on the legends of Dionysos, Aeschylus presented an Orpheus stricken with the devout love of one god greater than all the rest. Every day, at dawn, Orpheus scales the crags of Mount Pangaeus, the highest mountain in Thrace. He wishes to be the first to salute the Sun, who is for him "the greatest of the gods" and to whom he gives the name Apollo. Dionysos, it is said, is filled with resentment at this daily ritual. He sends to Orpheus women with a barbarian name, the Bassarai. They surround him, seize him, and dismember him, tearing him to pieces immediately. In fact, Dionysos takes an interest in Orpheus's activity because Pangaeus is Dionysos's own domain, an ambiguous region where Lykurgos, the king of the Edonians, is torn apart by wild horses. Pangaeus is also where Dionysos appears as an oracular deity whose prophetess recalls the Pythia in the temple of Apollo. Thus the Dionysos of Pangaeus has two faces, one of which is Apollonian. And the instruments of Orpheus's death are women, the fiercest and wildest representatives of the feminine gender (they appear armed with skewers, axes, stones, and hooks on Attic vases from between 480 and 430). These are women whom the voice of Orpheus is powerless to seduce, to tame, or to restrain. They would even have rejoiced in killing Orpheus—one of several details that show that they are outside the control of Dionysos, that they are not bacchanals but ferocious beasts who cause Orpheus to be destroyed by what he most deeply despises: the feminine, which brought to humans the disease of birth and death. In opposition to this feminine, Orpheus embodies the purely masculine, the *catharos* who is seen also in Apollo, the principle of unity, but Orpheus does so via the multiplicity of forms and by the roundabout path of Dionysian polymorphism.

TRACES OF ORPHISM IN NON-ORPHIC AUTHORS. Although Orphic literature was generally scorned in the classical age by writers closer to the religion of the state, some authors were interested in certain aspects of its message. Such philosophers as Parmenides and Empedocles, and above all the Pythagoreans and Plato, as well as lyric poets such as Pindar, seemed to know and accept certain features of the Orphic message. Plutarch claims to have been initiated into the mysteries and mentions several Orphic doctrines. The Orphic influence is present in Neoplatonism during the fifth and sixth centuries CE. There are also traces of Orphism in some Greek magical papyri and in Mithraism.

The so-called *Testament of Orpheus* reveals an Orphic influence on Hellenized Jews, and the early Christians exhibit two contradictory attitudes toward Orphism. Christians sometimes highlighted common features between Orphic and Christian beliefs in order to make their new message easier for pagans to adopt. Orpheus is represented in early Christian sarcophagi and is identified with the good shepherd in the catacombs. Early Christians also at times directly rejected the Orphic message, renouncing in particular the most reprehensible aspects of the Orphic myths, such as monsters, castration of gods, and incest.

SEE ALSO Apollo; Apotheosis; Baubo; Catharsis; Demeter and Persephone; Dionysos; Dualism; Eleusinian Mysteries; Eros; Hellenistic Religions; Magic, article on Magic in Greco-Roman Antiquity; Music, article on Music and Religion in Greece, Rome, and Byzantium; Mystery Religions; Neoplatonism; Plato; Platonism; Pythagoras; Soul, article on Greek and Hellenistic Concepts.

BIBLIOGRAPHY

Editions and Translations of Texts

Athanassakis, Apostolos N., trans. and ed. *The Orphic Hymns.* Missoula, Mont., 1977.

Bernabé, Alberto, ed. *Poetae Epici Graeci*, vol. 2: *Orphicorum et Orphicis similium testimonia et fragmenta.* Monachii et Lipsiae, 2003.

Colli, Giorgio. *La Sapienza greca.* Milan, Italy, 1977.

Halleux, Robert, and Jacques Schamp, eds. and trans. *Les lapidaires grecs.* Paris, 1985. French translation of the Orphic *Lithica.*

Kern, Otto, ed. *Orphicorum fragmenta.* Berlin, 1922; reprint, Dublin and Zürich, 1972.

Ricciardelli, Gabriella, trans and ed. *Inni orfici.* Milan, Italy, 2000.

Vian, Francis, trans. and ed. *Les argonautiques orphiques.* Paris, 1987.

Tablets of Olbia

Dubois, Laurent. *Inscriptions grecques dialectales d'Olbia du Pont.* Geneva, Switzerland, 1996. See pages 154–155.

West, Martin L. "The Orphics of Olbia." *Zeitschrift für Papyrologie und Epigraphik* 45 (1982): 17–29. A study of the tablets.

Zhmud, Leonid. "Orphism and Grafitti from Olbia." *Hermes* 120 (1992): 159–168.

Derveni Papyrus

Bernabé, Alberto. "La théogonie orhique du papyrus de Derveni." *Kernos* 15 (2002): 91–129. A reconstruction and analysis of the theogony.

Janko, Richard. "The Derveni Papyrus (Diagoras of Melos, *Apopyrgizontes Logoi?*: A New Translation." *Classical Philology* 96 (2001): 1–32.

Janko, Richard. "The Derveni Papyrus: An Interim Text." *Zeitschrift zur Papyrologie und Epigraphik* 141 (2002): 1–62.

Laks, André, and Glenn W. Most, eds. *Studies on the Derveni Papyrus.* Oxford, 1997.

Gold Leaves

Bernabé, Alberto, Jiménez San Cristóbal, and Ana Isabel. *Instrucciones para el Más Allá: Las laminillas órficas de oro.* Madrid, 2001.

Pugliese Carratelli, Giovanni. *Le lamine d'oro orfiche.* Milan, Italy, 2001.

Riedweg, Christoph. "Initiation-Tod-Unterwelt: Beobachtungen zur Komunikationssituation und narrativen Technik der orphisch-bakchischen Goldblättchen." In *Ansichten griechischer Rituale: Geburtstag-Symposium für Walter Burkert*, edited by Fritz Graf. Stuttgart and Leipzig, Germany, 1998. See pages 359–398.

Zuntz, Günther. *Persephone, Three Essays on Religion and Thought in Magna Graecia.* Oxford, 1971.

Cumae's Inscription

Pailler, Jean-Marie. *Bacchus: Figures et Pouvoirs.* Paris, 1995.

Turcan, Robert. "Bacchoi ou Bacchants: De la dissidence des vivants à la ségregation des morts." In *L'association Dianysiaque dans les societiés anciennes. Actes de la table ronde de l'école francaise de Rome.* Rome, 1986.

Overestimations of Orphism

Dieterich, Albrecht. *Nekyia.* Leipzig, Germany, 1913.

Eisler, Robert. *Orpheus the Fisher.* London, 1921.

Harrison, Jane Ellen. *Prolegomena to the Study of Greek Religion.* Cambridge, UK, 1903; 3d ed., Cambridge, UK, 1922.

Macchioro, Vittorio. *Zagreus: Studi intorno all'orfismo.* Florence, Italy, 1930. (See partial translation of this work that appeared as "Orphism and Paulism" in the *Journal of Religion* in 1928.)

Hypercritical Reaction

Dodds, E. R. *The Greeks and the Irrational.* Berkeley, Calif., 1951.

Linforth, Ivan M. *The Arts of Orpheus.* Berkeley, Calif., 1941; reprint, New York, 1973.

Wilamowitz-Moellendorff, Ulrich von. *Der Glaube der Hellenen.* Berlin, 1931; 3d rev. ed., Darmstadt, Germany, 1959.

Measured Points of View

Bianchi, Ugo. "Orfeo e l' orfismo nell' epoca classica." *Studi e materiali de storia delle religioni* 28 (1957): 151–156.

Bianchi, Ugo. "Péché originel et péché 'antécédent'." *Revue de l'Histoire des Religions* 170 (1966): 117–126.

Bianchi, Ugo. *Selected Essays on Gnosticism, Dualism, and Mysteriosophy.* Leiden, 1977.

Boyancé, Pierre. "Sur l' orphisme." *Revue des Études Anciennes* 40 (1938): 163–172.

Boyancé, Pierre. "Platon et les cathartes orphiques." *Revue des Études Grecques* 55, (1942): 217–235.

Boyancé, Pierre. "Xénocrate et les orphiques." *Revue des Études Anciennes* 50 (1948): 218–231.

Cumont, Franz. *Lux perpetua.* Paris, 1949.

Guthrie, W. K. C. *Orpheus and Greek Religion: A Study of the Orphic Movement.* London, 1935; 2d rev. ed., London, 1952; reprint, New York, 1967.

Kern, Otto. *Orpheus.* Berlin, 1920.

Keydell, Rudolf, and Karl Ziegler. "Orphische Dichtung." *Real Encyclopaedie* 18, no. 2 (1942): 1221–1417.

Lagrange, M.- J., *Les mystères: L'orphisme.* Paris, 1937. A Catholic approach.

Meuli, Karl. *Gesammelte Schriften.* Basle, 1975.

Nilsson, Martin P. "Early Orphism and Kindred Religious Movements." *Harvard Theological Review* 28 (1935): 181–230.

Nock, Arthur D. *Conversion: The Old and the New in Religion from Alexander the Great to Augustine of Hippo.* Oxford, 1933.

Prümm, Karl. "Die Orphik im Spiegel der neueren Forschung." *Zeitschrift für Katholische Theolologie* 78 (1956): 1–40.

Rohde, Erwin. *Psyche: Seelencult und Unterblichkeitsglaube der Griechen*, 4th ed. Tübingen, Germany, 1907.

Sabbatucci, Dario. *Saggio sul misticismo greco.* Rome, 1965 (French trans. *Essai sur le mysticisme grec.* Paris, 1982.)

Turcan, Robert. "L'âme oiseau et l'eschatologie orphique." *Revue de l'histoire des religions* 155 (1959): 33–40.

Turcan, Robert. "L'oeuf orphique et les quatre éléments." *Revue de l'histoire des religions* 160 (1961): 11–23.

New Approaches

Alderink, Larry J. *Creation and Salvation in Ancient Orphism.* Chico, Calif., 1981.

Bernabé, Alberto. "Platone e l' orfismo." In *Destino e salvezza: tra culti pagani e gnosi cristiana. Itinerari storico-religiosi sulle orme di Ugo Bianchi,* edited by Giulia Sfameni Gasparro, pp. 33–93. Cosenza, 1998.

Borgeaud, Philippe, ed. *Orphisme et orphée, en l'honneur de Jean Rudhardt.* Geneva, Switzerland, 1991. Papers discussing different aspects of Orphism.

Borgeaud, Philippe, Claude Calame, and André Hurst, eds. "L'Orphisme et ses écritures: Nouvelles recherches." *Revue de l'histoire des religions* 219 (2002): 379–516.

Brisson, Luc. *Orphée et l'orphisme dans l'antiquité gréco-romaine.* Aldershot, U.K., 1995. A collection of the author's papers about Orphism and the Neoplatonic reception of the movement.

Burkert, Walter. "Craft versus Sect: The Problem of Orphics and Pythagoreans." In *Jewish and Christian Self-Definition,* vol. 3: *Self-Definition in the Greco-Roman World,* edited by Ben F. Meyer and E. P. Sanders, pp. 1–22. Philadelphia, 1982.

Burkert, Walter. *Ancient Mystery Cults.* Cambridge, Mass., and London, 1987.

Burkert, Walter. *Da Omero ai Magi: La tradizione orientale nella cultura greca.* Venice, Italy, 1999.

Calame, Claude, "Qu' est-ce qui est orphique dans les *Orphica*? Une mise au point introductive." *Revue de l'histoire des religions* 219 (2002): 385–400.

Convegno di studi sulla Magna Grecia. *Orfismo in magna Grecia.* Naples, Italy, 1975. Papers about Orphism in southern Italy.

Detienne, Marcel. *Dionysos Slain.* Translated by Mireille Muellner and Leonard Muellner. Baltimore, Md., 1979.

Detienne, Marcel. *L'écriture d'Orphée.* Paris, 1989.

Graf, Fritz. *Eleusis und die orphische Dichtung Athens in vorhellenistischer Zeit.* Berlin and New York, 1974.

Masaracchia, Agostino, ed. *Orfeo e l'orfismo. Atti del Seminario Nazionale (Roma-Perugia 1985–1991).* Rome, 1993. Papers discussing different aspects of Orphism.

Parker, R. "Early Orphism." In *The Greek World,* edited by Powell Anton, pp. 483–510. London, 1995.

Tortorelli Ghidini, Marisa, Alfredina Storchi Marino, and Amedeo Visconti, eds. *Tra Orfeo e Pitagora.* Naples, Italy, 2000.

West, Martin L. *The Orphic Poems.* Oxford, 1983.

The Myth of Dionysos and the Titans

Bernabé, Alberto. "La toile de Pénélope: a-t-il existé un mythe orphique sur Dionysos et les Titans?" *Revue de l'histoire des religions* 219 (2002): 401–433.

Edmonds, Radcliffe G. "Tearing Apart the Zagreus Myth: A Few Disparaging Remarks on Orphism and Original Sin." *Classical Antiquity* 18 (1999): 35–73.

Marcel Detienne (1987)
Alberto Bernabé (2005)

ORPHIC GOLD TABLETS.

ORPHIC GOLD TABLETS. The Orphic Gold Tablets are thirty-five small pieces of gold foil that have been found in graves scattered throughout ancient Greece and Rome. The tablets are inscribed with texts in ancient Greek that vary in length from one word to sixteen lines of poetry. The longer texts provide instructions and information to guide the soul of the deceased as it makes its way through the underworld, and to ensure that it receives preferential treatment from the rulers there.

The tablets were labeled Orphic in the early twentieth century because scholars thought their statements reflected the tenets of a religious system the ancient Greeks and Romans believed was invented and promulgated by the legendary musician Orpheus. However, newer discoveries of tablets that refer to *bacchoi,* to the "Bacchic one," and to *thyrsoi* (staffs carried by worshippers of the god Bacchus) indicate that the tablets are associated with mystery cults in which Bacchus (also called Dionysos) and his mother Persephone were the most important deities. Calling the tablets Orphic is not completely erroneous, however, for verses engraved on the tablets probably were excerpted from a poem attributed to Orpheus. Some scholars now refer to the tablets as Orphic, some as Bacchic, and others simply as the Gold Tablets.

Most of the tablets have been found in southern Italy, northern Greece, or Crete, but one is from Sicily and another one from Rome. Most are from the fourth century BCE, although one from Hipponion (southern Italy) may be as early as the fifth century BCE and the tablet from Rome dates to the second or third century CE. Several were found on top of corpses, near a corpse's hand, or, in one case, in a corpse's mouth; another was found inside of an amulet case on a necklace. A list of all of the tablets, with notes and translations into Spanish, can be found in Bernabé and Jiménez San Cristóbal.

Gunther Zuntz divided the longer tablets that had been discovered by his time into two groups: A and B. Subsequently discovered tablets display qualities of both groups (prompting Bernabé and San Cristóbal to eschew the use of categories completely), but Zuntz's division still has heuristic value. The A tablets are distinguished by the soul's declaration of its purity and its kinship to the gods, its escape from the "circle of grief" (probably a reference to reincarnation), and its expectation that Persephone, the Queen of the Dead, will bestow special honors and rights upon it due to its initiation into Bacchic mysteries. There is a mention of death by lightning in three A tablets and a cryptic reference to animals falling into milk in four; the meanings of these statements are much debated. The B tablets are marked by descriptions of the underworld landscape, instructions to avoid drinking the subterranean waters of forgetfulness, and statements that the soul must pronounce to the guardians at a lake of memory before it is allowed to drink there.

There is no certainty about the ritual contexts in which the tablets were inscribed and given to the individuals in whose graves they were found, although it is certain that initiation into Bacchic mysteries was a prerequisite. It is possible that tablets were sometimes bestowed on an initiate at the time of initiation and subsequently buried with him or her, and that sometimes tablets were bestowed only at the time of burial, perhaps by an anxious family member.

The myth that underlies the tablets and the rituals connected with them, which is alluded to by some of the tablets' hexameters, concerns the birth of Dionysos to Zeus and his daughter Persephone; the subsequent murder, dismemberment, and consumption of the young Dionysos by jealous gods called Titans; Zeus's incineration of the Titans with lightning bolts; the emergence of humanity from their sooty remains (thus, humanity is largely composed of defective, Titanic material, although a bit of the consumed Dionysos lightens its composition); and Dionysos's miraculous rebirth from the womb of Semele, a mortal woman, made possible by the fact that the goddess Athena had snatched Dionysos's heart away from the hungry Titans.

The myth helps to explain why humanity must atone to Persephone, the grieving mother, for the deeds of the Titans (humanity's ancestors), lest Persephone make humans suffer in her realm, the underworld. They are able to do so by celebrating the mysteries of Persephone's son. It was probably during the mysteries that adherents were first given the directions about how to behave and what to do in the underworld that are found, in abbreviated form, on the Gold Tablets. The complete myth, as narrated above, must be pieced together from a number of ancient sources that span ten centuries, a fact that has sometimes caused scholars to question the relationship of individual episodes to each other, or even the very existence of the myth itself in antiquity. The 1990s saw attempts to dismiss the myth as either an allegorical invention by late antique Neoplatonic authors who were interested in alchemy or a projection of the Christian concept of original sin onto ancient Greece by nineteenth-century scholars. Yet in 2002, Alberto Bernabé offered a thorough re-analysis of the sources, showing that the myth was present already in the fifth century BCE and was central to Bacchic mysteries from an early period.

Other materials enhance our understanding of the doctrines and practices that lay behind the Gold Tablets, including numerous passages in ancient literary texts and small bone tablets from sixth or fifth century BCE Olbia (a city on the Black Sea), which are inscribed with the words "life-death-life" and "Dio [nysoi(?)] Orphikoi." Also important is a mid-fourth-century BCE funerary vase from Apulia in southern Italy, discussed by Johnston and McNiven, which shows Dionysos shaking hands with Hades, Lord of the Dead, while Persephone and other mythological characters look on; this can be interpreted as illustrating the promises made to those buried with the Gold Tablets.

BIBLIOGRAPHY

Bernabé, Alberto. "La toile de Pénélope: a-t-il existé un mythe orphique dur Dionysos et les Titans?" *Revue de l'histoire des religions* 219, no. 4 (2002): 401–433.

Bernabé, Alberto, and Ana Isabel Jiménez San Cristóbal. *Instrucciones para el más allá: Las laminillas órficas de oro.* Madrid, 2001.

Graf, Fritz. "Dionysian and Orphic Eschatology." In *Masks of Dionysus,* edited by Thomas Carpenter and Christopher Faraone. Ithaca, N.Y., 1993.

Johnston, Sarah Iles, and T. J. McNiven. "Dionysos and the Underworld in Toledo." *Museum Helveticum* 53 (1996): 25–36.

Zuntz, Gunther. *Persephone: Three Essays on Religion and Thought in Magna Graecia.* Oxford, 1971.

SARAH ILES JOHNSTON (2005)

ORTHODOX JUDAISM [FIRST EDITION]

is the branch of Judaism that adheres most strictly to the tenets of the religious law (*halakhah*). Its forebears may be identified in the eighteenth century, by which time the *qehillah,* the Jewish communal organization in each locality, had lost much of its authority in central and western Europe and its prestige in eastern Europe. This, in turn, undermined religious authority, which had heretofore relied not only on the faith of each Jew but also on communal consensus and the formal authority and prestige of communal leaders. The breakdown of the traditional community, coupled with the hope and expectation of political emancipation, encouraged new interpretations of Jewish life and new conceptions of appropriate relationships between Jews and non-Jews. These began to emerge by the end of the eighteenth century in central and western Europe and somewhat later in eastern Europe. Orthodoxy was born as the ideological and organizational response to these new conceptions.

The major tenets of Orthodoxy, like those of traditional Judaism, include the dogma that the Torah was "given from Heaven," that the *halakhah* derives directly or indirectly from an act of revelation, and that Jews are obligated to live in accordance with the *halakhah* as interpreted by rabbinic authority. But unlike traditional Judaism, Orthodoxy is conscious of the spiritual and cultural challenges of the modern world and especially of rival formulations of the meaning and consequences of being Jewish. Orthodoxy, in all its various manifestations and expressions, has never recognized any alternative conception of Judaism as legitimate. But it is aware of itself as a party, generally a minority party, within the Jewish world.

Orthodox Judaism received its earliest formulation in Hungary (then part of the Austro-Hungarian empire) in the first quarter of the nineteenth century and in Germany in the middle of the century. In both countries it constituted a response to the efforts of reformers to adapt the *halakhah* in general and the synagogue service in particular to currents in nineteenth-century culture. The reformers maintained that this was a condition for Jewish emancipation and civil equality. Orthodoxy developed in France and England at about this same time but in far less explicit and rigorous a manner. A major reason, no doubt, was that the challenge of Reform Judaism was so much weaker. The weakness of Reform Judaism in France and England may be attributable to the fact that it developed after, rather than before, the Jews had more or less obtained civil equality in those countries.

Orthodoxy arose in eastern Europe at the end of the nineteenth century, primarily in response to secular interpretations of Jewish life rather than in opposition to religious reform. The most important centers of Orthodoxy today are in Israel and the United States.

HUNGARIAN ORTHODOXY. The ideological and programmatic outlines of Hungarian Orthodoxy were formulated by Rabbi Mosheh Sofer (1762-1839), better known as the Ḥatam Sofer, the title of his seven-volume *responsa* to halakhic questions. This earliest variety of Orthodoxy is best described by the term *neotraditionalism* because it rejects any attempt at change and adaptation of the tradition. According to the Ḥatam Sofer, "all that is new is forbidden by the Torah"; the phrase is a play on the words of an injunction prohibiting consumption of "new" grain from each year's harvest until a portion is offered in the Temple in Jerusalem. Unlike some of his followers, the Ḥatam Sofer did not oppose all forms of secular education. A knowledge of some secular subjects, for example, is helpful in resolving certain halakhic problems. But in characteristically neotraditional fashion, he legitimated secular education in utilitarian terms, not as an end in itself.

The basic strategy of neotraditionalism was the sanctification of the rabbinic tradition in its entirety. Whereas traditional Judaism recognized different levels of sanctity and degrees of importance of halakhic injunctions (for example, acts prohibited by the Torah were in a more stringent category than acts prohibited by rabbinic legislation), neotraditionalists blurred the differences insofar as obligations to observe the injunctions were concerned. The tradition was self-consciously projected as woven of a single cloth, all parts of which were equally binding and sanctified. The two major instruments that the neotraditionalists fashioned to socialize the community to their ideology and values were a greatly expanded rabbinic authority and a new type of *yeshivah* (pl., *yeshivot*), or academy for intensive Talmudic study. These new and larger *yeshivot* were designed to exist in economic and ideological independence from the increasingly fragile local Jewish communities in which they were located. The *yeshivah* of the Ḥatam Sofer in Pressburg, where he served as communal rabbi from 1806 until his death, was the most important *yeshivah* in central Europe. His students, in turn, served as community leaders throughout Hungary, Galicia, and Bohemia-Moravia and in the Land of Israel (Erets Yisra'el), strengthening neotraditional influences in all these places.

The Ḥatam Sofer favored immigration to the Land of Israel. Many who favored immigration in those days were reacting to the reformers' rejection of nationalist elements in Judaism. The Ḥatam Sofer's espousal of an early form of Jewish nationalism and his projection of the importance of the Land of Israel in the Jewish tradition may also have been related to his negative attitude toward political emancipation. He feared its threat to religious authority. His followers believed they could establish a pure Jewish society, insulated from secularist modernizing influences, in the Land of Israel. They established a Hungarian subcommunity in the Land of Israel that played a major role within the old *yishuv* (the nineteenth-century settlement of religiously observant Jews, as distinct from the new *yishuv* of late-nineteenth- and twentieth-century settlers motivated by secular Jewish nationalism).

The distinctive instrument of Hungarian Orthodoxy in furthering its neotraditional objectives was the independent communal organization. In 1868 the Hungarian government convened a General Jewish Congress in order to define the basis for the autonomous organization of the Jewish community. The majority of the delegates were sympathetic to religious reform (Neologs), and most of the Orthodox delegates withdrew from the Congress. In 1870 the Hungarian parliament permitted the Orthodox to organize themselves in separate communal frameworks, which might coexist in the same locality with a Neolog community or a Status Quo community (the latter was composed of those who refused to join either the Orthodox or the Neolog community). Orthodox communities provided their members with the full gamut of religious services (kosher food, schools, religious courts, and, of course, synagogues) and represented Orthodox political interests to the government. Orthodox leaders discouraged contacts with members of the rival communities and prohibited entering their synagogues, and many Orthodox rabbis even enjoined intermarriage with them.

Hungarian Orthodoxy included both Hasidic and non-Hasidic elements. Hasidism, which originated in the eighteenth century, was bitterly opposed by the traditional religious elite, who feared that its folkishness, pietism, and ambivalence toward the central importance of Talmudic study undermined the tradition itself. Orthodoxy might have been born in opposition to Hasidism if not for leaders like the Ḥatam Sofer who sought a *modus vivendi*, recognizing that Hasidic leaders were no less antagonistic to basic changes in tradition than were the traditional religious elite. In fact, by the end of the century, the centers of Hasidic influence in the smaller Jewish communities remained least compromising in their attitude toward modernity. In the larger, more urbanized communities, one found signs of the growing attraction of German Orthodoxy with its more accommodating attitude toward modernity.

Even in an earlier period, not all Hungarian Orthodox rabbis were neotraditional in orientation. A minority were attracted by aspects of modern culture and/or believed that a more moderate approach might prove more attractive to potential deviators. Outstanding among such rabbis was German-born Esriel Hildesheimer, who served as a rabbi in Hungary until 1869. Although Hildesheimer was no less opposed to reform than his Hungarian colleagues, he aroused their particular antagonism when he established in the Austro-Hungarian community of Eisenstadt a *yeshivah* whose curriculum included secular studies. After leaving Hungary, Hildesheimer accepted the post of rabbi in an independent Orthodox congregation in Berlin. In 1873 he established a new rabbinical seminary in the more hospitable climate of German Orthodoxy.

GERMAN ORTHODOXY. The year 1850 marks the emergence of German Orthodoxy, with the establishment of the Israelitische Religionsgesellschaft in Frankfurt am Main, a congregation led by Samson Raphael Hirsch from 1851 until his death. But the distinctive ideological formulation of German Orthodoxy (often known as Neo-Orthodoxy) dates, at least in embryo, from the publication of Hirsch's *Nineteen Letters on Judaism* in 1836. The publication a few years later of an Orthodox weekly by Yaʿaqov Ettlinger (1798–1871) is also of significance.

Hirsch was the foremost proponent of the idea that Torah-true Judaism (to borrow a popular phrase of German Orthodoxy) was compatible with modern culture and political emancipation. Hirsch envisaged a divine order revealed in nature in which Jews could and should participate. But the divine order was also revealed in the Torah, many of whose commands were specific to Jews. The effect of Hirsch's conception, though not his intent, was the compartmentalization of life for the Orthodox Jew. Modern culture, patriotism, civil law—all become legitimate spheres for Jewish involvement since they were perceived as falling outside the realm proscribed by *halakhah*.

Hirsch and his followers directed their antagonism not at the Gentile world or its culture, but rather at religious reform, and in this respect they shared the outlook of the most intransigent of the Hungarian Orthodox. Reform Judaism, as a self-conscious movement in Jewish life, began in Germany with the establishment of the Hamburg temple in 1818. In the first few decades of the century it seemed that Reform conceptions of Judaism would replace those of traditional Judaism in Germany. Indeed, the major intellectual battle lines seemed to be drawn between the moderate reformers who sought changes in Jewish practice through the reinterpretation of Jewish law and the generally younger second generation of reformers who would abrogate the authority of the law entirely. Hirsch made no distinctions between moderate and radical reformers. Although in his *Nineteen Letters on Judaism* he was critical of traditional as well as Reform Judaism and seemed to advocate a position equidistant from both, some of his early endorsement of change was mitigated with the passage of time. What Hirsch never forgot was that the attraction of reform was an outgrowth of Jewish desire for emancipation and acceptance, that traditional Judaism appeared to be an obstacle to this goal, and that unless it could be reformulated as compatible with emancipation and modern culture, it had no future in Germany.

In addition to its educational system—day schools, religious schools, and seminaries around which German Orthodoxy united—the distinctive instrument that traditional Judaism forged to socialize its adherents to its values and conceptions was the autonomous congregation, even though it was only effective in a small number of localities. The heart of the congregational activity was the synagogue service itself, where the weekly or biweekly sermons by the rabbi, in German, represented a dramatic innovation. The traditional rabbi preached only a few times a year and never in the language of the state. The German Orthodox rabbi was likely to possess a university degree, an acquisition that distinguished him from his Hungarian and, as we shall see, his eastern European and Israeli counterparts. German Orthodox Jews were most attentive to the form of the service. Many Reform innovations, influenced in turn by the Christian churches, were adopted. German Orthodox rabbis, to the dismay of their traditional colleagues in other countries, officiated in clerical gowns, encouraged the participation of choirs (all male), and paid careful attention to musical arrangements in the service. In fact, some of their innovations would have been enough to identify a synagogue in Hungary as Neolog.

In addition to the synagogue itself, the autonomous congregation might sponsor a school, assume responsibility for the supervision of kosher foods, and provide opportunity for study and semisocial activity. Only political activity and sometimes welfare services remained outside its sphere of Jewish responsibilities, remaining the prerogatives of the more inclusive *Gemeinde* (the local Jewish community).

After the passage of a Prussian law in 1876 permitting Jews to secede, Hirsch insisted, as a matter of *halakhah*, that members of his congregation resign from the Frankfurt *Gemeinde*. Most of his congregants and certainly most Orthodox Jews in Germany refused to separate themselves and establish their own *Austrittsgemeinde* (seceded community).

Hirsch's demand for secession met opposition from traditionalists such as Rabbi Seligmann Ber Bamberger of Würzburg (1807–1878), probably the greatest contemporary Talmudist of Germany. It has recently been suggested that Bamberger harbored animosity toward the "modernizing ways" of Hirsch and his followers. The secession issue may have been a convenient opportunity to rebuke him and challenge his mastery of textual sources. Hirsch himself, in his lengthy response to Bamberger's opinion against secession, noted that the latter had never accepted Hirsch's ideal of *Torah ʿim derekh erets* (Torah and worldliness), which was the slogan of German Orthodoxy. Hildesheimer also favored secession and was not less antagonistic to Reform Judaism. Nevertheless, he differed from Hirsch, to whom he was personally close, on other issues. He was more favorable than Hirsch to integrating secular and sacred study. He and his followers did participate with non-Orthodox Jews in organizations dedicated to defending Jews against anti-Semitism. He was an enthusiastic supporter of the settlement of Jews and the establishment of Jewish institutions in the Land of Israel. To the chagrin of neotraditionalists, he sought means to raise the educational and vocational standards of Jews in the old *yishuv* and fought with them over this issue.

By the end of the century, Orthodoxy in both Germany and Hungary was well established, albeit with minority status within the Jewish world. Its exclusionary form of organization, its emphasis on those forms of observance that distinguished it from Reform Judaism, and its insistence that the core component of the authentic Jew's faith was the belief that God dictated the Torah to Moses suggested, in fact, that Orthodoxy was content to survive as a minority party in Jewish life, more concerned with maintaining its purity than extending its boundaries. The Orthodox camp in each country was reasonably well integrated and possessed its own organizational structure, periodicals, and schools. Its acknowledged leaders commanded deference in the general as well as the Jewish community. In fact, conservative governments, wary of radicals in general and aware of the attraction of political radicalism to so many Jews, often favored Orthodoxy, which it associated with tradition, law, and stability, over Reform. In short, by the end of the century it appeared that Orthodoxy, in one way or another, had withstood the challenge of modernity and emancipation and the blandishments of Reform. Jews in Hungary and Germany were increasingly assimilating and intermarrying. But this was a matter of greater immediate threat to Reform than to Orthodoxy.

In retrospect, Orthodoxy's strength was its ability to create small, meaningful, integrated communities that provided its adherents with a sense of identity and stability and mediated their involvement with the infinite. But Orthodoxy built upon certain assumptions. It was organized in a milieu in which one anticipated continued political and social freedom and in which the major threat to the tradition stemmed from religious reform. Its insularity from non-Orthodox Jews ill equipped it for a role in the defense of Jewish rights against a rising tide of anti-Semitism. Second, it had not yet developed ideological defenses against secular conceptions of Judaism. These, unlike Reform, argued not for religious alternatives to the tradition but for a totally new conception of the meaning of Jewishness. The most influential of these conceptions was Zionism, the notion that the Jews are a nation like other nations whose *sancta* are language, territory, and people rather than God and Torah. It was this last threat more than any other that led to the emergence of an international Orthodox organization—Agudat Yisra'el. Before such an organization could emerge, however, the level of Orthodox consciousness in eastern Europe had to undergo development.

ORTHODOXY IN EASTERN EUROPE. The vast majority of eastern European Jews continued to live in accordance with the religious tradition throughout the nineteenth century, although the institutions of traditional Judaism were severely undermined. Government law had destroyed many of the traditional privileges and responsibilities of the Jewish community. The charismatic authority of the *rebeyim* (Hasidic leaders) had further undermined the status of communal leaders. At the margins of society, the small party of radical *maskilim* (adherents of Jewish enlightenment) challenged traditional patterns of Jewish life. By the middle of the nineteenth century, changing economic conditions afforded new opportunities for a few, but further impoverished the masses and shook the moral consensus within the community. They also highlighted the importance of secular education, thereby undermining the alliance of the wealthy and the religious elite. They undermined the *battei midrash* ("houses of study"), once found in virtually every Jewish locality. There, small numbers of men had spent their day in study, supported, however meagerly, by the local housekeeper.

Traditional Judaism responded, however feebly and tentatively, to these developments, but the response cannot be labeled Orthodoxy, because it lacked one major distinguishing feature—self-awareness as one party among others in Jewish life. Traditional Jewish leaders who saw their authority questioned, Torah study abandoned, and new modes of behavior and belief increasingly legitimated differed among themselves as to how to meet the crisis. Their first concern tended to be the challenge to the primacy of textual study in the hierarchy of religious commandments. Hasidism had stressed the importance of religious experience and intention—adapting from earlier mystical Jewish conceptions the notion that in performing the commandments with true devotion and proper intent, the Jew was repairing the torn fabric of the cosmos. This stress on intention rather than behavior introduced a potential antinomianism and, no less seriously, suggested that the study of Talmud was of secondary importance in the hierarchy of religious injunctions.

The traditionalists' response was the establishment of central *yeshivot* supported by contributions solicited throughout the Jewish world. The first such *yeshivah* was established in 1802 in Volozhin (near Vilnius) by Rabbi Ḥayyim of Volozhin from his own funds. During the course of the century, *yeshivot* were founded throughout Lithuania and Belorussia (then still part of Russia). Leadership of a *yeshivah* rather than service as a communal rabbi marked one as a preeminent scholar automatically meriting deference and authority.

The *yeshivot* trained the Orthodox elite but generally failed to strengthen traditional Judaism among the masses. The Hasidic *rebeyim* filled a more important role in maintaining traditional norms, at least among their followers. But the decline of traditional patterns of observance until the last decades of the century must not be exaggerated. Rabbis such as Naftali Tsevi Yehudah Berlin (1817–1893), known as the Netsiv; Yisra'el Me'ir ha-Kohen (1838–1933), known as the Ḥafets Ḥayyim; and Yitsḥaq Elḥanan Spektor (1817–1896) retained authority and enormous prestige among the masses.

One measure of the continuing strength of the tradition was the failure of Rabbi Yitsḥaq Ya'aqov Reines (1839–1915), who later founded Mizraḥi, the Religious-Zionist movement, to establish a *yeshivah* in the 1880s. In 1881 Reines published a sharp critique of the method of study in traditional *yeshivot* and called for the reorganization of the institutions of eastern European Judaism. Jewish society, he maintained, was undergoing an ideological and institutional crisis. *Yeshivot* were crumbling, the rabbinate was weakened, and its authority was undermined because of its economic dependence on the wealthy. This, he argued, was a result of the loss of Jewish respect for the traditional leaders. His solution was the establishment of a new *yeshivah* to include secular studies in its curriculum and to produce graduates who would fill positions of Jewish leadership. Reines's view was supported by wealthy Russian Jews and Orthodox leaders from central Europe. But the opposition of the heads of the traditional *yeshivot* was enough to prevent the establishment of the new *yeshivah*.

A more successful effort at the reform of *yeshivot*, known as the Musar (ethical) movement, was initiated by Rabbi Yisra᾿el (Lipkin) Salanter (1810–1883). His call for ethical renewal was first addressed to the Jewish masses, businessmen and traders in particular, but failed to attract much enthusiasm. His doctrines were more influential in the *yeshivot*. While many of the heads of these academies initially resisted the introduction of the study of moral literature or discussions of moral issues at the expense of Talmudic study, the Musar movement was eventually co-opted. A limited amount of time was dedicated to the study of an ethical tract, and the custom of a weekly talk by the moral supervisor (a new position created in the *yeshivot* in response to the demands of the Musar movement) was introduced.

What traditional religious leaders did not do until the end of the century, either because they saw no need or because they did not know how to do it, was oppose the organization of rival parties with alternative conceptions of Judaism. But by the end of the nineteenth century this need was becoming apparent. In the 1870s an organization of Hasidic and non-Hasidic elements was formed to oppose the founding of a rabbinical seminary and the introduction of organizational changes in the community. In 1912 Agudat Yisra᾿el (Agudah for short) was established under the impetus of German Orthodox leaders, uniting the Orthodox leaders of central and eastern Europe in defense of the tradition.

Agudat Yisra᾿el never spoke for all religious Jews. Its greatest following was in Poland, the heartland of eastern European Jewry. Within Poland it functioned as a political party after World War I, rivaling the Zionists and the Bund (General Jewish Workers Union, a socialist Jewish party founded in 1897) for control of the Jewish street. Even within Poland it was opposed by the minority of religious Zionists and by the larger group of traditionalists, who remained indifferent to the needs that had led to its creation.

Agudah's primary strength came from the union of the Hasidic *rebe* of Ger (Avraham Mordekhai Alter, 1866–1948), whose followers numbered in the hundreds of thousands, with the leaders of the Lithuanian *yeshivot*, the most prominent of whom included Rabbi Ḥayyim ʿOzer Grodzinski of Vilnius (1863–1940). The latter carried enormous status in the world of religious Jewry. Nevertheless, in the Galician and Lithuanian regions, the masses remained aloof. The region around Warsaw and Lodz attracted Jews from the countryside. The struggle between religion and its opponents was most obvious and intense there, and Agudah prospered. In the older Jewish communities of Galicia, however, the Jewish tradition was less threatened, and religious Jews were content to leave political activity to non-Jews and secularists.

Agudah's own rabbinical authorities were, at best, tolerant of the necessity for political activity. Agudah was established to protect the traditional way of life, but political activity has an acculturating impact of its own. The Agudah press carried warnings from rabbis not to regard partisan politics as more than a temporary expedient.

Traditional religious leaders outside Agudah's ranks were impatient with the notion that some adaptation to modernity was necessary in the very defense of the tradition. Rabbi Yosef Yitsḥaq Schneersohn (1880–1950), leader of the Habad branch of Hasidism (better known as Lubavitcher Hasidism), attacked Agudah schools for including secular studies, accusing them of behaving no differently than the enemies of the tradition.

In addition to sponsoring schools whose curriculum included secular studies, Agudah established reading rooms where secular books were to be found, published a newspaper (though adherents were cautioned against reading it on the Sabbath), and organized a youth movement in which *yeshivah* students were warned not to spend too much time. Most damaging of all, Agudah's political survival required alliances with nonreligious parties, and when Agudah was the majority party in the local Jewish community, it bore at least indirect responsibility for nonreligious and even antireligious activity which the community funds supported.

Agudah, certainly in Poland, began as a neotraditionalist response to modernity. But its own efforts to defend the tradition through political instrumentalities and its own concern to control the environment within which the tradition had to function forced it into compromises that became particularly noticeable in the 1930s.

World War II brought the end to Agudah activity in eastern Europe. By the late 1930s it was apparent to many within Agudah itself that Jewish life in Poland was heading for catastrophe and that traditional responses were ineffective. Settlement in the Land of Israel became an increasingly attractive option, and Agudah muted its opposition to Zionism. Voices were increasingly heard, from within, for constructive efforts in the Land of Israel and for cooperation with the Zionists at the tactical level. Isaac Breuer (1883–1946), grandson of Samson Raphael Hirsch, a leading ideologue of German Orthodoxy, led the call for a reassessment of the Land of Israel in Agudah's program and ideology. The Balfour Declaration and the modern Zionist settlement of the land revealed, Breuer believed, the hand of providence. The Jews, he claimed, were a nation formed by

Torah, but as a nation they required their own land in order to renew themselves. In 1936 Breuer settled in Jerusalem. By the time other Agudah followers were prepared to reevaluate their position, the British had closed the gates of the land to world Jewry.

ORTHODOXY IN ISRAEL. Most Orthodox Jews today reside in Israel or the United States. Religiously observant Jews make up 15 to 20 percent of the Jewish population of Israel. The neotraditionalists, once quite marginal to Israeli society, play an increasingly important role. The most colorful and controversial group within their ranks is the successor to the old *yishuv*, the ʿEdah Ḥaredit (Community of the Pious), consisting of a few thousand families with thousands of sympathizers located primarily in Jerusalem and Benei Be-raq (on the outskirts of Tel Aviv). These are the most intransigent of the neotraditionalists. They relate to the state of Israel with varying degrees of hostility. They refuse to participate in its elections, the more extreme refuse to bear Israeli identification cards or utilize the state's services (their schools, for example, refuse government support), and the most extreme seek the imposition of Arab rule.

A more moderate neotraditionalism is found in Israeli Agudah circles. They are dominated by the heads of *yeshivot* and a number of Hasidic *rebeyim*. The most prominent continues to be the *rebe* of Ger. Agudat Yisraʾel generally obtains from 3 to 4 percent of the vote in Israeli elections. Although it has been a party to the ruling coalition, it continues to condemn ideological Zionism, that is, secular Jewish nationalism. It maintains that Israel's constitution must be based upon Torah and *halakhah* as interpreted by rabbinical authority. The leading rabbinical authorities, Agudah further claims, constitute its own Moʿetset Gedolei ha-Torah (Council of Torah Sages), to whom it turns for direction on basic policy issues.

Agudat Yisraʾel maintains its own network of elementary schools. Following graduation, boys continue their studies in *yeshivot qeṭannot* (minor *yeshivot*), whose curriculum consists almost exclusively of sacred text. They do not receive a high school degree. At the age of sixteen or seventeen they generally move on to advanced *yeshivot*, where study is devoted entirely to sacred writ, almost exclusively to Talmud. Girls pursue their high school studies in Beit Yaʿaqov, a network of girls' schools first established in Poland. The tendency is to prepare the girls to assume housewife-mother roles.

Beneficent government subsidy, largely for political reasons, has resulted in relative prosperity among Agudah-oriented institutions. Although the party itself is seriously troubled by personal and institutional conflicts and rivalries, and while it is the object of vociferous condemnation by more extreme neotraditionalists who charge it with selling out to the Zionists, the Agudah world appears relatively secure. It sponsors or supports a number of institutions for *baʿalei teshuvah*, Jews raised in nonreligious homes who have embraced Orthodoxy and are attracted by neotraditionalism rather than religious Zionism. Its *yeshivot* attract students from all over the world. Whereas a short time ago they were considered generally inferior to their counterparts in the United States, this is no longer true. The Agudah world is an international community with centers in New York, Montreal, London, Antwerp, and Zurich, to mention the major locations, but Jerusalem plays an increasingly important role. The young seem easily socialized to the values of the community, and their large families (seven and eight children are not at all uncommon) apparently assure continued communal growth. In fact, Israeli observers are rather surprised, given the size of Agudah families, that the party has not increased its proportion of the vote in recent elections—an indication that all may not be as well as it appears on the surface. One problem is Agudah's inability to integrate Sefardic Jews (Jews originating from Muslim countries) in their leadership groups. Sefardic Jews represent an important constituency of Agudah voters (some claim almost half), and in the summer of 1984 they bolted the party because they were excluded from its leadership. Another threat is economic. Agudah's educational institutions play a major role in the socialization of the Agudah community. The extended period of study for the men, often into their mid-twenties and beyond (they are exempted from Israeli army service as long as they remain in the *yeshivot*), requires public and/or private sources of support, which may not necessarily continue in the case of economic depression or a radical change in the Israeli political climate.

The Agudah world is in, but lives apart from, Israeli society. The religious Zionists are in a different category. They make up roughly 10 percent of the Jewish population but are in some sense the symbol of contemporary Israel. Israel's political culture, particularly since the 1970s, focuses on the Jewish people, the Jewish tradition, and the Land of Israel as objects of ultimate value. Symbols of traditional religion, though not traditional theology, pervade Israeli life. Religious Zionists are viewed by many of the nonreligious as most committed to and most comfortable with these values and symbols. The political elite, in particular, has been strongly influenced by the religious Zionists and their personal example of idealism and self-sacrifice. In fact, the success of religious Zionism makes the National Religious Party (their political organization) less attractive to voters, who no longer feel they need be as defensive about threats to religion from the secular parties.

In no other society do Orthodox Jews, religious Zionists in particular, feel quite so much at home. They are separated from the non-Orthodox population by their distinctive cultural and educational institutions (in the advanced religious Zionist *yeshivot*, students are required to fulfill their military obligations but generally do so in selected units) and their own friendship groups. There are political tensions between religious and non-religious Israelis over issues such as "Who is a Jew?," whether marriage and divorce law should be left to the rabbinate, Sabbath closing laws, and the sense of many secularists that they are subject to religious coercion. But most religious Zionists not only feel that they fully participate as equal members of the society but also sense a wholeness to their lives that they find missing outside of Israel. Nevertheless, they, too, confront the tension between tradition and modernity.

The founders of religious Zionism were influenced by modern currents of nationalism and the desire for political emancipation. Religious Zionists shared a concern for the physical as well as the spiritual welfare of Jews and an identification with nonreligious as well as religious Jews. Most of them believed that the modern settlement of the Land of Israel pointed to the beginning of divine redemption of the Jewish people. Unlike the neotraditionalists, they did not believe that Jews must patiently await the coming of the Messiah but rather that redemption was a process that Jews could initiate themselves. In other words, it was not only their espousal of Zionism that distinguished religious Zionists from the neotraditionalists, but also their acceptance of so many of the assumptions and values of modernity. Compartmentalization was an inadequate alternative. Although compartmentalization was and always will be a temptation for religious Jews who want to participate in worldly activity without compromising their religious principles, it is an inadequate ideology for religious Zionists. The establishment of the state of Israel and its public policies are to them matters of metaphysical significance intimately related to their religiously formed conceptions of reality. The reconciliation of tradition and modernity, therefore, requires other strategies.

One such strategy is adaptationism, sometimes labeled modern Orthodoxy. It affirms that the basic values of modernity are not also compatible with Judaism but partake of its essence. Freedom, the equality of man, rationalism, science, the rule of law, and nationalism are all found to be inherent in the Jewish tradition. Secular study is affirmed as a positive religious value—an instrument whereby man learns more about the divinely created world and therefore more about God. Adaptationism includes the effort to reinterpret the tradition, including those aspects of the *halakhah* that seem to stand in opposition to modern values. Adaptationism was a popular strategy among American Orthodox Jews. There are very few Israeli halakhic authorities whose rulings are adaptationist, and they lack the ideological self-consciousness or philosophical underpinning that is found among American Orthodox.

There are limits to the extent to which Orthodoxy can affirm every aspect of modernity, and there is an apologetic as well as an adaptive side to this strategy in practice. As in other religions, family law and relations between the sexes evoke the most conservative sentiments, though even here adaptationism has proved far more accommodating of modernity than other Orthodox strategies.

An alternative strategy for religious Zionism is expansionism. Expansionism affirms modernity by reinterpreting it through the prism of the Jewish tradition. It aspires, in theory, to bring all aspects of life under the rubric of its interpretation of Judaism. The program of religious Zionism, almost by definition, is expansionist. Since religious Zionism calls for a Jewish state in accordance with Jewish law, its adherents must believe, at least in theory, that Jewish law is a suitable instrument to guide a modern state. Me'ir Berlin (1880–1949), a major political leader of religious Zionism, claimed that the religious Zionist program was "not to content itself with a corner even if the Torah was there, but to capture Judaism, Jewish life, to impose the spirit of the Torah on the market, on the public, on the State." Anyone who reflects upon this statement must wonder whether, if this is indeed the task of religious Zionists, they would not have to reinterpret major motifs in the religious tradition and introduce rather radical changes in Jewish law. In other words, expansionism of this type bears within it the seeds of adaptationism. The leadership of the religious Zionist labor movement, the religious *kibbutsim* in particular, were prepared, at least in theory and sometimes in practice, for some halakhic adaptation. But they shied away from the final step that the realization of their goal would have required—the legitimation of religious changes through their adoption by the religious public rather than the assent of rabbinical authority. The ambivalent attitude toward adaptation by the leaders may help account for the permissive interpretation that many of their followers gave to *halakhah*. It may also help to account for the failure of this branch of expansionism to develop. It made no real effort to realize in practice its theoretical pretensions to adaptation, and it never legitimated the halakhic deviations that occurred under its roof.

Expansionism today is associated with the personality and philosophy of Rav Kook (Avraham Yitsḥaq Kook). This branch of expansionism, like neotraditionalism, is halakhically uncompromising. Unlike neotraditionalism, it abjures social and cultural isolation. Its goal is to sanctify all of life. The characteristic features of expansionism that support such a worldview and make its realization feasible, in addition to its commitment to Jewish nationalism, are a redefinition of secular-religious distinctions and a belief that divine redemption is imminent.

Expansionism is necessarily nationalistic since it argues that Jews must live a natural life in all its physical manifestations in order to invest all of life with the divine spirit. In the expansionist conception, as it has worked itself out in the last few years, the state itself assumes a special sanctity, its very creation being a sign of God's favor and a harbinger of the imminent redemption.

The religious conception of the state is challenged by three facts: that Israel was established by Jewish secularists, that the avowedly nonreligious constitute a majority of the population, and that the institutions of the state are controlled by secularists. The expansionists overcome this objection by their redefinition, following Rav Kook, of secularism. They blur distinctions not only between holy and profane but also between ostensibly religious and ostensibly secular

Jews. This enables the expansionists to break out of the traditional Orthodox perception, which viewed religious Jews as a beleaguered minority surrounded by hostile Jewish secularists with whom they might at best, and even then at their peril, cooperate at an instrumental level. The belief in imminent redemption that characterizes the expansionists' viewpoint reinforces their confidence in the eventual triumph of their position despite the apparent absence of support in the international arena. It also serves as a caution against any retreat or compromise that might interrupt and delay divine redemption. Finally, the belief in imminent redemption permits the evasion of troubling questions about the suitability of the *halakhah*, in its present state, to direct a modern society.

In addition to the neotraditionalists and religious Zionists, one still finds vestiges of pre-Orthodox traditionalism among some elderly Sefardic Jews of North African origin. They arrived in Israel before their own societies underwent modernization. They have no successors. Their descendants, in turn, tend to be deferential toward the tradition; they observe many of its customs and practices but are neither as punctilious or knowledgeable about the religion as are most Orthodox Jews. They categorize themselves and are categorized by others as "traditional," as distinct from the "religious" and "secular" segments of the population. They constitute a hinterland for Orthodox Jewry, though only time will tell whether they will continue to do so.

The state of Israel provides basic religious services such as religious schools, supervision over the *kashrut* of foods, religious courts, an established rabbinate with responsibility for marriage and divorce of Jews, ritual baths, and subsidies for synagogue construction and rabbis' salaries. The religious political parties act as intermediaries in the provision of welfare and educational services. Hence, the role of the synagogues proliferate in Israel, there is probably no country in the world where they play a less important role in the life of the Orthodox Jew.

ORTHODOXY IN THE UNITED STATES. American Orthodoxy bears the mark of two waves of immigrants and a native generation that combines characteristics of each. Many of the eastern European immigrants who came to the United States during the great wave of Jewish immigration between 1881 and 1924 were traditionalists. In the confrontation with American culture and the challenge of finding a livelihood, they abandoned many traditional patterns of religious observance. The dominant Orthodox strategy that emerged in the United States was adaptationism. In fact, in the first few decades of the twentieth century it appeared as though the difference between American Orthodox and Conservative Judaism was really the degree or pace of adaptation. The institutions and ideology of American Orthodoxy were severely challenged by neotraditionalist immigrants who arrived just prior to and immediately following World War II. They established their own *yeshivot*, Hasidic *rebeyim* among them reestablished their courts of followers, and they expressed disdain for the modern Orthodox rabbi. He was likely to be a graduate of Yeshiva University, the major institution for the training of Orthodox rabbis in the United States, where rabbinical students are required to have earned a college degree. The neotraditionalists were zealous and very supportive of their own institutions. In addition, they clustered in a few neighborhoods of the largest cities. Their concentration and discipline provided their leaders with political influence, which, in the heydays of the welfare programs of the 1960s and 1970s, was translated into various forms of government assistance.

The neotraditionalist challenge to modern Orthodoxy has had a decided impact on the native generation raised in modern Orthodox homes, and the American environment has left its mark on the generation raised in neotraditionalist homes. The American-born Orthodox Jew, regardless of the home in which he was raised, tends to be punctilious in religious observance, more so than his parents, and hostile to what he considers deviant forms of Judaism (i. e., Conservative or Reform). But he is sympathetic to many aspects of contemporary culture and accepting of secular education, if only for purposes of economic advancement. With the exception of pockets of neotraditional extremists who recall the ideology and attitudes of the ʿEdah Ḥaredit in Israel, the American Orthodox Jew, even the neotraditionalist, is familiar with, if not at home in, modern culture. Finally, there is a general willingness among most American Orthodox Jews to work with the non-Orthodox on behalf of general Jewish interests, those of Israel in particular.

Among the outstanding Orthodox figures in the United States is Rabbi Menahem Mendel Schneersohn (b. 1902), the present leader of Habad Hasidism. Habad is the Hasidic group with the largest number of sympathizers in the world. It is really a *sui generis* variety of Orthodoxy because it combines a neotraditional outlook with a conversionist impulse (toward other Jews, not non-Jews) and a unique belief system centering on the charismatic figure of the *rebe.*

Rabbi Moshe Feinstein (b. 1895), who came to the United States in 1937, is renowned in the Orthodox world as the outstanding *poseq* (adjudicator of religious law). Another significant Orthodox personality is Rabbi Joseph B. Soloveitchik (b. 1903), scion of a prominent rabbinical family and considered by many the greatest living Talmudic authority in the Orthodox world. Soloveitchik, who arrived in the United States in 1932, is particularly revered in modern Orthodox circles. He has a doctorate in philosophy and can communicate in the language of the world of ideas. His thought, which only began appearing in print in the last two decades of the twentieth century, is characterized by sensitivity to the tension between man, possessed of feelings and ideas connected to the divine within him, and the objective and demanding *halakhah* to which God also commands the Jew to subject himself.

The increasing importance of the neotraditional *yeshivot* has challenged the central role of the synagogue, but it is still the crucial mediator between most Orthodox Jews and their religious identity. Certainly, the synagogue plays a critical role in the lives of its members and recalls the importance of the autonomous congregations of German Orthodoxy. However, unlike the German congregations, the rabbi's role in the American Orthodox synagogue is more limited, though by no means negligible. The real strength of the Orthodox synagogue, which tends to be much smaller than the average Conservative or Reform synagogue, rarely exceeding 200 to 250 members, lies in the sense of community and mutual support that it offers rather than the network of services that it provides.

ORTHODOX JUDAISM TODAY. The dominant trend in Orthodoxy throughout the world, since the end of World War II, has been increased religious zealotry, punctiliousness in religious observance, and, with some exceptions, less explicit accommodation to modern values and contemporary culture. This is, at least in part, a result of the direction in which modern values and culture have moved. Increased permissiveness; challenges to authority, order, and tradition in general; and affirmation of self are inimical to all historical religions. But Orthodoxy has become far more skilled, after a century of experience, in developing institutions—such as schools, synagogues, political organizations, a press, and summer camps—to mute the threats of secularism and modernity. In some respects this means that Orthodoxy is more at ease with the world and tolerates certain forms of accommodation (advanced secular education is the outstanding example) that many Orthodox circles denounced in the past. But it also means an increased self-confidence and an absence of fear on the part of Orthodoxy to challenge and reject some of the basic behavioral and ideological assumptions upon which most of modern culture rests.

SEE ALSO Agudat Yisra'el; Hirsch, Samson Raphael; Judaism, article on Judaism in Northern and Eastern Europe since 1500; Musar Movement; Yeshivah; Zionism.

BIBLIOGRAPHY

Hebrew items are included only where English sources are inadequate and/or the Hebrew source is of major importance.

Hayim Halevy Donin's *To Be a Jew* (New York, 1972) is a practical guide to what it means to be an Orthodox Jew.

There is very little scholarly material in any language on most aspects of the social and religious history of Orthodox Judaism. The best material has been written recently; much is available only in the form of articles or doctoral dissertations.

On the background to Orthodoxy, see the last five chapters in Jacob Katz's *Tradition and Crisis: Jewish Society at the End of the Middle Ages* (New York, 1961) and *Out of the Ghetto: The Social Background of Jewish Emancipation* (Cambridge, Mass., 1973), particularly chapter 9, "Conservatives in a Quandary."

There is no general history of Orthodox Judaism. An outline of the topic is found in two articles by Moshe Samet, "Orthodox Jewry in Modern Times," parts 1 and 2, *Mahalakhim* (in Hebrew), nos. 1 and 3 (March 1969 and March 1970). Much can be learned from the two volumes of uneven biographical chapters edited by Leo Jung entitled *Jewish Leaders, 1750–1940* (New York, 1953) and *Guardians of Our Heritage, 1724–1953* (New York, 1958).

The best history of Hungarian Jewry covering the nineteenth and twentieth centuries and devoting considerable attention to Orthodoxy is Nathaniel Katzburg's "History of Hungarian Jewry" (in Hebrew), a lengthy introduction and bibliography to *Pinqas Qehillot Hungariyah* (Jerusalem, 1975). His article "The Jewish Congress of Hungary, 1868–1869," in *Hungarian Jewish Studies*, vol. 2, edited by Randolph Braham (New York, 1969), is the most significant study of a crucial aspect of the topic. The Ḥatam Sofer is the subject of Jacob Katz's major essay, "Contributions toward a Biography of R. Moses Sofer" (in Hebrew), in *Studies in Mysticism and Religion Presented to Gershom G. Scholem on His Seventieth Birthday, by Pupils, Colleagues and Friends*, edited by E. E. Urbach et al. (Jerusalem, 1967).

The English-language material on German Orthodoxy is more plentiful. Robert Liberles's *Between Community and Separation: The Resurgence of Orthodoxy in Frankfort, 1838–1877* (Westport, Conn., 1985) treats Hirsch and his community in detail. *Judaism Eternal: Selected Essays from the Writings of Rabbi Samson Raphael Hirsch*, vol. 2, translated from the German by I. Grunfeld (London, 1956), is probably the best place to start in reading Hirsch himself. On understanding some other leaders of German Orthodoxy, see David Ellenson, "The Role of Reform in Selected German-Jewish Orthodox Responsa: A Sociological Analysis," *Hebrew Union College Annual* (Cincinnati, 1982).

For a selection from Isaac Breuer, considered the most profound thinker of twentieth-century German Orthodoxy, see his *Concepts of Judaism*, edited by Jacob S. Levinger (Jerusalem, 1974).

There is no history of eastern European Orthodoxy, Emanuel Etkes's *R. Yisra'el Salanter ve-re'shitah shel tenu'at ha-musar* (Jerusalem, 1982) is an important source for understanding the Musar movement and the world of eastern European *yeshivot*. Eliyahu E. Dessler's *Strive for Truth* (New York, 1978), edited and translated by Aryeh Carmell, is an excellent example of Musar thought. *The Teachings of Hasidism*, edited by Joseph Dan (New York, 1983), provides some flavor of Hasidic literature.

On Zionism and Orthodox Judaism, see Ben Halpern's *The Idea of the Jewish State*, 2d ed. (Cambridge, Mass., 1969), pp. 65–95. On mainstream religious Zionism, see *Religious Zionism: An Anthology*, edited by Yosef Tirosh (Jerusalem, 1975).

The best study of the old *yishuv* and its confrontation with modern Zionism is Menachem Friedman's *Society and Religion: The Non-Zionist Orthodox in Eretz-Israel, 1918–1936* (Jerusalem, 1977; in Hebrew with English summary). An expression of the extreme neotraditionalist position is I. I. Domb's *The Transformation: The Case of the Neturei Karta* (London, 1958). On Rav Kook, see Avraham Yitsḥaq Kook's *The Lights of Penitence, The Moral Principles, Lights of Holiness, Essays, Letters, and Poems*, translated by Ben Zion Bokser (New York, 1978).

Charles S. Liebman and Eliezer Don-Yehiya's *Civil Religion in Israel: Judaism and Political Culture in the Jewish State* (Berkeley, Calif., 1983) reviews the role of traditional Judaism in Israel and devotes a chapter to the variety of Orthodox responses to Israel's political culture.

On American Orthodoxy, Charles S. Liebman's "Orthodoxy in American Jewish Life," *American Jewish Year Book* 66 (1965): 21–97, is the most extensive survey. An adaptation of Rabbi Soloveitchik's lectures is Abraham Besdin's *Reflections of the Rav* (Jerusalem, 1979), but Soloveitchik's work "The Lonely Man of Faith," *Tradition* 7 (Summer 1965): 5–67, is a better example of his speculative effort. Norman Lamm's *Faith and Doubt: Studies in Traditional Jewish Thought* (New York, 1971) illustrates the approach of a leading American Orthodox rabbi to problems of contemporary concern.

The halakhic literature remains the heart of the Orthodox enterprise. This literature is virtually closed to the nonspecialist, but the regular feature "Survey of Recent Halakhic Responses," appearing in each issue of *Tradition: A Journal of Orthodox Jewish Thought* (New York, 1958–), provides the nonspecialist with a good sense of that world. At a more academic level, see *The Jewish Law Annual* (Leiden, 1978–).

CHARLES S. LIEBMAN (1987)

ORTHODOX JUDAISM [FURTHER CONSIDERATIONS]. In a little more than fifty years, American Orthodox Judaism went from being a marginal phenomenon whose survival seemed to be in question to a religious option firmly established and at home in North America. There has, however, been a struggle among Orthodox Jews in the United States that has intensified since the early 1980s. The struggle concerns the definition of Jewish identity and the best way to assure its continuity. The traditionalist right wing of Orthodox Judaism, the so-called haredi movement, has not disappeared as many predicted it would but has instead been successful in building institutions, training rabbis, and asserting its place in the Orthodox world. This haredi approach appreciates American freedom of religion but wishes to remain separate from mainstream culture and values. This includes living in separate enclaves, dressing in demonstrably different ways (particularly noticeable among the men), downplaying the use of English, and eschewing a university education, while at the same time giving general secular cultural (which they consider toxic and defiling) a lower ontological meaning than the Jewish one. Instead, they value a life of Torah study above all else and scrupulous attention to ritual details, a life they sustain with many institutions that they have successfully built and sustained since the 1950s.

In contrast to the haredi, the so-called modern, or centrist, Orthodox have tried to stand with one foot in the world of strict observance and loyal faith and with the other foot in the outside world that they continue to view as valuable and essential for the survival of Orthodoxy into the future. At the same time, the people who once did little more than call themselves Orthodox because the synagogue they did *not* attend regularly was Orthodox, have stopped calling themselves Orthodox—in part because the demands of calling oneself Orthodox became much greater toward the end of the twentieth century.

As a result, Orthodox Jews who were once in the middle of the continuum found themselves on the outer edge, a place they were not used to inhabiting. They also faced an increasingly confident right wing, warning them that they were now more likely to fall prey to the defilements of the outside world to which they were powerfully drawn. Whereas in the past the modern or centrist Orthodox ignored these warnings and continued to participate in many different cultures at once, increasingly they were influenced by their haredi co-religionists and began to move back toward a more traditionalist position.

There are four major reasons that account for this change in the position of modern Orthodox Jews:

1. The perceived decline of American culture.
2. The complete handover by the family of the responsibility for education to Jewish day schools and yeshivas.
3. The lower proportion of modernists in the ranks of the Orthodox rabbinate and Jewish educators.
4. The emergence of study in Israeli *yeshivot* and women's seminaries, institutions that offer women an intensive course of religious study that excludes Talmud and that has a goal of socializing them into a haredi lifestyle and haredi values, which is seen as an essential part of Orthodox education.

To begin with the first reason, as long as American society and culture represented a positive model, the modern Orthodox ideal could be embraced without danger. The sexual revolution and the emergence of the university counterculture in the late 1960s, however, aroused doubts among many conservative elements in the population—including many who considered themselves Orthodox Jews. Consequently, the attraction of "making it in America" began to wear thin in some Orthodox circles. The growing secularization of public institutions, as well as the increasing moral relativism and tolerance of nontraditional lifestyles in mainstream society—from the cohabitation of unmarried heterosexuals to pressures for the legitimation of homosexual marriage—has only increased these doubts about the integrity of American culture.

However, Orthodox Jews in America were also becoming more self-confident in their ability to maintain their own standards of conduct and religious behavior without having to suffer persecution in America. As a result, a backlash developed not only against some of the cherished ideals of modern Orthodoxy but even against its very name. The quest for accommodation with modernity was increasingly regarded as a step down the slippery slope of compromise.

When the 1990 National Jewish Population Survey and the resulting debate within American Jewry about the continuity of tradition exposed the high rate of Jewish intermarriage and confirmed the continuing assimilation of American Jewry, modern Orthodox Jews became even more concerned about the cultural costs of modernity. The survey, and others like it, demonstrated that younger college graduates were among the most likely to marry non-Jews and become assimilated. This revelation of the unintended consequences of a college degree, which was so central to the ideological stance of modern Orthodox Jews, undermined their position.

The modern Orthodox then looked for more "Jewish insurance" that would protect them against the assimilationist tendency of American culture. This search led many of them to seek an "inoculation" against the diseases of assimilation and intermarriage. To many, that inoculation was to be found in a more intensively Jewish education. As a result, many of the modern Orthodox handed over the Jewish education of the young to those who had made it their vocation.

Increasingly, however, those educators were not modern Orthodox Jews. Even though the modern Orthodox were committed to full-time intensive Jewish education for their children, they had not obtained college degrees in order to become Jewish educators themselves. Day-school heads often admitted that harder than finding students to fill their classrooms was the critical quest for teachers who would provide instruction in Judaica and who shared the modern Orthodox ideological outlook. Those who had that outlook had pursued successful careers in the world outside Judaism. As a result, the Jewish educators to whom they handed over their children were the haredim who had remained in Jewish education. By one count, nearly two-thirds of the teachers of Judaica in the day schools of the early 2000s come from the haredi or fervently Orthodox world.

Moreover, once parents who were engaged in careers outside the Jewish world gave up a significant role in the education of their children in favor of placing them in schools where paid teachers provided the education, they became increasingly dependent upon those teachers. The teachers had control over the children throughout the entire day, from the earliest primary grades through the end of high school. Orthodox parents gave these teachers into whose hands they entrusted their children the right to supersede them. Even when the teachers pushed their students toward the haredi right wing of Orthodox Judaism and away from modernist values, the parents allowed this trend to grow because they had no alternative. In effect, these teachers inevitably undermined many modern Orthodox values related to acculturation. Yet the consumers of their teaching were given to understand, both by the heads of the schools and the larger Orthodox world, that these teachers were the guardians of the Jewish future. And the rabbi/teachers believed this no less—that was one of the reasons they were willing to step out of their enclaves into the defiled domains of the day school (although, to be sure, some did it because they needed the money).

A similar trend developed within the rabbinate. Few modernists chose to be rabbis, leaving the *yeshivot* that trained the rabbis to the haredi right wing. As a result, American Orthodox rabbis began to express haredi values and the worldview that underlay them. They entered the pulpits and the classrooms, serving as religious authorities to which all Orthodox Jews had no choice but to turn. They had a growing effect on the character of their congregations and students. These rabbis convinced their laity that their young people needed more powerful religious indoctrination in order to avoid the moral pitfalls of modern American culture.

The traditionalist rabbis believed that they would find the answer to their educational concerns in Israeli yeshivas and seminaries, and Orthodox Jewish parents accepted this line of reasoning. The Israeli institutions were, however, not simply educational; they were ideological training grounds engaged in fighting back against secular culture, and the instructors had their charges under continuous control for a year or longer. As a result, the Israeli teachers had a far greater influence than even haredi teachers on the faculties of Orthodox Jewish day schools in the United States. Moreover, the students who had spent more than one year in the Israeli schools tended to shun all those who remained outside their institutions. In time, as these young people matured and returned to America, they inserted their haredi values and behaviors into Orthodox Judaism in the United States, where increasingly right-wing younger rabbis were ready to serve them.

The long-term consequences of these trends remain an open question. While those who call themselves modern Orthodox may still be in the majority in North America, the center of gravity and confidence in the future appear to have moved toward the religious right.

Orthodox Judaism in the United States in the early twenty-first century finds most of its rabbinical leaders coming from its right wing. That right wing is defined both by those who embrace the values of the *yeshivot* and those whose political position favors a greater Israel. The latter group reflects the predominant role that the Orthodox, who constitute 22 percent of the Israeli population, have played in the settlement movement, the group that seeks to re-establish religious Jewish communities in the ancient biblical lands, many of which are in territories conquered in the 1967 war between Israel and the Arabs. This relationship has made the Orthodox in Israel an important part of the nationalist camp, while many of those in the Diaspora have become moral and financial supporters of Israel.

BIBLIOGRAPHY

Friedman, Menachem. "The Haredim and the Holocaust." *Jerusalem Quarterly* 53 (1990).

Heilman, Samuel. "The Many Faces of Orthodoxy, Part I." *Modern Judaism* 2 (1982): 23–51; and "The Many Faces of Orthodoxy, Part II." *Modern Judaism* 2 (1982): 171–198.

Heilman, Samuel. "The Ninth Siyum HaShas at Madison Square Garden: Contra-Acculturation in American Life." In *Americanization of the Jews*, edited by Norman Cohen and Robert Seltzer, pp. 311–338. New York, 1995.

Heilman, Samuel C., and Steven M. Cohen. *Cosmopolitans and Parochials: Modern Orthodox Jews in America.* Chicago, 1989.

Kaplan, Lawrence, and David Berger. "On Freedom of Inquiry in the Rambam—And Today." *The Torah U-Madda Journal* 2 (1990).

Keller, Chaim Dov. "Modern Orthodoxy: An Analysis and a Response." *Jewish Observer* 6, no. 8 (1970): 3–14.

Lichtenstein, Aaron. "A Consideration of General Studies from a Torah Point of View." *Gesher* 1 (1963).

Sacks, Jonathan. *Arguments for the Sake of Heaven: Emerging Trends in Traditional Judaism.* Northvale, N.J., 1991.

Samet, Moshe. "The Beginnings of Orthodoxy." *Modern Judaism* 8 (1988): pp, 123–137.

Wurzburger, Walter S. "Confronting the Challenge of the Values of Modernity." *The Torah U-Madda Journal* 1 (1989): pp. 26–32.

Zuroff, Efraim, and Yehuda Bauer. *The Response of Orthodox Jewry in the United States to the Holocaust.* New York, 2000.

SAMUEL C. HEILMAN (2005)

ORTHODOXY AND HETERODOXY. The concepts of orthodoxy and heterodoxy are found within all the major religious traditions, expressed by a variety of terms. In relation to religious life, *orthodoxy* means correct or sound belief according to an authoritative norm; *heterodoxy* refers to belief in a doctrine differing from the norm. The two terms originated in the patristic period of Christian history, when emphasis on belief rather than practice distinguished the concerns of Christian theologians.

Each of the major religious traditions has its own modes of determining orthodoxy. The extent to which heterodoxy is considered a serious deviance varies across traditions, and also within traditions at different phases of their history. From the perspective of an overview of the history of each tradition, one can discern that differing beliefs and/or practices have been considered of vital significance over the course of time. Further, some traditions allow for a wide variety of different perspectives within a wider unity, whereas others tend to split up into smaller groups competing as to which shall be considered the bearer of the authentic message or teaching.

Every major religious tradition has had to establish criteria for the acceptance or rejection of its members. In some cases, the civil power has supported the religious authorities, whereas in other cases, it has remained neutral or disinterested. Sometimes a group has insisted on rigid criteria of purity and conformity, whereas at other times, a great diversity of opinion and practice has been acceptable. Diversity of attitudes on such matters has existed at different times within each of the major traditions.

The scriptures normally serve to delineate the characteristics of acceptable, as opposed to unacceptable, persons. Later theological or philosophical or legal schools often take the scriptural indications as a basis for outlining systems. Elaborating the fixed systems usually involves decisions as to the canon of scriptures and the modes of authority, as well as the establishment of training institutions for those who are to impart and uphold the particular orthodoxy. The self-conscious articulation of an orthodox perspective tends to occur several generations after the establishment of a new perspective, or the successful renewal of an older tradition that has been challenged. The usual process is to project the newly proclaimed orthodox position backward onto the beginnings of the community's life.

In the past century, two opposite tendencies have manifested across traditions: There is both an active fundamentalism in every tradition and a new interest in reconciling divergent streams of thought and practice. The spread of literacy has enabled lay people to evidence new forms of interest and participation in religious leadership.

Those who lean toward fundamentalism tend to think the identity for the members of the community requires one exclusive interpretation of the tradition, and that particular interpretation must be imposed. The more traditional thinkers and the modernists, however, see the traditional tolerance of diverse interpretations as a source of strength rather than weakness.

NONLITERATE PEOPLES. Nonliterate peoples commonly affirm their group identity through myths that legitimate social relations within the group and orient the group toward the wider universe. Shamans or equivalent figures serve as mediators with sacred powers. Knowledge of the sacred mythology may be shared in diverse ways by members of the group. Changes in the mythology may come about through visions or insight. Ritual practice serves to maintain coherent identity among members.

Deviance usually involves breaking codes of behavior, particularly with respect to sexual or family matters. Deviants can sometimes be readmitted into a normal relationship with the group through rituals of purification, but sometimes they leave and join another group. Deviants are generally understood to be offending the sacred powers, and are therefore required to undergo rituals to transform them into acceptable persons.

HINDUISM. Classical Hindu philosophy of religion divides religious schools of thought into two types, *āstika* (usually translated as "orthodox") and *nāstika* (usually translated as "heterodox"). Those characterized as *nāstika* are the Jains, the Buddhists, and the materialists. The word *āstika* indicates the affirmation of being, whereas *nāstika* suggests nihilism, or denial of being.

The *Maitri Upaniṣad* expresses the importance of avoiding teachers of false doctrines. The same Upaniṣad uses the term *nāstika*, translated here as "atheism," to designate one of the characteristics emanating from the dark aspects of the unenlightened self in every individual.

There are no available sources available from the materialist or atheist schools of thought of ancient India, therefore the views of these schools are only known from the writings of their adversaries. But in the case of the Jains and the Buddhists, the sources still exist. The classical Hindu view is that the *nāstika* schools of thought are to be condemned because of their failure to accept the authority of the Vedas—a refusal that in practice means the rejection of their hereditary function as preservers and teachers of the Vedas, as well as in their duties as the priests responsible for ritual performances.

In time a principle of interpretation of the scriptures was developed that allowed for diversity: The interpretations varied according to which affirmations were deemed central. Hence more or less emphasis might be laid on ritual or other forms of religious life. Acceptance of the scriptures was, however, a necessary precondition for acceptance within the community. In his *History of Hindu Philosophy* (Cambridge, 1963), Surendranath Dasgupta has written: "Thus an orthodox Brahmin can dispense with image-worship if he likes, but not so with his daily Vedic prayers or other obligatory ceremonies."

The coherence of Hinduism derives from the discipline of the *brahmans* as transmitters and preservers of Vedic ritual and wisdom. The classical view is that the ancient seers (*ṛṣis*) who received the primal wisdom set in motion the oral transmission of the Vedas that is passed on through the educational system of the *brahmans.* The primary revelation is thus oral, *śruti.* The secondary level of sacred literature, *smṛti,* comprises the commentaries that explain the primal wisdom and give instruction on moral conduct and related matters.

Deviance within Hindu life can take many forms. The usual procedure for readmitting offenders is purification through ritual administered by a *brahman.* Offense is perceived as impurity that must be removed through the restorative power of ritual.

By the tenth century CE, the Buddhists had gradually disappeared from India, although their teaching had taken root in other countries. The Jains remained as a distinctive group, sometimes supported by local rulers. When the Abbé Sean-Antoine Dubois, in his *Hindu Manners, Customs and Ceremonies* (Oxford, 1928), wrote about India as he observed it in the late eighteenth century, he formed the impression that the Jains had been on occasion dominant in certain parts of India. By the twentieth century this was no longer the case: The Jains formed a relatively small minority community. Before the Muslim conquests of India, the local rulers probably helped determine whether the people tended toward the Buddhist, Jain, or Hindu perspectives. The last-named seems to have won out and to have remained dominant during the period of Muslim rule.

Diverse processes are taking place as the Hindu tradition confronts modernity. In the early twentieth century, several effective religious personalities—not all *brahmans*—attempted to articulate interpretations of Hinduism that would be acceptable to the modern age. Such writers as Vivekananda, Radhakrishnan, Tagore, Aurobindo, and Gandhi have exercised a great influence over modern Hindus.

A number of groups advocating particular interpretations of Hinduism also have come into being, such as the Brāhmo Samāj and the Ārya Samāj. These groups advocated reform of Hindu social practices. A fundamentalist interpretation of Hinduism has appealed to certain segments of the Hindu population, as evidenced most dramatically by the assassination of Mohandas Gandhi. India is a secular state; in practice, therefore, no religious group receives favored status from the government.

BUDDHISM. Buddhism emerged as one of the protest movements against orthodox Hinduism around the sixth century BCE. The monks and nuns who followed the teachings of the Buddha took those teachings as the only guide necessary for enlightenment. Present historians acknowledge that Buddhists held councils to resolve disputes, but because the various groups have their own versions of what occurred at those councils, there is no consensus now as to what councils were held and what issues were decided. The teachings were transmitted orally for several centuries. It is impossible to say when the oral tradition was written down. The Buddha taught that missionaries were to speak in the language of those they addressed. As a result, Buddhist teaching has moved rapidly from one language to another, and many varieties of the teaching have been handed down.

Tradition says that a council was held immediately after the Buddha's death. This council was concerned with the composition of the monastic discipline, Vinaya. A second council, held at Vaiśālī, is said to have been concerned with disputes about the severity of the monastic rules. A third council was reportedly called by the emperor Aśoka about 250 BCE. Some versions of the tradition say that this council completed the ratification of the canon of Buddhist scriptures and sent missionaries to various countries.

As source material for understanding the relationship between Buddhism and the state, and also the issues of orthodoxy and heterodoxy within Buddhism, the chronicles of Sri Lanka, whose earliest written form dates from approximately the fourth century CE, are useful. The norm for the monastic practices was the Vinaya, the code for monastic life believed to have been transmitted directly from the Buddha.

With respect to sectarianism, the Vinaya provides that, when four or more monks within a monastery differ from the others, they may leave and found their own monastery. This has made possible the development of many perspectives within Buddhism. It is the discipline of the order that maintains the unity. In Sri Lanka in the early period two large monasteries tended to dominate Buddhist life and practice: the Mahāvihāra and the Abhayagiri. In his *History of Buddhism in Ceylon* (Colombo, 1956) Walpola Rahula writes: "The Mahāvihāra . . . was faithful to the very letter of the orthodox teachings and traditions accepted by the Theravādins. The Abhayagiri monks, therefore, appeared in the eyes of the Mahāvihāra to be unorthodox and heretic" (p. 85).

At certain points in the history of Sri Lanka, one or the other of the major monasteries might be in favor, depending on the predilections of the ruler. These incidents indicate that in Buddhism, as in other traditions, the political leaders have exercised considerable control over what shall be deemed orthodox or acceptable. On the other hand, if the rulers unduly outrage the traditional values of the people, they can be in difficulty.

The sixth great Buddhist council was held in Rangoon, Burma, in 1954–1956. It reedited the Buddhist scripture and promoted movements of mutual understanding among Buddhists from different historical traditions. An ecumenical movement among Buddhists has developed, as indicated by the founding of the World Fellowship of Buddhists in 1950. Lay followers are more active in the modern period. Historically the monastic orders have dominated education and the transmission of the scriptures, but under modern conditions this is no longer the case.

Fundamentalism has been a prominent feature of the twentieth-century Sōka Gakkai. This group follows Nichiren's teaching as to the importance of one scripture only and advocates political activism as a way of imposing Buddhist virtues.

Chinese Religion. Religious life in China has been shaped since the earliest known dynasty (Shang, c. 1600 BCE) by cults of devotion to ancestors, and by a worldview that has affirmed the necessity of directing human activities toward harmony with the forces implicit in and beyond nature. Almost all schools of Chinese thought have assumed that an encompassing reality, the Dao, maintains balance and harmony among the divergent processes that constitute existence.

The emperor became a central legitimating figure, because he sanctioned the divine order and created or elevated new gods. Unlike in India, then, in China the legitimating power did not lie with priests.

The formative period of religious ferment was that of the Hundred Schools (sixth to third centuries BCE). The issues debated were generally concerned with how to develop individual character so as to overcome the divisive forces that led to social chaos. The two major schools of thought that emerged from these debates, the Confucian and the Daoist, shared the premise that the encompassing Dao existed, and that humans must learn to balance existence appropriately. They differed as to how the balance should be acquired, though neither perspective necessarily excluded the other.

The school that insisted on an exclusive orthodoxy of belief and practice was that of the Legalist, in power during the Qin dynasty (221–206 BCE). During this rigid regime, Confucian scholars were killed and books of traditional learning were burned. After this regime's collapse, the succeeding dynasties encouraged Confucianism as the state doctrine—a role it retained until modern times. During the Han period, Confucianism provided the government with a standard code of ritual and moral norms that regulated behavior among persons. Books were preserved, and provided a perspective from ancient days different from the immediate needs of the state. Under the emperor Wu (140–87 BCE) efforts were made to institute a national system of schools and a civil service examination system. Textual orthodoxy was established. The curriculum of the schools consisted of the Confucian classics. The aim was to produce Confucian sages to serve the emperor and the society as civil servants and moral exemplars.

Judaism. Around the beginning of the fourth century BCE the religious leader Ezra, a priest and a scribe, returned from among the exiles in Babylon to Jerusalem, where he effected a religious reform that shaped subsequent Judaism. These events are recorded in the biblical books of Ezra and Nehemiah. The reconstitution of Judaism that occurred at this time made the scriptures available through the institution of schools and the use of public occasions as opportunities for adult education. The Bible says: "And Ezra the priest brought the law before the assembly, both men and women and all who could hear with understanding . . . and the ears of the people were attentive to the book of the law" (*Neh.* 8:2–3).

This reconstitution of Judaism gives a teaching function to the scribes (the scholars of the Law), but it also implies that the people are to appropriate the teachings by their capacity to hear with understanding. Ezra's reforms are said to have reached a climax when the people engaged in solemn covenant to enter into no more mixed marriages, to refrain from work on the Sabbath, to support the Temple, and in general to comply with the demands of the Law. The school of scribes established by Ezra, or in his name, probably instituted a framework of orthodoxy that led eventually to the canonization of the Hebrew scriptures after the destruction of the Temple in 70 CE.

Subsequently, the locus of Judaism became a rabbinic program that stressed study of the scriptures, prayer, and works of piety. Under the leading rabbi, Yehudah ha-Nasi' (135–220?), an effort was made to standardize Jewish practice. The result was the collection of rabbinic lore titled the Mishnah, which became the primary source of reference and the basis around which the Talmud was later compiled.

Modern Hebrew uses the word *orthodox,* taken directly from the English, because no such term exists in earlier Hebrew. The word for *heterodox* is *min,* which tends to mean "individual deviant." Procedures exist for readmission of deviants. The philosopher Spinoza was excommunicated by rabbinic authorities in Holland in 1656 because of his allegedly dangerous attitudes toward biblical authority. The idea that individuals or groups might have beliefs and practices that threaten the well-being of the tradition has existed in Judaism as far back as is known. In Ezra's times, individuals and groups were excluded from the Temple for various practices considered impure, such as mixed marriages. However, the extent to which exclusion was exercised varied considerably in different historical periods. After the destruction of the Temple, the rabbis rarely excommunicated anyone. In the modern period, exclusion is not considered a significant problem.

Reform Judaism developed in Germany in the 1840s and later appeared in the United States, where it spread widely. The Reform Jewish group first used the term *Orthodox Judaism* to characterize their more traditional conservative opponents. Reform Judaism stressed the individual observance of the moral law rather than strict observance of the traditional legal codes.

CHRISTIANITY. In the pastoral epistles of the New Testament, the members of the church are called upon to live "in all holy conversation and godliness, looking for and hasting unto the coming of the day of God" (*2 Pt.* 3:11–12). They are warned against "false teachers among you, who privily shall bring in damnable heresies, even denying the Lord that bought them" (*2 Pt.* 2:1).

These and similar passages indicate divisiveness within the early generations of Christians. During the first three centuries, factionalism resulted from conflicts as to purity of conduct, steadfastness under persecution, gnosis, Christology, and practical matters such as the date of Easter. When the emperor Constantine became Christian in the fourth century, he attempted to further unite his territories by promoting a unified perspective among Christians. Under his auspices the Council of Nicaea was summoned in 325, and agreement was reached on disputed matters. Dissident opinions were held to be anathema.

Eastern orthodoxy. A schism took place in 1054 between the Roman Catholic church and the churches of the Eastern Byzantine Empire. The Eastern churches see themselves as a fellowship of churches governed by their own head bishops. Today there are fifteen such churches. They claim to have preserved the original apostolic faith, which they believe to have been expressed through the common Christian tradition of the first centuries. They recognize seven ecumenical councils.

Roman Catholicism. The perspective that emerged as orthodox envisaged the bishop of Rome as the primary authority. The authority of the bishops was legitimated by apostolic succession. The importance of the priesthood was linked to the centrality of the ritual of the Eucharist. The historian Eusebius, a contemporary of the emperor Constantine, wrote a history of the church that for centuries legitimated the view that the structures and doctrines of the fourth-century church were equivalent to the original practices and beliefs.

Protestantism. Reformers in the sixteenth century claimed to replace the authority of the Roman Catholic hierarchy with the authority of the Bible. They denied the doctrine of transubstantiation and held ministers to be competent to interpret the scriptures. The teachings of the church councils were to be supported only insofar as they conformed to the scriptures.

With the passage of time, the relationship between the state and the churches in Protestant countries became one of increasing separation. Therefore the differences among Christians were not linked to the need of the state for unity. If Christians differed, they had the option of leaving to establish different forms of Christianity. In the tract *A Plain Account of the People Called Methodist* (1749), John Wesley describes the early Methodists' protest against hierarchical authority legitimated by doctrine: "The points we chiefly insisted upon were four; First, that orthodoxy, or right opinion is, at best, but a very slender part of religion, if it can be allowed to be any part of it at all." The chief business of religion, according to Wesley, was to effect the transformation of consciousness, so that the believer might come to have the mind of Christ.

The Council of Trent. At the Council of Trent (1545–1563) the positions of the Roman Catholic church were reaffirmed. Many of the abuses that had preceded the Reformation were done away with, but the authority of the church hierarchy, the role of the priesthood, and the doctrine of transubstantiation were reasserted. At the same time, anathemas were pronounced against the respective Protestant opinions.

The modern period. Efforts have been made toward further mutual understanding among diverse Christian churches. At the Second Vatican Council (1962–1965), a number of studies reconsidered the roles of clergy and laity, and of biblical teaching with respect to the nature of the church. The forum for Protestant discussion of similar issues has been the World Council of Churches, which meets every six years since its establishment following World War II. It is attended by representatives of the majority of Protestant and Eastern Orthodox churches. Those who established the World Council held that mutual respect might better arise out of mutual knowledge and common action. They have envisaged a long-range process out of which a greater sense of mutuality may emerge, as a result of which historic conflicts may eventually be resolved.

Fundamentalism among Protestants usually affirms the inerrancy of the Bible and insists on one particular interpretation of scripture. Fundamentalist attitudes exist within all the major Protestant denominations.

ISLAM. One of the Arabic words used as an equivalent for orthodox is *mustaqīm.* It comes from the first *surāh* of the Qurʾān in which the believers are asked to follow the straight path, *al-sirāṭ al-mustaqīm.* In this respect, the straight path is primarily a way to live. Deviance would be a matter of rejecting the divine commands. From the Qurʾanic perspective, one who denies is called *kāfir* ("unbeliever," from *kufr,* "ingratitude; unbelief").

The first disputes among Muslims took place about thirty years after the death of the Prophet. These differences centered around the legitimate leadership of the community. After a brief civil war the members divided into two groups, Sunnīs and the Shīʿīs. The former acknowledged the actual leaders of the community to have been legitimate. The latter did not accept any leader apart from the caliph Ali, but rather waited for a divinely appointed leader to reappear and establish justice on the earth. A third group, the Khārijīs, attempted to enforce a strict puritanism as a criterion for membership in the community, but they failed to persuade the majority. With the passage of time, their perspective became insignificant.

Sunnī Islam and Shiism have each developed their own systems of religious law and theology, but neither explicitly excludes the other from Islam. Rather, each sees the other as misguided in its interpretations of particular aspects of Islam.

In one of the Sunnī theological statements commonly used as a basis for training scholar-jurists in the Middle Ages, and in traditional schools today—the *Commentary of al-Taftāzānī on the Creed of al-Nasafī* (trans. Edward Elder, New York, 1950)—heresy is characterized as *bāṭin* (esoteric interpretation of the Qurʾān). Such heresy is said to be equivalent to unbelief. The theologians commenting on the Qurʾān also equate unbelief with despair and with ridiculing the law. They are stating which attitudes they find unacceptable, rather than defining the characteristics that would lead to exclusion. Al-Taftāzānī deals with including great sinners in the community and affirms the Qurʾanic emphasis on the forgiveness of God. The community tended to leave final judgment of sinners to God's decision on Judgment Day.

The responsibility for guidance on matters respecting membership in the community lay with jurists rather than with theologians. On occasion, if the civil power was willing to support the opinions of particular scholar-jurists, persons were condemned for their views. More often, the condemnations of scholar-jurists with respect to dissenting opinions carried little force.

Deciding which practices and opinions were considered most adequate was a slow, informal process. There were no equivalents to the Buddhist or Christian councils. Only after the fact could it be determined that a particular perspective had gained widespread support. Even so, adherents of differing opinions were not normally excluded from participation in the community. Scholar-jurists often used abusive language about one another, but such rhetoric did not usually cause persons to be excluded from communal life.

The procedures by which the religious law, *sharīʿah*, was elaborated involved an appeal to chains of transmitters to legitimate the traditional narratives respecting the words and deeds of the prophet Muḥammad and his companions. This process of legitimation was similar to the Christian and Buddhist appeal to an unbroken line of trusted transmitters of the original teaching.

In the twentieth century Muslims threw off foreign domination in every major Muslim nation. The newly independent Muslim states varied in the ways by which they adapted the medieval religio-legal codes to modern conditions. A number of individuals wrote interpretations of Islam for modern times; two of the most influential were Syed Ameer Ali and Muḥammad Iqbal.

An active form of Muslim fundamentalism has developed in the Arab world, Iran, and the Indo-Pakistan subcontinent. Such groups affirm the urgency of agreement on one interpretation of Islam, and of imposing this interpretation by means of a state controlled by morally upright persons.

See Also Canon; Expulsion; Heresy; Orthopraxy; Schism; Theology, article on Christian Theology; Truth.

Bibliography

Peter Berger's *The Heretical Imperative* (Garden City, N.Y., 1979) offers a recent discussion of the issues of orthodoxy in the context of modernity across all traditions. With respect to ritual processes in the conflict between orthodoxy and heterodoxy among nonliterate peoples, see Victor Turner's *The Ritual Process: Structure and Anti-Structure* (1969; Ithaca, N.Y., 1977). A comprehensive survey of Indian religious thought is contained in Surendranath Dasgupta's *History of Indian Philosophy*, 3 vols. (1922–1940; Cambridge, 1963). For modern India, see *Religion in Modern India*, edited by Robert D. Baird (New Delhi, 1981). Sukumar Dutt's *Buddhist Monks and Monasteries of India* (London, 1962) offers a survey of Indian Buddhism. For Chinese thought, Wing-tsit Chan's *A Source Book in Chinese Philosophy* (Princeton, N. J., 1963) is excellent. Robert M. Seltzer's *Jewish People, Jewish Thought: The Jewish Experience in History* (New York, 1980) is a good source for Jewish intellectual history. Three books combined together give an excellent introduction to the complex issues of early Christian development: Robert M. Grant's *Augustus to Constantine* (New York, 1970); Robert L. Wilken's *The Myth of Christian Beginnings* (Garden City, N.Y., 1971); and Elaine H. Pagels's *The Gnostic Gospels* (New York, 1979). Kenneth Scott Latourette's *A History of Christianity* (New York, 1953) gives a comprehensive survey. With respect to Islam, Fazlur Rahman's *Islamic Methodology in History* (Karachi, Pakistan, 1965) explains the processes of Islamic reasoning. W. Montgomery Watt's *Islamic Philosophy and Theology*, 2d ed., rev. & enl. (Edinburgh, 1984) describes the main schools of thought. Noel J. Coulson's *A History of Islamic Law* (Edinburgh, 1971) discusses the religio-legal structures. For the modern period, see *Change and the Muslim World*, edited by Phillip H. Stoddard, David C. Cuthell, and Margaret W. Sullivan (Syracuse, N.Y., 1981).

New Sources

Metz, Johann Baptist, and Edward Schillebeeckx, eds. *Orthodoxy and Heterodoxy*. Edinburgh, 1987.

Sheila McDonough (1987)
Revised Bibliography

ORTHOPRAXY. Derived from the Greek *orthos* ("straight, right") and *praxis* ("doing, practice"), *orthopraxy* refers to "correctness of a practice or a body of practices accepted or recognized as correct," according to *Webster's Third International Dictionary of the English Language.* The term in English is rarely used, having been displaced by the related term *orthodoxy,* from the Greek *orthos* and *doxa* ("opinion, belief"). *Webster's Third* defines *orthodoxy* as "conformity to an official formulation or truth, esp. in religious belief or practice." Thus common English usage assumes that dogma governs practice.

The proclivity of English speakers to think in terms of orthodoxy rather than orthopraxy has historical roots. During the early centuries of the Christian church, the ecumenical councils defined and championed an orthodox creed to quell potentially divisive heresies. During the period of the Reformation, doctrinal interpretation became a battleground for orthodoxy as the various churches strove to reestablish stability in beliefs after a period of ferment and schism. In the modern world, traditional ideologies have their champions, who militantly defend orthodox views against maverick reinterpretations. As a result of this history, Westerners commonly assume that beliefs are the defining core of any religion.

Religions, however, do not begin and end with doctrine. They also entail liturgical, contemplative, or ethical practices as well as direct or mediated experiences of the sacred. If doctrines or beliefs remain the only yardstick by which a religious tradition is measured, other aspects of religious life and experience, which may in certain cases be far more important than belief, will be neglected or ignored.

Orthopraxy provides a nondoctrinal focus for analysis, an alternative model for understanding the functioning of religion in a given community. The concept of orthopraxy helps scholars to broaden their religious imaginations and enhance their religious "musicality," their sensitivity to the full scope and variety of the rhythms, patterns, and harmonies of religious life.

Orthopraxy is a particularly apt term for describing cases in which written codes of behavior for liturgy and daily life constitute the fundamental obligations of religion. Frederick Streng has called this religious modality "harmony with cosmic law," noting that the codes delineate not only the path of individual piety but also the hierarchical and complementary roles that build a harmonious society.

Judaism, Hinduism, Confucianism, and Islam exemplify Streng's "harmony with cosmic law." The primary religious obligation in these traditions is the observance of a code of ritual and social behavior minutely stipulated in religious texts and in scholarly commentaries as interpreted by the educated religious elite. The code has sacred authority because it was established in ancient times by a god or the revered founder or founders of the tradition. These religions have no creed, no officially sanctioned statement or dogma that holds a key place in liturgy or rites of passage. In these instances religiosity is not primarily a matter of holding correct opinions but of conforming to a set of behaviors.

Orthopraxy is central to the dynamics of religious life in Judaism, Hinduism, Confucianism, and Islam. For instance, in the first three traditions observance of the religious code (orthopraxy) establishes and reinforces the cultural or ethnic identity of the community. These religions do not claim to be universal; each is associated with a specific cultural group.

Cultural and ethnic groups perpetuate their communal identity through distinctive mores based on shared symbols and values that establish behavioral boundaries between themselves and other groups (Royce, 1982). In Judaism, Hinduism, and Confucianism, the practices mandated by the sacred law define the distinctive boundaries of the culture and the identity of the group within a larger world. In these cases religion defines and reaffirms one's cultural roots rather than one's beliefs; religious and cultural identity are inseparable. Observance of the written code also ensures a semblance of unity within each group despite considerable local variations caused by linguistic or regional differences.

At first glance, Islam does not appear to use orthopraxy to maintain an ethnic identity. Islam has not been bound to one ethnic or cultural group; like Christianity and Buddhism it has become a world religion, ranging extensively across the globe among a diversity of peoples. Originally, however, Islam was strongly tied to Arab culture and identity; to become a Muslim one had to join an Arab tribe if one were not favored by Arab birth. Perhaps the original cultural boundedness of Islam, its view of itself as the religion of a distinctive and chosen people, helps to account for the centrality of orthopraxy. To be a Muslim is to accept and observe the law of Allāh. Surrender to Allāh is not a matter of belief in a doctrine; it is a matter of obedience to his commands (Smith, 1963).

Although Qurʾanic law no longer maintains the original ethnic boundaries of Islam, it serves to create unity within the Islamic world, thus minimizing very real differences. Sunnī and Shīʿī interpretations of the law differ considerably, and there are local variations in the way in which the law is applied. Observance of the law, however, identifies each community as Muslim. A commitment to orthopraxy binds together all who surrender to Allāh.

In Judaism, Hinduism, Confucianism, and Islam, the sacred law also establishes a standard of religious purity that, along with knowledge of the law, defines a religious and social elite. All members of the culture traditionally were expected to observe the mores of the groups as encoded in the law, but meticulous observance was both the defining quality and the responsibility of the religious elite.

Gradations of ritual purity and observance define and perpetuate the hierarchical structure of Hindu society. Upper-caste Hindus have heavier ritual responsibilities and are expected to maintain an elevated standard of purity. Likewise, groups seeking recognition of increased social status in Hindu society must raise the level of their ritual purity. Thus in Hindu culture, the sacred law establishes a standard for both individuals and groups (Dumont, 1967).

Although Jewish, Confucian, and Islamic cultures were not characterized by the elaborately graduated ritual hierarchy of the Hindu caste system, scrupulous observance of the law and knowledge of tradition were the responsibility of the social and religious elite nonetheless. In China, the law or ritual code dealt primarily with social ethics, the standard of a humane and civilized society. However, it also prescribed ritual obligations in regard to the mourning and veneration of ancestors. The mandarin was to be the model of the civilized moral person, with a profound sense of obligation to family and community. In Judaism and Islam, the law defined a complete way of life: ritual observance, dietary code, ethics, familial and marriage practices. The rabbi in Judaism and the *ʿulamāʾ* in Islam were scholars and teachers who embodied and interpreted the law to their congregations.

In traditions in which the observance of the law is the central religious obligation, orthopraxy establishes and maintains ethnic or religious boundaries and gradations of social and religious purity. However, orthopraxy functions in a broad range of religious traditions and circumstances. An examination of selected examples will illustrate the variety of roles orthopraxy plays in the religions of the world.

In tribal cultures, orthopraxy defines not only religious obligations; it is also the law of the tribe. Its sacred and secular functions are barely distinguishable. The tribal rulers and the ritual specialists are usually two distinct groups; yet, because they share a common tradition and sense of orthopraxy, religion and government support each other. Religion and the state can cooperate in full harmony only in a religiously homogeneous community. When religious pluralism becomes the norm, secular law must develop along autonomous principles to apply equally to all citizens, whatever their religion.

Even in large-scale and complex societies, such as pre-Mughal India or traditional China, sacred law can have an intimate connection to sovereign authority and the secular law, if one religion is overwhelmingly dominant or has established an unassailable claim as the state ideology. The Indian and Chinese rulers were not themselves the religious elite, but their sovereignty and ruling effectiveness were shaped and supported by the sacred code.

In China, Confucianism remained the official state religion and ideology until 1911, and its values were enforced by law, although Buddhism, Daoism, Nestorianism, Islam, Judaism, and Christianity were present as well. The state accepted the existence of other religions as long as they made no claim to be the law of the land. When Daoists, Muslims, or Buddhists occasionally tried to supplant Confucian mores with their own, they were charged with rebellion and chastised by the full military power of the state.

The Chinese saw no threat in the coexistence of religions, even when two religions coexisted within the life of a single citizen. Most Chinese, in fact, combined Confucian values and practices with Buddhism, Daoism, or some other religion. Each religion, however, had its proper place in the hierarchy of the social order. As an old saying goes, "Daoism cures the body; Buddhism regulates the mind; Confucianism governs the state." Thus the Chinese found a means to reconcile religious pluralism with the maintenance of a sacred code and orthopraxy, a reconciliation that served as the basis of the Chinese social order for two millennia.

Orthodoxy and orthopraxy are also factors in the process of communal religious renewal. The history of religions offers endless variations on the theme of renewal as communities struggle to recapture the freshness and power of their tradition. Belief and practice are subject to continual reinterpretation by the religious elite, who revise their understanding of tradition according to ongoing experience, and by ordinary people, who believe and practice their religion in ways that reflect their individual, social, and historical circumstances. What makes beliefs or practices correct (*orthos*) is the consensus of the living community in a particular social and historical circumstance. In every religious drama, from everyday worship to grand ceremony, the actors negotiate the meanings and practices according to their collective and personal experiences.

Orthopraxy and orthodoxy become issues because religion and its meanings are social and shared. Private belief and experience neither mediated through the symbols of tradition nor authenticated by the living religious community isolate the individual; private belief is socially meaningless, often perceived as fantasy, or even madness. The ongoing process of religious socialization is the mediation of belief, the negotiation of significance. Collective perceptions, however, are fluid; they evolve with time and circumstances, and thus religious traditions are constantly renewed and reinterpreted.

Pluralistic cultures are torn by competing claims of orthodoxy and orthopraxy. The issue of orthopraxy dominates religious competition in sectarian groups that seek to separate themselves from a corrupt, misguided, and tainted society. Their members retreat into communities marked by a strict and demanding religious life. The Amish and the Shakers, among other groups, rejected the larger Christian culture, considering its laws and religious life fallen and depraved. They sought to live out their vision of a pure Christian life, abjuring the taint of sinful society. Members of their community who did not follow the discipline were first reproved, then shunned, and finally expelled. Correct living was the measure of the religious life.

Similar in some ways to the Amish and the Shakers, although not sectarian in intent, are the religious orders of the Roman Catholic church or the *saṃgha* of Buddhism. These communities of individuals choose the religious life in response to a special vocation; they renounce the pleasures and ties of the material world, such as sex and property, in order to live a life of purity and contemplation. Their exemplary lives of sacrifice and discipline were traditionally believed to benefit the broader community and not just themselves.

Orthopraxy can support the secular arm of the state or the rebellion of a sectarian movement. It can be a force for change or for repression of change. At times, the powerful forces for change threaten traditional values, and religious communities may hold tightly to an orthopraxy in order to maintain traditional values. At other times, orthopraxy evolves along with community acceptance of new realities and values, as in the loosening of regulations on drinking and card playing among American Methodists in the mid-twentieth century or the changes in Catholicism following Vatican II. An earlier example of this is the acceptance of married clergy among Pure Land Buddhists in Japan since the thirteenth century. Orthopraxy may even serve the cause of progressive social change, as it does for many liberation theologians. This group sees praxis, action, and reflection on action as the core of the Christian life and they believe that correct practice (orthopraxy) is directed toward liberating the oppressed and reducing suffering in the world.

The concept of orthopraxy helps the student of religion to avoid excessive emphasis on the doctrinal model of religions, but a word of caution is in order. In most cases orthopraxy and orthodoxy are intimately connected and represent two interrelated aspects of religious life. Belief and practice at once entail and support each other.

While orthopraxy is more important than orthodoxy in tribal religions, the "ways of the gods or ancestors" are based on stories or beliefs about what the gods or ancestors did or said. These practices are not merely a random set of behaviors; they express a worldview, a coherent story of the community and its relationship to the world it knows. Likewise, there is no motivation for following a ritually correct or pure life in Judaism, Hinduism, Confucianism, or Islam without belief in and about the God or gods or sages who handed down the law. The law is rooted in and implies a particular view of the sacred, of human life, and of the world. There is no ritual behavior that is not also the expression of certain beliefs about the relationship of the human and the divine, the relationship of ordinary action and sacred command.

While belief and practice are intimately connected, it is not the case that one always dominates the other. Some religions under certain conditions stress that belief leads to practice. Other religions, such as Confucianism, stress that practice leads to and deepens belief and understanding. The student of religion must carefully observe how doctrine and practice complement and correct each other in each unique historical circumstance.

See Also Heresy; Orthodoxy and Heterodoxy.

Bibliography

In his article "Orthodoxy," in the *Encyclopaedia of Religion and Ethics,* edited by James Hastings, vol. 9 (Edinburgh, 1917), William A. Curtis noted that ". . . since religion embraces feeling and activity as well as thought, orthodoxy becomes an inadequate criterion of its worth apart from right experience and right conduct. It ought to have for its correlatives such words as 'orthopathy' and 'orthopraxy,' the inward experience and outward exercise of piety." Wilfred Cantwell Smith argues forcefully that observance of the law, and not belief, is the sine qua non of Islam; see Smith's *The Meaning and End of Religion: A New Approach to Religious Traditions* (New York, 1963). Frederick J. Streng has gone further to define the religious modality of "harmony with cosmic law," in which orthopraxy dominates religious life; consult his *Understanding Religious Life,* 2d ed. (Encino, Calif., 1976).

A number of anthropologists have explored the ways in which religious practices and mores serve to define the ethnic or cultural boundaries of a community. In *Ethnic Identity: Strategies of Diversity* (Bloomington, Ind., 1982), Anya P. Royce provides a review of the literature and offers an articulate analysis of strategies for maintaining ethnic identity. Barbara E. Ward demonstrates how local regions and communities within cultures unified by a standard of behavior consider their variations on the universal mores in the realm of orthopraxy; see her "Varieties of the Conscious Model: The Fishermen of South China," in *The Relevance of Models for Social Anthropology,* edited by Michael Banton (New York, 1965).

Louis Dumont explores how standards of ritual and behavioral purity establish and maintain social differences in his now-classic *Homo Hierarchicus: An Essay on the Caste System,* rev. ed. (Chicago, 1980). For a Marxist analysis of orthopraxy, see Pierre Bourdien's *Outline of a Theory of Praxis* (Cambridge, U.K., 1979).

New Sources

Denny, Frederick M. "Orthopraxy in Islam and Judaism: Convictions and Categories." In *Studies in Islamic & Judaic Traditions: Papers Presented at the Institute for Islamic-Judaic Studies, Center for Judaic Studies, University of Denver,* edited by William M. Brinner and Stephen D. Ricks, vol. 2, pp. 83–95. Atlanta, 1989.

Schroeder, John. "Nagarjuna and the Doctrine of 'Skillful Means.'" *Philosophy East & West* 50, no. 4 (2000): 559–584.

Judith A. Berling (1987)
Revised Bibliography

OSAGE RELIGIOUS TRADITIONS.

OSAGE RELIGIOUS TRADITIONS. The Osage people (*wazhazhe* or *ni u ko^{n}shka*) were the aboriginal occupants of a large territory in the center of the present-day United States located between the Missouri and Arkansas Rivers west of the Mississippi, with reservation lands located today in northeastern Oklahoma. The Osage people are a part of a larger family of American Indian communities including the Poncas, Omahas, Kansas, and Quapaws and related linguistically to the Lakotas and Dakotas.

The Osage were the focus of study by an American Indian ethnographer who was fluent in a closely related dialect. Francis La Flesche, himself an Omaha, published some two thousand pages of ethnographic descriptions of the Osage for the Bureau of American Ethnography, recording substantial parts of many ceremonies. His publications include ceremonial descriptions and extensive recitations in Osage collected from several older practitioners with whom he worked in the early 1900s. His compilation has been called the most complete record of North American Indian ceremonies. Although La Flesche had the advantage of language skills in his study of the Osage, even these extensive documents need to be read with a critical and discerning eye.

La Flesche published five lengthy treatises describing seven significant ceremonial rites, but these are only a partial sampling of the full array of Osage ceremonial life, as he himself clearly notes. He only alludes, for instance, to the ceremony performed before engaging in a community buffalo hunt, commenting that it was in "all respects" similar to the war ceremony (namely, taking a period of some days to complete); likewise, he barely mentions the ceremonial structures attending to the agricultural activities of planting and harvesting. There are other key factors for which he fails to give any deeper explanation or interpretation, such as the central role of the sacred pipe (*no*ⁿ*nío*ⁿ*ba wako*ⁿ*dagi*) in all Osage proceedings.

Osage Ceremonial Structures. Like other indigenous nations in the Americas (and especially in North America), Osage people understood the world as an intricate and sophisticated, interconnected organic whole structured as a thoroughgoing dualism of reciprocity. They came to know the universe as a complementary pairing of above and below, sky and earth, the two great fructifying forces of the universe, and recognized a cosmic source of power that made itself manifest with the same dualistic reciprocity. As a result, they carefully modeled themselves—personally and socially—as a mirror-image reflection of this universe, dividing themselves and their clans between the two sociopolitical divisions of *tsízhu* (sky) and *hó*ⁿ*ga* (earth).

The numerous ceremonial structures of the Osage peoples, along with their underlying cultural philosophy, were remarkably complex, like those of most American Indian nations. They required enormous physical preparation and intense ceremonial acts as well as extensive memorization, since the ceremonies were detailed, lengthy, and required considerable verbatim recitation. Their religious traditions were thoroughly interlaced with their cultural values and daily practices, but were especially characterized in these carefully structured and intricately detailed ceremonies involving a widely dispersed number of key participants and leaders, upon whose cooperation the success of each ceremony depended.

There were ceremonies engaged in by the tribal community as a whole that involved key participants from all or many of the clans, such as ceremonies preparing for war or hunting, certain initiation ceremonies, or marking the beginning of a new year. Other ceremonies were personal, family, or clan ceremonies and might still involve a significantly large number of participants. The smoking of a sacred pipe might take a short period of time—an hour or less. The war ceremony might typically have taken up to a dozen days, while the ceremony for initiating someone into the ranks of the Little Old Ones could stretch over several years before its completion.

The importance of these ceremonies is already evident in the personal spiritual practices of Osage people, noticed historically by many Western observers. Daily prayers were a constant among the Osage, beginning with the personal song each member of the community sang to greet the rising of the sun, a discipline practiced by other Indian communities as far away as the Ojibwa in Minnesota. These personal prayers were then repeated at noon and sundown each day.

Osage Cosmology. Much of our knowledge of these ceremonies comes from La Flesche, who uses two translations that pose continuing problems for our understanding of Osage religious traditions. His use of certain convenient English language glosses as a device to connect with his readership of seventy or eighty years ago has biased understandings of Osage culture and religious traditions ever since. Each of these is a Western concept that is so loaded with connotative meaning as to render it less than helpful in talking about any non-Western culture. The first of these is his use of the word *god* to describe the Osage notion of the Sacred Other.

Spiritual concepts. *Wako*ⁿ*da* was the spiritual force or energy that Osages saw permeating the whole of the world, and which they experienced in a great variety of manifestations at any given moment and especially in any given place. This was the insight that lent itself to the Osage conception of the interrelationship of all things on the earth and in the universe. *Wako*ⁿ*da* was the Osage word used by the early missionaries to express their Christian concept of god, and indeed La Flesche most often translates *wako*ⁿ*da* as *god.* Treated thus, however, the word, like *great spirit,* is simply used as a popular gloss and conveys misinformation rather than real knowledge. La Flesche's second entry in his *Osage Dictionary* begins to get at the real heart of the matter: *wako*ⁿ*da* "is the name applied by the Osage to the mysterious, invisible, creative power which brings into existence all living things of whatever kind. They believe that this great power resides in the air, the blue sky, the clouds, the stars, the sun, the moon, and the earth, and keeps them in motion" (p. 193).

This *wako*ⁿ*da* is ultimately an unknowable mystery that only becomes knowable in particular manifestations. It makes itself manifest first of all as Above and Below, as *wako*ⁿ*da mo*ⁿ*shita* and *wako*ⁿ*da hiudseta,* corporealized as sky and earth, and called upon as Grandfather and Grandmother. *Wako*ⁿ*da,* which has no inherent or ultimate gender, becomes visible as the necessary reciprocity of male and female.

It needs to be emphasized that these two are not different *wako*ⁿ*da,* but rather manifestations of the one *wako*ⁿ*da,* even though they have specific personality traits similar to those which traditional Christian trinitarian doctrine asserts. While they are manifestations of the same *wako*ⁿ*da,* they represent power in different forms, both of which are necessary in order to have some balanced understanding of the Otherness that is the Sacred Mystery. Indeed, *wako^{n}da* has manifested itself in a great many other ways, all of which help the Osage people to better understand the Mystery, the world, themselves, and their place in the world. Since *wako^{n}da* permeates all life in the world, Osages readily conceived of themselves as kinfolk to the buffalo, eagles, spiders, rocks, and other manifestations of the cosmic energy that makes up the world. To assume that the simplistic gloss "god" somehow is adequate to translate and classify *wako^{n}da* in English immediately falsifies the internal cultural meaning of *wako^{n}da* for Osage peoples by imposing a historic Western category of cognition.

Leadership. The second problematic translation is La Flesche's use of the word *priest* to refer to a group of initiates who functioned as a village council. To get at this concern, we need to look at the structures of leadership in Osage civil and religious life, which was organized around a great diffusion of civil and religious leadership and authority. Osage cultural organization allowed for a variety of voices to be involved in each ceremony and any decision-making process and provided for the exercise of authority by different people in different community situations. While there were two appointed civil leaders (*gahiga,* called "chiefs" in English) in every village, one from each of the two principle divisions or moieties, they had only limited authority, which was exclusively focused on internal affairs and lacked any formal role in the external affairs of the tribe, such as military activities. The limitation of their authority can be seen implicitly in the practice of shared authority, with each taking leadership on alternate days during a tribal hunting expedition.

The most significant religious and political leadership (but not day-to-day governance) in an Osage village was exercised by a council called the Little Old Ones (*no^{n}ho^{n}zhi^{n}ga*), a group of mature adult men and always some women who coordinated the life of the community, conducted the ceremonies, and were the source and the keepers of the esoteric and abstract knowledge of the community. They held the greater decision-making power in key situations. Selected because of their character, intelligence, abilities, and spiritual gifts, members of this council had each gone through rigorous initiation rites into one or more of the different ranks of ceremonial responsibility and leadership. This council was, as a whole, the community's repository of wisdom and its members functioned as the principal ceremonial actors in every major ceremony. These council members are the public personalities that La Flesche calls priests.

In the course of a war-preparation ceremony and subsequent military expedition, more than a dozen different members of this council, each from different clans, would typically exercise leadership, either in the war ceremony itself or as tactical leaders in the actual engagement, with a sharp differentiation between the two. The one who is usually referred to as the war leader (*dodo^{n} ho^{n}ga*) was always a member of this council because of the religious function of the position, and was most critical to the success of the military endeavor. Most strikingly, this war leader was a noncombatant who had no responsibility or authority for determining actual battle strategy even though he (or occasionally she) accompanied the military detachment. The responsibility of this *dodo^{n} ho^{n}ga* was to be in constant prayer from the beginning of the war ceremony until the completion of the military engagement.

One of the most striking aspects of the Osage war ceremony was the commitment of this war leader to undertake a serious regimen of isolation, prayer, and dry-fasting (without food or water) for up to seven days in a ceremony called in English the Vision Quest or Rite of Vigil. His fast continued even while on the march until the excursion was fully completed and he returned home with the detachment. Then his role as war leader ended. The spiritual role of war leader could be filled by any one of a hundred or more *no^{n}ho^{n}zhi^{n}ga* who might potentially serve this function.

While the *no^{n}ho^{n}zhi^{n}ga* underwent significant rites of initiation into their formal eldership and held key roles in all the ceremonies, they were not priests, and the use of this word becomes terribly misleading. La Flesche reports the existence of two other categories of religious leadership, which seem to have had more day-to-day religious importance. These include those who were keepers of the Great Bundles and whose responsibilities extend to tattooing and certain kinds of healing. The other category is one that he only mentions, without interpretive description, but must have included those healers who are sometimes called "medicine" people by Western observers (whom James Dorsey calls "shaman," using the Tungusik word). Officially, La Flesche calls them the keepers of the "great medicine bundles." While these latter two categories might more logically fit the Western category of priest, neither of them had specific roles in the main public ceremonies of the tribe.

SOCIAL STRUCTURE. From all that can be pieced together of earlier Osage life, this was a diametric dualistic society, of the sort Lévi-Strauss contended did not exist, but which anthropologist Alfonso Ortiz demonstrated so thoroughly for his own Tewa community at San Juan (see *On Space, Time, Being, and Becoming in a Pueblo Society,* 1969). Every detail of social structure, even the geographic orientation of the old villages, reflected a reciprocal duality of all that is necessary for sustaining life. Like the Omahas, Poncas, Quapaws, and other related peoples, an Osage village was divided into two parts: the *tsízhu,* or sky moiety, and the *ho^{n}'ga,* or earth moiety.

An east-west roadway divided community architecture (both permanent towns and hunting camps), with the *tsízhu* constructing their lodges to the north and the *ho^{n}'ga* to the south. These two divisions represented female and male, matter and spirit, war and peace, but they functioned as a unified whole because they were always paired together as a reciprocal duality who together represented balance and completion. Spirit without matter is motion without substance; matter without spirit is motionless and meaningless. This spatial arrangement is carefully repeated in the seating of the *no^{n}ho^{n}zhi^{n}ga,* the council of elders, inside the lodge kept for their meetings and in all ceremonial observances.

Just as the Osage perceived the necessity of the two manifestations of *wako^{n}da* participating together to sustain life, so the two grand divisions sustained the life of the whole, so that what ethnographers would classify as "religion" pervaded marriage customs and even the habitual acts of sleeping and putting on clothing. To preserve the principles of spiritual and political unity in this duality, Osages were mandated to marry someone from the other grand division. To further enforce this religious sense of wholeness, the two grand divisions developed personal habits that helped each individual remember her or his part in this communal whole. Hence, those from the *ho^n'ga* grand division customarily slept on their right side and put on the right shoe first, while those from the *tsízhu* grand division functioned in the opposite manner, putting their left sleeve on first and sleeping on their left shoulder. As a result, even in sleep the two divisions performed a religious act that maintained their unity in division, as they lay facing each other asleep across the road that divided the whole community.

Much of the cosmological mythology of the tribe consists of accounts of the different origin of the two divisions and how they came to be together. The *tsízhu* division represents the tribe's origins in the sky itself, where the first Osages were created as incorporeal entities who needed to attain corporeality. In the course of this process they are eventually sent down to earth by *wako^{n}da,* "dropping like acorns from an oak tree." In their wanderings on the earth they soon discovered another community of *ho^n'ga* who called themselves the Isolated Earth People. After some negotiation these two decided to live together as one, bringing together the distinct qualities of each, and symbolically and functionally representing the whole of the Osage cosmology. To preserve the memory of their origins, the group maintained the division between sky and earth, and appointed two of three original divisions to live with the Isolated Earth People as the *ho^n'ga* moiety. Mandated intermarriage then functioned to hold the two divisions together. At the same time it symbolically held together the universe in microcosm and brought the opposites together both in the whole and in each individual. Thus it is that this dualism dominates even the material and ceremonial structures of Osage architectural geography and lends itself to the political and social cohesion and balance of every historic Osage community.

This symbiotic dualism, spatially configured, is not the oppositional dualism of good and evil that is typical in Judeo-Christian thought, but is, rather, a necessary reciprocity. It functions at a much more deeply spiritual level that still pertains for a great many American Indian people today, including Osages, even as they have abandoned the explicit structures of their historical past. While an Osage person may have been either *tsízhu* or *hon'ga,* she or he was always a child of parents who come from each of the divisions. Thus, each individual recognized herself or himself as a combination of qualities that reflected both sky and earth, spirit and matter, peace and war, male and female, and each struggled personally and communally to hold those qualities in balance with each other. These value structures begin with spatial designs of existence and are rooted in those spatial metaphors as fundamental mores of communal behavior and social organization.

Bibliography

Burns, Louis F. *Osage Customs and Myths.* Fallbrook, Calif., 1984.

Dorsey, James Owen. *An Account of the War Customs of the Osages.* Philadelphia, 1884.

Dorsey, James Owen. *Osage Traditions.* Washington, D.C., 1888.

Dorsey, James Owen. *Siouan Sociology.* Washington, D.C., 1897.

La Flesche, Francis. *The Osage Tribe: Rite of the Chiefs.* Washington, D.C., 1921.

La Flesche, Francis. *The Osage Tribe: The Rite of Vigil.* Washington, D.C., 1925.

La Flesche, Francis. *The Osage Tribe: Two Versions of the Child Naming Rite.* Washington, D.C., 1928.

La Flesche, Francis. *The Osage Tribe: Rite of Wa-xo'-be.* Washington, D.C., 1930.

La Flesche, Francis. *A Dictionary of the Osage Language* (1932). Phoenix, Ariz., 1975.

La Flesche, Francis. *War Ceremony and Peace Ceremony of the Osage Indians.* Washington, D.C., 1939.

La Flesche, Francis. *The Osage and the Invisible World: From the Works of Francis La Flesche.* Introduced and edited by Garrick Bailey. Norman, Okla., 1995.

Tink Tinker (2005)

OSIRIS

OSIRIS. Osiris is the Greek form of the name of the Egyptian god Wsjr, king of the afterworld. The Egyptian god Wsjr was often represented by a throne and an eye. He did not live with the other gods but among the dead, and therefore the Greeks identified him with Hades, as Plutarch (c. 46–after 199 CE) did in his *On Isis and Osiris.*

By the time of the Pyramid Texts (third millennium; fifth and sixth dynasties), the Egyptians believed that King Osiris once reigned in their land and was killed by his brother Seth. His corpse was saved and revified by his sister-wife Isis, his sister Nephthys, and other gods. Osiris's life continued in the next world, where he became king of the dead. The myth was the origin of rituals to preserve the deceased pharaohs. His was the prototypical death, and Osiris adopted the name Khentimentu (or Khentamenthes, Foremost of the Westerns).

According to the Greek version of the myth related by Plutarch in *On Isis and Osiris,* Typhon (the Greek name of

Seth) had a beautiful coffin made to Osiris's exact measurements and, with seventy-two conspirators at a banquet, promised it to the one who fit it. Each guest tried it for size, and of course Osiris fit exactly. Immediately Seth and the conspirators nailed the lid shut, sealed the coffin in lead, and threw it into the Nile. The coffin was eventually borne across the sea to Byblos, where Isis, who had been searching for her husband, finally located it. After some adventures of her own, Isis returned the body to Egypt, where Seth discovered it, cut it into pieces, and scattered the pieces throughout the country. Isis, however, found all the pieces (except the penis, which she replicated), reconstituted the body, performed the rituals to give Osiris eternal life, and founded his cult. The principal version of the story cited by Plutarch does not reveal how Isis gave birth to her son Horus, but according to the eighteenth-dynasty *Hymn to Osiris* and the iconography of several Egyptian monuments, she conceived Horus by the revivified corpse of her husband. The death of the god is often described by the Egyptian texts as a drowning at the end of a combat against Seth. Plutarch tells the story of the previous adultery of Osiris and Nephthys, Seth's sister and wife, the consequent birth of Anubis, and the wrath of Seth. The Pyramid Texts mention the "magic" acts performed by the gods to keep Osiris alive. Isis protected him with her wings, and Horus gave him an eye of his own to eat (Faulkner, 1969, nos. 579, 585).

Although Seth challenged the legitimacy of Isis's son, the gods decided in favor of Horus. The *Contendings of Horus and Seth,* preserved on a late New Kingdom papyrus and on a fragment of a Middle Kingdom one, indicates that Re, the chief god, favored Seth, but all the other great gods supported the cause of Horus. In the actual contest Horus proved himself the cleverer god. Horus succeeded and avenged his father without completely destroying Seth, toward whom Isis showed pity.

From the netherworld, Osiris granted the gifts of fertility and abundance to the earth and people. Droughts and the infertility of deserts were unavoidable as the god Seth was untamed, but the rituals in honor of Osiris assured the return of water and fertility.

CULT. Rituals of great political value included the balming, mummification, "opening of the mouth," and burial of the pharaohs to transform them into new beneficent gods following the Osirian pattern. The Pyramid Texts (e.g., nos. 219, 684) identify the dead pharaohs with Osiris and the living ones with Horus. The main purpose of the rituals was to keep the god alive, to preserve his vital might even in the realm of the dead. The condition of the god was sometimes described as asleep. In the Middle Kingdom period (2160–1580 BCE) the burial rituals of nobles identified them with Osiris, and during the New Kingdom period (1580–1090 BCE) the assimilation was widespread among the people. Relatively poor people could buy a cheap edition of the essential funerary texts in which their names were associated with Osiris. The name of the dead often included the name of Osiris before the personal name because he or she was like the god.

During the Middle Kingdom, Osiris's prevailing iconography was as a mummy bearing a wig, a crook, a flail, and sometimes a crown. Plutarch recorded in *On Isis and Osiris* that his body was dark. Later he was depicted lying on a lion-shaped bed flanked by Isis and Nephthys and backed by Anubis, the divine embalmer. In the *Book of the Dead,* Osiris is chairman at the soul's trial, when the heart of the dead is weighed.

One of the oldest centers of the Osirian cult was Abydos, where the kings of the earliest dynasties were buried and where many New Kingdom nobles were buried and represented face to face with Osiris. The Ramessides built many monuments in his honor. Here he was identified with the jackal god Khentimentu. His appellation "Lord of Busiris" witnesses an ancient cult location at Busiris, whose name signifies "house of Osiris." Osiris was identified with the funerary god Anedjti, but it is possible that Anedjti is simply the local name of Osiris. Memphis, Philae, and many other places pretended to keep a piece of the dismembered body of Osiris. His birth from Geb and Nut and his kinship to Isis, Seth, and Nephthys claim the ancient influence of the Heliopolite theology, in which he was one of the nine great gods of the Ennead.

Although each Egyptian district had its own specific cult, the rituals for Osiris were performed everywhere under pharaonic control. The most important one was the fall ritual in the month of Khoiak. At Dendera, twenty-three biers with various local forms of Osiris were venerated in the course of the local festival in Khoiak. People prepared mummiform figures molded from sand and barley that were later watered and allowed to germinate. Many mummiform figurines containing grains of corn or barley, most of them ithyphallic, have been discovered in excavations, and many images of Osiris show cornstalks sprouting from his corpse. In his honor the *djed* pillars, which were thought to represent the backbone of Osiris, were raised. In Abydos and Edfu the statue of the god was treated by the priests with secret substances, covered with a ram's skin, and kept in a special container. The idol of Osiris was also brought in the *Neshmet* ship. The papyrus Salt deals with those ceremonies. Plutarch, as evidenced in *On Isis and Osiris,* knew the Osirian Pamylia festival, which included a procession in which the phallus of the god was celebrated. That festival was celebrated in Alexandria in August to celebrate the birth of Osiris. Herodotos (c. 484–between 430 and 420 BCE) notes that at Sais, near a lake, some nocturnal performances called *mysteria* (mysteries) were organized. Diodorus (first century BCE) states that secrets surrounded the truth about Osiris's death. Noise was forbidden by him as a god of silence, and his burials were often surrounded by inaccessible precints (Assmann, 2001, p. 254). Herodotos identifies Osiris with Dionysos, and his opinion that the phallic processions of Greek Dionysiac festivals could have been influenced by Egyptian Osirian ceremonies has found modern acceptance (Burkert, 2002). In the Hellenistic Age (c. 200 BCE), Osiris also became the god who taught viticulture (Diodorus 1,17–18).

The motif of Osiris's life among the dead was specified and expanded in the solar character assumed by Osiris before the Amarna period (c.1370–c.1325 BCE). He was in fact joined to Amun-Ra. The *Book of the Dead* mentions "Osiris of sun-disk"; the Abydos stela of Ramses IV (twelfth century BCE) knows Osiris and Ra as "joined souls in the *Dat* (the realm of dead)." The mixed iconography of the Osirian mummy with the ram's head of Amun represented the joint nature of the gods. Osiris was therefore thought of as the sun during the night, when it visited the realm of dead, and his role as savior was bound to the vicissitudes of the sun. In this evolution there is no precise opposition between the solar theology of Heliopolis and chthonic religion as it has been thought (Kees, 1941).

Osiris's connections with the creator god Atum were strong. The lion-shaped funerary bed and the ram-shaped tool by which the mouths of the dead were opened were symbols of Atum. From the twenty-first dynasty, Osiris could be substituted as king and judge of the dead.

According to Plutarch's *On Isis and Osiris,* the fall festivals occurred when the days became shorter, the nights grew longer, and the level of the Nile began to recede. The fertility of the Egyptian earth depended on the Nile's inundation, and the cyclic burial and revival of Osiris were connected with the Nile's yearly phases. The inscription on the Shabaka's Stone (end of the eighth century) connects Osiris with the inundation of the Nile and its fructifying waters. The first century CE Egyptian priest Chaeremon attributed the same meaning to Osiris (fr.17 D van der Horst = Eusebius, *Evangelic Preparation* 3.11). Several later theologists contended that Osiris was the element of water, as Plutarch recorded in *On Isis and Osiris.* The papyrus *Jumilhac* informs us that people believed Osiris's sweat produced the Nile's flood and thus enabled the cultivation of cereals (Vandier, 1962).

The famous interpretation by James Frazer, *Adonis, Attis, Osiris* (1962), recognized in Osiris the spirit of the corn, and Osiris's mythology should be an interpretation of corn's annual cycle. The connection with agriculture is evident, but Osiris's actions covered a larger field in the social structure. An often adopted definition of Osiris is "suffering god" (or "dying and rising god"). The ancient (Diodorus's book 1) and modern (Sethe, 1930, pp. 94–95) euhemeristic explanations of Osiris as a deified ancient man are not suitable. The personality of this god goes back to the features of Neolithic religion, in which cults of the dead were strictly related to the agrarian rituals. A central feature of Osiris was his kingship over the dead, and this fact reproduced the structure of Egyptian society as a great monarchy (Griffiths, 1980). The dilemma of the dying god has worried many scholars, although Erik Hornung (1990) has stressed that death was the destiny of many Egyptian gods, whose beings were ever marked by cyclic death and life, as was the sun. A Greek god never looks older and never dies, whereas the eternity of Osiris consisted in a mysterious cycle of life and death. Nevertheless, in the coffin texts he was conceived as the immutable eternity.

HELLENISTIC AND ROMAN PERIODS. The Osirian mysteries acquired in imperial times a new philosophical dimension, and Osiris was thought of as the eternity. The priest-philosopher Heraiskos (fifth century CE) discovered that Aion of Alexandria was also Osiris and Adonis (Damascius, *Life of Isidorus,* p.174 Zintzen). Aion was the deity on perennial time, and the Alexandrian Aion was also the god of destiny. His image was that of a snake, and Osiris also was sometimes represented entwined with a snake. That image corresponds to the hieroglyph signifying eternity.

The Apis bull was thought of as the soul of Ptah and Osiris (Diodorus 1.85.4; Strabo 17.1.31; Plutarch, 1970, 20; 29), and the Greeks worshiped it at least from the beginning of the fifth century. The foundation of a Greek city at Alexandria and the creation of the Macedonian kingship in Egypt under Alexander (356–323 BCE) and later under the Ptolemies produced a restyling of the great god of the dead. The names of Osiris and Apis (Osor Apis) were joined and gave birth to the name of Sarapis (or Serapis). Perhaps Alexander knew this god, but the complete transformation of Osiris into Sarapis was conceived by Ptolemy I (367, 366, or 364–283 or 282 BCE), the Egyptian priest Manetho, and the Eleusinian priest Timotheos (fourth century BCE). The king saw in a dream a statue of Hades. His minister Sosibios discovered this statue at Sinope, and the Egyptians succeeded in taking it to Alexandria. That was the new image of Osiris identified with Hades, Dionysos, and Asklepios. Plutarch noted in *On Isis and Osiris* that he was seated on a throne and a snake stood on his hand and Cerberus by his feet. Over his head was the *kalathos* or *modius,* the measure of corn, to symbolize his attitude to produce fertility.

Sarapis's temple, the Serapeum, was built by Ptolemy III (d. 221 CE) and became the most famous one in Alexandria and one of the most important in the ancient world. Its destruction in 491 CE produced a pagan outburst. The Ptolemies attached a large library to the temple. The meter to measure the Nile's level (Nilometer) was kept by the Serapeum, and Aelius Aristides (129–c.189 CE) celebrated Sarapis as the one who "drives up the Nile in summertime, and calls him back in winter" (*Oration on Sarapis* 32).

The nature of Sarapis was that of an international god, and many Serapea were consecrated in the Hellenistic and Roman worlds with a major shift in the second century CE. The first phase (third to first centuries BCE) of his cult was marked by an evident Hellenization. During the first century BCE the Roman phase began, marked by a stronger Egyptian style. Because he was also the protector of the Ptolemaic dynasty, the spread of Sarapis's cult advanced in accord with the foreign policy of the Alexandrian royal house. Sarapis was a supreme god, whose cosmological place was over the top of the universe, which was conceived as a sphere. Many Jews and Christians venerated him as the image of their god (*Babylonian Talmud, Avodah Zarah;* Historia Augusta, *Life of Sa-*

turninus 8). The Greek translation of the Bible was kept in his temple (Iohannes Chrysostomus, *Patrologia Graeca* 48, 851), and he was often identified with the biblical Joseph (*Gn* 41:34–57) because this Jewish hero supplied the Egyptians with corn during the seven years of famine (Mussies, 1979). Sarapis often delivered oracles or performed miracles during dreams. The Roman Empire conceived of Sarapis as a solar god, the one god to whom the other divine entities owed their power (e.g., Iulian, *Hymn to Helios* 10; Macrobius 1.20.13). According to Erik Peterson (1926), he was often acclaimed, together with Zeus, as the only god.

Plutarch wrote that the cult of Osiris survived in the mysteries, and one can add that it was important in the doctrines and rituals of magic and that Sarapis was never substituted for him among Egyptian natives. The late mysteries of the Hellenistic and Roman worlds are scarcely known because of their secrecy. They were practiced in the temples of Sarapis and Isis. The most important text describing the ceremonies outside the temples is the eleventh book of Apuleius's (c. 124–after 170 CE) *Metamorphses.* The procession of the initiates carried an Osirian image in the form of a precious vessel an image of Osiris Hydreios that often had Osiris's head on top (the "Canopic Osiris") and held the sacred water of the Nile during the ceremonies. The bald-headed priests clad in linen held secret objects, wands and ivy used also in the Dionysiac cult, and in the temples water basins were regulated in the proper time to imitate the Nile flood. According to Julius Firmicus Maternus (fourth century CE) in *On the Error of Profane Religions,* the crucial rituals of the Isiac mysteries were the burial of Osiris, the mourning, the search for and discovery of his corpse, followed by the joy of the congregation.

Egyptian gem cutters produced series of hematite amulets that supposedly gave health to the womb. On them Osiris was represented alongside other fertility gods,such as Isis, Chnumis, Bes, the child Horus, and the mummiform Anubis, all standing on a schematic womb. These gods favored pregnancy and birth. In the magic practices several magicians acted as if they were Seth, threatened Osiris, and forced him to do what they wanted (e.g., *Papyri Graecae Magicae* 4,179–189; 12,121–143).

SEE ALSO Iconography, article on Egyptian Iconography; Kingship, article on Kingship in the Ancient Mediterranean World; Mystery Religions.

BIBLIOGRAPHY

Apuleius. *The Isis-Book (Metamorphoses, Book XI).* Translated and edited by John Gwyn Griffiths. Leiden, Netherlands, 1975.

Assmann, Jan. *Tod und Jenseits im Alten Ägypten.* Munich, 2001.

Beinlich, Horst. *Die "Osirisreliquien": Zum Motiv der Körperzergliederung in der altägyptischen Religion.* Wiesbaden, Germany, 1984.

Bergman, Jan. *Isis-Seele und Osiris-Ei.* Uppsala, Sweden, 1970.

Burkert, Walter. "Mysterien der Ägypter in griechischer Sicht." In *Ägyptische Mysterien?* edited by Jan Assmann and Martin Bommas, pp. 9–26. Munich, 2002.

Burkhard, Günter. *Spätzeitliche Osiris-Liturgien im Corpus der Asasif-Papyri.* Wiesbaden, Germany, 1995.

Cauville, Sylvie. *La théologie d'Osiris à Edfou.* Le Caire, Egypt, 1983.

Cauville, Sylvie. *Le temple de Dendara: Les chapelles osiriennes.* Le Caire, Egypt, 1997.

Derchain, Philippe. *Le Papyrus Salt 825 (B.M. 10051): Rituel pour la conservátion de la vie en Égypte.* Brussels, 1965.

Faulkner, Robert O. *The Ancient Egyptian Pyramid Texts.* Oxford, U.K., 1969.

Frazer, James G. *Adonis, Attis, Osiris.* 3d ed. *The Golden Bough,* pt. 4. London, 1962.

Griffiths, John Gwyn. *The Origins of Osiris and His Cult.* Rev. and enl. ed. Studies in the History of Religions, vol. 40. Leiden, Netherlands, 1980.

Helck, Wolfgang. "Osiris." In *Paulys realencyclopädie der klassischen,* Supp. 9 (1962): 469–513.

Horbostel, Wilhelm. *Sarapis.* Études préliminaires aux religions orientales dans l'empire romain (EPRO) 32. Leiden, Netherlands, 1973.

Hornung, Erik. *Der Eine und die Vielen: Ägyptische Gottesvorstellungen.* 4th ed. Darmstadt, Germany, 1990.

Kàkosi, Lazlo. "Osiris-Aion." *Oriens Antiquus* 3 (1964): 15–25.

Kees, Hermann. *Der Götterglaube im alten Aegypten.* Leipzig, Germany, 1941.

Merkelbach, Reinhold. *Isis regina, Zeus Sarapis: Die griechisch-ägyptische Religion nach den Quellen dargestellt.* Stuttgart and Leipzig, Germany, 1995.

Mussies, Gerard. "The Interpretation Judaica of Sarapis." In *Studies in Hellenistic Religions,* edited by Maarten J.Vermaseren, pp.189–214. Leiden, Netherlands, 1979.

Otto, Eberhard. *Osiris und Amun: Kult und heilige Stätten.* Munich, 1966. Translated by Kate Bosse Griffiths as *Ancient Egyptian Art: The Cults of Osiris and Amon* (New York, 1967).

Peterson, Erik. *Heis Theos.* Göttingen, Germany, 1926.

Plutarch. *On Isis and Osiris.* Translated and edited by John Gwyn Griffiths. Cardiff, Wales, 1970.

Raven, Maarten J. "Corn-Mummies." *Oudheidkundige mededelingen uit het rijksmuseum van oudheden te Leiden (OMRO)* 63 (1982): 7–38.

Sethe, Kurt. *Urgeschichte und älteste Religion der Ägypter.* Leipzig, Germany, 1930.

Stambaugh, John E. *Sarapis under the Early Ptolemies.* Leiden, Netherlands, 1972.

Tran, Vincent Tam Tinh. *Sérapis debout.* Études préliminaires aux religions orientales dans l'empire romain (EPRO) 84. Leiden, Netherlands, 1983.

Vandier, Jacques. *Le papyrus Jumilhac.* Paris, 1962.

Vidman, Ladislav. *Sylloge inscriptionum religionis Isiacae et Sarapiacae.* Berlin, 1969.

Vidman, Ladislav. *Isis und Sarapis bei den Griechen und Römern.* Berlin, 1970.

Wild, Robert A. *Water in the Cultic Worship of Isis and Sarapis.* Études préliminaires aux religions orientales dans l'empire romain (EPRO) 87. Leiden, Netherlands, 1981.

LEONARD H. LESKO (1987)
ATTILIO MASTROCINQUE (2005)

OSTIAK RELIGION SEE FINNO-UGRIC RELIGIONS; KHANTY AND MANSI RELIGION; SOUTHERN SIBERIAN RELIGIONS

OSTRACISM SEE EXPULSION

OTHERWORLD.

The belief that human beings are in touch with several dimensions of reality is nearly universal. Indeed, for many cultural groups and most religious ones, the nonphysical world is far more real and important than the material one. In most cultures it is believed that those who have died move into another dimension of reality and that the living can experience the presence of the deceased as well as other aspects of the nonphysical realm. Sometimes this belief is clearly articulated; sometimes it can best be observed by witnessing the rituals that people perform. Often, what people believe is better evaluated by what they do than by what they say they believe.

The available material on the nature and quality of the otherworld has grown to voluminous proportions as anthropological studies have added to the data over the last hundred years. There are only a limited number of disparate points of view concerning its essential nature, yet there is an amazing wealth of difference in specific details. Nearly every large cultural or religious group, from archaic times to the present, has one or another of these points of view concerning the otherworld. The attitude of the religious expert differs from that of the well-informed member of the group, and the latter in turn differs from the basically unconscious attitudes of the large majority of participants in a belief system. Some of the greatest works of literature describe this otherworld in detail, among them the *Epic of Gilgamesh* of Babylon, the *Bhagavadgītā* of India, the Tibetan *Book of the Great Liberation*, several of Plato's dialogues, Vergil's *Aeneid*, Dante's *Commedia*, and Goethe's *Faust*. On the other hand, B. F. Skinner's popular *Walden Two* (New York, 1948) presents a view of a world with no otherworld as counterpart.

In order to cover this enormous wealth of material, I shall deal first of all with seven quite different understandings of the otherworld. Communion with this dimension of reality on the part of specific groups will then be examined. Nonreligious studies and evidence for the reality of this domain will be surveyed, along with a brief discussion of the worldviews underlying these different conceptions.

VARIETIES OF BELIEF. In many cultures the otherworld is viewed as a shadowy state, gray and dull. In some groups the soul, or shade, of the person is believed to continue to live near the site of the burial. Ancient Roman and popular Chinese beliefs and rituals suggest that the ghost of the person is envious of living human beings and needs to be placated with offerings of food and other gifts. Some groups believe that the departed spirit of a person lingers near the corpse and renders it unclean. The Navajo practice of abandoning the dwelling in which a death occurs shows the fear with which many view the denizens of the otherworld. Furthermore, the modern fear of haunted places and the interest in ghosts found in nearly all cultures lingers in many of us.

In still another stratum of belief, these unhappy shades are collected together in one place, usually an underworld, to which they pass directly down from the grave. It is a dull, colorless place of half-existence. The Babylonians viewed the place of the dead very much as the Hebrews viewed She'ol, a place of diminished existence where there is no contact with Yahveh. The Homeric Hymns portray the same kind of place. For Dante, this place is described as limbo, where the righteous pagans must remain.

Edgar Herzog's excellent study *Psyche and Death* (New York, 1967) traces the psychological development of the understanding of afterlife from fear of the dead to a more happy view of the deceased and the otherworld. The life of the deceased from this view point is seen as being much the same as a full life in this world. The otherworld contains the best of human pleasures and joys. There is also a belief that the next world will be much better than this one, with greener grass, more beautiful flowers, and a more positive relation with the divine reality. Raymond Moody's *Life after Life* (Atlanta, 1975) and Karlis Osis's *At the Hour of Death* (New York, 1977) describe dying and near-death experiences, report contacts with deceased, and give a largely optimistic picture of the otherworld. This view is found throughout the world—among some Bantu-speaking peoples and many Polynesian tribes, as well as among some American Indians; it is represented in modern times by nonreligious research into the otherworld.

The most common view of the otherworld gives a picture of several different realms: a highly desirable heaven or heavens, many varieties of fearful and horrible states, and intermediate states through which one passes to arrive at the final destination. The quality of the dying person determines the realm of the otherworld into which he or she will pass. In some cultures the status of the deceased determines the outcome: a warrior killed in battle, a king, or a chief has easy access to the realm of bliss. In later Greek religion some of the heroes were able to escape Hades and enter the realm of the gods, a blissful otherworld. This view implies a soul that is immortal or at least long-lasting; the body is seen as only the temporary carrier of the soul. Mircea Eliade has demonstrated in his monumental study of archaic techniques of ecstasy, *Shamanism* (Princeton, 1964), that this view of a permanent core of humanness and a realm into which it can pass is found all over the globe and reaches back into prehistoric times. The shaman can leave the body through ecstasy and trance and enter the otherworld. The shaman can, therefore, become the guide of the dying, who must make a perilous journey into the otherworld. The dying can also step into this other dimension to bring back souls lost there and so bring healing to those whose sickness has been caused by a disturbed relation with the otherworld.

One enters this otherworld by way of a journey, passing through difficulties and tests, often crossing a bridge that is razor-sharp. In Hinduism, Islam, some forms of Buddhism, ancient Iranian religion, and Christianity, this journey and the places visited are described using earthly symbols, but the otherworld is perceived as another dimension of reality. Less reflective thinkers in these traditions retain a geocentric point of view, picturing heaven as above and hell as below the earth. Others believe that the entrance into the otherworld is put off until the end of time, when the dead will rise and take their places in a reconstituted heavenly earth or in the abyss or will even be annihilated.

Coming to the place of bliss and avoiding the state of torment can be accomplished in numerous ways. A skilled shaman may help to effect the passage. In Islam, knowing the right formula for acknowledging God may be more significant than the quality of moral or religious practice. In Christianity, having the last rites properly performed and confessing one's sins before death are important factors. The ultimate nature of the otherworld and the powers within it determine one's place there.

In both Hinduism and Buddhism, there is another important aspect of belief in the otherworld. The nonphysical, spiritual dimension is the only reality; religious illumination consists in coming to realize this truth and then, on the basis of this realization, becoming detached from the illusion (*māyā*) of this physical world, which keeps one from fulfillment in the real world. This is achieved by spiritual and moral discipline, well exemplified in the life of Gandhi. Much the same point of view is found in Gnosticism, in which the physical world is not only unreal but evil. It is irredeemable and can only be escaped by a process of knowledge (*gnōsis*) and asceticism. By the same process one enters progressively higher levels of an eternal spiritual dimension.

Belief in reincarnation or the transmigration of souls is found associated with both these points of view. Those who do not escape from the bondage of evil or the illusory material world are reborn again and again into this world. They are reborn according to their *karman*, a moral and spiritual accounting of one's life. *Karman* automatically determines the fate of the individual in the next reincarnation; rebirth can bring one into a higher or lower human state or even into an animal existence. The goal of this process is to be released from this agonizing, continuing reimmersion in the illusory material world, thus passing into heaven as a godlike being or entering *nirvāṇa*. This view has filtered down into popular thought in many Eastern cultures, and, as difficult as it is for Westerners to believe, for many of these people the otherworld is more real and important than this one.

Heaven is pictured in a welter of vivid images in the literature and in the art and sculpture characteristic of Hinduism and Buddhism. Hindu and Buddhist temples portray the real world of the gods throughout East Asia. This exciting, richly colored world is worth the moral and spiritual discipline required to become emotionally uninvolved and detached from concern with outer physical illusion. At the end of the great Hindu epic called the *Rāmāyaṇa*, the hero leaves his beloved wife so that he can come to the detachment necessary for spiritual advancement in the otherworld.

The Buddhist conception of *nirvāṇa* is unique and important; it presents a conception diametrically opposed to the richly sensuous picture of heaven presented by Hinduism and most other world religions. *Nirvāṇa* is described mainly in negatives. If, indeed, the physical world is illusion, so is the human ego, which clearly differentiates the contents of that world. According to Zen and many other schools of Buddhism, the distinction between subject and object disappears in the enlightened person. The individual becomes one with reality and merges into it. It is therefore impossible to give any significant descriptions of this ultimate state.

Many statements about *nirvāṇa* sound as if the individual was annihilated, whereas others describe *nirvāṇa* as a state of ecstatic bliss. Illumination is a taste of *nirvāṇa* for the living. Images can be another form of illusion. Thus, the path toward enlightenment leads through imageless (apophatic) prayer to an imageless fulfillment that cannot be described except in saying what the earthly condition is not.

The major world religions (with the exception of Buddhism) perceive inner and outer images as revealing reality rather than hiding it. Various schools in each tradition describe heaven as a place of transformation, where people are gradually or suddenly changed into the quality and likeness of the god image, becoming more and more like Allāh, Kṛṣṇa, Yahveh, or Christ. In some versions this process goes on into eternity; while in certain forms of Hinduism, after a very long time the universe returns to its divided condition, and the whole cycle repeats itself. Heaven and hell are understood by some religious thinkers as a process and by others as a static condition. Important thinkers in most traditions emphasize the inadequacy of all human descriptions of the otherworld.

The last major view about the otherworld is simply that there is none. This very important conception has dominated the Western world for several centuries and has deeply influenced Christianity. The same point of view has been held by the realistic philosophical schools in China described by Arthur Waley in *Three Ways of Thought in Ancient China* (New York, 1939). However, it is only in the cultures of Western Europe and those that derived from them that this worldview has been fully developed and has achieved wide acceptance. A few archaic cultures, including the people of Kiwai on the Fly River in New Guinea, the Fuegians, and some Bantu-speaking peoples, have little or no conception of any other world than this physical one.

The Western attitude is important because it is based on the philosophical premise that the only reality is physical or material. The only means of coming into contact with reality is through the five senses, which can be clearly differentiated, as described by Descartes in his *Discourse on the Meth-*

od of Rightly Conducting the Reason (1637). The major thrust of Western thought has been in this direction and is well exemplified in the writings of A. J. Ayer, B. F. Skinner, and Konrad Lorenz. Marxism denies the value of any world except the one created on this earth through revolution by the proleteriat. From this frame of reference, any concept of an otherworld is considered illusory, primitive (in the sense of infantile), premodern, and even dangerous. It is for this reason that the subject of otherworld is so largely ignored in modern Western culture and the modern evidence for the continued existence of the deceased is passed over and rejected.

If the materialistic worldview is accepted uncritically, it is quite natural to view all the data on the otherworld as of archaeological interest only. However, starting in about 1900, developments in scientific thought led to the questioning of rational materialism as a viable hypothesis. The materialist point of view is not able to account for the available data on many subjects and the evidence for otherworld in particular. In *Encounter with God* (Minneapolis, 1972) and *Afterlife* (New York, 1979), I have presented the development of this thought in detail.

Communion with the Dead. The basic worldview of a person or culture will largely determine the way the otherworld is viewed. From the point of view of Eastern religion and philosophy, the physical world is illusory and the otherworld real, and heaven or *nirvāṇa* is the goal to be sought. According to Platonism (the philosophical base for early Christianity) and the modern view of C. G. Jung, human beings participate both in a material universe and in a nonmaterial one. Thus, both the otherworld and this world are important aspects of total reality. Human wholeness depends on dealing adequately with each domain. Both moral actions (as in, for instance, learning to love) and specifically religious practices are essential to human wholeness.

In both of these points of view, the human person is more than just a physical organism operating mechanically or through conditioning. The psyche (or soul) is a complex nonphysical reality sharing the reality of a multifaceted nonphysical otherworld. The psyche can be viewed as preexistent (which leads to the idea of reincarnation) or as created at conception or birth. In both Islamic and Christian thinking, the soul is viewed as having vegetative, appetitive, intellectual, and spiritual aspects. In the views of some thinkers, only the spiritual or intellectual aspects survive in the otherworld. The Christian doctrine of the resurrection of the body maintains that most aspects of the personal nonphysical being are preserved and transformed.

In most cultures (not influenced by materialism), contact with the deceased is a part of religious practice. Eliade shows that one of the principal functions of living shamans is to pass over into the otherworld, return, and then help other people deal with both dimensions. Some shamans have mediumistic abilities and can bring back the dead, as the medium of Endor brought forth the ghost of Samuel at Saul's bidding (*1 Sm.* 28:6ff.). Once belief in an otherworld eroded in Christian cultures influenced by materialism, there was a spontaneous, popular resurgence of the practice of spiritualism, which brings the seeker into contact with the deceased through mediums and their controls.

The belief in ongoing contact with the spirits of the deceased is widespread in this and most countries. Sometimes these visitations are frightening, and at other times helpful or even numinous. J. B. Phillips, the British New Testament scholar, reports in *The Ring of Truth* (New York, 1967) that C. S. Lewis appeared to him and helped him translate a difficult passage of the Bible. The Christian doctrine of the communion of saints maintains that communion between the living and the dead is possible to those who are deeply rooted within the Christian fellowship. The same idea is found in Islam and Hinduism. These experiences of meeting the deceased, inhabitants of the otherworld, can occur either spontaneously, through religious rituals (particularly highly developed in China), through the trance condition, or through dreams and visions.

Modern Evidence. With the publication of Moody's *Life after Life* in 1975, a new surge of interest arose concerning reported experiences of an otherworld and of those who existed in it. Moody's study is a careful one; this well-trained philosopher and psychiatrist is cautious not to claim more than his evidence warrants. His work was followed by that of Karlis Osis and Elendur Haraldsson's *At the Hour of Death* (New York, 1977), Michael Sabom's *Recollections of Death* (New York, 1981), and Kenneth Ring's *Life at Death* (New York, 1980). This data has been collected by medical doctors and trained psychologists; Ring's work is a careful statistical study of the data.

Many different kinds of evidence can be studied once one is no longer bound by a materialistic worldview. Some people appear to die clinically and return to life, to report a series of experiences in which they go through a process of detachment from the body, experience an otherworld, sometimes meet deceased friends, relate to a being of light, and arrive at a boundary that they cannot cross if they are to return to life.

People who are at the point of death and who then die are occasionally observed to be participating in both this world and the other one simultaneously, and give reports similar to those who have had near-death experiences. Numerous reports have been studied of encounters with people from the other side. Supporting the possibility of these reports is the development of parapsychology, which suggests that we have faculties other than the five senses for obtaining information. In *Doors of Perception* (New York, 1970), Aldous Huxley suggests a theory of perception based on the thinking of Bergson, which states that we are in touch with many dimensions of reality but that the five senses block our contact with these dimensions, tying us to the physical world. Franz Riklin, a follower of C. G. Jung has stated that the dreams of the dying usually treat the physical death of the individual as of little significance. Within the framework of Einstein's theory of relativity, physical death loses its finality, because time appears to be relative and not absolute. Some who practice meditation maintain that they are in contact with an otherworld and experience much of what has been described here. Poetic imagination also seems to give access to some other dimension.

Christianity and the Afterlife. Little of the foregoing data has been discovered by those primarily interested in Christianity. Indeed, some of this evidence has been resisted by certain theologians who state that belief in the otherworld is based on faith and acceptance of dogma, rather than on experience. Some academic Christian thinkers maintain that profession of Christianity need not entail the belief in an afterlife or otherworld. Within the wide range of Christian belief and practice, one can find nearly all of the attitudes toward the otherworld that have been described above.

There is, first of all, an academic skepticism that either denies or ignores this aspect of reality. For some scholars, what is continuously ignored is usually of little value or concern. At the other extreme is the archaic belief in the dull, shadowy existence of the deceased and their ghostly presence at the place of death or burial. Many Christians have a view of the otherworld as a place only of bliss, which is unrelated to one's actions or beliefs. Others accept the traditional dichotomy between heaven and hell, while yet others believe in purgatory as a transitional state between the two. For some, the afterlife begins at the millennium, on a rejuvenated and transformed earth; others still imagine a heaven somewhere in the sky (although this image has become difficult to maintain, because of modern space travel). Others regard these different aspects of the otherworld as other dimensions of reality, seeing sensory images of it as purely symbolic. Still other Christians believe in reincarnation and all that it entails. Some see the otherworld as a place of continued growth and development in the presence of divine mind or divine love. This variety of beliefs is found in the other major world religions as well as Christianity.

There is almost total consensus among the religions and cultures of humankind that human beings are not totally extinguished at death and that there is continuing experience in an otherworld. Human beings are also given occasional experiences of this dimension and those continuing to exist in it. These varied views of the nature of an otherworld can be traced historically and cross-culturally; perhaps they may ultimately constitute different aspects of a reality too large for any one description.

See Also Afterlife; Heaven and Hell; Nirvāṇa; Supernatural, The; Underworld.

Bibliography

Culianu, I. P. *Out of this World: Otherworldly Journeys from Gilgamesh to Albert Einstein.* Boston, 1991.

Eliade, Mircea. *Shamanism.* Rev. & enl. ed. New York, 1964. The authoritative, although not universally accepted, study of the shaman and the technique of ecstasy by which the otherworld is mediated. Provides a cross-cultural worldview with a place for an otherworld.

Encyclopaedia of Religion and Ethics. 13 vols. Edited by James Hastings. Edinburgh, 1908–1926. Contains a wealth of detailed accounts of the otherworld in "State of the Dead" and many associated articles. Must be consulted with care because of its moralistic, Christian, and materialistic bias.

Herzog, Edgar. *Psyche and Death.* Translated by David Cox and Eugene Rolfe. New York, 1967. An excellent anthropological and psychological study of human concepts of death and the otherworld.

Jung, C. G. *Psychology and Religion: West and East.* Translated by R. F. C. Hull. New York, 1958. Provides a philosophical and psychological framework for understanding religious texts on the otherworld. Offers excellent commentary on the Tibetan *Book of the Dead* and the *Book of the Great Liberation.*

Kelsey, Morton. *Afterlife: The Other Side of Dying.* New York, 1979. The only modern Christian study providing a worldview for the otherworld and nonreligious evidence for continued existence. Presents a picture of the otherworld for a critical modern reader. Contains an extensive bibliography.

McGinn, Bernard. *Visions of the End.* New York, 1979.

Parabola (New York), vol. 2, no. 1 (1977). The entire issue deals with the subject of death and otherworld. A comprehensive cross-cultural, up-to-date overview.

Ring, Kenneth. *Life at Death.* New York, 1980. A comprehensive examination of the near-death experience with a careful statistical study.

Turner, Alice K. *The History of Hell.* New York, 1993.

Zaleski, Carol. *Otherworld Journeys: Accounts of Near-Death Experience in Medieval and Modern Times.* New York, 1987.

Morton Kelsey (1987)

OTOMÍ RELIGION.

The Otomí Indians of central Mexico, who speak a language of the Oto-Manguean phylum, number approximately 250,000. They occupy a vast territory located between 19° and 21° north latitude and 98° and 100° west longitude. This area, characterized by stark geographical contrasts, stretches from the steep mountain masses of the Sierra Gorda to the semiarid Mezquital plateaus, and from the Toluca Valley to the rolling hills of the Huastecan piedmont. In addition to the different sociocultural patterns that have emerged from this mosaic of environments, the blending of Indian culture with folk Catholicism from the colonial period to the present day has yielded a syncretic religion that is dominated by Christianity but includes specific forms of dualism that set the Otomí symbolic universe apart from its colonial influences.

There is little information on the origins of the Otomí, and their role in shaping the great Mesoamerican systems of thought remains unexplored. Subjects of the Aztec Empire from the fifteenth century to the conquest, the Otomí came under its sway everywhere except in the outlying eastern regions (Tutotepec, Huayacoctla). Since then, Otomí religious activities have been constrained to a clandestinity favored by the dispersal of their settlements. They have come to center primarily on local patrilineal cults (agrarian fertility rites and ancestor worship), while their ceremonial and liturgical calendar continues to reflect patterns of thought similar to those of the Aztecs on the eve of conquest.

Throughout the colonial period and down to the present, their particularly fluid social organization, built on a network of patrilineagical shrines, has allowed the Otomí to resist evangelization. Yet, devotions to Roman Catholic saints coexist with native rituals and sometimes, as in the Sierra Madre, serve to camouflage them. The focal points of this dual religious life are the home, the shrines, and the sacred mountain, on the one hand, and chapels and village churches, on the other. These different ritual spaces are arranged in a hierarchy that parallels a cosmic vision of different "skins" (*sí*), or sacred places (from the uterine cavity to the celestial vault), symbolically enclosed within each other.

At each level of the cosmic hierarchy there are correspondences based on fundamental male-female polarity. Thus, at the uppermost level of space, the sun and the moon form a complementary and antagonistic pair. The moon (Zâna), however, presents a complex and disquieting image to the Otomí. While in her syncretistic form Zâna is feminine and is associated with the Virgin of Guadalupe, in the indigenous cosmological system the moon displays a complex of complementary characteristics, including dual gender: It represents feminine characteristics (childbirth, sensuality, weaving, computing of time, death) as well as masculine ones (erection, mastery of women and their fertility). While the moon is the antagonistic counterpart to the masculine sun, it also embodies within itself the complementary forces. Further, as the heavenly counterpart to the earth goddess Hmûhoi, Zâna helps govern both creation and destruction.

The conception of a nighttime creation continues to power the Otomí imagination. One of the oldest Mesoamerican deities, the Otomí fire god known in the Aztec pantheon as Otontecuhtli ("the Otomí lord") is believed to govern, as he did in times past, the order of things. He is Šihta Sipi ("the ancestor who devours excrement"), the purifying principle whose presence marks the emergence of culture (associated with cooked food). He is also the preeminent lord of nocturnal spaces and grottoes, the realm of an imaginary world that mirrors in miniature the world of humans.

To understand the logic of the oppositions that inform Otomí cosmology, it is helpful to understand the model on which they are based: the human body. As a receptacle for the field of forces animating the universe, the body reveals the difference between a diurnal, masculine, "warm" world and a feminine, nocturnal, "cold" one and the process by which energy flows between the two (in the transfer of "energy" from the man's body to the woman's).

Otomí ritual is, in essence, a manifestation of a process of fusion between polarities of which the sexual distinction is the prototype. This is seen in rituals from fertility rites (*costumbres*) to the Feast of the Dead, which is both a mourning of ancestors and a celebration of the life force contained in their bones. The interdependence of life and death is revealed most completely in Carnival. During this time the major gods are represented by an ancestral couple, such as Old Father (Šihta) and Old Mother (Pømbe), whose function is to reenact the primordial creation. From their broken bodies they kindle life and youth in a supernatural society governed by devils, demons of vegetation, and lascivious women. Paradoxically, in Mezquital, where the erosion of indigenous tradition has been most complete, Carnival remains, despite its European origins, one of the last areas of resistance to cultural hybridization. Indigenous elements are also plainly evident in a number of rituals in the Catholic liturgical cycle, such as the Feast of the Finding of the Cross (Sierra Gorda) and the Feast of the Three Magi (Rio Laja Valley).

The richest complex of rituals is found on the eastern periphery of the Otomí region, in the foothills of the Sierra Madre. A distinctive feature of the religious life here is the use of hammered bark figurines that are fashioned and given their power by shamans. These figurines, rare evidence of pre-Hispanic iconography, are a precious source for interpreting the indigenous cosmological system. They are part of the essential paraphernalia of the healing and fertility rituals organized by shamans. As adepts possessed of specialized knowledge, shamans manipulate unseen forces and are thus able to cure (by restoring the body's equilibrium) and to afflict (by casting spells at a distance).

The *cargo* system—that is, the system of ritually based obligations to participate in the functioning of the community's civil and religious life—varies significantly from one community to another. This system is a primary cohesive force binding villages (*pueblos*) and their dependent peripheries (hamlets). Such cohesion is also promoted by regional pilgrimages to sacred mountains or Catholic sanctuaries (San Agustín Mezquititlán, Chalma, Tepeaca in Mexico City).

Through their many variants, Otomí rituals reveal certain obscure aspects of Otomí cosmology that are hardly brought to light by the myths themselves. Though known in a version little changed since pre-Hispanic times, the story of the creation of the sun and moon, the foundation of the dualistic order of the universe, is not often told anymore, except in villages deeply rooted in the Indian tradition. Yet the symbolic structure of this text remains, dimly outlined, in a number of tales that pit Christ against the Devil. Similarly, the theme of the Flood, in its variations, reveals how Mesoamerican symbols combine with biblical ones according to the importance each community gives to the two traditions.

In Otomí mythology today, the Devil appears as a predominant figure everywhere. Through a process of adjustment and reinterpretation, the medieval European figure of Satan has merged with indigenous representations of evil, fertility, and impurity. The Devil now sits enthroned at the apex of the pantheon, holding sway over a band of nocturnal deities and merging with the enigmatic lunar figure of Zâna.

BIBLIOGRAPHY

Carrasco, Pedro. *Los Otomies: Cultura e historia prehispánicas de los pueblos mesoamericanos de habla otomiana.* Mexico City, 1950. A comprehensive account of the ethnohistorical sources available on the subject.

Dow, James. *Santos y supervivencias: Funciones de la religion en una comunidad otomi.* Mexico City, 1974. A very detailed analysis of the religious obligation system in Santa Monica, a Sierra Madre village.

Galinier, Jacques. *N'yuhu: Les indiens Otomis.* Mexico City, 1979. An ethnographical study of the eastern Otomí area.

Manrique, Leonardo. "The Otomí." In *Handbook of Middle American Indians.* Austin, Tex., 1969. A brief synthesis of the main cultural features of the Otomí-Pame groups.

Soustelle, Jacques. *La famille Otomi-Pame.* Paris, 1937. The first study concerning the geographical distribution and linguistic characteristics of the Otomí, Mazahua, Atzinca, Pame, and Chichimeca languages, containing also valuable ethnographical data.

New Sources

Dow, James. "Symbols, Soul and Magical Healing among the Otomí Indians." *Journal of Latin American Lore* 10, no. 1 (1984): 3–21.

Dow, James. *Shaman's Touch: Otomí Indian Symbolic Healing.* Salt Lake City, 1986.

Galinier, Jacques. *Moitié du monde: le corps et le cosmos dans le rituel des Indiens Otomi.* Paris, 1997.

Pérez Lugo, Luis. *Visión del mundo otomi en correlato con la maya en torno al agro y al maiz.* Toluca, Mexico, 2002.

Sandstrom, Alan R. *Traditional Curing and Crop Fertility Rituals among Otomí Indians of the Sierra de Puebla, Mexico.* Bloomington, Ind., 1981.

JACQUES GALINIER (1987)
Translated from French by Robert Paolucci
Revised Bibliography

OTTO, RUDOLF.

OTTO, RUDOLF. Rudolf Otto (1869–1937) was a German systematic theologian who contributed especially to the philosophy and history of religion. As a liberal theologian or, more accurately, a *Vermittlungstheologe* (theologian of mediation), Otto conceived of systematic theology as a science of religion, whose components were the philosophy, psychology, and history of religions. In his view, philosophy identified the source of religion in a qualitatively unique experience for which he coined the term *numinous.* Descriptive psychology revealed the nonrational dimensions of this experience as a *mysterium tremendum et fascinans,* dimensions that, Otto said, were conjoined to rational or conceptual elements through a process that, loosely following Immanuel Kant, he called *schematization.* Otto's ideas became foundational for much twentieth-century work in the study of religion that claimed to be phenomenological or scientific rather than theological.

LIFE. Born on September 25, 1869, in Peine in the region of Hanover, Germany, Otto spent his childhood in Peine and Hildesheim, where his father owned malt factories. After graduating from the Gymnasium Adreanum in Hildesheim, he studied first at the University of Erlangen, a conservative neo-Lutheran institution, then at the University of Göttingen, where liberal theology and the historical-critical study of the Bible prevailed. He initially prepared for a ministerial career, but conservatives in the German church administration found him unsuitable. Instead of taking a German congregation in Paris, he opted for an academic career, where his prospects were only somewhat brighter. He became a *Privatdozent* at Göttingen in 1898 and something like a visiting associate professor there in 1906, but official opposition to his liberal views and popularizing activities plagued him for years.

In 1904 Otto adopted the philosophy of Jakob Friedrich Fries, helping to establish a neo-Friesian movement along with two Göttingen colleagues, the philosopher Leonard Nelson, who introduced him to Fries's thought, and the New Testament scholar Wilhelm Bousset, whom he recruited to the cause. In the same year, however, Otto fell into a deep depression and considered abandoning theology altogether. When his health finally recovered in 1907, Otto returned to teaching and writing, to ecclesiastical and liturgical activities with a group known as "The Friends of *Die Christliche Welt*" (*Die Christliche Welt* was a semipopular magazine for liberal theology), and to political activities, at that time in conjunction with a student-oriented group known as the Akademischer Freibund, the Göttingen chapter of which he, along with Nelson and Bousset, led. His most important publication from the period was *Kantisch-Fries'sche Religionsphilosophie und ihre Anwendung auf die Theologie* (The Philosophy of Religion Based on Kant and Fries, 1909).

In 1911 to 1912 Otto undertook a "world tour"—actually a journey from the Canary Islands to China and Japan—financed through the German government by the cosmopolitan French banker, Albert Kahn, for the purpose of preparing an introduction to the history of religions (never written). During a visit to a Moroccan synagogue on this trip he encountered in memorable fashion the *trisagion*—"Holy, holy, holy. . ." (*Is.* 6.3)—an encounter that he and his disciples later considered the moment when he discovered the Holy. Upon his return, Otto pursued the history of religions as part of a broader strategy of German cultural imperialism, commensurate with the ethical imperialism of the theologian and publicist Paul Rohrbach but in sharp contrast to the militaristic colonialism of organizations like the Naval and Pan-German Leagues. As part of this program he promoted the series *Quellen der Religionsgeschichte,* a German equivalent to the Sacred Books of the East. In 1913 he was elected to represent Göttingen in the Prussian state legislature, where in 1917 he led a faction of the National-Liberal Party in an attempt to abolish Prussia's notorious three-tier system of weighting votes. In 1915 he finally received a professoriate in systematic theology at the University of Breslau.

Otto wrote his most famous book, *Das Heilige* (The Idea of the Holy, 1917), during World War I. In part due to the attention this book received, he became professor of systematic theology at the University of Marburg in 1917, where he stayed until his death. During the 1920s he wrote two major comparisons of Indian religions and Christianity, *West-östliche Mystik* (Mysticism East and West, 1926), originally delivered as Haskell Lectures at Oberlin College in Ohio in 1924, and *Die Gnadenreligion Indiens und das Christentum* (India's Religion of Grace and Christianity, 1930), originally the Olaus Petri lectures in Uppsala, Sweden, in 1927. At Marburg Otto founded the *Religionskundliche Sammlung*, a museum of the world's religions, on behalf of which he made a second lengthy journey to South Asia in 1927 and 1928. He also attracted younger scholars as students and associates, including Heinrich Frick, Theodor Siegfried, Friedrich Heiler, Ernst Benz, and, more remotely, Gustav Mensching, Joachim Wach, and James Luther Adams. In the immediate aftermath of World War I he served on the commission to draft a new constitution, and in 1920 he organized a *Religiöser Menschheitsbund* (Religious league of humanity), an international nongovernmental organization that he saw as a necessary complement to the League of Nations. His time in Marburg was also marked by vehement antagonism to his thought from neoorthodox theologians, represented there by the New Testament scholar Rudolf Bultmann.

Although Otto retired early from teaching in 1929 for reasons of poor health, he continued to write and, after a brief hiatus, also to teach part time. In addition to pursuing interests in Indian religions, he discussed what he alleged were Persian roots of Christianity in *Reich Gottes und Menschensohn* (The Kingdom of God and the Son of Man, 1934). He intended his final major work, which was also to have been his Gifford Lectures, to be a system of ethics, but his scattered essays on the subject were not collected until 1981. Ever an ardent nationalist, Otto seems in 1933 to have taken an interest in the German Christian position, although he found German Christian leaders distasteful. He did not actively oppose the Nazi regime.

In October 1936 Otto fell some twenty meters from a tower, a fall that persistent but unconfirmed rumors identify as a suicide attempt. Whatever the cause, he suffered severely from his injuries and died of pneumonia on March 6, 1937.

THOUGHT. Otto's intellectual project grew from a desire to defend religion in general and Christianity more specifically from the attacks of nineteenth-century historians and natural scientists. As a result, although he taught dogmatics and ethics, most of his writing in systematic theology fell within a domain traditionally known as apologetics, albeit focused upon a general apologetics of religion rather than a defense of the superiority of Christianity. By 1909, however, Otto had abandoned these categories and had come to conceive of modern theology as a science of religion, a term whose apologetic utility is evident.

In the tradition of German idealism and, more remotely, of Cartesian dualism, Otto distinguished two realms, the mental and the material, a distinction that he took over from his teacher Hermann Schultz and developed in his first major book, *Naturalistische und religiöse Weltansicht* (Naturalism and Religion, 1904). Nineteenth-century naturalism made a major error, he thought, when it devalued the mental in favor of the material. Human beings had immediate access to and direct knowledge of only mental events, and such events always mediated knowledge of the material world. Along with some noted biologists, such as Emil Dubois-Reymond, Otto maintained that consciousness was a primary datum that in principle could not be explained in terms of material processes, such as neurophysiological events. Furthermore, he reversed the relationship between rational certainty and intuition that René Descartes had postulated. For him, the mental was not so much a rational realm of eternal ideas or pure reason as it was a realm of conscious experience whose rational representations rested ultimately on nonrational feelings and intuitions.

Although originally attracted to the thought of Friedrich Schleiermacher—as a young instructor, he edited the one-hundredth anniversary edition of Schleiermacher's famous *Speeches on Religion*—Otto came to believe that the thought of Fries provided a philosophically more satisfactory account of religion. He summarized that thought in *Kantisch-Fries'sche Religionsphilosophie*, and in doing so provided a philosophic critique (in the Kantian sense) of the possibility of religious experience, taking "experience" as much in an empirical as in an emotive sense (*Erfahrung* as well as *Erlebnis*). Unlike Kant, Fries thought that cognition takes place in the realms of practical and aesthetic as well as of theoretical reason, raising the possibility of a peculiar sort of religious cognition, too. Furthermore, in Fries's thought all knowledge depends upon feeling. For example, a *Wahrheitsgefühl*, or feeling of truth, is said to be responsible for one's judgment that the results of one's rational processes are correct. Even in the realm of science and mathematics it is possible to be convinced of the truth of a proposition without being able to demonstrate it, as Otto once illustrated with Fermat's last theorem: mathematicians could sense that the theorem was true, even if they could not prove it. But unlike scientific cognition, Otto claimed, religious cognition involves experiences that are in principle not subject to correction, or even full formulation and elaboration, by theoretical reason.

In his most famous book, *Das Heilige*, Otto turned from a critical philosophical account of the possibility of religious experience to a descriptive psychology of the content of that experience and its relationship to the "rational," symbolic dimension of religion. To designate religious feelings at their most distinctive he coined the word *numinous*, which referred, he said, to the Holy or Sacred minus the moral dimension. But he soon encountered a methodological limitation. Conscious experience is only available to the person who has it; therefore, it is possible to formulate a descriptive account of religious feelings only on the basis of introspection, informed by apparent similarities in what others have said. In other words, in order to study the experience that is the ultimate source of religion, a scholar must have a *sensus numinis,* an ability to experience numinous feelings—just as the description of color in painting or pitch in music requires certain kinds of perceptual abilities. Those who have such abilities, Otto suggested, experience the numinous as a *mysterium tremendum et fascinans.* As a *mysterium,* it is completely other, beyond the realm of ordinary existence, apprehensible but not comprehensible, evoking in human beings the feeling of stupor and stunned silence. People find this *mysterium* both attractive (*fascinans*) and repulsive (*tremendum*). On the one hand, it arouses the sense of grace, love, and mercy. On the other, it arouses feelings of terror and awe and the conviction that human beings are in reality nothing—feelings to which Otto, countering tendencies to equate genuine religion with love, gave a great deal of attention. Furthermore, this Holy is a category a priori, and as such beyond empirical criticism. (Otto's Kantianism is muddled.) It is, however, a complex category, consisting not just of the nonrational numinous but also of rational symbolic and ethical elements that "schematize" the numinous and result in relatively persistent but culturally variable religious forms.

Within the framework provided by these basic convictions in philosophy and psychology, Otto worked extensively in the history of religions. After his journey of 1911 to 1912 he learned Sanskrit and translated several religious texts into German. His most ambitious venture was a three-volume study of the *Bhagavadgītā* (one volume in English), which sought to reconstruct the poem's textual history and thus to recover its original inspiration. His two major comparative works, *West-östliche Mystik* and *Die Gnadenreligion Indiens und das Christentum,* also reflect his interest in Indian religions, as well as a division of religiosity common at the time into the mystical and the devotional. The former book compares the positions of the Advaita philosopher Śaṅkarācārya with the German mystic Meister Eckhart; the latter makes a similar comparison of *bhakti* movements with Christianity of a Pietist bent. Both works ascribe the distinctiveness and superiority of Christianity to a dynamism that derives from its Jewish roots. Otto's last major work, *Reich Gottes und Menschensohn,* is genealogical rather than comparative in intent and bridges what in the two major comparative studies is a divide between the Christian and the Indo-Iranian or, as that cultural region was called, Aryan. It examines the alleged Iranian roots of Christianity, although it still attributes the highest Christian insights to its Jewish ancestry.

Otto's work in the history of religions was not all descriptive. Influenced in particular by biology, he made modest attempts to identify processes at work in religious history, such as his account of parallels and convergences; that is, of similarities that derive not from common ancestry but from adaptation to similar environmental circumstances. But Otto did not expect comparative study to reveal the universal conceptual or symbolic content of religion, a point he made as early as his critique of Wilhelm Wundt (1910). Indeed, the structure of Otto's thought, oriented to a universal feeling beyond thought and expression, relegates symbols and ideas to a culturally determined rational schematization and so is fundamentally incompatible with later attempts by scholars such as C. G. Jung and Mircea Eliade to identify universal elements of religious or mythic thought. In old age Otto declined an invitation to participate in the first Eranos conference.

Otto's ethics, left incomplete, has received relatively little attention, but like his work on religion it builds upon a descriptive psychology of moral feelings, such as the feelings of guilt and responsibility. One might also note that Otto's thinking was never isolated from the world but always explicitly engaged with it, especially with the church and state. In the church, Otto strove to improve worship and ministry by encouraging liberal theology and incorporating moments of numinous experience into the liturgy. He was also convinced that his insights into religion could further the interests of the German state, which came into existence during his infancy, but his assessment of those interests changed over time. In religion as he understood it, he found the source of both German colonial greatness (his cultural imperialism before the first World War) and of international justice and equality between nations (the *Religiöser Menschheitsbund* afterward). In the Nazi period he claimed that the study of religions revealed the struggle of the German soul at its most profound and that dialogue between Protestants and Catholics was necessary to unify the German nation.

Impact and Assessment. When it appeared in late 1916 (dated 1917), Otto's account of the Holy created an immediate sensation, and it was quickly translated into English (1923), Swedish (1924), Spanish (1925), Italian (1926), Japanese (1927), Dutch (1928), and French (1929). The impact was especially pronounced in the English-speaking world, perhaps because of affinities between Otto's thought and English Romanticism (e.g., William Wordsworth's "Intimations of Immortality"). Otto's word *numinous,* his phrase *mysterium tremendum et fascinans* (occasionally cited as *fascinosum,* which means something different in Latin), and even the title of his book, "The Idea of the Holy," still enjoy a certain currency among English-speaking writers and artists, even apart from the details of Otto's thought.

Although himself a theologian, Otto's impact upon Protestant theology was muted, because his attempt to found religion on human experience went counter to the tenets of neoorthodoxy. Paul Tillich, however, made significant use of Otto's ideas, and recently some theologians interested in interreligious dialogue (e.g., Hans-Martin Barth) and feminism (e.g., Melissa Raphael) have engaged them, too. Otto's most significant impact was on the comparative study of religions, especially that form often known as phenomenology. Students and successors utilized Otto's analysis in far-reaching accounts that saw religion as the expression of an experience *sui generis.* Indeed, Otto's analysis became part of a standard rationale for founding independent academic units to study religion. With time, however, scholars have become suspicious that Otto's ideas improperly universalize structures that best fit Christianity. In addition, the widespread turn to culture and language that began in the 1960s tended to reject Otto's account of an experience that was autonomous, primary, and universal, and either to speak of experiences as shaped by particular cultural and symbolic environments or to ignore them altogether. Furthermore, a significant number of scholars have rejected Otto's insistence upon introspection and his prerequisite that in order to study the source of religion scholars possess a *sensus numinis* as a violation of scientific method. Among North American scholars, historical interest in Otto has been eclipsed by interest in William James.

The concurrence of neuropsychology, cognitive science, and the study of religion that took place in the 1990s returned in significant respects to themes that interested Otto, but in a way that reveals the difficulties of using Otto's thought today: For example, neuropsychologists such as Eugene d'Aquili and Andrew Newberg have studied religious experiences that are reminiscent of Otto's numinous experience, but unlike Otto they postulate a unitary mind-brain, and so seek to discover the basis for religious experiences in the structure and functioning of the physical brain. Some theologians have seen in such work a foundation and validation for human religiosity—a fulfillment of Otto's ultimate theological aim, if by a somewhat different route.

Cognitive scientists such as Pascal Boyer, Scott Atran, and Stewart Guthrie have had relatively little interest in religious experiences, even if they have on occasion mimicked Otto's phrases, perhaps unconsciously. Nevertheless, in significant respects their fundamental questions resemble Otto's. In a manner reminiscent of Kantianism they want both to identify the a priori, universal structures that shape intuitive, prerational cognition (folk physics, biology, and psychology) and to relate to those structures the cognitive processes that make religion possible. But they focus on mental representations rather than feelings and intuitions, and they embrace rather than reject evolutionary explanation. Like Otto they do postulate a plurality of distinct mental domains, but they define them in terms of content (inanimate object, living thing, animal, human) rather than varieties of rationality (theoretical, practical, aesthetic), and unlike Otto they do not consider religious cognition to constitute an independent, universal domain. Although they see religion as beyond adequate rational formulation, they attribute this to the symbolic rather than literal quality of religious representation and, unlike Otto, see it as a mark against the literal veracity of religious claims. Finally, they expect to test their claims not through introspection but through vigorous, cross-cultural experimentation. So long as presumptions such as these dominate, Otto's account of religious experience will remain data for the history of religious thought, but it will not be a live theoretical option within the study of religions.

BIBLIOGRAPHY

Works by Otto

Naturalistische und religiöse Weltansicht. Tübingen, Germany, 1904. Translated as *Naturalism and Religion* by J. Arthur Thomson and Margaret R. Thomson. London, 1907.

Kantisch-Fries'sche Religionsphilosophie und ihre Anwendung auf die Theologie. Tübingen, Germany, 1909. Translated as *The Philosophy of Religion Based on Kant and Fries* by E. B. Dicker. London, 1931.

Das Heilige: Über das Irrationale in der Idee des Göttlichen und sein Verhältnis zum Rationalen. Breslau, Germany, 1917. Translated as *The Idea of the Holy* by John W. Harvey. Oxford, 1923; 2d ed., 1950.

West-östliche Mystik. Gotha, Germany, 1926. Translated as *Mysticism East and West: A Comparative Analysis of the Nature of Mysticism* by Bertha L. Bracey and Richenda C. Payne. New York, 1932.

Die Gnadenreligion Indiens und das Christentum. Gotha, Germany, 1930. Translated as *India's Religion of Grace and Christianity Compared and Contrasted* by Frank Hugh Foster. New York, 1930.

Religious Essays: A Supplement to the Idea of the Holy. Translated by Brian Lunn. London, 1931.

Reich Gottes und Menschensohn. Munich, 1934. Translated as *The Kingdom of God and the Son of Man: A Study in the History of Religion* by Floyd V. Filson Bertram and Lee Wolff. Boston, 1943.

Aufsätze zur Ethik. Edited by Jack Stewart Boozer. Munich, 1981.

Autobiographical and Social Essays. Edited by Gregory D. Alles. Berlin, 1996.

Works about Otto

Alles, Gregory D. "Rudolf Otto (1869–1937)." In *Klassiker der Religionswissenschaft: Von Friedrich Schleiermacher bis Mircea Eliade,* edited by Axel Michaels, pp. 198–210. Munich, 1997.

Almond, Philip. *Rudolf Otto: An Introduction to His Philosophical Theology.* Chapel Hill, N.C., 1984.

Benz, Ernst, ed. *Rudolf Otto's Bedeutung für die Religionswissenschaft und für die Theologie Heute.* Leiden, 1971.

Davidson, Robert F. *Rudolf Otto's Interpretation of Religion.* Princeton, N.J., 1947.

Frick, Heinrich, Birger Forell, and Friedrich Heiler. *Religionswissenschaft in neuer Sicht: Drei Reden über Rudolf Ottos Persönlichkeit und Werk.* Marburg, Germany, 1951.

Gooch, Todd A. *The Numinous and Modernity: An Interpretation of Rudolf Otto's Philosophy of Religion.* Berlin, 2000.

Haubold, Wilhelm. *Die Bedeutung der Religionsgeschichte für die Theologie Rudolf Ottos.* Leipzig, 1940.

Schütte, Hans Walter. *Religion und Christentum in der Theologie Rudolf Ottos.* Berlin, 1969.

GREGORY D. ALLES (2005)

OTTO, WALTER F. Walter Friedrich Otto (1874–1958) was a German scholar of classical philology, mythology, and the history and philosophy of religions. The son of pharmacist Hermann Ernst Otto, Walter Otto was born in Hechingen, a small town below Mount Hohenzollern in Swabia. His family, marked by strong pietistic principles, soon moved to Stuttgart, where Otto attended secondary school at the humanistic Eberhard Ludwigs Gymnasium beginning in 1882. After winning the *Konkurs* in 1892, he was admitted to the Stift, an evangelical college in Tübingen that had been in earlier times the school of the poet Friedrich Hölderlin and the philosophers G. W. F. Hegel and Friedrich Schelling. The following year Otto switched to classical studies under Otto Crusius, Wilhelm Schmid, and Ludwig Schwabe. He continued these studies in 1894 in Bonn, where he was strongly influenced by Hermann Usener and Friedrich Bücheler. Under the supervision of the latter, he wrote his dissertation on the origin of Roman proper names, for which he was awarded a Ph.D. degree in 1897.

Following the *Staatsexamen* in the same year, he taught in a secondary school in Bonn for six months, and from 1898 onward he served as assistant of the *Thesaurus Linguae Latinae* in Munich. As part of this project he became editor of the *Onomasticon Latinum* from 1905 to 1911, continuing his work in the field of Latin onomastics. In 1905 Otto completed his *Habilitationsschrift on Juno* at the University of Munich under his former teacher in Tübingen, Otto Crusius. Other major essays on Roman religion appeared in the years 1900 to 1916, most of them in the *Real-Encyclopädie*. At the University of Munich he became *Privatdozent* in 1905; he gave Latin style exercises from 1907 on, and was appointed *außerordentlicher Professor* in 1910. Besides the philological work at the *Thesaurus*, which led Otto to the acquaintance of Ernst Diehl and Alfred Klotz, he attended the psychodiagnostic lectures of the Bachofen-influenced scholar Ludwig Klages. In 1911 he gave lectures at the University of Vienna, where his friendship with Hans von Arnim started.

In 1913 Otto was appointed *ordentlicher Professor* for Latin literature in Basel, and the next year he moved, with the same function, to Frankfurt am Main, where he wrote his main works, *The Homeric Gods* (1929) and *Dionysus* (1933). Here he was the leader of a major school in ancient culture and religion to which adhered important scholars, such as the classicist Karl Reinhardt and the ethnologist Leo Frobenius (who were Otto's best friends for his whole life), the Sinologist Richard Wilhelm, the philosopher Kurt Riezler and, among the younger generation, the Germanist Max Kommerell (who became Otto's son-in-law in 1936), the historian Franz Altheim, the religious historians Carl Koch and Károly Kerényi, the Iranist Hermann Lommel, and the ethnologist Adolf Ellegard Jensen. Most of these scholars wrote important works within the sixteen-volume series *Frankfurter Studien zur Religion und Kultur der Antike*, edited by Otto between 1932 and 1938. In those years Otto played a key role in Frankfurt's cultural life, attending both Wilhelm's China-Institut and Frobenius's Forschungsinstitut für Kulturmorphologie (Otto helped to transfer the latter from Munich to Frankfurt). He went several times to the exile residence of Kaiser Wilhelm II in Doorn (Netherlands), where scholars of Frobenius's entourage were invited regularly to hold conferences on myth-related topics. In his last years in Frankfurt, Otto put great efforts into advising the scientific edition of the unpublished works of Max Scheler and Friedrich Nietzsche. Otto was an important member of the scientific committee of the Nietzsche-Archiv in Weimar: together with Karl Schlechta and Martin Heidegger, both appointed to the committee by his suggestion, Otto tried to save Nietzsche's legacy from a mere political use.

Because of his connections with Kurt Riezler and his "clique," the Nazis forced Otto to move to Königsberg in 1934. Here he succeeded the Greek classicist Paul Maas, who had to leave his chair because of his Jewish origins, and became a good friend of the younger scholar Willy Theiler. He was also close to the philosopher Hans Heyse, the art historian Wilhelm Worringer, the musicologist Hans Engel, the archaeologist Guido von Kaschnitz-Weinberg, and the Indologist Helmut von Glasenapp. Besides his academic relationships, Otto took part in Königsberg's cultural life, becoming a member of the Königsberger Gelehrte Gesellschaft and the Kant-Gesellschaft, and attending the aristocratic society of Eastern Prussia (through the families Dohna and Dönhoff he was introduced to anti-Nazi milieus). During this period Otto wrote about Goethe's and Hölderlin's relationship to Greek religion, lectured on Nietzsche and Socrates, and edited the *Jahrbücher für die geistige Überlieferung* together with Karl Reinhardt and Ernesto Grassi. The second volume of this series was forbidden by the Nazis, who therefore decided to cancel the award of the Kant-Preis to Otto in 1943. In 1944 he escaped the disaster of Königsberg, leaving behind his library and several manuscripts. This heavy loss was important for Otto's shift to a more philosophical—and less philological—approach to classical myth, which goes back to the 1920s but is particularly characteristic of his works after 1945. Having spent the last year of war in Elmau (Bavaria), he obtained two teaching assignments in Greek literature in Munich and Göttingen (1945 and 1946), was visiting professor in Tübingen in 1946, and became emeritus in that university in 1955. During this period he was one of the founders of the Wissenschaftliche Buchgesellschaft and the Max-Scheler-Gesellschaft (the latter of which he directed), and lectured on various topics, including Apollo, Prometheus, the spirit of Greek religion, Greek tragedy, Socrates, and humanism.

Starting from studies in Latin onomastics strongly influenced by Usener's *Götternamen* (1896) and Bücheler's works on ancient Italic languages, Otto moved in his postdoctoral years to a comprehensive interpretation of Roman religion. As a challenge to Georg Wissowa's *Religion und Kultus der Römer* (1902), Otto concentrated on the autochthon (non-

Greek) aspects of the main Roman gods (Fatum, Faunus, Fides, Fortuna, Genius, Janus, and Juno), pointing out their chthonian, as well as their benign, character. In these years he also extended his cognition in the field of history of religions, on which he gave lectures at Munich University (thereby dwelling especially on Greek mystery cults). These interests directed his studies about soul-beliefs in ancient religions—a topic on which he lectured in Frankfurt and wrote his first book in 1923 (*Die Manen*).

In another book of the same year (*Der Geist der Antike und die christliche Welt*) Otto gave a strongly Nietzsche-influenced view of the Jewish and Christian religions in antithesis to the Greek Olympian world. Here, and in a series of articles leading to his main work, the *Homeric Gods* (1929; English translation, 1954), he supplied a philosophical interpretation of Greek religion, abandoning the philological method that had guided all his previous works. This methodological shift was due to Otto's classicistic conception of the uniqueness of Greek religion compared to any other. He maintained that the Homeric mode of seeing and thinking of the Olympian gods found continual expression within the Greek world "despite all temporal and individual variations, in the representative works of the Greek genius, whether in poetry, plastic art or philosophy" (Otto, 1929/1954, p. 20), being not only the very essence of Greek civilization, but indeed "the religious idea of the European spirit" and "one of humanity's greatest religious ideas" (p. 13). According to Otto, each Olympian god (he dwells on Athene, Apollo, Artemis, Aphrodite, and Hermes, not taking into account Zeus) is an *Urgestalt des Seins*, capable of revealing from its peculiar point of view the totality of reality—worldliness and naturalness—in human shape. Such are, for example, Apollo, the anthropomorphic revelation of spiritual freedom and distance from the mortal's world, and his twin sister Artemis, who represents "freedom of another sort—the feminine," which is "free nature with its brilliance and wildness, with its guiltless purity and its mysterious uncanniness" (p. 102). As Goethe had pointed out, Greek religion should therefore be considered as "theomorphic" and not as "anthropomorphic," with the divine in its human appearance being the model for mankind—and not the opposite.

Otto deepened his idea of the Greek divine as a revelation of "being" in human form in his other major work, *Dionysus* (1933; English translation, 1965). Relying on this conception, Otto was one of the few scholars of his time maintaining the Greek provenience of Dionysos, long before Michael Ventris and John Chadwick discovered the god's Mycaenean evidence in 1952. Though not belonging to the Olympian deities, this god discloses "a whole world, whose spirit presents itself again and again in new forms, connecting in an eternal unity the sublime with the simple, the human with the animal, the vegetal with the elemental" (Otto, 1933/1965, p. 188). The very essence of Dionysos lies therefore in the opposition between these incompatible poles; hence his madness, visible in his symbols: the mask (incarnating the simultaneity of presence and absence), the music (embodying both noise and silence), and the wine (symbol of the paradoxical unity of pleasure and pain). This madness, in which brightness and obscurity, and joy and horror, coincide, unifies also life and death, concealing in itself the mystery of procreation. For this reason, the Dionysian world is a feminine one, closely connected to women, as is clearly shown by the god's followers, the Maenads, and his spouse Ariadne.

SEE ALSO Greek Religion; Kerényi, Károly.

BIBLIOGRAPHY

Otto's Ph.D. work was written in Latin and published in 1898 in the *Fleckeisens Jahrbücher* (*Nomina propria latina oriunda a participiis perfecti*; Leipzig, 1898), pp. 745–932. His most important essays on Roman religion, which made him a renowned philologist, have been collected posthumously in the *Aufsätze zur römischen Religionsgeschichte* (Meisenheim a. G., 1975). Other major contributions to this topic can be found in volumes 6, 7, and 8 of August Pauly and Georg Wissowa's *Real-Encyclopädie der classischen Altertumswissenschaft* (Stuttgart, 1909–1913).

The shift to a comprehensive view of the history of religions is evident in Otto's editorial effort in the series *Religiöse Stimmen der Völker* (a German translation of the major religious texts of the world, published in Jena, 1915–1923), and in his monograph *Die Manen oder von den Urformen des Totenglaubens: Eine Untersuchung zur Religion der Griechen, Römer, und Semiten und zum Volksglauben überhaupt* (Berlin, 1923), which challenges Erwin Rohde's notion of psyche by showing the distinction between thymos, the life-spirit, and psyche—that is, the immaterial phantom of a person that remains when the life-spirit leaves the body at the moment of death (this distinction can be made in Roman and Jewish religions as well). In 1923 appeared also *Der Geist der Antike und die Christliche Welt* (Bonn; Italian trans., 1973), a book Otto didn't want republished, followed by his most widely known works, namely *Die Götter Griechenlands: Das Bild des Göttlichen im Spiegel des griechischen Geistes* (Bonn, 1929; English trans. by Moses Hadas: *The Homeric Gods: The Spiritual Significance of Greek Religion*, London, 1954; Italian trans.: Florence, 1941; Spanish trans: Buenos Aires, 1973; French trans. with a foreword by Marcel Détienne: Paris, 1981; Romanian trans.: Bucharest, 1995); and *Dionysos: Mythos und Kultus* (Frankfurt a. M., 1933; English trans. with an introduction by Robert B. Palmer: *Dionysus: Myth and Cult*, Bloomington, Ind., and London, 1965; French trans.: Paris, 1969; Italian trans.: Genoa, 1990; Greek trans.: Athens, 1991; Spanish trans.: Madrid, 1997).

Important writings to evaluate Otto's relationship to the Nazi regime are his booklet *Der junge Nietzsche* (Frankfurt a. M., 1936; reprinted in *Mythos und Welt*, Darmstadt and Stuttgart, 1963), and two volumes of the series *Geistige Überlieferung*, which he edited in Berlin in 1940 and 1942. Otto's literary bequest is evident in his books *Der Dichter und die alten Götter* (Frankfurt a. M., 1942; Italian trans.: Naples, 1991) and *Die Gestalt und das Sein: Gesammelte Abhandlungen über den Mythos und seine Bedeutung für die Menschheit* (Düsseldorf and Köln, 1954), where Hölderlin's topic of the "flight of the Divine" is analyzed in relation to the absence of the Olympian gods in modern times. According to Otto, in our epoch only poetry can save humankind from decay, poetry being the only possible approach to the truth of reality, as pointed out in *Die Musen und der göttliche Ursprung des Singens und Sagens* (Darmstadt, 1954). The importance of Greek myth from a philosophical perspective is pointed out as well in *Gesetz, Urbild, und Mythos* (Stuttgart, 1951; reprinted in *Die Gestalt und das Sein* [Dusseldorf and Koln, 1954], pp. 25–90, and in New York, 1978; Italian trans.: Rome, 1996), and in *Theophania: Der Geist der altgriechischen Religion* (Hamburg, 1956), with a biographical sketch by Ernesto Grassi; reprinted with a foreword by Friedrich Georg Jünger and a biographical note by Bernhard Wyß (Frankfurt a. M., 1934; Japanese trans.: Tokyo, 1966; Spanish trans.: Buenos Aires, 1968; Italian trans.: Genoa, 1983; French trans.: Paris, 1995).

Otto dedicated his last efforts to two major figures of Greek philosophy: Socrates (about whom he wrote 1,800 pages from 1940 to 1955, still unpublished) and *Epikur*, edited posthumously in *Das Wort der Antike* (Darmstadt and Stuttgart, 1962), pp. 293–333; Italian trans.: Parma, 2001). Also published after Otto's death were *Das Wort der Antike* (Darmstadt and Stuttgart, 1962) and *Mythos und Welt* (Darmstadt and Stuttgart, 1963), edited by Kurt von Fritz with a critical commentary on Otto's work and a bibliography of his publications by Egidius Schmalzriedt; and *Die Wirklichkeit der Götter: Von der Unzerstörbarkeit griechischer Weltsicht* (Hamburg, 1963), containing a deep appreciation on Otto's oeuvre by Károly Kerényi. The unpublished work of Otto that survived the flames of Königsberg lies in the *Deutsches Literaturarchiv* in Marbach; it includes roughly 25,000 handwritten pages, mostly stemming from lectures and conferences, and about 1,250 letters from and to Otto dating from 1944 to 1958.

Major biographical sketches of Otto include Karl Reinhardt, "Walter F. Otto," in *Vermächtnis der Antike* (Göttingen, 1966), pp. 87–90; Otto Weinreich, "Walter F. Otto zum 75: Geburtstag" and "Walter F. Otto zum 80: Geburtstag," both collected in *Ausgewählte Schriften* 1937–1970, vol. 3 (Amsterdam, 1979), pp. 275–277 and 361–363; Willy Theiler, "Walter F. Otto +" in *Gnomon* 32 (1960): 87–90; Viktor Pöschl, "Walter F. Otto und Karl Reinhardt," in *Literatur und geschichtliche Wahrheit* (Heidelberg, 1983), pp. 247–273; Gerhard Perl, "Walter F. Otto (1874–1958) in Königsberg," in *Eikasmos* 4 (1993): 283–285; and Hubert Cancik, "Walter Friedrich Otto," in *Neue Deutsche Biographie*, vol. 19 (Berlin, 1999), pp. 713–714. A biographical picture including information on Otto's unpublished work is supplied by Alessandro Stavru, "Il lascito di Walter Friedrich Otto nel Deutsches Literaturarchiv di Marbach," in *Studi e materiali di storia delle religioni* 64 (1998): 195–222. On Otto's gradual divergence from the ideas of his teacher Hermann Usener see the thorough study of Antje Wessels, *Ursprungszauber. Zur Rezeption von Hermann Useners Lehre von der religiösen Begriffsbildung*, New York- Berlin, 2003, pp. 185-225.

The only booklength work on Otto—Josef Donnenberg's dissertation *Die Götterlehre Walter Friedrich Ottos: Weg oder Irrweg moderner Religionsgeschichte?* (Innsbruck, 1961)—cannot be considered a comprehensive study, since it analyses only his writings on Greek religion and leaves out Otto's interpretation of Roman religion, which influenced profoundly his pupils Franz Altheim and Carl Koch, and was appreciated even by Ulrich von Wilamowitz-Moellendorff (*Der Glaube der Hellenen*, Berlin: vol. 1, 1931, pp. 11–12, 142, 313; vol. 2, 1932, pp. 328–329). In more recent times, following the reprint of Otto's main writings on Roman religion in 1975 by Reinhold Merkelbach, Wolfgang Fauth underlined their importance (*Anzeiger für die Altertumswissenschaft* 32 [1979]: 105–109), whereas George Dumézil criticized them in, for example, *La religion romaine archaïque* (Paris, 1974).

In a similar way, due to its nonphilological nature, Otto's approach to Greek religion encountered on one hand indifference (or even resistance), and on the other appreciation. This is evident in the reactions of major scholars to *Die Götter Griechenlands*, which encountered unfavorable criticism in the reviews by Martin Persson Nilsson, *Deutsche Literaturzeitung* 28 (1929): 1334–1337; Louis Gernet, *Revue de philologie, de litterature et d'histoire anciennes* 5 (1931): 91–94; Herbert Jennings Rose, *The Classical Review* 6 (1956): 162; Hubert Cancik, *Der altsprachliche Unterricht* 27 (1984): 71–89. *Die Götter Griechenlands* was assessed positively by Mario Untersteiner, *Il mondo classico* 1 (1931): 15–23; Bruno Snell, *Theologische Literaturzeitung* 3 (1955): 152–153; Arthur Hilary Armstrong, *The Hibbert Journal* 54 (1955–1956): 96–98; Françoise Frontisi-Ducroux, *Revue de l'histoire des religions* 200 (1983): 102–103. *Dionysus* was heavily attacked by Martin Persson Nilsson, *Gnomon* 11 (1935): 177–181, and Hubert Cancik in *Die Restauration der Götter*, edited by Richard Faber and Renate Schlesier (Würzburg, 1986), pp. 105–123; it was evaluated neutrally by Arthur William Hope Adkins, *The Classical Review* 21 (1971): 147–148; and was appreciated by Gustav van der Leeuw, *Nieuwe theologische Studien* 17 (1933): 87–94, and Mario Untersteiner, *Il mondo classico* 6 (1936): 297–305. Other interesting reviews on Otto's interpretation of Greek myth, extending beyond his main works, are those of Ludolf Malten, *Gnomon* 20 (1944): 113–126; Albin Lesky, *Gnomon* 24 (1952): 432–434; Walther Kraus, *Gnomon* 30 (1958): 561–566; Willy Theiler, *Gnomon* 35 (1963): 619–621, and Philip Merlan, *Gymnasium* 70 (1963): 424–429.

The influence of Otto's ideas is mostly evident in the oeuvre of Károly Kerényi, especially in his *Dionysos* (London, 1976), but it can also be noticed in such scholars as the philologists Bruno Snell (*Die Entdeckung des Geistes* [Hamburg, 1946], pp. 30–44) and Willy Theiler ("Der Mythos und die Götter Griechenlands" in *Untersuchungen zur antiken Literatur* [Berlin, 1970], pp. 130–147), as well as in the archaeologists Karl Schefold (*Griechische Kunst als religiöses Phänomen* [Hamburg, 1959]) and Erika Simon (*Die Götter der Griechen*, [Munich, 1969]). A much more indirect reception of Otto's thought can be caught in some writings of Walter Burkert (via his teacher Carl Koch) and, in a structuralistic frame, in the later works of Jean-Pierre Vernant and Marcel Détienne.

The importance of Otto's view of Greek Olympian religion for studies in the history of religion has been pointed out by Albert Henrichs, "Die Götter Griechenlands: Ihr Bild im Wandel der Religionswissenschaft," in *Thyssen-Vorträge: Auseinandersetzungen mit der Antike*, edited by Hellmut Flashar (Bamberg, 1987), pp. 3–49. The latter scholar contributed also to the success of Otto's interpretation of Dionysian duality in "Loss of Self, Suffering, Violence: The Modern View of Dionysus from Nietzsche to Girard," in *Harvard Studies in Classical Philology* 88 (1984): 205–240, making it become a popular hermeneutic paradigm (Anton Harald Bierl, *Dionysos und die griechische Tragödie* [Tübingen, 1991], pp. 1–20; Françoise Frontisi-Ducroux, *Le dieu-masque* [Paris and Rome, 1991], pp. 62–63; and Giovanni Casadio, *Il vino dell'anima* [Rome, 1999], pp. 79–81).

ALESSANDRO STAVRU (2005)

OUSPENSKY, P. D. Petyr Dem'ianovich Uspenskii (1878–1947) was a Russian philosopher, mathematician, teacher, and mystic. He is known as a conveyor and interpreter of the teachings of G. I. Gurdjieff (1866–1949), but was well established as an author even before he encountered Gurdjieff. Ouspensky has a lasting place in the early-twentieth-century Russian literary tradition, and as a writer of numerous books on human spiritual development.

Ouspensky was born in and grew up in Moscow. His mother was a painter, and his father a railroad surveyor who died when Ouspensky was a child. The precocious boy was dissatisfied with school. Even as a youth he discriminated between "ordinary knowledge" of worldly matters and "important knowledge" concerning questions about the nature of reality, human evolution and destiny, and the acquiring of higher consciousness. For this reason, he left the academic world and did not take any of the higher degrees for which he was qualified. These questions preoccupied him throughout his life. In 1905 he wrote a novel titled *Kinema-Drama*; it was not published until 1915 and was later was translated into English as *The Strange Life of Ivan Osokin*. The book, based on the idea of eternal recurrence popularized by Friedrich Nietzsche (1844–1900), dramatizes the notion that eternal recurrence, or living the same life again and again, can come to an end for a person who learns its secret. To escape "the trap called life," one must make sacrifices for many years, and even many lifetimes.

In 1907 Ouspensky's quest led him to Theosophy. After reading the works of Helena P. Blavatsky (1831–1891) and others, he joined the Theosophical Society in Saint Petersburg. However, Ouspensky became dissatisfied with Theosophy. Although invited to join the Inner Circle of initiates to study secret teachings, he declined and left the Theosophical Society in 1916. Ouspensky found that Theosophy was not a continuing path for him, but he acknowledged that it opened the door to esotericism and the study of higher dimensions.

In 1911 Ouspensky published a major work, the *Tertium Organum: The Third Canon of Thought, a Key to the Enigmas of the World*. This book, translated into English in 1920, argued that a new mode of thinking was needed in Western civilization. The classical mode had opened metaphysical inquiry. However, it also led to positivistic thought, which chose to suppress metaphysics in favor of empirical science. Aristotle (384–322 BCE) wrote the first *Organon*, a compendium of logic and a systematic means of communicating knowledge, exploring the principles of logic and discovery; Francis Bacon (1561–1626) wrote the *New Organum*, exposing the idols of the human intellect, which opened the way for further scientific exploration during the Renaissance. Ouspensky's *Tertium Organum* brought together theories of Eastern and Western mysticism, as well as sacred art and modern science, in a way that enlightened and moved the seeker toward a higher consciousness and a greater understanding of the principles of the universe.

Ouspensky's search for esoteric knowledge led him to travel to India and Ceylon in 1913. He was prevented from going to Persia and Central Asia because of the outbreak of World War I. He returned to Saint Petersburg via London, Norway, and Finland. Giving a lecture in Saint Petersburg in 1915, he met Sof'ia Grigor'evna Maksimenko, who became his wife. Ouspensky was told of another group engaged in the study of esoteric wisdom and occult phenomena; this was the circle around Gurdjieff. Ouspensky went to meet him in Moscow, and was accepted as a student of stature. Gurdjieff acknowledged that Ouspensky was a thinker and author in his own right. *In Search of the Miraculous: Fragments of an Unknown Teaching* (1949) contains an account of Ouspensky's conversations with Gurdjieff and a lucid systematic exposition of Gurdjieff's early ideas.

As early as 1918, Ouspensky began to become disillusioned with Gurdjieff's leadership. In a typescript for a meeting in 1937, Ouspensky explained that Gurdjieff had said years earlier, "First of all you must not believe anything, and second you must not do anything you do not understand." Ouspensky felt Gurdjieff was violating these principles, although the two men continued to work together. After immigrating to London to escape the Bolsheviks, Ouspensky developed his own circle of disciples. Gurdjieff joined him there in 1922 and acquired some of Ouspensky's pupils. In 1924 Ouspensky refused to stay at Gurdjieff's Institute at Prieuré des Basses Loges at Fontainebleau-Avon in France, and he announced the independent nature of his future work. The final break came in 1931 when Ouspensky was denied all access to Prieuré.

Undaunted, Ouspensky continued to teach and to write in London and founded the Historico-Psychological Society. However, World War II made life in London difficult. He also taught for a time in Lynn in Surrey, but decided to go to the United States, where he held large meetings in New York and New Jersey from 1941 to 1946. Although in failing health, he returned to England in 1947. Before his death in October of that year, he told his disciples that the work as they had known it could not continue without him. However, they were free to pursue the truth in their own way.

The Fourth Way (1957), consisting of records of Ouspensky's meetings from 1921 to 1947, was published under the supervision of Ouspensky's wife. The term "Fourth

Way" means bringing the life of the *fakir*, the monk, and the yogi into ordinary life, to experience eternity doing simple tasks. This fourth form of consciousness is the beginning of the transition to cosmic consciousness—the state of the spirit beyond time and the cycles of life and death.

Ouspensky's "Psychological Lectures," given from 1934 to 1940, were published posthumously as *The Psychology of Man's Possible Evolution* (1981). Here Ouspensky contends that living beings are progressing through levels of being from the one-dimensional (plants and lower animals), to the two-dimensional (higher animals), to the three-dimensional (ordinary humans). However, some humans who strive to do so can pass beyond the mere sensory consciousness of three dimensions in understanding time as the fourth dimension of space. There is a fifth dimension perpendicular to the line of time, which is the line of eternity, or an infinite number of finite points in time.

In a work published in 1931, *A New Model of the Universe: Principles of the Psychological Method in its Application to Problems of Science, Religion, and Art*, Ouspensky argues that to really understand non-Euclidian space, the seeker must expand his or her consciousness and experience directly the higher dimension. Ouspensky explained that the phenomenal universe is all most humans know. For example, a star is seen as a point of light, although astronomy contends it is a giant ball of gases. Ouspensky affirmed the idea of Immanuel Kant (1724–1804) that all phenomena have a noumenal substrate or real nature. Unlike Kant, Ouspensky's final message was that metageometrical laws could encompass noumena, the key to intuitive knowledge of the universe.

See Also Gurdjieff, G. I.

Bibliography

Driscoll, J. Walter. "P. D. Ouspensky: A Brief Bibliography." *Gurdjieff International Review*. 1999. Available from http://www.gurdjieff.org.

Ouspensky, P. D. *In Search of the Miraculous: Fragments of an Unknown Teaching*. New York, 1949.

Ouspensky, P. D. *The Fourth Way: A Record of Talks and Answers to Questions Based on the Teachings of G. I. Gurdjieff*. New York, 1957.

Ouspensky, P. D. *A New Model of the Universe: Principles of the Psychological Method in Its Application to Problems of Science, Religion, and Art*. New York, 1971.

Ouspensky, P. D. *The Psychology of Man's Possible Evolution*. New York, 1981.

Ouspensky, P. D. *Tertium Organum: The Third Canon of Thought, a Key to the Enigmas of the World*. New York, 1981.

Ouspensky, P. D. *The Strange Life of Ivan Osokin*. New York, 1988.

Presley, Michael. "A Brief Overview of Certain Aspects of the Thought of Petyr Demianovich Ouspensky." Available from http://www.sumeria.net/cosmo/ouspensky.html.

Taylor, Merrily E., ed. and comp. *Remembering Pyotr Demianovich Ouspensky*. New Haven, 1978.

Webb, James. *The Harmonious Circle: The Lives and Work of G. I. Gurdjieff, P. D. Ouspensky, and Their Followers*. Boston, 1980.

Judy D. Saltzman (2005)

OWLS. As a creature of two realms, the owl is a multivalent symbol admitting of both benevolent and malevolent interpretations. Like most birds, owls represent higher states of being (angels, spirits, supernatural aid, and wisdom), while their nocturnal nature and ominous hoot ally them with the instinctual world of matter, darkness, death, and blind ignorance. In a series of etchings he called *Los caprichos*, the Spanish painter Goya depicted owls as the dark forces of the irrational.

For many early peoples, owls were associated with the baleful, devouring nature of the Great Mother, and their sinister aspect as birds of ill omen prevailed over their benign connotations. In the Egyptian system of hieroglyphs, owls signify night, death, the sun that has sunk into darkness; in the Hindu tradition, they represent the soul and Yama, god of the dead; and in China, images of owls carved on funeral urns symbolize death. The owl was an attribute of the god of darkness for the Etruscans, a chthonic sign for the Celts, who called it the "corpse bird," and the taboo animal of early metallurgists. In the pagan religion of the Abyssinian Hamites, owls were sacred and were believed to embody the souls of those who had died unavenged.

Because of the owl's association with the otherworld and its mysteries, the bird was thought to be cognizant of future events and became an emblem of wisdom. Owls were regarded as auspicious in classical Greece, where they were sacred to Pallas Athena, the goddess of divine knowledge, human wisdom, and the arts; they were depicted on vases, coins, and monuments as her emblem and companion. A trace of totemism is detected in one of her epithets, Glaucopis ("owl"), which suggests that at one time the bird had been worshiped as a god and only later became an attribute of the goddess. The Romans allied the owl to Athena's counterpart Minerva, and also believed that it augured death. The funereal screech owl was anathema to the Romans, and its appearance at public auspices was deemed unpropitious. In Vergil's *Aeneid*, when Dido contemplates death upon learning that Aeneas is to abandon her, she hears the "deathly lamentations" of an owl. And Shakespeare has Lady Macbeth say "I heard the owl scream" when Duncan is murdered.

In Judaism the owl symbolizes blindness, and according to the Talmud it is an ill omen in dreams. The Hebrew scriptures classify owls among the unclean birds, and when God declares his vengeance against Zion, he condemns it to be "a habitation of dragons and a court for owls" (*Is.* 34:14). Job, in his despair, cries that he is "a companion to owls" (*Jb.* 30:29).

Throughout Christian Europe in the Middle Ages, owls were a sign of the darkness that prevailed before the advent of Christ and a symbol of those Jews who elected to dwell therein instead of in the light of the gospel. As a bird that shuns the light, the owl was equated with Satan, Prince of Darkness, who lures people into sin as the owl tricks birds into snares. A symbol of solitude when depicted with hermits at prayer, the owl denotes wisdom when it is shown at the side of Saint Jerome. Scenes of the crucifixion sometimes show the owl with Christ, whose sacrifice brought light to those in darkness.

Owls are considered the agents of magic among many peoples. Siberian and Inuit (Eskimo) shamans regard them as helping spirits, a source of powerful aid and guidance, and wear their feathers on caps and collars. Tatar shamans try to assume the bird's shape, and the Buriats keep an owl or hang up its skin to ward off evil spirits. The Ainu look on the owl as a deity. In one Samoan village the people believe that the owl incarnates their god. A malevolent pre-Columbian Aztec god is represented with a screech owl on his head.

Among certain American Indian tribes, it was believed that God's power was transmitted to the shaman through owls. The Kiowa thought that the medicine man became an owl after death, and Creek priests bore a stuffed owl as their insignia. Owl dances were performed as a magical rite, and in the Medicine Pipe Dance of the Crow tribes, the pipe stem was decorated with owl and woodpecker feathers to symbolize night and day. For some tribes the owl represented a psychopomp: The Ojibwa called the bridge over which the dead passed the "owl bridge," and the Pima believed that owl feathers facilitated the soul's flight to the world beyond.

BIBLIOGRAPHY

Cassirer, Ernst. *The Philosophy of Symbolic Forms,* vol. 2. Translated by Ralph Manheim. New Haven, Conn., 1955. The owl as a totemic animal. Basing his concept of totemism on the mythically experienced unity and equivalence of human and animal, the author accounts for totemism as a belief that the clan was not merely descended from the animal but united with it in a magical context of the energy flowing between them.

Eliade, Mircea. *Shamanism: Archaic Techniques of Ecstasy* (1964). Rev. & enl. ed. Reprint, Princeton, N.J., 1970. Owls as powerful guardians and helping spirits, bearers of instructions to sorcerers and shamans, symbolic of their power of flight.

Ovid. *Metamorphoses,* vol. 2. Translated by Frank Justus Miller. New York, 1916. The association of owls with the dark aspects of the goddesses of the underworld and their evocation of primitive fears.

New Sources

Cenzanto, Elena, and Fabio Santopietro. *Owls: Art, Legend, History.* Translated by Graham Fawcett. Boston, 1991.

Holmgren, Virginia. *Owls in Folklore and Natural History.* Santa Barbara, Calif., 1988.

Weinstein, Krystyna. *The Owl in Art, Myth, and Legend.* New York, 1991.

ANN DUNNIGAN (1987)
Revised Bibliography

P

PACHOMIUS (293?–346) was a Christian ascetic and founder of cenobitic monasticism. Information about Pachomius has been much confused in the many legends and biographies preserved in various versions and translations. Born of pagan parents in Upper Egypt, Pachomius encountered Christianity for the first time in the city of Latopolis (Copt., Esnen; modern-day Isna) while serving in the military. There he was impressed with the seemingly virtuous life of local Christians and by the love they showed for all people. After his conscription ended, Pachomius returned to his village, Chinoboskeia (Copt., Schneset), and was baptized. Because of his great love for God, he decided to become a monk and was placed under the spiritual guidance of the ascetic Palemon. In Egypt at the time the eremitic life as established by Antony of Egypt was dominant. After receiving divine exhortation, Pachomius decided to organize a monastic community.

In an abandoned village on the east bank of the Nile, near Dendera, Pachomius established a monastery surrounded by a wall and named it Tabennis (c. 318). The small number of ascetics there soon increased greatly, creating a need for other monasteries. Under his direction, nine monasteries for men and two for women were established. In order to administer the newly established monasteries more effectively, Pachomius moved the center from Tabennis to Pebu, where he was installed as general leader, or hegumen (Gr., *hēgoumenos*). His sister Mary became the first hegumen in one of the women's monasteries. A wealthy monk, Petronius, gave financial support to Pachomius to retain control of his institutions during a general meeting of the monks in Pebu at Easter. Pachomius died on May 9, 346, in an epidemic that took the lives of about a hundred monks.

In fourth-century Egypt three basic forms of monasticism appeared: (1) the severe eremitic form, which was based on Antony's life in the desert; (2) the anchoritic monasticism of Makarios, which employed Sunday worship as one of its common elements; and (3) cenobitic monasticism as developed and practiced by Pachomius. Cenobitic monasticism centered on life inside the walls of the monastery with all the hours of the day and night strictly regulated. Monastic rule governed all the needs and activities of the monks:

CLOCKWISE FROM TOP LEFT CORNER. Fifteenth-century woodcut depicting the burning of the Jews. *[©Bettmann/Corbis]*; Sixth-century BCE Laconian cup depicting Atlas and the punishment of Prometheus. Museo Gregoriano Etrusco, Vatican Museums. *[©Scala/Art Resource, N.Y.]*; The pyramids of Giza, Egypt: Menkaure (foreground), Khafre, and Khufu. *[©Yann Arthus-Bertrand/Corbis]*; The Temple of Poseidon in Sounion, Greece. *[©Jan Butchofsky-Houser/Corbis]*; Nineteenth-century carving of the Polynesian god Rongo, from the Gambier Islands. Museo Missionario Etnologico, Vatican Museums. *[©Scala/Art Resource, N.Y.]*.

common prayer, common table, common work, and common use of the products of labor. According to monastic legend and tradition, an angel dictated these rules to Pachomius. Regarded as equal to scripture, obedience to them was considered a great virtue.

The hegumen was the spiritual leader of the monks, also undertaking responsibility for the financial support of the monastery in order to relieve the monks of worldly cares. Thus the monks could turn their undivided attention to spiritual exercises and toward heaven. In fact, this was the most important difference between the monasticism of Pachomius and that of Makarios: the hegumen was not only responsible for the spiritual needs of the monks but also for all material needs (e.g., housing, clothing, food, health care). On the other hand, the eremitic, anchoritic, and cenobitic lives did have common elements—removal from the world, severe asceticism, work with the hands, prayers, and obedience to the hegumen and the canons.

Pachomius wrote his famous rules for monks in Coptic, but only Jerome's translation from Greek into Latin is extant. In Coptic and Greek, only fragments are preserved, but there are also Ethiopic and Arabic translations. The long version of his rules seems to be the original. Eleven letters of *Pachomius* are also preserved in translations by Jerome. *Admonitions* and a small section of *Catechetical Instructions* have also survived.

Pachomius was not a great theoretical teacher of asceticism, but he was a great organizer of its practice. His teachings were directed to the ordering of the monks' lives by strict canons. These canons were meant to insure the good operation of the cloister and to make the separation from the world pronounced, including regulating the travels of the monks and visits from the laity. The canons imposed uniformity on the monks' way of life, dress, and nourishment even when the monks were outside the monastery. Only the sick were exempt from the austere dietary rules. Pachomius's canons covered all hours of the day and night, which were strictly arranged and scheduled to cover work, prayer, and rest, as well as behavior in church and at the table.

The greatest influence Pachomius had on the history of monasticism was in the organizational thoroughness and effectiveness of his rules. He created a form of monasticism that was to extend beyond his own epoch: the development of monasticism in the East and West was largely based on his rules. He influenced such monastic leaders as Basil the Great, John Cassian, and Benedict of Nursia, either directly or indirectly, and his rules are still followed in the austere monastic life lived on Mount Athos.

BIBLIOGRAPHY

The Greek lives (i. e., biographies) of Pachomius are available in *Sancti Pachomii vitae Graecae,* edited by François Halkin, in "Subsidia Hagiographica," vol. 19 (Brussels, 1932). French and English translations of the "first Greek life" are *La première vie grecque de Saint Pachôme,* translated by A.-J. Festugière, in "Les moines d'Orient," vol. 4, no. 2 (Paris, 1965), and *The Life of Pachomius: Vita Prima Graeca,* translated by Apostolos N. Athanassakis (Missoula, Mont., 1975). A French translation of the Coptic lives is *Les vies coptes de Saint Pachôme et de ses premiers successeurs,* translated by L. T. Lefort, "Bibliothèque du Muséon," no. 16 (Louvain, 1943). See also the *Œuvres de S. Pachôme et ses disciples,* 2 vols., edited by L. T. Lefort, in "Corpus Scriptorum Christianorum Orientalium, Scriptores Coptici," vols. 23 and 24 (Louvain, 1956) for Coptic and French versions. The rule of Pachomius along with eleven letters are available in the Latin translation of Jerome in *Patrologia Latina,* edited by J.-P. Migne, vol. 23 (Paris, 1865), pp. 61–99.

Three relevant secondary works are Heinrich Bacht's "L'importance de l'idéal monastique de S. Pacôme pour l'histoire du monachisme chrétien," *Revue d'ascetique et de mystique* 26 (1950): 308–326; H. Idris Bell's *Egypt from Alexander the Great to the Arab Conquest* (Oxford, 1948), pp. 109ff.; and Karl Heussi's *Der Ursprung des Mönchtums* (Tübingen, 1936).

THEODORE ZISSIS (1987)
Translated from Greek by Philip M. McGhee

PACIFISM SEE NONVIOLENCE

PADMASAMBHAVA, an Indian Tantric adept of the eighth century who became a foremost Tibetan cultural hero, is the subject of greatly elaborated legends and serves as the eponymous source of much of the enormous corpus of revelatory textual "treasures" (*gter ma*). He remains, however, so obscure to historical research that it has even been proposed that he was an entirely mythical construction who in fact never lived. Though this extreme conclusion seems, in the light of the slim evidence that does exist, to be without merit, it does underscore that here, as with a great many founders of religious traditions, the religious view of the past cannot be readily reconciled with the demands of critical history.

THE LEGEND. According to traditional Tibetan accounts, the emperor Khri Srong lde btsan (Trhi Songdetsen, r. 755–c. 797), sometime after his adoption of Buddhism in 762, resolved to create the first monastic complex, Bsam yas (Samye), at which Tibetan aspirants could be ordained into the Buddhist *saṃgha.* To achieve this, he invited the renowned Indian monk and philosopher Śāntarakṣita to preside over the construction of Bsam yas, but whatever men built by day, the gods and demons of Tibet tore down by night. Śāntarakṣita then determined that such obstacles could be overcome only by great occult power, which he, as a monk who observed the Vinaya, could not deploy. He suggested therefore that the monarch extend an invitation to the great Indian master of esoteric Buddhism, Padmasambhava, who had been miraculously born in the land of Oḍḍiyāna and now practiced Tantric rites in Nepal. It is said that when

Khri Srong lde btsan's emissaries arrived at the frontier, Padmasambhava was already waiting for them and refused the gold that they offered, declaring that everything had been transformed into gold in his vision. When the progress of his journey was obstructed by Tibet's fierce local divinities, he waged miraculous competitions with them, converting them to become protectors of the Buddhist faith. In the most developed versions of the tale, these battles assume the character of an epic account of the taming of the land, converting it from a savage realm to a sphere of civilization.

On arriving in Central Tibet, Padmasambhava's charisma overwhelmed the ruler himself, so that he, together with the leading members of his court, became devoted disciples. A lady of the court, Ye shes mtsho rgyal (Yeshe Tsogyel), was taken as Padmasambhava's consort and in the developed legends she herself is divinized, becoming the spiritual mother of the Tibetan people. For his part, Padmasambhava worked wonders so as to turn deserts into rich, irrigated fields. By marking the outer wall of Bsam yas with his ritual dance he quelled the spirits that had obstructed the monastery's construction. The temple was built and consecrated, and soon became an outstanding center of Buddhist learning.

Padmasambhava, however, by gaining the favor of the king, became an object of jealousy among some factions of the aristocracy and these now plotted against him. The local divinities, too, although bound by oath to him, in some cases grew restive. With circumstances no longer propitious for his continued sojourn in Tibet, he departed, traveling to the southern island of Camara, where he will dwell as an immortal until the end of the present aeon. Prior to his departure from Tibet, however, accompanied by Ye shes mtsho rgyal, he traveled over every inch of the Tibetan plateau, everywhere concealing treasures specially intended for particular needs in the future. These treasures—images, ritual objects, and above all texts (for instance, the celebrated *Tibetan Book of the Dead*)—would be discovered by his own Tibetan disciples, perpetually reincarnating as "treasure-discoverers." Their continuing activity is a sign of the "Precious Guru" (*guru rinpoche*) Padmasambhava's special love for the Tibetan people, a love that may also be activated when the devotee summons him through prayer from his fortress on the isle of Camara.

The legend in history. The late-first-millennium Tibetan manuscripts discovered at Dunhuang contain only two mentions of Padmasambhava that have been noted so far. One of these is a mere annotation in a colophon, but the other provides a brief hagiography, in which certain of the elements that will inform the developed legend are already present. Here Padmasambhava is portrayed as a Tantric adept residing in Nepal who vanquishes demonic obstacles through his mastery of the occult rites of Vajrakīla (the "adamant spike"), one of the Tantric divinities with which he is indeed most closely associated in later tradition. His Tibetan disciples, instructed by him in accord with the progression of Tantric systems, realize a variety of miraculous abilities.

Considering this probably tenth-century account in the light of a second group of early traditions—those contained in the several redactions of the *Dba'* (or *Sba*) *bzhed,* dating to the early second millennium—we may conclude that these sources testify to the recollection of an eighth-century Tantric adept, a specialist in the Vajrakīla cycle of Tantric rites, who developed a following in Nepal and southern Tibet. He may have also met with the king, acted as an exorcist in connection with the construction of Bsam yas, and, because the control of rivers and irrigation figures prominently throughout the legends, it is not impossible that among the wonders he worked were elements of hydraulic engineering.

Given this, it becomes possible to imagine that the several lineages of lay Tantric practitioners that during the late tenth and early eleventh centuries traced their antecedents back to Padmasambhava, and that were devoted to the cult of Vajrakīla, would have laid great stress upon the royal meeting, whatever the real facts of the matter may have been, as this no doubt strengthened their sense of legitimacy and authority. Once these early Tibetan Tantric lineages started to come under attack by proponents of the newer lines of Tantrism being introduced from India from the late tenth century onwards, the tendency would have been to insist increasingly upon recollections of Padmasambhava's imperial connection, thereby reinforcing the ancient tradition against the upstart claims of the new teachings. Padmasambhava, perhaps a marginal *dharma*-master of the eighth century, in this way reemerged two centuries later as an emblem of Tibet's imperial greatness, the hero to a wide network of Tantric cults that had taken root and flourished during this time.

The tales of Padmasambhava's compassionate intercession in the Tibetan world were elaborated in epic narratives that were discovered as revealed treasures (*gter ma*). In the early development of this literature the treasure-finder Nyang ral Nyi ma 'od zer (Nyangrel Nyima Özer, 1124–1192) and his successor Guru Chos dbang (Guru Chöwang, 1212–1270) emerge as central figures in the formation of his cult. With the revelation by O rgyan gling pa (Orgyen Lingpa, fourteenth century) of the epic verse account of his life, the *Padma bka' thang shel brag ma,* as well as five supplementary works (*Bka' thang sde lnga*), all concerned with the conversion of the Tibetan empire to Buddhism, the legend of Padmasambhava arrives at its definitive form.

INFLUENCE ON DOCTRINE, RITUAL, AND ART. Throughout the second millennium Padmasambhava played an unusually significant role in the ongoing development of Tibetan Buddhism. Though it is impossible to securely assign any extant writings to his authorship, even after excluding the innumerable "treasures" as apocryphal works, a few texts do at least reflect beliefs regarding his teachings as formulated among the first generations of Tibetans owing allegiance to him. The most prestigious of these is the *Man ngag lta ba'i phreng ba* (Esoteric instruction: A garland of views), a survey of the nine vehicles of the Rnying ma (Nyingma) pa from the standpoint of the exegetical tradition of the *Guhyagarbha Tantra,* the fundamental Tantra of the Rnying ma pa esoteric system. This work has spawned a substantial commentarial literature and has much influenced the formulation of Rnying ma pa doctrine in general.

Besides being regarded as the source of the majority of treasure-texts, and hence of the ritual and contemplative systems they propound, Padmasambhava himself is frequently invoked as a principle figure in the liturgy, whether as the *guru* who is the object of devotion or as the central figure in the esoteric *maṇḍala* with whom the adept identifies. As such, Padmasambhava has inspired a tremendous body of liturgical poetry, iconic representation, and even sacred dance. To list the major Tibetan religious figures who have been among the leading contributors in this respect, as treasure-discoverers or authors, would require a virtual *Who's Who* of Tibetan religion. With the career of the fifth Dalai Lama (1617–1682), a fervent devotee of the Precious Guru, the cult of Padmasambhava was, in effect, given the sanction of the highest authority. Nevertheless, some sectarian factions regarded the entire revelatory corpus of treasures to be spurious and so sought its suppression. It is safe to say, however, that most Tibetan Buddhists, whether Rnying ma pa or not, count themselves among Padmasambhava's faithful adherents.

SEE ALSO Buddhism, article on Buddhism in Tibet; Buddhism, Schools of, article on Tibetan and Mongolian Buddhism.

BIBLIOGRAPHY

Bischoff, F. A. "Padmasambhava est-il un personnage historique?" In *Proceedings of the Csoma de Kőrös symposium,* edited by Louis Ligeti, pp. 27–33. Budapest, 1978. Skeptical assessment of the historical evidence.

Bischoff, F. A., and Charles Hartman. "Padmasambhava's Invention of the Phur-bu: Ms. Pelliot tibétain 44." In *Études tibétaines dédiées à la mémoire de Marcelle Lalou,* edited by Ariane Macdonald, pp. 11–28. Paris, 1971. The first study of the Dunhuang account.

Dudjom Rinpoche, Jikdrel Yeshe Dorje. *The Nyingma School of Tibetan Buddhism: Its Fundamentals and History.* 2 vols. Translated by Gyurme Dorje and Matthew Kapstein. Boston. 1991. Compendium of Rnying ma pa tradition, with much inter alia on the legends and teachings attributed to Padmasambhava.

Guenther, Herbert V. *The Teachings of Padmasambhava.* Leiden, 1996. An interesting compilation of texts attributed to Padmasambhava, though Guenther's historical speculations are implausible.

Kapstein, Matthew T. *The Tibetan Assimilation of Buddhism: Conversion, Contestation, and Memory.* Oxford, 2000. Includes comments on the Dunhuang and Sba bzhed traditions.

Karmay, Samten Gyaltsen. *The Great Perfection: A Philosophical and Meditative Teaching of Tibetan Buddhism.* Leiden, 1988. Includes a translation of the *Esoteric Instruction: A Garland of Views.*

Klaus, Christa. *Der aus dem Lotos Entstandene: Ein Beitrag zur Ikonographie und Ikonologie des Padmasambhava nach dem Rin chen gter mdzod.* Wiesbaden, Germany, 1982. Iconographical study of an important liturgical corpus.

Kunsang, Eric Pema, trans. *Dakini Teachings: Padma Sambhava's Oral Instructions to Lady Tsogyal.* Boston, 1990. Selections from a twelfth-century compilation.

Kunsang, Eric Pema, trans. *The Lotus-Born: The Life Story of Padmasambhava.* Boston, 1993. The influential version of the life by Nyang ral Nyi ma 'od zer.

Ngawang Zangpo, trans. *Guru Rinpoche: His Life and Times.* Ithaca, N.Y., 2002. Includes Tāranātha's influential "Indian" version of the life.

Thingo, Tsering T., and Gerd W. Essen. *Padmasambhava: Leben und Wundertaten des grossen tantrischen Meisters im Spiegel der tibetischen Bildkunst.* Cologne, Germany, 1991. An attractive collection of icons of Padmasambhava's varied forms.

Toussaint, Gustave-Charles, trans. *Le Dict de Padma: Padma thang yig, Ms. de Lithang.* Paris, 1933. Translated from the French by Kenneth Douglas and Gwendolyn Bays as *The Life and Liberation of Padmasambhava,* 2 vols. Emeryville, Calif., 1978. Though the French translation of O rgyan gling pa's epic sometimes goes astray, Toussaint had a richer poetic sense than any Western translator of Tibetan before or since.

Wangdu, Pasang, and Hildegard Diemberger. *dBa' bzhed: The Royal Narrative concerning the Bringing of the Buddha's Doctrine to Tibet.* Vienna, 2000. An early and important account of the adoption of Buddhism under Khri Srong lde btsan.

MATTHEW T. KAPSTEIN (2005)

PAGANISM, ANGLO-SAXON.

The "Anglo-Saxon" history of England stretches from the fifth to the eleventh centuries. Even before then, however, in 98 CE, Tacitus cites the "Angli" as one of seven tribes on the north-eastern German seaboard who worshiped "Nerthus, i.e., Earth the Mother" (Robinson, 1935, p. 317), a Bronze Age goddess borne about in a wagon. A formal comparison here with *Njörðr,* the name of a Norse god, may indicate that Tacitus mistakenly identified Nerthus with the earth when his informant treated them as divine husband and wife (North, 1997, pp. 19–25). When the Angles, Saxons, and other Germanic invaders settled in Britain they stayed heathen until various moments in the seventh century. It is hard to know what their beliefs were before this time (Owen, 1981). There is a dearth of evidence, and our literary sources consist of scraps found here and there in place-names, royal genealogies, and passages derived from a number of mostly Latin works concerned with Christian history and doctrine (Page, 1995).

Our chief sources are Northumbrian. Bede (c. 675–735), in his *History of the English Church and People* (c. 732), records the Anglo-Saxon conversion and its aftermath from 597 to the 640s (Colgrave and Mynors, 1969). He relates three crucial moments of conversion: when King Æthelberht of Kent gave Augustine permission to preach in 597; when

King Rædwald of East Anglia put a Christian altar at the center of his temple in the 610s; and when King Edwin of Deira, though he held off for eight years, had himself and his people baptized by Paulinus in 627. In this episode Bede refers to a man named Coifi, "first among the high priests" of Deira, who burned down the enclosure at Goodmanham after riding there unlawfully on a stallion and casting a spear at the idols inside. The same period is covered without this tale, but with some interesting additions, in the anonymous *Life of Pope Gregory the Great*, which was written in Whitby probably around 713 (Colgrave, 1968). Bede, in two works on *computus*, the calculation of the liturgical year, also claims that his heathen ancestors held a festival in honor of a "goddess" named Eostre at about the time of the Passion (Wallis, 1999, p. 54). Although the Modern English word *Easter*, a term for a time of year, comes from *eostre*, there is no other reason to personify the name in this way, and it looks as if Bede deified *eostre* on analogy with Februus, an invented Roman god whom he knew to be associated with the month of February (Wallis, 1999, p. 48). An older contemporary of Bede was Bishop Aldhelm of Sherborne (640s?–709), one of whose letters hints at the existence of priapic cults in Wessex in the early seventh century (Lapidge and Herren, 1979, p. 479). Still further south, according to *Life of Saint Wilfrid*, which was written between 710 and 720, there is an account of a heathen sorcerer defeated perhaps in the 680s by Bishop Wilfrid on a beach in Sussex (Mayr-Harting, 1991, p. 24).

Other sources derive from place-names, epigraphy, and archaeology. The gods' names Woden, Tiw, Thunor, and perhaps once the feminine Freo survive in place-names only in the south and midlands (Meaney, 1995). There Woden's name is the most common, and it was also used in Anglian royal genealogies of the eighth century (Dumville, 1976). Pre-Christian inscriptions of the Anglo-Saxons were written in runes. Aside from coin-legends, about ninety runic inscriptions survive from England and the associated Frisian region in the fifth to seventh centuries (Page, 1999). Now and then new texts are found, but no runes have turned up that might throw light on Anglo-Saxon paganism, unless the gibberish of three inscriptions can be taken to represent magic rituals. The names for a couple of runes, however, Tiw and Ing, do appear to refer to heathen gods, although anything about them more than their names is a matter for interpretation (Page, 1999, pp. 76–77). Within the wider archaeology, it is often assumed that some of the first English churches were built over heathen sites of worship, which had themselves been converted from Romano-British shrines (Blair, 1995). In 601 Pope Gregory commanded that heathen shrines should be reconsecrated rather than torn down, so that converts might hasten more readily to their accustomed places (Colgrave and Mynors, 1969, p. 106). To start with, at least, Anglo-Saxon heathens probably had no priesthood, but Old English place-name elements such as *weoh* and *hearh* show that they had, respectively, wayside and public shrines (Meaney, 1995), even if it is hard to recognize these in excavated ground plans (Wilson, 1992, pp. 44–46). Grave finds, on the other hand, are easily identified, the most significant being Sutton Hoo, a ship burial, or cenotaph, discovered in 1939 and dated to about 625, and probably meant for Rædwald. This find includes a whetstone mounted with a stag emblem, both of which might be pagan (Wilson, 1992, pp. 168–169). Made known in 2004, the grave find of another newly Christian king in Prittlewell, Essex, possibly the East Saxon Sæberht (d. 619?), will become a further rich source of research. The evidence from fifth- and sixth-century cemeteries also gives a picture of an imagined heathen afterlife in which earthly goods such as treasures and garments, horses, weapons, and even foodstuffs could accompany the dead as if into another version of the living world (Wilson, 1992, pp. 97–123).

It is not easy to make sense of all this. Most attempts involve comparisons with the rich mythological poetry and prose of tenth- to thirteenth-century Iceland (e.g., Dronke, 1992; Harris, 1975). In one such case, it is argued that heathen kingship was "sacral" and based on a presumed *hieros gamos* between Woden and the earth (Chaney, 1970); in another, that the husband was rather Ingui or Ing, not only a counterpart of the Norse gods Baldr and (Ingunar- or Yngvi-) Freyr, but also a progenitor god with a wagon, of whom mention is made in *The Old English Rune Poem* (North, 1997). Some scholars try to examine Anglo-Saxon paganism without recourse to the cognate mythology of Óðinn, Þórr, Frigg, Baldr, Freyr, and Freyja (Wilson, 1992). Yet Norse paganism remains relevant in another way in that its first purveyors, the Vikings, settled the east of England in the late ninth century, the northwest in the tenth, and the southwest in the early eleventh. Their paganism was kin to the Anglo-Saxon variety, and it seems likely that until their own conversion moments they helped to turn English superstitions back into cults. Most of the later evidence must be seen in this light. It is unclear, for example, whether or not an invocation to "Erce, mother earth" in the eleventh-century *Charm for Unfruitful Land*, which presents her as a bride in the embrace of God, is an Anglo-Saxon relic entirely free of Norse influence. On the other hand, it can be argued that Balder, who replaces the unrelated Baldæg in a genealogy in Æthelweard's Latin version of the *Anglo-Saxon Chronicle* (c. 975), is witness to a Norse myth imported into England (North, 1997, pp. 124–131). Abbot Ælfric of Eynsham (c. 950–c. 1010), in his *De falsis diis* (On the false gods), draws attention to Óðon, Þór, and Fricg (Johnson, 1995), where one might expect the native English names. Archbishop Wulfstan of York (d. 1023) rewrote this homily and also drafted laws for the Danish king Cnut in which he rendered some anti-pagan prohibitions of the sixth-century Bishop Martin of Braga into his own powerful West Saxon prose. This usage, above all, shows that heathen abuses were still rife in England as late as the eleventh century.

See Also Archaeology and Religion.

BIBLIOGRAPHY

Blair, John. "Anglo-Saxon Pagan Shrines and Their Prototypes." *Anglo-Saxon Studies in Archaeology and History* 8 (1995): 1–28.

Chaney, William A. *The Cult of Kingship in Anglo-Saxon England: The Transition from Paganism to Christianity.* Manchester, U.K., 1970.

Colgrave, Bertram, ed. *Vita Sancti Gregorii Magni: the Earliest Life of Gregory the Great.* Lawrence, Kans., 1968.

Colgrave, Bertram, and Roger Mynors, eds. and trans. *Bede's Ecclesiastical History of the English People.* Oxford, 1969; reprint with corrections, 1991.

Dronke, Ursula. "Eddic Poetry as a Source for the History of Germanic Religion." In *Germanische Religionsgeschichte: Quellen und Quellenprobleme,* edited by Heinrich Beck, Detlev Ellmers, and Kurt Schier, pp. 656–684. Berlin and New York, 1992.

Dumville, David N. "The Anglian Collection of Royal Genealogies and Regnal Lists." *Anglo-Saxon England* 5 (1976): 23–50.

Harris, Joseph. "Cursing with the Thistle: *Skírnismál* 31 and Old English *Metrical Charms* 9, 16–17." *Neuphilologische Mitteilungen* 76 (1975): 26–53.

Hofstra, Tette, Luuk A. J. R. Houwen, and Alasdair A. MacDonald, eds. *Pagans and Christians: The Interplay Between Christian Latin and Traditional Germanic Cultures in Early Medieval Europe.* Groningen, Netherlands, 1995.

Lapidge, Michael, and Michael Herren, trans. *Aldhelm: The Prose Works.* Cambridge, U.K. and Totowa, N.J., 1979.

Mayr-Harting, Henry. *The Coming of Christianity to Anglo-Saxon England.* 3d ed. London, 1991.

Meaney, Audrey L. "Pagan English Sanctuaries, Place-Names, and Hundred Meeting-Places." *Anglo-Saxon Studies in Archaeology and History* 8 (1995): 29–42.

North, Richard. *Heathen Gods in Old English Literature.* Cambridge Studies in Anglo-Saxon England 22. Cambridge, U.K., 1997.

Owen, Gale R. *Rites and Religions of the Anglo-Saxons.* Newton Abbot, U.K., 1981.

Page, R. I. *An Introduction to English Runes,* 2d ed. Woodbridge, U.K., 1999.

Robinson, Rodney P., ed. *The Germania of Tacitus.* Middletown, Conn., 1935.

Wallis, Faith, trans., with introduction, notes, and commentary. *Bede: the Reckoning of Time.* Translated Texts for Historians 29. Liverpool, 1999.

Wilson, David N. *Anglo-Saxon Paganism.* London, 1992.

RICHARD NORTH (2005)

PAIN. Most religious traditions seek to minimize suffering and explain its causes. At the same time, many religions around the world promote painful behavior in specific ritual contexts and produce influential discourse that praises the value of pain or glorifies those who either endure pain or willfully hurt themselves. Although such positive evaluation of pain in religious contexts is diminishing, it is still widely normative. In 1984, Pope John Paul II stated that "Christianity is not a system into which we have to fit the awkward fact of pain. . . . In a sense, it creates, rather than solves the problem of pain."

DEFINITIONS OF PAIN. The International Association for the Study of Pain defines *pain* as "an unpleasant sensory and emotional experience associated with actual or potential tissue damage or described in terms of such damage." The vast majority of people know pain directly and vividly as a noxious feeling located somewhere in the body. Despite the fact that pain is notoriously difficult to express in a verbal way, most languages do provide tropes for speaking about the sensation. Over seventy words are used in the McGill Pain Questionnaire, which is administered to patients who complain of pain. These include physical, emotional, and evaluative terms, such as piercing, burning, drilling, punishing, nagging, and terrifying. Other languages are equally rich in *pain* terms. Biblical Hebrew (the books of *Job* and *Jeremiah*) describes pain as tearing its victim, penetrating like arrows, and crushing like a storm. Similarly, Sanskrit and other Asian languages use terms that refer to tools or weapons, such as lances, darts, spears, or fire, in order to communicate the nature of the hurt.

The vocabulary of pain strongly suggests that pain and suffering are inseparable. In fact, the word *pain* is often used as a synonym for *suffering:* C. S. Lewis's famous book, *The Problem of Pain* (1940) is about emotional suffering. However, it is important to make a conceptual distinction between *nociception* (the perception of "physical" pain) and suffering. A back injury may be accompanied by suffering, for instance, due to isolation and loss of productivity leading to depression or anxiety. Other pains, however, may be experienced more ambiguously or even as desirable and joyful. A runner may report pleasant or desirable pain, and some cancer patients describe the severe discomfort of chemotherapy as healing. Similarly, most forms of suffering—the loss of a child to illness, for instance, or the fear of death—are not accompanied by pain.

Another distinction must be made: pain is distinct from either violence or death. Religious literature and rituals around the world describe violent executions, sacrifices, and the slaughter of nonbelievers and heretics as meaningful theological phenomena. A substantial body of scholarship is devoted to interpreting or analyzing violence and the sacred: Rene Girard's *Violence and the Sacred* (1977) stands out in this respect. The phenomenon of pain occupies a distinct domain of religious discourse and practice. The swift beheading of a heretic does not communicate the same information on the role of the body, power, self, and eschatology as the gradually increased and slow torment of a martyr who is given the option of ending the torture by conversion. Moreover, the self-willed pain of pilgrims and ascetics is different from both. Similarly, violent displays accompanied by heroic insensitivity to pain—the Malaysian piercers during the Thaipusam festival, for instance—are only indirectly linked to the subject of pain. Here pain is regarded as a meaningful existential category, but only to be transcended and ignored. Ritual analgesia is not pain behavior, but it is based on a profound religious evaluation of pain.

DISTRIBUTION AND CONTEXTS. The use of pain, or the praise of it, in religious contexts has been extremely widespread and diverse. Virtually every known tradition describes pain in spiritual terms, praises its effects, or prescribes it to adherents. This can be seen anywhere from ancient Near East religions, the three Western monotheistic traditions, and Greek and mystery cults to the major South and East Asian traditions and the religions of the Americas, Africa, and Australia. Pain figures either as an important feature of ritual performances or as the subject of extremely diverse and elaborate discourse. The performative use of pain includes pilgrimages, initiations (including shamans, secret societies, rites of passage, and puberty rites), mourning and funerary rituals, judicial ordeals, rites of possession and exorcism, specialized mystical disciplines, monastic guidelines, and modern mind-altering practices such as body-piercing and tattooing.

The most commonly practiced rituals in which pain figures prominently are pilgrimages, initiations, and rites of mourning. Pilgrims are often encouraged to walk barefoot on rocky or hot terrain, crawl on hands and knees or prostrate on the hard ground, sleep under difficult conditions, expose themselves to the heat or cold of the elements, and avoid refreshment and nourishment. Such discomforts are practiced in such places as Sabarai Malai in South India, Mount Kailash in Nepal, Lourdes in France, Guadalupe in Mexico, Karbala in Iraq, Jerusalem in Israel, Mecca in Saudi Arabia, and numerous lesser known centers of pilgrimage. Pilgrimage discomforts and pain are not incidental to the goals of the pilgrims' journey, or merely contingent on being on the road. They are central to the goal of pilgrimage. In Sabarai Malai, for example, a pilgrim was recorded as saying: "At one moment everything is pain. But at the next moment everything is love (*anpu*). . .for the Lord" (Daniel, 1984, p. 269).

Initiatory rituals, especially rites of passage for boys and girls at puberty, have been extremely common and are still widely practiced—often in a painful manner. Methods of hurting, applied to both sexes, commonly center on the genitals, with various forms of incision, insertion of objects such as twigs, and scraping or stabbing. Other types of initiatory pain include scarification, piercing of various body parts (e.g., nose, ears, cheeks), knocking out of teeth, the practice of kneeling on hot coals, suspension from hooks, and whippings and beatings. Similar and additional tortures are used in initiations to religious and military societies, as well as academic and athletic fraternities; such tortures are also associated with shamanic practices in Asia and the Americas. For instance, the Sun Dance rituals of the Arapahos, Cheyennes, Crows, and other Native Americans are lengthy and elaborate series of painful rites culminating with the piercing and tearing of tissue in the chest. Although ritual participants articulate numerous reasons for participating in the Sun Dance, the pain discourse focuses on self-sacrifice for the sake of the community, love, and compassion (Jorgensen, 1972).

Mourning rituals in which self-mutilation is practiced range from the merely symbolic tearing of the button in contemporary Judaism (a remnant of painful biblical practices) to self-beatings and head slashing by Muslim followers of the murdered Imam Ḥusayn. Mourning rituals involving self-mutilation also extend through numerous tribal religions in which such practices as tearing out one's hair, slashing the thighs with a knife, cutting the body with various objects, or banging one's head against the ground are ritually enacted (Durkheim, 1965/1912).

PAIN DISCOURSE. The discursive contexts in which pain is described, prescribed, or praised include scriptural teachings, myths, and folk narratives; biographies and hagiographies of mystics, saints, or martyrs; religious poetry; sermons; and ethnographic evidence. Unlike ritual performance, pain discourse explicitly addresses the nature and function of self-inflicted or involuntary pain. The literary and oral sources invariably couch their discussions of pain in tropes or elaborate models. These included juridical, medical, military, athletic, magical, communal, and psychotropic ways of conceptualizing pain. The tropes reveal both implicitly and explicitly a dual evaluation of the effects of pain on the agent. Pain is either a destructive force—a punishment—that causes aversion, or it is a necessary evil or even blessing, like medicine. In either case, pain in religious literature is a meaningful aspect of human experience, which either strengthens something of value (e.g., identity with God, community), or destroys something of perhaps lesser value (e.g., ego, self). Despite the varying cultural contexts in which religious discourse takes place, pain models always reveal this dualistic evaluation.

The juridical model. Narratives and discourses about pain that describe it in terms taken from the world of jurisprudence are included in this model. The clearest is pain as punishment, an obvious feature considering the etymology of the word from the Greek *poena,* meaning "payment" or "penalty." But pain may also be described as a debt or as damages owed, and it may be related to laws of evidence when it is linked to methods of eliciting truth. This model accounts for a large percentage of the cases found in religious literature, and many pain patients still use it today.

Pain is often described as a punishment by some personal agency (e.g., God, Satan, demons) or by some impersonal mechanism, such as karma. The punishment may be perceived as just, as the confessional writings of sinners and penitents indicate, or it may be entirely unwarranted and tragic. Such is the case of Job, or the cry of Prometheus, who rightly calls Zeus a tyrant.

Juridical pain straddles the boundary between *lex tallionis* (the law of retaliation) and the law of debts in a variety of cultures, from Judaism and ancient Greece to Hindu versions of karma. The difference between pain as punishment and an exchange of debts involves the legal distinction between owing something to a private party and being accountable to society as a whole. The strongest Jewish instance of this distinction may be found in the Yom Kippur (Day of Atonement) liturgy with its notion of redemption as exchange (*pidyon*) or a debt. This mechanism, the restoration of a balance through the perhaps magical or sacrificial mediation of pain, is also seen in the South Asian *vrata*—the vow that utilizes self-sacrifice to bring about desired results.

Juridical pain evokes the laws of evidence: Pain serves as the instrument for obtaining the truth from reluctant witnesses or the accused. This principle operates not just in cases of ordeals or religious inquisitions, as one might expect, but also in cases of initiatory ordeal and asceticism. This pain is a test. In the New Testament the agony that Jesus suffered in Gethsemane is characterized as a test, a type of ordeal or trial that reveals a hidden truth: "Because he himself was tested by what he suffered, he is able to help those who are being tested" (*Heb.* 2:12). Buddhist and Hindu texts (e.g., *Warrior Zen: The Diamond-hard Wisdom of Suzuki Shosan,* the *Bhagavadgītā,* and Patañjali's *Yoga Sūtra*) urge the practitioner to treat pain and pleasure alike in order to unmask the truth about the self.

Pain as medicine. Even though modern medical authorities characterize pain as an aversive sensation, religious sources often describe it as medical, and in so doing, evaluate it as a beneficial experience. A dramatic example comes from Prudentius, a fourth-century Christian poet who attributes to the martyr Saint Romanus the following words: "You will shudder at the handiwork of the executioners, but are doctors' hands gentler, when Hippocrates' cruel butchery is going on? The living flesh is cut and fresh-drawn blood stains lancers when festering matter is being scraped away." The claim, made forcefully by Saint Basil (d. 379) and others, is not that pain is pleasant, but that it benefits the soul. One need not seek it like a martyr, but if afflicted naturally, the pain ought to be taken as a spiritual sign—not just a reason for running to the doctor.

Medicine is both preventive and curative. It either cures diseases that have already been contracted (sin), or prevents ills to follow (punishment). In either case a familiar feature of classical medicine—and attendant aspects of this way of conceptualizing pain—is that the remedy is as bitter as the disease. In its Christian version this model may owe a great deal to the classic dictum that "medicine is the philosophy of the body, and philosophy is the medicine of the soul." This ideology can also be seen in Islamic metaphors for religious pain. The Ṣūfī poet Rūmī (1207–1273 CE) referred to "love" (of God) as pain without cure. *The Sea of Precious Virtues* (twelfth century) warns the man who seeks worldly gain that just as he is willing to suffer with a physician for physical health, so he must heed the health of the soul to avoid hell. And Shāhʿ Abdul Laṭīf, an eighteenth-century Indian Ṣūfī, wrote that the true lover of God does not seek out the medicine of the physician. The South Asian Muslim mystic Mirzā Asaduʾllāh Ghālib exclaimed: "When pain transgresses the limits, it becomes medicine."

Additional models of pain. Pain can also be conceptualized as a weapon used to destroy self-love in a spiritual battle. This is evident in the writings of such Christian theologians as Augustine of Hippo (354–430), as well as John Calvin (1509–1564), who conceived of the spiritual life as a battle against "the old man." Simon the Stylite (d. 459) battled his own body, and Macarius (d. 390) wrestled against the "fiends" that occupied his body. Muslim ascetics such as Abū Bakr Wāsiṭī claimed to be practicing jihad or holy war against the individual soul that deluded itself into thinking that it was divine.

The athletic model of pain is evident in the word *asceticism,* which Plato and Aristotle took to mean "training." The attitude revealed in the athletic model toward the body is softer than the military. *Hebrews* 12 describes pain as God's training for his faithful, and both Tertullian (third century) and Prudentius (fourth century) identified martyrdom with an athletic contest against false religion. Still, the strong aversion toward the flesh or individual ego is relatively mute here.

Pain can also be conceived as an alchemical purifier that transforms ordinary humans into saved souls. It acts like the fire that melts impure gold, in the words of Gregory of Nyssa (fourth century), or in Rūmī's words: "I am the fire!" Magical metaphors extend beyond alchemy or the blacksmith's trade to agricultural tropes, or in the case of the *tapas* (heat) of Hindu mysticism, the metaphor extends to a tool that bestows supernatural powers. Similarly, the idea that pain can miraculously transform consciousness and identity in an implicit passage is indicated by the charter of the Midwives Alliance of North America: "Labor. . .is a rite of passage, a psychospiritual training ground for both mother and child."

Central to the Christian conception of pain is the model of vicarious or communal suffering. *Colossians* 1:24 states: "Now I rejoice in my suffering for your sake." Indeed the painful death of Christ is a vicarious force that extends in effect to the entire community. Such too is the ritual destruction of the scapegoat in numerous cultures; in the *Zohar*'s addition to the Yom Kippur liturgy, for example, the death of the righteous atones for the sins of others.

In contemporary Western discourse on self-hurting, describing for instance the performances of "modern primitives," brain processes are often invoked to explain the heightened states of consciousness achieved. Although excitement and euphoria are often reported as a result of the secretion of beta-endorphins, the language of transcendence—unity of spirit and body, for instance—prevails: "It's an ecstasy state where no matter what happens in the body, no matter how much more intense the physical sensations become, I feel no more. Sensations just 'are'" (Mufasar, 1995, p. 5).

Meaning and Function of Pain. The methods of causing oneself or others pain in religious contexts, and the manner of articulating the nature of pain have been extremely diverse. Pain, itself a biological and psychological phenomenon, has been so deeply embedded in cultural expression that it has proven elusive and difficult to theorize. Few theorists have even attempted to focus on pain perception apart from its theoretical and ritual contexts. Four distinct approaches for understanding religious pain may be identified: cultural-symbolic, psychoanalytical, sociobiological-ethological, and psychodynamic. To simplify this range, one may say that religious pain has been reduced either to cultural interpretation or to biological analysis.

Mircea Eliade is preeminent among those theorists who refuse to "reduce" ritual performance or religious discourse to universal transcultural principles other than the sacred itself. Consequently, he argues that the pain inflicted on novices, for instance among Native Americans, is symbolic of specific cultural interpretations of the sacred, and the ritual hurt aims at "the spiritual transformation of the victim." The torture may represent a symbolic death and rebirth; the genital incisions symbolically de-sexualize the youngster to create an androgynous being for the state that precedes the new birth. In either case, the important religious phenomenon is not the sensation of pain itself but the symbolic value of its ritualized application.

Biological reductions, or ethological theories based on biology, address the question of aggression and dominance, access to females, or in some sophisticated versions, imposing ritual constraints on biological drives. For example, in *On Aggression* (1963) Konrad Lorenz regards the violent torture of initiates as an expression of such biological principles as the natural aggression of adults toward young sexual competitors. The highly respected theories of René Girard and Walther Burkhert ultimately resolve into such universal—"human nature"—principles. Freudian psychoanalytical theory explains the self-hurting of religious individuals, or the tortures of initiates, in broadly reductive terms. The former may represent masochistic pathology, or the ego's response to the anxiety of a profound sense of guilt. Sigmund Freud's *Civilization and Its Discontents* (1930) discusses how the torture of youngsters may be due to aggressive and erotic drives as they manifest in competition over sexual resources, or it may serve to curtail such potentially destructive drives.

While none of these approaches focuses exclusively on the perception of pain as a distinct area of interest, Elaine Scarry in *The Body in Pain* (1985) isolates pain as a unique phenomenon—an overwhelming "objectless," and therefore mute, experience that destroys the victim's ability to communicate and ultimately shatters his or her entire world, including even the self. Scarry's theory, which is based on the observation of torture victims, has had a significant influence on religious scholarship. Historians of religions, especially scholars of mysticism, including Maureen Flynn and Maureen A. Tilley, now believe that mortification of the flesh is designed to "unmake the world" and eradicate language and identity through the mute power of pain.

The most recent and extended analysis of pain in religious contexts is Ariel Glucklich's *Sacred Pain: Hurting the Body for the Sake of the Soul* (2001). This book argues, based on neuropsychological and cybernetic theories, that self-inflicted pain makes the agent transparent and thereby strengthens values, which are held in high regard. The voluntary mortifications and discomforts of such mystical practitioners as Maria Maddalena de' Pazzi and Henry Suso dissolve personal identity while fortifying a new telos or valued goal, such as God or community. Unwanted or natural pain (e.g., illness, accidents) can be transformed into "sacred" pain through the psychological mechanisms of self-sacrifice, or by subsuming one's personal identity within a broader and more highly valued center. The neuropsychological work of Ronald Melzack and Patrick D. Wall on phantom-limb pain offers a specific and sophisticated explanation of what may be taking place when the organism is over-stimulated with pain or irritation. A shutting down or diminution of output from the central nervous system results in phenomenal experiences, which diminishes the sense of self and reinforces the religious psychology that values other sources of identity: God, Christ, community, and others. Pain here is understood in terms of its phenomenal effects, not as a pathology or a political weapon.

See Also Healing and Medicine; Mortification; Ordeal; Suffering.

Bibliography

Bakan, David. *Disease, Pain, and Sacrifice: Toward a Psychology of Suffering.* Chicago, 1968. A psychoanalytical and phenomenological study of the two-fold effect of pain on the self: integrative and disintegrative (telic-centralizing and decentralizing).

Chittick, William C., trans. *The Sufi Path of Love: The Spiritual Teachings of Rumi.* Albany, N.Y., 1983.

Daniel, E. Valentine. *Fluid Signs: Being a Person the Tamil Way.* Berkeley, 1984. A sophisticated combination of ethnography, ethno-psychology, and traditional Indian philosophy as tools for understanding South Indian ritual.

Durkheim, Émile. *The Elementary Forms of the Religious Life* (1912). Translated by Joseph Ward Swain. New York, 1965. The foundational text for the sociology of religion, contains a large number of examples of ritualized pain, including in mourning and rites of expiation or penance.

Eliade, Mircea. *Rites and Symbols of Initiation: The Mysteries of Birth and Rebirth.* Translated by Willard R. Trask. New York, 1965. A comprehensive collection and symbolic interpretation of initiatory ordeals from around the world.

Flynn, Maureen. "The Spiritual Uses of Pain in Spanish Mysticism." *Journal of the American Academy of Religion* 64, no. 2 (1999): 257–278.

Freud, Sigmund. *Civilization and Its Discontents* (1930). Translated by James Strachey. New York, 1962. One of several cultural studies based on the psychology of biological drives. Useful primarily for the insight on the cultural curtailment of drives through ritual.

Girard, René. *Violence and the Sacred.* Translated by Patrick Gregory. Baltimore, Md., 1977. An extended and influential study of the religious and social psychology of the sacrifice.

Glucklich, Ariel. *Sacred Pain: Hurting the Body for the Sake of the Soul.* New York, 2001. A neuropsychological and psychodynamic study of the effect of self-hurting on states of consciousness sought by religious practitioners.

Jorgensen, Joseph G. *The Sun Dance Religion: Power for the Powerless.* Chicago, 1972. A comprehensive overview of several rituals and a number of ideologies and theories that explain them.

Lorenz, Konrad. *On Aggression.* New York, 1963. One of the early texts of ethology, the precursor to sociobiology.

Melzack, Ronald. "Pain: Past, Present, and Future." *Canadian Journal of Experimental Psychology* 47 (1993): 615–629. A relatively accessible explanation of the new theory of neuromatrix and neurosignature and its effect on the understanding and treatment of pain.

Melzack, Ronald, and Patrick D. Wall. *The Challenge of Pain.* New York, 1983.

Morris, David B. *The Culture of Pain.* Berkeley, 1991. A detailed literary and cultural study of pain, including one chapter on pain in religious contexts.

Mufasar, Fakir. "Editorial: Changes of Body-State." *Body Play: And Modern Primitives* 1, no. 3 (1995): 4–5.

Rey, Roselyne. *The History of Pain.* Translated by Louise Elliott Wallace, J. A. Cadden, and S. W. Cadden. Cambridge, Mass., 1993. A comprehensive study of pain in Western medical history and the interaction between medical theory and culture.

Scarry, Elaine. *The Body in Pain: The Making and Unmaking of the World.* New York, 1985. A literary and philosophical study of the destructive effect of extreme pain on consciousness and identity, and the creative potential embedded in this destruction.

Tilley, Maureen A. "The Ascetic Body and the Unmaking of the World of the Martyr." *Journal of the American Academy of Religion* 59, no. 3 (1990): 467–479.

ARIEL GLUCKLICH (2005)

PALEOLITHIC RELIGION. The term *Paleolithic* was coined more than a hundred years ago to distinguish the simple stone tools discovered in deep gravel pits or caves of the diluvial (or antediluvian) period from the polished stone tools of a later age, the Neolithic. Two incongruous criteria—geologic or climatological data and cultural or technological data—were used to distinguish the periods. Later the use of pottery became characteristic of the Neolithic age, and agriculture was seen as its chief distinguishing mark. Nowadays the term *Paleolithic* is understood in its strict sense, as the cultural equivalent of the geologic and climatological period known as the Ice Age (today usually called the Pleistocene), in which polished stones, pottery, and agriculture were still unknown. When it became clear that with few exceptions the characteristic traits of the Neolithic age appeared only some time after the end of the Pleistocene, phenomena dating from the postglacial (Holocene) period but prior to the Neolithic came to be known as Epipaleolithic or, rather unfortunately, as Mesolithic.

To be sure, the radical geologic and climatological changes that took place at this time of transition, more than ten thousand years ago, certainly affected the conditions of life and culture, but a truly epochal cultural transformation that indicates the beginning of the Upper Paleolithic period had occurred already about 35,000 years ago, that is, much earlier than the environmental change. In Europe, parts of Siberia, and southwestern Asia, and perhaps in some parts of Africa, the cultural transition is marked by the emergence of tools made of thin and slender stone blades and, in some areas, by the appearance of representational art. A more meaningful classification of periods would therefore merge the Lower and Middle Paleolithic into one period and distinguish it from the combined Upper Paleolithic and the Mesolithic. (Some scholars have proposed that terms *Protolithic* and *Miolithic* should be used, but the suggestion has not won acceptance.) Outside the context of Europe, and especially with reference to America, the term *Paleolithic* is, practically speaking, not used at all.

Although the end of the Paleolithic is usually identified by the beginning of the postglacial period (c. 8000 BCE), there were no highly significant distinctions between the two periods. As far as is known today, the Paleolithic was mainly a time during which food was acquired solely by hunting (including fishing) and gathering. But such methods of subsistence were used throughout broad areas of the world during the postglacial period, too, and continue to be used in a few restricted areas today. With certain reservations, then, it is possible to show continuity between the Paleolithic period and present-day "primitive" societies that follow a similar way of life.

In theory, the Paleolithic age begins with the first appearance of human beings. In practice, both occurrences are equally difficult to pinpoint. The beginning of the Stone Age—and therefore of all prehistory—is characterized by the appearance of artificial stone tools that could be used not only for immediate tasks but also to make additional tools (Henri Bergson's "tools for making tools"). The oldest tools discovered so far are from East Africa and are between two and two and one-half million years old. Whether East Africa is therefore the real cradle of civilization or whether accidents of preservation and of research and discovery only make this seem to be the case must for the present remain an open question.

In the course of time human beings appeared in other areas of Africa and, between one and one and one-half million years ago, in parts of southern and western Europe. Finds in southeastern and eastern Asia are probably as old or even older. As early as 300,000 years ago humans appeared in numerous other parts of Europe and Asia. Even in Australia there is evidence of human presence more than twenty thousand years ago, and it is likely that by that time human beings had already entered broad areas of America, although their presence becomes certain only about 10,000 BCE. Thereafter even the more northerly regions of Europe became increasingly populated.

Many developments and transformations occurred during this long stretch of time; very different cultures took shape in the various regions. It is questionable, therefore, whether *Paleolithic religion* is a meaningful concept at all. Rather, the point of departure for this article ought to be the existence of a variety of religions in the Paleolithic period. The nature and scarcity of the evidence (for the most part only fragmentary material remains) and its random character prevent researchers from convincingly distinguishing and defining any specific traits of these religions. The expression *Paleolithic religion* can really mean nothing more than the totality of ascertainable or inferred religious phenomena of the Paleolithic period. In addition, the term *religion* itself must be defined very broadly and be allowed to include everything that suggests dealings with a realm above and beyond natural phenomena.

SOURCES AND THEIR INTERPRETATION. Current knowledge of the Paleolithic period depends mainly on a functional interpretation of material remains, that is, a reconstruction of their use and cultural context in the life of prehistoric human beings. Such an interpretation relies, in turn, on a comparison of the available evidence with objects, facts, and processes that are directly known or have been transmitted in written, pictorial, or oral form from a relatively recent past. Since the situation in the prehistoric, and especially the Paleolithic, period is to be compared with that of present-day "primitive" societies rather than that of more "developed" ones, close attention must be given to conditions and modes of behavior examined in the studies of so-called primitive peoples. These studies can help in the interpretation of archaeological finds, but not infrequently they also show that similar material objects allow divergent functional interpretations.

These remarks about interpretation apply to a high degree to religion because it is primarily a spiritual phenomenon in which the sacred or supernatural word plays an important role. It is clear that manifestations of religion cannot be determined from archaeological research because material remains are silent. Only indirectly and in special circumstances do archaeological finds yield a religious meaning. Thus the first question that students of prehistoric religion must ask is "Which objects and findings can be regarded as signs of religious intentions, experiences, and activities?" Although religion is primarily a spiritual phenomenon, it nonetheless uses a wide range of material accessories: artifacts and places that have a cultic and ceremonial significance, images and symbols, sacrificial and votive offerings. In many cases religion makes use of art; to a certain extent inferences about religious conceptions can also be drawn from burial customs.

The interpretation of such sources by analogy with present-day religious practices implies that a more or less complete correspondence or at least a great similarity is inferred from an observed partial correspondence. But not infrequently particular findings can be interpreted in different ways. For example, it is often not clear to which religious category a find belongs; sacrifices and burials, cannibalism and human sacrifices, and animal sacrifices and animal cults are not clearly distinguishable by archaeological criteria. It is not enough, therefore, to select a few religious phenomena from contemporary primitive societies and apply them to the archaeological material. Instead, it is necessary to conduct comprehensive comparative studies in order to obtain a sufficiently wide range of correlations and establish a basic correspondence of meanings. Admittedly such studies make it possible to register only general characteristics and not concrete particularities. Even then it is still possible in many cases to give divergent interpretations, and it therefore becomes necessary to choose the one that is most likely.

The first rule, therefore, that must be observed in the interpretation of prehistoric finds is to compare them only with such recent phenomena as occur in a basically similar or corresponding context. For example, it is not possible to simply select a religious phenomenon connected with food cultivation (for example, feminine figurines of the Magna Mater type from Mediterranean and Eastern civilizations) and use it to explain one or another find connected with the culture of Paleolithic hunters and gatherers.

The vast stretch of time separating the Paleolithic period and today, the numerous opportunities for a shift in the meaning of things, and the modern dissemination and variety of phenomena all call for critical judgment in the use of ethnographic and historical analogies. One should be especially cautious in comparing prehistoric phenomena with contemporary primitive religions. On the other hand, as is clear from not a few cases, the very long interval of time that has passed does not necessarily mean that radical changes have occurred; often enough, strong tendencies toward stability are also observable. The lapse of time must be judged in relation to fundamental conditions; progressive development is accompanied by an acceleration. The first really epochal change took place only about 35,000 years ago, at the beginning of the Upper Paleolithic period. Thirty-five thousand years seems a short and insignificant span of time when compared with the hundreds of thousands of years' existence of the earliest human beings. It is therefore not as unimaginable as it might first appear that fundamental elements from a very early time should be preserved to the present day under comparable conditions. Furthermore, in comparison with the modern multiplicity and variety of phenomena, the number of possibilities realizable under simple conditions is limited.

A spiritual phenomenon such as religion does not develop in complete independence and isolation but depends to some degree on functional interrelations and limitations, including those of an economic and ecological kind. Careful account must be taken of duration and the interaction of tendencies toward stability or change, the multiplicity of possibilities and the limitation placed on them by general conditions, independent development, and functional interdependence. The divergent value judgments made of these criteria are the main reason for the debates among scholars about the significance and persuasiveness of the inferences they draw from comparisons.

Survey and Assessment. Current understanding of Paleolithic religion is essentially based on objects whose form and attributes themselves indicate religious or magical use or whose manner of deposition (burial, for example) or other contextual peculiarities suggests such a use, as well as on works of art whose content or situation reflects religious or magical meaning. For most of the Paleolithic (spatially as well as temporally) there are no such objects or artworks. Traces of these increase in Europe and some neighboring regions in the last part of the Paleolithic period. Previously, and outside these areas, they are scarce. Only in the immediately preceding time—the Middle Paleolithic (back to about 100,000 years ago)—does one find oneself on somewhat reliable ground.

The Middle Paleolithic. This discussion begins with finds from the Middle Paleolithic and not with the oldest finds, for one can make some useful statements about this period, especially on the basis of burials. In this context are human beings known as the Neanderthals. Because of their external appearance, Neanderthals were initially regarded as incapable of religious ideas, unlike the more recent *Homo sapiens.* But the picture of these early human beings has since changed substantially.

Neanderthal skeletons often exhibit severe injuries, but for the most part researchers are not able to say with certainty whether they resulted from fights and battles. Some of the head injuries had healed; others were evidently fatal, and the hipbone of a man from a site on Mount Carmel (Israel) apparently has been pierced by some lancelike object. Not a few Neanderthals survived not only wounds but also numerous illnesses. This was apparent also from the skeleton of the original Neanderthal—the find that gave the Neanderthals their name—who despite numerous afflictions had reached the age of fifty or so, a very advanced age for his time. Evidence of illnesses is also observable in other finds, especially that of an elderly Neanderthal at Shanidar (Iraq) who was probably blind from childhood and whose right forearm had been amputated. He had survived a number of illnesses and injuries, something possible only if he enjoyed the protection and care of a community, although he was probably of little economic value to it. There is no way of knowing whether this man had other abilities and knowledge that might have made him a respected member of the group. In any case, this instance, as well as others, indicates that Neanderthals were by no means the crude savages they are sometimes made out to be but lived in a kind of community in which not only the law of the jungle and economic utility carried weight.

Burials also provide evidence of the same situation. The dead are typically found with their legs slightly flexed, usually in elongated pits; in some Near Eastern finds, however, the dead are in a tightly crouched position, as though they had been forced down into narrow holes. With some regularity they are laid on an east-west axis, usually with the head to the east and, in the majority of cases, the body lying on its right side. It is not always possible to say with certainty whether animal bones and tools found near the corpse were burial gifts.

Noteworthy, however, is the little cemetery at La Ferrassie (France) where three fine stone artifacts, suited for adults, were found in the grave of three children, including a newborn or stillborn infant. Tools of the same kind were also found with adults, and some sites have yielded pits containing animal bones and artifacts, as well as reddish fragments. For example, the head of an elderly man found at La Chapelle aux Saints (France) was covered with large plates made of bone; his body was surrounded by pieces of jasper and quartz and fragments of a red material.

There are other instances in which the dead—and especially their heads, which were often protected by stones—were partly surrounded by large bones. For example, the grave of an approximately eight-year-old boy at Teshik-Tash in the foothills of the Tian Shan (Kyrgyzstan) was surrounded by a circle of horns. The corpse of a man found in the cave of Shanidar was surrounded by blossoms of flowers that are almost all used as curatives in popular medicine today. (Although graves containing flowers may have been more numerous, only one example has been discovered, thanks to a fortunate combination of circumstances and to modern investigative techniques.)

In all these cases are found clear signs that Neanderthals took care of their fellow human beings. The burial gifts really leave no reasonable doubt that the dead were thought to continue to live in some manner. This belief explains why objects were buried along with the dead, to be used in the future; even children were provided with objects that they certainly could not have used during their lifetime. What particular shape these general ideas took one cannot say. It can at least asserted, however, that the Neanderthals had an understanding of death and had somehow come to grips with it.

In the cemetery at La Ferrassie, a skull of a child was found in a burial pit about a meter away from the skeleton. Isolated skulls were also found elsewhere. In a cave on Monte Circeo, about a hundred kilometers southeast of Rome (Italy), a Neanderthal skull was found on the surface of the cave floor, with the basal opening (which had evidently been widened artificially) facing upward; it was surrounded by a circle of stones, and nearby there were three heaps of auroch and deer bones. The basal openings of most of the numerous skulls found in isolation—some from an even earlier period—are believed to have been artificially enlarged, probably to facilitate removal of the brain. This practice was probably connected with the consciousness of death and may indicate a special relationship between the living and the dead; researchers are not in a position, however, to hypothesize about the particulars of these ideas and activities.

In the burial site at Regourdou near Montignac (France), the skull and some other bones of a brown bear were found under a large block of stone. There are also reports of finds, not associated with human burials, of individual skulls of bears, especially of the great cave bear, together with some long bones. Stone chests containing the vertebrae of the neck still attached to the skulls were reportedly found in a few caves in Switzerland, but these finds are poorly documented and uncertain. Nonetheless it would not be wise to completely doubt the validity of these finds, as many do.

The specific meaning of such finds is again unclear. Perhaps they represent simple sacrifices of the especially important parts of the prey; perhaps Neanderthal hunters, like those of a later period, buried the bones in order to ensure the survival of the animals and their species. Such a theory may explain why parts of the skull, backbone, and long bones of a bovine were placed under a great stone at the entrance of the above-mentioned cave at La Chapelle.

The Lower Paleolithic. All in all, researchers find clear indications that the people of the Middle Paleolithic were concerned with the phenomenon of death and with existence in another world. Some of their practices display no secular meaning but, like burial rites, show a commitment to certain binding customs.

Hominids from the Lower Paleolithic period, who date as far back as over a half million years ago, have skulls with primitive proportions and generally smaller brains than modern man. These characteristics led some researchers to doubt that these hominids were capable of achievements comparable with those of human beings from later periods. But objective findings show that the way of life of these hominids must on the whole have been the same as that of the Neanderthals. Occasionally researchers have found shelters from the Lower Paleolithic that are superior to those of the Middle Paleolithic, although they have assumed, probably with justification, that the lack of such dwellings in later times should be attributed to the unfavorable conditions of preservation.

The opposite argument has been used to explain the lack of some kinds of finds from the Lower Paleolithic, especially the absence of burials. In fact, however, even burials from the Middle Paleolithic are found only in restricted areas and in caves. Because Lower Paleolithic archaeological finds have rarely been unearthed in caves, it is not surprising that researchers should know of no burials in caves dating from that period. It is not known whether the hominids of the Lower Paleolithic may have buried their dead elsewhere; if they did, perhaps the evidence has simply vanished. The spiritual background and ideas that can be inferred from burials may well have existed even if they have not manifested themselves in burials.

Skulls from the Lower Paleolithic, like those from the Middle Paleolithic, are often found in isolation, as with Java men, for example. Some of these as well as some of the skulls found at the site of Peking man have a basal opening that seems to have been artificially widened. Far more skulls, and especially tops of skulls, were found than other parts of the skeleton, suggesting that the skulls were buried apart from the rest of the body. (The fact that in some strata the skulls were found in no particular order as well as mingled with animal bones has led some to hypothesize that cannibalism was practiced. If so, the cannibalism must have been carried out elsewhere and the skulls and a few other bones subsequently brought to the site. But the bones could have just as well been brought to the site without cannibalism entering the picture.) The only thing researchers can say is that the skulls probably received special treatment and were deposited apart. As no convincing secular explanation of the phenomenon has been offered, it should simply be assumed that there existed practices in which the skull played a special role that transcended the life of the individual in question.

There are no similar indications for the earliest Paleolithic, which began at least two million years ago, perhaps even earlier. Yet even sites from this time have yielded artificial stone tools that are at least as complex as those of Peking man, as well as smashed and, in various places, collected bones of animals. Some finds from this period also suggest the presence of huts or shelters from the wind. Were these finds from a later date, no one would doubt such an interpretation. But because the hominids of the earliest Paleolithic had a very small brain, some researchers think that the archaeological finds of the period are not to be interpreted as they would be if they belonged to later human beings. (Although biological factors and archaeological evidence points to the existence of communities made up of small groups of nuclear families, many scholars think they should not assume that such "human" characteristics existed during the earliest Paleolithic.) If other explanations of these early finds are sought (they are not very convincing), it is for two reasons: The finds are very old and doubtless simple, and the hominids of that period were physically "more primitive" than Peking man or the Neanderthals. Whether these are persuasive reasons may be left unanswered for the moment, but it will be important for a general assessment of these early hominids.

The Upper Paleolithic. The people of the Upper Paleolithic are equal to present-day humans in physical appearance, and they are therefore given the same name, *Homo sapiens.* People of this time were still living as hunters and gatherers. Only in the course of the later Upper Paleolithic are more definite signs of specialization, differentiation, and an accumulation of cultural possessions to be seen. As an example is mentioned only the pronounced presence of personal ornaments, which are also to be found in graves. This fact differentiates the people of the Upper Paleolithic from those of the Middle Paleolithic, but it does not necessarily indicate any substantial distinction between them. Only rarely do individual dead persons seem to have been given more special attention than others.

Of special interest is the grave of a powerfully built man found at Brno (Czechoslovakia) and dating from the beginning of the Upper Paleolithic. A great deal of red material was used for the burial; near the skull were over six hundred cut, tubelike fossil mollusks (*Dentalium badense*). A find of particular importance at this site, however, is the only certainly masculine figurine thus far known from the Upper Paleolithic; it is distinguished by other characteristics as well. In addition, the grave contained two stone rings of a kind previously known from only a very few examples; perhaps all of them were connected with graves. Furthermore, the grave at Brno is the only one in which a large number of round disks made of stone, bone, and ivory have been found. Thus there are a number of objects that are rarely found elsewhere or at least rarely or never appear in graves (the anthropomorphic figurine, for example). It is hard not to think that the interred man was involved in some capacity with cultic or magical things.

The most important sources of information about religion during the Upper Paleolithic are works of art. Although the well-known paintings and drawings on the walls and roofs of caves are expressive, they do not display a great wealth of motifs. They primarily depict animals and only rarely, and then most often crudely, represent human beings. In many instances, moreover, the humans are not presented simply as humans but with animal attributes or as hybrid human-animal forms. Only a small number of the animals are depicted as prey, as indicated by the projectiles being thrown at them. Many anthropomorphic figures with animal attributes are regarded as masked dancers or sorcerers, but a good number are better described as composite figures. In any case, masking cannot be seen in images of animals that combine the attributes of various animals without any anthropomorphic element. There are even strange pictures for which no models could have been found in the fauna of the time. In many cases certain species predominate, but for the most part they are not the ones also found in the correlative strata of cultural relics.

A good deal of emphasis has been put on the fact that two species of animals or two groups of species frequently predominate in the pictures of a cave, but this dualism is by no means as clearly marked as is sometimes claimed. (At least there is no convincing evidence of a contrast between male and female.) At least as important is the fact that the pictures are generally unrelated to one another and that one will often cover and ruin another so that it has been possible to speak exaggeratedly of pictures being "consumed." By and large, it is the animal or, more rarely, an anthropomorphic being that is the focus of the artist's interest. The pictures are often drawn in parts of the caves that are dark and far from the entrances and, less frequently, in more accessible places. In some cases the old entrance has been blocked by a kind of stone wall. Often it is possible to view the pictures only with difficulty. Everything militates against the view that this is *l'art pour l'art,* "art for art's sake."

The pictures represent, above all, the essential character of the animal, sometimes in relation to the hunt, sometimes in relation to human beings or to anthropomorphic figures, especially when the latter show a mergence of human and animal forms. Animals clearly played an extremely important part in the mental world of these hunters, insofar as this world is reflected in their art. One may probably assume that to a certain extent the artworks mirror the real role of animals; they probably point even more clearly, however, to the special evaluation of animals and of certain species in particular. Paintings in which humans and animal forms and attributes are depicted together and in which the forms and attributes of various animal species are portrayed show the close connection between the animal world and other spheres of life.

It is probable that researchers are dealing, at least in principle, with a manifestation similar to one that still characterizes the mental world of numerous more developed hunting cultures. Central to this "animalism" are close relations between animals and humans and a heightened importance of the animal world even outside and above the natural realms. The animalist outlook is fleshed out and developed in ways that often differ widely in their details. Thus one often finds the notion of the animal as tutelary spirit and *alter ego,* the idea that human and animal forms are easily and often interchanged, and the idea of a higher being who is thought to have an animal shape or to be capable of changing and combining shapes and who is regarded as a kind of lord of animals, hunters, and the hunting grounds, as well as of the spirits of game and of the bush. Such zoomorphic higher beings are often group progenitors and culture heroes and appear also as mediators and as hypostases and personifications of a supreme god. In short, animalism is a widely found and dominant manifestation and yet, by its very nature, it should be seen as a lower or marginal sphere of religion, one that is frequently interspersed with other motifs and attitudes, including those of a magical type.

Because paintings and objects can be put in the service of both religion and magic, it is difficult and often impossible to distinguish between these two purposes. There is, however, no reason to regard rock paintings solely as instruments of magic. (This assumption arose when the study of Paleolithic art was in its infancy. The paintings were then regarded primarily as evidence of totemism; totemism, in turn, was seen as a manifestation of the magical mentality.) Researchers have no way of knowing which of the many possible uses was actually intended for Paleolithic painting.

A number of paintings of bears show peculiarities of one kind or another and occur in an unusual context. They may well have played a part in bear ceremonialism. Here the slain or to-be-slain bear is at the center of various rituals in which it is treated as a guest to whom respect is due or as an ancestor or mythical forefather. The climax of a festive meal is often the consumption of the bear's brain; the skull and long bones or even the entire skeleton are buried. Perhaps the bones and skulls of bears found at Paleolithic sites are to be interpreted along similar lines. Contemporary hunting peoples frequently bury parts of their prey to ensure a resuscitation of the animal and the preservation of its species. The deeper meaning of this ritual, however, is that it probably mystically returns the bear to the lord of the animals.

Bones of other animals are also occasionally found in circumstances indicating an intentional deposition that cannot be explained in secular terms. At some sites parts of reindeer have been discovered: head, neck, and the front part of the trunk, including the forelegs. A small scratch-drawing found at one site might depict a similar ceremony using a bovine. A deposition containing these parts of the skeleton was also found at the earlier-mentioned cave of La Chapelle. Once again, there is no way of determining whether there was a real sacrifice.

The significance of a painting of a birdlike man in the cave of Lascaux (France) has been much debated. The correct interpretation is probably that the picture depicts a man in a trance. His birdlike head and the bird shown on a pole may represent a shaman and a helping spirit. Anthropomorphic figures with the heads of birds may be interpreted similarly. The figurines of birds that have been found at sites in eastern Europe and Siberia and that were apparently nailed or hung remind observers of parts of a shaman's clothing. Other pictures may likewise depict shamans—for example, the drawing of the so-called Sorcerer of Les Trois Frères—but here as in most cases other interpretations are also possible.

Whether small scratch-drawings from the early Upper Paleolithic can be interpreted as pubic triangles or vulvas is uncertain. Only later do the so-called Venus figures make their appearance. These are distinguished for the most part by their ample bodies and large breasts, which perhaps indicate pregnancy in some cases; there is no special emphasis on the primary sexual characteristics. Most of the figures do not have feet, and their arms, which are always very thin, often display decorative bracelets. Frequently, too, care has been taken to represent the style of hair or a head covering, whereas the face is not developed at all. The emphasis is clearly on the areas of the body connected with pregnancy, birth, and nursing. It is reasonable therefore to assume that these little figures are associated with the idea of fertility, but this need not be their only significance. The fact that the figures always appear in dwellings or camps may indicate that they were protectors of dwellings. Even today there is frequently found, among peoples of the Northern Hemisphere, the idea of a higher feminine being who is, among other things, a mother or mistress of the animals, a divinity of the underworld (to which a shaman travels on his journey), a helper in the hunt and a provider of prey, a mistress of the land, of other regions, and of the powers of nature. But here again researchers cannot tie themselves down to details and specific traits. In the figures and scratch-drawings of a later period it is usually possible to conclude only indirectly that women are intended. Sexual characteristics often no longer play any part in these figures, but there is a great deal of emphasis on the buttocks. Whether these figures have the same meaning as the Venus figures is an open question. But perhaps the feminine need not always be expressed in such an extreme way.

Many other questions about religion during the Paleolithic remain mysterious and unexplained. Current knowledge covers only a small part of what once existed. It is clear enough, however, that one must rule out any attempt to impose a single general explanation on everything. Nonetheless, it also seems clear that animals and shapes with animal attributes, on the one hand, and a female principle, on the other, often played a part in the mental and spiritual world of the Paleolithic and fit in with the peculiar character of a world of gatherers and specialized hunters.

Theories about Paleolithic Religion. Finds from the Upper Paleolithic period, though relatively rich and potentially informative when compared with those of previous periods, surely reflect only a small part of the religious phenomena of the time. It is not even known whether the finds lead to the heart of the religion in question or simply represent marginal and secondary manifestations of it. Observations and conclusions about the Middle Paleolithic are much scantier; they are especially important, however, because here one leaves the world of human beings who are "modern" in their physical appearance and yet still finds clues pointing to ideas of a world beyond this one and to precise customs connected with such concepts. If one goes still farther back in time, the archaeological picture becomes more obscure. On the one hand, the conditions needed for the preservation and discovery of relics and traces of religious activities are much less favorable; on the other hand, one finds no break in the continuity of material remains that can be compared with the break between the Middle and the Upper Paleolithic in Europe. Any claim of division that separates later periods from an era in which religious ideas and activities were impossible is arbitrary. In this matter researchers are simply groping in the dark.

It may be asked whether early human beings possessed a religion, or it may even be asserted that a being, regardless of his appearance, who does not possess some form of religion cannot be regarded as truly human. (Humanity could also be determined by the development of language and other indicators.) The question becomes more pragmatic if one does not make religion the sole criterion for humanity but seek to discover whether there are other material manifestations pointing to a psyche, of a kind that allows researchers to infer some degree of what is specifically human and justifies their speaking of human beings in the true meaning of the word. In any event, the statement that early human beings did or did not possess a religion is an eminently anthropological one. But behind it, as behind all anthropological statements, lie fundamental anthropological assumptions.

The position researchers take on the question of early religion depends not least on their picture of early human beings. Some interpreters regard the earliest stone artifacts as evidence of low intelligence and a primitive mentality; nothing else, they claim, could be expected given the small brain of the hominids of that time. Others, however, will point out that stone artifacts indicate a mediated relation to nature, such as is characteristic of human beings, and reveal that these early hominids had human insight into the nature of things. This second group of researchers is therefore inclined to regard even the early hominids as fully human in principle, although they had not yet fully evolved in every respect and would undergo further developments. In any case, the earliest archaeological finds are such that they fit without difficulty into the picture of a group of hunters and gatherers of the *Homo sapiens* type. (The main argument to the contrary, whether or not it is expressed, is that early hominid toolmakers differed physically from modern man; in particular their brain was smaller and had different proportions from the brain of *Homo sapiens.* No one, however, is in a position to say what size and form a brain must have to develop religious ideas.)

These divergent points of view then become the basis on which other matters and questions are discussed and interpreted. For example, some researchers (who, in the final analysis, belong to the evolutionist tradition of the nineteenth century) think they must deny that early humans had permanent nuclear families, the basic form of human society. Scholars differ even more on whether beliefs in psychic phenomena and other forms of religion existed among early human beings.

In this type of discussion it is all too easy to forget that in dealing with other aspects of the early period, much is postulated that is not directly documented by finds. (For example, some scholars believe that at least half a million years ago human beings crossed parts of the Mediterranean where there was no land bridge and must therefore have had some kind of craft, although no remains of these have been found.) It is necessary in particular to avoid taking the simplicity of stone tools as the measure of everything else. For example, in the site at Huaca Prieta (Peru), equally primitive stone tools coexist later than 3000 BCE with cultivated plants and textiles. If one were to adopt that criterion, the presence of very simple stone tools in "more developed" cultures from later periods would almost certainly lead to erroneous judgments.

Two basic judgments on the nature of early human beings are thus possible; neither of them can be strictly demonstrated nor strictly refuted. So, too, are there two basic attitudes that can be adopted toward the question of early religion. One current view is that early human beings possessed no religion initially and only at a late date gradually moved beyond "low" conceptions of the supernatural and ascended to the level of "authentic" religion. Others, on the contrary, believe that the possession of some form of religion is a universal human trait. According to this position, if early hominids show human traits in the areas accessible through archaeological finds, they probably practiced some form of religion. No theory on the nature and development of the religion of early human beings can be based directly on these finds; all are hypotheses developed on the basis of later phenomena. The question in every case is whether the archaeological evidence from the Paleolithic can provide—and does provide—material grounds for these theories.

The nature and reciprocal relationship of religion and magic have played an important part in these discussions. Because the Upper Paleolithic was at one time widely regarded as a period in which belief in magic predominated, it was thought—and still is in many quarters—that researchers had a fixed point to which they could refer. To the extent that magic was considered to be an early form or a forerunner of authentic religion, the development of genuine religious forms could only have begun at a later time.

Another view, however, holds that belief in a personal god who creates and preserves the world and its order is the earliest and original form of religion; magic, according to this position, is a secondary form of religion and a product of decadence. To the extent that this view recognizes the special importance of magic in the Upper Paleolithic, it also sees authentic religion as having begun at a correspondingly earlier date. It is extremely unlikely, however, that magic occupied such a great role that it can be considered a stage in the development of religion, whether it is seen as a precursor to religion or as a degenerative form. However religion (in the strict sense) and magic are conceived and defined in detail, the two should be viewed as different types of attitudes toward the supernatural. Although these two attitudes are opposed, they are not always strictly distinguishable, with one capable of acquiring greater importance when the other regresses. When circumstances allow, both magic and religion use the same "artifacts," so that it is often impossible to distinguish between them at the archaeological level.

Even if one accepts that early human beings had a religion, a further question must be posed: Are there forms of religion that they could not have possibly had? It must be acknowledged that there is usually a close association between certain special manifestations of religion and the general conditions in which people live; the model on which society is actually based plays a part in determining it conceptions of the supernatural. Among simple hunters and gatherers who live in small and essentially egalitarian groups, there will hardly be a place for a proper hierarchy of divinities such as is found in hierarchically ordered civilizations.

These differences are in fact only differences of expression. This author does not see, however, why any of the fundamental religious categories cannot be ascribed to early humanity when one is trying to assess him as *homo religiosus.* In this area the criterion of early humanity's simplicity is sometimes invoked—but then one may ask: Is not the concrete and the personal more congenial to a simple mentality than abstractions of any kind? And if so, will not simple societies of hunters and gatherers, who are trying to achieve a basic understanding of things and processes for which they see no real explanation but on which they nonetheless depend, tend to think of personal supernatural beings (divinities) instead of more abstract powers and forces?

BIBLIOGRAPHY

General surveys of prehistory, including religion, can be found in my *Urgeschichte der Kultur* (Stuttgart, 1961) and in my *Handbuch der Urgeschichte,* vol. 1, *Ältere und mittlere Steinzeit: Jäger- und Sammlerkulturen* (Bern, 1966).

For early surveys of prehistory that assert the agnosticism of early humans, see John Lubbock's *Pre-Historic Times, as Illustrated by Ancient Remains, and the Manners and Customs of Modern Savages* (London, 1865) and Gabriel de Mortillet's *Le préhistorique: Antiquité de l'homme,* 2d ed. (Paris, 1885). Contrasting views regarding the religious thought of early man can be found in Thomas Lucien Mainage's *Les religions de la préhistoire: L'âge paléolithique* (Paris, 1921); Johannes Maringer's *De Godsdienst der Praehistorie* (Roermond en Masseik, 1952), translated by Mary Ilford as *The Gods of Prehistoric Man* (New York, 1960); and my "Approaches to the Religion of Early Paleolithic Man," *History of Religions* 4 (Summer 1964): 1–22. Mainage's book is still the essential work in this area, Maringer's discussion follows the view of the Vienna school, and my essay attempts a general evaluation.

The meaning and content of Paleolithic art are discussed in the following works.

Leroi-Gourhan, André. *Art et religion au paléolithique supérieur.* 2d ed. Paris, 1963.

Leroi-Gourhan, André. *Préhistoire de l'art occidental.* Paris, 1965. Translated by Norbert Guterman as *The Art of Prehistoric Man in Western Europe* (London, 1968). A dualistic interpretation in the sexual sense.

Narr, Karl J. "Bärenzeremoniell und Schamanismus in der Älteren Steinzeit Europas." *Saeculum* 10 (1959): 233–272.

Narr, Karl J. "Weibliche Symbol-Plastik der älteren Steinzeit." *Antaios* 2 (July 1960): 132–157.

Narr, Karl J. "Sentido del arte Paleolitico." *Orbis Catholicus: Revista Iberamericana Internacional* 4 (1961): 197–210.

Narr, Karl J. "Felsbild und Weltbild: Zu Magie und Schamanismus im jungpaläolithischen Jägertum." In *Sehnsucht nach dem Ursprung,* edited by Hans P. Duerr, pp. 118–136. Frankfurt, 1983.

Reinach, Salomon. "L'art et la magie: À propos des peintures et des gravures de l'âge du renne." *L'anthropologie* 14 (1903): 257–266. Starting from totemistic interpretation and asserting magic meaning.

Ucko, Peter J., and Andrée Rosenfeld. *Palaeolithic Cave Art.* New York, 1967. A critical review, neglecting animalism.

New Sources

Burkert, Walter. "The Problem of Ritual Killing." In *Violent Origins,* pp. 149–176. Stanford, Calif., 1987.

Dickson, D. Bruce. *The Dawn of Belief: Religion in the Upper Paleolithic of Southwestern Europe.* Tucson, 1990.

Leroi-Gourhan, André. *Les Religions de la préhistoire: paléolithique.* Paris, 1986.

Talalay, Lauren E., and Richard Handler. "The Present in the Past: Archaeological Objectivity and Interpetation of Stone Age Figurines." *American Journal of Archaeology* 90 (April 1986): 185.

Young, Dudley. *Origins of the Sacred: The Ecstasies of Love and War.* New York, 1991.

KARL J. NARR (1987)
Translated from German by Matthew J. O'Connell
Revised Bibliography

PALI TEXT SOCIETY. In 1881 British scholar Thomas William Rhys Davids (1843–1922) founded the Pali Text Society (PTS) to facilitate the study of Theravāda Buddhism by producing editions in roman characters of the Theravāda texts written in the language called *Pali,* and translations of as many as possible of them into English. Pali literature includes the Pali canon, a collection of texts the Theravāda Buddhists claim preserves the "words of the Buddha," and the commentaries on those canonical texts, as well as the subcommentaries on the commentaries, independent works of history and poetry, and works about ritual practice and monastic discipline.

Rhys Davids had learned Pali from Theravāda Buddhist monks during his years in the Ceylon Civil Service (1866–1872). In Ceylon (now Sri Lanka) he came to regard Theravāda as the oldest form of Buddhism, and its Pali literature as the repository of the most authentic Buddhist teachings. Upon his return to England, Rhys Davids continued his study of Buddhism and contributed to some of the earliest efforts by European scholars to edit, translate, and interpret Pali texts. He founded the PTS to complete this task. By doing so, he sought to deepen international understanding of Buddhism, and thereby to advance the study of the history of religion, language, and human culture. From the outset, the work of the PTS interested scholars in Europe, America, and Asia. It also appealed to the members of the growing middle class in Britain whose recent access to higher education, increased income, and leisure time enabled them to explore foreign religions as alternatives to what they saw as the empty materialism of modern science and the mindless dogmatism of the dominant religions of their own culture.

Rhys Davids succeeded in enlisting European and Asian scholars to edit and translate Pali texts. Although these scholars donated their services and subsidized the work by purchasing subscriptions to the Society, Rhys Davids needed more funds to cover the costs of printing the projected tens of thousands of pages. He obtained early support from the king of Siam (now Thailand), who funded the first volume, from private friends whose subscriptions supported the second, and from "poor men and scholars" (including Buddhist monks in Ceylon) who each paid a guinea (£1.05) a year to receive one copy of each of the PTS publications. Rhys Davids frequently urged "anyone intelligent enough" to see the significance of the Society's work to donate funds.

At first the PTS undertook the apparently finite task of completing the publication of roman-character editions of the canonical Pali texts, and translating into English as many of those texts as possible. The scope of the Society's work soon expanded to include editing the Pali commentaries. In 1896, Rhys Davids reported that in just twelve years the PTS had accomplished about half its work, having published thirty-four volumes. By the time of Rhys Davids's death in 1922, the PTS had issued sixty-four texts in ninety-four volumes, and had begun to publish a new Pali-English dictionary. Two years later, his wife and the second president of the PTS, Caroline Rhys Davids, reported that the original task of the PTS was completed—unless the Society undertook the translation of more texts into English or the editing of the Pali subcommentaries. The PTS carried on with this expanded mission, under the leadership of Caroline Rhys Davids and, after her death, of W. H. D. Rouse (president 1942–1950), then W. Stede (president 1950–1958), and I. B. Horner (hon. secretary 1942–1959, president 1959–1981).

In 1954, Horner reported that the PTS founder's dream of making the Pali literature available in the West was "all but realised," with the publication of 123 volumes of Pali texts and commentaries, plus the shorter texts and commentaries included in the Society's journal, forty-eight volumes of translations, and the publication (1921–1925) of the PTS *Pali-English Dictionary.* She noted that the Society had also begun to produce a concordance of the Pali canonical literature, a project originally envisioned by Caroline Rhys Davids. According to Horner, the "only" remaining tasks were to complete the last few editions of the Pali commentaries, to produce editions of one or two subcommentaries, as well as editions of a few "other and later works," and to translate more texts. Horner also considered it advisable, given the advances in the study of Pali in the first half of the twentieth century, to begin to re-edit and retranslate some of the earlier volumes, as well as to reprint texts and translations to keep available as many volumes as possible.

From the 1950s on—first under Horner and then during the successive tenures of PTS presidents K. R. Norman (1981–1994), Richard Gombrich (1994–2002), L. S. Cousins (2002–2003), and Rupert Gethin (beginning in 2003)—the work of the PTS has proven to be ever-expanding, while remaining remarkably true to Rhys Davids's original vision. The PTS now publishes new and revised editions and reprints of Pali texts in roman characters, English translations of these texts, dictionaries (including the multi-volume *Dictionary of Pali* by Margaret Cone), a concordance, grammars and other books for students of Pali language, and a journal. The Society has also collaborated with the Dhammakaya Foundation of Thailand to publish the entire PTS edition of the Pali canon on CD-ROM. In addition the PTS offers grants to scholars for research expected to foster future publications of Pali texts.

The foundational work of the PTS, like the initial development of Buddhist Studies as a separate field of academic research, took place in the context of western Europe's colonial domination of large portions of Buddhist Asia. Western scholars, as well as western-educated Asian scholars, who studied Buddhist traditions during that period tended to reflect colonial attitudes in the methods and aims of their work. In the widely accepted interpretive framework of their time, the beliefs and practices of living Asian Buddhists were seen as degenerate manifestations of a pure philosophy taught long ago by the Buddha, which had been developed legitimately into its full "classical" form, and subsequently corrupted by many centuries of unenlightened folk practices. Scholars who sought to recover the authentic Buddhist teaching focused on gaining access to and interpreting the written texts, which they saw as the most promising sources of Buddhism's "classical" formulations of the Buddha's wisdom. Quickly shipping whatever such texts they found in Asia off to the libraries of Europe for safe-keeping and careful study, they edited, translated, analyzed, and interpreted them to determine the shape and content of the real Buddhism—one that existed over and above the particular cultural contexts in which it appears.

Not surprisingly, for many decades the publications of the PTS reflected this narrowly intellectualized, exclusive understanding of Asia's Buddhist traditions. More recently, as Europe has moved beyond colonialism, scholars of Buddhism have developed more nuanced and inclusive ways of discussing their subject matter. Although the work of the PTS, by necessity, remains focused on texts, its publications continue to incorporate the latest developments in philology and to reflect the changing assumptions and methodological approaches of Buddhist Studies. By producing substantially revised editions and translations of previously published texts and expanding the range of new texts it publishes, the PTS continues to foster and promote the study of Pali literature in service of greater understanding of the history of religion, language, and human culture.

See Also Buddhism; Horner, I. B.

Bibliography

Carpenter, J. Estlin. "The Passing of the Founder." *Journal of the Pali Text Society* 7, no. 4 (1920–1923; reprint, London, 1978): 1–21.

Hallisey, Charles. "Roads Taken and Not Taken in the Study of Theravāda Buddhism." In *Curators of the Buddha: The Study of Buddhism Under Colonialism,* edited by Donald S. Lopez, pp. 31–61. Chicago and London, 1995.

Horner, I. B. "The Pali Text Society." *The Middle Way* 29, no. 3 (1954): 122–123.

Horner, I. B. "Early Days of Western Pali Studies." *The Middle Way* 39, no. 3 (1964): 109–112.

Lopez, Donald S. "Introduction." In his *Curators of the Buddha: The Study of Buddhism under Colonialism,* pp. 1–29. Chicago and London, 1995.

Norman, K. R. "The Pali Text Society: 1881–1981." In *Collected Papers.* Vol. 2, no. 47, pp. 194–199. Oxford, 1991.

Norman, K. R. "The Pali Text Society: 1981–86." In *Collected Papers.* Vol. 3, no. 62, pp. 108–114. Oxford, 1991.

Norman, K. R. "The Pali Text Society: Its Contribution to Buddhist Literature." *Jagajjyoti: Sanghanayak Dharmapal Mahathera Felicitation Volume,* pp. 89–94. Calcutta, 2000.

Pali Text Society homepage: www.palitext.demon.co.uk.

Rhys Davids, T. W. *Lectures on the Origin and Growth of Religion as Illustrated by Some Points in the History of Indian Buddhism* (The Hibbert Lectures, 1881). 2d ed. London, 1891.

Rhys Davids, T. W. *Buddhism: Its History and Literature* (American Lectures on the History of Religions, First Series, 1894–1895). New York and London, 1896.

Wickremeratne, L. Ananda. *The Genesis of an Orientalist: Thomas William Rhys Davids and Buddhism in Sri Lanka.* New Delhi, 1985.

GRACE G. BURFORD (2005)

PAN is a Greek god whose name, of Indo-European derivation, means "shepherd" (cf. Latin *pastor*). In appearance, he has the hooves, tail, hair, and head of a goat and the erect posture, upper body, and hands of a man. He is frequently depicted holding either a *lagobolon,* a kind of shepherd's crook used for hunting rabbits and controlling small flocks, or a syrinx, a flutelike instrument otherwise known as a panpipe.

Pan has his origins in ancient Arcadia, a remote and mountainous area of central Peloponnesus where an Archaic dialect is still spoken. Lord of Arcadia and guardian of its sanctuaries (according to Pindar), the goat-god is very much at home in this primitive region, with its essentially pastoral economy, where the political system of Classical Greece was slow in being established. The enclosure dedicated to Pan on Mount Lycaeus (Aelianus, *De natura animalium* 11.6) functions as a sanctuary where animals pursued by the wolf seek protection. Pan thus appears as a master of animals, protecting wild and domestic creatures, while watching over the human activities of hunting and animal breeding. His actions, whether they brought sterility or fertility, were of interest primarily to shepherds and hunters, who were concerned with reproduction in the animal world.

Theocritus in his *Idylls* (7.103–114) alludes to a rite performed by the Arcadians for Pan during periods when the animals were not reproducing: young men whipped his statue in order to call the inactive god back to life. The Arcadians pictured Pan as reigning over his own flocks in the mountainous lands that constituted his domain and his sanctuaries. Thus the whole of Mount Lampeia, where the Erymanthe has its source, is a sanctuary of Pan. So is the Menale, where people believed they could hear, in the mysterious and fearful sounds of the wilderness (echoes in particular), the music of this wild shepherd.

In Arcadia Pan was considered a major god. He had a cult on Mount Lycaeus, alongside that of Zeus. There is, however, no known figurative representation of the god antedating the diffusion on his cult outside Arcadia, nor does there exist any literary testimony, with the exception of some dedications that retain only the name of the god. Not until the beginning of the fifth century BCE, and after the introduction of his cult in Athens, does the image of Pan take shape. Although the god now loses some of his theological importance, as he assumes a marginal position in regard to Olympus and joins the host of minor gods, he nevertheless gains in symbolic richness, and his rites are no longer confined to the pastoral world. His cult, his mythology, and his iconography spread rapidly throughout the Greek world and were adapted to the local character of Attica, Boeotia, and especially the regions of Delphi and Macedonia.

In an account by Herodotus (6.105ff.), Pan became an official deity at Athens following his appearance in Arcadia to the messenger Philippides, whom the Athenians had sent to Sparta shortly before the Battle of Marathon (490 BCE). Pan asked Philippides why the Athenians did not dedicate a cult to him, since he had already been so benevolent toward them and would be again. Remembering this epiphany after the battle, the Athenians consecrated to Pan a small grotto on the northwest slope of the Acropolis.

The rapid spread of Pan's cult, from this time on, brought with it certain readjustments. A thorough reworking of symbolism gave this god, who was unknown to Homer and Hesiod, a complex but coherent form. In the poetry of the fifth century, numerous allusions are made to Pan. There are allusions to his natural habitat, Arcadia, which becomes a metaphor for the pastoral in contrast to the urban, the wild in contrast to the cultivated. The coexistence of the divine and the animal in Pan explains the ambiguity of a being whose power oscillates unceasingly between fear and seduction, disorder and harmony. Represented as shepherd, hunter, musician, and dancer, as an untiring and often unlucky pursuer of nymphs, Pan also appeared as the agent of "panic" fear (that collective, animal-like disorder that seizes military camps at rest, especially at night) and of a form of individual possession (panolepsy). Finally, some accounts describe the birth of Pan, whose monstrous appearance causes the gods to rejoice but sends his human nurse fleeing (Homeric *Hymn to Pan* 19). Other stories describe his unfruitful love affairs with Echo, Syrinx, or Pithys (in Alexandrine and post-Alexandrine poetry).

The philosophical destiny of the god, especially among the Stoics, is remarkable. By virtue of a Platonic play on words—the identification of Pan with *pan,* "all," in Plato's *Cratylus* (408c–d)—the goat-god becomes the personification of the All, the cosmic totality represented by the coexistence, in a single figure, of the animal (the material nature below) and the human (the spiritual nature above). Outside the Hellenic world his destiny is multiple: in Egypt he is assimilated to the god Min of the region of Coptos, lord of the routes of the eastern desert. At Rome he becomes the Greek version of Faunus, or of Inuus, because of the influence of the legend about the Arcadian origins of the town.

Plutarch provides the account of the death of Pan, announced by a mysterious voice to the pilot of a ship on its way from Greece to Italy under the reign of Tiberius. Pan's death upset the emperor so much that he called a committee of philologists to find out who this god was. The third-century bishop Eusebius of Caesarea believed that the death of the great Pan meant the death of all the demons of paganism, which occurred after the passion of Christ under Tiberius. Subsequently the account has been of interest to folklorists analyzing popular legends concerning "messages of death," legends that spread through northern Europe beginning with the sixteenth century, that is, at the same time that the ancient figure of Pan reappeared in literature (especially in Rabelais, in chapter 27 of his *Quart livre*).

BIBLIOGRAPHY

Cults, Myths, and Literary Destiny

Borgeaud, Philippe. "La mort du grand Pan: Problèmes d'interpretation." *Revue de l'histoire des religions* 200 (1983): 5–39.

Borgeaud, Philippe. *The Cult of Pan in Ancient Greece.* Chicago, 1988.

Merivale, Patricia. *Pan the Goat-God: His Myth in Modern Times.* Cambridge, Mass., 1969.

Iconography and Archaeology

Bernand, André. *Pan du désert.* Leiden, 1977.

Boardmann, John. "Pan." In *Lexikon iconographicum mythologiae classicae* VIII (1997): 923–941.

Cabanes, Pierre. "Le culte de Pan à Bouthrotos." Revue des études anciennes 90 (1988): 385–388.

Herbig, Reinhard. *Pan der griechische Bocksgott: Versuch einer Monographie.* Frankfurt, 1949.

Jost, Madeleine. *Sanctuaires et cultes d'Arcadie.* Paris, 1985.

Pouzadoux, Claude. "La dualité du dieu bouc: les épiphanies de Pan à la chasse et à la guerre dans la céramique apulienne." *Anthropozoologica* 33–34 (2001): 11–21.

Walter, Hans. *Pans Wiederkehr: Der Gott der griechischen Wildniss.* Munich, 1980.

PHILLIPE BORGEAUD (1987 AND 2005)
Translated from French by Mary Lou Masey

PANATHENAIA. One of the great pan-Hellenic festivals of the city of Athens and its tutelary deity, Athena, the Panathenaia can be seen as a commemorative celebration of the city's foundation. The great festival was performed every four years from 570 BCE onward, though there were yearly "small" Panathenaias as well. The date was the twenty-eighth day of the month Hekatombaion (mid-July to mid-August). The ceremonial elements are the same for both forms of the cyclical feast, consisting of the following acts: first, the bringing of new fire to the temple of Athena Polias, protector of peasants and craftsmen; second, a procession (*pompe*) with a new garment (*peplos*), carried on a shiplike float, to clothe the seated olivewood statue of Athena (the *xoanon*); third, large sacrifices (of more than one hundred animals for small festivals) of sheep and cattle to be distributed among and eaten by the assembly; and fourth, an ancient form of racing (*agon*).

During the first day, fire was kindled after sunset on the Akademos (the district outside the sacred Dipylon, or double gate), accompanied by sacrifices to Athena and Eros amid songs and dances by the youths. The fire was then carried by torch race through the Agora to the altar of Athena, where the cotton wick was lit. The mythic legitimation of this act, which was understood as the mystical significance of the rites, refers to the birth of the founding king of the city, Erichthonios: When Athena was pursued in love by Hephaistos, she preserved her virginity by having his seed spilled on her thigh, then wiping it with a cotton ball that she threw on the earth. From this seed sprang Erichthonios, a creature half human, half snake.

On the second and main day, a large procession started from the Dipylon, where the road from Eleusis entered Athens; the procession consisted of old men with olive branches, young girls with sacrificial vessels and sacred baskets, and the sacrificial animals. The focus of the procession was the large *peplos,* woven during the previous nine months by the women of Athens under the guidance of the virginal attendants of the temple of Athena (the Arrephoroi). Weaving had started at the Chalkeia festival for Athena Ergane ("Athena, patroness of crafts and craftiness"). The *peplos* was draped around the wooden statue, which had been ritually washed at an earlier celebration (the festival Plynteria in the month Thargelion, mid-April to mid-May).

While the Panathenaia can be fully appreciated only in relation to all other festivals of the agricultural year, its importance is to mark the ancient founding of the city and the start of a fertile year: It is a New Year festival. The great chariot race, during which fully clad warriors had to jump from their wagons and race on, recalls its originator, Erichthonios. Many more references are made to Athena as founder, protector, and virgin deity with strong chthonic features: Central to the meaning are the multiple snake symbols. Both Erichthonios and the earlier autochthonous king Kekrops are depicted on vases as snakes winding around olive trees. Kekrops had three daughters, to whom Athena handed a closed basket in which she had secreted the snake-child Erichthonios. All three girls' names refer to fertility, containing the word for "dew," which also connotes "semen." One daughter, Pandrosos, also received sacrifices during the Panathenaia. The gist of the festival seems to be the symbolic association between fertility and autochthony, which accords well with the structural logic of the myths surrounding Athena: The goddess who was born without mother gives birth to progeny without her virginal status being violated.

SEE ALSO Athena.

BIBLIOGRAPHY

Burkert, Walter. *Griechische Religion der archaischen und klassischen Epoche.* Stuttgart, 1977. Emphasizes strongly the central rite of dressing the statue of the goddess. Coherently integrates this festival into a rhythm of festivals of the city of Athens, in particular the constellation between goddess and primeval king.

Kerényi, Károly. *Athene, die Jungfrau und Mutter der griechischen Religion.* Zurich, 1952. Translated as *Athene, Virgin and Mother* (Irving, Tex., 1978). A thorough but often disorganized attempt to show the consistency of the myths around the many forms of Athena; often comes close to later structural analysis. Some daring philological derivations that nevertheless seem to capture the underlying logic of mythic narratives.

New Sources

Brulé, Pierre. "Fêtes grecques: périodicité et initiations: Hyakinthies et Panathénées." In *L'initiation: actes du colloque international de Montpellier, 11–14 avril 1991,* vol. 1. *Les rites d'adolescence et les mystères,* pp. 19–38. Montpellier, 1992.

Brulé, Pierre. "La cité en ses composantes." *Kernos* 9 (1996): 37–63.

Neils, Jenifer. *Worshipping Athena: Panathenaia and Parthenon.* Madison, Wis., 1996.

Piblis, Spyros. *Panathenaea: The Greatest Festival of Ancient Athens.* Athens, 1970.

Robertson, Noel. "The Origin of the Panathenaea." *Rheinisches Museum f. Philologie* 128 (1985): 231–295.

Sfyroeras, Pavlos. "Fireless Sacrifices." *American Journal of Philology* 114 (1993): 1–26.

KLAUS-PETER KÖPPING (1987)
Revised Bibliography

PAÑCATANTRA. The *Pañcatantra* is a collection of animal stories, in Sanskrit, compiled by an unknown author some time prior to the sixth (possibly as early as the fourth) century CE. Many of the stories were doubtless drawn from the great mass of Indian oral tradition, and part at least are of Buddhist origin, as may be seen from their close affinities to the Jātakas, or stories of the prior births of the Buddha. The *Pañcatantra* belongs in part to a class of works known as *nītiśāstra* ("science of right conduct") and partly also to the closely allied *arthaśāstra* ("science of polity"), which involves the practical and shrewd knowledge needed by an Indian king to rule his kingdom and conduct its internal and extermal affairs efficiently. Because of their practical and worldly purpose, the *Pañcatantra* fables are often amoral in tone, in contrast to the fables of the Greek storyteller Aesop, the connection with which, though much discussed, seems most unlikely on a number of grounds.

The stories of the *Pañcatantra* are set in a frame story in which a learned brahman named Viṣṇuśarman undertakes to impart political and social propriety to the ignorant and dissolute sons of King Amaraśakti of Mahilaropya. The Pañcatantra consists of five (*pañca*) books (*tantra*) of varying length. Its characters are, for the most part, animals, birds, and fish whose behavior is like that of human beings. So contrived as to lead from one to the other in a continuous series, the stories are emboxed in one another, each being introduced by a character in the foregoing story who recites a verse of general wisdom or one about a situation similar to the matter at hand. This leads to a request by one of the other characters for an explanation, which then follows in the form of an illustrative story.

Typical of the fables of the *Pañcatantra* is that of the two geese and their friend the tortoise. Because there is a scarcity of water in the lake where the three have been living happily, the geese are about to leave for another lake. The tortoise begs them to take him along. They agree to transport him if he grasps with his mouth a stick they will hold in their beaks, and warn him not to say anything if he hears people below expressing wonder at the sight. In spite of his promise, the tortoise opens his mouth to reply to the comments of the people on the ground and falls to his death. The moral of this tale is that he who fails to heed the exhortation of his friends and well-wishers comes to grief.

Because of its widespread popularity the *Pañcatantra* has been endlessly recopied and recast over the centuries, leading to many recensions. Its fables were also variously abbreviated or condensed for incorporation into other works, as for example the *Kathasāritsāgara* of Somadeva and the *Bṛhatkathāmañjarī* of Kṣemendra, both of the eleventh century. One of the most famous abridgments is that contained in the *Hitopadeśa* (Instruction in What Is Salutary), whose author states that he drew his work "from the *Pañcatantra* and another book." Many of the fables are common parlance among Indians of all classes today, who are often unaware of a particular story's connection with the Sanskrit *Pañcatantra,* because one version or another will have been translated into almost every vernacular of India. The original *Pañcatantra* has, of course, long since perished, superseded by these countless variations and metamorphoses, whose mutual interrelations are often difficult, if not impossible, to establish with certitude.

At an early time fame of the *Pañcatantra* began to extend far beyond the borders of India, and scarcely a land can be named to which a translation of all or part of it has not come, whether centuries ago or in recent times. The oldest translation outside India is that into Pahlavi (c. 550) made, according to the traditional account, by a physician named Burzūye, who had been sent from Persia by the Sasanid king Khusrū Anūshīrvān for the purpose of translating the *Pañcatantra* and other works of Indian wisdom. Although this translation, like the original *Pañcatantra,* has long since disappeared, two translations from it have survived. By far the more important of the two is that made into Arabic around 750 by ʿAbd Allāh ibn al-Muqaffaʿ; its title, *Kitāb Kalīlah wa-Dimnah* (The Book of Kalilah and Dimnah), contains the arabicized names of the two jackals called Karataka and

Damanaka in the *Pañcatantra.* The *Kalīlah wa-Dimnah* quickly became diffused everywhere in the Arab world from Spain to India through translations into its principal languages. Of all these translations the Hebrew by Rabbi Jōʿēl has an especially significant place in the westward migration of the fables, as it was from this Hebrew version that they were finally brought into Latin and so made accessible to Europeans. The Latin translation, by a converted Jew named John of Capua, entitled *Liber Kelile et Dimne, Directorium Vite Humane,* about two centuries later became one of the earliest books printed in Europe, for its first edition appeared in 1480, barely three decades after the invention of movable types by Gutenberg. An Italian translation of the Latin *Directorium* by Antonio Francesco Doni, *La moral Filosophia del Doni,* in turn was rendered into English in 1570 as *The Morall Philosophie of Doni* by Sir Thomas North. Thus did the *Pañcatantra* fables come into English more than a thousand years after their composition, in a version standing in the seventh degree from the original.

See Also Śāstra Literature.

Bibliography

Complete and selective translations of the *Pañcatantra* have been made by Arthur W. Ryder under the titles *The Panchatantra, Translated from the Sanskrit* and *Gold's Gloom: Tales from the Panchatantra* (both Chicago, 1925). An attempt was made by Franklin Edgerton in *The Panchatantra Reconstructed,* 2 vols. (New Haven, Conn., 1924), to restore the lost original *Pañcatantra* by a painstaking comparison of the oldest surviving derivatives. The first volume contains a detailed discussion of his method and the interrelationships of the various derivatives in addition to an English translation of the reconstructed *Pañcatantra;* the second volume has the reconstructed Sanskrit text and critical apparatus. The English translation has been separately published as *The Panchatantra, Translated from the Sanskrit* by Franklin Edgerton (London, 1965). In *Quellen des Pañcatantra* (Wiesbaden, 1978), Harry Falk compares the *Pañcatantra* fables with parallel versions in the Buddhist Jātakas and the *Mahābhārata.* This work is much influenced by Ruprecht Geib's *Zur Frage nach der Urfassung des Pañcatantra* (Wiesbaden, 1969).

A translation that is antiquated in a number of respects yet remains of great intrinsic value to the student of the *Pañcatantra* and its diffusion is Theodor Benfey's *Pantschatantra: Fünf Bücher indischer Fabeln, Märchen und Erzählungen, aus dem Sanskrit übersetzt mit Einleitung und Anmerkungen,* 2 vols. (1859; reprint, Hildesheim, 1966). A convenient and readable discussion of the fables and their progression from language to language outside India is contained in *Kalīlah and Dimnah, or the Fables of Bidpai: Being an Account of Their Literary History, with an English Translation of the Later Syriac Version of the Same, and Notes* by I. G. N. Keith-Falconer (Cambridge, 1885). Following the introduction there is a genealogical table of the principal translations that have descended from the Sanskrit original outside India. A much more detailed and accurate table, prepared by Franklin Edgerton, is to be found in *The Ocean of Story, Being C. H. Tauney's Translation of Somadeva's Kathā Sarit Sāgara,* edited by N. M. Penzer, vol. 5 (1926; reprint, Delhi, 1968), app. 2, pp. 232–242. Another general account of the migration of the fables, though much less detailed, is given by Joseph Jacobs in *The Earliest English Version of the Fables of Bidpai* (London, 1888), which reproduces Sir Thomas North's English translation, *The Morall Philosophie of Doni* (1570).

New Sources

Olivelle, Patrick, trans. *Pañcatantra: The Book of India's Folk Wisdom.* New York, 1997.

Sternback, L. *Hindu Legends of Justice: Panchantantra & Smrti.* Delhi, 2002.

Walter Harding Maurer (1987)
Revised Bibliography

PANTHEISM AND PANENTHEISM.

In Greek *pan* means "all," *theos* means "god," and *en* means "in." *Pantheism* means that all is God; *panentheism,* that all is in God. The two doctrines can be definitely distinguished. When considered together they may be called the pan-doctrines.

Although theism is often contrasted with pantheism and panentheism, the idea of all, or totality, is prominent in every form of theism as a doctrine of the high religions. Thus it occurs in the terms *all-knowing, all-powerful, creator of all,* and still others. Nevertheless, the most usual form of Western theology, sometimes called classical theism, holds or implies that the world of creatures is outside God. Yet it is also said by those in this tradition that in God is knowledge of all things. Can anything be outside knowledge-of-all-things? To many great minds this has seemed an unendurable paradox. To escape this apparent absurdity of a knowing that does not include the known and yet also to avoid including the world in the divine life, Aristotle denied knowledge of particular things to God, who, he held, was aware only of universal forms or ideas. Divine thought then knows only itself: it is pure thinking of thinking. Therewith Aristotle fell into other paradoxes, including that of exalting as divine a being ignorant of us and our world and hence, it seems, inferior to us. Yet classical theists accepted Aristotle's formula "unmoved mover" (meaning unchanged changer) as descriptive of God. This conception implies that there can be nothing changing in God. Was then Paul, who said, referring to God, "For in him we live and move, and have our being" (*Acts* 12:28), a pan-theologian?

When we human beings know things other than our own minds and bodies, the known things seem to be outside us. However, our knowledge of these outside things is extremely incomplete and uncertain. God must know everything at least as well and as certainly as we know our own pains and pleasures. Nothing can be so external to an all-knowing God as most things are to us. Accordingly, Plato, the first great philosophical theologian, believing in a divine Soul of the World (who knows us and whose body is the universe), made it clear that nothing was simply outside this deity: the universe as divine body is "in" the divine soul rather than the reverse. Plato was certainly a pan-theologian.

The essential difference between the two forms of pantheology is manifest in their answers to the question "Do the creatures have genuine freedom of decision making, or does God determine everything?" Classical pantheism was a form of theological determinism: God decides or determines everything, including our supposed decisions. Both the ancient Greek Stoics and Spinoza (1632–1677) held this view. Panentheists object that, if one power determines all, there is, causally speaking, only one agent in all action. The Stoic-Spinozistic doctrine is an extreme monism rather than a genuine pluralism. Or, at best, its pluralism is unclear or ambiguous, for reality is active agency or nothing. As Plato said, "being is power"; for him every soul is "self-moved." This agrees with panentheism, which admits a plurality of active agents within the reality of the supreme agent.

The medieval tradition, following Aristotle's wisdom in this, admitted that—at least in all cases apart from God—to know something is one thing; to determine or make it is quite another. If this applies to God, there is no absurdity in holding that God knows and in that sense includes all things but does not fully determine their actions. Panentheism avoids both extreme monism and extreme pluralism, and it does this, it claims, without obvious paradox. Indeed, it sees in extremes a chief source of philosophical paradox. Also, since God does not determine all, the problem of evil is less formidable for panentheism than for either classical theism or pantheism as usually formulated. For, as one can see in Augustine, Thomas Aquinas, and many others, classical theism was always tempted by—and, in the case of the early American theologian Jonathan Edwards, frankly adopted—theological determinism.

The possible ideas of God and the created world can be classified with a precision not customary in the past by using the "modal" concepts of necessity and contingency (see table 1). Classical theism contrasts the contingency of the world (meaning that it might not have existed as it actually does) with the necessary existence of God, who, it is held, could not have failed to exist. In table 1 it is assumed that both God and a world exist. Also assumed is that *God* is a religious term, in that it is appropriate to speak of worshiping, serving, and loving God with all one's mind, heart, soul, and strength.

Let *N* stand for necessity in God, *C* for contingency in God; let *n* and *c* stand for the same in creatures. Also let > mean that God includes the creatures and ≯ mean that God does not include the creatures. In views 4 and 6 the question mark instead of the inclusion symbol means that, so far as the table goes, it is indefinite what contingent things God, as a wholly contingent being, does or does not include.

View 1 has been long and widely held; view 9 has recently become important. View 1 consists of the view that God, who is wholly necessary, does not include the creatures, who are wholly contingent. View 9 refers to the belief that God (in different respects, otherwise there would be contradiction) is necessary and also contingent and that God includes the creatures, who, in different respects, are contingent and necessary.

Model Table of Views of God and the Creatures

I	II	III
(1) N≯c	(4) C?c	(7) NC>c
(2) N>n	(5) C>n	(8) NC>n
(3) N≯cn	(6)C?cn	(9) NC>cn

TABLE 1.

The reversal of the order of *NC* and *cn* (3, 6, 7, 8, 9) symbolizes the greater importance of necessity in God and of contingency in creatures. God, except according to views 4, 5, and 6, exists necessarily but may also (7, 8, 9) have some qualities that might have been otherwise. In contrast, a particular creature, according to six of the views (1, 3, 4, 6, 7, and 9), exists contingently. The *n* in *cn* (third row) is best taken to mean only that there must be some creatures or other. The *C* standing alone (column II) symbolizes that God might not have existed at all. The *c* alone (first row) means that there might have been no creatures at all, while *n* alone (second row) means that the creatures are entirely necessary.

The two definite noninclusions (1, 3) result from the law of modal logic according to which there can be nothing contingent in the wholly necessary. Three definite inclusions (2, 5, and 8) express the modal law that the necessary is in everything. The inclusions in views 7 and 9, although not required by modal logic, are permitted by it and, because of the paradox of putting the known outside the all-inclusive and infallible knowledge, are appropriate.

In column I are the three views that take God to be wholly necessary. Classical theism is expressed in view 1; classical pantheism in view 2. View 3 was held by Aristotle. The views that take God to be wholly contingent (column II) include what is usually meant by a "finite God," one entirely without any necessary, absolute, eternal, infinite, or self-sufficient aspect; this is the view held by Charles Renouvier, John Stuart Mill, William James, and others. (John Hick would be among these, except for his attempt to find a meaning for the divine preeminence that implies eternal existence and a necessary support for other existing things but is compatible with the possibility that God might not have existed.) Column III shows the modal possibilities for allowing in God a contrast between necessary and contingent qualities.

Classical pantheism, view 2, derives an advantage from the laws of modal logic, which do not allow a wholly necessary God to include the creatures if they are (even in part) contingent, but do require such a deity to include the creatures if they are wholly necessary. Thus classical pantheism has no problem on this score; but classical theism (in its usual *N, c* form) does, since it attributes omniscience to God. Precisely for this reason, Spinoza was scornful of classical theism. He was its first severe critic, although Aristotle would have preceded him had classical theism been known in his time.

The fact that the three views in column I were the chief forms of belief during the first two millennia after Plato may be explained in two ways. First, views 1 and 2 are the simplest of the nine views, except for 4 and 5, which reduce God to a mere accident of existence, a "fetish" according to Charles S. Peirce. Second, views 1 and 3 have an advantage over 2 and 4 in that they honor the principle of contrast (Wittgenstein), or polarity (Morris Cohen), which says that one pole of an ultimate contrast, such as necessary-contingent, has meaning only because the other does and that both must apply to reality if either does. Where all is necessary or all is contingent, both concepts lose their distinctive meanings. Hegel had a similar idea. Yet the paradox of an all-inclusive knowledge possessed by a non-all-inclusive being favors view 2, classical pantheism, as against view 1. Thus is explained the recurring opposition between first the Stoics, then Spinoza, and then the German theologian Schleiermacher on the one hand and the countless classical theists on the other. Although views 1 and 2 are perhaps the two simplest religious doctrines that can be made plausible, each has advantages and serious disadvantages when compared with the other. For several centuries, however, the determinism of early modern (Newtonian) science favored view 2.

The unpopularity of view 3 is readily accounted for. It lacks the simplicity of 1 and 2, and it either, with Aristotle and Gersonides (Levi ben Gershom, 1288–1344), denies concrete knowledge to God or shares, with view 1, the paradox of the wholly necessary God knowing something contingent—whether contingent in all or only some respects does not alter this difficulty. (Knowledge of a contingent aspect of something must itself have a contingent aspect. If proposition *p* is contingent, it could have been false, and then there would have been no such knowledge as knowledge-that-*p*.)

Aristotle, by clear implication, held view 3 but saw that he must pay the price of denying concrete worldly knowledge to God. The Scholastics and some of the Jewish and Islamic thinkers refused to pay this price yet insisted on the knowledge; but, as Spinoza saw, they failed to pay the equally obligatory logical price of *that* decision—either by admitting contingency in God as well as in the world (as the Italian Fausto Sozzini later did) or by affirming the sheer necessity of the world (as Spinoza and the Stoics did). Modal law excludes divine cognition from views 1 and 3; both the principle of modal contrast and the need to admit real freedom (therefore contingency) in God and the creatures render view 2 problematic; some would say impossible.

If we eliminate column II as dishonoring deity by making it wholly contingent, we have left column III. View 8 seems absurd—if there is any contingency at all, there must be some in the creatures. View 7 agrees with view 1, or classical theism, that God must be free not only to decide among different kinds of worlds but also to decide upon no world. Yet what good, one may ask, is this freedom to create nothing? Is not anything better than nothing? "Being as such is good" was a traditional doctrine, from Plato down. Why should one suppose it exalts divine power to think of it as capable of creating nothing as well as of creating something? This is another paradox of classical theism. So we are left with 9 as the view that retains the advantages of the others without their disadvantages. Clearly the five positive ideas of the table are all present in 9 and only in 9. Wilmon Sheldon, like Leibniz (both classical theists), held that the mistakes of philosophers were in what they denied, not in what they asserted. If so, it is view 9 that should be preferred. It symbolizes the modal structure of panentheism, or (as I call my version) neoclassical theism.

Besides the polarity of necessary-contingent, there are other ultimate contrasts that play similar roles: absolute-relative, infinite-finite, eternal-temporal, potential-actual, abstract-concrete, object-subject. Each of these yields a set of nine views subject to similar laws, except that while there are modal logics, there are no worked-out logics for the other polarities, although in my writings there are informal indications of what the logics would be like. The ninth combination, I hold, is logically favored for all pairs of universal contraries. If this is so, the American philosopher E. S. Brightman (1884–1952) did well to use the phrases "finite-infinite" and "temporal-eternal" of God.

If the *N* and the *C* in *NC*, or if infinite and finite, were to be applied to God in the same respect, column III would represent self-inconsistent views. But this is not the intention. Whitehead, for example, makes this clear by distinguishing the "primordial" and the "consequent" natures of God, describing the former as abstract, absolute, infinite, and strictly eternal and the latter as concrete, relative (dependent), finite, and "in a sense temporal." The two natures form one being by the "ontological," or "Aristotelian," principle that abstract entities are real only in the concrete. By no logical rule can view 9 be declared contradictory simply because the same being is assigned characters that would be contradictory if both were on the same level of abstractness or concreteness.

Historically, classical theism has been represented by Philo Judaeus (Jewish theologian of the first century CE), Augustine, Anselm, al-Ghazālī (Islamic theologian, 1058–1111), Thomas Aquinas, and countless other scholastics. More recently, Calvin, Luther, Descartes, Leibniz, Kant (in his *Ethics*), and the Americans Jonathan Edwards and Wilmon Sheldon—the list could be very long—have been in this tradition.

In this century classical pantheism has been losing ground. Its universal necessity is a doctrine of Brand Blanshard, but Blanshard is not a theist in any clear sense. F. H. Bradley, by one interpretation, was a pantheist (see W. L. Reese's article on Bradley in the *Dictionary of Religion and Philosophy*, 1980). Josiah Royce could also be so classified.

His deity is inclusive and all-knowing, and he says that relations are universally and exclusively internal or essential to their terms, which implies universal necessity; however, the implication is never clearly admitted in so many words, as it is by Blanshard, who was influenced by Royce. Royce's favorite pupil, W. E. Hocking, was a panentheist or a neoclassical theist, although he did not spell out the matter so clearly as some do.

Plato's theism has been rather poorly understood. Plato affirms self-determination ("self-motion") of those creatures that have souls and by implication also conceives the all-inclusive World Soul as self-moved. This implies some contingency in God and the world. As for necessity, Plato never suggests that not existing or not having a world was a possibility for God. In the *Timaeus* he speaks of two gods, the eternal God, the Demiurge or Creator, and "the God that was to be," the World Soul. There are hints that the Demiurge is a mythical figure, but the World Soul, with its cosmic body, seems intended more literally. The Plato scholar Francis M. Cornford suggests that the World Soul is the actual deity (Ronald Levinson says "Plato's real God") while the Demiurge is only an abstract aspect of the World Soul, its eternal envisagement of the form of the Good, according to which it acts creatively. In this interpretation, which might have somewhat surprised Plato, he can be considered the first panentheist. The Neoplatonists, however, including Plotinus, seem too unclear to be usefully classified. Their emanations from the One are apparently outside it and, as in classical theism, contribute nothing to it; and the World Soul is held less real than the One. Yet we are not told that the emanations might not have taken place or are contingent.

For two thousand years Plato's suggestion of a soul-and-body structure in God was ignored (or misunderstood), first by Aristotle and Plotinus and then by the Scholastics. More recently it was underestimated even by Whitehead. But about 1600 the heretical doctrine Socinianism, named for its founder, Socinus, proposed that God does not know or determine our decisions eternally (they are not eternally there to be known); rather, God knows them only as or after they occur. By making free decisions, we give divine knowledge new content and thus change God. Socinus may not have held that divine knowledge includes the things known, but he might as well have. At any rate his view conforms to *NC, cn.* A Socinian theologian defined the eternity of God in modal terms, "God is eternal in that he cannot not exist." This was a deliberate avoidance of the well-known medieval doctrine that God is immutable and impassable (meaning that no creature can influence God). This momentous event of three centuries ago—the rejection of a central doctrine of classical theism, a rejection made on behalf of the self-motion, or freedom, of souls—was passed over by historians and scholars until recently. It is still not to be found in encyclopedias and histories. Only a German book on Socinianism (by Otto Fock) tells the story.

The term *pantheism* goes back to the English writer John Toland (1670–1722), and the term *panentheism* to the German philosopher K. F. Krause (1781–1832), a student of Hegel and Fichte. Krause thought of the deity as a divine organism inclusive of all lesser organisms. He said that God is more than and includes nature and man. Consciously or not, he was to some extent returning to Plato's *Timaeus.* Toland coined the word *pantheist* and held that the universe is God. Similarly, Spinoza had spoken of "God or nature." There seems no evidence that either Toland or Krause had much influence on later doctrines, apart from funishing a label; they were minor figures in the history of thought. Oddly enough, Krause's chief influence was in Spain.

Hegel (1770–1831) must be regarded as a panentheist if he is any definite kind of theist. He holds that contraries must be united to express truth, and he uses both terms, necessity and contingency. Yet, what precisely he means by these is difficult to determine. He certainly holds that the unity of *necessary* and *contingent,* infinite and finite, universal and particular, is the truth of both. But how the unity is to be described is the problem. On this issue Hegel is, for me, unclear. Friedrich Schelling (1775–1854), Hegel's fellow student at Tübingen, in his later writings seems a panentheist in a clearer, more definite sense than Hegel, although he is still not notably clear. He did affirm change and freedom of both God and creatures and certainly did not regard either the creator or the existence of some created order as merely contingent.

After Schelling, the German physicist, psychologist, and philosopher G. T. Fechner (1801–1887) developed a rather neat system that easily fits *CN* > *cn*: both God and creatures have some freedom; both face an open future; and there is no suggestion that God exists contingently or could have lacked creatures. (Here is an unusually clear case of the ninth view.) As with Socinus, most scholars gave no heed. In France, however, Jules Lequier (1814–1862), aware of the Socinians, took freedom as his "first principle," addressing God thus: "Thou hast created me creator of myself." In this he anticipated Whitehead's "self-created creature." Of course Lequier had no such idea as that the divine existence was a mere logical accident, nor did he imply divine freedom to have no creatures at all. He also clearly affirmed that our decisions make a difference to God, that they "make a spot in the absolute." That the deity includes the creatures in knowing them is not clearly stated, but it seems to be implied.

In Italy Bernardino Varisco (1850–1933) affirmed some freedom of indeterminacy for every creature (which Plato, Socinus, Lequier, and, probably, Hegel had not done) and affirmed that God includes the creatures. Varisco also held that every creature is sentient: there is no dead, mindless matter. This only Fechner, of the previous European writers in this tradition, had proposed. In America Charles S. Peirce (1839–1914) also (after about 1880) asserted that every creature has some freedom and sentience, that chance, or piecemeal contingency, is pervasive in nature, and that the future is partly indeterminate, not simply for our knowledge but in reality. He accepted the characterization of God as the "necessary being" but was not satisfied with the unqualified description of God as eternal or immutable. He did not believe that our thoughts about God could be made very precise and hence left his theological ideas somewhat indefinite and not altogether consistent. But, if he had a definite position, it could only be the ninth view.

Alfred North Whitehead (1861–1947), an English mathematician, logician, physicist, and philosopher who moved to America in 1924, soon thereafter developed a comprehensive metaphysical system, clearly theistic, and, in most respects, clearly a panentheism. The polar principle, which in application to God may be called "dual transcendence," is, as already remarked, quite clear in his writing (apart from the label, which is an invention of mine). His "category of the ultimate," creativity, implies universal freedom, with an open future even for God. Sentience, or "feeling," is taken as universal (from atoms to people), and God is characterized as "the unification of all things" (in the divine "consequent nature"). Although the divine existence is not said to be necessary, still, since God as primordial is taken as the necessary seat of the "pure potentials" without which nothing would even be possible, what "the possibility of the divine nonexistence" could mean is not apparent.

Whitehead's remarkable saying "Every creature transcends God" I take to mean that the becoming of the creature is not divinely determined and that, until the becoming is accomplished, the creature is not yet prehended by, and thus taken into, the divine consciousness, thereby enriching the latter.

I have tried to draw out, clarify, and systematize the entire development as sketched above. Whitehead was somewhat aware of the partial Platonic precedent, but he may have had little or no knowledge of some of the others. Besides using Krause's panentheism for my view, I also call it neoclassical theism. I give many arguments for this form of theism, including six theistic proofs, arguments that are convincing for those who accept the premises on which they are based.

Paul Weiss (b. 1901) seems a panentheist of some kind, since he affirms human freedom and says that, in prayer, both God and the worshiper are transformed. He implies that deity is a unity somehow inclusive of all things so far as they are good. He does not say that God is wholly necessary or that the world is wholly contingent. John Findlay (b. 1903) is similarly heretical from the classical standpoint. W. P. Montague (1873–1963) and J. E. Boodin (1869–1950) are among the recent American nonclassical theists more or less close to panentheism.

The old issues have been partly left behind. The mere contrasts—necessary versus contingent, infinite versus finite, absolute versus relative, or even eternal versus temporal—no longer serve to define deity. Divine love must be sensitive to the weal and woe of the creatures and far from a purely independent, self-sufficient, unrelative, mere absolute. Paul Tillich (1886–1965) was no classical theist, and, in the third volume of his *Systematic Theology* (3 vols., 1951–1963), he admits that the creatures contribute to the divine life. This had already been said by Nikolai Berdiaev (1874–1948), who called himself a "mystical pantheist" but spoke of a "divine time" and of creaturely freedom undetermined by God. He was essentially a panentheist, except that, like Tillich, he thought that theological truth cannot be stated literally. Schubert Ogden (b. 1928), a theologian who defends panentheism, partly agrees with Tillich and Berdiaev about the irreducibly symbolic, or nonliteral, functioning of religious language.

Among living philosophers whom I know at all well, the nearest to a classical theist is the logician Richard M. Martin, who holds that all truth is timelessly known to God. Yet since Martin (together with the influential logician W. V. O. Quine, b. 1908) thinks that modal concepts are an affair of our language rather than of the nature of things, it is hard to classify his doctrine in modal terms.

The nine views in our modal table do not exhaust possible beliefs about God or the extraordinary, supreme reality. Various forms of atheism, for example, have been omitted. An important omitted view is that the supreme reality is the only reality: what may seem to us nonsupreme, ordinary realities are only appearances of the supreme reality, appearances that we in ignorance wrongly take as realities. To the questions "To whom do the appearances appear?" and "Who wrongly takes them as more than mere appearances?" the reply of some seems to be that the questions, too, are wrong or ignorant. Really, there are no wrongly thinking realities, only the one utterly good and real absolute, or *brahman.* This is the extreme version of Hinduistic monism, called Advaita Vedānta (*advaita* means "nondual"; Vedānta refers to the Vedas, ancient hymns and other sacred documents of Hinduism.) Its greatest formulator was Śaṅkara (788–820).

That the doctrine makes sense is more than most Westerners can see and also more than many Hindus—Rāmānuja (eleventh century) and Aurobindo Ghose (1872–1950), for example—can or could see. But it has had countless adherents. The *Bhagavadgītā* is indefinite or ambiguous on the relationship between *advaita* (also called "acosmism," implying the unreality of the cosmos) and pantheism or panentheism. Together with Robert Whittemore, a contemporary American philosopher who went to India to inquire into the matter, I consider that the *Bhagavadgītā* can equally well be interpreted panentheistically as acosmically.

Medieval Islam was classically theistic, with an even greater tendency to deny or belittle creaturely freedom. Yet a great poet in what is now Pakistan, Muhammad Iqbal (1877–1938), a disciple of Henri Bergson, accepted the ideas of a divine becoming and of creaturely freedom.

One branch of Hinduism, the Bengali school, may, according to some of its representatives, be close to the neoclassical view. For example, it has been reported that a disciple of the school's founder, Jiva Goswami, said, "God, although perfect in love, [yet] grows without ceasing." There seems to be no sharp contradiction between this Indian view and Whiteheadian or (in many respects, at least, the same) Hartshornean theology.

Buddhism appears superficially to be entirely nontheistic. It is certainly not classically theistic, with realities outside the supreme reality. In certain forms of Mahayana Buddhism in China, there is some movement toward classical pantheism (the Hua-yen tradition of Fa-tsang, 643–712). In Theravada Buddhism (in Burma, Sri Lanka, and Thailand), there is nothing like theism, although the tendency to deify the Buddha seems to haunt all Buddhism. Whitehead spoke of "the diffuse God of Buddhism," but the standard theism of the medieval or Renaissance West is simply not to be found in Buddhism.

Confucianism was vaguely theistic but hardly further classifiable in Western terms. To relate Taoism to pantheism or panentheism would be even more difficult.

A sharply formulated doctrine of determinism, theological or otherwise, is a largely Western affair. (The idea of *karman* suggests it, but vaguely.) So is a sharply formulated doctrine of timeless omniscience, as in classical theism. Plato and Aristotle did not have it. Classical theism (which many scholars say is not biblical) is a largely Western (or Near Eastern) invention of the first Christian centuries. Perhaps Madhva (1197–1276) in India most nearly resembles scholastic theology.

So far, almost nothing has been said about the saying "God is love." Whitehead says that God "prehends" the creatures; since he defines prehension (so far as the prehended entity is concrete) as "feeling of feeling" and also as "empathy," which can be taken as the universal kernel of love, he is saying that God (in "perfect" or unsurpassable fashion) feels the feelings of all. What is that but to say that God (in the best possible sense) loves all? Precisely this is the final meaning of neoclassical theism. The idea of divine love is biblical for Jews and Christians, is far from unknown to Muslims and Hindus, and is, perhaps, not so alien to Buddhists as some may think.

The long reign of classical theism and the considerable appeal (for shorter periods of time and to more limited groups) of classical pantheism have, perhaps, not been adequately explained in this essay. Many arguments for one or another of these views have been omitted, partly because of space limitations and partly, no doubt, from bias, as have some objections that partisans of other views could make to neoclassical theism, or, as it is called by some, "process theism." But then, many arguments for the neoclassical and against the classical views have also been omitted. For these deficiencies, further research by the reader is the only remedy.

See Also Attributes of God; Monism; Theism.

Bibliography

For historical examples of the doctrines discussed, see William L. Reese's and my *Philosophers Speak of God* (1953; reprint, Chicago, 1976). In Alfred North Whitehead's *Process and Reality* (1929; corr. ed., New York, 1978), part 5 should be consulted, as should the index references under *God.* I have presented my view in *The Divine Relativity: A Social Conception of God* (1948; reprint, New Haven, 1982) and in chapters 11–14 of *Creative Synthesis and Philosophic Method* (1970; reprint, Lanham, Md., 1983). Also recommended are *The Reality of God, and Other Essays* (New York, 1966) by Schubert Ogden, *Hartshorne and Neoclassical Metaphysics* (Lincoln, Nebr., 1970) by Eugene H. Peters, and *Process Theology: An Introductory Exposition* (Philadelphia, 1976) by John B. Cobb, Jr., and David R. Griffin. About Whitehead's theism, there are many books. For an able discussion of my reasons for believing as I do about God, see *Charles Hartshorne and the Existence of God* (Albany, N.Y., 1984) by Donald W. Viney.

See also, in *Encyclopaedia Britannica,* 15th ed. (Chicago, 1982), the article "Pantheism and Panentheism" and, in the *Dictionary of Philosophy and Religion: Eastern and Western Thought* (Atlantic Highlands, N.J., 1980), edited by William L. Reese and others, the articles on Cournot, Fechner, Iqbal, Krause, Lequier, Plato, Plotinus, and Whitehead (secs. 16–21).

New Sources

Christ, Carol P. *She Who Changes. Re-Imagining the Divine in the World.* New York and Basingstoke, England, 2003.

Janssens, David. "The Problem of the Enlightenment: Strauss, Jacobi, and the Pantheism Controversy." *Review of Metaphysics,* 56 (March 2003): 605–632.

Levine, Michael P. *Pantheism: A Non-Theistic Concept of Deity.* New York, 1994.

Levine, Michael P. "Pantheism, Theism, and the Problem of Evil." *International Journal for Philosophy of Religion* 35 (June 1994): 129–152.

Melamed, Yitzhak. "Solomon Maimon and the Rise of Spinozism in German Idealism." *Journal of the History of Philosophy* 42 (January 2004): 67–97.

Thomson, Curtis L. "From Presupposing Pantheism's Power to Potentiating Panentheism's Personality: Seeking Parallels between Kierkegaard's and Martensen's Theological Anthropologies. " *Journal of Religion* 82 (April 2002): 225–252.

Zoetmulder, P. S. M. C. Ricklefs, ed. and trans. *Pantheism and Monism in Javanese Suluk Literature: Islamic and Indian Mysticism in an Indonesian Setting.* Leiden, 1995.

Charles Hartshorne (1987)
Revised Bibliography

PAPACY.

PAPACY. The papacy is the central governing institution of the Roman Catholic church under the leadership of the pope, the bishop of Rome. The word *papacy* (Lat., *papatus*) is medieval in origin and derives from the Latin *papa,* an affectionate term for "father."

The Early Period. This era, extending from the biblical origins of Christianity to the fifth century, was marked by the ever-increasing power and prestige of the bishop of Rome within the universal church and the Roman empire.

Scriptural foundation. Traditional Roman Catholic teaching holds that Jesus Christ directly bestowed upon the apostle Peter the fullness of ruling and teaching authority. He made Peter the first holder of supreme power in the universal church, a power passed on to his successors, the bishops of Rome. (See table 1.) Two biblical texts are cited to substantiate this claim. In *Matthew* 16:18 there is the promise of Jesus: "You are Peter, and on this rock I will build my church, and the gates of Hades shall not prevail against it." In *John* 21:15–16, this promise is fulfilled in the admonition of Jesus to Peter: "Feed my lambs. . . . Look after my sheep." Modern Roman Catholic biblical scholars affirm the genuine authority of Peter among the Twelve but make the following observations: there is no New Testament evidence that Peter was ever a bishop or local administrator of any church (including Rome and Antioch); there is no direct biblical proof that Jesus established the papacy as a permanent office within the church; but there is other cogent evidence that Peter arrived in Rome late in his life and was martyred and buried there.

Catholic scholars insist, however, that even though the idea of an abiding Petrine ministry is not explicitly found in scripture, it is not contrary to the biblical tradition and indeed is implicitly rooted in it. Peter had a preeminent role in the New Testament, where he is described as the most prominent apostolic witness and missionary among the Twelve. He is the model of the shepherd-pastor, the receiver of a special revelation, and the teacher of the true faith. Gradually Christians, through the providential direction of the Holy Spirit, recognized the papacy, the office of headship in the church, to be the continuation of that ministry given by Christ to Peter and exercised through the historic Roman episcopate. Although other Christian scholars would accept many of these conclusions, they would generally deny the Roman Catholic belief that the papacy is an absolutely essential element of the church.

First three centuries. The early Christian churches were not organized internationally. Yet Rome, almost from the beginning, was accorded a unique position, and understandably so: Rome was the only apostolic see in the West; it was the place where Peter and Paul were martyred; and it was the capital of the empire. Ignatius of Antioch, in his letter to the Romans (c. 110), called the Roman church the church "presiding in love" (4.3), and Irenaeus, in his *Against Heresies* (c. 180), referred to its "more imposing foundation" (3.3.2). Although these controverted texts may not be a proof of Roman primacy, they at least indicate the lofty stature of the see of Rome.

The exact structure of the very early Roman church is not known, but it seems that by the middle of the second century monepiscopacy (the rule of one bishop) was well established. The memory of Peter was kept alive in Rome, and its bishops were often involved in the affairs of churches outside their own area. Clement I (c. 90–c. 99), for example, sent a letter from the church of Rome to the church of Corinth to settle a dispute over the removal of several church officials. Victor I (c. 189–c. 198) sought, under threat of excommunication, to impose on the churches of Asia Minor the Roman custom for the celebration of Easter. Finally, Stephen I (254–257) reinstated two Spanish bishops who had been deposed by their colleagues and also decided, contrary to the custom in Syria and North Africa, that repentant heretics did not have to be rebaptized. Although Cyprian, bishop of Carthage (d. 258), objected to Stephen's decisions, he was able to call Rome the "principal church" (letter 59, addressed to Cornelius, bishop of Rome) and to insist that for bishops to be legitimate they must be in communion with Rome.

The bishops of Rome in the third century claimed a universal primacy, even though it would be another 150 years before this idea was doctrinally formulated. Rome attracted both orthodox and heterodox teachers—some to have their views heard, others to seek confirmation. More and more, the bishop of Rome, either on his own initiative or by request, settled doctrinal and disciplinary disputes in other churches. Roman influence was felt as far away as Spain, Gaul, North Africa, and Asia Minor. The see of Peter was looked upon as the guarantor of doctrinal purity even by those who found fault with its leadership.

Fourth and fifth centuries. With the Edict of Milan (313) the empire granted toleration of all religions and allowed Christians to worship freely. This policy ended the era of persecution, increased the number of Christians, and shaped the institutional development of the papacy. Once Emperor Constantine decided to move the seat of the empire to Constantinople in 324, the papacy began to play a larger role in the West. By the time Christianity became the official religion of the empire in 381, several popes were already affirming papal primatial authority. The critical period in the doctrinal systematization of Roman primacy took place in the years between Damasus I (366–384) and Leo I (440–461). In that period, the popes explicitly claimed that the bishop of Rome was the head of the entire church and that his authority derived from Peter.

Damasus I, the first pope to call Rome the apostolic see, made Latin the principal liturgical language in Rome and commissioned Jerome to revise the old Latin version of the New Testament. At the Council of Rome (382), he declared that the primacy of the bishop of Rome is based on continuity with Peter. He deposed several Arian bishops. His successor, Siricius (384–399), whose decretal letters are the earliest extant, promoted Rome's primatial position and imposed his decisions on many bishops outside Italy.

It was Leo I, the first of three popes to be called the Great, who laid the theoretical foundation of papal primacy. Leo took the title Pontifex Maximus, which the emperors no longer used, and claimed to possess the fullness of power *(plenitudo potestatis).* Governing the church through a tumultuous period of barbarian invasions and internal disputes, he relentlessly defended the rights of the Roman see. He rejected Canon 28 of the Council of Chalcedon (451), which gave the bishop of New Rome (Constantinople) privileges equal to those of the bishop of Old Rome and a rank second only to that of the pope. A favorite theme for Leo was the relationship between Peter and the pope. This idea had been advanced by earlier popes, but Leo elaborated it, in his sermons calling himself "Peter in Peter's see" (2.2) and his "unworthy heir" (3.4). Thus, as he noted, a particular pope may be sinful, but the papacy as such still retains its Petrine character. The Leonine distinction between person and office has proved to be of immense value and has helped the papacy survive unsuitable popes. Leo believed that Peter's successors have "the care of all the churches" (*Sermons* 3.4), and he exercised his authority over Christian churches in Italy, Africa, and Gaul. The Western Roman empire ended in 476. The successors of Leo, especially Felix III (483–492) and Gelasius I (492–496), applied his principles, but the imperial government in Constantinople exerted continual pressure on the papacy.

For centuries the popes did not change their names. The first name change occurred when a Roman called Mercury, having been elected pope, chose the more suitable appellation of John II (533–535). From the time of Sergius IV (1009–1012)—his name had been Peter Buccaporca (Peter Pigmouth)—the taking of a new name has continued to the present, with two exceptions: Adrian VI (1522–1523) and Marcellus II (1555). The most popular papal names have been John, Gregory, Benedict, Clement, Innocent, Leo, and Pius. There has never been a Peter II or a John XX. John Paul I was the first pope to select a double name. The legend that a woman pope—Pope Joan—reigned between Leo IV (847–855) and Benedict III (855–858) has long been rejected by historians.

The accompanying list is based generally on the catalog of popes given in the *Annuario pontificio*, the official Vatican yearbook, with some changes dictated by recent scholarly research. It should be noted that the legitimacy of certain popes—for example, Dioscorus (530), Leo VIII (963–965), Benedict V (964), Gregory VI (1045–1046), and Clement II (1046–1047)—is still controverted. Although Stephen (752) is mentioned in the list, he died three days after his election without being consecrated a bishop.

THE MEDIEVAL PAPACY. The eventful period from the sixth to the fifteenth century demonstrated the unusual adaptability of the papal office. Successive popes opposed imperial control, attempted to reform the papacy and the church, and brought papal authority to its peak in the twelfth and thirteenth centuries. A severe decline followed.

The struggle for independence. The popes of the sixth and seventh centuries resisted excessive encroachments but were still subservient to the power of the emperor. The most notable pope at this time was Gregory I, the Great (590–604), a deeply spiritual man who called himself "the servant of the servants of God." A skilled negotiator, he was able to conclude a peace treaty with the Lombards, who threatened Rome; the people of Rome and the adjacent regions considered him their protector. Gregory was respectful of the rights of individual bishops, but he insisted, nevertheless, that all churches, including Constantinople, were subject to the apostolic see of Rome. He realized that direct confrontation with the emperor would be futile, and so he concentrated on developing the church in territories outside imperial jurisdiction. He established links with the Frankish monarchs that proved to be of great significance in the later Middle Ages; he also sent forty missionaries to Britain. The break with the East began when Gregory II (715–731) condemned the iconoclastic decrees of Emperor Leo I, who had prohibited the use of images in liturgical ceremonies. The gap widened when Stephen II (752–757), the first pope to cross the Alps, met with Pépin, king of the Franks. Pépin agreed to defend the pope against the invading Lombards and apparently promised him sovereignty over large areas in central Italy. The Donation of Pépin was an epoch-making event; it marked the beginning of the Papal States, in existence until 1870. Stephen became the first of a long line of popes to claim temporal rule. Through his alliance with the Frankish kingdom, Stephen was virtually able to free the papacy from the domination of Constantinople. The last step in the division of Rome from the Eastern Empire was when Pope Leo III (795–816) crowned Charlemagne emperor of the West at Saint Peter's Basilica in 800. As a result of their new status, the popes minted their own coins, and they no longer dated papal documents according to imperial years. The primatial prominence of Rome increased when the Muslim conquests destroyed the church in North Africa and ended the strong influence of Rome's great rivals: the patriarchates of Alexandria, Antioch, and Jerusalem. By the middle of the ninth century, Nicholas I, the Great (858–867), was able to act as the supreme judge and lawmaker for the entire church. He resisted Carolingian interference and dealt severely with recalcitrant archbishops, deposing several and overruling the decisions of others. In his relations with the Byzantine church he was less successful because he failed to resolve adequately the dispute with Photios, the patriarch of Constantinople. The assertion of primatial claims by John VIII (872–882) also met Byzantine opposition. The tenth century was a bleak one for the papacy. After the Carolingian rulers lost power, the papacy was scandalously dominated, first by the Roman nobility and then by the German emperors Otto I and his successors. The so-called Ottonian privilege restricted the freedom of papal electors and allowed the emperor the right of ratification. There were some two dozen popes and antipopes during this period, many of low moral caliber. Depositions and impositions of popes became commonplace. Clearly, then, by the beginning of the eleventh century, the need for radical reform was urgent.

The reform movement. Advocates of reform found a dedicated leader in Leo IX (1049–1054). He traveled extensively throughout Italy, France, and Germany, presiding over synods that issued strong decrees dealing with clerical marriage, simony, and episcopal elections. Only six months of his entire pontificate were spent in Rome. Further reforms

Name	Date	Name (continued)	Date
St. Peter	?-64/7	Boniface II	22 Sep. 530-17 Oct. 532
St. Linus	64/7-79?	[Dioscorus]	[22 Sep.-14 Oct. 530]
St. Anacletus (Cletus)	79?-90/2	John II	2 Jan. 533-8 May 535
St. Clement I	90/2-99/101	St. Agapitus I	13 May 535-22 Apr. 536
St. Evaristus	99/101-107?	St. Silverius	1 Jun. 536-11 Nov. 537
St. Alexander I	107?-116?	Vigilius	29 Mar. 537-7 Jun. 555
St. Sixtus I	116?-125?	Pelagius I	16 Apt. 556-4 Mar. 561
St. Telesphorus	125?-136?	John III	17 Jul. 561-13 Jul. 574
St. Hyginus	136?-140/2	Benedict I	2 Jun. 575-30 Jul. 579
St. Pius I	140/2-154/5	Pelagius II	26 Nov. 579-7 Feb. 590
St. Anicetus	154/5-166?	St. Gregory I, the Great	3 Sep. 590-12 Mar. 604
St. Soter	166?-174?	Sabinian	13 Sep. 604-22 Feb. 606
St. Eleutherius	174?-189?	Boniface III	19 Feb.-12 Nov. 607
St. Victor I	189?-198?	St. Boniface IV	25 Aug. 608-8 May 615
St. Zephyrinus	198?-217?	St. Deusdedit (Adeodatus I)	19 Oct. 615-8 Nov. 618
St. Callistus I	217?-222	Boniface V	23 Dec. 619-25 Oct. 625
[St. Hippolytus]	[217?-235]	Honorius I	27 Oct. 625-12 Oct. 638
St. Urban	I 222-230	Severinus	28 May-7 Aug. 640
St. Pontian	21 Jul. 230-28 Sep. 235	John IV	24 Dec. 640-12 Oct. 642
St. Anterus	21 Nov. 235-3 Jan. 236	Theodore I	24 Nov. 642-14 May 649
St. Fabian	10 Jan. 236-20 Jan. 250	St. Martin I	July 649-16 Sep. 655
St. Cornelius	Mar. 251-Jun. 253	St. Eugene I	10 Aug. 654-2 Jun. 657
[Novatian]	[251-258?]	St. Vitalian	30 Jul. 657-27 Jan. 672
St. Lucius I	25 Jun. 253-5 Mar. 254	Adeodatus II	11 Apr. 672-17 Jun. 676
St. Stephen I	12 May 254-2 Aug. 257	Donus	2 Nov. 676-11 Apr. 678
St. Sixtus II	30 Aug. 257-6 Aug. 258	St. Agatho	27 Jun. 678-10 Jan. 681
St. Dionysius	22 Jul. 259-26 Dec. 268	St. Leo II	17 Aug. 682-3 Jul. 683
St. Felix I	5 Jan. 269-30 Dec. 274	St. Benedict II	26 Jun. 684-8 May 685
St. Eutychian	4 Jan. 275-7 Dec. 283	John V	23 Jul. 685-2 Aug. 686
St. Gaius (Caius)	17 Dec. 283-22 Apr. 296	Conon	21 Oct. 686-21 Sep. 687
St. Marcellinus	30 Jun. 296-25 Oct. 304	[Theodore]	[687]
St. Marcellus I	27 May 308-16 Jan. 309	[Paschal]	[687]
St. Eusebius	18 Apr.-17 Aug. 309	St. Sergius I	15 Dec. 687-8 Sep. 701
St. Miltiades 2	Jul. 311-11 Jan. 314	John VI	30 Oct. 701-11 Jan. 705
St. Sylvester I	31 Jan. 314-31 Dec. 335	John VII	1 Mar. 705-18 Oct. 707
St. Mark	18 Jan.-7 Oct. 336	Sisinnius	15 Jan.-4 Feb. 708
St. Julius I	6 Feb. 337-12 Apr. 352	Constantine	25 Mar. 708-9 Apr. 715
Liberius	17 May 352-24 Sep. 366	St. Gregory II	19 May 715-11 Feb. 731
[Felix II]	[355-22 Nov. 365]	St. Gregory III	18 Mar. 731-Nov. 741
St. Damasus I	1 Oct. 366-11 Dec. 384	St. Zachary	10 Dec. 741-22 Mar. 752
[Ursinus]	[366-367]	Stephen (II)	23-25 Mar. 752
St. Siricius	15 Dec. 384-26 Nov. 399	Stephen II (III)	26 Mar. 752-26 Apt. 757
St. Anastasius I	27 Nov. 399-19 Dec. 401	St. Paul I	29 May 757-28 Jun. 767
St. Innocent I	22 Dec. 401-12 Mar. 417	[Constantine II]	[28 Jun. 767-769]
St. Zosimus	18 Mar. 417-26 Dec. 418	[Philip]	[31 Jul. 768]
St. Boniface I	28 Dec. 418-4 Sep. 422	Stephen III	(IV) 7 Aug. 768-24 Jan. 772
[Eulalius]	[27 Dec. 418-419]	Adrian I	1 Feb. 772-25 Dec. 795
St. Celestine I	10 Sep. 422-27 Jul. 432	St. Leo III	26 Dec. 795-12 Jun. 816
St. Sixtus III	31 Jul. 432-19 Aug. 440	Stephen IV	(V) 22 Jun. 816-24 Jan. 817
St. Leo I, the Great	29 Sep. 440-10 Nov. 461	St. Paschal I	25 Jan. 817-11 Feb. 824
St. Hilary	19 Nov. 461-29 Feb. 468	Eugene II	Feb. 824-Aug. 827
St. Simplicius	3 Mar. 468-10 Mar. 483	Valentine	Aug.-Sep. 827
St. Felix III (II)	13 Mar. 483-1 Mar. 492	Gregory IV	827-Jan. 844
St. Gelasius I	1 Mar. 492-21 Nov. 496	[John]	[Jan. 844]
Anastasius II	24 Nov. 496-19 Nov. 498	Sergius II	Jan. 844-27 Jan. 847
St. Symmachus	22 Nov. 498-19 Jul. 514	St. Leo IV	Jan. 847-17 Jul. 855
[Lawrence]	[498; 501-505]	Benedict III	Jul. 855-17 Apr. 858
St. Hormisdas	20 Jul. 514-6 Aug. 523	[Anastasius]	[Aug.-Sep. 855]
St. John I	13 Aug. 523-18 May 526		
St. Felix IV (III)	12 Jul. 526-22 Sep. 530	(continued)	

TABLE 1. *The Popes.* A Roman numeral in parentheses after a pope's name indicates differences in the historical sources. The names of the antipopes and their dates are given in brackets. The first date for each pope refers to his election; the second date refers to his death, deposition, or resignation. Dates for the first two hundred years are uncertain. Abbreviations: Bl. = Blessed; St. = Saint.

Name (continued)	Date
St. Nicholas I, the Great	24 Apt. 858-13 Nov. 867
Adrian II	14 Dec. 867-14 Dec. 872
John VIII	14 Dec. 872-16 Dec. 882
Marinus I	16 Dec. 882-15 May 884
St. Adrian III	17 May 884-Sep. 885
Stephen V (VI)	Sep. 885-14 Sep. 891
Formosus 6	Oct. 891-4 Apr. 896
Boniface VI	Apr. 896
Stephen VI (VII)	May 896-Aug. 897
Romanus	Aug.-Nov. 897
Theodore II	Dec. 897
John IX	Jan. 898-Jan. 900
Benedict IV	Jan. 900-Jul. 903
Leo V	Jul.-Sep. 903
[Christopher]	[Jul. 903-Jan. 904]
Sergius III	29 Jan. 904-14 Apr. 911
Anastasius III	Apt. 911-Jun. 913
Lando	Jul. 913-Feb. 914
John X	Mar. 914-May 928
Leo VI	May-Dec. 928
Stephen VII (VIII)	Dec. 928-Feb. 931
John XI	Feb. 931-Dec. 935
Leo VII 3	an. 936-13 Jul. 939
Stephen VIII (IX)	14 Jul. 939-Oct. 942
Marinus II	30 Oct. 942-May 946
Agapetus II	10 May 946-Dec. 955
John XII	16 Dec. 955-14 May 964
Leo VIII	4 Dec. 963-1 Mar. 965
Benedict V	22 May-23 Jun. 964
John XIII	1 Oct. 965-6 Sep. 972
Benedict VI	19 Jan. 973-Jun. 974
[Boniface VII]	[Jun.-Jul. 974; Aug. 984-Jul. 985]
Benedict VII	Oct. 974-10 Jul. 983
John XIV	Dec. 983-20 Aug.'984
John XV	Aug. 985-Mar. 996
Gregory V	3 May 996-18 Feb. 999
[John XVI]	[Apr. 997-Feb. 998]
Sylvester II	2 Apr. 999-12 May 1003
John XVII	Jun.-Dec. 1003
John XVIII	Jan. 1004-Jul. 1009
Sergius IV	31 Jul. 1009-12 May 1012
Benedict VIII	18 May 1012-9 Apr. 1024
[Gregory]	[1012]
John XIX	Apt. 1024-1032
Benedict IX	(first time) 1032-1044
Sylvester III	20 Jan.-10 Feb. 1045
Benedict IX	(second time) 10 Apt.-1 May 1045
Gregory VI	May 1045-20 Dec. 1046
Clement II	24 Dec. 1046-9 Oct. 1047
Benedict IX	(third time) 8 Nov. 1047-17 Jul. 1048
Damasus II	17 Jul.-9 Aug. 1048
St. Leo IX	12 Feb. 1049-19 Apr. 1054
Victor II	16 Apt. 1055-28 Jul. 1057
Stephen IX (X)	3 Aug. 1057-29 Mar. 1058
[Benedict X]	[5 Apt. 1058-24 Jan. 1059]
Nicholas II	24 Jan. 1059-27 Jul. 1061
Alexander II	1 Oct. 1061-21 Apr. 1073
[Honorius II]	[28 Oct. 1061-1072]
St. Gregory VII	22 Apt. 1073-25 May 1085
[Clement III]	[26 Jun. 1080-8 Sep. 1100]
Bl. Victor III	24 May 1086-16 Sep. 1087
Bl. Urban II	12 Mar. 1088-29 Jul. 1099
Paschal II	13 Aug. 1099-21 Jan. 1118
[Theodoric]	[1100]
[Albert]	[1102]
[Sylvester IV]	[18 Nov. 1105-1111]
Gelasius II	24 Jan. 1118-28 Jan. 1119
[Gregory VIII]	[8 Mar. 1118-1121]
Callistus II	2 Feb. 1119-13 Dec. 1124
Honorius II	5 Dec. 1124-13 Feb. 1130
[Celestine II]	[Dec. 1124]
Innocent II	14 Feb. 1130-24 Sep. 1143
[Anacletus II]	[14 Feb. 1130-25 Jan. 1138]
[Victor IV]	[Mar.-29 May 1138]
Celestine II	26 Sep. 1143-8 Mar. 1144
Lucius II	2 Mar. 1144-15 Feb. 1145
Bl. Eugene III	15 Feb. 1145-8 Jul. 1153
Anastasius IV	12 Jul. 1153-3 Dec. 1154
Adrian IV	4 Dec. 1154-1 Sep. 1159
Alexander III	7 Sep. 1159-30 Aug. 1181
[Victor IV]	[7 Sep. 1159-20 Apt. 1164]
[Paschal III]	[26 Apt. 1164-20 Sep. 1168]
[Callistus III]	[Sep. 1168-29 Aug. 1178]
[Innocent III]	[29 Sep. 1179-1180]
Lucius III	1 Sep. 1181-25 Sep. 1185
Urban III	25 Nov. 1185-20 Oct. 1187
Gregory VIII	21 Oct.-17 Dec. 1187
Clement III	19 Dec. 1187-Mar. 1191
Celestine III	30 Mar. 1191-8 Jan. 1198
Innocent III	8 Jan. 1198-16 Jul. 1216
Honorius III	18 Jul. 1216-18 Mar. 1227
Gregory IX	19 Mar. 1227-22 Aug. 1241
Celestine IV	25 Oct.-10 Nov. 1241
Innocent IV	25 Jun. 1243-7 Dec. 1254
Alexander IV	12 Dec. 1254-25 May 1261
Urban IV	29 Aug. 1261-2 Oct. 1264
Clement IV	5 Feb. 1265-29 Nov. 1268
Bl. Gregory X	1 Sep. 1271-10 Jan. 1276
Bl. Innocent V	21 Jan.-22 Jun. 1276
Adrian V	11 Jul.-18 Aug. 1276
John XXI	8 Sep. 1276-20 May 1277
Nicholas III	25 Nov. 1277-22 Aug. 1280
Martin IV	22 Feb. 1281-28 Mar. 1285
Honorius IV	2 Apt. 1285-3 Apt. 1287
Nicholas IV	22 Feb. 1288-4 Apt. 1292
St. Celestine V	5 Jul.-13 Dec. 1294
Boniface VIII	24 Dec. 1294-11 Oct. 1303
Bl. Benedict XI	22 Oct. 1303-7 Jul. 1304
Clement V	5 Jun. 1305-20 Apr. 1314
John XXII	7 Aug. 1316-4 Dec. 1334
[Nicholas V]	[12 May 1328-25 Aug. 1330]
Benedict XII	20 Dec. 1334-25 Apt. 1342
Clement VI	7 May 1342-6 Dec. 1352
Innocent VI	18 Dec. 1352-12 Sep. 1362
Bl. Urban V	28 Sep. 1362-19 Dec. 1370
Gregory XI	30 Dec. 1370-26 Mar. 1378
Urban VI	8 Apt. 1378-15 Oct. 1389

(continued)

Name (continued)	Date
Boniface IX	2 Nov. 1389- 1 Oct. 1404
Innocent VII	17 Oct. 1404-6 Nov. 1406
Gregory XII	30 Nov. 1406-4 Jul. 1415
[Clement VII, Avignon]	[20 Sep. 1378-16 Sep. 1394]
[Benedict XIII, Avignon]	[28 Sep. 1394-23 May 1423]
[Clement VIII, Avignon]	[10 Jun. 1423-26 Jul. 1429]
[Benedict XIV, Avignon]	[12 Nov. 1425-1430]
[Alexander V, Pisa]	[26 Jun. 1409-3 May 1410]
[John XXIII, Pisa]	[17 May 1410-29 May 1415]
Martin V	11 Nov. 1417-20 Feb. 1431
Eugene IV	3 Mar. 1431-23 Feb. 1447
[Felix V]	[5 Nov. 1439-7 Apr. 1449]
Nicholas V	6 Mar. 1447-24 Mar. 1455
Callistus III	8 Apt. 1455-6 Aug. 1458
Plus II	19 Aug. 1458-15 Aug. 1464
Paul II	30 Aug. 1464-26 Jul. 1471
Sixtus IV	9 Aug. 1471-12 Aug. 1484
Innocent VIII	29 Aug. 1484-25 Jul. 1492
Alexander VI	11 Aug. 1492-18 Aug. 1503
Pius III	22 Sep.-18 Oct. 1503
Julius II	31 Oct. 1503-21 Feb. 1513
Leo X	9 Mar. 1513-1 Dec. 1521
Adrian VI	9 Jan. 1522-14 Sep. 1523
Clement VII	19 Nov. 1523-25 Sep. 1534
Paul III	13 Oct. 1534-10 Nov. 1549
Julius III	7 Feb. 1550-23 Mar. 1555
Marcellus II	9 Apt.-1 May 1555
Paul IV	23 May 1555-18 Aug. 1559
Plus IV	25 Dec. 1559-9 Dec. 1565
St. Pius V	7 Jan. 1566-1 May 1572
Gregory XIII	13 May 1572-10 Apr. 1585
Sixtus V	24 Apr. 1585-27 Aug. 1590
Urban VII	15 Sep.-27 Sep. 1590
Gregory XIV	5 Dec. 1590-16 Oct. 1591
Innocent IX	29 Oct.-30 Dec. 1591
Clement VIII	30 Jan. 1592-3 Mar. 1605
Leo XI	1 Apt.-27 Apt. 1605
Paul V	16 May 1605-28 Jan. 1621
Gregory XV	9 Feb. 1621-8 Jul. 1623
Urban VIII	6 Aug. 1623-29 Jul. 1644
Innocent X	15 Sep. 1644-7 Jan. 1655
Alexander VII	7 Apt. 1655-22 May 1667
Clement IX	20 Jun. 1667-9 Dec. 1669
Clement X	29 Apt. 1670-22 Jul. 1676
Bl. Innocent XI	21 Sep. 1676-12 Aug. 1689
Alexander VIII	6 Oct. 1689-1 Feb. 1691
Innocent XII	12 Jul. 1691-27 Sep. 1700
Clement XI	23 Nov. 1700-19 Mar. 1721
Innocent XIII	8 May 1721-7 Mar. 1724
Benedict XIII	29 May 1724-21 Feb. 1730
Clement XII	12 Jul. 1730-6 Feb. 1740
Benedict XIV	17 Aug. 1740-3 May 1758
Clement XIII	6 Jul. 1758-2 Feb. 1769
Clement XIV	19 May 1769-22 Sep. 1774
Pius VI	15 Feb. 1775-29 Aug. 1799
Pius VII	14 Mar. 1800-20 Aug. 1823
Leo XII	28 Sep. 1823-10 Feb. 1829
Pius VIII	31 Mar. 1829-30 Nov. 1830
Gregory XVI	2 Feb. 1831-1 Jun. 1846
Pius IX	16 Jun. 1846-7 Feb. 1878
Leo XIII	20 Feb. 1878-20 Jul. 1903
St. Pius X	4 Aug. 1903-20 Aug. 1914
Benedict XV	3 Sep. 1914-22 Jan. 1922
Pius XI	6 Feb. 1922-10 Feb. 1939
Pius XII	2 Mar. 1939-9 Oct. 1958
John XXIII	28 Oct. 1958-3 Jun. 1963
Paul VI	21 Jun. 1963-6 Aug. 1978
John Paul I	26 Aug.-28 Sep. 1978
John Paul II	16 Oct. 1978-

were made under Nicholas II (1059–1061), whose coronation, perhaps the first ever, was rich in monarchical symbolism. His decree on papal elections (1059), which made cardinal bishops the sole electors, had a twofold purpose: to safeguard the reformed papacy through free and peaceful elections and to eliminate coercion by the empire or the aristocracy. By not granting the emperor the right of confirmation, he directly opposed the Ottonian privilege. Nicholas also introduced feudalism into the papacy when he enfeoffed the Normans; the papacy invested them with the lands they had conquered and received the oath of fealty. This feudal contract—actually made to the apostle Peter through the pope—was the first of many. By the twelfth century, the papacy had more feudal vassals than any other European power.

The most famous of the reform popes was Gregory VII (1073–1085), surnamed Hildebrand. Endowed with great gifts, he had learned much about the papacy from his years of service under Leo IX, Nicholas II, and Alexander II (1061–1073). His ambitious program of reform focused on three areas. The first task was to restore prestige to the papacy, to resurrect it from the sorry state to which it had descended in the previous two centuries. In his letters and especially in his *Dictates of the Pope,* Gregory, like Leo I before him, identified himself with Peter; claimed universal authority over bishops, clerics, and councils; and asserted his right to make law, to render judgments that allow no appeal, and even to depose emperors. The second area of reform was directed against clerical corruption, particularly simony and incontinence. The third area concerned lay investiture—a practice whereby feudal lords, princes, and emperors bestowed spiritual office through the selection of pastors, abbots, and bishops. Gregory's determination to root out this evil brought him into direct conflict with Emperor Henry IV, whom he consequently excommunicated (and later absolved in the famous winter scene at Canossa in 1077). The Gregorian reform movement met fierce resistance and achieved only limited success, but it was an important milestone in papal history. For the first time the extensive theoretical principles of papal power were tested in practice. Henceforth, the papacy exercised a new style of leadership:

The pope emerged not only as the undisputed head of the church but also as the unifying force in medieval western Europe.

The height of papal authority. The papacy reached its zenith in the twelfth and thirteenth centuries. Six general councils between 1123 and 1274 issued many doctrinal and disciplinary decrees aimed at reform and left no doubt that the popes were firmly in control of church policy. During the pontificate of Innocent III (1198–1216), one of the most brilliant of all the popes, the papacy reached the summit of its universal power and supervised the religious, social, and political life of the West. Some of the greatest popes at this time were canonists who proclaimed a pontifical world hegemony. Under Innocent III, the first official collection of canon law was published (1209), and the kingdoms of Bulgaria, Portugal, and England were made papal fiefs. Honorius III (1216–1227) further centralized papal administration and finances and approved the establishment of the Franciscan and Dominican orders. In theory, papal authority extended also to non-Christians. Innocent IV (1243–1254) believed that every creature is subject to the pope—even infidels, Christ's sheep by creation though not members of the church. This idea of a world theocracy under the popes was to be part of the theological and political justification for the Crusades.

The medieval popes took stringent action against such heretics as the Waldensians and the Cathari. Gregory IX (1227–1241) made the Inquisition a permanent tribunal to combat heresy, selecting Dominicans and Franciscans to serve as inquisitors, or judges. Heresy was considered not only a grave sin but also a crime against the state. Thus Innocent IV approved the use of torture by the state to force heretics to confess.

Two significant changes were made in the procedures for papal elections. At the Third Lateran Council (1179), Alexander III (1159–1181) decreed that all cardinals—not just cardinal bishops—could vote and that a two-thirds majority was required. The Second Council of Lyons (1274), under Gregory X (1271–1276), established the law of the conclave, whereby the cardinal electors had to assemble in the papal palace and remain in a locked room until the election was completed.

Decline of the papacy. The death of Boniface VIII (1294–1303) marked the end of the grandiose idea of a theocratic world order with all power, spiritual and temporal, emanating from the pope. Several factors contributed to the decline of the papacy: high taxation, the inappropriate conferral and control of benefices, corruption in the Roman bureaucracy, and, above all, the failure of the popes to foresee the effect of nationalism on church-state relations. The effort to construct a Christian commonwealth under papal leadership was unsuccessful, but it must be judged in context. The popes struggled to protect the independence of the church, but their temporal involvements complicated the situation. Europe at that time was a mosaic of feudal territories; nations, as they are known today, were only in the process of formation. It was a turbulent time. Yet in the Middle Ages, the papacy was the only institution in the West with the authority and stability to provide law and order. At times it went to excess, but medieval Europe owed it a considerable debt.

In 1308, Clement V (1305–1314) moved the papal residence to Avignon, which then belonged to the king of Naples, a vassal of the pope. Several factors prompted this decision: the upcoming general council of Vienne (1311–1312); the tension between the pope and the king of France; and the unsafe and chaotic political situation in Rome and Italy. The popes remained in Avignon for seventy years. During their so-called Babylonian Captivity, the popes were French, but the papacy was not a puppet of the French rulers. Centralization and administrative complexity increased, especially under John XXII (1316–1334). The cardinals assumed greater power that at times bordered on oligarchy. They introduced the practice of capitulation—an agreement made by electors of the pope to limit the authority of the person chosen to be pope—and thus tried to restrict papal primacy. The Avignon popes worked to reform the clergy and religious orders; they also promoted missionary activity in China, India, and Persia.

No sooner had Gregory XI (1370–1378) returned to Rome in 1377 than the papacy faced another crisis, the great Western schism. The election of Urban VI (1378–1389) was later disputed by some of the cardinals, who claimed coercion. Five months after Urban's election, they rejected him and elected Clement VII (1378–1394), who went back to Avignon. The two popes had their own cardinals, curial staffs, and adherents among the faithful. A council was held at Pisa in 1409 to resolve the problem, but instead still another pope was elected, Alexander V, who in less than a year was succeeded by John XXIII (1410–1415). The general council of Constance (1414–1418) confronted the scandal of three would-be popes and pledged to reform the church in head and members. Unity was restored with the election of Martin V (1417–1431). The council deposed both Benedict XIII (1394–1423) of Avignon and John XXIII of Pisa; Gregory XII (1406–1415) of the Roman line abdicated. What makes the Council of Constance important in the history of the papacy is the theological principle that dictated its actions, namely conciliarism, enunciated in the council's decree *Haec sancta*, the dogmatic validity of which is still debated. The theory of conciliarism, that a general council is the supreme organ of government in the church, was later condemned by several popes, but it did not die. It resurfaced again in the seventeenth and eighteenth centuries in the form of Gallicanism and Febronianism.

FROM THE RENAISSANCE TO THE ENLIGHTENMENT. Papal authority was severely challenged between the fifteenth and eighteenth centuries. It had to face the massive religious and societal repercussions brought about by the Renaissance, the Protestant Reformation, and the Enlightenment.

The Renaissance. Martin V tried to fulfill the provisions of the decree *Frequens* (1417) that emanated from the Council of Constance, which mandated that a general council should be held in five years, another seven years later, and then one regularly every ten years. He convened a council at Siena that later moved to Pavia (1423–1424), but the plague forced its dissolution. Seven years later another council was held, meeting first at Basel and later at Ferrara and Florence (1431–1445), under Eugene IV (1431–1447). Greek and Latin prelates attended, and they were able to agree on several thorny doctrinal issues including the primacy of the pope. The decree *Laetentur caeli* (1439), the first dogmatic definition of papal primacy by a council, stated: "We define that the holy apostolic see and the Roman Pontiff have primacy over the whole world, and that the same Roman Pontiff is the successor of Saint Peter, prince of the Apostles, the true vicar of Christ, the head of the church." Unfortunately, the union between the Greeks and Rome was short-lived.

Nicholas V (1447–1455) and his successors made Rome a center of the arts and scholarship. Humanistic concerns and involvement in Italian politics dominated their pontificates. Pius II (1458–1464), one of the most notable examples of papal humanism, in the bull *Exsecrabilis* (1460) prohibited any appeals to future general councils, thus striking at conciliarism. The same oligarchic spirit of the earlier Avignon cardinals appeared again at the election of Paul II (1464–1471). The cardinals drew up a capitulation requiring consultation with them before any major papal appointment, but after his election Paul promptly rejected this limitation. Sixtus IV (1471–1484) concerned himself mostly with the restoration of Rome and the expansion of the Papal States; he is responsible for building the magnificent Sistine Chapel in the Vatican. The Borgian pope, Alexander VI (1492–1503), has gone down in history as one of the most notorious of the Renaissance popes although his exploits have been exaggerated. The papacy, moreover, was engaged in almost continual warfare. The most famous of the warrior popes was Julius II (1503–1513), known as Il Terribile. A capable and energetic leader, Julius became the patron of Michelangelo, Raphael, and Bramante; he commissioned the construction of the new basilica of Saint Peter's. Adrian VI (1522–1523) was an exception among the Renaissance popes; in his short pontificate he tried to introduce reform measures, but these met persistent opposition from both civil rulers and highly placed ecclesiastics. In sum, the Renaissance popes were generally more interested in politics, the arts, and the ostentatious display of wealth than in providing genuine religious leadership. Their artistic achievements were outstanding, their neglect of spiritual concerns tragic.

The Reformation and Counter-Reformation. By the beginning of the sixteenth century the papacy was severely weakened by internal decay and a loss of supernatural vision. The faithful throughout Europe were asked to contribute alms to the extravagant building projects in Rome. These factors, coupled with deep-seated religious, social, and economic unrest in Europe, set the stage for the Protestant Reformation. Martin Luther's challenge in 1517 caught the papacy unprepared. Leo X (1513–1521) and his successors badly underestimated the extent and intensity of antipapal sentiment in Europe. The popes neither adequately comprehended the religious intentions of Luther nor understood the appeal that the reformers' ideas had for many who were outraged at both the policies and the conduct of church leaders. What began in the Reformation as a movement to restore genuine apostolic integrity to the church of Rome ended with the creation of a separate church. Luther, Calvin, and Zwingli eventually repudiated all papal claims. By the time of Clement VII (1523–1534), millions of Catholics in Germany, Scandinavia, the Low Countries, Switzerland, and Britain had departed from the Roman communion. A new era in church history had dawned.

The rapid rise of Protestantism had a sobering effect on the papacy: It forced the popes to concentrate on church affairs. Paul III (1534–1549), for example, appointed competent cardinals to administrative posts, authorized the establishment of the Society of Jesus (1540), and reformed the Roman Inquisition (1542). The church's most wide-ranging answer to the Protestant Reformation was the Council of Trent (1545–1563), convoked by Paul III and concluded by Pius IV (1559–1565). In its twenty-five sessions, the council discussed the authority of scripture and of tradition, original sin and justification, the sacraments, and specific reform legislation. It did not, strangely enough, treat explicitly the theology of the church or the papacy. The council refused to accept demands for a married clergy, Communion under both species, and a vernacular liturgy. The principles of conciliarism did not affect the Council of Trent, at which the reigning popes were in control of the proceedings.

One of the effects of the Tridentine reform was a reorganization of the church's central administrative system. The Curia Romana, which had existed, at least functionally, since the first century, was plagued by nepotism, greed, and abuse of authority. Sixtus V (1585–1590), who was committed to a reform of the Curia, established fifteen congregations of cardinals to carry out church administration. The popes endeavored to consider moral character and ability in selecting cardinals, whose number was set at seventy in 1588. Under Gregory XIII (1572–1585), papal nuncios to Catholic countries proved most valuable in implementing the ideals of Trent and in supervising the activities of the local bishops. For forty years after Trent, zealous popes strengthened papal authority and prestige. They increased centralization, mandated uniformity in liturgical ritual, and renewed priestly life and seminary training. The bishops of dioceses, who now had to submit regular reports to Rome and visit it at specified intervals, became much less independent. The success of the Counter-Reformation resulted from sound papal governance and the extraordinary contributions of the Jesuits and other religious orders. Yet union with the Protestants was not accomplished; the Christian church in the West had a divided membership.

Seventeenth and eighteenth centuries. The papacy had to face new problems caused by radical shifts in the political and intellectual climate of Europe during the seventeenth and eighteenth centuries. Skepticism, rationalism, and secularism became pervasive during the Enlightenment, and many intellectuals were violently opposed to the Catholic church and the papacy. As a result, the popes were often on the defensive. In actions reminiscent of the medieval papacy, Paul V (1605–1621) in 1605, in the wake of the Gunpowder Plot, forbade Catholics to take a loyalty oath to the king of England, and in 1607 he put Venice under interdict—a penalty largely ignored. The lengthy and often acrimonious debate between Dominicans and Jesuits over grace and free will, a question not settled at Trent, was terminated during Paul's reign. In 1597 Clement VIII (1592–1605) had established a special papal commission (the Congregatio de Auxiliis) to examine the orthodoxy of the two views. Paul received the final report, and in 1607 he declared that both orders could defend their positions, that neither side should censure the opposite opinion, and that all should await the final decision of the Holy See. This decision has not yet been made.

The Thirty Years War (1618–1648), a series of religious and dynastic wars that involved most of Europe, embroiled the papacy in conflict. Paul V and Gregory XV (1621–1623) had little influence on the conduct of Catholic rulers. Innocent X (1644–1655) protested, albeit futilely, against the Peace of Westphalia (1648), because he felt that Catholics were treated unjustly. This war and its aftermath showed how ineffective the papacy had become in European politics. The spirit of patriotism contributed to the problem. Furthermore, conciliarism revived in France in the form of Gallicanism, in Germany in the form of Febronianism, and in Austria in the form of Josephism. Although each of these movements had its own particular characteristics, all had two things in common: a strong nationalistic feeling and an antipapal bias. All reflected resentment of Roman centralism, urged greater autonomy for national churches, and advocated state control of ecclesiastical matters. The Holy See had also to contend with the absolutist ambitions of Louis XIV of France. Innocent XI (1676–1689) engaged in a protracted struggle with Louis over the king's claim to the right of revenues from vacant benefices (the *régale*) and over royal support of Gallicanism. Innocent's major achievement was his diplomatic role in preventing the fall of Vienna to the Turks in 1683, thus halting Muslim expansion into Europe.

During the following decades the popes were active in many areas. Innocent XII (1691–1700) forbade nepotism and Clement XII (1730–1740) condemned Freemasonry. Benedict XIV (1740–1758) finally ended the so-called Chinese and Malabar rites controversy, which had lasted nearly two centuries. Jesuit missionaries in China and South India had adapted certain indigenous customs and rites to Christianity. Benedict XIV condemned this practice and required the missionaries to take an oath rejecting the rites. The oath remained in force until the pontificate of Pius XII (1939–1958).

In the theological area, Innocent X repudiated five propositions on the theology of grace found in the writings of the Flemish bishop Cornelis Jansen; Alexander VII (1655–1667) rejected laxism as a moral system; and Alexander VIII (1689–1691) acted similarly against rigorism. The spiritual teaching of Quietism also received papal disapproval, when Innocent XII proscribed the views of Miguel de Molinos. The most dramatic papal action of the eighteenth century occurred when Clement XIV (1769–1774), bending to pressure from the Bourbon monarchies and fearing possible schism in France and Spain, suppressed the Society of Jesus in 1773.

THE MODERN PERIOD. Dramatic shifts in the prestige and authority of the papacy have occurred between the era of the French Revolution and the twentieth century. The popes of this period, faced with the demanding challenges of a new age, have attempted to restore their spiritual authority.

Revolution and restoration. The French Revolution, which began in 1789, and the subsequent actions of Napoleon created a new political order in Europe that adversely affected the Roman Catholic church. With nationalistic fervor, France's new revolutionary government became an instrument of dechristianization, secularization, and anticlericalism. Pius VI (1775–1799), who had little sympathy with the ideals of the revolution, was unable to deal effectively with such vehement defiance of the Holy See and such massive threats to the very existence of religion. At times it seemed as if the papacy itself would be destroyed. The octogenarian and infirm Pius was taken prisoner by Napoleon and died in exile on his way to Paris. Resistance to Napoleonic aggression continued during the pontificate of Pius VII (1800–1823). The Concordat of 1801 with Napoleon, which for over a century regulated the relationship between France and the church, revealed that Pius was willing to make concessions for the sake of peace. Yet in 1809 Napoleon captured Rome, annexed the Papal States, and arrested the pope and held him prisoner until 1814. The Catholic restoration began after the defeat of Napoleon: the Congress of Vienna (1814–1815) returned most of the papal territory to the church, and in 1814 Pius restored the Society of Jesus.

The fall of the monarchy in France and its impact on the rest of Europe weakened Gallicanism, Febronianism, and Josephism. Ultramontanism—a propapal movement that began early in the nineteenth century—advocated greater centralization of church government and a vigorous exercise of papal primacy. It gained strength under Gregory XVI (1831–1846), who opposed all revolutionary movements and defended papal primacy, infallibility, and the independence of the church from the state. A great missionary pope, Gregory fully controlled Catholic mission work.

The thirty-two-year pontificate of Pius IX (1846–1878), the longest in history, was significant. Initially hailed as a liberal, he soon showed his advocacy of ultramontanism. Pius believed that rationalism and secularism eroded both the faith and human society, and he considered a constitutional government for the Papal States to be a threat to the independence of the Holy See. Although many of his ideas isolated the church from the world, he gave the Roman Catholic faithful, with whom he was immensely popular, a new sense of spiritual identity. He restored the Catholic hierarchies of England (1850) and the Netherlands (1853), began a renewal of Marian devotion by his definition of the Immaculate Conception of Mary (1854), and supported extensive missionary activity. His greatest disappointment was the loss of the Papal States in 1870, which ended a millennium of temporal sovereignty. The popes became voluntary prisoners in the Vatican for the next sixty years. Pius's greatest triumph was the First Vatican Council (1869–1870), which ended abruptly when Italian troops occupied Rome. It produced two constitutions: *Dei filius*, a reaffirmation of the centrality of revelation, and *Pastor aeternus*, a definition of papal primacy and infallibility.

Vatican I and modernity. The most formal and detailed exposition of papal prerogatives is found in *Pastor aeternus*. In regard to primacy it taught that Jesus conferred upon Peter a primacy of both honor and jurisdiction; that by divine right Peter has perpetual successors in primacy over the universal church; that the Roman pontiff is the successor of Peter and has supreme, ordinary (not delegated), and immediate power and jurisdiction over the church and its members; and that the Roman pontiff is the supreme judge who is not subject to review by anyone. In regard to infallibility, Vatican I taught that by divine assistance the pope is immune from error when he speaks *ex cathedra*—that is, when "by virtue of his supreme apostolic authority he defines a doctrine concerning faith or morals to be held by the universal church." Such definitions are "irreformable of themselves and not from the consent of the church." This last phrase is directed against Gallicanism, even though by 1870 it was no longer a major problem. The formidable conception of the papacy at Vatican I was a victory for ultramontanism. Using juridical and monarchical language, it asserted the universal spiritual authority of the pope. The council, however, did not, because of its premature termination, present the papacy within the full context of the theology of the church, and it failed to discuss the relationship between the pope and the bishops.

The popes between Vatican I and Vatican II, individuals of superior quality, had much in common. First, they were all committed to the spiritual restoration of Catholicism, using their magisterial and jurisdictional authority to that end. A profusion of encyclical letters, addresses, and disciplinary decrees helped shape Catholic thought. Second, the popes continued to centralize church administration in Rome by increasing the power of the Roman Curia and the diplomatic corps. The movement toward uniformity in theology, liturgy, and law discouraged particularism. Third, the papal office actively promoted missionary endeavors; newly converted Catholics and immigrants to North America displayed great loyalty to the Holy See. Fourth, the popes, at times reluctantly and unsuccessfully, tried to respond to the demands of a changing world. They sought amicable relations with secular governments, especially through concordats, and worked devotedly for social justice and peace.

The popes of this period continued the ultramontanist policies of the nineteenth century, but with a difference. Leo XIII (1878–1903), for example, was more open to the positive aspects of modernity. Although he denied the validity of Anglican priestly orders in 1896, he was a pioneer in ecumenism. He supported the revival of Thomism (*Aeterni patris*, 1879), encouraged Catholic biblical studies (*Providentissimus Deus*, 1893), and presented the church's position on labor (*Rerum novarum*, 1891). His successor, Pius X (1903–1914), desired to renew the interior life of the church, as is shown by his teachings on the Eucharist, the liturgy, and seminary education. The most serious crisis he faced was modernism—a complex movement supported by Catholic thinkers in France, England, Germany, and Italy who sought to adapt Catholic doctrine to contemporary intellectual trends. Calling modernism "the synthesis of all heresies," Pius condemned it in *Pascendi* (1907). During World War I, the complete impartiality of Benedict XV (1914–1922) brought criticism from all sides. In 1917 he promulgated the first Code of Canon Law. The pope of the interwar years was Pius XI (1922–1939), noted for his encyclicals on marriage (*Casti connubii*, 1930) and social thought (*Quadragesimo anno*, 1931), for his promotion of missionary work, and most importantly, for concluding the Lateran Pacts (1929). Under these pacts Italy recognized the temporal sovereignty of the pope over Vatican City. Finally, Pius XII (1939–1958), a trained diplomat with broad interests, addressed almost every aspect of church life, and in a prodigious number of pronouncements applied Catholic doctrine to contemporary problems. In *Humani generis* (1950), Pius XII gave a wide-ranging critique of the theology that followed World War II. Although he encouraged theological speculation, he reaffirmed, for example, the traditional Catholic interpretation of creation, original sin, and transubstantiation and warned against the relativizing of dogma, the neglect of the teaching authority of the church *(magisterium)*, and scriptural exegesis that ignored the tradition of the church. Under Pius, the modern papacy reached an unprecedented level of respect.

Vatican II and postconciliar developments. John XXIII (1958–1963), elected when he was nearly seventy-seven, began a new era for Roman Catholicism. His open style of papal leadership, enhanced by his appealing personality, was warmly welcomed by Catholics and non-Catholics alike. Although he is well known for his efforts in promoting ecumenism and world peace (*Pacem in terris*, 1963), the pope's greatest accomplishment was the unexpected convocation of the Second Vatican Council (1962–1965). John designed the council to foster reform and reunion, believing that a contemporary reformulation of the Christian tradition would revitalize the Catholic church and ultimately benefit all humankind. Paul VI (1963–1978) skillfully maintained the council's pastoral orientation. To implement its program, he established the Synod of Bishops, internationalized and increased the number of cardinals, reformed the Curia, and promoted liturgical reform. He made nine trips outside Italy.

Vatican II supplied what was lacking in Vatican I. Its doctrine of collegiality described the relationship between the pope and the bishops. The Constitution on the Church (*Lumen gentium*) stated: "Together with its head, the Roman Pontiff, and never without this head, the episcopal order is the subject of supreme and full power in relation to the universal church. But this power can be exercised only with the consent of the Roman Pontiff" (Article 22). The college of bishops, then, exists only under the leadership of the pope, himself a bishop. The pope is not the executor of the bishops' wishes (Gallicanism), nor are the bishops vicars of the pope (papal absolutism). Both the papacy and the episcopacy have their own legitimate authority, and the purpose of collegiality is to unite the bishops with the pope. Yet there remains the difficult theological problem of reconciling papal primacy with episcopal authority. Many theologians argue that there is only one subject of supreme authority in the church—the college of bishops—and that it can operate in two ways: through a collegial action or through a personal act of the pope as head of the college. Thus every primatial action of the pope is always collegial. The council did not establish any legal norms that would require the pope to consult with the bishops, but nevertheless it posed the moral ideal of cooperation and collaboration that should govern the relationship between the pope and the bishops.

The theory of collegiality has altered the style of papal leadership, making it far less monarchical. The closer relationship between the pope and the bishops is best exemplified by the Synod of Bishops, a consultative body that meets once every three years. Collegiality has made the papacy less objectionable to other Christians since it fosters the idea of authority as service and not domination. This aspect has been noted in the fifth dialogue of the Lutheran-Roman Catholic discussions (1974) and in the Final Report of the Anglican-Roman Catholic International Commission (1982). Both groups recognized the value of a universal Petrine ministry of unity in the Christian church and foresaw the possibility of the bishop of Rome exercising that function for all Christians in the future.

Vatican II significantly changed the Catholic Church. Along with progressive reforms, however, there were also reactions that resulted in doctrinal and disciplinary confusion. Thousands of priests and nuns left the active ministry, and some misguided experiments occurred. Dissent over Paul VI's prohibition against artificial birth control in *Humanae vitae* (1968) caused acute pastoral problems and raised serious questions about the credibility of the papal office.

In 1978 two popes died and two were elected. The pontificate of John Paul I, the successor of Paul VI, lasted only thirty-three days. Breaking a tradition that had endured for more than nine hundred years, John Paul I was not installed by a rite of coronation or enthronement. He rejected the obvious symbols of temporal and monarchical authority and was inaugurated at a solemn mass. Instead of the tiara, he was given the pallium, a white woolen stole symbolizing his spiritual and pastoral ministry. His successor, John Paul II, became the first non-Italian pope in 456 years, the first Polish pope, and the first pope from a Communist country. The most-traveled pope in history, John Paul II earned huge popular appeal with his international pastoral visits. As of May 2003, he had made ninty-nine trips outside of Italy. He personalized the papal office to an extent never before attempted. He had also written fourteen encyclicals, three of which were devoted to social justice and peace, major themes in his teaching: *Laboren exercens* (1981); *Sollicitudo rei socialis* (1987), and *Centesimus annus* (1991). One of the main goals of his pontificate has been the restoration of traditional Roman Catholicism and the promotion of Christian unity. Uneasy with theological dissent (he has censured some theologians), moral laxity, and arbitraty innovations, John Paul II has taken forceful steps to invigorate the Catholic Church. In 1983 he promulgated the revised Code of Canon Law. In an effort to encourage collegiality, he has presided over twenty-one international Synods of Bishops. In October 2003 at the age of eighty-three he celebrated the twenty-fifth anniversary of his election to the papacy. He has survived two assasination attempts and has become severly affected by Parkinson's disease. John Paul II will undoubtably be judged as one of the most illustrious holders of the Chair of Peter.

The papacy has had a complex but intriguing history. For nearly two millennia, showing remarkable resiliency, it has continued through times of growth and decline, glory and shame, internal and external conflicts, and radical social upheavals. In an age of widespread unbelief and unsettling technological change, the papacy can work to rekindle the spiritual aspirations of humanity.

See Also Canon; Church; Councils, article on Christian Councils; Crusades, article on Christian Perspective; Ecumenical Movement; Gallicanism; Inquisition, The; Modernism, article on Christian Modernism; Reformation; Schism, article on Christian Schism; Trent, Council of; Ultramontanism; Vatican Councils.

Bibliography

Historical Works

Two standard works on papal history are Johannes Haller's *Das Papsttum: Idee und Wirklichkeit*, 5 vols. (1950–1953; reprint, Esslingen am Neckar, 1962), and Franz Xaver Seppelt's *Geschichte der Päpste von den Anfängen bis zur Mitte des zwan-*

zigsten Jahrhunderts, 5 vols. (Munich, 1954–1959). Dated in some respects but still very useful are two monumental studies: Horace K. Mann's *The Lives of the Popes in the Early Middle Ages*, 18 vols. in 19, 2d ed. (London, 1925–1969), which covers the period from 590 to 1304; and Ludwig von Pastor's *The History of the Popes from the Close of the Middle Ages*, 40 vols. (London, 1891–1953), which concerns the years from 1305 to 1799. Walter Ullmann's *A Short History of the Papacy in the Middle Ages* (London, 1972) and Guillaume Mollat's *The Popes at Avignon, 1305–1378*, translated from the 9th French edition by Janet Love (London, 1963), can be recommended. The papacy in the eighteenth, nineteenth, and twentieth centuries is discussed in Owen Chadwick's *The Popes and European Revolution* (Oxford, 1981); Roger Aubert's *Le pontificat de Pie IX, 1846–1878*, 2d ed. (Paris, 1964); and J. Derek Holmes's *The Papacy in the Modern World, 1914–1978* (New York, 1981). More recent histories of the papacy and of the popes include: J. N. D. Kelly, *The Oxford Dictionary of Popes* (Oxford, N.Y., 1986); Eamon Duffy, *Saints and Sinners: A History of the Popes* (New Haven, Conn., 1997); Richard P. McBrien, *Lives of the Popes: The Pontiffs from St. Peter to John Paul II* (New York, 1997); and Bruno Steiner and Michael G. Parkers, eds., *Dictionary of Popes and the Papcy* (New York, 2001). General histories of the church contain much information on the papal office. One of the most comprehensive and reliable is *Histoire de l'Église depuis les origines jusqu'à nos jours*, 21 vols. (Paris, 1934–1964), edited by Augustin Fliche et al. There is valuable material on papal documentation in Carl Mirbt's *Quellen zur Geschichte des Papsttums und des Rö-mischen Katholizismus*, 5th ed. (1895; reprint, Tübingen, 1934), and James T. Shotwell and Louise R. Loomis's *The See of Peter* (New York, 1927).

Theological Works

An analysis of the biblical evidence is found in Raymond E. Brown et al., *Peter in the New Testament* (Minneapolis, 1973). For a detailed study of the theology of the papacy see my two works, *The Papacy in Transition* (Garden City, N. Y., 1980), and *The Church Limits of the Papacy: Authority and Autonomy in the Church* (New York, 1987). Both books contain full bibliographies. Various theological points are discussed in *Papal Primacy in the Church, Concilium*, vol. 64 (New York, 1971), edited by Hans Küng; in Karl Rahner and Joseph Ratzinger's *The Episcopate and the Primacy* (New York, 1962); in Gustave Thils's *La primauté pontificale* (Gembloux, 1972); and in Jean-Marie R. Tillard's *The Bishop of Rome* (Wilmington, Del., 1983). For a discussion of the ecumenical dimension of the papacy, see *Das Papstamt: Dienst oder Hindernis für die Ökumene?* (Regensburg, 1985), by Vasilios von Aristi et al. Excellent articles on the same topic are contained in the following: *Papal Primacy and the Universal Church* (Minneapolis, 1974), edited by Paul C. Empie and T. Austin Murphy; *Teaching Authority and Infallibility in the Church* (Minneapolis, 1980), edited by Paul C. Empie et al.; *The Anglican-Roman Catholic International Commission: The Final Report, Windsor, Sept. 1981* (London, 1982); and John Meyendorff et al., *The Primacy of Peter* (London, 1963).

PATRICK GRANFIELD (1987 AND 2005)

PARABLES AND PROVERBS.

Proverbs are brief, memorable sayings that offer ethical direction in specific situations from generation to generation. They are a feature of almost all cultures, historically, as well as today. The proverb is tailor-made for primary oral cultures where, with no system of inscription, what cannot be remembered is lost, but even in contemporary literary cultures new sayings continue to be coined. A parable is a more expansive cousin to the proverb. It is a short narrative fiction that expresses a moral or religious lesson. Like the proverb, parables are memorable and inspire listener participation: applying the parable to situations in one's daily life.

KEY FEATURES OF PROVERBS. Proverbs arise out of the experience and observation of repeated patterns in daily life. A famous definition attributed to Miguel de Cervantes holds that "a proverb is a short sentence founded upon long experience." Proverbs are useful in contexts outside of their time and place of origin, most often serving to inculcate traditional values of self-control, hard work, and cautious speech. They are, however, also capable of subverting traditional wisdom. A proverb which, though of rather recent coinage, reflects traditional values, "Life is short, play hard," is subverted by "Life is short, pray hard."

A key quality of a proverb is that it is able to transcend the situation of its origins to illuminate situations in the lives of contemporary hearers. This ability is ascribable to several linguistic features. They include brevity, generalized syntax, and vivid imagery. Many proverbs employ metaphor and imagery: "A city set on a hill cannot be hid." Nonmetaphorical proverbs are often called maxims ("What can't be cured must be endured"), whereas widely known sayings whose author we know are called aphorisms.

Proverbs are context-transcending on account of their inclusion of several memorable features of oral communication. These include repetition ("All's well that ends well"), alliteration and rhyming ("Haste makes waste"), use of opposites, ("What goes up must come down"), and use of the present tense. From this context-transcending quality comes the eloquent anonymous definition of the proverb as "a winged word, outliving the fleeting moment."

Nonetheless, proverbs express only a partial truth appropriate for certain situations and not for others. As proverbs scholar Alan Dundes points out in *Folklore Matters* (1989), proverbs are a genre that expresses the worldviews of the social group from which they come. Paremiologist (collector and analyst of proverbs) Wolfgang Mieder, in his extensive research on American proverbs, has explored the ways in which sayings like "The grass is always greener on the other side," "Money talks," and "There's more where that came from" convey much about, respectively, American discontent, the tendency to reduce everything to its monetary value, and the belief in limitless abundance. In the United States, proverbs often express and inculcate the secular gospel that initiative and self-reliance lead to the good life, defined narrowly as financial prosperity: "Do unto others before they do unto you"; "It's no sin to be rich"; "If you need a helping hand, look on the end of your arm." In any culture, proverbs, though brief, are by no means innocuous. They both reflect and shape how we experience our world.

African Proverbs. More than a thousand languages are spoken in Africa, and proverbs have been found in every African language studied so far. African proverbs often employ animal metaphors and point out the foibles of human conduct: "The higher the ape climbs the more he shows his tail" (Yoruba proverb). Historically, proverbs have been the most important expression of human wisdom and knowledge of nature, psychology, and reality for the traditional cultures of Africa. They cover topics such as family relationships, luck, and survival by one's wits in a harsh environment. They are used for teaching and correcting the young and for consoling the suffering.

Jan Knappert, in *The A–Z of African Proverbs* (1989), points out that, even among the literate peoples of Africa, such as the Zulus, the Yorubas, the Swahili, and the North African Arabs, proverbs are a vital part of conversation in everyday life, conveying the condensed experience of past generations. The function of proverbs in some African societies is so fundamental that no negotiations can take place without them (Knappert, 1989, p. 6).

In his book *Swahili Proverbs* (1997), Knappert points out that religious proverbs are especially prevalent among the Swahili. Many of their proverbs refer to the rituals and philosophy of Islam: "God does not forget the hour" (meaning the hour of death, prayers, or other duties that people tend to forget); "Mortal man cannot erase what has been written," meaning that God has written down our fate and destiny in a secret Book in Heaven. The Swahili view this life as a preparation for the next: "Happiness is obeying God's will, for following His law will open the gates of Paradise." Many Swahili proverbs stress the importance of avoiding dangerous habits and the value of trusting in God (Knappert, 1997, p.21).

Religious proverbs are widely found among other African peoples as well. They emphasize the sovereignty of God: "There is no appeal against an act of God" (Kenya); "Planning is man's, doing is God's" (Yoruba); "God does not sleep" (Congo). Another theme is God's care for the helpless: "God will prevent flies from stinging the tailless cow" (Yoruba); "God does not put a brave man to shame" (Somali). Yet another is the need for human action and our accountability for what we do: "God gave us the seed of every plant, but we must sow it" (Zande); "God will not save the man who breaks the ties of brotherhood and friendship" (Guinea) (Knappert, 1989, pp. 52–53).

Henry H. Mitchell and Nicholas C. Cooper-Lewter, in their book *Soul Theology* (1986), point out that brief sayings and lines from scripture, hymns, and spirituals were used proverbially in the religion of the slave quarters among Africans transported to America during the fifteenth through nineteenth centuries. They expressed trust in God the Creator, who gives the people strength to cope with their suffering. Many of these sayings persist in African American communities today. For example, the goodness of God and creation is expressed in the proverb, "Well, I wouldn't take nothing for my journey now." The omnipotence of God is expressed in the saying, "My God is so high, you can't git over him; He's so low, you can't git under him; He's so wide, you can't git around him" (Mitchell and Cooper-Lewter, 1986, p. 44). Such proverbial wisdom informs the autobiographical reflections of contemporary poet and novelist Maya Angelou.

Native American Proverbs. Native American proverbs reflect reverence for the earth, concern the gifts and expectations of the Great Spirit, and outline the types of conduct that should be avoided or embraced: "It is easy to be brave from a distance" (Omaha); "We will be known forever by the tracks we leave" (Dakota); "Each person is his own judge" (Shawnee); "The Great Spirit is always angry with those who shed innocent blood" (Iowa); "Dreams count, the Spirits have pitied us and guided us" (Cree); "The Rainbow is a sign of Him who is in all things" (Hopi); "God gives us each a song" (Ute). The worldview constructed by Native American proverbs is one in which personal and communal harmony is achieved when individuals live in harmony with the Great Spirit. That plays itself out in words and actions that evince a respect for the sacredness of nature, animals, and other human beings. Such a manner of living is undergirded by the realization that one is responsible for one's actions in the present that form one's legacy for the future.

Proverbs and Parables in World Religions. Proverbial discourse characterizes the sacred writings of a broad spectrum of world religions, including Bahāʾī, Buddhism, Confucianism, Hinduism, Islam, Jainism, Judaism, Christianity, Shintoism, Sikhism, Sufism, and Daoism (see Griffin, 1991, for a broad sampling of religious proverbs). Major religious texts in which proverbs play an essential part include the *Analects* (Confucianism), the *Dhammapada* (Buddhism), the Qurʾān (Islam), the Upaniṣads (Hinduism), Ibn ʿAṭāʾ Allāh's *The Book of Wisdom* (Sufism), the Hebrew Scriptures and Talmud (Judaism), the *Dao de jing* (Daoism), the *Nihongi* (Shintoism), the *Gurū Granth Sāhib* and the songs of Kabīr (Sikhism), and the Old and New Testaments (Christianity).

The proverbs embedded in these sacred writings commend attitudes and actions that align one's life with the presence of the divine and lead to individual and communal harmony. On some topics, their advice sounds remarkably similar. For example, a compilation of proverbs from various world religions lists twenty-four versions of the Golden Rule ("Treat others as you would like to be treated") (Griffin, 1991, pp. 67–69).

Likewise parables are a form found across the board in various religions of the world. They are often reported as having been uttered by the religion's founder. Like proverbs, they express aspects of the worldview of that particular religion and offer guidance to individuals wishing to become disciples.

CONFUCIAN PROVERBS. Buddhism, both in India and Japan, featured proverbs that spark questions rather than provide answers: "When you reach the top, keep climbing"; "When you are ready to learn, a teacher will appear." However, no religion has given a more central role to proverbs than Confucianism. Confucius, born in China in 551 BCE, taught moral ideals through sayings and anecdotes in an attempt to redress the ill effects of the social anarchy that plagued his country: "Human beings are by nature good"; "What you do not wish done to yourself, do not do to others"; "Do not wish for quick results, nor look for small advantages." Confucius's sayings commend a mature respect for others: "Measure the feelings of others by one's own"; "Approach others not asking 'What can I get from you?' But 'How can I accommodate you?'." They also encourage the honorable fulfillment of one's social roles, moderation in personal habits ("nothing to excess"), and respecting others in familial relationships, especially the aged ("The duty of children to their parents is the fountain from which all virtues spring"). Confucius and his followers believed that a society could thrive peaceably if it abided by these guidelines. Their teachings developed an intellectual, philosophical, and spiritual foundation for familial and social dealings. Generations of Chinese school children have memorized his sayings and stories (see Smith, 1994, pp. 102–111). Half a century after Confucius's death, his disciples compiled dialogues between the Master and his disciples in the *Analects (Lunyu).*

PROVERBS AND PARABLES OF THE HEBREW PEOPLE. The Hebrew people were by no means the only Ancient Near Eastern people to cherish proverbs. In fact, scholars have long noted the evident debt *Proverbs* 22:17–24:22 owes to the *Instruction of Amenemope,* an Egyptian wisdom collection (Murphy, 1990, p. 23).

Proverbs occur most frequently in what is known as the wisdom literature of the Hebrew Bible, a genre whose focus is on practical strategies for daily living in the present. In the last quarter of the twentieth century, biblical scholars of both the Old and New Testaments began to pay more attention to wisdom genres.

Hebrew biblical wisdom literature is primarily identified with the books of *Job, Proverbs,* and *Ecclesiastes.* Proverbs and parables in the Hebrew Scriptures are a subset of a wisdom genre that comes under the heading of the Hebrew noun *mashal,* the root of which (*m-sh-l*) means "to be like" (Scott, 1989, p. 9). This term is used in the Hebrew Scriptures to refer to a number of literary forms that arise from the close observation of daily life and are characterized by vivid, evocative language. These forms include similitudes, popular sayings, literary aphorisms, taunt songs, bywords, riddles, allegories, and short narrative fictions or parables. The proverb, a wisdom sentence based on observation of experience, is the most common form of *mashal* in the Hebrew Bible. It is far more common there than the parable.

The *Book of Proverbs,* traditionally ascribed to Solomon, is a collection of wisdom sayings culled from hundreds of years of Jewish experience. Proverbs represents the wisdom passed down by the older and wiser to the young, and emphasize attitudes and behaviors that make for communal harmony and order. Such proverbs are often antithetical in their form—that is, they oppose wise and foolish behavior in the sharpest of terms: "A wise child makes a glad father, but the foolish despise their mothers" (*Prov.* 15:20). They may also express the superiority of wisdom to folly: "Better is a dry morsel with quiet, that a house full of feasting with strife" (*Prov.* 17:1). They may also come in the form of rhetorical questions that beg an obvious answer: "Can fire be carried in the bosom without burning one's clothes?" (*Prov.* 6:27). Yet another form is that of the beatitude, or statement of blessing. It affirms that wise activities bestow on the doer a condition of spiritual blessing: "Happy [or blessed] is the one who is never without fear, but one who is hard-hearted will fall into calamity" (*Prov.* 24:18).

Wise behavior includes measured speech, control of one's temper and appetites for food, drink, and sex, kindness to the poor, and avoidance of foolish companions: "A soft answer turns away wrath, but a harsh word stirs up anger" (*Prov.* 15:1); "Can one walk on hot coals without scorching the feet?" (*Prov.* 6:28); "One who is slow to anger is better than the mighty, and one whose temper is controlled than one who captures a city" (*Prov.* 16:32).

The parable is a narrative variation on the *mashal* theme, sharing the proverb's rootedness in daily life and its evocative language. No *mashal* in the Hebrew Bible, however, not even Ezekiel's tale of the eagle (*Ezek.* 17:3–10) or Nathan's warning to David (*2 Sam.* 12:1–6), offers an exact parallel, in terms of its narrative structure and purpose, to the parables of the New Testament Jesus.

RABBINIC PARABLES. In the literary work of the rabbis (second through fourth centuries CE), parables take center stage. They are narratives, usually told in the first person, that focus on the action of a main character and describe a general situation, not a specific past event. These vivid narratives were usually told to illuminate a particular verse in Scriptures. They do not normally include elements of paradox and hyperbole. The term *midrash* describes the body of exegesis of scriptural texts as well as the activity of interpretation as it was practiced during the third and fourth centuries CE.

Medieval Jewish philosophers employed the parable, most notably Moses Maimonides (1135/8–1204) in his "Parable of the Palace" (Stern, 1991, p. 226).

The literature of Qabbalah, Jewish mysticism as it developed in Spain in the thirteenth century, employed parables that mimicked earlier rabbinic parables in form, but were mystical and esoteric in content.

In the eighteenth and nineteenth centuries, Eastern European rabbis continued the rabbinic parabolic tradition. Three names associated with this tradition are Eliyyahu ben

Shelomoh Zalman (Vilna Gaon; 1720–1797), Maggid of Dubno (1740/41–1804), and Rabbi Naḥman of Bratslav (1772–1810) (see Naveh, 2000, pp. 107ff).

The Proverbs and Parables of Jesus. Jesus as a teacher of proverbs and parables is particularly emphasized in the *Gospel of Matthew.* Together, the Synoptic Gospels *(Matthew, Mark,* and *Luke)* contain over 102 proverbial sayings and 40 parables (see Carlston, 1980, pp. 87–105).

The proverbs. Jesus' proverbs do not counsel moderation or advocate seeking security. They eschew negative assessments of women as sources of temptation and trouble in life, to be avoided by the wise man. Jesus' most distinctive use of proverbs seems to be the way in which he infuses the traditional proverbial form with paradox and hyperbole. Sometimes he points to a dramatic future reversal of human conditions: "Many are first that will be last, and the last will be first" (*Mark* 10:31; *Matt.* 19:30; 20:16; *Luke* 13:30); "Whoever would be great among you must be your servant, and whoever would be first among you must be slave of all" (*Mark* 19:43–44; *Luke* 22:26; *Matt.* 20:26–27).

Jesus' distinctive wisdom voice seems to come through most clearly when he takes an antithesis or oppositional saying and intensifies it to the point that it equates opposites. The result is a paradox, a form (interestingly, absent from *Proverbs*) that goes to extremes to make a point: "Those who want to save their life will lose, and those who lose their life will save it" (*Luke* 17:33; *Mark* 8:35; *John* 12:25); "To those who have will more be given, but to those who have not, even what they have will be taken away" (*Luke* 8; 18; 12:48b; *Matt.* 13:12; *Mark* 4:25); "What is prized by humans is an abomination in the sight of God" (*Luke* 16:15b).

Jesus' beatitudes (*Matt.* 5:1–11; *Luke* 6:20–26) continue the pattern of pairing what is viewed as negative by conventional wisdom (being poor, mourning, being persecuted, being hungry and thirsty) with a state of blessedness. Jesus' versions of Old Testament admonitions are extreme, vivid, and specific, portraying a specific scene and making a command relative to it. In *Matthew's* sermon on the mount (chapters 5–7) such admonitions concerns judging others (*Matt.* 7:3–5), inward motives and outward behavior (*Matt.* 5:21–26; 5:27–30), retaliation (*Matt.* 5:39–42), and private piety and public opinion (*Matt.* 6:1–7).

Jesus also employs what some scholars have called "impossible questions" as part of his proverbial repertoire: "Which of you by being anxious can add one cubit to his span of life?" (*Matt.* 6:27; *Luke* 12:25); "What does it profit a man to gain the whole world and forfeit his life?" (*Mark* 8:35; *Matt.* 16:26; *Luke* 9:25).

The parables. Jesus' parables, like his aphorisms, subvert traditional wisdom by the use of paradox and hyperbole and make metaphorical connections between everyday life and a new reality, the kingdom of God (Scott, 1989, p. 14).

While parables can be allegories, stories in which everything stands for something else, recent parables scholars agree that parables are better described as narratives with metaphorical qualities. In his *Parables of the Kingdom* (1935), biblical scholar C. H. Dodd defined a parable as " a metaphor or simile drawn from nature or common life, arresting the hearer by its vividness or strangeness, and leaving the mind in sufficient doubt about its precise application to tease it into active thought" ([1935] 1961, p. 5).

Dodd's definition expresses the force of the New Testament parables: they are realistic, yet strange, metaphorical, paradoxical, challenging, and open-ended. The paradox in Jesus' parables lies in their strange twists, often an equation of something we normally think of as odd or negative with something positive—something, in fact, that points to an aspect of God's presence and power in the world: someone looked down on and despised is the one who acts as the neighbor (*Luke* 10:30–35); a wily steward's dubious business practices are commended to those who would enter the kingdom of God (*Luke* 16:18a); workers who work for one hour are paid the same as those who have worked all day (*Matt.* 20:1–15).

Proverbs and Parables in the Modern Era. Philosopher and theologian Søren Kierkegaard (1813–1855) considered parabolic communication an integral part of his philosophic method, which held that the truth is to be found in the process of reflection and appropriation of insights that arise from experience. His parables are intended to increase the reader's capacity for self-examination, leading in turn to increased moral sensitivity and intensified spirituality (Oden, 1978, p. xv). He ranks among the best of the great parabolists of the Western tradition.

Many poets, philosophers, and religious thinkers in modern Western culture have attached great importance to proverbial thinking. They include Blaise Pascal (1623–1662), Georg Christoph Lichtenberg (1742–1799), Jean Paul (Jean Paul Friedrich Richter; 1763–1825), Friedrich Nietzsche (1844–1900), Oscar Wilde (1854–1900), Franz Kafka (1883–1924), Karl Kraus (1874–1936), Paul Valéry (1871–1945), and Stanislaw Jerzy Lec (1909–1966). A deliberately proverbial style informs the work of Martin Buber (1878–1965), Abraham Joshua Heschel (1907–1972), and Norman O. Brown (1913–2002) (Williams, 1981, pp. 13–14).

Kahlil Gibran (1883–1931), the Lebanese philosopher, artist, and poet, expressed his insights in parables, most notably in the volume *The Madman: His Parables and Poems* (1918). Other recent parabolists include Argentinean novelist Jorge Luis Borges (1899–1986), Italian novelist and short story writer Italo Calvino (1923–1985), and Israeli novelist S. Y Agnon (1888–1970).

In the twentieth century Franz Kafka, through his parables, expressed the radical estrangement of human kind from the divine. One of his most famous parables is a story entitled "An Imperial Message," in which a message from a dying emperor symbolically represents his own impossible quest for knowledge (Naveh, 2000, p. 150).

Proverbs continue to be important bearers and shapers of meaning in more recent times. New proverbs, sometimes subversive versions of existing proverbs, are continually being coined. "A woman's place is in the home" has recently been subverted by "A woman's place is in the House and in the Senate!" The value of both proverbs and parables for the instruction of children and youth is appreciated across a spectrum of faiths and cultures. The continuing vitality of proverbs and parables in contemporary religions and cultures is a tribute to their pithy, poetic, participatory qualities.

See Also African Religions; Jesus; Kierkegaard, Søren; Literature, article on Literature and Religion; Rabbinic Judaism in Late Antiquity.

Bibliography

Proverbs

Beck, Charlotte J. *Everyday Zen: Love and Work.* San Francisco, 1989.

Camp, Claudia V. *Wisdom and the Feminine in the Book of Proverbs.* Sheffield, U.K., 1985.

Carlston, Charles E. "Proverbs, Maxims, and the Historical Jesus." *Journal of Biblical Literature* 99 (March 1980): 87–105.

Confucius. *The Analects of Confucius (Lun You).* Translated by Chichung Huang. Oxford, 1997.

Cordry, Harold V. *The Multicultural Dictionary of Proverbs: Over 20,000 Adages from More Than 120 Languages, Nationalities, and Ethnic Groups.* Jefferson, N.C., 1997.

Dundes, Alan. *Folklore Matters.* Knoxville, Tenn., 1989.

Griffin, Albert Kirby, ed. *Religious Proverbs: Over 1,600 Adages from 18 Faiths Worldwide.* Jefferson, N.C., 1991.

Knappert, Jan. *The A–Z of African Proverbs.* London, 1989.

Knappert, Jan. *Swahili Proverbs.* Burlington, Vt., 1997.

McKenzie, Alyce M. *Preaching Proverbs: Wisdom for the Pulpit.* Louisville, Ky., 1996.

Mieder, Wolfgang. *American Proverbs: A Study of Texts and Contexts.* New York, 1989.

Mieder, Wolfgang, ed. *The Prentice-Hall Encyclopedia of World Proverbs: A Treasury of Wit and Wisdom through the Ages.* Englewood Cliffs, N.J., 1986.

Mitchell, Henry H., and Nicholas C. Cooper-Lewter. *Soul Theology: The Heart of American Black Culture.* San Francisco, 1986.

Williams, James G. *Those Who Ponder Proverbs: Aphoristic Thinking and Biblical Literature.* Sheffield, U.K., 1981.

Zona, Guy. *Soul Would Have No Rainbow if the Eye Had No Tears and Other Native American Proverbs.* New York, 1994.

Parables

Burlingame, Eugene Watson, ed. and trans. *Buddhist Parables.* New Haven, Conn., 1922; reprint, Delhi, 1999.

Buttrick, David. *Speaking Parables: A Homiletic Guide.* Louisville, Ky., 2000.

Dodd, C. H. *Parables of the Kingdom.* London, 1935; rev. 2d ed., New York, 1961.

Feldman, Reynold, and Cynthia Voelke, eds. *A World Treasury of Folk Wisdom.* New York, 1992.

Herzog, William R., II. *The Parables as Subversive Speech: Jesus as Pedagogue of the Oppressed.* Louisville, Ky., 1994.

Murphy, Roland. *The Tree of Life: An Exploration of Biblical Wisdom Literature.* New York, 1990.

Naveh, Gila Safran. *Biblical Parables and Their Modern Re-Creations.* Albany, N.Y., 2000.

Oden, Thomas C., ed. *Parables of Kierkegaard.* Princeton, N.J., 1978.

Outcalt, Todd. *Candles in the Dark: A Treasury of the World's Most Inspiring Parables.* New York, 2002.

Scott, Bernard Brandon. *Hear Then the Parable: A Commentary on the Parables of Jesus.* Minneapolis, 1989.

Smith, Huston. *The Illustrated World's Religions: A Guide to Our Wisdom Traditions.* San Francisco, 1994.

Stern, David. *Parables in Midrash: Narrative and Exegesis in Rabbinic Literature.* Cambridge, Mass., 1991.

Tanahashi, Kazuaki, and Peter Levitt. *A Flock of Fools: Ancient Buddhist Tales of Wisdom and Laughter from the One Hundred Parable Sutra.* Translated by Tanahashi; adapted by Levitt. New York, 2004.

Wineman, Aryeh. *Beyond Appearances: Stories from the Kabbalistic Ethical Writings.* Philadelphia, 1988.

Wineman, Aryeh. *The Hasidic Parable.* Philadelphia, 2001.

Alyce M. McKenzie (2005)

PARACELSUS (1493?–1541) was a German alchemist, mystic, and physician. Philippus Aureolos Theophrastus Bombastus von Hohenheim was one of the most bizarre characters in the history of science. Commonly known as Paracelsus because in his own estimation he was greater than the great Greek physician Celsus, he was a paranoid, uncouth, abusive, and usually drunken genius, whose reputation varied widely. While his supporters dubbed him the "Luther of science," his detractors denounced him as a heretic and condemned him as the disreputable black magician who provided the model for Faust. His considerable writings offer a strange blend of medicine, religion, philosophy, cosmology, alchemy, magic, and astrology, a synthesis of natural and mystical philosophy typical of other writers before the scientific revolution separated science from religious and philosophical speculation.

Neither modest in presenting his opinions nor restrained in his language, Paracelsus launched an acrimonious attack on the medical and scientific establishment of his day. He rejected the prevailing Galenic theory that attributed disease to an imbalance of the four humors and replaced it with his own dynamic theory of diseases as specific entities attacking specific organs.

Paracelsus was an idealist and a visionary who considered chemistry the key to the universe. In his view, God was the divine alchemist who created the world by calcinating, congealing, distilling, and sublimating the elements of chaos. The alchemist had only to read the reactions in his laboratory on a grand scale to fathom the mysteries of creation. By turning alchemy away from gold-making, Paracelsus and his followers transformed it into a universal science of matter concerned with every aspect of material change.

Paracelsus's thought was shaped by both the Renaissance and the Reformation. Although he rejected the aesthetics and classicism of Renaissance humanists, he shared their anthropocentric and individualistic outlook. As Walter Pagel (1958, p. 36) has pointed out, there was a decentralizing tendency throughout Paracelsus's work. An enormous variety of noncorporeal forces (vital spirits, demons, subhumans, superhumans) work below the surface of the Paracelsian universe. Paracelsus drew his vitalist and pantheist ideas from the occult philosophies and sciences revived by Renaissance scholars—Neoplatonism, Gnosticism, Qabbalah, magic, alchemy, and astrology. The analogy between the macrocosm and the microcosm characteristic of these philosophies shaped Paracelsus's theory of knowledge. He rejected scholastic rationalism in favor of a kind of psychological empiricism. Because humans are the microcosm they contain within themselves all the elements of the greater world, or macrocosm. Knowledge therefore consists in an intuitive act of recognition, in which the knower and the known become one.

Because Paracelsus's theory of knowledge approximates Luther's doctrine of the "inner light," the two men have been compared. Each attacked established ideologies and institutions, wrote in the vernacular, and was a master of scurrilous invective. Both enjoyed theatrics: Luther burned the papal bull excommunicating him; Paracelsus burned the works of Galen and Ibn Sina (Avicenna). The comparison between the two men is, however, superficial. Luther preached the bondage of the human will, while Paracelsus was an ardent advocate of free will; Luther made grace the prerequisite of salvation, while Paracelsus emphasized charitable acts; Luther sided with sovereigns, while Paracelsus's sympathies remained with the people. Although Paracelsus was in contact with many reformers, sharing their criticism of church abuses, he eventually became disillusioned and charged that the reformers were as autocratic as their Catholic counterparts. Paracelsus's religious ideas were more compatible with nondogmatic reformers such as Hans Denck (1495?–1527) and Sebastian Franck (1499?–1542?).

Religion and philosophy provided the sources for both the progressive and the obscurantist aspect of Paracelsus's thought. His repudiation of reason led him to embrace empiricism; it also made much of his writing incomprehensible. On the basis of his vitalist philosophy, he rejected mechanical explanations of biological processes in favor of an organic, holistic approach that allowed for psychological factors. The same vitalism taken to extremes, however, resulted in proliferation of the number of active, independent forces to the point that classification became impossible and causality meaningless.

With his penchant for oracular and aphoristic statements, Paracelsus was more a prophet than a scientist. His most vociferous critic, Thomas Lüber (Thomas Erastus), denounced him as a gnostic heretic. Paracelsus did believe he was divinely inspired. In this sense, he was the "spiritual man" or "knowing one" who had achieved *gnōsis.*

See Also Occultism; Rosicrucians.

Bibliography

The critical standard edition of Paracelsus's *Sämtliche Werke,* 15 vols., edited by Karl Sudoff and Wilhelm Mattiessen (Munich, 1922–1933), includes copious annotations and bibliographic references. Walter Pagel's *Paracelsus: An Introduction to Philosophical Medicine in the Era of the Renaissance* (New York, 1958) has an excellent bibliography and provides a thorough discussion of Paracelsus's sources. In his *The Chemical Philosophy: Paracelsian Science and Medicine in the Sixteenth and Seventeenth Centuries,* 2 vols. (New York, 1977), Allen G. Debus discusses Paracelsus's legacy and influence on later scientists. English translations of selected treatises can be found in Arthur Edward Waite's *The Hermetic and Alchemical Writings of Aureolus Philippus Theophrastus Bombast, called Paracelsus the Great,* 2 vols. (1894; reprint, New Hyde Park, N. Y., 1967); Henry Sigerist's *Four Treatises of Theophrastus von Hohenheim* (Baltimore, 1941); and Jolande Jacobi's *Paracelsus: Selected Writings* (New York, 1951).

Allison Coudert (1987)

PARADISE.

The word *paradise* originated from Old Persian *pairidaeza,* which meant "walled enclosure, pleasure park, garden." *Pairidaeza* came into Hebrew, Aramaic, and Greek retaining its original meanings. It appears three times in the Hebrew scriptures (*Neh.* 2:8, *Eccl.* 2:5, *Sg.* 4:13) and also in later rabbinic literature. In the Septuagint, the Hebrew word for "garden" was usually translated by the Greek *paradeisos.* In *Genesis* 2–3 *paradeisos* refers to the original Garden of Eden (lit., "delight").

The earliest known description of a paradisial garden appears on a cuneiform tablet from protoliterate Sumer. It begins with a eulogy of Dilmun, a place that is pure, clean, and bright, a land of the living who do not know sickness, violence, or aging. It lacks one thing only: fresh water. This, however, is soon supplied by the sun god Utu at the command of the Sumerian water god Enki. Dilmun is thereby transformed into a garden with fruit trees, edible plants, and green meadows. Dilmun is a garden of the gods, not for humans, although one learns that Ziusudra, the Sumerian Noah, was exceptionally admitted to the divine paradise.

The Garden of Eden. According to the mythical narrative in *Genesis* 2–3, God planted a garden in Eden and therein placed man to till and keep it. God also caused trees to grow in the garden. The Edenic paradise was mainly arboreal, thereby providing food for man. The original human diet seems to have been vegetarian. According to *Genesis* 9, it was only later—after the Flood—that the descendants of Adam (Noah and his family) were permitted to eat flesh. A dietary restriction remained, however, for flesh containing blood was not to be eaten (*Gn.* 9:4).

The garden was the source of the world's sweet waters. A river not only watered the garden but flowed out of it to become four rivers (Pishon, Gihon, Tigris, and Euphrates), apparently to water the four directions or quarters of the world (*Gn.* 2:10–14).

The myth recognizes a deficiency in man's life in Eden: He is alone. This solitariness is soon relieved, for God forms beasts and birds. These living creatures are brought to man to be named. The naming signifies his mastery of the animals. Still, it is said, man does not have a suitable companion. The account of the creation of woman (Eve) follows. She is said to have been created from the rib (bone) of Adam, perhaps reflecting an archaic religious identification of the essence of life with bone (rather than with blood, as in *Genesis* 9). Adam and Eve become "one flesh."

One of the creatures of God, the serpent, approaches Eve and inquires whether God has placed any limits on the trees from which the couple may eat. Earlier in the narrative (2:9), there is reference to the Tree of Life and the Tree of the Knowledge of Good and Evil, and the warning to humans that they will die if he eats of the latter (2:17). When Eve reveals the prohibition, the serpent denies that death will result and insists instead that eating the fruit will result in likeness to God in that humans will then know good and evil. Both Eve and Adam eat the forbidden fruit, popularly thought to have been an apple. The knowledge they obtain is of their own nakedness; in shame they fashion simple garments.

At the sound of God walking in the garden, the couple hide among the trees. When discovered and questioned, they reveal that they have violated the divine prohibition. Sentence is passed on them as well as the serpent. Henceforth, Eve will experience pain in childbirth and subordination to her husband. Adam is condemned to till the soil under difficult conditions and ultimately to return to the soil or dust from which he originally came, that is, to die.

The concluding verses of the narrative refer to the second of the trees—the Tree of Life—which is earlier said to be in the midst (center?) of the garden. The deity appears concerned that humans, if allowed to remain in the garden, will eat also of the Tree of Life and live forever. It may be that the myth intends to say that the Tree of Life was hidden among the many trees of the garden and that humans, having eaten of the Tree of Knowledge, might find it. At any rate, Adam and Eve are driven from the garden, and an angel and a flaming sword are placed at the entrance to guard the way to the Tree of Life.

The first human habitat was, according to the narrative of Eden, a fertile, well-watered garden or orchard that supplied all things required by its inhabitants for nutrition and ease. The garden was a veritable oasis, perhaps to be contrasted with the desert or the wilderness, as it was in Jewish, Christian, and Islamic thought (see, e.g., Williams, 1962). The taking of life was not necessary for human sustenance. The animals and birds of Eden, while under the mastery of humans, seem to have lived in more or less peaceful and harmonious relationship with them and one another. Similarly, the relationship between man and woman seems to have been harmonious. Sexual tension had not yet appeared. The original nudity of the pair and the lack of shame signified paradisial innocence. In general, the conditions of life were ideal.

The significance of the serpent is not clear. It has been suggested that the serpent hoped through Adam and Eve to discover the Tree of Life and thus secure immortality for himself. In many interpretations of the *Genesis* narrative the serpent is given a negative valuation as the tempter and deceiver of women. In some other religious traditions (e.g., Hinduism), the serpent is associated with the very things symbolized by the two special trees of paradise: wisdom and immortality.

The turning point of the narrative is the act of disobedience. It has serious consequences. That Adam and Eve should recognize their nakedness is indicative of their loss of innocence. Also, the divine-human communication possible when God walks in the garden and converses with humans becomes problematic. The consequences of disobedience are profound changes in the conditions of human life: Pain, toil, and mortality are specifically mentioned (*Gn.* 3:16–19). It is the loss of paradise that gives the narrative its poignancy. However one may interpret the details, the essential meaning of the myth of the Garden of Eden is that, in the beginning, life was paradisial but something happened that changed it into what it has been since that time.

The lost paradise of Eden has sometimes been thought actually to have existed somewhere on earth. Because the Bible nowhere indicates its destruction, some people have assumed that the garden, or traces of it, could be discovered. Thus it has been imagined to exist at the headwaters of the Tigris and Euphrates rivers. It has also been "discovered" far from the Middle East. Christopher Columbus, for example, believed that the freshwater currents he detected in the Gulf of Paria between Trinidad and the South American coast had their source in the four rivers flowing out of the biblical Eden. The luxuriant vegetation and the mild climate as well as the scents of tropical flowers seemed proof enough to confirm his speculations. Paradise has also been "found" in the most improbable places, as, for example, the Arctic Pole (see William F. Warren, *Paradise Found: The Cradle of the Human Race at the North Pole,* 1885).

THE PRIMORDIALITY OF PARADISE. The Edenic paradise was primordial. Paradise is frequently thought to have been primordial, that is, to have existed in the fabulous time of beginnings.

Hermann Baumann (1936) has called attention to African myths concerning a primordial paradise. In these myths, human beings understand the language of animals and are at peace with them. They have no need to work, and food is plentiful at hand. Disease and death are unknown. However, an event occurs that terminates these paradisial conditions and makes human life what it is today.

Myths of primordial paradise, broadly conceived, include the large number of myths in which, in the beginning, Heaven and Earth are in close proximity and, also, myths according to which Heaven is easily accessible by a concrete means such as a tree, ladder, vine, or mountain that can be climbed. As the result of the separation of Heaven and Earth or the removal of the link between them, easy communication is lost. A rupture occurs. It signifies the end of paradise and entry into the ordinary human condition.

Characteristics of the Primordial Paradise. Among the marks or characteristics of the primordial paradise are perfection, purity, plenitude, freedom, spontaneity, peace, pleasure, beatitude, and immortality. Each contrasts with the characteristics of ordinary, postparadisial human life. To this list could appropriately be added harmony and friendship with the animals, including knowledge of their language, and, as well, ease of communication with the gods and the world above.

Unlike a Darwinian view with its stress on rudimentary, imperfect beginnings, the myths of primordial paradise envision the perfection of beginnings. Moreover, the original purity of all things is preserved. Myths of primordial paradise affirm plenitude, often in terms of extraordinary abundance. Freedom and spontaneity are expressed by the absence or minimalization of constraints; there are few if any laws in paradise. As for peace, the typical scenario creates an atmosphere of ease, rest, tranquillity, the absence of tension and conflict. As noted above, human beings and animals live peaceably, sexual tension has not yet appeared, and labor is unnecessary. Indeed, things seem to be in easy equilibrium, perhaps even static. Pleasure abounds, whether described in sensual terms or as spiritual satisfactions. Beatitude, consummate bliss, is the happy lot of all the inhabitants of paradise. Paradise is outside ordinary, historical time. Hence there can be no aging or death. Humans are immortal, for death has not yet appeared. Nor has sickness or disease or sin or injustice or any of the ills that postparadisial man is heir to.

Nostalgia for Paradise. Although the primordial paradise has been lost, it has not been forgotten. One finds expressions of the desire to recover the essential condition, the condition that would still obtain if all had gone as it should. The image of a place and time of perfect and endless peace and plenty has the power to make historical existence significant and bearable and its transitoriness acceptable. A Freudian interpretation would speak of wish fulfillment and the desire to return to the womb, but such an interpretation would be both limited and reductive. More significant than wishes, although they may be present, is the nostalgia, the haunting sense of loss and the powerful desire for recovery. The nostalgia for paradise is among the powerful nostalgias that seem to haunt human beings. It may be the most powerful and persistent of all. A certain longing for paradise is evidenced at every level of religious life.

An unusually well documented example of an actual quest for paradise is provided by the Guaraní Indians of Brazil. For more than four centuries, the Guaraní have engaged in a series of migrations in search of the "land without evil." It is thought actually to exist in this world but to be well hidden. Mircea Eliade has suggested that the paradisial images used by shamans in recounting their dreams and ecstasies have helped to keep alive the centuries-old quest (*The Quest,* 1969).

Recurring Paradises. Paradises are found in cosmically oriented as well as historically oriented religions, that is, in religions in which time is cyclical as well as in those in which it is linear and historical. In the former, paradise is not only lost but recurs, from time to time, in step with the ever-turning wheel of time.

The most impressive example in the history of religion is the Hindu doctrine of the world ages (*yugas*). It is cast in mythical terms by relating the ages of the life of the god Brahmā. Briefly, each world cycle is subdivided into four world ages. They are comparable to the four ages of Greco-Roman tradition. That tradition used the names of metals—gold, silver, bronze, and iron—to designate the successive ages. Hinduism uses the four throws of the Indian game of dice: *kṛta* (4), *tretā* (3), *dvāpara* (2), and *kali* (1). Decline and deterioration proceed as age follows age.

Kṛtayuga is the perfect age, the age of four (the winning throw in the dice game). The number four is a frequent symbol of totality, plenitude, and perfection in Hinduism. The age is known also as the *satya* ("real, true, authentic") *yuga.* During the *kṛta* age *dharma* (the fundamental universal moral order) is observed totally and spontaneously. It is the golden age, the age of truth, justice, prosperity, and human fulfillment. In other words, it is equivalent to the primordial, paradisial age of other religious traditions.

Unfortunately, the *kṛtayuga* inevitably ends and is followed by the three ages of increasing decline, culminating in the *kaliyuga,* the dark age, in which only one-quarter of *dharma* remains. In the dice game *kali* is the losing throw. In the *kali* age the nadir is reached. The world and humans are at their worst. Also unfortunately, today's world is now in the *kaliyuga,* which, according to one reckoning, will last 432,000 human years. Even so, it will eventually come to an end and will be followed by the return of the *kṛtayuga,* the perfect, golden age. In other words, paradise will reappear. In the meanwhile, it exists as an image, a powerful image of perfection, plenitude, and prosperity.

Buddhism adopted essentially the Hindu cyclical view of ages, relating it to the Buddhas and *bodhisattvas.* Here, too, paradisial motifs appear, as in Mahāyāna texts describing the world at the time of the birth of the expected next Buddha, Maitreya, in this world system. In the *Maitreyavyākaraṇa* the world—more specifically, India—is described as remarkably different at the time of Maitreya's appearing. Its innumerable inhabitants will commit no crimes or evil deeds and will delight in doing good. People will be without blemishes. They will be strong, large, and joyful, and few will be the illnesses among them. The soil will be free of thorns, covered with green grass, and will produce rice without any work. Into this paradisial, or near-paradisial, world, Maitreya will come to proclaim the true Dharma.

Hesiod in the *Theogony* writes of five ages, inserting an age of heroes after the bronze age in the usual Greco-Roman sequence of gold, silver, bronze, and iron ages. He describes the golden age in paradisial terms. Men live like gods. They do not work or experience sorrow. Neither do they grow old. Though they are mortal, death comes as sleep. The fertile land is fruitful. Men are at peace and have every want supplied. They are succeeded, however, by a lesser, silver race of men.

Plato in the *Politicus* (269c ff.) speaks of cyclical return that includes times of regeneration. The time comes when ordinary processes are reversed. Thus human beings begin to grow younger rather than older, returning to infancy and finally ceasing to be. There appears then the age of Kronos in which a new race ("Sons of Earth") is born. Human beings rise out of the earth. Trees provide them with fruits in abundance. They sleep naked (in paradisial nudity) on the soil. The seasons are mild, and all animals are tame and peaceable.

PARADISE AS THE ABODE OF THE RIGHTEOUS. The biblical conception of paradise is not limited to the primordial Garden of Eden. With the emergence of Jewish belief in the resurrection of the dead, perhaps around 200 BCE, paradise could be taken to refer not only to the original Garden of Eden but also to the eternal abode of the righteous. That is, the righteous dead could expect to have the Garden of Eden, or paradise, as their postresurrection abode (rather than Gehenna, the fiery place of punishment of the wicked). Thus Garden and Gehenna constituted a contrasting pair. Moreover, the garden of paradise could refer as well to the intermediate abode of the righteous until their resurrection.

The location of the paradisial abode of the righteous, whether before or after the resurrection, could still be taken as earthly, as it was by some, but the tendency was to locate it above, either in heaven or in one of the multiple heavens (e.g., the third heaven).

In the New Testament, the myth of the Garden of Eden is interpreted as the account of the "fall" of humans through willful disobedience, thus emphasizing the need for and appropriateness of a savior who effects the restoration of fallen humans. In this regard, characteristically Christian interpretations of the myth of Eden have differed from Jewish interpretations. The former have emphasized estrangement from the divine and "original sin." The latter have not.

The New Testament contains three specific references to paradise (*2 Cor.* 12:3, *Lk.* 23:43, *Rv.* 2:7). These indicate experiential and eschatological conceptions of paradise. In *2 Corinthians* 12:3 a man is said to have been caught up into paradise, which in the preceding verse is identified with the third heaven. Paradise appears to be thought of as a celestial or heavenly level entered through ecstasy. Paradise may also be entered by privileged persons (for example, martyrs and the "good thief" of *Luke* 23:43). The third reference to paradise is *Revelation* 2:7, addressed to the church in Ephesus. The promise is given that one who conquers will be granted to eat of the tree of life in God's paradise. It is said in the context of a call for patient endurance and appears to link an eschatological paradise with the primordial, earthly Eden.

In the Islamic religion the Arabic word for "garden"—*janna*—is used to refer to the Garden of Eden and, as well, to the heavenly Paradise in which the God-fearing will dwell. In the Qur'ān it more commonly refers to the latter. As in the Jewish religion, there is a contrasting pair of terms: garden (*janna*) and Gehenna (Jahannam). In *sūrah* 2:25 those who believe and do works of righteousness are promised gardens with flowing rivers and abundant fruit, therein to dwell forever. *Sūrah* 47:15 promises the God-fearing a garden not only with rivers of water but rivers of milk, wine, and honey as well as every kind of fruit. The garden is a luxuriant oasis, an appealing image to any desert-dwelling people such as the first hearers of the Qur'ān. "Gardens of delight" are promised in *sūrah* 56. The inhabitants will recline on couches where they will be served from a pure spring by immortal youths. They will eat as they desire of fruit and the flesh of fowl. With them will be the *ḥūrīs*, described (56:36f.) as chastely amorous virgins.

REPRESENTATIONS OF PARADISE. Paradise is susceptible to a variety of specific representations. Something that belongs to the actual world is used to refer to an ideal world.

Garden. The garden is the most common representation of paradise. This representation is not limited to religions originating in the Middle East. There is, for example, a Mahāyāna Buddhist paradise, Sukhāvatī, the "pure land" of the Buddha Amitābha. In the *Sukhāvativyūha,* the paradise of Amitābha is described as fertile, rich, comfortable, and delightful. It is filled with a great variety of flowers and fruits. Many deep, broad rivers flow through it. Birds sing pleasantly. Calm and peace pervade this garden paradise.

In Greek mythology one finds the garden, or orchard, of Hesperides, located in the far west, not far from the Isles of the Blessed. It is renowned for its golden apples. A guard stands at the entrance. There are, as well, the Elysian Fields, where, according to Homer's *Odyssey* (4.564ff.), the climate is wonderfully mild, as there is no winter. The ocean provides refreshing breezes for mortals. Their lives are said to be the easiest.

The association of garden with paradise has been persistent, as shown by Elizabeth Moynihan in *Paradise as a Gar-*

den: In Persia and Mughal India (1979). She demonstrates the continuity of the tradition and symbolic topography of the paradise garden. She points especially to the relationship between water, the central and most essential element in the Persian garden, and trees, symbolizing regeneration or immortality and the possibility of ascension. The blissful Paradise—the reward in the afterlife—was the model for the Persian garden. The latter, with its trees reaching symbolically upward and its rippling water and fragrant flowers, never became entirely secular.

A rather different kind of example is found in the symbolization of America as a garden paradise. Charles L. Sanford has studied the depth of the search for paradise in American civilization in *The Quest for Paradise* (1961). It is well known that the early explorers and settlers of the New World spoke of it in terms of Eden. Its virgin forests, fertile soil, abundant game, aboriginal inhabitants, and freedom from the restraints of the Old World encouraged this identification. Here humankind, having left behind the Old World of Europe, could make a new beginning, as R. W. B. Lewis makes clear in *The American Adam* (1955). Moreover, particular parts of America were identified with Eden, illustrating the possibility of a multiplicity of paradises. Thus George Alsop identified Maryland as the terrestrial paradise, saying that its trees, plants, flowers, fruits, and even its roots were signs of Adam's realm, special evidence of its innocence. John Smith believed he had discovered Eve in the Powhatan tribe and that he had chanced on a land that was as God made it, a place where heaven and earth best agreed as a land for human habitation. In a 1609 farewell sermon given for Virginia adventurers by Daniel Price, Virginia was described as the garden of the world, a land flowing with milk and honey. When the frontierspeople crossed the mountains through the Cumberland Gap into Kentucky, they saw it not only as "the dark and bloody ground" but, paradoxically, as a veritable Eden, rich in forests and game and fertile in soil. The same sort of thing was happening in Puritan New England, though often in terms of future expectations. Thus Edward Johnson considered Massachusetts a place where a new heaven and a new earth will be created by the Lord. Later, Jonathan Edwards could speak of the Great Awakening as a glorious work that would make New England a heaven on earth.

It is not difficult to understand why the garden has often provided the setting for the primordial paradise and, as well, the paradise of the dead. Whether cultivated (as it was after the discovery of agriculture) or provided by nature, a garden is a striking phenomenon. Typically, it is in evident contrast with the surrounding territory, sometimes dramatically. It seems to constitute another world, different from the ordinary one, a world in which seed, soil, and water combine in evident manifestation of fertility, vitality, and abundance. For humans it provides refreshment as well as nourishment, and signalizes an alluring mode of human existence.

Island. Gardens are not the sole representations of paradise. It is also represented in other ways, frequently as an island or a mountain. These several representations are sometimes combined, as in a gardenlike island paradise. Such is the case with the Pacific Ocean island paradises of novels and the lush, vividly colored island paradises of Gauguin's paintings.

The Isles of the Blessed in Greek mythology are well known. They are an insular counterpart to Olympus, the mountain of the gods. One finds parallels in Celtic mythology, where isle as well as garden is used as an image of paradise. Moreover, the myth of the submerged world, comparable to Plato's Atlantis, is also found. Here one has the motif of a more or less paradisial world in which something went wrong, resulting in its disappearance beneath the waves.

Perhaps even more effectively than the garden, the island symbolizes a world. Its limits and contours are in sharp relief in the midst of the sea, and its microcosmic nature is evident.

An island suggests isolation. It can readily symbolize the remoteness and difficulty of access of paradise. Often a river or an ocean has to be traversed. Paradise cannot easily be found, entered, recovered. In this context the motif of journey, especially of difficult or perilous journey, appears.

Mountain. The mountain is also sometimes associated with paradise, as, for example, in connection with Jerusalem (Mount Zion) in its paradisial dimensions, or with Mount Meru of Hindu mythology. John Milton in book 4 of *Paradise Lost* describes paradise as a mountain. In fact, Milton brings together several images, for in his description the paradisial mountain is also a garden and the origin of the four rivers that course down its sides.

The distinctive characteristic of the mountain is its height. It towers above the earth and therefore can readily symbolize transcendence. Thus when paradise is thought of as a transcendental realm, the mountain is an appropriate image.

Eschatological Paradises. While paradise is usually thought of as in the past, it also figures in some eschatologies. In the *Book of Revelation* there is envisioned a new heaven and a new earth and, as well, a new Jerusalem, which will come down from God (*Rv.* 21:1ff.). God will then dwell among humans, and henceforth mourning, crying, pain, and death will be no more. In Jewish messianism the coming age is frequently described in terms strongly reminiscent of paradisial existence (e.g., *Is.* 11:6–8, *Ez.* 47:1–12). Norman Cohn in *The Pursuit of the Millennium* (1957) found paradisial elements in his study of revolutionary messianism in medieval and Reformation Europe.

In modern times "cargo cults" of Melanesia and Micronesia have been especially generative of paradisial motifs. Briefly, these cults are typically based on myths that prophesy that soon an ancestor-bearing ship will arrive with a wonderful cargo to be received by those who have expected and prepared for its arrival. The return of the ancestors and the arrival of cargo signal profound changes. Not only will poverty be abolished but all that belongs to the old world will be destroyed. A series of reversals will take place: Servants will become masters, the old will become young, yams will grow on trees, and coconuts will grow in the ground. After all that belongs to the old world has been changed or destroyed, a new world will appear. In this world there will be freedom from laws, traditions, work, poverty, disease, ageing, and death. In other words, this radical transformation or renewal of the world signifies paradise.

SECULAR PARADISES. Most of the paradises referred to have been explicitly religious. However, paradisial motifs and nostalgias for paradise have appeared, especially in the modern world, in other guises. Utopias, some of which, but not all, are explicitly religious, typically have some of the characteristics of paradise, often to a lesser degree and with some concessions to actuality. It could be said that utopias are efforts to actualize the image of paradise, under the conditions of this world.

The strong interest in communes in recent decades, especially among the young, may be understood as a quest for a secular paradise, as may the more pervasive and continuing interest in returning to the land, evidenced first by the creation of suburbia but extending subsequently to the truly rural countryside.

SEE ALSO Bones; Cargo Cults; Fall, The; Gardens, overview article; Heaven and Hell; Mountains; Utopia.

BIBLIOGRAPHY

Armstrong, John H. S. *The Paradise Myth.* London, 1969. Seeks an alternative to the *Genesis* paradise myth in elements of Sumerian and Greek myths and in themes in Renaissance literature and art.

Baumann, Hermann. *Schöpfung und Urzeit des Menschen im Mythus der afrikanischer Völker.* Berlin, 1936. Myths of beginning and end in Africa.

Cohn, Norman. *The Pursuit of the Millennium.* 3d ed. New York, 1970. Revolutionary messianism in medieval and Reformation Europe and its bearing on modern totalitarian movements.

Lewis, R. W. B. *The American Adam.* Chicago, 1955. The new Adam in American literature of the nineteenth century as an expression of a native American mythology.

Lincoln, Andrew T. *Paradise Now and Not Yet.* Cambridge, U.K., 1981. Paradise in Saint Paul's eschatology.

Moynihan, Elizabeth B. *Paradise as a Garden: In Persia and Mughal India.* New York, 1979. The oldest surviving garden tradition. Richly illustrated.

Sanford, Charles L. *The Quest for Paradise.* Urbana, Ill., 1961. Origins and meaning of "the Garden of America" and its broader applications to aspects of American civilization.

Smith, Henry Nash. *Virgin Land.* Cambridge, Mass., 1950. The American West as myth and symbol.

Stevens, Henry Bailey. *The Recovery of Culture.* New York, 1949. Argues that humans once lived in a horticultural paradise before the "fall" into hunting and the subsequent sacrifice-linked agricultural period.

Sylvia Mary, Sr. *Nostalgia for Paradise.* London, 1965. A somewhat comparative study of the longing for paradise done from a Christian religious and theological perspective.

Williams, George H. *Wilderness and Paradise in Christian Thought.* New York, 1962. The ambivalent meanings of wilderness, garden, and desert in the Bible and subsequent appearances of these themes in Christian thought and literature.

New Sources

Bernheim, Pierre-Antoine. *Paradis, Paradis.* Paris, 1991.

Bockmuehl, Markus. "Strawberries, the Food of Paradise: A Study in Christian Symbolism." *Crux* 27/3 (1991): 9–21.

Brockway, Robert W. "The Eden Myth: Archetypal Vision of Paradise." *Faith and Freedom: A Journal of Progressive Religion* 44 (1991): 33–34; 39–42.

Buck, Christopher. *Paradise and Paradigm: Key Symbols in Persian Christianity and the Bahâi Faith.* Albany, N.Y., 1999.

Heinberg, Richard. *Memories and Visions of Paradise: Exploring the Universal Myth of a Lost Golden Age.* Los Angeles, 1989.

Luttikhuizen, Gerard P., ed. *Paradise Interpreted: Interpretations of Biblical Paradise in Judaism and Christianity.* Leiden and Boston, 1999.

Miller, James E. *Western Paradise: Greek and Hebrew Traditions.* San Francisco, 1997.

Zaleski, Carol. "When I Get to Heaven: Picturing Paradise." *Christian Century* 120, no. 7 (2003): 22–31.

HARRY B. PARTIN (1987)
Revised Bibliography

PARADOX AND RIDDLES.

PARADOX AND RIDDLES. Although paradoxes can seem enigmatic and riddles paradoxical, they are fundamentally different realities. Riddles are mainly instrumental and performance-oriented, whether used in sacred or secular contexts, whereas paradoxes are rooted in the heart of being and language, touching on the crux of experience and expression. Riddles are to be solved; a paradox is to be transcended, or, rather, lived.

RIDDLES. A riddle was called *griphos* (lit., "fishing creel," or something intricate) or *ainigma* ("dark saying") in Greek and *aenigma* ("problem") in Latin. The modern meaning of enigma, "that which is unknown and remains obscure," reflects this ancestry. Riddles may or may not have solutions. As the English saying "It remains a riddle" indicates, what cannot be known remains a mystery. In Greek, *mustērion* meant something beyond the comprehension of human intelligence.

Riddles have been known since antiquity and throughout the world. The oldest recorded riddles are found in Babylonian school textbooks, in which one finds such riddles as: "Who becomes pregnant without conceiving, who gets fat without eating?" The answer, not given in the textbook, is probably a "rain cloud." (Taylor, 1948, pp. 12–13) The Greek poet Pindar called the Sphinx's question a riddle (*ainigma*); Plato alludes to the punning riddles common in his time (*Republic* 5.479). Riddles may be both playful and serious—playful as a humorous diversion or pastime, or serious as in the riddle of the Sphinx, failure to solve which would cost a person's life. German philologists referred to such a riddle as a *Halsrätsel* (capital riddle). By the same token, Yudhiṣṭhira in the Indian epic of *Mahābhārata* restored his brothers to life by successfully solving the riddles posed by a *yakṣa*, a demi-god (chapter 41, "The Enchanted Pool"). Although of modern creation, Bilbo Baggins's interaction with Gollum in *The Hobbit* by J. R. R. Tolkien preserves the life-staking seriousness of the riddles as a performing act (see ch. 5, "Riddles in the Dark").

In Vedic India, riddles were posed as part of such rituals as the *rājasūya* (coronation of a king) and the *aśvamedha* (horse sacrifice). The exchange of questions and answers between the sacrificial priests was highly formalized, as in this pair: "What is it that walketh singly?" "It is yonder sun, doubtless, that walks singly, and he is spiritual luster" (*Śatapatha Brāhmaṇa* 8.2.6.9ff.). Brahmans competed in *jātavidyā* (knowledge of the origins) and *brahmodya* (theological or philosophical discussion about brahman). Cosmological questions were often the topics of riddles, as in the *Ṛgveda*: "I ask you about the furthest limit of earth. Where, I ask, is the center of the world? I ask you about the Stallion's prolific seed; I ask you about high heaven where abides the Word" (1.164.34). This suggests that philosophical inquiry developed in the form of posing riddles (see *Ṛgveda* 1.164.46; 10.129; *Atharvaveda* 9.9–10; 10.7). A verse in the *Atharvaveda* asks: "How does the wind not cease to blow? How does the mind take no repose? Why do the waters, seeking to reach truth, never at any time cease to flow?" (10.7.37; cited in Bloomfield, 1969, pp. 210–218; Huizinga, 1949, pp. 105–107).

Dealing with the mystery of existence and the universe, riddles were often considered to have a special power. The possession of esoteric knowledge meant the possession of power (Huizinga, 1949, p. 108). Moreover, a magical power was associated with riddles: the idea that a spoken word has a direct influence on the world order is at the heart of the ritualistic use of riddles, such as those used at the time of rice planting and growing (but that were strictly forbidden between harvest and the laying out of new fields), and those used on certain occasions such as funerals.

To the authors of the Hebrew scriptures, riddles were closely connected with wisdom, which the Lord conferred as a blessing (see Samson's riddle in *Judges* 14:13–18; on the Lord's blessing, see *Judges* 13:24). Solomon's wisdom, which "God had put in his heart" (1 *Kgs.* 10:24), was challenged by the queen of Sheba with "hard questions" (1 *Kgs.* 10:1–13; 2 *Chr.* 9:1–12). The authors of medieval *midrashim* elaborated on such questions in detail, as for instance: "Who were the three that ate and drank on the earth, yet were not born of male and female?" "The three angels who revealed themselves to our father Abraham, peace be unto him," and so on (Schechter, 1891, pp. 354–356). Riddles were "most characteristic of Jewish table-amusements in the middle ages" that "great Hebrew poets of the middle ages composed acrostics and enigmas of considerable merit" (Abrahams, 1896, pp. 384–387, 133).

Riddles were actively employed in Christian missionary activities during the middle ages. It was in this context that the bishop Boniface (ca. 675–754) chose ten virtues and ten vices as a theme for riddles (Taylor, 1948, pp. 63–64). Biblical passages often provided allegorical riddles (*ibid.*, pp. 61–65).

KŌAN. *K'an* (Chin., *gong'an*, "public document, authoritative statute") are a series of questions that Zen masters give to their students as an aid to their meditation practice. *Kōan* are still actively utilized to train students in the Japanese Rinzai lineage of Zen tradition, which belongs to Mahāyāna Buddhism. The popularized version of *kōan*, such as "What is the sound of one hand clapping?" or "What was your original face before your parents were born?", may initially appear to be riddle-like, but they are actually not riddles and have a distinct function to free the mind from its conventional habits beset by the subject-object dichotomy.

The practice of *kōan* became widespread among the disciples of the Chinese Chan (Jpn., Zen) master Dahui Zonggao (Jpn., Daie Sōkō; 1089–1163). The *kōans* often consist of questions and answers (known as *mondō* in Japanese) exchanged between masters and students during the Tang and early Song periods in China, as well as questions put forward by teachers and anecdotes of famous masters.

The *kōan* traditionally given to the beginners is known as "Zhaozhu and the dog," which is a dialogue between a monk and the master Zhaozhu (Jpn., Jōshū). A monk asked Master Zhaozhu: "Does the dog have a Buddha nature?" The Master replied: "No." A variation of this *kōan* continues: on another occasion, another monk asked Master Zhaozhu: "Does the dog have a Buddha nature?" The Master replied: "Yes." Baffling it may be, this particular *kōan* is not about the concept of emptiness or nothingness, nor does it deal with the opposition of existence and non-existence (Izutsu, p. 176). *Kōans* point beyond the discursive level of yes and no to the very reality of the world in which all beings are vitally interrelated.

D. T. Suzuki notes that *kōans* are intended as themes for meditation, as "the means for opening one's mind to the truth of Zen"; and further: "*kōan* and *zazen* [seated meditation] are the two handmaids of Zen; the first is the eye and the second is the foot." Thus without thorough training in seated meditation, Zen students will not attain spiritual awakening (Suzuki, 1964, pp. 101–102).

Zen teaching may appear to deny discursive thinking, but it actually brings the practitioners face to face with the primordial reality that is prior to conceptualization. The following statement by a Chinese master Qingyuan (Jpn., Seigen) illustrates the inner dynamics of Zen/Chan training:

> Thirty years ago, before this aged monk got into Chan training, I used to see a mountain as a mountain and a river as a river. Thereafter I had the chance to meet enlightened masters and, under their guidance, I could attain enlightenment to some extent. At this stage, when I saw a mountain: lo! it was not a mountain. When I saw a river: lo! it was not a river. But in these days I have settled down to a position of final tranquility. As I used to do in my first years, now I see a mountain just as a mountain and a river just as a river. (Izutsu, p. 208)

The first stage is characteristic of the ordinary way of looking at the world: the knower (subject) and the known (object) are separated, and the mountain is perceived as a thing standing out there. The second stage is the experience of the oneness of the knower and the known. The third stage is the recognition of the world as is, based on the experience of the oneness (second stage) and overcoming the subject-object dichotomy (first stage) of the knower and the known (Izutsu, pp. 208–209). Riddle-like statements often found in Zen/Chan literature thus have an epistemological foundation.

PARADOX. The original Greek meaning of *para doxa*, "contrary to received opinion or expectation," cuts through various meanings of paradox. In classical Greek, *paradoxia* meant "marvelousness" and *paradoxologeō*, "to tell marvels." Thus, paradox was more than just a contradiction; *paradoxos* meant "incredible"—contrary to one's expectation or a generally held notion (*doxa*). This was the sense of the word retained in the New Testament passage about Jesus healing a palsied man: people were "all amazed, and they glorified God, and were filled with fear, saying, we have seen strange things [*paradoxa*] today" (*Lk.* 5:26). In this particular passage, *paradoxos* thus means "miraculous."

Definitions of paradox. The word *paradox* has been understood variously as a logical contradiction, absurdity, enigma, or seeming contradiction. Hamlet said, "This was sometime a paradox, but now the time gives it proof" (*Hamlet* 3.1.114–115). Some define paradox as a unique form of thinking, "a dynamic, bi-polar thought which bespeaks a vital tension involving both the opposition and reciprocation of ideas" (Slaatte, p. 132). Others see paradox, "playing with human understanding," as "primarily a figure of thought, in which the various suitable figures of speech are inextricably impacted" (Colie, pp. 7, 22). Kierkegaard, on the other hand, asserted that the paradox, arising from the "relation between an existing cognitive spirit and eternal truth . . . is not a concession but a category, an ontological definition" (ed. Bretall, p. 153).

Kinds of paradox. There are logical, visual, psychological, rhetorical, and other types of paradoxes, such as epistemological and existential. Logical paradox has preoccupied logicians and mathematicians since olden times. The paradoxes associated with Zeno of Elea go back to the fifth century BCE. Many logical paradoxes are considered solvable by applying different conceptual frameworks as for instance Russell's "barber paradox," which runs: in a certain town the barber shaves everyone who does not shave himself; does the barber shave himself? If the barber does not shave himself, he must shave himself, and if he does shave himself, he cannot shave himself. Some other logical paradoxes are considered antinomies, and still others are mind-twisters. Evaluations as to the kinds of paradoxes are by no means uniform. For instance, Quine considers the paradox by Eubulides of Epimenides the Cretan, who said "All Cretans are liars," untidy and therefore solvable, while Poundstone considers it to be a genuine paradox (Quine, p. 86; Poundstone, p. 18).

Visual paradoxes, such as the picture that presents a duck from one view and a rabbit from another, have come to be regarded more in relation to the psychology of representation (Gombrich, 1960). The rhetorical paradox as a literary genre was extremely popular during the Renaissance. *The Praise of Folly* (1509) by Erasmus set the tone; the genre was also practiced by the poet John Donne, the satirist Joseph Hall, among others.

Functions of paradox. Fundamentally connected with the problem of language and being, paradoxes function variously. Paradoxes in mathematics or physical science are puzzles to be solved by "putting the conceptual framework in a new perspective," so that "the limitations of the old concept are revealed" (Rapoport, p. 56). Challenging the limits of reason, paradoxes may function as gateways to a new and more comprehensive paradigm of reality. Indeed, "paradoxes have played a dramatic part in intellectual history, often foreshadowing revolutionary developments in science, mathematics and logic" (Rapoport, p. 50). In the field of logic and mathematics the confrontation with paradoxes—such as Russell's paradoxes—greatly stimulated studies of the foundations of mathematics (Quine, p. 84). Contradictions are regarded as a fertile soil for the development of theories in physical science. A. N. Whitehead holds that "in the formal logic, a contradiction is the signal of a defeat: but in the evolution of real knowledge it marks the first step in progress towards a victory" (p. 260).

Some consider paradox as a higher form of expression of truth that defies a logical or linear mode of description as it involves a contradictory juxtaposition of images rather than of logical ideas (Slater, p. 115). Just as metaphor and images point beyond words, so do paradoxes point beyond a logical linguistic construct, and open up the domain of experience itself. They make accessible religious experiences, poetic intuitions, artistic creativities, and much of everyday experience.

Paradox and religious discourse. Heraclitus described God as "day night, winter summer, war peace, satiety hunger" (frag. 67). And the Japanese Zen master Daitō described religious truth as "Separated by an eternity, yet not separated even an instant; face to face the whole day, yet not face to face even an instant." Paradoxical statements are often oxymoronic in style, combining contradictions. Descriptions of the religious reality and religious experience are frequently dressed in contradictory language such as *plenum/nihilum,* *personal/impersonal, immanent/transcendent, affirmation/negation, sin/redemption.* Out of the tension between these terms emerges a meaning that is characteristic of religious experiences. Rudolf Otto described the dimension of numinous as "*mysterium tremendum et fascinosum,*" and considered that "these two qualities, the daunting and the fascinating, now combine in a strange harmony of contrasts, and the resultant dual character of the numinous consciousness, to which the entire religious development bears witness, at any rate from the level of the 'daemonic dread' onwards, is at once the strangest and most noteworthy phenomenon in the whole history of religion" (Otto, p. 31).

There is a correlation between types of experience and types of expression. "Between logical contradiction (or seeming contradiction) and certain forms of religious feeling there is a close relation," observes Arthur Lovejoy (p. 279). Some consider paradox to be a more suitable, if not essential, form of expression of religious experience (see Calhoun; Stace). To say God is immanent/transcendent is more than just a simple placing of these two qualities side by side; rather it describes the character of religious experience itself.

In the Christian mystical tradition or in the Zen tradition, linguistic expressions are regarded with suspicion, because of the basic assumption of the limitation of language—or at least of certain forms of statement—and the hierarchy of intelligibility, which is not confined to logical thinking. But all the same the need for affirming the reality beyond human thoughts and language remains strong.

Chinese Chan master Wumen (Jpn., Mumon), whose collection of *gong'an* (*kōan*) is known as *The Gateless Barrier* (Chin., *Wumenguan*, Jpn., *Mumonkan*, 1228), made full use of paradoxical language, as the title of his collection indicates. He wrote in his preface: "The Buddha Mind is the basis, and gateless is the Dharma Gate. If it is gateless, how can you pass through it?" And again: "to cling to words and phrases and thus try to achieve understanding is like trying to strike the moon with a stick, or scratching a shoe because there is an itchy spot on the foot" (Shibayama, p. 9).

Ninian Smart considers "paradoxical pronouncements" to "fulfill such a number of functions that by understanding the gist of them one can penetrate to the heart of the philosophy of religion" (Smart, 1958, p. 20). Citing a passage "It is far, and It is near. It is within all this, And It is outside of all this" (*Īśā Upaniṣad* 5) as a case in point, Smart notes that the objective, transcendent, numinous, far, brahman, and "wholly other" belong to the strand of worship, whereas the subjective, immanent, mystical, near, *ātman*, and "within" belong to the strand of mystical experience. Moreover, these two are woven together in a way characteristic of religious experience, as shown by the exhilarating yet self-effacing experience of the mystic (Smart, 1958; see also Austin). Paradoxical expressions may also be considered as rhetorical devices or "therapeutic paradoxes" (Ramsey and Smart, 1959, p. 220).

***Coincidentia oppositorum,* a paradoxical logic.** The expression *coincidentia oppositorum* or "coincidence of opposites" explains why paradoxical descriptions of themselves belong to the nature of ultimate reality. Although this idea of coincidence of opposites goes back to Proclus and even Heraclitus, it is today generally associated with Nicholas of Cusa (1401–1464), the German churchman, scholar, philosopher, and astronomer. He observed in *De docta ignorantia* (On Learned Ignorance):

> For whatsoever things are apprehended by the senses, by reason, or by intellect both within themselves and in relation to one another—[differ] in such way that there is no precise equality among them. Therefore, Maximum Equality, which is neither other than nor different from anything, surpasses all understanding. Hence, since the absolute Maximum *is* all that which can be, it is *altogether* actual. And just as there cannot be a greater, so for the same reason there cannot be a lesser, since it is all that which can be. But the Minimum is that than which there cannot be a lesser. And since the Maximum is also such, it is evident that the Minimum coincides with the Maximum. (1.4; trans. Hopkins, p. 53)

The logic of *coincidentia oppositorum* presupposes a unifying ground of the many, that is, equality. "Therefore, opposing features belong only to those things which can be comparatively greater or lesser" (*ibid.*), that is, to the relative world of plurality of things.

Mahāyāna Buddhism also deals with *coincidentia oppositorum* and maintains the unity of the one and the many. In unity there is multiplicity, and in multiplicity there is unity. A favorite simile is that of the ocean water (the one) and innumerable waves (the many). Paradoxical is the character of the ultimate. The *Heart Sutra*, the summation of the Prajñāpāramitā corpus, proclaims "all the phenomenal world of experience is empty, and empty is the whole phenomenal world of experience." Suzuki, in discussing this kind of logic of simultaneous negation and affirmation, calls it *sokuhi no ronri*, or "the logic of *prajñā*" (Suzuki, 1951, p. 18). Contrasting *prajñā* ("intuition") with the workings of *vijñāna* ("reason"), he notes: "Paradoxical statements are characteristic of *prajñā*-intuition. As it transcends *vijñāna* or logic it does not mind contradicting itself; it knows that a contradiction is the outcome of differentiation, which is the work of *vijñāna*. *Prajñā* negates what it asserted before, and conversely; it has its own way of dealing with this world of dualities" (*ibid.*, p. 24). Such insight into the paradoxical character of reality marks the Japanese Kyoto School of philosophy, of which Nishida Kitarō (1870–1945) was the formative presence.

***Docta ignorantia:* The paradoxical knowledge of the ultimate.** The Socratic tradition of knowledge is a paradoxical mode of knowing: I know that I do not know. Again, "We desire to know that we do not know," wrote Nicholas of Cusa in *De docta ignorantia.* "If we can fully attain unto this [knowledge of our ignorance], we will attain unto learned ignorance" (1.1). By examining the mode of inquiry and observing that it proceeds by means of a comparative relation and "hence the infinite *qua* infinite is unknown, for it escapes all comparative relation" (1.1), he concluded that "reason cannot leap beyond contradictories." Moreover, "as regards the movement of reason, plurality or multiplicity is opposed to oneness" (1.24). To recognize reason in this way is to attain "learned ignorance" or "sacred ignorance," which knows that "the precise truth shines incomprehensibly within the darkness of our ignorance" (1.26). Learned ignorance takes people beyond the apprehension of plurality of things, and they also see in their self-knowledge "that there is precise truth which we cannot comprehend" (2, prologue). One also reads in the *Kena Upaniṣad*: "it is not understood by those who understand it. It is understood by those who understand it not" (11).

Christian mystics also fondly cherished this intuition. John of the Cross held that if it is not by way of reason, then it is by way of non-knowing that one may arrive at what one knows not (*The Ascent of Mount Carmel* 1.14). In his poem, "I Entered I Knew Not Where," the reader encounters such lines:

> I entered I knew not where
> and remained without knowing,
> transcending all knowledge . . .
>
> I did not know where I entered,
> but when I saw myself there,
> not knowing where I was
> I understood great things . . .
>
> The higher one rose,
> the less was understood,
> for it was the dark cloud
> that illuminated the night. . . .
> (Krabbenhoft, pp. 25–29)

The idea of learned ignorance or recognition of the inability of reason to comprehend the ultimate reality has not been foreign to many Western thinkers. Pascal said, "There is nothing so consistent with reason as this denial of reason" (*Pensées* 182), or, again, "Reason's last step is the recognition that there are an infinite number of things which are beyond it. It is merely feeble if it does not go as far as to realize that. If natural things are beyond it, what are we to say about supernatural things?" (*Pensées* 188). And Kierkegaard held that "it is the duty of the human understanding to understand that there are things which it cannot understand, and what those things are" (ed. Bretall, p. 153).

The paradox and the *via negativa*. Dionysius the Areopagite noted that the ultimate reality, the Deity, was beyond human thought and therefore could only be approximated by negative predication. The medieval German mystic Meister Eckhart, a faithful adherent of this method, wrote: "It is God's nature to be without a nature. To think of his goodness, or wisdom, or power is to hide the essence of him, to obscure it with thoughts about him. Even one single thought or consideration will cover it up" (frag. 30). The famous beginning of the *Dao de jing* echoes this tradition: "The Way that can be spoken of is not an eternal way." In the Upaniṣadic tradition, *ātman* is "not this, not that [*neti, neti*]. It is unseizable, for it is not seized. It is indestructible, for it is not destroyed. It is unattached, for it does not attach itself. It is unbound. It does not tremble. It is not injured" (*Bṛhadāraṇyaka Upaniṣad* 3.9.26, 4.2.4, 4.4.22, 4.5.15).

The *via negativa*, or apophatic path, is in fact a paradoxical method of affirming the ultimate, which is considered a superlogical reality. Aquinas pointed out the contradiction inherent in this method: "The meaning of a negation always is found in an affirmation, as appears from the fact that every negative proposition is proved by an affirmative one; consequently, unless the human understanding knew something of God affirmatively, it could deny nothing of God; and such would be the case if nothing of what it says of God could be verified affirmatively" (*De potentia Dei* 7.5). The approach of mystical theology, however, has a paradoxical rather than a logical interest. Dionysius the Areopagite concluded his *Mystical Theology* thus: "We can neither affirm nor deny Him [God], inasmuch as the all-perfect and unique Cause of all things transcends all affirmation, and the simple preeminence of His absolute nature is outside of every negation—free from every limitation and beyond them all." One is thus left with the *docta ignorantia*—one knows that one does not know the divine reality.

The paradox of faith. Referring to the *Book of Job*, "the paradox of the best man in the worst fortune," G. K. Chesterton wrote that human beings are "most comforted by paradoxes" (p. 237). A. O. Lovejoy explored the psychological need for paradoxical expression in relation to religious salvation in his essay on *felix culpa*, "the fortunate fall." He argues that Adam's sin was fortunate and as such constitutes the *conditio sine qua non* of the Christian redemptive drama. This theme "had its own emotional appeal to many religious minds—partly, no doubt, because its very paradoxicality, its transcendence of the simple logic of common thought, gave it a kind of mystical sublimity" (p. 279). His study reveals that this theme in Milton's *Paradise Lost* actually goes back to du Bartas, Francis of Sales, Gregory the Great, Leo the Great, and Ambrose (pp. 294–295; see also Weisinger, 1953).

The paradox of sin and redemption deeply marks the thinking of religious figures. Luther held that "God conceals his eternal mercy and loving-kindness beneath eternal wrath, his righteousness beneath unrighteousness" (Althaus, p. 279). Again, "If sin is abolished, then Christ has also been done away with for there would no longer be any need for him" (*ibid.*, p. 258). Shinran, the founder of the Japanese True Pure Land school, said: "If the good are saved, how much more the wicked" (*Tannishō* 3). The paradox of redemption is sustained by faith. The Christian doctrine of the incarnation was for Kierkegaard the paradox *par excellence:* it is, he wrote, "the 'absolute Paradox,' the paradox of God in time. If one is to believe this paradox, God himself must give him the condition for doing so by giving him 'a new organ' of apprehension—that of Faith" (ed. Bretall, p. 154). The presence of paradox in religious writings can be understood as an integral part of the time-honored question of faith and reason.

Paradox, riddles, and enigma. Both paradox and riddles grapple with the enigma of the universe, of human existence. If something remains a riddle to human intelligence, it remains mysterious or else is understood only paradoxically.

The mystery of existence, the paradox of life, took a concrete expression in an ancient Chinese story. There was an old man living with his son and a very mangy horse near a fortress in a remote border region. One day this horse, the family's only possession, ran away. The villagers all sympathized with the old man for his loss, but he was not a bit perturbed, saying, "This could be a blessing in disguise." The following spring the horse came back with a mare, and they gave the old man many foals. The villagers now congratulated him, but he remained unperturbed. His son broke his leg while riding one of the horses. A war broke out, and nine out of ten men fighting the battle were killed, but his son was spared because he was lame. This Daoist story from the collection of *Huainanzi*, illustrates the inscrutability of what any event may lead to. This practical wisdom sees a complementary, dynamic interflow of the positive and the negative. It takes the enigma of existence and articulates it in a paradoxical way: It "conceptualizes" it in a "spherical" language. Paradox can be seen as one of the ways in which the human mind rationalizes the nonrational, the inscrutable, the unknown.

Paradoxes are baffling, striking, surprising, or nonsensical to linear thinking. But they are also free, creative, and playful, a form of expression conducive to a "spherical thinking" that expands and contracts freely "across terminal and categorical boundaries" (Colie, p. 7). A host of thinkers have directly or indirectly recognized paradox as an integral aspect of reality. From Heraclitus, Socrates, Plato, ancient sages, numerous mystics, to thinkers such as Pascal, Kierkegaard, Whitehead, Nishida, and Suzuki, the list encompasses seminal thinkers.

SEE ALSO Nishida Kitarō; Transcendence and Immanence; Via Negativa.

BIBLIOGRAPHY

For a comprehensive exposition of riddles, see James A. Kelso's "Riddle," in the *Encyclopaedia of Religion and Ethics*, edited by James Hastings, vol. 10 (Edinburgh, 1918). For close to nine hundred bibliographical entries on riddles, see Archer Taylor's *A Bibliography of Riddles* (Helsinki, 1939). Taylor's *The Literary Riddle before 1600* (Berkeley, 1948) is an invaluable cross-cultural study of riddles with an excellent bibliography on this subject. For an overview of riddles, see Mathilde Hain's *Rätsel* (Stuttgart, 1966) and Roger D. Abrahams's *Between the Living and the Dead* (Helsinki, 1980). Johan Huizinga's *Homo Ludens: A Study of the Play-Element in Culture* (London, 1949) offers a perceptive account of riddles.

For the Jewish and Arab fondness for riddles during the middle ages, see Israel Abrahams's *Jewish Life in the Middle Ages* (New York, 1896). Solomon Schechter's "The Riddles of Solomon in Rabbinic Literature," *Folklore* 1 (September 1891): 349–358, gives a full account of fifteenth-century midrash on the Solomon Riddle. Volumes 3, 7, and 9 of James G. Frazer's *The Golden Bough: A Study in Magic and Religion*, 3d ed. rev. & enl. (London, 1911–1915), contain accounts of riddles. On Vedic riddles, see Maurice Bloomfield's *The Religion of the Veda* (New York, 1969), pp. 210–218. For the *Ṛgveda* and other Hindu texts, see Raimon (var. Raimundo) Panikkar's *The Vedic Experience* (Berkeley, 1977).

On religion and paradox, see I. T. Ramsey and Ninian Smart's "Paradox in Religion," *Aristotelian Society Supplementary Volume* 33 (1959): 195–232. See also Smart's *Reasons and Faiths* (London, 1958). William H. Austin's *Waves, Particles and Paradoxes* (Houston, 1967) applies the principle of complementarity to explaining theological discourse. For the idea of the numinous, see Rudolf Otto's *The Idea of the Holy* (Oxford, 1928). W. T. Stace's *Mysticism and Philosophy* (Philadelphia, 1960) has an extensive section on religious discourse and paradox. Religious language and paradox are discussed in Robert L. Calhoun's "The Language of Religion," in *The Unity of Knowledge*, edited by Lewis Leary (Garden City, N.Y., 1955), pp. 248–262. For Heraclitus's writings, see *The Cosmic Fragments*, edited by G. S. Kirk (Cambridge, 1954). For a translation of Nicholas of Cusa's *De docta ignorantia*, see Jasper Hopkins's *On Learned Ignorance* (Minneapolis, 1981). On John of the Cross, see Kin Krabbenhoft, trans., *The Poems of St. John of the Cross* (New York, San Diego, London, 1999) (the translation was slightly altered in the text). Pascal's *Pensées* have been translated by, among others, A. J. Krailsheimer (Harmondsworth, 1966).

On the *kōan*, see *The Kōan: Texts and Contexts in Zen Buddhism*, Steven Heine and Dale Wright, ed. (Oxford and New York, 2000); *The World of Zen*, edited by Nancy W. Ross (New York, 1960); and Daisetz T. Suzuki's *An Introduction to Zen Buddhism* (New York, 1964). On the *Mumonkan* (*Wumenguan*) text, see Shibayama Zenkei's *Zen Comments on the Mumonkan*, trans. by Sumiko Kudo (New York, 1974). Toshihiko Izutsu's *Toward a Philosophy of Zen Buddhism* (Tehran, 1977) provides a philosophical exposition of *kōan*.

On Buddhism and paradox, see D. T. Suzuki's "Reason and Intuition in Buddhist Philosophy," in *Essays in East-West Philosophy*, edited by Charles A. Moore (Honolulu, 1951), pp. 17–48; see also Suzuki's "Basic Thoughts Underlying Eastern Ethical and Social Practice," in *Philosophy and Culture: East and West*, edited by Charles A. Moore (Honolulu, 1962), pp. 428–447. For representative works of the Kyoto School, see Nishida Kitarō, *An Inquiry into the Good* (New Haven, Conn. 1990) and "The Logic of *Topos* and the Religious Worldview," trans. by Michiko Yusa, *Eastern Buddhist*, 19.2 (1986), 1–29 and 20.1 (1987), 81–119, and Nishitani Keiji, *Religion and Nothingness* (Berkeley, 1982). Robert Slater's *Paradox and Nirvana* (Chicago, 1951) is a study on the religious ultimate with reference to Burmese Buddhism.

The philosophy of paradox is extensively discussed in Howard A. Slaatte's *The Pertinence of the Paradox* (New York, 1968). For an accessible coverage of paradox, see William Poundstone, *Labyrinths of Reason, Paradox, Puzzles, and the Frailty of Knowledge* (New York, London, Toronto, Sydney, Auckland, 1988). On paradox and faith, see *The Book of Job*, edited by G. K. Chesterton (London, 1916), an introduction to which may be found in *The Dimensions of Job*, edited by Nahum N. Glatzer (New York, 1969), pp. 228–238. For Kierkegaard's writings, see *A Kierkegaard Anthology*, edited by Robert W. Bretall (Princeton, 1946). Luther's ideas are studied in Paul Althaus's *The Theology of Martin Luther* (Philadelphia, 1966). On the idea of *felix culpa*, see Arthur O. Lovejoy's "Milton and the Paradox of the Fortunate Fall," in his *Essays in the History of Ideas* (Westport, Conn., 1978), pp. 277–295. See also Herbert Weisinger's *Tragedy and the Paradox of the Fortunate Fall* (London, 1953).

For logical paradox, see John van Heijenoort's "Logical Paradoxes," in *The Encyclopedia of Philosophy* (New York, 1967). W. V. O. Quine gives a cogent exposition of the topic in "Paradox," *Scientific American* 206 (April 1962): 84–96. Anatol Rapoport's "Escape from Paradox," *Scientific American* 217 (July 1967): 50–56, offers another excellent view of the subject, especially in relation to decision theory. Augustus De Morgan's *A Budget of Paradoxes*, 2d ed., 2 vols. (Chicago, 1915), presents extensive materials on "paradoxers."

On science and paradox, see Alfred North Whitehead's *Science and the Modern World* (New York, 1925). Thomas S. Kuhn's *The Structure of Scientific Revolutions*, 2d ed., rev. (Chicago, 1970), deals with the shift of conceptual scheme in the sciences. Bernard Bolzano's *Paradoxes of the Infinite* (1851; London, 1950) is one of the classical studies on the topic. On the nature of knowing and paradoxes, see Elizabeth H. Wolgast's *Paradoxes of Knowledge* (Ithaca, N. Y., 1977).

On the paradoxical tradition of the Renaissance, see Rosalie Littell Colie's *Paradoxia Epidemica* (Princeton, 1966). Nicholas Falletta's *The Paradoxicon* (Garden City, N. Y., 1983) gives a concise account while presenting wide-ranging examples of paradoxes with an extensive bibliography. On art and paradox, see Ernst H. Gombrich's *Art and Illusion* (New York, 1960).

MICHIKO YUSA (1987 AND 2005)

PARAMĀRTHA was the religious name of Kulanātha (499–569), an Indian monk and translator of Sanskrit texts. Paramārtha was a central figure in the introduction of the Buddhist Yogācāra, or Vijñānavāda (idealist), doctrines to China. Born in Ujjain, India, Paramārtha traveled widely as a Buddhist missionary and was probably living in Cambodia prior to arriving in Canton, baggage full of sūtras, in 546. Two years later he reached the Liang capital at Jiankang, present Nanjing, and was summoned to audience by Emperor Wu, a great patron of Buddhism. Impressed by both the knowledge and volume of sūtras Paramārtha possessed, the emperor had decided to appoint him director of an ambitious translation project when the Hou Jing rebellion forced him to abandon his plan.

Fleeing to the coastal provinces, Paramārtha wandered about translating and teaching and for a year or so enjoyed the patronage of Lu Yuanzhe, the governor of Fuchun in the Fuyang district of Zhejiang. In 552 he was recalled to the capital by a victorious Hou Jing. After only 120 days on the throne, Hou jing was overthrown by Xiao I (Emperor Yuan), during whose three-year reign Paramārtha enjoyed imperial support and resided at the Zhenguan temple in Nanking, translating the *Suvarṇaprabhāsa Sūtra* (*Jinguangming jing*). After three years in Nanjing, Paramārtha was forced by the unsettled political situation to resume the life of a wanderer, which, however, did not inhibit his prodigious translation activities. Yet despite such apparent energy he was depressed by his unstable circumstances, was constantly nostalgic for India, and repeatedly attempted to return home, only to be dissuaded each time by disciples and friends.

One of the more fateful of these attempts occurred in 562, when he managed to board a ship and journey the open sea for two months before a storm blew the boat into Canton. Ouyang Wei, the governor there, and his son Ouyang Ho, old acquaintances from Paramārtha's previous days in Canton, came to his aid and soon became his disciples. Under their patronage he translated many texts, including the *Mahāyānasaṃgraha* (Compendium of the Mahāyāna; Chin., *Shedasheng lun*), that were central to the development of uniquely Chinese traditions in Buddhism. The completion of these works brought him evident satisfaction, but nevertheless he lapsed into depression again, and his disciples had to thwart a suicide attempt in 568.

Hoping to brighten his outlook, his followers planned to return him to the capital, but the monks already entrenched there, fearing that Paramārtha might threaten their status, convinced the emperor of the newly founded Chen dynasty that his doctrines were a threat to the government. Paramārtha therefore stayed on in Canton until he succumbed to illness at the age of seventy.

A number of Paramārtha's translations proved influential in the development of indigenous Chinese Buddhist traditions during the Sui (581–618) and Tang (618–907) periods. These include the *Abhidharmakośa* (*Epidamozhushe lun*, Treasury of the Abhidharma), *Madhyāntavibhāga* (*Zhongbian fenbie lun*, On distinguishing the extremes from the middle), *Viṃśatikā*, and *Triṃśikā*, by Vasubandhu; the *Mahāyānasaṃgraha*, the *Saptadaśabhūmikaśāstra (Youjia shidi lun qishi lun)* portion of the *Yogācārabhūmi;* and Vasubandhu's treatise on Asaṅga's *Mahāyānasaṃgraha*, the *Mahāyānasaṃgraha-bhāṣya*. The last text provided the foundation for Paramārtha's own Shelun school, which came to be patronized during the Sui by Emperor Wen, and was championed and modified during the Tang by the monk Xuanzang. Paramārtha's work was the point of departure for Zhiyi (538–597) and Fazang (738?–838?), the principal masters of the Tiantai and Huayan schools, respectively. His thought was also important to the development of the Faxiang and Chan (Zen) schools of the Tang dynasty.

Bibliography

An important source for information on the life and thought of Paramārtha is Ui Hakuju's *Shindai sanzōden no kenkyū*, volume 6 of *Indo tetsugaku kenkyū* (Tokyo, 1965). For a superb review of Paramārtha's influence on the development of Chinese Buddhism, including a complete bibliography of modern critical studies, see Diana Y. Paul's *Philosophy of Mind in Sixth Century China: Paramārtha's "Evolution of Consciousness"* (Stanford, Calif., 1984).

MIYAKAWA HISAYUKI (1987)

PĀRAMITĀS. The term *pāramitā*, Sanskrit and Pali for "perfection," refers to the virtues that must be fully developed by anyone aspiring to become a Buddha, that is, by a *bodhisattva*. The practice of the *pāramitās* makes the career of a *bodhisattva* exceedingly long, but their fulfillment transforms the enlightenment process from one that benefits only the individual to one that is, in the words of the *Visuddhimagga*, "for the welfare and benefit of the whole world."

The idea of the *pāramitās* as a group is not found in the oldest Buddhist literature. Such a notion developed in the general expansion of Buddhist thought and practice before the beginning of the common era, which movement gave new recognition to types of religion other than renunciation. The *pāramitās* provided an alternative scheme of religious practice more in tune with newly developed conceptions of the Buddha and the nature of a *bodhisattva* than were the older schemes of morality, meditation, and wisdom (*śīla*, *samādhi*, *prajñā*) and the Noble Eightfold Path.

When the *pāramitās* appear as a group, their number varies; six and ten occur most often, but lists of five and seven are also found. It is sometimes suggested that six may have been the original number, because of an apparent progression in difficulty in such enumerations. The six are "giving" (*dāna*), "morality" (*śīla*), "patience" (*kṣānti*), "vigor" (*vīrya*), "contemplation" (*dhyāna*), and "wisdom" (*prajñā*). Such lists are found in early Mahāyāna texts (e.g., the *Saddharmapuṇḍarīka Sūtra* and the Prajñāpāramitā literature) and in the *Mahāvastu* of the Mahāsaṃghika school. The lists of ten, which include the additional virtues of "skill-in-means" (*upāya* or *upāyakauśalya*), "resolution" (*praṇidhāna*), "strength" (*bala*), and "knowledge" (*jñāna*), occur in later texts, for example, the *Daśabhūmika Sūtra* (fourth century). In such texts, the *pāramitās* are correlated with the ten stages (*bhūmi*) of a *bodhisattva*'s career.

Other independent and relatively early enumerations of the perfections are found in the *Cariyāpiṭaka* and the *Buddhavaṃsa*, both written in Pali and considered canonical by the Theravāda school. While the *Cariyāpiṭaka* lists seven perfections, the *Buddhavaṃsa* gives ten. These have become standard in the Theravāda traditions: "giving" (*dāna*), "morality" (*śīla*), "renunciation" (*nekkhamma*), "wisdom" (*paññā*), "vigor" (*viriya*), "patience" (*khanti*), "truthfulness" (*sacca*), "determination" (*adhiṭṭhāna*), "loving kindness" (*mettā*), and "equanimity" (*upekkhā*).

The Sanskrit and Pali noun *pāramitā* is derived from the adjective *parama*, meaning "high, complete, perfect." The Thervāda has consistently understood the term in this way and has commonly used another derivative, *pāramī*, as a synonym. In contrast, the Mahāyāna tradition has analyzed the term as consisting of two words, *pāram ita*, meaning "gone to the beyond," indicating its character as a scheme of spiritual progress. The Chinese and Tibetan translations of the term *pāramitā* (*tu* and *pha rol tu phyin pa*, respectively) reflect this latter understanding of its meaning.

These interpretations may differ along sectarian lines, but the applications they suggest are found in each of the Buddhist schools. In the Theravāda, the perfections afford the practitioner one way of celebrating the significance and superiority of the Buddha, whose fulfillment of them is often said to be incomparable. Similarly, Mahāyāna devotees focus their reverence on the enormous toils of great *bodhisattvas* such as Avalokiteśvara, who are engaged in practicing the perfections.

The *pāramitās* also provide a set of norms to structure the reading of the Jātakas, the collection of stories about the Buddha's previous lives. These tales, often non-Buddhist in origin and obscure in meaning, assume a Buddhist character when read with the *pāramitās* as guidelines. The *Cariyāpiṭaka*, the *Buddhavaṃsa*, and later Theravāda works (e.g., the *Nidānakathā*, the fifth-century introduction to the Jātaka collection) group and order some of the stories according to the practice and attainment of each perfection. We also see this template for reading in Mahāyāna works such as the *Mahāprajñāpāramitā Śāstra*.

The same pattern guides the illustrations of Jātakas as evidenced by such Buddhist art forms as the friezes on religious monuments of ancient India and the paintings decorating temples in modern Sri Lanka and Southeast Asia. In short, the *pāramitās* transformed the Jātakas into effective and popular sources for didactic art and literature. As Richard Gombrich observed in his study of Buddhism in modern Sri Lanka, *Precept and Practice* (Oxford, 1971), "There is a general tendency for those *Jātakas* which are canonically associated with the Bodhisattva's acquisition of a particular perfection to be more widely known" (p. 93).

The superposition of the *pāramitās* on the Jātakas, in turn, altered the perception of the perfections themselves. As gradations of the virtues became apparent, it proved practical to subdivide the ten perfections into thirty. Each *pāramitā* was divided into three degrees: an ordinary perfection (*pāramī*), an inferior perfection (*upapāramī*), and a superior perfection (*paramatthapāramī*). For example, in the Theravāda, the ordinary perfection of giving is "sacrifice of limbs," the inferior perfection is "sacrifice of external goods or property," and the superior perfection is "sacrifice of life."

The Jātakas also provide models for practicing the *pāramitās*. Through these stories about the Bodhisattva's—and thus, the Buddha's—involvement in the world, the virtues represented by the perfections are inculcated and come to be highly valued as qualities in individuals.

As the Mahāyāna analysis of the term suggests, these virtues are not merely a random assortment but are an ordered group leading to a goal. When the Mahāyāna replaced the notion of the *arhat* with the idea of the *bodhisattva* as the religious ideal to which all should aspire, the *pāramitās* provided a practical program that could be followed by new aspirants. This replacement altered some of the basic assumptions of spiritual progress. Under this new dispensation, as the *arhat* follows the Noble Eightfold Path he destroys the defilements that perpetuate rebirth but becomes enlightened only to the degree necessary to obtain release from rebirth. The *bodhisattva,* in contrast, renounces the enlightment of the *arhat* in order to pursue what is perceived as the higher and more complete enlightenment attained by Buddhas. The *bodhisattva* prepares himself for this attainment by practicing the perfections, which represent a program of positive moral development for the benefit of others. The Mahāyāna devotees negatively assess the practice of the *arhats,* claiming that it is based on restraint and removal and is without overt altruism. The perfections project the attainment of the goal into an inconceivable future and displace the sense of urgency and immediacy that motivates the *arhat's* quest. As a result, virtues such as patience, resolution, strength, and determination, which had a small place in early Buddhism, became prominent as *pāramitās.* Vigor, for instance, which had complemented the urgency felt by the disciple following the Eightfold Path, became an antidote to fatigue and despair during the *bodhisattva's* long career.

The idea of the perfections as a graduated soteriological path was developed and emphasized in the Mahāyāna, but it had a place in the Theravāda as well. This can be seen in a lengthy discussion in the *Cariyāpiṭaka* commentary by Dhammapāla, the sixth-century Pali commentator, where the perfections are treated as a spiritual path accessible to all. Some of the perfections (e.g., renunciation and equanimity) reinforce the basic assumptions of the *arhat* program, which the Theravāda never rejected.

To function as a progressive scheme leading to the final goal of enlightenment all of the perfections must be fulfilled. We can see, however, that certain perfections have assumed a greater importance. Doctrinally, wisdom (*prajñā*), the last of the six perfections, is often given pride of place in Mahāyāna writings. The *Bodhicaryāvatāra* says that "the Buddha taught that this multitude of virtues is all for the sake of wisdom"(Matics, 1970, p. 211). *Prajñā* is said to be greater than all the other virtues and to be that perfection that makes all others effective. Practically, the perfection of giving (*dāna*) has great importance. Emotive stories of the practice of this perfection (e.g., the Jātaka stories of King Śibi and Prince Viśvantara) are enormously popular throughout the Buddhist world and have been favorite subjects for Buddhist art and literature. As the first and easiest of the *pāramitās, dāna* is accessible to the humblest Buddhist when he or she aspires to enter the path to enlightenment. Its importance as a preparation for enlightenment is amply attested by the *Viśvantara* (*Vessantara*) *Jātaka,* in which the future Buddha perfects *dāna* in his penultimate birth.

See Also Avalokiteśvara; Bodhisattva Path; Eightfold Path; Prajñā.

Bibliography

A survey of the *pāramitās* in Mahāyāna literature may be found in Har Dayal's *The Bodhisattva Doctrine in Buddhist Sanskrit Literature* (London, 1932; reprint, Delhi, 1975). It provides detailed interpretations of each of the perfections and relates them to other aspects of Buddhist thought. A beautiful account of the *pāramitās* and their place in the career of a *bodhisattva,* as understood by the Indian Mādhyamika tradition, is Śantideva's *Bodhicaryāvatāra,* translated by Marion Matics as *Entering the Path of Enlightenment* (New York, 1970). The *Cariyāpiṭaka* and the *Buddhavaṃsa* have been translated by both B. C. Law (Oxford, 1938) and I. B. Horner (London, 1975) in volumes 11 and 31, respectively, of the "Sacred Books of the Buddhists" series. Dhammapāla's "Treatise on the *Pāramīs,*" from the *Cariyāpiṭaka* commentary is available in translation in *The Discourse on the All-Embracing Net of Views: The Brahmajāla Sutta and Its Commentarial Exegesis,* translated by Bhikkhu Bodhi (Kandy, 1978). A *summa* of Buddhist thought on the perfections is the *Mahāprajñāpāramitā Śāstra,* attributed to Nāgārjuna and translated from the Chinese by Étienne Lamotte as *Le traité de la grande vertu de sagesse* (Louvain, 1944–1980). This is an indispensable source for the study of the *pāramitās.* Lamotte's annotations themselves are a mine of information for literacy references to the *pāramitās* and for references to the many publications that treat their iconography.

New Sources

Aitken, Robert. *The Practice of Perfection: The Paramitas from a Zen Buddhist Perspective.* New York, 1994.

Sanam Richen, Geshe. *The Six Perfections: An Oral Teaching.* Translated and edited by Ruth Sonam. Ithaca, N.Y., 1998.

Charles Hallisey (1987)
Revised Bibliography

PARENTALIA.

PARENTALIA. The term *Parentalia* designates the period of nine days during which Roman families would visit the tombs of the dead to honor them. This novena, private in character, began on February13 and ended with the public feast of the Feralia on February 21. This cycle of days received its most extended comment from the Roman poet Ovid. He interchangeably calls them the *parentales dies* (*Fasti* 2.548) or the *ferales dies* (*Fasti* 2.34). The word *Feralia* gave the ancients occasion to coin etymological puns. The word could stem either "from the action of bringing food" *(a ferendis epulis)* or "from the action of sacrificing animals" (*a feriendis pecudibus;* Paulus-Festus, ed. Lindsay, 1913, p. 75 L.). The scholar M. Terentius (Varro, *De lingua Latina* 6.13) preferred to compare the term *Feralia* to both *inferi* and *ferre,* adding, "because the ones having the right to *parentare* bring then some food to the tomb" ("quod ferunt tum epulas ad sepulcrum quibus ius ibi parentare").

Parentare, "to celebrate the Parentalia," consisted in honoring the *di parentes,* or dead, with offerings. Ovid (*Fasti* 2.537–539) was glad to list such offerings: garlands, grains of wheat, salt, bread softened with wine, a few violets. These modest offerings were appropriate for the *manes,* the shades or spirits of the dead.

One may note the variations in vocabulary used by the various authors to refer to the dead: *inferi* (Varro, *De lingua Latina* 6.13); *dis manibus* (Festus, op. cit., p. 75 L.); *manes* (Ovid, *Fasti* 2.534). *Manes* or *di manes* is very likely explained as a euphemism: "the *inferi* are called *di manes,* that is, "good ones" with whom one should be reconciled out of fear of death" (Festus, op. cit., p. 132 L.). Use of the term corresponds to a later usage (first century BCE) that substituted for the ancient expression *di parentes* or *di parentum,* as had appeared already (specifically, in the form *divis parentum;* Festus, op. cit., p. 260 L.) in a "royal" law. A deceased person was regarded as having joined the collectivity of the *di parentes* (in the funerary inscriptions, it is written in the dative or the genitive along with the collective term). The formulation of Cornelia's letter to her son Gaius Sempronius Gracchus gives evidence of the link between the verb *parentare* and the corresponding noun: "Ubi mortua ero, parentabis mihi et invocabis deum parentem" ("When I am dead, you will honor me at the Parentalia and call on the parental shade"). By this *pietas*—the expression is Ovid's (*Fasti* 2.535)—toward the dead, the Parentalia were differentiated from the Lemuria of May 9, 11, and 13, which consisted of rites in which evil spirits were expelled (ibid., 5.429–444). On February 22, the day after the Feralia, which commemorated a family's dead, there followed the Caristia or Cara Cognatio, which united the living members of the family in a banquet (ibid., 2.677).

Bibliography

Bömer, Franz. *Ahnenkult und Ahnenglaube im alten Rom.* Bonn, 1943.

Dumézil, Georges. *Archaic Roman Religion.* 2 vols. Translated by Philip Krapp. Chicago, 1970.

Schilling, Robert. *Rites, cults, dieux de Rome.* Paris, 1979. See pages 11–15 for a discussion of Feralia and Lemuria.

Wagenvoort, Hendrik. *Studies in Roman Literature, Culture and Religion.* Leiden, 1956. Pages 290–297 treat the *parentatio* in honor of Romulus.

Wissowa, Georg. *Religion und Kultus der Römer.* 2d ed. Munich, 1912. See pages 232–235.

New Sources

Gessel, Wilhelm. "Reform von Märtyrenkult und Totengedächtnis. Die Bemühungen des Presbyters Augustinus gegen die laetitia und parentalia vom J. 395." In *Reformatio Ecclesiae. Beiträge zu kirchlichen Reformbemühungen von der alten Kirche bis zur Neuzeit. Festgabe Erwin Iserloh,* edited by Remigius Bäumer, pp. 61–73. Paderborn, 1980.

Lejeune, Michel. "Capoue: iovilas de terre cuite et iovilas de tufi." *Latomus* 49 (1990): 785–791.

Littlewood, R. J. "Ovid among the Family Dead." *Latomus* 60 (2001): 916–935.

Radke, Gerhardt. "Anmerkungen zu den ersten fünf Feriae Publicae der römischen Fasten." In *Religio graeco-romana. Festschrift für Walter Pötscher,* ed. by Joachim Dalfen, Gerhard Petersmann and Franz Ferdinand Schwarz, pp. 177–193. Horn, 1993.

Rüpke, Jörg. "Wann feierte Ovid die Feralia." *Museum Helveticum* 51 (1994): 97–102.

Scheid, John. "Die Parentalien für die verstorbenen Caesaren als Modell für den römischen Totenkult." *Klio* 75 (1993): 188–201.

ROBERT SCHILLING (1987)
Translated from French by Paul C. Duggan
Revised Bibliography

PARMENIDES. A Greek philosopher who lived between the second half of the sixth century BCE and the first half of the fifth century BCE, Parmenides was born in and lived in Elea, an Ionic colony on the coast of Campania, in an area then inhabited by the Lucani, who called the city Velia. He was a pupil of Xenophanes as well as a Pythagorean. Charged with the governance of the city, he gave Elea a long-lasting constitution regarded as the principal reason for its power. He also founded a philosophical school, which was monist and has become known historically as the Eleatic school. His closest followers were Zeno and Melissus. Parmenides wrote a long poem in hexameters titled *On Nature,* a difficult text even for his contemporaries. The work was lost in the early Middle Ages, and about twenty fragments of around 150 to 160 verses survive. Thus modern interpretation of his work is even more controversial. Parmenidean doctrine denies the real existence of diversity and change and asserts the unity of being. This doctrine has been regarded from time to time as the foundation of metaphysics, of logic, and of the theory of predication and as the methodology of scientific research based upon the principle of correspondence, that is, of "invariance."

Whatever the intention, it is a passionate espousal of *l'esprit de géométrie,* a radical departure from the normal manner of ethical or political discourse, despite the significant political role played by Parmenides in his native city. It is particularly revealing that, all this notwithstanding, Parmenides's discourse is set out in clear theological and religious terms from various related perspectives.

The doctrine is presented in the proem as the "revelation" of a goddess, in fact of the Goddess, probably Persephone, the titular goddess of the celebrated mystery cult of Demeter at Elea. Parmenides tells of a fantastic journey in a horse-drawn chariot, guided by the Heliades, the daughters of Helios, the Sun, who guide it to the Gate of Night and Day. When they reach there, they ask the gatekeeper, Dike, Justice, to open up and allow their charge to pass through. The poet thus manages to enter into the presence of the

Goddess, who welcomes him and invites him to listen to her explain both "the unshakeable heart of well-rounded Truth" and "the opinions of mortals, in which there is no certainty at all"

In terms of the conventions particular to archaic Greece, the image of the chariot in the proem is a clear metaphor for poetry, often guided by the Muses, who steer the poet in the "right" direction. For Parmenides the chariot symbolizes poetic wisdom, *sophia,* encompassing as it does the tension regarding the Truth and the absolute poetic skill necessary to express this. The route here is "the way of the goddess," which takes the "wise man" in the direction of the "Ultimate Truth." The chariot is not guided by the Muses, the daughters of Memory, but by the Heliades, goddesses related to the light of the Sun, because Parmenides was not attempting to set out a mythical tale, like any other poet, but rather a scientific account. The motif of the gate is made still more complex because it is a specific gate that had always played a central part in the sphere of myth and cosmology, that is, the Gate of Day and Night, also called the Gate of the Sun, and is identified with the Gate of Hades. It towered in the extreme west, far from the region inhabited by humankind. Beyond this, just as in Parmenides, yawned the abyss, in Greek *berethron,* chaos, (*chasma*), in other words the world of the dead, the realm of Hades and Persephone, the god and goddess of the netherworld, but also, according to Hesiod, the cosmic location in which were gathered the first principles of everything, the "roots," the "sources," the "limits," that is, the elements of matter.

After the proem, throughout the poem every abstract concept, every natural entity is represented in divine terms. Physical law becomes Justice (Dike) or Themis, the goddess of justice regarded by the Greeks as older and with greater authority than Dike, or Necessity (Ananke), the goddess of Homer and Hesiod, who ruled over the most powerful gods, or Moira (Fate), the ancient goddess of birth, life, and death. The abstract luminance was Truth (Aletheia), the epic goddess of truthfulness. Being itself was represented in the likeness of an imprisoned god in shackles, a obvious allusion to Prometheus in chains. In Parmenides, in complete form, the unique union that was to be characteristic of subsequent Greek cultural development is evident, a synthesis of absolute intellectual rationalism and the religious symbolism of the polytheistic tradition.

The astronomical section of the poem, following in the footsteps of Anaximander, sets out a map of the heavens in the form of spherical concentric bands on which individual stars were set out. These, or at least some of these, were clearly divine in form. The outer surface, the farthest away, including all the bands in order nearest to the earth, which was located in the center, was called in lay terms *ouranos,* "heaven," but also theologically *Olympus eschatos,* "the final Olympus." This alludes to the mountain on the summit of which, myth said, was situated the abode of the gods. In the center band, perhaps the heaven of Hesperus-Lucifer, correctly identified by Parmenides as one and the same star, is "the goddess who controls all things," especially regarding sexual congress, the source of life, thus a supreme goddess, probably Aphrodite. Eros also plays an important role. It is clear that the doctrine of divine intelligence and astral influences has already made its appearance.

There is no doubt that the pantheon of Parmenides is predominantly feminine. In particular the two principal divinities, the inspired revelatrix of the proem and the omnipotent one in the center of the heavens, are goddesses. Being, in Greek, Eon, single unchanging matter, which has no space in which to move, is neuter gender. The masculine, theologically speaking, is of marginal importance. This causes a difficulty of interpretation that is impossible to resolve because of the scarcity of available information. Some see the survival or reemergence in Parmenides of an ancient pre-Greek Mediterranean religion with a matriarchal basis (Untersteiner, 1958).

See Also Empedocles; Metaphysics; Monism; Muses; Plato; Pythagoras; Xenophanes.

Bibliography

Burkert, Walter. "Das Proömium des Parmenides und die Katabasis des Pythagoras." *Phronesis* 14 (1969): 1–30.

Cerri, Giovanni. "Cosmologia dell'Ade in Omero, Esiodo e Parmenide." *Parola del passato* 50 (1995): 437–467.

Cerri, Giovanni. *Poema sulla natura, Parmenide di Elea: Introduzione, testo, traduzione, e note.* Milan, 1999.

Couloubaritsis, Lambros. *Mythe et philosophie chez Parménide.* Brussels, 1990.

Coxon, A. H. *The Fragments of Parmenides: A Critical Text with Introduction, Translation, the Ancient Testimonia, and a Commentary.* Assen, Netherlands, 1986.

Diels, Hermann, and Walther Kranz. *Die Fragmente der Vorsokratiker,* vol. 1. Berlin, 1951. See pp. 217–246. Reference edition.

Frère, Jean. "Aurore, Eros, et Ananke: Autour des dieux parméniennes." *Études philosophiques* 60 (1985): 459–470.

Jaeger, Werner Wilhelm. *Theology of the Early Greek Philosophers.* Oxford, 1947. See chap. 6.

Kingsley, Peter. *In the Dark Places of Wisdom.* Inverness, Calif., 1999.

Pellikaan-Engel, Maja E. *Hesiod and Parmenides: A New View on Their Cosmologies and on Parmenides' Proem.* Amsterdam, 1974.

Pugliese Carratelli, Giovanni. "La Theà di Parmenide." *Parola del passato* 43 (1988): 337–346.

Tarán, Leonardo. *Parmenides: A Text with Translation, Commentary, and Critical Essays.* Princeton, N.J., 1965.

Untersteiner, Mario. *Parmenide:, Testimonianze e frammenti:* Introduzione, traduzione, e commento. Florence, 1958.

West, Martin L. *Early Greek Philosophy and the Orient.* Oxford, 1971.

Giovanni Cerri (2005)
Translated from Italian by Paul Ellis

PARSIS (Pārsis, also rendered as Parsees), "Persians," or Zoroastrians, from Iran who settled in the Indian subcontinent during the tenth century CE, and their descendents.

ORIGINS. Zoroastrians in Iran had contact with people in the Indian subcontinent from at least the fifth century BCE through overland and maritime trade. After the Arab Muslim conquest of Iran in the seventh century CE, there were many small, poorly documented migrations by Zoroastrians away from that country over both land and sea. The one relocation that gained a historiography probably occurred in the tenth century and produced the Parsi community in India. That particular migration is recorded as the Parsi community's founding legend, known as the *Qessa-e Sanjān* (Story of Sanjan), a New Persian narrative poem based upon an older oral tradition, composed in 1600 CE. It forms the basis—idealized and augmented—for much of the Parsis' early history. According to the text, during the reign of the Samanid kings (892–1005) many Zoroastrians from the northeastern Iranian province of Khorasan relocated overland via the mountains of Kuhestan to the Persian Gulf port of Hormuz, then by ship via the Persian Gulf and the Indian island of Diu to Gujarat in western India. Their date of arrival at Gujarat is assigned by tradition to 992 Vikram Samvat (an Indian calendar begun in 58 BCE equivalent to 936 CE). Owing to uncertainty resulting from parallels between the local script and Devanagari numbers, the date came to be read as 772 Vikram Samvat or 716 CE—an inaccuracy still accepted by some Parsis and scholars. Yet the maritime migration to Gujarat and relocation there along the coastal region does not explain adequately accounts by Muslim travelers during the tenth century CE of groups that they referred to as *gabr* (hollow or empty, hence "one lacking faith, infidel"), a derogatory designation by Muslims for Zoroastrians, living in the hinterland of north India. The number and size of such inland communities suggest strongly that other Zoroastrians must have entered India via land routes from the northwest and, in time, fallen under the rubric of Parsis.

The *Qessa-e Sanjān* goes on to claim that a local raja or ruler named Jādi Rānā (Vajjardevrai or Vajjadadeva) of the Silhara dynasty agreed to grant the Zoroastrians safe haven in Gujarat on the condition that the newcomers explain their beliefs to the Hindus, adopt the Gujarati language, refrain from bearing weapons, perform weddings only at night, and ensure that their women blend with Hindu counterparts by wearing the local garb, the sari. Gujarat, as a result, became the region in India where most Zoroastrians settled. A complementary folk tale claims that the raja had shown the newcomers a pitcher full of milk to signify that India was already heavily populated, with little room for new settlers, but that a magus who was present deposited something worthwhile into the milk—sugar, a coin, or a ring, depending on the version—to indicate that Zoroastrians would coexist harmoniously with Indians, become Indianized, and enhance Indian society. Interestingly, neither the *Qessa-e Sanjān* nor the early folk tales mention any agreement or understanding between the Zoroastrians and the Hindu barring the former from proselytizing their faith.

SETTLEMENT PATTERNS. The Parsis founded the town of Sanjan. About five years after their arrival, the Parsis consecrated an *ātash bahrām*—a "victory fire," the highest level of ritual fire—named Irān Shāh (king of Iran), which remained their main flame for more than eight hundred years. Most religious rituals were performed using *dādgāh* (hearth) fires. During the first three hundred years after the arrival in Gujarat, as the community prospered and its population increased, some Parsis moved to Navsari on the banks of the Varoli River in 1142. They also spread to the towns of Surat, Anklesar, Cambay, and Broach. In each of those towns they worked as farmers, toddy brewers, carpenters, weavers, and merchants. Magi continued to dress in white robes and turbans as they had in Iran. Parsi laymen adopted Indian dress but wore white on ritual occasions. Parsi women wore the Indian sari, with minor variations in the manner of wrapping it around the body that became distinctive to Zoroastrians.

Clusters of families had their spiritual needs tended to by an individual magus, and those devotional clusters came to be known as the priest's *panthak.* In time, this association of particular lay or *behdin* families with a specific magian or *athōrnān* priest and his descendants as *panthaki* became hereditary. Around 1290 the Parsi magi divided Gujarat into five *panths* (ecclesiastic groups) based on location: the Sanjānas at Sanjan, the Bhagarias serving Navsari, the Godavras based at Anklesar, the Bharuchas controlling rites in Broach, and the Khambattas of Cambay. Each *panth* regulated its own clergy, laity, and religious matters through an *anjoman* (association). At many locales over the centuries, under the direction of priests and lay patrons, an *ateshgah* (fire precinct) was established for rituals by the living, as was a *dakhma* (funerary tower) for exposure of the dead.

DOCTRINES AND RITES IN MEDIEVAL TIMES. The *jizya* (poll tax) was imposed on non-Muslims in 1297 when the Delhi Muslim sultanate conquered Gujarat. Economic hardship created by payment of the *jizya,* plus the stigma of designation as a *dhimmī* (protected religious minority) resulted in conversion of portions of the Parsi population to Islam. Yet the community persisted in its beliefs and praxes, so that early European travelers in the region began to encounter them; in 1350, for example, the Dominican friar Jordanus commented on the exposure of Parsi corpses. In 1741, after a few previous relocations, the Irān Shāh *ātash bahrām* was brought to the city of Udwada, where it continued to burn at the beginning of the twenty-first century. The Bhagarias consecrated their own *ātash bahrām* at Navsari in 1765. Thereafter, six other fires of the *ātash bahrām* ritual level were established—two at Surat in 1823 and four at Bombay (later Mumbai) in 1783, 1830, 1845, and 1897.

As they assimilated into Indian society, pressure from Hindus compelled the Parsis to accept certain socioreligious transformations. For example, the ritual slaughter of cattle had to be discontinued gradually in accordance with Hindu veneration for that animal, although goats and sheep continued to be offered, with a portion of their bodies or fat being deposited in holy fires. As Parsis settled in parts of the Indian subcontinent where their numbers were insufficient to maintain funerary towers, they began adopting the custom of burial in an *āramgāh* (place of repose, cemetery, graveyard). Perhaps most important in terms of socioreligious change was that, over time, Parsis came to be regarded as a caste within Hindu society. So, despite accepting some converts from among Hindus who had close contact through friendship or work, the religion slowly became hereditary in an Indian context, with no converts being accepted. Parsis also had to mingle with members of other faiths in India and to explain their doctrines and praxes. For instance, in 1578 the emperor Akbar summoned a Bhagaria priest named Meherji Rāna to the Mogul court for a symposium. That contact proved beneficial to the Parsis, as the *jizya* on them was lifted a few years later.

In 1746 a disagreement relating to the calendar caused division of the community into Kadmīs, who accept the *qadīmī* (ancient) Iranian calendar, and the Shenshaīs, or Rasimīs (traditionalists), who maintain the original Parsi calendar. Since 1906 another group, the Fasalīs, or Faslīs, have formed, and its members utilize a *fasl* (seasonal) calendar for rituals. The majority of Parsis remain Shenshaī, but calendrical preferences have maintained those communal divisions and have produced minor variations in liturgies and rites.

Contact between Zoroastrians in India and Iran—the Parsis and the Iranis—gained momentum in the thirteenth century. Several religious texts were sent from Iran to India for safekeeping, and as a result, most of the oldest extant copies of Zoroastrian scripture and exegesis remained in India until the eighteenth century onward, when some of those documents were obtained by Western museums and universities. Just as important, Parsis began seeking religious advice from magi in Iran. A collection of treatises on religious observances, sent from Iran to India between 1478 and 1773 and known collectively as the *Persian Revāyats*, attests to the close ties that were developing as Parsi emissaries were welcomed, lived among, and educated by their Iranian coreligionists before returning to India.

TRANSFORMATION IN PREMODERN AND MODERN TIMES. Contact between the Parsis and Europeans grew with the establishment of trading posts in the seventeenth century. European eyewitness accounts note that at first the Parsis enforced their own customs, with violators being excommunicated or even, occasionally, executed. But as trade increased, so did the Parsi community's economic and social diversity. The port of Surat grew into a settlement of over 100,000 Parsi Zoroastrians between the seventeenth and eighteenth centuries. Then, in 1661, the port of Bombay came under the British East India Company's administration and Parsis moved there to trade. Parsis flourished in Bombay, led by the commercial successes of individuals such as Lowji Nassarwanji Wadia (1702–1744) and Sir Jamsetji Jijibhai (1783–1859) in shipbuilding and the opium and cotton trades between India, England, and China. Parsis also established themselves quickly in textile manufacture and the bankingindustry. Steadily, Parsis became the mercantile arm of the British in India, serving in that capacity for over two hundred years. Members of the community then went on to play central roles in establishing the industrial base of modern India. Pioneers included Jamshedji N. Tata (1839–1904), who founded the iron and steel industries, early hydroelectric power plants in India, and the Indian Institute of Science, and Homi J. Bhabha (1909–1966), who pioneered research in atomic energy. Others, such as Lieutenant General Sam H. F. J. Manekshaw (1914–), led India's post-independence military during the late twentieth century.

Socioeconomic success would transform the community in many different ways. The Parsi Panchāyat, initially a council of elders, was established in 1728 to regulate community affairs. It did so not through law but through edicts and codes of conduct that were enforced by communal pressure. Since the question of religious freedom in Iran occupied the thoughts of Parsis, in 1854 they sent an emissary named Manekji Limji Hataria (1813–1890) to Iran. Hataria lived in Iran for four decades, married an Irani Zoroastrian woman, and even visited the Qajar court to intercede on behalf of Zoroastrians. Hataria's mission, coupled with pressure on the Qajar dynasty from the British Raj on behalf of prominent Parsis like Dadabhai Naoroji (1825–1917), succeeded in having the *jizya* abolished in Iran in 1882. Wealthy Parsis also began to look after the secular needs of their coreligionists in Iran by building schools, hospitals, orphanages, and retirement homes, in addition to renovating several *ātashkada* (fire temples) and *dakhma* and *āramgāh* funerary sites there.

Secular education, in particular, fundamentally reoriented the Parsis. In the nineteenth century, Parsis founded English-style schools, libraries, and educational trusts for their sons and daughters. Following mores that were emerging in Europe at the time, the Parsis began encouraging educated men and women to take up careers in public, multicommunal, workplaces. This development played a major role in fueling a demographic shift among Parsis—away from the coastal villages and orchards of Gujarat to large cities like Bombay, Delhi, Calcutta, Karachi, and Colombo. Rapid urbanization began in the 1900s, reaching 94 percent by 1961 among Parsis (compared to 27 percent for Muslims, 23 percent for Christians, and 16 percent for Hindus) on the Indian subcontinent. Parsi Zoroastrians, consequently, became a highly urbanized middle and upper class. As part of westernization and urbanization, the ritual slaughter of animals was slowly phased out by the late 1930s, as was the *ātash-zōhr* (offering to fire) of animal flesh, fat, and butter. Likewise, marriages arranged by relatives declined in frequency after the 1920s as women exercised their greater freedom to select their own spouses. At the same time, educated women in the community began to choose careers over marriage, family, and domesticity—close to 25 percent of Parsi women remained unmarried after the 1970s, and the community's birthrate declined drastically. Moreover, by the end of the twentieth century, women's expectations had begun to exceed the reality represented by potential male partners within the community—again reinforcing the trend in declining marital and reproductive rates.

Parsis began entering politics, with Naoroji, an architect of Indian independence, becoming the first president of the Indian National Congress in 1885. Other Parsis closely associated with the Indian nationalist movement were Sir Pherozeshah Mehta (1845–1915), Sir Dinshaw Wacha (1844–1936), and Madam Bhikaji Cama (1861–1936). In England, several Parsis have held elected office at various levels of government, starting with three members of the British Parliament—Naoroji of the Liberal Party mentioned previously, Sir Muncherji Bhownagree (1851–1933) of the Conservative Party, and Shapurji Saklatvala (1874–1936), who was a Communist. This trend in political involvement continues among Parsis globally. In Sri Lanka, Kairshasp Choksy (1932–) became minister of constitutional and state affairs and subsequently minister of finance. Jamsheed Marker (1922–) became a prominent diplomat, first for Pakistan and then for the United Nations. Loyalty and service to the countries and cultures in which they reside have emerged as important attitudes among Parsis.

International Dispersal and Its Consequences. During the time of the British Empire, Parsis began traveling to England for commerce and education, especially after the mid-nineteenth century. By 1861 a Zoroastrian Association had been founded there. However, a major international dispersion of Parsis from India occurred for a variety of socioeconomic reasons only after the early 1950s. A few left India to join the descendants of relatives who had immigrated earlier to England. Some departed India, Pakistan, and Sri Lanka to avoid rising nationalism and religious fundamentalism in those countries. Others went to Australia, Hong Kong, and countries in sub-Saharan Africa seeking economic opportunities. From the 1960s, migration has been for education and employment in the United States and Canada. Nonetheless, Parsis still dwell in most major cities of India, particularly Bombay (subsequently Mumbai), Delhi, and Calcutta.

Largely English-speaking, with many older Parsis still bilingual in English and Gujarati, Parsis number approximately 69,200 in India (in 2001), 10,000 in the United States (in 2000), 6,000 in Canada (in 2000), 4,000 in England and Scotland (in 2000), 3,000 in the European Union (in 2002), 2,200 in Pakistan (in 2003), 2,000 in Australia (in 2000), and 1,000 in the United Arab Emirates (in 2000). (Zoroastrian communities in each country consist of two broad groups: the Iranis, or Iranian Zoroastrians, and members of that group who have settled in many countries, and the Parsis, or Indian Zoroastrians, who are discussed in this entry. The demographic numbers refer to the Parsis only, not to overall Zoroastrian communities in each country.) Smaller communities live in New Zealand (200 in 2000), Hong Kong (190 in 2000), Singapore (150 in 2000), Bahrain (130 in 1996), Democratic Republic of the Congo (100 in 2000), South Africa (70 in 2000), and Sri Lanka (63 in 2001). The communities in Pakistan, Sri Lanka (then Ceylon), Singapore, and Hong Kong date from British colonial times as a legacy of trade. Even smaller groups are found in countries as diverse as Japan, China, Malaysia, Myanmar, Yemen, Seychelles, Bermuda, and Venezuela. In most of those countries, there are other Zoroastrians as well.

In most countries where Parsi diasporas exist, each community has at least one fire temple of the *dādgāh* ritual level, a community hall associated with the temple, and a graveyard to bury the dead (although cremation by electricity is becoming popular as a means of avoiding long-term ritual pollution of earth and fire), expect in India and in the Pakistani city of Karachi, where the funerary towers—now commonly called "towers of silence"—are still utilized amidst ongoing debate about how to ensure swift desiccation and decomposition of corpses placed therein. The communities have religious classes for children, and ceremonies of *navjote* (initiation) are conducted regularly for them. However, a low birthrate as individuals defer marriage in favor of professional careers, a widespread prohibition of the acceptance of converts, and a discouraging level of intermarriage with members of other sectarian groups have contributed to a gradual overall decline in numbers.

On the other hand, following a pattern common to many minorities, the international diasporas have been economically and socially successful in professions such as law, medicine, and academia, and in entrepreneurial endeavors from computer programming to watch manufacture. The arts, too, have caught the attention of a number of Parsis, including the American conductor Zubin Mehta (1936–), born in Bombay; the English rock musician Freddy Mercury (1946–1991), born in Zanzibar as Farrokh Bulsara; and the Canadian writer Rohinton Mistry (1952–), born in Bombay. As a direct result of westernization and secularization, educated women have come to wield leadership positions within Parsi diasporas, including editorial positions at widely read Zoroastrian newsletters, such as the *FEZANA Journal* in North America and *Parsiana* in South Asia, wherein issues of societal change are hotly debated.

Other Major Contemporary Issues. During the eighteenth and nineteenth centuries, European scholars concluded that the founder of the Parsis' religion, Zarathushtra, or Zoroaster, had preached a monotheistic faith that was debased by his followers. This viewpoint gained the acceptance of many Parsis, who sought to structure their religion into its allegedly pristine form based on the *Gāthās* (Devotional poems) ascribed to Zarathushtra. Zoroastrians who follow the teachings of Minocher Pundol (1908–1975) combine such trends with mysticism. The introduction of theosophy further attenuated doctrinal unity among the Parsis. Lack of doctrinal concord and a concomitant decline in theological education continue in the twenty-first century.

Poor wages, substandard living conditions, and the lure of secular professional careers have steadily sapped enrollment in the two *madrasahs* (seminaries)—the Athornan Boarding Madrasa at Dadar and the M. F. Cama Athornan Institute at Andheri—where Zoroastrian priests are trained in India. Thus, the number of priests available to perform rituals continues to decline. Therefore, rites in many instances have been abbreviated and in certain locales are restricted to the basic ones of passage—initiation, marriage, and death—and to *jashan* (thanksgiving) services. Likewise, the number of women who weave the *kustī* (holy cord) has also diminished as their priestly families take up secular occupations.

Other, interrelated topics of much debate worldwide within Parsi communities include the issues of who the Parsis are, whether intermarriage with non-Zoroastrians should be recognized, and whether converts can be accepted. As the Parsis became a de facto caste within Indian society, they diverged from their Iranian coreligionists by abjuring conversion to the faith. By the nineteenth century, magi who initiated as Zoroastrians the children of non-Parsi fathers or the adopted children (from non-Zoroastrian parents) of Parsis were subjected to censure by their clerical *anjomans*. Eventually, guidelines were set in India by that country's civil judiciary in 1909 and 1925 as the result of court cases seeking to exclude non-Parsi wives from fire temples and community institutions. Through those legal decisions, the civil courts upheld the community's restriction of its properties to the children of Parsi and Irani Zoroastrians plus duly initiated children of Parsi fathers by non-Zoroastrian wives. So in India and, as a result of colonial rule, in Pakistan and Sri Lanka, a Parsi Zoroastrian—male or female—is defined as a person whose father was or is a Parsi Zoroastrian. Converts are not accepted. The children of a Parsi woman who is married to a non-Zoroastrian are regarded as neither Parsis or Zoroastrians. They cannot enter fire temples, benefit from communal funds, or even have Zoroastrian last rites. Not all priests and laity accept that position, however, either in South Asia or elsewhere. For example, during the late twentieth in the United States (as previously in India), there were occasional instances when individuals who wished to join Zoroastrianism were initiated by Parsi priests. Moreover, enhanced contact between Zoroastrians and members of other faiths, especially in Europe, North America, and Australia, has led to an increase in the frequency of marriage across confessional boundaries. On this issue, the diaspora communities in the West have increasingly diverged from the Parsis on the Indian subcontinent by permitting non-Zoroastrian spouses to attend rituals at fire temples and cemeteries and to participate fully in community activities and governance. In so doing, Parsis living in the West have come closer to the long-standing position of Iranian Zoroastrians and Irani Zoroastrian immigrants to the West on those issues.

SEE ALSO Ateshgah; Gender and Religion, article on Gender and Zoroastrianism; Zoroastrianism.

BIBLIOGRAPHY

Axelrod, Paul. "A Social and Demographic Comparison of Parsis, Saraswat Brahmins, and Jains in Bombay." Ph.D. diss., University of North Carolina, 1974.

Axelrod, Paul. "Myth and Identity in the Indian Zoroastrian Community." *Journal of Mithraic Studies* 3, nos. 1–2 (1980): 150–165.

Choksy, Jamsheed K. *Purity and Pollution in Zoroastrianism: Triumph over Evil.* Austin, Tex., 1989.

Choksy, Jamsheed K. *Evil, Good, and Gender: Facets of the Feminine in Zoroastrian Religious History.* New York, 2002.

Daryaee, Touraj. "The Persian Gulf Trade in Late Antiquity." *Journal of World History* 14, no. 1 (2003): 1–16.

Desai, Sapur F. *History of the Bombay Parsi Punchayet, 1860–1960.* Bombay, 1977.

Hinnells, John R. "Parsis and the British." *Journal of the K. R. Cama Oriental Institute* 46 (1978): 1–92.

Hinnells, John R. *Zoroastrians in Britain.* Oxford, 1996.

Hinnells, John R. *Zoroastrian and Parsi Studies: Selected Works of John R. Hinnells.* Aldershot, U.K., 2000.

Hodivala, Shahpurshah H. *Studies in Parsi History.* Bombay, 1920.

Kennedy, Robert E., Jr. "The Protestant Ethic and the Parsis." *American Journal of Sociology* 68, no. 1 (1962): 11–20.

Kreyenbroek, Philip G., and Shehnaz N. Munshi. *Living Zoroastrianism: Urban Parsis Speak about Their Religion.* Richmond, U.K., 2001.

Kulke, Eckehard. *The Parsees in India: A Minority as Agent of Social Change.* Delhi, 1974.

Langstaff, Hilary A. *Indian Parsis in the Twentieth Century.* Karachi, Pakistan, 1987.

Luhrmann, Tanya M. *The Good Parsi: The Fate of a Colonial Elite in a Postcolonial Society.* Cambridge, Mass., 1996.

Maneck, Susan S. *The Death of Ahriman: Culture, Identity, and Theological Change among the Parsis of India.* Bombay, 1997.

Menant, Delphine. *The Parsis.* Edited and translated by M. M. Murzban and A. D. Mango. 3 vols. Bombay, 1994–1996.

Mistree, Khojeste P. "The Breakdown of the Zoroastrian Tradition as Viewed from a Contemporary Perspective." In *Irano-Judaica,* vol. 2, edited by S. Shaked and A. Netzer, pp. 227–254. Jerusalem, 1990.

Palsetia, Jesse S. *The Parsis of India: Preservation of Identity in Bombay City.* Leiden, 2001.

Rose, Jennifer. "The Traditional Role of Women in the Iranian and Indian (Parsi) Zoroastrian Communities from the Nineteenth to the Twentieth Century." *Journal of the K. R. Cama Oriental Institute* 56 (1989): 1–103.

Seervai, Khurshedji N., and Bomanji B. Patel. "Gujarat Parsis from Their Earliest Settlement to the Present Time (A.D. 1898)." *Gazetteer of the Bombay Presidency* 9, no. 2 (1899): 183–254.

Taraporevala, Sooni. *Parsis, the Zoroastrians of India: A Photographic Journey.* Mumbai, India, 2000.

Whitehouse, David, and Andrew Williamson. "Sasanian Maritime Trade." *Iran* 11 (1973): 29–49.

Whitehurst, James E. "The Zoroastrian Response to Westernization: A Case Study of the Parsis of Bombay." *Journal of the American Academy of Religion* 37, no. 3 (1969): 224–236.

Writer, Rashna. *Contemporary Zoroastrians: An Unstructured Nation.* Lanham, Md., 1994.

"The Zarathushti Odyssey." *FEZANA Journal* (Winter 2000).

JAMSHEED K. CHOKSY (2005)

PARTHEV, SAHAK SEE SAHAK PARTHEV

PĀRVATĪ SEE GODDESS WORSHIP, *ARTICLE ON* THE HINDU GODDESS

PASCAL, BLAISE

PASCAL, BLAISE (1623–1662), French mathematician, religious thinker, and philosopher, was one of the greatest minds in modern intellectual history. He was educated at home by his father, Étienne, who, when living in Paris from 1631 to 1639, belonged to the society of scientists organized by Mersenne. A precocious genius, Pascal in 1639 wrote a mathematical work of which a part, *Essai sur les coniques,* has been preserved and published. From 1642 to 1644, when in Normandy with his father, he constructed a calculating machine. His mathematical and physical works include a treatise, based on experiments, disproving the theory of the impossibility of vacuum, as well as works on cycloids and on the theory of probability.

JANSENISM. In Normandy Pascal was in touch with priests who were disciples of the Abbé of Saint-Cyran, and in 1646 he went through a religious conversion, but he neither abandoned his scientific work nor renounced mundane life. However, in November 1654, he experienced a second conversion, a kind of violent shock about which he wrote a short and remarkable memoir; he kept this reminder of his experience on his person to the end of his days. For some years before his conversion Pascal had been under Jansenist influence, in particular in Port-Royal. There Pascal became acquainted with the main figures of Jansenism—Antoine Arnauld, Pierre Nicole, Le Maistre de Saci—and became himself one of the leading writers and polemicists of this political as well as religious movement.

Cornelius Jansen, also called Jansenius (1585–1638), in his posthumously published *Augustinus* (1640), elaborated a theory of grace that was antagonistic to the Jesuit soteriology known as Molinism, after the Jesuit theologian Luis de Molina (1535–1600), and which contributed to the reform of the church in the spirit of moral rigorism and theocentric piety. The Molinists were attacked for making the efficacy of divine grace dependent on human free choice and thus falling into Pelagian or semi-Pelagian heresy and for encouraging moral laxity, dangerous self-confidence, and "easy devotion." Jansenius, following Augustine, emphasized the deep corruption of human nature, its inability both to know God and to help us in obeying his commandments; he praised the omnipotence of divine grace, which is presented in his writings as the condition, not only necessary but sufficient as well, of salvation. In 1643, Arnauld published his treatise on the Eucharist, *De la fréquente communion,* which became a kind of Jansenist manifesto. The battle between the two camps was carried on with ferocity in the 1650s. As a result of pressure by the Jesuits, Innocent X, in his bull *Cum occasione* (1653), condemned five of Jansenius's statements in which the Molinists detected the Calvinist heresy; Jansenius was accused of saying that some divine commandments are for humans impracticable, that Jesus Christ sacrificed himself for the elect only and not for all people, and that divine grace works irresistibly. The Jansenists argued that the condemned statements could not be found in *Augustinus* and that the pope was not infallible in the matter-of-fact question of whether or not a given book included a certain theological doctrine. In 1656, Alexander VII renewed the condemnation in a separate constitution and asserted that the heretical statements were in fact in the book; earlier Arnauld had been condemned by the Sorbonne for theological and factual errors.

Pascal intervened in the battle by publishing pseudonymously, from January 1656 until March 1657, eighteen successive writings known collectively as the *Lettres provinciales,* a literary masterpiece which, notwithstanding its listing in the Index of Forbidden Books, was to become a classic of French literature. In this pamphlet Pascal attacked the Jesuits' moral doctrine, as it was taught in the works of known writers (Le Moine, Escobar, and Bauny, among others), as well as the theory of grace on which Jesuit "laxism" and moral permissiveness were supposedly based. The letters display to some extent the influence of Cartesianism, an influence not unusual among Jansenists, insofar as they imply the separation of faith from secular reason and assert the latter's autonomy; they denounce Jesuit casuistry and educational technique, claiming that through it all kinds of sins and vices could be exculpated easily or turned into virtues; they attack the Molinist teaching that sufficient grace has been given to all, and thus, by virtue of a free decision, anyone can make it efficient and perfectly fulfill the divine law.

PENSÉES. In the 1650s, apart from producing a number of short theological, philosophical, and scientific texts, all of them published posthumously *(Préface d'un traité du vide, Entretien avec M. de Saci, Comparaison des chrétiens des premiers temps avec ceux d'aujourd'hui, De l'esprit géométrique, De l'art de persuader, Écrits sur la grâce, Histoire de la roulette),* Pascal worked on *Apologie de la religion chrétienne.* This major apologetical work was to be addressed to libertines, probably of the kind he knew well personally: people who were religiously indifferent, skeptical, or incredulous, rather than committed atheists; the apology was to convince them of the truth of Christianity. He did not complete this work, and the first edition (1670) of the fragments he left was incomplete and arbitrarily ordered. In a number of subsequent printings, the editors of *Pensées,* as the work came to be known, arranged the text according to its logical order as they saw it. The edition of Brunschwig (1897) was used for several decades as a standard text, yet Louis Lafuma proved that the text left by Pascal was less chaotic and better arranged than had been previously assumed; since 1952 his edition has been considered superior to all others in existence.

Pensées is beyond doubt one of the major texts in the history of philosophical and religious ideas. This extremely rich and challenging work can be read as the depiction of the ambiguity of human destiny in the face of God, who is both hidden and manifest, and in the face of our own corruption and frailty. To Pascal, nature does not lead us to God unambiguously: "Why, do not you say yourself that the sky and the birds prove God?—No—Does your religion not say so?—No. For though it is true to some souls whom God has enlightened in this way, yet it is untrue for the majority." There are no "proofs" of faith, which is God's gift. "Our religion is wise and foolish: wise because it is the most learned and most strongly based on miracles, prophecies, etc., foolish, because it is not all this which makes people belong to it. This is a good enough reason for condemning those who do not belong, but not for making those who do belong believe. What makes them believe is the Cross."

Reason is not to be condemned—a person's entire dignity consists in thinking—but it ought to be looked upon with suspicion, and it is crucial that it knows its limitations. Pascal was the reader of Epictetus and Montaigne; the former stressed the strength of human nature, the latter its weakness and fragility. Both are right in part, but to take only one side amounts to falling either into hubris and dogmatic self-confidence or into despair. "We have an incapacity for proving anything which no amount of dogmatism can overcome. We have an idea of truth which no amount of skepticism can overcome." It is proper that God should be hidden in part and revealed in part, and it is proper that we should know both God and our misery. Therefore to know Jesus Christ is essential, as it is in him that we find both God and our misery. Indeed, our greatness consists in being aware of our misery. The position of man as a creature located between angels and animals by no means gives us, in Pascal's eyes, a quiet abode in our natural place; being "in the middle," we are torn between incompatible desires, and our natural state is the most opposed to our higher inclinations. It is the immobility of tension, rather than of satisfaction, that distinguishes us; we are incomprehensible to ourselves, our reason and our senses deceive us, no certainty is accessible to us. Christianity, with all its "foolishness," is the only way the human condition can become intelligible and meaningful. Indeed, the mystery of original sin, the core of the Christian worldview, according to Pascal, is an outrage to reason, and yet without this mystery we cannot understand ourselves. "Acknowledge then the truth of religion in its very obscurity, in the little light we can throw on it, in our indifference regarding knowledge of it."

Although, as Pascal argues both in *Pensées* and in *De l'esprit géométrique,* human reason cannot achieve any certitude, there is a separate power, the heart, which has "reasons of its own, unknown to reason" and which is a practical, rather than intellectual, faculty whereby a choice between equally valid arguments for and against Christianity can be made. In the famous passage on the wager (*pari*), Pascal appeals to a kind of practical reasoning in order to compel the libertine to admit that he cannot avoid the choice between religion and irreligion. It is impossible to suspend the question of immortality and of our eternal destiny: our happiness is at stake, and the search for happiness is an aspect of our nature. God being infinite and therefore inaccessible to our reason, one cannot rationally affirm or deny his existence, but neither can one suspend judgment. One has to bet, as in a game of chance: If one bets on God having even the slightest chance of existence, one may gain an eternal life of happiness, whereas only one's finite life on earth is at stake; betting against God one risks the loss of eternal life, and the possible gain is finite; it is therefore practically rational to opt for God.

It needs stressing that the wager is a way to persuade skeptics that they ought to bet on God, however uncertain of God's existence they might be; it is neither the expression of Pascal's own uncertainty nor another "proof" of a theological truth. It is practical advice, and Pascal is aware that by itself it cannot produce genuine faith. He wants to show libertines that they ought to behave as if God were real, and this means taming their passions and even "stultifying" themselves by complying, without real faith, with external Christian rules. The new way of life eventually will make them realize that they have lost nothing in abandoning their sinful habits, and they will be converted to a true Christian faith.

By the standards of human nature, religion is uncertain, and humanity cannot get rid of its nature. A tension between the attraction of the world and participation in the eternal is unavoidable. Human history and social life do not offer any solution; history is the prey of insignificant accidents ("Cleopatra's nose: if it had been shorter the whole face of the earth would have been different"); social reality has no intrinsic value and cannot be improved. Therefore Pascal, on the one hand, sneers at all titles and ranks, reduces laws and justice to pure conventions and property to a superstition, and, on the other hand, recommends a conservative acceptance of social hierarchy and external respect for monarchy, rank, and wealth. His worldview is essentially nonhistorical.

Pascal, not surprisingly, was attacked by the eighteenth-century *philosophes* Voltaire, Diderot, and Condorcet; his skeptical view of science, to which he (unlike his critics) made very serious contributions, his belief in the naturally incurable corruption of human nature, his pessimistic assessment of the human quest for happiness, were, of course, unacceptable to the prophets of the Enlightenment. He has remained one of the main figures in the history of conflict between Christianity and modernity, and his analyses sound astonishingly fresh in the present time.

Bibliography

Works by Pascal

Œuvres complètes. Edited by Louis Lafuma. With a preface by Henri Gouhier. New York and Paris, 1963.

Pensées. Translated into English by A. J. Krailsheimer. Harmondsworth, 1966.

Works about Pascal

Blaise Pascal, l'homme et l'œuvre. Cahiers de Royaumont, Philosophie, no. 1. Paris, 1956.

Brunschvicg, Léon. *Le génie de Pascal.* Paris, 1924.

Brunschvicg, Léon. *Descartes et Pascal, lecteurs de Montaigne.* Paris, 1944.

Goldmann, Lucien. *Le dieu caché.* Paris, 1955. Translated by Philip Thody as *The Hidden God* (New York, 1964).

Jovy, Ernest. *Études pascaliennes.* 9 vols. Paris, 1927–1936.

Laporte, Jean. *Le cœur et la raison selon Pascal.* Paris, 1950.

Mesnard, Jean. *Pascal, l'homme et l'œuvre.* Paris, 1951. Translated by G. S. Fraser as *Pascal, His Life and Works* (London, 1952).

Russier, Jeanne. *La foi selon Pascal.* Paris, 1949.

Strowski, Fortunat. *Pascal et son temps.* 3 vols. Paris, 1907–1922.

Leszek Kolakowski (1987)

PASSOVER is the joyous Jewish festival of freedom that celebrates the Exodus of the Jews from their bondage in Egypt. Beginning on the fifteenth day of the spring month of Nisan, the festival lasts for seven days (eight days for Jews outside Israel). The Hebrew name for Passover, Pesaḥ, refers to the paschal lamb offered as a family sacrifice in Temple times (*Ex.* 12:1–28, 12:43–49; *Dt.* 16:1–8), and the festival is so called because God "passed over" (*pasaḥ*) the houses of the Israelites when he slew the Egyptian firstborn (*Ex.* 12:23). The annual event is called Ḥag ha-Pesaḥ, the Feast of the Passover, in the Bible (*Ex.* 34:25). Another biblical name for it is Ḥag ha-Matsot or the Feast of the Unleavened Bread, after the command to eat unleavened bread and to refrain from eating leaven (*Ex.* 23:15, *Lv.* 23:6, *Dt.* 16:16). The critical view is that the two names are for two originally separate festivals, which were later combined. Ḥag ha-Pesaḥ was a pastoral festival, whereas Ḥag ha-Matsot was an agricultural festival. In any event, the paschal lamb ceased to be offered when the Temple was destroyed in 70 CE, and although the name Passover is still used, the holiday is now chiefly marked by the laws concerning leaven and, especially, by the home celebration held on the first night—the Seder ("order, arrangement").

Prohibition on Leavening. On the night before the festival the house is searched thoroughly for leavened bread. Any found is gathered together and removed from the house during the morning of 14 Nisan. This is based on the biblical injunction that not only is it forbidden to eat leaven, but no leaven may remain in the house (*Ex.* 12:15, 12:19). On Passover, observant Jews do not employ utensils used during the rest of the year for food that contains leaven. Either they have special Passover utensils or they remove the leaven in the walls of their regular utensils by firing or boiling them in hot water. Only food products completely free from even the smallest particle of leaven are eaten. In many communities, rabbis supervise the manufacture of packaged Passover foods to verify that they are completely free from leaven, after which they attach their seal of fitness to the product. There was at first considerable rabbinical opposition to machine-made *matsah* on the grounds that pieces of dough might be left in the machine and become leaven. Nowadays, with vastly improved methods of production, the majority of Jews see no objection to machine-made *matsah.*

The biblical reason given for eating unleavened bread (*matsah*) and refraining from eating leaven (*ḥamets*) is that during the Exodus the Israelites, having left Egypt in haste, were obliged to eat unleavened bread because their dough had had insufficient time to rise (*Ex.* 12:39). *Matsah* is therefore the symbol of freedom. A later idea is that leaven—bread that has risen and become fermented—represents pride and corruption, whereas unleavened bread represents humility and purity.

Great care is consequently taken when baking *matsah* for Passover. The process is speeded up so that no time is allowed for the dough to rise before it is baked. The resulting *matsah* is a flat bread with small perforations (an extra precaution against the dough's rising). Some Jews prefer to eat only round *matsah,* because a circle is unbounded, representing the unlimited need to strive for freedom.

Synagogue Service. The synagogue liturgy for Passover contains additional prayers and hymns suffused with the themes of freedom and renewal. On the first day there is a prayer for dew; the rainy season now over, supplication is made for the more gentle dew to assist the growth of the produce in the fields. The scriptural readings are from passages dealing with Passover. On the seventh day, the anniversary of the parting of the sea (*Ex.* 14:17–15:26), the relevant passage is read; some Jews perform a symbolic reenactment to further dramatize the event. On the Sabbath in the middle of Passover, the Prophetic reading is Ezekiel's vision of the dry bones (*Ez.* 37:1–14). On this Sabbath, too, there is a reading of the *Song of Songs* (interpreted by the rabbis as a dialogue between God and his people), in which there is a reference to the spring (2:11–13) and to the Exodus (1:9).

The Seder and the Haggadah. The Seder, celebrated in the home on the first night of Passover (outside Israel, also on the second night), is a festive meal during which various rituals are carried out and the Haggadah is read or chanted. The Haggadah ("telling") is the traditional collection of hymns, stories, and poems recited in obedience to the command for parents to tell their children of God's mighty deeds in delivering the people from Egyptian bondage (*Ex.* 13:8). The main features of the Haggadah are already found in outline in the Mishnah (*Pes.* 10) with some of the material going back to Temple times. It assumed its present form in the Middle Ages, with a few more recent additions. The emphasis in the Haggadah is on God alone as the deliverer from bondage. It is he and no other, neither messenger nor angel, who brings his people out from Egypt. Even Moses is mentioned by name only once in the Haggadah, and then only incidentally, at the end of a verse quoted for other purposes.

A special dish is placed on the Seder table upon which rest the symbolic foods required for the rituals. These are three *matsot,* covered with a cloth; *maror,* bitter herbs that serve as a reminder of the way the Egyptian taskmasters embittered the lives of their slaves (*Ex.* 1:14); *ḥaroset,* a paste made of almonds, apples, and wine, symbolic of the mortar the slaves used as well as of the sweetness of redemption; a bowl of salt water, symbolic of the tears of the oppressed; parsley or other vegetables for a symbolic dipping in the salt water; a roasted bone as a reminder of the paschal lamb; and a roasted egg as a reminder of the animal sacrifice, the *ḥagigah* offered in Temple times on Passover, Shavu'ot, and Sukkot. During the Seder, four cups of wine are partaken of by all the celebrants, representing the four different expressions used for redemption in the narrative of the Exodus. Since in ancient times the aristocratic custom was to eat and drink while reclining, the food and drink are partaken of in this way as a symbol of the mode of eating of free people. Some medieval authorities held that since people no longer recline at meals, there is no longer any point in the symbolic gesture, but their view was not adopted.

The Seder begins with the Qiddush, the festival benediction over the first cup of wine. The middle *matsah* is then broken in two, one piece being set aside to be eaten as the *afiqoman* ("dessert"), the last thing eaten before the Grace after Meals, so that the taste of the *matsah* of freedom might linger in the mouth. It is customary for the grown-ups to hide the *afiqoman,* rewarding the lucky child who finds it with a present. The parsley is first dipped in the salt water and then eaten. The youngest child present asks the Four Questions, a standard formula beginning with "Why is this night different from all other nights?" The differences are noted in four instances, such as, "On all other nights we eat either leaven or unleaven, whereas on this night we eat only unleaven." The head of the house and the other adults then proceed to reply to the Four Questions by reading the Haggadah, in which the answers are provided in terms of God's deliverances. When they reach the section that tells of the ten plagues, a little wine from the second cup is poured out to denote that it is inappropriate to drink a full cup of joy at the delivery, since in the process the enemy was killed. This section of the Haggadah concludes with a benediction in which God is thanked for his mercies, and the second cup of wine is drunk while reclining.

The celebrants then partake of the meal proper. Grace before Meals is recited over two of the three *matsot* and a benediction is recited: "Blessed art thou, O Lord our God, who has sanctified us with thy commandments and commanded us to eat *matsah.*" The bitter herbs (horseradish is generally used) are then dipped in the *ḥaroset* and eaten. There is a tradition that in Second Temple times the famous sage Hillel would eat *matsah,* bitter herbs, and the paschal lamb together. In honor of Hillel's practice, a sandwich is made of the third *matsah* and the bitter herbs. In many places the first course is a hard-boiled egg in salt water, a further symbol of the tears of the slaves in Egypt and their hard bondage.

At the end of the meal the *afiqoman* is eaten, and the Grace after Meals is recited over the third cup of wine. The Hallel (consisting of *Psalms* 113–118) and other hymns of thanksgiving are then recited over the fourth cup of wine. Before the recital of Hallel, a cup is filled for the prophet Elijah, the herald of the Messiah, who is said to visit every Jewish home on this night. The door of the house is opened to let Elijah in, and the children watch eagerly to see if they can notice any diminution in Elijah's cup as the prophet quickly sips the wine and speeds on his way to visit all the other homes. At this stage there is a custom dating from the Middle Ages of reciting a number of imprecations against those who oppressed the Jews and laid the Temple waste. Nowadays, many Jews either do not recite these verses or substitute prayers more relevant to the contemporary situation, such as prayers for freedom to be established for all people.

The Seder concludes with the cheerful singing of table hymns, most of them jingles for the delight of the children present, such as *Ḥad Gadya'* (One kid), constructed on the same lines as *This Is the House That Jack Built,* the cat devouring the kid, the dog devouring the cat, and so on until the Angel of Death devours the final slaughterer and then God slays the Angel of Death. Commentators to the Haggadah have read into this theme various mystical ideas about the survival of Israel and the ultimate overcoming of death itself in eternal life. All join in singing these songs, for which there are many traditional melodies. This night is said to be one of God's special protection so that the usual night prayers on retiring to bed, supplicating God for his protection, are not recited since that protection is granted in any event.

SEE ALSO Leaven.

BIBLIOGRAPHY

J. B. Segal's *The Hebrew Passover: From the Earliest Times to A.D. 70* (London, 1963), with a comprehensive bibliography, deals with the history and development of the festival through the Temple period and surveys the various critical theories on the origins of the festival. For the later period the best work is Chaim Raphael's *A Feast of History: Passover through the Ages as a Key to Jewish Experience* (New York, 1972). This book also attractively presents one of the very many editions of the Haggadah. Isaac Levy's little book *A Guide to Passover* (London, 1958) provides a useful summary of the traditional laws and customs of the festival. An anthology of teachings with a comprehensive bibliography is Philip Goodman's *The Passover Anthology* (Philadelphia, 1961). For an insightful look at the history of the printed Haggadah one may consult Yosef H. Yerushalmi's *Haggadah and History* (Philadelphia, 1975).

New Sources

Anisfield, Sharon Cohen, Tara Mohr, and Catherine Spector, eds. *The Women's Passover Companion: Women's Reflections on the Festival of Freedom.* Woodstock, Vt., 2003.

Bergant, Dianne. "An Anthropological Approach to Biblical Interpretation: The Passover Supper in *Exodus* 12:1–20 as a Case Study." *Semeia* 67 (1994): 43–62.

Parnes, Stephan O., ed. *The Art of Passover.* New York, 1994.

Prosic, Tamara. "Origin of Passover." *SJOT* 13 (1999): 78–94.

Safran, Eliyahu. *Kos Eliyahu: Insights on the Haggadah and Pesach.* Hoboken, N.J., 1993.

LOUIS JACOBS (1987)
Revised Bibliography

PATAÑJALI THE GRAMMARIAN (fl. c. 140 BCE) was a Sanskrit grammarian and author of the *Mahābhāṣya,* the major commentary on Pāṇini's *Aṣṭādhyāyī.* Patañjali's *bhāṣya* ("commentary") focuses on Pāṇini's work both directly and indirectly, for it evaluates both Pāṇini's verses and those of Kātyāyana's *Vārttika,* the first notable commentary on the *Aṣṭādhyāyī.* Pāṇini, Kātyāyana, and Patañjali have often been grouped together in a kind of grammatical lineage; Pāṇini and Patañjali, however, remain by far the foremost authorities on the Sanskrit language.

Scholars vary in opinion as to Patañjali's purpose in composing his *Mahābhāṣya.* Most agree, however, that the very fact that Patañjali chose to fashion his observations not in an independent grammar but in a commentary on Pāṇini's work indicates great deference to the original grammarian; it was not Patañjali's purpose to attempt to surpass him or disprove his authority. In his work Patañjali mentions directly his indebtedness to the *mahācārya* ("great teacher").

Many social changes were occurring in India during Patañjali's time. There was an influx of different peoples from bordering lands; intellectual, commercial, and political contact with regions as far as Greece was common; and class structure was undergoing substantial transitions. Social change was reflected in language: The use of classical Sanskrit (i.e., the *saṃskṛta* or "perfected" language of Pāṇini) became restricted more and more to the social and literary elite, while the rest of the population spoke one of the many Prakrits (i.e., the *prakṛta,* or "natural, unpolished" languages and dialects) that were rapidly developing.

Even spoken Sanskrit was beginning to include *apaśabda,* "vulgar, imperfect speech." For example, social stratification had reduced women to a much lower status than that which they had enjoyed during the Vedic and early Upaniṣadic periods; this was reflected in speech by a growing irregularity of feminine forms and endings that all but eliminated the feminine honorific. Patañjali observed that the grammar of Pāṇini was by now being retained almost artificially; when he observed that even some of the most respected pandits, while meticulous in religious recitation, would resort to an occasional *apaśabda* term in their ordinary speech, he realized that certain modifications were in order. Patañjali thus became the first Indian grammarian to address the difference between *laukikabhāṣya* ("empirical language") and *śāstrīyabhāṣya* ("sacred language").

Patañjali's intent was not to reflect in grammar every form of imperfect speech, but rather to incorporate some of the changes that were occurring in spoken Sanskrit so that the language could thereby be preserved in a viable form. He chose to revalidate Pāṇini's dictums and expand them where necessary. If, for example, Pāṇini allowed that three classes of nouns conformed to a certain rule, Patañjali might revise the rule to incorporate an additional class. In Pāṇini's time the Vedic *ṛ* and *ḷ* were still commonly used vocalically. Within a few centuries the two letters had shifted, with very few exceptions, to the status of consonants; this was another type of change that Patañjali accommodated.

Patañjali believed that the grammarian should stay in touch with the contemporary language and provide for reasonable changes, adhering as closely as possible to the classical rules. In this way the populace would continue to turn to the grammarians for guidance in all matters of speech.

When Pāṇini composed his grammar he was more concerned with the forms of words (*padas*) than with syntax and sentence meaning. By Patañjali's time, Mimāṃsā and other philosophical schools had introduced a shift in emphasis whereby speech (*vākya*) and the complete thought expressed in a sentence represented the true basis of language. Patañjali's contact with these other views influenced his expansion of Pāṇini's grammar, and he thus introduced the concept of *vākyasphota,* that is, the concept that the eternal element of sounds and words, and the true vehicle of an idea, flash on the mind when a sound is uttered. This indicates an inherent *nityatva* ("infinitude") in *śabda* ("correct grammatical speech"); even *apaśabda* ("incorrect speech") can partake of this in varying degrees.

By incorporating the notion of *nityatva* into *vyākaraṇa* ("grammar"), Patañjali helped to elevate the status of the science of grammar. Pāṇini's *Aṣṭādhyāyī,* revered as it was for its insurmountable contributions to the preservation of the sacred Vedic speech and classical Sanskrit, did not belong to any particular category of Sanskrit literature before Patañjali's time. It was variously considered Dharmaśāstra, *smṛti,* Āgama, or, occasionally, Vedāṅga ("limb of the Veda"). Patañjali's observations and syntheses, in addition to his frequent reiteration that the study of *vyākaraṇa* is a religious duty, served to elevate Pāṇini's *Aṣṭādhyāyī* permanently to the sacred status of Vedāṅga.

SEE ALSO Vedāṅgas.

BIBLIOGRAPHY

Patañjali's *Mahābhāṣya* is available in English translation in *Patañjali's Vyākaraṇa-mahābhāṣya,* 8 vols., translated and edited by S. D. Joshi and J. A. F. Roodbergen (Poona, 1968–1980); the edition also offers a valuable introductory section. Useful secondary works include K. Madhava Krishna Sarma's *Pāṇini, Kātyāyana, and Patañjali* (Delhi, 1968) and Franz Kielhorn's *Kātyāyana and Patañjali: Their Relation to Each Other and to Pāṇini* (1876; 2d ed., Varanasi, 1963).

New Sources

Benson, James W. *Patañjali's Remarks on Anga.* Oxford University South Asian studies series. Delhi and New York, 1990.

Coward, Harold G., and K. Kunjunni Raja, eds. *Encyclopedia of Indian Philosophies,* vol. 5: *The Philosophy of the Grammarians.* Princeton, N.J., 1990.

Filliozat, Pierre-Sylvain. *An Introduction to Commentaries on Patañjali's Mahabhasya.* Poona, 1991.

CONSTANTINA BAILLY (1987)
Revised Bibliography

PATRIARCHATE, or *Nesi'ut,* was the leading Jewish communal office in the Late Roman and Byzantine Empires, emerging soon after the destruction of the city and Temple of Jerusalem in 70 CE and disappearing in the first part of the fifth century. At its peak, the Patriarchate, a hereditary office passing from father to son, wielded authority throughout Roman-Byzantine Palestine as well as the Roman diaspora.

Our knowledge of the Patriarchate is relatively extensive. Rabbinic sources are especially rich in this regard, as the patriarch was an integral part of rabbinic circles from the late first century until the mid-third century. A number of archaeological sites from the third through the fifth centuries relate to this office: the Bet She'arim necropolis; the Hammat Tiberias synagogue; and diaspora inscriptions from Stobi (Macedonia), Venosa, Sicily, and Argos. A number of Church Fathers take note of the Patriarchate as well, though usually in a negative vein; several, however, are quite informative. Finally, Roman sources—Julian, Libanius, and especially the Theodosian Code—are of cardinal importance for understanding the office during the fourth and early fifth centuries, and perhaps even earlier.

Although there is some dispute as to when this office first crystallized, with the minimalists claiming that it emerged as late as Rabbi Judah I at the turn of the third century and the maximalists as early as Hillel several centuries earlier, the general consensus dates its origin to the late first century and the figure of Rabban Gamaliel II. He appears to have maintained ongoing relations with Roman officials, as there are records of a number of trips he took to Rome and Antioch, and rabbinic sources refer on occasion to his relations with imperial authorities. However, Gamaliel's son, Rabbi Simeon, functioned after the Bar Kokhba revolt (132–135) and seems to have operated in a void. There is no evidence of any contact with Rome, and his authority and influence in Jewish society of his time appear severely limited.

The Patriarchate undoubtedly achieved new heights of prestige and authority in the days of Rabbi Judah I (often referred to as "the Prince," or simply "Rabbi"). Under the sympathetic Severan dynasty (193–235), he garnered a great deal of economic wealth and political influence that, when combined with his intellectual and religious stature, all but guaranteed him an undisputed position of leadership. His close relations with one Antoninus, possibly the emperor Caracalla (r. 211–217) himself, contributed to his accrued influence and means, and this in turn propelled the Patriarchate to an entirely new plane of power and responsibility. The testimony of Origen, who lived in Caesarea only a few years later, is rather dramatic; according to him, the Jewish ethnarch (another term for patriarch) functioned almost like a king, enjoying, inter alia, the power of capital punishment. Additional powers attributed to the third-century patriarchs in rabbinic literature include judicial appointments, some sort of control over educational institutions, and collecting taxes.

Given this enhanced status, and in line with the policy adopted by the Romans themselves throughout the East, the patriarch began to forge new alliances, the most important of which was with the wealthy Jewish urban aristocracies of Tiberias and Sepphoris. The need and desire of patriarchs to cultivate ties with those who were in a position to help them implement their policies were natural. These ties, however, often came at the expense of the sages. Time and again, the latter complained that the wealthy received judicial appointments in their stead and that the patriarchal taxation system affected them adversely.

The rabbis, for the most part, kept their distance from the patriarch as well, critiquing his policies, judgments, and decisions. The number of references to the patriarch drops precipitously in rabbinic sources after the early third century. Whereas Rabbi Judah I is mentioned some twelve hundred times, his grandson Judah II (c. 250 CE) is noted only fifty times, and the latter's grandson, Judah III (c. 300 CE), but twenty times. Fourth-century patriarchs are rarely mentioned in rabbinic sources.

The patriarch cultivated his own "rabbinic" circles, whose counsel he sought and on whom he relied to formulate and implement his policies. Those close to the patriarch were often buried in Bet She'arim, a central necropolis famous for its association with this office, but practically no sages mentioned in rabbinic literature were interred there. As a result of this growing dichotomy, both the Patriarchate and sages became more and more peripheral to each other's agenda.

Fourth-century non-Jewish sources clearly indicate that the Patriarchate enjoyed extensive prestige and recognition. The Theodosian Code is particularly revealing in this regard. One decree, issued by the emperors Arcadius and Honorius in 397, stipulates that:

> those who are subject to the rule of the Illustrious Patriarchs, that is the archisynagogues, the patriarchs (*sic!*),

> the presbyters and the others who are occupied in the rite of that religion, shall persevere in keeping the same privileges that are reverently bestowed on the first clerics of the venerable Christian Law. For this was decreed in divine order also by the divine Emperors Constantine and Constantius, Valentinian and Valens. Let them therefore be exempt even from the curial liturgies, and obey their laws. (Theodosian Code 16, 8, 13, in Linder, *The Jews in Roman Imperial Legislation,* no. 27)

This decree clearly spells out the dominance of the patriarch in a wide range of synagogue affairs: he stood at the head of a network of officials, including archisynagogues, patriarchs, presbyters, and others who were in charge of the religious dimension of the synagogue, all of whom had privileges on a par with the Christian clergy. Moreover, this arrangement is said to date from the time of Constantine, over sixty years earlier. When added to other areas of authority noted in earlier rabbinic literature, such as calendrical decisions (determining the time of a new month and when to add an additional month to the year), declaring public fast days, and issuing bans, then the prominence of this office in Jewish communal and religious life becomes quite evident.

With the Patriarchate's demise around 425 CE (for reasons unknown), the last vestige of a unifying public office for Jews living under Roman domination disappeared. Local autonomy, which had always been an important factor in Jewish society, now reigned supreme for a number of centuries.

SEE ALSO Rabbinic Judaism in Late Antiquity; Sanhedrin; Talmud.

BIBLIOGRAPHY

Cohen, Shaye J. D. "Pagan and Christian Evidence on the Ancient Synagogue." In *The Synagogue in Late Antiquity,* edited by Lee I. Levine, pp. 159–181. Philadelphia, 1987. On the basis of Roman and Christian fourth-century sources, Cohen asserts the growing patriarchal control of diaspora affairs, especially in the latter half of the century.

Goodman, Martin. "The Roman State and the Jewish Patriarch in the Third Century." In *The Galilee in Late Antiquity,* edited by Lee I. Levine, pp. 127–139. New York, 1992. This study argues that the *Nasi'* was a religious leader in third-century Galilee who wielded certain secular powers as well. He was recognized as such by Rome and for the most part fit Roman provincial patterns of rule.

Jacobs, Martin. *Die Institution des jüdischen Patriarchen.* Tübingen, Germany, 1995. Jacobs presents all primary sources relating to the Patriarchate, together with an extensive commentary and a suggested reconstruction of the history of this institution.

Levine, Lee I. "The Jewish Patriarch (Nasi) in Third Century Palestine." In *Aufstieg und niedergang der römischen Welt (ANRW)* II, 19.2, edited by Hildegard Temporini and Wolfgang Haase. pp. 649–688. Berlin and New York, 1979. The article focuses on the areas of authority, religious and secular, of the third-century patriarchs.

Levine, Lee I. *The Rabbinic Class of Roman Palestine in Late Antiquity.* Jerusalem and New York, 1989. The volume includes a detailed treatment of the relationships between the third-century patriarchs and contemporary sages.

Levine, Lee I. "The Status of the Patriarch in the Third and Fourth Centuries: Sources and Methodology." *Journal of Jewish Studies* 47 (1996): 1–32. Levine provides a methodological study of the various sources regarding the patriarchs and a suggested reconstruction of their status in the third to fifth centuries.

Linder, Amnon. *The Jews in Roman Imperial Legislation.* Detroit, 1987. This is a collection of Roman-Byzantine laws relating to the Jews. Each law is accompanied by an introduction, text, translation, and commentary.

Schwartz, Seth. "The Patriarchs and the Diaspora" *Journal of Jewish Studies* 50 (1999): 208–222. Focusing on the fourth century, Schwartz claims that the patriarch was primarily a diaspora-related institution with regard to whom it served and where it found support.

Stern, Sacha. "Rabbi and the Origins of the Patriarchate," *Journal of Jewish Studies* 54 (2003): 193–215. The article presents a somewhat radical proposal that the Patriarchate was created under Rabbi Judah I, who hailed from the Galilean aristocracy. Rabbi Judah, Stern maintains, was unrelated to any previous rabbinic personality (e.g., Rabban Gamaliel).

LEE I. LEVINE (2005)

PATRIARCHY AND MATRIARCHY.

Patriarchy may be defined as the "rule of the father" that extends beyond the confines of the family to include the governance of men and the dominance of male values in society as a whole. Patriarchal dominance, whether that of male heads of extended families or the *andrarchy* of senior men within a given political dispensation, gives men control over the familial and political economy; limits women's freedom of sexual expression and alliance; marginalizes or excludes them from political and religious leadership; and limits their education and sometimes their freedom of movement. Specific phenomena associated with the patriarchal privileging of the masculine include female economic disadvantage, the coerced genital mutilation experienced by an estimated two million girls a year, the sex selection practices and female infanticide in parts of India and China, and the preferential care of boys in developing or underdeveloped countries leading to a higher mortality rate for girls.

Since the mid-nineteenth century, first and then second wave feminisms have sharply challenged patriarchy as a primary injustice to be remedied by women's educational, professional, and political emancipation from the familial sphere. By the end of the 1970s patriarchy had been judged not only the primary and general cause of female suffering, but the appropriation, accumulation, and consumption of all bodily and natural territory and resources (often cast as female) by male elites in the consolidation and expansion of their own power. Second wave radical feminism launched the most uncompromising critique of patriarchy. Kate Millett's *Sexual Politics* (New York, 1970) argued that patriarchy, with "God on its side," ideologically exaggerates male and female difference in the interests of maintaining roles that produce male dominance and female subordination. Marilyn French, in *Beyond Power: On Women, Men, and Morals* (New York, 1985), also cast patriarchy as the paradigmatic social oppression that produces all others.

However, a postmodern unease with cumbersome "grand narratives" and absolute moral dualities (even when conceived by feminists) has seen a number of feminist theorists either relinquish the universalizing term *patriarchy,* or relativize it by using it in the plural to theorize the relation between different social, historical, geographic, economic, and ethnic hierarchies. It is now recognized that patriarchies vary and that they intersect with complex factors of class and race. It is clear that not all women suffer equally (if at all) under patriarchy since it can reward cooperative women closely associated with powerful men through marriage or birth. As black women have pointed out, not all women are powerless: black women have been oppressed not only by men but by white women as well. It is also clear that while political and religious structures traditionally serve male interests, not all men personally oppress women, and some men feel less than comfortable with the heterosexism and machismo pervasive in patriarchal cultures.

For these reasons, recent feminist scholarship has proposed a new terminology by which to account for the normativity and privileging of the masculine. In her book *But She Said* (1992) Elisabeth Schüssler Fiorenza coined the term *kyriarchy* to denote the rule of the emperor, lord, master, and husband over all their subordinates, including women, in order to demonstrate that not all men have the same sort of power over all women, and that elite men exercise power over nonelite men. Other commentators prefer the term *masculinist* to *patriarchal* since the former suggests that certain practices, categories, and values defer to the masculine but that men as such are not essentially culpable for all social ills. More typical of French feminist theory is the term *phallocentric.* Here, feminism rejects the Freudian phallocentrism in which power and agency is signified by the phallus, thereby casting the female as the merely receptive or as that which lacks the active procreative agency of the male. In opposition to the patriarchal preoccupation with mortality, Grace Jantzen borrows the term *natalist* from Hannah Arendt to describe how feminist values demonstrate an active commitment to the nurturing of life.

Despite the introduction of a more nuanced and contextualized terminology, most religious feminists would still want to claim that patriarchal religious traditions, that is almost the whole of the world's religious traditions, are founded, interpreted, represented, and mediated by men and from the perspective of the male subject. Religious feminist scholars have been unanimous in their view of the world's religions as the engines and regulators of patriarchal societies. It was the radical, post-Christian feminist Mary Daly who, in her early books *Beyond God the Father* (1985) and *Gyn/Ecology* (1991), was to insist that the male God's transcendent power was the source of all female disempowerment. The possibility of female authenticity, vitality, or "lust" was to be predicated on women's exodus from patriarchal religious practice and consciousness with its derogation of the natural and emphasis on "female" reproductivity. Christian feminists also argued that the patriarchal model of God as King, Lord, Father, and Husband of the Church and of the people of Israel founds and symbolizes a hierarchical sacred order whose political power sanctions the marginalization or exclusion of women and of the distinctively female experience, however socially and historically diverse that might be.

Patriarchy has been, and remains, a psychological, spiritual, and political impediment to emotional reciprocity and mutuality. Scripture, theology, and religious rituals not only often discriminate against women but can also sanction contempt for and violence against women. Patriarchal religion characteristically valorizes feminine spiritualities of self-sacrifice, submission, and silence; its ascetic dimension typically devalues or repudiates female sexuality as a locus and occasion of cultic and moral impurity or chaos and blames women for their subordination.

Feminist scholars of religion therefore interpret religious phenomena with a critical "hermeneutic of suspicion." This need not amount to a repudiation of religion: religious feminism stands in moral judgment on patriarchy as the definitive or "original" sin while also recognizing that religion can countermand its own patriarchy. By the early 1990s feminist scholarship had conceded that patriarchal religion can both protect and limit women's rights; it is both liberative and oppressive. Feminist literature, historiography, and ethics demonstrate that women may be the victims of patriarchy but can also be the agents of their own spiritual and practical resistance. In short, the term *patriarchy* remains central to the feminist interpretation and, more, to the feminist-prophetic criticism of religion, even though the latter's generalization of religion is no longer academically or intellectually entirely persuasive.

MATRIARCHY. Contemporary anthropologists agree that there is no known matriarchal society in which women were or are accorded political power or hierarchical dominance over men by virtue of being female. Admittedly, some cultures—especially those of South America—offer myths of prehistorical female dominance, and instances may be found of matrilinearity (where name, inheritance, and other statuses pass through the maternal line) and matrilocality (where men reside in their wives' or mothers' homes). This does not, however, amount to conclusive evidence for matriarchy. Belief in the replacement of matriarchy by patriarchy belongs rather to a nineteenth-century progressivist account of cultural evolution in which the instinctive "primitive" veneration of female generative power was gradually succeeded by the rational knowledge of the role of male paternity. Since Johann Jakob Bachofen published his *Das Mutterrecht* (Mother-right) in 1861, arguing that women enjoyed social power in prehistorical societies because only a woman is demonstrably the parent of her child, anthropologists and feminists have, for different political reasons, sought to demonstrate the possibility of an original or surviving society dominated or governed by women.

While matriarchal theory has since become profoundly unfashionable, some spiritual feminists persist in its promotion. The feminist archaeologist Marija Gimbutas is the best known of those who have presented (hotly contested) archaeological evidence that women enjoyed socioreligious preeminence in peaceable prehistoric Goddess-worshiping cultures prior to their destruction between the fifth and third centuries BCE by the military and agricultural technologies and patriarchal religious systems of invading warrior horsemen.

While it is evident that the worship of goddesses in various of the world's religions does not necessarily or usually entail the social ascendancy of feminine values, some contemporary post-Christian feminists, especially Wiccan feminists, associate matriarchy with the worship of the Great Goddess. Inspired by the existence of a very few small, women-led, primal religions (see Sered, 1994), these spiritual feminists have sought to recover the power of a female divine principle in the conviction that it is this which will underpin the possibility of female social power and the decline of patriarchy. Nonetheless, it should be noted that very few religious feminists have used the term *matriarchy* to denote a simple reversal of power from men to women. Some post-Christian feminists have preferred the less hierarchical term *matrifocal* to symbolize religious practice inspired by the practical authority of mothers as opposed to fathers, but not as a bid for social dominance.

SEE ALSO Androcentrism; Gender and Religion, overview article and article on History of Study; Gender Roles; Goddess Worship, overview article; Gynocentrism; Women's Studies.

BIBLIOGRAPHY

Bamberger, Joan. "The Myth of Matriarchy: Why Men Rule in Primitive Society." In *Women, Culture, and Society,* edited by Michelle Zimbalist Rosaldo and Louise Lamphere, pp. 263–280. Stanford, Calif., 1974.

Brown, Donald E. *Human Universals.* Philadelphia, 1991.

Eller, Cynthia. "The Rise and Fall of Women's Power." In her *Living in the Lap of the Goddess: The Feminist Spirituality Movement in America.* New York, 1993.

Gage, Matilda Joslyn. *Woman, Church, and State: A Historical Account of the Status of Woman through the Christian Ages, with Reminiscences of the Matriarchate.* Chicago, 1983; reprint, Amherst, N.Y., 2002.

Gimbutas, Marija. *The Language of the Goddess: Unearthing the Hidden Symbols of Western Civilization.* New York, 1989.

Jantzen, Grace M. *Becoming Divine: Towards a Feminist Philosophy of Religion.* Manchester, U.K., 1998.

Juschka, Darlene, ed. *Feminism in the Study of Religion.* New York, 2001.

Lerner, Gerda. *Women and History.* Vol. 1: *The Creation of Patriarchy.* New York, 1986.

Raphael, Melissa. "Is Patriarchal Theology Still Patriarchal? Reading Theologies of the Holocaust from a Jewish Feminist Perspective." *Journal of Feminist Studies of Religion* 18 (2002): 105–113.

Ruether, Rosemary Radford. "Patriarchy." In *An A to Z of Feminist Theology,* edited by Lisa Isherwood and Dorothea McEwan, pp. 173–174. Sheffield, U.K., 1996.

Sanday, Peggy Reeves. *Female Power and Male Dominance: On the Origins of Sexual Inequality.* Cambridge, U.K., 1981.

Schüssler Fiorenza, Elisabeth. *But She Said: Feminist Practices of Biblical Interpretation.* Boston, 1992.

Sered, Susan Starr. *Priestess, Mother, Sacred Sister: Religions Dominated by Women.* New York, 1994.

Sjöö, Monica, and Barbara Mor. *The Great Cosmic Mother: Rediscovering the Religion of the Earth.* 2d ed. New York, 1991.

MELISSA RAPHAEL (2005)

PATRICK (c. 390–c. 460), called the "apostle of the Irish," was a Christian Briton sent by his church as a missionary bishop to Ireland. During thirty years of evangelistic and pastoral work, Patrick laid foundations for the Roman church in Ireland and for the wide influence it later came to have in Europe.

Apart from numerous traditions and legends about Patrick, historians are dependent on two documents, his *Confession* and *Letter to the Soldiers of Coroticus.* Scholars agree that these are authentic but have differed as to their implications. Patrick was evidently born and raised in Roman Britain. His father, Calpornius, a Roman citizen, a well-to-do landholder, and a member of a district council, was responsible for collecting taxes in his area. From childhood Patrick spoke two languages, British (a Celtic language) and a commercial, unscholarly form of Latin. Behind him were at least two generations of Christians: His paternal grandfather was a presbyter, or priest, and his father was a deacon. Yet, during his childhood, Patrick's own faith seems to have been only nominal.

During the fourth century the invading Anglo-Saxons had pushed the Britons into the western part of England and into Wales. For generations the Irish tribes had raided the west coast of Britain for slaves. With Roman protection growing weaker toward the end of the fourth century, these raids became more frequent. About 406, when Patrick was sixteen years old, the raiders descended on the estate of Patrick's father. Along with hundreds of others, Patrick was carried off to the west coast of Ireland to work as a herdsman. For one accustomed to the culture of Roman civilization and the privileges of rural aristocracy, the hardship of enslavement by an uncouth people was a traumatic experience. Yet it kindled Patrick's faith such that it grew into a warm piety with a vivid awareness of the presence and friendship of God. He wrote, "In a single day I would say as many as a hundred prayers, and almost as many at night." After six years of captivity, when he was about twenty-two, Patrick fled his captors and made his way back to his family in Britain. The next years were probably spent in one of the monasteries of Britain. Some scholars have held that these years, or part of them, were spent in France, but from his ideas and practices and the quality of his Latin, recent scholarship has concluded that Patrick was a thoroughgoing representative of British Christianity. If he spent any time in Gaul, it was probably brief.

Sometime in the 420s Patrick dreamed that his former Irish captors were calling him back: "We ask thee, boy, come and walk among us once more" (*Confession* 23). During his slave days he had learned the Irish language (a Celtic language akin to British) and now felt drawn by God to return. His monastic years had provided him neither higher education nor fluency in Latin, but there was much evidence of his Christian dedication and ability as a leader. The British church had already sent at least one mission to a neighboring territory (led by Ninian). So they concurred with Patrick's call, appointed him bishop, and around 431 sent him and some assistants to Ireland. He was then about forty years old. He traveled to the northeast of Ireland, was welcomed by the regional king, and probably made his headquarters at Armagh, near the king's estate.

Other Christians had preceded Patrick to Ireland. The slave raids, the Irish settlers returned from Britain, and commerce with Christian tribes had brought Christian influence to the country. But the Christian presence was scattered. A year or so before Patrick's trip, Rome had sent a bishop, Palladius, to southern Ireland. His work may have overlapped that of Patrick; in any event, it was cut short by his early death. Patrick was thus the pioneer missionary in the area.

Amid the traditional religion of the druids and among the unlettered Irish, Patrick's work was typical of a fifth-century missionary bishop. He made friends, preached, baptized, confirmed, celebrated the Eucharist, encouraged the formation of monasteries, and prepared and ordained clergy. This meant that he developed a written language and taught his ordinands to read and write. He excommunicated where he felt it necessary and assumed that a bishop's authority was paramount in the church (later influence on the Celtic church shifted authority to the monasteries and the abbots). Patrick distributed relief goods supplied by the British church. He was not an academic theologian but an activist bishop.

Inevitably opposition arose from the druids and at times from within the Irish and British churches. In later years Patrick wrote his *Confession* to explain his activities. Some of his personality and message are reflected in his two writings. One finds a disarming honesty and modesty, a deep pastoral concern, frequent quotations from the Bible, a sense of unworthiness, and gratitude toward a merciful and sovereign God, who cares for people and wants their responding faith and a behavior that is just and merciful. His theology was orthodox trinitarian and evangelical. He saw himself as an evangelist, a "fisher of men." He was a vigorous defender of his flock. He once wrote to "the Soldiers of Coroticus," a group of his own British people, Christians and Roman citizens, to rebuke them for raiding an Irish settlement and carrying away newly baptized youths. His ministry in Ireland seems to have lasted about thirty years, until his death, around 460. Details of Patrick's travels and work in Ireland are not available, but legends about him attest to the love and respect he must have received. Later the Irish church that he helped found contributed substantially to the evangelization of Scotland, northern England, and western Europe.

BIBLIOGRAPHY

The best of the older biographies is John B. Bury's *The Life of Saint Patrick and His Place in History* (New York, 1905). A useful translation of Patrick's writings is in Ludwig Bieler's *The Works of Saint Patrick by Saint Secundinus* (Westminster, Md., 1953). The scholarly debates, with a convincing contribution on the dates, places, and movements in the life of Patrick, are in Richard P. C. Hanson's *Saint Patrick: His Origins and Career* (Oxford, 1968). An attractive collection of maps, photographs, and drawings with a very readable text is Tom Corfe's *Saint Patrick and Irish Christianity* (Cambridge, 1973).

H. MCKENNIE GOODPASTURE (1987)

PAUCK, WILHELM (1901–1981), was a German-American historian and theologian. Born in Westphalia, Germany, on January 31, 1901, Pauck was reared in Berlin, where his father taught physics. He studied at the universities of Berlin and Göttingen, taking his licentiate in theology at Berlin in 1925 with a dissertation on Martin Bucer. The decisive influences on his intellectual development were two Berlin professors of renown, Ernst Troeltsch and Karl Holl. It was Troeltsch who first turned him to the study of theology and impressed upon him the nature of Christianity as a historical movement that must be interpreted by means of the historical method. From Holl he received magisterial instruction in Reformation history and theology, above all in studies of Martin Luther. He also heard lectures by two other giants of modern Protestant thought: Adolf von Harnack (at Berlin) and Karl Barth (at Göttingen).

Pauck came to the United States in 1925, was ordained to the ministry of the Congregational Church in 1928, and became an American citizen in 1937. His teaching career, which bore remarkable fruit, spanned fifty years: at the Chicago Theological Seminary and, chiefly, at the divinity school and history department of the University of Chicago (1926–1953); at Union Theological Seminary, New York City (1953–1967); at Vanderbilt University (until 1972); and as professor emeritus at Stanford University (until 1976). He died in Palo Alto, California, on September 3, 1981.

Pauck's thought has been aptly described as an ellipse with two foci, one in the Reformation interpretation of the

Christian gospel and the other in the modern historical understanding of reality. This dual commitment led him to reject two strategies that he considered equally ahistorical: either a simple "repristination" of Reformation theology (as attempted by Protestant neoorthodoxy) or a facile "accommodation" of the Christian tradition to modernity (as practiced by radical theological liberalism). His own approach to the Reformation was at once critical and conserving—the latter because Reformation religion was biblical and evangelical and thus foundational to authentic Protestantism; the former because the permanent truth of the Christian gospel cannot be identified with any of its temporary historical forms, all of which are necessarily relative to their immediate contexts and thus must be constantly refashioned in response to new historical situations. Hence Pauck maintained that the future of Protestantism lay with the historical-critical interpretation of Christianity articulated by such premier liberal theologians as Troeltsch and Harnack, rather than with the traditional "dogmatic" viewpoint espoused by the neoorthodox theologians, especially Barth.

Pauck's writings, distinguished by the vast learning and literary felicity evinced by them, moved with ease from the Reformation era through nineteenth-century liberal Protestantism to contemporary theology. Two collections of his seminal essays are of special importance: *The Heritage of the Reformation* (2d ed., rev. and enl., 1961) and *From Luther to Tillich: The Reformers and Their Heirs*, edited by Marion Pauck (1984). His preeminence as a Luther scholar is displayed in his new edition and translation of Luther's *Lectures on Romans* with a masterly general introduction (1961). Other representative publications are *Das Reich Gottes auf Erden: Utopie und Wirklichkeit* (The Kingdom of God on earth: utopia and reality, 1928), a still valuable study of Bucer; *Karl Barth: Prophet of a New Christianity?* (1931); *Harnack and Troeltsch: Two Historical Theologians* (1968); and, in collaboration with his wife Marion Pauck, *Paul Tillich: His Life and Thought* (1976).

Pauck's most important achievement and enduring legacy is that he transmitted to North America the great tradition of Reformation scholarship that had emerged in his native Germany during the first half of the twentieth century. Famed as a virtuoso lecturer and a wise director of graduate students, he trained, at Chicago and New York, two generations of the leading American historical theologians and Reformation scholars. Thus, through his writings and classroom teaching, Pauck exercised an extraordinary influence on American Protestantism, enabling it to recover its Reformation roots in a form suited to its contemporary situation.

BIBLIOGRAPHY

For additional information, see Marion Pauck's "Wilhelm Pauck: A Biographical Essay" and "Bibliography of the Published Writings of Wilhelm Pauck," in *Interpreters of Luther: Essays in Honor of Wilhelm Pauck*, edited by Jaroslav Pelikan (Philadelphia, 1968), in which there appears also Pelikan's "Wilhelm Pauck: A Tribute." Other tributes to Pauck and appraisals of his career are collected in *In Memory of Wilhelm Pauck (1901–1981)*, edited by me (New York, 1982). Pauck's thought, in midcareer, was considered by David Wesley Soper in *Major Voices in American Theology*, vol. 2, *Men Who Shape Belief* (Philadelphia, 1955), pp. 980–1111.

New Sources

Kingdon, Robert M. "Reformation Studies." In *Century of Church History*, edited by Henry W. Bowden, pp. 98–118. Carbondale, Ill., 1988.

Pauck, Marion Hausner. "Reinhold Niebuhr, Wilhelm Pauck, and Paul Tillich: Public and Private." *Union Seminary Quarterly Review* 53, nos. 1–2 (1999): 29–45.

Pauck, Marion Hausner. "Wilhelm Pauck: Church Historian and Historical Theologian 1901–1981: Précis of a Memoir." *Zeitschrift für neuere Theologiegeschichte* 6, no. 1 (1999): 50–68.

DAVID W. LOTZ (1987)
Revised Bibliography

PAUL VI (Giovanni Battista Montini, 1897–1978), was pope of the Roman Catholic Church during most of the Second Vatican Council and the years immediately after it. Born to influential and prosperous parents in Concesio, near Brescia, Italy, the sickly young Giovanni was nurtured in an encompassing church environment and groomed for leadership beginning with his seminary career. By the time he was ordained in 1920 he had already begun making friends and adopting styles that were to be conducive to a diplomatic career in the church.

Pius XII wanted to name Montini a cardinal in 1953, but he declined this honor until 1958, when John XXIII endowed him with the title. Pius had earlier appointed the scholarly, diplomatic-minded cleric archbishop of Milan, a key post. Yet it was his years in the Vatican Secretariat of State, to which he had been related through various positions for three decades, that best prepared Montini for the papal vocation to which his colleagues in the cardinalite named him on June 21, 1963.

The first and generally disappointing session of the Second Vatican Council, called by John XXIII to effect reform and renewal in the church, had occurred in autumn of 1962. It now fell to Paul VI to authorize its continuation and to preside over it through three more sessions. Montini's previous reputation would have seen him acting far more in continuity with the conservative, cautious ways of Pius XII than with the bold and disruptive styles of John XXIII. Yet, though he always remained conservative and cautious, he did help create a climate in which the bishops undertook actions that promoted *aggiornamento*, the creative shaking up and rearrangement that John had hoped for from the council.

Through the three remaining sessions, council decrees supported ecumenism, a more open attitude toward other religions (*Nostra aetate*), a collegiality of a sort that implied a sharing of papal power with the bishops, and many internal reforms. Paul seemed to sense more than did many of the reformers that it would not be easy to administer and lead a church in transition to the modern world. While Paul shared a passion to make the church at home in this world, he also felt distanced from secular life and warned against an easy embrace for contemporary value.

Though Paul VI was instinctively reluctant to be an iconoclast, his papacy did initiate many practices that assured continuance of conciliar styles. He worked continuously to reform the Curia, the network of Vatican congregations and offices that surrounds the pope. He changed the often repressive Congregation of the Holy Office to a somewhat more judicious Sacred Congregation for the Doctrine of Faith. He gave it more positive assignments than the old Holy Office, which had been associated chiefly with prohibiting suspicious books through the Index of Forbidden Books (*Index prohibitorum librorum*).

More important, Paul continued renewal by establishing a Synod of Bishops, whose second meeting in 1969 was as successful as its first one in 1967 had been fumbling and inauspicious. Subsequent meetings of this synod occurred in 1971, 1974, and 1977. At each of these the pope found means to exert pressure for more change and then to counterbalance it, by example and injunction, to hold to tradition where possible.

Reform of the Curia and promotion of synods, his most important works inside the Vatican, were less visible to the church or to the public than other activities for which Paul VI is remembered and through which he left an indelible stamp on the papacy. Most visible was his personal manner. The second regularly televised pope, he was the first to be televised throughout his entire papal career, and he was the first pope to ride in an airplane. He was the subject of extensive media coverage because of the way Vatican II had projected the papacy into the center of religious and political affairs. The pope's image was that of a studious academic, a sober and often mournful figure who bore the weight of many burdens, a leader who cautioned against reckless change.

Of change there was plenty. Priests by the thousands were leaving the priesthood to go into secular work and often to marry. Their move depleted the work force and symbolized decline in the older-style clerical church. Paul took these losses personally and warned remaining priests not to have romantic notions that the church could live without faithful priests or that those who left the priesthood—or the convent, for that matter, since many members of religious orders of women were also leaving them—could accomplish as much for Christ outside their office as in them. Yet he was not able to slow the exodus from the priesthood and the orders.

Paul compensated for some of these losses by giving the church a far more positive image in the eyes of those who had once regarded it, and especially its papal leadership, as alien and self-enclosed. He became the "pilgrim pope," who in a sequence of travels deftly displayed the best his church and he as pope had to offer. In 1964 Paul broke precedent by embracing Patriarch Athenagoras during a trip to Israel, a pilgrimage rich in symbolism for both Judaism and Orthodox Christianity. The papacy had long symbolized to Jews the focus of anti-Jewish thought and action. Paul VI made efforts to enlarge upon the Vatican Council's new spirit toward Jews. Meanwhile, Roman Catholicism and Eastern Orthodoxy, having been severed from each other for nine hundred years, in symbol and in spirit came closer together through the papal and patriarchal embrace in Israel than they had at any previous time during those centuries.

Paul's early travels, during which he reached out to Judaism and, more, to Orthodoxy, showed the thrust of his papacy: For all his cautions, he is remembered as an ecumenical pioneer. First, he encouraged "secular ecumenism" by inaugurating a Vatican Secretariat for Nonbelievers and reached to other faiths in 1964 by appointing a Secretariat for Relations with Non-Christian Religions. He followed up his approach to Orthodoxy with a stop in Turkey in 1967, again to see Athenagoras. He also visited the headquarters of the Orthodox and Protestant World Council of Churches in Geneva, Switzerland, in 1969. His words and actions showed that he saw great differences between Roman Catholic and other Christians, yet he would not let these hinder his efforts to improve relations.

Second, the pilgrim pope's travels let him indicate other directions he would take the church. At the council he clearly wanted to be known as the pope of the poor and, after it, a pope of peace. To this end, in another trip without precedent, he traveled to New York to address the United Nations in 1965. Diplomats were constantly welcomed at the Vatican, always with an interest in seeing whether Paul VI's interventions might promote justice, distribution of resources, and peace. To anyone who observed, it was clear that the papacy henceforth would not be perceived as participating in world affairs only to advance its own ends. His letter *Populorum progressio* in 1967 revealed his lifelong interest in social justice and seemed to be such a departure from Vatican conservatism that in America the *Wall Street Journal* called it "warmed-over Marxism." Needless to say, Paul was radically removed from the religious or antireligious ideology of Marxism, against which he constantly cautioned.

Third, his travels allowed Paul to combine ecumenical and internationalist issues by showing his interest in church and society in developing nations. His trips were to take him to Asia in 1964, to Colombia in 1968, to Uganda in 1969, and to a number of nations (including the Philippines, where an assassin threatened him) in 1970. His efforts to deal with the poor in these nations and elsewhere were compromised in the eyes of his critics by his resistance to birth control and population planning as means of limiting hunger and misery.

Birth control was a controversial issue also within the church. In 1968 Paul went against the advice of the majority of his chosen counselors on the subject and in his letter *Hu-*

manae vitae upheld the tradition of his predecessors, who had condemned what they called "artificial" birth control. Theologians in many nations subsequently spoke out in open revolt. Many bishops and priests had difficulties administering the church in congruence with *Humanae vitae.* Polls showed that in several nations the large marjority of Roman Cathoic couples did practice such birth control—a sign, to the pope, of a disobedience that became as great a burden as did the defection of priests.

Humanae vitae symbolized the efforts of Paul VI to slow change in the church. In 1967 his *Sacerdotalis caelibatus* emphatically insisted on celibacy for Latin-rite priests and dashed the hopes of those who desired some change in this concept. It was clear through these letters that the pope wanted to balance his ecumenical and diplomatic image as a flexible leader with an internal or churchly posture that would resist many kinds of compromise with the modern world. In a disciplined way, however, he also set the church on a fresh course, making it impossible for his successors to return it to its sequestered and self-defensive pre–Vatican II styles.

Bibliography

The collected writings and addresses of Paul VI to the midway point in his papacy are to be found in *The Teachings of Pope Paul VI,* 11 vols. (New York, 1968–1979), but a more condensed version of these is *The Mind of Paul VI on the Church and the World,* edited by James Walsh (Milwaukee, 1964), with emphasis on Montini's religious ideas prior to his election as pontiff. The most readable of the early biographies is Corrado Pallenberg's *The Making of a Pope* (New York, 1964), which avoids hagiographical tendencies if not uncritical enthusiasms; Michael Serafian's *The Pilgrim* (New York, 1964) avoids neither but provides ample detail for an understanding of Paul's 1964 embrace of Eastern Orthodoxy and the "third world" of developing nations. Insight into the pope's character, personality, and theological thought is provided by a series of interviews entitled *The Pope Speaks: Dialogues of Paul VI with Jean Guitton,* translated by Anne Fremantle and Christopher Fremantle (London, 1968). An interesting and informative study of the administrative aspect of Paul's papacy and its link with previous administrations is Peter Nichols's *The Politics of the Vatican* (London, 1968). The best English-language source compiling contemporary evaluations of Paul's major contributions and/or missteps is *Paul VI: Critical Appraisals,* edited by James F. Andrews (New York, 1970). After the pontiff's trip to New York and the United Nations, a number of pictorial essays and journalistic accounts of the event appeared. None is outstanding, but Bill Adler's *Pope Paul in the United States: His Mission for Peace on Earth, October 4, 1965* (New York, 1965) is as good as any.

Martin E. Marty (1987)

PAUL THE APOSTLE (d. 62 CE), also called Paul of Tarsus, known to Jewish Christians as Saul, was a Christian apostle and saint. A controversial missionary, Paul provoked intense opposition both during his career and after. His letters, which make up a substantial portion of the New Testament canon, stimulated diverse reactions and attracted problematic adherents to his beliefs. Modern research has uncovered the efforts of the post-Pauline church to soften his legacy of theological radicalism.

Some of Paul's letters, such as *1 Corinthians* and *2 Corinthians,* were edited a generation after Paul's death in an effort to mold them in directions suitable for the conservative consolidation of Christianity. Other letters, for example, *1 Timothy, 2 Timothy,* and *Titus,* were composed in Paul's name to serve the same purposes. In addition, several interpolations, such as *1 Corinthians* 14:33b–36 and *Romans* 16:17–20, skew Paul's message in authoritarian and sexually chauvinistic directions. *Acts of the Apostles* also presents a conservative picture of Paul.

The result is that the indisputably genuine letters (*Romans, 1 Corinthians, 2 Corinthians, Galatians, Philippians, Philemon, 1 Thessalonians,* and, with less unanimity, *2 Thessalonians*) have traditionally been interpreted in light of the later writings. This has resulted in serious confusions concerning Paul's theology, his relations with his churches and with other early Christian leaders, his outlook on major ethical issues, and the chronology of his life. Scholars have tended to be divided along ideological lines in resolving these issues, eliminating the possibility of consensus even on the most elemental facts about Paul's life.

Another problem is the tradition of theological abstraction in interpreting the Pauline letters. Because Christian theology has been shaped so largely by Pauline thought, the tendency has been to argue over every nuance, on the premise that Paul was a systematic theorist setting down doctrinal truth for all time. In fact, his letters are highly situational responses to complex congregational problems. The letters should be interpreted in light of those social realities, requiring the interpreter to reconstruct the situation largely on the basis of evidence within the letters themselves. This is rendered more difficult by traditional scholarly biases against the charismatic, sectarian, apocalyptic, and mystical experiences that animated Paul and his communities. Modern scholarship has detected the long-standing "fallacy of idealism," to use Bengt Holmberg's expression in *Paul and Power* (Philadelphia, 1978), by which Paul's theological response to problems arising from these sectarian communities has been wrongly interpreted as if it were the structuring principle of those communities.

The application of modern research techniques has allowed the apostle Paul to emerge from the mists of later orthodoxy and hagiography so that the fusion of his charismatic religious experience, his cooperative missionary activities, and his dialogical theology can be grasped. In contrast to traditional preferences that still persist among interpreters, Paul's view of salvation was cosmic rather than individualistic. His worldview was apocalyptic rather than bourgeois. He participated along with his churches in sectarian experiences of radical transformation, spiritual enthusiasm, and the expectation of future vindication. The preaching that evoked those experiences is accessible only by inferences from his letters, while his theology was the inspired but largely impromptu response to missional and congregational imperatives. The vitality and profundity of Paul's occasional remarks in the letters led to recognition of "the genius of Paul," which is the title of Samuel Sandmel's significant study (Philadelphia, 1979).

In order to break from the framework of *Acts* and the later writings of the Pauline school, it is necessary to reconstruct Paul's career primarily from the authentic letters.

From Pharisee to Christian missionary. The evidence in *Philippians* 3:3–4 and *Galatians* 1:13–24 indicates that Paul came from a Hellenistic-Jewish family in the Diaspora. His zeal for the law and his persecution of early Christians in Diaspora synagogues as heretics place him close to the school of Shammai in the Pharisee party. If he ever studied under Gamliʾel the Elder as reported in *Acts* 22:3, he rejected his teacher's tolerance. Because he was a complete stranger to residents of Judaea (*Gal.* 1:22), it is likely that Paul was educated in Tarsus rather than Jerusalem. His Roman citizenship and his mastery of Greek, including a sophisticated grasp of Greco-Roman rhetoric, indicate he came from a prominent family that had rendered loyal service to the empire and was in a position to offer him a classical as well as a Hebrew education. Paul's trade of tent making, probably learned in the family shop, allowed him thereafter a degree of independence as a journeyman leatherworker, according to Ronald F. Hock in *The Social Context of Paul's Ministry* (Philadelphia, 1980).

In the two laconic references to his conversion in 34 CE (*1 Cor.* 15:8, *Gal.* 1:15–17), Paul alludes to a theophanic experience of encountering the risen Christ on the road to Damascus. In the context of his persecution of diaspora Christians as violators of synagogal legalism, this encounter indicated that Jesus, who had been crucified for lawlessness and blasphemy, was indeed the promised Messiah. The correctness of Jesus' message and the sin of his persecutors were proven by his resurrection and appearance to Paul. Paul's robust and confident commitment to legal obedience as the path to the messianic kingdom, characteristic of Phariseeism, was therefore shattered and replaced by a mystical identification with the Messiah (*Phil.* 3:4–8).

Krister Stendahl is correct in insisting that Paul's references to the Damascus experience preclude any interpretation in terms of resolving guilt concerning Paul's previous performance as a Pharisee. "There is no indication that psychologically Paul had some problem of conscience," producing a conversion along the lines of Augustine or Luther, Stendahl writes in *Paul among Jews and Gentiles* (Philadelphia, 1976, p. 13). Paul speaks of being "called" rather than converted, impelled by the encounter with the risen Christ to become a missionary to lawless Gentiles (*Gal.* 1:15–16). Paul's zeal for the law changed into its opposite: a commitment to the inclusion of Gentiles in the messianic community without imposing the burden of the law. Paul's previous intolerant exclusion of "heretics" was transformed into a lifelong commitment to messianic pluralism so offensive to zealous legalists that from that moment on Paul became the target of reprisals (*1 Thes.* 2:2, 14–16).

In the seven to eight years after his Damascus experience, Paul was aligned with the Hellenistic Christians of Arabia, Syria, and Cilicia who had been driven out of Jerusalem after the martyrdom of Stephen (*1 Thes.* 1:15, *Acts* 8:1–4). Accepting their version of Christianity, which was critical of the Temple cult, legalistic obedience, and racial-religious zealotism, Paul became an artisan-missionary involved in creating charismatic communities of faith consisting of Jews and Gentiles (*Gal.* 1:23, 2:12–16). Troubles with political authorities, which began quite early in his career (cf. *2 Cor.* 11:32–33), were probably provoked by the highly charged, sectarian apocalypticism that marked these radical communities. For a brief period of fifteen days, he visited the apostle Peter in Jerusalem (*Gal.* 1:18–20), but in Paul's letters there is no evidence of theological influence from the more conservative branch of early Christianity. By the early 40s, Paul was working in cooperation with the dynamic center of Hellenistic Christianity in Antioch. Sharing their commitment to interracial, charismatic leadership (*Acts* 13:1), to intense community life of prayer and ecstatic worship (*Acts* 13:2–4), and to the eucharistic meal as an expression of unity (*Gal.* 2:12–16), Paul became one of the leaders in the first organized mission to Cyprus and southern Galatia around the years 43–45 (*Acts* 13–14).

Judging from Paul's earliest references to his missionary preaching (*1 Thes.* 1:9–10, 2:9–13), his message centered in the apocalyptic dawn of a new age that opened salvation to Gentiles. The "gospel of God" included an exposure of idolatry and a promise of escape "from the wrath to come." The resurrection of Jesus and the expectation of his return are given prominent expression. The invitation of Gentiles to "faith in God" (*1 Thes.* 1:8) without the imposition of the law implies a substantial break with Pharisaic Judaism as well as with conservative Jewish Christianity in Jerusalem. Yet at this early stage there is no indication of a systematic critique of the law; in fact, a positive assessment of legal holiness is visible as late as 50 CE in *1 Thessalonians* 4:1–8, a position consistent with the negative view of "lawlessness" in *2 Thessalonians* 2:3, 7, 8. The hostile reactions of Jewish zealots to Paul's early preaching (*1 Thes.* 2:15–16; *Acts* 13:45, 13:50, 14:2–5, 14:19) can be understood on the grounds of the inclusion of despised Gentiles, without assuming the abrasive rhetoric of Paul's later teaching about freedom from the law.

Beginning in approximately 46 CE, Paul entered a fully independent phase of missionizing. While two earlier colleagues traveled to Cyprus, apparently with the support of the Antioch church, Paul, Silas, and Timothy struck off for the west (*1 Thes.* 1:1, *Acts* 16:6–12). Revisiting the churches of Cilicia and southern Galatia, they spent as much as a year in the northern Galatia cities of Ancyra, Pessinus, and Germa founding several churches (*Gal.* 1:2) of purely Gentile members of Gallo-Grecian background (*Gal.* 3:1) despite an illness that Paul suffered at this time (*Gal.* 4:13–15). A period of shifting plans followed, in which Paul and his colleagues were dissuaded from traveling to the populous provinces of Asia and Bithynia. They ended up in Troas, where a church was founded (*Acts* 16:8–10, 20:6–12) and where they were joined by the author, traditionally identified as Luke, of the "we-source" material in the second half of *Acts.*

Sailing to Europe in the spring of 48 CE, they founded the important congregation in Philippi. Predominantly Gentile in background, this church entered into a formal arrangement with Paul, forming what Paul J. Sampley has called "a consensual partnership in Christ for preaching the gospel" (*Pauline Partnership in Christ,* Philadelphia, 1980, p. 51). Paul thereafter received financial support from Philippi for the extended activities of an increasing circle of missionary colleagues while continuing to work as a tent maker. Among the male and female co-workers whose names are known to us from this period are Timothy, Titus, Silas, Luke, Epaphroditus, Clement, Euodia, and Syntyche, along with local patrons and patronesses such as the Philippian jailor and Lydia. The charismatic, apocalyptic piety of this congregation contained some divisive tendencies (*Phil.* 4:2–3) and it experienced a traumatic expulsion of heretical libertinists during the founding mission (*Phil.* 3:17–20). The Philippian mission came to an end in the spring or summer of 49 with a humiliating episode of mob violence followed by judicial beating and imprisonment (*1 Thes.* 2:2, *Acts* 16:19–40).

Continuing in a westward direction after the expulsion from Philippi, Paul and his traveling companions arrived in Thessalonica, where a rapidly expanding ministry was cut short after several months by riotous opposition from the local synagogue (*Acts* 17:1–9; *1 Thes.* 2:14–17). A congregation marked by enthusiastic radicalism was formed out of Jewish and Gentile converts, including a house-church patron by the name of Jason and several prominent women. Because the Thessalonian letters were composed so quickly after Paul's departure, one gains a vivid picture of a freshly established congregation. It was troubled by conflicts over sexual irregularities (*1 Thes.* 4:1–8), the status and control of ecstatic forms of worship (*1 Thes.* 5:19–22), and tensions between leaders and followers (*1 Thes.* 5:12–13). A key factor in these troubles was the misunderstanding of Pauline apocalypticism (*1 Thes.* 5:1–11, *2 Thes.* 2:1–12), which ultimately led to the incredible announcement by a Thessalonian ecstatic that "the day of the Lord has already come" (*2 Thes.* 2:2). Apparently the radicals interpreted their experience of the spirit in a way that made them believe that history had come to an end. Some of these leaders had dropped out of their daily occupations to be supported by the congregation as full-time charismatics, free from restraint (*1 Thes.* 5:14, *2 Thes.* 3:6–15). This highly inflated enthusiasm was severely shaken by the unexpected violence that had forced Paul to leave Thessalonica and thereafter resulted in the harassment and death of congregational members. Having erroneously concluded that the age of the spirit had released them from the risks of history, these shock waves led to the crisis addressed by Paul's first congregational letters composed in the spring of 50 CE.

Paul's letters were written as a substitute for his personal presence, as emergency efforts to resolve congregational issues that neither he nor his traveling colleagues could deal with in person. The creativity and power of these letters are the result of his efforts to improvise responses to the unique and highly volatile situations that marked the sectarian congregations he had helped to found. In the case of *1 Thessalonians,* the innovations are immediately apparent. Building the argument into the most broadly extended thanksgiving in the annals of Greco-Roman or Hebrew letter-writing, Paul clarified the realistic potential of the charismatic faith, hope, and love that the congregation had experienced (*1 Thes.* 1:2–3:13). Rather than eliminating the "old" age of persecution and labor for daily bread, such ecstatic experiences provided the means to face life with courage and realism. But Paul's confident statements of hope and his effort to explain a traditional Judaic apocalyptic scheme to a Hellenistic audience led to the misunderstanding of the first letter, which was taken to support the view that the end of history had indeed occurred (*2 Thes.* 2:2). Paul's second letter to the Thessalonians was apparently composed shortly thereafter to summarize the message of the earlier letter and to squelch the ecstatic understanding of eschatology.

The Thessalonian crisis shows that Paul's missionary success was in part the cause of the troubles that marked his career (see *2 Cor.* 11:23–29, 6:3–10). The intense religious fervor evoked by his proclamation broke down traditional restraints to create interracial and multiclass congregations with strong but immediately divisive charismatic leadership. Sectarian congregations with this level of social innovation and a consciousness of having been redeemed from a corrupt environment naturally became the target of reprisals by synagogal and civil authorities as well as by neighbors and family members. This pattern of successful mission, provoking strong local opposition, repeated itself in the short Beroean ministry in the early fall of 49 CE (*Acts* 17:10–14). After a less successful effort to establish a congregation in Athens (*Acts* 17:33–34), Paul came in the winter to Corinth, where he began a ministry of eighteen months with the most formative and troubled congregation in his career.

The Corinthian ministry appears to have had a decisive influence on the evolution of Paul's theology. The scope of this evolution can be measured by comparing the Thessalonian letters, written at the beginning of the Corinthian ministry, with the Corinthian correspondence, which was composed five to six years later. The Corinthian correspondence deals in part with conflicts between forms of apostolic teaching. Many of Paul's most distinctive ideas appear to have arisen out of the interaction with the Corinthians: the church as the "body of Christ"; marriage as mutual submission "in the body"; respect for conscience even when it is ill-informed; the theology of the cross in dialectic with human wisdom on the one side and human weakness on the other; and the superiority of love over faith or hope.

The social context for Paul's Corinthian ministry was a series of house churches under the patronage of middle- or upper-class leaders such as Prisca and Aquila, Jason, Chloe, Stephanas, and Titius Justus. According to Gerd Theissen in *The Social Setting of Pauline Christianity* (Philadelphia, 1982), it is likely that these socially superior leaders practiced a kind of loving patriarchalism in their sponsorship of socially diverse churches. Competition between house churches came to focus on their different attachments to early Christian missionaries who functioned alongside Paul. This helps to explain the subsequent evolution of parties that boasted the superiority of their particular traditions: "'I belong to Paul' or 'I belong to Apollos' or 'I belong to Cephas' [i. e., Peter] or 'I belong to Christ'" (*1 Cor.* 1:12). The latter group, claiming to transcend human leaders, was most likely protognostic in outlook, providing radical challenges to Pauline teachings and ethics. The forces dividing the Corinthians also included racial and cultural diversity, as well as the lack of space for all the house churches to meet together regularly, as shown by the archaeological evidence of Jerome M. O'Connor (*St. Paul's Corinth,* Wilmington, Del., 1983, pp. 155–158). The strategic location of Corinth as a commercial and transit center and the large crowds drawn to the biennial Isthmian Games contributed to the recruitment of co-workers and the establishment of churches in satellite cities, for example, Cenchreae under the patronage of Phoebe (see *Rom.* 16:1–2). The Corinthian ministry ended with a judicial hearing of charges raised by influential members of the local synagogue. Paul was arraigned before Gallio, the proconsul of Achaea (*Acts* 18:12–17) whose tenure in Corinth provides one of the reliable dates in the reconstruction of Pauline chronology. Because Paul was free to return to Corinth, he must have been exonerated, but he left Corinth soon after the hearing to take part in the apostolic conference at Jerusalem, one of the crucial events in the history of first-century Christianity.

The Judaizer crisis and its aftermath. The background of the apostolic conference (51 CE) was a campaign to circumcise Gentile Christians and thus incorporate them into a Jewish-Christian mode of adherence to the Torah. *Acts* 15:1 provides a reliable account of the origin and content of this campaign: "But some men came down [to Antioch] from Judaea and were teaching the brethren, 'Unless you are circumcised according to the custom of Moses, you cannot be saved.'" Paul's account of the conference in *Galatians* 2:1–10 reflects the mortal threat this campaign posed against the "freedom" of Gentile Christians to live without the burden of the Torah and to enjoy an inclusive fellowship with Jewish Christians despite differences in lifestyle. Some of the motivations for the sudden interest of the Judean Christians in the affairs of the Antioch church are alluded to with considerable sarcasm in *Galatians* 6:12–13. Wishing to avoid persecution "for the cross of Christ," the Judeans wanted to "make a good showing" to some unnamed third party by getting the Gentiles circumcised. The most likely explanation for the Judaizer campaign was the Zealot pressure that was intensifying during the procuratorship of Ventidius Cumanus (48–52), enforcing conformity with the law and acceptance of circumcision along with noncommunication with the uncircumcised. That the Christian communities in Judaea had experienced such violent pressures is revealed in *2 Thessalonians* 1:14–16. The promotion of circumcision among Gentile Christians thus promised to relieve the threat of persecution. But Paul saw that this temporary expedient would shatter the hopes of a successful Gentile mission and destroy the inclusive quality of Christian fellowship between Jews and Gentiles. His key doctrine of justification by faith rather than by works such as circumcision emerged out of this crisis, providing a distinctive and radical cast to all of his later theology. While claiming in *Galatians* 2:15–16 that all Christians, including Jewish Christians, "know that a man is not justified by works of the law but through faith in Jesus Christ," Paul insists on the antithesis "not by works" as the essential premise of "freedom."

In Paul's version of the apostolic conference, he was supported by Barnabas, the key leader of the Antioch church, and Titus, an uncircumcised Gentile Christian, in providing an account of "the gospel which I preach among the gentiles" (*Gal.* 2:2). The leaders of the Judean churches—James, Peter, and John—acknowledged the truth of this message and the fact that its success among Gentiles provided divine confirmation (*Gal.* 2:8). They agreed on a practical division of the mission along cultural lines, "that we should go to the Gentiles and they to the circumcised" (*Gal.* 2:9), but that the Gentile churches would undertake a financial campaign to aid the impoverished Christians in Judaea. Despite the continued opposition of a Judaizer faction, which Paul castigates as "false brethren," the integrity of the Gentile mission was preserved.

The question of coexistence of Jews and Gentiles in the worship life of local churches was left unresolved. Herein lay the seeds of later controversies, because Paul understood the agreement in principle on the legitimacy of his gospel to mean the acceptance of equality and solidarity between Jewish and Gentile Christians. Shortly after the apostolic conference this issue came to a head when a delegation sent by James prevailed on Peter not to eat with Gentile Christians at Antioch. Paul accused Peter and the other Jewish Christians at Antioch of insincerity and inconsistency in forsaking the common meal that had been a crucial element of the inclusive form of the faith at Antioch. The repercussions of this conflict are visible throughout Paul's subsequent ministry in his attempts to defend the integrity of his gospel and his apostolicity against pressures ranging from political expediency to violent opposition against the doctrine of freedom from the law.

Paul's letter to the Galatians, written in 53 CE, reflects an intensification of the Judaizer crisis after the apostolic conference. A delegation of Judaizers was sent by the "false brethren" in Judaea to the exclusively Gentile churches in northern Galatia, arriving there shortly after Paul had revisited these congregations on his journey from Antioch to Ephesus. As reconstructed from his highly polemical defense in *Galatians,* the emissaries proposed circumcision as a means to gain perfection and enter into the mystical promise of being "sons of Abraham" (*Gal.* 3:6–18). They advocated conformity to Jewish festivals by sanctioning their role in appeasing the astrological powers (*Gal.* 4:9–10). They insinuated that Paul himself had previously preached such conformity to the law as derived from the Jerusalem apostles, but that he had trimmed the gospel to win quick converts (*Gal.* 1:10–14, 1:18–2:2, 5:11).

Paul angrily refuted these allegations and provided a systematic defense of the freedom of the gospel. He contended that the charismatic experience of the Galatians proved that salvation comes through faith in the gospel rather than by works of the law (*Gal.* 3:1–5). Scripture itself reveals the correctness of this message, because Abraham's faith "was reckoned to him as righteousness" (*Gen.* 15:6) and the principle from *Habakkuk* 2:4 is that the just shall live by faith (*Gal.* 3:6–14). Paul went on to show that the status of being "sons of God" was conferred by faith through baptism so that a new relationship of solidarity developed among racially, economically, and sexually distinct groups (*Gal.* 3:26–29). To accept the law as binding for salvation was therefore to repudiate Christ and to again become enslaved to the principalities and powers of paganism (*Gal.* 4:1–11).

An explosive allegory concerning the two sons of Abraham was developed to show that the slave Hagar corresponds to the Jerusalem of the Judaizers, bringing a flesh-bound oppression against the children of the free woman, Sarah (*Gal.* 4:21–31). Thus the antitheses of flesh versus spirit, slavery versus freedom, and law versus promise were related to an ongoing political and ideological struggle in the church, now seen as a conflict between "the present Jerusalem" and the "Jerusalem above." The crucial issue of freedom was then used as the leitmotiv of the moral exhortation of *Galatians* 5:1–6:10. According to Hans Dieter Betz, the thrust of this argument is that "'freedom in Christ' is a gift of God, but a delicate one. It is a gift, but it is not to be taken for granted. Freedom exists only insofar as people live in freedom. . . . Those who were liberated by the Spirit can protect their freedom only by 'walking by the Spirit'. . ." (*A Commentary on Paul's Letter to the Churches in Galatia,* Philadelphia, 1979, p. 32).

Whether Paul's powerful argument was convincing to the Galatians is an open question, in light of their nonparticipation in the Jerusalem offering and the lack of evidence about their later activities. The Judaizer movement continued to be a threat to Pauline congregations, as evidenced by the polemical warning in Paul's next letter, the letter to the Philippians (3:2–6), probably written from an Ephesian prison in the winter of 54–55. A modified form of the Galatian argument also appears in Paul's last extant letter, the letter to the Romans. The political pressures from the increasingly violent Zealot movement in the diaspora communities as well as in Judaea also directly affected Paul's mission. The results were riots, charges of subversion, and plots against his life (e.g., *Acts* 20:3, 23:12–22).

The ministry in Asia. From the latter part of 52 CE through the next several years, Paul's center of missionary activities was Ephesus, the administrative and commercial hub of the province of Asia. An intensification of the collegial mission during these years involved Prisca and Aquila, who had moved from Corinth to establish their business in the new location in support of the expanding activities. Other colleagues, such as Apollos, Archippus, Aristarchus, Demas, Epaenetus, Epaphras, Erastus, Jesus Justus, Luke, Mark, Silas, Timothy, Titus, Trophimus, and Tychichus, are mentioned in the writings deriving from this period. Their activities account for the establishment of satellite churches in such cities as Laodicea, Hierapolis, and Colossae.

Perhaps for the first time in his career Paul had access in Ephesus to a larger facility, the Hall of Tyrannus (*Acts* 19:9), but he appears to have maintained his regimen as a self-supporting artisan. The availability of rapid communications between Ephesus and the cities of the Aegean Sea as well as of the hinterland brought Paul into the vortex of competing leaders, church conflicts, and societal pressures that marked the first generation of Christianity. This vivid description pertains to the Asian years:

> danger from my own people, danger from gentiles, danger in the city, danger in the wilderness, danger at sea, danger from false brethren; in toil and hardship, through many a sleepless night, in hunger and thirst, often without food, in cold and exposure. And, apart from other things, there is the daily pressure upon me of my anxiety for all the churches. Who is weak, and I am not weak? Who is made to fall, and I am not indignant? (*2 Cor.* 11:26–29)

The controversies involving the "weak" and the "falling," as well as the threats from Jews and Gentiles, resulted in Paul's writing a number of letters during the Asian period, including those to the Galatians, the Philippians, the Colossians, Philemon, and the Corinthians. *Philippians* was drafted during an incarceration that apparently followed the riot described in *1 Corinthians* 15:32 and *Acts* 19:23–41. It reflects conflicts with heretical libertinists, roving Judaizers, and rival missionaries who took advantage of Paul's imprisonment by insinuating that his inflammatory gospel imperiled the future of the church. In the opening chapter, Paul gives thanks that the Philippians have shared in the suffering, conflicts, and growth of the gospel. Then on the basis of an early Christian hymn cited in *Philippians* 2:6–11, Paul develops a theology of self-emptying love and solidarity capable of resolving conflicts and enduring persecution. He requests cooperation with his emissary Epaphroditus, who is visiting Macedonia while Paul is detained.

After warning about the threat of Judaizers from outside the community (3:2–11) and from libertinists within Philippi itself (3:17–21), Paul urges local leaders Euodia and Syntyche to be reconciled. The theme of apocalyptic urgency and joy is expressed with the memorable lines "Rejoice in the Lord always; again I will say, Rejoice. Let all men know your forbearance. The Lord is at hand" (*Phil.* 4:4–5). The letter ends with thanks for the financial support the Philippians have provided for the activities of the Pauline mission. Resilient joy in the midst of tribulation is the note struck repeatedly in the letters of the Asian period.

The extensive Corinthian correspondence allows one to grasp the issues raised by that congregation as well as the evolving shape of Paul's theology. References in *1 Corinthians* 5:9 and *2 Corinthians* 2:3–9 make it likely that at least four and perhaps as many as seven separate letters are contained in the canonical *1 Corinthians* and *2 Corinthians*. Reconstructions of the interaction between Paul and the controversialists make it likely that the opening issues related to shifts in sexual roles, disturbances in the celebrations of the Lord's Supper, and the rise of sectarian divisiveness. In *1 Corinthians* 11:2–34 Paul argues the abandonment of sexual differentiation in the form of women adopting male hairstyles to express their powerful new sense of equality in the church. Paul argues that men and women should retain culturally determined indications of sexual differentiation even while leading Christian worship, but he does not question the right of women to play an equal part.

The problem of sacramental disorder was closely related to class differences that arose in connection with the common meal. In *The Social Setting of Pauline Christianity,* Gerd Theissen has related this problem to the pattern of Greco-Roman banquets in which upper-class hosts treated guests "differently depending on their social status" (p. 58). Since poorer members of the congregation would be humiliated by such practices, Paul is indignant at the violation of the unity of the church. The peculiar warning that those eating and drinking without "discerning the body" would fall under divine judgment (*1 Cor.* 11:29) makes it likely that theological issues were mixed with sociological factors in this instance. Walter Schmithals has suggested that spiritualists critical of the bodily elements in the sacramental meal aimed "to sabotage the cultic observation and to transform it into . . . a profane feast" (*Gnosticism in Corinth,* Nashville, 1971, p. 255). This is rendered more likely by Paul's assertion that the disruptions were connected with theological factions in the congregation (see *1 Cor.* 11:18–19).

The next phase of the Corinthian controversy involved resistance against traditionally Judaic sexual ethics, a rejection of the doctrine of the bodily resurrection, and an interpretation of the sacrament as a kind of spiritual medicine of immortality. Paul responds to the report of these developments brought by Stephanas, Fortunatus, and Achaicus (*1 Cor.* 16:17) by developing a concept of the body as the basis of human identity and relationship. Against the gnostic tendency to downplay the significance of bodily relations, Paul insists that "the body is for the Lord and the Lord is for the body" (*1 Cor.* 6:13), which means that casual sexual liaisons are excluded. Bodily disciplines are therefore required by faith (*1 Cor.* 9:24–27). Sacramental experiences do not relieve persons from such responsibilities (*1 Cor.* 10:1–13) because "sharing in the body of Christ" creates a unity between believers and their Lord that excludes immoral relations with pagan prostitutes and temples (*1 Cor.* 10:14–22).

Gnostic skepticism about the Christian tradition of bodily resurrection is countered by reiterating the early Christian gospel, warranted by the firsthand witnesses of the resurrection of Christ (*1 Cor.* 15:1–19). A new concept of the "spiritual body" is developed to render the doctrine of resurrection less vulnerable to the charge of mindless crudity. The gnostic teaching about the original spiritual Adam of *Genesis* 1 degenerating into the bodily Adam of *Genesis* 2–3 is repudiated by insisting that Christ is the second Adam, the spiritual redeemer from heaven (*1 Cor.* 15:35–41). The hope of Christians is that "as we have borne the image of the man of dust, we shall also bear the image of the man from heaven," that is, Christ (*1 Cor.* 15:49).

Responding to reports from "Chloe's people" (*1 Cor.* 1:12) about divisions in the congregation and to a list of controversial questions they had brought, Paul wrote the so-called answer letter from Ephesus just prior to Pentecost in 54 CE. The prideful wisdom that lay behind the competition among house churches in Corinth was contrasted with the word of the cross and the experience of humble hearers transformed by it. "God chose what is low and despised in the world, even things that are not, to bring to nothing things that are, so that no human being might boast in the presence of God" (*1 Cor.* 1:28–29). The gospel of grace brought and nurtured by various apostles aimed at creating a new, unified community animated by the spirit rather than by pride (*1 Cor.* 2:1–4:7). As for the gnostic leader living in arrogant incest, rather than taking pride in his capacity to transcend moral compunctions, the congregation should ban him in the hope that he would see his error (*1 Cor.* 5:1–13).

Responding to questions from the Ephesian congregation about the preferability of platonic marriages, Paul defends marriage as a permanent and mutual covenant to fulfill bodily needs (*1 Cor.* 7:1–24). Paul's own gift of celibacy is well suited to the uncertain conditions of missionizing in the end time, but he insists that each Christian should discover the path of personal responsibility in such matters (*1 Cor.* 7:25–40).

The difficult question about whether Christians should eat food offered to idols is dealt with by a new doctrine of the autonomous conscience. Paul argues that while conscience is socially conditioned, it must be followed as the guarantor of personal integrity. Those whose conscience allows them to eat such food are cautioned not to use their freedom irresponsibly so that the weak are led into destructive violations of their integrity (*1 Cor.* 8:1–13, 10:23–11:1). On the issue of whether glossolalia is the supreme gift or whether it ought to be repressed, Paul develops a doctrine that "there are varieties of gifts, but the same spirit," so that members of the congregation should exercise their various gifts in love for the sake of the common good (*1 Cor.* 12:4–14:40).

After Paul's departure from Ephesus under conditions that made it impossible for him to return, he wrote the later portions of the Corinthian correspondence. In that correspondence he dealt with the revolt stimulated by the arrival of "super-apostles" with a success-oriented theology. The humiliating circumstances of an Ephesian riot and imprisonment, the latter reflected in *Philippians,* may have rendered Paul more vulnerable to the charge that his misfortunes showed the inadequacies of his gospel. Paul admits his limitations on the principle that the treasure of the gospel resides "in earthen vessels" (*2 Cor.* 4:7), but pleads for reconciliation (*2 Cor.* 5:18–6:13, 7:2–4). He then revisited Corinth at the height of the controversy and was summarily dismissed by the congregation, thereupon writing the so-called letter of tears (*2 Cor.* 10:1–13:13), which apparently caused a softening of heart. The plans for collecting the Jerusalem offering were reactivated (*2 Cor.* 9:1–15), and the final phase of the correspondence reflects the "comfort of Christ," which Paul experienced upon meeting Titus in Macedonia the following year with news that the revolt was over (*2 Cor.* 1:3–2:13, 7:5–8:24).

In the meantime Paul had suffered the "affliction in Asia" (*2 Cor.* 1:8), probably the imprisonment reflected in the letter to Philemon, a tactful plea for the freedom of the converted slave Onesimus. During this same imprisonment, Paul apparently helped to plan the letter to the Colossians, which dealt with the threat of gnostic syncretism in churches founded by Paul's missionary colleagues not far from Ephesus.

From Corinth to Rome as diplomat and prisoner. While wintering in Corinth and its neighboring city of Cenchreae in 56–57, Paul developed the plan to deliver the offering to Jerusalem and then to begin a mission westward to Rome and Spain. Working under the patronage of Phoebe (*Rom.* 16:1–2), Paul undertook extensive preparations to become informed about the fragmented and suspicious churches in Rome so as to make possible a cooperative mission in the thoroughly gentile and nonhellenized area of Spain. The letter to the Romans was written to elicit support for this mission, proclaiming the triumphant power of God manifested in the gospel, which reveals that all humans are equal in sin but also in unmerited grace (*Rom.* 1:16–3:31). Although it proved to be Paul's most influential theological statement, the letter to the Romans served the practical purpose of finding a common basis in faith to further cooperation between conservative and liberal factions in Rome.

In contrast to the Corinthian letters, which are a jumbled composite of correspondence over a lengthy period of time, *Romans* is a well-organized and brilliantly composed essay on the theme of the righteousness of God revealed through faith (*Rom.* 1:16–17). That divine righteousness is impartial (*Rom.* 2:11) is the premise on which the status of Jew and Gentile is shown to be equal, so that Abraham becomes the "father of all who have faith" (*Rom.* 4:11) rather than merely the progenitor of circumcised Jews. Since all humans are saved by faith rather than by works of self-justification, the baptism of Christians is described as the inauguration of a new life in which slavery to sin and the law has been broken (*Rom.* 6:1–23).

The problem Paul finds with the Jewish law is that it lures humans into aggressive self-righteousness that produces death in place of life (*Rom.* 7:1–25). True righteousness is the gift of God in Christ, inaugurating the new age of the spirit in which the good is accomplished not because it gains something but because it expresses the new status of belonging to "Abba, Father" (*Rom.* 8:1–16). Yet this new life occurs in the midst of a fallen world of decay, sin, and hostility, so faith is sustained by an eschatological hope in the triumph of righteousness by the ongoing experience of the love of God that death itself cannot thwart (*Rom.* 8:17–39). That the bulk of Paul's fellow Jews had not accepted this message does not negate the power of the gospel or the freedom of God over creation (*Rom.* 9:1–29). Despite the zealous resistance of legalists, the gospel will achieve its goal of converting first Gentiles and then Jews, unifying the human race under grace: "For God has consigned all men to disobedience, that he may have mercy upon all" (*Rom.* 11:32).

Paul's great letter then takes up the question of ethics, arguing for the principles of responsible love and charismatic equality derived from the shared experience of the "mercies of God" (*Rom.* 12:1–13:14). The special problems of intolerance among the Roman house churches are dealt with by the admonition to pass on the same welcome to each other that they had already experienced in Christ (*Rom.* 14:1–15:7). If that occurs, the world mission that Paul had already brought as far west as Illyricum would have a chance of succeeding in uniting Jews and Gentiles, Greeks and barbarians from Jerusalem to Spain, the end of the Mediterranean world (*Rom.* 15:8–33). Paul closes his letter by greeting a wide variety of Roman house churches, leaders, and missionaries, giving diplomatic expression to his lifelong commitment to messianic pluralism (*Rom.* 16:3–23).

Paul's final journey to Jerusalem, in the spring of 57 CE, was undertaken against dangerous opposition in order to deliver the offering and thereby seal the unity of the church, which had been fractured by tensions between Jewish and Gentile Christians of various persuasions. His plan was to sail from there to Rome. Paul construed the offering as a sign of mutual indebtedness between Jews and Gentiles (*Rom.* 15:27), which explains the hostile reactions of Jewish Zealots who plotted his assassination. A substantial delegation of

Gentile Christians sailed with Paul (*Acts* 20:4) in this diplomatic venture, but the Jerusalem church refused to accept the offering without a legalistic subterfuge (*Acts* 21:24). The Zealot pressure against collaboration with Gentiles expressed itself also in a Temple riot when Paul and his delegation arrived, and in a subsequent plot to assassinate him before he could reach the safety of the Roman garrison at Caesarea. Paul suffered an imprisonment of two years duration in Caesarea, at the end of which he appealed his case to the emperor in Rome. Thus he arrived at his desired destination in the spring of 60 CE, but in chains. Two years later, when Nero restored the treason law, Paul was summarily executed.

INFLUENCE OF PAUL. The riotous opposition that marked the end of Paul's life was a formative element in the final decades of the first century and in the shaping of the New Testament itself. Right-wing and left-wing factions vied for the legacy of Paul in a struggle that had many counterparts in later Christian history. The splits already visible within Paul's lifetime evolved into full-scale conflicts between gnostic and orthodox congregations, both of which called on Paul as their apostle.

Written in the latter decades of the first century, *Acts* devotes about half its length to a depiction of Paul as a successful missionary who warned against heretics who would later arise (*Acts* 20:28–30). The author of *Acts* includes no references to Paul's controversial letters, his radical doctrines, or his involvement in church conflicts at Corinth, Galatia, Ephesus, Philippi, or Thessalonica. The use of Paul's letters and ideas by left-wing factions was countered by the composition of *1 Timothy, 2 Timothy,* and *Titus* by the Pauline school toward the end of the first century. The Paul of these letters is authoritarian, sober, uncharismatic, and morally conformist, teaching faith as a set of beliefs to be learned rather than as a revolutionary relationship based on unmerited grace. Other epistles, such as *Jude, James,* and *2 Peter,* were drafted to counter libertinistic and gnostic interpretations of Pauline doctrine. The fact that about half the New Testament is directly related to Paul and his story or is written in the epistolary form that he popularized makes it clear that his theology and example provided the raw materials of later controversies. Down to the time of the Christian gnostic Marcion (d. 160?) and beyond, pro- and anti-Paulinists vied for the domination of the Christian mind.

The impact of Pauline thought on later theological revolutions is well known. Augustine, Luther, Calvin, and Wesley, as well as moderns like Barth, Brunner, Bonhoeffer, and Bultmann, were decisively shaped by rediscovering Paul's doctrine of grace, his analysis of the problem of the law, and his revolutionary grasp of the righteousness of God. Their opponents in many instances cited the same materials both within and outside the authentic Pauline corpus that traditionalists in the early church had used. These conflicts leave a permanent stamp on the interpretation of Pauline materials, as shown by Krister Stendahl in *Paul among Jews and Gentiles* (Philadelphia, 1976). Although it is a mistake to view Paul as the second founder of the Christian church, it is true that he remains at the center of its most vital controversies.

SEE ALSO Biblical Literature, article on New Testament; Biblical Temple; Israelite Law; Messianism; Persecution; Pharisees; Rabbinic Judaism in Late Antiquity.

BIBLIOGRAPHY

The best nontechnical introduction to the problem of understanding Paul is Leander E. Keck's *Paul and His Letters* (Philadelphia, 1979). An excellent supplement in more technical style is available in the essays of Nils A. Dahl collected in *Studies in Paul: Theology for the Early Christian Mission* (Minneapolis, 1977). For the sequence of Paul's activities, see my *A Chronology of Paul's Life* (Philadelphia, 1979). A competent though somewhat dated introduction to the problem of interpreting epistolographic materials is William G. Doty's *Letters in Primitive Christianity* (Philadelphia, 1973). A stimulating sketch of Pauline theology is available in Robin Scroggs's *Paul for a New Day* (Philadelphia, 1977), while more detailed treatments from innovative viewpoints are available in J. Christiaan Beker's *Paul the Apostle: The Triumph of God in Life and Thought* (Philadelphia, 1980) and Daniel Patte's *Paul's Faith and the Power of the Gospel: A Structural Introduction to the Pauline Letters* (Philadelphia, 1983). For a more traditional overview, see Frederick F. Bruce's *Paul: Apostle of the Free Spirit* (Exeter, Pa., 1977). Ralph P. Martin explores a theme with broad implications in *Reconciliation: A Study of Paul's Theology* (Atlanta, 1981). Hans Hübner's *Law in Paul's Thought* (Edinburgh, 1983) is a basic study comparable to Victor P. Furnish's *Theology and Ethics in Paul* (Nashville, 1968) and my own work *Paul's Anthropological Terms* (Leiden, 1971). See also Halvor Moxnes's *Theology in Conflict: Studies in Paul's Understanding of God in Romans* (Leiden, 1980) and my *Christian Tolerance: Paul's Message to the Modern Church* (Philadelphia, 1982).

Alongside works cited in the article above by Holmberg, Hock, O'Connor, Sampley, and Theissen, basic explorations of the social context for Paul's ministry are provided in John H. Schütz's *Paul and the Anatomy of Apostolic Authority* (New York, 1975) and Wayne A. Meeks's *The First Urban Christians: The Social World of the Apostle Paul* (New Haven, 1982). Explorations of the Hebraic setting in W. D. Davies's *Paul and Rabbinic Judaism,* 4th ed. (Philadelphia, 1981) and E. P. Sanders's *Paul and Palestinian Judaism: A Comparison of Patterns of Religion* (Philadelphia, 1977) are matched by Helmut Koester's *Introduction to the New Testament,* 2 vols. (Philadelphia, 1982), which offers the best current summary of the Pauline letters in the context of Greco-Roman culture. Technical articles dealing with the identification of Pauline opponents and the later evolution of his tradition are accessible in *Paul and Paulinism: Essays in Honour of C. K. Barrett,* edited by M. D. Hooker and Stephen G. Wilson (London, 1982). The struggle over the Pauline legacy is reflected in Elaine H. Pagels's *The Gnostic Paul: Gnostic Exegesis of the Pauline Letters* (Philadelphia, 1975) and Dennis R. MacDonald's *The Legend and the Apostle: The Battle for Paul in Story and Canon* (Philadelphia, 1983).

The most significant recent commentaries on Paul's letters are Ernst Käsemann's *Commentary on Romans* (Grand Rapids,

Mich., 1980), with bibliographies mainly in German; C. K. Barrett's *A Commentary on the First Epistle to the Corinthians,* 2d ed. (London, 1971), written in nontechnical style; Victor P. Furnish's *II Corinthians* (Garden City, N. Y., 1984), a technical, comprehensive but readable study; Hans Dieter Betz's *Galatians: A Commentary on Paul's Letter to the Churches in Galatia* (Philadelphia, 1979), the definitive commentary on Galatians; and Ralph P. Martin's *Colossians and Philemon* (London, 1974) and Eduard Schweizer's *The Letter to the Colossians: A Commentary* (Minneapolis, 1981), both standard works. Ernest Best's *The First and Second Epistles to the Thessalonians* (London, 1972) and F. W. Beare's *A Commentary on the Epistle to the Philippians* (New York, 1959) are the best available on those letters.

ROBERT JEWETT (1987)

PEACE. In a negative sense religious traditions speak of peace as freedom from war and unrest. Peace can also take a positive meaning of well-being and fulfillment as goals of religious and social life. In ancient Greece the word for peace, *eirēnē,* meant primarily the opposite of war, and even when personified as a goddess, Eirene had no mythology and little cult. The Roman Pax was also a vague goddess, scarcely heard of before the age of Augustus and then taken as the representation of quiet at home and abroad. The Pax Romana expressed the absence of internal strife, although Seneca remarked that whole tribes and peoples had been forced to change their habitats.

In ancient Hebrew thought, peace (*shālōm*) was not only the absence of war but well-being if not prosperity. A famous passage that appears twice in the Bible (*Is.* 2:2–4, *Mi.* 4:1–3) describes all nations going to Jerusalem to learn the divine law, beating their swords into plowshares and their spears into pruning hooks, abandoning their swords, and learning war no more. Micah adds that every man would sit under his vine and fig tree, an ideal picture of a small landholder in a tiny state between rival superpowers. In expectation of a better future the ideal Davidic king is called Prince of Peace, and his government is described as having boundless dominion and peace (*Is.* 9:6–7).

The Israelites used the Hebrew word *shālōm* to refer to material and spiritual conditions that were joined together. Psalm 85 envisages God speaking peace to his people, righteousness and peace united, and the land yielding its increase. It is not only war that destroys peace but also covetousness, false dealing, and priests and prophets who practice abominations and say "Peace, peace, when there is no peace" (*Jer.* 6:14). To the Israelites peace was a social concept; it was visible and produced a harmonious relationship in the family, in local society, and between nations. The salutation *shālōm* expressed the positive aim of encouraging friendly cooperation and living together for mutual benefit, and such a greeting, in use from the times of the judges and David, was later employed by both Jews and Christians.

The Arabic word *salām,* meaning "peace" or "health," has been in general use as a greeting or salutation since the time of the Qurʾān. One of its oldest chapters speaks of the coming down of the Qurʾān on "the Night of Power" and concludes that "it is peace until the rising of the dawn" (97:5). God calls people to the "abode of peace" (*dār al-salām*), both in this life and in the next (10:26).

It is as a salutation that the Qurʾān has most to say about *salām.* The prophet Muḥammad said "Peace be upon you" (*al-salām ʿalaykum*) at the beginning of a message, and this was reckoned to be the greeting given to the blessed when they entered Paradise. It became the common salutation in the Islamic world, and the Qurʾān recommends its use. The *salām* formula, thought to be used by angels, is uttered after the names of previous prophets—Noah, Abraham, Moses, Jesus, and the like.

In Islamic ritual, the prayer for the blessing of God and peace on the Prophet, the worshiper, those present, and pious servants of God precedes the confession of faith. At the end of formal prayer the worshiper turns to the right and to the left, invoking the peace and mercy of God. Liturgical use helped to make the peace formula characteristic of Islam, and it is recommended to return the greeting with an additional blessing, following the Qurʾanic verse "When you receive a greeting, respond with a better" (4:86–88).

Islamic eschatology, in popular tradition, has held to the hope of a future deliverer who would rule according to the example of the Prophet and give stability to Islam for a short millennium before the end of all earthly things: The Mahdi, "the guided one," would descend from heaven and fill the earth with equity and justice.

In the New Testament both the Gospels and the epistles use the Greek word *eirēnē* for "peace," although Jesus must have used the Aramaic equivalent of the Hebrew *shālōm,* and *eirēnē* is given the positive sense of the Hebrew. When the apostles were sent out they were instructed to say "Peace be to this house," on entering any house, and, "If a son of peace is there, your peace shall rest upon him; but if not, it shall return to you again" (*Lk.* 10:6). The peacemaker was blessed, and the struggling early church was exhorted to "follow after things which make for peace, to edify one another" (*Rom.* 14:19).

The reconciliation of Jews and Gentiles was sought through Christ: "He is our peace, who made both one" (*Eph.* 2:14). For those under external pressures, peace was a spiritual calm as well as a social benefit, as promised by Christ in his parting words, according to John, "Peace I leave with you, my peace I give you, not as the world gives it" (*Jn.* 14.27). This led on to Paul's view of the peace of God that passes human understanding, and the "fruits of the Spirit" included peace among virtues such as patience, kindness, and forbearance.

In New Testament eschatology there is little detail of the future, except in the *Apocalypse of John* (*Revelation*). Instead there are general statements about the ultimate triumph of good, when "God shall be all in all." Meanwhile the kingdom of God is "righteousness and peace and joy in the Holy Spirit" (*Rom.* 14:17).

In the history of the church peace has been seen on the one hand as calm for the soul and on the other as social and political reconciliation and the establishment of a just order. This has led to doctrines of a just war or to judgments on social change, but more general statements speak of individual and communal well-being. Augustine of Hippo in his *City of God* (*De civitate Dei* 413–426) remarks that peace is the purpose of war between nations, for no one would seek war by peace, but as the peace of humankind is an orderly obedience to the eternal law of God, so the peace of God's city is "the perfect union of hearts, in the enjoyment of God and of one another in God" (19.13). Peace is our final good; eternity in peace, or peace in eternity, for the good of peace is the greatest wish of the world and the most welcome when it comes.

The salutation *Peace* is frequent in the New Testament, and it entered into the liturgy. In the traditional canon of the Latin Mass the priest said or chanted both "Dominus vobiscum" ("The Lord be with you") and "Pax Domini sit semper vobiscum" ("The Peace of the Lord be always with you"). In modern times there has been a revival of "the peace," or "giving the peace," in many churches. For example, the peace may be given throughout the congregation with the words "the peace of the Lord," and this is often accompanied by the shaking of hands or even kissing in peace.

Both social and personal ideals of peace have been important concerns of Chinese religious leaders and thinkers. The Daoist classic *Dao de jing* comments that one who seeks to help a ruler by the Dao will oppose all conquest by force of arms. Not only will the Daoist be against war and weapons, but will object to imposed rules and government, even to morality and wisdom, because the Daoist believes that in simplicity and fewness of desires evil would disappear.

The Daoist should adopt a peaceful or passive attitude, "actionless activity" *(wuwei),* and by such wordless teaching will control all creatures, and everything will be duly regulated. Colin A. Ronan (1978) has noted that Joseph Needham rejected the customary translation of *wuwei* as "inaction" (p. 98). The Daoist, he maintained, is not idle or passive, but is natural. He or she should refrain from acting against the grain, from trying to make things perform unsuitable functions, from exerting force when a perceptive person would see that force must fail. There is support for this view in *The Book of Huainan* (120 BCE), which criticizes those who claim that the person who acts with *wuwei* does not speak or move or will not be driven by force. No sages, it says, gave such an interpretation, but the proper view of such quiet activity is that no personal prejudice should check the Dao, and no desires lead the proper courses of techniques astray. Nonaction does not mean doing nothing; it means allowing everything to act according to its nature.

In popular Daoism the ideals of a past golden age of peace, and of one yet to come, were expressed in the Taiping Dao, the Way of great peace, which arose about 175 CE. Some of its doctrines had been stated in a lost scripture decades earlier, the *Taiping jing* (Classic of great peace). Its writer, Yu Ji, was a preacher and healer in Shantung province who was executed about 197, although his followers believed that he had become an immortal.

The new movement, the Way of Great Peace, was established by Zhang Jue, who founded in 175 CE an organization of which he was the "Heavenly General." He held vast public ceremonies at which the sick confessed their sins and were healed by faith. What is just as important, Zhang Jue sent missionaries to convert people in central and eastern China to the way of peace and healing. Crowds flocked to this movement, probably because the troubled times of warfare gave rise to the longing for a millenarian era reminiscent of the mythical golden age of peace. There was also dissatisfaction with the coldness of state Confucianism, and a yearning for a more personal religion and a more just society.

The Way of Great Peace became very popular, and eight provinces were converted by its missionaries. The central government was alarmed and prepared countermeasures. The Daoists were warned, and on the day that the governmental action began they decided to revolt. The rebels wore yellow kerchiefs on their heads, thus giving rise to the movement's other name, Yellow Turbans. Zhang Jue and his brothers were caught and executed, but it was many years before the rebellion was finally suppressed.

In the nineteenth century the Taiping Rebellion swept across China and almost destroyed the crumbling Manzhu dynasty. It raged from 1850 to 1865 and was put down only with the help of foreign powers, notably the British, and with a catastrophic loss of some twenty million lives. The leader of the rebellion, Hong Xiuquan, sought to establish the Taiping, the Great Peace, under a purely Chinese dynasty, but he was inspired by both Chinese and Christian ideas. The Taiping would come in the cycle of history but would resemble the kingdom of heaven, where all people would worship the heavenly father.

Hong proclaimed his regime the Heavenly Kingdom of Great Peace and himself took the title Heavenly King. Nanjing was captured in 1853 and renamed Heavenly Capital, but internal divisions and external attacks led to its collapse. By 1864 Hong had despaired of his cause; he took poison and died, and his followers were overwhelmed. Later Chinese attempts at reform and peace through strength occurred, but not all were inspired by Daoist ideals.

Indian views of peace are both personal and social, positive and negative. Many sacred Hindu texts open with the sacred syllable *oṃ,* followed for invocation and meditation by a threefold repetition of the Sanskrit word for peace: *śāntiḥ, śāntiḥ, śāntiḥ.* (These three words appear at the end of T. S. Eliot's famous poem *The Waste Land,* 1922.) The peace invoked in the Sanskrit texts is one of tranquillity, quiet, calmness of mind, absence of passion, aversion of pain, and indifference to the objects of pleasure and pain.

In the *Bhagavadgītā* the despondency of the warrior Arjuna, with which the poem opens, comes from envisaging the destruction of human beings and order (*dharma*) that war would bring. Arjuna is moved by compassion, declares that he would rather be killed than kill other beings, and lays down his weapons. His charioteer, the god Kṛṣṇa, gives several answers to Arjuna's problems, the chief one of which is that a soldier may kill the body but cannot kill the soul, or self, which is indestructible and immortal, without beginning or end. This answer ignores the question of Arjuna's compassion. The true yogin, whether he be a warrior or not, should be detached; he should act but remain unmoved by the result of his actions. Thus he can "attain the peace that culminates in *nirvāṇa* and rests in me [i.e., God]" (6.15). Kindness to all beings is occasionally suggested in the *Gītā*, but the general picture is one of peace and tranquillity unmoved by the affairs of the world.

The Jains in India have been noted for their advocacy of nonviolence, or not killing (*ahiṃsā*), and some of their temples today bear the inscription (in English as well as in Sanskrit), "Nonviolence is the highest religion." They teach that *nirvāṇa* is an indescribable and passionless state beyond this world, at the ceiling of the universe. The Buddhists, contemporary with the Jains, have also taught *nirvāṇa* and have done so in negative terms. A Buddhist compendium of teachings, *The Questions of King Milinda,* agrees that *nirvāṇa* cannot be indicated in form or shape, in duration or size, by simile or argument. Yet it does exist: "There is *nirvāṇa*"; it is lofty and exalted, inaccessible to the passions and unshakable, bringing joy and shedding light.

Positive social efforts for peace were illustrated in the words and actions of the most famous Indian ruler, the Buddhist emperor Aśoka, in the third century BCE, as revealed by extant inscriptions on pillars and rocks. After thousands of people had been killed in his war against the Kalingas, Aśoka felt remorse, renounced war, sought reconciliation, and wished that "all beings should be unharmed, self-controlled, calm in mind, and gentle." Fighting was forbidden, as was all killing of animals for food or sacrifice. Medical services were provided for human beings and animals, useful herbs were planted, wells were dug, and trees were planted along roads to shelter people and animals. Local rulers were instructed to tour among their people and teach the *dharma* of obedience to parents, generosity to priests, prohibition of killing, ownership of "the minimum of property."

In modern times Mohandas Gandhi (1869–1948) was noted for teaching *ahiṃsā,* but not just as a negative way to peace and justice. He coined the term *satyāgraha* (literally, "truth insistence"), defining it as "soul force" or "the force which is born of truth and love or nonviolence." Gandhi sought to follow the New Testament injunction to return good for evil as well as to follow the Jain command of nonviolence. He argued that soul force was the only method by which home rule could be regained for India and that it was "superior to the force of arms." Further, in a message to Hindus and Muslims on communal unity Gandhi insisted that politics should be approached in a religious spirit. He ended his speech with these words: "I ask all lovers of communal peace to pray that the God of truth and love may give us both the right spirit and the right word, and use us for the good of the dumb millions."

SEE ALSO Ahiṃsā; Nonviolence; Taiping; War and Warriors, overview article.

BIBLIOGRAPHY

Biblical teaching about peace can be found in many books, and useful articles are included in *A Dictionary of Christian Spirituality* (London, 1983) and *A Dictionary of Christian Ethics* (Philadelphia, 1967). Islamic texts are listed in the *Shorter Encyclopaedia of Islam* (1953; reprint, Leiden, 1974). Indian and Chinese teachings with selections from texts are easily found in *Sources of Indian Tradition* and *Sources of Chinese Tradition* (New York, 1958 and 1960), edited by Wm. Theodore de Bary and others. Daoist movements are described by Holmes Welch in *The Parting of the Way: Lao Zu and the Daoist Movement* (London, 1957), and informative chapters on Daoism, Confucianism, and Buddhism are included in Colin A. Ronan's *Shorter Science and Civilisation in China* (New York, 1978), an abridgment of Joseph Needham's text from volumes 1 and 2 of the larger work.

GEOFFREY PARRINDER (1987)

PEARL. The making of the natural pearl commences when a grain of sand from the ocean or river floor works its way into the body of a pearl-bearing mollusk. To protect itself from this alien source of agitation, the mollusk secretes a substance (nacre, or mother-of-pearl) that slowly and cumulatively coats the foreign body until it loses its abrasive contours and becomes smooth and spherical in shape. On account of its singular origin, the pearl has been a symbol of sacred power since ancient times.

In many archaic cultures the marine shell, because of its appearance, is associated with the female genitalia, and the pearl is believed to be both the sacred product and the emblem of the feminine generative power. The pearl thus symbolizes both the life that is created and the mysterious force that begets life. One example of this reproductive symbolism is found in *Beiya,* a Chinese text of the eleventh century CE. The author of *Beiya* likens the pearl to a developing fetus and calls the oyster "the womb of the pearl." The anthropomorphic image for this sacred power is the goddess of love. In the ancient Mediterranean world, shells and pearls were often symbols for the great goddesses. In a manner analogous to the pearl's origin in an oyster, Aphrodite was born from a marine conch, and the Syrian goddess was known as the Lady of Pearls.

It is through this connection with feminine generative power that the pearl becomes a symbol for regeneration and rebirth as well. As a regenerative force, the pearl is often thought to have the power to heal or protect from harm. Throughout the Middle Ages and into the seventeenth century, a debate flourished among European physicians concerning the best way to prepare a pearl for healing purposes: Should it be ground or dissolved? In either case, an elixir containing a pearl was prescribed for numerous physical ailments. An Eastern example of the belief in the power of the pearl to protect life is found in the iconography of the *bodhisattva* Kṣitigarbha, who is especially venerated in Japanese Buddhism by pregnant women and young children as the protector of all weak and suffering humanity; statues and images depict Kṣitigarbha holding a pearl, his emblem, in his left hand. Because of their connection with rebirth and resurrection, pearls have been found in the tombs of rulers in lands as far apart as Egypt and the Americas. In Laos, a pearl is inserted into each orifice of a corpse to effect safe passage into the next world.

Finding and obtaining the natural pearl is both hard work and a hazardous undertaking. Pearl fishers are known to work in pairs: One dives deep into the sea while a partner stays above to hold the other end of the fisher's lifeline and, after a predetermined time, to haul both pearl fisher and catch to the surface. The difficulties of locating and harvesting the natural pearl give rise to a second level of symbolism: The pearl represents the hard-won goal of spiritual striving. For example, in the parable about the merchant who found a pearl of special value and so went to sell everything he owned in order to purchase it, Jesus compares the kingdom of God to a pearl. In medieval European alchemy, one of the many names for the philosophers' stone is *margarita pretiosa,* or "precious pearl." In *The Pearl,* a Middle English tale by an anonymous author, the hero laments the disappearance of his pearl in a grassy meadow. Seeking it, he falls into another world, where he experiences spiritual renewal and regains the balance of his own inner nature. Zhuangzi, the legendary Daoist mystic, reports how the Yellow Emperor lost his "night-pearl" during an excursion to the edge of the world. He sought for it by means of every resource at hand: by science, by analysis, by logic. But only when, in despair, the emperor turned to the "emptiness" (*xu*) that is the ground of all things was the pearl restored to him.

The search for the pearl is also the theme of the Gnostic *Hymn of the Pearl,* which relates how a prince leaves his heavenly home to recover a pearl that lies buried in Egypt in the possession of a giant serpent. The prince is sent forth by his father, mother, and brother, who watch over his journey in a way reminiscent of the second fisherman who holds the lifeline at the surface of the sea. The prince inevitably succumbs to the spell that governs all Egypt (a Gnostic symbol for the illusion of cosmic existence). He loses all memory of his origins and of the pearl (i. e., he becomes spiritually ignorant or unconscious). But his watchful parents send forth a message to awaken him and to remind him of his identity and his mission to recover the pearl.

Especially in the East, from India to Japan, the pearl is often depicted in the possession of a dragon or sea monster. These mythological beings, like the serpent in the *Hymn of the Pearl,* are common symbols for chaos, that admixture of forces both cosmic and spiritual that oppose the establishment of a meaningful and inhabitable order. Thus, the search for the pearl often entails a heroic confrontation with the demonic.

Wherever the cultivation or liberation of the soul is regarded as the goal of spiritual striving, the pearl may symbolize the soul itself. This belief may have historical roots in the mythological thinking of the Hellenistic world, from which has come the formula "Ho sōma, hē sarx" ("The body is the tomb"). In this view, the subject of spiritual and eternal life is the immortal soul that exists within an alien and perishable body. According to the Mandaeans, the pearl's temporary home within the oyster provides an allegory for the temporary dwelling of the soul within the body. A variation of this imagery is found in the Coptic *Kephalaia,* a Manichaean text that relates how the soul is like a raindrop that falls into the sea and enters the body of an oyster in order to develop into a pearl. So, too, the soul acquires permanent definition and individuality by enduring life in the body. The pearl as a symbol for the actualized soul found its way into the poetry of the Ṣūfī mystic Farīd al-Dīn ʿAṭṭār:

> Out of the ocean like rain clouds come and travel—
> For without traveling, you will never become a pearl!

BIBLIOGRAPHY

Bausani, Alessandro. *Persia religiosa: Da Zaratustra a Baha'ullah.* Milan, 1959.

Bausani, Alessandro. *Storia della letteratura persiana.* Milan, 1959.

Cirlot, J. E. *A Dictionary of Symbols.* 2d ed. New York, 1971.

Eliade, Mircea. *Images and Symbols: Studies in Religious Symbolism.* New York, 1961. Contains a comprehensive bibliography.

Jonas, Hans. *The Gnostic Religion: The Message of the Alien God and the Beginnings of Christianity.* 2d ed., rev. & enl. Boston, 1963.

New Sources

Donkin, R. A. *Beyond Price: Pearls and Pearl-Fishing: Origins to the Age of Discoveries.* Philadelphia, 1998.

Hackney, Ki, and Diana Edkins. *People and Pearls: The Magic Endures.* New York, 2000.

Landman, Neal, Rudiger Bieler, Paula Mikkelson, and Bennet Bronson. *Pearls: A Natural History.* New York, 2001.

Malaguzzi, Sylvia. *The Pearl.* New York, 2001.

BEVERLY MOON (1987)
Revised Bibliography

PECHAM, JOHN (c. 1230–1292) was a Franciscan theologian, scientist, and educator; a provincial minister of the Franciscans and archbishop of Canterbury. Pecham was born in Sussex, in the vicinity of Lewes. Educated initially at the priory of Lewes and the University of Oxford, he joined the Franciscan order about 1250 and later in the decade was sent to the University of Paris for theological studies, earning the doctorate in 1269. Pecham was regent master in theology at Paris from 1269 to 1271, lecturer in theology for the Franciscan school in Oxford from about 1272 to 1275, provincial minister of the order from 1275 to 1277, master in theology to the papal Curia from 1277 to 1279, and archbishop of Canterbury from 1279 until his death in 1292.

Pecham's theology was typically Franciscan: conservative and centered on the teachings of Augustine. Indeed, Pecham became a leader in the opposition to the new—and in his opinion heterodox—Aristotelian and Averroist ideas circulating in the universities. For example, he took strong exception to Thomas Aquinas's views on the unity of substantial form. He defended such doctrines as the divine illumination of the intellect, complete hylomorphism (the idea that everything is a composite of form and matter), and plurality of forms. Pecham also became involved in the power struggle between secular and mendicant clergy, writing a series of pamphlets in defense of the mendicants. As an educator, Pecham followed Robert Grosseteste and Roger Bacon by incorporating mathematical science into the university curriculum (including the theological curriculum). He wrote two books on optics, one of which, *Perspectiva communis*, became the standard university textbook for several centuries. An energetic, reform-minded archbishop, Pecham fought for the preservation of ecclesiastical privileges against royal encroachment and campaigned against a variety of clerical abuses, such as nonresidence and the holding of multiple benefices.

BIBLIOGRAPHY

On Pecham's ecclesiastical career, see David Knowles's "Some Aspects of the Career of Archbishop Pecham," *English Historical Review* 57 (1942): 1–18, 178–201, and Decima Douie's *Archbishop Pecham* (Oxford, 1952). For Pecham's philosophy, the most succinct and convenient source is D. E. Sharp's *Franciscan Philosophy at Oxford in the Thirteenth Century* (Oxford, 1930). On Pecham's scientific efforts see two works of my own: *John Pecham and the Science of Optics: Perspectiva communis* (Madison, Wis., 1970) and "Pecham, John," in the *Dictionary of Scientific Biography*, vol. 10 (New York, 1974), pp. 473–476. See the latter for additional bibliographic information.

DAVID C. LINDBERG (1987)

PELAGIANISM. The term *Pelagianism* designates both the teachings of Pelagius, a fourth-century Christian monk, and any teaching that minimizes the role of divine grace in salvation. Few of the ideas associated with Pelagianism in the latter sense can be directly traced to Pelagius, but because he was opposed by the great North African bishop Augustine, whose influence on Western Christian theology has been far-reaching, he has come to stand for an insufficient and erroneous doctrine of grace. Some have suggested that Pelagianism was the creation of Augustine and not Pelagius. But it was Pelagius's views on the Christian life, his moral rigorism, his high regard for the law, and his emphasis on discipline and the human will that laid the foundation for the controversy that gave birth to what has come to be known as Pelagianism.

Pelagius (d. 418), a monk from Britain, was living in Rome at the end of the fourth century when he came in contact with wealthy and aristocratic Romans who had lapsed into Christianity through marriage or political expedience. Adopting Christianity had done little to change their lives. Baptism, which had been thought to signify a clean break with one's past, was becoming a polite convention. Only the ascetics seemed to take seriously the radical demands of the gospel. Pelagius, however, believed that the law of the gospel should be imposed on all members of the church, not just on the monks. The word of Jesus, "Be ye perfect as your father in heaven is perfect," was addressed to all Christians; thus, according to Pelagius, "since perfection is possible for humans, it is obligatory."

As a moral reformer Pelagius met with success among a circle of supporters in Rome, but his notion of the church as a society of pure and authentic Christians had an old-fashioned ring to it at a time when the level of commitment among Christians was in decline because of a large influx into the church of merely nominal converts. He was offended when he read in Augustine's *Confessions* that humans must necessarily and inevitably sin even after baptism. Augustine's phrase "Give what you command and command what you will" seemed to him to undermine the moral law and the quest for perfection, because it placed responsibility for righteousness on God rather than on the human will.

Pelagius did not, as is often thought, deny the necessity of grace. Grace was to be understood as the revelation of God's purpose and will, the wisdom by which humans are stirred to seek a life of righteousness. It was God's way of helping humankind and was found in (1) the endowment of a rational will and the capacity to choose good or evil, (2) the law of Moses, (3) the forgiveness of sins in the redemptive death of Christ, (4) the teaching of Christ, and (5) the example of Christ. Pelagius saw no opposition between the laws of the old covenant and the gospel. He saw grace as precept and example, a view that led him to overestimate human capability and thus to invite criticism.

The controversy began in 412, at a council in Carthage, in North Africa, with the condemnation of Celestius, a supporter of Pelagius, for holding the views that (1) Adam was created mortal and would have died whether or not he was a sinner; (2) Adam's sin injured himself alone, and not the human race; (3) infants at birth are in that state in which Adam was before his sin; (4) the whole human race neither died on account of Adam nor rises on account of Christ; (5) the law as well as the gospel admits a person to the kingdom of heaven; (6) before the advent of Christ there were humans who did not sin; (7) a person can be without sin and keep the divine commands. This is not Pelagianism, but Pelagius would have agreed with some of these propositions—for example, that sinless human beings had lived before the coming of Christ. He pointed to "gospel men before the gospel" such as Noah, Melchizedek, Abraham, and Job.

As a result of the condemnation of Celestius, Pelagius, who had traveled to Palestine, was forced to defend himself in the East. His most vehement critics, however, were Westerners such as Jerome. Significantly, at two councils in Palestine in 415 he was acquitted by bishops from the East. In the meantime Augustine opened up a literary campaign against Pelagius, and this led Augustine to produce the theological works that would define Pelagianism for Western Christian theology and to formulate the objections that would lead to Pelagius's condemnation. Under Augustine's influence Pelagius was condemned by two African councils, and in 417 Pope Innocent I ratified the anathema.

After Pelagius's death in 418 (or shortly thereafter) his followers, often under much hardship, continued to defend his teachings. One of these, the gifted and articulate bishop Julian of Eclanum, a town in Apulia (southeastern Italy), though banished from his see, traveled and wrote extensively. He vigorously opposed the new ideas of Augustine, seeing in them the specter of Manichaean dualism. In a modified form Pelagius's teachings were embraced by John Cassian (360–435), a monastic writer from Marseilles (France) who is sometimes called the founder of semi-Pelagianism, though this term only came to be used in the sixteenth century. Other exponents were Vincent of Lerins (d. 450) and Faustus of Riez (408–490), both from southern France. The focus of discussion centered on the necessity of human cooperation with divine grace in salvation, and since then these questions have been central to the history of theology in the West. The dispute finally ended at the Council of Orange (429), which condemned the writings of Faustus and upheld most of the teachings of Augustine.

Only in recent years has there been a serious effort to understand the historical Pelagius and the circumstances surrounding his teaching. More often Pelagianism has been used as an epithet to vilify one's foes whenever there is a suggestion that human efforts displace the role of grace. In the Middle Ages Thomas Bradwardine (1290–1349), archbishop of Canterbury, wrote against the "Pelagians," meaning those of his contemporaries who subverted God's grace by stressing free will. Peter Abelard (1079–1142) has sometimes been called a Pelagian because of his view of the exemplary as distinct from the redemptive character of Christ's life and death. In the sixteenth century the Protestant reformers charged their opponents with Pelagianism because of their belief that one could prepare for grace by doing good works: Martin Luther called Erasmus a Pelagian. In Roman Catholicism Luis de Molina, a sixteenth-century Jesuit, was suspected of Pelagian convictions because he taught that God's foreknowledge of human cooperation is itself a sign of grace. The term *semi-Pelagian* arose from this controversy. Although Pelagianism has had little direct influence on Eastern Christian thought, which also never adopted Augustine's ideas, aspects of Orthodox Christian theology have been held to possess a Pelagian tinge from the perspective of Western Christian theology.

See Also Augustine of Hippo; Pelagius.

Bibliography

Bonner, Gerald. *Augustine and Modern Research on Pelagianism.* Villanova, Pa., 1972.

Brown, Peter. *Religion and Society in the Age of Saint Augustine.* London, 1972.

Evans, Robert F. *Pelagius: Inquiries and Reappraisals.* New York, 1968.

Robert L. Wilken (1987)

PELAGIUS (d. 418) was a Christian monk whose name has become synonymous with doctrines of human cooperation in salvation at the expense of divine grace. The historical figure is more complex than the teachings associated with his name. Pelagius was born in Britain in the middle of the fourth century. Nothing is known of his background or upbringing, but he seems to have received an excellent education. He was highly regarded for his exemplary life, and even his great opponent, Augustine of Hippo, acknowledged that he was a "holy man who had made no small progress in the Christian life." He went to live in Rome sometime toward the end of the fourth century, perhaps as early as the 380s.

Pelagius was first and foremost a monk and an ascetic, a tutor to men and women seeking the life of perfection. His primary concern was moral and spiritual, not theological. He had been influenced by earlier Christian moral and ascetic literature, for example *Sentences of Sextus,* a collection of moral maxims from the second century, and the writings of Origen, the great third-century Christian teacher. From these works he learned the importance of freedom of the will, discipline, the quest for perfection, and righteousness through the doing of good deeds.

In the world of fifth-century Rome, however, moral rigorism, which had once marked the entire Christian community, was now practiced chiefly by the ascetics. Pelagius continued to believe that there should be no double standard and that the precepts of the gospel were applicable to all. For a time he was successful in urging these ideas in Rome, but as his writings became known outside of Rome, in Africa, where Augustine lived, and in Palestine, where Jerome lived, he came to be vigorously opposed.

Pelagius left Rome in 410 with his disciple Celestius to travel to Africa. Celestius was condemned by a council in Carthage in 412. In Palestine Pelagius was brought before councils in Jerusalem and Lydda in 415, but he ably defended himself and was acquitted. In the West, however, through the efforts of Augustine, he was condemned by a council in Carthage in 416 and again by Pope Innocent in 417. After being briefly vindicated by Zosimus, Innocent's successor, he was eventually condemned by a great council at Carthage in 418 and by the pope and was banished by the Roman emperors. He died in 418 or sometime thereafter.

He wrote widely, but few of his works are extant in their entirety. The most important is a commentary on the epistles of Paul, a close verse-by-verse exposition of the text of the letters with an eye to the Christian life. The influence of Origen, transmitted through Latin translations, is evident in the commentary. His major theological works, *De natura* and *De libero arbitrio,* written only after he had traveled to Palestine in 412 and come into contact with Jerome, are extant only in fragments in the writings of Augustine. Besides these works there are a number of shorter tractates and letters, some of which have only recently been shown to be genuine.

SEE ALSO Pelagianism.

BIBLIOGRAPHY

Ferguson, John. *Pelagius.* Cambridge, 1956.

Plinval, Georges de. *Pelage: Ses écrits, sa vie et sa reforme.* Lausanne, 1943.

ROBERT L. WILKEN (1987)

PENANCE SEE REPENTANCE; SACRAMENT, *ARTICLE ON* CHRISTIAN SACRAMENTS

PENATES.

In the Latin world *di penates* (always in the plural) were spirits protecting a house or a city. The etymological connection with *penus* in the sense of "storing-place of the household" raises problems. The cult of the *penates* was associated with that of Vesta; both were linked to the hearth. During family meals offers of food were made to them and burned on the fireplace. Plautus speaks in *Mercator* (1.834) of the *penates* as "gods of the parents" (*di penates meum parentum*) and distinguishes them from the *lar* (singular) of the household (*familia*).

The *penates* were originally aniconic. In the late republican period images of them were put on the table. By a further development the notion of *penates* came to include all the gods worshiped in the household, beginning with Vesta and the *lar familiaris* (later also lares in general). In the first century CE Pompeii and even Jupiter, Venus, Vulcanus, and Fortuna were counted among the *penates.* City *penates* are known also outside Rome.

The peculiarity of Rome was that the *penates* of the city were worshiped both within the city, in a temple on the Velia not far from the Forum (on the site of the later Church of Saints Cosma and Damianus) and in the Latial city of Lavinium. According to tradition, Aeneas had brought his own *penates* from Troy to Lavinium. The *penates* had refused to move to Alba Longa when it was founded by Aeneas's son Ascanius. Toward the end of the fourth century BCE, the Greek historian Timaeus was told that the *penates* of Lavinium were aniconic objects. As soon as they were elected, Roman consuls, dictators, and praetors went to Lavinium to make sacrifices to them. Respect was still paid by Roman emperors to the Lavinium *penates.*

The aniconic *penates* worshiped on the Velia acquired human features in the late republic and were often identified with the Dioscuri (Castor and Pollux), an identification apparently repudiated by Varro (*De lingua Latina* 5.58). It is doubtful whether the *penates* preserved at Lavinium were at any time identified with the Dioscuri. According to Tacitus (*Annals* 15.41.1), *penates* of the Roman people were also preserved in the temple of Vesta on the Palatine, but this is an obscure piece of information. Equally problematic is the mention of a "priest of the *di penates*" (*sacerdos deum penatium*) in two inscriptions of Rome (*Corpus inscriptionum Latinarum,* Berlin, 1863, vol. 6, no. 7283).

BIBLIOGRAPHY

Alföldi, András. *Early Rome and the Latins.* Ann Arbor, Mich., 1965. See pages 258–271.

Latte, Kurt. *Römische Religionsgeschichte.* Munich, 1960. See pages 89 and 416.

Radke, Gerhard. *Die Götter Altitaliens.* Münster, 1965. See pages 247–252.

Radke, Gerhard. "Die *di penates* und Vesta im Rom." In *Aufstieg und Niedergang der römischen Welt,* vol. 2.17.1, pp. 343–373. Berlin and New York, 1981. Includes bibliography.

Weinstock, Stanley. "*Penates.*" In *Real-Encyclopädia der classischen Altertumswissenschaft,* vol. 19, cols. 417–447. Stuttgart, 1937.

New Sources

Dubourdieu, Annie. *Les origines et le développement du culte des Pénates à Rome.* Paris, 1989.

Palombi, Domenico. "Aedes Deum Penatium in Velia. Note di topografia e storia." *Mitteilungen des Deutschen Archäologischen Instituts. Römische Abteilung* 104 (1997): 435–463.

Poucet, Jacques. "Troie, Lavinium, Rome et les Pénates." *Antiquté Classique* 61 (1992): 260–267.

ARNALDO MOMIGLIANO (1987)

PENN, WILLIAM

(1644–1718), Quaker religious leader and theologian, was a proponent of religious and political rights, and founder of Pennsylvania. Educated at Oxford, the French Protestant academy at Saumur, and, briefly, at Lincoln's Inn, Penn came under Dissenter influence and renounced a life of social prominence for Quakerism in 1667. Intent on transforming England into a more truly Christian society, he wrote many of his more than 140 books, pamphlets, and broadsides from 1668 to 1680, when he spent virtually all of his time working to organize, spread, and protect the Quaker movement, also known as the Society of Friends. Having found England resistant to change, he secured a charter for a colony he envisioned as both a haven for persecuted Friends and a model consensual society that would demonstrate to a skeptical world the fruitfulness and practicality of Quaker principles. Pennsylvania received most of his time and energy from 1680 to 1685, and Penn's duties as proprietor were his major concern the rest of his life. He remained active as a Quaker leader in England and played a central role in the successful attempt to demonstrate that Quakers were sufficiently orthodox to be acceptable under the terms for toleration established after the Glorious Revolution of 1688.

Although a source of controversy at times within the Quaker movement, Penn was at the center of the network of Quaker leaders and was probably the most effective mediator between Friends and the rest of the world. He was a close friend and collaborator of George Fox, the founder of the movement; his wife Margaret Askew Fell Fox; and Robert Barclay, the movement's major theologian. Penn traveled extensively as a preacher and organizer throughout England and in Ireland, Germany, and Holland and from 1672 was active in the London Morning Meeting, the Quakers' informal executive body. In favor of the disciplinary practices and organizational structure espoused by Fox, he was active in upholding the authority of the central leadership against the individualistic conception of authority favored by schismatics. Penn's unique contribution as a leader of Friends was his injection of a prophetic activism into the movement at a time when many first-generation leaders were settling into a more quietist, sectarian posture. He helped organize the Meeting for Sufferings in 1675 as a committee for the legal and political defense of indicted Quakers and led it into political activity in support of sympathetic candidates in parliamentary elections. His toleration treatises of the 1670s and 1680s had wide influence in the battle for religious liberty for all English Christians and effectively stated his views of mixed constitutional government and fundamental English rights.

Penn was one of the most prolific and theologically knowledgeable exponents of Quaker thought, and he distilled the visions and experiences of Fox and the "First Publishers of Truth" into the theological language of the times. His works include exhortatory letters, ethical treatises, refutations of schismatics, historical accounts of the movement, expositions of Quaker thought, and defenses against the attacks of Anglicans, Presbyterians, Independents, Baptists, and spiritualists. His distinctive approach to Quaker thought was his understanding of the "inner light" or "Christ within" as an epistemological principle making divine knowledge available in a manner that bypassed the indirect sense-knowledge emphasized in sacramental Roman Catholicism and scripture-based Protestantism. His Platonic rationalism, identification of Christ with the universal Logos, critique of scripture as a comprehensive source of revelation, and corresponding insistence on the metaphorical and symbolic nature of Christian theological formulas, such as those for the Trinity and atonement, linked him with such liberal Anglicans of his day as the Cambridge Platonists. These same ideas have had many echoes in subsequent theology.

SEE ALSO Quakers.

BIBLIOGRAPHY

Penn's correspondence, journals, religious and political papers, and business and legal records have been published in microfilm form by the Historical Society of Pennsylvania, *The Papers of William Penn,* 14 reels, 1975. The first two volumes of a projected four-volume edition of the most important of these materials have appeared, *The Papers of William Penn,* vol. 1, *1644–1679,* and vol. 2, *1680–1684,* edited by Mary Maples Dunn and Richard S. Dunn (Philadelphia, 1981–1982). A fifth volume containing a definitive annotated bibliography is also in preparation. *The Papers of William Penn* do not include the published works, which are available in a two-volume edition, *A Collection of the Works of William Penn, To Which Is Prefixed a Journal of His Life,* edited by Joseph Besse (London, 1726). Selections from this incomplete collection with many textual problems were reprinted in 1771, 1782, and 1825. No adequate biography exists; the most useful is William I. Hull's *William Penn: A Topical Biography* (New York, 1937). Penn's religious life and thought are comprehensively discussed in my *William Penn and Early Quakerism* (Princeton, 1973).

MELVIN B. ENDY, JR. (1987)

PENTATEUCH

SEE BIBLICAL LITERATURE, *ARTICLE ON* HEBREW SCRIPTURES; TORAH

PENTECOSTAL AND CHARISMATIC CHRISTIANITY.

This form of Christianity centers on the emotional, mystical, and supernatural: miracles, signs, wonders, and "the gifts of the Spirit" (charismata), especially "speaking in tongues" (glossolalia), faith healing, and "casting out demons" (exorcism). Supreme importance is attached to the subjective religious experience of being filled with or possessed by the Holy Spirit.

The name *Pentecostal* derives from the account of the day of Pentecost as described in chapters 1 and 2 of the *Acts of the Apostles,* when the Holy Spirit descended upon the first Christians: "And they were all filled with the Holy Spirit and began to speak in other tongues, as the Spirit gave them utterance" (*Acts* 2:1–4). *Charismatic* derives from the Greek *charism,* meaning supernatural gifts of the Spirit, which are most often considered those listed in *1 Corinthians* 12–14.

BIBLICAL AND HISTORICAL BASES. Pentecostals trace the beginnings of their movement to the day of Pentecost described in *Acts.* They believe that the experience of Spirit Baptism and the practice of the gifts of the Spirit that occurred on that day were meant to be normative in the life of the church and of each believer. They maintain that although the charismata ceased in the main body of the church soon after the apostolic age, one can trace an intermittent history of charismatic practices among sectarians like the Montanists, Anabaptists, Camisards, Shakers, Irvingites, Mormons, and various nineteenth-century Holiness groups. The twentieth-century Pentecostal and charismatic movements, therefore, mark the restoration of the charismata to the church.

THE ORIGINS OF PENTECOSTALISM IN THE UNITED STATES. The Pentecostal movement developed within the radical, separatist wing of the late nineteenth-century Holiness movement in the United States. It represented an amalgam of extremist Wesleyan and Keswick views on premillennialism, dispensationalism, faith healing, and "the Baptism in the Spirit" as an enduement of miraculous powers. Charles Fox Parham, an independent Holiness preacher and former Methodist, is generally regarded as the founder of the modern Pentecostal movement. Speaking in tongues and other ecstatic behavior broke out in Parham's Bethel Bible "College" in Topeka, Kansas, in January 1901. Parham asserted that glossolalia was the evidence of "the true Baptism in the Spirit." On the basis of this teaching and faith healing, Parham's Apostolic Faith movement had some success in the lower Midwest. William Joseph Seymour, a black Holiness preacher converted by Parham, carried the movement to Los Angeles in 1906. Seymour's Azusa Street Apostolic Faith Mission became the center of a great revival, in which visitors to the Azusa mission spread the movement across the nation and around the world in only a few years.

The movement was condemned and ostracized by all other Christian churches, and it at first consisted of a few small schismatic offsprings of the Holiness sects and many independent congregations. The movement's center of strength lay in the region stretching from lower Appalachia to the Ozarks, and in the urban centers of the North and West. Adherents were drawn from vastly different religious, racial, ethnic, and cultural backgrounds. In time, these differences divided the movement into a bewildering array of small, hostile sects that were constantly splitting and resplitting. By 1916, the American Pentecostal movement had divided into three major doctrinal camps, and by the early 1930s, each of these had split along racial lines.

FINISHED WORK, OR BAPTISTIC, PENTECOSTALS. Originally, all Pentecostals believed in three acts of grace: conversion, sanctification, and Baptism in the Spirit. Beginning about 1908, William H. Durham introduced his "Finished Work of Calvary" doctrine, in which conversion and sanctification were declared a single act of grace. A majority of American Pentecostals accepted this doctrine; it was especially strong among those of Baptist and Keswick backgrounds. In 1914, a Finished Work denomination was organized: the Assemblies of God.

SECOND WORK, OR WESLEYAN, PENTECOSTALS. Those who held to the original three acts of grace were called "Second Work Pentecostals." They were predominantly from Wesleyan backgrounds and were concentrated in the South. The largest such denominations are the Church of God in Christ, the Church of God (Cleveland, Tenn.), and the Pentecostal Holiness Church.

ONENESS, OR "JESUS ONLY," PENTECOSTALS. From 1913 to 1916, the Finished Work group was torn asunder by a controversy over the proper water baptismal formula and the nature of the godhead. Advocates of the "Oneness" position rejected traditional Trinitarianism, maintaining that Father, Son, and Holy Ghost are simply different titles or offices of the one God whose name is Jesus. A number of small Oneness denominations were organized, the most important of which was Garfield T. Haywood's interracial Pentecostal Assemblies of the World. The movement consisted mostly of the very poorest Pentecostals and was strongest in the urban centers of the upper Midwest. In 1945 most white Oneness Pentecostals were brought together in the United Pentecostal Church.

PENTECOSTAL REVIVAL GOES GLOBAL. Within a very few years, visitors to the Azusa Street revival carried the movement all around the world. Thomas Ball Barratt, an English-born Methodist minister and pastor of an independent free church in Oslo, Norway (then Kristiania), was converted to Pentecostalism in New York City in 1906. His church, Kristiania Bymission, became the center of a revival in 1907 from which Pentecostalism spread throughout Scandinavia. The movement's greatest appeal was to evangelical and Holiness believers of the poorer classes.

In the United Kingdom, the Anglican clergyman Alexander A. Boddy attended Thomas Barratt's meetings in 1907 and then established his All Saints Church in Sunderland, England, as a Pentecostal center from which the movement spread through the British Isles. Leadership of the movement soon passed to the Welsh miners W. J. and D. P. Williams and Stephen and George Jeffreys. Overall in the United Kingdom, Pentecostalism had only modest success until the 1950s, when many West Indian and other colonial immigrants were converted to it. A Pentecostal revival in Germany began in Kassel-Hesse under the preaching of female evangelists from Barratt's church in 1907. Luigi Francescon and other Italian-Americans from Chicago established Pentecostalism in Italy in 1908, primarily among poor peasants in the South and in the major cities. In 1910, the movement was established in Brazil by Francescon and the Swedish-American steelworkers Daniel Berg and Gunnar Vingren, from which it spread elsewhere in South America. In Chile in 1907, the American Willis C. Hoover's conversion to Pentecostalism led to his eviction from the pastorate of a Methodist church in Valparaíso. Hoover then founded the Pentecostal Methodist Church. Pentecostalism was brought to Bulgaria, Romania, and Russia in the early 1920s by Ivan E. Voronaev, founder in 1919 of the First Russian Pentecostal Church in New York City.

The Pentecostal message was brought to India in 1907 by American and European missionaries. The movement spread widely but had little impact before the 1940s, when the indigenous churches, founded in the 1920s and 1930s, began to grow rapidly. In Indonesia in the early 1920s, American missionaries established the Pentecostal movement on the island of Bali, and German missionaries introduced it at Bandung, Java. The Pentecostal movement was brought to China in 1908. The movement in Japan began in 1913 but had very little growth until the 1950s.

The American missionaries John G. Lake and Thomas Hezmalhalch, converts to Pentecostalism from John Alexander Dowie's Christian Catholic Apostolic Church in Zion, Illinois, won most of Dowie's South African churches to the new movement following a revival in 1908 in Johannesburg. A former Dutch Reformed minister, Pieter Louis leRoux, emerged as the leader of the Apostolic Faith Mission of South Africa. The segregationist policies of this and other Pentecostal mission churches led to the early loss of most of their black adherents. As a result, numerous schismatic "Zionist" churches arose—so-called because nearly all use the word Zion in their official names. In addition, many independent, indigenous Pentecostal churches were founded by prophets who have often been regarded as demi-gods by their followers. Missionaries from South Africa, Europe, and North America had established the movement throughout most of sub-Saharan Africa by the 1920s, but it was the evangelizing efforts of native preachers that account for Pentecostalism's great success. The distribution of American Pentecostal literature in Nigeria led to the indigenous *Aladura* (praying people) movement beginning in the early 1920s, which spread all through western Africa in the wake of a revival in 1928. The preaching of Simon Kimbangu in the lower Congo in 1921 led to his life imprisonment, but the church founded in his name by his followers grew throughout central Africa.

The "Deliverance," or Healing, Revival. The institutionalization of the American Pentecostal movement, together with generational changes and the rise of many into the middle classes, brought a decline in the fervor of Pentecostal worship, especially in the larger, white denominations. This led to a renewal movement in the late 1940s. The New Order of the Latter Rain began with a revival in an independent church in North Battleford, Saskatchewan, in 1948, and soon spread throughout the world. The revival placed a new emphasis on the "laying on of hands" for the reception of Holy Spirit Baptism, healing, and other charismata. A group of faith-healing evangelists arose to deliver the faithful from formalism, sickness, and demon possession. The healers reintroduced tent revivals and attracted multitudes of non-Pentecostals.

William Branham, a Oneness Pentecostal from an impoverished Indiana family, was at first the most renowned leader of the revival. But Oral Roberts (1918–), a Pentecostal Holiness preacher from Oklahoma, soon overshadowed Branham and became the most prominent Pentecostal in the United States (he became a member of the Methodist Church in 1968). Many of the leaders of the Pentecostal denominations turned against the healers, who formed their own organizations and radio and television ministries.

The Charismatic Revival. Many non-Pentecostals first became aware of Pentecostalism through the highly publicized Deliverance revival. In the 1960s, a Neo-Pentecostal, or charismatic, movement emerged in nearly all the Protestant denominations, the Roman Catholic Church, and in Eastern Orthodox communions.

In 1951, Oral Roberts encouraged Demos Shakarian, a wealthy Pentecostal dairyman from California, to found the Full Gospel Business Men's Fellowship, International (FGBMFI) for the purpose of providing lay support for the healers. Hundreds of FGBMFI luncheon and dinner meetings were held in fashionable hotels across the nation. Many converts to the charismatic movement were first brought into contact with Pentecostalism through FGBMFI, which served as a bridge from the Deliverance revival to the charismatic revival.

In 1961, Father Dennis Bennett, pastor of an Episcopal church in Van Nuys, California, announced that he had received the Baptism in the Spirit and had spoken in tongues. Widespread media coverage followed, and a charismatic revival in the Protestant denominations took off, actively promoted by the FGBMFI. Fears of denominational leaders diminished when the charismatics proved to be neither schismatic nor fanatical. Their meetings were marked by restraint, and they were careful not to challenge the established doctrines and practices of their communions.

In 1967, charismatic practices emerged among Roman Catholic students and faculty at Duquesne, Notre Dame, and Michigan State universities. The movement grew rapidly by means of prayer groups and local, national, and international conferences. It soon surpassed its Protestant counterpart, numbering among its adherents many religious and bishops and at least one cardinal, Leon Joseph Cardinal Suenens of Belgium.

Protestant charismatics regard Spirit Baptism as a distinct act of grace, as do all Pentecostals, but many Protestant and all Roman Catholic charismatics regard it as a renewal or actualization of the baptism in the Spirit, which all Christians receive in water baptism or on their conversion. Some Protestant charismatics hold the "initial evidence" view of glossolalia; other Protestant and all Roman Catholic charismatics reject this view.

The Gospel of Health and Wealth. As the healing revival began to wane and many middle-class people were embracing the charismatic movement, a new movement began in the 1970s under the leadership of Kenneth Hagin and Kenneth Copeland. The "Word of Faith" teaching proclaimed that every true Christian believer could have health, happiness, and prosperity by simply claiming it. It was a gospel entirely congenial to upwardly mobile middle classes, not only in the United States, but those emerging middle classes in some parts of Asia and Africa as well. It coincided with the global expansion of capitalism and consumerism, and became a major trend in the Pentecostal/charismatic movement.

THE THIRD WAVE. This term refers to some new movements in the United States in the 1980s and 1990s, but also to indigenous movements in the Third World that had been developing for many decades. The unifying element is their rejection of Pentecostal/charismatic language and heritage while preserving the practice of the charismata.

In 1975, C. Peter Wagner and John Wimber, instructors at Fuller Theological Seminary, taught a course on "Signs and Wonders" in which they held that the key to evangelism was demonstrating the power of the gospel through performing signs and wonders. They minimized Spirit Baptism and glossolalia. Wimber organized the Association of Vineyard Churches in 1985. A revival in the Toronto Airport Vineyard Church began in 1994 under the leadership of John Arnott. Its extreme bodily manifestations like dancing, laughing, and bellowing like animals earned it the condemnation of many, and it was evicted from the Vineyard Association. A similar revival marked by jerking and twitching began the following year in a Brownsville church in Pensacola, Florida. Both revivals have attracted many thousands. Wagner founded the New Apostolic Church movement in 1996. It emphasizes the authority of apostles and prophets and the loose association of entirely independent congregations.

The Shepherding/Discipleship movement, led by a group of Pentecostal preachers in Fort Lauderdale, Florida, also began in the 1970s. It taught the submission of every believer to the authority of a shepherd who would direct all aspects of his or her life, including choice of spouse and management of finances. The movement was rejected by most and withered away by 1986.

By far the most dramatic aspect of the Third Wave is its explosive growth in Africa, Latin America, and Asia, especially since the 1970s. These movements have taken root among peoples whose traditional beliefs were animistic, and therefore quite compatible with those of Pentecostals and charismatics. But they are not fully accepted by many more traditional Pentecostals and charismatics because some of their beliefs and practices, like ancestor worship and polygyny, are considered heretical or non-Christian. Their forms of worship, however, are virtually indistinguishable from those of the Pentecostals and charismatics.

There are four types of Pentecostalism in Asia, Africa, and Latin America:

1. Mission churches established by missionaries from the Pentecostal denominations of North America and Europe.
2. charismatic movements in the mainstream non-Pentecostal denominations.
3. Independent schismatic offspring of the mission churches.
4. Wholly indigenous movements growing out of traditional religions.

The great expansion of Pentecostalism in Africa, Latin America, and Asia since the 1960s has coincided with the global evangelizing campaigns of American healers and preachers of the Prosperity Gospel. These have made many converts among the masses of people disoriented and socially disrupted by the process of decolonization, by the penetration of capitalist market relations, and by the breakdown of traditional religions, family relationships, and community ties.

WORSHIP. The heart of Pentecostalism is the worship service. In the early years of the Pentecostal movement, nearly every meeting was marked by speaking in tongues, prophesying, healings, exorcisms, hand-clapping, uncoordinated praying aloud, running, jumping, falling, dancing "in the Spirit," crying, and shouting with great exuberance. Very quickly these practices were subjected to unwritten but clearly understood conventions concerning what was appropriate and when; however, Pentecostal services still appeared chaotic to the uninitiated. In the larger, white Pentecostal denominations these practices have all but disappeared. Charismatics have always maintained a high degree of decorum. The original character of Pentecostal worship, however, is still much in evidence among racial and ethnic minorities in North America and Europe and throughout sub-Saharan Africa, Latin America, and parts of Asia.

BELIEF AND PRACTICE. Experience, not doctrine, has been the principal concern of Pentecostals. There is no unanimity on doctrine, polity, or any matter whatsoever except Spirit Baptism and the practice of the charismata. The early Pentecostals were heirs to the evangelical faith of the late-nineteenth-century Holiness movement. Most American Pentecostals subscribe to the tenets of Fundamentalism. Their only distinctive doctrine is that of Baptism in the Spirit. Many American Pentecostal denominations believe that the "initial evidence" of Spirit Baptism is always glossolalia. Other Pentecostals believe that it may be evidenced by any one of the charismata. Speaking in tongues was originally believed to be miraculously speaking a language completely unknown to the speaker. Many Pentecostals continue to hold this view, even though linguistic analysis has refuted it. Some acknowledge its nonlinguistic character but continue to assert its divine signification.

The charismatics have rejected nearly all of the Holiness and fundamentalist heritage of the Pentecostal movement. They have concentrated on integrating the experience of Spirit Baptism and the practice of the charismata into the traditional beliefs and practices of their respective traditions. Despite differences in forms of expression, worship, for all Pentecostals, is the ritual reenactment of *Acts 2*—the recapturing of awe, wonder, and joy in the immediate experience of the Holy Spirit, and immersion in mystery and miracle. Worship provides the believer with an opportunity for individual expression, forges an emotional bond with the spiritual community, brings consolation and assurance, and lifts one into the sublime. The believer's objective is "to feel the moving of the Spirit," or, in psychological terms, to experience intense arousal and discharge of emotion. The goal is infilling, or possession, by the Holy Spirit.

The Third Wavers only connection with the Pentecostals and charismatics is in their style of worship: the emotional and physical expression of the charismata.

SOCIAL CHARACTER. The Pentecostal movement originated in the United States as a protest against the increasing formalism, "modernism," and middle-class character of the mainstream denominations. It was a movement of the poor, the uprooted, the socially and culturally deprived, recent immigrants, blacks, Hispanics, and other minorities in America. The movement's leaders were poor and lower-middle-class clergy and religious workers with little advanced education, generally from the outermost fringes of American Christendom. With few exceptions, the social character of the movement in all the countries to which it spread was analogous, and it is still overwhelmingly so in those indigenous movements that are most dynamic in Africa, Latin America, and Asia. Pentecostalism has played a role in easing the transit of some of those who have suffered most from the transformation of preindustrial societies into modern urbanizing, industrializing ones. Pentecostalism has shown an ability to incorporate elements of both traditional and modern modes of thought and behavior into a subculture that has served as a bridge between the two. Its pre-scientific outlook gives it an affinity with many non-Christian religions. Its emphasis on subjectivity, emotional expression, Spirit Baptism, healing, exorcism, and miracles makes it highly congenial to adherents of traditional religions that are characterized by animism, spirit possession, divination, shamanism, and prophetism. On the other hand, Pentecostalism has inculcated in its adherents an ethic of hard work, discipline, obedience to authority, sobriety, thrift, and self-denial—the qualities of the ideal proletarian in modernizing societies. These qualities have enabled some adherents to rise into the middle classes. It has also attracted new converts from those already moving into the middle classes, for whom the charismatic movement and the Prosperity Gospel serve as vehicles for upward mobility.

MORES. The early American Pentecostals were markedly ascetic, with prohibitions against tobacco, alcohol, dancing, gambling, movies, coffee, tea, Coca-Cola, cosmetics, and jewelry. Such prohibitions are no longer typical of white, middle-class American Pentecostals, but they are typical of other American Pentecostals. European Pentecostals have generally taken a more liberal position. Charismatics regard all such taboos as irrelevant. Nonwhite Pentecostals often tend more toward asceticism.

SOCIAL ETHICS. The dominance of millenarianism among the early Pentecostals and their identification of the Social Gospel with the mainstream churches led to wholesale rejection of social activism by the Pentecostal denominations. They have always approved of individual acts of charity but have avoided corporate church involvement in social or political action. Pentecostals tend strongly toward conservative and reactionary views. They believe that society can be improved by the conversion and Spirit Baptism of individuals within it, but only the Second Coming can bring the good society—and the signs of that Coming are an increase in immorality, conflict, and general social chaos. Such beliefs militate against any real social ethic.

A few Pentecostal academics have worked to develop a Pentecostal social ethic, a move which has been welcomed by some, especially nonwhite and Third World adherents, but frowned upon by most, who are still convinced of the futility of bettering the world before its imminent apocalyptic destruction and the Second Coming of Jesus.

POLITICAL ORIENTATION. Most American Pentecostals were hostile to any involvement in politics until the 1970s, when they were politicized around the New Right reaction against the social and cultural changes brought about by the 1960s and 1970s protest movements. They lent support to the candidacy of Jimmy Carter, a self-proclaimed "born again" Christian whose sister was a prominent charismatic, in 1976; to Ronald Reagan in 1980 and 1984; to the prominent Pentecostal television evangelist Pat Robertson in 1988; and to George W. Bush in 2000. After his failed bid for the Republican nomination, Robertson founded the Christian Coalition, which eventually settled into the right wing of the Republican Party.

Pentecostals and charismatics in other nations tend to support or at least accommodate any government—Left, Right, or Center—on the basis of the belief that "the powers that be are ordained of God" and should therefore not be resisted. Their only concern is that they be free to practice and proselytize their religion. However, they do tend to be more favorably disposed toward conservative, authoritarian governments. In Latin America, Pentecostalism has been favored by parties and governments who see their growth as a force to weaken the political power of the Roman Catholic Church.

POLITY AND INTERCHURCH RELATIONS. The early Pentecostals opposed all "man-made" organizations; they called only for spiritual unity based on Spirit Baptism. Soon, however, they created a multitude of tight denominational structures of widely differing polities. But whether episcopal, presbyterian, congregational, or mixed in form, in practice all Pentecostals have tended toward the authoritarianism of the national leader(s) in denominational matters and that of the pastor in congregational matters.

American Pentecostal denominations were at first strongly separatist in their relations with one another, as well as with non-Pentecostal churches. A break in the isolationism of American Pentecostals came in 1943, when several Pentecostal denominations joined the National Association of Evangelicals. In 1948, the largest white Pentecostal denominations organized the Pentecostal Fellowship of North America, a racially segregated organization of Finished Work and Second Work Pentecostals. In 1994 this was disbanded and reorganized as the racially integrated Pentecostal and charismatic Churches of North America.

European Pentecostals engaged in various regional and national cooperative efforts from an early point; they held the first All-Europe Pentecostal Conference in 1939 and the first Pentecostal World Conference in 1947, which soon included many Pentecostal churches from around the world. While fellowship with other Pentecostals and evangelicals has become common, attempts at theological agreement and organizational unity have been resisted.

Since 1961 several Pentecostal churches have joined the World Council of Churches, though none from the United States. However, some American Pentecostal clergy have attended meetings of this organization, often against the official positions of their churches. charismatics, in contrast to Pentecostals, are ardently ecumenical, being active in nearly all interchurch organizations at all levels. Adherents in Africa, Latin America, and Asia stand somewhere in between—separatism and independency are quite strong, but several denominations have joined ecumenical organizations, including the World Council of Churches. In 1972 the first General Conference on charismatic Renewal was held in Kansas City; subsequent ones have been held periodically. The North American Congress of the Holy Spirit and Evangelization has met annually since 1986.

GLOBAL DIMENSIONS. Because of the great number of Pentecostal organizations, the variety of names, and the amorphous character of many groups, it is impossible to accurately estimate the totals of Pentecostal/charismatic/"Third Wave" adherents. However, the *World Christian Encyclopedia* (2001), edited by David B. Barrett, estimates the global total of Pentecostals of all types at 535 million, including 65 million Pentecostals, 175 million charismatics, and 295 million Third Wavers (whom Barrett calls "Neo-charismatics"). Total adherents to these three groups (in the millions) are estimated at 79.6 in North America, 37.5 in Europe, 141.4 in Latin America, 126 in Africa, 134.8 in Asia, and 4.2 in Oceania.

SEE ALSO Charisma; Shavuʿot.

BIBLIOGRAPHY

The seminal work on the origins of the Pentecostal movement is Robert M. Anderson's *Vision of the Disinherited: The Making of American Pentecostalism* (Oxford, 1979; Hendrickson, rev. ed., 1992). Anderson provides a thorough narrative, analytical, and interpretative treatment of the American movement from its origins to the 1930s. Many of the major historical, sociological, psychological, and theological issues involved in the study of Pentecostal Christianity as a whole are addressed in this work.

A useful overview of developments since the movement's origins is Vinson Synan's (editor and contributor) *The Century of the Holy Spirit: 100 Years of Pentecostal and Charismatic Renewal, 1901–2001* (Nashville, Tenn., 2001). The various works of Walter Hollenweger, who pioneered in the scholarly research of Pentecostalism, are well worth consulting, including *Pentecostals after a Century: Global Perspectives on a Movement in Transition* (Sheffield, U.K., 1999), edited in collaboration with Alan Anderson. Much useful information and many extensive bibliographies may be found in *New International Dictionary of Pentecostal Charismatic Movements* (Grand Rapids, Mich., 2002), edited by Stanley M. Burgess and written primarily by Pentecostals. The bibliographies compiled by Charles Edwin Jones, including *A Guide to the Study of the Pentecostal Movement,* 2 volumes (Metuchen, N.J., 1983), and *The Charismatic Movement,* 2 volumes (Metuchen, N.J., 1995), are indispensable for the researcher. Also indispensable is Sherry Sherrod DuPree's *African American Holiness Pentecostal Movement: An Annotated Bibliography* (New York, 1996), which also includes a wealth of information on many churches and prominent leaders.

Pneuma: The Journal of the Society for Pentecostal Studies (semiannual, 1979–) and the *Newsletter of the Society for Pentecostal Studies* are essential for keeping up with the flood of literature about Pentecostalism.

For an eyewitness account by a leader in the Los Angeles, California, revival, see Frank Bartleman's *Azusa Street* (Plainfield, N.J., 1980). This edition has an excellent foreword by the Pentecostal historian Vinson Synan. The complete editions of the Azusa Street mission's publication, *The Apostolic Faith,* have been edited by Wayne Warner as the *Azusa Street Papers* (Foley, Ala., 1997). Larry Martin is reprinting many of the earliest accounts of the movement in an ongoing series, titled the *Complete Azusa Street Library* (Joplin, Mo., 1994–), which covers more than the title suggests. James R. Goff's *Fields White unto Harvest* (Fayetteville, Ark., 1988), a biography of Charles F. Parham, is an important study of the first prominent leader of the movement. The African and African American influences are explored in Iain MacRobert's *The Black Roots and White Racism of Early Pentecostalism in the U. S. A.* (New York, 1988). The origins of what is the largest African American Pentecostal church in America is explored by Ithiel C. Clemmons in *Bishop C. H. Mason and the Roots of the Church of God in Christ* (Bakersfield, Calif., 1996). Also important is the sociological study of Arthur E. Paris, *Black Pentecostalism: Southern Religion in an Urban World* (Amherst, Mass., 1982), which shows how Pentecostalism serves the needs of rural-to-urban migrants, and the perceptive study by an insider, Cheryl J. Sanders' *Saints in Exile: The Holiness Pentecostal Experience in African American Religion and Culture* (New York, 1996). For more information about membership statistics for the Pentecostal/charismatic churches, see the *World Christian Encyclopedia,* edited by David B. Barrett, (New York, 2d ed., 2001).

The development of the largest Finished Work church is perceptively related in Edith L. Blumhofer's *Restoring the Faith: The Assemblies of God, Pentecostalism, and American Culture* (Urbana, Ill., 1993). In *Heaven Below: Early Pentecostals and American Culture* (Cambridge, Mass., 2001), Grant Wacker describes what it was like to be a Pentecostal in the early years; it is a valuable work despite its insupportable contention that first generation Pentecostals were a "cross section of the American population."

Mickey Crews's *The Church of God: A Social History* (Knoxville, Tenn., 1993), Vinson Synan's *The Holiness Pentecostal Tradition* (Grand Rapids, Mich., 2d. ed., 1997), and Dennis Covington's *Salvation on Sand Mountain: Snake Handling and Redemption in Southern Appalachia* (Reading, Mass., 1995) are important histories of the Second Work wing. For the "Jesus Only" wing, see Talmadge L. French's *Our God Is One: The Story of the Oneness Pentecostals* (Hazelwood, Mo., 2000).

The origins of the Pentecostal movement in Europe may be found in Nils Bloch-Hoell's *The Pentecostal Movement* (Oslo, 1964), which is best on Scandinavia. Donald Gee's *Wind and Flame* (London, 1967), on the United Kingdom, should be supplemented by Peter D. Hocken's *Streams of Renewal* (Washington, D.C., and Exeter, U.K., 1997); both treatments are theological as well as historical. The life and writings of the founder of the movement are found in *The Work of T. B. Barratt* (New York, 1985), edited by Donald W. Dayton.

For the New Order of the Latter Rain movement of the 1940s, see Richard M. Riss's *Latter Rain* (Mississauga, Ontario, 1987). The story of the Deliverance and charismatic revivals is told with scholarship and verve in David Edwin Harrell, Jr.'s *All Things Are Possible* (Bloomington, Ind., 1975), and his *Oral Roberts: An American Life* (Bloomington, Ind., 1985). Also important is C. Douglas Weaver's *The Healer-Prophet: William Marion Branham* (Macon, Ga., 2d ed., 2000).

Indispensable on the charismatic revival are Richard Quebedeaux's *The New Charismatics II* (San Francisco, Calif., 1983) and the collection of essays edited by Russell P. Spittler, *Perspectives on the New Pentecostalism* (Grand Rapids, Mich., 1976). Historical and theological assessments of the Catholic charismatic movement include Edward D. O'Connor's *The Pentecostal Movement in the Catholic Church* (Notre Dame, Ind., 1971) for the American scene, and René Laurentin's *Catholic Pentecostalism,* (Garden City, N.Y., 1977) for the European. The resurgence of the more extreme forms of Pentecostalism is explored in *"Toronto" in Perspective* (Waynesboro, Ga., 2001), edited by David Hilborn. The affinity of many Pentecostal/charismatics for right-wing politics is examined in David Edwin Harrell, Jr.'s *Pat Robertson* (San Francisco, Calif., 1987).

Among the many important studies of world Pentecostalism are David Martin, *Pentecostalism: The World Their Parish* (Oxford, and Malden, Mass., 2002), Simon Coleman, *The Globalisation of Charismatic Christianity: Spreading the Gospel of Prosperity* (Cambridge, U.K., and New York, 2000), Stephen Hunt et al., eds., *Charismatic Christianity: Sociological Perspectives* (New York, 1997), Andre Corten and Ruth Marshall-Fratani, eds., *Between Babel and Pentecost: Transnational Pentecostalism in Africa and Latin America* (Bloomington, Ind., 2001), and, from the Pentecostal perspective, Murray Dempster et al., eds. *The Globalization of Pentecostalism* (Irvine, Calif., 1999).

Latin American Pentecostalism has attracted more scholars than any other region, and they have produced an impressive body of work, beginning with Emile Willems, *Followers of the New Faith* (Nashville, Tenn., 1967), and Christian Lalive d'Epinay, *Haven of the Masses* (London, 1969) who first laid bare the social roots of Latin American Pentecostalism, and by extension, those of Pentecostalisms throughout the Third World. Among other studies are Edward L. Cleary and Hannah Stewart-Gambino, eds., *Power, Politics, and Pentecostals in Latin America* (Boulder, Colo., 1998), R. Andrew Chesnut, *Born Again in Brazil* (New Brunswick, N.J., 1997), Frans Kamsteeg, *Prophetic Pentecostalism in Chile* (Lanham, Md., 1998), Karl-Wilhelm Westmeier, *Protestant Pentecostalism in Latin America* (Madison, N.J., and London, 1999), and Barbara Boudewijnse et al., eds., *More than Opium: An Anthropological Approach to Latin American and Caribbean Pentecostal Praxis* (Lanham, Md., 1998).

The mainstream Pentecostal position on Spirit Baptism and the charismata is presented by the first-generation Pentecostal Ralph M. Riggs in his work *The Spirit Himself* (Springfield, Mo., 1949). More moderate charismatic positions are laid out by the Presbyterian J. Rodman Williams in *The Gift of the Holy Spirit Today* (Plainfield, N.J., 1980), and the Roman Catholic theologian Donald L. Gelpi in *Pentecostalism* (New York, 1971).

The clinical psychologist John P. Kildahl, in his *The Psychology of Speaking in Tongues* (New York, 1972), presents a generally favorable assessment of the mental health of glossolalists. In *Speaking in Tongues* (Chicago, Ill., 1972), the anthropologist Felicitas D. Goodman concludes on the basis of her cross-cultural study that the practice involves an altered mental state. The sociolinguist William J. Samarin's *Tongues of Men and Angels* (New York, 1972) demonstrates the nonlinguistic character of the phenomenon and views it as learned behavior.

ROBERT MAPES ANDERSON (1987 AND 2005)

PERCUSSION AND NOISE. The role of percussion and noise in the evolution of the human species remains the subject of ongoing debate and speculation. That manufactured sound commands inexhaustible fascination and enjoins relentless exploration seems patent from the historical record. *Homo sapiens* is also *homo* "per-soni-fication"—a creature summoned by and summoning "what sounds through." There is a dense intersection between percussion and ritual repetition that goes by the name of religion in the ceaseless quest of humanity to express, comprehend, control, free, fecundate, and otherwise elaborate its experience of meaning by way of rhythm. Examples of various uses of noise and sound ground speculative musing on the ritual fusing of myth, music, and dance—the body in contemplation and in motion—and the ascribed effects such sonic textures arouse in consciousness and community alike.

Percussive sound is here understood as a rhythmic patterning of noise, a precise structure and ordering of both pitch and timing, produced primarily by instruments of the idiophone and membranophone families, or indeed by the human body itself (in forms of clapping, stomping, or aspirating). Noise refers to sound that is unspecifiable in pitch and duration, from virtually any source, that nonetheless gains employment in ritual soundings of the cosmos. Firecrackers, vocal cries, grunts and growls and howls imitating nature, or even certain aspects of material culture, are examples. The line between noise and percussion depends, perhaps now more than ever, on cultural context and political purpose: any sound shortened enough in duration is noise; any noise given enough time and space for repetition can be comprehended as rhythm. In the last half of the twentieth century, the introduction of electronic media quickly revolutionized the human probe of the soundscape as aural symbol: hip-hop scratching of records, machinelike inflections of the human voice by means of synthesizer, and digitalized fracturing and suturing of sound into a surround of trancelike droning invaded world musics both secular and sacred. Postmodern literature and music together ask if spirit can be found inside the machine as well as in the mosque (or in mammal and mineral, in older belief), in the chip as well as in the chirp or church. Industrial noise may itself emerge in hindsight as a new kind of "god" (or "demon") and Adam Smith's "invisible hand" (guiding market choice), the animism of the modern hour.

PERCUSSION. Percussion appears across the worldscape as a primary modality of both experiencing and expressing ritual solemnity and religious intensity. Gong strikes, drumrolls, bell rings, palm beats, cymbal crashes, stick clicks, and stone clacks have served the religious interrogation of things invisible around the planet. Paleolithic culture divulges mammoth-jaw scrapers, reindeer-antler beaters, and bone and seashell wrist-rattles. Skin-covered drums and musical bows were common in cultures as ancient and divergent as Neolithic Bulgaria, Bronze Age China, Babylonia-on-the-rise, and Buddha's India. Bull-roarers (a bull-roarer is a piece of bone or wood attached to a long string) swung around the head to create "vortices of sonic monstrosity" effected initiation in Australia, Nigeria, Navajo Arizona, and Inuit Canada. Goat-hoof rattle-belts called *manjur* are combined with tin can rattles (*ashukhshaykhah*) in the Zar cults of Egypt, and springbok ears filled with pebbles and tied around the ankles serve the same the need to rattle in South Africa. There is perhaps no object found or manufactured that is not sooner or later annexed to the drive to syncopate, vibrate, resonate, or orchestrate matter into an aural augury of ultimate mystery. The land itself is drafted into the divination in some places: slit drums of the Lokele people of Zaire take advantage of the acoustical properties of natural formations to make river basins and valley passages speak an African tongue like a modern telegraph. Here the drum-as-spirit-mouth of a local place was the subject of ritual care, sheltered in a hut, offered sacred milk daily, warmed continuously by fire, replenished in power by cattle sacrifice and beer. Indeed, this effort at aural enchantment may even predate humanity, insofar as gorilla chest-pounds or beaver-tailed water-slaps of warning sought to use sharp sound to alter awareness. That human consciousness could be sonically shocked or "rocked" into perception of an "otherworld" is one of the primordial intuitions of religious practice in the memory of the species.

But there is little agreement about the exact nature of percussive triggers (e.g., drum rhythms) for this altered consciousness. Certainly the nearly universal congruence of ritual percussion and rites of transition (like those for birth, puberty, marriage, and death) is well established. But ethnomusicology has raised issue with any easy neurobiological explanation of trance behavior as drum-driven. The lab experiments conducted by neurobiologists too radically alter the performance context, too uncritically limit alpha brainwave effects to the trance music in question (nontrance music can also cause the same effect), and too abstractly ignore the cultural specificity of the psychological conditioning in evidence. At most, we can say religious experience of an "otherworld" sometimes seems to involve ritually mediated, drum-triggered "possession-states" that are communally embraced and culturally interpreted in quite particular ways.

What such an "otherworld" might consist of is a core riff of human cultures. Science today makes us aware of the primacy of the Big Bang, the first beat, the explosion of time and space in din and chaos that sets matter in motion as vibration. Hindus call the seed sound *Nada Brahma*; the *Tibetan Book of the Dead* speaks of the essence of reality as a "reverberating like a thousand distant thunders." Percussive exploration—whether as a mode of taming the terror of volcano and thunder, titillation accompanying the rhythmic "cracking" of stone tool-making, or merely observation of the undulations of natural phenomena (spiders drumming their webs, termites clicking the ground in march, waves on beaches)—finds careful and playful elaboration in the myths of origins of percussion instruments. The Buria people of Siberia trace the single-headed shaman's drum to a retaliatory lightning strike that split the two-headed drum ridden by their chief shaman, Morgon-Kara, after successfully raiding heaven to retrieve a soul stolen by the High God. The Dan people of Africa track the advent of the wooden drum to a dancing-versus-drumming battle to the death won by an orphan village boy avenging the death of his brother at the hands of the termite-mound genie who originally owned the drum. Among the Sioux, the powwow drum is thought to have been the contrivance of the Great Spirit, revealed to Tailfeather Woman, as an instrument to tease whites out of their wanton violence towards natives by entrancing them with the secret of the powwow dance. Whatever the explanation, power, both terrible and tantalizing, was obviously, early on in human history, found in sound. Mastery of the mystery of producing rhythmic patterns may be one of the defining capacities of human evolution.

But the history of the drum, in particular, also reveals the ambiguity of the religious valuing of sound. Based on artifactual evidence and artistic imagery dating back to at least 2200 BCE, the drum appears to have been widely embraced around the planet as a means of ritual concourse with the spirit-dimension—and its use, as often as not, a realm of women's work. In the cultural genealogy of the West, however, sacred drum use was increasingly replaced by new melodic instruments such as the trumpet, harp, lyre, and shawm beginning with the emergence of Sumerian civilizations in the third century BCE, and hitting a nadir with the early Roman Christian evaluation of percussion as "the devil's music." Whether this was an effect of an ideological shift accompanying the suppression of agricultural-based goddess religions by male-controlled transcendental orientations, or some deep psychosocial antipathy to lower frequency, the larger kettle and cylinder drums were gradually displaced from temple to battlefield, from magical power to martial. (In the breach, however, clappers, ratchets, castanets, whirring discs, and xylophones were all used percussively to chase away evil spirits and attract goods ones, and eventually bells were hung in church towers to gather believers or toll warnings.) Only in encounters with Muslim invaders in the Middle Ages, and later with indigenous cultures in the course of colonization, did the deep bass "boom" of big drum sounds slowly reinvest European sensibilities of the sacred. In the New World, beginning in the nineteenth century, West African modalities of spirit possession articulated by rhythmic aggression percolated up from freed-slave communities into the heart of American societies as a kind of return of the repressed—jazz, blues and gospel, samba, bomba, and mambo exercising white fascination despite (and indeed because of) widespread fear that rhythm leads to insurrection, or percussive beat to sexual heat. The thirst for trance evident in this rhythmic revelry in contemporary Western societies may well belie their self-naming as secular.

Elsewhere, percussion has been articulated in concert with quite varied cultural cues as to what constitutes acceptable clues of the sacred. Among the Mapuche of Chile and Argentina, the *kultrún* drum used by the *machi* medicine man or woman anchors a kind of cosmogram of the universe, with drawings on its sides that map good (east, south) and evil (west, north). It harbors within its resonant belly the earth products (coins, seeds of medicinal plants, animal hair, wheat, and corn) that augur fertility, and in its bay wood body it partakes of the sacred "world-tree" substance believed to project its shaman-player to the heavens (Grebe, 1973). Drumming instruments in many South American Indian cultures are medicine as well as tocsin and prayer: together with the singing voice of the shaman, they fight evil actively, aid in diagnosis, serve as prophylaxis, and reinforce cure. Spirits are thought to echo through the throbbing skins, and mythologies ascribe to the instruments an origin as pristine as creation itself (Béhague, 1993). Pre-Columbian high Indian cultures throughout Meso- and South America bear similar witness. Carvings on and codices about Aztec *teponaztles* (slit drums) and *huehuetls* (upright, cylindrical drums) reveal instruments that were "instrumental" in giving cosmic structure to the universe from its mythic genesis to its apocalyptic end in ancient Mexico. Maya murals at the eighth-century CE Bonampak temple in Chiapas evince the ritual import of drums and rattles. Incan *tinya*—small double-headed drums carrying ritually activated magical powers—are honored up to the present in successor Indian communities in Peru in Carnival parades and ceremonies of cattle branding. The magical sound properties of the *tinya* are produced by cloves of garlic and red peppers inserted in the drum body, activated by the zoomorphic mallet with which it is struck, and (in Puno at least) reinforced by accoutrements worn by drummers that are associated with the mythical condor (Béhague, 1993).

In India, the folk drum *dholak* (double-headed, barrel-shaped) underwrites birth and marriage ceremonies, stimulates devotion, and announces news of good omen from village to village. In the south of the country, the *mrdanga* drum (similar to the *dholak*) aids in ordinary religious instruction; North Indian *kīrtan* chanting (in praise of Kṛṣṇa), popularized by the Vaisnava Caitanya (1486–1533), is made accessible to everyone through use of the clay *khola* drum and the brass *karatala* cymbals that are affordable even by the poor. Aspiring Punjabi *tabla* players are encouraged to make three vision-quest-like *chilla* retreats of forty days each, sequestered in huts, fed little, drumming fifteen or more hours per day, until trance-images come and the drum "talks." In Chinese cultures, where preference for more subdued rhythms reflects a valuing of calmness and serenity, myth tells of a maid who sought to spare her father's life by fulfilling an augury that the bell he was struggling to cast for the Son of Heaven would only turn out right if mingled with the blood of a maid. She cast herself into the molten metal at the last minute, and the bell so produced ever after tolled a sad "Ko-ngai" sounding of her name. Fritz Kuttner, a scholar of Chinese music and explorer of secret metallophone production techniques, tells of the Metropolitan Museum of Art's testing of an ancient Chinese *tam-tam* gong, which when tapped only once issued a soft hum for ten seconds, followed by a gradual crescendo for thirty-five seconds, until a colossal triple fortissimo peak was reached after a full minute, terrifying all the museum bystanders who heard it.

In Korea, two-headed drums used in shamanist practice may sport the eight primary trigrams of the Yi jing, and in Sri Lanka *geiji* bells are strung onto leather knee pads to knock out rhythmic accompaniment in ritual dance. Huge *taiko* drums in Japan punctuate Zen meditation and Shintō reverence with a reverberance that reinforces the perception of silence. Tibetan *damaru* (double-headed drums, made from halved human skulls) are power instruments said to be capable of rousing the dead, and *gang-san* gongs with human jawbone handles are used among the Bontoc Igorot people of the Philippines as part of their grief rituals. *Tabl* drums in Qatar are not only sounded, but also touched in certain dances to solicit healing, and Dubai performances of Mawlid (the celebration of the birth and death of the prophet Muḥammad) commemorations invoke memory of a saint's death day by means of frame drums. Ṣūfī trance-seeking through dervish-dancing may involve entrainment with *dar* (frame) drumming and flute playing.

Africa holds a special place in the percussive praise song, as homeland of the species and motherland of the polyrhythmic paradigm writ large. African peoples across the globe invoke ancestral memory and communal vitality in the key of contrastive sound. San peoples of South Africa clap and stomp out an intricate rhythm to collectively "face the gods" and effect cure. The Minianka of Mali hoe their fields in time to accompanying drumbeats. Venda adults of South Africa syncopate every child's least banging of some object with a counterrhythm designed to inculcate sensitivity to the polyrhythmic proclivities of their communal cult. The talking drum called *dundun* by the Ewe of Togo and Ghana is used to tell proverbs as well as to crack jokes by emulating tonal qualities in the language through varying the pitch of the drumhead by squeezing its webbing as it is played. In Yorubaland, every major *orisha* (ancestral spirit-persona) has its own rhythm to which it responds when drummed and into which it plunges its human "horse" in possession-dance. Vodou, Santería, and Candomblé—in syncretic cooperation with Catholic ritual elements—reiterate and amplify the possession vocabularies of these spirit-dances in Haiti, Cuba, and Brazil, respectively.

Creative adaptation under the duress of slavery led to divergence in details of practice and belief. For instance, the *batá* (double-headed, horizontally played) drums of the Yoruba Shango cult in Nigeria morphed in Cuba into a trio (from largest to smallest, *iya, itótele,* and *okónkolo*) that must be harvested together from the same tree trunk and played together as the sound organs of the god Aña. In the Lucumi (Cuban) context, the threesome is animated by an *afóuobó*-secret, known to the priests of Ana alone, physically signified by sacred seeds, cowrie shells, and other objects placed in a small bag inside the largest drum body, and inspirited by *éggüe*-plants (and other objects determined by divination) deposited in the drum cavity during construction that crumble into a powder over time and consecrate the sound. Sacrificial foods and blood further reinforce the potency in an annual offering. Shared ideas of "drum baptism" among West African and Afro-Cuban and Afro-Brazilian traditions mandate animal sacrifice and sacred food offerings while baptizing the instruments into potency to call gods and provoke possession. But the actual associations in each tradition are quite culture specific. In the Americas in particular, historically, they shifted in reference under different plantation regimes and racist polities that force distinct African tribal groups to intermingle bodies, beliefs, and practices in order to survive.

West African idiophone use and understanding likewise bridge the Atlantic. For example, the Yoruban double bell *adjá,* shaken before any speech by the priests of *Ogún,* the god of war and iron, is thought to personify aspects of this god and indeed to "ventriloquize" his voice; in Bahia, Brazil, the same instrument, here called *xerê,* is shaken over initiates' heads to summon all the *orixá* (ancestral spirit-persona) and to facilitate response, through possession, to the varied voices of the gods, articulated in each one's particular drum rhythm. In Yoruba-Fon inspired Candomblé funeral rites in Brazil known as *axêxê* (in the Nagô cult) or *azeri* (in the Gege cult), stick-struck calabash drums or fan-struck pottery jars, respectively, drive the spirit of Iku (Death) away and ensure transformation of the dead initiate into the realm of ancestors. All artifacts of the ceremony are eventually broken to signify severance of all ties between cult center and dead member and become part of the *carrego* (load of death).

NOISE. By comparison, noise in ritual is often used to mark moments that call for special attention or abrupt transition. Firecrackers, for instance, are employed in Chinese Confucian commemorations of ancestral dead to exorcise evil influence around the gravesite. In Mexican performances of the pre-Columbian *danza de los voladores* (dance of the flyers), these same noisemakers signal the crossover from ascent of "shaman-flyers" up the sacred post (or "tree of life") to flight downwards as symbolic birds, bringing divine messages and fertility to earth (Béhague, 1993). Similarly, during the public ceremony of *Xirê* in Bahia, Brazil, the entry of the gods (in the form of possessed initiates) into the main dance hall of the cult center is announced with a mixture of happiness and awe by a sudden burst of firecrackers.

Somewhere between percussion and noise is the old practice of "tattooing" a wooden board or metal plate (called a *semantron* or *simandron* in Greek, or *klepalo* in Slavic contexts) with sharp pulsing sounds by means of a stick or mallet. The urgency and solemnity of the clatter assumes an aspect of holy summons to prayer or, sometimes, fearful alarm at the approach of some untoward event (e.g., fire, invasion). Common to both Eastern and Western Christian traditions before the seventh-century advent of the church bell in the West, today the practice remains enshrined in Orthodox and Eastern church practices, especially in monasteries such as those on Mount Athos or the island of Patmos.

Vocalized shouts and ritualized groans also can oscillate between noise and rhythm—punctuating the precise moment of possession in both Brazil and Yorubaland with the cry of the arriving god, or laying down something more like a pattern of hyperventilation in "trumping" circles associated with the Afro-Christian Pukkumina cults of Jamaica or the noisy inhaling and exhaling of (non-Christian) Afro-Cuban Ronconeo worship. In each of these latter two instances, the rhythmic breathing accompanied by trunk and arm motions establishes an alternating high (inspiration) and low (expiration) pitch level, functioning like a form of "opaque, bitonal drumming" (Béhague, 1984; Ortiz, 1952–1954). A somewhat similar use of breathing signals the "code-switch," according to Morton Marks (1974), when African American "gospel" preaching suddenly shifts from a European monotone beginning to a higher velocity, African possession-cadence known as "whooping." Indeed, the percussive breathing and body language is recognizable across religious communions—for example, a Pentecostal preacher gesturing (unconsciously) for a visiting Candomblé or Santería devotee a message of Shàngó or Oshun (spirits common to the two West African-derived religions) as well as articulating a word of Jesus.

Indian Kuṇḍalinī meditation traditions recognize a form of discipline called *shubda yoga* that works with percussive sound to open the knots of energy called *cakra* that run up the spinal column. Hard consonants in particular are vocalized to release "male" energies associated especially with the second "sexual" *cakra*—a practice that one Indian teacher recently likened to certain forms of rap rhyming that work the harder sounds explosively to achieve a particular kind of "manhood."

Handclapping is another action that works the edge between abrupt punctuation and patterned rhythm. In addition to reinforcing or embroidering upon musical instrumentation, handclaps in many cultures serve as a symbolic expression of collective emotion. In Central Africa, some peoples interpret rhythmic clapping as an exalted (and exalting) modality of direct contact between the gods and the human spirit. In Ifa divination practices common to West Africa and Brazil, readings of positive signs by the *babalawo* (diviner) provokes affirmation and rejoicing in the form of exuberant clapping.

Finally, in African American contexts, even the percussion agent *par excellence*, the drum itself, is sometimes shifted out of its role of time-keeping and rhythm-patterning to "drop bombs" (as jazz legend Max Roach used to say) of exclamation and fury.

BIBLIOGRAPHY

Béhague, Gerard. "Patterns of Candomblé Music Performance: An Afro-Brazilian Religious Setting." In *Performance Practice: Ethnomusicological Perspectives*, edited by Gerard Béhague, pp. 222–254. Westport, Conn., 1984. Illustrates the functions of drums and other percussion in an African-related religion, providing detailed information on drums' sacralization and drummers' social status within the group.

Béhague, Gerard. "Percussion and Noise." In *Encyclopedia of Religion*, edited by Mircea Eliade, vol. 11. New York, 1987. A suggestive and succinct survey of uses of percussion and noise across the globe.

Deva, F. Chaitanya. *Musical Instruments of India: Their History and Development.* Calcutta, 1978. A very comprehensive study on Indian organology relating the history of musical instruments to many other relevant sources.

Eliade, Mircea. *Shamanism: Archaic Techniques of Ecstasy*, translated by Willard R. Trask. Princeton, N.J., 1964. The classic text on shamanism; encyclopedic in its discussion and examples.

Grebe, Maria Ester. "El Kultrún mapuche: Un microcosmo simbólico." *Revista musical chilena* 27 (July–December 1973): 3–42. This study presents an excellent model of integration of analysis of belief systems and symbolism as encapsulated in a ritual object.

Marks, Morton. "Uncovering Ritual Structures in Afro-American Music." In *Religious Movements in Contemporary America*, edited by Irving I. Zaretsky and Mark P. Leone, pp. 60–134. Princeton, N.J., 1974. A probing phenomenological and philosophical exploration of "code-switching" in Afro-disaporic rituals, including gospel preaching and samba and carnival dancing.

Needham, Rodney. "Percussion and Transition." *Man* (1967): 606–614. A classic example of an attempt to relate drum sounds (i.e., percussion itself) to trance phenomena in Haitian vodou in strictly physiological terms.

Ortiz, Fernando. *Los instrumentos de la música afrocubana*, vols. 1 and 4. Havana, Cuba, 1952–1954. The most comprehensive study on Afro-Cuban organology.

Pinn, Anthony, ed. *Noise and Spirit: The Religious and Spiritual Sensibilities of Rap Music.* New York and London, 2003. An anthology of articles probing lyrical developments, ritual uses, and percussive effects of hip-hop from a broad range of disciplines.

Rouget, Gilbert. *Music and Trance: A Theory of the Relations between Music and Possession.* Chicago, 1985. A thorough study, drawing on cross-cultural illustrations in the attempted formulation of a theory.

Walker, Sheila. *Ceremonial Spirit Possession in Africa and Afro-America: Forms, Meanings, and Functional Significance for Individuals and Social Groups.* Leiden, 1972. A social anthropological examination of possession phenomena combining insights from ethnography, biopsychological theory, and sociological and cultural perspectives, and referencing materials from Balinese and Zar cult possession as well as West Africa and the African diaspora in the Americas.

JAMES W. PERKINSON (2005)

PERFECTIBILITY.

The etymology of the word *perfect* indicates the centrality of the idea of perfectibility in religion. Derived from the Latin *per facere*, the English word *perfect* implies completion or being thoroughly made. Also the Greek word *teleios* is translated as "perfect," and it lends to the concept the idea of attaining a goal or end (*telos*). Aristotle saw human perfectibility as the capacity to achieve the goal of fulfilling or realizing one's nature. Drawing on these definitions, we can say that perfection as the goal of actualizing the highest human potential plays an important role in religion.

Anders Nygren (1960) has described the dynamic of religion as fourfold. First, religion reveals the eternal, the ultimate reality, which represents perfection in the sense of wholeness, completeness, and integrity. Second, this revelation of a perfect ultimate reality throws into sharp relief the imperfect nature of humanity. The human predicament becomes visible in its separation from the eternally perfect. Third, religion seeks to provide a means of overcoming this separation. Having judged human nature to be radically imperfect when compared with ultimate perfection, religion nevertheless declares that human beings are perfectible. Ways of purification or atonement have been made known and can be followed by the members of the religion. This affirmation of human perfectibility and the provision of means to achieve it stand at the heart of religion. As Nygren writes, "A religion which did not claim to make possible the meeting between the eternal and man, a religion which did not claim to be the bridge over an otherwise impassable gulf, would be a monstrosity" (p. 44). Religious traditions provide for the bridging of this gulf to take place in two opposite directions: either from the human side, by human initiative, or from the divine side. The final characteristic of religion results from this mediation between the human and the divine: religion makes possible the union of the soul with the eternal. Variously phrased in different religious traditions, the perfectibility of human beings is realized by identification or union with the perfection of the ultimate reality. This dynamic of religion as a means to perfection inheres in all religions but may be seen clearly in the biblical traditions of the West and in the Hindu and Buddhist traditions of the East.

PERFECTIBILITY IN BIBLICAL RELIGIONS. For the biblical traditions, God represents perfection, the embodiment of all wisdom and virtue. God possesses transcendental and metaphysical perfection. In the Middle Ages Anselm, archbishop of Canterbury (1093–1109), declared God to be "that than which nothing greater can be conceived." By contrast, human beings are separated from and judged by this divine perfection. When Isaiah saw the Lord seated upon his throne, his response was to say, "Woe is me! For I am lost; I am a man of unclean lips" (*Is.* 6:5). The Hebrew scriptures depict this understanding of God's perfection and man's imperfection in terms of the covenant. God is righteous and desires to establish his covenant with humanity. But, as the primeval history (*Gn.* 1–11) indicates, humanity, beginning with Adam and Eve, was unrighteous and violated the covenantal relationship. Eternally righteous and loving, God reestablishes his covenant with Abraham and the patriarchs. But even the chosen people continually fall short of the demands for perfection, as the Pentateuch shows. Later, the Hebrew prophets declare that only God is holy, and all human beings have turned away from God.

The New Testament and Christianity inherited and developed this understanding of human nature as fallen, sinful, or imperfect. The apostle Paul set the stage for much of later Christian theology when he described human sin as having come "into the world through one man," Adam. Whether taken literally or figuratively, the fall depicts the human condition. And when this condition is compared with the perfection revealed in Christ, Christians perceive the imperfection that is the human predicament.

Both the Hebrew scriptures and the New Testament, however, proclaim that the human predicament can be resolved; the fallen state need not be permanent since human beings are perfectible. In the Torah, God's desire to restore the covenant with the Israelites indicates the possibility of rapprochement with the divine. This covenantal relationship is not something impossible for human beings; as *Deuteronomy* says, "This commandment is not too hard for you, neither is it far off. . . . But the word is near you, it is in your mouth and in your heart, so that you can do it" (30:11–14).

The New Testament attributes to Jesus the straightforward demand, "You, therefore, must be perfect *[te-leioi]* as your heavenly father is perfect" (*Mt.* 5:48). In its context, this demand follows Jesus' reformulation of the major commandments, in which he requires inner purity, radical obedience to the spirit of the Law over and above the letter of the Law. When Jesus summarized all the commandments with the two love commandments (*Mt.* 22:37–40), he also summed up the essence of this demand for perfection. He further described perfection in the same radical fashion in his dialogue with the young man who asked what he must do to gain eternal life (*Mt.* 19:16–21). When Jesus responded that he must keep the commandments, the young man, replying that he had kept them, asked what more he lacked. Jesus answered by placing before him the radical demand of love: "If you would be perfect, go and sell what you own and give to the poor, and you will have treasure in heaven."

Although the New Testament seems clearly to demand perfection as the way out of the human predicament, the Christian tradition has debated at length the meaning of perfection and the question of human perfectibility. Augustine questioned the possibility of human perfection for two reasons. First, only God has perfection in an ontological sense; human beings are far lower in being and power. Second, because of original sin, human beings cannot now even will finite perfection. It is the human predicament that a person cannot on his own fulfill the demands stated in *Matthew* 5:48 (quoted above). The only way that progress can be made toward moral perfection and salvation is by God's grace. Without grace, people experience the situation that Paul described when he said, "I do not do the good I want, but the evil that I do not want" (*Rom.* 7:19). Thus, Augustine held that such perfectibility as humans have results from the prior action of God. God predetermines who shall receive salvation, but this predetermination does not obviate human free will. Salvation is possible for those who receive grace, but full perfection lies beyond this life even for the saints. This view, placing the initiative for perfection on God's side, has its parallel in the Hebrew scriptures and in Jewish tradition also. In his vision, Isaiah received purification from one of the seraphim who touched his mouth with a burning coal (*Is.* 6:6–7).

Pelagius, a fifth-century English lay monk, questioned Augustine's views, however, saying that God would not have commanded anything (i.e., perfection) that was impossible for man to achieve. He was much more sanguine about the human exercise of free will to achieve perfection. This commonsense approach has appealed to many Christians, and as R. N. Flew observes, the history of Christianity—and of the notion of perfectibility—can be told as the swing "between the extremes of Pelagianism and the extremes of dual predestination" (Flew, 1968, p. 99).

Thomas Aquinas agreed theologically with Augustine, although he held out much more hope for human perfectibility. Absolute perfection, he said, belongs to God alone and cannot be possessed by human beings, but a lower perfection is not only possible but incumbent upon them. This "evangelical perfection" involves removing all mortal sin and cultivating the love of God. It was with regard to this kind of perfection that the Catholic church interpreted Jesus' dialogue with the young man (cited above) to imply two standards of virtuous conduct. The first consists in following the commandments, as the young man said he had done. This is the standard for ordinary virtue and salvation. Jesus' response, "If you would be perfect . . . ," sets out a higher standard, a "counsel of perfection" for those who wish to ensure salvation by works of supererogation. The church traditionally interpreted these counsels of perfection to imply the vows of poverty, chastity, and obedience.

Within Christianity, this distinction between spiritual foot soldiers and a spiritual elite provided the constitution for the anchorite and monastic movements. Mystics and ascetics of various kinds have flourished in the Christian tradition alongside mainstream Christianity. The quest of the mystics was the quest for perfection, both in the sense of freedom from sin and, even more important, in the sense of the contemplation of and union with God. Renouncing the body, they frequently employed severe asceticism to subdue the desires of the flesh. John of the Cross, for example, wore knotted ropes under his clothing in his quest for the vision of God.

The Reformation marked a swing of the Christian pendulum away from Pelagianism and back toward predestination. Martin Luther developed a radically theocentric theology in which human salvation as well as perfection depend on the grace of God. For Luther, free will could not be regarded as a means to perfection because human beings, in their fallen state, had only self-will, which was alienated from God. John Calvin also regarded humanity as totally alienated from God and unable to do anything on its own to achieve perfection. Calvin and the other reformers, however, still believed that humanity reflected the image of God and was thus perfectible by God's grace. In this world, however, even with grace, one can do no more than make progress toward perfection, for final perfection can come only in the afterlife or in the Kingdom. Modern Protestant theologians have tended to reaffirm these reformers' views of perfectibility. Reinhold Niebuhr, for example, wrote, "The ethical demands of Jesus are incapable of fulfillment in the present existence of man . . . their final fulfillment is possible only when God transmutes the present chaos of this world into its final unity" (*An Interpretation of Christian Ethics*, 1936, p. 56).

The most significant exception to the Protestant Reformation's reluctance to accept perfectibility was pronounced by John Wesley. Preaching in eighteenth-century England, Wesley placed perfection at the center of his theology. He based Methodism on the idea that all Christians should strive for perfection in this life. By perfection he seems to have meant primarily evangelical or ethical perfection, but, at times, he also described it as an absolute perfection that unites one with the love of God. Wesley was not a Pelagian, however: he believed that perfection came only by grace through faith. But he held that Christians must seek that grace and faith by following the commandments and "taking up the cross daily."

PERFECTIBILITY IN INDIAN RELIGIOUS TRADITIONS. Turning from the West to the East, we find that the great religious traditions of Asia that began in India have affirmed human perfectibility in similiar ways. The Hindu tradition has taught that absolute perfection represents the nature of the ultimate reality. The Hindus who composed the Upaniṣads (c. 800 BCE) reflected on *brahman*, the Absolute, the source of the universe. *Brahman* transcends the world and yet is also immanent in all things in the world. The Upanisadic thinkers described its perfection positively by saying that it is higher than the "great" and higher than even the "unmanifest." Mainly, however, the Upanisadic thinkers described *brahman* by negation, "*neti neti*," saying *brahman* is "not this, not this." Because it transcends the world, it cannot be described by any terms—even positive ones—appropriate to worldly things. Later theistic Hindus, for example the author of the *Bhagavadgītā*, adapted this language to describe deities such as Kṛṣṇa as "unborn, beginningless" and generally splendid to a degree that human beings could not comprehend.

The Buddhists, although they discarded the notion of a deity, took over the idea of a transcendent absolute. This absolute can be seen as either *nirvāṇa*, the blissful state of transcendent enlightenment, or as *dharma*, the truth that both underlies and transcends all existence.

In comparison with this perfect absolute, human beings, according to the Hindu and Buddhist traditions, lack perfection in three ways. First, they lack perfection in wisdom: they do not comprehend the absolute and their relation to it. For Hinduism, especially in the Vedanta tradition, this means that individuals do not know that they too are one with *brahman.* Second, human beings lack perfection in action: because they have a wrong perception of reality, people act in ways that are contrary to the absolute truth. The term *karman* denotes for both the Hindu and Buddhist traditions this idea of action. *Karman*, or action, whether positive or negative, is based on desire and generates a causal force that must come to fruition. Finally, because of *karman* and its consequences, human beings lack perfection in their existence: they are bound up in cycles of *saṃsāra*, or reincarnation. In these cycles they are separated from the absolute reality.

Despite humanity's threefold imperfection, the Indian traditions hold that perfectibility is possible. For the Hindus, human beings are perfectible because, although they may not be aware of it, ultimately they are sparks of the divine or drops of water from the infinite ocean. The human soul (*ātman*) is one with the Absolute (*brahman*). In the Buddhist tradition, human perfectibility stands as the basic presupposition for all of the Buddha's teachings. He told people to "be refuges for themselves" and to "work out your liberation with diligence" (*Dīgha Nikāya* 2.100, 2.120). Those who did so, he proclaimed, could reach their highest human potential just as the *arhats*, or Perfected Ones, had.

To bridge the gulf to perfection, the Hindu and Buddhist traditions set out various paths, some requiring human initiative, others requiring divine action. In the Hindu tradition, human initiative is required to follow the two paths called *karma-mārga,* the path of action, and *jñāna-mārga,* the path of wisdom. *Karma-mārga,* expounded and popularized by the *Bhagavadgītā,* requires that people perform their actions in life without attachment. By so doing, they will free themselves from *karman* and desire. *Jñāna-mārga* represents the classic Hindu path of meditation to achieve the wisdom that overcomes separation from the Absolute. With its counsels of asceticism and solitary meditation, this path resembles the way of the mystics in the biblical traditions. The early Buddhists' path follows this model of meditation.

Buddhism, especially in its South Asian forms, divided the path to perfection or purification into three stages: *śīla,* ethical conduct; *samādhi,* concentration; and *prajñā* (Pali, *paññā*), wisdom. These constitute a gradual path to perfection that a person can pursue over many lifetimes. At the first stage, the Buddhists said, a person must develop his ethical conduct by refraining from killing, stealing, and lying, as well as by abstaining from wrong sexual conduct and from intoxicants. Further, Buddhist ethical conduct, as spelled out in elaborate lists of precepts incumbent upon monks, nuns, and the laity, required "right livelihood": following a way of life that brings no harm to oneself or others. The highest form of ethical conduct, Buddhists taught, consists in controlling not only one's outer actions but also one's inner desires.

The second aspect of the Buddhist path is *samādhi,* trance, or, more properly, concentration. At this stage, the Buddhist, having already controlled his conduct, seeks to control and calm his mind. The mind is focused on "one point" so that it may be trained to sever its attachments to the world. The culmination of *samādhi* comes in the development of the *dhyāna*s (Pali, *jhāna*s), or higher trance states. Finally, the advanced follower reaches the stage of the development of wisdom (*prajñā*) in meditation. Here, the Buddhist achieves perfection by overcoming ignorance and seeing the truth, *dharma.* The attainment of wisdom represents the highest human potential, and Buddhists proclaim that the Buddha and countless *arhat*s have achieved this state, called *nirvāṇa.* Buddhist descriptions of these perfected individuals declare that they overcame such imperfections as egocentricity, desire, sensuality, doubt, pride, and, finally, ignorance.

Despite an emphasis on individual initiative, the Buddhist and Hindu traditions also set forth ways to perfection comparable to the Christian notion of grace. Among the Hindus, the way of *bhakti,* or devotion to a deity, represents an important example of this path to perfection and salvation. In the *Bhagavadgītā,* Kṛṣṇa, the divine embodiment of perfection, declares that if a person will worship and love him, that person will be united with him. For millions of Hindus, devotion constitutes the most accessible and plausible path to perfection.

The Buddhist tradition also knows paths to perfection and liberation that depend on extra-human grace rather than human initiative. The most striking example of this kind of path is found in the Pure Land sect of Mahāyāna Buddhism, with its worship of the Buddha Amida. Buddhist teachers such as Hōnen and Shinran in Japan proclaimed that since in this age the meditative path to purification was too difficult for most people, people must rely on the grace of Amida Buddha. They taught people the *mantra "Namu Amida Butsu,"* which invokes the mercy of Amida, as the only requirement for salvation. As in Christianity, debates have raged within Pure Land Buddhism over the relationship between divine grace and human effort in the process of salvation.

To sum up: human perfectibility represents an ideal central to Asian and Western religious traditions. Perfectibility signifies the possibility of transcending the human predicament of separation from the perfection of the ultimate reality. In religious traditions, perfectibility involves ethical purification but goes beyond that to some degree of absolute perfection in harmony with the ultimate reality. Most Asian and biblical traditions maintain that human beings progress gradually toward the ideal of perfection although some have declared that more rapid or sudden progress is possible. Many Christian theologians have held that perfection can never be fully realized in this life, while Indian thinkers have viewed the process of reincarnation as the context for perfectibility.

SEE ALSO Arhat; Free Will and Predestination; ʿIṣmah; Mahāsiddhas; Pelagianism; Sainthood; Tathāgata; Walāyah; Zhenren.

BIBLIOGRAPHY

Anders Nygren's *Essence of Christianity: Two Essays* (London, 1960) analyzes the structure of religion in a way that illuminates the importance of perfectibility. Two books particularly trace the notion of perfectibility in the West: John Passmore's *The Perfectibility of Man* (London, 1970) examines the history of the idea from the Greeks to modern science, while R. N. Flew's *The Idea of Perfection in Christian Theology* (New York, 1968) restricts its scope to Christian theology. The history of the idea of perfectibility in Asian religions has not been written, but two books provide a comparison of Asian and Western concepts: Shanta Ratnayaka's *Two Ways of Perfection: Christian and Buddhist* (Colombo, 1978) compares Theravāda Buddhist thought with the theology of John Wesley, and the anthology *Sainthood in World Religions,* edited by George D. Bond and Richard Kieckhefer (Berkeley, 1985), surveys notions of the perfected individual in the major religious traditions.

GEORGE D. BOND (1987 AND 2005)

PERFORMANCE AND RITUAL. Theater, dance, drama, dance drama, dance theater, and similar activities known by other terms that vary according to language and historical circumstance are universal. Unless otherwise specified, herein the term *ritual* refers to both secular and sacred rituals. *Performance* is an inclusive term meaning the activities of actors, dancers, musicians, and their spectators and audiences. *Theater, dance,* and *music* are equivalent terms, each referring to a specific genre of performance. Theater emphasizes narrative, dance emphasizes movement, and music emphasizes sound. Performance may also be understood as "restored behavior," the organized re-enactment of mythic or actual events as well as the role-playing of religious, political, professional, familial, and social life.

Performances have occurred among all the world's peoples from the dawn of human cultures. Dancing, singing, wearing masks and costumes; impersonating other people, animals, or supernaturals (or being possessed by these others); acting stories, retelling the hunt; re-presenting alternative histories; rehearsing and preparing special places and times for these presentations—these are all coexistent with the human condition. Concrete archaeological evidence of performances date at least from Paleolithic times. Whether to categorize these first performances as ritual or entertainment is an unanswerable problem. Most likely, these performances functioned as both ritual and entertainment. In fact, all known performances incorporate both ritual and entertainment. Throughout historical time, based on archaeological as well as anthropological evidence, both secular and sacred rituals have usually involved one or more of the performance genres of theater, dance, and music. These ritual performances are not only efficacious, but they are also often beautiful and pleasure-giving: Efficacy, pleasure, and aesthetics are tightly bound to each other in performances.

Furthermore, ritual performances have an economic aspect and impact on the communities enacting them. In premodern, as well as modern and postmodern societies, a sizable proportion of a community's wealth, time, and energy is dedicated to ritual performances. The performers and arrangers of rituals are paid for their services either directly or indirectly. Although some ritual performances take place in simple, even private spaces, many others are pointedly enacted in a grand manner in spectacular venues. Erecting and maintaining these venues is an expensive undertaking. Ritual centers are also frequently commercial centers—the market, the money-changers, and the church have long shared neighborhoods, each benefiting from the presence of the other. Many ritual sites are truly multipurpose locations and constructions, like traditional performing arts centers. One need think only of the uses of such world-renowned edifices and public spaces as the pyramids of Egypt or Mexico, the Borobudur temple complex of Cambodia, or the Mall of Washington, D.C.

PALEOLITHIC PERFORMANCES. Performance and ritual were conjoined at the very earliest periods of human cultures. Dancers, musicians, shamans, actors, painters, and sculptors used the caves of southwest Europe as long ago as thirty thousand years. Because paint and stone endure, whereas gestures, dance steps, and music disappear, the scholarly emphasis has been on the visual arts of these caves. But these places of such difficult access and long-term use were certainly not art museums or silent ceremonial centers. In some caves, footprints are found in a circular pattern indicating dancing. Also surviving are bone and ivory pieces that were probably percussive musical instruments. Caves and rock shelters in every habitable continent attest to the ancient, worldwide, and persistent presence of human ritual performing arts.

These performance spaces—simultaneously theaters, shrines, pilgrimage destinations, and temples, hidden in the earth and illuminated by torch—almost certainly were sites for rituals concerning hunting and fertility, which have long been closely associated. For example, among the hunters of the Kalahari Desert, traditionally when a large animal is taken, a brief ritual entreats the gods to replenish the game. As it is with animals, so it is also with humans. The erotic temple sculptures at Konarak (thirteenth century, located in Orissa, India) are but one example among many of the joining together of fertility/sexuality, dancing, and music. This ancient and abiding association of the performing arts with sexuality is one of the reasons churches and governments have tried to repress performers as the fine line between licit and illicit celebrations of fertility is often crossed. Perhaps the illicit suggests the dangerous, the concealed, the difficult of access. These kinds of performances would focus a group's material resources, employ the skills of its performance, artistic, and religious specialists while also transforming, educating, and entertaining the participants.

The difficulty of access to many of the Paleolithic performance sites indicates a secrecy surrounding the shows. This practice of rationing ritual performance knowledge continues in the twenty-first century. Many performance specialists guard not only what they do but how they do it. Secret techniques are passed on within a family as, for example, in Japanese Nō (an aesthetic form of theater with roots in farming rituals, Buddhism, and Shintō that reached its peak in the fourteenth century) or the lifelong pledges of adherence to the faith, guild, or tribe required before a neophyte is taught the techniques and tricks of the craft or the dances and songs of the community, often associated with initiation rites. This secrecy, which also guarantees a strong line of oral transmission, may partly explain the continuity of basic performance conventions from Paleolithic times to the twenty-first century. But along with this conservatism, ritual performances also bring about, as the anthropologist Victor Turner emphasized, individual and social change—what is conservative procedurally can be radical in terms of consciousness, individual behavior, and social process and structure.

THE EFFICACY–ENTERTAINMENT DYAD. Ritual emphasizes efficacy—getting something done (e.g., a prayer answered, a god propitiated). Entertainment emphasizes the pleasurable and aesthetic qualities of a performance. One can depict the distinction between efficacious (ritual) performances and entertainment (aesthetic) performances as a binary:

Efficacy–Ritual	Entertainment–Aesthetic
Human and nonhuman audience	Human audience
Audience participates	Audience observes
Audience believes	Audience appreciates
Serving the divine	Serving the market
Eternal present	Historical time
Revealed truths	Invented fictions
Transformation possible	Transformation unlikely
Trance possession	Self-awareness
Nonrepresentational roles	Character roles
Virtuosity downplayed	Virtuosity valued
Collective creativity	Individual creativity
Criticism discouraged	Criticism flourishes

However, efficacy and entertainment are not opposites, but rather they are dancing partners along a continuum connecting each of the above qualities. Ritual performances tend toward the efficacy end of the continuum, and aesthetic performances tend toward the entertainment end. But all ritual performances have some aesthetic qualities, and all aesthetic performances have some ritual qualities.

At any given point in time, in every part of the world, and in every culture, people were, and are, making dance, music, and theater. People use performances for a variety of purposes, including ritual, community building, healing, making money, and socializing. These functions operate as dynamic tensions and creative interactions between efficacy and entertainment.

Varieties of Performance. Performance and ritual interrelate in a myriad of combinations: in initiations and shamanic healings and exorcisms; in public sacred and secular ceremonies such as the Mass celebrated in St. Peter's Square (or in any number of humbler parishes), the inauguration of the American president or the installation of a judge, the Hindu temple service, the daily facing to Mecca of Muslims, and the raising and lowering of the national flag in Mexico City's Zocalo; in great cycle plays, parades, and public celebrations of power; and in the daily rituals that individuals perform to maintain the continuity of their individual, family, and professional roles. There are ritual performances, rituals in performances, the ritual frames separating performance reality from the ordinary, and the ritual process underlying how performances are made. There is also the conscious invention of new rituals, a postmodern attempt to sacralize ordinary experience.

The ways performance permeates religious ceremony is obvious. Ritual, as Émile Durkheim (1858–1917) noted in 1915, is a "doing," and therefore inherently performative. Universally, music, dance, storytelling, and dramatic enactment are at the core of observances. The acts of a religion's most important figures, both human and divine, are transformed into shared living deeds by means of performance. The Mass is not only a source of medieval and Renaissance European theater, but also is itself inherently theatrical. To make a pilgrimage, to light candles, to offer food, to sing or chant prayers, to "fall out" in a trance in the aisles of a church, or to be "ridden" by a Yoruba *orisha* are all performances, as are the nearly silent meditations of Buddhist monks seated on cushions in a Kyoto temple. The participatory gestures of different religions—circumambulating (walking around) the Kaʿbah at Mecca, making the sign of the cross, eating matzoh and bitter herb during Passover Seder—are each performances. Particularly among especially African and Asian religions, the performing arts are highly regarded and enthusiastically practiced. Through performance, superhuman beings and forces manifest themselves. In the western hemisphere, where African religions not only thrive on their own but have also fused with Christianity, a vital part of religious services consists of performing: vivid preaching infused with enacted storytelling, individual and choral singing, trance dancing, healing by means of laying on of hands, and individual testimony.

Frequently, worship, theater, dance, music, and healing overlap. Many secular performances include a sacral dimension, and almost all sacred activities involve performing. In India this connection is rooted in the fundamental religious–aesthetic belief that performing is an offering to the gods and that daily reality is itself a *līlā* (performance). While the Hindu god Śiva dances his *Tandava*, the present existence continues—the known world is Śiva's dance. In the Vaishnavite tradition, the incarnations of the god Viṣhu (especially Rāma and Kṛṣṇa) manifest themselves in annual theatrical performances of the Rāma-līlās and Ras-līlā. From ancient times until the middle decades of the twentieth century, *devadāsī*s (servants of God) danced in the temples to entertain the deities. On special annual occasions, gods are carried through the streets where ordinary people admire and worship them. During Durgā Puja celebrating the goddess Durgā's victory over the the buffalo demon Mahiasura, millions of clay Durgās are created by artists and common people alike. After worshiping and parading these *mūrtis* (images of the divine), they are immersed in the sacred Ganges River or in the ocean where they dissolve.

In West Africa and in the African diaspora, the deities—*loas* and *òrìṣà* —possess, or "mount," adepts in the trance dances and dramatic performances of the Gẹlẹdẹ, vodou, Camdomblé, and Umbanda. In Native American cultures, performance and religion are also completely in harmony with each other. Many of these traditions also fuse indigenous and Christian practices. The Yaqui of the Sonoran Desert enact a yearly six-week passion play combining Native American and European ritual performance traditions. Annually in the Jewish tradition, Ḥasidim mask and take to the streets to perform Purim plays (*Purimshpil*), which tell the Bible story of Esther's triumph over Haman. Examples such as these can be drawn from all parts of the world, from every inhabited place. Obviously, ritual masking, dancing, music making, and storytelling by means of theater is a universal phenomenon. Throughout the world, rituals are made from all the varieties of aesthetic performance. Both practically and theoretically, it is not possible to think about ritual except as a category of performance.

Theater flourishes even among traditions that officially reject it. The popular theater of the Middle East (Turkey and Iran, in particular) is rich in a variety of both human and puppet forms. Indonesia, the world's most populous Islamic nation, abounds with masked, live, and puppet theater and dance—many of which are both rituals and entertainments. The *taʿziyah* of the Shīʿī Muslims is an intense religious ritual and passion play that reenacts in bloody detail the martyrdom at Karbala (in Iraq) of Ḥusayn, the grandson of the prophet Muḥammad. So involved are *taʿziyah* audiences that many spectators weep and flail themselves in sympathy with Ḥusayn's fate. Among Muslim mystics, the legendary dancing of the Mevlevis (known in the west as the "whirling dervishes") arose in Anatolia under the inspiration of the poetic-religious philosophy of the thirteenth-century Ṣūfī sage Jalāluddīn Rūmī (known also as Mawlana). The intentions and mood of Mevlevi dancing is something like that of the Shakers, a Christian religious sect of the nineteenth and twentieth centuries. However, by no means are all performances in the Islamic world sacred. In Iran, alongside *taʿziyah* is *ru-huzi*, a slapstick folk theater with connections to both commedia dell'arte and the popular theater of north India. Paradoxically, *wayang kulit*, the leather shadow puppetry of Indonesia, enacts stories from the Sanskrit-Hindu epics *Rāmāyaṇa* and *Mahābhārata* to delighted, devout Muslim audiences. The *dalang*, the puppeteer, is both an entertainer and a shaman, who is sometimes called on to perform for sheer pleasure and sometimes to accompany life-cycle rituals and important public events.

In India itself, the prejudice against theater voiced by the *Manusm˙ti* (second century CE) is more than overcome by the enormously influential *Nāṭya Śāstra* of Bhārata Muni (dates vary from second century BCE to second century CE). If anything, Hinduism is biased in favor of performance. The whole creation is in fact theorized as performance. Sometimes this is expressed in the metaphor of Śiva's *tandava* dance; sometimes it is worked out in the well-developed theory of *māyā-līlā* (terms meaning illusion and play). In *māyā-līlā*, the cosmos is a theatrical event, the play of the gods. In this theory, human performing arts are models of the reality of the cosmos—plays within the larger play of existence. Thus Hinduism enjoys a profusion of dance, music, and theater.

The anti-theatrical prejudice. The situation in the West and in Islam is full of irony. The reasons for this anti-theatrical prejudice are many, varying according to social circumstances and historical period. The codifiers and interpreters of Judaic, Christian, and Islamic traditions and laws often bitterly opposed—and in some instances, still oppose—the visual arts and theater. The theater is especially distrusted because it is mimetic whereas music and dance may not be. Judaism, Christianity, and Islam share a common root in the Old Testament in which it is written that no one should make a graven image of god. In the West, this injunction has been reinforced by a philosophical antipathy to the visual arts and theater that goes back to Plato's *Republic,* composed in Athens in the fifth century BCE at the close of the first great age of Western theater. The Greek philosopher wanted to chase all visual, poetic, and theatrical artists from his ideal republic. Plato's arguments were later elaborated and ingrained into church doctrine by Tertullian (North Africa writer, c. 200 CE) and Augustine of Hippo (354–430). Their ideas, in turn, have operated, sometimes strongly and sometimes more mildly, throughout Western history and, by means of colonialism and globalization, in all areas of the world. Despite their condemnation of the theater, both Plato and Augustine were passionately involved in it. Plato's dialogues are philosophical dramas, and Augustine the saint repented Augustine the avid theatergoer.

Plato argued that the arts are doubly removed from ultimate truth and are mere shadows cast on the wall of the cave of human ignorance. But underneath his philosophical argument, an authoritarian political and ideological program is operating. Plato felt that the arts of representation in general, and theater in particular, are dangerous because they enact alternative realities that may be in conflict with those of the established political and philosophical authorities. Thus, it is not only that the performing arts are dangerous, but also that (and perhaps more important) they are extremely powerful persuaders of opinion and arousers of feelings. The established authorities wish to control these powerful media and employ them for their own uses. What in tribal settings is the preservation of the secrecy of rites becomes in Judaism, Christianity, and Islam—religions with historical and ideological similarities—a dedicated program of maintaining a monopoly of performance techniques.

Western and Islamic religious leaders have not treated the performing arts equally. They have been most uneasy about theater, ambivalent about dance, but friendly to music. Theater is censored because it can be subversive; dance, when not closely managed as among the Shakers, can be (sexually) immoral. Music, being abstract, can most easily suit the ceremony at hand and is generally accepted by Western and Islamic religious authorities.

Still, despite all suspicions and condemnations, Western churches and branches of Islam have used theater and dance. A somewhat parallel example to the *taʿziyah* are the great cycle plays of medieval Europe, which performed a complete history of humankind from the creation and the fall in the Garden of Eden to the flood, the coming of Christ and his crucifixion, on to the Last Judgment. Beginning at dawn and going until dusk, the performances took place in the streets, while richly detailed scenes mounted on wagons proceeded along fixed routes. The enactments were replete with angels, devils, hellmouth, and Eden. Various cycles consisted of a number of individual plays. For example, at York, England, in 1554, fifty-seven plays were put on at twelve to sixteen locations. These extraordinary cycles arose out of a confluence of the Mass, the *Quem quaeritis* trope (a tenth-century Easter drama), and popular entertainments that never died out from Roman times and whose shamanistic origins date back to prehistory. The cycles peaked in the fourteenth through sixteenth centuries. Although most were extinguished by the Renaissance, some remnants persisted, not only in the famed performances that take place every ten years in Oberammergau, Germany, but also among Native American and Hispanic peoples who have fused European traditions with indigenous performance practices.

The Yaqui *Waehma*. The Yaqui of the Sierra Madre and Sonoran Desert of northwestern Mexico and the southwestern United States celebrate a six-week Lenten cycle play that fuses native American and European elements. The *Waehma* begins at Lent and intensifies week by week, climaxing on Good Friday and Holy Saturday. *Waehma* retells the story of Christ's passion in Yaqui terms. It incorporates indigenous performance techniques into the religious theater brought from Europe by the Jesuits in the seventeenth and eighteenth centuries. Much of what the Yaqui of northwestern Mexico and the southwestern United States perform took shape during the century after 1767, when the Jesuits were withdrawn from the New World.

Waehma consists of many episodes and observances enacted over the six-week span from Lent to Easter. The story focuses on the actions of masked figures called *Chapayekam* who join the Soldiers of Rome—a group of up to fifty men dressed in black—in the pursuit and crucifixion of Jesus. The *Chapayekam* wear helmet masks similar to those of the Zuni and other tribal peoples of the Sonoran Desert and adjoining areas. Their ritual practices, which includes farce and parody, are similar to those of other Native American tribal nations. On Good Friday, a large group of wailing women, including the Marys, follow Jesus—represented by an eighteen-inch figure—around the stations of the cross, which the Yaqui call the *Konti Vo'o*. At the eleventh cross, the symbolic Christ is tied to a cross as nails are driven into the figure's "flesh." The Christ figure is then taken into the church, which is occupied by the *Chapayekam* and the Soldiers of Rome. Later that night, Jesus is resurrected and the church is liberated. The *Chapayekam* and the Soldiers of Rome are infuriated. They set out to recover Jesus and recapture the church. On Holy Saturday morning the climatic battle takes place that pits the *Chapayekam* and the Soldiers of Rome against the forces of good represented by sacred Deer and *Pascola* (ritual clowns) dancers, *Matachin* dancers (a dance society of men and boys), and "little angels" (i.e., Yaqui children armed with cottonwood switches). The Deer and *Pascolas* are unique to the Yaqui and allied native peoples; the *Matachins* derive from Europe.

Waehma takes place everywhere in a Yaqui town: in the church, in the plaza, in private households, and along the *Konti Vo'o*. Although the *Chapayekam* are successful in capturing and killing Jesus, they are unable to impose their rule permanently on the church or the people. On Holy Saturday morning, the *Chapayekam* and the Soldiers of Rome attempt to recapture Jesus, whose resurrected figure has been placed on the altar. Three times they storm the church. From inside the church the little angels rush forward to beat the attackers with their sticks. Close by the Deer and the *Matachins* dance while the *Pascolas* throw flower petals on the attackers. The flowers, which are sacred to the Yaqui, represent both the blood of Jesus and the sacred *huya aniya*, the desert "flower world" of the Yaqui. Each time the *Chapayekam* and the Soldiers of Rome are driven back they are further weakened by the power of the flowers, the dancing, and the vigorous clanging of the church bell. The defense of the Yaqui village is a complete cacophony-synthesis of Native American and European cultures. Finally defeated, the *Chapayekam* throw off their masks, and the *Chapayekam* and the Soldiers of Rome are transformed, liberated themselves from the awesome holy work they have dedicated themselves to perform annually. After casting their masks on the pyre, the Yaqui men rush back into the church to kneel in thanks before the altar. At this point, the year's greatest fiesta commences, continuing long into Saturday night. The Deer, *Pascolas*, and *Matachins* dance; other native dances and entertainments are also featured. The people eat their fill. Not until Easter Sunday morning Mass does an official representative of the Roman Catholic Church appear.

Carnivals. Like *Waehma*, carnivals mark the Easter season. But unlike *Waehma*, carnivals do not enact the passion or the resurrection directly. They collapse ritual time, as they simultaneously struggle against Lenten prohibitions and predict Easter's life-returning fertility. To some degree, carnivals may be classified as antireligious religious performances, because they could not exist without being in oppositional reference to religious and civil authorities. But, at the same time, there is much going on that is officially sanctioned, well-organized, and tourist-friendly.

Carnivals are characterized by an exuberant outburst of public and private masking, partying, dancing, parading, music making, and drinking. Taking over the streets during the days before Lent, carnivals are a tumultuous acting out of permitted festivity, inebriation, and lewdness that, traditionally, yield to a season of sorrow ultimately redeemed by the resurrection. Carnivals are celebrated primarily in Europe and the Western Hemisphere, but their performance practices in the New World and West Indian diasporic communities include elements from Africa, Asia, and Native America. Taken as a whole, the carnival complex is a ritual performance of great magnitude. Days or weeks are spent celebrating as the festivities take over entire cities. In Trinidad, after months of preparations in the neighborhoods, a large stadium is filled for several nights to witness fierce competitions that award prizes for the best masks, calypsos, and steel-drum bands.

Carnivals have multiple roots, depending on the specific carnival. European carnivals combine Roman, pagan, and Christian elements; Western Hemispheric carnivals such as those in Trinidad, Rio de Janeiro, and New Orleans (i.e., Mardi Gras) fuse African performance traditions with European and, to a lesser degree, Native American and Asian. The Trinidad carnival is also widely celebrated by members of the West Indian diaspora in New York, Toronto, London, and elsewhere. Because these diasporic carnivals are celebrated in the summer, detached from the church calendar, can they still be considered ritual performances? They do not signal the onset of Lent, but in every other quality they express the meanings of carnival. In fact, the diasporic carnivals prove the non- or pre-Christian core of this kind of celebration: a rebellion against authority resulting in a temporary triumph of excess.

The Trinidad Carnival emerged in the nineteenth century from the celebrations of liberated African slaves embodying African ways and values and the carnival traditions of Catholic Europe as carried to the Caribbean by Spanish and French planters and slave owners. Ironically, the Trinidad Carnival is a celebration of former slaves and former masters enjoying—and to some degree satirizing—each other's cultural heritages. As the Trinidad Carnival continues to develop in the twenty-first century, its cultural complexity multiplies to include—and rebroadcast to the world-at-large—musical and visual performance languages that are of an Afro-Caribbean, Euro-Caribbean, South Asian, and global nature.

THE *RĀMA-LĪLĀ* OF RAMNAGAR. A rich example of the fusion of ritual and theater is the *Rāma-līlā* of Ramnagar, Uttar Pradesh, India. Thousands of *Rāma-līlās* are performed annually throughout the Hindi language belt of north India. But the Ramnagar *Rāma-līlā*, sponsored and personally overseen by the Maharaja of Banaras, is recognized by Indians to be in a class by itself because of its scale, its deeply devotional qualities, and the theatrical detail of its staging, singing, and acting. *Rāma-līlās,* in some ways like the *Waehma,* are cycle plays dramatizing the life and acts of Rāma, the seventh incarnation of Viṣṇu, as related first in Valmiki's Sanskrit epic, the *Rāmāyaṇa,* and in Tulasidas' sixteenth-century Hindi redaction, the *Ramcaritmanas.* Both the Valmiki and the Tulasidas poems are regarded as sacred. During the Ramnagar *Rāma-līlā* the entire *Ramcaritmanas* is chanted by a chorus of twelve Brahmin priests. This chanting alternates during the performance with *samvads,* spoken dialogue by a cast of more than fifty actors, all Brahmin men. The principal roles of Rāma, his queen Sītā, and his brothers Bharat, Lakshman, and Shatrughna are all played by boys whose voices have not yet changed. All five of these boys are regarded as *swarups,* the actual living form of the gods they enact. However, there is no doubt that Rāma and Sītā are the main gods being worshiped during *Rāma-līlā.* Often persons attending the *Rāma-līlā* press the feet of Rāma and Sītā and gratefully receive blessed lotus blossoms and tulasi leaves from them.

Most *Rāma-līlās* are performed over a span of six to twenty-one daily episodes, each called a *līlā* (the play or sport of the gods) staged in simple locations within a local neighborhood. The Ramnagar *Rāma-līlā* is unique because it extends for thirty-one episodes that are meticulously staged in full-scale environments deployed over many square miles and incorporating all the town of Ramnagar. On big days—such as when Rāma wins Sītā's hand in marriage by lifting and then breaking Śiva's bow, or when Rāma slays his principle antagonist (the ten-headed demon king Rāvaṇa)—the crowds at Ramnagar *Rāma-līlā* swell to eighty thousand. These spectators include a broad cross-section of the regional population ranging from farmers, urban laborers, storekeepers, and professionals to itinerant *sādhus* (holy men) devoted to Rāma and Sītā. The multitudes come for *darshan* of the *swarups,* a ritually beneficial view of the gods-on-earth. They also attend to watch a drama and enjoy the *mela* (fair) that arises next to the *Rāma-līlā* sites. At the *mela,* people enjoy the many snack stands, games, and a wide variety of items for sale.

The Ramnagar *Rāma-līlā*'s principal spectator is the Māharājā of Banaras, who oversees the ritual drama while atop his royal elephant, riding in a black carriage drawn by a pair of horses, or from his vintage Cadillac. The Māharājā attends all but three of the episodes. He does not watch the argument between King Dasaratha and Queen Kaikeyi that leads to Rāma's exile, the kidnapping of Sītā, or the climax of the story when Rāma slays the demon king Rāvaṇa. Of these absences, Māharājā Vibhuti Narain Singh (1927–2000) said, "It is only a rule, not a tradition, so I sometimes break the rule" (Schechner, 1985, 193). His son and successor, Ananda Narain Singh, has continued this tradition. Regarded by the people of Varanasi as an incarnation of Śiva, the Maharaja enacts one principle Hindu deity worshiping another. Although the Maharaja's role is found neither in the *Rāmāyaṇa* nor the *Ramcaritmanas,* during the final several episodes, he actively participates in the *Rāma-līlā* as a performer. He enters the drama as a king and god inviting Rāma, his queen Sītā, and his brothers Bharat, Lakshman, and Shatrughna to a feast in the inner courtyard of the Fort, an enormous, if somewhat rundown, palace constructed in the eighteenth and nineteenth centuries along the banks of the sacred Ganges (Gangā) River. The honor the Māharājā shows Rāma, Sītā, and the other deities is reciprocated by the presence of the gods in the Fort. Once the *Rāma-līlā* is over, the Maharaja receives the boys playing the *swarups* and pays them each a sum of rupees—thereby reestablishing the ordinary social relationship between king and subjects.

Particular *Rāma-līlā* environments are given special care. Ayodhya, Rāma's birthplace, is a large walled courtyard right next to the Fort. Janakpur, Sītā's birthplace, includes two temples sacred to the goddess and a splendid garden. The *kshir sagar,* the endless ocean of milk where Viṣṇu sleeps atop Sesha, the thousand-headed cobra, is a very large pool that is more than one-thousand feet on each side and faces a three-hundred-year-old Durga temple that predates Ramnagar *Rāma-līlā.* Chitrakut, Rāma, Sītā, and Lakshman's first stop during their twelve-year exile is an enormous butterfly tent erected next to the *kshir sagar.* A small hill marks Panchavati, where Sītā is kidnapped by Rāvaṇa. The bridge from Ramesvaram, on the south Indian coast, to Lanka, hundreds of miles away, is, paradoxically, a few planks across less than ten feet of shallow, murky water. Lanka itself is a huge field triangulated by Mount Meru (where Rāma's army, led by Hanuman, the monkey god, set up headquarters), the Ashoka Garden where Sītā is held prisoner, and Rāvaṇa's earthen fort. In short, the *Rāma-līlā* environments are a large-scale model of mythic India, from the Himalayan north to the Gangetic plains, on through the forests of central India and on to the south and what has become the country of Sri Lanka. Throughout the thirty-one days, spectators follow the action from place to place. For many, attending *Rāma-līlā* is to take part in a pilgrimage not only to the holy city of Kashi (Vārāṇasī) but also to all the places that *Rāma-līlā* represents. The logic is unassailable: If the *swarups* are the actual gods-on-earth for a month, then the ground they transverse is really that of India and Lanka.

Rāma-līlā of Ramnagar enacts a complexly interactive relationship among ritual, theater, religion, and politics. In the late eighteenth century, the seat of the Raja of Banaras (not made a Māharājā until after the Indian uprising of 1857) was moved by the British across the Ganges River out of the city to Ramnagar. The move was a militarily and politically strategic. The fort was built at a point where troops could prevent an attack from the south by Mughal forces. By the third decade of the nineteenth century, the Ramnagar *Rāma-līlā* was already a grand spectacle. As the century advanced, the annual enactment of the religious cycle drama was a concrete example of a growing Hindu nationalism and pride expressed directly against the Muslim Mughal potentates and, indirectly, against the Māharājā's British sponsors. During the struggle for Indian independence, Rāma was held up by Mohandas Gandhi (1869–1948) as an example of an effective and just indigenous ruler—a king who would unite Hindus and Muslims against the British colonial force. Religion was brought into the struggle especially by Gandhi, who often framed his campaigns in religious terms. *Rāma-līlā* was a very powerful instance of the conflation of religion, politics, and theater.

Traditionally, in *Rāma-līlā* of Ramnagar, Muslims operate behind the scenes constructing all of the large effigies of gods and demons, managing the fireworks and the flares that illuminate the Hindu temple service that concludes each night's *līlā,* and caring for the elephants used by the Māharājā and his guests. Some Muslims attend the *Rāma-līlā,* but they do not make their presence publicly known. From the 1990s onward, *Rāma-līlā* of Ramnagar has been caught up in Hindu–Muslim tensions despite the Māharājā's wish to keep *Rāma-līlā* purely devotional-theatrical. These tensions flared in 1992 when Hindu militants destroyed the 1528 Babri Mosque in Ayodhya, Rāma's birthplace, vowing to erect a temple to Rāma in its place (archaeological evidence indicates that there once was a temple at this site). The destruction of the mosque ignited Hindu–Muslim hostilities that claimed more than two thousand lives—with deadly tensions remaining high into the twenty-first century. Many of the *sādhus* attending Ramnagar *Rāma-līlā* spend the rest of the year in Ayodhya. Their presence at *Rāma-līlā*—as well as increasing Hindutva activities (the call for a Hindu religious state in India)—injected a nationalist edge into the *Rāma-līlā.*

Other Religious Cycle Plays. The medieval European plays, the Yaqui *Waehma,* and Ramnagar *Rāma-līlā* are part of an historical and contemporary cluster of such works. In Irian Barat (Indonesian New Guinea) until the 1930s, the *Elema hevehe* cycle of dances, festivities, and ritual observances sometimes took more than thirty years to enact and complete. An extreme extension of time and space—a vast temporal and spatial encirclement—is characteristic of ritual cycles. In the late twentieth century, artists began to invent ritual cycles. Anna Halprin started making new rituals in the 1960s. Her *Planetary Dance,* first performed in 1981, is an annual ritual for global peace and healing, "moving in a wave around the globe, going west with the sun" (Halprin, 1995, 226). In 2004, hundreds of people in thirty-six countries on six continents performed the circle dance of walking, running, and standing still in relation to the four cardinal directions. Since the late 1950s the visual artist Christo has been wrapping buildings, trees, and small islands in cloth, erecting cloth gates, giant umbrellas, and miles-long fences in an ongoing project he calls "public art." Halprin and Christo are but two examples in a widespread practice outside of organized religion of ritualizing and sacralizing. Their works are contemporary versions of cathedrals and ritual dramas.

Such performances are not mimetic: They symbolize and actualize simultaneously. In doing so they mesh the ordinary lives of the performers with the extraordinary activities of culture heroes. Far from being a "leisure activity"—as much modern theater and dance is—the medieval Christian cycles, the *Waehma,* the *Rāma-līlā,* the *Hevehe* cycle, and Halprin's and Christo's work are obligatory as well as celebratory. They demand a big share of a community's attention, energy, and wealth. Such a price is paid because these performances are the dynamic constructions of reality by means of which a whole community knows itself.

Ritual Frames. All performances, sacred and secular, are ritually framed. Frames mark and modulate transformations of time, space, and consciousness, signaling that a performance is about to begin or that a return to the ordinary is imminent. Sometimes frames are so conventional they are all but forgotten: the dimming of houselights, the lighting of candles, the final applause, the sprinkling of holy water. There is a continuum between religious frames and aesthetic ones, with many intermediate cases.

In the *Ẹ̀fẹ̀-Gẹ̀lẹ̀dẹ́* performances of the Yoruba, Ogbagba (The Divine Mediator) and Arabi Ajigbale (The Sweeper) always appear first, clearing the way for the dances and ceremonies that will follow. The closing dance brings forward a special mask and costume representing the community's deified ancestress. Her dancing brings blessings and concludes the festival. These opening and closing figures effect a transition from ordinary daily life to the intense spiritual world of the festival and back again to the ordinary.

In the *kathakali* of India, even when danced as a tourist entertainment, performances begin by the lighting of the *kalivilakku*, a bronze oil lamp identical to that used in Hindu temple services. The *kalivilakku* burns throughout the performance, reminding all that *kathakali* is an offering to the gods, who are the first and most important spectators. Every performance closes with the *dhanasi*, a short prayer-dance. *Kathakali* developed in the seventeenth century from antecedents reaching back to the Sanskrit theater of the fifth to tenth centuries. One form of Sanskrit theater, *kutiyattam*, is still performed in temples. *Kathakali's* other roots are the martial art *kalarippayattu* and the *teyyam* masked folk ritual. Most of a *kathakali* performance, which can last from less than an hour at a tourist hotel to all night in a Kerala village, is made of stories taken from the Sanskrit-Hindu epics, *Rāmāyaṇa* and *Mahābhārata*, or from the Purāṇas, collections of stories and myths. During a *kathakali* performance in a village, as in *Rāma-līlā*, people commonly rise with hands clasped in front of them in the devotional pose, worshipfully honoring the performer playing a god as if the performer were the god incarnate. Thus, the theater and the temple meet.

The ritual frames of Japanese Nō are very strong, combining religious and aesthetic qualities. As Nō developed in the fourteenth and fifteenth centuries, it drew on shamanism, Shintō, Buddhism, and *sarugaku*, a popular entertainment featuring magic, songs, and dances. All these sources continue to operate in the twenty-first century. Every program alternates the solemn Nō plays with the comic *kyogen* plays. There are ritualized procedures for entering and leaving the stage. Ghosts and spirits are summoned by the sound of the performers' stamping feet, which is amplified by large earthen jugs placed beneath the polished wooden stage floor. The action of many Nō plays is an exorcism. Nō theater architecture retains many qualities of a Shinto shrine.

Entering the Nō stage is a two-part process. In the *kagami no ma* (mirror room) the *shite* (doer) gazes at himself in the mirror. He simultaneously merges with his mask and distances himself from it. The *shite* seeks an incomplete transformation, a dialectical tension between the power of the mask and his skills as an actor. But even when the *shite* achieves a proper state of mind, he cannot enter the stage directly. He must first cross the *hashigakari* (literally, suspension bridge) that links the mirror room to the stage. When the play is over, the *shite* returns to the mirror room via the *hashigakari*, removes his mask, and carefully studies it before putting it away. This double framing (in the mirror room and on the *hashigakari*) reminds performers and spectators alike of the aesthetic ritual quality of Nō.

How different are the ritual frames of *Ẹ̀fẹ̀-Gẹ̀lẹ̀dẹ́, kathakali*, Nō and other ritual theaters from what modern actors do? Konstantin Stanislavsky, the most influential of European actor trainers, instructed actors to prepare for their first entrance on the stage while still at home. A performance day ought to be uncluttered. When the actors arrive at the theater, there is to be no gossip but a quiet intensity combined with specific relaxation and concentration exercises. The actors put aside their ordinary lives and focus on the life they will call into existence on stage. As with the *shite* in the mirror room, the Stanislavsky-trained actor concentrates on the being into which he or she is transforming. These secular rituals help modern actors separate from ordinary life and successfully enact their roles.

SHAMANIC AND TRANCE PERFORMANCE. Shamans cure, prophesy, exorcise, and entertain by means of trance performance, storytelling, dancing, singing, magic, masks, and costumes. The word *shaman* is of Tungus (Siberian) origin, but shamanism is a phenomenon that occurs all over the world. The similarities of the shamanism of Eurasia, South Asia, Southeast Asia, and the Americas is not coincidental. The migrations from Siberia to the Western Hemisphere and the links between India, Southeast Asia, Tibet, China, Korea, and Japan are demonstrable by means of archaeology, historical records, and similarities in performance practices, and shamanic elements are visible in ancient Greek rituals. The exact work of any given shaman will vary from society to society, for shamans enact and retain a community's knowledge. They are able to separate their souls from their bodies and enlist animal or spirit helpers as they journey to nonhuman worlds in pursuit of demons or in search of cures. The shamanic rituals of the Kwakiutl, Bella Bella, and Haida, who live along the Gulf of Alaska were once complex dance theater performances employing transformation masks—at the climax of a performance, the outer mask sprang open revealing an interior mask. The recently revived *hamatsa* performance uses transformation masks, and participants and spectators are entertained as well as ritually cleansed.

Often, shamans perform in trance, and they may even induce trance in their patients and spectators. But what is trance? In trance, performers are possessed by nonhuman beings—gods, spirits, animals, or objects. Trance performers enact actions not of their own devising. These actions belong to specific cultural performance texts—specific gestures, dance steps, utterances, songs, and whole ritual patterns. Trance occurs not only in shamanism but in a variety of other performative circumstances such as "falling out" in African American churches, being possessed by the *loa* of Haitian vodou or the *orixa* of Brazilian Umbanda. Hypnotic trance has been used both medically and as entertainment. The experience of being in trance varies. In Bali, where people can be possessed by ordinary things such as brooms, pot lids, and potatoes as well as by gods and demons, trancers may remember what they do while in trance, whereas in other cultures the entranced have no idea of what they have done.

Neurologically, the experience of trance is how one feels when both hemispheres (frontal lobes) of the brain are simultaneously stimulated. In brief, the left lobe guides logical thought and speech; the right lobe guides spacial and tonal perceptions. Stimulating the right lobe loosens the ego, dissolving boundaries between the self and others; stimulating the left energizes a person. By various means, including repetitive rhythmic drumming and dancing, the ingestion of drugs, and sleep and food deprivation, both hemispheres are stimulated. Usually, one or the other hemisphere is dominant—a person cannot ordinarily be tranquil and excited at the same time. But when one side of the brain is fully in play, it "rebounds," bringing the other side into play also. When this occurs—as it can in trance, sexual orgasm, and Zen mediation—a person is both excited and released simultaneously. At the height of maximum bi-hemispheric arousal, people are weightless, egoless, outside their bodies, or "oceanic"—at one with the universe or with god. Extreme trance experience may be the specialty of shamans and other performance experts, but light trance is common, occurring during such activities as social dancing, marching, cheering at a sports match, or being taken over by the crowd. This experience is what Victor Turner termed "spontaneous *communitas*" (see Turner, 1969, pp. 96, 125–65).

Animal Rituals, Human Rituals. The evolutionary source of human ritual in animal behavior is demonstrable. This has become increasingly clear since 1914, when Julian Huxley noted that in the course of phylogeny certain animal movement patterns lose their specific function and become symbolic. To the ethologists who came after Huxley, a ritual is a behavior sequence genetically transformed over the course of evolutionary time. Behavior is rearranged, condensed, sped up or slowed down; functions change so that, for example, threat behavior becomes part of a "mating dance." In animal ritual, as in human ritual, movements are exaggerated or simplified, becoming rhythmical and repetitive, often freezing into postures. In animals, along with behavioral changes, conspicuous body structures develop, such as a peacock's feathers or a moose's antlers. Among humans, ornate costumes, masks, architectural structures, and other means are used to make ritual special. Despite these similarities and the clear evolutionary development of ritualized behavior, analogies between animal behavior and human rituals must be put forward cautiously. The "dances" of bees are not dances in the human sense. Where everything is genetically determined, there is no art.

Rituals in nonhuman animals do not occur haphazardly. They improve communication in situations that are contested and dangerous, such as issues of territory, hierarchy, mating, and access to food. Human ritual performances, which develop many of their particular details individually and socially rather than genetically, also cluster around troublesome life and social crises, such as birth, puberty, marriage, sickness, healing, and death; war; hierarchy; hunting, fertility, and food; the seasonal cycle of planting, harvest, and fallow; rain and drought; and the predictability or unpredictability of natural disasters and upheavals. Animal ritual is nonideological, operating through pure action. Human rituals, although also actions, are totally infused with thought and ideology. At the same time, human rituals share with animal rituals qualities of repetition, exaggeration, condensation, simplification, and spectacle. Human ritual performances enact the plea, explicit or implicit, for success in living and dying. Such universal practices as singing, dancing, marching, mass displays, flag waving, masking, cheering, clapping, stamping, sharing of sacred foods, offering sacrifices actually or symbolically, processions, incense burning, and bell ringing may be individually or socially constructed and inflected while also being ethologically based.

Ethological and neurological theories answer some very important questions. They help explain not only the extraordinary persistence of performance conventions and the need for ritual frames to manage such powerful forces, but also the apparently identical experiences of performer, audience, and participant down through many epochs and across cultures, genres, ideologies, and religious systems. The universality of trance—whether associated with dancing, singing, speaking in tongues, shamanizing, meditation, or hypnosis, and whether individual or collective—is at least partly explained by the neurological spillover theory.

What the ethological and neurological theories cannot explain are the unique, creative qualities of ritual performance. For ritual is not just a conservator of evolutionary behavior and thought, it is also a generator of new images, ideas, and practices. Victor Turner thought that if ritual had a biogenetic foundation, then while meaning is passed on culturally by means of learning, the creative processes that generate new cultural knowledge result from a coadaptation of genetic and cultural information.

Ritual Process and Liminality. Victor Turner was among the first to emphasize the generative, creative, and antistructural qualities of ritual by uncovering deep links among ritual, theatrical, and social processes. Developing the ideas put forward by Arnold van Gennep in *The Rites of Passage* (1909), Turner explored the three phases of the ritual process: separation, transition or liminal, and reincorporation. Turner was especially interested in the liminal phase in which people temporarily inhabit a realm "betwixt and between" personal and social categories (Turner, 1967, pp. 93–111; 1969, pp. 94–130) Liminal space-times are where and when known social structures are dissolved or put aside and new identities emerge that allow for the performance of new social structures and identities. During liminality, communities, artists, and even individuals liberate their thoughts, feelings, and creativity from ordinary social constraints. Van Gennep felt that rituals integrate individuals into a set social order, whereas Turner explored ritual as a motor for profound individual and community change.

Two seemingly contradictory results are achieved during the liminal phase of a ritual: individuals are liberated from prior constraints on creativity and socially deviant behaviors, and, when this period of license ends, new statuses or norms are established or older ones are reestablished. This describes perfectly the actions and importance of the *Chapayekam* among the Yaqui. Turner saw this process as channeling the living magma upwelling in all human societies: a periodic, temporary, molten creativity. It is also analogous to the training, workshop, and rehearsal process of many if not all performance genres. Through this process all the "givens" or "ready-mades"—such as accepted texts, accepted ways of using the body, and accepted feelings—are deconstructed or broken down into malleable bits of behavior, feeling, thought, and text. These bits are later reconstructed into a new order: the performance.

In traditional genres such as *kathakali*, Nō, or ballet, neophytes begin training early in life. Training involves learning new ways of speaking, gesturing, and moving, and maybe even new ways of thinking and feeling—new for the trainee, that is, but traditional for the genre. An important feature of *kathakali* training is the deep massage that actually reorients muscles and bones to the extreme turn-out and arched back necessary to perform *kathakali*. A no less radical reconstruction of the body is required for ballet. As in initiation rites, the mind and body are made ready to be written on in the language of the form being learned. Training enables the performer to "speak" Nō, *kathakali*, or ballet as he or she is incorporated into the tradition, no longer a neophyte but an initiated member.

Turner went far beyond van Gennep in suggesting that the rites of tribal, agrarian, and traditional societies are analogous to the artworks and leisure activities of industrial and postindustrial societies. These activities Turner called "liminoid" (Turner, 1982, 20–60). Liminal rites are collective and obligatory; liminoid activities are individualized and voluntary. Thus, the workshops of experimental theater and dance are liminoid means of psychophysical retraining. Whereas in liminal rites traditional behavior is inscribed, in liminoid arts new behaviors are created. But on close inspection of liminoid arts or leisure activities, most of what appears to be new or original consists of ready-mades and already-behaved behaviors, arranged in new combinations or presented in new contexts. Thus, although the avant-garde always appears to be advancing, it is in fact most often rearranging what already exists. Taking the view from 1875 to the twenty-first century, it is clear that elements of earlier avant-garde movements are recycled. And taking the very long view—from Paleolithic times to the twenty-first century—art does not advance at all in the ways science and technology do. Arts develop in cyclically, rather than linearly, progressive ways.

SOCIAL DRAMA. Victor Turner developed his theory of liminality into that of social drama, a four-phase sequence of breach, crisis, redress, and reintegration (or schism). A breach is an underlying fault in social life (e.g., the Montague–Capulet feud in *Romeo and Juliet*; the mix of hatred, fear, and envy that many in the world feel for the United States); a crisis is a precipitating event that must be dealt with (e.g., Romeo and Juliet falling in love; the September 11, 2001, attack on the United States); the redress is what is done to resolve the crisis (e.g., the lovers flight to Mantua; the American "War on Terrorism"); and the reintegration or schism are the two outcomes of a social drama (e.g., "O brother Montague, give me thy hand;" an unending war). The ritual process and liminality operate during the redress, the third phase of a social drama. Actions taken during the redress are often symbolic and performative—demonstrations or symbolic displays. They are what they are, but they are also more than what they are. As Turner noted, such actions are performed in the cultural subjunctive mood, in the "as if," the "might be," and the "ought to be." Even the bombing of a city is done to "show something" to the inhabitants and to the onlookers—both allies and enemies—who are watching. On a more peaceful level, crises are often explored and resolved by means of ritual performances of both religious and secular kinds.

If universality is the advantage of Turner's theories, reductivism is their weakness. Turner's social drama theory is tethered to Western aesthetics' appetite for conflict, crisis, and resolution. Birth, puberty, marriage, gaining power and losing it, familial strife, sickness, death, natural disasters, and the like, are all, of course, universal events. But the ritual performances used to cope with, mark, or celebrate these events vary widely from culture to culture. What in the West is often perceived of as a crisis (e.g., a sickness or death) may to a Buddhist sensibility be an expected part of the life process. The social drama and liminality models are valuable; but they are not universally applicable.

INVENTING RITUALS. Influenced by the earlier path-breaking writings of James G. Frazer, the twentieth-century Cambridge anthropologists Gilbert Murray, Jane Ellen Harrison, and Francis Cornford and allied scholars of the ancient Mediterranean and Middle East asserted that Greek theater and, by inference, all theater came from ritual. The line of the Cambridge theory was developed further by propounders of the theory of archetypes of C. G. Jung and Joseph Campbell. Susanne K. Langer and Northrop Frye took the Cambridge thesis in a parallel direction. The underlying idea is that tragedy and comedy show evidence of an earlier violent sacrificial ritual of struggle, sacrifice, dismemberment, reassembling of the body, and resurrection. In other words, Christ's Divine Comedy. This theory of an ur-ritual (i.e., the conquest of life over death) underlying tragedy and comedy is attractively comprehensive. But, if true at all, the Cambridge theory is regional rather than universal. Over time, the theory has never been proved, and no actual ur-ritual has been discovered.

The Cambridge theory marches on in the generally held belief that ritual (some ritual, any ritual) is the first genre of human performance, that from ritual all subsequent forms have evolved. However, demonstrably the opposite is also true. New rituals are continuously being invented, and the source of these new rituals can be theater, dance, or music—the aesthetic genres whose function is to entertain. Other new rituals are devised for political reasons. For centuries, rulers, judges, and governments have invented rituals such as saluting the flag, singing anthems, and swearing oaths to reinforce a given order of society. Associations such as the Masons, Kiwanis, Lions, Elks, and sororities and fraternities also employ invented rituals during initiations and ceremonies. Corporations display emblems, enunciate slogans, enforce uniform or other dress codes, and require workers to perform company rituals. Since at least the 1960s, many artists, mostly Western but also African and Asian, have invented rituals that are practiced by large numbers of people.

These artists work with both professional performers and with amateurs, and they offer both public performances and workshops. The venues for these events and encounters vary: rooms in which participants can work in seclusion, beaches, forests, city streets, department stores, theaters, art galleries, churches, synagogues, and many other places. Sometimes artists transform rituals from Asia, Europe, Native America, Australia, Micronesia, and Africa, drawing on ethological and anthropological research. Sometimes they compose new movements, songs, and spoken or sung texts. They try to forge links between the personal and the archetypal. Their work is linked to that of New Age shamanic and therapeutic practices. Frequently, their works and techniques are hybrids of new and traditional materials and techniques.

Jerzy Grotowski (1933–1999) was an enormously influential inventor of theatrical rituals. From 1959 to 1967 he propagated his ideas of the "holy actor"—a rigorously trained artist who offers his body as a symbolic public sacrifice, thereby performing "secular holiness." Grotowski's theatre productions of the 1950s and early 1960s—especially *The Constant Prince*, *Akropolis*, and *Apocalypsis cum Figuris*—were regarded both as artworks and as ritual performances. In his later work, Grotowski explored a direct relationship between performers and audiences. There was no play performed, just sheer ritualized interactions. Next, Grotowski tried to identify core "objective" gestures, movements, chants, and songs that were the distilled essence of ritual performance. He researched the rituals and spiritual practices of China, India, Latin America, the Caribbean, and ancient Egypt as well as western psychology, anthropology, and the history of religion. Grotowski and his small group of followers explored trance, vodou, the Baul singing of Bengal, Balinese dance, and tai chi. He was also influenced by the American human potential movement. Some of the actions Grotowski used included extended silent vigils, improvised chanting and movement, running in total darkness through the woods, and the passing of fire from person to person. Grotowski sought spontaneous *communitas* detached from any specific religious practice. In his final phase, during the 1990s, with a few adherents (primarily Thomas Richards), Grotowski developed a ritual performance work titled simply *Action,* which was performed mostly by one man, "Doer." This work, which serves as a living ritual and is always evolving, has continued to be presented by Richards and those he teaches into the twenty-first century.

Anna Halprin's example is different from Grotowski's but parallel in its basic direction. As noted earlier, Halprin has been inventing rituals since the 1960s. Her goal is initiatory transformation and healing—to change those who participate in her dances. Halprin believes that dance can be more than entertainment—it can be transformative ritual. The titles of some of Halprin's works from the 1960s and 1970s clearly show her intention: *Ceremony of Us*, *Animal Ritual*, *Trance Dances*, and *Initiations and Transformations*. Halprin explained that the "chief intention of these works was to understand how the process of creation and performance could be used to accomplish concrete results: social change, personal growth, physical alignment, and spiritual attunement" (Halprin, 1995, p. 228). She often works with large groups of fifty to one hundred persons moving in circles and spirals. These "archetypal movements trace out the forms and patterns of a larger organism, communicating with and being moved by a group body-mind or spirit" (Halprin, 1995, p. 229) In addition to her work in ritual, Halprin is recognized as a seminal figure of postmodern dance.

There are many others involved in similar work, blurring the distinctions between sacred and secular, ritual and art. A major theorist and practitioner is Allan Kaprow (b. 1927), who since the 1980s has practiced Zen-like actions such as walking in the desert and retracing one's footsteps. This kind of activity Kaprow terms "lifelike art." According to Kaprow, lifelike art weaves "meaning-making activity with any or all parts of our lives . . . embracing religious, philosophical, scientific, and social/personal exploration" (Kaprow, 1993, p. 216).

CONCLUSIONS. The varieties of ritual performances are uncountable, and ritual is part of the warp and woof of every kind of performance, whether religious or secular. There are no universal performative themes, actions, or patterns other than the ethological and neurological processes that shape the formal qualities and special experiences of the performer and spectator. All performances are ritually framed, but what these frames are and what they signify varies from culture to culture, even from one performance to another. Individual performances do not tell universal stories so much as provide observers with ways of understanding particular cultural and subcultural circumstances. Performers give participants a concrete, sensuous, and sometimes overwhelmingly powerful experience of cultural values. The similarity of the initiation and ritual process to the training, workshop, and rehearsal process makes it probable that not only will religious ritual be secularized but that aesthetic performances will be sacralized. It is a complicated but fruitful two-way system.

What is it that makes a person human? A nexus of circumstances: speech, bipedal locomotion, brain size and complexity, and social organization—but more as well. A performance of a nightmare, of yesterday's hunt or encounter with a strange band, of a sound heard in the forest—each are second actualities that when performed well rival the first in detail and presence. This second actuality has additional qualities that even make it superior to the first—it can be based on *what is not* as easily as on *what is* because the recalled or restored dream, hunt, encounter, or sound may actually be imaginary. Therefore, it can be elaborated on and improved through repetition. What counts is how well it is performed and how neatly it fits, or adds to, an existing or emerging worldview. Thus, three classes of performance events are possible: what was, what is imagined, and what falls between history and imagination. This third class of events, which shares both in the authority of recollection and the creativity of the imagination, is most powerful. Moreover, once such a realm of virtual actuality is given concrete existence in performance, it can lead to a third, a fourth, and so on.

In these ways performance has always and everywhere stood in relation to religion. Sometimes this relationship has been mutually supportive and other times it has been hostile. There is nothing in performance that is inherently pro-religious or anti-religious. Archaeological and anthropological evidence indicates a coexistence of performance and religion at least since Paleolithic times. And the ethological and neurological evidence suggests that, among humans, ritual and performance are close enough to be considered identical: they are repetitive, condensed, intense, and communicative displays and doings. Articulated religious beliefs, aesthetic enjoyment and theories, and political ideologies and manipulations are some of the uses people have found for ritual-performance behavior. As Victor Turner was fond of pointing out, to make believe is to make belief.

SEE ALSO Darwīsh; Ritual; Ritual Studies; Rūmī, Jalāl al-Dīn; Shakers; Taʿziyah.

BIBLIOGRAPHY

Aristotle was the first to propose an intimate connection between ritual, dance, music, and theater. In the *Poetics*, Aristotle expressed the opinion that Greek tragedy arose from the improvisations of those who led the dithyrambs, while comedy arose from the improvisations of those who led the phallic songs. Eric R. Dodds, in *The Greeks and the Irrational* (Berkeley, Calif., 1951), investigates the relationship between shamanism and the Greeks, thereby linking the sources of European culture with Asia. E. T. Kirby, in *Ur-Drama: The Origins of Theater* (New York, 1975), theorizes that all theater is originally shamanistic. Other important works on shamanism include Mircea Eliade, *Shamanism: Archaic Techniques of Ecstasy* (New York, 1964); Sergei M. Shirokogoroff, *Psychomental Complex of the Tungus* (London, 1935); and Laurel Kendall, *Shamans, Housewives, and Other Restless Spirits: Women in Korean Ritual Life* (Honolulu, 1987). The ancient Sanskrit theory of theater is contained in Bharata-muni, *The Natyasastra* (New Delhi, 1996). Discussions of the ritual performances of Paleolithic Europe are found in John E. Pfeiffer, *The Creative Explosion: An Inquiry into the Origins of Art and Religion* (New York, 1982); Weston La Barre, *The Ghost Dance* (Garden City, N.Y., 1970); and Yann Pierre Montelle, *Paleoperformance: The Emergence of Theatricality in the Deep Caves of the Upper Paleolithic* (Providence, R.I., 2004).

The first attempt in modern times to make a comparative survey of rituals, mythologies, and religions was James G. Frazer's *The Golden Bough*, 2 vols. (London, 1890), which he eventually expanded to twelve volumes and a supplement. Frazer's work influenced Jane Ellen Harrison's *Themis*, with contributions by Gilbert Murray and Francis Macdonald Cornford (Cambridge, UK, 1912) and *Ancient Art and Ritual* (London, 1913), Gilbert Murray's "Excursus on the Ritual Forms Preserved in Greek Tragedy," in *Themis* by Jane Ellen Harrison, pp. 341–363 (Cambridge, U.K., 1912), and Francis M. Cornford's *The Origin of Attic Comedy* (London, 1914). These scholars believed they had discovered a "primal ritual"—a seasonal death–rebirth drama common to the ancient Near East. However, the existence of the primal ritual cannot be proved, throwing into doubt any presumed relationship between it and succeeding Western theater (i.e., Greek, Elizabethan, modern). A convincing critique of the primal ritual theory is offered by Sir Arthur Wallace Pickard-Cambridge, *Dithyramb, Tragedy and Comedy*, 2d ed., rev. (Oxford, 1962). Despite this, the theory remains popular among those who believe ritual patterns underly tragedy and comedy. Among the most notable works of this kind are Susanne Langer's *Feeling and Form* (New York, 1953) and Northrop Frye's *Anatomy of Criticism* (Princeton, N.J., 1957). A similar, if not identical, trend in thinking is the theory of archetypes as propounded by Carl G. Jung and elaborated on by Joseph Campbell. See Jung's *Man and His Symbols* (Garden City, N.Y., 1964 and *The Portable Jung*, edited by Joseph Campbell (New York, 1971); and Campbell's *The Hero with a Thousand Faces* (Princeton, N.J., 1949) and *The Masks of God* (4 vols.; New York, 1959–1968).

The relationship between ritual and performance has been fruitfully investigated by anthropologists and performance theorists doing fieldwork among existing societies. Under the anthropological aegis the discussion shifts to eyewitness and even participatory accounts of actual performances. These data form the basis for theories of ritual process. Basic ritual theory exploring the relationships among aesthetic, religious, and social performances can be found in a number of texts, including Arnold van Gennep, *The Rites of Passage* (Chicago, 1909; reprint, 1960); Emile Durkheim, *The Elementary Forms of Religious Life*, (London, 1915; reprint, New York, 2001); Mircea Eliade, *Rites and Symbols of Initiation* (New York, 1958); Victor Turner, *The Forest of Symbols* (Ithaca, N.Y., 1967), *The Ritual Process* (Chicago, 1969), *Dramas, Fields, and Metaphors* (Ithaca, N.Y., 1974), *From Ritual to Theater* (New York, 1982), and *On the Edge of the Bush* (Tucson, Ariz., 1985); Erving Goffman, *The Presentation of Self in Everyday Life* (Garden City, N.Y., 1959) and *Interaction Ritual* (Chicago, 1967); Edith Turner, *Experiencing Ritual* (Philadelphia, 1992); Clifford Geertz, *The Interpretation of Cultures* (New York, 1973); Richard Schechner, *Between Theater and Anthropology* (Philadelphia, 1985), *The Future of Ritual* (London, 1993), and *Performance Theory* (London,

2003); James Redmond, ed., *Drama and Religion* (Cambridge, U.K., 1983); Sally F. Moore and Barbara G. Myerhoff, eds., *Secular Ritual* (Assen, Netherlands, 1977); Catherine Bell, *Rituals: Perspectives and Dimensions* (New York, 1997) and *Ritual Theory, Ritual Practice* (New York, 1992); Roy A. Rappaport, *Ecology, Meaning, and Religion* (Berkeley, Calif., 1979); Robert P. Armstrong, *The Powers of Presence: Consciousness, Myth, and Affecting Presence* (Philadelphia, 1981); Ronald Grimes, ed., *Readings in Ritual Studies* (Upper Saddle River, N.J., 1996); and John Emigh, *Masked Performance: The Play of Self and Other in Ritual and Theatre* (Philadelphia, 1996).

New or invented rituals are discussed in Anna Halprin, *Moving Toward Life* (Hanover, N.H., 1995) and *Dance as a Healing Art* (Mendocino, Calif., 2000); Suzanne Lacy, *Mapping the Terrain: New Genre Public Art* (Seattle, 1995); Allan Kaprow, *The Blurring of Art and Life* (Berkeley, Calif., 1993); and David H. Brown, *Santeria Enthroned* (Chicago, 2003).

For ethological and neurological approaches to ritual focus on the continuities between animal and human behavior and the relation of brain structure-function to ritual action and felt experience, see Desmond Morris, *Primate Ethology* (Garden City, N.J., 1969); Mario von Cranach, Klaus Foppa, Wolf Lepenies, and Detlev Ploog, eds., *Human Ethology* (Cambridge, U.K., 1979); and Eugene G. d'Aquili, Charles D. Laughlin Jr., and John McManus, *The Spectrum of Ritual* (New York, 1979). Also relevant in this regard are studies of trance, including Jane Belo, *Trance in Bali* (New York, 1960), Maya Deren, *Divine Horsemen: The Living Gods of Haiti* (London, 1953), and Gilbert Rouget, *Music and Trance* (Chicago, 1985).

Ritual, carnival, festival, and related performances are described and theorized in Victor Turner, *Celebration—Studies in Festivity and Ritual* (Washington, D.C., 1982), John J. MacAloon, ed., *Rite, Drama, Festival, Spectacle* (Philadelphia, 1984), Alessandro Falassi, *Time Out of Time: Essays on the Festival* (Albuquerque, 1987), and Milla Riggio, ed., *Carnival: Culture in Action—The Trinidad Experience* (London, 2004).

In addition to comprehensive and intercultural works, there are also many studies of ritual performances in individual cultures. See, for example, Baldwin Spencer and F. J. Gillen, *The Native Tribes of Central Australia* (London, 1899); Gregory Bateson, *Naven*, 2d ed. (Stanford, Calif., 1958); Raymond Firth, *Tikopia Ritual and Belief* (London, 1967); Victor Turner, *The Drums of Affliction* (London, 1968); Kenneth E. Read, *The High Valley* (New York, 1965); Richard A. Gould, *Yiwara: Foragers of the Australian Desert* (New York, 1969); F. E. Williams, *The Drama of the Orokolo* (London, 1940); Clifford Geertz, *Negara: Theater State in Nineteenth Century Bali* (Princeton, N.J., 1980); Anuradha Kapur, *Actors, Pilgrims, Kings, and Gods* (Calcutta, 1990); Edward L. Schieffelin, *The Sorrow of the Lonely and the Burning of the Dancers* (New York, 1976); Simon Ottenberg, *Masked Rituals of Afikpo* (Seattle, 1975); Charlotte J. Frisbie, ed., *Southwestern Indian Ritual Drama* (Albuquerque, N.M., 1980); Hanay Geiogamah and Jaye T. Darby, eds., *American Indian Performance* (Los Angeles, 2000); Edward Spicer, *The Yaqui* (Tucson, Ariz., 1980); Henry John Drewal and Margaret T. Drewal, *Gelede: Art and Female Power among the Yoruba* (Bloomington, Ind., 1983); Margaret T. Drewal, *Yoruba Ritual* (Bloomington, Ind., 1992); Frits Staal, ed., *Agni: The Vedic Ritual of the Fire Altar*, 2 vols. (Berkeley, Calif., 1983); and Bruce Kapferer, *A Celebration of Demons: Exorcism and the Aesthetics of Healing in Sri Lanka* (Bloomington, Ind., 1983).

RICHARD SCHECHNER (1987 AND 2005)

PĒRKONS

PĒRKONS. In Baltic languages, the proper noun *Pērkons* (Latv.) or *Perkūnas* (Lith.) corresponds exactly to the common noun meaning "thunder." There is no agreement among linguists about the word's original meaning. In earlier research the essence of the god who bears this name was determined purely through etymology. Consequently, three different schools of thought emerged, each claiming a different Indo-European root as the base.

The first school, using **perg-* as the root, regarded Pērkons as the sky god who controlled rain and storm. Typologically he was then likened to the Vedic Parjanya ("rain cloud"). The second school, deriving the god's name from **pergu(o)*, asserted that *Pērkons* is linked with *perkuu-s*, or *ozols*, meaning "oak tree." Pērkons was then considered to be the god of trees, in particular the oak, which was his symbol of power. The third school claimed that *Pērkons* is related to the Hittite *peruaš*, from *pirua-* (*perua-*), meaning "cliff" or "mountain." As a result Pērkons was regarded as the god of mountains. These various hypotheses, based only on etymology, did not give a clear conception of the true nature of this god. From these hypotheses, however, emerged the definite conclusion that the name *Pērkons* is derived from Proto-Indo-European.

An examination of the Pērkons cult offers valuable insights. Peter von Dusburg, in a discussion of the history of Old Prussians in the Chronicle of 1326, notes that Pērkons was worshiped. That the Latvians also recognized him as their god is demonstrated by a reference in the statutes of the Church Synod of 1428: *"a tonitruo, quod deum suum appellant"* ("from the thunder, which they name their god"). These older sources, however, do not give more detailed information about the nature of the cult itself. They merely contain standard condemnations of pagan worship of natural phenomena, for which Innocent III had earlier criticized the Latvians in his papal bull of 1199. Not until the seventeenth century was a specific rite from the Pērkons cult described, by the pastor Dionysius Fabricius in his *Livonicae Historicae Series* (1611–1620):

> At times of great drought when there is no rain, neighbors gather in densely wooded hills. They slaughter a she-calf, a black goat, and a black rooster. In accordance with their sacrificial rite a great number of people gather together and hold a communal feast. They drink together and invoke Pērkons, i. e. the thunder god. After filling the first cup of beer, they ecstatically march around the bonfire three times. They then pour the beer

> into the fire and pray to Pērkons (Percuum) to send them rain. (Mannhardt, 1936, p. 458; author trans.)

It should be noted, as this description of the feast clearly shows, that this rite was openly performed long after these peoples had formally been christianized. The gathering of worshipers in the thick forests can be explained by the fear of reprisals from the ruling German colonial church against non-Christian traditions.

This seventeenth-century account can be supplemented with another description, written 250 years later by an eyewitness who took part in the autumn threshing celebrations:

> On beginning the threshing, a rooster was slain in a niche of the open oven and a cross was painted with the rooster's blood on the oven. The meat was cooked and eaten. On completing the threshing another rooster was slain in the same spot. A vessel containing meat, brandy, and bread was placed on the oven. . . . On Saturday evening relatives and friends were invited to a communal feast, which ended in singing and dancing.

This description shows significant differences from the seventeenth-century account in that it contains syncretistic elements; the cross, the bread, and the brandy. Nevertheless, the feast is the same, even though Pērkons is not mentioned by name in the description.

Folk songs from the same time, however, do mention the god: "What shall we give to Pērkons for last summer's thunder? A large quantity [laste] of rye, a large quantity [*laste*] of barley, and a large quantity [*birkava*] of hops." This text, like the previous one, refers to a sacrificial feast after the harvest. It is a feast of thanksgiving to Pērkons. His cult thus appears to have remained strong throughout the centuries.

A bloody animal sacrifice also has a central place in the cult. There is also mention of bread and the sacral drink of the Balts, beer, which is poured into the fire. Typologically the rite appears as a sacrificial feast shared by gods and men. On the one hand it is associated with a supplication, asking for assistance during hard times; on the other hand, it is a thanksgiving for a plentiful harvest. During the thanksgiving the peasant experiences ecstatic joy because he stands in a right relation with his god and because the god, in turn, provides for him. The singing and dancing associated with the feast, which lasts well into the night, even until morning, also shows this joy. The ecstatic joy may climax in the participation of the gods in the festivities, as expressed in the following folk song: "Dievs [the Baltic god of heaven] is dancing with Pērkons; I am dancing with my brother; Pērkons has the whole earth in his possession; I have nine brothers."

The function of Pērkons is clearly defined: he is a fertility god. Hence, all etymologically based guesswork is superfluous. So also are any attempts to explain his essence and character by referring to analogical divinities in other religions. It is in this connection that Pērkons has also been regarded as a war god (he has especially been likened to Jupiter Fulminans, one of the aspects of the Roman sky god) and as a guardian of justice. Such assertions lack evidence in Baltic sources. If these and similar aspects appear to be connected with his function, then this can be explained as a later modification of ancient religious tradition, or by the influence of Christianity, which may have led to the perception of Pērkons as a slayer of demons and a guardian of morality.

BIBLIOGRAPHY

Balys, Jonas. *Perkunas lietuviuh liaudes tikejimuose.* Kaunas, 1937. Complete folkloristic material with a critical introduction.

Biezais, Haralds. *Die himmlische Götterfamilie der alten Letten.* Uppsala, 1972. The only up-to-date and complete historico-phenomenological and critical study, with an extensive bibliography. See especially part 3, "Der Donner," on pages 92–179.

Funk and Wagnalls Standard Dictionary of Folklore, Mythology and Legend. New York, 1950.

Ivanov, Vyacheslav, and Vladimir Toporov. *Issledovania v oblosti slavianskih drevnostei.* Moscow, 1974.

Mannhardt, Wilhelm. *Lettopreussische Götterlehre.* Riga, 1936. The best sourcebook on Baltic religion.

Skardzius, Pranas. "Dievas ir Perkunas." In *Aidai,* pp. 311–318. Chicago, 1953. A comparative linguistic analysis.

Šmits, Pēteris. *Latviešu mitoloģija.* (Latvian Mythology). Rīga, 1926.

Zicāns, Eduards. "Der altlettische Gott Pērkons." In *In Piam memoriam A. von Bulmerincq,* pp.189–217. Riga, 1938. A comparative analysis of the Latvian folkloristic material.

New Sources

Jones, Prudence, and Nigel Pennick. *A History of Pagan Europe.* Routledge, 1995.

Mitoloģijas enciklopēdija 2. (Encyclopedia of Mythology, vol.2.) Riga, 1994.

HARALDS BIEZAIS (1987)
Revised Bibliography

PERSECUTION

This entry consists of the following articles:

PERSECUTION: JEWISH EXPERIENCE

The related terms *religious persecution* and *martyrdom* are difficult to define rigorously. The notion of religious persecution cannot be confined simply to assaults on religious ritual and belief; the intertwining of religion with every facet of premodern existence sometimes made attacks on religious life an outlet for economic, social, and political grievances and sometimes diverted religious antipathy into economic, social, and political channels. The ambiguity of religious animosity and violence complicates the definition of *martyrdom* as well, forcing religious communities to examine and reexamine specific claims on behalf of those reputed to have chosen death in response to religious persecution and in testimony to the truth of their faith.

Religious Persecution in the History of Judaism. Biblical literature shows some instances of religious persecution, usually set in a political context. Thus the Philistine capture of the Ark of the Covenant and the Babylonian razing of the Jerusalem Temple both represent, in essence, politically motivated attacks on religious institutions and symbols. The biblical *Book of Daniel* presents two purported incidents of more purely religious persecution. In chapter 3, King Nebuchadnezzar is alleged to have erected a golden statue and ordered all his officials to prostrate themselves before it. Three Jewish lads were reported to the king for having contravened his royal order. As punishment, they were thrown into a blazing furnace, from which they miraculously emerged alive. Impressed by both their steadfastness and their salvation, the king was supposed to have prohibited any blasphemy of the God of the three young men. In chapter 6 a similar incident is told of Daniel, with the same outcome.

During the period of Hellenistic hegemony in the Near East, there was considerable tension between Jews and their neighbors, and this expressed itself in both political and religious terms. Particularly striking is the story of the Seleucid king Antiochus IV and his prohibition of basic Jewish religious practices. A group powerfully devoted to the fulfillment of covenantal law rose in rebellion against the effort to limit Jewish religious practice and belief. Modern scholarship has raised serious questions concerning these alleged Antiochene injunctions, which it has found totally at variance with Hellenistic custom. As an alternative, some scholars have proposed an essentially political motive for the decrees, a parallel to the earlier Philistine and Babylonian assaults on Judaism. A similarly political attack on Judaism is reflected in the Roman burning of the Second Temple in 70 CE. By this time there was already a strong tradition of Greco-Roman animus toward Jews and Judaism. Nonetheless, the policy of the Roman authorities at the close of the Great War basically reflects a desire to suppress the political rebellion that had broken out in Palestine, not to deliver a death blow to the Jewish religious faith. Similar considerations motivated the Hadrianic decrees at the close of the Bar Kokhba Revolt of 132–135 CE. Disturbed by ongoing Jewish unrest in Palestine, the Romans decided to quell permanently the rebelliousness of these Jews by attacking its seeming wellspring, Judaism.

With the emergence of Christianity as the authoritative religion of the Roman Empire in the fourth century and Islam as the ruling faith of a vast state in the seventh century, persecution of the Jews and Judaism took a decidedly new turn. Both these religions ultimately negated in theory the legitimacy of all other faiths, although each carved out a theoretical and practical status of limited tolerance for the other monotheisms, including Judaism. In many ways the situation of the Jews in the Muslim world was somewhat better than in medieval Christendom. Critical factors accounting for this difference included the ethnic and religious heterogeneity of the Muslim world, the size and antiquity of the Jewish communities within the orbit of Islam, the absence of any unique role for the Jews in the development of Islam, and the absence of any potent anti-Jewish symbolism at the core of the religion. There was, to be sure, occasional persecution of the Jews; sometimes this occurred at the official level, as with the Almohad rulers of North Africa and Spain during the mid-twelfth century, and sometimes at the popular level, as with the uprising in Granada in 1066, triggered by popular resentment of the Ibn Nagrela family of Jewish viziers. As the Muslim world increasingly lost the impressive vitality it had exhibited during the early centuries of the Middle Ages, the situation of its Jewish minority deteriorated, and instances of governmental persecution and popular violence multiplied.

It was in the medieval Christian world, however, that persecution of the Jews and Judaism was especially notable. Two factors in particular account for this prominence: (1) the central place of Jews in the Christian drama of crucifixion and resurrection, and (2) the relative newness and smallness of the Jewish communities in most—although not all—areas of medieval Christendom. At the official level, Judaism was in theory a tolerated faith, although its practice was limited in order to ensure the well-being of the ruling religion. Occasionally, concern with the impact of Judaism upon the spiritual health of Christendom could lead to persecution of the Jews or could be used to justify such persecution. Thus, for example, Christian persecution of Jews emerged in the early eleventh century from anxiety over the appearance of purported heresy in northern Europe and at the end of the fifteenth century from dismay over the alleged backsliding of New Christians in Spain to their original Jewish faith. In both situations Jews were viewed as contributors to the perceived dangers and were forced into conversion or exile.

In medieval Christendom popular persecution was the more common form of anti-Jewish behavior. Anti-Jewish animosities often developed within large-scale socioeconomic upheavals. During the First Crusade spiritual exhilaration produced powerful anti-Jewish sentiment in certain fringe bands of the crusading masses. The result was a set of devastating attacks on a number of the main centers of nascent German Jewry. During the last decade of the thirteenth century and the first decade of the fourteenth, powerful social discontent in Germany unleashed wide-ranging assaults against a series of Jewish communities. The hysteria occasioned by the uncontrollable Black Death of the mid-fourteenth century once again produced massive anti-Jewish violence, as did social and religious ferment in Spain in 1391. During the mid-seventeenth century the popular uprising of Ukrainian peasants against their Polish overlords occasioned repeated massacres in the Jewish communities of the area. In all these instances, long-nurtured stereotypes of Jewish enmity and malevolence served as the backdrop for the explosion of popular violence. The imagery of Jewish malevolence, rooted in the New Testament account of the Crucifixion, was embellished during the Middle Ages with notions of ritual murder, Jewish use of Christian blood, Host desecration, and the poisoning of wells. At points of religious exhilaration or social unrest, such imagery served alternately as the spark or the rationale for popular persecution of the Jews.

With the breakdown of the corporate premodern society and with the increasing restriction of the role of religion in modern Western civilization, the older patterns of religious persecution have generally given way. To be sure, there has been little sign of diminishing anti-Jewish hostility or anti-Jewish violence, but its religious nature is even more difficult to identify than heretofore. New definitions of Jewishness have emerged, and with them anti-Jewish activity has taken on an enhanced political, economic, social, and ethnic cast. The late-nineteenth-century racial definition of Jewishness produced the new term *anti-Semitism* for anti-Jewish attitudes and behavior. Those inclined to see anti-Semitism as a new phenomenon and to remove traditional Christian thinking from association with this new phenomenon have coined the term *anti-Judaism* as a foil. Debate has raged as to the Christian roots of anti-Semitism.

The seeming ubiquity of anti-Jewish violence has led to the conceptualization of the Jewish past as one long sequence of persecution and suffering. This perception emerged in the medieval Jewish polemical confrontation with Christianity, as Jewish polemicists insisted that Isaiah's suffering servant figure prefigured the travails of the Jewish people, in the process negating Christian claims for Jesus as fulfillment of this pivotal prophesy. At the close of the Middle Ages a number of Jewish authors organized narrative portraits of the Jewish past in terms of suffering intended to lead to eventual redemption. These views were secularized by the distinguished nineteenth-century Jewish historian Heinrich Graetz (1817–1891), who conceptualized the Jewish past in terms of suffering and the capacity to rise above suffering through the life of the mind. Modern Zionist historiography accepted the notion of suffering as the leitmotif of the Jewish past but rejected the valorization of such suffering. The young Salo Baron (1895-1989), embarking in the 1920s on his career as a major historian of the Jewish people, attacked what he called the "lachrymose conception of Jewish history," arguing that the Jewish past constitutes a rich, variegated, and creative saga. The eruption of the Holocaust did much to rehabilitate the earlier sense of the Jewish past as a vale of tears.

MARTYRDOM IN THE HISTORY OF JUDAISM. In Jewish tradition the notion of martyrdom has been expressed in the commandment of *qiddush ha-shem,* the requirement to sanctify the divine name. This commandment has broad meaning, as seen in *Leviticus* 22:31–33: "You shall faithfully observe my commandments: I am the Lord. You shall not profane my holy name, that I might be sanctified in the midst of the Israelite people—I the Lord who sanctify you, I who brought you out of the land of Egypt to be your God, I the Lord." Sanctification of the divine name could be and has been interpreted as any noble action undertaken out of commitment to the divine will and thus reflecting glory upon the God of Israel. Not surprisingly, however, a more restricted meaning of *qiddush ha-shem* has developed as well: it has been applied in particular to those who give up their most precious possession—life itself—out of this sense of submission to God's will, and who thus serve as ringing testimony to the reality and truth of their deity.

The Hebrew Bible certainly features the importance of submission to the divine will, as seen in Abraham's response to the command that he sacrifice his beloved son Isaac, in Moses' acceptance of God's call, and in repeated prophetic acquiescence to divinely imposed missions. Generally, however, this steadfastness involves the suppression of internal psychological blocks to the divine will; only rarely does it require the overcoming of external pressures, most notably with the two incidents recounted in the *Book of Daniel.* The Antiochene persecution, whatever its motivations may have been, produced a Jewish response of martyrological resistance to the external threat and created a set of figures whose deeds were subsequently retold as paradigms of heroic human behavior. The war of 66 to 70 CE elicited a similar sense of martyrdom, a desire to reject uncompromisingly the reimposition of Roman rule. Perhaps out of an awareness of the heavily political motivations on both sides, subsequent Jewish sources by and large overlooked this group of militant resisters and relegated the heroism of Masada to a position of relative neglect.

Entirely different was the response to the resistance against the Hadrianic persecution of the late 130s CE. Here the essentials of Jewish religious life were at stake, and the resisters were at the center of the Jewish community. The martyrdom of ʿAqivaʾ ben Yosef and his associates was accorded a major place in the Jewish liturgy and undoubtedly served to encourage succeeding generations of Jews to undertake, when required, the same commitment. Jewish law eventually codified the essentials of martyrdom by specifying key issues on which there could be no compromise.

> R[abbi] Yohanan said in the name of R[abbi] Shimʿon ben Yehotsadaq: "By a majority vote it was resolved in the upper chambers of the house of Nithza in Lydda that, for every [other] law of the Torah, if a man is commanded: 'Transgress and suffer not death,' he may transgress and not suffer death, excepting idolatry, incest, and murder." (Babylonian Talmud, *Tractate Sanhedrin* 74a)

This important statement limits the number of infringements upon Jewish law for which life is to be sacrificed. At the same time, it strongly reaffirms the basic principle of *qiddush ha-shem* when the infringement is major.

The persecutions cited here all reflect an assault on Judaism out of essentially political motivations. It is only with the development of Christianity and Islam and their rise to positions of political authority that the stage was set for direct confrontation between militant monotheistic faiths. In this regard the Jewish martyrdoms during the First Crusade assume special significance. The Crusader assaults of 1096 were couched in almost purely religious terms; there were no political aspects to this persecution, and socioeconomic issues were distinctly secondary. At their core the attacks on Rhineland Jewry were triggered by a radical desire to rid the world of all infidels. This was not, of course, the papal view of the crusade; it was, however, the yearning that animated the fringe bands of German Crusaders. The Jewish communities that suddenly found themselves under assault were spiritually as intense as their attackers. The result was a remarkable Jewish willingness to perish in defiance of Christian pressure and in testimony to the truth of the Jewish faith. The following utterance, imputed to the martyrs of Mainz on the verge of their deaths, captures the intensity of the period—the conviction of the absolute truth of Judaism; the sense that their actions represent *qiddush ha-shem,* a means of sanctifying the divine name in this world; and the resultant certainty of rich celestial reward:

> Ultimately one must not question the qualities of the Holy One, blessed be he, who gave us his Torah and commanded that we be put to death and be killed for the unity of his sacred name. Fortunate are we if we do his will and fortunate are all who are killed and slaughtered and die for the unity of his name. Not only do they merit the world to come and sit in the quarter of the righteous pillars of the world, but they exchange a world of darkness for a world of light, a world of pain for a world of joy, a transitory world for an eternal world. (Chazan, 1987, p. 237)

The martyrs of 1096 created a compelling set of symbols to sustain themselves in the face of the terrible test imposed upon them. These included a sense of identification with the great hero figures of the Jewish past, such as Abraham, Daniel and his companions, and ʿAqivaʾ ben Yosef and his associates; recollection of the divinely ordained sacrificial system with the conviction that God had called upon these martyrs to offer themselves up as surrogate sacrifices on a new-style altar; introduction of rituals of purity to underscore the sanctity of the acts they were about to undertake; and lavish descriptions of the celestial glories awaiting those who died on behalf of the divine name.

As the medieval synthesis disintegrated, religious persecution seemingly declined, and with it the possibility of martyrdom. Whether animosity and persecution grounded in prior religious thinking has in fact disappeared is a matter of deep dispute. What is clear is that the victims of modern anti-Semitism have not often been in a position to exercise choice in rejecting or accepting death. While choice seems to have been a critical factor in earlier notions of martydom, the martyr's mantle has nonetheless been accorded to the victims of the Holocaust out of a sense that they too died as a result of their Jewish identity.

See Also Anti-Semitism; Holocaust, The, article on History; Marranos; Suffering.

Bibliography

A useful general history of the Jews is Salo W. Baron, *A Social and Religious History of the Jews,* 2d ed., 18 vols. (New York, 1952–1983); Baron's footnotes are invaluable guides to major topics in Jewish history. The multivolume study by Léon Poliakov, *The History of Anti-Semitism,* translated by Richard Howard, 4 vols. (New York, 1965–1985). Studies of specific persecutions include, for the Antiochene persecution, Victor Tcherikover, *Hellenistic Civilization and the Jews* (Philadelphia, Pa., 1959); for the persecution of 1096, Robert Chazan, *European Jewry and the First Crusade* (Berkeley, Calif., 1987); for that of 1391, Yitzhak F. Baer, *A History of the Jews in Christian Spain,* 2 vols. (Philadelphia, Pa., 1961–1966); for that of 1648–1649, Bernard D. Weinryb, *The Jews of Poland* (Philadelphia, Pa., 1972). The studies of Tcherikover, Chazan, Baer, and Weinryb all analyze patterns of Jewish response to persecution along with their descriptions of the oppression itself. Shalom Spiegel's *The Last Trial* (New York, 1967) is a brilliant study of the imagery of testing and submission to divine will throughout Jewish history. Depictions of Nazi persecution and modern Jewish martyrdom abound. See especially Lucy S. Dawidowicz's *The War against the Jews, 1933–1945* (New York, 1975); Raul Hilberg's *The Destruction of the European Jews,* rev. and enl. ed., 3 vols. (New York, 1985); Alan Mintz's *Hurban: Responses to Catastrophe in Hebrew Literature* (New York, 1984); and David G. Roskies's *Against the Apocalypse* (Cambridge, Mass., 1984).

Robert Chazan (1987 and 2005)

PERSECUTION: CHRISTIAN EXPERIENCE

The atoning and vicarious nature of Jesus' sacrifice provides the main link between Jewish and Christian outlooks toward persecution and martyrdom. In *Mark* 10:45, a possible reminiscence from *Isaiah* 53:10–12, Jesus proclaims that he "came not to be served but to serve and to give his life as a ransom for many." It is, however, in the Johannine literature that the term *martyr* ("witness") moves quickest from its ordinary secular meaning to the Christian sense of "blood-witness." Numerous passages (e.g., *Jn.* 3:11, 5:30–33, 18:37, and 1 *Jn.* 5:10) present Jesus in terms of witness to the truth or to his Father, while others associate witness to Jesus with the Paraclete (*Jn.* 15:26, cf. also 14:26) standing in opposition to the world, convincing the world of sin and judgment. Witness to the Crucifixion was revealed in "blood and water," and had in addition the missionary purpose "that you also may believe" (*Jn.* 19:34–35).

The association of the Holy Spirit with suffering and persecution because of witness to Christ was emphasized in the synoptic Gospels (*Mk.* 13:11 and parallel *Mt.* 10:19). By the end of the first century CE, these ideas had become fused into a single idea of martyrdom. Martyrs conquered (Satan) "by the blood of the Lamb and by the word of their testimony [*marturias*], for they loved not their lives even unto death" (*Rev.* 12:11). Theirs was a personal witness to the truth of Christ's claim to be Messiah and a token of the closest possible identification with their Lord. In the early years of the second century, Ignatius of Antioch in his letter to the Christians in Rome said that he would be truly a disciple of Christ when he had been found "pure bread of Christ" (chap. 4). "It is better," he urged, "to die in Christ Jesus than to be king over the ends of the earth" (6.1).

The concept of martyrdom formulated in these years proved to be long lasting. In particular, its association with the spirit of prophecy, opposition to the world (not only to the Roman Empire), and its connection with the coming of the end of this world can be seen in the *Acta martyrum* of the second and early third centuries. Thus, in 177, the anonymous writer of the *Acta* of the martyrs of Lyon understood the persecution that assailed the congregation there as "foreshadowing the coming of Antichrist" (that would precede the end of this age). (See Eusebius's *Ecclesiastical History,* hereafter cited as *H.E.,* 5.1.5 and following.) As for the martyrs, one was described in the anonymous letter as the "Paraclete of the Christians" (5.1.9). Their witness and confession placed them in direct contact with Jesus himself, and while not "perfected" until dead, they were able to "bind and loose" as partakers in Christ's sufferings. The martyrs of Lyon were not followers of Montanus, whose movement, which began in Phrygia in 172, illustrated the close connection between prophecy, eschatology, and martyrdom. Their recorded outlook, however, indicates the strong undercurrent in the same direction among orthodox communities during this period. At the end of the century, this can be illustrated from the church in North Africa. Around 197, Tertullian proclaimed in *Apologeticum* 50.16 that martyrdom, as the baptism of blood, wiped away all postbaptismal sin. A decade later (c. 207), as a Montanist, he asserted in *De fuga in persecutione,* chapter 9, that it was the only form of death worthy of a Christian, for in that event Christ, who had suffered for the Christians, might be glorified.

The idea of martyrdom developed against the background of occasional severe, if local, persecutions. Jesus had warned his followers to expect persecution (*Mt.* 10:17). Like that of the prophets of Israel, his blood would be poured out. Until the Gospels attained their final form with the passion narrative, the suffering servant of *Isaiah* 53:1–12 was the perfect type of Christ. The earliest enemies of the Christians were the Jews, who regarded them as belonging to a dangerous, subversive movement in their midst. The martyrdom of Stephen in about 35 was followed by the persecution under Herod Agrippa around 42. Although Agrippa died in 44, over the next fifteen years Jews did everything possible to impede the preaching of Christianity by Paul and his friends among the synagogues of the Diaspora. They portrayed Paul as "a mover of sedition among the Jews throughout the world" (*Acts* 24:5), and first in Corinth and then in Jerusalem attempted to have him executed by the Roman authorities.

Luke and *Acts* show that the authorities themselves were by no means hostile to Paul and his preaching but rather regarded Christianity as an internal Jewish matter that was not their concern. What then was the cause of the Neronian persecution in Rome in 64 CE?

PERSECUTION AND TOLERATION IN THE ROMAN EMPIRE. Little is known of the Christian community in Rome during Nero's reign, but three factors seem relevant. First, Nero was desperate to find a scapegoat for the conflagration that he was suspected of causing. Second, official and popular opinion in Rome reprobated any threat to the majesty of the Roman gods by foreign cults, including Judaism. Jews were also suspected of misanthropy and incendiarism. Finally, by 60 CE, Jewish hostility toward Christianity had spread to Rome.

Tacitus's account of the savage repression of Christianity (*Annales* 15.44), written some sixty years later, may have been influenced by Livy's detailed account of the suppression of the Bacchanal conspiracy of 186 BE (Livy, *History of Rome* 39.8–19). The Christian movement was also regarded as a conspiracy by adherents of a foreign "false religion" (*prava religio*), one of whose aims was to set fire to Rome. In both cases, self-confessed adherents were put to death; in particular, the Christians were executed in a cruel and theatrical way, their death designed as a human sacrifice to appease the wrath of the gods. A generation later, the writer of *1 Clement* appeared to blame this catastrophe on the "envy and jealousy" of the internal enemies of the church, namely, the Jews.

Although the Neronian persecution was not extended to Italy and the provinces, it put the Christians on the wrong side of the law. Tacitus believed that Pontius Pilate was justified in ordering Jesus' execution, and that the "deadly superstition" of Christianity deserved punishment. His contemporary, Suetonius, listed the repression of the Christians among Nero's police actions of which he approved (*Nero* 16.2). For him the Christians were guilty of practicing black magic as well as of introducing a "novel and dangerous religion." Suetonius did not, however, connect the persecution with the fire at Rome.

In the second century, Melito of Sardis and Tertullian named Domitian (r. 81–96) as the second persecuting emperor. Domitian's repressive measures, however, in 95 aimed at discouraging forcibly members of the Roman nobility from "lapsing into Jewish ways." By this time, however, the authorities were distinguishing between Jews and non-Jews "who were living like Jews," a group that must have included Christians, and Christianity was illegal. The *Book of Revelation* indicates savage persecutions by Jews, the local populace, and the authorities in the province of Asia (western Asia Minor). In 112, the correspondence between the emperor Trajan and his special commissioner (*legatus pro praetore*) in the Black Sea province of Bithynia shows that Christians were liable to summary execution if denounced to the authorities. Pliny reports that their obstinacy in the face of questioning was an aggravating circumstance. Faced with apostasies, Pliny asked the emperor what he was to do, giving his opinion that Christianity was nothing worse than a perverse superstition and suggesting that leniency would restore the situation. Trajan replied that while Christians were not to be sought out like common criminals they were to be punished if they persisted in their refusal "to worship our gods." If they recanted, however, they were to be freed.

Instructions (*rescripta*) issued in 124/5 by Trajan's successor, Hadrian (r. 117–138), directed the proconsul of Asia, C. Minicius Fundanus, to condemn Christians only if found guilty of criminal offenses in a court of law. They were not to be subjected to clamorous denunciations, and they had the right of turning against their accusers a charge that proved to be false. These two decisions established the policy of the imperial authorities for the remainder of the century. They had the effect of discouraging prosecutions, and Christians enjoyed relative tranquillity until the reign of Marcus Aurelius (161–180). By then, however, the official reluctance to pursue Christians had begun to yield to the force of popular suspicion of them, as reflected in charges of incest, cannibalism, and atheism. They were also held responsible for natural disasters that demonstrated, it was believed, the anger of the gods. The result was a series of severe local persecutions, such as the martyrdom of Polycarp of Smyrna in about 166 and the "pogrom" of Lyon in 177. In about 178 an informed Platonist writer, Celsus, without mentioning specific popular accusations directed against the Christians, mentions membership in an illegal organization, lack of civic sense, and subversion of traditional social structures through active proselytism as additional grounds for unpopularity and justification for oppression.

In the first decade of the third century, the increase in the number of Christians resulting from a more aggressive missionary policy resulted in persecutions in Carthage, Alexandria, Rome, Antioch, Corinth, and Cappadocia. In Carthage and Alexandria the rage of the mob seems to have been directed against converts. Eusebius associated these persecutions with the emperor Septimius Severus (r. 193–211), and it is possible that that emperor reacted against the rising tide of mob outbreaks in some of the main cities of the empire by prohibiting conversion either to Judaism or to Christianity.

Between 212 and 235 Christians enjoyed a further period of quasi toleration under the emperors of the Severan dynasty. The revolution that removed Alexander Severus on March 22, 235, saw the beginnings of a new policy. Severus's supplanter, Maximinus Thrax (235–238), liquidated the Christian servants and officeholders at his predecessor's court and struck at the Christian leadership, sending the pope, Pontian (235–236), and the antipope, Hippolytus, into exile in Sardinia, where they both died.

In 238 Maximinus fell to a revolution inspired by landowning interests in North Africa. The next dozen years saw a period of Christian expansion and prosperity that provoked growing antipathy on the part of the pagans. In 248 there was a massive popular assault on the Christians in Alexandria, but the change of emperor that took place in the autumn of 249 resulted in the first empire-wide persecution. C. Quintus Messius Decius, who took the surname *Trajan* (r. 249–251), was a good general and believed firmly in the traditional values of the Roman state. He was convinced that the Christians were responsible for the disasters that had befallen his predecessor. In January 250, he ordered that the yearly sacrifice made to the Roman gods on the Capitoline hill should be repeated throughout the empire, and almost simultaneously he had prominent Christians seized, whether clergy or laity. On January 21, Pope Fabian was tried before him and executed. A similar fate befell Bishop Babylas of Antioch; Cyprian of Carthage and Dionysius of Alexandria escaped only by going into hiding. This phase was followed by the establishment of commissions in the towns of each province to supervise sacrifices to the gods of the empire and the emperor's genius. The process extended from February and March in Asia Minor and North Africa to June and July in Egypt. Some forty-three *libelli* (certificates) given to those who sacrificed have survived on Egyptian papyri. Few Christians resisted. If Decius had been able to give his undivided attention to the repression, the church might have been in serious danger. The peril, however, was already over when the emperor met his death at the hands of the Goths in June 251.

Hostility was continued under the emperors Gallus and Volusian in 252 and 253, but in 257 their successor Valerian (253–260) made a massive effort to force Christians to acknowledge and respect the Roman gods. This was the object of Valerian's first edict (summer 257), although the contributory factors may have included a desire on the part of the authorities to lay hands on the wealth that the church was believed to have accumulated. The church's leaders were arrested, interrogated, and deported. The edict also forbade Christians to hold services and to frequent their cemeteries, but otherwise left them alone. A year later, however, the emperor decided on severer measures. An imperial order reached Rome early in August 258, ordering that clergy should be executed, that Christian senators should forfeit their status and property, that a similar fate should befall highborn women, and that civil servants should be reduced to slavery. On September 14, 258, Cyprian of Carthage was summoned from his relatively comfortable place of exile to confront the proconsul of Africa. After a brief trial he was condemned as the ringleader of "an unlawful association" and as "an open enemy of the gods and the religion of Rome" (*Acta proconsularia*).

Persecution continued through 259, but ended with Valerian's capture by the Persians near Edessa in June 260. His son and successor, Gallienus, sent instructions in 260 and 261 to provincial governors to restore the property of the church and free its members from further molestation. The church, though not technically *religio licita* ("lawful religion"), had at last achieved a recognized status.

For more than forty years this situation continued. Church and empire moved closer together. In Nicomedia, the capital of the emperor Diocletian (284–305), the cathedral stood in full view of the emperor's palace. Why Diocletian decided to force the issue with the Christians nearly twenty years after he had seized power is not known; but the connection with the anti-Christian sentiments of his caesar, Galerius, and with his own policy of bringing uniformity in every aspect of the life of the peoples of the empire through the establishment of a common currency, prices, taxation, and legal framework seems clear. The great nonconformists, the Christians, could not be allowed to opt out. The Great Persecution of 303–312 (303–305 in the West) was preceded by a number of repressive acts (298–302) designed to remove Christians from public positions. On February 23, 303, the emperor posted an edict at Nicodemia, ordering the surrender of all copies of the Christian scriptures for burning and the dismantlement of all churches. No meetings for Christian worship were to be held. Christians were also disbarred from being plaintiffs in lawsuits, and lost all honors and privileges, but there was no death penalty, for Diocletian wanted no more Christian martyrs. In the summer of 303 other edicts followed, first directing that Christian clergy should be arrested and imprisoned, and then that they should be forced to sacrifice and thereafter freed.

So far only the clergy had been seriously affected, but in the winter of 303–304 Diocletian became incapacitated by illness following a visit to Rome to celebrate his twenty years' rule. Galerius took over control of the government and in the spring of 304 issued an edict ordering everyone to sacrifice to the immortal gods. This phase of the persecution saw numerous martyrs in North Africa, especially in Numidia, and a hardening of attitudes between Christians and pagans. Diocletian recovered from his illness, but was persuaded to retire from the government, which he did on May 1, 305, to live another eleven years in a magnificent military palace at Spalatum (Split) on the Adriatic coast.

The new emperors, Constantius in the West and Galerius (with Maximinus as his caesar) in the East, pursued contrasting religious policies. Persecution ceased in the West, but was restarted in the East after Easter 306. Successive edicts were accompanied by efforts by Maximinus to reorganize the pagan cult on a hierarchical basis. However, enthusiasm among the pagans was waning, and Galerius, struck down in the spring of 311 by a mysterious, deadly illness, issued an edict of toleration on April 30, a week before he died. This "Palinode of Galerius" accepted the fact that the great majority of Christians could not be brought back to the worship of the Roman gods, considered it better for the empire that they should worship their own god than that they worship no god at all, and accorded them contemptuous toleration. "Christians may exist again, and may establish their meeting houses, provided they do nothing contrary to good order." They were also asked "to pray to their god for our good estate and their own, so that the commonwealth may endure on every side unharmed."

Meantime, in the West Constantius had died at York on July 25, 306, and his son Constantine had been acclaimed augustus by the soldiers. Though he had to be content with lesser honors for the time being, Constantine gradually increased his power, until in the spring of 312 he was ready to bid for the control of the whole of the West. He invaded Italy, defeated the usurper Maxentius at the battle of the Milvian Bridge, just north of Rome (October 28, 312), and was hailed "senior augustus" by the Senate the next day. He was already strongly influenced by Christianity and, whatever the vision he saw on the day before the decisive battle, he was determined to end the era of persecution. In February 313 he met his fellow augustus at Milan, and together they published the famous Edict of Milan. Christians received, together with all the other subjects of the empire, complete freedom of religion, but they and the *Summus Deus* were regarded as the positive force and contrasted with "all others." Insensibly the scales had tipped toward Christianity as the official religion of the empire. By the time Constantine moved east, in 324, to challenge Licinius for control over the whole Roman world, the "immortal gods" of the Romans had been displaced as patrons and protectors of the empire. The religious revolution was complete. The church's intensive ramifications through town and countryside alike, coupled with a firm organization and a continued underlying enthusiasm for martyrdom, at least among a minority of the faithful, had proved too strong for the pagan empire.

Persecution of Heretics and Dissenters. Constantine's religious policy was founded on unity. The Christian God could not be served by two or more rival groups of ministers. Only one such group could be accepted as representing the true catholic (universal) church. At the same time, however, the strains and tensions resulting from the Great Persecution had exacerbated existing divisions in the church and caused new ones. In the West, the North African church had been divided since 311 between factions supporting or opposed to the new bishop of Carthage, Caecilian. In Egypt, there were divisions between the Melitians and adherents of Alexander, bishop of Alexandria. Persecution directed against opponents of the church supported by Constantine was not slow in coming.

Constantine and his sons saw themselves as the *custodes fidei* ("guardians of the faith") of the empire. This involved the suppression of paganism and dissenting views such as those of the Donatists in 346–347, and measures against individuals, like Athanasius of Alexandria, who was exiled in 356. A generation later, after the free-for-all toleration under Julian (r. 361–363), the emperor Theodosius I in 380 published the general edict Cunctos Populos, by which the Christian religion as adhered to by Pope Damasus and Peter of Alexandria was decreed to be the sole legitimate religion of the empire.

Cunctos Populos is one of the turning points in the grim story of religious persecution. Those who did not accept that law forfeited their civil rights and were liable to punishment by the state. It was followed by a series of laws reiterating penalties against heretics, which reached a climax in June 392, when the emperor ordered heretical clergy to be fined ten pounds of gold and decreed that places where forbidden practices were occurring should be confiscated if the owner had connived. Pagans fared equally badly. In February 391 a law sent from Milan to Albinus, the praetorian prefect of the East, took up the legislation against paganism by the emperors Constantius II and Valens by prohibiting all sacrifices and fining people of high rank or official position who entered temples. This paved the way for a more comprehensive law late in 392 that banned every sort of pagan practice under very severe financial penalties. Informers were to be encouraged.

This framework of imperial legislation provided the means by which leaders of the catholic church were able to suppress their opponents. If, in the East, church and state formed one integrated whole under the emperor, in the West the "two swords" theory of the separate authority of church and state required the church to regard the secular power as its protector and sword against its enemies. In his long struggle against the Donatists, which lasted from 393 to 421, Augustine gradually built up a justification for the repression of religious dissent by the state. In 399 he identified the Donatists as heretics and urged that if kings could legislate against pagans and prisoners they could legislate against heretics. In 405 Augustine had imperial legislation against heretics applied to the Donatists. Denial of testamentary rights and floggings with lead whips were to be meted out to the obdurate. In 408, Augustine confessed that he was now convinced that Donatists should be coerced into the unity of Christ and quoted the Lucan text "Compel them to come in." After the proscription of the Donatists by law in 412, Augustine added to his arguments justifying persecution the statement that coercion in this world would save the heretics from eternal punishment in the next.

"No salvation outside the church," a doctrine preached by Augustine in 418 in his sermon addressed to the people of the church of Caesarea (chap. 6), implied a right to convert forcibly or otherwise the church's opponents. The precedents established in the Donatist controversy by Augustine passed into the armory of the catholic church through the Middle Ages and into Reformation times. The Albigensian crusades of 1212 and 1226–1244 witnessed terrible massacres in centers such as Béziers and Carcassonne where the heresy flourished. In 1244 the defenders of the last Abigensian stronghold, Mont Ségur, were burned alive by their victorious enemies. More than a century and a half later, in 1415, the same punishment was inflicted on Jan Hus at Prague.

In the Reformation, persecution of opposing churches was accepted by all parties. Henry VIII burned the Protestants Thomas Bilney and Robert Barnes; Mary Tudor sent some three hundred Protestants to the stake between 1555 and her death in November 1558; Calvin ordered the burning of Servetus in 1541. Unwillingness in the Roman Catholic Church to concede that "error has any rights over truth" prolonged the period of persecution of Protestants into the eighteenth century. The bloody repression of the Calvinist Camisards in the Cévennes following the revocation of the Edict of Nantes in 1685 and the repression of Protestants in the Palatinate in 1715 and in the diocese of Salzburg in 1732 are reminders that religious persecution did not end with the formal conclusion of hostilities between Protestants and Catholics at the Peace of Westphalia in 1648. Even in World War II, the Ustasi government in Croatia unleashed what may be hoped to be the final spasm of religious persecution against the Orthodox minority in Bosnia. On the other hand, Christianity itself has been the object of persecution by the Hitlerite and Communist regimes. These persecutions have so far failed in their aims, but among Christians themselves it is to be hoped that the growth of the ecumenical movement and the decrees of Vatican II may help banish this blot from history.

SEE ALSO Cathari; Constantine; Constantinianism; Cult of Saints; Donatism; Heresy, article on Christian Concepts; Reformation.

BIBLIOGRAPHY

Sources

The Acts of the Christian Martyrs. Translated by Herbert A. Musurillo. Oxford, 1972. Includes useful introductions and bibliographical notes.

Lanata, Giuliana. *Gli atti dei martiri come documenti processuali.* Milan, 1973. No English translation, but contains excellent bibliographical notes and evaluation of manuscript traditions.

Lawlor, Hugh J., and John E. L. Oulton. *Eusebius, Bishop of Caesarea: The Ecclesiastical History and the Martyrs of Palestine (1927–1928).* 2 vols. Reprint, London, 1954. The best English text of Eusebius's *Martyrs of Palestine.*

Secondary Literature

Barnes, Timothy D. "Legislation against the Christians." *Journal of Roman Studies* 58 (1968): 32–50.

Barnes, Timothy D. "Pre-Decian Acta Martyrum." *Journal of Theological Studies,* n.s. 19 (October 1968): 509–531.

Baynes, N. H. "The Great Persecution." In *The Imperial Crisis and Recovery, A.D. 193–324,* vol. 12 of *Cambridge Ancient History,* edited by S. A. Cook et al., pp. 646–677. Cambridge, 1939.

Brown, Peter R. *Religion and Society in the Age of Saint Augustine.* London, 1972. Contains important studies of Augustine's attitude toward religious coercion.

Emery, Richard W. *Heresy and Inquisition in Narbonne.* New York, 1941.

Frend, W. H. C. *Martyrdom and Persecution in the Early Church: A Study of a Conflict from the Maccabees to Donatus.* Oxford, 1965. Includes a bibliography of works published before 1964.

Grégoire, Henri. *Les persécutions dans l'Empire romain. In Mémoires de l'Académie Royale de Belgique,* vol. 46, fasc. 1. Brussels, 1951. Stimulating, like everything Grégoire wrote, though occasionally wrong-headed.

Hardy, E. G. *Christianity and the Roman Government: A Study in Imperial Administration (1894).* Reprint, London, 1925. Fine piece of work by a classical scholar.

King, Noel Q. *The Emperor Theodosius and the Establishment of Christianity.* Philadelphia, 1960.

Kitts, Eustace J. *Pope John the Twenty-Third and Master John Hus of Bohemia.* London, 1910.

Knipfing, John R. "The Libelli of the Decian Persecution." *Harvard Theological Review* 16 (October 1923): 345–390.

Moreau, Jacques. *La persécution du christianisme dans l'Empire romain.* Paris, 1956. Revised and published in German as *Die Christenverfolgung im römischen Reich,* "Aus der Welt der Religion," n. s. 2 (Berlin, 1961). A perceptive and stimulating statement by one of Grégoire's pupils.

Shannon, Albert C. *The Popes and Heresy in the Thirteenth Century.* Villanova, Pa., 1949.

Sherwin-White, Adrian Nicholas. "The Early Persecutions and Roman Law Again." *Journal of Theological Studies,* n.s. 3 (October 1952): 199–213.

Ste. Croix, G. E. M. de. "Why Were the Early Christians Persecuted?" *Past and Present* 26 (November 1963): 6–38. The best short account of the persecutions and their causes.

Vogt, Joseph, and Hugh Last. "Christenverfolgung: 1, Historisch" and "Christenverfolgung: 2, Juristisch." In *Reallexikon für Antike und Christentum,* edited by Theodor Klauser, vol. 2. Stuttgart, 1954.

New Sources

Bowerstock, Glen Warren. *Martyrdom and Rome.* The Wiles lectures at the Queen's University at Belfast. Cambridge, U.K., and New York, 1995.

Cassidy, Richard J. *Paul in Chains: Roman Imprisonment and the Letters of St. Paul.* New York, 2001.

Cavanaugh, William T. *Torture and Eucharist: Theology, Politics, and the Body of Christ.*Oxford and Malden, Mass., 1998.

Ellis, Jane. *The Russian Orthodox Church: A Contemporary History.* Bloomington, Ind., 1986.

Ferguson, Everett, ed. *The Church and State in the Early Church.* New York, 1993.

Hillar, Marian. *The Case of Michael Servetus (1511–1553): The Turning Point in the Struggle for Freedom of Conscience.* Lewiston, N.Y., 1997.

Loades, David M., ed. *John Foxe and the English Reformation.* Proceedings of a Colloquium held July 4–6, 1995, at Magdalene College, Cambridge. Aldershot, U.K., and Brookfield, Vt., 1997.

Waugh, Scott L., and Peter D. Dieh, eds. *Christendom and Its Discontents: Exclusion, Persecution, and Rebellion.* Cambridge, U.K., and New York, 1996.

W. H. C. FREND (1987)
Revised Bibliography

PERSEPHONE

SEE DEMETER AND PERSEPHONE

PERSONIFICATION

SEE ANTHROPOMORPHISM; HYPOSTASIS

PERUN was the thunder god of the heathen Slavs. A fructifier, a purifier, and an overseer of right and order, he was the adversary of the Slavic "black god" (Chernobog, Veles). His actions were perceived by the senses: he was seen in the thunderbolt, he was heard in the crackling rattle of stones or the thunderous bellow of the bull or he-goat, and he was felt in the sharp touch of an ax blade.

The cult of Perun among the Baltic Slavs is attested by the Byzantine historian Procopius in the sixth century CE. In the Russian *Primary Chronicle,* compiled circa 1111, Perun is invoked by name in the treaties of 945 and 971, and his name is first in the list of gods compiled by Vladimir I in 980. As Prone, Perun was worshiped in oak groves by West Slavs, and he is so named in Helmold's *Chronica Slavorum* of the twelfth century. Saxo Grammaticus mentions Perun's son, whom he calls Porenutius, in his *Gesta Danorum* of the early thirteenth century.

The root *per-/perk-,* meaning "to strike, to splinter," is common to Indo-European languages. Close relatives to the Slavic name *Perun* are the Lithuanian *Perkūnas,* Prussian *Perkonis,* Latvian *Pērkons,* Old Icelandic *Fjǫr-gynn,* and Greek *Zeus keraunos* (from a taboo **peraunos*). Common nouns derived from the same Indo-European root—Sanskrit *parjanyah* ("cloud, thunder"), Hittite *peruna* ("mountaintop"), Gothic *fairguni* ("oak forest"), Celtic *hercynia* (from *silva,* "oak forest"), and Latin *quercus* (from **perkus,* "pine" or, earlier, "oak")—suggest prehistoric ties between Indo-European thunder gods and clouds (i.e., rain), oaks, oak forests, and mountaintops. The veneration of the Slavic **pergynja* (Russian *peregynia,* Polish *przeginia*), meaning "oak forest," is attested by Russian literary sources. West Slavic and South Slavic personal names and place-names with the root *per-* are mostly linked with "oak," "oak forest," and "hill": *Perun gora* (Serbian), *Perunowa gora* (Polish), and *Porun,* the name of a hill in Istria. The word for "Thursday" (Thor's day) in the Polabian dialect is *peründan,* which literally means "lightning."

In the Christian period, worship of Perun was gradually transferred to the old, white-bearded Saint Elijah (Russian, Il'ia), who traveled across the sky in a fiery chariot (as the Lithuanian thunder god, copper-bearded Perkunas, is still believed to do). In folk beliefs, Perun's fructifying, life-stimulating, and purifying functions are still performed by his traditional instruments: ax, bull, he-goat, dove, and cuckoo. Sacrifice of a bull and a communal feast on Saint Il'ia's Day, July 20, in honor of Perun or Il'ia were last recorded in northern Russia in 1907, when they were combined with Christian hymns and blessings. The meat was prepared entirely by men and then taken into the church and divided among the villagers (see Otto Schrader, *Die Indogermanen,* 1907).

BIBLIOGRAPHY

Darkevich, V. P. "Topor kak simvol Peruna v drevnerusskom iazychestve." *Sovetskaia arkheologiia* 4 (1961): 91–102.

Duridanov, I. "Urslav: Perun und seine Spuren in der Toponymie." *Studia Slavica Academiae Scientiarum Hungaricae* 12 (1966): 99–102.

Gimbutas, Marija. "Perkūnas/Perun: The Thunder God of the Balts and the Slavs." *Journal of Indo-European Studies* 1 (1973): 466–478.

Ivanov, J. "Kul't Peruna u iuzhnykh slavian." *Izvestiia* 8, no. 4 (1903): 140–174.

Rozniecki, Stan. "Perun und Thor: Ein Beitrag zur Quellenkritik der russischen Mythologie." *Archiv für slawische Philologie* (Berlin) 23 (1901): 462–520.

New Sources

Yoffe, Mark, and Joseph Krafczik. *Perun: The God of Thunder.* New York, 2003.

MARIJA GIMBUTAS (1987)
Revised Bibliography

PESHER. The Hebrew noun *pesher* (pl. *pesharim*) is an Aramaic loanword that entered late biblical Hebrew (*Qoheleth* 8:1) and is current in the Hebrew of the Qumran scrolls in the sense of "meaning, explanation, interpretation." Since this term is mostly employed by a particular type of Qumran biblical interpretation, it came to be the nomenclature of Qumran works, which in their literary character and their structure engaged in such interpretation. In Qumran research the term *pesher* has therefore four distinct usages: (1) as the name of the genre that contemporizes biblical prophecies according to the worldview of the Qumran ascetic community; (2) as the name attached to individual Qumran works or literary units containing such interpretations; (3) as a formula introducing the exposition of a given biblical text according to the said method; (4) as the name of the particular exegetical method applied in this kind of interpretation.

1. THE *PESHER* GENRE. One of the first scrolls to be discovered was a *pesher* of Habakkuk exhibiting a particular type of commentary. It consisted of reading into biblical prophecies allusions to various historical circumstances and events contemporary with and related to the Qumran community, often placed in the perspective of the approaching *eschaton* and the final redemption. Among the extant *pesharim* are interpretations of the prophets and other biblical passages (e.g., the Blessings of Bileam [*Num.* 24:17] in CD VII, 19 and 1QM XI, 6; the Song of the Well [*Num.* 21:18] in CD VI, 2–11; and occasionally also legal texts; *cf.* discussion of *pesher* Melchizedek below). Also included in this group are the *Psalms of David* and the vision contained in the *Book of Daniel,* both viewed as prophetic (for Psalms see 11QPs^{a} 27:11 and for *Daniel* see 4Q174 1–3 ii 3). This selection shows that various biblical texts were deemed prophetic and were subjected to *pesher* interpretation even when appearing in non-prophetic literary contexts. Nevertheless, running *pesharim* on large textual passages are extant only for the prophets and *Psalms.* All the *pesharim* from Qumran display the same fundamental structure and exegetical method, but they vary in technical formulae. The running *pesharim* on large passages are found mostly in copies dated to the second half of the first century BCE. But a copy of pesher of Isaiah, 4QpIs^{c}(4Q163) dates to the beginning of the first century BCE. Also, single *pesher* units, embedded in different literary contexts, appear in the earliest works of the community, the so-called *Rule of the Community* (1QS VIII, 13–16) and the *Damascus Document* (e.g., CD VI, 3–11; VII, 14–21). Moreover, historical allusions in the *pesharim* cover a century, approximately from 150 to 50 BCE. In addition, the *pesher* of Habakkuk attributes this technique to the founder of the community, the Teacher of Righteousness, a claim that may have a historical kernel (*cf.* below). Another piece of evidence suggesting the antiquity of the method is provided by the *Apocryphon of Joshua,* which produces a *pesher* on the curse of Joshua; (cf. below). So the *pesher* method was practiced by the community since its inception. Perhaps certain *pesharim,* especially the running ones, committed much earlier interpretative traditions to writing. Given the antiquity of the pesher method, the running *pesharim* could hardly be autographs as claimed because the extant specimens do not overlap.

Reading contemporary circumstances into old prophecies, the *pesharim* contain numerous allusions to real historical figures and events. This is evident from many details contained in the *pesher* comments that do not stem from the biblical texts or its exegetical problems and may only be explained as references to real circumstances. Accordingly, the *pesharim* are the main source for historical data of the Qumran community and its history.

2. INDIVIDUAL *PESHARIM.* The *pesharim* appear in four distinct forms.

Continuous *pesharim.* Thus labeled are works citing large running prophetic texts with detailed expositions. The citations consist of one or two phrases each, followed by a comment, usually introduced by the formula *pesher hadaver* ("the interpretation of it") or *pishro* ("its interpretation"). The available specimens of this type are the following:

1QpHab. A *pesher* of Habakkuk chapters 1–2, found in Qumran cave 1, preserved almost intact. It offers consecutive *pesher* on the first two chapters of Habakkuk, containing allusions to historical figures and events from the middle of the second century BCE to the first third of the first century BCE. Among the persons referred to is the Teacher of Righteousness, known from CD (I, 10–15) to be the founder of the community. The *pesher* attributes to him a special understanding of the mysteries embedded in the prophetic message, divulged by divine revelation: "And when he [i.e., Habakkuk] says so that the reader can read it easily (Habakkuk 2:2) its interpretation concerns the Teacher of Righteousness to whom God made known all the mysteries of the words of his servants the prophets" (1QpHab VII, 3–5). The Teacher's identity remains a mystery. His major political opponent was the Wicked Priest, who is usually identified with the Hasmonean Jonathan (152–142 BCE) or Simon (142–134 BCE). The Teacher's ideological rival is referred to by the sobriquet "the Spouter of Lie" (1QpHab X, 9; *cf.* CD VIII, 13), probably identical with "the Man of Lie" (1QpHab II, 2; V, 11; cf. CD I, 15; XX, 15) or "the Man of Mockery" (cf. CD I, 14). This person was the leader of an opponent group (1QpHab X, 10), perhaps the one dubbed in other pesharim "the Seekers after Smooth Things" (4QpNah 3–4 i 2,7; ii 2, 4; cf. CD I, 18) or "the Men of Mockery" (4QpIs^b ii 6, 10; cf. CD XX, 11). All are derogatory epithets for those who, according to the view of the sectaries, practiced false exposition of Scriptures. Most scholars identify them with the Pharisees. A different type of group is labeled by the pesher as "the Kittim." In the Hebrew Bible the Kittim designate western peoples, from Greece or Cyprus (*Gen.* 10:4; *Isa.* 23:1, 12; *Ezek.* 27:6–7), but in the *pesharim* they stand for the Romans. This is clear from the assertions that they sacrifice to their standards (1QpHab VI, 4), a well-known practice of the Roman army, and are governed by rulers appointed by their council (1QpHab IV, 10–12), probably the Roman Senate.

4QpNahum (= 4Q169). The fragments of this running *pesher* of *Nahum* provide a typical illustration of the *pesher* method. One comment sees in the lion, mentioned in *Nahum* 2:12, an allusion to the Greek king Demetrius (4QpNah 3–4 i 2), probably the Seleucid ruler Demetrius III Eukerus (95–88 BCE). This pesher makes a clear distinction between the "kings of Greece" (4QpNah 3–4 i 2), namely the Seleucids, and the "rulers of the Kittim" (4QpNah 3–4 i 3), namely the Roman rulers, perhaps their military commanders. Most scholars see in this last reference an allusion to Pompey's capture of Jerusalem (63 BCE), which marked the end of the independent Hasmonean kingdom. The *pesher* also refers to a rift within Judaism, which it reads into the prophecy of Nahum: "the lion tears victims for his cubs and strangles prey for his lionesses (*Nahum* 2:13a) [. . . its interpretation] concerns the Lion of Wrath who would strike his great ones and his men of counsel [. . . and as for what he (i.e., Nahum) said And it fills up with prey] its lair and its den with mangled flesh [*Nahum* 2:13b] its interpretation concerns the Lion of Wrath [. . . who will take ven]geance of the Seekers of Smooth Things and he would hang men up alive" (4QpNah 3–4 i 4–7). The prophetic verse is understood to refer to the Hasmonean king Alexander Jannaeus (103–76 BCE), here dubbed "the Lion of Wrath," who crucified eight hundred partisans of the Pharisees for joining the army of his enemy Demetrius Eukeros (see Josephus, *Antiquities of the Jews.*, xiii, 389–391; *Jewish War,* i, 92–95). Other continuous pesharim have survived, mostly very fragmentary. There are six *pesharim* of *Isaiah:* 3QpIs (= 3Q4), 4QpIs^a (= 4Q161), 4QpIs^b (= 4Q162), 4QpIs^c (= 4Q163), 4QpIs^d (= 4Q164), and 4QpIs^e (= 4Q165). 4QpIs^c (= 4Q163) merits special attention since it is not only the oldest specimen of running pesher but also the only one written on papyrus. It also cites other prophets (Zechariah and probably Jeremiah), and apparently comments only on a selection of *Isaiah* passages. Significant for understanding the community's self-image is 4QpIs^d, which explains the description of Jerusalem in *Isaiah* 54 as a symbol of the community and its leadership. Two texts contain a *pesher* of *Hosea:* 4QpHos^a (= 4Q166), 4QHos^b (= 4Q167). Of interest is the first. Expounding *Hosea* 2:10–14, it criticizes the calendar practiced in Israel at the time (4QHos^a ii 16), thus adding evidence to the well-known polemics on this issue in the Qumran writings. Other exemplars of continuous *pesharim* are poorly preserved: two interpret *Micah,* 1QpMic (= 1Q14) and 4QpMic (= 4Q168), and two expound *Zephaniah,* 1Q15 and 4QZeph (= 4Q170). A *pesher* of Malachi may also be extant (5Q10). The Psalms seem to be a favorite subject for the *pesher* authors. Three texts contain a *pesher* of *Psalms:* 1QpPs (= 1Q16), 4QpPs^a (= 4Q171), and 4QPs^b (= 4Q173). Substantial fragments of a pesher on Psalm 37 are preserved in 4QPs^a (4Q171), expressing the sectaries' hopes for the eschatological age, when the wicked will perish and the righteous will take possession of their inheritance. But contemporary controversies also occupy the pesher. The opponent of the Teacher of Righteousness, the Man of Lie, is accused of "misleading many with deceptive words for they have chosen light things" (4QpPs^a 1–10 i 26–27), probably another reference to the Pharisees and criticism of their method of interpreting biblical law. Various verses of *Psalms* are commented by other Qumran texts (cf. 4QFlorilegium and 4QCatena below).

Thematic *pesharim.* Thematic pesharim are works containing *pesher* interpretations arranged around central themes rather than producing a running commentary on a single text. Significantly, some of them, such as the *pesher* of Melchizedek, date to the first half of the first century BCE. So this form of *pesher* may have been created earlier than the running *pesharim.*

4QForilegium (4Q174). Structured around citations from 2 Samuel 7:10–14 (*1 Chron.* 17:9–13), *Exodus* 15:17–18, *Amos* 9–11, *Psalms* 1:1, *Isaiah* 8:11, *Ezekiel* 37:23, and *Psalms* 2:1, the work expounds various eschatological themes. Reflecting the Qumranites' criticism of the contemporary temple, the pesher, explaining *2 Samuel* 7, likens the reality of the Qumranites to a "Temple of Men" (*mqdš 'dm*) in which "deeds of Torah," namely practicing the Torah commandments, replace animal sacrifices (4QFlor 1–2 i 6–7). It expresses the hope for a future temple, established by divine initiative (4QFlor 1–2 i 3–5).

4QCatena A (4Q177). This text dated to the mid-first century BCE concerns the circumstances of the Qumran covenanters in the final redemptive age (4Q177 1–4 + 14 + 24 + 31 5). It strings together pesher comments on a selection of Psalms (*Ps.* 6, 11, 12, 13, 16, 17), developing each exposition with the help of additional allusions to other biblical passages. It has been recently suggested that 4QFlorileguim and 4QCatena A are copies of the same work (by A. Steudel). However, the absence of overlapping between the two and their different literary structure excludes this suggestion.

11QMelchizedek (11Q13). This single manuscript, dated to 75–50 BCE, takes its starting point from the Torah laws mandating the liberation of slaves and the return of the possessions in the jubilee year (*Lev.* 25: 10, 13; *cf. Deut.* 15:2). Linking them with additional Psalms (*Ps.* 82:1, 7:8–9, 82:2) and prophetic texts (*Isa.* 52:7, *Dan.* 9:25), the *pesher* explains it as a redemption of the righteous from the yoke of evil forces in the eschatological jubilee, under the guidance of Melchizedek, a supernatural figure of the eschatological judge. This *pesher* provides interesting examples of *pesher* exegesis applied to legal texts from *Leviticus* and *Deuteronomy.* In the biblical books these passages are formulated as part of the speech of Moses, a prophet already by biblical statement (*Deut.* 34:10), and hence apt for *pesher* exegesis. Of significance is the special eschatological role of Melchizedek in this *pesher,* not found in the biblical references (*Gen.* 14:18; *Ps.* 110:4) but it probably lies in the background to the *Letter to the Hebrews* 7, where Melchizedek prefigures Jesus as the divine and eternal high priest.

***Pesher* units in non-*pesher* works.** Smaller *pesharim,* of one or more sentences, are interwoven into compositions of different literary genres. Such are the *pesharim* occurring in the *Rule of the Community* (1QS VIII 12–16 expounding *Isa.* 40:3) and the *Damascus Document* (e.g., the *pesher* of *Hos.* 4:16 in CD I, 13–14, the *pesher* of *Ezek.* 44:15 in CD III, 21–IV,1–6, and the *pesher* of *Amos* 5:26–27 in CD VII, 14–18). Another example of an isolated *pesher* unit is provided by the *Commentary on Genesis A* (4Q252). This work contains commentary by various exegetical methods on a selection of passages from *Genesis,* but only a single comment of the *pesher* type. It interprets the pericope about Judah in the Blessing of Jacob (*Gen.* 49:10) as applying to the Qumranites at the End of Days (4Q252 V 1–7). The *Apocryphon of Joshua* offers another significant instance. Since this work lacks any explicit sectarian terminology, it is noteworthy that it contains a *pesher* on Joshua's curse of the builder of Jericho (*Josh.* 6:26), understood as referring to contemporary historical figures (4Q379 22 ii 7–15). This piece of *pesher* exegesis must be quite old, since it is cited by 4QTestimonia (4Q175), dated to around 100 BCE.

Sobriquets as allusions to *Pesher.* A special category is presented by sobriquets applied to figures and groups who played central roles in the life of the Qumran community. They appear in several sectarian compositions without explanation, thus indicating that they were already known and accepted nicknames. Yet they were not invented at random, for most are condensed expressions taken from particular biblical locutions; each epithet functions as a cryptogram for a full *pesher* to a given biblical paragraph. For instance, the epithet "the Teacher of Righteousness" (mentioned in CD, 1QpHab, 4QpPs^{a}), alludes to *Hosea* 10:12 and *Joel* 2:23. The sobriquet "Spouter of Lie" (mentioned in CD, 1QpHab, 1QpMic, and 4QpPs^{a}) refers to *Micah* 2:11. The appellation "Seekers of Smooth Things" (appearing in CD, 4QpIs^{c}, 4QpNah) is based on *Isaiah* 30:10 (*cf. Dan.* 11:32). "The Man of Mockery" or "the Men of Mockery" (occurring in CD and 4QpIs^{b}) alludes to *Isaiah* 28:14. Being intimately connected with the community's image of its history, these sobriquets occur only in the *pesharim* and in the *Damascus Document.* In this respect the *Damascus Document* has a special place within the library of Qumran, for its narrative text interweaves not only explicit *pesher* units but also numerous nonexplicit *pesharim,* namely citations without introductory formulae.

3. THE TERM *PESHER* AS INTRODUCTORY FORMULA. The use of the term *pesher* to introduce the comment after a citation is typical of the continuous *pesharim* and is also sporadically employed in the thematic *pesharim.* However, it appears only once in the *Damascus Document* (CD IV, 14). This distribution shows that this term was not constituent for the genre. In fact, in several Qumran texts of sectarian provenance (1Q30 1 6; 4Q180 1 1,7; 4Q252 IV 5; note also 4Q464 3 ii 7 and 4Q159 5 1, 5), the term *pesher* occurs in a general sense of "meaning, interpretation," without the specific adaptation to contemporary events known from the major *pesharim.* The absence of the term *pesher* from the earliest exemplar of running *pesher,* 4QpIsc (4Q163), and from examples of *pesharim* in the *Rule of the Community* and the *Damascus Document,* suggests that the genre went through various phases of development, still detected in the sectarian works.

4. THE *PESHER* EXEGETICAL METHOD. The *pesher* exegetical procedure can be summarized as follows: (1) The first step consists of equating one or more nouns of the biblical citation with nonbiblical nouns connected with the community's life and historical or contemporary circumstances. This initial equation is usually quite arbitrary. (2) The second step is to apply all or some of the remaining words of this phrase to the nonbiblical noun. (3) At times one detail is extracted from the citation for additional interpretation. In thematic *pesharim,* adducing other biblical quotations that share one element or more with the main citation often accomplishes such amplification. Since the connection between the citation and the interpretation is not obvious, in fact, quite obscure, the writers of the *pesharim* followed a number of exegetical procedures to bridge the gap. They modeled the interpretation on the syntactical and lexical patterns of the citation, selected lexical synonyms of words in the citation, made puns on words in the citation, atomized certain words (that is, disconnected the syntactical links), and vocalized or grouped the words of the citation in a different way. Many of these procedures were known and applied in antiquity to interpretations of dreams and dreamlike visions. The *pesher* exegesis, which appeared so unique to Qumran manuscripts when the first scrolls were published, cannot be considered the sole creation of the Qumranites. Actualizing interpretations, reading into biblical prophecies intimations of later historical events, appear in the *Book of Daniel* (*Dan.* 9:2–19, interpreting *Jer.* 25:11, 29:10, and *Dan.* 11: 30 interpreting *Num.* 24:24) and in the Gospels (e.g., *Matt.* 3:3, *Luke* 3:3–4, and *John* 1:23, commenting on *Isa.* 40:3; *Matt.* 21:4 and

John 12:14–15, citing *Zech.* 9:9). The antiquity of this method, attested as early as *Daniel* (around 164 BCE), suggests that it predates the emergence of the Qumran community, and that the Qumranites, like the first Christians later, received it from older tradents and appropriated it to their own purposes.

SEE ALSO Biblical Exegesis; Dead Sea Scrolls; Midrash and Aggadah.

BIBLIOGRAPHY

Text Editions

The first full edition of the cave 4 *pesharim* can be found in John M. Allegro, *Qumran Cave 4, I* (*DJD* V) (Oxford, 1968). It is to be used with the corrections and additions by J. Strugnell, "Notes en marge du volume V des Discoveries in the Judaean Desert of Jordan," *Revue de Qumran* 7 (1969–1971): 183–186. A fresh edition of the Allegro volume is now being prepared by G. J. Brooke and M. Bernstein. Fresh editions with introductions and commentaries of all the continuous *pesharim,* incorporating Strugnell's contributions and summarizing previous research, can be found in M. Horgan's *Pesharim: Qumran Interpretations of Biblical Books* (Washington, D.C., 1979). This is the most thorough collection of its kind and with due updating is still indispensable for the study of *pesharim.* For fresh editions and translations of all the continuous *pesharim* (mostly by M. Horgan; see previous reference) and thematic *pesharim,* together with texts the editors considered related to them (not justifiably in every case), see J. H. Charlesworth, ed., *Pesharim, Other Commentaries, and Related Documents* (*The Dead Sea Scrolls* 6B) (Tübingen and Louisville, 2002). The collection takes into account previous editions but provides no proper commentaries. It includes updated bibliographies and references to recent discussions, which place the *pesharim* in context of the contemporary Qumran research.

Surveys and Studies

An updated edition of the classical study first published in 1958 (one of the first to be published and one that can still be read with profit) is F. M. Cross's *The Ancient Library of Qumran,* 3d ed. (Minneapolis, 1995), pp. 88–120. For a thorough investigation of 4QForilegium and its exegetical methods in the context of ancient Jewish exegesis, see G. J. Brooke, *Exegesis at Qumran* (*JSOT Supp* 29) (Sheffield, 1985). B. Nitzan has a perceptive analysis of the *pesher* technique and structure contained in the introductory chapters of the Hebrew edition of the *pesher* of Habakkuk in "Creating Pesharim," in *Pesher Habakkuk* (Jerusalem, 1986; in Hebrew), pp. 29–79. For a survey of the research on the *pesharim* at the time of publication, see D. Dimant, "Pesharim, Qumran," in *The Anchor Bible Dictionary,* edited by D. N. Freedman, vol. 5 (New York, 1992), pp. 244–251. A. Steudel, *Der Midrasch zur Eschatologie aus der Qumran-gemeinde (4QMidrEschat^{a,b})* (STDJ 13) (Leiden, 1994), offers a fresh, improved edition of 4QFlorilegium [4Q174] and 4QCatena [4Q177] with detailed comments and discussion. However, the underlying assumption that both are copies of the same work is not supported by evidence. S. L. Berrin, "Pesharim," in *The Encyclopedia of the Dead Sea Scrolls,* edited by L. H. Schiffman and J. C. VanderKam, vol. 6 (Oxford, 2000), pp. 644–647, has a short survey of the subject. T. H. Lim, *Pesharim* (London and New York, 2002), offers a review of the *pesharim* and their study, aimed at students and the general public. Scholarly issues are often reviewed with a polemical edge.

DEVORAH DIMANT (2005)

PETER DAMIAN SEE DAMIAN, PETER

PETER LOMBARD (c. 1100–1160), also known as Peter the Lombard, was a Christian theologian and teacher. There is little precise knowledge of Peter Lombard's origin except that he was born in northern Italy at Lumellogno in Novarre before 1100. Peter was a student at Bologna (or perhaps Vercelli) before he went to France to study, first in Reims and then in Paris and its environs (c. 1134). While it is believed that he returned to Italy, visiting Rome in 1154, all of Peter Lombard's professional life and work is associated with a career in northern France, especially Paris, where he taught at the Cathedral School of Notre Dame. By 1143 his reputation was widespread. Sometime in 1144 or 1145 he became a canon at Notre Dame, and his teaching continued to influence students, among whom were Herbert of Bosham and Peter Comestor.

Peter Lombard participated in two significant ecclesiastical investigations concerning the orthodoxy of the teachings of Gilbert of Poitiers; the first was held in Paris on April 21, 1147, the second at the Council of Reims on March 21, 1148. By 1156 Peter was archdeacon of Paris, and on June 29, 1159, he was consecrated its bishop. He died the following year.

Today only four works attributed to Peter are considered authentic: a collection of sermons, two biblical commentaries, and the *Book of Sentences.* The thirty-three sermons were composed by Peter during the twenty years that he exercised leadership in Paris (c. 1140–1160). Until recently, many of these were attributed to Hildebert of Lavardin. Peter begins each sermon with a scriptural citation, and his homilies, although clear and precise, give little evidence of the academic interest in exegesis as a science that was developing at the time. Instead, Peter's instructions emphasize a moral and spiritual exposition.

The same approach to exegesis appears to characterize the Lombard's first biblical commentary, on *Psalms* (*Commentarius in psalmos Davidicos*), completed by 1138. Peter follows the method of the teachers at Laon (northern France), glossing the biblical word with a series of patristic teachings. The prologue to the commentary, however, does include the *accessus ad auctores* formula (author, text, subject matter, intention, and *modus tractandi)* that had only recently been appropriated to scriptural exposition in some of the school works. But because this work shows no influence of the anonymous *Summa sententiarum,* which dates from circa 1137–1138, it is usually seen as an early writing of the Lombard.

Peter Lombard's *Commentary on the Pauline Epistles* (1139–1141) brings a new dynamic to his teachings. Although composed shortly after his work on the psalter these glosses reflect the doctrine and exegetical methods from the schools. For example, he includes a wider variety of patristic sources; and the contemporary teachings of both the *Summa sententiarum* and of Gilbert of Poitiers appear as well. In addition, the *Commentary* shows some influence of the discursive inquiry associated with the new theological method, which brought questions to the text in an effort to discern meaning. However, Peter Lombard remained a cautious theologian, and although this work is more didactic than its predecessor he continued to stress spiritual exegesis.

It is the Lombard's last major work, the *Book of Sentences,* that sets his teachings apart in the twelfth century. The text provided his students with a systematic and comprehensive presentation of Christian doctrine in an orderly and accessible format: book 1 examines the Trinity; book 2 discusses creation, grace, and sin; book 3 presents the doctrines of incarnation and redemption; and book 4 considers the sacraments and eschatology. Although the work is a concise synthesis, Peter's citations of authorities provided a vast range of critically selected resources on distinctions and questions that were pertinent and timely. Understandably, Augustine was favored; but accepted contemporary works were also included, such as the *Glossa ordinaria,* the *Decretum* of Gratian, and the Lombard's own scriptural commentaries. Peter also confronted the vigorous inquiry of the school theologians, such as Hugh of Saint-Victor, Peter Abelard, and Gilbert of Poitiers. Peter's responses to the issues offered a moderate, orthodox position and met the needs of the times more adequately than the numerous other collections available. The final form of the *Sentences* was completed by 1157 or 1158.

The significance of Peter Lombard for the development of theology is due to the place of the *Sentences* in the medieval curriculum. What the *Glossa ordinaria* did for scripture, and what Gratian's *Decretum* did for law, the *Sentences* did for Christian doctrine. Peter would, in fact, be remembered as the "Master of the Sentences." His student Peter of Poitiers continued to use the *Sentences* for teaching his own classes in theology, and in about 1222 Alexander of Hales officially incorporated the text into the course of studies at the University of Paris. Thenceforth all students were required to comment on the *Sentences* for a degree in theology. In this way, all medieval theologians became disciples of the Lombard, and the format, method, and distinctions of the *Sentences* continued to shape theology for more than four hundred years.

BIBLIOGRAPHY

Critical editions of the Lombard's writings can be found in volumes 191 and 192 of J.-P. Migne's *Patrologia Latina* (1879–1880; reprint, Turnhout, 1975). His sermons, attributed to Hildebert of Lavardin, are edited in volume 171 of that series (1854; reprint, Turnhout, 1978). However, the best text of the *Sentences* is *Sententiae in IV libris distinctae,* 3d ed. (Rome, 1971).

A comprehensive and critical study of Peter Lombard's writings remains to be done. One standard reference for his life and teaching is the extensive essay by Joseph de Ghellinck, "Pierre Lombard," in the *Dictionnaire de théologie catholique* (Paris, 1903–1950). Several more recent studies have brought precision to this essay. For example, Philippe Delhaye's *Pierre Lombard: Sa vie, ses œuvres, sa morale* (Montreal, 1961) summarizes the major themes of the Lombard's writings: human nature, grace, freedom, the theological and cardinal virtues, the gifts of the Holy Spirit, sin, and penance. Ignatius Brady's major essay "Pierre Lombard" in the *Dictionnaire de spiritualité* (Paris, 1985) continues these scholarly efforts. Brady's article includes an extensive, up-to-date bibliography. Another significant resource is the journal *Pier Lombardo: Revista di teologia, filosofia e varia cultura* (Novarre, 1953–1962).

John van Dyk's study of the *Sentences,* "Thirty Years since Stegmüller: A Bibliographic Guide to the Study of Medieval Sentence Commentaries since the Publication of Stegmüller's *Repertorium* (1947)," *Franciscan Studies* 39 (1979): 255–315, updates previous bibliographies and compiles the best research on this text and its influence. Van Dyk's study includes many articles in English and organizes information into significant categories: texts and editions; philosophy, theology, history; and two indexes.

EILEEN F. KEARNEY (1987)

PETER THE APOSTLE (d. 64? CE) was one of the twelve apostles of Jesus and, according to Roman Catholic tradition, the first pope. The earliest sources of information about Peter are such that it is not possible to draw an altogether clear distinction between those elements in the image of Peter that are derived from his role in the church prior to his death and those that derive from the Peter of later Christian remembrance and tradition. None of the surviving sources is primarily interested in Peter. Only a few, *Galatians* and *1 Corinthians,* were written while Peter was still alive and by someone who certainly knew him. Those sources that give a more circumstantial account of Peter were written some years, often some decades, after his death. They incorporate the story of Peter into the story of Jesus and of the early church in such a way as to raise questions about the historicity of some of the details. Are accounts of Peter's prominent role among the apostles an accurate recollection of the way things actually happened, or are they a retrojection into the time of Jesus' ministry of the role that Peter would later play in the early church? No one denies that there is a substratum of fact or event behind the New Testament descriptions of Peter, but there is considerable disagreement about what that substratum is. These problems are neither so complex nor so heavy with consequences as the problems connected with "the historical Jesus," but they are similar in type.

THE APOSTLE. Symeon or Simon (Hebrew and Greek names, respectively) was, with his brother Andrew, a fisherman at the Sea of Galilee when they were both called to follow Jesus of Nazareth. They may have been the first called, and were to be among the closest of Jesus' followers. Simon was also called Kepha (or Kephas), which is Aramaic for "rock," the Greek form of which is *Petra* or *Petros,* whence the name *Peter.* According to both *Mark* 3:16 and *John* 4:42, it was Jesus who gave Simon this additional name, but the fact that the two accounts are quite different has led some to suggest that the name may have been given only subsequently, in view of his work in the early church, and then retrojected into the time of Jesus' ministry.

Various New Testament sources present Peter as playing a special role among the disciples during Jesus' lifetime. He is named first among the disciples (*Mk.* 3:16 and parallels, *Acts* 1:13). He is often presented as speaking on their behalf (*Mk.* 8:29, 10:28, 11:21, 16:7, and their parallels). Along with James and John, he is one of an inner circle among the disciples (*Mk.* 5:37, 9:2ff., 14:33, and their parallels).

In different ways *Matthew, Luke,* and *John* all relate that Jesus entrusted to Peter some special role in the community that Jesus was to leave behind. He is the rock on which the church is to be built (*Mt.* 16:18). Jesus prays for him that, after having been tested himself, he may strengthen his brethren (*Lk.* 22:31). Jesus takes him aside and specially commissions him to feed his lambs and his sheep (*Jn.* 21:15–17). Here again there is disagreement as to whether these narratives report events that actually took place or are efforts to legitimate Peter's later role in the early church by anchoring it in the actions of Jesus. A middle position is, of course, possible: that Jesus did entrust some special responsibility to Peter, and that this was later elaborated on by the evangelists.

Peter is also the disciple whose failures are most fully described in the New Testament. When he objects to Jesus' prediction of his own suffering and death, Jesus calls him Satan (*Mt.* 16:23, *Mk.* 8:33). When Jesus' final sufferings have already begun, Peter publicly denies any association with him (*Mk.* 14:66–72 and parallels). In addition, he is described, not unsympathetically, as being impetuous (*Jn.* 21:7).

Several different strands of New Testament tradition testify that Peter was the first of the apostles to see Jesus after he was raised from the dead. Many judge *1 Corinthians* 15:5 to be part of a traditional confessional formula. If this is correct, then well before the mid-fifties of the first century it was part of Christian tradition that Jesus appeared first to Kephas. In the Lucan account it is the women who first see the risen Jesus, but then Peter is the first of the apostles to see him after the women, and his seeing is clearly more important than theirs (*Lk.* 24:1–34). In *John,* Peter is the first to enter the empty tomb. Mary Magdalene is the first to see Jesus, and only subsequently a group of the apostles (all but Thomas) are together when they first see Jesus (*Jn.* 20:1–25).

Throughout the early chapters of *Acts* (chaps. 1–12), Peter plays the leading role in the formation and expansion of the church. He is the leading preacher and wonder-worker (2:14–36; 3:1–10, 11–26; 9:32–43). He is the first to extend the Christian mission to the Gentiles (10:1–11, 18).

To judge from Paul's letter to the Galatians, Peter was the most important figure in the church at Jerusalem in the late thirties (*Gal.* 1:18). According to the same source he was still one of the pillars of that church in the late forties but now is mentioned between James and John (2:9). It is in this same letter that Paul speaks of Peter as being raised up to preach to the Jews as he, Paul, had been sent to the gentiles (2:7–8). Paul provides no detailed information about Peter's work as apostle to the Jews, but the fact that he speaks of him in this way suggests that it must have been fairly extensive, and not confined merely to his work in the church at Jerusalem. It is known that Peter was in Antioch (*Gal.* 2:11–14), and it seems likely that he was in Corinth as well (*1 Cor.* 1:12). The fact that somewhat later in the first century the pseudonymous *1 Peter* is addressed to Christians in Pontus, Galatia, Asia, and Bithynia (*1 Pt.* 1:1) suggests that these regions were associated with Peter's ministry. Also, the fact that the letter is ostensibly sent from Rome (referred to in *1 Peter* 5:13 as "Babylon") suggests that a Roman activity of Peter was also a tradition at this time.

In the disputes over the obligation of gentile Christians to conform to Jewish law, Peter probably adopted a position somewhere between that of Paul and Paul's opponents. In theory he seems to have sided with Paul, but his practice apparently was not always consistent with his ideas (*Gal.* 2:11–14).

Peter's activity at Rome would later be of great importance in Christian tradition, and so has attracted considerable attention. There is no evidence linking him with Rome in the documents written during his lifetime, but the tradition that he preached at Rome is widely attested in the late first and second centuries. Because at this time the matter had not yet become important in church politics, there seems to be no good reason to question this early tradition. Equally early is the tradition of Peter's martyrdom (*Jn.* 21:18–19) and of his martyrdom in Rome (*1 Clement* 5). Archaeological investigation has not settled the question of Peter's burial place, but it has shown that by the middle of the second century Roman Christians honored a particular place as the location of Peter's burial.

PETER IN CHRISTIAN TRADITION. Peter remained prominent in a variety of Christian traditions in the second and third centuries. Several writings were ascribed to him, either directly or indirectly, and in several others he played a leading role. Early in the second century it was asserted that the gospel according to Mark was a compendium of Peter's teaching, a view that would be generally accepted in later orthodoxy. A *Gospel of Peter,* of heretical cast according to the bishop of Antioch, was in use in Syria in the second half of the century. The *Kerygma of Peter,* a work with some similarities to the writing of the second-century Christian apologists, may have been written before midcentury. An *Apocalypse of*

Peter dates from about the same time, and *The Acts of Peter* from not much later. The gnostic library from Nag Hammadi likewise contains several works in which Peter is featured: another *Apocalypse of Peter,* an *Acts of Peter and the Twelve Apostles,* and a *Letter of Peter to Philip.* These works probably date from the third century. None of these writings reveals much that is likely to be historically reliable about Peter, but taken together they indicate the importance accorded to Peter in the polymorphous Christianity of this period.

Another work, the *Kerugmata Petrou,* has been reconstructed by some scholars as among the earliest sources of the later pseudo-Clementine literature. (Some scholars deny that such a document ever existed.) This reconstructed document, of a strikingly Jewish-Christian character, describes a Peter who, along with James, takes the lead in defending Christianity against such perverters of the truth as Simon Magus and Paul of Tarsus.

It was within what would subsequently be identified as orthodox Christianity that the figure of Peter has exercised its most widespread and long-lasting influence. Within this orthodox tradition his influence has been especially important in the West. Peter has been seen as the archetypal Christian, as the prototype of episcopal church order, and as the first pope. The last has been the most influential—but also the most controverted—part of the Petrine tradition.

As early as the late first century the tradition arose that Peter (along with Paul) had made special provision for the leadership in the Roman church after their departure or death (see the authentic first letter of Clement of Rome to the Corinthians, chaps. 42 and 44). In the course of the subsequent controversy over gnosticism, the issue of the apostolic foundations of the church became very important. The same writers who stressed the apostolic authorship of the books of the New Testament also laid great stress on the apostolic foundations of particular churches. The church at Rome, because of the role allegedly played there by Peter and Paul, was singled out and came to see itself as the apostolic church *par excellence* (see Irenaeus, *Against Heresies* 3.3.1–3). Gradually this tradition of the Petrine origin of the Roman church (Paul gradually fades from the picture) is combined with the New Testament image of Peter as the first and even the leader of the apostles. On this basis, the Roman church is seen as the first and even the leader among the churches. At first, original succession ideas (in Irenaeus, for example) emphasized that the bishop was successor to the apostle-founder of the particular church as preacher of the apostolic gospel. By the late fourth century (some would say earlier), the claim is made that the bishop of Rome succeeds as well to Peter's apostolic primacy. It is on this basis that Rome claims authority over the entire church.

These views seem to have developed first within the Roman church itself and to have spread from there only slowly throughout the West. The Christian East had a different tradition and never fully accepted the Roman interpretation of Petrine authority. Traditionally the East too recognized a Petrine primacy within the New Testament and a kind of Roman primacy within the church universal. The nature of this latter primacy has been the subject of much dispute, and the East has fairly consistently refused to see it as involving a Roman authority over other churches, or at least over the churches of the East.

Other images of Peter have also flourished over the centuries. Peter as the keeper of the keys to the kingdom of heaven has played an important role in Christian art and folklore, taking its point of departure from the same New Testament text, *Matthew* 16:18, that has been so important in sustaining the image of Peter as the first pope. Similarly, the many images of Peter to be found in the New Testament—Peter as shepherd, as fisher of men, as confessor of true faith against false teaching, as weak and impetuous—have all been reflected at various times and places within the Christian tradition.

SEE ALSO Discipleship.

BIBLIOGRAPHY

The classic modern study of Peter from a conservative Protestant perspective is Oscar Cullman's *Peter, Disciple, Apostle, Martyr: A Historical and Theological Study,* 2d edition. (Philadelphia, 1953). Cullman gives a generally conservative reading of the New Testament texts, but he rejects the idea of successors to Peter. Less negative on this latter point is Rudolf Pesch's *Simon-Petrus: Geschichte und geschichtliche Bedeutung des ersten Jungers Jesu Christi* (Stuttgart, 1980). A very useful survey of the roles of Peter in the New Testament and of the methodological problems involved is given by Raymond Brown and others in *Peter in the New Testament* (Minneapolis, 1973). Eastern Christian perspectives on Peter are presented by John Meyendorff and others in *Peter in the New Testament* (Minneapolis, 1973). Eastern Christian perspectives on Peter are presented by John Meyendorff and others in the *Primacy of Peter* (London, 1963). See especially Meyendorff's contribution, "St. Peter in Byzantine Theology, " pp. 7–29.

On the matter of the archeological evidence for Peter at Rome, see Daniel W. O'Conner's *Peter in Rome: The Literacy, Liturgical and Archeological Evidence* (New York, 1969) and more briefly his "Peter in Rome: A Review and Position," in *Christianity, Judism, and Other Graeco-Roman Cults, edited by Jacob Neusner* (Leiden, 1975), pt. 2, pp. 146–160. For bibliographical information, see the section "Petrus" in the bibliography in *Archivum Historiae Pontificae* (Rome, 1968–).

JAMES F. MCCUE (1987)

PETRE, MAUDE DOMINICA.

PETRE, MAUDE DOMINICA. Maude Dominica Petre (1863–1942) is best remembered as the biographer of George Tyrrell, one of the main protagonists of Catholic modernism in England, a Roman Catholic reform movement between 1890 and 1910. The leaders of this movement tried to respond theologically and pastorally to the intellectual developments of modern culture, but they were suppressed by the Vatican. Petre was a participant in the modernist movement as well as one of its first historians and critics who long survived its demise. As a writer, editor, and translator of over a dozen books and more than one hundred articles on a wide range of religious, philosophical, and literary topics (always published under the name of M. D. Petre), she was a prolific theological author in her own right who has never been given the full recognition and critical attention she deserves.

Maude Petre was born, the seventh of eleven children, on August 4, 1863, on the Essex estate of the Petres, an old English Catholic family, resident there since 1539 and prominent in post-Reformation Catholic history. Her father was a younger son of the thirteenth Lord Petre, her mother was the daughter of the earl of Wicklow and a convert to Catholicism. Born on the feast of Saint Dominic, the child was given the middle name Dominica. She grew up in the stern but religious atmosphere of an aristocratic environment, described in detail in her autobiography *My Way of Faith* (1937). Petre received a wide education at home that included literature, history, philosophy, and several languages, later used in her extensive translation work. In 1882 both of her parents died. Deeply religious, she was nonetheless plagued by recurrent religious doubt. In order to overcome this insecurity in her Catholic belief, she went to Rome in 1885 to study Thomistic theology privately for a year, a decision that her aunt explained as having gone there "to study for the priesthood."

Hesitating between marriage and the religious life, she decided in 1890 to enter the novitiate of the Society of the Daughters of the Heart of Mary (*Filles de Marie*), founded during the French Revolution along freer lines than traditional women's orders because members were free to live alone rather than in community and did not wear distinctive dress. Petre became first a local and later a provincial superior of this congregation for England and Ireland. Much involved with practical social work, she promoted orphanages and settlement houses for the poor and instructed converts in Catholicism while at the same time pursuing her own writing, begun in 1895 with essays on literary figures such as Thomas Carlyle and Victor Hugo.

By 1900 Petre had met the Jesuit George Tyrrell at a retreat and had begun corresponding with him and other modernists, namely Henri Bremond and Baron Friedrich von Hügel. On Tyrrell's suggestion she began to keep a diary, and in these personal journals are found "not only the intellectual turmoil of a theological movement, but the personal torment of a great-hearted and deeply spiritual woman as well" (Crews, 1984, p. 11). Petre became so deeply attached to Tyrrell that an intimate personal friendship and correspondence developed and changed the course of her life. Tyrrell was impressed by the freedom of mind expressed in her writings, and their growing friendship led to closer collaboration. They exchanged their manuscripts for mutual criticism, published some texts together, and shared their readings, including some studies of Buddhism.

When Tyrrell left the Society of Jesuits, he found refuge in a small cottage on Petre's property in Storrington, Essex, where he died in 1909. He had appointed her as his literary executor, and it was in this capacity that she posthumously edited some of his writings and letters but especially his autobiographical fragment supplemented by her own account of his life under the title *Autobiography and Life of George Tyrrell* (1912). This remains an indispensable source for Tyrrell's personal development, although some critics judge it as lacking in distance and objectivity. The Catholic Church soon placed the two volumes on the Index of Forbidden Books, causing Petre further trouble after an earlier controversy occasioned by her *Catholicism and Independence: Being Studies in Spiritual Liberty* (1907), published at the height of the modernist crisis. This book explored the possible conflict between personal conscience and religious authority, outlining the qualities needed for a genuine reformer of the church. The controversies surrounding its publication made Petre decide to cut all ties with her religious congregation and work independently from then onward.

Petre had a healthy respect for civil and religious authority but was sharply critical of its abuse, especially in the church. She was the only woman asked to take the antimodernist oath, but she refused to do so. Her modernist views motivated her bishop to exclude her from taking Communion in her parish church, a decision she considered an unwarranted "pseudo-excommunication," but she got around this by worshiping in another diocese. After Tyrrell's death, Petre not only dealt with his literary estate but developed new social and political interests through her association with a center of international relations in Pontigny, France, and began to write about democracy, international developments, war and peace, socialism, and fascism. Her book *Modernism: Its Failures and Its Fruits* (1918) is significant in that it provides one of the earliest histories of this movement from an insider's perspective. Her closeness to the events and people gives it a lively directness without lacking critical analysis and objectivity. She returned to reflections on modernism twenty years later in her autobiography *My Way of Faith*, a moving account largely motivated by the need to show why she, as a trenchant critic of the church, had remained a loyal believer within it, revealing her love for the sacramental and mystical dimensions of the Christian faith. She published further books on von Hügel and Tyrrell's friendship and on Alfred Loisy, but she died suddenly on December 16, 1942, in London, where she resided during the last years of her life. Her active community involvement until the end was evident from her concern for many social causes, including her volunteer nursing and her work as a nighttime fire warden during World War II in London, just as she had nursed soldiers in France during World War I.

Assessing Maude Petre's full significance remains a scholarly task to be undertaken. With her books out of print and no longer widely read, she is a largely forgotten figure. Yet she was a remarkable, courageous woman of faith and a productive essayist and writer for a wider public, rather than a scholar. She took an active role in the modernist crisis and wrote on the burning issues of her day, whether religious, social, or political, a Christian believer who saw herself as both passionately religious and innately skeptical, offering limited obedience in the face of ecclesiastical pressure. Petre was not only deeply involved with modernism as a force of change in her church, but she responded to the dynamic patterns of a changing society by addressing questions on the changing views of women and on contemporary politics and ideology. Her writings on a broad range of topics from philosophy to theology, spirituality, history, and politics make her difficult to categorize. She wrestled with the great themes of the church in its relationship to modern culture, including questions of spirituality, asceticism, mission, and reform, and ultimately she judged the problems that modernism had tried to address as fundamentally challenges of spirituality and pastoral care that had not yet been met. She saw the need for a fuller and more spiritual Christianity, for a Copernican revolution in religion.

Petre also insisted on the spiritual independence of each person, and she had a deep respect for pluralism. In some ways she anticipated the emphases on reform and renewal proclaimed by the Second Vatican Council, of an *ecclesia semper reformanda*, but also a church "subservient to the religious and spiritual needs of humanity" (Petre, 1918, p. 67). Ellen Leonard (1991) has rightly seen Petre's theology and spirituality as deeply rooted in her own experience, that of a passionate faith in God, of her involvement in the world, and of the consciousness of herself as a woman. Petre said it had been her ambition when young to become a saint, a philosopher, and a martyr. She became a loyal critic, rebel, and pioneer instead, perhaps even a prophet. She considered religious experience as primary, believed in the separation of faith from certainty, the autonomous realms of secular knowledge, allegiance to the church as largely a matter of choice, and the possibility of salvation and revelation outside the Catholic Church. She even spoke of the possible coming of a new religion and believed fervently in the spiritual unity of humanity, still in search of its social and political embodiment. The rich legacy of her writings invites further scrutiny and study.

See Also Hügel, Friedrich von; Loisy, Alfred; Modernism, article on Christian Modernism; Tyrrell, George.

Bibliography

Maude Petre's publications date from 1885 to 1944 and cover a wide range of topics.

An extensive, though incomplete, list of her published and unpublished writings is in the first major study on Petre, Clyde F. Crews, *English Catholic Modernism: Maude Petre's Way of Faith* (Notre Dame, Ind., 1984). Ellen Leonard has made a start in examining Petre from a contemporary woman's perspective in *Unresting Transformation: The Theology and Spirituality of Maude Petre* (Lanham, Md., New York, and London, 1991), but a comprehensive critical analysis of Petre's significance within a larger framework of gender history and feminist theology is still outstanding.

Only a few of Petre's writings can be listed here, beginning with her first book on the work of the seventeenth-century Jesuit Peter Claver among African slaves in South America, *Aethiopum Servus: A Study in Christian Altruism* (London, 1896). A significant publication during the height of the modernist crisis was her controversial book *Catholicism and Independence: Being Studies in Spiritual Liberty* (London, 1907), followed more than ten years later by one of the earliest critical analyses of this movement, *Modernism: Its Failure and Its Fruits* (London, 1918). As her own life and works have been little studied, her reputation rests primarily on what she wrote on other modernists, especially the two-volume *Autobiography and Life of George Tyrrell* (London, 1912), the account *Von Hügel and Tyrrell: The Story of a Friendship* (London, 1937), and the posthumously published *Alfred Loisy: His Religious Significance* (Cambridge, U.K., 1944). However, Alec R. Vidler's *A Variety of Catholic Modernists* (Cambridge, U.K., 1970) lists Petre as a modernist in her own right, and readers can judge this for themselves by studying Petre's autobiography *My Way of Faith* (London, 1937) and her unpublished journals from 1900 to 1942 (see Maude Petre Papers, Add. MSS 52372–79, British Library, London).

Helpful introductory surveys are in Charles J. Healey, "Maude Petre: Her Life and Significance," *Recusant History* 15, no. 1 (May 1979): 23–42; and Clyde F. Crews, "Maude Petre's Modernism," *America* 144, no. 19 (May 16, 1981): 403–406. J. J. Kelly has published *The Letters of Baron Friedrich von Hügel and Maude D. Petre* (Louvain, Belgium, 2003).

Ursula King (2005)

PETR MOGHILA

PETR MOGHILA (1596–1646), also known as Petr Mohyla, or Movila, was an Orthodox metropolitan of Kiev. As head of the Orthodox church in the Ukraine, at that time under Polish rule, Petr Moghila was chiefly responsible for the revival of Orthodoxy in southwestern Russia following the Union of Brest-Litovsk (1596), at which a large part of the Orthodox population submitted to Rome. Although willing to consider possible schemes for union with Rome, Moghila devoted his energies to strengthening the position of the Orthodox who chose to remain independent of the papacy.

Of Romanian princely descent, Moghila was born in Moldavia and educated at the Orthodox school in Lwów. He may have continued his studies in the West, possibly at the University of Paris. Widely read in classical Latin literature and scholastic theology, dynamic and authoritarian by nature, Moghila became abbot of the important Monastery of the Caves at Kiev in 1627 and was made metropolitan of Kiev in 1633, a position he held until his death.

The thirteen years of Moghila's episcopate constitute a decisive cultural turning point for Orthodoxy in southwestern Russia. In the schools that he opened for Orthodox clergy and laity, the teaching was based on Western models and was given predominantly in Latin, not in Greek or Slavonic. Western secular and religious writings were studied together with modern science. The college that Moghila established at Kiev reached a standard of excellence unequaled elsewhere in the Orthodox world of the time and continued to play a formative role throughout the seventeenth century; many of the Russians who collaborated closely with Peter the Great had been educated there. Seeking to create an "Occidental Orthodoxy," Moghila opened Little Russia to Western influences half a century before this happened in Great Russia.

Moghila's latinizing approach is evident in the wide-ranging liturgical reforms that he imposed, for example in the Sacrament of Confession, where he replaced the deprecative formula used at absolution in the Greek manuals ("May God forgive you . . .") with an indicative formula taken directly from the Roman Catholic ritual ("I absolve you . . ."). *The Orthodox Confession of Faith* that he composed in 1639–1640 was based on Latin catechisms by Peter Canisius and others. Here Moghila not only employed the term *transubstantiation* but taught explicitly that the moment of consecration in the Eucharist occurs at the Words of Institution, not at the Epiclesis of the Holy Spirit; and when discussing the state of the departed he virtually adopted the Latin doctrine of purgatory. After extensive alterations had been made in the *Orthodox Confession* by the Greek theologian Meletios Syrigos, it was approved by the Council of Jassy (1642) and by the four Eastern patriarchs (1643). Moghila himself was displeased by these changes. In his Little Catechism (1645) he continued to affirm consecration by Words of Institution, although he was more guarded on the question of purgatory.

The *Orthodox Confession* represents the high-water mark of Roman Catholic theological influence upon the Christian East. But the extent of Moghila's Latinisms should not be exaggerated, for on questions such as the *filioque* and the papal claims, he adheres to the traditional Orthodox viewpoint, although he expresses this viewpoint in a moderate form.

BIBLIOGRAPHY

Works by Petr Moghila

The original Latin version of the *Orthodox Confession,* as drawn up by Moghila in 1640, is now lost; an intermediate Latin version, embodying many of the changes made by Meletios Syrigos in 1642 but sometimes adhering to the 1640 text, has been edited by Antoine Malvy and Marcel Viller, *La Confession Orthodoxe de Pierre Moghila métro-polite de Kiev, 1633–1646,* "Orientalia Christiana," vol. 10 (Rome, 1927). For the Greek text, as revised by Syrigos and adopted at Jassy, see part 1 of Ernest Julius Kimmel's *Monumental Fidei Ecclesiae Orientalis* (Jena, 1850), pp. 56–324; see also Ioannis N. Karmiris's *Ta dogmatika kai sumbolika mnemeia tes Orthodoxou Katholikes Ekklesias,* vol. 2 (Athens, 1953), pp. 593–686, translated into English as *The Orthodox Confession of the Catholic and Apostolic Eastern Church* (London, 1762); see also the new edition by J. J. Overbeck and James N. W. B. Robertson (London, 1898).

Works about Petr Moghila

On the cultural and educational aspects of his career, see William K. Medlin and Christos G. Patrinelis's *Renaissance Influences and Religious Reforms in Russia: Western and Post-Byzantine Impacts on Culture and Education, Sixteenth-Seventeenth Centuries* (Geneva, 1971), pp. 124–149; on his theological position, see part 1 of Georges Florovsky's *Ways of Russian Theology,* volume 5 of his *Collected Works,* edited by Richard S. Haugh (Belmont, Mass., 1979), pp. 64–78. Earlier studies include S. I. Golubev's classic work, *Kievskii Mitropolit Petr Mogila i ego spodvizhniki* (Kiev, 1883–1898); Émile Picot's "Pierre Movila (Mogila)," in *Bibliographie hellénique, ou Description raisonnée des ouvrages publiés par des Grecs au dix-septième siècle,* vol. 4, edited by Émile Legrand (Paris, 1896), pp. 104–159; and Téofil Ionesco's *La vie et l'œuvre de Pierre Movila, métropolite de Kiev* (Paris, 1944).

KALLISTOS WARE (1987)

PETTAZZONI, RAFFAELE (1883–1959), an Italian historian of religions, was "one of the very few historians of religion who took seriously the dimensions of his discipline: as a matter of fact, he attempted to master the entire field of *allgemeine Religionswissenschaft*" (Eliade, 1963, pp. 104–105). He founded and promoted historical religious studies in Italy in the first half of the twentieth century and presided over the International Association for the History of Religions from 1950 to his death.

LIFE. Pettazzoni was born in San Giovanni in Persiceto (Bologna) on February 3, 1883. He attended high school and university in Bologna, and during those years, under the influence of a positivist and Carduccian cultural background, he lost his Catholic faith. But he kept his love for religion and felt a vocation for the history of religions, a discipline absent in Italian universities at that time and in which he trained by himself, subordinating his philological, archaeological, and ethnological studies to it.

At the university in Bologna, Pettazzoni received useful suggestions for the study of myths and religions from Vittorio Puntoni, a Greek scholar also skilled in Oriental languages and literatures. Pettazzoni addressed problems of mythology and the history of religions in his M.A. degree thesis in Greek literature, "Le origini dei Kabiri nelle isole del Mar Tracio."After he received his degree (June 1905), he attended the Italian School of Archaeology of Rome (1905–1908). He then earned a general certificate of education in archaeological studies and subsequently worked as an inspector at the Prehistorical and Ethnographical Museum in Rome from August 1909 to October 1914, five years that were decisive for his scholar training. During that time he completed his classical education with the study of primitive civilizations, going from archaeology to paleoethnology, to ethnology, to the history of religions.

Pettazzoni took his first steps in the new discipline in an unfavorable political and cultural situation. Whereas in other European countries the scientific study of religions was flourishing, in Italy, after the abolition of theological departments in state universities (1873), there had been only sporadic official teaching of religious studies. At the beginning of the twentieth century the traditional indifference toward this subject was broken by the Catholic modernists' movement, which wanted to be a sound reaction against the supremacy of old ideas but which had "its own particular congenital deficiency: modernism, for its religious Catholic origins, for the very essence of its general aspirations, was fatally obliged to be much more interested in some religious problems than in others; the philosophy of religion particularly gained modernists' attention; in the history of religions first of all and above all they saw the history of Christianity" (Pettazzoni, 1912, p. viii). The hostility of the Catholic Church not only to modernistic ferments but also to the study of religious events using independent criteria along with the lack of understanding, or the opposition, of an important representative of Italian culture, Benedetto Croce, denied autonomous value to religion and thereby also denied its own autonomy to the historical-religious discipline.

In 1912 Pettazzoni published *La religione primitiva in Sardegna* about the primitive religion in Sardinia, the first monograph of a series he dedicated to single religions. In the same year, for the first time, he attended the Fourth International Congress on the History of Religions in Leiden, Netherlands. The following year he qualified to teach the history of religions at the university in Rome. (Before him only one other scholar, Uberto Pestalozza, had qualified in 1911. He qualified for the university in Milan, which established the conditions for the creation of another center for research on religions, the so-called Scuola mediterranea.)

In 1913–1914 Pettazzoni taught a free course at the university in Rome. He then taught with a temporary appointment at the university in Bologna until 1923, with an interruption for military service during World War I. At the end of 1923, after competitive examination, he became a full professor of the history of religions in Rome, the first such position for the subject founded in Italy, and he held this chair for thirty years, until 1953. In Rome from January 1937 to December 1939 he taught ethnology and so introduced this discipline into the faculties of letters and philosophy. Ethnology as historical science separated from anthropology and joined the history of religions. For Pettazzoni this union was a fundamental need, "since between the so-called historical civilizations (both ancient and modern) and the civilisations on an ethnologic level there is neither break nor substantial heterogeneity: but there is continuity and adhesion, in a dynamic development that goes from the most archaic forms of civilization to the most modern ones, with no solution of continuity" (Lanternari, 1959, p. 286). Pettazzoni gave concrete expression to this unity, founding the Institute for Primitive Civilization at the university in 1942.

From 1910 to 1924 Pettazzoni also faced problems connected with the methodology used in the study of religions. He explained his position about the matter in the preface to the volume of 1912, later in essays, and in his opening lecture of January 17, 1924. He advocated the historical-comparative method by which religious phenomena are not compared in themselves but in their historical, dynamic development; "a history embracing both inferior and superior religions, dead and living, primitive and contemporary, including Christianity, for also the history of Christianity as religious history, cannot be understood if it is not placed inside the whole religious history" (Pettazzoni, *Svolgimento e carattere della storia delle religioni,* 1924, p. 14).

In his works of that period and in his methodologic essays Pettazzoni's historiographic inclination is clear. In his writings he often returned to the foundations of his method, which he brought to maturity through his scientific work. For example, in a lecture to the Seventh International Congress on the History of Religions he clearly explained his method of comparison:

> But comparison must neither be made following the method of the old comparative mythology (Max Müller), which compared *only* what was comparable *from a linguistic point of view,* nor following the one of the anthropological school (E. B. Tylor), which compared *all* that appeared *morphologically* alike, even if only externally and superficially. Only what is *historically* comparable can be rightly compared. From a historical point of view, in principle we can compare culturally homogeneous facts, that is belonging to similar historical-cultural situations. The religion of a rural civilization can only be radically different from the religion of a nomadic one. (Pettazzoni, "Le due fonti della religione greca," 1951, pp. 123–124)

To the history of the comparative method and to his own comparative method, Pettazzoni dedicated the last article of his life, "Il metodo comparativo," published in *Numen* (1959).

His historicist ideas did not prevent him from appreciating some positive aspects of the phenomenology of religion. In the 1920s and 1930s, reviewing Gerardus van der Leeuw's works, Pettazzoni criticized the abstract nature and the classifying character of the typological methodology, but in the success of this school, from Rudolf Otto to the Dutch scholar, he saw the remarkable symptom of the need, more and more perceived by the history of religions, of overcoming the crisis of atomism and of collecting in a unifying synthesis.

In the 1950s Pettazzoni developed a personal relationship with Mircea Eliade (the first exchange of letters is dated 1926). Eliade favored Pettazzoni's approach to phenomenological positions.

> In systematic terms, it means to overcome the unilateral positions of phenomenology and of historicism integrating them mutually, that is strengthening the religious phenomenology with the historicist idea of development and the historicist historiograhy with the phenomenological requirement of the autonomous value of religion, so defining phenomenology in history

> and at the same time recognizing the character of qualified historical science to the religious history. (Pettazzoni, "Il metodo comparativo," 1959, p. 14)

Instead, until his last days he maintained a strong opposition to the fundamentally antihistoricist currents and to the irrationalistic conceptions of religion.

After 1945 Pettazzoni also expressed his political and social thoughts. For example, he stood up for the defense of freedom of culture, of religious freedom and toleration, and of laic principles. In the 1950s he worked for the advancement of religious-historical studies on a worldwide scale. In 1950 the International Association for the Study of the History of Religions (later the International Association for the History of Religions) was founded, and in the same year, after van der Leeuw's death, Pettazzoni became its president. He helped found the review *Numen* and the series *Studies in the History of Religions* (Supplements to *Numen)* in 1954. Also in 1954, during his presidency, the *International Bibliography of the History of Religions* began to be published under the supervision of C. J. Bleeker. Pettazzoni organized the Eighth International Congress on the History of Religions in Rome in April 1955. In the summer of 1958 he attended the congress in Tokyo, the first outside Europe.

Pettazzoni's last works worsened his already weak health, and he died in Rome on December 8, 1959. During the last months of his life some scholars, either trained at his school or in touch with it, held the chairs of history of religions in Rome (Angelo Brelich), in Cagliari (Ernesto de Martino), and in Messina (Ugo Bianchi), and some years later another pupil of his, Vittorio Lanternari, held a chair of ethnology, a discipline Pettazzoni strongly fought to have included in university faculties. In the early twenty-first century many more scholars refer to Pettazzoni's teaching, even if with different individual positions and different approaches.

WORK. After he published the volume about the primitive religion in Sardinia (1912), Pettazzoni in the 1920s published other works dedicated to single religions, studied in their historical-cultural backgrounds. His book on the religion of Zarathushtra in the religious history of Iran (1920) was the first volume of the series *Storia delle religioni,* which Pettazzoni founded and directed. This collection, fourteen volumes in all, including three other works by Pettazzoni and works by other authors, was published between 1920 and 1940. Pettazzoni also published a monograph on the religion of ancient Greece, *La religione nella Grecia antica fino ad Alessandro* (1921); an essay on mysteries, *I Misteri* (1924); and a small book on Japanese mythology, *La Mitologia giapponese secondo il I libro del Kojiki* (1929), the first of the second series he founded and directed, *Testi e documenti per la storia delle religioni,* seven volumes published between 1929 and 1937. In these monographs Pettazzoni based his research on the principle, expressed in his opening lecture in 1924, that every single religious event is a forming and, as such, is the ending—and therefore the indication—of a precious development and at the same time the starting point of a further one. Several years later he wrote: "History ignores revelations; she only knows formations. Every *phainómenon* is a *genómenon* for history" (Pettazzoni, "Les deux sources de la religion grecque," 1951, p. 2).

In addition to directing the two collections, Pettazzoni founded the School of Historical-Religious Studies and the review *Studi e Materiali di Storia delle Religioni,* which he edited from the first year (1925) to the double volume of 1953–1954. The programmed line of the review is on the second page of every issue: "Studies and Materials of History of Religions pursue scientific and cultural aims in their specific field. They give a contribution to the historical science as they consider religion in its development as a subject of history. They open larger horizons to culture promoting Italian thinkers' greater knowledge of less recent and less known forms and events."

Pettazzoni accepted contributions from Italian and foreign scholars who specialized in civilizations and occasionally studied the associated religions. "So, from the very beginning the review had assumed a twice as hybrid character, just as the other few periodicals of history of religions, then existing in the world, had: on the one hand, accepting articles of comparatists ('historians of religions'), of historians of single religions and of scholars of single civilisation in general; on the other hand accepting very different, if not often opposite methodological trends in each of these classes of contributors"; all this in order "to make events and problems of his discipline known in their largest variety, since he considered his discipline of the greatest importance; to arouse interest in it, and somehow to get its recognition in Italy, not only officially" (Brelich, 1969, pp. 6–7).

In 1910 Pettazzoni planned to develop *Dio: Formazione e sviluppo del monoteismo nella storia delle religioni* in three parts: the first part regarding the beings of the sky in primitive peoples' beliefs, the second part about the supreme gods of the polytheistic religions, the third part on the gods of the monotheistic religions. He finished only the first part, which was not published until 1922 because of World War I.

The problem of the Supreme Beings and of the origin of the idea of God was particularly discussed in the first half of the twentieth century. Andrew Lang's thesis, declaring that the first form of religiousness had been a rudimentary monotheism based on the faith in a Supreme Being conceived as "All-Father" and as creator, was asserted again by the ethnologist Wilhelm Schmidt, who, in the first volume of his monumental work *Der Ursprung der Gottesidee* (1912), "emphasized the exceptionally high character of the belief in the supreme being and, at the same time, its absolute primitivity and priority in comparison with any other belief, and therefore also its uniqueness" (Pettazzoni, 1922, p. 51). Pettazzoni, on the basis of this extensive work to verify ethnographic materials referring to uncultured peoples' religious beliefs, asserted that the claimed *Urmonotheismus* (primitive monotheism) could be reduced "to the more modest proportions of belief in a heavenly being, perceived as a personal figure of the sky, according to the forms of the mythical thought that is over to any form of primitive religiousness" (Pettazzoni, 1922, p. xvi).

The controversy between the two scholars continued into the 1950s. In Pettazzoni's opinion this belief in a being of uranic nature could be "seen also in the religions of most ancient peoples as the idea of a real God, and more precisely of a supreme God, according to the generally polytheistic character of the old religions." Moreover he asserted "that this universal belief in a celestial being was also of the greatest importance, later, in the historical development of the true monotheism" (Pettazzoni, 1922, p. xvi). In his works at the beginning of the 1920s he considered monotheism historically characterized as a revolution against polytheism: "*Logically* monotheism is the negation of polytheism, just as *historically* it presupposes a polytheism from which it derived as negation, that is as revolution" (Pettazzoni, 1923, p. 200).

Pettazzoni's research about the idea of God in his historical development advanced in a different way in comparison to the theory expressed in his 1922 volume. His attention increasingly concentrated on the Supreme Being's attributes, particularly on all-seeingness and omniscience. The study "Allwissende höchste Wesen bei primitivsten Völkern," published in *Archiv für Religionswissenschaft* (1931), is about the omniscient Supreme Beings of primitive peoples. The research was later enlarged to divine omniscience in different religions, a work that took up the author's time in the 1930s and 1940s and that was crowned with the systematic treatment published in Italian in 1955 and in English in 1956. Pettazzoni modified the thesis of the identity and unicity of the (uranic) nature of supreme beings, considering their nature conditioned by the cultural environment in which each supreme being was formed; hence the need for their own typology:

> The primitive notion of the Supreme Being is no abstract *a priori* idea but rises in men's thoughts from the very conditions of human existence; and since these conditions vary in the different phases and forms of primitive culture, the form of the Supreme Being varies accordingly within these phases. As in farming cultures the Supreme Being is Mother Earth, because man's sustenance comes from the earth, and as in pastoral communities he is Father Sky, since it is from the sky that there comes the rain to make the grass, which is needful for the pasture of the cattle and therefore for human life, spring up and grow, so in a hunting-culture the Supreme Being is the Lord of animals, because on him depends the capture of game and the result of the hunt, which is of vital consequence for man. (Pettazzoni, 1956, p. 445)

The project of another work of phenomenological character dates back to 1914; Pettazzoni realized this project in the decade 1925–1935, studying the confessional practice in non-Christian religions (but Christianity was not excluded from the plan) in a systematic way for the first time. Numerous articles and books were the fruit of this ten-year research. In a few pages in the essay "La confessione dei peccati: Metodo e risultati," published in *Scientia* (1937), Pettazzoni explained the method followed in the research and the results obtained. These results, expressed either in final form or as a temporary hypothesis, can be summarized so:

> The confession of sins appeared to him as a cathartic rite, essentially similar to the eliminating practices that usually accompany it. The elimination of the sin is obtained by evoking it orally, considering this, in the original phase, as a magic operation (the magic of the word). Nor did he see solution of continuity between the primitive magic operation and the confessional rite of the superior religions, giving both the elementary redeeming function: liberation from the miasma linked to the sin, first, and liberation from the repentance of the sin (or from the condition of sinner with regard to a god, or to God) later (Sabbatucci, 1963, p. 22).

The work on the confession of sins, as generally all the other works, received gratifying judgments from several scholars. The abundance and the clear exposition of the data collected were appreciated also by Adolfo Omodeo, who, however, denied any historical value to their interpretation, repeating his criticism, already expressed in other situations, to the position of the "science of religions," because "in it is possible only a process of generical synthesis of sociologic type, instead of the historical synthesis following an organized process of development" (Omodeo, 1937, p. 368). Pettazzoni replied to his colleague's criticism some years later, confirming his historicist position and the validity of historical-religious studies as historical science (Pettazzoni, 1946, pp. xvi–xvii).

"Pettazzoni is the scientist of great works," wrote Eliade (Eliade, 1938, p. 226). After the enormous research on the confession of sins, Pettazzoni undertook another important work that he had been planning since 1931: a wide anthology of the myths and legends of the peoples who did not know writing in order to divulge the voices of a primitive humanity. He worked on it in the first half of the 1940s and continued in the following years with the collaboration of Tullio Tentori (vol. 4, 1959) and Vittorio Lanternari, who completed it, supervising and finishing the second volume (1963).

This work persuaded Pettazzoni to return to a subject that had interested him during his youth: the interpretation of myth, the relation between myth and religion. In the preface of the first volume of *Miti e leggende* (1948) and in successive essays he expressed his idea of the "truth of myth":

> It is thus evident that the myth is not pure fiction; it is not fable but history, a "true story" and not a "false" one. It is a true story because of its contents, which are an account of events that really took place, starting from those impressive happenings which belong to the beginnings of things, the origin of the world and of mankind, that of life and death, of the animal and vegetable species, of hunting and of tilling the soil, of worship, of ini-

tiation-rites, of the associations of medicine-men and of their powers of healing. All these events are far removed in time, and from them our present life had its beginning and its foundation, from them came the present structure of society, which still depends on them. The divine or other superhuman persons who play their parts in the myth, their remarkable exploits and surprising adventures, all this world of wonders is a transcendent reality which may not be doubted, because it is the antecedent, the *sine qua non* of present reality. Myth is true history because it is sacred history, not only by reason of its contents but also because of the concrete sacral forces which it sets going. The recital of myths of beginnings is incorporated in cult because it is cult itself and contributes to the ends for which cult is celebrated, these being the preservation and increase of life. (Pettazzoni, 1954, p. 15)

In his works of the 1950s Pettazzoni's methodological idea came to complete maturity. For example, in his writings about divine omniscience, compared to the volume on the celestial being, he "articulates his interpretation to the different cultural situations considered in their heterogeneous contexts, with coherently appropriate and different meanings." And in his introduction to the new edition of the book about the Greek religion "for the first time the historicist planning, that links the religious history to the social-economic history, appears in articulated terms" (Lanternari, 1997, p. 16).

SEE ALSO Historiography, overview article; Monotheism; Schmidt, Wilhelm; Study of Religion, overview article; Supreme Beings.

BIBLIOGRAPHY

A rich and important collection of bibliographic and documentary literature about Pettazzoni's life and work is Mario Gandini, "Il Fondo Pettazzoni della Biblioteca comunale 'G. C. Croce' di San Giovanni in Persiceto (Bologna)," *Archaeus* 7 (2003). Pettazzoni's main publications include "Le origini dei Kabiri nelle isole del Mar Tracio," *Memorie della R. Accademia nazionale dei Lincei: Classe di scienze morali*, vol. 12 (Rome, 1909), pp. 635–740; *La religione primitiva in Sardegna* (Piacenza, Italy, 1912); *La religione di Zarathustra nella storia religiosa dell'Iran* (Bologna, Italy, 1920); *La religione nella Grecia antica fino ad Alessandro* (Bologna, Italy, 1921; new ed., Turin, Italy, 1953; French translation, Paris, 1953); *Dio: Formazione e sviluppo del monoteismo nella storia delle religioni*, vol. 1, *L'essere celeste nelle credenze dei popoli primitivi* (Rome, 1922); "La formation du monothéisme," *Revue de l'Histoire des Religions* 44, no. 88 (1923): 193–229; *I Misteri: Saggio di una teoria storico-religiosa* (Bologna, Italy, 1924); *Svolgimento e carattere della storia delle religioni* (Bari, Italy, 1924); *La mitologia giapponese secondo il I libro del Kojiki* (Bologna, Italy, 1929); *La confessione dei peccati*, 3 vols. (Bologna, Italy, 1929, 1935, 1936; French edition of vol. 1, Paris, 1931–1932); "Allwissende höchste Wesen bei primitivsten Völkern," *Archiv für Religionswissenschaft* 29 (1931): 108–129, 209–243; "La confessione dei peccati: Metodo e risultati," *Scientia* 31, no. 61 (1937): 226–232; *Saggi di storia delle religioni e di mitologia* (Rome, 1946); *Miti e leggende*, vol. 1, *Africa, Australia* (Turin, Italy, 1948), vol. 2, with Vittorio Lanternari, *Oceania* (Turin, Italy, 1963), vol. 3, *America settentrionale* (Turin, Italy, 1953), vol. 4, with Tullio Tentori, *America centrale e meridionale* (Turin, Italy, 1959); "Le due fonti della religione greca," in *Proceedings of the Seventh Congress on the History of Religions, Amsterdam, 4th–9th September 1950* (Amsterdam, 1951), pp. 123–124; "Les deux sources de la religion grecque," *Mnemosyne* 4, no. 4 (1951): 1–8; *Italia religiosa* (Bari, Italy, 1952); *Essays on the History of Religions*, translated by H. J. Rose (Leiden, 1954); *L'onniscienza di Dio* (Turin, Italy, 1955; English translations, London, 1956, New York, 1978; Polish translation, Warsaw, 1967); *L'essere supremo nelle religioni primitive (L'onniscienza di Dio)* (Turin, Italy, 1957; German translation Frankfurt am Main and Hamburg, 1960); *Letture religiose* (Florence, Italy, 1959); "Il metodo comparativo," *Numen* 6 (1959): 1–14; and *Religione e società*, edited by Mario Gandini (Bologna, Italy, 1966), reprints of the most significant essays of the years 1948–1959.

For a bibliography of Pettazzoni's writings and a list of writings on him and on religious-historical studies in Italy up to 1969, see Mario Gandini, "Nota bibliografica degli scritti di Raffaele Pettazzoni," *Studi e Materiali di Storia delle Religioni* 31 (1960): 3–21, and "Il contributo di Raffaele Pettazzoni agli studi storico-religiosi," *Strada maestra* 2 (1969): 1–48. Other bibliographic supplements are in Gandini, "Presenza di Pettazzoni," *Strada maestra* 3 (1970): 1–69. These bibliographic lists are reprinted in Jacques Waardenburg, *Classical Approaches to the Study of Religion*, vol. 2, *Bibliography* (The Hague and Paris, 1973), pp. 209–215.

For detailed and documented notes on Pettazzoni's life, his published and unpublished writings, his scientific and teaching activities, the critical valuation of his works, his relations with Italian and foreign scholars up to 1940, see the eighteen instalments (over 1,800 pages) of Mario Gandini, "Raffaele Pettazzoni. Materiali per una biografia," *Strada maestra* 27 (1989)–55 (2003). On Pettazzoni's thought and work see disciples' writings: Vittorio Lanternari, *Rivista di Antropologia* 46 (1959): 283–286; Angelo Brelich, *Studi e Materiali di Storia delle Religioni* 31 (1960): 23–28, 191–202; Dario Sabbatucci, *Numen* 10 (1963): 1–41; and Ugo Bianchi, *The History of Religions* (Leiden, 1975), pp. 199–200, and "Between Positivism and Historicism: The Position of R. Pettazzoni," in *Religionswissenschaft und Kulturkritik*, edited by Hans G. Kippenberg and Brigitte Luchesi (Marburg, Germany, 1991), pp. 259–263.

See also Delio Cantimori, *Nuova rivista storica* 44 (1960): 179–187; Alphonse Dupront, *La Table Ronde* 154 (1960): 129–133; Charles Picard, *Revue de l'Histoire des Religions* 79, no. 157 (1960): 260–266; Ugo Bianchi, Claas Jouco Bleeker, and Alessandro Bausani, eds., *Problems and Methods of the History of Religions* (Leiden, 1972), especially Geo Widengren, "La méthode comparative: Entre philologie et phénomenologie," pp. 5–14, in which the Swedish scholar expresses a number of reservations about Pettazzoni's historical-comparative method; Eric J. Sharpe, *Comparative Religion: A History* (London, 1975), pp. 184–185; Ugo Casalegno, *Dio, Esseri Supremi, Monoteismo nell'itinerario scientifico di Raffaele Pettazzoni* (Turin, Italy, 1979); Olof Pettersson and Hans Åkeberg, *Interpreting Religious Phenomena: Studies with Reference to the Phenomenology of Religion* (Stockholm, 1981), pp. 46–49; *Studi e Materiali di Storia delle Religioni* 49 (1983): 1; Nicola Gasbarro and Paola Pisi, *Studi e Materiali di Storia delle Religioni* 56 (1990): 1; Frank Whaling, "Comparative Approaches," in *Contemporary Approaches to the Study of Religion,* vol. 1, edited by Frank Whaling (Berlin and New York, 1983–1984), pp. 262–264; Sonia Giusti, *Storia e mitologia* (Rome, 1988); Mircea Eliade and Raffaele Pettazzoni, *L'Histoire des Religions a-t-elle un sens? Correspondance 1926–1959,* edited by Natale Spineto (Paris, 1994); Walter H. Capps, *Religious Studies: The Making of a Discipline* (Minneapolis, 1995), pp. 89–93; Natale Spineto, "Raffaele Pettazzoni e la verità del mito," *Rivista di storia della storiografia moderna* 17 (1996): 59–65, and "Raffaele Pettazzoni e la comparazione, fra storicismo e fenomenologia," *Storiografia* 6 (2002): 27–48; Riccardo Nanini, "Raffaele Pettazzoni e la fenomenologia della religione," *Studia Patavina* 50 (2003): 377–413; Mircea Eliade, *Zalmoxis* 1 (1938): 226, and "The History of Religions in Retrospect 1912–1962," *Journal of Bible and Religion* 31, no. 2 (1963): 98–109, 104–105; Angelo Brelich, "Premessa," *Studi e Materiali di Storia delle Religioni* 40 (1969): 3–26; Angelo Brelich, ed., "Gli ultimi appunti di Raffaele Pettazzoni," *Studi e Materiali di Storia delle Religioni* 31 (1960): 23–55; and Adolfo Omodeo, *La Critica* 35 (1937): 367–371.

For an explanation of religious anthropology in Italy, see Vittorio Lanternari, "La parole des exclus de l'histoire: Débuts de l'anthropologie religieuse en Italie," *Ethnologie française* (1994): 497–513, and *Antropologia religiosa: Etnologia, storia, folklore* (Bari, Italy, 1997), pp. 7–71. See also Gianfranco Bertagni, *Lo studio comparato delle religioni: Mircea Eliade e la Scuola italiana* (Bologna, Italy, 2002); and Giuseppe Mihelcic, *Una religione di libertà: Raffaele Pettazzoni e la scuola romana di storia delle religioni* (Rome, 2003). For a review of contemporary studies, see Natale Spineto, "Storici delle religioni italiani del '900: Notizie e osservazioni sugli studi recenti (1995–2000)," *Storiografia* 3, special issue (1999): 63–82.

Mario Gandini (2005)

PEUHL RELIGION See FULBE RELIGION

PEYOTE CULTS See PSYCHEDELIC DRUGS

PHALLUS AND VAGINA. The historical religious traditions and the modern critical study of religion share at least one thing in common: they both display an abiding fascination with the sexual organs and their power to shape religious language, social life, human thought, and the experience of the sacred itself. Historically speaking, both this history and this modern study have been controlled largely by male actors, that is, by human beings with penises, and so these discourses have tended to be phallic discourses that implicitly or explicitly erase, ignore, or simply deny the vagina, whose internal and external anatomy, sexual function, and means of arousal male actors have seldom, if ever, really understood. This situation, however, has changed dramatically since the 1960s. As women and female perspectives have increasingly entered the center of the study of religion and enriched, deepened, and complicated our understandings, the phallus has, in one sense, only become more important—though in ways that depart considerably from the earlier male views and positions—within a broad critical discourse that Jan Campbell has humorously but quite accurately called "arguing with the phallus." At the same time, the vagina has entered more and more into both the discussion and the historical analyses, particularly through the foundational philosophical work of Luce Irigaray and other French and Anglo-American feminist writers, enriching further and correcting what has long been a very one-sided and inadequate sexual perspective on the history of religions. Since most of the scholarship has in fact focused on the phallus, the relative coverage of the phallus and the vagina in the present entry will replicate this unevenness, but with the important caveat that this state of things is neither intellectually desirable nor historically faithful to the realities of roughly half the planet's past and present human inhabitants.

Before writing a history of the phallus and the vagina in the world's religions, however, it would be helpful to distinguish between what might be called implicit and explicit histories. This distinction takes us immediately into the realm of contemporary theory, an inevitable step, since there are no adequate sexual histories without developed sexual theories. Implicit sexual phenomena include all those common symbols or institutions of religion that imply the phallus or vagina but do not actually display them as such. Explicit sexual phenomena include all those that do. To take a few very simple examples, the Jewish and Islamic practices of circumcision (the ritual cutting of the foreskin to signal God's covenant with the community), the Hindu *liṅga-yoni* (an iconic representation of the divine phallus and vagina in union), and the Christian language about those who have willingly "castrated themselves for the kingdom of heaven" (*Matt.* 19:11–12) all focus explicitly and obviously on the sexual organs as central to the religious meanings of the act, figure, or saying, even if these same sexual meanings have been suppressed or euphemistically reinterpreted at different points by the traditions themselves. On the other hand, any prayer, devotional sigh, scriptural text, or sacred story that understands the divine as a "father" is an implicitly phallic expression, since, biologically speaking, it is the phallus that constitutes a father as a father, that is, as a procreative parent of a child ("father" and "phallus," of course, imply both "mother" and "vagina," but the latter have traditionally been erased in religious language and consciousness, particularly in the monotheistic West, where the One God can have no consort or spouse).

The point is a simple but important one: the semiotic reach of the vagina and the phallus in the history of religions is far greater than the casual reader or common wisdom might first suppose. Once both implicit and explicit sexual phenomena and their relationships are recognized, it is remarkably easy to see how central the sexual organs are to the history of religions. Indeed, from the innumerable creation myths of antiquity that employ the trope of human sexuality to express cosmic origins to the moral debates surrounding genetic engineering and human cloning (that is, conception outside the female womb), from the first recorded crisis in early Christian churches over the necessity of circumcising Gentiles (that is, ritually cutting their adult penises) to the most recent Christian debates about the ordination of women (who lack the penis that Jesus had) or gay men (who have one but allegedly use it wrongly), the history of religions is, on one level at least, a history of the phallus, the vagina, and their (dis)unions. The case is overstated here for the sake of illumination, as there are other factors clearly at work in all of these examples, from communal identity and purity sensibilities surrounding menstruation, birth, and anal intercourse to philosophical understandings of "nature" and "the natural," but the point remains: the history of religions has been deeply informed by basic sexual physiology.

THE SEXUAL IGNORANCE OF THE RELIGIONS. This same history, it turns out, is also a relatively ignorant one, for when it comes to the actual biological workings of the vagina and the phallus, the history of religions is defined by at least two forms of sexual ignorance. The first involves the wildly incorrect agricultural metaphor of "seed and soil" that implicitly identifies the male as the sower of the person or soul and the owner of the field, and likewise likens the female role to a kind of passive dirt (so that if there is infertitlity in a couple it is ascribed to the woman, who is said to be "barren"). Within this same broad agricultural complex appears the astonishingly common pattern of likening the male or masculine to spirit, soul, seed, and culture and the female or feminine to the body, sexuality, soil, nature, and death. Biological knowledge of the mathematically even (23/23) genetic contribution of male and female chromosomal material via the event of ovum fertilization and subsequent cell division is entirely modern and would likely weaken the legitimacy and meaningfulness of both the symbolism of seed and soil and its dramatic asymmetrical gender implications, were these genetic facts fully understood and appropriated. They, of course, have not been, but the point remains: the sexual-agricultural symbolism of religious history rests on a serious biological error that has had profound, and profoundly asymmetrical, gender implications for religious consciousness.

The second form of sexual ignorance involves the practical impossibility, again until very recently, of guaranteeing correct paternity and, therefore, a definite lineage or flow of inheritance (*pater semper incertus est,* "the father is always uncertain," as one Latin proverb had it; or, in a more modern south Chicago version, "mama's baby, papa's maybe"). This particular inability to know the identity of the father has in turn produced any number of purity code systems and other, often extreme, cultural measures designed to guarantee paternity and so control the smooth flow of inheritance and family line from one generation to the next. Male anxieties over female (but seldom male) virginity, the actual control of women and their physical movement or location, the marriage of young women or girls shortly after or even before puberty—all of these common cultural practices are designed to ensure paternity; that is, to guarantee that the owner of the "field," and only the owner of the field, sows his "seed" there.

Behind both of these broad cultural patterns, moreover, lies a material and political economy that understands female sexuality to be a kind of male possession in need of control and protection and capable of being traded among other male social actors—hence that immense swath of cultural practices from the institutions of prostitution, in which (primarily female) sexual acts are literally bought and sold, and the multiple practices of dowry, or bride price, in which a marriage arranged by male actors is accompanied by a negotiated exchange of economic goods, to the modern Western practices of the father "giving away the bride" and the bride taking on the surname of the groom's family line. Once these two broad metaphorical discourses are in place—the male seed and both the female farm and its fruit as male sexual possessions—much of the traditional religious systems develop, almost logically, around them.

Much, but by no means all. In actual historical fact, the phallus and the vagina have not been restricted to procreative symbolism in the history of religions, and so the agricultural frame of reference, although indeed often central, is hardly the only one to consider. For strictly procreative purposes, the phallus may physiologically imply the vagina and vice versa, but one would be seriously mistaken to reduce all religious sexual symbolism or activity to procreative meanings and heterosexual patterns. In actual historical fact, vaginas and phalluses come to express multiple meanings in the history of religions, and many, perhaps even most, of these have little, if anything, to do with physical procreation or, for that matter, heterosexuality. Indeed, in many cases, it is some form of homosexual expression or homoerotic symbolism that is implicitly or explicitly normative. Moreover, and perhaps even more importantly, aggression and submission are often more primary than any literal sexual code; that is, like their primate cousins, human beings use penile and posterior displays to express both social and religious power.

In writing a dual history of the vagina and the phallus, then, it is important to learn to see these highly coded semiotic organs as physiologically related on at least two levels (via heterosexual intercourse and the sexological fact that the penis and the clitoris are biological transformations of one another), but also as quite independent and perfectly capable of multiple and diverse pairings, erotic directions, and expressive acts. As in documented human sexual behavior, the vagina of religious symbolism does not always imply the phallus, nor the phallus the vagina. With one's perspective shifted toward this kind of complementarity *and* independence, the history of religions becomes a remarkably dramatic expression of erotic diversity constituted by sexual expressions, repressions, aggressions, sublimations, cuts, castrations, and orgasmic states of altered consciousness that people have only begun to admit and identify, much less understand, analyze, and evaluate.

PREHISTORY. Much ink has been spilled discussing just what prehistoric communities knew or did not know about the details of sexual reproduction. Many writers, particularly within popular feminist circles since the 1970s, have inferred from the impressive consistency of the female genitalia and the exaggerated breasts and hips of the Paleolithic "Venus figurines" found in Europe that prehistoric peoples worshiped women as fertility goddesses and did not yet understand the role of the male and the phallus in human procreation. Beginning with Johann Jakob Bachofen's *Das Mutterrecht* (1861), some have even gone so far as to suggest an early matriarchal culture that preceded a later patriarchal revolution, with each successive evolutionary stage defined by a respective sexual organ; that is, the primordial vagina and the later, secondary phallus. As numerous anthropologists and historians of religions have pointed out, however, there simply is no solid evidence for any such matriarchal culture. As Cynthia Eller has powerfully pointed out, no such society is known of, anywhere or at any time; much of the Paleolithic evidence can be read in other ways, including explicitly phallic and even pornographic ways (some of the figurines and drawings do vaguely resemble sexual positions used to this day in pornographic contexts); and both the anthropological evidence and the findings of primate studies strongly suggest quite the opposite. Primate communities, for example, which cultural historians inclined toward evolutionary models would presumably identify as "older" than any human cultures, display very strong patterns of male dominance. Moreover, as Sherry Ortner has shown in a classic essay, "Is Female to Male as Nature Is to Culture?," human cultures across the globe have shown a remarkably consistent tendency to analogize maleness to culture and femaleness to nature—and consequently to subordinate and devalue women (see Ortner, 1996).

In any case, it remains generally true that Paleolithic art found on the European continent displays the vagina and phallus and what sometimes appear to be their symbolic equivalents, in ways that suggest strong cultural interest in, if not an overriding obsession with, these same sexual organs.

ANCIENT GREECE AND ROME. In what is arguably the definitive study of the phallus in ancient Greek culture to date, Eva Keuls has pointed out that classicists teaching Aristophanes routinely tell their students that if they cannot detect an obscenity in any particular phrase, they are probably not understanding the passage properly, and that a previous German encyclopedia entry on "Phallos," which did not even approach completeness, covered sixty-eight pages of dense columns. No culture, she suggests, has been more imbued with phallic meanings than the Greek world, even if much of modern classicist scholarship has striven mightily to subdue this truth or, more concretely, lock its painted ceramic evidence away in secret museum cabinets or behind euphemistic translations and obfuscating readings.

It seems difficult to argue with Keuls's point. This, after all, was a male culture that created an elaborate system of prostitution, legally understood women and slaves as sexual possessions, developed a pottery tradition portraying almost every sexual act imaginable (including vaginal, intercrural, anal, same-sex, pederastic, and via dildos), and encouraged pederastic sexual intercourse with the sons of each other's social peers as a means of organizing social life and its elaborate sexual-social hierarchies. They commonly and proudly displayed their genitals in public—to the amazement (and laughing ridicule) of foreigners—and studded their cities with "Herms," those abstract stone representatives of the god Hermes that marked boundaries and doorways—much like the Japanese Shintō phallic stones used to mark boundaries or the Yoruba phallic images of the god Legba established before every house—and boasted only two detailed characteristics: a bearded head and an erect phallus (the head and the phallus are thus iconically connected very early). Moreover, as Keuls points out, the entire Dionysiac religion, and along with it the Western origins of both tragedy and comedy, sprang out of the "systematic veneration of the male generative principle" (1985, p. 78). Nor can such historical readings be safely fended off as functions of our own modern obsessions, as if every Greek "phallic symbol" were really nothing but our own anachronistic Freudian projection. What to do, after all, with all those playful Greek representations of birds, horses, and plants that commonly sport anatomically accurate penises in place of their heads? What to do when the head or bird (compare the English "cock") is not a phallic symbol but an actual phallus? The Greek joke, it appears, is very much still Freud's.

But all was not humor. There was violence as well, real violence, hence the cultural resonance of the *Amazonomachia,* the "battle of the sexes" enacted between Greek males and Amazon women so obsessively dwelt on by Greek writers and artists. In pottery illustrations of these battles, the phallus is a kind of weapon, with the male swords and spears held in obviously phallic positions and aimed at women's genitals or breasts. In this same context, Keuls also sees reflected the elaborate mythologies of rape (with Zeus playing the central rapist), Attic warmongering, and the misogynistic myth of Pandora's "box": whereas the phallus is displayed and openly celebrated in myth and ritual, the vagina is mythologized here as the primordial source of all evil and suffering. The phallus too carries a real ambivalence in Greek culture and in the general history of religions, alternating consistently between the two poles of sexuality and aggression, that is, as organ of fertility, ecstasy, and life, and as weapon of anger, domination, threat, and violence.

It was Hermes's son, the half-man, half-goat shepherd Pan, who, like the Greek satyrs, was associated with natural fertility, along with Priapus, who later becomes so popular with the Romans as the god of the garden, despite (or because of) what the Greeks considered his exaggerated and quite ugly phallus (as Keuls has pointed out, the Greeks liked theirs small and dainty). It is worth noting that Pan is particularly important for the later history of religions, primarily through his morphing into the Christian devil, himself often connected, implicitly or explicitly, to sexuality, the initiatory insemination of witches, and the antinomian counterstructures of sexual magic from medieval witchcraft trials to Aleister Crowley. Not surprisingly, then, when the English poet William Blake wanted to celebrate the transgressive sacrality and poetic potency of sexuality, he did so through what he called "the voice of the Devil." That is, after all, what the religious phallus of antiquity (Hermes, Dionysius, Pan, and Priapus) had become in the Christian imagination. In the Christian demonization of sexuality and the phallus one can perhaps hear psychosexual echoes of earlier castration motifs (witches were said to collect penises) that are found in such abundance in the mythologies of the Egyptian Osiris (whose dismembered body gathered together by his wife/sister Isis lacked only the penis), the Greek Ouranos (violently castrated by his children in Hesiod's *Theogony*), and the Greek and Roman Attis (the gentle lover self-castrated in sorrow for his unfaithfulness to the mother goddess Cybele).

JUDAISM. All three Western monotheistic traditions (Judaism, Christianity, and Islam) locate the origin point of their faith communities in a religious event explicitly focused on the phallus—God's covenant with Abraham that was to be "marked" or "cut" on the procreative penis. This was no tangential or accidental sign that just happened to be located on the male sexual organ, a curiously anxious choice indeed if the covenant could have just as easily been cut into the ear, nose, or forearm. No, the circumcised (literally "cut around") penis was *the* symbol or sign that marked a man as a member of the covenant community, and lacking such a marked penis could be quite literally deadly: God tries to kill Moses in *Exodus* 4:24–26 for just such a lack.

Most likely originally an adult fertility ritual—thought to increase male fertility by exposing the penis, rather like a pruned plant—practiced before weddings in the ancient Near Eastern world (see Eilberg-Schwartz, 1990), the symbolic act of circumcision was adopted by the Hebrew community to capture the essence of God's dual promise to them recorded in *Genesis* 17, the promise of land (always deeply connected to human fertility in the ancient Hebrew imagination) and offspring, who were thought to come, as seed, through this same fertile organ. Both concerns—land and progeny—were absolutely central to ancient Judaism, and many of its ritual practices and purity codes, and particularly those that were concerned with the acts of the phallus, were designed explicitly to ensure certain and acceptable lines of descent and inheritance—that is, how the land, wealth, and family heritage were passed on from generation to generation. Hence the overwhelming cultural preference for a male child as heir; the agricultural symbolism of the male "seed," believed to contain the essence of the person and "planted" in the passive soil of the womb, the latter owned by the male, like a farm; the horror of infertility, always, it appears, likened to barren soil and blamed on the woman; the radical sexual ploys sometimes used to ensure a proper male heir; the cultural concern over female sexual activity as a male possession to be controlled and contained; the prohibition of any sexual activity that might either confuse family lines and the smooth flow of inheritance (such as incest or adultery) or prevent the production of a male heir (such as sexual intercourse with a menstruating woman or male same-sex activity); and the law of Levi, which ruled that if a man died before producing a male heir his younger brother was required to copulate with the deceased man's widow, to ensure a proper male heir for the older brother's family line. Such a list could be expanded indefinitely, but the point is made: there is no way to understand ancient Judaism and its scriptural texts without understanding the centrality of the religious phallus and vagina, and their respective control.

The same point is only radicalized further through consideration of the biblical visionary patterns that Howard Eilberg-Schwartz has studied in *God's Phallus*. In ancient Israel, he points out, God is male, Israel is his bride, and therefore any male representative of that corporate bride (rabbi, prophet, priest, or visionary) is necessarily cast in what amounts to a homoerotic relationship with God:

> The primary relationships in Israelite imagination were between a male God and individual male Israelites, such as Moses, the patriarchs, and the prophets. . . . Men were encouraged to imagine themselves as married to and hence in a loving relationship with God. A homoerotic dilemma was thus generated, inadvertently and to some degree unconsciously, by the superimposition of heterosexual images on the relationship between human and divine males. (Eilberg-Schwartz, 1994, p. 99)

Hence the well-known biblical prohibition against seeing God's body, particularly his front side (that is, his exposed penis). Similar homoerotic patterns are developed further by Elliot Wolfson, who uncovers striking phallic patterns in medieval Jewish Qabbalah in such mystical tropes as the circumcised penis as organ of vision, the crowned corona/head of the qabbalist, the phallic rainbow, the ritual arousal of the divine phallus via the sexual union of the qabbalist and his wife, and the vaginal amorphousness of the *shekhinah,* that "speculum that does not shine." Indeed, in what certainly must count as one of the most provocative and radical of contemporary insights, Wolfson demonstrates that what the qabbalist envisions with his phallic vision through the sexual crevices of this feminine *shekhinah* is not the internal mysteries of the divine womb but the divine phallus hidden within and at the very top of the sefirotic pleroma. Phallic vision thus encounters the phallic pleroma within a striking homoerotic metaphysics that Wolfson has described as a kind of mystical ocular phallocentrism.

Finally, it also seems important to mention that much of ancient Jewish, and all of early Christian, understandings developed largely within cultural matrices that these religions did not create or control. That is to say, they were minority traditions within a broad cultural world defined by the regional politics of the time, in this case controlled largely by the Persian, Greek, and Roman Empires. This fact had profound consequences for the early Jewish communities, and often these political differences were focused precisely on the circumcised penis, that mark or sign that so clearly distinguished a Jew from a non-Jew, and so prevented full assimilation into the broader Gentile culture. This became a particularly potent problem under Greek rule when the Greek gymnasium and its nude male social bathing (*gymnos* means "naked") became a source of debate among the Jewish community. Once again, it was the cut penis that marked a man as a member of the Jewish community.

CHRISTIANITY. These phallic identity problems were only further exacerbated with the rise of early Christianity, which originated very much as a Jewish sect but eventually split from Judaism, largely through the early Pauline rejection of the purity codes that had separated Jews from non-Jews for centuries. Foremost among Christian concerns was the central issue of whether converts to the new faith were required to be circumcised. In other words, in the early Christian communities, just as today, one of the most contentious debates involved the penis. Largely under the influence of Paul, the Jerusalem Council, as described in the *Acts of the Apostles* 15, determined that circumcision would not be required. The tradition thus effectively broke with its own Jewish origins and, with it, the literal requirements of physical progeny, inheritance, and land.

Such a move was both a radical break from and a development of the teachings of Jesus, at least as they were recorded in the canonical gospels. Jesus certainly never spoke of abrogating the requirements of circumcision and understood himself and his mission as thoroughly Jewish, but both his recorded acts and teachings were often aimed at a radical rejection of traditional notions of holiness defined by purity, especially sexual purity. Hence an unclean menstruating woman is cured by touching him, Jesus socializes with known prostitutes and sinners, the despised eunuch (a castrated man associated in the Mediterranean world with physical deformation, passive homosexuality, sexual license, and imperial administration) is made the model disciple of the kingdom of heaven both in *Matthew* and in later Christian tradition, a centurion's slave and probable male lover is healed, and, perhaps most striking of all, Jesus himself appears to have a male lover both in the *Gospel of John,* as Theodore Jennings has recently argued, and in an early Gnostic fragment, as Morton Smith suggested in the 1970s. Such readings, of course, are hardly universal, and other scholars have advanced counter, conservative readings that seek to question, if not deny, the sexual radicalism of the gospels, particularly with reference to homosexual practice (see especially Gagnon)—but this modern debate itself is instructive, since it only underscores the fact that intense controversy, including controversy about sexual matters, was central to the gospel traditions from the very beginning.

Elements of Christian theology, moreover, can easily be read in vaginal and phallic terms. The early doctrine of the virgin birth, for example, represents a clear attempt to remove the human phallus (but, curiously, not the human vagina) entirely from the central event of Christian salvation history (the conception and birth of Jesus). This doctrine is entirely absent in *Mark* and *John* and most likely represents a transformation of an earlier illegitimacy motif, seduction or rape narrative, or biblical dual-parentage trope (with the divine inspiring or participating in the usual sexual means of procreation) (see Schaberg, 1990). As the same doctrine developed, its original focus on an inspired conception, or even virgin birth, was radicalized further to an assumption of Mary's perpetual virginity (despite surprisingly clear biblical references to Jesus' siblings) and eventually to theological speculations about a miraculously unbroken hymen. In other words, as Mariology developed, the Virgin's vagina became more and more protected from any kind of phallic penetration. This same sexual complex also had the long-range effect of helping to privilege virginity and celibacy over active sexuality as the surest mark of Christian holiness, thus essentially reversing the Jewish practice of circumcision, which focused on human fertility.

Similar patterns of elaborate sexual symbolism and extreme asceticism appear in the Gnostic communities of the first few centuries of the common era. Hence the famous "bridal chamber" ritual of the Nag Hammadi texts, the precise nature of which scholars are still divided over; the seeming obsession with "virginal" male spirits and entities; the outrageous stories of Simon Magus and his harlot-consort-goddess Helen; the radical acosmic dualisms of the texts (which seemed to have led to both ascetic and libertine practices); and the heresiological rumors of the Gnostic use of sexual fluids as sacramental substances. It also seems relevant here that the image of the "seed" (*spora* or *sperma*) is omnipresent in the Gnostic texts, particularly within that branch scholars dub Sethian Gnosticism, with its notion of the "seed of Seth" as a kind of mystical substance that carries divinity across the generations, from Adam to Jesus to the Sethian Gnostics themselves. What we have in this latter case is essentially a cult of mystical semen that, once again, locates religious identity in the seed instead of the soil.

Such sexual themes hardly end with the Gnostics after their suppression, although they do clearly morph into other, more homoerotic, patterns. Indeed, it is a fascinating mark of later Christian mysticism, particularly in its more erotic modes that derive from the Hebrew *Song of Songs* and its Christian commentaries from Origen to John of the Cross, that only one man can have a functioning phallus and employ it as an organ of mystical communion: Christ himself. Every other mystic, by theological necessity (since God is overwhelmingly imagined as male), is either biologically a woman or must become one in the religious imagination.

For Christian male mystics, then, a rich homoeroticism develops, disguised in the orthodox heteroerotic code of bridal mysticism. Indeed, in the context of normative Christian mysticism, male heterosexuality, at least any acted on or expressed toward the divine, is both symbolically impossible and theologically heretical (see Kripal, 2001). One, after all, would need a goddess for this, and there can be no true goddess in orthodox Christianity, at least not one who would be interested in the phallus. Every orthodox Christian mystic that chose to employ sexual language to express his or her love for God, then, was essentially seeking a divine phallus and acting within a vaginal mode. Hence Don Cupitt's mischievous observation in *Mysticism and Modernity* that male Christian mystical union with God "is described *exactly* as if it were female orgasm, by people who are not merely of the wrong sex, but not supposed to have any personal experience of such things anyway" (1998, p. 25). The French psychoanalytic and feminist category of *jouissance*—defined as pleasure, mystical rapture, or (female) orgasm—that is so evident in the works of such thinkers as Jacques Lacan and Catherine Clément is also worth mentioning in this context.

One of the more remarkable sexual developments within Christianity occurred in Renaissance art as it grappled with the theological implications of the Incarnation, which it symbolically expressed through the penis, as against the Gnostic tendency to deny the carnal flesh and the real suffering of Christ. As Leo Steinberg puts it in his classic study of this phenomenon, *The Sexuality of Christ in Renaissance Art and Modern Oblivion*, "the genuineness of the Incarnation is put to proof in the sexual member" (1983, p. 58). Commenting on over one hundred images out of nearly a thousand available to him, Steinberg demonstrates an elaborate *ostentatio genitalium* or ritual "display of the genitals" through artistic renditions of women playing with the child's penis, the god-baby masturbating, the Virgin touching or pointing to her infant son's organ, the magi staring at it, the dead Christ reaching for his penis, and the risen Christ displaying a clear erection under the folds of his tunic or suggestively sitting on a bull with its horned head emerging from between his legs. Here we even see the "blood-hyphen," a concept invented by the Church Fathers and developed further by artists that linked the blood of Christ's circumcision to that of His passion: "Christ's redemptive Passion, which culminates on the cross in the blood of the sacred heart, begins in the blood of the penis" (1983, p. 58).

The displayed adult penis, so evident in the work of Michelangelo, for example, is also a sign of redemption here, for if the sin of Adam resulted in the shame of the genitals (*pudendum* was a traditional term for the female genitals and meant literally "to be ashamed of"), then Christ's redemption must have removed that same shame and returned humanity to the sexual innocence before the fall. Unlike the Dionysian phallus as organ of fertility, however, Christ's penis is controlled and continent, since there is no longer any need of procreation after his victory over death, the latter being, within the Christian imagination, the result of sin. The Christian phallus, then, is a symbol of anti-death, but in a different key than that of Dionysius and the Greek phallus of fertility and life.

As with classicists embarrassed by Greek ceramics and phallic texts, Christian post-Renaissance culture would become ashamed of this redemptive shamelessness and would paint or sculpt tunics over the god-man's penis or simply lock the images away. Once again, the male member could not be mentioned, much less openly depicted in public art. A certain Bowdlerism ensued, perhaps most dramatically displayed by Pope Paul IV, who "castrated" the antique statues of Rome by literally chopping off their penises.

ISLAM. In its various approaches to the phallus and the vagina, Islam seems much closer to Judaism than to Christianity. Its elaborate concern over ritual and sexual (particularly female) purity, its ritual treatment of menstruation as a purity and religious issue, its continued practice of circumcision, its qualified acceptance of polygamy, its overwhelming concern with law *(sharīʿah)* and a legal approach to religious and social life, and its general rejection of celibacy (with the important exceptions of some Ṣūfī communities) all suggest very close connections to the ancient Jewish traditions to which the religion seems particularly indebted, even as it no doubt changed and transformed these ancient sexual and social customs for its own cultural milieus and theological purposes.

There are, however, real variations and alternative sexual traditions within Islam, as many scholars and cultural observers have noted. For example, the homoerotic patterns so evident in ancient Jewish biblical tradition and medieval Christian bridal mysticism have been studied in Islamic traditions as well, but it remains true that such phallic phenomena have been both marginal and heretical in the context of orthodox Islam. The heterosexual "seed and soil" symbolisms we noted above seem to have been far more determinative of both actual gender relations and general Islamic religious understandings of the phallus/plow and vagina/field.

INDIA. Keuls's humorous point about obscene Greek texts and unseeing classicist translators carries over into Indology as well, where Sanskritists working on ancient Indian materials sometimes share the joke that any Sanskrit word can refer to at least three things: its literal meaning, some aspect of sexual intercourse, and some part of an elephant. The joke, like many jokes, is clearly an exaggeration, but also a very instructive one, pointing as it does to the omnipresent tendency of ancient Indian culture to load the meaning of words with sexual connotations long before Freud taught us to look for such things.

Unlike their orthodox Jewish or Muslim counterparts, who tended to use the phallus as a literally "cut" marker of communal and religious identity, Indian thinkers were inclined to see the phallus as transformer of consciousness and connected the profundities of sexual pleasure with religious rapture and contemplative accomplishment very early, primarily through the Sanskrit category of *ānanda* or "bliss," as it is usually euphemistically translated. In an important essay, "Orgasmic Rapture and Divine Ecstasy: The Semantic History of Ānanda," Patrick Olivelle has demonstrated that there exists in the ancient Sanskrit texts an "explicit and unambiguous connection between *ānanda* as orgasmic rapture and *ānanda* as the experience of *brahman/ātman*" (1997, p. 154). The Upaniṣads, for example, clearly identify the organ of *ānanda* as the penis: precisely as the eye is identified as the organ of sight and the ear the organ of hearing, the penis is identified as the organ of *ānanda*. Similarly, *ānanda* is equated with nocturnal experiences of divine sexual intercourse, the ejaculation of semen, and the production of male offspring. Hence Olivelle's glossing of the term as "orgasmic rapture" and the swoon of ejaculation—that *petit mort* that somehow participates in and signals, as a kind of sacrament, the even more extreme phenomenology of mystical ecstasy. Because Being *(sat)* is essentially blissful, one of the best ways to come to know it is through that preeminent organ of (male) bliss, the aroused phallus. Such meanings, however, would not survive unchallenged and were eventually ignored, suppressed, or simply lost in many of the later Indic textual traditions. In the process, male celibacy became a *sine qua non* of the monastic traditions that would come to control the production and interpretation of many of these same philosophical texts, including those dealing with the *ānanda* of *brahman*. Not surprisingly, *ānanda* as an expressed "orgasmic rapture" was no longer commonly seen as a sexual sacrament of Being.

This same profound cultural ambivalence over the phallus as both site of erotic *ānanda* and something to renounce is particularly evident in the mythology of Śiva, the great lord of yoga and paradigm of virile power. In Wendy Doniger O'Flaherty's memorable phrase, Śiva is "the erotic ascetic" whose mythology alternates between seeming paradoxical cycles of eroticism and asceticism that never quite resolve the cultural dilemma but, in the process, express the profound metaphysical and psychological connections that appear to exist between sexual and ascetic energies. Certainly the mythological origins of Śiva's *liṅgam*, or iconic phallus, are located in some explicitly phallic behavior and in a dramatic castration. After Śiva seduces their wives, the forest sages curse his phallus and cause it to fall off. As it falls to the earth, the *liṅgam* threatens to destroy all in its flames until the forest sages promise to restore peace by worshiping it.

And indeed it is worshiped to this day in millions of shrines and stone images across India, often in the form of the *liṅga-yoni*, the dual icon of Śiva's phallus (*liṅga*) set in the vagina or womb *(yoni)* of his consort-goddess. Conditioned by over two centuries of colonial criticism, imported Victorian sensibilities, and subsequent Hindu reform movements (not to mention the original and quite ancient ambivalences expressed in the origin myth of the forest sages' curse and subsequent forced worship), many might deny the sexual connotations of such popular ritual expressions, but the mythological and historical records are clear enough. Here, then, we can speak of a kind of incomplete "historical sublimation," a historical process that gradually disassociated the categories of *ānanda, liṅgam,* and *yoni* from the physiological organs they were originally linked to, the phallus and the vagina. Their meanings (and no doubt their experiential correlates) were progressively spiritualized into *yantras* or abstract geometric shapes (such as up-turned and down-turned equilateral triangles), until the latter often presupposed the renunciation or denial of the very physicality that originally created, as it were, the categories in the first place—that is, the experience of male and female intercourse, orgasm, and ejaculation.

But the repressed always returns, and the return of the repressed in Hindu and Buddhist cultures is best represented by the efflorescence of Tantric traditions starting around the sixth century CE and continuing throughout the medieval and early modern periods, up until their gradual, if ineffective, suppression during the colonial and postcolonial eras. Certainly both the vagina and the phallus were central to many Tantric traditions. Each, for example, received extensive ritual attention, both in their actual physiological forms and as abstract triangular *yantras* (the famous *Śrīvidyā yantra*) or abstract iconic forms (the *liṅga-yoni*). Indeed, we have at least one entire text dedicated to the worship of the vagina, the *Yoni Tantra,* and numerous others treating the mythology and cultural meanings of the phallus (O'Flaherty's *Śiva: The Erotic Ascetic* and Bhattacharya's *Śaivism and the Phallic World* constitute treasuries of these). Moreover, as David Gordon White has argued in *Kiss of the Yoginī,* early medieval Kaula Tantra appears to have been organized around the production, distribution, and oral ingestion of real sexual fluids within Tantric clans. White suggests that such sexual rituals were designed to produce semen, which was then fed to the clan goddess or *yoginī* through the upper or lower "mouths" (a kind of ancient upward displacement of the vagina in Tantric symbolism). Similarly, female sexual fluids, including menstrual blood, were used in elaborate ritual contexts to transfer mystical energies *(śakti)* from the goddess/*yoginī* to the *yogin* (Irigaray's rich meditations on the morphology of female lips, the kiss, and the one who "thinks through mucous" seem especially apt here [*An Ethics,* 1993, p. 110]). Moreover, in numerous medieval Siddha alchemical contexts, the "power substances" of both semen and female sexual fluids, along with any number of symbolic or chemical equivalents (especially semen as *rasa*/mercury and menstrual blood or sexual emissions as sulfur/mica/red arsenic), were used to transubstantiate or sublimate mundane forms of consciousness and metals into ecstatic and divine ones (see White, 1996). On a side note, such rich material should give serious pause to historians of Gnosticism who wish to read accounts of similar practices in early Christian history simply as pure heresiological rumor.

Finally, before we leave ancient India, it also seems necessary to at least mention here the Jain traditions that placed such an enormous religious weight on male nudity as a sign of asceticism and renunciation. Certainly, neither Jain iconography nor Jain theology dwelt on the swollen phallus, since sexual desire was understood to entrap one further in the karmic webs of *saṃsāra,* but it nevertheless remains true that the ritual and iconic display of the *tīrthaṃkara's* penis was and remains central to the tradition, not as a phallus per se, but as an almost casual sign of the male monk's indifference to social custom and victory over the psychological and physical webs of attachment and action *(karma).* Significantly, just as early Christianity broke with Judaism over the phallic question of the circumcised penis, early Jainism split into two separate traditions (the *Digambaras* or "sky-clad" [that is, naked] and *Śvetāmbaras* or "white-clad"), largely over the implicit phallic questions of ascetic (male) nudity, which of course involves the ritual display of the penis, and of the ability of women (that is, people without penises) to achieve salvation. Significantly, whereas the Śvetāmbaras defended the possibility of female salvation on the grounds that such salvation is an internal state not to be measured by the external criterion of clothes, both sects agreed that women could not practice ritual nudity—that, in other words, the vagina could not be publicly displayed like the penis (see Jaini).

BUDDHIST AND DAOIST ASIA. Bernard Faure has written of what he calls the "red thread" of human sexuality that binds individuals to the family and the concerns of lineage, reproduction, and inheritance. Strikingly, whereas in Judaism and Islam the penis is cut to sacralize these lineage markers and in Brahmanism various sexual rituals are instituted for the same ends, within the Buddhist *Vinaya* (monastic regulations) the penis and vagina early on become veritable battlegrounds for the attempted cutting of this "red thread"—even if later, within Mahāyāna and Buddhist Tantra, they become mystical organs for this same thread's intimate weaving into the very natures of enlightenment, emptiness, and *nirvāṇa.* The discourses and semiotic patterns of what might be called the Buddhist phallus and vagina, in other words, are by no means singular or simple, and there are clearly many mythological and philosophical resources (the central doctrine of *śūnyatā,* or emptiness, foremost among them) for the deconstruction of gender and patriarchy. Still, these discourses, at least in their more normative forms, do seem to move within what many Buddhologists have identified as a profoundly androcentric, if not actually misogynistic, structure that identifies the female body as the paradigmatic example of impermanence, disgust, and suffering (see Wilson); that sees heterosexuality as the clearest threat to the stability and sanctity of the monastic community (homosexuality is quite another matter, as it can support and even strengthen monastic ties); and that even defines Tantric transgression itself as a dominantly male domain. Hence the Chinese Buddhist debates about whether one can be enlightened as a woman—that is, as a human being possessing a vagina or, perhaps more accurately, *not* possessing a penis. In some cases, at least, reincarnation was invoked as the preferred means of gender switching over multiple lives, or, alternately, as an explanation for gender-bending within an individual life ("I really *am* a man in a woman's body").

In some very literal fashion, the boundaries of the Buddhist monastery are drawn with the vagina and the phallus—by what they do, or, more precisely, do not do. Serinity Young, for example, has explored some of the gender implications of the early biographies of the Buddha and their claims that the Buddha was encased in a bejeweled box inside his mother's womb to avoid pollution; that he was born through her side instead of through the impure vaginal canal; and that his mother had to die seven days after he was born, since it is inappropriate for the mother of a Buddha to ever have sex again (we are reminded here of similar themes in early Christian Mariology and its fixation on Mary's perpetual virginity). As Faure has pointed out, although later developments would certainly bring to the fore the rhetorics of purity and pollution that were omnipresent in ancient India, Vinaya regulations generally approached the phallic penetration of the vagina and its psychophysical effects (the presence or absence of pleasure was very much part of the discourse and helped determine the act's legal ramifications), not as a dangerous loss of spiritual energy, as we find in Brahmanic Hinduism, Daoism, and later Tantrism, but as a serious breach of the social integrity of the monastic community. Indeed, the slightest insertion of the penis into the vagina, "even to a sesame seed," resulted in expulsion. The community and its boundaries are thus largely determined by the (in)actions of the sexual organs. Other sexual acts (solitary male or female masturbation, anal or oral sex, the use of dildos, etc.) were also treated in great detail but were generally not judged as harshly as heterosexual intercourse. Little wonder, then, that in Japanese Buddhist culture a punning etymology links the terms for penis *(mara),* obstacle *(māra),* and the lord of Death himself (Māra) (Faure, 1998, p. 22), or that the Buddha named his first and only son *Rāhula,* or "Obstacle." Here too we might consider the famous "cryptorchidy" of the Buddha—the belief that the Buddha's penis was hidden in a sheath.

Much of this would be challenged by later philosophical developments, particularly within the Mahāyāna and Vajrayāna turnings of the wheel, in which radical forms of nondualism would identify *nirvāṇa* and *saṃsāra* and, consequently, the passions and awakening. Young, for example, has pointed out that during the Kushan dynasty the genitals of both male and female figures were clearly displayed in the art, and that male figures from the same period "emphasize the penis under the folds of their lower garments, even statues of the Buddha and the future Buddha Maitreya" (Young, 30). In many Tantric forms, moreover, the traditions would go even further to assert that the powerful energies of the passions are in fact necessary for awakening, or that orgasm itself is a subtle mental state compatible with reason and inducive of profound mystical states of consciousness (see Hopkins, 1998).

In China, Korea, and Japan, moreover, these developments were often synthesized with Daoist alchemical practices and symbolisms, particularly the famous yin-yang icon that was often read in sexual terms—with the "stem of yang" *(yang xing),* or penis, representing semen, hardness, light, mountain heights, and the masculine, and the "path of yin" *(yin dao),* or vagina, representing the womb, softness, darkness, valley lows, and the feminine.

SEXUAL SYMBOLS IN "MODERN OBLIVION." In his own always eloquent terms, the art historian Leo Steinberg explored the phallic dimensions of Christian theology and art "before everybody was educated into incomprehension." The result of the latter process he dubbed "modern oblivion" (1983, p. 108). Steinberg's expression connotes a certain tendency of modern thought to see sexuality as an entirely natural or biological affair and, consequently, to banish it from the sacred, or, in the reverse of the same move, to reduce all forms of religious eroticism to simple sexuality. Here a pious amnesia or prudish censorship easily beds down with modern Freudian reductionism to render a category like a resurrected erection, a ritually worshiped phallus-in-a-vagina, or an enlightening orgasm impossible, offensive, embarrassing, or, at the very least, simply in bad taste. However briefly and inadequately sketched, the comparative history of the religious vagina and phallus should make one very wary of both this embarrassment and this "modern oblivion."

It is often assumed that the act of reading sexual meanings into religious or cultural symbols originates with Freud. Indeed, the history of the religious vagina or phallus often reads like a Freudian textbook, with the hole, box, house, triangle, cave, or garden commonly evoking the vagina, and the snake, bird, head, nose, plow, pillar, thigh, spear, knife, arrow, foot, stalk, and flute all standing in for the omnipresent but not quite present phallus (one needs to be careful here, though, for there are many "reversals," such as the Indic serpent, which is often coded female).

Consider, for example, the alleged "Freudian" reading of the foot as a symbolic phallus. A modern Freudian invention? Hardly. Already in the eighteenth century, specifically erotic hermeneutics were being developed in Europe to interpret religious phenomena. Sir William Hamilton, for example, tried to visit a church near Mount Vesuvius where the faithful were bringing wax *voti* of the male organ to their churches for the women to kiss (for fertility?), only to learn that the local bishop had since suppressed the practice. Hamilton left the district with some of the waxen phalli, euphemistically dubbed "big toes." Similarly, Marsha Keith Schuchard notes that Richard Payne Knight's 1786 *Treatise on the Worship of Priapus and Its Connexion with the Mystic Theology of the Ancients* describes the phallus as the "Great Toe," that both Jewish Qabbalah and the Bible have long employed the foot as a euphemism for the phallus (the two most oft-cited biblical expressions are *Isaiah* 6:2, where four of the seraphim's six wings are described as covering their faces and "feet" before the divine presence, and the phrase "uncovering the feet," which functions as a euphemism for sexual intercourse), and that the foot and toe return again in the diaries of the great Swedish mystic Emanuel Swedenborg, who believed that there was an actual pathway or nerve connecting the two protruding organs. And, it turns out, there actually is. Cognitive science has established that different body parts are mapped onto different parts of the brain, and that when a specific body part is amputated an adjacent neural system will often take over. It turns out, moreover, that the feet and the genitals occupy adjacent neural systems, and there is at least one documented case of a man with an amputated lower leg who reported immense orgasms in his phantom foot when he had sex (Ramachandran and Blakeslee, 1998). It is certainly true that Freud's psychoanalysis has helped us immeasurably to admit, come to terms with, and better understand these remarkable and remarkably ambivalent histories, but nothing could be further from the truth than the assumption that vaginal and phallic readings of religious phenomena begin (or end) with Sigmund Freud. Moreover, to the extent that psychoanalysis encourages the reading of phallic symbols in purely biological or materialistic terms, classical psychoanalytic hermeneutics can only serve to obfuscate and prevent a deeper understanding of these same religious and sexual phenomena. The Hindu *liṅgam* or *yoni* and the Buddhist Tantric *vajra* (jewel, lightning bolt, or phallus) and *padma* (lotus or vagina), after all, are not simply penises and vaginas; they are also mystical organs capable of radically altering human consciousness and producing non-ontological bliss. Similarly, the circumcised Jewish or Muslim penis is not an arbitrary sign on an arbitrary organ: it is a cut phallus intended to be used and so pass on, quite literally, particular religious, social, political, and economic resources. So too with the Virgin's vagina: it matters a great deal to the celibate structures of Roman Catholicism whether a human phallus ever penetrated its depths, just as it is a matter of great theological and moral import to contemporary Christians whether Jesus ever actually used his phallus (and, if so, with whom). Until we can read such classical religious phenomena and modern debates as carriers of both biological and deep religious meanings, as phenomena "both natural and mysterial," as Steinberg put it so well, we have failed to grasp their full range and have only reproduced our own modern assumptions, our own modern oblivion, be it social-scientifically or spiritually defined. To close with Steinberg again, "[t]reated as illustrations of what is already scripted," that is, as purely spiritual or as purely sexual phenomena, the religious phallus and vagina can only "withhold their secrets" (1983, p. 108).

SEE ALSO Atum; Castration; Circumcision; Dionysos; Masculine Sacrality; Osiris; Pan; Priapus; Sexuality, overview articles; Śiva; Yoni.

BIBLIOGRAPHY

Bhattacharya, B. *Śaivism and the Phallic World.* 2 vols. New Delhi, 1975.

Boyarin, Daniel. *Carnal Israel: Reading Sex in Talmudic Culture.* Berkeley, Calif., 1993.

Campbell, Jan. *Arguing with the Phallus: Feminist, Queer, and Postcolonial Theory: A Psychoanalytic Contribution.* London, 2000.

Clément, Catherine. *Syncope: The Philosophy of Rapture.* Translated by Sally O'Driscoll and Deirdre M. Mahoney. Minneapolis, 1994.

Countryman, L. William. *Dirt, Greed, and Sex: Sexual Ethics in the New Testament and Their Implications for Today.* Philadelphia, 1988.

Cupitt, Don. *Mysticism and Modernity.* Oxford, 1998.

Daniélou, Alain. *The Phallus: Sacred Symbol of Male Creative Power.* Translated by Jon Graham. Rochester, Vt., 1995.

Delaney, Carol. *Abraham on Trial: The Social Legacy of Biblical Myth.* Princeton, N.J., 1998.

Eilberg-Schwartz, Howard. *The Savage in Judaism: An Anthropology of Israelite Religion and Ancient Judaism.* Bloomington, Ind., 1990.

Eilberg-Schwartz, Howard. *God's Phallus and Other Problems for Men and Monotheism.* Boston, 1994.

Eller, Cynthia. *The Myth of Matriarchal Prehistory: Why an Invented Past Won't Give Women a Future.* Boston, 2000.

Faure, Bernard. *The Red Thread: Buddhist Approaches to Sexuality.* Princeton, N.J., 1998.

Gagnon, Robert A. J. *The Bible and Homosexual Practice: Texts and Hermeneutics.* Nashville, 2001.

Hopkins, Jeffrey. *Sex, Orgasm, and the Mind of Clear Light: The Sixty-four Arts of Gay Male Love.* Berkeley, Calif., 1998.

Irigaray, Luce. *Speculum de l'autre femme.* Paris, 1974. Translated by Gillian C. Gill as *Speculum of the Other Woman* (Ithaca, N.Y., 1985).

Irigaray, Luce. *An Ethics of Sexual Difference.* Translated by Carolyn Burke and Gillian C. Gill. Cornell, N.Y., 1993.

Jaini, Padmanabh S. *Gender and Salvation: Jaina Debates on the Spiritual Liberation of Women.* Berkeley, Calif., 1991.

Jamison, Stephanie W. *Sacrificed Wife, Sacrificer's Wife: Women, Ritual, and Hospitality in Ancient India.* New York, 1996.

Jennings, Theodore W., Jr. *The Man Jesus Loved: Homoerotic Narratives in the New Testament.* Cleveland, Ohio, 2003.

Jordan, Mark. *The Silence of Sodom: Homosexuality in Modern Catholicism.* Chicago, 2000.

Keuls, Eva C. *The Reign of the Phallus: Sexual Politics in Ancient Athens.* New York, 1985.

Kripal, Jeffrey J. *Roads of Excess, Palaces of Wisdom: Eroticism and Reflexivity in the Study of Mysticism.* Chicago, 2001.

O'Flaherty, Wendy Doniger. *Śiva: The Erotic Ascetic.* London, 1973.

Olivelle, Patrick. "Orgasmic Rapture and Divine Ecstasy: The Semantic History of Ānanda." *Journal of Indian Philosophy* 25 (1997): 153–180.

Ortner, Sherry B. *Making Gender: The Politics and Erotics of Culture.* Boston, 1996.

Paul, Diana Y. *Women in Buddhism: Images of the Feminine in the Mahāyāna Tradition.* 2d ed. Berkeley, Calif., 1985.

Ramachandran, V. S., and Sandra Blakeslee. *Phantoms in the Brain: Probing the Mysteries of the Mind.* New York, 1998.

Rancour-Laferriere, Daniel. "Some Semiotic Aspects of the Human Penis." *Versus: Quaderni di studi semiotico* 24 (1979): 37–82.

Schaberg, Jane. *The Illegitimacy of Jesus: A Feminist Theological Interpretation of the Infancy Narratives.* New York, 1990.

Schuchard, Marsha Keith. "'Why Mrs. Blake Cried': Swedenborg, Blake, and the Sexual Basis of Spiritual Vision." *Esoterica* 2 (2000): 45–93. Available from http://www.esoteric.msu.edu.

Smith, Morton. *The Secret Gospel.* New York, 1973.

Steinberg, Leo. *The Sexuality of Christ in Renaissance Art and in Modern Oblivion.* Chicago, 1983.

White, David Gordon. *The Alchemical Body: Siddha Traditions in Medieval India.* Chicago, 1996.

White, David Gordon. *Kiss of the Yoginī: "Tantric Sex" in Its South Asian Contexts.* Chicago, 2003.

Wilson, Liz. *Charming Cadavers: Horrific Figurations of the Feminine in Indian Buddhist Hagiographic Literature.* Chicago, 1996.

Wolfson, Elliot R. *Through a Speculum That Shines: Vision and Imagination in Medieval Jewish Mysticism.* Princeton, N.J., 1994.

Young, Serinity. *Courtesans and Tantric Consorts: Sexualities in Buddhist Narrative, Iconography, and Ritual.* New York, 2004.

JEFFREY J. KRIPAL (2005)

PHENOMENOLOGY OF RELIGION. Philosophical phenomenology is one of the major twentieth-century philosophies, and the phenomenology of religion is one of the major approaches within religious studies. Although the phenomenology of religion emerges as both a major field of study and an extremely influential approach to religion, formulating an essay on this subject poses serious difficulties. The term has become very popular and is used by numerous scholars who share little if anything in common.

USES OF THE TERM. For the sake of organization, it is possible to differentiate four major groups of scholars who use the term *phenomenology of religion.* First, there are works in which *phenomenology of religion* is used in the vaguest, broadest, and most uncritical of ways. Often the term seems to mean nothing more than an investigation of the phenomena of religion. Second, from the Dutch scholar P. D. Chantepie de la Saussaye (1848–1920) to such contemporary scholars as the Scandinavian historians of religions Geo Widengren (1907–1996) and Åke Hultkrantz (b. 1920), *phenomenology of religion* means the comparative study and the classification of different types of religious phenomena. There is little if any regard for specific phenomenological concepts, methods, or procedures of verification.

Third, numerous scholars, such as W. Brede Kristensen (1867–1953), Gerardus van der Leeuw (1890–1950), Joachim Wach (1898–1955), C. Jouco Bleeker (1898–1983),

Mircea Eliade (1907–1986), and Jacques Waardenburg (b. 1935), identify the phenomenology of religion as a specific branch, discipline, or method within *Religionswissenschaft*. This is where the most significant contributions of the phenomenology of religion to the study of religion have been made.

Fourth, there are scholars whose phenomenology of religion is influenced by philosophical phenomenology. A few scholars, such as Max Scheler (1874–1928) and Paul Ricoeur (b. 1913), explicitly identify much of their work with philosophical phenomenology. Others, such as Rudolf Otto (1869–1937), van der Leeuw, and Eliade, use a phenomenological method and are influenced, at least partially, by phenomenological philosophy. There are also influential theological approaches, as seen in the works of Friedrich Schleiermacher (1768–1834), Paul Tillich (1886–1965), Edward Farley (b. 1929), and Jean-Luc Marion (b. 1946), that utilize phenomenology of religion as a stage in the formulation of theology.

The terms *phenomenon* and *phenomenology* are derived from the Greek word *phainomenon* (that which shows itself, *or* that which appears). As Herbert Spiegelberg (1904–1990) establishes in the first volume of *The Phenomenological Movement: A Historical Introduction* (1982), the term *phenomenology* has both philosophical and nonphilosophical roots.

One encounters nonphilosophical phenomenologies in the natural sciences, especially in the field of physics. With the term *phenomenology*, scientists usually want to emphasize the descriptive, as contrasted with the explanatory, conception of their science. (In the phenomenology of religion, a similar emphasis will be seen, as phenomenologists submit that their approach describes, but does not explain, the nature of religious phenomena.)

A second nonphilosophical use of phenomenology appears in the descriptive, systematic, comparative study of religions in which scholars assemble groups of religious phenomena in order to disclose their major aspects and to formulate their typologies. This phenomenology-as-comparative-religion has roots independent of philosophical phenomenology.

The first documented philosophical use of the term *phenomenology* is by the German philosopher Johann Heinrich Lambert (1728–1777) in his *Neues Organon* (1764). In a use unrelated to later philosophical phenomenology and to the phenomenology of religion, Lambert defines the term as "the theory of illusion."

In the late eighteenth century, the German philosopher Immanuel Kant (1724–1804) devoted considerable analysis to "phenomena" as the data of experience, things that appear to and are constructed by human minds. Such phenomena, which Kant distinguishes from "noumena," or "things-in-themselves" independent of our knowing minds, can be studied rationally, scientifically, and objectively. A similar distinction between religious phenomena as appearances and religious reality-in-itself, which is beyond phenomenology, is found in the "descriptive phenomenologies" of many phenomenologists of religion.

Of all the uses of *phenomenology* by philosophers before the twentieth-century phenomenological movement, the term is most frequently identified with the German philosopher G. W. F. Hegel (1770–1831) and especially with his *Phenomenology of Spirit* (1807). Hegel is determined to overcome Kant's phenomena-noumena bifurcation. Phenomena are actual stages of knowledge—manifestations in the development of Spirit—evolving from undeveloped consciousness of mere sense experience and culminating in forms of absolute knowledge. Phenomenology is the science by which the mind becomes aware of the development of Spirit and comes to know its essence—that is, Spirit as it is in itself—through a study of its appearances and manifestations.

During the nineteenth and early twentieth centuries, a number of philosophers used *phenomenology* to indicate a merely descriptive study of a subject matter. Thus William Hamilton (1788–1856), in his *Lectures on Metaphysics* (1858), used phenomenology to refer to a descriptive phase of empirical psychology; Eduard von Hartmann (1842–1906) formulated several phenomenologies, including a descriptive "phenomenology of moral consciousness"; and the American philosopher Charles Sanders Peirce (1839–1914) used phenomenology to refer to a descriptive study of whatever appears before the mind, whether real or illusory.

As Richard Schmitt points out in his entry on "Phenomenology" in *The Encyclopedia of Philosophy* (1967), the philosophical background led to two distinct senses of *phenomenology*. There is the older, wider sense of the term as any descriptive study of a given subject matter or as a discipline describing observable phenomena. There is also a narrower twentieth-century sense of the term as a philosophical approach utilizing a phenomenological method. It is to the latter sense that this entry now turns.

PHILOSOPHICAL PHENOMENOLOGY. As one of the major schools, movements, or approaches in modern philosophy, phenomenology takes many forms. One can distinguish, for example, the "transcendental phenomenology" of Edmund Husserl (1859–1938), the "existential phenomenology" of Jean-Paul Sartre (1905–1980) and Maurice Merleau-Ponty (1908–1961), and the "hermeneutic phenomenology" of Martin Heidegger (1889–1976) and Paul Ricoeur. Since phenomenology is so complex and diverse, every phenomenologist does not accept all that follows.

The phenomenological movement. The primary aim of philosophical phenomenology is to investigate and become directly aware of phenomena that appear in immediate experience, and thereby to allow the phenomenologist to describe the essential structures of these phenomena. In doing so, phenomenology attempts to free itself from unexamined presuppositions, to avoid causal and other explanations, to utilize a method that allows it to describe that which appears, and to intuit or decipher essential meanings.

An early formulation of the phenomenological movement appears as a statement in the *Jahrbuch für Philosophie und phänomenologische Forschung,* published from 1913 to 1930 with Edmund Husserl as editor in chief. Coeditors included leading phenomenologists Moritz Geiger (1880–1937), Alexander Pfänder (1870–1941), Adolf Reinach (1883–1917), Max Scheler, and, later, Martin Heidegger and Oskar Becker (1889–1964).

Husserl is usually identified as the founder and most influential philosopher of the phenomenological movement. The earliest phenomenologists worked at several German universities, especially at Göttingen and Munich. Outside of Husserl's predominant influence on phenomenology, the most significant phenomenologists are Scheler, an independent and creative thinker in his own right, and Heidegger, who emerged as one of the major twentieth-century philosophers.

The initial flourishing of the phenomenological movement is identified with the "Göttingen Circle" and the "Munich Circle" during the period leading up to World War I, and phenomenology remained an overwhelmingly German philosophy until the 1930s when the center of the movement begins to shift to France. Through the works of Sartre, Merleau-Ponty, Gabriel Marcel (1889–1973), Ricoeur, and others, French phenomenology established itself as the leading development in phenomenological philosophy, beginning in the 1930s and continuing at least until the 1960s. Particularly noteworthy was the French attempt to integrate the concerns and insights of phenomenology with those of existentialism.

Characteristics of philosophical phenomenology. One may delineate five characteristics of philosophical phenomenology that have particular relevance for the phenomenology for religion.

Descriptive nature. Phenomenology aims to be a rigorous, descriptive science, discipline, or approach. The phenomenological slogan "Zu den Sachen!" ("To the things themselves!") expresses the determination to turn away from philosophical theories and concepts toward the direct intuition and description of phenomena as they appear in immediate experience. Phenomenology attempts to describe the nature of phenomena, the way appearances manifest themselves, and the essential structures at the foundation of human experience. As contrasted with most schools of philosophy, which have assumed that the rational alone is real and which have a philosophical preoccupation with the rational faculties and with conceptual analysis, phenomenology focuses on accurately describing the totality of phenomenal manifestations in human experience. A descriptive phenomenology, attempting to avoid reductionism and often insisting on the phenomenological *epoché* (see below), describes the diversity, complexity, and richness of experience.

Antireductionism. Phenomenological antireductionism is concerned with freeing people from uncritical preconceptions that prevent them from becoming aware of the specificity and diversity of phenomena, thus allowing them to broaden and deepen immediate experience and provide more accurate descriptions of this experience. Husserl attacked various forms of reductionism, such as "psychologism," which attempts to derive the laws of logic from psychological laws and, more broadly, to reduce all phenomena to psychological phenomena. In opposing the oversimplifications of traditional empiricism and other forms of reductionism, phenomenologists aim to deal faithfully with phenomena as phenomena and to become aware of what phenomena reveal in their full intentionality.

Intentionality. A subject always "intends" an object, and intentionality refers to the property of all consciousness as consciousness of something. All acts of consciousness are directed toward the experience of something, the intentional object. For Husserl, who took the term from his teacher Franz Brentano (1838–1917), intentionality was a way of describing how consciousness constitutes phenomena. In order to identify, describe, and interpret the meaning of phenomena, phenomenologists must be attentive to the intentional structures of their data; to the intentional structures of consciousness with their intended referents and meanings.

Bracketing. For many phenomenologists, the antireductionist insistence on the irreducibility of the intentional immediate experience entails the adoption of a "phenomenological *epoché*." This Greek term literally means "abstention" or "suspension of judgment" and is often defined as a method of "bracketing." It is only by bracketing the uncritically accepted "natural world," by suspending beliefs and judgments based on an unexamined "natural standpoint," that the phenomenologist can become aware of the phenomena of immediate experience and can gain insight into their essential structures. Sometimes the *epoché* is formulated in terms of the goal of a completely presuppositionless science or philosophy, but most phenomenologists have interpreted such bracketing as the goal of freeing the phenomenologist from unexamined presuppositions, or of rendering explicit and clarifying such presuppositions, rather than completely denying their existence. The phenomenological *epoché*, whether as the technical Husserlian "transcendental reduction" or in its other variations, is not simply "performed" by phenomenologists; it must involve some method of self-criticism and intersubjective testing allowing insight into structures and meanings.

Eidetic vision. The intuition of essences, often described as "eidetic vision" or "eidetic reduction," is related to the Greek term *eidos*, which Husserl adopted from its Platonic meaning to designate "universal essences." Such essences express the "whatness" of things, the necessary and invariant features of phenomena that allow us to recognize phenomena as phenomena of a certain kind.

For all of their differences, the overwhelming majority of phenomenologists have upheld a descriptive phenomenology that is antireductionist, involves phenomenological bracketing, focuses on intentionality, and aims at insight into essential structures and meanings. The following is a brief formulation of a general phenomenological procedure for gaining insight into such essential structures and meanings with application to the phenomena of religious experience.

In the "intuition of essences" (*Wesensschau*), the phenomenologist attempts to disengage essential structures embodied in particular phenomena. One begins with particular data: specific phenomena as expressions of intentional experiences. The central aim of the phenomenological method is to disclose the essential structure embodied in the particular data.

One gains insight into meaning by the method of "free variation." After assembling a variety of particular phenomena, the phenomenologist searches for the invariant core that constitutes the essential meaning of the phenomena. The phenomena, subjected to a process of free variation, assume certain forms that are considered to be accidental or inessential in the sense that the phenomenologist can go beyond the limits imposed by such forms without destroying the basic character or intentionality of one's data. For example, the variation of a great variety of religious phenomena may disclose that the unique structures of monotheism do not constitute the essential core or universal structure of all religious experience.

The phenomenologist gradually sees that phenomena assume forms that are regarded as essential in the sense that one cannot go beyond or remove such structures without destroying the basic "whatness" or intentionality of the data. For example, free variation might reveal that certain intentional structures of "transcendence" constitute an invariant core of religious experience. When the universal essence is grasped, the phenomenologist achieves the eidetic intuition or the fulfilled *Wesensschau.*

Husserl proposed that all phenomena are constituted by consciousness and that, in the intuition of essences, we can eliminate the particular, actual given datum and move on to the plane of "pure possibility." Most phenomenologists who have used a method of *Wesensschau* have proposed that historical phenomena have a kind of priority, that one must substitute for Husserl's imaginary variation an actual variation of historical data, and that the particular phenomena are not constituted by an individual but are the source of one's constitution and judgment.

Though relatively few philosophical phenomenologists had much interest in religious phenomena during most of the twentieth century, some of the vocabulary of philosophical phenomenology and, in several cases, some of its methodology have influenced the phenomenology of religion.

PHENOMENOLOGY OF RELIGION AS PART OF HISTORY OF RELIGIONS (RELIGIOUS STUDIES). The modern scholarly study of religion probably had its beginnings in the late eighteenth century, largely as a product of the rational and scientific attitude of the Enlightenment, but the first major figure in this discipline was F. Max Müller (1823–1900). Müller intended *Religionswissenschaft* to be a descriptive, objective science free from the normative nature of theological and philosophical studies of religion.

The German term *Religionswissenschaft* has been given no adequate English equivalent, although the International Association for the History of Religions has adopted the term *history of religions* as synonymous with the term *general science of religions.* Thus *history of religions* is intended to designate a field of studies with many specialized disciplines utilizing different approaches.

P. D. Chantepie de la Saussaye is sometimes considered the founder of phenomenology of religion as a special discipline of classification. Phenomenology of religion occupied an intermediary position for him between history and philosophy and is a descriptive, comparative approach involving "the collecting and grouping of various religious phenomena." One of the founders of *Religionswissenschaft,* the Dutch historian C. P. Tiele (1830–1902), considered phenomenology to be the first stage of the philosophical part of the science of religion.

Scholars of religion point to the phenomenology of religion's sense of generality, with its approach invariably characterized as systematic. For Widengren, the phenomenology of religion aims at "a coherent account of all the various phenomena of religion, and is thus the systematic complement of the history of religion" (1945, p. 9). The historical approach provides a historical analysis of the development of separate religions; phenomenology provides "the systematic synthesis."

The Italian historian of religions Raffaele Pettazzoni (1883–1959) attempted to formulate the diverse methodological tendencies and tensions, defining *Religionswissenschaft* in terms of these two complementary aspects: the historical and the phenomenological. On the one hand, the history of religions attempts to uncover "precisely what happened and how the facts came to be," but it does not provide the deeper understanding of the meaning of what happened, nor "the sense of the religious": these come from phenomenology. On the other hand, phenomenology cannot do without ethnology, philology, and other historical disciplines. Therefore, according to Pettazzoni, phenomenology and history are two complementary aspects of the integral science of religion.

MAJOR PHENOMENOLOGISTS OF RELIGION. What follows are brief formulations of the approaches and contributions of eight influential phenomenologists of religion: Max Scheler, W. Brede Kristensen, Rudolf Otto, Gerardus van der Leeuw, Friedrich Heiler, C. Jouco Bleeker, Mircea Eliade, and Ninian Smart. Included are criticisms of perhaps the three most influential phenomenologists of religion within religious studies: Otto, van der Leeuw, and Eliade.

Max Scheler. Of the major philosophers who founded and developed philosophical phenomenology, Max Scheler had the greatest focus on religion. After Husserl, he may have been the most influential philosophical phenomenologist during the 1920s. In many ways, he can be considered the most significant early phenomenologist of religion. Influenced by Brentano, Husserl, Kant, Nietzsche, Dilthey, and Bergson, among others, Scheler developed his own original phenomenological approach. Among his books, *Vom Ewigen im Menschen* (1921, translated as *On the Eternal in Man,* 1960) and *Der Formalismus in der Ethik und die materiale Wertethik* (2 vols., 1913–1916, translated as *Formalism in Ethics and Non-Formal Ethics of Values,* 1973) bring out his phenomenological method, his description and analysis of sympathy, love, and other values, and key characteristics of his phenomenology of religion.

Although Scheler's detailed epistemology, ethics and axiology, metaphysics, and philosophical anthropology are very complex and his phenomenology of religion goes through several radical changes, it is possible to delineate a few influential characteristics of his phenomenological approach to religion. Reminiscent of Schleiermacher and Otto, Scheler focused on a phenomenological description and analysis of human experience: the unique religious human mode of experience and feeling; the being of the human being for whom structures and essences of religious values are presented to consciousness. Within the phenomenology of religion, phenomenological disclosure, focusing on what is "given" to consciousness as the Absolute, the Divine Person, or God, is not achieved through reason but only through the love of God as orienting one toward experiential realization of the Holy.

Philosophical phenomenologists of religion are greatly indebted to Scheler, although it is not clear the extent to which scholars within religious studies have been influenced by him, even if some of their approaches can be related to his phenomenological analysis. The turn to religion in some of philosophical phenomenology and other forms of continental philosophy at the end of the twentieth century often exhibited characteristics similar to Scheler's phenomenological orientation.

W. Brede Kristensen. From Chantepie de la Saussaye and Tiele, through van der Leeuw and the Norwegian expatriate Kristensen, and up to the writings of Bleeker and others, much of the field has been dominated by a Dutch tradition of phenomenology of religion. Sometimes this is broadened to encompass a Dutch-Scandinavian tradition in order to include phenomenologists such as Nathan Söderblom (1866–1931).

W. Brede Kristensen, a specialist in Egyptian and ancient historical religions, illustrates an extreme formulation of the descriptive approach within phenomenology. As a subdivision of the general science of religion, phenomenology is, according to Kristensen, a systematic and comparative approach that is descriptive and not normative. In opposing the widespread positivist and evolutionist approaches to religion, Kristensen attempted to integrate historical knowledge of the facts with phenomenological "empathy" and "feeling" for the data in order to grasp the "inner meaning" and religious values in various texts.

The phenomenologist must accept the faith of the believers as the sole "religious reality." In order to achieve phenomenological understanding, scholars must avoid imposing their own value judgments on the experiences of believers and must assume that the believers are completely right. In other words, the primary focus of phenomenology is the description of how believers understand their own faith. One must respect the absolute value that believers ascribe to their faith. An understanding of this religious reality is always approximate or relative, since one can never experience the religion of others exactly as the believers experience it. After describing the "belief of the believers," the scholar may classify the phenomena according to essential types and make comparative evaluations. But all investigations into the essence and evaluations of phenomena entail value judgments by the interpreter and are beyond the limits of a descriptive phenomenology.

Rudolf Otto. Two interdependent methodological contributions made by Rudolf Otto deserve emphasis: his experiential approach, which involves the phenomenological description of the universal, essential structure of religious experience, and his antireductionism, which respects the unique, irreducible, "numinous" quality of all religious experience.

In *Das Heilige* (1917, translated as *The Idea of the Holy,* 1923), Otto presents what is probably the best-known phenomenological account of religious experience. In attempting to uncover the essential structure and meaning of all religious experience, Otto describes the universal "numinous" element as a unique a priori category of meaning and value. By *numen* and *numinous,* Otto means the concept of "the holy" minus its moral and rational aspects. With such an emphasis on this nonmoral, nonrational aspect of religion, he attempts to isolate the "overplus of meaning," beyond the rational and conceptual, which constitutes the universal essence of the religious experience. Since such a unique nonrational experience cannot be defined or conceptualized, the symbolic and analogical descriptions are meant to evoke within the reader the experience of the holy. The religious experience of the numinous, as an a priori structure of consciousness, can be reawakened or recognized by means of our innate sense of the numinous, that is, our capacity for this a priori knowledge of the holy.

In this regard, Otto formulates a universal phenomenological structure of religious experience in which the phenomenologist can distinguish autonomous religious phenomena by their numinous aspect and can organize and analyze specific religious manifestations. He points to our "creature feeling" of absolute dependence in the experiential presence of the holy. This sui generis religious experience is described as the experience of the "wholly other" (*ganz Andere*), which is qualitatively unique and transcendent.

This insistence on the unique a priori quality of the religious experience points to Otto's antireductionism. Otto rejects the one-sidedly intellectualistic and rationalistic bias of most interpretations and the reduction of religious phenomena to the interpretive schema of linguistic analysis, anthropology, sociology, psychology, and various historicist approaches. This emphasis on the autonomy of religion, with the need for a unique, autonomous phenomenological approach that is commensurate with interpreting the meaning of the irreducibly religious phenomena, is generally accepted by major phenomenologists of religion.

Various interpreters have criticized Otto's phenomenological approach for being too narrowly conceived. According to these critics, Otto's approach focuses on nonrational aspects of certain mystical and other "extreme" experiences, but it is not sufficiently comprehensive to interpret the diversity and complexity of religious data, nor is it sufficiently concerned with the specific historical and cultural forms of religious phenomena. Critics also object to the a priori nature of Otto's project and influences of personal, Christian, theological, and apologetic intentions on his phenomenology. Van der Leeuw, while agreeing with Otto's antireductionism, attempts to broaden his phenomenology by investigating and systematizing a tremendous diversity of religious phenomena.

Gerardus van der Leeuw. In his *Comparative Religion*, Eric J. Sharpe writes that "between 1925 and 1950, the phenomenology of religion was associated almost exclusively with the name of the Dutch scholar Gerardus van der Leeuw, and with his book *Phänomenologie der Religion*" (1986, pp. 229–230). Especially notable among the many influences on his phenomenology acknowledged by van der Leeuw are the writings of the German philosopher Wilhelm Dilthey (1833–1911) on hermeneutics and the concept of "understanding" (*Verstehen*).

In several writings, especially the epilogue of *Phänomenologie der Religion* (1933, translated as *Religion in Essence and Manifestation*, 2d ed., 1963), which contains the chapters "Phenomenon and Phenomenology" and "The Phenomenology of Religion," van der Leeuw defines the assumptions, concepts, and stages of his phenomenological approach. According to van der Leeuw, the phenomenologist must respect the specific intentionality of religious phenomena and simply describe the phenomenon as "what appears into view." The phenomenon is given in the mutual relations between subject and object; that is, its "entire essence" is given in its appearance to someone.

Van der Leeuw proposed a subtle and complex phenomenological method with which the phenomenologist goes far beyond a descriptive phenomenology. His method involves systematic introspection—"the interpolation of the phenomenon into our lives"—as necessary for understanding religious phenomena. In the first volume of his *Classical Approaches to the Study of Religion* (1973–1974), Jacques Waardenburg describes this phenomenological-psychological method as "an 'experiential' method to guide intuition and to arrive at immediate understanding" and as the "classification of religious phenomena by means of ideal types which are constituted by a psychological technique of re-experiencing religious meanings" (p. 57).

According to van der Leeuw, phenomenology must be combined with historical research, which precedes phenomenological understanding and provides the phenomenologist with sufficient data. Phenomenology must be open to "perpetual correction by the most conscientious philological and archaeological research," and "it becomes pure art or empty fancy" (van der Leeuw, 1963, vol. 2, p. 677) when it removes itself from such historical control. Special note may be taken of van der Leeuw's emphasis on the religious aspect of "power" as the basis of every religious form and as defining that which is religious. "Phenomenology describes how man conducts himself in his relation to Power" (1963, vol. 1, p. 191). The terms *holy, sanctus, taboo*, and so on, taken together, describe what occurs in all religious experience: "a strange, 'Wholly Other,' Power obtrudes into life" (1963, vol. 2, p. 681).

Influences from van der Leeuw's own Christian point of view are often central to his analysis of the phenomenological method for gaining understanding of religious structures and meanings. For example, he claims that "faith and intellectual suspense (the *epochē*) do not exclude each other," and "all understanding rests upon self-surrendering love" (1963, vol. 2, pp. 683–684). Indeed, van der Leeuw above all considered himself a theologian, positing that phenomenology of religion leads to both anthropology and theology. Numerous scholars have concluded that much of his phenomenology of religion must be interpreted in theological terms.

Critics, while often expressing admiration for *Religion in Essence and Manifestation* as an extraordinary collection of religious data, offer many objections to van der Leeuw's phenomenology of religion: his phenomenological approach is based on numerous theological and metaphysical assumptions and value judgments; it is often too subjective and highly speculative; and it neglects the historical and cultural context of religious phenomena and is of little value for empirically based research.

Friedrich Heiler. Born in Munich, Friedrich Heiler (1892–1967) is known for his studies on prayer, great religious personalities, ecumenism, the unity of all religion, and a kind of global phenomenology of religion.

According to Heiler, the phenomenological method proceeds from the externals to the essence of religion. Although every approach has presuppositions, the phenomenology of religion must avoid every philosophical a priori and utilize only those presuppositions that are consistent with an inductive method. Heiler's phenomenology of religion, which is theologically oriented, emphasizes the indispensable value of "empathy": the phenomenologist must exercise respect, tolerance, and sympathetic understanding for all religious experience and the religious truth expressed in the data. Indeed, the phenomenologist's personal religious experience is a precondition for an empathic understanding of the totality of religious phenomena.

C. Jouco Bleeker. Bleeker distinguished three types of phenomenology of religion: the descriptive phenomenology that restricts itself to the systematization of religious phenomena, the typological phenomenology that formulates the different types of religion, and the specific sense of phenomenology that investigates the essential structures and meanings of religious phenomena. In terms of this more specific sense, phenomenology of religion has a double meaning: it is an independent science that creates monographs and handbooks, such as van der Leeuw's *Religion in Essence and Manifestation* and Eliade's *Patterns in Comparative Religion* (1958), but it is also a scholarly method that utilizes such principles as the phenomenological *epoché* and eidetic vision. Although Bleeker frequently used such technical terms in gaining insight into religious structures and acknowledged that these terms were borrowed from the philosophical phenomenology of Husserl and his school, he claimed that they were used by the phenomenology of religion in only a figurative sense.

According to Bleeker, the phenomenology of religion combines a critical attitude and concern for accurate descriptions with a sense of empathy for the phenomena. It is an empirical science without philosophical aspirations, and it should distinguish its activities from those of philosophical phenomenology and of anthropology. He warned that historians and phenomenologists of religion should not dabble in philosophical speculations on matters of method, stating that "phenomenology of religion is not a philosophical discipline, but a systematization of historical fact with the intent to understand their religious meaning" (Bleeker, in Bianchi et al., 1972, pp. 39–41, 51).

Probably the best-known formulation in Bleeker's reflections on phenomenology is his analysis of the task of phenomenology of religion as an inquiry into three dimensions of religious phenomena: *theoria, logos,* and *entelecheia.*

The *theoria* of phenomena "discloses the essence and significance of the facts." It has an empirical basis and leads to an understanding of the implications of various aspects of religion. The Logos of phenomena "penetrates into the structure of different forms of religious life." This provides a sense of objectivity by showing that hidden structures "are built up according to strict inner laws," and that religion "always possesses a certain structure with an inner logic" (Bleeker, 1963, pp. 14, 17).

Most original is Bleeker's position that the *entelecheia* of phenomena "reveals itself in the dynamics, the development which is visible in the religious life of mankind," or in "the course of events in which the essence is realized by its manifestations." Phenomenology, it is frequently stated, abstracts from historical change and presents a rather static view of essential structures and meanings. By the *entelecheia,* Bleeker wants to stress that religion is not static but is "an invincible, creative and self-regenerating force." The phenomenologist of religion must work closely with the historian of religions in studying the dynamics of phenomena and the development of religions (Bleeker, 1963, pp. 14, 16–24).

Mircea Eliade. According to the Romanian scholar Mircea Eliade, one of the major interpreters of religious symbol and myth, religion "refers to the experience of the sacred." The phenomenologist works with historical documents expressing *hierophanies,* or manifestations of the sacred, and attempts to decipher the existential situation and religious meaning expressed through the data. The sacred and the profane express "two modes of being in the world," and religion always entails the attempt of *homo religiosus* to transcend the relative, historical-temporal, profane world by experiencing a "superhuman" sacred world of transcendent values.

In Bleeker's first sense of phenomenology of religion as an independent discipline that creates monographs that describe and classify essential structures and meanings, one may note Eliade's many morphological studies of different kinds of religious symbolism; his interpretations of the structure and function of myth, with the cosmogonic myth and other creation myths functioning as exemplary models; his treatment of rituals, such as those of initiation, as reenacting sacred mythic models; his structural analysis of sacred space, sacred time, and sacred history; and his studies of different types of religious experience, such as yoga, shamanism, alchemy, and other "archaic" phenomena.

In Bleeker's second sense of phenomenology of religion as a specific method, there are three key methodological principles underlying Eliade's approach: his assumption of the "irreducibility of the sacred," his emphasis on the "dialectic of the sacred" as the universal structure of sacralization, and his uncovering of the structural systems of religious symbols that constitute the hermeneutical framework in terms of which he interprets religious meaning.

The assumption of the irreducibility of the religious is a form of phenomenological *epoché.* In attempting to understand and describe the meaning of religious phenomena, the phenomenologist must utilize an antireductionist method commensurate with the nature of the data. Only a religious frame of reference or "scale" of interpretation does not distort the specific, irreducible religious intentionality expressed in the data.

The universal structure of the dialectic of the sacred provides Eliade with essential criteria for distinguishing religious from nonreligious phenomena. There is always a sacred-profane dichotomy and the separation of the hierophanic object, such as a particular mountain or tree or person, since this is the medium through which the sacred is manifested; the sacred, which expresses transcendent structures and meanings, paradoxically limits itself by incarnating itself in something ordinarily finite, temporal, historical, and profane; the sacred, in its dialectical movement of disclosure and revelation, always conceals and camouflages itself; and the religious person, in resolving existential crises, evaluates and chooses the sacred as powerful, ultimate, normative, and meaningful.

The central position of symbolism, with the focus on coherent systems of symbolic structures, establishes the phenomenological grounds for Eliade's structural hermeneutics. Among the characteristics of symbols are: (1) their "logic," which allows various symbols to fit together to form coherent symbolic systems; (2) their "multivalence," through which they express simultaneously a number of structurally coherent meanings not evident on the level of immediate experience; and (3) their "function of unification," by which they integrate heterogeneous phenomena into a whole or a system. These autonomous, universal, coherent systems of symbols usually provide the phenomenological framework for Eliade's interpretation of religious meaning. For example, he interprets the meaning of a religious phenomenon associated with the sun or moon by reintegrating it within its solar or lunar structural system of symbolic associations.

Although Eliade was extremely influential, many scholars ignore or are hostile to his history and phenomenology of religion. The most frequent criticism is that Eliade is methodologically uncritical, often presenting sweeping, arbitrary, subjective generalizations not based upon specific historical and empirical data. Critics also charge that his approach is influenced by various normative judgments and an assumed ontological position that is partial to a religious, antihistorical mode of being and to certain Eastern and archaic phenomena.

Ninian Smart. Smart (1927–2001), who was born in Cambridge, England, to Scottish parents, had a major impact on the field of religious studies. He was committed to phenomenology as the best way to study religion. His phenomenology of religion avoids what were two dominant approaches to religion: (1) ethnocentric, normative, especially Christian, theological approaches in the study of religion; and (2) normative philosophical approaches with their exclusive focus on belief and conceptual analysis to the exclusion of other dimensions of religious phenomena. Smart was capable of technical scholarly analysis, as seen in his *Doctrine and Argument in Indian Philosophy* (1964), but he is probably better known as a popularizer in his study of religion, as seen in *The Religious Experience of Mankind* (1969). He believed that profound insights can be presented in simple understandable language and ordinary phenomenological categories.

Smart emphasized many points that became easily recognizable and widely accepted in the phenomenology of religion and other approaches to religious phenomena during the last decades of the twentieth century. He emphasized suspension of one's own value judgments and the need for phenomenological empathy in understanding and describing the religious phenomena of others. He endorsed a liberal humanistic approach that upholds the value of pluralism and diversity. In Smart's phenomenological approach, one recognizes that religion expresses many dimensions of human experience. Such an approach is "polymethodic," multiperspectival, comparative, and cross-cultural. The phenomenologist of religion needs to take seriously the contextual nature of diverse religious phenomena; to ask questions, engage in critical dialogue, and maintain an open-ended investigation of religion; and to recognize that religions express complex, multidimensional, interconnected worldviews. This focus on religions in terms of worldview analysis leads to the contemporary interest in the globalization of religion and global pluralism.

CHARACTERISTICS OF PHENOMENOLOGY OF RELIGION. The following features, some of which have already been mentioned, are characteristic of much of the phenomenology of religion: its identification as a comparative, systematic, empirical, historical, descriptive discipline and approach; its antireductionist claims and its autonomous nature; its adoption of philosophical phenomenological notions of intentionality and *epoché;* its insistence on the value of empathy, sympathetic understanding, and religious commitment; and its claim to provide insight into essential structures and meanings. Several of these characteristics are associated primarily with the phenomenology of religion; others, while accepted by most phenomenologists of religion, are shared by other historians of religions.

Comparative and systematic approach. As previously noted, there is widespread agreement that the phenomenology of religion is a very general approach concerned with classifying and systematizing religious phenomena. There is also widespread agreement that this discipline uses a comparative approach. Various phenomenologists simply define their phenomenology of religion as equivalent to comparative religion. But even those scholars who reject such a simple identification maintain that phenomenologists are able to gain insight into essential structures and meanings only after comparing a large number of documents expressing a great diversity of religious phenomena.

Empirical approach. Bleeker, Eliade, and most phenomenologists of religion insist that they use an empirical approach that is free from a priori assumptions and judgments. Such an empirical approach, which is often described as "scientific" and "objective," begins by collecting religious documents and then goes on to decipher the religious phenomena by describing just what the empirical data reveal. Phenomenologists usually maintain that their discoveries of essential typologies and universal structures are based on empirical, inductive generalizations.

One of the most frequent attacks on the phenomenology of religion is that it is not empirically based and that it is therefore arbitrary, subjective, and unscientific. Critics charge that the universal structures and meanings are not found in the empirical data and that the phenomenological discoveries are not subject to empirical tests of verification.

Historical approach. Phenomenologists of religion usually maintain not only that their approach must cooperate with and complement historical research but also that phenomenology of religion is profoundly historical. All religious data are historical; no phenomena may be understood outside their history. The phenomenologist must be aware of the specific historical, cultural, and socioeconomic contexts within which religious phenomena appear.

Critics, however, charge that not only is the phenomenology of religion not historical, it is even antihistorical, both in terms of a phenomenological method that neglects the specific historical and cultural context and with regard to the primacy—methodologically and even ontologically—it grants to nonhistorical and nontemporal universal structures.

Descriptive approach. Unlike Müller, who intends the modern scholarly study of religion (*Religionswissenschaft*) to be a descriptive science attaining the autonomy and objectivity of the descriptive natural sciences, and Kristensen, who conceives of phenomenology of religion as "purely descriptive," almost all phenomenologists of religion today do not restrict themselves to mere description of religious phenomena. While cognizant of Kristensen's concerns about the subjective nature of much past scholarship in which interpreters filtered data through their own assumptions and value judgments, phenomenologists go far beyond the severe methodological restrictions of his descriptive phenomenology.

And yet these same phenomenologists invariably classify their discipline and approach as a descriptive phenomenology of religion; at the minimum, it is "essentially descriptive," and sometimes it is presented as "purely descriptive." They claim to utilize a descriptive approach and see their classifications, typologies, and structures as descriptive. Sometimes phenomenologists of religion distinguish the collection and description of religious data, which is objective and scientific, from the interpretation of meaning, which is at least partially subjective and normative.

Antireductionism. Philosophical phenomenology, in defining itself as a radically descriptive philosophy, opposes various kinds of reductionism. Phenomenologists oppose reductionism, which imposes uncritical preconceptions and unexamined judgments on phenomena, in order to deal with phenomena simply as phenomena and to provide more accurate descriptions of just what the phenomena reveal.

More than any other approach within the modern study of religion, phenomenology of religion insists that investigators approach religious data as phenomena that are fundamentally and irreducibly religious. Otto, Eliade, and other phenomenologists of religion often defend their strong antireductionism by criticizing past reductionist approaches. Many of these reductionist interpretations, for example, are based on "positivist" and "rationalist" norms and force religious data into preconceived unilinear, evolutionary explanatory frameworks. Phenomenologists criticize the reductions of religious data to fit nonreligious perspectives, such as those of sociology, psychology, or economics. Such reductionisms, it is argued, destroy the specificity, complexity, and irreducible intentionality of religious phenomena. In attempting sympathetically to understand the experience of the other, the phenomenologist must respect the "original" religious intentionality expressed in the data.

Autonomy. Directly related to the antireductionist claim of the irreducibility of the religious is the identification of phenomenology of religion as an autonomous discipline and approach. If there are certain irreducible modes by which religious phenomena are given, then one must utilize a specific method of understanding that is commensurate with the religious nature of the subject matter, and one must provide irreducibly religious interpretations of religious phenomena.

The phenomenology of religion is autonomous but not self-sufficient. It depends heavily on historical research and on data supplied by philology, ethnology, psychology, sociology, and other approaches. But it must always integrate the contributions of other approaches within its own unique phenomenological perspective.

Intentionality. Phenomenology analyzes acts of consciousness as consciousness of something and claims that meaning is given in the intentionality of the structure. In order to identify, describe, and interpret the meaning of religious phenomena, scholars must be attentive to the intentional structure of their data. For Otto, the a priori structure of religious consciousness is consciousness of its intended "numinous object." Van der Leeuw's phenomenological-psychological technique and Eliade's dialectic of the sacred are methods for capturing the intentional characteristics of religious manifestations. The major criticism made by phenomenologists of religion of reductionist approaches involves the latter's negation of the unique intentionality of religious phenomena.

Religious experiences reveal structures of transcendence in which human beings intend a transcendent referent, a supernatural metaempirical sacred meaning. Such intentionality is always historically, culturally, and linguistically situated. Religious language points beyond itself to intended sacred structures and meanings that transcend normal spatial, temporal, historical, and conceptual categories and analysis. That is why religious expressions are highly symbolic, analogical, metaphorical, mythic, and allegorical. Reductive explanations tend to destroy the intentional structure of religious meaning, invariably pointing to the transcendent sacred.

At the same time, no intentional referent and meaning is unmediated. For meaningful religious experience and communication, the intended transcendent referent must be mediated and brought into an integral human relation with our limited spatial, temporal, historical, cultural world with its intended objects and meanings. This is why symbolism, in its complex and diverse structures and functions, is essential for revealing, constituting, and communicating religious intentional meaning. Religious symbolic expressions serve as indispensable mediating bridges. On the one hand, they always point beyond themselves to intended transcendent meanings. On the other hand, by necessarily using symbolic language drawn from the spatial, temporal, natural, historical world of experience, they mediate the transcendent referent, limit and incarnate the sacred, allow the disclosure of the transcendent as imminent, and render sacred meanings humanly accessible and relevant to particular existential situations.

This specific religious intentionality ensures that the structures of religious experience, as well as interpretations and understandings, will remain open-ended with no possible closure. The necessary structural conditions for religious experience, the construction of religious texts, and the formulation of scholarly interpretations ensure that meaningful human understandings necessarily reveal limited intentional perspectives. And such relative, situated, intentional, religious perspectives always point beyond themselves to structures of transcendence; to inexhaustible possibilities for revalorizing symbolic expressions, for bursting open self-imposed perspectival closures, and for new, creative, self-transcending experiences, interpretations, and understandings.

***Epoché*, empathy, and sympathetic understanding.** Most philosophical phenomenologists present the phenomenological *epoché* as a means of bracketing beliefs and preconceptions normally imposed on phenomena. It is important to clarify that Husserl and other philosophers who formulate a "phenomenological reduction" as *epoché* do not intend a narrowing of perspective and negation of the complexity and specificity of phenomena. The phenomenological reduction is intended to achieve the very opposite of reductionism: by suspending one's unexamined assumptions and ordinary preconceptions and judgments, it allows one to become attentive to a much fuller disclosure of what manifests itself and how it manifests itself in experience; it allows for greater awareness of phenomena experienced on prereflective, emotive, imaginative, nonconceptual levels of intentional experience, thus leading to new insights into the specific intentionality and concrete richness of experience.

The phenomenological *epoché*, with an emphasis on empathy and sympathetic understanding, is related to methodological antireductionism. If the phenomenologist is to describe the meaning of religious phenomena as they appear in the lives of religious persons, she or he must suspend all personal preconceptions as to what is "real" and attempt to empathize with and imaginatively reenact these religious appearances. By insisting on the irreducibility of the religious, phenomenologists attempt sympathetically to place themselves within the religious "life-world" of others and to grasp the religious meaning of the experienced phenomena.

There are, of course, limitations to this personal participation, since the other always remains to some extent the "other." Phenomenologists insist that empathy, a sympathetic attitude, and personal participation in no way undermine the need for a critical scholarly approach with rigorous criteria of interpretation. This phenomenological orientation may be contrasted with the ideal of detached, impersonal scientific objectivity that characterizes almost all nineteenth-century approaches within the scholarly study of religion and that continues to define many approaches today.

In assuming a sympathetic attitude, the phenomenologist is not claiming that religious phenomena are not "illusory" and that the intentional object is "real." (As a matter of fact, many phenomenologists make such theological and metaphysical assumptions and judgments, but these usually violate the self-defined limits of their phenomenological perspectives.) The phenomenological bracketing entails the suspension of all such value judgments regarding whether or not the holy or sacred is actually an experience of ultimate reality.

With a few exceptions, it seems that phenomenologists of religion, while generally upholding an *epoché* or similar values, have not subjected such concepts to a rigorous analysis. Often they give little more than vague appeals to abstain from value judgments and to exercise a personal capacity for empathetic participation, but without scholarly criteria for verifying whether such sympathetic understanding has been achieved.

Many phenomenologists argue for the necessity of religious commitment, a personal religious faith, or at least personal religious experience in order for a scholar to be capable of empathy, participation, and sympathetic understanding. Other phenomenologists argue that such personal religious commitments generally produce biased descriptions that rarely do justice to the religious experience of others. It seems that a particular faith or theological commitment is not a precondition for accurate phenomenological descriptions. Rather it is a commitment to religious phenomena, manifested in terms of intellectual curiosity, sensitivity, and respect, that is indispensable for participation and understanding. Such a commitment may be shared by believers and nonbelievers alike.

Insight into essential structures and meanings. No subject matter is more central to philosophical phenomenology than analyses of the eidetic reduction and eidetic vision, the intuition of essences, the method of free variation, and other techniques for gaining insight into the essential structures and meanings of phenomena. By contrast, the phenomenology of religion, even in the specific sense of an approach concerned with describing essential structures and meanings, tends to avoid such methodological formulations. There are, of course, notable exceptions, as evidenced in the works of Max Scheler, Paul Ricoeur, and a relatively small number of other philosophers who incorporate phenomenology of religion as part of their philosophical phenomenology.

One generally finds, however, that most phenomenologists of religion accept both Bleeker's qualification that such terms as *eidetic vision* are used only in a figurative sense and his warning that phenomenology of religion should avoid philosophical speculations and not meddle in difficult philosophical questions of methodology. The result is that one is frequently presented with phenomenological typologies, "universal structures," and "essential meanings" of religious phenomena that lack a rigorous analysis of just how the phenomenologist arrived at or verified these discoveries. In short, in its claims concerning insight into essential structures and meanings, much of the phenomenology of religion appears to be methodologically uncritical.

Phenomenologists aim at intuiting, interpreting, and describing the essence of religious phenomena, but there is considerable disagreement as to what constitutes an essential structure. For some phenomenologists, an "essential structure" seems to be the result of an empirical inductive generalization, expressing a property that different phenomena have in common. For others, "essential structures" refer to types of religious phenomena, and there is debate concerning the relationship between historical types and phenomenological types. In the sense closest to philosophical phenomenology, *essence* refers to deep or hidden structures, which are not apparent on the level of immediate experience and must be uncovered and decoded or interpreted through the phenomenological method. These structures express the necessary invariant features allowing us to distinguish religious phenomena and to grasp religious phenomena as phenomena of a certain kind.

CONTROVERSIAL ISSUES. The examination of the major phenomenologists of religion and the major characteristics of the phenomenology of religion has raised many controversial issues. This section elaborates on several of these controversial issues and introduces a few others.

Descriptive versus normative claims. There are many controversial issues regarding the claim that the phenomenology of religion is a descriptive discipline with a descriptive method, especially since almost all phenomenologists go far beyond a mere description of the data, offering comparisons and evaluations of phenomena, universal structures, and essential meanings.

Many of these issues arise from the acceptance of a rather traditional descriptive-normative distinction. The adoption by many phenomenologists of religion of a radical, at times absolute, descriptive-normative dichotomy has been consistent with the classical empiricism of such philosophers as David Hume (1711–1776), with the Kantian philosophical framework, and with most nineteenth- and twentieth-century approaches in the history of religions.

Even those phenomenologists of religion who go far beyond Kristensen's descriptive restrictions frequently adopt a clear distinction between the collection and description of religious data, which is seen as objective and scientific, and the interpretation of meaning, which is at least partially subjective and normative. Despite its rejection of earlier models of positivism, it may be that the phenomenology of religion has unintentionally retained some of the positivistic assumptions regarding the investigation and "pure" description of unconstructed, uninterpreted, objective "facts."

Much of recent philosophy, however, challenges this absolute dichotomy. What is taken as objective and scientific is historically, culturally, and socially situated, based on presuppositions, and constructed in terms of implicit and explicit value judgments. For example, how does one even begin the investigation? What facts should be collected as religious facts? One's very principles of selectivity are never completely value-free. Indeed, philosophical phenomenologists have never accepted this sharp dichotomy, since the entire phenomenological project is founded on the possibilities of describing meanings. The challenge to the phenomenology of religion is to formulate a phenomenological method and framework for interpretation that allows the description of essential structures and meanings with some sense of objectivity.

Understanding versus explanation claims. Often related to controversies arising from the sharp descriptive-normative dichotomy are controversial issues involving the sharp understanding-explanation dichotomy. Phenomenology often claims that it aims at understanding, which involves describing meanings, and avoids explanation, which involves uncovering historical, psychological, and other causal relationships. Phenomenologists describe what appears and how it appears, and they interpret the meaning of such phenomena, but they do not provide causal explanations of the phenomena. This "understanding" often has the sense of *Verstehen* as formulated by Dilthey and others as the method and goal of hermeneutics. Phenomenologists aim at interpreting meaning and understanding the nature of religious and other "human" phenomena—as opposed to scientific, reductionistic approaches that give causal and other explanations and do not grasp the irreducibly human and irreducibly religious dimension of the phenomena they investigate.

Critics challenge such methods and goals as unscholarly and unscientific, and many scholars question whether phenomenological understanding and nonphenomenological explaining can be so completely separated. Explanatory approaches always involve understanding, and understanding is not possible without critical explanatory reflection. For example, even in terms of phenomenological understanding, the expressions of the religious other are not the final word, absolute and inviolable. The other may have a limited understanding of phenomena shaping her or his religious lifeworld, provide false explanations, talk nonsense, and engage in blatantly unethical behavior. Phenomenology of religion necessarily involves critical reflection, including contextual awareness and scholarly interpretations, understandings, and explanations that go beyond describing the expressed position of the religious other.

This in no way denies the value of phenomenological approaches that are self-critical in rendering explicit one's own presuppositions, that suspend one's own value judgments, that empathize and hear the voices of the religious other, and that describe as accurately as possible the religious phenomena and intended meanings of the religious other. Such phenomenology of religion aims at finding ways to allow other voices to be heard and is informed by a history of dominant, critical, normative approaches and reductionistic explanations that ignore, silence, and misinterpret the religious phenomena of others.

Antireductionist claims. Many critics attack phenomenology of religion's antireductionism, arguing that it is methodologically confused and unjustified and that it arises from the theological intention of defending religion against secular analysis. The most general criticism of this antireductionism is based on the argument that all methodological approaches are perspectival, limiting, and necessarily reductionistic. The assumption of the irreducibility of the religious is itself reductionistic, since it limits what phenomena will be investigated, what aspects of the phenomena will be described, and what meanings will be interpreted. Phenomenologists of religion cannot argue that other reductionistic approaches are necessarily false and that their approach does justice to all dimensions of religious phenomena.

The phenomenology of religion must show that its religious antireductionism is not methodologically confused, does not beg serious scholarly questions, does not simply avoid serious scholarly challenges, and may even be granted a certain methodological primacy on the basis of such key notions as intentionality and insight into essential structures and meanings. It must show, in terms of a rigorous method with procedures for verification, that its particular perspective is essential in shedding light on such religious structures and meanings.

Empirical and historical claims. Critics often claim that the phenomenology of religion starts with a priori nonempirical assumptions, utilizes a method that is not empirically based, and detaches religious structures and meanings from their specific historical and cultural contexts. Such critics often assume a clear-cut dichotomy between an empirical, inductive, historical approach and a nonempirical, often rationalist, deductive, antihistorical approach. They identify their approaches with the former and the phenomenology of religion with versions of the latter. They conclude that the phenomenology of religion cannot meet minimal empirical, historical, inductive criteria for a scientific approach, such as rigorous criteria for verification and falsification. (It may be simply noted that much of recent philosophy has been directed not only at critiquing classical empiricism but also at undermining this absolute dichotomy.)

Much of philosophical phenomenology is conceived in opposition to traditional empiricism. Husserl called for a "phenomenological reduction" in which the phenomenologist "suspends" the "natural standpoint" and its empirical world in order to become more attentive to phenomena and to intuit the deeper phenomenological essences. Although such a phenomenology has been described as a radical empiricism, it employs a critique of traditional empiricism adopted by most of the history of religions.

Controversies arise from criticisms that phenomenology of religion is highly normative and subjective because it makes nonempirical, nonhistorical, a priori, theological, and other normative assumptions, and because it grants an ontologically privileged status to religious phenomena and to specific kinds of religious experience. Thus, critics charge that Kristensen, Otto, van der Leeuw, Heiler, Eliade, and others have nonempirical and nonhistorical, extraphenomenological, theological, and other normative assumptions, intentions, and goals that define much of their phenomenological projects, taking them beyond the domain of a descriptive phenomenology and any rigorous scientific approach.

The status granted to essential religious structures and meanings is also controversial insofar as they exhibit the peculiarity of being empirical—that is, based on investigating a limited sample of historical data—and, at the same time, universal. These structures are therefore empirically contingent and yet also the essential necessary features of religious phenomena.

Finally, there is controversy regarding the insistence by many phenomenologists of religion that they proceed by some kind of empirical inductive inference that is not unlike the classical formulations of induction developed by John Stuart Mill (1806–1873) and others. Critics charge that they cannot repeat this inductive inference, that the phenomenological structures do not appear in the empirical data, and that phenomenologists read into their data all kinds of essential meanings.

One response by phenomenologists, as expressed in Guilford Dudley's *Religion on Trial* (1977), is to give up their empirical and historical claims and turn to a nonempirical, nonhistorical, rationalist, deductive approach. A different response, as expressed in Douglas Allen's *Structure and Creativity in Religion* (1978), is to formulate a method of "phenomenological induction" different from classical empirical induction, in which essential structures and meaning are based on, but not found fully in, the empirical data. This response involves a process of imaginative construction and idealization by phenomenologists, and the essential structures must then be rigorously tested in terms of the light that they shed on the empirical-historical data.

Questions of verification. As has been repeatedly noted, there are many different criticisms of the phenomenology of religion for being methodologically uncritical. The phenomenology of religion cannot continue to avoid basic methodological questions raised by philosophical phenomenology and other disciplines if it is to overcome these criticisms. Many of these criticisms involve questions of verification. Phenomenological "intuition" does not free one from the responsibility of ascertaining which interpretation of a given phenomenon is most adequate nor of substantiating why this is so. Fueling this controversy is the observation that different phenomenologists, while investigating the same phenomena and claiming to utilize the phenomenological method, continually present different eidetic intuitions. How does one resolve this contingency introduced into phenomenological insights? How does one verify specific interpretations and decide between different interpretations?

Such questions pose specific difficulties for a phenomenological method of *epoché* and intuition of essences. A phenomenological method often suspends the usual criteria of "objectivity" that allow scholars to verify interpretations and choose between alternative accounts. Does this leave the phenomenology of religion with a large number of very personal, extremely subjective, hopelessly fragmented interpretations of universal structures and meanings, each relativistic interpretation determined by the particular temperament, situation, and orientation of the individual phenomenologist?

The phenomenologist of religion can argue that past criteria for verification are inadequate and result in a false sense of objectivity, but phenomenology of religion must also overcome the charges of complete subjectivity and relativism by struggling with questions of verification. It must formulate rigorous procedures for testing its claims of essential structures and meanings, and these procedures must involve criteria for intersubjective verification.

Response to controversial issues. Many writers describe the phenomenology of religion as being in a state of crisis. They usually minimize the invaluable contributions made by phenomenology to the study of religion, such as the impressive systematization of so much religious data and the raising of fundamental questions of meaning often ignored by other approaches.

If the phenomenology of religion is to deal adequately with its controversial issues, the following are several of its future tasks. First, it must become more aware of historical, philological, and other specialized approaches to, and different aspects of, its religious data. Second, it must critique various approaches of its critics, thus showing that its phenomenological method is not obliged to meet such inadequate criteria for objectivity. And most importantly, it must reflect more critically on questions of methodology so that phenomenology of religion can formulate a more rigorous method, allowing for the description of phenomena, the interpretation of their structures and meanings, and the verification of its findings.

RECENT DEVELOPMENTS IN PHENOMENOLOGY OF RELIGION. Developments within the phenomenology of religion during the last decades of the twentieth century and the early years of the twenty-first century convey a very mixed and confusing picture about the present status and future prospects for the field.

Within religious studies. Phenomenology of religion continues as a major discipline and approach within the general scholarly study of religion. Phenomenologists of religion are influenced by earlier major phenomenologists, and they share the general phenomenological orientation defined by the major characteristics previously delineated. The phenomenology of religion has also been successful to the extent that many other scholars, who do not consider themselves phenomenologists, adopt a phenomenological approach during early stages of their scholarly investigations because it has great value in allowing them to assemble data and do justice to the religious perspectives of religious persons.

At the same time, phenomenology of religion, as has been noted, is sometimes described as being in a state of crisis. There are no contemporary phenomenologists of religion who enjoy the status and influence once enjoyed by a van der Leeuw or an Eliade. Some scholars, doing phenomenology of religion, are uncomfortable with the term since it carries so much past baggage from Husserlian philosophical foundations and from Eliadean and other phenomenology of religion they consider outdated. In general, contemporary phenomenologists of religion within religious studies attempt to be more contextually sensitive and more modest in their phenomenological claims.

Recent challenges. Most of the scholarly challenges to the phenomenology of religion continue the major criticisms previously described. Robert Segal and other leading scholars of religion, usually identified with social scientific and reductionist approaches, repeatedly criticize the phenomenology of religion for being unscientific, highly subjective, and lacking scholarly rigor. Scholars identifying with reductionistic cognitive science and claiming that this is the only rigorous method and model for gaining objective knowledge provide a recent illustration of such challenges.

There are also a tremendous variety of other challenges to the phenomenology of religion that are often classified as postmodernist and narrativist. In many ways, they offer opposite challenges from the above social scientific reductionist approaches. They criticize the phenomenology of religion's claim to uncover universal structures and essences as being too reductionistic in denying the diversity and plurality of religious phenomena. Included here are a tremendous variety of approaches often described by such terms as postmodernist, deconstructionist, post-structuralist, narrativist, pragmatist, feminist, and relativist.

For example, in *Beyond Phenomenology: Rethinking the Study of Religion* (1999), Gavin Flood argues that the inadequate presuppositions, central concepts, and models of philosophical phenomenology, an impact identified almost exclusively with Husserl's transcendental phenomenology, have dominated the study of religion. By way of extreme contrast, Flood, influenced primarily by Mikhail Bakhtin's dialogical analysis and Paul Ricoeur's hermeneutical analysis, proposes a dialogical, narrativist, interactional, dynamic model for rethinking the study of religion. This model includes: recognition of signs and language as a starting point; rejection of essentializing hegemonic approaches with their universalizing claims to objectivity; recognition that self or subject is always embodied and embedded, relational and interactive, contextualized, constituted and constituting subject; recognition of the complex narrativist situatedness of both investigator and subject matter with dialogical, mutually interactive relations between the two perspectives; and affirmation of open-ended, perspectival nature of all knowledge with emphasis on nonclosure of interpretations and explanations.

In response, one can submit that Flood greatly exaggerates the impact that Husserlian transcendental phenomenology has had on the study of religion, and that most of the critiques of phenomenology and the antiphenomenological features he formulates can be found within later developments of philosophical phenomenology and phenomenology of religion.

PHILOSOPHICAL PHENOMENOLOGY OF RELIGION. The emphasis in this entry has been on phenomenology of religion as a discipline and method within *Religionswissenschaft* (the general history of religions or religious studies). The emphasis has not been on philosophical phenomenology with its limited focus on religion and its limited influence on phenomenology of religion within religious studies.

However, there has been a remarkable development, beginning in the last part of the twentieth century: continental philosophy, frequently identified with phenomenology and hermeneutics, has often taken a religious turn. It is not always clear whether to classify such developments under "the phenomenology of religion." Most of these key philosophers are deeply influenced by Husserl's phenomenology, but they often seem to transgress phenomenology's boundaries and express ambiguous relations to phenomenology. They are sometimes classified under the "new phenomenology" or under postphenomenological variations.

Special mention may be made of several of the most influential European philosophers of the twentieth century. Emmanuel Levinas (1906–1995), a student of Husserl with deep roots in phenomenology, became one of the dominant continental philosophers in the late twentieth century. With his major focus on ethics, spirituality, and Jewish philosophy, Levinas emphasized radical alterity and the primacy of the "other," thus reversing earlier phenomenological self–other emphasis on the privileged status of the epistemic constituting self or ego. Paul Ricoeur, also with deep roots in Husserl and phenomenology, has made invaluable contributions to our understanding of religious phenomena with his analysis of philosophy as the hermeneutical interpretation of meaning and with his focus on religious language, symbolism, and narrative.

Two of the most influential European philosophers are Martin Heidegger and Jacques Derrida (1930–2004). Heidegger's writings on "phenomenology of religion," based on lectures and courses he gave in 1920 and 1921, were published in German in the 1990s and translated as *Phenomenology of Religious Life* (2004). Derrida, whose early work is on Husserl, is the major figure of deconstructionist philosophy, which can be viewed as a rejection of philosophical phenomenology and traditional philosophy. Starting in the late 1990s, Derrida increasingly turned his focus to religion. His works may be described as a hermeneutic of the desire for God, deeply shaped by a return to Husserl but more of a postphenomenological critique of presence with an affirmation of the religious other.

There are several other influential philosophers who are more easily classified under the renewed interest in the philosophical phenomenology of religion. Special mention may be made of Michel Henry, with such books as *The Essence of Manifestation* (1973), *Incarnation* (2000), and *I Am the Truth* (2003); and Jean-Luc Marion, with deep roots in Husserl, who is the most influential figure within the recent religious turn in the "new phenomenology," with such books as *God without Being* (1991), *Reduction and Givenness* (1998), and *Being Given* (2002).

In the late twentieth century, significant developments in continental philosophy, usually influenced by Husserl and philosophical phenomenology, increasingly focused on religion. It is not yet clear whether such philosophical developments will have a significant influence on the phenomenology of religion within religious studies.

Several recent contributions. Finally, there are three interrelated contributions to the phenomenology of religion that often contrast with earlier dominant characteristics: the focus on the "other," givenness, and contextualization.

From their very beginnings, philosophical phenomenology and phenomenology of religion have emphasized the need to become aware of one's presuppositions, suspend one's value judgments, and accurately describe and interpret the meaning of phenomena as phenomena. Past philosophy, theology, and other normative approaches have been critiqued for ignoring or distorting the intentional structures and meanings of the religious phenomena of the "other." More recent phenomenologists recognize that earlier phenomenology, with its essentializing projects and universalizing claims, often does not pay sufficient attention to the diverse experiences and meanings of the other. One sometimes learns more about the scholar's phenomenological theory of religion than about the particular religious phenomena of the other. Recent phenomenology has been much more sensitive to providing a methodological and hermeneutical framework for becoming attentive to the tremendous diversity of the religious voices of others.

Related to this is the focus on givenness. Philosophical phenomenology and phenomenology of religion emphasize the need to become attentive to what is given in experience. Phenomenological reflection involves an active openness and deeper kind of attentiveness to how religious phenomena appear or are given to us in experience. Over the decades, phenomenology of religion has become much broader, more self-critical, and much more sophisticated in recognizing the complexity, ambiguity, and depth of our diverse modes of givenness. For example, in their very dynamic of givenness, religious phenomena both reveal and conceal structures and meanings; are multidimensional and given meaning through pre-understandings, the pre-reflective, the emotive, and the imaginative, as well as rational and conceptual analysis; are not disclosed as bare givens but as highly complex, inexhaustible, constituted, self-transcending givens; and are given in ways that affirm the open-ended perspectival nature of all knowledge and the nonclosure of descriptions, interpretations, and explanations.

Finally, phenomenologists of religion are much more sensitive to the complex, mediated, interactive, contextual situatedness of their phenomenological tasks. Unlike the earlier emphasis on doing justice to experiential givenness and the phenomena of the other, philosophical phenomenology and phenomenology of religion are continually criticized for claiming to uncover nonhistorical, nontemporal, essential structures and meanings largely detached from their specific contexts within which religious phenomena have been expressed.

More recent phenomenologists of religion tend to be more sensitive to the perspectival and contextual constraints of their approach and more modest in their claims. There is value in uncovering religious essences and structures, but as embodied and contextualized, not as fixed, absolute, ahistorical, eternal truths and meanings.

In this regard, a more self-critical and modest phenomenology of religion may have much to contribute to the study of religion, including an awareness of its presuppositions, its historical and contextualized situatedness, and its limited perspectival knowledge claims, while also not completely abandoning concerns about the commonality of human beings and the value of unity, as well as differences. Such a self-critical and modest phenomenology of religion may attempt to formulate essential structures and meanings through rigorous phenomenological methods, including intersubjective confirmation of knowledge claims, while also attempting to formulate new, dynamic, contextually sensitive projects involving creative encounter, contradiction, and synthesis.

SEE ALSO Comparative Religion; Study of Religion, overview article; World Religions.

BIBLIOGRAPHY

The most comprehensive general introduction to philosophical phenomenology remains Herbert Spiegelberg's *The Phenomenological Movement: A Historical Introduction*, 2 vols., 3d ed. (The Hague, 1982). Richard Schmitt's "Phenomenology" in *The Encyclopedia of Philosophy* (New York, 1967), vol. 5, pp. 133–151, provides another introduction, although it tends to be formulated primarily on the basis of Husserl's approach and often is more of a critical philosophical essay rather than a survey of the field. Of the anthologies of phenomenological philosophers and their different philosophical approaches, *Phenomenology and Existentialism*, edited by Robert C. Solomon (Washington, D.C., 1972), is highly recommended.

There is no major comprehensive survey of the phenomenology of religion. Jacques Waardenburg's *Classical Approaches to the Study of Religion: Aims, Methods, and Theories of Research*, 2 vols. (The Hague, 1973–1974), provides a general introduction to scholars identified with the modern study of religion, including selections from the leading phenomenologists of religion and fairly extensive bibliographies of their works. A number of books have a chapter or section surveying the phenomenology of religion, including Eric J. Sharpe's *Comparative Religion: A History* (London, 1975; 2d ed. La Salle, Ill., 1986) and John Macquarrie's *Twentieth-Century Religious Thought*, 4th ed. (London and New York, 1988). See also Ursula King, "Historical and Phenomenological Approaches to the Study of Religion," in *Contemporary Approaches to the Study of Religion*, edited by Frank Whaling, 2 vols. (Berlin and New York, 1983–1984), and *Experience of the Sacred: Readings in the Phenomenology of Religion*, edited by Summer B. Twiss and Walter H. Conser (Hanover, N.H., 1992).

The following are selected works by the major phenomenologists of religion considered in this entry. As the first major philosophical phenomenologist with a focus on religion, Max Scheler's important translated works include *On the Eternal in Man*, translated by Bernard Noble (London, 1960), and *Formalism in Ethics and Non-Formal Ethics of Values*, 5th ed., translated by Manfred S. Frings and Roger L. Funk (Evanston, Ill., 1973). William Brede Kristensen's *The Meaning of Religion: Lectures in the Phenomenology of Religion*, translated by John B. Carman (The Hague, 1960), illustrates a very restricted descriptive phenomenology. Rudolf Otto's *The Idea of the Holy: An Inquiry into the Non-Rational Factor in the Idea of the Divine and Its Relation to the Rational*, 2d English ed., translated by John W. Harvey (Oxford, 1950), is the best-known account of religious experience. Gerardus van der Leeuw's *Religion in Essence and Manifestation: A Study in Phenomenology*, 2 vols., 2d ed., translated by J. E. Turner (New York, 1963), is often considered the classic work in phenomenology of religion. Friedrich Heiler's *Prayer: A Study in the History and Psychology of Religion* (Oxford, 1932), is available in English in a translation by Samuel McComb, but the complete edition of his *Erscheinungsformen und Wesen der Religion* (Stuttgart, 1961) has not been translated. Of C. Jouco Bleeker's many writings on the phenomenology of religion, one may cite *Problems and Methods of the History of Religions*, edited by Ugo Bianchi, C. Jouco Bleeker, and Alessandro Bausani (Leiden, 1972), which contains Bleeker's essay, "The Contribution of the Phenomenology of Religion to the Study of the History of Religions." as well as Bleeker's *The Sacred Bridge: Researches into the Nature and Structure of Religion* (Leiden, 1963), which contains the essays "The Phenomenological Method" and "Some Remarks on the 'Entelecheia' of Religious Phenomena."

Of more than thirty books by Mircea Eliade available in English, *Patterns in Comparative Religion*, translated by Rosemary Sheed (New York, 1958), is his systematic morphological work that best illustrates his hermeneutical framework of symbolic systems necessary for interpreting religious meaning. *The Quest: History and Meaning in Religion* (Chicago, 1969), a collection of Eliade's important essays, provides insight into his phenomenological method and discipline. Of Ninian Smart's many books, *The Phenomenon of Religion* (London, 1973), *The Science of Religion and the Sociology of*

Knowledge: Some Methodological Questions (1973), and *Dimensions of the Sacred: An Anatomy of the World's Beliefs* (Berkeley, 1996) provide a good background on his phenomenological approach.

The following are a wide variety of books focusing on the phenomenology of religion. Jacques Waardenburg's *Reflections on the Study of Religion* (The Hague, 1978) includes an essay on the work of van der Leeuw and two other essays on the phenomenology of religion. *Science of Religion: Studies in Methodology*, edited by Lauri Honko (The Hague, 1979), includes essays under the title "The Future of the Phenomenology of Religion." Douglas Allen's *Structure and Creativity in Religion: Hermeneutics in Mircea Eliade's Phenomenology and New Directions* (The Hague, 1978), written from a perspective informed by philosophical phenomenology, surveys approaches in the phenomenology of religion and argues that Eliade has a sophisticated phenomenological method. Two works, written from perspectives often quite critical of the phenomenology of religion, are Olof Pettersson and Hans Akerberg's *Interpreting Religious Phenomena: Studies with Reference to the Phenomenology of Religion* (Atlantic Highlands, N.J., 1981) and António Barbosa da Silva's *The Phenomenology of Religion as a Philosophical Problem* (Uppsala, Sweden, 1982). See also Henry Duméry, *Phenomenology and Religion; Structures of the Christian Institution* (Berkeley, 1975), and Thomas Ryba, *The Essence of Phenomenology and Its Meaning for the Scientific Study of Religion* (New York, 1991).

Raffaele Pettazzoni and Geo Widengren write about the complementary nature of the history and phenomenology of religion. See Pettazzoni's "The Supreme Being: Phenomenological Structure and Historical Development," in *The History of Religions: Essays in Methodology*, edited by Mircea Eliade and Joseph M. Kitagawa (Chicago, 1959) and Widengren's *Religionens värld* (Stockholm, 1945) and German translation: *Religionsphänomenologie* (Berlin, 1969).

Numerous works by critics of phenomenology of religion, claiming that it is unscientific, lacks methodological rigor, and is subjective, include important studies by such scholars as Robert Segal, Hans Penner, and Donald Wiebe. See, for example, *Religion and Reductionism: Essays on Eliade, Segal, and the Challenge of the Social Sciences for the Study of Religion*, edited by Thomas A. Idinopulos and Edward A. Yonan (Leiden, 1994), which includes Segal's essay "In Defense of Reductionism." Other challenges to philosophical phenomenology and phenomenology of religion have been offered by scholars identified with postmodernist, poststructuralist, deconstructionist, feminist, pragmatist, narrativist, and relativist approaches. See, for example, Gavin Flood, *Beyond Phenomenology: Rethinking the Study of Religion* (London and New York, 1999).

Paul Ricoeur and Emmanuel Levinas are extremely influential continental philosophers, deeply rooted in phenomenology and with a major focus on religion, even if the relation of many of their works to phenomenology is often ambiguous. See, for example, Ricoeur's *Husserl: An Analysis of His Phenomenology*, translated by Edward G. Ballard and Lester E. Embree (Evanston, 1967), and *The Symbolism of Evil*, translated by Emerson Buchanan (New York, 1967); and Levinas's *Totality and Infinity: An Essay on Exteriority*, translated by Alphonso Lingis (Pittsburgh, 1969) and *Otherwise Than Being or Beyond Essence*, translated by Lingis (The Hague, 1981).

There has been a turn toward religion in much of continental philosophy. Some of this has been shaped by phenomenology, whether it remains within the phenomenology of religion or goes beyond the boundaries of phenomenology. See *Phenomenology and the "Theological Turn": The French Debate* (New York, 2000) with essays by Dominique Janicaud, Jean-François Courtine, Paul Ricoeur, Jean-Louis Chrétien, Jean-Luc Marion, and Michel Henry. Another volume, focusing on Derrida-Marion debates, with some discussion on phenomenology in this religious turn, is *God, the Gift, and Postmodernism*, edited by John D. Caputo and Michael J. Scanlon (Bloomington, Ind., 1999). Two influential French scholars deeply influenced by phenomenology are Michel Henry and Jean-Luc Marion. See Henry's *The Essence of Manifestation*, translated by Girard Etzkorn (The Hague, 1973), and *I Am the Truth: Toward a Philosophy of Christianity*, translated by Susan Emanuel (Stanford, Calif., 2003); and Marion's *Reduction and Givenness: Investigations of Husserl, Heidegger, and Phenomenology*, translated by Thomas Carlson (Evanston, Ill., 1998), and *Being Given: Toward a Phenomenology of Givenness*, translated by Jeffrey Kosky (Stanford, Calif., 2002).

DOUGLAS ALLEN (1987 AND 2005)

PHILARET OF MOSCOW SEE FILARET OF MOSCOW

PHILISTINE RELIGION. The original arrival of the Philistines to the Near East seems to have occurred during the end of the thirteenth century BCE as the waves of the "Sea Peoples"—so called in Egyptian texts—appeared in the eastern Mediterranean and spread throughout the whole area. For instance, the inscriptions accompanying the battle reliefs of the great mortuary temple of Medinet Habu at Thebes mention six different foreign peoples that tried to invade Egypt during the eighth year of the reign of Ramses III (twelfth century BCE): the Peleset (*prst* or *plst*); the Tjeker (*tkr*); the Shekelesh (*škrš* or *šklš*); the Danuna (*dnjn*); the Sherden (*šrdn*); and the Weshesh (*wšš*). Some of these ethnonyms, along with a few additional ones (e.g., Lukka or *Rwkw*, probably connected to Lycia), occur in other Egyptian documents, such as the Great Papyrus Harris (from the reign of Ramses III), and earlier, at the end of the Late Bronze Age, in the Merneptah inscription at Karnak (late thirteenth century). Many of these peoples are mentioned also in Hittite and Ugaritic texts and Akkadian letters found in Amarna, all from the end of the Late Bronze Age. All these peoples seem to have had their roots in Anatolia and the Aegean. The Weshesh probably came from western Anatolia, like another group of the "Sea Peoples," the Tursha or Teresh (*trš*), cited in an inscription from Deir el-Medinah (Egypt) and identified with the *Tursēnoi* in Greek texts (perhaps the ancestors of the Etruscans). The island of Sardinia may owe its name to the Sherden or Shardanu. The Danuna are frequently identified with the Danuniyim mentioned in Phoenician inscriptions and with the Danaoi of Greek texts. Sicily may have been named after the Shekelesh or Sicels. The Tjeker or Zakkala eventually settled south of Carmel, and Dor was their capital. Finally, the Peleset or Purasti must be identified with the Philistines.

Centuries after Ramses III and as part of the originally Yahwistic materials eventually added to the Priestly genealogy (*tôledôt*) known as the "Table of the Nations" in *Genesis* 10, the Philistines are mentioned as originating from Kaphtor (*Gn.* 10:14: "and the Kaphtorim, from whom the Philistines came," cf. *Am.* 9:7; *Jer.* 47:4; *Dt.* 2:23)—Hebrew Kaphtor (*kaptôr,* Egyptian *kftjw,* Akkadian *kaptaru*) is usually identified with Crete. The people labeled in the Hebrew Bible as Philistines (*pĕlištîm*) occupied a rather larger territory (*Jos.* 13:2–3) that included a Pentapolis: Gaza, Ashqelon, Ashdod, Eqron, and Gath. Along with this Pentapolis, the Bible mentions other smaller Philistine settlements, called "villages" (*ḥăṣērîm*) or "daughters" (*banôt*), such as Ziklag, Timna, and Jabneh. Furthermore, there were other important cities identified as Philistine in some biblical passages, such as Gerar in the Yahwistic story of Isaac's encounter with Abimelek, king of the Philistines (*Gn.* 26)—but in the Elohistic story of Abraham (*Gn.* 20), Gerar is not associated with the Philistines. In terms of material culture, it is important to point out that the early (twelfth century BCE, Iron Age I) strata of some of these Philistine sites (Eqron, Ashdod) have yielded a sizeable amount of mostly locally produced Mycenaean pottery (specifically, type Mycenaean IIIC.1b).

Almost everything the Bible tells us about the Philistines is likely to refer to later groups (Carians, Ionians, Lydians, and probably Cretans), rather than to any possible original Iron-Age-II descendants of a particular branch of the Late-Bronze and Iron-Age-I "Sea Peoples." Nevertheless, the biblical traditions constitute the main source of information (even if anachronistic) about the Philistines. According to the Bible (*Jos.* 13:3; *Jgs.* 3:3; 16; *1 Sm.* 5–7; 29; *1 Chr.* 12:20; *Sir.* 46:18), the ruler of a Philistine city was called **seren* (a word attested only in plural, *sĕrānîm*). Two different proposals have been put forward in order to explain this term.

First, **seren* would be related to Greek *túrannos* and perhaps to the Neo-Hittite word for ruler in Hieroglyphic Luwian, *tarwani-*; but this does not point to a direct Indo-European connection, as early Greek words concerning authority positions (*túrannos, wánax/ánax, basileús*), even if attested already in Linear B (*wa-na-ka, qa-si-re-u*), have no good Indo-European etymologies.

Second, **seren* would come from the Anatolian root **sar-/*ser-* meaning "above, superior." The root appears in some Anatolian substantives: Hittite *šarli-* [sarli-] "outstanding"; Luwian *šarlaimi-* [sarlaimi-] "lofty"; Lydian *serli-/selli-* "authority." A suffix *-ēn* is present in designations of political authorities in Anatolian languages: Phrygian *ballēn,* "king"; Lycian *essēn,* "king" and *palēn,* "chief."

Both etymologies present problems. Nonetheless, the Anatolian (albeit not necessarily Indo-European) connection seems a recurrent theme in what is known about the Philistines. The case of the name of the champion of the Philistines in the Davidic narratives (*1 Sm.* 17; 21–22; *2 Sm.* 21:19; *1 Chr.* 20:5), Goliath (*golyāt*), is even more complicated. It has been suggested that Goliath's name is somehow related to the name of the Lydian king Alyattes (ca. 610–560 BCE), the grandson of Gyges (Greek *Gúgēs,* Assyrian *Gugu*). Gyges may be the historical figure behind the legendary northern king Gog (*gôg*) in *Ez.* 38–39 (cf. *Ap.* 20:7, whose kingdom is called Magog (*māgôg,* the name Gog with a prefix for place-names). In the *Qurʾān* (18:94, 21:96), Gog (*Yājūj*) and Magog (*Mājūj*) are both reinterpreted as tribal names, and later Islamic sources (such as the Ḥadīth corpus) identified them either with two branches of Turks or with the Scythians. In spite of this complicated tapestry of relations, a connection between Goliath and Alyattes (even if only typological) poses serious linguistic problems.

THE PHILISTINE PANTHEON. The main god of the biblical Philistines was Dagon (*Dāgôn*). There were temples dedicated to him in Ashdod (*1 Sm.* 5:1–7; *1 Mc.* 10: 83–84; 11:4), Gaza (*Jgs.* 16), and probably Beth-Shan (*1 Chr.* 10:10; *1 Sm.* 31:10). The toponym Beth-Dagon (*Bêt Dāgôn,* "The House of Dagon") may imply the presence of temples dedicated to Dagon in the two homonymous towns, one in the Shephelah (lowlands) of Judah, near Lakhish (Jos 15:41), and another on the southern border of the tribal area of Asher (*Jos.* 19:27). Beth-Dagon is mentioned among the cities captured by the Neo-Assyrian king Sennacherib (704–681) during his second campaign (Chicago Prism II 69: *Bīt-Daganna,* and appears also in Egyptian (*bt-jdqn, byt-jdqn*), Phoenician (*bt dgn*), and perhaps even Greek texts (*Bētagōn*)—the Greek form seems misinterpreted as a deity in the gloss in the *Etymologicum magnum* (Kallierges [Venice, 1499] 196.52: *ho Krónos hupò Phoiníkōn,* "Kronos by the Phoenicians"). The identification of this Beth-Dagon in Assyrian, Egyptian, Phoenican, and Greek sources with one of the two biblical Beth-Dagons (in Judah and in Asher) remains problematic. As in the case of other terms associated with the Philistines, Dagon may have an Indo-European etymology (related to the word for earth, **dʰeʰom*). However, this god (Dagon/Dagan) was worshiped in Syria in the second half of the third millennium already, a fact that can hardly find a place in the web of alleged connections between the Philistines and the Anatolian and Aegean worlds. Moreover, in spite of their direct and prominent association with the cult of Dagon, it is quite likely that the Philistines limited themselves to taking over the preexisting worship of a deity that was already popular in Syria and the Levant for over two thousand years.

It is clear that the Philistines did not introduce the cult of Dagon/Dagan to the Levant. In fact, the name of a prince in Late Bronze Age southern Palestine occurring in two letters from the archive of international diplomatic correspondence found in Amarna (Egypt) is Dagan-takala (Knudtzon, EA 317, 318). This theophoric name implies the presence of the cult of Dagan in the area long before the arrival of the Philistines. Nonetheless, the cult of Dagon would seem central in the Philistine pantheon. According to *1 Samuel* 5:1–7, the Philistines brought the Ark of the Covenant into the temple of Dagon at Ashdod. This was intended to signal submission to the Philistine god. However, in a typical theopolitical twist to show the superiority of Israel's national god, the move backfired, and apparently the statue of Dagon fell down—that is, Dagon prostrated himself in the presence of the Ark—and broke into pieces. In *Judges* 16:23, the Philistine rulers (*sarnê Pĕlištîm,* the *sĕrānîm* of the Philistines) gathered in what seems to be a temple of Dagon in Gaza, in order to offer a thanksgiving sacrifice ("a great sacrifice," *zebaḥ gādôl*) to Dagon for the capture of Samson. Likewise, according to *1 Chronicles* 10:10, the head of Saul was displayed by the Philistines as a war trophy in a temple of Dagon, probably at Beth-Shan (*1 Sm.* 31:10). During the Second Temple period, the cult of Dagon seems to have survived. In *1 Maccabees* 10:83–84, the high priest Jonathan burns down the temple of Dagon in Azotus (i.e., Ashdod), which was providing shelter to the cavalry of Apollonius, the Seleucid governor of Koile Syria.

The other two deities linked with the Philistines in the Hebrew Bible are Baal Zebub and Ashtoret. Baal Zebub, or Baalzebub (*baʿal zĕbûb*), is attested only four times in the Hebrew Bible, all in *2 Kings* 1:2–16, a section that describes how Ahaziah, the king of Israel, consulted the oracle of Baal Zebub, god of Eqron (*baʿal zĕbûb ʾĕlohê ʿeqrôn*). The apparent meaning of the name Baab Zebub is "lord of the flies," but this may be the result of a folk etymology that ended up transforming the name itself. The spelling in the Hebrew text does match the interpretation contained in the Greek translation of the Hebrew Bible known as the Septuagint (*Baal muîa* "Baal the fly"), the interpretation by the Hellenistic Jewish historian Flavius Josephus (*Jewish Antiquities* 9.2.1), and the Latin transliteration in the Vulgate (*Beelzebub*). However, a fragmentarily preserved Greek translation of the Hebrew Bible by Symmachus uses *Beezeboul,* and the manuscripts of the New Testament use *Beelzeboul* (*Mt.* 10:25; 12:24, 27; *Mk.* 3:22; *Lk.* 11:15, 18–19). Moreover, the name is accompanied by the epithet "head of the demons" (*árkhōn tôn daimoníōn*) in several New Testament passages (*Mt.* 12:24; *Mk.* 3:22; *Lk.* 11:15). Symmachus and the New Testament are likely to preserve an oral tradition. Furthermore, second-millennium BCE texts from Ugarit (Ras Shamra, in Syria) exhibit two common titles of the god *Baʿlu* (literally "lord"): *zbl bʿl* ("prince Baʿlu") and *zbl bʿl ʾarṣ* ("prince *Baʿlu*/Lord of the earth"). Thus, Baal Zebub is most likely the result of a folk etymology ("lord of the flies"), as the original Baal Zebul ("Prince Baal/Lord") seemed to contain a word that was rather uncommon in Hebrew (*zĕbûl* "dominion, lordship").

The Semitic goddess Astarte appears in the Hebrew Bible as Ashtoret (*ʿaštōret*). In fact, Ashtoret may be the Phoenician form corresponding to Hebrew Ashtarot (*ʿaštārôt*), the latter being usually interpreted as a plural of Ashtoret. In *1 Samuel* 31:10, the armor of Saul is said to be hung on the walls of the temple of Astarte (or perhaps "the temple of the Astartes"): "they deposited his armor in the house of Astarte (*bêt ʿaštārôt*), his corpse they nailed to the wall of Beth-Shan." In the retelling of this episode in *1 Chronicles* 10:10, "the house of Astarte" becomes "the house of their gods" (*bêt ʾĕlōhêhem*). Moreover, Herodotus (I 105.2) mentions the sanctuary of Aphrodite Ourania (*tês ouraníēs Aphrodítēs tò hirón*) in Ashqelon (a Philistine city), a goddess frequently assimilated to Astarte (see also Herodotus 1.131.3). This may be the same goddess Ctesias (Jacoby, *FGrH* 688 F I (4) 2-3) connected with Hierapolis and equated with Atargatis as a Phoenician goddess: Derceto (*Derketō*); see also *De dea syria* 14; Strabo, *Geography* 16.4.27; Diodorus, *History* 2.4. Nevertheless, the use of Ashtarot in the Hebrew Bible is to be regarded most of the time as a generic label for goddesses, whose worship and worshipers were fiercely attacked by the eventually monotheistic layers of Israelite mainstream religion. The biblical emphasis on the demonization of all these deities worshiped by the Philistines and other peoples in the area should not be regarded as part of an ethnic or political antagonism. The theo-political discourse of the official and centralized cult anathematized most manifestations of popular and peripheral religion in ancient Israel.

THE INSCRIPTION FROM EQRON. New light on Philistine religion and history has been shed by an inscription that was found in the cella of the Late Iron Age II temple at Tel Miqne (Ḫirbet al-Muqannaʿ, ancient ʿEqrôn) in 1996. The temple was most likely built after Sennacherib's campaign in Palestine (towards the very end of the eighth century), and the inscription probably dates to the seventh century. This Phoenician inscription contains what seems to be a mention of mysterious deity, for whom a temple (*bt*) was build by the prince or lord of Eqron (*šr ʿqrn*), Akayuš, son of Padi (*ʾkyš. bn. pdy*): "for PTGYH, his lady" (*lptgy.h. ʾdth*). Akayuš and Padi are mentioned in several Assyrian historical accounts as *i-ka-ú-su* and *pa-di-i* (or *pa-de-e*). The same Akayuš, king of Eqrôn, is mentioned in the Bible (*ʾākîš, 1 Sm.* 21:11; *1 Kgs.* 2:39–40). It has been suggested that the name Akayuš/Akayuś (*ʾkyš*) may be related to *Akhaios,* meaning "the Achaean," "the Greek." Although written in Phoenician, the Tel Miqne inscription seems historically and culturally Philistine. In fact, this is somehow the first Philistine inscription ever recovered, although there is a small fragment of a seventh-century Phoenician inscription found in Guadalhorce (Málaga, Spain), which may contain the toponym Eqron (*ʿqrn*). Among several proposals concerning the interpretation of the theonym *Ptgyh,* three deserve particular attention:

1. Pidrayu, as in Ugaritic *pdry,* daughter of Baʿlu, probably due to a scribal mistake or the like (so, one would have to read *ptryh*). This may be connected to Ugaritic *pdr,* which, depending on the context, may be an epithet of Baʿlu or simply another form of *pdry.* Nonetheless, both

Ugaritic names have been connected with Ugaritic *pdr* (town, city), which may have a Hurro-Urartian origin. The existence of some irregular correspondences between the various Semitic cognates (Syriac *pdorā,* Arabic *baðr*) supports the idea that this word may be ultimately Hurro-Urartian. The Mycenaean Greek form *po-to-ri-jo* is probably unrelated and corresponds to /*p(t)ólis/ > Greek *polis* (city). According to this, *Ptgyh* would be either a scribal mistake for *Pdryh,* or the result of a complex and unlikely chain of phonetic changes.

2. Potnia (Greek *pótnia* "lady, mistress," Mycenaean *po-ti-ni-ja*), which requires assuming a scribal mistake and emending the phrase to *lptnyh ʾdth.* Thus, the scribe would have started an *n,* but left it unfinished as a *g*—in this Phoenician script, an *n* resembles a *g,* but with a longer vertical stroke.
3. Pythogaia (**putho-gaia Puthō* + *Gaîa*), an unattested form reconstructed on the basis of Greek (already Mycenaean) words, "(in) Pytho (i.e., Delphi, as in a synecdoche) the goddess Gaia."

Although option three, Pythogaia, is particularly interesting, no interpretation of this name on the Tel Miqne inscription seems convincing enough. Furthermore, one could connect the final *-yh* element in this theonym with the *-yh* found in seemingly non-Semitic anthroponyms in two ostraca from Tell Jemmeh, dated to the period of Assyrian occupation in Iron Age II (*qsryh, brsyh*).

Philistine Temples and Cultic Objects. Besides the aforementioned sanctuaries, alluded to in several Biblical passages, there is direct archaeological information concerning the Philistines and their religious life. The main sources of evidence for Philistine material culture are the excavations at Ashdod, Eqron, and Tell Qasile (on the northern fringe of modern Tel Aviv). The apsidal structure with adjacent rooms and a courtyard found at Ashdod may have fulfilled a religious function, but this is rather speculative. At Tell Qasile, an original temple was twice rebuilt and enlarged, so generating three superimposed temples that were excavated within the sacred precinct: Stratum XII (end of the twelfth century BCE), Stratum XI (eleventh century), and Stratum X (beginning of the tenth century). These successively built sanctuaries at Tell Qasile included raised mud-brick platforms, pillars, mud-brick benches, and small chambers at their back, which could have been used as treasuries or were perhaps a holy-of-holies.

At Eqron (Tel Miqne), a monumental building (Building 350) that may have been a palace with shrines was unearthed in the center of the city. These shrines were not simple palace rooms as they contain mud-brick altars as well as a few bronze, iron, and ivory objects, possibly for cultic use. The shrines opened onto a hall in which there was a circular hearth with two pillar bases on each side. Hearths like this played an essential role in the structure of the megaron in the Aegean and Cyprus, whereas mud-brick altars existed in Canaan before the Iron Age (but were also common in Cyprus and the Aegean during Mycenaean times). Likewise, at Tell Qasile, a building near the earliest temple (Stratum XII, end of the twelfth century BCE) also included a hearth and two pillars, which resembled those in Building 350 at Eqron.

The Aegean connections of Philistine material culture and sites are reinforced by the presence of seemingly cult-related objects, such as the famous "Ashdoda," a ceramic figurine found in Ashdod, which is a hybrid of a chair or a throne and most likely a goddess (the top of the chair's back continues into an elongated neck ending in a head and other body parts are painted or embedded in the surface of the chair). Fragments of "Ashdoda"-like figurines have been found in Eqron and Tell Qasile as well. This seems to be a local version of the Mycenaean female figurines seated on a throne and sometimes holding a child. At Ashdod, Eqron, Gezer, and Megiddo, locally produced *kernoi* have been found. A *kernos* is an originally Aegean cultic libation vessel, consisting of a hollow ceramic ring on which the potter placed figurines of animals (such as birds, rams' or bulls' heads), pomegranates, and the like. On the other side, the Philistines had also their own style of cult vessel: a kind of lion-headed rhyton with one handle, of which examples have been uncovered in Eqron, Megiddo, Tell Qasile, and other sites. Moreover, there is also textual information about some cultic objects. Although they do not seem to correspond to any materials excavated to date, the biblical story of the return of the Ark (*1 Sm.* 6:4–16) refers to the compensation or fine (*ʾāšām*) the Philistines had to pay to the god of Israel: images or figurines of tumors (*ḥămiššāh ʿĕpolê zāhāb,* "five golden tumors"; *ṣalmê ʿĕpolêkem,* "images of your tumors") and figurines of mice (*ḥămiššāh ʿakberê zāhāb,* "five golden mice"; *ṣalmê ʿakbĕrêkem hammašḥîtim ʾet-hāʾāreṣ,* "images of your mice that are wasting the land").

It is obvious that the archaeological remains found at the Philistine sites abound in connections with Aegean material culture and that the scarce linguistic items linked to the Philistines seem to all point to Anatolia and the Aegean (the world of the "Sea Peoples"). However, with the exception of the recently discovered Phoenician inscription from Eqron, the Philistine pantheon and the general setting of its worship (such as the use of mud-brick altars) are essentially local, rooted in Canaanite religious traditions. In this respect and aside from the specific narratives of the legends of Saul and David, the theo-political biblical discourse antagonizing and demonizing the Philistines is not specific to this ethnic group. Similar intellectual constructs targeted diverse (otherwise autochthonous) groups, such as the Edomites, the Moabites, and the bulk of the rural population of ancient Israel, who were all engaged in traditional Canaanite religious practices long after the centralization and monopolization of an exclusive and monotheistic cult in Jerusalem. This theological elaboration contrasts with many details in the Davidic narratives. For instance, the name of David's special mercenary units (his "Praetorian guard" of sorts) is Kerethites (*kĕretîm,* e.g., *2 Sm.* 8:18, *1 Chr.* 18:17), which should be connected with Kaphtor (see above) and therefore understood as "Cretans." In fact, these troops of David were equated with the Philistines by some prophets (*Ez.* 25:16; *Zep.* 2:5). To a great extent, the deep religious and ethnic rivalry injected into the Davidic narratives did not have its roots in a historical setting of interaction between Philistines and Israelites, but rather in the subsequent articulation of a political theology justifying the later status quo.

SEE ALSO Astarte; Dagan.

BIBLIOGRAPHY

On the Philistines and the "Sea Peoples," see Trude Dothan and Moshe Dothan, *People of the Sea: The Search for the Philistines* (New York, 1992); Gösta W. Ahlström, *The History of Ancient Palestine* (Minneapolis, Minn.,1993), pp. 288–333; Donald B. Redford, *Egypt, Canaan, and Israel in Ancient Times* (Princeton, N.J., 1992), pp. 241–280; Carl S. Ehrlich, *The Philistines in Transition: A History from ca. 1000–730 BCE* (Leiden, the Netherlands, 1996); Symour Gitin, et al. (eds.), *Mediterranean Peoples in Transition: Thirteenth to Early Tenth Centuries* BCE (Jerusalem, 1998); Israel Finkelstein, "The Philistines in the Bible: A Late-Monarchic perspective," *Journal for the Study of the Old Testament* 27 (2002): 131–167. For citations of Ctesias, see F. Jacoby, *Die Fragmente der griechischen Historiker* (Leiden, the Netherlands, 1923–1958). The Amarna letters are quoted according to J. A. Knudtzon, *Die El-Amarna-Tafeln* (Leipzig, 1915).

On Philistine *seren*, see Franco Pintore, "Seren, tarwanis, tyrannos," in *Studi orientalistici in ricordo di Franco Pintore,* edited by Onofrio Carruba, and others, (Pavia, Italy, 1983), pp. 285–322; Giovanni Garbini, "The Hebrew-Philistine Word Seren," in *Semitic Studies in Honor of Wolf Leslau,* edited by A. S. Kaye, (Wiesbaden, 1991), vol. 1, pp. 516–519.

On the new inscription from Eqron, see Seymour Gittin, and others, "A Royal Dedicatory Inscription from Eqron," *Israel Exploration Journal* 47 (1997): 1–16; Aaron Demsky, "The Name of the Goddess of Ekron: A New Reading," *Journal of the Ancient Near Eastern Society* 25 (1997): 1–5; Reinhard G. Lehmann, "Studien zur Formgeschicte der ʿEqron-Inschrift des ʾKŠY und den phönizischen Dedikationstexten aus Byblos," *Ugarit-Forschungen* 31 (1999): 255–306; Christa Schäfer-Lichtenberger, "The Goddess of Ekron and the Religious-Cultural Background of the Philistines," *Israel Exploration Journal* 50 (2000): 82–91; Ryan Byrne, "Philistine Semitics and Dynastic History at Ekron," *Ugarit-Forschungen* 34 (2002): 1–23.

On the Tell Jemmeh names, see Joseph Naveh, "Writing and Scripts in Seventh-Century BCE Philistia: The New Evidence from Tell Jemmeh," *Israel Exploration Journal* 35 (1985): 8–21; Aharon Kempinski, "Some Philistine Names from the Kingdom of Gaza," *Israel Exploration Journal* 37 (1987): 20–24.

GONZALO RUBIO (2005)

PHILO JUDAEUS (c. 20 BCE–50 CE), Hellenistic Jewish thinker, author of an elaborate synthesis of Jewish religious thought and Greek philosophy. Although the church fathers know him as Philo Judaeus (Jerome, *De viris illustribus* 11), modern scholars often designate him Philo of Alexandria, to distinguish him from various pagan Greek authors of the same name. Philo's work marks the climax of a long chain of Hellenistic Jewish writings. His mildly atticized Greek, which is marked by a strong Platonic coloring, is unexceptionable; his encyclopedic knowledge of Greek literature and rhetoric is impressive. Disdaining a philosophically systematic exposition of his reinterpretation of Judaism, Philo assumed instead the role of scriptural exegete. He may have believed that the success of his entire enterprise was largely dependent on his ability to convince his readers that the mystical Platonism through which his Jewish understanding was refracted was no arbitrary construct imposed on the Mosaic text, but could readily be deduced from every one of its verses.

Although fully acquainted with the Greek philosophical texts firsthand and in no way restricted to manuals or digests, Philo is clearly not to be regarded as an original philosopher. He saw his task more modestly, as that of the great reconciler who would bridge two apparently disparate traditions. Although there is still no consensus, the view is gaining ground that the apparent eclecticism of his thought is in fact representative of the Middle Platonic tradition (stretching from c. 80 BCE to c. 220 CE), a highly stoicized form of Platonism, streaked with Neo-Pythagorean concerns, which included a large dose of arithmology, or number symbolism.

LIFE AND WORKS. Philo belonged to a wealthy, aristocratic Jewish family (of priestly descent, if Jerome is to be credited) that was readily attracted by the glitter of the Hellenistic world. His brother Alexander was an *alabarch* (usually equated with *arabarch*), or customs agent, for the collection of dues on all goods imported into Egypt from the East, and his wealth was such that he could grant Agrippa, the grandson of Herod the Great, a loan of two hundred thousand drachmas (equivalent to fifty-four thousand dollars); thus was established a connection that ultimately led to the betrothal of Agrippa's daughter Berenice to Alexander's son Marcus. His great wealth is further attested by his provision of silver and gold plates for nine gates of the Jerusalem Temple. His other son, Tiberius Julius Alexander, to whom Philo addressed his dialogue *On Providence* and who was described by Josephus Flavius as "not remaining true to his ancestral practices," served as procurator of the province of Judaea (46–48 CE) and as prefect of Egypt under Nero.

Of Philo himself, aside from the fact that he headed the embassy to (Gaius) Caligula in 39–40 CE and visited the Jerusalem Temple, very little is known. Though silent with regard to his Jewish education, he speaks enthusiastically of his Greek training and with engaging melancholy of his having been torn at some point from his "heavenly lookout," where he had consorted with divine principles and doctrines, to be hurled into a vast sea of civil cares. His constant use of athletic imagery, including references to specific athletic and theatrical events that he himself had attended and a triple reference to God as the "president of the games," shows him to have been an *aficionado* of the sports world. When this trait is coupled with his passionate devotion to speculative philosophy, one recognizes the presence of a Diaspora Jewish intellectual of a type utterly foreign to his Palestinian counterpart.

The Philonic corpus may be divided into three groups: historical or apologetic, philosophical (comprising four treatises, two of which are in dialogue form and preserved only in Armenian and some Greek fragments), and exegetical. The last is subdivided into three Pentateuchal commentaries: the Allegory of the Law or those treatises which begin with a scriptural passage; the Exposition of the Law or those treatises whose structure is shaped by a broad theme indicated in their title; and Questions and Answers on Genesis and Exodus. There are also references in Philo to a number of his treatises that are no longer extant. The question of the chronology of Philo's works remains problematic but the earlier tendency to assign his philosophical works to a youthful period is no longer accepted.

EXEGETICAL TECHNIQUE. Philo's attempt to read Greek philosophy into Mosaic scripture was no innovation on his part. He was fully aware of the earlier and less ambitious attempts by Pseudo-Aristeas (c. 130 BCE) and Aristobulus (c. 175 BCE), though he was also undoubtedly heir to a rich body of scholastic tradition that has vanished but to which he frequently makes allusion. He was also fully alert to the techniques employed by many Middle Platonists in their attempt to foist post-Pythagorean doctrines, including even their own, on Pythagoras (fifth century BCE) himself. Following in their footsteps, Philo put Moses forward as the greatest authority of all, as the teacher of Pythagoras and, indeed, of all Greek philosophers and lawgivers.

The main exegetical technique for Philo's vast enterprise, however, was provided by the Greek allegorical tradition, which had been initiated by Theagenes of Rhegium (sixth century BCE) in order to defend Homer against the detractors of his theology; the gods' names were made to refer to various dispositions of the soul, and their internecine struggles to the opposition between the natural elements. The Stoics expanded the Cynics' employment of Homeric allegory in the interests of a philosophical system and made much use of the etymologizing of names (of the gods, though not of the heroes), a procedure that had much appeal for Philo. For an important reassessment of Stoic allegorizing, see A. A. Long, "Stoic Readings of Homer," in *Homer's Ancient Readers*, ed. Robert Lamberton and John J. Keaney (Princeton, 1992) 41–66. Moreover, his preoccupation with the "allegory of the soul" is very similar to the later Neoplatonic allegories clustering around Odysseus, which detect in his adventures the mystical history of the soul on its way to its homeland.

John Dillon in 1977 noted the essential unity in the tradition of commentary that Philo's exegetical works and the Neoplatonic commentaries exemplify and has concluded that their common source was the Stoic exegesis of the last two centuries BCE, especially that by Crates of Mallus and Herodicus of Babylon. Thomas H. Tobin pointed out in 1983 that Stoic and Middle Platonic allegory did not include the recognition of different levels of interpretation: the allegorical interpretations involved either a rejection of the literal or complete obliviousness to it. Philo is the earliest extant example of a writer who tries to maintain the validity of both levels; thus he involved himself in a controversy with other Jewish allegorists.

A novice in the use of Hebrew texts, Philo relied on the Septuagint, which he happily considered inspired. D. W. Gooding has demonstrated that Philo shows no awareness of the Hebrew underlying the Greek translation of the Hebrew Bible, for he uniformly cites the Septuagint, which, given its frequent inadequacy, he would surely not have done without explanation had he known the underlying Hebrew, and he occasionally offers expositions of the Greek that the Hebrew would have forbidden (see David Winston and John Dillon, *Two Treatises of Philo of Alexandria*, Chico, 1983, pp. 119–125).

THOUGHT AND INFLUENCE. Philo's understanding of biblical thought is rooted in his abiding confidence in the existence of God as a supremely transcendent being, one absolutely without quality, whose pervasive immanence rules and directs all. The first half of this seemingly paradoxical concept of transcendent immanence has its source in the Old and Middle Academies, apparently going back to Plato's successor Speusippus (d. 339/8 BCE), and was more fully elaborated by some of the Neo-Pythagoreans as well as by the Middle Platonist Eudorus of Alexandria (fl. 25 BCE), who postulated a supranoetic First Principle above a pair of opposites, the Monad and the Dyad. The second half derives from a central emphasis of Stoic teaching, which envisions the omnipresent vitality of an all-traversing Logos whose highest terrestrial manifestation is the human intellect, which is identified by both Philo and the Stoics as an inseparable portion of the divine mind. Humans are thus akin to the divine and has unbroken access to it from within.

Philo defines two paths that lead to a knowledge of God's existence. In *On Rewards and Punishments* 41 he speaks of those who have apprehended God through his works as advancing on a sort of heavenly ladder and conjecturing his existence through plausible inference. The true friends of God, however, "are those who have apprehended him through himself without the cooperation of reasoned inference, as light is seen by light" (ibid.), a formula later used by Plotinus. Although there is no consensus concerning the precise significance of Philo's second way to God, it is very likely based on his notion of humanity's direct access to God from within and may perhaps be viewed as an early form of the ontological argument. A similar argument for God's existence seems to be found in both the works of the Stoics and in Plotinus.

Philo's theory of creation is based on Plato's Timaeus as interpreted by Middle Platonism. God created the universe out of a relatively nonexistent and qualityless primordial matter that contains nothing lovely and is utterly passive and lifeless. All things were created simultaneously, and the sequential account of creation in Genesis is only meant to indicate the logical order in God's design.

Although the human soul, as a fragment of the Logos, might be thought to have a natural claim on immortality, the latter can be forfeited if the soul is not properly assimilated into its divine source. From Philo's Platonist perspective, the body is a corpse entombing the soul, which at its death returns to its own proper life. The gradual removal of the psyche from the sensible realm and its ascent to a life of perfection is represented for Philo by two triads of biblical figures: Enoch, Enosh, and Noah; Abraham, Isaac, and Jacob. The Abraham of Philo's allegory is a mystical philosopher who, after having mastered the encyclical or general studies (symbolized by Hagar), in which stage all he could produce was sophistry (Ishmael), abandoned the realm of sense (symbolized in his parting with Lot) for the brighter regions of intelligible reality and, despite his initial flirtation with Chaldean pantheism, has attained to the highest vision of deity, resulting in his transformation into a perfect embodiment of natural law.

In a 1965 work, *Pagan and Christian in an Age of Anxiety,* E. R. Dodds has correctly noted that the ecstatic form of prophecy as defined by Philo is not a description of mystical union but a state of temporary possession (p. 71f.). Philo, however, speaks also of another form of prophecy, which may be designated "hermeneutical" and is mediated not through ecstatic possession but through the divine voice. Whereas in the state of possession the prophet's sovereign mind is entirely preempted, it is clear from Philo's analysis of the giving of the Decalogue, the paradigm of hermeneutical, or divine-voice, prophecy, that in the latter the inspired mind is extraordinarily quickened. Since ecstatic possession is employed by Philo for the explanation of predictive prophecy alone, whereas the core of the Mosaic prophecy, the special laws, is delivered by him in his role of hermeneutical prophet, it is in this form of prophecy that one must locate Philo's conception of mystical union. In his allegorical interpretation of the divine voice as the projection of a special "rational soul full of clearness and distinctness" making unmediated contact with the inspired mind that "makes the first advance," it is not difficult to discern a reference to the activation of human intuitive intellect (*On the Decalogue* 33, 35). In Philo's hermeneutical prophecy, then, one may detect the union of the human mind with the divine mind, or, in Dodd's terms, a psychic ascent rather than a supernatural descent.

Philo's mystical passages contain most of the characteristic earmarks of mystical experience: knowledge of God as humanity's supreme bliss and separation from him as the greatest of evils; the soul's intense yearning for the divine; its recognition of its nothingness and of its need to go out of itself; attachment to God; the realization that it is God alone who acts; a preference for contemplative prayer; a timeless union with the All and the resulting serenity; the suddenness with which the vision appears; the experience of sober intoxication; and, finally, the ebb and flow of mystical experience. Philo was thus, at the very least, an intellectual, if not a practicing, mystic.

Philo never had a major impact on Jewish thought. His name appears nowhere in rabbinic literature, and were it not for the preservation of his works by the church, they would surely have perished. In the Middle Ages Jews had access at best to an Arabic or Syriac translation of a small portion of his works. It was not until the sixteenth century that Philo was rediscovered, by ʿAzaryah dei Rossi, who read his work in a Latin translation and outlined a number of his characteristic doctrines in his Me'or ʿeinayim (Mantua, 1573). His attitude toward Philo, however, though appreciative, is at best ambivalent. Yosef Shelomoh Delmedigo (1591–1655) read Philo in the original Greek and made a Hebrew translation of excerpts from his writing, which unfortunately was stolen from him and never recovered. Simone Luzzatto, in his *Italian Discorso* (1638) on the Jews of Venice, admired Philo, whom he cited from a Latin version, and believed that his motive for allegorizing the scriptures was to attract his pagan audience. Finally, Nahman Krochmal (1785–1840) includes in his *Moreh nevukhei ha-zeman* (Guide for the Perplexed of the Time, 1851) a Hebrew translation of the account of Philo by J. A. W. Neander (1789–1850, née David Mendel), a baptized Jew who was a professor of church history in Berlin.

SEE ALSO Logos.

BIBLIOGRAPHY

The older literature on Philo is fully detailed in Erwin R. Goodenough's *The Politics of Philo Judaeus* (1938; reprint, Hildesheim, 1967), pp. 127–348. An excellent annotated bibliography for the years 1937–1962 is provided by Louis H. Feldman in *Scholarship on Philo and Josephus, 1937–1962* (New York, 1963). Earle Hilgert's "Bibliographia Philoniana, 1935–1975" appears in volume 2.21.1 *of Aufstieg und Niedergang der römischen Welt* (Berlin and New York, 1984) a volume completely devoted to Philo.

Exhaustive bibliographies of Philo with annotation are provided by Roberto Radice and David T. Runia, *Philo of Alexandria: An Annotated Bibliography 1937–1986* (Leiden, 1988); and David T. Runia, *Philo of Alexandria: An Annotated Bibliography 1987–1996* (Leiden, 2000). These two annotated bibliographies of Philo are continued in *The Studia Philonica Annual* ed. by D. T. Runia and Gregory E. Sterling (1989–). Günter Mayer's *Index Philoneus* (Berlin, 1974), and Peder Borgen et al., *The Philo Index: A Complete Greek Word Index to the Writings of Philo of Alexandria* (Grand Rapids, 2d ed., 2000)] supplement Hans Leisegang's index (vol. 7) of the *Editio maior of Philo,* 7 vols. in 4, edited by Leopold Cohn and Paul Wendland (Berlin, 1896–1930).

For German, French, and English translations of Philo, with very useful notes, see *Die Werke Philos von Alexandria,* 7 vols., edited by Leopold Cohn et al. (Breslau, 1909–1964); *Les œuvres de Philon d'Alexandrie*, 36 vols., edited by Roger Arnaldez et al. (Paris, 1961–); and *Philo*, with an English translation by F. H. Colson and G. H. Whitaker, "Loeb Classical Library" (Cambridge, Mass., 1929–1962), plus two supplementary volumes translated by Ralph Marcus (Cambridge, Mass., 1953). Fully annotated editions of Philo's works include *In flaccum*, by Herbert Box (Oxford, 1939); *Legatio ad Gaium*, by E. Mary Smallwood (Leiden, 1961); *De animalibus*, by Abraham Terian (Chico, Calif., 1981); *De gigantibus* and *Quod Deus sit immutabilis*, by David Winston and John Dillon (Chico, Calif., 1983); and David T. Runia, *Philo of Alexandria: On the Creation of the Cosmos according to Moses, Introduction, Translation and Commentary* (Leiden, 2001), which has become the definitive commentary of this work. A useful anthology of Philo's writings, translated by the author of this entry, is *Philo of Alexandria: The Contemplative Life, Giants, and Selections* (New York, 1981).

The most balanced general book on Philo is Émile Bréhier's *Les idées philosophiques et religieuses de Philon d'Alexandrie*, 2d ed., rev. (Paris, 1925). The large monographs by Walther Völker, *Fortschritt und Vollendung bei Philo von Alexandrien* (Leipzig, 1938), and Harry A. Wolfson, *Philo: Foundations of Religious Philosophy in Judaism, Christianity and Islam*, 2 vols., rev. ed. (Cambridge, Mass., 1962), are indispensable for their very rich presentations of data but are somewhat one-sided in their interpretations. Philon d'Alexandrie: *Colloque, Centre national de la recherche scientifique*, Lyon, 11–15 septembre 1966 (Paris, 1967) offers a splendid series of articles on Philo.

Valentin Nikiprowetzky's *Le commentaire de l'écriture chez Philon d'Alexandrie* (Leiden, 1977) is a rich study of Philo's exegetical approach. It is now supplemented by David T. Runia, *Exegesis and Philosophy* (Variorum, 1990); Peder Borgen, *Philo of Alexandria: An Exegete for His Time* (Leiden, 1997); David M. Hay, ed., *Both Literal and Allegorical: Studies in Philo of Alexandria's Questions and Answers on Genesis and Exodus* (Atlanta, 1991); John P. Kenney, *The School of Moses: Studies in Philo snd Hellenistic Religion In Memory of H. R. Moehring* (Atlanta, 1995); and A. Kamesar, "The Literary Genres of the Pentateuch as Seen from the Greek Perspective: The Testimony of Philo of Alexandria," in *The Studia Philonica Annual* 9 (1997) 143–189. For Philo's etymologizing of biblical names, see Lester L. Grabbe's thoroughgoing study *Etymology in Early Jewish Interpretation: The Hebrew Names in Philo* (Atlanta, 1988). Excellent accounts of Philo's Platonism are John Dillon's *The Middle Platonists* (London, 1977), pp. 139–183, and David T. Runia's *Philo of Alexandria and the Timaeus of Plato* (Leiden, 1986). A very stimulating study of the exegetical sources of Philo's cosmological exegesis is Thomas H. Tobin's *The Creation of Man: Philo and the History of Interpretation* (Washington, D.C., 1983).

Important studies of Philo's relationship to Judaism are Isaak Heinemann's *Philons griechische und jüdische Bildung* (1929; reprint, Hildesheim, 1962); Yehoshua Amir, *Die hellenistische Gestalt des Judentums bei Philon von Alexandrien* (Neukirchen-Vluyn, 1983); Ellen Birnbaum, *The Place of Judaim in Philo's Thought: Israel, Jews, and Proselytes* (Atlanta, 1996); Naomi G. Cohen, *Philo Judaeus: His Universe of Discourse* (Frankfurt am Main, 1995); Alan Mendelsson, *Philo's Jewish Identity*; Jutta Leonhardt, *Jewish Worship in Philo of Alexandria* (Tübingen, 2001); and Maren R. Niehoff, *Philo on Jewish Identity and Culture* (Tübingen, 2001). For a study of Philo's mysticism, see E. R. Goodenough, *By Light Light: The Mystic Gospel of Hellenistic Judaism* (New Haven, 1935; reprint by Philo Press, Amsterdam, 1969), which is very stimulating but highly speculative; my book *Logos and Mystical Theology in Philo of Alexandria* (Cincinnati, 1985); and Christian Noak, *Gottesbewusstsein* (Tübingen, 2000).

For Philo's theory of Mosaic prophecy, see the excellent study of Helmut Burkhardt, *Die Inspiration heiliger Schriften bei Philo von Alexandrien* (Giessen, 1988); D. Winston, "Two Types of Mosaic Prophecy According to Philo," *Journal for the Study of the Pseudepigrapha* 4 (1989): 49–67; "Philo and the Wisdom of Solomon on Creation, Revelation, and Providence," in James L. Kugel, *Shem in the Tents of Japhet: Essays on the Encounter of Judaism and Hellenism* (Leiden, 2002) 109–130, esp. 116–127. For Philo's views of sex, see Dorothy Sly, *Philo's Perception of Women* (Atlanta, 1990); Gregory E. Sterling, ed., *The Ancestral; Philosophy in Second Temple Judaism: Collected Essays of David Winston* (Providence, 2001) 199–219. For Philo's rhetoric, see T. M. Conley, "Philo of Alexandria," in *A Handbook of Classical Rhetoric in the Hellenistic Period*, ed. S. E. Porter (Leiden, 1997); and Manuel Alexandre, Jr., *Rhetorical Argumentation in Philo of Alexandre* (Atlanta, 1999). For the role of the encyclical studies in Philo, see the good study by Alan Mendelson, *Secular Education in Philo of Alexandria* (Cincinnati, 1982), and for Philo and the Sophists, see Bruce W. Winter, *Philo and Paul Among the Sophists* (2d ed.,Grand Rapids, Mich., 2002). A good account of Philo's doctrine of divine providence is Peter Frick, *Divine Providence in Philo of Alexandria* (Tübingen, 1999). A very useful account of Philo's works and the manuscript tradition is that of Jenny Morris in Emil Schürer, *The History of the Jewish People in the Age of Christ* (Edinburgh, 1987), revised and edited by Geza Vermes, Fergus Millar, and Martin Goodman, vol. 3.2, pp. 809–870.

DAVID WINSTON (1987 AND 2005)

PHILOSOPHY

This entry consists of the following articles:

AN OVERVIEW
PHILOSOPHY AND RELIGION
PHILOSOPHY OF RELIGION

PHILOSOPHY: AN OVERVIEW

One of the questions most intriguing to the philosopher is the question "What is philosophy?" Perhaps no other discipline has quite so much difficulty explaining what it is about, and in no other discipline is the question of what it is so germane to the discipline itself. Some sort of answer to this question lies close at hand in the case of the natural and human sciences: Biology is the study of life, anthropology the study of human beings, psychology the study of the psyche. Granted that these answers are not very satisfactory or edifying, they at least provide us with a point of departure; they state the specific area or realm being studied. Philosophy lacks even this point of departure, because it has no special area or realm as its subject matter.

Etymologically, *philosophy* means "the love of wisdom." Wisdom is some sort of knowledge, although it might well take some time and thought before one could say what kind of knowledge it constitutes. Perhaps one can begin by stating three things about wisdom that are quite simple and uncontroversial. (1) Wisdom does not primarily have to do with specific facts or information. (2) Wisdom is not usually to be found in a very young person; it presupposes a good deal of experience and, above all, the ability to learn from experience. (3) Wisdom must have something to do with the manner of living one's life; it must include *praxis.*

The gathering of facts or information does not automatically produce wisdom or make a person wise. Someone who reads newspapers and listens to news reports will at best be well-informed (depending on the sources), but will not on that account be wise. At the other end of the scale, individuals who study logic and the rules of critical thinking will not automatically become wise either. They will be able to argue well; their thinking will be coherent and well-organized; they will be able to pick out flaws in the arguments of others. These are fine and necessary tools, but not wisdom. It has been pointed out that logic has no content. It is like a sausage grinder; one gets out of it what is put into it, only in a better, more palatable form.

As Aristotle pointed out in his *Nicomachean Ethics,* ethics and politics are not suitable studies for the young, be they young in years or in character. Understood in Aristotle's original sense of how best to govern a city, ethics and politics require the observation of human nature and the formulation of general, flexible principles. Above all, it is necessary to recognize the fact that these sciences can never be exact in the way that the natural sciences are; to expect the kind of precision possible in natural science merely betrays false expectations and a lack of understanding of the subject matter.

Finally, one would probably expect of someone who is wise that he would lead a certain kind of life. This is meant not exclusively or, for that matter, even primarily in a moral sense, but rather in the sense of practical knowledge, of understanding. A wise person would have judgment without being judgmental. There are many great, dramatic figures in history whom one would probably not wish to call wise. In fact, Plato was most likely right: The best and wisest life is the unpretentious and undramatic life of an ordinary citizen.

One of the most illuminating statements about the nature of philosophy was made by Immanuel Kant when he said that there were three fundamental questions of concern to human beings: (1) What can I know? (2) What ought I to do? (3) What may I hope? These questions, taken together, add up to a final question: What is humanity? Kant attempted to answer them in his three main works: the question of knowledge in the *Critique of Pure Reason,* the question of ethics in the *Critique of Practical Reason,* and the question of what may be hoped for in the *Critique of Judgment.*

Having found the question "What is philosophy?" impervious to instant answers, one might pose the question "Who is the philosopher?" In a broad sense, everybody is. Every thinking human being asks certain fundamental questions: What am I doing in the world? Wow did I get here? What am I supposed to be doing? What is going to happen to me? What does it all mean? Some ask themselves more abstract questions, such as whether the world has a beginning or not. The philosopher is the person who thinks and asks; he does not necessarily write books. Three of the greatest thinkers of history, Socrates, Buddha, and Jesus, wrote nothing. One could cite many more.

In a less general sense, the philosopher is the one who asks what is real. This question led the Greeks, with whom philosophy as is known today began, to inquire into the nature of change and the relation of being (what does not change) to becoming. At least three of the most philosophical questions of all were staked out by the Greeks: the relation of (1) being to becoming; (2) reality to appearance; and (3) being to thinking. This leads to a brief look at the history of philosophy.

HISTORY. There are some philosophers who say that philosophy is a specifically Western (Greek) phenomenon and that the East does not have "philosophy" in the strict sense of that term. This seems too biased a view; Eastern thought will be briefly discussed in this article. However, Western philosophy does have its roots in the Greeks, and this article turns now to a consideration of them.

Western philosophy began with the pre-Socratics, so called because they lived before Socrates. These thinkers, often erroneously thought to be somewhat "primitive," searched for the first principle (*archē*) in things. Thales, for instance, found that principle in water, Anaximander in the boundless (*apeiron*), Heraclitus in the *logos,* Parmenides in being. The simplicity and profundity of their vision is splendid and their influence on the two greatest of Greek thinkers, Plato and Aristotle, extensive. Thus began the tradition of the history of philosophy, of thinkers learning from each other, often disagreeing and being stimulated to formulate their own ideas. It is not the case, as has been alleged, that philosophers never come up with any definitive answers because they all disagree with one another, canceling one another out, so to speak, so the end result is nothing at all. Each thinker learns from his predecessors; without Socrates there would never have been a Plato; without Plato, no Aristotle. Thus, the history of philosophy can be viewed as a long critical dialogue tracing shifting conceptions of reality.

Socrates was the true model of a philosopher. Contrasting himself with the Sophists, who claimed to have knowledge and the ability to teach it and who took money for their services, Socrates said that he knew that he knew nothing, and he therefore also taught nothing. In Plato's dialogue *Theatetus,* Socrates compares himself to a midwife who is herself barren but who helps others to give birth. The Sophists were the natural enemies of Socrates (and Plato). They taught a kind of empty rhetoric that enabled their pupils to sound impressive and win arguments, but the real philosophical issues and questions were lost to them.

These issues and questions eventually led Plato to formulate his famous theory of Forms, or Ideas (*idea, eidos*). A just person becomes just by imitating or participating in the perfect, eternal, changeless reality of justice itself. Justice itself is by no means a mere mental concept; it is what is really real. This, in a nutshell, is what is generally meant by the term *Platonism.* Reality lies in the Form, or Idea, which can be known only by the mind, not the senses. Reality is not in the mind, but it is accessible only to the mind.

If one accepts Whitehead's somewhat oversimplified, dramatic statement that "the whole history of philosophy is nothing but a series of footnotes on Plato," this thumbnail sketch may suffice to indicate the direction that the history of philosophy was to take. Two major periods followed the Greek one: the medieval, when philosophy came together with the Judeo-Christian tradition, and the modern, beginning with Descartes. In the medieval period, philosophy went hand in hand with theology and was employed in working out proofs of God's existence or in clarifying the status of the Platonic Forms, then known as "universals."

With his well-known dictum "Cogito, ergo sum" ("I think, therefore I am"), Descartes opened up what is called the modern period of philosophy. The term *modern,* in this case, indicates the belief that the unshakable foundation of all knowledge lies in the thinking subject. By isolating the subject as what alone is real, Descartes ushered in the era of subjectivism, with its concomitant dualisms of mind-body, mind-matter, and subject-object—dualisms that contemporary philosophers are still struggling to overcome and that permeate everyday language and life.

AREAS OF PHILOSOPHY. Having stated that philosophy has no specifiable subject matter peculiar to it, this article will take a look at some of the areas it prefers to deal with. These areas are articulated into what might be called different branches of philosophy. It would be well to preface this discussion with the remark that the phrase "philosophy of" can precede almost anything. "The philosophy of sport" and "the philosophy of fashion" impart a special perspective on an independent subject matter.

As primary branches of philosophy, one might cite ethics, epistemology, logic, aesthetics, metaphysics, and ontology; on a secondary level, philosophy of law, philosophy of politics, philosophy of science, philosophy of language, and philosophy of religion. With the exception of philosophy of religion, this article shall not discuss these secondary branches.

The primary branches are as old as philosophy itself—they go back to Plato. The first four are easily delineated; the last two are more problematic. An ethic is something that every human being has; it is an idea of how they want to live their lives. Even if some have ethics that one would call highly unethical, even if their concern is solely for their own interests, this view still constitutes their ethic, their idea of the best way to go through life. The question of this "unethical" ethic is discussed in detail by Plato in his *Republic:* Is the unjust person better off than the just one? Plato concludes that the height of justice is to appear unjust but to be just; the height of injustice is to appear just but to be unjust. Justice is a matter of inner balance and harmony; it has nothing to do with gain, riches, or power.

Epistemology and logic are more specialized and technical branches of philosophy. They deal with theories of how one knows things and the laws of thought. Finally, although the term *aesthetics* (philosophy of art) was coined by Alexander Baumgarten only in the eighteenth century, Western inquiry into the nature of art goes back as far as Plato and Aristotle. Aesthetics and the philosophy of art reached a culmination as the meeting place of nature and spirit in the philosophy of Kant, Schiller, and the other German Idealists. The work of art, they believed, is nature transformed by spirit.

Perhaps the most intelligible way to order terms unfamiliar to the nonphilosopher such as *metaphysics* and *ontology* is initially to adopt the classification set forth by Christian Wolff (1679–1754). *Metaphysics* generally refers to that which goes beyond (*meta*) the physical, although Aristotle's book of that name is so titled simply because he wrote it after the *Physics;* the two books, the *Physics* and the *Metaphysics,* have roughly the same (metaphysical) subject matter. To put it briefly, metaphysics is supposed to deal with what is ultimate.

Wolff divided metaphysics into two branches: general metaphysics (*metaphysica generalis*) and special metaphysics (*metaphysica specialis*). General metaphysics is equivalent to ontology, the study of being, or what is (in Greek, *to on*) in its generic traits. Special metaphysics consists of three parts: rational psychology (study of the soul), rational cosmology (study of the cosmos or world), and rational theology (study of God). Immanuel Kant called these three parts the Ideas of Pure Reason. By this he meant that these were the ultimate ideas that reason arrived at in its inherent attempt to unify the manifold (synthesize).

PHILOSOPHY AND RELIGION. Whereas in the East the relation of philosophy and religion is generally so unproblematic that there is often no clear-cut distinction between the two, the situation in the West is not so simple. The mainstream of Western philosophy was closely involved with religious questions until the late nineteenth century; there was certainly never a question of major conflict. The Greeks in general and Plato in particular pursued questions that are usually taken to be religious (e.g., the immortality of the soul, transmigration and the possibility of a future life or lives, the existence of the godlike), although there was no emphasis on the human relation to a personal deity. When philosophy joined hands with the Judeo-Christian tradition in late antiquity, it became almost indissolubly linked to theology. With that union arose the problem of reconciling philosophical thought with established dogma. For example the eternity of the world and transmigration of souls are incompatible with Christian dogma. When Descartes laid the foundation for knowledge in the thinking subject (in reason as opposed to faith), the possibility was created for the eventual parting of ways between philosophy and religion.

This parting took place in the nineteenth century with such thinkers as Feuerbach, Marx, and, especially, Nietzsche, with his pronouncement that God is dead. Since that time, philosophers may or may not have religious concerns. For example, the twentieth-century movement labeled existentialism can be divided into two camps: a theistic one (Marcel, Maritain) and an atheistic one (Sartre, Camus). Then there are those thinkers whom one could call religious but who have nothing to do with explicitly theological questions; their religious sense provides a background for their philosophizing (Heidegger, Wittgenstein). Finally, there are thinkers who believe that religious questions are not the business of philosophy, the main function of which is to develop critical argument (Russell, Moore). A twentieth-century thinker and theologian who sought to mediate between philosophy and religion, Paul Tillich, defines humankind in terms of its ultimate concern, which is a truly religious, but not a theological, definition. Instead of defining the human being as the animal with reason (*zoon logon echon*), as Aristotle and virtually everyone after him did, Tillich defines the human being in terms of his or her link to something ultimate or divine. In a similar vein, Heidegger speaks of humanity in terms of its relation to being.

It was, however, chiefly theology, as distinct from religion, that joined with philosophy, by using such concepts as Plato's Good (*agathon*) and Aristotle's Unmoved Mover to interpret theological ideas. *Religion* would appear to be a broader and less sharply defined term than *theology*. The etymological root of the word *religion* is the same as that of *yoga;* the root means "to join or link," and *yoga* comes to mean "to join (man to something transcending him)."

Thus, perhaps the main question with regard to the relation of philosophy to religion is whether humans are conceived as a self-contained and self-sufficient physical beings whose essences coincide with their material existence or as spiritual beings whose existence points beyond themselves and the "human-all-too-human." In the latter case, philosophy and religion coalesce; in the former, they diverge.

Not only is the question of belief in a divine being or some kind of transcendence at stake in the question of religion, but also the question of the nature of humanity. If the human being is conceived purely as a natural being, there seems to be no need or perhaps no room for anything godlike. One can draw a certain parallel between religion and art here. One can conceive of art, as did Freud, as a surrogate for more basic (more real) sexual drives. This conception makes a mockery of any kind of transcendence; transcendence is utterly fabricated, a futile, self-deluding, and mildly ridiculous attempt to escape the urgency of ultimately insatiable appetites. This view posits one's animality, one's body, as the very basis of one's being and renders one's spiritual side superfluous, not to say suspect. In this view, humans cannot be defined as Aristotle's rational animal; they are the botched-up animal. Animals do not suffer from doubts, despair, depression; they are totally what they are. They are "innocent." But man is "the disease of nature" (Nietzsche). "He is not what he is and is what he is not"; he is "a useless passion" (Sartre). His so-called spirituality serves only to estrange him from himself. Certainly, if individuals cannot achieve a certain transcendence, not just of their bodies, but of themselves, their spirituality will only disturb the comforts of animal existence. The plays of Samuel Beckett are among the most powerful presentations of what human life utterly lacking in transcendence is like.

DIVERSE PHILOSOPHICAL POSITIONS. Some mention must be made of the diversity of philosophical positions with regard to the nature of reality. These positions lie between the two opposite poles of idealism and empiricism, between stressing the importance of reason and of the senses. Humans seem to have two main accesses to the nature of the world and reality: their senses, which tell them about colors, sounds, and so forth, and reason, which tells them about concepts such as mathematical truths and the existence of God. Those philosophers who feel that the senses are the most important access to reality tend to downplay the activity of the mind, restricting it to combining and relating sense impressions. The most influential exponent of this view was the empiricist John Locke. At the other end of the scale, there is the rationalist or idealist who mistrusts the senses because they are often deceptive and who looks to reason or the mind for the foundation of knowledge. Plato was the first to articulate fully this view, which has had a long and varied history.

Many gradations exist between these two extremes of empiricism and rationalism. Some philosophers combine them in various ways; for example, Berkeley, who is both empirical and idealist (he is the philosopher who denied the existence of matter), or Kant, who insisted that one needs both sense experience and the understanding in order to have knowledge. More recently, there have been such movements as pragmatism and phenomenology, which seek to overcome the duality—pragmatism by turning its attention away from such purely theoretical questions to more practical ones (if it works, it is "true"), and phenomenology by looking at the "things themselves" as they show themselves prior to any such division. In any case, these "isms" never exhaust the philosopher's thought; they are convenient labels that can help individuals to orient themselves initially; more they cannot and should not be intended to do.

EASTERN PERSPECTIVES. The time is approaching when Western philosophers will no longer be able to neglect Eastern thought with impunity. Hinduism and Buddhism in India, Buddhism, Daoism, and Confucianism in China, to name just two cultures, form a vast tradition from which the

West can learn. But because these traditions are so vast, it will take time to get all the material translated, make it available, and assimilate it. The following brief comments are broad and sweeping.

In general, Eastern thought does not separate philosophy and religion. The main concern of its philosophy as well as its religion can be said to be soteriological, focusing on some kind of salvation of the individual. *Salvation* means literally "to make whole." In India, salvation can be conceived as union of the self (*ātman*) with the Absolute (*brahman*) in Hinduism or as the attainment of *nirvāṇa* (liberation, enlightenment) in Buddhism. In both of these religions, salvation means the cessation of rebirths and release from *saṃsāra,* the round of birth and death perpetuated by the individual's craving or ignorance. The Indian philosophical tradition is richly speculative, and many rather elaborate metaphysical systems have been developed. In particular, Indian theories of consciousness are intriguingly elaborate and subtle, far outstripping anything of this sort the West has produced. For example, certain Buddhist schools enumerate as many as one hundred elements of consciousness.

As Buddhism gradually lost ground in India, it moved on to China, where it was assimilated to the indigenous religions of Daoism and Confucianism. Chinese thought manifests a more practical and concrete temperament than the Indian, and much of the Buddhist metaphysical speculation was discarded. This tendency continued as Buddhism was later transmitted to Japan.

Thus far, Eastern influence on Western thinkers has been minimal. Leibniz (1646) was probably one of the first philosophers to show an interest in China. This is no mere coincidence; there are truly remarkable affinities between his *Monadology* and Huayan Buddhism. In the nineteenth century, Hegel referred to Eastern thought in his *History of Philosophy,* but his thoroughly Western bias resulted in a rather condescending treatment. Schopenhauer made use of both Hindu and Buddhist ideas, weaving them into a remarkable fabric with Platonism and Kantianism. And Nietzsche, in his attack on traditional philosophy and religion, lumped Buddhism together with Christianity, pronouncing them both "religions of exhaustion." A serious, fruitful dialogue has yet to take place.

CURRENT TRENDS. In conclusion, one might well raise the timely questions of where philosophers are heading now and what sorts of issues attract their attention. The answers will, of course, vary with different countries and areas of specialization. But a few general, tentative observations can be made.

The interest in metaphysics seems to be definitely on the wane. With the great figures of German Idealism (Fichte, Hegel, Schelling) and their British counterparts, metaphysics may have exhausted its possibilities. The era of systems and of the dominance of reason and rationality would appear to lie in the past. A lingering and self-perpetuating interest in Marx and Freud is still evident in an emphasis on the human being as a natural being and a sexual being. If there is one trend that is dominant today, it is that philosophers are preoccupied with the question of language, though in the most diverse ways imaginable. From Wittgenstein's philosophy of ordinary language to Heidegger's poetic, noncalculative thinking to the intricacies of the French schools, philosophers are taking a hard look at the way people use and structure language or the way it structures them. These are problems that religious thinkers have long been aware of in their own province. Their particular formulation of the problem asks how one can use finite language, the language naming finite things (there is no other), to speak about something neither finite nor a thing.

It is to be hoped that the philosophers will not encapsulate themselves in technical areas of academic specialization, but will be able to face and grapple with the issues looming today. The gloomiest of the existentialists seem to have played themselves out without having found much solace for the predicaments they delineated, but the force of what they expressed still continues in literature, drama, and art in a more vivid, aesthetic form.

If philosophy stays aloof from the existential concerns of the human being, as it did and does in movements so vastly different as Scholasticism and logical positivism, it loses its original (Platonic) sense of a quest for something transcending humanity. Aristotle said that philosophy begins in wonder. Perhaps in times of spiritual destitution such as the present, wonder could be the beginning of the end of thoughtlessness. As Heidegger, quoting his favorite German poet, Hölderlin, says: Where the danger grows, there also grows the saving power. The philosopher must strive to avoid the extremes of petulant pessimism and mindless optimism.

SEE ALSO Aesthetics; Apologetics; Cosmology; Henotheism; Knowledge and Ignorance; Morality and Religion; Pantheism and Panentheism; Religious Experience; Revelation; Soteriology; Soul; Theism; Theodicy; Transcendence and Immanence; Truth.

BIBLIOGRAPHY

The following works, given in chronological order, represent classics in the development of Western philosophical thought.

Plato. *Collected Dialogues.* Edited by Edith Hamilton and Huntington Cairns. New York, 1963.

Aristotle. *The Basic Works of Aristotle.* Edited by Richard McKeon. New York, 1941.

Augustine. *The Confessions of St. Augustine.* Translated by Edward B. Pusey. New York, 1961.

Thomas Aquinas. *Concerning Being and Essence.* Translated by George G. Leckie. New York, 1965.

Descartes, René. *Meditations on First Philosophy.* Translated by Donald A. Cress. Indianapolis, 1979.

Spinoza, Barukh. *Ethics.* Translated by William Hale White, revised by Amelia Hutchinson Stirling. New York, 1949.

Leibniz, G. W. *Discourse on Metaphysics, Correspondence with Arnauld, and Monadology.* Translated by George R. Montgomery. Chicago, 1962.

Locke, John. *An Essay concerning Human Understanding.* Edited by Peter H. Nidditch. Corr. ed. Oxford, 1979.

Berkeley, George. *Three Dialogues between Hylas and Philonous.* Edited by Colin M. Turbayne. New York, 1954.

Hume, David. *A Treatise on Human Nature.* 3 vols. London, 1739.

Kant, Immanuel. *Critique of Pure Reason.* Translated by Norman Kemp Smith. New York, 1929.

Hegel, G. W. F. *Phenomenology of Spirit.* Translated by A. V. Miller. Oxford, 1977.

Heidegger, Martin. *Being and Time.* Translated by John Macquarrie and Edward Robinson. New York, 1962.

Wittgenstein, Ludwig. *Tractatus logico philosophicus.* Translated by C. K. Ogden. London, 1958.

New Sources

Bourdieu, Pierre. *Practical Reason.* Translated by Randal Johnson. Stanford, Calif., 1998.

Bourgeois, Patrick L. *Philosophy at the Boundary of Reason: Ethics and Postmodernity.* Albany, 2001.

Coetzee, P.H., and A.P.J. Roux. *The African Philosophy Reader.* 2nd ed. New York, 2003.

Lakoff, George, and Mark Johnson. *Philosophy in the Flesh: The Embodied Mind and Its Challenge to Western Thought.* New York, 1999.

Lloyd, Genevieve. *Feminism and the History of Philosophy.* New York, 2002.

Mohanty, Jitendra Nath. *Reason and Tradition in Indian Thought: An Essay on the Nature of Indian Philosophical Thinking.* Oxford, 1992.

Nichol, Lee, ed. *The Essential David Bohm.* New York, 2003.

Rorty, Richard. *Philosophy and Social Hope.* New York, 1999.

JOAN STAMBAUGH (1987)
Revised Bibliography

PHILOSOPHY: PHILOSOPHY AND RELIGION

The two enduring forms of spiritual expression designated by the terms *religion* and *philosophy* quite obviously never confront each other as such; they enter into relations with one another only in historical and specific terms. It is in the visions of individual philosophers as they intersect with the beliefs and the practices of particular religious traditions that one finds the living relations between religion and philosophy.

THE NATURE OF RELIGION AND PHILOSOPHY AND THEIR RELATION TO EACH OTHER. A fine example of the interaction between religion and philosophy is found in the thought of Clement (150?–215?) and Origen (c. 185–c. 254), usually known as the Christian Platonists of Alexandria because their school was located in that ancient center of Hellenistic culture. As this appellation implies, they were engaged in interpreting the basic beliefs of Christianity concerning God, Christ, human beings, and the world in terms of the insights of the Neoplatonic philosophy current in their time. More than a century earlier, the Jewish philosopher Philo Judaeus (d. 45–50 CE) carried out much the same enterprise for the Hebraic tradition, drawing chiefly on the thought of the Greek philosopher Plato (c. 429–347 BCE), and the Pythagorean and Stoic schools. This type of interpreting—or dialogue, if you will—involving the use of the Greco-Roman philosophical systems for formulating the ideas and elucidating the religious insights of the biblical tradition, continued throughout the Middle Ages and lasted until the end of the Renaissance.

Despite the fact that the historical interactions between religion and philosophy must always be concrete—because it is the thought of a particular philosopher or school of philosophy that is interacting with a specific religious tradition—both are themselves enduring forms to be found in every culture, and they are marked by general features that serve to distinguish one from the other. It is on this account that one not only can but must come to some theoretical understanding of how religious faith and philosophical reflection are related not only as a matter of historical fact but as one of principle. To speak of principle means to approach the task of reaching down to the roots of these two spiritual forms, universal in the experience of humankind, in an attempt to grasp what they essentially are and to determine how they should be related to each other. That the task is not easy should be obvious in view of the enormous variety of religious experiences and of philosophical outlooks recorded in human history. The task is, nevertheless, inescapable if one is to understand one's self, and therefore one must not be dissuaded by the knowledge that no one characterization of either religion or philosophy can capture everything or satisfy everybody.

The American philosopher and psychologist William James (1842–1910), in his epoch-making study *The Varieties of Religious Experience* (1902), quite rightly described religion as concerned chiefly with a strategy for redemption calling all human beings away from the snares and illusions of natural existence and back to their true selves. That such a strategy is needed follows from the fact, not always sufficiently recognized, that every religion offers a diagnosis of the human predicament, a judgment focusing attention on some flaw or defect in natural existence that stands as an obstacle between one's self and the ideal life envisioned by the particular religion in question. Redemption, in short, means being delivered from that flaw through a divine power capable of overcoming it. And the nature of the deliverance is determined in every religious faith by the character of the flaw envisaged. Both the diagnosis and the strategy of redemption derive from the lives and insights of the founders, sages, and prophets upon which the religious tradition rests. The articulated beliefs and practices that define a particular religious tradition are transmitted from age to age through historical communities of faith. Individuals owe their life to the tradition in which they stand, but the tradition owes its life to the continuing community sustained by the spiritual bonds existing between the members.

Philosophy, on the other hand, has as its chief concern the attainment of a comprehensive theoretical understanding of the many types and levels of being in the universe and their relations to each other, including a conception of the place to be assigned in the cosmic scheme to human beings and their experience. As far as Western philosophy is concerned, two different lines of inquiry manifested themselves in the earliest stages of development. On one side curiosity was directed toward the discovery of the most pervasive or universal traits exhibited by everything that is. Such features as unity and plurality, identity and difference, spatial and temporal location, acting and being acted upon were singled out as constituting the universal order holding sway throughout the universe. This line of inquiry can be called the quest for the categories ingredient in both the world and the structure of human thought and knowledge about it. Without pushing the identification too far, one may say that this side of philosophy is one that it shares with science. The affinity is nicely illustrated by the fact that what is called science today went by the name of "natural philosophy" in the seventeenth and eighteenth centuries, as can be seen from the full title of the famous treatise written by the English physicist Isaac Newton (1642–1727), *Principia mathematica philosophiae naturalis* (1687).

On its other side, philosophy meant a bolder and more speculative inquiry prompted by wonder about the being of things. Wonder in the face of the fact that there is anything at all and wonder about what there might be about things that sustains them and causes them to stand out against nothingness and the void. This concern for what came to be called metaphysics in one of its senses has expressed itself in the quest for a ground not only of the being of things but of human being as well; the latter concern led to the inclusion of speculative insight about the good and ideal human existence within the scope of philosophy. Understood in this sense, philosophy shows its affinity with the concerns of religion, an overlap of interest that has in the past occasioned both fruitful cooperation as well as conflict between them. The two, however, remain distinct by virtue of their different aims and approaches. This difference may be summed up in a way that is symbolic for both: The reality of the divine, however conceived, is always the initial conviction of the religious outlook, while for philosophy that reality remains the final or ultimate problem.

There is yet another difference between religion and philosophy, and its meaning becomes clear when one takes into account what was said previously about the role of the religious community. Philosophical analyses and visions are the products of solitary thinkers whose doctrines have indeed formed the basis of traditions and schools of thought, witness Plato and the Greek philosopher Aristotle (384–322 BCE), but such schools do not perform the same functions as a religious community. The latter exists to bring together many individuals in a spiritual unity that transfigures life; schools of thought are primarily focal points of understanding and a place for the meeting of minds.

Much of the foregoing analysis has, of course, been based entirely on the situation in the West, where the three major faiths—Judaism, Islam, and Christianity—found themselves confronted with the autonomous philosophical systems developed in the classical world. These systems were autonomous in the sense that they were not developed under the special aegis of religious belief, even if they were sometimes influenced by religious ideas. They represent the reflections of individual minds attempting to articulate a comprehensive vision of what there truly is above and beyond appearances and mere opinions. The case of Aristotle, although in some respects unique, provides a clear illustration. His thought, ranging as it does over the entire spectrum of experience and existence, embraces a profound conception of God as, among other things, the Unmoved Mover. There is, as has often been pointed out, no essential connection between this conception of God and religion. In fact the thought of Aristotle on this point has often been described as the paradigm of conceptions of God without religion.

It is necessary to emphasize the autonomous nature of the classical philosophical systems for at least two reasons. One is the tension resulting from the fact that these philosophies, while useful in providing the concepts and principles through which primary religious experience and insight could be precisely expressed, stood at the same time as rival interpretations of reality to which the biblically based religions had to come to terms. To appeal to Aristotle again for an illustration, his conception of the world as eternal, or as not having come into being in time, posed a serious problem with regard to so central a doctrine of biblical religion as that of creation. Religious thinkers, therefore, could not avail themselves of his thought as a framework for theology without first reinterpreting it at crucial points. It is noteworthy that the tension thus introduced, plus the fear of distorting the religious message by expressing it in philosophical terms, led some thinkers, especially representatives of early Latin Christianity, to reject philosophy as an alien medium and to declare, with Tertullian (160?–225?), that "Jerusalem has nothing to do with Athens." This negative attitude, however, did not prevail, and the subsequent course of Western religious thought, at least until the Reformation, was marked by a continuous interaction between philosophical and religious ideas.

The second reason for dwelling on the autonomy of the philosophies that figured so largely in the religious thought of the West is that it opens to view a most important contrast with much Eastern thought. It is generally admitted that there is not to be found in the Hindu and Buddhist traditions, for example, any sharp and clear distinction between religion and philosophy. The two are closely interwoven, and there is no clear historical counterpart in the history of these traditions to the situation in the West, where more or less clearly defined religions encountered distinctive and already formed philosophies. It must, of course, be borne in mind that this is speaking in very general terms; one cannot say dogmatically that no distinction whatever was drawn between religion and philosophy in the Eastern cultures, especially in view of some difficult cases such as Confucianism and Daoism. The former is often described not as a religion but as a philosophical system of ethics, and the latter seems to have had its roots primarily in philosophical reflections that in time assumed religious form. Contemporary historical scholars, moreover, in rewriting the history of Indian thought, for example, are putting more emphasis, possibly under Western influence, on the strictly philosophical theories represented by the classical systems of thought and distinguishing them from "salvation doctrines" said to be representative of religion. Be this as it may, the important point is that the problems faced by Western thinkers in relating religion and philosophy were quite different from those confronting their counterparts in the East. It is one thing to attempt to relate two forms of insight to each other starting within a historical situation in which they meet each other as quite distinct, and another to confront the problem of their interconnections in cultures where the two were never clearly separated from the outset.

IMPACT OF KANT'S PHILOSOPHY AND THE EMPIRICIST CRITERION OF MEANING. Concentrating on Western civilization, where the interaction between religious faith and philosophical inquiry has so largely determined the history of both, it is necessary to understand the impact of two decisive developments that greatly disrupted the sort of exchange that had resulted in the monumental philosophico-religious syntheses represented by such thinkers as Augustine of Hippo (354–430); Anselm of Canterbury (1033–1109); Philo Judaeus; Moses Maimonides, the medieval Jewish philosopher (1135–1204); Bonaventure, the scholastic theologian and philosopher (1217–1274); Duns Scotus, Scottish philosopher and theologian (1265?–1308); and Thomas Aquinas, author of the monumental *Summa theologiae* (1226–1274); as well as such Muslim thinkers as Ibn Rushd (Averroës, 1126–1198) and Ibn Sina (Avicenna, 980–1037), who sustained for Islamic religion the same kind of dialogue with Aristotle carried on for Christianity by Albertus Magnus, the German scholastic philosopher (1200–1280) and Thomas Aquinas. The first of these developments was the attack by the German philosopher Immanuel Kant (1724–1804) on the traditional metaphysics that had so long served as a medium of expression for religious belief; the second was the claim, stemming from the philosophies of empiricism, that there is a single criterion for determining the meaning and truth value of all statements, and that this criterion is found in sense experience and the knowledge represented by science. Relations between philosophy and religion had been determined since the beginning of the nineteenth century by the response to Kant and since early in the twentieth century have been characterized by attempts on the part of religious thinkers to deal with what came to be known as the empiricist criterion of meaning.

Three strategies have been proposed for overcoming the obstacles that arose and impeded a continuation of the classical dialogue between religious insight and philosophical reflection. The first is represented by those religious thinkers who accepted the Kantian thesis that knowledge extends no further than mathematics and what he called the general science of nature, so that metaphysics, and especially the classical proofs for the existence of God, become invalid, because they transcend the limits of what the human understanding can know. Because these thinkers were committed to upholding the validity of religion, their task was to find some new basis for it other than metaphysics and philosophy. The second strategy found expression in those who accepted the theory of one criterion of meaning and who, insofar as they were concerned with religion at all, identified it with emotion, feeling, and attitudes, all of which were said to be devoid of cognitive significance. This was the position of positivism or logical empiricism. Finally, there was the alternative associated chiefly with the name of the Austrian philosopher Ludwig Wittgenstein (1889–1951), who saw the limitations of the empiricist criterion of meaning and the difficulties involved in justifying it. Consequently, he proposed instead to focus attention not on meaning but on the use of language in different contexts of experience—aesthetic, economic, religious, moral, and so forth. These different uses of language were called "language games," and he described the language of religion as distinctive because it expresses what he called a "form of life." Just as in the preceding alternative, however, no cognitive status can be claimed for religious utterance, although it must be admitted that in shifting from meaning to use Wittgenstein intended to criticize positivism for having gone too far.

It should be evident that each of these alternatives represents a response to the Kantian philosophy, with its restriction of reason to the bounds of sense and of knowledge to science. The proponents of all three alternatives basically accepted Kant's analysis as valid, but with important differences. Those who adopted the first strategy had the strongest concern for preserving religion, and they consequently sought to find new foundations for it, while at the same time leaving Kant's position intact. The positivists, on the whole, regarded religion as outmoded and its utterances as without meaning; in this they went beyond Kant in abolishing his distinction between what can be meaningfully thought and what can be known. Kant, that is to say, held that individuals can validly think the idea of God, because reason demands that they do, but that knowledge of the reality meant is not possible. In identifying meaning with the possibility of verification in sense experience, the positivists had to deny that the idea of God is meaningful in any sense. Wittgenstein, though not alone in his criticism, had, nevertheless, the most influential voice in turning back the positivist approach. He claimed, in effect, that the use of language in theoretical science is not its only use; account must be taken as well of the functions of language in other contexts of experience, including the religious. Thus, he argued, instead of stopping inquiry before it begins by invoking the positivist criterion of meaning and declaring religious expression meaningless, the task is to understand the grammar and the logic of the language and forms of expression actually used by the members of religious communities. One very significant consequence of this approach was the discovery that "religious language" embraces a considerable variety of types of expression and that careful distinctions are necessary if each type is to be understood in terms proper to itself. The devotional language of worship, for example, differs in important respects from the conceptual language needed for theology, which in turn differs from the languages represented by myth, parable, exhortation, and prophetic insight.

Invaluable as this sort of clarification has been in fostering a better understanding of what religion is and means, it does not engage the problem of validity in religion, nor does it go very far in relating religion to other dimensions of experience. In fact the language-game approach in the hands of Wittgenstein and his followers has tended to encapsulate religion in a sphere of sheer faith—fideism—cut off from all forms of knowledge. So great a gap between reason and faith has been brought about that Wittgenstein could find no way of overcoming it. On the contrary, he even claimed that if there were a single scrap of "empirical" evidence to support what is intended to be a religious statement, it would thereby cease to be "religious." The major difficulty with such a position is that it fails to deal with the most important fact about religious belief, which is that those who adhere to it do so with the firm conviction that it is true, that reality is in accord with it, even if they are unable to give an account of what this precisely means in philosophical terms.

Enough has been said about the second and third alternatives to indicate that they are not ultimately satisfactory. This author should now like to return to the first alternative and mention briefly a number of the proposals that have been made to find a new basis for religion without violating the limits imposed by Kant. It shall be suggested that each of these proposals expresses something important, but that no one of them achieves a satisfactory relation between religion and philosophy. Finally, this article will propse a fourth alternative that is actually a new version of the ancient dialogue between religion and philosophy.

One of the most important religious responses to Kant was the thought of the German theologian Albrecht Ritschl (1822–1889) and his school, which made its appearance at the middle of the nineteenth century. He sought to free theology from dependence on metaphysics by stressing the essentially moral meaning of religious conceptions. Following Kant in stressing the primacy of practical reason, Ritschl envisaged Christianity as a faith aimed at the realization of a practical ideal of human life. While it is correct to say that Ritschl found the basis of theology not in metaphysics but in a value judgment expressing the practical significance of a divine reality, the value judgment in question is of a complex sort. Jesus, the object in human experience possessing the value of Godhead, is the occasion upon which individuals apprehend him as the bearer of grace, the one who reveals God as love. Insofar as individuals experience and evaluate the action of Jesus in revealing God, they see him as God. According to Ritschl, however, it is not through command or authority that Jesus is effective, but only through his moral teachings. In realizing God's goal, Jesus also realizes one's own goal, which is the fulfillment of one's purpose in life. Ritschl saw in this fundamental evaluation the justification whereby individuals gain admission to the kingdom of God through Jesus in the church. In making the moral dimension central, Ritschl was able to retain a theology unaffected by Kant's elimination of classical metaphysics.

This proposed solution of the relation between philosophy and religion is not, however, without difficulties. Granted that Ritschl's position involves something more than a simple reduction of the religious to the moral, the fact remains that the latter is too limited in scope to do justice to the religious concern. Morality is concerned primarily with what a person is to do, while religion aims at what a person is to be, and the problem of being presents itself at this point in the form of the need to find a basis for the unity and integrity of the person, something not to be resolved within the confines of morality and values. There is, in addition, the fact that the biblical message involves other theological concepts requiring an articulation that takes one beyond the resources of morality and valuation.

A second, and far more influential, attempt to resolve the problem was made by the brilliant Danish thinker Søren Kierkegaard (1813–1855). Using the philosophy of Absolute Spirit set forth by the German philosopher G. W. F. Hegel (1770–1831) as both a foil and the focal point of his attack, and declaring that "Kant is my philosopher," Kierkegaard insisted that Christianity is concerned primarily with the relation of faith between God and human beings and that on this account it stands over against speculative philosophy and all efforts to make Christian doctrine "rational." According to Kierkegaard, the central Christian claim that the eternal has entered time is the "absolute paradox," defying all mediation and rational explanation; God confronts human pride and refusal to acknowledge his status as a creature, so that religion is and must always appear as an "offense." If it does not, says Kierkegaard, then it is inauthentic and conventional for having been made "palatable" or consonant with human reason. From this perspective, rooted in the primacy of *existence*—that is, the individual who finds himself "there" in a time and place confronting the problem of salvation—attempts like that of Hegel to use speculative reason to break through the mystery of the eternal entering time succeed only in distorting the essential religious message, for, Kierkegaard insisted, this message is simply "absurd" when considered from the standpoint of human reason. Although not without philosophical acumen of his own, Kierkegaard devoted himself, through his genius for irony, wit, paradox, and profound psychological insight, to the confounding of philosophy, thus opening a wide gap between reason and religion. Kierkegaard could well afford to accept the strictures on theoretical reason dictated by Kant's philosophy, because he was firmly convinced that Christianity neither can nor need be made "rational."

For all of its undoubted insights into the human condition and the meaning of God and faith, Kierkegaard's position is ultimately unstable. In the face of Hegel's massive rationalism, Kierkegaard was undoubtedly right in seeking to discover the reality of the individual and the need to appropriate Christian faith in a personal commitment, something that does not happen by understanding alone. But in equating thought with possibility, so that it necessarily abstracts from existing (the individual's being and situation), Kierkegaard not only lost the basis upon which thought can be said to penetrate and illuminate human life, but he was forced as well to turn existence into a "surd" element—"what thought cannot think." As subsequent developments proved, the step from the "surd" to the "absurd" is quite short and contains a pitfall. The withdrawal of reflective thought from existence led ultimately to the declaration that religion is illusory because human existence itself is absurd. That is to say, existence came to be thought absurd, not in the ironic and paradoxical Kierkegaardian sense, but rather in the sense established by the French philosopher Jean-Paul Sartre (1905–1980), according to which religion is abolished and no meaning attaches to human existence in itself but is found only in what individuals, through the heroic human will, can succeed in creating for themselves. Kierkegaard, to be sure, is not to be held accountable for this later development, but in his insistence on the irreconcilability of religion and philosophy, he left religion open to dissolution by those who could see no rationality in it and were unpersuaded by his modern version of the ancient proclamation, "I believe because it is absurd."

Yet another alternative framework for the articulation of religious insight took the form of an appeal to "sacred history," or the history of divine redemption. From this standpoint, theology has to do not with the classical doctrine of God expressed, as in the case of the medieval theologians, through philosophical categories, but with the activity of God, discernible through the eyes of faith, in accomplishing the redemption of the whole creation through history. This position finds strong support in the undoubtedly valid, even if sometimes exaggerated, distinction between the fundamental patterns exhibited by Hebraic and Greek thought. The latter, stressing form and the timelessness attached to being and truth, found itself, insofar as attention was focused on history at all, interpreting the course of human events in essentially cyclical terms after the fashion of the continual recurrence of forms in the natural world. Hebraic thought, by contrast, was marked not only by a powerful sense of the reality of time and a linear history, but by the belief that historical development is itself the medium through which the nature, and especially the will, of God is revealed.

Numerous attempts have been made, going back to the German theologians Wilhelm Herrmann (1846–1922) and Ernst Troeltsch (1865–1923), to establish the primacy of history as the medium for understanding and interpreting religion; no brief discussion, however, could possibly do justice to all the shades of opinion and differences of emphasis that have been expressed. If these attempts, and those represented more recently by the thought of such theologians as H. Richard Niebuhr (1894–1962), Rudolf Bultmann (1884–1976), Friedrich Gogarten (1887–1967), and John Macquarrie have anything in common, it is the belief that not philosophy but historical experience and the course of history provide both the foundation of Christian faith and the interpretative framework within which it is to be understood. It is, of course, true that this approach has deep roots in the biblical tradition; Christianity followed the faith of the Hebrew scriptures (Old Testament) in recognizing the unique conception of a linear history in and through which the will of God becomes manifest. Wolfhart Pannenberg, the contemporary German theologian, writes, "Indeed, if it is at all possible . . . to compress [the] biblical understanding of reality into a single word, that word would certainly be 'history'" (*Faith and Reality,* Philadelphia, 1977, p. 10). The strength of this position is found in what it positively accomplishes in highlighting the essential contribution of the temporal and historical—the incarnation as the disclosure of God in history—as opposed to all static conceptions of reality, wherein no provision is made either for history as a medium of revelation or for the novel and creative increment represented by the course of history itself. If, however, whether under the influence of an exaggerated contrast between the Hebraic and Greek views of the historical, or in an effort to remain within the limits of Kant's philosophy alone, proponents of the history-as-medium view hope to replace philosophy with history, serious problems arise. For, on the one hand, there is the philosophical problem of understanding the nature of historical events, the relation between interpreting and explaining them and, consequently, of having some theory about the connections between history, nature, and God. These are essentially philosophical concerns not to be resolved on the basis of the historical dimension alone. Moreover, there is no avoiding the theological issue posed by the mediating function history is to perform, for it is not only the so-called brute historical datum that is involved, but the all-important fact that this datum—especially the historicity of Jesus—must mean or point to God. This fact leads directly to the vexing problems stemming from the need to appeal to a "sacred" history that bears the religious meaning without thereby losing the historicity assumed to belong *ipso facto* to the "secular" account of the events in question. Once again, an attempt to respect what the Swiss theologian Karl Barth (1886–1968) has called the "Kantian terms for peace" in the relations between philosophy and religion, and to find a medium for religious thought other than metaphysics, turns, after the fashion of Hegel's logic, into its opposite, so that new philosophical and theological problems arise in the effort to establish this medium as the successor of metaphysics.

Other religious thinkers, sometimes called the "theologians of encounter," have maintained that religion finds its foundation neither in metaphysics, history, nor morality, but in an immediate encounter establishing a relation with a divine Thou, somewhat analogous to the situation in which two persons are related to each other through intimate bonds of love, compassion, and concern. Central to this outlook is a contrast similar to that between meeting and being acquainted with a person in direct encounter and "knowing about" that person indirectly through abstract concepts.

The small classic written by the Jewish philosopher Martin Buber (1878–1965), *I and Thou,* gave moving expression to this way of understanding the relation between humankind and God and exerted a powerful influence on Jewish and Christian thought alike. Buber, by no means a foe of philosophy, did, however, under the influence of Kant, draw a sharp distinction between the theoretical, conceptual knowledge of objects—what he called the "it-world"—and the experienced relations between persons who meet and acknowledge each other as such—the world of the "thou." Accordingly, Buber interpreted religion as the special relation established between the "I" and the divine "Thou." Theoretical knowing Buber saw as nullifying the "I-thou" relations precisely because it objectifies its content and leaves the world of persons out of account.

The approach to God through encounter has had its representatives among Christian theologians as well, with, of course, certain transformations necessary to accommodate that tradition. *The Divine-Human Encounter,* by the Swiss theologian Emil Brunner (1889–1966), is a paradigm of the view that human meets God in a faith that is essentially an "answering" acceptance of the divine word, something that is neither a thinking "about" God nor the communication of information. H. H. Farmer has expressed a similar idea in *The World and God,* where he declares that the experience of divine encounter "must be self-authenticating and able to shine in its own light, independently of the abstract reflections of philosophy. . . ." Barth, although his theological system is far too complex to be subsumed under the encounter thesis, nevertheless insists that God remains forever a subject, and that through the incarnation in Christ he makes himself available to be apprehended in the personal knowledge of encounter.

Some contemporary religious thinkers, influenced by the concerns of developing nations, of minorities and the disinherited, by new and more permissive attitudes in morality, and by conflicts in social relations, have turned away completely from traditional philosophical approaches to God and religion and have looked instead to the social sciences as the appropriate medium for expressing what they take to be relevant in religious belief for dealing with these concerns. A fine example of this trend of thought is found in what has come to be called "liberation theology," which focuses attention on the concerns of the oppressed. There is no doubt that this development has been playing an important role in bringing religious faith into the arena of social, economic, and political problems of the utmost urgency. In the context of the present discussion, however, it is necessary to call attention to a basic problem. A liberation theology must be, whatever else it is, a theology, which is to say that it must remain in touch with both religious and philosophical thought concerning God, because the social sciences themselves do not provide this content.

The most radical position as regards the relation between religion and philosophy finds expression in the claim that religion is exclusively a matter of revelation—the word of God—and stands in no need of mediation through secular knowledge, including philosophy. The theology of neoorthodoxy, as it was called, represented chiefly by the massive work of Barth, is based on the proposition that there is no "point of contact" between reason and revealed truth; every philosophical position is equally distant from and thus equally irrelevant to the theological articulation of religious faith. To take but one example, a secular philosopher discussing the meaning of nothingness, according to Barth, could, *ipso facto,* not be referring to the same nothing from which, in the biblical account, the creation was called forth. The rupture is complete; philosophy and religion must dwell in two separate and noncommunicating spheres.

The responses to Kant do not exhaust the interplay between religion and philosophy in the period under consideration. One must take into account as well the impact on religion of logic-analytic philosophies, as represented by Rudolf Carnap (1891–1970) and the proponents of logical empiricism, and A. J. Ayer, whose *Language, Truth and Logic* had serious repercussions not only for religious thought, but for metaphysics, ethics, and aesthetic theory as well. In fairness to Ayer, it should be noted that he no longer holds the views expressed in his epoch-making book; on the other hand, one cannot afford to ignore the sort of positivism expressed there because it was those ideas that, so to speak, did the work.

Central to the thought of both Carnap and Ayer is what has been called the empiricist criterion of meaning, or the thesis that the meaningfulness of any utterance is to be determined solely by verification (or verifiability) in sense experience, where experience is understood according to the conception of experience made classic by the Scottish philosopher David Hume (1711–1776). This view conflates meaning and truth in such a way that, in the absence of the sense datum that would verify an utterance, its constituent terms are said to be without meaning. By implication, the position includes the further thesis that with regard to any utterance it is necessary to specify what datum would count against its supposed truth, or, in short, would falsify it.

It is not difficult to envision what the consequences of applying this monolithic criterion to religious statements would be. Basic theological concepts such as God, atonement, sin, salvation, and faith, along with metaphysical concepts like being, reality, necessary existence, personality, and creativity would all be deprived of cognitive meaning, so that statements involving these and similar terms could not even be called false, because they are supposed to be, quite literally, nonsense. Those who accepted the full authority of the one-meaning criterion for all utterances, insofar as they attended to religious utterances at all, had no alternative but to identify religion wholly with emotion, feeling, or attitudes of a certain kind, with the clear understanding that these have no cognitive significance. It should be obvious that no positive or creative interaction between religion and philosophy is possible from this point of view, because it reduces religion to an emotive level at which no articulation of religious ideas is possible. The underlying assumption determining this outcome was that the only knowledge people possess derives from science. The interesting fact, however, is that subsequent discussion of the empiricist criterion of meaning led to its erosion when it became clear that positivism is itself philosophy and cannot appropriate the credentials of science.

The credit for resolving this situation in a way that allowed both for a mode of interpreting religious insight and the preservation of the linguistic approach to philosophy must go to Wittgenstein. He interpreted religion primarily in practical terms as the legitimate expression of a "form of life," but religious language carries with it no cognitive claim. For this reason religion had to become a matter of sheer faith—fideism—with the consequence that no religious utterance can be construed as making any assertion purporting to be true or false about any realities whatever. The position is a singular one indeed. Wittgenstein was, on the one hand, rightly aware of the difference between the type of significance—purpose, value, aim—embodied in religious language and the theoretical assertions and explanatory theories of science that provided the model for the empiricist criterion of meaning. Hence the shift from meaning to use. On the other hand, this shift was made with the meaning criterion still hovering in the background, so that in the end it remained the determining factor in defining the sphere of the "cognitive," and religion was excluded.

Recovery of the Dialogue between Religion and Philosophy. Nevertheless, as was noted earlier on, the linguistic analysis of religious language proposed by Wittgenstein made one important contribution to current understanding. It served to call attention to the fact that "religious language," though it purports to express a distinctive dimension of experience, is by no means to be regarded as a single, homogeneous form of discourse. The literature of the world's religions manifests a plurality of "uses," or types of expression, and great care must be exercised in distinguishing them. The language of devotion and liturgy, for example, must be distinguished from that of theology, and likewise from the languages of parable, exhortation, lamentation, myth, legend, and historical report. Each has a distinctive function, and only confusion can result from a failure to understand what each purports to express. To take but one typical example, when confronted with parabolic speech, it is a gross misunderstanding to seek the so-called literal meaning of such expressions, because their intent is of a quite different sort. A parable is a vivid and engaging story drawing on familiar experiences and things—putting a new patch on an old garment, a widow losing her last coin, tares among the wheat—for the purpose of dramatizing some religious or moral insight. Expressing the point prosaically or "literally" can never have the same effect. Important as this source of clarification may be, however, it does not go far enough, because it does not engage those theological questions that stand at the interface of philosophy and religion, nor does a purely critical philosophy provide any basis for determining the relation between religion and cultural life. What limits all critical philosophies in this regard is the absence of any but the most implicit (and sometimes hidden) metaphysics, or general theory of reality and experience, in accordance with which the various dimensions of life can be related to each other. As is learned from history, a truly fruitful interplay between religion and philosophy takes place when philosophy is represented, not by critical methods and analytic programs, but by a substantive vision of reality such as one finds in Hegel or Whitehead.

There remains yet another alternative different from all the preceding, and it is suggested by the point just made about metaphysics. An attempt must be made to recover the classical interaction between religion and philosophy in such a way that the former will once again be intelligible despite the skepticism of the age, and the latter will find its way back to those speculative questions that human beings will never cease to raise. The rationale for such a recovery can be given by showing the adverse consequences that follow for both religion and philosophy from their separation and loss of communication. First, however, it is necessary to challenge a number of philosophical assumptions, assumptions that have been in force for a century and have served to bring about the present unsatisfactory situation. It is an error to suppose that Kant's critical philosophy must be accepted as the final word about the capacity of reason and the possibility of metaphysics while attempts are made to insert religion and theology into what Barth has called the "gaps" in Kant's thought. A more radical approach is called for, which means adopting a far more critical stance to the critical philosophy itself. As Hegel saw so well, Kant's ultimate conclusion is dogmatic in the precise sense that he simply opted for the priority of understanding over reason, and in so doing he employed mathematics and physics as the criterion of knowledge, thus judging the validity of metaphysics in accordance with an alien standard.

The underlying issue is an ancient one, going back to the difference of opinion expressed in the thought of Plato and Aristotle: Is there, as Plato held, one universal method and criterion governing all thought, or, is it not the case, as Aristotle claimed, that method and standards of judgment must follow the particular subject matter in question? It is only the latter position that makes it possible to do justice to the many different spheres of meaning and dimensions of experience that actually exist, and at the same time to develop standards appropriate to a given type of thought. Speculative philosophy is not a special science, like physics or geology, and its aims and criteria of adequacy must not be thought of and judged in terms appropriate for experimental inquiries. The same is true of religion and theology; any attempt to understand either is bound to fail if no attention is paid to the special sort of meaning both purport to express. Clearly what is called for is a broader conception of reason, one that is not modeled on the most abstract patterns of thought, which, essential though they are, must exclude the most concrete and important human concerns. A reason, in short, that extends no further than the spheres of formal logic and empirical science forces beyond the bounds of rationality not only philosophy but religion and morality as well.

Earlier on, it was suggested that the rationale for seeking to recover a positive and fruitful interplay between religion and philosophy is to be found in the unfortunate consequences for both that come as the result of their separation from each other. Consider, first, the impact on religion that follows from this separation. Without the benefit of careful, conceptual articulation and the discipline of critical reflection—whether in the form of a philosophical theology or a philosophy of religion—religion is in danger of becoming obscurantist or fanatical in its basic orientation. While the central religious insights that define a tradition must be preserved and transmitted in each historical period, the culture in which the tradition finds itself and the people to whom it speaks are constantly changing. New knowledge is forthcoming, novel patterns of thought and behavior emerge, social and political conditions arise that are very different from those prevailing when the religion was first established. The world in which Augustine proclaimed the Christian message, for example, has little in common with the situation in which that same message was set forth by such thinkers as the German theologian Paul Tillich (1886–1965) or Barth in the twentieth century. A living religion must come to terms with this all-important fact and not seek to preserve itself either by refusing to confront the problems posed by the intellectual climate of the time or by retreating into an inner sanctuary untouched by secular thought and experience. It has, moreover, been persuasively argued that it is precisely through a dialogue engaging the entire spectrum of a culture that a religious tradition comes to realize previously undiscovered implications of its basic faith that further illuminate and help to transform human life. The need to relate the enduring insights of religion to new historical situations and to new generations of people who confront them presents a salutary challenge not only to obscurantism and disdain for intelligence in religion but to fanaticism as well. Having to respond seriously to the critic's question or the skeptic's doubt, as well as to the believer's plea for guidance, must engender in the religious thinker a measure of humility and circumspection not to be reconciled with the fanatic posture, which, as William James was so well aware, is the greatest evil perpetrated by religion wherever it exists. The great ages of faith in Western religion have been those in which faith and intelligence went hand in hand. That religion and philosophy should be separated must be, for religion, the greatest of disasters.

Consider now the consequences of the separation from the side of philosophy. The presence of the religious questions—the problem of God and transcendence, the place of humanity in the cosmic order and its final destiny, the issue of freedom and responsibility, the problem of evil—has repeatedly served as a goad to philosophy, orienting the thinking of philosophers in the direction of speculative themes. As has been seen, especially in the twentieth century, philosophers motivated by the desire to be scientific and to show that philosophy makes progress have worked to reduce the subject to purely critical proportions, with major emphasis falling on technical issues concerning method, knowledge, logic, and language. Speculative questions were often ignored as either without significance or beyond human intellectual capacities. Without the goad of religion (unfortunately not very powerful in the period under consideration), philosophy runs the risk of formalizing itself and of abandoning its constructive task in treating the most important human concerns. Concentration on technique alone has little value when philosophers fail to confront these concerns. A recovery of the dialogue between religion and philosophy would serve the double purpose of bringing philosophy back to the task of constructive metaphysics and of keeping religious thought within the scope of rationality, thus guarding it from the evils of dogmatism and obscurantism.

That such a recovery is a real possibility finds support in two developments of recent decades whose importance must not be overlooked or discounted. The first was the philosophical theology of Tillich, with its method of correlating philosophical questions and theological resolutions; the second was the process philosophy of the English philosopher Alfred North Whitehead (1861–1947), who emigrated to America in 1924, and the several types of theologies inspired by it. Tillich's theological method not only called for a creative exchange with metaphysical thought, but it was accompanied as well by a substantive metaphysical position in the classical mode of correlating the concepts of being and God. While Tillich's thought was marked by an undoubted originality, its appropriation was somewhat hampered because of its dependence on the philosophy of the German contemporary of Hegel, F. W. Schelling (1775–1854)—by far the least known on the American scene of the exponents of German Idealism. Despite this handicap, however, Tillich was a major force in sustaining a theologico-philosophical dialogue, and he did much to counteract the powerful antiphilosophical bias within Protestantism that had its origins in the dogmatic theology of Barth.

Like Tillich, Whitehead had a well-developed metaphysical scheme, including a network of categories for interpreting the many dimensions of experience. In Whitehead one can see how, on the one hand, religious experience and insight were brought into relation to current patterns of thought, scientific as well as philosophical, and how, on the other, these insights were incorporated into his metaphysics as part of the evidence that must be taken into account by a speculative scheme intended to be relevant for understanding everything that happens. The fruitfulness of the interplay between philosophy and religion in this particular case is all the more striking because it coincided with the recovery within the biblical tradition of an emphasis upon time, life, and history in the conception of God, features which had been eclipsed by the great stress previously placed on God as absolute, that is, unrelated to the cosmic process, and as "pure actuality," or a perfection to which the novel increment of history could make no difference.

On the basis of the foregoing analysis, one must conclude that the proper and most satisfactory relation between religion and philosophy is that of dialogical exchange, an exchange of a sort that existed for centuries until it was interrupted by the critical philosophy of Kant and the authority of the empiricist criterion of meaning. But, as has been seen, Kant's reduction of reason to the limits of understanding need not be the last word on the matter, nor should anyone continue to think that it is possible to accept Kant's position while at the same time attempting to find some loophole through which religion can pass. The monolithic criterion of meaning also need not be accepted, because it so clearly fails to do justice to dimensions of meaning not to be fitted into the pattern of thought exemplified by natural science. With these obstacles surmounted, the way is clear for the renewal of the mutual exchange between religion and metaphysics that has borne fruit in the past.

SEE ALSO Analytic Philosophy; Aristotelianism; Deism; Empiricism; Enlightenment, The; Existentialism; Humanism; Idealism; Logical Positivism; Materialism; Naturalism; Neoplatonism; Nominalism; Platonism; Positivism; Scholasticism; Skeptics and Skepticism.

BIBLIOGRAPHY

This bibliographic essay focuses on some books dealing with positions and trends noted in the foregoing article. No effort is made to include such thinkers as Kant, Kierkegaard, Hegel, James, Barth, Tillich, and Whitehead, because they are the subjects of separate articles.

James Collins's *The Emergence of Philosophy of Religion* (New Haven, Conn., 1967), both in its historical treatment and its systematic focus on underlying issues, serves to set the stage for the modern discussion concerning the intersection of philosophy and religion. Collins takes note of the important fact that prior to the eighteenth century, philosophical reflection on religious and theological topics took place for the most part within the ambit of the Judeo-Christian tradition and its fundamental doctrines. As Collins shows, however, by discussing three representative thinkers—Hume, Kant, and Hegel—in the succeeding century and a half, the situation was to change radically.

James Alfred Martin, Jr.'s *The New Dialogue between Philosophy and Theology* (New York, 1966), a clear, well-informed, and perceptive study, is the best overall account of the response by religious thinkers both in America and Britain to analytic and linguistic philosophy and to the orientation of the later Wittgenstein. Martin does not only expose the error of identifying analytic philosophy with logical positivism; he skillfully shows how the twentieth-century dialogue between analytic philosophy and theology is connected with the historical dialogue within Christendom that started with Origen and Tertullian and continued through the centuries into the discussions of Tillich, Barth, and Heidegger. In addition to critical accounts of the major writers, religious and philosophical, the book contains a useful bibliography.

Ian T. Ramsey's *Religious Language: An Empirical Placing of Theological Phrases* (London, 1957) begins with an account of what situations can legitimately be called "religious" and considers how some traditional phrases in theology—"first cause," "infinitely wise," "infinitely good"—can be given a logical structure appropriate to these religious situations. Echoing the idea that "religious language" is multiple in character, Ramsey distinguishes the language of the Bible from the language of Christian doctrine, describing each in terms of its functions and aims. In this way he hopes to avoid the many confusions resulting from lumping together under the rubric of "religious language" such diverse forms of expression as that of devotion, on the one hand, and that of theological conceptualization, on the other.

John Macquarrie's *God-Talk: An Examination of the Language and Logic of Theology* (New York, 1967), in addition to an appraisal of the impact of logical empiricism on theological discourse, includes illuminating chapters on different types of such discourse based on case-study analyses of a classical theological text—Athanasius's *On Incarnation*—and of Heidegger's philosophical theory of interpretation. The result is the delineation in theology of a plurality of meaning devices, including mythology, symbolism, analogy, indirect language, existential discourse, ontological discourse, the language of authority, appeal to direct experience, and, finally, the language of paradox.

John Hick's *Faith and Knowledge,* 2d ed. (Ithaca, N.Y., 1966), is concerned primarily with problems of religious knowledge, the distinction between belief and knowledge, and the relation of both to different conceptions of faith. It is representative of a general trend, which is the attempt to combine an analytically oriented philosophy with a neoorthodox approach to religion generally and to Christianity in particular.

E. L. Mascall's *The Secularization of Christianity* (New York, 1965) offers an extraordinarily thorough and acute analysis of J. A. T. Robinson's *Honest to God* (Philadelphia, 1963) and Paul Van Buren's *The Secular Meaning of the Gospel* (New York, 1963) in an attempt to show that, while it is essential that Christianity be presented in terms that are both intelligible and relevant to the present day, it is not necessary to jettison centuries of accumulated Christian wisdom for the purpose of communicating what in fact may prove to be merely a substitute for Christian doctrine. Whether one agrees or not with Mascall's conclusions, it is unquestionable that no better account of the topic is to be found.

Ninian Smart's *The Science of Religion and the Sociology of Knowledge* (Princeton, 1973) surveys the broad theme of the relation of religion to rationality in light of phenomenology, history, sociology, and anthropology. The author notes, quite rightly, the difference between theology as the systematic expression of the faith of a religious community and various ways of studying religion as a phenomenon involved in the total pattern of life and culture throughout the world. Although too short for an extended treatment, the discussion ranges over a very wide body of material, including references to Weber, Lévy-Bruhl, Otto, Wach, Kierkegaard, Tillich, Barth, Marx, Freud, Eliade, Berger, Jayatilleke, and Wilfred Cantwell Smith.

H. D. Lewis's *Our Experience of God* (London, 1959) decries the idea that it is the task of philosophy to construct some form of philosophical substitute for religion, or to provide proofs for religious beliefs supposedly held on inadequate grounds. The positive role of philosophy in relation to religion is to make clearer the meaning and status of religious beliefs actually held and at the same time to show their relation to the larger experiential setting in which they occur.

In *The Person God Is* (London, 1970), Peter Bertocci, a chief representative of the philosophy and theology of personalism, carries on the tradition of interpreting religious insight in philosophical terms by viewing God, the cosmic person, as the creator of "co-creators." The author considers whether the goodness of God can be empirically grounded, whether grace can be discovered in freedom, and whether religion itself can be understood in terms of the pursuit of creativity.

In the works of Charles Hartshorne, including *Man's Vision of God, and the Logic of Theism* (New York, 1941), *The Divine Relativity: A Social Conception of God* (New Haven, Conn., 1948), *The Logic of Perfection* (La Salle, Ill., 1962), *Anselm's Discovery* (La Salle, Ill., 1965), and *Omnipotence and Other Theological Mistakes* (Albany, N.Y., 1984), the critical interchange on philosophical and theological issues is sustained. Hartshorne's thought may be understood as concentrating on two distinct but closely related focal points. The first is his "neoclassical" theism based on what he calls the "principle of Dual Transcendence," according to which God contrasts with creatures not as an abstract infinite against the finite, but as a concrete "infinite-and-finite," each aspect of which contrasts with fragmentary creatures who are neither relative nor absolute in themselves. In short, Hartshorne finds that despite the great emphasis placed by the biblical tradition on time, individuality, personal responsibility, and historical development, much classical theology neglected these features by conceiving of God, not as living, but as already complete or perfect. The other focus in Hartshorne's writing is restatement and reassessment of the ontological argument as first proposed by Anselm. Here he reoriented the centuries-long discussion of this oft "refuted" argument, not by concentrating on the usual question of whether "existence is a predicate," but by directing attention to what had largely been neglected by a host of previous thinkers, namely, what is to be understood by the idea of God—the *what* of the matter—and its expression in Anselm's formula. An informative commentary on Hartshorne's work can be found in *Existence and Actuality: Conversations with Charles Hartshorne,* edited by John B. Cobb, Jr., and Franklin I. Gamwell (Chicago, 1984).

Experience, Reason and God, edited by Eugene T. Long (Washington, D.C., 1980), provides a broad spectrum of opinion by twelve authors concerning the intersection of philosophy and religion on the contemporary scene.

New Sources

Alston, William. *Perceiving God: The Epistemology of Religious Experience.* Ithaca, 1991.

Brooke, John Hedley. *Science and Religion: Some Historical Perspectives.* New York, 1991.

Bunge, Mario. *Finding Philosophy in Social Science.* New Haven, 1996.

Faulconer, James. *Transcendence in Philosophy and Religion.* Bloomington, Ind., 2003.

Kunin, Seth. *Religion: The Modern Theories.* Baltimore, 2003.

Pals, Daniel. *Seven Theories of Religion.* New York, 1996.

Schiffer, Stephen. *The Things We Mean.* New York, 2003.

Store, David. *The Plato Cult, and Other Philosophical Follies.* Malden, Mass., 1991.

Swinburne, Richard. *The Evolution of the Soul* (1997). Reprint, New York, 2003.

Thagard, Paul. *Conceptual Revolutions.* Princeton, N.J., 1992.

Ward, Graham. *Theology and Contemporary Critical Theory.* New York, 2000.

Warner, Martin, ed. *Religion and Philosophy.* Philosophy and Religion series. New York, 1992.

JOHN E. SMITH (1987)
Revised Bibliography

PHILOSOPHY: PHILOSOPHY OF RELIGION

The idea of a philosophy of religion is a recent one, and it assumes a differentiation between philosophy and religion that has emerged chiefly in the modern West. Much that is included under that rubric, however, dates back to ancient philosophical analysis and speculation. Philosophy of religion is the philosophical scrutiny of religion, but the meaning of those terms and the proper method and content of the field are subject to considerable dispute. Current work in the field can be divided into two types: (1) assessment of the rationality of religious beliefs, with attention to their coherence and to the cogency of arguments for their justification; and (2) descriptive analysis and elucidation of religious language, belief, and practice with particular attention to the rules by which they are governed and to their context in the religious life. The boundary between these two types is not always clear, but they can be illumined by considering their origins and some paradigmatic arguments from each.

JUSTIFICATION OF RELIGIOUS BELIEFS. The first type of philosophy of religion has been concerned chiefly with theism, but analogues can be found in nontheistic traditions. Rational arguments are proposed and assessed in order to justify or to criticize religious beliefs. Because the philosophy of religion has its provenance in the West, theistic issues have dominated the discussion, but neither type should be restricted to the consideration of theism.

Most of the classical topics in the philosophy of religion are topics in philosophical theism or natural theology. Foremost among these are the existence and nature of God. Analyses of the concept of God, discussion of the divine nature and its attributes, and arguments that purport to demonstrate the existence of God constitute the principal subject matter of philosophical theism. Such attributes as unity, simplicity, omniscience, perfection, eternity, and immutability require analysis in order to clarify their meanings, to assess their compatibility, and to consider the implications of applying them outside of the contexts in which individuals normally ascribe knowledge, power, and goodness to persons. Many of the classical issues and arguments derive from medieval philosophy and theology.

Immanuel Kant (1724–1804) classified the arguments for the existence of God as the ontological argument, the cosmological argument, and the teleological argument, or argument from design. This classification has become canonical, though not everyone would agree with Kant's claim that these three kinds of argument exhaust the logical possibilities.

The original formulation of the ontological argument, and the one that has continued to command the attention of philosophers, was given by Anselm of Canterbury (1033–1109) in his *Proslogion* (1077–1078). Anselm argues that the existence of God can be demonstrated by a proper analysis of the concept of God. He begins by claiming that what is meant by the word *God* is "something than which nothing greater can be thought." Even one who would doubt or deny the existence of God, says Anselm, understands this concept, and thus something than which nothing greater can be thought exists in his mind. But that than which no greater can be thought cannot exist in the mind alone. Were it to exist only in the mind, it would be possible to think of it as existing outside the mind as well, and that would be even greater. Then that which existed in the mind alone would not be something than which no greater could be thought. Therefore, that than which no greater can be thought must exist both in the mind and in reality.

The monk Gaunilo, a contemporary of Anselm, criticized the argument by claiming that it could be used to demonstrate the existence of a perfect island, or of any other thing in which the requirement of existence was embedded in the idea of perfection or greatness. Anselm replied that the concept of an island is already the concept of something limited, and thus cannot contain unlimited greatness. In what has been viewed as the standard refutation, Kant argued that existence is not a property that can be added or subtracted in order to make comparisons of worth. To say that a table exists is not to add anything to the concept of table, but is to say that the concept is instantiated.

The ontological argument differs from the cosmological and teleological arguments in that it appears to depend entirely on conceptual analysis. But the argument is embedded in a prayer in which Anselm asks God for faith in order that he might understand. This context has prompted some commentators to suggest that Anselm was not offering an argument at all, but was reflecting on a faith that was derived solely from divine revelation. The *Proslogion* opens, however, with Anselm's expression of joy at having discovered a single argument that would suffice to prove that both God exists and all that is believed about the divine nature. Philosophical treatments often consider the argument in isolation from its religious context and from Anselm's claim that divine omnipotence, mercy, impassibility, simplicity, eternity, and other attributes could be derived from the same concept.

Recently there has been renewed interest in the ontological argument. In an influential article (1960), Norman Malcolm claims that Kant had refuted the argument set forth in the second chapter of the *Proslogion,* but that the following chapter and the reply to Gaunilo contain another argument that has been overlooked and that is successful. This is an argument not for God's existence but for his necessary existence. Malcolm contends that Anselm has demonstrated that the concept of God is such that God cannot fail to exist. Were he not to exist, or were his existence contingent rather than necessary, he would not satisfy the human concept of God. Malcolm claims that Anselm was engaged in an elucidation of the concept that is implicit in the religious life of those in theistic traditions. He was analyzing the grammar by which that concept is governed. Alvin Plantinga (1974) has employed the very different techniques of modal logic to reformulate Anselm's argument to demonstrate the rationality of belief in the existence of God, though he holds that it cannot justify that belief.

The classical statement of the cosmological argument is found in the *Summa theologiae* (1268–1273) of Thomas Aquinas. Thomas offers five proofs of the existence of God, the first three of which are versions of the cosmological argument. Each begins with some characteristic of things in the world (e.g., change, causation, contingency) and argues that a proper explanation of this phenomenon requires that one posit a first cause or something whose existence is not dependent upon anything other than itself. Thomas begins the first way with the observation that some things in the world are changing. He then asserts that anything that is in the process of change is being changed by something else, a controversial premise that he defends and glosses by appeal to conceptions of actuality and potentiality derived from the Aristotelian tradition. But this other thing, he says, if in the process of change, is itself being changed by something else, and so on. Unless this potentially infinite series is halted, there will be no first cause of the change, thus no subsequent cause, and therefore no change. So there must be some first cause of change not itself being changed by anything, and this is what everyone understands by God.

The second of Thomas's ways begins from the relation between cause and effect, and proceeds in a manner parallel to the first. The third way takes its departure from the observation that some things in the world are contingent, and thus might not have existed. Thomas argues that it is impossible for everything to be contingent, because anything that need not be was once nonexistent. If everything were contingent, then there must have been a time at which there was nothing. If that were the case there would be nothing now, for something that does not exist can be brought into being only by something that already exists. But there is something now. So there must be something the existence of which is not contingent but necessary.

Thomas's five ways are fraught with difficulties, most deriving from their dependence upon Aristotelian physics and metaphysics. The observation that some things are changing is not a controversial one unless change is understood in Aristotelian terms. If it is understood in those terms, much metaphysical baggage is packed into what appears to be an ordinary observation, and the rest of the proof turns on unpacking that baggage. If it is not understood in those terms, the argument does not succeed. The same dilemma holds for the observation that some things are contingent. Current theorists are aware, as Thomas was not, of the controversial science and metaphysics that are assumed by the proofs.

The five ways, like Anselm's argument, are embedded in a theological context. Thomas says that Christian theology is a science that takes its principles on faith in God's revelation. Some have argued that he intended only to elucidate a faith based on revelation, but Thomas asserts that some truths about God can be known by natural reasoning and are presupposed by faith. Like Anselm, he continues, after presenting his arguments for the existence of God, to derive the manner of God's existing and certain characteristics of the divine nature.

Versions of the cosmological argument have been offered by Jewish, Christian, and Islamic philosophers, and the belief that the world cannot be accounted for without reference to the existence and activity of God seems to be a part of the religious life of any theist. Doctrines of God as creator and preserver, which are central to each of these traditions, are closely connected with the cosmological argument.

Recently, renewed attention has been given to an eighteenth-century version of the cosmological argument offered by Samuel Clarke (1675–1729). Clarke argued that Thomas incorrectly assumed that there must be a first cause to account for change, causation, or contingent being. There could be an infinite series of causes. But Clarke held that such a series would still require an explanation. In order to account for the existence of this series rather than another or none at all, one must posit a cause for the series as a whole. Clarke's argument has stimulated interest because it seems to depend neither on Thomas's assumption that there can be no infinite series of causes nor on his employment of Aristotelian science and metaphysics.

The most influential statement of the argument from design comes from a critic rather than a proponent. In *Dialogues concerning Natural Religion* (1779) by David Hume (1711–1776), the interlocutor Cleanthes sets forth a version of the argument, and much of the work is an analysis of its weaknesses and of the resulting implications for religious belief. Cleanthes argues that the order that is found in the universe, and "the curious adaptation of means to ends," can only be explained by positing some kind of mind that is analogous to human minds. The universe is one great machine. No such intricate pattern and order could be accounted for by chance. A designer must be posited, and some of his attributes can be inferred from the order one observes. Like the cosmological argument, this is a formalization of an aspect of ordinary theistic belief. God is the creator, and the world shows evidence of his handiwork.

Hume raises a number of problems for Cleanthes's argument, chief among them the weakness of the analogy between the order individuals discover in the universe and the order or design in a machine, other explanations that are as or more plausible on the basis of evidence, and the religious inadequacy of the God that Cleanthes's argument permits him to infer. Hume is particularly persuasive in showing that naturalistic hypotheses are as well supported by the evidence as is the theistic hypothesis.

The *Dialogues* also contain a clear presentation of a classical argument against theistic belief, the argument from evil. Hume offers two forms of this argument, emphasizing logical and empirical problems. The logical form consists in the claim that theists are committed to the inconsistent conjunction of three propositions: (1) God is omnipotent; (2) God is wholly good; and (3) evil exists. As Hume puts it: "Epicurus's old questions are yet unanswered. Is he willing to prevent evil, but not able? then is he impotent. Is he able, but not willing? then he is malevolent. Is he both able and willing? whence then is evil?" The claim is that theism is incoherent. Consistency can be restored by giving up any one of the three beliefs, and examples can be found for each of these alternatives. The traditional solutions, however, have been either to deny that there really is evil when viewed from a proper perspective, or to offer what has become known as the free will defense. The first is a denial of (3) on the grounds that what seems from one's parochial perspective to be evil can be seen from the divine viewpoint as contributing to the greater good. The free will defense is a clarification of the meaning and limits of (1). Free will defenders argue that it was better for God to have created a world in which some creatures have free will than one in which their actions are totally determined, that evil results from human free will, and that if God creates such a world there are certain outcomes that he cannot control, but that this fact does not compromise his omnipotence.

The second form of the argument from evil is not a matter of logical compatibility. Unlike the first form, it arises from the inference articulated in the design argument. Hume says that even though one might be able to demonstrate the consistency of theism, the evil and suffering one finds in the world blocks any inference to an all-powerful and benevolent designer. While the logical form of the problem of evil has dominated the discussion, those whose theism is grounded upon an inference from the world to a benevolent creator must consider how the evil and suffering in the world affects that inference.

Some contributors to this first type of philosophy of religion have employed the techniques of modal logic (Plantinga, 1974) and confirmation theory (Swinburne, 1977, 1979, 1981) to address classical questions of the coherence and rationality of theistic belief and the arguments for and against that belief.

Description and Analysis of Religious Language, Practice, and Belief. Those who constructed arguments for or against the existence of God did not suppose that religious faith is adopted or discarded for these reasons. Anselm wrote of his task as faith seeking understanding. These were attempts to employ reason to understand and to justify or criticize beliefs that had been received from tradition. While work on the coherence of theism and arguments for the existence of God continue, new interpretations of the classical texts have been offered that challenge the assumption that the authors of those texts were seeking to justify religious belief. Malcolm takes Anselm to be elucidating the faith of a believer rather than proposing an argument that is meant to convince the nonbeliever. Victor Preller (1967) and David Burrell (1979) argue that when restored to their theological context the five ways of Thomas Aquinas will be seen as relatively unimportant and as displaying occasions for the application of religious grammar rather than offering proofs for the existence of God. Alvin Plantinga (1974) reconstructs the ontological argument and the free will defense in order to refute challenges by critics who argue that theism is inconsistent or irrational. Despite important differences, in each of these cases the proper task of the philosophy of religion is viewed as the elucidation of religious belief rather than as the justification or refutation of that belief.

The second type of philosophy of religion consists of reflection on the distinctive character of the religious life and the placing of religious practice and belief with respect to other sets of beliefs and practices, especially those of science and of morals. This conception of the task of philosophy of religion stems from the conviction that religious doctrine and beliefs should not be subject to criteria of rationality and justification that derive from such other pursuits as science, metaphysics, or morals. Religious practices and beliefs require no justification from outside the religious life. The task of the philosopher is to understand them rather than to subject them to heteronomous criteria.

Though there are precursors, philosophical reflection on religion began in earnest in the eighteenth century. Hume distinguished two kinds of inquiry about religion, the first concerning its foundation in reason, and the second its origin in human nature. The first of these questions was addressed in the *Dialogues,* and the second in *The Natural History of Religion* (1777), in which he sketched a naturalistic account of the origin of religious belief and practice. Speculation about the origin of religion and its relation to other aspects of culture flourished in the eighteenth century.

The agenda for much subsequent philosophy of religion was set by Kant and by responses to his work. Kant held that traditional arguments purporting to demonstrate or to refute the existence of God were flawed. More important, however, he held that such arguments were bound to fail. They were illegitimate extensions beyond experience of categories and forms of judgment that are valid only within the bounds of experience. Philosophical debate about such issues is futile, leads to antinomies, and can never be resolved. The traditional topics of philosophical theism are ill-formed, and any semblance of progress is an illusion.

Kant argued that the task of the philosopher is not to contribute to the substance of science, morals, art, or religion, but to reflect critically on the kinds of judgments that are employed in each of these areas, to map the limits of their proper application, to describe the problems that result from exceeding those limits, and to offer an account of how such judgments are possible. The moral philosopher, for instance, cannot add to or detract from the sense of moral obligation that is accessible to all rational beings, but he can describe that obligation and the structure of moral judgments. The philosopher of religion ought not to argue for or against religious beliefs, but ought to restrict himself to mapping the structure of religious concepts, beliefs, and practices, and to offering an account of their origin in practical reason.

In *Religion within the Limits of Reason Alone* (1793), Kant situated religious concepts, beliefs, and practices within the moral life. He argued that people schematize or represent in imaginative terms the experience of moral obligation. The obligation to obey the moral law is viewed as if it were a duty imposed by a divine lawgiver. This kind of schematism cannot be avoided, and thus morality leads ineluctably to religion. Religious experience and practice derive from the moral life. Religious doctrines are not to be assessed for their truth or falsity. That would be to misconstrue them. They are expressions of aspects of moral experience. Kant offered an account of the concept of God and of major Christian doctrines as schemata of the moral law and of issues that arise from attempts to act in accord with it. Religious beliefs can never conflict with scientific beliefs because they serve very different functions. Religious beliefs cannot yield knowledge, but they are a necessary outgrowth of the moral life.

Friedrich Schleiermacher (1768–1834) accepted Kant's critique of metaphysics and of traditional natural theology, and he agreed that religious doctrine ought not to be viewed as making scientific or metaphysical claims, but he rejected the assimilation of religion to morality. He argued that religious doctrine and practice express an autonomous and irreducible moment in human experience that cannot be reduced to belief or action. Piety is neither science nor morals, but an affective moment in experience with its own integrity. Philosophy of religion is reflection on this moment as it is shaped by different traditions and cultures, and as it is expressed in various doctrines and practices. Schleiermacher described the religious moment as a sense of finitude or dependence. While it can be understood only by acquaintance, it is a universal moment in human experience that is accessible to all. Because religious doctrine is not a matter of belief but an expression of this affective moment as it is shaped by particular traditions, religious doctrines can never conflict with the findings of science. Religious beliefs require no justification because they are independently grounded in an autonomous moment of experience.

Following Kant and Schleiermacher, representatives of the second type have embedded the philosophy of religion within a broader philosophy of culture. The focus has shifted from the justification of religious beliefs to the identification of the distinctive character of religious experience, religious language, or religious practice. The task of the philosopher of religion is to describe that experience, language, and practice, to elucidate them, and to place them with respect to other cultural phenomena. G. W. F. Hegel (1770–1831) showed that religious concepts and beliefs are embedded in particular traditions of thought and practice and can be understood only in the light of those traditions. Søren Kierkegaard (1813–1855) continued Kant's emphasis on the will as central to the religious life but differentiated that life from a life characterized by aesthetic immediacy and one defined by Kantian morality. He explored the role of religious language both in expressing that life and in providing the occasion for an individual to confront the absolute paradox that he took to be the heart of the Christian gospel. Ludwig Feuerbach (1804–1872) and Karl Marx (1818–1883) offered accounts of religious belief and practice as idealized projections of hopes, fears, and desires that originally had more palpable objects in the material and social worlds.

Hume had located his discussion of theism within a sketch of the natural history of religion, and Hegel had traced the development of the religious consciousness through different cultural traditions. By the beginning of the twentieth century, research in the history of religions was sufficiently advanced that many philosophers of religion realized that their descriptions and analyses of religious experience, practice, and belief must, in principle at least, take account of traditions beyond Christianity and even beyond theism. Philosophy of religion could no longer be merely prolegomena to Christian theology. Most contemporary philosophers of religion would agree, but the reorientation of the discipline implied by that recognition has yet to be achieved in practice.

During the nineteenth century, work in the history of religions had been informed by Schleiermacher's claim that religion is an experiential matter that is expressed in doctrines and practices reflecting different cultures, but that is universal at the core. In the early years of the twentieth century, William James (1842–1910) and Rudolf Otto (1869–1937) both attempted to describe the distinctive characteristics of religious experience and to examine the implications for religious belief. Both drew on illustrative material from other religious traditions and viewed the object of their inquiry as religious experience considered generally, but both were chiefly influenced by Christianity.

James held that religion is principally a matter of feeling and not of belief, but that there is no distinctively religious affection. Religious fear, love, awe, and joy are ordinary fear, love, awe, and joy associated with religious objects. In *The Varieties of Religious Experience* (1902), James provided both a taxonomy of kinds of religious experience and astute philosophical analysis of such problems for the philosophy of religion as the relation between the scientific study of religion and the assessment of its meaning, significance, or value. He explored the implications of the identification of religion with a feeling or sense, and, especially in his chapter on mysticism, considered the authority of such experiences for the persons who have them and for those who do not. He argued that widespread testimony provides some evidence in support of what he took to be the common element in religious experience, a belief or sense that there is something more beyond this mundane world and that it can have a benevolent effect on the lives of individuals.

In contrast to James, and in explicit indebtedness to Schleiermacher, Otto argued that there is a distinctive moment in religious experience. That moment is not properly characterized as feeling, but it is unmistakably specific and peculiar. Otto described it as the nonrational and ineffable moment in religious experience. He coined a special term, the *numinous,* to refer to "the holy" minus its moral and rational factors. He claimed that there is a unique numinous category of value and a numinous state of mind that is *sui generis* and irreducible. The numinous moment in experience cannot be communicated but can only be known by acquaintance. Otto portrays that moment as one of creaturely feeling and a sense of finitude, of awe and fascination in response to something "wholly other." Otto later went on to study non-Western religious traditions, and particularly some strands of the religions of India, but his characterization of the numinous moment in religious experience is clearly derivative from the monotheism of the Hebrew scriptures and of Lutheran Christianity.

Philosophers of religion have drawn on material from the history of religions to investigate what appear to be common beliefs or practices. Mysticism, ritual, sacrifice, prayer, and a sense of the holy or of the sacred have been subjects of such inquiry. James held that religious thoughts and beliefs vary from culture to culture, but that feelings and conduct are invariant. Many have shared this assumption and have looked to the study of mysticism, prayer, or a sense of the sacred as a way to approach the heart of the religious life. It has become clear, however, that one cannot identify an emotion or a practice without reference to the concepts and beliefs that can be ascribed to the person who has that emotion or engages in that practice. Attempts by Schleiermacher, James, and Otto to characterize a core religious experience that is independent of those concepts, beliefs, and practices are bound to fail. James's assumption that beliefs vary while feelings and actions are invariant reflects his inability to appreciate the fact that any emotion or action must be identified under a description, and that that description must be one that can be properly attributed to the subject of the emotion or action.

In Anglo-American philosophy in the mid-twentieth century, the focus shifted from religious experience to religious language. A. J. Ayer (1936), developing his version of logical positivism, contended that religious statements, along with moral statements, were incapable of verification or falsification and therefore were not cognitively meaningful. They were to be understood as expressive utterances without cognitive content. The verifiability criterion of cognitive meaningfulness was soon abandoned because of problems that were independent of its application to religious statements, but the inquiry into the proper status of religious language continued. Some philosophers, drawing on the later philosophy of Ludwig Wittgenstein (1889–1951), argued that religious language ought not to be subject to criteria derived from such other forms of discourse as scientific or moral discourse. Rather, the task of the philosopher of religion ought to be to map the peculiar grammar governing religious uses of language. Problems arise, however, when one attempts to discriminate between distinctively religious uses and other uses of particular words and sentences.

Attempts to identify a distinctive grammar of religious language in such a way as to make that language autonomous and independent of other concepts and beliefs resemble Schleiermacher's claim that there is a distinctive and autonomous moment in religious experience. In both forms, the claim is motivated by apologetic considerations as well as by the aim for descriptive adequacy. If Schleiermacher is correct in his portrayal of religious language as expressive of a moment that is independent of concepts and beliefs, then a religious statement can never conflict with a scientific statement or a moral claim. The same words function entirely differently in a religious context from their use in a scientific or metaphysical context. "God created the world" as a doctrinal statement can never conflict with any scientific or metaphysical statement about the origin of the world. The words have different meanings in the different settings. This sharp distinction constitutes a protective strategy that precludes any conflict between religious beliefs and scientific or ordinary beliefs about the world. That strategy is continued by those who claim that religious uses of language are governed by their own peculiar grammar and are not subject to criteria from outside the sphere of religious discourse. Such strategies show that the second type of philosophy of religion, while allegedly concerned with description and elucidation in contrast to justification, may be used for apologetic purposes as well. It may serve to justify religious belief and practice by ascribing to those beliefs and practices a status that precludes any conflict with scientific knowledge or claims in other areas of culture.

Both types of philosophy of religion are represented in the contemporary literature. After a desultory period, there is renewed interest in philosophical theism. Chief among the tasks facing contemporary philosophers of religion is the need for the discipline to be sufficiently comprehensive to be accountable to other religious traditions, but to avoid the distortion that results from wrenching statements and phenomena out of their historical and cultural contexts in order to serve some comparative or apologetic purpose. This task is further complicated by the fact that the concept of religion prevalent in philosophy of religion has its provenance in the modern West. Theistic assumptions are embedded in the criteria by which individuals identify an experience or a phenomenon as religious. These assumptions may be masked by claims that the philosophy of religion ought to concern itself with description and analysis while remaining neutral with respect to the justification of religious beliefs and practices.

BIBLIOGRAPHY

Anselm of Canterbury. *St. Anselm's Proslogion.* Translated by M. J. Charlesworth. Oxford, 1965.

Ayer, A. J. *Language, Truth, and Logic* (1936). 2d ed. London, 1946.

Burrell, David B. *Aquinas: God and Action.* Notre Dame, Ind., 1979.

Craig, William L. *The Cosmological Argument from Plato to Leibniz.* New York, 1980.

Hume, David. *Dialogues concerning Natural Religion.* Edited by Norman Kemp Smith. Oxford, 1935.

Hume, David. *The Natural History of Religion.* Edited by H. E. Root. London, 1956.

James, William. *The Varieties of Religious Experience.* New York, 1902.

Kant, Immanuel. *Religion within the Limits of Reason Alone.* Translated by Theodore M. Greene and Hoyt H. Hudson. La Salle, Ill., 1960.

Katz, Steven T., ed. *Mysticism and Philosophical Analysis.* Oxford, 1978.

Kenny, Anthony. *The Five Ways: St. Thomas Aquinas' Proofs of God's Existence.* New York, 1969.

Mackie, J. L. *The Miracle of Theism.* Oxford, 1982.

Malcolm, Norman. "Anselm's Ontological Arguments." *Philosophical Review* 69 (January 1960): 41–62.

Otto, Rudolf. *The Idea of the Holy.* Translated by John W. Harvey. Oxford, 1928.

Plantinga, Alvin. *The Nature of Necessity.* Oxford, 1974.

Preller, Victor. *Divine Science and the Science of God: A Reformulation of Thomas Aquinas.* Princeton, N.J., 1967.

Schleiermacher, Friedrich. *The Christian Faith.* Edited by H. R. Mackintosh and J. S. Stewart. Edinburgh, 1929.

Schleiermacher, Friedrich. *On Religion.* Translated by John Oman, with an introduction by Rudolf Otto. New York, 1955.

Swinburne, Richard. *The Coherence of Theism.* Oxford, 1977.

Swinburne, Richard. *The Existence of God.* Oxford, 1979.

Swinburne, Richard. *Faith and Reason.* Oxford, 1981.

Thomas Aquinas. *Summa theologiae,* vols. 1 and 2. Translated and edited by Thomas Gilby. New York, 1964. See especially questions 1–11.

Wainwright, William J. *Philosophy of Religion: An Annotated Bibliography of Twentieth-Century Writings in English.* New York, 1978.

New Sources

Anderson, Pamela Sue. *A Feminist Philosophy of Religion: The Rationality and Myths of Religious Belief.* Oxford, 1998.

Arrington, Robert, and Mark Addis. *Wittgenstein and the Philosophy of Religion.* New York, 2001.

Bryden, Mary, ed. *Deleuze and Religion.* New York, 2001.

Carrette, Jeremy. *Foucault and Religion: Spiritual Corporality and Political Spirituality.* New York, 2000.

Faulconer, James, ed. *Transcendence in Philosophy and Religion.* Bloomington, Ind., 2003.

Gilson, Étienne. *The Philosophy of St. Thomas Aquinas.* New York, 1993.

Peterson, Michael, William Hasker, Bruce Reichenach, and David Basinger, eds. *Reason and Religious Belief: An Introduction to the Philosophy of Religion.* 3d ed. New York, 2002.

Stump, Eleonore, ed. *Reason Faith.* Ithaca, N.Y., 1993.

Swinburne, Richard. *The Resurrection of God Incarnate.* New York, 2003.

Ward, Graham. *Cities of God.* New York, 2000.

WAYNE PROUDFOOT (1987)
Revised Bibliography

PHOENICIAN RELIGION [FIRST EDITION].

The names *Phoenicia* and *Phoenician* come from the Greek *phoinikē* and *phoinikias,* respectively. These terms were used by the Greeks to designate the coastal strip on the eastern shores of the Mediterranean and its hinterland, and the Semitic-speaking inhabitants of that territory. The terms may correspond etymologically to the biblical (*kena'an*) and cuneiform (*kinahhu*) names for Canaan; both the Greek and Semitic names may derive from words that refer to a reddish-purple dye for which the Phoenician dyeing industry was renowned. But there is not a precise correspondence in usage between *Phoenicia* and *Canaan.* There is, moreover, no clear evidence for what the people in question called themselves; affiliation by individual city was more likely than any pervasive national consciousness.

There is no reason to doubt the ancient claim that the Phoenicians were autochthonous, but before the late second millennium BCE there is little evidence for a distinctive Phoenician culture in the Levant. At the beginning of the Iron Age (c. 1200 BCE), though, the great political and social unrest in the Levant seems to have forced the Phoenicians into some sort of cultural coherence. This period witnessed the collapse of the Egyptian and Hittite empires and the concomitant demise of the Levantine city-states that had been their allies or vassals. At the same time, several invading groups (Philistines, Arameans, Hebrews) appeared on the scene, ultimately to establish the nation-states that would occupy the Levant throughout most of the first millennium BCE.

The Phoenicians found themselves confined to the coast, in a territory nowhere more than 60 kilometers wide, bounded by mountains to the east and the sea to the west. The northern and southern borders varied considerably, but basically the Phoenicians occupied the central portion of the coastal strip, from Tartus (Antaradus) in the north to 'Akko (Acre) in the south. The most important cities in the Phoenician homeland were, from north to south, Arvad (Aradus), Gebal (Byblos), Beirut (Berytus), Sidon, and Sur (Tyre).

Since they were generally cut off politically and geographically from the interior, the Phoenicians turned their attention to the sea. Even within their homeland, the Mediterranean provided them with the safest and surest path for transportation and communications. And the Phoenician mastery of navigation led them to establish a series of colonies, trading posts, and settlements across the Mediterranean to the west. These colonies, the most famous of which was Carthage (probably founded by Tyre in the late ninth century), are often called "Punic" (the Latin equivalent of Phoenician), to distinguish them from mainland Phoenicia. The colonies generally shared the two most important virtues of the mainland cities: they provided safe anchorage and they were easily defensible. Some of the Phoenician ports (e.g., Palermo and Cadiz) have remained continuously in use, but most of them (e.g., Tyre and Carthage) are too small for modern ships.

Phoenician political power was at its height in the tenth and ninth centuries BCE, with Tyre emerging as the most important city. The alliance between King Hiram of Tyre and King Solomon of Israel represents the political zenith of both nations. Close relations between Phoenicia and the Israelite kingdoms, including alliance by marriage, lasted into the ninth century. By the second quarter of the ninth century, however, all the main Phoenician cities were paying tribute to Assyrian overlords. Several uprisings, including one in alliance with Egypt in the 670s, failed to overthrow the Assyrian yoke, although Tyre itself was never actually captured. After Assyria fell to the Babylonians in 612, the Babylonians moved into the Levant; they captured Jerusalem in 587/6, and defeated Tyre thirteen years later. Nebuchadrezzar's siege of Tyre is depicted in *Ezekiel* 26:7–12.

After the fall of Tyre, Sidon emerged as the chief mainland city. When the Persians defeated the Babylonians in 539, they made Phoenicia part of their fifth satrapy, and built a royal palace in Sidon. During the period of Persian rule, the Phoenician fleets acted in Persia's interest against the Greeks. In general, however, both the Phoenician mainland and the colonies moved closer to the Greek cultural sphere. Finally, Alexander conquered Phoenicia in 332, thanks in part to a remarkable feat of military engineering (Diodorus Siculus, *Bibliotheca historica* 17.40–46). Only vestiges of Phoenician autonomy remained in the Seleucid and subsequent Roman periods.

Until the middle of the nineteenth century CE, the Phoenicians were known exclusively from non-Phoenician sources—products of the Phoenician encounters with the Greeks, Romans, and Israelites. Since that time, there has been extensive archaeological work both in Phoenicia proper and in the colonies. Material discoveries have supplied considerable data about Phoenician sacrificial and funerary practices. But native Phoenician and Punic texts (mostly funerary and dedicatory inscriptions) do not provide a sufficient context for the interpretation of those data. Any coherent account of Phoenician religion, therefore, must still rely heavily on biblical and classical sources, especially the *Phoenician History* of Philo Byblius and *The Syrian Goddess*, attributed to Lucian of Samothrace.

Two additional factors make a general description of Phoenician religion difficult, if not impossible. First, there seems never to have been a unified national religious consciousness. As a result, the major centers had their own pantheons and idiosyncratic practices. Second, Phoenician religion tended to be adaptive rather than exclusive; in particular, Egyptian, Aramean, and Greek elements are evident, as are local influences in the western colonies. It has often been claimed that there is a Phoenician "core" that can be isolated from the external influences, on the assumption that Phoenician religion substantially perpetuated second-millennium Canaanite religion. That assumption, which is mostly based on a comparison of Phoenician evidence with the second-millennium religious texts excavated at Ras Shamra (ancient Ugarit), is fraught with difficulties. Despite some important elements of continuity, Phoenician religion seems to have been far more innovative than is generally allowed. This innovation and change continued throughout the first millennium, as the Phoenician gods, beliefs, and practices evolved in response to changing circumstances.

DEITIES. The Phoenicians worshiped three main types of gods under different names in different places. These gods are well characterized in the treaty drawn up in 677 BCE between the Assyrian king Esarhaddon and his newly conquered vassal, King Baal of Tyre. The fourth column of the treaty contains the traditional treaty curses, invoking the wrath of the gods against any Tyrian breach of the treaty's terms. The curses are divided into two sections. The first mentions Esarhaddon's own gods, as well as two additional gods associated with Aram or North Syria. Then the Phoenician gods are invoked: Baal-Shamem, Baal-Malage, and Baal-Safon are to raise a tempest and destroy the Phoenician ships; Melqart and Eshmun are to deprive the Phoenicians of their sustenance and clothing; and Astarte is to lead them to defeat in battle.

The epithet *Baal-Shamem* ("lord of heaven") denotes the high god of any local Phoenician pantheon. In the tenth-century inscription of King Yehimilk of Byblos, the god is summoned to bless the king for having restored the local temples. He is presumably the El ("god") of Byblos (not to be confused with the El of Ugarit) who is identified with Kronos by Philo Byblius. In the eighth-century inscription of King Azitawadda (found at Karatepe, in southern Anatolia), Baal-Shamem takes precedence over the rest of the gods. He is the Elioun/Hypsistos ("highest one") of Philo Byblius, and the Olympian Zeus venerated in Tyre, according to Dio's *History of the Phoenicians* (see Josephus Flavius, *Against Apion* 1.113). A bilingual Palmyrene inscription makes the equation of Baal-Shamem with Zeus Hypsistos absolutely certain.

In the Esarhaddon treaty, Baal-Shamem is clearly the lord of the storm, and he is appropriately identified with the old Canaanite Baal of Mount Tsafon, the weather god who was the Baal of Ugarit in the second millennium. According to Philo Byblius, the primordial inhabitants of Phoenicia considered Baal-Shamem "the sole god, the ruler of heaven," and appealed to him in times of drought. It is precisely Baal-Shamem's power to alleviate a drought that is challenged by the prophet Elijah in *1 Kings* 18. The other title of this Baal, *Baal-Malage*, probably means "lord of mariners," and refers to the god's role as patron of Phoenician seafaring. This title may be compared with the Zeus Meilichios ("gentle Zeus") of Philo Byblius; that god is identified with Chousor/Hephaistos ("first of all men to sail"), inventor of fishing equipment and the raft. Philo's Chousor, in turn, must be descended from the old Canaanite craftsman god, Kothar.

While the high god is the leading deity in the pantheon, he is not the principal object of cultic veneration. That situation is paralleled at Ugarit, where Il (El) is head of the pantheon, but he is neither the most active god in the myths nor the most popular god in the cult. The other two types of gods mentioned in the Esarhaddon treaty were evidently regarded as the protective geniuses of the individual cities, and cultic activity centered around them.

The treaty shows that Eshmun and Melqart were gods who guaranteed the fertility of the land and the fecundity of the flocks. The prophet Hosea (especially in 2:10–15) calls this type of god *ba'al* (pl., *ba'alim*), and condemns the Northern Israelites for thus identifying their own national god (cf. 2:18–19). Melqart was the city god of Tyre; his cult later spread to Egypt, Cyprus, Carthage, and elsewhere. According to Menander of Ephesus (see Josephus, *Antiquities* 8.146), the tenth-century King Hiram of Tyre (Solomon's famous ally) built a new temple for Melqart (Herakles), and innovated the celebration of the "awakening" (i.e., resurrection) of Melqart. This testimony shows that Melqart was a dying and reviving god; his life cycle evidently corresponded to the seasons of the agricultural year. Melqart's name literally means "king of the city." Since the word *city* is a widespread Semitic euphemism for the netherworld (i.e., the infernal city), the name is a further indication of Melqart's chthonic character.

Eshmun, who is linked with Melqart in the Esarhaddon treaty, was the dying and reviving god venerated at Sidon. He was later identified with the healer god Asklepios. The association of healer gods with the chthonic cycle is a common phenomenon in the ancient Near East. At Ugarit, the patron of the deified dead was Rapiu ("healer"), and his name survives in those of the late first-millennium Phoenician deities Shadrafa ("healing spirit") and Baal-Merappe ("healer Baal").

The third important dying and reviving god was Adonis, whose cult was prominent in Byblos, and especially at the spring of Aphaca, near Beirut. This god's name is attested by classical authors, and does not appear in Phoenician texts; the name is, however, clearly derived from the Canaanite *adoni* or *adonai*, which means "my lord." The well-known story of the death of Adonis (e.g., Ovid, *Metamorphoses* 10.710–739) is undoubtedly of Semitic origin.

The most prominent deity in the Phoenician and Punic cults was the goddess Astarte. In the Esarhaddon treaty she is invoked as a war goddess, but her personality was more complex; she was also a fertility goddess, a mother goddess, and a goddess of love, having assimilated her many characteristics from various older goddesses such as the Canaanite triad of Athirat, Anat, and Athtart; the Egyptian Hathor; and the Mesopotamian Ishtar. Astarte's character was so diverse, in fact, that she was identified with several Greek goddesses: Aphrodite, goddess of love and fertility; Hera, queen of heaven; and the mother goddess Cybele. In Byblos, Astarte was worshiped simply as Baalat, "lady" (feminine form of Baal), and in Carthage she was identified with Tanit (origin uncertain). She was also venerated at Tyre (as consort of Baal-Shamem), Sidon, Arvad, and Ashkelon, as well as in the colonies on Cyprus, Sicily, and Malta. She is the Ashtoret/ Ashtarot so detested by the biblical authors.

In the fifth-century inscription of King Eshmunazor of Sidon, Astarte bears the epithet "name of Baal"; similarly, in Carthage, Tanit is styled "face of Baal." These epithets suggest that the Phoenicians saw Astarte as the manifestation of Baal-Shamem's numinous power. The cult of Astarte, then, was the means of access to the high god; the great mother served as a sort of mediator between the people and the heavenly Baal.

It has often been suggested that the divine triad described above—high god, great goddess, and dying and reviving god—constituted the basis of all Phoenician pantheons. Attractive as that suggestion is, it must be considered no more than tentative in light of the evidence. The cult of Beirut, for example, seems only to possess a divine couple (Poseidon and Aphrodite/ Astarte), and the Tyrian Melqart seems to be both a high god and a dying and reviving god. In addition, the precise relationship between the goddess and the dying and reviving god is often uncertain.

Various other gods comprise the "assembly of the gods," the "holy ones" (so the Yehimilk inscription), or the "whole family of the children of the gods" (Azitawadda). The main feature of the different local pantheons is their diversity. In the Karatepe inscription, for example, King Azitawadda's patron god is the otherwise unknown Baal-*krntrysh* (significance uncertain). The inscription also mentions Rashap (Reshef), one of the most important West Semitic gods from the third millennium onward; but the epithet assigned to Azitawadda's Rashap is unique and problematic. In his curse against anyone who would remove the great portal he has just dedicated, Azitawadda specifically invokes Baal-Shamem, El-Creator-of-the-World, and Eternal Sun. All of these divine titles evoke numerous Near Eastern parallels, but nowhere else do they occur in this form or juxtaposition.

Another problematic deity of great importance bears the epithet *Baal-Hammon* ("lord of the brazier"). He is later identified with Saturn, but the Phoenician divine name that underlies his epithet cannot be determined, nor can anything definite be said about the god's character. He is mentioned once in the ninth- or eighth-century inscription of King Kilamuwa of Ya'adi (Zinjirli, in southern Anatolia), and later becomes enormously popular in the Punic cults of North Africa, Malta, and Sicily. In Carthage, votive stelae are regularly dedicated "To the lady, Tanit-Face-of-Baal, and to the lord, Baal-Hammon." (Elsewhere, Baal-Hammon is generally mentioned first.) In view of the close relationship between Tyre and Carthage, it is tempting to equate Tanit and Baal-Hammon with Astarte and Melqart. While some assimilation is certain, however, absolute identity is not.

Throughout the first millennium, the Phoenician divine world becomes increasingly complex. Innovations do not, however, appear to be organic developments. They stem, rather, primarily from syncretism—incorporation of external influences. Compound divine names, which appear in profusion after the middle of the first millennium, are good indications of syncretism and assimilation. For example, Eshmun-Melqart is attested in several fourth-century inscriptions from Kition (Cyprus). Milk-Astarte, whose name is probably a combination of *Melqart* and *Astarte*, is prominent in the third- and second-century texts from Umm el-Awamid (near Tyre); the significance of the combination, however, is unclear.

In addition, a number of old gods from different places appear in various cults. The old Canaanite storm god Hadad, for example, is found together with the "Syrian goddess" Atargatis in a second-century Greek inscription from Kfar Yassif, near Acre. In general, though, the old gods belong to a shadowy world of protective geniuses and malevolent demons. The proliferation of divine and semidivine guardians and healers (usually chthonic, like Shadrafa) is one of the most important developments within Phoenician religion. Early evidence comes from the two extraordinary seventh-century apotropaic plaques from Arslan Tash in north Syria, which name several of these figures. One of the plaques invokes the protection of Baal-Lord-of-the-Earth (i.e., the netherworld) and of the chthonic god Horon, who is also prominent in two second-millennium Canaanite incantation texts. And later Phoenician and Punic cults venerate the Egyptian Osiris and Bes, the Babylonian Nergal (Rashap), and the Canaanite Mekal and Anat (identified with Athena), among others.

Finally, some Phoenician gods are only attested by their Greek "equivalents," so that their Phoenician identities can only be surmised. An important case in point is the high god of Beirut, who was "Poseidon," perhaps to be identified with El-Creator-of-the-Earth.

Beliefs and Practices. Phoenician religion was certainly rooted in a rich mythological tradition. That tradition, unfortunately, does not survive in native texts. The main source is Philo Byblius's *Phoenician History*, which is supposedly a Greek translation of a Phoenician account by a priest named Sanchuniaton. Most of the extant portions of Philo's work are in book 1 of Eusebius's *Praeparatio evangelica*, and variant versions of some parts can be found in other late classical texts.

Despite the indubitable value of Philo's work, its reliability should not be overstressed. It is composed of numerous sources, and is replete with internal confusion and duplication. It conflates originally independent local traditions, and it imposes an alien euhemeristic framework on the material. Still, as Albert I. Baumgarten concludes in his important study (1981) of Philo Byblius, "behind the distortions one can see traces of a more traditional mythology and religion" (p. 268).

At the very least, Philo's work demonstrates that the Phoenicians had a cosmogonic creation myth that was combined with the generations of the gods and an account of the origin of culture. The traditions are generally comparable to such texts as the Babylonian epic *Enuma elish* and Hesiod's *Theogony* (according to Philo, Hesiod appropriated the Phoenician stories and "decked them out in every way"); they all provide etiologies and apologies for the supremacy of particular gods and cults in particular places. Thus, for example, the high god Kronos/El (Baal-Shamem?) assigns Phoenicia to Astarte and Zeus-Demarous/Adad ("Baal," that is, a dying and reviving god), constituting the divine triad (cf. *Dt.* 32:8 with Baumgarten, p. 214). Astarte herself then consecrates her shrine at Tyre. The text continues with etiologies of human sacrifice (see below) and circumcision, explaining that Kronos gave his beloved son up as a wholly burned offering during a time of "pestilence and death," and later circumcised himself.

In Phoenician religion, three kinds of cultic activity predominated: (1) rituals associated with the dying and reviving god, (2) sacrificial rites, and (3) funerary rites. There were three centers of cultic activity: (1) undeveloped natural sites, especially mountains, rivers, and groves of trees, which for one reason or another were considered sacred (cf. *Is.* 57:3–13); (2) open-air shrines, usually featuring a sacred grove, a small chapel, a sacrificial altar (the biblical "high place"), and one or more conical stone pillars, called betyls, that symbolized divine presence (to be compared with the wooden asherah poles mentioned in the Bible); and (3) fully enclosed temples with large courtyards for public ceremonies, such as Solomon's Phoenician-designed sanctuary. When the Phoenicians established a colony, they generally built a temple to serve as a center of both religious and mercantile activity. Their commercial ventures and dealings with foreigners thus came under divine protection (see the excellent discussion by Guy Bunnens, 1979, pp. 282–285).

The cult of the dying and reviving god was associated with sacred natural sites. The temple of Eshmun in Sidon was located on a hillside near the Asklepios River (modern Nahr el-Awali), and the famous shrine of Adonis at Aphaca was in the mountains outside Beirut at the source of the Adonis River (modern Nahr Ibrahim), near the sacred grove and shrine of Astarte. Lucian (*Syrian Goddess* 6–8) describes some of the rites and traditions associated with Adonis. In an annual celebration of his death, the people of Byblos would perform mourning rites and lamentations. Then they would offer sacrifices to Adonis "as if to a dead person," following which they would proclaim his revival. Celebrants were required, according to Lucian, to shave their heads; the many ritual razors found in Punic tombs may be connected with this rite, as are biblical proscriptions of such shaving. Women who refused to shave had to act as prostitutes for a day, turning the proceeds over to Aphrodite (Astarte).

Other sources confirm Lucian's general description of the feast of Adonis. It entailed a dramatic enactment of the god's funeral, a mournful procession to the temple of Astarte where sacrifices were offered, and an orgiastic banquet that celebrated the god's resurrection. It can be surmised that similar festivals took place in other Phoenician cities (see especially Édouard Lipinski's brilliant study [1970] of the festival of the burial and resurrection of Melqart).

The ultimate source of the festival is clearly the seasonal cycle; the dying and reviving god, whose demise comes with the withering summer heat, personifies that cycle. The return of the god guarantees the return of fertility to the land. To the archaic fertility cult, however, the Phoenicians appear to have added a personal soteriological dimension, which became increasingly important in the late first millennium. In this new theological context, Adonis personifies the vicarious sacrificial victim whose life is forfeit for the benefit of the individual celebrant. Noel Robertson (1982) rightly calls the god's death "a mythical paradigm of an act of personal atonement" (p. 359). The believer performs a private sacrifice (cf.

Syrian Goddess 55) and a rite whereby he identifies himself with the victim. He then participates in the public displays of mourning for Adonis, who is the mythic projection of the sacrificial victim, and he ultimately rejoices at the god's (and, vicariously, his own) "salvation."

The concept of the vicarious victim finds its fullest expression in the Phoenician and (especially) Punic sacrificial cults. In Phoenicia proper, animal and vegetable offerings were made at the various shrines, especially in conjunction with the seasonal festivals, and in fulfillment of personal vows; human sacrifices were apparently offered in times of crisis. In the Punic cults, sacrifice was the primary (not to say only) religious act; there is no evidence for the sort of temple ceremonies and religious feasts found in the homeland.

The evidence for the Punic sacrificial cults comes primarily from Carthage, with comparable evidence from other sites in Sardinia, Sicily, and North Africa. The sacrificial precinct was known as the *tofet* (cf. the biblical sources of this term: *2 Kings* 23:10; *Isaiah* 30:33; *Jeremiah* 7:30–32, 19:6–14); the *tofet* of Carthage covered as much as 6,000 square meters. Excavations in the area have turned up thousands of urns containing the cremated remains of birds, animals, and small children. The urns have been found in three distinct archeological strata, indicating that the precinct was in continuous use from around 750 BCE until the Romans destroyed the city in 146 BCE.

Many urns were buried under stelae that were engraved either with inscriptions or designs. The designs are usually crude representations of betyls, figures of Tanit, or symbols of Tanit and Baal-Hammon: the upraised right hand, the caduceus (crescent and disk atop a staff), the disk surmounted by a crescent, and the enigmatic "Tanit sign," basically a triangle topped by a horizontal bar upon which a disk rests. The inscriptions are typically of the votive type, such as the following: "To the Lady, Tanit-Face-of-Baal, and to the Lord, Baal-Hammon, that which Matonbaal, wife of Abdmilqart son of Baalhanno son of Bodashtart vowed, because he [the god] heard his [the votary's] voice and blessed him" (Donner and Röllig, 1966–1969, no. 88).

The dedicators of these stelae evidently repaid their vows to the gods with live sacrifices, mainly of children. And while it is often suggested that child sacrifice took place only in times of duress (cf. Diodorus Siculus 20.14.4–7), the archeological evidence points toward regular, institutionalized practice. Sacrificial animals, in fact, were probably substitutes for the preferred human victims (cf. *Genesis* 22, which is, among other things, an etiology of the substitute offering).

The sacrifice was called a *mulk*-offering; the term *mulk* (biblical *Molech*) is derived from the West Semitic word for "king," and it is evidently an epithet of the god who was the recipient of the offering. This god would have been either an autonomous god of death, like the old Canaanite Mot, or, more likely, the dying and reviving god (Baal-Hammon?) in his chthonic aspect. The location of the Jerusalem *tofet* outside the city's eastern wall, at the traditional entrance to the netherworld, explicitly connects child sacrifice with the cult of death. Offering up an innocent child as a vicarious victim was a supreme act of propitiation, probably intended to guarantee the welfare of family and community alike.

Another aspect of the Phoenician attitude toward death shows up in funerary practices. The preferred mode of burial was inhumation, although there were some cremations (aside from sacrificial victims). Wealthier Phoenicians were buried in decorated coffins, in rock-cut tombs of various types. Egyptian influence is often discernible in the design of both tombs and coffins. In later times, funerary monuments were sometimes built above the tombs. The deceased were buried together with all sorts of practical and ritual objects: utensils for food, cosmetic containers, toilet articles, clothing, jewelry, coins, masks, and figurines. As Donald Harden (1980) remarks in his excellent discussion of Phoenician tombs and burial customs (pp. 96–104), "were it not for the burials, we should know little of the pottery and other things which the Phoenicians used in their day-to-day existence" (p. 104).

The funerary practices strongly imply Phoenician belief in an afterlife. That impression is confirmed by Phoenician royal tomb inscriptions, which level curses against anyone who would disturb the tombs. In the fifth-century inscriptions of both King Tabnit of Sidon and his son Eshmunazor II, part of the curse would deny the tomb violator his "rest with the Refaim." This term, meaning literally "healers," denotes the deified dead of second-millennium Ugarit (also the depotentialized shades of the Bible). As at Ugarit, presumably, dead Phoenician notables assumed a new role as chthonic healers. A first-century- CE bilingual inscription from Lybia contains a dedication "to the divine Refaim." There is insufficient evidence to permit the reconstruction of a Phoenician cult of the dead, but a first-century- BCE text from Piraeus (Greece) does mention a Sidonian *marzih* feast—the ritual banquet of the cult of the dead.

The many Phoenician religious shrines were staffed by various cultic officials, including priests, scribes, musicians, barbers (probably for the ritual shaving mentioned above), and male and female cult prostitutes. The titular head of the cult, in all likelihood, was the king (in those cities that had one). Tabnit refers both to himself and to his father as "priest of Astarte, king of the Sidonians." The word for "priest," *khn*, is common West Semitic; it occurs frequently in the inscriptions to designate the most important cultic officials, as does the feminine form *khnt*, "priestess." The priesthood was hereditary: one stela from Carthage lists seventeen generations of priests of Tanit. Since the stela is probably from the late fourth century, that line of priests might date back to the very founding of Carthage (see Harden, 1980, p. 283, n. 31, and corresponding plate 31).

Artistic representations of the priests show them bringing offerings (in one case an infant) and giving benedictions. They wear a squarish cap or a head scarf, with a stole over one shoulder and a close-fitting tunic. Something of the priests' livelihood can be determined from lists of the sacrificial tariffs of third- and second-century Carthage, of which several broken copies have survived. These tariffs detail the payments the priests received for performing various sacrifices—both in money and in portions of the sacrificial animal (cf. the opening chapters of *Leviticus*). The two main types of offering were apparently the "whole gift-offering" and the "substitute offering" (for a child?), although both terms are problematic. The priest's fee was higher for the latter; the fee also varied according to the type of animal sacrificed. Bird offerings, oblations, and meal offerings constitute separate categories in the tariff, and there is also a provision for free sacrifices for the poor.

In addition to performing their sacerdotal functions, the priests were probably the conservators and transmitters of Phoenician culture. Through their activity, the Phoenician language and traditions survived even in the most unpromising circumstances. Poignant evidence of that survival is the one extant Phoenician prayer, an improvised personal prayer recited by a merchant named Hanno, which is preserved in Latin transcription at the beginning of the fifth act of the *Poenulus* of Plautus.

Bibliography

There are two excellent general works on the Phoenicians in English: Donald B. Harden's *The Phoenicians*, 2d ed. (New York, 1980), and Sabatino Moscati's *The World of the Phoenicians*, translated by Alastair Hamilton (New York, 1968). Both are well illustrated and contain extensive bibliographies of older works (which will, therefore, not be listed here). The definitive edition of the Phoenician and Punic inscriptions, still in progress, is the *Corpus Inscriptionum Semiticarum*, part 1 (Paris, 1881–). A thoroughly annotated English translation of Phoenician (but not Punic) texts is John C. L. Gibson's *Textbook of Syrian Semitic Inscriptions*, vol. 3, *Phoenician Inscriptions* (Oxford, 1982). A good selection of both Phoenician and Punic inscriptions with German translations, commentary, and glossary is *Kanaanäische und aramäische Inschriften*, 2d ed., 3 vols., edited by Herbert Donner and Wolfgang Röllig (Wiesbaden, 1966–1969). Of the utmost importance for students of the inscriptions is Javier Teixidor's "Bulletin d'épigraphie sémi-tique," which has appeared more or less regularly in the journal *Syria* since 1967 (vols. 44–). There is also a fine dictionary available in English: Richard S. Tomback's *A Comparative Semitic Lexicon of the Phoenician and Punic Languages* (Missoula, Mont., 1978). The standard survey of the Phoenician gods is Marvin H. Pope and Wolfgang Röllig's "Syrien: Die Mythologie der Ugariter und Phönizier," in *Wörterbuch der Mythologie*, vol. 1, edited by H. W. Haussig (Stuttgart, 1965), pp. 219–312. Phoenician and Punic personal names are collected and analyzed in Frank L. Benz's *Personal Names in the Phoenician and Punic Inscriptions* (Rome, 1972).

The student interested in the state of the art in Phoenician and Punic studies must learn Italian, the primary language of scholarly publication. The most important scholarly journal is the *Rivista di studi fenici* (Rome, 1973–). Fundamental treatments of key issues are Sabatino Moscati's *Problematica della civiltà fenicia* (Rome, 1974) and the essays of Giovanni Garbini collected in *I Fenici, storia e religione* (Naples, 1980). An excellent introduction to the present state of scholarship is the conference volume *La religione fenicia: Matrici orientali e sviluppi occidentali* (Rome, 1981). This volume includes, among a number of important studies, two seminal programmatic statements: Paolo Xella's "Aspetti e problemi dell'indagine storico-religiosa" (pp. 7–25) and Giovanni Garbini's "Continuità e innovazioni nella religione fenicia" (pp. 29–43; also in *I Fenici*, cited above, pp. 151–159).

There are many recommendable studies on special topics. Javier Teixidor's *The Pagan God* (Princeton, 1977) is a brilliant analysis of popular religion in the Greco-Roman Near East, with special attention to Phoenicia, Syria, North Arabia, and Palmyra. Two volumes of essays filled with learning and interest are Robert Du Mesnil du Buisson's *Études sur les dieux phéniciens hérités par l'empire romain* (Leiden, 1970) and *Nouvelles études sur les dieux et les mythes de Canaan* (Leiden, 1973). The two essays that reconstruct the pantheons of Byblos (*Études*, pp. 56–116) and Tyre (*Nouvelles études*, pp. 32–69) are *tours de force*. A characteristically insightful and controversial study of Phoenician religion in relation to the Bible is William F. Albright's *Yahweh and the Gods of Canaan* (London, 1968), pp. 208–264. On the dying and reviving god, two recent studies of extraordinary interest are Édouard Lipinski's "La fête de l'ensevelissement et de la résurrection de Melqart," in *Actes de la Dix-septième Rencontre Assyriologique Internationale*, edited by André Finet (Brussels, 1970), pp. 30–58 (exhaustively annotated), and Noel Robertson's "The Ritual Background of the Dying God in Cyprus and Syro-Palestine," *Harvard Theological Review* 75 (July 1982): 313–359.

A splendid account of the Phoenician colonization of the west is Guy Bunnens's *L'expansion phénicienne en Méditerranée* (Brussels, 1979). A popular account of recent excavations at Carthage that emphasizes the issue of child sacrifice is Lawrence E. Stager and Samuel R. Wolff's "Child Sacrifice at Carthage: Religious Rite or Population Control?" *Biblical Archaeology Review* 10 (January-February 1984): 31–51. The article is generally more sober than the title would suggest, and it is magnificently illustrated. For a powerful argument against the existence of institutionalized child sacrifice, see Moshe Weinfeld's "The Worship of Molech and of the Queen of Heaven and Its Background," *Ugarit-Forschungen* 4 (1972): 133–154.

On Philo Byblius's *Phoenician History*, there is a first-rate translation and commentary by Albert I. Baumgarten, *The Phoenician History of Philo of Byblos* (Leiden, 1981). No similar up-to-date study of *The Syrian Goddess* exists, although there is a readable English translation with brief introduction by Harold W. Attridge and R. A. Oden, Jr., *The Syrian Goddess* (*De dea Syria*) (Missoula, Mont., 1976). For a fuller commentary, *Lu-kians Schrift über die syrische Göttin*, edited and translated by Carl Clemen (Leipzig, 1938), is still useful.

Finally, space must be found for Gustave Flaubert's novel of Carthage, *Salammbô*, corr. ed. (Paris, 1879), inspired by his visit to the site in 1858. The chapter entitled "Moloch" includes Flaubert's gruesome account of child sacrifice.

ALAN M. COOPER (1987)

PHOENICIAN RELIGION [FURTHER CONSIDERATIONS]. With regard to the *mlk*-sacrifice, both the definition of the word *mlk* and the nature of the actual sacrifice are still under debate. There was an underworld deity named *M-l-k* (variously vocalized) in many Mesopotamian and Syro-Palestinian god lists and personal names from the late third millennium BCE on, and there existed an Akkadian term *maliku* designating shades of the dead or chthonic deities who received funeral offerings in texts from the same time period. However, there is no evidence that either the god or the shades are to be connected to child sacrifice or to the later Phoenician sacrificial term *mlk*. It is not necessary to assume that, by his nature, a god of the netherworld would receive such a sacrifice, and indeed the god *Mlk* at Ugarit (possibly pronounced *Milku*) receives only typical animal offerings (e.g., *KTU* 1.111). In addition, the later Phoenician or Punic *mlk*-sacrifice is given to more than one god and never to one called *Mlk*; for example, to the god Kronos in classical texts, to Baʿl Hammon and Tanit at Carthage and elsewhere in the western Mediterranean, and perhaps to Eshmun in the only Punic *mlk* text from Palestine (third or second century BCE). It is only in the Bible that human sacrifices are given to a god Molech (or Molek). This may be the result of a confusion on the part of the biblical text between the sacrificial term *mlk* and the divine designation *Mlk*, which was perhaps triggered by an antagonistic and rather defamatory view of non-Israelite religions.

It seems most likely that the term *mlk/mlkt* is a causative nominal form with the pattern *maqtil(at)*, meaning "thing presented" or "the act of presenting," from the causative of the root *ylk* (*wlk*), meaning "to offer, present" (*cf.* *mtnt*, "gift," from *ntn*, "to give," or *mṣʾ* "place or act of going forth," from *yṣʾ*, "to go forth"). The *mlk*-sacrifice is thus not connected to the root *mlk*, "to rule" (*cf.* biblical *melek*, "king"), even if the divine name *Mlk* may be.

Moreover, there have been new discussions about whether or not the *mlk*-sacrifice could sometimes actually indicate a human offering. Scholars have tried to distinguish between the sacrifices in the Punic realm and those on the Phoenician mainland. The large cemetery containing the burned bones and ashes of small children at Carthage, as well as the several occurrences of *mlk ʾdm* (sacrifice of a human) in Punic texts—in contrast to the almost total lack of archaeological and textual evidence in the Palestinian Levant—have led to the understanding of some scholars that there were no human sacrifices in Phoenicia. However, an unpublished basalt stela from İnçirli in southeastern Turkey found in 1993, written in standard Phoenician from the late eighth century BCE, may indicate that *mlk*-sacrifices of firstborn human sons were made there along with those of sheep and horses (Zuckerman and Kaufman, 1998).

One may still wonder whether *mlk ʾdm* denotes the literal sacrifice of a human. Some have proposed that the Carthage cemetery may simply contain burials of stillborn or short-lived infants whose bodies were cremated and then placed in an urn and buried. According to this view, the children buried in the special sacred precinct were symbolically "offered" to a deity in hopes for the divine protection or survival of others. Other scholars have suggested that the textual occurrences of *mlk ʾdm* could but did not necessarily mean the sacrifice of a human, and that the substitution of an animal would often occur, as is the case with, for example, the *mlk bʿl* (sacrifice in place of an infant) or with the *mlk bšr* (sacrifice in place of flesh). At any rate, the majority opinion among European scholars is that the immolation of humans may not have existed at all, or that, at best, it was a limited phenomenon in the Phoenician and Punic world. Nevertheless, other scholars tend to argue that human sacrifice played a somewhat essential role in non-Israelite religions. At this point, however, it seems that still more evidence is needed before the *mlk*-sacrifice is fully understood.

THE SPECIALIZED RELIGION OF PHOENICIAN MARINERS. That Phoenician mariners had a specialized religion is demonstrated by excavations of harbor shrines and ancient shipwrecks, burials of sailors, iconographic representations of seafaring activity, and classical texts. In addition to the gods Baʿl Šamem, Baʿl Malage, and Baʿl Ṣapon mentioned in the treaty between Esarhaddon and the king of Tyre, all of whom seem to be aspects of the weather god, one notes that Libyan Ammon and Baʿl Roʾš ("lord of the promontory") were invoked concerning control of the winds and weather. The goddesses ʾAsherah and Tanit, known mostly from their cults on land, were also believed to help in navigation. Many promontories, islands, and harbors were named after the god Melqart, and, on the basis of the attributes of his Greek counterpart, Herakles, it was probably believed that he was a god of travelers who also conquered sea monsters. Ships were thought to possess protective spirits, sometimes represented on the prow, and archaeologists can isolate promontory shrines that seemed to have served as landmarks for navigation and as indicators of freshwater sources. Maritime votive offerings such as model ships and dedicatory anchors in harbor shrines were presumably offered by sailors.

SEE ALSO Baal; Heracles; Melqart.

BIBLIOGRAPHY

Recent discussions of the *mlk*-sacrifice include: J. Day, *Molech: A God of Human Sacrifice in the Old Testament* (Cambridge, 1989), G. C. Heider, *The Cult of Molek: A Reassessment* (Sheffield, 1985); D. Pardee, "Review of Heider, *Cult of Molek*," *Journal of Near Eastern Studies* 49 (1990): 370–372; K. A. D. Smelik, "Moloch, Molech or Molk-Sacrifice? A Reassessment of the Evidence Concerning the Hebrew Term Molekh," *Scandinavian Journal of the Old Testament* 9 (1995): 133–192. G. C. Heider, "Molech," in *Dictionary of Deities and Demons in the Bible,* edited by Karel van der Toorn, Bob Becking, and Pieter W. van der Horst, pp. 581–585 (Leiden, 1999); H.-P. Müller, "Mōlek," in the *Theological Dictionary of the Old Testament,* vol. 8, (edited by G. J. Botterweck et al., Grand Rapids, Mich., 1997), pp. 375–388. Otto Eissfeldt's classic article is now reprinted in a bilingual edition by C. González Wagner and L. A. Ruiz Cabrero, *El Molk como concepto del sacrificio punico y hebreo y el final del dios Moloch* (Madrid, 2002), and in the same volume an article by Edward Lipinski (pp. 141–157) sums up the strongest arguments for the occurrence of actual, non-symbolic, human *mlk*-sacrifices. For counterarguments against *mlk* as a child sacrifice, see M. Gras, P. Rouillard, and J. Teixidor, *L'univers phénicien* (Paris, 1989).

For a preliminary description of the as-yet unpublished İnçirli Inscription, see Bruce Zuckerman and Stephen Kaufman, "Recording the Stela: First step on the road to decipherment," available from http://www.humnet.ucla.edu/humnet/nelc/stelasite/zuck.html (last updated June 21, 1998). For a brief notice, see H. Shanks, "Who—or what—was Molech? New Phoenician Inscription May Hold Answer," *Biblical Archaeology Review* 22, no. 4 (1996): 13.

On the specialized religion of Phoenician mariners, see Aaron Jed Brody, *"Each Man Cried Out to His God": The Specialized Religion of Canaanite and Phoenician Seafarers* (Atlanta, 1998); see also the review by Ignacio Márquez Rowe, *Orientalistische Literaturzeitung* 97 (2002): 369–372. For an up-to-date edition and detailed commentary of Lucian's *On the Syrian Goddess,* see now that of J. L. Lightfoot (Oxford, 2003).

For works on the relation between Phoenician religion and the Bible, Albright's *Yahweh and the Gods of Canaan* is now surpassed by Mark S. Smith's *The Early History of God: Yahweh and the Other Deities in Ancient Israel,* 2nd ed. (Grand Rapids, Mich., 2002), and John Day's *Yahweh and the Gods and Goddesses of Canaan* (Sheffield, 2000). For general matters on Phoenicians, see *The Phoenicians,* edited by Sabatino Moscati (New York, 1988) and Corinne Bonnet, *Melqart: Cultes et mythes de l'Héraclès tyrien en Méditerranée* (Leuven, 1988). For the Ugaritic texts (*KTU*), see now Manfried Dietrich, Oswald Loretz, and Joaquín Sanmartín. *The Cuneiform Alphabetic Texts from Ugarit, Ras Ibn Hani and Other Places (KTU)* (Münster, 1995, 2nd edition of *Die keilalphabetischen Texte aus Ugarit,* Neukirchen, 1976).

TAWNY L. HOLM (2005)

PHOTIOS (c. 820–891), patriarch of Constantinople, saint of the Orthodox church, was a scholar, public minister, diplomat, professor, organizer of missions, ecclesiastical writer, and hierarch. Photios was born into a noble family. His father, Sergius, was the brother of the patriarch Tarasios. Three of Photios's four brothers held high civil offices; because of his family's social position, he was able to obtain an advanced education.

In 850, when the university of Constantinople was reorganized (by Photios at the empress's request), Photios was one of the first professors called there to teach. He was sent to Baghdad in 851, together with Constantine the Philosopher, as diplomatic representative of the emperor to the caliph al-Mutawakkil. After intervention in 858 by the caesar Bardas, uncle of Michael III, the conservative patriarch Ignatius resigned. Photios as a layman was elected patriarch. Although he was eventually ordained, Nicholas I refused to recognize his election, and, under pressure from Ignatius's supporters, he officially condemned Photios in Rome (863). After the intervention of the new emperor, Basil I, in 867, Photios was deposed and Ignatius once again became patriarch.

A synod convened in 869, comprised of only a limited number of bishops, condemned Photios and definitively justified Ignatius. As Francis Dvornik has said, this synod was used exclusively by the Latins to define their attitude against Photios (Dvornik, 1948). However, ten years later, in 879, at the request of John VIII, another synod was held that canceled all decisions of the previous one and reelected Photios as patriarch. He died in the Monastery of Amoniakon, probably on February 6, 891.

Photios's most important theological views are expressed in his *Mystagogy of the Holy Spirit,* which is a detailed analysis of the doctrine of the Holy Spirit. According to Photios, the *filioque* clause, which claims that the Holy Spirit proceeds from the Father "and from the Son," was theologically unacceptable because it introduced a new principle into the Trinity. If the procession of the Holy Spirit was dependent upon procession from the Son, then this would create an unequal union among the three divine persons, destroying the balance.

Within the church, Photios thought true communion impossible without the coexistence of dogma and ethos. However, he saw the importance of accepting a diversity of institutions and ecclesiastical customs, a diversity that would be made whole by the effects of the Spirit. As a result of mission work, there were new Slavic churches demanding autonomy, which was giving impetus to changes in ecclesiastical organizations that had until that time remained uniform.

According to Photios, political authority is equal to ecclesiastical authority in the governance of a people; the functions of the emperor and patriarch are parallel. Photios's theory, known as the dual control theory, places responsibility for the subjects' material well-being in the emperor's hands; the patriarch is held accountable for their spiritual welfare. In other words, governance is equally distributed between the emperor and the patriarch, who work harmoniously for the good of the world.

Photios's theological and literary works continued to influence others long after his death. His theological work has had the most influence, especially his detailed presentation of the doctrine of the Holy Spirit, which was identical to that put forth by his successors. Photios's interest and participation in the theological and political discussions of his time directly determined the field of jurisdiction of the early Christian rulers in Slavic countries and contributed to the formation of laws and to the regulation of relations between church and state. Photios was, in fact, the first patriarch of Constantinople to initiate missionary work among the Slavs. He chose Cyril and Methodius from Thessalonica to preach Christianity in Russia, Bulgaria, Moravia, Croatia, and

Slovenia. At the same time, Photios struggled to protect the rights of the ecumenical throne from the interference of the ambitious Nicholas I in southern Italy, Sicily, and on the Balkan peninsula.

Photios's corpus includes poetic and prose writings, literary works, and theological works. His most significant works are *Lexicon, Ecclesiastic History Compendium,* and *Myriobiblion* (or *Bibliotheca*), which contains the literary analyses of 280 works studied by Photios, many of which are no longer extant. Photios's *Amphilochia* is an important collection of dogmatic essays, whereas his *Mystagogy of the Holy Spirit,* an anti-filioque essay, presents all the arguments related to the teaching about the procession of the Holy Spirit from the Father alone. His *Against the Manichaeans* refutes the Manichaean heresy and warns about the dangers it holds for the orthodox faith. Although the *Nomocanon* and the *Epanagoge* certainly reflect Photios's opinions and were for years attributed to him, they were most likely written by his students.

BIBLIOGRAPHY

Only a few of Photios's works have been translated. See, for example, in English, *The Homilies of Photius, Patriarch of Constantinople,* translated, with commentary, by Cyril Mango (Cambridge, Mass., 1958), and, in Russian, *Patriarkha Fotiia XLV neizdannykh pisem,* edited and translated by Athanasios Papadopoulos-Kerameus (Saint Petersburg, 1896). Photios's writings are collected in *Patrologia Graeca,* edited by J.-P. Migne, with Joseph Hergenröther, vols. 101–104 (Paris, 1857–1866), and in *Epistolai,* edited by Ioannou Balettas (London, 1864). For critical discussion, see Francis Dvornik's "Photius, Father of Schism or Patron of Reunion?" in *Report of the Proceedings at the Church Unity Octave, 1942* (Oxford, 1942), pp. 19–32, and the same author's *The Photian Schism: History and Legend* (Cambridge, 1948), which includes a full bibliography and explicates the false legends about Photios. In Greek, see my *Theologia kai diaprosopikai skheseis kata ton M. Photion* (Thessaloniki, 1974); in German, Joseph Hergenröther's *Photius, Patriarch von Konstantinopel,* 3 vols. (Regensburg, 1867–1869).

VASILEIOS YIOULTSIS (1987)

PHYSICS AND RELIGION. Physics describes the material world on the basis of repeatable observation and in terms of concepts such as mass, energy, space, and time. As the earliest of the modern scientific disciplines, physics has played a central role in establishing the approach that characterizes modern science in general. At the heart of this approach lies the quest for precise mathematical "laws," which can be used to explain, predict, and control the natural world. The historical roots of this quest lie in the musings of the ancient Greeks, most notably those of Pythagoras (sixth century BCE) and his followers. The writings of the Pythagorean tradition, as well as those of Aristotle and other Greek philosophers, were re-introduced to late medieval Europe by Islamic scholars such as Ibn Sīnā (known also as Avicenna; 980–1037). This collection of writings had a profound impact on European history, precipitating many of the intellectual shifts that led to the birth of modern physics during the Renaissance and the Enlightenment. Because of these historical connections, the impact of modern physics upon religious ideas has been most enduringly felt and evaluated from the perspective of Western Christian thought. This article thus focuses primarily on Christian responses, though works relating to other religions are included in the bibliography.

Galileo Galilei (1564–1642) stands at the center of one of the first encounters between physics and Christianity. The Roman Catholic Church is commonly perceived to have put forward theological objections to the sun-centered, or heliocentric, account of planetary motion first developed by Nicolaus Copernicus (1473–1543) and later promoted by Galileo. However, historians now generally agree that the church's hostility toward heliocentrism resulted more from Reformation controversies over authority and biblical interpretation, as well as the various personalities involved in the encounter, than from any real theological difficulties stemming from the earth's motion. In retrospect, the lasting theological significance of physics' emerging worldview proved to be its comprehensive account of physical motion in terms of deterministic laws. If every moment in history had been completely determined by physical laws acting upon what came before it, could one still conceive of God's ongoing activity in the world? And equally important, in such a world could one still conceive of human thought and action as genuinely free?

NEWTONIAN MECHANISM. The deterministic worldview of early modern physics solidified around the grand synthesis of Isaac Newton (1642–1727), which united celestial and terrestrial motion into a single conceptual scheme. The heavens were no longer the abode of spiritual beings but merely another part of the physical world that could be understood mathematically in terms of its parts. In this key respect, Newton's account of physical motion, his "mechanics," shaped the character of modern science in general. All of the early scientists in Europe, including Newton, were at least nominally Christian, though many held unorthodox beliefs. Some, like Johannes Kepler (1571–1630), took it as their task and reward to "think God's thoughts after him" and thought of their investigations as a hymn of praise to the Creator. Others, like Galileo, attempted to distance scientific ideas from theological ones by describing science and the church as two distinct authorities, each controlling separate spheres of knowledge. Quoting the respected cardinal and Counter-Reformation historian Césare Baronio (1538–1607), Galileo wrote in his own defense that "the intention of the Holy Ghost is to teach us how one goes to heaven, not how the heavens go." But distinguishing religion from science in this way obscured, at least initially, the far-reaching consequences of replacing the medieval view of the world as an organism open to divine interaction with physics' developing view of the world as a lifeless and autonomous clocklike mechanism closed to any "external" influence.

At the heart of this new worldview lay the idea of determinism, which has become a synonym for classical (i.e., Newtonian) physics signifies the impossibility of any genuine novelty in the world. As the French mathematician Pierre-Simon de Laplace (1749–1827) famously stated, "Given for one instant an intelligence which could comprehend all the forces by which nature is animated and the respective situation of the beings who compose it. . . , for [this intelligence] nothing would be uncertain and the future, as the past, would be present to its eyes" (Laplace, 1917, p. 4). Newtonian mechanism also reinforced the strategy of reductionism, by which an object's behavior is explained solely in terms of the behavior of its parts. Embracing both determinism and reductionism, Newtonian physicists and other scientists came to eschew explanations that appealed to purpose, or *telos.* Instead, they sought to provide explanations solely in terms of efficient causes. This mechanistic outlook continues to oppose religious perspectives that speak of the meaningfulness and purposefulness of the world.

In response to the rise of mechanistic physics, Western philosophers and theologians of the Enlightenment focused much of their effort on protecting human freedom. One of the first to deal with this issue was René Descartes (1596–1650), who divided reality into two realms: the material world of mechanical necessity *(res extensa)* and the mental world of human free willing *(res cogitans).* Immanuel Kant (1724–1804) subsequently advanced a more nuanced dualism, distinguishing between the determinism of the perceived world (the realm of *phenomena*) and the freedom of the world in and for itself (the realm of *noumena*). Following Descartes and Kant, many Protestant theologians abandoned the physical world and retreated into the "inner" world of the human spirit. Friedrich Schleiermacher (1768–1834) was one of the first to push this agenda, removing religion from the realm of knowledge and relocating it in the realm of feeling. By the end of the nineteenth century, Albrecht Ritschl (1822–1889) could write, "theology has to do, not with natural objects, but with states and movements of man's spiritual life." In its first interactions with modern physics, Christian thought had managed to protect human freedom from physical determinism only by severing human existence from its physical foundation.

Classical physics also posed a serious challenge to notions of God's ongoing activity in the world. In response to determinism, Christian thinkers developed three markedly different theories of divine action. According to the first, the universe does not have the causal powers within itself necessary to bring about its present configuration. Newton espoused an early version of this approach, claiming that the planets' orbits were inherently unstable and thus in need of occasional divine adjustment. Locating God's activity as Newton did in events allegedly lying beyond the ken of scientific explanation has been called the *God of the gaps* approach. Such explanations rely problematically on scientific ignorance and must retreat whenever science fills an explanatory gap. Others pursued a more compelling version of this approach, often called *interventionism,* in which God breaks the laws of nature when acting in a specific event. God, on this view, creates gaps in an otherwise deterministic world to make "room" for particular divine acts. Deists rejected this theory because they felt that the most honest and reasonable response to determinism was to relinquish the God who continues to act, in favor of a God who brings the world into existence and then desists. (Newton's account of inertial, or self-sustaining, motion helped to discredit the idea that the world depends upon God's ongoing activity for its continued existence.) Finally, nineteenth-century Protestant liberals eliminated from their theory of divine action all objectively special acts and miracles, speaking only of God's one great uniform act: the entire history of creation. On the liberal account, one might *perceive* God acting specially in some particular physical event, but this would be merely a matter of one's own subjective perception.

The three responses—interventionism, deism, and liberalism—differ sharply from one another, yet they brook a common theological constraint. Each accepts that a God who brings about change in the world must be treated on a par with any other object entering into human experience. Thus, all concede to classical physics that if the world is deterministic then there is no "room" within its structures for God to act. Deism and liberalism infer from this that God does not act specially at particular moments in history. Interventionism retains the idea of an active God, but it sees God acting by breaking the world's natural structures. The far-reaching consequences of this constraint cannot be overemphasized. Prior to the rise of physics, theologians had no difficulty harmonizing a God who acts with a world that manifests its own causal integrity. While few would accept a return to prescientific notions of divine action, the virtues and liabilities of the notion that objectively special divine acts are incompatible with physical determinism, or *theological incompatibilism,* have not been discussed extensively by contemporary theologians.

Recent developments in physics have led to a new (but still theologically incompatibilist) approach to divine action. On the one hand, this approach agrees with the liberal theological tradition that God must be understood to act with the grain of natural processes—after all, it is noted, God is the one who established these processes—though it rejects the liberals' purely subjective view of special divine action. On the other hand, it agrees with interventionism that God acts objectively at particular moments in the world, though it rejects the interventionist view that God thereby violates the laws of nature. This new *noninterventionist* strategy attempts to straddle the traditional divide by turning to developments in twentieth-century physics, many of which can be seen to undercut the determinism and reductionism of the classical paradigm.

The Twentieth-Century Revolution. As the nineteenth century drew to a close, physicists' work seemed nearly complete. Classical mechanics described the motion of physical masses under the influence of mechanical forces, electromagnetic theory described the interaction of electrical charges and currents, and thermodynamics described the phenomena of temperature and heat. The eminent Victorian physicist Lord Kelvin (1824–1907), who was instrumental in the development of thermodynamics, saw nothing new on the horizon for future generations of physicists to discover. He professed to see only a few inconsequential clouds obscuring the "beauty and clearness" of Newtonian physics. But in truth, behind these clouds lay deep puzzles regarding the nature of light and the behavior of atoms. Contrary to Kelvin's expectations, attempts to solve them ushered in the greatest revolution in physical science since the time of Newton. This revolution came in the form of two new theoretical paradigms, both of which seemed at odds with the worldview of classical physics: the theory of relativity developed by Albert Einstein (1879–1955) and the theory of atomic behavior called *quantum theory* developed by a host of scientists in the 1920s. New views of space, time, and causation prompted by these theories encouraged renewed theological reflection on the nature of God, the world, and humanity.

Newton had conceived of space as God's means of experiencing the world and of time as an absolute structure with an endless past and future, as well as a uniformly moving present. Einstein, in his special theory of relativity, reconceptualized space and time as a single reality, *spacetime*, and postulated that the speed of light, not space or time, was the true invariant of the universe. Accordingly, measurements of distance and time vary from different perspectives depending upon the different observers' relative motion. This understanding denies the existence of a universal "now" and raises questions about traditional notions of the relation between divine eternity and creaturely temporality. Additionally, the portrayal of time as a fourth dimension has led some to interpret Einstein's theory as hostile to the very idea of temporal flow. According to proponents of the *block universe* interpretation, our spacetime universe exists timelessly as a four-dimensional whole, challenging the reality of human freedom and our general sense of temporal becoming.

After publishing his special theory of relativity, Einstein turned to the problem of developing a new theory of gravity (the general theory of relativity) based on his account of spacetime. His new theory treated gravity geometrically as the curvature of spacetime rather than in Newtonian terms as a force acting on a mass. According to Einstein, matter curves spacetime, and spacetime tells matter how to move. It is within this conceptual framework that physicists developed the cosmological theory of the origin, structure, and development of the universe known as the Big Bang theory. Extrapolating backwards from the present expansion of the universe, physicists arrived at the notion of a primordial explosion, or *big bang*. This notion led Pope Pius XII to suggest in 1951 that physics had finally confirmed the Christian doctrine of creation. Much discussion has ensued as to whether such connections can be made and whether the concept of *creation* entails an absolute beginning or only the more general notion of ontological dependence. Recent scientific proposals such as *eternal inflation* and *quantum cosmology* suggest that the beginning of our universe may have been only one event in a much longer series. Consequently, the Big Bang now looks less and less like an absolute beginning.

Contemporary cosmology has also reinvigorated the design argument for the existence of God. Although earlier forms of this argument focused on the intricacy and beauty of living organisms, Darwin's case against design—it was only "apparent"—shifted the debate to the level of physics. According to the so-called anthropic principle argument, the structure and processes of the universe are finely tuned for the requirements of our own existence. In its strongest form, this argument leads to the existence of a divine tuner. In its weaker form, however, our existence is seen merely as the result of a process of cosmic Darwinism: we can only live in a particular domain of the universe where its structures and processes are hospitable to life. This weaker version avoids the theistic conclusion, but much disagreement remains as to whether or not it amounts to a scientific explanation. The design argument runs into further difficulties with the far future of the universe, which appears doomed either to endless expansion and cooling, the *freeze* scenario, or to eventual recollapse and implosion, the *fry* scenario. Neither offers much comfort for an eschatological perspective that clings to the notion of future fulfillment. It is at least conceivable that life, suitably transformed, could extend itself far into the future, though this kind of pseudo-immortalization does not satisfy the Christian vision of a creation ultimately assumed into the divine life.

While Einstein was rewriting Newton's account of space and time, as well as reshaping our understanding of the universe at the largest scales, another even more radical revolution was taking place at the very smallest scales. In 1900 the physicist Max Planck (1858–1947) turned his attention to one of the most puzzling of the remaining "clouds," a problem having to do with the emission and absorption of electromagnetic radiation by atoms. He solved this problem theoretically by introducing the curious notion that energy comes only in discrete units, called *quanta,* not in continuously varying amounts as classical physicists had supposed. This and other breakthroughs led physicists such as Niels Bohr (1885–1962), Werner Heisenberg (1901–1976), Erwin Schrödinger (1887–1961), and Paul Dirac (1902–1984) to develop quantum theory, which achieved great successes in describing the behavior of atoms and their components. These successes, however, came at the expense of classical intuitions regarding basic physical concepts such as causality, determinism, separability, and the wave-particle distinction. At the quantum level, objects can change their state over time without any sufficient mechanical cause, evolve in a purely random or indeterministic manner, remain intimately connected to one other over large distances, and behave like waves in one setting but like particles in another. Theologians have responded to the quantum perspective on the physical world in a variety of ways. Some have connected Bohr's notion of *complementarity*, the idea that mutually incompatible descriptions like *wave* and *particle* are necessary for a complete description of the same reality, to issues such the relation between religion and science. Others have appealed to quantum indeterminism to resolve the question of divine action. According to their arguments, an indeterministic ontology makes it possible to conceive of God (and perhaps human beings as well, though by different means) as acting directly in the physical world without breaking physical laws by determining otherwise underdetermined quantum events. Still others are exploring quantum nonseparability or entanglement, which suggests that creation is a place not only of immense times and distances but also of deep and subtle connections.

The remarkable subtlety of physical processes is additionally highlighted by chaos theory, a third significant theoretical development within twentieth-century physics. Strictly speaking, chaos theory fits within the Newtonian deterministic paradigm. However, it reveals how even processes described by deterministic mathematical laws, such as weather patterns, can develop in seemingly random and unpredictable ways. Because the theory is deterministic, it does not appear to offer any straightforward opportunities for those pursuing a noninterventionist account of divine or human action. Still, some have argued that, despite being presently deterministic, the theory points to a genuine form of openness in nature; this openness, they aver, will eventually be reflected in a future version of the theory. If this were to happen, chaos theory would provide yet another example of physics moving beyond its Newtonian origins.

Physicists are currently struggling to unite the various theoretical developments surveyed here under one conceptual framework, but at present the theory of relativity, quantum theory, and chaos theory each provide quite distinct lenses onto the world's physical structures and processes. Although both relativity theory and chaos theory transform various aspects of Newton's account of space, time, and causation, they also essentially sustain the determinism of the classical tradition. Quantum theory, on the other hand, at least according to the most widely held interpretation, dramatically overturns this tradition. Physics is a scientific discipline presently at odds with itself, presenting us with remarkable but fractured insights into the nature of the physical world. The resolution of this tension will no doubt lead to further opportunities for conversation with religious perspectives. The human quest for meaning and transcendence cannot be reduced to physical explanation, but it can be enriched by the deeper understanding of the world's natural processes that physics provides.

See Also Chaos Theory; Cosmology, article on Scientific Cosmologies.

Bibliography

General

Introductory theological texts include a collection edited by Robert J. Russell, William R. Stoeger, S.J., and George V. Coyne, S.J., *Physics, Philosophy, and Theology: A Common Quest for Understanding* (Vatican City, 1988), and Mark W. Worthing's *God, Creation, and Contemporary Physics* (Minneapolis, 1996). Twentieth-century developments in physics are surveyed in Paul C. Davies's *God and the New Physics* (New York, 1983), and in his *The Mind of God: The Scientific Basis for a Rational World* (New York, 1992). For a more detailed analysis of epistemological issues, see Philip Clayton's *Explanation from Physics to Theology: An Essay in Rationality and Religion* (New Haven, Conn., 1989) and Roy D. Morrison's *Science, Theology, and the Transcendental Horizon: Einstein, Kant, and Tillich* (Atlanta, 1994), as well as a collection of essays edited by Jan Hilgevoord, *Physics and Our View of the World* (Cambridge, U.K., 1994). Apologetic concerns dominate in Stephen M. Barr's *Modern Physics and Ancient Faith* (Notre Dame, Ind., 2003) and Victor J. Stenger's *Has Science Found God? The Latest Results in the Search for Purpose in the Universe* (Amherst, N.Y., 2003). In one of the first popular works to explore the religious implications of modern physics, *The Tao of Physics: An Exploration of the Parallels between Modern Physics and Eastern Mysticism,* 3d ed. (Berkeley, Calif., 1975), Fritjof Capra focuses on connections to the Eastern traditions. Essays written from a wide variety of perspectives are contained in a collection edited by Henry Margenau and Roy A. Varghese, *Cosmos, Bios, Theos: Scientists Reflect on Science, God, and the Origins of the Universe, Life, and Homo Sapiens* (La Salle, Ill., 1992), and in another edited by Clifford N. Matthews and Roy A. Varghese, *Cosmic Beginnings and Human Ends: Where Science and Religion Meet* (Chicago and La Salle, Ill., 1995). Other general works include Arthur Peacocke's *Theology for a Scientific Age: Being and Becoming: Natural, Divine, and Human* (Minneapolis, 1993), John C. Polkinghorne's *The Faith of a Physicist: Reflections of a Bottom-up Thinker* (Minneapolis, 1996), Michael Heller's *The New Physics and a New Theology* (Vatican City, 1996), Guy Consolmagno's *The Way to the Dwelling of Light: How Physics Illuminates Creation* (Vatican City, 1998), Peter Hodgson's *Theology and the New Physics* (Oxford, 1998), and Andreas Benk's *Moderne Physik und Theologie: Voraussetzungen und Perspektiven eines Dialogs* (Mainz, Germany, 2000). See also Pierre-Simon de Laplace, *A Philosophical Essay on Probabilities, 2d* ed., translated from the 6th French edition by Frederick Wilson Truscott and Frederick Lincoln Emory (New York, 1917).

Historical

Studies of religious and philosophical developments accompanying the rise of modern physics include Edwin A. Burtt's *The Metaphysical Foundations of Modern Physical Science: A Historical and Critical Essay,* rev. ed. (Atlantic Highlands, N.J., 1952); Amos Funkenstein's *Theology and the Scientific Imagination: From the Middle Ages to the Seventeenth Century* (Princeton, N.J., 1986); Michael J. Buckley's *At the Origins of Modern Atheism* (New Haven, Conn., 1987); and John

Hedley Brooke's *Science and Religion: Some Historical Perspectives* (Cambridge, UK, 1991). Carolyn Merchant examines the social and ecological impact of mechanistic thinking in *The Death of Nature: Women, Ecology, and the Scientific Revolution* (San Francisco, 1980), and Margaret Wertheim compares the historical marginalization of women in religious institutions to their exclusion from the physics academy in *Pythagoras' Trousers: God, Physics, and the Gender Wars* (New York, 1995). N. Max Wildiers examines the impact of modern science on religious cosmology in *The Theologian and His Universe: Theology and Cosmology from the Middle Ages to the Present* (New York, 1982). The preservation and expansion of early science in Islamic society is discussed in Muzaffar Iqbal's *Islam and Science* (Burlington, Vt., 2002). Other works deal with particular concepts or historical figures: Jerome Langford discusses recent scholarship on Galileo in *Galileo, Science, and the Church,* 3d ed. (Notre Dame, Ind., 1998); Wolfhart Pannenberg treats the religious significance of the concept of *inertia* in *Toward a Theology of Nature: Essays on Science and Faith,* edited by Ted Peters (Louisville, Ky., 1993); J. L. Heilbron recounts the use of churches for astronomical observation in *The Sun in the Church: Cathedrals as Solar Observatories* (Cambridge, Mass., 1999); Max Jammer examines Einstein's views in *Einstein and Religion: Physics and Theology* (Princeton, N.J., 1999); and Richard Cross reconstructs one medieval perspective in *The Physics of Duns Scotus: The Scientific Context of a Theological Vision* (Oxford, UK, 1998).

Special Relativity and Temporality

Paul Davies introduces the scientific and philosophical issues in *About Time: Einstein's Unfinished Revolution* (New York, 1996). Treatments of the religious implications include Lawrence W. Fagg's *The Becoming of Time: Integrating Physical and Religious Time* (Atlanta, 1995), Jürgen Heinze's *"Gott im Herzen der Materie": Die Struktur der Zeit als Grundlage christlicher Rede von Gott im Kontext der modernen Physik* (Bonn, Germany, 1996), and William Lane Craig's *Time and Eternity: Exploring God's Relationship to Time* (Wheaton, Ill., 2001). The relation between eternity and temporality is the topic of several of the essays in a collection edited by Robert J. Russell, Nancey C. Murphy, and Chris J. Isham, *Quantum Cosmology and the Laws of Nature: Scientific Perspectives on Divine Action,* 2d ed. (Vatican City and Berkeley, Calif., 1996).

General Relativity and Cosmology

Popular scientific introductions include Stephen W. Hawking's *A Brief History of Time: From the Big Bang to Black Holes* (New York, 1988) and Robert Jastrow's *God and the Astronomers,* 2d ed. (New York, 2000). Discussions of the religious implications can be found in Stanley L. Jaki's *God and the Cosmologists* (Edinburgh, 1989); in a collection edited by Ted Peters, *Cosmos as Creation: Theology and Science in Consonance* (Nashville, 1989); in another edited by Robert J. Russell, Nancey C. Murphy, and Chris J. Isham, *Quantum Cosmology and the Laws of Nature: Scientific Perspectives on Divine Action,* 2d ed. (Vatican City and Berkeley, Calif., 1996); and in Willem B. Drees's *Beyond the Big Bang: Quantum Cosmologies and God* (La Salle, Ill., 1990), Owen Gingerich's *Space, Time, and Beyond: The Place of God in the Cosmos* (Valparaiso, Ind., 1993), and Jeffrey G. Sobosan's *Romancing the Universe: Theology, Science, and Cosmology* (Grand Rapids, Mich., 1999). The anthropic principle is discussed in John D. Barrow and Frank J. Tipler's *The Anthropic Cosmological Principle* (Oxford, 1985) and John Leslie's *Universes* (London, 1989); its theological implications are further explored in Nancey C. Murphy and George F. R. Ellis's *On the Moral Nature of the Universe: Theology, Cosmology, and Ethics,* (Minneapolis, 1996). Cosmological arguments for and against the existence of God are presented in William Lane Craig and Quentin Smith's *Theism, Atheism, and Big Bang Cosmology* (New York, 1993). Attempts to harmonize scientific and biblical accounts of creation can be found in Hugh Ross's *Beyond the Cosmos: The Extra-Dimensionality of God,* 2d ed. (Colorado Springs, Colo., 1999), Gerald L. Schroeder's *Genesis and the Big Bang: The Discovery of Harmony between Modern Science and the Bible* (New York, 1990), and Howard Van Till's *The Fourth Day: What the Bible and the Heavens Are Telling Us about Creation* (Grand Rapids, Mich., 1986). Scientific and theological considerations are enlisted to support a philosophical cosmology in Arthur Gibson's *God and the Universe* (New York, 2000) and Nancy Howell's *A Feminist Cosmology: Ecology, Solidarity, and Metaphysics* (Amherst, N.Y., 2000). The far future of the universe is the topic of a collection edited by John C. Polkinghorne and Michael Welker, *The End of the World and the Ends of God: Science and Theology on Eschatology* (Harrisburg, Pa., 2000); Arnold Benz's *The Future of the Universe: Change, Chaos, God?* (New York, 2000); and a volume edited by George F. R. Ellis, *The Far-Future Universe: Eschatology from a Cosmic Perspective* (Philadelphia, 2002). The possibilities for life continuing into the distant future are explored in Freeman J. Dyson's *Infinite in All Directions* (New York, 1988) and Frank J. Tipler's *The Physics of Immortality: Modern Cosmology, God, and the Resurrection of the Dead* (New York, 1994).

Quantum Theory

Popular scientific introductions include Nick Herbert's *Quantum Reality: Beyond the New Physics* (Garden City, N.Y., 1985) and John Polkinghorne's *Quantum Theory: A Very Short Introduction* (Oxford, 2002). Early theological reflections on quantum theory include Karl Heim's *The Transformation of the World* (London, 1953) and William G. Pollard's *Chaos and Providence* (London, 1958). The noninterventionist approach to divine action is assessed in a book edited by Robert J. Russell, Philip Clayton, Kirk Wegter-McNelly, and John Polkinghorne, *Quantum Mechanics: Scientific Perspectives on Divine Action* (Vatican City and Berkeley, Calif., 2001); see also earlier volumes in the VO/CTNS series. Metaphysical perspectives are constructed in David Bohm's *Wholeness and the Implicate Order* (London, 1980) and John A. Jungerman's *World in Process: Creativity and Interconnection in the New Physics* (Albany, N.Y., 2000). An Islamic perspective is developed in Bint al-Shati's *The Subatomic World in the Qur'an* (Norwich, UK, 1980). A Buddhist perspective is presented in Matthieu Ricard and Trinh Xuan Thuan's *The Quantum and the Lotus: A Journey to the Frontiers Where Science and Buddhism Meet* (New York, 2001). John Losee discusses methodological parallels in *Religious Language and Complementarity* (Lanham, Md., 1992).

Chaos Theory

A popular scientific introduction is James Gleick's *Chaos: Making a New Science* (New York, 1988). John Polkinghorne argues for the relevance of chaos theory to divine action in, for example, *Reason and Reality: The Relationship between Science and Theology* (London, 1991). Its relevance is examined critically in a book edited by Robert J. Russell, Nancey C. Murphy, and Arthur Peacocke, *Chaos and Complexity: Scientific Perspectives on Divine Action* (Vatican City and Berkeley, Calif., 1995).

Spirituality

Numerous works have been written from a variety of religious perspectives. Some of the more prominent include Daniel Liderbach's *The Numinous Universe* (New York, 1989); B. Alan Wallace's *Choosing Reality: A Contemplative View of Physics and the Mind* (Boston, 1989); John L. Hitchcock's *The Web of the Universe: Jung, the "New Physics," and Human Spirituality* (New York, 1991); Kevin O'Shea's *Person in Cosmos: Metaphors of Meaning from Physics, Philosophy, and Theology* (Bristol, Ind., 1995); Brian Hines's *God's Whisper, Creation's Thunder: Echoes of Ultimate Reality in the New Physics* (Brattleboro, Vt., 1996); Daniel C. Matt's *God and the Big Bang: Discovering Harmony between Science and Spirituality* (Woodstock, Vt., 1996); Diarmuid O'Murchu's *Quantum Theology: Spiritual Implications of the New Physics* (New York, 1997); Lothar Schäfer's *In Search of Divine Reality: Science as a Source of Inspiration* (Fayetteville, Ark., 1997); David Toolan's *At Home in the Cosmos* (Maryknoll, N.Y., 2001); and Ken Wilber's *Quantum Questions: Mystical Writings of the World's Great Physicists,* rev. ed. (Boston, 2001).

KIRK WEGTER-MCNELLY (2005)

PICO DELLA MIRANDOLA, GIOVANNI (1463–1494), philosopher of the Italian Renaissance, was the youngest son of Francesco Pico, count of Mirandola and Concordia, a small feudal territory just west of Ferrara. He was named papal protonotary at the age of ten and was sent to study canon law at Bologna in 1477. Two years later he began the study of philosophy at Ferrara, and from 1480 to 1482 he studied at Padua, one of the main centers of Aristotelianism. He visited Paris, where he encountered Scholastic theology, returned to Florence, and then moved to Perugia, where he studied Hebrew and Arabic with several Jewish teachers. In Perugia, Pico developed an interest in Ibn Rushd (Averroës) and the mystical Jewish Qabbalah. In his late twenties, after a carefree youth, Pico's life took a more serious turn. He gave up his share of his patrimony and planned to give away his personal property in order to take up the life of a poor preacher. During his final years Pico came under the influence of the Dominican friar Savonarola. He died of a fever in Florence on November 17, 1494, the very day on which Charles VIII of France made his entry into Florence, after the expulsion of its ruler, Piero de' Medici.

A brilliant young philosopher, Pico is best known as the author of *Oration on the Dignity of Man,* which is considered to be the manifesto of Renaissance humanism. "I have read in Arabian books," Pico wrote, "that nothing in the world can be found that is more worthy of admiration than man." To support this humanistic assertion of the first part of the *Oration* he cites a broad array of ancient sources—the mystical writings ascribed to Hermes Trismegistos, various Persian writers, David, Moses, Plato, Pythagoras, Enoch, the qabbalists, Muhammad, Zarathushtra, the apostle Paul, and many others. Unlike Marsilio Ficino, his friend and mentor at the Platonic academy in Florence, Pico did not give humans a fixed place in the great chain of being; he described humanity as the object of special creation and the focal point of the world with no fixed place, outline, or task, but free to make its own choices and to seek what is heavenly and above the world, free to become a veritable angel. The *Oration* served as the rhetorical introduction to his *Conclusiones* (1486), nine hundred "theses" providing a summation of all learning, which Pico offered for public disputation. Upon publication in Rome, seven of the theses were found by a commission of Innocent VIII to be heretical and six of them dubious. Pico's apologia for them was not accepted, but Alexander VI subsequently vindicated his orthodoxy.

Pico's mature philosophical writings include the *Heptaplus* (1489), a sevenfold interpretation of *Genesis* 1:1–27; *Of Being and Unity* (1491), on the harmony of Plato and Aristotle; and a long treatise attacking astrology as demeaning to human liberty and dignity. He allowed for sidereal influence only because of heat and light, but not because of any occult power of the stars. His thought was notable for its synthesis of Aristotelianism and Platonism, its combination of scholastic and humanist elements, and for the fascination with Qabbalah that it reflects.

BIBLIOGRAPHY

Although Pico's *Opera* (Basel, 1572) is not readily accessible, Eugenio Garin has published editions of various texts: *De hominis dignitate, Heptaplus, De ente et uno, e Scritti vari* (Florence, 1942) and the *Disputationes adversus astrologiam divinatricem,* 2 vols. (Florence, 1946–1952). For a translation of the *Oration,* see *The Renaissance Philosophy of Man,* edited by Ernst Cassirer et al., translated by Josephine L. Burroughs (Chicago, 1948), pp. 223–254. For Pico's life and thought, see Eugenio Garin's *Giovanni Pico della Mirandola* (Florence, 1937) and *La cultura filosofica del Rinascimento italiano* (Florence, 1961); Eugenio Anagnine's *Giovanni Pico della Mirandola* (Bari, 1937); and Paul O. Kristeller's *Eight Philosophers of the Italian Renaissance* (Stanford, Calif., 1964), pp. 54–71, the best brief treatment in English.

LEWIS W. SPITZ (1987)

PIETISM. Pietism has been and remains an identifiable religious orientation within the churches of the Reformation. As the name indicates, it emphasizes the life of personal piety according to the model it finds in the primitive Christian community. By doing so it has hoped to complete the Reformation, which, in the judgment of many of its adherents, has never become a movement to reform the religious life of individuals. The roots of Pietism are found, on the one hand, in the mystical spirituality of an earlier day and, on the other, in the writings of Martin Luther and John Calvin, as well as other reformers such as Caspar Schwenckfeld and the prominent Anabaptists.

It is difficult to fix precisely the boundaries of Pietism, either in terms of chronology or distribution. While scholars have associated Pietism largely with Lutheranism, it has been customary to date its beginning from the publication of Philipp Jakob Spener's *Pia desideria* in 1675, two years after which his followers were referred to as "Pietists." The present tendency, growing out of a great deal of recent research, is to expand the term so as to include what is now widely perceived as the same development within other communions, notably the Reformed, as well as Protestants who questioned the need for any kind of church affiliation because they found a lack of religious devotion and ethical urgency within the churches of the day. Under the circumstances, the classical phase of the Pietist movement should now be loosely regarded as a Protestant phenomenon of the seventeenth and early eighteenth centuries. It is bounded, on the one hand, by the age of post-Reformation orthodoxy, to which it reacted both negatively and positively, and, on the other, by the Enlightenment, which rejected some of its insights and incorporated others. In the sense of a prominent undercurrent within the religious self-understanding of large segments of Protestantism, Pietism as a historical entity has never ceased to exist.

The basic characteristics of the movement can be most easily isolated with reference to its classical phase. Pietists of the day believed that religiousness within the Christian tradition, if it is to be meaningful, must involve the complete religious renewal of the individual believer. The experience of such a renewal need not follow any prescribed pattern, but it must consist in a conscious change of humanity's relationship to God so as to bring certainty concerning divine forgiveness, acceptance, and continued concern. The fruit of such a renewal must become visible in the form of "piety," that is, a life expressive of love for God and humanity and built on a vivid sense of the reality of God's presence in all situations of life. Pietists believed that those in whom this religious perspective becomes actualized constitute an inclusive fellowship, namely the *koinōnia,* that was so profoundly cherished by the primitive Christian community. This fellowship was perceived to transcend every barrier of church affiliation, race, class, and nationality—even that of time. Thus Pietists characteristically addressed one another as "brother" or "sister," terms symbolic of a common experience of profound spiritual unity. This sense of religious solidarity was enhanced by an awareness of the fact that they were called upon to live in a society that chose to adhere to a value system different from their own, though it was widely supported by the major Christian communions. Hence they often assembled in conventicles of like-minded people within local parishes. Furthermore, Pietism during its classical period centered its concept of religious authority in a biblicism set originally against the formidable but lifeless theological systems of Protestant orthodoxy. Later it was opposed to the Enlightenment attempt to reduce Christian commitment to the acceptance of a few propositions held to be rationally demonstrable. In tension between these poles, Pietists strove to restore to Protestantism a theology based on a commonsense, untortured, more-or-less literal, and basically devotional interpretation of the Bible. Lastly, Pietists hoped to reform society through the efforts of renewed individuals, thus stemming the moral decay that, in their judgment, afflicted both the churches and the body politic.

EARLY PIETISM. The rise of Pietism is best discussed with reference to five early groupings.

1. Pietism's manifestation within the Reformed territories of the Low Countries is sometimes still referred to as "Precisianism," though it may be best to drop that designation because of the difficulty of distinguishing it conceptually from Pietism as it is here understood. Pietism within Dutch Reformed churches had certain natural affinities with Puritanism, which historically comes from the same source. It is attached to such illustrious names as Willem Teellinck (1579–1629), who may be regarded as its father; William Ames, or Amesius, as he called himself (1576–1633), who, although born and educated in England, chose to teach at the University of Franeker; and Jodocus van Lodensteyn (1620–1677). Within German Reformed territories its chief theological spokesman became Friedrich Adolph Lampe (1683–1729).

2. The branch of early Pietism that has received the greatest attention is the Spener-Halle type. It was strictly a Lutheran phenomenon, profoundly indebted to Johann Arndt (1555–1621) and counting among its outstanding representatives Philipp Jakob Spener (1635–1705) and August Hermann Francke (1663–1727). Although its concern encompassed men and women in all walks of life, it addressed itself especially to the nobility.

3. Swabian Pietism, on the other hand, exhibited a somewhat different ecclesiastical, as well as social, profile. Its chief spokesman, Johann Albrecht Bengel (1687–1752), was a convinced Lutheran and partially indebted to Spener. Yet he and his followers steered the Pietist development so as to make it dominantly a movement of the people. For that reason Württemberg witnessed the eventual rise of various Pietist fellowships, made up of peasants and artisans, that often resonated to the mysticism of Jakob Boehme and hence were only loosely associated with Lutheranism. A typical fellowship was the Hahnische Gemeinschaft, named after its founder, Johann Michael Hahn (1758–1819).

4. A fourth branch of early Pietism arose within Lutheranism but followed the theological leadership of Count Nikolaus Ludwig von Zinzendorf und Pottendorf (1700–1760). This strain ultimately became the Renewed Moravian Church.

5. Not to be overlooked is the radical wing of Pietists, which was often very critical of the major communions and their close ties to the state. Especially prominent among these critics were the young Gottfried Arnold (1666–1714) and Johann Konrad Dippel (1673–1734), while the saintly Ernst Christoph Hochmann von Hochenau (1670–1721) and Gerhard Tersteegen (1697–1769) were among the radical wing's more irenical representatives.

The eighteenth century. During the second part of the eighteenth century the face of Pietism was considerably altered by the spirit of the times. In its reaction against the Enlightenment philosophy of Christian Wolff (1679–1754), who greatly influenced continental Protestantism, Pietism was forced to align itself theologically with Protestant orthodoxy, its former antagonist, while espousing at the same time the ethical sensitivity of the Enlightenment. Interacting also with the literary movement usually referred to as Sturm und Drang, which tried to legitimize the inner human experience, the freedom of the individual vis-à-vis the accepted norms of the day, and especially the place of feeling, it tended to become sentimentalized and suspicious of rational conclusions.

In one form or another Pietism eventually reached both Switzerland and Scandinavia. By various emissaries, among them Henry Melchior Muhlenberg (1711–1787), Theodor J. Frelinghuysen (1691–1748), Michael Schlatter (1718–1790), Philip W. Otterbein (1726–1813), Peter Becker (1687–1758), and Zinzendorf, it was brought to the American colonies. Its Moravian phase strongly influenced the Wesley brothers and hence the Methodist movement in America. Thus Pietism, along with Puritanism, must now be considered one of the major religious traditions that shaped American Protestantism.

HERITAGE OF PIETISM IN THE PROTESTANT TRADITION.

The influence of Pietism on world Protestantism has been pervasive and far-reaching. With respect to the ministry, it stressed the religious and ethical qualifications of the minister above his ecclesiastical status. In the area of Protestant worship, it greatly expanded Protestant hymnody, deemphasized ritual, and tended to make the sermon central. It helped to make religious commitment the major aim of Protestant worship. Its advocacy of the devotional reading of the Bible made the latter a book of the people and produced a large corpus of edificatory literature. It was instrumental in reorienting theological education by enthroning the concept of biblical theology and by advocating the religious formation of the whole person, which inevitably resulted in the establishment of theological seminaries for prospective clergy. Its deep concern for the plight of the poor and the sick made for a massive effort to establish homes and schools that would meet their needs, and it projected the hope of a better world brought about through the involvement of concerned Christians. Its vision of a humanity in need of the gospel of Christ made for the initiation and rapid expansion of foreign and domestic missionary enterprises. Its contribution to the rise of the ecumenical ideal is clear, as is its impact on the development of modern theology, notably through the work of Friedrich Schleiermacher and his disciples. Not to be forgotten is the fact that the chief representatives of the intellectual movement known as German Idealism grew up in a Pietist environment. Its genius is discernible also in a variety of later religious movements, such as American evangelicalism.

SEE ALSO Devotion; Francke, August Hermann; Schleiermacher, Friedrich; Spener, Philipp Jakob; Wesley Brothers; Zinzendorf, Nikolaus.

BIBLIOGRAPHY

The first extensive historical study of Pietism was Albrecht Ritschl's *Geschichte des Pietismus,* 3 vols. (Bonn, 1880–1886). Although it was an unfriendly, strongly biased treatment, it brought into focus the whole Pietist movement in both the Lutheran and Reformed communions as well as among radicals. This was followed by Paul Grünberg's thorough and scholarly work, *Philipp Jakob Spener,* 3 vols. (Göttingen, 1893–1906). Subsequently there were many local histories, but only sporadic attempts to examine the general phenomenon of Pietism. There was a growing tendency to disregard Ritschl's broad concept and to limit the study to Lutheranism, specifically to Philipp Jakob Spener and August Hermann Francke, Spener's well-known successor at Halle.

After decades of neglect, Erich Beyreuther concentrated some of his prodigious energies upon the subject, notably upon Francke and Zinzendorf. His first volume in this effort was *August Hermann Francke, 1663–1727* (Marburg, 1956). A new era of Pietism study commenced when Martin Schmidt, the outstanding Pietism scholar of the day, published the first of a series of works in the field, *Das Zeitalter des Pietismus* (Bremen, 1965), edited by Wilhelm Jannasch. The present very intense interest in Pietism study was given tremendous impetus when, under the leadership of Martin Schmidt and the Francke scholar Erhard Peschke, the Kommission zur Erforschung des Pietismus was founded in Germany in 1965. On the basis of its findings the concept of Pietism was once again broadened, and under its auspices a series of volumes was published under the title "Arbeiten zur Geschichte des Pietismus" (Bielefeld, 1967–), edited by Kurt Aland, Erhard Peschke, and Martin Schmidt. In 1972, it brought out the first volume, *Abteilung 3: August Hermann Francke,* of *Texte zur Geschichte des Pietismus* (Berlin, 1972), and later the first yearbook, titled *Pietismus und Neuzeit* (Bielefeld, 1974).

During the same period I attempted to generate interest in the study of Pietism in the English-speaking world through *Rise of Evangelical Pietism* (Leiden, 1965), *German Pietism during the Eighteenth Century* (Leiden, 1973), and *Continental Pietism and Early American Christianity* (Grand Rapids, Mich., 1976). In the meantime Theodore G. Tappert had translated into English and edited Spener's *Piadesideria* (Philadelphia, 1964), based on Kurt Aland's treatment of the same work. James Tanis followed with *Dutch Calvinistic Pietism in the Middle Colonies* (The Hague, 1967); J. Steven O'Malley with *Pilgrimage of Faith: The Legacy of the Otterbeins* (Metuchen, N. J., 1973); Dale W. Brown with *Understanding Pietism* (Grand Rapids, Mich., 1978), which is limited largely to an exposition of the views of Spener and Francke; and Gary R.

Stattler with *God's Glory, Neighbor's Good: A Brief Introduction to the Life and Writings of August Hermann Francke* (Chicago, 1982).

F. Ernest Stoeffler (1987)

PIGS. The pig is an animal at once unclean and sacred. Dear to demons, it is used as bait to divert them from tormenting humans, but at the same time it has particular associations with sacrifices of expiation and purification. The pig is strikingly chthonic in nature, for it is usually offered to the divinities and powers of the underworld. When pigs are so bred as to grow tusks that are curved or crescent in shape, they assume the lunar symbolism of the renewal of life or of rebirth after death. Pigs are sometimes believed to be the transformations of certain divine beings.

In ancient Mesopotamia the pig was domesticated in very early times, but its use in the temple cult was extremely rare. As an Assyrian fable puts it, "The pig is not acceptable in the temples, and it is an abomination to the gods." However, it played a very important role in healing rituals and the exorcism of demons. One healing ritual prescribed the immolation of a piglet: The bed of a sick person is rubbed with its blood, the beast is dismembered, and its limbs are applied to the limbs of the sick person. In this way, the piglet substitutes for the sick person. Pigs were especially employed against the demoness Lamashtu, the enemy of pregnant women, young mothers, and their babies. In the rite of exorcism a piglet was immolated and its heart placed at the mouth of a figure of Lamashtu. In Egypt, the pig appeared most notably in connection with the myths and rituals of Seth, the god who killed his brother Osiris and who represented the forces of evil. According to the *Book of Going Forth by Day* (chap. 112), Seth changed himself into a black pig during his fight with Horus, the son of Osiris. Whenever a pig was sacrificed to Horus and its related divinities, it symbolized the forces of evil.

Pigs were sacrificed in ancient Greece for the purification of the sacred field, the sanctuary, and the house of the priestess; they were sacrificed partly because of their association with dirt, with which evil spirits were often equated, and partly because of their association with fertility. Especially noteworthy is the use of pigs in the festivals connected with the goddess Demeter and her daughter Persephone. In the Eleusinian mysteries, for example, each initiate had to sacrifice a piglet for the specific purpose of purifying himself. Because the piglet was as symbolic of the celebration as were the torch and the *kernos* (the sacred vessel used in the Eleusinian cult), in a number of works of art it is represented in the arms of the initiates. Small pigs played a part also in the Thesmophoria, the annual fertility festival honoring Demeter and Persephone. Together with wheat cakes in the shape of serpents and human beings, pigs were thrown, probably alive, into underground chambers (*megara*), where they were left to rot for a year, while the bones from the year before were brought up aboveground and placed upon an altar.

In the cult of Attis and Adonis as well as in the festivals of Demeter, each worshiper sacrificed a pig as an individual offering. According to mythic tradition, Attis was gored by a wild boar, and likewise Adonis was killed by a wild boar while out hunting. In commemoration of these tragic events boars were sacrificed in the Levant in the domestic rite of mourning, in which the sacrificer acted as if he had been deprived of his own life. The boar sacrifice was a vicarious offering for the life of the worshiper.

For the Jews, the pig is an unclean animal and its flesh may not be eaten nor its carcass touched (see *Lv.* 11:7, *Dt.* 14:8). In ancient times, Jews did not hesitate to risk their lives for their devotion to the Torah in this regard (e.g., *2 Mc.* 6:18–31); in the middle of the second century BCE, they stood against the Seleucid king Antiochus IV when he defiled the Temple of Jerusalem by dedicating it to Olympian Zeus, immolating pigs and other unclean animals and offering them in sacrifice. His religious policy was dictated by his concern to unify the beliefs and practices of his empire (*1 Mc.* 1:41–42), and the cult of Zeus seemed to him an appropriate focus for the religious allegiance of all his subjects. In order to break down the resistance, the king directly attacked the things that expressed Jewish faith: the Torah and its prescriptions, circumcision, the Sabbath, the ritual of sacrifices, and finally the prohibition against immolating and eating pigs.

The dietary prohibition of the Torah is pre-Israelite in origin, for abstinence from the meat of the pig was a widespread, religiously motivated custom that is well attested among the Phoenicians, the Cypriots, the Syrians, the Arabs, and in fact among all Semitic peoples with the exception of the Babylonians. Although its religious origins have sunk into oblivion, the custom has been preserved: Jews and Muslims of today abstain from eating pork in accordance with its strict prohibition by the Torah and the Qurʾān.

In the Hindu tradition, the boar appears again as an avatar of the god Viṣṇu. When a demon, Hiraṇyākṣa, cast the earth into the depths of the cosmic ocean, Viṣṇu assumed the form of an enormous boar, killed the demon, and retrieved the earth with his tusk. This mythic scenario probably developed through a primitive non-Aryan cult of the sacred pig.

The pig continues to play a highly significant role in the myths and rituals of Southeast Asia and Melanesia. Among the Ngaju of South Borneo, when cosmic order has been destroyed by violation of the divine commandments, by incest, for example, the guilty parties must slaughter a pig as a vicarious sacrifice. The entire village community in which they live (the people, houses, fields, animals, plants, and so on) is smeared with the blood of the pig, and then a "tree of life" is erected at the center of the village square before cosmic order is restored. According to the aborigines of the Melanesian island Malekula, the journey to the land of the dead starts with the offering of a pig to the female divinity who guards the cavernous entrance to the otherworld. The pig can be no ordinary one; it must have been raised by the sacrificer's own hands and ritually consecrated time and again. Especially important is the shape of its tusks: They should be curved or crescent, symbolizing the waxing and waning moon. While the pig's black body, consumed by the divinity, corresponds to the new, or "black," invisible moon, its crescent-shaped tusks symbolize the continuance of life after death, rebirth, or resurrection. The killing of pigs is understood by the Ceramese in New Guinea as a reenactment of their ancestors' murder of the maiden divinity Hainuwele, which occurred at the mythical time of beginning. Hainuwele was killed, but her dismembered body was miraculously transformed into tuberous plants (such as coconuts, bananas, and yams) and into pigs, neither of which had previously existed. Pigs are thus Hainuwele in disguise.

Bibliography

The best single study of the pig in the ancient Near East is Roland de Vaux's "Les sacrifices de porcs en Palestine et dans l'ancien Orient," in *Von Ugarit nach Qumran,* 2d ed., edited by W. F. Albright et al. (Berlin, 1961), pp. 250–265, which is now translated by Damian McHugh in de Vaux's *The Bible and the Ancient Near East* (London, 1972), pp. 252–269. See also Noel Robertson's "The Ritual Background of the Dying God in Cyprus and Syro-Palestine," *Harvard Theological Review* 75 (1982): 313–359. On pigs in the myths, symbols, and rituals of Southeast Asia and Melanesia, see Hans Schärer's classic study, *Die Gottesidee der Ngadju Dajak in Süd-Borneo* (Leiden, 1946), translated by Rodney Needham as *Ngaju Religion: The Conception of God among a South Borneo People* (1946; reprint, The Hague, 1963); John Layard's *Stone Men of Malekula* (London, 1942); and Adolf E. Jensen's *Die getötete Gottheit: Weltbild einer frühen Kultur* (Stuttgart, 1966).

New Sources

Hendel, Ronald S. "Of Sacred Leopards and Abominable Pigs: How Common Practice Becomes Ritual Law." *Bible Review* 16, no. 5 (2000): 8.

Hesse, Brian, and Paula Wapnish. "Pig Use and Abuse in the Ancient Levant: Ethnoreligious Boundary-building with Swine." In *Ancestors for the Pigs: Pigs in Prehistory,* edited by Sarah M. Nelson, pp. 123–135. Philadelphia, 1998.

Landau, Paul S. "The Spirit of God, Pigs and Demons: The 'Samuelites' of Southern Africa." *Journal of Religion in Africa* 29, no. 3 (1999): 313–340.

Nihom, Max. "On Buffalos, Pigs, Camels, and Crows." *Wiener Zeitschrift für die Kunde Südasiens und Archiv für indische Philosophie* 31 (1987): 75–109.

Rappaport, Roy. *Pigs for the Ancestors: Ritual in the Ecology of a New Guinea People.* Rev. ed. New Haven, 1985.

MANABU WAIDA (1987)
Revised Bibliography

PILGRIMAGE

This entry consists of the following articles:

PILGRIMAGE: AN OVERVIEW

A religious believer in any culture may sometimes look beyond the local temple, church, or shrine, feel the call of some distant holy place renowned for miracles and the revivification of faith, and resolve to journey there. The goal of the journey, the sacred site, may be Banaras, India (Hindu); Jerusalem, Israel (Jewish, Christian, Muslim); Mecca, Saudi Arabia (Muslim); Meiron, Israel (Jewish); Ise, Japan (Shintō); Saikoku, Japan (Buddhist); or one of a hundred thousand others. Whatever the site, whatever the culture, the general features of a pilgrim's journey are remarkably similar. A generalized account of one woman's pilgrimage may thus serve to illustrate the process.

> Once, in a place apart, there appeared a very holy person; miracles occurred at that place and drew multitudes of pilgrims. Later, a shrine was built by devotees. Now, in the present, those who are afflicted make a promise to the holy person in their hearts: "If you help me, I will make the journey to your shrine and perform devotions there." The journey will be arduous and inconvenient, but the goal beckons, the source out there that heals both body and soul, and worldly considerations fall away. The pilgrim sets out lightheartedly. As she travels, she joins with many others who are bound in the same direction, and bonds of friendship develop between them. During her journey the pilgrim calls at sacred way stations, each of which strengthens her faith further. When she nears her goal, and can make out the shrine from afar, she weeps for joy. When she enters the sacred domain she is conscious of actually seeing with her own eyes the place of those holy events, while her feet touch the very ground the holy one trod. At last she is in the presence of the sacred—and is in awe. She touches the shrine with her hand, then remains there a long time in bliss and prayer. Afterward, she gives offerings and makes the rounds of the lesser shrines that cluster about the main one. Before leaving she eats holy food and calls at the market for pious presents to take home. Her return journey is cheerful, for her affliction is lifted. When she arrives home, her family and neighbors feel and share in the blessings that have come to her.

THE EXPERIENCE OF PILGRIMAGE. Pilgrimage has the classic three-stage form of a rite of passage: (1) separation (the start of the journey), (2) the liminal stage (the journey itself, the sojourn at the shrine, and the encounter with the sacred), and (3) reaggregation (the homecoming). It differs from initiation in that the journey is to a center "out there," not through a threshold that marks a change in the individual's social status (except in the case of the pilgrimage to Mecca).

The middle stage of a pilgrimage is marked by an awareness of temporary release from social ties and by a strong sense of *communitas* ("community, fellowship"), as well as by a preference for simplicity of dress and behavior, by a sense of ordeal, and by reflection on the basic meaning of one's religion. Movement is the pilgrim's element, into which she or he is drawn by the spiritual magnetism of a pilgrimage center.

Freedom from social structure. The temporary release from social ties that characterizes a pilgrim's journey is shared by other travelers who have an affinity with pilgrims, especially tourists and mystics. Tourists may, at heart, be pilgrims, for many serious-minded ones, perhaps alienated from their own society, find an elective center in the periphery of society, in a place of power that affects them in a personal way. Like pilgrims, they switch worlds, and they may even experience transcendence in the situation of liminality, in the special state of being freed from social structure. Their outward journey, like pilgrimage, may thus be a form of exteriorized mysticism. Mystics, on the other hand, make an inward sacred journey, an interior pilgrimage. Pilgrims, tourists, and mystics are, all three, freed for a time from the nets of social structure.

Communitas. Pilgrims typically experience the sentiment of *communitas,* a special sense of bonding and of humankindness. Many pilgrims claim of their own company that "here is the only possible classless society." Yet, in each case, this *communitas* is channeled by the beliefs, values, and norms of a specific historical religion. The rules and norms that develop in pilgrimage are essential to the sense of flow that pilgrims feel when they act with total involvement. They need the frame to focus action. So pilgrimage, in its specificity, can foster exclusiveness between the religions, the sense that "ours is the only one."

Here one encounters the fact that pilgrims are usually social conservatives, while their critics are often liberals. More often than not, pilgrimage is a phenomenon of popular religion. The populations from which pilgrims are drawn tend to cling jealously to their traditional rights and customs. Thus there occurs the paradox that they have often rallied for national independence under pilgrimage banners such as Our Lady of Guadalupe in Mexico and the Virgin of Częstochowa in Poland.

Pilgrimage has been of concern to the orthodox hierarchies of many religions, for pilgrimage draws the faithful away from the center of organization. A devotion may arise spontaneously, not in a consecrated place, and may not keep the strictest rules of the structured religion. Once started, it is democratic, rich in symbolism of its own and in *communitas.* From the point of view of social structure such manifestations of *communitas* are potentially subversive.

SPIRITUAL MAGNETISM OF PILGRIMAGE CENTERS. A number of factors may be involved in the spiritual magnetism of a pilgrimage center. A sacred image of great age or divine origin may be the magnet. Such images show great variety, from a painted picture such as that of the Virgin of Częstochowa, to a lovingly clothed doll as at Tlaxcala, Mexico, to a colossal statue of the Buddha in Sri Lanka. They induce awe and devotion, for they have the power to touch the religious instinct. There is an ambivalence in such objects. Are they themselves divine or not? The ambivalence only intensifies the wonder.

Miracles of healing also endow pilgrimage centers with a powerful spiritual magnetism. Such miracles seem to occur when there are both a heightened sense of the supernatural and a profound sense of human fellowship, of shared experience. Although the study of neurological effects of religious experience is in its infancy, there appears to be a healing factor in the unitary experience that is central to religion. The repeated stories of miracles at pilgrimage centers may thus constitute more important material than has been hitherto recognized.

Many pilgrimage centers are sites of apparitions, places where supernatural beings have appeared to humans. The appearance of a supernatural being imparts magnetic power to a site whether or not it has independent beauty or significance. Pilgrims endeavor to touch objects as close as possible to the site of apparition. Through the concreteness of touch, they experience connection with the original event.

The birthplace, location of life events, or tomb of a holy person may be a pilgrimage magnet in the same way, and the land itself in certain places has power to move the spirit, so that rivers, mountains, caves, islands, and strange features of the landscape may radiate spiritual magnetism. A cave at Amarnath, India, is an example. The magically beautiful ice formation within it is worshiped as an incarnation of Śiva. Nature, at the margins of the mundane, may represent a threshold into the spiritual.

Generally, the numinosity of a pilgrimage center is palpable. After the inception of the center it takes on a longterm character, gradually unfolding throughout history.

HISTORICAL CLASSIFICATION OF PILGRIMAGES. Pilgrimages have arisen in different periods of history and have taken different paths. According to one typology, based largely in a Western view of history, pilgrimages can be classified as archaic, prototypical, high-period, and modern. Although this typology is most fruitful in examining Christian pilgrimage, it can be extended to other religious traditions as well.

Archaic pilgrimage. Certain pilgrimage traditions have come down from very ancient times, and little or nothing is known of their foundation. Some of these archaic traditions, like that of the Huichol Indians of Mexico, retain a complex symbolic code. Others have been overlaid by the trappings of a later religion, although archaic customs can still be discerned; the *communitas* of past ages also carries on, providing energy for the new establishment. Such syncretism occurred at Mecca and Jerusalem in the Middle East, at Izamal and Chalma in Mexico, and at Canterbury in England.

At Canterbury it was officially sanctioned; Augustine of Canterbury received a message from Pope Gregory the Great that he should "baptize" the Anglo-Saxon customs, bringing them into the fold and harnessing them for the new religion.

Prototypical pilgrimage. Pilgrimages established by the founder of a religion, by his or her first disciples, or by important evangelists of the faith may be called "prototypical." As in all new pilgrimage traditions, the foundation is marked by visions and miracles and by the advent of a swarm of fervent pilgrims. They make spontaneous acts of devotion, praying, touching objects at the site, leaving tags on trees, and so on. As the impulse for *communitas* grows, a strong feedback system develops, further increasing the popularity of the pilgrimage center. A prototypical pilgrimage tradition soon manifests charter narratives and holy books about the founder. A shrine is built and an ecclesiastical structure develops. The Jerusalem and Rome pilgrimages are prototypical for Christianity, Jerusalem for Judaism, Mecca for Islam, Banaras and Mount Kailash for Hinduism, Bodh Gayā and Sārnāth, India, for Buddhism, and Ise for Shintō. Pilgrims at these sites often reenact events of the founding times.

High-period pilgrimage. In the heyday of a pilgrimage tradition an elaborate shrine, crowded with symbols, is created; side shrines, a market, a fairground, and hostels spring up near the center, and professional pilgrims make their appearance. In the Middle Ages, when the growth of Muslim power in the Mediterranean hampered Christian pilgrimage to the Holy Land, the loss was compensated by the creation of shrines all over Europe. A holy relic was commonly the focus of devotion, as, for example, at Chartres, France, where the Virgin's veil is enshrined. New World pilgrimages resembled their medieval forerunners, although New World shrines lacked relics—one of the reasons for the prevalence of images as a substitute in this region.

Meanwhile, at many European centers routinization and decline had set in. The shrines became so choked with symbolic objects that meaning was being forgotten. Thus, during the Reformation and the era of Puritanism many of them became targets of iconoclasts and were suppressed. Walsingham in England is a prime example.

Desiderius Erasmus, William Langland, John Wyclif, Hugh Latimer, and John Calvin were reformers who opposed pilgrimage and the excessive veneration of images. In recent years opposition has come from the Vatican, which denied approval to pilgrimages to Joazeiro, Bahia, in Brazil and to Necedah, Wisconsin, in the United States; miraculous or apparitional events may be ratified only after exhaustive examination by clerical officials. In Israel the rabbinate keeps watch for irregularities at the many popular pilgrimages to the tombs of *tsaddiqim* ("holy persons").

Modern pilgrimage. All over the world in the last two centuries a new type of pilgrimage, with a high devotional tone and bands of ardent adherents, has developed. Modern pilgrimage is frankly technological; pilgrims travel by automobile and airplane, and pilgrimage centers publish newspapers and pamphlets. The catchment areas of modern pilgrimage are the great industrial cities. However, the message of the shrine is still traditional, at variance with the values of today. Many Roman Catholic pilgrimages have been triggered by an apparition of the Virgin Mary to some humble visionary with a message of penance and a gift of healing, as at Lourdes, France.

Other centers have arisen from the ashes of some dead pilgrimage shrine. A devotee has a vision of the founder, which heralds new miracles and a virtually new pilgrimage, as at Aylesford, England. Both apparitional and saint-centered pilgrimages in other parts of the modern world abound, as in Japan and at the tomb of the holy rabbi Huri of Beersheva, Israel.

CONCLUDING REMARKS. Pilgrimage is a process, a fluid and changing phenomenon, spontaneous, initially unstructured and outside the bounds of religious orthodoxy. It is primarily a popular rite of passage, a venture into religious experience rather than into a transition to higher status. A particular pilgrimage has considerable resilience over time and the power of revival. Pilgrims all over the world attest to the profundity of their experience, which often surpasses the power of words.

SEE ALSO Relics.

BIBLIOGRAPHY

Aradi, Zsolt. *Shrines to Our Lady around the World.* New York, 1954. A remarkably full listing of world Marian pilgrimages, illustrated, and with short descriptions.

Bhardwaj, Surinder Mohan. *Hindu Places of Pilgrimage in India: A Study in Cultural Geography.* Berkeley, 1973. A much-discussed analysis of levels or rank-order among pilgrimages in India.

Janin, Hunt. *Four Paths to Jerusalem: Jewish, Christian, Muslim, and Secular Pilgrimages, 1000 BCE to 2001 CE.* Jefferson, N.C., 2002.

Kamal, Ahmad. *The Sacred Journey, Being Pilgrimage to Makkah; the Traditions, Dogma, and Islamic Ritual That Govern the Lives and the Destiny of More Than Five Hundred Million who Call Themselves Muslim: One Seventh of Mankind.* London, 1964. This volume, which is a primary source, was written in response to the request of eminent Shiʿites in Baghdad.

Kitagawa, Joseph M. "Three Types of Pilgrimage in Japan." In *Studies in Mysticism and Religion Presented to Gershom G. Scholem,* edited by E. E. Urbach, R. J. Zwi Werblowsky, and Chaim Wirszubski, pp. 155–164. Jerusalem, 1967. Analyzes pilgrimages to sacred mountains, to temples and shrines, and to places hallowed by holy men. A pioneer article.

Morinis, E. Alan, ed. *Sacred Journeys: The Anthropology of Pilgrimage.* New York, 1992. An essential reference covering many types and aspects of pilgrimage throughout the world, using an advanced theoretical framework.

Palestine Pilgrims Text Society (London). Volumes 1, 3, and 10 (1891–1897) are classic primary sources, constituting the texts of the earliest pilgrims to the Holy Land.

Preston, James J. "Spiritual Magnetism: An Organizing Principle for the Study of Pilgrimage." In *Sacred Journeys,* edited by E. Alan Morinis, pp.47–61. New York, 1992. A careful and enlightened essay introducing pilgrimage in all its aspects.

Turner, Victor. "Pilgrimage as Social Process." In his *Dramas, Fields, and Metaphors,* pp. 167–230. Ithaca, N.Y., 1974. The first modern anthropological essay on pilgrimage, introducing the role of pilgrimage in the generation of *communitas* and the sentiment of humankindness. Turner views religious pilgrimage as a moving process, not an arrangement of structures.

Turner, Victor, and Edith Turner. *Image and Pilgrimage in Christian Culture.* New York, 1978. An anthropological study of the cultural, symbolic, and theological aspects of pilgrimage, using Mexican, Irish, medieval, and Marian examples.

EDITH TURNER (1987 AND 2005)

PILGRIMAGE: ROMAN CATHOLIC PILGRIMAGE IN EUROPE

During the Middle Ages the concept of Christian pilgrimage became a reality in Europe, with varied significance. Pilgrimage, making one's way to holy places, is above all an ascetic practice that lets the Christian find salvation through the difficulties and dangers of a temporary exile. It is also a means of coming in contact with that which is divine and thereby obtaining grace because of the accumulation of supernatural power in the pilgrimage site. However, there are occasions where the blessing requested has already been received, and the pilgrimage is then an act of gratitude. One can therefore distinguish two kinds of journey: the journey of the pilgrim seeking blessing and the journey of the pilgrim giving thanks. Important in both cases, however, is the interchange between God and man through the medium of the saints. It works like an exchange: a material offering (often symbolic, such as a candle) and a self-imposed mortification, the journey to the shrine, correspond to a spiritual or material favor bestowed upon the faithful, who considers it a miracle.

PRINCIPAL TYPES OF SHRINE. The first type of shrine for pilgrimage evident in Europe was the sanctuary for relics, centered on a tomb or reliquary containing the remains of a saint or a fragment thereof. Usually initiated by mass devotion, such worship was validated by the bishop up to the thirteenth century and thereafter by the pope. Among these shrines, the tomb of Peter in Rome and that attributed to James the Greater at Santiago de Compostela in Spain were by far the most frequently visited. But there were also thousands of small churches frequented mainly by local pilgrims, most of which were brought to life only once a year, on the feast day of the patron saint.

The second large category of centers of pilgrimage is that of the Marian shrines. From the twelfth century onward, the worship of Mary developed greatly in Europe, worship that continues to draw the faithful right up to the present. Two main types of Marian shrines have evolved. First are those based on the veneration of a miraculous statue, sometimes called the Black Madonna; important examples of the type are found at Chartres, Le Puy, and Rocamadour in France; Montserrat and Guadalupe in Spain; Mariazell in Austria; Einsiedeln in Switzerland; and Częstochowa in Poland. All these shrines have been frequented since the Middle Ages. A variation on this type is represented by the two locations where homage is paid in a place where the Virgin Mary was miraculously transported or resurrected: Loreto in Italy and Walsingham in England.

The second main category of Marian shrine consists of places sanctified by an apparition of the Virgin and the transmission of a message to a believer chosen by her. These apparitions are evident mainly in the nineteenth and twentieth centuries. The principal ones took place in the rue du Bac in Paris (1830), at La Salette (1846), Lourdes (1858), Pontmain (1871), and at Pellevoisin (1876) in France; at Fátima in Portugal (1917); and at Beauraing and Banneux in Belgium (1932). Of all the shrines, those dedicated to the Virgin Mary still attract the greatest number of believers.

THE EVOLUTION OF PILGRIMAGE IN EUROPE. There have been six main stages in the evolution of pilgrimage in Europe beginning with the Middle Ages. The period encompassing the eleventh to the fourteenth centuries saw a dramatic increase in the number of centers of pilgrimage and a corresponding rise in the number of pilgrims. During the fifteenth century and above all the sixteenth century (at the time of the Reformation), the practice of pilgrimage underwent a crisis in which its very usefulness was called into serious question (in the context of the rise of the iconoclastic movement in the churches). With the Council of Trent (1545–1563) there began a period of resurgence, the duration of which varied from country to country. The impulse was halted in France at the beginning of the eighteenth century, but it continued in the Germanic and Slavic countries right up to the time of the French Revolution. Generally speaking, the pilgrim movement became victim to the philosophy of the Enlightenment, which favored reason above religion, and victim as well to the wish to purge the faith. (The pilgrimage is interpreted by the Roman Catholic hierarchy at this time as a form of superstition to be discouraged.) In the nineteenth century, Catholicism underwent another renewal of faith, which brought with it a renewed impulse for pilgrimage, slow in the first half of the century, then gathering momentum and reaching a peak between 1850 and 1875, probably due to the development of rail travel coinciding with a rise in the influence of the papacy. Since the end of World War I, pilgrimage has been at a notable level, while undergoing sociological change: collective pilgrimages have taken the lead over individual journeys, and more than ever before, young people are taking part in pilgrimages, previously more of an adult occupation. This contributes a notably more universal and ecumenical tone to pilgrimage. However, the modern-day pilgrimage continues, as in previous centuries, to temporarily dissolve the normal lines between social classes. It has also kept its popular nature, even if some of the folklore and customs attached to it have disappeared.

The current record for the number of visits to a shrine is held by Lourdes, to which three million pilgrims journey each year. Next comes Fátima with two million visitors. There are several shrines that annually receive more than one million pilgrims: the Chapel of the Miraculous Medallion at the rue du Bac in Paris, Our Lady of Rocamadour, Our Lady of Scherpenheuvel (French, Montaigu) in Belgium, Our Lady of Montserrat in Spain, the Sacré-Coeur at Montmartre in Paris and Mont-Saint-Michel in northwestern France. With regard to pilgrimages to Rome, the greatest number of believers come in the Holy Years.

Today, as during previous centuries, the pilgrimage is a manifestation of collective devotion in which are mingled the two great concerns of the faithful: the salvation of the soul and the thirst for miracles. The pilgrimage is also an opportunity for human contacts of all sorts and for economic, artistic, and religious interchanges, making it one of the most vital elements of European Catholicism.

See Also Relics.

Bibliography

For a general view of the meaning of Christian pilgrimage, see Victor Turner and Edith Turner's *Image and Pilgrimage in Christian Culture: Anthropological Perspectives* (New York, 1978). A more detailed work on Roman Catholic pilgrimage in Europe, and particularly in France, is the recent and well-informed publication edited by Jean Chelini and Henry Branthome, *Les chemins de Dieu: Histoire des pèlerinages chrétiens des origines à nos jours* (Paris, 1982). With regard to the medieval period, a good study in English is Jonathan Sumption's *Pilgrimage: An Image of Mediaeval Religion* (London, 1972). More recent developments are described in the work edited by Bernard Plongeron and Robert Pannet, *Le christianisme populaire* (Paris, 1976). Finally, a good work on the greatest European contemporary pilgrimage, the pilgrimage to Lourdes, is that of Bernard Billet and Pierre Lafourcade, *Lourdes pèlerinage* (Paris, 1981).

New Sources

Dahlberg, Andrea. "The Body as a Principle of Holism: Three Pilgrimages to Lourdes." In *Contesting the Sacred: The Anthropology of Christian Pilgrimage,* edited by John Eade and Michael J. Sallnow. New York, 1991.

Dunn, Maryjane, and Linda Kay Davidson, eds. *The Pilgrimage to Campostela In the Middle Ages.* New York, 1996.

Nolan, Mary Lee, and Sidney Nolan. *Christian Pilgrimage In Modern Western Europe.* Chapel Hill, N.C., 1989.

Kessler, Herbert L., and Johanna Zacharias. *Rome 1300: On the Path of the Pilgrims.* New Haven, Conn., 2000.

Webb, Diana. *Pilgrims and Pilgrimages in the Medieval West.* London, 1999.

Pierre André Sigal (1987)
Translated from French by P. J. Burbidge
Revised Bibliography

PILGRIMAGE: ROMAN CATHOLIC PILGRIMAGE IN THE NEW WORLD

Roman Catholic pilgrimage shrines are found from Alaska and Canada to Tierra del Fuego. The oldest shrine in the Americas is probably Our Lady of Mercy at Santo Cerro in the Dominican Republic. Here, according to tradition, Christopher Columbus erected a cross in thanks for a victory over local Indians in the mid-1490s. The original image of the Virgin Mary is said to have been a gift from Isabella I, queen of Castile (1474–1504), and a pilgrimage chapel may have been erected as early as 1505. Thereafter, Catholic shrines spread through the Americas with Spanish, Portuguese, and French colonization. In some cases, as at Guadalupe, Amecameca, and Chalma in Mexico; Esquipulas, Guatemala; Caranqui, Ecuador; and Copacabana, Bolivia, indigenous holy places were christianized. More often, however, the establishment of shrines involved events leading to the sanctification of places not previously conceptualized as holy.

Missionaries and immigrants to the Americas from various parts of Catholic Europe introduced their own special devotions as well as regionally specific ideas about shrines and pilgrimages. Iberian and French influences were particularly important during the sixteenth through eighteenth centuries, as were ideas brought by missionaries from Habsburg Germanic regions. Diversity increased with mass migrations from other parts of Europe during the nineteenth and twentieth centuries. For example, areas of Italian settlement in Argentina, Chile, and southern Brazil have important shrines dedicated to the fifteenth-century Marian apparition at Caravaggio in northern Italy and to the Virgin of Pompei, a late-nineteenth-century cult that originated near Naples. Similarly, eight shrines of the Byzantine rite are found in the diocese of Curitiba, Brazil, where 95 percent of the population are persons of Ukrainian descent, and a shrine at Doylestown, Pennsylvania, honors the Polish Virgin of Częstochowa. As a result of multiple influences from different parts of Europe at different time periods, the pattern of pilgrimage circulation in the Americas is rich in variety.

The New World's most famous shrine is the Basilica of the Virgin of Guadalupe on the outskirts of Mexico City. Here, according to tradition, the Virgin Mary appeared in 1531 to an Indian named Juan Diego. As proof of the apparition's validity, Diego's cloak was miraculously imprinted with an image of the Virgin in the guise of an Indian maiden. The Mexican Virgin of Guadalupe has been proclaimed patroness of Mexico and of the Americas.

Other apparitional shrines of sixteenth-century origin are at San Bartolo, Naucalpan, Tlaxcala, and Zacatecas, Mexico; Cisne, Ecuador; and Chiantla, Guatemala. Later colonial-period shrines of this type are located at Chirca, Bolivia; Lima, Peru; Ambato, Ecuador; Segorbe, Colombia; San Cristóbal, Venezuela; and Higüey, Dominican Republic. One of the most recent accounts of a New World Marian apparition came from Cuapa, Nicaragua, in 1980.

Numerous American shrines commemorate European apparitions of the Virgin Mary, particularly the 1858 event at Lourdes, France. Some of the more important New World Lourdes shrines are at Mar del Plata, Argentina; Santiago, Chile; Montevideo, Uruguay; Maiquetía, Venezuela; Euclid, Ohio; Brooklyn, New York; San Antonio, Texas; and Rigaud, Canada. American shrines celebrating the 1917 apparitions at Fátima, Portugal, are found at Campo Grande and other places in Brazil as well as at Cojutepeque, El Salvador, and Youngstown, New York. A shrine at Mayo, near Buckingham, Canada, commemorates the 1879 Marian apparitions at Knock, Ireland, and several shrines in the United States and Canada are dedicated to a manifestation of the Virgin Mary at La Salette, France, in 1846.

Many New World shrines came into being when a newly acquired relic or an image of Mary, Christ, or a saint was credited with miracles. Some of these images were probably brought by early missionaries. Examples are found at Itati and Laguna de los Padres, Argentina; Monserrate, Colombia; and Zapopan and Querétaro in Mexico. Other images, such as those honored at Cedros, Honduras; Guanajuato, Mexico; Lima, Peru; La Estrella, Colombia; and Cuenca, Ecuador, were sent as gifts by Spanish royalty. Mysterious strangers are said to have left miraculous images in such places as Cuernavaca, Mexico, and Nátago, Colombia. Elsewhere, as at Banos, Ecuador, and Saltillo and Oaxaca, Mexico, the image is said to have been brought by a mule that refused to move any farther. A variation on this theme comes from Luján, Argentina. Here, at the greatest of all Argentine shrines, an ox cart carrying a statue of Mary from church to church for veneration became stuck in 1630, thus indicating the proper place for the shrine.

Shipwrecks, or the "refusal" of ships to leave harbors, resulted in the acquisition of important cult objects at Antón and Portobelo, Panama, and at Montecristi, Ecuador. The image of Christ at Bom Jesus de Lapa, Brazil, was brought in 1690 by a workman who spent years of penitence in a grotto before becoming a missionary priest, and the image of Santa Rosa of Lima venerated at Pelequén, Chile, was brought south from Lima by a soldier in 1840. Shrines of this type in the United States include those at Dickinson, Texas, where a relic of the True Cross was enshrined in 1936; San Juan del Valle, Texas, where an image of Mary was brought from Mexico by the local priest in 1949; and Miami, Florida, where a modernistic pilgrimage church has been built in honor of the "exiled" image of Our Lady of Charity that arrived from Cuba in 1961.

Many New World shrines trace their origins to the finding of relics or images, usually under mysterious circumstances, similar to events dating to early Christian times in Europe. Stories of such discoveries account for some of the most important shrines in the Americas. Among those of sixteenth-century origin was the dark image of Christ that "appeared" in a cave at Chalma, Mexico, around 1540.

Fishermen at Cobre, Cuba, found a statue of Mary floating on the waters of the bay in 1601. An image of Mary was found on a lake shore after a 1603 flood at Caacupé, Paraguay. Early in the seventeenth century, some Indians found a statue of Mary in a cave at Catamarca, Argentina. At Cartago, Costa Rica, in 1635 an Indian woman found an image of Mary in the woods. Boys found a faded painting of Mary in a hut at Táchira, Venezuela, in 1654, and the painting was miraculously restored. In 1685, just south of Bogotá, Colombia, a man looking for lost treasure found a statue of Mary.

At Yauca, Peru, in about 1700, a group of farmers found an image of Mary in some bushes. A woman on her way back from a pilgrimage to the shrine of Coromoto at San Cristóbal, Venezuela, in 1702 found an image of Mary in a tree at Acarigua. At Aparecida do Norte, Brazil, fishermen found a black image of Mary in a river in 1717. An elderly peasant man found an image of Mary buried in the ground at Suyapa, Honduras, in 1747. At Ipiales, Colombia, in 1754, a young girl saw a painting of the Virgin on a rock face. In 1780, an image of Mary was found after a rainstorm on the edge of a solar, a usually dry lake bed, at Copiapó, Chile.

In 1807, a flash of lightning revealed a damaged image of Mary in the corner of a convent room in Guadalajara, Mexico, and in 1868 a rustic wooden cross was found on a mountain with pagan associations near Motupe, Peru.

Other shrine-generating images are said to have been found in oak tree branches, inside trees being cut for timber or firewood, in fountains, under stones in rivers, in thorn thickets, under magueys, and in ruined churches. At least one, at Sopo, Colombia, appeared in an eroded stone.

Other important New World shrines came into being as the result of a miraculous transformation of an already existent image. For example, in 1586, the cult of the Colombian Virgin of Chiquinquirá emerged when a painting of the Madonna was mysteriously restored. Similar stories are told about once-faded copies of this image that have been venerated since the mid-eighteenth century at Aregue and Maracaibo, Venezuela. Similarly, at Talpa, Mexico, a deteriorating corn-paste image of Mary is said to have been miraculously restored in about 1644. Weeping and sweating images of the Virgin Mary have given rise to the establishment of pilgrimage shrines in several places, including Lima, Peru (1591), and Santa Fe, Argentina (1636). Pilgrimages began to the Colegio San Gabriel in Quito, Ecuador, in 1906 after students reported that a painting of Mary opened and closed its eyes several times, and a similar event in 1888 encouraged the development of pilgrimages to a Marian shrine in Cap de la Madeleine, Canada. One of the most recent examples of this type of phenomenon is a plaster image of the Virgin in the cathedral at Managua, Nicaragua, reported to be sweating copiously in 1980.

The most important devotion for northern Mexicans, at San Juan de los Lagos in the state of Jalisco, began attracting devotees in 1623 after a traveling acrobat's daughter, thought to be dead after falling onto upright knives, came back to life when an old woman touched her with an ancient image of the Virgin. Pilgrimages generated by sudden cures have also emerged in Quinche, Ecuador (1589); Sainte Anne de Beaupré, Canada (1659); San Felipe, Guatemala (1820); and numerous other places. Shrines to which there have been a declining number of pilgrimages have often been regenerated by spectacular cures, as happened at Andacollo, Chile, in 1860 and San Juan Parangaricutiro, Mexico, in 1869.

Frequently shrines were established as community thank offerings for salvation from catastrophe. Survival of Indian attack or victory in battle has given rise to shrines in such places as Jujuy, Argentina; Recife, Brazil; Coroico, Bolivia; Villa Vieja, Uruguay; and Maipú, Chile. Riobamba, Ecuador, and San Miguel, El Salvador, are among the shrine centers that commemorate the end of earthquakes and/or volcanic eruptions. Others, like that at Yaguachi, Ecuador, emerged in the wake of epidemics, or, like that at Biblián, Ecuador, in the aftermath of threatened famine.

Votive shrines have also been created by individuals. For example, the venerated image at Guadalupe, Peru, was brought from the Spanish shrine of the same name in the mid-sixteenth century in thanks for the donor's release from prison, and a shrine at Hormigueros, Puerto Rico, is said to have been promoted by a man who was saved from a bull. The famous shrine at Chimayo, New Mexico, was established in the early nineteenth century by Don Bernardo Abeyta in thanks for health and prosperity.

Shrines also emerge in places sanctified through association with saints or exemplary, but uncanonized, persons. This type of holy place is more common in Europe than in the Americas, but there are several New World examples. These include the burial places of Santa Rosa and San Martín de Porres in Lima, Peru; the Aracanian Indian Ceferino Namuncura in Pedro Luro, Argentina; San Pedro Claver in Cartagena, Colombia; Saint John Neumann in Philadelphia, Pennsylvania; the Blessed Philippine Duchesne in Saint Charles, Missouri; and the Italian missionary nun Mother Cabrini in New York City.

Mother Cabrini is also honored at a site in the Rocky Mountain foothills near Denver, Colorado. Here, in 1912, the first citizen-saint of the United States struck a rock with her staff, whereupon a spring emerged with waters since reported to be curative. Other examples include a shrine at Midland, Canada, near the place where French Jesuit missionaries were killed by Huron Indians in the 1640s, and the Coronado Cross erected in 1976 near Dodge City, Kansas, at the place on the Arkansas River where Father Juan Padilla offered a mass for members of the Coronado expedition. Killed by Indians in 1542, this Franciscan friar was the first priest martyred in what is now the United States.

Pilgrimages have also developed at a number of places known primarily for their historical significance. Examples include the "La Leche" shrine in Saint Augustine, Florida, at the site of the first Spanish mission in America north of Mexico (established 1565); the Sacred Heart Mission church at Cataldo, Idaho; and several of the Spanish mission churches in the southwestern United States. Although not a pilgrimage center in a conventional sense, Boys Town, Nebraska, established as a home for wayward boys by Father Edward Flanagan in the early twentieth century, provides another example of a religiously significant site. It draws more than one million visitors a year and is considered an important place of inspiration.

Finally, many New World shrines, especially in North America, are of purely devotional origin. They came into being because an individual or a group believed that a pilgrimage center should be created in a particular place and set about to make it happen. Examples of such shrines include the National Shrine of the Immaculate Conception in Washington, D. C.; the Shrine of the Miraculous Medal in Perryville, Missouri; the Sanctuary of Our Sorrowful Mother at The Grotto in Portland, Oregon; and the National Shrine of the Sacred Heart at Pointe aux Trembles, Canada.

In 1983 a number of North American churches not previously conceptualized as pilgrimage shrines were scenes of pilgrimages for the 1983–1984 Holy Year of the Redemption. Given the late-twentieth-century interest in pilgrimage on the part of many American Catholics, it is possible that some of these places will become permanent centers for the devotion of pilgrims, especially if miraculous events are perceived to occur there. Certainly, shrines will continue to emerge in the hemisphere as religious significance is attached to relief from environmental stress ranging from natural disasters to political upheavals.

BIBLIOGRAPHY

No comprehensive study of Roman Catholic pilgrimages in the Americas has yet been published. Much of the information in this article comes from letters, pamphlets, booklets, photocopies of accounts in diocesan handbooks, and simiiar materials acquired in response to mail queries directed to Latin American bishops in 1979 and North American bishops in 1983. These materials are on file in the Department of Geography, Oregon State University, Corvallis, Oregon. Numerous descriptive works on individual New World shrines exist, but they are difficult to obtain except on site or by direct correspondence with shrine administrators. An exception is a work edited by Donald Demarest and Coley Taylor, *The Dark Virgin: The Book of Our Lady of Guadalupe; A Documentary Anthology* (Freeport, Maine, 1956).

Some of the more important shrines and those that are interesting for the folklore attached to them are mentioned in travel guidebooks and travelers' accounts. Occasional publications by national tourism agencies, such as the Mexican Government Tourism Department's *Fiestas in Mexico* (Mexico City, n. d.), provide useful information. A thorough search of the ethnographic literature in all relevant languages would undoubtedly yield a rich body of information on shrines and pilgrimages that happened to attract the attention of anthropologists, cultural geographers, and other field investigators.

Compendiums of selected shrine descriptions form a devotional point of view include Joseph L. Cassidy's *Mexico: Land of Mary's Wonders* (Paterson, N.J., 1958); Ralph Louis Woods and Henry Fitzwilliam Woods's *Pilgrim Places in North America: A Guide to Catholic Shrines* (New York, 1939); Francis Beauchesne Thornton's *Catholic Shrines in the United States and Canada* (New York, 1954); Nectario María Hermano's *Venezuela Mariana, o Sea relación histórica compendiada de las imagenes más celebradas de las Santísima Virgen en Venezuela* (Madrid, 1976); Francisco García Huidobro's *Santuarios Marianos del Ecuador* (Quayaquil, 1978); and the mammoth two-volume compilation on Marian shrines in Latin America by Rubén Vargas Ugarte, *Historia del culto de María en Iberoaméri-cá y de sus imagenes y santuarios más celebrados* (Madrid, 1956). Folklore-oriented descriptions of several Middle American shrines can be found in Frances Toor's *A Treasury of Mexican Folkways* (New York, 1947) and in Edith Hoyt's *The Silver Madonna: Legends of Shrines, Mexico-Guatemala* (Mexico City, 1963). Short descriptions of important Canadian churches are provided in *L'almanach populaire catholique* 1984 (Sainte Anne de Beaupré, 1983), but this source does not consistently differentiate between pilgrimage churches and other notable ecclesiastical structures.

I have undertaken preliminary attempts to provide an analysis of Mexican shrines in "The Mexican Pilgrimage Tradition," *Pioneer America* 5 (1973): 13–27, as did Victor Turner in "The Center Out There: Pilgrim's Goal," *History of Religions* 12 (February 1973): 191–230. Victor Turner and Edith Turner included an overview of New World, primarily Mexican, pilgrimages in their pioneer effort to interpret Christian pilgrimage, *Image and Pilgrimage in Christian Culture: Anthropological Perspectives* (New York, 1978). Most other published works by social scientists deal with one pilgrimage center or a few regionally interrelated shrines. Examples of such studies include Daniel R. Gross's "Ritual and Conformity: A Religious Pilgrimage to Northeastern Brazil," *Ethnology* 10 (April 1971): 129–148, and N. Ross Crumrine's "Three Coastal Peruvian Pilgrimages," *El Dorado* 2 (1977): 76–86. Numerous shrine and regionally specific pilgrimage studies undertaken during the 1970s were just beginning to be published in the early 1980s. A collection of papers on Latin American pilgrimage, edited by E. Alan Morinis and N. Ross Crumrine, was in the final stages of review as of June 1985.

New Sources

Office of Pastoral Care for Migrants and Refugees. *Catholic Shrines and Places of Pilgrimage In the United States.* Rev. ed. Washington, D.C., 1994.

Griffith, James S. *Beliefs and Holy Places: A Spiritual Geography of the Primería Alta.* Tucson, 1992.

Olivas Weston, Marcela. *Peregrinaciones en le Perú Antigua Rutas Devocionales.* Lima, 1999.

Quiroz Malca, Haydée. *Fiestas, Peregrinaciones y Santuarios en México: los viajes para el pago de las mandas.* Mexico City, 2000.

Salazar Medina, Richard. *El Santuario de la Virgen de la Quinche: Peregrinacion en un Espacio Sagrado Milenario.* Quito, 2000.

Sallnow, Michael J. *Pilgrims of the Andes: Regional Cults in Cusco.* Smithsonian Series in Ethnographic Inquiry. Washington, D.C., 1987.

MARY LEE NOLAN (1987)
Revised Bibliography

PILGRIMAGE: EASTERN CHRISTIAN PILGRIMAGE

Christian pilgrimage is rooted in the eastern domain of Christianity, primarily in Palestine, where Jesus was born and accomplished his mission, and secondarily in Egypt, the cradle of Christian monasticism. The fact that Jerusalem became the focal point of Christian pilgrimage is not surprising. For the Israelites, the Temple in Jerusalem had long served as the locus of the pilgrimage prescribed by their religious tradition.

The meaning of pilgrimage in ancient Israel and in early Christianity is similar yet differs markedly in one point: for the Israelite, a visit to the Temple was a requirement of faith to be fulfilled annually; for the Christian, that requirement had been fulfilled once and for all by Jesus Christ in his own final pilgrimage to the Temple. Therefore, the Christian pilgrimage became a journey to fulfill personal needs of piety rather than collective requirements. Understanding Christian pilgrimage and appreciating forms of Eastern Christian pilgrimage that have persisted for centuries necessitates, nevertheless, an examination of the meaning and form of pilgrimages in the Old Testament as well as in the New Testament.

PILGRIMAGE IN THE OLD TESTAMENT. Ancient pilgrimage sites in the history of Israel were usually linked to a marvellous event in the life of an individual Israelite or in the collective history of the community. The site for a sanctuary was not arbitrarily chosen but was designated by God in a theophany (or divine manifestation) as, for example, Jacob's dream on his way to Haran (*Gn.* 28:10–22). The memory of the glorious event was made concrete by the erection of an altar. The journeys of Abraham, Moses, and the other patriarchs, the exile of the Israelites from Egypt and their forty-year journey through the desert were all pilgrimages, in the sense that they were the means to an end: the possession of the land where milk and honey flows and where God has made his rest (*Dt.* 12:9; *Ps.* 95:11, 132:8–14). After the building of the Temple, in which rested the ark of the covenant, Jerusalem became the goal for Israelite pilgrims. It was the sacred obligation of each Israelite to make an annual pilgrimage to Jerusalem, anticipating in this way the eschatological pilgrimage to God's city where all the nations of the world would gather at the end of time to inaugurate the kingdom of God.

SIGNIFICANCE OF PILGRIMAGE IN THE NEW TESTAMENT. The importance and meaning of pilgrimage is not explicit in the New Testament. The Synoptic Gospels ascribe to Christ only one journey to Jerusalem on the occasion of the

Passover feast (except for Luke's account of Jesus' pilgrimage with his parents at age twelve). John, however, assumes the regular participation of Christ in the pilgrimage feasts (*Jn.* 2:13, 6:4, 11:55, 7:2, and 10:22). The four evangelists are in accord in their messianic interpretation of Jesus Christ's final journey to Jerusalem, which culminates in the events of his crucifixion and resurrection. In this way, Christ fulfills for all time the eschatological pilgrimage into the city of God and inaugurates the kingdom of God. In this kingdom, one no longer needs to buy and sell sacrificial animals for the offering at the temple; according to the Pauline epistles, Christ has eliminated the need for sacrifice, having become himself both the sacrificed lamb and the high priest who entered behind the veil into the Holy of Holies (*Heb.* 6:9–20).

The theme of exile occurs again and again in the New Testament writings (*1 Pt.* 1:1–17, 2:11; *Heb.* 13:14; cf. *Gn.* 23:3–4; *Ps.* 39:12–13, 119:19; *Acts* 7:6–29.) For the early Christians viewed their lives as the time of pilgrims in exile, and the destination of this journey was the heavenly city of Jerusalem. So powerful was this idea that the Greek word *paroikia,* which means "sojourning in a foreign land," came to designate the fundamental unit of the Christian community, the parish.

EARLY CHRISTIAN PILGRIMAGE. Imperial influence and not religious obligation became the greatest single motivating force in the growth and development of Christian pilgrimage to Jerusalem. Constantine's church-building program on the holy sites of Jerusalem (begun after the Council of Nicaea in 325) invited many Christians to go and see the sacred places where Jesus was born, lived, worked, and was crucified and raised.

As pilgrimage to the holy places of Christendom became more common, the corporate life of the church was affected as well, through liturgical development. Many of the early pilgrims came to Palestine with a desire to see the places described in biblical episodes, a desire that combined historical curiosity and pious zeal. The pattern of worship conducted at each site by the pilgrims, the central feature of which was the reading of the relevant passage from the Bible, gave rise eventually to an annually recurring cycle of liturgical festivals in commemoration of the life of Christ. In these celebrations too, the central feature remained a reading of the biblical narrative, appropriately chosen to suit not only the place but also the liturgical season.

Another significant feature of Christian pilgrimage liturgies was the practice of numerous processions. "The desire to embrace all the principal holy places in the course of the celebrations, combined with the possibility of commemorating the events of the gospel at the actual places where they were believed to have occurred, produced a form of worship distinguished by its constant movement and its arduous length" (Hunt, p. 114). These processions remind one of *ḥag,* the Hebrew word for pilgrimage feasts, the root meaning of which is "to dance" or "to move in circles."

It is noteworthy that the churches that have maintained a strong liturgical tradition, particularly all of the ancient churches of the East, have lived these pilgrimage themes symbolically through their cyclical liturgical celebrations. As pilgrims they need not fulfill either the pilgrimage to the Temple or to the holy places of Christendom; rather, a spiritual participation in the life of Christ, expressed through liturgical celebrations, is their pilgrimage. For example, Gregory of Nyssa maintains that Bethlehem, Golgotha, the Mount of Olives, and the empty tomb should always be before the eyes of the true Christian as spiritual pointers to the godly life.

The same attitude gave rise to another form of pilgrimage: visits to the holy men and women who had chosen to give themselves to a life of perpetual prayer—the monks and ascetics. Basil of Caesarea, who in 351 made the journey to Palestine and later to Egypt, Syria, and Mesopotamia, hardly mentions the holy places; he states that the object of his journey was to visit the monks and ascetics, to stay with them in order to learn the secret of their holy lives. Basil wanted to learn the method of the personal spiritual pilgrimage, the destination of which was the heavenly city of God experienced on an inner level.

The pilgrim Egeria (late fourth century) refers to another tradition, that of the pilgrimages to martyria (churches that have been built on the tomb of a saint or a martyr). She notes that the monks in Charra, a region of Mesopotamia, rarely come out of seclusion but that they do so on Easter and on the feast of the martyr to celebrate the Divine Liturgy in the martyrium.

This tradition still continues. Many pilgrims go to the monasteries of Mount Athos in Greece and to monasteries in Egypt, Syria, and other parts of the world. Among these monasteries there are many that were built near martyria or near sites that have biblical importance. In Egypt there is the monastery of Dair al-Muharraq, the site where the holy family rested and took refuge in their flight from Herod. Each year in Dair al-Muharraq, as at all martyria, on the feast day of the saint, pilgrims come to commemorate liturgically and later through festivities the saint in whose name the martyrium or shrine was built.

Thus, personal piety for the Eastern Christian has found expression beyond the liturgical life. Pilgrimage to Jerusalem, to martyria, and to the cells of monks has given rise to numerous customs and traditions that symbolically perpetuate the main theme of pilgrimage: the yearning of the exile to reach his destination, the promised land, the city where God rests and encounters his people.

CUSTOMS AND TRADITIONS ASSOCIATED WITH PILGRIMAGE. Armenians, Copts, Greeks, Russians, Syrians, Ethiopians, and other Eastern Christians share common traditions of pilgrimage.

The pilgrimage to Jerusalem. There is no particularly appropriate time in one's life when one ought to make a pilgrimage. However, the pilgrimage *par excellence,* the journey to Jerusalem, generally becomes possible late in one's life. Once in Jerusalem, a pilgrim considers that the serious occupations of his or her life have ended. Having seen "death conquered" at the site of Christ's resurrection (the holy sepulcher), the pilgrim looks forward to his or her own death, sometimes desiring to die in Jerusalem. The Armenian term *mahdesi* ("one who has seen death") aptly describes this state. This title of honor is given to a pilgrim returning from a pilgrimage to Jerusalem. Russian pilgrims also acknowledge the overcoming of death by taking white shrouds to Jerusalem. They bathe in the Jordan River, the scene of John's baptisms, shrouded in white, in evocation of the awakened dead on Resurrection Morning. Other Eastern Christians bring their white shrouds and on Holy Friday place them on Christ's tomb, anoint them with oil from the lamps burning there, and perfume them with sweet-smelling incense. A pilgrim designated as a *mahdesi* is one who has seen the Holy Fire on Easter and who has received a tattoo on the inner right wrist, depicting most often a cross and the date of the pilgrimage.

The ceremony of the Holy Fire. Conducted jointly by all of the Eastern churches at midday on Easter Eve in the Church of the Holy Sepulcher, the ceremony of the Holy Fire is of uncertain origin, but it derives from the ritual and symbolism of the primitive church. It symbolizes the triumph of the Christian faith. The Eastern Orthodox patriarch and the Armenian patriarch (representing also the Copts, the Ethiopians, and the Syrians) enter through the door over the tomb, then emerge, each carrying a sheaf of lighted candles. This light quickly spreads among the people present, who light their own candles from it. It is said that some pilgrims take pains to carry the flame home unextinguished, preserving it in a lantern.

It is also the custom of the Armenian patriarch to distribute wafers with the resurrection imprint to all the pilgrims. This may be a symbolic vestige of a custom of hospitality that was practiced by the monks in Egypt and elsewhere in the East. Isolated in the desert, monks had to provide pilgrims with both food and lodging. As the number of pilgrims increased, the monks began to give tokens of hospitality, most often in the form of the fruit they had grown. The pilgrim Egeria called this the monks' "blessing."

Vows, offerings, and healing. Whether rich or poor, the pilgrims carry gifts of offering to the churches on the holy sites. Many bring their work or the work of skillful craftsmen; vessels and vestments to be used for the liturgical rites. Some contribute toward the building of guest rooms in the holy city where pilgrims can stay. Traditionally, pilgrims spend many months, as much as a whole year, in pilgrimage. Originally, they would come before Christmas and stay until after Easter in order to participate in the events commemorating the life of Christ. Gradually, that time has been shortened to the season of Lent and Easter.

Pilgrims come often to fulfill vows they have made. Some also bring with them the petitions of friends. If the request is for healing, they bring silver charms that represent the part of the body in need of healing. These they leave on or near the icon of the saint to whom they pray.

Returning home. The return of pilgrims to their homes has been marked ceremoniously in some Armenian communities. Usually a group of pilgrims make the journey together. Upon their return, they go to the parish church, where prayers of thanksgiving are offered on their behalf for having been able to fulfill their pilgrimage. At the conclusion of the service, the pilgrims distribute to the congregation objects of devotion that they have brought home.

They bring home oil from the lanterns that have been lighted in holy places to use for anointing and healing. Olives from two-thousand-year-old trees in the garden of Gethsemane are treasured also. Most valuable, however, are the candles that were lighted in various holy places, especially from the Holy Fire on Easter.

BIBLIOGRAPHY

L. M. Orrieux's "Le pèlerinage dans la Bible," *Lumière et vie* 15 (September–October 1966): 5–34, is a concise yet comprehensive study of the meaning of pilgrimage in the Old and New Testaments. The rise and development of Christian pilgrimage are presented in two important works: E. D. Hunt's *Holy Land Pilgrimage in the Later Roman Empire, AD 312–460* (Oxford, 1984), a thorough study that takes into account the historical, political, and liturgical aspects of Christian pilgrimage, and John Wilkinson's excellent translation of Egeria's account of her travels, with exhaustive commentary, *Egeria's Travels* (London, 1971). While the pilgrim routes and churches are discussed in Wilkinson's book, the study of the Jerusalem liturgy holds an important place and is based on the detailed information given by Egeria. L. G. A. Cust's *The Status Quo in the Holy Places* (Jerusalem, 1980) is a descriptive account of the holy places and the practices that are carried out by their principal caretakers, the Greeks, the Armenians, and the Roman Catholics. For a description of the ceremony of the Holy Fire, see pages 66–70. Concerning pilgrimage sites of the most ancient monasteries and shrines, see Otto F. A. Meinardus's *Monks and Monasteries of the Egyptian Desert* (revised ed., Cairo, 1989) and Erhart Kaestner's *Mount Athos* (London, 1961).

New Sources

Meinardus, Otto Friedrich August. *Coptic Saints and Pilgrimages.* Cairo and New York, 2002.

Smith, Mark. S., and Elizabeth Block-Smith. *The Pilgrimage Pattern in Exodus.* Sheffield, U.K., 1997.

SIRARPI FEREDJIAN-AIVAZIAN (1987)
Revised Bibliography

PILGRIMAGE: MUSLIM PILGRIMAGE

The annual pilgrimage of Muslims to Mecca, in west-central Arabia, is known by the term *ḥājj.* As a religious duty that is the fifth of the Five Pillars of Islam, the *ḥājj* is an obligation for all Muslims to perform once in their adult lives, provided they be of sound mind and health and financially able at the time. In 1982, from an estimated world Islamic population of 750 million, approximately 3 million Muslims were reported to have made the journey. The nature and size of this annual ingathering of Muslims from countless ethnic, linguistic, and political backgrounds, combined with the common sacred status that ideally makes princes indistinguishable from paupers, render the *ḥājj* experience an important expression of social and religious unity in Islamic culture.

ḤĀJJ IN THE CONTEXT OF MIDDLE EASTERN WORLDVIEWS. The duty of performing the *ḥājj* rests on the authority of scripture (Qurʾān) and the recorded practice of the prophet Muḥammad (*sunnah*), as these are interpreted by the orthodox schools of Islamic law; Shīʿī Muslims rely in addition on the teachings of the early *imāms*, leaders descended from the family of the Prophet through the lineage of ʿAlī. The *manāsik al-ḥājj*, manuals that explain the rituals and prayers required at each of the *ḥājj* stations, are adduced from these authorities. More than the symbolism found in the other religious duties of Islam, however, *ḥājj* symbolism carries overtones of ancient Arab and Judeo-Christian cosmologies, which resonate in the appointed times and places of the ritual performances.

For Muslims, the shrine in Mecca comprehends several notions: for example, that creation began at Mecca; that the father of the prophets, Ibrāhīm (Abraham), constructed the first house of worship (Kaʿbah, Bayt Allāh) at Mecca; that the pagan practices of the Arabs at the Kaʿbah were displayed by God's final revelation through Muḥammad, his Messenger to the Arabs and to all of humankind. Indeed, the Kaʿbah determines the ritual direction, or *qiblah,* the focal point toward which canonical prayers (*ṣalāt*) and places of prayer (*masjid,* mosque) are physically oriented, the direction in which the deceased are faced in their graves, and the focus of other ritual gestures as well. The Kaʿbah is regarded as the navel of the universe, and it is the place from which the prayers of the faithful are believed to be most effective. For Muslims, Mecca has been the site of divine, angelic, prophetic, and auspicious human activity since the primordial moment of creation.

Ḥājj manuals commonly begin with the following Qurʾanic epigraph: "Truly, the first House of Worship established for humankind is the one at Bakkah [Mecca], a blessing and guidance to all realms of being. In it are clear signs, such as the Place of Ibrāhīm, and whoever enters [the Meccan precincts] is safe. The *ḥājj* to the House is a duty humankind owes to God, that is, for those who are able to journey to it" (3:96–97). The significance of the prophet Ibrāhīm to the sacred origins of the *ḥājj* sites is attested widely in Islamic literature. Ibrāhīm symbolizes the pure monotheism that the ancient communities subsequently perverted or forgot. In the Muslim view, the period of Arabian history that intervened between the prophets Ibrāhīm and Muḥammad was one of religious ignorance, Jahilīyah—a period during which monotheism was abandoned and the pilgrim stations were made to serve pagan nature deities. Yet, the pre-Islamic *ḥājj* provided important precedents of ritual sites and gestures that continued to be auspicious in Islamic times.

By the sixth century CE, the bedouin tribes of central Arabia were undergoing political and social changes, reflected especially in the growing commercial importance of settled markets and caravansaries at Mecca. Muḥammad's tribe, the Quraysh, dominated caravan trading through the use of force and lucrative arrangements with other tribes. Such trading centers were also pilgrimage sites to which Arabs journeyed annually during sacred months constituting a moratorium of tribal feuding. Although the pilgrimage remained a dangerous undertaking in the face of banditry and unpacified tribal rivalry, the special months and territories provided sanctuary for many of the shared sacred and profane activities of Arab tribal culture. The auspicious times and places of pilgrimage, along with the annual fairs and markets held at nearby locales along the pilgrims' routes, appear to have played significant roles in stabilizing the segmented polity of Arab tribalism.

The term *ḥājj* itself, like its Hebrew cognate *ḥag,* seems to reflect an ancient Semitic notion of "going around" or "standing" in the presence of a deity at a sacred mountain or shrine, or the journey to it (see *Ex.* 23:14; also *Ex.* 23:17 and 24:22, *Jgs.* 21:19, and *1 Kgs.* 8:2). The pilgrimage stations at Arafat, Muzdalifah, and Minā on the road east of Mecca appear to have been associated with solar and mountain deities prior to the rise of Islam; the "standing" at Arafat, the "hurry" to Muzdalifah, and the stoning of the pillars at Minā—the Islamic significance of which will be discussed below—were all ancient rites among the Arabs.

Islam did not destroy the pre-Islamic *ḥājj* rituals, but it infused them with new symbols and meanings. In its own conceptual terms, Islam asserted (or reasserted) monotheism over the polytheism of Jahilīyah. The Qurʾān also declared that the sacred months of pilgrimage should be calculated according to a lunar calendar that could not be adjusted every few years—as it had been in pagan times—and the Qurʾanic injunction against intercalation resulted in a lunar year of twelve months approximately every 354 days, thus distinguishing the *ḥājj* and other Muslim festivals from the fixed seasonal celebrations characteristic of pagan astral and agricultural (fertility) religions. Following the Muslim calendar, the *ḥājj* and other ceremonials rotate throughout the seasons of the year.

According to Islamic tradition, the Abrahamic origins of *ḥājj* sites and rituals had been taught by the prophet Muḥammad to the nascent Islamic community during the pilgrimage he performed just before the end of his life (632 CE). The sermon he delivered on the Mount of Mercy, at Arafat, and his removal of all pagan idols from the Kaʿbah in Mecca are recollected annually during the *ḥājj* ceremonies. The imputed Abrahamic origins of the *ḥājj* ceremonies constitute a deeper, complementary layer of symbolism that serves to underpin Muḥammad's treatment of the *ḥājj* as a monotheistic ritual. Ibrāhīm's duty to sacrifice Ismāʿīl (Ishmael; not Isaac as in the biblical tradition), Satan's three attempts to dissuade Ibrāhīm from following God's command, and the divine substitution of a ram for the blood sacrifice are celebrated at Minā during the festival of the Greater Sacrifice and the ritual stoning of the three pillars (see below). Mecca itself is believed to have been the wilderness sanctuary to which the banished Ḥājar (Hagar) and her infant son Ismāʿīl were escorted by Ibrāhīm. The Kaʿbah stands on the site of a primordial temple where Adam is said to have prayed after his expulsion from Paradise. Destroyed by the deluge, the Kaʿbah was rebuilt by Ibrāhīm and Ismāʿīl: during the deluge, the sacred Black Stone from the primordial Kaʿbah had been sealed in a niche in Mount Qubays (east of Mecca), then brought by the angel Jibrīl (Gabriel) to Ibrāhīm for the reconstruction of the present Kaʿbah, where it was set into the eastern corner. The sacred hillocks of al- Ṣafā and al-Marwah situated near the Kaʿbah symbolize the points between which Ḥājar is said to have run in desperate search of water, and the gushing forth of water next to the Kaʿbah is a Muslim symbol of God's providential relief to Ḥājar and Ismāʿīl.

The historic seventh-century shift at Mecca from a polytheistic to a monotheistic cosmology—of which the *ḥājj* is the supreme ritual expression—is significant for the comparative study of religions and civilizations. Urban geographer Paul Wheatley (*The Pivot of the Four Corners,* 1971) argues that archaeological and textual evidence on the rise of cities throughout the ancient world point to the importance of shrines and cults that stood at the center of urban complexes. Wheatley suggests that cities such as Mecca, by focusing sacredness on cult symbols of cosmic and moral order, were able to organize the previous tribal polities into larger, more efficient economic, social, and political systems. Urban-based great traditions evolved and were perpetuated by literati who canonized the technical requirements and meanings of ritual performance at the shrines. In this way, such traditions provided for the continuity of culture over time and geographic space; they ensured that the cosmic center (*omphalos, axis mundi*) continued to be enshrined and celebrated within the sacred city. The seventh-century shift from local deities and tribal morality to a monotheistic cosmic and moral order in Islam coincided with a period of Arabian hegemony over larger neighboring civilizations. With the Islamization of the Arabian *ḥājj* during this process, therefore, the pilgrimage to Mecca came to symbolize for Muslim peoples and lands across Asia, the Middle East, and North Africa the sacred origins and center of their common confessional heritage.

REQUIREMENTS AND PREPARATIONS FOR THE ḤĀJJ. Muslim authorities generally agree on the following requirements of eligibility for the *ḥājj*: (1) one must be a confessing Muslim who (2) has reached the age of puberty, (3) is of rational and sound mind, (4) is a freed man or woman, and (5) has the physical strength and health to undertake the rigors of the journey. Islamic law also provides that a pilgrim must be in possession of sufficient and honest funds not only for the expenses of the *ḥājj* but also for the care of dependents who remain at home.

From figures available on *ḥājj* participation in relation to total Muslim population, it is clear that only a small percentage of Muslims make the pilgrimage in any given year, and that many never undertake the journey at all. In addition to the above qualifications, one is not expected to risk life, limb, or possessions if war and hostility are known to exist along the pilgrim's path. Living at great distances from Mecca has tended to make fulfillment of the duty of *ḥājj* less likely for many Muslims for obvious reasons, although in modern times some Muslim countries such as Malaysia have instituted programs to assist Muslims in saving and preparing for the journey. Children, to whom the obligation of *ḥājj* does not apply, may nonetheless accompany their parents. The schools of law generally agree that women should be accompanied by their husbands or by two male relatives who are ineligible to marry them (first-cousin marriages are common in Islam). Although legal consensus and practical considerations discourage women from making the journey without appropriate male chaperons, the law does not allow males to prevent female Muslims from fulfilling the *ḥājj* if proper arrangements can be made. The Prophet is cited as having approved of Muslims' making the *ḥājj* on behalf of deceased relatives who intended, but were unable, to do so themselves. The feeble and desperately ill may send others to Mecca on their behalf.

Thus, although *ḥājj* is a duty one owes to God, the decision as to whether and when one should undertake the "journey to the House" belongs ultimately to each individual Muslim. The authorities insist that *ḥājj* is valid at any stage of adult life. The *ḥājj*, therefore, is not a rite of passage in the sense of the ritual celebrations of birth, circumcision, marriage, and death, which have their appointed times within the human life cycle, and this aspect of the *ḥājj* duty allows Muslims, including the very pious, to delay the decision to make the *ḥājj*, in many cases indefinitely. Islam recognizes that conditions may exist that will cause postponement of the journey and charges apostasy or heresy only to those who deny that *ḥājj* is a duty to God.

A pilgrim's separation from familiar social and cultural surroundings constitutes a moment of prayerful anxiety and joyful celebration for all concerned. On the eve of departure, it is traditional for family and friends to gather for prayers, Qur'ān recitation, food, and perhaps poetry and singing about the *ḥājj*. (So, too, when the *ḥājj* rites have been completed, the pilgrim's return home will be celebrated by family and friends; in some parts of the Islamic world the homes of returning pilgrims are decorated with symbols of the *ḥājj*, reflecting local popular art forms.) Many pilgrims follow the practice of setting out from home on the right foot, a symbol of good omen and fortune. Similarly, it is auspicious to enter mosques, including the Sacred Mosque in Mecca, on the right foot and depart on the left; the right/left symbolism is associated with several ritual gestures in Islam as well as in other traditions. As on so many occasions during the *ḥājj*, the actual moment of departure calls for the recitation of a particular verse from the Qurʾān, and departing pilgrims recite the words of Noah, uttered to those escaping the deluge: "Board [the Ark]; in God's name be its course and mooring. My Lord is forgiving, merciful" (11:41). Indeed, the symbolism of separation, salvation, and safe passage is found in the pilgrimage rituals of many religious traditions. Those who complete the *ḥājj* will be entitled to the epithet *ḥājj* or *ḥājji* (*ḥajjah* or *ḥajjiyah* if female). This honorific title indicates socially perceived status enhancement in the sense of recognition by one's peers that a sacred duty has been fulfilled, and this is a matter of universal value, if not universal achievement, in Islam.

Most pilgrims require assistance in arranging for travel, lodging, and proper guidance in the execution of rites and prayers within the Meccan precincts. During the Middle Ages, caravans of pilgrims assembled and traveled together from Egypt, South Arabia, Syria, and Iraq. Their common wayfaring experiences on the road have not produced an *Islamic Canterbury Tales,* although one Muslim writer has observed that material for such a literature abounds within the communities of pilgrims who journey each year to Mecca. During the Middle Ages hospices and hostels were established along the pilgrimage routes from religious endowments given by those in possession of both piety and wealth. In recent times, *ḥājj* travel organizations in Muslim countries have helped to arrange for chartered air, sea, and overland travel and for local accommodations in Mecca.

Of considerable importance throughout the centuries have been the *ḥājj* guides (known as *muṭawwifs*). The responsibilities of these guides and their agents include leading groups of pilgrims through the proper performance of rituals and prayers at each pilgrimage station as well as seeing to food and lodging needs. Employing a trustworthy guide is a major concern for pilgrims, as attested in *ḥājj* manuals and in conventional wisdom about preparing for the *ḥājj*. Since the rise of Islam in the seventh century CE, the Muslims of Arabia, especially the Meccans, have served a growing "*ḥājj* industry" of services for pilgrims from around the world. Recognizing that opportunities invariably arise to take advantage of those who are far from home and in a state of intense piety, in modern times the government of Saudi Arabia has sought to regulate the offering of religious, material, and health services to the millions of visitors who enter its national boundaries each year to fulfill the sacred duty.

Travel accounts by pilgrims reveal other dimensions of the *ḥājj*, such as opportunities for adventure, business, education, and even marriage. The intention to engage in business with other pilgrims is lawful, especially if it is meant to help defray the costs of the journey. *Ḥājj* manuals nonetheless caution wariness of unscrupulous sellers of goods and services, even those who may be found within the sacred precincts. Marriage among pilgrims is also permitted, and the *ḥājj* provides occasions for establishing friendships and personal relationships, although marriage and sexual contact are forbidden during the period of sacred observance at the Meccan precincts. In former times, when travel was considerably more difficult, many pilgrims followed an open itinerary and lingered at towns and cities along the way; those who thirsted for knowledge found opportunities to attend the lectures of famous teachers at mosque colleges. Biographical literature in Islam indicates that the *ḥājj* has been for many individuals an important moment or phase of life that has had numerous ramifications of lasting personal, if not social, significance.

IḤRĀM, THE CONDITION OF CONSECRATION. The *ḥājj* season lasts from the beginning of the tenth month of the Muslim calendar, Shawwal, until the tenth day of the twelfth month, Dhū al-Ḥijjah. Although the actual *ḥājj* rites do not begin until the eighth of Dhu al-Hijjah, the two-and-a-half-month period known as *al-miqat al-zamanīyah* is reserved for travel and ritual preparations for the *ḥājj* ceremonies. The rites of preparation and consecration are comprehended by the term *iḥrām.* Pilgrims assume the condition of *iḥrām* before they pass the territorial markers, *al-mīqāt al-makānīyah,* that are situated several miles outside of Mecca along the ancient routes for caravans from Syria, Medina, Iraq, and the Yemen. Within the territory bounded by these markers lie the sacred precincts of Mecca. For the vast majority of Muslims who in modern times disembark from air and sea travel at the west Arabian port of Jidda, the rites of *iḥrām* are begun on board before arrival, or at Jidda itself. Muslims may enter Mecca and its vicinity at any time without assuming the condition of *iḥrām,* but if their intention is to perform the rites of *ḥājj* or *ʿumrah* (see below), *iḥrām* is required.

Assuming the condition of *iḥrām* before passing the territorial markers has several aspects.

1. *Iḥrām* requires a state of ritual purity, and pilgrims who enter it must perform ablutions much the same as they do for the daily canonical prayers, *ṣalāt.* The special condition of *iḥrām* also requires pilgrims to trim their fingernails and remove underarm and pubic hair, and men must shave off beards and mustaches. The further cutting of nails and hair is part of the rite of deconsecration, *taḥallul,* and is not permitted until the *ḥājj* and/or *ʿumrah* rites have been completed. A pilgrim in the state of *iḥrām* is also forbidden to use perfumes or carry symbols of personal wealth, such as silk and gold jewelry.

2. *Iḥrām* is initiated and sustained by prayers of several kinds. (a) The *nīyah* is the prayer by which each pilgrim declares his or her intention in the rites that follow. At any time of the year except during the three days of the *ḥājj* itself, Muslim visitors may enter the Meccan precincts with the intention of performing rites at the Sacred Mosque of Mecca, which enshrines the Kaʿbah. This is known as the *ʿumrah,* or "lesser pilgrimage." Pilgrims making the *ḥājj*, or "greater pilgrimage," will declare a *nīyah* also to visit Arafat, Muzdalifah, and Minā on the eighth through the tenth of Dhū al-Ḥijjah. Their prayers must stipulate whether or not they intend to interrupt the state of *iḥrām* during the interval that may lapse between the performances of *ʿumrah* and *ḥājj*. (b) A second form of prayer is the *ṣalāt*, which includes the formal prostrations in the direction (*qiblah*) of the Kaʿbah in Mecca. When pilgrims assume *iḥrām*, they perform a *ṣalāt* of two prostrations before entering the sacred territories. During the *ḥājj*, including the days of travel to and from Mecca, the five daily performances of *ṣalāt* assume the following pattern: once at dawn, the noon and afternoon prayers together at midday, and the sunset and evening prayers at dusk. (c) A third form of prayer is called *duʿāʾ*, "supplication." *Duʿāʾ* is a less formalized, more individualized expression of communication with God. A supplication is normally offered after the *ṣalāt*, especially the *ṣalāt* of *iḥrām*, and thereafter frequently at each of the pilgrimage sites. The texts of supplications recommended in the *ḥājj* manuals reveal something of the meanings these shrines and performances hold for Muslims. (d) The fourth type of prayer, the *talbiyah*, belongs to *iḥrām* alone. The *talbiyah* is uttered in a loud voice as pilgrims pass the markers of the sacred territory and frequently during the days of consecration. The brief lines of *talbiyah* begin with a phrase that means roughly "Here I am, O Lord! What is Thy command?"

3. In addition to the ablutions and prayers, *iḥrām* requires each pilgrim to exchange normal clothing for special garments. The *iḥrām* garb is simple, a visual symbol of the ideal of universal Islamic brotherhood that the *ḥājj* and *ʿumrah* rites celebrate. For males the *iḥrām* attire consists of two seamless white pieces of cloth, one attached around the waist and reaching to the knees, the other worn over the left shoulder and attached around the torso, leaving the right shoulder and arm free for ritual gesturing. Males may not wear any head covering, and their footwear is restricted to sandals that leave the backs of the heels exposed. Females wear plain dresses that extend from neckline to ankles and cover the arms. A head covering is required of females, but veiling the face is not permitted during the period of consecration. *Ḥājj* manuals are less than sanguine about the comfort of the *iḥrām* attire, especially in summer and winter seasons.

Iḥrām, then, is a state of consecration that each pilgrim must assume before he or she may enter the sacred precincts. The state of consecration exemplifies the concept of egalitarian brotherhood, or *communitas*, that many religious traditions establish ritually during pilgrimages and other rites. The *ḥaram*, or "sacred precincts," is a place in which those who enter expect to feel nearness to God, and *iḥrām* is a special moment and condition of brotherhood for all pilgrims. Within the spatial and temporal boundaries of *iḥrām*, it is forbidden to uproot plants, kill animals, or foment any social violence. Husbands and wives are enjoined to refrain from sexual intercourse, and women are counseled to conduct themselves modestly so as not to attract male attention. Familiar sociocultural identities and structures are reduced drastically, for pilgrims are now approaching the navel of creation, the primordial house where Adam and Ibrāhīm worshiped, a hallowed ground where Muḥammad recited God's final revelation to humankind.

ʿ*UMRAH*, THE LESSER PILGRIMAGE. All accounts of the experience of the final approach to Mecca indicate that it is a moment of high emotions attending the realization of a lifelong ambition. The practical matter of securing lodging and the care of a pilgrim guide is usually the first order of business; the most valued and anticipated task, however, is a visit to the Kaʿbah for the rites of *ʿumrah*.

From ancient times, the Kaʿbah and its environs have been symbols of refuge from violence and pursuit, a sacred space in which wayfaring pilgrims could find sanctuary with the divine. The Kaʿbah is now enclosed within the roofless courtyard of the Sacred Mosque of Mecca, al-Masjid al-Ḥāram. Arriving pilgrims approach the mosque through streets teeming with the traffic of other pilgrims, vendors, and merchants, whose shops and stalls compact the urban space that surrounds the ancient shrine.

Twenty-four gates lead into the mosque courtyard. The four corners of the outer walls of the Sacred Mosque as well as the four corners of the Kaʿbah in the center of its grounds are oriented approximately in the cardinal directions. The Kaʿbah is surrounded by a circle of stone flooring called the *maṭāf*, the place of circumambulations. Set within the eastern corner of the Kaʿbah is the sacred Black Stone, encased by a silver rim; another auspicious stone is encased in the southern corner. The four walls of the Kaʿbah are covered with a gigantic black curtain, called the *kiswah*, which is decorated in bands of Arabic calligraphy embroidered in gold. The Gate of Peace near the northern corner of the Sacred Mosque is the traditional entrance for the performance of *ʿumrah*. Again, emotions rise at the first glimpse of the haunting specter of the Kaʿbah.

Once they have entered the Gate of Peace, pilgrims move to a position east of the Kaʿbah and face the corner with the Black Stone. The rite of *ṭawāf*, or circumambulation, begins from this point with a supplication followed by a kiss, touch, or gesture of touching the black stone. The pilgrim turns to the right and begins the seven circumambulations, moving counterclockwise around the Kaʿbah. Each circuit has a special significance with recommended prayers that the pilgrim may recite either from *ḥājj* manuals or by following the words of the *ḥājj* guide leading the group. When passing the stone in the southern corner and the sacred Black Stone in the eastern corner, it is traditional to touch or make a gesture of touching each stone with uplifted right arm and a verbal supplication. Male pilgrims are admonished to take the first three laps at a quickened pace and the remaining four more slowly.

Following the *ṭawāf*, pilgrims visit shrines adjacent to the Kaʿbah. An area along the northeastern wall of the Kaʿbah between its sole door and the Black Stone is the *multazim* or "place of pressing." With uplifted arms, resting if possible on the *multazim* wall, pilgrims offer a supplication. Another place of visitation is the Maqām Ibrāhīm, which symbolizes the place from which Abraham is said to have prayed toward the Kaʿbah. From within or near the covered shrine of Ibrāhīm, pilgrims perform a prayer of two prostrations. Near Maqām Ibrāhīm to the east of the Kaʿbah is the well of Zamzam. A drink of its water, said to have a brackish taste, is sought by every pilgrim. On the northwestern side of the Kaʿbah, a low semicircular wall encloses a space. The enclosure is known as al-Ḥijr, and it is thought to be the site of the graves of Ḥājar and Ismāʿīl. Al-Ḥijr is also said to be the spot beside the Kaʿbah where Muḥammad slept on the night of his miraculous journey from Mecca to Jerusalem.

After the circumambulations and visitations, pilgrims leave the Sacred Mosque (leading with the left foot) through the Gate of Purity on the southeast side. A few yards outside the Gate of Purity is the small hillock of al-Ṣafā. From al-Ṣafā begins the *saʿy,* the rite of trotting seven laps to and from the hillock of al-Marwah, which is located some four hundred and fifty yards to the northeast of the Sacred Mosque. The *saʿy* commemorates Ḥājar's desperate search for water in the Meccan wilderness and ends the rites of *ʿumrah.* Year-round visitors to Mecca who intend to perform *ʿumrah* only, or pilgrims who arrive early for the *ḥajj,* deconsecrate themselves at this time by a ritual of haircutting and by doffing the *iḥrām* garb (see below).

ḤĀJJ, THE GREATER PILGRIMAGE. The *ḥājj* proper begins on the eighth of Dhū al-Ḥijjah, the day of setting out for Arafat, which is located some thirteen miles east of Mecca. Many pilgrims spend the first night at Minā, as the prophet Muḥammad himself is said to have done, while others push on to Arafat. The goal of all pilgrims is to reach Jabal al-Raḥmah, the Mount of Mercy, located on the eastern plain of Arafat, by noon on the ninth of Dhū al-Ḥijjah.

Arafat. Muslim authorities agree that "there is no *ḥājj* without Arafat," that is, the rite of *wūquf* or "standing" at the Mount of Mercy. According to legend, Adam and Eve first met and "knew" (*ʿarafū*) one another at Arafat after the long separation that followed their expulsion from Paradise. Tradition also teaches that Ibrāhīm went out to Arafat and performed *wūquf.* The prophet Muḥammad addressed a multitude of followers performing *wuquf* during his farewell pilgrimage, and the following words are attributed to him on that occasion: "O people, hear what I have to say, for I know not whether I shall again be with you here after this day. . . . Truly, all Muslims are brothers . . . and your Lord is one." Tradition also accords to this occasion the revelation of the final verse of the Qurʾān recited by Muḥammad: "This day I have perfected your religion for you and have chosen for you Islam as your religion" (5:3). On the Day of Standing at Arafat, pilgrims perform an ablution and canonical prayer at a mosque located near the western entrance to the plain. When the sun passes the noon meridian, the Mount of Mercy is covered with pilgrims. The themes of brotherhood and repentance dominate the afternoon sermons and supplications.

Muzdalifah. At sundown the somber scene of prayer changes abruptly as pilgrims scramble to break camp and begin the "hurrying" to Muzdalifah. This rite is called the *ifaḍāh* ("pouring forth") or *nafrah* ("stampede") and is described in pilgrim diaries as a moment of urgent confusion. Like the preceding period of respectful standing, however, the hurry to Muzdalifah is a rite of ancient significance; it is not simply undisciplined mass behavior. At Muzdalifah, a few miles on the road back toward Mecca, pilgrims halt for a combined observance of the sunset and evening *ṣalāt* prayers. The *sunnah* of the Prophet established the tradition of staying overnight at Muzdalifah, although it is permissible after the halt in Muzdalifah to push on closer to Minā. The Qurʾān admonishes: "When you hurry from Arafat, remember God at the Sacred Grove (*al-mashʿar al-ḥaram*)," that is, at Muzdalifah (2:198). Today a mosque marks the place in Muzdalifah where pilgrims gather to perform the special *ṣalāt.* Also during the halt at Muzdalifah, pilgrims gather small stones for the ritual lapidations at Mina the next day.

Minā. The tenth of Dhū al-Ḥijjah is the final official day of the *ḥājj* season. Most of the ritual activities of this day take place in Minā and include (1) the casting of seven small stones at the pillar of Aqaba, (2) the feast of the major sacrifice (ʿId al-Aḍḥā), (3) the rite of deconsecration from the condition of *iḥrām,* and (4) the visit to Mecca for the *ṭawāf,* called *al-ifāḍah.*

The story of Ibrāhīm's duty to sacrifice Ismāʿīl provides the symbolic significance of the rites of lapidation and blood sacrifice. It is said that on his return from Arafat, Ibrāhīm was given the divine command to sacrifice that which was most dear to him, his son Ismāʿīl. Along the way to Mina, Satan whispered to him three times (or to Ibrāhīm, Ismāʿīl, and Ḥajār), tempting him (or them) not to obey the heavy command. The legendary response was a hurling of stones to repulse the Tempter. Three brick and mortar pillars stand in the center of Minā as symbols of Satan's temptations, and the pillar called Aqaba is the site where pilgrims gather early on the morning of the tenth of Dhū al-Ḥijjah to cast seven stones. Following the lapidations, those pilgrims who can afford it offer a blood sacrifice of a lamb or goat (sometimes a camel) to commemorate the divine substitution of a ram for Ibrāhīm's sacrifice. *Ḥājj* manuals recommend supplications that express the pilgrim's willingness to sacrifice for the sake of God that which is dear. The meat is consumed by family and friends, with unused portions given to the poor. The festival of the major sacrifice is also celebrated on this day by Muslims around the world in gatherings of family and friends.

Ṭawāf al-ifāḍah and taḥallul. After the sacrifice and feast, the process of *taḥallul,* or deconsecration, is begun with the rite of clipping the hair. Many men follow the tradition of having the head shaved, although for women, and for men if they prefer, the cutting of three hairs meets the ritual requirement. This is followed by a visit to Mecca for another rite of circumambulation known as *ṭawāf al-ifāḍah.* Pilgrims who have not yet performed the complete rites of *ʿumrah* may do so at this time.

The Kaʿbah itself undergoes purification and ritual renewal during the three days of *ḥājj.* Shortly before the *ḥājj* begins, the black *kiswah*—weathered and worn by a year of exposure to the open air—is replaced by a white one, suggestive of the *iḥrām* garb worn by pilgrims. After pilgrims go out to Arafat, Meccan authorities open the door of the Kaʿbah for the purpose of washing its interior, an act symbolic of the Prophet's cleansing of idols from the sacred house. Pilgrims returning for *ṭawāf al-ifāḍah* on the tenth of Dhū al-Ḥijjah are greeted by the sight of a lustrous new black *kiswah.* In the early Islamic period, the new *kiswah* and other presents for the shrines of Mecca and Medina were sent annually by the caliphs; these offerings were borne by camel caravan in an ornate box called a *maḥmal.* From the thirteenth century until 1927, the Egyptian *maḥmal.* brought the new *kiswah* each year. Since 1927 the *kiswah* has been made at a factory in Mecca.

When the *ṭawāf al-ifāḍah* has been completed, the dissolution of the condition of consecration is made final by doffing the pilgrim garb and wearing normal clothing. All the prohibitions of *iḥrām* are now lifted, and most pilgrims return to Minā for days of social gathering on the eleventh to the thirteenth of Dhū al-Ḥijjah. On each of these days it is *sunnah* to cast seven stones at each of the three pillars in Minā. This vast amalgam of pilgrims, dwelling in a river of tents pitched along the narrow valley of Minā, eases into a more relaxed atmosphere of friendly exchanges of religious greetings and visiting with Muslims from around the world. By sundown on the thirteenth, the plain of Minā must be vacated. Though many will choose to spend additional time in Mecca, all pilgrims make a last visit to the Kaʿbah for the final circumambulation, *ṭawāf al-qūdum,* which is permissible without the condition and attire of *iḥrām.* The *ḥajj* is thus complete, and each pilgrim leaves the sacred precincts with the honorific title of *ḥajjī.*

THE ZIYĀRAH, OR VISITATION TO HOLY PLACES. The Sacred Mosque in Mecca, the Prophet's Mosque in Medina, and the mosque of al-Aqṣā in Jerusalem are the three most sacred shrines in Islamic belief, and the three cities are especially holy to Muslims. Thus an additional pilgrimage to the Prophet's mosque and tomb in Medina is made by many Muslim visitors to Arabia each year, usually preceding or following the *ḥājj.* Although such visitations do not have the weight of religious duty in Islamic law and are not a formal part of the *ḥājj, ziyārah,* or visitation to holy places, is nonetheless an essential aspect of traditional Muslim piety. There are many monuments in both Mecca and Medina that mark the homes, graves, and events associated with the Prophet, his family, and his closest companions. Guides for *ziyārah* conduct pilgrims to these sites, where prayers and meditation are offered.

The most auspicious visitation is the one to the Mosque of the Prophet in Medina. Under the guidance of a shaykh, visitors enter the mosque through a passage called the Gate of Peace, uttering a supplication. Inside the mosque as it stands today is a brass railing that marks out the smaller boundaries of the original home and mosque of the Prophet, and within this brass railing pilgrims perform a *ṣalāt* of two prostrations followed by supplications. Nearby is the green-domed mausoleum of the Prophet, where pilgrims offer supplications and praises for the Prophet. The Prophet's mausoleum also enshrines the graves of the first two caliphs of Islam, Abū Bakr and ʿUmar, for whom prayers may also be said.

THE ḤĀJJ INTERPRETED. The meaning of the pilgrimage to Mecca, in general and in its many particulars, has been the subject of numerous books by Muslims throughout the centuries and by non-Muslim scholars in modern times. Although *ḥājj* is a duty that is carefully delimited by Islamic law, the great diversity of Muslims with differing degrees and kinds of piety are accommodated remarkably well within the structures of traditional interpretations. For example, the various schools of law differ in the degree of stringency each suggests for the length of time one must perform the rite of standing at Arafat. The more pious pilgrims seek to emulate what the Prophet recommended and practiced at each station within the sacred precincts, while others may choose to follow the minimal requirements of the more lenient interpretations of the schools of law. For virtually every rite, such as the blood sacrifice at Minā, physical or economic inability to meet the literal requirement can be compensated by the substitution of prayer and fasting.

The continual process of interpreting *ḥājj* meanings and requirements within the framework of Islamic symbols can be witnessed in the writings of contemporary Muslims. One problem under increasing discussion is the size of the pilgrim gathering in relation to available physical space for performance of the rites. The press of more than two million pilgrims to cast stones at the pillars of Minā, for example, has prompted Saudi *ḥājj* authorities to devise ways of organizing and regulating the social space within which the rite is performed. The mass slaughtering of hundreds of thousands of animals at Minā within a limited space and time creates a considerable health problem, particularly when the *ḥājj* occurs during the hot summer months. Some authorities have speculated on alternative ways for pilgrims to accomplish the root meaning of the sacrifice, namely, giving up that which is dear. Others, on the basis of statements drawn from the *sunnah* and the schools of law, have proposed that greater latitude should be given to the time permitted for the completion of such rites as the lapidations and the blood sacrifice.

The problem of interpretation and meaning must also be seen in relation to the political and technological changes that have affected the Islamic world. For example, the rise of nationalism has added a new dimension to the quest for ritual unity with the sacred precincts. Mass transportation has made travel to Mecca available to vastly larger numbers of pilgrims. The traditional experiences of adventure and hospitality along the *ḥājj* routes are being exchanged for the benefits of faster and safer passage by a growing majority of contemporary pilgrims. The ability to have media coverage of the *ḥājj* at home affords the Muslim community at large an audio and visual experience of the pilgrimage rites. Thus the *ḥājj* is becoming an ever more visible event to the world of Islam in modern times.

SEE ALSO Kaʿbah.

BIBLIOGRAPHY

A readable modern Muslim *ḥajj* manual is Ahmad Kamal's *The Sacred Journey* (New York, 1961). A pictorial essay with color photographs and accompanying text has been expertly prepared by Mohamed Amin, *Pilgrimage to Mecca* (Nairobi, 1978). Both the old and new editions of *The Encyclopaedia of Islam* (Leiden, 1913–1938 and 1960–) are valuable sources of information about the *ḥajj*; see especially the articles "Ḥadjdj" and "Kaʿba."

Among the works that attempt to analyze and interpret the *ḥajj* from a history-of-religions and social-science perspective, the most substantial is Maurice Gaudefroy-Demombynes's *Le pèlerinage à la Mekke* (Paris, 1923). On the *ḥajj* in relation to the study of ritual in the history of religions, see the articles by Frederick M. Denny and William R. Roff in *Islam and the History of Religions*, edited by Richard C. Martin (Berkeley, Calif., 1983). David Edwin Long's *The Hajj Today: A Survey of the Contemporary Makkah Pilgrimage* (Albany, N.Y., 1979) analyzes various social and health problems and modern attempts by the Saudi Arabian government to resolve them; it includes a useful bibliography.

Numerous accounts of the *ḥajj* by travelers and adventurers provide useful historical information about the pilgrimage at specific times in the past. The best known of this genre is Richard F. Burton's *Personal Narrative of a Pilgrimage to al-Madinah and Meccah*, 2 vols. (London, 1893). Eldon Rutter's *The Holy Cities of Arabia*, 2 vols. (London and New York, 1928), is a work written about the 1925 *ḥājj*—the period of Ibn Saud's incursion into western Arabia—and contains considerable geographical information and descriptions of the major *ḥajj* sites as well as the numerous points of visitation in and near Mecca. The role of Mecca and the Meccans in relation to the *ḥajj* was studied in Christiaan Snouck Hurgronje's *Mekka in the Latter Part of the Nineteenth Century* (Leiden, 1931).

RICHARD C. MARTIN (1987)

PILGRIMAGE: CONTEMPORARY JEWISH PILGRIMAGE

Jewish pilgrimages in Israel may be classified into three main types: (1) those that originated during the biblical period or that have as their goals historical sites from the biblical period located in Jerusalem and its surroundings; (2) pilgrimages to the tombs of Talmudic and qabbalistic sages, mainly located in the Galilee; and (3) emerging new centers of pilgrimage in various parts of the country dedicated to Diaspora sages and saints.

The tradition of pilgrimage, *ʿaliyyah le-regel* (literally, going up on foot), has been institutionalized in Jewish culture since the beginning of nationhood, with the religious prescription that committed all males to "go up" annually to the Temple in Jerusalem on three festivals (Passover; Shavuʿot or Pentecost; and Sukkot, the Feast of Tabernacles; see *Ex.* 23:17, 34:23; *Dt.* 16:16). The essence of the pilgrimage was the entry of the pilgrims into the Temple to worship, particularly through the offering of sacrifices. After the destruction of the Temple in 70 CE, pilgrimage to the holy site in Jerusalem continued until modern times, though it lost its convivial characteristics. The Western Wall (often referred to as the Wailing Wall), which survived the destruction of the Temple, became the symbol of Jewish historical continuity, recalling the tragedy of destruction and dispersion as well as the hope of the exiles to return to Erets Yisraʾel (the Land of Israel).

Other sites related to the biblical period have gradually become centers of pilgrimage. The most venerated are the Cave of Machpelah in Hebron (the reputed burial ground of the patriarchs); the reputed tomb of Rachel, Jacob's wife (and symbol of Jewish motherhood), in Bethlehem; and the reputed tomb of King David in Jerusalem. For most of the past nineteen hundred years, however, it was usually difficult, if not impossible, for Jews to visit most of the biblical sites because of obstructions set up by the local authorities. The Western Wall was for many centuries under Muslim *Waqf* administration, and Jews were not allowed to enter the Cave of Machpelah. Free entrance and worship at these sites became possible for Jews only after the Israeli army gained control of them during the 1967 war.

In later years, however, the free presence of Jews in the site of the Temple Mount in Jerusalem that hosts two monumental Muslim shrines (the mosques of Al-Aqsa and Dome of the Rock) as well as the competition for control over the Hebron Cave of the Patriarchs gradually raised tensions that culminated in extreme violence between Israelis and Palestinians. These two centers of pilgrimage became major symbols of contesting national aspirations, as well as obstacles to reconciliation and a territorial accommodation between two independent states. But less-central sites also gained popularity after 1967 and gradually caused violent conflicts, in particular the reputed tomb of Joseph in the Palestinian town of Nablus (the biblical location of Shechem).

A second center for pilgrimages developed in the Galilee, at Safad and Tiberias, where many Talmudic sages (first to fifth centuries) and qabbalist sages (particularly during the sixteenth century) lived and were reputedly buried. The first evidence of pilgrimage to these sites dates from the thirteenth century. The most famous site is the reputed tomb of Rabbi Shimʿon bar Yoḥʾai, since the sixteenth century the most venerated postbiblical figure in Jewish folk tradition. Bar Yoḥʾai, who lived during the second century, was a scholar and patriot who opposed the Roman occupation and who has been accredited by popular tradition with the authorship of the *Zohar,* the classic text of Jewish mysticism. According to tradition, Bar Yoḥʾai was buried with his son Elʿazar in Meron, a village on a hill near Safad. For at least four centuries a ceremony and a popular festival have been held at Meron on the holiday of Lag ba-ʿOmer, the eighteenth day of the Jewish month of Iyyar. Pilgrims to Meron usually also celebrate at the tomb of Rabbi Meʾir Baʿal ha-Nes in Tiberias. The latter is believed by many to have been a distinguished scholar and saint, also from the second century.

Regular pilgrimages to the tombs of the sages and saints have been particularly popular in North Africa, where Muslim and Jewish beliefs have often been shared and exchanged. Among Moroccan Jewry (formerly the largest Jewish community in the Muslim world), many individuals were devoted to a particular family saint. Some of these saints' tombs acquired wide reputations throughout Morocco and became centers for large annual festivals *(hillulot;* singular, *hillula).* A number of these shrines have been symbolically transferred to the state of Israel, to which the majority of Moroccan Jews immigrated. Synagogues or memorial rooms were dedicated on spots indicated by the saints themselves, as revealed to certain individuals in dreams. Also a few venerated North African rabbis who died in Israel have gained the popularity of saints and attract large crowds of pilgrims (in particular the *hillula* at the tomb of Baba Sali in the Negev town of Netivot). The new shrines, often located in poor immigrant towns, have become new centers for convivial pilgrimages.

Contemporary pilgrims often visit, at the appropriate annual dates, the biblical, the Talmudic-qabbalistic, and the new centers of pilgrimage. But they demonstrate at the various sites different patterns of devotional activity. Visits to biblical sites are shorter than visits to other sites (a few hours at most), more specifically oriented, more formally ritualized, and less convivial.

The pilgrimage and the festivities carried out on Lag ba-ʿOmer in Meron are the most elaborate. More than 100,000 pilgrims assemble on that day, and many stay for several days. Boys are brought to the Meron pilgrimage for their first haircuts, and the hair is burned in the fire kindled on the roof of the tomb to commemorate the saint's spirit. Into the same fire people also throw small personal belongings, such as scarves and handkerchiefs. Money and candles are thrown onto the tomb itself; the money is later used for charity. Sheep and goats are slaughtered on the spot to provide food for the congregating people, including the poor, who are invited to take a share. A variety of ethnic groups, including Jews of Ashkenazic (eastern and central European), Middle Eastern, and North African extraction, meet convivially at the site, which is reputed to have miraculous powers. Structural liminality and feelings of Israeli *communitas* reach their peaks here.

In contrast, the North African immigrants who participate in *hillulot* at the new shrines, though aspiring toward similar religious and moral goals, display more noticeable feelings of ethnic solidarity. Through the commemoration of North African Jewish cultural heroes, they seem to express symbolically their shared experience of emigration and their position in Israeli society.

Contemporary Israelis also go on pilgrimage to Jewish sites outside of their country. They visit the graves of famous rabbis and saints left behind in eastern Europe (Naḥman of Bratslav [1772–1810] in the Ukraine in particular), in Morocco, and, since the late 1990s, to the grave in New York of the last venerated leader of the Habad Hasidic movement, Menaḥem Mendel Schneersohn (1902–1994).

All pilgrimages to holy sites, tombs, and shrines, during the major annual festivals or on other occasions, are deemed to carry good luck and remedy for particular misfortunes. The pilgrims pray, make offerings, and sometimes write requests on notes that they leave at the site. With the exception of the Western Wall in Jerusalem, where prayers are addressed to God, pilgrims tend to call on the ancestors and saints associated with the holy site to intercede for divine help. The belief in this practice has been expressed by a Moroccan immigrant, who stated: "We travel to the saint who will ask God for mercy. When you can't get to the mayor, you approach the deputy and ask for his help."

SEE ALSO Culture Heroes; Folk Religion, article on Folk Judaism.

BIBLIOGRAPHY

Ben-Ami, Issachar. *Yahadut Maroko.* Jerusalem, 1975. See pages 110–117 and 171–197.

Ben-Ami, Issachar. "Le-heqer folqlor ha-milhamah: Motiv ha-qedoshim." In *Sefer Dov Sadan,* edited by Samuel Werses, Nathan Rotenstreich, and Chone Shmeruk, pp. 87–104. Tel Aviv, 1977.

Ben-Ari, Eyal, and Yoram Bilu. "Saints' Sanctuaries in Israeli Development Towns." *Urban Anthropology* 16 (1987): 243–272. This article is also in *Israeli Judaism: The Sociology of Religion in Israel,* edited by Shlomo Deshen, Charles S. Liebman, and Moshe Shokeid, pp. 255–284. New Brunswick, N.J., 1995.

Bilu, Yoram. "Dreams and Wishes of the Saint." In *Judaism Viewed from Within and from Without,* edited by Harvey E. Goldberg, pp. 285–314. Albany, N.Y., 1987.

Braslavi, Joseph. *Studies in Our Country, Its Past and Remains.* Tel Aviv, 1954. See pages 342–358.

Deshen, Shlomo. "The Memorial Celebrations of Tunisian Immigrants." In *The Predicament of Homecoming: Cultural and Social Life of North African Immigrants in Israel,* by Shlomo Deshen and Moshe Shokeid, pp. 95–121. Ithaca, N.Y., 1974.

Levy, André. "To Morocco and Back: Tourism and Pilgrimage among Moroccan-Born Israelis." In *Grasping Land: Space and Place in Contemporary Israeli Discourse and Experience,* edited by Eyal Ben-Ari and Yoram Bilu, pp. 25–46. Albany, N.Y., 1997.

Shokeid, Moshe. "An Anthropological Perspective on Ascetic Behavior and Religious Change." In *The Predicament of Homecoming: Cultural and Social Life of North African Immigrants in Israel,* by Shlomo Deshen and Moshe Shokeid, pp. 64–94. Ithaca, N.Y., 1974.

Shokeid, Moshe. "The Moroccan Jewish Cult of Saints in Israel Revisited" (in Hebrew). *Israeli Sociology* 1, no. 1 (1998): 39–54.

Vilnay, Zev. *Matsevot qodesh be-Erets-Yiśra'el.* Jerusalem, 1963.

Weingrod, Alex. *The Saint of Beersheba.* Albany, N.Y., 1990.

MOSHE SHOKEID (1987 AND 2005)

PILGRIMAGE: BUDDHIST PILGRIMAGE IN SOUTH AND SOUTHEAST ASIA

Victor and Edith Turner, in their book *Image and Pilgrimage in Christian Culture* (New York, 1978), have written that "if mysticism is an interior pilgrimage, pilgrimage is exteriorized mysticism." In the Buddhist tradition, one undertakes a pilgrimage in order to find the Buddha in the external world; one undertakes meditation to discover the Buddha nature within oneself. The internal pilgrimage brings one closer to the goal of *nirvāṇa* (Pali, *nibbāna*) than does the external pilgrimage, but the turning toward the Buddha who is iconically represented in the marks of his presence on earth or in relics constitutes an important preliminary step along the path to enlightenment. That the Buddha actually existed in the world, and continues to exist through traces (Skt., *caitya;* Pali, *cetiya*), must be acknowledged before one begins to follow his teachings (Skt., *dharma;* Pali, *dhamma*).

The question of the persistence of the Buddha in the world arose as he approached his physical death and his *parinirvāṇa* (*parinibbāna*), or "final cessation." During his lifetime, the Buddha had attracted many followers, among whom were those who came to constitute the *saṃgha,* the order of mendicants devoted to his teachings. While the *saṃgha* could be entrusted with the responsibility of perpetuating the Dharma through practice and teaching after the Buddha's death, there remained still the problem of how people were to be attracted in the first place to the Buddhist message. This problem was resolved when the Buddha charged his disciple Ananda to arrange for his cremated remains to be enshrined in stupas. In the *Mahāparinibbāna Sutta* it is recorded how, after the death of the Buddha, his body was cremated, and his remains were divided into eight parts, each enshrined in a separate stupa. Two more stupas were also erected; one, built by the *brahman* who had divided the relics, enshrined the Master's alms bowl, and another, erected by those who had arrived too late to receive a portion of the remains, enshrined the ashes of the funerary pyre.

According to ancient legend, after the great Mauryan king Aśoka (c. 270–232 BCE) converted to Buddhism he had all but one (which was protected by *nāgas*) of the original reliquary shrines opened and the relics divided into eighty-four thousand parts, each destined for a new stupa. Although this number must be interpreted symbolically, there is historical evidence that Aśoka did, in fact, erect a number of new stupas. Moreover, the tradition that relics of the Buddha had been, as it were, placed into circulation by Aśoka served to legitimate claims that true relics of the Buddha were to be found wherever Buddhism became established.

In addition to bodily relics (Pali, *sarīradhātu*), Buddhist tradition also recognizes two other forms of relics that are taken as indicative of the Buddha's presence in the world. In Pali these are termed *paribhogikadhātu* and *uddesikadhātu,* the former referring to objects that the Buddha used (as, for example, his alms bowl) or marks (such as a footprint or shadow) that he left on earth, and the latter referring to votive reminders, such as images and stupas known not to contain actual relics.

From the edicts of Aśoka is obtained the first historical evidence of Buddhist pilgrimage, even though it is probable that the practice began before Aśokan times. In Rock Edict 8, he says that, while previously he used to go out on *vihārayātrās* ("excursions for enjoyment"), ten years after his coronation he undertook a *dharmayātrā* ("journey for truth") to the place where the Buddha attained enlightenment, that is, to Bodh Gayā. This pilgrimage appears to constitute the beginning of Aśoka's search for the true Dharma and for the significance of the Dharma in his own life as emperor.

From the time of Aśoka to the present, Bodh Gayā has remained the most important Buddhist pilgrimage site in India. It is often grouped with three other sites—Lumbini in Nepal, where Siddhārtha Gautama, the future Buddha, was born; the Deer Park at Sārnāth near Banaras, where he "turned the Wheel of the Law," that is, preached his first sermon; and Kuśinagara in Uttar Pradesh, where he passed into the state of *nirvāṇa.* None of these other sites, nor any other in India where he was reputed to have performed miracles during his life, however, holds the significance for Buddhists that Bodh Gayā does. Bodh Gayā represents the birth of Buddhism, the place where the Tathāgata realized the fundamental truth that lies at the base of Dharma.

The quest for the Dharma appears to have been the primary motivation for perhaps the most famous of Buddhist pilgrims, the Chinese monks who journeyed from their homeland to India in the fifth century and again in the seventh century CE. Faxian, the earliest of these pilgrims to have left a detailed record, departed from his home in Chang'an in 399 and traveled by land through Central Asia and then across northern India. From northern India he then traveled by ship to Sri Lanka and to Java and finally returned to China in 412. While Faxian's pilgrimage, like those of subsequent Chinese monks, was undertaken for the purpose of acquiring the Dharma, it reveals also another model of Buddhist pilgrimage, one much more popular with lay persons, namely a pilgrimage centered on the cult of the relics.

From his first encounter with Buddhist communities in Central Asia, Faxian found not only monks but also stupas and images of the Buddha that were the foci of popular cults. He himself visited a number of places associated with incidents in the life of the Buddha, and his account serves as a brief version of the life of the Buddha. Of particular interest, given the later development of Buddhist pilgrimage in lands outside India, Faxian observed "footprints" of the Buddha in areas as far removed from the region where the Buddha actually lived as the Punjab and Sri Lanka.

Shrines marking traces left by the Buddha in his supernatural visits to lands that were to become Buddhist as well as shrines enclosing relics that had been transported—naturally or supernaturally—from India to such lands often became pilgrimage centers in their own right. Indeed, for the long period between the decline of Buddhism in India in the latter part of the first millennium CE and the late nineteenth century, when cheap travel and Buddhist revival together stimulated renewed interest in the sacred Buddhist sites in India, Buddhist pilgrimage was confined mainly to Buddhist lands outside India. The emerging importance of certain sites—the so-called sixteen great places in Sri Lanka and the twelve shrines associated with the twelve-year cycle in northern Thailand—was associated primarily with the linking of political and moral communities in the world to a sacred Buddhist cosmos.

Buddhist pilgrims have long traveled to such important shrines as those housing the Buddha's footprints on Siripada (Adam's Peak) in Sri Lanka and at Saraburi in Thailand and those housing famous Buddhist relics, such as the Temple of the Tooth in Kandy, Sri Lanka; the Shwe Dagon in Rangoon, Myanmar; the That Luang temple in Vientiane, Laos; and Doi Suthep near Chiang Mai, Thailand. Pilgrims visited these and other holy sites in order to acquire merit or to gain access to the presumed magical power associated with them. While some have made pilgrimages to shrines associated with traces of the Buddha as an end in itself, most have continued, as did Aśoka and Faxian, to see pilgrimage as a means for orienting themselves toward the Buddha as a preliminary step along the path to enlightenment. The pilgrimage that begins by turning toward the Buddha in this world finds its culmination in an inner pilgrimage that leads to a true understanding of the Dharma.

SEE ALSO Aśoka; Faxian; Stupa Worship; Xuanzang; Yijing.

BIBLIOGRAPHY

The scriptural source for Buddhist pilgrimage is to be found in the *Mahāparinibbāna Suttānta,* a text that has been translated by T. W. Rhys Davids in "Sacred Books of the East," vol. 11 (Oxford, 1881), pp. 1–136. A discussion of Aśokan pilgrimage, together with translations of the edicts in Aśoka, appears in *Aśoka* (London, 1928) by Radhakumud Mookerji. The travels of Faxian have been translated by James Legge in *A Record of Buddhistic Kingdoms* (1886; reprint, New York, 1965). The *locus classicus* for an understanding of the cosmological significance of Buddhist stupas is Paul Mus's *Barabadur* (1935; reprint, New York, 1978). Marilyn Stablein has provided an overview of Buddhist pilgrimage among Tibetans in her "Textual and Contextual Patterns of Tibetan Buddhist Pilgrimage in India," *Tibet Society Bulletin* 12 (1978): 7–38. For discussions of Buddhist pilgrimage in Sri Lanka, see Gananath Obeyesekere's "The Buddhist Pantheon in Ceylon and Its Extensions," in *Anthropological Studies in Theravada Buddhism,* edited by Manning Nash et al. (New Haven, Conn., 1966), pp. 1–26; Bryan Pfaffenberger's "The Kataragama Pilgrimage: Hindu-Buddhist Interaction and Its Significance in Sri Lanka's Polyethnic Social System," *Journal of Asian Studies* 38 (1979): 253–270; and H. L. Seneviratne's *Rituals of the Kandyan State* (Cambridge, 1978). Buddhist pilgrimage in Thailand has been examined in my article "Buddhist Pilgrimage Centers and the Twelve Year Cycle: Northern Thai Moral Orders in Space and Time," *History of Religions* 15 (1975): 71–89, and in James B. Pruess's "Merit-Seeking in Public: Buddhist Pilgrimage in Northeastern Thailand," *Journal of the Siam Society* 64 (1976): 169–206.

New Sources

Cohen, Paul T. "Lue across Borders: Pilgrimage and the Muang Sing Reliquary in Northern Laos." In *Where China Meets Southeast Asia: Social & Cultural Change in the Border Regions,* edited by Grant Evans, Chris Hutton, and Kuah Khun Eng, pp. 145–161. Singapore, 2000.

Doyle, Tara Nancy. "Bodh Gaya: Journeys to the Diamond Throne and the Feet of Gayasur." Ph.D. diss., Harvard University, 1997.

Leoshko, Janice. "On the Construction of a Buddhist Pilgrimage Site." *Art History* 19 (1996): 573–597.

Pruess, James B. "Sanctification Overland: The Creation of a Thai Buddhist Pilgrimage Center." In *Sacred Journeys: The Anthropology of Pilgrimage,* edited by Alan Morinis, pp. 211–231. Westport, Conn., 1992.

Walters, Jonathan S. "Pushing Poson: The Politics of a Buddhist Pilgrimage in Postcolonial Sri Lanka." In *Sri Lanka: Collective Identities Revisited,* edited by Michael Roberts, pp. 133–162. Colombo, 1998.

CHARLES F. KEYES (1987)
Revised Bibliography

PILGRIMAGE: BUDDHIST PILGRIMAGE IN EAST ASIA

Pilgrimage, especially to sacred mountain sites, has long been a popular religious practice in both China and Japan. Since the entry of Buddhism into China in the first centuries of the common era, and since its entry into Japan through China several centuries later, pilgrimage in East Asia has become associated with Buddhist religious beliefs.

PILGRIMAGES IN CHINA. In mainland China there have been various pilgrimage sites, related to both Buddhism and Daoism. As for the former, there existed the following four major sites: Mount Wutai, sacred to Mañjuśrī (Skt.; known in Chinese as Wenshu); Mount Emei, sacred to Samantabhadra (Chin., Puxian); Mount Putuo, sacred to Avalokiteśvara (Guanyin); and Mount Jiu Hua, sacred to Kṣitigarbha (Dizang). In the case of Daoist pilgrimages, one of the most famous sites is Mount Dai. This article shall deal with Mount Wutai and Mount Dai.

Mount Wutai. Located in northeastern China, Mount Wutai consists of five peaks. This sacred mountain has attracted a great number of pilgrims over the centuries, not only from every part of China but also from Manchuria, Mongolia, Central Asia, India, and Japan. It has, therefore, been referred to as the most eminent pilgrimage site in Asia. Although it was famous as the sacred site of Mañjuśrī, it is said to have been originally a sacred place related to the spiritual tradition of Daoism. It was not until the Northern Wei dynasty (386–535) that Buddhist influence became widespread in China, predominating over the indigenous Daoist tradition, and from this time Mount Wutai became a site holy to Mañjuśrī. In the Tang dynasty (618–907), it was so popular as a pilgrimage site that many pilgrims even came to visit the mountain from foreign countries, including Tibet and India. During the same period, many books were published, collecting stories of the miracles and wonders performed by Mañjuśrī. Drawings sketching Mount Wutai were also widely distributed. These drawings were usually put up on the walls of either Buddhist temples or individual houses all over China.

It is said to have been during the Yuan dynasty (1271–1366), when China was invaded and ruled by the Mongols, that Tibetan Buddhism, which the Mongols preferred to Chinese Buddhism, started to spread its influence at Mount Wutai. Soon Chinese Buddhism and Tibetan Buddhism came to coexist on this sacred mountain. In other words, the mountain became an important pilgrimage site for two different religious traditions simultaneously. During the Qing dynasty (1644–1912), Tibetan Buddhism gradually came to predominate at Mount Wutai, partly because the Manzhu Qing rulers, who were not ethnically Chinese, began to take a conciliatory policy toward other non-Chinese groups such as the Mongols, who believed in Tibetan Buddhism. As a result, Mount Wutai became the most holy religious site of the Mongols. According to the reports of Japanese scholars who visited Mount Wutai in the 1930s, many fervent Mongolian pilgrims were to be witnessed there. In the case of Chinese Buddhist pilgrimage sites, it is quite common for other religious traditions, including indigenous ones like Daoism, to have been closely related to the history of the sites.

Mount Dai. Long famous as a Daoist pilgrimage site, Daishan has been continually associated with Buddhism in various ways. In Chinese history, this sacred moutain has been well known as one of the so-called Five Peaks, designated as indispensable for the protection of the whole country. The history of Mount Dai can be separated into three phases.

In ancient times, Chinese emperors were supposed to visit Daishan when they ascended the throne and were supposed to perform a special ritual for declaring their ascension, worshiping all the divinities in the sky and on the earth as well. At the same time, the emperors were said to pray for their own individual wishes, such as longevity.

It was probably toward the end of the Latter Han dynasty (25–220 CE) that Daishan came to be regarded as having some connection with the world of the dead, although this was diametrically opposed to the previous belief in longevity. As time went on, therefore, Mount Dai was thought to be related to Hell. It was believed, then, that the dead received judgment at Mount Daishan as to whether they should go to Hell or not. This idea of Hell was introduced by Buddhism.

From the Song dynasty (960–1279) up until the modern period, another new belief was associated with Mount Dai: that of a goddess. This goddess was worshiped as one who presided over the birth and rearing of children. This special characteristic of the goddess attracted a great number of pilgrims because of its familiarity and closeness with the common people. Accordingly, miniature statues of this particular goddess were enshrined all over China in modern times.

Pilgrimage in modern China. Pilgrimages in China seemed to have disappeared after Communist China was established in 1949. Moreover, many temples and shrines belonging to various pilgrimage sites all over China were seriously damaged during the Cultural Revolution in the 1960s and 1970s. However, in recent years, pilgrimage sites have been rapidly restored and have reopened their doors to pilgrims both from China and from overseas. The majority of the foreign pilgrims are Chinese merchants living abroad. As a result of a rapid growth in the living standards of the Chinese people, there seems to be a tendency for famous pilgrimage sites to become targets of tourism.

PILGRIMAGES IN JAPAN. In Japanese religious tradition, both Shintō and Buddhism have various pilgrimage sites. In Japan, pilgrimages can be divided into two general types. The first is the type exemplified by the Pilgrimage to the Thirty-three Holy Places of Kannon (Avalokiteśvara) in the Western Provinces and by the Pilgrimage to the Eighty-Eight Temples of Shikoku, in which one makes a circuit of a series of temples or holy places in a set order. The individual holy places that the pilgrim visits may be separated by great distances, as in the case of the Shikoku pilgrimage, in which eighty-eight temples are scattered along a route of about 1,200 kilometers (746 miles). The order of visitation is an important feature of this type of pilgrimage. The second type is a journey to one particular holy place. Pilgrimage to the Kumano Shrines and Ise Shintō Shrine, as well as to certain holy mountains, belong to this type. In common usage, the term *junrei,* the Japanese word for "pilgrimage," usually refers to the first type only.

It is thought that pilgrimages were first undertaken in the Nara period (710–794), although the custom did not become popular until the Heian period (794–1185). With the increasing popularity of religions involving mountain worship, members of the imperial family, the nobility, and Buddhist monks made pilgrimages to remote holy mountains. Among them, Kumano in the southern part of Wakayama prefecture is the most famous, having at that early time already developed into a large center for the adherents of mountain worship. Besides Kumano, Hasedera Temple, Shitennoji, Mount Koya, and Mount Kinpu were also popular pilgrimage sites. Early forms of the pilgrimage circuits for the western provinces and Shikoku were also established by the late Heian period. It can be surmised that many of these places were centers where Buddhist monks and ascetics engaged in austerities. Such pilgrimages continued throughout the Kamakura period (1185–1333) and the Muromachi period (1333–1568).

In the Edo period (1600–1868) an unprecedented number of people began to visit pilgrimage centers. While the vast majority of pilgrims had previously been member of the upper classes, such as monks, aristocrats, and warriors, in the Edo period the number of pilgrims from the general populace greatly increased. This change was largely owing to the peace established by the Tokugawa feudal regime and to the improvement in the economic condition of both the farming and the merchant classes. Transportation improved, and although government policy restricted travel between provinces, an exception was made for pilgrimages. The number of pilgrims who made journeys to the western provinces, Shikoku, Kotohira Shrine, Zenkoji, Ise, and Mount Fuji increased rapidly, and many new pilgrimage centers developed in various parts of the country. During this period, pilgrims tended to travel in groups, and as more and more people participated for recreational as well as for religious purposes, temple and shrine towns sprang up with facilities for accommodating these people. One should also note an increase in the number of so-called beggar-pilgrims who wandered from one center to another. The Shikoku circuit was particularly frequented by criminals, lepers, and beggars.

Travel since the Meiji period (1868–1912) has basically preserved the Edo period pattern of pilgrimage. Even today, many travelers include visits to famous temples and shrines in their itineraries. Even pilgrimage circuits that lack any other attraction, such as the Shikoku pilgrimage, have once again become popular. Behind this phenomenon perhaps lies a nostalgia for the past, a resurging interest in religion, and a desire for temporary escape from urban life.

SEE ALSO Avalokiteśvara; Kṣitigarbha; Mañjuśrī; Mountains; Shugendō; Worship and Devotional Life, article on Buddhist Devotional Life in East Asia.

BIBLIOGRAPHY

Adachi K., and Shioiri Ryodo, eds. *Nittō guhō junrei kōki.* 2 vols. Tokyo, 1970–1985. An annotated edition of Ennin's account of his travels in Tang China.

Kitagawa, Joseph M. "Three Types of Pilgrimage in Japan." In *Studies in Mysticism and Religion Presented to Gershom G. Scholem on His Seventieth Birthday by Pupils, Colleagues and Friends,* edited by E. E. Urbach, R. J. Zwi Werblowsky, and Chaim Wirszubski, pp. 155–164. Jerusalem, 1967.

Maeda Takashi. *Junrei no shakaigaku.* Kyoto, 1971.

Ono Katsutoshi. *Nittō guhō junrei gyōki no kenkyū.* 4 vols. Tokyo, 1964–1969. A translation and study of Ennin's account of his travels in Tang China.

Ono Katsutoshi, and Hibino Takeo. *Godaisan.* Tokyo, 1942.

Reischauer, Edwin O., trans. *Ennin's Diary: The Record of a Pilgrimage to China in Search of the Law.* New York, 1955.

Shinjō Tsunezō. *Shaji-sankei no shakai-keizaishiteki kenkyū.* Rev. ed. Tokyo, 1982.

New Sources

Birnbaum, Raoul. "The Manifestation of a Monastery: Shenying's Experiences on Mount Wu-t'ai in T'ang Context." *Journal of the American Oriental Society* 106, no. 1 (1986): 119–138.

Huber, Toni. *The Cult of Pure Crystal Mountain: Popular Pilgrimage and Visionary Landscape in Southeast Tibet.* New York, 1999.

McKay, Alex, ed. *Pilgrimage in Tibet.* Richmond, Va., 1998.

Naquin, Susan, and Chün-fang Yü, eds. *Pilgrims and Sacred Sites in China.* Berkeley, 1992.

Swanson, Paul, and Ian Reader. "Editor's Introduction: Pilgrimage in the Japanese Religious Tradition." *Japanese Journal of Religious Studies* 24 (1997): 225–270.

HOSHINO EIKI (1987)
Revised Bibliography

PILGRIMAGE: TIBETAN PILGRIMAGE

Pilgrimage, in the sense of an extended journey to a sacred place, has long been central to Tibetan life. The word for pilgrim is *gnas skor ba,* "one who circles a sacred place." Thus the lexicon defines pilgrims by the rite they perform at the end of their journey. Although one may ride a horse to the pilgrimage site, one must as a rule walk around (or circumambulate) the sacred place on foot. In fact, in the Buddhist world it is said that the merit accrued by the pilgrim for the pious act of pilgrimage is far smaller if the circumambulation is performed on horseback.

PILGRIMAGE SITES. Since the conversion of Tibet to Buddhism, which began in the seventh century CE, Tibetans have venerated the holy places of Buddhist India. During the eleventh and twelfth centuries Tibetans traveled to India to receive Buddhist teachings and to visit Buddhist sacred sites. Buddhist institutions, and Buddhism in general, in India ended after the twelfth century. The Tibetan practice of pilgrimage to India was not revived until the late nineteenth century and early twentieth century, following the archaeological discovery of sites associated with the life of the Buddha, such as Bodh Gayā, where he was enlightened, and Sarnath, where he preached his first sermon. Tibetans also travel to Indian sites associated with the history of Tibetan Buddhism, such as Lotus Lake (Mtsho Padma) in Himachal Pradesh. There, Padmasambhava, a key figure in the introduction of Buddhism to Tibet, is said to have appeared from a lotus in the middle of a lake.

Also outside the borders of Tibet, the stupa of Bodnath, in the Kathmandu Valley of Nepal, is a primary pilgrimage destination for Tibetans in the southern Himalayan region. It has attracted pilgrims for centuries and, following the Chinese occupation of Tibet that began in the 1950s, became a place of refuge for many Tibetans. Its fame derives from the legend of its founding. The Tibetan king Khri sron lde btsan, the Indian Buddhist abbot Śāntirakṣita, and the tantric master Padmasambhava (who together played important roles in establishing Buddhism in Tibet in the eighth century CE) were said in a previous life to have been brothers who built the Bodnath stupa.

In Tibet itself, two types of pilgrimage sites can be distinguished. The first are man-made. These include cities, the most famous of which is the Tibetan capital Lhasa, the "place of gods." Within the city the most famous temple is the Jo khang, or "house of the Lord," which shelters a statue of Śākyamuni Buddha said to have been brought by the Chinese princess Wengcheng in the seventh century CE. Buddhist monasteries are also important destinations for pilgrims. Some of the more famous include Bsam yas, the first Buddhist monastery built in central Tibet; Bkra sis lhun po in the city of Gzi ka rtse, the seat of the Panchen Lamas; and sKu 'bum in present-day Qinghai province, birthplace of Tsong kha pa (1357–1419), the "founder" of the Dge lugs school.

Pilgrimage sites may also be natural phenomena. The lake Lha mo bla mtsho (Central Tibet), for example, is traditionally visited to receive visions of the birthplace of the next Dalai Lama. The caves where the saint Mi la ras pa (1028/40–1111/23) practiced meditation are considered powerful pilgrimage sites. The most important of the natural pilgrimage places, however, are sacred mountains, like Mount Kailash in Western Tibet, Tsa ri in Southeast Tibet, and A myes rma chen in Qinghai province. A mountain associated with a lake—with the mountain considered the father and the lake the mother—is regarded as the ideal sacred place.

Beginning long before the introduction of Buddhism, the mountains of Tibet were regarded as territorial gods (*yul lha*). In Buddhist Tibet many mountains have retained this status and its cult, according to which only males were permitted to perform rituals of offering on the slope. Many of these mountains were incorporated into the Buddhist cosmography through the deeds of a Buddhist saint. This transformation typically occurred when a great religious figure "opened the pilgrimage" (*gnas skor phyed ba*) by subduing the negative forces that prevented access to the site. It was then a Buddhist site, and the practice of circumambulation was performed by men and women alike to consolidate this metamorphosis. The popularity of such sacred sites has waxed and waned over time through competition between Buddhist schools to gain real and symbolic control over them.

A rarer type of pilgrimage takes the form of great millenarian migrations toward "hidden lands" *(sbas yul)*, revealed by Padmasambhava, where Tibetans can take refuge when dangers threaten the country. The most well known of these is Gnas Padma bkod in Southeast Tibet. Finally, Tibetans have set off on pilgrimages to mythical kingdoms like Shambhala, said to be in the north, the cradle of the Kālacakra teachings.

LITERATURE. A wide variety of Tibetan texts have been designated by Western scholars with the term *pilgrimage guides*. Some of these are indeed guidebooks in the ordinary sense of the term. They provide concrete information, indicate directions to follow, and sometimes even give the approximate time it takes to go from one point to another. A great number of texts, however, are not conventional guidebooks. They are dedicated to a single site and present a tantric vision of the sacred place. These works describe, in more or less detail, the subjugation of the local deities and the transformation of the place into a maṇḍala, the multistoried palace of a Buddhist deity. These texts are literary projections of an internal vision onto the physical landscape, intended to convey the pilgrim toward a higher level of spiritual insight. Pilgrims, many of whom have traditionally been illiterate, know these texts from monks, nuns, and lamas met along the pilgrimage routes. Thus these written sources, passed on orally, superimpose the sacred landscape onto the land for those who have not yet gained the insight to see its true nature for themselves.

PRACTICES AND BENEFITS. Through pilgrimage, Tibetans seek purification, the accumulation of merit, and blessings. Some of these are gained through the rituals they perform along the way. Yet the place itself has its own power, often derived from the past presence of a saint, and pilgrims often take water, stones, earth, and plants home with them from their pilgrimages. Drinking the water or wearing the earth or the stone inside an amulet around the neck is said to aid in finding a better rebirth in the next lifetime. But it also brings more immediate rewards, such as prosperity, long life, and protection from harm.

Despite the pervasive influence of Buddhism in Tibet, pilgrimage remains a mixture of Buddhist and non-Buddhist, Tibetan and non-Tibetan elements. Pilgrimage guides state where along the route pilgrims must circumambulate, bow down, make offerings, and recite sacred mantras, the most popular being oṃ maṇi padme hūṃ, the mantra of Avalokiteśvara, the bodhisattva protector of Tibet. Circumambulation derives from the Indian practice of keeping revered objects to one's right; there is evidence of this ritual act being practiced in Tibet during the final centuries of the monarchy (seventh to ninth centuries CE). Buddhists must move in a clockwise direction; adherents of the Bon religion move counterclockwise. In order to accrue special merit, pilgrims sometimes perform prostrations (lying face down, rising, taking a step, and lying face down again) along the entire route. There are also particularly auspicious times to perform pilgrimage during the twelve-year cycle of the Tibetan calendar. Upon arrival at the sacred site, pilgrims make Buddhist offerings of money, butter lamps, or ceremonial scarves. But they also perform non-Buddhist rituals, like burning juniper branches and adding stones to a cairn. Other practices mix Buddhist and non-Buddhist elements in a single act, like weighing sins by hanging from a projection of a rock or crossing the *smyal lam*, the "path to hell," in order to overcome the fear of facing the intermediate state (*bar do*) between death and the next rebirth.

Social, Political, and Economic Implications. Pilgrimage routes link the sacred sites of Tibet and provide pathways for the expression of political and cultural identity. The long pilgrimages so typical in Tibet lead to large movements of population into new regions where all forms of social interaction occur. Pilgrims not only visit sacred sites, they also meet people (leading sometimes to marriage), they carry news, and they transmit forms of knowledge. The practice of pilgrimage in Tibet helped in breaking down cultural separatism and building political integration.

Along the pilgrimage routes all the ranks of the society are encountered, yet social distinctions and hierarchies do not fade. In some cases women are not permitted to enter monastic spaces or set foot on certain segments of the ritual route. At the same time, pilgrimage offers the opportunity to escape from a variety of political constraints and social obligations. Since the 1980s, for example, pilgrimage has sometimes provided a pretext for escaping from Chinese oppression; numerous refugees who have gone on pilgrimage to Mount Kailash in Western Tibet have then continued on to Nepal.

In the Tibetan world, pilgrimage is a collective practice. Groups of pilgrims from the same family, the same locality, or the same monastery typically gather together. Often monks or lamas will serve as guides for lay people, providing information along the way. Upon arrival at the sacred site, these groups of pilgrims do not mix with one another, and conversation is limited to requests for information from a local person or a religious figure. But pilgrimage is also a festive occasion, with groups stopping along the way for song and dance and people dressed in their most beautiful clothes and jewelry.

The economic implications of pilgrimage are also significant. It promotes trade, both large-scale and small-scale, and thus the redistribution of wealth. Pilgrims typically are asked by family members to carry gifts and make offerings on their behalf at the sacred destination in order that they might share in the merit of the pilgrimage. The monastery or temple, so often located near the pilgrimage place (if it is not the sacred site itself), provides consecrated items (ceremonial scarves, consecrated pills, and sometimes food) in return for these donations.

Modernization. Since the Chinese occupation of Tibet, many changes have occurred in the Tibetan practice of pilgrimage. Numerous roads have been constructed, so it is not unusual to see pilgrims performing the circumambulation of a sacred lake in a bus. Roads have also redefined pilgrimage routes. In 2002 many Tibetans completed only half of the traditional pilgrimage around A myes rma chen Mountain, stopping at the end of the road construction.

Tourism, encouraged by the Chinese authorities, has also had an influence on some sacred sites, affecting not only the economic and political conditions but also the sense of local identity of the Tibetan residents. In general, the tremendous influx of tourists, most of them Han Chinese seeking an idyllic place populated by "authentic Tibetans," has led to a decline of the practice of more traditional pilgrimage to the region.

See Also Circumambulation; Mantra; Worship and Devotional Life, article on Buddhist Devotional Life in Tibet.

Bibliography

Buffetrille, Katia. *Pèlerins, lamas, et visionnaires: Sources orales et écrites sur les pèlerinages tibétains.* Vienna, 2000. A translation of several pilgrimage guides, biographies of religious figures, and prayers, with Tibetan text and French translation.

Ekvall, Robert B., and James F. Downs. *Tibetan Pilgrimage.* Tokyo, 1987. A survey, with numerous examples, of many aspects of Tibetan pilgrimage.

Huber, Toni. *The Cult of Pure Crystal Mountain: Popular Pilgrimage and Visionary Landscape in Southeast Tibet.* New York, 1999. A study of the representations, ritual practices, and participants of the pilgrimage around Tsa ri Mountain in Southeast Tibet.

Huber, Toni, ed. *Sacred Places and Powerful Places in Tibetan Culture: A Collection of Essays.* Dharamsala, 1999. Essays regarding sacred space in Tibet, Nepal, Sichuan, Qinghai, North India, and other Tibetan areas.

Mcdonald, Alexander W., ed. *Mandala and Landscape.* New Delhi, India, 1997. Essays on the relationship between the conception of the maṇḍala and physical landscapes.

McKay, Alex, ed. *Pilgrimage in Tibet.* Richmond, Surrey, U.K., 1998. Essays on the theory and practice of pilgrimage in Tibet and Sikkim as practiced by Indians and Tibetans.

Katia Buffetrille (2005)

PILGRIMAGE: HINDU PILGRIMAGE

Over the millennia, Hindus have developed an enormous number of pilgrimage places, pilgrimage-related practices, and texts extolling the virtues of, and benefits to be gained by, pilgrimages to powerful places and persons. Some of the more prominent themes that emerge in Hindu pilgrimage are the importance of water, the effects of powerful persons on particular places, the centrality of purity and asceticism, the association of pilgrimage with death, and the growing popularity and commercialization of pilgrimage as it becomes associated with tourism.

In Sanskrit and related languages, the central term for pilgrimage place is *tīrtha*, a crossing place or a ford where one leaves the mundane world and crosses over into a more powerful or spiritual location. The term already points to the centrality of water, rivers, and bathing in Hinduism. It is possible that this centrality was already present in the ancient Indus Valley Civilization, in which bathing seems to have been of central ritual importance. The Indus River itself is highly praised in the Vedas (where it is called the Sindhu), as are seven other "mother-rivers," originally located in Punjab in the northwest of India. The practice of Hindu pilgrimage always involves bathing, so that the pilgrim is purified before entering the sacred place or approaching the divinities there. From ancient times until the present, rivers have been prominent pilgrimage places, along with the numerous temples and other religious places along their banks.

The great Hindu epics *Rāmāyaṇa* and *Mahābhārata* already mention the practice of pilgrimage, and many of the places visited by their protagonists subsequently became important pilgrimage places. In the *Tīrthayātrāparvan* (the episode relating to the pilgrimage to the *tīrthas*) of the *Mahābhārata*, numerous sites throughout the subcontinent are mentioned that have continued to be prominent pilgrimage places to the present day: rivers like the Ganges, the Godāvarī, and the Narmadā; as well as places such as Badrināth, Gayā, Puṣkara, and Prayāga.

There is no comparable listing of pilgrimage places in Vālmīki's *Rāmāyaṇa*; however, many of the places visited by Rāma and his entourage in this epic have subsequently become important places of pilgrimage for Hindus, such as Ayodhyā, the city of Rāma's birth; Citrakuṭ, where he paused with Sītā on his journey; and Rāmeśvaram, in the far South, where he allegedly worshiped Śiva before crossing to Rāvaṇa's island of Laṅkā.

The Hindu Purāṇas, written roughly between the fourth and the eleventh centuries CE, have preserved a large number of names of pilgrimage places, along with a system classifying them into "divine" (*daiva*), "demonic" (*āsura*), "sage" (*ārṣa*), and "human" (*mānuṣa*) sites. The Purāṇas also contain extensive *māhātmyas*, passages extolling the virtues of particular pilgrimage places and the benefits to be obtained by pilgrimage to them. This *māhātmya* literature continues to be produced today, by those interested in promoting the fame and virtue of particular sites.

Later sources like the *Kṛtyakalpataru* of Bhaṭṭa Lakṣmīdhara (early twelfth century) and the *Triṣṭhalīsetu* of Bhaṭṭa Nārāyaṇa (mid-sixteenth century) rework the Purāṇic material and develop detailed rules and regulations for the behavior of pilgrims. It has been suggested that such literature was developed in reaction to the appearance of conquering Islamic armies in the subcontinent, as Hindus sought to codify and systematize their own practices. Both works stress that one of the virtues of pilgrimage is that it is accessible to all. Whereas Vedic sacrifice requires great wealth, the merit of pilgrimage is available to everyone, including the poor. Lakṣmīdhara says that even the lowest-caste *caṇḍāla* can obtain the fruits of pilgrimage. Both works emphasize the importance of purity and an ascetic lifestyle during pilgrimage, in order to obtain its fruits. Practices such as bathing, fasting, and shaving are recommended, and Lakṣmīdhara says that it is these practices, as much as the place itself, that bring benefit, arguing that the best of all *tīrthas* is a pure heart.

Both works stress the connection of *tīrthas* with death and the ancestors, and they give instructions on how to perform special rituals for throwing the bones of deceased persons into sacred rivers. Important Hindu rituals such as piṇḍa-dāna (feeding the ancestors), tarpaṇa (offering water to them), and Śrāddha (regular worship of them) are enjoined at *tīrthas*. More than one-third of the *Triṣṭhalīsetu* is devoted to such death-associated rituals. In addition, Lakṣmīdhara recommends living at a *tīrtha* until one dies, so that its special power will help the pilgrim to achieve a better birth. Elsewhere in the dharmaśastra literature, the *mahāprasthāna*, or "pilgrimage unto death," is allowed for those who have committed a heinous crime, or have an incurable disease. Sometimes, particular *tīrthas* are recommended as places for such religious suicide, and there are numerous historical accounts of this being practiced, by kings and others. These citations tend to confirm what has been suspected by many scholars, that Hindu pilgrimage in the medieval period was in many cases positively valued as a way for sick and infirm people to die with dignity.

Many of these ideas and practices are very much alive today. In general, Hindu pilgrims refrain from sex, as well as from the consumption of meat, fish, liquor, and other impure substances during their journeys. Numerous pilgrimages throughout the subcontintent are strongly associated with the assumption of a "temporarily ascetic" lifestyle, for example the pilgrimage to Sabari Mallai in Kerala in South India. Men participating in this pilgrimage temporarily become "renouncers" for a period ranging from forty-five to sixty days, adding the energy of their asceticism to the power of the sacred place. Similar practices are followed by the so-called kāvarīwālās, pilgrims who carry Ganges water from Hardwār in North India back to their local Śiva shrines in time to offer it on the annual festival of Śivarātrī, observing strict asceticism on their journey.

Death- and ancestor-related rituals also remain important in contemporary Hindu pilgrimage. Some of the most famous and well-attended *tīrthas*, such as Kāśī (Banaras) and Gayā, are strongly associated with the performance of these rituals. For those lacking the time or opportunity for such a long pilgrimage, local and regional *tīrthas* serve as places for the performance of such rituals. People still come to Banaras for "Kāśīmokṣ(a)"—the liberation obtained by dying there—while the immersion of the bones of the dead remains a common practice.

Certain particularly famous *tīrthas* became important in the political and economic history of India. Kauṭilya, in his *Arthaśāstra* (written at the beginning of the common era), had already advised kings that they should send spies to pilgrimage places in order to ascertain the mood of the populace and to be on the lookout for enemies of the state. Pilgrims were not traditionally subject to taxation, but the commercial activities that grew up around large pilgrimage centers attracted the attention of rulers. In later times certain pilgrimage places became objects of contention amongst various rulers and religious orders, for commercial reasons as well as for the prestige that accrued to those who controlled them.

Caitanya (1486–1533), Guru Nānak (1469–1539; the founder of Sikhism), and many other sect-founders are said in their hagiographies to have performed extensive pilgrimages throughout South Asia, in the course of which they converted the adherents of rival sects to their cause.

One of the oldest and best-known Hindu *tīrthas* is the city of Kāśī (Benaras), which has pride of place in Lakṣmīdhara's book. By the twelfth century it had become the premier pilgrimage place in India. Lying on an unusual north-turning bend of the Ganges River, the entire riverfront of Kāśī is lined with *ghāṭs,* stone steps that lead pilgrims from the city's lanes to the edge of the river to bathe. Images of these *ghāṭs* have become almost synonymous with India and Hinduism in the tourist literature. Originally a sacred forest, Kāśī is a large city filled with perhaps the greatest concentration of *tīrthas* anywhere in India. It has always been regarded as Śiva's city, and it is believed that those who die there obtain mokṣa when Śiva whispers a liberating mantra into their ear.

In addition to Kāśī, there are two other great *kṣetras* or "pilgrimage fields" located in north India: Gayā and Prayāga. Gayā is above all a *pitṛ-tīrtha,* a pilgrimage place where the ancestors are worshiped. The Śrāddha ritual mentioned above is believed to have special merit when performed in this place, and even today hundreds of thousands of pilgrims gather there every year during the *pitṛ-pakṣa,* the time of year especially set aside for this practice, in order to perform the Śrāddha and related rituals.

The third great pilgrimage field of North India is Prayāga, even more ancient than Kāśī. It is located at the saṅgama (confluence) of the two sacred rivers—the Ganges and the Yamunā—along with an invisible third river, the Sarasvatī. At Prayaga, one is not only allowed, but in fact, enjoined to commit religious suicide by drowning, and there are historical records of such suicides there by ancient Hindu kings. Prayāga is the site of the Kumbha Melā, the largest religious gathering in the world, as well as a pilgrimage fair that occurs there once every twelve years.

There are many other systems of pilgrimage places in India. The most encompassing of these are the "four dhāms," four pilgrimage places at the corners of kite-shaped India. Badrināth in the central Himalayas of North India, sacred to Viṣṇu, was already known to the redactors of the Mahābhārata; Jagganāth to the East in Orissa is, like Badrināth, sacred to Viṣṇu and was of great importance during the late medieval period in India as a source of authoritative religious practice and doctrine. Rāmeśvaram in the South, the only Śaiva temple of the four dhāms, is where Rāma is believed to have worshiped Śiva before crossing to Rāvaṇa's fortress city of Laṅkā; and Kṛṣṇa's temple-city of Dvārakā in the West. It is widely believed that the great philosopher Śaṅkarācārya (c. eighth–ninth centuries) made a circumambulatory pilgrimage of the subcontinent and established these four shrines, though there is no reliable historical evidence of this.

Another well-known system of pilgrimage places is the so-called Saptapurī, or "seven cities" (also known as the *saptamahātīrtha* or seven great pilgrimage places), where liberation may be obtained. These include Dvāraka in Gujarat (already mentioned as one of the four dhām); Ayodhyā, the birthplace of Rāma; Mathurā, where Kṛṣṇa spent much of his life; Kāśī (mentioned below); Ujjain (associated with the Mahākala jyotirliṅga mentioned below); and Haridvār, on the Ganges at the foot of the Himalaya. Some say that Kāñcīpuram in the South is the seventh city, others say it is Prayāga in the north. Other sectarian pilgrimage systems include the twelve jyotirliṅga or "liṅgas of light" sacred to Śiva. According to the Śivapurāṇa, these are: Somanātha in Saurāṣṭra, Mallikārjuna on Śrīsaila hill, Mahākala in Ujjayinī, Parameśvara in Oṃkārakṣetra (an island in the Narmadā river), Kedāra in the Himalayas, Bhīmaśaṅkara at the source of the Godāvarī River, Viśveśvara in Kāśī, Tryambakeśvara on the Godāvarī River near Nāsik (another site of the periodic Kumbha Melā), Vaidyanātha in Citābhūmī, Nāgeśa in Dārukāvana, Rāmeśvara (mentioned above as one of the four dhām), and Ghṛṣṇeśa (near present-day Daulatābād).

The system of Śaktipīṭhas, or seats of power sacred to the goddess, is said to have been created after the goddess Satī immolated herself on the sacrificial fire of her father Dakṣa. Crazed with grief, Śiva picked up her corpse and began performing his world-destroying dance, the *ānanda-tāṇḍava,* or dance of bliss. Viṣṇu, understanding that the entire world was threatened by Śiva's dance, cut Satī's body into pieces with his discus, and the places where they fell became the Śaktipīṭhas. Currently, the most powerful of these is believed to be Kāmarūpa in Assam, where the goddess's vulva fell to earth.

The sectarian aspect of pilgrimage systems is, in any case, not terribly relevant for contemporary Hindu pilgrimage. Hindus have in the past been famous for their tolerance. Sectarian differences among Hindus are not very important, and most Hindu pilgrims readily visit the shrines of a variety of gods. This kind of openness extends to the pilgrimage places of different religions as well. Kataragama in Sri Lanka, for example, is visited by Hindus, Buddhists, Christians, and Muslims; the tomb of the Muslim saint Niẓām al-Dīn Awliyā' (AH 636–725 /1238–1325 CE) in Delhi is regularly visited by Sikhs and Hindus; and the Sikh pilgrimage place of Amritsar attracts numerous pilgrims from other religions, including Hinduism.

In addition to the all-India level of pilgrimage places and systems discussed above, each region within the subcontinent has its own important pilgrimage places. A complete list of such places would be very long; however, some of the more notable shrines in India that have not been mentioned above include the following: the goddess temple of Jwālāmukhi, near Kāṅgaḍā in Himachal Pradesh; Kurukṣetra, near Ambālā in Punjab, thought to be the site of the great battle in which the Mahābhārata culminated;

Mount Kailāsa in Tibet, thought of as the home of Lord Śiva; Amarnāth in Kashmir, a liṅga of ice that is the goal of a very large annual pilgrimage; Amarakaṇṭaka in Madhya Pradesh on the banks of the Narmadā River; Nāthadvāra, near Udaipur, associated with Kṛṣṇa; Somanātha in Gujarat, destroyed by Maḥmūd in 1026 and now an important shrine for Hindu nationalists; Nāsik in Maharashtra, where one of the periodic Kumbha Melās is held; Pāndharpur, associated with Viṭṭhobā, the "Maharashtrian Viṣṇu"; the goddess Kālī's temple of Kālīghāṭ in Kolkatta, West Bengal; the temple of Śṛṅgerī in Karnataka, one of the four headquarters of the Daśanāmī order of Śaiva monks believed to have been founded by Śaṅkarācārya; Uḍipi, also in Karnataka, birthplace of the dualist philosopher Madhvācārya; and in Tamil Nadu, the city of Madurai with its temple of the "fish-eyed" goddess Mīnākṣī, the famous Śaiva pilgrimage place Cidambaram, and the city of Kāñcīpuram. The state of Andhra Pradesh includes the Vaiṣṇava temple of Tirupati, quite possibly the wealthiest shrine in India.

Pilgrimage activity is often associated with certain dates or times of the year. Gayā is visited especially during the pitṛ-pakṣa, the annual half-month period that is reserved for ancestor rituals. The sanctity of the four sites at which the Kumbha Melās are held on a rotating basis is also connected to particular astrologically determined times. In many places throughout the subcontinent, it is believed that a conjunction of heavenly bodies releases a kind of power that can in turn be tapped or absorbed by pilgrims at sacred places for a limited time. Therefore, throughout India, one finds pilgrimage fairs (melās) that draw huge crowds of pilgrims, but only for a limited time.

The motivations for pilgrimage are often rather mundane: success in business or studies; curing of sickness; and birth of children (especially sons). These desired objects are called fruits (Skt., *phala*). Typically, one takes a vow, promising that if the desired fruit is obtained, one will perform a pilgrimage; or one performs a pilgrimage in the hope that the desired fruit will be obtained. The power of the sacred place, along with the energy that is generated by the ascetic practices associated with pilgrimage and the grace of the god for whom the pilgrimage is performed, are believed to result in the attainment of the desired object. Such a "this-worldly" orientation has been an object of criticism for Hindu theologians and reformers for centuries. For example, the poet-saint Kabīr lamented the many pilgrims who wander the earth lost and parched, not realizing that the true Ganges lies within.

Hindus also engage in many kinds of practices that are quite similar to pilgrimage. For example, Hindus often journey to have the darśan (auspicious sight) of a holy person. This may be done on the occasion of a special ritual, or during a melā or other festival. Such journeys are not called pilgrimages *(tīrtha-yātrā)*, but the similarity of holy place and holy person is implicitly recognized by the fact that a holy person is often called a tīrtha.

The ritual processions that occur throughout South Asia are also pilgrimage-like activities. Many pilgrimage temples are associated with annual festivals where the god or goddess emerges from his or her temple and circumambulates the town or visits another deity. Ritual processions in which one deity visits another are common in the Himalayas, and in these processions the deity is normally accompanied by priests and pilgrims who tend the deity during the procession and worship him regularly.

Sādhus, or holy men, are often seen wandering in India, and they are particularly prevalent at pilgrimage places, so that one easily thinks of them as "perpetual pilgrims." However, their own understandings of these journeys are rather different. They may think of themselves variously as gods' soldiers, as novices undergoing initiation, as members of a travelling monastery, or as ascetics who are roaming for pleasure or merely wandering aimlessly.

With the rapid growth of tourism and transport in the past few decades, pilgrimage activity in India is exploding. It is now quite common to combine religious pilgrimage with tourism, and this occurs at all economic levels, from the inexpensive bus tours organized for a clientele of peasant or lower-middle-class Hindus to the five-star pilgrimage tours organized for overseas Hindus and increasingly promoted by the government of India. The video bus coach, in which pilgrims en route to a tīirtha sthān watch Bollywood movies rather than singing religious hymns, has existed for some time. Other new forms of pilgrimage include "web pilgrimages," where one may have *darśan* (sight) of the deity online, and even order some *prasād,* or blessed food, from the temple.

SEE ALSO Banaras; Ganges River; Kumbha Melā; Kurukṣetra; Rivers; Sarasvatī; Vṛndāvana; Worship and Devotional Life, article on Hindu Devotional Life.

BIBLIOGRAPHY

The best general introduction to the concept of *tīrtha* is still Diana Eck's "India's *Tīrthas*: 'Crossings' in Sacred Geography," *History of Religions* 20 (4): 323–344. Excellent sources on the medieval classification of *tīrthas*, their particular qualities, and the rules and practices associated with them can be found in the *Kṛtyakalpataru* of Bhaṭṭa Lakṣmīdhara (Gaekwad's Oriental Series, Vol. XCVIII, Baroda, India, 1942) and the *Tristhalīsetu* of Bhaṭṭa Nārāyaṇa (translated with commentary by Richard Salomon as *The Bridge to the Three Holy Cities* (Delhi, India, 1985). Further information on the history of Hindu pilgrimage can be found in P. V. Kane's *History of Dharmaśastra* (in five volumes, Pune, India, 1930–1962).

The most comprehensive modern listing of pilgrimage places is found in a special issue of *Kalyāṇa* 31, no. 1 (1957), titled *Tīrthāṅk.* The best source for the Śaktipīṭhas is still D. C. Sircar's "The Śakta Pīṭhas," *Jounal of the Royal Asiatic Society of Bengal Letters* 14 (1948): 1–108 (republished Delhi, India, 1973). Other contemporary lists of pilgrimage places with commentary include S. M. Bhardwaj's *Hindu Places of Pil-*

grimage in India: A Study in Cultural Geography (Berkeley, Calif., 1973), which maps the pilgrimage places mentioned in the *Mahābhārata*; Agehananda Bharati's "Pilgrimage in Indian Tradition," *History of Religions* 3 (Summer, 1963): 135–167 and his "Pilgrimage Sites and Indian Civilization," *in* Joseph W. Elder, ed., *Chapters in Indian Civilization* (Dubuque, Iowa, 1970). Discussions of "pilgrimage unto death" include von Stietencron's "Suicide as a Religious Institution," *Bhāratīya Vidyā* XXVII (1969) and William Sax's "Pilgrimage Unto Death," in *To Strive and Not to Yield: Essays in Honour of Colin Brown,* edited by Jim Veitch (Wellington, New Zealand, 1992). One of the most remarkable studies of an important pilgrimage center is to be found in Anncharlott Eschmann, et al., *The Cult of Jagganath and the Regional Tradition of Orissa* (New Delhi, India, 1978).

Anthropological accounts of pilgrimage include Ann Gold's *Fruitful Journeys: The Ways of Rajasthani Pilgrims* (Berkeley, Calif., 1988), E. Valentine Daniel's "Equilibrium Regained," chapter five of his *Fluid Signs: Being a Person the Tamil Way* (Berkeley, Calif., 1984); David Haberman's *Journey Through the Twelve Forests: An Encounter with Krishna* (New York, 1994); Alan Morinis's *Pilgrimage in the Hindu Tradition* (Delhi 1984), and William S. Sax's *Mountain Goddess: Gender and Politics in a Himalayan Pilgrimage* (New York, 1991).

WILLIAM S. SAX (2005)

PIḶḶAI LOKĀCĀRYA (1264–1369) was an early formulater of Teṅkalai theology for Śrī Vaiṣṇava Hindus of South India. Born in the sixth generation of disciples of Ramanuja, and from a family learned in Sanskrit and Tamil, he lived his long life in the temple complex of Śrī Raṅgam. His father was known simply as Vaṭakku Tiruvīti Piḷḷai, "the Piḷḷai of North Street," and his mother was Śrī Raṅga Nācciyār. The couple was childless until, tradition says, Piḷḷai's *gurū,* Nampiḷḷai, ordered him to give up his ascetic chastity. When subsequently a son was born, the couple named him Lokācārya ("teacher of the world") after one of Nampiḷḷai's own titles. Piḷḷai Lokācārya himself never married, but rather devoted himself to the service of Nārāyaṇa in his iconic forms and to teaching. In 1309, when northern Muslims raided the temple, tradition relates that he walled in the immovable icons and escaped with the movable ones to a distant village, sustaining their worship until they could be safely returned.

Teaching shaped his scholarship from an early age. Whereas his father recorded Nampiḷḷai's comments on Nammāḻvār's *Tiruvāymoḻi* in the *Bhagavat Viṣayam,* and his younger brother, the ascetic Aḻakiya Māṇavāḷa Perumāḷ Nāyaṉār, one of his own disciples, likewise composed an important commentary on Nammāḻvār's poems, the *Ācārya Hṛdayam* (The heart of the teacher), Piḷḷai Lokācārya produced theological textbooks such as the *Aṣṭadaśa Rahasyam* (Eighteen Secrets), a compendium of succinct treatises that systematically explain the esoteric teachings Śrī Vaiṣṇavas receive from their *gurūs.* The work is written in the Śrī Vaiṣṇava *brahman* dialect, Maṇipravāḷam, and is addressed to "women and ignorant men," to free them from their painful bondage to the world and to deliver them into the joyful service of Nārāyaṇa. After the sect had divided into two schools, the Teṅkalai and the Vaṭakalai, the *Aṣṭadaśa Rahasyam* served the Teṅkalais through commentaries by the school's paramount theologian, Māṇavāḷa Māmuṉikaḷ (1370–1443).

Of the eighteen treatises, three have been highly significant for Śrī Vaiṣṇavas: *Mumukṣuppaṭi* (The means for those who desire freedom), *Tattvatrayam* (The three realities), and *Śrī Vacana Bhūṣanam* (The auspicious ornament of instruction). Piḷḷai Lokācārya teaches Viśiṣṭādvaita Vedānta but stresses one aspect—that of God's grace and the relative helplessness of embodied souls to emancipate themselves. As various scriptures reveal, Nārāyaṇa's consort, Śrī, or Lakṣmī, is the mediating agent between the majestic Lord and the numberless souls entangled in self-created bondage. She is compassionate toward all sentient beings and perfectly subservient to her Lord. Being totally dependent, she thus is able to influence him on behalf of those souls whom she touches with her grace. Surrender to the Goddess is all that is required for emancipation.

Piḷḷai Lokācārya thus teaches that the devotee—whether male or female of any caste whatever—who cannot fulfill the scriptural requirements of ritual, wisdom, and devotion can nevertheless attain the Lord, either through the grace that enables the devotee to give up this world out of impatient longing for God, or through such absolute trust in Nārāyaṇa and Śrī that he relinquishes the burden of his salvation to them. Furthermore, even the devotee who cannot surrender to God can still surrender to a *gurū.* Regarding the refugee as helpless, the properly qualified *gurū,* by virtue of his own wisdom and Śrī's activity within him, can assume his disciple's burden. Any ritual and devotional acts performed after surrender to God or *gurū* are to derive from the refugee's desire to please God and as a witness to his neighbor, not from his desire for merit. A contemporary of Piḷḷai Lokācārya, Vedānta Deśika (1268–1369) of the rival Vaṭakalai school, took issue and taught that in addition to Śrī's activity, ritual and devotional efforts, too, are important for emancipation.

SEE ALSO Śrī Vaiṣṇavas.

BIBLIOGRAPHY

A good exposition of *Śrī Vacana Bhūṣanam* by a modern Hindu *gurū* is *Sree Srivachana Bhushanam by Sri Pallai Lokacharya: An English Glossary* by Sri Satyamurthi Swami (Gwalior, India, 1972). The differences between Piḷḷai Lokācārya and Vedānta Deśika are discussed succinctly in *Srimad Rahasyatrayasara of Sri Vedantadesika,* translated with introduction and notes by M. R. Rajagopala Aiyangar (Kumbakonam, India, 1956). John B. Carman provides an excellent discussion of the concept of surrender and its relation to Rāmānuja's thought in chapter 17 of *The Theology of Rāmānuja: An Essay in Interreligious Understanding* (New Haven, 1974). The most recent discussion of Piḷḷai

Lokācārya in the history of Tamil literature is given in Tamil by M. Aruṇācalam in *Tamiḻ ilakkiya varalāṟu,* 6 vols. (Tirucirrampalam, India, 1969–1972).

D. DENNIS HUDSON (1987)

PINARD DE LA BOULLAYE, HENRI (1874–1958),

was a French Jesuit theologian, preacher, and writer on theology, comparative religion, and the spirituality of Ignatius Loyola. Born in Paris in 1874, Pinard entered the Society of Jesus in 1893. He was subsequently appointed professor of theology at a Jesuit institution in Enghien, Belgium, a position that he held from 1910 to 1927. During his professorship at Enghien he became interested in the study of comparative religion. He introduced a course in the history of religions that he later offered at the Gregorian University in Rome, where he lectured from 1927 to 1934.

Earlier, in 1913, Pinard had printed privately for the use of his students a manual entitled *De vera religione.* In this work he endorsed the theory of a primitive monotheism (*Urmonotheismus*) proposed by the priest-ethnologist Wilhelm Schmidt, and the theory of cultural cycles of Fritz Graebner, also an ethnologist. The manual was a detailed study of comparative problems, a foretaste of the intellectual style of his later, more important work, *L'étude comparée des religions,* the two volumes of which appeared in 1922 and 1925. Several editions were published subsequently, for Pinard continued to revise the work.

Volume 1 of *L'étude comparée des religions,* subtitled *Son histoire dans le monde occidentale,* evidenced Pinard's erudition. By means of detailed historical, biographical, and bibliographical research, he lucidly presented the periods and personages relevant to the comparative study of religion, broadly conceived, in the West. Almost an encyclopedia, the volume was followed by an extensive double index (names and topics) that appeared in 1931. The second volume, subtitled *Ses méthodes,* studied numerous methods of classification and comparison, and the associated theories of explanation and interpretation of religion, that had appeared during the past century. Pinard analyzed the philosophical positions and presuppositions of the various methods and defined precisely what each could bring to the understanding of religion on the historical plane, as well as their defects and limits. He gave considerable attention to the method of the historico-cultural school of Graebner and Schmidt, but he preferred Schmidt's rationalism to his parallel emphasis on primordial revelation. Further, Pinard emphasized the importance of the several human sciences (history, ethnology, philology, psychology, and sociology) in the comparative study of religion, calling for the convergence of these disciplines in such study. Moreover, he insisted on the unity of science and faith.

In 1937 Pinard returned to Enghien, where he devoted himself exclusively to the study of comparative religion, intending to prepare a massive dictionary; the project was interrupted, however, by the outbreak of World War II. Pinard then turned to the study of the *Spiritual Exercises* of Ignatius Loyola. Several books and articles on Ignatian spirituality appeared between 1940 and 1956. He died at Lille on February 9, 1958.

Pinard prided himself on rigorous logic and objectivity, holding irrationality, sentiment, and subjectivity in suspicion. He asserted that religion comes into existence on the basis of reason: That is, it is on the rational, deductive plane that religion first imposes itself on humans ("Dieu se conclut avant d'être vu"). Religious experience, on which he wrote several articles during his tenure at Enghien, he considered to be a complement to religion arrived at rationally.

BIBLIOGRAPHY

Pinard's major work is *L'étude comparée des religions,* 2 vols. (Paris, 1922–1925). Attention should also be directed to his early work on religious experience, *La théorie de l'expérience religieuse: Son évolution de Luther à W. James* (Louvain, 1921), and to his much later writings on Ignatian spirituality: *Exercices spirituels, selon la méthode de saint Ignace,* 4 vols. (Paris, 1944–1947), *Saint Ignace de Loyola: Directeur d'âmes* (Paris, 1947), and *La spiritualité ignatienne* (Paris, 1949).

HARRY B. PARTIN (1987)

PINDAR.

The links between poetry and religion were tight in ancient Greece, and Pindar (c. 518–c. 438 BCE) was no exception. Born in Cynoscephalae (near Thebes) and educated in Thebes and Athens, he had a special relationship with the Sicilian tyrants and the Aeginetan aristocratic families, but his reputation was Panhellenic. Some of Pindar's odes allude to the most relevant historical event of his lifetime: the Persian invasion, which was put to an end by Greek victories at Salamis in 480 and Plataia in 479. In odes for the Sicilian victors, Pindar emphasized the triumphs of the local rulers against the Carthaginians (*Himera,* 480) and the Etruscans (*Kyme,* 474). Ancient biographies of Pindar, in which he is described as *theophilés* (loved by the Gods), highlight certain "prodigious" episodes of his life. The biographies claim, for example, that a bee made a honeycomb on his mouth as he was sleeping on Mount Helikon (a symbol of his inspiration), that the goddess Demeter reproached him for having ignored her in his hymns, and that the god Pan was heard singing one of Pindar's songs in the mountains near Thebes.

The ancient editors classified the Pindaric poems into seventeen books containing hymns, paeans (a variety of hymn, mostly in honor of Apollo), dithyrambs (Dionysiac hymns), processional odes, maiden songs and others "separate from the maiden songs," dance-odes, eulogies, dirges, and victory odes.

The victory odes were grouped, according to the kind of contest they celebrated, as Olympian, Pythian, Isthmian, or Nemean (a class to which two odes of a different origin have been added). Although the essential aim of the victory odes is to praise the victor and his exploits, the religious elements that pervade them can be explained in terms of the festivals, which were dedicated to the important gods Zeus (Olympian and Nemean), Apollo (Pythian), and Poseidon (Isthmian). The poems' religious elements also reflect the belief that victory was proof of a divine predilection for the victor and his family, as well as the ritual context of the celebration that followed the triumph, and the immortalizing power of poetry. The poet contributed to this extraordinary religious atmosphere through a wide range of means: music and choreography; formal resources, such as poetical and rhetorical devices that shared traits with religious hymns or prayers; maxims; and mythical narratives or allusions.

More than half of Pindar's forty-six victory songs begin with a short prayer or an invocation to a divinity. Thirty-three of Pindar's odes describe one or more myths that give a solemn tone to the poet's praise for the victor, who appears in a remarkably heroic light. Seventeen of those myths deal with local traditions of the victor's homeland: the myths of the Aeacids in the eleven odes for Aeginetans, with many episodes from the old epic poetry; Apollo's love for the nymph Cyrene, eponym of this city (*Pythian Odes* 9, for Telesicrates of Cyrene); the origin of Rhodes (*Olympian Odes* 7, for the Rhodian Diagoras); and so on. Another ten either underline the parallel between the victors and some mythical hero, or they display an ad hoc narrative fitting the hero's personal circumstances, or they even adopt a paradigmatic tone. Thus the young hero Perseus is a perfect model for the child Hippocles of Thessaly (*Pythian Odes* 10); Heracles for a pancratium winner (*Isthmian Odes* 4, 5, and 6); and Philoctetes for a pain-suffering Hieron of Syracuse (*Pythian Odes* 1). Eschatological myths, which are related to Orphic beliefs, are significant in an ode for the Sicilian victor Theron of Acragas (*Olympian Odes* 2), where for the first time in Western literature an afterlife with prizes and punishments is described, as is the Island of the Blessed, a destiny for exceptional heroes. Finally, there are other myths that are included in the poems because of the type of victory or traditions about the origins of the festival. This is the case with the well-known myth of Pelops, the mythical paradigm of winners in the chariot race (*Olympian Odes* 1), or with Herakles as founder of the Olympian games (*Olympian Odes* 10).

The odes are full of moral advice regarding religious conceptions and other values. The poet is a *sophós*, an inspired wise artist. A victory is proof of the nature of the winner, a gleam of inborn excellence, but also a result of effort. Poets contribute to the winner's glory and fame among mortals but also proclaim the necessity of being prudent and of following the Delphic precept "know thyself": mortals must be aware of their limits and not fall into *hybris* (wanton violence). Humans must fear the justice of Zeus, be aware of Apollo's infinite wisdom, and recognize the immense powers of all divine beings. Stories about the shameful conduct of the Gods are wrong, and the poet must look for the truth in all of them. Moreover, destiny is mutable, as many mythical paradigms show, and mortals must grasp the fragility of human existence: "a dream of a shadow is man" (*Pythian Odes* 8, 95, tr. Race). Fortunately, the celebration of triumph spreads a particular *aglaia* (brilliance) upon the victors and their families. The Graces preside on those moments, and the *charis* (grace) of the song contributes to this hopeful joy.

Other types of songs with special significance for Greek religion are paeans, dithyrambs, and dirges. Pindar adapted his paeans to the requirements of audience and performance. In the Delian paeans either he sings the origins of Delos (7b), the birth of the God in the island (12, for the Naxians), and its colonization (5, for the Athenians), or he exemplifies, with relevant heroes, faith in the Gods and love for the homeland, as in, for instance, Euxanthios and Melampous (4, for the Keans). Among the Delphic paeans (3, 6, 8, 10), it is worth mentioning the myth of the successive temples (8), which symbolically exemplifies the evolution of prophetic activity, whereas in *Paean* 6 the epic past and the sanctuary are linked by the myth of Neoptolemos's death (his tomb was at Delphi). Neoptolemos was an important hero for the Aeginetans, who were attendants at this celebration. *Paean* 10 probably included the foundation myth of Python's killing and the purification of the god. Paeans 1 (for Apollo Ismenios), 7 (with the myth of Apollo and Melia), and 9 (motivated by an eclipse) were composed for the Apollonian cult of Thebes.

As was the case with paeans, Pindar's dithyrambs stressed the links between the current festival and the divine world using a rich variety of resources. The degree to which the words, music, and contents fit the spirit and tradition of a festival is clearly apparent in the impressive beginning of *Dithyramb* 2 (for the Thebans), which is rich in orgiastic and religious evocations (the heavenly festival mirrors the present rite). It is also apparent in the first stanza of *Fragment* 75 (for the Athenians), where the alliterative effects echo the sound of musical instruments. Perhaps it is not a coincidence that the myths included in the dithyrambs were apt to enhance local trends of Dionysiac religion. Herakles' descent to the underworld and the introduction into Thebes of the Eleusynian mysteries were commemorated in *Dithyramb* 2. Myths having Perseus as protagonist appeared in at least two dithyrambs (1 and 4) and were probably composed for the city of Argos, where stories told that the hero fought against the god, with whom he was finally reconciled.

The dirges illustrate the importance of the consolatory function of poetry and the wide range of beliefs concerning the afterlife that were current in the fifth century BCE. Along with a description of a delightful paradise reserved for the pious in Hades (*Threni* 7, *Fragment* 129), the dirges also contain one of the first literary testimonies of Orphic beliefs (*Fragment* 133) concerning the destiny of souls and the role of Persephone in their expiation process.

BIBLIOGRAPHY

The best bibliographies on Pindar can be found in Douglas E. Gerber, *A Bibliography of Pindar, 1513–1966* (Cleveland, Ohio, 1969); "Pindar and Bacchylides 1934–1987," *Lustrum* 31 (1989): 97–269, and *Lustrum* 32 (1990): 7–67. An excellent edition (with a good translation) of Pindar's works is William H. Race's *Pindar* (Cambridge, Mass., and London, 1997), vol. 1: *Olympian Odes, Pythian Odes*; vol. 2: *Nemean Odes, Isthmian Odes, Fragments*. The paeans have been edited, with full commentary and introduction, by Ian Rutherford in *Pindar's Paeans: A Reading of the Fragments with a Survey of the Genre* (Oxford, 2001). For the dithyrambs, see Salvatore Lavecchia, *Pindari dithyramborum fragmenta* (Rome, 2000), and for the dirges, Maria Cannatà Fera, *Pindarus threnorum fragmenta* (Rome, 1990).

Some important works for the understanding of Pindar's poetical technique are Elroy L. Bundy, *Studia Pindarica (I–II)* (Berkeley, Calif., 1962; reprint, 1986); Richard Hamilton, *Epinikion: General Form in the Odes of Pindar* (The Hague, Netherlands, 1974); Deborah Steiner, *The Crown of Song: Metaphor in Pindar* (London, 1986); Gregory Nagy, *Pindar's Homer: The Lyric Possession of an Epic Past* (Baltimore, Md., and London, 1990); and William H. Race, *Style and Rhetoric in Pindar's Odes* (Atlanta, 1990). Interesting analyses on the role of myth can be found in Adolf Köhnken, *Die Funktion des Mythos bei Pindar* (Berlin, 1974), and Paola A. Bernardini, *Mito e attualità nelle odi di Pindaro* (Rome, 1983). On the specific religious questions in Pindar, see Erik Thummer, *Die Religiosität Pindars* (Innsbruck, Austria, 1957); Luigi Lehnus, *L'inno a Pan di Pindaro* (Milan, 1979); Hugh Lloyd-Jones, "Pindar and the After-Life" in *Pindare* (Vandoeuvres-Genève, 1985), pp. 245–279; Eveline Krummen, *Pyrsos Hymnon: Festliche Gegenwart und mythisch-rituelle Tradition bei Pindar* (Berlin, 1990); Emilio Suárez de la Torre, "Píndaro y la religión griega," *Cuadernos de Filología Clásica (egi)* 3 (1993): 67–97; and Michael Theunissen, *Pindar: Menschenlos und Wende der Zeit* (Munich, 2000), an important essay on the concept of time in Pindar, with religious implications.

EMILIO SUÁREZ DE LA TORRE (2005)

ISBN 0-02-865743-8
90000
9 780028 657431